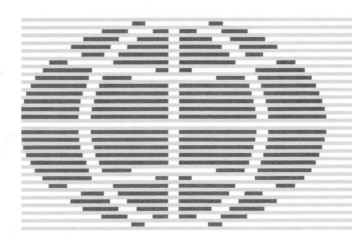

The
World Book
Atlas

Published by
World Book Encyclopedia, Inc.

A subsidiary of World Book–Childcraft International, Inc.
Chicago London Paris Sydney Tokyo Toronto

The World Book Atlas

Copyright © 1979 by Rand McNally & Company

Our Planet Earth section, pages 1A-73A inclusive,
Copyright © by Mitchell Beazley Publishers Limited 1973
as The Good Earth. Fully revised 1976

Printed in the United States of America

Library of Congress Card Number 78-58583
ISBN 0-7166-2029-4

Preface

The World Book Atlas serves both the specific needs of students and the general needs of the office and home. It is an atlas designed to meet the educational needs of those in school, and also to provide an opportunity for browsing and informal study.

The use of maps is essential to a thorough understanding of the world in which we live. The World Book Atlas brings together different kinds of maps, demonstrating meaningful relationships that make it possible for a user to study a particular area of the Earth and compare it with other areas. The World Book Atlas is also designed to be an effective reference tool that answers specific questions about the land forms, weather, and climate of the Earth, and about the location of countries, cities, rivers, mountains, and other geographic features.

The World Book Atlas combines thematic and general reference maps with charts, tables, and special illustrative material to tell the story of our Earth. Special emphasis has been given to world metropolitan areas, which have become vital in today's increasingly urbanized environment.

The World Book Atlas is divided into six major sections. It opens with the exciting story of Our Planet Earth, told with fascinating illustrations and informative text. This section deals with subjects ranging from the solar system to the control of pollution. Next, a comprehensive section of World Thematic Maps uses maps and other graphics to present information on the world distribution of major geographic, social, and economic elements. The third section is devoted to maps of 62 of the world's Major Cities. The main section of the Atlas is devoted to Country and Regional Maps of the world arranged continent by continent. Appropriate thematic maps are also included in this section. The final map section—Ocean Floor Maps—provides the reader with a view of one of the Earth's last great frontiers, the ocean floors. Handy reference tables and indexes—including up-to-date population tables, a glossary of foreign geographical terms, a separate index for the major city maps, and a pronouncing index for the reference maps—complete the Atlas.

Each section of the Atlas has a separate introduction. Appropriate legends for the maps in the major city, country, and regional sections appear there.

The World Book Atlas represents the combined efforts of the cartographic and research staff of Rand McNally and Company and the editors, designers, and researchers of The World Book Encyclopedia.

The world thematic maps and country and regional maps originally appeared in the well-known Goode's School Atlas, first published more than 50 years ago.

Cartographic Editors

Edward B. Espenshade, Jr., Ph.D.
Professor of Geography at Northwestern University. Dr. Espenshade has served as President of the Association of American Geographers; Chairman of the Earth-Science Division of the National Academy of Sciences—National Research Council; and Chairman of the Commission on College Geography of the Association of American Geographers.

Joel L. Morrison, Ph.D.
Associate Professor of Geography and Director of the Cartographic Laboratory of the University of Wisconsin at Madison. Dr. Morrison's specialties include cartographic communication and automation in map-making.

Contents

Scale
and
Projection

Map Scale. A map can only show a reduced representation of the Earth's surface or any part of it. Therefore, the reader has to answer the question: What is the relationship between the size of the map and the actual size of the portion of the Earth it depicts? This proportional relationship is the *scale* of a map. To help the reader, most maps in this Atlas give the scale in three ways—as a ratio, in written form, and graphically.

As a *ratio*, the scale of a map is expressed as, for example, 1:4,000,000. This means one inch on the map represents four million inches on the Earth. In *written form*, this ratio is expressed as: "one inch to sixty-four miles." This means one inch on the map represents sixty-four miles on the Earth. *Graphically*, scale is shown with a bar scale, on which distance calculations may be made directly.

Map Projections. There is no way to represent the curved surface of the globe on the flat surface of a map without some distortion of distance, direction, shape, or area. Only a globe can show the Earth without distortion. On large-scale maps that cover only a few square miles, this distortion is negligible. However, on maps that represent large areas, such as a large country, a continent, or the whole world, the distortion is considerable. Unless understood, distortion may result in serious misconceptions on the part of the reader.

A *map projection* is a way to transfer locations on the Earth to locations on a map. The number of possible projections is unlimited and several hundred of them are used by cartographers. None avoids some distortion of the spatial relationships that only a globe can show truthfully. No single flat map can accurately show area, shape, angle, and scale. However, a cartographer can select a projection that will accurately depict a particular property, such as shape. It is also possible to compromise by limiting the distortion of one or more properties at the expense of the others.

Most of the maps used in this Atlas are drawn on projections that give equality of area, good land and ocean shapes, and parallels of latitude that are parallel. However, the maps do have distortions and the reader should make allowances for them. One of the best ways to understand the nature of a map's distortion is to compare the latitude and longitude grid lines of the flat map with the grid of the globe. To do this, the reader should understand the basic characteristics of a globe grid:

1. All meridians of longitude are equal in length and meet at the poles.

2. All parallels of latitude are parallel.

3. The length, or circumference, of the parallels decreases from the equator to the poles. At 60° latitude, the circumference of the parallel is half the circumference of the equator.

4. Distances along the meridians between any two parallels are equal.

5. All parallels and meridians meet at right angles.

For example, the map on page 47 uses a projection that produces meridians and parallels that are straight lines which meet at right angles. But all the parallels are the same length, which is not true on a globe. This results in considerable exaggeration of areas in the higher latitudes, near the poles. For example, northern Canada looks much larger in proportion to the rest of the world than it really is. In the projection used on pages 4-5, parallels and meridians meet at oblique angles in higher latitudes, which distorts land shapes in such areas as Alaska and Greenland. Their areas, however, are accurately portrayed in relation to each other.

Some of the more commonly used projections and an indication of their properties are shown on the following pages.

PROJECTIONS

A map projection is merely an orderly system of parallels and meridians on which a flat map can be drawn: There are hundreds of projections, but no one represents the earth's spherical surface without some distortion. The distortion is relatively small for most practical purposes when a small part of the sphere is projected. For larger areas, a sacrifice of some property is necessary.

Most projections are designed to preserve on the flat map some particular property of the sphere. By varying the systematic arrangement or spacing of the latitude and longitude lines, a projection may be made either equal-area or conformal. Although most projections are derived from mathematical formulas, some are easier to visualize if thought of as projected upon a plane, or upon a cone or cylinder which is then unrolled into a plane surface. Thus, many projections are classified as plane (azimuthal), conic, or cylindrical.

For a fuller discussion of map projections, see Preface. Figures with asterisks indicate projections used in this atlas.

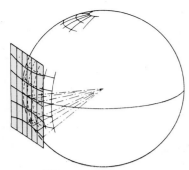

(A) GNOMONIC PROJECTION

A geometric or perspective projection on a tangent plane with the origin point at the center of the globe. Shapes and distances rapidly become increasingly distorted away from the center of the projection. Important in navigation, because all straight lines are great circles.

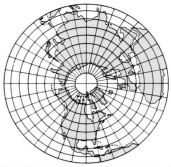

(B) LAMBERT EQUAL AREA PROJECTION*

A mathematically designed azimuthal equal-area projection. Excellent for continental areas. For larger areas away from the center, distortion of distances and shapes is appreciable.

FIGURE 1.–TYPICAL PLANE PROJECTIONS

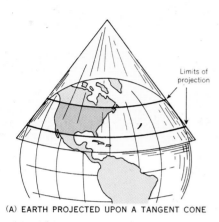

(A) EARTH PROJECTED UPON A TANGENT CONE

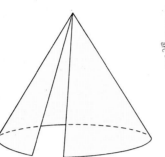

(B) CONE CUT FROM BASE TO APEX

A perspective projection on a tangent cone with the origin point at the center of the globe. At the parallel of tangency, all elements of the map are

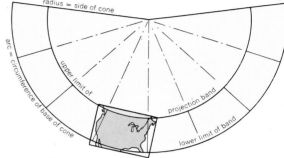

(C) CONE DEVELOPED INTO A PLANE SURFACE

true- angles,distances,shapes,areas.   Away from the tangent parallel, distances increase rapidly, giving bad distortion of shapes and areas.

FIGURE 2.–SIMPLE CONIC PROJECTIONS

(A) EARTH PROJECTED UPON AN INTERSECTING CONE

This modification of the conic has two standard parallels, or lines of intersection. It is not an equal-area projection, the space being reduced in size between the standard parallels and

(B) CONIC PROJECTION WITH TWO STANDARD PARALLELS*

progressively enlarged beyond the standard parallels. Careful selection of the standard parallels provides, however, good representation for areas of limited latitudinal extent.

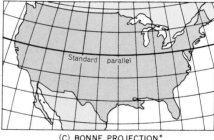

(C) BONNE PROJECTION*

An equal-area modification of the conic principle. Distances are true along all parallels and the central meridian; but away from it, increasing obliqueness of intersections and longitudinal distances, with their attendant distortion of shapes, limits the satisfactory area.

FIGURE 3.–MODIFIED CONIC PROJECTIONS

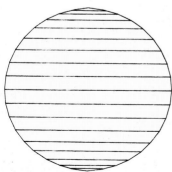

(A) EARTH CONSIDERED AS FORMED BY BASES OF CONES

(B) DEVELOPMENT OF THE CONICAL BASES

This variation is not equal-area. Parallels are non-concentric circles truly divided. Distances along the straight central meridian are also true, but along the curving meridians are increasingly exaggerated. Representation is good near the central meridian, but away from it there is marked distortion.

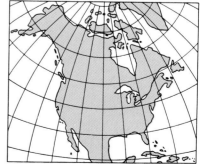

(C) POLYCONIC PROJECTION*

FIGURE 4.–POLYCONIC PROJECTION

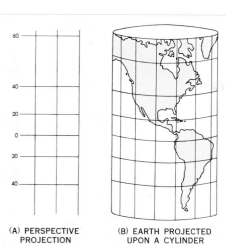

(A) PERSPECTIVE PROJECTION

(B) EARTH PROJECTED UPON A CYLINDER

A perspective projection on a tangent cylinder. Because of rapidly increasing distortion away from the line of tangency and the lack of any special advantage, it is rarely used.

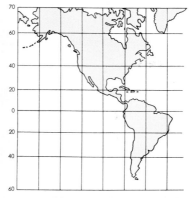

(C) MERCATOR CONFORMAL PROJECTION

Mercator's modification increases the latitudinal distances in the same proportion as longitudinal distances are increased. Thus, at any point shapes are true, but areas become increasingly exaggerated. Of value in navigation, because a line connecting any two points gives the true direction between them.

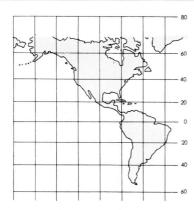

(D) MILLER PROJECTION*

This recent modification is neither conformal nor equal-area. Whereas shapes are less accurate than on the Mercator, the exaggeration of areas has been reduced somewhat.

FIGURE 5.– CYLINDRICAL PROJECTIONS

(A) MOLLWEIDE'S HOMOLOGRAPHIC PROJECTION

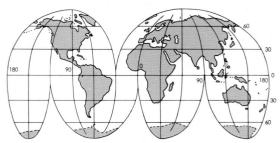

(B) GOODE'S INTERRUPTED HOMOLOGRAPHIC PROJECTION

(C) SINUSOIDAL PROJECTION*

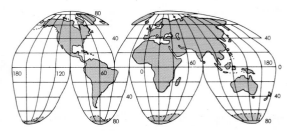

(D) GOODE'S INTERRUPTED HOMOLOSINE PROJECTION*

Although each of these projections is equal-area, differences in the spacing and arrangement of latitude and longitude lines result in differences in the distribution and relative degree of the shape and distance distortion within each grid. On the homolographic, there is no uniformity in scale. It is different on each parallel and each meridian. On the sinusoidal, only distances along all latitudes and the central meridian are true. The homolosine combines the homolographic, for areas poleward of 40°, with the sinusoidal. The principle of interruption permits each continent in turn the advantage of being in the center of the projection, resulting in better shapes.

FIGURE 6.– EQUAL AREA PROJECTIONS OF THE WORLD

A conformal projection in which a selected great circle of the globe is considered as the "equator" of the ordinary Mercator projection, with the cylinder tangent along the great circle. It is used chiefly for charts of great-circle air routes between distant cities.

FIGURE 7.– TRANSVERSE MERCATOR PROJECTION

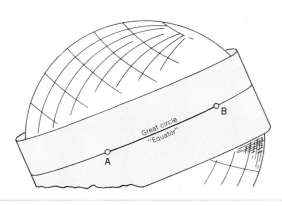

Our Planet Earth

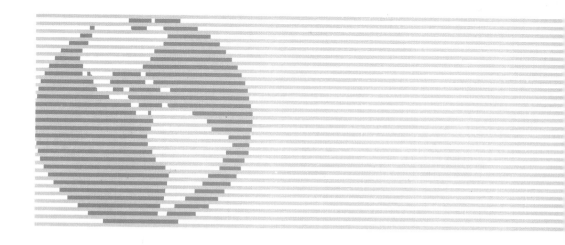

Our home is the Earth, a small planet that revolves around the Sun. The Sun is a star, but only one of the hundred thousand million which exist in the local system of stars, or galaxy, of which we are a part. Our own galaxy, we now know, is just one of millions of other galaxies in the universe.

Scientists generally believe that the Earth was formed about 4.5 billion years ago. Since that time the planet's surface has been ceaselessly altered and its present physical features are the result of numerous processes that interact with each other, usually very slowly, but sometimes very violently. The land is eroded by the wind and rain, washed away by the rivers and seas, and reduced to sediment that builds up elsewhere. Other changes are created by more spectacular events, such as explosive volcanic eruptions and vast out-pourings of molten lava. The records of these processes can be seen in the rocks themselves.

There are various theories about the exact origin of life on Earth. But one thing is certain, the planet upon which life came into being was very different from the world we know now. With agonizing slowness, through hundreds of millions of years, life gradually changed with the environment. The struggle to stay alive produced new plants and animals of millions of varieties, from tiny bugs to giant whales and from speck-like algae to towering trees. These formed a thin frosting of life over the surface of the planet. It was into this world that human beings eventually emerged.

Because of the vast size of the Earth, people long believed that its natural resources could never be exhausted. However, the dramatic growth in population and industrial and agricultural demands has made it obvious that our planet has limits, and in some instances these limits are being fast approached. Of course some new sources remain to be discovered and others will be replaced by man-made material, but we no longer can afford to waste our heritage.

The Sun is the controlling body of the solar system and is far more massive than all its planets combined. Even Jupiter, much the largest of the planets, has a diameter only about one-tenth that of the Sun. The solar system is divided into two main parts. The inner region includes four relatively small, solid planets: Mercury, Venus, the Earth and Mars. Beyond the orbit of Mars comes a wide gap in which move many thousands of small minor planets or asteroids, some of which are little more than rocks. Further out come the four giants: Jupiter, Saturn, Uranus and Neptune. Pluto, on the fringe of the system, is a curious little planet; it appears to be in a class of its own, but at present very little is known about it and even its size is a matter for conjecture. Maps of the solar system can be misleading in that they tend to give a false idea about distance. The outer planets are very widely separated. For example, Saturn is further away from Uranus than it is from the Earth.

The contrasting planets

The inner, or terrestrial, planets have some points in common, but a greater number of differences. Mercury, the planet closest to the Sun, has almost no atmosphere and that of Mars is very thin; but Venus, strikingly similar to the Earth in size and mass, has a dense atmosphere made up chiefly of carbon dioxide, and a surface temperature of over 400°C. The giant planets are entirely different. At least in their outer layers they are made up of gas, like a star; but, unlike a star, they have no light of their own and shine only by reflecting the light of their star, the Sun. Several of the planets have moons. The Earth has one (or it may be our partner in a binary system), Jupiter has at least 13, Saturn 10 (discounting its rings), Uranus five and Neptune two. Mars also has two satellites but these are less than 15 mi (24 km) in diameter and of a different type from the Earth's Moon. The Earth is unique in the solar system in having oceans on its surface and an atmosphere made up chiefly of nitrogen and oxygen. It is the only planet suited to life of terrestrial type. It is not now believed that highly evolved life can exist on any other planet in the Sun's family, though it is still possible that some primitive life forms may exist on Mars.

Observing the planets

Five of the planets, Mercury, Venus, Mars, Jupiter and Saturn, were known to the inhabitants of the Earth in very ancient times. They are starlike in aspect but easy to distinguish because, unlike the stars, they seem to wander slowly about the sky whereas the true stars appear to hold their position for century after century. The so-called proper motions of the stars are too slight to be noticed by the naked eye, but they can be measured by modern techniques. Mercury and Venus always appear to be in the same part of the sky as the Sun. Mercury is never prominent but Venus is dazzlingly bright, partly because its upper clouds are highly reflective and partly because it is close; it can come within 25,000,000 mi (40,000,000 km), only about 100 times as far as the Moon. Jupiter is generally very bright, as is Mars when it is well placed. Saturn is also conspicuous to the naked eye, but Uranus is only just visible and Neptune and Pluto are much fainter.

The Sun's active surface *right*

The structure of a star, such as the Sun, is immensely complex. The very concept of its surface is hard to define, and the size of the Sun depends on the wavelength of the light with which it is viewed. Using the 'hydrogen alpha' wavelength the bright surface of the Sun, known as the photosphere, appears as shown right, above. The surface, at about 5500 °C, is dotted with light and dark patches as a result of the violent upcurrents of hotter gas and cooler areas between them. Larger, darker regions are sunspots (right), temporary but very large disturbances.

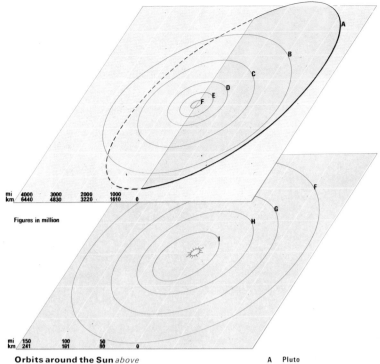

Orbits around the Sun *above*
The Sun's nine known planets, and the asteroids, describe heliocentric orbits in the same direction. But some planetary orbits are highly eccentric, while some asteroids are both eccentric and steeply inclined. The outermost planet, Pluto, passes within the orbit of Neptune, while one asteroid reaches almost to the radius of Saturn. Over 350 years ago Johannes Kepler showed that the planets do not move in perfect circles, and found that the line joining each planet to the Sun sweeps out a constant area in a given time, so that speed is greatest close to the Sun.

A	Pluto
B	Neptune
C	Uranus
D	Saturn
E	Jupiter
F	Mars
G	Earth
H	Venus
I	Mercury

mi 4000 3000 2000 1000 0
km 6440 4830 3220 1610 0

Figures in million

mi 150 100 50 0
km 241 181 80 0

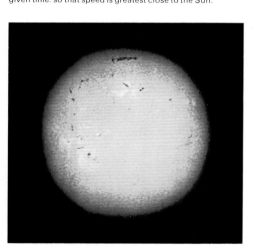

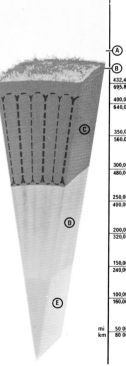

The Sun's structure *right*

The Sun is made up of highly dissimilar regions. This narrow sector includes the inner part of the corona (A) which, though very diffuse, has a temperature of some 1,000,000 °C. Into it leap solar prominences, 'flames' thousands of miles long which arch along the local magnetic field from the chromosphere (B), the outer layer of the Sun proper, which covers the visible photosphere with a layer of variable, highly mobile and rarefied gas about 6000 mi (10000 km) thick. Inside the Sun the outer layer (C) of gas is in constant movement and transfers heat from the interior. Inner region D is thought to transfer energy mainly by radiation. The innermost zone of all (E), the conditions of which can only be surmised but are thought to include a temperature of some 15,000,000 °C, sustains the energy of the Sun (and its planets) by continuous fusion of hydrogen into helium.

mi 1,250,00
2,000,00

A
B
432,475
695,80
400,000
640,00
C
350,00
560,00
300,000
480,00
D
250,000
400,00
200,000
320,00
E
150,000
240,00
100,000
160,00
mi 50 000
km 80 000

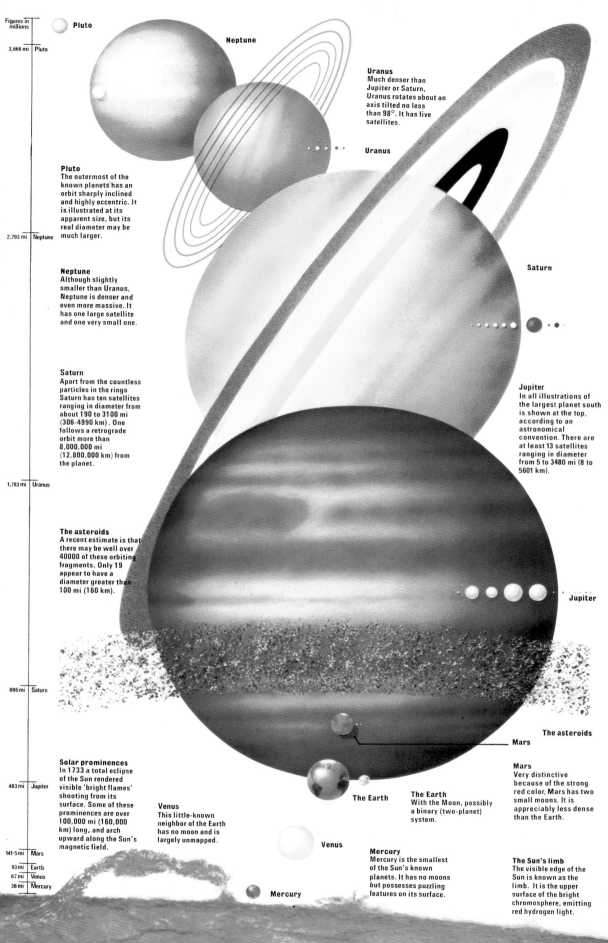

Figures in millions

3,666 mi | Pluto

2,793 mi | Neptune

1,783 mi | Uranus

886 mi | Saturn

483 mi | Jupiter

141·5 mi | Mars
93 mi | Earth
67 mi | Venus
36 mi | Mercury

Pluto

Neptune

Uranus
Much denser than
Jupiter or Saturn,
Uranus rotates about an
axis tilted no less
than 98°. It has five
satellites.

Uranus

Pluto
The outermost of the
known planets has an
orbit sharply inclined
and highly eccentric. It
is illustrated at its
apparent size, but its
real diameter may be
much larger.

Saturn

Neptune
Although slightly
smaller than Uranus,
Neptune is denser and
even more massive. It
has one large satellite
and one very small one.

Saturn
Apart from the countless
particles in the rings
Saturn has ten satellites
ranging in diameter from
about 190 to 3100 mi
(306-4990 km). One
follows a retrograde
orbit more than
8,000,000 mi
(12,800,000 km) from
the planet.

Jupiter
In all illustrations of
the largest planet south
is shown at the top,
according to an
astronomical
convention. There are
at least 13 satellites
ranging in diameter
from 5 to 3480 mi (8 to
5601 km).

The asteroids
A recent estimate is that
there may be well over
40000 of these orbiting
fragments. Only 19
appear to have a
diameter greater than
100 mi (160 km).

Jupiter

The asteroids

Mars

Mars
Very distinctive
because of the strong
red color, Mars has two
small moons. It is
appreciably less dense
than the Earth.

Solar prominences
In 1733 a total eclipse
of the Sun rendered
visible 'bright flames'
shooting from its
surface. Some of these
prominences are over
100,000 mi (160,000
km) long, and arch
upward along the Sun's
magnetic field.

Venus
This little-known
neighbor of the Earth
has no moon and is
largely unmapped.

The Earth

The Earth
With the Moon, possibly
a binary (two-planet)
system.

Venus

Mercury
Mercury is the smallest
of the Sun's known
planets. It has no moons
but possesses puzzling
features on its surface.

Mercury

The Sun's limb
The visible edge of the
Sun is known as the
limb. It is the upper
surface of the bright
chromosphere, emitting
red hydrogen light.

The solar system *left*
The Sun is the major body in the solar
system. It lies 30000 light-years from
the center of our galaxy and takes about
200 million years to complete one
journey around it. There are nine planets
and their satellites in the system, as well
as comets and various minor bodies such
as meteoroids. The diagram on the
left shows the upper limb of the
Sun (bottom) and the main
constituent members of the solar
system very greatly condensed into a
smaller space. To indicate the amount of
the radial compression, the limb of the
Sun is drawn for a near-sphere of 5 ft
(1.52 m) diameter. On this scale the Earth
would be about 420 ft (127 m) away
and the outermost planet Pluto, no less
than 3 mi (4.9 km) distant.

Pluto, discovered in 1930, has a very
eccentric orbit, with a radius varying
between 2766 and 4566 million mi
(4500 and 7400 million kilometers).
Being so far from the Sun, it is extremely
cold, and probably has no atmosphere.

Neptune, discovered in 1846, has a
diameter of 30760 mi (49500 km) and is
made up of gas, although little is known
of its interior. It orbits the Sun once in
164¾ years. Seen through binoculars
it is a small bluish disk.

Uranus, discovered in 1781, is
apparently similar to Neptune, but less
massive. Although faintly visible to
the naked eye, even large telescopes
show little detail upon its greenish surface.

Saturn is the second largest planet, its
equatorial diameter being 75100 mi
(120,900 km). Visually it is unlike any
other heavenly body, because of its
equatorial system of rings made up of
particles of various sizes. The planet itself
is less dense than water and at least its
outer layers are gaseous.

Jupiter, the largest planet, has an
equatorial diameter of 88700 mi
(142,700 km), but its rapid spin, once
every 9¾ hours, makes it very flattened
at the poles. It appears to have cloud
belts, possibly of liquid ammonia,
and various spots, of which the great red
spot seems to be permanent.

The asteroids, a mass of apparent
planetary material ranging in size from
dust up to one lump about as large as the
British Isles, orbit mainly between Mars
and Jupiter, though some have eccentric
orbits which approach the Earth.

Mars is about 4200 mi (6760 km) in
diameter. It has a thin atmosphere, mainly
of carbon dioxide, and its surface is
pitted with Moon-like craters. It is not
thought today that the planet contains
any life.

The Earth/Moon system is today
regarded as a double planet rather than a
planet and satellite. The Moon has an
average distance from Earth of
238,857 mi (384,403 km) and it is now
known that it has never contained life.

Venus is almost the twin of the Earth in
size and mass. It is too hot to contain
life, and its very dense atmosphere is
mainly carbon dioxide. It has a year of
224¾ Earth days, and it spins on its axis
once every 243 Earth days.

Mercury, the innermost planet, is only
about 3100 mi (5000 km) in diameter,
and has lost almost all of its atmosphere.
Like Venus it shows phases, but it is
always close to the Sun when viewed
from the Earth and cannot be seen clearly.

Earth's Companion: The Moon

The Moon is our companion in space. Its mean distance from the Earth is less than a quarter of a million miles – it varies between 221,460 miles (356,410 km) and 252,700 miles (406,685 km) – and it was the first world other than our Earth to come within the range of man's space probes. At first mere masses, these then became instrument packages and finally spacecraft carrying men. With their aid our knowledge of the Moon has been vastly increased in the past decade. Astronauts Neil Armstrong and Edwin Aldrin made the first human journey to the lunar surface in July 1969, and the Moon has since been subjected to detailed and direct investigation.

The mean diameter of the Moon is 2158 miles (3473 km), and its mass is 1/81st as much as that of the Earth. Despite this wide difference the ratio is much less than that between other planets and their moons, and the Earth/Moon system is now widely regarded as a double planet rather than as a planet and satellite. The Moon's mean density is less than that of the Earth, and it may lack a comparable heavy core. Escape velocity from the lunar surface is only 1.5 mi/sec (2.4 km/sec), and this is so low that the Moon has lost any atmosphere it may once have had. To Earth life it is therefore an extremely hostile world. Analysis of lunar rock brought back to Earth laboratories and investigated by Soviet probes on the Moon has so far revealed no trace of any life. The Moon appears to have always been sterile.

Much of the surface of the Moon comprises large grey plains, mis-called 'maria'(seas), but most of it is extremely rough. There are great ranges of mountains, isolated peaks and countless craters which range from tiny pits up to vast enclosures more than 150 miles (240 km) in diameter. Many of the craters have central mountains or mountain-groups. Some of the larger craters show signs of having been produced by volcanic action, while others appear to have resulted from the impacts of meteorites.

The Moon rotates slowly, performing one complete turn on its axis every 27 days, 7 hours, 43 minutes. It always presents the same face to the Earth. But in October 1959 the Soviet probe *Lunik 3* photographed the hidden rear hemisphere and it has since been mapped in detail. It contains no large 'seas'. The appearance of the lunar surface depends strongly on the angle at which it is viewed and the direction of solar illumination. In the photograph on the right, taken from a height of about 70 miles (115 km) with the Earth having once more come into full view ahead, the lunar surface looks deceptively smooth; in fact, there is practically no level ground any where in the field of vision. The lunar horizon is always sharply defined, because there is no atmosphere to cause blurring or distortion. For the same reason, the sky seen from the Moon is always jet black.

Full Moon *below*
This striking photograph was taken by the *Apollo 11* astronauts in July 1969. It shows parts of both the Earth-turned and far hemispheres. The dark plain near the center is the Mare Crisium.

Earthrise *above*
This view of the Earth rising was visible to the crew of *Apollo 10* in May 1969 as they orbited the Moon 70 miles (112 km) above the surface. They had just come round from the Moon's rear hemisphere.

Eclipses

Once regarded as terrifying actions of angry gods, eclipses are today merely useful. They provide a different view of the Sun and Moon that opens up fresh information. In a lunar eclipse the Earth passes directly between the Sun and Moon; in a solar eclipse the Moon passes between Sun and Earth. Both the Earth and Moon constantly cast a shadow comprising a dark inner cone surrounded by a region to which part of the sunlight penetrates. A body passing through the outer shadow experiences a partial eclipse, while the inner cone causes a total eclipse in which all direct sunlight is cut off.

A total solar eclipse is magnificent. The bright star is blocked out by a black Moon, but around it the Sun's atmosphere flashes into view. The pearly corona of thin gas can be seen extending a million miles from the Sun. Closer to the surface huge 'prominences' of red hydrogen leap into space and curve back along the solar magnetic field. In a partial solar eclipse these things cannot be seen, while in a total eclipse caused by the Moon at its greatest distance from Earth a ring of the Sun is left visible. As the Moon's orbit is not in the same plane as the Earth's, total solar eclipses occur very rarely, on occasions when the tip of the Moon's dark shadow crosses the Earth as a spot 169 miles (272 km) wide.

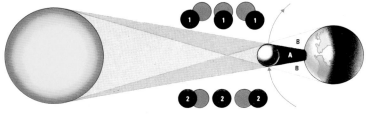

Eclipses *left and below*
When the Moon passes in front of the Sun as in sequence 1 its shadow B causes a partial solar eclipse (below, left, taken 21 November 1966). But in the case of sequence 2, shadow cone A gives a total eclipse (below, right, 15 February 1961).

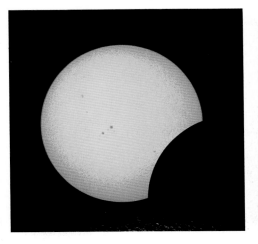

1 According to the most widely accepted theory, (the 'accretion' theory) the solar system originally consisted only of a mass of tenuous gas, and dust. There was no true Sun, and there was no production of nuclear energy. The gas was made up chiefly of hydrogen, with occasional random condensations.

2 Gravitational forces now cause the cloud to shrink and assume a more regular shape. Its density and mass near the center increase, but there are still no nuclear processes.

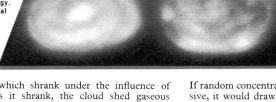

3 The gas cloud begins to assume the form of a regular disk. The infant Sun begins to shine - by the energy from gravitational shrinkage.

4 Material is thrown off from the Sun to join that already in the solar cloud, whose condensations have become more noticeable.

How did the Earth come into existence? This question has intrigued mankind for centuries, but it was not until the start of true science that plausible theories were advanced. Although some theories held sway for many years, they were eventually deposed by the discovery of some fatal flaw. Even today, it is impossible to be sure that the main problem has been solved, but at least some concrete facts exist as a guide. It is now reasonably certain that the age of the Earth is of the order of 4550-4700 million years. The other planets are presumably about the same age, since they were probably formed by the same process in the same epoch.

Several centuries ago Archbishop Ussher of Armagh maintained that the world had come into being at a definite moment in the year 4004 BC. This estimate was made on purely religious grounds, and it soon became clear that the Earth is much older. In 1796 the French astronomer Laplace put forward the famous Nebular Hypothesis, according to which the Sun and the planets were formed from a rotating cloud of gas which shrank under the influence of gravitation. As it shrank, the cloud shed gaseous rings, each of which condensed into a planet. This would mean that the outer planets were older than those closer to the Sun which itself would represent the remaining part of the gas cloud.

The Nebular Hypothesis was accepted for many years, but eventually serious mathematical weaknesses were found in it. Next came a number of tidal theories according to which the Earth and other planets were formed from a cigar-shaped tongue of matter torn from the Sun by the gravitational pull of a passing star. The first plausible theory of this kind came from the English astronomer Sir James Jeans, but this too was found to be mathematically untenable and the idea had to be given up.

Most modern theories assume that the planets were formed by accretion from a rotating solar cloud of gas and finely-dispersed dust. If the Sun were originally attended by such a cloud, this cloud would, over a sufficiently long period of time, become a flat disk. If random concentration had become sufficiently massive, it would draw in extra material by virtue of its gravitational attraction, forming 'proto-planets'. When the Sun began to radiate strongly, part of the mass of each proto-planet would be driven off due to the high temperatures, leaving a solar system of the kind that exists today.

The fact that such an evolutionary sequence can be traced emphasizes that in talking about the origin of the Earth we are considering only a small part of a continuous story. What will become of the Earth in the far future? The Sun is radiating energy because of the nuclear process within it: hydrogen is being converted into helium causing mass to be lost with a resulting release of energy. However, when the supply of hydrogen begins to run low, the Sun must change radically. It will move towards a red giant stage swelling and engulfing the Earth. Fortunately, this will not happen for at least another 6000 million years, but eventually the Sun which sustains our planet will finally destroy it.

Alternative theories

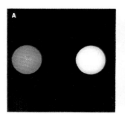

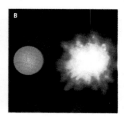

Contracting nebula *above*
Laplace suggested that a contracting nebula might shed gas which then condensed.

Tidal theories *above*
In 1917 Sir James Jeans postulated that Sun A was attracted to another star B which passed at close range. A cloud of matter was drawn off by their gravitational attraction. Star B moved on while the cloud condensed to form planets circling our Sun at C.

A violent beginning *above*
One of the theories of how the solar system came to be formed assumes that the Sun once had a binary companion star. This exploded as a supernova (above) and was blown off as a white dwarf

16 As the 'fuel' runs out, the radiation pressure falls, and under internal gravity the Sun will collapse inwards changing in only 50000 years from a red giant into a super-dense white dwarf.

17 As a white dwarf, the Sun will continue to radiate feebly for an immense period. At last all radiation must cease, and the Sun will remain as a dead, dark globe - a black dwarf.

15 By now all the inner planets will have long since been destroyed. The Sun will become unstable, reaching the most violent stage of its career as a red giant, with a vast, relatively cool surface and an intensely hot, dense core.

14 When the center of the Sun has reached another critical temperature, the helium will begin to 'burn' giving the so-called 'helium flash'. After a temporary contraction the Sun will then swell out to a diameter 400 times that at present.

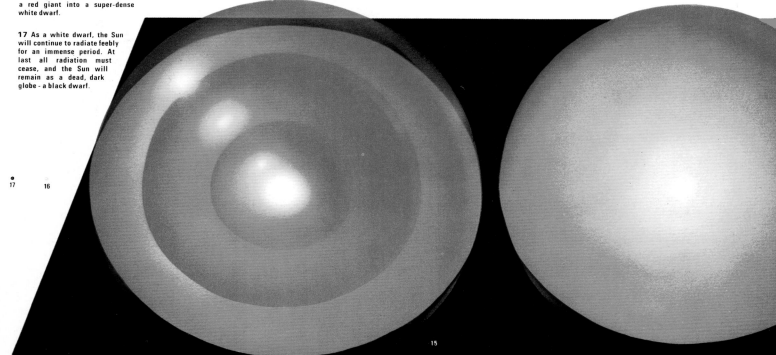

17 16

15

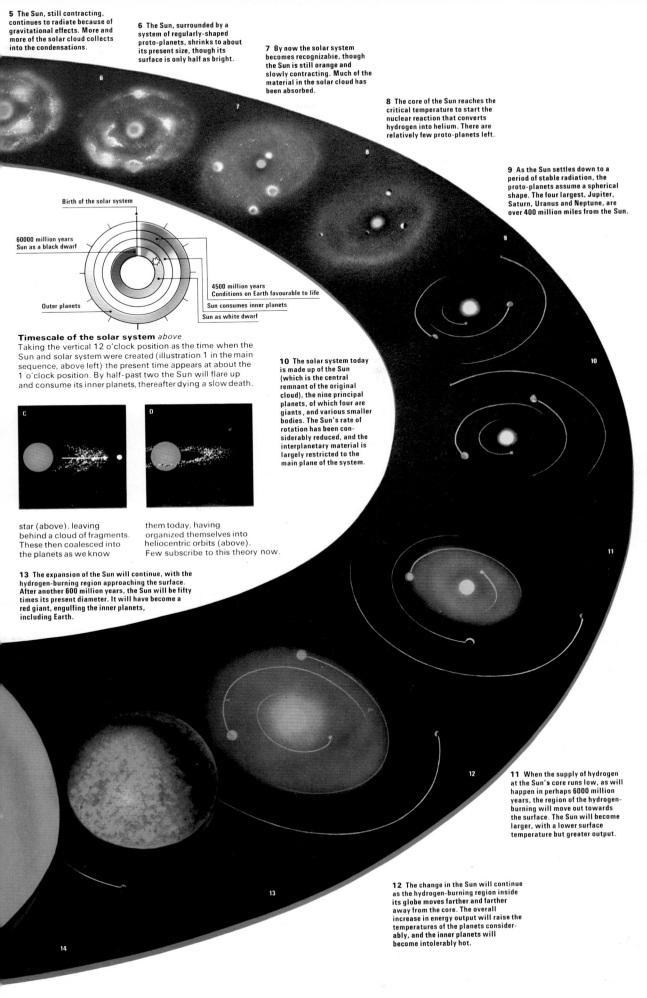

5 The Sun, still contracting, continues to radiate because of gravitational effects. More and more of the solar cloud collects into the condensations.

6 The Sun, surrounded by a system of regularly-shaped proto-planets, shrinks to about its present size, though its surface is only half as bright.

7 By now the solar system becomes recognizable, though the Sun is still orange and slowly contracting. Much of the material in the solar cloud has been absorbed.

8 The core of the Sun reaches the critical temperature to start the nuclear reaction that converts hydrogen into helium. There are relatively few proto-planets left.

9 As the Sun settles down to a period of stable radiation, the proto-planets assume a spherical shape. The four largest, Jupiter, Saturn, Uranus and Neptune, are over 400 million miles from the Sun.

Birth of the solar system

60000 million years
Sun as a black dwarf

Outer planets

4500 million years
Conditions on Earth favourable to life

Sun consumes inner planets

Sun as white dwarf

Timescale of the solar system *above*
Taking the vertical 12 o'clock position as the time when the Sun and solar system were created (illustration 1 in the main sequence, above left) the present time appears at about the 1 o'clock position. By half-past two the Sun will flare up and consume its inner planets, thereafter dying a slow death.

10 The solar system today is made up of the Sun (which is the central remnant of the original cloud), the nine principal planets, of which four are giants, and various smaller bodies. The Sun's rate of rotation has been considerably reduced, and the interplanetary material is largely restricted to the main plane of the system.

C

D

star (above), leaving behind a cloud of fragments. These then coalesced into the planets as we know

them today, having organized themselves into heliocentric orbits (above). Few subscribe to this theory now.

13 The expansion of the Sun will continue, with the hydrogen-burning region approaching the surface. After another 600 million years, the Sun will be fifty times its present diameter. It will have become a red giant, engulfing the inner planets, including Earth.

11 When the supply of hydrogen at the Sun's core runs low, as will happen in perhaps 6000 million years, the region of the hydrogen-burning will move out towards the surface. The Sun will become larger, with a lower surface temperature but greater output.

12 The change in the Sun will continue as the hydrogen-burning region inside its globe moves farther and farther away from the core. The overall increase in energy output will raise the temperatures of the planets considerably, and the inner planets will become intolerably hot.

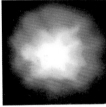

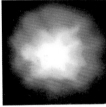

The lifespan of the Earth

The Earth was produced from the solar cloud (1-6 on main diagram). It had no regular form, but, as more and more material was drawn in, it began to assume a spherical shape (7-8).

When it had reached its present size (9), the Earth had a dense atmosphere; not the original hydrogen atmosphere but one produced by gas from the interior. Life had not started.

The Earth today (10), moving in a stable orbit, has an equable temperature and oxygen-rich atmosphere, so that it alone of all the planets in the solar system is suitable for life.

When the Sun nears the red giant stage (11-13), the Earth will be heated to an intolerable degree. The atmosphere will be driven off, the oceans will boil and life must come to an end.

As the Sun reaches the peak of its violence (14-15) it will swell out until the Earth is engulfed. Its natural life is probably no more than 8000 million years: its end is certain

Man's most powerful nuclear weapons pale into insignificance beside the violence of an earthquake or the destructive and indiscriminate force of a volcano. These cataclysmic phenomena frequently occur along the same belts of instability in the Earth's crust and are often only different manifestations of the same fundamental processes. About 800 volcanoes are known to have been active in historical times, and many are extremely active today. All the mid-ocean ridges are volcanic in origin, and many underwater eruptions occur along these submarine mountain ranges. Spectacular volcanic eruptions sometimes break the ocean surface, such as during the formation in 1963 of the island of Surtsey, south of Iceland (photograph, right). Some islands, such as Iceland itself, are the products of continued outpourings of lava along the crest of the mid-ocean ridge.

Oceanic earthquakes caused by sudden sea-floor displacements may result in tsunamis or giant sea waves. About 80 per cent of the shallow earthquakes and almost all deep ones take place along the belt around the Pacific. Clear evidence of the large scale movements of the mantle are provided by the zones within which earthquake shocks are generated along some Pacific island arc systems. These zones plunge down from sea-floor level to depths as great as 400 miles (640 km) beneath the adjacent continents and mark the positions of downward flow of the mantle convection currents (page 11A). The corresponding upwelling regions lie along the mid-ocean ridges, where new basic volcanic material is continually being added to the ocean crust as outward movement takes place away from the ridges.

These sea-floor spreading movements act as 'conveyor belts' for the continents, and constitute the basic mechanism for the large displacements involved in continental drifting. Geological data confirm the former close fits of the margins of the reassembled continental jig-saw puzzle, and also corroborate the detailed paleomagnetic evidence visible in today's rocks of the movements of the continents relative to the geographic poles.

Geysers
Ground water and mud heated by volcanic activity can lie on the surface as puddles and hot springs, rendered colorful by dissolved minerals, or be pumped out in the form of geysers. The latter are connected to extensive underground reservoirs in which steam pressure builds up above the hot water. Intermittently the system discharges high into the air.

Fissure eruption
In this type of eruption freely flowing molten basaltic material exudes from apertures forced in the crust. The surface crack may be several miles in length and the more or less horizontal flow has on occasion covered more than 200 square miles (500 km²).

Hawaiian-type eruption
In this case large, shallow cones, often containing lakes of molten lava, generally release gas and vapor in a relatively passive way. But sometimes glowing lava is expelled as a fine spray which in a high wind can be drawn out into fine threads called Pelée's hair.

Emissions
Incandescent lava issues from the main cone or from side vents, while dense vapors pour from every crevice. Water vapor is the main gaseous component, but nitrogen and sulphur dioxide are also important.

Layering
Most volcanoes have a history extending back thousands or even millions of years. Over this time the main cone has built up in many stratified layers, sometimes of contrasting types of lava. Each fresh eruption produces at least one additional layer.

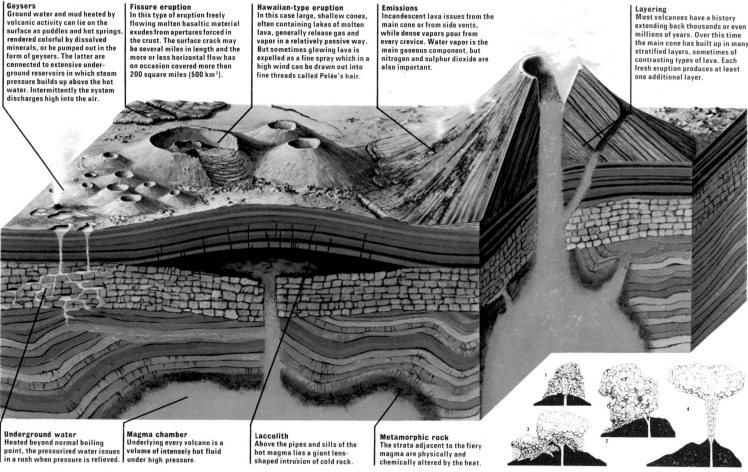

Underground water
Heated beyond normal boiling point, the pressurized water issues in a rush when pressure is relieved.

Magma chamber
Underlying every volcano is a volume of intensely hot fluid under high pressure.

Laccolith
Above the pipes and sills of the hot magma lies a giant lens-shaped intrusion of cold rock.

Metamorphic rock
The strata adjacent to the fiery magma are physically and chemically altered by the heat.

Where the Earth seems active *right*
Although we live on a white-hot globe with a thin cool crust, the fierce heat and energy of the interior is manifest only along fairly clearly defined belts. Around the Pacific, volcanoes and earthquakes are frequent. Another belt traverses the mountains from southeast Asia through the Middle East to the Mediterranean. Every site is an external expression of activity within the crust and upper mantle. The underlying cause is a slow flowing of the rocks of the mantle in response to changes in temperature and density.

• Volcanoes
◦ Earthquake foci

Types of eruption *above*
Volcanic cones differ in both shape and activity. The Strombolian (1) erupts every few minutes or hours; the Peléan form (2) gives a hot avalanche; the Vesuvian (3) is a fierce upward expulsion, while the Plinian (4) is the extreme form.

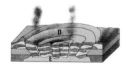

A caldera *left*
Expulsion of lava (A) from the magma chamber (B) may leave the central core (C) without support. A collapse results in a large, steep-sided caldera (D). The magma chamber may cool and solidify (E), and water may collect inside the caldera (F).

Earthquake *right*

Along lines of potential movement, such as fault planes, stresses may build up over many years until the breaking strength of some part of the rock is exceeded (A). A sudden break occurs and the two sides of the fault line move, generating shock-waves which travel outward in all directions from the focus at the point of rupture (B). The point on the surface directly above the focus is the epicenter (C). While the fault movement reaches its fullest extent, the shockwaves reach the surface (D). Far right the aftermath of an earthquake.

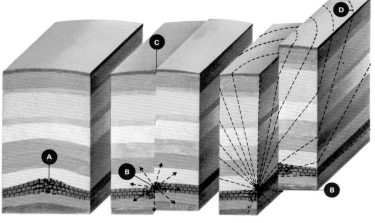

Destructive waves *right*

The Japanese, who have suffered severely from them, have given the name tsunami to the terrifying waves which follow earthquakes. Their character depends on the cause. In the case of a sudden rift and slump in the ocean bed (A) the wave at the surface is initially a trough, which travels away to both sides followed by a crest and subsequent smaller waves (B). A fault causing a sudden changed level of sea bed (C) can generate a tsunami that starts with a crest (D). Travelling at 400 miles (650 km) per hour or more the tsunami arrives at a beach as a series of waves up to 200 feet (60 m) high (E), the 'trough first' variety being heralded by a sudden withdrawal of the ocean from the shore. Warning stations ring the Pacific (far right) and the concentric rings show tsunamic travel time from an earthquake site to Hawaii at the center.

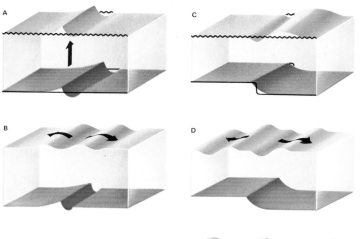

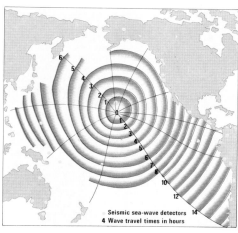

Seismic sea-wave detectors
4 Wave travel times in hours

Tsunami warning *above*

Numerous seismographic warning stations around the earthquake belt of the Pacific Ocean maintain a continuous alert for earthquake shocks and for the tsunami waves that may follow it. Possible recipients of such waves plot a series of concentric rings, such as these centered on the Hawaiian Islands, which show the time in hours that would be taken for a tsunami to travel from any earthquake epicenter. Aircraft and satellites are increasingly helping to create a globally integrated life-saving system.

Seismic waves *right*

An earthquake caused by a sudden movement in the crust at the focus (A) sends out a pattern of shock waves radiating like ripples in a pond. These waves are of three kinds. Primary (P) waves (full lines) vibrate in the direction of propagation, and thus are a rapid succession of high and low pressures. Secondary (S) waves (broken lines), which travel only 60 per cent as fast, shake from side to side. Long waves (L) travel round the crust. In a belt around the world only waves of the L-type occur, giving rise to the concept of a shadow zone (B and shaded belt in inset at lower right). But intermittent records of P waves in this zone led seismologists to the belief that the Earth must have a very dense fluid core (D, lower drawing) capable of strongly refracting P waves like a lens. Seismic waves are almost man's only source of knowledge about the Earth's interior.

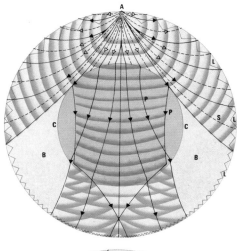

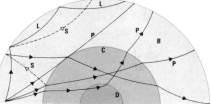

Seismology *right*

Seismic waves of all three types (P, S and L) are detected and recorded by seismographs. Usually these contain a sprung mass which, when an earthquake shock passes, stays still while the rest of the instrument moves. Some seismographs detect horizontal waves (A) while others detect vertical ones (B). The pen in the instrument leaves a distinctive trace (P-S-L). P (primary) waves are a succession of rarefactions and compressions, denoted by the packing of the dots; S (secondary) waves are a sideways shaking, shown here in plan view.

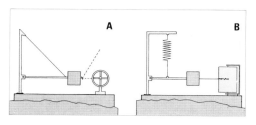

P. waves (longitudinal)

← Rarefaction → ← Compression →

Direction of travel

S. waves (transverse)

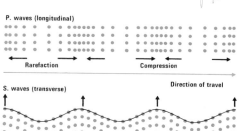

A fundamental mystery that still confronts science even today is the detailed internal structure of the planet on which we live. Although Jules Verne's intrepid 'Professor Otto Lindenbrock was able to journey to the center of the Earth, this is one scientific fantasy that will never be achieved. The deepest boreholes and mines do little more than scratch the surface and so, deprived of direct observation, the geologist is forced to rely almost entirely on indirect evidence to construct his picture of the Earth's anatomy. In spite of these drawbacks, he can outline with some confidence the story of the planet's development from the time of its formation as a separate body in space some 4550 million years ago.

Since that time the Earth has been continuously evolving. The crust, mantle and inner core developed during its first 1000 million years, but there is only scant evidence of how they did so. Probably the original homogenous mass then partly or completely melted, whereupon gravitational attraction caused the densest material to form a part-liquid, part-solid central core overlaid by the less dense mantle. The extremely thin outermost layer of 'scum' began to form at an early stage and as long ago as 3500 million years parts of it had reached almost their present state. But most of the crust evolved in a complex way through long-term cyclic changes spanning immense periods of time. The evidence of today's rocks can be interpreted in different ways; for example, the core, mantle and crust could have separated out quickly at an early stage or gradually over a longer period.

Today's restless Earth

Many of the changes which have taken place in the Earth's structure and form have been very gradual. For example, although it may well be that our planet has been getting larger (as illustrated below), the rate of increase in radius has been no more rapid than $2\frac{1}{2}$ inches (65 mm) per century. But this does not alter the fact that the Earth is very far from being a mere inert sphere of matter. Although it is not possible faithfully to portray it, almost the whole globe is at brilliant white heat. If the main drawing were true to life it would contain no color except for a thin band, about as thick as cardboard, around the outer crust in which the color would change from white through yellow and orange to red. With such high temperatures the interior of the Earth is able to flow under the influence of relatively small differences in density and stress. The result is to set up convection currents which are now believed to be the main driving force behind the formation of mountain ranges and the drifting apart of continents. But the fact remains that our knowledge of the interior of our planet is derived almost entirely from indirect evidence, such as the passage of earthquake shock waves through the mantle (page 13A). Direct exploration is confined to the surface and to boreholes which so far have never penetrated more than about five miles (8 km) into the crust. It is difficult to imagine how man could ever devise experiments that would greatly enhance and refine his knowledge of the Earth's interior. Indeed, he knows as much about the Moon and other much more distant heavenly bodies as he does about the Earth below a depth of a mere 20 miles (32 km).

The crust (A)
This varies in thickness from 20 miles (32 km) in continental regions, where it is largely granitic, to 5 miles (8 km) under the oceans, where it is basaltic.

The upper mantle (B, C)
From the crust down to 375 miles (600 km), this layer is divided into upper and lower zones with differing P wave speeds (see page 39).

The lower mantle (D¹, D²)
Made of peridotite, as is the upper mantle, this zone extends down to a depth of 1800 miles (2900 km). P wave speeds increase still further.

The outer core (E, F)
Largely iron and nickel, this molten zone reaches to 3200 miles (5120 km). Dynamo action of convection currents may cause the Earth's magnetic field.

Not a true sphere *below*
The Earth's shape is controlled by equilibrium between inward gravitational attraction and outward centrifugal force. This results in the average radius at the equator of 3963 miles (6378 km) slightly exceeding that at the poles of 3950 miles (6356 km).

An expanding Earth?
During its history the Earth may have gradually expanded. Some 4500 million years ago it may have been wholly covered with crust equal in area to today's continents. An intermediate stage with a radius of 2735 miles is suggested by the worn-down stumps of ancient mountain folds, while the symmetry of younger fold-mountains indicates that the radius when they were formed was approximately 3730 miles. If the shapes of the modern continents are preserved as nearly as possible they would fit a globe about 2600 miles in radius, which may be the size at which the crust was formed.

	A	B	C	D	E
Age Million years ago.	4500	3500	2800	600	present.
Size ratio	1.000	1.210	1.360	1.820	1.930
Radius in km.	3300	4000	4400	6000	6371

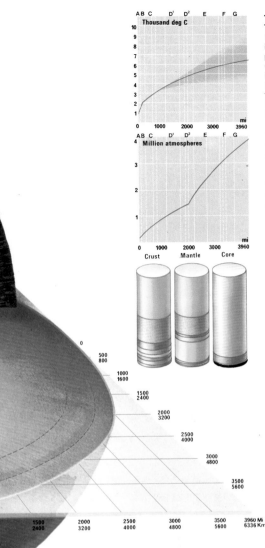

Temperature *left*
Temperature inside the Earth increases with depth, initially at a rate of 48°C per mile (30°C/km) so that 60 miles (100 km) down it is white hot. The rate of increase then falls, and the shaded area indicates how uncertain is man's knowledge of great depths.

Pressure *left*
This likewise increases with depth. Only 200 miles (320 km) down it reaches 100,000 atmospheres, 1200 times the pressure at the deepest point in the ocean. A change of state at the discontinuity between the mantle and core shows as a kink on the graph.

Crust   Mantle   Core

O₂	OXYGEN
Si	SILICON
Al	ALUMINUM
Fe	IRON
Ni	NICKEL
Co	COBALT
Mg	MAGNESIUM
Ca	CALCIUM
Na	SODIUM
K	POTASSIUM

Chemical composition *above*
The crust is made of mainly light elements and has relatively low density. Towards the base of the crust the composition is probably richer in iron and magnesium. The mantle is composed of heavier elements and the core is probably of iron and nickel.

Density *left*
Virtually all man's knowledge of the interior of the Earth stems from measuring the transit of earthquake waves. The resulting data indicate sharp increases in density at the boundaries of both the outer core and the 'solid' inner core, with several intermediate zones.

The inner core (G)
The pressure of 3½ million atmospheres (35000 kg/mm²) keeps this a solid ball of 800 miles (1300 km) radius. Its density varies from 14 to about 16.

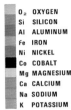

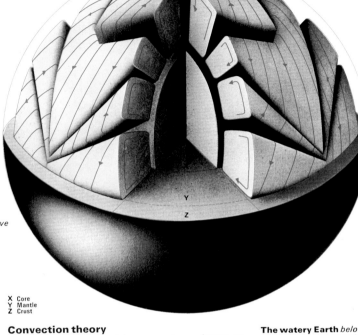

X Core
Y Mantle
Z Crust

Convection currents
The fundamental pattern of movement in the mantle (A) is modified by the Earth's rotation (B) and also by friction between adjacent cells as shown in the main figure, below, in which core (X) and mantle (Y) are shown but crust (Z) is removed.

Convection theory
Geologists and geophysicists are not unanimous on the question of whether there are convection currents present in the Earth's mantle or not, nor on the part these could play in providing the driving mechanism for major movements of the continents. Slow movement of 'solid' rocks can occur over long periods of time when the temperature is high and only relatively small density differences would be required to trigger them. Another matter for debate is whether convection is confined to the upper mantle or is continuous throughout the whole. It is not certain whether changes of physical state at different levels would constitute barriers to mantle-wide convection. The convection cells above are highly schematic but could largely explain the formation of some of the major geosynclinal fold mountains in the crust over the past thousand million years. Large-scale convection current systems in the mantle could also be the driving force for sea floor spreading and the associated continental drift.

The watery Earth *below*
Almost three-quarters of the Earth is covered by water. Basically the continents are rafts of relatively light crust 'floating' on generally denser oceanic crust. They comprise not only the visible land but also the adjacent continental shelves covered by shallow water. Oceanic crust underlies the deep sea platforms and ocean trenches. The areas of the major lands and seas (below, left) do not take into account the continental shelves but are the gross areas reckoned in terms of the land and water distribution at mean sea level. Extra area due to terrain is not included.

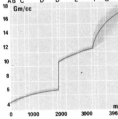

The watery Earth *right*
Key to numbered areas.

Oceans	Area (x 1000)	
	Sq mi	km²
1 Arctic	5541	14350
2 Pacific	63,800,000	165,200,000
3 Atlantic	31530	81660
4 Indian	28,356,000	73,441,700
Continents		
5 Americas	16,301,000	42,219,000
6 Europe (excluding USSR)	1903	4929
7 Asia (excluding USSR)	10661	27611
8 USSR	8649	22402
9 Africa	11,707,000	30,320,000
10 Oceania	3286	8510
11 Antarctica	5 100,000	13,209,000

Measured against the time standards of everyday life, the major forces that shape the face of the Earth seem to act almost unbelievably slowly. But in geological terms the erosion of rock formations by river, marine or ice action is in fact rather rapid. Indeed, in isolated locations, on coasts or below waterfalls, visible erosion can take place in a period of months or even days.

Over large regions of the Earth the rates of river erosion, expressed as the mass of material removed from each unit of land area in a given time, range between 34 and 6720 short tons per square mile per year (12–2354 metric tons/km²/year). The main factor determining the rate at any place is the climate. The average rate of erosion for Eurasia, Africa, the Americas and Australia, a land area of some 50 million sq. mi. (130 million km²), has been calculated to be about 392 short tons per sq. mi. per year (137 metric tons/km²/year). This corresponds to a general lowering of the surface of the land by about 40 inches (one meter) every 22000 years. At this rate these continents would be worn down to sea level in less than 20 million years, which in geological terms is a fairly short span of time.

In practice, the surface of the land would be most unlikely to suffer such a fate. Although isolated areas could be worn away, worldwide erosion on this scale and at a steady rate would be balanced or prevented by a number of factors, one of which is the continuing large-scale uplift of the land in other regions. Nevertheless long-term estimates do emphasize the cumulative effects of the apparently slow processes of erosion. Even man's own structures wear away. Already the portland stone of St. Paul's cathedral in London has lost half an inch (13 mm) overall in 250 years, aided by the additional force of atmospheric pollution.

Where do all the products of this erosion go? By far the largest accumulations of sediments occur in river deltas, and at many periods in the geological past great thicknesses of such deposits have been laid down in extensive subsiding troughs called geosynclines. A rate of deposition of 1/250 inch (0.1 millimeter) per year is enough to lay down 12 miles (20 km) of strata in 200 million years.

The cycle of rock change

The agents of weathering
Gross break-up of the Earth's surface rocks is caused by earthquakes, the ceaseless cycle of diurnal and annual heating and cooling, and by the freezing of water trapped in fissures and crevices. The water of the seas, rivers and rain dissolves some rocks and in others leaches out particular minerals. Water is especially powerful as a weathering agent when it contains dissolved acidic chemicals. Today's main sources are plants and animals (1), but in the primeval world such chemicals were evolved mainly by volcanoes (2).

Erosion of the land
Only the material exposed at the surface of the Earth by volcanic action (2) or uplift (3) is subjected to erosion, but this material is constantly changing. Chemical erosion is an extension of the weathering process, converting the surface material into different and usually physically degraded substances. Physical erosion (4) is effected by running water and the wind (in both cases accelerated by the presence of an abrasive load) and by ice action and frost shattering.

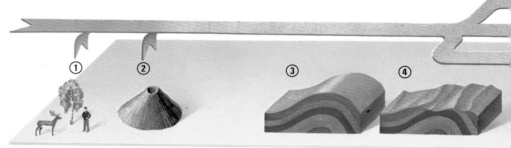

Extrusions
Most lavas are at a temperature of 900-1200°C. Acidic (granitic) lava is fairly viscous, but basic (basalt) lava flows relatively freely and when extruded from surface fissures or volcanoes can cover large areas (15). Lavas which have originated from partial melting of crustal rocks can also be erupted.

Basic magmas
Basic magma generated by partial melting in the mantle (14) may rise into and through the crust to be extruded from surface volcanoes. Basic magmas are the hottest, as well as the most freely flowing, and are often generated at very considerable depth. In their ascent they can intrude large areas of the crust and finally extrude through fissures in the surface.

Intrusions
Contact metamorphism is a form of baking and re-crystallization caused by the intrusion of hot magma into existing strata (13).

Granitic magmas
Partial melting deep in the crust generates new granitic magma—hot, rather viscous molten rock of an acidic nature which is able to migrate both upwards and laterally (12). This may then inject and mix with the surrounding rocks to form a migmatite complex.

Slow uplift
Strata can be slowly uplifted (11) until they once more appear at the surface; continued or violent uplift results in mountain-building. In either case, erosion begins afresh.

Deep metamorphism
If the strata are depressed far down, to depths up to about 25 miles (40 km), deep metamorphism at high pressures and high temperatures (10) results in complete re-crystallization. This gradually converts the original sediments into a complex of new rock types.

Erosion

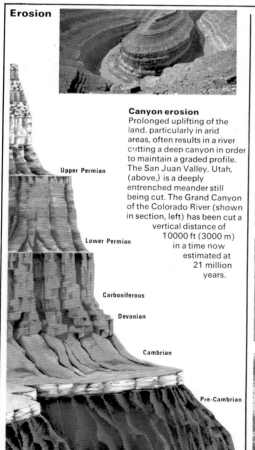

Canyon erosion
Prolonged uplifting of the land, particularly in arid areas, often results in a river cutting a deep canyon in order to maintain a graded profile. The San Juan Valley, Utah, (above,) is a deeply entrenched meander still being cut. The Grand Canyon of the Colorado River (shown in section, left) has been cut a vertical distance of 10000 ft (3000 m) in a time now estimated at 21 million years.

Upper Permian

Lower Permian

Carboniferous

Devonian

Cambrian

Pre-Cambrian

Wind erosion
Laden with grains of sand and other air-transportable debris, the wind exerts a powerful sculpturing effect. Rate of erosion varies with rock hardness, giving rise to odd effects (Mushroom Rock, Death Valley, California, left). Desert sand forms 'barchan' dunes (right), which slowly travel points-first.

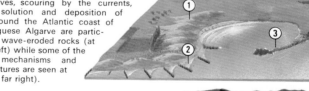

Sculpture by the sea
The ocean shapes the land by the pounding of the waves, scouring by the currents, chemical solution and deposition of debris. Around the Atlantic coast of the Portuguese Algarve are particularly fine wave-eroded rocks (at Piedade, left) while some of the principle mechanisms and coastal features are seen at right (key, far right).

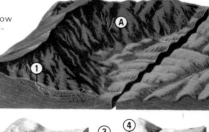

River development
The youthful river flows fast, eroding a narrow channel in an otherwise unchanged landscape. In maturity the channel is wider; flow is slower and some transported debris is deposited. The old river meanders across a broad flood plain (River Wye near Goodrich, left), some meanders becoming cut off as ox-bow lakes.

Glacial action
Briksdal Glacier, Norway (left), is a remnant of the Ice Ages, carving U-shaped valleys (2) in the pre-glacial rock (1). The bergschrund (3) forms close to the back wall, while other crevasses (4) form at gradient changes. Eroded rocks form a longitudinal moraine (5).

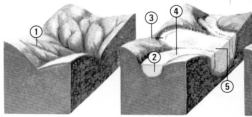

Transportation
As material is worn away from the surface rocks it is carried away by various processes. The most important transport system is flowing water (5), which can move sediments in suspension, in solution or carried along the beds of river channels. In open country, and especially over deserts, much solid debris is blown by the wind (6). Even slow-moving glaciers (7) perform a significant erosion and transport role by bearing heavy burdens of rock debris.

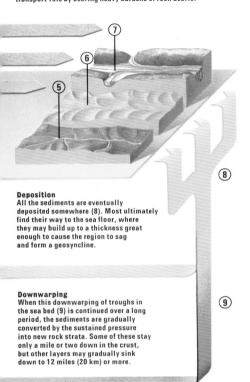

Deposition
All the sediments are eventually deposited somewhere (8). Most ultimately find their way to the sea floor, where they may build up to a thickness great enough to cause the region to sag and form a geosyncline.

Downwarping
When this downwarping of troughs in the sea bed (9) is continued over a long period, the sediments are gradually converted by the sustained pressure into new rock strata. Some of these stay only a mile or two down in the crust, but other layers may gradually sink down to 12 miles (20 km) or more.

250 million years ago
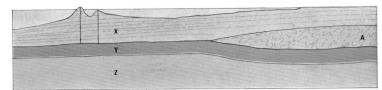

180 million years ago
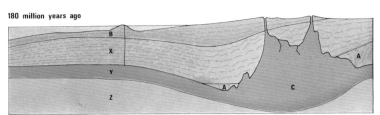

130 million years ago

Present day
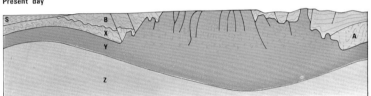

Late Paleozoic *left*
The formation of a geosyncline begins with the laying down of heavy sediments. In the creation of the Sierra Nevada range sediments X were deposited by the primeval ocean on top of Precambrian rock A, basalt crust Y and peridotite mantle Z.

Jurassic *left*
Downwarping of the crust causes the deposition of Mesozoic sediments B and carries the lower basalt crust and sediments into the zone of the mantle's influence. The bottom of the bulge is gradually converted into hot, fluid magma C.

Cretaceous *left*
In this period the geosynclinal process is in a mature stage. The inner rocks reach their maximum downward penetration into the mantle and are metamorphosed by high temperature and pressure. The deep metamorphism spreads (curved shading).

Present day *left*
Uplift and cooling opens the way to a new cycle of formation. The metamorphic rocks are exposed at the surface and subsequently eroded to yield today's complex landscape structure. Final withdrawal of the sea exposes marine sediments S.

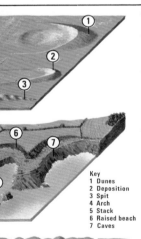
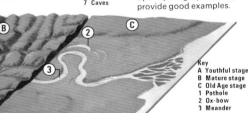

Wind-blown sand *left*
Sand deserts exhibit dunes of various forms. Unlike a barchan the parabolic blowout (1) travels with points trailing. In elongated form this becomes a parabolic hairpin (2), and a third form is the longitudinal ridge (3), known in the Sahara as a seif dune.

Emerging coastline *right*
Where the shoreline is rising, the continental shelf becomes exposed. River silt accumulates and forms an offshore bar, pierced by the river flow. Eventually infilling forms a tidal salt marsh through which the braided river reaches a new shore. Spain (far right) and Italy provide good examples.

Key
1 Dunes
2 Deposition
3 Spit
4 Arch
5 Stack
6 Raised beach
7 Caves

Key
A Youthful stage
B Mature stage
C Old Age stage
1 Pothole
2 Ox-bow
3 Meander

Glaciated landscape *left*
The landscape shows evidence of former ice coverage. Broken rock debris forms valley-floor moraines (6), the peaks are sharp and knife-edged (7), and hanging valleys (8) mark the entry of the glacier's tributaries. Terminal moraines (9) are a characteristic feature.

Key
A Initial stage
B Late youth
C Early maturity
1 Cut-off
2 Spit
3 4 Bars
5 Lagoon

Key
A Initial stage
B Bar development
C Emergence complete

Key
1 Esker
2 Recessional moraine
3 Drumlin
4 Lake
5 Terminal moraine
6 Outwash delta
7 Lake deposits
8 Kettle lake
9 Outwash plain
10 Kettle hole

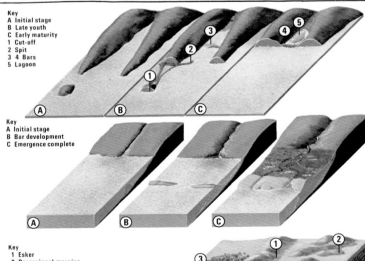
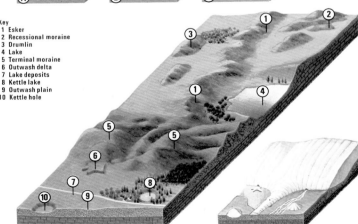

Subsiding coastline *left*
Most coastal regions undergoing submergence are highly irregular. Drowned hills are eroded by the waves to form cliff headlands, or cut-offs; spits and bars cross the submerged valleys, enclose them and form lagoons. Finally all these features wear back to a new shoreline.

Area previously sea
Mediterranean Sea
Neapolis
SPAIN

Glaciated landforms *left*
Throughout a vast area of the temperate lands evidence of past glacial action is abundant. A geomorphologist, studying the landscape shown in the larger illustration, would deduce the former glacial situation depicted in the inset. Weight and sculpture by the ice carved out characteristic depressions, some later filled with water. Subglacial streams left alluvial deposits in the form of eskers and an outwash fan or delta, while the limit of the glacier is suggested by rocks deposited as a terminal moraine. Kettle holes result from the melting of ice within moraine debris.

The Active Oceans

The surface of the oceans presents an infinite variety of contrasts ranging from glassy calm to terrifying storms with towering waves and wind-whipped wraiths of spray. But no part of the oceans is ever really still. Together the oceans comprise 300 million cubic miles (1250 million km³) of ever-active water. The whole mass ebbs and flows on a global scale with the tides. The surface is disturbed by winds into great patterns of waves which eventually break on the shores of the land. And the largest and most far-reaching movements of all are the ocean currents, some on or near the surface and others at great depths, which profoundly alter not only the oceans but also the weather.

Best known of all these currents is the Gulf Stream, which was discovered in late medieval times when early navigators found that their ships were consistently not in the place predicted by their calculations of course and estimated speed. Some 500 years ago it had become customary for Spanish captains voyaging to the New World to keep well south of the Gulf Stream on their outward journey and then use its swift four or five knot (8–9 km/hr) current to help them along on the return. The Gulf Stream brings mild weather to northwest Europe, and a corresponding role is played on the other side of the globe by the Kuroshio, a warm current which flows northeastward off Japan. Conversely, in the southeastern Pacific the Peru Current brings cold water from the sub-Antarctic region northward towards the equator. The surface flow is accompanied during most months of the year by an 'upwelling' of water rich in nutrients along the coast of Chile and Peru, and this, like many other cold currents elsewhere, supports great fisheries.

In coastal seas the water movements are often dominated by the currents that accompany the rise and fall of the tide. Because of the friction of the tides, the Moon is moving slowly further from the Earth.

Wave generation *right*
Waves are generated on the surface by the wind. Once a slight undulation has been formed it will react on the air flow so that an eddying motion, with a reduced pressure, is produced on the lee side (A) of each crest. Combined with the wind pressure on the windward side (B), this causes the waves to grow in height. The wave travels forward in the direction of the wind, but the individual water particles (X) move in almost closed orbits (C).

Internal motion *right*
On the surface of deep water these orbits are almost circular. Below the surface the radii of the orbits decrease with depth and become very small at a depth equal to half a wavelength. In shallow water the orbits are ellipses, becoming flatter towards the bottom.

Shore and rip currents *below*
In addition to its circular movement, each water particle slowly moves in the direction of propagation. When waves approach a coast water tends to pile up at the shoreline. This leads to a return flow seaward (X) which is concentrated in narrow, fast-flowing rip currents (Y). Beyond the breaker zone these spread out into a head and gradually disperse (Z).

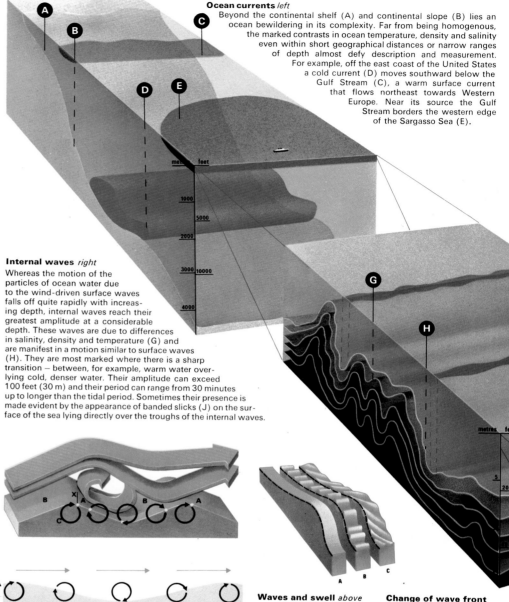

Ocean currents *left*
Beyond the continental shelf (A) and continental slope (B) lies an ocean bewildering in its complexity. Far from being homogenous, the marked contrasts in ocean temperature, density and salinity even within short geographical distances or narrow ranges of depth almost defy description and measurement. For example, off the east coast of the United States a cold current (D) moves southward below the Gulf Stream (C), a warm surface current that flows northeast towards Western Europe. Near its source the Gulf Stream borders the western edge of the Sargasso Sea (E).

Internal waves *right*
Whereas the motion of the particles of ocean water due to the wind-driven surface waves falls off quite rapidly with increasing depth, internal waves reach their greatest amplitude at a considerable depth. These waves are due to differences in salinity, density and temperature (G) and are manifest in a motion similar to surface waves (H). They are most marked where there is a sharp transition — between, for example, warm water overlying cold, denser water. Their amplitude can exceed 100 feet (30 m) and their period can range from 30 minutes up to longer than the tidal period. Sometimes their presence is made evident by the appearance of banded slicks (J) on the surface of the sea lying directly over the troughs of the internal waves.

Waves and swell *above*
Ocean swell (A) is invariably present and travels hundreds of miles. On it the wind can superimpose small waves (B), which die out relatively rapidly. These smaller waves may be at any angle to the original swell (C).

Change of wave front *left, below*
When waves from the open sea pass into a region of shallow water where the depth is less than about half a wavelength their forward velocity is progressively reduced. One consequence of this is that the wave fronts are refracted so that they turn towards the shallower water, and the wave crests tend to line up parallel to the shore. In the diagram X-X is the original frontal axis of the waves coming in from the ocean. When the depth of water varies along a coast, waves tend to become focused on the shallower areas (Y) and to diverge from the deeper ones such as the head of a submarine valley or canyon (Z). For the same reason large waves can often be seen breaking on a headland while the breakers in an area of originally deeper water, leading to a bay, are relatively much smaller.

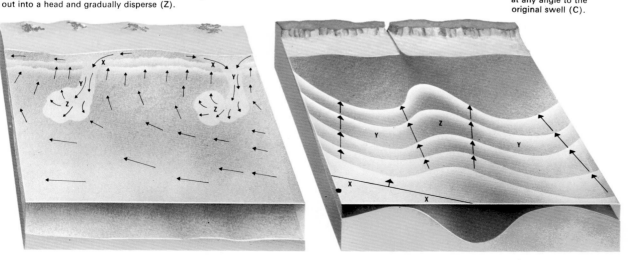

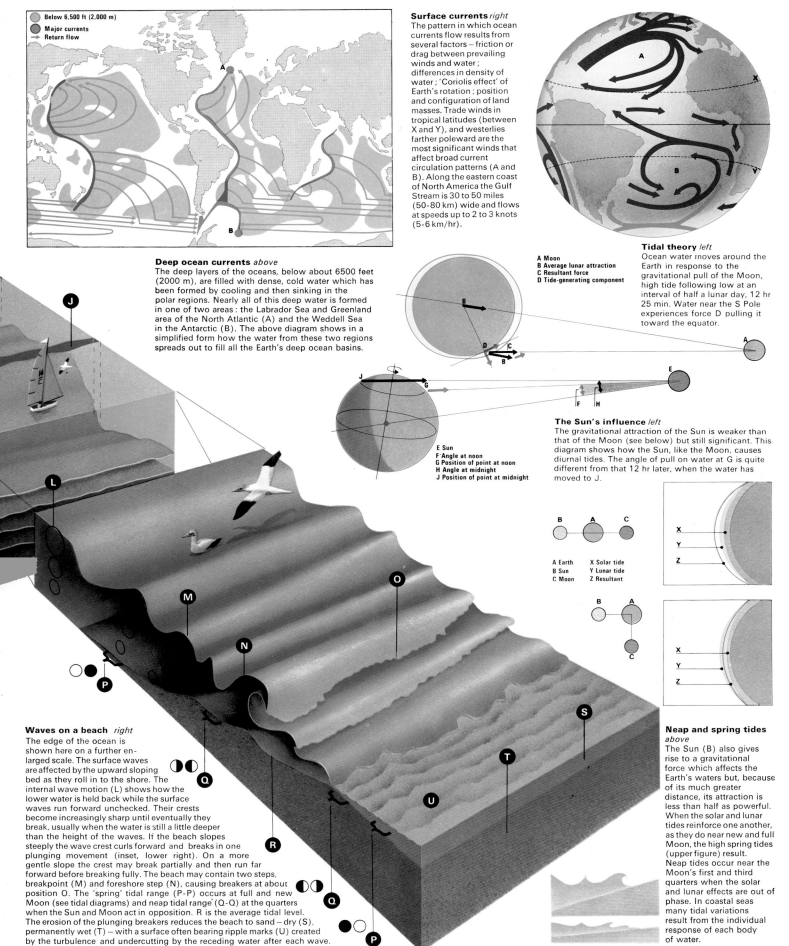

Below 6,500 ft (2,000 m)
Major currents
Return flow

Surface currents *right*
The pattern in which ocean currents flow results from several factors – friction or drag between prevailing winds and water; differences in density of water; 'Coriolis effect' of Earth's rotation; position and configuration of land masses. Trade winds in tropical latitudes (between X and Y), and westerlies farther poleward are the most significant winds that affect broad current circulation patterns (A and B). Along the eastern coast of North America the Gulf Stream is 30 to 50 miles (50-80 km) wide and flows at speeds up to 2 to 3 knots (5-6 km/hr).

Deep ocean currents *above*
The deep layers of the oceans, below about 6500 feet (2000 m), are filled with dense, cold water which has been formed by cooling and then sinking in the polar regions. Nearly all of this deep water is formed in one of two areas: the Labrador Sea and Greenland area of the North Atlantic (A) and the Weddell Sea in the Antarctic (B). The above diagram shows in a simplified form how the water from these two regions spreads out to fill all the Earth's deep ocean basins.

A Moon
B Average lunar attraction
C Resultant force
D Tide-generating component

Tidal theory *left*
Ocean water moves around the Earth in response to the gravitational pull of the Moon, high tide following low at an interval of half a lunar day, 12 hr 25 min. Water near the S Pole experiences force D pulling it toward the equator.

E Sun
F Angle at noon
G Position of point at noon
H Angle at midnight
J Position of point at midnight

The Sun's influence *left*
The gravitational attraction of the Sun is weaker than that of the Moon (see below) but still significant. This diagram shows how the Sun, like the Moon, causes diurnal tides. The angle of pull on water at G is quite different from that 12 hr later, when the water has moved to J.

A Earth   X Solar tide
B Sun   Y Lunar tide
C Moon   Z Resultant

Waves on a beach *right*
The edge of the ocean is shown here on a further enlarged scale. The surface waves are affected by the upward sloping bed as they roll in to the shore. The internal wave motion (L) shows how the lower water is held back while the surface waves run forward unchecked. Their crests become increasingly sharp until eventually they break, usually when the water is still a little deeper than the height of the waves. If the beach slopes steeply the wave crest curls forward and breaks in one plunging movement (inset, lower right). On a more gentle slope the crest may break partially and then run far forward before breaking fully. The beach may contain two steps, breakpoint (M) and foreshore step (N), causing breakers at about position O. The 'spring' tidal range (P-P) occurs at full and new Moon (see tidal diagrams) and neap tidal range' (Q-Q) at the quarters when the Sun and Moon act in opposition. R is the average tidal level. The erosion of the plunging breakers reduces the beach to sand – dry (S), permanently wet (T) – with a surface often bearing ripple marks (U) created by the turbulence and undercutting by the receding water after each wave.

Neap and spring tides *above*
The Sun (B) also gives rise to a gravitational force which affects the Earth's waters but, because of its much greater distance, its attraction is less than half as powerful. When the solar and lunar tides reinforce one another, as they do near new and full Moon, the high spring tides (upper figure) result. Neap tides occur near the Moon's first and third quarters when the solar and lunar effects are out of phase. In coastal seas many tidal variations result from the individual response of each body of water.

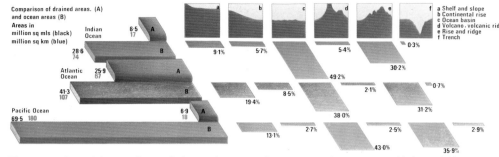

Comparison of drained areas. (A) and ocean areas (B)
Areas in
million sq mls (black)
million sq km (blue)

Indian Ocean	6·5 / 17	A
	28·6 / 74	B
Atlantic Ocean	25·9 / 67	A
	41·3 / 107	B
Pacific Ocean	6·9 / 18	A
69·5 / 180		B

a Shelf and slope
b Continental rise
c Ocean basin
d Volcano. volcanic ridge
e Rise and ridge
f Trench

a
9·1%
b
5·7%
c
5·4%
d
0·3%
e
30·2%
f

49·2%
8·5%
2·1%
0·7%
19·4%
38·0%
31·2%
13·1%
2·7%
2·5%
2·9%
43·0%
35·9%

The water planet *left*
From directly over Tahiti the Earth appears to be covered by water. The Pacific averages 2.5 miles (4 km) deep, with great mountains and trenches.

Ocean drainage *above*
The ratio between the areas of the oceans and the land they drain varies greatly. Many large rivers feed the Atlantic but few discharge into the Pacific.

Ocean proportions *above*
The major oceans show a similarity in the proportions of their submarine topography. By far the greatest areas contain deep plains with rises and ridges. More prominent features, the mid-ocean volcanic ridges and trenches, occupy much smaller areas. About one tenth of each ocean is continental shelf.

At present the sea covers about 71 per cent of the Earth's surface. But if the continents could be sliced away and put into the deep oceans to make a perfectly uniform sphere the sea would have an average depth of about 8000 feet (2500 m) over the whole planet. In the distant past the level of the sea has fluctuated violently. The main cause has been the comings and goings of the ice ages. Glaciers and ice-caps lock up enormous volumes of water and the advance and recession of ice has alternately covered the continental shelves with shallow seas and revealed them as dry land. If the Earth's present polar ice-caps and glaciers were to melt, the mean sea level would rise by about 200 feet (60 m), which would submerge half the world's population. Average depth of the sea is more than 12000 feet (3600 m), five times the average height of the land above sea level.

The deep oceans

Below the level of the continental shelf lies the deep ocean floor with great topographical contrasts ranging from abyssal plains at a depth of about 13000 feet (4 km) to towering submarine mountain ranges of the mid-ocean ridges which reach far up toward the surface. Great advances have recently been made in exploring the ocean floors which were previously unknown. Most of the ocean area is abyssal plain which extends over about 78 million square miles (200 million km²). But a more remarkable feature of the deep ocean is the almost continuous mid-ocean mountain range which sweeps 40000 miles (64000 km) around the globe and occasionally – as at Iceland – is seen above sea level in the form of isolated volcanic islands. The basic symmetry of the oceans is the central ridge flanked by abyssal plain sloping up to the continental shelves. On the deep floor sediments accumulate at a rate of 30–35 feet (10 m) per million years; they also build up more slowly at the central ridges. No ocean sediments have been found older than 150 million years, which suggests that the material which now makes up the floors of the deep oceans was formed comparatively recently. Exploration and detailed mapping of the ocean bed is still in its infancy.

Submarine landscape

Principal features of the bed of the oceans can be grouped into a much smaller space than they would actually occupy. Although each ocean differs in detail, all tend to conform to the general layout of a central volcanic ridge (which can break the surface in places), broad abyssal plains with occasional deep trenches and shallow slopes and shelves bordering the continents.

Submarine relief *below*
The bottom of the sea is very far from being flat. If the ocean waters were removed a new landscape would become visible, with immense relief features.

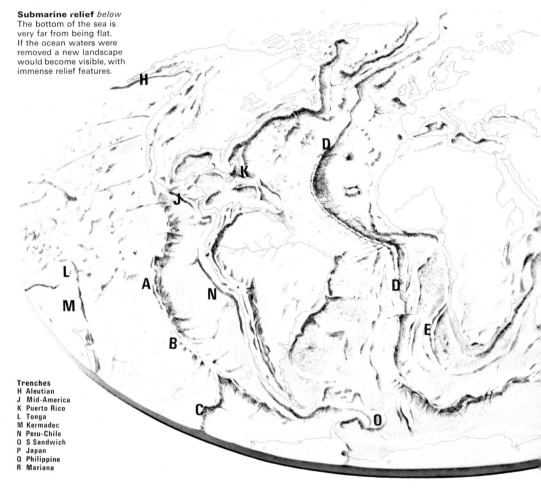

Trenches
H Aleutian
J Mid-America
K Puerto Rico
L Tonga
M Kermadec
N Peru-Chile
O S Sandwich
P Japan
Q Philippine
R Mariana

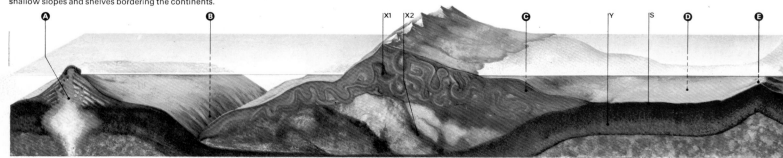

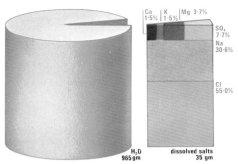

Composition of sea-water *above*
The water of the Earth's oceans is an exceedingly complex solution of many organic and inorganic salts, together with suspended solid matter. In a typical kilogram of sea-water there are 35 grams of chlorine, sodium, sulphates, magnesium, potassium and calcium.

Ca 1·5% K 1·5% Mg 3·7%
SO₄ 7·7%
Na 30·6%
Cl 55·0%

H₂O 965 gm   dissolved salts 35 gm

Rises and Ridges
A E Pacific
B SE Pacific
C Pacific-Antarctic
D Mid-Atlantic
E Walvis
F Indian Ocean
G SE Indian

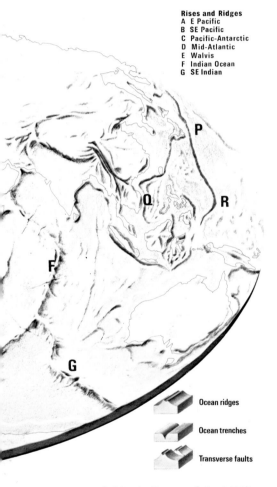

P
Q   R
F
G

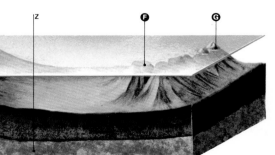

Ocean ridges

Ocean trenches

Transverse faults

A Volcano in mid-ocean ridge
B Deep oceanic trench
C Continental shelf
D Abyssal plain
E Mid-ocean ridge
F Guyots
G Oceanic islands
X1 Upper granitic crust and sediments
X2 Lower granitic crust
Y Basaltic crust
Z Mantle

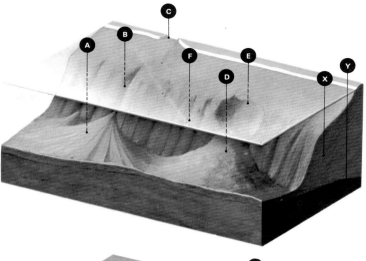

Continental shelf *left*
The submerged continental fringes lie at depths to about 450 feet (135 m) and have a total area of some 11 million square miles (28 million km²). The surface of the land is eroded and carried by rivers to form sedimentary deposits on the shelf. At its outer margin it slopes down to the abyssal plains of the deep ocean at about 2½ miles (4 km) below sea level.

A Scree fan
B Gully opposite river
C River delta
D Slump (turbidite) mass
E Scar left by (D)
F Continental slope
X Granite
Y Basalt

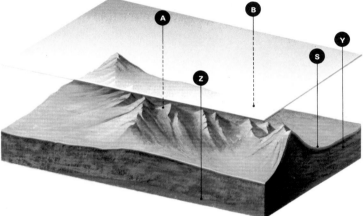

Mid-ocean ridge *left*
Well-marked ridges are found along the centers of the major oceans and form an extensive worldwide system. The central part of the ridge may have a double crest with an intervening deep trough forming a rift valley, or there may be several ridges. They are volcanic in nature and along them is generated new basaltic ocean crust. The volcanoes become progressively younger as the mid-ocean ridge is approached.

A Mid-ocean ridge
B Abyssal plain
S Ocean floor sediments
Y Basalt crust
Z Mantle

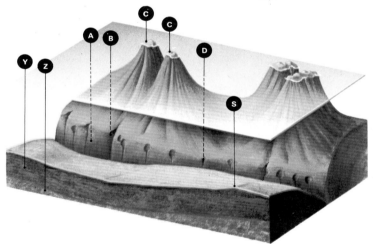

Oceanic trench *left*
These long and relatively narrow depressions are the deepest portions of the oceans, averaging over 30,000 feet (10 km) below sea level. Around the Pacific they lie close to the continental margins and in the western Pacific are often associated with chains of volcanic islands. Some trenches are slowly becoming narrower as the ocean floor plates on either side converge.

A Trench wall
B Canyon
C Island arc
D Trench
S Sediment
Y Basalt
Z Mantle

A sinking island *below*
A pre-requisite to the formation of a coral atoll is an island that is becoming submerged by the sea. Such islands are formed by the peaks of the volcanic mountains which are found on the flanks of the great mid-oceanic ridges.

Coral grows *below*
Millions of polyps, small marine animals, secrete a substance which forms the hard and often beautiful coral. The structure grows round the island in shallow water and extends above the sinking island to form an enclosed and shallow salt-water lagoon.

The mature atoll *below*
Continued submergence of the volcano results in the disappearance of the original island, but the upward growth of the coral continues unabated. The reef is then worn away by the sea and the coral debris fills in the central part of the lagoon.

A guyot *below*
Eventually the coral atoll itself begins to sink beneath the ocean surface. By this time the lagoon is likely to have become completely filled in by debris eroded from the reef, and the result is a submerged flat island, known as a guyot.

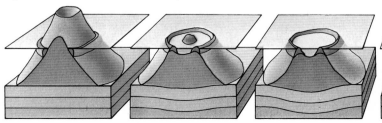

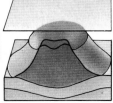

The Evolution of Land and Sea

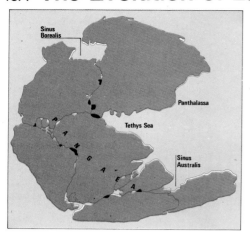

Pangaea *above*
About 200 million years ago there was only a single land mass on Earth, named Pangaea. The map shows how today's continents can be fitted together, with the aid of a computer, at the edge of the continental shelf at a depth of 1000 fathoms (6000 ft, 1830 m).

Although land and water first appeared on the Earth's surface several thousand million years before anyone could be there to watch, modern man has a very good idea of how it came about. The Earth's gravitational field caused the lighter, more volatile elements gradually to move outwards through the mantle and form a solid crust on the surface. By far the largest proportion of material newly added to the crust is basaltic volcanic rock derived from partial melting of the mantle beneath; in fact the oceanic crust which underlies the Earth's great water areas is made of almost nothing else. So the earliest crust to form was probably volcanic and of basaltic composition.

Air and water appear

The earliest records of the existence of an atmosphere of air and a hydrosphere of water are to be found in sediments laid down some 3300 million years ago from the residue of erosion of previously existing rocks. These sediments could not have been formed without atmospheric weathering, water transport and water deposition. The atmosphere was probably originally similar to the fumes which today issue from volcanoes and hot springs and which are about three-quarters water vapor. Once formed, the primitive atmosphere and oceans could erode the crust to produce vast layers of sediments of new chemical compositions. Gradually the oceans deepened and the land took on a more varied form. Convection in the mantle produced mountain ranges which in turn eroded to generate new sedimentary rocks. The ceaseless cycles of growth and decay had started, causing continually changing patterns of seas, mountains and plains. And in the past few years man has discovered how the continents and oceans have developed over the most recent 200 million years of geological time. The results of this research are to be seen in the maps on this page.

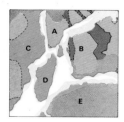

Another arrangement *left*
India (A) may have been separated by Australia (B) from East Antarctica (E) more than 200 million years ago on the evidence of today's geological deposition zones. Africa (C) and Madagascar (D) complete this convincing fit.

Migrant Australia *left*
By measuring the direction of magnetization of old Australian rocks it is possible to trace successive positions of that continent with respect to the Earth's magnetic pole. It appears to have moved across the world and back during the past 1000 million years.

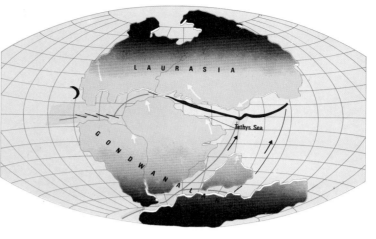

180 million years ago
At this time the original Pangaea land mass had just begun to break up. The continents first split along the lines of the North Atlantic and Indian Oceans. North America separated from Africa and so did India and Antarctica. The Tethys Sea, between Africa and Asia, closed somewhat, and the super continents of Laurasia to the north and Gondwanaland to the south became almost completely separated. In effect the Earth possessed three super landmasses, plus an India that had already begun to move strongly northward.

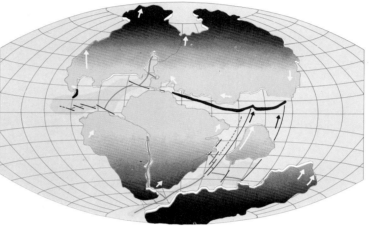

135 million years ago
After a further 45 million years of drifting, the world map had still not taken on a form that looks familiar today. But the two original splits, the North Atlantic and the Indian Ocean, have continued to open out. The North Atlantic is now about 600—650 miles (1000 km) wide. Rifting is extending towards the split which opened up the Labrador Sea and this will eventually separate Greenland from North America. India has firmly launched itself on its collision course with the southern coast of Asia, which is still 2000 miles (3200 km) away.

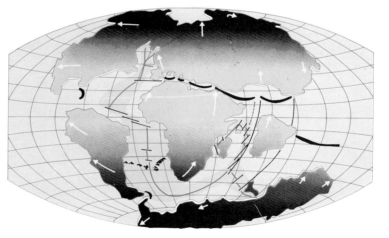

65 million years ago
Some 135 million years after the start of the drifting process the continents have begun to assume their present configuration. South America has at last separated from Africa and in Gondwanaland only Australia and Antarctica have yet to move apart. A continuation of the North Atlantic rifting will shortly bring about another big separation in Laurasia. Greenland will move apart from Europe and eventually North America will separate completely from the Eurasian landmass. The pink area (below) shows the extent of the crustal movements.

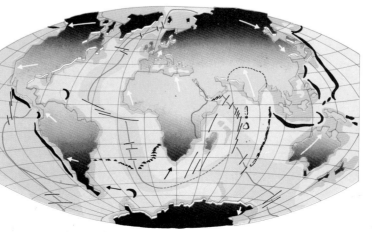

Today's positions
The Atlantic is now a wide ocean from Arctic to Antarctic, the Americas have joined and Australia has separated from Antarctica and moved far to the north. India has likewise moved northwards and its collision with Asia and continued movement has given rise to the extensive uplift of the Himalayas. All the continents which formerly made up the great land mass of Pangaea are now separated by wide oceans. Comparison of areas shows how much of India has been submerged by sliding underneath the crust of Asia (see facing page, far right).

Plate tectonics

This theory has revolutionized the way the Earth's crust – continents and oceans – is interpreted on a global scale. The crust is regarded as being made up of huge plates which converge or diverge along margins marked by earthquakes, volcanoes and other seismic activity. Major divergent margins are the mid-ocean ridges where molten lava forces its way upward and escapes. This causes vast regions of crust to move apart at a rate of an inch or two (some centimeters) per year. When sustained for up to 200 million years this means movements of thousands of miles or kilometers. The process can be seen in operation today in and around Iceland. Oceanic trenches are margins where the plates are moving together and the crust is consumed downward. The overall result is for the crustal plates to move as relatively rigid entities, carrying the continents along with them as if they were on a giant conveyor belt. Over further considerable periods of geologic time this will markedly change today's maps.

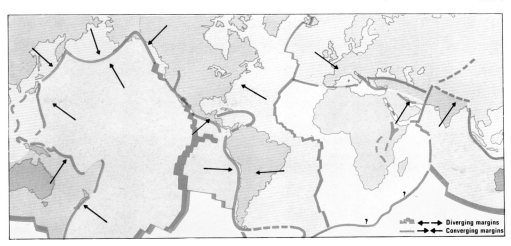

Diverging margins
Converging margins

Sea-floor spreading *left*
Arrows show how the lava flows on the ocean bed spread out on each side of a mid-ocean ridge. Evidence for such movement is provided by the fact the rock is alternately magnetized in opposing directions (coloured stripes).

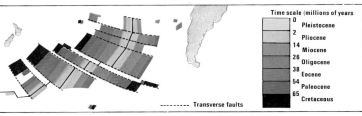

Time scale (millions of years

0	Pleistocene
2	Pliocene
14	Miocene
26	Oligocene
38	Eocene
54	Paleocene
65	Cretaceous

- - - - - - Transverse faults

Plate movements
above and left
The Earth's crust is a series of large plates 'floating' on the fluid mantle. At their edges the plates are either growing or disappearing. Magnetic measurements in the S. Pacific (left) show rock ages on each side of the mid-ocean ridges.

Plate movements in cross-section *above*
The basic mechanism of plate movements is illustrated above in simplified form with the vertical scale greatly exaggerated. This figure is explained in detail in both of the captions below.

Crustal divergence
above and right
The Earth's crust (1) behaves as a series of rigid plates which move on top of the fluid mantle (2). At their mating edges some of these plates are moving apart (3). This was the mechanism that separated North America (A) from Europe (B). The plates moved to the north and also away from each other under the influence of convection currents in the mantle (C). Between the land areas appeared an oceanic gap with a mid-ocean ridge (D) and lateral ridges (E). The movements continued for some 200 million years, fresh volcanoes being generated by igneous material escaping through the plate joint (F) to add to the lateral ridges which today cross the Atlantic (G). The volcanoes closest to the median line in mid-Atlantic are still young and active — whereas those nearer to the continents are old and extinct.

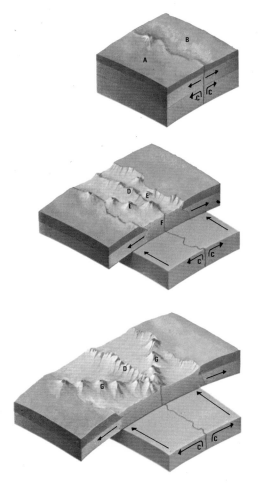

Crustal convergence
above and right
Diverging plate margins occur only in the centers of the major oceans (see map above) but plates are converging on both sea and land. Where an oceanic plate (4, above) is under-riding a continental plate (5) a deep ocean trench is the result (6). Such trenches extend around much of the Pacific; those around the northwest Pacific include the deepest on Earth where the sea bed is almost seven miles below the ocean surface. The continental margin is squeezed upward to form mountains such as the Andes or Rockies (7). If continental masses converge, such as India (A, right) and Asia (B), the convection in the mantle (C) pulls the plates together so hard that the upper crust crumples (D). Sedimentary deposits between the plates (E) are crushed and squeezed out upward (F), while the mantle on each side is turned downward, one side being forced under the other (G). Continued movement causes gross deformation at the point of collision. The static or slow-moving crust is crushed and tilted, and giant young mountains (the Himalayas, H) are thrust upward along the collision just behind the edge of the crumpled plate.

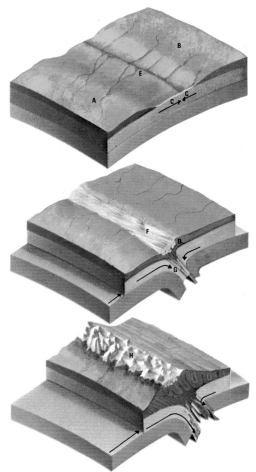

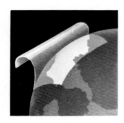

A thin coating *left*
The protective atmospheric shell around the Earth is proportionally no thicker than the skin of an apple. Gravity compresses the air so that half its mass lies within 3.5 miles (5.5 km) of the surface and all the weather within an average depth of 12 miles (20 km).

Space exploration has enabled man to stand back and take a fresh look at his Earth. Even though we, like all Earth life, have evolved to suit the Earth environment, we can see today as never before how miraculous that environment is. And by far the most important single factor in determining that environment is the atmosphere.

The Earth orbits round the Sun in a near-total vacuum. So rarefied is the interplanetary medium that it contains little heat energy, but the gas molecules that are present are vibrating so violently that their individual temperature is over 2000°C. And the surface of the Sun, at some 6000°C, would melt almost everything on the surface of the Earth, while the tenuous chromosphere around the Sun is as hot as 1,000,000°C. From the chromosphere, and from millions of other stars and heavenly objects, come radio waves. Various places in the universe, most of them far beyond the solar system, send us a penetrating kind of radiation known as cosmic rays. The Earth also receives gamma rays, X-rays and ultraviolet radiation, and from the asteroid belt in the solar system (see page 3A) comes a stream of solid material. Most of these are small micrometeorites, no more than flying specks, but the Earth also receives meteors and meteorites.

A meteorite is a substantial mass that strikes the Earth; fortunately, none has yet hit in a populous area. Apart from these extremely rare objects, every other influence from the environment that would be dangerous to life is filtered out by the atmosphere. Meteors burn up through friction as they plunge into the upper parts of the atmosphere. To avoid burning up in the same way, spacecraft designed to return to the Earth from lunar or interplanetary flight require a special re-entry shield.

Much of the ultraviolet radiation is arrested many miles above the Earth and creates ionized layers known as the ionosphere which man uses to reflect radio waves. Much of the infra-red (heat) radiation is likewise absorbed, lower down in the atmosphere, and most of the cosmic radiation is broken up by collisions far above the ground into such particles as 'mu-mesons'. Only a few cosmic rays, harmless radio waves and visible light penetrate the blanket of air to reach the planetary surface and its teeming life.

Credit for our vital atmosphere rests with the Earth's gravitational attraction, which both prevents the molecules and atoms in the atmosphere from escaping into space and also pulls them down tightly against the Earth. As a result nearly all the atmosphere's mass is concentrated in a very thin layer; three-quarters of it lies below 29000 feet (8840 m), the height of Mount Everest. The highest-flying aircraft, 19 miles (30 km) up, are above 99 per cent of the atmosphere. The total weight of the atmosphere is of the order of 5000 million million tons. In the lower parts are some 17 million million tons of water vapor.

The water vapor plays a great part in determining the weather on Earth, the only way in which the atmosphere consciously affects daily human life. All the weather is confined to the lower parts of the atmosphere below the tropopause. In this region, temperature falls away sharply with increasing altitude. The Sun heats up the Earth's surface, water is evaporated from the surface of the oceans and an immensely complicated pattern of global and local weather systems is set up. Every part of the air in the troposphere is in motion. Sometimes the motion is so slow as to be barely perceptible, while on other occasions, or at the same time in other places, the air roars over the surface with terrifying force at speeds of 200 miles (320 km) per hour or more. It erodes the land, lashes the surface with rain and clogs cold regions with snow. Yet it is man's shield against dangers, an ocean of air without which we could not exist.

Characteristics of the atmosphere *right*
Basically the Earth's atmosphere consists of a layer of mixed gases covering the surface of the globe which, as a result of the Earth's gravitational attraction, increases in density as the surface is approached. But there is very much more to it than this. Temperature, composition and physical properties vary greatly through the depth of the atmosphere. The Earth's surface is assumed to lie along the bottom of the illustration, and the various major regions of the atmosphere—which imperceptibly merge into each other—are indicated by the numbers on the vertical scale on the facing page.

Exosphere (1)
This rarefied region is taken to start at a height of some 400 miles (650 km) and to merge above into the interplanetary medium. Atomic oxygen exists up to 600 mi (1000 km); from there up to about 1500 mi (2400 km) helium and hydrogen are approximately equally abundant, with hydrogen becoming dominant above 1500 mi. The highest auroras are found in this region. Traces of the exosphere extend out to at least 5000 mi (8000 km).

Ionosphere (2)
This contains electrically conducting layers capable of reflecting radio waves and thus of enabling radio signals to be received over great distances across the Earth. The major reflecting layers, designated D, E, F1 and F2, are at the approximate heights shown. Meteors burn up brightly at heights of around 100 mi (160 km). Charged particles coming in along the lines of force of the Earth's magnetic field produce aurorae in the ionosphere at high latitudes, some of them of the corona type with a series of radial rays; and the ionosphere's structure alters from day to night and according to the influence of the solar wind and incoming streams of other particles and radiation.

Stratosphere (3)
This lies above the tropopause which varies in altitude from about 10 mi (16 km) over the equator to just below 7 mi (11 km) in temperate latitudes. The lower stratosphere has a constant temperature of −56°C up to 19 mi (30 km); higher still the 'mesosphere' becomes warmer again. One of the vital properties of the stratosphere is its minute ozone content which shields the Earth life from some harmful short-wave radiations which, before the Earth's atmosphere had developed, penetrated to the surface.

Troposphere (4)
Within this relatively very shallow layer is concentrated about 80 per cent of the total mass of the atmosphere, as well as all the weather and all the Earth's life. The upper boundary of the troposphere is the tropopause, which is about 36000 ft (11000 m) above the surface in temperate latitudes; over the tropics it is higher, and therefore colder, while it is at a lower altitude over the poles. Air temperature falls uniformly with increasing height until the tropopause is reached; thereafter it remains constant in the stratosphere. Composition of the troposphere is essentially constant, apart from the vital factor of clouds and humidity.

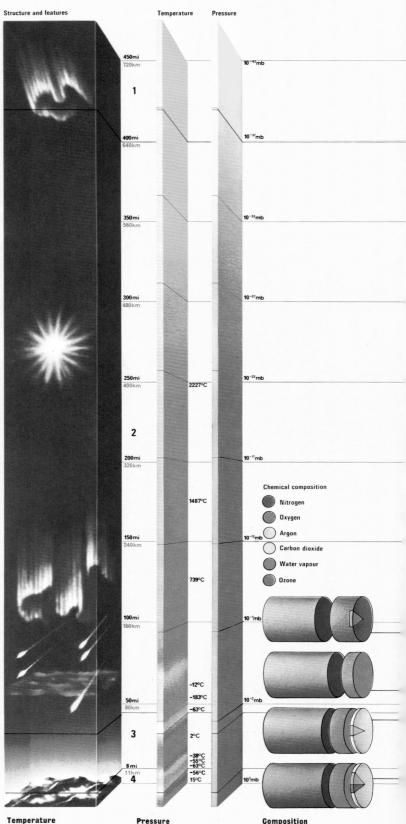

Structure and features

Temperature Pressure

450 mi / 720 km		10^{-42} mb
1		
400 mi / 640 km		10^{-37} mb
350 mi / 560 km		10^{-32} mb
300 mi / 480 km		10^{-27} mb
250 mi / 400 km	2227°C	10^{-22} mb
2		
200 mi / 320 km		10^{-17} mb
	1487°C	
150 mi / 240 km	739°C	10^{-12} mb
100 mi / 160 km		10^{-7} mb
	−12°C	
50 mi / 80 km	−183°C	10^{-2} mb
	−63°C	
3	2°C	
8 mi / 11 km	−38°C / −55°C / −63°C	
4	−56°C / 15°C	10^3 mb

Chemical composition
- Nitrogen
- Oxygen
- Argon
- Carbon dioxide
- Water vapour
- Ozone

Temperature
The mean temperature at the Earth's surface is about 15°C. As height is gained the temperature falls swiftly, to −56°C at the tropopause. It remains at this value to 19 miles (30 km), becomes warmer again, and then falls to a very low value around 60 miles (100 km). It rises once again in space.

Pressure
At sea level the pressure is some 1000 millibars, or about 14.7 pounds per square inch. The total force acting on the surface of an adult human body is thus of the order of 20 tons. But only 10 miles (16 km) above the Earth the pressure, and the atmospheric density, have both fallen by some 90 per cent.

Composition
Chemical composition of the atmosphere varies considerably with altitude. In the troposphere the mixture of nitrogen, oxygen and other gases is supplemented by water vapor, which exerts a profound influence on the weather. Ozone in the stratosphere shields life from harmful ultraviolet rays.

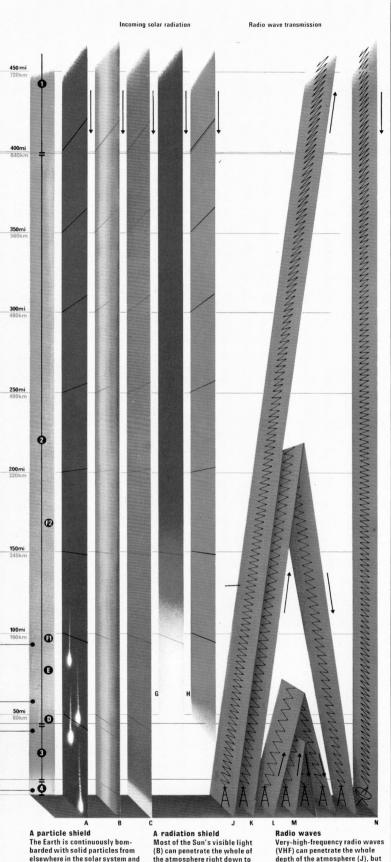

Incoming solar radiation   Radio wave transmission

450 mi / 720 km
400 mi / 640 km
350 mi / 560 km
300 mi / 480 km
250 mi / 400 km
200 mi / 320 km
150 mi / 240 km
100 mi / 160 km
50 mi / 80 km

A particle shield
The Earth is continuously bombarded with solid particles from elsewhere in the solar system and possibly from more distant parts of the universe. Only the largest meteors (A) reach the surface. Small meteorites generally burn up through friction caused by passage through the thin air more than 40 miles (65 km) up.

A radiation shield
Most of the Sun's visible light (B) can penetrate the whole of the atmosphere right down to the Earth's surface, except where cloud intervenes. But only some of the infra-red radiation gets through (C); the rest (G) is cut off, along with the harmful ultraviolet radiation (H), by atmospheric gases.

Radio waves
Very-high-frequency radio waves (VHF) can penetrate the whole depth of the atmosphere (J), but short-wave transmissions are reflected by the Appleton F2 layer (K). Medium (L) and long waves (M) are reflected at lower levels by the D, E or F1 layers. Yet radio waves from distant stellar sources can be received (N).

The circulation of the atmosphere *left*
The atmosphere maintains its equilibrium by transferring heat, moisture and momentum from low levels at low latitudes to high levels at high latitudes where the heat is radiated to space. This circulation appears to comprise three distinct 'cells' in each hemisphere. In the tropical (A) and polar (B) cells the circulations are thermally direct — warm air rises and cold air sinks — but the mid-latitude circulation, the Ferrel cell (C), is distorted by the polar front as shown in greater detail below.

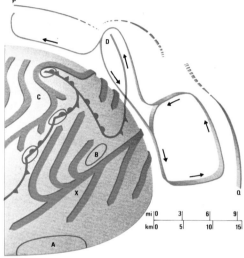

Frontal systems *left*
Although the figure above shows a true general picture, the actual circulation is more complicated. A portion of the Earth on a larger scale shows how frontal systems develop between the polar and tropical air masses. The tropopause, the demarcation between the troposphere in which temperature falls with height, and the stratosphere above, is much higher in the tropics than in the polar cell. Between the cells the polar front causes constant successions of warm and cold fronts and changeable weather. Surface winds are shown, together with areas of low pressure and high pressure. The scale along the bottom, although exaggerated, indicates the greater height of the tropical tropopause compared with that in polar regions. Conventional symbols indicate warm and cold fronts.

Warm front / Cold front

A Area of low pressure
B Area of high pressure
C Area of low pressure
D Polar front
P Polar cell tropopause
Q Tropical tropopause

Precipitation *left*
This map shows the mean annual rain, hail and snow over the Earth.

0 / 25 / 50 / 100 / 200 Cm per year

Evaporation *left*
Accurate estimates of evaporation can be made only over the oceans.

0 / 60 / 100 / 150 / 200 / 250 Cm per year

Surface radiation *left*
Variations in heat output over the Earth's surface affect air and ocean circulations.

60 / 40 / 20 / 0 / −20 / −40 / −60 K/cal per cm² per year

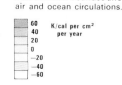

The Structure of Weather Systems

Until recently there were few scientists in the tropics or the polar regions, and the science of meteorology therefore evolved in the mid-latitudes. Likewise, the early concepts of meteorology were all based on observations of the mid-latitude atmosphere. Originally only two types of air mass were recognized: polar and tropical. Today a distinct equatorial air mass has been identified, as well as Arctic and Antarctic masses at latitudes even higher than the original polar ones. The concept of a 'front' between dissimilar air masses dates from as recently as 1919, and three years later the development of a cyclone – a large system of air rotating around an area of low pressure– was first described. Today satellite photographs have confirmed the validity of these early studies and enable the whole Earth's weather to be watched on daily computer processed photo-charts as it develops.

Why the weather varies

Anywhere in the Earth's mid-latitudes the climate is determined mainly by the frequency and intensity of the cyclones, with their frontal systems and contrasting air masses, which unceasingly alter the local temperature, wind velocity, air pressure and humidity. In turn, the frequency of the cyclonic visits is governed principally by the behavior of the long waves in the upper westerlies. When these waves change their shape and position the cyclonic depressions follow different paths. The major changes are seasonal, but significant variations also occur on a cycle of 5–6 weeks. It is still proving difficult to investigate the long wave variations. As a front passes, a fairly definite sequence of cloud, wind, humidity, temperature, precipitation and visibility can be seen. The most obvious change is the type of cloud, of which nine are shown opposite. Each cyclone contains numerous cloud types in its structure. Within these clouds several forms of precipitation can form; raindrops are the most common, but ice precipitation also forms, with snow in winter and hail in the summer when intense atmospheric instability produces towering cumulonimbus clouds topped by an 'anvil' of ice crystals.

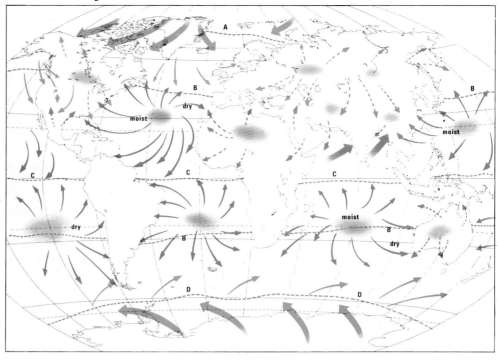

Air masses and convergences *above*
An air mass is an extensive portion of the atmosphere in which, at any given altitude, the moisture and temperature are almost uniform. Such a mass generally arises when the air rests for a time on a large area of land or water which has uniform surface conditions. There are some 20 source regions throughout the world. A second pre-requisite is large-scale subsidence and divergence over the source region. The boundary between air masses is a convergence or front. (A Arctic, B Polar, C Equatorial, D Antarctic.) The polar front is particularly important in governing much of the weather in mid-latitudes. The pattern depicted provides a raw framework for the world's weather. It is considerably modified by the air's vertical motion, by surface friction, land topography, the Earth's rotation and other factors.

Arctic	Equatorial
Polar maritime	Tropical maritime
Polar continental	Tropical continental
Cold air masses	Warm air masses

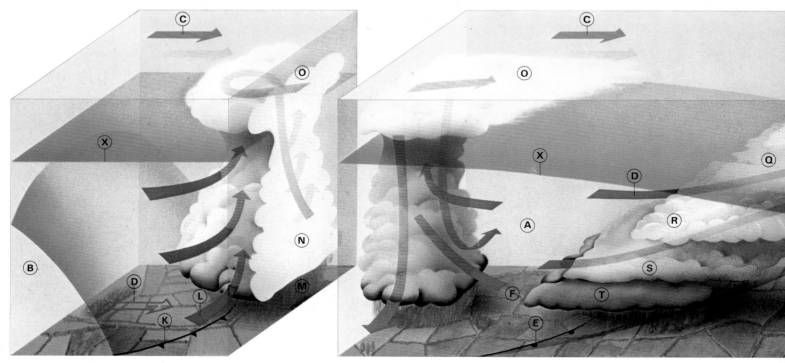

Anatomy of a depression
Seen in cross section, a mature mid-latitude cyclone forms a large system which always follows basically the same pattern. Essentially it comprises a wedge of warm air (A) riding over, and being undercut by; cold air masses (B). (Page 23A shows full development.) The entire cyclone is moving from left to right, and this is also the basic direction of the winds (C) and (D). To an observer on the ground the warm front (E) may take 12-24 hours to pass, followed by the warm sector (F) perhaps 180 miles (300 km) wide.

The cold front (K)
As this frontal zone, about one mile (1-2 km) wide, passes overhead the direction of the wind alters (L) and precipitation (M) pours from cumuliform clouds (N). If the air above the frontal surface is moving upwards then giant cumulonimbus (O) may grow, with heavy rain or hail. Cirrus clouds then form in air above the freezing level (X). Sometimes the front is weak with subsidence of air predominant on both sides of it. In this case there is little cloud development and near-zero surface precipitation.

The warm front (E)
The front is first heralded by cirrus clouds (P), followed by cirrostratus (Q), altocumulus (R), stratus (S) and finally nimbostratus (T). The descending layers are due partly to humidity distribution and partly to the warm air rising over the sloping frontal surface. Precipitation may be steady and last for hours. Alternatively some warm fronts have a predominantly subsident air motion, with the result that there is only a little thin cloud and negligible precipitation. Air temperature increases as the front passes.

Development of a depression *right*

Most mid-latitude depressions (cyclones) develop on the polar front (map above). An initial disturbance along this front causes a fall in pressure and a confluence at the surface, deforming the front into a wave (1, right). The confluence and thermal structure accelerate the cyclonic spin into a fully developed depression (2). The depression comprises a warm sector bounded by a sharp cold front (A) and warm front (B). The fast-moving cold front overtakes the warm front and eventually the warm sector is lifted completely clear of the ground resulting in an occlusion (3). The continued overlapping of the two wedges of cold air eventually fills up the depression and causes it to weaken and disperse (4). By the time this occurs the warm sector has been lifted high in the atmosphere. In this way, depressions fulfil an essential role in transferring heat from low to high levels and from low to high latitudes.

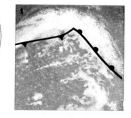
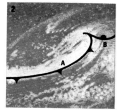
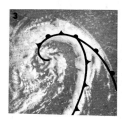
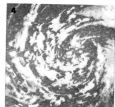

Plan view *left*

A developing cyclone will appear this way on the 'synoptic' weather chart. Lines of equal pressure (isobars) are nearly straight within the warm sector but curve sharply in the cold sector to enclose the low pressure focus of the system.

Examples of the three major cloud groups

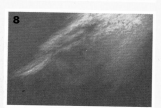

Low cloud *top*

Stratocumulus (1) is a grey or white layer of serried masses or rolls. Cumulus (2) is the familiar white cauliflower. It can develop into cumulonimbus (3), a large, threatening cloud, characterized by immense vertical development topped by an 'anvil' of ice crystals. These produce heavy rain or hail.

Medium cloud *left*

Nimbostratus (4) is a ragged grey layer producing drizzle or snow. Altocumulus (5) comprises rows of 'blobs' of ice and water forming a sheet at a height of 1.5-4.5 miles (2-7 km). Altostratus (6) occurs at similar heights but is a water/ice sheet either uniform, striated or fibrous in appearance.

High cloud *right*

Cirrus (7) is the highest cloud and appears as fine white ice filaments at 8-10 miles (13-16 km), often hair-like or silky. Cirro-cumulus (8) forms into thin white layers made up of very numerous icy globules or ripples. Cirrostratus (9) is a high-level veil of ice crystals often forming a halo round the Sun.

Four kinds of precipitation

Rain

Most rain results from the coalescence of microscopic droplets (1) which are condensed from vapor onto nuclei in the atmosphere. The repeated merging of small droplets eventually forms water droplets (2) which are too large to be kept up by the air currents. Rain drops may also form from melting of ice crystals in the atmosphere.

Glaze

In completely undisturbed air it is possible for water to remain liquid even at temperatures well below freezing point. So air above the freezing level (X) may contain large quantities of this 'supercooled water'. This can fall as rain and freeze on impact with objects, coating them with ice.

Dry snow

The origin of snow differs from that of rain in that the vapor droplets (1) settle on microscopic crystals of ice and freeze. The result is the growth of a white or translucent ice crystal having a basically hexagonal form (photomicrograph below). The crystals then agglomerate into flakes (2).

Hail

In cumulonimbus clouds raindrops (formed at 1,2) may encounter up-currents strong enough to lift them repeatedly back through a freezing level (X). On each pass (3) a fresh layer of ice is collected. The hailstone builds up like an onion until it is so heavy (4) that it falls to the ground.

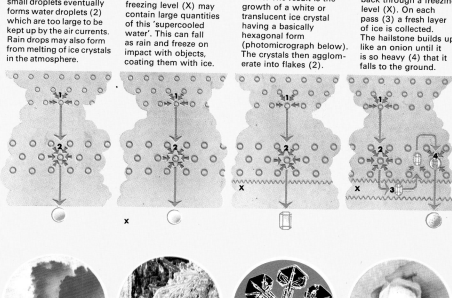

Tropical weather, between the Tropic of Cancer at 23½°N and the Tropic of Capricorn at 23½°S, differs fundamentally from that at higher latitudes. Overall there is a considerable surplus of heat, giving high mean temperatures; and the 'Coriolis force' due to the Earth's rotation, which deflects air currents to the right in the northern hemisphere and to the left in the southern, is almost non-existent. As a result, tropical weather hardly ever contains distinct air masses, fronts and cyclones. Instead the region is occupied mainly by the tradewinds, which are laden with moisture and potentially unstable. Thunderstorms are frequent, especially over land, and the pattern of land and sea leads to local anomalies, such as the monsoon of southeast Asia. This particular anomaly, too big to be called local, changes the prevailing wind over a vast area. It is superimposed on the apparently simple global circulation near the Equator.

Polar weather

At very high latitudes the atmosphere radiates heat to space. The Arctic is essentially an ocean surrounded by land, whereas the Antarctic is land surrounded by ocean. The land around the Arctic quickly takes up solar heat but the southern oceans transfer heat to deeper water to make the Antarctic the coldest region on Earth. Because the air is so intensely cold it can hold very little moisture, so the south polar region is a freezing desert with exceptionally clean air.

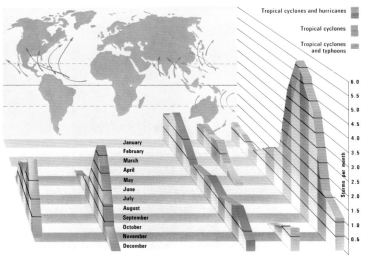

The afflicted areas *above* Tropical cyclones build up over the warm oceans, and many of them—about half over the Caribbean and four-fifths over the western Pacific—develop into hurricanes. Precisely how a hurricane is triggered is still not fully known, but there is no doubt it is a thermodynamic engine on a giant scale which either misfires completely or runs with catastrophic effect.

Hurricanes *left* These violent storms form over ocean warm enough (27°C) to maintain strong vertical circulation, except for the belt closest to the equator where lack of a Coriolis force prevents cyclonic spin from building up. Condensation of the moisture taken up from the ocean surface releases latent heat and thus provides energy to drive the storm. The daily energy can be equivalent to that released by several hundred H bombs. Despite their formidable power hurricanes are penetrated by specially equipped aircraft whose mission is both to provide early warning and to gather data enabling the storm's mechanism to be better understood.

Hurricane structure
A Spiral rainbands.
B High-altitude winds.
C Easterly tradewinds.

Structure of a hurricane *above*
A hurricane consists of a huge swirl of clouds rotating around a calm center known as the eye. This cyclonic circulation may be as much as 250 miles (400 km) in diameter, and it extends right through the troposphere which is about 9-12 miles (15-20 km) thick. The clouds, nearly all of the cumulonimbus type, are arranged in bands around the eye. The largest form the wall of the eye and it is here that precipitation is heaviest. The whole system is usually capped by streamers of cirrus. Wind speeds range from about 110 mph (180 kmh) at 20–25 miles (30–40 km) from the eye wall down to about 45 mph (72 kmh) at a distance of 90 miles (140 km). Warm, calm air in the eye is sucked downwards.

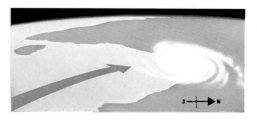

Hurricane development *below*

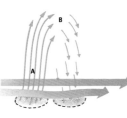

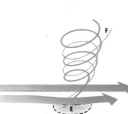

Nature's giant energy *left and above*
A hurricane such as that which killed over half a million people in Bangladesh in November 1970 (left) dissipates thousands of millions of horsepower. The spiral structure is clearly visible from a satellite (above).

Birth of a storm.
Hurricanes usually have their origin in a low-pressure disturbance directing part of an easterly wind (A) to the north. The air rises to some 40,000 ft (12 km) where it releases heat and moisture (B) before descending.

The young hurricane
The Earth's rotation imparts a twist to the rising column which becomes a cylinder (C) spiralling round a relatively still core (D). Warm, moist air off the sea picks up speed and feeds energy at a very high rate to intensify the rising column.

Dying of starvation
The hurricane does not begin to die until it moves over colder water or over land (E). Then, cut off from its supply of energy, the speed of the spiralling winds falls away. The eye begins to fill with clouds, the hurricane expands (F) and dissipates.

The monsoon *right*
In principle the processes which give rise to the monsoon are the same as those causing a sea breeze but on a vastly larger scale in space and time. In southeast Asia each May and June warm, moist air streams in from the south causing heavy rain and occasional violent storms. In winter the circulation is reversed and winds come mainly from high pressure over Siberia. In detail the monsoon is considerably modified by the Himalayas and the positions of the waves in the westerlies in the atmosphere's upper levels, but its mechanism is not fully known.

Duststorm *right*
In arid regions strong wind circulations can become filled with dust and extend over considerable areas. The storm typically arrives in the form of an advancing wall of dust possibly five miles (8 km) long and 1000 ft (300 m) high. The haboobs of the Sudan, a recurrent series of storms, are most frequent from May to September and can approach from almost any direction. They usually occur, after a few days of rising temperature and falling pressure, where the soil is very dry. Dust-devils, small local whirlwinds forming pillars of sand, can dot the land.

Nacreous cloud *right*
At high latitudes, when the Sun is below the horizon, these clouds sometimes come into view as fine filmy areas containing regions of bright spectral color. They look rather like a form of cirrus, but are far higher. Nacreous cloud in the Antarctic—such as that in the photograph, taken in Grahamland—has been measured at heights from 8.5 to 19 miles (13.5-30 km), and Scandinavian observations lie in the 20-30 km range. Despite their great altitude, nacreous clouds are undoubtedly formed as a result of air being lifted by passage across high mountains.

The monsoon seasons *below*
In summer an intense low-pressure area over northwest India overcomes the equatorial low pressure region. In winter an intense high over central Asia blows cold, dry air in the reverse direction.

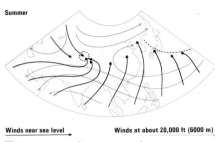

Summer

Winds near sea level ➝   Winds at about 20,000 ft (6000 m)

Winter

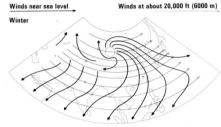

Flash flood *below*
In historic times floods have drowned millions. Even in a modern advanced country a major flood is a national disaster. The scene below is a flooded crossing on the road from Lake Grace to Dumbleyung, W Australia. It is a 'flash flood', caused by heavy rain and poor drainage.

After the hurricane *left*
Whereas a tornado can cause buildings to explode, as a result of the sudden violent difference in pressure between inside and outside, a hurricane just blows. But the wind can demolish sound houses, such as this residence in Biloxi, Mississippi.

Blown snow *above*
When the wind blows in polar regions it soon begins to lift dry powdery snow and ice granules from the surface. As the wind increases in strength this drifting snow forms a thicker layer, as at this British base in Antarctica. When the entrained material reaches eye level it is known as blown snow. Any further rise in wind velocity swiftly increases the concentration of particulate matter, causing the visibility rapidly to fall to zero. When this is the case the term blizzard is appropriate, as it also is when high winds are combined with a heavy snowfall.

All the past history of the Earth since the original formation of the crust is there to be discovered in the rocks existing today if only the appropriate techniques are used to find it. Sedimentary, igneous and metamorphic – the three basic types of rock – all have an enormous amount of information stored within them on such diverse aspects of the Earth's history as, for example, the variations of past climates in space and in time, the incidence of ice ages and the positions of former mountain ranges. The migrations of the ancient geo-magnetic poles at different periods of time can be discovered by studying some sedimentary and igneous rocks, while other types can yield their ages of formation or metamorphism – their changed character over long periods. The prevailing wind directions over certain regions, the direction of stream flow in river deltas that have long since vanished, or the ways in which the ice flowed in some past ice age are all there to be discovered. So are the past distributions of land and sea, areas of deposition, periods of uplift and the raising of great mountain chains (see pages 12–13A and 18-19A). Even lightning strikes millions of years old can be clearly seen.

The first task of the geologist is to make a map showing the positions and relative ages of the various rock types in a region. It is around this basic information incorporated in the geological map that all else is built, whether it is to be studies of the geological history and evolution of the region, or detailed investigations of the flora and fauna, or any of many other lines of research – such as the disentangling of various periods of deformation which have affected the region during which the rocks may have been folded or faulted (foot of this page) or eroded down to sea level. Two of the most important methods of dating, by which the age of rock is determined, are the study of fossils and the use of radiometric methods in which age is calculated by analyzing radioactive minerals having a known half-life (opposite page). Using a combination of 'correlation' techniques and either method of dating it is possible for a skilled geologist to compare the relative time sequences of geological events in any regions in the world.

A geological map *below*
A geological map records the outcrop pattern and the structural features of each region as they are today, corresponding with the final stage of the reconstruction—right.

How the story unfolds
right
The complex 3500 million year story of the rocks is very far from being superficially obvious. Even a skilled geologist can do no more than study the land as it is today, plot a geological map and then try to think backward over periods of millions of years in an endeavor to determine the sequences which produced the present terrain. On the right is depicted such a sequence, which might reasonably be arrived at after studying the map below, left. The history begins (A) with the landmass rising and the sea retreating, leaving behind 'off-lap' sediments. The landmass continues to rise and is folded by compressive forces, the fold tops then being eroded (B). Over a long period the landmass then subsides and tilts; the sea once more advances, laying down 'on-lap' sediments (C). Then a great upheaval causes the sea to retreat completely. The landmass is strongly uplifted and faulted, and the higher mass is at once attacked by erosion (D). Continued erosion gradually reduces the region to a more or less common level. Rivers, formed at stage C, carry eroded materials away and deposit them at lower levels (left side of E). Finally, the northeast part of the region is invaded by an extrusive mass of volcanic material. Of course, the processes of change would continue even now.

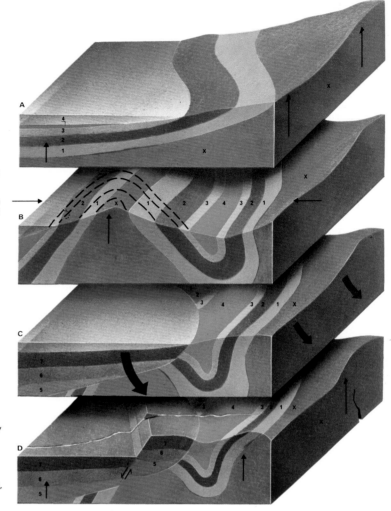

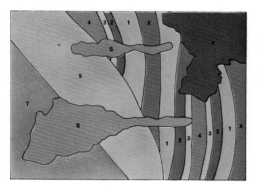

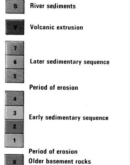

S	River sediments
V	Volcanic extrusion
7	
6	Later sedimentary sequence
5	Period of erosion
4	
3	Early sedimentary sequence
2	
1	Period of erosion
x	Older basement rocks

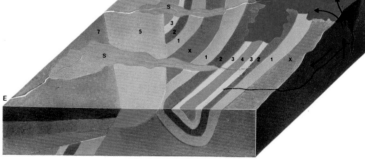

The language of geology

Plane of movement of a normal fault (1) displacing strata to right (downthrow side) relative to left (upthrow side).

Block of strata (2) dropped between two tensional faults forming a rift valley. Other strata are compressional.

Normal anticline (3) and syncline (4) with symmetrically dipping limbs on either side of the axial plane of the strata.

Positions of the axial planes (5, 6) passing through an asymmetrical anticline (5) and an asymmetrical syncline (6).

Compressional reversed fault (7). In this case the left side of the fault is over-riding basically horizontal strata on the right.

Monoclinal fold (8), with a relatively steep limb separating basically horizontal areas of strata at two levels.

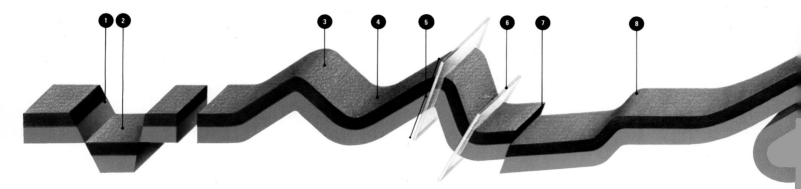

Geological dating

The relative dating of geological strata is found from the sequence in which the layers were deposited, the oldest being at the base of a local sequence and the youngest at the top. On this basis, together with correlations over wide areas based on the fossil evidence of the forms of life at different stages of the 'geological column', the main periods and sub-divisions can be worked out.

Prior to the Cambrian, the oldest epoch of the Paleozoic era (see scale at right), evidence of life is seldom found in the rocks. The extremely primitive earliest forms of life have generally not been preserved in the form of fossils, and so correlations by palaeontological methods cannot be applied to the Precambrian.

In recent years the progressive evolution of radio-metric dating has enabled geologists to assign actual dates to the relative sequences of strata. Since the formation of the Earth's crust various isotopes have been present in it which are radioactive, spontaneously decaying over a precisely fixed period of time into a different element. For example a large number of geological dates have been based on the decay of potassium (K^{40}) to argon (A^{40}) and on that of rubidium (Rb^{87}) to strontium (Sr^{87}). The manner in which these valuable geological time-clocks decay over many millions of years is depicted below. No radioactive isotope is ever completely used up; millions of years later atoms are still present of both the original isotope and the end-product of its disintegration.

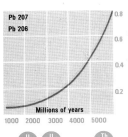

Half-life *left*
Radioactive materials decay according to a law. Each isotope has a characteristic half-life, the time required for the number of radioactive atoms to decay to half the original number. The half-life for each element is unalterable.

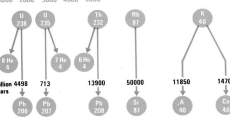

Degeneration *above and left*
Some of the isotopes, shown above with their half-lives and end-products can be used for dating over the whole age of the Earth. For more recent dating, radio-carbon with a half-life of 5570 years is used (left).

1 Neutron
2 Nitrogen 14
3 Proton
4 Carbon 14
5 Nitrogen 14
6 β particle

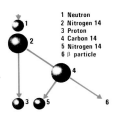

Overturned anticline (9) overlying an overturned syncline in a system distinguished by isoclinal (almost parallel) limbs.

Plane of thrusting (10) causes the overturned anticline (11) to ride over lower strata in form of a horizontally displaced 'nappe'.

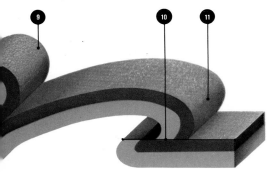

Quaternary

This most recent period of geological history leads up to the appearance of man and the present day. Changes of climate took place which brought on the great ice ages with glacial periods alternating with warmer sequences between them. And, of course, the period is still in progress.

Tertiary

A complex history of changes took place, each epoch of the Tertiary period from Paleocene to Pliocene showing a diverse sequence of volcanism and mountain-building in different regions. Shallow seas alternated with sub-tropical delta flats harboring the precursors of today's life.

Cretaceous

The Tethys Sea spread over large areas of the adjacent continents. Fossil evidence reveals a diverse flora and fauna. The South Atlantic reached a width of some 1900 miles (3000 km) and only Antarctica and Australia and the northern lands of the North Atlantic remained unseparated.

Jurassic

The North Atlantic had opened to a width of some 600 miles (1000 km). Sedimentary deposits formed marginal belts around the continents which had separated, and deeper-water sediments were deposited in the Tethys Sea. Extensive eruption of basalts accompanied the rifting of the South Atlantic.

Triassic

This was the period in which the continental drift began. The progressive opening of the North Atlantic was accompanied by rift-valley faulting and large outpourings of basalt along the eastern seaboard of what is today North America. Gondwanaland in the south began to break up.

Permian

Many areas were characterized by arid or semi-arid climates, with frequent salt lakes giving rise to evaporite deposits and red desert sandstones. Much volcanic activity took place on a local scale. This was the last period in which Pangaea remained a single continental mass. New flora were abundant.

Carboniferous

Extensive forest and deltaic swamp conditions led to the eventual formation of coal basins in North America and Europe. Phases of folding and mountain formation occurred in many places. In Gondwanaland widespread glaciation occurred, with glaciers radiating from a great central ice-cap.

Devonian

Large areas of arid continental and sandstone deposits formed, partly as the products of erosion of the mountains formed previously. Intervening basins of shallow sea or lagoonal deposits occurred, with abundant fossil fish. Distinct faunal provinces have been recognized from this period.

Silurian

In this period further widespread basins of thick sedimentary deposits were laid down. Many of these are characterized by the abundance of marine fossils, including corals. The Caledonian mountains were formed in Laurasia in which enormous volumes of granitic rocks were later emplaced.

Ordovician

Graptolites and trilobites continued to be important forms of marine life. Thick marine sediments continued to be laid down, and there were extensive and widespread outbursts of volcanic activity. In some regions deformation and uplift of the rocks created major mountain ranges.

Cambrian

Rocks of this period contain the earliest fossilized remnants of more complex forms of life such as graptolites, brachiopods, trilobites and gastropods. In many regions the Cambrian period was characterized by the deposition of thick sequences of sedimentary rocks, usually on an eroded basement.

Precambrian

By far the longest period of geological time is included in the Precambrian. This encompasses a complex history of sedimentation, mountain-building, volcanism, and granitic intrusions. Precambrian rocks form basements to many sedimentary deposits, and make up the nuclei of continents.

Chart columns

Million years	Major periods	Period scale	Million years	Period
	Cenozoic		65	Quaternary / Tertiary
500	Mesozoic / Palaeozoic		100	
	Upper Proterozoic		136	Cretaceous
1000	Lower Proterozoic		190 / 200	Jurassic
1500			225	Triassic
2000	Archaean		280 / 300	Permian
2500			345	Carboniferous
3000	Katarchaean		395 / 400	Devonian
3500	Oldest known crust		430	Silurian
4000			500	Ordovician
4500	formation of the earth		570 / 600	Cambrian / Precambrian

Isotope decay chains (half-lives in million years):

Isotope	End product	Half-life (Million years)
U 238 → 8 He 4	Pb 206	4498
U 235 → 7 He 4	Pb 207	713
Th 232 → 6 He 4	Pb 208	13900
Rb 87	Sr 87	50000
K 40	A 40	11850
K 40	Ca 40	1470

Pb 207 / Pb 206 — 0.8 0.6 0.4 0.2 — Millions of years — 1000 2000 3000 4000 5000

In 1833 Charles Lyell courageously proposed that the fragments of bones of animals and men that persistently cropped up in deep geological strata could mean only one thing: that the Earth had been created long before the date of 4004 BC accepted by Christianity. Since then practically the whole of our knowledge of man's early development has come from systematic digging. At first a lone archaeologist could do the whole job, but today digging for early man involves a team of specialized archaeologists, geologists, technologists and laboratory workers. They hope to identify everything significant, study it in relation to its resting place, the history of the region and nearby finds, and also subject chosen items to detailed laboratory tests – such as accurate age determination by the potassium/argon method (p.27A). A major dig needs experts on rocks, on soils and on plant pollen.

Although there are remarkable instances of well-preserved human bodies being found (for example, in peat bogs) and of woolly mammoths whose flesh could be eaten after a million years in frozen Siberia, almost all archaeology rests on bones and on man's artifacts. Gradually, from small fragments of jaw, teeth, skull and other bones, it has been possible to piece together what appears to be a fairly complete history of human evolution. The artist can then cover a deduced skeleton with tissue, as has been done in these pages. But pigmentation of skin and degree of hairiness is still a matter for conjecture.

Among the significant factors studied in early man are his brain size, jaw structure, posture and loco-motion. Today's great apes have a stooping, occasionally four-legged posture. So did ape-men from 20 million down to five million years ago; then, gradually, the hominid line learned to walk upright. Its members also learned to use tools, and to make them progressively better. Even later, true men began to leave behind evidence of their growing culture in their burials, their artifacts and their art. All these things can be studied in bone caves, such as the imaginary one illustrated on the right, and in excavation sites.

The cave in use
The cave is modeled after European examples of the Upper Paleolithic period of the order of 25000 years ago. It was at about this time that cave paintings appear to have become widespread. The river was then close to its present level, but the rock falls and piles of debris were still to come.

A bone cave *above and right*
From about 100,000 years ago caves provided many types of early men with a ready-made refuge. Probably most of these caves still exist. Although many are buried under later strata, and virtually all are greatly changed by subsequent developments, it is still possible with experience to read the message contained in them.

River level
In general, the lowest geological sediments are the oldest, but it is unwise to jump to this conclusion. In this hypothetical cave the earliest of all the deposits is a river terrace A above the cave on the hillside, indicating that the whole cave was originally submerged. At about this period insoluble limestone residue was settling on the cave floor at B. As the river cut its valley its level fell to C, leaving silt bed D. Continued deepening of the valley brought the river to its present level, leaving the cave dry and eroding the thick layer of silt at the mouth of the cave.

An obstructed mouth
Early man sheltered in the mouth of the cave and lit fires there for warmth and to cook food. The ashes of these fires gradually accumulated in three main layers, each denoting a long period of use. The 'contemporary' inset illustrates the third of these periods. Later the cave was abandoned by man and the mouth gradually became blocked by a pile of rock debris.

A burrow in the cave
Here a small animal has burrowed into the floor. It was deflected sideways by the hard flowstone until it could continue on down, throwing fossil bones up on to the floor above. Finally it died at the end of its burrow.

A buzzard's nest?
Just inside the lip of the cave mouth a bird of prey built its nest. Directly beneath it on the slope of the rock debris are scattered small rodent bones.

Mesolithic
About 10,000 years ago
About 20000 years ago the great ice sheets began slowly to recede, a process that is still continuing. As the climate grew warmer the Late Paleolithic people gave way to the Mesolithic (transitional) about the year 8000 BC. Milder conditions allowed man to exploit the rivers and seas, using fishing nets and even elaborate barricades and weirs made of woven saplings. The family had by now become a firm social unit, while people also explored the territory of their neighbors. For the first time there is evidence of large groups combining in habitation, hunting, art and making useful articles. Although farming of crops and animals had yet to come, the Mesolithic period saw a great enrichment of life and—probably—the development of a social conscience.

Neolithic
8000 years ago
The scene below depicts the greatest revolution ever wrought on Earth. The Neolithic ('new stone') people discovered some of the basic secrets of life—how animals can be reared in captivity and how plants can be grown from seed. The keeping of pets by children may have provided the key to animal husbandry by their parents. As a result men no longer had to risk their lives in finding and killing their prey; they kept them in a herd. And the organized growing of crops at last freed man from the role of passive and often desperate scavenger, and instead set him on his great path leading to mastery over his environment. Unlike all other Earth life he became able to shape the whole world around him and, to an increasing degree, become master of his life and future destiny. Many of the inhabitants of today's world still live in a basically Neolithic way.

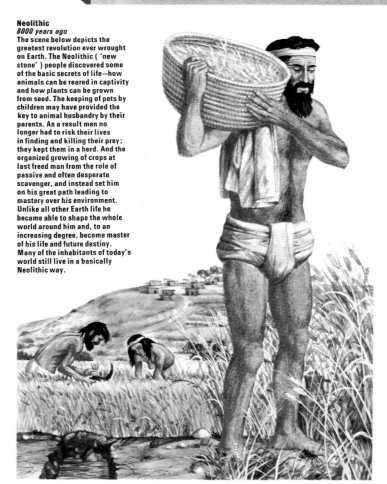

Cave art
Many well preserved cave paintings are masterpieces. Most show animals being hunted by early man, and their power, color and dynamic energy can be startling. But they are often in difficult, inaccessible places, and appear to have been part of the hunter's semi-religious efforts to insure his success and safety in finding and then killing a powerful and dangerous opponent.

The bear cult
Another manifestation of early man's hunting superstitions is to be found in carefully prepared arrangements of cave bear skulls, leg bones and other fragments. Men could hardly have chosen a more dangerous opponent, and they could find meat much more easily; yet the cave bear cult is evident in many forms, such as this stone compartment filled with skulls.

Human burial
Early men buried their own kind in various ways. Some societies buried skulls only, arrayed with possessions or ornaments; others buried men but left female corpses on refuse heaps. This skeleton shows evidence of careful burial in a sleeping posture similar to that of the Grimaldi remains in the Grotte des Enfants, Monaco. Later the grave was overlain by rock debris, here removed.

Petrification
Even the interior of a structurally stable cave changes over a long period, and in this case a sudden gross alteration has resulted from a large fall of rock from the roof. Subsequent to this, slow seepage through the limestone roof of water containing dissolved minerals, especially calcium carbonate, caused gradual growth of pendulous stalactites and upright stalagmites.

Animal remains
The cave is littered to a depth of well over a foot (0.3 m) with the debris of the food and other refuse of carnivores. The great cone above the fall of rock is littered with the remains of animals which fell in through the hole above; and on top of the cone is a pile of bat dung.

A rock fall
A massive collapse of the cave roof left a pile of rock on the floor of the cave and a gaping open shaft above. New layers of flowstone accumulated, earth and rock debris built up above the growing cone reached the roof. Sediments then filled the shaft.

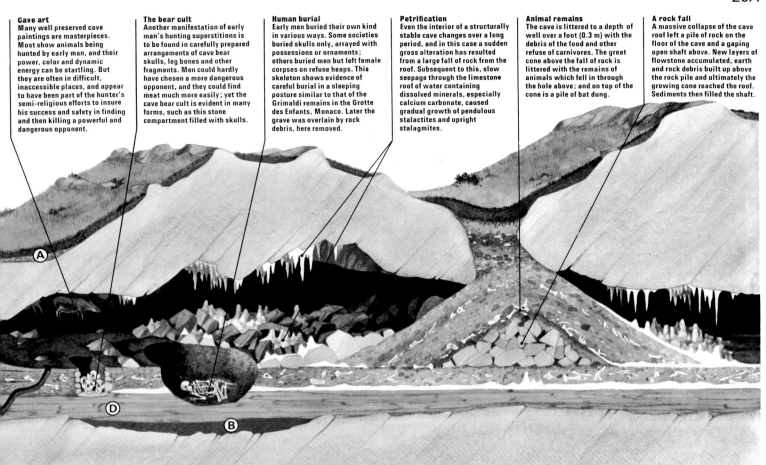

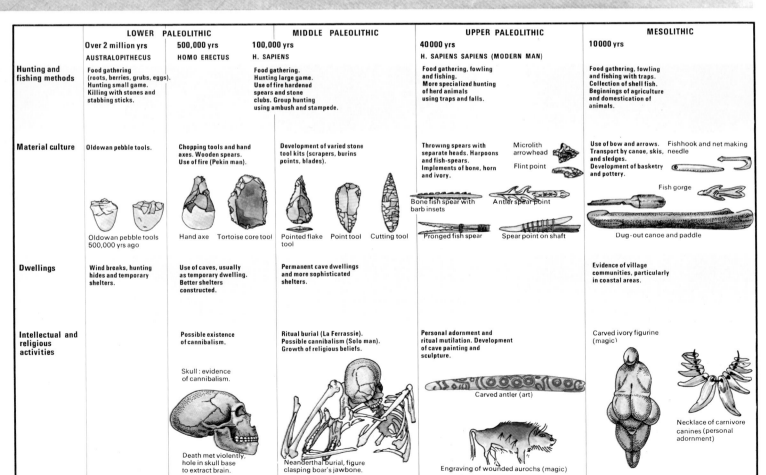

	LOWER PALEOLITHIC			MIDDLE PALEOLITHIC	UPPER PALEOLITHIC	MESOLITHIC
	Over 2 million yrs	500,000 yrs	100,000 yrs		40000 yrs	10000 yrs
	AUSTRALOPITHECUS	HOMO ERECTUS	H. SAPIENS		H. SAPIENS SAPIENS (MODERN MAN)	
Hunting and fishing methods	Food gathering (roots, berries, grubs, eggs). Hunting small game. Killing with stones and stabbing sticks.		Food gathering. Hunting large game. Use of fire hardened spears and stone clubs. Group hunting using ambush and stampede.		Food gathering, fowling and fishing. More specialized hunting of herd animals using traps and falls.	Food gathering, fowling and fishing with traps. Collection of shell fish. Beginnings of agriculture and domestication of animals.
Material culture	Oldowan pebble tools. Oldowan pebble tools 500,000 yrs ago	Chopping tools and hand axes. Wooden spears. Use of fire (Pekin man). Hand axe Tortoise core tool	Development of varied stone tool kits (scrapers, burins points, blades). Pointed flake tool Point tool Cutting tool		Throwing spears with separate heads. Harpoons and fish-spears. Implements of bone, horn and ivory. Bone fish spear with barb insets Antler spear point Pronged fish spear Spear point on shaft Microlith arrowhead Flint point	Use of bow and arrows. Transport by canoe, skis, and sledges. Development of basketry and pottery. Fishhook and net making needle Fish gorge Dug-out canoe and paddle
Dwellings	Wind breaks, hunting hides and temporary shelters.	Use of caves, usually as temporary dwelling. Better shelters constructed.	Permanent cave dwellings and more sophisticated shelters.			Evidence of village communities, particularly in coastal areas.
Intellectual and religious activities		Possible existence of cannibalism. Skull : evidence of cannibalism. Death met violently, hole in skull base to extract brain.	Ritual burial (La Ferrassie). Possible cannibalism (Solo man). Growth of religious beliefs. Neanderthal burial, figure clasping boar's jawbone.		Personal adornment and ritual mutilation. Development of cave painting and sculpture. Carved antler (art) Engraving of wounded aurochs (magic)	Carved ivory figurine (magic) Necklace of carnivore canines (personal adornment)

One of the wonders of the Earth must be the subtle interplay between light and structure that transforms common minerals into precious jewels. In most cases man's hand can be detected in their creation, but even in the natural state many minerals have a range of color, shape, texture and form that makes them the treasures of the Earth.

By popular definition, anything that is mined is called a mineral and on this basis coal and oil are the most important minerals (pages 34–35A). However, geologists reserve the term for naturally occurring materials which have an unvarying chemical composition and crystalline structure. The basic structural elements are arranged in a rigid pattern within three-dimensional crystal matrices.

Each crystal grows from a nucleus by adding atoms layer by layer. A freely growing crystal assumes one of seven basic forms, depending on the relative angles of its faces and the distances between opposite parallel pairs. But in practice the shape of naturally occurring crystals is generally influenced by the space in which it is constrained to grow. Thus in nature crystals develop characteristic habits or overall shapes. The faces may be all of the same size or unequal. They may occur in narrow layers or grow like a bunch of grapes.

Minerals can be identified by their structure, habit, hardness, density, and the ease with which they can be cleaved along particular planes. Hardness, for example, is normally measured against a scale of increasing hardness from talc to diamond, devised in 1822 by the German mineralogist, F. Mohs. Color is frequently the result of minute proportions of impurities. These often result in minerals of such startling beauty that they are coveted by man as gemstones. The brilliance of transparent gems is due to the way light is reflected inside the stone, and man has learned how to cut gems to enhance their optical properties. The stone is cut or ground to a precise external form with face angles arranged to insure the maximum brilliance based on the refractive index of the material. Rocks (below) are composed of different combinations of a limited number of minerals

Basic igneous rock
Dolerite, a basic igneous rock, is composed of laths of plagioclase (grey and black), pyroxene (yellow and orange) and oxides of iron and titanium (blackish regions).

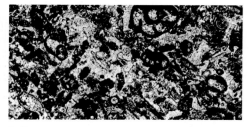

Sedimentary rock *above*
Limestone is composed of finely crystalline calcite. It shows the fossilized remains of foraminifera.

Acid igneous rock *below*
Granite is a hard igneous rock made up of quartz, potassium feldspar and red-brown crystals of biotite.

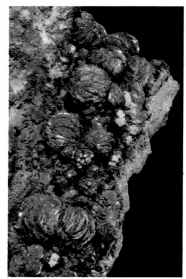

Azurite
Carbonate of copper, possibly the first metal used by man.

Malachite
Hydrated carbonate of copper; used as both ore and ornament.

Cerussite
Very clearly defined crystals of lead carbonate.

Opal
Amorphous silicon dioxide with a variable content of water.

Hemimorphite
A zinc silicate, botryoidal crystal found with other zinc deposits.

Pyromorphite
A bed of fine hexagonal columns of lead chlorophosphate.

Sphene
Silicates are abundant; sphene is calcium titanium silicate.

Crystal size
Although crystal shapes are governed by internal structure, individual sizes are controlled only by conditions of growth. For example, plates of mica—seen as minute biotite flakes in granite sections (lower left)— have reached 33ft (10m) by 14ft (4.3m) wide as in one 90-ton example discovered in Canada.

Quartz
Columnar crystals of silicon dioxide.

Torbernite
Hydrous copper uranium
phosphate; a uranium source.

Beryl
Beryllium aluminium silicate is
known in crystals of 25 tons.

Pyrite on calcite
Crystals of iron disulphide,
on calcium carbonate.

Wavelite
Crystals of hydrous basic
aluminium phosphate.

Cassiterite
Tin was one of man's earliest
metals; this is the dioxide ore.

Calcite
Often occurs as stalactites and
stalagmites.

Citrine
The yellowish variety of quartz
(silicon dioxide).

Ruby in host rock
The deep red variety of
corundum (aluminium oxide).

Diamonds in kimberlite
Native diamonds (crystalline
carbon) in their original rock.

Polished diamond
For use as a gemstone the
diamond is skilfully cut.

Polished ruby
Large rubies are among the most
precious of all gemstones.

Sulphur
Crystalline sulphur (brimstone)
occurs in nature.

Blue John
Calcium fluoride (fluorite),
occurs in various colorful forms.

Galena
Cubic crystals of lead sulphide,
a major ore of lead.

Minerals Under the Land

Of about 2000 minerals in the Earth's crust only 100 or so are of economic importance. These are distributed very irregularly, so that no country today can boast all the minerals it needs. As a result minerals are a source of great national wealth, exploitation and even of rivalry. And the strife is likely to intensify as man's demands grow, because the total of the Earth's minerals is limited.

Against this background of uneven distribution, economic warfare and sharply increasing demand, man's use of minerals constantly changes. Coal, in 1920 the most important mineral in the world on a tonnage basis, is today unable to compete in several of its former markets because of the high cost of transporting it, and its use is increasingly changing from that of a fuel to that of a raw material for plastics and chemicals. Nitrates for fertilizers and explosives sustained the economy of Chile until 1914, when Germany found a way to 'fix' nitrogen from the atmosphere. **Aluminum, one the most abundant** minerals, was costly and little used until a large-scale refining process was discovered which made use of **cheap hydroelectricity.**

Taking the broad view, the Earth's minerals are seen as a stern test of man's ability to make proper use of the resources available to him. Already some nations have amassed enormous stockpiles of what are today considered to be strategically important minerals. Nickel is one such metal, and the bulk of the world's supply comes from Canada. Another is manganese, and in this case the dominant supplier is the Soviet Union; but manganese is one of the many minerals which might be dredged from the sea bed.

Uneven distribution of minerals is paralleled by uneven consumption. Paradoxically, the industrialized countries which owed their original development to the presence of mineral resources, particularly iron and coal, now rely for their continued prosperity on developing nations. If the latter were to develop a similar demand for materials a mineral famine would ensue which would have repercussions throughout the world.

World output *right*
The most important commercial minerals and main producers. At the foot of each column is annual world output in millions of long tons. Precious mineral outputs (asterisked) are : gold 52 million fine troy ounces ; silver 240 m.f.t.o. ; platinum 3.4 m.f.t.o. ; diamonds 30 million metric carats.

Key to mineral producers

1 Soviet Union	15 Zambia
2 USA	16 Australia
3 France	17 Spain
4 S Africa	18 Italy
5 Philippines	19 Malaysia
6 Congo (Kinshasa)	20 United Kingdom
7 Canada	21 Thailand
8, Morocco	22 Argentina
9 Brazil	23 Uganda
10 Chile	24 India
11 New Caledonia	25 Mexico
12 SW Africa	26 Peru
13 Finland	27 Congolese Rep.
14 China (People's Rep.)	28 Ghana

Ferro-alloy metals								Non-ferrous metals					Light metals		Nuclear fuels		Precious metals			
Iron ore	Chromite	Cobalt	Manganese	Molybdenum	Nickel	Vanadium	Tungsten	Copper	Lead	Mercury	Tin	Asbestos	Aluminum	Beryllium	Uranium	Thorium	Gold	Silver	Platinum	Diamonds
	1	1		1			14	2	2		17				22		2		7	27
	2		6		2	7		1	1	16	18	19	7	2	23			24	25	1	
	3	4		4			2	15				20		1	9		1	19	26		4
				9		11				1	21			7		7				28
		5	7	8		4							9				9		1		
					7		12						4							4	
			10	1		13										7			7		
661	4.7	0.019	18	0.11	0.5	0.01	0.04	5.3	2.9	0.01	0.21	3.47	7.7	0.003	0.024	0.0006	*	*	*	*

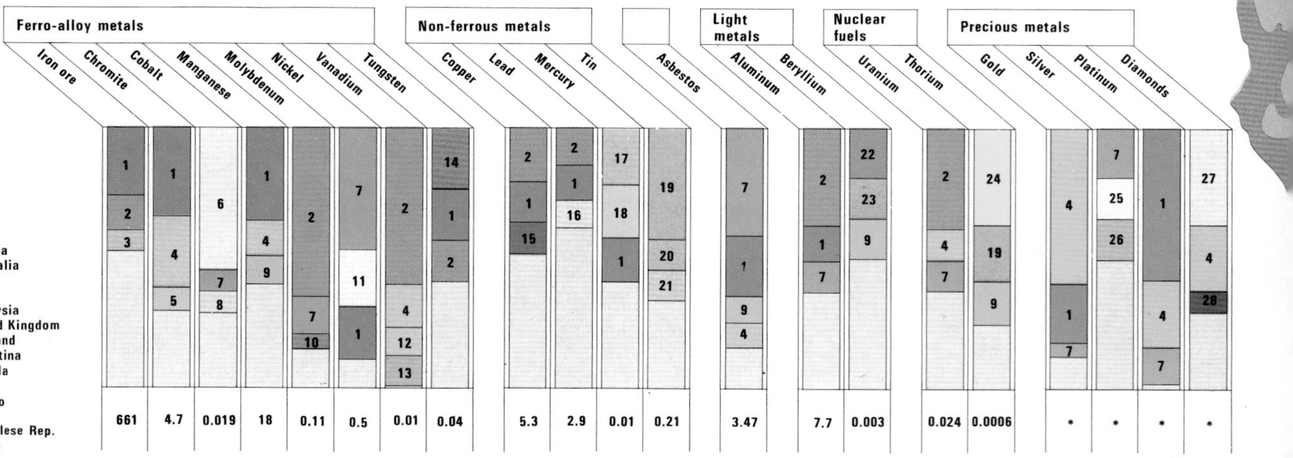

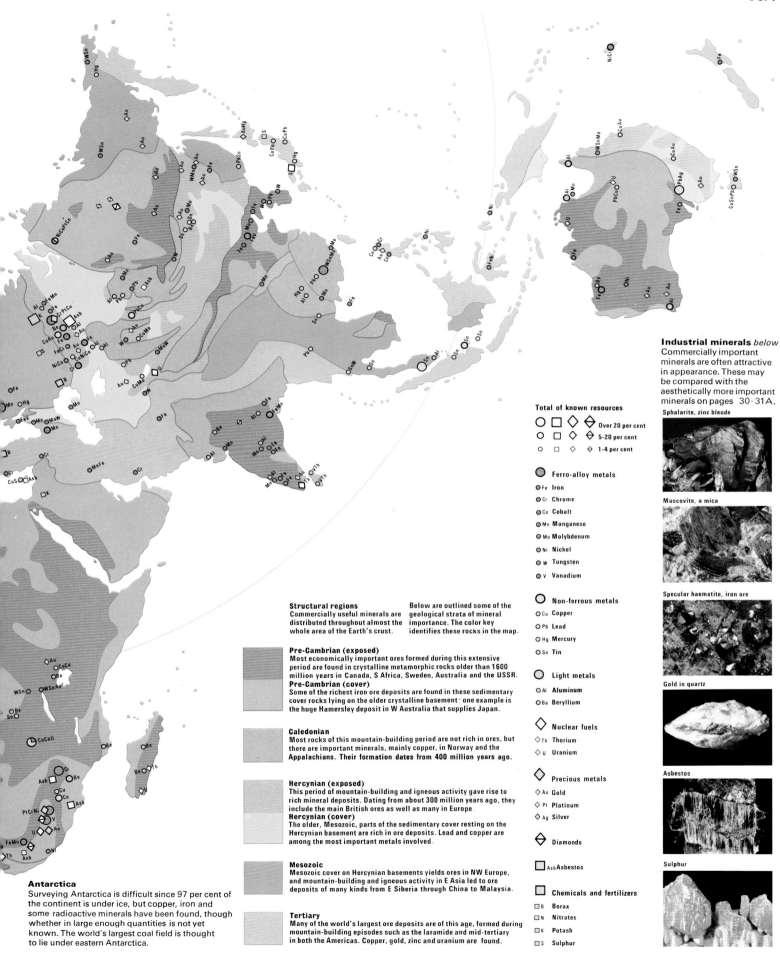

Total of known resources

| | Over 20 per cent |
| 5-20 per cent |
| 1-4 per cent |

Ferro-alloy metals

- Fe Iron
- Cr Chrome
- Co Cobalt
- Mn Manganese
- Mo Molybdenum
- Ni Nickel
- W Tungsten
- V Vanadium

Non-ferrous metals

- Cu Copper
- Pb Lead
- Hg Mercury
- Sn Tin

Light metals

- Al Aluminum
- Be Beryllium

Nuclear fuels

- Th Thorium
- U Uranium

Precious metals

- Au Gold
- Pt Platinum
- Ag Silver

Diamonds

Asb **Asbestos**

Chemicals and fertilizers

- B Borax
- N Nitrates
- K Potash
- S Sulphur

Structural regions
Commercially useful minerals are distributed throughout almost the whole area of the Earth's crust.

Below are outlined some of the geological strata of mineral importance. The color key identifies these rocks in the map.

Pre-Cambrian (exposed)
Most economically important ores formed during this extensive period are found in crystalline metamorphic rocks older than 1600 million years in Canada, S Africa, Sweden, Australia and the USSR.
Pre-Cambrian (cover)
Some of the richest iron ore deposits are found in these sedimentary cover rocks lying on the older crystalline basement: one example is the huge Hamersley deposit in W Australia that supplies Japan.

Caledonian
Most rocks of this mountain-building period are not rich in ores, but there are important minerals, mainly copper, in Norway and the Appalachians. Their formation dates from 400 million years ago.

Hercynian (exposed)
This period of mountain-building and igneous activity gave rise to rich mineral deposits. Dating from about 300 million years ago, they include the main British ores as well as many in Europe.
Hercynian (cover)
The older, Mesozoic, parts of the sedimentary cover resting on the Hercynian basement are rich in ore deposits. Lead and copper are among the most important metals involved.

Mesozoic
Mesozoic cover on Hercynian basements yields ores in NW Europe, and mountain-building and igneous activity in E Asia led to ore deposits of many kinds from E Siberia through China to Malaysia.

Tertiary
Many of the world's largest ore deposits are of this age, formed during mountain-building episodes such as the laramide and mid-tertiary in both the Americas. Copper, gold, zinc and uranium are found.

Antarctica
Surveying Antarctica is difficult since 97 per cent of the continent is under ice, but copper, iron and some radioactive minerals have been found, though whether in large enough quantities is not yet known. The world's largest coal field is thought to lie under eastern Antarctica.

Industrial minerals *below*
Commercially important minerals are often attractive in appearance. These may be compared with the aesthetically more important minerals on pages 30-31A.

Sphalarite, zinc blende

Muscovite, a mica

Specular haematite, iron ore

Gold in quartz

Asbestos

Sulphur

Earth's Energy Resources

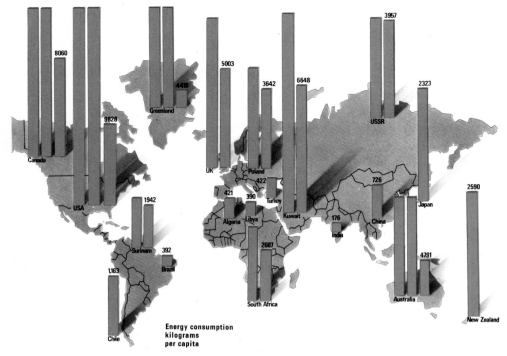

Energy consumption
kilograms
per capita

The concept of energy arose only very recently in the period of man's life on Earth, but already it dominates the whole quality of this life. Early man had no mechanical energy but that of his muscles. By about 2500 years ago he had learned to harness draft animals, such as the ox and horse, and to devise crude water wheels to harness part of the energy of the flow of water in a river. Soon afterwards he added sails to make the fickle wind propel his ships, and by 1000 years ago had started to dot his landscape with windmills. By this time he was adept at burning combustible materials, and during the past 500 years his energy has been increasingly based upon fire, first using wood, and subsequently coal, gas made from coal, petroleum, and natural gas.

All these energy sources, including animal muscle and the wind, are based on the energy radiated by the Sun. Although modern man has begun to use this energy directly in a few trivial installations in hot countries, almost all his energy is derived from solar heat locked up in fossil fuels. The known reserves of these fuels are tending to increase, as a result of prospecting, even faster than man is burning them up. But if no more were discovered most of man's world would come to a halt inside 20 years.

But there should be no energy gap. The promise of nuclear energy is such that, by using fast reactors that breed more fuel than they consume, energy should become one of the very few really plentiful and cheap commodities in man's world of the future. The challenges reside in extracting the fuels and using them effectively.

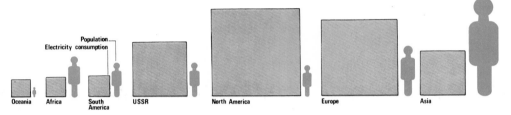

Population
Electricity consumption

Oceania | Africa | South America | USSR | North America | Europe | Asia

Power and people *above*
World consumption of energy is very uneven. One way of measuring it is to reduce all forms of energy to an equivalent weight of coal burned. The columns on the world map are proportional to the 'coal equivalent' of selected national consumptions expressed in kilograms per head. Electricity consumption is even more disproportionate, as witness the square areas and figure heights immediately above.

Fuels and energy *right*
The caloric value of a fuel is the quantity of heat generated by burning a unit mass. Figures are in British Thermal Units per pound. The surrounding curve shows the increase in the rate at which man is consuming energy; one joule (j) per second is equal to one watt.

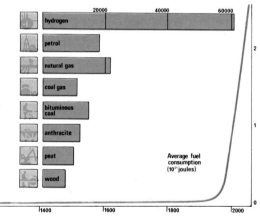

	20000	40000	60000
hydrogen			
petrol			
natural gas			
coal gas			
bituminous coal			
anthracite			
peat			
wood			

Average fuel consumption
(10^{22} joules)

1000 | 1200 | 1400 | 1600 | 1800 | 2000

Sources of power *below*
For many centuries the only alternative sources of power to muscles were wood fires, waterwheels and windmills — and the latter had too slight an effect to be shown on the figure below. The left portion shows the way in which, since 1850, the United States has enjoyed successive new sources of energy. In 1920 the US economy was not untypical in being based on coal, but since then more energetic, cleaner and more efficiently used fuels have dominated the picture. In the future, nuclear power, shown in the right-hand figure, promises to make good shortages of fossil fuels.

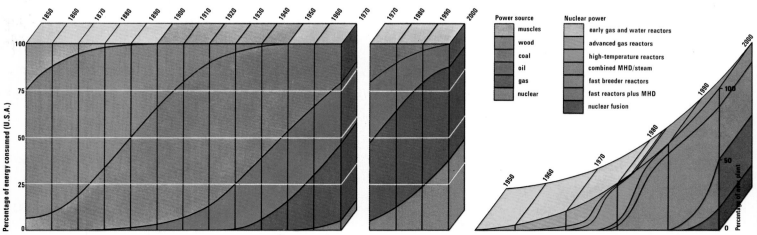

Percentage of energy consumed (U.S.A.)

Power source	Nuclear power
muscles	early gas and water reactors
wood	advanced gas reactors
coal	high-temperature reactors
oil	combined MHD/steam
gas	fast breeder reactors
nuclear	fast reactors plus MHD
	nuclear fusion

Coal into electricity
To reduce costs modern coal-fired generating stations are sited on coalfields ; Lea Hall colliery feeds Rugeley power station (background).

Flare in the desert
Once oil has been struck, harmful gases are burned off in the atmosphere. Similar 'flares' are a prominent feature of petroleum refineries.

Drilling for gas
To reach natural gas trapped in submarine strata a drill rig is used to bore a hole at a location determined by the prospectors

Nuclear power station
Nearly all today's nuclear energy is used to generate electricity. One of the largest stations is Wylfa, Wales, rated at 1180 million watts.

Coal

For three centuries the most important of the fossil fuels, coal is the result of some 300 million years of subterranean decay of vegetation. Many thousands of generations of the Carboniferous trees have become compressed and hardened, first into peat, then into lignite, then into bituminous coal and finally into anthracite. Until this century coal was used inefficiently as a source of heat. Today it is becoming equally important as a raw material producing plastics, heavy chemicals, insecticides, perfumes, antiseptics, road surfaces and many other products. Great advances have been made in automating the mining of coal, but it remains a laborious task and is therefore becoming increasingly expensive. However, coal mining remains a worldwide industry that passes on to modern man the products of the solar energy captured by a younger Earth.

Petroleum

Like coal, oil is a mixture of fossil remains, but yields few clues as to its origin. Crude oil, from the locations shown on the map at right, is carried by tanker ships to refineries in the user countries. Here it is heated in pipe stills until the various constituent 'fractions' are boiled off. The result is a wide range of products from gasoline through kerosene and gas oil to heavy fuel oils, lubricants and vaseline, with a wide range of other by-products used in many thousands of chemicals and plastics materials. Petroleum fuels are replacing coal in heating and transport applications, partly owing to their easier handling and partly to reduce air pollution by sulphurous compounds. LPG, liquefied pertroleum gas, is even cleaner burning and may become more important than gasoline and kerosene in road vehicles and aircraft over the next 25 years.

Gas

In 1807 a London street was lit by town gas, a mixture of hydrogen (about 50%), methane, carbon monoxide and dioxide and other gases, formed by cooking coal at high temperature in a retort. By 1950 this manufactured gas was an important fuel, but in many advanced countries its place is now being taken by natural gas, a primary fuel consisting mainly of methane piped straight from deposits sometimes conveniently sited from the user's point of view (right). Intensive prospecting is discovering natural gas faster than it is being used, and during the past 20 years natural gas has become man's largest single source of energy. In refrigerated form, as a compact liquid, it promises to become an attractive fuel for transport vehicles. A major benefit is that the exhaust from such a vehicle would contain less pollutants than from those using gasoline.

Nuclear energy

In 1956 Britain opened the world's first electricity generating station using the heat of nuclear fission. It was fuelled with rods of natural uranium, a heavy silvery metal containing a small proportion of atoms capable of spontaneous fission when struck by a free neutron. Fission releases further neutrons capable of sustaining a continuous chain reaction. Such a reaction generates heat which is used to provide steam for turbines. The prime advantage of nuclear power is that the fuel is used extremely slowly. Now the fast reactor, which uses raw 'fast' neutrons instead of ones artificially slowed down, has been developed. Not only can the fast reactor generate great energy from a small bulk but it creates fresh fuel faster than the original (plutonium) fuel is consumed. Fast reactors, using uranium from granite, could provide limitless cheap energy.

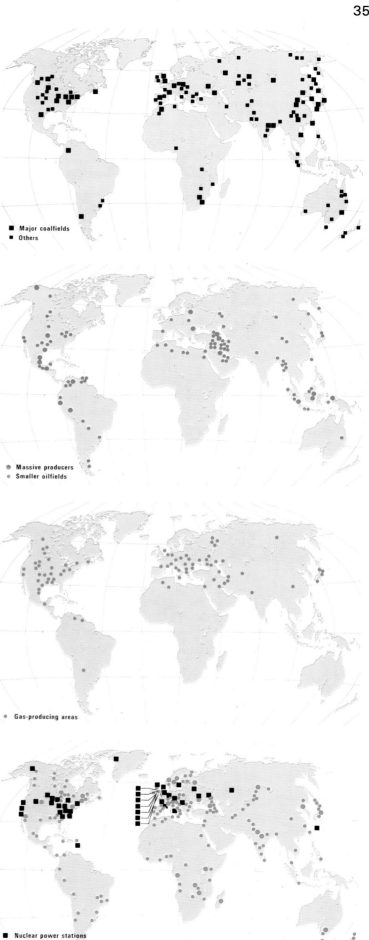

Earth's Water Resources

Without water there would be no life as we know it on the Earth. Life began in the oceans and the life of the land, both plant and animal, still remains utterly dependent on water for its survival. The atmosphere plays a vital role in the terrestrial water system. Spurred by the energy of the Sun, the moist layer surrounding the globe forms a vast heat engine, operating at a rate of billions of horsepower. All the exposed water surface is constantly being converted into vapor. Eventually the air holding the vapor cools, and the vapor condenses as rain, hail or snow. Most of this precipitation falls into the sea, but nearly a quarter of it falls on the land. Altogether about two-thirds of it evaporates back into the air, or is transpired by plants; the rest runs off in rivers, or filters through the ground to the water table beneath.

Satisfying the collective thirst of man and his industry grows daily more difficult. Almost always the demand is for fresh water; but the proportion of the Earth's water in rivers and streams is less than one part in a million. If the Antarctic ice cap were to melt, it would feed all the rivers for 800 years. Although schemes have been suggested for towing giant fresh-water icebergs from Antarctica to the Californian coast, man is unlikely to make extensive use of the ice cap. Far more promising is the large supply of subterranean water. At the same time great strides are being made in desalination of sea water, using a variety of methods. Management of the Earth's water resources is seen ever more clearly as a technical challenge of the greatest magnitude.

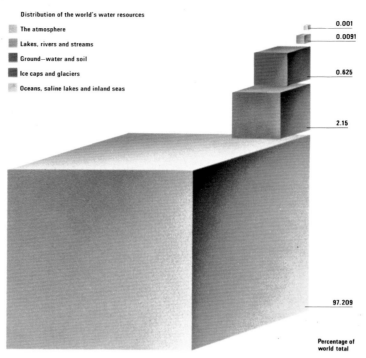

Distribution of the world's water resources

- The atmosphere
- Lakes, rivers and streams
- Ground—water and soil
- Ice caps and glaciers
- Oceans, saline lakes and inland seas

0.001
0.0091
0.625
2.15
97.209

Percentage of world total

The world's water *left*
The total volume of the Earth's water is about 326 million cubic miles (1400 million km³). Practically all of it is in the oceans, in a form rich in dissolved salts. Solar heating is constantly evaporating this mass, converting it ultimately into precipitation of fresh water which falls back to the surface. Run-off from the surface in rivers and streams is one of the forms of terrestrial water most visible to man, but it accounts for a negligible fraction of the total. Some 80 times as much water lies in salt lakes and inland seas, 90 times as much in fresh-water lakes, more than 6000 times as much in ground water beneath the land surface, and almost a quarter-million times as much in ice caps and glaciers. So far man has made little attempt to use these sources of fresh water. Instead he interrupts the hydrologic cycle in the easy places: the rivers and lakes, where, because of the small volumes and flows available, he causes significant pollution.

A valued resource *above*
Shiupur head, the head-waters of the Gang canal in Rajasthan province, India. This and other canal systems are gradually bringing to this arid province an assured supply of irrigation water from the Himalayas.

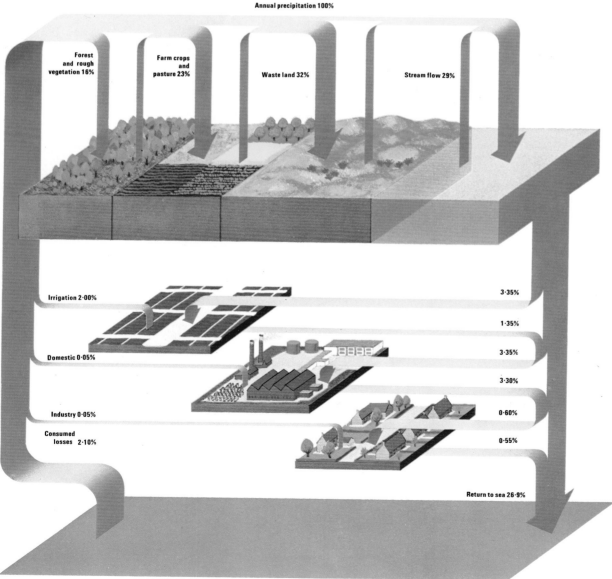

Annual precipitation 100%

Forest and rough vegetation 16%
Farm crops and pasture 23%
Waste land 32%
Stream flow 29%

Irrigation 2·00% — 3·35%
1·35%
Domestic 0·05% — 3·35%
3·30%
Industry 0·05% — 0·60%
Consumed losses 2·10% — 0·55%

Return to sea 26·9%

The hydrologic cycle *left*
This diagram is drawn for United States, but the basic features of the cycle are common to most of the Earth's land. Just over three-quarters of the rain snow and hail falls on the oceans. The usual measure for water in huge quantities is the acre-foot (one acre of water, one foot deep). Each year about 300 thousand million acre-feet of water falls on the oceans and 80 thousand million on the land. In the diagram all the figures are percentages. In the US, which is not unusual in its proportion of farmland, less than one-quarter of the water falling on the land falls directly on crops or pasture. A greater amount falls into rivers and streams, from which man takes varying small fractions for his own purposes. It can be seen that, even in the US, the total quantity of water withdrawn for use is only 7.3 per cent of the fraction of water falling on the land. Yet, to attain even this performance, Americans spend more than $10000 million each year on improving their water supplies.

Domestic use of water

In some countries the total consumption of water is less than one gallon per head, but in the United States more than 70 US gallons are consumed by each person daily, on average, in domestic use alone. The way this consumption is split up varies greatly, but these percentages, for 'an average home in Akron, Ohio' are typical for modern urban areas having piped water to flush toilets. Total domestic water consumption in the industrially advanced countries is usually between five and 30 per cent of the national total.

Flushing toilet 41%

Washing and bathing 37%

Kitchen use 6%

Drinking 5%

Laundry 4%

Household cleaning 3%

Garden 3%

Cleaning car 1%

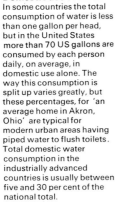

Process	Requirement
1 Family car	100,000 gals
2 Filling radiator	2 gals
3 One gallon of gas	70 gals
4 One tire	42 000 gals
5 One ton of steel	44 000 gals
6 One ton of glass	130 gals

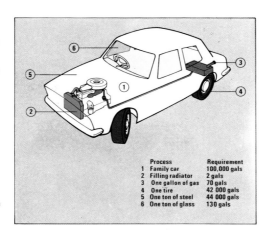

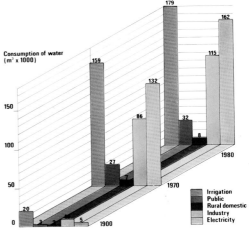
Consumption of water (m³ x 1000)

Irrigation / Public / Rural domestic / Industry / Electricity

Rising demand above
Civilized man needs more water every year. Plotted graphically, the rising demand for water in the United States is startling; the rate of increase is about three times the rate of population growth. Rural domestic supplies are from wells; others are piped.

Irrigation below
Irrigation of land by man is at least 7000 years old, yet still in its infancy. The grey areas on the world map are virtually without irrigation. The last column of data shows the percentage of each continent irrigated. Only Japan and the UAR exceed 50 per cent.

Continent	Area : million acres (1 acre = 4047m²) Total	Cultivated (A)	Irrigated (B)	Ratio of B to A (x 100)
Africa	898	37	11.2	30
Asia	5062	1289	296.9	23
Australia	1900	38	3	8
Europe	288	122	5.8	5
N America	2809	485	49	10
S America	4620	187	13	7
USSR	5540	568	23	4
Grand total	21117	2726	401.9	15

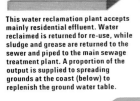

Most liquid wastes are generated by mixed human concentrations-including habitations, businesses and industry. Before reclamation, any wastes having excessive or toxic mineral content must be segregated from the main flow.

Oilfields on the land invariably generate large and varied liquid wastes, particularly including concentrated brines, which must be excluded from conventional reclamation processes.

This water reclamation plant accepts mainly residential effluent. Water reclaimed is returned for re-use, while sludge and grease are returned to the sewer and piped to the main sewage treatment plant. A proportion of the output is supplied to spreading grounds at the coast (below) to replenish the ground water table.

Liquid wastes from residential and business areas normally comprise sewage suitable for reclamation without pre-treatment or segregation.

This water reclamation plant supplies water to the city (above) and to agriculture and industry (below, right). Sludge and grease are returned to the sewer (route, far right).

Reclaimed waters may be used to maintain underground supplies by spreading them on percolation beds (above), where the water filters down to the storage basin.

Below, the main sewage treatment plant can operate by a variety of methods, including long-term open storage, aeration, mechanical filtration and softening.

Reclaiming used water
In almost every country the quality of the water pumped into domestic supplies is subject to precise controls, and the proportion of some substances may not exceed one or two parts per million. National water systems make maximum use of water reclaimed close to the point of consumption by plant which returns the heavy sludges and greases to the sewer for treatment at a large sewage works. This facilitates effluent quality control and also provides an emergency outlet for a temporarily overloaded or faulty reclamation plant. In the example here the main treatment plant discharges wastes into an ocean outfall (left), while the fresh water spreading grounds just inshore replenish the water table and thus prevent infiltration by the ocean water.

Desalination
Man's growing demand for fresh water cannot readily be met without an enormous increase in his capacity to desalinate salt water. A choice between several ways of doing this is invariably made on economic grounds. Nearly all the large installations in use are multi-stage flash evaporators in which some form of heat – if possible, heat otherwise wasted - is used to convert sea water to steam which is condensed by the incoming salt water. But in some circumstances more economic results can be obtained by freezing, reverse osmosis or other methods.

GROWTH OF DESALTING CAPACITY 1961 TO 1968

Year Ending	Municipal water use M gal per day	Industrial/other uses M gal per day	Total
1961	17.6	42.2	59.8
1962	20.9	45.5	66.4
1963	28.4	50.4	78.8
1964	32.5	53.5	86.0
1965	39.3	58.9	98.2
1966	52.6	101.6	154.2
1967	102.2	115.3	217.5
1968	121.4	125.8	247.2
Historical annual growth %	32	17	23
Projection to 1975	835	415	1250
Projected annual growth %	32	19	26

SIZE RANGES OF THE WORLD'S DESALTING PLANTS

Size range M gal per day	Number of Plants	Total capacity M gal per day
0.025–0.1	351	17.8
0.1–0.3	218	35.3
0.3–0.5	34	13.0
0.5–1.0	31	21.3
1.0–5.0	46	95.4
5.0–7.5	3	17.5
over 7.5	3	46.9
TOTAL	686	247.2

The Oceans' Mineral Resources

A submerged land almost equal to the area of the Moon is being urgently explored for its store of minerals. The continental shelf around the Earth's land has the proportions of a seventh continent; around Britain or Japan its area is several times larger than that of the land itself. The shelf is rich in minerals, some of which are accumulating faster than man can at present use them.

By far the most important resources of the shallow seas are the deposits of oil and gas locked in the strata below the bed. About 200 drilling rigs are constantly looking for new deposits, and already nearly 20 per cent of the world's supplies, worth annually $4800 million, are taken from under the sea. Geologists estimate that oil and gas resources under the oceans are at least as great as those under the land. Next to oil and gas the most important marine minerals are lowly sand and gravel. It is becoming increasingly difficult and costly to extract these from the land, and marine deposits are fast becoming of great commercial importance. Often their extraction is combined with land reclamation. The Dutch, for example, have devised several systems that help to create new land and, as at Europoort, deep-water channels.

Last in importance, but very high in speculative interest, come the heavy minerals. Some, such as gravels rich in ilmenite, rutile and zircon, have been concentrated by the sorting action of the waves. Others, including tin, gold and diamonds, have been derived from igneous deposits. But in most cases these minerals can still be obtained more cheaply on land, except in one or two freak instances where concentrated deposits can be easily reached.

Exploiting the shallow sea

One of the most important recent discoveries of oil and natural gas has occurred in the North Sea, on the very doorstep of industrial Western Europe. The North Sea gas is found mainly in layers of a porous sandstone deposited under desert conditions. Since both natural gas and oil are thought to have originated from the compressed remains of animals and plants that swarmed in the warm seas of the Carboniferous period, the gas could not have formed in the rocks where it is now found.

Immediately below the sandstone lie thick coal measures, and the gas appears to have risen from these into the porous sandstone until halted by a thick layer of salt and limestone. Where the limestone is broken and porous, the gas has risen into it and become trapped under salt domes. In the Gulf of Mexico these domes have themselves become a source of minerals. While drilling down to a promising dome an oil company came across the third largest sulphur deposit in the United States.

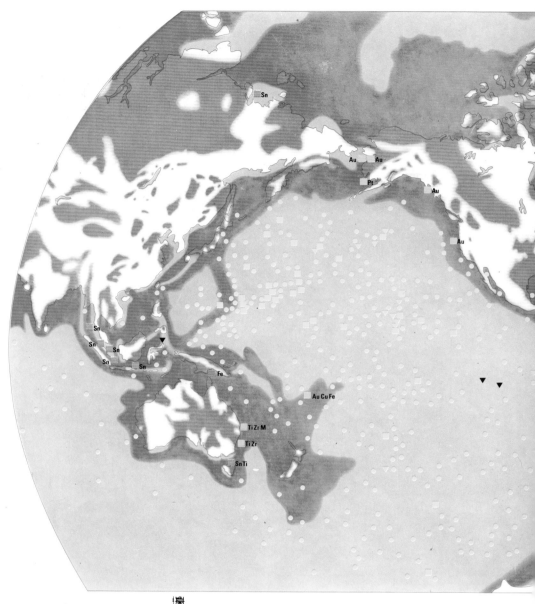

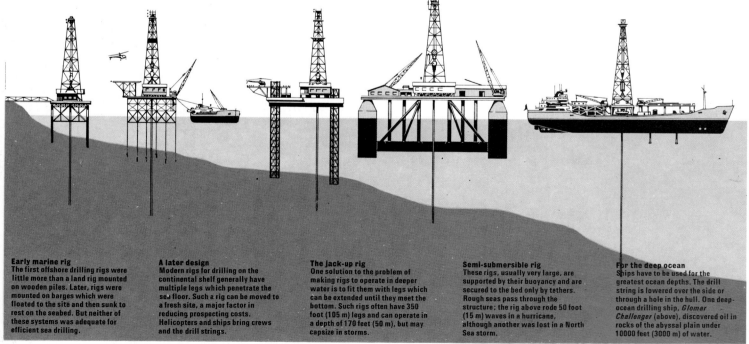

Early marine rig
The first offshore drilling rigs were little more than a land rig mounted on wooden piles. Later, rigs were mounted on barges which were floated to the site and then sunk to rest on the seabed. But neither of these systems was adequate for efficient sea drilling.

A later design
Modern rigs for drilling on the continental shelf generally have multiple legs which penetrate the sea floor. Such a rig can be moved to a fresh site, a major factor in reducing prospecting costs. Helicopters and ships bring crews and the drill strings.

The jack-up rig
One solution to the problem of making rigs to operate in deeper water is to fit them with legs which can be extended until they meet the bottom. Such rigs often have 350 foot (105 m) legs and can operate in a depth of 170 feet (50 m), but may capsize in storms.

Semi-submersible rig
These rigs, usually very large, are supported by their buoyancy and are secured to the bed only by tethers. Rough seas pass through the structure; the rig above rode 50 foot (15 m) waves in a hurricane, although another was lost in a North Sea storm.

For the deep ocean
Ships have to be used for the greatest ocean depths. The drill string is lowered over the side or through a hole in the hull. One deep-ocean drilling ship, *Glomar Challenger* (above), discovered oil in rocks of the abyssal plain under 10000 feet (3000 m) of water.

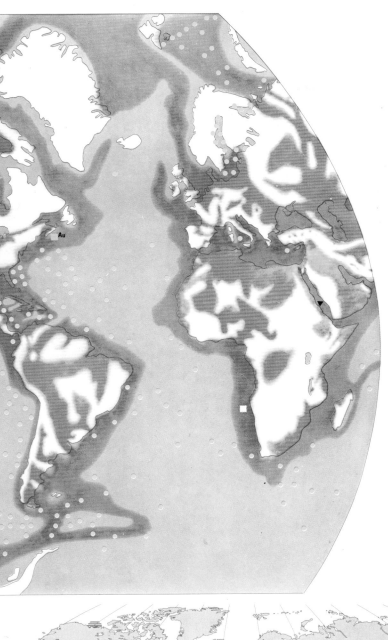

Undersea resources *left*

- **Deep ocean basins**
- **Sedimentary basins locally favourable for petroleum**
- Au: gold
- Sn: tin
- Fe: iron
- Ti: titanium
- D: diamonds
- Mn sampled
- Mn photo 25+ per cent.
- Mn photo 25− per cent.
- ▼ Metal-bearing muds

The large map gives a broad general picture of the distribution of petroleum resources, shown as favorable sedimentary basins, and of major subsea mineral deposits, but does not attempt to indicate commercial value or even which regions are worth exploiting. These are multi-billion dollar questions which are taxing mining companies in many countries. The manganese oxide deposits are shown only where they have been sampled or photographed (with symbols to indicate whether the nodules cover more or less than one-quarter of the sea floor). The metal-bearing muds are a recent exciting discovery. Deep down in the Red Sea, off Indonesia and elsewhere, prospectors have discovered concentrated brines rich in valuable industrial metals.

Mining the oceans *below*

For 20 years industry has been tantalized by the prospect of literally sucking or sweeping valuable minerals off the ocean floor. But the most widespread loose nodules (see photograph below) have a composition ill-matched to world demand (foot of page), and even the mining system sketched below, in which ships operate what is in effect a giant vacuum cleaner, has yet to be used on a commercial scale. The technical, economic and political problems associated with such ventures are immense: but the potential rewards are great enough to sustain interest.

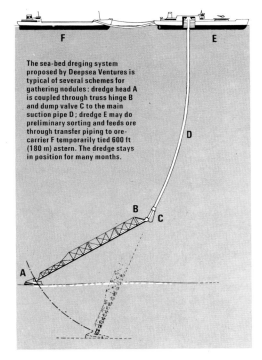

The sea-bed dreging system proposed by Deepsea Ventures is typical of several schemes for gathering nodules: dredge head A is coupled through truss hinge B and dump valve C to the main suction pipe D; dredge E may do preliminary sorting and feeds ore through transfer piping to ore-carrier F temporarily tied 600 ft (180 m) astern. The dredge stays in position for many months.

Manganese nodules

One of the most tempting concepts is to scoop minerals off the bed of the ocean. One of the few products which could thus be harvested is manganese, which is found in the form of potato-sized nodules scattered on the ocean floor.

Unfortunately not only are there technical difficulties standing in the way of such an operation but production would be out of step with world needs. The undersea production of the world's needs of manganese, equivalent to more than 18.6 million tons of ore, would lead to a 453 per cent glut of cobalt. Similarly, if all the world demand for copper were met from the same source, the glut of cobalt would be no less than 11335 per cent (right).

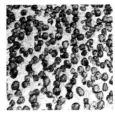

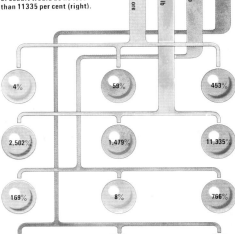

Manganese 18,650,000 tons ore | Copper 11,189,377,000 lb | Nickel 1,007,943,000 lb | Cobalt 32,390,000 lb

4%	59%	453%
2,502%	1,479%	11,335%
169%	8%	766%
22%	0.9%	13%

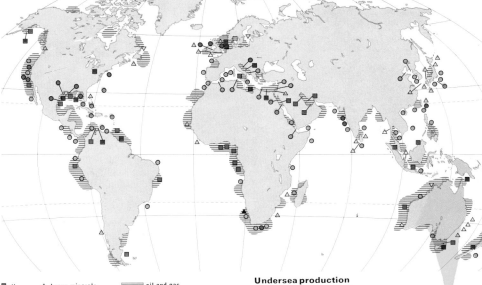

Undersea production

Man's commercial use of the ocean minerals is so far confined almost entirely to the continental shelves around the land.

- ■ oil
- ■ gas
- △ tin
- ▽ iron
- △ coal
- ▽ salt
- △ heavy minerals
- ▽ sulphur
- ▲ diamonds
- ▣ magnesium
- ⊙ fresh water
- ⊙ other minerals
- ▦ oil and gas exploration

Fish and shellfish were probably the first marine resources to be exploited by man. Many of his early settlements in coastal and estuarine areas bear witness to this with their ancient mounds of oyster and mussel shells. Even now, coastal fisheries remain a vital source of high quality protein for numerous primitive communities. And yet, in spite of this long history of coastal fishing, the commercial fisheries have been dominated by a mere handful of nations until recent times. Three-quarters of the world fish catch is still accounted for by only 14 countries.

The world fish catch is the only source of food that has managed to increase dramatically since the end of World War II. In the decade from 1958-68 alone, it rose from below 34 million tons to 64 million tons. Although the catch fell by two per cent in 1969, it is expected to continue to improve and may even top the 120 million ton mark by the mid-1980s.

The steady growth of the commercial fisheries since the war has relied on improvements in technology and boats, and the spread of these modern techniques from traditional northern fisheries to newer ones being developed in the southern oceans. Peru, for example, now has the world's largest single species fishery, catching some 10 million tons of anchoveta a year: in 1958 the catch was only 960,000 tons. However, the time is fast approaching when few fish stocks will remain unexploited.

Already many established fisheries are beginning to suffer from the effects of over-fishing with too many boats pursuing too few fish, leading to the capture of younger, smaller fish and a decline in the fish stocks and the fisheries that they support. Only the briefest respite may be needed for the fish to recover: a single female fish can lay thousands of eggs in a single season. Over-exploitation of the whales and turtles is a much more serious matter. Already several species of whale are on the verge of extinction and, with one young born to a female every two years, the prospects for their recovery are poor.

The living resources of the oceans must be conserved and managed if they are to continue to provide mankind with food. It is now clear that the world fish catch has a finite limit, possibly about 200 million tons. With adequate international agreement and controls, this limit might one day be approached. The productivity of the oceans could be increased further only by harvesting animals lower than fish in the marine food chain or by artificially fertilizing and farming the seas. Some of the first steps in this direction are now in progress. Perhaps in the future a new pattern of exploitation will emerge, with fleets harvesting the oceanic fish while other fish, shellfish and crustaceans such as lobster and prawn are farmed in the shallow coastal waters.

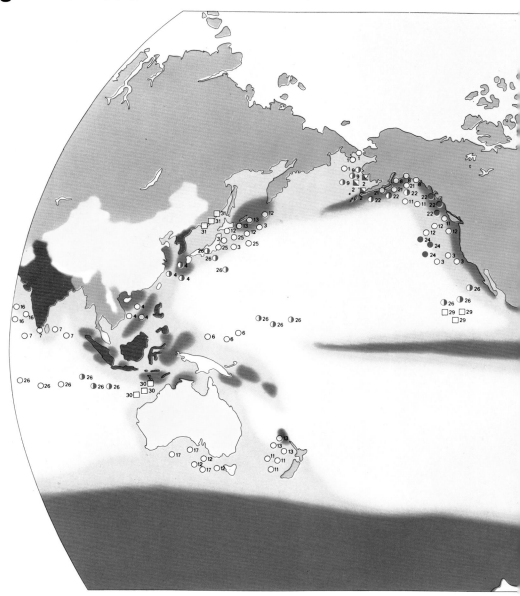

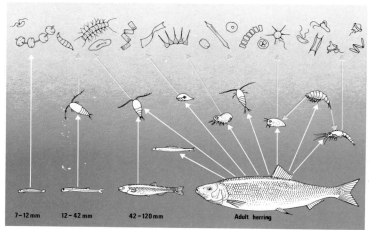

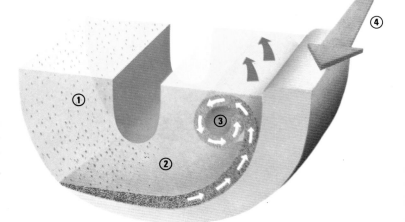

Marine food web *above*
The path leading to food fish such as the herring involves a succession of feeding and energy levels. The plants drifting in the plankton first convert the Sun's energy into a usable form through the process of photosynthesis (top band). The plants are then eaten by small planktonic animals (middle band). These in turn are eaten by the fish during its growth (bottom band). However, as the arrows indicate, the path from plant to fish is far from simple. At each point in the web, energy is exchanged and lost so that the adult fish receives less than a thousandth of the original energy captured in photosynthesis. This loss of energy has prompted suggestions for short-circuiting the process by harvesting members of the plankton itself — either the plants or the small crustaceans and other animals that feed on them.

Upwelling *above*
Most of the world's great fisheries occur in regions of upwelling where nutrient-rich water rises to the surface and supports prolific marine life. Deep ocean waters accumulate the remains of dead and decaying organisms (1) that rain down from the surface. When this nutrient-rich water (2) rises to the surface (3) it contains all the minerals and salts necessary for plant growth in approximately the ratio best suited to stimulate maximum growth. The actual mechanism which causes the water to rise to the surface can vary, but a common source is the inter-action between surface winds and ocean currents running along the edge of continents. The wind (4) causes the surface water to move away from the coast, enabling the deep water to swirl up to the surface where it renews the supplies of plant nutrients.

7-12mm   12-42mm   42-120mm   Adult herring

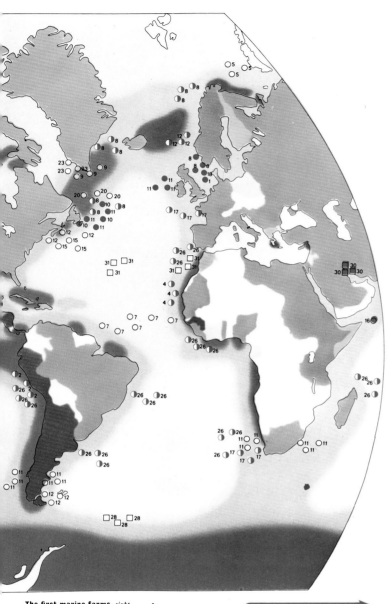

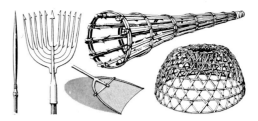

World fisheries *left*

With more nations claiming a share of the oceans' living resources few productive regions remain unexplored by fishing fleets. Already many fisheries show signs of over-exploitation and some coastal states are demanding exclusive rights to very large areas of sea, e.g. Iceland's demand for a 50 mile limit.

Biological productivity

■ Very favorable conditions for the growth of marine life

▨ Moderately favorable conditions for the growth of marine life

Exploitation of fish stocks

● Over-exploited by 1949

◐ Over-exploited by 1968

○ Under-exploited

Exploitation of crustaceans

◣ Over-exploited by 1968

□ Under-exploited

Key to numbers

1 Alaska pollack	17 Pilchard
2 Anchoveta	18 Plaice
3 Anchovy	19 Pamfret
4 Demersal fish	20 Red fish
5 Capelin	21 Rock fish
6 Carangidae	22 Salmon
7 Clupeidae	23 Sand eel
8 Cod	24 Sardine
9 Flat fish	25 Saury
10 Haddock	26 Tuna
11 Hake	27 King crab
12 Herring	28 Krill
13 Jack mackerel	29 Red crab
14 Mackerel	30 Shrimp
15 Menhaden	31 Squid
16 Pelagic	

Fishing limits

□ Nations claiming a 3 mile exclusive zone

▨ Nations claiming a 6 mile exclusive zone

▨ Nations claiming a 12 mile exclusive zone

■ Nations claiming more than 12 miles

Fishing gear

Primitive fisheries use a wide range of techniques (above) including spears, nets and basket traps.

Mainstays of the modern commercial fisheries (below) are the gill net (top), the seine net and the otter trawl (bottom).

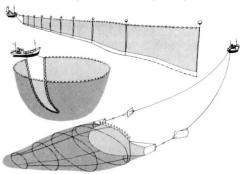

Anchoveta
5 in, 13 cm
2-3 oz, 85 g

Herring
12 in, 30 cm
8 oz, 227 g

Commercial fish

Although the oceans contain many thousands of different fish species, very few of these support large commercial fisheries. The anchoveta supplies the largest single species fishery in the world with an annual catch of about 10 million tons. This is slightly greater than the total catch of the other species illustrated here.

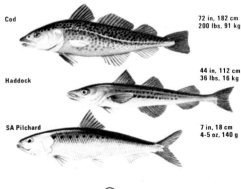

Cod
72 in, 182 cm
200 lbs, 91 kg

Haddock
44 in, 112 cm
36 lbs, 16 kg

SA Pilchard
7 in, 18 cm
4-5 oz, 140 g

The first marine farms, *right*

An early use of marine stockades was to keep alive fish caught at sea until they were needed for eating (A). An advance on this is to catch young fish and then fatten them in fertile coastal waters (B). But marine farming really begins with the production of 'seed fish' which can be reared until they are large enough to survive at sea (C). Such a scheme was proposed in the early 1900s as a means of increasing the productivity of the North Sea fisheries. The proposal was rejected, although marine fish hatcheries existed at the time. These hatcheries, however, were unable to feed their young fish once the yolk sacs had become exhausted. Success became possible with the discovery that brine shrimps, hatched in large numbers, could be used as fish food and that antibiotics would prevent marine bacteria from coating the eggs and killing or weakening the fish embryos inside. The point has now been reached at which fish farming is possible, although fish reared in this way are still too expensive to compete with those caught at sea. In one scheme, eggs collected from adult fish kept in ponds are hatched and the young fed on diatoms and brine shrimps until large enough to be put into marine enclosures (D).

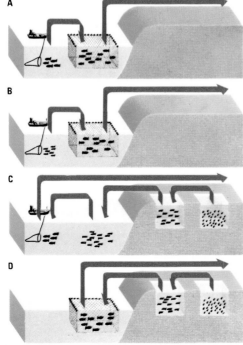

Enriching the sea *right, below*

Some marine farms in the future will exploit the store of nutrients that lie in the cold, deep ocean water. The value of this marine 'fertilizer' is clearly seen in areas where deep water rises to the surface. One project to create an artificial upwelling was started in the Virgin Islands in 1970. When completed it could include both a marine farm and provide fresh water supplies. In this system the cold nutrient-rich water (1) would be raised to the surface by a pump (2) driven by the warm, humid, prevailing winds (3). The cold water would then pass through a condenser (4) where it would be used to cool the wind and release its store of fresh water (5). Finally, the water, now warmed to the temperature of the surface waters, would be used to promote the growth of marine plants and animals such as shellfish, prawn and valuable food fish within net enclosures (6). Deep ocean water may also be used to combat thermal pollution, particularly in tropical areas where marine organisms live close to their upper temperature limit. The cold water would cool down the warm effluent discharged from power stations as well as provide valuable nutrients for marine aquiculture.

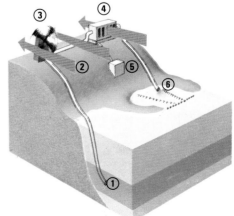

Combine harvester discharging wheat into trailer

Agriculture has always been a cornerstone of human civilization. Until man was able to give up the life of a nomadic hunter he could not be called civilized, and it was the settled life based on the land which enabled progress toward modern society to begin. Today agriculture is the occupation of more people than all other industries, but the pattern of their work varies greatly. In poor or developing lands as many as 90 per cent of the population live directly off the land, whereas in the most industrialized countries the proportion can be as low as three per cent.

The underlying purpose of farming is to convert the energy of sunlight into a form in which it can be assimilated by humans. Initially this can be done only by photosynthesis in green plants, and here the efficiency of the conversion process – expressed in terms of assimilable food energy obtained from a given amount of sunlight – varies from about two per cent down to less than one part in 1000. Further stages involve the consumption of plants by livestock to provide meat and other food for man, or the direct consumption of fruit, vegetables and cereals by man himself. Each additional step in this food chain involves large losses in energy, lowering the overall 'efficiency' of the process.

For many years research has led to improved methods of producing crops, by developing new plant strains with a higher edible yield or greater resistance to disease, by increasing both the area of land under cultivation and the nutritional value of the soil, by devising swifter and surer techniques of cultivation and by reducing the labor effort needed. Improved methods are especially needed in regions of poor farming. The 'Green Revolution' of SE Asia has already shown how yields can be increased dramatically, although at a greater cost in terms of agricultural chemicals and water supplies. Another promising way of increasing food supplies is to extract protein from plants such as soybean and even grass, and to convert them into forms that have the texture and taste of meat. For the more distant future there are prospects of growing single-cell protein and other revolutionary foods which in theory could at least double the Earth's ability to produce food.

World crop production and trade *right above*
In the large map, symbols and shading indicate the pattern of distribution of a selection of the most important crops used for human food. The distribution shown is that of growing area. This is often far removed from the plant's original center, and today the world crop pattern is being subjected to dramatic changes. For example, enormous increases have taken place in Italy's yield of maize (corn) and the United States' production of rice. Pie diagrams are used to show world crop trade, the pie area giving output and the color segments the products (key, far right).

Some important crops *right*
Eight of the world's chief human food crops are described individually at right. The figure below the name is the aggregate world production expressed in metric tons (1 m. ton is 0.984 British ton and 1.12 US tons). The pie diagrams in the form of segmented drums show the percentage of the world total raised by the three largest producing countries (in each case China is the People's Republic). The sketches illustrate the mature plant and its fruit, a form often unfamiliar to consumers. Similar panels on the next two pages deal with livestock, fish and oils.

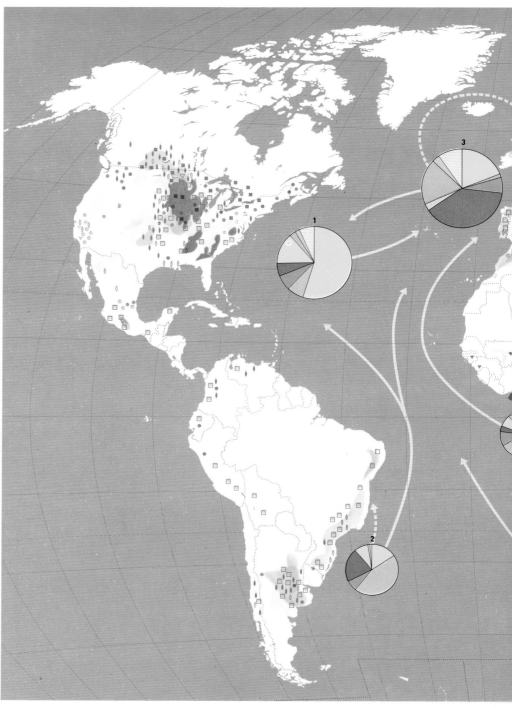

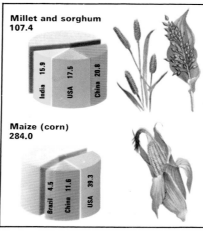

Millet and sorghum
107.4

India 15.9 | USA 17.5 | China 20.8

Several species of plant of the millet family form staple food crops throughout the Earth's warmer countries. The main genuses are *Panicum, Pennisetum,* and *Sorghum* or African millet. Chief growing regions are tropical and warm temperate Asia and Africa.

Maize (corn)
284.0

Brazil 4.5 | China 11.6 | USA 39.3

Maize was originally brought from America by Columbus. Although it needs a growing period of 140 days in a soil rich in nitrogen, it can be made into bread and is the subsistence diet of much of Asia and Africa and is important in North America and Britain.

Potatoes
352.0

China (M) 10.4 | Poland 14.4 | USSR 29.0

Grapes
53.7

USSR 8.4 | France 18.4 | Italy 19.2

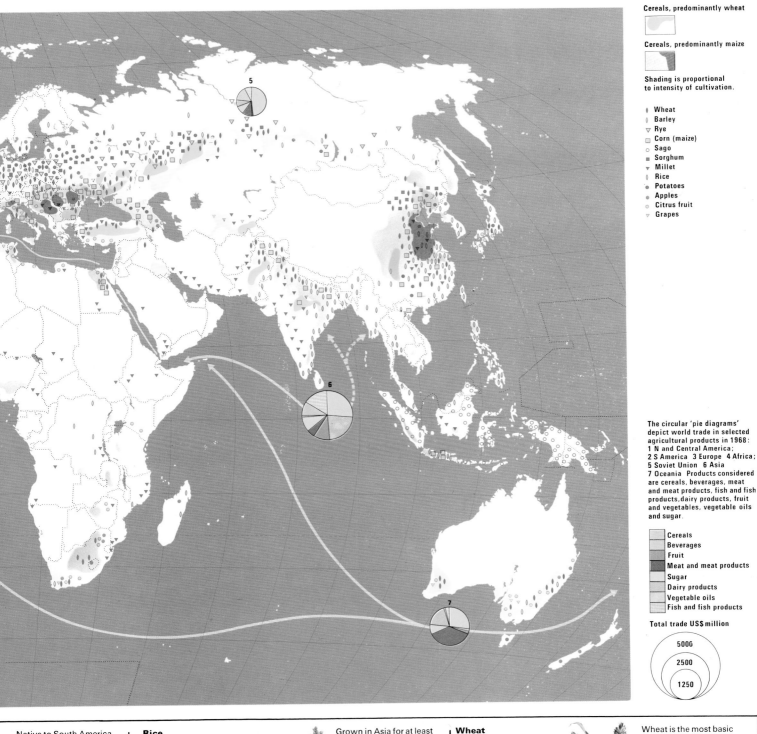

Cereals, predominantly wheat

Cereals, predominantly maize

Shading is proportional
to intensity of cultivation.

- ↓ Wheat
- ↓ Barley
- ▽ Rye
- ☐ Corn (maize)
- ○ Sago
- ■ Sorghum
- Millet
- ◊ Rice
- Potatoes
- Apples
- ○ Citrus fruit
- ▽ Grapes

The circular 'pie diagrams'
depict world trade in selected
agricultural products in 1968:
1 N and Central America;
2 S America 3 Europe 4 Africa;
5 Soviet Union 6 Asia
7 Oceania Products considered
are cereals, beverages, meat
and meat products, fish and fish
products, dairy products, fruit
and vegetables, vegetable oils
and sugar.

- Cereals
- Beverages
- Fruit
- Meat and meat products
- Sugar
- Dairy products
- Vegetable oils
- Fish and fish products

Total trade US$ million

5000

2500

1250

Native to South America,
the potato was introduced
by Spanish explorers to an
intrigued Europe about
1572. Although it needs a
long, cool growing season,
and a high nutrient level, it
yields more food per area of
land than cereals. It is a
source of alcohol.

The vine thrives in warm,
temperate areas, although
the quality of its rootstock
is critical to its nutrient
demand and its resistance
to disease and drought.
About 80 per cent of the
world crop is made into
wine, but large quantities
are dried for raisins.

Rice
284.2

Pakistan 7.1 India 21.0 China 32.0

Rye
33.4

W Germany 9.5 Poland 25.5 USSR 42.2

Grown in Asia for at least
5000 years, rice was
introduced into Europe by
the Arabs. Irrigation or a
very heavy rainfall is
essential for growing rice,
with the fields being flooded
for most of the season. The
main source of vitamins, the
husk, is removed in milling.

Gradually giving way to
other cereals, rye is
important where soils are
sandy and acid and the
winters long and harsh.
From Britain deep into
Siberia it remains a staple
foodstuff used for animal
feeds, for various forms of
bread and for whisky.

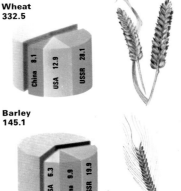

Wheat
332.5

China 8.1 USA 12.9 USSR 28.1

Barley
145.1

USA 6.3 China 9.9 USSR 19.9

Wheat is the most basic
human food of the
temperate zone. It flourishes
in well-drained, fertile
conditions, but can rapidly
exhaust the soil. New breeds
have been genetically
tailored to improve yield
and resistance to disease

Barley has a very short
growing season and so can
be produced further north
and at a higher altitude than
any other cereal. It needs
good drainage and non-
acid soil. More than half the
world crop is eaten by
livestock, and 12 per cent
goes into making beer.

Unloading frozen lamb carcasses.

Beverages
Coffee, cocoa and tea are grown in the tropics for export to economically advanced countries where their chief role is to add flavor than to provide nutrition. Tea is the cheapest at present.

- Coffee
- Cocoa
- Tea

Spices
Invariably these are pungent, aromatic vegetable products. They have been important European imports since pre-Roman times, and a major source today is Indonesia. Spices are extracted from buds, bark and pods.

- Pimento
- Ginger
- Nutmeg
- Mace
- Pepper
- Cloves
- Cinnamon
- Cassia
- Vanilla

Alcohol and tobacco
Originally native to South America, tobacco was brought to Europe by the Spanish 400 years ago. Today, it is grown all over the world in various climates and soils. The US is the biggest producer.

- Beer
- Wine
- Spirits
- Tobacco

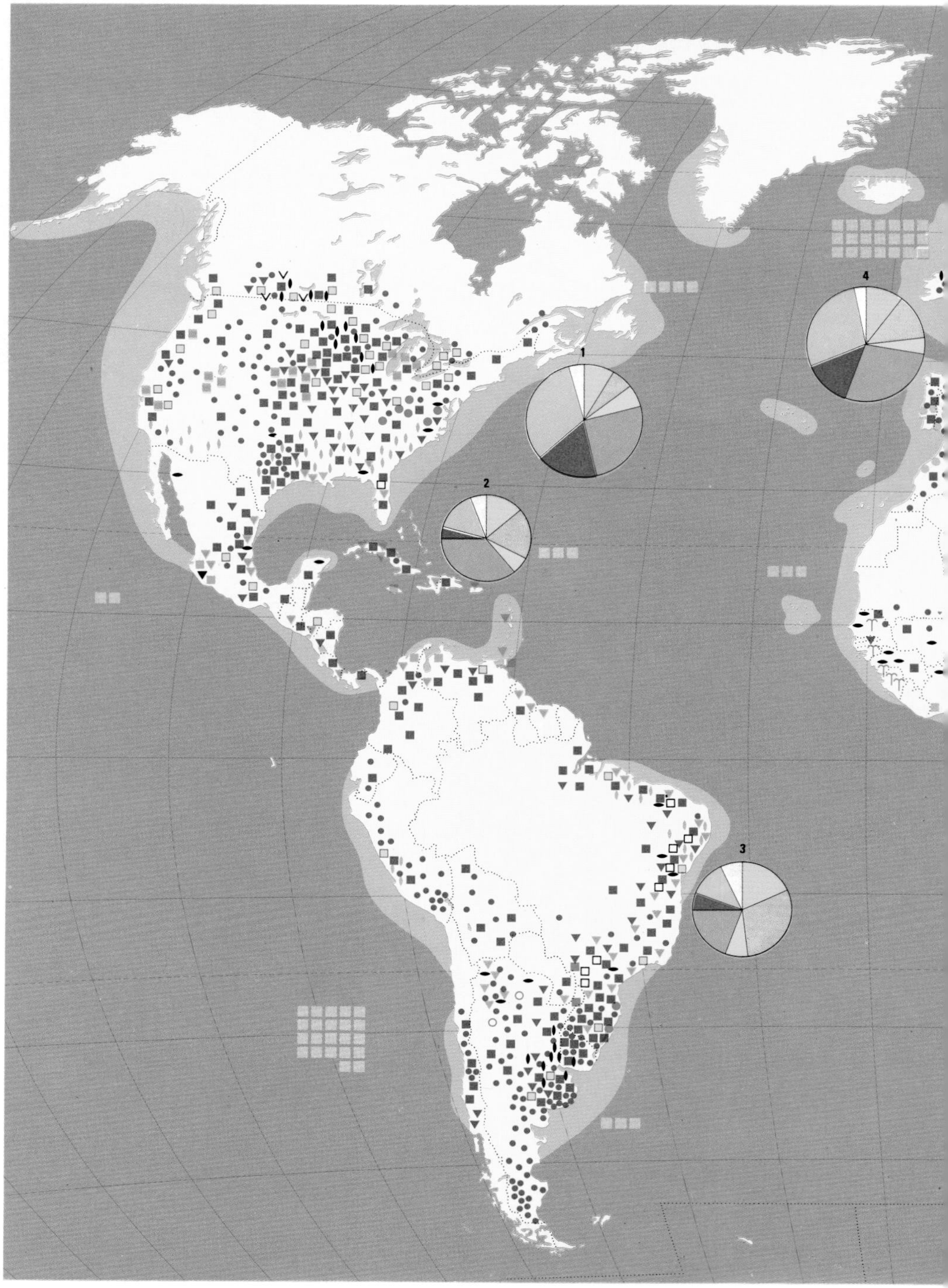

Beef cattle
Beef 29.7

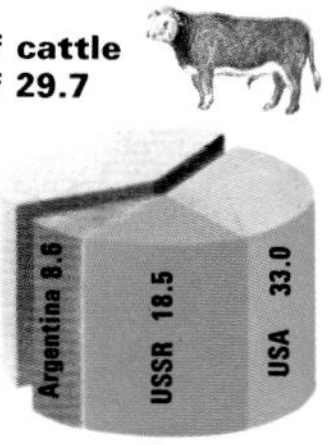

Argentine 8.6 | USSR 18.5 | USA 33.0

The two principal types of domestic cattle, the Eurpopean and the tropical Zebu or humped type, are found all over the world in every type of climate. There is an urgent need in the developing countries for better breeding, disease control and management.

Dairy cattle
415.8

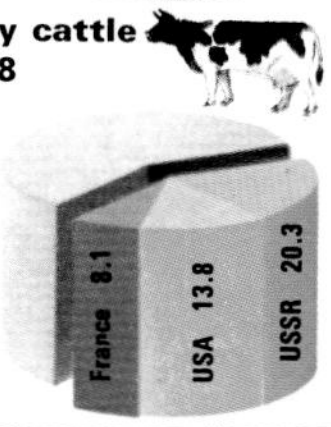

France 8.1 | USA 13.8 | USSR 20.3

Specialized dairy farming takes place mainly near densely populated urban areas with a high standard of living, though there is an increasing trend towards combined milk/meat herds. Various forms of processing, such as canning and freezing, extend product life.

Sheep
Mutton 4.5

India 8.2 | Australia 15.0 | USSR 22.3

Sheep are kept mainly for meat and wool, although in southern Europe they may be milked and in the tropics the hides are the most important product. Sheep do not lend themselves readily to 'factory farming' and are raised on marginal land only.

Pigs
Pork 24.5

China 11.0 | USSR 16.7 | USA 24.1

Because they are often kept indoors, the distribution of pigs depends more on food supply than on the climate. They are often found on mixed farms where they are fed on by-products such as skim milk. Their breeding cycle is complete in about six months.

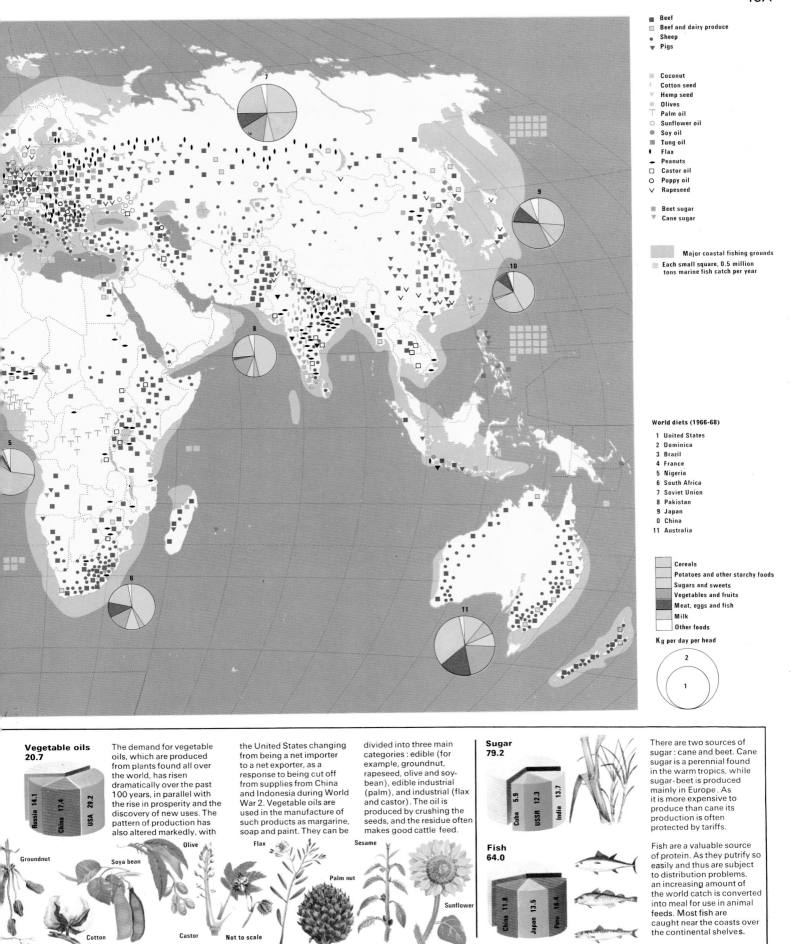

Beef
Beef and dairy produce
Sheep
Pigs

Coconut
Cotton seed
Hemp seed
Olives
Palm oil
Sunflower oil
Soy oil
Tung oil
Flax
Peanuts
Castor oil
Poppy oil
Rapeseed

Beet sugar
Cane sugar

Major coastal fishing grounds
Each small square, 0.5 million tons marine fish catch per year

World diets (1966-68)

1 United States
2 Dominica
3 Brazil
4 France
5 Nigeria
6 South Africa
7 Soviet Union
8 Pakistan
9 Japan
0 China
11 Australia

Cereals
Potatoes and other starchy foods
Sugars and sweets
Vegetables and fruits
Meat, eggs and fish
Milk
Other foods

Kg per day per head

Vegetable oils 20.7

The demand for vegetable oils, which are produced from plants found all over the world, has risen dramatically over the past 100 years, in parallel with the rise in prosperity and the discovery of new uses. The pattern of production has also altered markedly, with the United States changing from being a net importer to a net exporter, as a response to being cut off from supplies from China and Indonesia during World War 2. Vegetable oils are used in the manufacture of such products as margarine, soap and paint. They can be divided into three main categories: edible (for example, groundnut, rapeseed, olive and soy-bean), edible industrial (palm), and industrial (flax and castor). The oil is produced by crushing the seeds, and the residue often makes good cattle feed.

Russia 14.1 China 17.4 USA 29.2

Groundnut Soya bean Olive Flax Sesame Palm nut Sunflower Cotton Castor Not to scale

Sugar 79.2

Cuba 5.9 USSR 12.3 India 13.7

There are two sources of sugar: cane and beet. Cane sugar is a perennial found in the warm tropics, while sugar-beet is produced mainly in Europe. As it is more expensive to produce than cane its production is often protected by tariffs.

Fish 64.0

China 11.8 Japan 13.5 Peru 16.4

Fish are a valuable source of protein. As they putrify so easily and thus are subject to distribution problems, an increasing amount of the world catch is converted into meal for use in animal feeds. Most fish are caught near the coasts over the continental shelves.

To survive, animals must be adapted to their environment. They must be able to resist cold if they live in polar regions, drought if they live in deserts. They must find food, escape from predators and reproduce. Their offspring must mature and reproduce in turn. Adaptations of anatomy, physiology and behavior have evolved, so that today animals are found in all the Earth's diverse environments.

Ecologists divide the Earth into natural zones or 'biomes', each with its own highly adapted and integrated animal and plant communities. Inside each broad climatic zone animals have become adapted to various local environments or habitats. In tropical forests, for example, there are several layers of vegetation from the ground up to the tallest trees, and different animals with contrasting ways of life live in different layers. One species eats leaves and another eats berries, and so they avoid competition. Indeed the animals and plants of a community are interdependent. Herbivores eat plants, and carnivores eat herbivores. Food chains and the whole balance of a natural community can be altered by destroying one part of it. Thus, insecticides kill insects but also poison other animals in the area and the predators which prey on them.

Today's animals and plants are those whose ancestors survived immense changes. Continents drifted apart and moved together, seas rose and fell, mountains erupted and were levelled by erosion, glaciers advanced and retreated. Life evolved. Some animals became extinct; others adapted to the changes and spread to new areas. Sometimes they met impassable oceans, mountains and deserts. Groups of animals then became isolated and continued to evolve independently. Marsupials, mammals with pouches, were isolated in Australia before placental mammals, whose young are nourished for a long time in the mother's uterus, evolved in Europe and Asia. Placental mammals then supplanted marsupials everywhere but in Australia. Scientists divide the world into six zoogeographical realms each containing animals not found elsewhere. Some animals mix in transitional zones such as the Sahara Desert and the Himalayas.

Environmental factors

Climate is determined by the Sun's radiation on the Earth's atmosphere, oceans and continents. It varies with the time of day and season. Winds generated by the solar heating carry moisture inland, and heat away from the tropics. Ocean currents affect the prevailing temperature over large regions. Solar radiation, winds and ocean currents, together with latitude, altitude and the form of the land, combine to produce each local climate.

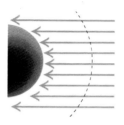

Solar heating *left*
The tropics are hotter than the poles because the Sun's rays pass almost vertically through a shallow depth of atmosphere and so are less attenuated. The Sun's vertical rays shift seasonally between the Tropics of Cancer and Capricorn, altering the length of daylight.

Wind and weather *left*
Hot air at the equator rises and moves north and south to higher latitudes. It subsides, producing trade winds, deflected by the rotation of the Earth, back again to the tropics. Westerly winds blow from the sub-tropics highs poleward toward the sub-polar lows.

Oceans *left*
Surface currents created by prevailing winds and variations in the density of the water are deflected by landmasses and the Coriolis effect' of rotation. Onshore winds across ocean currents are a major climatic control.

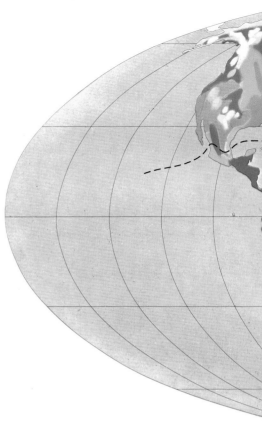

The zoogeographical classification of environments

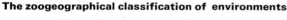

Roe deer
Flycatcher
Warbler
Dunnock
Wild ass
Hedgehog
Edible dormouse
Wild Sheep

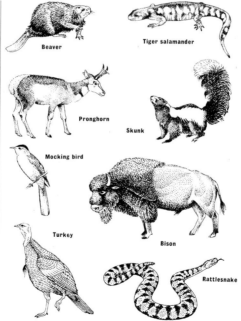

Beaver
Pronghorn
Mocking bird
Skunk
Turkey
Bison
Rattlesnake

Tiger salamander
Orangutan
Tree shrew
Gibbon
Fairy bluebird
Tiger
Peacock
Indian elephant

Palearctic (A)
This zoogeographical realm, the extent of which is shown on the map at right, is often grouped with the Nearctic to form the so-called Holarctic region. Roe deer, hedgehogs, dormice and the Asian wild ass are all unique here. Ancestors of modern horses crossed into it from North America during an ice age when the continents were bridged with ice.

Nearctic (B)
Covering the whole of North America from Greenland to the high plateau of Mexico, this realm contains beavers, elk and caribou. The prairie buffalo, which were slaughtered in their millions by 19th century man, have been saved from total extinction. And the American wild turkey has now been very successfully domesticated.

Oriental (C)
Comprising the southern part of Asia, Indonesia and the Philippines, this realm is largely isolated from the Palearctic realm to the north by the great folded barrier of the Himalayas, thrown up when the Indian subcontinent collided with Asia. Indigenous animals include tree shrews, tarsiers, gibbons, orangutans and the Indian elephant.

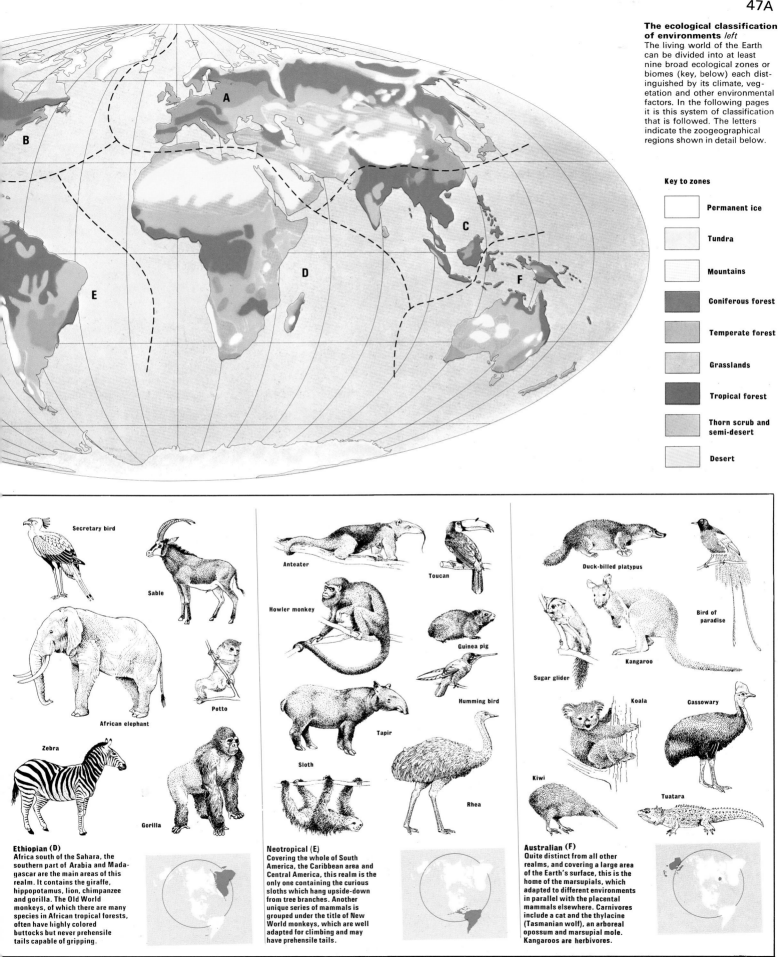

The ecological classification of environments *left*

The living world of the Earth can be divided into at least nine broad ecological zones or biomes (key, below) each distinguished by its climate, vegetation and other environmental factors. In the following pages it is this system of classification that is followed. The letters indicate the zoogeographical regions shown in detail below.

Key to zones

- Permanent ice
- Tundra
- Mountains
- Coniferous forest
- Temperate forest
- Grasslands
- Tropical forest
- Thorn scrub and semi-desert
- Desert

Ethiopian (D)

Africa south of the Sahara, the southern part of Arabia and Madagascar are the main areas of this realm. It contains the giraffe, hippopotamus, lion, chimpanzee and gorilla. The Old World monkeys, of which there are many species in African tropical forests, often have highly colored buttocks but never prehensile tails capable of gripping.

Secretary bird, Sable, African elephant, Potto, Zebra, Gorilla

Neotropical (E)

Covering the whole of South America, the Caribbean area and Central America, this realm is the only one containing the curious sloths which hang upside-down from tree branches. Another unique series of mammals is grouped under the title of New World monkeys, which are well adapted for climbing and may have prehensile tails.

Anteater, Toucan, Howler monkey, Guinea pig, Humming bird, Tapir, Sloth, Rhea

Australian (F)

Quite distinct from all other realms, and covering a large area of the Earth's surface, this is the home of the marsupials, which adapted to different environments in parallel with the placental mammals elsewhere. Carnivores include a cat and the thylacine (Tasmanian wolf), an arboreal opossum and marsupial mole. Kangaroos are herbivores.

Duck-billed platypus, Bird of paradise, Sugar glider, Kangaroo, Koala, Cassowary, Kiwi, Tuatara

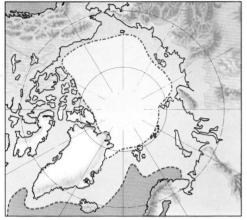

Pack ice limit ..... Drifting ice limit ----

The Arctic ice cap is the opposite of Antarctica in much more than mere location. It is principally an area of permanently frozen sea ice, although it also includes part of Greenland. It has an indigenous human population, despite the average annual temperature of −24°F on the Greenland ice cap, who have managed to adapt themselves to a ferocious environment by copying the animals around them. Just as the seals and polar bears shelter under the snow, bearing their cubs in dens, the Eskimos developed the igloo built from blocks of wind-packed snow. These ice homes are windproof and the temperature inside can rise to 59°F.

Fur and feathers are good heat insulators because each hair or feather is surrounded by air, which conducts heat poorly and thus lessens the amount of body heat escaping. Polar animals have very thick fur. Eskimos wear two layers of skins, one fur side in and the other fur side out. But fur is less efficient if it is wet, so seals and walruses have a thick layer of fatty blubber under the skin. Fat, like air, is a poor heat

conductor. Circulation can be restricted so that some animals maintain two body temperatures: one normally warm-blooded inside the body and one as cold as the environment in the feet, flippers and nostrils, which must be free of fur or blubber to function. Extremities from which heat is easily lost, such as ears, are small in polar bears and absent in seals. Heat lost through radiation is proportional to the body's surface. Relative to its volume, a large animal has less surface area than a small one. So a large animal will lose heat more slowly. Polar bears, for instance, are bigger than bears in more temperate regions.

Few eskimos are still hunters of seals, walruses and whales. There has been mass slaughter of seals for their skins, and the population has rapidly declined. Life in the Arctic is changing. Uranium, titanium and other minerals have been discovered. In Alaska oil is bringing prosperity and industrialization. Much of the energy devoted to opening up these great 'lands of tomorrow' has been triggered by military needs. Now the main spur is becoming an economic one.

Polar bears
Bigger animals have less surface area for each unit of body weight than small animals, and thus lose heat less rapidly. Polar bears are among the largest bears. The adult male (top right) can be 11 feet (3.4 m) long, compared with the 9-10 ft (2.7-3 m) of the brown grizzly (center right) and 4-4.5 ft (1.2-1.4 m) of the sun bear (bottom right). Most polar bears winter in a den roughly eight feet (2.4 m) long, but two-room dens have been found.

Vulnerable *right*
On land the polar bear is supreme, even on slippery ice. But if a bear is forced to enter deep water it becomes much more vulnerable and can be harried even by young seals. A big bull walrus, illustrated, can kill it swiftly.

Walrus bulls *below*
Weighing up to 3000 pounds. the 12 foot (3.7 m) bull walrus uses its tusks for digging out shellfish, breaking air-holes in the ice and fighting. One-third of its weight is blubber, in a 2½ inch (63.5 mm) thick layer under the skin (right).

Dermis
Follicle
Gland
Fat projections
Blubber with blood vessels
Muscle

Pack ice *above*
Open pack ice, stretching as far as the eye can see, reflects the pink rays of the low Sun. Such ice is seldom more than one year old and usually gets crushed or melted in a shorter time. Unlike the dangerous bergs, it is no hazard to navigation.

Seal and tern *below*
The shores of the Irish Sea are among the wide areas of rocky coast on both sides of the North Atlantic inhabited by the grey seal (female illustrated : the male is larger) and sandwich tern (once common at Sandwich in Kent).

Arctic tern *below*
Distinguished from other terns by its vivid beak and feet, the Arctic tern migrates down the coasts of Europe and Africa to the Antarctic before returning to the Arctic to nest. The round trip (left) can be a remarkable 22000 miles (35000 km).

Sandwich tern

Female grey seal

Antarctic

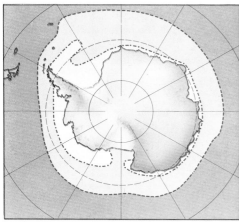

Pack ice limit (March) .... Pack ice limit (September)

In complete contrast to the North Polar region, the Antarctic is a frozen continent encircled by ocean. Mountains surround low-lying land covered with ice so thick that it forms a high plateau. It is the coldest region on Earth. Throughout almost all of Antarctica no monthly average temperature exceeds 0°C, and the average annual temperature at the South Pole is –60°C. Blizzards blow when a shallow layer of colder air over the ice-sheet flows downslope, and the snow is packed into a hard pavement.

Around the continental edges, icebergs up to 1000 feet (300 m) thick break off the ice caps or valley glaciers and fall into the sea. The ice, formed of compacted and recrystallized snow, is only slightly less dense than sea-water, so icebergs float low in the ocean with five-sixths to eight-ninths of their bulk below the surface. The Antarctic icebergs are tabular, with flat tops and cliff-like sides; Arctic bergs from the Greenland ice cap are peaked and rarely break off in the sizes common in Antarctica, where the floating ice islands can be as much as ten miles (16 km) long.

Until 450 million years ago the Earth had no ice caps. In the Antarctic, ice formed in the center of the continent and moved out towards the sea. Cooling at the North Pole probably occurred later.

In summer, when the ice breaks up and the amount of daylight increases, there is a rapid growth of tiny floating plants called phytoplankton. These plants provide 'grazing' for the zooplankton, small animals of which the shrimp-like krill are the most numerous, which in turn are eaten by the larger animals, among them seals and whalebone whales. One of these whales, the blue whale, is the largest animal ever to inhabit the Earth. A variety of birds live in the Antarctic, including penguins and the skuas which prey on them, snow petrels and albatrosses. These warm-blooded animals all have to keep their body temperature well above that of the environment. Many birds avoid the polar winter by migrating to temperate lands. But emperor penguins stay, and in an Antarctic blizzard colonies of them huddle tightly together to reduce the exposed surface area of their bodies.

18in, 45cm

Adélie penguins *above*
They make devoted parents and may, as shown here, produce two chicks at different times in one season.

Emperor penguin *right*
Easily the largest penguin, the emperor (about 4 ft, 120 cm) breeds on Antarctic sea ice and coasts (see below).

Seals *left and below*
Seals abound in the Antarctic. The crab-eater (left) bears the scars of an encounter with a killer whale. The Weddell seal (below left) is guarding its three-week pup. South Georgia elephant seals (below) are wallowing among tussock grass.

Fjord *above*
A scene of rare beauty north of Marguerite Bay in the Antarctic Peninsula (Grahamland). Here the rock of the continent is visible, with a glacier at the right and brash ice at the left floating on water ruffled only by the gentle passage of the ship.

Incubating *above*
The male emperor hatches the eggs, which rest on the feet beneath a warm brood flap of fatty skin.

Macaroni *left*
There are several species of crested penguins. Tallest is the macaroni, here seated on its nest. (18 in, 45 cm)

Great skua *right*
Skuas are scavengers. They steal food and eggs, kill young chicks and prey on weak adults.

Lichen *below*
The red lichen on this rock could be 1000 years old. Its slow metabolism survives the cold.

The Cold Lands: Tundra

The cold lands *above*
In the northern hemisphere there are vast areas of land at latitudes higher than 60°. The warmer parts of these regions are colonized by immense numbers of conifers (facing page) which extend right across the Earth's widest land mass. Where the climate is too severe for trees, the forest gives way to tundra.

Permanent residents of the tundra

Life is hard in the Arctic tundra, but a great variety of animal life is adapted to it. Grass and other plant food grows for no more than two out of each 12 months, but many animals live off it all the year round and even eat the roots while the surface is covered with snow. Carnivores depend to a great degree on the population of lemmings (below) which reaches a peak about every third year. In spring the land becomes ablaze with flowers, and birds abound.

Lemmings
These small rodents are about five inches (125 mm) long. They have short tails, and ears hidden by thick fur. Every three or four years a population explosion triggers a mass migration in which thousands of lemmings die.

Seasonal plumage
Many of the Arctic birds and animals change their appearance to blend into the contrasting summer and winter backgrounds. For example, the rock ptarmigan is mottled brown in July (left) but white in winter until May (below). Both hunted animals, such as

Surrounding the Arctic Ocean are the Arctic tundra and, further south, the coniferous forest. There is no land at such high latitude (60°-70°) in the southern hemisphere. Seasonal changes are extreme. The Sun may shine continuously in summer and not at all in mid-winter. Winter cold and summer heat are greatest in the continental interiors, where it is also drier than around the coasts. Interaction between polar and tropical air masses causes storms.

In the treeless tundra the average temperature of the warmest month is below 10°C (50°F). The land is forested where the average for at least one month is above that temperature. In some places the tundra and forest are divided by a distinct tree-line; in other regions the true coniferous forest is preceded by grasses, sedges and lichens. The soils are affected by 'permafrost' and are almost permanently frozen. In summer the surface becomes waterlogged and often flooded, but the seasonal thaw reaches a depth of only 4-24 inches (100-600 mm). Soil water under the plants melts, and a thick mud forms which may

flow downslope making bulging terraces. Because of recent glaciation there are many lakes and swamps, called muskeg in Canada.

Lemmings feed on the vegetation of the tundra. In winter they dig for roots in an underground network of tunnels where it is about 10°C (18°F) warmer than on the surface. If their population increases so much that there is competition for space, masses of lemmings move into the forest and cross streams, lakes and rivers as they go. Many drown.

Herds of American caribou and closely related European reindeer migrate up to several hundred miles from their summer pasture on the tundra to find winter food on the forest fringes. Nomadic Lapps follow the reindeer and use them for transport, food and clothing. They milk them and make cheese. In contrast, the caribou have never been domesticated: the Indians of northern Canada were hunters. Their skill as trappers was exploited by the European fur trade. And in the Siberian tundra every resource is being vigorously exploited; a new land is opening up.

Winter and summer
above and left
In winter the cold lands are dull and seemingly barren, although at the edges of the tundra stunted conifers are dotted among the lakes. But in summer the plant life flourishes. Reindeer graze among flowers from Norway to the Pacific.

the Arctic hare, and their predators change their color. The Arctic fox, which preys on the rock ptarmigan, is white or very pale in winter (above) but changes into a summer coat which is usually brown but in the so-called "blue-foxes" is deep blue-grey (right).

Arctic color *below*
Tundra is not always dull. In the Alaskan September plant life is in full bloom.

Early blooms *above*
The Pasque flower is in evidence throughout Alaska as early as May.

The Coniferous Forests

Except for the Siberian larch, which sheds its needles in winter, the trees of the coniferous forest are evergreen. Spruce, fir, pine and hemlock (associated near water with mountain ash, poplar, balsam, willow and birch) are widespread through Eurasia and North America. The similarity between the distribution of plants and animals is the result of frequent freezing of the Bering Strait which allowed migration between the continents.

The forest animals depend on the trees for food. Beavers eat bark, and squirrels and birds eat buds and seeds. In summer, when there is more food, multitudes of birds migrate to the forest to nest.

The cold forests are of enormous extent. Lumbering is a major industry, and the numerous rivers are used to transport the logs to the sawmills. Great volumes of softwoods are consumed every year, mainly in the building industry and for papermaking. Minerals are now being mined in the cold lands. Iron ore is mined in Labrador and Quebec, and Alaska's gold, copper, iron, oil and gas are being exploited.

The beaver's handiwork
Throughout northern America, and in northern Europe and Asia, the beaver gnaws through trees to secure the soft inner bark from the upper branches. It stores these in a still pool formed by damming a river, and nearby constructs a remarkable lodge with as many as eight underwater entrances.

Ventilation shaft
Beaver lodge
Dam   Raised water level   Food store   Entrances

Tree types *above*
Temperate broad-leaved trees could not survive the northern winter. Most cold forest trees are conifers, with needle-like leaves. From the left : scots pine ; larch, which sheds its leaves ; Norway spruce ; Douglas fir.

Contrasting diets
above and right
Despite its formidable appearance the moose lives on small plants, berries and tree shoots. Only the male has antlers. But the lynx (right) is a carnivore, whose population follows that of its principal prey, the hare.

Burrowers *right and below*
The woodchuck (right) is one of the cold forest dwellers that hibernates. Its winter metabolism falls almost to a standstill ; then it awakens in March and is busy until fall. The European polecat (below) sometimes kills marmots and uses their burrows.

Grizzlies *above*
Although a carnivore, the giant brown bear often digs for roots, as here.

Ground squirrel *below*
The striped ground squirrel does not climb trees but eats roots, leaves and insects.

South of the coniferous forest is extensive deciduous woodland of oak, beech and chestnut which flourishes wherever there is an annual rainfall of 30-60 inches (750-1500mm) distributed throughout the year. Woodland once covered large areas of the northern hemisphere, but most has now been cleared for agriculture. There are different mid-latitude climates on the east and west sides of continents: east coast climates are continental, with hot summers and cold winters, while winds blowing off the ocean bring rain to the more equable west coasts.

In winter the deciduous trees shed their broad leaves which would be vulnerable to frost. The leaves slowly rot to a rich humus, and in boggy places peat forms. Nutrients circulate by water draining through the soil and then being drawn up by evaporation and transpiration through the leaves.

Tree types

In North America and Asia the oak, beech, hickory and maple dominate; in Europe the oak, ash, lime and chestnut, with beech in cool moist areas. On damp ground near rivers willow, alder, ash and elm are found. Conifers grow faster so that they often supplant deciduous trees in managed forests. They form the natural forest on the west coast of North America, where some of the largest trees are found.

Near the tropics are the broadleaf evergreen forests. In Japan and the southeast of the United States there are evergreen oaks, laurel and magnolia, with palms, bays and ferns in the swamps of the Mississippi delta. The warm wet forest of New Zealand's South Island contains conifers, podocarp and evergreen beeches, with tree ferns, palms and bamboos. In a Mediterranean type of climate the summers are hot and dry. Cork oaks have hard, leathery leaves covered with a thick cuticle to minimize water loss. The Mediterranean forest is now only a narrow coastal belt. Tree felling and frequent summer fires have left scrub known as the maquis. The chaparral of California and Mexico is similar.

Redwoods *above*
Along the west coast of the United States is a foggy coastal belt where the redwood forests flourish. The giant redwoods and sequoias may be several thousand years old and up to 400 feet (120 m) high. They are among the Earth's oldest living things.

Beechwoods *left*
Typical of the cool northern deciduous forest, Burnham Beeches, near London, generates millions of beech leaves each year. Littering the ground, they decompose into a rich humus which overlies the soil and supports plant life, worms and a variety of insects.

Little owl *above*
Predator of woodland animals, its forward-facing eyes give good binocular vision for judging distance in dim light.

Luna moth *above*
Found in American deciduous forest, the moth prefers a diet of rhododendrons. India has a tropical variety.

Animal variety
above and left
Woodland inhabitants of the New England states are the box turtle and wood frog (above). The Yugoslavian four-lined snake (left) has the slender body and angled scales common to snakes which need to obtain purchase on bark.

Forest birds
The crossbill (left) can pry open tough pine cones; the pheasant (below,) of which there are 49 species, is concealed on the ground by its camouflage.

The ecology of an oak

Oaks of various sub-species are among the most important trees in the northern deciduous forests, and they play a major role in local wildlife. Oaks have a history dating back over 50 million years, and 7000 years ago covered vast tracts of temperate land. Throughout recorded history man has prized the oak for its hard, durable wood, which has been favored above all others for making houses, ships, furniture and other artifacts. The oak population has thus dwindled, and in modern managed forests the faster-growing conifers are preferred. But each remaining oak is a microcosm of nature. The autumn leaf-fall returns valuable nutrients to the soil, providing a source of humus. In the spring up to a quarter of a million new leaves grow, providing an area for photosynthesis as great as 10000 sq ft (930 m²). Small streamers of flowers are pollinated by wind-borne pollen, leading in midsummer to the crop of acorns which are stored by grey squirrels, badgers and many other animals for the coming winter. As many as 200 species of insect can feed on one tree. Largest is the leaf-eating stag beetle, and the most prominent the gall wasp whose marble gall houses the larva. The damage insects inflict often results in the tree producing a second crop of midsummer leaves. The serotine bat and tawny owl are the main nocturnal predators of the oak forest. The former takes winged insects in flight, while small rodents form the staple diet of the owl.

Marble gall showing larva of gall wasp

Serotine bat

Tawny owl

Stag beetle

Grey squirrel

Badger

The mature oak *right*

The extensive buttressed roots of an old oak can provide the portal through which a fox (1) tunnels to its lair. Low on the trunk a beefsteak fungus (2) may grow, providing fruiting bodies upon which feed many kinds of animals and insects. The trunk often decays locally (3), providing a home for both bats and owls. The fallow deer (female, 4) and jay (5) collect acorns, while in the branches a clump of mistletoe (6) grows, nurtured by the tree on which it is a parasite.

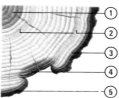

Record in the rings *above*
In deciduous trees each year's growth adds a ring of new tissue to the trunk, as shown by this section segment from an oak with an age of 24 years. Within the first five years is the dark heartwood (1). Between years 7-10 growth was slowed (2), possibly by drought or the crowding of other trees. Growth was also slow in years 19-22, and in the 21st year part of the tree was burned, leaving a scar (4) which gradually heals with further growth. Present growth takes place in the cambium (3) just inside the bark (5).

Paper wasp
The queen starts the football-like nest, which is made of chewed wood and has a paper-like consistency. Her subjects enlarge it.

Mole
Moles live in burrows excavated underground by their strong front claw-feet. Emerging into the open, their eyes see poorly.

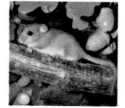

Dormouse
Most of the forest rodents store food for the winter, but the dormouse hibernates, at a reduced body temperature.

Dormouse nest
Although the dormouse lives deep in the undergrowth, it is very agile, and builds a spherical nest above ground level.

Sparrowhawk
Like many birds of prey the sparrowhawk makes a substantial nest of twigs and forest debris high in a tree, where its young are safe.

Blue tit
A favorite choice of home for the blue tit is a hole in a tree. Inside the cavity it constructs a nest of moss and soft debris.

Common oak
Widespread and important to commerce and forest life, the oak grows slowly and is yielding to other species.

Silver birch
Mature at 50, the silver-barked birch is found in all temperate forest and extends far into the tundra.

Beech
Big and densely packed, the beech is very beneficial. Essentially a forest tree, it prefers drained chalky soil.

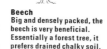

Ash
Although it exhausts soil, the ash produces tough wood. Its multi-leaflet leaves are one foot (0.25 m) long.

Sweet chestnut
Originally from Asia Minor, the sweet chestnut fruit is a preferred food of many forest animals.

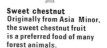

Sycamore
One of the maple family, the sycamore prefers exposed positions where its seeds can travel on the wind.

Alder
The inconspicuous alder prefers marshy ground and river banks. Although not a conifer, it bears cone fruit.

The hot, humid conditions in equatorial rainforests which encourage a profusion of life, change very little over the year, daily variations being greater than seasonal ones. The average temperature is about 27°C, while the rainfall, which is as high as 80-160 inches (2000-4000 mm) a year, falls regularly in heavy thunderstorms.

Tropical forests are the highest, densest and most varied on Earth, in spite of having infertile soil. This is because nutrients are contained in the plants which grow, flower and fruit throughout the year. As leaves and fruits fall to the ground and decay, the minerals are rapidly taken up again by the roots of the growing shrubs and trees. The crowns of the tall, broad-leaved trees form a canopy of foliage. Underneath, it is shady and the tree trunks are smooth and unbranched, while lianas and creepers thrust upwards to the light.

Forest animals find a variety of habitats in the different layers. Monkeys, apes, sloths, lizards and frogs are adapted to climbing or swinging through trees. Multitudes of birds feed on nectar, insects or fruit. Many animals browse on the forest floor, and a vast number of animal and plant species co-exist.

Lianas *below*
Long rope-like stems loop from tree to tree, ever climbing toward the light that pierces the canopy.

Deep rainforest *right*
The hot, humid atmosphere of tropical rainforest encourages most luxuriant plant growth.

Flowers *right and below*
Tropical blooms are famed for their size and beauty. The very small seasonal variation in climate means plants can germinate, grow and flower without interruption throughout the year. Right, blossoms of Royal Poinciana; below, Strelitzia, native to Africa.

Contrasting predators *right and below*
Tropical forests are the home of the largest spiders and largest snakes. But, whereas the monkey spider of Trinidad (right) kills its prey by a venomous bite, the 30 foot (10 m) royal python (below) crushes and suffocates its victim.

Butterflies *right and below*
There are more butterflies and moths in the rainforest than in all the rest of the Earth; typical species are the Ulysses butterfly (right), *Precis almana* (below right) and Rajah Brooke's bird-wing *Trogonoptera brookiana* (below).

Hovering jewel *right*
Hummingbirds, such as Pucheran's emerald variety illustrated here, are found only in the Americas. Their wings, which beat about 100 times a second and allow them to hover while drinking nectar, are covered with iridescent feathers of brilliant hues.

Forest amphibians *above and right*
As large as a man, the iguana (above) has feet with long digits provided with hard scales and curved claws adapted to tree-climbing. Another climber is the African grey tree frog (right) whose nest of foam overhangs the water.

Indian crested swift

Spinetail swift

White rumped swift

Harpy eagle

The emergents
Some trees break through the canopy formed by the main tree population. Many of these emergent trees reach to 150 ft (46 m), although all tree heights are reduced with increasing altitude or distance from the equator. Life at this topmost level is almost wholly insects and birds. The swifts, which fly above the forest at over 100 mph (160 kmh), catch insects on the wing. The harpy eagle preys on animals in the upper branches.

100 feet
30 m

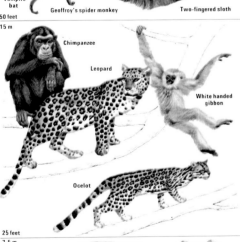

Indian langur

Chameleon

Great hornbill

Bird of paradise

Birdwing butterfly

Flying lizard

Pit viper

Flying fox

Violet-ear hummingbird

Toco toucan

Emerald tree boa

White-plumed marmoset

Vampire bat

Geoffroy's spider monkey

Two-fingered sloth

The canopy
This is one of the major life zones of the tropical forest, and it exerts a powerful effect on all the lower levels. Most of the forest trees grow to 100-120 ft (30-37 m) and form an almost continuous layer of leafy vegetation at this height, cutting off direct sunlight from below and markedly altering the climate inside' the forest to a shady coolness. Most of the trees of tropical forests have straight stems which do not branch until quite close to the canopy; emergent tree (1) passes straight through without branching. Many tropical trees are cauliflorous—they produce flowers which grow directly out of the trunks and branches and frequently dot the canopy with color (2). Inside the forest is a tangle of creepers and climbers which tend to bind the branches of the canopy into a tight mass. The fauna of the canopy is adapted to specialized feeding from particular flowers, fruit or other food. Winged insects and animals range readily through the whole stratum. Many of the birds (for example, the great hornbill and toucan) have long bills with which they can reach food through the mat of vegetation. The non-flying animals are invariably adapted to running along branches, swinging from one branch to another and even leaping 50 ft (15 m) or more.

50 feet
15 m

Chimpanzee

Leopard

White handed gibbon

Ocelot

The middle layer
There may be no sharp division between this layer and the canopy, but in general the middle is made up of smaller trees whose crowns do not form a continuous mat. In this layer are found nest epiphytes (3), non-parasitic plants growing in sunlight on trees where they seed in cracks in the bark. Some store water while others absorb it through hanging roots (4). Cauliflorous growths (5) hang from some trees, while many trunks are covered in vines and lianas (6). The trees are sturdy enough to bear heavy animals. Whereas many inhabitants of the canopy seldom if ever come down to ground level, a considerable proportion of the middle-level animals spend part of their life on the forest floor.

25 feet
7.5 m

Mandrill

Tiger

Bay duiker

Red jungle fowl

Giant armadillo

Jaguar

Red rumped agouti

The lower levels
The bottom strata of the humid tropical forest can be divided into a shrub layer below 15 ft (4.5 m), a herb layer below 3 ft (1 m) and a fungus layer on the surface. The fallen tree (7) may have died from strangulation by parasitic vegetation. At the right air roots (8) pick up moisture, while a trunk (9) is almost hidden by two types of epiphyte. Fungi (10) cover the ground near a massive buttressed tree root (11), while in the rear is a stilt root (12) of a kind common in swamp forest. The ground here is covered in sparse vegetation (13) typical of the shady floor. The features illustrated are typical of hot rain forest throughout the tropics, but the elephant (14) is Indian.

The Grasslands

Flat or rolling grasslands lie between the forests and deserts in the dry interiors of all the continents, in the transitional zones where dry and moist climates merge into each other. There are two major types of grassland, the temperate which is hot in summer and cold in winter and the tropical which has a fairly uniform high temperature all the year round. The Russian steppe, North American prairie, South American pampas, South African veld and Australian downland are examples of temperate grassland, while more than one third of Africa is covered by tropical savanna.

The height of the grass is dependent upon the annual rainfall. There are few trees on these wide plains to break the wind or provide shelter. In spring or summer there is a short rainy season when the grasses and shrubs flourish and there is rich grazing; then the long dry season comes and growth halts as a severe drought develops. The grasslands may result from frequent fires during this period, which kill the trees and shrubs leaving grass-roots unharmed.

Animal life

Throughout most of the tropical grasslands the climate is semi-arid, the soil poor, yet their meager grazing supports a rich and varied assortment of animals. In most grassland regions the fauna has been used by man with care for the future, but in the biggest savanna of all, that of Africa, man has done little but misuse and destroy the grassland animals. To a considerable degree this has been the result of emphasis by both Africans and white ranchers, on domestic cattle. Such beasts graze only on certain species of grass, and have been bred principally for the temperate regions of Europe. In contrast, the natural fauna makes full use of the whole spectrum of vegetation, grazing selectively at different levels and in different places. As a result there is no deterioration of the environment despite the large numbers of animals supported by each area of land. Moreover, the wild animals need not be fed or sheltered, nor inoculated against the sleeping sickness carried by the tsetse fly which ravages cattle. Now that game can be seen to have a distinct commercial value the grassland animals, particularly easily domesticated species such as the eland, are at last being more generally preserved so that controlled game-cropping can provide an additional source of high quality protein.

The dust bowls

Man has often interfered in the grassland environment sometimes with disastrous consequences. The American grassland soil is rich and farmers have turned the wetter tall-grass prairie into the corn belt and the short-grass prairie into the wheat belt. Further west is the cattle country. But in years of drought crops fail and the valuable topsoil, lacking the protective cover of grass, blows away in great dust clouds, leaving behind large areas of barren land.

Venomous snakes *left*
Grasslands in every continent harbor dangerous snakes. The Egyptian cobra (far left) is the largest cobra in Africa. The prairie rattlesnake (near left) is the most common venomous snake in the United States and causes many deaths each year.

African savanna *above*
The Serengeti plains of Tanzania are among the most beautiful areas of big game country in the world. Here animals of a great range of species graze on fine grassland amongst the kopjes — rocky outcrops which are characteristic of central Africa.

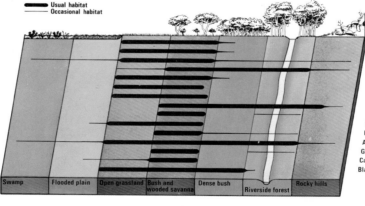

Usual habitat
Occasional habitat

Lion
Spotted hyena
Griffon vulture
Anubis (olive) baboon
Grant's zebra
Brindled gnu (wildebeest)
White rhinoceros
Impala
Giraffe
Cape eland
Kirk's long-snouted dik-dik
African elephant
Gerenuk
Cape buffalo
Black rhinoceros

Swamp | Flooded plain | Open grassland | Bush and wooded savanna | Dense bush | Riverside forest | Rocky hills

Ecological co-existence *above*
The African savanna supports a very large and varied animal population. Most of the animals are herbivores which have each adapted to a particular habitat and a particular section of the available food. These sections are divided geographically, as shown here, and also into different feeding levels above the ground.

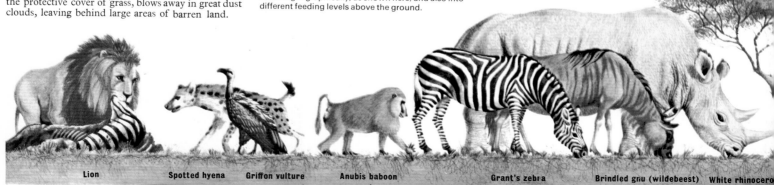

Lion | Spotted hyena | Griffon vulture | Anubis baboon | Grant's zebra | Brindled gnu (wildebeest) | White rhinoceros

Buffalo *above*
African buffalo at Manyara, Tanzania. Buffalo live in herds of up to 100 or more males and females of all ages, with a firm hierarchy among the males. They use their horns and horn-bosses in pushing contests that help to decide their ranks.

Impala *below*
African grassland has 72 species of antelope, weighing from a few pounds to 1800 lb (800 kg).

Tick bird *left*
The yellow-billed oxpecker rides on the backs of rhinos and other large animals and eats ticks and flies living in or on the hide. Sometimes the birds swoop off their perch to take large insects which have been disturbed by the animal.

Leopard *right*
Stealthy and athletic, the leopard is found through most of Africa and southern Asia. It often rests in trees, and this fine specimen has pulled its prey, a reedbuck, onto a high branch.

Giraffes *left*
Tallest of all land animals, the giraffe eats acacia leaves and other greenery high above the ground (see large illustration below). Here a group gallops past zebras across a bare patch of ground.

7ft, 213cm

Griffon vulture *left*
Vultures soar at high altitudes on their large wings while searching to the horizon for carrion.

Jackrabbit *above*
Big ears are not only for keen hearing: they help radiate heat and control body temperature.

Ostrich *below*
The tall ostrich can see for miles across the African plains and run swiftly from danger.

8ft, 240cm

Feeding habits
The great grasslands of Africa, and to a lesser degree those of other continents, teem with wild life of remarkable variety. In this wide open environment conceal ment is difficult and the majority of animals survive by having good long-distance vision and by being fleet of foot. Some of the smaller plant eaters escape their preda tors by burrowing. The key to the co-existence of the herbivores is that they tend to feed at different levels. The elephant can reach up to 15 feet (4·5 m) above the ground to tear at broad-leafed trees, while the giraffe can feed on its favored acacias at even higher levels. The rhino, buffalo, gerenuk and eland eat not only low shrubs and trees but also grass. Only the gnus, zebras and some rhinos com pete for the same areas, but these areas are so large that there is little fear of over-grazing. The baboon delves for roots and what ever it can find, while the carni vores include the carrion-eating hyenas and vultures and the pre datory lion, cheetah and leopard. Left to themselves, the wild animals of the savanna do little harm to their habitat, but the growing herds of domesticated cattle and goats pose a threat. Whereas the native fauna leaves living shoots which can sprout into a fresh plant, the cattle and goats eat the whole of the grass and tree shoots so that the vegetation is soon eradicated. Over-grazing and poor range management are encouraged by the fact that some African tribes still regard cattle as symbols of wealth. The value of the indigen ous savanna animals has been forcefully demonstrated in parts of South Africa and Rhodesia where ranges run down by domestic cattle have been restored by grazing 10 to 12 varieties of antelope in their place.

Impala   Giraffe   Cape eland   Kirk's dik-dik   African elephant   Gerenuk   Cape buffalo   Black rhinoceros

The Deserts

The desert is a harsh, arid and inhospitable environment of great variety where the average rainfall for a year is less than five inches (125 mm) and in some years there is none at all. The cloudless sky allows the Earth's surface to heat up to 40°C (104°F) by day and cool near to freezing at night. Relative humidity is low. On the basis of temperature arid lands are divided into low-latitude hot deserts and mid-latitude deserts. The latter, in central Asia and the Great Basin of the United States, are bitterly cold in winter. In the coastal deserts of Peru and Chile the cold offshore current flowing northward from the Antarctic Ocean cools the moist air producing a swirling sea fog.

Landscapes are rocky, and weathered to strange shapes by the winds and sudden rains (pp. 12-13A). Sand dunes shifted and shaped by the wind are common in Saudi Arabia and the Sahara. The dunes are almost sterile, but most deserts have some sparse plant cover. Stems and leaves are hard, to prevent loss of water and protect the plant from sand erosion. Succulent cacti and euphorbias store water in fleshy stems or leaves, and have widespread shallow roots to absorb the dew. Sahara oases were probably cultivated 7000 years ago, producing grain, olives, wine, figs and dates. The Egyptians channelled the waters of the flooding Nile to irrigate the land, and today the Imperial Valley of the Californian desert and the Arizona desert near Phoenix are highly productive agricultural land.

Water in the desert
Most of the world's deserts are neither billowing sand dunes (such as that on the opposite page) nor totally devoid of water. But in all deserts water, especially fresh water, is a precious commodity. In the great stony deserts brief rains allow stunted vegetation to provide a basis for animal life. The neighborhood of Monument Valley, Utah (above) is surprisingly full of life which has adapted to arid conditions. Some life is also found in the Sahara, where sudden torrential rains cause flash flood erosion (south of Ouargla, left) leaving smooth ridges and deep gullies Sometimes

the water table is at the surface. The water may be brackish and undrinkable, as in Cyrenaica west of the Siwa Oasis (below), but the true oasis contains fresh water at which a camel can drink copiously (right). Even the meager dew is stored by plants – nothing is wasted.

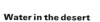

Desert plants *right*
Deserts test the ability of plants to adapt to a near absence of water. Plants survive by throwing out large catchment areas for dew at night, minimizing water loss by evaporation during the day, growing deep roots to find water far below the surface, storing what water they find, and in extreme cases by lying dormant during dry years and springing to life as soon as it rains.

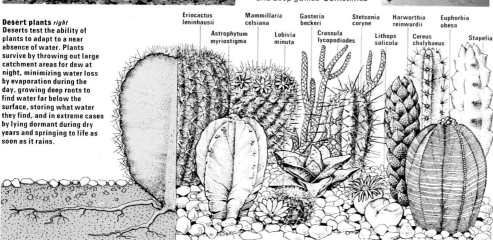

Eriocactus leninhausii
Astrophytum myriostigma
Mammillaria celsiana
Lobivia minuta
Gasteria beckeri
Crassula lycopodiodes
Stetsonia coryne
Lithops salicola
Harworthia reinwardii
Cereus chalybaeus
Euphorbia obesa
Stapelia

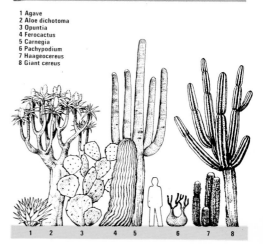

1 Agave
2 Aloe dichotoma
3 Opuntia
4 Ferocactus
5 Carnegia
6 Pachypodium
7 Haageocereus
8 Giant cereus

1 2 3 4 5 6 7 8

Desert animals

Many animals are so well adapted to retain water that they survive on the moisture in their food. Some, such as the armadillo lizard, scorpions, insects and spiders, have hard, impenetrable skins to reduce water loss. The urine of camels and gazelles is very concentrated to minimize excretion of water. Arabian camels can lose 30 per cent of their body weight (which would be lethal for a man) without distress, and then regain it by drinking up to 27 gallons (120 liters) at a time. This does not dilute their blood dangerously. A camel does not sweat until its body temperature reaches 40°C, and it loses heat easily during the cold night because it stores its fat in the hump and not as a layer under the skin. Its fur insulates against the heat, as do the loose clothes of the people. Snakes hide in crevices, and sand-swimming lizards burrow to avoid extreme temperatures. Jerboas and kangaroo rats hop along, and some lizards run on their hind legs to keep their bellies off the ground. As soon as it rains, swarms of dormant life surge into activity.

Desert Burrowers

White-footed mouse • Burrow taken over by horned lizard • Horned lizard • American badger • Pocket mouse • Kit fox • Kangaroo rat in nest • Food store • Green-collared lizard • Kangaroo rat

Ant lions *right and below*
Some types of ant lion catch their prey — mainly ants — by digging a smooth conical pit and waiting at the bottom ; others bury themselves in the sand with only eyes and jaws protruding. The larval stage (right) precedes the winged adult (below).

8in, 21cm

Sand desert *above*
Only one-seventh of the Sahara looks like this Hollywood-style vista of giant dunes in Algeria.

Dung beetles *left*
These female scarabs are rolling a pellet of animal dung into a ball containing an egg.

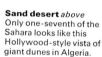

Painted lady *above*
N African desert thistles provide nectar for their migration through Europe as far as Iceland.

Gila monster *right*
This venomous N American lizard tracks its prey with the aid of a sensor in its mouth (right, lower).

20in, 51cm

Nasal cavity • External nostril • Sensory part of Jacobsons organ • Duct • Internal nostril

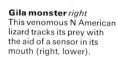

Scorpion and snake
When scorpions mate, the male deposits a patch of sperm on the ground and then contrives to maneuver a female over it in what looks like a square dance (above, left). The dangerous rattlesnake (above) senses the heat radiated by its prey using organs on its face.

Plants and predator
The leopard tortoise (left) enjoys a meal of cactus, a plant which stores water and minimizes evaporation (Ferocactus of Arizona, right). Other desert blooms include Echinopsis rhodatricia and Chamacerus silvestri (far right, upper and lower).

The mountain environment varies enormously with height and the direction of the prevailing wind. Temperature falls about 2°C (3.4°F) for each 1000 feet (300 m) increase in altitude. Barometric pressure also falls until lack of oxygen makes any human exertion cause shortness of breath. Before people adjust to the conditions they often suffer from mountain sickness —headache, weakness and nausea.

Sun temperature may be 28°C (83°F) hotter than in the shade or at night, and the slope of a mountain facing the equator is warmer than the other sides. Mountains force rain-bearing winds to rise, so that they cool and have to release moisture. Clouds form, and rain falls on the windward slope; on the opposite slope the descending winds are drying.

High-altitude life

Altitude has the same effect on vegetation as latitude. At about 5000 feet (1500 m) tropical rainforest changes to montane forest resembling a temperate rainforest. At twice this height the broad-leaved trees disappear but there are conifers and shrubs such as laurel. Above the treeline, where the average monthly temperature never exceeds 10°C, is alpine tundra or heath. The snowline at the equator is at about 15000 feet (4500 m). In Peru irrigated sugar and cacao cover the lower slopes, and above the timberline corn grows at 11000 feet, wheat at 12000, barley at 13000 and potatoes up to 14000 feet. The Incas had terraced the Andes and had an efficient agricultural system by 1000 AD.

The mountain life zone which is unique is that above the treeline. The animal communities are isolated, since mountains act as a barrier to migration. Most plants and insects on mountain tops can withstand freezing. Some animals burrow or shelter under rocks where temperature variations are smaller. Ibexes, yaks, deer and sheep all have thick coats but move down the mountain-side in winter. Mountain animals have enlarged hearts and lungs and extra oxygen-carrying red blood corpuscles to make the most of the thin air. The vicuna, for example, has nearly three times the number of red corpuscles per cubic millimeter of blood as man.

Near Murren *above right*
The environment on a high mountain is essentially polar, even in a tropical country. Above the timberline ice and snow replace animals and plants, and the conditions are further modified by intense solar radiation and low atmospheric pressure.

Lichens *above and right*
Lichens comprise a fungus and an alga in close association. The alga govern the color (page 49A for red lichen). The metabolism of lichens is exceedingly slow ; barely alive, they can subsist on mountain rock in harsh conditions for hundreds of years.

Altitude and latitude *right*
At extreme latitudes – for example, in the Antarctic – the climate is so severe at sea level that no very pronounced change takes place even as one climbs a mountain, although the mountain's presence can strongly modify the local weather. In contrast, mountains near the equator rise from hot, steamy forests into freezing, arid peaks, with almost every kind of Earth environment in between. To most kinds of terrestrial life large mountains are barriers. As altitude increases, plants and animals become adapted to the environment and then peter out entirely.

Tundra	Coniferous / deciduous forest	Temperate evergreen
Alpine	Mixed temperate	Mountain forest
Boreal	Cloud forest	Tropical rainforest

21000 ft / 6400 m
18000 ft / 5500 m
15000 ft / 4570 m
12000 ft / 3650 m
9000 ft / 2750 m
6000 ft / 1830 m
3000 ft / 910 m
0

1   2   3   4   5

Mountain zones *above*
At high latitudes a mountain offers fewer contrasts; much of New Zealand (1) has cool, humid cloud forest, topped by alpine heath and tundra. In SE Australia, SE Africa and S Brazil (2) the cloud forest extends to a greater altitude, with only tundra above. The high tropical Andes (3) afford contrasts surpassed only by the mountainous regions of the eastern Himalayas and SE Asia (4), where six distinct regions overlie one another, with very local regions of tropical mountain forest. Mountains of Europe (5) lie in regions where there are already great contrasts in climate at sea level. Boreal is a north-facing mountain region.

Tortoise *above*
The margined tortoise is native to mountainous regions in Greece and the Balkans.

Plants *left*
Purple gentian and (upper) auricula are typical of mountain dwarf perennials ; some can resist freezing.

Butterflies
Mountains are often rich in insects. The six-spot burnet (mating, left) is common. Some Apollo butterflies (below) are found above 17000 feet (5200 m) in the Himalayas. Erebia (right) is carrying an orange mite, a parasite which can survive freezing. Mountain insects rely for much of their food on pollen, seeds and even insects swept up in the frequent updraft of winds from the warm lowlands.

4in, 8cm

African birds of prey
Small mountain rodents make a tasty meal for the jackal buzzard (left), a bird with exceedingly acute vision. The black eagle (with three-week chick, right) lives on rats and lizards but can tackle animals as large as the 7 lb (3.2 kg) rock hyrax. It nests in July.

Rodents
Whereas the alpine marmot (below) hibernates in winter, the pika of Tibet (in group, below right) stores its supplies. The chinchilla and cavy both come from South America. Above 10000 ft (3000 m) rodents outnumber all other animals.

Salamander *right*
This Pyrenean salamander is climbing out of a cool mountain stream, but the true alpine salamander has had to become adapted to an arid habitat. Much darker than the lowland varieties, it does not lay its eggs in water but bears its young alive. It remains amphibious.

American cougar *left*
Also known as the puma or mountain lion, the cougar hunts by day above the timberline. When it makes a large kill it is able to store the carcass for weeks at sub-zero temperature. Most of these beasts range over a fixed area, although some wander down to lower levels.

Yak *right*
Domesticated in its native Tibet, the shaggy yak is still found in local wild herds in central Asia. It is a hardy animal, adapted to eating snow in the absence of water, and moss and lichens when no better vegetation is available. It is found up to 20000 ft (6000 m).

Grazers
Sure-footed, the mountain goat (left) inhabits the northern Rockies. The chamoix (above) is scattered through mountain regions of soutnern Europe, while ibexes (right) are a very widespread family. Specialized sheep also graze at high altitudes.

The Lakes and the Rivers

Freshwater environments range from puddles to lakes which cover thousands of square miles, from small streams to rivers that stretch hundreds of miles from mountain source to the ocean. Together, they provide a diversity of habitats that supports a wide range of plant and animal life.

In rivers the type and variety of life is controlled by the depth and speed of water. Fast mountain streams have few plants and the fish are either fast swimmers or shelter among stones. The slower, wider lowland rivers are rich in vegetation and many of the fish have mouths adapted to sucking food from the rich silt of the river bed. In the brackish waters of the estuary few freshwater animals can survive because of the increasing salinity. But migratory fish, such as eels and Atlantic salmon, adapt to fresh and salt water at different stages of their life cycles.

In standing water the surface is often much warmer than the depths. This produces layers which are so distinct that separate habitats are created. The deeper waters may be completely devoid of oxygen because they do not mix with the well-aerated surface layers. Lakes go through three stages of development: oligotrophic with barren sides and clear water; eutrophic when the lake has begun to silt up and is rich in life; and, finally, dystrophic with decayed organic matter developing into swamp or peat bog. This natural process of eutrophication normally takes thousands of years, but man can, by his indiscriminate pollution and over-enrichment of some lakes condense this process dangerously into a few decades.

Near its source a river is cold, clear and well oxygenated, and flows swiftly.

In the middle reaches the river runs deep, but is still clear and fast-flowing.

A mature river is broad and sluggish; it may be clouded and polluted.

Fish of the river *below*
In the swift-flowing upper reaches only the powerful swimming fish can survive, although small fish nestle near the bottom. The water is well oxygenated, and remains so into the less tumultuous middle reaches. The sluggish lowland river contains deep-bodied fish.

Trout stream

Salmon
Brown trout
Stone loach
Bullhead

Minnow reach

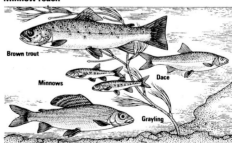

Brown trout
Minnows
Dace
Grayling

Lowland river

Pike
Perch
Barbel
Roach

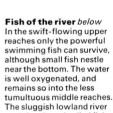

Salmon leaping *above*
Mature salmon return from the ocean to the rivers in which they hatched. Swimming against the current, and leaping up rapids and waterfalls, they finally gain the upper reaches where they spawn. After 1-3 years, the next generation migrates to the sea.

Kingfisher *above*
These colorful birds are by far the most numerous of the many species that take fish while on the wing. Plunging across the surface in a shallow dive, they seize in their long beaks prey they had spotted while on the branch of a tree. Average size 7 in (18 cm).

Teeming with life *left*
Most lakes begin life in the oligotrophic stage, barren of life and with clear, bright waters. After a time the water is colonized, and gradually a community rich in plant and animal species occupies the freshwater habitat. Such a lake is eutrophic.

A swamp *left*
The Indian name of Lake Okeefenokee, Georgia, means 'land of trembling earth'. Measuring some 30 miles by 40 (48 by 64 km), it is a region of perfect mirror-like reflections and teeming wild life.

Swamp butterfly *above*
There are many sub-species of swallowtail; this is the eastern tiger swallowtail from the marshes of Georgia. Average size 4 in (10 cm).

Tree frog *above*
Devouring flies and gnats by the million, green tree frogs breed in the warm swamp waters. Average size is 2½in (6 cm).

Lubber grasshopper *left*
Bigger even than the majority of desert locusts, it makes a tasty meal for birds and young alligators.

Alligator *above*
Generally not aggressive, they keep open the channels in American swamps. Average size is 10 ft (3 m).

Terrapin *above*
The Suwannee river terrapin is sometimes found in the Gulf of Mexico. Average size is 7 in (18 cm).

Swamp turtle *above*
The soft-shelled turtles have a leathery skin without an outer covering of horny plates. Size 14 in (36 cm).

The pond environment *left*
1 Common frog (male, × 0.5)
2 Starwort (× 0.5)
3 Water crowfoot (× 0.25)
4 Aplecta hypnorum (× 2)
5 Wandering snail (× 0.75)
6 Keeled ramshorn snail (× 0.5)
7 Curled pondweed (× 0.25)
8 Bithynia (× 1)
9 Ramshorn snail (× 0.3)
10 Water lily root (× 0.25)
11 Great pond snail (× 0.8)

Pond life *below*
The essential characteristic of pond life is adaptation to a fresh-water environment without a flowing current. As in almost every other habitat on Earth the life is divided into distinct zones —atmosphere, surface film, middle depths and bed—although many species cross from one zone to another. The newt, for example, is active everywhere from the bed of a pond to dry land. Throughout the ecology of freshwater life all food is manufactured by green plants. First-order animals, such as zooplankton and many fish and insects, feed directly on the plants; everything else feeds on predators lower in the food chain or web. The water itself is very far from being a pure compound of hydrogen and oxygen. It contains dissolved oxygen and nitrogen salts and much organic material. The life of the pond establishes ecological cycles which constantly balance inputs and outputs between water, air, and life. For example, the supply of nitrates washed in from the land is aug-mented by the decomposition of dead organisms in the water itself

Near the surface
12 Pond skater (× 0.5)
13 Whirligig beetle (× 0.25)
14 Water boatman (× 1)
15 Non-biting midge (× 5)
16 Mosquito pupa (× 5)
17 Dragonfly (male, × 0.65)
18 China-marks moth (× 0.75)
19 Mayfly (female, × 0.2)

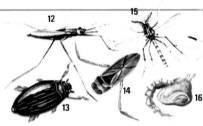

Middle depths
20 Water flea (Daphnia, × 2.5)
21 Smooth newt (male, × 0.5)
22 Cyclops (typical of species, × 8)
23 Flagellate (× 650)
24 Great diving beetle (male, × 1)
25 Hydra (× 4)
26 Stickleback (male, × 0.5)
27 Common frog tadpole (× 1.5)
28 Flagellate (Euglena, × 180)
29 Water mite (× 5)

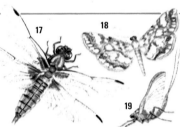

The bottom
30 Caddis-fly larva in case
31 Chaetonotus (× 150)
32 Horny-orb shell (× 1)
33 Tubifex worms (× 0.2)
34 Midge larva (× 3.5)
35 Pond sponge (× 0.2)
36 Leech (Helobdella sp., × 4)
37 Water hog-louse (× 2.5)
38 Flatworm (× 2)

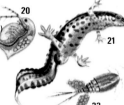

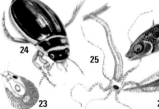

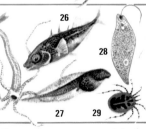

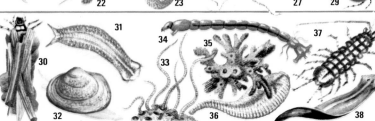

The oceans are a continuous mass of 5000 million million tons of water; but variations in light, pressure, salinity, temperature, currents, waves, and tides interact to create numerous regions each with its own typical forms of life.

Plants are the basis of ocean food chains, just as they are on land. Since all plants need sunlight they are found only in the upper layer of the sea. Myriads of tiny marine plants called phytoplankton are eaten by the small floating zooplankton and by tiny fish, which in turn support a succession of predators. Deep-water animals are adapted to great pressure and to darkness. Most are predators but some of them are scavengers which depend on a rain of food debris from above.

Some ocean islands are coral, built by millions of polyps resembling sea anemones which produce a hard stony skeleton (p. 17A). But most are thrust up by volcanic eruptions. They are completely isolated and were never joined to a continent. Such islands are usually wet and windswept.

Island plant and animal communities evolved from the few original forms which crossed the ocean and colonized. Island colonization is difficult, and is seldom accomplished by land mammals apart from bats, nor even by amphibians. Land and freshwater animals may have evolved from sea-dwelling ancestors. Once a species has colonized an island it interbreeds, because of its isolation, and adapts to its new conditions and competitors. Often new endemic species evolve.

The first colonizers are usually sea birds. They bring nutrients, so seeds and the spores of mosses, lichens and ferns carried by the wind can take root. The wind also brings insects, spiders and bats, and occasionally land birds in storms, but such birds rarely establish themselves. Reptiles and some land animals may cross the sea on driftwood rafts. Many island reptiles, perhaps because of the lack of mammals, have become unusually large. Examples include such creatures as the Komodo dragon and the giant tortoises of the Galapagos.

The ocean layers

sea level

1000 m
3300 ft

3000 m
10000 ft

6000 m
20000 ft

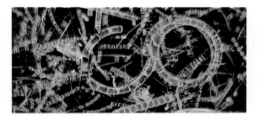

Phytoplankton *above*
All marine life depends ultimately on microscopic plant plankton, which is mostly single-celled. (x 20)

Tiger cowrie *right*
Cowries are tropical marine snails. This spotted example is feeding, with its mantle extended below.

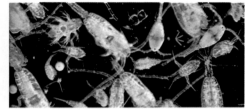

Zooplankton *above*
These microscopic animals feed on the phytoplankton and on each other. In turn they support fish. (x 8)

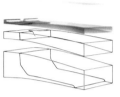

Leopard coral *right*
The derivation of the name of this hard coral is obvious. Each 'spot' is an individual in the colony.

Air and surface life
The seabirds (right) are typical of a range of species, some of them exceptionally large birds, which navigate unerringly over thousands of miles of ocean. Most have wide wingspans and use favourable airflow over the waves to soar apparently without effort. Sunlight penetrates the warm upper layers of the ocean to provide energy for photosynthesis, permitting the prolific growth of the phytoplankton (plant life). This is the starting point for the whole complex web of marine life which leads ultimately to large predatory fish such as the tuna and marlin, and to human foods.

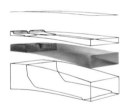

Near the surface
above and right
Seabirds generally keep below 1000 ft (300 m) but can be found much higher. The upper layer of ocean is taken to extend down to 3300 ft (1000 m). Water temperature is about 10 °C and sunlight may reach to 650 ft (200 m).

Soft coral *above*
Photographed in Mauritius, a bluish coral has almost finished reproducing by splitting into two.

Sea urchin *below*
This 'slate pencil' variety from Mozambique coral reefs contrasts with spiny types. Size 10 in (25 cm).

Sea slug *above*
Many of these marine relatives of land slugs are colorful. This one from the Indian Ocean is 4 in (10 cm).

Feather star *below*
Another of the starfish and sea urchin group from Mozambique, this has four inch (10 cm) arms.

Middle dwellers
In this range of depths, most of which (down to 6000 ft) is known as the bathyal or bathypelagic zone, the water cools to 4 °C, the temperature at which the density of water reaches its peak. Little or no light penetrates, and the life is made up of free-swimming fish, crustaceans and cephalopods (squids, for example) possessing body fluids at the same hydrostatic pressure as the environment and having approximately the same degree of salinity. At night some middle dwellers migrate to the surface to feed on other animals which in turn congregate to 'graze' on the plankton.

Middle depths
above and right
The horizontal 'slice' of ocean water in which live the middle-depth species illustrated opposite is taken to extend from 3300 down to 10000 ft (1000-3000 m). Here the temperature falls from 10 °C down to below 4 °C at the lower level.

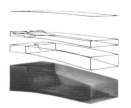

The abyss
above and right
The bottom layer of the ocean is here taken to extend down to about 20000 ft (6000 m). Temperature is always below 4 °C, hydrostatic pressure is enormous and the environment is perpetually devoid of sunlight.

Bottom dwellers
Below 3000 meters the life comprises a range of animals, most of them very small, adapted to living in near-freezing water at extremely high pressures. The only light in this region comes from the curious luminescent organs common to many deep-sea creatures. Although the deep waters contain abundant salts and nutrient minerals, these are useless without the energy of sunlight. Every abyssal organism is therefore either a scavenger, depending for its supply of food on a 'rain' of debris from above, or a predator. Yet the abyssal zone supports a surprising variety of life.

Great Shearwater
span 8½ in 0.2 m

Wandering albatross
span 11 ft 3.35 m

Red-billed tropic bird
span 1 ft 0.3 m

Magnificent frigate bird
span 8 ft 2.45 m

Portuguese man o'war
11 in 0.28 m
(tentacles 100 ft 30 m)

sea level

Flying fish
9 in 0.23 m

Marlin
10 ft 3 m

Ocean sunfish
10 ft 3 m

Anchovies
6 in 0.15 m

Basking shark
40 ft 12 m

Dolphin fish
4 ft 1.2 m

Squid
1 ft 0.3 m

Bluefin tuna
7 ft 2 m

Ocean bonito
2 ft 0.6 m

Diretmus argentus
2 in 0.05 m

Mackerel shark
12 ft 3.6 m

Lantern fish
3 in 0.075 m

Photostomias guerni
7 in 0.18 m

1000 m
3300 ft

Giant squid
55 ft 17 m

Hatchet fish
1 in 0.025 m

Oarfish
20 ft 6 m

Ghost shark
4 ft 1.2 m

Chiasmodus niger
3 in 0.075 m

Gulper eel
4 ft 6 in 1.4 m

3000 m
10000 ft

Angler fish
3 in 0.075 m

Deep sea swimming cucumber
4 in 0.1 m

Prawn
4 in 0.1 m

Viper fish
1 ft 0.3 m

Angler fish
2 in 0.05 m

Pelican eel
10 in 0.25 m

Deep sea jellyfish
3 in 0.075 m

Rat tail
18 in 0.45 m

Tripod fish
10 in 0.25 m

Abyssal octopus
4 in 0.1 m

Brotulid
6 in 0.15 m

Sea snail
9 in 0.23 m

Abyssal sea cucumber
¾ in 0.02 m

Brittle star 3 in 0.075 m

The story of man's use of the land is one of increasing diversity and complexity. Preagricultural man developed perhaps six land uses; hunting, trapping, fishing, gathering wild fruits, fashioning tools and sheltering in caves. Modern man has developed several thousand forms, and frequently concentrates hundreds within a single square mile. For most of them he has created distinctive environments; one can tell at a glance whether the land is being used to grow carrots, make cement, repair ships, treat sewage, sell antiques, mine coal or educate children.

Although every place is unique in the ways its land uses intermingle, we can nevertheless recognize five major land-use patterns. Each has sprung into prominence at some major crossroads in human history. The first of the five is wildscape, which man uses so lightly and so rarely that nature is still in chief control. Some of it is still almost wholly natural, as in the remote parts of the Antarctic icecap. Other areas have been quite profoundly changed, as on the Pennine moorlands where generations of sheep have nibbled away tree seedlings and prevented the regeneration of forest, or where polluted air is now preventing the growth of sphagnum moss. But these areas are still wildscape. Man uses their resources but he leaves nature to replenish them.

The rural landscape evolves

Farmscape dates from man's first great technical advance, the Neolithic agricultural revolution of about 8000 years ago. For the first time he began to alter the landscape and live with the results instead of moving on; he ploughed and harvested, enclosed fields and diverted water for irrigation. During subsequent millennia this more controlled form of land-use spread over enormous areas of every continent, with a cumulative stream of diversifications as man applied his ingenuity to it in different environments. The rural landscape was now distinctively divided into the wild and the cultivated.

Townscape also existed from an early date, but had to await man's second great technical advance before it could develop at all extensively. Not until the twin agrarian and industrial revolutions of the 18th century did agriculture develop sufficiently to support a vastly greater population than its own labor force, or industry develop sufficiently to be able to employ a vast non-agricultural population. Once this possibility was established as a world trend, townscape began to develop rapidly.

Conflicts in land use

There are now three 'scapes' of increasing artificiality and complexity, respectively dominated by nature, the individual farmer and the public authority. So different are these three 'scapes' that problems tend to arise where they confront and interact with each other. Unfortunately such fringes of conflict have been intensified as side effects of two otherwise beneficial transport revolutions.

The first, or long-distance, transport revolution began with the steamship and the train in the 19th century. It opened up competition in foodstuffs on a global scale: the benefit was cheaper food from more favored areas, and the cost was the decline of less-favored areas. Some farmscape reverted to wildscape, resolving the problem. Elsewhere, the land remained good enough to reclaim in times of booming prices but too poor to be profitable in times of recession. The result in such areas is recurrent farm poverty.

The long-distance transport revolution also had a similar effect upon less competitive mining areas which tended to become derelict as a result, forming rurban (rural-urban) fringe. The main growth of rurban fringe, however, was stimulated by the second, or personal, transport revolution, in which the car gave city workers the opportunity to live in the country and commute daily to a neighboring city. The result was an unprecedented intermingling of urban areas and farmland, and an unprecedented degree of conflict between the two. Farmland became fragmented and subjected to many kinds of urban pressures so that much of it became uneconomic to farm. The urban area, on the other hand, experienced many difficulties in service facilities, because its sprawling layout multiplied distances and costs. Thus both marginal fringe and rurban fringe have become areas of patchy, conflicting landuses.

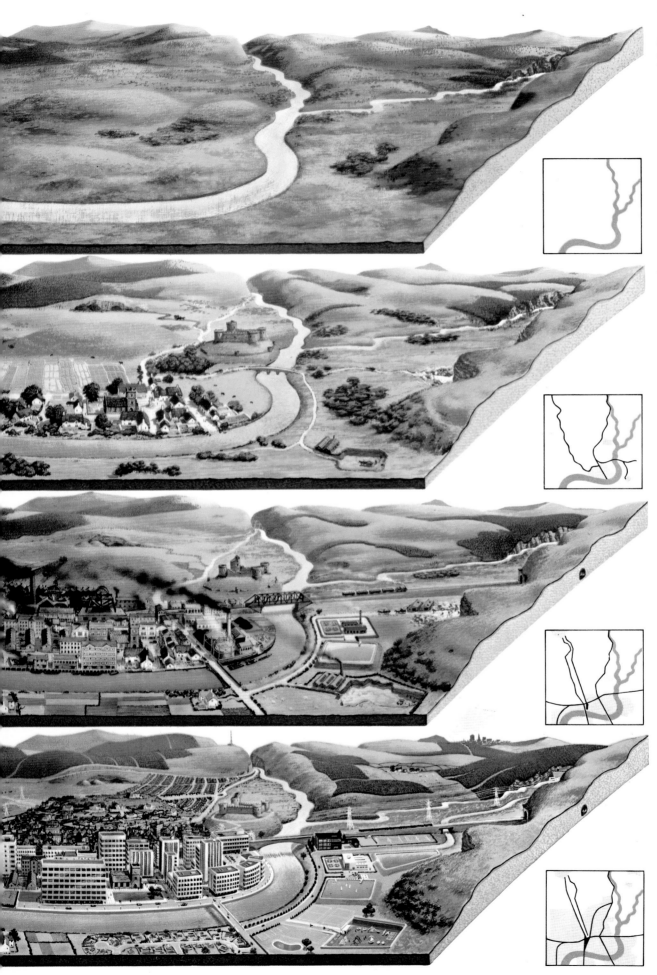

Prehistoric landscape
The natural prehistoric landscape consisted of a series of wildscape ecosystems wherein all forms of life interacted in a stable balance of nature. The land falls from distant hills to a coastal plain where the river widens into a broad estuary. Woodlands partially cover the plains, thinning into scrub on the hills. Stone age man used this wildscape in diffuse and restricted ways. He roamed the forest and heath hunting game but, apart from a cave shelter or toolmaking floor, rarely set aside land for a particular use. He exerted no perceptible influence upon the landscape apart from the fact that grazing animals gradually retarded the regeneration of the forest and led to a more open vegetation. But the presence of flat land, water, coal, stone and good access were ideal for later man.

Medieval
After he had developed agriculture man was able to use the land in more ways. It is possible by this time to detect at least a dozen types of stable land use. This was basically an age of slowly developing farmscape, when wildscape was reclaimed for food production and most settlement was designed to serve agricultural communities. Villagers are cultivating open strip fields in rotation for winter corn, spring corn and fallowing, surrounded by common grazing lands. The improved standard of shelter is reflected in clearance of forest to obtain timber, and the land is quarried for clay (near left), stone (left) and iron ore (background). With such burdens man has improved his transport methods. And the river is now becoming polluted.

19th Century
The industrial revolution was a marked change in man's use of land. Coal was deep-mined as a source of unprecedented power which led to the concentration of crafts in large factories. Gasworks, flour mills and textile mills were basic industries, in turn leading to an industrial townscape. Different types of land use can be measured by the score. Building stone and brick-making continue to flourish, but imports have replaced the old ironworkings. Agriculture plays its part by more efficient production from larger fields to support the growing population. Greatly improved communications are evident. But there is marked pollution of both the river and the atmosphere, and filter beds and clean-water reservoirs are necessary.

Modern
Land uses are now so differentiated as to be countless. Many hundreds of new uses are service functions, ranging from financial institutions to children's playgrounds (the former brick pit) and hairdressers. Dwellings abound in great variety, many of them made of new materials by new methods Electricity has wrought a revolution that extends to virtually every human construction, and the urgent demand for better transport has led to a complete transformation of the scene on this ground alone. A more subtle effect of better transport is that uneconomic local farming has given way to imported food, and much of the land is being reforested. Perhaps most important of all is the fact that man has become concerned about his environment.

Pollution is harmful waste. All living creatures produce waste, often with marked effects on the environment. Pine leaves blanket out the flowers which would otherwise grow on the forest floor; the droppings of seabirds can cover nesting islands meters deep in guano. Plants as well as road vehicles give off carbon dioxide; volcanoes as well as power stations emit sulphur dioxide.

What turns man's waste into pollution? First, we produce too much waste: only man lives in such vast communities that his excreta de-oxygenates whole rivers. Secondly, the unwanted by-products of man's industrial metabolism change so rapidly that the environment has little hope of accommodating it. African grassland has evolved over millions of years to accept piles of elephant dung, with many species of animals specially adapted to living inside dungheaps and helping to decompose them. But the ecosystem is often unable to cope with our latest pollutants: few bacteria are able to digest plastics. Thirdly, man's waste is often extremely persistent: DDT may remain unchanged for decades, passing from one animal to another, poisoning and weakening them all.

Pollution may harm man directly: smoke causes bronchitis, and fouled drinking water can spread typhoid. Pollution may harm us indirectly, reducing the capacity of the land, rivers and seas to supply us with food. But perhaps the most insidious effects are the least obvious. Small doses of separate pollutants, each harmless by itself, may together weaken wild populations of animals so that they cannot recover from natural disasters. Acute pollution kills tens of thousands of animals; chronic pollution gradually reduces the quality of the entire human environment.

Pollution is wasteful. Too often modern technology painstakingly extracts a metal from the crust, uses it once and then discards it. For example, once unwanted chromium or mercury is released into the seas it will be diluted many millions of times and is unlikely ever to be recoverable except at prohibitive expense. If man is not to face raw material famines in the foreseeable future, he must learn to recycle everything from air and water to the rarer elements.

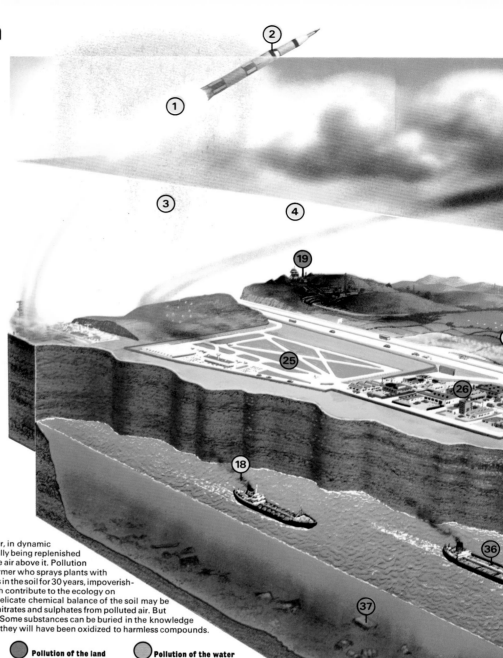

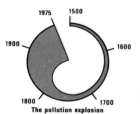

1975 1500
1900 1600
1800 1700

The pollution explosion

Pollution of the land

The soil is a living organic layer, in dynamic equilibrium with, and continually being replenished by, the rocks beneath it and the air above it. Pollution affects it in many ways. The farmer who sprays plants with insecticides may leave residues in the soil for 30 years, impoverishing the micro-organisms which contribute to the ecology on which his crops depend. The delicate chemical balance of the soil may be disrupted by rain loaded with nitrates and sulphates from polluted air. But the land is also a de-pollutant. Some substances can be buried in the knowledge that before they can re-appear they will have been oxidized to harmless compounds.

Pollution of the air

1 Rocket exhaust contains a variety of combustion products.

2 Space launchings leave jettisoned propellants and other debris orbiting above the atmosphere.

3 Nuclear weapon testing can leave fall-out on a global scale.

4 Increased air traffic creates noise pollution over wide areas.

5 Jet efflux contains kerosene combustion products, unburned fuel and particles of soot.

6 Nuclear weapons can cause radioactive contamination; together with chemical and biological devices they could eradicate all life on Earth.

7 Jet aircraft cause intense local noise, and supersonic aircraft create a shock-wave boom.

8 Large-scale aerial transport of pollutants distributes particles and gaseous matter.

9 Carbon dioxide build-up and 'greenhouse effect' traps solar heat within the atmosphere.

10 Pesticide spraying can cause widespread contamination, and organochlorine residues (such

as DDT) can build up in animals and disrupt natural food chains.

11 Nuclear power station is potential source of escaping radioactive or liquid coolant.

12 Thermal (coal or oil fired) power station causes thermal and chemical pollution from exhaust stacks.

13 Power station cooling towers transfer waste heat to the air.

14 Sulphur dioxide from high roof-level chimneys falls into 'canyon streets' causing irritation to eyes and lungs.

15 Refinery waste gases burned in the air cause heavy pollution unless the flame is extremely hot.

16 Road vehicle exhausts and crankcase gases contain lead, unburned hydrocarbons, carbon monoxide and oxides of nitrogen, and can cause widespread pollution; action of sunlight on nitrogen oxides causes smog.

17 Most domestic fuels are very inefficiently burned, causing smoke and chemical pollution.

18 Steam boilers or diesel smoke can cause persistent trails of gaseous and particulate matter.

Pollution of the land

19 Coal mining leaves unsightly and potentially dangerous tips.

20 Electricity transmission pylons are a classic of visual pollution.

21 Powerful air-conditioning cools buildings in summer by heating the immediate surroundings.

22 Visual pollution of highways is accentuated by billboards.

23 Unreclaimed wastes are often dumped and not recycled.

24 Quarrying leaves unsightly scars.

25 Growth of air traffic is reflected in increasing size and number of airports which occupy otherwise valuable land.

26 Even modern industrial estates invariably cause chemical and thermal pollution, and pose waste-disposal problems.

27 Large motorways, especially intersections, occupy large areas of land.

28 Caravan and chalet sites may cause severe local chemical, as well as visual, pollution.

29 Modern litter includes high proportion of non-biodegradable plastics materials.

Pollution of the water

30 Nuclear power station discharges waste heat into river and can cause radioactive contamination.

31 Industrial wastes are often poured into rivers without treatment.

32 Cooling water from thermal power stations can cause very large-scale heating of rivers, changing or destroying the natural fauna and flora.

33 Refinery and other chemical plants generate waste heat and liquid refuse which may be discharged directly into the river.

34 Oil storage installation can cause intermittent pollution.

35 When it reaches the sea the river is heavily polluted by nitrates and phosphates from fertilizers and treated sewage, as well as by heavy toxic metals.

36 Tanker too close inshore risks severe beach pollution from accidental release of cargo.

37 Radioactive and corrosive wastes often dumped without enough knowledge of local conditions to insure that the containers will not leak before contents

have decomposed; nothing should be dumped on continental shelf and adequate dilution is essential.

38 The main influx of pollutants into the sea is via rivers; typical categories include agricultural and industrial chemicals, waste heat, treated and untreated sewage and solid matter.

39 Excess nutrients from untreated sewage, agricultural chemicals and nuclear wastes can lead to 'blooms' of toxic marine plankton or, through their oxidation and decay, to severely reduced oxygen levels in the water.

40 Sewage sludge dumped at sea contains persistent chemicals such as PCB (polychlorinated biphenyl) compounds, toxic heavy metals and nutrients.

41 Large oil slicks are released by tanker accidents or deliberate washing at sea, and by oil-rig blow-outs.

42 Sediments stirred by mineral exploitation, dumped from ships or carried by rivers may form thick layers on the ocean floor which suffocate the organisms living there.

43 Clouds of particulate matter, both organic and inorganic wastes, reduce the penetration of sunlight and sharply curtail marine productivity.

44 Oil rigs suffer explosive blow-outs, a serious problem off the California coast.

45 In some waters wrecks, many of them uncharted, pose hazards to shipping which may lead to further pollution.

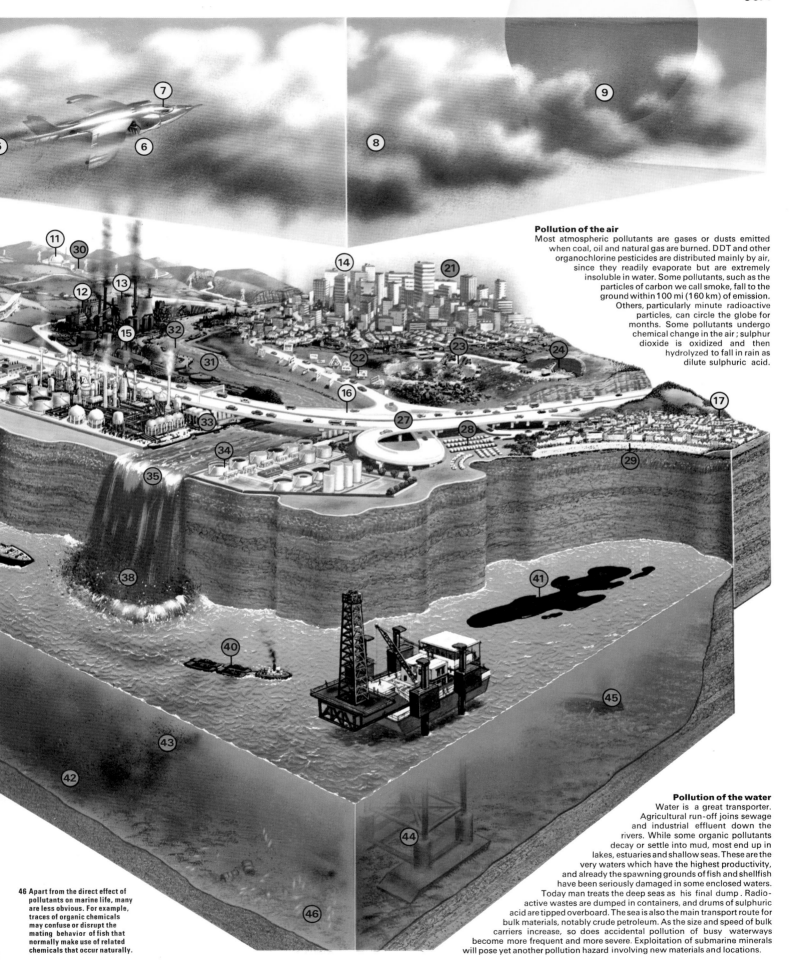

Pollution of the air

Most atmospheric pollutants are gases or dusts emitted when coal, oil and natural gas are burned. DDT and other organochlorine pesticides are distributed mainly by air, since they readily evaporate but are extremely insoluble in water. Some pollutants, such as the particles of carbon we call smoke, fall to the ground within 100 mi (160 km) of emission. Others, particularly minute radioactive particles, can circle the globe for months. Some pollutants undergo chemical change in the air; sulphur dioxide is oxidized and then hydrolyzed to fall in rain as dilute sulphuric acid.

Pollution of the water

Water is a great transporter. Agricultural run-off joins sewage and industrial effluent down the rivers. While some organic pollutants decay or settle into mud, most end up in lakes, estuaries and shallow seas. These are the very waters which have the highest productivity, and already the spawning grounds of fish and shellfish have been seriously damaged in some enclosed waters. Today man treats the deep seas as his final dump . Radioactive wastes are dumped in containers, and drums of sulphuric acid are tipped overboard. The sea is also the main transport route for bulk materials, notably crude petroleum. As the size and speed of bulk carriers increase, so does accidental pollution of busy waterways become more frequent and more severe. Exploitation of submarine minerals will pose yet another pollution hazard involving new materials and locations.

46 Apart from the direct effect of pollutants on marine life, many are less obvious. For example, traces of organic chemicals may confuse or disrupt the mating behavior of fish that normally make use of related chemicals that occur naturally.

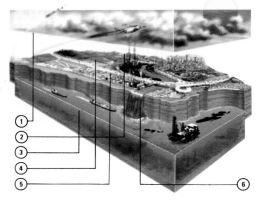

Pollution often travels along strange pathways, and these must be unravelled if the menace is to be controlled and its effects predicted. It is unwise ever to assume the obvious. DDT was found in the soil of apple orchards in Kent months after spraying, and it was also detected in local rivers. The obvious conclusion was that it was leaching down through the soil into the groundwater. But analysis of the springs and wells showed no DDT at all. In fact the insecticide was leaving the surface by evaporation and falling again as rain.

Pollution can be distributed over vast distances. The insecticide BHC is carried by the prevailing westerly winds from the Soviet Union across China and N America and to Europe. Water likewise carries contaminants down rivers to oceans. But the most important pathway is the food chain. A pollutant is released into the air, soil or sea. It is absorbed by plants. These are eaten by a herbivore, which in its turn is eaten by a carnivore which is itself eaten by a predator. The chain may have many links or only a few, but at every stage the pollutant is more concentrated. If a hawk eats 100 birds which each ate 100 insects it may die from pollution 10000 times the strength met by the insect.

Pollution and health

Eyes

Ozone from various industrial processes is extremely toxic and irritates the eyes

Sulphur dioxide is generated by burning all sulphurous fuels: coal, oil and gas

Smoke is mainly particulate carbon plus mixed carbohydrate molecules, some of them carcinogenic

Dust, varied particulate and fibrous matter, is caused by ash, mineral extraction and abrasion

Photochemical smog is a suspension of irritant and carcinogenic molecules of nitro-oxide origin

Nose

Carbon monoxide, formed when anything is incompletely burned, inactivates blood hemoglobin in humans

Nitrogen oxides, caused by almost all fuel burning, combine with other elements to form harmful compounds

Smoke particles inhaled by humans form a black oily coating on the lungs; cigarettes are the main source

Sulphur dioxide is a choking irritant in high concentrations. Its action on the lungs is complex

Mineral particles are released by clothing and other fabrics and have an irritant effect on the lungs

Lead compounds, often from gasoline vapor, are inhaled and then washed from the lungs to the throat and stomach

Ears

30 decibels: watch ticking

60 db: normal conversation

90 db: close heavy truck

102 db: modern big jetliner

110 db: car horn, football crowd

120 db: older jet at 500 ft (180 m)

130 db: loud pop group, air raid siren

150 db: laboratory rats paralysed

180 db: presumed lethal to humans

Skin

Dieldrin is used to make woollen cloth mothproof and is thus brought into prolonged contact with the skin

Detergents and enzyme compounds generally pass into or through the skin, causing dermatitis

Insecticides can usually enter the body through the skin, in extreme cases having harmful effects

Organophosphorus insecticides, such as Dieldrin, invariably penetrate the skin and require protective clothing

Mouth (water)

Pesticides can become concentrated to dangerous or lethal levels (see opposite page)

Heavy metals, such as cadmium, zinc and nickel, are difficult to eliminate from water and foodstuffs

Chlorine, fluorine, selenium and copper compounds in drinking water can have complex adverse effects

Pathogenic bacteria are released mainly from raw sewage, causing typhoid, diarrhea and other ills

Mouth (food)

Pesticides enter the body mainly on food, and are particularly prevalent on the skins of fruit and vegetables

Dyes of many kinds are added to restore what the public considers to be a desirable color to food

Mercury, in organic compounds, is one of the few really dangerous elements to humans (see diagram below)

Modern processed foodstuffs contain numerous forms of flavoring and preservatives in small quantities

① Radiation *right*

No pollutant has been so continuously monitored as nuclear radiation. But it is not a problem created solely by modern man. In the modern world nearly all the radioactivity issues from the rocks, and, as far as humans are concerned, from the body.

Rocks	50 %
Cosmic	25 %
Body	$23\frac{1}{4}$ %
Tests	$1\frac{1}{2}$ %
Waste	$\frac{1}{4}$ %

② Radiation and life *right*

Living cells concentrate radiation. In an above-ground nuclear-weapon test all heavy radioactive particles drop within hours in a narrow region down-wind of the explosion. Their residence time in the atmosphere varies from four weeks in the troposphere to ten years in the mesosphere. One such product, strontium 90, is taken up from the soil by plants. Eaten by cattle and released in their milk, it ends up in human bone where it is only slowly liquidated. As it decays it can destroy the marrow which produces red blood cells, in extreme cases causing death through pentaemia. Radiation pollution can also arise from power reactors or nuclear waste. Plankton can concentrate radioactivity a thousandfold. Fish eat plankton, and on migration can disperse the radiation far from its source. In the 1950s this mechanism caused radiation sickness in Japanese fishermen hundreds of miles from US test sites in the Pacific.

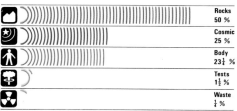

Concentration of atomic waste (phosphorus 32) in animal food chains

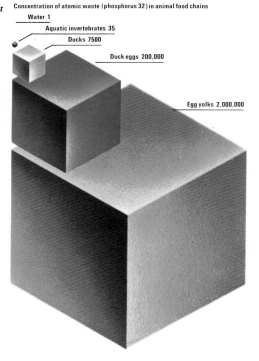

Water 1

Aquatic invertebrates 35

Ducks 7500

Duck eggs 200,000

Egg yolks 2,000,000

③ Deadly mercury *right*

Compounds of mercury have for 1000 years been known to be highly toxic. An industrial plant often discharges such compounds, but it was thought these rested at the sea bed. Man has now learned that bacteria can convert inorganic mercury compounds to deadly methyl mercury, which can then be successively concentrated in marine food chains. Shellfish are particularly good concentrators of methyl mercury. When eaten by humans they cause severe disabling of the central nervous system, and in extreme cases cause death (below).

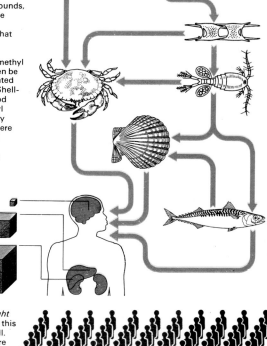

brains

liver

kidneys

Minimata tragedy *right*

In 1953 people living in this Japanese city became ill. Ultimately over 120 were afflicted, and 43 (black) died. The cause was methyl mercury concentrated in seafoods. Some acetaldehyde plants still emit methyl mercury.

④ The DDT menace *right*
Introduced during World War 2, DDT appeared to be ideal. It would kill lice on soldiers weeks after the treatment of their clothes. Houses sprayed against malaria remained lethal to mosquitoes long after the health teams had departed. But the persistence brought its own problems. DDT and other organochlorine pesticides, such as BHC, Dieldrin, Endosulfan and Heptachlor, are only slightly broken down by animal metabolism. An insect receiving a non-lethal dose of DDT retains it in its body and passes it on up the food chain. Animals at the head of the chain often build up large residues in their fatty tissues. Under stress these residues can be released and fatally damage the liver, kidney and brain. DDT can evaporate from soil, travelling round the globe, before being adsorbed on to dust and falling as rain. The organochlorines soon penetrate every corner of an ecosystem.

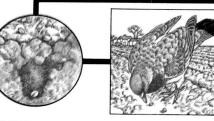

DIELDRIN

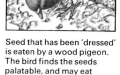   

Seed that has been 'dressed' is eaten by a wood pigeon. The bird finds the seeds palatable, and may eat dozens to hundreds in a day.

The pigeon is devoured by a badger (or a cat, fox, hawk or other predator). The badger may build up poison from eating many pigeons.

In this case the pesticide-soaked grain is attractive to a yellowhammer, typical of many small birds which pick seeds off the land.

The yellowhammer has fallen prey to a sparrowhawk. In a few weeks dieldrin may build up causing death or inability to breed.

DDT

Sap-sucking insects, such as aphids, feed on sprayed wheat and build up a DDT concentration not sufficiently high to kill them.

A predator ladybird climbs wheat grain devouring aphids in large numbers. It soon builds up a very large residue of DDT in its body.

On a nettle at the edge of the field the ladybird is in turn eaten by a whitethroat, spotted flycatcher or other insect-eating bird.

Finally the bird suffering from severe DDT toxicity, is devoured by a hawk. In many countries birds of prey have almost vanished.

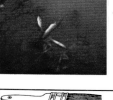

⑥ Misuse of a river by overloading *above and left*
In moderation, man can safely pour his effluents into the rivers. A farmhouse beside a river (above) causes a little local pollution which is soon oxidized; the fish population does not suffer. A village causes no lasting pollution but merely a depression of the dissolved oxygen in the water for a mile or two downstream. But a large city pours out so much effluent that the river is completely de-oxygenated. All the fish and plants are killed and the river becomes foul in an irreversible way (left). Whereas a river may be capable of processing pollutants from 50000 people, pollutants from 100000 may destroy the ecological cycle.

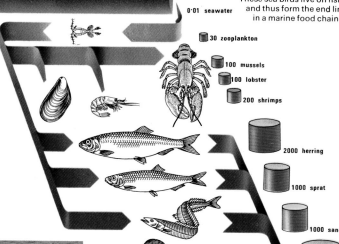

⑤ The PCB problem
PCBs (polychlorinated biphenyls) are persistent and can be scattered in smoke from burning or washed down a drain adsorbed on dust particles. Virtually all these molecules end up in the sea in the form of non-biodegradable particles which can be intensely concentrated as they move within the marine food chain. Their lethal effect was first driven home when the population of Irish sea birds, especially guillemots, crashed in 1969. Almost all the corpses were found to have liver and kidney lesions characteristic of PCB poisoning. Fat, healthy birds can carry a large PCB load safely, but the Irish birds were starving and had drawn on their fatty reserves, where the PCB was stored. Passing into the circulation, the chemical accumulated in the birds' organs in lethal amounts.

PCB uses *left*
Polychlorinated biphenyls have numerous uses in modern industry. They serve as plasticizers in paints, as fillers in plastics and in electrical capacitors.

Guillemots *right*
These sea birds live on fish and thus form the end link in a marine food chain.

0.01 seawater
30 zooplankton
100 mussels
100 lobster
200 shrimps
2000 herring
1000 sprat
1000 sand-eel
3400 guillemot

Thin guillemot *below*
When a guillemot with 3400 ppb of PCB in its body becomes emaciated it draws on its reserves of fat. The chemical becomes concentrated in its organs, reaching a lethal level of 60000 ppb.

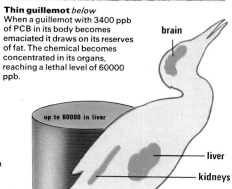

brain

up to 60000 in liver

liver

kidneys

Fat guillemot *left*
Healthy guillemots (feeding at sea, far left) can have 3400 parts per billion (ppb) of PCBs in the body but only 400 in the liver.

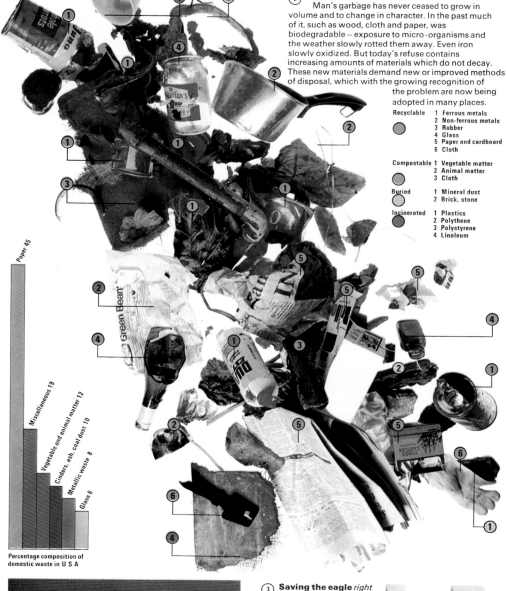

② **Domestic waste**
Man's garbage has never ceased to grow in volume and to change in character. In the past much of it, such as wood, cloth and paper, was biodegradable – exposure to micro-organisms and the weather slowly rotted them away. Even iron slowly oxidized. But today's refuse contains increasing amounts of materials which do not decay. These new materials demand new or improved methods of disposal, which with the growing recognition of the problem are now being adopted in many places.

Recyclable 1 Ferrous metals
2 Non-ferrous metals
3 Rubber
4 Glass
5 Paper and cardboard
6 Cloth

Compostable 1 Vegetable matter
2 Animal matter
3 Cloth

Buried 1 Mineral dust
2 Brick, stone

Incinerated 1 Plastics
2 Polythene
3 Polystyrene
4 Linoleum

Pollution is a global problem. It affects the land, the sea and the atmosphere in an inter-related way that is incredibly complex and often very subtle. At least in the industrially developed countries man has learned that he must do better than merely bury his unwanted materials in the ground, pour them into the rivers or burn them to pollute the air. But learning the best ways of disposing of them – or, preferably, of storing them until they can be used again – is a difficult, long-term process; and time is not on man's side.

Once pollutants are dispersed, controlling them becomes extremely costly or even impossible. The answer is to prevent their release, wherever possible, into the arterial pathways of water and air. The growing awareness of this is reflected in the legislation of many countries. It is seen in the Clean Air Act of Great Britain, the German convention banning harmful detergents, the tight California restrictions on car exhaust gases, and so on. But this is only the start of the movement to clean-up the environment and conserve its resources.

Much of the action against pollution has been piecemeal in nature, often in response to particular disasters. Now comes the promise, in no small part due to the public mood, for more widespread action against pollutants that are already known to be harmful to the environment and man. For example, public health authorities in most countries are alive to the hazard of mercury contamination in fish and other foods. At the international level, the convention on oil pollution is being strengthened and the permissible levels of radioactive discharges reviewed. At the same time, industry is slowly becoming persuaded that waste should be regarded as a valued resource which is often capable of being recycled over and over again instead of discarded.

Paper 45
Miscellaneous 19
Vegetable and animal matter 12
Cinders, ash, coal dust 10
Metallic waste 8
Glass 6

Percentage composition of domestic waste in U S A

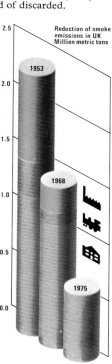

2.5
2.0
1.5
1.0
0.5
0.0

Reduction of smoke emissions in UK Million metric tons

1953
1968
1975

① **Air pollution in cities**
Smoke is one of the commonest, most dangerous and most visible of all air pollutants. It is the direct cause of bronchitis and other respiratory diseases. But many nations are cleaning their urban atmosphere by introducing smokeless zones. Since 1956 winter sunshine in British city centers has increased by over 50 per cent. Smoke from railways (violet segment, right) has dwindled as steam traction has been superseded. Industrial smoke has likewise been reduced, although iron oxide dust from steelworks (above) remains a problem as do domestic coal fires.

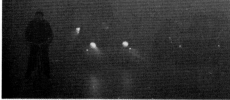

The menace of the car *below*
Dramatic reductions in air pollution will result as soon as simple alterations are universally adopted. One of the worst sources, the crankcase breather (1), is not opened to the air but piped through a vacuum-sensing valve (2) back to the intake. Fuel-tank vapor (3) is filtered and similarly dealt with. The exhaust is made oxygen-rich with extra fresh air (4) to burn up all but a few combustion products; the residue is oxidized to harmless compounds by passage through a high temperature furnace (5) in the presence of a chemical catalyst which promotes the desired reactions.

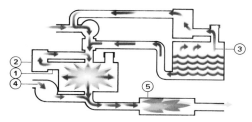

③ **Saving the eagle** *right*
In the early 1960s ecologists became sure that organo-chlorine insecticides (DDT and Dieldrin, for example) were the cause of the sudden drop in breeding success of many predatory birds. But the charge could not be proved, and in most countries the use of these pesticides continued. One bird affected was the golden eagle. Scottish highland sheep were dipped in Dieldrin to kill ticks. The chemical became dissolved in the mutton fat, and this eagle lives largely on sheep carrion. In one area the proportion of eagle eyries producing young fell from 72 to 29 per cent, following the introduction of Dieldrin sheep dips in 1960. Scotland's 300 pairs of eagles seemed doomed. But in 1966 Britain banned Dieldrin sheep-dips. By the early 1970s more than enough young survived to maintain the eagle population.

1960 1963 1966 1969
Golden eagle: percentage breeding successes

④ Oil pollution

Every year millions of tons of oil enter the oceans either directly through spills, accidents and deliberate discharge or indirectly via air and water from the land. Hardly any part of the ocean remains free from contamination. Some oil pollution is the disturbing result of industrial society's dependence on an oil-based technology. Equally, there is no doubt that much oil pollution is unnecessary and can be controlled or prevented. One of the earliest attempts to do this occurred in 1926 when the United States tried to obtan international agreement to limit the discharge of oil. This and later attempts by the United Kingdom failed and it was not until 1958 that the International Convention for the Preventionof Pollution of the Sea by Oil came into force – four years after it was agreed. Even then, the Convention did not ban completely the release of oil into the sea. This must be the ultimate goal. However, even if this is achieved, the problem will persist – oil pollution from sources on land is more than double that occurring directly at sea. One of the chief offenders are gasoline and diesel engines. The crankcases of such engines contribute at least 2.8 million metric tons of oil to the sea every year. A serious waste of a vital resource, steps are at last being taken in some countries to curb it.

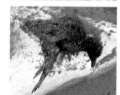

The Torrey Canyon disaster
In 1967 the sea had its first major case of oil pollution when the Torrey Canyon ran aground off the Cornish coast (above left). Within a few days the first oil began to sweep onto the beaches. To disperse it, large quantities of detergent were sprayed both from boats (above) and on the shore, turning the sea creamy white with a froth of oily emulsion (center left). Unfortunately the use of these detergents probably caused more damage to marine life than did the oil – except for the early kill of seabirds (bottom left). The oil also drifted across to France coating the shore with congealed oil (right).

Major oil routes

Oil movements *left*
Increased transport is reflected in the percentage growth of the world tanker fleet (below).

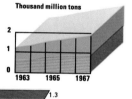

Thousand million tons

	1963	1965	1967

Oil tankers' new load-on-top system *below*
Before the introduction of this system, ballast water and tank washings, along with a hundred or so tons of oil which had originally stuck to the internal steelwork, were discharged into the sea before taking on a new cargo. In the load-on-top system, one cargo compartment (A) is used as a 'slop tank'. Water in a ballast tank (B) is run off until only oil and oily water remains (C). The residue together with washings from the tanks are collected in the slop tank (D). Here the mixture is finally separated before running clean water off (E). The load goes on top of the remaining oil.

Oil entering the oceans — Million metric tons

Industrial machine waste	1.3
Motor vehicle waste	1.8
Refineries	0.3
Accidental spillage	0.2
Offshore drilling	0.1
Tanker operations	0.53
Other ships	0.5

Sources of oil pollution *left*
Although the spectacular incidents such as tanker collisions and drilling rig accidents receive most publicity, they release little oil compared with motor vehicles and industrial machines.

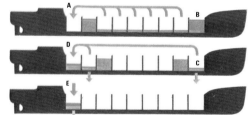

⑤ Thermal pollution *above and below*

Man throws away a great deal of unwanted heat into rivers. This is done on the largest scale by electricity generating stations whose condensers cycle cooling water in vast quantities. In Britain the hot effluent is spread as a thin film on an otherwise cool river, causing visible steam (above, River Trent) but minimal disturbance to river life. The problem is accentuated by the spread of very large nuclear stations (in the US, below), which for safety reasons have so far generally been sited miles from urban areas on rivers which previously were quite unpolluted. In Britian all such stations are on the sea shore or wide estuaries.

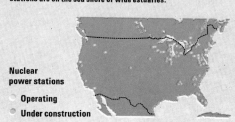

Nuclear power stations
○ **Operating**
○ **Under construction**

⑥ Lake pollution

Lakes pass through a sequence of physical and chemical states from youth to maturity (p66A). Man's sewage and industrial effluents accelerate the intake of nutrient salts — such as the phosphates and nitrates shown in the bar chart above the map — which feed the natural population of algae. Combined with sunny weather the result can be an algal 'bloom'. Billions of algae use up the water's dissolved oxygen, killing fish and other life. The aerobic (oxygen-breathing) bacteria needed to degrade sewage and other organic matter are replaced by anaerobic forms which decompose the refuse not to carbon dioxide and water but to foul gases and black slimes. Eventually the bloom is replaced by an algal 'crash' and the countless bodies, often visible as a colored tide, evolve toxic decomposition products which, concentrated in food chains, can prove lethal to sea birds and even humans. The answer is better water treatment plants, possibly combined with new forms of fertilizers, detergents and other products of modern civilization which contain smaller quantities of nutrient salts.

Main pollutants: percentages

Phosphate	20	43	37	
Nitrate	9	17	74	

☐ Lakeshore sewage
☐ Sewage from tributaries
■ Natural inflow from rivers

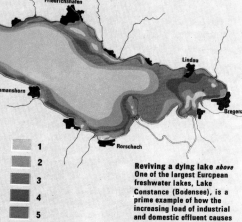

Ludwigshafen, Überlingen, Radolfzell, Konstanz, Friedrichshafen, Kreuzlingen, Steckborn, Lindau, Romanshorn, Rorschach, Bregenz

| 1 |
| 2 |
| 3 |
| 4 |
| 5 |
| 6 |
| 7 |

Numbers indicate increasing pollution

Reviving a dying lake *above*
One of the largest European freshwater lakes, Lake Constance (Bodensee), is a prime example of how the increasing load of industrial and domestic effluent causes serious pollution. The aim now is to install treatment plant at source rather than use the lake as a liquid refuse dump.

World Thematic Maps

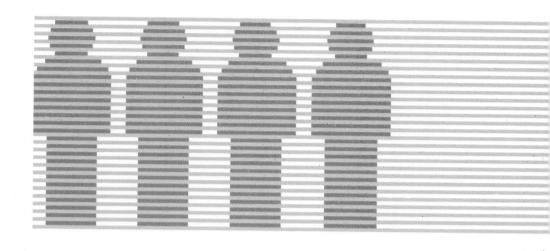

This section contains more than 50 thematic maps that present world patterns and distributions in visual form. Together with accompanying graphs, these maps communicate basic information on mineral resources, agricultural products, trade, transportation, and other selected aspects of the natural and human environment.

The thematic map uses symbols to communicate information. Generally, each map tells about only one class of geographical information, such as climate or population. This "theme" of a thematic map is placed over a map that gives basic geographic information, such as coastlines, country boundaries, rivers, and oceans. A thematic map's primary purpose is to give the reader a general idea of the subject. For example, the map on page 37 shows the distribution of cattle by the use of dot symbols. From this, the reader can learn that cattle are distributed much more uniformly throughout the United States than in China. The reader can also see that America has more cattle than China. But there is no way to tell the exact number in each country.

This is true of most thematic maps. They are not intended to provide exact statistical information. A reader who wants precise statistics should consult the bar graphs that appear with the thematic maps in this Atlas or other sources, such as encyclopedias or almanacs.

Thematic maps use point, line, and area symbols, singly and in combination. These can show both *qualitative differences* (differences in kind) and *quantitative differences* (differences in amount). For example, the Natural Vegetation map (page 16) uses color and pattern symbols to show the kind of vegetation that grows naturally in various parts of the world. This is qualitative information. Quantitative information is shown on the Annual Precipitation map (page 14). By means of lines that connect points of equal rainfall, the reader can tell, in general, how much rain an area receives in a year. Color is used to show the area between the lines. Thus, the thematic maps communicate general information far better than could volumes of words and tables.

One of the most important uses of the thematic maps section is to show comparisons and relationships. For example, a reader can compare the relationship of population density (page 20) with agriculture (page 28) and annual precipitation (page 14).

The maps and graphs in this section also give an idea of the relative importance of countries in the distributions mapped. The maps are based on recent statistics gathered by the United Nations and various governmental and nongovernmental sources. However, no single year affords a realistic base for production, trade, and certain economic and demographic statistics; averages of data for three or four years are used.

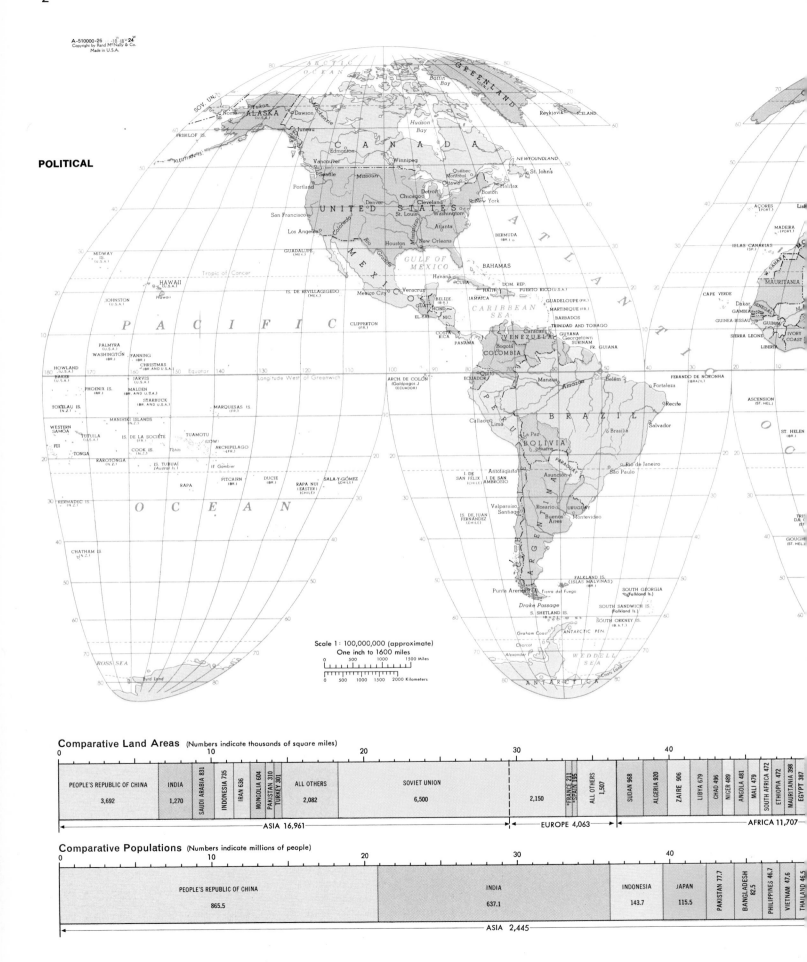

A-510000-26
Copyright by Rand McNally & Co.
Made in U.S.A.

POLITICAL

Scale 1 : 100,000,000 (approximate)
One inch to 1600 miles
0   500   1000   1500 Miles
0   500   1000   1500   2000 Kilometers

Comparative Land Areas (Numbers indicate thousands of square miles)

| PEOPLE'S REPUBLIC OF CHINA 3,692 | INDIA 1,270 | SAUDI ARABIA 831 | INDONESIA 735 | IRAN 636 | MONGOLIA 604 | PAKISTAN 310 | TURKEY 301 | ALL OTHERS 2,082 | SOVIET UNION 6,500 | 2,150 | FRANCE 211 | SPAIN 195 | ALL OTHERS 1,507 | SUDAN 968 | ALGERIA 920 | ZAIRE 906 | LIBYA 679 | CHAD 496 | NIGER 489 | ANGOLA 481 | MALI 479 | SOUTH AFRICA 472 | ETHIOPIA 472 | MAURITANIA 398 | EGYPT 387 |

ASIA 16,961   EUROPE 4,063   AFRICA 11,707

Comparative Populations (Numbers indicate millions of people)

| PEOPLE'S REPUBLIC OF CHINA 865.5 | INDIA 637.1 | INDONESIA 143.7 | JAPAN 115.5 | PAKISTAN 77.7 | BANGLADESH 82.5 | PHILIPPINES 46.7 | VIETNAM 47.6 | THAILAND 46.5 |

ASIA 2,445

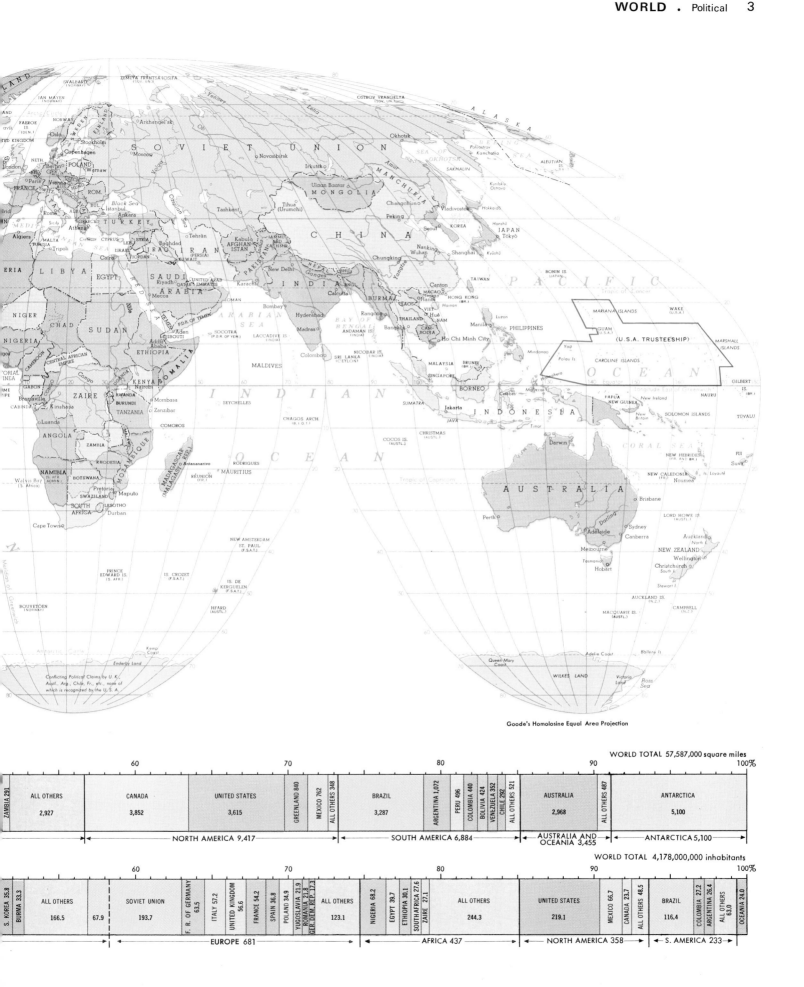

Goode's Homolosine Equal Area Projection

WORLD TOTAL 57,587,000 square miles

| | ALL OTHERS 2,927 | CANADA 3,852 | UNITED STATES 3,615 | GREENLAND 840 | MEXICO 762 | ALL OTHERS 348 | BRAZIL 3,287 | ARGENTINA 1,072 | PERU 496 | COLOMBIA 440 | BOLIVIA 424 | VENEZUELA 352 | CHILE 292 | ALL OTHERS 521 | AUSTRALIA 2,968 | ALL OTHERS 487 | ANTARCTICA 5,100 |

ZAMBIA 291

NORTH AMERICA 9,417 — SOUTH AMERICA 6,884 — AUSTRALIA AND OCEANIA 3,455 — ANTARCTICA 5,100

WORLD TOTAL 4,178,000,000 inhabitants

| | ALL OTHERS 166.5 | 67.9 | SOVIET UNION 193.7 | F. R. OF GERMANY 63.5 | ITALY 57.2 | UNITED KINGDOM 56.6 | FRANCE 54.2 | SPAIN 36.8 | POLAND 34.9 | YUGOSLAVIA 21.9 | ROMANIA 21.8 | GER. DEM. REP. 17.3 | ALL OTHERS 123.1 | NIGERIA 68.2 | EGYPT 39.7 | ETHIOPIA 30.1 | SOUTH AFRICA 27.6 | ZAIRE 27.1 | ALL OTHERS 244.3 | UNITED STATES 219.1 | MEXICO 66.7 | CANADA 23.7 | ALL OTHERS 48.5 | BRAZIL 116.4 | COLOMBIA 27.2 | ARGENTINA 26.4 | ALL OTHERS 63.0 | OCEANIA 24.0 |

S. KOREA 35.8
BURMA 33.3

EUROPE 681 — AFRICA 437 — NORTH AMERICA 358 — S. AMERICA 233

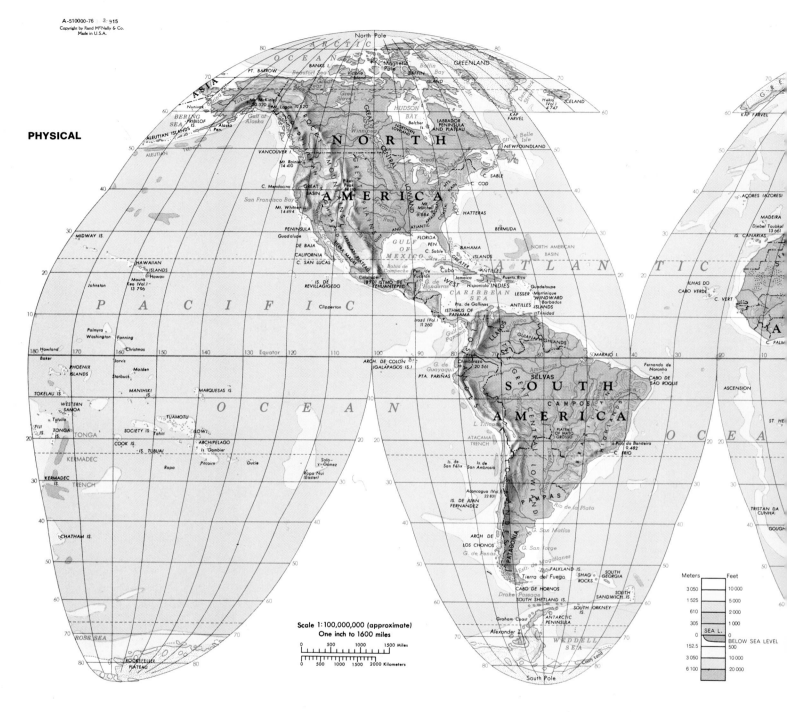

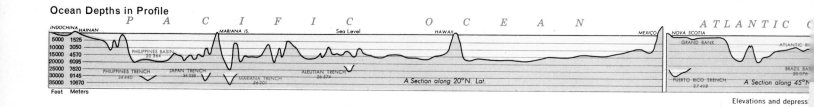

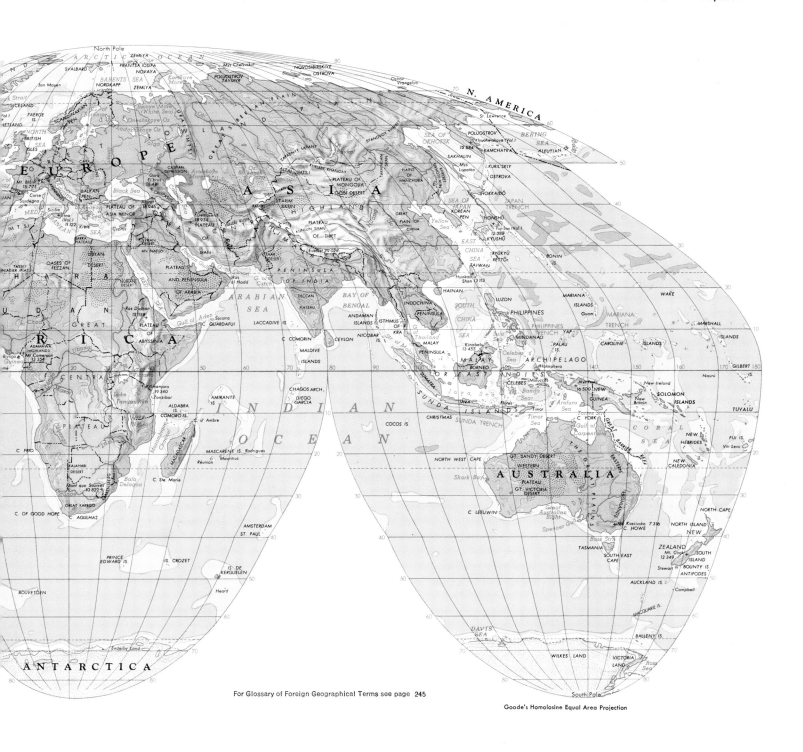

For Glossary of Foreign Geographical Terms see page 245

Goode's Homolosine Equal Area Projection

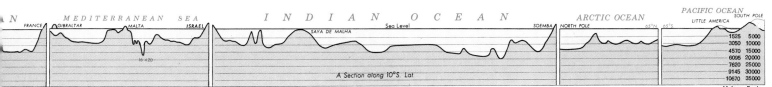

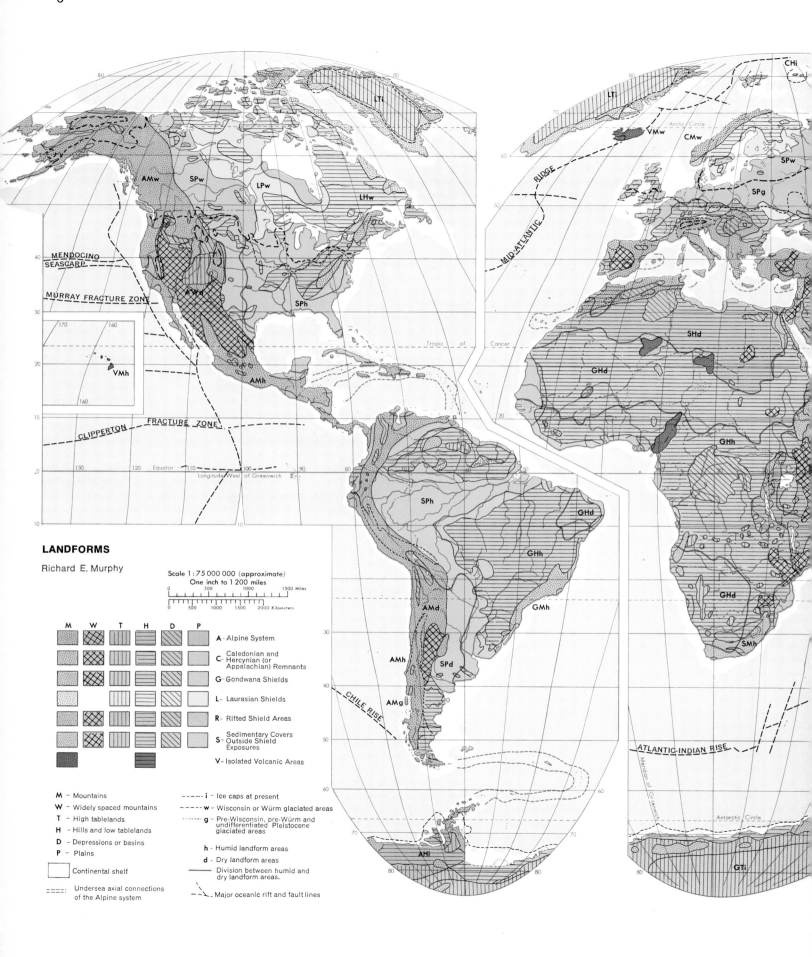

LANDFORMS

Richard E. Murphy

Scale 1 : 75 000 000 (approximate)
One inch to 1 200 miles

| 0 | 500 | 1000 | 1500 Miles |

| 0 | 500 | 1000 | 1500 | 2000 Kilometers |

	M	W	T	H	D	P	
							A – Alpine System
							C – Caledonian and Hercynian (or Appalachian) Remnants
							G – Gondwana Shields
							L – Laurasian Shields
							R – Rifted Shield Areas
							S – Sedimentary Covers Outside Shield Exposures
							V – Isolated Volcanic Areas

M – Mountains
W – Widely spaced mountains
T – High tablelands
H – Hills and low tablelands
D – Depressions or basins
P – Plains

Continental shelf

Undersea axial connections of the Alpine system

- - - - **i** – Ice caps at present
- - - - **w** – Wisconsin or Würm glaciated areas
· · · · **g** – Pre-Wisconsin, pre-Würm and undifferentiated Pleistocene glaciated areas
h – Humid landform areas
d – Dry landform areas
——— Division between humid and dry landform areas.
- - - Major oceanic rift and fault lines

MENDOCINO SEASCARP

MURRAY FRACTURE ZONE

CLIPPERTON FRACTURE ZONE

CHILE RISE

ATLANTIC-INDIAN RISE

MID-ATLANTIC RIDGE

Tropic of Cancer

Equator

Longitude West of Greenwich

Arctic Circle

Antarctic Circle

Meridian of Greenwich

SPg

SHh

AMg

SPh

SPd

ADd

SHd

AMh

SHd

GHh

OWEN FRACTURE ZONE

CARLSBURG RIDGE

AMh

Tropic of Cancer

GMh

Longitude East of Greenwich

Equator

WEST INDIAN RIDGE

MID-INDIAN RIDGE

Tropic of Capricorn

GHd

SPd

CHh

AMh

AMg

AUSTRALIAN-ANTARCTIC RISE

GTi

Goode's Homolosine Equal Area Projection (Condensed)

A-510000-9A6 2-3-4

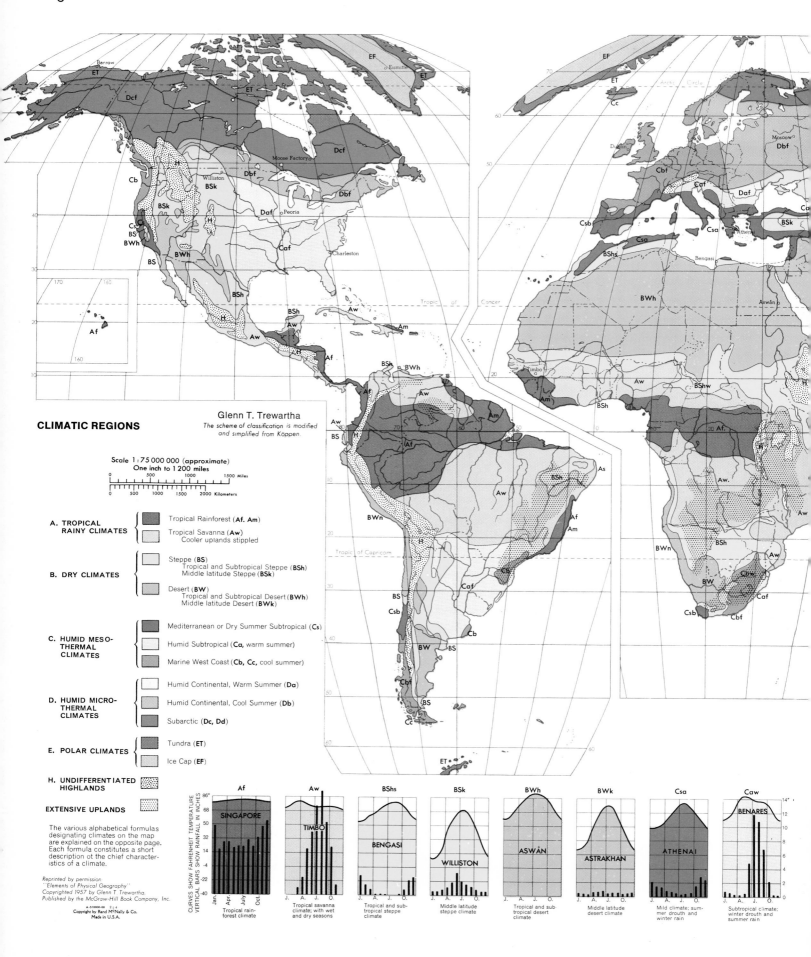

8

CLIMATIC REGIONS

Glenn T. Trewartha
*The scheme of classification is modified
and simplified from Köppen.*

Scale 1 : 75 000 000 (approximate)
One inch to 1 200 miles

A. TROPICAL
RAINY CLIMATES
- Tropical Rainforest (**Af. Am**)
- Tropical Savanna (**Aw**)
  Cooler uplands stippled

B. DRY CLIMATES
- Steppe (**BS**)
  Tropical and Subtropical Steppe (**BSh**)
  Middle latitude Steppe (**BSk**)
- Desert (**BW**)
  Tropical and Subtropical Desert (**BWh**)
  Middle latitude Desert (**BWk**)

C. HUMID MESO-
THERMAL
CLIMATES
- Mediterranean or Dry Summer Subtropical (**Cs**)
- Humid Subtropical (**Ca**, warm summer)
- Marine West Coast (**Cb, Cc**, cool summer)

D. HUMID MICRO-
THERMAL
CLIMATES
- Humid Continental, Warm Summer (**Da**)
- Humid Continental, Cool Summer (**Db**)
- Subarctic (**Dc, Dd**)

E. POLAR CLIMATES
- Tundra (**ET**)
- Ice Cap (**EF**)

H. UNDIFFERENTIATED
HIGHLANDS

EXTENSIVE UPLANDS

The various alphabetical formulas
designating climates on the map
are explained on the opposite page.
Each formula constitutes a short
description ot the chief characteristics of a climate.

Reprinted by permission of
"Elements of Physical Geography"
Copyrighted 1957 by Glenn T. Trewartha.
Published by the McGraw-Hill Book Company, Inc.

A-510000-88 8¼4
Copyright by Rand M⁵Nally & Co.
Made in U.S.A.

CURVES SHOW FAHRENHEIT TEMPERATURE
VERTICAL BARS SHOW RAINFALL IN INCHES

Af	Aw	BShs	BSk	BWh	BWk	Csa	Caw
SINGAPORE	TIMBO	BENGASI	WILLISTON	ASWÂN	ASTRAKHAN	ATHENAI	BENARES
Tropical rain-forest climate	Tropical savanna climate; with wet and dry seasons	Tropical and sub-tropical steppe climate	Middle latitude steppe climate	Tropical and sub-tropical desert climate	Middle latitude desert climate	Mild climate; summer drouth and winter rain	Subtropical climate; winter drouth and summer rain

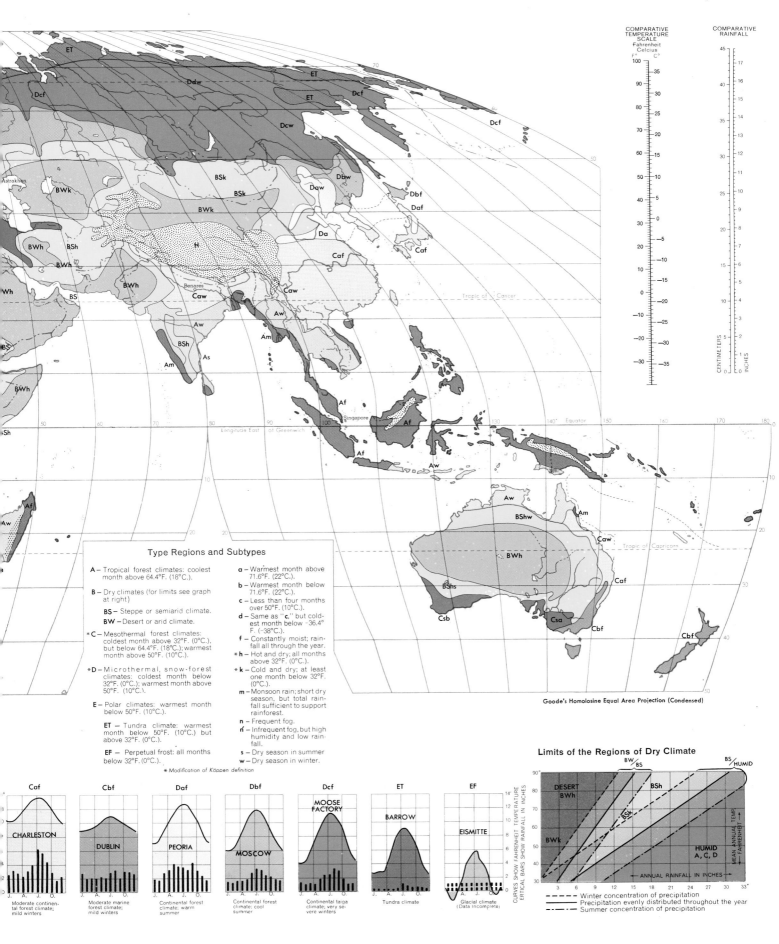

COMPARATIVE
TEMPERATURE
SCALE
Fahrenheit
Celsius

COMPARATIVE
RAINFALL

Type Regions and Subtypes

A – Tropical forest climates: coolest month above 64.4°F. (18°C.).

B – Dry climates (for limits see graph at right)

  BS – Steppe or semiarid climate.

  BW – Desert or arid climate.

*C – Mesothermal forest climates: coldest month above 32°F. (0°C.), but below 64.4°F. (18°C.); warmest month above 50°F. (10°C.).

*D – Microthermal, snow-forest climates: coldest month below 32°F. (0°C.); warmest month above 50°F. (10°C.).

E – Polar climates: warmest month below 50°F. (10°C.).

  ET – Tundra climate: warmest month below 50°F. (10°C.) but above 32°F. (0°C.).

  EF – Perpetual frost: all months below 32°F. (0°C.).

a – Warmest month above 71.6°F. (22°C.).

b – Warmest month below 71.6°F. (22°C.).

c – Less than four months over 50°F. (10°C.).

d – Same as "c," but coldest month below −36.4°F. (−38°C.).

f – Constantly moist; rainfall all through the year.

*h – Hot and dry; all months above 32°F. (0°C.).

*k – Cold and dry; at least one month below 32°F. (0°C.).

m – Monsoon rain; short dry season, but total rainfall sufficient to support rainforest.

n – Frequent fog.

ń – Infrequent fog, but high humidity and low rainfall.

s – Dry season in summer.

w – Dry season in winter.

*Modification of Köppen definition

Goode's Homolosine Equal Area Projection (Condensed)

Limits of the Regions of Dry Climate

BW/BS

BS/HUMID

DESERT
BWh

BSh

BSk

BWk

HUMID
A, C, D

CURVES SHOW FAHRENHEIT TEMPERATURE
VERTICAL BARS SHOW RAINFALL IN INCHES

MEAN ANNUAL TEMP.
FAHRENHEIT

ANNUAL RAINFALL IN INCHES

– – – – Winter concentration of precipitation
———— Precipitation evenly distributed throughout the year
– · – · – Summer concentration of precipitation

Caf
CHARLESTON
Moderate continental forest climate; mild winters

Cbf
DUBLIN
Moderate marine forest climate; mild winters

Daf
PEORIA
Continental forest climate; warm summer

Dbf
MOSCOW
Continental forest climate; cool summer

Dcf
MOOSE FACTORY
Continental taiga climate; very severe winters

ET
BARROW
Tundra climate

EF
EISMITTE
Glacial climate
(Data incomplete)

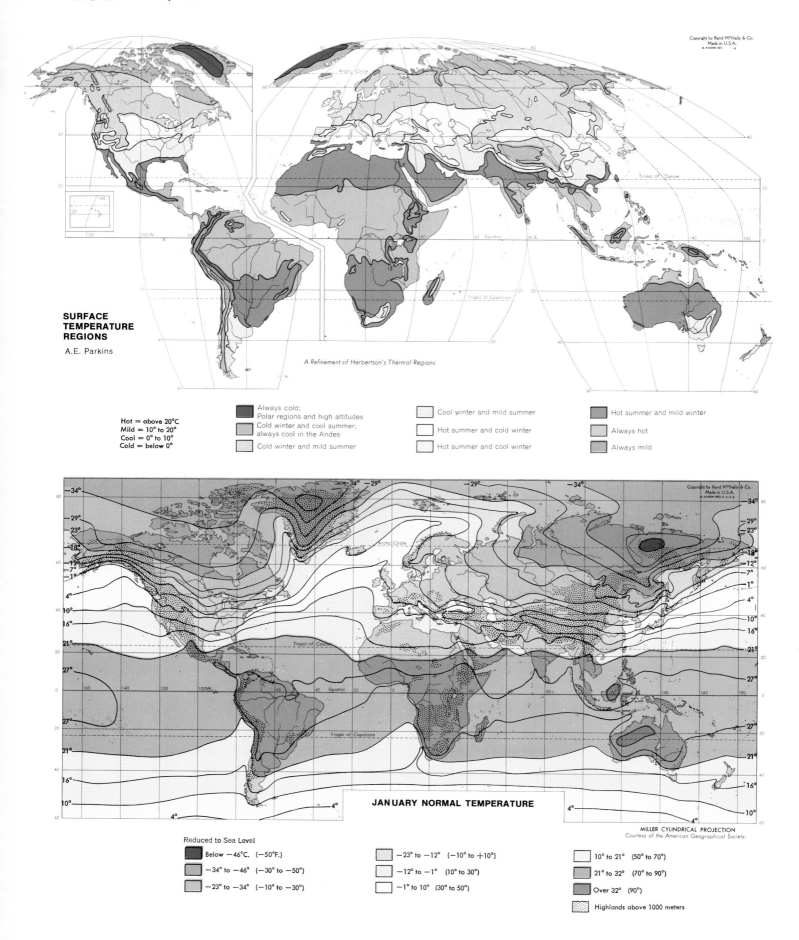

**SURFACE
TEMPERATURE
REGIONS**

A.E. Parkins

A Refinement of Herbertson's Thermal Regions

Hot = above 20°C
Mild = 10° to 20°
Cool = 0° to 10°
Cold = below 0°

Always cold;
Polar regions and high altitudes

Cold winter and cool summer;
always cool in the Andes

Cold winter and mild summer

Cool winter and mild summer

Hot summer and cold winter

Hot summer and cool winter

Hot summer and mild winter

Always hot

Always mild

JANUARY NORMAL TEMPERATURE

MILLER CYLINDRICAL PROJECTION
Courtesy of the American Geographical Society.

Reduced to Sea Level

Below −46°C. (−50°F.)

−34° to −46° (−30° to −50°)

−23° to −34° (−10° to −30°)

−23° to −12° (−10° to +10°)

−12° to −1° (10° to 30°)

−1° to 10° (30° to 50°)

10° to 21° (50° to 70°)

21° to 32° (70° to 90°)

Over 32° (90°)

Highlands above 1000 meters

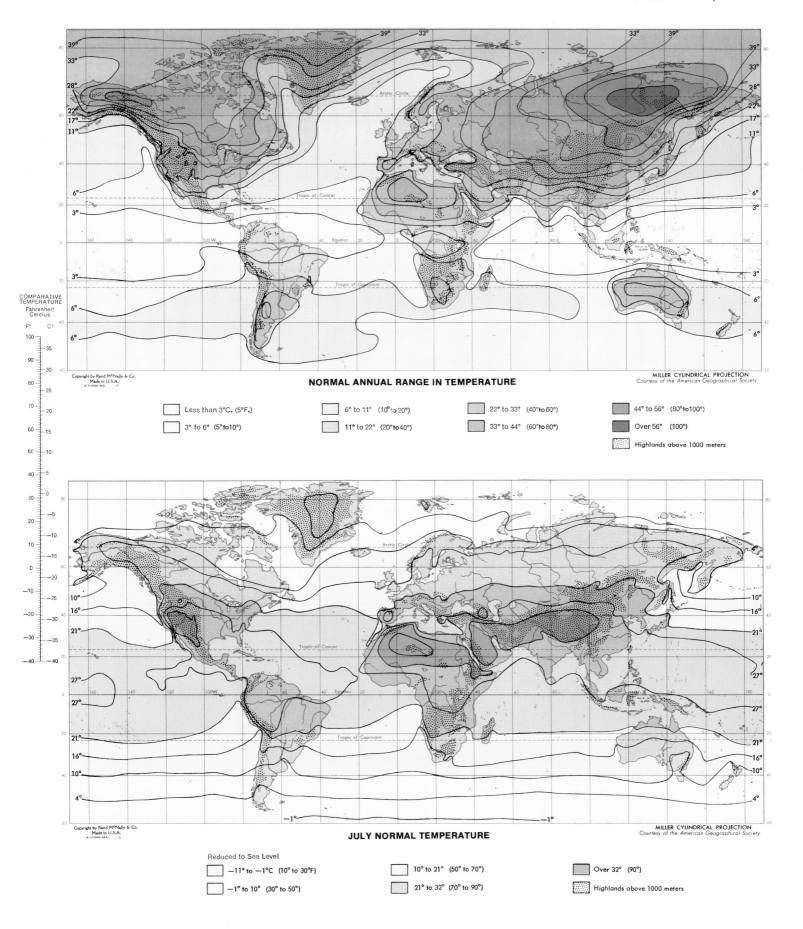

COMPARATIVE
TEMPERATURE
Fahrenheit
Celcius

NORMAL ANNUAL RANGE IN TEMPERATURE

MILLER CYLINDRICAL PROJECTION
Courtesy of the American Geographical Society.

Copyright by Rand McNally & Co.
Made in U.S.A.
A-510000-882   -5

Less than 3°C. (5°F.)	
3° to 6° (5° to 10°)	
6° to 11° (10° to 20°)	
11° to 22° (20° to 40°)	
22° to 33° (40° to 60°)	
33° to 44° (60° to 80°)	
44° to 56° (80° to 100°)	
Over 56° (100°)	
Highlands above 1000 meters	

JULY NORMAL TEMPERATURE

MILLER CYLINDRICAL PROJECTION
Courtesy of the American Geographical Society.

Copyright by Rand McNally & Co.
Made in U.S.A.
A-510000-884   -5

Reduced to Sea Level

−11° to −1°C (10° to 30°F)	
−1° to 10° (30° to 50°)	
10° to 21° (50° to 70°)	
21° to 32° (70° to 90°)	
Over 32° (90°)	
Highlands above 1000 meters	

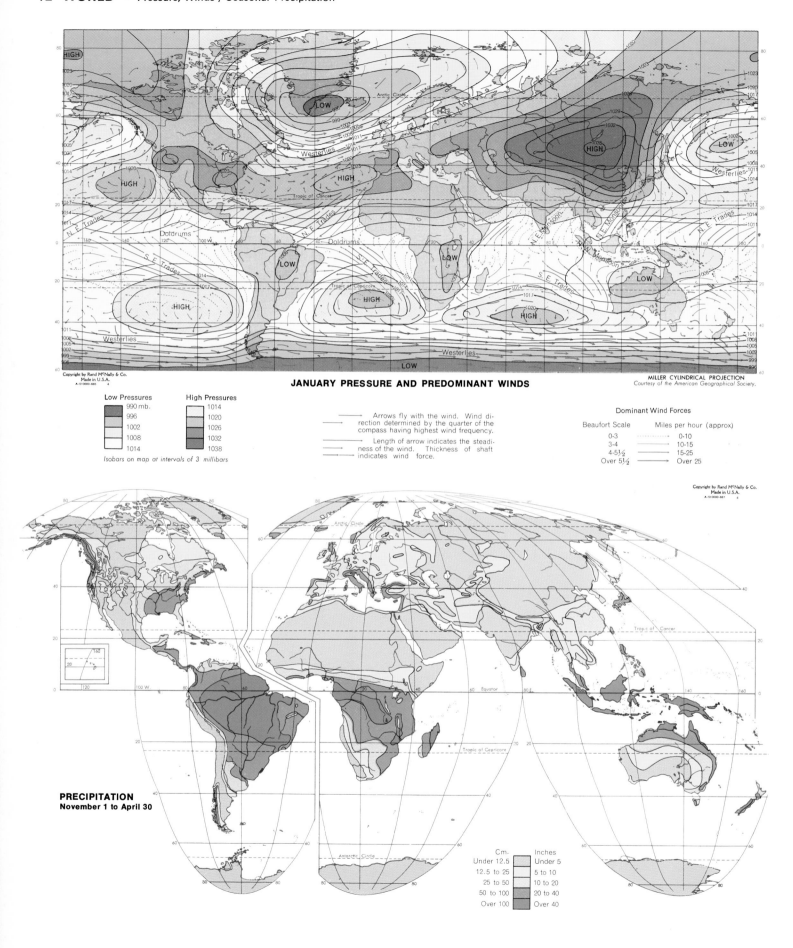

JANUARY PRESSURE AND PREDOMINANT WINDS

MILLER CYLINDRICAL PROJECTION
Courtesy of the American Geographical Society.

Copyright by Rand McNally & Co.
Made in U.S.A.
A-510000-665   4

Low Pressures
990 mb.
996
1002
1008
1014

High Pressures
1014
1020
1026
1032
1038

Isobars on map at intervals of 3 millibars

Arrows fly with the wind. Wind direction determined by the quarter of the compass having highest wind frequency.

Length of arrow indicates the steadiness of the wind. Thickness of shaft indicates wind force.

Dominant Wind Forces

Beaufort Scale	Miles per hour (approx)
0-3	0-10
3-4	10-15
4-5½	15-25
Over 5½	Over 25

Copyright by Rand McNally & Co.
Made in U.S.A.
A-510000-667   4

PRECIPITATION
November 1 to April 30

Cm.	Inches
Under 12.5	Under 5
12.5 to 25	5 to 10
25 to 50	10 to 20
50 to 100	20 to 40
Over 100	Over 40

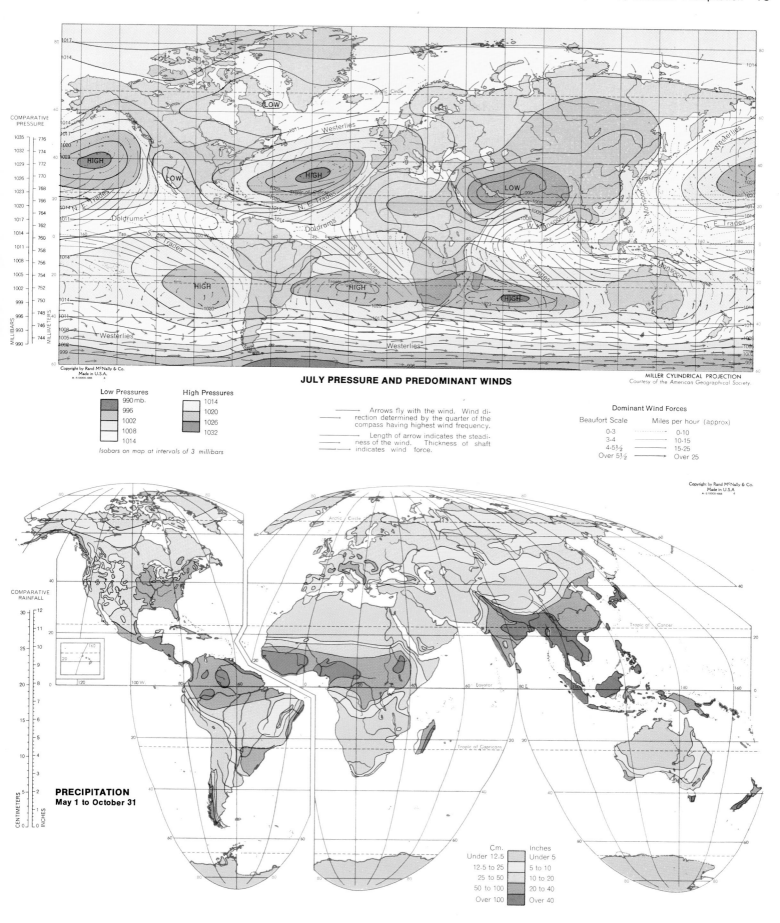

COMPARATIVE
PRESSURE

1035	776
1032	774
1029	772
1026	770
1023	768
1020	766
1017	764
1014	762
1011	760
1008	758
1005	756
1002	754
999	752
996	750
993	748
990	746
	744

MILLIBARS   MILLIMETERS

Copyright by Rand McNally & Co.
Made in U.S.A.
A-510000-668   4

JULY PRESSURE AND PREDOMINANT WINDS

MILLER CYLINDRICAL PROJECTION
Courtesy of the American Geographical Society.

Low Pressures
990 mb.
996
1002
1008
1014

High Pressures
1014
1020
1026
1032

Isobars on map at intervals of 3 millibars

Arrows fly with the wind. Wind direction determined by the quarter of the compass having highest wind frequency.

Length of arrow indicates the steadiness of the wind. Thickness of shaft indicates wind force.

Dominant Wind Forces

Beaufort Scale	Miles per hour (approx)
0-3	0-10
3-4	10-15
4-5½	15-25
Over 5½	Over 25

Copyright by Rand McNally & Co.
Made in U.S.A.
A-510000-668   4

COMPARATIVE
RAINFALL

30	12
	11
25	10
	9
20	8
	7
15	6
	5
10	4
	3
5	2
	1
0	0

CENTIMETERS   INCHES

PRECIPITATION
May 1 to October 31

Cm.	Inches
Under 12.5	Under 5
12.5 to 25	5 to 10
25 to 50	10 to 20
50 to 100	20 to 40
Over 100	Over 40

ANNUAL PRECIPITATION AND OCEAN CURRENTS

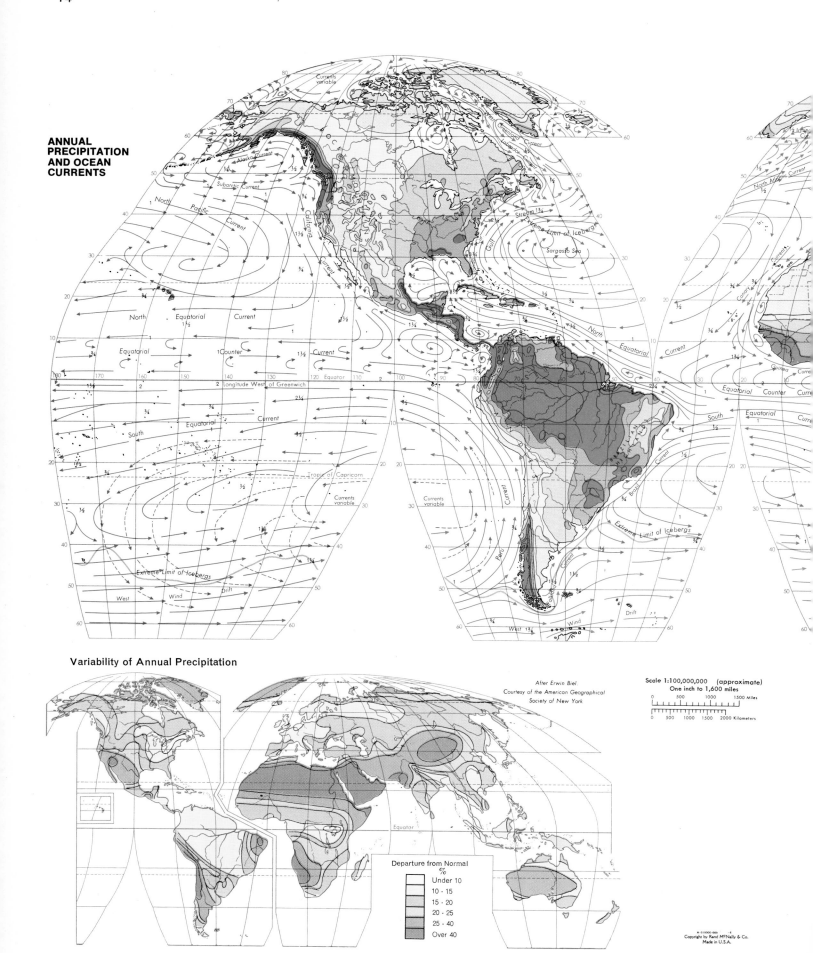

Variability of Annual Precipitation

After Erwin Biel.
Courtesy of the American Geographical
Society of New York

Scale 1:100,000,000 (approximate)
One inch to 1,600 miles

0   500   1000   1500 Miles

0   500   1000   1500   2000 Kilometers

Departure from Normal
%
Under 10
10 - 15
15 - 20
20 - 25
25 - 40
Over 40

A-510000-669
Copyright by Rand McNally & Co.
Made in U.S.A.

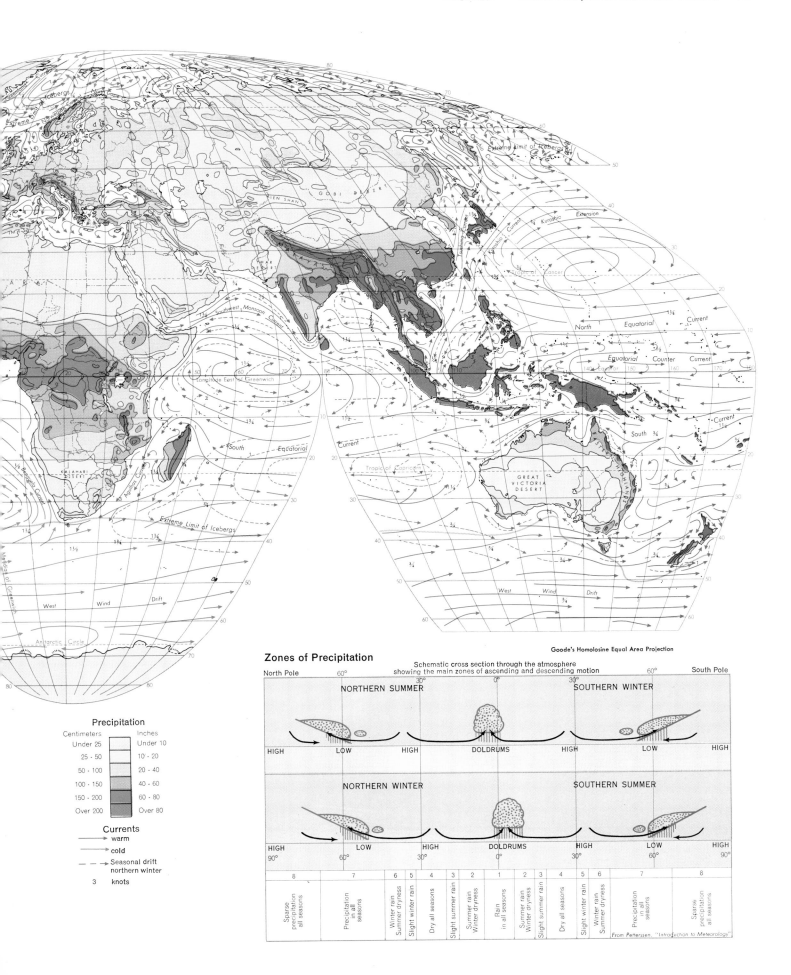

Goode's Homolosine Equal Area Projection

Zones of Precipitation

Schematic cross section through the atmosphere
showing the main zones of ascending and descending motion

North Pole 60° 30° 0° 30° 60° South Pole

NORTHERN SUMMER   SOUTHERN WINTER

HIGH   LOW   HIGH   DOLDRUMS   HIGH   LOW   HIGH

NORTHERN WINTER   SOUTHERN SUMMER

HIGH   LOW   HIGH   DOLDRUMS   HIGH   LOW   HIGH
90°   60°   30°   0°   30°   60°   90°

8	7	6	5	4	3	2	1	2	3	4	5	6	7	8
Sparse precipitation all seasons	Precipitation in all seasons	Winter rain Summer dryness	Slight winter rain	Dry all seasons	Slight summer rain	Summer rain Winter dryness	Rain in all seasons	Summer rain Winter dryness	Slight summer rain	Dry all seasons	Slight winter rain	Winter rain Summer dryness	Precipitation in all seasons	Sparse precipitation all seasons

From Petterssen, "Introduction to Meteorology"

Precipitation

Centimeters		Inches
Under 25		Under 10
25 - 50		10 - 20
50 - 100		20 - 40
100 - 150		40 - 60
150 - 200		60 - 80
Over 200		Over 80

Currents

→ warm
→ cold
– – –→ Seasonal drift
       northern winter

3 knots

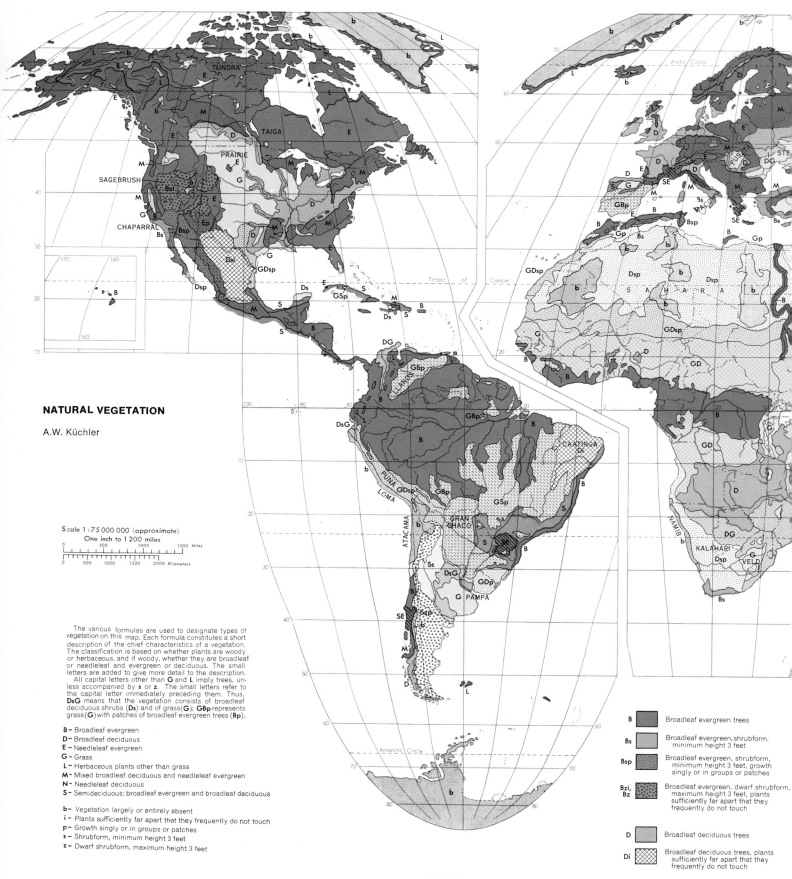

NATURAL VEGETATION

A.W. Küchler

Scale 1:75 000 000 (approximate)

One inch to 1 200 miles

| 0 | 500 | 1000 | 1500 | Miles |

| 0 | 500 | 1000 | 1500 | 2000 | Kilometers |

The various formulas are used to designate types of vegetation on this map. Each formula constitutes a short description of the chief characteristics of a vegetation. The classification is based on whether plants are woody or herbaceous, and if woody, whether they are broadleaf or needleleaf and evergreen or deciduous. The small letters are added to give more detail to the description.

All capital letters other than **G** and **L** imply trees, unless accompanied by **s** or **z**. The small letters refer to the capital letter immediately preceding them. Thus, **DsG** means that the vegetation consists of broadleaf deciduous shrubs (**Ds**) and of grass (**G**); **GBp** represents grass (**G**) with patches of broadleaf evergreen trees (**Bp**).

B – Broadleaf evergreen
D – Broadleaf deciduous
E – Needleleaf evergreen
G – Grass
L – Herbaceous plants other than grass
M – Mixed broadleaf deciduous and needleleaf evergreen
N – Needleleaf deciduous
S – Semideciduous: broadleaf evergreen and broadleaf deciduous

b – Vegetation largely or entirely absent
i – Plants sufficiently far apart that they frequently do not touch
p – Growth singly or in groups or patches
s – Shrubform, minimum height 3 feet
z – Dwarf shrubform, maximum height 3 feet

B	Broadleaf evergreen trees
Bs	Broadleaf evergreen, shrubform, minimum height 3 feet
Bsp	Broadleaf evergreen, shrubform, minimum height 3 feet, growth singly or in groups or patches
Bzi, Bz	Broadleaf evergreen, dwarf shrubform, maximum height 3 feet, plants sufficiently far apart that they frequently do not touch
D	Broadleaf deciduous trees
Di	Broadleaf deciduous trees, plants sufficiently far apart that they frequently do not touch

Goode's Homolosine
Equal Area Projection
(Condensed)

	Broadleaf deciduous, shrubform, minimum height 3 feet	
	Broadleaf deciduous, shrubform, minimum height 3 feet, plants sufficiently far apart that they frequently do not touch	
	Broadleaf deciduous, shrubform, minimum height 3 feet, growth singly or in groups or patches	
	Broadleaf deciduous, dwarf shrubform, maximum height 3 feet, growth singly or in groups or patches	
	Broadleaf deciduous, shrubform, minimum height 3 feet Grass and other herbaceous plants	
	Broadleaf deciduous trees Grass and other herbaceous plants	
	Broadleaf deciduous trees Broadleaf evergreen, shrubform, minimum height 3 feet	

E	Needleleaf evergreen trees	
Ep	Needleleaf evergreen trees, growth singly or in groups or patches	
G	Grass and other herbaceous plants	
Gp	Grass and other herbaceous plants, growth singly or in groups or patches	
GBp	Grass and other herbaceous plants Broadleaf evergreen, shrubform, minimum height 3 feet	
GD	Grass and other herbaceous plants Broadleaf deciduous trees	
GDp	Grass and other herbaceous plants Broadleaf deciduous trees, growth singly or in groups or patches	

GDsp	Grass and other herbaceous plants Broadleaf deciduous, shrubform, minimum height 3 feet, growth singly or in groups or patches	
GSp	Grass and other herbaceous plants Semideciduous: broadleaf evergreen and broadleaf deciduous trees, growth singly or in groups or patches	
L	Herbaceous plants other than grass	
M	Mixed: broadleaf deciduous and needleleaf evergreen trees	
N	Needleleaf deciduous trees	
ND	Needleleaf deciduous trees Broadleaf deciduous trees	

S	Semideciduous: broadleaf evergreen and broadleaf deciduous trees	
Ss	Semideciduous: broadleaf evergreen and broadleaf deciduous, shrubform, minimum height 3 feet	
SsG	Semideciduous: broadleaf evergreen and broadleaf deciduous, shrubform, minimum height 3 feet Grass and other herbaceous plants	
Szp	Semideciduous: broadleaf evergreen and broadleaf deciduous, dwarf shrub-form, maximum height 3 feet, growth singly or in groups or patches	
SE	Semideciduous: broadleaf evergreen and broadleaf deciduous trees Needleleaf evergreen trees	
b	Vegetation largely or entirely absent	

18

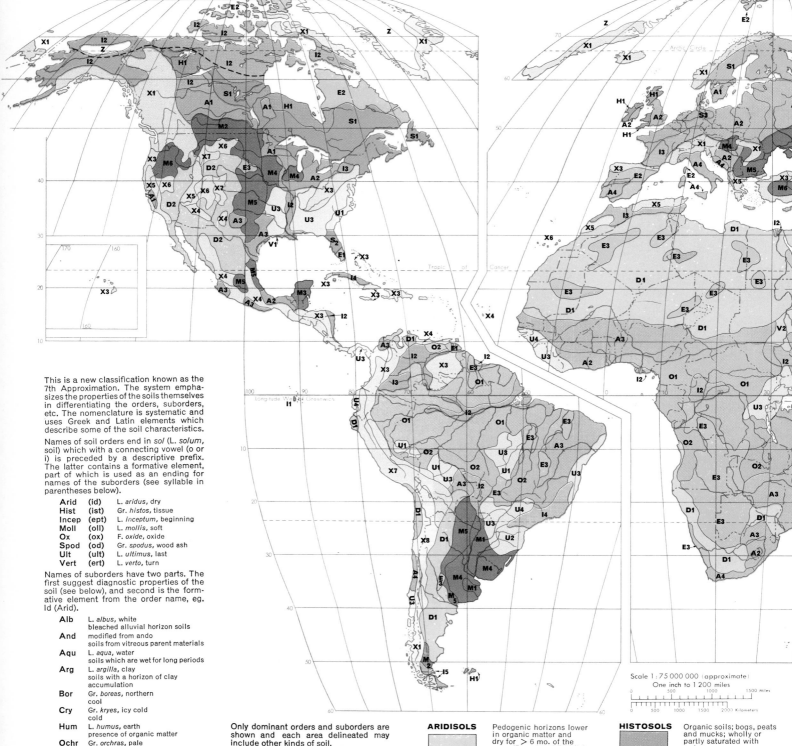

This is a new classification known as the 7th Approximation. The system emphasizes the properties of the soils themselves in differentiating the orders, suborders, etc. The nomenclature is systematic and uses Greek and Latin elements which describe some of the soil characteristics.

Names of soil orders end in *sol* (L. *solum*, soil) which with a connecting vowel (o or i) is preceded by a descriptive prefix. The latter contains a formative element, part of which is used as an ending for names of the suborders (see syllable in parentheses below).

Arid	(id)	L. *aridus*, dry
Hist	(ist)	Gr. *histos*, tissue
Incep	(ept)	L. *inceptum*, beginning
Moll	(oll)	L. *mollis*, soft
Ox	(ox)	F. *oxide*, oxide
Spod	(od)	Gr. *spodus*, wood ash
Ult	(ult)	L. *ultimus*, last
Vert	(ert)	L. *verto*, turn

Names of suborders have two parts. The first suggest diagnostic properties of the soil (see below), and second is the formative element from the order name, eg. Id (Arid).

Alb	L. *albus*, white bleached alluvial horizon soils
And	modified from ando soils from vitreous parent materials
Aqu	L. *aqua*, water soils which are wet for long periods
Arg	L. *argilla*, clay soils with a horizon of clay accumulation
Bor	Gr. *boreas*, northern cool
Cry	Gr. *kryes*, icy cold cold
Hum	L. *humus*, earth presence of organic matter
Ochr	Gr. *orchras*, pale soils with little organic matter
Psamm	Gr. *psammas*, sand sandy soils
Rend	from Rendzina high carbonate content
Torr	L. *torridus*, hot and dry soils of very dry climate
Ud	L. *udus*, humid soils of humid climate
Umbr	L. *umbra*, shade dark color reflecting relatively high organic matter
Ust	L. *ustus*, burnt soils of dry climates with summer rains
Xer	Gr. *xeros*, dry soils of dry climates with winter rains

Only dominant orders and suborders are shown and each area delineated may include other kinds of soil.

ALFISOLS — Podzolic soils of middle latitudes; soils with gray to brown surface horizons; subsurface horizons of clay accumulation; medium to high base supply.

Boralfs A1	Cool to cold, freely drained.
Udalfs A2	Temperate to hot; usually moist (Gray-brown Podzolic*)
Ustalfs A3	Warm subhumid to semi-arid; dry > 90 days (some Reddish Chestnut and Red & Yellow Podzolic soils*)
Xeralfs A4	Warm, dry in summer; moist in winter.

ARIDISOLS — Pedogenic horizons lower in organic matter and dry for > 6 mo. of the year. (Desert and Reddish Desert*) Salts may accumulate on or near surface.

Aridisols D1	Undifferentiated.
Argids D2	With horizon of clay accumulation.

ENTISOLS — Soils without pedogenic horizons on recent alluvium, dune sands, etc.; varied in appearance.

Aquents E1	Seasonally or perennially wet; bluish or gray and mottled.
Orthents E2	Shallow; or recent erosional surfaces (Lithosols*). A few on recent loams.
Psamments E3	Sandy soils on shifting and stabilized sands.

HISTOSOLS — Organic soils; bogs, peats and mucks; wholly or partly saturated with water.

INCEPTISOLS — Immature, weakly developed soils; pedogenic horizons show alteration but little illuviation; usually moist.

Andepts I1	Soil formed on amorphous clay or vitric volcanic ash.
Aquepts I2	Seasonally saturated with water (includes some Humic Gley, alluvial tundra soils*).
Ochrepts I3	Thin, light-colored surface horizons; little organic matter.
Tropepts I4	Continuously warm to hot; brownish to reddish.
Umbrepts I5	Dark colored surface horizons; rich in organic matter; medium to low base supply.

Scale 1:75 000 000 (approximate)
One inch to 1 200 miles

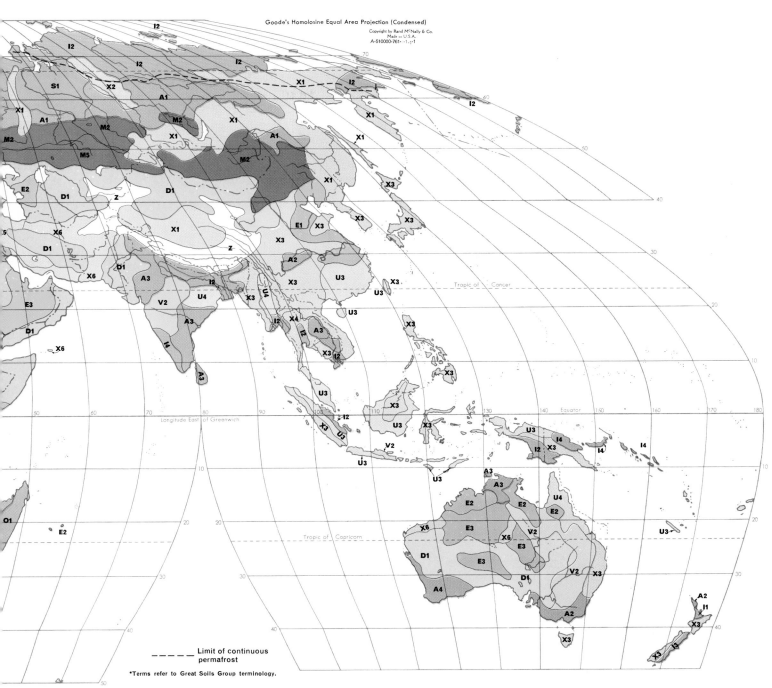

Goode's Homolosine Equal Area Projection (Condensed)

Copyright by Rand McNally & Co.
Made in U.S.A.
A-510000-761- -1-;-1

———— Limit of continuous
permafrost

*Terms refer to Great Soils Group terminology.

	MOLLISOLS	Soils of the steppe (incl. Chernozem and Chestnut soils*). Thick, black organic rich surface horizons and high base supply.
	Albolls **M1**	Seasonally saturated with water; light gray subsurface horizon.
	Borolls **M2**	Cool or cold (incl. some Chernozem, Chestnut and Brown soils*).
	Rendolls **M3**	Formed on highly calcareous parent materials (Rendzina*).
	Udolls **M4**	Temperate to warm; usually moist (Prairie soils*).
	Ustolls **M5**	Temperate to hot; dry for > 90 days (incl. some Chestnut and Brown soils*).
	Xerolls **M6**	Cool to warm; dry in summer; moist in winter.

	OXISOLS	Deeply weathered tropical and subtropical soils (Laterites*); rich in sesquioxides of iron and aluminum; low in nutrients; limited productivity without fertilizer.
	Orthox **O1**	Hot and nearly always moist.
	Ustox **O2**	Warm or hot; dry for long periods but moist > 90 consecutive days.

	SPODOSOLS	Soils with a subsurface accumulation of amorphous materials overlaid by a light colored, leached sandy horizon.
	Spodosols **S1**	Undifferentiated (mostly high latitudes).
	Aquods **S2**	Seasonally saturated with water; sandy parent materials.
	Humods **S3**	Considerable accumulations of organic matter in subsurface horizon.
	Orthods **S4**	With subsurface accumulations of iron, aluminum and organic matter (Podzols*).

	ULTISOLS	Soils with some subsurface clay accumulation; low base supply; usually moist and low in organic matter; usually moist and low in organic matter; can be productive with fertilization.
	Aquults **U1**	Seasonally saturated with water; subsurface gray or mottled horizon.
	Humults **U2**	High in organic matter; moist, warm to temperate all year.
	Udults **U3**	Low in organic matter; moist, temperate to hot (Red-Yellow Podzolic; some Reddish-Brown Lateritic soils*).
	Ustults **U4**	Warm to hot; dry > 90 days.

	VERTISOLS	Soils with high content of swelling clays; deep, wide cracks in dry periods dark colored.
	Uderts **V1**	Usually moist; cracks open < 90 days.
	Usterts **V2**	Cracks open > 90 days; difficult to till (Black tropical soils*).

	MOUNTAIN SOILS	Soils with various moisture and temperature regimes; steep slopes and variable relief and elevation; soils vary greatly within short distance.
	X1	Cryic great groups of Entisols, Inceptisols and Spodosols.
	X2	Boralfs and Cryic groups of Entisols and Inceptisols.
	X3	Udic great groups of Alfisols, Entisols and Ultisols; Inceptisols.
	X4	Ustic great groups of Alfisols, Entisols, Inceptisols, Mollisols and Ultisols.
	X5	Xeric great groups of Alfisols, Entisols, Inceptisols, Mollisols and Ultisols.
	X6	Torric great groups of Entisols; Aridisols.
	X7	Ustic and cryic great groups of Alfisols, Entisols; Inceptisols and Mollisols; ustic great groups of Ultisols; cryic great groups of Spodosols.
	X8	Aridisols; torric and cryic great groups of Entisols, and cryic great groups of Spodosols and Inceptisols.

Z	Areas with little or no soil; icefields, and rugged mountain.

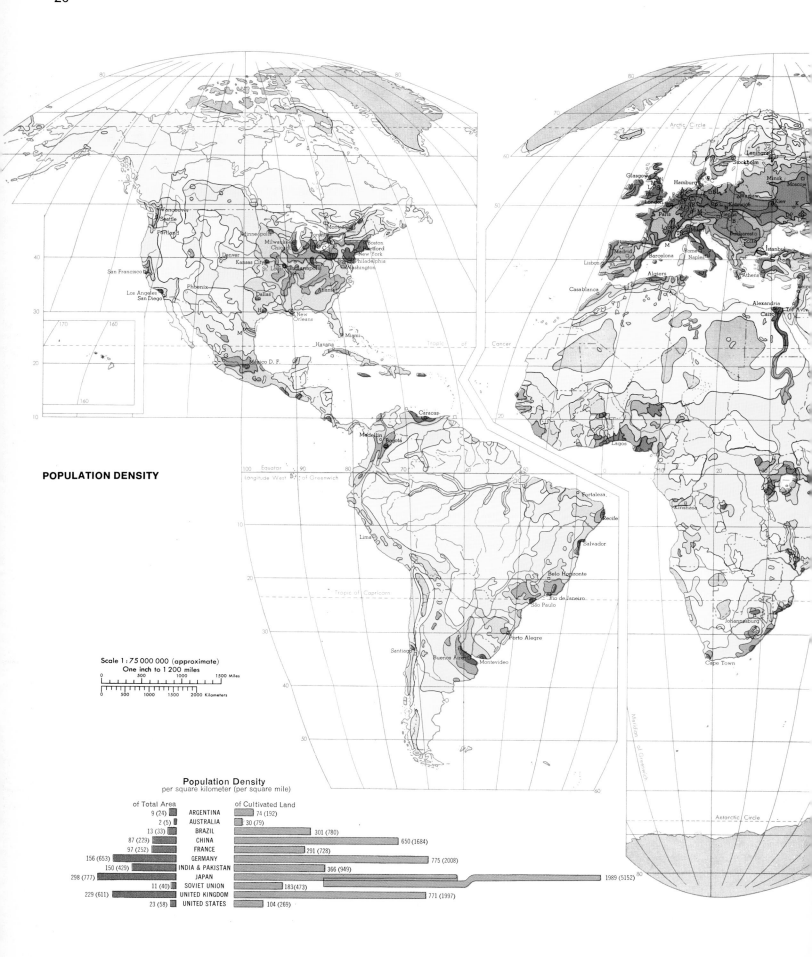

POPULATION DENSITY

Scale 1 : 75 000 000 (approximate)
One inch to 1 200 miles

0   500   1000   1500 Miles

0   500   1000   1500   2000 Kilometers

Population Density
per square kilometer (per square mile)

of Total Area		of Cultivated Land	
9 (24)	ARGENTINA	74 (192)	
2 (5)	AUSTRALIA	30 (79)	
13 (33)	BRAZIL	301 (780)	
87 (229)	CHINA	650 (1684)	
97 (252)	FRANCE	291 (728)	
156 (653)	GERMANY	775 (2008)	
150 (429)	INDIA & PAKISTAN	366 (949)	
298 (777)	JAPAN	1989 (5152)	
11 (40)	SOVIET UNION	183 (473)	
229 (611)	UNITED KINGDOM	771 (1997)	
23 (58)	UNITED STATES	104 (269)	

Rural/Urban Population Ratios

	Rural		Urban	
ARGENTINA	17%			83%
AUSTRALIA	14			86
BRAZIL	44			56
CANADA	24			76
CHINA	71		29	
FRANCE	30			70
INDIA	80		20	
JAPAN	43			57
SOVIET UNION	44			56
TURKEY	65		35	
UNITED KINGDOM	22			78
UNITED STATES	26			74

Goode's Homolosine Equal Area Projection (Condensed)

Per Sq. Km.	Per Sq. Mile
Uninhabited	Uninhabited
Under 1	Under 2
1-10	2-25
10-25	25-60
25-50	60-125
50-100	125-250
Over 100	Over 250

□ Metropolitan areas over 2,000,000 population
○ Metropolitan areas 1,000,000 to 2,000,000 population

*Not all cities are named and some
are identified by initial letter only.*

A-510000-16- 5-2-7
Copyright by Rand M°Nally & Co.
Made in U.S.A.

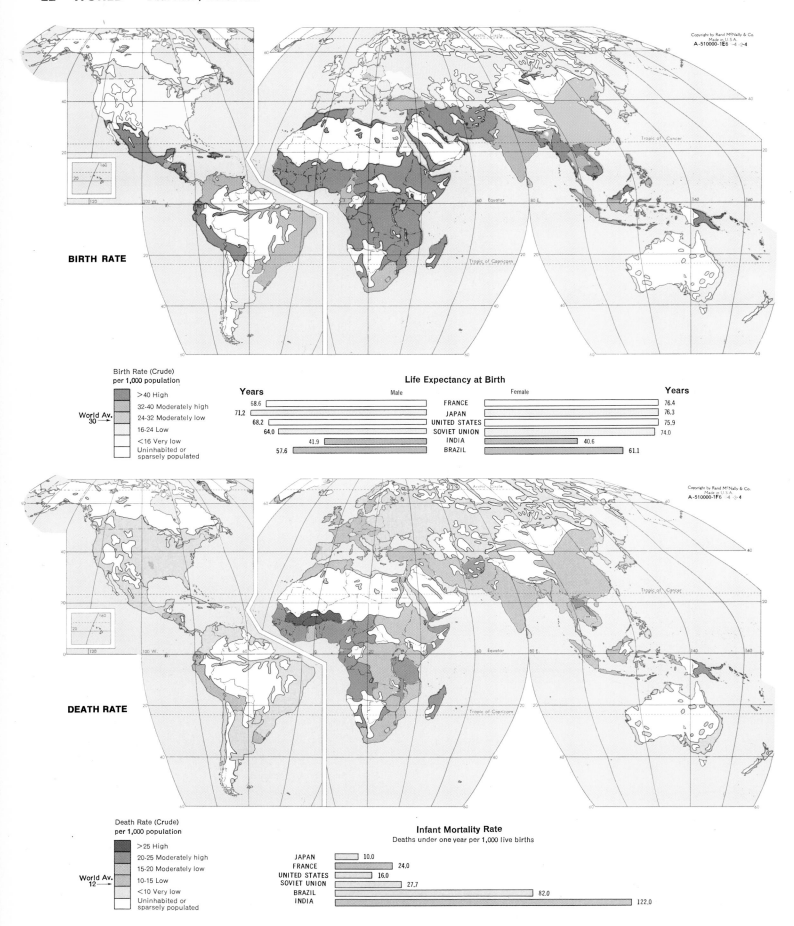

BIRTH RATE

Birth Rate (Crude)
per 1,000 population

- >40 High
- 32-40 Moderately high
- 24-32 Moderately low
- 16-24 Low
- <16 Very low
- Uninhabited or sparsely populated

World Av.
30 →

Life Expectancy at Birth

	Years	Male		Female	**Years**
FRANCE	68.6				76.4
JAPAN	71.2				76.3
UNITED STATES	68.2				75.9
SOVIET UNION	64.0				74.0
INDIA	41.9			40.6	
BRAZIL	57.6				61.1

DEATH RATE

Death Rate (Crude)
per 1,000 population

- >25 High
- 20-25 Moderately high
- 15-20 Moderately low
- 10-15 Low
- <10 Very low
- Uninhabited or sparsely populated

World Av.
12 →

Infant Mortality Rate
Deaths under one year per 1,000 live births

JAPAN	10.0
FRANCE	24.0
UNITED STATES	16.0
SOVIET UNION	27.7
BRAZIL	82.0
INDIA	122.0

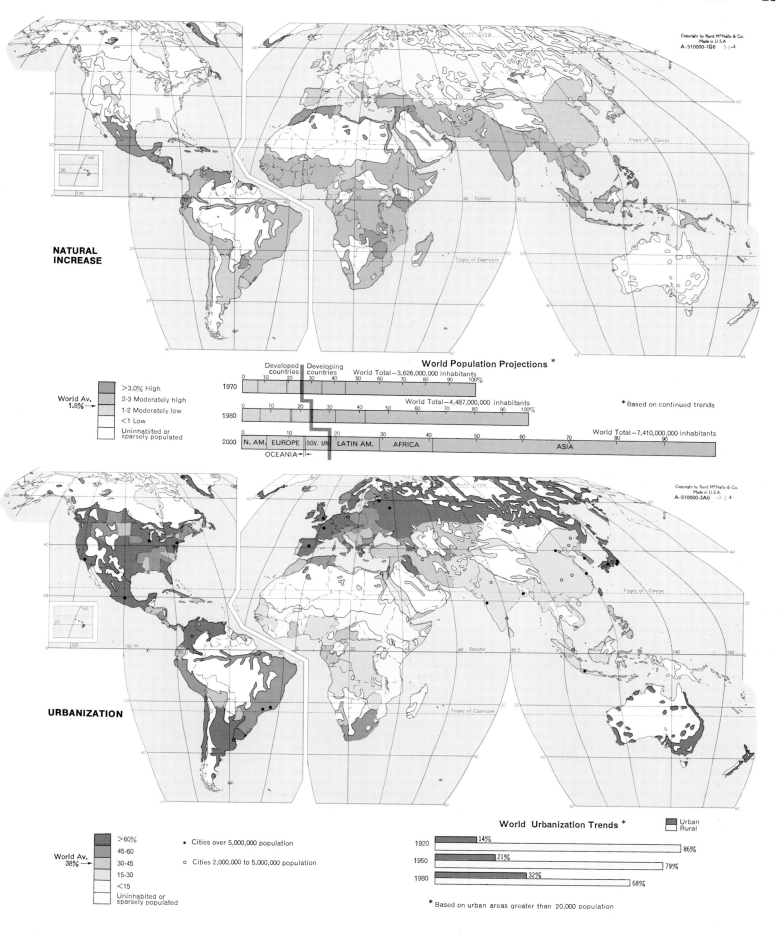

Copyright by Rand McNally & Co.
Made in U.S.A.
A-510000-1G6   3 g-4

**NATURAL
INCREASE**

World Av.
1.8% →

>3.0% High
2-3 Moderately high
1-2 Moderately low
<1 Low
Uninhabited or
sparsely populated

World Population Projections *

Developed countries   Developing countries

1970   World Total—3,626,000,000 inhabitants

1980   World Total—4,487,000,000 inhabitants

* Based on continued trends

2000   N. AM. EUROPE SOV. UN. LATIN AM. AFRICA ASIA   World Total—7,410,000,000 inhabitants

OCEANIA →

Copyright by Rand McNally & Co.
Made in U.S.A.
A-510000-3A6   -3 g 4

URBANIZATION

World Av.
38% →

>60%
45-60
30-45
15-30
<15
Uninhabited or
sparsely populated

• Cities over 5,000,000 population

○ Cities 2,000,000 to 5,000,000 population

World Urbanization Trends *

Urban
Rural

1920   14%   86%

1950   21%   79%

1980   32%   68%

* Based on urban areas greater than 20,000 population

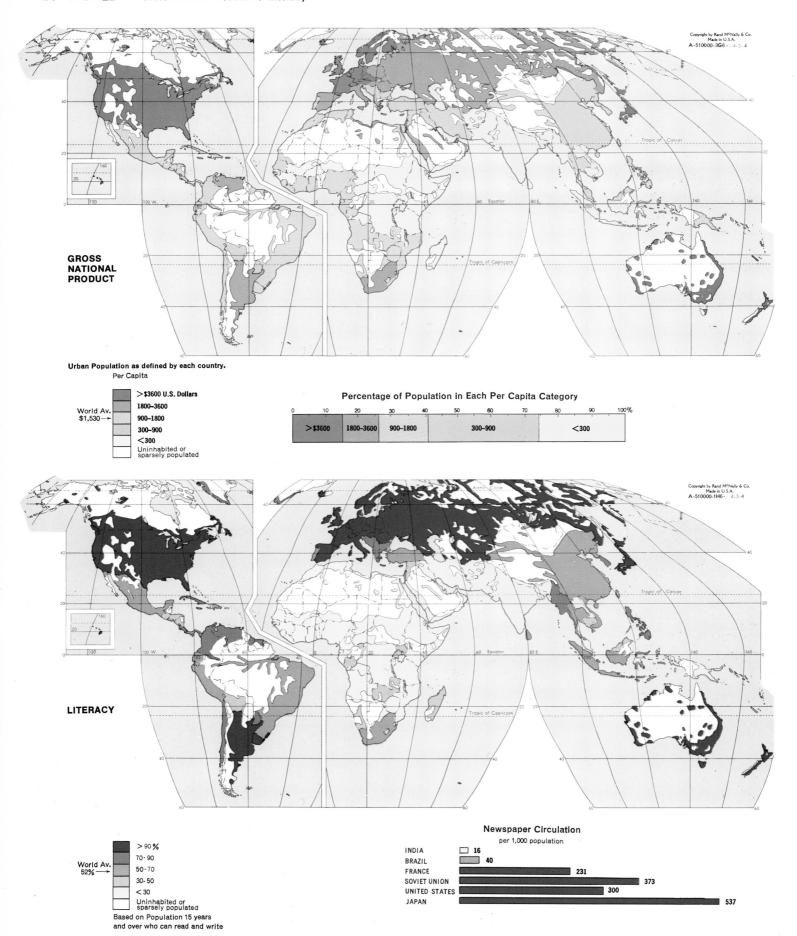

**GROSS
NATIONAL
PRODUCT**

Copyright by Rand McNally & Co.
Made in U.S.A.
A-510000-3G6 - 4-3-4

Urban Population as defined by each country.

Per Capita

> $3600 U.S. Dollars
1800–3600
World Av.
$1,530 → 900–1800
300–900
< 300
Uninhabited or
sparsely populated

Percentage of Population in Each Per Capita Category

0	10	20	30	40	50	60	70	80	90	100%
> $3600	1800–3600	900–1800	300–900				< 300			

LITERACY

Copyright by Rand McNally & Co.
Made in U.S.A.
A-510000-1H6 - 4-3-4

> 90 %
70- 90
World Av.
52% → 50- 70
30- 50
< 30
Uninhabited or
sparsely populated

Based on Population 15 years
and over who can read and write

Newspaper Circulation

per 1,000 population

INDIA	16
BRAZIL	40
FRANCE	231
SOVIET UNION	373
UNITED STATES	300
JAPAN	537

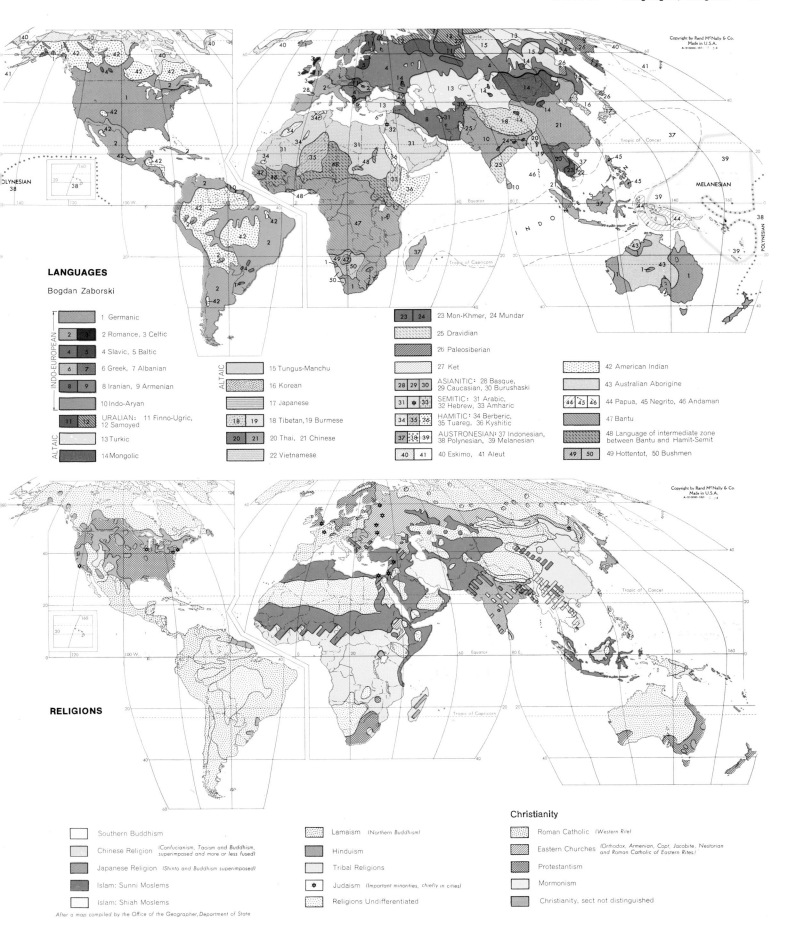

LANGUAGES

Bogdan Zaborski

INDO-EUROPEAN
1 Germanic
2 Romance, 3 Celtic
4 Slavic, 5 Baltic
6 Greek, 7 Albanian
8 Iranian, 9 Armenian
10 Indo-Aryan

URALIAN: 11 Finno-Ugric, 12 Samoyed

ALTAIC
13 Turkic
14 Mongolic
15 Tungus-Manchu
16 Korean
17 Japanese

18 Tibetan, 19 Burmese
20 Thai, 21 Chinese
22 Vietnamese

23 Mon-Khmer, 24 Mundar
25 Dravidian
26 Paleosiberian
27 Ket
ASIANITIC: 28 Basque, 29 Caucasic, 30 Burushaski
SEMITIC: 31 Arabic, 32 Hebrew, 33 Amharic
HAMITIC: 34 Berberic, 35 Tuareg, 36 Kyshitic
AUSTRONESIAN: 37 Indonesian, 38 Polynesian, 39 Melanesian
40 Eskimo, 41 Aleut

42 American Indian
43 Australian Aborigine
44 Papua, 45 Negrito, 46 Andaman
47 Bantu
48 Language of intermediate zone between Bantu and Hamit-Semit
49 Hottentot, 50 Bushmen

RELIGIONS

Southern Buddhism
Chinese Religion *(Confucianism, Taoism and Buddhism, superimposed and more or less fused)*
Japanese Religion *(Shinto and Buddhism superimposed)*
Islam: Sunni Moslems
Islam: Shiah Moslems

Lamaism *(Northern Buddhism)*
Hinduism
Tribal Religions
Judaism *(Important minorities, chiefly in cities)*
Religions Undifferentiated

Christianity
Roman Catholic *(Western Rite)*
Eastern Churches *(Orthodox, Armenian, Copt, Jacobite, Nestorian and Roman Catholic of Eastern Rites.)*
Protestantism
Mormonism
Christianity, sect not distinguished

After a map compiled by the Office of the Geographer, Department of State

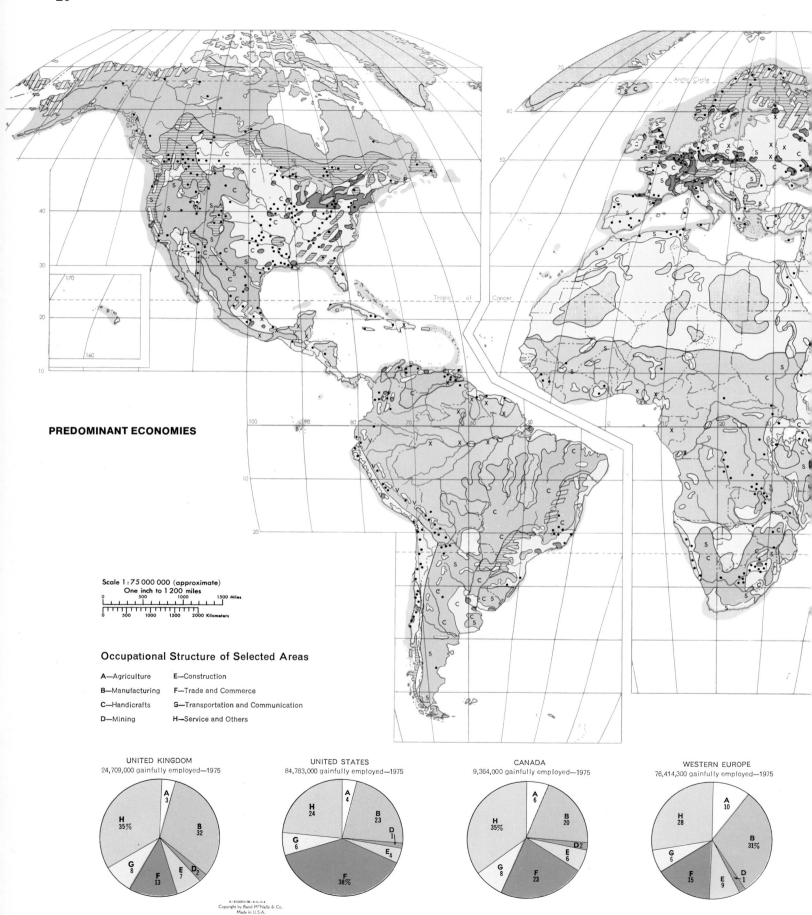

PREDOMINANT ECONOMIES

Scale 1 : 75 000 000 (approximate)
One inch to 1 200 miles

Occupational Structure of Selected Areas

A—Agriculture   E—Construction

B—Manufacturing   F—Trade and Commerce

C—Handicrafts   G—Transportation and Communication

D—Mining   H—Service and Others

UNITED KINGDOM
24,709,000 gainfully employed—1975

A 3
B 32
D 2
E 7
F 13
G 8
H 35%

UNITED STATES
84,783,000 gainfully employed—1975

A 4
B 23
D 1
E 4
F 38%
G 6
H 24

CANADA
9,364,000 gainfully employed—1975

A 6
B 20
D 2
E 6
F 23
G 8
H 35%

WESTERN EUROPE
76,414,300 gainfully employed—1975

A 10
B 31%
D 1
E 9
F 15
G 6
H 28

A-810000-36-4-4-3-4
Copyright by Rand McNally & Co.
Made in U.S.A.

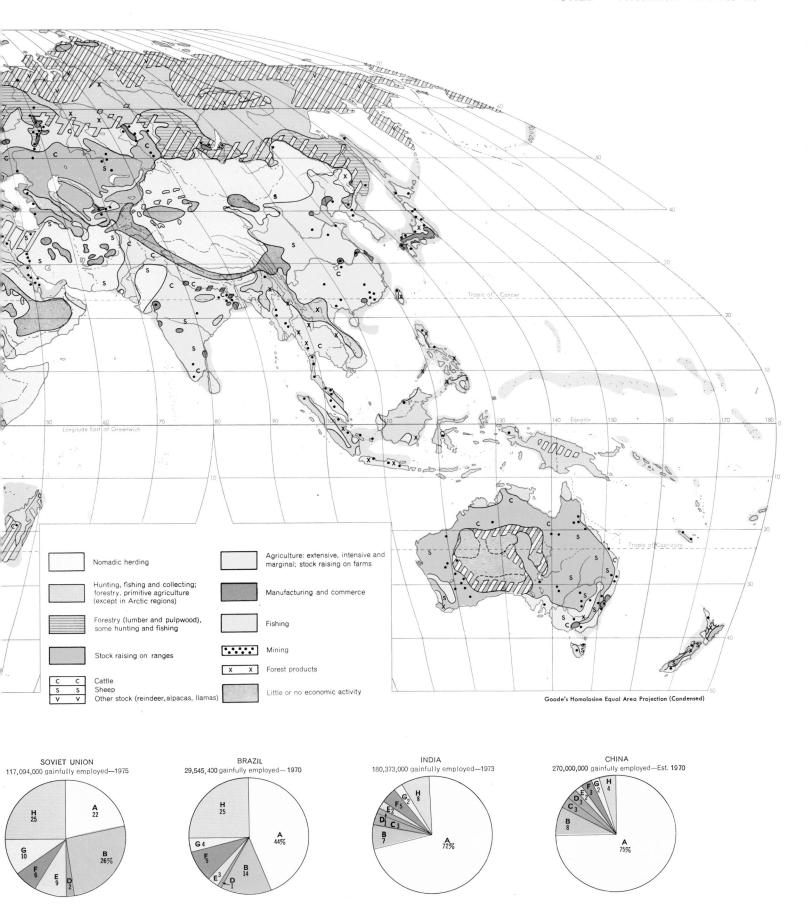

Nomadic herding

Hunting, fishing and collecting; forestry, primitive agriculture (except in Arctic regions)

Forestry (lumber and pulpwood), some hunting and fishing

Stock raising on ranges

C	C	Cattle
S	S	Sheep
V	V	Other stock (reindeer, alpacas, llamas)

Agriculture: extensive, intensive and marginal; stock raising on farms

Manufacturing and commerce

Fishing

| • • • | • • • | Mining |

| X | X | Forest products |

Little or no economic activity

Goode's Homolosine Equal Area Projection (Condensed)

SOVIET UNION
117,094,000 gainfully employed—1975

A 22
B 26%
D 2
E 9
F 6
G 10
H 25

BRAZIL
29,545,400 gainfully employed—1970

A 44%
B 14
D 1
E 3
F 9
G 4
H 25

INDIA
180,373,000 gainfully employed—1973

A 72%
B 7
C 3
D 1
E 2
F 5
G 2
H 8

CHINA
270,000,000 gainfully employed—Est. 1970

A 75%
B 8
C 3
D 2
E 2
F 2
G 3
H 4

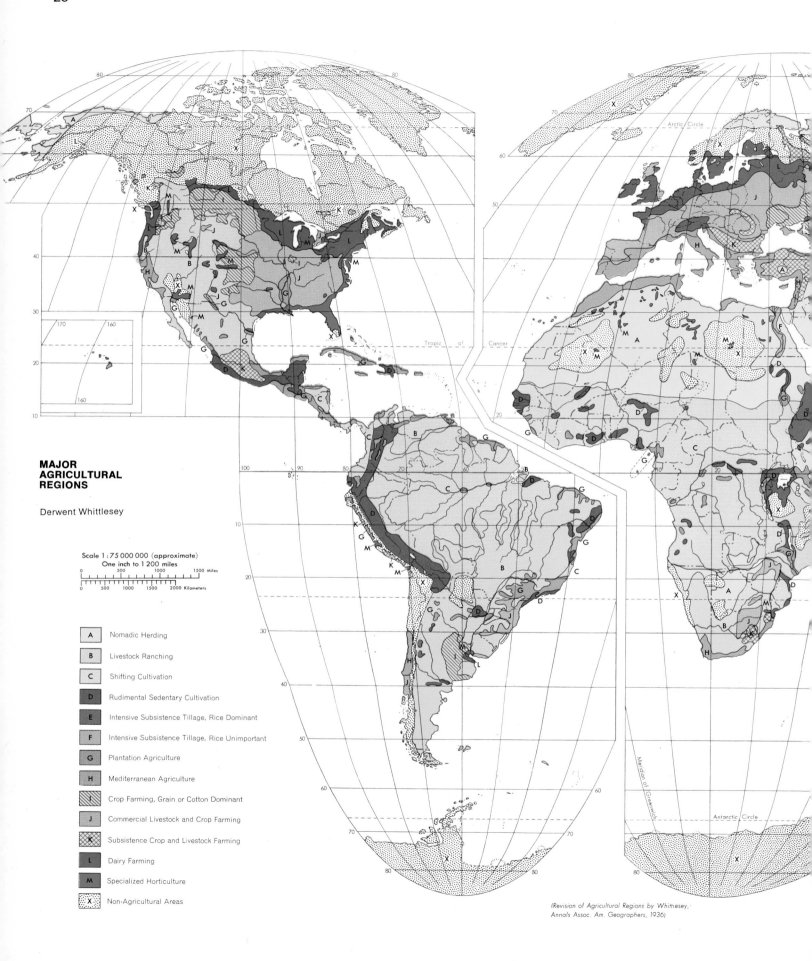

**MAJOR
AGRICULTURAL
REGIONS**

Derwent Whittlesey

Scale 1 : 75 000 000 (approximate)
One inch to 1 200 miles

0	500	1000		1500 Miles
0	500	1000	1500	2000 Kilometers

A	Nomadic Herding
B	Livestock Ranching
C	Shifting Cultivation
D	Rudimental Sedentary Cultivation
E	Intensive Subsistence Tillage, Rice Dominant
F	Intensive Subsistence Tillage, Rice Unimportant
G	Plantation Agriculture
H	Mediterranean Agriculture
I	Crop Farming, Grain or Cotton Dominant
J	Commercial Livestock and Crop Farming
K	Subsistence Crop and Livestock Farming
L	Dairy Farming
M	Specialized Horticulture
X	Non-Agricultural Areas

(Revision of Agricultural Regions by Whittlesey,
Annals Assoc. Am. Geographers, 1936)

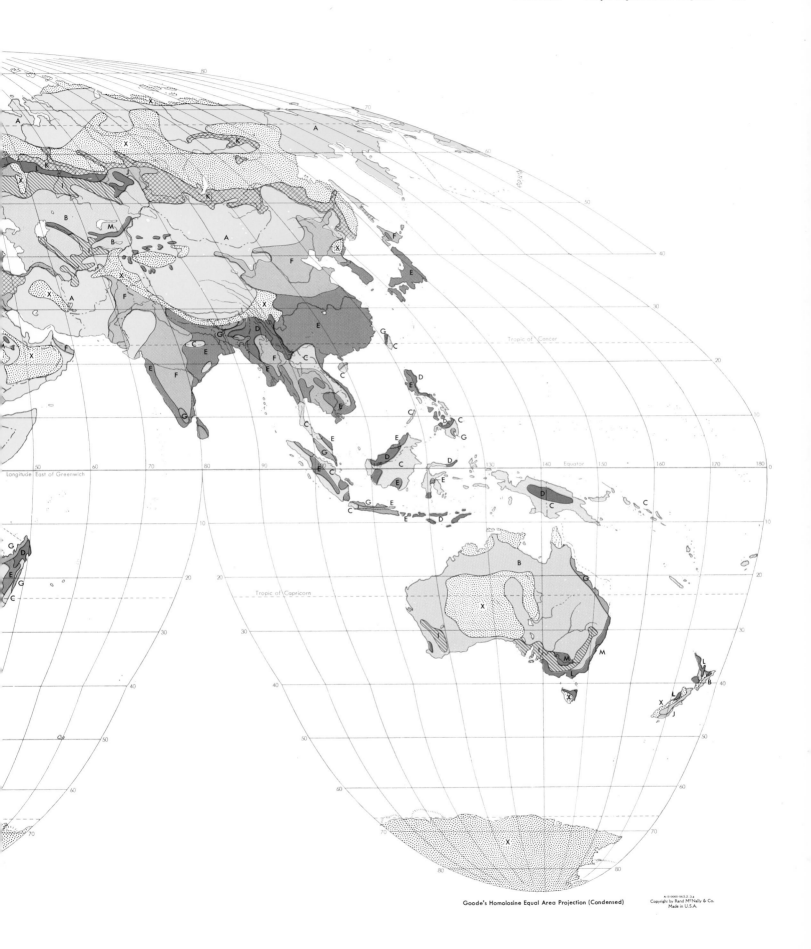

Goode's Homolosine Equal Area Projection (Condensed)

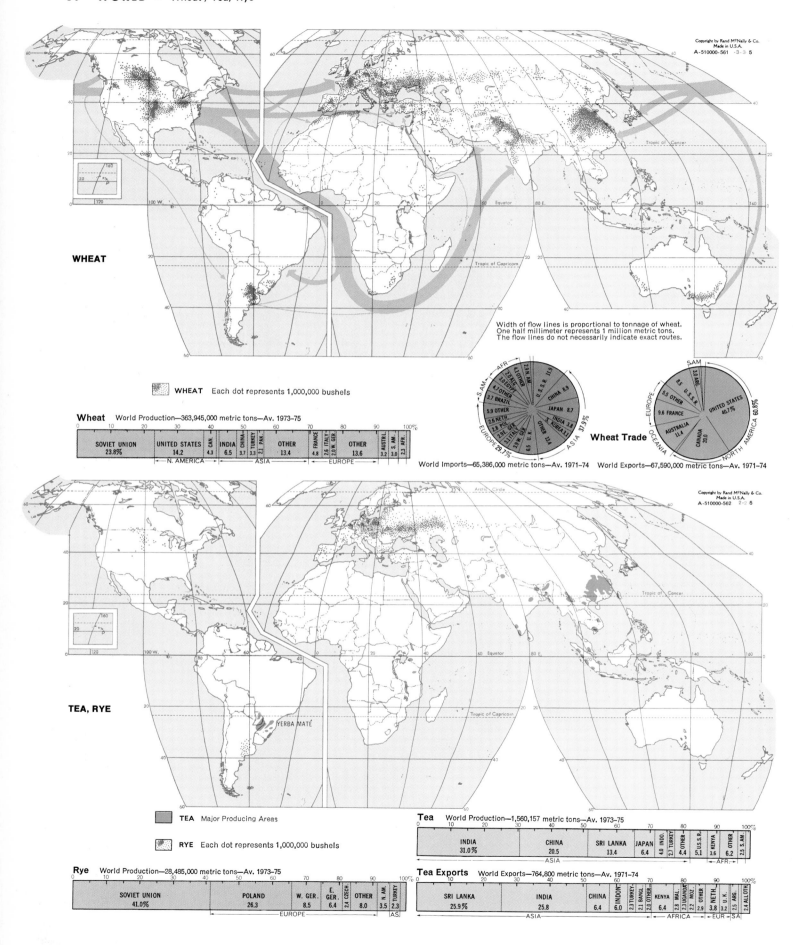

Copyright by Rand McNally & Co.
Made in U.S.A.
A-510000-561 -3-3 5

WHEAT

Width of flow lines is proportional to tonnage of wheat.
One half millimeter represents 1 million metric tons.
The flow lines do not necessarily indicate exact routes.

WHEAT Each dot represents 1,000,000 bushels

Wheat World Production—363,945,000 metric tons—Av. 1973–75

	0	10	20	30	40	50	60	70	80	90	100%

| SOVIET UNION 23.8% | UNITED STATES 14.2 | CAN. 4.3 | INDIA 6.5 | CHINA 3.7 | TURKEY 3.3 | PAK. 2.1 | OTHER 13.4 | FRANCE 4.8 | ITALY 2.6 | W.GER. 2.0 | OTHER 13.6 | AUSTRL. 3.2 | S. AM. 3.0 | AFR. 2.3 |

N. AMERICA — ASIA — EUROPE

Wheat Trade

World Imports—65,386,000 metric tons—Av. 1971–74

U.S.S.R. 11.3
CHINA 8.9
JAPAN 8.7
INDIA 3.8
S. KOREA 3.1
OTHER 13.4
U.K. 6.5
E. GER. 3.9
W. GER. 3.1
SE. GER. 2.5
POL. 2.8
NETH. 2.6
OTHER 5.9
BRAZIL 3.3
EGYPT 3.7
ITALY 2.7
OTHER 4.1
N. AM. 2.9
ASIA 37.9%
EUROPE 29.7%

World Exports—67,590,000 metric tons—Av. 1971–74

UNITED STATES 40.7%
CANADA 20.0
AUSTRALIA 11.4
FRANCE 9.6
OTHER 5.5
U.S.S.R. 8.5
ARG. 3.0
NORTH AMERICA 60.8%

Copyright by Rand McNally & Co.
Made in U.S.A.
A-510000-562 2-2 5

TEA, RYE

YERBA MATÉ

TEA Major Producing Areas

RYE Each dot represents 1,000,000 bushels

Tea World Production—1,560,157 metric tons—Av. 1973–75

	0	10	20	30	40	50	60	70	80	90	100%

| INDIA 31.0% | CHINA 20.5 | SRI LANKA 13.4 | JAPAN 6.4 | INDO. 4.0 | TURKEY 4.4 | OTHER 5.1 | U.S.S.R. 3.6 | KENYA 6.2 | OTHER | S. AM. 2.5 |

ASIA — AFR.

Rye World Production—28,485,000 metric tons—Av. 1973–75

	0	10	20	30	40	50	60	70	80	90	100%

| SOVIET UNION 41.0% | POLAND 26.3 | W. GER. 8.5 | E. GER. 6.4 | CZECH. 2.4 | OTHER 8.0 | N. AM. 2.3 | TURKEY 2.3 |

EUROPE — ASJ

Tea Exports World Exports—764,800 metric tons—Av. 1971–74

| SRI LANKA 25.9% | INDIA 25.8 | CHINA 6.4 | INDON. 6.0 | TURKEY 2.3 | BANGL. 2.1 | OTHER 2.0 | KENYA 6.4 | MAL. 2.8 | UGANDA 2.3 | MOZ. 2.2 | OTHER 2.9 | NETH. 3.8 | U.K. 3.2 | ARG. 2.3 | ALL OTH. 2.4 |

ASIA — AFRICA — EUR — SA

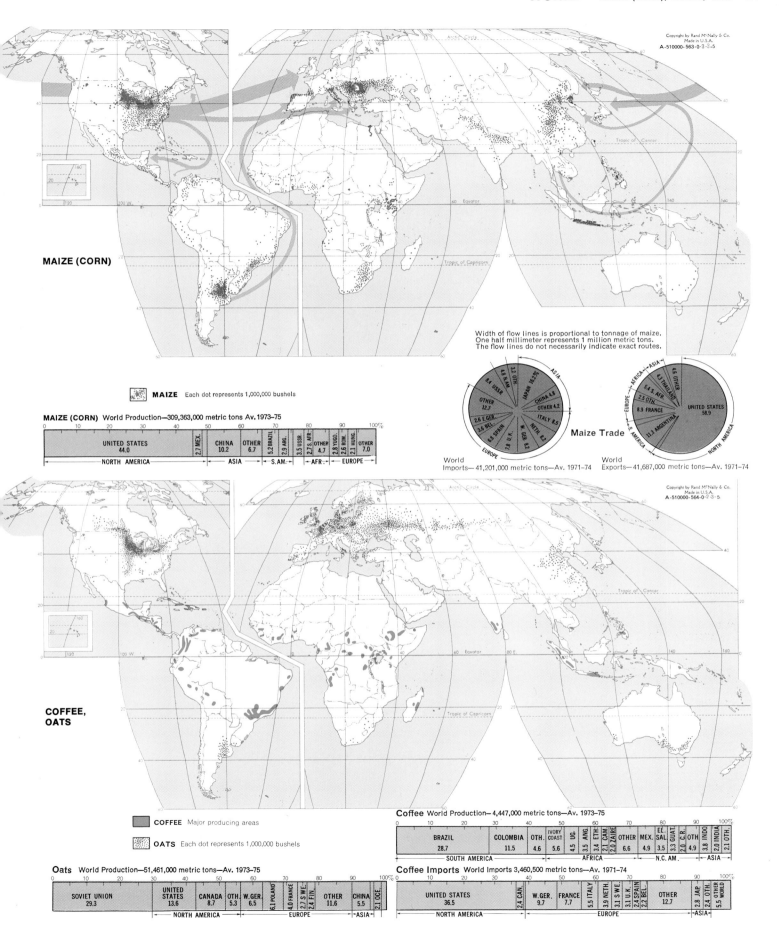

Copyright by Rand McNally & Co.
Made in U.S.A.
A-510000-563-0-3-3-5

MAIZE (CORN)

Width of flow lines is proportional to tonnage of maize.
One half millimeter represents 1 million metric tons.
The flow lines do not necessarily indicate exact routes.

MAIZE   Each dot represents 1,000,000 bushels

MAIZE (CORN) World Production—309,363,000 metric tons Av.1973-75

UNITED STATES 44.0	2.7 MEX.	CHINA 10.2	OTHER 6.7	5.2 BRAZIL	2.9 ARG.	3.5 USSR	2.7 S. AFR.	OTHER 4.7	2.8 YUGO.	2.6 ROM.	2.1 HUNG.	OTHER 7.0	
NORTH AMERICA		ASIA		S.AM.		AFR.		EUROPE					

Maize Trade

World Imports— 41,201,000 metric tons—Av. 1971-74

World Exports— 41,687,000 metric tons—Av. 1971-74

Copyright by Rand McNally & Co.
Made in U.S.A.
A-510000-564-0-2-3-5.

COFFEE, OATS

COFFEE   Major producing areas

OATS   Each dot represents 1,000,000 bushels

Coffee World Production— 4,447,000 metric tons—Av. 1973-75

BRAZIL 28.7	COLOMBIA 11.5	OTH. 4.6	IVORY COAST 5.6	UG. 4.5	ANG. 3.5	ETH. 3.4	CAM. 2.1	ZAIRE 2.0	OTHER 6.6	MEX. 4.9	EL. SAL. 3.5	GUAT. 3.3	C.R. 2.0	OTH 4.9	INDO. 3.8	INDIA 2.0	OTH. 2.1
SOUTH AMERICA			AFRICA							N.C. AM.					ASIA		

Oats World Production—51,461,000 metric tons—Av. 1973-75

SOVIET UNION 29.3	UNITED STATES 13.6	CANADA 8.7	OTH. 5.3	W.GER. 6.5	POLAND 6.1	FRANCE 4.0	S WE. 2.7	FIN 2.4	OTHER 11.6	CHINA 5.5	OCE. 2.1
	NORTH AMERICA			EUROPE						ASIA

Coffee Imports World Imports 3,460,500 metric tons—Av. 1971-74

UNITED STATES 36.5	CAN. 2.4	W.GER. 9.7	FRANCE 7.7	ITALY 5.5	NETH. 3.9	U.K. 3.1	S WE. 3.1	SPAIN 2.4	BEL. 2.2	OTHER 12.7	JAP. 2.8	OTH. 2.4	OTHER WORLD 5.5
NORTH AMERICA		EUROPE									ASIA	

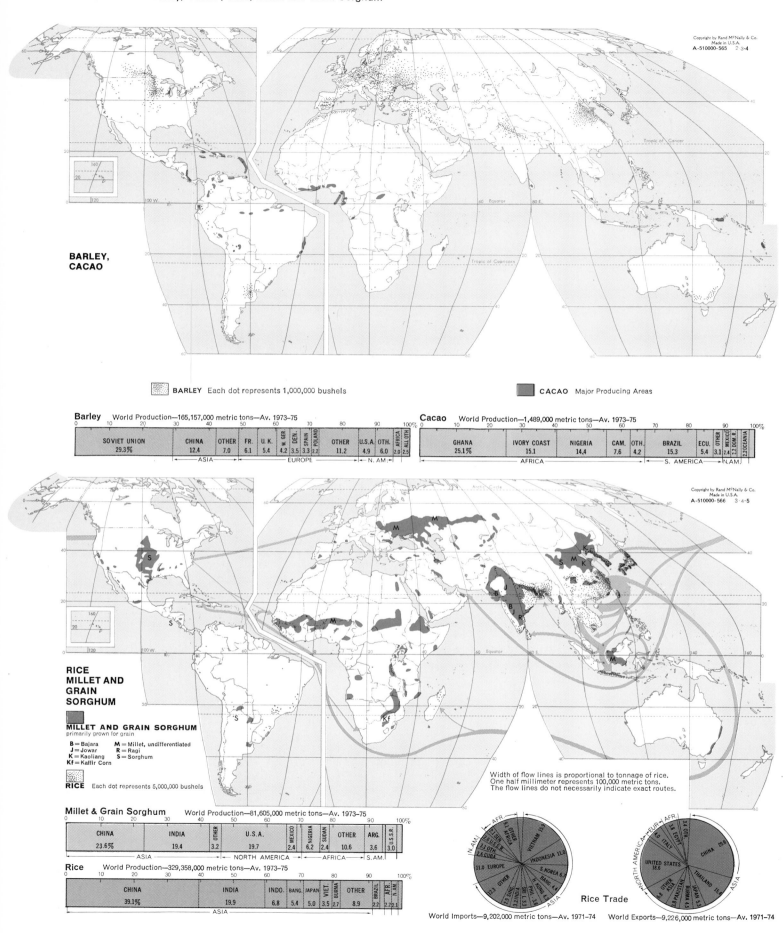

Copyright by Rand McNally & Co.
Made in U.S.A.
A-510000-565   2-3-4

BARLEY, CACAO

▦ **BARLEY** Each dot represents 1,000,000 bushels

▬ **CACAO** Major Producing Areas

Barley World Production—165,157,000 metric tons—Av. 1973-75

SOVIET UNION 29.3%	CHINA 12.4	OTHER 7.0	FR. 6.1	U.K. 5.4	W. GER. 4.2	DEN. 3.5	SPAIN 3.3	POLAND 2.2	OTHER 11.2	U.S.A. 4.9	OTH. 6.0	AFRICA 2.0	ALL OTH 2.5
	ASIA				EUROPE					N. AM.			

Cacao World Production—1,489,000 metric tons—Av. 1973-75

GHANA 25.1%	IVORY COAST 15.1	NIGERIA 14.4	CAM. 7.6	OTH. 4.2	BRAZIL 15.3	ECU. 5.4	OTHER 3.1	MEXICO 2.4	DOM. R. 1.2	OCEANIA 2.2
	AFRICA					S. AMERICA		N.AM.		

Copyright by Rand McNally & Co.
Made in U.S.A.
A-510000-566   3-4-5

**RICE
MILLET AND
GRAIN
SORGHUM**

▬ **MILLET AND GRAIN SORGHUM**
primarily grown for grain

B = Bajara   M = Millet, undifferentiated
J = Jowar   R = Ragi
K = Kaoliang   S = Sorghum
Kf = Kaffir Corn

▦ **RICE** Each dot represents 5,000,000 bushels

Width of flow lines is proportional to tonnage of rice.
One half millimeter represents 100,000 metric tons.
The flow lines do not necessarily indicate exact routes.

Millet & Grain Sorghum World Production—81,605,000 metric tons—Av. 1973-75

CHINA 23.6%	INDIA 19.4	OTHER 3.2	U.S.A. 19.7	MEXICO 2.4	NIGERIA 6.2	SUDAN 2.4	OTHER 10.6	ARG. 3.6	U.S.S.R. 3.0
	ASIA		NORTH AMERICA		AFRICA			S. AM.	

Rice World Production—329,358,000 metric tons—Av. 1973-75

CHINA 39.1%	INDIA 19.9	INDO. 6.8	BANG. 5.4	JAPAN 5.0	VIET 3.5	BURMA 2.7	OTHER 8.9	BRAZIL 2.2	AFR. 2.2	N.AM. 2.1
	ASIA									

Rice Trade

World Imports—9,202,000 metric tons—Av. 1971-74

World Exports—9,226,000 metric tons—Av. 1971-74

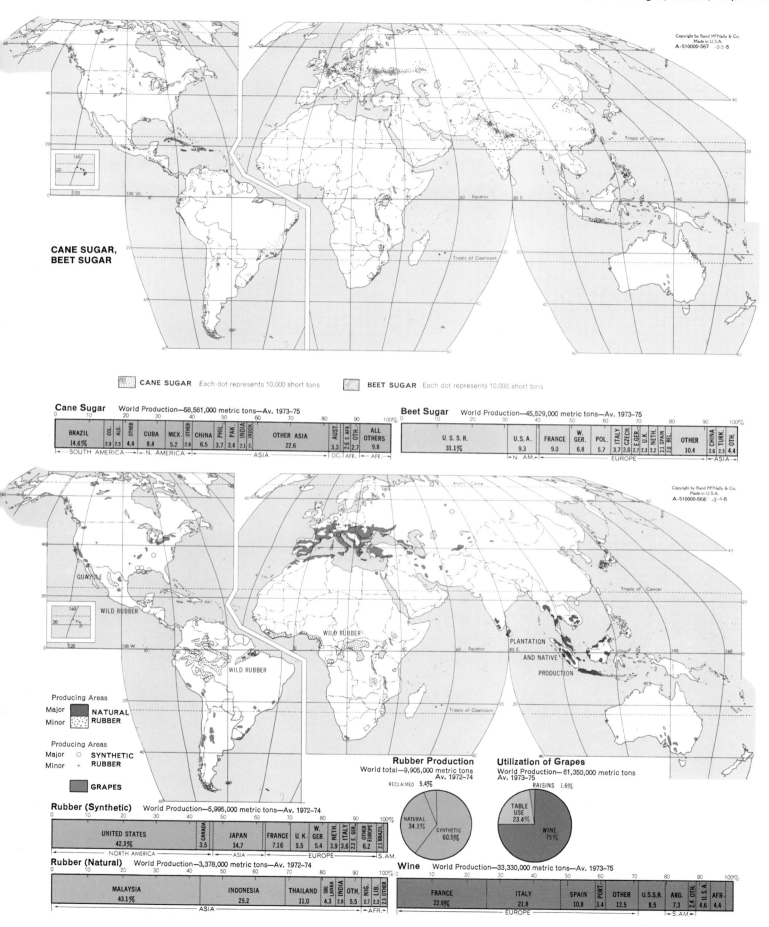

CANE SUGAR,
BEET SUGAR

CANE SUGAR Each dot represents 10,000 short tons

BEET SUGAR Each dot represents 10,000 short tons

Cane Sugar World Production—58,561,000 metric tons—Av. 1973–75

BRAZIL 14.6%	COL. 2.9	ALG. 2.5	OTHER 4.4	CUBA 8.4	MEX. 5.2	OTHER 2.8	CHINA 6.5	PHIL. 3.7	PAK. 3.4	INDIA 2.1	INDON. 2.	OTHER ASIA 22.6	AUST. 3.3	S. AFR. 2.6	OTH. 2.7	ALL OTHERS 9.8

SOUTH AMERICA — N. AMERICA — ASIA — OC. AFR. — AFR.

Beet Sugar World Production—45,529,000 metric tons—Av. 1973–75

U. S. S. R. 31.1%	U.S.A. 9.3	FRANCE 9.0	W. GER. 6.8	POL. 5.7	ITALY 3.7	CZECH. 3.0	E.GER. 2.3	U.K. 2.2	NETH. 2.1	SPAIN 2.0	BEL. 1	OTHER 10.4	CHINA 2.6	TURK. 2.3	OTH. 4.4

N. AM. — EUROPE — ASIA

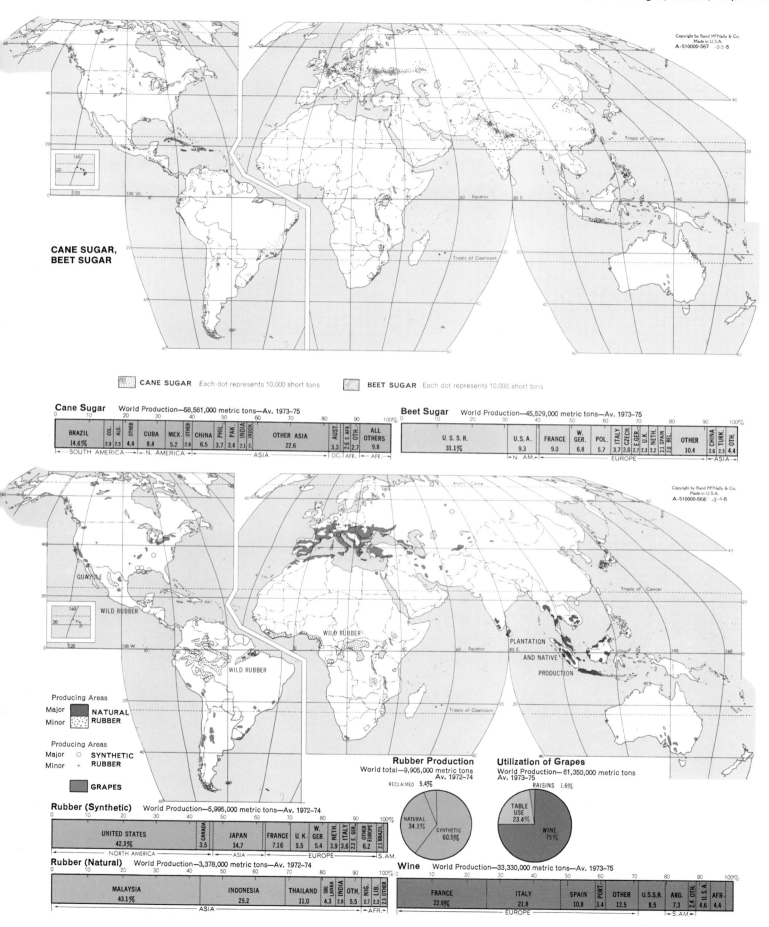

GUAYULE
WILD RUBBER
WILD RUBBER
WILD RUBBER

PLANTATION
AND NATIVE
PRODUCTION

Producing Areas
Major NATURAL
Minor RUBBER

Producing Areas
Major ○ SYNTHETIC
Minor + RUBBER

GRAPES

Rubber Production
World total—9,905,000 metric tons
Av. 1972–74

RECLAIMED 5.4%
NATURAL 34.1%
SYNTHETIC 60.5%

Utilization of Grapes
World Production—61,350,000 metric tons
Av. 1973–75

RAISINS 1.6%
TABLE USE 23.4%
WINE 75%

Rubber (Synthetic) World Production—5,995,000 metric tons—Av. 1972–74

UNITED STATES 42.3%	CANADA 3.5	JAPAN 14.7	FRANCE 7.16	U.K. 5.5	W. GER. 5.4	NETH. 3.9	ITALY 3.6	E.GER. 2.3	OTHER EUROPE 6.2	BRAZIL 2.1

NORTH AMERICA — ASIA — EUROPE — S.AM.

Rubber (Natural) World Production—3,378,000 metric tons—Av. 1972–74

MALAYSIA 43.1%	INDONESIA 25.2	THAILAND 11.0	SRI LANKA 4.3	INDIA 2.8	OTH. 5.5	NIG. 2.7	LIB. 2.3	OTHER 2.3

ASIA — AFR.

Wine World Production—33,330,000 metric tons—Av. 1973–75

FRANCE 22.6%	ITALY 21.8	SPAIN 10.8	PORT. 3.4	OTHER 12.5	U.S.S.R. 8.5	ARG. 7.3	OTH. 2.4	U.S.A. 4.6	AFR. 4.4

EUROPE — S.AM.

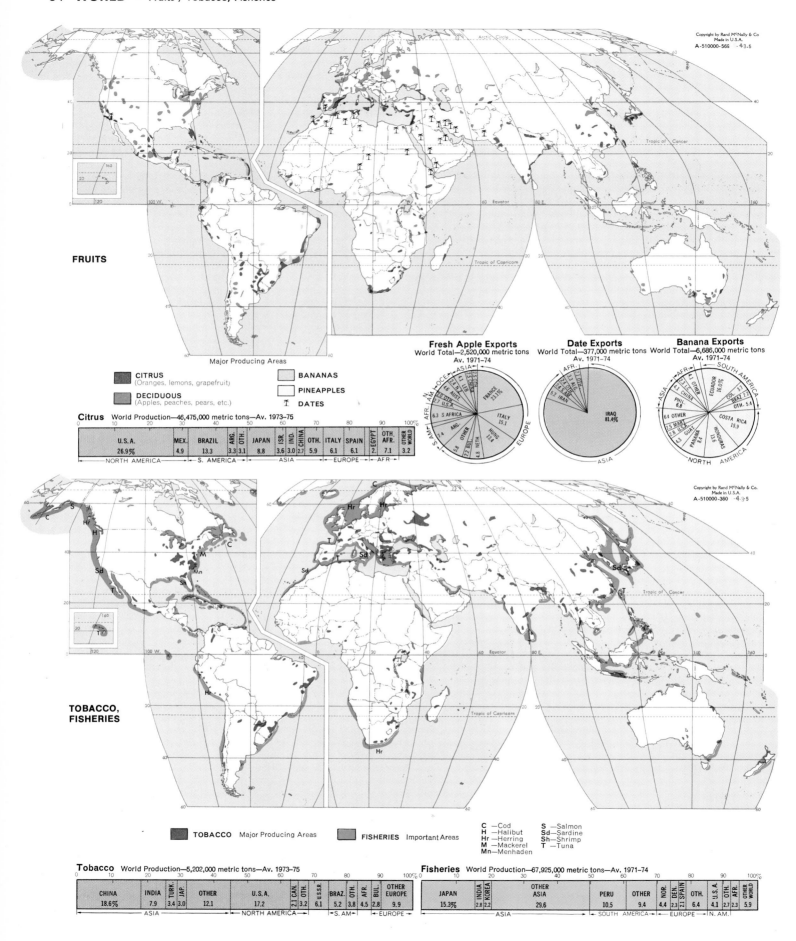

FRUITS

Major Producing Areas

CITRUS
(Oranges, lemons, grapefruit)

DECIDUOUS
(Apples, peaches, pears, etc.)

BANANAS

PINEAPPLES

Ⓣ DATES

Fresh Apple Exports
World Total—2,520,000 metric tons
Av. 1971-74

Date Exports
World Total—377,000 metric tons
Av. 1971-74

Banana Exports
World Total—6,686,000 metric tons
Av. 1971-74

Citrus World Production—46,475,000 metric tons—Av. 1973-75

U.S.A. 26.9%	MEX. 4.9	BRAZIL 13.3	ARG. 3.3	OTH. 3.1	JAPAN 8.8	ISR. 3.6	IND. 3.0	CHINA 2.7	OTH. 5.9	ITALY 6.1	SPAIN 6.1	EGYPT 2.	OTH. AFR. 7.1	OTHER WORLD 3.2
NORTH AMERICA		S. AMERICA			ASIA					EUROPE			AFR.	

TOBACCO, FISHERIES

TOBACCO Major Producing Areas

FISHERIES Important Areas

C —Cod
H —Halibut
Hr —Herring
M —Mackerel
Mn—Menhaden

S —Salmon
Sd—Sardine
Sh—Shrimp
T —Tuna

Tobacco World Production—5,202,000 metric tons—Av. 1973-75

CHINA 18.6%	INDIA 7.9	TURK. 3.4	JAP. 3.0	OTHER 12.1	U.S.A. 17.2	CAN. 2.1	OTH. 3.2	U.S.S.R. 6.1	BRAZ. 5.2	OTH. 3.8	AFR. 4.5	BUL. 2.8	OTHER EUROPE 9.9
ASIA					NORTH AMERICA			S. AM.		EUROPE		

Fisheries World Production—67,925,000 metric tons—Av. 1971-74

JAPAN 15.3%	INDIA 2.8	KOREA 2.2	OTHER ASIA 29.6	PERU 10.5	OTHER 9.4	NOR. 4.4	DEN. 2.3	SPAIN 2.1	OTH. 6.4	U.S.A. 4.1	OTH. 2.7	AFR. 2.3	OTHER WORLD 5.9
ASIA				SOUTH AMERICA		EUROPE				N. AM.		

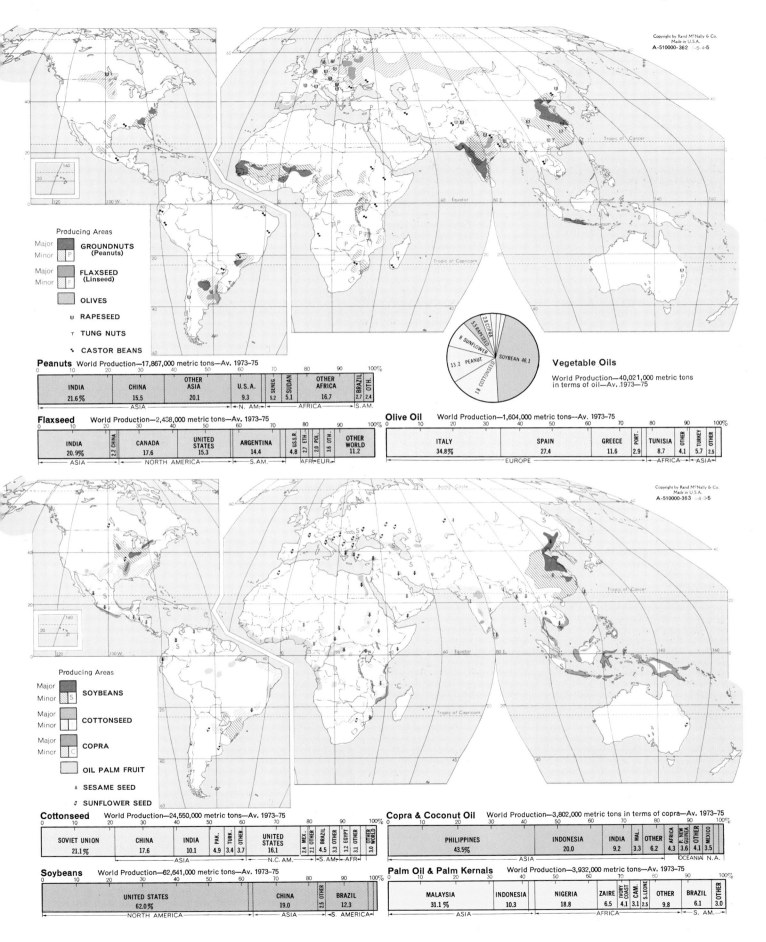

Producing Areas

Major / Minor		
	GROUNDNUTS (Peanuts)	P
	FLAXSEED (Linseed)	F
	OLIVES	
ш	RAPESEED	
т	TUNG NUTS	
ᕷ	CASTOR BEANS	

Vegetable Oils

World Production—40,021,000 metric tons in terms of oil—Av. 1973–75

Pie chart: SOYBEAN 46.1, PEANUT 13.2, COTTONSEED 11.8, SUNFLOWER 8, RAPESEED 5.3, COPRA 2.8

Peanuts   World Production—17,867,000 metric tons—Av. 1973–75

INDIA 21.6%	CHINA 15.5	OTHER ASIA 20.1	U.S.A. 9.3	SENEG. 5.2	SUDAN 5.1	OTHER AFRICA 16.7	BRAZIL 2.7	OTH. 2.4
ASIA			N. AM.	AFRICA			S. AM.	

Flaxseed   World Production—2,438,000 metric tons—Av. 1973–75

INDIA 20.9%	CHINA 2.2	CANADA 17.6	UNITED STATES 15.3	ARGENTINA 14.4	U.S.S.R. 4.8	ETH. 2.7	POL. 2.0	OTH. 3.6	OTHER WORLD 11.2
ASIA		NORTH AMERICA		S. AM.	AFR.	EUR.			

Olive Oil   World Production—1,604,000 metric tons—Av. 1973–75

ITALY 34.8%	SPAIN 27.4	GREECE 11.6	PORT. 2.9	TUNISIA 8.7	OTHER 4.1	TURKEY 5.7	OTHER 2.5
EUROPE				AFRICA		ASIA	

Producing Areas

Major / Minor		
	SOYBEANS	S
	COTTONSEED	
	COPRA	C
	OIL PALM FRUIT	
ᕷ	SESAME SEED	
ᕷ	SUNFLOWER SEED	

Cottonseed   World Production—24,550,000 metric tons—Av. 1973–75

SOVIET UNION 21.1%	CHINA 17.6	INDIA 10.1	PAK. 4.9	TURK. 3.4	OTHER 3.7	UNITED STATES 16.1	MEX. 2.4	OTHER 2.1	BRAZIL 4.5	OTHER 3.3	EGYPT 3.2	OTHER 3.1	OTHER WORLD 3.0
ASIA						N.C. AM.			S. AM.		AFR.		

Soybeans   World Production—62,641,000 metric tons—Av. 1973–75

UNITED STATES 62.0%	CHINA 19.0	OTHER 2.5	BRAZIL 12.3
NORTH AMERICA	ASIA		S. AMERICA

Copra & Coconut Oil   World Production—3,802,000 metric tons in terms of copra—Av. 1973–75

PHILIPPINES 43.5%	INDONESIA 20.0	INDIA 9.2	MAL. 3.3	OTHER 6.2	AFRICA 4.3	N. GUINEA 3.6	OTHER 4.1	MEXICO 3.5
ASIA					OCEANIA			N. A.

Palm Oil & Palm Kernals   World Production—3,932,000 metric tons—Av. 1973–75

MALAYSIA 31.1%	INDONESIA 10.3	NIGERIA 18.8	ZAIRE 6.5	IVORY COAST 4.1	CAM. 3.1	S. LEONE 2.5	OTHER 9.8	BRAZIL 6.1	OTHER 3.0
ASIA		AFRICA						S. AM.	

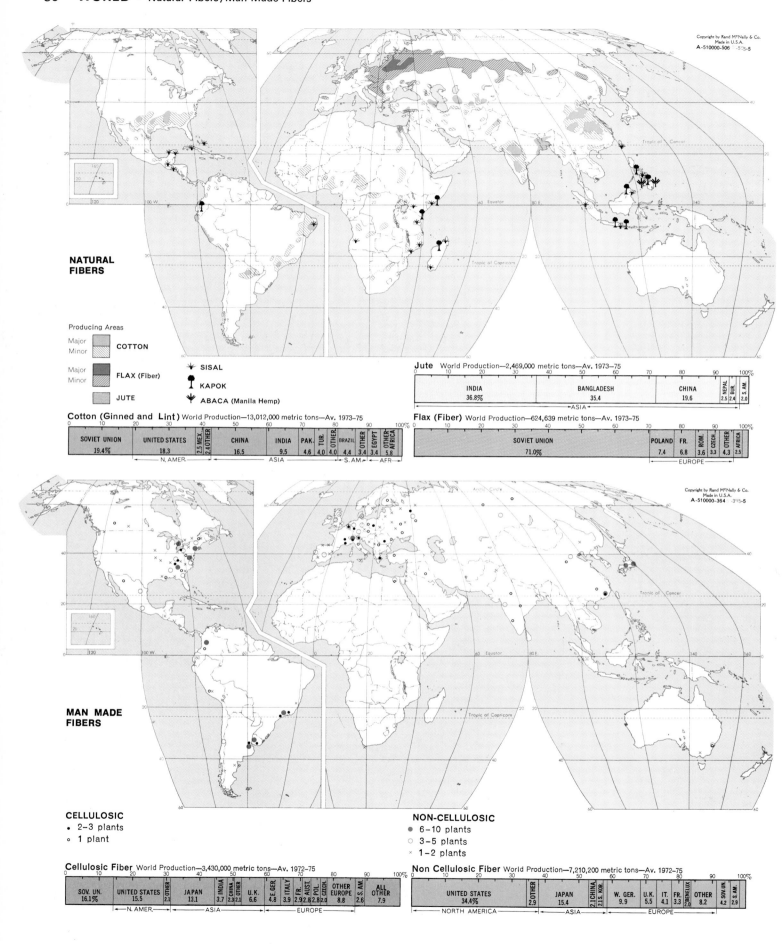

**NATURAL
FIBERS**

Producing Areas

Major / Minor	COTTON
Major / Minor	FLAX (Fiber)
	JUTE

☥ SISAL
⸷ KAPOK
☥ ABACA (Manila Hemp)

Jute World Production—2,469,000 metric tons—Av. 1973–75

0	10	20	30	40	50	60	70	80	90	100%

INDIA 36.8%	BANGLADESH 35.4	CHINA 19.6	NEPAL 2.5	BUR. 2.4	S. AM. 2.0

←————————ASIA————————→

Cotton (Ginned and Lint) World Production—13,012,000 metric tons—Av. 1973–75

0	10	20	30	40	50	60	70	80	90	100%

SOVIET UNION 19.4%	UNITED STATES 18.3	MEX. 2.5	OTHER 2.4	CHINA 16.5	INDIA 9.5	PAK. 4.6	TUR. 4.0	OTHER 4.0	BRAZIL 4.4	OTHER 3.4	EGYPT 3.4	OTHER AFRICA 5.8

←N. AMER.→ ←————ASIA————→ ←S. AM.→ ←AFR.→

Flax (Fiber) World Production—624,639 metric tons—Av. 1973–75

0	10	20	30	40	50	60	70	80	90	100%

SOVIET UNION 71.0%	POLAND 7.4	FR. 6.8	ROM. 3.6	CZECH 3.3	OTHER 4.3	AFRICA 2.5

←————————EUROPE————————→

**MAN MADE
FIBERS**

CELLULOSIC
● 2–3 plants
○ 1 plant

NON-CELLULOSIC
● 6–10 plants
○ 3–5 plants
× 1–2 plants

Cellulosic Fiber World Production—3,430,000 metric tons—Av. 1972–75

0	10	20	30	40	50	60	70	80	90	100%

SOV. UN. 16.1%	UNITED STATES 15.5	OTHER 2.1	JAPAN 13.1	INDIA 3.7	CHINA 2.3	OTHER 2.1	U.K. 6.6	E. GER. 4.8	ITALY 3.9	FR. 2.9	AUST. 2.8	POL. 2.8	CZECH. 2.0	OTHER EUROPE 8.8	S. AM. 2.6	ALL OTHER 7.9

←N. AMER.→ ←————ASIA————→ ←————EUROPE————→

Non Cellulosic Fiber World Production—7,210,200 metric tons—Av. 1972–75

0	10	20	30	40	50	60	70	80	90	100%

UNITED STATES 34.4%	OTHER 2.9	JAPAN 15.4	CHINA 2.1	S. KOR. 2.1	W. GER. 9.9	U.K. 5.5	IT. 4.1	FR. 3.3	BENELUX	OTHER 8.2	SOV. UN. 4.2	S. AM. 2.9

←————NORTH AMERICA————→ ←——ASIA——→ ←————EUROPE————→

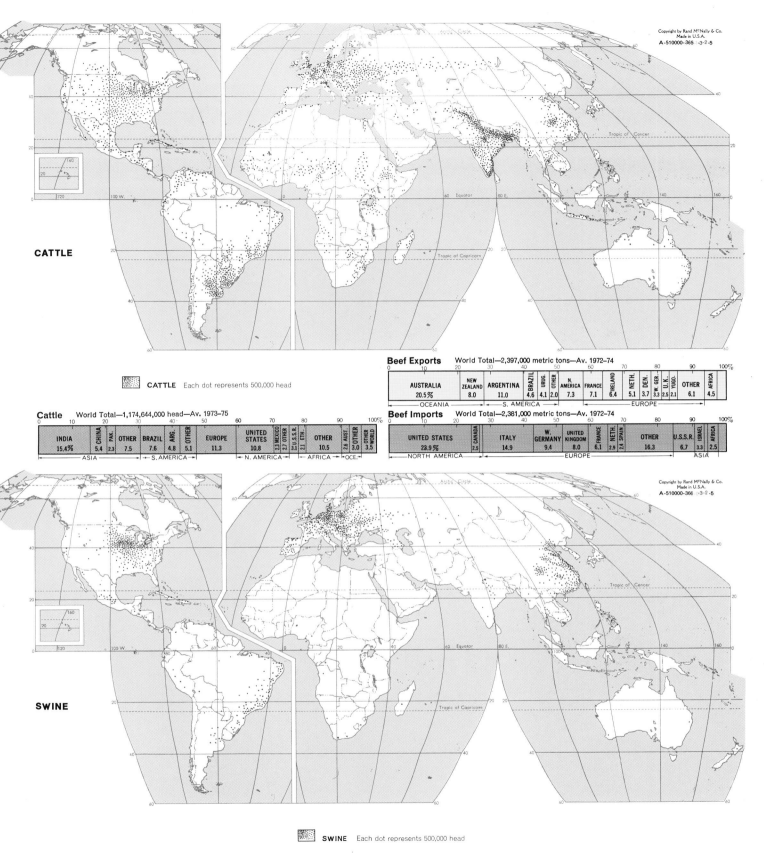

CATTLE

CATTLE Each dot represents 500,000 head

Cattle World Total—1,174,644,000 head—Av. 1973–75

	0	10	20	30	40	50	60	70	80	90	100%

| INDIA 15.4% | CHINA 5.4 | PAK. 2.3 | OTHER 7.5 | BRAZIL 7.6 | ARG. 4.8 | OTHER 5.1 | EUROPE 11.3 | UNITED STATES 10.8 | MEXICO 2.3 | OTHER 2.7 | U.S.S.R. 3.1 | ETH. 2.1 | OTHER 10.5 | AUST. 2.6 | OTHER 3.0 | OTHER WORLD 3.5 |

— ASIA — — S. AMERICA — — N. AMERICA — — AFRICA — OCE.—

Beef Exports World Total—2,397,000 metric tons—Av. 1972–74

	0	10	20	30	40	50	60	70	80	90	100%

| AUSTRALIA 20.5% | NEW ZEALAND 8.0 | ARGENTINA 11.0 | BRAZIL 4.6 | URUG. 4.1 | OTHER 2.0 | N. AMERICA 7.3 | FRANCE 7.1 | IRELAND 6.4 | NETH. 5.1 | DEN. 3.7 | W. GER. 3.3 | U.K. 2.5 | YUGO. 2.1 | OTHER 6.1 | AFRICA 4.5 |

— OCEANIA — — S. AMERICA — — EUROPE —

Beef Imports World Total—2,381,000 metric tons—Av. 1972–74

	0	10	20	30	40	50	60	70	80	90	100%

| UNITED STATES 23.9% | CANADA 2.5 | ITALY 14.9 | W. GERMANY 9.4 | UNITED KINGDOM 8.0 | FRANCE 6.1 | NETH. 2.9 | SPAIN 2.4 | OTHER 16.3 | U.S.S.R. 6.7 | ISRAEL 3.3 | AFRICA 2.5 |

— NORTH AMERICA — — EUROPE — ASIA

SWINE

SWINE Each dot represents 500,000 head

Swine World Total—665,273,000 head—Av. 1973–75

	0	10	20	30	40	50	60	70	80	90	100%

| CHINA 35.9% | OTHER 8.5 | POLAND 11.8 | W. GER. 3.0 | OTHER 8.4 | U.S.S.R. 10.5 | UNITED STATES 8.8 | OTHER 2.1 | BRAZIL 5.1 | OTHER 2.4 |

— ASIA — — EUROPE — N. AM. S. AM.

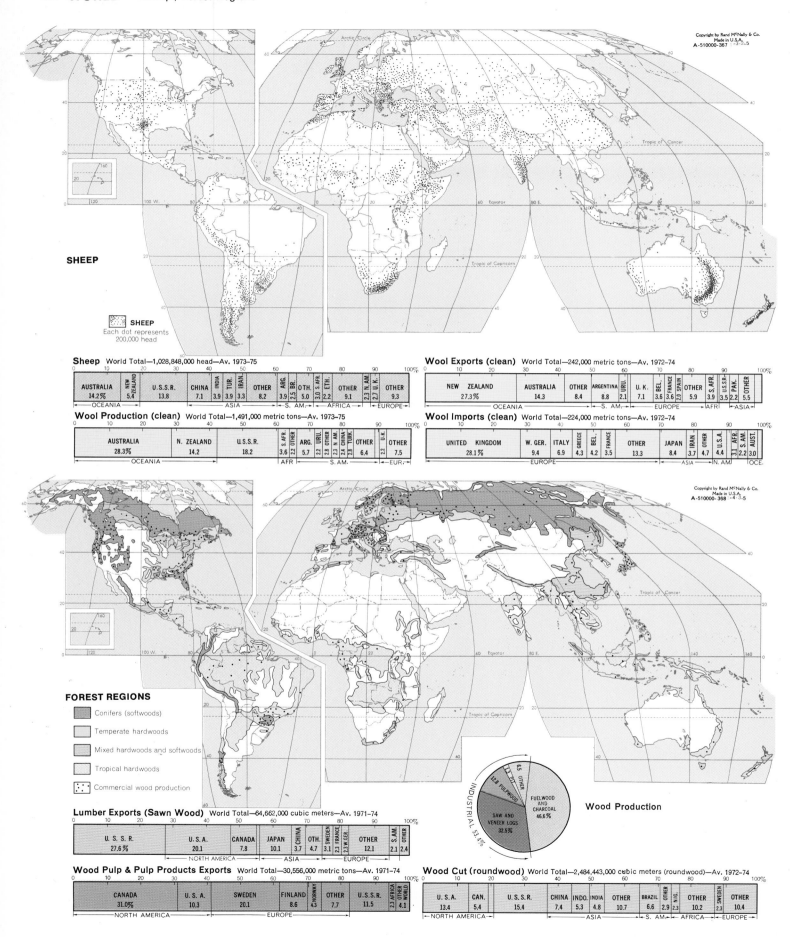

Copyright by Rand McNally & Co.
Made in U.S.A.
A-510000-367 -3-2-5

SHEEP

SHEEP
Each dot represents
200,000 head

Sheep World Total—1,028,848,000 head—Av. 1973-75

AUSTRALIA 14.2%	NEW ZEALAND 5.4	U.S.S.R. 13.8	CHINA 7.1	INDIA 3.9	TUR. 3.9	IRAN 3.3	OTHER 8.2	ARG. 3.9	BR. 2.5	OTH. 5.0	S. AFR. 3.0	ETH. 2.2	OTHER 9.1	N. AM. 2.3	U.K. 2.7	OTHER 9.3
OCEANIA			ASIA					S. AM.			AFRICA			EUROPE		

Wool Production (clean) World Total—1,491,000 metric tons—Av. 1973-75

AUSTRALIA 28.3%	N. ZEALAND 14.2	U.S.S.R. 18.2	S. AFR. 3.6	OTHER 2.2	ARG. 5.7	URU. 2.2	OTHER 2.8	CHINA 2.8	TURK. 2.3	OTHER 6.4	U.K. 2.2	OTHER 7.5
OCEANIA			AFR.		S. AM.						EUR.	

Wool Exports (clean) World Total—242,000 metric tons—Av. 1972-74

NEW ZEALAND 27.3%	AUSTRALIA 14.3	OTHER 8.4	ARGENTINA 8.8	URU. 2.1	U.K. 7.1	BEL. 3.6	FRANCE 3.6	SPAIN 2.0	OTHER 5.9	S. AFR. 3.9	U.S.S.R. 3.5	PAK. 2.2	OTHER 5.5
OCEANIA			S. AM.		EUROPE					AFR.		ASIA	

Wool Imports (clean) World Total—224,000 metric tons—Av. 1972-74

UNITED KINGDOM 28.1%	W. GER. 9.4	ITALY 6.9	GREECE 4.3	BEL. 4.2	FRANCE 3.5	OTHER 13.3	JAPAN 8.4	IRAN 3.7	OTHER 4.7	U.S.A. 4.4	S. AFR. 3.1	S. AM. 2.2	AUST. 3.0
EUROPE							ASIA			N. AM.			OCE.

Copyright by Rand McNally & Co.
Made in U.S.A.
A-510000-368 -4-3-5

FOREST REGIONS

- Conifers (softwoods)
- Temperate hardwoods
- Mixed hardwoods and softwoods
- Tropical hardwoods
- Commercial wood production

Wood Production

INDUSTRIAL 53.4%
6.5 OTHER
13.8 PULPWOOD
FUELWOOD AND CHARCOAL 46.6%
SAW AND VENEER LOGS 32.5%

Lumber Exports (Sawn Wood) World Total—64,662,000 cubic meters—Av. 1971-74

U.S.S.R. 27.6%	U.S.A. 20.1	CANADA 7.8	JAPAN 10.1	CHINA 3.7	OTH. 4.7	SWEDEN 3.1	FRANCE 2.3	W.GER. 2.3	OTHER 12.1	S. AM. 2.1	OTHER 2.4
	NORTH AMERICA		ASIA			EUROPE					

Wood Pulp & Pulp Products Exports World Total—30,556,000 metric tons—Av. 1971-74

CANADA 31.0%	U.S.A. 10.3	SWEDEN 20.1	FINLAND 8.6	NORWAY 4.3	OTHER 7.7	U.S.S.R. 11.5	AFRICA 2.3	OTHER WORLD 4.1
NORTH AMERICA		EUROPE						

Wood Cut (roundwood) World Total—2,484,443,000 cubic meters (roundwood)—Av. 1972-74

U.S.A. 13.4	CAN. 5.4	U.S.S.R. 15.4	CHINA 7.4	INDO. 5.3	INDIA 4.8	OTHER 10.7	BRAZIL 6.6	NIG. 2.9	OTHER 2.3	OTHER 10.2	SWEDEN 2.3	OTHER 10.4
NORTH AMERICA		ASIA					S. AM.		AFRICA		EUROPE	

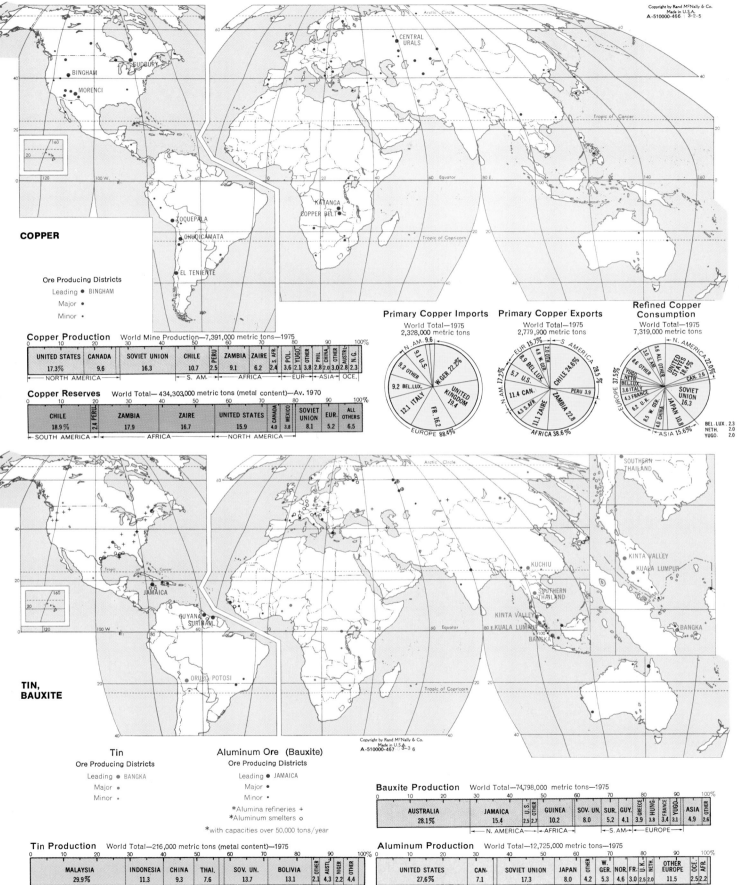

COPYRIGHT by Rand McNally & Co.
Made in U.S.A.
A-510000-466 3-2-5

COPPER

Ore Producing Districts
Leading ● BINGHAM
Major ●
Minor ·

Copper Production World Mine Production—7,391,000 metric tons—1975

UNITED STATES 17.3%	CANADA 9.6	SOVIET UNION 16.3	CHILE 10.7	PERU 2.5	ZAMBIA 9.1	ZAIRE 6.2	S. AFR. 2.4	POL. 3.6	YUGO. 2.1	OTHER 3.8	PHIL. 2.8	CHINA 3.0	OTHER 2.8	AUSTRL. 2.3	N.G. 2.3

NORTH AMERICA — S. AM. — AFRICA — EUR. — ASIA — OCE.

Copper Reserves World Total—434,303,000 metric tons (metal content)—Av. 1970

CHILE 18.9%	PERU 2.4	ZAMBIA 17.9	ZAIRE 16.7	UNITED STATES 15.9	CANADA 4.0	MEXICO 3.8	SOVIET UNION 8.1	EUR. 5.2	ALL OTHERS 6.5

SOUTH AMERICA — AFRICA — NORTH AMERICA

Primary Copper Imports
World Total—1975
2,328,000 metric tons

Primary Copper Exports
World Total—1975
2,779,900 metric tons

Refined Copper Consumption
World Total—1975
7,319,000 metric tons

TIN, BAUXITE

Copyright by Rand McNally & Co.
Made in U.S.A.
A-510000-467 3-3 6

Tin
Ore Producing Districts
Leading ● BANGKA
Major ●
Minor ·

Aluminum Ore (Bauxite)
Ore Producing Districts
Leading ● JAMAICA
Major ●
Minor ·
*Alumina refineries +
*Aluminum smelters o
*with capacities over 50,000 tons/year

Bauxite Production World Total—74,798,000 metric tons—1975

AUSTRALIA 28.1%	JAMAICA 15.4	U.S. 2.5	OTHER 2.7	GUINEA 10.2	SOV. UN. 8.0	SUR. 5.2	GUY. 4.1	GREECE 3.9	HUNG. 3.8	FRANCE 3.4	YUGO. 3.1	ASIA 4.9	OTHER 2.6

N. AMERICA — AFRICA — S. AM. — EUROPE

Tin Production World Total—216,000 metric tons (metal content)—1975

MALAYSIA 29.9%	INDONESIA 11.3	CHINA 9.3	THAI. 7.6	SOV. UN. 13.7	BOLIVIA 13.1	OTHER 2.1	AUSTL. 4.3	NIGER 2.2	OTHER 4.4

ASIA — S. AM. — OCE. — AFR.

Aluminum Production World Total—12,725,000 metric tons—1975

UNITED STATES 27.6%	CAN. 7.1	SOVIET UNION 17.3	JAPAN 8.0	OTHER 4.2	W. GER. 5.3	NOR. 4.6	FR. 3.0	U.K. 2.5	NETH. 2.0	OTHER EUROPE 11.5	OCE. 2.5	AFR. 2.2

NORTH AMERICA — ASIA — EUROPE

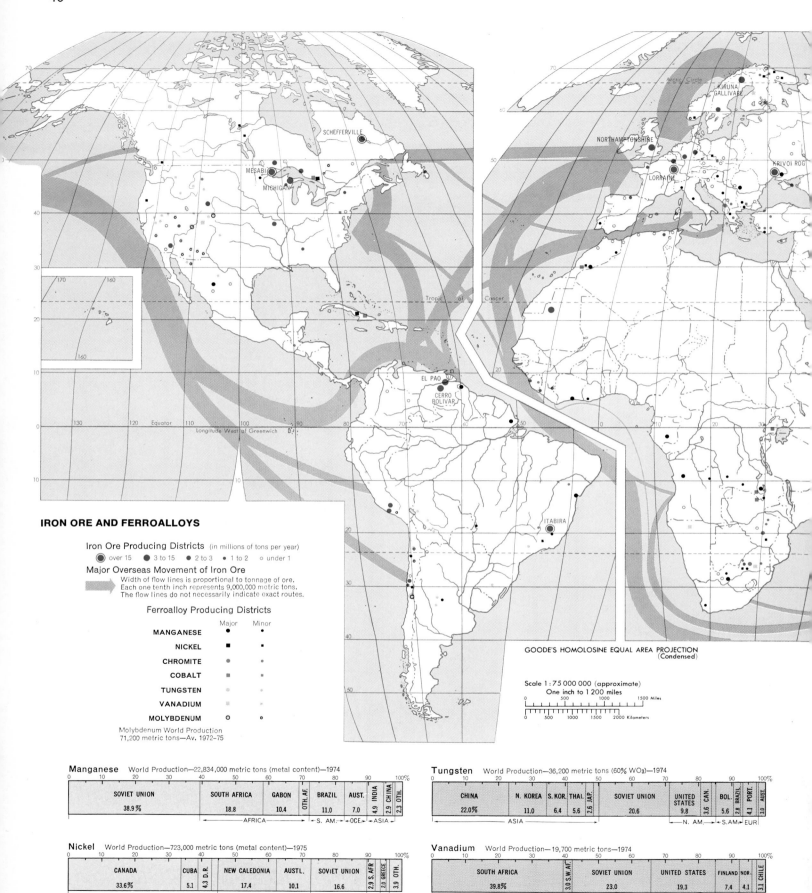

IRON ORE AND FERROALLOYS

Iron Ore Producing Districts (in millions of tons per year)
⬤ over 15   ● 3 to 15   ● 2 to 3   • 1 to 2   ○ under 1

Major Overseas Movement of Iron Ore
Width of flow lines is proportional to tonnage of ore.
Each one tenth inch represents 9,000,000 metric tons.
The flow lines do not necessarily indicate exact routes.

Ferroalloy Producing Districts

	Major	Minor
MANGANESE	●	•
NICKEL	■	▪
CHROMITE	●	•
COBALT	■	▪
TUNGSTEN	●	•
VANADIUM	■	▪
MOLYBDENUM	○	○

Molybdenum World Production
71,200 metric tons—Av. 1972-75

SCHEFFERVILLE
MESABI
MICHIGAN
EL PAO
CERRO BOLIVAR
ITABIRA
KIRUNA
GALLIVARE
NORTHAMPTONSHIRE
LORRAINE
KRIVOI ROG

Tropic of Cancer
Equator
Longitude West of Greenwich

GOODE'S HOMOLOSINE EQUAL AREA PROJECTION
(Condensed)

Scale 1 : 75 000 000 (approximate)
One inch to 1 200 miles

0   500   1000   1500 Miles
0   500   1000   1500   2000 Kilometers

Manganese World Production—22,834,000 metric tons (metal content)—1974

SOVIET UNION 38.9%	SOUTH AFRICA 18.8	GABON 10.4	OTH. AF.	BRAZIL 11.0	AUST. 7.0	INDIA 4.9	CHINA 2.9	OTH. 2.3
	←——— AFRICA ———→			S. AM.→	OCE.→	←— ASIA —→		

Nickel World Production—723,000 metric tons (metal content)—1975

CANADA 33.6%	CUBA 5.1	D.R. 4.3	NEW CALEDONIA 17.4	AUSTL. 10.1	SOVIET UNION 16.6	S. AFR 2.9	GREECE 2.0	OTH. 3.9
←——— NORTH AMERICA ———→			←——— OCEANIA ———→			AFR	EU	

Tungsten World Production—36,200 metric tons (60% WO₃)—1974

CHINA 22.0%	N. KOREA 11.0	S. KOR. 6.4	THAI. 5.6	JAP. 2.6	SOVIET UNION 20.6	UNITED STATES 9.8	CAN. 3.6	BOL. 5.6	BRAZIL 2.8	PORT. 4.1	AUST 3.0
←——————— ASIA ———————→							N. AM.→	←S.AM.→		EUR→	

Vanadium World Production—19,700 metric tons—1974

SOUTH AFRICA 39.8%	S.W. AF. 3.0	SOVIET UNION 23.0	UNITED STATES 19.3	FINLAND 7.4	NOR. 4.1	CHILE 3.1
←——— AFRICA ———→			←— N. AM. —→	←—— EUROPE ——→		

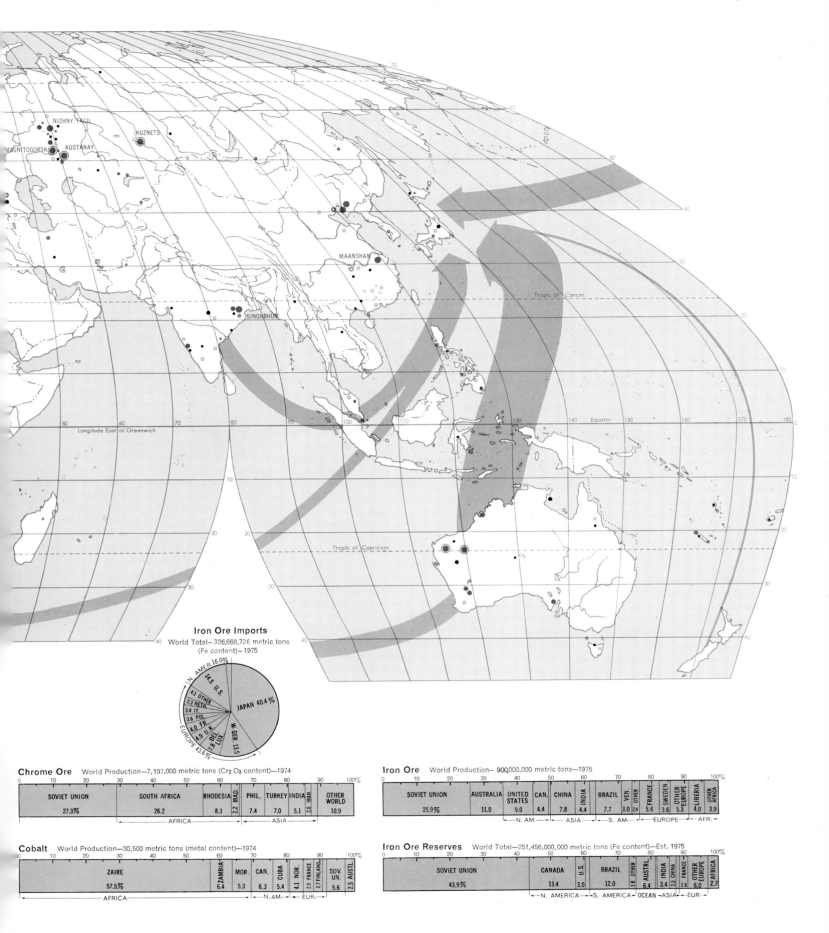

NIZHNY TAGIL

MAGNITOGORSK KUSTANAY

KUZNETS

MAANSHAN

SINGHBHUM

Tropic of Cancer

Longitude East of Greenwich

Equator

Tropic of Capricorn

Iron Ore Imports
World Total—326,668,726 metric tons
(Fe content)—1975

N. AMER. 16.0%
14.5 U.S.
4.1 OTHER
2.3 NETH.
3.4 IT.
3.6 POL.
4.0 FR.
4.9 U.K.
1.8 BEL. LUX.
EUROPE 43.6%
W. GER. 13.5
JAPAN 40.4%

Chrome Ore World Production—7,197,000 metric tons (Cr₂O₃ content)—1974

	SOVIET UNION 27.3%	SOUTH AFRICA 26.2	RHODESIA 8.3	MAD. 2.2	PHIL. 7.4	TURKEY 7.0	INDIA 5.1	IRAN 2.0	OTHER WORLD 10.9
		← AFRICA →			← ASIA →				

Iron Ore World Production— 900,000,000 metric tons—1975

SOVIET UNION 25.9%	AUSTRALIA 11.0	UNITED STATES 9.0	CAN. 4.4	CHINA 7.8	INDIA 4.4	BRAZIL 7.7	VEN. 3.0	OTHER 2.4	FRANCE 5.6	SWEDEN 3.6	OTHER EUROPE 5.3	LIBERIA 4.0	OTHER AFRICA 3.9
		← N. AM. →		← ASIA →		← S. AM. →			← EUROPE →			← AFR. →	

Cobalt World Production—30,500 metric tons (metal content)—1974

ZAIRE 57.5%	ZAMBIA 6.4	MOR. 5.3	CAN. 6.3	CUBA 5.4	NOR. 4.1	FRANCE 2.7	FINLAND 2.7	SOV. UN. 5.6	AUSTL. 2.5
← AFRICA →			← N. AM. →		← EUR. →				

Iron Ore Reserves World Total—251,456,000,000 metric tons (Fe content)—Est. 1975

SOVIET UNION 43.9%	CANADA 13.4	U.S. 3.0	BRAZIL 12.0	OTHER 1.6	AUSTRL. 6.4	INDIA 3.4	CHINA 2.3	FRANCE 2.6	OTHER EUROPE 6.0	AFRICA 2.7
	← N. AMERICA →		← S. AMERICA →		← OCEAN →	← ASIA →		← EUR. →		

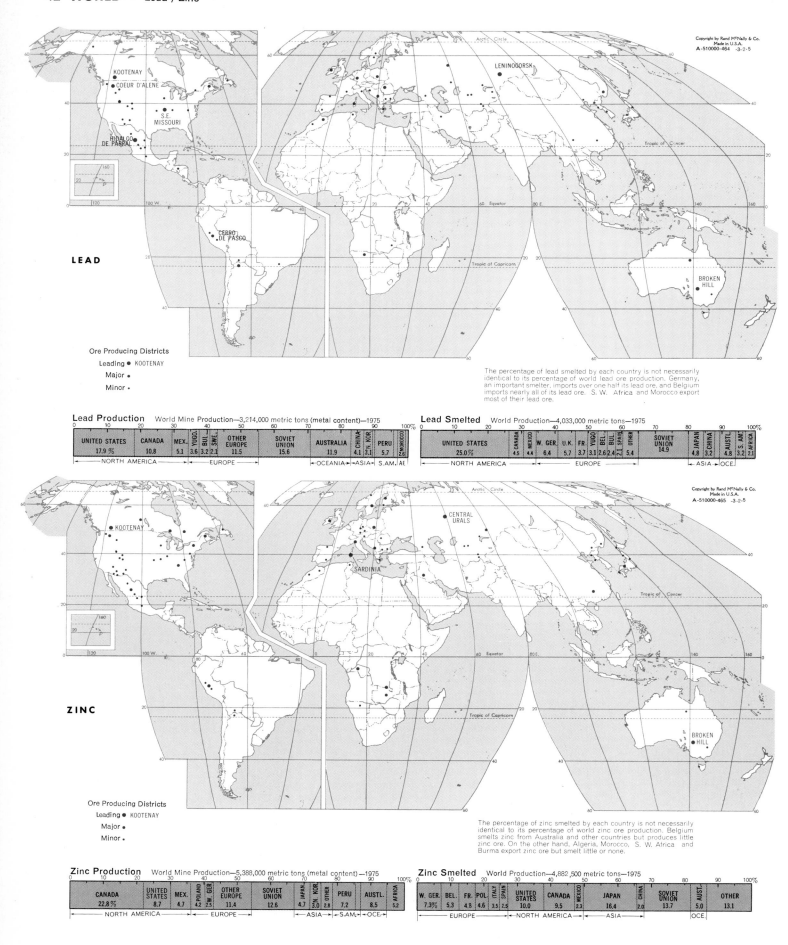

LEAD

Copyright by Rand McNally & Co.
Made in U.S.A.
A-510000-464 -3-2-5

KOOTENAY
COEUR D'ALENE
S.E. MISSOURI
HIDALGO DE PARRAL
CERRO DE PASCO
LENINOGORSK
BROKEN HILL

Ore Producing Districts

Leading ● KOOTENAY

Major •

Minor ·

The percentage of lead smelted by each country is not necessarily identical to its percentage of world lead ore production. Germany, an important smelter, imports over one half its lead ore, and Belgium imports nearly all of its lead ore. S. W. Africa and Morocco export most of their lead ore.

Lead Production — World Mine Production—3,214,000 metric tons (metal content)—1975

UNITED STATES 17.9 %	CANADA 10.8	MEX. 5.1	YUGO. 3.6	BUL. 3.2	SWE. 2.1	OTHER EUROPE 11.5	SOVIET UNION 15.6	AUSTRALIA 11.9	CHINA 4.1	N. KOR. 3.1	PERU 5.7	MOROCCO 2.6
NORTH AMERICA			EUROPE					OCEANIA	ASIA		S.AM.	AF.

Lead Smelted — World Production—4,033,000 metric tons—1975

UNITED STATES 25.0%	CANADA 4.5	MEXICO 4.4	W. GER. 6.4	U.K. 5.7	FR. 3.7	YUGO. 3.1	BEL. 2.6	BUL. 2.4	SPAIN 2.1	OTHER 5.4	SOVIET UNION 14.9	JAPAN 4.8	CHINA 3.2	AUSTL. 4.8	S. AM.	AFRICA 2.1
NORTH AMERICA			EUROPE									ASIA		OCE.		

ZINC

Copyright by Rand McNally & Co.
Made in U.S.A.
A-510000-465 -3-2-5

KOOTENAY
CENTRAL URALS
SARDINIA
BROKEN HILL

Ore Producing Districts

Leading ● KOOTENAY

Major •

Minor ·

The percentage of zinc smelted by each country is not necessarily identical to its percentage of world zinc ore production. Belgium smelts zinc from Australia and other countries but produces little zinc ore. On the other hand, Algeria, Morocco, S. W. Africa and Burma export zinc ore but smelt little or none.

Zinc Production — World Mine Production—5,388,000 metric tons (metal content)—1975

CANADA 22.8%	UNITED STATES 8.7	MEX. 4.7	POLAND 4.2	W. GER 3.0	OTHER EUROPE 11.4	SOVIET UNION 12.6	JAPAN 4.7	N. KOR. 3.0	OTHER 2.8	PERU 7.2	AUSTL. 8.5	AFRICA 5.2
NORTH AMERICA			EUROPE				ASIA			S.AM.	OCE.	

Zinc Smelted — World Production—4,882,500 metric tons—1975

W. GER. 7.3%	BEL. 5.3	FR. 4.8	POL. 4.6	ITALY 3.5	SPAIN 2.5	UNITED STATES 10.0	CANADA 9.5	MEXICO 2.3	JAPAN 16.4	CHINA 2.0	SOVIET UNION 13.7	AUST. 5.0	OTHER 13.1
EUROPE						NORTH AMERICA			ASIA			OCE.	

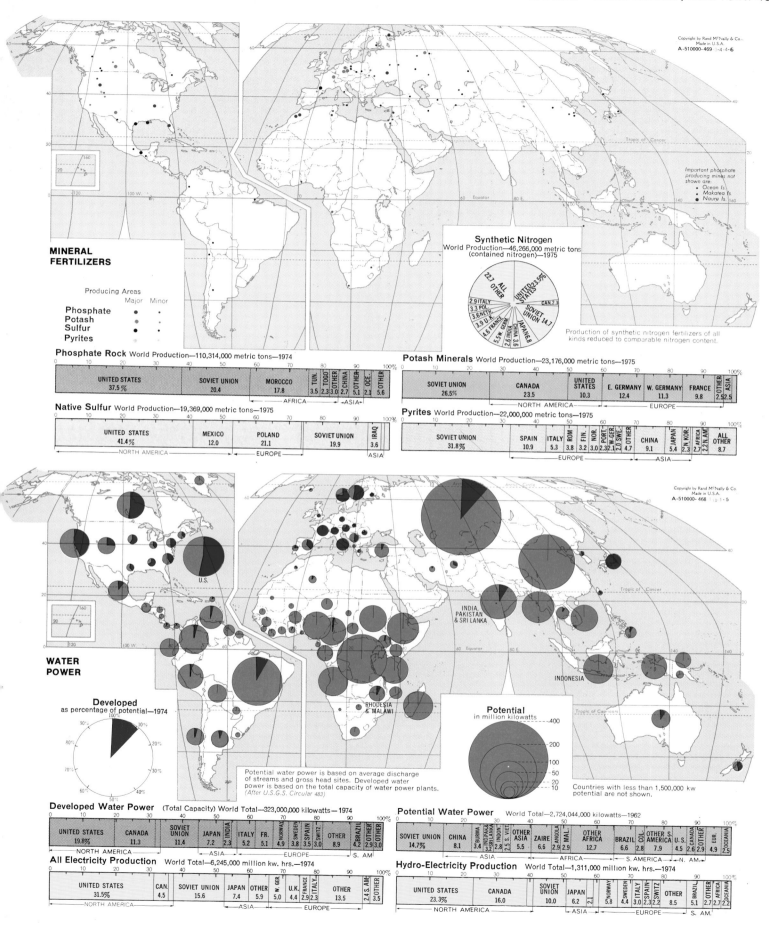

MINERAL FERTILIZERS

Producing Areas

	Major	Minor
Phosphate		
Potash		
Sulfur		
Pyrites		

Important phosphate producing mines not shown are:
• Ocean Is.
• Makatea Is.
• Nauru Is.

Synthetic Nitrogen

World Production—46,266,000 metric tons
(contained nitrogen)—1975

UNITED STATES 23.5%
CAN. 2.3
SOVIET UNION 14.7
JAPAN 6.8
CHINA 3.6
INDIA 2.6
W. GER. 5.5
FRANCE 4.6
U.K. 3.9
NETH. 3.6
POL. 3.3
ITALY 2.9
ALL OTHER 22.7

Production of synthetic nitrogen fertilizers of all kinds reduced to comparable nitrogen content.

Phosphate Rock World Production—110,314,000 metric tons—1974

0	10	20	30	40	50	60	70	80	90	100%

UNITED STATES 37.5%	SOVIET UNION 20.4	MOROCCO 17.8	TUN. 3.5	TOGO 2.3	OTHER 3.0	CHINA 2.7	OTHER 5.1	OCE. 2.1	OTHER 5.6

AFRICA — ASIA

Potash Minerals World Production—23,176,000 metric tons—1975

0	10	20	30	40	50	60	70	80	90	100%

SOVIET UNION 26.5%	CANADA 23.5	UNITED STATES 10.3	E. GERMANY 12.4	W. GERMANY 11.3	FRANCE 9.8	OTHER 2.5	ASIA 2.5

NORTH AMERICA — EUROPE

Native Sulfur World Production—19,369,000 metric tons—1975

0	10	20	30	40	50	60	70	80	90	100%

UNITED STATES 41.4%	MEXICO 12.0	POLAND 21.1	SOVIET UNION 19.9	IRAQ 3.6

NORTH AMERICA — EUROPE — ASIA

Pyrites World Production—22,000,000 metric tons—1975

0	10	20	30	40	50	60	70	80	90	100%

SOVIET UNION 31.8%	SPAIN 10.9	ITALY 5.3	ROM 3.8	FIN. 3.2	NOR. 3.0	PORT. 2.3	W.GER. 2.1	SWE. 2.0	OTHER 4.7	CHINA 9.1	JAPAN 5.4	N. KOR. 2.3	AFRICA 2.2	N. AM. 2.2	ALL OTHER 8.7

EUROPE — ASIA

WATER POWER

Developed
as percentage of potential—1974

Potential
in million kilowatts
400
200
100
50
10

Countries with less than 1,500,000 kw potential are not shown.

Potential water power is based on average discharge of streams and gross head sites. Developed water power is based on the total capacity of water power plants.
(After U.S.G.S. Circular 483)

Developed Water Power (Total Capacity) World Total—323,000,000 kilowatts—1974

0	10	20	30	40	50	60	70	80	90	100%

UNITED STATES 19.8%	CANADA 11.3	SOVIET UNION 11.4	JAPAN 7.2	INDIA 2.3	ITALY 5.2	FR. 5.1	NORWAY 4.9	SWEDEN 3.8	SPAIN 3.5	OTHER 3.0	OTHER 8.9	BRAZIL 4.2	OTHER 2.9	OTHER 3.0

NORTH AMERICA — ASIA — EUROPE — S. AM.

Potential Water Power World Total—2,724,044,000 kilowatts—1962

0	10	20	30	40	50	60	70	80	90	100%

SOVIET UNION 14.7%	CHINA 8.1	BURMA 3.4	INDIA,PAK.& SRI LANKA 2.8	INDON. 2.5	S. VIET 2.5	OTHER ASIA 5.5	ZAIRE 6.6	ANGOLA 2.9	MAL. 2.9	OTHER AFRICA 12.7	BRAZIL 6.6	COL. 2.9	OTHER S. AMERICA 7.9	U.S. 4.5	CANADA 2.6	OTHER 4.9	EUR.	OCEANIA

ASIA — AFRICA — S. AMERICA — N. AM.

All Electricity Production World Total—6,245,000 million kw. hrs.—1974

0	10	20	30	40	50	60	70	80	90	100%

UNITED STATES 31.5%	CAN. 4.5	SOVIET UNION 15.6	JAPAN 7.4	OTHER 5.9	W. GER. 5.0	U.K. 4.4	FRANCE 2.9	ITALY 2.3	OTHER 13.5	S. AM. 2.4	OTHER 3.5

NORTH AMERICA — ASIA — EUROPE

Hydro-Electricity Production World Total—1,311,000 million kw. hrs.—1974

0	10	20	30	40	50	60	70	80	90	100%

UNITED STATES 23.3%	CANADA 16.0	SOVIET UNION 10.0	JAPAN 6.2	2.1	NORWAY 5.8	SWEDEN 4.4	ITALY 3.0	SPAIN 2.3	SWITZ. 2.2	OTHER 8.5	BRAZIL 5.1	OTHER 2.7	AFRICA 2.7	OCEANIA 2.2

NORTH AMERICA — ASIA — EUROPE — S. AM.

44

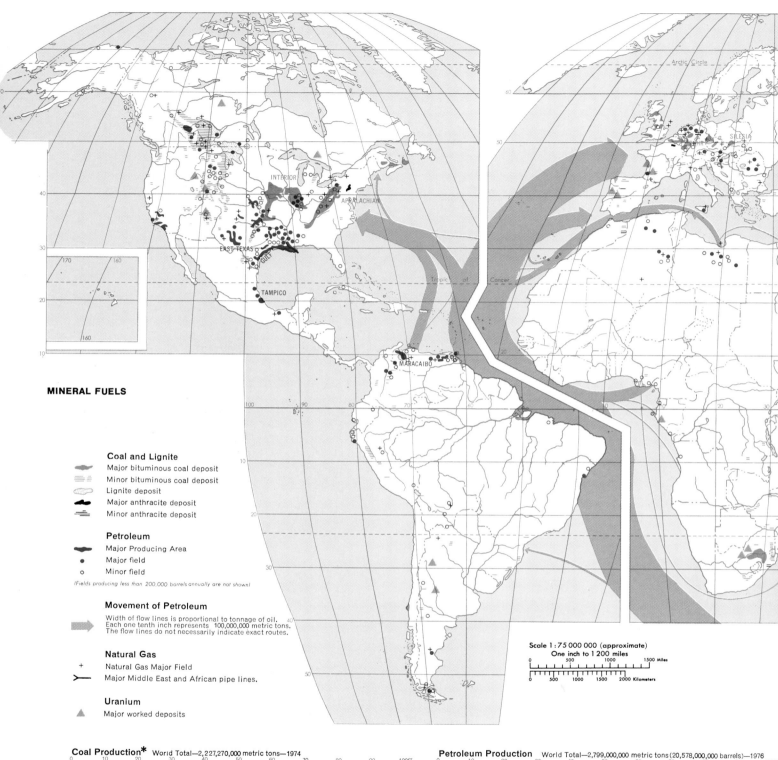

MINERAL FUELS

Coal and Lignite
Major bituminous coal deposit
Minor bituminous coal deposit
Lignite deposit
Major anthracite deposit
Minor anthracite deposit

Petroleum
Major Producing Area
● Major field
○ Minor field

(Fields producing less than 200,000 barrels annually are not shown)

Movement of Petroleum
Width of flow lines is proportional to tonnage of oil.
Each one tenth inch represents 100,000,000 metric tons.
The flow lines do not necessarily indicate exact routes.

Natural Gas
+ Natural Gas Major Field
➤ Major Middle East and African pipe lines.

Uranium
▲ Major worked deposits

Scale 1 : 75 000 000 (approximate)
One inch to 1 200 miles

INTERIOR
APPALACHIAN
EAST TEXAS
GULF
TAMPICO
MARACAIBO
SILESIA

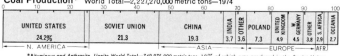

Coal Production* World Total—2,227,270,000 metric tons—1974

UNITED STATES	SOVIET UNION	CHINA	INDIA	OTHER	POLAND	UNITED KINGDOM	W. GERMANY	OTHER	S. AFRICA	OCEANIA
24.2%	21.3	19.3	3.7	3.6	7.3	4.9	4.5	3.8	2.9	2.7
← N. AMERICA →		← ASIA →			← EUROPE →				← AFR. →	

Bituminous and Anthracite Lignite World Total—749,975,000 metric tons, 19% of which was produced in the Soviet Union.

Coal Reserves** World Total—1,417,048,000,000 metric tons—1975

UNITED STATES	CHINA	OTHER	SOVIET UNION	W. GER.	UNITED KINGDOM	POLAND	E. GER.	AUSTRALIA	AFRICA
25.6%	21.1	2.8	19.3	7.1	7.0	2.7	2.1	3.5	5.2	2.1
← N. AMER. →	← ASIA →			← EUROPE →				OCE.	

Petroleum Production World Total—2,799,000,000 metric tons (20,578,000,000 barrels)—1976

SOVIET UNION	SAUDI ARABIA	IRAN	IRAQ	KUWAIT	U.A.E.	INDONESIA	CHINA	OTHER	UNITED STATES	VENEZUELA	CANADA	OTHER	NIG.	LIBYA	OTHER	EUROPE
18.2%	14.7	10.5	3.7	3.0	2.4	2.8	2.7	3.8	14.4	2.3	3.5	3.5	3.6	3.1	2.3	
← ASIA →										← W. HEMISPHERE →			← AFRICA →			

Petroleum Reserves World Total—75,530,000 metric tons (555,368,000,000 barrels)—Av. 1974

SAUDI ARABIA	KUWAIT	IRAN	IRAQ	U.A.E.	CHINA	INDO.	SOVIET UNION	UNITED STATES	VEN.	OTHER	NIG.	OTHER	U.K.
19.6%	13.7	12.3	6.2	4.6	2.8	2.1	8.7	6.1	2.4	3.2	3.5	6.7	2.2
← ASIA →								← W.HEMIS. →		← AFRICA →		← EUR. →	

**Including lignite and coke

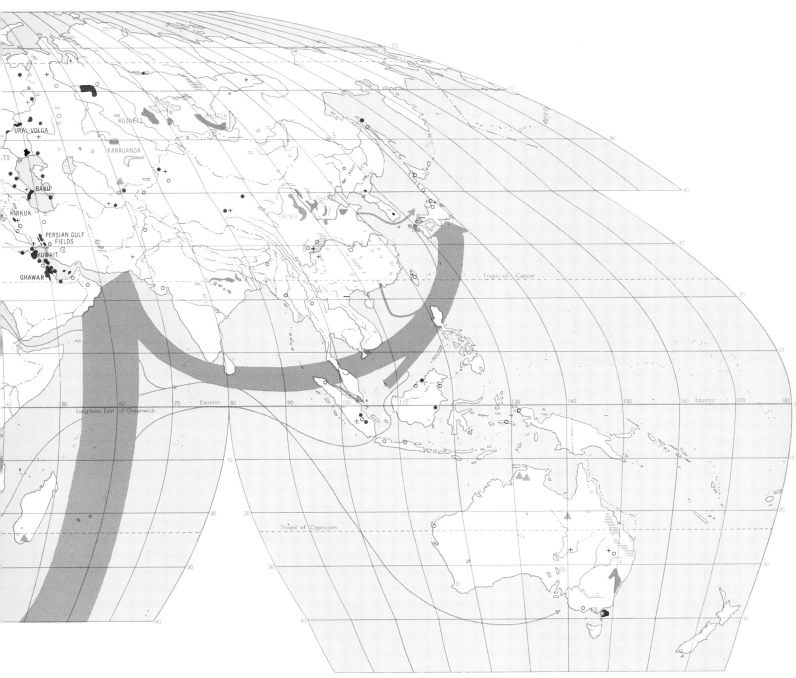

Goode's Homolosine Equal Area Projection (Condensed)

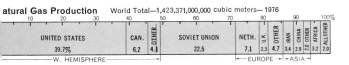

atural Gas Production World Total—1,423,371,000,000 cubic meters—1976

UNITED STATES 39.7%	CAN. 6.2	OTHER 4.1	SOVIET UNION 22.5	NETH. 7.1	U.K. 2.3	OTHER 4.7	IRAN 3.4	CHINA 2.8	OTHER 2.0	AFRICA 3.2	ALL OTHER 2.0

W. HEMISPHERE — EUROPE — ASIA

atural Gas Reserves World Total—59,195,000,000,000 cubic meters—1974

SOVIET UNION 33.5%	IRAN 17.9	SAUDI ARABIA 2.9	OTHER 8.5	UNITED STATES 11.3	CAN. 2.7	VEN. OTHER 3.7 2.1	ALGERIA 4.7	NIG. 2.4	OTHER 2.2	NETH. 3.7	OTHER 4.4

ASIA — W. HEMIS. — AFRICA — EUROPE

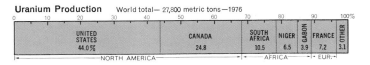

Uranium Production World total— 27,800 metric tons—1976

UNITED STATES 44.0%	CANADA 24.8	SOUTH AFRICA 10.5	NIGER 6.5	GABON 3.9	FRANCE 7.2	OTHER 3.1

NORTH AMERICA — AFRICA — EUR.

Uranium Reserves World Total—1,080,000 metric tons—1975

UNITED STATES 29.6%	CANADA 13.3	AUSTRALIA 22.5	SOUTH AFRICA 17.2	NIGER 3.7	ALGERIA 2.6	OTHER 2.8	FRANCE 3.4	OTHER 2.0	ALL OTHER 2.9

N. AMERICA — AFRICA — EUR.

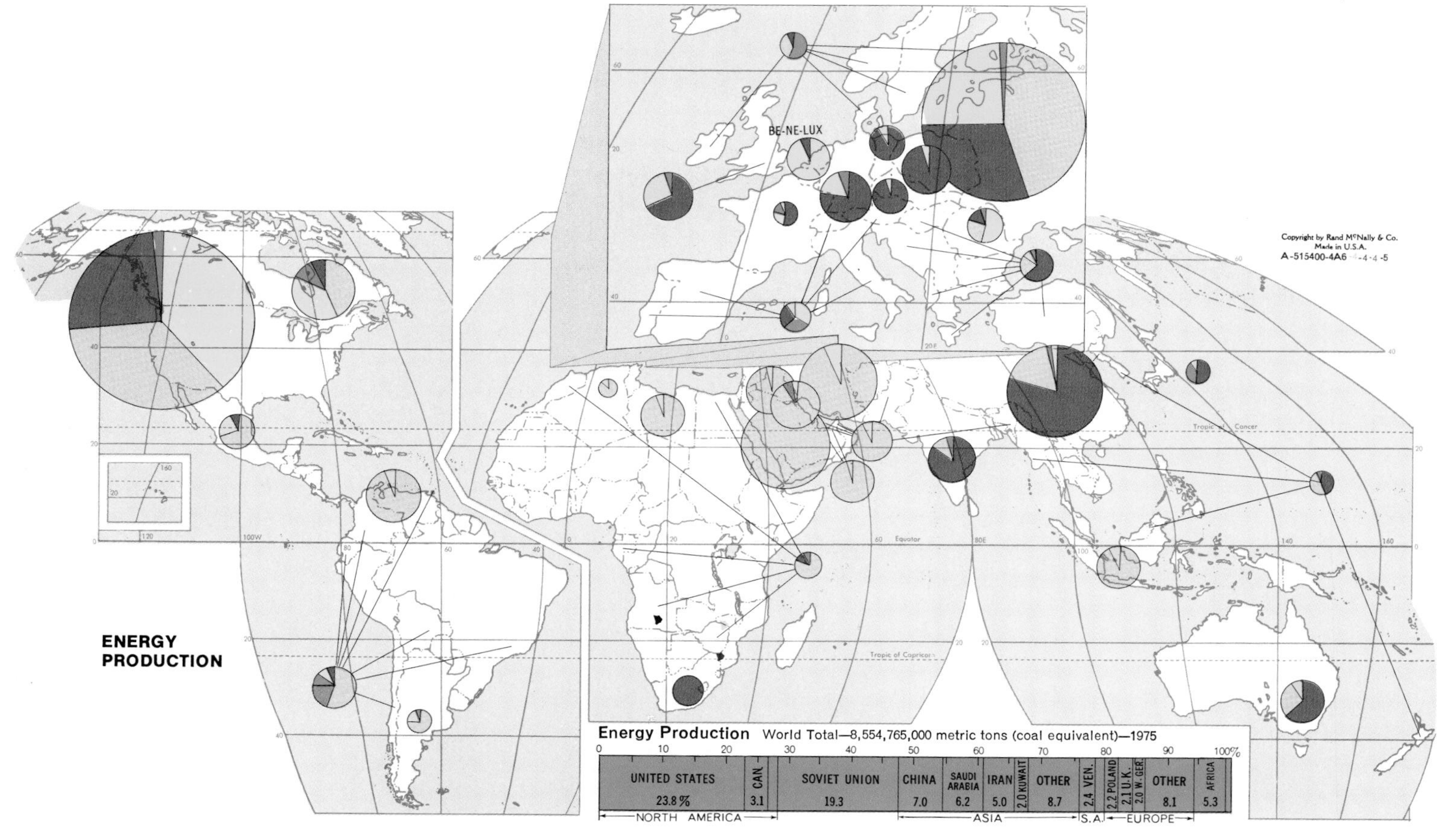

Copyright by Rand McNally & Co.
Made in U.S.A.
A-515400-4A6 -4-4-5

**ENERGY
PRODUCTION**

Energy Production World Total—8,554,765,000 metric tons (coal equivalent)—1975

0	10	20	30	40	50	60	70	80	90	100%		

| UNITED STATES 23.8% | CAN. 3.1 | SOVIET UNION 19.3 | CHINA 7.0 | SAUDI ARABIA 6.2 | IRAN 5.0 | KUWAIT 2.0 | OTHER 8.7 | VEN. 2.4 | POLAND 2.2 | U.K. 2.1 | W. GER. 2.0 | OTHER 8.1 | AFRICA 5.3 |

NORTH AMERICA — ASIA — S.A. — EUROPE

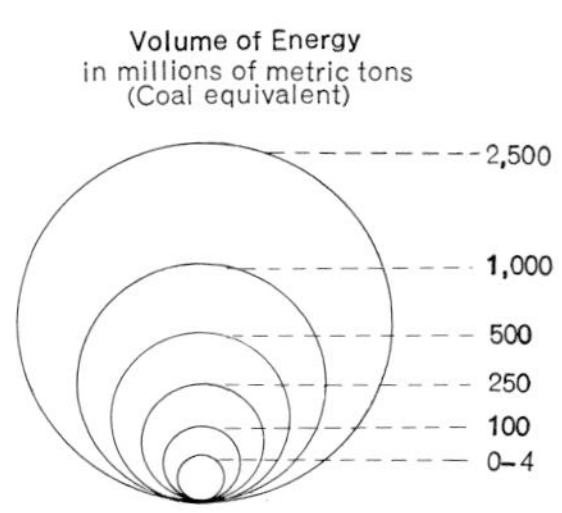

Volume of Energy
in millions of metric tons
(Coal equivalent)

- 2,500
- 1,000
- 500
- 250
- 100
- 0–4

All countries with less than 0.5 million metric tons
(Coal Equivalent) are not shown.

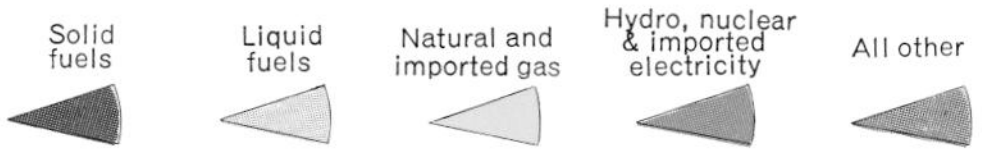

Composition of Energy
(Data based on 1975)

Solid fuels | Liquid fuels | Natural and imported gas | Hydro, nuclear & imported electricity | All other

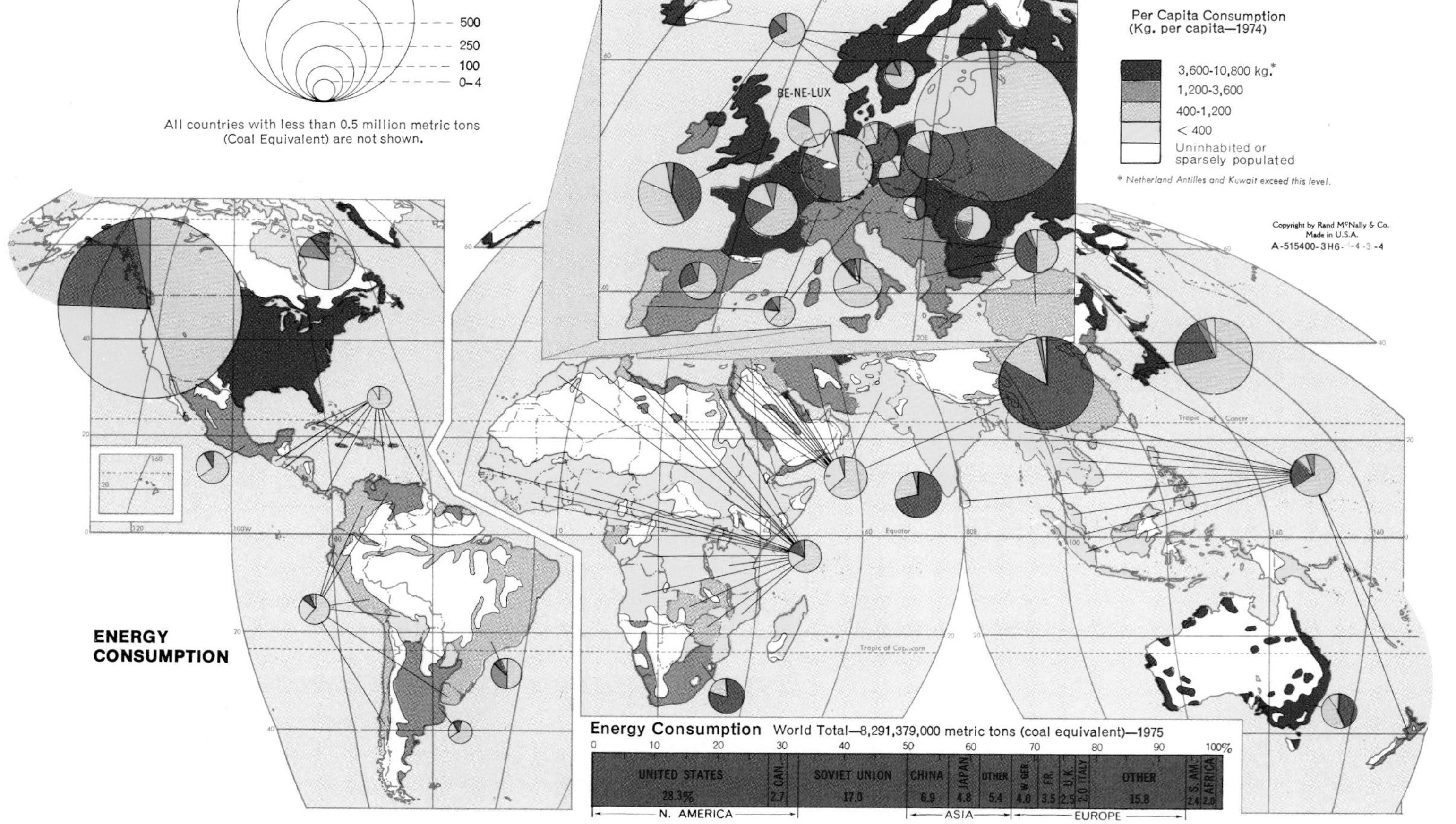

Per Capita Consumption
(Kg. per capita—1974)

- 3,600-10,800 kg.*
- 1,200-3,600
- 400-1,200
- < 400
- Uninhabited or sparsely populated

* Netherland Antilles and Kuwait exceed this level.

Copyright by Rand McNally & Co.
Made in U.S.A.
A-515400-3H6- -4-3-4

**ENERGY
CONSUMPTION**

Energy Consumption World Total—8,291,379,000 metric tons (coal equivalent)—1975

0	10	20	30	40	50	60	70	80	90	100%	

| UNITED STATES 28.3% | CAN. 2.7 | SOVIET UNION 17.0 | CHINA 6.9 | JAPAN 4.8 | OTHER 5.4 | W. GER. | FR. 3.5 | U.K. | ITALY 2.0 | OTHER 15.8 | S. AM. 2.4 | AFRICA 2.0 |

N. AMERICA — ASIA — EUROPE

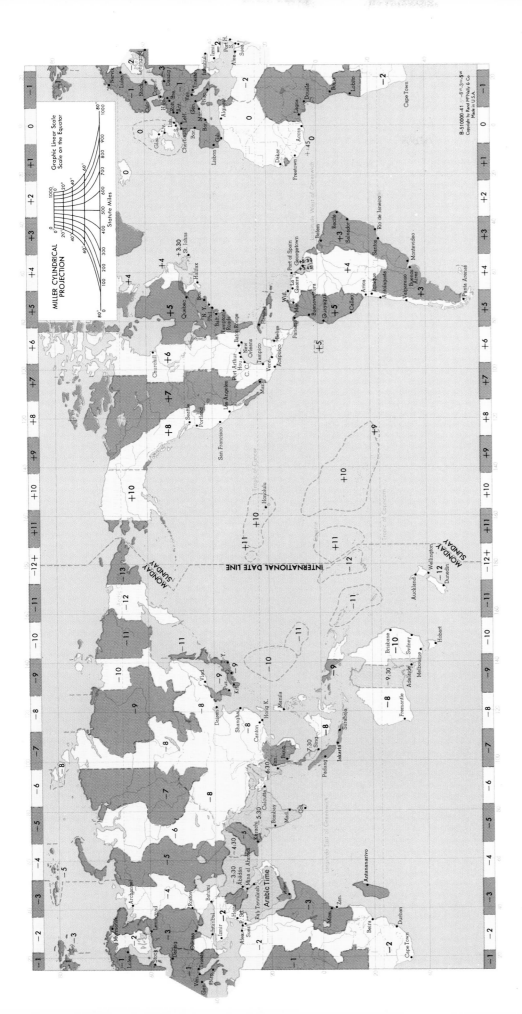

Time Zones

The surface of the earth is divided into 24 time zones. Each zone represents 15° of longitude or one hour of time. The time of the initial, or zero, zone is based on the central meridian of Greenwich and is adopted eastward and westward for a distance of 7½° of longitude. Each of the zones in turn is designated by a number representing the hours (+ or −) by which its standard time differs from

Greenwich mean time. These standard time zones are shown by bands of brown and yellow. Orange indicates areas which have a fractional deviation from standard time. The irregularities in the zones and the fractional deviations are due to political and economic factors.

(Revised to 1973. After U.S. Oceanographic Office)

MILLER CYLINDRICAL PROJECTION

Graphic Linear Scale
Scale on the Equator

Statute Miles

INTERNATIONAL DATE LINE

MONDAY SUNDAY

Arabic Time

Longitude West of Greenwich

Longitude East of Greenwich

Tropic of Cancer

Tropic of Capricorn

B-510000-41
Copyright by Rand McNally & Co.
Made in U.S.A.

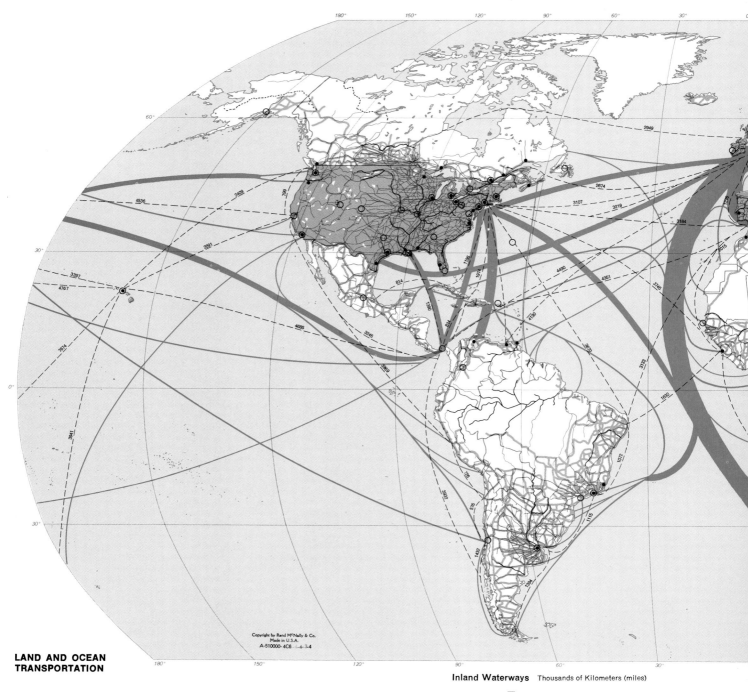

LAND AND OCEAN TRANSPORTATION

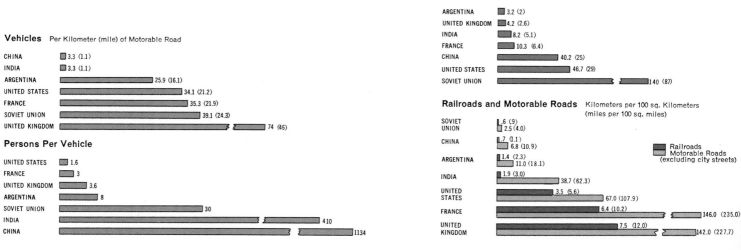

Vehicles Per Kilometer (mile) of Motorable Road

CHINA	3.3 (1.1)
INDIA	3.3 (1.1)
ARGENTINA	25.9 (16.1)
UNITED STATES	34.1 (21.2)
FRANCE	35.3 (21.9)
SOVIET UNION	39.1 (24.3)
UNITED KINGDOM	74 (46)

Persons Per Vehicle

UNITED STATES	1.6
FRANCE	3
UNITED KINGDOM	3.6
ARGENTINA	8
SOVIET UNION	30
INDIA	410
CHINA	1134

Inland Waterways Thousands of Kilometers (miles)

ARGENTINA	3.2 (2)
UNITED KINGDOM	4.2 (2.6)
INDIA	8.2 (5.1)
FRANCE	10.3 (6.4)
CHINA	40.2 (25)
UNITED STATES	46.7 (29)
SOVIET UNION	140 (87)

Railroads and Motorable Roads Kilometers per 100 sq. Kilometers (miles per 100 sq. miles)

	Railroads	Motorable Roads (excluding city streets)
SOVIET UNION	.6 (.9)	2.5 (4.0)
CHINA	.7 (1.1)	6.8 (10.9)
ARGENTINA	1.4 (2.3)	11.0 (18.1)
INDIA	1.9 (3.0)	38.7 (62.3)
UNITED STATES	3.5 (5.6)	67.0 (107.9)
FRANCE	6.4 (10.2)	146.0 (235.0)
UNITED KINGDOM	7.5 (12.0)	142.0 (227.7)

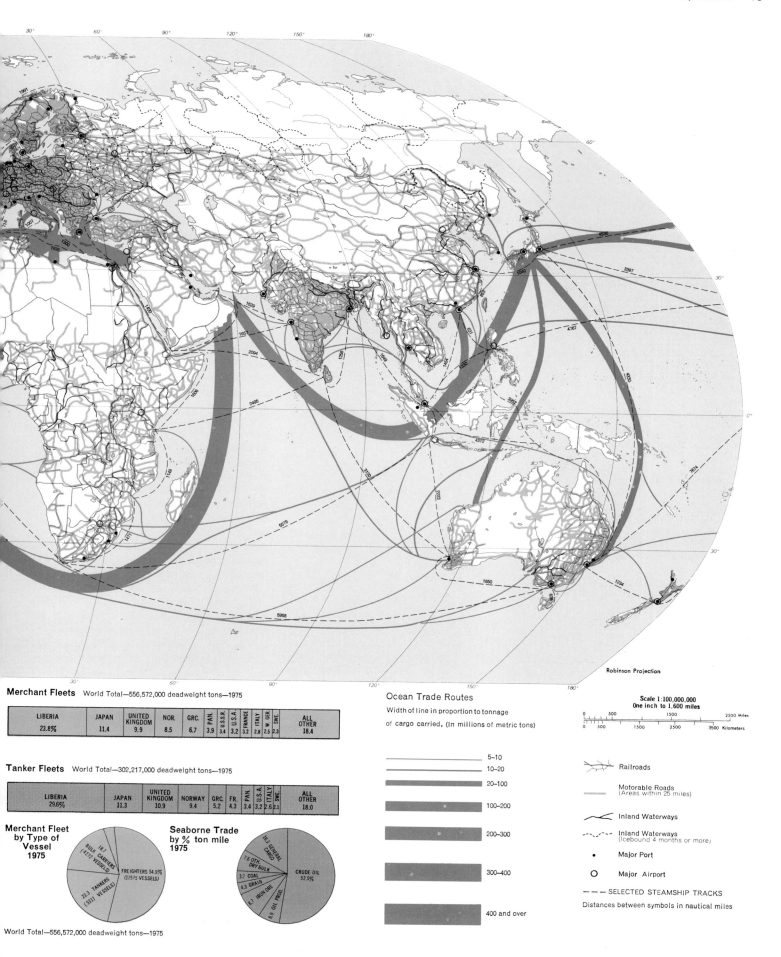

Robinson Projection

Merchant Fleets   World Total—556,572,000 deadweight tons—1975

LIBERIA 23.8%	JAPAN 11.4	UNITED KINGDOM 9.9	NOR. 8.5	GRC. 6.7	PAN. 3.9	U.S.S.R. 3.4	U.S.A. 3.2	FRANCE 3.2	ITALY 2.8	W. GER. 2.5	SWE. 2.3	ALL OTHER 18.4

Tanker Fleets   World Total—302,217,000 deadweight tons—1975

LIBERIA 29.6%	JAPAN 11.3	UNITED KINGDOM 10.9	NORWAY 9.4	GRC. 5.2	FR. 4.3	PAN. 3.4	U.S.A. 3.2	ITALY 2.6	SWE. 2.1	ALL OTHER 18.0

Merchant Fleet by Type of Vessel 1975

- BULK CARRIERS 18.7 (4272 VESSELS)
- FREIGHTERS 54.9% (17575 VESSELS)
- TANKERS 23.3 (5311 VESSELS)

World Total—556,572,000 deadweight tons—1975

Seaborne Trade by % ton mile 1975

- GENERAL CARGO 16.3
- OTH. DRY BULK 7.6
- COAL 3.7
- GRAIN 4.3
- IRON ORE 8.7
- OIL PROD. 6.9
- CRUDE OIL 52.5%

Ocean Trade Routes

Width of line in proportion to tonnage of cargo carried. (In millions of metric tons)

————	5–10
————	10–20
————	20–100
————	100–200
————	200–300
————	300–400
————	400 and over

Scale 1:100,000,000
One inch to 1,600 miles

0   500   1500   2500 Miles
0   500   1500   2500   3500 Kilometers

- ∿∿ Railroads
- ——— Motorable Roads (Areas within 25 miles)
- ⌇⌇ Inland Waterways
- – – – Inland Waterways (Icebound 4 months or more)
- • Major Port
- ○ Major Airport
- – – – SELECTED STEAMSHIP TRACKS
  Distances between symbols in nautical miles

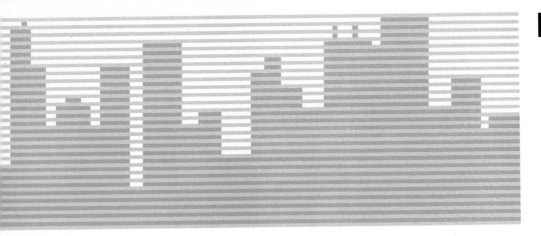

Major Cities

This section consists of 62 maps of the world's most populous metropolitan areas. In order to make comparisons easier, all the metropolitan areas are shown at the same scale, 1:300,000. An index to the places shown on the maps in this section can be found on page 232. The names of many large settlements, towns, suburbs, and neighborhoods can be located in these large-scale maps. For the symbols used on the maps, see the legend on the facing page.

The world is becoming increasingly urbanized as people move from country areas to city areas. This makes the study of metropolitan areas more important than ever before. The maps in this section enable the reader to study and compare urban extent, major industrial areas, parks, public land, wooded areas, airports, shopping centers, streets, and railroads. A special effort has been made to portray the various metropolitan areas in a manner as standard and comparable as possible.

Notable differences occur in the way cities are laid out. In most of North America, cities developed from a rectangular pattern of streets, with well-defined residential, commercial, and industrial zones. Most European cities are different and more complex. They have irregular street patterns and less well-defined land-use zones. In Asia, Africa, and South America the form tends to be even more irregular and complex, partly due to widespread dispersion of craft and trade activities. Some cities have no identifiable city centers, and some cities have both old and modern city centers.

Major City Map Legend

Inhabited Localities

The symbol represents the number of inhabitants within the locality

- •　　0—10,000
- ○　　10,000—25,000
- ⊙　　25,000—100,000
- ⊡　　100,000—250,000
- ▣　　250,000—1,000,000
- ■　　>1,000,000

The size of type indicates the relative economic and political importance of the locality

Écommoy
Trouville　　　　**St.-Denis**
Lisieux　　　　　**PARIS**

Hollywood　　Section of a City,
Westminster　Neighborhood
Northland ■
Center　　　　Major Shopping Center

 Urban Area (area of continuous industrial, commercial, and residential development)

 Major Industrial Area

Wooded Area

Political Boundaries

International (First-order political unit)

— — — —　Demarcated, Undemarcated, and Administrative

— — — —　Demarcation Line

Internal

　　　　　State, Province, etc.
　　　　　(Second-order political unit)

　　　　　County, Oblast, etc.
　　　　　(Third-order political unit)

– – – – –　Okrug, Kreis, etc.
　　　　　(Fourth-order political unit)

– – – – – –　City or Municipality
　　　　　(may appear in combination with another boundary symbol)

Capitals of Political Units

BUDAPEST　Independent Nation

Recife　State, Province, etc.

White Plains　County, Oblast, etc.

Iserlohn　Okrug, Kreis, etc.

Transportation

Road

PASSAIC EXPWY.　(I-80)　Primary

BERLINER RING　Secondary

Tertiary

Railway

CANADIAN NATIONAL　Primary

Secondary

Rapid Transit

Airport

LONDON (HEATHROW) AIRPORT

Rail or Air Terminal

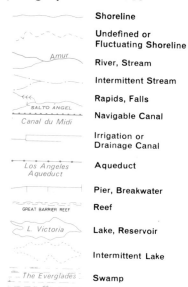

■ SÜD BAHNHOF

REICHS-BRÜCKE　Bridge

GREAT ST. BERNARD TUNNEL　Tunnel

Houston Ship Channel　Shipping Channel

Canal du Midi　Navigable Canal

TO MALMÖ　Ferry

Hydrographic Features

Shoreline

Undefined or Fluctuating Shoreline

Amur　River, Stream

Intermittent Stream

Rapids, Falls

SALTO ANGEL　Navigable Canal

Canal du Midi　Irrigation or Drainage Canal

Los Angeles Aqueduct　Aqueduct

Pier, Breakwater

GREAT BARRIER REEF　Reef

L. Victoria　Lake, Reservoir

Intermittent Lake

The Everglades　Swamp

Miscellaneous Cultural Features

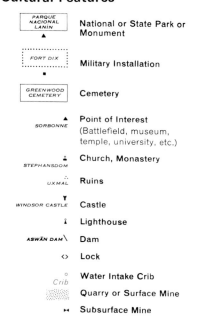

PARQUE NACIONAL LANÍN
▲　National or State Park or Monument

FORT DIX
■　Military Installation

GREENWOOD CEMETERY　Cemetery

SORBONNE ▲　Point of Interest (Battlefield, museum, temple, university, etc.)

STEPHANSDOM　Church, Monastery

UXMAL　Ruins

WINDSOR CASTLE　Castle

Lighthouse

ASWĀN DAM \　Dam

< >　Lock

Crib　Water Intake Crib

Quarry or Surface Mine

Subsurface Mine

Topographic Features

Mt. Kenya 5199　△　Elevation Above Sea Level

Elevations are given in meters

★　Rock

A N D E S
KUNLUNSHANMAI　Mountain Range, Plateau, Valley, etc.

BAFFIN ISLAND　Island

POLUOSTROV KAMČATKA
CABO DE HORNOS　Peninsula, Cape, Point, etc.

a

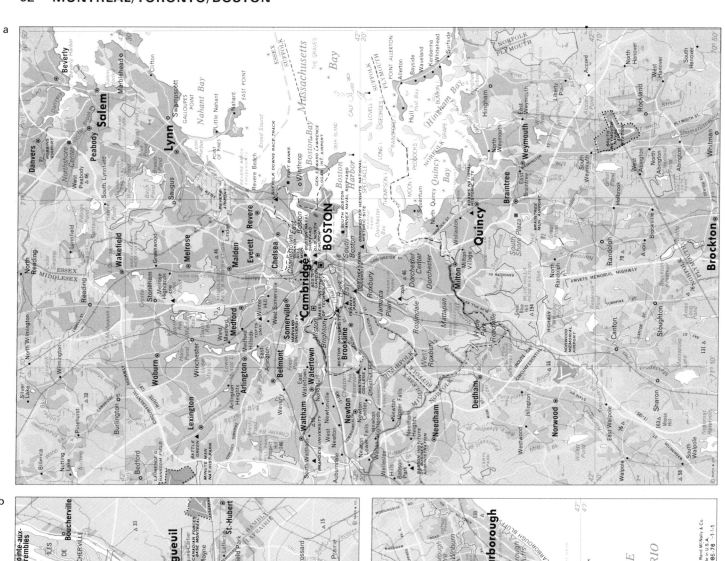

b

c

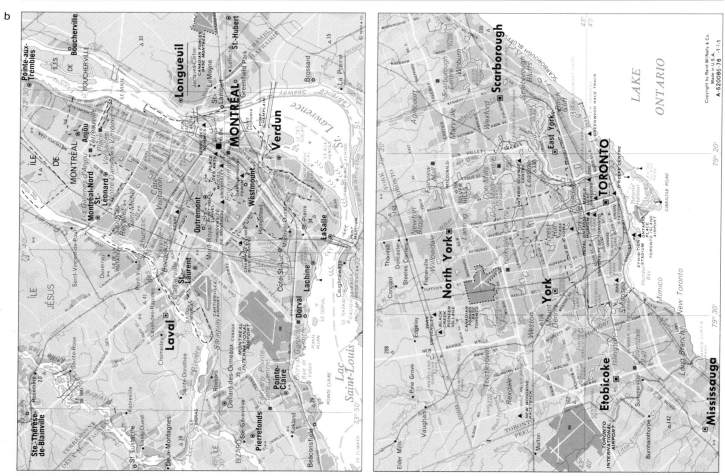

Scale 1:300,000; one inch to 4.7 miles.

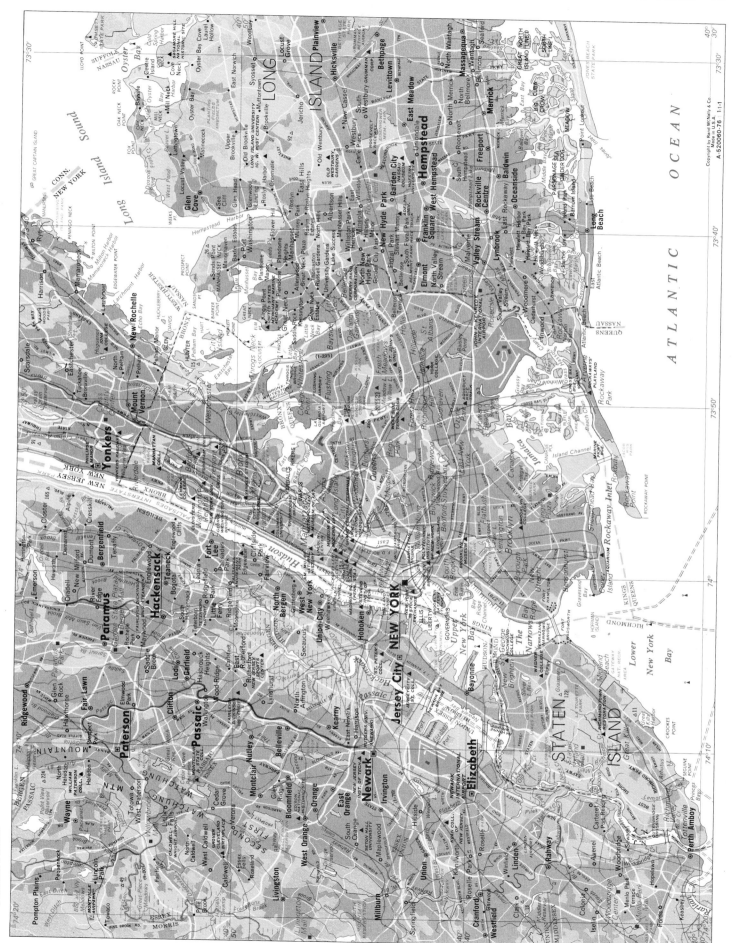

Scale 1:300,000; one inch to 4.7 miles.

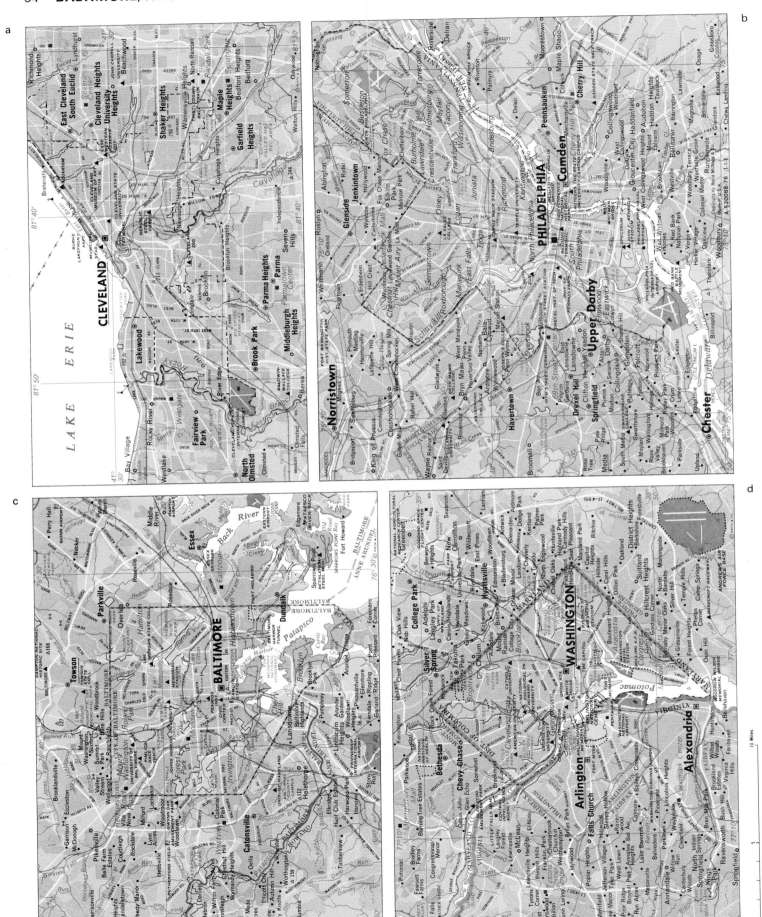

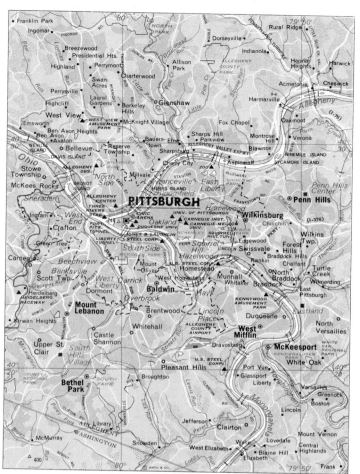

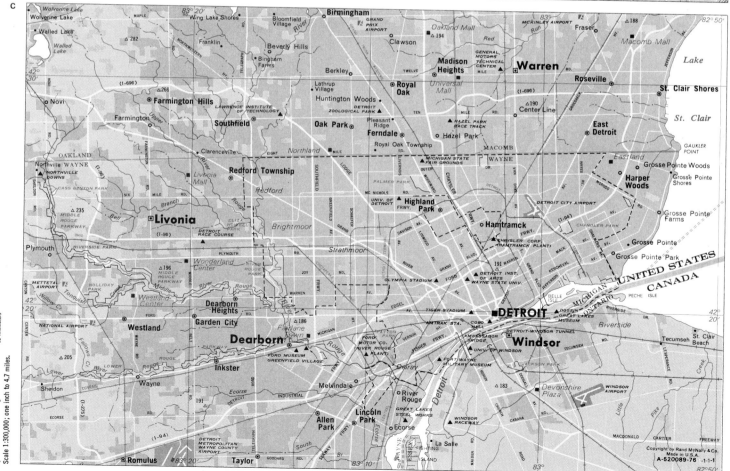

a

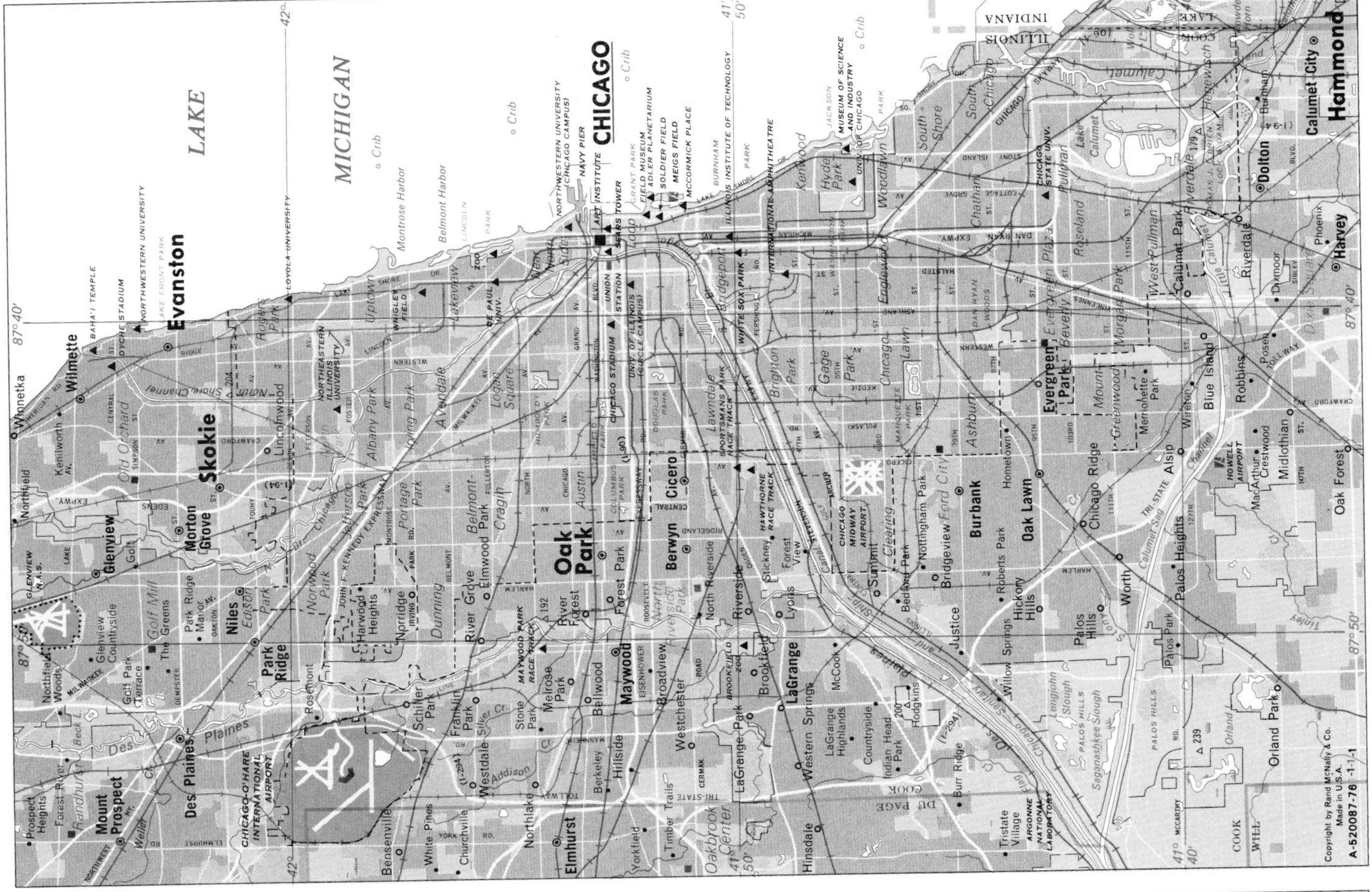

CHICAGO

LAKE MICHIGAN

Evanston
Wilmette
Winnetka
Skokie
Glenview
Morton Grove
Niles
Park Ridge
Mount Prospect
Des Plaines
Oak Park
Cicero
Berwyn
Maywood
Riverside
LaGrange
Elmhurst
Burbank
Oak Lawn
Evergreen Park
Blue Island
Harvey
Dolton
Hammond
Calumet City

CHICAGO-O'HARE INTERNATIONAL AIRPORT
CHICAGO MIDWAY AIRPORT

COOK
DU PAGE

INDIANA
ILLINOIS
COOK

Copyright by Rand McNally & Co.
Made in U.S.A.
A-520087-76-1-1-1

b

SAN FRANCISCO

San Rafael
Richmond
Berkeley
OAKLAND
Alameda
San Leandro
SAN FRANCISCO
South San Francisco
Daly City
San Bruno
Millbrae
Burlingame
Hillsborough
San Mateo
Foster City
San Carlos
Belmont
Redwood City
Pacifica

San Francisco Bay
PACIFIC OCEAN

Golden Gate
GOLDEN GATE BRIDGE
SAN FRANCISCO-OAKLAND BAY BRIDGE
SAN MATEO BRIDGE
RICHMOND-SAN RAFAEL BRIDGE

SAN FRANCISCO INTERNATIONAL AIRPORT
METROPOLITAN OAKLAND INTERNATIONAL AIRPORT

ALAMEDA
SAN MATEO
CONTRA COSTA
SAN FRANCISCO

10 Miles
10 Kilometers

Scale 1:300,000; one inch to 4.7 miles.

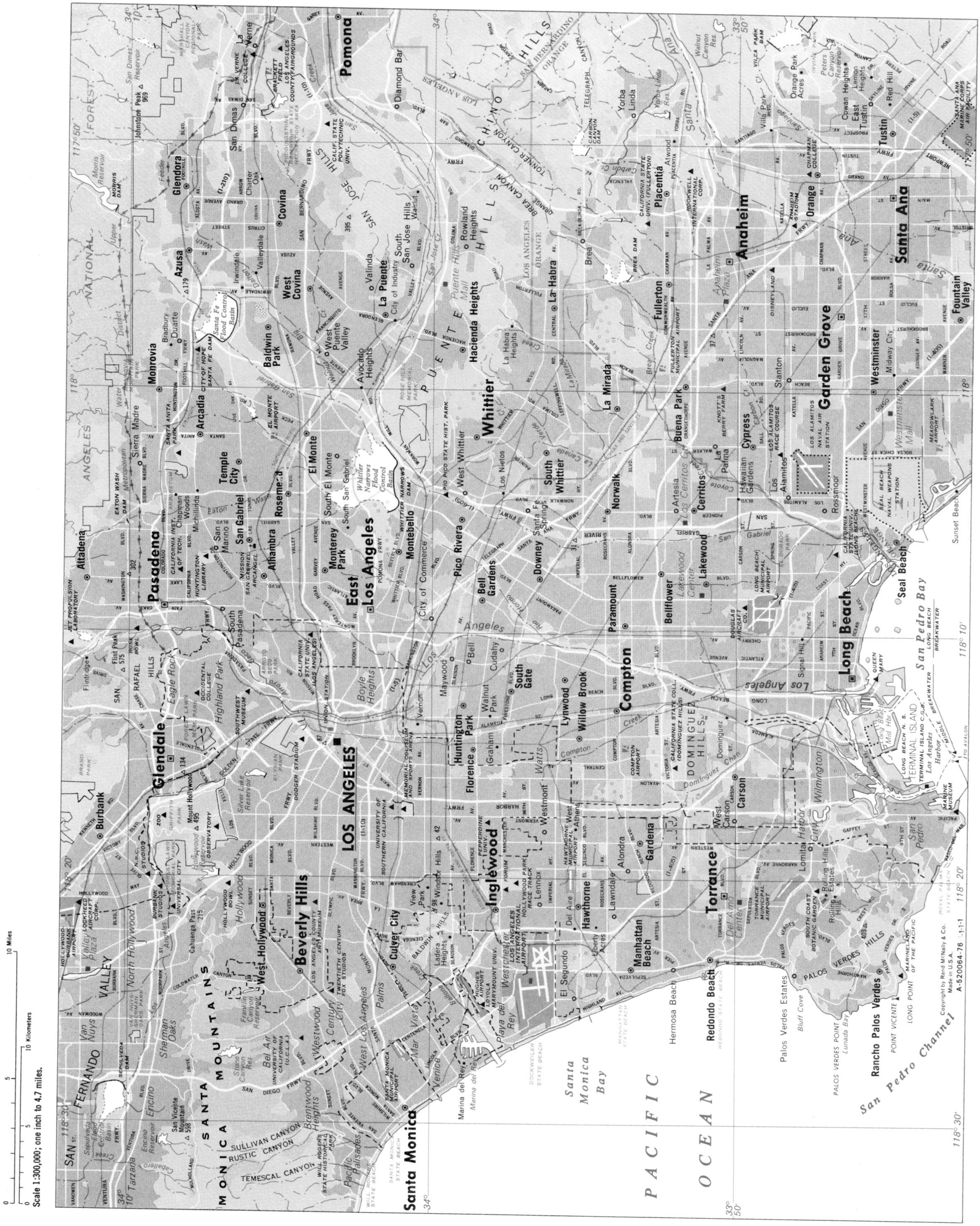

Scale 1:300,000; one inch to 4.7 miles.

10 Miles
10 Kilometers

PACIFIC OCEAN

Santa Monica
Los Angeles
Pasadena
Glendale
Burbank
Beverly Hills
West Hollywood
Inglewood
Culver City
Torrance
Compton
Long Beach
Anaheim
Santa Ana
Garden Grove
Pomona
Whittier
East Los Angeles
Fullerton
Glendora
Covina
West Covina
Azusa
Baldwin Park
Monrovia
Arcadia
Temple City
El Monte
San Gabriel
Rosemead
Alhambra
Monterey Park
Montebello
Pico Rivera
Downey
Norwalk
Cerritos
Lakewood
Bellflower
Paramount
South Gate
Huntington Park
Florence Park
Gardena
Hawthorne
Manhattan Beach
Redondo Beach
Palos Verdes
Rancho Palos Verdes
Cypress
Westminster
Fountain Valley
Buena Park
La Habra
Placentia
Orange
Brea
La Mirada
La Puente
Hacienda Heights
Rowland Heights
San Dimas
Altadena

Santa Monica Bay
San Pedro Bay
San Pedro Channel
Santa Monica Mountains
San Fernando Valley
Angeles National Forest
Puente Hills
San Jose Hills
Chino Hills

Copyright by Rand McNally & Co. Made in U.S.A.
A-520064-76 -1-1-1

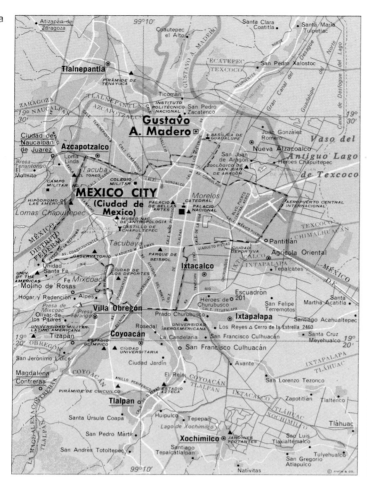

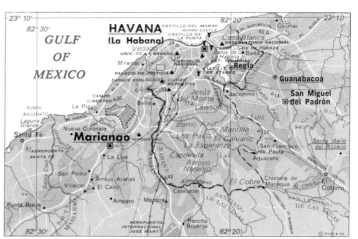

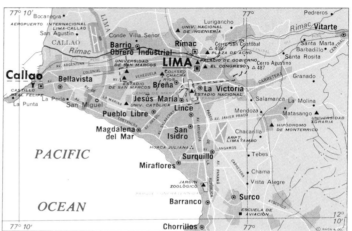

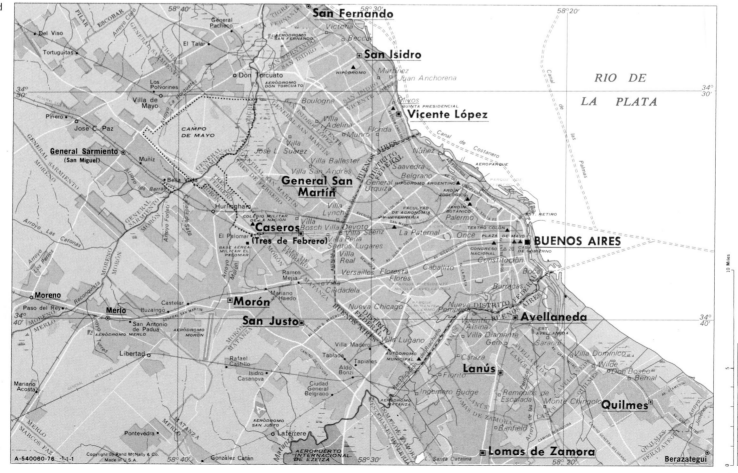

a

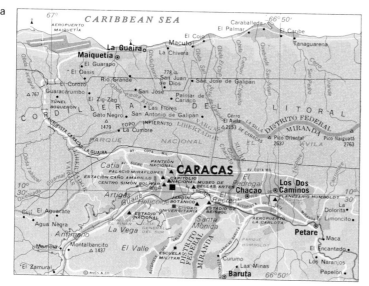

b

c

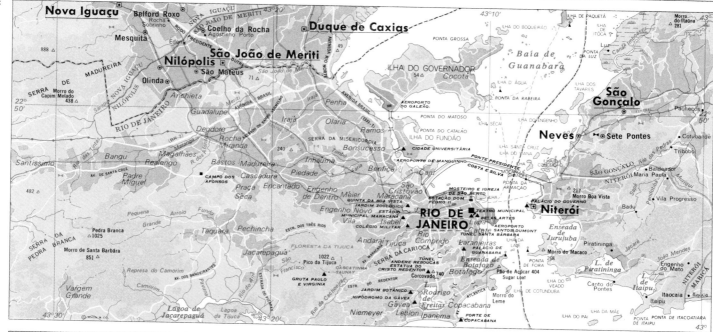

d

Scale 1:300,000; one inch to 4.7 miles.

A-550052-76 -1-1

Copyright by Rand McNally & Co. Made in U.S.A.

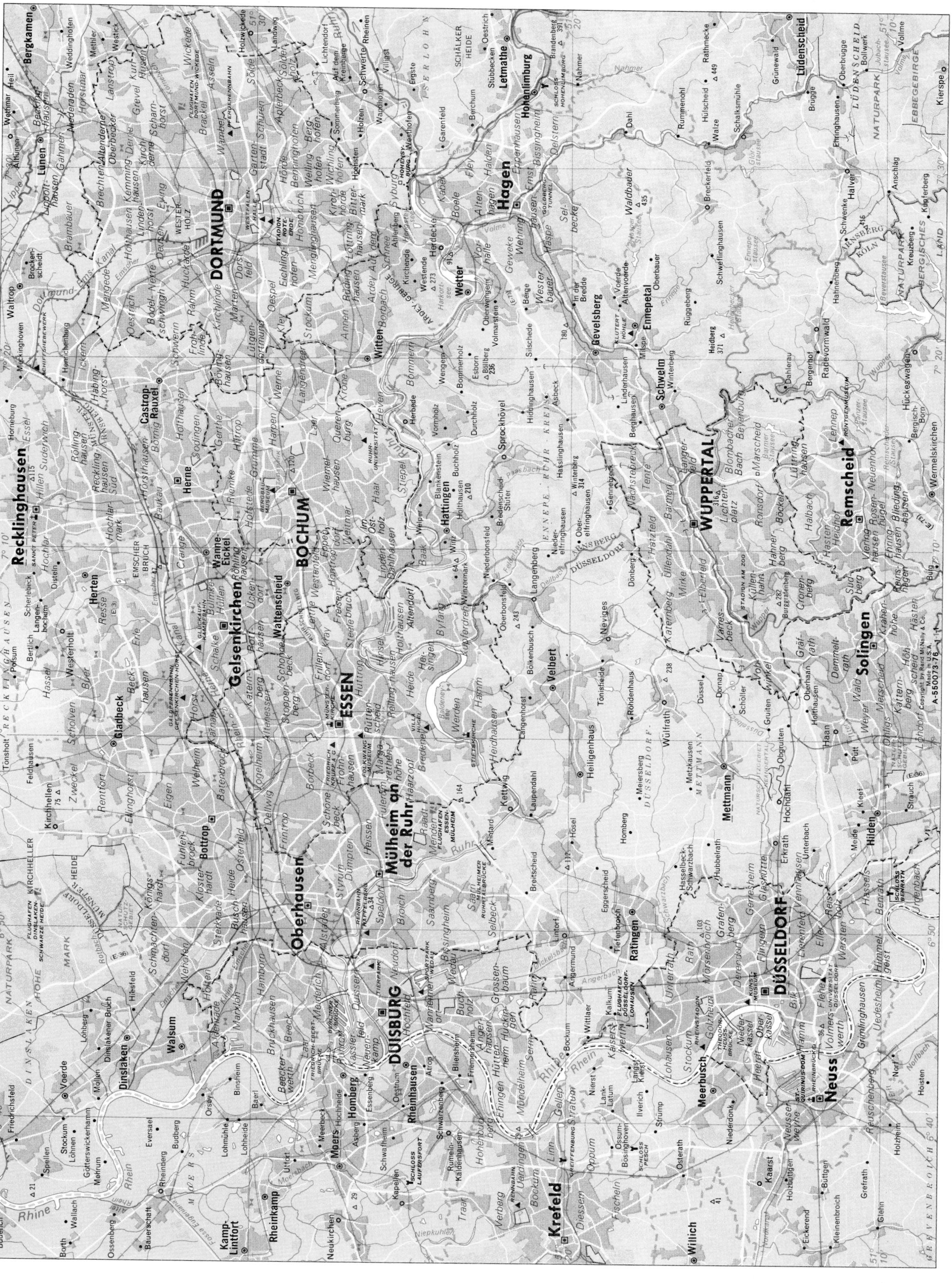

Scale 1:300,000; one inch to 4.7 miles.

10 Miles

10 Kilometers

DORTMUND

Recklinghausen

BOCHUM

Gelsenkirchen

ESSEN

Mülheim an der Ruhr

Oberhausen

DUISBURG

Hagen

Wetter

Witten

Hattingen

Wattenscheid

Wanne-Eickel

Herne

Castrop-Rauxel

Gladbeck

Bottrop

Herten

Waltrop

Lünen

Bergkamen

Letmathe

Hohenlimburg

Lüdenscheid

Gevelsberg

Schwelm

Ennepetal

WUPPERTAL

Remscheid

Solingen

DÜSSELDORF

Neuss

Krefeld

Meerbusch

Ratingen

Mettmann

Velbert

Hilden

Walsum

Dinslaken

Voerde

Moers

Rheinberg

Kamp-Lintfort

Rheinkamp

Homberg

a

b

c

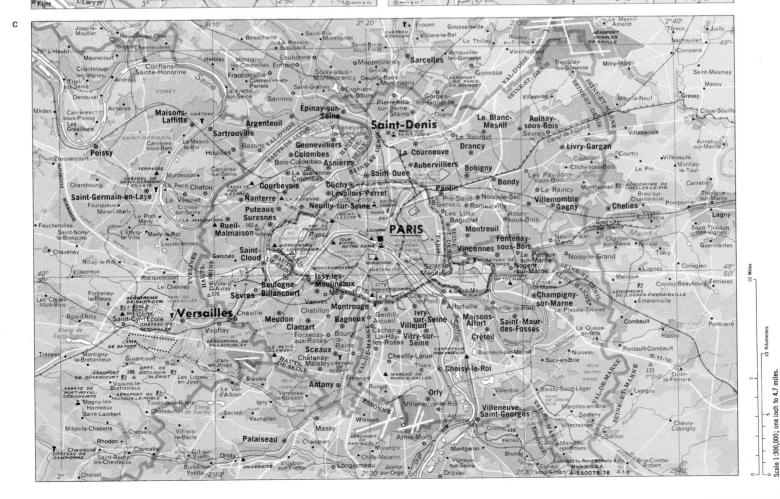

Scale 1:300,000; one inch to 4.7 miles.

a

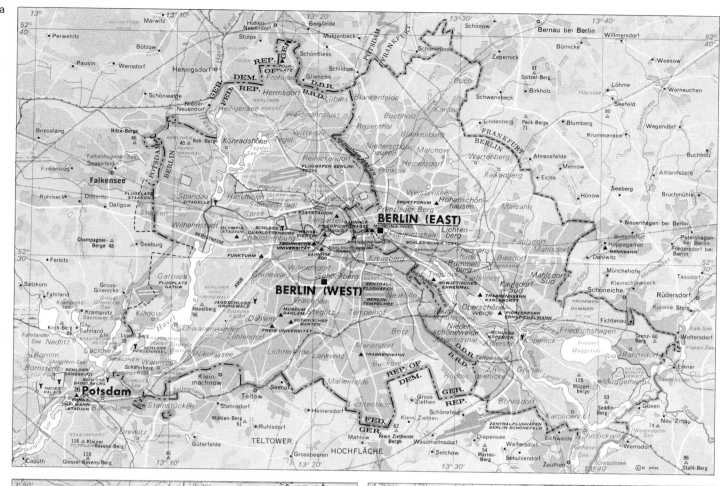

b

c

d

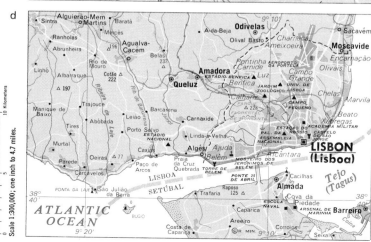

e

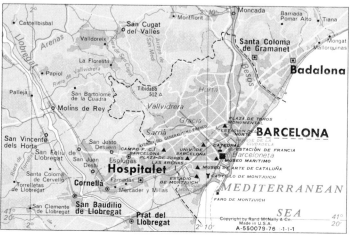

Scale 1:300,000; one inch to 4.7 miles.

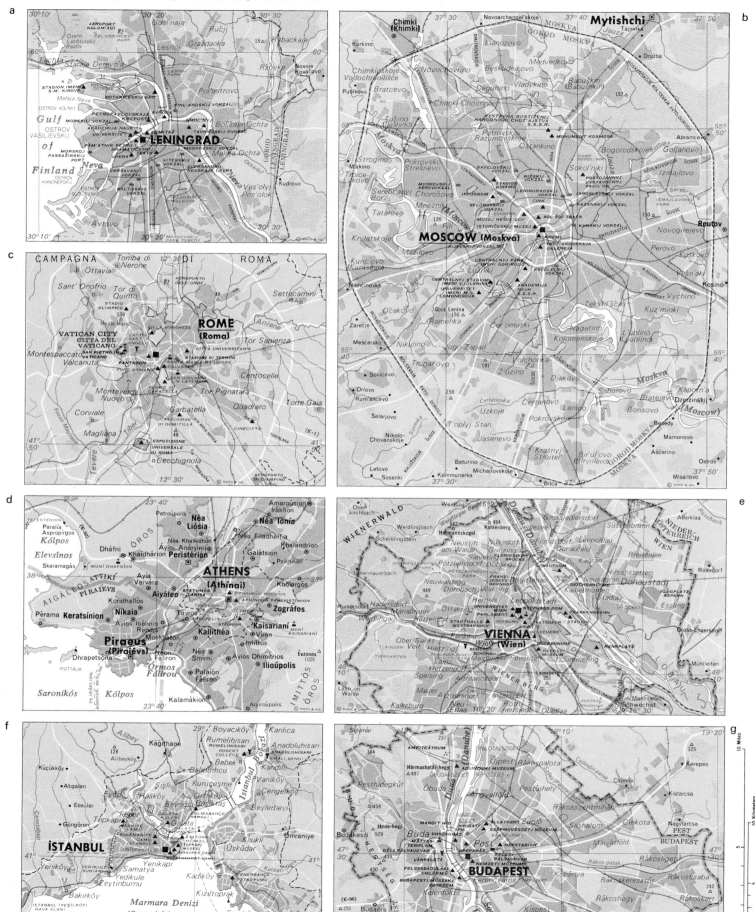

Scale 1:300,000; one inch to 4.7 miles.

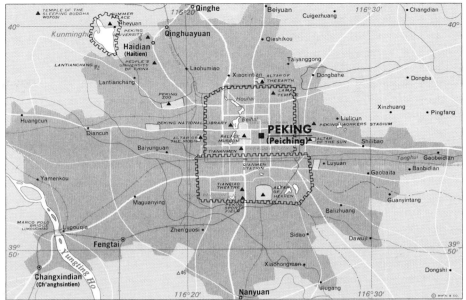

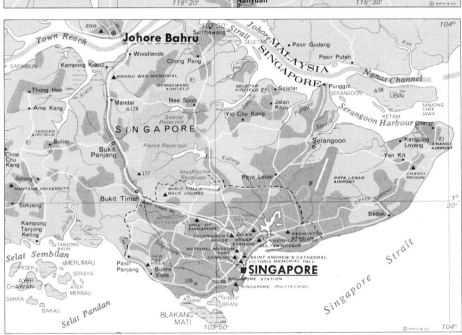

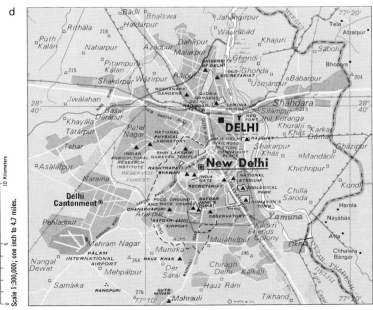

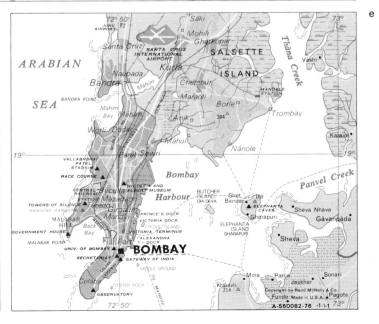

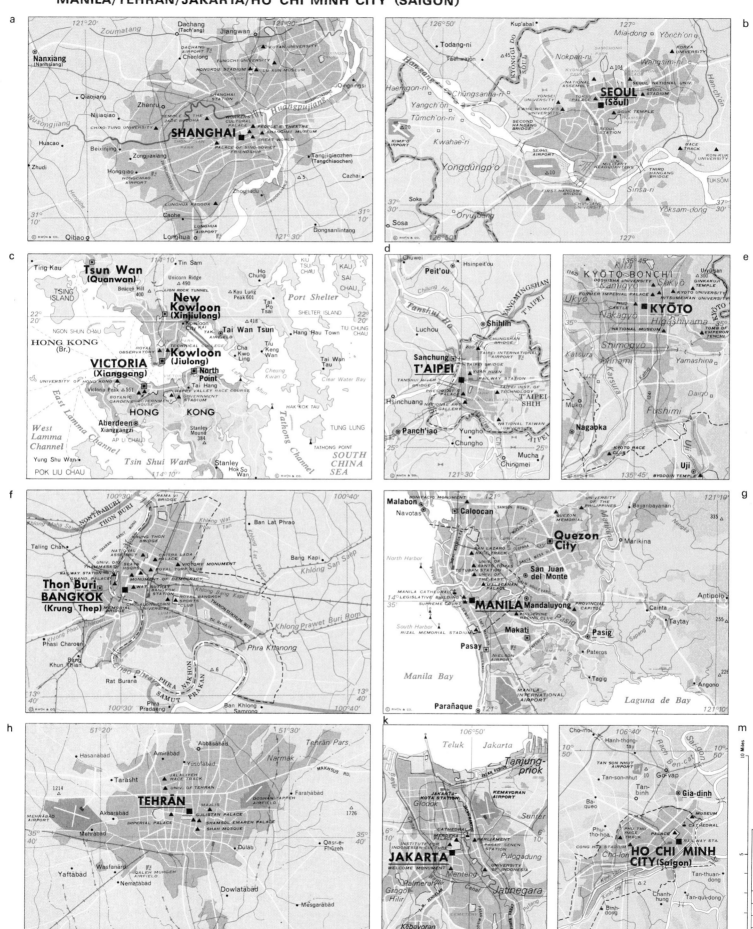

a

b

Scale 1:300,000; one inch to 4.7 miles.

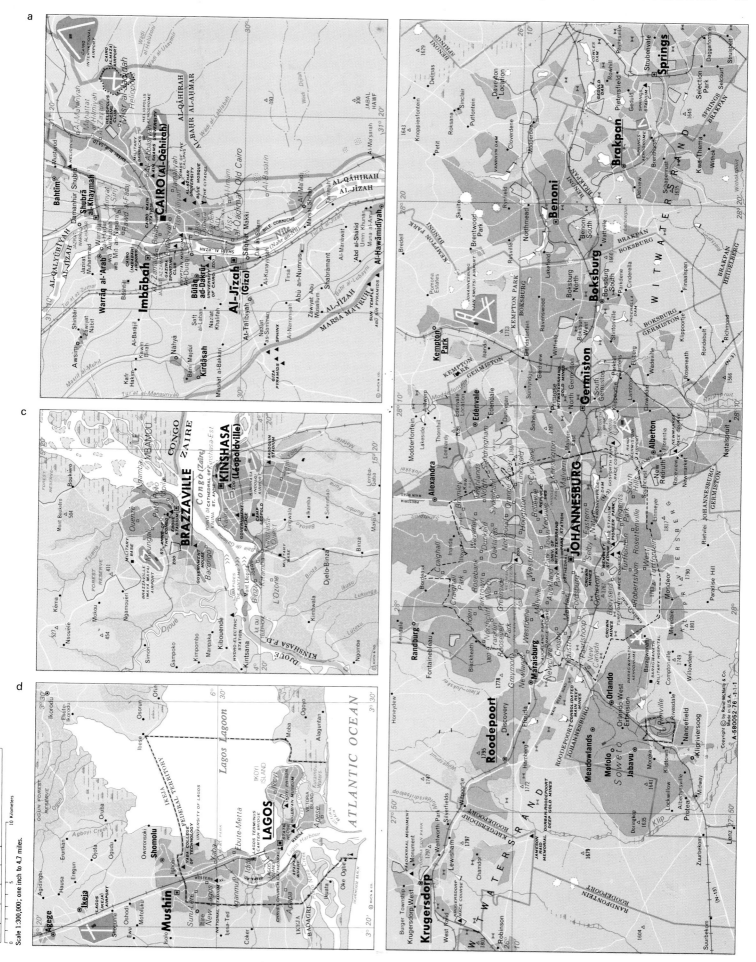

Country and Regional Maps

This section provides the reader with basic continental, regional, and country reference maps of the world's land areas. The maps are arranged by continents: North America, South America, Europe, Asia, Australia, and Africa. Each section begins with a series of basic thematic maps dealing with the environment, culture, and economy of each continent. Place names on the reference maps are listed in the unique pronouncing index, the last section of the Atlas. A complete legend on the facing page provides a key to the symbols on the reference maps in this section.

To aid the reader in making comparisons, uniform scales for comparable areas were used whenever possible. All continental maps are at the same scale, 1:40,000,000. In addition, most of the world is covered by a series of regional maps at scales of 1:16,000,000 and 1:12,000,000.

Maps at 1:10,000,000 provide even greater detail for parts of Europe, Africa, and Southeast Asia. The United States, parts of Canada, and much of Europe and the Soviet Union are mapped at 1:4,000,000. Seventy-six urbanized areas are shown at 1:1,000,000.

The reference maps use different colors (layer tints) to show general elevation above and below sea level. A legend on each map provides a key to the colors used for elevation.

The maps also provide the reader with a three-dimensional impression of the way the land looks. This terrain representation, superimposed on the layer tints, provides a realistic and readily visualized impression of the surface.

This Atlas generally uses a *local name* policy for naming cities and towns and local land and water features. However, for a few major cities the Anglicized name is preferred and the local name given in parentheses, for instance, Moscow (Moskva), Vienna (Wien), Cologne (Köln). Names in Chinese, Japanese, and other nonalphabetic languages are transliterated into the Roman alphabet. In countries where more than one official language is used, the name is in the dominant local language. The generic parts of local names for land and water features are usually self-explanatory. A complete glossary of foreign geographical terms is given on page 245.

Country and Regional Map Legend

Cultural Features

Political Boundaries

International
(Demarcated, Undemarcated, and Administrative)
(over water)

Disputed de facto

Disputed de jure

Indefinite or Undefined

Secondary, State, Provincial, etc.
(over water)

Parks, Indian Reservations

City Limits   Built-up Areas

Cities, Towns and Villages

PARIS 1,000,000 and over
(Metropolitan Area Population)

Ufa 500,000 to 1,000,000
(Metropolitan Area Population)

Győr 50,000 to 500,000

Agadir 25,000 to 50,000

Moreno 0 to 25,000

TŌKYŌ National Capitals

Boise Secondary Capitals

Note: On maps at 1:20,000,000 and smaller, and on maps at 1:1,000,000, the type size indicates the relative importance of cities, not the specific population classification shown above.

Transportation

Railroads

Railroads
On 1:1,000,000 scale maps

Railroad Ferries

Roads
Major
On 1:1,000,000 scale maps
Other

Major
On 1:4,000,000 scale maps
Other

On other scale maps

Caravan Routes

Airports

Other Cultural Features

Dams

Pipelines

Pyramids

Ruins

Land Features

Peaks, Spot Heights

Passes

Sand

Contours

Water Features

Lakes and Reservoirs

Fresh Water

Fresh Water: Intermittent

Salt Water

Salt Water: Intermittent

Other Water Features

Salt Basins, Flats

Swamps

Ice Caps and Glaciers

Rivers

Intermittent Rivers

Aqueducts and Canals

Ship Channels

Falls

Rapids

Springs

Water Depths

Fishing Banks

Sand Bars

Reefs

GREENLAND

Arctic Circle

Godthab

Labrador Sea

A R C T I C   O C E A N

North Pole

Baffin Bay

ELLESMERE ISLAND

BAFFIN ISLAND

UNGAVA PENINSULA

DEVON ISLAND

Hudson Bay

MELVILLE ISLAND

VICTORIA ISLAND

Cambridge Bay

BANKS ISLAND

Churchill

Beaufort Sea

Great Slave Lake

Peace

Edmonton

Regina

BROOKS RANGE

Calgary

Bering Strait

Fairbanks

R O C K Y   M O U N T A I N S

Yukon

Nome

ALASKA RANGE

Anchorage

Juneau

Prince Rupert

Columbia

Gulf of Alaska

Vancouver

Seattle

Bering

Portland

Sea

P A C I F I C   O C E A N

A L E U T I A N   I S L A N D S

Scale 1:24,000,000; one inch to 380 miles. Lambert Azimuthal Equal-Area Projection

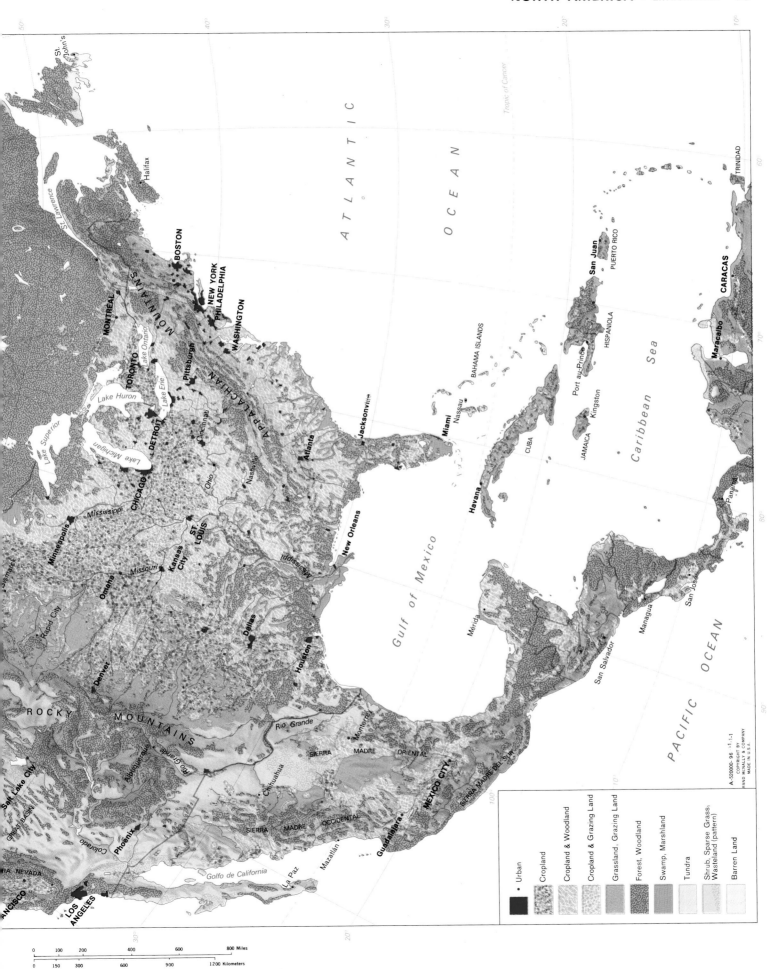

ATLANTIC

OCEAN

Tropic of Cancer

St. John's

Halifax

St. Lawrence

BOSTON

NEW YORK
PHILADELPHIA
WASHINGTON

MONTREAL

TORONTO

Pittsburgh

Lake Ontario

Lake Erie

Cincinnati

APPALACHIAN MOUNTAINS

DETROIT

Lake Huron

Lake Superior

Lake Michigan

Nashville

Atlanta

Jacksonville

CHICAGO

Ohio

Mississippi

Minneapolis

ST. LOUIS

Omaha

Kansas City

Missouri

Bismarck

Rapid City

Denver

Dallas

Houston

New Orleans

Mississippi

Miami

Nassau

BAHAMA ISLANDS

Havana

CUBA

JAMAICA

Kingston

HISPANIOLA

Port au-Prince

San Juan

PUERTO RICO

Caribbean Sea

CARACAS

Maracaibo

TRINIDAD

Merida

Gulf of Mexico

Monterrey

Rio Grande

SIERRA MADRE ORIENTAL

Chihuahua

SIERRA MADRE OCCIDENTAL

Albuquerque

Rio Grande

ROCKY MOUNTAINS

GREAT BASIN

SIERRA NEVADA

Salt Lake City

Phoenix

Colorado

MEXICO CITY

SIERRA MADRE DEL SUR

Guadalajara

Mazatlan

La Paz

Golfo de California

Managua

San Salvador

San Jose

Panama

PACIFIC OCEAN

SAN FRANCISCO

LOS ANGELES

A-520000-96 -1-1-1
COPYRIGHT BY
RAND McNALLY & COMPANY
MADE IN U.S.A.

• Urban
Cropland
Cropland & Woodland
Cropland & Grazing Land
Grassland, Grazing Land
Forest, Woodland
Swamp, Marshland
Tundra
Shrub, Sparse Grass, Wasteland (pattern)
Barren Land

0   100   200   400   600   800 Miles

0   150   300   600   900   1200 Kilometers

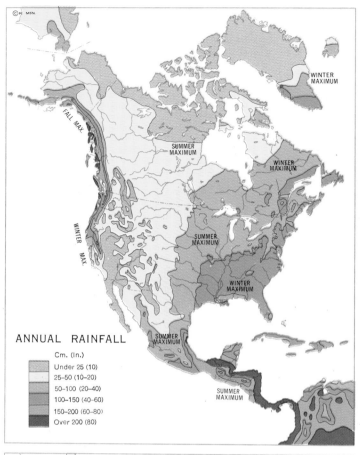

ANNUAL RAINFALL

Cm. (In.)

- Under 25 (10)
- 25–50 (10–20)
- 50–100 (20–40)
- 100–150 (40–60)
- 150–200 (60–80)
- Over 200 (80)

FALL MAX.

WINTER MAX.

WINTER MAX.

SUMMER MAXIMUM

SUMMER MAXIMUM

WINTER MAXIMUM

WINTER MAXIMUM

SUMMER MAXIMUM

SUMMER MAXIMUM

SUMMER MAXIMUM

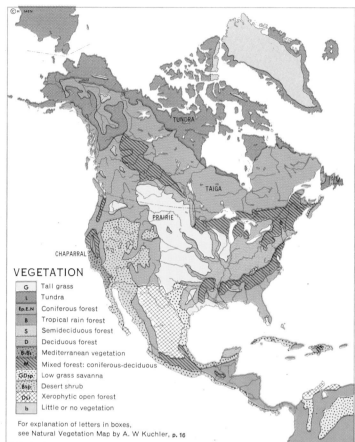

VEGETATION

G	Tall grass
L	Tundra
Ep.E.N	Coniferous forest
B	Tropical rain forest
S	Semideciduous forest
D	Deciduous forest
B-Bs	Mediterranean vegetation
M	Mixed forest: coniferous-deciduous
GDsp	Low grass savanna
Bsp	Desert shrub
Dxi	Xerophytic open forest
b	Little or no vegetation

For explanation of letters in boxes,
see Natural Vegetation Map by A. W Kuchler, p. 16

TUNDRA

TAIGA

PRAIRIE

CHAPARRAL

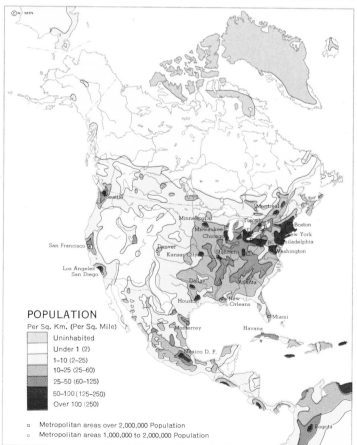

POPULATION

Per Sq. Km. (Per Sq. Mile)

- Uninhabited
- Under 1 (2)
- 1–10 (2–25)
- 10–25 (25–60)
- 25–50 (60–125)
- 50–100 (125–250)
- Over 100 (250)

□ Metropolitan areas over 2,000,000 Population
○ Metropolitan areas 1,000,000 to 2,000,000 Population

Seattle

Montreal

Minneapolis

Toronto

Milwaukee

Chicago

Boston

New York

San Francisco

Denver

St. Louis

Philadelphia

Washington

Kansas City

Los Angeles
San Diego

Dallas

Atlanta

Houston

New Orleans

Monterrey

Miami

Havana

Mexico D. F.

Bogota

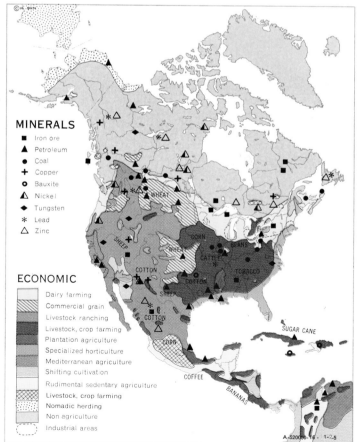

MINERALS

- ■ Iron ore
- ▲ Petroleum
- ● Coal
- + Copper
- ○ Bauxite
- ▲ Nickel
- ◆ Tungsten
- ＊ Lead
- △ Zinc

ECONOMIC

- Dairy farming
- Commercial grain
- Livestock ranching
- Livestock, crop farming
- Plantation agriculture
- Specialized horticulture
- Mediterranean agriculture
- Shifting cultivation
- Rudimental sedentary agriculture
- Livestock, crop farming
- Nomadic herding
- Non agriculture
- Industrial areas

WHEAT

WHEAT

SHEEP

CORN

BEANS

COTTON

CATTLE

COTTON

TOBACCO

SHEEP

COTTON

CORN

COFFEE

SUGAR CANE

BANANAS

A-520000-16 - 1-2-5

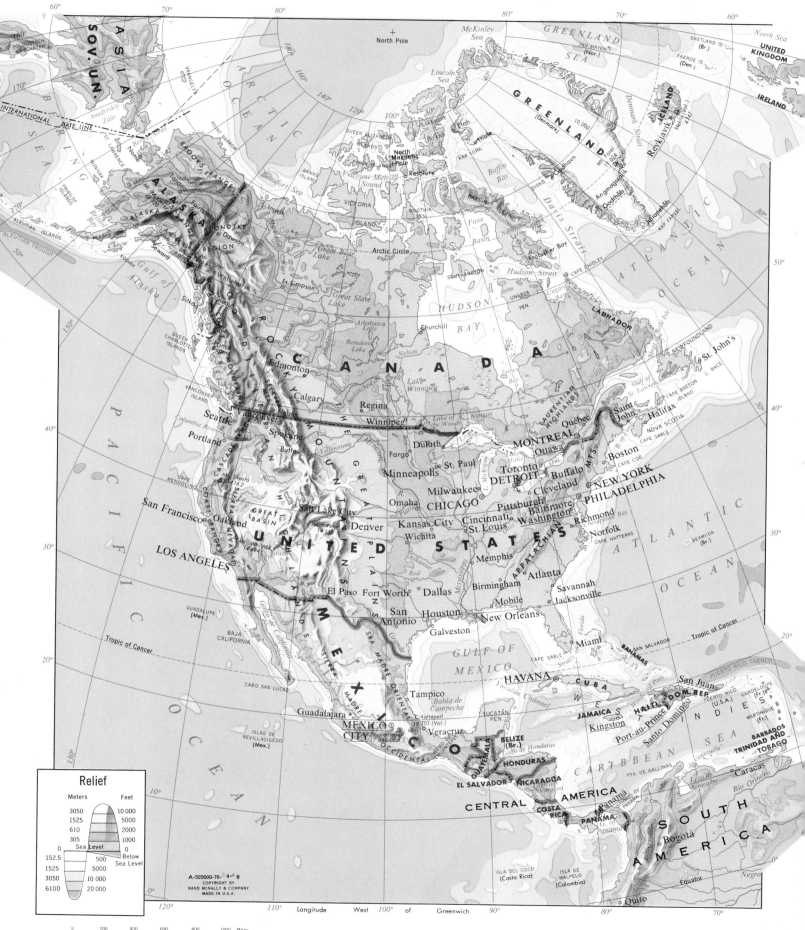

ASIA
SOV. UN.

GREENLAND
SEA

UNITED
KINGDOM

IRELAND

ICELAND

GREENLAND
(Denmark)

ARCTIC OCEAN

ALASKA

North Pole

North
Magnetic
Pole

Arctic Circle

HUDSON
BAY

C A N A D A

LABRADOR

ATLANTIC
OCEAN

Edmonton

Calgary

Vancouver

Seattle

Spokane

Portland

Winnipeg

Regina

Duluth

Fargo

Minneapolis

St. Paul

Milwaukee

CHICAGO

Omaha

MONTREAL

Ottawa

Toronto

DETROIT

Cleveland

Buffalo

Boston

NEW YORK

PHILADELPHIA

Québec

Saint
John

Halifax

San Francisco

Oakland

LOS ANGELES

Salt Lake City

Denver

Kansas City

St. Louis

Cincinnati

Pittsburgh

Baltimore

Washington

Richmond

Norfolk

Wichita

Memphis

UNITED   STATES

GREAT   BASIN

Dallas

Fort Worth

El Paso

San
Antonio

Houston

Galveston

Birmingham

Atlanta

Savannah

Jacksonville

Mobile

New Orleans

Miami

GULF OF
MEXICO

Tropic of Cancer

M E X I C O

Guadalajara

MEXICO
CITY

Veracruz

Tampico

HAVANA

CUBA

BAHAMAS

San Juan

JAMAICA

Kingston

HAITI

DOM. REP.

Port-au-Prince

Santo Domingo

PUERTO RICO
(U.S.A.)

W E S T   I N D I E S

CARIBBEAN
SEA

GUATEMALA

BELIZE
(Br.)

HONDURAS

EL SALVADOR

NICARAGUA

COSTA
RICA

PANAMA

CENTRAL   AMERICA

Caracas

Bogotá

SOUTH
AMERICA

Quito

Equator

PACIFIC
OCEAN

Relief

Meters		Feet
3050		10 000
1525		5000
610		2000
305		1000
0	Sea Level	0
152.5		500
1525		5000
3050		10 000
6100		20 000

Below
Sea Level

A-520000-76- 4-4 B
COPYRIGHT BY
RAND McNALLY & COMPANY
MADE IN U.S.A.

0   200   400   600   800   1000   Miles
0   400   800   1200   1600   Kilometers

Scale 1:40 000 000; one inch to 630 miles. Lambert's Azimuthal Equal Area Projection
Elevations and depressions are given in feet

Longitude   West   of   Greenwich

PACIFIC

OCEAN

Vancouver

Seattle

Spokane

Portland

CASCADE RANGE

Columbia

Medford

Boise

Reno

GREAT BASIN

Great Salt Lake

Salt Lake City

SIERRA NEVADA

Fresno

Las Vegas

SAN FRANCISCO

LOS ANGELES

San Diego

Colorado

Phoenix

PACIFIC

OCEAN

Gulf of California

Hermosillo

SIERRA MADRE OCCIDENTAL

Chihuahua

Torreon

ROCKY MOUNTAINS

Calgary

Regina

Billings

Rapid City

Casper

Denver

Albuquerque

Amarillo

El Paso

Odessa

Rio Grande

San Antonio

SIERRA MADRE ORIENTAL

Rio Grande

Monterrey

Lake Winnipeg

Winnip

Bismarck

Missouri

Omaha

Wichita

Oklahoma City

Red

Dalla

ROCKY MOUNTAINS

50°

45°

40°

35°

30°

25°

125°

120°

115°

110°

A-520500-96 -1-1-1
COPYRIGHT BY
RAND MCNALLY & COMPANY
MADE IN U.S.A.

Urban

Cropland

Cropland & Woodland

Cropland & Grazing Land

Grassland, Grazing Land

Forest, Woodland

Swamp, Marshland

Shrub, Sparse Grass; Wasteland (pattern)

Barren Land

Scale 1:12,000,000; one inch to 190 miles. Polyconic Projection

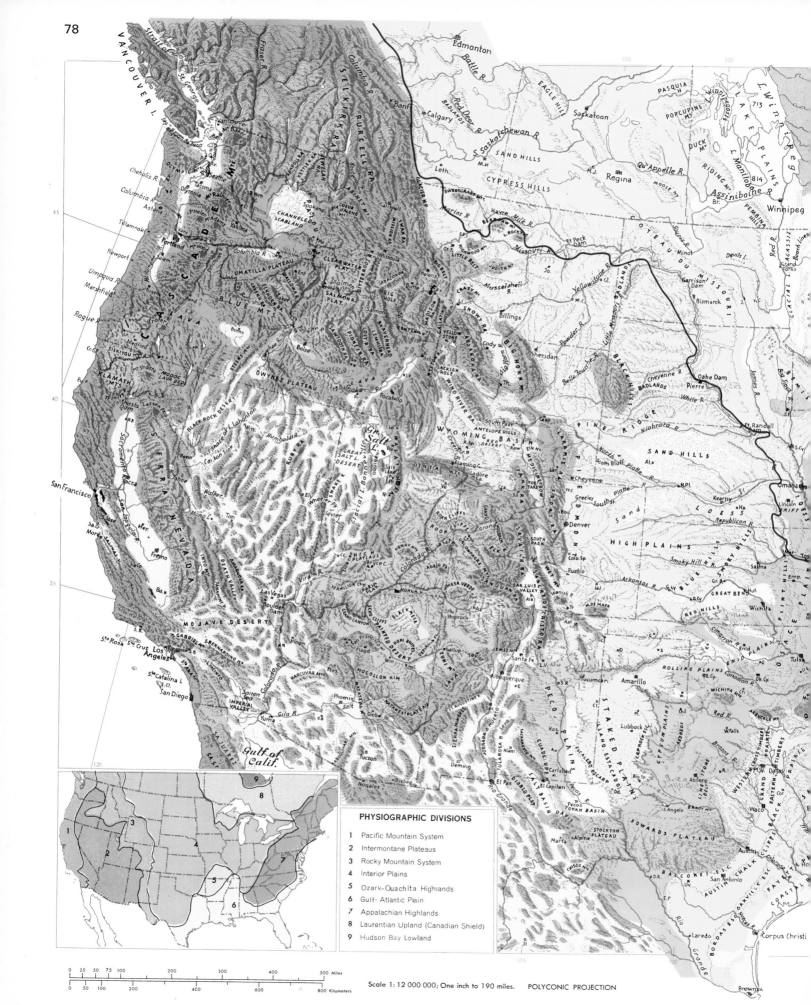

PHYSIOGRAPHIC DIVISIONS

1   Pacific Mountain System
2   Intermontane Plateaus
3   Rocky Mountain System
4   Interior Plains
5   Ozark-Ouachita Highlands
6   Gulf- Atlantic Plain
7   Appalachian Highlands
8   Laurentian Upland (Canadian Shield)
9   Hudson Bay Lowland

0 25 50 75 100   200   300   400   500 Miles
0   50   100   200   400   600   800 Kilometers

Scale 1: 12 000 000; One inch to 190 miles.   POLYCONIC PROJECTION

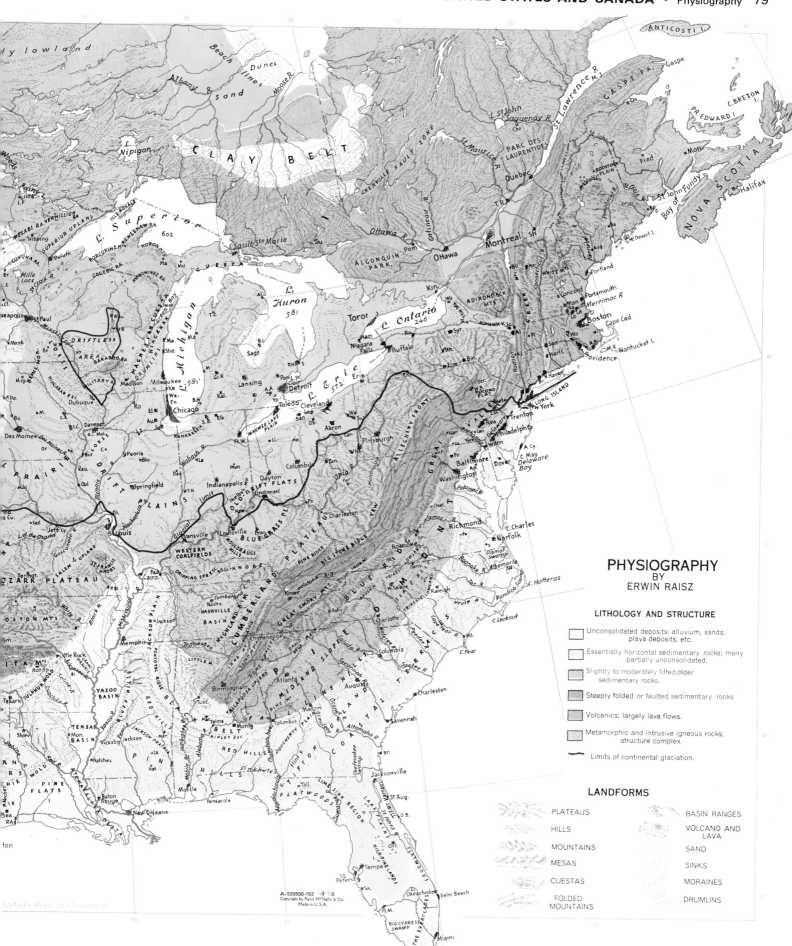

PHYSIOGRAPHY
BY
ERWIN RAISZ

LITHOLOGY AND STRUCTURE

Unconsolidated deposits: alluvium, sands, playa deposits, etc.

Essentially horizontal sedimentary rocks; many partially unconsolidated.

Slightly to moderately tilted, older sedimentary rocks.

Steeply folded or faulted, sedimentary rocks

Volcanics; largely lava flows.

Metamorphic and intrusive igneous rocks; structure complex.

Limits of continental glaciation.

LANDFORMS

PLATEAUS	BASIN RANGES
HILLS	VOLCANO AND LAVA
MOUNTAINS	SAND
MESAS	SINKS
CUESTAS	MORAINES
FOLDED MOUNTAINS	DRUMLINS

A-520500-762 -3- -5
Copyright by Rand McNally & Co.
Made in U.S.A.

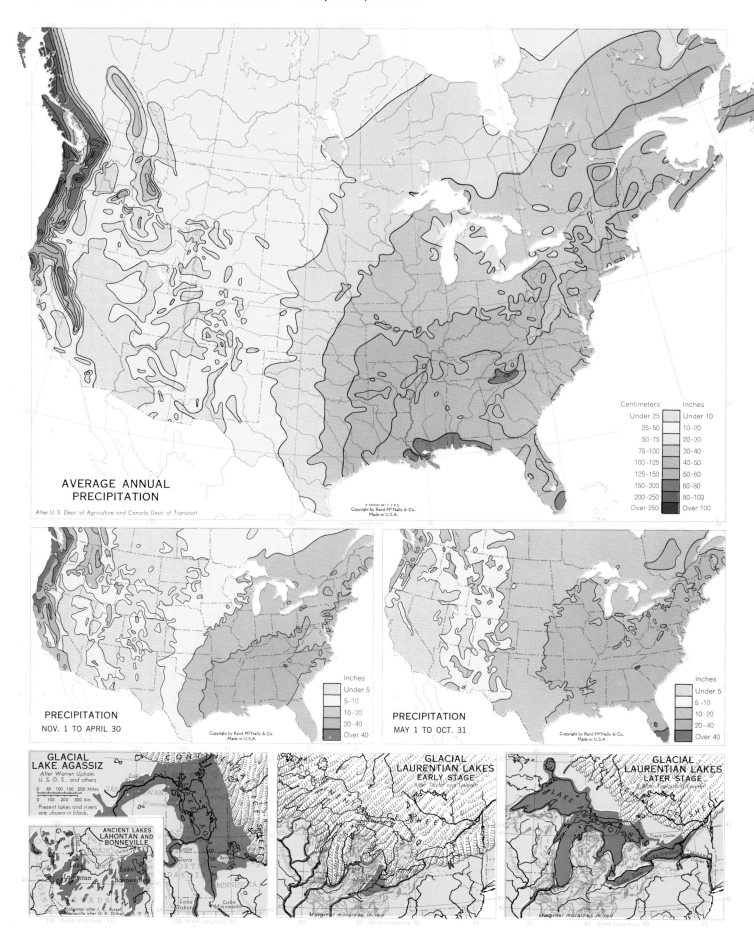

AVERAGE ANNUAL PRECIPITATION

After U.S. Dept. of Agriculture and Canada Dept. of Transport

A-520500-96i 1. 2·2·3
Copyright by Rand McNally & Co.
Made in U.S.A.

Centimeters	Inches
Under 25	Under 10
25-50	10-20
50-75	20-30
75-100	30-40
100-125	40-50
125-150	50-60
150-200	60-80
200-250	80-100
Over 250	Over 100

PRECIPITATION

NOV. 1 TO APRIL 30

Copyright by Rand McNally & Co.
Made in U.S.A.

Inches
Under 5
5-10
10-20
20-40
Over 40

PRECIPITATION

MAY 1 TO OCT. 31

Copyright by Rand McNally & Co.
Made in U.S.A.

Inches
Under 5
5-10
10-20
20-40
Over 40

GLACIAL LAKE AGASSIZ

*After Warren Upham,
U.S.G.S. and others*

0 50 100 150 200 Miles
0 100 200 300 Km.

*Present lakes and rivers
are shown in black.*

ANCIENT LAKES LAHONTAN AND BONNEVILLE

*Lahontan after I. C. Russell
Bonneville after G. K. Gilbert, U.S.G.S.*

GLACIAL LAURENTIAN LAKES EARLY STAGE

After Taylor and Leverett

Precipital moraines in red

GLACIAL LAURENTIAN LAKES LATER STAGE

After Taylor and Leverett

Marginal moraines in red

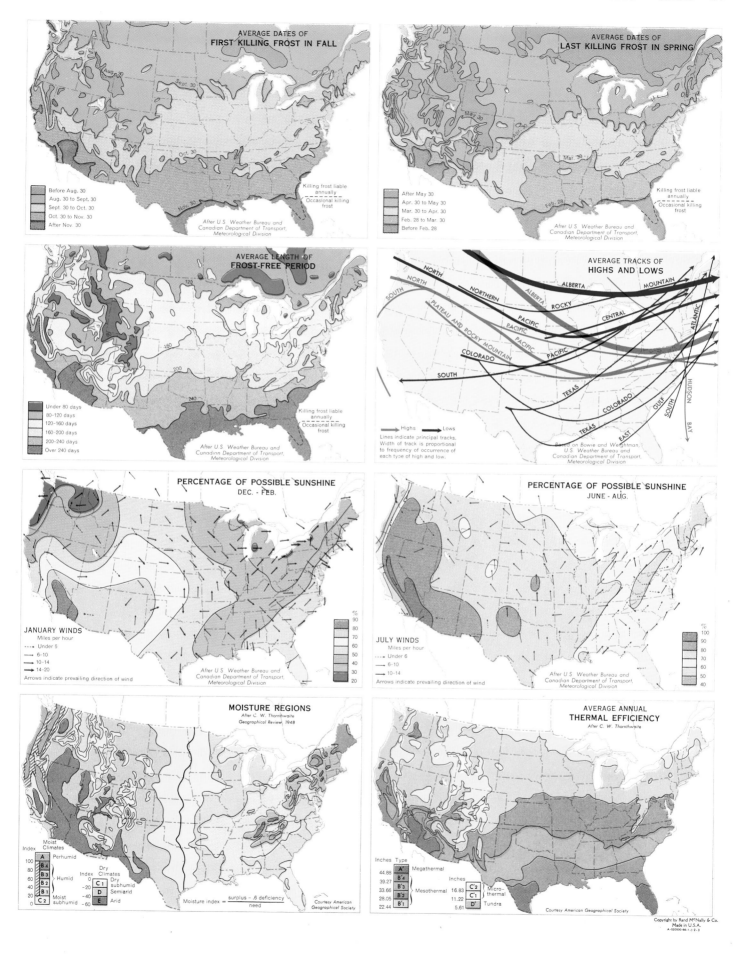

AVERAGE DATES OF
FIRST KILLING FROST IN FALL

Before Aug. 30
Aug. 30 to Sept. 30
Sept. 30 to Oct. 30
Oct. 30 to Nov. 30
After Nov. 30

Killing frost liable annually
Occasional killing frost

After U.S. Weather Bureau and Canadian Department of Transport, Meteorological Division

AVERAGE DATES OF
LAST KILLING FROST IN SPRING

After May 30
Apr. 30 to May 30
Mar. 30 to Apr. 30
Feb. 28 to Mar. 30
Before Feb. 28

Killing frost liable annually
Occasional killing frost

After U.S. Weather Bureau and Canadian Department of Transport, Meteorological Division

AVERAGE LENGTH OF
FROST-FREE PERIOD

Under 80 days
80–120 days
120–160 days
160–200 days
200–240 days
Over 240 days

Killing frost liable annually
Occasional killing frost

After U.S. Weather Bureau and Canadian Department of Transport, Meteorological Division

AVERAGE TRACKS OF
HIGHS AND LOWS

NORTH
NORTH
SOUTH
NORTHERN
PLATEAU AND ROCKY MOUNTAIN
PACIFIC
PACIFIC
PACIFIC
PACIFIC
ALBERTA
ROCKY
MOUNTAIN
CENTRAL
ATLANTIC
COLORADO
SOUTH
TEXAS
COLORADO
GULF
SOUTH
HUDSON BAY
TEXAS
EAST

→ Highs   ← Lows
Lines indicate principal tracks. Width of track is proportional to frequency of occurrence of each type of high and low.

Based on Bowie and Weightman, U.S. Weather Bureau and Canadian Department of Transport, Meteorological Division

PERCENTAGE OF POSSIBLE SUNSHINE
DEC. - FEB.

JANUARY WINDS
Miles per hour
---- Under 5
→ 6–10
→ 10–14
→ 14–20
Arrows indicate prevailing direction of wind

%
90
80
70
60
50
40
30
20

After U.S. Weather Bureau and Canadian Department of Transport, Meteorological Division

PERCENTAGE OF POSSIBLE SUNSHINE
JUNE - AUG.

JULY WINDS
Miles per hour
---- Under 6
→ 6–10
→ 10–14
Arrows indicate prevailing direction of wind

%
100
90
80
70
60
50
40

After U.S. Weather Bureau and Canadian Department of Transport, Meteorological Division

MOISTURE REGIONS
*After C. W. Thornthwaite
Geographical Review, 1948*

Index	Moist Climates		Index	Dry Climates
100	A	Perhumid	0	
80	B4		-20	C1 Dry subhumid
60	B3	Humid	-40	D Semiarid
40	B2		-60	E Arid
20	B1			
0	C2	Moist subhumid		

Moisture index = surplus − .6 deficiency / need

Courtesy American Geographical Society

AVERAGE ANNUAL
THERMAL EFFICIENCY
After C. W. Thornthwaite

Inches	Type	
44.88	A'	Megathermal
39.27	B'4	
33.66	B'3	Mesothermal
28.05	B'2	
22.44	B'1	

Inches		
16.83	C'2	Microthermal
11.22	C'1	
5.61	D'	Tundra

Courtesy American Geographical Society

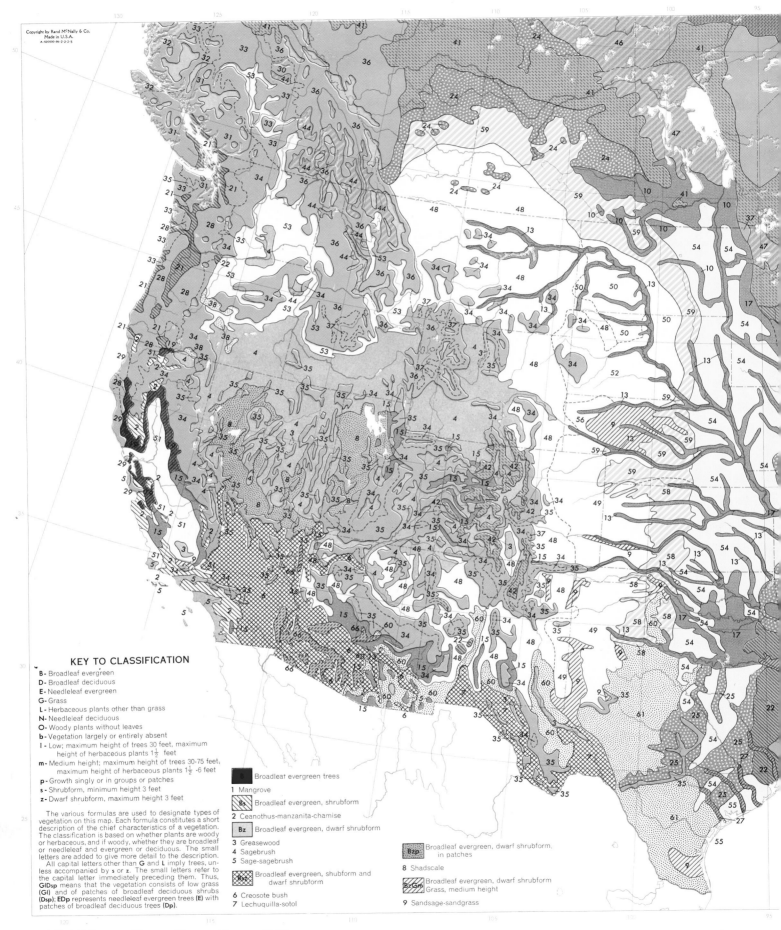

Copyright by Rand McNally & Co.
Made in U.S.A.
A-520500-86-2-2-2-5

KEY TO CLASSIFICATION

B - Broadleaf evergreen
D - Broadleaf deciduous
E - Needleleaf evergreen
G - Grass
L - Herbaceous plants other than grass
N - Needleleaf deciduous
O - Woody plants without leaves
b - Vegetation largely or entirely absent
l - Low; maximum height of trees 30 feet, maximum
       height of herbaceous plants $1\frac{1}{2}$ feet
m - Medium height; maximum height of trees 30-75 feet,
       maximum height of herbaceous plants $1\frac{1}{2}$ -6 feet
p - Growth singly or in groups or in patches
s - Shrubform, minimum height 3 feet
z - Dwarf shrubform, maximum height 3 feet

The various formulas are used to designate types of
vegetation on this map. Each formula constitutes a short
description of the chief characteristics of a vegetation.
The classification is based on whether plants are woody
or herbaceous, and if woody, whether they are broadleaf
or needleleaf and evergreen or deciduous. The small
letters are added to give more detail to the description.
All capital letters other than **G** and **L** imply trees, unless accompanied by **s** or **z**. The small letters refer to
the capital letter immediately preceding them. Thus,
GlDsp means that the vegetation consists of low grass
(**Gl**) and of patches of broadleaf deciduous shrubs
(**Dsp**); **EDp** represents needleleaf evergreen trees (**E**) with
patches of broadleaf deciduous trees (**Dp**).

8 Broadleaf evergreen trees
1 Mangrove

Bs Broadleaf evergreen, shrubform
2 Ceanothus-manzanita-chamise

Bz Broadleaf evergreen, dwarf shrubform
3 Greasewood
4 Sagebrush
5 Sage-sagebrush

Bsz Broadleaf evergreen, shubform and
       dwarf shrubform
6 Creosote bush
7 Lechuquilla-sotol

Bzp Broadleaf evergreen, dwarf shrubform,
       in patches
8 Shadscale

Bz:Gm Broadleaf evergreen, dwarf shrubform
        Grass, medium height
9 Sandsage-sandgrass

0 25 50 75 100   200   300   400   500 Miles

0 50 100   200   400   600   800 Kilometers

Scale 1:14 000 000;   One inch to 220

NATURAL VEGETATION

BY A. W. KÜCHLER

Based on "A Physiognomic Classification of Vegetation"
Annals of the Assoc. of American Geographers, Vol. 39, September, 1949

BERT CONFORMAL CONIC PROJECTION

D Broadleaf deciduous trees

10 Aspen-oak
11 Beech-maple
12 Beech-tulip tree-maple-basswood
13 Cottonwood-willow
14 Maple-basswood
15 Oak
16 Oak-ash-maple
17 Oak-hickory
18 Oak-tulip tree

DB Broadleaf deciduous trees
Broadleaf evergreen trees

19 Oak-madrone

DE Broadleaf deciduous trees
Needleleaf evergreen trees

20 Maple-yellow birch-hemlock-pine
21 Oak-Douglas fir
22 Oak-pine
23 Maple-beech-hemlock

D / Gmp Broadleaf deciduous trees
Grass, medium height, in patches

24 Aspen-needle grass-wheat grass
25 Oak-hickory-bluestem

DN Broadleaf deciduous trees
Needleleaf deciduous trees

26 Bay trees-bald cypress
27 Tupelo-gum-bald cypress

E Needleleaf evergreen trees

28 Douglas fir
29 Douglas fir-redwood
30 Hemlock-arbor vitae
31 Hemlock-arbor vitae-Douglas fir
32 Hemlock-arbor vitae-fir
33 Hemlock-spruce
34 Pine
35 Pine-juniper
36 Pine-spruce
37 Spruce-fir

Esp Needleleaf evergreen, shrubform,
in patches

38 Juniper

EDp Needleleaf evergreen trees
Broadleaf deciduous trees, in patches

39 Douglas fir-pine-aspen
40 Pine-spruce-birch
41 Spruce-aspen
42 Spruce-fir-aspen
43 Spruce-poplar-birch

EN Needleleaf evergreen trees
Needleleaf deciduous trees

44 Hemlock-arbor vitae-Douglas fir-larch
45 Pine-bald cypress
46 Pine-spruce-larch
47 Spruce-larch

Gl Grass, low

48 Grama grass
49 Grama grass-buffalo grass
50 Grama grass-needle grass
51 Needle grass-blue grass
52 Wheat grass
53 Wheat grass-blue grass

Gm Grass, medium height

54 Bluestem
55 Broom grass-water grass
56 Marsh grass
57 Saw grass

Gml Grass, medium and low height

58 Bluestem-bunch grass
59 Needle grass-wheat grass

Gl / Dsp Grass, low
Broadleaf deciduous, shrubform, in patches

60 Bunch grass-oak

Gm / Dsp Grass, medium height
Broadleaf deciduous, shrubform, in patches

61 Mesquite grass-mesquite

L Herbaceous plants other than grass

62 Lichens, etc.

LEp Herbaceous plants other than grass
Needleleaf evergreen trees, in patches

63 Lichens-spruce

LEp / Np Herbaceous plants other than grass
Needleleaf evergreen trees, in patches
Needleleaf deciduous trees, in patches

64 Lichens-spruce-larch

N Needleleaf deciduous trees

65 Bald cypress

Op Woody plants without leaves, in patches

66 Palo verde-cacti-ocotillo

b Vegetation largely or entirely absent

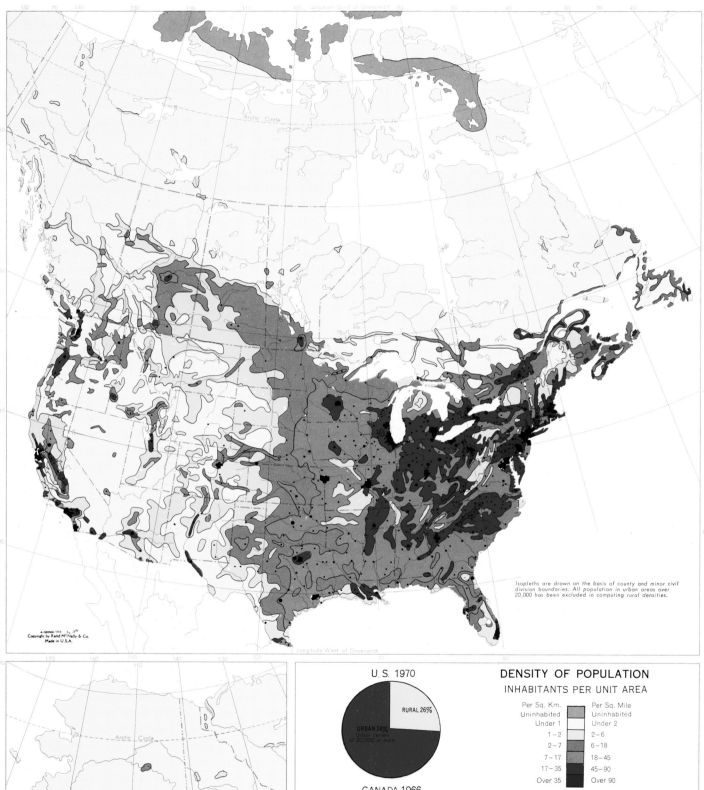

Isopleths are drawn on the basis of county and minor civil division boundaries. All population in urban areas over 20,000 has been excluded in computing rural densities.

A-520500-1A6   3,   3W
Copyright by Rand M⁰Nally & Co.
Made in U.S.A.

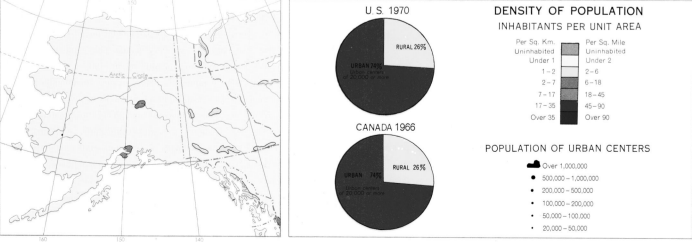

U.S. 1970

RURAL 26%

URBAN 74%
Urban centers
of 20,000 or more

CANADA 1966

URBAN 74%
Urban centers
20,000 or more

RURAL 26%

DENSITY OF POPULATION
INHABITANTS PER UNIT AREA

Per Sq. Km.	Per Sq. Mile
Uninhabited	Uninhabited
Under 1	Under 2
1–2	2–6
2–7	6–18
7–17	18–45
17–35	45–90
Over 35	Over 90

POPULATION OF URBAN CENTERS

Over 1,000,000
500,000 – 1,000,000
200,000 – 500,000
100,000 – 200,000
50,000 – 100,000
20,000 – 50,000

Scale 1:32 000 000; One inch to 500 miles.   LAMBERT CONFORMAL CONIC PROJECTION

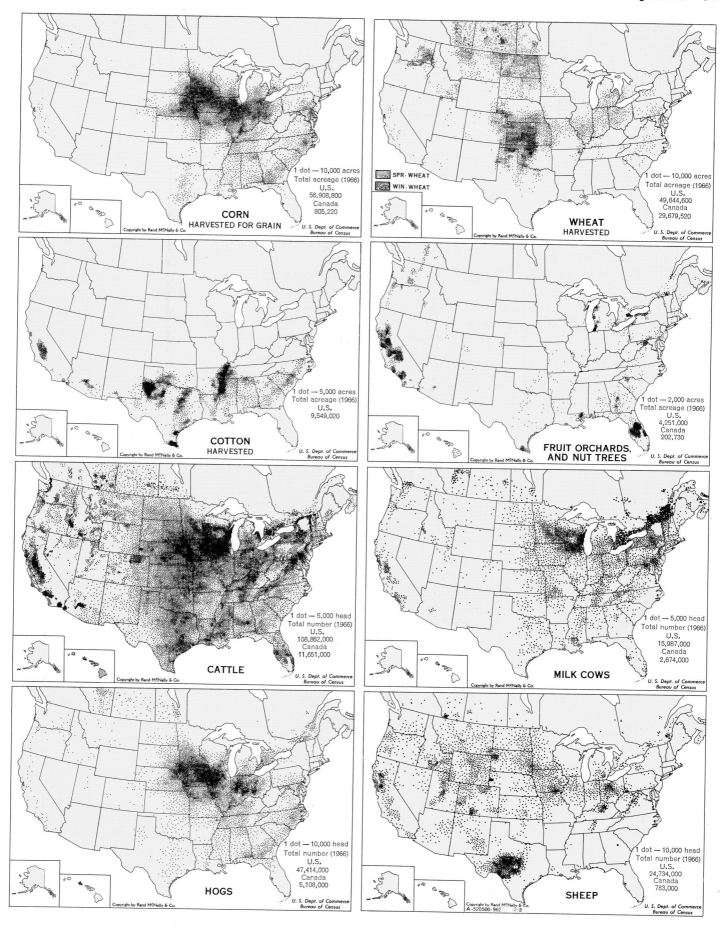

1 dot — 10,000 acres
Total acreage (1966)
U.S.
56,908,800
Canada
805,220

CORN
HARVESTED FOR GRAIN

Copyright by Rand McNally & Co.

U. S. Dept. of Commerce
Bureau of Census

SPR. WHEAT
WIN. WHEAT

1 dot — 10,000 acres
Total acreage (1966)
U.S.
49,844,800
Canada
29,679,520

WHEAT
HARVESTED

Copyright by Rand McNally & Co.

U. S. Dept. of Commerce
Bureau of Census

1 dot — 5,000 acres
Total acreage (1966)
U.S.
9,549,020

COTTON
HARVESTED

Copyright by Rand McNally & Co.

U. S. Dept. of Commerce
Bureau of Census

1 dot — 2,000 acres
Total acreage (1966)
U.S.
4,251,000
Canada
202,730

**FRUIT ORCHARDS,
AND NUT TREES**

Copyright by Rand McNally & Co.

U. S. Dept. of Commerce
Bureau of Census

1 dot — 5,000 head
Total number (1966)
U.S.
108,862,000
Canada
11,651,000

CATTLE

Copyright by Rand McNally & Co.

U. S. Dept. of Commerce
Bureau of Census

1 dot — 5,000 head
Total number (1966)
U.S.
15,987,000
Canada
2,674,000

MILK COWS

Copyright by Rand McNally & Co.

U. S. Dept. of Commerce
Bureau of Census

1 dot — 10,000 head
Total number (1966)
U.S.
47,414,000
Canada
5,108,000

HOGS

Copyright by Rand McNally & Co.

U. S. Dept. of Commerce
Bureau of Census

1 dot — 10,000 head
Total number (1966)
U.S.
24,734,000
Canada
783,000

SHEEP

Copyright by Rand McNally & Co.
A-520500-962 -2-3

U. S. Dept. of Commerce
Bureau of Census

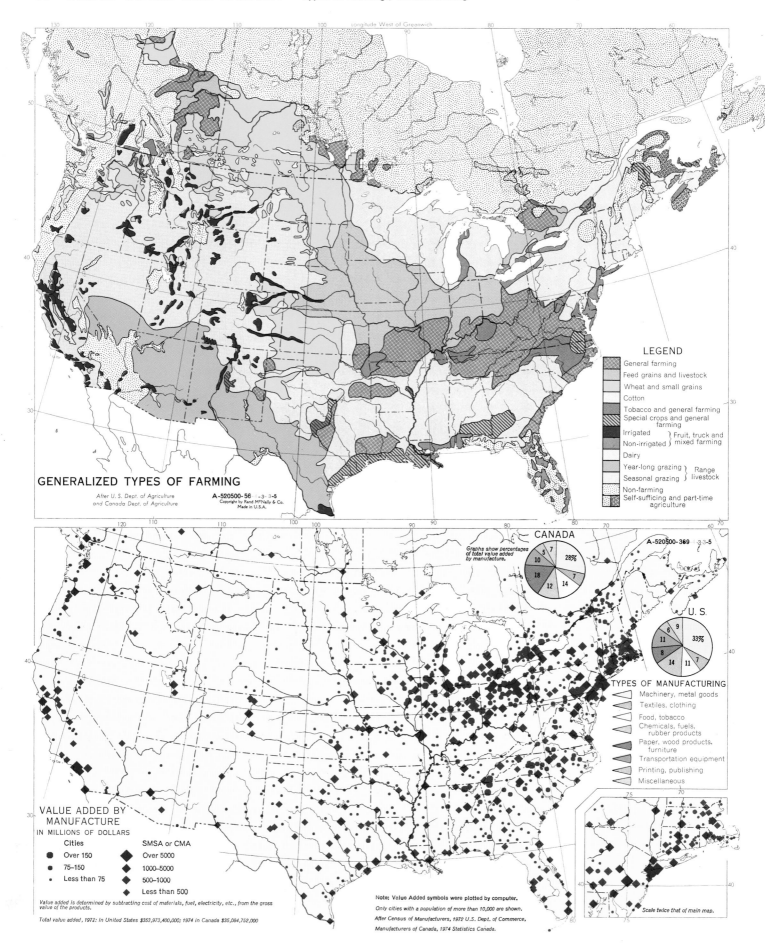

GENERALIZED TYPES OF FARMING

After U. S. Dept. of Agriculture
and Canada Dept. of Agriculture

A-520500-56   -3-3-5
Copyright by Rand M⁰Nally & Co.
Made in U.S.A.

LEGEND

General farming
Feed grains and livestock
Wheat and small grains
Cotton
Tobacco and general farming
Special crops and general farming
Irrigated } Fruit, truck and
Non-irrigated } mixed farming
Dairy
Year-long grazing } Range
Seasonal grazing } livestock
Non-farming
Self-sufficing and part-time agriculture

CANADA

Graphs show percentages
of total value added
by manufacture.

5 7
10   28%
18   7
12 14

A-520500-369 -3-3-5

U.S.

6 9
11   33%
8   7
14 11

TYPES OF MANUFACTURING

Machinery, metal goods
Textiles, clothing
Food, tobacco
Chemicals, fuels, rubber products
Paper, wood products, furniture
Transportation equipment
Printing, publishing
Miscellaneous

VALUE ADDED BY MANUFACTURE

IN MILLIONS OF DOLLARS

Cities	SMSA or CMA
Over 150	Over 5000
75–150	1000–5000
Less than 75	500–1000
Less than 500

Value added is determined by subtracting cost of materials, fuel, electricity, etc., from the gross value of the products.

Total value added, 1972: In United States $353,973,400,000; 1974 in Canada $35,084,752,000

Note: Value Added symbols were plotted by computer.

Only cities with a population of more than 10,000 are shown.

After Census of Manufactures, 1972 U.S. Dept. of Commerce,

Manufacturers of Canada, 1974 Statistics Canada.

Scale twice that of main map.

Scale 1: 28 000 000; One inch to 440 miles.   LAMBERT CONFORMAL CONIC PROJECTION

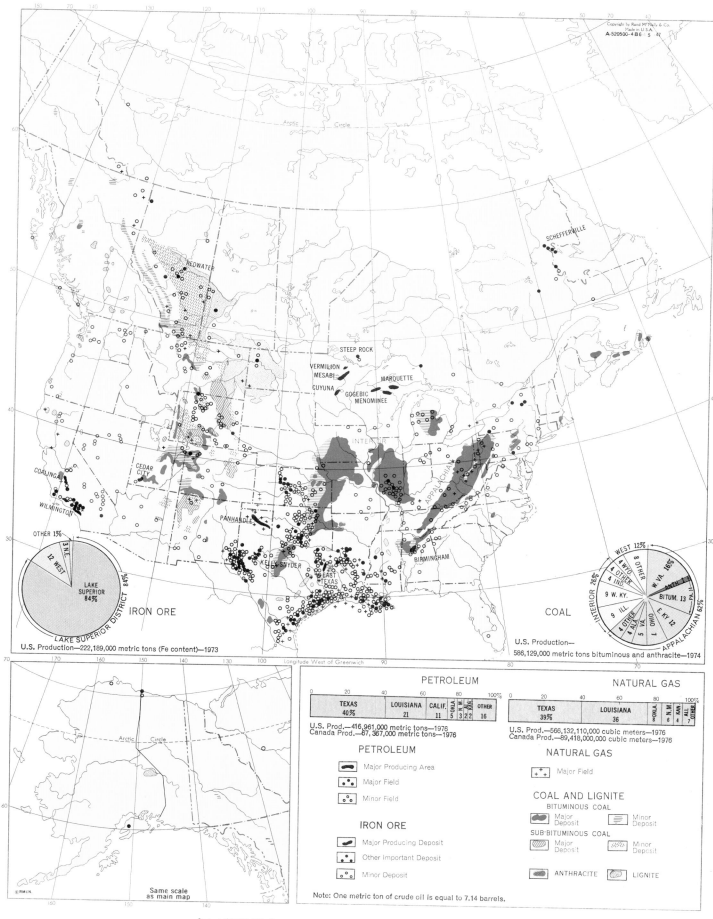

Copyright by Rand McNally & Co.
Made in U.S.A.
A-520500-4 B 6   5   47

SCHEFFERVILLE

REDWATER

STEEP ROCK

VERMILION
MESABI
CUYUNA
GOGEBIC
MENOMINEE

MARQUETTE

INTERIOR

APPALACHIAN

COALINGA
WILMINGTON

CEDAR
CITY

PANHANDLE

KELLY-SNYDER

EAST
TEXAS

BIRMINGHAM

IRON ORE

OTHER 1%
3 N.E.
12 WEST
LAKE SUPERIOR 84%
LAKE SUPERIOR DISTRICT 84%

U.S. Production—222,189,000 metric tons (Fe content)—1973

COAL

WEST 12%
8 OTHER
4 WYO.
4 OTHER
4 IND.
9 W. KY.
9 ILL.
4 OTHER
4 ALA.
5 OHIO
7 E. KY 12
INTERIOR 26%
W. VA. 18%
ANTH.
BITUM. 13
PA. 14
APPALACHIAN 62%

U.S. Production—
586,129,000 metric tons bituminous and anthracite—1974

Arctic Circle

Longitude West of Greenwich

Arctic Circle

Same scale
as main map

©RMCN.

PETROLEUM

0	20	40	60	80		100%
TEXAS 40%	LOUISIANA 21	CALIF. 11	OKLA. 5	N.M. 3	KAN. 2	OTHER 16

U.S. Prod.—416,961,000 metric tons—1976
Canada Prod.—67,367,000 metric tons—1976

NATURAL GAS

0	20	40	60	80	100%
TEXAS 39%	LOUISIANA 36	OKLA. 8	N.M. 6	KAN. 4	ALL OTHER 7

U.S. Prod.—566,132,110,000 cubic meters—1976
Canada Prod.—89,418,000,000 cubic meters—1976

PETROLEUM

Major Producing Area

Major Field

Minor Field

IRON ORE

Major Producing Deposit

Other Important Deposit

Minor Deposit

NATURAL GAS

Major Field

COAL AND LIGNITE

BITUMINOUS COAL
Major Deposit   Minor Deposit

SUB-BITUMINOUS COAL
Major Deposit   Minor Deposit

ANTHRACITE   LIGNITE

Note: One metric ton of crude oil is equal to 7.14 barrels.

Scale 1:32 000 000; One inch to 500 miles.   LAMBERT CONFORMAL CONIC PROJECTION

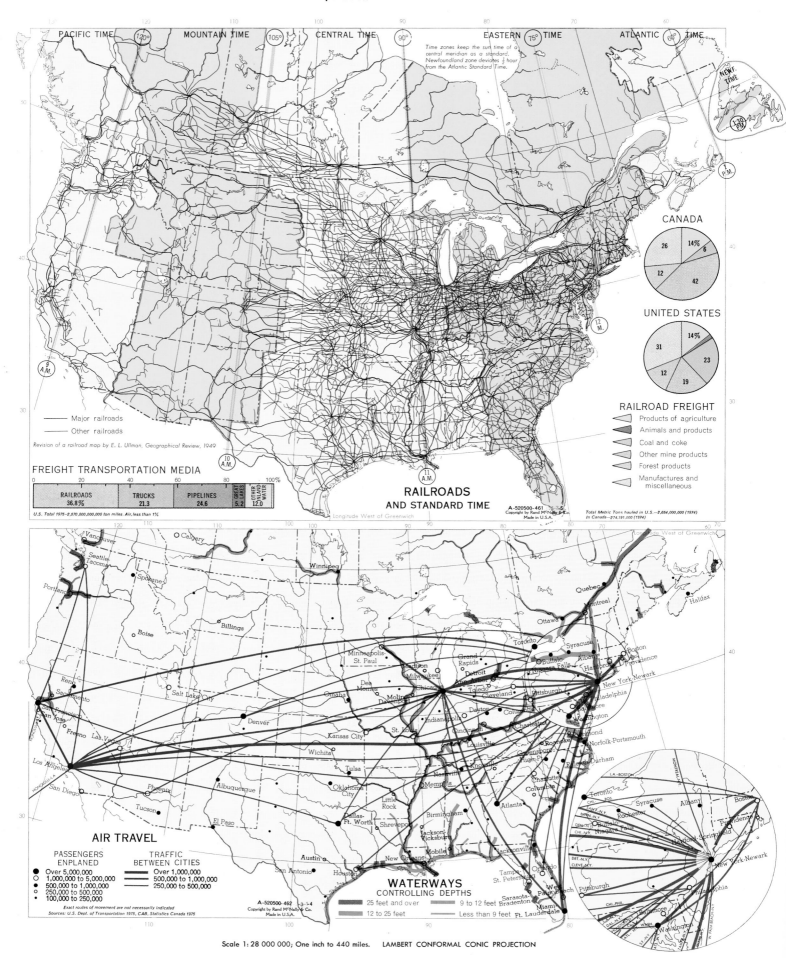

PACIFIC TIME ⟨120°⟩ MOUNTAIN TIME ⟨105°⟩ CENTRAL TIME ⟨90°⟩ EASTERN ⟨75°⟩ TIME ATLANTIC ⟨60°⟩ TIME

NEWF. TIME

Time zones keep the sun time of a central meridian as a standard. Newfoundland zone deviates ½ hour from the Atlantic Standard Time.

CANADA

26 | 14% | 6
12 | 42

UNITED STATES

31 | 14% | 23
12 | 19

RAILROAD FREIGHT

Products of agriculture
Animals and products
Coal and coke
Other mine products
Forest products
Manufactures and miscellaneous

—— Major railroads
—— Other railroads

Revision of a railroad map by E. L. Ullman, Geographical Review, 1949

FREIGHT TRANSPORTATION MEDIA

| RAILROADS 36.8% | TRUCKS 21.3 | PIPELINES 24.6 | GREAT LAKES 5.2 | OTHER INLAND WATER 12.0 |

U.S. Total 1975–2,070,000,000,000 ton miles. Air, less than 1%

RAILROADS
AND STANDARD TIME

A-520500-461
Copyright by Rand McNally & Co.
Made in U.S.A.

Total Metric Tons hauled in U.S.—2,654,000,000 (1974)
In Canada—274,191,000 (1974)

Longitude West of Greenwich

Vancouver
Seattle-Tacoma
Portland
Calgary
Winnipeg
Spokane
Billings
Boise
Quebec
Ottawa
Montreal
Halifax
Toronto
Syracuse
Boston
Reno
Sacramento
Salt Lake City
Minneapolis-St. Paul
Madison
Milwaukee
Grand Rapids
Detroit
Buffalo Falls
Albany Providence
Hartford
New York-Newark
San Francisco
San Jose
Fresno
Las Vegas
Denver
Omaha
Des Moines
Moline Davenport
Chicago
Toledo
Cleveland
Pittsburgh
Philadelphia
Baltimore
Washington
Los Angeles
Kansas City
St. Louis
Indianapolis
Dayton
Columbus
Cincinnati
Richmond
Norfolk-Portsmouth
Wichita
Louisville
Greensboro
High Pt.
Roanoke
Raleigh Durham
San Diego
Phoenix
Albuquerque
Tulsa
Oklahoma City
Little Rock
Nashville
Knoxville
Charlotte
Columbia
Atlanta
Tucson
El Paso
Dallas-Ft. Worth
Shreveport
Birmingham
Jackson Vicksburg
Mobile
Jacksonville
Austin
New Orleans
San Antonio
Houston
Tampa
St. Petersburg
Orlando
Sarasota Bradenton
West Palm Beach
Miami
Ft. Lauderdale

AIR TRAVEL

PASSENGERS ENPLANED
● Over 5,000,000
○ 1,000,000 to 5,000,000
○ 500,000 to 1,000,000
○ 250,000 to 500,000
○ 100,000 to 250,000

TRAFFIC BETWEEN CITIES
══ Over 1,000,000
══ 500,000 to 1,000,000
── 250,000 to 500,000

Exact routes of movement are not necessarily indicated
Sources: U.S. Dept. of Transportation 1975, CAB, Statistics Canada 1975

A-520500-462
Copyright by Rand McNally & Co.
Made in U.S.A.

WATERWAYS
CONTROLLING DEPTHS

25 feet and over | 9 to 12 feet
12 to 25 feet | Less than 9 feet

Toronto
Syracuse
Albany
Boston
Buffalo
Rochester
Niagara Falls
Providence
Hartford Springfield
New York-Newark
Philadelphia
Baltimore
Washington
W. Palm Beach

Scale 1: 28 000 000; One inch to 440 miles. LAMBERT CONFORMAL CONIC PROJECTION

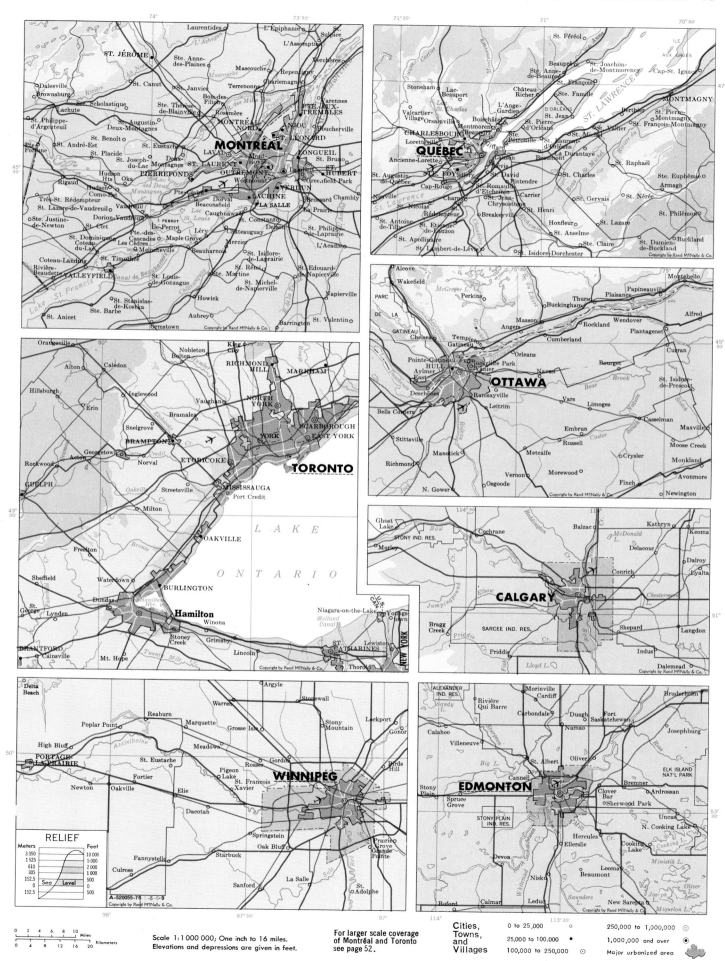

CANADA • Cities and Environs

MONTRÉAL

ST. JÉRÔME

Laurentides
L'Épiphanie
St. Sulpice
L'Assomption
Ste. Anne-des-Plaines
Mascouche
Repentigny
Verchères
Charlemagne
Terrebonne
Dalesville
Brownsburg
St. Canut
St. Janvier
Bois-des-Filion
Rosemère
Ste. Thérèse-de-Blainville
PTE. AUX-TREMBLES
Lachute
St. Scholastique
Ste. Anne-des-Plaines
MONTRÉAL NORD
ANJOU
St. Philippe-d'Argenteuil
St. Augustin-Deux-Montagnes
ST. LÉONARD
Boucherville
St. Benoît
St. Eustache
LAVAL
St. André-Est
St. Placide
Oka
Mont-Royal
LONGUEUIL
St. Bruno
PIERREFONDS
ST. LAURENT
OUTREMONT
ST. HUBERT
Hudson Hts.
Rigaud
Como-Est
Deux Montagnes
Westmount
Greenfield Park
Très-St. Rédempteur
Hudson
Pte. Claire
VERDUN
Brossard Chambly
St. Lazare-de-Vaudreuil
Vaudreuil
Dorval
Beaconsfield
LACHINE
Ste. Justine-de-Newton
Dorion-Vaudreuil
Île Perrot
LA SALLE
La Prairie
St. Clet
Pte.-des-Cascades
Léry
St. Constant
St. Philippe-de-Laprairie
Ste. Dominique-Coteau-du-Lac
Les Cèdres
Maple Grove
St. Isidore-de-Laprairie
Coteau-Landing
St. Timothée
Beauharnois
Chateauguay
Delson
Mercier
L'Acadie
Rivière-Beaudette
VALLEYFIELD
Melocheville
St. Louis-de-Gonzague
Ste. Martine
St. Michel-de-Napierville
St. Édouard-de-Napierville
St. Stanislas-de-Koska
Howick
Napierville
Ste. Barbe
St. Anicet
Aubrey
Ormstown
Barrington
St. Valentin

QUÉBEC

St. Féréol
St. Joachim-de-Montmorency
Cap-St. Ignace
ÎLE AUX GRUES
Stoneham
Lac-Beauport
Beaupré
Ste. Anne-de-Beaupré
Château Richer
Ste. Famille
St. François
MONTMAGNY
Valcartier-Village
Orsainville
Boischâtel
D'ORLÉANS
Berthier
St. Pierre-Montmagny
CHARLESBOURG
Montmorency
Beauport
St. Pierre d'Orléans
St. Laurent d'Orléans
St. Vallier
St. François-Montmagny
Loretteville
Ste. Pétronille
St. Michel
Ancienne-Lorette
QUÉBEC
Giffard
Neuville
STE. FOY
Sillery
Lévis
St. David
La Durantaye
St. Raphaël
Ste. Euphémie
St. Augustin-de-Québec
Cap-Rouge
Charny
St. Romuald-d'Etchemin
Carrier
St. Charles
Armagh
St. Nicolas
Rédempteur
St. Jean-Chrysostome
St. Gervais
St. Nérée
St. Antoine-de-Tilly
St. Étienne-de-Lauzon
Breakeyville
St. Henri
St. Philémon
Honfleur
St. Lazare
St. Apollinaire
St. Anselme
St. Lambert-de-Lévis
Ste. Claire
St. Damien-de-Buckland
St. Isidore-Dorchester
Buckland

TORONTO

Orangeville
Nobleton
King City
RICHMOND HILL
MARKHAM
Alton
Caledon
Bolton
Hillsburgh
Inglewood
Vaughan
NORTH YORK
SCARBOROUGH
EAST YORK
Erin
Snelgrove
Bramalea
BRAMPTON
YORK
Rockwood
Georgetown
Acton
Norval
ETOBICOKE
GUELPH
Streetsville
MISSISSAUGA
TORONTO
Milton
Port Credit
LAKE ONTARIO
Sheffield
Waterdown
OAKVILLE
St. George
Lynden
Freelton
BURLINGTON
Dundas
Hamilton Hbr.
Niagara-on-the-Lake
Youngstown
BRANTFORD
Cainsville
Mt. Hope
Stoney Creek
Hamilton
Winona
Grimsby
Lincoln
Welland Canal
Lewiston
NEW YORK
ST. CATHARINES
Thorold

OTTAWA

Alcove
Wakefield
McGregor L.
Perkins
Thurso
Plaisance
Papineauville
Montebello
PARC DE LA GATINEAU
Buckingham
Masson
Angers
Rockland
Wendover
Alfred
Chelsea
Templeton
Gatineau
Cumberland
Plantagenet
Pointe-Gatineau
HULL
Rockcliffe Park
Vanier
Orleans
Bourget
Curran
Aylmer East
OTTAWA
Navan
St. Isidore-de-Prescott
Deschênes
Ramsayville
Leitrim
Vars
Limoges
Casselman
Bells Corners
Maxville
Stittsville
Embrun
Russell
Moose Creek
Manotick
Metcalfe
Crysler
Monkland
Richmond
Vernon
Morewood
Avonmore
N. Gower
Osgoode
Finch
Newington

CALGARY

Ghost Lake
Bow
Cochrane
Balzac
McDonald L.
Kathryn
Keoma
STONY IND. RES.
Morley
Conrich
Dalroy
Lyalta
CALGARY
Jumpingpound
Elbow
Chestermere
Bragg Creek
Shepard
Langdon
Priddis
SARCEE IND. RES.
Priddis
Indus
Lloyd L.
Dalemead

WINNIPEG

Delta Beach
Argyle
Stonewall
Warren
Poplar Point
Reaburn
Marquette
Grosse Isle
Stony Mountain
Lockport
Gonor
High Bluff
Meadows
Birds Hill
PORTAGE LA PRAIRIE
St. Eustache
Assiniboine
Gordon
Rosser
Fortier
Pigeon Lake
St. François Xavier
WINNIPEG
Newton
Oakville
Elie
Prairie Grove
Dacotah
Springstein
Oak Bluff
Culross
Starbuck
La Salle
Fannystelle
Sanford
St. Adolphe

EDMONTON

ALEXANDER IND. RES.
Morinville
Cardiff
Bruderheim
Sandy L.
Rivière Qui Barre
Carbondale
Duagh
Fort Saskatchewan
Calahoo
Villeneuve
Namao
Josephburg
Big L.
St. Albert
Oliver
Sturgeon
ELK ISLAND NAT'L PARK
Stony Plain
Cannell
EDMONTON
Bremner
Ardrossan
Spruce Grove
Clover Bar
Sherwood Park
STONY PLAIN IND. RES.
Uncas
Hercules
N. Cooking Lake
Devon
Ellerslie
Cooking Lake
Nisku
Looma
Ministik L.
Beaumont
Buford
Calmar
Leduc
New Sarepta

RELIEF

Meters	Feet
3 050	10 000
1 525	5 000
610	2 000
305	1 000
152.5	500
0 Sea Level	Level
152.5	500

A-520055-76
Copyright by Rand McNally & Co.

0 2 4 6 8 10 Miles
0 4 8 12 16 20 Kilometers

Scale 1:1 000 000; One inch to 16 miles.
Elevations and depressions are given in feet.

For larger scale coverage of Montréal and Toronto see page 52.

Cities, Towns, and Villages

0 to 25,000
25,000 to 100,000
100,000 to 250,000
250,000 to 1,000,000
1,000,000 and over
Major urbanized area

Relief

Meters		Feet
3050		10 000
1525		5000
610		2000
305		1000
152.5		500
0	Sea Level	0
152.5		500
1525		5000

A-520220-76-- 4-1-5
COPYRIGHT BY
RAND McNALLY & COMPANY
MADE IN U.S.A.

Continued on pages 110–111

Longitude West of Greenwich

Scale 1:4 000 000; one inch to 64 miles. Conic Projection
Elevations and depressions are given in feet.

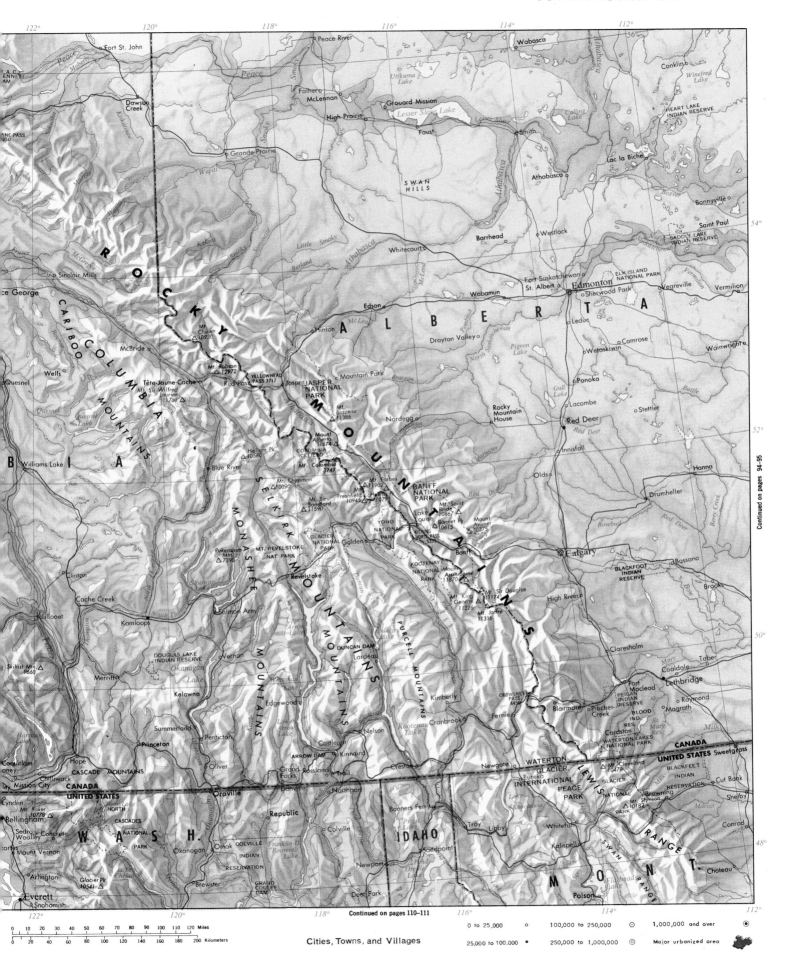

Continued on pages 94-95

Continued on pages 110–111

Cities, Towns, and Villages

0 to 25,000 ○
25,000 to 100,000 ●
100,000 to 250,000 ◍
250,000 to 1,000,000 ◎
1,000,000 and over ◉

Major urbanized area

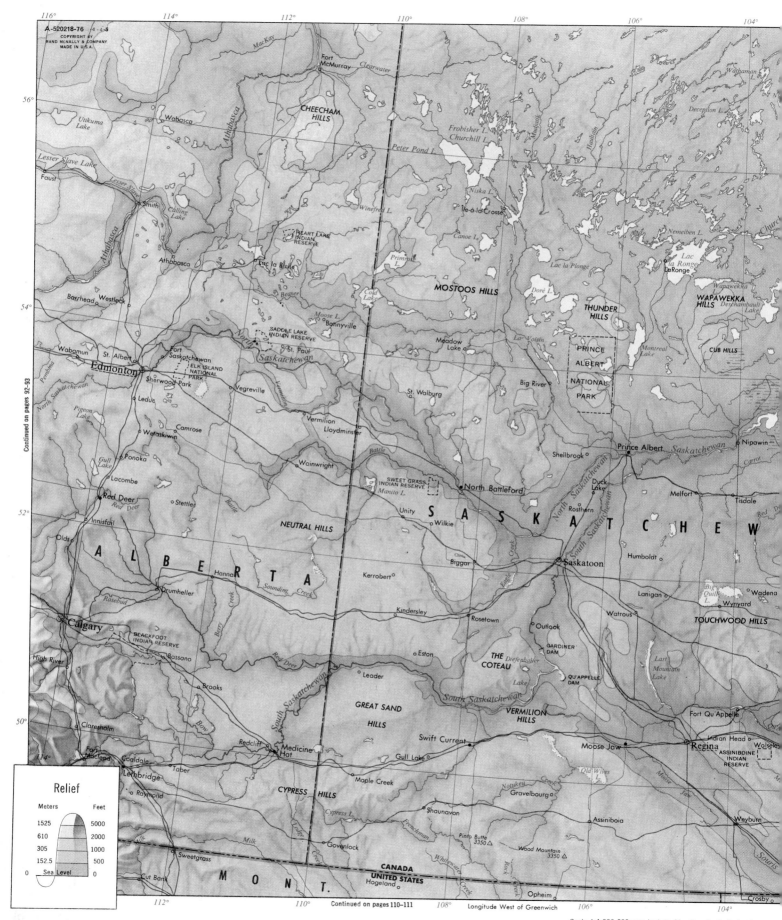

A-520218-76 |4-4-5
COPYRIGHT BY
RAND McNALLY & COMPANY
MADE IN U.S.A.

Continued on pages 92-93

Relief

Meters		Feet
1525		5000
610		2000
305		1000
152.5		500
0	Sea Level	0

Continued on pages 110–111

Longitude West of Greenwich

Scale 1:4 000 000; one inch to 64 miles. Conic Projection

Elevations and depressions are given in feet.

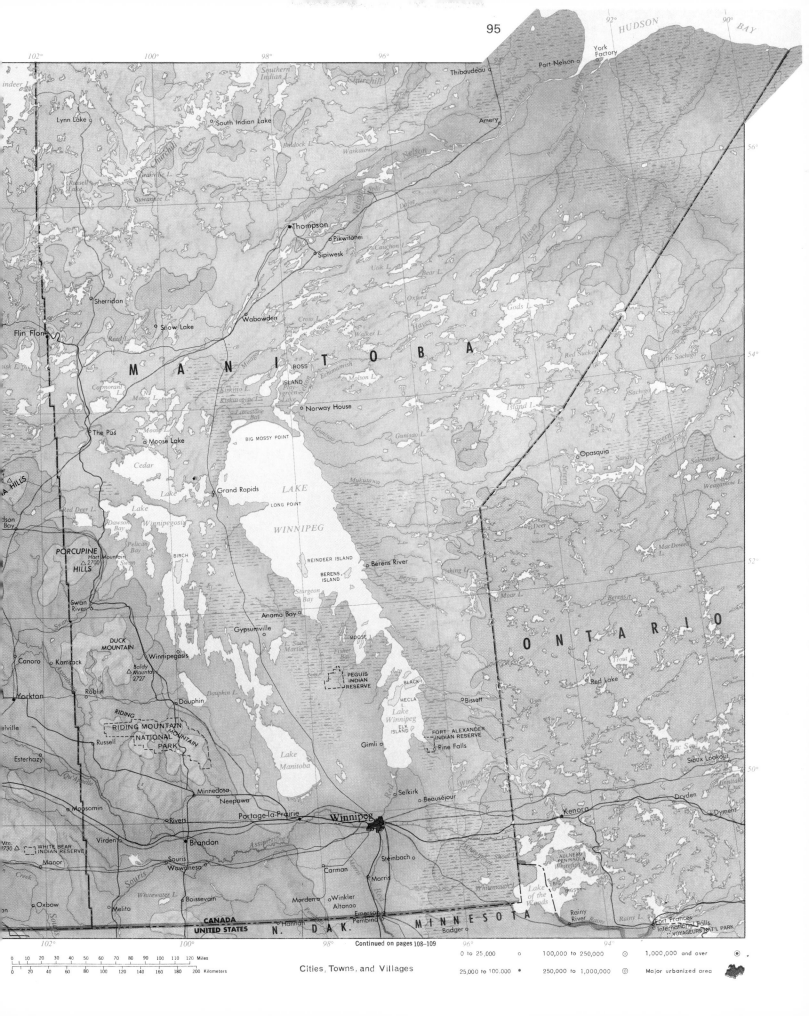

HUDSON BAY

Port Nelson
York Factory
Thibaudeau
Amery
56°

Lynn Lake
South Indian Lake
Baldock L.
Waskaiowaka L.
Nelson
Southern Indian L.
Churchill
55°

Granville L.
Russell Lake
Suwannee L.
56°

Sherridon
Thompson
Pikwitonei
Sipiwesk
Sipiwesk L.
Utik L.
Caughon L.
Bear L.
Oxford L.
Gods L.
Snow Lake
Wabowden
Cross L.
Walker L.
Hayes
Red Sucker L.
Little Sachigo
54°

MANITOBA
Flin Flon
Cormorant L.
Minago
ROSS
ISLAND
Playgreen
Lake
Molson L.
Echimamish
Island L.
Sachigo
Kiskitto L.
Kiskittogisu L.
Limestone Bay
Norway House
Guniso L.
Opasquia
Sand
Salway L.
Weagamow L.
The Pas
Moose Lake
Moose L.
BIG MOSSY POINT
LAKE
Mukutawa
MacDowell L.
52°

Cedar
Lake
Grand Rapids
LONG POINT
WINNIPEG
Deer
Red Deer L.
Dawson Bay
Pelican L.
Swan L.
BIRCH L.
REINDEER ISLAND
BERENS ISLAND
Berens River
Berens
Fishing L.
Berens
52°

PORCUPINE
HILLS
Hart Mountain
△ 2700
Sturgeon Bay
Moar L.
Canora
Kamsack
Winnipegosis
Baldy Mountain △ 2727
Anama Bay
Gypsumville
L. Saint Martin
Fisher Bay
MOOSE I.
Trout L.
ONTARIO
Yorkton
Roblin
Dauphin L.
Dauphin
PEGUIS INDIAN RESERVE
BLACK I.
HECLA I.
Lake Winnipeg
Red Lake
Bissett
RIDING
RIDING MOUNTAIN
NATIONAL PARK
Russell
Lake Manitoba
ELK ISLAND
FORT ALEXANDER INDIAN RESERVE
Gimli
Pine Falls
Sioux Lookout
Minnedosa
Neepawa
Selkirk
Beauséjour
50°

Moosomin
Rivers
Portage-la-Prairie
Winnipeg
Kenora
Dryden
Dyment
Virden
Brandon
Assiniboine
WHITE BEAR INDIAN RESERVE
Mtn. △ 730
Manor
Souris
Wawanesa
Carman
Steinbach
Morris
AULNEAU PENINSULA Whitefish
BIGSBY
Oxbow
Melita
Boissevain
Whitewater L.
Morden
Winkler
Altona
Emerson
Pembina
Lake of the Woods
Rainy River
Fort Frances
International Falls
VOYAGEURS NAT'L PARK
CANADA
UNITED STATES
Hannah
Pembina
N. DAK.
Badger
MINNESOTA
Rainy L.

Continued on pages 108–109

0 10 20 30 40 50 60 70 80 90 100 110 120 Miles
0 20 40 60 80 100 120 140 160 180 200 Kilometers

Cities, Towns, and Villages

| 0 to 25,000 | ○ | 100,000 to 250,000 | ⊙ | 1,000,000 and over | ◉ |
| 25,000 to 100,000 | ● | 250,000 to 1,000,000 | ◎ | Major urbanized area | |

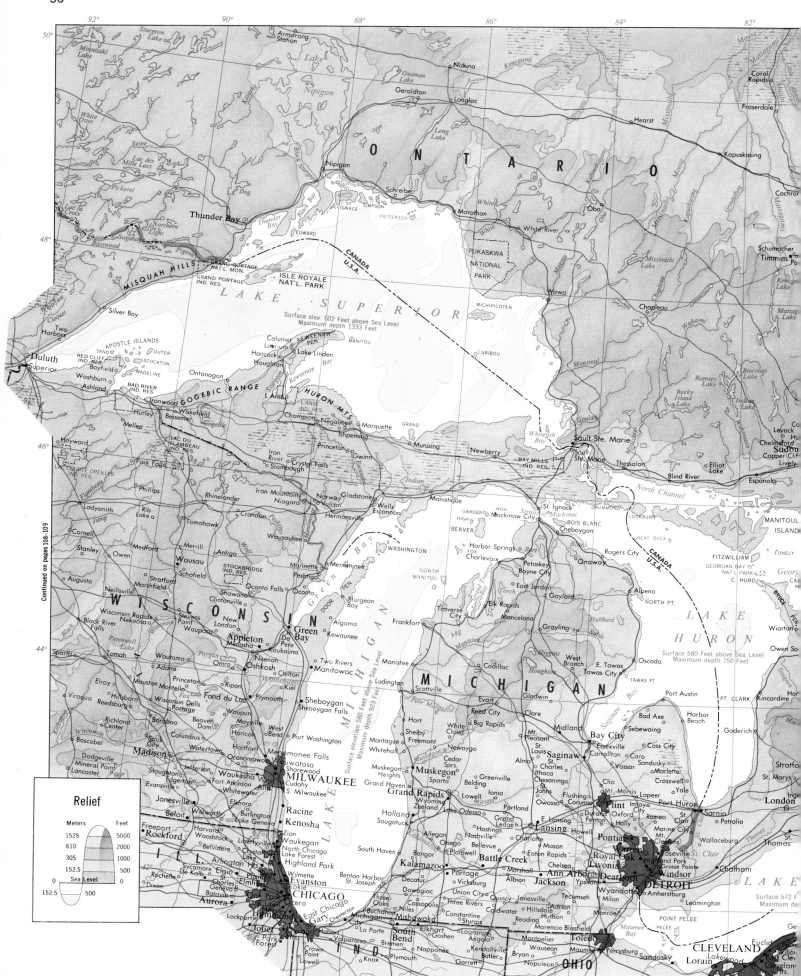

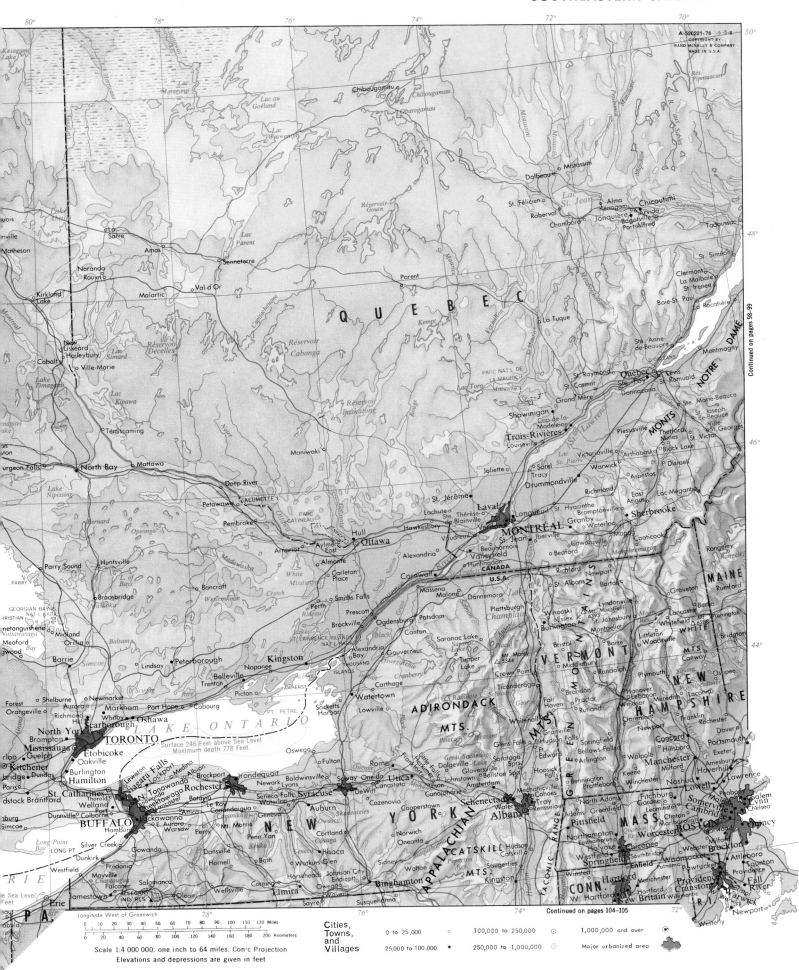

Continued on pages 98-99

Continued on pages 104-105

Cities,
Towns,
and
Villages

| 0 to 25,000 ○ | 100,000 to 250,000 ⊙ | 1,000,000 and over ◉ |
| 25,000 to 100,000 ● | 250,000 to 1,000,000 ⊚ | Major urbanized area |

Longitude West of Greenwich

0 10 20 30 40 50 60 70 80 90 100 110 120 Miles
0 20 40 60 80 100 120 140 160 180 200 Kilometers

Scale 1:4 000 000; one inch to 64 miles. Conic Projection
Elevations and depressions are given in feet

A-520221-76 -5-5-8
COPYRIGHT BY
RAND McNALLY & COMPANY
MADE IN U.S.A.

Scale 1:4 000 000, one inch to 64 miles. Conic Projection
Elevations and depressions are given in feet.

Longitude West of Greenwich

Continued on pages 104–105

Relief

Meters		Feet
1525		5000
610		2000
305		1000
152.5		500
	Sea Level	0
152.5	500	
1525	5000	

LABRADOR SEA

GULF OF ST. LAWRENCE

NEWFOUNDLAND

LONG RANGE MTS.

ANNIEOPSQUOTCH MTS.

St. John's

ST. PIERRE & MIQUELON (Fr.)

PRINCE EDWARD ISLAND

CAPE BRETON HIGHLANDS NAT'L PARK

NOVA SCOTIA

CAPE BRETON ISLAND

OCEAN

Scale 1:1 000 000

MASSACHUSETTS BAY

BOSTON

Worcester

Merrimack R.

A-510705-76 4-5-6-10
COPYRIGHT BY
RAND McNALLY & COMPANY
MADE IN U.S.A.

Cities, Towns, and Villages

| 0 to 25,000 | 100,000 to 250,000 | 1,000,000 and over |
| 25,000 to 100,000 • | 250,000 to 1,000,000 ○ | Major urbanized area |

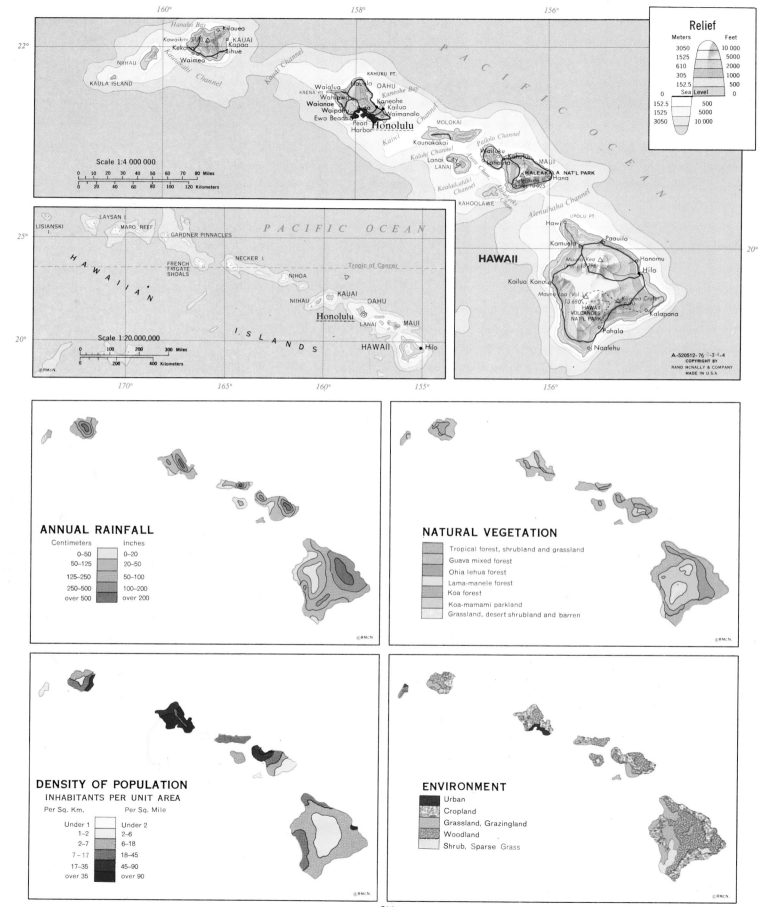

Relief

Meters	Feet
3050	10 000
1525	5000
610	2000
305	1000
152.5	500
0	Sea Level	0
152.5	500
1525	5000
3050	10 000

Scale 1:4 000 000

0 10 20 30 40 50 60 70 80 Miles
0 20 40 60 80 100 120 Kilometers

PACIFIC OCEAN

Hanalei Bay
Kilauea
Kawaikini 5170
KAUAI
Kekaha
Kapaa
Lihue
Waimea
NIIHAU
KAULA ISLAND

KAHUKU PT.
Waialua
Haula
OAHU
KAENA PT.
Wahiawa
Kaneohe Bay
Waianae
Kaneohe
Waipahu
Kailua
Ewa Beach
Waimanalo
Pearl Harbor
Honolulu

MOLOKAI
Kaunakakai
Pailolo Channel
Kalohi Channel
Lanai City
LANAI
Wailuku
Kahului
Lahaina
MAUI
HALEAKALA NAT'L PARK
Haleakala Crater 10 025
Hana
Kealaikahiki Channel
KAHOOLAWE
Alenuihaha Channel

UPOLU PT.
Hawi
Paauilo
Kamuela
Mauna Kea (Vol.) 13 796
Honomu
Kailua Kona
Hilo
Mauna Loa (Vol.) 13 680
Kilauea Crater
HAWAII VOLCANOES NAT'L PARK
Kalapana
Pahala
Naalehu

HAWAII

A-520512-76-3-4-4
COPYRIGHT BY
RAND McNALLY & COMPANY
MADE IN U.S.A.

PACIFIC OCEAN

LISIANSKI I.
LAYSAN I.
MARO REEF
GARDNER PINNACLES
HAWAIIAN
FRENCH FRIGATE SHOALS
NECKER I.
Tropic of Cancer
NIHOA
ISLANDS
NIIHAU
KAUAI
OAHU
Honolulu
LANAI
MAUI
HAWAII
Hilo

Scale 1:20,000,000
0 100 200 300 Miles
0 200 400 Kilometers
©RMcN.

ANNUAL RAINFALL

Centimeters	Inches
0–50	0–20
50–125	20–50
125–250	50–100
250–500	100–200
over 500	over 200

NATURAL VEGETATION

Tropical forest, shrubland and grassland
Guava mixed forest
Ohia lehua forest
Lama-manele forest
Koa forest
Koa-mamami parkland
Grassland, desert shrubland and barren

DENSITY OF POPULATION
INHABITANTS PER UNIT AREA

Per Sq. Km.	Per Sq. Mile
Under 1	Under 2
1–2	2–6
2–7	6–18
7–17	18–45
17–35	45–90
over 35	over 90

ENVIRONMENT

Urban
Cropland
Grassland, Grazingland
Woodland
Shrub, Sparse Grass

Cities, Towns, and Villages

0 to 25,000   ○
25,000 to 100,000   •
100,000 to 250,000   ⊙
250,000 to 1,000,000   ◎
1,000,000 and over   ◉
Major urbanized area

Relief

Meters		Feet
3050		10 000
1525		5000
610		2000
305		1000
152.5		500
0	Sea Level	0
152.5		500
1525		5000
3050		10 000
6100		20 000

Scale 1:12 000 000; one inch to 190 miles. Conic Projection

Elevations and depressions are given in feet

Longitude East of Greenwich   Longitude West of Greenwich   Same scale as main map

Cities, Towns, and Villages

0 to 25,000 ○   100,000 to 250,000 ◉   1,000,000 and over ◉

25,000 to 100,000 •   250,000 to 1,000,000 ◎   Major urbanized area

A-520502-76- :.4-:5.6
COPYRIGHT BY
RAND McNALLY & COMPANY
MADE IN U.S.A.

Longitude West of Greenwich

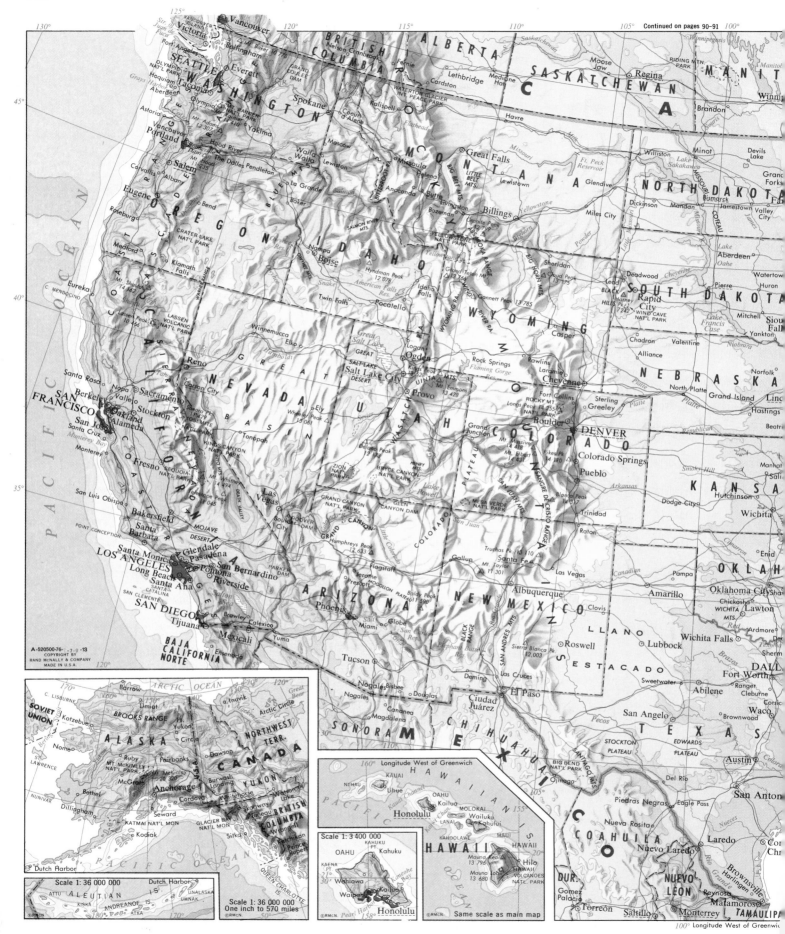

Continued on pages 90–91

Scale 1:12 000 000; one inch to 190 miles. Polyconic Projection
Elevations and depressions are given in feet

Scale 1:36 000 000

Scale 1:36 000 000
One inch to 570 miles

Scale 1:3 400 000

Same scale as main map

100° Longitude West of Greenwich

Relief

Meters		Feet
3050		10 000
1525		5000
610		2000
305		1000
152.5		500
Sea Level	0	0
		Below
152.5	500	Sea Level
1525	5 000	
3050	10 000	
6100	20 000	

Continued on pages 108–109

Continued on pages 120–121

Longitude West of Greenwich

Scale 1:4 000 000; one inch to 64 miles.   Conic Projection
Elevations and depressions are given in feet

Continued on pages 96–97

Relief

Meters		Feet
1525		5000
610		2000
305		1000
152.5		500
0	Sea Level	0
152.5		500
1525		5000
3050		10 000

A-520596-76 5-7-10
COPYRIGHT BY
RAND McNALLY & COMPANY
MADE IN U.S.A.

LAKE ONTARIO
Surface 246 Feet above Sea Level
maximum depth 778 Feet

0   20   40   60   80   100   120 Miles
0   20   40   60   80   100   120   140   160   180   200 Kilometers

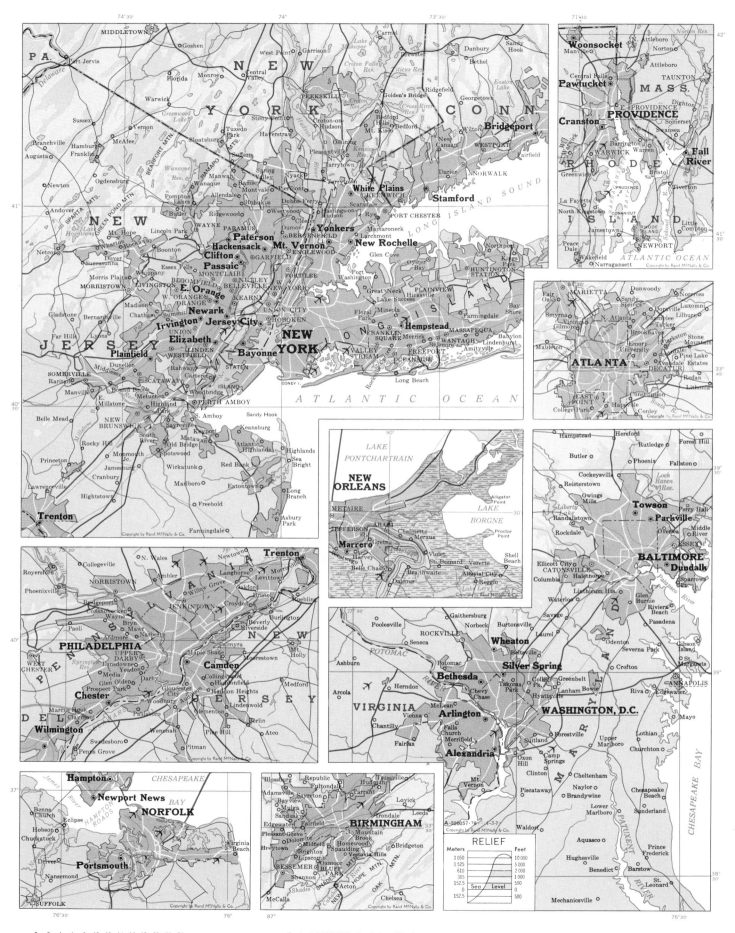

For larger scale coverage of New York, Baltimore,
Washington, D. C. and Philadelphia see pages 53 and 54.

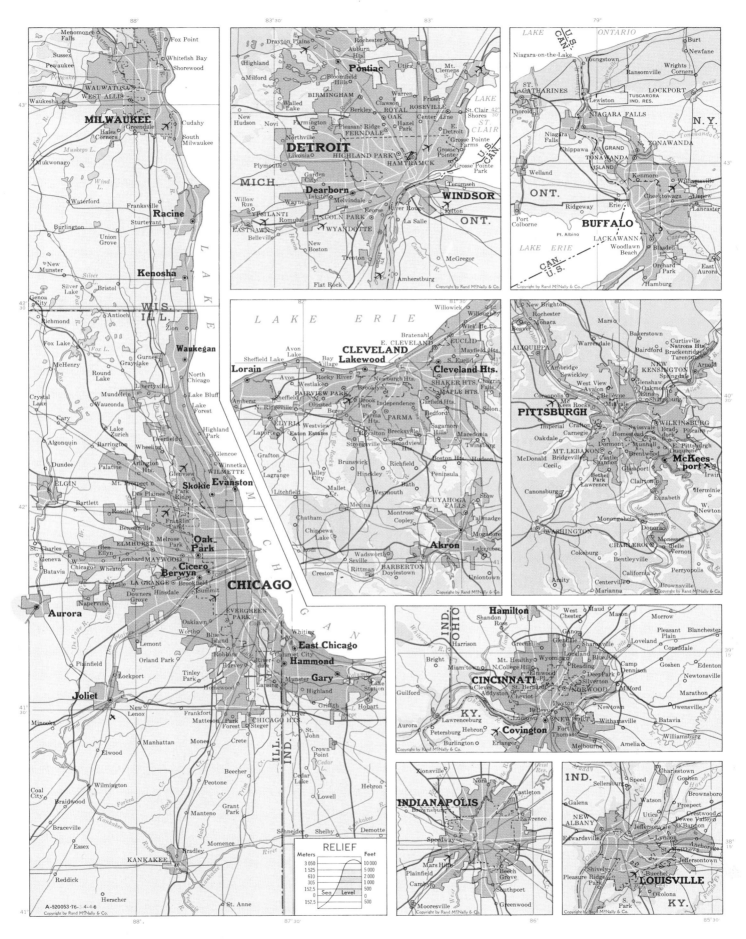

RELIEF

Meters		Feet
3 050		10 000
1 525		5 000
610		2 000
305		1 000
152.5		500
0	Sea Level	0
152.5		500

Scale 1:1 000 000; One inch to 16 miles.
Elevations and depressions are given in feet.

For larger scale coverage
of Chicago see page 56.

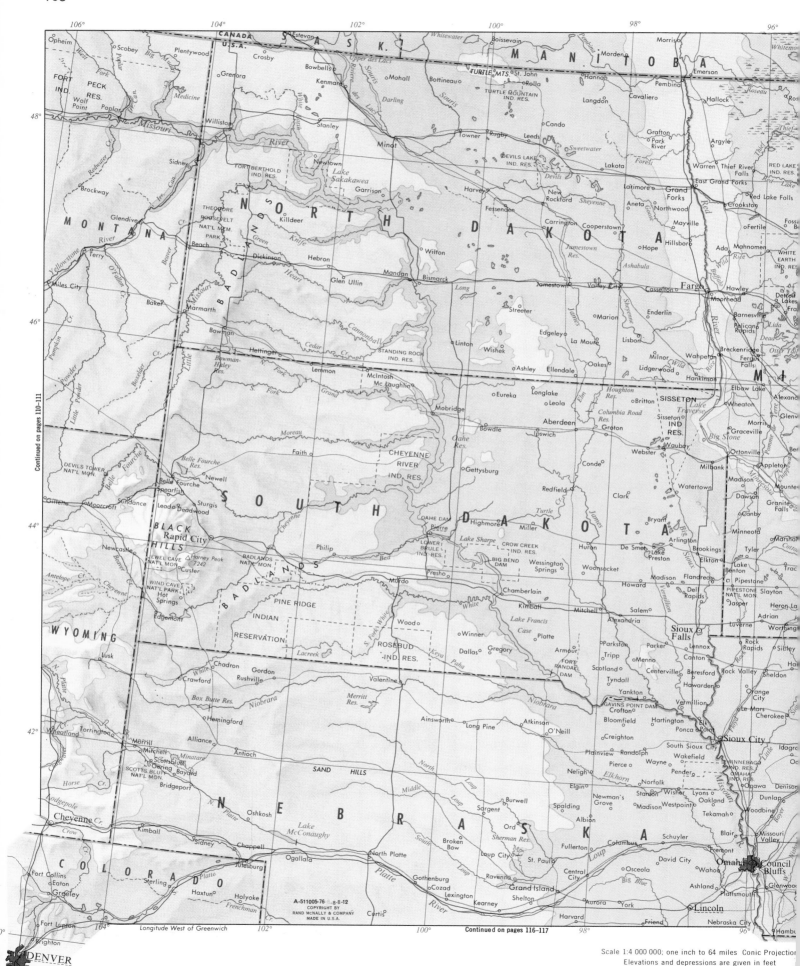

Continued on pages 110-111

Continued on pages 116-117

A-511005-76 -8-8-12
COPYRIGHT BY
RAND McNALLY & COMPANY
MADE IN U.S.A.

Longitude West of Greenwich

Scale 1:4 000 000; one inch to 64 miles Conic Projection
Elevations and depressions are given in feet

DENVER

Relief

Meters	Feet
1525	5000
610	2000
305	1000
152.5	500
0	Sea Level 0
152.5	500

Continued on pages 104–105

Continued on pages 116–117

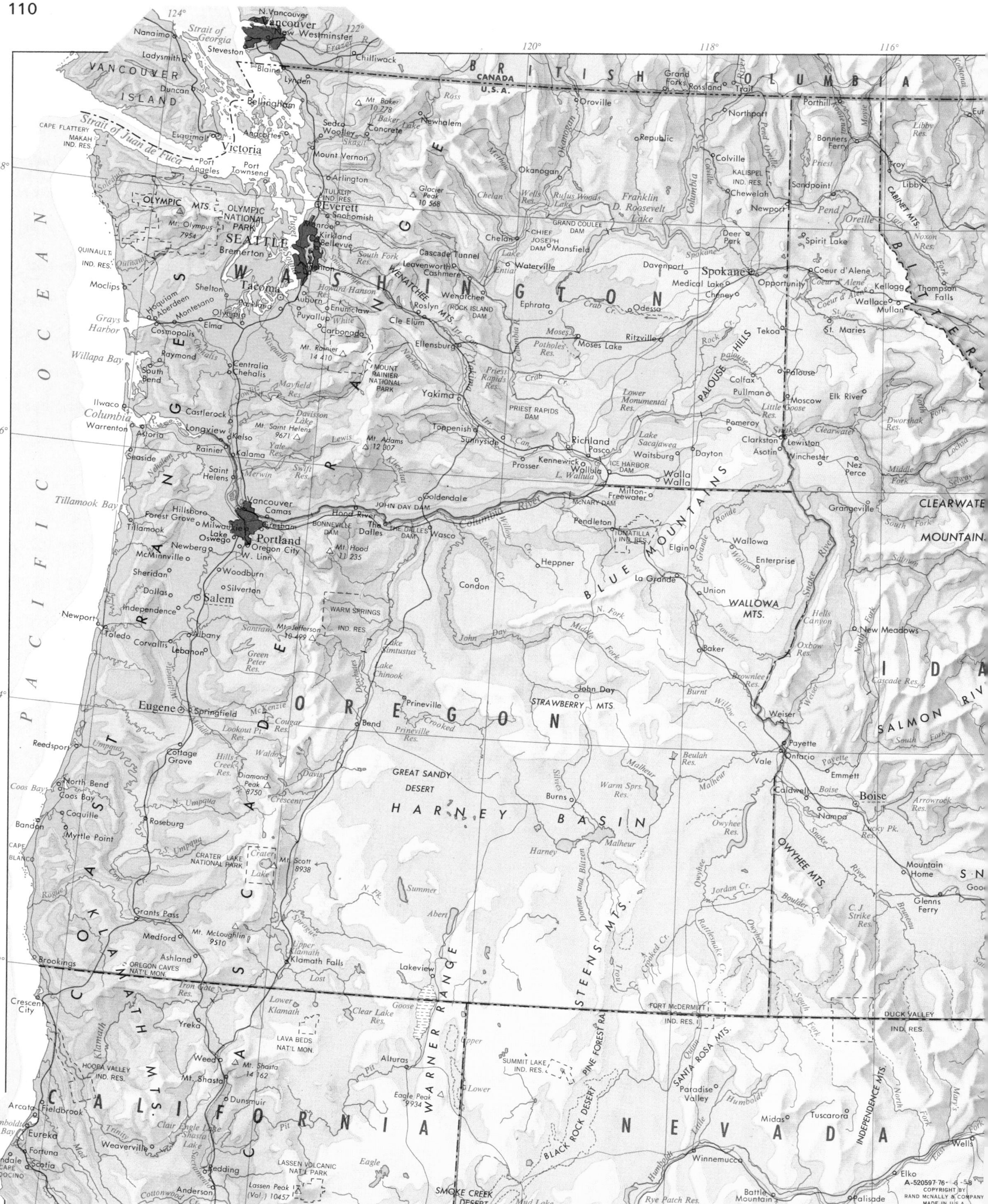

124° · 122° · 120° · 118° · 116°

BRITISH COLUMBIA
CANADA
U.S.A.

N. Vancouver
Vancouver
New Westminster
Nanaimo
Ladysmith
Steveston
Blaine
Lynden
Chilliwack
Fraser
Grand Forks
Rossland
Trail
Porthill
Libby Res.
Troy
Libby
Cut

Strait of Georgia
Duncan
VANCOUVER ISLAND
Bellingham
Esquimalt
Victoria
Andacortes
Mount Vernon
Sedro Woolley
Concrete
Baker Lake
Mt. Baker 10,778
Newhalem
Ross
Oroville
Republic
Northport
Colville
KALISPEL IND. RES.
Chewelah
Newport
Bonners Ferry
Deer Park
Spirit Lake
Noxon Res.
Pend Oreille
CABINET MTS.

CAPE FLATTERY
Strait of Juan de Fuca
MAKAH IND. RES.
Port Angeles
Port Townsend
Arlington
TULALIP IND. RES.
Everett
Snohomish
Glacier Peak 10,568
Chelan
Okanogan
Wells Res.
Rufus Woods Lake
Franklin D. Roosevelt Lake
GRAND COULEE DAM
Davenport
Spokane
Medical Lake
Cheney
Opportunity
Coeur d'Alene
Kellogg
Wallace
Mullan
Thompson Falls

48°

OLYMPIC MTS.
Mt. Olympus 7,954
OLYMPIC NATIONAL PARK
QUINAULT IND. RES.
Quinault
SEATTLE
Bremerton
Kirkland
Bellevue
Monroe
Leavenworth
Cashmere
Cascade Tunnel
CHIEF JOSEPH DAM
Mansfield
Waterville
Entiat
Lake Chelan
St. Joe
St. Maries

Moclips
Hoquiam
Aberdeen
Montesano
Elma
Olympia
TACOMA
Auburn
Enumclaw
Puyallup
South Fork Res.
Howard Hanson Res.
Roslyn
Cle Elum
Ellensburg
Wenatchee
ROCK ISLAND DAM
WENATCHEE MTS.
Ephrata
Moses Lake
Potholes Res.
Ritzville
Odessa
Crab Cr.
Tekoa
Palouse
Colfax
Moscow
Pullman
Elk River
Dworshak Res.

Grays Harbor
Cosmopolis
Centralia
Chehalis
Carbonado
Mt. Rainier 14,410
MOUNT RAINIER NATIONAL PARK
Naches
Yakima
Toppenish
PRIEST RAPIDS RES.
PRIEST RAPIDS DAM
Lower Monumental Res.
PALOUSE HILLS
Pomeroy
Little Goose

46°

Ilwaco
South Bend
Raymond
Willapa Bay
Mayfield Res.
Davisson Lake
Mt. Saint Helens 9,671
Yale Res.
Mt. Adams 12,307
Sunnyside
Richland
Pasco
Kennewick
Prosser
Wallula
ICE HARBOR DAM
L. Wallula
Waitsburg
Dayton
Clarkston
Lewiston
Asotin
Winchester
Nez Perce
Middle Fork

Columbia
Warrenton
Astoria
Seaside
Castlerock
Longview
Kelso
Kalama
Rainier
Saint Helens
Lewis
Merwin
Swift Res.
Klickitat
Goldendale
JOHN DAY DAM
Columbia River
McNARY DAM
Milton-Freewater
Walla Walla
CLEARWATER MOUNTAIN

COAST RANGE
Tillamook Bay
Hillsboro
Forest Grove
Tillamook
McMinnville
Newberg
Sheridan
Dallas
Woodburn
Silverton
Salem
Vancouver
Camas
Portland
Oregon City
W. Linn
Lake Oswego
Milwaukie
Gresham
Hood River
BONNEVILLE DAM
The Dalles
THE DALLES DAM
Wasco
Mt. Hood 11,235
Condon
Heppner
UMATILLA IND. RES.
Pendleton
Elgin
La Grande
Union
Wallowa
Enterprise
WALLOWA MTS.
BLUE MOUNTAINS
Grangeville
Salmon

Newport
Independence
Albany
Corvallis
Lebanon
Green Peter Res.
Mt. Jefferson 10,499
WARM SPRINGS IND. RES.
Lake Simtustus
Lake Chinook
John Day
N. Fork
Middle Fork
Powder
STRAWBERRY MTS.
John Day
Burnt
Baker
Hells Canyon
Brownlee Res.
New Meadows
Cascade Res.
SALMON RIVER

44°

Eugene
Springfield
McKenzie
Cougar Res.
Lookout Pt. Res.
Bend
Prineville
Crooked
Prineville Res.
Deschutes
GREAT SANDY DESERT
John Day
Warm Sprs. Res.
Malheur
Beulah Res.
Oxbow Res.
Weiser
Payette
Ontario
Emmett
IDAHO

Reedsport
Umpqua
Cottage Grove
Hills Cr. Res.
Waldo
Davis
Crescent
Diamond Peak 8,750
HARNEY BASIN
Burns
Harney
Malheur
Owyhee Res.
Vale
Caldwell
Boise
Nampa
Arrowrock Res.
Lucky Pk.

Coos Bay
North Bend
Coos River
Coquille
Bandon
Myrtle Point
Roseburg
N. Umpqua
S. Umpqua
CRATER LAKE NATIONAL PARK
Crater Lake
Mt. Scott 8,938
Summer
Donner und Blitzen
STEENS MTS.
Jordan Cr.
OWYHEE MTS.
C.J. Strike Res.
Boulder
Mountain Home
Glenns Ferry
SNAKE

42°

CAPE BLANCO
Rogue
Grants Pass
Medford
Ashland
OREGON CAVES NAT'L MON.
Mt. McLoughlin 9,510
Upper Klamath Lake
Klamath Falls
Lakeview
Abert
Summer
WARNER RANGE
Crooked Cr.
Rattlesnake
Owyhee
River
North Fork

Brookings
KLAMATH MTS.
Iron Gate Res.
Lost
Lower Klamath
Clear Lake Res.
Goose
FORT McDERMITT IND. RES.
DUCK VALLEY IND. RES.

Crescent City
Yreka
Weed
Mt. Shasta 14,162
Mt. Shastina
LAVA BEDS NAT'L MON.
Alturas
Pit
Upper
Lower
Eagle
PINE FOREST RANGE
SUMMIT LAKE IND. RES.
SANTA ROSA MTS.
Paradise Valley
INDEPENDENCE MTS.

Arcata
Fieldbrook
Humboldt Bay
Eureka
Fortuna
Scotia
Ferndale
CAPE MENDOCINO
Dunsmuir
Clair Engle Lake
Shasta Lake
Trinity
Weaverville
HOOPA VALLEY IND. RES.
CALIFORNIA
Eagle Peak 9,934
Lower
BLACK ROCK DESERT
Humboldt
Midas
Tuscarora
NEVADA
Wells

Anderson
Redding
LASSEN VOLCANIC NAT'L PARK
Lassen Peak (Vol.) 10,457
Lassen Pk.
Eagle
Mud Lake
SMOKE CREEK DESERT
Winnemucca
Battle Mountain
Rye Patch Res.
Palisade
Elko

Cottonwood Cr.
Mad

PACIFIC OCEAN

Scale 1: 4,000,000; one inch to 64 miles. Conic Projection
Elevations and depressions are given in feet

A-520597-76 · 6-58
COPYRIGHT BY
RAND McNALLY & COMPANY
MADE IN U.S.A.

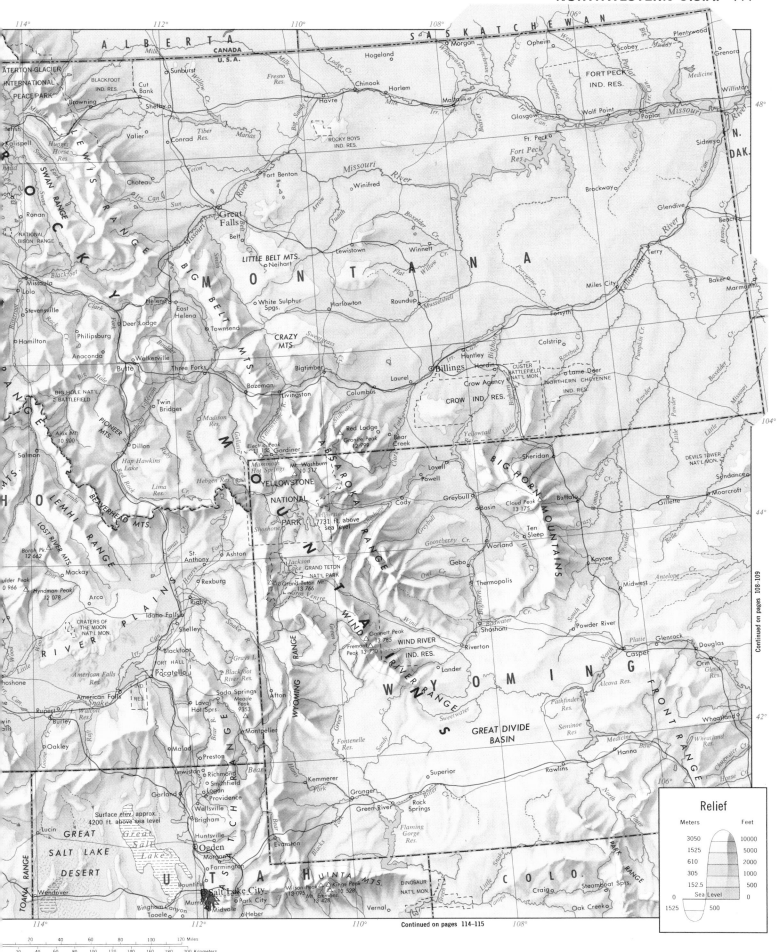

Continued on pages 108-109

Continued on pages 114-115

Relief

Meters		Feet
3050		10000
1525		5000
610		2000
305		1000
152.5		500
Sea Level		0
1525		500

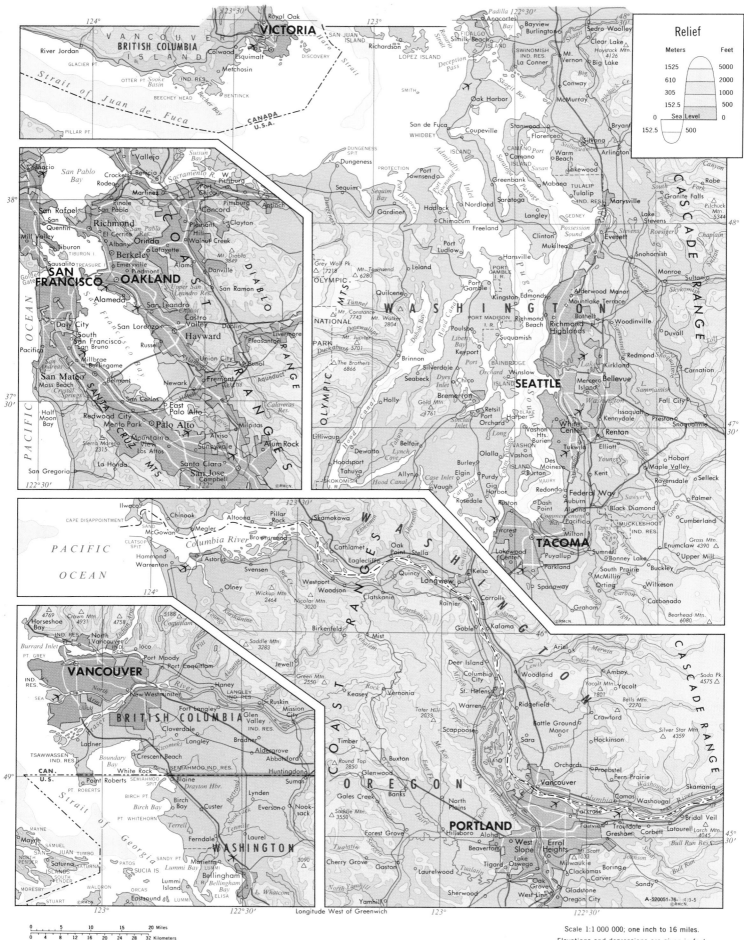

Longitude West of Greenwich

Scale 1:1 000 000; one inch to 16 miles.
Elevations and depressions are given in feet.

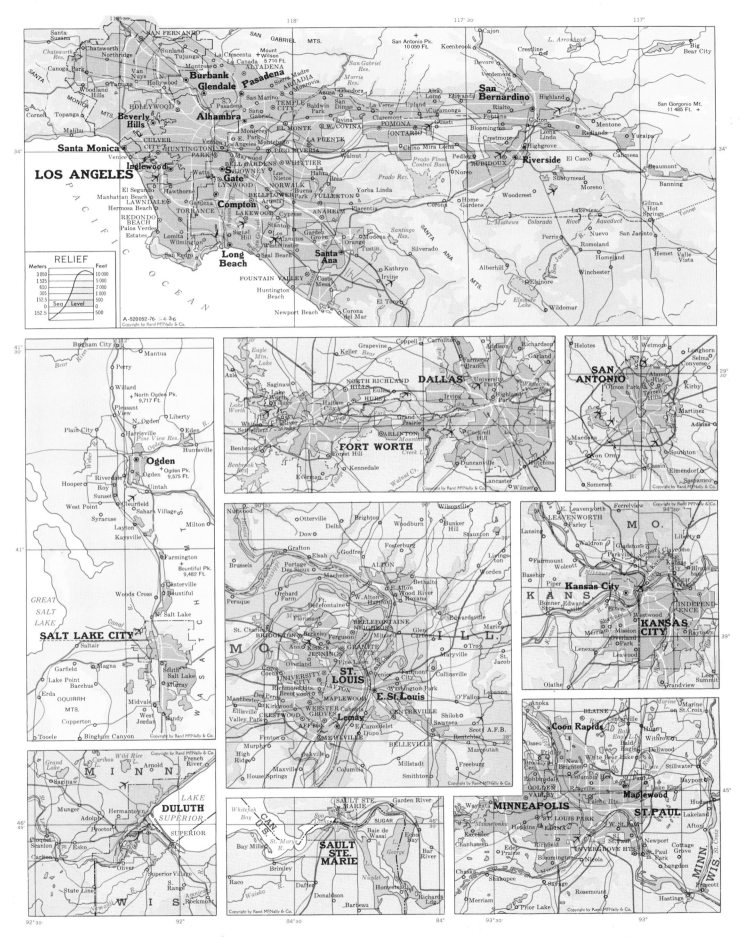

Scale 1:1 000 000; One inch to 16 miles.
Elevations and depressions are given in feet.

For larger scale coverage
of Los Angeles see page 57.

Continued on pages 110–111

Relief

Meters		Feet
3050		10000
1525		5000
610		2000
305		1000
152.5		500
0	Sea Level	0
		Below
152.5		500 Sea Level
1525		5000
3050		10000

SAN DIEGO

Scale 1:1 000 000

0   5   10 Miles

0 4 8 12 16 Kilometers

®RMcN.

A-520599-76   -7-10
COPYRIGHT BY
RAND McNALLY & COMPANY
MADE IN U.S.A.

Scale 1:4 000 000; one inch to 64 miles. Conic Projection
Elevations and depressions are given in feet

Longitude West of Greenwich

0   20   40   60   80   100   120 Miles

0 20 40 60 80 100 120 140 160 180 200 Kilometers

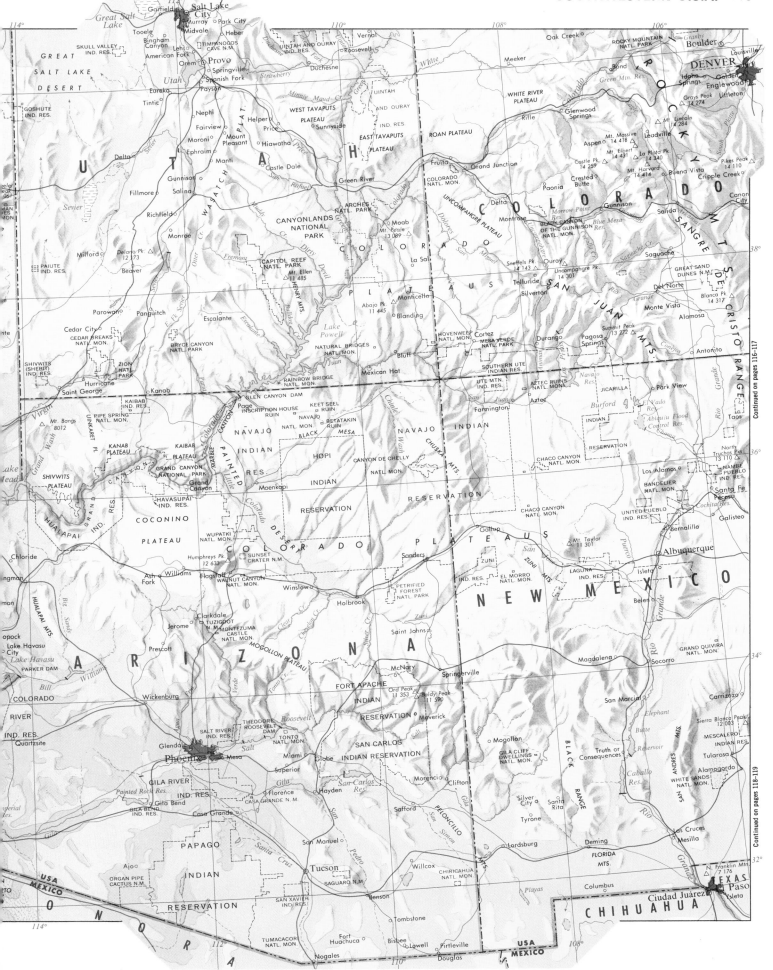

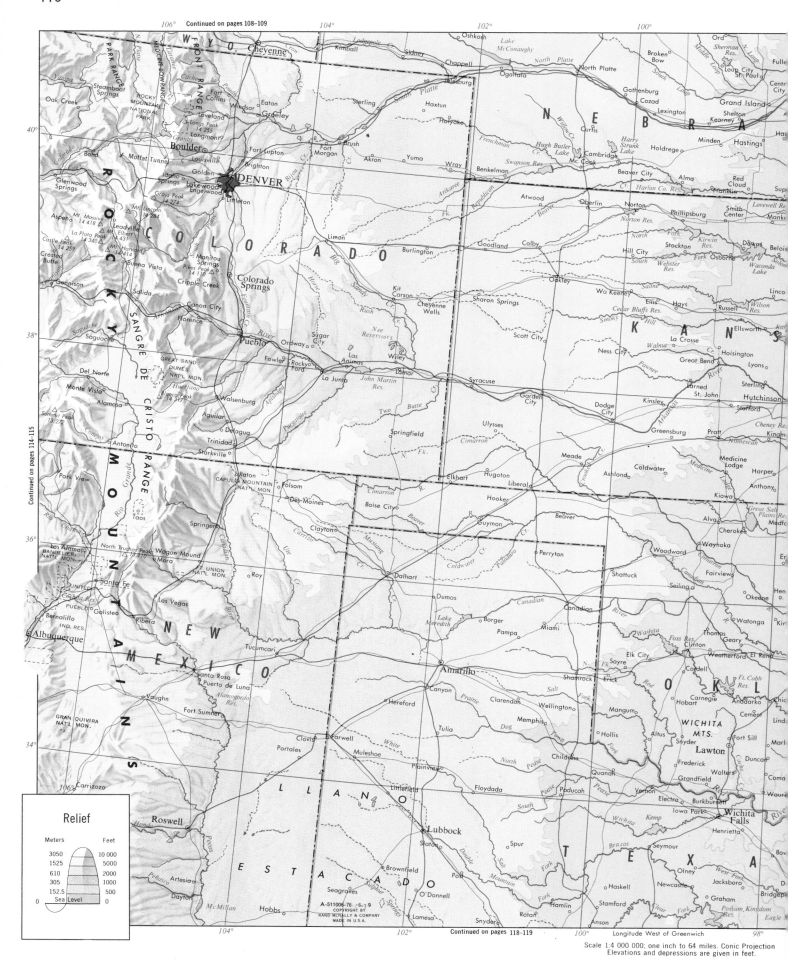

116

Continued on pages 108–109

Continued on pages 114–115

W Y O   Cheyenne

N E B R A

C O L O R A D O

R O C K Y

S A N G R E   D E   C R I S T O   R A N G E

DENVER

Boulder

Colorado Springs

Pueblo

K A N S

M O U N T A I N S

N E W   M E X I C O

Albuquerque

Santa Fe

O K L A

Amarillo

Lubbock

WICHITA MTS.

L L A N O   E S T A C A D O

T E X A S

Roswell

Relief

Meters		Feet
3050		10 000
1525		5000
610		2000
305		1000
152.5		500
0	Sea Level	0

A-511005-76-6-7-9
COPYRIGHT BY
RAND MCNALLY & COMPANY
MADE IN U.S.A.

Continued on pages 118–119

Longitude West of Greenwich

Scale 1:4 000 000; one inch to 64 miles. Conic Projection
Elevations and depressions are given in feet.

Continued on pages 108-109

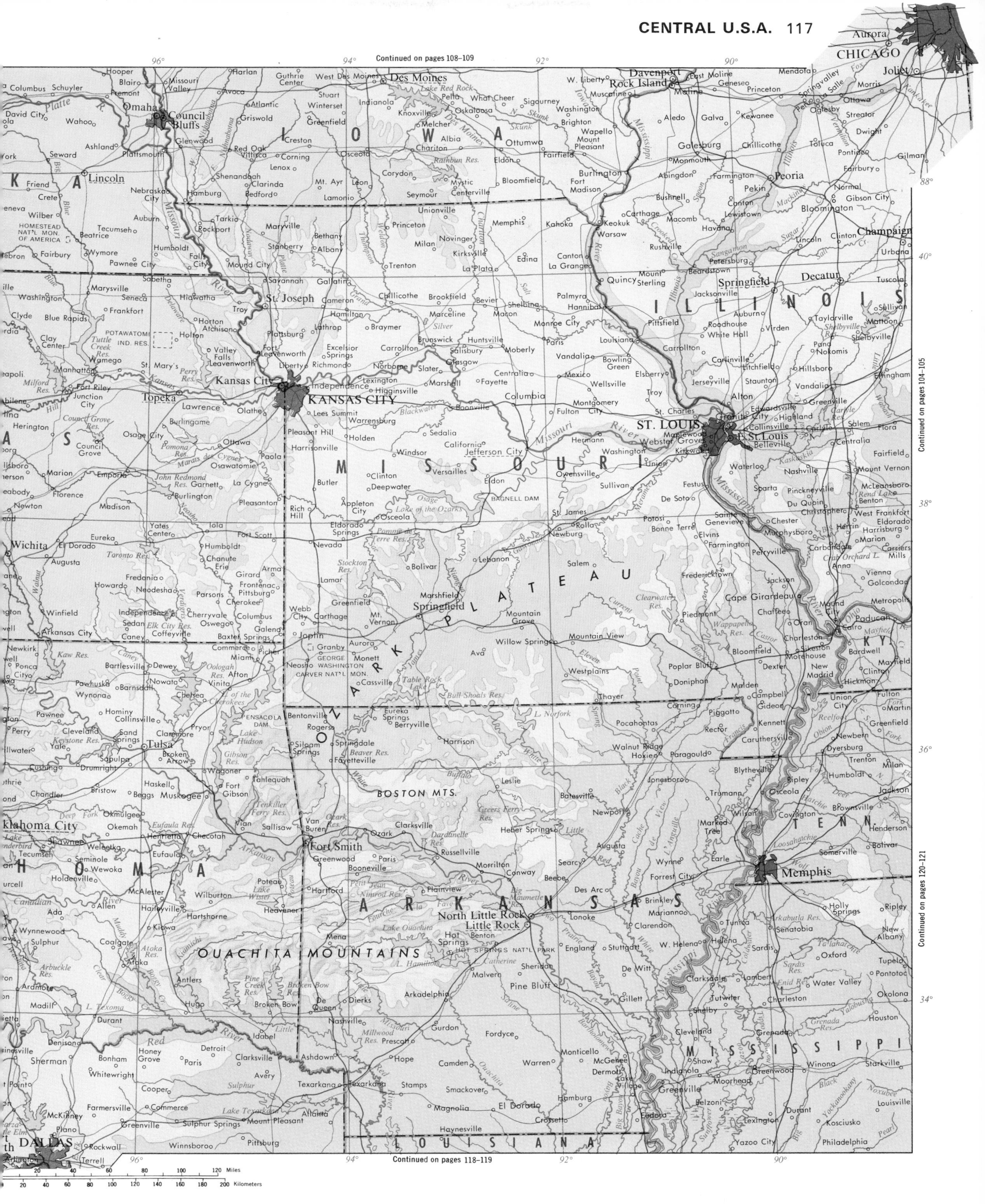

CHICAGO
Aurora
Joliet

IOWA

Des Moines

Omaha
Council Bluffs

Lincoln

ILLINOIS

Peoria
Champaign

Springfield
Decatur

MISSOURI

Kansas City
KANSAS CITY
Topeka

ST. LOUIS
E. St. Louis

Jefferson City
Columbia

KANSAS

Wichita

OZARK PLATEAU

Springfield

BAGNELL DAM
Lake of the Ozarks

Cape Girardeau
Paducah

Tulsa

OKLAHOMA

Oklahoma City

BOSTON MTS.

Fort Smith

ARKANSAS

Memphis

TENN.

OUACHITA MOUNTAINS

North Little Rock
Little Rock
Hot Springs
HOT SPRINGS NAT'L PARK

DALLAS

LOUISIANA

MISSISSIPPI

Continued on pages 104-105
Continued on pages 120-121
Continued on pages 118-119

20 40 60 80 100 120 Miles
20 40 60 80 100 120 140 160 180 200 Kilometers

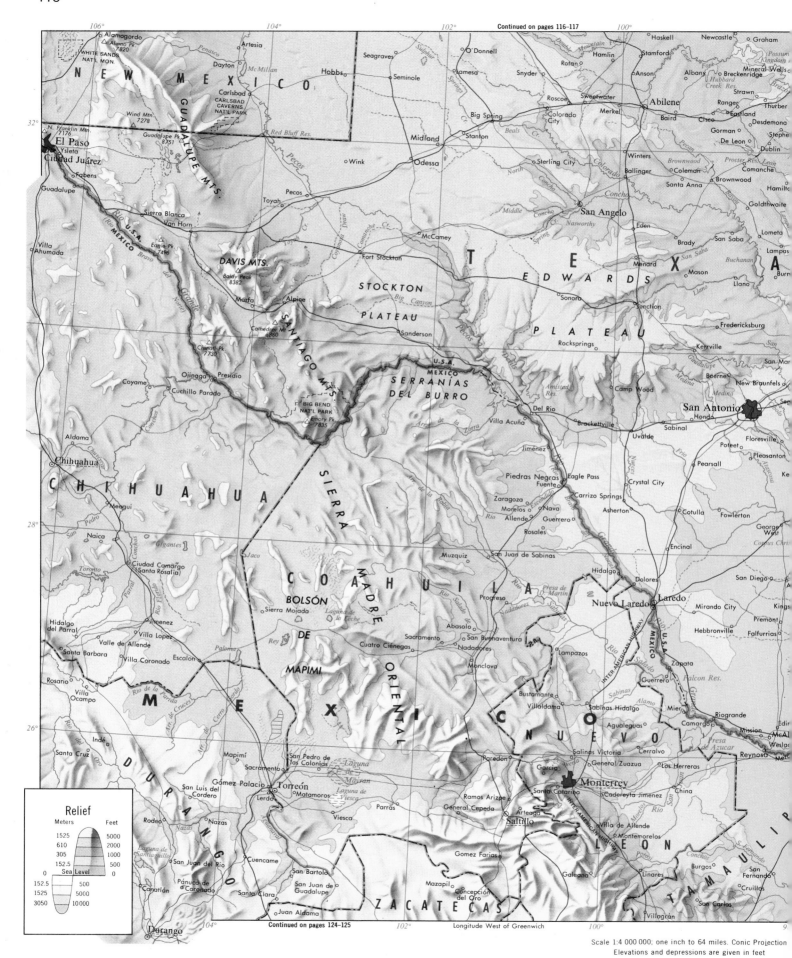

118

Continued on pages 116–117

NEW MEXICO

32°

Alamogordo
Alamo Pk.
7820
WHITE SANDS
NAT'L MON.

Penasco
Artesia

Carlsbad
CARLSBAD
CAVERNS
NAT'L PARK

Dayton
McMillan

Seagraves

O'Donnell
Double Mountain
Haskell
Newcastle
Graham

Hobbs
Seminole
Lamesa
Hamlin
Stamford
Anson
Albany
Breckenridge
Mineral Wells

Wind Mtn.
7278
Guadalupe Pk.
8751

Red Bluff Res.

Snyder
Rotan
Roscoe
Sweetwater
Merkel
Abilene
Baird
Ranger
Thurber
Strawn
Hubbard
Creek Res.
Brad

N. Franklin Mtn.
7176
El Paso
Ysleta
Ciudad Juárez
Fabens

Pecos

Midland
Big Spring
Stanton
Colorado
City
Winters
Ballinger
Gorman
De Leon
Dublin
Stephe
Eastland
Desdemona

Guadalupe

Sierra Blanca
Van Horn

Eagle Pk.
7496

Wink
Odessa
Sterling City
Coleman
Brownwood
Santa Anna
Comanche
Hamilto
Goldthwaite

Villa
Ahumada

MEXICO
U.S.A.
Rio
Bravo
del
Norte

Toyah

Pecos

Coyanosa Draw
McCamey

North
Concho
San Angelo
Eden
Brady
San Saba
Lometa
Lampas
Burn

DAVIS MTS.
Baldy Peak
8382

Marfa
Alpine
Fort Stockton

STOCKTON
PLATEAU

Sanderson

Sonora
Junction
Menard
Mason
Llano

EDWARDS
PLATEAU

Fredericksburg
Kerrville
San Mar

Chihuahua

Coyame
Cuchillo Parado

Ojinaga
Presidio

SANTIAGO MTS.
Cathedral Mt.
6860
Chinati Pk.
7730

BIG BEND
NAT'L PARK
Emory Pk.
7835

USA
MEXICO
SERRANÍAS
DEL BURRO

Del Rio
Villa Acuña

Rocksprings

Camp Wood
Brackettville
Sabinal
Hondo
Uvalde

San Antonio
New Braunfels
Boerne

Floresville
Poteet
Pleasanton

CHIHUAHUA

Meoqui
Naica

San
Pedro

Gigantes
Jaco

Jimenez
Piedras Negras
Fuente
Zaragoza
Morelos
Nava
Allende
Guerrero
Rosales

Eagle Pass
Carrizo Springs
Asherton
Crystal City

Pearsall
Cotulla
Fowlerton

George
West
Corpus Chri
Encinal

28°

Aldama

Conchos

Muzquiz
San Juan de Sabinas

SIERRA

COAHUILA

MADRE

Hidalgo
Dolores
San Diego

Hidalgo
del Parral
Jimenez
Villa Lopez

Santa Barbara
Valle de Allende
Villa Coronado
Escalon

Sierra Mojada
Laguna de
la Leche

Progreso
Abasolo
Sacramento
Cuatro Ciénegas
Nadadores
San Buenaventura
Monclova

Presa de
Martin

Nuevo Laredo
Laredo
Mirando City
Kings

Hebbronville
Premont
Falfurrias

MEXICO

BOLSÓN
DE
MAPIMI

ORIENTAL

Rey

Paloma

Rosario
Villa
Ocampo

Hidalgo
Rio de la Parida

26°

Indé
Santa Cruz

Mapimí
San Pedro de
las Colonias
Sacramento

Lampazos
Bustamante
Villaldama
Sabinas Hidalgo
Aguaguas
Guerrero
Mier
Camargo
Riogrande
Zapata
Falcon Res.

DURANGO

Rodeo
Nazas

Gómez Palacio
San Luis del
Cordero
Torreón
Lerdo
Matamoros

Laguna de
Mayran

Paredon
Garcia
General Zuazua
Salinas Victoria
Cerralvo
Los Herreros
China
Cadereyta Jimenez

Mission
McAl
Weslac
Reynosa

Viesca
Parras

Ramos Arizpe
Santa Catarina
Monterrey

Villa de Allende
Montemorelos

Presa
de Azucar

Cuencame

San Juan del Rio

Canatlán
Pánuco de
Coronado

Laguna de
Santiaguillo

Gómez Farias
General Cepeda
Saltillo
Arteaga

LEON

Linares

San
Fernando
Cruillas

Durango

San Bartolo
San Juan de
Guadalupe
Mazapil
Concepción
del Oro
Juan Aldama

ZACATECAS

Galeana
Burgos

Villagrán
San Carlos

TAMAULIP

Continued on pages 124–125

Longitude West of Greenwich

Scale 1:4 000 000; one inch to 64 miles. Conic Projection
Elevations and depressions are given in feet

Relief

Meters	Feet
1525	5000
610	2000
305	1000
152.5	500
0	Sea Level	0
152.5	500
1525	5000
3050	10 000

Continued on pages 116–117

Continued on pages 120 121

GULF OF MEXICO

Scale 1:1 000 000

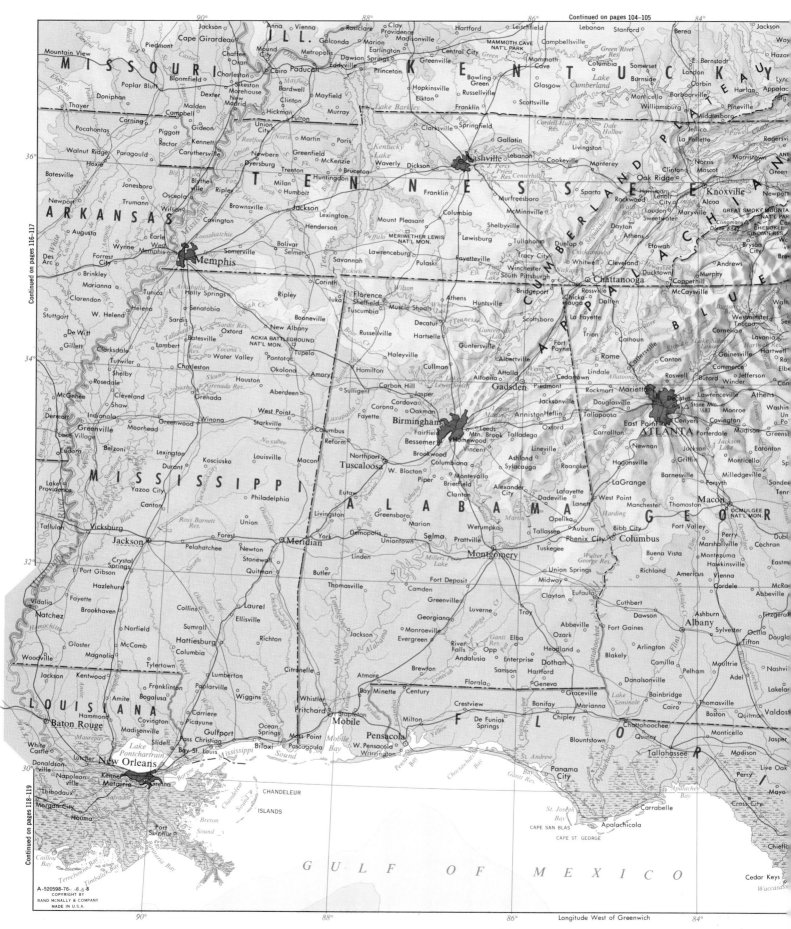

Continued on pages 104–105

Continued on pages 116–117

Continued on pages 118–119

A-520598-76-6.6-8
COPYRIGHT BY
RAND McNALLY & COMPANY
MADE IN U.S.A.

GULF OF MEXICO

Longitude West of Greenwich

Scale 1:4 000 000; one inch to 64 miles. Conic Projection
Elevations and depressions are given in feet

Relief

Meters	Feet
1525	5000
610	2000
305	1000
152.5	500
Sea Level	0
152.5	500
1525	5000

Same scale as main map

122

Scale 1:16 000 000; one inch to 250 miles. Polyconic Projection
Elevations and depressions are given in feet

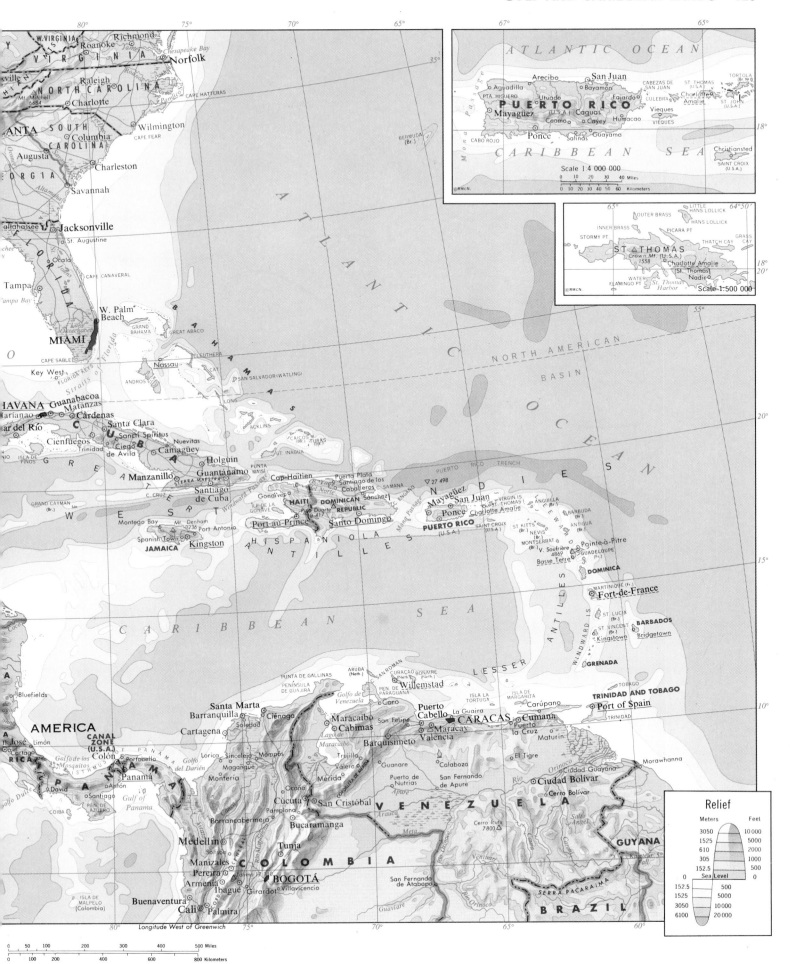

Inset map (upper right):

ATLANTIC OCEAN

Aguadilla   Arecibo   San Juan   CABEZAS DE   ST. THOMAS   TORTOLA (Br.)
PTA. HIGUERO   Utuado   Bayamón   SAN JUAN   (U.S.A.)   Charlotte
Mayagüez   Caguas   Fajardo   CULEBRA   Amalie
PUERTO RICO   Coamo   Cayey   Humacao   ST. JOHN (U.S.A.)
(U.S.A.)   VIEQUES
Cabo Rojo   Ponce   Salinas   Guayama   VIEQUES

CARIBBEAN SEA   Christiansted
SAINT CROIX (U.S.A.)

Scale 1:4 000 000

0   10   20   30   40 Miles
0   10 20 30 40 50 60 Kilometers
© RMcN.

Inset map (middle right):

LITTLE HANS LOLLICK
OUTER BRASS   HANS LOLLICK
INNER BRASS   PICARA PT   GRASS CAY
STORMY PT   THATCH CAY
ST THOMAS (U.S.A.)
Crown Mt.   Charlotte Amalie
1558   (St. Thomas)   Nadir
WATER   St. Thomas
FLAMINGO PT   Harbor
Scale 1:500 000
© RMcN.

Relief

Meters		Feet
3050		10 000
1525		5000
610		2000
305		1000
152.5		500
0	Sea Level	0
152.5		500
1525		5000
3050		10 000
6100		20 000

0   50   100   200   300   400   500 Miles
0   100 200   400   600   800 Kilometers

Longitude West of Greenwich

Continued on pages 118-119

106° 104° 102° 100°

24°

DURANGO

San Dimas
El Salto
Nombre de Dios
Pánuco
Siqueros
Concordia
Villa Unión
Rosario
Escuinapa
Huajicori
Acaponeta
Tecuala
San Felipe
Rosamorada

SINALOA

Miguel Auza
Juan Aldama
Durango
Nieves
Río Grande
Muleros
Sombrerete
Mezquital
Chalchihuites
Sain Alto
Cañitas
Fresnillo
Valparaíso
Calera
Víctor Rosales
Zacatecas
Morelos
Troncoso
Ramos

ZACATECAS

Gruñidora

NUEVO LEÓN

Ascensión
Aramberri
Zaragoza
Hidalgo
Jiménez
Padilla
Abasolo
Ciudad Victoria
Soto la Marina
Doctor Arroyo
Miquihuana
Jaumave
Llera
Xicoténcatl

TAMAULIPAS

SIERRA MADRE

SAN LUIS POTOSÍ

Vanegas
Cedral
Catorce
La Paz
Matehuala
Charcas
Venado
Moctezuma
Villa de Guadalupe
Guadalcázar
Cerritos
Peotillos
Bocas

Laguna de Agua Brava

Ruiz
Tuxpan
San Blas
Jalisco
Tepic

NAYARIT

Pochotitán
Sta. María del Oro
San Pedro Lagunillas
Compostela
Jomulco
Ixtlán del Río
Ahuacatlán

SIERRA MADRE DE NAYARIT

Huejuquilla el Alto
Mezquitic
Monte Escobedo
Huejúcar
Villanueva
Luis Moya
Asientos
Tepezalá
Villa García
Colotlán
Sta. María de los Ángeles
Rincón de Romos
Calvillo

AGUASCALIENTES
Aguascalientes

ALTIPLANICIE MEXICANA

Ojocaliente
Salinas
Zaragoza
Pozos
San Luis Potosí
Soledad Díez Gutiérrez
Pastora
Ciudad Fernández
Sta. María del Río
Ríoverde
Rayón
Cárdenas
El Ebano
Tamuín
Cd. de Valles
General Pedro Antonia Santos
Xilitla
Tamazunchale

SAN LUIS POTOSÍ

Tabasco
Jalpa
Villa Hidalgo
Teocaltiche
Nochistlán
Encarnación de Díaz
Lagos de Moreno
San Felipe
Villa de Reyes
Villa Pedro Montoya
Lagunillas
Arroyo Seco
Jalpan
Tolimán
Zimapán
Cadereyta
Colón
Amealco
Tequisquiapan
Tecozautla
Ixmiquilpan
Huichapan

QUERÉTARO

Jiménez del Téul
Juchipila
Moyahua
Yahualica
Jalostotitlán
Unión de San Antonio
San Francisco del Rincón
León
Silao
Guanajuato
San Miguel de Allende
San José Iturbide
Querétaro
Cayetano Rubio

GUANAJUATO

Bolaños
Chimaltitán
García de la Cadena
Cuquío
San Miguel el Alto
Tepatitlán de Morelos
Ciudad Manuel Doblado
Romita
Comonfort

JALISCO

SIERRA DE VALLEJO

Punta de Mita
Bahía de Banderas
Puerto Vallarta
Mascota
Talpa de Allende
Cabo Corrientes

Ezatlán
Ahualulco
Amatlán de Cañas
Ameca
Tequila
Zapopan
Guadalajara
Tlaquepaque
Tonalá
Zapotlanejo
Arandas
Atotonilco el Alto
Ayo el Chico
San Juan de los Lagos
Jalpa
Pénjamo
Irapuato
Salamanca
Cortazar
Celaya
Juventino Rosas
Valle de Santiago
Jaral del Progreso
Salvatierra
Tequisquiapan
Tecozautla
San Juan del Río
Amealco

SIERRA MADRE OCCIDENTAL

Cocula
Tecolotlán
Tenamaxtlán
Ayutla
Zacoalco de Torres
Jocotepec
Tlajomulco de Zúñiga
Ocotlán
Chapala
La Barca
Degollado
La Piedad
Cabadas
Yurécuaro
Angamacutiro
Penjamillo
Puruándiro
Moroleón
Yuriria
Acámbaro
Contepec
Maravatío
El Oro
Tlalpujahua
Angangueo
Zitácuaro

HIDALGO
Pachuca
Mixquiahuala
Actopan
Tezontepec de Aldama
Tula
Tepeji del Río
Tezontepec
Zumpango
Otumba

Tototlán
Tomatlán
Autlán
Unión de Tula
Venustiano Carranza
El Grullo
Purificación
Casimiro Castillo
Tamazula de Gordiano
Zapotiltic
Ciudad Guzmán
Tuxpan
Tecalitlán

Lago de Chapala

Jiquilpan
Sahuayo de Díaz
Chavinda
Zamora
Tangancícuaro
Purépero
Chilchota
Zacapu
Coeneo de la Libertad
Zináparo
Quiroga
Morelia
Pátzcuaro
Ciudad Hidalgo

MICHOACÁN

Cotija de la Paz
Los Reyes
Tingüindín
Paracho
Cherán
Uruapan
Villa Escalante
Acuitzio del Canje

Lago de Pátzcuaro

Nevada de Colima 13,993
de Colima 12,620

Minatitlán
Comala
Villa de Álvarez
Colima
Cuyutlán

COLIMA

Bahía de Manzanillo
Manzanillo
Tecomán

Coalcomán de Matamoros
Aguililla
Tepalcatepec
Tancítaro
Apatzingán de la Constitución
Tacámbaro de Codallas
Turicato
Carácuaro de Morelos
Tacámbaro

Cerro Tancítaro 12,660
V. Parícutin 9,210

SIERRA DE COALCOMÁN

Churumuco
Huetamo de Núñez
Cutzamala de Pinzón
Zirándaro
Ciudad Altamirano
Coyuca de Catalán
Ajuchitlán del Progreso
Coahuayutla

Presa de Infiernillo

Tumbiscatío

Arcelia
Tlapehuala
Apipilulco
Cuetzala del Progreso
Teloloapan
Cuetzala
Iguala
Huitzuco
Tepecoacuilco de Trujano
Taxco de Alarcón
Ixcateopan
Acapetlahuaya
Tlatlaya
Teloloapan

GUERRERO

Tlacotepec
Atliaca
Tixtla de Guerrero
Chilapa
Apango
Zitlala
Mochitlán
Chilpancingo
Olinalá
Huamuxtitlán
Tlapa
Silacayoapan
Zapotitlán

SIERRA MADRE

Tecpan de Galeana
Atoyac de Álvarez
San Jerónimo de Juárez
Coyuca de Benítez
Acapulco
Petatlán
Tlacotepec

Cuautepec
San Marcos
Ayutla
Cozoyoapan
Azoyú
Ometepec
Tecoanapa
Pinotepa Nacional
Puerto Minis

PACIFIC OCEAN

Punta de Mita
Pta. Farallón
Punta Tejupan
Bahía de Petacalco
La Unión

DISTRITO FEDERAL
MÉXICO CITY
Azcapotzalco
Coyoacán
Tlalpan
Toluca
Metepec
Lerma
Tenango
Tenancingo
Valle de Bravo
Temascaltepec
Texcaltitlán
Sultepec
Zacualpan
Cuernavaca
Yautepec
Cuautla

MORELOS

Nevado de Toluca 15,409
Popocatépetl 17,887
Ixtaccíhuatl 17,343

TLAXCALA

Apizaco
Calpulalpan
Huamantla
Puebla

PUEBLA

Huejotzingo
Cholula
Atlixco
Huaquechula
Huatlatla
Axochiapan
Chiautla
Tulcingo
Xochihuehuetla
Acatlán de Osorio
Chiautla
Tehuitzingo

Laguna Papagayo

Laguna Catarina

22°

20°

18°

16°

Longitude West of Greenwich

104° 102° 100°

Scale 1:4 000 000; one inch to 64 miles. Conic Projection
Elevations and depressions are given in feet

Relief

Meters		Feet
3050		10 000
1525		5000
610		2000
305		1000
152.5		500
0	Sea Level	0
152.5		500
1525		5000
3050		10 000

Inset Map — Mexico City

Morelos
Nicolás Romero
Cuautitlán
Tutitlán
Tecamac
Teotihuacán
Acolman
Otumba
HIDALGO
Apan

Cahuacán
San Bartolo
Coacalco
Pyramids of Teotihuacán
Calpulalpan

MÉXICO
Ixtlahuaca
Atizapán
Tepexpan
Tepetlaoxtoc
TLAXCALA

Jiquipilco
Cerro La Catedral 13 000
Tlalnepantla
Gustavo A. Madero
San Jerónimo
Texcoco
Nanacamilpa

Atzcapotzalco
Naucalpan
Lago de Texcoco (Dry Lake)
Coatlinchán

Temoaya
Mimiapan
Chimalpa
MEXICO CITY
Chicoloapan

Mazatla
Ixtacalco
Los Reyes

Huixquilucan
Cuajimalpa
Ixtapalapa
Ayotla
INTER - AMERICAN
Río Frío
HY.

Toluca
Lerma
Villa Obregón Contreras
Coyoacán
Ixtapaluca
Texmelucan

Capultitlán
San Andrés
Tlalpan
Xochimilco
Tláhuac
PUEBLA

Metepec
Mexicalcingo
Cerro Muneca 12 655
Ajusco
Topilejo
Tecómitl
Chalco

Almoloya
Cerro Ajusco 12 850
Milpa Alta
Tlalmanalco
Iztaccihuatl △ 17 343

Nevado de Toluca △ 14 409
Coatepec
Oxtotepec
Tenango
Amecameca

Tenango
Tres Cumbres
Ozumba
Volcán Popocatépetl 17 887

Scale 1:1 000 000
Huitzilac
Tepoztlán
Tlalnepantla

0   10 Miles
0 4 8 12 16 Kilometers

MORELOS
Tlayacapan

©RMcN
Cuernavaca

Main Map

Laguna Almagre
Tropic of Cancer

TA. JEREZ

Laguna de San Andrés

ra

ad Madero
ampico
a Cuauhtémoc
mpico Alto

Laguna Tamiahua
CABO ROJO
ARRECIFE BLANQUILLA
ISLA DE LOBOS

ma

ancoco
Tamiahua

Alamo
ARRECIFE TANQUIJO
ARRECIFE TÚXPAN

Túxpan

GULF OF MEXICO

pan
Poza Rica
Tecolutla
Gutiérrez Zamora

Furbero
Coyutla
Nautla

Coxquihui
Vega de Alatorre

Cuetzalan del Progreso
Tlapacoyan
Misantla

án
axtla
Atempan
Teziutlán
Jalacingo
Altotonga
Naolinco

Libres
Las Vigas
Perote
△14 048
Jalapa Enríquez
Punta Zempoala

ΒΑΗÍΑ   DE   CAMPECHE

Teocelo
Coatepec
Antigua Veracruz

a
Teocelo
Veracruz
ARRECIFE CABEZA

atzingo
Huatusco
Coscomatepec

o Hidalgo
atempan
Maltrata
Orizaba
Heroica Córdoba
Medellín
Tlalixcoyan
Alvarado

otepec
Nogales
Omealca Cotaxtla
Laguna

Tehuacan
Ajalpan
Zoquitlán
San Martín (Vol.) △ 6000
PTA ZAPOTLÁN

San Gabriel Chilac
Zinacatepec
Tlacotalpan
Santiago Tuxtla
San Andrés Tuxtla
Catemaco

Chazumba
Huatla de Jiménez
Ojitlán (S. Lucas)
Tuxtepec
Pajápan
Coatzacoalcos (Puerto México)

alcingo
S. Miguel
Teotitlán del Camino
Jalapa de Díaz (San Felipe)
Cosamaloapan
Chacaltianguis
Soteapan

Tepelmeme
San Juan Evangelista
Jaltipan
Texistepec

ajuapan de León
Coixtlahuaca
Cuicatlán
Acayucan
Minatitlán
Sayula

ogreso
Tejúpan (Santiago)
Playa Vicente

dro y San Pablo
Nochixtlán (Asunción)
Talea de Castro (San Miguel)
Jesús Carranza
Pueblo Viejo

Tlaxiaco
Sta. María Asunción
Ixtlán de Juárez
Villa Alta (San Ildefonso)
ISTMO
Presa de Malpaso

ero
Chalcatongo (Sta. Catarina)
San Mateo (Etlatongo)
Talea de Castro
Zempoaltepetl △11 742
Zacatepec (Santiago)

lotlán (Sta. María)
Yosonotú
Zaachila
Tlacolula de Matamoros
Oaxaca de Juárez
Mazatlán (San Juan)
DE

niltepec
Sola de Vega (S. Miguel)
Zimatlán de Álvarez
Ocotlán de Morelos
Guichicovi (San Juan)
Ixtepec
TEHUANTEPEC

Tóviche
INTER - AMERICAN HY.
Jalapa del Marqués
Ixtaltepec (Asunción)
Zanatepec (Sto. Domingo)

Loxicha (Sta. Catarina)
Miahuatlán
Ejutla de Crespo
Las Vacas
Juchitán de Zaragoza
Unión Hidalgo
Ixhuatán (San Francisco)

Pluma Hidalgo
Tehuantepec (Sto. Domingo)
Laguna Superior
Laguna Inferior
Mar Muerto

Pochutla (San Pedro)
Salina Cruz
Tonalá

Puerto Ángel
Golfo de Tehuantepec

Eastern section

Sisal
Hunucmá
YUCATÁN

Maxcanú
Halachó

Calkini
Dzitbalché

Hecelchakán

Lerma
Campeche

Seybaplaya

Champotón

Pustunich

Sabancuy
CAMPECHE

Chicbul

San Pedro
ISLA DEL CARMEN
Ciudad del Carmen
Laguna de Términos
Mamantel

PUNTA FONTERA
Frontera
Palizada

Paraíso
Allende
Arroyo Caribe

San Pedro
Comalcalco
TABASCO

Huimanguillo
Jalpa
Cunduacán
Januta

Cárdenas
Villahermosa
San Carlos
Balancán
**MEXICO
GUATEMALA**

Pichucalco
Tacotalpa
Teapa
Emiliano Zapata
Palenque

Chapultenango
Pantepec
Simojovel
Yajalón
Tenosique

Tecpatán
Compaialá
Jitotol
Bachajón
Ococingo

9 400
Cancuc
Oxchuc
MESETA DE AGUA ESCONDIDA

Berriozábal
Ozocoautla
Chiapa de Corzo
Ciudad de las Casas
Acala

Tuxtla Gutiérrez
Bohom
Teopisca
Amatenango

Cintalapa
Suchiapa
Las Rosas

Las Cruces
Venustiano Carranza
Socoltenango
Comitán

8202
Villa Flores
La Concordia
Trinitaria

Tapanatepec
Arriaga
**SIERRA
CUCHUMATANES**

CORD. DE CHIAPAS
La Concordia
GUATEMALA

Cuauhtémoc
Jacatenango

Pijijiapan

Mapastepec
San Miguel

For larger scale coverage of Mexico City see page 58.

Continued on pages 126-127

0 20 40 60 80 100 120 Miles
0 20 40 60 80 100 120 140 160 180 200 Kilometers

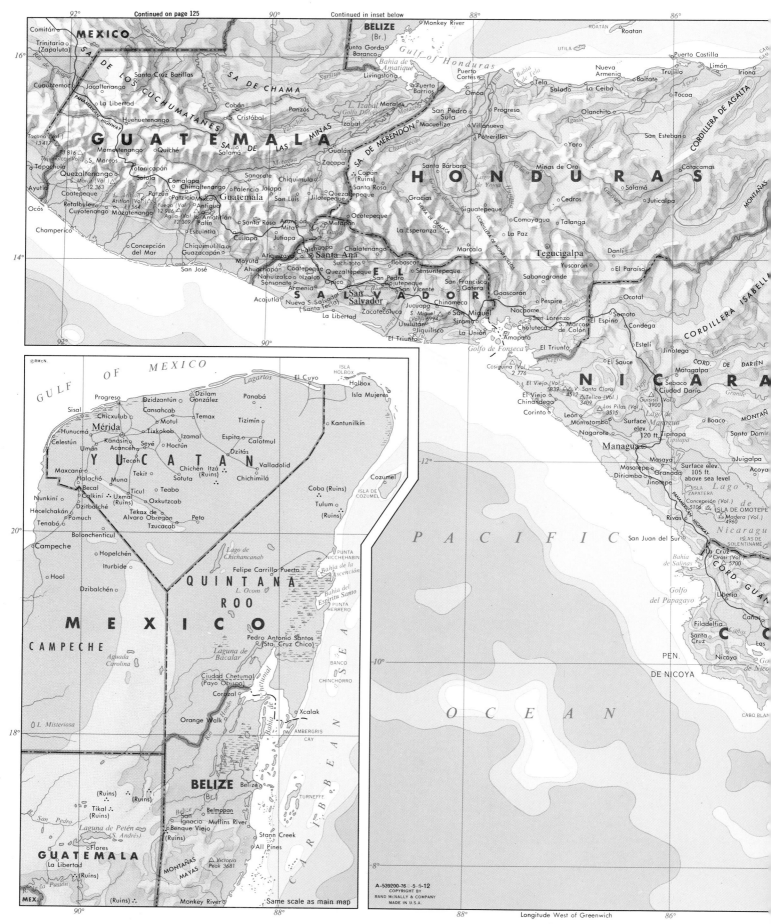

126

Continued on page 125
Continued in inset below

MEXICO

BELIZE
(Br.)

GUATEMALA

HONDURAS

EL SALVADOR

NICARA

GULF OF MEXICO

YUCATAN

QUINTANA ROO

MEXICO

CAMPECHE

BELIZE
(Br.)

GUATEMALA

CARIBBEAN SEA

PACIFIC OCEAN

PEN. DE NICOYA

A-539200-76 -5-4-12
COPYRIGHT BY
RAND McNALLY & COMPANY
MADE IN U.S.A.

Longitude West of Greenwich

Scale 1:4 000 000; one inch to 64 miles. Sinusoidal Projection

Elevations and depressions are given in feet

Same scale as main map

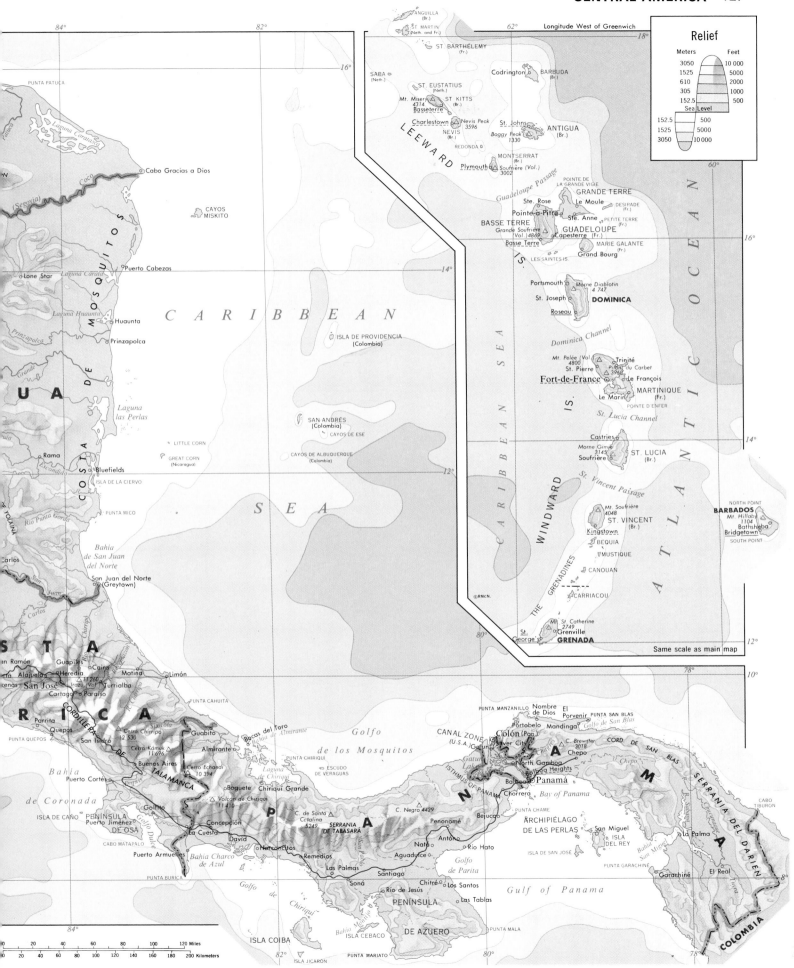

Longitude West of Greenwich

Relief

Meters	Feet
3050	10 000
1525	5000
610	2000
305	1000
152.5	500
Sea Level	
152.5	500
1525	5000
3050	10 000

ANGUILLA (Br.)
ST. MARTIN (Neth. and Fr.)

ST. BARTHÉLEMY (Fr.)

SABA (Neth.)
ST. EUSTATIUS (Neth.)
Codrington BARBUDA (Br.)

Mt. Misery 4314 ST. KITTS (Br.)
Basseterre
Charlestown Nevis Peak 3596 St. Johns ANTIGUA (Br.)
NEVIS (Br.) Boggy Peak 1330

REDONDA (Br.)

MONTSERRAT (Br.)
Plymouth Soufrière (Vol.) 3002

LEEWARD IS.

Guadeloupe Passage
POINTE DE LA GRANDE VIGIE
GRANDE TERRE
Ste. Rose Le Moule DESIRADE (Fr.)
Pointe-à-Pitre Ste. Anne PETITE TERRE (Fr.)
BASSE TERRE Grande Soufrière (Vol.) 4869 GUADELOUPE
Basse Terre Capesterre (Fr.)
MARIE GALANTE (Fr.)
LES SAINTES IS. Grand Bourg

Portsmouth Morne Diablotin 4 747
St. Joseph DOMINICA
Roseau

Dominica Channel

Mt. Pelée (Vol.) 4800 Trinité
St. Pierre Pitons du Carbet 3960
Fort-de-France Le François
Le Marin MARTINIQUE (Fr.)
POINTE D'ENFER

CARIBBEAN SEA

St. Lucia Channel

Castries
Morne Gimie 3145 ST. LUCIA (Br.)
Soufrière

WINDWARD IS.

St. Vincent Passage

Mt. Soufrière 4048
ST. VINCENT (Br.)
Kingstown
BEQUIA
MUSTIQUE

NORTH POINT
BARBADOS
Mt. Hillaby 1104
Bathsheba
Bridgetown
SOUTH POINT

CANOUAN

THE GRENADINES

CARRIACOU

Mt. St. Catherine 2749
St. George's Grenville
GRENADA

Same scale as main map

©RMcN.

ATLANTIC OCEAN

PUNTA PATUCA

Laguna Caratasca
Coco (Segovia)
Cabo Gracias a Dios

CAYOS MISKITO

CARIBBEAN

Lone Star
Laguna Caratá Puerto Cabezas

Huaunta
Laguna Huaunta
Prinzapolca
Prinzapolca

Laguna las Perlas

ISLA DE PROVIDENCIA (Colombia)

SEA

Rama
Bluefields
ISLA DE LA CIERVO

SAN ANDRÉS (Colombia)
CAYOS DE ESE

LITTLE CORN
GREAT CORN (Nicaragua)

CAYOS DE ALBUQUERQUE (Colombia)

Punta Mico

SEA

Bahía de San Juan del Norte
San Juan del Norte (Greytown)

San Carlos

CARIBBEAN SEA

San Ramón Guápiles Caira
Alajuela Heredia Matina
San José Irazú 11 260 (Vol.) Turrialba Limón
Cartago Paraíso
CORDILLERA
Parrita
Quepos
Punta Quepos
San Isidro

Cerro Chirripó 12 530
Cerro Kámuk 11 696
Buenos Aires
Cerro Echandi 10 394

DE TALAMANCA

Bahía de Coronada

Puerto Cortés

PENÍNSULA DE OSA
Puerto Jiménez
CABO MATAPALO

Golfito
Golfo Dulce

La Cuesta
Concepción
David
Horconcitos
Puerto Armuelles
PUNTA BURICA

PUNTA CAHUITA

Guabito
Almirante
Bocas del Toro
Bahía de Almirante
PUNTA CHIRIQUÍ

Golfo de los Mosquitos

Chiriquí Grande

Boquete
Volcán de Chiriquí 11 410
C. de Santa Catalina 8249
SERRANÍA DE TABASARA

Laguna de Chiriquí
ESCUDO DE VERAGUAS

ISTMO DE PANAMÁ

C. Negro 4429

La Palma
Remedios
Las Palmas
Soná
Santiago
Río de Jesús
Chitré
Los Santos
Las Tablas

PENÍNSULA DE AZUERO

ISLA COIBA
ISLA CEBACO
PUNTA MALA
PUNTA MARIATO
ISLA JICARÓN

Bahía Montijo
Chiriquí

Golfo de Montijo

PUNTA MANZANILLO Nombre de Dios El Porvenir PUNTA SAN BLAS
CANAL ZONE (U.S.A.) Portobelo Mandinga Golfo de San Blas
Colón (Pan.) Gatún Silver City
Gatún Lake C. Brewster 3018 CORD. DE SAN BLAS
North Gamboa Chepo
Balboa Heights
Balboa Panamá
Chorrera
Bay of Panama

PANAMÁ

Bejuco
PUNTA CHAME

Penonomé
Antón
Aguadulce
Río Hato
Natá

Golfo de Parita

Golfo de Panamá

Gulf of Panama

ARCHIPIÉLAGO DE LAS PERLAS
San Miguel
ISLA DEL REY
ISLA DE SAN JOSÉ
PUNTA GARACHINÉ

SERRANÍA DEL DARIÉN

CABO TIBURÓN

La Palma
El Real
Garachiné

Chepo

Bahía de San Miguel

COLOMBIA

| 0 20 40 60 80 100 120 Miles |
| 0 20 40 60 80 100 120 140 160 180 200 Kilometers |

Relief

Meters		Feet
3050		10 000
1525		5000
610		2000
305		1000
152.5		500
0	Sea Level	0
152.5		500
1525		5000
3050		10 000
6100		20 000

A-533200-76 5-4-8
COPYRIGHT BY
RAND McNALLY & COMPANY
MADE IN U.S.A.

Longitude West of Greenwich

Scale 1:4 000 000; one inch to 64 miles. Conic Projection
Elevations and depressions are given in feet.

Scale 1:1 000 000

HAVANA
(La Habana)

Playa de Guanabo
Cojimar
Guanabacoa
Regla
Campo Florido
Playa de Santa Fé
Marianao
San Francisco de Paula
Baracoa
Cotorro
Arroyo Arena
Calabazar
Cuatro Caminos
Bauta
Rancho Boyeros
Managua
Caimito del Guayabal
Santiago de las Vegas
San José de las Lajas
La Sabina
Bejucal
Ceiba del Agua
San Antonio de los Baños
Buenaventura
San Antonio de las Vegas
L. de Ariguanabo
△ 950
©RMcN.

JAMES PT.
Governor's Harbour
PALMETTO PT.
ELEUTHERA
Rock Sound

A T L A N T I C

O C E A N

HERA PT.
Arthur's Town
NORTHEAST PT.
LITTLE SAN SALVADOR
CAT

Old Bight
HAWKS NEST PT.
COLUMBUS PT.
SAN SALVADOR (WATLING)
(Columbus, Oct. 12, 1492)
SOUTHWEST PT.

GREAT
UANA CAY
CONCEPTIÓN

LEE STOCKING
Rolleville
CAPE STA. MARIA
RUM CAY

GREAT EXUMA
George Town
LITTLE EXUMA
HOG CAY
LONG
Clarence Town
SAMANÁ OR ATWOOD CAY

Tropic of Cancer

JUMENTO CAYS
WATER CAY
FLAMINGO CAY
CAP VERDE
BIRD ROCK
CROOKED
NORTHEAST PT.

Man of War Channel
JAMAICA CAY
SEAL CAYS
FORTUNE
DIANA BANK
FISH CAY
The Bight of Acklins
ACKLINS
PLANA OR FLAT CAYS

CHINOS
ANKS
NURSE CAY
RACCOON CAY
SALINA PT.
CASTLE
Abraham's Bay
MAYAGUANA

GREAT RAGGED
MIRA POR VOS ISLETS
CAY VERDE
Mayaguana Passage

COLUMBUS BANK
CAY STA. DOMINGO
HOGSTY REEF
Caicos Passage
PROVIDENCIALES
NORTH CAICOS
GRAND CAICOS
CAPE COMETE
EAST CAICOS

BROWN BANK
WEST CAICOS
CAICOS IS. (Br.)
CAICOS BANK
GRAND TURK
Grand Turk
TURKS IS. (Br.)

LITTLE INAGUA
NORTHEAST PT.
WEST SAND SPIT
SOUTH CAICOS
AMBERGRIS CAYS
SALT CAY

PALMETTO PT.
Ocean Bight
The Lake
GREAT INAGUA
SEAL CAYS
Turks I. Passage
Mouchoir Passage
MOUCHOIR BANK

CABO LUCRECIA
Man of War Bay
Matthew Town
South Bay
Silver Bank Passage
SILVER BANK

Holguin
Banes
Antilla
Bahia de Nipe
NAVIDAD BANK

OLGUÍN
Mayari
Sagua de Tánamo
CUCHILLAS DE TOAR
△3700
Baracoa

SANTIAGO DE CUBA
Alto Songo
SA. DE PURIAL
PUNTA MAISÍ

STRA
Soriano
San Luis
Caney
△Gran Piedra 4011
Guantánamo
Bahia de Ovando
ÎLE DE LA TORTUE
CABO ISABELA

Santiago de Cuba
Chimaneyo
Yateras
Naval Station (U.S.A.)
Bahia de Guantánamo
Canal de la Tortue
Port de Paix
Le Borgne
Monte Cristi
Puerto Plata
CORDILLERA SEPTENTRIONAL
Pico Diego △4009
CABO FRANCÉS VIEJO

CAP ST. NICOLAS
Le Môle
Limbé
Grande Rivière du Nord
Fort
Guayubin
Mao
Dajabón
Santiago Rodríguez
Gaspar Hernández
Bahia Escocesa

PTE. PLATEFORME
Gonaïves
St. Michel-de-l'Atalaye
Valliére
Santiago de los Caballeros
Salcedo
Nagua
CABO SAMANÁ

GOLFE DES GONAÏVES
Hinche
DOMINICAN
Riva
Bahia de Samaná
CABO SAN RAFAEL

H A I T I
St. Marc
Pic Bonhomme △5883
Mte. Mio △7445
Pico Duarte △10417
CORDILLERA CENTRAL
Jarabacoa
Cotuí
Sabana de la Mar
Miches

POINT OUEST
ÎLE DE LA GONÂVE
△2546
Étang Saumâtre
SIERRA DE NEIBA
Lago Enriquillo
Bánica
San Juan
△2285
Yamasá
Haiti Mayor
Bayaguana
Los Llanos
Sejbo

Jérémie
ÎLE GRANDE CAYÉMITE
Mirebalais
Lascahobas
CORDILLERA ORIENTAL
Higüey

CAP DAME MARIE
CAP DES IROIS
Canal du Sud
Port-au-Prince
Léogâne
Pétionville
R E P U B L I C
Azua
San Cristóbal
Santo Domingo
La Romana

FORMIGAS BANK
Anse d'Hainault
Baie des Baraderes
Anse à Veau
MASSIF DE LA SELLE
△6793
SIERRA DE NEIBA
Neiba
Baní
CATALINA

NAVASSA (U.S.A.)
MASSIF DE LA HOTTE
Pico de Macaya △7920
Miragoâne
Petit Goâve
Duvergé
Barahona
Bahia de Ocoa
PTA. PALENQUE

t Antonio
Tiburon
Coteaux
Aquin
Jacmel
Belle-Anse
SIERRA DE BAHORUCO
Enriquillo
SAONA

Roche à Bateau
Les Cayes
ÎLE À VACHE
S E A
POINTE À GRAVOIS
Duvergé
H I S P A N I O L A

MORANT PT.
CABO FALSO
Oviedo
Il. Trujin
BEATA
CABO BEATA
ALTO VELO

10 20 30 40 50 60 70 80 90 100 110 120 Miles
20 40 60 80 100 120 140 160 180 200 Kilometers

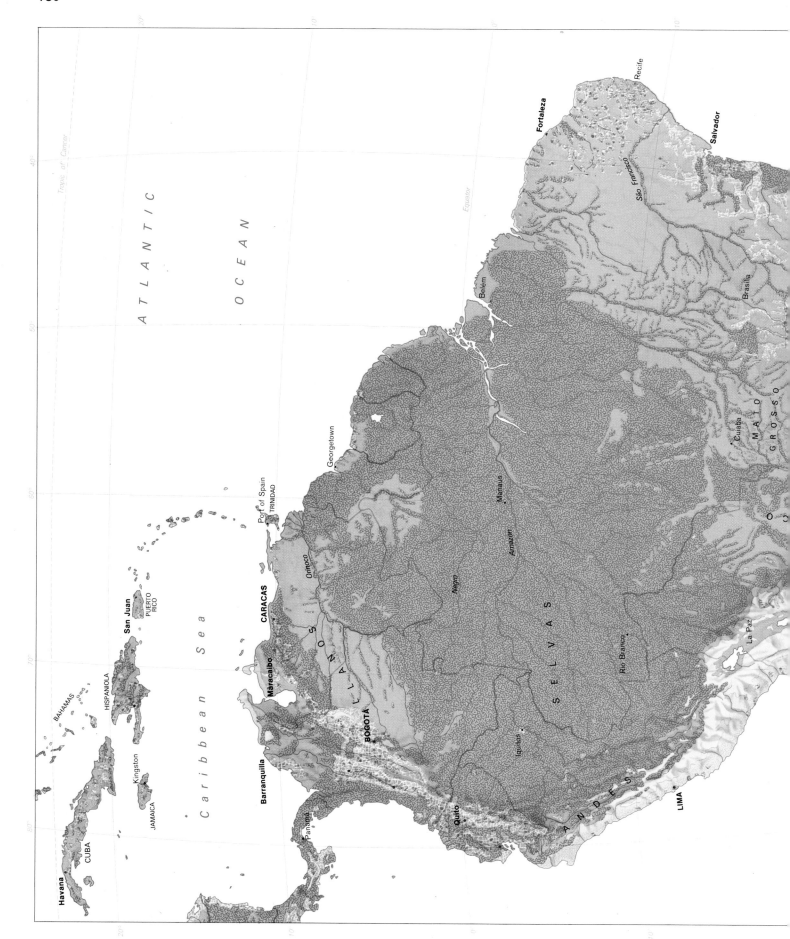

A T L A N T I C

O C E A N

Tropic of Cancer

Equator

Fortaleza

Recife

Salvador

São Francisco

Brasília

Belém

Cuiabá

M A T O   G R O S S O

Georgetown

Manaus

Amazon

S E L V A S

Port of Spain
TRINIDAD

Orinoco

Negro

Rio Branco

La Paz

San Juan

PUERTO
RICO

CARACAS

L L A N O S

Maracaibo

BOGOTÁ

Iquitos

A N D E S

LIMA

Barranquilla

Quito

C a r i b b e a n   S e a

BAHAMAS

HISPANIOLA

Kingston

JAMAICA

Panamá

Havana

CUBA

Scale 1:24,000,000; one inch to 380 miles. Lambert Azimuthal Equal-Area Projection

ATLANTIC

OCEAN

RIO DE JANEIRO

SÃO PAULO

Paraná

Porto Alegre

Asunción

Montevideo

SOUTH
GEORGIA

PAMPAS

BUENOS AIRES

Bahia Blanca

San Miguel de Tucumán

Córdoba

GRAN

FALKLAND
ISLANDS

Drake Passage

ANDES

PATAGONIA

TIERRA
DEL FUEGO

ANTARCTIC PENINSULA

SANTIAGO

Puerto Montt

Punta Arenas

PACIFIC

OCEAN

A-540000-96   -1-2
COPYRIGHT BY
RAND McNALLY & COMPANY
MADE IN U.S.A.

- Urban

Cropland

Cropland & Woodland

Cropland & Grazing Land

Grassland, Grazing Land

Forest, Woodland

Swamp, Marshland

Shrub, Sparse Grass,
Wasteland (pattern)

Barren Land

| 0 | 100 | 200 | 400 | 600 | 800 Miles |

| 0 | 150 | 300 | 600 | 900 | 1200 Kilometers |

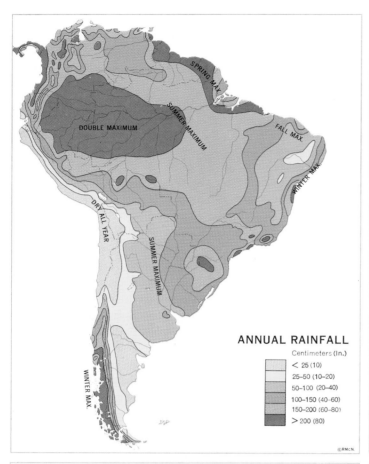

DOUBLE MAXIMUM

SPRING MAX.

SUMMER MAXIMUM

FALL MAX.

WINTER MAX.

DRY ALL YEAR

SUMMER MAXIMUM

WINTER MAX.

ANNUAL RAINFALL

Centimeters (In.)

	< 25 (10)
	25–50 (10–20)
	50–100 (20–40)
	100–150 (40–60)
	150–200 (60–80)
	> 200 (80)

©RMcN.

For explanation of letters in boxes,
see Natural Vegetation Map
by A. W. Küchler, p.16

LLANOS

SELVAS

CAATINGA

LOMA

PUNA

GRAN CHACO

ATACAMA

PAMPA

VEGETATION

B	Tropical rain forest
B'	Mediterranean vegetation
S	Semideciduous forest
D	Broadleaf deciduous (galeria forest)
SE	Araucaria forest
M	Beech, cedar forest
Di	Xerophytic open forest
Szp	Desert shrub
G	Tall grass
Gsp	Tall grass, galleria forest
DsG	Low grass, desert shrub
GDsp	Montane grass, tola shrub
b	Little or no vegetation

©RMcN.

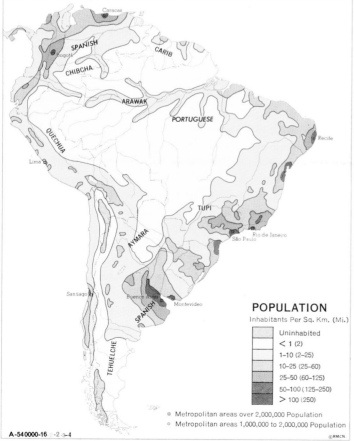

Caracas

SPANISH

Bogotá

CHIBCHA

CARIB

ARAWAK

PORTUGUESE

QUECHUA

Lima

Recife

TUPI

AYMARA

Rio de Janeiro

São Paulo

Santiago

Buenos Aires

Montevideo

SPANISH

TEHUELCHE

POPULATION

Inhabitants Per Sq. Km. (Mi.)

	Uninhabited
	< 1 (2)
	1–10 (2–25)
	10–25 (25–60)
	25–50 (60–125)
	50–100 (125–250)
	> 100 (250)

□ Metropolitan areas over 2,000,000 Population
○ Metropolitan areas 1,000,000 to 2,000,000 Population

A-540000-16 -2-3-4

©RMcN.

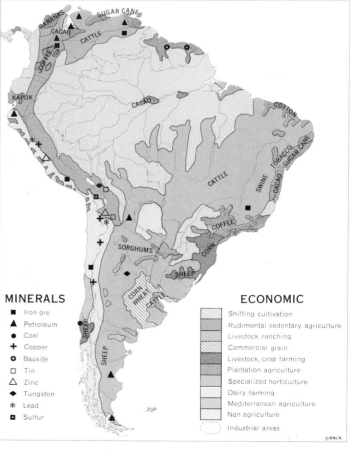

BANANAS

CACAO

SUGAR CANE

CATTLE

COFFEE

KAPOK

CACAO

CACAO

COTTON

CATTLE

SWINE

TOBACCO

SUGAR CANE

CACAO

CORN

COFFEE

SORGHUMS

SHEEP

CORN WHEAT

CATTLE

SHEEP

SHEEP

MINERALS

■	Iron ore
▲	Petroleum
●	Coal
✛	Copper
○	Bauxite
□	Tin
△	Zinc
◆	Tungsten
✳	Lead
▣	Sulfur

ECONOMIC

	Shifting cultivation
	Rudimental sedentary agriculture
	Livestock ranching
	Commercial grain
	Livestock, crop farming
	Plantation agriculture
	Specialized horticulture
	Dairy farming
	Mediterranean agriculture
	Non agriculture
	Industrial areas

©RMcN.

HAVANA

CENTRAL

AMERICA

NORTH AMERICAN BASIN

ATLANTIC OCEAN

CARIBBEAN SEA

Barranquilla
Cartagena
Panama
Maracaibo
Valencia CARACAS
Port of Spain
TRINIDAD AND TOBAGO

Medellín BOGOTÁ
Mérida Ciudad Bolívar
VENEZUELA
Georgetown
Paramaribo
GUYANA
SURINAM
FR. GUIANA
Cayenne

COLOMBIA
Boa Vista do Rio Branco
GUIANA HIGHLANDS

Quito
ECUADOR
Guayaquil
Cotopaxi

Equator
ILHA DE MARAJÓ
Belém (Pará)
São Luís (Maranhão)
ROCEDOS SÃO PEDRO E SÃO PAULO (Brazil)

Manaus (Manáos)
Rio Negro
Rio Amazonas

Iquitos
Leticia
Rio Solimões (Amazonas)

PERU
Fortaleza (Ceará)
ARQUIPÉLAGO FERNANDO DE NORONHA (Brazil)

Chiclayo
Trujillo
Rio Branco
Pôrto Velho
Teresina
Natal
João Pessoa (Paraíba)
RECIFE (Pernambuco)
Maceió

LIMA
Callao
Cuzco
B R A Z I L
CHAPADA DE MATO GROSSO
Cuiabá
Brasília
Salvador (Bahia)

Arequipa
La Paz
BOLIVIA
Sucre
Potosí
Belo Horizonte
Diamantina
Vitória

Mollendo
Iquique
GRAN CHACO
PARAGUAY
SÃO PAULO
Santos
RIO DE JANEIRO
CABO FRIO

Antofagasta
Salta
Tucumán
Asunción
Iguassú Falls

Copiapó
Corrientes
Florianópolis

Coquimbo
Córdoba
Santa Fe
Salto
Pôrto Alegre

Valparaíso
SANTIAGO
Mendoza
Rosario
URUGUAY
BUENOS AIRES
Rio Grande

Concepción
A R G E N T I N A
La Plata
MONTEVIDEO

PAMPAS

Valdivia
Bahía Blanca

Puerto Montt
Viedma
Golfo San Matías

Comodoro Rivadavia
Golfo San Jorge

Río Gallegos
Stanley
SOUTH GEORGIA (Falkland Is.)

Punta Arenas
TIERRA DEL FUEGO
ISLA DE LOS ESTADOS

CABO DE HORNOS (CAPE HORN)

Drake Passage

PACIFIC OCEAN

ATLANTIC OCEAN

SOUTH SHETLAND ISLANDS (B.A.T.)
SOUTH ORKNEY IS. (B.A.T.)
SOUTH SANDWICH ISLANDS (Falkland Is.)

Antarctic Circle

Relief		
Meters		Feet
3050		10 000
1525		5000
610		2000
305		1000
0	Sea Level	0
152.5		500
1525		5000
3050		10 000
6100		20 000

Longitude West of Greenwich

Scale 1:40 000 000, one inch to 630 miles. Lambert's Azimuthal, Equal Area Projection
Elevations and depressions are given in feet

0   200   400   600   800   1000 Miles
0   400   800   1200   1600 Kilometers

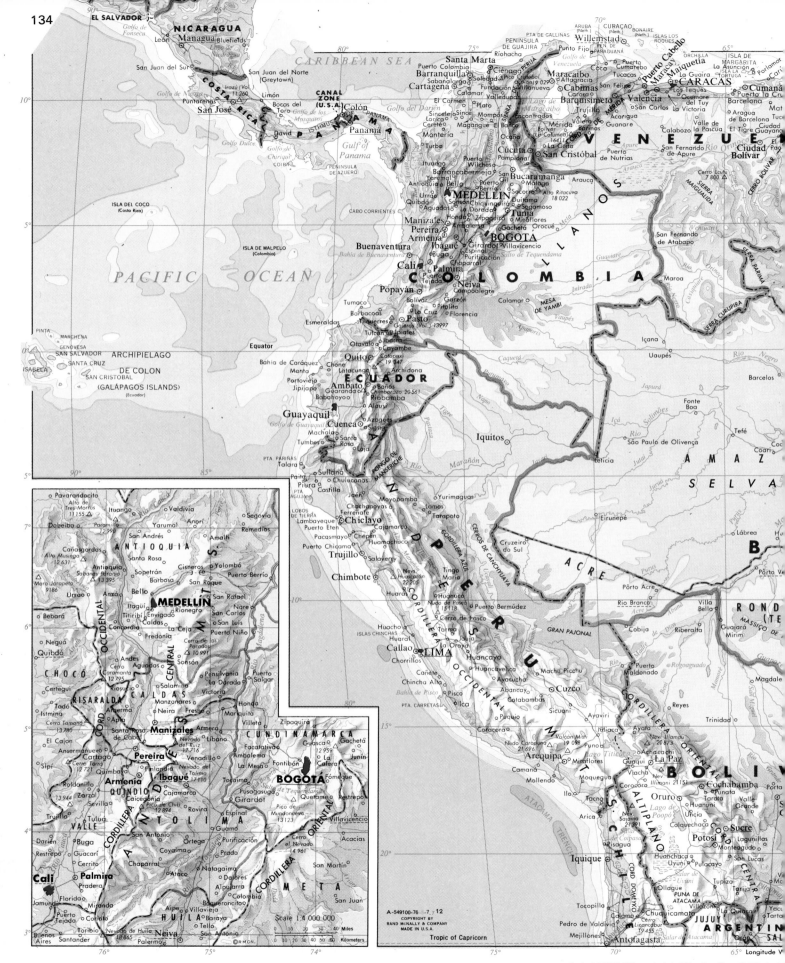

Scale 1:16 000 000, one inch to 250 miles. Sinusoidal Projecti
Elevations and depressions are given in feet

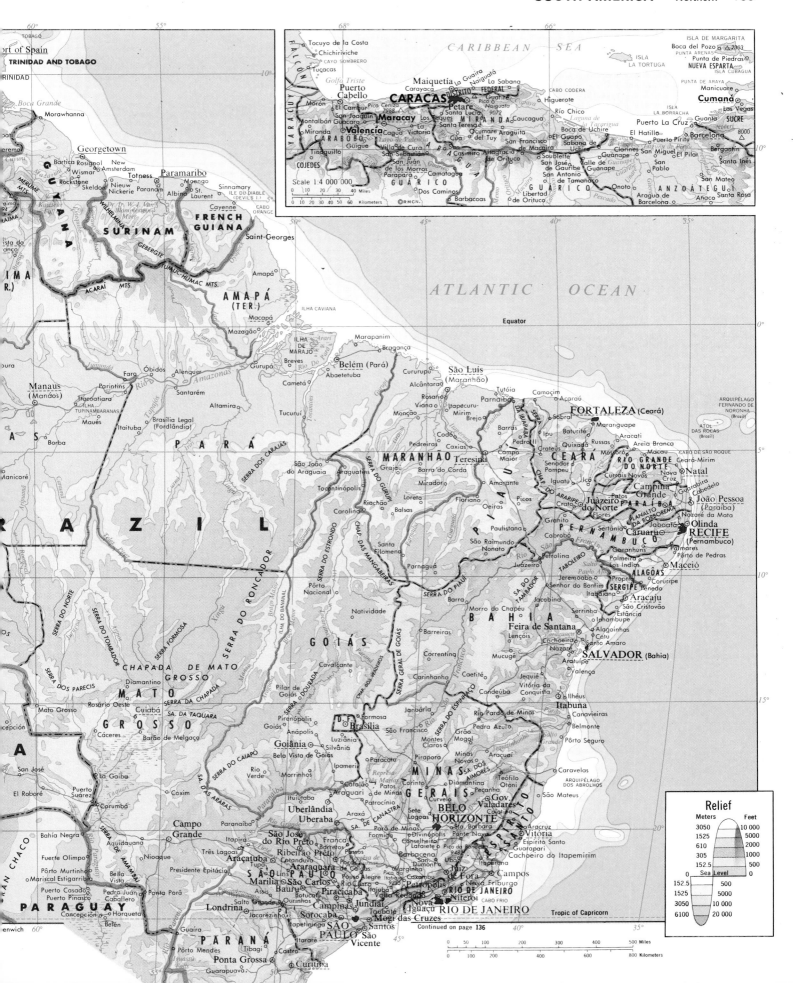

Port of Spain
TRINIDAD AND TOBAGO
TRINIDAD

Boca Grande
Morawhanna

Georgetown
Bartica Rosignol New
Wismar Amsterdam
Rockstone Skeldon
Nieuw Paranam
Nickerie Albina St.
Laurent
Totness Cayenne
Paramaribo Moengo
Sinnamary
ILE DU DIABLE
(DEVIL'S I.)
CABO
ORANGE

SURINAM
FRENCH GUIANA
GEBERGTE
Saint-Georges
TUMUC-HUMAC MTS.
ACARAÍ MTS.

Amapá

AMAPÁ (TER.)
Macapá
ILHA CAVIANA
Mazagão

ILHA DE MARAJO
Marapanim
Breves Arari Rio
Bragança
Gurupá Do Belém (Pará)
Cametá Cururupu
Abaetetuba São Luís (Maranhão)
Alcântara Tutóia
Rosário Camocim Acaraú

ATLANTIC OCEAN

Equator

ARQUIPÉLAGO DE
NORONHA
(Brazil)
ATOL
DAS ROCAS
(Brazil)

Manaus (Manáos)
Itacoatiara
ILHA
TUPINAMBARANAS
Faro Óbidos Alenquer
Parintins Santarém
Maués Borba Altamira

Brasília Legal
(Fordlândia)
Itaituba

P A R Á

Viana
Monção
Itapecurú-Mirim
Brejo
Parnaíba
Barras
Ipu
Baturité
FORTALEZA (Ceará)
Maranguape

São João
do Araguaia
SERRA DOS CARAJÁS
Tucuruí
Tocantins
Pedreiras
Codó
Caxias
Campo Maior
Teresina
Grajaú Barra do Corda
Pedro II
Quixadá
Grateús
Russas
Mossoró
Aracati
Areia Branca

CEARÁ
RIO GRANDE DO NORTE
Ceará-Mirim
CABO DE SAO ROQUE

B R A Z I L

MARANHÃO

SERRA DO GURUPI
Araguatins
Miradoro
Amarante
Picos
Iguatu
Icó
Currais Novos
Nova Cruz Natal

Riachão
Loreto
Floriano
Oeiras
Juàzeiro
do Norte
Crato
Flores
Campina
Grande
João Pessoa
(Paraíba)
PARAÍBA

Carolina
Balsas
Paulistana
São Raimundo
Nonato
Granito
Cabrobó
Sertânia
Jaboatão
Olinda
RECIFE (Pernambuco)

PERNAMBUCO
PLANALTO DA BORBOREMA

Santa
Filomena
Parnaguá
Juàzeiro
Petrolina
Garanhuns
Palmares
Pôrto de Pedras
Pôrto
Nacional

SERRA DO PIAUÍ
Barra
ALAGÔAS
Penedo
Maceió

G O I Á S
Natividade
Jeremoabo
Senhor do Bontim
Corurípe
SERGIPE
Propriá
São Cristóvão
Aracaju

Cavalcante
Barreiras
Morro do Chapéu
Serrinha
Alagoinhas
Estância

Dourada
Correntina
Jacobina
Catu
Santo Amaro

B A H I A
Feira de Santana
Cachoeira
Nazaré

Pilar de Goiás
Lençóis
Mucugê
Maragogipe
SALVADOR (Bahia)

Carinhanha
Caetité
Yalença

Janbária
Condeúba
Vitória da
Conquista
Jequié
Itabuna
Ilhéus

CHAPADA DE MATO GROSSO
Diamantino
SERRA DA CHAPADA
M A T O
G R O S S O
Cuiabá
SA. DA TAQUARA
Rosário Oeste
Barão de Melgaço

SERRA DO CAIAPÓ
Pirenópolis
Goiás
Anápolis
Luziânia
Silvânia
Formosa
São Francisco
Brasília
Montes
Novas
Grão
Mogol
Pedra Azul
Canavieiras
Belmonte
Pôrto Seguro

G O I Á S
Rio Pardo de Minas
ARQUIPÉLAGO
DOS ABROLHOS
Caravelas
São Mateus

Cáceres

Goiânia
Ipameri
Bela Vista de Goiás
Pirapora
Diamantina
Teófilo
Otoni
Peçanha

San José
La Gaiba
Puerto
Suárez
Corumbá
Coxim
Rio
Verde
Morrinhos
Catalão
Araguari
Patos
de Minas
Paracatu
Corinto
M I N A S
Gov.
Valadares
Aracruz

CHAPADA DE MATO GROSSO
Campo
Grande
Aquidauana
Itapira
Uberlândia
Uberaba
Araxá
Sete
Lagoas
SA. DE CANASTRA
GERAIS
BELO HORIZONTE
Ponte Nova
Vitória
Espírito Santo
Guarapari
Cachoeiro de Itapemirim

PARAGUAY
Bahía Negra
Fuerte Olimpo
Pôrto Murtinho
Mariscal Estigarribia
Puerto Casado
Pedro Juán
Caballero
Bella
Vista
Presidente Epitácio
Assis
Bauru
Marília
São Carlos
São José
do Rio Prêto
Ribeirão Prêto
Franca
Barretos
Catanduva
Pirassununga
Passos
Barbacena
Juiz
de Fora
Campos

S Ã O
P A U L O
Piracicaba
Campinas
Jundiaí
Taubaté
Nova
Friburgo
Petrópolis
RIO DE JANEIRO
Niterói
CABO FRIO

Concepción
Horqueta
Londrina
Jacarezinho
Salto Grande
Sorocaba
Mogi das Cruzes
SÃO PAULO
São
Vicente
Santos
RIO DE JANEIRO
Tropic of Capricorn

P A R A N Á
Pôrto Mendes
Tibagi
Castro
Guaíra
Iguassú
Ponta Grossa
Curitiba
Guarapuava

Continued on page 136

Relief

Meters	Feet
3050	10 000
1525	5000
610	2000
305	1000
152.5	500
0 Sea Level	0
152.5	500
1525	5000
3050	10 000
6100	20 000

Inset map (top right):

CARIBBEAN SEA
ISLA DE MARGARITA
Boca del Pozo
PUNTA ARENAS
Punta de Piedras
NUEVA ESPARTA
ISLA CUBAGUA
Tocuyo de la Costa
Chichiriviche
CAYO SOMBRERO
Tucacas
Golfo Triste
Guaira
Naiguatá
La Sabana
ISLA
LA TORTUGA
PUNTA DE ARAYA
Manicuare
Cumaná
Los Vegas
Maiquetía
Puerto Cabello
CARACAS
DISTRITO FEDERAL
Higuerote
Río Chico
Boca de Uchire
ISLA
LA BORRACHA
Puerto La Cruz
Guanta
SUCRE
Morón El Campur Pico Ceniza
Montalbán Guacara
Santa Lucía
Petare
Ocumare
del Tuy
El Guapo
Sabana de Uchire
Barcelona
El Hatillo
Puerto Píritu
Maracay
Los Teques
MIRANDA
Caucagua
Clarines
San
Pablo
Valencia
Cagua
Santa Teresa
San Francisco
de Macaira
El Pilar
Santa Inés
CARABOBO
Güigue
Villa de Cura
Ocumare
del Tuy
Soublette
Valle de Guanape
Tinaquillo
Ouguri
Allagracia
de Orituco
San José
de Guanape
San
Antonio
Bergantín
COJEDES
San Juán
de los Morros
Parapara
Camatagua
Onoto
ANZOÁTEGUI
San Mateo
Santa Rosa
GUÁRICO
Dos Caminos
Barbacoas
Libertad
de Orituco
Aragua de
Barcelona
Anaco

Scale 1:4 000 000
Miles
Kilometers
©RMcN.

Continued on pages 134–135

Relief

Meters	Feet
3050	10 000
1525	5000
610	2000
305	1000
152.5	500
Sea Level	Level
0	0
152.5	500
1525	5000
3050	10 000
6100	20 000

Below Sea Level

BUENOS AIRES

Scale 1:1 000 000
0 4 8 12 16 Kilometers
0   4   8   10 Miles
©RMCN.

RIO DE JANEIRO

SERRA DAS ARARAS

RIO DE JANEIRO

Scale 1:1 000 000
0 4 8 12 16 Kilometers
0   4   8   10 Miles
©RMCN.

FALKLAND IS.
(ISLAS MALVINAS)
(Br.)

Stanley

A-549200-76 -10 -9
COPYRIGHT BY
RAND MCNALLY & COMPANY
MADE IN U.S.A.

Scale 1:16 000 000: one inch to 250 miles. Sinusoidal Projection
Elevations and depressions are given in feet

0 50 100 200 300 400 500 Miles
0   100 200   400   600   800 Kilometers

For larger scale coverage of Buenos Aires,
Rio de Janeiro, and São Paulo see pages 58 and 59

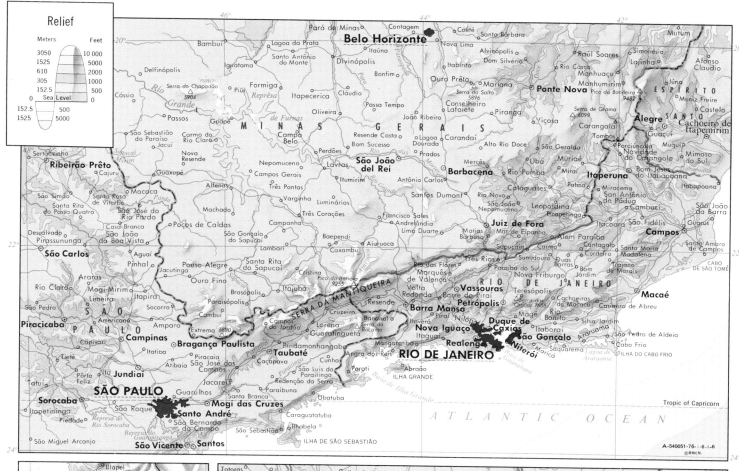

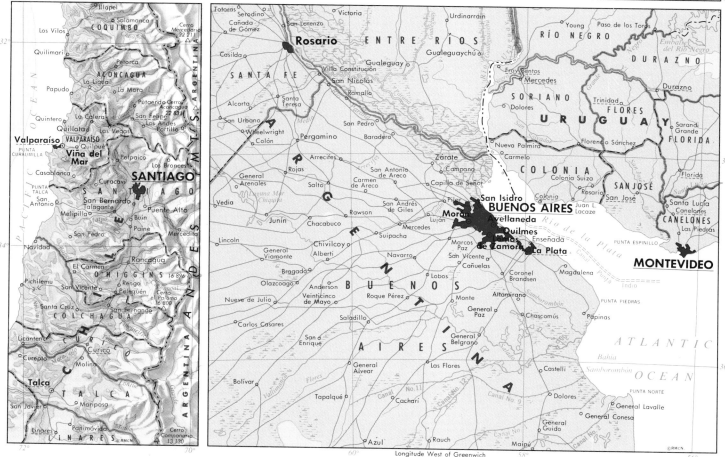

Scale 1:4 000 000; one inch to 64 miles.
Elevations and depressions are given in feet.

Longitude West of Greenwich

Urban
Cropland
Cropland & Woodland
Cropland & Grazing Land
Grassland, Grazing Land
Forest, Woodland
Swamp, Marshland
Tundra
Shrub, Sparse Grass,
Wasteland (pattern)
Barren Land
Oasis

ATLANTIC OCEAN

North Sea

Baltic Sea

Gulf of Bothnia

Mediterranean Sea

Tyrrhenian Sea

Adriatic Sea

Aegean Sea

Bay of Biscay

Reykjavik
Narvik
Murmansk
Ume
Trondheim
Bergen
Oslo
Helsinki
LENINGRAD
Tallinn
Stockholm
Göteborg
Rīga
Copenhagen
Kaliningrad
Minsk
Glasgow
Belfast
MANCHESTER
Dublin
LONDON
Amsterdam
Hamburg
Elbe
BERLIN
Oder
Pripyat
Warsaw
Antwerp
Essen
Leipzig
Frankfurt
Kraków
L'vov
PARIS
Seine
Strasbourg
Prague
Loire
Rhine
Danube
CARPATHIANS
Dnestr
Munich
VIENNA
Brest
Tisza
Zürich
BUDAPEST
Lyon
Rhône
ALPS
MILAN
Zagreb
La Coruña
Bordeaux
Garonne
Venice
Sava
Belgrade
Bilbao
PYRENEES
Ebro
Genoa
Bucharest
Douro
Marseille
Danube
MADRID
Lisbon
BARCELONA
CORSICA
ROME
Sofia
Sevilla
Tirane
ISLAS BALEARES
SARDINIA
Naples
Tanger
Palermo
Algiers
Athens
Oran
SICILY
Casablanca
Tunis
ATLAS MOUNTAINS
MALTA
CRETE

20° 10° 0° 10° 20° 30°
60°
50°
50°
10°
10°
20°

Longitude West of Greenwich   0°   Longitude East of Greenwich

Scale 1: 16,000,000; one inch to 250 miles. Conic Projection

0 50 100   200   300   400   500 Miles
0   100   200   400   600   800 Kilometers

Nar'yan-Mar

White Sea

Pechora

Ob'

Ob'

Novosibirsk

Archangelsk

Irtysh

Omsk

URALS

SVERDLOVSK

Perm'

Karaganda

Kirov

Vologda

Kama

Ufa

Balkhash

Volga

Kazan

Magnitogorsk

Gorki

MOSCOW

Kuybyshev

Orsk

Kzyl-Orda

Tula

Volga

Syr-Dar'ya

Saratov

Ural

Aral'skoye
More
(Aral Sea)

DEPRESSION

PESKI
KYZYLKUM

Khar'kov

Don

VOLGOGRAD

CASPIAN

Kiev

Volga

Amu Dar'ya

Dnepropetrovsk

Donetsk

Astrakhan'

MANYCH   DEPRESSION

PESKI KARAKUMY

Dnepr

Odessa

Krasnodar

Caspian

Ashkhabad

CAUCASUS MTS.

Sea

BAKU

Black   Sea

TBILISI

Yerevan

İSTANBUL

ELBURZ   MTS.

Ankara

TEHRAN

DASHT-E-KAVIR

TOROS

AĞRI

Kerman

Nicosia

Tigris

ZAGROS

CYPRUS

Euphrates

Baghdad

MOUNTAINS

Beirut

Ābādān

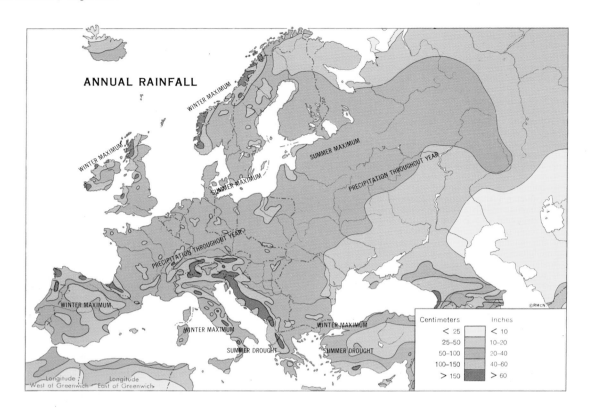

ANNUAL RAINFALL

Centimeters	Inches
< 25	< 10
25–50	10–20
50–100	20–40
100–150	40–60
> 150	> 60

VEGETATION

E	Coniferous forest
B,Bs	Mediterranean vegetation
M	Mixed forest: coniferous-deciduous
S	Semi-deciduous forest
D	Deciduous forest
Dg	Wooded steppe
G	Grass (steppe)
Gp	Short grass
Dsp	Desert shrub
L	Heath and moor
L	Alpine vegetation tundra
b	Little or no vegetation

For explanation of letters in boxes,
see Natural Vegetation Map
by A. W. Kuchler, p. 16

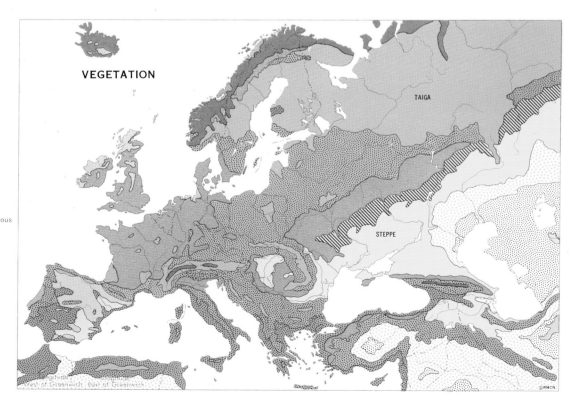

VEGETATION

TAIGA

STEPPE

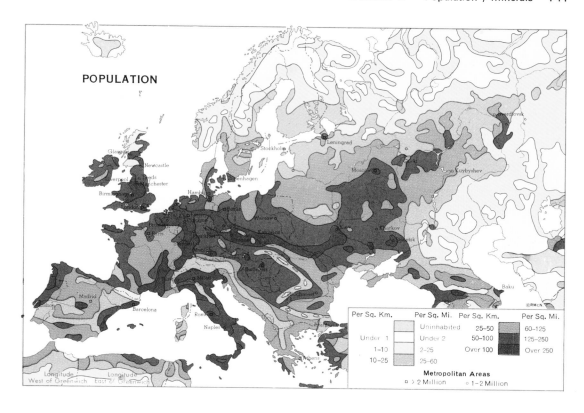

POPULATION

Per Sq. Km.	Per Sq. Mi.	Per Sq. Km.	Per Sq. Mi.
	Uninhabited	25–50	60–125
Under 1	Under 2	50–100	125–250
1–10	2–25	Over 100	Over 250
10–25	25–60		

Metropolitan Areas
□ > 2 Million ○ 1–2 Million

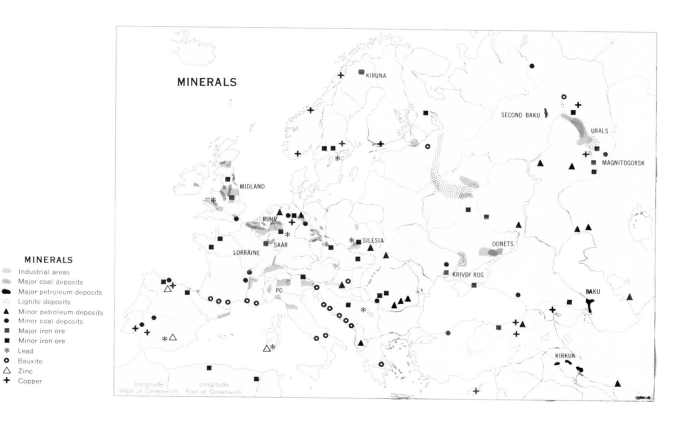

MINERALS

KIRUNA
SECOND BAKU
URALS
MAGNITOGORSK
MIDLAND
RUHR
SAAR
SILESIA
LORRAINE
DONETS
PO
KRIVOI ROG
BAKU
KIRKUK

MINERALS

- Industrial areas
- Major coal deposits
- Major petroleum deposits
- Lignite deposits
- ▲ Minor petroleum deposits
- ● Minor coal deposits
- ■ Major iron ore
- ■ Minor iron ore
- ✳ Lead
- ○ Bauxite
- △ Zinc
- ✛ Copper

Longitude West of Greenwich Longitude East of Greenwich

142

Scale 1:16 000 000; one inch to 250 miles. Conic Projection
Elevations and depressions are given in feet.

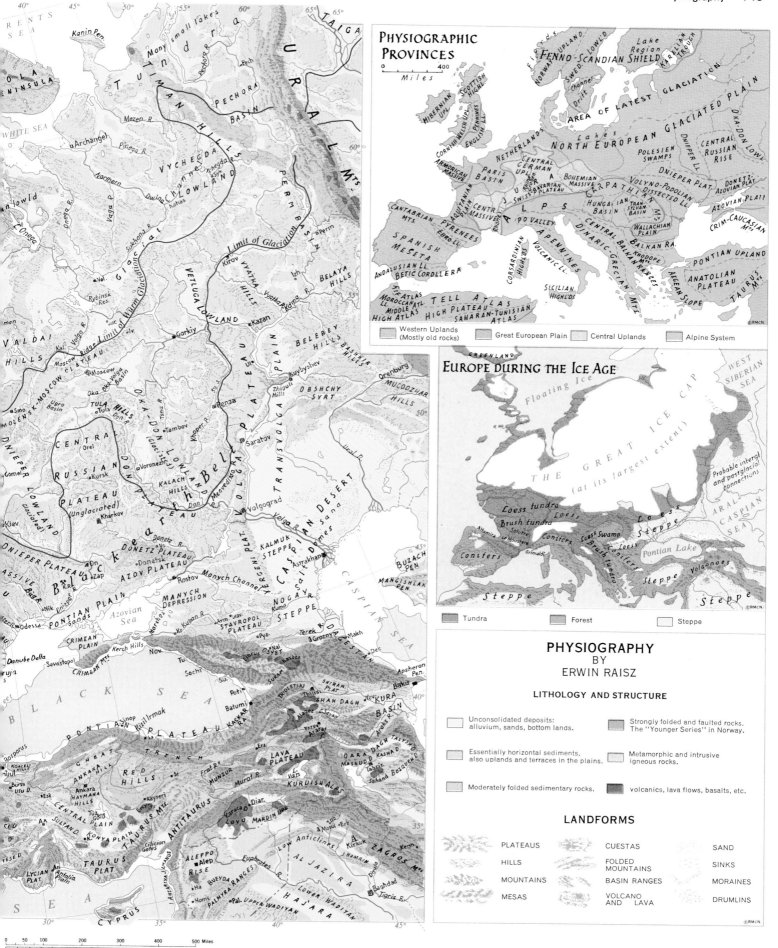

PHYSIOGRAPHIC PROVINCES

Miles 0 — 400

Legend:
- Western Uplands (Mostly old rocks)
- Great European Plain
- Central Uplands
- Alpine System

EUROPE DURING THE ICE AGE

THE GREAT ICE CAP (at its largest extent)

Legend:
- Tundra
- Forest
- Steppe

PHYSIOGRAPHY
BY ERWIN RAISZ

LITHOLOGY AND STRUCTURE

- Unconsolidated deposits: alluvium, sands, bottom lands.
- Essentially horizontal sediments, also uplands and terraces in the plains.
- Moderately folded sedimentary rocks.
- Strongly folded and faulted rocks. The "Younger Series" in Norway.
- Metamorphic and intrusive igneous rocks.
- volcanics, lava flows, basalts, etc.

LANDFORMS

- PLATEAUS
- HILLS
- MOUNTAINS
- MESAS
- CUESTAS
- FOLDED MOUNTAINS
- BASIN RANGES
- VOLCANO AND LAVA
- SAND
- SINKS
- MORAINES
- DRUMLINS

0 50 100 200 300 400 500 Miles
0 100 200 400 600 800 Kilometers

EUROPE LANGUAGES
BY
BOGDAN ZABORSKI

Longitude West of Greenwich Longitude East of Greenwich

0   100   200   300   400   500   600 Miles
0   200   400   600   800   1000 Kilometers

Scale 1:16,500,000; one inch to 260 miles Conic Projection

B-550000-108-54-14
COPYRIGHT BY
RAND MCNALLY & COMPANY
MADE IN U.S.A

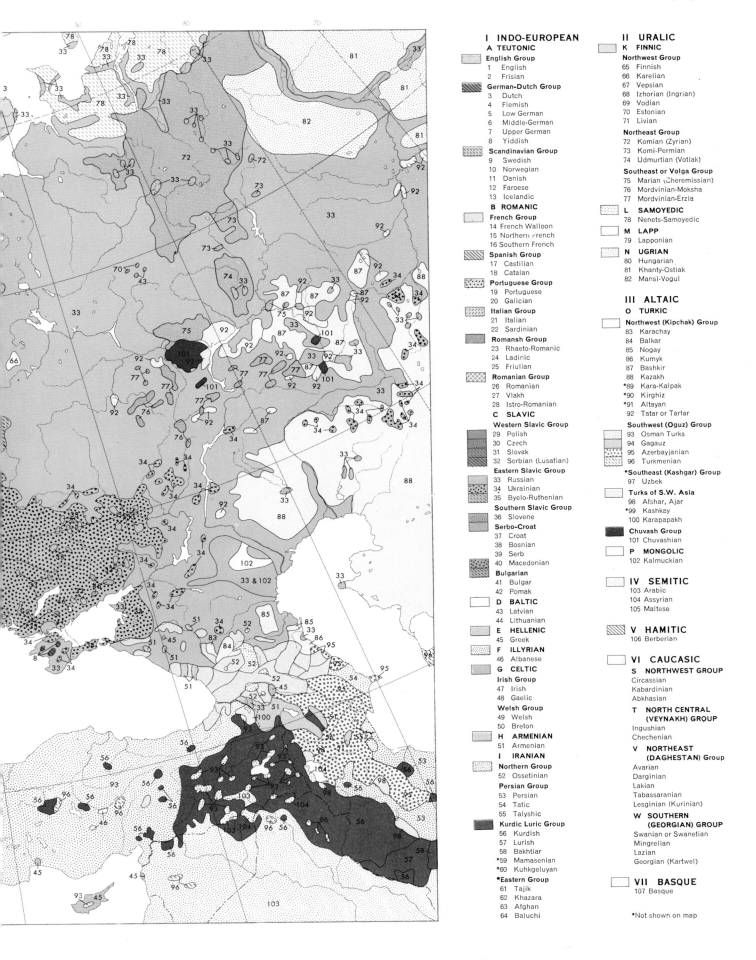

I INDO-EUROPEAN

A TEUTONIC

English Group
1 English
2 Frisian

German-Dutch Group
3 Dutch
4 Flemish
5 Low German
6 Middle-German
7 Upper German
8 Yiddish

Scandinavian Group
9 Swedish
10 Norwegian
11 Danish
12 Faroese
13 Icelandic

B ROMANIC

French Group
14 French Walloon
15 Northern French
16 Southern French

Spanish Group
17 Castilian
18 Catalan

Portuguese Group
19 Portuguese
20 Galician

Italian Group
21 Italian
22 Sardinian

Romansh Group
23 Rhaeto-Romanic
24 Ladinic
25 Friulian

Romanian Group
26 Romanian
27 Vlakh
28 Istro-Romanian

C SLAVIC

Western Slavic Group
29 Polish
30 Czech
31 Slovak
32 Sorbian (Lusatian)

Eastern Slavic Group
33 Russian
34 Ukrainian
35 Byelo-Ruthenian

Southern Slavic Group
36 Slovene

Serbo-Croat
37 Croat
38 Bosnian
39 Serb
40 Macedonian

Bulgarian
41 Bulgar
42 Pomak

D BALTIC
43 Latvian
44 Lithuanian

E HELLENIC
45 Greek

F ILLYRIAN
46 Albanese

G CELTIC

Irish Group
47 Irish
48 Gaelic

Welsh Group
49 Welsh
50 Breton

H ARMENIAN
51 Armenian

I IRANIAN

Northern Group
52 Ossetinian

Persian Group
53 Persian
54 Tatic
55 Talyshic

Kurdic Luric Group
56 Kurdish
57 Lurish
58 Bakhtiar
*59 Mamasenian
*60 Kuhkgeluyan

*Eastern Group
61 Tajik
62 Khazara
63 Afghan
64 Baluchi

II URALIC

K FINNIC

Northwest Group
65 Finnish
66 Karelian
67 Vepsian
68 Izhorian (Ingrian)
69 Vodian
70 Estonian
71 Livian

Northeast Group
72 Komian (Zyrian)
73 Komi-Permian
74 Udmurtian (Votiak)

Southeast or Volga Group
75 Marian (Cheremissian)
76 Mordvinian-Moksha
77 Mordvinian-Erzia

L SAMOYEDIC
78 Nenets-Samoyedic

M LAPP
79 Lapponian

N UGRIAN
80 Hungarian
81 Khanty-Ostiak
82 Mansi-Vogul

III ALTAIC

O TURKIC

Northwest (Kipchak) Group
83 Karachay
84 Balkar
85 Nogay
86 Kumyk
87 Bashkir
88 Kazakh
*89 Kara-Kalpak
*90 Kirghiz
*91 Altayan
92 Tatar or Tartar

Southwest (Oguz) Group
93 Osman Turks
94 Gagauz
95 Azerbayjanian
96 Turkmenian

*Southeast (Kashgar) Group
97 Uzbek

Turks of S.W. Asia
98 Afshar, Ajar
*99 Kashkay
100 Karapapakh

Chuvash Group
101 Chuvashian

P MONGOLIC
102 Kalmuckian

IV SEMITIC
103 Arabic
104 Assyrian
105 Maltese

V HAMITIC
106 Berberian

VI CAUCASIC

S NORTHWEST GROUP
Circassian
Kabardinian
Abkhasian

T NORTH CENTRAL (VEYNAKH) GROUP
Ingushian
Chechenian

V NORTHEAST (DAGHESTAN) Group
Avarian
Darginian
Lakian
Tabassaranian
Lesginian (Kurinian)

W SOUTHERN (GEORGIAN) GROUP
Swanian or Swanetian
Mingrelian
Lazian
Georgian (Kartwel)

VII BASQUE
107 Basque

*Not shown on map

Relief

Meters		Feet
3050		10 000
1525		5000
610		2000
305		1000
152.5		500
0	Sea Level	0
152.5		500	Below
1525		5000	Sea Level
3050		10 000

Scale 1: 16 000 000; one inch to 250 miles. Conic Projection
Elevations and depressions are given in feet

Continued on pages 210–211

| 0 | 50 | 100 | 200 | 300 | 400 | 500 Miles |
| 0 | 100 | 200 | 400 | 600 | 800 Kilometers |

Continued on pages 172-173

Continued on pages 186-187

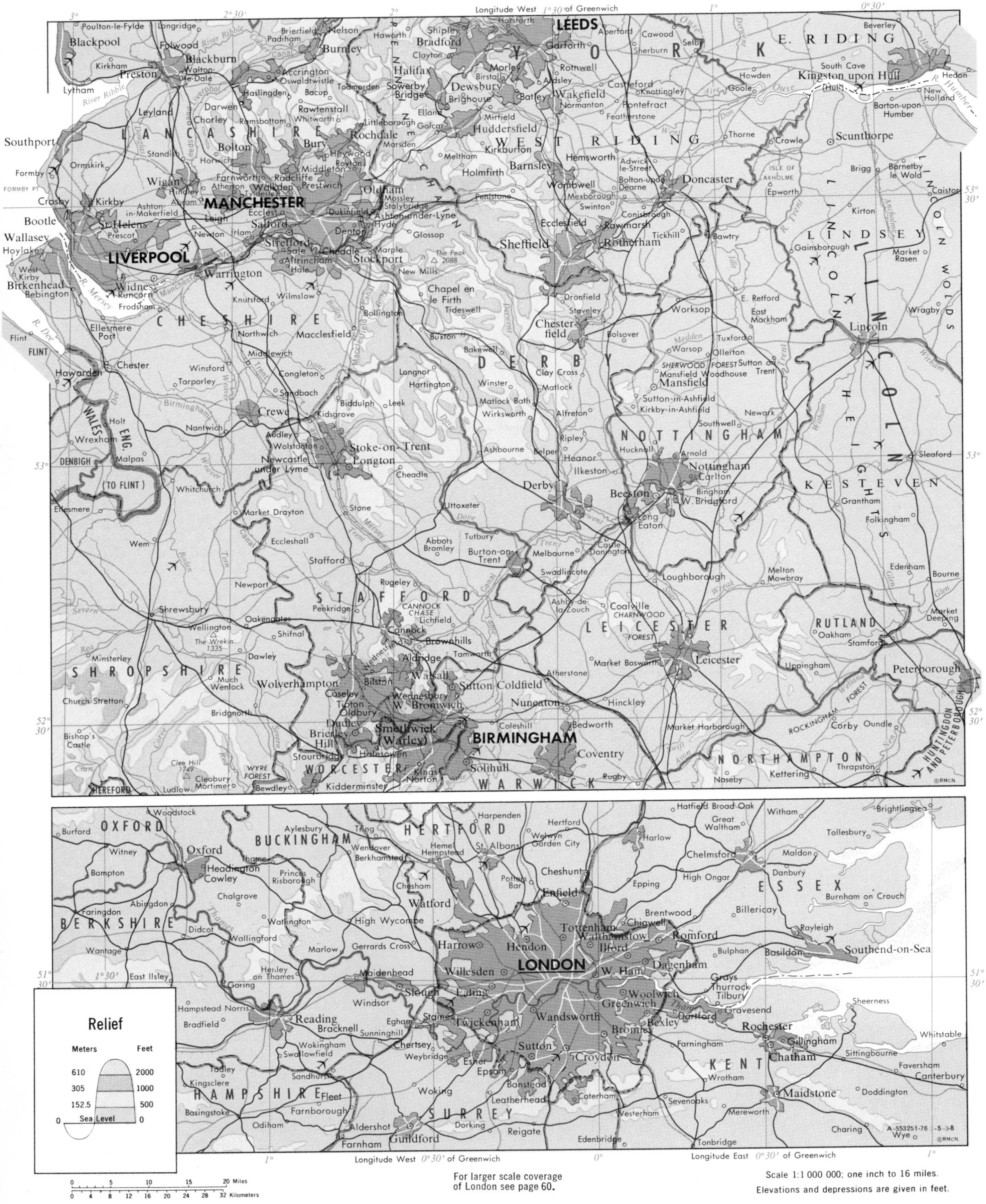

Longitude West 1°30' of Greenwich

LEEDS

E. RIDING

Kingston upon Hull (Hull)

LANCASHIRE

WEST RIDING

YORK

LINDSEY

Scunthorpe

MANCHESTER

LIVERPOOL

Sheffield

LINCOLN

Lincoln

CHESHIRE

DERBY

Chesterfield

KESTEVEN

WALES

ENG.

FLINT

DENBIGH

Stoke-on-Trent

NOTTINGHAM

Nottingham

The Peak 2088

Derby

SHROPSHIRE

STAFFORD

LEICESTER

RUTLAND

The Wrekin 1335

Cannock

Leicester

Peterborough

Wolverhampton

Walsall

NORTHAMPTON

Clee Hill 1749

W. Bromwich

BIRMINGHAM

Coventry

WYRE FOREST

WORCESTER

WARWICK

HEREFORD

OXFORD

HERTFORD

ESSEX

BUCKINGHAM

Oxford

BERKSHIRE

Watford

Southend-on-Sea

Reading

LONDON

Croydon

HAMPSHIRE

SURREY

KENT

Maidstone

Relief

Meters	Feet
610	2000
305	1000
152.5	500
0 Sea Level	0

20 Miles

0 4 8 12 16 20 24 28 32 Kilometers

Longitude West 0°30' of Greenwich

Longitude East 0°30' of Greenwich

For larger scale coverage of London see page 60.

Scale 1:1 000 000; one inch to 16 miles.
Elevations and depressions are given in feet.

A-553251-76 -5-3-8
©RMcN

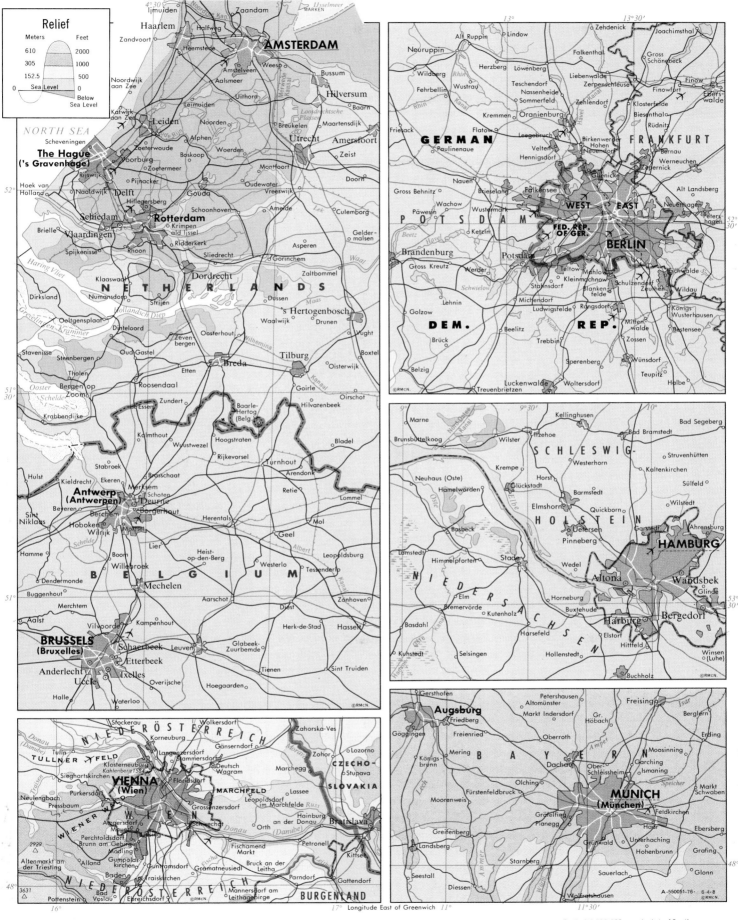

Relief

Meters	Feet
610	2000
305	1000
152.5	500
0 Sea Level	0
	Below Sea Level

NORTH SEA

Ijmuiden Zaandam Marken
Zandvoort Haarlem Halfweg
Heemstede Weesp Bussum
AMSTERDAM
Noordwijk aan Zee Amstelveen Hilversum
Aalsmeer Uithorn Baarn
Katwijk aan Zee Leimuiden Noorden Loosdrechtsche Plassen
Scheveningen Leiden Alphen Maartensdijk Amersfoort
The Hague ('s Gravenhage) Voorburg Boskoop Woerden Utrecht Zeist
Rijswijk Zoeterwoude Zoetermeer Montfoort Doorn
Hoek van Holland Naaldwijk Delft Hillegersberg Oudewater Vreeswijk
Pijnacker Gouda Schoonhoven Amide Culemborg
Brielle Schiedam **Rotterdam** Krimpen aid IJssel Lek Gelder-malsen
Vlaardingen Rhoon Ridderkerk Asperen
Spijkenisse Sliedrecht Gorinchem Zaltbommel Waal
Klaaswaal Dordrecht Dussen Maas
Dirksland Numansdorp Strijen 's Hertogenbosch
Ooltgensplaat **NETHERLANDS** Waalwijk Drunen Vught
Stavenisse Dinteloord Oosterhout Zevenbergen Boxtel
Steenbergen Oud Gastel Wilhelmina **Tilburg** Oisterwijk
Bergen op Zoom Roosendaal **Breda** Oirschot
Krabbendijke Essen Zundert Baarle-Hertog (Belg) Goirle Kanaal
Tholen Kalmthout Hoogstraten Hilvarenbeek
Wuustwezel Rijkevorsel Bladel
Hulst Stabroek Turnhout Arendonk Retie
Kieldrecht Ekeren Merksem Schoten Herentals Mol
Sint Niklaas Beveren **Antwerp (Antwerpen)** Deurne Borgerhout Geel Leopoldsburg
Hoboken Berchem Lier Heist-op-den-Berg Westerlo Tessenderlo Albert Kanaal
Hamme Boom **BELGIUM** Aarschot Zonhoven
Dendermonde Willebroek Mechelen Diest Herk-de-Stad Hasselt
Buggenhout Merchtem Kampenhout Sint Truiden
Aalst Vilvoorde Leuven Glabbeek-Zuurbemde
BRUSSELS (Bruxelles) Schaerbeek Tienen
Anderlecht Etterbeek Ixelles Overijsche Hoegaarden
Halle Uccle Waterloo

Vienna area

Stockerau Wolkersdorf **NIEDERÖSTERREICH** Zahorska-Ves
Tulln Korneuburg Gänserndorf Lozorno
TULLNER FELD Langenzersdorf Deutsch Wagram CZECHO- Stupava
Klosterneuburg Kahlenberg 1584 Floridsdorf **MARCHFELD** Marchegg **SLOVAKIA**
Sieghartskirchen **VIENNA (Wien)** Lassee
Neulengbach Purkersdorf **WIEN** Leopoldsdorf im Marchfelde Russ
Pressbaum Grossenzersdorf Hainburg an der Donau **Bratislava**
WIENERWALD Atzgersdorf Schwechat Orth Donau (Danube) Petronell
Mauer Perchtoldsdorf Fischamend Markt Kittsee
Brunn am Gebirge Mödling Bruck an der Leitha
2929 Gumpolds-kirchen Gramatneusiedl Parndorf
Altenmarkt an der Triesting Baden Traiskirchen Mannersdorf am Leithagebirge
3631 **NIEDERÖSTERREICH** Gattendorf
Pottenstein Vöslau Ebreichsdorf **BURGENLAND**

Berlin area

Alt Ruppin Lindow Zehdenick Joachimsthal
Neuruppin Herzberg Löwenberg Falkenthal Gross Schönebeck
Wildberg Wustrau Teschendorf Liebenwalde Finow Ebers-walde
Fehrbellin Nassenheide Zerpenschleuse Finowfurt
Sommerfeld Zehlendorf Klosterfelde **FRANKFURT**
GERMAN Flatow Oranienburg Birkenwerder Hohen Neuendorf Biesenthal Rüdnitz
Friesack Leegebruch Velten Werneuchen
Paulinenaue Nauen Hennigsdorf Zepernick
Gross Behnitz Wachow Brieselang **WEST EAST** Alt Landsberg
Päwesin Wustermark Falkensee Neuenhagen
POTSDAM **FED. REP. OF GER.** Glienicke Petershagen
Brandenburg Ketzin **BERLIN** Eichwalde
Gross Kreutz Werder Potsdam Teltow Mahlow Schulzendorf Bernau Wildau
Schwielow Kleinmachnow Blankenfelde Zeuthen Königs Wusterhausen
DEM. Lehnin Michendorf Ludwigsfelde Rangsdorf Bastensee
Golzow Beelitz **REP.** Mitten-walde
Brück Trebbin Zossen Wünsdorf Teupitz
Belzig Sperenberg Woltersdorf Halbe
Luckenwalde Treuenbrietzen

Hamburg area

Marne Kellinghusen Bad Segeberg
Brunsbüttelkoog Nord-Ostsee Kanal Wilster Itzehoe Bad Bramstedt
Neuhaus (Oste) Krempe Horst Westerhorn **SCHLESWIG-** Kaltenkirchen Sülfeld
Hamelwörden Glückstadt Barmstedt Quickborn Wilstedt
Basbeck Elmshorn Uetersen Garstedt **HOLSTEIN** Ahrensburg
Lamstedt Pinneberg **HAMBURG**
Himmelpforten Stade Wedel Altona Wandsbek Glinde
NIEDERSACHSEN Horneburg Harburg Bergedorf
Bremervörde Buxtehude Hittfeld
Basdahl Kutenholz Harseberg Elstorf Winsen (Luhe)
Kuhstedt Selsingen Hollenstedt Buchholz

Munich area

Gersthofen Petershausen Freising Isar
Augsburg Friedberg Altomünster Markt Indersdorf Berglern
Göggingen Freienried Oberroth Gr. Höbach
Königs-brunn Mering Dachau **BAYERN** Moosinning Erding
Moorenweis Olching Ober-Schleissheim Garching Ismaning
Fürstenfeldbruck Gröbenzell Speicher
Greifenberg Planegg **MUNICH (München)** Markt Schwaben
Landsberg Gräfelfing Haar Feldkirchen
Starnberg Grünwald Unterhaching Ebersberg
Seestall Hohenbrunn Grafing
Diessen Sauerlach Glonn
Wolfratshausen

A-550051-76— 6-4-8

Scale

0 5 10 15 20 Miles
0 4 8 12 16 20 24 28 32 Kilometers

16° 17° Longitude East of Greenwich 11° 11°30'

Scale 1:1 000 000; one inch to 16 miles.
Elevations and depressions are given in feet.

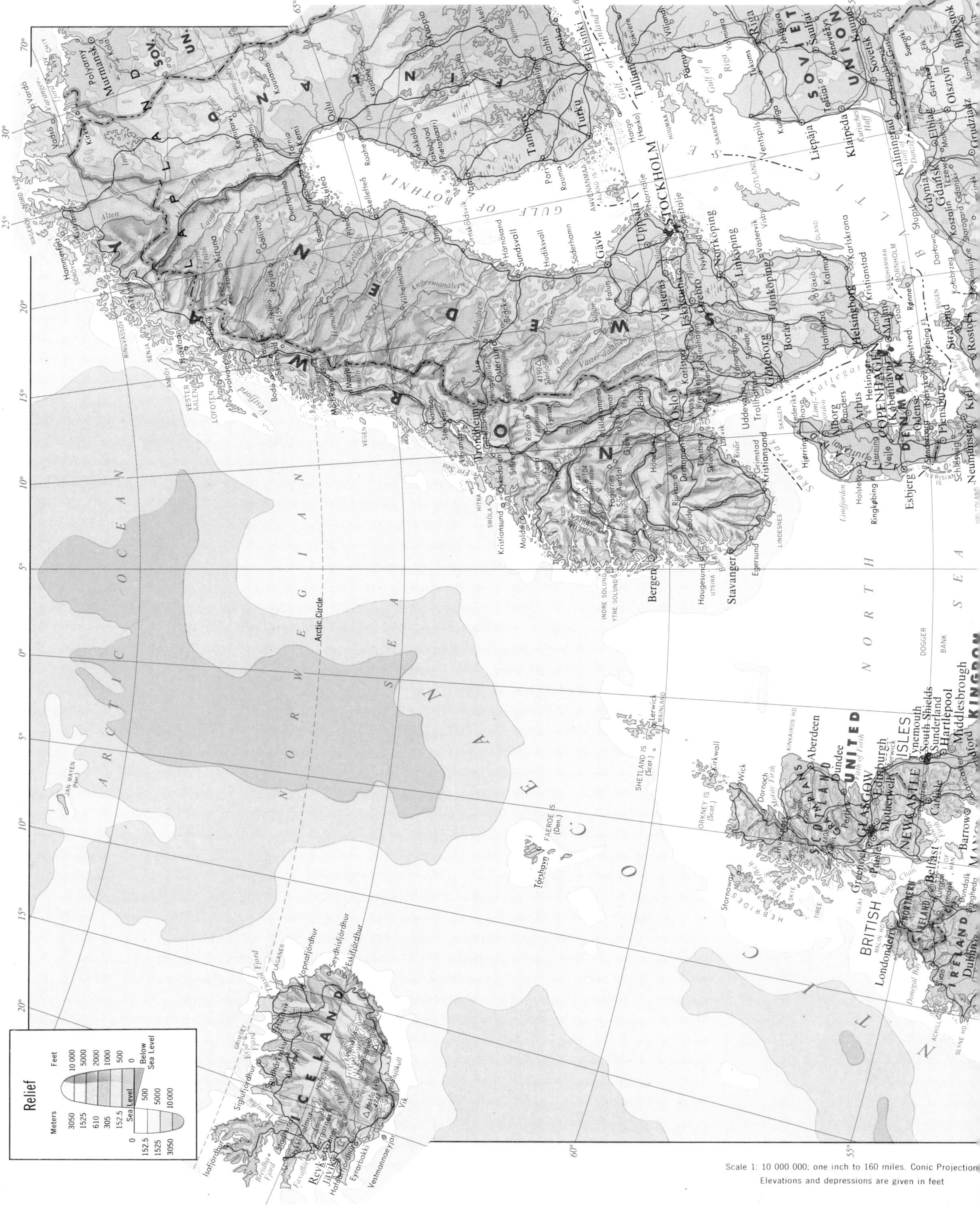

SOVIET UNION

FINLAND

LAPLAND

SWEDEN

NORWAY

DENMARK

ICELAND

BRITISH ISLES

UNITED KINGDOM

SCOTLAND

NORTHERN IRELAND

IRELAND

ARCTIC OCEAN

NORWEGIAN SEA

NORTH SEA

GULF OF BOTHNIA

Arctic Circle

Murmansk · Polyarny · Kola

Vardø · Vadsø · Kirkenes

Oulu · Kemi · Tornio · Rovaniemi

Helsinki · Turku · Tampere · Lahti

Tallinn · Riga · Šiauliai

Klaipeda · Kaliningrad · Gdynia · Gdansk

STOCKHOLM · Uppsala · Gävle

Norrköping · Linköping · Jönköping

Göteborg · Helsingborg · Borås

Oslo · Drammen · Bergen · Stavanger

Trondheim · Namsos · Molde · Kristiansund

COPENHAGEN · Odense · Esbjerg · Ålborg · Århus

Rostock · Flensburg · Schleswig

Reykjavík · Vík

GLASGOW · Edinburgh · Aberdeen · Dundee

Newcastle · Middlesbrough · Sunderland · Hartlepool

Belfast · Londonderry · Dublin

Lerwick · SHETLAND IS. (Scot.)

ORKNEY IS. (Scot.) · Kirkwall · Wick

FAEROE IS. (Den.) · Tórshavn

JAN MAYEN (Nor.)

Stornoway · HEBRIDES

DOGGER BANK

GRAMPIANS

Relief

Meters	Feet
3050	10 000
1525	5000
610	2000
305	1000
152.5	500
0	Sea Level
	Below Sea Level

Sea Level	
152.5	500
1525	5000
3050	10 000

Scale 1: 10 000 000; one inch to 160 miles. Conic Projection
Elevations and depressions are given in feet

POLAND

CZECHOSLOVAKIA

BUDAPEST

HUNGARY

ROMANIA

YUGOSLAVIA

ALBANIA

GERMANY
FEDERAL
REPUBLIC

BERLIN

PRAGUE (Praha)

VIENNA (Wien)

MUNICH

STUTTGART

FRANKFURT

MANNHEIM

DÜSSELDORF
COLOGNE

NETHERLANDS
AMSTERDAM
The Hague
Rotterdam
's Gravenhage

BELGIUM
BRUSSELS

SWITZERLAND

MILAN

VENICE

ROME
Vatican City

NAPLES

ITALY

ADRIATIC SEA

IONIAN SEA

TYRRHENIAN SEA

LIGURIAN SEA

CORSICA (Fr.)
Ajaccio

SARDINIA (It.)
Sassari
Cagliari

SICILY
Palermo
Catania
Messina

MALTA (Valletta)

MEDITERRANEAN SEA

TUNISIA
Tunis
Bizerte

ATLAS MOUNTAINS

ALGERIA
Algiers

MOROCCO

FRANCE
PARIS
Versailles
Orléans
Tours
Lyon
Marseille
Toulon
Cannes
MONACO
Nice
Bordeaux
Toulouse
Nantes
Rennes
Brest
Le Havre
Cherbourg
Calais
Lille
Reims
Dijon
Nancy
Strasbourg
Perpignan
Montpellier

ENGLISH CHANNEL

ENGLAND
LONDON
BIRMINGHAM
Cardiff
Swansea
Bristol
Plymouth
Exeter
Portsmouth
Brighton
Southampton
Norwich
Cambridge
Leicester
Nottingham

WALES

BAY OF BISCAY

SPAIN
MADRID
BARCELONA
Valencia
Zaragoza
Bilbao
San Sebastián
Sevilla
Málaga
Granada
Murcia
Cartagena
Alicante
Córdoba
Cádiz
Gibraltar (Br.)
Almería
Valladolid
León
Burgos
Pamplona
Santander
Gijón
La Coruña
Vigo

PORTUGAL
LISBON
Pôrto
Coimbra

BALEARES (Sp.)
Palma de Mallorca
I. DE MENORCA
I. DE MALLORCA
I. DE IBIZA

ANDORRA

STRAIT OF GIBRALTAR

Ceuta (Sp.)
Melilla (Sp.)
Tangier

ATLANTIC

Longitude West of Greenwich
Longitude East of Greenwich

0 50 100 150 200 250 300 Miles
0 100 200 300 400 500 Kilometers

A-559400-A 7-5-12
COPYRIGHT BY
RAND McNALLY & COMPANY
MADE IN U.S.A.

ATLANTIC
OCEAN

BAY OF BISCAY

FRANCE

SPAIN

PORTUGAL

LISBON

MADRID

BARCELONA

MEDITERRANEAN SEA

LIGURIAN SEA

CORSICA (Fr.)

SARDINIA (It.)

TYRRHENIAN SEA

ITALY

ROME

NAPLES

VATICAN CITY

SICILY

MALTA

MOROCCO

ALGERIA

TUNISIA

HAUT ATLAS

MOYEN ATLAS

SAHARAN ATLAS

MONTS DES OULED NAIL

MONTS DE LUARSENS MOUNTAINS

MONTS DES ATLAS

GRAND ERG OCCIDENTAL

GRAND ERG ORIENTAL

EL HAMADA

TARABULUS (TRIPOLITANIA)

HAMMÂDAH AL HAMRÂ

Tripoli (Tarâbulus)

Relief

Meters		Feet
3050		10000
1525		5000
610		2000
305		1000
152.5		500
0	Sea Level	0
152.5		500 Below Sea Level
1525		5000
3050		10000

A-558300-76
COPYRIGHT BY
RAND MCNALLY & COMPANY
MADE IN U.S.A.

Longitude West of Greenwich 0° Longitude East of Greenwich

Scale 1: 10 000 000; one inch to 160 miles. Bonne's Projection
Elevations and depressions are given in feet

Same scale as main map

ATLANTIC

SHETLAND
St. Magnus Bay
ISLANDS
(Br.)
Lerwick
FOULA

HERMA NESS
UNST
YELL
MAINLAND

OCEAN

SUMBURGH HD.

FAIR

WESTRAY   N RONALDSAY
ROUSAY   SANDAY
STRONSAY
Kirkwall   ORKNEY
HOY   MAINLAND   ISLANDS
(Br.)
S RONALDSAY
Thurso   Pentland   Firth
DUNCANSBY HD.
SCOTLAND

©RMcN.

HOY   S. RONALDSAY
Pentland   Firth
DUNCANSBY HD.
Thurso   Wick

ATLANTIC

OCEAN

BUTT OF LEWIS   CAPE WRATH
FLANNAN IS.
LEWIS
Stornoway   The Minch
ST KILDA   HARRIS
HEBRIDES   NORTH UIST
Ben Hope 3040
Loch Shin
NORTHWEST HIGHLANDS
Ben More Assynt 3273
Dornoch Firth   TARBAT NESS
Dingwall   Moray Firth
Ben Dearg 3547   Nairn   Inverness   Elgin   Buckie   Banff   KINNAIRDS HD.
Fraserburgh
Peterhead

OUTER   SOUTH UIST
BARRA
The Little Minch   SKYE   INNER
Cuillin Hills
Sea of   RHUM
The Hebrides   HEBRIDES   Ben Attow 3383
Fort William   Ben Nevis 4406
SCOTLAND   Macdhui 4296   Ballater   Aberdeen
Forfar   Stonehaven
Montrose

COLL   TIREE   MULL
Oban   Loch
Firth of Lorn   COLONSAY   Loch Lomond   Perth   Buckhaven   St. Andrews   FIFE NESS
Dundee   Arbroath
GRAMPIAN MTS.
Firth of Tay

STANTON BANKS

Passage of Oronsay   Stirling   Dunfermline   Kirkcaldy
Helensburgh   Dumbarton   Firth of Forth   Dunbar
ISLAY   Greenock   Clydebank   EDINBURGH   Musselburgh
Paisley   GLASGOW   Motherwell   Falkirk
Rothesay   Kilmarnock   Lanark   Peebles   Galashiels   Berwick
Campbeltown   Irvine   HOLY
Ayr   SOUTHERN UPLANDS   Hawick   FARNE IS.
MALIN HD.   Girvan   Tweed
Lough Swilly   RATHLIN   Dumfries   CHEVIOT HILLS
TORY   Carndonagh   ANTRIM   Stranraer   Luce Bay   Solway Firth   NEWCASTLE-ON-TYNE   Tynemouth
ERRIGAL 2466   Coleraine   MTS.   Belfast Lough   Carlisle   Gateshead   South Shields
MTS OF DONEGAL   Londonderry   SPERRIN   Sunderland
MALINMORE HD.   Strabane   MTS.   Newtownards   Workington   Durham   Hartlepool
Donegal   Omagh   BELFAST   Whitehaven   LAKE DISTRICT   Stockton   Middlesbrough
Donegal Bay   ULSTER   Lurgan   Strangford Lough   ST. BEES HD.   Windermere   Northallerton   Darlington (Teesside)
MULLET PEN.   Sligo   Enniskillen   Armagh   ISLE OF MAN   Kendal   NORTH YORK MOORS   Scarbo
Killala   Lough Erne   Monaghan   MOURNE   (Br.)   Ramsey   Barrow   Lancaster   YORKSHIRE WOLDS
Ballina   NORTHERN   Cavan   MTS.   Dundrum Bay   Douglas   WALNEY   York   Hull
ACHILL   OX MTS.   IRELAND   Dundalk   IRISH   Morecambe Bay   Beverley
MTS OF MAYO   Boyle   Lough Allen   Dundalk Bay   Blackpool   Blackburn   Burnley   Halifax   LEEDS   Gri
CLARE   Clew B.   Castlebar   Longford   Drogheda   SEA   Preston   Bolton   Rochdale   Huddersfield   Wakefield   Doncaster   Lincoln
Westport   CONNACHT   Sheelin   Southport   Wigan   Oldham
Clifden   MTS.   Claremorris   Lough Ree   SKERRIES   LIVERPOOL   Bootle   MANCHESTER   Sheffield   Chesterfield
CONNEMARA   Lough   Mullingar   Boyne   Holyhead   ANGLESEY   Birkenhead   St Helens   Stockport
Galway   Lough Corrib   Athlone   Royal Canal   Llandudno   Chester   Crewe   Stoke-on-Trent   Nottingham
SLYNE HEAD   Ballinasloe   Grand Canal   Bangor   Denbigh   Wrexham   Stafford   Burton-on-Trent   Derby   Grantham
Galway Bay   DUBLIN   Caernarvon Bay   Snowdon   Shrewsbury   Walsall   Leicester
ARAN IS.   (Baile Atha Cliath)   Caernarvon   LLEYN PROMONTORY   Welshpool   Wolverhampton   BIRMINGHAM   Peterbo
IRELAND   Tullamore   Dun Laoghaire   Festiniog   RADNOR   Dudley   Coventry   Northampton
(EIRE)   Kildare   Bray   BARDSEY   Trenadog Bay   FOREST   SOUTH SHROPSHIRE HILLS   Leamington   Bedford   Cambr
Mal Bay   Ennis   Athy   Cardigan   Aberystwyth   Worcester   Warwick   Stratford
LOOP HEAD   Nenagh   Lugnaquilla 3039   KINGDOM   Hereford   St. Albans
Limerick   WICKLOW MTS.   Cardigan Bay   CAMBRIAN MTS.   Aylesbury   Hertford
MUNSTER   Tipperary   Cill Mhantain   High   London
Brandon Hill 3127   Thurles   LEINSTER   (Wicklow)   BRECON BEACONS   Gloucester   Oxford   Wycombe   Willesd
Dingle   Kilkenny   Arklow   Merthyr   Cheltenham   LONDON
GREAT BLASKET   Tralee   CALTY MTS.   Carlow   ST DAVID'S HD.   Carmarthen   Tydfil   Croydon
Dingle Bay   Clonmel   Enniscorthy   St. Brides Bay   Abergavenny   COTSWOLD HILLS   Swindon   Reading   Windsor   Guildfor
VALENCIA   Mallow   KNOCKMEALDOWN   New Ross   Llanelly   Aberdare   Newbury
Carrahill 3414   Killarney   MTS.   Waterford   Wexford   Milford Haven   Neath   Rhondda   Newport   Aldershot
MTS. OF KERRY   Blackwater   Suir   CARNSORE PT.   Pembroke   Swansea   Cardiff   Bath   HAMPSHIRE   Tunbridge
SHEHY MTS.   Fermoy   Dungarvan   Carmarthen Bay   Swansea Bay   Bristol   DOWNS   THE W
Cork   Youghal   Nymphe   Bristol Channel   Weston-super-Mare   Salisbury   Winchester   SOUTH DOWNS   Hove
Bantry   Lee   Youghal Bay   Bank   LUNDY   Ilfracombe   EXMOOR   SALISBURY PLAIN   Southampton   Portsmouth   Brigh
Bantry Bay   Cobh   St. GEORGE'S CHANNEL   HARTLAND PT.   Barnstaple   Taunton   Yeovil   BLACKDOWN   DOWNS   Cowes   Worthing
Cork Harbor   Nymphe   Bank   Exeter   HILLS   Dorchester   Poole   ISLE OF WIGHT
Skibbereen   Kinsale Harbor   Launceston   DARTMOOR   Honiton   Bournemouth   Ryde   St. ALBANS HD.   Newport
C. CLEAR   Clonakilty Bay   OLD HEAD OF KINSALE   BODMIN   Torquay   Exmouth   Weymouth
MOOR   Bodmin   (Torbay)   START PT.
Camborne   Truro   Plymouth   Dartmouth
Penzance   LAND'S END   ENGLISH
Falmouth
SCILLY IS.   LIZARD PT.

Relief

Meters		Feet
610		2000
305		1000
152.5		500
0	Sea Level	0
152.5		500
1525		5000

Sea Level
Below Sea Level

A-559700-76   -6-12
COPYRIGHT BY
RAND McNALLY & COMPANY
MADE IN U.S.A.

Longitude West of Greenwich

Scale 1: 4 000 000; one inch to 64 miles. Conic Projection
Elevations and depressions are given in feet

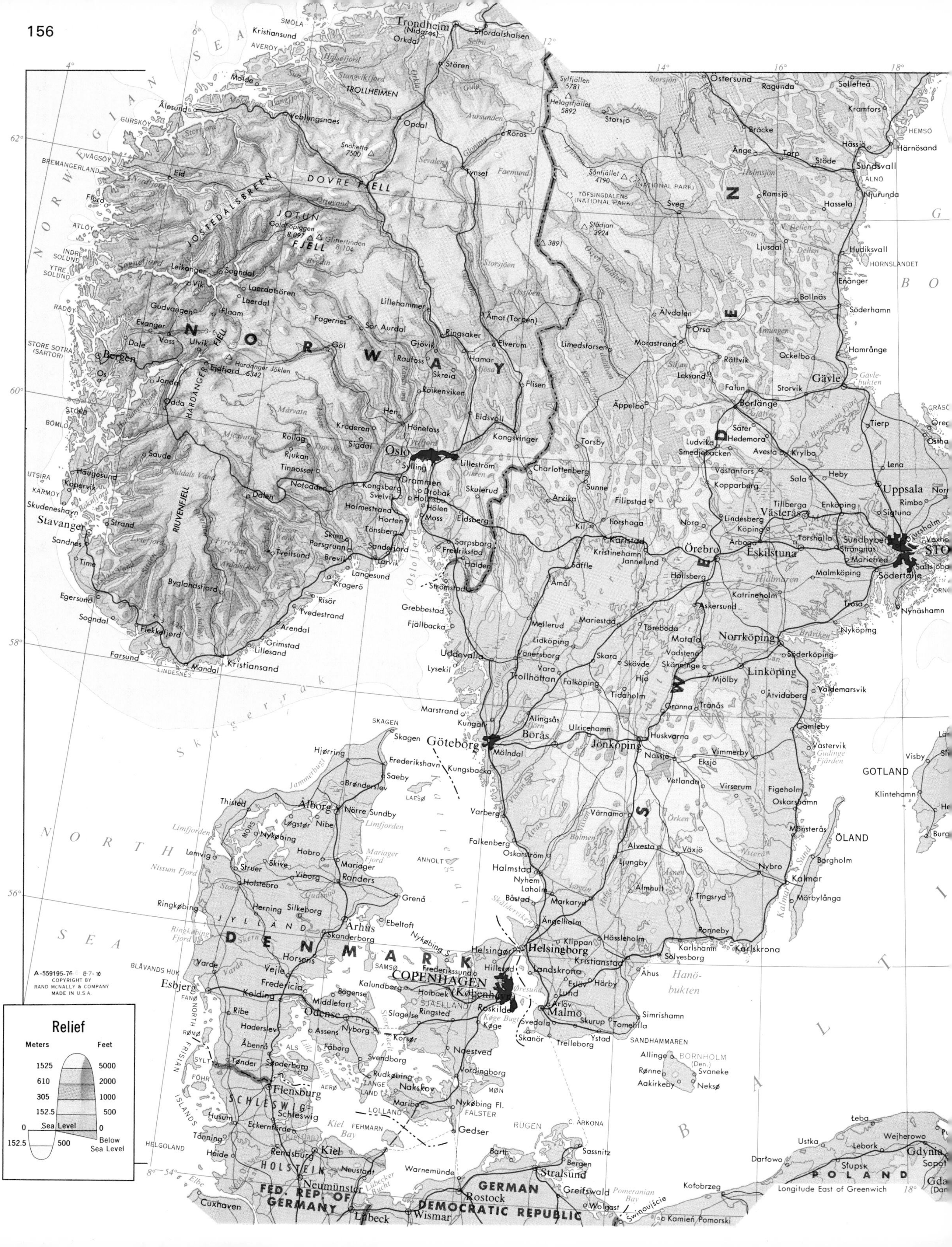

NORWEGIAN SEA

NORWAY

SWEDEN

DENMARK

NORTH SEA

BALTIC SEA

Skagerrak

Kattegat

GERMAN DEMOCRATIC REPUBLIC

FED. REP. OF GERMANY

POLAND

GOTLAND

ÖLAND

BORNHOLM (Den.)

Trondheim (Nidaros)

Oslo

Bergen

Stavanger

Kristiansand

Göteborg

COPENHAGEN (København)

Stockholm (STO...)

Uppsala

Malmö

Helsingborg

Copyright by RAND McNALLY & COMPANY
MADE IN U.S.A.
A-559195-76   8-7-10

Relief

Meters	Feet
1525	5000
610	2000
305	1000
152.5	500
0 Sea Level	0
152.5	500 Below Sea Level

Longitude East of Greenwich

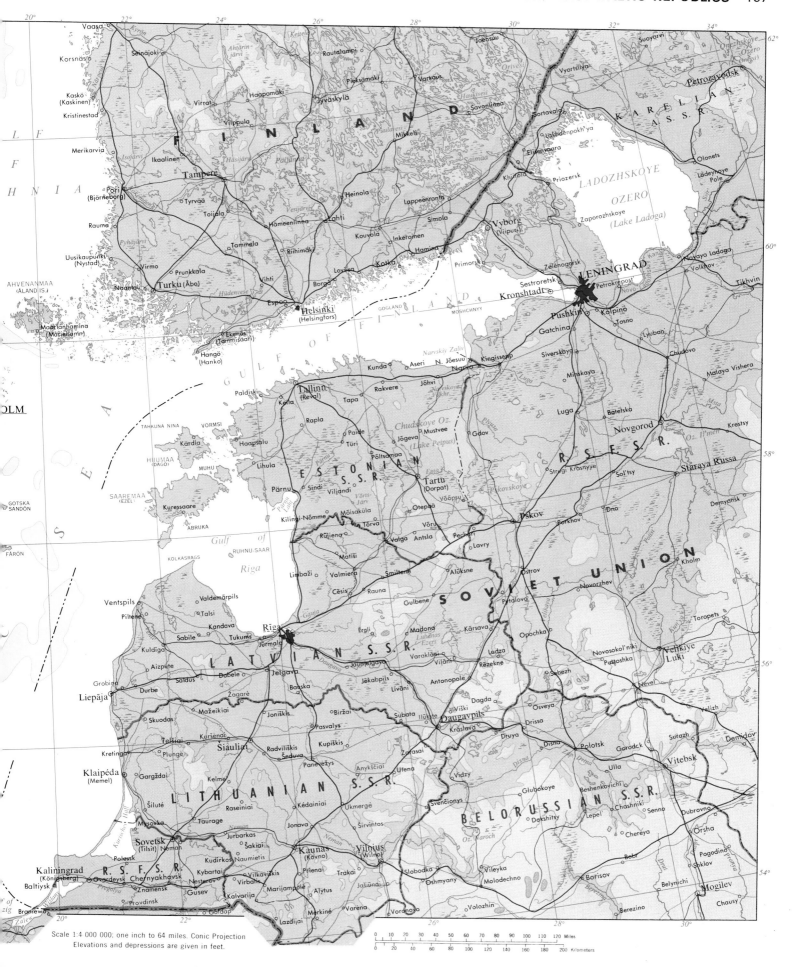

Scale 1:4 000 000; one inch to 64 miles. Conic Projection
Elevations and depressions are given in feet.

Scale 1:4 000 000, one inch to 64 miles. Conic Projection
Elevations and depressions are given in feet.

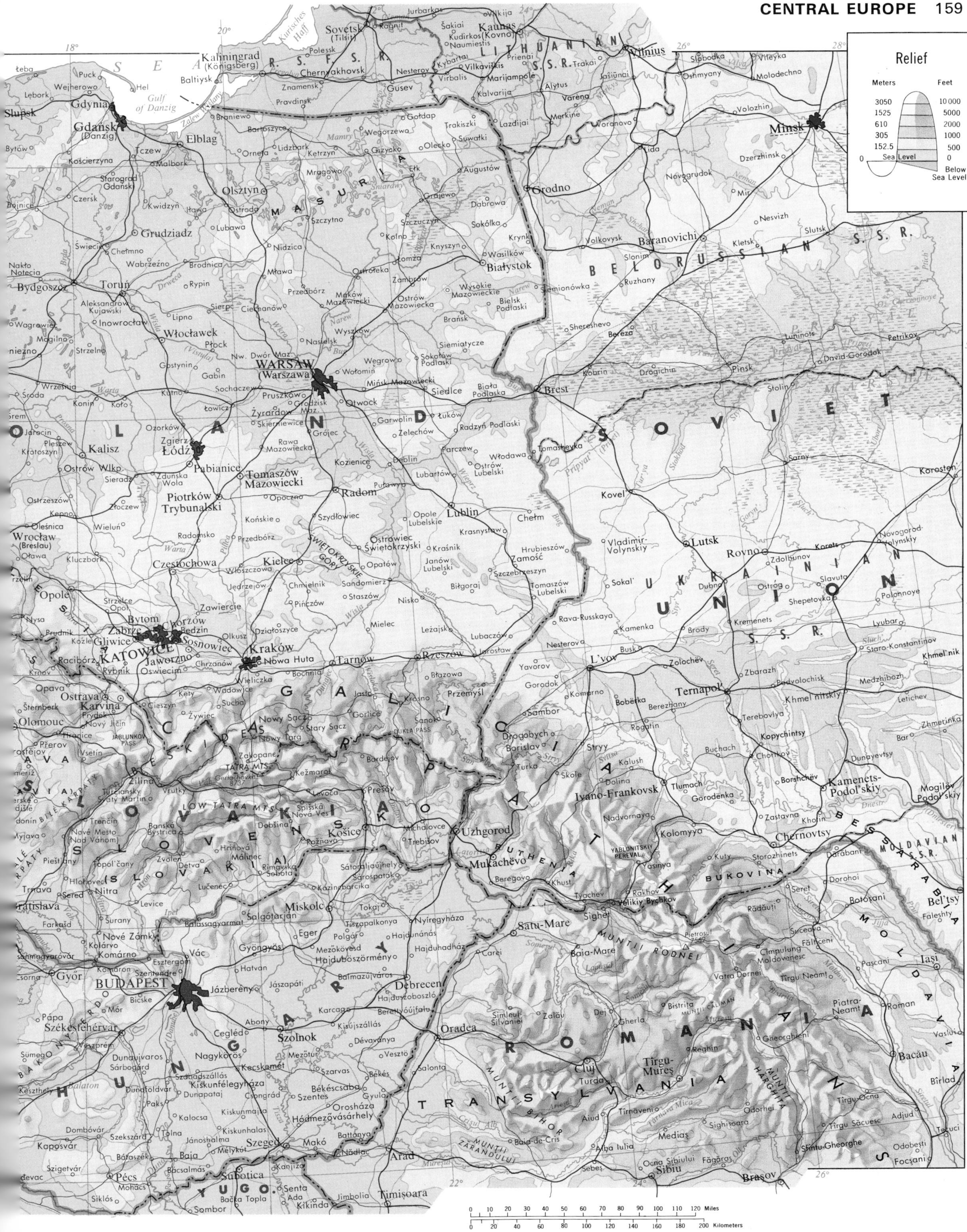

Relief

Meters		Feet
3050		10 000
1525		5000
610		2000
305		1000
152.5		500
0 Sea Level		0
		Below Sea Level

Continued on pages 170-171

SEA

Gulf of Danzig

R.S.F.S.R.

LITHUANIAN S.S.R.

Kaliningrad (Königsberg)

Vilnius

Minsk

BELORUSSIAN S.S.R.

MASURIA

P O L A N D

WARSAW (Warszawa)

SOVIET

Łódź

UKRAINIAN UNION S.S.R.

G A L I C I A

L'vov

C Z E C H O S L O V A K I A

S L O V A K I A (SLOVAKIA)

TATRA MTS.

LOW TATRA MTS.

BESKIDES

C A R P A T H I A N S

RUTHENIA

BUKOVINA

MOLDAVIAN S.S.R.

BESSARABIA

MOLDAVIA

H U N G A R Y

BUDAPEST

R O M A N I A

T R A N S Y L V A N I A

MUNTII RODNEI

MUNTII CALIMAN

MUNTII HARGHITA

MUNTII BIHOR

MUNTII ZARANDULUI

Y U G O.

Krków, Katowice, Wrocław (Breslau), Bydgoszcz, Toruń, Gdańsk (Danzig), Gdynia, Słupsk, Lublin, Radom, Kielce, Częstochowa, Białystok, Grodno, Brest, Pinsk, Baranovichi, Slonim, Kovel, Lutsk, Rovno, Ternopol, Ivano-Frankovsk, Chernovtsy, Uzhgorod, Mukachevo, Satu-Mare, Baia-Mare, Oradea, Cluj, Tîrgu-Mures, Sibiu, Brasov, Timişoara, Arad, Szeged, Debrecen, Miskolc, Košice, Bratislava, Nitra, Wien

Kaunas, Vilnius, Minsk

NETH.
Maastricht
COLOGNE
(Köln)
Siegen
Düren
Aachen
Liège
Bonn
Siegburg
Wetzlar
Verviers
WESTERWALD
Neuwied
Andernach
Koblenz
Limburg
Bad Ems
FRANKFURT AM MAIN
EIFEL
Cochem
Wiesbaden
Mainz
Wittlich
Bad Kreuznach
Bingen
Echternach
LUX.
Trier
HUNSRÜCK
Worms
Luxembourg
Esch-sur-Alzette
MANNHEIM
Merzig
Kaiserslautern
Ludwigshafen
Thionville
SAAR
Speyer
Neunkirchen
Zweibrücken
Landau
Saarbrücken
Forbach
Karlsruhe
Metz
Sarreguemines
Wissembourg
Rastatt
Pont-à-Mousson
Sarrebourg
Saverne
Haguenau
Baden Baden
Nancy
Schiltigheim
Bischheim
Strasbourg
Lunéville
Baccarat
Offenburg
Charmes
St. Dié
Erstein
Mirecourt
Thaon-les-Vosges
Sélestat
Épinal
Ste. Marie aux Mines
Colmar
MONTS FAUCILLES
Remiremont
Freiburg
SCHWARZWALD
Guebwiller
Thann
Luxeuil
Mulhouse
Lörrach
Belfort
Vesoul
Basel
Montbéliard
Beaucourt
Audincourt
Porrentruy
Olten
Aarau
Gray
Besançon
Solothurn
Biel
Langenthal
Luzern
Neuchâtel
Burgdorf
Salins-les-Bains
Bern
Pontarlier
Thun
Thuner See
Poligny
Yverdon
Moudon
SWITZERLAND
Jungfrau 13 668
Lons-le-Saunier
Lausanne
BERNER ALPEN
Vevey
L. Geneva
Brig
Geneva
(Genève)
Thonon-les-Bains
Sion
SIMPLON PASS
Annemasse
Martigny
Matterhorn 14 685
Bourg
PENNINE ALPS
Chamonix
Annecy
Mt. Blanc 15 771
GT. ST. BERNARD PASS
Monte Rosa 15 200
Albertville
Mt. Blanc Tunnel
Aosta
Aix-les-Bains
LITTLE ST. BERNARD PASS
Moûtiers
Ivrea
GRAIAN ALPS
Levanna 11 874
Voiron
Villard-Bonnot
Mt. Cenis 6835
Chivasso
Grenoble
MT. CENIS PASS
Mt. Pelvoux 12 920
TURIN
(Torino)
La Mure
Briançon
COTTIAN
Mt. Viso 12 602
Saluzzo
Embrun
ALPS
Gap
Veynes
Barcelonnette
Cuneo
Mt. Pelat 10079
MARITIME ALPS
Sisteron
Mt. Mounier 9246
Digne
Breil
San Remo
Manosque
Menton
Nice
MONACO
Grasse
Cagnes
Draguignan
Cannes
Antibes
Fréjus
Aix-en-Provence
Marseille
Aubagne
St. Tropez
Hyères
La Seyne-sur-Mer
Toulon
ILES D'HYÈRES
ERRANEAN SEA
0 10 20 30 40 50 60 70 80 90 100 110 120 Miles
0 20 40 60 80 100 120 140 160 180 200 Kilometers

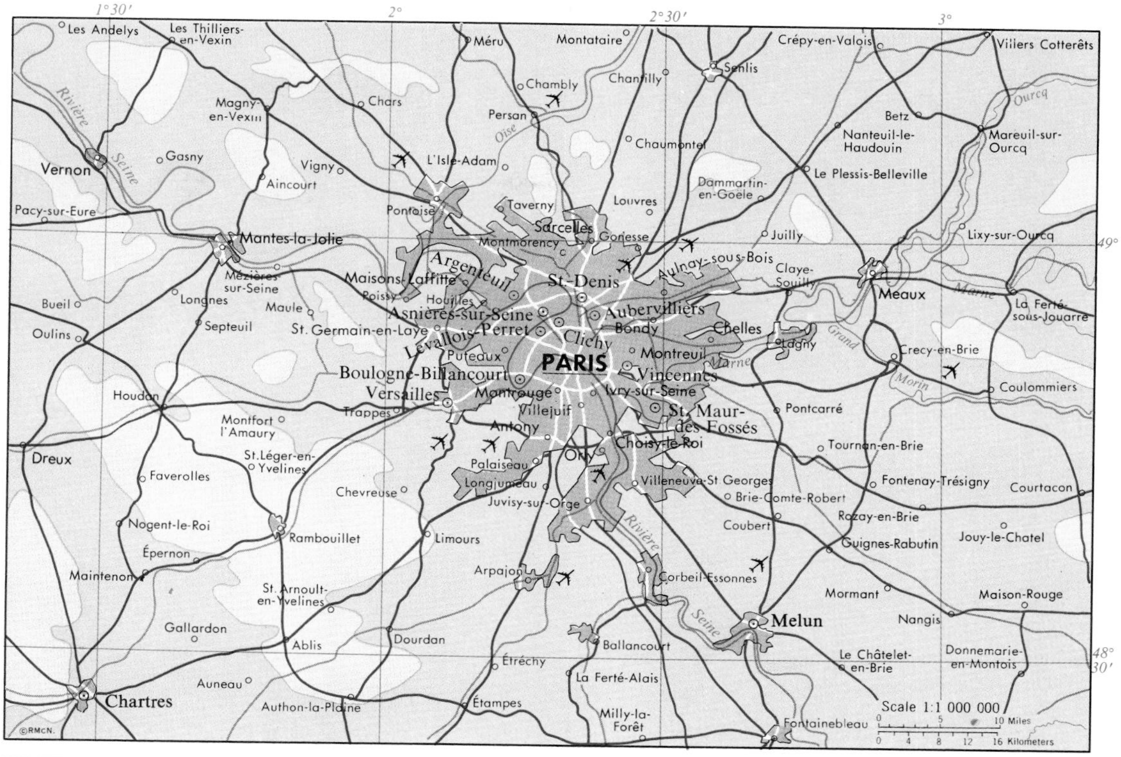
Les Andelys
Les Thilliers-en-Vexin
Méru
Montataire
Crépy-en-Valois
Villers Cotterêts
Senlis
Chambly
Chantilly
Magny-en-Vexin
Chars
Persan
Betz
Nanteuil-le-Haudouin
Mareuil-sur-Ourcq
Vernon
Gasny
Vigny
L'Isle-Adam
Chaumontel
Aincourt
Dammartin-en-Goële
Le Plessis-Belleville
Pacy-sur-Eure
Pontoise
Taverny
Louvres
Sarcelles
Gonesse
Juilly
Lixy-sur-Ourcq
Mantes-la-Jolie
Montmorency
Argenteuil
St.-Denis
Aulnay-sous-Bois
Claye-Souilly
Mézières-sur-Seine
Maisons-Laffitte
Poissy
Houilles
Meaux
Bueil
Longnes
Maule
Asnières-sur-Seine
Aubervilliers
La Ferté-sous-Jouarre
Oulins
Septeuil
St. Germain-en-Laye
Levallois-Perret
Clichy
Bondy
Chelles
Lagny
Puteaux
PARIS
Montreuil
Crecy-en-Brie
Boulogne-Billancourt
Vincennes
Coulommiers
Houdan
Versailles
Montrouge
Ivry-sur-Seine
Trappes
Villejuif
St. Maur-des-Fossés
Pontcarré
Montfort l'Amaury
Antony
Choisy-le-Roi
Dreux
St.Léger-en-Yvelines
Palaiseau
Orly
Tournan-en-Brie
Faverolles
Chevreuse
Longjumeau
Villeneuve-St Georges
Fontenay-Trésigny
Courtacon
Juvisy-sur-Orge
Brie-Comte-Robert
Nogent-le-Roi
Rambouillet
Limours
Rozay-en-Brie
Coubert
Jouy-le-Chatel
Guignes-Rabutin
Épernon
Maintenon
Arpajon
Corbeil-Essonnes
St. Arnoult-en-Yvelines
Mormant
Maison-Rouge
Nangis
Melun
Gallardon
Ablis
Dourdan
Ballancourt
Le Châtelet-en-Brie
Donnemarie-en-Montois
Étréchy
Auneau
La Ferté-Alais
Chartres
Authon-la-Plaine
Étampes
Milly-la-Forêt
Fontainebleau
Seine
Marne
Oise
Ourcq
Scale 1:1 000 000
0 5 10 Miles
0 4 8 12 16 Kilometers
©RMCN.

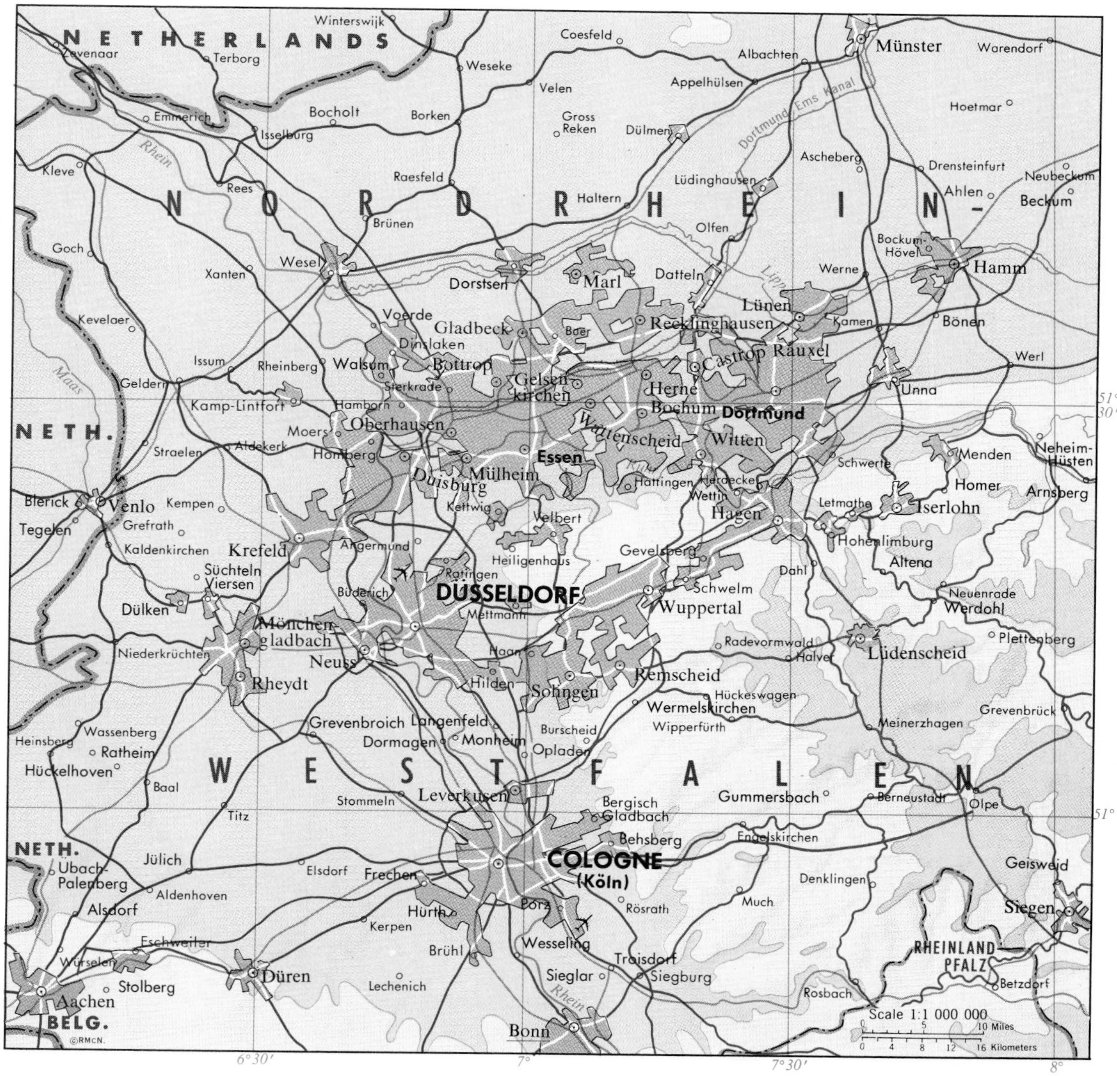
NETHERLANDS
Winterswijk
Coesfeld
Münster
Zevenaar
Terborg
Weseke
Albachten
Warendorf
Velen
Appelhülsen
Emmerich
Bocholt
Borken
Hoetmar
Gross Reken
Dülmen
Isselburg
Ascheberg
Kleve
Raesfeld
Drensteinfurt
Rees
Lüdinghausen
Neubeckum
NORDRHEIN-
Haltern
Ahlen
Beckum
Brünen
Olfen
Goch
Bockum-Hövel
Hamm
Wesel
Xanten
Dorsten
Marl
Datteln
Werne
Voerde
Lünen
Kevelaer
Gladbeck
Recklinghausen
Kamen
Dinslaken
Bönen
Issum
Rheinberg
Walsum
Bottrop
Castrop Rauxel
Werl
Gelsenkirchen
Herne
Unna
Geldern
Sterkrade
Bochum
Dortmund
Kamp-Lintfort
Hamborn
Moers
Oberhausen
Wattenscheid
Witten
NETH.
Essen
Schwerte
Menden
Neheim-Hüsten
Straelen
Aldekerk
Homberg
Mülheim
Hattingen
Herdecke
Homer
Arnsberg
Duisburg
Wetter
Blerick
Venlo
Kempen
Kettwig
Velbert
Hagen
Letmathe
Iserlohn
Tegelen
Grefrath
Hohenlimburg
Kaldenkirchen
Krefeld
Angermund
Gevelsberg
Altena
Heiligenhaus
Süchteln
Viersen
Ratingen
Dahl
Schwelm
Neuenrade
Büderich
DÜSSELDORF
Werdohl
Dülken
Wuppertal
Mettmann
Mönchen-gladbach
Plettenberg
Radevormwald
Niederkrüchten
Neuss
Halver
Lüdenscheid
Haan
Remscheid
Rheydt
Hilden
Solingen
Hückeswagen
Wermelskirchen
Grevenbroich
Langenfeld
Meinerzhagen
Grevenbrück
Wassenberg
Burscheid
Wipperfürth
Heinsberg
Ratheim
Dormagen
Monheim
Opladen
Hückelhoven
WESTFALEN
Baal
Stommeln
Leverkusen
Bergisch Gladbach
Gummersbach
Berneustadt
Olpe
Titz
Behsberg
NETH.
Engelskirchen
Jülich
Ubach-Palenberg
Elsdorf
Frechen
COLOGNE
(Köln)
Denklingen
Geisweid
Porz
Aldenhoven
Much
Hürth
Rösrath
Siegen
Alsdorf
Kerpen
Eschweiler
Wesseling
RHEINLAND PFALZ
Würselen
Brühl
Troisdorf
Düren
Sieglar
Siegburg
Betzdorf
Stolberg
Lechenich
Aachen
Rosbach
BELG.
Bonn
Rhein
Maas
Lippe
Dortmund Ems Kanal
Scale 1:1 000 000
0 5 10 Miles
0 4 8 12 16 Kilometers
©RMCN.

Relief

Meters		Feet
3050		10000
1525		5000
610		2000
305		1000
152.5		500
0	Sea Level	0
152.5		500
1525		5000
3050		10000

A-552900-76--5 4-7-
COPYRIGHT BY
RAND McNALLY & COMPANY
MADE IN U.S.A.

Scale 1:4 000 000, one inch to 64 miles. Conic Projection
Elevations and depressions are given in feet

Longitude West of Greenwich

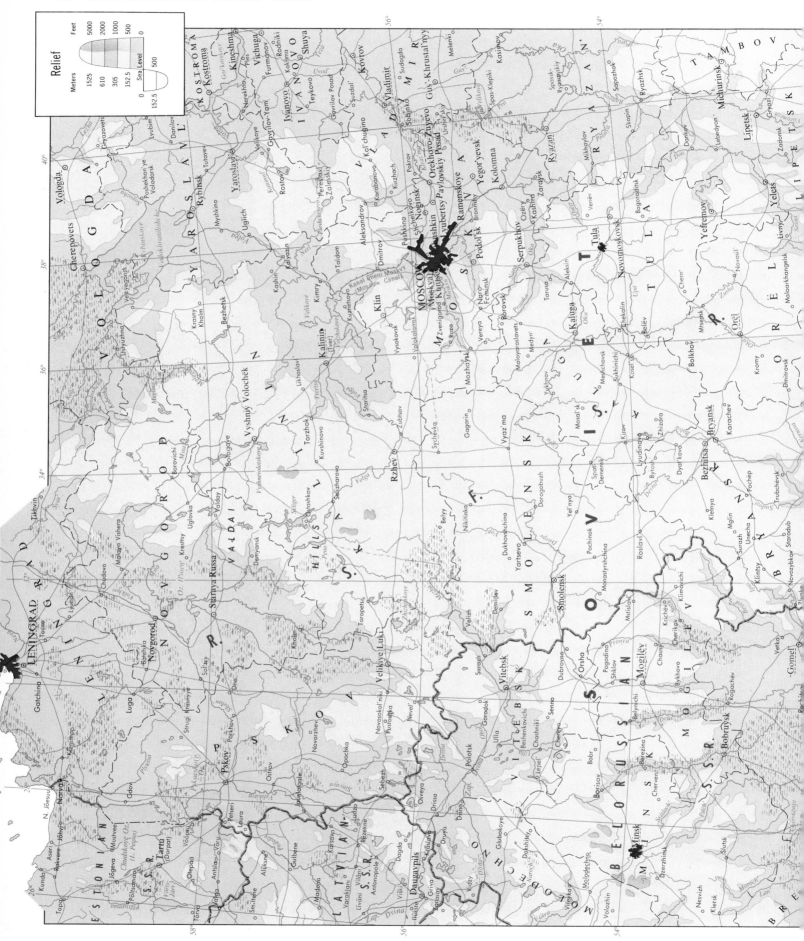

Scale 1:4 000 000; one inch to 64 miles. Conic Projection
Elevations and depressions are given in feet

Scale 1:20 000 000; one inch to 315 miles.
Lambert's Azimuthal, Equal Area Projection
Elevations and depressions are given in feet

Continued on pages 150–151

Scale 1:10 000 000; one inch to 160 miles. Conic Projection
Elevations and depressions are given in feet.

Continued on pages 152–153

Continued on pages 146-147

Scale 1:16 000 000; one inch to 250 miles Conic Projection
Elevations and depressions are given in feet.

Continued on pages 188–189

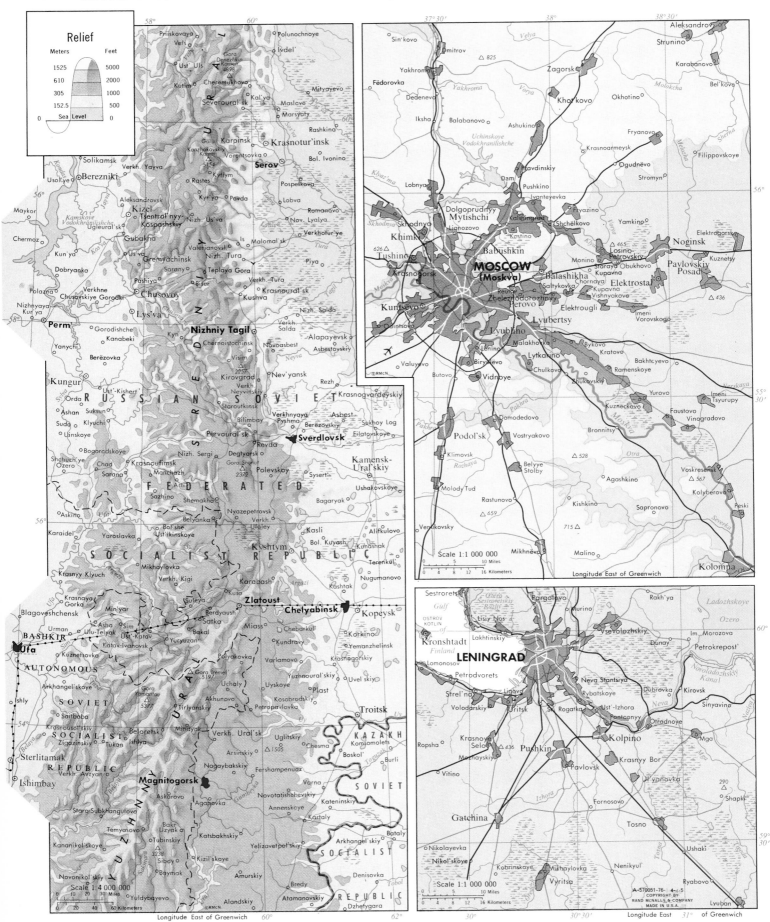

For larger scale coverage of Moscow see page 64.

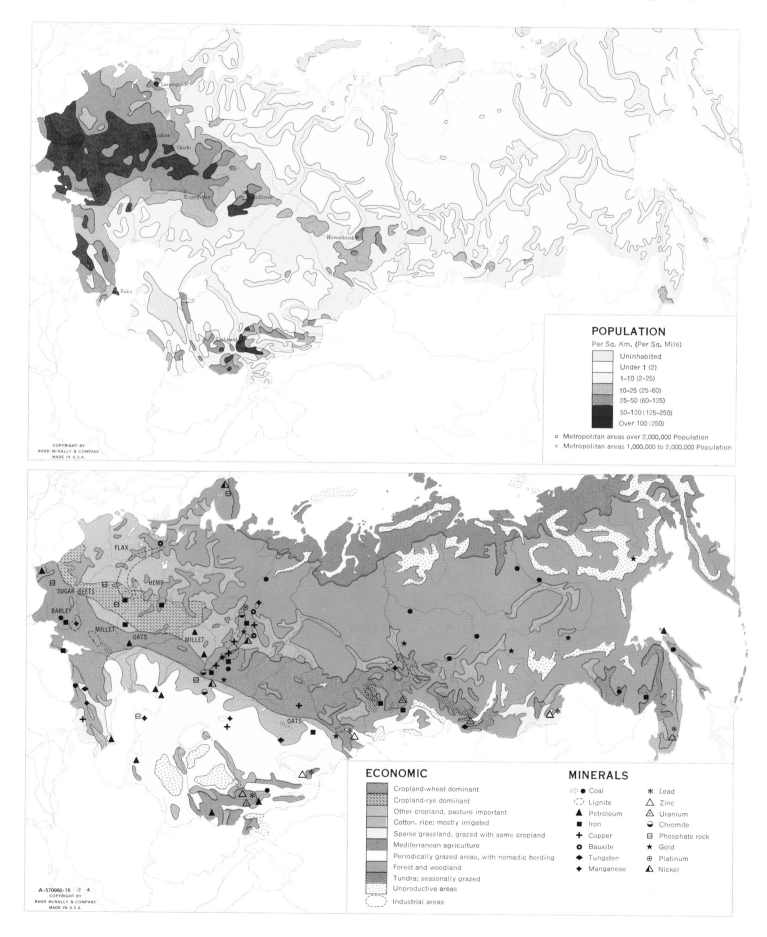

POPULATION

Per Sq. Km. (Per Sq. Mile)

Uninhabited
Under 1 (2)
1–10 (2–25)
10–25 (25–60)
25–50 (60–125)
50–100 (125–250)
Over 100 (250)

▫ Metropolitan areas over 2,000,000 Population
◦ Metropolitan areas 1,000,000 to 2,000,000 Population

COPYRIGHT BY
RAND MCNALLY & COMPANY
MADE IN U.S.A.

ECONOMIC

Cropland-wheat dominant
Cropland-rye dominant
Other cropland, pasture important
Cotton, rice; mostly irrigated
Sparse grassland, grazed with some cropland
Mediterranean agriculture
Periodically grazed areas, with nomadic herding
Forest and woodland
Tundra; seasonally grazed
Unproductive areas

Industrial areas

MINERALS

● Coal   ✳ Lead
Lignite   △ Zinc
▲ Petroleum   ◬ Uranium
■ Iron   ◠ Chromite
+ Copper   ⊟ Phosphate rock
◉ Bauxite   ★ Gold
◆ Tungsten   ⊙ Platinum
◆ Manganese   ◮ Nickel

A-570000-16 -2 4
COPYRIGHT BY
RAND MCNALLY & COMPANY
MADE IN U.S.A.

Ocean Floor Maps

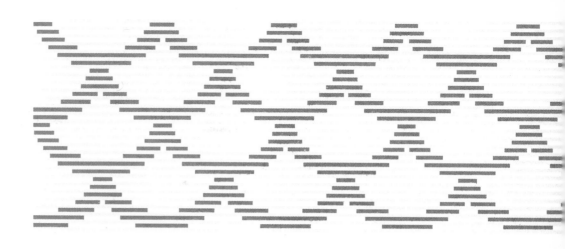

The maps in this section give an artist's view of what the land beneath the surface of the world's oceans looks like. In general, colors used are those which scientists believe may exist on the ocean floor. For continental shelves or shallow inland seas, grayish-green corresponds to sediments washed from the continental areas. Layers of mud, which scientists call *oozes*, cover the ocean bottom. In deeper parts of the oceans, the oozes consist largely of the skeletons of marine life. These appear in white. The fine mud from land is red. In the Atlantic Ocean, materials accumulate relatively rapidly and have a high iron content. These are shown in a brighter red than elsewhere. Slower accumulation in the Pacific and Indian oceans results in more manganese, which results in darker colors. Undersea ridges are shown in black to suggest that they were formed relatively recently from molten rock. Around certain islands white is used to show coral reefs.

The ocean floor has towering mountain ranges, vast canyons, broad plains, and a variety of features that often exceed anything found on the continents. One of the most dramatic features of the ocean floor is the Mid-Atlantic Ridge, a chain of mountains that extends down the middle of the Atlantic Ocean. One distinct characteristic of this ridge is a *trough*, or valley, that runs along the center of the ridge, in effect producing a double line of ridges.

Scientists believe that the ocean ridges mark lines where molten materials from the earth's interior rise to the ocean floor, to form gigantic plates that move slowly apart. This theory, called Continental Drift, suggests that the continents are moving away from each other, having been a single land mass in ancient times. The matching curves of the Atlantic Ocean shorelines of South America and Africa have long been cited as support for this theory.

Where the subsea plates meet certain continental areas or island chains, the ridges plunge downward to form deep trenches. Some of the deepest known trenches are found along the northern and western edges of the Pacific Ocean. These include the Mariana, Tonga, and Kuril trenches.

Deep trenches also parallel the western coasts of Central and South America, the northern coast of Puerto Rico and the Virgin Islands, and other coastal areas. Other identifiable ocean floor features include great submarine canyons that lead from the edges of the continents; seamounts that rise above the ocean floor to form islands; and the continental shelves, which appear to be underwater extensions of the continents.

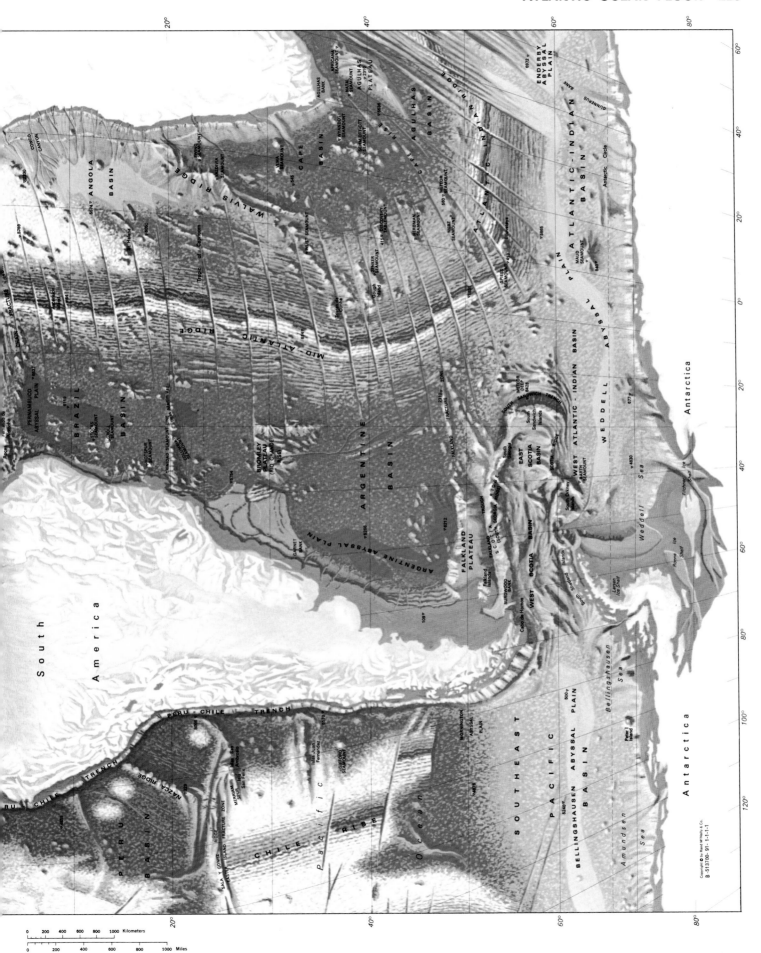

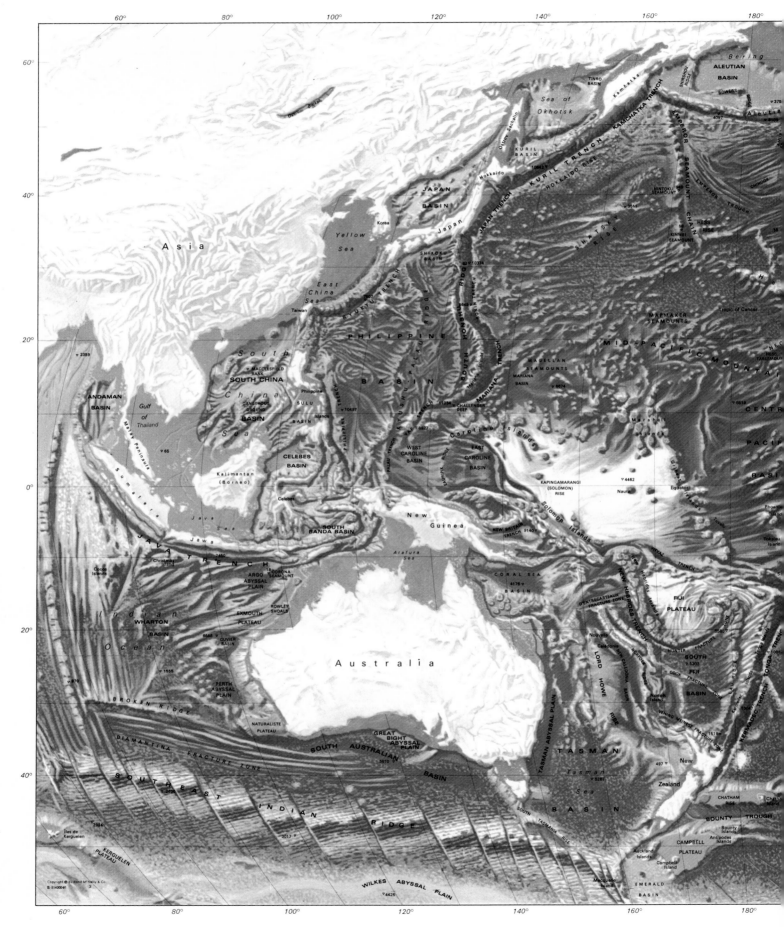

Scale 1:58 000 000; one inch to 900 miles (approx.)
Modified Cylindrical Projection   ▽ Depths in meters.

60°
40°

LABRADOR
BASIN

Hudson
Bay

Great
Lakes

North America

NORTH

AMERICAN

BASIN

▽6399

LEUTIAN TRENCH
ALEUTIAN
YSSAL PLAIN

KODIAK
GUYOT
(SEAMOUNT)

ALASKA
ABYSSAL
PLAIN

TUFTS
ABYSSAL
PLAIN

▽3828

▽5257

7022
URVEYOR
LNO

FRACTURE   ZONE

FRACTURE   ZONE

MUSICIANS
SEAMOUNTS

▽6298

PIONEER   FRACTURE   ZONE

DELGADA
FAN

▽5120

MONTEREY
FAN

MURRAY   FRACTURE   ZONE

▽1765

MOLOKAI FRACTURE ZONE

Isla de
Guadalupe

▽3008

BAJA CALIFORNIA
SEAMOUNT
PROVINCE

40°

PEDRO
TRENCH

MOLOKAI

1057
PENSACOLA
SEAMOUNT

EAST

CLARION   FRACTURE   ZONE

4808

CLARION FRACTURE ZONE

▽6720

CLARION FRACTURE ZONE

480

SUITCASE
SEAMOUNTS

RIVERA FRACTURE
ZONE

Isla de
Revillagigedo

OROZCO
FRACTURE ZONE

Gulf of

MEXICO BASIN
SIGSBEE
KNOLLS ▽4023
Mexico

WEST FLORIDA SHELF

CAMPECHE
BANK

BLAKE PLATEAU

CAYMAN TRENCH
Caribbean
Sea
11
BEATA RIDGE

20°

PACIFIC

BASIN

CHRISTMAS RIDGE

IDGE

MOLOKAI

HAWAIIAN

Islands

Christmas
Island

5349

5029

Îles
Marquises

6486

CLIPPERTON   FRACTURE   ZONE

MATHEMATICIANS

Île
Clapperton

SIQUEIROS FRACTURE ZONE

20
GERMAINE
BANK

TEHUANTEPEC FRACTURE ZONE

MIDDLE AMERICA TRENCH

▽4085

GUATEMALA
BASIN

GALAPAGOS
RISE

PANAMA
BASIN
420
Isla del
Malpelo

PERU
BASIN

▽4399

PERU-CHILE TRENCH

COCOS RIDGE

EAST PACIFIC RISE (ALBATROSS CORDILLERA)

GALAPAGOS   FRACTURE   ZONE

5851

Galapagos
Islands

CARNEGIE RIDGE

Île
Tahiti

MARQUESAS   FRACTURE   ZONE

Îles de la
Société

Îles
Tuamotu

7314

Cook Islands

apic of Capricorn

Îles Tubai

Raga

Pitcairn
Island

Sala y Gomez

Isla de
Pascua
(Easter Island)

SALA Y GOMEZ RIDGE

EASTER ISLAND   FRACTURE   ZONE

BAUER   FRACTURE   ZONE

▽4525

CHILE

BASIN

Isla San
Feliz
Isla San
Ambrosio

NAZCA RIDGE

329

8066

20°

▽3841

C
H
I
L
E
R
I
S
E

Isla Juan
Fernandez

GIFFORD
SEAMOUNT

EAST   PACIFIC   CORDILLERA

(ALBATROSS CORDILLERA)

CHALLENGER   FRACTURE   ZONE

FERNANDEZ   FRACTURE   ZONE

SOUTHEAST
PACIFIC
BASIN

▽4876

South America

40°

▽1006

OUTHWEST   PACIFIC   BASIN

ELTANIN   FRACTURE   ZONE

▽4785

3977

1447

▽3841

Atlantic
Ocean

109

Falkland
Islands

FALKLAND
PLATEAU

50°

SCOTIA RIDGE
(SOUTH GEORGIA RIDGE)

WEST SCOTIA
BASIN

0   400   800   1200 Kilometers

0   400   800   1200 Miles

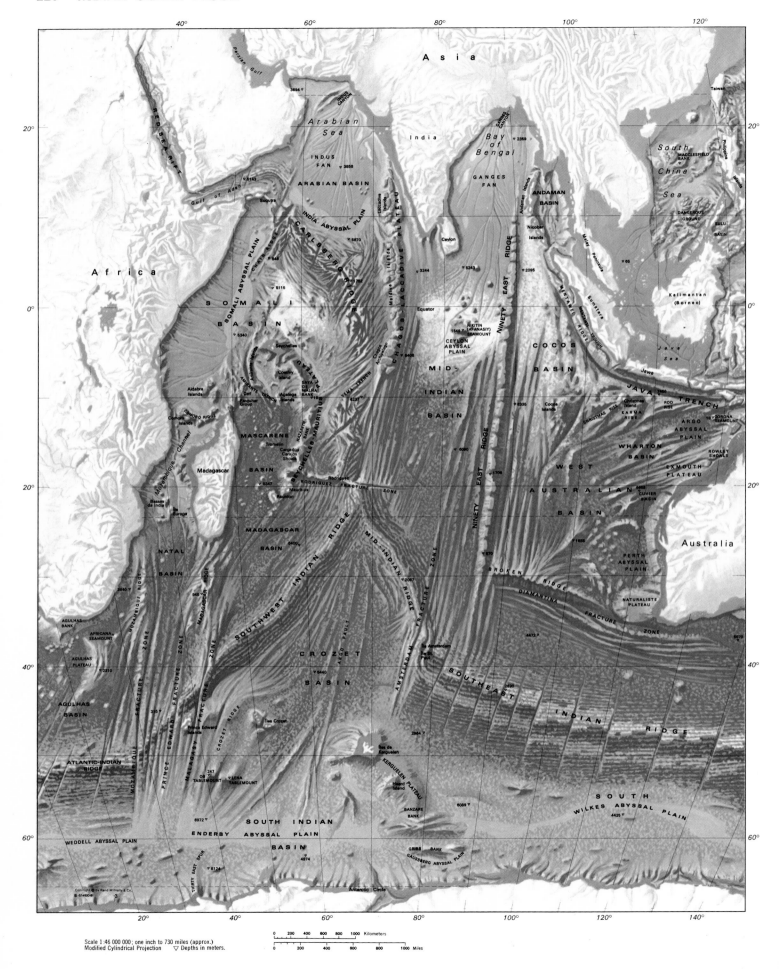

Scale 1:46 000 000; one inch to 730 miles (approx.)
Modified Cylindrical Projection   ▽ Depths in meters.

0 200 400 600 800 1000 Kilometers
0 200 400 600 800 1000 Miles

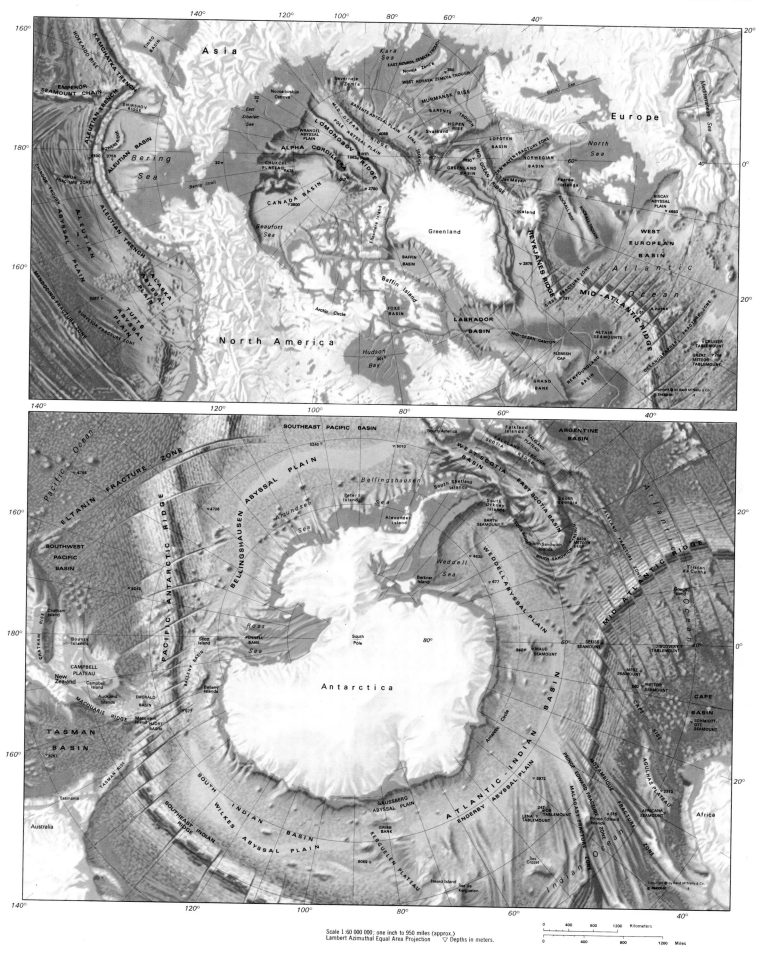

Scale 1:60 000 000; one inch to 950 miles (approx.)
Lambert Azimuthal Equal Area Projection   ▽ Depths in meters.

Index
and World Facts

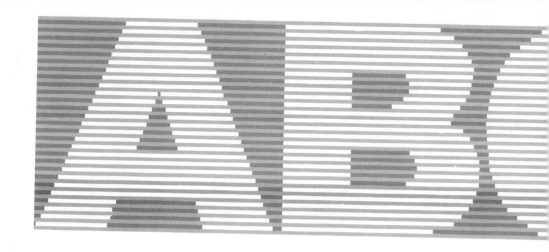

The following pages provide a vast store of factual information of geographical interest on the world, the continents, individual countries, and the 50 U.S. states.

Presented in tabular form, this information supplements the maps with data not readily available from the maps themselves. Here are answers to many of the questions raised by those who use the Atlas, particularly questions that ask "How large?" "How many?" and "Where?"

Two indexes are included, one for major cities, and a pronouncing index to the main body of reference maps. The pronouncing index also features latitude and longitude to make it easier for readers to locate places on the maps.

Other aids to the Atlas usage are populations, areas in both square miles and square kilometers, a glossary of foreign terms, and abbreviations.

principal countries and regions of the world

Political Unit	Area in sq. miles	Area in km^2	Population*
Afghanistan	250,000	647,497	20,666
Africa	11,707,000	30,320,000	437,000
Alabama (U.S.)	51,609	133,667	3,614
Alaska (U.S.)	586,412	1,518,800	352
Albania	11,100	28,748	2,730
Alberta (Can.)	255,285	661,185	1,838
Algeria	919,595	2,381,741	18,460
American Samoa (U.S.)	76	197	36
Andorra	175	453	27
Angola	481,354	1,246,700	6,265
Antarctica	5,100,000	13,209,000	....
Antigua (incl. Barbuda) (U.K.)	171	442	74
Argentina	1,072,163	2,776,889	26,378
Arizona (U.S.)	113,909	295,023	2,224
Arkansas (U.S.)	53,104	137,539	2,116
Asia	16,979,000	43,976,000	2,445,000
Australia (Comm.)	2,967,909	7,686,848	14,213
Austria	32,374	83,849	7,680
Azores (Port.)	905	2,344	273
Bahamas (Comm.)	5,380	13,935	230
Bahrain	240	622	275
Bangladesh (Comm.)	55,598	143,998	82,453
Barbados (Comm.)	166	431	251
Belgium	11,781	30,513	9,962
Belize (U.K.)	8,867	22,965	154
Benin	43,484	112,622	3,422
Bermuda (U.K.)	21	53	59
Bhutan	18,147	47,000	1,245
Bolivia	424,165	1,098,581	6,061
Botswana (Comm.)	231,805	600,372	756
Brazil	3,286,488	8,511,965	116,418
British Columbia (Can.)	366,255	948,596	2,406
Brunei (U.K.)	2,226	5,765	173
Bulgaria	42,823	110,912	8,889
Burma	261,218	676,552	33,326
Burundi	10,747	27,834	4,070
California (U.S.)	158,693	411,013	21,185
Cambodia	69,898	181,035	8,809
Cameroon	183,569	475,442	6,773
Canada (Comm.)	3,851,809	9,976,139	23,671
Canal Zone (U.S.)	647	1,676	40
Canary Is. (Sp.)	2,808	7,273	1,365
Cape Verde	1,557	4,033	316
Cayman Is. (U.K.)	100	259	11
Central African Empire	240,535	622,984	2,870
Central America	201,976	523,115	20,833
Chad	495,755	1,284,000	4,291
Channel Is. (U.K.)	75	195	130
Chile	292,258	756,945	11,131
China (excl. Taiwan)	3,691,523	9,561,000	865,493
Colombia	439,737	1,138,914	27,168
Colorado (U.S.)	104,247	269,998	2,534
Comoros	838	2,171	337
Congo	132,047	342,000	1,484
Connecticut (U.S.)	5,009	12,973	3,095
Cook Is. (N.Z.)	93	241	17
Costa Rica	19,575	50,700	2,137
Cuba	44,218	114,524	9,762
Cyprus (Comm.)	3,572	9,251	649
Czechoslovakia	49,371	127,869	15,042
Delaware (U.S.)	2,057	5,328	579
Denmark	16,629	43,069	5,167
Dist. of Columbia (U.S.)	68	176	757
Djibouti	8,494	22,000	114
Dominica	290	751	77
Dominican Republic	18,816	48,734	5,115
Ecuador	109,484	283,561	7,946
Egypt	386,662	1,001,449	39,729
El Salvador	8,260	21,393	4,480
England (U.K.)	50,338	130,375	46,996
Equatorial Guinea	10,830	28,051	321
Ethiopia	471,778	1,221,900	30,067
Europe	4,063,000	10,523,000	681,000
Faeroe Is. (Den.)	540	1,399	42
Falkland Is. (excl. Deps.) (U.K.)	4,618	11,961	2
Fiji (Comm.)	7,055	18,272	604
Finland	130,120	337,009	4,757
Florida (U.S.)	58,560	151,670	8,357
France	211,208	547,026	54,208
French Guiana (Fr.)	35,135	91,000	67
French Polynesia (Fr.)	1,544	4,000	142
Gabon	103,347	267,667	1,029
Gambia (Comm.)	4,361	11,295	563
Georgia (U.S.)	58,876	152,488	4,926
German Democratic Republic (East)	41,768	108,178	17,304
Germany, Fed. Rep. of (West)	95,934	248,468	63,544
Ghana (Comm.)	92,100	238,537	10,687
Gibraltar (U.K.)	2.3	6	33
Gilbert Is. (U.K.)	278	720	52
Greece	50,944	131,944	9,143
Greenland (Den.)	840,004	2,175,600	52
Grenada (Comm.)	133	344	98
Guadeloupe (Fr.)	687	1,779	373
Guam (U.S.)	212	549	103
Guatemala	42,042	108,889	6,360
Guinea	94,926	245,857	4,741
Guinea-Bissau	13,948	36,125	549
Guyana (Comm.)	83,000	214,969	844
Haiti	10,714	27,750	4,810
Hawaii (U.S.)	6,450	16,705	865
Honduras	43,277	112,088	3,431
Hong Kong (U.K.)	1,126	2,916	4,563
Hungary	35,919	93,030	10,678
Iceland	39,769	103,000	226
Idaho (U.S.)	83,557	216,412	820
Illinois (U.S.)	56,400	146,075	11,145
India (incl. part of Kashmir) (Comm.)	1,269,346	3,287,590	637,082
Indiana (U.S.)	36,291	93,993	5,311
Indonesia	741,035	1,919,270	143,732
Iowa (U.S.)	56,290	145,790	2,870
Iran	636,296	1,648,000	35,687
Iraq	167,925	434,924	12,258
Ireland	27,136	70,283	3,224
Isle of Man (U.K.)	227	588	67
Israel	7,992	20,700	3,742
Italy	116,314	301,253	57,154
Ivory Coast	124,504	322,463	5,260
Jamaica (Comm.)	4,244	10,991	2,137
Japan	145,711	377,389	115,486
Jordan	37,738	97,740	3,036
Kansas (U.S.)	82,264	213,063	2,267
Kentucky (U.S.)	40,395	104,623	3,396
Kenya (Comm.)	224,961	582,646	14,874
Korea, North	46,540	120,538	17,175
Korea, South	38,025	98,484	35,793
Kuwait	7,768	20,118	1,155
Laos	91,429	236,800	3,581
Lebanon	4,015	10,400	3,321
Lesotho (Comm.)	11,720	30,355	1,108
Liberia	43,000	111,369	1,831
Libya	679,362	1,759,540	2,766
Liechtenstein	61	157	23
Louisiana (U.S.)	48,523	125,674	3,791
Luxembourg	998	2,586	372
Macao (Port.)	6	16	286
Madagascar	226,658	587,041	7,971
Madeira Is. (Port.)	308	797	245
Maine (U.S.)	33,215	86,026	1,059
Malawi (Comm.)	45,747	118,484	5,409
Malaysia (Comm.)	127,316	329,749	12,830
Maldives	115	298	127
Mali	478,767	1,240,000	6,138
Malta (Comm.)	122	316	320
Manitoba (Can.)	251,000	650,087	1,022
Martinique (Fr.)	425	1,102	381
Maryland (U.S.)	10,577	27,394	4,098
Massachusetts (U.S.)	8,257	21,385	5,828
Mauritania	397,956	1,030,700	1,435
Mauritius (Comm.)	790	2,045	899
Mexico	761,605	1,972,547	66,692
Michigan (U.S.)	58,216	150,779	9,157
Midway Is. (U.S.)	2	5	5
Minnesota (U.S.)	84,068	217,735	3,926
Mississippi (U.S.)	47,716	123,584	2,346
Missouri (U.S.)	69,686	180,486	4,763
Monaco	0.58	1.49	25
Mongolia	604,250	1,565,000	1,579
Montana (U.S.)	147,138	381,086	748
Montserrat (U.K.)	38	98	12
Morocco	172,414	446,550	19,290
Mozambique	302,330	783,030	9,889
Namibia (S. Afr.)	318,261	824,292	1,027
Nauru (Comm.)	8	21	7
Nebraska (U.S.)	77,227	200,017	1,546
Nepal	54,362	140,797	13,545
Netherlands	15,892	41,160	14,091
Neth. Antilles (Neth.)	383	993	256
Nevada (U.S.)	110,540	286,297	592
New Brunswick (Can.)	28,354	73,437	677
New Caledonia (incl. Deps.) (Fr.)	7,335	18,998	141
Newfoundland (Can.)	156,185	404,517	558
New Hampshire (U.S.)	9,304	24,097	818
New Hebrides (Fr.-U.K.)	5,700	14,763	104
New Jersey (U.S.)	7,836	20,295	7,316
New Mexico (U.S.)	121,666	315,113	1,147
New York (U.S.)	49,576	128,401	18,120
New Zealand (Comm.)	103,747	268,704	3,264
Nicaragua	50,193	130,000	2,373
Niger	489,191	1,267,000	4,979
Nigeria (Comm.)	356,669	923,768	68,160
Niue (N.Z.)	100	259	4
Norfolk I. (Austl.)	14	36	1
North America	9,417,000	24,390,000	358,000
North Carolina (U.S.)	52,586	136,197	5,451
North Dakota (U.S.)	70,665	183,021	635
Northern Ireland (U.K.)	5,452	14,120	1,566
Northwest Ters. (Can.)	1,304,903	3,379,683	43
Norway	125,182	324,219	4,100
Nova Scotia (Can.)	21,425	55,490	829
Ohio (U.S.)	41,222	106,764	10,759
Oklahoma (U.S.)	69,919	181,089	2,712
Oman	82,030	212,457	840
Ontario (Can.)	412,582	1,068,582	8,264
Oregon (U.S.)	96,981	251,180	2,288
Pac. Is. Tr. Ter. (U.S.)	717	1,857	115
Pakistan (incl. part of Kashmir) (Comm.)	310,404	803,943	77,674
Panama	29,209	75,650	1,857
Papua New Guinea (Comm.)	178,260	461,691	2,826
Paraguay	157,048	406,752	2,714
Pennsylvania (U.S.)	45,333	117,412	11,827
Peru	496,225	1,285,216	17,449
Philippines	115,831	300,000	46,660
Poland	120,725	312,677	34,920
Portugal	35,553	92,082	8,805
Prince Edward I. (Can.)	2,184	5,657	118
Puerto Rico (U.S.)	3,435	8,897	3,385
Qatar	4,247	11,000	101
Quebec (Can.)	594,860	1,540,680	6,234
Reunion (Fr.)	969	2,510	539
Rhode Island (U.S.)	1,214	3,144	927
Rhodesia	150,804	390,580	7,000
Romania	91,699	237,500	21,796
Rwanda	10,169	26,338	4,622
St. Helena (incl. Deps.) (U.K.)	162	419	6
St. Kitts-Nevis-Anguilla (U.K.)	138	357	66
St. Lucia (U.K.)	238	616	114
St. Pierre & Miquelon (Fr.)	93	242	5
St. Vincent (U.K.)	150	388	121
San Marino	24	61	19
Sao Tome & Principe	372	964	85
Saskatchewan (Can.)	251,700	651,900	921
Saudi Arabia	831,313	2,153,090	9,799
Scotland (U.K.)	30,415	78,774	5,190
Senegal	75,750	196,192	4,744
Seychelles (Comm.)	145	376	65
Sierra Leone (Comm.)	27,699	71,740	2,873
Singapore (Comm.)	224	581	2,374
Solomon Is. (Comm.)	10,983	28,446	203
Somalia	246,201	637,657	3,424
South Africa	471,445	1,221,037	27,615
South America	6,884,000	17,829,000	233,000
South Carolina (U.S.)	31,055	80,432	2,818
South Dakota (U.S.)	77,047	199,551	683
Soviet Union	8,649,500	22,402,000	261,565
Spain	194,885	504,750	36,818
Sri Lanka (Comm.)	25,332	65,610	14,982
Sudan	967,500	2,505,813	19,122
Surinam	63,037	163,265	455
Svalbard (Nor.)	23,958	62,050	....
Swaziland (Comm.)	6,704	17,363	540
Sweden	173,732	449,964	8,292
Switzerland	15,941	41,288	6,798
Syria	71,498	185,180	8,109
Taiwan (Natl. China)	13,885	35,961	17,009
Tanzania (Comm.)	364,900	945,087	16,408
Tennessee (U.S.)	42,244	109,411	4,188
Texas (U.S.)	267,338	692,402	12,237
Thailand	198,457	514,000	46,532
Togo	21,622	56,000	2,406
Tokelau Is. (N.Z.)	4	10	2
Tonga (Comm.)	270	699	110
Trinidad & Tobago (Comm.)	1,980	5,128	1,113
Tunisia	63,170	163,610	6,202
Turkey	301,382	780,576	43,009
Turks & Caicos Is. (U.K.)	166	430	7
Tuvalu	10	26	6
Uganda (Comm.)	91,134	236,036	12,721
United Arab Emirates	32,278	83,600	243
United Kingdom	94,223	244,035	56,555
United States	3,615,122	9,363,123	219,103
Upper Volta	105,869	274,200	6,459
Uruguay	68,536	177,508	3,176
Utah (U.S.)	84,916	219,931	1,206
Vatican City	0.17	0.44	1
Venezuela	352,145	912,050	13,143
Vermont (U.S.)	9,609	24,887	471
Vietnam	128,402	332,559	47,588
Virginia (U.S.)	40,817	105,716	4,967
Virgin Is. (U.S.-U.K.)	192	497	132
Wales (incl. Monmouthshire) (U.K.)	8,018	20,766	2,803
Washington (U.S.)	68,192	176,616	3,544
Western Sahara	102,703	266,000	152
Western Samoa (Comm.)	1,097	2,842	168
West Virginia (U.S.)	24,181	62,628	1,803
Wisconsin (U.S.)	56,154	145,438	4,607
World	57,605,000	149,196,000	4,178,000
Wyoming (U.S.)	97,914	253,596	374
Yemen	75,290	195,000	7,262
Yemen, People's Dem. Rep. of	128,560	332,968	1,733
Yugoslavia	98,766	255,804	21,925
Yukon (Can.)	207,076	536,324	22
Zaire	905,568	2,345,409	27,051
Zambia (Comm.)	290,586	752,614	5,410

* Populations are given in thousands.
Population and area figures are from the 1978 edition of *The World Book Encyclopedia*. They are based on censuses and estimates from official government and United Nations sources.
Membership of the Commonwealth of Nations is indicated by the abbreviation (Comm.).

Accra, Ghana (★738,498)..........564,194
Addis Ababa, Ethiopia..........1,161,267
Adelaide, Australia..........809,466
Āgra, India (★634,622)..........591,917
Ahmadābād, India (★1,741,522)..1,585,544
Albany, New York (★777,977).....115,781
Aleppo (Halab), Syria..........639,428
Alexandria (Al Iskandarīyah), Egypt..........2,259,000
Algiers (Alger), Algeria..........1,503,720
Al Jīzah (Giza), Egypt..........933,900
Alma-Ata, Soviet Union..........753,000
'Ammān, Jordan..........500,000
Amsterdam, Netherlands (★990,790)..........757,958
Ankara (Angora), Turkey (★1,553,897)..........1,522,350
Anshan, China..........1,500,000
Antwerp (Antwerpen), Belgium (★657,485)..........243,426
Asunción, Paraguay..........392,753
Athens (Athínai), Greece (★2,540,241)..........867,023
Atlanta, Georgia (★1,595,517).....497,421
Auckland, New Zealand (★649,746).151,580

Baghdad, Iraq..........2,183,760
Baku, Soviet Union (★1,292,000)...870,000
Baltimore, Maryland (★2,071,016)..905,787
Bandung, Indonesia..........1,282,121
Bangalore, India (★1,653,779)....1,540,741
Bangkok (Krung Thep), Thailand..........1,867,297
Barcelona, Spain..........1,745,142
Barquisimeto, Venezuela..........459,000
Barranquilla, Colombia..........664,533
Beirut, Lebanon (★938,940).......474,870
Belém, Brazil (★656,351)..........572,654
Belfast, No. Ireland..........360,150
Belgrade (Beograd), Yugoslavia...746,105
Belo Horizonte, Brazil (★1,613,305)..........1,126,368
Berlin, East, Ger. Dem. Rep. (★Berlin)..........1,086,374
Berlin, West, Fed. Rep. of Ger...2,122,346
Bern, Switzerland (★288,100).......152,800
Birmingham, Alabama (★767,230)..300,910
Birmingham, England (★2,275,300)..........1,006,760
Bogotá, Colombia (★3,143,200)...2,850,000
Bologna, Italy..........493,639
Bombay, India..........5,970,575
Bonn, Fed. Rep. of Ger..........299,400
Boston, Massachusetts (★2,899,101)..........641,071
Brasília, Brazil..........277,005
Bremen, Fed. Rep. of Ger..........607,200
Brisbane, Australia..........816,987
Bristol, England..........421,580
Brussels (Bruxelles), Belgium (★1,050,787)..........153,405
Bucharest (București), Romania (★1,574,536)..........1,488,328
Budapest, Hungary..........2,038,787
Buenos Aires, Argentina (★8,925,000)..........2,976,000
Buffalo, New York (★1,349,211)...462,768

Cairo (Al Qāhirah), Egypt.......5,715,000
Calcutta, India (★7,031,382).....3,148,746
Calgary, Canada..........469,917
Cali, Colombia (★1,133,500).......898,253
Canberra, Australia..........156,334
Canton (Kuangchou), China.....2,300,000
Cape Town, South Africa (★1,096,597)..........691,296
Caracas, Venezuela (★2,755,000)..1,309,000
Cardiff, Wales..........274,960
Casablanca, Morocco..........1,506,373
Ch'angch'un (Hsinking), China..1,500,000
Ch'angsha, China..........850,000
Chelyabinsk, Soviet Union..........891,000
Chengchou, China..........1,500,000
Ch'engtu, China..........2,000,000
Chicago, Illinois (★7,084,700)....3,369,357
Ch'ich'ihaerh (Tsitsihar), China..1,500,000
Chittagong, Bangladesh..........889,760
Chungking (Ch'ungch'ing), China.3,500,000
Cincinnati, Ohio (★1,385,103)......451,455
Cleveland, Ohio (★2,063,729).......750,879
Cologne (Köln), Fed. Rep. of Ger..866,300
Colombo, Sri Lanka..........562,160
Columbus, Ohio (★1,017,847)......540,025
Copenhagen (København), Denmark (★1,384,411)..........625,678
Córdoba, Argentina..........798,663
Curitiba, Brazil (★767,879)........497,626

Dacca, Bangladesh..........1,679,572
Dakar, Senegal..........580,000
Dallas, Texas (★2,378,353)..........844,401
Damascus (Dimashq), Syria......836,668
Davao, Philippines (★591,500).......515,520
Dayton, Ohio (★852,531)..........242,917
Delhi, India (★3,647,023)........3,287,883
Denver, Colorado (★1,239,477).....514,678
Detroit, Michigan (★4,435,051)...1,513,601
Dnepropetrovsk, Soviet Union.....882,000
Donetsk (Stalino), Soviet Union....891,000
Dortmund, Fed. Rep. of Ger......648,900
Dresden, Ger. Dem. Rep..........501,508

Dublin (Baile Atha Cliath), Ireland (★679,748)..........567,866
Durban, South Africa (★843,327)...495,458
Düsseldorf, Fed. Rep. of Ger......680,800

Edinburgh, Scotland..........472,000
El Paso, Texas (★359,291)..........322,261
Eșfahān, Iran..........618,000
Essen, Fed. Rep. of Ger..........704,800

Florence (Firenze), Italy..........460,248
Fortaleza, Brazil (★973,452).......529,933
Frankfurt am Main, Fed. Rep. of Ger..........660,400
Fuchou (Foochow), China..........900,000
Fukuoka, Japan..........853,270
Fushun, China..........1,700,000

Geneva (Genève), Switzerland (★323,000)..........159,200
Genoa (Genova), Italy..........815,708
Glasgow, Scotland (★1,698,231)....984,000
Gorki (Gorkiy), Soviet Union....1,189,000
Guadalajara, Mexico (★1,455,825)..........1,193,601
Guatemala, Guatemala..........700,504
Guayaquil, Ecuador..........814,064

Haerhpin (Harbin), China.......2,750,000
Hamburg, Fed. Rep. of Ger.....1,817,100
Hangchou, China..........1,100,000
Hannover (Hanover), Fed. Rep. of Ger..........517,800
Hanoi, Vietnam (★643,576)........414,620
Hartford, Connecticut (★720,581)..........148,576
Havana (La Habana), Cuba.....1,900,240
Helsinki, Finland (★817,370)......513,254
Hiroshima, Japan..........541,998
Ho Chi Minh City (Saigon), Vietnam..........1,761,335
Hong Kong, Hong Kong........4,563,000
Honolulu, Hawaii (★630,528)......324,871
Houston, Texas (★1,999,316)......1,232,802
Hsian (Sian), China..........1,900,000
Hsüchou (Süchow), China.......1,500,000
Hyderābād, India (★1,796,339)...1,607,396

Ibadan, Nigeria..........885,300
Inch'ŏn, Korea (South)..........646,013
Indianapolis, Indiana (★1,111,352)..746,302
Indore, India..........543,381
Irkutsk, Soviet Union..........462,000
Istanbul, Turkey (★3,135,354)....2,487,100
İzmir, Turkey (★819,276)..........619,150

Jacksonville, Florida (★621,827)....528,865
Jakarta (Batavia), Indonesia....5,490,000
Jerusalem, Israel..........326,400
Johannesburg, South Africa (★1,432,643)..........654,682

Kābul, Afghanistan..........597,000
Kānpur, India (★1,275,242)......1,154,388
Kansas City, Missouri (★1,273,926)..........507,330
Kaohsiung, Taiwan..........828,191
Karāchi, Pakistan..........3,515,402
Kātmāndu, Nepal..........332,982
Katowice, Poland..........305,600
Kawasaki, Japan..........973,486
Kazan', Soviet Union..........885,000
Khar'kov, Soviet Union..........1,248,000
Khartoum, Sudan..........852,000
Kiev, Soviet Union..........1,693,000
Kingston, Jamaica (★506,200).......117,900
Kinshasa, Zaire..........2,202,333
Kitakyūshū, Japan..........1,042,321
Kōbe, Japan..........1,288,937
Kowloon, Hong Kong..........716,272
Kraków, Poland..........589,900
Kuala Lumpur, Malaysia..........451,728
K'unming, China..........1,700,000
Kuybyshev, Soviet Union..........1,069,000
Kyōto, Japan..........1,419,165

Lagos, Nigeria..........1,149,200
Lahore, Pakistan..........2,169,742
Lanchou (Lanchow), China......1,500,000
La Paz, Bolivia..........660,700
La Plata, Argentina..........506,287
Leeds, England (★1,735,350).......498,790
Leipzig, Ger. Dem. Rep..........584,365
Leningrad, Soviet Union (★4,243,000)..........3,512,974
Lille, France (★935,882)..........172,280
Lima, Peru (★3,254,789)..........2,941,473
Lisbon (Lisboa), Portugal (★1,635,400)..........757,700
Liverpool, England (★1,245,520)...588,600
Łódź, Poland..........764,100
London, England..........7,281,080

Los Angeles, California (★6,999,600)..........2,809,813
Louisville, Kentucky (★867,330)...361,706
Luanda, Angola..........600,000
Lucknow, India (★813,982)........749,239
Lüta (Dairen), China..........4,000,000
Luxembourg, Luxembourg..........76,143
L'vov, Soviet Union..........564,000
Lyallpur, Pakistan..........823,343
Lyon, France (★1,170,660)..........456,716

Madras, India (★3,169,930)......2,469,449
Madrid, Spain..........3,520,320
Managua, Nicaragua..........364,337
Manchester, England (★2,389,220).531,270
Mandalay, Burma..........417,266
Manila, Philippines (★4,904,262)..1,455,272
Mannheim, Fed. Rep. of Ger......330,900
Maracaibo, Venezuela..........845,000
Marseille, France (★1,070,912)......908,600
Mecca (Makkah), Saudi Arabia....250,000
Medan, Indonesia..........700,363
Medellín, Colombia..........1,064,741
Melbourne, Australia..........2,388,941
Memphis, Tennessee (★834,103)....623,530
Mexico City, Mexico (★11,339,774)..........8,591,750
Miami, Florida (★1,267,792)........334,859
Milan (Milano), Italy..........1,738,487
Milwaukee, Wisconsin (★1,403,884)..........669,022
Minneapolis, Minnesota (★1,965,391)..........434,400
Minsk, Soviet Union (★955,000)..........907,000
Mogadisho (Mogadiscio), Somalia..444,882
Monterrey, Mexico (★1,213,497)...858,107
Montevideo, Uruguay..........1,229,750
Montreal, Canada (★2,758,780)...1,060,033
Moscow (Moskva), Soviet Union (★7,528,000)..........6,941,961
Mukden (Shenyang), China.....3,750,000
Multān, Pakistan..........538,949
Munich (München), Fed. Rep. of Ger..........1,326,300

Nagoya, Japan..........2,080,000
Nāgpur, India (★930,459)..........866,076
Nairobi, Kenya..........535,200
Nanking (Nanching), China.....2,000,000
Naples (Napoli), Italy..........1,223,659
Newark, New Jersey (★2,057,468)..381,930
Newcastle-on-Tyne, England (★797,750)..........217,220
New Delhi, India..........301,801
New Orleans, Louisiana (★1,046,470)..........593,471
New York, New York (★9,943,800)..........7,895,563
Norfolk, Virginia (★732,600).......307,951
Novosibirsk, Soviet Union.......1,243,000
Nürnberg (Nuremberg), Fed. Rep. of Ger..........477,10)

Odessa, Soviet Union..........913,000
Oklahoma City, Oklahoma (★699,092)..........368,377
Omaha, Nebraska (★542,646)......346,929
Omsk, Soviet Union..........850,000
Osaka, Japan..........2,780,000
Oslo, Norway (★556,377)..........477,476
Ottawa, Canada (★693,288).......304,462

Palembang, Indonesia..........642,416
Palermo, Italy..........650,113
Panamá, Panama..........418,013
Paris, France (★8,549,898).......2,299,830
Peking (Peiching), China........7,570,000
Perm', Soviet Union..........863,000
Perth, Australia..........639,622
Philadelphia, Pennsylvania (★4,824,110)..........1,949,996
Phnom Penh, Cambodia..........200,000
Phoenix, Arizona (★969,425).......581,562
Pittsburgh, Pennsylvania (★2,401,362)..........520,117
Port-au-Prince, Haiti (★525,380)...386,250
Portland, Oregon (★1,007,130).....379,967
Pôrto (Oporto), Portugal (★1,341,000)..........304,000
Pôrto Alegre, Brazil (★1,531,168)...887,338
Poznań, Poland..........473,300
Prague (Praha), Czechoslovakia..1,078,096
Pretoria, South Africa (★561,703)..543,950
Providence, Rhode Island (★908,887)..........179,116
Pune, India (★1,135,034)..........856,105
Pusan, Korea (South)..........1,880,710
P'yŏngyang, Korea (North).....2,500,000

Québec, Canada (★542,158).......177,082
Quezon City, Philippines..........960,341
Quito, Ecuador..........597,133

Rabat, Morocco..........367,620
Rangoon, Burma..........1,351,911
Rawalpindi, Pakistan..........614,809

Recife (Pernambuco), Brazil (★1,699,079)..........1,070,078
Rīga, Soviet Union..........743,000
Rio de Janeiro, Brazil (★7,094,211)..........4,315,746
Riyadh, Saudi Arabia..........300,000
Rochester, New York (★961,516)...296,233
Rome (Roma), Italy..........2,868,248
Rosario, Argentina..........810,840
Rostov-na-Donu, Soviet Union....808,000
Rotterdam, Netherlands (★1,032,152)..........620,867

Sacramento, California (★803,793)..257,105
St. Louis, Missouri (★2,410,492)....622,236
St. Paul, Minnesota (★1,965,391)..........309,714
Salisbury, Rhodesia..........557,000
Salt Lake City, Utah (★705,458)...175,885
Salvador, Brazil (★1,095,274).....1,017,591
San Antonio, Texas (★888,179)....654,153
San Bernardino, California (★1,141,307)..........102,303
San Diego, California (★1,357,854).697,027
San Francisco, California (★3,108,782)..........715,674
San José, Costa Rica (★438,658)...215,441
San Juan, Puerto Rico (★936,693)..........452,749
San Salvador, El Salvador........378,531
Santiago, Chile..........3,168,500
Santo Domingo, Dominican Rep...673,470
São Paulo, Brazil (★8,062,130)...5,241,232
Sapporo, Japan..........1,010,123
Saratov, Soviet Union..........773,000
Seattle, Washington (★1,424,605)...530,831
Semarang, Indonesia..........689,832
Sendai, Japan..........545,065
Seoul, Korea (South)..........6,889,470
Sevilla, Spain..........548,072
Shanghai, China..........10,820,000
Sheffield, England..........513,310
Singapore, Singapore..........2,074,507
Sofia (Sofiya), Bulgaria (★1,064,712)..........965,729
Soochow (Wuhsien), China......1,300,000
Stockholm, Sweden (★1,352,359)...723,688
Stuttgart, Fed. Rep. of Ger......628,400
Surabaya, Indonesia..........1,660,355
Sverdlovsk, Soviet Union........1,048,000
Sydney, Australia..........2,717,069

Tabrīz, Iran..........571,000
Taegu, Korea (South)..........1,082,750
T'aipei, Taiwan..........1,839,640
T'aiyüan (Yangkū), China......2,725,000
Tangshan, China..........1,200,000
Tashkent, Soviet Union..........1,424,000
Tbilisi, Soviet Union..........907,000
Tegucigalpa, Honduras..........267,754
Tehrān, Iran..........4,716,000
Tel Aviv-Yafo, Israel..........367,600
The Hague ('s Gravenhage), Netherlands (★678,905)..........482,879
Tientsin (T'ienching), China.....4,280,000
Tiranë, Albania..........175,000
Tōkyō, Japan (★11,622,651).....8,640,000
Toronto, Canada (★2,081,521).....633,318
Tripoli (Tarābulus), Libya.......551,477
Tsinan (Chinan), China.........1,500,000
Tsingtao (Ch'ingtao), China.....1,900,000
Tunis, Tunisia (★647,640)..........468,997
Turin (Torino), Italy..........1,172,476

Ufa, Soviet Union..........796,000
Ulaan Baatar, Mongolia..........267,400

Valencia, Spain..........653,690
Valencia, Venezuela..........471,000
Vancouver, Canada (★1,166,348)...410,188
Vārānāsi (Benares), India (★606,271)..........583,856
Venice (Venezia), Italy..........363,540
Viangchan (Vientiane), Laos......130,000
Victoria, Hong Kong..........520,932
Vienna (Wien), Austria..........1,614,841
Vladivostok, Soviet Union........456,000
Volgograd (Stalingrad), Soviet Union..........834,000

Warsaw (Warszawa), Poland....1,317,000
Washington, D.C. (★2,925,521)....756,668
Wellington, New Zealand (★184,669)..........135,677
Winnipeg, Canada (★578,217).....560,874
Wrocław (Breslau), Poland..........527,600
Wuhan, China..........4,250,000
Wuppertal, Fed. Rep. of Ger......414,700

Yerevan, Soviet Union..........791,000
Yokohama, Japan..........2,620,000

Zagreb, Yugoslavia..........566,224
Zaragoza (Saragossa), Spain.......479,845
Zürich, Switzerland (★720,800).....396,300

★ Population of metropolitan area, including suburbs.
Population figures are from the 1978 edition of *The World Book Encyclopedia.* They are based on censuses and estimates from official government and United Nations sources.

This index includes the more important cities, towns and other localities that appear on the maps on pages 52–69. For a complete list of abbreviations, see page 246. If a page contains several maps, a lowercase letter identifies the particular map to which the entry is indexed.

Page	Name Region	Lat. ° ′	Long. ° ′
58d	Berazategui	34·45 S	58·12 W
61	Berchum	51·23 N	7·32 E
54a	Berea	41·22 N	81·52 W
53	Bergenfield	40·55 N	74·00 W
63a	Bergfelde	52·40 N	13·19 E
61	Berghausen	51·18 N	7·17 E
55a	Bergholtz	43·06 N	78·53 W
61	Bergisch-Born	51·09 N	7·15 E
61	Bergkamen	51·38 N	7·38 E
56b	Berkeley, Ca.	37·57 N	122·18 W
56a	Berkeley, Il.	41·53 N	87·55 W
55b	Berkeley Hills	40·32 N	80·00 W
60	Berkhamsted	51·46 N	0·35 W
55c	Berkley	42·31 N	83·10 W
63a	Berlin (East)	52·30 N	13·25 E
63a	Berlin (West)	52·30 N	13·20 E
63a	Bernau bei Berlin	52·40 N	13·35 E
61	Bertlich	51·37 N	7·04 E
56a	Berwyn	41·50 N	87·47 W
54d	Berwyn Heights	38·59 N	76·54 W
64b	Besedy	55·37 N	37·47 E
64f	Beşiktaş (Neigh.)	41·03 N	29·01 E
64b	Beskudnikovo (Neigh.)	55·52 N	37·34 E
63e	Besós (R.)	41·25 N	2·04 E
55b	Bethel Park	40·18 N	80·02 W
54d	Bethesda	38·59 N	77·06 W
60	Bethnal Green (Neigh.)	51·32 N	0·03 W
53	Bethpage	40·45 N	73·29 W
60	Betsham	51·25 N	0·19 E
52a	Beverly	42·33 N	70·53 W
68a	Beverly Hills, Austl.	33·57 S	151·05 E
57	Beverly Hills, Ca.	34·03 N	118·26 W
55c	Beverly Hills, Mi.	42·32 N	83·15 W
68a	Bexley	33·57 S	151·08 E
60	Bexley (Neigh.)	51·26 N	0·10 E
61	Beyenburg (Neigh.)	51·15 N	7·18 E
64f	Beylerbeyi (Neigh.)	41·03 N	29·03 E
64f	Beyoğlu (Neigh.)	41·02 N	28·59 E
62c	Bezons	48·56 N	2·13 E
65a	Bhadreswar	22·50 N	88·21 E
65d	Bhalswa (Neigh.)	28·44 N	77·10 E
65a	Bhātpāra	22·52 N	88·24 E
65d	Bhopura	28·42 N	77·20 E
62b	Bickerstaffe	53·32 N	2·50 W
60	Bickley (Neigh.)	51·24 N	0·03 E
62b	Bidston	53·24 N	3·05 W
63a	Biesdorf (Neigh.)	52·31 N	13·33 E
62c	Bièvres	48·45 N	2·13 E
54a	Big Cr.	41·27 N	81·41 W
60	Biggin Hill (Neigh.)	51·18 N	0·04 E
60	Billericay	51·38 N	0·25 E
54b	Billingsport	39·51 N	75·14 W
55c	Bingham Farms	42·32 N	83·16 W
66m	Binh-dong	10·43 N	106·39 E
61	Binsheim	51·31 N	6·42 E
62b	Birch	53·34 N	2·13 W
62b	Birkenhead	53·24 N	3·02 W
63a	Birkholz	52·38 N	13·34 E
60	Birling	51·19 N	0·25 E
55c	Birmingham	42·33 N	83·15 W
61	Bissingheim (Neigh.)	51·24 N	6·49 E
61	Bittermark (Neigh.)	51·27 N	7·28 E
68b	Blackburn	37·49 S	145·09 E
52c	Black Creek Pioneer Village (P. Int.)	43·47 N	79·32 W
62b	Blackley (Neigh.)	53·31 N	2·13 W
60	Blackmore	51·41 N	0·19 E
68b	Black Rock	37·59 S	145·01 E
68b	Black Springs	37·46 S	145·19 E
68a	Blacktown	33·46 S	150·55 E
54d	Bladensburg	38·56 N	76·55 W
55b	Blaine Hill	40·16 N	79·53 W
65c	Blakang Mati (I.)	1·15 N	103·50 E
68a	Blakehurst	33·59 S	151·07 E
63a	Blankenburg (Neigh.)	52·35 N	13·28 E
63a	Blankenfelde (Neigh.)	52·37 N	13·23 E
61	Blankenstein	51·24 N	7·14 E
55b	Blawnox	40·29 N	79·52 W
61	Bliedinghausen (Neigh.)	51·09 N	7·12 E
61	Bliersheim	51·23 N	6·43 E
61	Blombacher Bach (Neigh.)	51·15 N	7·14 E
53	Bloomfield	40·48 N	74·12 W
55c	Bloomfield Village	42·33 N	83·15 W
56a	Blue Island	41·40 N	87·41 W
69a	Blue Mosque (P. Int.)	30·02 N	31·15 E
60	Bobbingworth	51·44 N	0·13 E
62c	Bobigny	48·54 N	2·27 E
58d	Boca (Neigh.)	34·38 S	58·21 W
58c	Bocanegra	12·01 S	77·07 W
61	Bochum	51·28 N	7·13 E
61	Böckel (Neigh.)	51·13 N	7·12 E
61	Bockum	51·20 N	6·44 E
61	Bockum (Neigh.)	51·21 N	6·38 E
61	Bodelschwingh (Neigh.)	51·33 N	7·22 E
64b	Bogorodskoje (Neigh.)	55·49 N	37·44 E
53	Bogota	40·53 N	74·02 W
63a	Böhnsdorf (Neigh.)	52·24 N	13·33 E
62c	Bois-Colombes	48·55 N	2·16 E
62c	Boissy-Saint-Léger	48·45 N	2·31 E
69b	Boksburg	26·12 S	28·14 E
69b	Boksburg North	26·12 S	28·15 E
69b	Boksburg South	26·14 S	28·15 E
69b	Boksburg West	26·13 S	28·14 E
61	Bölkenbusch	51·21 N	7·06 E
63c	Bollate	45·33 N	9·07 E
63a	Bollensdorf	52·31 N	13·43 E
62b	Bollington	53·22 N	2·25 W
61	Bollwerk	51·10 N	7·35 E
64a	Bol'šaja Ochta (Neigh.)	59·57 N	30·25 E
64b	Bol'šoj Teatr (P. Int.)	55·46 N	37·37 E
62b	Bolton	53·35 N	2·26 W
65e	Bombay	18·58 N	72·50 E
61	Bommerholz	51·23 N	7·18 E
61	Bommern (Neigh.)	51·25 N	7·20 E
59d	Bom Retiro (Neigh.)	23·32 S	46·38 W
54b	Bon Air	39·58 N	75·19 W
68a	Bondi	33·53 S	151·17 E
62c	Bondy	48·54 N	2·28 E
62c	Bonneuil-sur-Marne	48·46 N	2·29 E
68a	Bonnyrigg	33·54 S	150·54 E
59c	Bonsucesso (Neigh.)	22·52 S	43·15 W
62b	Boothstown	53·30 N	2·25 W
62b	Bootle	53·28 N	3·00 W
69b	Booysens (Neigh.)	26·14 S	28·01 E
61	Borbeck (Neigh.)	51·29 N	6·57 E
69b	Bordeaux	26·06 S	28·01 E
52b	Bordeaux (Neigh.)	45·33 N	73·41 W
60	Borehamwood	51·40 N	0·16 W
65e	Borle (Neigh.)	19·02 N	72·55 E
63a	Bornim (Neigh.)	52·26 N	13·00 E
63a	Bornstedt (Neigh.)	52·25 N	13·02 E
64f	Anadoluhisarı (P. Int.)	41·04 N	29·03 E
60	Borough Green	51·17 N	0·19 E
53	Borough Park (Neigh.)	40·38 N	74·00 W
61	Borth	51·36 N	6·33 E
68a	Bossley Park	33·52 S	150·54 E
64f	Bostancı (Neigh.)	40·57 N	29·05 E
52a	Boston, Ma.	42·21 N	71·04 W
55b	Boston, Pa.	40·18 N	79·49 W
52a	Boston B.	42·22 N	70·54 W
52a	Boston Garden (P. Int.)	42·22 N	71·04 W
52a	Boston Har.	42·20 N	70·58 W
59c	Botafogo (Neigh.)	22·57 S	43·11 W
59c	Botafogo, Enseada de (B.)	22·57 S	43·10 W
68a	Botany	33·57 S	151·12 E
60	Botany Bay (Neigh.)	51·41 N	0·07 W
68a	Botany B.	33·59 S	151·12 E
61	Bottrop	51·31 N	6·55 E
63a	Bötzow	52·39 N	13·08 E
52b	Boucherville	45·36 N	73·27 W
52b	Boucherville, Îles de (Is.)	45·37 N	73·28 W
69c	Boukiéro	4·12 S	15·18 E
58d	Boulogne (Neigh.)	34·31 S	58·34 W
62c	Boulogne-Billancourt	48·50 N	2·15 E
62c	Bourg-la-Reine	48·47 N	2·19 E
60	Bournebridge	51·38 N	0·11 E
60	Bourne End	51·45 N	0·32 W
61	Böwinghausen (Neigh.)	51·31 N	7·19 E
62b	Bowdon	53·23 N	2·22 W
68b	Box Hill	37·49 S	145·08 E
60	Boxmoor	51·45 N	0·29 W
64f	Boyacıköy (Neigh.)	41·06 N	29·02 E
55b	Braddock	40·25 N	79·50 W
55b	Braddock Hills	40·25 N	79·51 W
62b	Bradshaw	53·36 N	2·24 W
52a	Braintree	42·13 N	71·00 W
69b	Brakpan	26·14 S	28·22 E
62b	Bramhall	53·22 N	2·10 W
63a	Brandenburger Tor (P. Int.)	52·31 N	13·23 E
64b	Bratcevo (Neigh.)	55·51 N	37·24 E
54a	Bratenahl	41·35 N	81·33 W
68b	Braybrook	37·47 S	144·51 E
69c	Brazzaville	4·16 S	15·17 E
57	Brea	33·55 N	117·54 W
61	Brechten (Neigh.)	51·35 N	7·28 E
61	Breckerfeld	51·16 N	7·28 E
62b	Bredbury	53·25 N	2·06 W
69b	Bredell	26·05 S	28·17 E
61	Bredeney (Neigh.)	51·24 N	6·59 E
61	Bredenscheid-Stüter	51·22 N	7·11 E
55b	Breezewood	40·34 N	80·03 W
61	Breitscheid	51·22 N	6·52 E
58c	Breña	12·04 S	77·04 W
54d	Bren Mar Park	38·48 N	77·09 W
60	Brentford (Neigh.)	51·29 N	0·18 W
69b	Brenthurst	26·16 S	28·23 E
60	Brentwood, Eng.	51·38 N	0·18 E
54d	Brentwood, Md.	38·56 N	76·57 W
55b	Brentwood, Pa.	40·22 N	79·59 W
57	Brentwood Heights (Neigh.)	34·04 N	118·30 W
69b	Brentwood Park	26·08 S	28·18 E
63c	Bresso	45·32 N	9·11 E
54b	Bridesburg (Neigh.)	40·00 N	75·04 W
54b	Bridgeport	40·06 N	75·21 W
56a	Bridgeport (Neigh.)	41·51 N	87·39 W
56a	Bridgeview	41·45 N	87·48 W
62c	Brie-Comte-Robert	48·41 N	2·37 E
55c	Brightmoor (Neigh.)	42·24 N	83·14 W
68b	Brighton	37·55 S	145·00 E
52a	Brighton (Neigh.)	42·21 N	71·08 W
68a	Brighton le Sands	33·58 S	151·09 E
54d	Brightwood (Neigh.)	38·58 N	77·02 W
64e	Brigittenau (Neigh.)	48·14 N	16·22 E
54d	Brilyn Park	38·54 N	77·10 W
60	Brindley Heath	51·12 N	0·03 W
54c	Brinkleigh	39·18 N	76·50 W
56b	Brisbane	37·41 N	122·24 W
62b	Broadheath	53·24 N	2·21 W
60	Broadley Common	51·45 N	0·04 E
68b	Broadmeadows	37·40 S	144·54 E
56b	Broadmoor	37·41 N	122·29 W
61	Brockenscheidt	51·38 N	7·25 E
52a	Brockton	42·05 N	71·01 W
61	Broich (Neigh.)	51·25 N	6·51 E
62b	Bromborough	53·19 N	2·59 W
60	Bromley (Neigh.)	51·24 N	0·02 E
60	Bromley Common (Neigh.)	51·22 N	0·03 E
53	Bronx (Neigh.)	40·49 N	73·56 W
53	Bronxville	40·56 N	73·50 W
56a	Brookfield	41·49 N	87·51 W
54b	Brookhaven	39·52 N	75·23 W
54d	Brookland (Neigh.)	38·56 N	76·59 W
54c	Brooklandville	39·26 N	76·41 W
54b	Brooklawn	39·53 N	75·08 W
52a	Brookline	42·21 N	71·07 W
54a	Brooklyn	41·25 N	81·49 W
54c	Brooklyn (Neigh.)	39·14 N	76·36 W
54a	Brooklyn Heights	41·24 N	81·40 W
54c	Brooklyn Park	39·14 N	76·36 W
60	Brookmans Park	51·43 N	0·12 W
54d	Brookmont	38·57 N	77·07 W
54a	Brook Park	41·24 N	81·48 W
60	Brook Street	51·37 N	0·17 E
68a	Brookvale	33·46 S	151·17 E
52a	Brookville, Ma.	42·08 N	71·01 W
53	Brookville, NY.	40·49 N	73·35 W
54b	Broomall	39·59 N	75·22 W
60	Broomfield	51·14 N	0·38 E
52b	Brossard	45·26 N	73·29 W
55b	Broughton	40·21 N	79·59 W
62c	Brou-sur-Chantereine	48·53 N	2·38 E
60	Broxbourne	51·45 N	0·01 W
63a	Bruchmühle	52·33 N	13·47 E
61	Bruckhausen (Neigh.)	51·29 N	6·44 E
61	Brügge	51·13 N	7·34 E
63c	Brugherio	45·33 N	9·18 E
62c	Brunoy	48·42 N	2·30 E
68b	Brunswick	37·46 S	144·58 E
54b	Bryn Mawr	40·01 N	75·19 W
62c	Buc	48·46 N	2·08 E
63a	Buch (Neigh.)	52·38 N	13·30 E
63a	Buchholz	52·35 N	13·47 E
61	Buchholz (Neigh.), F.R.G.	51·23 N	6·46 E
63a	Buchholz (Neigh.), G.D.R.	52·36 N	13·26 E
55a	Buckhorn Island State Park (P. Int.)	43·03 N	78·59 W
60	Buckingham Palace (P. Int.)	51·30 N	0·08 W
63a	Buckow (Neigh.)	52·25 N	13·26 E
64g	Buda (Neigh.)	47·30 N	19·02 E
64g	Budai-hegység (Mts.)	47·31 N	19·57 E
64g	Budakeszi	47·31 N	18·56 E
64g	Budaörs	47·27 N	18·58 E
64g	Budapest	47·30 N	19·05 E
61	Budberg	51·32 N	6·38 E
61	Büderich	51·37 N	6·34 E
61	Buderus	51·33 N	7·38 E
57	Buena Park	33·52 N	118·00 W
58d	Buenos Aires	34·36 S	58·27 W
61	Buer (Neigh.)	51·36 N	7·03 E
55a	Buffalo	42·54 N	78·53 W
55a	Buffalo Har.	42·51 N	78·52 W
65c	Bukit Panjang	1·23 N	103·46 E
65c	Bukit Timah	1·20 N	103·47 E
65c	Bulim	1·23 N	103·43 E
61	Bulmke-Hüllen (Neigh.)	51·31 N	7·06 E
60	Bulpham	51·33 N	0·22 E
60	Bumbles Green	51·44 N	0·02 E
68b	Bundoora	37·42 S	145·04 E
52a	Bunker Hill Monument (P. Int.)	42·22 N	71·04 W
67a	Bunkyō (Neigh.)	35·43 N	139·45 E
65c	Buona Vista	1·16 N	103·47 E
57	Burbank	34·12 N	118·18 W
62c	Bures-sur-Yvette	48·42 N	2·10 E
61	Burg	51·08 N	7·09 E
69b	Burger Township	26·05 S	27·46 E
60	Burgh Heath	51·18 N	0·13 W
54b	Burholme (Neigh.)	40·03 N	75·05 W
56b	Burlingame	37·35 N	122·22 W
52a	Burlington	42·30 N	71·12 W
62b	Burnage	53·26 N	2·12 W
56a	Burnham	41·39 N	87·34 W
52c	Burnhamthorpe	43·37 N	79·36 W
54d	Burning Tree Estates	39·01 N	77·12 W
60	Burrowhill	51·21 N	0·36 W
56a	Burr Ridge	41·46 N	87·55 W
62b	Burton	53·16 N	3·01 W
68b	Burwood, Austl.	37·51 S	145·06 E
62b	Bury	53·36 N	2·17 W
61	Buschhausen (Neigh.)	51·30 N	6·51 E
60	Bushey	51·39 N	0·22 W
60	Bushey Heath	51·38 N	0·20 W
54d	Bush Hill	38·48 N	77·07 W
53	Bushwick (Neigh.)	40·42 N	73·55 W
54b	Bustleton (Neigh.)	40·05 N	75·02 W
59d	Butantã (Neigh.)	23·34 S	46·43 W
61	Butendorf (Neigh.)	51·33 N	6·59 E
61	Büttgen	51·12 N	6·36 E
65e	Byculla (Neigh.)	18·58 N	72·49 E
61	Byfang (Neigh.)	51·24 N	7·06 E
60	Byfleet	51·20 N	0·29 W
68a	Bynea Bay	34·03 S	151·06 E
	C		
58d	Caballito (Neigh.)	34·37 S	58·27 W
54d	Cabin John	38·58 N	77·09 W
68a	Cabramatta	33·54 S	150·56 E
62c	Cachan	48·48 N	2·20 E
63d	Cacilhas	38·41 N	9·09 W
62b	Cadishead	53·25 N	2·26 W
69a	Cairo (Al-Qāhirah)	30·03 N	31·15 E
59c	Caju (Neigh.)	22·53 S	43·13 W
58b	Calabazar	23·01 N	82·22 W
65a	Calcutta	22·32 N	88·22 E
53	Caldwell	40·51 N	74·17 W
63d	Calhariz (Neigh.)	38·44 N	9·12 W
57	California, University of (U.C.L.A.) (P. Int.)	34·04 N	118·26 W
58c	Callao	12·02 S	77·05 W
66g	Caloocan	14·39 N	120·59 E
56a	Calumet, L.	41·41 N	87·35 W
56a	Calumet City	41·37 N	87·31 W
56a	Calumet Park	41·44 N	87·33 W
56a	Calumet Sag Chan.	41·42 N	87·57 W
68b	Camberwell	37·50 S	145·04 E
52a	Cambridge	42·22 N	71·06 W
59d	Cambuci (Neigh.)	23·34 S	46·37 W
54b	Camden	39·57 N	75·07 W
60	Camden (Neigh.)	51·33 N	0·10 W
68b	Campbellfield	37·41 S	144·57 E
63d	Campo Grande (Neigh.)	38·45 N	9·09 W
68a	Campsie	33·55 S	151·06 E
54d	Camp Springs	38·48 N	76·55 W
53	Canarsie (Neigh.)	40·38 N	73·53 W
63b	Canillas (Neigh.)	40·28 N	3·38 W
63b	Canillejas (Neigh.)	40·27 N	3·37 W
57	Canoga Park (Neigh.)	34·12 N	118·35 W
68b	Canterbury, Austl.	37·49 S	145·05 E
54d	Canterbury Woods	38·49 N	77·15 W
59c	Canto do Pontes	22·58 S	43·04 W
52a	Canton	42·09 N	71·09 W
56b	Canyon	37·49 N	122·09 W
59d	Capão Redondo (Neigh.)	23·40 S	46·46 W
63d	Caparica	38·40 N	9·12 W
62b	Capenhurst	53·15 N	2·57 W
54d	Capitol Heights	38·53 N	76·55 W
54d	Capitol View	39·01 N	77·04 W
68a	Captain Cook Bridge (P. Int.)	34·00 S	151·08 E
59d	Capuáva	23·39 S	46·29 W
63a	Caputh	52·21 N	13·00 E
59a	Caraballeda	10·37 N	66·50 W
63b	Carabanchel Alto (Neigh.)	40·22 N	3·45 W
63b	Carabanchel Bajo (Neigh.)	40·23 N	3·47 W
59a	Caracas	10·30 N	66·56 W
59d	Carapicuíba	23·31 S	46·50 W
68a	Caringbah	34·03 S	151·08 E
68a	Carlingford	33·47 S	151·03 E
53	Carlstadt	40·50 N	74·06 W
63d	Carnaxide	38·43 N	9·15 W
55b	Carnegie Institute (P. Int.)	40·27 N	79·57 W
62c	Carnetin	48·54 N	2·42 E
63d	Carnide (Neigh.)	38·46 N	9·11 W
62c	Carrières-sous-Bois	48·57 N	2·07 E
62c	Carrières-sous-Poissy	48·57 N	2·03 E
62c	Carrières-sur-Seine	48·55 N	2·11 E
62b	Carrington	53·26 N	2·24 W
60	Carshalton (Neigh.)	51·22 N	0·10 W
57	Carson	33·50 N	118·16 W
54d	Carsondale	38·57 N	76·50 W
53	Carteret	40·35 N	74·13 W
52c	Casa Loma (P. Int.)	43·41 N	79·25 W
58d	Caseros (Tres de Febrero)	34·36 S	58·33 W
63e	Castellbisbal	41·29 N	1·59 E
68a	Castlecrag	33·48 S	151·13 E
68a	Castle Hill	33·44 S	151·00 E
55b	Castle Shannon	40·22 N	80·02 W
62b	Castleton	53·35 N	2·11 W
61	Castrop-Rauxel	51·34 N	7·19 E
63e	Cataluña, Museo de Arte de (P. Int.)	41·23 N	2·09 E
60	Caterham	51·17 N	0·04 W
59c	Catete (Neigh.)	22·55 S	43·10 W
60	Catford (Neigh.)	51·27 N	0·01 W
59a	Catia (Neigh.)	10·31 N	66·57 W
54c	Catonsville	39·16 N	76·44 W
52b	Caughnawaga	45·25 N	73·41 W
68b	Caulfield	37·53 S	145·03 E
63d	Caxias	38·42 N	9·16 W
64c	Cecchignola (Neigh.)	41·49 N	12·29 E
68a	Cecil Park	33·52 S	150·51 E
54b	Cedarbrook	40·05 N	75·10 W
53	Cedar Grove	40·51 N	74·14 W
54b	Cedar Heights	40·05 N	75·17 W
53	Cedarhurst	40·38 N	73·44 W
55c	Center Line	42·29 N	83·03 W
64c	Centocelle (Neigh.)	41·53 N	12·34 E
55b	Central Highlands	40·16 N	79·50 W
54d	Central Intelligence Agency (P. Int.)	38·57 N	77·09 W
53	Central Park (P. Int.)	40·47 N	73·58 W
53	Centre Island	40·54 N	73·32 W
59a	Centro Simón Bolívar (P. Int.)	10·30 N	66·55 W
57	Century City (Neigh.)	34·03 N	118·26 W

Page	Name Region	Lat. °′	Long. °′
64b	Čer'omuski (Neigh.)	55·41 N	37·35 E
64b	Čertanovo (Neigh.)	55·38 N	37·37 E
63c	Cesano Boscone	45·27 N	9·06 E
59a	Chacao	10·30 N	66·51 W
62b	Chadderton	53·33 N	2·08 W
68b	Chadstone	37·53 S	145·05 E
60	Chadwell Saint Mary	51·29 N	0·22 E
65a	Chakdaha	22·20 N	88·20 E
60	Chaldon	51·17 N	0·07 W
55b	Chalfant	40·25 N	79·52 W
60	Chalfont Common	51·38 N	0·33 W
60	Chalfont Saint Giles	51·38 N	0·34 W
60	Chalfont Saint Peter	51·37 N	0·33 W
60	Chalk	51·26 N	0·25 E
62c	Chambourcy	48·54 N	2·03 E
65a	Champdāni	22·48 N	88·21 E
62c	Champigny-sur-Marne	48·49 N	2·31 E
62c	Champlan	48·43 N	2·16 E
62c	Champs-sur-Marne	48·51 N	2·36 E
65a	Chāmrāil	22·38 N	88·18 E
65a	Chandannagar	22·51 N	88·21 E
60	Chandler's Cross	51·40 N	0·27 W
65b	Changdian	40·01 N	116·32 E
65c	Changi	1·23 N	103·59 E
65b	Changxindian	39·49 N	116·12 E
66m	Chang-hung	10·43 N	106·41 E
62c	Chanteloup-les-Vignes	48·59 N	2·02 E
66f	Chao Phraya (R.)	13·39 N	100·31 E
54d	Chapel Oaks	38·54 N	76·55 W
62b	Chapeltown	53·38 N	2·24 W
57	Chapman Woods	34·08 N	118·05 W
58a	Chapultepec, Castillo de (P. Int.)	19·25 N	99·11 W
62c	Charenton-le-Pont	48·49 N	2·25 E
52a	Charles (R.)	42·22 N	71·03 W
62c	Charles de Gaulle, Aéroport (Arpt.)	49·00 N	2·34 E
63a	Charlottenburg (Neigh.)	52·31 N	13·16 E
63a	Charlottenburg, Schloss (P. Int.)	52·31 N	13·14 E
60	Charlton (Neigh.)	51·29 N	0·02 E
63d	Charneca (Neigh.)	38·47 N	9·08 W
55b	Charterwood	40·33 N	80·00 W
62c	Châteaufort	48·44 N	2·06 E
62c	Châtenay-Malabry	48·46 N	2·17 E
62c	Châtillon	48·48 N	2·17 E
62c	Chatou	48·54 N	2·09 E
65a	Chatpur (Neigh.)	22·36 N	88·23 E
68a	Chatswood	33·48 S	151·12 E
62c	Chavenay	48·51 N	1·59 E
62c	Chaville	48·48 N	2·10 E
62b	Cheadle	53·24 N	2·13 W
62b	Cheadle Hulme	53·22 N	2·12 W
60	Cheam (Neigh.)	51·21 N	0·13 W
55a	Cheektowaga	42·55 N	78·46 W
62b	Cheetham Hill (Neigh.)	53·31 N	2·15 W
63d	Chelas (Neigh.)	38·45 N	9·07 W
62c	Chelles	48·53 N	2·36 E
60	Chelmsford	51·44 N	0·28 E
52a	Chelsea	42·24 N	71·02 W
68b	Cheltenham, Austl.	37·58 S	145·03 E
65e	Chembūr (Neigh.)	19·04 N	72·54 E
60	Chenies	51·41 N	0·32 W
62c	Chennevières	49·00 N	2·07 E
55b	Cherry City	40·29 N	79·58 W
54b	Cherry Hill	39·55 N	75·01 W
54c	Cherry Hill (Neigh.)	39·15 N	76·38 W
60	Chertsey	51·24 N	0·30 W
60	Chesham	51·43 N	0·38 W
60	Chesham Bois	51·41 N	0·37 W
60	Cheshunt	51·43 N	0·02 W
60	Chessington (Neigh.)	51·21 N	0·18 W
54b	Chester	39·51 N	75·21 W
54d	Chesterbrook	38·55 N	77·09 W
52a	Chestnut Hill, Ma.	42·20 N	71·10 W
54c	Chestnut Hill, Md.	39·17 N	76·47 W
55b	Cheswick	40·32 N	79·47 W
60	Chevening	51·18 N	0·08 E
54d	Cheverly	38·55 N	76·55 W
62c	Chevilly-Larue	48·46 N	2·21 E
62c	Chevreuse	48·42 N	2·03 E
54d	Chevy Chase	38·58 N	77·05 W
54d	Chevy Chase View	39·01 N	77·05 W
65d	Chhalera Bāngar	28·33 N	77·20 E
65a	Chhināmor	22·48 N	88·18 E
56a	Chicago	41·53 N	87·38 W
56a	Chicago, North Branch (R.)	41·53 N	87·38 W
56a	Chicago Lawn (Neigh.)	41·47 N	87·41 W
56a	Chicago-O'Hare International Arpt.	41·59 N	87·54 W
56a	Chicago Ridge	41·42 N	87·47 W
56a	Chicago Sanitary and Ship Canal (Can.)	41·42 N	87·58 W
60	Chignall Saint James	51·46 N	0·25 E
60	Chigwell	51·38 N	0·05 E
60	Chigwell Row	51·37 N	0·07 E
62b	Childer Thornton	53·17 N	2·57 W
54d	Chillum	38·58 N	76·59 W
62c	Chilly-Mazarin	48·42 N	2·19 E
64b	Chimki	55·54 N	37·26 E
64b	Chimki-Chovrino (Neigh.)	55·51 N	37·30 E
56b	Chinatown (Neigh.)	37·48 N	122·26 W
60	Chingford (Neigh.)	51·38 N	0·01 E
66d	Chingmei	24·59 N	121·32 E

Page	Name Region	Lat. °′	Long. °′
60	Chipperfield	51·42 N	0·29 W
60	Chipping Ongar	51·43 N	0·15 E
60	Chipstead, Eng.	51·18 N	0·10 W
60	Chipstead, Eng.	51·17 N	0·09 E
65d	Chirāgh Delhi (Neigh.)	28·32 N	77·14 E
60	Chislehurst (Neigh.)	51·25 N	0·04 E
60	Chiswellgreen	51·44 N	0·22 W
60	Chiswick (Neigh.)	51·29 N	0·16 W
65c	Choa Chu Kang	1·22 N	103·41 E
60	Chobham	51·21 N	0·36 W
67a	Chōfu	35·39 N	139·33 E
62c	Choisel	48·41 N	2·01 E
62c	Choisy-le-Roi	48·46 N	2·25 E
66m	Cho-lon (Neigh.)	10·46 N	106·40 E
66m	Cho Moi	10·51 N	106·38 E
65c	Chong Pang	1·26 N	103·50 E
60	Chorleywood	51·39 N	0·31 W
62b	Chorlton-cum-Hardy (Neigh.)	53·27 N	2·17 W
64b	Chorošovo (Neigh.)	55·47 N	37·28 E
58b	Chorrera de Managua	23·02 N	82·19 W
58c	Chorrillos	12·12 S	77·02 W
66b	Chŭngsanha-ri (Neigh.)	37·35 N	126·54 E
67a	Chūō (Neigh.)	35·40 N	139·47 E
55b	Churchill, Pa.	40·27 N	79·51 W
54d	Churchill, Va.	38·54 N	77·10 W
60	Church Street	51·26 N	0·28 E
56a	Cicero	41·51 N	87·45 W
69b	Cinderella	26·15 S	28·16 E
63c	Cinisello Balsamo	45·33 N	9·13 E
64g	Cinkota (Neigh.)	47·31 N	19·14 E
63c	Cisliano	45·27 N	8·59 E
53	City College of New York (P. Int.)	40·49 N	73·57 W
53	City Island (Neigh.)	40·51 N	73·47 W
54d	City of Baltimore	39·18 N	76·37 W
57	City of Baltimore	33·59 N	118·08 W
57	City of Industry	34·01 N	117·57 W
60	City of London (Neigh.)	51·31 N	0·05 W
60	City of Westminster (Neigh.)	51·30 N	0·09 W
58a	Ciudad de Naucalpan de Juárez	19·28 N	99·14 W
58a	Ciudad Deportiva (P. Int.)	19·24 N	99·06 W
58d	Ciudad General Belgrano	34·44 S	58·32 W
63b	Ciudad Lineal (Neigh.)	40·27 N	3·40 W
63b	Ciudad Universitaria (Neigh.)	40·27 N	3·44 W
55b	Clairton	40·18 N	79·53 W
62c	Clamart	48·48 N	2·16 E
60	Claremont	51·21 N	0·22 W
53	Clark	40·38 N	74·19 W
52c	Clarkson	43·31 N	79·37 W
55c	Clawson	42·32 N	83·09 W
62c	Claye-Souilly	48·57 N	2·42 E
60	Claygate	51·22 N	0·20 W
60	Claygate Cross	51·16 N	0·19 E
56a	Clearing (Neigh.)	41·47 N	87·47 W
54a	Cleveland	41·30 N	81·41 W
54a	Cleveland Heights	41·30 N	81·34 W
54a	Cleveland Museum of Art (P. Int.)	41·31 N	81·37 W
54d	Cleveland Park (Neigh.)	38·56 N	77·04 W
62c	Clichy	48·54 N	2·18 E
62c	Clichy-sous-Bois	48·55 N	2·33 E
53	Cliffside Park	40·49 N	73·59 W
52a	Clifton, Ma.	42·29 N	70·53 W
53	Clifton, NJ.	40·53 N	74·08 W
54b	Clifton Heights	39·56 N	75·18 W
68a	Clontarf	33·48 S	151·16 E
53	Closter	40·59 N	73·58 W
69b	Cloverdene	26·09 S	28·22 E
65b	Coal Hill Park (P. Int.)	39·56 N	116·23 E
60	Cobham	51·23 N	0·24 E
68b	Coburg	37·45 S	144·58 E
60	Cockfosters (Neigh.)	51·39 N	0·09 W
59c	Cocotá (Neigh.)	22·49 S	43·11 W
59c	Coelho da Rocha	22·47 S	43·23 W
58b	Cojímar	23·10 N	82·18 W
69d	Coker	6·29 N	3·20 E
65e	Colāba (Neigh.)	18·54 N	72·48 E
60	Coldblow (Neigh.)	51·26 N	0·10 E
54d	College Park	39·00 N	76·55 W
53	College Point (Neigh.)	40·47 N	73·51 W
60	Collier Row (Neigh.)	51·36 N	0·10 E
54b	Collingdale	39·55 N	75·17 W
54b	Collingswood	39·55 N	75·04 W
68b	Collingwood	37·48 S	145·00 E
60	Colnbrook	51·29 N	0·31 W
60	Colney Heath	51·44 N	0·15 W
60	Colney Street	51·42 N	0·20 W
63c	Cologno Monzese	45·32 N	9·17 E
62c	Colombes	48·55 N	2·15 E
53	Colonia	40·35 N	74·18 W
54b	Colonial Manor	39·51 N	75·09 W
54c	Colonial Park	39·19 N	76·45 W
64c	Colosseo (P. Int.)	41·54 N	12·29 E
54c	Columbia	39·13 N	76·52 W
53	Columbia University (P. Int.)	40·48 N	73·58 W
54b	Colwyn	39·55 N	75·15 W
58c	Comas	11·57 S	77·04 W
68a	Como	34·00 S	151·04 E
62c	Compans	49·00 N	2·40 E

Page	Name Region	Lat. °′	Long. °′
57	Compton	33·54 N	118·13 W
59b	Conchalí	33·24 S	70·39 W
68a	Concord, Austl.	33·52 S	151·06 E
52c	Concord, Can.	43·48 N	79·29 W
68a	Concord West	33·51 S	151·05 E
53	Coney Island (Neigh.)	40·34 N	74·00 W
62c	Conflans-Sainte-Honorine	48·59 N	2·06 E
69c	Congo (Zaïre) (R.)	0·00	0·00
54d	Congress Heights (Neigh.)	38·51 N	77·00 W
54b	Connaughton	40·05 N	75·19 W
54b	Conshohocken	40·05 N	75·18 W
59d	Consolação (Neigh.)	23·33 S	46·39 W
69b	Consolidated Main Reef Mines (P. Int.)	26·11 S	27·56 E
58d	Constitución (Neigh.)	34·37 S	58·23 W
68b	Coode Can.	37·49 S	144·55 E
68a	Coogee	33·55 S	151·16 E
68b	Cook, Pt.	37·55 S	144·48 E
60	Cooksmill Green	51·44 N	0·22 E
60	Coopersale Common	51·42 N	0·08 E
59c	Copacabana (Neigh.)	22·58 S	43·11 W
63c	Cormano	45·33 N	9·10 E
62c	Cormeilles-en-Parisis	48·59 N	2·12 E
63e	Cornellá	41·21 N	2·04 E
60	Corringham	51·31 N	0·28 E
63d	Corroios	38·38 N	9·09 W
63c	Corsico	45·26 N	9·07 E
56b	Corte Madera	37·55 N	122·31 W
63b	Cortes (P. Int.)	40·25 N	3·41 W
64c	Corviale (Neigh.)	41·52 N	12·25 E
63d	Costa de Caparica	38·38 N	9·14 W
58d	Costanero, Canal de (Can.)	34·34 S	58·22 W
52b	Côte-Saint-Luc	45·28 N	73·40 W
52b	Côte Visitation (Neigh.)	45·33 N	73·36 W
54d	Cottage City	38·56 N	76·57 W
60	Coulsdon (Neigh.)	51·19 N	0·08 W
62c	Courbevoie	48·54 N	2·15 E
62c	Courcelle	48·42 N	2·06 E
54c	Courtleigh	39·22 N	76·46 W
62c	Courtry	48·55 N	2·36 E
63d	Cova da Piedade	38·40 N	9·10 W
53	Cove Neck	40·53 N	73·31 W
57	Covina	34·05 N	117·53 W
57	Cowan Heights	33·47 N	117·47 W
60	Cowley (Neigh.)	51·32 N	0·29 W
58a	Coyoacán	19·20 N	99·10 W
55b	Crafton	40·26 N	80·04 W
69b	Craighall (Neigh.)	26·07 S	28·02 E
69b	Craighall Park (Neigh.)	26·08 S	28·01 E
53	Cranford	40·39 N	74·19 W
62b	Crank	53·29 N	2·45 W
60	Creekmouth (Neigh.)	51·31 N	0·06 E
54b	Crescentville (Neigh.)	40·02 N	75·05 W
53	Cresskill	40·57 N	73·57 W
54d	Crest Haven	39·02 N	76·59 W
56a	Crestwood	41·39 N	87·44 W
62c	Créteil	48·48 N	2·28 E
59c	Cristo Redentor, Estatua do (P. Int.)	22·57 S	43·13 W
60	Crockenhill	51·23 N	0·10 E
62c	Croissy-Beaubourg	48·50 N	2·40 E
62c	Croissy-sur-Seine	48·53 N	2·09 E
68a	Cromer	33·44 S	151·17 E
61	Cronenberg (Neigh.)	51·12 N	7·08 E
62b	Cronton	53·23 N	2·46 W
62b	Crosby	53·30 N	3·02 W
69b	Crosby (Neigh.)	26·12 S	27·59 E
62c	Crosne	48·43 N	2·28 E
68a	Cross Roads	33·58 S	150·53 E
55b	Crouse Run (R.)	40·35 N	79·58 W
68a	Crows Nest	33·50 S	151·12 E
60	Croxley Green	51·39 N	0·27 W
68b	Croydon, Austl.	37·48 S	145·17 E
60	Croydon (Neigh.)	51·23 N	0·06 W
54b	Crum Lynne	39·52 N	75·20 W
55a	Crystal Beach	42·52 N	79·04 W
64g	Csömör	47·33 N	19·14 E
58b	Cuatro Caminos	22·54 N	82·23 W
58a	Cuautepec el Alto	19·34 N	99·08 W
60	Cudham (Neigh.)	51·19 N	0·05 E
60	Cuffley	51·47 N	0·07 W
65b	Cuigezhuang	40·01 N	116·28 E
54d	Culmore	38·51 N	77·08 W
57	Culver City	34·01 N	118·24 W
60	Culverstone Green	51·20 N	0·21 E
54c	Curtis B.	39·13 N	76·35 W
63c	Cusano Milanino	45·33 N	9·11 E
60	Cuxton	51·22 N	0·27 E
54a	Cuyahoga (R.)	41·30 N	81·42 W
54a	Cuyahoga Heights	41·26 N	81·39 W
57	Cypress	33·50 N	118·01 W
69b	Cyrildene (Neigh.)	26·11 S	28·06 E

D

Page	Name Region	Lat. °′	Long. °′
66a	Dachang	31·18 N	121·25 E
65e	Dadar (Neigh.)	19·01 N	72·50 E
60	Dagenham (Neigh.)	51·32 N	0·10 E
69b	Daggafontein	26·18 S	28·28 E
65d	Dahīrpur (Neigh.)	28·43 N	77·12 E
61	Dahl	51·18 N	7·31 E
63a	Dahlem (Neigh.)	52·28 N	13·17 E
61	Dahlerau	51·13 N	7·19 E
63a	Dahlwitz	52·30 N	13·38 E
67b	Daitō	34·42 N	135·38 E
63a	Dallgow	52·32 N	13·05 E
62b	Dalton	53·34 N	2·46 W
56b	Daly City	37·42 N	122·29 W
68b	Dandenong	37·59 S	145·12 E
54c	Daniels	39·26 N	77·03 W
52a	Danvers	42·34 N	70·56 W
66h	Darakeh	35·48 N	51·23 E
69a	Dār as-Salām	29·59 N	31·13 E
66h	Darband	35·49 N	51·26 E
54b	Darby	39·54 N	75·15 W
60	Dartford	51·27 N	0·14 E
60	Datchet	51·29 N	0·34 W
69b	Daveyton Location	26·09 S	28·25 E
62b	Davyhulme	53·27 N	2·22 W
65b	Dawuji	39·51 N	116·30 E
62b	Dean Row	53·20 N	2·11 W
55c	Dearborn	42·18 N	83·10 W
55c	Dearborn Heights	42·19 N	83·14 W
52a	Dedham	42·15 N	71·10 W
68a	Deewhy	33·45 S	151·17 E
54b	Delair	39·59 N	75·03 W
54b	Delaware (R.)	39·50 N	75·23 W
65d	Delhi	28·40 N	77·13 E
65d	Delhi Cantonment	28·36 N	77·08 E
61	Dellwig (Neigh.)	51·29 N	6·56 E
69b	Delmas	26·06 S	28·26 E
54b	Delran	40·02 N	74·58 W
58d	Del Viso	34·26 S	58·46 W
53	Demarest	40·57 N	73·58 W
61	Demmeltrath (Neigh.)	51·11 N	7·03 E
67a	Denenchōfu (Neigh.)	35·35 N	139·41 E
62b	Denshaw	53·35 N	2·02 W
62b	Denton	53·27 N	2·07 W
60	Deptford (Neigh.)	51·28 N	0·02 W
61	Derendorf (Neigh.)	51·15 N	6·48 E
61	Derne (Neigh.)	51·34 N	7·31 E
56a	Des Plaines	42·02 N	87·54 W
56a	Chicago Sanitary and Ship Can.	41·42 N	87·58 W
55c	Detroit	42·20 N	83·03 W
55c	Detroit (R.)	42·06 N	83·08 W
55c	Detroit Metropolitan-Wayne County Arpt.	42·13 N	83·22 W
62c	Deuil-la-Barre	48·59 N	2·20 E
61	Deusen (Neigh.)	51·33 N	7·26 E
52b	Deux-Montagnes	45·23 N	73·53 W
64d	Dhāfni	37·48 N	22·01 E
68b	Diamond Creek	37·41 S	145·09 E
65b	Diancun	39·55 N	116·14 E
62b	Didsbury (Neigh.)	53·25 N	2·14 W
63a	Diepensee	52·22 N	13·31 E
61	Diersfordt	51·42 N	6·33 E
61	Diessem (Neigh.)	51·20 N	6·35 E
62b	Digmoor	53·32 N	2·45 W
65a	Digra	22·50 N	88·20 E
54d	Dillon Park	38·52 N	76·56 W
62b	Dingle (Neigh.)	53·23 N	2·57 W
61	Dinslaken	51·34 N	6·44 E
61	Dinslakener Bruch	51·35 N	6·43 E
69b	Dinwiddie	26·16 S	28·10 E
69b	Discovery	26·10 S	27·54 E
57	Disneyland (P. Int.)	33·48 N	117·55 W
61	Disteln	51·36 N	7·09 E
54d	District Heights	38·51 N	76·53 W
60	Ditton, Eng.	51·18 N	0·27 E
52c	Dixie	43·36 N	79·36 W
64b	Djakovo (Neigh.)	55·39 N	37·40 E
69c	Djelo-Binza	4·23 S	15·16 E
69c	Djoué (R.)	4·19 S	15·14 E
64e	Döbling (Neigh.)	48·15 N	16·22 E
60	Doddinghurst	51·40 N	0·18 E
52b	Dollard-des-Ormeaux	45·29 N	73·49 W
56a	Dolton	41·39 N	87·37 W
57	Dominguez	33·50 N	118·13 W
64c	Domitilla, Catacombe di (P. Int.)	41·52 N	12·31 E
52c	Don (R.)	43·39 N	79·21 W
64e	Donaufeld (Neigh.)	48·15 N	16·25 E
64e	Donaustadt (Neigh.)	48·13 N	16·30 E
64e	Donauturm (P. Int.)	48·14 N	16·25 E
61	Dönberg	51·18 N	7·10 E
58d	Don Bosco (Neigh.)	34·42 S	58·19 W
68b	Doncaster, Austl.	37·47 S	145·08 E
52c	Doncaster, Can.	43·48 N	79·25 W
68b	Doncaster East	37·47 S	145·10 E
65b	Dongba	39·58 N	116·32 E
65b	Dongbahe	39·58 N	116·27 E
65b	Dongshi	39·49 N	116·34 E
58d	Don Torcuato	34·30 S	58·40 W
52a	Dorchester Heights National Historic Site (P. Int.)	42·20 N	71·03 W
55b	Dormont	40·24 N	80·03 W
61	Dornap	51·15 N	7·04 E
55b	Dorseyville	40·35 N	79·53 W
61	Dorstfeld (Neigh.)	51·31 N	7·25 E
61	Dortmund	51·31 N	7·28 E

Page	Name Region	Lat. °′	Long. °′
52b	Dorval	45·27 N	73·44 W
68a	Dover Heights	33·53 S	151·17 E
68b	Doveton	38·00 S	145·14 E
66h	Dowlatābād	35·37 N	51·27 E
57	Downey	33·56 N	118·08 W
62c	Drancy	48·56 N	2·27 E
62c	Draveil	48·41 N	2·25 E
55b	Dravosburg	40·21 N	79·51 W
63a	Drewitz (Neigh.)	52·22 N	13·08 E
54b	Drexel Hill	39·57 N	75·19 W
62b	Droylsden	53·29 N	2·10 W
68a	Drummoyne	33·51 S	151·09 E
64b	Družba	55·53 N	37·45 E
57	Duarte	34·08 N	117·58 W
62c	Dugny	48·57 N	2·25 E
61	Duisburg	51·25 N	6·46 E
61	Duissern (Neigh.)	51·26 N	6·47 E
62b	Dukinfield	53·29 N	2·05 W
60	Dulwich (Neigh.)	51·26 N	0·05 W
65a	Dum-Dum	22·35 N	88·24 E
53	Dumont	40·56 N	74·00 W
61	Dümpten (Neigh.)	51·27 N	6·54 E
54c	Dundalk	39·15 N	76·31 W
68a	Dundas	33·48 S	151·02 E
62b	Dunham Town	53·23 N	2·24 W
68a	Dunheved	33·45 S	150·47 E
54d	Dunn Loring	38·53 N	77·14 W
60	Dunton Green	51·18 N	0·11 E
60	Dunton Wayletts	51·35 N	0·24 E
69b	Dunvegan	26·09 S	28·09 E
63c	Duomo (P. Int.)	45·27 N	9·11 E
59c	Duque de Caxias	22·47 S	43·18 W
55b	Duquesne	40·21 N	79·51 W
69b	Durban Roodepoort Deep Gold Mines (P. Int.)	26·10 S	27·51 E
61	Durchholz	51·23 N	7·17 E
61	Düssel	51·16 N	7·03 E
61	Düsseldorf	51·12 N	6·47 E
64b	Dzeržinskij	55·38 N	37·50 E

E

Page	Name Region	Lat. °′	Long. °′
57	Eagle Rock (Neigh.)	34·09 N	118·12 W
60	Ealing (Neigh.)	51·31 N	0·20 W
53	East (R.)	40·48 N	73·48 W
52a	East Arlington	42·25 N	71·08 W
60	East Barnet (Neigh.)	51·38 N	0·09 W
60	East Bedfont (Neigh.)	51·27 N	0·26 W
52a	East Braintree	42·13 N	70·58 W
68b	East Burwood	37·51 S	145·09 E
60	Eastbury	51·37 N	0·25 W
53	Eastchester	40·57 N	73·49 W
54a	East Cleveland	41·32 N	81·35 W
68b	East Coburg	37·45 S	144·59 E
60	Eastcote (Neigh.)	51·35 N	0·24 W
55c	East Detroit	42·28 N	82·56 W
69b	Eastern Native (Neigh.)	26·13 S	28·05 E
54b	East Falls (Neigh.)	40·01 N	75·11 W
62b	Eastham	53·19 N	2·58 W
60	East Ham (Neigh.)	51·32 N	0·03 E
68a	East Hills, Austl.	33·58 S	150·59 E
53	East Hills, NY.	40·47 N	73·38 W
66c	East Lamma Chan.	22·15 N	114·07 E
54b	East Lansdowne	39·56 N	75·16 W
55b	East Liberty (Neigh.)	40·27 N	79·55 W
68a	East Lindfield	33·46 S	151·11 E
57	East Los Angeles	34·01 N	118·09 W
60	East Malling	51·17 N	0·26 E
53	East Meadow	40·43 N	73·34 W
60	East Molesey	51·24 N	0·21 W
53	East Newark	40·45 N	74·10 W
53	East New York (Neigh.)	40·40 N	73·53 W
53	East Norwich	40·50 N	73·32 W
53	East Orange	40·46 N	74·13 W
55b	East Pittsburgh	40·24 N	79·48 W
56b	East Richmond	37·57 N	122·19 W
53	East Rockaway	40·39 N	73·40 W
60	East Tilbury	51·28 N	0·26 E
57	East Tustin	33·46 N	117·49 W
52a	East Walpole	42·10 N	71·13 W
52a	East Watertown	42·22 N	71·10 W
52a	East Weymouth	42·13 N	70·55 W
54b	Eastwick (Neigh.)	39·55 N	75·14 W
60	East Wickham (Neigh.)	51·28 N	0·07 E
68a	Eastwood	33·48 S	151·05 E
52c	East York	43·41 N	79·20 W
62c	Eaubonne	49·00 N	2·17 E
67a	Ebina	35·26 N	139·25 E
69d	Ebute-ikorodu	6·37 N	3·30 E
62b	Eccles	53·29 N	2·21 W
62b	Eccleston, Eng.	53·27 N	2·47 W
54c	Eccleston, Md.	39·24 N	76·44 W
55c	Ecorse	42·15 N	83·09 W
67a	Eda (Neigh.)	35·34 N	139·34 E
59c	Éden	22·48 S	43·24 W
69b	Edendale	26·09 S	28·09 E
69b	Edenvale	26·08 S	28·09 E
69b	Edenvale Location	26·08 S	28·11 E
62b	Edge Hill (Neigh.)	53·24 N	2·57 W
54c	Edgemere	39·14 N	76·27 W
53	Edgewater, NJ.	40·50 N	73·58 W
55a	Edgewater, NY.	43·03 N	78·55 W
60	Edgware (Neigh.)	51·37 N	0·17 W
62b	Edgworth	53·39 N	2·24 W
56a	Edison Park (Neigh.)	42·01 N	87·49 W
54d	Edmonston	38·57 N	76·56 W
60	Edmonton (Neigh.)	51·37 N	0·04 W
67a	Edo (R.)	35·41 N	139·53 E
67a	Edogawa (Neigh.)	35·42 N	139·52 E
60	Egham	51·26 N	0·34 W
67a	Egota (Neigh.)	35·43 N	139·40 E
61	Ehingen (Neigh.)	51·22 N	6·42 E
61	Ehringhausen	51·11 N	7·33 E
61	Ehringhausen (Neigh.)	51·09 N	7·11 E
63a	Eiche	52·34 N	13·36 E
61	Eichlinghofen (Neigh.)	51·29 N	7·24 E
63a	Eichwalde	52·22 N	13·37 E
61	Eickerend	51·13 N	6·34 E
62c	Eiffel, Tour (P. Int.)	48·51 N	2·18 E
61	Eigen (Neigh.)	51·33 N	6·57 E
61	Eilpe (Neigh.)	51·21 N	7·29 E
65a	Eksāra	22·38 N	88·17 E
59a	El Aguacate	10·28 N	66·59 W
69b	Elandsfontein	26·10 S	28·12 E
61	Elberfeld (Neigh.)	51·16 N	7·08 E
58b	El Calvario (Neigh.)	23·05 N	82·20 W
63b	El Campamento (Neigh.)	40·24 N	3·46 W
59a	El Caribe	10·37 N	66·49 W
56b	El Cerrito	37·55 N	122·18 W
59a	El Cojo	10·37 N	66·53 W
59a	El Corozo	10·35 N	66·58 W
58b	El Cotorro	23·03 N	82·16 W
52c	Elder Mills	43·49 N	79·38 W
59a	El Encantado	10·27 N	66·47 W
65e	Elephanta I. (Ghārāpuri)	18·57 N	72·55 E
56b	El Granada	37·30 N	122·28 W
59a	El Guarapo	10·36 N	66·58 W
53	Elizabeth, NJ.	40·40 N	74·11 W
55b	Elizabeth, Pa.	40·16 N	79·53 W
54b	Elkins Park	40·05 N	75·08 W
54c	Elkridge	39·13 N	76·42 W
62b	Ellesmere Park	53·29 N	2·20 W
62b	Ellesmere Port	53·17 N	2·54 W
54c	Ellicott City	39·16 N	76·48 W
59a	El Limoncito	10·29 N	66·47 W
61	Ellinghorst (Neigh.)	51·34 N	6·57 E
56a	Elmhurst	41·53 N	87·56 W
53	Elmhurst (Neigh.)	40·44 N	73·53 W
58a	El Molinito	19·27 N	99·15 W
53	Elmont	40·42 N	73·42 W
54b	Elmwood (Neigh.)	39·56 N	75·14 W
56a	Elmwood Park	41·55 N	87·49 W
59a	El Palmar	10·38 N	66·52 W
59a	El Pedregal (Neigh.)	10·30 N	66·51 W
63b	El Plantío (Neigh.)	40·28 N	3·49 W
59a	El Recreo (Neigh.)	10·30 N	66·53 W
58a	El Reloj	19·18 N	99·08 W
59b	El Rincón de La Florida	33·33 S	70·34 W
69b	Elsburg	26·15 S	28·12 E
57	El Segundo	33·55 N	118·24 W
61	Elsey	51·22 N	7·34 E
60	Elstree	51·39 N	0·16 W
60	Eltham (Neigh.)	51·27 N	0·04 E
62b	Elton	53·16 N	2·49 W
58a	El Toreo (P. Int.)	19·27 N	99·13 W
59a	El Valle (Neigh.)	10·27 N	66·55 W
59a	El Zamural	10·27 N	67·00 W
59a	El Zig-Zag	10·33 N	66·58 W
59d	Embu	23·39 S	46·51 W
62c	Émerainville	48·49 N	2·37 E
53	Emerson	40·58 N	74·02 W
56b	Emeryville	37·50 N	122·17 W
69b	Emmarentia (Neigh.)	26·10 S	28·01 E
61	Emst (Neigh.)	51·21 N	7·30 E
55b	Emsworth	40·30 N	80·04 W
63d	Encarnação (Neigh.)	38·47 N	9·06 W
57	Encino (Neigh.)	34·09 N	118·30 W
68a	Enfield	33·53 S	151·06 E
59c	Engenho de Dentro (Neigh.)	22·54 S	43·18 W
59c	Engenho do Mato	22·52 S	43·01 W
59c	Engenho Nôvo (Neigh.)	22·55 S	43·17 W
62c	Enghien-les-Bains	48·58 N	2·19 E
60	Englefield Green	51·26 N	0·35 W
53	Englewood	40·54 N	73·59 W
56a	Englewood (Neigh.)	41·47 N	87·39 W
53	Englewood Cliffs	40·53 N	73·57 W
61	Ennepetal	51·18 N	7·22 E
62c	Épinay-sous-Sénart	48·42 N	2·31 E
62c	Épinay-sur-Seine	48·57 N	2·19 E
61	Eppendorf (Neigh.)	51·27 N	7·11 E
61	Eppenhausen (Neigh.)	51·21 N	7·31 E
68a	Epping, Austl.	33·46 S	151·05 E
60	Epping, Eng.	51·43 N	0·07 E
60	Epping Green, Eng.	51·44 N	0·05 E
60	Epping Upland	51·43 N	0·06 E
60	Epsom	51·20 N	0·16 W
64f	Erenköy (Neigh.)	40·58 N	29·04 E
61	Ergste	51·25 N	7·34 E
60	Erith (Neigh.)	51·29 N	0·10 E
61	Erkrath	51·13 N	6·55 E
61	Erle (Neigh.)	51·33 N	7·05 E
62c	Ermont	48·59 N	2·16 E
68a	Erskine Park	33·49 S	150·47 E
61	Esborn	51·23 N	7·20 E
58a	Escuadrón 201	19·22 N	99·06 W
60	Esher	51·23 N	0·22 W
63e	Esplugas	41·23 N	2·06 E
61	Essel (Neigh.)	51·37 N	7·15 E
61	Essen	51·28 N	7·01 E
61	Essenberg	51·26 N	6·42 E
68b	Essendon	37·46 S	144·55 E
54c	Essex	39·18 N	76·29 W
53	Essex Fells	40·50 N	74·17 W
54b	Essington	39·52 N	75·18 W
64e	Essling (Neigh.)	48·13 N	16·32 E
58a	Estrella, Cerro de la (Mtn.)	19·21 N	99·05 W
55b	Etna	40·30 N	79·57 W
52c	Etobicoke	43·39 N	79·34 W
60	Eton	51·31 N	0·37 W
56a	Evanston	42·02 N	87·42 W
52a	Everett	42·24 N	71·03 W
56a	Evergreen Park	41·43 N	87·42 W
62b	Everton (Neigh.)	53·25 N	2·58 W
61	Eving (Neigh.)	51·33 N	7·29 E
60	Ewell	51·21 N	0·15 W
69d	Ewu	6·33 N	3·19 E
60	Eynsford	51·22 N	0·13 E
64f	Eyüp (Neigh.)	41·03 N	28·55 E
69a	Ezbekīyah (Neigh.)	30·03 N	31·15 E

F

Page	Name Region	Lat. °′	Long. °′
52b	Fabreville (Neigh.)	45·34 N	73·50 W
63a	Fahrland	52·28 N	13·01 E
62b	Failsworth	53·31 N	2·09 W
68a	Fairfield, Austl.	33·52 S	150·57 E
53	Fairfield, NJ.	40·53 N	74·17 W
68a	Fairfield West	33·52 S	150·55 E
54d	Fairhaven	38·47 N	77·05 W
53	Fair Lawn	40·56 N	74·07 W
54d	Fairlee	38·52 N	77·16 W
54d	Fairmount Heights	38·54 N	76·55 W
60	Fairseat	51·20 N	0·20 E
53	Fairview	40·49 N	74·00 W
54a	Fairview Park	41·27 N	81·51 W
63a	Falkensee	52·33 N	13·04 E
54d	Falls Church	38·53 N	77·11 W
63e	Famadas	41·21 N	2·05 E
66h	Farazād	35·47 N	51·21 E
55c	Farmington	42·28 N	83·22 W
55c	Farmington Hills	42·28 N	83·23 W
60	Farnborough (Neigh.)	51·21 N	0·04 E
60	Farningham	51·23 N	0·13 E
62b	Farnworth	53·33 N	2·24 W
53	Far Rockaway (Neigh.)	40·36 N	73·45 W
64e	Favoriten (Neigh.)	48·11 N	16·23 E
60	Fawkham Green	51·22 N	0·17 E
68b	Fawkner	37·43 S	144·58 E
54d	Fawsett Farms	38·59 N	77·14 W
65b	Fengtai	39·51 N	116·16 E
63a	Ferbitz	52·30 N	13·01 E
64g	Ferencváros (Neigh.)	47·28 N	19·06 E
54c	Ferndale, Md.	39·11 N	76·38 W
55c	Ferndale, Mi.	42·28 N	83·08 W
68b	Ferntree Gully	37·53 S	145·18 E
68b	Ferny Creek	37·53 S	145·21 E
59d	Ferraz de Vasconcelos	23·32 S	46·22 W
62c	Ferrières	48·49 N	2·42 E
55a	Ferry Village	43·58 N	78·57 W
60	Fetcham	51·17 N	0·22 W
63a	Fichtenau	52·27 N	13·42 E
60	Fiddlers Hamlet	51·41 N	0·08 E
64b	Fili (Neigh.)	55·45 N	37·31 E
69b	Finaalspan	26·17 S	28·15 E
60	Finchley (Neigh.)	51·36 N	0·10 W
63a	Finkenkrug	52·34 N	13·03 E
62b	Firgrove	53·37 N	2·08 W
61	Fischeln (Neigh.)	51·18 N	6·35 E
56b	Fisherman's Wharf (P. Int.)	37·48 N	122·25 W
52c	Fisherville	43·47 N	79·28 W
62b	Fishpool	53·35 N	2·17 W
68b	Fitzroy	37·48 S	144·59 E
68a	Five Dock	33·52 S	151·08 E
53	Flatbush (Neigh.)	40·39 N	73·56 W
60	Flaunden	51·42 N	0·32 W
61	Flehe (Neigh.)	51·12 N	6·47 E
61	Fley (Neigh.)	51·23 N	7·30 E
61	Flingern (Neigh.)	51·14 N	6·49 E
53	Floral Park	40·43 N	73·42 W
57	Florence	33·58 N	118·15 W
69b	Florentia	26·16 S	28·08 E
58d	Flores (Neigh.)	34·38 S	58·28 W
58d	Floresta (Neigh.)	34·38 S	58·29 W
69b	Florida	26·11 S	27·55 E
58a	Flotantes, Jardines (P. Int.)	19·16 N	99·06 W
54b	Flourtown	40·07 N	75·13 W
53	Flower Hill	40·49 N	73·41 W
53	Flushing (Neigh.)	40·45 N	73·49 W
54b	Folcroft	39·54 N	75·17 W
54b	Folsom	39·54 N	75·19 W
69b	Fontainebleau	26·07 S	27·59 E
62c	Fontenay-aux-Roses	48·47 N	2·17 E
62c	Fontenay-le-Fleury	48·49 N	2·03 E
62c	Fontenay-sous-Bois	48·51 N	2·29 E
68b	Footscray	37·48 S	144·54 E
59c	Fora, Ponta de (C.)	22·57 S	43·07 W
65b	Forbidden City (P. Int.)	39·55 N	116·23 E
53	Fordham University (P. Int.)	40·51 N	73·53 W
53	Fords	40·32 N	74·19 W
69b	Fordsburg (Neigh.)	26·13 S	28·02 E
60	Forest Gate (Neigh.)	51·33 N	0·02 E
54d	Forest Heights	38·49 N	77·00 W
68b	Forest Hill	37·50 S	145·11 E
52c	Forest Hill (Neigh.)	43·42 N	79·24 W
55b	Forest Hills	40·26 N	79·52 W
53	Forest Hills (Neigh.)	40·42 N	73·51 W
56a	Forest Park	41·53 N	87·50 W
54c	Forest Park (Neigh.)	39·19 N	76·41 W
68a	Forestville, Austl.	33·46 S	151·13 E
54d	Forestville, Md.	38·50 N	76·52 W
62b	Formby	53·34 N	3·05 W
62b	Formby Pt.	53·33 N	3·06 W
65e	Fort (Neigh.)	18·56 N	72·50 E
55a	Fort Erie	42·54 N	78·56 W
54c	Fort Howard	39·12 N	76·27 W
53	Fort Lee	40·51 N	73·58 W
54c	Fort McHenry National Monument (P. Int.)	39·16 N	76·35 W
54d	Fort McNair (P. Int.)	38·52 N	77·04 W
55c	Fort Wayne Military Museum (P. Int.)	42·18 N	83·06 W
65a	Fort William (P. Int.)	22·33 N	88·20 E
56b	Foster City	37·34 N	122·16 W
62c	Fourqueux	48·53 N	2·04 E
55b	Fox Chapel	40·30 N	79·55 W
68a	Fox Valley	33·45 S	151·06 E
62c	Franconville	48·59 N	2·14 E
55b	Frank	40·16 N	79·48 W
62b	Frankby	53·22 N	3·08 W
54b	Frankford (Neigh.)	40·01 N	75·05 W
55c	Franklin	42·31 N	83·18 W
56a	Franklin Park, Il.	41·56 N	87·49 W
55b	Franklin Park, Pa.	40·35 N	80·06 W
54d	Franklin Park, Va.	38·55 N	77·09 W
69b	Franklin Roosevelt Park (Neigh.)	26·09 S	27·59 E
53	Franklin Square	40·43 N	73·40 W
55c	Fraser	42·32 N	82·57 W
63a	Fredersdorf bei Berlin	52·31 N	13·44 E
53	Freeport	40·39 N	73·35 W
61	Freisenbruch (Neigh.)	51·27 N	7·06 E
68a	French's Forest	33·45 S	151·14 E
62b	Freshfield	53·34 N	3·04 W
53	Fresh Meadows (Neigh.)	40·44 N	73·48 W
63a	Friedenau (Neigh.)	52·28 N	13·20 E
61	Friedrichsfeld	51·38 N	6·39 E
63a	Friedrichsfelde (Neigh.)	52·31 N	13·31 E
63a	Friedrichshagen (Neigh.)	52·27 N	13·38 E
63a	Friedrichshain (Neigh.)	52·31 N	13·27 E
61	Friemersheim	51·23 N	6·42 E
65d	Friends Colony (Neigh.)	28·34 N	77·16 E
54c	Friendship International Arpt.	39·11 N	76·40 W
60	Friern Barnet (Neigh.)	51·37 N	0·10 W
61	Frillendorf (Neigh.)	51·28 N	7·05 E
62b	Frodsham	53·18 N	2·44 W
63a	Frohnau (Neigh.)	52·38 N	13·18 E
61	Frohnhausen (Neigh.)	51·27 N	6·58 E
60	Fryerning	51·41 N	0·22 E
67a	Fuchū	35·40 N	139·29 E
63b	Fuencarral (Neigh.)	40·30 N	3·41 W
61	Fuhlenbrock (Neigh.)	51·32 N	6·54 E
67b	Fujiidera	34·34 N	135·36 E
67a	Fukagawa (Neigh.)	35·40 N	139·48 E
67b	Fukiai (Neigh.)	34·42 N	135·12 E
67b	Fukushima (Neigh.)	34·42 N	135·29 E
61	Fulerum (Neigh.)	51·26 N	6·57 E
57	Fullerton	33·52 N	117·55 W
60	Fulmer	51·33 N	0·34 W
67b	Funasaka	34·49 N	135·17 E
59c	Fundão, Ilha do (I.)	22·51 S	43·14 W
65e	Funde	18·54 N	72·58 E
67a	Futatsubashi	35·28 N	139·30 E
60	Fyfield	51·45 N	0·16 E

G

Page	Name Region	Lat. °′	Long. °′
62c	Gagny	48·53 N	2·32 E
61	Gahmen (Neigh.)	51·36 N	7·32 E
64f	Galata (Neigh.)	41·01 N	28·58 E
64f	Galata Köprüsü (P. Int.)	41·00 N	28·57 E
64d	Galátsion	38·01 N	23·45 E
68b	Galvin	37·51 S	144·49 E
65b	Gaobaita	39·53 N	116·30 E
65b	Gaobeidian	39·54 N	116·33 E
63c	Garbagnate Milanese	45·35 N	9·05 E
64c	Garbatella (Neigh.)	41·52 N	12·29 E
62c	Garches	48·51 N	2·11 E
57	Gardena	33·53 N	118·18 W
55c	Garden City, Mi.	42·20 N	83·20 W
53	Garden City, NY.	40·43 N	73·37 W
53	Garden City Park	40·44 N	73·40 W
57	Garden Grove	33·46 N	117·57 W
65a	Garden Reach	22·33 N	88·17 E
61	Garenfeld	51·24 N	7·31 E
53	Garfield	40·53 N	74·07 W
54a	Garfield Heights	41·26 N	81·37 W
62c	Garges-lès-Gonesse	48·58 N	2·25 E
54c	Garland	39·11 N	76·39 W
54c	Garrison	39·24 N	76·45 W
60	Garston	51·41 N	0·23 W
62b	Garston (Neigh.)	53·21 N	2·53 W
61	Gartenstadt (Neigh.)	51·30 N	7·26 E
65a	Garulia	22·49 N	88·22 E
53	Garwood	40·39 N	74·19 W
62b	Gateacre (Neigh.)	53·23 N	2·51 W

Page	Name Region	Lat. °′	Long. °′
65e	Gateway of India (P. Int.)	18·55 N	72·50 E
62b	Gatley	53·23 N	2·14 W
59a	Gato Negro	10·33 N	66·57 W
65e	Gāvanpāda	18·57 N	73·01 E
59c	Gávea (Neigh.)	22·58 S	43·14 W
62b	Gayton	53·19 N	3·06 W
62b	Gee Cross	53·26 N	2·04 W
61	Gellep-Stratum (Neigh.)	51·20 N	6·41 E
68b	Gellibrand, Pt.	37·52 S	144·54 E
61	Gelsenkirchen	51·31 N	7·07 E
58d	General Pacheco	34·28 S	58·40 W
58d	General San Martín	34·35 S	58·30 W
58d	General Sarmiento (San Miguel)	34·33 S	58·43 W
58d	General Urquiza (Neigh.)	34·34 S	58·29 W
61	Gennebreck	51·19 N	7·12 E
62c	Gennevilliers	48·56 N	2·18 E
62c	Gentilly	48·49 N	2·21 E
68a	Georges Hall	33·55 S	150·59 E
54d	Georgetown (Neigh.)	38·54 N	77·03 W
54d	Georgetown University (P. Int.)	38·54 N	77·04 W
69b	Gerdview	26·10 S	28·11 E
58d	Gerli (Neigh.)	34·41 S	58·23 W
54b	Germantown (Neigh.)	40·03 N	75·11 W
69b	Germiston	26·15 S	28·05 E
60	Gerrards Cross	51·35 N	0·34 W
63b	Getafe	40·18 N	3·43 W
55a	Getzville	43·01 N	78·46 W
61	Gevelsberg	51·19 N	7·20 E
61	Geweke (Neigh.)	51·22 N	7·25 E
65e	Ghārāpuri	18·54 N	72·56 E
65e	Ghātkopar (Neigh.)	19·05 N	72·54 E
65d	Ghāzipur (Neigh.)	28·38 N	77·19 E
65d	Ghonda (Neigh.)	28·41 N	77·16 E
65d	Ghondi (Neigh.)	28·42 N	77·16 E
65a	Ghushuri	22·37 N	88·22 E
66m	Gia-dinh	10·48 N	106·42 E
54b	Gibbsboro	39·50 N	74·58 W
52c	Gibraltar Pt.	43·36 N	79·23 W
60	Gidea Park (Neigh.)	51·35 N	0·12 E
62c	Gif-sur-Yvette	48·42 N	2·08 E
67a	Ginza (Neigh.)	35·40 N	139·47 E
65e	Girgaum (Neigh.)	18·57 N	72·48 E
69a	Giza Pyramids (P. Int.)	29·59 N	31·08 E
61	Gladbeck	51·34 N	6·59 E
68a	Gladesville	33·50 S	151·08 E
54b	Gladwyne	40·02 N	75·17 W
61	Glashütte (Neigh.)	51·13 N	6·52 E
54d	Glassmanor	38·49 N	76·59 W
55b	Glassport	40·19 N	79·54 W
61	Glehn	51·10 N	6·35 E
54d	Glenarden	38·56 N	76·52 W
53	Glen Cove	40·52 N	73·37 W
57	Glendale	34·10 N	118·17 W
57	Glendora, Ca.	34·08 N	117·52 W
54b	Glendora, NJ.	39·50 N	75·04 W
54d	Glen Echo	38·58 N	77·08 W
68a	Glenfield	33·58 S	150·54 E
53	Glen Head	40·50 N	73·37 W
68b	Glenhuntly	37·54 S	145·03 E
54c	Glenmore	39·11 N	76·36 W
54b	Glenolden	39·54 N	75·17 W
53	Glen Ridge	40·49 N	74·13 W
53	Glen Rock	40·58 N	74·08 W
68b	Glenroy	37·42 S	144·55 E
55b	Glenshaw	40·31 N	79·57 W
54b	Glenside	40·06 N	75·09 W
56a	Glenview	42·04 N	87·48 W
68b	Glen Waverley	37·53 S	145·10 E
53	Glenwood Landing	40·50 N	73·39 W
63a	Glienicke	52·37 N	13·19 E
54b	Gloucester City	39·54 N	75·07 W
60	Goff's Oak	51·43 N	0·05 W
65a	Golabāri	22·36 N	88·20 E
56b	Golden Gate (Str.)	37·49 N	122·29 W
60	Golders Green (Neigh.)	51·35 N	0·12 W
56a	Golf	42·03 N	87·48 W
56a	Golf Park Terrace	42·03 N	87·51 W
62c	Gonesse	48·59 N	2·27 E
58d	González Catán	34·46 S	58·39 W
68a	Gordon (Ku-ring-gai)	33·45 S	151·08 E
54d	Gordons Corner	38·50 N	76·57 W
68a	Gore Hill	33·49 S	151·11 E
62b	Gorton (Neigh.)	53·27 N	2·10 W
63a	Gosen	52·24 N	13·43 E
67a	Gotanno (Neigh.)	35·46 N	139·49 E
61	Götterswickerhamm	51·35 N	6·40 E
63a	Göttin	52·27 N	12·54 E
62c	Gournay-sur-Marne	48·52 N	2·34 E
62c	Goussainville	49·01 N	2·28 E
66m	Go-vap	10·49 N	106·42 E
59c	Governador, Ilha do (I.)	22·48 S	43·12 W
61	Grafenberg (Neigh.)	51·14 N	6·50 E
58a	Gran Canal del Desagüe (Can.)	19·29 N	99·05 W
55a	Grand Island	43·01 N	78·58 W
55a	Grand I.	43·02 N	78·58 W
55a	Grandyle	43·00 N	78·57 W
60	Grange Hill	51·37 N	0·05 E
54c	Granite	39·21 N	76·51 W
56a	Grant Park (P. Int.)	41·52 N	87·37 W
68a	Granville	33·50 S	151·01 E
62b	Grassendale (Neigh.)	53·21 N	2·54 W
60	Gravesend	51·27 N	0·24 E
60	Grays	51·29 N	0·20 E
62b	Greasby	53·23 N	3·07 W
62b	Great Altcar	53·33 N	3·01 W
60	Great Bookham	51·16 N	0·22 W
60	Great Burstead	51·36 N	0·25 E
62b	Great Crosby	53·29 N	3·01 W
54d	Great Falls	39·00 N	77·17 W
53	Great Kills (Neigh.)	40·33 N	74·10 W
53	Great Neck	40·47 N	73·44 W
60	Great Oxney Green	51·44 N	0·25 E
60	Great Parndon	51·45 N	0·05 E
62b	Great Sutton	53·17 N	2·56 W
60	Great Warley	51·35 N	0·17 E
63c	Greco (Neigh.)	45·30 N	9·13 E
54d	Greenbelt	39·01 N	76·53 W
56b	Greenbrae	37·57 N	122·31 W
52b	Greenfield Park	45·29 N	73·29 W
60	Greenhithe	51·27 N	0·17 E
54d	Green Meadows	38·58 N	76·57 W
62b	Greenmount	53·37 N	2·20 W
68b	Greensborough	37·42 S	145·06 E
69b	Greenside (Neigh.)	26·09 S	28·01 E
60	Greenstead	51·42 N	0·14 E
60	Green Street	51·40 N	0·16 W
60	Green Street Green (Neigh.)	51·21 N	0·04 E
53	Greenvale	40·49 N	73·38 W
68a	Green Valley	33·54 S	150·53 E
68a	Greenwich	33·50 S	151·11 E
60	Greenwich (Neigh.)	51·28 N	0·02 E
60	Greenwich Observatory (P. Int.)	51·28 N	0·00
53	Greenwich Village (Neigh.)	40·44 N	74·00 W
52a	Greenwood	42·29 N	71·04 W
61	Greiffenburg (P. Int.)	51·20 N	6·38 E
61	Grevel (Neigh.)	51·34 N	7·33 E
68a	Greystanes	0·00	0·00
61	Grimlinghausen (Neigh.)	51·10 N	6·44 E
64e	Grinzing (Neigh.)	48·15 N	16·21 E
63a	Grossbeeren	52·21 N	13·18 E
61	Grossenbaum (Neigh.)	51·22 N	6·47 E
64e	Gross-Enzersdorf	48·12 N	16·33 E
55c	Grosse Pointe	42·24 N	82·55 W
55c	Grosse Pointe Farms	42·25 N	82·53 W
55c	Grosse Pointe Park	42·23 N	82·56 W
55c	Grosse Pointe Woods	42·27 N	82·55 W
64e	Grossjedlersdorf (Neigh.)	48·17 N	16·25 E
63a	Gross Ziethen	52·24 N	13·27 E
61	Gruiten	51·14 N	7·01 E
61	Grumme (Neigh.)	51·30 N	7·14 E
63a	Grünau (Neigh.)	52·25 N	13·34 E
61	Grünewald	51·13 N	7·37 E
63a	Grunewald (Neigh.)	52·30 N	13·17 E
58a	Guadalupe, Basílica de (P. Int.)	19·29 N	99·07 W
59d	Guaianazes (Neigh.)	23·33 S	46·25 W
59a	Guaire (R.)	10·25 N	66·46 W
58b	Guanabacoa	23·07 N	82·18 W
59c	Guanabara, Baía de (B.)	22·50 S	43·10 W
65b	Guanyintang	39·52 N	116·31 E
59a	Guaracarumbo	10·34 N	66·59 W
59d	Guarulhos	23·28 S	46·32 W
62c	Guermantes	48·51 N	2·42 E
68a	Guildford	33·51 S	150·59 E
54b	Gulph Mills	40·04 N	75·21 W
58a	Gustavo A. Madero	19·29 N	99·07 W
53	Guttenberg	40·48 N	74·01 W
62c	Guyancourt	48·46 N	2·04 E

H

Page	Name Region	Lat. °′	Long. °′
61	Haan	51·11 N	7·00 E
61	Haar (Neigh.)	51·26 N	7·13 E
68a	Haberfield	33·53 S	151·08 E
67a	Hachiōji	35·39 N	139·20 E
57	Hacienda Heights	33·58 N	117·58 W
53	Hackensack	40·53 N	74·03 W
60	Hacketts	51·45 N	0·05 W
60	Hackney (Neigh.)	51·33 N	0·03 W
54b	Haddonfield	39·54 N	75·02 W
54b	Haddon Heights	39·52 N	75·02 W
64e	Hadersdorf (Neigh.)	48·13 N	16·14 E
68b	Hadfield	37·42 S	144·56 E
66b	Haemgon-ni (Neigh.)	37·35 N	126·49 E
61	Hagen	51·22 N	7·28 E
61	Hahnenberg	51·12 N	7·24 E
65d	Haidārpur (Neigh.)	28·43 N	77·09 E
65b	Haidian	39·59 N	116·18 E
67a	Haijima	35·42 N	139·21 E
60	Hainault (Neigh.)	51·36 N	0·06 E
61	Halden (Neigh.)	51·23 N	7·31 E
62b	Hale, Eng.	53·23 N	2·21 W
62b	Halebarns	53·22 N	2·19 W
53	Haledon	40·56 N	74·11 W
54c	Halethorpe	39·15 N	76·41 W
62b	Halewood	53·22 N	2·49 W
64f	Haliç (B.)	41·02 N	28·58 E
68b	Hallam	38·01 S	145·06 E
60	Halstead	51·20 N	0·08 E
61	Halver	51·11 N	7·30 E
60	Ham (Neigh.)	51·26 N	0·19 W
69b	Hamberg	26·11 S	27·53 E
61	Hamborn (Neigh.)	51·29 N	6·46 E
61	Hamm (Neigh.), F.R.G.	51·12 N	6·44 E
60	Hammersmith (Neigh.)	51·30 N	0·14 W
56a	Hammond	41·36 N	87·30 W
68a	Hammondville	33·57 S	150·57 E
60	Hampstead (Neigh.)	51·33 N	0·11 W
60	Hampstead Heath (P. Int.)	51·34 N	0·10 W
68b	Hampton	37·56 S	145·00 E
60	Hampton (Neigh.)	51·25 N	0·22 W
54c	Hampton National Historic Site (P. Int.)	39·25 N	76·35 W
55c	Hamtramck	42·24 N	83·03 W
62b	Handforth	53·21 N	2·13 W
66b	Han-gang (R.)	37·36 N	126·47 E
66c	Hang Hau Town	22·19 N	114·16 E
66m	Hanh-thong-tay	10·50 N	106·40 E
54c	Hanover	39·11 N	76·42 W
60	Hanworth (Neigh.)	51·26 N	0·23 W
62b	Hapsford	53·16 N	2·48 W
67a	Haramachida	35·33 N	139·27 E
57	Harbor City (Neigh.)	33·48 N	118·17 W
68a	Harbord	33·45 S	151·26 E
53	Harbor Isle	40·36 N	73·40 W
60	Harefield (Neigh.)	51·36 N	0·29 W
60	Haringey (Neigh.)	51·35 N	0·07 W
54b	Harker Village	39·51 N	75·09 W
53	Harlem (Neigh.)	40·49 N	73·56 W
60	Harlesden (Neigh.)	51·32 N	0·15 W
60	Harlington (Neigh.)	51·29 N	0·26 W
55b	Harmar Heights	40·33 N	79·49 W
55b	Harmarville	40·32 N	79·51 W
65d	Harola	28·36 N	77·19 E
60	Harold Hill (Neigh.)	51·36 N	0·13 E
60	Harold Wood (Neigh.)	51·36 N	0·14 E
61	Harpen (Neigh.)	51·29 N	7·16 E
55c	Harper Woods	42·24 N	82·55 W
62b	Harpurhey (Neigh.)	53·31 N	2·13 W
53	Harrison, NJ.	40·45 N	74·10 W
53	Harrison, NY.	40·58 N	73·43 W
54c	Harrisonville	39·23 N	77·50 W
68a	Harris Park	33·49 S	151·01 E
60	Harrow (Neigh.)	51·35 N	0·21 W
60	Harrow on the Hill (Neigh.)	51·34 N	0·20 W
60	Hartley	51·23 N	0·19 E
60	Harvel	51·21 N	0·22 E
56a	Harvey	41·37 N	87·39 W
55b	Harwick	40·34 N	79·48 W
62b	Harwood, Eng.	53·35 N	2·23 W
54c	Harwood, Md.	38·52 N	76·37 W
56a	Harwood Heights	41·59 N	87·48 W
54c	Harwood Park	39·12 N	76·44 W
66h	Ḩasanābād	35·44 N	51·19 E
53	Hasbrouck Heights	40·52 N	74·04 W
62b	Haskayne	53·34 N	2·58 W
64f	Hasköy (Neigh.)	41·02 N	28·58 E
61	Hasselbeck-Schwarzbach	51·16 N	6·53 E
61	Hassels (Neigh.)	51·10 N	6·53 E
61	Hasslinghausen	51·20 N	7·17 E
61	Hästen (Neigh.), F.R.G.	51·09 N	7·06 E
61	Hasten (Neigh.), F.R.G.	51·12 N	7·09 E
60	Hastingwood	51·45 N	0·09 E
61	Hattingen	51·23 N	7·10 E
60	Hatton (Neigh.)	51·28 N	0·25 W
67b	Hattori	34·46 N	135·27 E
61	Hatzfeld (Neigh.)	51·17 N	7·11 E
62b	Haughton Green	53·27 N	2·06 W
65d	Hauz Rāni (Neigh.)	28·32 N	77·13 E
58b	Havana	23·08 N	82·22 W
63a	Havel-Kanal (Can.)	52·36 N	13·12 E
54b	Haverford	40·01 N	75·18 W
60	Havering (Neigh.)	51·34 N	0·14 E
60	Havering-atte-Bower (Neigh.)	51·37 N	0·11 E
60	Havering's Grove	51·38 N	0·23 E
54b	Havertown	39·59 N	75·18 W
57	Hawaiian Gardens	33·50 N	118·04 W
69a	Ḩawf, Jabal (Hills)	29·55 N	31·21 E
60	Hawley	51·25 N	0·14 E
53	Haworth	40·58 N	73·59 W
68b	Hawthorn	37·49 S	145·02 E
57	Hawthorne, Ca.	33·55 N	118·21 W
53	Hawthorne, NJ.	40·57 N	74·09 W
60	Hayes (Neigh.), Eng.	51·23 N	0·01 E
62b	Hazel Grove	53·23 N	2·08 W
60	Headley	51·17 N	0·16 W
62b	Heald Green	53·22 N	2·14 W
68b	Heathmont	37·49 S	145·15 E
62b	Heaton Moor	53·25 N	2·11 W
60	Heaverham	51·18 N	0·15 E
62b	Heaviley	53·24 N	2·09 W
54c	Hebbville	39·20 N	77·46 W
61	Heerdt (Neigh.)	51·13 N	6·43 E
61	Heide (Neigh.), F.R.G.	51·31 N	6·52 E
68b	Heidelberg, Austl.	37·45 S	145·04 E
55b	Heidelberg, Pa.	40·23 N	80·05 W
61	Heil	51·38 N	7·35 E
61	Heiligenhaus	51·19 N	6·59 E
63a	Heiligensee (Neigh.)	52·36 N	13·13 E
63a	Heinersdorf	52·23 N	13·20 E
63a	Heinersdorf (Neigh.)	52·34 N	13·27 E
61	Heisingen (Neigh.)	51·25 N	7·04 E
69a	Heliopolis, see Miṣr al-Jadīdah (Neigh.)	30·06 N	31·20 E
69a	Heliopolis (P. Int.)	30·08 N	31·17 E
62b	Helsby	53·16 N	2·46 W
60	Hemel Hempstead	51·46 N	0·28 W
53	Hempstead	40·42 N	73·37 W
63a	Hennigsdorf	52·38 N	13·13 E
61	Herbede	51·25 N	7·16 E
61	Herdecke	51·24 N	7·26 E
64e	Hermannskogel (Mtn.)	48·16 N	16·18 E
57	Hermosa Beach	33·52 N	118·24 W
63a	Hermsdorf (Neigh.)	52·37 N	13·18 E
64e	Hernals (Neigh.)	48·13 N	16·20 E
61	Herne	51·32 N	7·13 E
54c	Hernwood Heights	39·22 N	77·50 W
58a	Héroes Chapultepec	19·28 N	99·04 W
58a	Héroes de Churubusco	19·22 N	99·06 W
60	Herongate	51·36 N	0·21 E
60	Heronsgate	51·38 N	0·31 W
60	Hersham	51·22 N	0·23 W
61	Herten	51·35 N	7·07 E
62b	Heswall	53·20 N	3·06 W
64e	Hetzendorf (Neigh.)	48·10 N	16·18 E
61	Heven (Neigh.)	51·26 N	7·17 E
53	Hewlett	40·38 N	73·42 W
53	Hewlett Harbor	40·38 N	73·41 W
60	Hextable	51·25 N	0·11 E
62b	Heywood	53·36 N	2·13 W
56a	Hickory Hills	41·43 N	87·49 W
53	Hicksville	40·46 N	73·32 W
61	Hiddinghausen	51·22 N	7·17 E
61	Hiesfeld	51·33 N	6·46 E
64e	Hietzing (Neigh.)	48·11 N	16·18 E
67b	Higashi (Neigh.)	34·41 N	135·31 E
67a	Higashimurayama	35·46 N	139·29 E
67b	Higashinada (Neigh.)	34·43 N	135·16 E
67a	Higashinakano	35·38 N	139·25 E
67b	Higashinari (Neigh.)	34·40 N	135·33 E
67a	Higashiōizumi (Neigh.)	35·45 N	139·36 E
67b	Higashiōsaka	34·39 N	135·35 E
67b	Higashisumiyoshi (Neigh.)	34·37 N	135·32 E
66e	Higashiyama (Neigh.)	34·52 N	135·48 E
67b	Higashiyodogawa (Neigh.)	34·44 N	135·29 E
60	Higham Upshire	51·26 N	0·28 E
60	High Beach	51·39 N	0·02 E
55b	Highcliff	40·32 N	80·03 W
62b	Higher Broughton (Neigh.)	53·30 N	2·15 W
55b	Highland	40·33 N	80·04 W
54d	Highland Park, Md.	38·54 N	76·54 W
55c	Highland Park, Mi.	42·24 N	83·06 W
69b	Highlands North (Neigh.)	26·09 S	28·05 E
60	High Laver	51·45 N	0·13 E
60	High Ongar	51·43 N	0·16 E
62b	Hightown	53·32 N	3·04 W
61	Hilden	51·10 N	6·56 E
69b	Hillbrow (Neigh.)	26·11 S	28·03 E
54b	Hill Crest	40·05 N	75·11 W
54d	Hillcrest Heights	38·52 N	76·57 W
61	Hillen (Neigh.)	51·37 N	7·13 E
60	Hillingdon (Neigh.)	51·32 N	0·27 W
54d	Hillside	38·52 N	76·55 W
53	Hillside (Neigh.)	40·42 N	73·47 W
54d	Hillwood	38·52 N	77·10 W
61	Hiltrop (Neigh.)	51·30 N	7·15 E
61	Himmelgeist (Neigh.)	51·10 N	6·49 E
52a	Hingham	42·14 N	70·53 W
52a	Hingham	42·17 N	70·55 W
67a	Hino	35·41 N	139·24 E
56a	Hinsdale	41·48 N	87·56 W
61	Hinsel (Neigh.)	51·26 N	7·05 E
67b	Hirota	34·45 N	135·21 E
64e	Hirschstetten (Neigh.)	48·14 N	16·29 E
60	Hither Green (Neigh.)	51·27 N	0·01 W
53	Hoboken	40·45 N	74·03 W
68b	Hobsons B.	37·51 S	144·56 E
61	Hochdahl	51·13 N	6·56 E
61	Hochheide	51·27 N	6·41 E
66m	Ho Chi Minh City (Saigon)	10·45 N	106·40 E
61	Hochlar (Neigh.)	51·36 N	7·10 E
61	Höchsten	51·27 N	7·29 E
56a	Hodgkins	41·46 N	87·51 W
64e	Hofburg (P. Int.)	48·12 N	16·22 E
58a	Hogar y Redención	19·22 N	99·13 W
61	Hohenlimburg	51·21 N	7·35 E
63a	Hohen-Neuendorf	52·40 N	13·16 E
63a	Hohenschönhausen (Neigh.)	52·33 N	13·30 E
61	Hohensyburg (P. Int.)	51·25 N	7·29 E
61	Höhscheid (Neigh.)	51·09 N	7·04 E
61	Hoisten	51·08 N	6·42 E
60	Holborn (Neigh.)	51·31 N	0·07 W
52a	Holbrook	42·09 N	71·01 W
62b	Hollins	53·34 N	2·17 W
53	Hollis (Neigh.)	40·43 N	73·46 W
57	Hollywood (Neigh.)	34·06 N	118·21 W
57	Hollywood Bowl (P. Int.)	34·07 N	118·20 W
54b	Holmes	39·54 N	75·19 W
54d	Holmes Run Acres	38·51 N	77·13 W
68a	Holroyd	33·50 S	150·58 E
61	Holten (Neigh.)	51·31 N	6·48 E
61	Holthausen (Neigh.)	51·34 N	7·26 E
61	Holzen	51·26 N	7·31 E
61	Holzheim	51·09 N	6·39 E
61	Holzwickede	51·30 N	7·36 E
61	Homberg, F.R.G.	51·28 N	6·43 E

Page	Name Region	Lat. °′	Long. °′
58d	Mariano Acosta	34·40 S	58·50 W
58d	Mariano J. Haedo	34·39 S	58·36 W
59c	Maria Paula	22·54 S	43·02 W
68b	Maribyrnong	37·46 S	144·54 E
63a	Mariendorf (Neigh.)	52·26 N	13·23 E
63a	Marienfelde (Neigh.)	52·25 N	13·22 E
66g	Marikina	14·37 N	121·06 E
57	Marina del Rey	33·59 N	118·28 W
57	Marina del Rey (B.)	33·58 N	118·27 W
56b	Marin City	37·52 N	122·21 W
57	Marineland of the Pacific (P. Int.)	33·44 N	118·24 W
62c	Marly-le-Roi	48·52 N	2·05 E
62c	Marne (R.)	48·49 N	2·25 E
62c	Marolles-en-Brie	48·44 N	2·33 E
68a	Maroubra	33·57 S	151·16 E
62b	Marple	53·24 N	2·03 W
68a	Marrickville	33·55 S	151·09 E
61	Marscheid (Neigh.)	51·14 N	7·14 E
68a	Marsfield	33·47 S	151·07 E
61	Marten (Neigh.)	51·31 N	7·23 E
58d	Martínez (Neigh.)	34·29 S	58·30 W
63d	Marvila (Neigh.)	38·44 N	9·06 W
63a	Marwitz	52·41 N	13·09 E
54d	Maryland Park	38·53 N	76·54 W
63a	Marzahn (Neigh.)	52·33 N	13·33 E
68a	Mascot	33·56 S	151·12 E
54d	Masonville	38·51 N	77·12 W
53	Maspeth (Neigh.)	40·43 N	73·55 W
52a	Massachusetts B.	42·20 N	70·50 W
52a	Massachusetts Institute of Technology (P. Int.)	42·21 N	71·06 W
53	Massapequa	40·40 N	73·29 W
62c	Massy	48·44 N	2·17 E
67b	Matsubara	34·34 N	135·33 E
67a	Matsudo	35·47 N	139·54 E
64g	Mátyásföld (Neigh.)	47·31 N	19·13 E
64g	Mátyas-Templom (P. Int.)	47·30 N	19·02 E
59d	Mauá	23·40 S	46·27 W
64e	Mauer (Neigh.)	48·09 N	16·16 E
62c	Maurecourt	49·00 N	2·04 E
54b	Mayfair (Neigh.), Pa.	40·02 N	75·03 W
69b	Mayfair (Neigh.), S. Afr.	26·12 S	28·01 E
69b	Mayfair West (Neigh.)	26·12 S	28·00 E
57	Maywood, Ca.	33·59 N	118·11 W
56a	Maywood, Il.	41·53 N	87·51 W
53	Maywood, NJ.	40·56 N	74·04 W
64b	Mazilovo (Neigh.)	55·44 N	37·26 E
58b	Mazorra	23·01 N	82·24 W
69b	Meadowlands	26·13 S	27·54 E
61	Meckinghoven	51·37 N	7·19 E
52a	Medford	42·25 N	71·07 W
52a	Medford Hillside	42·24 N	71·07 W
54b	Media	39·54 N	75·23 W
64b	Medvedkovo (Neigh.)	55·53 N	37·38 E
61	Meerbusch	51·15 N	6·41 E
67a	Meguro (Neigh.)	35·38 N	139·42 E
65d	Mehpālpur (Neigh.)	28·33 N	77·08 E
66h	Mehrābād	35·40 N	51·20 E
65d	Mehram Nagar (Neigh.)	28·34 N	77·07 E
63a	Mehrow	52·34 N	13·37 E
61	Mehrum	51·35 N	6·37 E
61	Meide	51·11 N	6·55 E
61	Meiderich (Neigh.)	51·28 N	6·46 E
64e	Meidling (Neigh.)	48·11 N	16·20 E
61	Meiersberg	51·17 N	6·57 E
67a	Meiji Shrine (P. Int.)	35·41 N	139·42 E
68b	Melbourne	37·49 S	144·58 E
62b	Melling	53·30 N	2·56 W
52a	Melrose	42·27 N	71·04 W
52a	Melrose Highlands	42·28 N	71·04 W
56a	Melrose Park	41·54 N	87·51 W
61	Menden (Neigh.)	51·24 N	6·54 E
61	Mengede (Neigh.)	51·34 N	7·23 E
61	Menglinghausen (Neigh.)	51·28 N	7·25 E
53	Menlo Park Terrace	40·32 N	74·20 W
68b	Mentone	37·59 S	145·05 E
60	Meopham	51·22 N	0·22 E
60	Meopham Station	51·23 N	0·21 E
63e	Mercader y Millás	41·21 N	2·05 E
63d	Mercês	38·47 N	9·19 W
66k	Merdeka Palace (P. Int.)	6·10 S	106·49 E
62b	Mere	53·20 N	2·25 W
69b	Meredale	26·17 S	27·59 E
54b	Merion Station	40·00 N	75·15 W
58d	Merlo	34·40 S	58·45 W
68b	Merlynston	37·43 S	144·58 E
53	Merrick	40·40 N	73·33 W
54d	Merrifield	38·52 N	77·14 W
56a	Merrionette Park	41·41 N	87·42 W
68a	Merrylands	33·50 S	150·59 E
61	Merscheid (Neigh.)	51·10 N	7·01 E
62b	Mersey (R.)	53·26 N	3·01 W
60	Merton (Neigh.)	51·25 N	0·12 W
64b	Meščerskij	55·40 N	37·25 E
59c	Mesquita	22·48 S	43·26 W
62c	Messy	48·58 N	2·42 E
53	Metropolitan Museum of Art (P. Int.)	40·47 N	73·58 W
61	Mettmann	51·15 N	6·58 E
62c	Meudon	48·48 N	2·14 E
58a	Mexico City (Ciudad de México)	19·24 N	99·09 W
66b	Mia-dong (Neigh.)	37·37 N	127·01 E
64b	Michajlovskoje	55·35 N	37·35 E
57	Michillinda	34·07 N	118·05 W
54a	Middleburgh Heights	41·22 N	81·48 W
54c	Middle River	39·19 N	76·27 W
62b	Middleton	53·33 N	2·13 W
53	Midland Beach (Neigh.)	40·34 N	74·05 W
56a	Midlothian	41·38 N	87·42 W
69b	Midway	26·18 S	27·51 E
57	Midway City	33·45 N	118·00 W
63c	Milan (Milano)	45·28 N	9·12 E
54c	Milford	39·21 N	76·44 W
54b	Millbourne	39·58 N	75·15 W
56b	Millbrae	37·36 N	122·24 W
53	Millburn	40·44 N	74·20 W
60	Mill Green	51·41 N	0·22 E
60	Mill Hill (Neigh.)	51·37 N	0·13 W
53	Mill Neck	40·52 N	73·34 W
55b	Millvale	40·29 N	79·58 W
56b	Mill Valley	37·54 N	122·32 W
54b	Milmont Park	39·53 N	75·20 W
62b	Milnrow	53·37 N	2·06 W
62c	Milon-la-Chapelle	48·44 N	2·03 E
61	Milspe	51·18 N	7·21 E
52a	Milton	42·15 N	71·05 W
66e	Minami (Neigh.), Jap.	34·58 N	135·45 E
67a	Minamisenju (Neigh.)	35·44 N	139·48 E
67a	Minato (Neigh.), Jap.	35·39 N	139·45 E
67b	Minato (Neigh.), Jap.	34·39 N	135·26 E
53	Mineola	40·45 N	73·38 W
67b	Minō	34·50 N	135·28 E
61	Mintard	51·22 N	6·54 E
68a	Minto	34·01 S	150·51 E
54b	Miquon	40·04 N	75·16 W
58c	Miraflores	12·08 S	77·03 W
58b	Miramar (Neigh.)	23·07 N	82·25 W
68a	Miranda	34·02 S	151·06 E
65a	Mirzāpur	22·50 N	88·24 E
64b	Misailovo	55·34 N	37·49 E
69a	Mişr al-Jadīdah (Heliopolis) (Neigh.)	30·06 N	31·20 E
69a	Mişr al-Qadīmah (Old Cairo) (Neigh.)	30·00 N	31·14 E
52c	Mississauga	43·35 N	79·37 W
67a	Mitaka	35·40 N	139·33 E
68b	Mitcham	37·49 S	145·12 E
60	Mitcham (Neigh.)	51·24 N	0·10 W
62c	Mitry-Mory	48·59 N	2·37 E
63a	Mitte (Neigh.)	52·31 N	13·24 E
58a	Mixcoac (Neigh.)	19·23 N	99·12 W
67b	Miyakojima (Neigh.)	34·43 N	135·33 E
67a	Mizonokuchi	35·36 N	139·37 E
67a	Mizonuma	35·48 N	139·36 E
67a	Mizue (Neigh.)	35·41 N	139·54 E
67a	Mizuho	35·46 N	139·21 E
64b	Mnevniki (Neigh.)	55·45 N	37·28 E
69d	Moba	6·27 N	3·28 E
69b	Modderbee	26·10 S	28·24 E
69b	Modderfontein	26·06 S	28·09 E
57	Modjeska	33·43 N	117·37 W
64e	Mödling	48·05 N	16·17 E
61	Moers	51·27 N	6·37 E
69b	Mofolo	26·14 S	27·53 E
65e	Mohili (Neigh.)	19·06 N	72·53 E
58a	Molino de Rosas	19·22 N	99·13 W
63e	Molins de Rey	41·25 N	2·01 E
61	Möllen	51·35 N	6·42 E
63e	Moncada	41·29 N	2·11 E
69b	Mondeor	26·17 S	28·00 E
63e	Mongat	41·28 N	2·17 E
60	Monken Hadley (Neigh.)	51·40 N	0·11 W
55b	Monongahela (R.)	40·27 N	80·00 W
57	Monrovia	34·09 N	118·03 W
59a	Montalbancito	10·28 N	66·59 W
56b	Montara	37·33 N	122·31 W
57	Montclair, Ca.	34·06 N	117·41 W
53	Montclair, NJ.	40·49 N	74·13 W
57	Montebello	34·01 N	118·06 W
58d	Monte Chingolo (Neigh.)	34·45 S	58·20 W
57	Monterey Park	34·04 N	118·07 W
64c	Montespaccato (Neigh.)	41·54 N	12·23 E
64c	Monteverde Nuovo (Neigh.)	41·51 N	12·27 E
62c	Montfermeil	48·54 N	2·34 E
63e	Montflorit	41·29 N	2·08 E
62c	Montgeron	48·42 N	2·27 E
54c	Montgomery Knolls	39·14 N	76·48 W
62c	Montigny-le-Bretonneux	48·46 N	2·02 E
62c	Montigny-lès-Cormeilles	48·59 N	2·12 E
63e	Montjuich, Castillo de (P. Int.)	41·22 N	2·10 E
62c	Montmagny	48·58 N	2·21 E
62c	Montmartre (Neigh.)	48·53 N	2·21 E
68b	Montmorency, Austl.	37·43 S	145·07 E
62c	Montmorency, Fr.	49·00 N	2·20 E
52b	Montréal	45·31 N	73·34 W
52b	Montréal-Nord	45·36 N	73·38 W
52b	Montréal-Quest	45·27 N	73·39 W
62c	Montreuil	48·52 N	2·27 E
68b	Montrose	37·49 S	145·21 E
55b	Montrose Hill	40·30 N	79·51 W
62c	Montrouge	48·49 N	2·19 E
52b	Mont-Royal	45·31 N	73·39 W
63c	Monza	45·35 N	9·16 E
59d	Moóca (Neigh.)	23·33 S	46·35 W
53	Moonachie	40·50 N	74·03 W
68b	Moorabbin	37·56 S	145·02 E
68a	Moorebank	33·56 S	150·56 E
54b	Moorestown	39·58 N	74·57 W
68b	Mooroolbark	37·47 S	145·19 E
62b	Moorside	53·34 N	2·04 W
62c	Morangis	48·42 N	2·20 E
68b	Mordialloc	38·00 S	145·05 E
58a	Morelos (Neigh.)	19·27 N	99·07 W
58d	Moreno	34·39 S	58·48 W
62b	Moreton	53·24 N	3·07 W
67b	Moriguchi	34·44 N	135·34 E
63c	Morivione (Neigh.)	45·26 N	9·12 E
62b	Morley Green	53·20 N	2·16 W
54d	Morningside	38·50 N	76·53 W
58d	Morón	34·39 S	58·37 W
58b	Morro, Castillo del (P. Int.)	23·09 N	82·21 W
61	Mörsenbroich (Neigh.)	51·15 N	6·48 E
68a	Mortlake	33·51 S	151·07 E
60	Mortlake (Neigh.)	51·28 N	0·16 W
54b	Morton	39·55 N	75·20 W
56a	Morton Grove	42·02 N	87·47 W
63d	Moscavide	38·47 N	9·06 W
64b	Moscow (Moskva)	55·45 N	37·35 E
64d	Moskhāton	37·57 N	23·41 E
68a	Mosman	33·49 S	151·14 E
62b	Moss Bank	53·29 N	2·44 W
56b	Moss Beach	37·32 N	122·31 W
54d	Moss Crest	38·55 N	77·15 W
62b	Mossley	53·32 N	2·02 W
62b	Mossley Hill (Neigh.)	53·23 N	2·55 W
60	Mottingham (Neigh.)	51·26 N	0·03 E
57	Mount Baldy	34·14 N	117·40 W
52c	Mount Dennis (Neigh.)	43·42 N	79·30 W
68a	Mount Druitt	33·46 S	150·49 E
54b	Mount Ephraim	39·53 N	75·06 W
56a	Mount Greenwood (Neigh.)	41·42 N	87·43 W
54c	Mount Hebron	39·18 N	76·50 W
55b	Mount Lebanon	40·23 N	80·03 W
60	Mountnessing	51·39 N	0·21 E
55b	Mount Oliver	40·28 N	79·59 W
68a	Mount Pritchard	33·54 S	150·54 E
56a	Mount Prospect	42·04 N	87·56 W
54d	Mount Rainier	38·56 N	76·58 W
53	Mount Vernon, NY.	40·54 N	73·50 W
55b	Mount Vernon, Pa.	40·17 N	79·48 W
54c	Mount Washington (Neigh.)	39·22 N	76·40 W
54c	Mount Washington Summit	39·23 N	76·40 W
68b	Mount Waverley	37·53 S	145·08 E
54b	Moylan	39·54 N	75·23 W
60	Mucking	51·30 N	0·26 E
63a	Mühlenbeck	52·40 N	13·22 E
64e	Lower New York B.	48·10 N	16·34 E
65d	Mujāhidpur (Neigh.)	28·34 N	77·13 E
66e	Mukō	34·56 N	135·42 E
61	Mülheim an der Ruhr	51·24 N	6·54 E
63a	Münchehofe	52·30 N	13·40 E
61	Mündelheim (Neigh.)	51·21 N	6·41 E
55b	Munhall	40·24 N	79·53 W
65d	Munirka (Neigh.)	28·34 N	77·10 E
58d	Munro (Neigh.)	34·32 S	58·31 W
67a	Murayama	35·45 N	139·23 E
63d	Murtal	38·42 N	9·22 W
67a	Musashino	35·42 N	139·34 E
69d	Mushin	6·32 N	3·22 E
69a	Musturud	30·08 N	31·17 E
64b	Mytischi	55·55 N	37·46 E

N

Page	Name Region	Lat. °′	Long. °′
61	Nächstebreck (Neigh.)	51·18 N	7·14 E
67b	Nagao	34·50 N	135·43 E
66e	Nagaoka	34·55 N	135·42 E
67b	Nagata (Neigh.)	34·40 N	135·09 E
64b	Nagatino (Neigh.)	55·41 N	37·41 E
67a	Nagatsuta (Neigh.)	35·32 N	139·30 E
64g	Nagytarcsa	47·32 N	19·17 E
52a	Nahant	42·25 N	70·55 W
52a	Nahant B.	42·27 N	70·55 W
61	Nahmer	51·20 N	7·35 E
69a	Nāhyā	30·03 N	31·07 E
65a	Naihāti	22·54 N	88·25 E
67a	Naka (R.)	35·39 N	139·51 E
66e	Nakagyō (Neigh.)	35·01 N	135·45 E
67a	Nakajima	35·26 N	139·56 E
67a	Nakanobu (Neigh.)	35·36 N	139·43 E
67a	Namamugi (Neigh.)	35·29 N	139·41 E
69b	Nancefield	26·17 S	27·53 E
67b	Naniwa (Neigh.)	34·39 N	135·30 E
65e	Nānole (Neigh.)	19·01 N	72·55 E
62c	Nanterre	48·53 N	2·12 E
62c	Nantouillet	49·00 N	2·42 E
66a	Nanxiang	31·17 N	121·18 E
65b	Nanyuan	39·48 N	116·23 E
65a	Naoābād	22·28 N	88·27 E
65a	Naopukuria	22·55 N	88·16 E
65a	Nārāyanpāra	22·54 N	88·19 E
54b	Narberth	40·01 N	75·18 W
68a	Narrabeen	33·43 S	151·18 E
68a	Narraweena	33·45 S	151·16 E
68b	Narre Warren North	37·59 S	145·19 E
67b	Naruo	34·43 N	135·23 E
65a	Nātāgarh	22·42 N	88·25 E
69b	Natalspruit	26·19 S	28·09 E
54b	National Park	39·51 N	75·12 W
65e	Naupada (Neigh.)	19·04 N	72·50 E
60	Navestock	51·39 N	0·13 E
60	Navestock Side	51·39 N	0·16 E
66g	Navotas	14·40 N	120·57 E
65d	Nayābās	28·35 N	77·19 E
69a	Nazlat as-Sammān	29·59 N	31·08 E
69a	Nazlat Khalīfah	30·01 N	31·10 E
69c	Ndjili (Neigh.)	4·20 S	15·22 E
64d	Néa Ionía	38·02 N	23·45 E
64d	Néa Liósia	38·02 N	23·42 E
56a	Near North Side (Neigh.)	41·54 N	87·38 W
64d	Néa Smírni	37·57 N	23·43 E
63a	Nedlitz (Neigh.)	52·26 N	13·03 E
52a	Needham	42·17 N	71·14 W
52a	Needham Heights	42·18 N	71·14 W
65c	Nee Soon	1·24 N	103·49 E
66h	Nematābād	35·38 N	51·21 E
64b	Nemčinovka	55·43 N	37·23 E
64d	Néon Psikhikón	38·00 N	23·47 E
62b	Ness	53·17 N	3·03 W
62b	Neston	53·18 N	3·04 W
62b	Netherton	53·30 N	2·58 W
61	Nette (Neigh.)	51·33 N	7·25 E
61	Neudorf (Neigh.)	51·25 N	6·47 E
63a	Neuenhagen bei Berlin	52·32 N	13·41 E
61	Neuenhof (Neigh.)	51·10 N	7·13 E
61	Neuenkamp (Neigh.)	51·26 N	6·44 E
64e	Neu-Erlaa (Neigh.)	48·08 N	16·19 E
63a	Neu Fahrland	52·26 N	13·03 E
62c	Neuilly-sur-Marne	48·51 N	2·32 E
62c	Neuilly-sur-Seine	48·53 N	2·16 E
61	Neukirchen-Vluyn	51·27 N	6·33 E
61	Neuss	51·12 N	6·41 E
61	Neusserweyhe (Neigh.)	51·13 N	6·39 E
64e	Neustift am Walde (Neigh.)	48·15 N	16·18 E
62c	Neuville-sur-Oise	49·01 N	2·04 E
64e	Neuwaldegg (Neigh.)	48·14 N	16·17 E
64a	Neva (R.)	59·55 N	30·15 E
59c	Neves	22·51 S	43·06 W
61	Neviges	51·19 N	7·05 E
55b	Neville I.	40·31 N	80·08 W
65a	Newabāgam	22·48 N	88·24 E
60	New Addington (Neigh.)	51·21 N	0·01 W
53	Newark	40·44 N	74·10 W
62b	New Brighton	53·26 N	3·03 W
53	New Brighton (Neigh.)	40·38 N	74·06 W
54a	Newburgh Heights	41·27 N	81·40 W
54d	New Carrollton	38·58 N	76·53 W
69b	Newclare (Neigh.)	26·11 S	27·58 E
65d	New Delhi	28·36 N	77·12 E
60	New Eltham (Neigh.)	51·26 N	0·04 E
62b	New Ferry	53·22 N	2·59 W
60	Newgate Street	51·44 N	0·07 W
60	Newham (Neigh.)	51·32 N	0·03 E
62b	New Hey	53·36 N	2·06 W
53	New Hyde Park	40·44 N	73·41 W
60	New Hythe	51·19 N	0·27 E
66c	New Kowloon (Xinjiulong)	22·20 N	114·10 E
69d	New Lagos (Neigh.)	6·30 N	3·22 E
69b	Newmarket	26·17 S	28·08 E
53	New Milford	40·56 N	74·01 W
68b	Newport	37·51 S	144·53 E
69b	New Redruth	26·16 S	28·07 E
53	New Rochelle	40·55 N	73·47 W
52a	Newton	42·21 N	71·11 W
52c	Newton Brook (Neigh.)	43·48 N	79·24 W
52a	Newton Highlands	42·19 N	71·13 W
52a	Newton Lower Falls	42·19 N	71·23 W
52a	Newton Upper Falls	42·19 N	71·13 W
52a	Newtonville	42·21 N	71·13 W
68a	Newtown (Neigh.)	33·54 S	151·11 E
53	New Utrecht (Neigh.)	40·36 N	73·59 W
53	New York	40·43 N	74·01 W
67b	Neyagawa	34·46 N	135·38 E
69c	Ngamouéri	4·14 S	15·14 E
69c	Ngombe	4·24 S	15·11 E
55a	Niagara Falls, Can.	43·06 N	79·04 W
55a	Niagara Falls, NY.	43·06 N	79·02 W
61	Niederaden (Neigh.)	51·36 N	7·34 E
61	Niederbonsfeld	51·23 N	7·08 E
61	Niederdonk	51·14 N	6·41 E
61	Niederelfringhausen	51·21 N	7·10 E
63a	Nieder-Neuendorf	52·37 N	13·12 E
63a	Niederschöneweide (Neigh.)	52·27 N	13·31 E
63a	Niederschönhausen (Neigh.)	52·35 N	13·23 E
59c	Niemeyer (Neigh.)	23·00 S	43·15 W
61	Nierst	51·19 N	6·43 E
67a	Nihonbashi (Neigh.)	35·41 N	139·47 E
67a	Niiza	35·48 N	139·34 E
64d	Níkaia	37·58 N	23·39 E
64b	Nikolo-Chovanskoje	55·36 N	37·27 E
56a	Niles	42·01 N	87·49 W
65a	Nilgani	22·46 N	88·26 E
59c	Nilópolis	22·49 S	43·25 W
60	Nine Ashes	51·42 N	0·18 E
67b	Nishi	34·41 N	135·30 E
67b	Nishinari (Neigh.)	34·38 N	135·28 E
67b	Nishinomiya	34·43 N	135·20 E
67b	Nishiyodogawa (Neigh.)	34·42 N	135·27 E

Page	Name Region	Lat. °′	Long. °′
63b	Prado, Museo del (P. Int.)	40·25 N	3·41 W
58a	Prado Churubusco	19·21 N	99·07 W
68b	Prahran	37·51 S	144·59 E
63d	Praia da Cruz Quebrada	38·42 N	9·14 W
63e	Prat del Llobregat	41·20 N	2·06 E
60	Pratt's Bottom (Neigh.)	51·20 N	0·07 E
62b	Prenton	53·22 N	3·03 W
63a	Prenzlauer Berg (Neigh.)	52·32 N	13·26 E
62b	Prescot	53·26 N	2·48 W
59d	Presidente Roosevelt, Estação (P. Int.)	23·33 S	46·36 W
56b	Presidio of San Francisco (P. Int.)	37·48 N	122·28 W
68b	Preston	37·45 S	145·01 E
62b	Prestwich	53·32 N	2·17 W
54b	Primos	39·55 N	75·18 W
69b	Primrose	26·12 S	28·10 E
68a	Prospect	33·48 S	150·56 E
56a	Prospect Heights	42·06 N	87·56 W
53	Prospect Park, NJ.	40·56 N	74·10 W
54b	Prospect Park, Pa.	39·53 N	75·19 W
69b	Protea	26·17 S	27·51 E
59b	Providencia	33·26 S	70·37 W
62b	Puddington	53·15 N	3·00 W
58c	Pueblo Libre	12·08 S	77·05 W
63b	Pueblo Nuevo (Neigh.)	40·26 N	3·39 W
56a	Pullman (Neigh.)	41·43 N	87·36 W
54c	Pumphrey	39·13 N	76·38 W
68a	Punchbowl	33·56 S	151·03 E
65c	Punggol	1·25 N	103·55 E
58b	Punta Brava	23·01 N	82·30 W
60	Purfleet	51·29 N	0·15 E
64e	Purkersdorf	48·12 N	16·11 E
60	Purley (Neigh.)	51·20 N	0·07 W
62c	Puteaux	48·53 N	2·14 E
69b	Putfontein	26·08 S	28·24 E
65d	Puth Kalān (Neigh.)	28·43 N	77·05 E
64b	Putilkovo	55·52 N	37·23 E
60	Putney (Neigh.)	51·28 N	0·13 W
61	Pütt	51·11 N	6·59 E
68a	Pymble	33·45 S	151·09 E
60	Pyrford	51·19 N	0·30 W

Q

Page	Name Region	Lat. °′	Long. °′
66h	Qaṣr-e Fīrūzeh	35·40 N	51·32 E
66a	Qibao	31·09 N	121·20 E
65b	Qieshikou	39·59 N	116·24 E
65b	Qinghe	40·01 N	116·20 E
65b	Qinghuayuan	40·00 N	116·19 E
64c	Quadraro (Neigh.)	41·51 N	12·33 E
68a	Quakers Hill	33·43 S	150·53 E
63d	Queluz	38·45 N	9·15 W
61	Querenburg (Neigh.)	51·27 N	7·16 E
66g	Quezon City	14·38 N	121·00 E
58d	Quilmes	34·43 S	58·15 W
52a	Quincy	42·15 N	71·01 W
52a	Quincy B.	42·17 N	70·58 W
59b	Quinta Normal	33·27 S	70·42 W
63c	Quinto Romano (Neigh.)	45·29 N	9·05 E
59d	Quitaúna	23·31 S	46·47 W

R

Page	Name Region	Lat. °′	Long. °′
61	Raadt (Neigh.)	51·24 N	6·56 E
64e	Raasdorf	48·15 N	16·34 E
62b	Raby	53·19 N	3·02 W
69b	Raceview	26·17 S	28·08 E
62b	Radcliffe	53·34 N	2·20 W
61	Radevormwald	51·12 N	7·21 E
60	Radlett	51·42 N	0·20 W
54b	Radnor	40·02 N	75·21 W
58d	Rafael Castillo	34·42 S	58·37 W
61	Rahm (Neigh.)	51·21 N	6·47 E
63a	Rahnsdorf (Neigh.)	52·26 N	13·42 E
53	Rahway	40·37 N	74·17 W
62b	Rainford	53·30 N	2·48 W
62b	Rainhill	53·26 N	2·46 W
62b	Rainhill Stoops	53·24 N	2·45 W
65d	Rājpur (Neigh.)	28·41 N	77·12 E
64g	Rákoscsaba (Neigh.)	47·29 N	19·17 E
64g	Rákoshegy (Neigh.)	47·28 N	19·14 E
64g	Rákoskeresztúr (Neigh.)	47·29 N	19·15 E
64g	Rákosliget (Neigh.)	47·30 N	19·16 E
64g	Rákospalota (Neigh.)	47·34 N	19·08 E
64g	Rákosszentmihály (Neigh.)	47·32 N	19·11 E
64b	Ramenka (Neigh.)	55·41 N	37·30 E
62b	Ramsbottom	53·40 N	2·19 W
60	Ramsden Heath	51·38 N	0·28 E
68a	Ramsgate	33·59 S	151·08 E
54c	Ranchleigh	39·22 N	76·40 W
57	Rancho Palos Verdes	33·45 N	118·24 W
54c	Randallstown	39·22 N	76·48 W
69b	Randburg	26·06 S	27·59 E
52a	Randolph	42·10 N	71·03 W
68a	Randwick	33·55 S	151·15 E
63d	Ranholas	38·47 N	9·22 W
55b	Rankin	40·25 N	79·53 W
61	Rath (Neigh.)	51·17 N	6·49 E
61	Rathmecke	51·15 N	7·38 E
61	Ratingen	51·18 N	6·51 E
69b	Ravenswood	26·11 S	28·15 E

Page	Name Region	Lat. °′	Long. °′
54d	Ravensworth	38·48 N	77·13 W
54d	Ravenwood	38·52 N	77·09 W
52a	Reading	42·31 N	71·07 W
52a	Readville (Neigh.)	42·14 N	71·08 W
58c	Real Felipe, Castillo (P. Int.)	12·04 S	77·09 W
54b	Rebel Hill	40·04 N	75·20 W
61	Recklinghausen	51·36 N	7·13 E
61	Recklinghausen-Süd (Neigh.)	51·34 N	7·13 E
58d	Reconquista (R.)	34·27 S	58·36 W
54b	Red Bank	39·52 N	75·10 W
60	Redbridge (Neigh.)	51·34 N	0·05 E
62b	Reddish	53·26 N	2·09 W
55c	Redford (Neigh.)	42·25 N	83·16 W
55c	Redford Township	42·25 N	83·16 W
57	Red Hill	33·45 N	117·48 W
57	Redondo Beach	33·51 N	118·23 W
56b	Redwood City	37·29 N	122·13 W
68a	Regents Park	33·53 S	151·02 E
60	Regent's Park (P. Int.)	51·32 N	0·09 W
58b	Regla	23·08 N	82·20 W
53	Rego Park (Neigh.)	40·44 N	73·52 W
61	Reh	51·22 N	7·33 E
61	Reisholz (Neigh.)	51·11 N	6·52 E
58d	Remedios de Escalada (Neigh.)	34·43 S	58·23 W
61	Remscheid	51·11 N	7·11 E
59b	Renca	33·24 S	70·44 W
59b	Renca, Cerro (Mtn.)	33·23 S	70·43 W
57	Reseda (Neigh.)	34·12 N	118·31 W
68b	Reservoir	37·43 S	145·00 E
61	Resse (Neigh.)	51·34 N	7·07 E
63b	Retiro, Parque del (P. Int.)	40·25 N	3·41 W
61	Reusrath	51·06 N	6·57 E
64b	Reutov	55·46 N	37·52 E
52a	Revere	42·24 N	71·01 W
68a	Revesby	33·57 S	151·01 E
66h	Rey	35·35 N	51·25 E
61	Rheinberg	51·33 N	6·35 E
61	Rheinen	51·27 N	7·38 E
61	Rheinhausen	51·24 N	6·44 E
61	Rhein-Herne-Kanal (Can.)	51·27 N	6·47 E
61	Rheinkamp	51·30 N	6·37 E
61	Rhine (Rhein) (R.)	51·52 N	6·02 E
63c	Rho	45·32 N	9·02 E
68a	Rhodes, Austl.	33·50 S	151·05 E
62b	Rhodes, Eng.	53·33 N	2·14 W
62c	Rhodon	48·43 N	2·04 E
68b	Richmond, Austl.	37·49 S	145·00 E
56b	Richmond, Ca.	37·57 N	122·22 W
60	Richmond (Neigh.), Eng.	51·28 N	0·18 W
54b	Richmond (Neigh.), Pa.	39·59 N	75·06 W
54a	Richmond Heights	41·33 N	81·29 W
53	Richmond Hill (Neigh.)	40·42 N	73·49 W
53	Richmondtown Restoration (P. Int.)	40·34 N	74·09 W
53	Richmond Valley (Neigh.)	40·31 N	74·13 W
68b	Ricketts Pt.	38·00 S	145·02 E
60	Rickmansworth	51·39 N	0·29 W
60	Ridge	51·41 N	0·15 W
53	Ridgefield	40·50 N	74·00 W
53	Ridgefield Park	40·51 N	74·01 W
53	Ridgewood	40·59 N	74·07 W
53	Ridgewood (Neigh.)	40·42 N	73·53 W
54b	Ridley Park	39·53 N	75·19 W
61	Riemke (Neigh.)	51·30 N	7·13 E
69b	Rietvlei	26·18 S	28·03 E
58c	Rímac	12·02 S	77·03 W
58c	Rímac (R.)	12·02 S	77·09 W
58b	Rincón	22·57 N	82·25 W
68b	Ringwood	37·49 S	145·14 E
68b	Ringwood North	37·48 S	145·14 E
59c	Rio Comprido (Neigh.)	22·55 S	43·12 W
59c	Rio de Janeiro	22·54 S	43·15 W
63d	Rio de Mouro	38·46 N	9·20 W
59a	Río Grande	10·35 N	66·57 W
60	Ripley	51·18 N	0·29 W
65a	Rishra	22·43 N	88·21 E
54d	Ritchie	38·52 N	76·52 W
65d	Rithāla (Neigh.)	28·43 N	77·06 E
54d	Riverdale	38·58 N	76·55 W
53	Riverdale (Neigh.)	40·54 N	73·54 W
53	River Edge	40·56 N	74·02 W
56a	River Forest	41·53 N	87·49 W
56a	River Grove	41·56 N	87·50 W
60	Riverhead	51·17 N	0·10 E
56a	Riverside, Il.	41·50 N	87·49 W
54b	Riverside, NJ.	40·02 N	74·58 W
56a	Robbins	41·39 N	87·42 W
69b	Robertsham (Neigh.)	26·15 S	28·00 E
69b	Robinson	26·09 S	27·43 E
59c	Rocha Miranda (Neigh.)	22·52 S	43·22 W
59c	Rocha Sobrinho	22·47 S	43·25 W
53	Rochelle Park	40·55 N	74·04 W
53	Rockaway Park (Neigh.)	40·35 N	73·50 W
53	Rockaway Point (Neigh.)	40·33 N	73·55 W
54d	Rock Creek Park (P. Int.)	38·58 N	77·03 W
68a	Rockdale, Austl.	33·57 S	151·08 E

Page	Name Region	Lat. °′	Long. °′
54c	Rockdale, Md.	39·21 N	76·46 W
53	Rockefeller Center (P. Int.)	40·45 N	74·00 W
62b	Rock Ferry	53·22 N	3·00 W
52a	Rockland	42·08 N	70·55 W
54b	Rockledge	40·03 N	75·05 W
53	Rockville Centre	40·40 N	73·37 W
54a	Rocky (R.)	41·30 N	81·49 W
66c	Rocky Hbr.	22·20 N	114·19 E
54a	Rocky River	41·30 N	81·40 W
62c	Rocquencourt	48·50 N	2·07 E
60	Roehampton (Neigh.)	51·27 N	0·14 W
68a	Rogans Hill	33·44 S	151·01 E
56a	Rogers Park (Neigh.)	42·01 N	87·40 W
61	Rohdenhaus	51·18 N	7·01 E
61	Röhlinghausen (Neigh.)	51·36 N	7·14 E
63a	Rohrbeck	52·32 N	13·02 E
62c	Roissy	48·47 N	2·39 E
62c	Roissy-en-France	49·00 N	2·31 E
69b	Roksana	26·07 S	28·04 E
67a	Rokugō (Neigh.)	35·33 N	139·43 E
54c	Rolling Acres	39·17 N	76·52 W
61	Röllinghausen (Neigh.)	51·31 N	7·08 E
57	Rolling Hills	33·46 N	118·21 W
62c	Romainville	48·53 N	2·26 E
64c	Rome (Roma)	41·54 N	12·29 E
62b	Romiley	53·25 N	2·05 W
69b	Rondebult	26·18 S	28·14 E
61	Ronsdorf (Neigh.)	51·14 N	7·12 E
69b	Roodepoort-Maraisburg	26·10 S	27·52 E
53	Roosevelt	40·41 N	73·36 W
68a	Rooty Hill	33·46 S	150·50 E
68b	Rosanna	37·45 S	145·04 E
69b	Rosebank (Neigh.)	26·09 S	28·02 E
68a	Rosebury (Neigh.)	33·55 S	151·12 E
52c	Rosedale (Neigh.), Can.	43·41 N	79·22 W
53	Rosedale (Neigh.), NY.	40·39 N	73·45 W
56a	Roseland (Neigh.)	41·42 N	87·38 W
53	Roselle	40·40 N	74·16 W
57	Rosemead	34·04 N	118·03 W
52b	Rosemère	45·38 N	73·48 W
56a	Rosemont, Il.	41·59 N	87·52 W
54b	Rosemont, Pa.	40·01 N	75·19 W
69b	Roseneath	26·17 S	28·11 E
63a	Rosenthal (Neigh.)	52·36 N	13·23 E
54b	Rose Tree	39·56 N	75·23 W
68a	Roseville, Austl.	33·47 S	151·11 E
55c	Roseville, Mi.	42·30 N	82·56 W
53	Roslyn, NY.	40·48 N	73·39 W
54b	Roslyn, Pa.	40·07 N	75·08 W
53	Roslyn Estates	40·47 N	73·40 W
53	Roslyn Heights	40·47 N	73·39 W
62c	Rosny-sous-Bois	48·53 N	2·29 E
68a	Rossmore	33·57 S	150·46 E
54c	Rossville	39·20 N	76·29 W
62b	Rostherne	53·21 N	2·23 W
64e	Roth-neusiedl (Neigh.)	48·08 N	16·23 E
57	Rowland Heights	33·59 N	117·54 W
68b	Rowville	37·56 S	145·14 E
52b	Roxboro	45·31 N	73·48 W
54b	Roxborough (Neigh.)	40·02 N	75·13 W
53	Roxbury (Neigh.)	40·34 N	73·54 W
60	Royal Albert Hall (P. Int.)	51·30 N	0·11 W
60	Royal Naval College (P. Int.)	51·29 N	0·01 W
55c	Royal Oak	42·30 N	83·08 W
55c	Royal Oak Township	42·27 N	83·10 W
52c	Royal Ontario Museum (P. Int.)	43·40 N	79·24 W
62b	Royton	53·34 N	2·08 W
68a	Rozelle	33·52 S	151·10 E
63a	Rüdersdorf	52·29 N	13·47 E
59d	Rudge Ramos	23·41 S	46·34 W
61	Rüdinghausen (Neigh.)	51·27 N	7·25 E
63a	Rudow (Neigh.)	52·25 N	13·30 E
62c	Rueil-Malmaison	48·53 N	2·11 E
61	Rüggeberg	51·16 N	7·22 E
63a	Ruhlsdorf	52·23 N	13·16 E
61	Ruhr (R.)	51·27 N	6·44 E
61	Ruhrort (Neigh.)	51·26 N	6·45 E
60	Ruislip (Neigh.)	51·34 N	0·25 W
64b	Rum'ancevo	55·38 N	37·26 E
64f	Rumelihisarı (Neigh.)	41·05 N	29·03 E
61	Rumeln-Kaldenhausen	51·24 N	6·40 E
63a	Rummelsburg (Neigh.)	52·30 N	13·29 E
61	Rummenohl	51·17 N	7·32 E
62b	Runcorn	53·20 N	2·44 W
54b	Runnemede	39·51 N	75·04 W
60	Runnymede (P. Int.)	51·26 N	0·34 W
55b	Rural Ridge	40·35 N	79·50 W
62b	Rusholme (Neigh.)	53·27 N	2·12 W
53	Russell Gardens	40·47 N	73·43 W
69b	Rusville	26·10 S	28·18 E
53	Rutherford	40·49 N	74·07 W
54b	Rutledge	39·54 N	75·20 W
61	Rüttenscheid (Neigh.)	51·26 N	7·00 E
60	Ryarsh	51·19 N	0·24 E
54b	Rydal	40·06 N	75·06 W
68a	Rydalmere	33·49 S	151·02 E
68a	Ryde	33·49 S	151·06 E
53	Rye	40·59 N	73·41 W
69b	Rynfield	26·09 S	28·20 E

S

Page	Name Region	Lat. °′	Long. °′
61	Saarn (Neigh.)	51·24 N	6·53 E
61	Saarnberg (Neigh.)	51·25 N	6·53 E
64b	Saburovo (Neigh.)	55·38 N	37·42 E
63d	Sacavém	38·47 N	9·06 W
62c	Sacré-Cœur (P. Int.)	48·53 N	2·21 E
63a	Sacrow (Neigh.)	52·26 N	13·06 E
53	Saddle Brook	40·54 N	74·06 W
53	Saddle Rock	40·48 N	73·45 W
65d	Safdar Jang's Tomb (P. Int.)	28·36 N	77·13 E
67a	Sagamihara	35·32 N	139·23 E
66m	Saigon, see Ho Chi Minh City	10·45 N	106·40 E
68b	Saint Albans, Austl.	37·45 S	144·48 E
60	Saint Albans, Eng.	51·46 N	0·21 W
53	Saint Albans (Neigh.)	40·42 N	73·46 W
60	Saint Albans Cathedral (P. Int.)	51·45 N	0·20 W
69c	Saint Anne of the Congo (P. Int.)	4·16 S	15·17 E
62c	Saint-Brice-sous-Forêt	49·00 N	2·21 E
52c	Saint-Bruno	45·32 N	73·21 W
55c	Saint Clair Shores	42·30 N	82·54 W
62c	Saint-Cloud	48·51 N	2·13 E
62c	Saint-Cyr-l'Ecole	48·48 N	2·04 E
54b	Saint Davids	40·02 N	75·22 W
62c	Saint-Denis	48·56 N	2·22 E
52b	Sainte-Dorothée (Neigh.)	45·32 N	73·49 W
52b	Saint-Eustache	45·33 N	73·53 W
52b	Sainte-Geneviève	45·29 N	73·52 W
53	Saint George (Neigh.)	40·39 N	74·05 W
62c	Saint-Germain-en-Laye	48·54 N	2·05 E
62c	Saint-Gratien	48·58 N	2·17 E
52b	Sainte-Hélène, Île (I.)	45·31 N	73·32 W
62b	Saint Helens	53·28 N	2·44 W
52b	Saint-Hubert	45·30 N	73·25 W
68a	Saint Ives	33·44 S	151·10 E
55a	Saint Johnsburg	43·05 N	78·53 W
53	Saint John's University (P. Int.)	40·43 N	73·48 W
68b	Saint Kilda	37·52 S	144·59 E
52c	Saint-Lambert	45·30 N	73·30 W
52b	Saint Laurent	45·30 N	73·40 W
62c	Saint-Mandé	48·50 N	2·25 E
60	Saint Mary Cray (Neigh.)	51·23 N	0·07 E
60	Saint Marylebone (Neigh.)	51·31 N	0·10 W
68a	Saint Marys	33·47 S	150·47 E
62c	Saint-Maur-des-Fossés	48·48 N	2·30 E
62c	Saint-Maurice	48·49 N	2·25 E
62c	Saint-Mesmes	48·59 N	2·42 E
52b	Saint-Michel	45·35 N	73·35 W
62c	Saint-Nom-la-Bretèche	48·51 N	2·01 E
62c	Saint-Ouen	48·54 N	2·20 E
60	Saint Pancras (Neigh.)	51·32 N	0·07 W
60	Saint Paul's Cathedral (P. Int.)	51·31 N	0·06 W
60	Saint Paul's Cray (Neigh.)	51·24 N	0·07 E
52b	Saint-Pierre	45·27 N	73·39 W
62c	Saint-Prix	49·01 N	2·16 E
62c	Saint-Rémy-lès-Chevreuse	48·42 N	2·04 E
52b	Sainte-Rose (Neigh.)	45·36 N	73·47 W
52b	Sainte-Thérèse-de-Blainville	45·38 N	73·51 W
62c	Saint-Thibault-des-Vignes	48·52 N	2·41 E
52b	Saint-Vincent-de-Paul (Neigh.)	45·37 N	73·39 W
67b	Sakai	34·35 N	135·28 E
62b	Sale	53·26 N	2·19 W
52a	Salem	42·31 N	70·55 W
62b	Salford	53·28 N	2·18 W
65a	Salkhia	22·35 N	88·21 E
65d	Samāika (Neigh.)	28·32 N	77·05 E
58a	San Andrés Totoltepec	19·15 N	99·10 W
59a	San Antonio de Galipán	10·33 N	66·53 W
57	San Antonio Heights	34·10 N	117·40 W
63e	San Bartolomé de la Cuadra	41·26 N	2·02 E
63e	San Baudilio de Llobregat	41·21 N	2·03 E
56b	San Bruno	37·37 N	122·25 W
56b	San Carlos	37·31 N	122·16 W
66d	Sanchung	25·04 N	121·29 E
63e	San Clemente de Llobregat	41·20 N	2·00 E
63e	San Cugat del Vallés	41·28 N	2·05 E
60	Sanderstead (Neigh.)	51·20 N	0·05 W
57	San Dimas	34·06 N	117·49 W
68b	Sandringham	37·57 S	145·00 E
69b	Sandringham (Neigh.)	26·09 S	28·07 E
53	Sands Point	40·51 N	73·43 W
58a	San Felipe Terremotos	19·22 N	99·04 W
63e	San Feliu de Llobregat	41·23 N	2·03 E
58d	San Fernando	34·26 S	58·34 W
56b	San Francisco	37·48 N	122·24 W
56b	San Francisco B.	37·43 N	122·17 W
58a	San Francisco Culhuacán	19·20 N	99·06 W
58b	San Francisco de Paula	23·04 N	82·18 W

glossary of foreign geographical terms

Annam ... Annamese
Arab ... Arabic
Bantu ... Bantu
Bur ... Burmese
Camb ... Cambodian
Celt ... Celtic
Chn ... Chinese
Czech ... Czech
Dan ... Danish
Du ... Dutch
Fin ... Finnish
Fr ... French
Ger ... German
Gr ... Greek
Hung ... Hungarian
Ice ... Icelandic
India ... India
Indian ... American Indian
Indon ... Indonesian
It ... Italian
Jap ... Japanese
Kor ... Korean
Mal ... Malayan
Mong ... Mongolian
Nor ... Norwegian
Per ... Persian
Pol ... Polish
Port ... Portuguese
Rom ... Romanian
Rus ... Russian
Siam ... Siamese
So. Slav ... Southern Slavonic
Sp ... Spanish
Swe ... Swedish
Tib ... Tibetan
Tur ... Turkish
Yugo ... Yugoslav

å, *Nor., Swe* ... brook, river
aa, *Dan., Nor* ... brook
aas, *Dan., Nor* ... ridge
āb, *Per* ... water, river
abad, *India, Per* ... town, city
ada, *Tur* ... island
adrar, *Berber* ... mountain
air, *Indon* ... stream
akrotírion, *Gr* ... cape
älf, *Swe* ... river
alp, *Ger* ... mountain
altipiano, *It* ... plateau
alto, *Sp* ... height
archipel, *Fr* ... archipelago
archipiélago, *Sp* ... archipelago
arquipélago, *Port* ... archipelago
arroyo, *Sp* ... brook, stream
ås, *Nor., Swe* ... ridge
austral, *Sp* ... southern
baai, *Du* ... bay
bab, *Arab* ... gate, port
bach, *Ger* ... brook, stream
backe, *Swe* ... hill
bad, *Ger* ... bath, spa
bahía, *Sp* ... bay, gulf
bahr, *Arab* ... river, sea, lake
baia, *It* ... bay, gulf
baía, *Port* ... bay
baie, *Fr* ... bay, gulf
bajo, *Sp* ... depression
bak, *Indon* ... stream
bakke, *Dan., Nor* ... hill
balkan, *Tur* ... mountain range
bana, *Jap* ... point, cape
banco, *Sp* ... bank
bandar, *Mal., Per.* ... town, port, harbor
bang, *Siam* ... village
bassin, *Fr* ... basin
batang, *Indon., Mal* ... river
ben, *Celt* ... mountain, summit
bender, *Arab* ... harbor, port
bereg, *Rus* ... coast, shore
berg, *Du., Ger., Nor., Swe.* ... mountain, hill
bir, *Arab* ... well
birkat, *Arab* ... lake, pond, pool
bit, *Arab* ... house
bjaerg, *Dan., Nor* ... mountain
bocche, *It* ... mouth
boğazı, *Tur* ... strait
bois, *Fr* ... forest, wood
boloto, *Rus* ... marsh
bolsón, *Sp* ... flat-floored desert valley
boreal, *Sp* ... northern
borg, *Dan., Nor., Swe* ... castle, town
borgo, *It* ... town, suburb
bosch, *Du* ... forest, wood
bouche, *Fr* ... river mouth
bourg, *Fr* ... town, borough
bro, *Dan., Nor., Swe* ... bridge
brücke, *Ger* ... bridge
bucht, *Ger* ... bay, bight
bugt, *Dan., Nor., Swe* ... bay, gulf
bulu, *Indon* ... mountain
burg, *Du., Ger* ... castle, town
buri, *Siam* ... town
burun, burnu, *Tur* ... cape
by, *Dan., Nor., Swe* ... village
caatinga, *Port. (Brazil)* ... open brushland
cabezo, *Sp* ... summit
cabo, *Port., Sp* ... cape
campo, *It., Port., Sp* ... plain, field
campos, *Port. (Brazil)* ... plains
cañón, *Sp* ... canyon
cap, *Fr* ... cape
capo, *It* ... cape
casa, *It., Port., Sp* ... house
castello, *It., Port* ... castle, fort
castillo, *Sp* ... castle
càte, *Fr* ... hill
çay, *Tur* ... stream, river
cayo, *Sp* ... rock, shoal, islet
cerro, *Sp* ... mountain, hill
champ, *Fr* ... field
chang, *Chn* ... village, middle
château, *Fr* ... castle
chen, *Chn* ... market town
chiang, *Chn* ... river
chott, *Arab* ... salt lake
chou, *Chn* ... capital of district; island
chu, *Tib* ... water, stream
cidade, *Port* ... town, city
cima, *Sp* ... summit, peak
città, *It* ... town, city
ciudad, *Sp* ... town, city
cochilha, *Port* ... ridge
col, *Fr* ... pass
colina, *Sp* ... hill
cordillera, *Sp* ... mountain chain
costa, *It., Port., Sp* ... coast
côte, *Fr* ... coast
cuchilla, *Sp* ... mountain ridge
dağ, *Tur* ... mountain(s)
dake, *Jap* ... peak, summit
dal, *Dan., Du., Nor., Swe* ... valley
dan, *Kor* ... point, cape
danau, *Indon* ... lake
dar, *Arab* ... house, abode, country
darya, *Per* ... river, sea
dasht, *Per* ... plain, desert
deniz, *Tur* ... sea
désert, *Fr* ... desert
deserto, *It* ... desert
desierto, *Sp* ... desert
détroit, *Fr* ... strait
dijk, *Du* ... dam, dike
djebel, *Arab* ... mountain
do, *Kor* ... island
dorf, *Ger* ... village
dorp, *Du* ... village
duin, *Du* ... dune
dzong, *Tib.* ... fort, administrative capital
eau, *Fr* ... water
ecuador, *Sp* ... equator
eiland, *Du* ... island
elv, *Dan., Nor* ... river, stream
embalse, *Sp* ... reservoir
erg, *Arab* ... dune, sandy desert
est, *Fr., It* ... east
estado, *Sp* ... state
este, *Port., Sp* ... east
estrecho, *Sp* ... strait
étang, *Fr* ... pond, lake
état, *Fr* ... state
eyjar, *Ice* ... islands
feld, *Ger* ... field, plain
festung, *Ger* ... fortress
fiume, *It* ... river
fjäll, *Swe* ... mountain
fjärd, *Swe* ... bay, inlet
fjeld, *Nor* ... mountain, hill
fjord, *Dan., Nor* ... fiord, inlet
fjördur, *Ice* ... fiord, inlet
fleuve, *Fr* ... river
flod, *Dan., Swe* ... river
flói, *Ice* ... bay, marshland
fluss, *Ger* ... river
foce, *It* ... river mouth
fontein, *Du* ... a spring
forêt, *Fr* ... forest
fors, *Swe* ... waterfall
forst, *Ger* ... forest
fos, *Dan., Nor* ... waterfall
fu, *Chn* ... town, residence
fuente, *Sp* ... spring, fountain
fuerte, *Sp* ... fort
furt, *Ger* ... ford
gang, *Kor* ... stream, river
gangri, *Tib* ... mountain
gat, *Dan., Nor* ... channel
gàve, *Fr* ... stream
gawa, *Jap* ... river
gebergte, *Du* ... mountain range
gebiet, *Ger* ... district, territory
gebirge, *Ger* ... mountains
ghat, *India* ... pass, mountain range
gobi, *Mong* ... desert
gol, *Mong* ... river
göl, gölü, *Tur* ... lake
golf, *Du., Ger* ... gulf, bay
golfe, *Fr* ... gulf, bay
golfo, *It., Port., Sp* ... gulf, bay
gomba, gompa, *Tib* ... monastery
gora, *Rus., So. Slav* ... mountain
góra, *Pol* ... mountain
gorod, *Rus* ... town
grad, *Rus., So. Slav* ... town
guba, *Rus* ... bay, gulf
gundung, *Indon* ... mountain
guntō, *Jap* ... archipelago
gunung, *Mal* ... mountain
haf, *Swe* ... sea, ocean
hafen, *Ger* ... port, harbor
haff, *Ger* ... gulf, inland sea
hai, *Chn* ... sea, lake
hama, *Jap* ... beach, shore
hamada, *Arab* ... rocky plateau
hamn, *Swe* ... harbor
hāmūn, *Per* ... swampy lake, plain
hantō, *Jap* ... peninsula
hassi, *Arab* ... well, spring
haus, *Ger* ... house
haut, *Fr* ... summit, top
hav, *Dan., Nor* ... sea, ocean
havn, *Dan., Nor* ... harbor, port
havre, *Fr* ... harbor, port
háza, *Hung* ... house, dwelling of
heim, *Ger* ... hamlet, home
hem, *Swe* ... hamlet, home
higashi, *Jap* ... east
hisar, *Tur* ... fortress
hissar, *Arab* ... fort
ho, *Chn* ... river
hoek, *Du* ... cape
hof, *Ger* ... court, farmhouse
höfn, *Ice* ... harbor
hoku, *Jap* ... north
holm, *Dan., Nor., Swe* ... island
hora, *Czech* ... mountain
horn, *Ger* ... peak
hoved, *Dan., Nor* ... cape
hsien, *Chn* ... district, district capital
hu, *Chn* ... lake
hügel, *Ger* ... hill
huk, *Dan., Swe* ... point
hus, *Dan., Nor., Swe* ... house
île, *Fr* ... island
ilha, *Port* ... island
indsö, *Dan., Nor* ... lake
insel, *Ger* ... island
insjö, *Swe* ... lake
irmak, irmagi, *Tur* ... river
isla, *Sp* ... island
isola, *It* ... island
istmo, *It., Sp* ... isthmus
järvi, jaur, *Fin* ... lake
jebel, *Arab* ... mountain
jima, *Jap* ... island
jökel, *Nor* ... glacier
joki, *Fin* ... river
jökull, *Ice* ... glacier
kaap, *Du* ... cape
kai, *Jap* ... bay, gulf, sea
kaikyō, *Jap* ... channel, strait
kalat, *Per* ... castle, fortress
kale, *Tur* ... fort
kali, *Mal* ... creek, river
kand, *Per* ... village
kang, *Chn* ... mountain ridge; village
kap, *Dan., Ger* ... cape
kapp, *Nor., Swe* ... cape
kasr, *Arab* ... fort, castle
kawa, *Jap* ... river
kefr, *Arab* ... village
kei, *Jap* ... creek, river
ken, *Jap* ... prefecture
khor, *Arab* ... bay, inlet
khrebet, *Rus* ... mountain range
kiang, *Chn* ... large river
king, *Chn* ... capital city, town
kita, *Jap* ... north
ko, *Jap* ... lake
köbstad, *Dan* ... market-town
kol, *Mong* ... lake
kólpos, *Gr* ... gulf
kong, *Chn* ... river
kopf, *Ger* ... head, summit, peak
köpstad, *Swe* ... market-town
körfezi, *Tur* ... gulf
kosa, *Rus* ... spit
kou, *Chn* ... river mouth
köy, *Tur* ... village
kraal, *Du. (Africa)* ... native village
ksar, *Arab* ... fortified village
kuala, *Mal* ... bay, river mouth
kuh, *Per* ... mountain
kum, *Tur* ... sand
kuppe, *Ger* ... summit
küste, *Ger* ... coast
kyo, *Jap* ... town, capital
la, *Tib* ... mountain pass
labuan, *Mal* ... anchorage, port
lac, *Fr* ... lake
lago, *It., Port., Sp* ... lake
lagoa, *Port* ... lake, marsh
laguna, *It., Port., Sp* ... lagoon, lake
lahti, *Fin* ... bay, gulf
län, *Swe* ... county
landsby, *Dan., Nor* ... village
liehtao, *Chn* ... archipelago
liman, *Tur* ... bay, port
ling, *Chn* ... pass, ridge, mountain
llanos, *Sp* ... plains
loch, *Celt. (Scotland)* ... lake, bay
loma, *Sp* ... long, low hill
lough, *Celt. (Ireland)* ... lake, bay
machi, *Jap* ... town
man, *Kor* ... bay
mar, *Port., Sp* ... sea
mare, *It., Rom* ... sea
marisma, *Sp* ... marsh, swamp
mark, *Ger* ... boundary, limit
massif, *Fr* ... block of mountains
mato, *Port* ... forest, thicket
me, *Siam* ... river
meer, *Du., Ger* ... lake, sea
mer, *Fr* ... sea
mesa, *Sp* ... flat-topped mountain
meseta, *Sp* ... plateau
mina, *Port., Sp* ... mine
minami, *Jap* ... south
minato, *Jap* ... harbor, haven
misaki, *Jap* ... cape, headland
mont, *Fr* ... mount, mountain
montagna, *It* ... mountain
montagne, *Fr* ... mountain
montaña, *Sp* ... mountain
monte, *It., Port., Sp.* ... mount, mountain
more, *Rus., So. Slav* ... sea
morro, *Port., Sp* ... hill, bluff
mühle, *Ger* ... mill
mund, *Ger* ... mouth, opening
mündung, *Ger* ... river mouth
mura, *Jap* ... township
myit, *Bur* ... river
mys, *Rus* ... cape
nada, *Jap* ... sea
nadi, *India* ... river, creek
naes, *Dan., Nor* ... cape
nafud, *Arab* ... desert of sand dunes
nagar, *India* ... town, city
nahr, *Arab* ... river
nam, *Siam* ... river, water
nan, *Chn., Jap* ... south
näs, *Nor., Swe* ... cape
nez, *Fr* ... point, cape
nishi, nisi, *Jap* ... west
njarga, *Fin* ... peninsula
nong, *Siam* ... marsh
noord, *Du* ... north
nor, *Mong* ... lake
nord, *Dan., Fr., Ger., It., Nor., Swe* ... north
norte, *Port., Sp* ... north
nos, *Rus* ... cape
nyasa, *Bantu* ... lake
ö, *Dan., Nor., Swe* ... island
occidental, *Sp* ... western
ocna, *Rom* ... salt mine
odde, *Dan., Nor* ... point, cape
oedjoeng, *Mal* ... point, cape
oeste, *Port., Sp* ... west
oka, *Jap* ... hill
oost, *Du* ... east
oriental, *Sp* ... eastern
óros, *Gr* ... mountain
ost, *Ger., Swe* ... east
öster, *Dan., Nor., Swe* ... eastern
ostrov, *Rus* ... island
oued, *Arab* ... river, stream
ouest, *Fr* ... west
ozero, *Rus* ... lake
pää, *Fin* ... mountain
padang, *Mal* ... plain, field
pampas, *Sp. (Argentina)* ... grassy plains
pará, *Indian (Brazil)* ... river
pas, *Fr* ... channel, passage
paso, *Sp* ... mountain pass, passage
passo, *It., Port.* ... mountain pass, passage, strait
patam, *India* ... city, town
pei, *Chn* ... north
pélagos, *Gr* ... open sea
pegunungan, *Indon* ... mountains
peña, *Sp* ... rock
peresheyek, *Rus* ... isthmus
pertuis, *Fr* ... strait
peski, *Rus* ... desert
pic, *Fr* ... mountain peak
pico, *Port., Sp* ... mountain peak
piedra, *Sp* ... stone, rock
ping, *Chn* ... plain, flat
planalto, *Port* ... plateau
planina, *Yugo* ... mountains
playa, *Sp* ... shore, beach
pnom, *Camb* ... mountain
pointe, *Fr* ... point
polder, *Du., Ger* ... reclaimed marsh
polje, *So. Slav* ... plain, field
poluostrov, *Rus* ... peninsula
pont, *Fr* ... bridge
ponta, *Port* ... point, headland
ponte, *It., Port* ... bridge
pore, *India* ... city, town
porthmós, *Gr* ... strait
porto, *It., Port* ... port, harbor
potamós, *Gr* ... river
p'ov, *Rus* ... peninsula
prado, *Sp* ... field, meadow
presqu'île, *Fr* ... peninsula
proliv, *Rus* ... strait
pu, *Chn* ... commercial village
pueblo, *Sp* ... town, village
puerto, *Sp* ... port, harbor
pulau, *Mal* ... island
punkt, *Ger* ... point
punt, *Du* ... point
punta, *It., Sp* ... point
pur, *India* ... city, town
puy, *Fr* ... peak
qal'a, qal'at, *Arab* ... fort, village
qasr, *Arab* ... fort, castle
rann, *India* ... wasteland
ra's, *Arab* ... cape, head
reka, *Rus., So. Slav* ... river
reprêsa, *Port* ... reservoir
rettō, *Jap* ... island chain
ría, *Sp* ... estuary
ribeira, *Port* ... stream
riberão, *Port* ... river
rio, *It., Port* ... stream, river
río, *Sp* ... river
rivière, *Fr* ... river
roca, *Sp* ... rock
rt, *Yugo* ... cape
rūd, *Per* ... river
saari, *Fin* ... island
sable, *Fr* ... sand
sahara, *Arab* ... desert, plain
saki, *Jap* ... cape
sal, *Sp* ... salt
salar, *Sp* ... salt flat, salt lake
salto, *Sp* ... waterfall
san, *Jap., Kor* ... mountain, hill
sat, satul, *Rom* ... village
schloss, *Ger* ... castle
sebkha, *Arab* ... salt marsh
see, *Ger* ... lake, sea
şehir, *Tur* ... town, city
selat, *Indon* ... stream
selvas, *Port. (Brazil)* ... tropical rain forests
seno, *Sp* ... bay
serra, *Port* ... mountain chain
serranía, *Sp* ... mountain ridge
seto, *Jap* ... strait
severnaya, *Rus* ... northern
shahr, *Per* ... town, city
shan, *Chn* ... mountain, hill, island
shatt, *Arab* ... river
shi, *Jap* ... city
shima, *Jap* ... island
shōtō, *Jap* ... archipelago
si, *Chn* ... west, western
sierra, *Sp* ... mountain range
sjö, *Nor., Swe* ... lake, sea
sö, *Dan., Nor* ... lake, sea
söder, södra, *Swe* ... south
song, *Annam* ... river
sopka, *Rus* ... peak, volcano
source, *Fr* ... a spring
spitze, *Ger* ... summit, point
staat, *Ger* ... state
stad, *Dan., Du., Nor., Swe.* ... city, town
stadt, *Ger* ... city, town
stato, *It* ... state
step', *Rus* ... treeless plain, steppe
straat, *Du* ... strait
strand, *Dan., Du., Ger., Nor., Swe* ... shore, beach
stretto, *It* ... strait
strom, *Ger* ... river, stream
ström, *Dan., Nor., Swe* ... stream, river
stroom, *Du* ... stream, river
su, suyu, *Tur* ... water, river
sud, *Fr., Sp* ... south
süd, *Ger* ... south
suidō, *Jap* ... channel
sul, *Port* ... south
sund, *Dan., Nor., Swe* ... sound
sungai, sungei, *Indon., Mal* ... river
sur, *Sp* ... south
syd, *Dan., Nor., Swe* ... south
tafelland, *Ger* ... plateau
take, *Jap* ... peak, summit
tal, *Ger* ... valley
tandjung, tanjong, *Mal* ... cape
tao, *Chn* ... island
târg, târgul, *Rom* ... market, town
tell, *Arab* ... hill
teluk, *Indon* ... bay, gulf
terra, *It* ... land
terre, *Fr* ... earth, land
thal, *Ger* ... valley
tierra, *Sp* ... earth, land
tō, *Jap* ... east; island
tonle, *Camb* ... river, lake
top, *Du* ... peak
torp, *Swe* ... hamlet, cottage
tsangpo, *Tib* ... river
tsi, *Chn* ... village, borough
tso, *Tib* ... lake
tsu, *Jap* ... harbor, port
tundra, *Rus* ... treeless arctic plains
tung, *Chn* ... east
tuz, *Tur* ... salt
udde, *Swe* ... cape
ufer, *Ger* ... shore, riverbank
umi, *Jap* ... sea, gulf
ura, *Jap* ... bay, coast, creek
ust'ye, *Rus* ... river mouth
valle, *It., Port., Sp* ... valley
vallée, *Fr* ... valley
valli, *It* ... lake
vár, *Hung* ... fortress
város, *Hung* ... town
varoš, *So. Slav* ... town
veld, *Du* ... open plain, field
verkh, *Rus* ... top, summit
ves, *Czech* ... village
vest, *Dan., Nor., Swe* ... west
vik, *Swe* ... cove, bay
vila, *Port* ... town
villa, *Sp* ... town
villar, *Sp* ... village, hamlet
ville, *Fr* ... town, city
vostok, *Rus* ... east
wad, wādī, *Arab.* ... intermittent stream
wald, *Ger* ... forest, woodland
wan, *Chn., Jap* ... bay, gulf
weiler, *Ger* ... hamlet, village
westersch, *Du* ... western
wüste, *Ger* ... desert
yama, *Jap* ... mountain
yarimada, *Tur* ... peninsula
yug, *Rus* ... south
zaki, *Jap* ... cape
zaliv, *Rus* ... bay, gulf
zapad, *Rus* ... west
zee, *Du* ... sea
zemlya, *Rus* ... land
zuid, *Du* ... south

abbreviations of geographical names and terms

Afg.............Afghanistan
Afr.................Africa
Ak..................Alaska
Al.................Alabama
Alb................Albania
Alg...............Algeria
And...............Andorra
Ang...............Angola
Ant.............Antarctica
Ar...............Arkansas
Arch..........Archipelago
Arc. O.......Arctic Ocean
Arg..............Argentina
A. S. S. R.
   Autonomous Soviet
   Socialist Republic
Atl. O........Atlantic Ocean
Aus...............Austria
Austl...........Australia
Aut.............Autonomous
Az................Arizona

B...........Bay, Bahia
Ba...............Bahamas
Bngl...........Bangladesh
Barb............Barbados
Bdy.............Boundary
Bel..............Belgium
Bg..................Berg
Bhu...............Bhutan
Bk.................Bank
Bol...............Bolivia
Bots............Botswana
Br................British
Braz..............Brazil
Bru...............Brunei
Bul..............Bulgaria
Bur................Burma

C..........Cerro, Cape
Ca..............California
Cam............Cameroon
Camb..........Cambodia
Can......Canal, Canada
Can. Is......Canary Is.
Cen. Afr. Emp.
  Central African Empire
Chan............Channel
Co......County, Colorado
Col..............Colombia
Con...............Congo
Comm........Commonwealth
C. R..........Costa Rica
Cr.................Creek
Ct..............Connecticut
C. V...........Cape Verde
C. Z............Canal Zone
Czech......Czechoslovakia

DC......District of Columbia
De..............Delaware
Den.............Denmark
Dept..........Department
Des..............Desert
D. F.......Distrito Federal
Dist.............District
Div...............Division
Dom. Rep.
   Dominican Republic

E...................East
Ec...............Ecuador
Eng.............England
Equat. Gui..Equatorial Guinea
Eth.............Ethiopia
Eur...............Europe

Faer...........Faeroe Is.
Falk. Is.....Falkland Is.
Fd..................Fjord
Fed. Rep. of Ger., F.R.G.
  Federal Republic of Germany
Fin...............Finland
Fk...................Fork
Fl................Florida
For...............Forest
Fr.................France
Fr. Gu.......French Guiana
Ft...................Fort

G...................Gulf
Ga...............Georgia
Gam..............Gambia
Ger. Dem. Rep., G.D.R.
  German Democratic Republic
Gib.............Gibraltar
Grc................Greece
Grnld..........Greenland
Gt..................Great
Gt. Brit......Great Britain
Guad..........Guadeloupe
Guat..........Guatemala
Gui...............Guinea
Guy..............Guyana

Hai................Haiti
Har., Hbr....Harbor, Harbour

Hd...................Head
Hi..................Hawaii
Hond...........Honduras
Hts..............Heights
Hung............Hungary

I....................Island
Ia...................Iowa
Ice...............Iceland
Id..................Idaho
Il................Illinois
In......Inset, Indiana
Ind. O.......Indian Ocean
Indon.........Indonesia
Ind. Res...Indian Reservation
Int., Intl...International
Ire...............Ireland
Is................Islands
Isr...............Israel
Isth............Isthmus
It..................Italy

Jam..............Jamaica
Jap................Japan
Jc...............Junction

Ken................Kenya
Km....Kilometer, Kilometers
Kor................Korea
Ks................Kansas
Kuw..............Kuwait
Ky..............Kentucky

L.....Lake, Loch, Lough
La.............Louisiana
Lat..............Latitude
Leb.............Lebanon
Leso............Lesotho
Lib..............Liberia
Liech......Liechtenstein
Long............Longitude
Lux..........Luxembourg

M............Mile, Miles
Ma.........Massachusetts
Mad...........Madagascar
Mad. Is...Madeira Islands
Mala...........Malaysia
Mand............Mandate
Mart..........Martinique
Max.............Maximum
Max. surf. elev.
   Maximum surface
     elevation
Md..............Maryland
Me..................Maine
Medit........Mediterranean
Mex.............Mexico
Mi.....Mile, Miles, Michigan
Mn............Minnesota
Mo.............Missouri
Mong..........Mongolia
Mor............Morocco
Moz..........Mozambique
Ms.........Mississippi
Mt....Mount, Montana
Mtn.............Mountain
Mts............Mountains

N. A......North America
Natl.............National
Natl. Mon.
   National Monument
Ne..............Nebraska
NC........North Carolina
N. Cal....New Caledonia
ND..........North Dakota
Neigh.......Neighborhood
Nep...............Nepal
Neth.........Netherlands
New Hebr.....New Hebrides
NH.........New Hampshire
Nic............Nicaragua
Nig.............Nigeria
N. Ire.....Northern Ireland
NJ............New Jersey
NM...........New Mexico
Nor...............Norway
Nv................Nevada
NY............New York
N. Z........New Zealand

O..................Ocean
Obs.........Observatory
Oh..................Ohio
Ok............Oklahoma
Om.................Oman
Or.................Oregon
O-va.............Ostrova

P...................Pass
Pa...........Pennsylvania
Pac. O......Pacific Ocean
Pak.............Pakistan
Pan...............Panama

Pap. N. Gui.........Papua
   New Guinea
Par.............Paraguay
Pass.............Passage
P.D.R. of Yem....Yemen,
   People's Democratic
     Republic of
Pen.............Peninsula
Phil..........Philippines
P. Int.......Point of Interest
Pk...........Peak, Park
Plat.............Plateau
Pln.................Plain
Pol................Poland
Port............Portugal
P-Ov..........Poluostrov
P. R.........Puerto Rico
Prov............Province
Pt..................Point
Pta................Punta
Pte................Pointe

R.........River, Rio, Rivière
Ra.........Range, Ranges
Reg...............Region
Rep............Republic
Res....Reservation, Reservoir
Rf...................Reef
Rh..............Rhodesia
RI..........Rhode Island
Rom............Romania
R. R........Railroad
R. S. F. S. R...Russian Soviet
  Federated Socialist
     Republic
Rw................Rwanda
Ry..............Railway
Rys.............Railways

S..........San, Santo, South
Sa.........Serra, Sierra
S. A........South America
S. Afr.......South Africa
Sal..........El Salvador
SC........South Carolina
Scot...........Scotland
SD..........South Dakota
Sd..................Sound
S. L........Sierra Leone
Sol. Is.......Solomon Is.
Som.............Somalia
Sov. Un.......Soviet Union
Sp..................Spain
Spr., Sprs.....Spring, Springs
S. S. R......Soviet Socialist
     Republic
St...................Saint
Sta................Santa
Ste................Sainte
Str.................Strait
Strm.............Stream
Sud................Sudan
Sur.............Surinam
Swaz..........Swaziland
Swe..............Sweden
Switz........Switzerland
Swp.............Swamp
Syr................Syria

Tan..............Tanzania
Tas.............Tasmania
Ter............Territory
Thai...........Thailand
Tn.............Tennessee
Trin...Trinidad and Tobago
Tun..............Tunisia
Tur...............Turkey
Tx..................Texas

U.A.E...United Arab Emirates
Ug..............Uganda
U. K..........United Kingdom
  of Gt. Brit. and N. Ire.
Ur..............Uruguay
U. S., U. S. A.
   United States of America
Ut..................Utah

Va..............Virginia
Val...............Valley
Ven...........Venezuela
Viet.............Vietnam
Vir. Is.........Virgin Is.
Vol..............Volcano
Vt...............Vermont

Wa............Washington
Wi.............Wisconsin
W. Sah......Western Sahara
W. Sam.....Western Samoa
WV.........West Virginia
Wy..............Wyoming

Yugo............Yugoslavia

pronunciation of geographical names

Key to the Sound Values of Letters and Symbols
Used in the Index to Indicate Pronunciation

ă—ăt, căt, băttle
ȧ—ȧppeal, finȧl
ā—rāte, elāte
â—inanimâte, senâte
ä—cälm, ärm
à—àsk, bàth
ȧ—mȧrine, sofȧ (short neutral or indeterminate sound)
â—fâre, prepâre
ch—church, choose
dh—as th in other, either
ē—bē, ēve
ê—crêate, êvent
ĕ—bĕt, ĕnd
ĕ—recĕnt (short neutral or indeterminate sound)
ẽ—cratẽr, cindẽr
g—gō, gāme
gh—guttural g
ĭ—wĭll, bĭt
ĭ—short neutral or indeterminate sound
ī—rīde, bīte
κ—guttural k as ch in German ich
ng—sing
ŋ—baŋk, liŋger
N—indicates nasalized preceding vowel
ŏ—nŏd, ŏdd
ȯ—cȯmmit, cȯnnect
ō—ōld, bōld
ô—ôbey, hôtel
ô—ôrder, nôrth
oi—boil
oo—fōod, rōot
ŏŏ—fŏŏt, wŏŏd
ou—thou, out
s—as in soft, so, sane
sh—dish, finish
th—thin, thick
ū—pūre, cūre
ů—ůnite, ůsurp
û—ûrn, fûr
ŭ—stŭd, ŭp
ū—as in French tu or as "y" in study
ŭ—circŭs, sŭbmit
zh—as z in azure
'—indeterminate vowel sound

In many cases the spelling of foreign geographic names does not even remotely indicate the pronunciation to an American, i. e., Słupsk in Poland is pronounced swoopsk; Jujuy in Argentina is pronounced hoo-hwē'; La Spezia in Italy is lä-spĕ'zyä.

This condition is hardly surprising, however, when we consider that in our own language Worcester, Massachusetts, is pronounced woos'tẽr; Sioux City, Iowa, soo sĭ'tĭ; Schuylkill Haven, Pennsylvania, skool'kĭl hä-vĕn; Poughkeepsie, New York, pǒ-kĭp'sĕ.

The indication of pronunciation of geographic names presents several peculiar problems:

(1) Many foreign tongues use sounds that are not present in the English language and which an American cannot normally articulate. Thus, though the nearest English equivalent sound has been indicated, only approximate results are possible.

(2) There are several dialects in each foreign tongue which cause variation in the local pronunciation of names. This also occurs in identical names in the various divisions of a great language group, as the Slavic or the Latin.

(3) Within the United States there are marked differences in pronunciation, not only of local geographic names, but also of common words, indicating that the sound and tone values for letters as well as the placing of the emphasis vary considerably from one part of the country to another.

(4) A number of different letter and diacritical combinations could be used to indicate essentially the same or approximate pronunciations.

Some variation in pronunciation other than that indicated in this index may be encountered, but such a difference does not necessarily indicate that either is in error, and in many cases it is a matter of individual choice as to which is preferred. In fact, an exact indication of pronunciation of many foreign names using English letters and diacritical marks is extremely difficult and sometimes impossible.

a pronouncing index
of over 30,000 geographical names

This universal index includes in a single alphabetical list all important names that appear on the reference maps. Each place name is preceded by the page number of the map on which it appears. Place names are followed by the pronunciation of the name (see facing page for an explanation of the pronunciation system); the location; and the approximate geographic coordinates.

State locations are listed for all places in the United States. All other place name entries show only country locations. When a name is only shown on an inset map the name of the inset on which it appears is listed.

All minor political divisions are followed by a descriptive term (Dist., Reg., Prov., State, etc.) and by the country in which they are located.

The names of physical features and points of interest that are shown on the maps are listed in the index. Each entry is followed by a descriptive term (Bay, Hill, Mtn., Is., Plat., etc.) to indicate its nature.

The system of alphabetizing used in the index is standard. When more than one name with the same spelling is shown, including both political and physical names, the order of precedence is as follows: *first*, place names; *second*, political divisions; and *third*, physical features.

Local official names are used on the maps for nearly all cities and towns, with the exception of about 50 major world cities for which Anglicized conventional names have been preferred. For these exceptions, the index gives a cross-reference to the official local name.

Page	Name	Pronunciation	Region	Lat. °′	Long. °′
161	Aachen	(ä′kĕn)	F.R.G. (Ruhr In.)	50·46 N	6·07 E
156	Aakirkeby	(ô-kír′kĕ-bü)	Den.	55·04 N	15·00 E
158	Aalen	(ä′lĕn)	F.R.G.	48·49 N	10·08 E
149	Aalsmeer		Neth. (Amsterdam In.)	52·16 N	4·44 E
149	Aalst		Bel. (Brussels In.)	50·58 N	4·00 E
158	Aarau	(är′ou)	Switz.	47·22 N	8·03 E
149	Aarschot		Bel. (Brussels In.)	50·59 N	4·51 E
215	Aba		Nig.	5·06 N	7·21 E
217	Aba		Zaïre	3·52 N	30·14 E
186	Ābādān	(ä-bä′-dän′)	Iran	30·15 N	48·30 E
135	Abaetetuba	(ä′bȧĕ-tĕ-tōō′bä)	Braz.	1·44 S	48·45 W
115	Abajo Pk.	(ä-bä′hŏ)	Ut.	37·51 N	109·28 W
215	Abakaliki		Nig.	6·21 N	8·06 E
172	Abakan	(ŭ-bä-kän′)	Sov. Un.	53·43 N	91·28 E
172	Abakan	(R.)	Sov. Un.	53·00 N	91·06 E
134	Abancay	(ä-bän-kä′ė)	Peru	13·44 S	72·46 W
194	Abashiri	(ä-bä-shē′rē)	Jap.	44·00 N	144·13 E
124	Abasolo	(ä-bä-sō′lô)	Mex.	24·05 N	98·24 W
118	Abasolo		Mex.	27·13 N	101·25 W
	Abay (R.), see Blue Nile				
211	Abaya L.	(ä-bä′yä)	Eth.	6·24 N	38·22 E
218	'Abbāsah, Tur'at al (Can.)		Egypt (Suez In.)	30·45 N	32·15 E
120	Abbeville	(ăb′ê-vĭl)	Al.	31·35 N	85·15 W
160	Abbeville	(ȧb-vēl′)	Fr.	50·08 N	1·49 E
120	Abbeville	(ăb′ê-vĭl)	Ga.	31·53 N	83·23 W
119	Abbeville		La.	29·59 N	92·07 W
121	Abbeville		S.C.	34·09 N	82·25 W
164	Abbiategrasso	(äb-byä′tȧ-gräs′sō)	It.	45·23 N	8·52 E
148	Abbots Bromley	(ăb′ŭts brŭm′lḕ)	Eng.	52·49 N	1·52 W
112	Abbotsford	(ăb′ŭts-fērd)	Can. (Vancouver In.)	49·03 N	122·17 W
218	Abd Al Kuri (I.)	(äbd-ĕl-kōō′rè)	P.D.R. of Yem. (Horn of Afr. In.)	12·12 N	51·00 E
170	Abdulino	(äb-dōō-lē′nō)	Sov. Un.	53·40 N	53·45 E
211	Abéché	(ȧ-bĕ-shä′)	Chad	13·48 N	20·39 E
214	Abengourou		Ivory Coast	6·44 N	3·29 W
156	Åbenrå	(ô′bĕn-rô)	Den.	55·03 N	9·20 E
215	Abeokuta	(ä-bà-ô-kōō′tä)	Nig.	7·10 N	3·26 E
	Abercorn, see Mbala				
154	Aberdare	(ăb-ēr-dâr′)	Wales	51·45 N	3·35 W
120	Aberdeen	(ăb-ēr-dēn′)	Ms.	33·49 N	88·33 W
154	Aberdeen		Scot.	57·10 N	2·05 W
108	Aberdeen		S.D.	45·28 N	98·29 W
110	Aberdeen		Wa.	47·00 N	123·48 W
148	Aberford	(ăb′ēr-fērd)	Eng.	53·49 N	1·21 W
154	Abergavenny	(ăb′ēr-gȧ-vĕn′ĭ)	Wales	51·45 N	3·05 W
110	Abert L.	(ā′bērt)	Or.	42·39 N	120·24 W
154	Aberystwyth	(ă-bēr-ĭst′wĭth)	Wales	52·25 N	4·04 W
174	Abestovskiy	(ä-bĕs′tôv-skĭ)	Sov. Un. (Urals In.)	57·46 N	61·23 E
186	Abhā		Sau. Ar.	17·47 N	42·29 E
214	Abidjan		Ivory Coast	5·19 N	4·02 W
195	Abiko	(ä-bē-kō)	Jap. (Tōkyō In.)	35·53 N	140·01 E
117	Abilene	(ăb′ĭ-lēn)	Ks.	38·54 N	97·12 W
118	Abilene		Tx.	32·25 N	99·45 W
148	Abingdon		Eng. (London In.)	51·38 N	1·17 W
109	Abingdon	(ăb′ĭng-dŭn)	Il.	40·48 N	90·21 W
121	Abingdon		Va.	36·42 N	81·57 W
99	Abington	(ăb′ĭng-tŭn)	Ma. (In.)	42·07 N	70·57 W
115	Abiquiu Res.		N.M.	36·26 N	106·42 W
91	Abitibi (L.)	(ăb-ĭ-tĭb′ĭ)	Can.	48·27 N	80·20 W
91	Abitibi (R.)		Can.	49·30 N	81·10 W
171	Abkhaz A.S.S.R.		Sov. Un.	43·10 N	40·45 E
161	Ablis	(ȧ-blē′)	Fr. (Paris In.)	48·31 N	1·50 E
218	Abnûb	(äb-nōōb′)	Egypt (Nile In.)	27·18 N	31·11 E
	Åbo, see Turku				
184	Abohar		India	30·12 N	74·13 E
214	Aboisso		Ivory Coast	5·28 N	3·12 W
215	Abomey	(ȧb-ô-mā′)	Benin	7·11 N	1·59 E
159	Abony	(ŏ′bô-ny′)	Hung.	47·12 N	20·00 E
215	Abou Deïa		Chad	11·27 N	19·17 E
197	Abra (R.)	(ä′brä)	Phil (In.)	17·16 N	120·38 E
137	Abraão	(äbrȧ-oun′)	Braz. (Rio de Janeiro In.)	23·10 S	44·10 W
129	Abraham's B.		Ba.	22·20 N	73·50 W
148	Abram	(ā′brăm)	Eng.	53·31 N	2·36 W
162	Abrantes	(ȧ-brän′tĕs)	Port.	39·28 N	8·13 W
135	Abrolhos, Arquipélago dos (Arch.)	(ä-rōōê-pĕ′lä-gô dôs ä-brô′l-yōs)	Braz.	17·58 S	38·40 W
157	Abruka (I.)	(ȧ-brōō′kȧ)	Sov. Un.	58·09 N	22·30 E
164	Abruzzi E Molise (Reg.)	(ä-brōōt′sē, mô′lê-zā)	It.	42·10 N	13·55 E
111	Absaroka Ra. (Mts.)	(ȧb-sȧ-rō-kȧ)	Wy.	44·50 N	109·47 W
184	Abu Road	(ȧ′bōō)	India	24·38 N	72·45 E
186	Abū Arīsh	(ä-bōō á-rēsh′)	Sau. Ar.	16·48 N	43·00 E
211	Abu Ḥamad	(ä′bōō hä′-mĕd)	Sud.	19·37 N	33·21 E
186	Abū Kamāl		Syr.	34·45 N	40·46 E
153	Abūksāh		Egypt	29·30 N	30·40 E
134	Abunã (R.)	(ȧ-bōō-nä′)	Bol.-Braz.	10·25 S	67·00 W
218	Abū Qīr	(ä′bōō kēr′)	Egypt (Nile In.)	31·18 N	30·06 E
218	Abū Qurqāṣ	(ä′bōō kōōr-käs′)	Egypt (Nile In.)	27·57 N	30·51 E
183	Abū Qurūn, Ra's (Mtn.)		Egypt (Palestine In.)	30·22 N	33·32 E
195	Aburatsu	(ȧ′bōō-rät′sōō)	Jap.	31·33 N	131·20 E
218	Abū Tīj		Egypt (Nile In.)	27·03 N	31·19 E
186	Abū Ẓaby		U. A. E.	24·15 N	54·28 E
183	Abū Zanīmah		Egypt (Palestine In.)	29·03 N	33·08 E
	Abyad, Al-Bahr al- (R.), see White Nile				
173	Abyy		Sov. Un.	68·24 N	134·00 E
134	Acacias	(ä-kä′sēäs)	Col. (In.)	3·59 N	73·44 W
98	Acadia Natl. Park	(ȧ-kā′dĭ-ȧ)	Me.	44·19 N	68·01 W
126	Acajutla	(ä-kä-hōōt′lä)	Sal.	13·37 N	89·50 W
125	Acala	(ä-kä′lä)	Mex.	16·38 N	92·49 W
216	Acalayong		Equat. Gui.	1·05 N	9·40 E
124	Acámbaro	(ä-käm′bä-rō)	Mex.	20·03 N	100·42 W
126	Acancéh	(ä-kän-sĕ′)	Mex. (In.)	20·50 N	89·27 W
124	Acapetlahuaya	(ä-kä-pĕt′lä-hwä′yä)	Mex.	18·24 N	100·04 W
124	Acaponeta	(ä-kä-pô-nā′tä)	Mex.	22·31 N	105·25 W
124	Acaponeta (R.)		Mex.	22·47 N	105·23 W
124	Acapulco	(ä-kä-pōōl′kô)	Mex.	16·49 N	99·57 W
135	Acaraí Mts.		Braz.	1·30 N	57·40 W
135	Acaraú	(ä-kärhȧ-ōō′)	Braz.	2·55 S	40·04 W
134	Acarigua	(ä-kä-rē′gwä)	Ven.	9·29 N	69·11 W
124	Acatlán de Osorio	(ä-kät-län′ dā ô-sō′rē-ō)	Mex.	18·11 N	98·04 W
125	Acatzingo de Hidalgo	(ä-kät-zǐn′gô dā ê-dhäl′gō)	Mex.	18·58 N	97·47 W
125	Acayucan	(ä-kä-yōō′kän)	Mex.	17·56 N	94·55 W
104	Accoville	(ăk′kô-vĭl)	W.V.	37·45 N	81·50 W
214	Accra	(ä′krà)	Ghana	5·33 N	0·13 W
148	Accrington	(ăk′rĭng-tŭn)	Eng.	53·45 N	2·22 W
163	Acerra	(ä-chĕ′r-rä)	It. (Naples In.)	40·42 N	14·22 E
134	Achacachi	(ä-chä-kä′chè)	Bol.	16·11 S	68·32 W
194	Acheng	(ä′chĕng′)	China	45·32 N	126·59 E
154	Achill	(ȧ-chĭl′)	Ire.	53·55 N	10·05 W
172	Achinsk	(ȧ-chēnsk′)	Sov. Un.	56·13 N	90·32 E
164	Acireale	(ä-chê-rä-ä′lä)	It.	37·37 N	15·12 E
120	Ackia Battle Ground Natl. Mon.	(ä-kyū′)	Ms.	34·22 N	89·05 W
129	Acklins (I.)	(ăk′lĭns)	Ba.	22·30 N	73·55 W
129	Acklins, The Bight of (B.)		Ba.	22·35 N	74·20 W
125	Acolman	(ä-kôl-mä′n)	Mex. (In.)	19·38 N	98·56 W
137	Aconcagua (Prov.)	(ä-kôn-kä′gwä)	Chile (Santiago In.)	32·20 S	71·00 W
137	Aconcagua, Cerro (Mtn.)		Arg. (Santiago In.)	32·38 S	70·00 W
137	Aconcagua (R.)		Chile (Santiago In.)	32·43 S	70·53 W
210	Açores (Azores) (Is.)	(ä-zō′rĕs)	Atl. O.	37·44 N	29·25 W
126	Acoyapa	(ä-kô-yä′pä)	Nic.	11·54 N	85·11 W
164	Acqui	(äk′kwē)	It.	44·41 N	8·22 E
134	Acre (State)	(ä′krä)	Braz.	8·40 S	70·45 W
134	Acre (R.)		Braz.	10·33 S	68·34 W
106	Acton	(ăk′tŭn)	Al. (Birmingham In.)	33·21 N	86·49 W
89	Acton		Can. (Toronto In.)	43·38 N	80·02 W
99	Acton		Ma. (In.)	42·29 N	71·26 W
124	Actopan	(äk-tô-pän′)	Mex.	20·16 N	98·57 W
125	Actopan (R.)	(äk-tô′pän)	Mex.	19·25 N	96·31 W
124	Acuitzio del Canje		Mex.	19·28 N	101·21 W
129	Acul, Baie de l' (B.)	(ȧ-kōōl′)	Hai.	19·55 N	72·20 W
108	Ada	(ā′dȧ)	Mn.	47·17 N	96·32 W
104	Ada		Oh.	40·45 N	83·45 W
117	Ada		Ok.	34·45 N	96·43 W
165	Ada	(ä′dä)	Yugo.	45·48 N	20·06 E
195	Adachi		Jap. (Tōkyō In.)	35·50 N	39·36 E
101	Adak	(ȧ-dăk′)	Ak.	56·50 N	176·48 W
101	Adak (I.)		Ak.	51·45 N	176·28 W
101	Adak Str.		Ak.	51·42 N	177·16 W
	Adalia, see Antalya				
215	Adamaoua (Mts.)		Cam.-Nig.	6·30 N	11·50 E
93	Adams (R.)		Can.	51·30 N	119·20 W
105	Adams (ăd′ȧmz)		Ma.	42·35 N	73·10 W
109	Adams		Wi.	43·55 N	89·48 W
110	Adams, Mt.		Wa.	46·15 N	121·19 W
106	Adamsville	(ăd′ȧmz-vĭl)	Al. (Birmingham In.)	33·36 N	86·57 W
171	Adana	(ä′dä-nä)	Tur.	37·05 N	35·20 E
171	Adapazari	(ä-dä-pä-zä′rè)	Tur.	40·45 N	30·20 E
211	Adarama	(ä-dä-rä′mä)	Sud.	17·11 N	34·56 E
164	Adda (R.)	(äd′dä)	It.	45·43 N	9·31 E
211	Ad Dabbah		Sud.	18·04 N	30·58 E
186	Ad Dahnā (Des.)		Sau. Ar.	26·05 N	47·15 E
211	Ad-Dāmir	(ad-dä′mēr)	Sud.	17·38 N	33·57 E
186	Ad Dammām		Sau. Ar.	26·27 N	49·59 E
183	Ad Dāmūr		Leb. (Palestine In.)	33·44 N	35·27 E
186	Ad Dawhah		Qatar	25·02 N	51·28 E
186	Ad Dilam		Sau. Ar.	23·47 N	47·03 E
218	Ad Dilinjāt		Egypt (Nile In.)	30·48 N	30·32 E
211	Addis Abeba		Eth.	9·00 N	38·44 E

ng-sing; ŋ-baŋk; N-nasalized n; nŏd; cŏmmit; ōld; ôbey; ôrder; fōōd; fŏŏt; ou-out; s-soft; sh-dish; th-thin; pūre; ûnite; ûrn; stŭd; circ*u*s; ü-as "y" in study; '-indeterminate vowel.

248 Addison — Al Batrun PRONOUNCING INDEX

Page	Name	Pronunciation	Region	Lat. °′	Long. °′
113	Addison	(ă'dĭ-sŭn)	Tx. (Dallas, Fort Worth In.)	32·58 N	96·50 W
213	Addo	(ădō)	S. Afr. (Natal In.)	33·33 S	25·43 E
211	Ad Duwaym	(dōō-ām')	Sud.	13·56 N	32·22 E
107	Addyston	(ăd'ē-stŭn)	Oh. (Cincinnati In.)	39·09 N	84·42 W
120	Adel	(ā-dĕl')	Ga.	31·08 N	83·55 W
203	Adelaide	(ăd'ē-lād)	Austl.	34·46 S	139·08 E
213	Adelaide	(ăd-ĕl'ād)	S. Afr. (Natal In.)	32·41 S	26·07 E
220	Adelaide I.		Ant.	67·15 S	68·40 W
186	Aden	(ä'dĕn)	P. D. R. of Yem.	12·48 N	45·00 E
186	Aden, G. of		Asia	11·45 N	45·45 E
197	Adi (I.)	(ä'dē)	Indon.	4·25 S	133·52 E
164	Adige, Fiume (R.)	(fyōō'mĕ ä'dē-jā)	It.	46·38 N	10·43 E
152	Adige R.	(ä'dē-jā)	Aus.-Switz.	46·34 N	10·51 E
184	Adilābād	(ŭ-dĭl-ä-bäd')	India	19·47 N	78·30 E
105	Adirondack, Mts.	(ăd-ĭ-rŏn'dăk)	NY	43·45 N	74·40 W
211	Adi Ugri	(ä-dē ōō'grē)	Eth.	14·54 N	38·52 E
159	Adjud	(äd'zhōōd)	Rom.	46·05 N	27·12 E
113	Adkins		Tx. (San Antonio In.)	29·22 N	98·18 W
101	Admiralty (I.)		Ak.	57·50 N	133·50 W
112	Admiralty Inlet	(ăd'mĭrăl-tē)	Wa. (Seattle In.)	48·10 N	122·45 W
197	Admiralty Is.		Pap. N. Gui.	1·40 S	146·45 E
215	Ado-Ekiti		Nig.	7·38 N	5·12 E
113	Adolph	(ā'dolf)	Mn. (Duluth In.)	46·47 N	92·17 W
185	Ādoni		India	15·42 N	77·18 E
160	Adour (R.)	(à-dōōr')	Fr.	43·43 N	0·38 W
162	Adra	(ä'drä)	Sp.	36·45 N	3·02 W
164	Adrano	(ä-drä'nō)	It.	37·42 N	14·52 E
164	Adria	(ä'drē-ä)	It.	45·03 N	12·01 E
104	Adrian	(ā'drĭ-ăn)	Mi.	41·55 N	84·00 W
108	Adrian		Mn.	43·39 N	95·56 W
	Adrianople, see Edirne				
164	Adriatic Sea		Eur.	43·30 N	14·27 E
210	Adrir		Alg.	27·53 N	0·15 W
211	Adwa		Eth.	14·02 N	38·58 E
148	Adwick-le-Street	(ăd'wĭk-lē-strēt')	Eng.	53·35 N	1·11 W
173	Adycha (R.)	(ä'dĭ-chà)	Sov. Un.	66·11 N	136·45 E
167	Adzhamka	(ád-zhäm'ká)	Sov. Un.	48·33 N	32·28 E
214	Adzopé		Ivory Coast	6·06 N	3·52 W
170	Adz'va (R.)	(ädz'vá)	Sov. Un.	67·00 N	59·20 E
153	Aegean Sea	(ē-jē'ăn)	Asia-Eur.	39·04 N	24·56 E
155	Aerø (I.)	(âr'ö)	Den.	54·52 N	10·22 E
113	Affton		Mo. (St. Louis In.)	38·33 N	90·20 W
182	Afghanistan	(ăf-găn-ĭ-stăn')	Asia	33·00 N	63·00 E
218	Afgoi	(äf-gô'ĭ)	Som. (Horn of Afr. In.)	2·08 N	45·08 E
215	Afikpo		Nig.	5·53 N	7·56 E
210	Aflou	(ä-flōō')	Alg.	33·59 N	2·04 E
101	Afognak (I.)	(ä-fŏg-nák')	Ak.	58·28 N	151·35 W
163	Afragola	(ä-frá'gō-lä)	It. (Naples In.)	40·40 N	14·19 E
209	Africa	(ăf'rĭ-kà)			
113	Afton	(ăf'tŭn)	Mn. (Minneapolis, St. Paul In.)	44·54 N	92·47 W
117	Afton		Ok.	36·42 N	94·56 W
111	Afton		Wy.	42·42 N	110·52 W
183	'Afula	(ä-fōō'lá)	Isr. (Palestine In.)	32·36 N	35·17 E
171	Afyonkarahisar	(ä-fē-ōn-kä-rá-hē-sär')	Tur.	38·45 N	30·20 E
215	Agadem	(ä'gá-dĕm)	Niger	16·50 N	13·17 E
215	Agadez	(ä'gá-dĕs)	Niger	16·58 N	7·59 E
210	Agadir	(ä-gá-dēr)	Mor.	30·30 N	9·37 W
126	Agalta, Cord. de (Mts.)	(kôr-dēl-yĕ'rä-dĕ-ä-gä'l-tä)	Hond.	15·15 N	85·42 W
174	Agapovka	(ä-gä-pôv'kä)	Sov. Un. (Urals In.)	53·18 N	59·10 E
184	Agartala		India	23·53 N	91·22 E
185	Agāshi		India (In.)	19·28 N	72·46 E
174	Agashkino	(ä-gäsh'kĭ-nô)	Sov. Un. (Moscow In.)	55·18 N	38·13 E
101	Agattu (I.)	(á'gä-tōō)	Ak.	52·14 N	173·40 E
167	Agayman	(á-gä-ē-män')	Sov. Un.	46·39 N	34·20 E
214	Agboville		Ivory Coast	5·56 N	4·13 W
171	Agdam	(äg'dăm)	Sov. Un.	40·00 N	47·00 E
160	Agde	(ägd)	Fr.	43·19 N	3·30 E
160	Agen	(á-zhäN')	Fr.	44·13 N	0·31 E
173	Aginskoye	(ä-hĭn'skō-yĕ)	Sov. Un.	51·15 N	113·15 E
197	Agno	(äg'nō)	Phil. (In.)	16·07 N	119·49 E
197	Agno (R.)		Phil. (In.)	15·42 N	120·28 E
164	Agnone	(än-yō'nā)	It.	41·49 N	14·23 E
214	Agogo		Ghana	6·47 N	1·04 W
184	Agra	(ä'grä)	India	27·18 N	78·00 E
164	Agri (R.)	(ä'grē)	It.	40·15 N	16·21 E
165	Agrínion	(à-grē'nyôn)	Grc.	38·38 N	21·06 E
126	Agua (Vol.)	(ä'gwä)	Guat.	14·28 N	90·43 W
124	Agua Blanca, Río (R.)	(rē'ō-ä-gwä-blä'n-kä)	Mex.	21·46 N	102·54 W
124	Agua Brava, Laguna de (L.)	(lä-gōō'nä-dĕ-ä'gwä-brä'vä)	Mex.	22·04 N	105·40 W
114	Agua Caliente Ind. Res.	(ä'gwä kal-yĕn'tä)	Ca.	33·50 N	116·24 W
128	Aguada	(ä-gwä'dá)	Cuba	22·25 N	80·50 W
126	Aguada L.		Mex. (In.)	18·46 N	89·40 W
134	Aguadas	(ä-gwä'-dás)	Col. (In.)	5·37 N	75·27 W
123	Aguadilla	(ä-gwä-dēl'yä)	P. R. (Puerto Rico In.)	18·27 N	67·10 W
127	Aguadulce	(ä-gwä-dōōl'sä)	Pan.	8·15 N	80·33 W
125	Agua Escondida, Meseta de (Plat.)	(mĕ-sĕ'tä-dĕ-ä'gwä-ĕs-kōn-dē'dä)	Mex.	16·54 N	91·35 W
115	Agua Fria (R.)	(ă'gûá frĭ'á)	Az.	33·43 N	112·22 W
137	Aguai	(ägwä-ē')	Braz. (Rio de Janeiro In.)	22·04 S	46·57 W
118	Agualeguas	(ä-gwä-lā'gwäs)	Mex.	26·19 N	99·33 W
118	Aguanaval, R.	(á-guä-nä-väl')	Mex.	25·12 N	103·28 W
126	Aguán R.	(ä-gwä'n)	Hond.	15·22 N	87·00 W
99	Aguanus (R.)	(á-gwä'nŭs)	Can.	50·45 N	62·03 W
124	Aguascalientes	(ä'gwäs-käl-yĕn'tās)	Mex.	21·52 N	102·17 W
124	Aguascalientes (State)		Mex.	22·00 N	102·18 W
162	Agueda	(ä-gwā'dá)	Port.	40·36 N	8·26 W
162	Agueda (R.)	(ä-gĕ-dä)	Sp.	40·50 N	6·44 W
214	Aguelhok		Mali	19·28 N	0·52 E
116	Aguilar	(ä-gē-lär')	Co.	37·24 N	104·38 W
162	Aguilar		Sp.	37·32 N	4·39 W
162	Aguilas	(ä-gē-läs)	Sp.	37·26 N	1·35 W
124	Aguililla	(ä-gē-lēl-yä)	Mex.	18·44 N	102·44 W
124	Aguililla (R.)		Mex.	18·30 N	102·48 W
134	Aguja, Pta. (Pt.)	(pŭn'tä á-gōō' hä)	Peru	6·00 S	81·15 W
212	Agulhas, C.	(ä-gōōl'yäs)	S. Afr.	34·47 S	20·00 E
196	Agung, Gunung (Mtn.)	(ä-gōōng')	Indon.	8·28 S	115·07 E
197	Agusan (R.)	(ä-gōō'sän)	Phil.	8·12 N	126·07 E
210	Ahaggar (Mts.)	(à-hä-gär')	Alg.	23·14 N	6·00 E
161	Ahlen	(ä'lĕn)	F.R.G. (Ruhr In.)	51·45 N	7·52 E
184	Ahmadābād	(ŭ-mĕd-ä-bäd')	India	23·04 N	72·38 E
184	Ahmadnagar	(ä'mûd-nû-gûr)	India	19·09 N	74·45 E
218	Ahmar Mts.		Eth. (Horn of Afr. In.)	9·22 N	42·00 E
121	Ahoskie	(ā-hŏs'kē)	NC	36·15 N	77·00 W
149	Ahrensburg	(ä'rĕns-bōōrg)	F.R.G. (Hamburg In.)	53·40 N	10·14 E
158	Ahrweiler	(är'vī-lĕr)	F.R.G.	50·34 N	7·05 E
157	Ahtärin-järvi (L.)		Fin.	62·46 N	24·25 E
124	Ahuacatlán	(ä-wä-kät-län')	Mex.	21·05 N	104·28 W
126	Ahuachapan	(ä-wä-chä-pän')	Sal.	13·57 N	89·53 W
124	Ahualulco	(ä-wä-lōōl'kō)	Mex.	20·43 N	103·57 W
124	Ahuatempan	(ä-wä-tĕm-pän)	Mex.	18·11 N	98·02 W
156	Åhus	(ô'hōōs)	Swe.	55·56 N	14·19 E
186	Ahvāz		Iran	31·15 N	48·54 E
157	Ahvenanmaa (Åland Is.)	(ä'vĕ-nàn-mô) (ô'länd)	Fin.	60·36 N	19·55 E
199	Aiea		Hi. (In.)	21·18 N	157·52 W
121	Aiken	(ā'kĕn)	SC	33·32 N	81·43 W
135	Aimorès, Serra dos (Mts.)	(sĕ'r-rä-dôs-ī-mō-rĕ's)	Braz.	17·40 S	42·38 W
195	Aimoto	(ī-mô-tō)	Jap. (Ōsaka In.)	34·59 N	135·09 E
210	Aïn Beïda	(ä'ēn bā-dä')	Alg.	35·57 N	7·25 E
161	Aincourt	(âN-kōō'r)	Fr. (Paris In.)	49·04 N	1·47 E
163	Aïne Ousséra	(ĕn ōō-sā-rá)	Alg.	35·25 N	2·50 E
210	Aïn Salah		Alg.	27·13 N	2·22 E
108	Ainsworth	(ānz'wûrth)	Ne.	42·32 N	99·51 W
152	Aïn Taïba	(ä'ēn tä'ē-bä)	Alg.	30·20 N	5·30 E
151	Aïn-Temouchent	(ä'ĕntĕ-mōō-shaN')	Alg.	35·20 N	1·23 W
134	Aipe	(ī'pĕ)	Col. (In.)	3·13 N	75·15 W
215	Aïr (Mts.)		Niger	18·00 N	8·30 E
160	Aire	(âr)	Fr.	43·42 N	0·17 W
148	Aire (R.)		Eng.	53·42 N	1·00 W
183	Airhitam, Selat (Str.)		Indon. (Singapore In.)	0·58 N	102·38 E
160	Aisne (R.)	(ĕn)	Fr.	49·28 N	3·32 E
197	Aitape	(ä-ē-tä'pā)	Pap. N. Gui.	3·00 S	142·10 E
109	Aitkin	(āt'kĭn)	Mn.	46·32 N	93·43 W
165	Aitolikón	(ā-tō'lĭ-kŏn)	Grc.	38·27 N	21·21 E
165	Aitos	(ä-ē'tōs)	Bul.	42·42 N	27·17 E
199	Aitutaki (I.)	(ī-tōō-tä'kē)	Cook Is.	19·00 S	162·00 W
159	Aiud	(ä'ē-ōōd)	Rom.	46·19 N	23·40 E
137	Aiuruoca	(äē'ōō-rōōō'-kä)	Braz. (Rio de Janeiro In.)	21·57 S	44·36 W
137	Aiuruoca (R.)		Braz. (Rio de Janeiro In.)	22·11 S	44·35 W
160	Aix-en-Provence	(ĕks-prô-väNs)	Fr. (In.)	43·32 N	5·27 E
161	Aix-les-Bains	(ĕks'-lā-baN')	Fr.	45·42 N	5·56 E
165	Aíyina		Grc.	37·37 N	22·12 E
165	Aíyina (I.)		Grc.	37·43 N	23·35 E
165	Aíyion		Grc.	38·13 N	22·04 E
157	Aizpute	(ä'ēz-pōō-tĕ)	Sov. Un.	56·44 N	21·37 E
195	Aizuwakamatsu		Jap.	37·27 N	139·51 E
164	Ajaccio	(ä-yät'chō)	Fr.	41·55 N	8·42 E
125	Ajalpan	(ä-häl'pän)	Mex.	18·21 N	97·14 W
204	Ajana	(ăj-ăn'ĕr)	Austl.	28·00 S	114·45 E
111	Ajax Mt.	(ā'jăks)	Mt.	45·19 N	113·43 W
211	Ajdābiyah		Libya	30·56 N	20·16 E
183	'Ajmah, Jabal al (Mts.)		Egypt (Palestine In.)	29·12 N	34·03 E
186	Ajman		U. A. E.	25·15 N	54·30 E
184	Ajmer	(ŭj-mēr')	India	26·26 N	74·42 E
115	Ajo	(ä'hō)	Az.	32·20 N	112·55 W
124	Ajuchitlán del Progreso	(ä-hōō-chet-lân)	Mex.	18·11 N	100·32 W
125	Ajusco	(ä-hōō's-kō)	Mex. (In.)	19·13 N	99·12 W
125	Ajusco, Cerro (Mtn.)	(sĕ'r-rô-ä-hōō's-kō)	Mex. (In.)	19·12 N	99·16 W
195	Akaishi-dake (Mtn.)	(ä-kī-shē dä'kä)	Jap.	35·30 N	138·00 E
195	Akashi	(ä'kä-shē)	Jap. (Ōsaka In.)	34·38 N	134·59 E
216	Aketi	(ä-kå-tē)	Zaire	2·44 N	23·46 E
171	Akhaltsikhe	(äkä'l-tsĭ-kĕ)	Sov. Un.	41·40 N	42·50 E
211	Akhdar, Al Jabal al (Mts.)		Libya	32·00 N	22·00 E
165	Akhelóös (R.)	(ä-hĕ'lō-ōs)	Grc.	38·45 N	21·26 E
171	Akhisar	(äk-hĭs-sär')	Tur.	38·58 N	27·58 E
167	Akhtarskaya, Bukhta (B.)	(bōōk'tä äK-tär'skä-yà)	Sov. Un.	45·53 N	38·22 E
165	Akhtopol	(äK'tô-pōl)	Bul.	42·08 N	27·54 E
167	Akhtyrka	(äK-tür'kà)	Sov. Un.	50·18 N	34·53 E
174	Akhunovo	(ä-kû'nô-vô)	Sov. Un. (Urals In.)	54·13 N	59·36 E
195	Aki	(ä'kē)	Jap.	33·31 N	133·51 E
101	Akiak	(äk'yàk)	Ak.	61·00 N	161·02 W
91	Akimiski (I.)	(ä-kĭ-mĭ'skĭ)	Can.	52·54 N	80·22 W
194	Akita	(ä'kē-tä)	Jap.	39·40 N	140·12 E
214	Akjoujt		Mauritania	19·45 N	14·23 W
183	'Akko		Isr. (Palestine In.)	32·56 N	35·05 E
90	Aklavik	(äk'lä-vĭk)	Can.	68·28 N	135·26 W
214	'Aklé 'Âouâna (Dunes)		Mali-Mauritania	18·07 N	6·00 W
195	Ako	(ä'kô)	Jap.	34·44 N	134·22 E
184	Akola	(à-kô'lä)	India	20·47 N	77·00 E
211	Akordat		Eth.	15·34 N	37·54 E
91	Akpatok (I.)	(ák'pá-tŏk)	Can.	60·30 N	67·10 W
150	Akranes		Ice.	64·18 N	21·40 W
165	Akrítas, Akr. (C.)		Grc.	37·45 N	22·00 E
116	Akron	(ăk'rŭn)	Co.	40·09 N	103·14 W
107	Akron		Oh. (Cleveland In.)	41·05 N	81·30 W
171	Aksaray	(äk-sá-rī')	Tur.	38·30 N	34·05 E
171	Aksehir	(äk'shà-hēr)	Tur.	38·20 N	31·20 E
171	Aksehir (L.)		Tur.	38·40 N	31·30 E
173	Aksha	(äk'shà)	Sov. Un.	50·28 N	113·00 E
	Aksu, see Wensu				
188	Ak Su (R.)		China	40·34 N	77·15 E
171	Aktyubinsk	(äk'tyōō-bĕnsk)	Sov. Un.	50·20 N	57·00 E
195	Akune	(ä'kōō-nå)	Jap.	32·03 N	130·16 E
150	Akureyri	(ä-kōō-rå'rē)	Ice.	65·39 N	18·01 W
101	Akutan (I.)	(ä-kōō-tän')	Ak. (In.)	53·58 N	169·54 W
214	Akwatia		Ghana	6·04 N	0·49 W
103	Alabama (State)	(ăl-à-băm'à)	U. S.	32·50 N	87·30 W
120	Alabama (R.)		Al.	31·20 N	87·39 W
197	Alabat (I.)	(ä-lä-bät')	Phil. (In.)	14·14 N	122·05 E
171	Alacam	(ä-lä-chäm')	Tur.	41·30 N	35·40 E
128	Alacranes	(ä-lä-krä'nås)	Cuba	22·45 N	81·35 W
186	Al Aflaj (Des.)		Sau. Ar.	24·00 N	44·47 E
135	Alagôas (State)	(ä-lä-gō'äzh)	Braz.	9·50 S	36·33 W
135	Alagoinhas	(ä-lä-gō-ēn'yäzh)	Braz.	12·13 S	38·12 W
162	Alagón	(ä-lä-gōn')	Sp.	41·46 N	1·07 W
162	Alagón (R.)		Sp.	39·53 N	6·42 W
124	Alahuatán (R.)	(ä-lä-wä-tá'n)	Mex.	18·30 N	100·00 W
127	Alajuela	(ä-lä-hwa'lä)	C.R.	10·01 N	84·14 W
172	Alakol (L.)		Sov. Un.	45·45 N	81·13 E
199	Alalakeiki Chan.	(ä-lä-lä-kā'kē)	Hi. (In.)	20·40 N	156·30 W
211	Al 'Alamayn		Egypt	30·53 N	28·52 E
112	Alameda	(ăl-à-mā'dà)	Ca. (San Francisco In.)	37·46 N	122·15 W
112	Alameda (R.)		Ca. (San Francisco In.)	37·36 N	122·02 W
197	Alaminos	(ä-lä-mē'nōs)	Phil. (In.)	16·09 N	119·58 E
153	Al 'Amiriyah		Egypt	31·01 N	29·52 E
112	Alamo	(ă'lá-mō)	Ca. (San Francisco In.)	37·51 N	122·02 W
125	Alamo	(ä'lä-mô)	Mex.	20·55 N	97·41 W
114	Alamo	(ă'lá-mō)	Nv.	37·22 N	115·10 W
118	Alamo, R.	(ä'lä-mō)	Mex.	26·33 N	99·35 W
115	Alamogordo	(ăl-à-mō-gôr'dō)	NM	32·55 N	106·00 W
113	Alamo Heights	(ă'lá-mō)	Tx. (San Antonio In.)	29·28 N	98·27 W
118	Alamo Pk.	(ă'lá-mō pēk)	NM	32·50 N	105·55 W
115	Alamosa	(ăl-à-mō'sá)	Co.	37·25 N	105·50 W
174	Alandskiy	(ä-länt'skĭ)	Sov. Un. (Urals In.)	52·14 N	59·48 E
217	Alanga Arba		Ken.	0·07 N	40·25 E
171	Alanya		Tur.	36·40 N	32·10 E
213	Alaotra (L.)	(ä-lä-ō'trá)	Mad.	17·15 S	48·17 E
174	Alapayevsk	(ä-lä-pä'yĕfsk)	Sov. Un. (Urals In.)	57·50 N	61·35 E
183	Al 'Aqabah		Jordan (Palestine In.)	29·32 N	35·00 E
124	Alaquines	(ä-lá-kē'nás)	Mex.	22·07 N	99·35 W
183	Al 'Arīsh	(a-rēsh')	Egypt (Palestine In.)	31·08 N	33·48 E
192	Ala Shan (Mts.)	(ä'lä-shän')	China	38·02 N	105·20 E
75	Alaska (State)	(à-lăs'kà)	U. S.	64·00 N	150·00 W
101	Alaska, G. of		Ak.	57·42 N	147·40 W
101	Alaska Hy.		Ak.	63·00 N	142·00 W
101	Alaska Pen.		Ak.	55·50 N	162·10 W
101	Alaska Ra.		Ak.	62·00 N	152·18 W
211	Al-'Aṭrūn		Sud.	18·13 N	26·44 E
170	Alatyr'	(ä'lä-tür)	Sov. Un.	54·55 N	46·30 E
134	Alausí	(ä-lou-sē')	Ec.	2·15 S	78·45 W
218	Al 'Ayyāṭ	(ä-ē-yät')	Egypt (Nile In.)	29·38 N	31·18 E
164	Alba	(äl'bä)	It.	44·41 N	8·02 E
162	Albacete	(äl-bä-thā'tā)	Sp.	39·00 N	1·49 W
161	Albachten	(äl-bá'K-tĕn)	F.R.G. (Ruhr In.)	51·55 N	7·31 E
218	Al Badārī		Egypt (Nile In.)	26·59 N	31·29 E
162	Alba de Tormes	(äl-bá dā tôr'mās)	Sp.	40·48 N	5·28 W
218	Al Bahnasā		Egypt (Nile In.)	28·35 N	30·30 E
159	Alba Iulia	(äl-bä yōō'lyá)	Rom.	46·05 N	23·32 E
163	Albalate	(äl-bä-lä'tä)	Sp.	41·07 N	0·34 W
218	Al Ballaḥ	(bä'lä)	Egypt (Suez In.)	30·46 N	32·20 E
218	Al Balyanā		Egypt (Nile In.)	26·12 N	32·00 E
146	Albania	(ăl-bā'nĭ-à)	Eur.	41·45 N	20·00 E
163	Albano, Lago (L.)	(lä'-gō äl-bä'nō)	It. (Rome In.)	41·45 N	12·44 E
163	Albano Laziale	(äl-bä'nō lät-zē-ä'lā)	It. (Rome In.)	41·44 N	12·43 E
204	Albany	(ôl'bá-nĭ)	Austl.	35·00 S	118·00 E
112	Albany		Ca. (San Francisco In.)	37·54 N	122·18 W
120	Albany		Ga.	31·35 N	84·10 W
117	Albany		Mo.	40·14 N	94·18 W
105	Albany		NY	42·40 N	73·50 W
110	Albany		Or.	44·38 N	123·06 W
118	Albany		Tx.	32·43 N	99·17 W
91	Albany (R.)		Can.	51·45 N	83·30 W
186	Al Baṣrah		Iraq	30·35 N	47·59 E
183	Al Batrūn	(bä-trōōn')	Leb. (Palestine In.)	34·16 N	35·39 E

ăt; finăl; rāte; senâte; ärm; àsk; sofá; fâre; ch-choose; dh-as th in other; bē; ēvent; bĕt; recĕnt; cratēr; g-go; gh-guttural g; bĭt; ĭ-short neutral; rīde; K-guttural k as ch in German ich;

PRONOUNCING INDEX

Al Bawiti — Al Mabrak 249

Page	Name Pronunciation Region	Lat. °′	Long. °′
211	Al Bawīţī, Egypt	28·19 N	29·00 E
121	Albemarle (ăl'bē-märl), NC	35·24 N	80·36 W
121	Albemarle Sd., NC	36·00 N	76·17 W
164	Albenga (äl-bĕŋ'gä), It.	44·04 N	8·13 E
162	Alberche (R.) (äl-bĕr'chā), Sp.	40·08 N	4·19 W
204	Alberga, The (R.) (ăl-bŭr'gȧ), Austl.	27·15 S	135·00 E
162	Albergaria a-Velha (äl-bĕr-gȧ-rē'ȧ-ä-vāl'yȧ), Port.	40·47 N	8·31 W
113	Alberhill (ăl'bĕr-hĭl), Ca. (Los Angeles In.)	33·43 N	117·23 W
160	Albert (ȧl-bâr'), Fr.	50·00 N	2·49 E
217	Albert (L.) (ăl'bĕrt) (ȧl-bâr'), Afr.	1·50 N	30·40 E
217	Albert, Parc Natl. (Natl. Pk.), Zaire	0·05 N	29·30 E
90	Alberta (Prov.) (ăl-bûr'tȧ), Can.	54·33 N	117·10 W
93	Alberta, Mt., Can.	52·18 N	117·28 W
197	Albert Edward, Mt. (ăl'bĕrt ĕd'wĕrd), Pap. N. Gui.	8·25 S	147·25 E
137	Alberti (ȧl-bĕ'r-tē), Arg. (Buenos Aires In.)	35·01 S	60·16 W
149	Albert Kanal (Can.), Bel. (Brussels In.)	51·07 N	5·07 E
109	Albert Lea (ăl'bĕrt lē'), Mn.	43·38 N	93·24 W
217	Albert Nile (R.), Ug.	3·25 N	31·35 E
98	Alberton (ăl'bĕr-tŭn), Can.	46·49 N	64·04 W
213	Alberton, S. Afr. (Johannesburg & Pretoria In.)	26·16 S	28·08 E
120	Albertville (ăl'bĕrt-vĭl), Al.	34·15 N	86·10 W
161	Albertville (ȧl-bĕr-vēl'), Fr.	45·42 N	6·25 E
	Albertville, see Kalemie		
160	Albi (äl-bē'), Fr.	43·54 N	2·07 E
109	Albia (ăl-bĭ-ȧ), Ia.	41·01 N	92·44 W
135	Albina (äl-bē'nä), Sur.	5·30 N	54·33 W
216	Albina, Ponta (Pt.), Ang.	15·51 S	11·44 E
107	Albino, Pt. (äl-bē'nō), Can. (Buffalo In.)	42·50 N	79·05 W
104	Albion (ăl'bĭ-ŭn), Mi.	42·15 N	84·50 W
108	Albion, Ne.	41·42 N	98·00 W
105	Albion, NY	43·15 N	78·10 W
162	Alboran, Isla del (I.) (ē's-lä-dĕl-äl-bō-rä'n), Sp.	35·58 N	3·02 W
162	Alboran Sea, Afr.-Eur.	35·54 N	4·26 W
156	Ålborg (ôl'bŏr), Den.	57·02 N	9·55 E
162	Albox (äl-bōk'), Sp.	37·23 N	2·08 W
218	Al Buḩayrah al Murrah al Kubrā (Great Bitter) (Salt L.), Egypt (Suez In.)	30·24 N	32·27 E
218	Al Buḩayrah al Murrah aş Şughrā (Little Bitter) (Salt L.), Egypt (Suez In.)	30·10 N	32·36 E
115	Albuquerque (ăl-bŭ-kûr'kē), NM	35·05 N	106·40 W
127	Albuquerque, Cayus de (I.) (äl-bû-kûr'kē), Col.	12·12 N	81·24 W
186	Al Buraymī, Om.	23·45 N	55·39 E
162	Alburquerque (äl-bōōr-kĕr'kā), Sp.	39·13 N	6·58 W
203	Albury (ôl'bĕr-ē), Austl.	36·00 S	147·00 E
163	Alcabideche (äl-kȧ-bē-dā'chā), Port. (Lisbon In.)	38·43 N	9·24 W
162	Alcacer do Sal (äl-kä'sĕr dōō säl'), Port.	38·24 N	8·33 W
163	Alcalá de Chivert (äl-kä-lä'dā chē-vĕrt'), Sp.	40·18 N	0·12 E
163	Alcalá de Henares (äl-kä-lä' dā ā-na'rās), Sp. (Madrid In.)	40·29 N	3·22 W
162	Alcalá de los Gazules (äl-kä-lä' dā lōs gä-thōō'lås), Sp.	36·29 N	5·44 W
162	Alcalá la Real (äl-kä-lä'lä rā-äl'), Sp.	37·27 N	3·57 W
164	Alcamo (äl'kȧ-mō), It.	37·58 N	13·03 E
163	Alcanadre (R.) (äl-kä-nä'drā), Sp.	41·41 N	0·18 W
163	Alcanar (äl-kä-när'), Sp.	40·35 N	0·27 E
163	Alcañiz (äl-kän-yēth'), Sp.	41·03 N	0·08 W
135	Alcântara (äl-kän'tȧ-rȧ), Braz.	2·17 S	44·29 W
162	Alcaraz (äl-kä-räth'), Sp.	38·39 N	2·28 W
162	Alcaudete (äl-kou-dhā'tā), Sp.	37·38 N	4·05 W
162	Alcazar de San Juan (äl-kä'thär dā sän hwän'), Sp.	39·22 N	3·12 W
163	Alcira (ä-thē'rä), Sp.	39·09 N	0·26 W
120	Alcoa (ăl-kō'ȧ), Tn.	35·45 N	84·00 W
163	Alcobendas (äl-kō-bĕn'dås), Sp. (Madrid In.)	40·32 N	3·39 W
163	Alcochete (äl-kō-chā'ta), Port. (Lisbon In.)	38·45 N	8·58 W
163	Alcora (äl-kō'rä), Sp.	40·05 N	0·12 W
163	Alcorisa (äl-kō-rē'sä), Sp.	40·53 N	0·20 W
163	Alcorón (äl-kô-rô'n), Sp. (Madrid In.)	40·22 N	3·50 W
137	Alcorta (ȧl-kôr'tä), Arg. (Buenos Aires In.)	33·32 S	61·08 W
111	Alcova Res. (ăl-kō'vȧ), Wy.	42·31 N	106·33 W
89	Alcove (ăl-kōv'), Can. (Ottawa In.)	45·41 N	75·55 W
163	Alcoy (äl-koi'), Sp.	38·42 N	0·30 W
163	Alcudia, Bahia de (B.) (bä-ē'ä-dĕ-äl-kōō-dhē'å), Sp.	39·48 N	3·20 E
213	Aldabra Is. (äl-dä'brä), Afr.	9·16 S	46·17 E
124	Aldama (äl-dä'mä), Mex.	22·54 N	98·04 W
118	Aldama, Mex.	28·50 N	105·54 W
173	Aldan, Sov. Un.	58·46 N	125·19 E
173	Aldan (R.), Sov. Un.	63·30 N	132·14 E
173	Aldan Plat., Sov. Un.	57·42 N	130·28 E
173	Aldanskaya, Sov. Un.	61·52 N	135·29 E
161	Aldekerk (äl'dĕ-kĕ'rk), F.R.G. (Ruhr In.)	51·26 N	6·26 E
161	Aldenhoven (ȧl'dĕn-hō'vĕn), F.R.G. (Ruhr In.)	50·54 N	6·18 E
112	Aldergrove (ôl'dĕr-grōv), Can. (Vancouver In.)	49·03 N	122·28 W
160	Alderney (I.) (ôl'dĕr-nĭ), Guernsey	49·43 N	2·11 W
148	Aldershot (ôl'dĕr-shŏt), Eng. (London In.)	51·14 N	0·46 W
104	Alderson (ôl-dĕr-sŭn), WV	37·40 N	80·40 W
112	Alderwood Manor (ôl'dĕr-wŏŏd măn'ŏr), Wa. (Seattle In.)	47·49 N	122·18 W
148	Aldridge-Brownhills, Eng.	52·38 N	1·55 W
117	Aledo (ȧ-le'dō), Il.	41·12 N	90·47 W
214	Aleg, Mauritania	17·03 N	13·55 W
137	Alegre (älĕ'grĕ), Braz. (Rio de Janeiro In.)	20·41 S	41·32 W
136	Alegre (R.), Braz. (Rio de Janeiro In.)	22·22 S	43·34 W
136	Alegrete (ä-lå-grā'tā), Braz.	29·46 S	55·44 W
174	Aleksandrov (ä-lyĕk-sän' drôf), Sov. Un. (Moscow In.)	56·24 N	38·45 E
174	Aleksandrovsk (ä-lyĕk-sän'drôfsk), Sov. Un. (Urals In.)	59·11 N	57·36 E
173	Aleksandrovsk, Sov. Un.	51·02 N	142·21 E
159	Aleksandrow Kujawski (ä-lĕk-säh'drōōv kōō-yav'skē), Pol.	52·54 N	18·45 E
167	Alekseyevka (ä-lyĕk-sā-yĕf'kȧ), Sov. Un.	50·39 N	38·40 E
166	Aleksin (ä-lyĕk-sĕn), Sov. Un.	54·31 N	37·07 E
165	Aleksinac (ȧ-lyĕk-sē-nȧk'), Yugo.	43·33 N	21·42 E
137	Alem Paraíba (ä-lĕ'm-pȧ-räē'bȧ), Braz. (Rio de Janeiro In.)	21·54 S	42·40 W
160	Alençon (ȧ-läɴ-sôɴ'), Fr.	48·26 N	0·08 E
135	Alenquer (ä-lĕŋ-kĕr'), Braz.	1·58 S	54·44 W
162	Alenquer, Port.	39·04 N	9·01 W
162	Alentjo (Reg.) (ä-lĕŋ-tā'zhōō), Port.	38·05 N	7·45 W
199	Alenuihaha Chan. (ä'lȧ-nōō-ē-hä'hä), Hi. (In.)	20·20 N	156·05 W
153	Aleppo (ȧ-lĕp-ō), Syr.	36·10 N	37·18 E
160	Alès (ä-lĕs'), Fr.	44·07 N	4·06 E
164	Alessandria (ä-lĕs-sän'drē-ä), It.	44·53 N	8·35 E
	Alessio, see Lesh		
156	Ålesund (ô'lĕ-sōōn'), Nor.	62·28 N	6·14 E
101	Aleutian Is. (ȧ-lu'shăn), Ak.	52·40 N	177·30 W
101	Aleutian Trench, Ak.	50·40 N	177·10 E
173	Alevina, Mys (C.), Sov. Un.	58·49 N	151·44 E
101	Alexander Arch. (ăl-ĕg-zăn'dĕr), Ak.	57·05 N	138·10 W
120	Alexander City, Al.	32·55 N	85·55 W
89	Alexander Ind. Res., Can. (Edmonton In.)	53·47 N	114·00 W
220	Alexander I., Ant.	71·00 S	71·00 W
213	Alexandra (ăl-ex-ăn'drȧ), S. Afr. (Johannesburg & Pretoria In.)	26·07 S	28·07 E
204	Alexandria (ăl-ĕg-zăn'drĭ-ȧ), Austl.	19·00 S	136·56 E
105	Alexandria, Can.	45·50 N	74·35 W
104	Alexandria, In.	40·20 N	85·20 W
119	Alexandria, La.	31·18 N	92·28 W
108	Alexandria, Mn.	45·53 N	95·23 W
165	Alexandria, Rom.	43·55 N	25·21 E
213	Alexandria (ăl-ĕx-ăn-drĭ-ȧ), S. Afr. (Natal In.)	33·40 S	26·26 E
108	Alexandria, SD	43·39 N	97·45 W
106	Alexandria (ăl-ĕg-zăn'drĭ-ȧ), Va. (Baltimore In.)	38·50 N	77·05 W
	Alexandria, see Al Iskandarīyah		
105	Alexandria Bay, NY	44·20 N	75·55 W
165	Alexandroúpolis (Dedeagats) (ä-lĕk-sän-drōō'pō-lĭs) (de'dĕ-ä-gäts), Grc.	40·51 N	25·51 E
162	Alfaro (äl-färō), Sp.	42·08 N	1·43 W
211	Al-Fāshir (fä'shĕr), Sud.	13·38 N	25·21 E
218	Al Fashn, Egypt (Nile In.)	28·47 N	30·53 E
211	Al Fayyūm, Egypt	29·14 N	30·48 E
137	Alfenas (äl-fĕ'nås), Braz. (Rio de Janeiro In.)	21·26 S	45·55 W
165	Alfiós (R.), Grc.	37·33 N	21·50 E
218	Al Firdān (fer-dän'), Egypt (Nile In.)	30·43 N	32·20 E
137	Alfonso Claudio (äl-fōn'sô-klou'dēō), Braz. (Rio de Janeiro In.)	20·05 S	41·05 W
89	Alfred (ăl'frĕd), Can. (Ottawa In.)	45·34 N	74·52 W
148	Alfreton (ăl'fēr-tŭn), Eng.	53·06 N	1·23 W
162	Algarve (Reg.) (äl-gär'vĕ), Port.	37·15 N	8·12 W
162	Algeciras (äl-hä-thē'räs), Sp.	36·08 N	5·25 W
210	Alger (Algiers) (äl-zhā') (ăl-jēr), Alg.	36·51 N	2·56 E
209	Algeria (ăl-gē'rĭ-ȧ), Afr.	28·45 N	1·00 E
163	Algete (äl-hā'tā), Sp. (Madrid In.)	40·36 N	3·30 W
164	Alghero (äl-gâ'rō), It.	40·32 N	8·22 E
	Algiers, see Alger		
119	Algoa (ăl-gō'ȧ), Tx. (In.)	29·24 N	95·11 W
213	Algoabaai (B.) (ăl'gōȧ), S. Afr. (Natal In.)	33·51 S	24·50 E
112	Algoma, Wa. (Seattle In.)	47·17 N	122·15 W
109	Algoma, Wi.	44·38 N	87·29 W
109	Algona, Ia.	43·04 N	94·11 W
104	Algonac (äl'gō-năk), Mi.	42·35 N	82·30 W
107	Algonquin (ăl-gŏŋ'kwĭn), Il. (Chicago In.)	42·10 N	88·17 W
105	Algonquin Provincial Park, Can.	45·50 N	78·20 W
162	Alhama (äl-hä'mä), Sp.	37·00 N	3·59 W
162	Alhama, Sp.	37·50 N	1·24 W
113	Alhambra (ăl-hăm'brȧ), Ca. (Los Angeles In.)	34·05 N	118·08 W
153	Al Ḩammām, Egypt	30·46 N	29·42 E
163	Alhandra (äl-yän'drȧ), Port. (Lisbon In.)	38·55 N	9·01 W
186	Al Hasā (Plain), Sau. Ar.	27·00 N	47·48 E
162	Alhaurín el Grande (ä-lou-rēn'ĕl-grä'n-dĕ), Sp.	36·40 N	4·40 W
186	Al Ḩijāz (Reg.), Sau. Ar.	23·45 N	39·08 E
183	Al Hirmil, Leb. (Palestine In.)	34·23 N	36·22 E
163	Alhos Vedros (äl'yōs'vā'drōs), Port. (Lisbon In.)	38·39 N	9·02 W
162	Alhucemas, Baie d' (B.), Mor.	35·18 N	3·50 W
186	Al Hudaydah, Yemen	14·43 N	43·03 E
186	Al Hufūf, Sau. Ar.	25·15 N	49·43 E
165	Aliákmon (R.) (äl-ê-äk'mōn), Grc.	40·26 N	22·17 E
215	Alibori (R.), Benin	11·40 N	2·55 E
163	Alicante (ä-lê-kän'tä), Sp.	38·20 N	0·30 W
163	Alicante, Bahia de (B.) (bä-ē'ä-dĕ-ä-lê-kän'tä), Sp.	38·12 N	0·22 W
213	Alice (ăl-ĭs), S. Afr. (Natal In.)	32·47 S	26·51 E
118	Alice (ăl'ĭs), Tx.	27·45 N	98·04 W
92	Alice Arm, Can.	55·29 N	129·29 W
213	Alicedale (ăl'ĭs-dāl), S. Afr. (Natal In.)	33·18 S	26·04 E
204	Alice Springs (ăl'ĭs), Austl.	23·38 S	133·56 E
164	Alicudi (I.) (ä-lē-kōō'dē), It.	38·34 N	14·21 E
174	Alifkulovo (ä-lĭf-kû'lô-vô), Sov. Un. (Urals In.)	55·57 N	62·06 E
184	Alīgarh (ä-lê-gŭr'), India	27·58 N	78·08 E
156	Alingsås (ȧ'lĭŋ-sôs), Swe.	57·57 N	12·30 E
107	Aliquippa (ăl-ĭ-kwĭp'ȧ), Pa. (Pittsburgh In.)	40·37 N	80·15 W
218	Al Iskandarīyah (Alexandria), Egypt (Nile In.)	31·12 N	29·58 E
	Al Ismā'īlīyah, see Ismailia		
212	Aliwal North (ä-lē-wäl'), S. Afr.	31.09 S	28·26 E
186	Al-Jabal Al-Akhḑar (Mts.), Om.	23·30 N	56·43 W
183	Al Jafr, Qa'al (L.), Jordan (Palestine In.)	30·15 N	36·24 E
211	Al Jaghbūb, Libya	29·46 N	24·32 E
211	Al Jawf, Libya	24·14 N	23·15 E
186	Al Jawf, Sau. Ar.	29·45 N	39·30 E
162	Aljezur (äl-zhā-zōōr'), Port.	37·18 N	8·52 W
218	Al Jīzah, Egypt (Nile In.)	30·01 N	31·12 E
210	Al Jufrah (Oasis), Libya	29·30 N	15·16 E
162	Aljustrel (äl-zhōō-strĕl'), Port.	37·44 N	8·23 W
218	Al Kāb, Egypt (Suez In.)	30·56 N	32·19 E
211	Al Kāmilin (käm-lēn'), Sud.	15·09 N	33·06 E
183	Al Karak (kĕ-räk'), Jordan (Palestine In.)	31·11 N	35·42 E
218	Al Karnak (kär'nak), Egypt (Nile In.)	25·42 N	32·43 E
186	Al Khābūrah, Om.	23·45 N	57·30 E
183	Al Khalil (Hebron), Jordan (Palestine In.)	31·31 N	35·07 E
211	Al Khandaq (kän-däk'), Sud.	18·38 N	30·29 E
211	Al Khums, Libya	32·35 N	14·10 E
186	Al Khurmah, Sau. Ar.	21·37 N	41·44 E
211	Al Khurţūm (Khartoum) (kär-tōōm'), Sud.	15·34 N	32·36 E
211	Al-Khurţūm Baḩrī, Sud.	15·43 N	32·41 E
183	Al Kiswah, Syr. (Palestine In.)	33·31 N	36·13 E
155	Alkmaar (älk-mär'), Neth.	52·39 N	4·42 E
218	Al Kūbrī (kōō'brē), Egypt (Suez In.)	30·01 N	32·35 E
211	Al Kufrah (Oasis), Libya	24·45 N	22·45 E
183	Al Kuntillah, Egypt (Palestine In.)	29·59 N	34·42 E
186	Al Kuwayt (Kuwait) (kōō-wit), Kuw.	29·04 N	47·59 E
153	Al Lādhiqīyah (Latakia), Syr.	35·32 N	35·51 E
98	Allagash (R.) (ăl'ȧ-găsh), Me.	46·50 N	69·24 W
184	Allāhābād (ŭl-ŭ-hä-bäd'), India	25·32 N	81·53 E
114	All American Can. (âl ȧ-mĕr'ĭ-kăn), Ca.	32·43 N	115·12 W
149	Alland, Aus. (Vienna In.)	48·04 N	16·05 E
162	Allariz (äl-yä-rēth'), Sp.	42·10 N	7·48 W
120	Allatoona (R.) (ăl'ȧ-tōōn'ȧ), Ga.	34·05 N	84·57 W
160	Allauch (ä-lĕ'ōō), Fr. (In.)	43·21 N	5·30 E
173	Allaykha (ä-lĭ'kȧ), Sov. Un.	70·32 N	148·53 E
96	Allegan (ăl'ē-găn), Mi.	42·30 N	85·55 W
105	Allegany Ind. Res. (ăl-ē-gā'nĭ), NY	42·05 N	78·55 W
105	Allegheny (R.), Pa.	41·10 N	79·20 W
105	Allegheny Front (Mts.), U. S.	38·12 N	80·03 W
103	Allegheny Mts., U. S.	37·35 N	81·55 W
104	Allegheny Plat, U. S.	39·00 N	81·15 W
105	Allegheny Res., Pa.	41·50 N	78·55 W
117	Allen (ăl'ĕn), Ok.	34·51 N	96·26 W
154	Allen, Lough (B.) (lŏk ăl'ĕn), Ire.	54·07 N	8·09 W
106	Allendale (ăl'ĕn-dāl), NJ (New York In.)	41·02 N	74·08 W
121	Allendale, SC	33·00 N	81·19 W
125	Allende (äl-yĕn'då), Mex.	18·23 N	92·49 W
118	Allende, Mex.	28·20 N	100·50 W
105	Allentown (ăl'en-toun), Pa.	40·35 N	75·30 W
185	Alleppey (ȧ-lĕp'ē), India	9·33 N	76·22 E
158	Aller R. (äl'ēr), F.R.G.	52·43 N	9·50 E
108	Alliance (ȧ-lĭ'ăns), Ne.	42·06 N	102·53 W
104	Alliance, Oh.	40·55 N	81·10 W
186	Al Lidām, Sau. Ar.	20·45 N	44·12 E
160	Allier (R.) (ȧ-lyā'), Fr.	46·43 N	3·03 E
106	Alligator Pt. (al'ĭ-gā-tēr), La. (New Orleans In.)	30·57 N	89·41 W
156	Allinge (äl'ĭŋ-ĕ), Den.	55·16 N	14·48 E
126	All Pines (ôl pīnz), Belize (In.)	16·55 N	88·15 W
186	Al Luḩayyah, Yemen	15·58 N	42·48 E
106	Alluvial City, La. (New Orleans In.)	29·51 N	89·42 W
112	Allyn (ăl'ĭn), Wa. (Seattle In.)	47·23 N	122·51 W
98	Alma (ăl'mȧ), Can.	45·36 N	64·59 W
98	Alma, Can.	48·29 N	71·42 W
121	Alma, Ga.	31·33 N	82·31 W
104	Alma, Mi.	43·25 N	84·40 W
116	Alma, Ne.	40·08 N	99·21 W
218	Alma, S. Afr. (Johannesburg & Pretoria In.)	24·30 S	28·05 E
109	Alma, Wi.	44·21 N	91·57 W
172	Alma-Ata (ăl'mȧ ȧ'tȧ), Sov. Un.	43·19 N	77·08 E
183	Al Mabrak (R.), Sau. Ar. (Palestine In.)	29·16 N	35·12 E

ng-sing; ŋ-baŋk; ɴ-nasalized n; nŏd; cŏmmit; ōld; ôbey; ôrder; fōōd; fŏŏt; ou-out; s-soft; sh-dish; th-thin; pūre; ûnite; ûrn; stŭd; circŭs; ü-as "y" in study; '-indeterminate vowel.

Page	Name Pronunciation Region	Lat. °′	Long. °′
163	Almada (äl-mä′dä) Port. (Lisbon In.)	38·40 N	9·09 W
162	Almadén (äl-mȧ-dhän′) Sp.	38·47 N	4·50 W
186	Al Madīnah (Medina) Sau. Ar.	24·26 N	39·42 E
183	Al Mafraq..Jordan (Palestine In.)	32·21 N	36·13 E
125	Almagre, Laguna (L.) (lä-gōō′nä-äl-mä′grĕ) Mex.	23·48 N	97·45 W
162	Almagro (äl-mä′grō) Sp.	38·52 N	3·41 W
218	Al Maḥallah al Kubrā Egypt (Nile In.)	31·00 N	31·10 E
186	Al Manāmah Bahrain	26·01 N	50·33 E
114	Almanor (R.) (ăl-măn′ôr) Ca.	40·11 N	121·20 W
162	Almansa (äl-män′sä) Sp.	38·52 N	1·09 W
218	Al Manshāh Egypt (Nile In.)	26·31 N	31·46 E
162	Almansor (R.) (äl-män-sôr) Port.	38·41 N	8·27 W
218	Al Manṣūrah Egypt (Nile In.)	31·02 N	31·25 E
218	Al Manzilah (män′za-la) Egypt (Nile In.)	31·09 N	32·05 E
162	Almanzora (R.) (äl-män-thō′rä) Sp.	37·20 N	2·25 W
218	Al Marāghah Egypt (Nile In.)	26·41 N	31·35 E
163	Almargem (äl-mär-zhĕn) Port. (Lisbon In.)	38·51 N	9·16 W
211	Al-Marj Libya	32·44 N	21·08 E
186	Al Maṣīrah (I.) Om.	20·43 N	58·58 E
186	Al Mawsil Iraq	36·00 N	42·53 E
162	Almazán (äl-mä-thän′) Sp.	41·30 N	2·33 W
183	Al Mazār...Jordan (Palestine In.)	31·04 N	35·41 E
183	Al Mazra′ah Jordan (Palestine In.)	31·17 N	35·33 E
162	Almeirim (äl-māĭ-rēn′) Port.	39·13 N	8·31 W
155	Almelo (äl′mē-lō) Neth.	52·20 N	6·42 E
162	Almendralejo (äl-mān-drä-lā′hō) Sp.	38·43 N	6·24 W
162	Almería (äl-mā-rē′ä) Sp.	36·52 N	2·28 W
162	Almería, Golfo de (G.) (gôl-fô-dĕ-äl-māĭ-rēn′) Sp.	36·45 N	2·26 W
162	Almería (R.) Sp.	37·00 N	2·40 W
156	Älmhult (ĕlm′hōōlt) Swe.	56·35 N	14·08 E
162	Almina, Pta. (äl-mē′nä) Mor.	35·58 N	5·17 W
218	Al Minyā Egypt (Nile In.)	28·04 N	30·45 E
127	Almirante (äl-mē-rän′tā) Pan.	9·18 N	82·24 W
127	Almirante, Bahía de (B.) (bä-ē′ä-dĕ-äl-mē-rän′tā) Pan.	9·22 N	82·07 W
165	Almirós Grc.	39·13 N	22·47 E
162	Almodóvar (äl-mō-dhō′vär) Sp.	38·43 N	4·10 W
184	Almoi India	29·41 N	79·42 E
124	Almoloya (äl-mō-lō′yä) Mex.	19·32 N	99·44 W
125	Almoloya Mex. (In.)	19·11 N	99·28 W
105	Almonte (ăl-mŏn′tē) Can.	45·15 N	76·15 W
162	Almonte (äl-mōn′tā) Sp.	37·16 N	6·32 W
162	Almonte (R.) Sp.	39·35 N	5·50 W
184	Almora India	29·20 N	79·40 E
186	Al Mubarraz Sau. Ar.	22·31 N	46·27 E
183	Al Mudawwarah Jordan (Palestine In.)	29·20 N	36·01 E
186	Al Mukallā P. D. R. of Yem.	14·27 N	49·05 E
186	Al Mukhā Yemen	13·43 N	43·27 E
162	Almuñécar (äl-mōōn-yā′kär) Sp.	36·44 N	3·43 W
156	Alnö (I.) Swe.	62·20 N	17·39 E
112	Aloha (ä′lō-hä)..Or. (Portland In.)	45·29 N	122·52 W
197	Alor (I.) (ä′lôr) Indon.	8·07 S	125·00 E
162	Álora (ä′lō-rä) Sp.	36·49 N	4·42 W
183	Alor Gajah..Mala (Singapore In.)	2·23 N	102·13 E
196	Alor Setar (ä′lôr stär) Mala.	6·24 N	100·08 E
188	Alot′ai (ä̤lōt′ī) China	47·52 N	86·50 E
112	Alouette (R.) (ä-lōō-ĕt′) Can. (Vancouver In.)	49·16 N	122·32 W
104	Alpena (ăl-pē′nȧ) Mi.	45·05 N	83·30 W
149	Alphen....Neth. (Amsterdam In.)	52·07 N	4·38 E
162	Alpiarca (äl-pyär′sȧ) Port.	39·38 N	8·37 W
118	Alpine (ăl′pīn) Tx.	30·21 N	103·41 W
152	Alps (Mts.) (ălps) Eur.	46·18 N	8·42 E
134	Alpujarra (äl-pōō-ĸä′rä) Col. (In.)	3·23 N	74·56 W
162	Alpujarras (Mts.) (äl-pōō-här′räs) Sp.	36·55 N	3·25 W
211	Al Qaḍārif Sud.	14·03 N	35·11 E
218	Al Qāhirah (Cairo) Egypt (Nile In.)	30·00 N	31·17 E
218	Al Qanṭarah.....Egypt (Suez In.)	30·51 N	32·20 E
211	Al Qaryah ash Sharqiyah...Libya	30·36 N	13·13 E
186	Al Qaṭīf Sau. Ar.	26·30 N	50·00 E
186	Al Qayṣūmah Sau. Ar.	28·15 N	46·20 E
183	Al Qunaytirah Syr. (Palestine In.)	33·09 N	35·49 E
186	Al Qunfudhah Sau. Ar.	19·08 N	41·05 E
183	Al Quṣaymah Egypt (Palestine In.)	30·40 N	34·23 E
211	Al Quṣayr Egypt	26·14 N	34·11 E
183	Al Qusayr...Egypt (Palestine In.)	34·32 N	36·33 E
156	Als (I.) (äls) Den.	55·06 N	9·40 E
161	Alsace (Reg.) (äl-sȧ′s) Fr.	48·25 N	7·24 E
190	Al Shan (Mts.) (äī′shän) China	37·27 N	120·35 E
156	Alsterån (R.) Swe.	56·54 N	15·50 E
113	Altadena (ăl-tă-dē′nä) Ca. (Los Angeles In.)	34·12 N	118·08 W
136	Alta Gracia (äl′tä grä′sē-a) Arg.	31·41 S	64·19 W
134	Altagracia Ven.	10·42 N	71·34 W
135	Altagracia de Orituco (ä′l-tȧ-grȧ′sēȧ-dĕ-ôrē-tōō′kô) Ven. (In.)	9·53 N	66·22 W
188	Altai Mts. (äl′tī′) Asia	49·11 N	87·15 E
113	Alta Loma (ăl′tă lō′mä) Ca. (Los Angeles In.)	34·07 N	117·35 W
119	Alta Loma (ăl′tȧ lō-mȧ)..Tx. (In.)	29·22 N	95·05 W
121	Altamaha (R.) (ôl-tȧ-mȧ-hô′)..Ga.	31·50 N	82·00 W
135	Altamira (äl-tä-mē′rä) Braz.	3·13 S	52·14 W
125	Altamira Mex.	22·25 N	97·55 W
136	Altamirano (äl-tä-mē-rä′nō)..Arg.	35·26 S	58·12 W
164	Altamura (äl-tä-mōō′rä) It.	40·40 N	16·35 E
173	Altan Bulag Mong.	50·18 N	106·31 E
121	Altavista (ăl-tä-vēs′tȧ) Va.	37·08 N	79·14 W
150	Alten (R.) (äl′tĕn) Nor.	69·40 N	24·09 E
158	Altenburg (äl-tĕn-bōōrgh) .G.D.R.	50·59 N	12·27 E
149	Altenmarkt an der Triesting Aus. (Vienna In.)	48·02 N	16·00 E
162	Alter do Chão (äl-tĕr′dōō shäɴ′ōɴ). Port.	39·13 N	7·38 W
124	Altiplanicie Mexicana (Plat.) (äl-tē-plä-nē′syĕ-mĕ-ĸē-kȧ-nä) Mex.	22·38 N	102·33 W
134	Altiplano (Plat.) (äl-tē-plȧ′nō) Bol.	18·38 S	68·20 W
149	Alt Landsberg (ält länts′bĕrgh) G.D.R. (Berlin In.)	52·34 N	13·44 E
119	Alto (ăl′tō) La.	32·21 N	91·52 W
134	Alto Marañón, Río (R.) (rē′ō-ȧl′tō-mä-rän-yō′n). Peru	8·18 S	77·13 W
217	Alto Molócuè Moz.	15·38 S	37·42 E
149	Altomünster (äl′tō-mün′stĕr) F.R.G. (Munich In.)	48·24 N	11·16 E
89	Alton (ôl′tŭn)..Can. (Toronto In.)	43·52 N	80·05 W
113	Alton Il. (St. Louis In.)	38·53 N	90·11 W
202	Altona.....Austl. (Melbourne In.)	37·52 S	144·50 E
95	Altona Can.	49·06 N	97·33 W
149	Altona (äl′tō-nȧ) F.R.G. (Hamburg In.)	53·33 N	9·54 E
120	Altoona (ăl-tōō′nȧ) Al.	34·01 N	86·15 W
105	Altoona Pa.	40·25 N	78·25 W
112	Altoona.......Wa. (Portland In.)	46·16 N	123·39 W
137	Alto Rio Doce (äl′tô-rē′ô-dō′sĕ) Braz. (Rio de Janeiro In.)	21·02 S	43·23 W
129	Alto Songo (äl-fō-sôŋ′gō)....Cuba	20·10 N	75·45 W
125	Altotonga (äl-tō-tôŋ′gä).....Mex.	19·44 N	97·13 W
216	Alto-Uama Ang.	12·14 S	15·33 E
129	Alto Velo (I.) (äl-tō-vĕ′lō) Dom. Rep.	17·30 N	71·35 W
148	Altrincham (ôl′trĭng-ăm) Eng.	53·18 N	2·21 W
149	Alt Ruppin (ält rōō′ppēn) G.D.R. (Berlin In.)	52·56 N	12·50 E
110	Alturas (ăl-tōō′rȧs) Ca.	41·29 N	120·33 W
116	Altus (ăl′tŭs) Ok.	34·38 N	99·20 W
211	Al-Ubayyiḍ Sud.	13·15 N	30·15 E
211	Al-Uḍayyah Sud.	12·06 N	28·16 E
211	Al-′Ugaylah Libya	30·15 N	19·07 E
166	Alūksne (ä′lōōks-nĕ).....Sov. Un.	57·24 N	27·04 E
218	′Alula (ä-lōō′lä) Som. (Horn of Afr. In.)	11·53 N	50·40 E
105	Alumette I. (ȧ-lü-mĕt′) Can.	45·50 N	77·00 W
112	Alum Rock Ca. (San Francisco In.)	37·23 N	121·50 W
218	Al Uqṣur (Luxor). Egypt (Nile In.)	25·38 N	32·59 E
167	Alushta (ä′lshōō-tȧ).....Sov. Un.	44·39 N	34·23 E
116	Alva (ăl′vȧ) Ok.	36·46 N	98·41 W
125	Alvarado (äl-vä-rä′dhō).....Mex.	18·48 N	95·45 W
125	Alvarado, Luguna de (L.) (lä-gōō′nä-dĕ-äl-vä-rä′dô)..Mex.	18·44 N	96·45 W
156	Älvdalen (ĕlv′dä-lĕn) Swe.	61·14 N	14·04 E
163	Alverca (al-vĕr′kȧ) Port. (Lisbon In.)	38·53 N	9·02 W
156	Alvesta (äl-vĕs′tä) Swe.	56·55 N	14·29 E
119	Alvin (ăl′vĭn) Tx. (In.)	29·25 N	95·14 W
137	Alvinópolis (äl-vēnō′pō-lēs) Braz. (Rio de Janeiro In.)	20·07 S	43·03 W
112	Alviso (ăl-vī′sō) Ca. (San Francisco In.)	37·26 N	121·59 W
186	Al Wajh Sau. Ar.	26·15 N	36·32 E
184	Alwar (ŭl′wŭr) India	27·39 N	76·39 E
218	Al Wāsiṭah Egypt (Nile In.)	29·21 N	31·15 E
157	Alytus (ä′lê-tōōs) Sov. Un.	54·25 N	24·05 E
124	Amacuzac (R.) (ä-mä-kōō-zȧk) Mex.	18·00 N	99·03 W
204	Amadeus, (L.) (ăm-ȧ-dē′ŭs). Austl.	24·30 S	131·25 E
91	Amadjuak (L.) (ä-mädj′wäk). Can.	64·50 N	69 20 W
195	Amagasaki (ä′mä-gä-sä′kê) Jap. (Ōsaka In.)	34·43 N	135·25 E
195	Amakusa-Shimo (I.) (ämä-kōō′sä shē-mō). Jap.	32·24 N	129·35 E
156	Åmål (ô′môl) Swe.	59·05 N	12·40 E
134	Amalfi (ä-mä′l-fē)......Col. (In.)	6·55 N	75·04 W
163	Amalfi (ä-mä′l-fē). It. (Naples In.)	40·23 N	14·36 E
165	Amaliás (ȧ-măl′yȧs) Grc.	37·48 N	21·23 E
184	Amalner India	21·07 N	75·06 E
135	Amambai, Serra de (Mts.) Braz.	20·06 S	57·08 W
194	Amami Guntō (Is.) (ä′mä′mē gōōn′tō′). Jap.	28·25 N	129·00 E
194	Amamio (I.) (ä-mä′mē-ō).....Jap.	28·10 N	129·55 E
135	Amapá (ä-mä-pá′) Braz.	2·14 N	50·48 W
135	Amapá (Ter.) Braz.	1·15 N	52·15 W
126	Amapala (ä-mä-pä′lä)......Hond.	13·16 N	87·39 W
135	Amarante (ä-mä-rän′tä).....Braz.	6·17 S	42·43 W
114	Amargosa (R.) (ȧ′mär-gō′sȧ)..Ca.	35·55 N	116·45 W
116	Amarillo (ăm-ȧ-rĭl′ō) Tx.	35·14 N	101·49 W
164	Amaro, Mt. (ä-mä′rō) It.	42·07 N	14·07 E
171	Amasya (ä-mä′sê-ȧ) Tur.	40·40 N	35·50 E
125	Amatenango (ä-mä-tä-naŋ′gō) Mex.	16·30 N	92·29 W
101	Amatignak (I.) (ä-mȧ′tê-näk)..Ak.	51·12 N	178·30 W
126	Amatique, Bahía de (B.) (bä-ē′ä-dĕ-ä-mä-tē′kä) Belize-Guat.	15·58 N	88·50 W
126	Amatitlán (ä-mä-tê-tlän′)...Guat.	14·27 N	90·39 W
124	Amatlán de Cañas (ä-mät-län′dā kän-yäs). Mex.	20·50 N	104·22 W
134	Amazonas (State) (ä-mä-thō′näs). Braz.	4·15 S	64·30 W
135	Amazonas, Rio (R.) (rē′ō-ä-mä-thō′näs). Braz.	2·03 S	53·18 W
184	Ambāla (ŭm-bä′lŭ) India	30·31 N	76·48 E
134	Ambalema (äm-bä-lā′mä) Col. (In.)	4·47 N	74·45 W
173	Ambarchik (ŭm-bär′chĭk). Sov. Un.	69·39 N	162·18 E
185	Ambarnāth...India (Bombay In.)	19·12 N	73·10 E
134	Ambato (äm-bä′tō) Ec.	1·15 S	78·30 W
213	Ambatondrazaka Mad.	17·58 S	48·43 E
158	Amberg (äm′bĕrgh) F.R.G.	49·26 N	11·51 E
126	Ambergris Cay (I.) (ăm′bĕr-grēs kāz). Belize	18·04 N	87·43 W
129	Ambergris Cays (Is.) Turks & Caicos Is.	21·20 N	71·40 W
161	Ambérieu (äɴ-bā-rê-u′) Fr.	45·57 N	5·21 E
160	Ambert (äɴ-bĕr′) Fr.	45·32 N	3·41 E
197	Ambil (I.) (äm′bēl).....Phil. (In.)	13·51 N	120·25 E
106	Ambler (ăm′blĕr) Pa. (Philadelphia In.)	40·09 N	75·13 W
197	Amboina (ăm-boi′nȧ) Indon.	3·45 S	128·17 E
160	Amboise (äɴ-bwăz′) Fr.	47·25 N	0·56 E
197	Ambon (I.) Indon.	4·50 S	128·45 E
213	Ambositra (äɴ-bô-sē′trä)....Mad.	20·31 S	47·28 E
104	Amboy (ăm′boi) Il.	41·41 N	89·15 W
112	Amboy........Wa. (Portland In.)	45·55 N	122·27 W
213	Ambre, Cap d′ (C.) Mad.	12·06 S	49·15 E
107	Ambridge (ăm′brĭdj) Pa. (Pittsburgh In.)	40·36 N	80·13 W
205	Ambrim (I.) New Heb.	16·25 S	168·15 E
216	Ambriz Ang.	7·50 S	13·06 E
216	Ambrizete Ang.	7·14 S	12·52 E
101	Amchitka P. (ăm-chĭt′kȧ).....Ak.	51·30 N	179·36 W
184	Amdo Tsonag Tsho (L.)....China	31·38 N	91·18 E
124	Amealco (ä-mā-äl′kō) Mex.	20·12 N	100·08 W
124	Ameca (ä-mĕ′kä) Mex.	20·34 N	104·02 W
125	Amecameca (ä-mȧ-kä-mä′kä) Mex. (In.)	19·06 N	98·46 W
149	Ameide...Neth. (Amsterdam In.)	51·57 N	4·57 E
155	Ameland (I.) Neth.	53·29 N	5·54 E
107	Amelia (ȧ-mēl′yȧ) Oh. (Cincinnati In.)	39·01 N	84·12 W
114	American (R.) (ȧ-mĕr′ĭ-kăn)...Ca.	38·43 N	120·45 W
137	Americana (ä-mĕ-rê-kȧ′nȧ) Braz. (Rio de Janeiro In.)	22·46 S	47·19 W
111	American Falls (ȧ-mĕr-ĭ-kăn)..Id.	42·45 N	112·53 W
111	American Falls Res. Id.	42·56 N	113·18 W
115	American Fork Ut.	40·20 N	111·50 W
220	American Highland Ant.	72·00 S	79·00 E
120	Americus (ȧ-mĕr′ĭ-kŭs) Ga.	32·04 N	84·15 W
149	Amersfoort (ä′mĕrz-fōrt) Neth. (Amsterdam In.)	52·08 N	5·23 E
95	Amery (ā′mĕr-ê) Can.	56·34 N	94·03 W
109	Amery Wi.	45·19 N	92·24 W
109	Ames (āmz) Ia.	42·00 N	93·36 W
99	Amesbury (āmz′bĕr-ê)...Ma. (In.)	42·51 N	70·56 W
165	Amfissa (ȧm-fĭ′sȧ) Grc.	38·32 N	22·26 E
173	Amga (ŭm-gä′) Sov. Un.	61·08 N	132·09 E
173	Amga (R.) Sov. Un.	61·41 N	133·11 E
173	Amgun (R.) Sov. Un.	53·33 N	137·57 E
211	Amhara (Prov.) (äm-hä′rä)...Eth.	11·30 N	36·45 E
98	Amherst (ăm′hĕrst) Can.	45·49 N	64·14 W
107	Amherst......Oh. (Cleveland In.)	41·24 N	82·13 W
97	Amherst (I.) Can.	44·08 N	76·45 W
160	Amiens (ä-myăɴ′) Fr.	49·54 N	2·18 E
220	Amirante Is. Sey.	6·02 S	52·30 E
95	Amisk L. Can.	54·35 N	102·13 W
118	Amistad Res. Tx.	29·20 N	101·00 W
119	Amite (ă-mēt′) La.	30·43 N	90·32 W
119	Amite R. La.	30·45 N	90·48 W
107	Amity (ăm′ĭ-tĭ) Pa. (In.)	40·02 N	80·11 W
106	Amityville (ăm′ĭ-tĭ-vĭl) NY (New York In.)	40·41 N	73·24 W
101	Amlia (I.) (ȧ′m-lêä) Ak.	52·00 N	173·28 W
183	′Ammān (äm′man) Jordan (Palestine In.)	31·57 N	35·57 E
149	Ammer L. (äm′mĕr) F.R.G. (Munich In.)	48·00 N	11·08 E
113	Amnicon R. (ăm′nê-kŏn) Wi. (Duluth In.)	46·35 N	91·56 W
	Amnok (R.), see Yalu		
165	Amorgós (I.) (ä-môr′gōs).....Grc.	36·47 N	25·47 E
120	Amory (ăm′o-rē) Ms.	33·58 N	88·27 W
97	Amos (ā′mŭs) Can.	48·31 N	78·04 W
156	Åmot (Torpen) (ô′mōt) (tôr′pĕn) Nor.	61·08 N	11·17 E
	Amoy, see Hsiamen		
137	Amparo (äm-pȧ′-rô) Braz. (Rio de Janeiro In.)	22·43 S	46·44 W
149	Amper R. (äm′pĕr) F.R.G. (Munich In.)	48·18 N	11·32 E
163	Amposta (äm-pōs′tä) Sp.	40·42 N	0·34 E
98	Amqui Can.	48·28 N	67·28 W
184	Amrāvati India	20·58 N	77·47 E
184	Amritsar (ŭm-rĭt′sŭr) India	31·43 N	74·52 E
149	Amstelveen Neth. (Amsterdam In.)	52·18 N	4·51 E
149	Amsterdam (äm-stĕr-däm′) Neth. (Amsterdam In.)	52·21 N	4·52 E
105	Amsterdam (ăm′stĕr-dăm)....NY	42·55 N	74·10 W
158	Amstetten (äm′stĕt-ĕn) Aus.	48·09 N	14·53 E
211	Am Timan (äm′tê-män′)....Chad	11·18 N	20·30 E
186	Amu Darya (R.) (ä-mōō-dä′rēä). Asia	40·40 N	62·00 E
101	Amukta P. (ä-mōōk′tȧ) Ak.	52·30 N	172·00 W
197	Amulung (ä′mōō′lōōng) Phil. (In.)	17·51 N	121·43 E
90	Amundsen G. (ä′mŭn-sĕn)....Can.	70·17 N	123·28 W
220	Amundsen Sea Ant.	72·00 S	110·00 W
156	Amungen (L.) Swe.	61·07 N	16·00 E
192	Amur R. (ä-mōōr′) China and Sov. Un.	49·38 N	127·25 E
174	Amurskiy (ä-mûr′skĭ) Sov. Un. (Urals In.)	52·35 N	59·36 E
194	Amurskiy, Zaliv (B.) (zä′lĭf ä-mōōr′skĭ). Sov. Un.	43·20 N	131·40 E
124	Amusgos (San Pedro) (ä-mōō′s-gôs) (sän-pĕ′drō). Mex.	16·39 N	98·09 W
197	Amuyao, Mt. (ä-mōō-yä′ō) Phil. (In.)	17·04 N	121·09 E

PRONOUNCING INDEX

Amvrakikos — 'Arabah 251

Page	Name Pronunciation Region	Lat. °'	Long. °'
165	Amvrakikos Kólpos (G.)..... Grc.	39·00 N	21·00 E
183	Amyun....... Leb. (Palestine In.)	34·18 N	35·48 E
173	Anabar (R.) (ăn-à-bär') Sov. Un.	71·15 N	113·00 E
135	Anaco (ä-nà'kô)........ Ven. (In.)	9·29 N	64·27 W
111	Anaconda (ăn-à-kŏn'dà)...... Mt.	46·07 N	112·55 W
112	Anacortes (ăn-à-kôr'tĕz) Wa. (Seattle In.)	48·30 N	122·37 W
116	Anadarko (ăn-à-där'kō)....... Ok.	35·05 N	98·14 W
173	Anadyr' (ŭ-nà-dĭr')...... Sov. Un.	64·47 N	177·01 E
173	Anadyr (R.)............ Sov. Un.	65·30 N	172·45 E
183	Anadyrskiy Zaliv (B.)... Sov. Un.	64·10 N	178·00 W
113	Anaheim (ăn'à-hīm) Ca. (Los Angeles In.)	33·50 N	117·55 W
119	Anahuac (ä-nä'wäk)..... Tx. (In.)	29·46 N	94·41 W
185	Ānai Mudi (Mtn.).......... India	10·10 N	77·00 E
95	Anama Bay................ Can.	51·56 N	98·05 W
128	Ana María, Cayos (Is.) (kä'yōs-ä'nà mà-rē'à). Cuba	21·55 N	78·50 W
196	Anambas, Kepulauan (Is.) (ä-näm-bäs). Indon.	2·41 N	106·38 E
109	Anamosa (ăn-à-mō'sà)......... Ia.	42·06 N	91·18 W
167	Anan'yev (à-nä'nyĕf).... Sov. Un.	47·43 N	29·59 E
167	Anapa (à-nä'pä)......... Sov. Un.	44·54 N	37·19 E
135	Anápolis (ä-nà'pō-lēs)....... Braz.	16·17 S	48·47 W
136	Añatuya (à-nyä-tōō'yà)...... Arg.	28·22 S	62·45 W
160	Ancenis (äN-sē-nē')........... Fr.	47·24 N	1·12 W
136	Anchieta (àn-chyĕ'tä) Braz. (Rio de Janeiro In.)	22·49 S	43·24 W
193	Anching (än'kĭng')......... China	30·32 N	117·00 E
101	Anchitka (I.) (än-chē't-kä).... Ak.	51·25 N	178·10 E
190	Anch' iu (än'chē).......... China	36·26 N	119·12 E
148	Ancholme (R.) (ăn'chŭm).... Eng.	53·28 N	0·27 W
101	Anchorage (ăŋ'kēr-āj)........ Ak.	61·12 N	149·48 W
107	Anchorage.... Ky. (Louisville In.)	38·16 N	85·32 W
89	Ancienne-Lorette (äN-syĕn' lō-rĕt') Can. (Quebec In.)	46·48 N	71·21 W
122	Ancon (ăŋ-kōn')...... C. Z. (In.)	8·55 N	79·32 W
164	Ancona (än-kō'nä)............ It.	43·37 N	13·32 E
136	Ancud (äŋ-kōōdh')......... Chile	41·52 S	73·45 W
136	Ancud, G. de (gôl-fô-dĕ-äŋ-kōōdh'). Chile	41·15 S	73·00 W
136	Andalgalá (á'n-däl-gä-lá').... Arg.	27·35 S	66·14 W
162	Andalucia (Reg.) (än-dä-lōō-sē'ä). Sp.	37·35 N	5·40 W
120	Andalusia (ăn-dà-lōō'zhĭà)..... Al.	31·19 N	86·19 W
196	Andaman Is. (ăn-dà-măn') Andaman & Nicobar Is.	11·38 N	92·17 E
196	Andaman Sea............... Asia	12·44 N	95·45 E
149	Anderlecht (än'dēr-lĕkt) Bel. (Brussels In.)	50·49 N	4·16 E
158	Andernach (än'dēr-näk).... F.R.G.	50·25 N	7·23 E
137	Anderson (ä'n-dĕr-sōn) Arg. (Buenos Aires In.)	35·15 S	60·15 W
110	Anderson (ăn'dēr-sŭn)........ Ca.	40·28 N	122·19 W
104	Anderson.................... In.	40·05 N	85·50 W
121	Anderson.................... SC	34·30 N	82·40 W
90	Anderson (R.).............. Can.	68·32 N	125·12 W
133	Andes Mts. (ăn'dēz) (än'dās).. S. A.	13·00 S	75·00 W
185	Andheri............. India (In.)	19·08 N	72·50 E
185	Andhra Pradesh (State)...... India	16·00 N	79·00 E
153	Andikíthira (I.)............ Grc.	35·50 N	23·20 E
172	Andizhan (än-dē-zhän').. Sov. Un.	40·51 N	72·39 E
194	Andong (än'dŭng')......... Kor.	36·31 N	128·42 E
163	Andorra (än-dôr'rä)......... And.	42·38 N	1·30 E
151	Andorra.................. Eur.	42·30 N	2·00 E
99	Andover (ăn'dō-vēr)..... Ma. (In.)	42·39 N	71·08 W
106	Andover...... NJ (New York In.)	40·59 N	74·45 W
150	Andöy (I.) (änd-ûē)......... Nor.	69·12 N	14·58 E
163	Andraitx (än-drà-ītsh')........ Sp.	39·34 N	2·25 E
101	Andreanof Is. (än-drâ-ä'nôf)... Ak.	51·10 N	177·00 W
137	Andrelândia (än-drĕ-lä'n-dyà) Braz. (Rio de Janeiro In.)	21·45 S	44·18 W
120	Andrew Johnson Natl. Mon. (ăn'drōō jŏn'sŭn). Tn.	36·15 N	82·55 W
120	Andrews (ăn'drōōz).......... NC	35·12 N	83·48 W
121	Andrews.................... SC	33·25 N	79·32 W
167	Andreyevka (än-drâ-yĕf'kà) Sov. Un.	48·03 N	37·03 E
164	Andria (än'drē-ä)............ It.	41·17 N	15·55 E
165	Andros (än'dhrôs)........... Grc.	37·50 N	24·54 E
128	Andros I. (ăn'drŏs).......... Ba.	24·30 N	78·00 W
165	Andrós (I.) (än'drôs)........ Grc.	37·59 N	24·55 E
98	Androscoggin (R.) (ăn-drŭs-kŏg'ĭn). Me.	44·25 N	70·45 W
162	Andújar (än-dōō'här).......... Sp.	38·04 N	4·03 W
214	Anefis i-n-Darane............ Mali	18·03 N	0·36 E
195	Anegasaki (ä'nâ-gä-sä'kē) Jap. (Tōkyō In.)	35·29 N	140·02 E
205	Aneityum (I.) (ä-nâ-ē'tē-ŭm) New Hebr.	20·15 S	169·49 E
108	Aneta (ă-nē'tà)............. ND	47·41 N	97·57 W
197	Angadanan (äŋ-gà-dä'nàn) Phil. (In.)	16·45 N	121·45 E
197	Angaki (än-gä'kē)...... Phil. (In.)	17·10 N	120·40 E
124	Angamacutiro (än'gä-mä-kōō-tē'rô). Mex.	20·08 N	101·44 W
192	Angangchi (än'gäng'kē').... China	47·05 N	123·58 E
124	Angangueo (än-gäŋ'gwä-ō)... Mex.	19·36 N	100·18 W
	Angara (R.), see Verkhnyaya Tunguska		
172	Angarsk............... Sov. Un.	52·48 N	104·15 E
156	Ange (ông'ā)................. Swe.	62·31 N	15·39 E
134	Angel, Salto (Falls) (säl'tō-à'n-hĕl). Ven.	5·44 N	62·27 W
122	Angel De La Guarda (I.) (á'n-hĕl-dĕ-lä-gwä'r-dä). Mex.	29·30 N	113·00 W
197	Angeles (än'hâ-lās)..... Phil. (In.)	15·09 N	120·35 E
156	Ängelholm (ĕng'ĕl-hôlm)..... Swe.	56·14 N	12·50 E
119	Angelina R. (ăn-jē lē'nà)..... Tx.	31·30 N	94·53 W
114	Angels Camp (ān'jĕls kămp')... Ca.	38·03 N	120·33 W
150	Angermanälven (R.)......... Swe.	64·02 N	17·15 E
161	Angermund (än'ngĕr-mŭnd) F.R.G. (Ruhr In.)	51·20 N	6·47 E
158	Angermünde (äng'ĕr-mûn-dĕ) G.D.R.	53·02 N	14·00 E
89	Angers (äN-zhā') Can. (Ottawa In.)	41·31 N	75·29 W
160	Angers...................... Fr.	47·29 N	0·36 W
196	Angkor (Ruins) (äng'kôr).. Camb.	13·52 N	103·50 E
154	Anglesey (I.) (ăŋ'g'l-sē)..... Wales	53·35 N	4·28 W
119	Angleton (aŋ'g'l-tŭn).... Tx. (In.)	29·10 N	95·25 W
75	Angmagssalik (àŋ-mà'sà-lĭk) Grnld.	65·40 N	37·40 W
217	Angoche, Ilha (I.) (ē'lä-ăn-gō'châ). Moz.	16·20 S	40·00 E
136	Angol (aŋ-gōl')............ Chile	37·47 S	72·43 W
104	Angola (ăŋ-gō'là)............ In.	41·35 N	85·00 W
209	Angola..................... Afr.	14·15 S	16·00 E
	Angora, see Ankara		
160	Angoulême (äŋ-gōō-lâm')...... Fr.	45·40 N	0·09 E
137	Angra dos Reis (aŋ'grä dōs rā'ēs) Braz. (Rio de Janeiro In.)	23·01 S	44·17 W
163	Angri (ä'n-grê).... It. (Naples In.)	40·30 N	14·35 E
128	Anguilla, Cays (Is.) (ăŋ-gwĭl'à) Ba.	23·30 N	79·35 W
127	Anguilla (I.) St. Kitts-Nevis-Anguilla (In.)	18·15 N	62·54 W
99	Anguille, C. (äŋ-gē'yĕ)....... Can.	47·55 N	59·25 W
156	Anholt (I). (än'hŏlt)........ Den.	56·43 N	11·34 E
188	Anhsi..................... China	40·36 N	95·49 E
189	Anhwei (Anhui) (Prov.).... China	31·30 N	117·15 E
101	Aniak (ä-nyà'k).............. Ak.	61·32 N	159·35 W
115	Animas (R.) (ä'nê-màs)....... Co.	37·03 N	107·50 W
165	Anina (ä-nē'nä)............ Rom.	45·03 N	21·50 E
105	Anita (à-nē'à)............... Pa.	41·05 N	79·00 W
194	Aniva, Mys (Pt.) (mĭs à-nē'và) Sov. Un.	46·08 N	143·13 E
194	Aniva, Zaliv (B.) (zä'lĭf à-nē'và) Sov. Un.	46·28 N	143·30 E
89	Anjou........ Can. (Montreal In.)	45·37 N	73·33 W
213	Anjouan (I.) (äN-zhwäN) Comoros	12·14 S	44·47 E
192	Ank'ang................. China	32·38 N	109·10 E
171	Ankara (Angora) (än'kà-rà) (ăn-gō'rà). Tur.	39·55 N	32·50 E
158	Anklam (än'kläm)........ G.D.R.	53·52 N	13·43 E
217	Ankoro (ăŋ-kō'rō)........... Zaire	6·45 S	26·57 E
190	Ankuo (an'gōō ŭ).......... China	38·27 N	115·19 E
214	Anloga.................. Ghana	5·47 N	0·50 E
193	Anlu (än'lōō')............. China	31·18 N	113·40 E
193	Anlung................... China	25·01 N	105·32 E
105	Ann, C. (ăn)................ Ma.	42·40 N	70·40 W
117	Anna (ăn'à).................. Il.	37·28 N	89·15 W
167	Anna (än'ä)........... Sov. Un.	51·31 N	40·27 E
210	Annaba (Bône)............. Alg.	36·57 N	7·39 E
158	Annaberg-Bucholz (än'ä-bĕrgh). G.D.R.	50·35 N	13·02 E
186	An Nafūd (Des.)........ Sau. Ar.	28·30 N	40·30 E
186	An Najaf (än nä-jäf')......... Iraq	32·00 N	44·25 E
183	An Nakhl... Egypt (Palestine In.)	29·55 N	33·45 E
196	Annamitic Cordillera (Mts.) (ä-nà-mĭt'ĭk kôr-dĭl-yä'rà) Laos-Viet.	17·34 N	105·38 E
106	Annapolis (ă-năp'ô-lĭs) Md. (Baltimore In.)	39·00 N	76·25 W
98	Annapolis Royal........... Can.	44·45 N	65·31 W
104	Ann Arbor (ăn är'bēr)........ Mi.	42·15 N	83·45 W
186	An Nāşirīyah................ Iraq	31·08 N	46·15 E
211	An Nawfalīyah)............ Libya	30·57 N	17·38 E
161	Annecy (àn sē')............... Fr.	45·54 N	6·07 E
161	Annemasse (än'mäs')........... Fr.	46·09 N	6·13 E
174	Annenskoye (ä-nĕn'skô-yĕ) Sov. Un. (Urals In.)	53·09 N	60·25 E
92	Annette I.................... Ak.	55·13 N	131·30 W
99	Annieopsquotch Mts.......... Can.	48·37 N	57·17 W
120	Anniston (ăn'ĭs-tŭn).......... Al.	33·39 N	85·47 W
160	Annonay (à-nô-nē').......... Fr.	45·16 N	4·36 E
128	Annotto Bay (än-nō'tō)..... Jam.	18·15 N	76·45 W
211	An-Nudūd.................. Sud.	12·39 N	28·18 E
113	Anoka (à-nō'kà) Mn. (Minneapolis, St. Paul In.)	45·12 N	93·24 W
134	Anori (á-nō'rê)......... Col. (In.)	7·01 N	75·09 W
165	Áno Theológos............. Grc.	40·37 N	24·41 E
164	Áno Viánnos.......... Grc. (In.)	35·02 N	25·26 E
193	Anp'u.................... China	21·28 N	110·00 E
158	Ansbach (äns'bäk)........ F.R.G.	49·18 N	10·35 E
129	Anse à Veau (äNs' ä-vō')..... Hai.	18·30 N	73·25 W
129	Anse d' Hainault (äNs'dĕnō).. Hai.	18·45 N	74·25 W
134	Anserma (á'n-sĕ'r-mà)... Col. (In.)	5·13 N	75·47 W
134	Ansermanuevo (á'n-sĕ'r-mà-nwĕ'vō). Col. (In.)	4·47 N	75·59 W
192	Anshan................... China	41·00 N	123·00 E
193	Anshun (än-shōōn')........ China	26·12 N	105·50 E
118	Anson (ăn'sŭn)................ Tx.	32·45 N	99·52 W
204	Anson B.................. Austl.	13·10 S	130·00 E
194	Ansŏng (än'sŭng')........... Kor.	37·00 N	127·12 E
214	Ansongo................... Mali	15·40 N	0·30 E
105	Ansonia (ăn-sō'nĭ-à)........... Ct.	41·20 N	73·05 W
171	Antakya (än-täk'yä).......... Tur.	36·20 N	36·10 E
171	Antalya (Adalia) (än-tä'lē-ä) (ä-dä'lē-ä). Tur.	37·00 N	30·50 E
171	Antalya Körfezi (G.)......... Tur.	36·40 N	31·20 E
213	Antananarivo.............. Mad.	18·51 S	47·40 E
220	Antarctica.......................	80·15 S	127·00 E
220	Antartic Pen............... Ant.	70·00 S	65·00 W
111	Antelope Cr. (ăn'tê-lōp)...... Wy.	43·29 N	105·42 W
162	Antequera (än-tĕ-kĕ'rä)........ Sp.	37·01 N	4·34 W
116	Anthony (ăn'thō-nē).......... Ks.	37·08 N	98·01 W
210	Anti Atlas (Mts.)........... Mor.	28·45 N	9·30 W
161	Antibes (äN-tēb')............. Fr.	43·36 N	7·12 E
99	Anticosti, Île d' (I.) (ăn-tĭ-kŏs'tē). Can.	49·30 N	62·00 W
109	Antigo (ăn'tĭ-gō)............. Wi.	45·09 N	89·11 W
99	Antigonish (ăn-tĭ-gô-nēsh')... Can.	45·35 N	61·55 W
126	Antigua (än-tē'gwä)........ Guat.	14·32 N	90·43 W
123	Antigua.................. N. A.	17·15 N	61·15 W
125	Antigua (R.)............... Mex.	19·16 N	96·36 W
125	Antigua Veracruz (än-tē'gwä vā-rä-krōōz'). Mex.	19·18 N	96·17 W
129	Antilla (än-tē'lyä).......... Cuba	20·50 N	75·50 W
123	Antilles, Greater (Is.)....... N. A.	20·30 N	79·15 W
123	Antilles, Lesser (Is.)........ N. A.	12·15 N	65·00 W
112	Antioch (ăn'tĭ-ŏk) Ca. (San Francisco In.)	38·00 N	121·48 W
107	Antioch......... Il. (Chicago In.)	42·29 N	88·06 W
108	Antioch.................... Ne.	42·05 N	102·36 W
134	Antioquia (än-tê-ō'kêä).. Col. (In.)	6·34 N	75·49 W
134	Antioquia (Dept.)...... Col. (In.)	6·48 N	75·42 W
117	Antlers (ănt'lērz)............ Ok.	34·14 N	95·38 W
136	Antofagasta (än-tô-fä-gäs'tä) Chile	23·32 N	70·21 W
136	Antofalla, Salar de (Des.) (sà-làr'de àn'tō-fä'lä). Arg.	26·00 S	67·52 W
127	Antón (än-tōn')............. Pan.	8·24 N	80·15 W
213	Antongil, Baie d' (B.) (äN-tôN-zhēl'). Mad.	16·15 S	50·15 E
137	Antônio Carlos (än-tō'nêōō-kà'r-lôs) Braz. (Rio de Janeiro In.)	21·19 S	43·45 W
217	António Enes (ăn-to'nyŏ ĕn'ēs) Moz.	16·14 S	39·58 E
116	Antonito (ăn-tô-nē'tō)........ Co.	37·04 N	106·01 W
166	Antonopole (än'tô-nô-pō lyĕ) Sov. Un.	56·19 N	27·11 E
154	Antrim Mts. (ăn'trĭm)..... N. Ire.	55·00 N	6·10 W
213	Antsirabe (änt-sê-rä'bā)..... Mad.	19·49 S	47·16 E
166	Antsla (änt'slà)......... Sov. Un.	57·49 N	26·29 E
136	Antuco (Vol.) (än-tōō'kō)... Chile	37·30 S	72·30 W
192	Antung (än'tŏŏng')......... China	40·10 N	124·30 E
190	Antungwei (ändŏŏngwā).... China	35·08 N	119·19 E
	Antwerp, see Antwerpen		
149	Antwerpen (Antwerp) (ănt'wērpĕn). Bel. (Brussels In.)	51·13 N	4·24 E
192	Antz'u.............. China (In.)	39·23 N	116·44 E
184	Anūpgarh (ŭ-nŏŏp'gŭr)..... India	29·22 N	73·20 E
185	Anuradhapura (ŭ-nōō'rä-dŭ-pōō'rŭ) Sri Lanka	8·24 N	80·25 E
190	Anyang (än'yäng).......... China	36·05 N	114·22 E
157	Anykščiai (anĭksh-chà'ê). Sov. Un.	55·34 N	25·04 E
134	Anzá (ân-zà')........... Col. (In.)	6·19 N	75·51 W
172	Anzhero-Sudzhensk (än'zhâ-rô-sŏŏd'zhĕnsk). Sov. Un.	56·08 N	86·08 E
163	Anzio (änt'zē-ō).... It. (Rome In.)	41·28 N	12·39 E
135	Anzoátegui (State) (än-zôà'tĕ-gê) Ven. (In.)	9·38 N	64·45 W
194	Aomori (äô-mō'rê)........... Jap.	40·45 N	140·52 E
164	Aosta (ä-ôs'tä).............. It.	45·45 N	7·20 E
211	Aouk, Bahr (R.) (ä-ŏŏk')..... Chad	9·30 N	20·45 E
214	Aoukâr (Pln.)........ Mauritania	18·00 N	9·40 W
120	Apalachicola (ăp-à-lăch-ĭ-kō'là) Fl.	29·43 N	84·59 W
125	Apan (ä-pà'n)......... Mex. (In.)	19·43 N	98·27 W
124	Apango (ä-päŋ'gō).......... Mex.	17·41 N	99·22 W
134	Apaporis (R.) (ä-pä-pô'rĭs).... Col.	0·48 N	72·32 W
196	Aparri (ä-pär'rē)............ Phil.	18·15 N	121·40 E
124	Apasco (ä-pà's-kō).......... Mex.	20·33 N	100·43 W
165	Apatin (ŏ'pŏ-tĭn)........... Yugo.	45·40 N	19·00 E
124	Apatzingán de la Constitución (ä-pät-zĭŋ-gän'dā lä cōn-stĭ-tōō-sē-ōn'). Mex.	19·07 N	102·21 W
155	Apeldoorn (ä'pĕl-dōōrn)..... Neth.	52·14 N	5·55 E
134	Apía (à-pē'ä).......... Col. (In.)	5·07 N	75·58 W
124	Apipilulco (ä-pĭ-pĭ-lōōl'kō)... Mex.	18·09 N	99·40 W
165	Apíranthos................ Grc.	37·07 N	25·32 E
116	Apishapa (R.) (ăp-ĭ-shä'pà)... Co.	37·40 N	104·08 W
124	Apizaco (ä-pê-zä'kō)........ Mex.	19·18 N	98·11 W
197	Apo (Mtn.) (ä'pō)............ Phil.	6·56 N	125·05 E
121	Apopka (ă-pŏp'kà)....... Fl. (In.)	28·37 N	81·30 W
121	Apopka (L.)............ Fl. (In.)	28·38 N	81·50 W
109	Apostle Is. (ă-pŏs'l)......... Wi.	47·05 N	90·55 W
120	Appalachia (ăpà-lăch'ĭ-à)..... Va.	36·54 N	82·49 W
103	Appalachian Mts. (ăp-à-lăch'ĭ-àn). U. S.	37·20 N	82·00 W
120	Appalachicola R. (ăpà-lăch'ĭ-cōlā) Fl.	30·11 N	85·00 W
156	Äppelbo (ĕp-ĕl-bōō)......... Swe.	60·30 N	14·02 E
161	Appelhülsen (ä'pĕl-hül'sĕn) F.R.G. (Ruhr In.)	51·55 N	7·26 E
164	Appennino (Mts.) (äp-pĕn-nē'nô) It.	43·48 N	11·06 E
158	Appenzell (äp'ĕn-tsĕl)...... Switz.	47·19 N	9·22 E
108	Appleton (ăp'l-tŭn).......... Mn.	45·10 N	96·01 W
109	Appleton.................... Wi.	44·14 N	88·27 W
117	Appleton City.............. Mo.	38·10 N	94·02 W
121	Appomattox (R.) (ăp-ō-măt'ŭks) Va.	37·22 N	78·09 W
163	Aprília (à-prē'lyà).. It. (Rome In.)	41·36 N	12·40 E
171	Apsheronskiy, P-Ov. (Pen.) Sov. Un.	40·20 N	50·30 E
161	Apt (äpt).................... Fr.	43·54 N	5·19 E
	Apulia (Reg.), see Puglia		
134	Apure (R.) (ä-pōō'rä)........ Ven.	8·08 N	68·46 W
134	Apurimac (R.) (ä-pōō-rē-mäk') Peru	11·39 S	73·48 W
153	Aqaba, G. of (ä'kà-bà)....... Asia	28·30 N	34·40 E
183	Aqabah, Wādī al (R.) Egypt (Palestine In.)	29·48 N	34·05 E
106	Aquasco (à'gwă'scō) Md. (Baltimore In.)	38·35 N	76·44 W
135	Aquidauana (ä-kē-däwä'nä).. Braz.	20·24 S	55·46 W
162	Aquilianos, Montes (Mts.) (mô'n-tĕs-ä-kē-lyä'nôs). Sp.	42·27 N	6·35 W
129	Aquin (ä-kăn')............... Hai.	18·20 N	73·25 W
195	Ara (R.) (ä-rä).. Jap. (Tōkyō In.)	35·40 N	139·52 E
211	Arab, Bahr al- (R.).......... Sud.	9·46 N	26·52 E
218	'Arabah, Wādī... Egypt (Nile In.)	29·02 N	32·10 E

ng-sing; ŋ-baŋk; N-nasalized n; nŏd; cŏmmit; ōld; ôbey; ôrder; fōōd; fŏŏt; ou-out; s-soft; sh-dish; th-thin; pūre; ûnite; ûrn; stŭd; circŭs; ū-as "y" in study; '-indeterminate vowel.

252 Arabatskaya — Ascent PRONOUNCING INDEX

Page	Name Pronunciation Region	Lat. °′	Long. °′
167	Arabatskaya Strelka (Tongue of Arabat) (Spit) (ä-rä-băt′ skȧ-yȧ strĕl′kȧ) (ȧ-rȧ-băt′). Sov. Un.	45·50 N	35·05 E
106	Arabi...... La. (New Orleans In.)	29·58 N	90·01 W
211	Arabian Des. (Aş Şaḥrā'ash Sharqīyah (ȧ-rā′bĭ-ăn) (Nile In.)	27·06 N	32·49 E
209	Arabian Pen. .... Asia	28·00 N	40·00 E
182	Arabian Sea (ȧ-rā′bĭ-ăn) ..... Asia	16·00 N	65·15 E
135	Aracaju (ä-rä′kä-zhōō′) ..... Braz.	11·00 S	37·01 W
135	Aracati (ä-rä′kä-tē′) .... Braz.	4·31 S	37·41 W
135	Araçatuba (ä-rä-sȧ-tōō′bä) ... Braz.	21·14 S	50·19 W
135	Aracruz (ä-rä-krōō′s) .... Braz.	19·58 S	40·11 W
135	Araçuaí (ä-rä-sōō-ä-ē′) ...... Braz.	16·57 S	41·56 W
183	'Arad .... Isr. (Palestine In.)	31·20 N	35·15 E
159	Arad (ŏ′rŏd) .... Rom.	46·10 N	21·18 E
198	Arafura Sea (ä-rä-fōō′rä) .. Oceania	8·40 S	130·00 E
163	Aragon (Reg.) (ä-rä-gōn′) ..... Sp.	40·55 N	0·45 W
162	Aragón (R.) .... Sp.	42·35 N	1·10 W
135	Aragua (State) (ä-rä′gwä) . Ven. (In.)	10·00 N	67·05 W
135	Aragua de Barcelona (ä-rä′gwä dā bär-thā-lō′nä) Ven. (In.)	9·29 N	64·48 W
135	Araguaía (R.) (ä-rä-gwä′yä) . Braz.	8·37 S	49·43 W
135	Araguari (ä-rä-gwä′rē) ...... Braz.	18·43 S	48·03 W
135	Araguatins (ä-rä-gwä-tēns) .. Braz.	5·41 S	48·04 W
135	Aragüita (ärȧ-gwē′tȧ) ... Ven. (In.)	10·13 N	66·28 W
153	Araj (Oasis) (ä-räj′) .... Egypt	29·05 N	26·51 E
186	Arāk .... Iran	34·08 N	49·57 E
188	Arakan Yoma (Mts.) (ŭ-rŭ-kŭn′yō′mȧ) . Bur.	19·51 N	94·13 E
165	Arakhthos (R.) (är′äĸ-thôs) .. Grc.	39·10 N	21·05 E
	Aral Sea, see Aral'skoye More		
172	Aral'sk (ȧ-rälsk′) .... Sov. Un.	46·47 N	62·00 E
147	Aral'skoye More (Aral Sea) Sov. Un.	45·17 N	60·02 E
171	Aralsor (L.) (ȧ-räl′sôr′) .. Sov. Un.	49·00 N	48·20 E
124	Aramberri (ä-rȧm-bĕr-rē′) .... Mex.	24·05 N	99·47 W
154	Aran (I.) (ăr′ăn) .... Ire.	54·58 N	8·33 W
154	Aran Is. .... Ire.	53·04 N	9·59 W
162	Aranda de Duero (ä-rän′dä dā dwā′rō) . Sp.	41·43 N	3·45 W
124	Arandas (ä-rän′däs) .... Mex.	20·43 N	102·18 W
162	Aranjuez (ä-rän-hwāth′) ...... Sp.	40·02 N	3·24 W
119	Aransas Pass (ȧ-răn′sȧs pȧs) ... Tx.	27·55 N	97·09 W
214	Araouane .... Mali	18·54 N	3·33 W
171	Arapkir (ä-räp-kēr′) .... Tur.	39·00 N	38·10 E
135	Araraquara (ä-rä-rä-kwä′rä) . Braz.	21·47 S	48·08 W
137	Araras (ä-rȧ′răs) Braz. (Rio de Janeiro In.)	22·21 S	47·22 W
135	Araras, Serra das (Mts.) (sĕ′r-rä-däs-ä-rä′räs) . Braz.	18·03 S	53·23 W
136	Araras, Serra das (Mts.) .... Braz.	23·30 S	53·00 W
136	Araras, Serra das (Mts.) . Braz. (In.)	22·24 S	43·15 W
203	Ararat (ăr′ȧrăt) .... Austl.	37·17 S	142·56 E
171	Ararat (Mtn.) .... Tur.	39·50 N	44·20 E
135	Arari (L.) (ä-rä′rē) .... Braz.	0·30 S	48·50 W
135	Araripe, Chapada do (Plain) (shä-pä′dä-dō-ä-rä-rē′pĕ) . Braz.	5·55 S	40·42 W
137	Araruama (ä-rä-rōō-ä′mä) Braz. (Rio de Janeiro In.)	22·53 S	42·19 W
137	Araruama, Lagoa de (L.) (lȧ-gôä-dĕ-ä-rä-rōō-ä′mä) Braz. (Rio de Janeiro In.)	23·00 S	42·15 W
171	Aras (R.) (ȧ-räs) .... Iran-Sov. Un.	39·15 N	47·10 E
135	Aratuípe (ä-rä-tōō-ē′pĕ) ..... Braz.	13·12 S	38·58 W
134	Arauca (ä-rou′kä) .... Col.	6·56 N	70·45 W
134	Arauca (R.) .... Ven.	7·13 N	68·43 W
184	Aravalli Ra. (ä-rä′vŭ-lē) ..... India	24·15 N	72·40 E
135	Araxá (ä-rä-shä′) .... Braz.	19·41 S	46·46 W
135	Araya, Punta de (Pt.) (pŭn′tȧ-dĕ-ä-rä′yȧ) . Ven. (In.)	10·40 N	64·15 W
197	Arayat (ä-rä′yät) ...... Phil. (In.)	15·10 N	120·44 E
211	'Arbi .... Sud.	20·36 N	29·57 E
156	Arboga (är-bō′gä) .... Swe.	59·26 N	15·50 E
164	Arborea (är-bō-rē′ä) .... It.	39·50 N	8·36 E
154	Arbroath (är-brōth′) .... Scot.	56·36 N	2·25 W
160	Arc (R.) (ärk) .. Fr. (Marseille In.)	43·34 N	5·17 E
160	Arcachon (är-kä-shôɴ′) .... Fr.	44·39 N	1·12 W
160	Arcachon, Bassin d' (Basin) (bä-sĕn′ där-kä-shôn′) . Fr.	44·42 N	1·50 W
113	Arcadia (är-kā′dĭ-ȧ) Ca. (Los Angeles In.)	34·08 N	118·02 W
121	Arcadia .... Fl. (In.)	27·12 N	81·51 W
119	Arcadia .... La.	32·33 N	92·56 W
109	Arcadia .... Wi.	44·15 N	91·30 W
110	Arcata (är-kȧ′tȧ) .... Ca.	40·54 N	124·05 W
114	Arc Dome Mtn. (ärk dōm) .... Nv.	38·51 N	117·21 W
124	Arcelia (är-sā′lē-ä) .... Mex.	18·19 N	100·14 W
105	Archbald (ärch′bôld) .... Pa.	41·30 N	75·35 W
115	Arches Natl. Park (är′ches) ... Ut.	38·45 N	109·35 W
134	Archidona (är-chē-do′nä) ...... Ec.	1·01 S	77·49 W
162	Archidona (är-chē-dô′nä) ...... Sp.	37·08 N	4·24 W
164	Arcila (är-sē′lä) .... Mor.	35·30 N	6·05 W
160	Arcis-sur-Aube (är-sēs′sûr-ōb′) Fr.	48·31 N	4·04 E
111	Arco (är′kō) .... Id.	43·39 N	113·15 W
106	Arcola (är′cōlȧ) Va. (Baltimore In.)	38·57 N	77·32 W
119	Arcola .... Tx. (In.)	29·30 N	95·28 W
162	Arcos de la Frontera (är′kōs-dĕ-lä-frôn-tĕ′rä) . Sp.	36·44 N	5·48 W
219	Arctic Ocean (ärk′tĭk)		
165	Arda (R.) (är′dä) .... Bul.	41·36 N	25·18 E
186	Aradabīl .... Iran	38·15 N	48·00 E
171	Ardahan (är-dȧ-hän′) .... Tur.	41·10 N	42·40 E
156	Ardals Fd. (är-däls) .... Nor.	58·53 N	7·55 E
170	Ardatov (är-dȧ-tôf′) ..... Sov. Un.	54·58 N	46·10 E
155	Ardennes (Mts.) (är-dĕn′) .... Bel.	50·01 N	5·12 E
162	Ardila (R.) (är-dē′lȧ) .... Port.	38·10 N	7·15 W
117	Ardmore (ärd′mōr) .... Ok.	34·10 N	97·08 W
106	Ardmore .... Pa. (Philadelphia In.)	40·01 N	75·18 W

Page	Name Pronunciation Region	Lat. °′	Long. °′
89	Ardrossan (är-dros′ăn) Can. (Edmonton In.)	53·33 N	113·08 W
148	Ardsley (ärdz′lē) .... Eng.	53·43 N	1·33 W
150	Åre .... Swe.	63·12 N	13·12 E
162	Arecena (ä-rē-sē′nä) .... Sp.	37·53 N	6·34 W
123	Arecibo (ä-rā-sē′bō) P. R. (Puerto Rico In.)	18·28 N	66·45 W
135	Areia Branca (ä-rĕ′yä-brȧ′n-kă) Braz.	4·58 S	37·02 W
114	Arena, Pt. (ä-rā′nȧ) .... Ca.	38·57 N	123·40 W
135	Arenas, Punta (Pt.) (pōō′n′tä-rĕ′näs) . Ven. (In.)	10·57 N	64·24 W
162	Arenas de San Pedro (ä-rā′nȧs dā sän pā′drō) . Sp.	40·12 N	5·04 W
156	Arendal (ä′rĕn-däl) .... Nor.	58·29 N	8·44 E
149	Arendonk ...... Bel. (Brussels In.)	51·19 N	5·07 E
134	Arequipa (ä-rā-kē′pä) .... Peru	16·27 S	71·30 W
164	Arezzo (ä-rĕt′sō) .... It.	43·28 N	11·54 E
162	Arga (R.) (är′gä) .... Sp.	42·35 N	1·55 W
163	Arganda (är-gän′dä) Sp. (Madrid In.)	40·18 N	3·27 W
174	Argazi (L.) (är′gä-zĭ) Sov. Un. (Urals In.)	55·24 N	60·37 E
174	Argazi R. .... Sov. Un. (Urals In.)	55·33 N	57·30 E
160	Argentan (ȧr-zhäɴ-täɴ′) .... Fr.	48·45 N	0·01 W
160	Argentat (ȧr-zhäɴ-tä′) .... Fr.	45·07 N	1·57 E
161	Argenteuil (är-zhäɴ-tû′y′) Fr. (Paris In.)	48·56 N	2·15 E
133	Argentina (är-jĕn-tē′nȧ) ..... S. A.	35·30 S	67·00 W
136	Argentino (L.) (är-ĸĕn-tē′nō) . Arg.	50·15 S	72·45 W
160	Argenton-sur-Creuse (är-zhäɴ′tôɴ-sür-krôs) . Fr.	46·34 N	1·28 E
165	Arges (R.) (ȧr′zhĕsh) .... Rom.	44·27 N	25·22 E
165	Argolikos Kólpos (G.) .... Grc.	37·20 N	23·00 E
160	Argonne (Mts.) (ä′r-gôn) ...... Fr.	49·21 N	5·54 E
165	Argos (är′gŏs) .... Grc.	37·38 N	22·45 E
165	Argostólion (är-gŏs-tŏ′lē-ŏn) .. Grc.	38·10 N	20·30 E
114	Arguello, Pt. (är-gwĕl′yō) ..... Ca.	34·35 N	120·40 W
173	Argun R. (ȧr-gōōn′) China-Sov. Un.	50·15 N	118·45 E
215	Argungu .... Nig.	12·45 N	4·31 E
89	Argyle (är′gīl) . Can. (Winnipeg In.)	50·11 N	97·27 W
108	Argyle .... Mn.	48·21 N	96·48 W
156	Århus (ôr′hōōs) .... Den.	56·09 N	10·10 E
195	Ariakeno-Umi (Sea) (ä-rē′ä-kä′nō ōō′nē) . Jap.	33·03 N	130·18 E
195	Ariake-Wan (B.) (ä′rē-ä′kä wän) Jap.	31·19 N	131·15 E
164	Ariano (ä-rē-ä′nō) .... It.	41·09 N	15·11 E
134	Ariari (ä-ryȧ′rē) (R.) .... Col. (In.)	3·34 N	73·42 W
214	Aribinda .... Upper Volta	14·14 N	0·52 W
134	Arica (ä-rē′kä) .... Chile	18·34 S	70·14 W
99	Arichat (ä-rĭ-shät′) .... Can.	45·31 N	61·01 W
160	Ariège (R.) (ȧ-rē-ĕzh′) .... Fr.	43·26 N	1·29 E
112	Ariel (ā′rĭ-ĕl) .. Wa. (Portland In.)	45·57 N	122·34 W
159	Arieşul (R.) (ȧ-rē-ā′shōōl) ... Rom.	46·25 N	23·15 E
129	Ariguanabo, L. de (lä′gô-dĕ-ä-rē-gwä-nä′bô) Cuba (In.)	22·17 N	82·33 W
183	Arīḥā (Jericho) Jordan (Palestine In.)	31·51 N	35·28 E
116	Arikaree (R.) (ă-rĭ-kȧ-rē′) .... Co.	39·51 N	102·18 W
195	Arima (ä′rē-mä′) . Jap. (Ōsaka In.)	34·48 N	135·16 E
197	Aringay (ä-rĭŋ-gä′ē) .... Phil. (In.)	16·25 N	120·20 E
135	Arinos (R.) (ä-rē′nŏzh) ...... Braz.	12·09 S	56·49 W
135	Aripuanã (R.) (ȧ-rē-pwän′yȧ) Braz.	7·06 S	60·29 W
183	'Arīsh, Wādī al (R.) (ȧ-rēsh′) Egypt (Palestine In.)	30·36 N	34·07 E
92	Aristazabal I. .... Can.	52·30 N	129·20 W
102	Arizona (State) (ăr-ĭ-zō′nȧ) .. U. S.	34·00 N	113·00 W
162	Arjona (är-hō′nä) .... Sp.	37·58 N	4·03 W
173	Arka (R.) .... Sov. Un.	60·12 N	142·30 E
120	Arkabutla Res. (är-kȧ-bŭt′lā) .. Ms.	34·48 N	90·00 W
117	Arkadelphia (är-kȧ-dĕl′fĭ-ȧ) .... Ar.	34·06 N	93·05 W
103	Arkansas (State) (är′kăn-sô) (är-kăn′sȧs) . U. S.	34·50 N	93·40 W
117	Arkansas City .... Ks.	37·04 N	97·02 W
117	Arkansas R. .... Ok.	35·20 N	94·56 W
170	Arkhangelsk (Archangel) (ȧr-ĸän′gĕlsk) . Sov. Un.	64·30 N	40·25 E
174	Arkhangel'skiy (är-kän-gĕl′skĭ) Sov. Un. (Urals In.)	52·52 N	61·53 E
174	Arkhangel'skoye (är-kän-gĕl′skô-yĕ) Sov. Un. (Urals In.)	54·25 N	56·48 E
154	Arklow (ärk′lō) .... Ire.	52·47 N	6·10 W
156	Arkona, C. (är′kō-nä) ..... G.D.R.	54·43 N	13·43 E
185	Arkonam (är-kō-näm′) ...... India	13·05 N	79·43 E
162	Arlanza (R.) (är-län-thä′) ..... Sp.	42·08 N	3·45 W
162	Arlanzón (R.) (är-län-thōn′) ... Sp.	42·12 N	3·58 W
158	Arlberg Tun. (ärl′bĕrgh) ...... Aus.	47·05 N	10·15 E
160	Arles (ärl) .... Fr.	43·42 N	4·38 E
120	Arlington (är′lĭng-tun′) .... Ga.	31·25 N	84·42 W
99	Arlington .... Ma. (In.)	42·26 N	71·13 W
108	Arlington (är′lĕng-tŭn) .... SD	44·23 N	97·09 W
119	Arlington (är′lĭng-tŭn) Tx. (Dallas, Fort Worth In.)	32·44 N	97·07 W
218	Arlington . S. Afr. (Johannesburg & Pretoria In.)	28·02 S	27·52 E
105	Arlington .... Vt.	43·05 N	73·05 W
106	Arlington ..... Va. (Baltimore In.)	38·55 N	77·10 W
112	Arlington .... Wa. (Seattle In.)	48·11 N	122·08 W
107	Arlington Heights (är′lĕng-tŭn-hī′ts) Il. (Chicago In.)	42·05 N	87·59 W
156	Arlöv (är′lûf) .... Swe.	55·38 N	13·05 E
204	Arltunga (ärl-tŏŏŋ′gȧ) ...... Austl.	23·19 S	134·45 E
117	Arma (är′mȧ) .... Ks.	37·34 N	94·43 W
89	Armagh (är-mä′) (är-mäĸ′) Can. (Quebec In.)	46·45 N	70·36 W
154	Armagh .... N. Ire.	54·21 N	6·25 W

Page	Name Pronunciation Region	Lat. °′	Long. °′
218	Armant (ȧr-mänt′) Egypt (Nile In.)	25·37 N	32·32 E
134	Armaro (är-mȧ′rō) ...... Col. (In.)	4·58 N	74·54 W
171	Armavir (ȧr-mȧ-vĭr′) ..... Sov. Un.	45·00 N	41·00 E
134	Armenia (ȧr-mĕ′nē-ä) .... Col. (In.)	4·33 N	75·40 W
126	Armenia (är-mā′nē-ä) .... Sal.	13·44 N	89·31 W
168	Armenian, S. S. R. .... Sov. Un.	41·00 N	44·39 E
160	Armentières (ȧr-mäɴ-tyâr′) .... Fr.	50·43 N	2·53 E
124	Armeria, Rio de (R.) (rē′ō-dĕ-är-mȧ-rē′ä) . Mex.	19·36 N	104·10 W
107	Armherstburg (ärm′hĕrst-bōōrgh) Can. (Detroit In.)	42·06 N	83·06 W
203	Armidale (är′mĭ-dāl) .... Austl.	30·27 S	151·50 E
108	Armour (är′mẽr) .... SD	43·18 N	98·21 W
96	Armstrong Station (ärm′strŏng) . Can.	50·21 N	89·00 W
167	Armyansk (ärm′yȧnsk) ... Sov. Un.	46·06 N	33·42 E
162	Arnedo (är-nā′dō) .... Sp.	42·12 N	2·03 W
155	Arnhem (ärn′hĕm) .... Neth.	51·58 N	5·56 E
204	Arnhem, C. .... Austl.	12·15 S	137·00 E
204	Arnhem Land, (Reg.) (ärn′hĕm-lănd) . Austl.	13·15 S	133·00 E
164	Arno (R.) (ä′r-nô) .... It.	43·45 N	10·42 E
148	Arnold (är′nŭld) .... Eng.	53·00 N	1·08 W
113	Arnold (ȧr′nŭld) Mn. (Duluth In.)	46·53 N	92·06 W
107	Arnold .... Pa. (Pittsburgh In.)	40·35 N	79·45 W
105	Arnprior (ärn-prī′ẽr) .... Can.	45·25 N	76·20 W
155	Arnsberg (ärns′bĕrgh) ...... F.R.G.	51·25 N	8·02 E
158	Arnstadt (ärn′shtät) ...... G.D.R.	50·51 N	10·57 E
212	Aroab (är′ō-ȧb) .... Namibia	25·40 S	19·45 E
98	Aroostook (R.) (ȧ-rōōs′tŏŏk) .. Me.	46·44 N	68·15 W
197	Aroroy (ä-rô-rô′ē) ...... Phil. (In.)	12·30 N	123·24 E
161	Arpajon (ăr-pä-jô′n) Fr. (Paris In.)	48·35 N	2·15 E
136	Arpoador, Ponta do (Pt.) (pô′n-tä-dŏ-är′pôä-dō′r) Braz. (In.)	22·59 S	43·11 W
162	Arraiolos (är-rī-ō′lōzh) ...... Port.	38·47 N	7·59 W
186	Ar Ramādī .... Iraq	33·30 N	43·12 E
154	Arran (I.) (ă′răn) .... Scot.	55·39 N	5·30 W
211	Ar Rank .... Sud.	11·45 N	32·53 E
160	Arras (ȧ-räs′) .... Fr.	50·21 N	2·40 E
218	Ar Rawḍah .... Egypt (Nile In.)	27·47 N	30·52 E
137	Arrecifes (är-rā-sē′fās) Arg. (Buenos Aires In.)	34·03 S	60·05 W
137	Arrecifes (R.) Arg. (Buenos Aires In.)	34·07 S	59·50 W
160	Arrée, Mts. d' (är-rā′) .... Fr.	48·27 N	4·00 W
125	Arriaga (är-rēȧ′gä) .... Mex.	16·15 N	93·54 W
	Ar Riyāḍ, see Riyadh		
163	Arrone (R.) .... It. (Rome In.)	41·57 N	12·17 E
113	Arrowhead, L. (lăk ăr′ōhĕd) Ca. (Los Angeles In.)	34·17 N	117·13 W
111	Arrow R. (ăr′ō) .... Mt.	47·29 N	109·53 W
110	Arrowrock Res. (ăr′ō-rŏk) ..... Id.	43·40 N	115·30 W
129	Arroya Arena (är-rô′yä-rē′nä) Cuba (In.)	23·01 N	82·30 W
162	Arroyo de la Luz (är-rō′yō-dĕ-lä-lōō′z) . Sp.	39·39 N	6·46 W
124	Arroyo Grande (R.) (är-rō′yō-grä′n-dĕ) . Mex.	23·30 N	98·45 W
124	Arroyo Seco (är-rō′yō sā′kō) . Mex.	21·31 N	99·44 W
186	Ar Rub' Al Khālī (Des.) .. Sau. Ar.	20·30 N	49·15 E
211	Ar-Ruşayriş .... Sud.	11·38 N	34·42 E
173	Arsen'yev .... Sov. Un.	44·13 N	133·32 E
174	Arsinskiy (är-sĭn′skĭ) Sov. Un. (Urals In.)	53·46 N	59·54 E
165	Árta (är′tä) .... Grc.	39·08 N	21·02 E
118	Arteaga (är-tā-ä′gä) .... Mex.	25·28 N	100·50 W
173	Artëm (ȧr-tyôm′) .... Sov. Un.	43·28 N	132·29 E
128	Artemisa (är-tā-mē′sä) ...... Cuba	22·50 N	82·45 W
167	Artëmovsk (ȧr-tyŏm′ŏfsk) Sov. Un.	48·37 N	38·00 E
116	Artesia (är-tē′sĭ-ȧ) .... NM	32·44 N	104·23 W
203	Artesian Basin, The (är-tē′zhăn) . Austl.	26·45 S	141·40 E
98	Arthabaska .... Can.	46·03 N	71·54 W
129	Arthur's Town .... Ba.	24·40 N	75·40 W
174	Arti (är′tĭ) ... Sov. Un. (Urals In.)	56·20 N	58·38 E
129	Artibonite (R.) (är-tē-bô-nē′tā) Hai.	19·00 N	72·25 W
197	Aru, Kepulauan (Is.) ...... Indon.	6·20 S	133·00 E
217	Arua (ä′rōō-ä) .... Ug.	3·01 N	30·55 E
134	Aruba (ä-rōō′bȧ) (I.) Neth. Antilles	12·29 N	70·00 W
188	Arunachal Pradesh (Union Ter.) India	27·35 N	92·56 E
217	Arusha (ȧ-rōō′shä) .... Tan.	3·22 S	36·41 E
97	Arvida .... Can.	48·26 N	71·11 W
156	Arvika (är-vē′kȧ) .... Swe.	59·41 N	12·35 E
170	Arzamas (är-zä-mäs′) .... Sov. Un.	55·20 N	43·52 E
163	Arzew (är-zȧ-ōō′) .... Alg.	35·50 N	0·20 W
162	Arzua (är-thōō′ä) .... Sp.	42·54 N	8·19 W
158	As (äsh′) .... Czech.	50·12 N	12·13 E
195	Asahi-Gawa (Strm.) (ä-sä′hē-gä′wä) . Jap.	35·01 N	133·40 E
194	Asahikawa .... Jap.	43·50 N	142·09 E
195	Asaka (ä-sä′kä) .. Jap. (Tōkyō In.)	35·47 N	139·36 E
184	Asansol .... India	23·45 N	86·58 E
174	Asbest (äs-bĕst′) Sov. Un. (Urals In.)	57·02 N	61·28 E
98	Asbestos (ăs-bĕs′tōs) .... Can.	45·49 N	71·52 W
106	Asbury Park (ăz′bĕr-ĭ) NJ (New York In.)	40·13 N	74·01 W
126	Ascención, Bahía de la (B.) (bä-ē′ä-dĕ-lä-äs-sĕn-sē-ōn′) Mex. (In.)	19·39 N	87·30 W
124	Ascensión (äs-sĕn-sē-ōn′) .... Mex.	24·21 N	99·54 W
209	Ascension (I.) (ȧ-sĕn′shŭn) . Atl. O.	8·00 S	13·00 W
218	Ascent (ăs-ĕnt′) .... S. Afr. (Johannesburg & Pretoria In.)	27·14 S	29·06 E

ăt: finăl; rāte; senâte; ärm; ȧsk; sofȧ; fâre; ch-choose; dh-as th in other; bē; ēvent; bĕt; recĕnt; cratẽr; g-go; gh-guttural g; bĭt; ĭ-short neutral; rīde; ĸ-guttural k as ch in German ich:

PRONOUNCING INDEX

Aschaffenburg — Authon 253

Page	Name / Pronunciation / Region	Lat. °′	Long. °′
158	Aschaffenburg (ä-shäf'ĕn-bŏŏrgh) F.R.G.	49·58 N	9·12 E
161	Ascheberg (ä'shĕ-bĕrg) F.R.G. (Ruhr In.)	51·47 N	7·38 E
158	Aschersleben (äsh'ĕrs-lā-bĕn) G.D.R.	51·46 N	11·28 E
164	Ascoli Piceno (äs'kō-lēpē-chā'nō) It.	42·50 N	13·55 E
218	Aseb......Eth. (Horn of Afr. In.)	12·52 N	43·39 E
165	Asenovgrad Bul.	42·00 N	24·49 E
166	Aseri (ä'sĕ-rĭ) Sov. Un.	59·26 N	26·58 E
	Asfi, see Safi		
174	Asha (ä'shä) Sov. Un. (Urals In.)	55·01 N	57·17 E
108	Ashabula (L.) (ăsh'ă-bū-lă) ND	47·07 N	97·51 W
174	Ashan (ä'shän) Sov. Un. (Urals In.)	57·08 N	56·25 E
148	Ashbourne (ăsh'bŭrn) Eng.	53·01 N	1·44 W
120	Ashburn (ăsh'bŭrn) Ga.	31·42 N	83·42 W
106	Ashburn Va. (Baltimore In.)	39·02 N	77·30 W
204	Ashburton (R.) (ăsh'bûr-tŭn) Austl.	22·30 S	115·30 E
148	Ashby-de-la-Zouch (ăsh'bĭ-dē-lȧ zōōsh') Eng.	52·44 N	1·23 W
183	Ashdod Isr. (Palestine In.)	31·46 N	34·39 E
117	Ashdown (ăsh'doun) Ar.	33·41 N	94·07 W
121	Asheboro (ăsh'bŭr-ō) NC	35·41 N	79·50 W
118	Asherton (ăsh'ēr-tŭn) Tx.	28·26 N	99·45 W
121	Asheville (ăsh'vĭl) NC	35·35 N	82·35 W
115	Ash Fork Az.	35·13 N	112·29 W
195	Ashikaga (ä'shē-kä'gä) Jap.	36·22 N	139·26 E
195	Ashiya (ä'shē-yä') Jap.	33·54 N	130·40 E
195	Ashiya Jap. (Ōsaka In.)	34·44 N	135·18 E
195	Ashizuri-Zaki (Pt.) (ä-shē-zōō-rē zä-kē) Jap.	32·43 N	133·04 E
147	Ashkhabad (ŭsh-kä-bät') Sov. Un.	39·45 N	58·13 E
120	Ashland (ăsh'lănd) Al.	33·15 N	85·50 W
116	Ashland Ks.	37·11 N	99·46 W
104	Ashland Ky.	38·25 N	82·40 W
98	Ashland Me.	46·37 N	68·26 W
99	Ashland Ma. (In.)	42·16 N	71·28 W
108	Ashland Nb.	41·02 N	96·23 W
104	Ashland Oh.	40·50 N	82·15 W
110	Ashland Or.	42·12 N	122·42 W
105	Ashland Pa.	40·45 N	76·20 W
109	Ashland Wi.	46·34 N	90·55 W
108	Ashley (ăsh'lē) ND	46·03 N	99·23 W
105	Ashley Pa.	41·15 N	75·55 W
196	Ashmore Rf. (ăsh'mōr) Indon.	12·08 S	122·45 E
218	Ashmūn (ȧsh-mōōn') Egypt (Nile In.)	30·19 N	30·57 E
183	Ashqelon (äsh'kĕ-lōn) Isr. (Palestine In.)	31·40 N	34·36 E
211	Ash Shabb (shĕb) Egypt	22·34 N	29·52 E
218	Ash Shallūfah (shäl'lōō-fā) Egypt (Suez In.)	30·09 N	32·33 E
186	Ash Shaqrā' Sau. Ar.	25·10 N	45·08 E
183	Ash Shawbak Jordan (Palestine In.)	30·31 N	35·35 E
186	Ash Shihr P.D.R. of Yem.	14·45 N	49·32 E
104	Ashtabula (ăsh-tȧ-bū'lȧ) Oh.	41·55 N	80·50 W
111	Ashton (ăsh'tŭn) Id.	44·04 N	111·28 W
148	Ashton-in-Makerfield (ăsh'tŭn-ĭn-māk'ēr-fēld) Eng.	53·29 N	2·39 W
148	Ashton-under-Lyne (ăsh'tŭn-ŭn-dēr-līn') Eng.	53·29 N	2·04 W
91	Ashuanipi (L.) (ăsh-wȧ-nĭp'ĭ) Can.	52·40 N	67·42 W
174	Ashukino (ȧ-shōō'ki-nô) Sov. Un. (Moscow In.)	56·10 N	37·57 E
182	Asia (ā'zhȧ)		
147	Asia Minor (ā'zhȧ) Asia	38·18 N	31·18 E
124	Asientos (ä-sē-ĕn'tōs) Mex.	22·13 N	102·05 W
164	Asinara, Golfo di (G.) (gôl'fō-dē-ä-sē-nä'rä) It.	40·58 N	8·28 E
164	Asinara (I.) (ä-sē-nä'rä) It.	41·02 N	8·22 E
186	Asīr (Reg.) (ä-sēr') Sau. Ar.	19·30 N	42·00 E
218	Asir, Ras (C.) Som. (Horn of Afr. In.)	11·55 N	51·30 E
174	Askarovo (äs-kä-rô'vô) Sov. Un. (Urals In.)	53·21 N	58·32 E
156	Askersund (äs'kĕr-sōōnd) Swe.	58·43 N	14·53 E
174	Askino (äs'kĭ-nô) Sov. Un. (Urals In.)	56·06 N	56·29 E
211	Asmera (äs-mä'rä) Eth.	15·17 N	38·56 E
161	Asnieres-sur-Seine (ä-nyâr'sür-sĕ'n) Fr. (Paris In.)	48·55 N	2·18 E
211	Asosa Eth.	10·13 N	34·28 E
110	Asotin (ȧ-sō'tĭn) Wa.	46·19 N	117·01 W
115	Aspen (ăs'pĕn) Co.	39·15 N	106·55 W
149	Asperen Neth. (Amsterdam In.)	51·52 N	5·07 E
99	Aspy B. (ăs'pē) Can.	46·55 N	60·25 W
218	Aş Şaff Egypt (Nile In.)	29·33 N	31·23 E
	Aş Şahrā' al Lībīyah, see Libyan Des.		
	Aş Şahrā' ash Sharqīyah, see Arabian Des.		
211	As Sallūm Egypt	31·34 N	25·09 E
183	As Salt Jordan (Palestine In.)	32·02 N	35·44 E
184	Assam (State) (ăs-săm') India	26·00 N	91·00 E
156	Assens (äs'sĕns) Den.	55·16 N	9·54 E
218	As Sinbillāwayn Egypt (Nile In.)	30·53 N	31·37 E
210	Assini (ȧ-sē-nē') Ivory Coast.	4·52 N	3·16 W
94	Assiniboia Can.	49·38 N	105·59 W
94	Assiniboine (R.) (ă-sĭn'ĭ-boin) Can.	50·03 N	97·57 W
93	Assiniboine, Mt. Can.	50·52 N	115·39 W
135	Assis (ä-sē's) Braz.	22·39 S	50·21 W
164	Assisi It.	43·04 N	12·37 E
211	As-Sudd (Reg.) Sud.	8·45 N	30·45 E
186	As Sulaymānīyah Iraq	35·47 N	45·23 E
186	As Suwaydā' Syr.	32·41 N	36·41 E
218	As Suways (Suez) Egypt (Suez In.)	29·58 N	32·34 E
165	Astakós (äs'tä-kôs) Grc.	38·42 N	21·00 E
171	Astara Sov. Un.	38·30 N	48·50 E
164	Asti (äs'tē) It.	44·54 N	8·12 E
188	Astin Tagh (Mts.) China	36·58 N	85·09 E
153	Astipálaia (I.) Grc.	36·31 N	26·19 E
162	Astorga (äs-tôr'gä) Sp.	42·28 N	6·03 W
112	Astoria (ăs-tō'rĭ-ȧ) Or. (Portland In.)	46·11 N	123·51 W
171	Astrakhan' (äs-trȧ-kän') Sov. Un.	46·15 N	48·00 E
212	Astrida (äs-trē'dȧ) Rw.	2·37 S	29·48 E
162	Asturias (Reg.) (äs-tōō'ryäs) Sp.	43·21 N	6·00 W
136	Asunción (ä-sōōn-syōn') Par.	25·25 S	57·30 W
	Asunción, see Ixtaltepec		
	Asunción, see Nochixtlán		
126	Asunción Mita (ä-sōōn-syŏ'n-mē'tä) Guat.	14·19 N	89·43 W
155	Åsunden (L.) (ô'sōōn-dĕn) Swe.	57·46 N	13·16 E
218	Aswān (ä-swän') Egypt (Nile In.)	24·05 N	32·57 E
218	Aswān High Dam Egypt (Nile In.)	23·58 N	32·53 E
218	Asyūţ (ä-syōōt') Egypt (Nile In.)	27·10 N	31·10 E
136	Atacama, Puna de (Reg.) (pōō'nä-dē-ätä-kà'mä) Chile	23·15 S	68·45 W
134	Atacama, Puna de (Plat.) (pōō'nä-dē-ä-tä-kà'mä) Bol.	21·35 S	66·58 W
133	Atacama, Desierto de (Des.) (dĕ-syĕ'r-tō-dĕ-ä-tä-kà'mä) Chile-Peru	23·50 S	69·00 W
136	Atacama, Salar de (L.) (sà-lär'dĕ-ätä-kà'mä) Chile	23·38 S	68·15 W
136	Atacama Trench S.A.	25·00 S	71·30 W
134	Ataco (ä-tà'kŏ) Col. (In.)	3·36 N	75·22 W
214	Atacora, Chaîne de l' (Mts.) Benin	10·15 N	1·15 E
183	Atā 'itah, Jabal al (Mts.) Jordan (Palestine In.)	30·48 N	35·19 E
214	Atakpamé (ä'tȧk-pȧ-mā') Togo	7·32 N	1·08 E
174	Atamanovskiy (ä-tä-mä'nôv-skĭ) Sov. Un. (Urals In.)	52·15 N	60·47 E
218	'Atāqah, Jabal (Mts.) Egypt (Suez In.)	29·59 N	32·20 E
210	Atar (ä-tär') Mauritania	20·45 N	13·16 W
114	Atascadero (ăt-ăs-kȧ-dâ'rō) Ca.	35·29 N	120·40 W
118	Atascosa R. (ăt-ăs-kō'sȧ) Tx.	28·50 N	98·17 W
211	'Aţbarah (ät'bȧ-rä) Sud.	17·45 N	33·15 E
211	Atbara R. Sud.	17·14 N	34·27 E
172	Atbasar (ät'bä-sär') Sov. Un.	51·42 N	68·28 E
119	Atchafalaya B. (ăch-ȧ-fȧ-lī'ȧ) La.	29·25 N	91·30 W
119	Atchafalaya R. La.	30·53 N	91·51 W
117	Atchison (ăch'ĭ-sŭn) Ks.	39·33 N	95·08 W
106	Atco (ăt'kō) NJ (Philadelphia In.)	39·46 N	74·53 W
125	Atempan (ä-tĕm-pà'n) Mex.	19·49 N	97·25 W
124	Atenguillo (R.) (ä-tĕn-gē'l-yō) Mex.	20·18 N	104·35 W
90	Athabasca (ăth-ȧ-băs'kȧ) Can.	54·43 N	113·17 W
90	Athabasca (L.) Can.	59·04 N	109·10 W
93	Athabasca (R.) Can.	56·00 N	112·35 W
120	Athens (ăth'ĕnz) Al.	34·47 N	86·58 W
120	Athens Ga.	33·55 N	83·24 W
104	Athens Oh.	39·20 N	82·10 W
105	Athens Pa.	42·00 N	76·30 W
120	Athens Tn.	35·26 N	84·36 W
119	Athens Tx.	32·13 N	95·51 W
	Athens, see Athinai		
148	Atherstone (ăth'ēr-stŭn) Eng.	52·34 N	1·33 W
148	Atherton (ăth'ēr-tŭn) Eng.	53·32 N	2·29 W
205	Atherton Plat. (ădh-ĕr-tŏn) Austl.	17·00 S	144·30 E
217	Athi (R.) (ä'tē) Ken.	2·43 S	38·30 E
165	Athinai (Athens) (ä-thē'nĕ) Grc.	38·00 N	23·38 E
154	Athlone (ăth-lōn') Ire.	53·24 N	7·30 W
165	Athos (Mtn.) (ăth'ŏs) Grc.	40·10 N	24·15 E
183	Ath Thamad Egypt (Palestine In.)	29·41 N	34·17 E
154	Athy (ȧ-thī) Ire.	52·59 N	7·08 W
215	Ati Chad	13·13 N	18·20 E
137	Atibaia (ä-tē-bà'yȧ) Braz. (Rio de Janeiro In.)	23·08 S	46·32 W
91	Atikonak (L.) Can.	52·34 N	63·49 W
197	Atimonan (ä-tē-mō'nän) Phil. (In.)	13·59 N	121·56 E
126	Atiquizaya (ä'tē-kē-zä'yä) Sal.	14·00 N	89·42 W
126	Atitlan (Vol.) (ä-tē-tlän') Guat.	14·35 N	91·11 W
126	Atitlan L. (ä-tē-tlän') Guat.	14·38 N	91·23 W
125	Atizapán (ä'tē-zà-pän') Mex. (In.)	19·33 N	99·16 W
101	Atka (ăt'kȧ) Ak.	52·18 N	174·18 W
101	Atka (I.) Ak.	51·58 N	174·30 W
171	Atkarsk (ät-kärsk') Sov. Un.	51·50 N	45·00 E
108	Atkinson (ăt'kĭn-sŭn) Ne.	42·32 N	98·58 W
106	Atlanta (ăt-lăn'tȧ) Ga. (Atlanta In.)	33·45 N	84·23 W
117	Atlanta Tx.	33·09 N	94·09 W
109	Atlantic (ăt-lăn'tĭk) Ia.	41·23 N	94·58 W
121	Atlantic NC	34·54 N	76·20 W
106	Atlantic Highlands NJ (New York In.)	40·25 N	74·04 W
105	Atlantic City NJ	39·20 N	74·30 W
6	Atlantic Ocean		
210	Atlas Mts. (ăt'lăs) Alg.-Mor.	31·22 N	4·57 W
124	Atliaca (ät-lē-ä'kä) Mex.	17·38 N	99·24 W
90	Atlin (L.) (ăt'lĭn) Can.	59·34 N	133·20 W
124	Atlixco (ät-lēz'kō) Mex.	18·52 N	98·27 W
156	Atlöy (I.) (ät-lûê) Nor.	61·24 N	4·46 E
120	Atmore (ăt'mōr) Al.	31·01 N	87·31 W
117	Atoka (ȧ-tō'kȧ) Ok.	34·23 N	96·07 W
117	Atoka Res. Ok.	34·30 N	96·05 W
124	Atotonilco el Alto (ä'tô-tô-nēl'kō ĕl äl'tō) Mex.	20·35 N	102·32 W
124	Atotonilco el Grande (ä'tō-tō-nēl-kō ĕl grän'dā) Mex.	20·17 N	98·41 W
210	Atoui R. (ȧ-tōō-ē') Mauritania-W. Sah.	21·00 N	15·32 W
124	Atoyac (ä-tô-yäk') Mex.	20·01 N	103·28 W
125	Atoyac (R.) Mex.	16·27 N	97·28 W
124	Atoyac (R.) Mex.	18·35 N	98·16 W
124	Atoyac de Alvarez (ä-tô-yäk'dā äl'vä-rāz) Mex.	17·13 N	100·29 W
125	Atoyatempan (ä-tô'yȧ-tĕm-pän') Mex.	18·47 N	97·54 W
186	Atrak (R.) Iran	37·45 N	56·30 E
156	Atran (R.) Swe.	57·02 N	12·43 E
134	Atrato, Rio (R.) (rē'ō-ä-trä'tō) Col.	7·15 N	77·18 W
134	Atrato (R.) (ä-trä'tō) Col. (In.)	5·48 N	76·19 W
183	Aţ Ţafīlah (tä-fē'la) Jordan (Palestine In.)	30·50 N	35·36 E
186	Aţ Ţā'if Sau. Ar.	21·03 N	41·00 E
120	Attalla (ȧ-tăl'yȧ) Al.	34·01 N	86·05 W
91	Attawapiskat (R.) (ăt'ȧ-wȧ-pĭs'kăt) Can.	52·31 N	86·22 W
158	Atter See (L.) (Kammer) Aus.	47·57 N	13·25 E
105	Attica (ăt'ĭ-kȧ) NY	42·55 N	78·15 W
106	Attleboro (ăt''l-bŭr-ō) Ma. (Providence In.)	41·56 N	71·15 W
154	Attow, Ben (Mtn.) (bĕn ăt'tō) Scot.	57·15 N	5·25 W
119	Attoyac Bay (ă-toi'yăk) Tx.	31·45 N	94·23 W
101	Attu (I.) (ät-tōō') Ak.	53·08 N	173·18 E
153	Aţ Ţūr Egypt	28·09 N	33·47 E
186	Aţ Ţurayf Sau. Ar.	31·32 N	38·30 E
156	Åtvidaberg (ôt-vē'dȧ-bĕrgh) Swe.	58·12 N	15·55 E
116	Atwood (ăt'wŏŏd) Ks.	39·48 N	101·06 W
125	Atzcapotzalco (ät'zkä-pō-tzäl'kō) Mex. (In.)	19·29 N	99·11 W
149	Atzgersdorf Aus. (Vienna In.)	48·10 N	16·17 E
100	Auau Chan. (ä'ōō-ä'ōō) Hi. (In.)	20·55 N	156·50 W
161	Aubagne (ō-bän'y') Fr.	43·18 N	5·34 E
160	Aube (R.) (ōb) Fr.	48·42 N	3·49 E
160	Aubenas (ōb-nä') Fr.	44·37 N	4·22 E
161	Aubervilliers (ō-bĕr-vē-yā') Fr. (Paris In.)	48·54 N	2·23 E
160	Aubin (ō-băN') Fr.	44·29 N	2·12 E
89	Aubrey (ô-brē') Can. (Montreal In.)	45·08 N	73·47 W
120	Auburn (ô'bŭrn) Al.	32·35 N	85·26 W
114	Auburn Ca.	38·52 N	121·05 W
117	Auburn Il.	39·36 N	89·46 W
104	Auburn In.	41·20 N	85·05 W
98	Auburn Me.	44·04 N	70·24 W
99	Auburn Ma. (In.)	42·11 N	71·51 W
117	Auburn Ne.	40·23 N	95·50 W
105	Auburn NY	42·55 N	76·35 W
112	Auburn Wa. (Seattle In.)	47·18 N	122·14 W
107	Auburn Hts. Mi. (Detroit In.)	42·37 N	83·13 W
160	Aubusson (ō-bü-sôN') Fr.	45·57 N	2·10 E
160	Auch (ōsh) Fr.	43·38 N	0·35 E
120	Aucilla (R.) (ô-sĭl'ȧ) Fl.-Ga.	30·15 N	83·55 W
205	Auckland (ôk'lănd) N. Z. (In.)	36·53 S	174·45 E
220	Auckland Is. N. Z.	50·30 S	166·30 E
160	Aude (R.) (ōd) Fr.	42·55 N	2·08 E
160	Audierne (ō-dyĕrn') Fr.	48·02 N	4·31 W
161	Audincourt (ō-dăn-kōōr') Fr.	47·30 N	6·49 E
148	Audley (ôd'lĭ) Eng.	53·03 N	2·18 W
218	Audo Ra. Eth. (Horn of Afr. In.)	6·58 N	41·18 E
109	Audubon (ô'dŏŏ-bŏn) Ia.	41·43 N	94·57 W
106	Audubon NJ (Philadelphia In.)	39·54 N	75·04 W
158	Aue (ou'ē) G.D.R.	50·35 N	12·44 E
203	Augathella (ôr'gȧ'thĕ-lȧ) Austl.	25·49 S	146·40 E
212	Augrabiesvalle (Falls) S. Afr.	28·30 S	20·00 E
149	Augsburg (ouks'bŏŏrgh) F.R.G. (Munich In.)	48·23 N	10·55 E
117	Augusta (ô-gŭs'tȧ) Ar.	35·16 N	91·21 W
121	Augusta Ga.	33·26 N	82·00 W
117	Augusta Ks.	37·41 N	96·58 W
104	Augusta Ky.	38·45 N	84·00 W
98	Augusta Me.	44·19 N	69·42 W
106	Augusta NJ (New York In.)	41·07 N	74·44 W
109	Augusta Wi.	44·40 N	91·09 W
159	Augustow (ou-gōōs'tōōf) Pol.	53·52 N	23·00 E
161	Aulnay-sous-Bois (ō-nĕ'sōō-bwä') Fr. (Paris In.)	48·56 N	2·30 E
160	Aulne (R.) (ōn) Fr.	48·08 N	3·53 W
161	Auneau (ō-nō) Fr. (Paris In.)	48·28 N	1·45 E
212	Auob (R.) (ä'wŏb) Namibia	25·00 S	19·00 E
183	Aur (I.) Mala. (Singapore In.)	2·27 N	104·51 E
184	Aurangābād (ou-rŭŋ-gä-bäd') India	19·56 N	75·19 E
160	Auray (ō-rĕ') Fr.	47·42 N	3·00 W
160	Aurillac (ō-rē-yäk') Fr.	44·57 N	2·27 E
97	Aurora Can.	43·59 N	79·25 W
107	Aurora (ō-rō'rȧ) Il. (Chicago In.)	41·45 N	88·18 W
107	Aurora In. (Cincinnati In.)	39·04 N	84·55 W
109	Aurora Mn.	47·31 N	92·17 W
117	Aurora Mo.	36·58 N	93·42 W
116	Aurora Ne.	40·54 N	98·01 W
156	Aursunden (L.) (äur-sûndĕn) Nor.	62·42 N	11·10 E
104	Au Sable (R.) (ô-sā'b'l) Mi.	44·40 N	84·25 W
105	Ausable (R.) NY	44·25 N	73·50 W
109	Austin (ôs'tĭn) Mn.	43·40 N	92·58 W
114	Austin Nv.	39·30 N	117·05 W
119	Austin Tx.	30·15 N	97·42 W
204	Austin (L.) Austl.	27·45 S	117·30 E
119	Austin Bayou (ôs'tĭn bī-ōō') Tx. (In.)	29·17 N	95·21 W
204	Australia (ôs-trā'lĭ-ȧ)		
203	Australian Alps (Mts.) Austl.	37·10 S	147·55 E
203	Australian Capital Ter. (ôs-trā'lĭ-ăn) Austl.	35·30 S	148·40 E
146	Austria (ôs'trĭ-ȧ) Eur.	47·15 N	11·53 E
161	Authon-la-Plaine (ō-tōN-lă-plĕ'n) Fr. (Paris In.)	48·27 N	1·58 E

ng-sing; ŋ-baŋk; N-nasalized n; nŏd; cŏmmit; ōld; ôbey; ôrder; fōōd; fŏŏt; ou-out; s-soft; sh-dish; th-thin; pūre; ûnite; ûrn; stŭd; circŭs; ü-as "y" in study; '-indeterminate vowel.

Page	Name Pronunciation Region	Lat. °′	Long. °′
124	Autlán (ä-o͞ot-län′)....Mex.	19·47 N	104·24 W
160	Autun (ō-tŭN′)....Fr.	46·58 N	4·14 E
160	Auvergne (Mts.) (ō-vĕrn′y′)...Fr.	45·12 N	2·31 E
160	Auxerre (ō-sâr′)....Fr.	47·48 N	3·32 E
117	Ava (ā′vȧ)....Mo.	36·56 N	92·40 W
217	Avakubi (ä-vä-ko͞o′bē)....Zaire	1·20 N	27·34 E
160	Avallon (ȧ-vȧ-lôN′)....Fr.	47·30 N	3·58 E
107	Avalon (ăv′ȧ-lŏn) Pa. (Pittsburgh In.)	40·31 N	80·05 W
114	Avalon....Ca.	33·21 N	118·22 W
162	Aveiro (ä-vā′ro͝o)....Port.	40·38 N	8·38 W
136	Avelar (ä′vĕ-lä′r) Braz. (Rio de Janeiro In.)	22·20 S	43·25 W
136	Avellaneda (ä-vĕl-yä-nā′dhä) Arg. (Buenos Aires In.)	34·25 S	58·23 W
163	Avellino (ä-vĕl-lē′nō) It. (Naples In.)	40·40 N	14·46 E
156	Averöy (I.) (ävĕr-ûē)....Nor.	63·40 N	7·16 E
164	Aversa (ä-vĕr′sä)....It.	40·58 N	14·13 E
117	Avery (ā′vēr-ĭ)....Tx.	33·34 N	94·46 W
156	Avesta (ä-vĕs′tä)....Swe.	60·16 N	16·09 E
160	Aveyron (R.) (ä-vâ-rôN)....Fr.	44·07 N	1·45 E
164	Avezzano (ä-vât-sä′nō)....It.	42·03 N	13·27 E
164	Avigliano (ä-vēl-yä′nō)....It.	40·45 N	15·44 E
160	Avignon (ȧ-vē-nyôN′)....Fr.	43·55 N	4·50 E
162	Ávila (ä-vē-lä)....Sp.	40·39 N	4·42 W
162	Avilés (ä-vē-lās′)....Sp.	43·33 N	5·55 W
117	Avoca (ȧ-vō′kȧ)....Ia.	41·29 N	95·16 W
105	Avon (ā′vŏn)....Ct.	41·40 N	72·50 W
99	Avon (ā′vŏn)....Ma. (In.)	42·08 N	71·03 W
107	Avon....Oh. (Cleveland In.)	41·27 N	82·02 W
154	Avon (R.) (ā′vŭn)....Eng.	52·05 N	1·55 W
106	Avondale....Ga. (Atlanta In.)	33·47 N	84·16 W
107	Avon Lake....Oh. (Cleveland In.)	41·31 N	82·01 W
89	Avonmore (ā′vōn-mōr) Can. (Ottawa In.)	45·11 N	74·58 W
121	Avon Park (ā′vŏn pärk′) Fl. (In.)	27·35 N	81·29 W
160	Avranches (ȧ-vräNsh′)....Fr.	48·43 N	1·34 W
195	Awaji-Shima (I.) (ä′wä-jê shē-mä) Jap. (Osaka In.)	34·32 N	135·02 E
154	Awe, Loch (L.) (lŏk ôr)....Scot.	56·22 N	5·04 W
211	Awjilah....Libya	29·07 N	21·21 E
160	Ax-les-Thermes (åks′lā tĕrm′) Fr.	42·43 N	1·50 E
124	Axochiapan (äks-ō-chyä′pän). Mex.	18·29 N	98·49 W
160	Ay (ȧ′ē)....Fr.	49·05 N	3·58 E
170	Ay (R.)....Sov. Un.	55·55 N	57·55 E
195	Ayabe (ä′yä-bē)....Jap.	35·16 N	135·17 E
136	Ayacucho (ä-yä-ko͞o′chō)....Arg.	37·05 S	58·30 W
134	Ayacucho....Peru	12·12 S	74·03 W
172	Ayaguz (ä-yä-go͞oz′)....Sov. Un.	48·00 N	80·12 E
162	Ayamonte (ä-yä-mô′n-tě)....Sp.	37·14 N	7·28 W
173	Ayan (ȧ-yän′)....Sov. Un.	56·26 N	138·18 E
134	Ayata (ä-yä′tä)....Bol.	15·17 S	68·43 W
134	Ayaviri (ä-yä-vē′rē)....Peru	14·46 S	70·38 W
167	Aydar (R.) (ī-där′)....Sov. Un.	49·15 N	38·48 E
121	Ayden (ā′dĕn)....NC	35·27 N	77·25 W
171	Aydın (āĭy-dĕn)....Tur.	37·40 N	27·40 E
99	Ayer (âr)....Ma. (In.)	42·33 N	71·36 W
183	Ayer Hitam Mala. (Singapore In.)	1·55 N	103·11 E
165	Ayiá (ā-yē′ȧ)....Grc.	39·42 N	22·47 E
165	Ayiassos....Grc.	39·06 N	26·25 E
165	Áyion Óros (Mount Athos) (Reg.) Grc.	40·20 N	24·15 E
165	Áyios Evstrátion (I.)....Grc.	39·30 N	24·58 E
148	Aylesbury (ālz′bēr-ĭ) Eng. (London In.)	51·47 N	0·49 W
90	Aylmer (L.) (āl′mēr)....Can.	64·27 N	108·22 W
93	Aylmer, Mt....Can.	51·19 N	115·26 W
89	Aylmer East (āl′mēr) Can. (Ottawa In.)	45·24 N	75·50 W
124	Ayo el Chico (ä′yô el chē′kō) Mex.	20·31 N	102·21 W
173	Ayon (I.) (ī-ôn′)....Sov. Un.	69·50 N	168·40 E
214	Ayorou....Niger	14·44 N	0·55 E
125	Ayotla (ä-yōt′lä)....Mex. (In.)	19·18 N	98·55 W
214	Ayoun el Atrous....Mauritania	16·40 N	9·37 W
154	Ayr (âr)....Scot.	55·27 N	4·40 W
154	Ayr (L.)....Scot.	55·25 N	4·20 W
218	Aysha....Eth. (Horn of Afr. In.)	10·48 N	42·32 E
126	Ayutla (ȧ-yo͞ot′lä)....Guat.	14·44 N	92·11 W
124	Ayutla....Mex.	16·50 N	99·16 W
124	Ayutla....Mex.	20·09 N	104·20 W
196	Ayutthaya (ȧ-yo͞ot′hē′ä)....Thai.	14·16 N	100·37 E
165	Ayvalik (āĭy-wă-lĭk)....Tur.	39·19 N	26·40 E
214	Azaouad (Dunes)....Mali	18·00 N	3·20 W
214	Azaouak, Vallée de l′ (Val.)..Mali	15·50 N	3·10 E
215	Azare....Nig.	11·40 N	10·11 E
210	Azemmour (ȧ-zē-mo͞or′)....Mor.	33·20 N	8·21 W
168	Azerbaydzhan (Azerbaijan) (S. S. R.) (ä′zĕr-bä-ê-jän′) Sov. Un.	40·38 N	47·25 E
113	Azle (ăz′lē) Tx. (Dallas, Fort Worth In.)	35·54 N	97·33 W
134	Azogues (ä-sō′gās)....Ec.	2·47 S	78·45 W
	Azores (Is.), see Açores		
167	Azov (ȧ-zôf′)....Sov. Un.	47·07 N	39·19 E
	Azov, Sea of, see Azovskoye More		
167	Azovskoye More (Sea of Azov) (ȧ-zôf′skô-yě mô′rě).Sov. Un.	46·00 N	36·20 E
124	Azoyú (ä-zō-yo͞o′)....Mex.	16·42 N	98·46 W
	Azraq, Al-Bahr al- (R.), see Blue Nile		
115	Aztec (ăz′tĕk)....NM	36·40 N	108·00 W
115	Aztec Ruins Natl. Mon....NM	36·50 N	108·00 W
129	Azua (ä′swä)....Dom. Rep.	18·30 N	70·45 W
162	Azuaga (ä-thwä′gä)....Sp.	38·15 N	5·42 W
127	Azuero, Peninsula de (Pen.) (ä-swā′rō).Pan.	7·30 N	80·34 W
118	Azucar, Presa de (Res.) (prĕ′sä-dĕ-ä-zo͞o′kär).Mex.	26·06 N	98·44 W
136	Azufre, Cerro (Copiapó) (Vol.) (sĕr′rō ä-so͞o′frā) (kō-pē-äpō′) Chile	26·10 S	69·00 W
137	Azul (ä-so͞ol′) Arg. (Buenos Aires In.)	36·46 S	59·51 W
124	Azul, Sierra (Mts.) (sē-ĕ′r-rä-zo͞o′l) Mex.	23·20 N	98·28 W
134	Azul, Cordillera (Mts.) (kô′r-dē-lyĕ′rä-zo͞o′l).Peru	7·15 S	75·30 W
113	Azusa (ȧ-zo͞o′sȧ) Ca. (Los Angeles In.)	34·08 N	117·55 W
183	Az Zabdānī....Syr. (Palestine In.)	33·45 N	36·06 E
186	Az Ẓahrān (Dhahran) (dä-rän′) Sau. Ar.	26·13 N	50·00 E
218	Az Zaqāzīq....Egypt (Nile In.)	30·36 N	31·36 E
183	Az Zarqā′..Jordan (Palestine In.)	32·03 N	36·07 E
211	Az Zawiyah....Libya	32·28 N	11·55 E

B

Page	Name Pronunciation Region	Lat. °′	Long. °′
161	Baal (bäl)....F.R.G. (Ruhr In.)	51·02 N	6·17 E
197	Baao (bä′ō)....Phil. (In.)	13·27 N	123·22 E
149	Baarle-Hertog..Bel. (Brussels In.)	51·26 N	4·57 E
149	Baarn....Neth. (Amsterdam In.)	52·12 N	5·18 E
165	Babaeski (bä′bä-ĕs′kĭ)....Tur.	41·25 N	27·05 E
134	Babahoyo (bä-bä-ō′yō)....Ec.	1·56 S	79·24 W
215	Babana....Nig.	10·36 N	3·50 E
213	Babanango....S. Afr. (Natal In.)	28·24 S	31·11 E
211	Babanūsah....Sud.	11·30 N	27·55 E
197	Babar (I.) (bä′bär)....Indon.	7·50 S	129·15 E
218	Bab-el-Mandeb, Str. of (bäb′ĕl män-dĕb′) Afr.-Asia (Horn of Afr. In.)	13·17 N	42·49 E
118	Babia, Arroyo de la (är-rō′yō dā lä bä′bē-ȧ).Mex.	28·26 N	101·50 W
92	Babine (R.)....Can.	55·10 N	127·00 W
92	Babine L. (băb′ēn)....Can.	54·45 N	126·00 W
186	Bābol....Iran	36·30 N	52·48 E
173	Babushkin (bä′bo͝osh-kĭn) Sov. Un.	51·47 N	106·08 W
174	Babushkin.Sov. Un. (Moscow In.)	55·52 N	37·42 E
196	Babuyan Is. (bä-bo͞o-yän′)...Phil.	19·30 N	122·38 E
165	Babyak (bäb′zhåk)....Bul.	41·59 N	23·42 E
106	Babylon (băb′ĭ-lŏn) NY (New York In.)	40·42 N	73·19 W
186	Babylon (Ruins)....Iraq	32·15 N	45·23 E
126	Bacalar, Laguna de (L.) (lä-go͞o-nä-dĕ-bä-kä-lär′) Mex. (In.)	18·50 N	88·31 W
197	Bacan (I.)....Indon.	0·30 S	127·00 E
193	Bacarra (bä-kär′rä)....Phil.	18·22 N	120·40 E
159	Bacău....Rom.	46·34 N	27·00 E
161	Baccarat (bȧ-kȧ-rȧ′)....Fr.	48·29 N	6·42 E
113	Bacchus (băk′ŭs) Ut. (Salt Lake City In.)	40·40 N	112·06 W
125	Bachajón (bä-chä-hōn′)....Mex.	17·08 N	92·18 W
90	Back (R.)....Can.	65·30 N	104·15 W
165	Bačka Palanka (bäch′kä pälän-kä) Yugo.	45·14 N	19·24 E
165	Bačka Topola (bäch′kä tô′pô-lä′) Yugo.	45·48 N	19·38 E
185	Back Bay (băk)....India (In.)	18·55 N	72·45 E
204	Backstairs Pass. (băk-stârs′) Austl.	35·50 S	138·15 E
193	Bac Ninh (bäk′nēn″)....Viet.	21·10 N	106·02 E
197	Bacnotan (bäk-nō-tän′).Phil. (In.)	16·43 N	120·21 E
197	Baco, Mt. (bä′kō)....Phil. (In.)	12·50 N	121·11 E
163	Bacoli (bä-kō-lē′)..It. (Naples In.)	40·33 N	14·05 E
196	Bacolod (bä-kō′lōd)....Phil.	10·42 N	123·03 E
159	Bácsalmás (bäch′ôl-mäs)...Hung.	46·07 N	19·18 E
148	Bacup (băk′ŭp)....Eng.	53·42 N	2·12 W
108	Bad (R.) (băd)....SD	44·04 N	100·58 W
162	Badajoz (bȧ-dhä-hōth′)....Sp.	38·52 N	6·56 W
163	Badalona (bä-dhä-lō′nä)....Sp.	41·27 N	2·15 E
186	Badanah....Sau. Ar.	30·49 N	40·45 E
104	Bad Axe (băd′ ăks)....Mi.	43·50 N	82·55 W
149	Bad Bramstedt (bät bräm′shtĕt) F.R.G. (Hamburg In.)	53·55 N	9·53 E
161	Bad Ems (bät ĕms)....F.R.G.	50·20 N	7·45 E
149	Baden (bä′dĕn)..Aus. (Vienna In.)	48·00 N	16·14 E
158	Baden....Switz.	47·28 N	8·17 E
158	Baden-Baden (bä′dĕn-bä′dĕn) F.R.G.	48·46 N	8·11 E
158	Baden Württemberg (State) (bä′dĕn vür′tĕm-bĕrgh).F.R.G.	48·38 N	9·00 E
158	Bad Freienwalde (bät frī′ĕn-väl′dĕ).G.D.R.	52·47 N	14·00 E
158	Bad Hersfeld (bät hĕrsh′fĕlt) F.R.G.	50·53 N	9·43 E
155	Bad Homberg (bät hōm′bĕrgh) F.R.G.	50·14 N	8·35 E
121	Badin (bă′dĭn)....NC	35·23 N	80·08 W
184	Badin....Pak.	24·47 N	69·51 E
158	Bad Ischl (bät ĭsh′'l)....Aus.	47·46 N	13·37 E
158	Bad Kissingen (bät kĭs′ĭng-ĕn) F.R.G.	50·12 N	10·05 E
158	Bad Kreuznach (bät kroits′näk) F.R.G.	49·52 N	7·53 E
108	Badlands (Reg.) (băd′ lănds).ND	46·43 N	103·22 W
108	Badlands (Reg.)....SD	43·43 N	102·36 W
108	Badlands Natl. Mon....SD	43·56 N	102·37 W
185	Badlāpur....India (In.)	19·12 N	73·12 E
214	Badogo....Mali	11·02 N	8·13 W
158	Bad Oldeslow (bät ōl′dĕs-lōē) F.R.G.	53·48 N	10·21 E
158	Bad Reichenhall (bät rī′kĕn-häl) F.R.G.	47·43 N	12·53 E
109	Bad River Ind. Res. (băd)....Wi.	46·41 N	90·36 W
149	Bad Segeberg (bät sĕ′gĕ-bo͞orgh) F.R.G. (Hamburg In.)	53·56 N	10·18 E
158	Bad Tölz (bät tûltz)....F.R.G.	47·46 N	11·35 E
185	Badulla....Sri Lanka	6·55 N	81·07 E
149	Bad Vöslau....Aus. (Vienna In.)	47·58 N	16·13 E
111	Badwater Cr. (băd′wô-tēr)...Wy.	43·13 N	107·55 W
162	Baena (bä-ā′nä)....Sp.	37·38 N	4·20 W
137	Baependi (bä-å-pĕn′dĭ) Braz. (Rio de Janeiro In.)	21·57 S	44·51 W
75	Baffin B. (băf′ĭn)....Can.	72·00 N	65·00 W
119	Baffin B....Tx.	27·11 N	97·35 W
75	Baffin I....Can.	67·20 N	71·00 W
214	Bafoulabé (bä-fo͞o-lä-bā′)....Mali	13·48 N	10·50 W
186	Bāfq (bäfk)....Iran	31·48 N	55·23 E
171	Bafra (bäf′rä)....Tur.	41·30 N	35·50 E
197	Bagabag (bä-gä-bäg′)...Phil. (In.)	16·38 N	121·16 E
185	Bāgalkot....India	16·14 N	75·40 E
217	Bagamoyo (bä-gä-mō′yō)....Tan.	6·26 S	38·54 E
174	Bagaryak (bå-går-yäk′) Sov. Un. (Urals In.)	56·13 N	61·32 E
217	Bagbele....Zaire	4·21 N	29·17 E
136	Bagé (bä-zhā′)....Braz.	31·17 S	54·07 W
186	Baghdād (bågh-däd′) (băg′dăd) Iraq	33·14 N	44·22 E
164	Bagheria (bä-gȧ-rē′ä)....It.	38·03 N	13·32 E
108	Bagley (băg′lē)....Mn.	47·31 N	95·24 W
164	Bagnara (bän-yä′rä)....It.	38·17 N	15·52 E
117	Bagnell Dam (băg′nĕl)....Mo.	38·13 N	92·40 W
160	Bagnères-de-Bigorre (băn-yâr′dĕ-bē-gor′).Fr.	43·40 N	0·70 E
160	Bagnères-de-Luchon (băn-yâr′ dĕ-lu chôN′) Fr.	42·46 N	0·36 E
160	Bagnols (bä-nyôl′)....Fr.	44·09 N	4·37 E
210	Bagoé R. (bȧ-gō′ā)....Mali	12·22 N	6·34 W
97	Bagotville (bȧ-gô-vēl′)....Can.	48·21 N	70·53 W
188	Bagrash Köl (L.)....China	42·06 N	88·01 E
197	Baguio (bä-gê-ō′)....Phil. (In.)	16·24 N	120·36 E
215	Bagzane, Monts (Mtn.)....Niger	18·40 N	8·40 E
123	Bahamas (bȧ-hä′mȧs)....N. A.	26·15 N	76·00 W
183	Bahau....Mala. (Singapore In.)	2·48 N	102·25 E
184	Bahāwalpur (bŭ-hä′wŭl-po͞or).Pak.	29·29 N	71·41 E
217	Bahi Swp....Tan.	6·05 S	35·10 E
	Bahia, see Salvador		
135	Bahia (State)....Braz.	11·05 S	43·00 W
122	Bahía, Islas de la (I.) (ē′s-lās-dĕ-lä-bä-ē′ä).Hond.	16·15 N	86·30 W
136	Bahia Blanca (bä-ē′ä bläŋ′kä).Arg.	38·45 S	62·07 W
134	Bahía de Caráquez (bä-ē′ä dā kä-rä′kĕz).Ec.	0·45 S	80·29 W
135	Bahía Negra (bä-ē′ä nā′grä)..Par.	20·11 S	58·05 W
136	Bahias, Cabo dos (C.) (kå′bô-dôs-bä-ē′äs).Arg.	44·55 S	65·35 W
129	Bahoruco, Sierra de (Mts.) (sē-ĕ′r-rä-dĕ-bä-ō-ro͞o′kô) Dom. Rep.	18·10 N	71·25 W
186	Bahrain (bä-rān′)....Asia	26·15 N	51·17 E
211	Baḥr al Ghazāl (Prov.) (bär ĕl ghä-zäl′).Sud.	7·56 N	27·15 E
153	Baḥrīyah (Oasis) (bȧ-hȧ-rē′yä) Egypt	28·34 N	29·01 E
183	Baḥrīyah, Jabal Jalālah al (Plat.) Egypt (Palestine In.)	29·15 N	32·20 E
159	Baia de Cris (bä′yä dā krēs′) Rom.	46·11 N	22·40 E
216	Baía dos Tigres....Ang.	16·36 S	11·43 E
159	Baia-Mare (bä′yä-mä′rā)....Rom.	47·40 N	23·35 E
196	Bai-Bung Mui (C.)....Viet.	8·36 N	104·43 E
218	Baidoa....Som. (Horn of Afr. In.)	3·19 N	44·20 E
184	Baidyabāti....India (In.)	22·47 N	88·21 E
98	Baie-Comeau....Can.	49·13 N	68·10 W
113	Baie de Wasai (bā dē wä-sä′ē) Mi. (Sault Ste. Marie In.)	46·27 N	84·15 W
97	Baie-St. Paul (bā′sånt-pôl′)..Can.	47·27 N	70·30 W
	Baikal Mts., see Baykal′skiy Khrebet		
	Baikal, L., see Baykal, Ozero		
	Baile Atha Cliath, see Dublin		
162	Bailén (bä-ê-lān′)....Sp.	38·05 N	3·48 W
165	Băileşti (bŭ-ĭ-lĕsh′tē)....Rom.	44·01 N	23·21 E
120	Bainbridge (bān′brĭj)....Ga.	30·52 N	84·35 W
112	Bainbridge I....Wa. (Seattle In.)	47·39 N	122·32 W
118	Baird (bârd)....Tx.	32·22 N	99·28 W
107	Bairdford (bârd′fŏrd) Pa. (Pittsburgh In.)	40·37 N	79·53 W
101	Baird Mts....Ak.	67·35 N	160·10 W
203	Bairnsdale (bârnz′dāl)....Austl.	37·50 S	147·39 E
160	Baïse (R.) (bä-ēz′)....Fr.	43·52 N	0·23 E
159	Baja (bŏ′yŏ)....Hung.	46·11 N	18·55 E
122	Baja California Norte (State) (bä-hä).Mex.	30·15 N	117·25 W
122	Baja California Sur (State) Mex.	26·00 N	113·30 W
174	Bakal (bä′kål).Sov. Un. (Urals In.)	54·57 N	58·50 E
111	Baker (bā′kēr)....Mt.	46·21 N	104·12 W
110	Baker....Or.	44·46 N	117·52 W
198	Baker (I.)....Oceania	1·00 N	176·00 W
90	Baker (L.)....Can.	63·51 N	96·10 W
110	Baker, Mt....Wa.	48·46 N	121·52 W
107	Baker Cr....Il. (Chicago In.)	41·13 N	87·47 W
114	Bakersfield (bā′kērz-fēld)....Ca.	35·23 N	119·00 W
107	Bakerstown (bā′kerz-toun) Pa. (Pittsburgh In.)	40·39 N	79·56 W
148	Bakewell (bāk′wĕl)....Eng.	53·12 N	1·40 W

PRONOUNCING INDEX

Bakhchisaray — Barlee 255

Page Name Pronunciation Region Lat. °′ Long. °′

167 Bakhchisaray (bȧk′chĕ-sȧ-rī′) Sov. Un. 44·46 N 33·54 E
167 Bakhmach (bȧĸ-mäch′) Sov. Un. 51·09 N 32·47 E
186 Bakhtegan, Daryācheh-ye (L.) Iran 29·29 N 54·31 E
174 Bakhteyevo (bȧk-tyĕ′yĕ-vô) Sov. Un. (Moscow In.) 55·35 N 38·32 E
211 Bako (bä′kö) Eth. 5·47 N 36·39 E
159 Bakony-Erdo (Mts.) (bȧ-kōn′y′) Hung. 46·57 N 17·30 E
214 Bakoye (R.) (bȧ-kô′ê) Mali 12·47 N 9·35 W
174 Bakr Uzyak (bȧkr o͞oz′yȧk) Sov. Un. (Urals In.) 52·59 N 58·43 E
171 Baku (bȧ-ko͞o′) Sov. Un. 40·28 N 49·45 E
Bakwanga, see Mbuji-Mayi
196 Balabac (I.) (bä′lä-bäk) Phil. 8·00 N 116·28 E
196 Balabac Str. Indon.-Phil. 7·23 N 116·30 E
183 Ba′labakk Leb. (Palestine In.) 34·00 N 36·13 E
196 Balabalagan, Kepulauan (Is.) (bä-lä-bä′lä-gän) Indon. 2·00 S 117·15 E
174 Balabanovo (bȧ-lȧ-bä′nô-vô) Sov. Un. (Moscow In.) 56·10 N 37·44 E
172 Balagansk (bä-lä-gänsk′) Sov. Un. 53·58 N 103·09 E
163 Balaguer (bä-lä-gĕr′) Sp. 41·48 N 0·50 E
172 Balakhta (bȧ′lȧk-tȧ′) Sov. Un. 55·22 N 91·43 E
167 Balakleya (bȧ′lȧ-klā′yȧ) Sov. Un. 49·28 N 36·51 E
171 Balakovo (bȧ′lȧ-kô′vô) Sov. Un. 52·00 N 47·40 E
125 Balancán (bä-läŋ-kän′) Mex. 17·47 N 91·32 W
197 Balanga (bä-läŋ′gä) Phil. (In.) 14·41 N 120·31 E
197 Balaoan (bä-lou′än) Phil. (In.) 16·49 N 120·24 E
174 Balashikha (bȧ-lȧ′shĭ-kȧ) Sov. Un. (Moscow In.) 55·48 N 37·58 E
171 Balashov (bȧ′lȧ-shôf) Sov. Un. 51·30 N 43·00 E
184 Balasore (bä-lȧ-sōr′) India 21·38 N 86·59 E
159 Balassagyarmat (bô′lôsh-shô-dyôr′môt) Hung. 48·04 N 19·19 E
159 Balaton L. (bô′lô-tôn) Hung. 46·47 N 17·55 E
197 Balayan (bä-lä-yän′) Phil. (In.) 13·56 N 120·44 E
197 Balayan B. Phil. (In.) 13·46 N 120·46 E
122 Balboa (bäl-bô′ä) C. Z. (In.) 8·55 N 79·34 W
127 Balboa Heights C. Z. 8·59 N 79·33 W
122 Balboa Mt. C. Z. (In.) 9·05 N 79·44 W
136 Balcarce (bäl-kär′sā) Arg. 37·49 S 58·17 W
165 Balchik Bul. 43·24 N 28·13 E
113 Bald Eagle (bôld ē′g′l) Mn. (Minneapolis, St. Paul In.) 45·06 N 93·01 W
113 Bald Eagle L. Mn. (Minneapolis, St. Paul In.) 45·08 N 93·03 W
95 Baldock L. Can. 56·33 N 97·57 W
113 Baldwin Park (bôld′wĭn) Ca. (Los Angeles In.) 34·05 N 117·58 W
105 Baldwinsville (bôld′wĭns-vĭl) NY 43·10 N 76·20 W
95 Baldy Mtn. Can. 51·28 N 100·44 W
115 Baldy Pk. (bôl′dê) Az. 33·55 N 109·35 W
118 Baldy Pk. (bôl′dê pēk) Tx. 30·38 N 104·11 W
163 Baleares, Islas (Balearic Is.) (e′s-läs bä-lĕ-ä′rĕs) Sp. 39·25 N 1·28 E
Balearic Is., see Baleares, Islas
163 Balearic Sea (băl-ê-ăr′ĭk) Eur. 39·40 N 1·05 E
91 Baleine, Grande Rivière de la (R.) Can. 54·45 N 74·20 W
197 Baler (bä-lar′) Phil. (In.) 15·46 N 121·33 E
197 Baler B. Phil. (In.) 15·51 N 121·40 E
197 Balesin (I.) Phil. (In.) 14·28 N 122·10 E
173 Baley (bȧl-yā′) Sov. Un. 51·29 N 116·12 E
126 Balfate (bäl-fä′tē) Hond. 15·48 N 86·24 W
218 Balfour (băl′fo͝or) S. Afr. (Johannesburg & Pretoria In.) 26·41 S 28·37 E
196 Bali (I.) (bä′lê) Indon. 8·00 S 115·22 E
171 Balikesir (balĭk′ĭysĭr) Tur. 39·40 N 27·50 E
196 Balikpapan (bä′lêk-pä′pän) Indon. 1·13 S 116·52 E
196 Balintang Chan. (bā-lĭn-täng′) Phil. 19·50 N 121·08 E
Balkan Mts., see Stara Planina
187 Balkh (bälk) Afg. 36·48 N 66·50 E
172 Balkhash (bȧl-käsh′) Sov. Un. 46·58 N 75·00 E
172 Balkhash, Ozero (L.) Sov. Un. 45·58 N 72·15 E
167 Balki (bäl′kĭ) Sov. Un. 47·22 N 34·56 E
161 Ballancourt (bä-län-ko͞or′) Fr. (Paris In.) 48·31 N 2·23 E
203 Ballarat (băl′ȧ-răt) Austl. 37·37 S 144·00 E
204 Ballard (L.) (băl′ȧrd) Austl. 29·15 S 120·45 E
154 Ballater (băl′ȧ-tĕr) Scot. 57·05 N 3·06 W
214 Ballé Mali 15·20 N 8·35 W
220 Balleny Is. (băl′ĕ nê) Ant. 67·00 S 164·00 E
203 Ballina (băl-ĭ-nä′) Austl. 28·50 S 153·35 E
154 Ballina Ire. 54·06 N 9·05 W
154 Ballinasloe (băl′ĭ-nȧ-slō′) Ire. 53·20 N 8·09 W
118 Ballinger (băl′ĭn-jĕr) Tx. 31·45 N 99·58 W
105 Ballston Spa (bôls′tŭn spä′) NY 43·05 N 73·50 W
159 Balmazújváros (bŏl′mŏz-o͞o′y′vä′rôsh) Hung. 47·35 N 21·23 E
217 Balobe Zaire 0·05 N 28·00 E
203 Balonne (R.) (băl-ōn′) Austl. 27·00 S 149·10 E
184 Bālotra India 25·56 N 72·12 E
203 Balranald (băl′-rȧn-ăld) Austl. 34·42 S 143·30 E
165 Balş (bälsh) Rom. 44·21 N 24·05 E
105 Balsam (L.) (bôl′sȧm) Can. 44·30 N 78·50 W
135 Balsas (bäl′säs) Braz. 7·09 S 46·04 W
122 Balsas (R.) Mex. 18·00 N 103·00 W
167 Balta (bäl′tȧ) Sov. Un. 47·57 N 29·38 E
150 Baltic Sea (bôl′tĭk) Eur. 55·20 N 16·50 E
218 Baltīm (bȧl-tēm′) Egypt (Nile In.) 31·33 N 31·04 E
106 Baltimore (bôl′tĭ-môr) Md. (Baltimore In.) 39·20 N 76·38 W
157 Baltiysk (bäl-tēysk′) Sov. Un. 54·40 N 19·55 E
124 Baluarte, Río del (rē′ō-dĕl-bä-lo͞o′r-tĕ) Mex. 23·09 N 105·42 W
187 Baluchistān (Reg.) (bȧ-lo͞o-chĭ-stän′) Pak. 27·30 N 65·30 E
89 Balzac (bôl′zăk) Can. (Calgary In.) 51·10 N 114·01 W
215 Bama Nig. 11·30 N 13·41 E
214 Bamako (bä-mä-kō′) Mali 12·39 N 8·00 W
197 Bambang (bäm-bäng′) Phil. (In.) 16·24 N 121·08 E
211 Bambari (bäm-bȧ-rē) Cen. Afr. Emp. 5·44 N 20·40 E
158 Bamberg (bäm′bĕrgh) F.R.G. 49·53 N 10·52 E
121 Bamberg (băm′bûrg) SC 33·17 N 81·04 W
137 Bambuí (bä′m-bo͞o-ē) Braz. (Rio de Janeiro In.) 20·01 S 45·59 W
215 Bamenda Cam. 5·56 N 10·10 E
215 Bamingui (R.) Cen. Afr. Emp. 7·35 N 19·45 E
215 Bamingui Bangoran, Parc Nat′l. du (Natl. Park) Cen. Afr. Emp. 8·05 N 19·35 E
148 Bampton (băm′tŭn) Eng. (London In.) 51·42 N 1·33 W
186 Bampūr (bŭm-po͞or′) Iran 27·15 N 60·22 E
215 Bam Yanga, Ngao (Mts.) Cam. 8·20 N 14·40 E
197 Banahao, Mt. (bä-nä-hä′ō) Phil. (In.) 14·04 N 121·45 E
216 Banalia Zaire 1·33 N 25·20 E
214 Banamba Mali 13·33 N 7·27 W
137 Bananal (bä-nä-näl′) Braz. (Rio de Janerio In.) 22·42 S 44·17 W
135 Bananal, Ilha do (I.) (ē′lä-dô-bä-nä-näl′) Braz. 12·09 S 50·27 W
184 Banās (R.) (bän-äs′) India 25·20 N 74·51 E
211 Banās, Ra′s (C.) Egypt 23·48 N 36·39 E
165 Banat (Reg.) (bä-nät′) Rom.-Yugo. 45·35 N 21·05 E
196 Ban Bangsaphan Thai. 11·19 N 99·27 E
105 Bancroft (băn′krôft) Can. 45·05 N 77·55 W
Bancroft, see Chililabombwe
184 Bānda (bän′dä) India 25·36 N 80·21 E
196 Banda Aceh Indon. 5·10 N 95·10 E
203 Banda Banda, Mt. (băn′dȧ băn′dȧ) Austl. 31·09 S 152·15 E
197 Banda Besar (I.) Indon. 4·40 S 129·56 E
197 Banda Laut (Banda Sea) Indon. 6·05 S 127·28 E
214 Bandama Blanc (R.) (bän-dä′mä) Ivory Coast 6·15 N 5·00 W
186 Bandar ′Abbās (Hbr.) (bän-där′ ȧb-bäs′) Iran 27·04 N 56·22 E
186 Bandar-e Lengeh (Hbr.) Iran 26·44 N 54·47 E
186 Bandar-e Shāh Iran 37·05 N 54·08 E
186 Bandar-e-Shāhpūr (Hbr.) Iran 30·27 N 48·45 E
183 Bandar Maharani (bän-där′ mä-hä-rä′nê) Mala. (Singapore In.) 2·02 N 102·34 E
196 Bandar Seri Begawan Bru. 5·00 N 114·59 E
137 Bandeira, Pico da (Pk.) (pē′ko͞o dä bän-dā′rä) Braz. (Rio de Janeiro In.) 20·27 S 41·47 W
115 Bandelier Natl. Mon. (băn-dĕ-lēr′) NM 35·50 N 106·45 W
124 Banderas, Bahía de (B.) (bä-ē′ä dĕ bän-dĕ′räs) Mex. 20·38 N 105·35 W
171 Bandirma (bän-dĭr′mȧ) Tur. 40·25 N 27·50 E
162 Bando (bä′n-dô) Sp. 42·02 N 7·58 W
110 Bandon (băn′dŭn) Or. 43·06 N 124·25 W
185 Bāndra India (In.) 19·04 N 72·49 E
216 Bandundu Zaire 3·18 S 17·20 E
196 Bandung Indon. 7·00 S 107·22 E
129 Banes (bä′näs) Cuba 21·00 N 75·45 W
93 Banff (bănf) Can. 51·10 N 115·34 W
154 Banff Scot. 57·39 N 2·37 W
93 Banff Natl. Park Can. 51·38 N 116·22 W
136 Bānfield (bä′n-fē′ld) Arg. (Buenos Aires In.) 34·44 S 58·24 W
214 Banfora Upper Volta 10·38 N 4·46 W
185 Bangalore (băŋ′gȧ′lôr) India 13·03 N 77·39 E
197 Bangar (bäŋ-gär′) Phil. (In.) 16·54 N 120·24 E
211 Bangassou (bäɴ-gȧ-so͞o′) Cen. Afr. Emp. 4·47 N 22·49 E
215 Bangé Cam. 3·01 N 15·07 E
197 Bangeta, Mt. Pap. N. Gui. 6·20 S 147·00 E
197 Banggai, Kepulauan (Is.) (bäng-gī′) Indon. 1·05 S 123·45 E
196 Banggi (I.) Mala. 7·12 N 117·10 E
211 Banghāzī (bĕn-gä′zē) Libya 32·08 N 20·06 E
196 Bangka (I.) (bäŋ′kȧ) Indon. 2·24 S 106·55 E
196 Bangkalan (bäng-kȧ-län′) Indon. 6·07 S 112·50 E
Bangkok, see Krung Thep
187 Bangladesh Asia 24·15 N 90·00 E
98 Bangor (băn′gĕr) Me. 44·47 N 68·47 W
104 Bangor Mi. 42·20 N 86·05 W
105 Bangor Pa. 40·55 N 75·10 W
154 Bangor (băŋ′ĕr) (băn′ôr) Wales 53·13 N 4·05 W
115 Bangs, Mt. (băngs) Az. 36·45 N 113·50 W
197 Bangued (bäŋ-gād′) Phil. (In.) 17·36 N 120·38 E
215 Bangui (bäɴ-gē′) Cen. Afr. Emp. 4·22 N 18·35 E
217 Bangweulu, L. (băng-wê-o͞o′lo͞o) Zambia 10·55 S 30·10 E
217 Bangweulu Swp. Zambia 11·25 S 30·10 E
218 Banhā Egypt (Nile In.) 30·24 N 31·11 E
129 Bani (bä′-nê) Dom. Rep. 18·15 N 70·25 W
197 Bani (bä′nē) Phil. (In.) 16·11 N 119·51 E
214 Bani (R.) Mali 13·07 N 6·15 W
129 Bánica (bä′-nē-kä) Dom. Rep. 19·00 N 71·35 W
218 Banī Mazār Egypt (Nile In.) 28·29 N 30·48 E
218 Banī Suwayf Egypt (Nile In.) 29·05 N 31·06 E
196 Banjak, Kepulauan (I.) Indon. 2·08 N 97·15 E
164 Banja Luka (bän-yä-lo͞o′kȧ) Yugo. 44·45 N 17·11 E
196 Banjarmasin (bän-jĕr-mä′sĕn) Indon. 3·18 S 114·32 E
214 Banjul (Bathurst) Gam. 13·28 N 16·39 W
196 Ban Kantang (bän-kän′tăng′) Thai. 7·26 N 99·28 E
213 Bankberg (Mts.) (băŋk′bûrg) S. Afr. (Natal In.) 32·18 S 25·15 E
112 Banks (bănks) Or. (Portland In.) 45·37 N 123·07 W
205 Banks (Is.) Austl. 10·10 S 143·08 E
202 Banks, C. Austl. (Sydney In.) 34·01 S 151·17 E
92 Banks I. Can. 53·25 N 130·10 W
75 Banks I. Can. 73·00 N 123·00 W
205 Banks Is. New Hebr. 13·38 S 168·23 E
203 Banks Str. Austl. 40·45 S 148·00 E
196 Ban Kui Nua Thai. 12·04 N 99·50 E
154 Bann (R.) (băn) N. Ire. 54·50 N 6·29 W
113 Banning (băn′ĭng) Ca. (Los Angeles In.) 33·56 N 116·53 W
121 Bannister (R.) (băn′ĭs-tĕr) Va. 36·45 N 79·17 W
202 Bannockburn Austl. (Melbourne In.) 38·03 S 144·11 E
184 Bannu Pak. 33·03 N 70·39 E
134 Baños (bä′-nyōs) Ec. 1·30 S 78·22 W
159 Banská Bystrica (bän′skä bē′strē-tzä) Czech. 48·46 N 19·10 E
165 Bansko (bän′skō) Bul. 41·51 N 23·33 E
148 Banstead (băn′stĕd) Eng. (In.) 51·18 N 0·09 W
197 Banton (bän-tōn′) Phil. (In.) 12·54 N 121·55 E
154 Bantry (băn′trĭ) Ire. 51·39 N 9·30 W
154 Bantry B. Ire. 51·25 N 10·09 W
196 Banyuwangi (bän-jo͞o-wäŋ′gê) Indon. 8·15 S 114·15 E
211 Banzyville (bäɴ-zê-vēl′) Zaire 4·14 N 21·11 E
213 Bapsfontein (băps-fŏn-tān′) S. Afr. (Johannesburg & Pretoria In.) 26·01 S 28·26 E
134 Baqueroncito (bä-kĕ-rô′n-sē-tô) Col. (In.) 3·18 N 74·40 W
167 Bar (bär) Sov. Un. 49·02 N 27·44 E
172 Barabinsk (bȧ′rȧ-bĭnsk) Sov. Un. 55·18 N 78·00 E
109 Baraboo (bâr′ȧ-bo͞o) Wi. 43·29 N 89·44 W
129 Baracoa (bä-rä-kō′ä) Cuba 20·20 N 74·25 W
129 Baracoa Cuba (In.) 23·03 N 82·34 W
137 Baradeo (bä-rä-dĕ′ō) Arg. (Buenos Aires In.) 33·50 S 59·30 W
129 Baradères, Baie des (B.) (bä-rä-dâr′) Hai. 18·35 N 73·35 W
129 Barahona (bä-rä-ô′nä) Dom. Rep. 18·15 N 71·10 W
163 Barajas de Madrid (bä-rȧ′häs dā mä-drēdh′) Sp. (Madrid In.) 40·28 N 3·35 W
184 Baranagar India (In.) 22·38 N 88·25 E
126 Baranco (bä-räŋ′kō) Belize 16·01 N 88·55 W
101 Baranof (I.) (bä-rä′nôf) Ak. 56·48 N 136·08 W
159 Baranovichi (bä′rä-nô-vē′chê) Sov. Un. 53·08 N 25·59 E
183 Baranpauh Indon. (Singapore In.) 0·40 N 103·28 E
136 Barão de Juperanã (bä-rou′ɴ-dĕ-zho͞o-pe-rȧ′nȧ) Braz. (Rio de Janeiro In.) 22·21 S 43·41 W
135 Barão de Melgaço (bä-rouɴ-dĕ-mĕl-gä′sō) Braz. 16·12 S 55·48 W
184 Bārāsat India (In.) 22·42 N 88·29 E
119 Barataria B. La. 29·13 N 89·90 W
134 Baraya (bä-rȧ′yä) Col. (In.) 3·10 N 75·04 W
137 Barbacena (bär-bä-sā′nȧ) Braz. (Rio de Janeiro In.) 21·15 S 43·46 W
134 Barbacoas (bär-bä-kō′äs) Col. 1·39 N 78·12 W
135 Barbacoas (bär-bä-kō′äs) Ven. (In.) 9·30 N 66·58 W
123 Barbados (bär-bā′dōz) N. A. 13·30 N 59·00 W
211 Barbar Sud. 18·11 N 34·00 E
163 Barbastro (bär-bäs′trō) Sp. 42·05 N 0·05 E
113 Barbeau (bȧr-bō′) Mi. (Sault Ste. Marie In.) 46·17 N 84·16 W
107 Barberton (bär′bĕr-tŭn) Oh. (Cleveland In.) 41·01 N 81·37 W
212 Barberton S. Afr. 25·48 S 31·04 E
160 Barbezieux (bärb′zyû′) Fr. 45·30 N 0·11 W
120 Barboorville (bär′bĕr-vĭl) Ky. 36·52 N 83·58 W
134 Barbosa (bär-bô′-sä) Col. (In.) 6·26 N 75·19 W
104 Barboursville (bär′bĕrs-vĭl) WV 38·20 N 82·20 W
123 Barbuda (I.) (bär-bo͞o′dȧ) Antigua 17·45 N 61·15 W
205 Barcaldine (bär′kôl-dĭn) Austl. 23·33 S 145·17 E
163 Barcarena (bär-kä-rĕ′-nä) Port. (Lisbon In.) 38·29 N 9·17 W
162 Barcarrota (bär-kär-rō′tä) Sp. 38·31 N 6·50 W
164 Barcellona (bär-chĕl-lō′nä) It. 38·07 N 15·15 E
163 Barcelona (bär-thȧ-lō′nä) Sp. 41·25 N 2·08 E
135 Barcelona (bär-sȧ-lō′nä) Ven. (In.) 10·09 N 64·41 W
161 Barcelonnette (bär-sĕ-lô-nĕt′) Fr. 44·24 N 6·42 E
134 Barcelos (bär-sĕ′lōs) Braz. 1·04 S 63·00 W
162 Barcélos (bär-thȧ′lōs) Port. 41·34 N 8·39 W
186 Bardar-e Pahlavī Iran 37·16 N 49·15 E
183 Bardawīl, Sabkhat al (B.) Egypt (Palestine In.) 31·20 N 33·24 E
159 Bardejov (bär′dyĕ-yôf) Czech. 49·18 N 21·18 E
218 Bardera (bär-dā′rä) Som. (Horn of Afr. In.) 2·13 N 42·24 E
154 Bardsey (I.) (bärd′sē) Wales 52·45 N 4·50 W
104 Bardstown (bärds′toun) Ky. 37·50 N 85·30 W
120 Bardwell (bärd′wĕl) Ky. 36·51 N 88·57 W
168 Barents Sea (bä′rĕnts) Sov. Un. 72·14 N 37·28 E
211 Barentu (bä-rĕn′to͞o) Eth. 15·06 N 37·39 E
160 Barfleur, Pte. de (Pt.) (bȧr-flûr′) Fr. 49·43 N 1·17 W
173 Barguzin (bär′go͞o-zĭn) Sov. Un. 53·44 N 109·28 E
98 Bar Harbor (bär här′bĕr) Me. 44·22 N 68·13 W
164 Bari (bä′rē) It. 41·08 N 16·53 E
134 Barinas (bä-rē′näs) Ven. 8·36 N 70·14 W
90 Baring, C. (bâr′ĭng) Can. 70·07 N 119·48 W
196 Barisan, Pegunungan (Mts.) (bä-rê-sän′) Indon. 2·38 S 101·45 E
196 Barito (Strm.) (bä-rē′tō) Indon. 2·10 S 114·38 E
211 Barka (R.) Eth. 16·44 N 37·34 E
92 Barkley Sd. Can. 48·53 N 125·20 W
213 Barkly East (bärk′lē ēst) S. Afr. (Natal In.) 30·58 S 27·37 E
204 Barkly Tableland (Plat.) (bär′klê) Austl. 18·15 S 137·05 E
160 Bar-le-Duc (băr-lē-dük′) Fr. 48·47 N 5·05 E
204 Barlee (L.) (bär-lē′) Austl. 29·45 S 119·00 E

ng-sing; ŋ-baŋk; ɴ-nasalized n; nŏd; cŏmmit; ōld; ôbey; ôrder; fo͞od; fo͝ot; ou-out; s-soft; sh-dish; th-thin; pūre; ûnite; ûrn; stŭd; circŭs; ü-as "y" in study; ′-indeterminate vowel.

256 Barletta — Beaver PRONOUNCING INDEX

Page	Name Pronunciation Region	Lat. °'	Long. °'
164	Barletta (bär-lĕt'tä) It.	41·19 N	16·20 E
149	Barmstedt (bärm'shtĕt) F.R.G. (Hamburg In.)	53·47 N	9·46 E
172	Barnaul (bär-nä-ōōl') Sov. Un.	53·18 N	83·23 E
105	Barnesboro (bärnz'bēr-ô) Pa.	40·45 N	78·50 W
120	Barnesville (bärnz'vĭl) Ga.	33·03 N	84·10 W
108	Barnesville Mn.	46·38 N	96·25 W
104	Barnesville Oh.	39·55 N	81·10 W
105	Barnet (bär'nĕt) Vt.	44·20 N	72·00 W
148	Barnetby le Wold (bär'nĕt-bĭ) Eng.	53·34 N	0·26 W
128	Barnett Hbr. Ba.	25·40 N	79·20 W
117	Barnsdall (bärnz'dôl) Ok.	36·38 N	96·14 W
148	Barnsley (bärnz'lĭ) Eng.	53·33 N	1·29 W
154	Barnstaple (bärn'stā-p'l) Eng.	51·06 N	4·05 W
121	Barnwell (bärn'wĕl) SC	33·14 N	81·23 W
215	Baro (bä'rô) Nig.	8·37 N	6·25 E
211	Bāro (R.) Eth.	7·40 N	34·17 E
184	Baroda (bä-rō'dä) India	22·21 N	73·12 E
216	Barotse Pln. Zambia	15·50 S	22·55 E
211	Barqah (Cyrenaica) (Prov.) Libya	31·09 N	21·45 E
134	Barquisimeto (bär-kē-sê-mä'tō) Ven.	10·04 N	69·16 W
135	Barra (bär'rä) Braz.	11·04 S	43·11 W
203	Barraba Austl.	30·22 S	150·36 E
135	Barra do Corda (bär'rä dōō cōr-dä) Braz.	5·33 S	45·13 W
154	Barra Is. (băr'ră) Scot.	57·00 N	7·30 W
137	Barra Mansa (bär'rä män'sä) Braz. (Rio de Janeiro In.)	22·35 S	44·09 W
134	Barrancabermeja (bär-räṇ'kä-bēr-mā'hä) Col.	7·06 N	73·49 W
134	Barranquilla (bär-rän-kēl'yä) Col.	10·57 N	75·00 W
135	Barras (bå'r-räs) Braz.	4·13 S	42·14 W
105	Barre (băr'ē) Vt.	44·15 N	72·30 W
137	Barre do Piraí (bär'rĕ-dô-pē'rä-ē') Braz. (Rio de Janeiro In.)	22·30 S	43·49 W
135	Barreiras (bär-rā'räs) Braz.	12·13 S	44·59 W
163	Barreiro (bär-rĕ'ê-rōō) Port. (Lisbon In.)	38·39 N	9·05 W
203	Barren, C. (băr'ĕn) Austl.	40·20 S	149·00 E
213	Barren, Îles (Is.) Mad.	18·18 S	43·57 E
120	Barren (R.) Ky.	37·00 N	86·20 W
135	Barretos (bär-rā'tōs) Braz.	20·40 S	48·36 W
93	Barrhead (băr-hĕd) (băr'ĭd) Can.	54·08 N	114·24 W
105	Barrie (băr'ĭ) Can.	44·25 N	79·45 W
89	Barrington (bă-rēng-tŏn) Can. (Montreal In.)	45·07 N	73·35 W
107	Barrington Il. (Chicago In.)	42·09 N	88·08 W
106	Barrington RI (Providence In.)	41·44 N	71·16 W
203	Barrington Tops (Mtn.) Austl.	32·00 S	151·25 E
113	Bar River (bär) Can. (Sault Ste. Marie In.)	46·27 N	84·02 W
109	Barron (băr'ŭn) Wi.	45·24 N	91·51 W
101	Barrow (băr'ō) Ak.	71·20 N	156·00 W
154	Barrow Eng.	54·10 N	3·15 W
204	Barrow (I.) Austl.	20·50 S	115·00 E
204	Barrow Creek Austl.	21·23 S	133·55 E
101	Barrow Pt. Ak.	71·20 N	156·00 W
154	Barrow R. (bå-rå) Ire.	52·35 N	7·05 W
162	Barruelo de Santullán (bär-rōō-å-lō dā sän-tōō-lyän') Sp.	42·55 N	4·19 W
114	Barstow (bär'stō) Ca.	34·53 N	117·03 W
106	Barstow Md. (Baltimore In.)	38·32 N	76·37 W
158	Barth (bärt) G.D.R.	54·20 N	12·43 E
117	Bartholomew Bay (bär-thŏl'ô-mū bī-ōō') Ar.	33·53 N	91·45 W
98	Barthurst (băr-thŭrst') Can.	47·38 N	65·40 W
135	Bartica (bär'tĭ-kå) Guy.	6·23 N	58·32 W
171	Bartin (bär'tĭn) Tur.	41·35 N	32·12 E
205	Bartle Frere, Mt. (bärt''l frēr') Austl.	17·30 S	145·46 E
117	Bartlesville (bär'tlz-vĭl) Ok.	36·44 N	95·58 W
107	Bartlett (bärt'lĕt) Il. (Chicago In.)	41·59 N	88·11 W
119	Bartlett Tx.	30·48 N	97·25 W
105	Barton (bär'tŭn) Vt.	44·45 N	72·05 W
148	Barton-upon-Humber (bär'tŭn-ŭp'ŏn-hŭm'bēr) Eng.	53·41 N	0·26 W
159	Bartoszyce (bär-tô-shĭ'tså) Pol.	54·15 N	20·50 E
121	Bartow (bär'tō) Fl. (In.)	27·51 N	81·50 W
167	Barvenkovo (bär'vĕn-kô'vô) Sov. Un.	48·55 N	36·59 E
203	Barwon (R.) (bär'wŭn) Austl.	29·45 S	148·25 E
202	Barwon Heads Austl. (Melbourne In.)	38·17 S	144·29 E
158	Barycz R. (bä'rĭch) Pol.	51·30 N	16·38 E
211	Basankusu (bä-sän-kōō'sōō) Zaire	1·14 N	19·45 E
149	Basbeck (bäs'bĕk) F.R.G. (Hamburg In.)	53·40 N	9·11 E
149	Basdahl (bäs'däl) F.R.G. (Hamburg In.)	53·27 N	9·00 E
113	Basehor (bās'hôr) Ks. (Kansas City In.)	39·08 N	94·55 W
158	Basel (bä'z'l) Switz.	47·32 N	7·35 E
213	Bashee (R.) (bă-shē') S. Afr. (Natal In.)	31·47 S	28·25 E
193	Bashi Chan (băsh'ē) Phil.	21·20 N	120·22 E
170	Bashkir (A.S.S.R.) (båsh-kēr') Sov. Un.	54·12 N	57·15 E
167	Bashtanka (båsh-tän'kå) Sov. Un.	47·32 N	32·31 E
196	Basilan (I.) Phil.	6·37 N	122·07 E
164	Basilicata (Reg.) (bä-zē-lē-kä'tä) It.	40·30 N	15·55 E
111	Basin (bā'sĭn) Wy.	44·22 N	108·02 W
148	Basingstoke (bā'zĭng-stōk) Eng. (London In.)	51·14 N	1·06 W
164	Baška (bäsh'ka) Yugo.	44·58 N	14·44 E
171	Baskale (bäsh-kä'lĕ) Tur.	38·10 N	44·00 E
97	Baskatong Res. Can.	46·50 N	75·50 W
171	Baskunchak (L.) Sov. Un.	48·20 N	46·40 E
211	Basoko (bå-sō'kō) Zaire	0·52 N	23·50 E
93	Bassano (bäs-sän'ō) Can.	50·47 N	112·28 W
164	Bassano It.	45·46 N	11·44 E
214	Bassari Togo	9·15 N	0·47 E
213	Bassas da India (I.) (bäs'säs dä ēn'dê-å) Afr.	21·23 S	39·42 E
196	Bassein (bŭ-sēn') Bur.	16·46 N	94·47 E
127	Basse Terre (bås' târ') Guad. (In.)	16·00 N	61·43 W
127	Basseterre St. Kitts-Nevis-Anguilla (In.)	17·20 N	62·42 W
127	Basse Terre I. Guad. (In.)	16·10 N	62·14 W
121	Bassett (băs'sĕt) Va.	36·45 N	81·58 W
104	Bass Is. (băs) Oh.	41·40 N	82·50 W
203	Bass Str. Austl.	39·40 S	145·40 E
109	Basswood (L.) (băs'wŏŏd) Can.-Mn.	48·10 N	91·36 W
156	Båstad (bô'stät) Swe.	56·26 N	12·46 E
164	Bastia (bäs'tē-ä) Fr.	42·43 N	9·27 E
155	Bastogne (bäs-tôn'y') Bel.	50·02 N	5·45 E
119	Bastrop (băs'trŭp) La.	32·47 N	91·55 W
119	Bastrop Tx.	30·08 N	97·18 W
119	Bastrop Bayou Tx. (In.)	29·07 N	95·22 W
216	Bata (bä'tä) Equat. Gui.	1·51 N	9·45 E
128	Batabanó (bä-tä-bä-nō') Cuba	22·45 N	82·20 W
128	Batabano, Golfo, de (G.) (gôl-fô-dĕ-bä-tä-bå'nô) Cuba	22·10 N	83·05 W
184	Batāla India	31·54 N	75·18 E
174	Bataly (bå-tä'lĭ) Sov. Un. (Urals In.)	52·51 N	62·03 E
183	Batam I. (bä-täm') Indon. (Singapore In.)	1·03 N	104·00 E
193	Batan Is. (bä-tän') Phil.	20·58 N	122·20 E
193	Batangan, C. Viet.	15·18 N	109·10 E
197	Batangas (bä-tän'gäs) Phil. (In.)	13·45 N	121·04 E
159	Bátaszék (bä'tå-sĕk) Hung.	46·07 N	18·40 E
107	Batavia (bå-tā'vĭ-å) Il. (Chicago In.)	41·51 N	88·18 W
105	Batavia NY	43·00 N	78·15 W
107	Batavia Oh. (Cincinnati In.)	39·05 N	84·10 W
167	Bataysk (bå-tīsk') Sov. Un.	47·08 N	39·44 E
121	Batesburg (bāts'bûrg) SC	33·53 N	81·34 W
117	Batesville (bāts'vĭl) Ar.	35·46 N	91·39 W
104	Batesville In.	39·15 N	85·15 W
120	Batesville Ms.	34·17 N	89·55 W
166	Batetska (bå-tĕ'tskå) Sov. Un.	58·36 N	30·21 E
98	Bath (båth) Can.	46·31 N	67·36 W
154	Bath Eng.	51·24 N	2·20 W
98	Bath Me.	43·54 N	69·50 W
105	Bath NY	42·25 N	77·20 W
107	Bath Oh. (Cleveland In.)	41·11 N	81·38 W
127	Bathsheba Barb. (In.)	13·13 N	60·30 W
205	Bathurst (båth'ŭrst) Aust.	33·28 S	149·30 E
213	Bathurst (băt-hûrst) S. Afr. (Natal In.)	33·26 S	26·53 E
	Bathurst, see Banjul		
101	Bathurst, C. (båth'ŭrst) Can.	70·33 N	127·55 W
204	Bathurst (I.) Austl.	11·19 S	130·13 E
90	Bathurst Inlet Can.	68·10 N	108·00 W
214	Batia Benin	10·54 N	1·29 E
197	Batian (I.) Indon.	1·07 S	127·52 E
186	Bāṭlāq-E Gāvkhūnī (L.) Iran	31·40 N	52·48 E
148	Batley (băt'lĭ) Eng.	53·43 N	1·37 W
210	Batna (bät'nä) Alg.	35·41 N	6·12 E
119	Baton Rouge (băt'ŭn rōōzh') La.	30·28 N	91·10 W
215	Batouri Cam.	4·26 N	14·22 E
196	Battambang (bát-tám-bäng') Camb.	13·14 N	103·15 E
185	Batticaloa Sri Lanka	8·40 N	81·10 E
93	Battle (R.) Can.	52·20 N	111·59 W
94	Battle (R.) Can.	53·05 N	109·40 W
104	Battle Creek (băt''l krēk') Mi.	42·20 N	85·15 W
112	Battle Ground (băt''l ground) Wa. (Portland In.)	45·47 N	122·32 W
91	Battle Harbour (băt''l här'bēr) Can.	52·17 N	55·33 W
110	Battle Mountain Nv.	40·40 N	116·56 W
159	Battonya (bät-tô'nyä) Hung.	46·17 N	21·00 E
196	Batu Kepulauan (I.) (bä'tōō) Indon.	0·10 S	99·55 E
171	Batumi (bŭ-tōō'mē) Sov. Un.	41·40 N	41·30 E
183	Batu Pahat Mala. (Singapore In.)	1·51 N	102·56 E
183	Batupanjang Indon. (Singapore In.)	1·42 N	101·35 E
135	Baturité (bä-tōō-rē-tā') Braz.	4·16 S	38·47 W
197	Bauang (bä'wäng) Phil. (In.)	16·31 N	120·19 E
215	Bauchi (bå-ōō'chē) Nig.	10·19 N	9·50 E
212	Baudouinville (bō-dwăN-vēl') Zaire	7·12 S	29·39 E
99	Bauld, C. Can.	51·38 N	55·25 W
184	Bāuria India (In.)	22·29 N	88·08 E
135	Bauru (bou-rōō') Braz.	22·21 S	48·57 W
157	Bauska (bou'skå) Sov. Un.	56·24 N	24·12 E
129	Bauta (bå'ōō-tä) Cuba (In.)	22·14 N	82·33 W
158	Bautzen (bout'sĕn) G.D.R.	51·11 N	14·27 E
	Bavaria (State), see Bayern		
203	Baw Baw, Mt. (bå-bå) Austl.	37·50 S	146·17 E
196	Bawean (I.) (bå'vē-än) Indon.	5·50 S	112·40 E
148	Bawtry (bô'trĭ) Eng.	53·26 N	1·01 W
121	Baxley (băks'lĭ) Ga.	31·47 N	82·22 W
202	Baxter (băks'tēr) Austl. (Melbourne In.)	38·12 S	145·10 E
117	Baxter Springs (băks'tēr sprĭngs') Ks.	37·01 N	94·44 W
129	Bayaguana (bä-yä-gwä'nä) Dom. Rep.	18·45 N	69·40 W
152	Bay al Kabīr Wadi (R.) Libya	29·52 N	14·28 E
197	Bayambang (bä-yäm-bäng') Phil. (In.)	15·50 N	120·26 E
128	Bayamo (bä-yä'mō) Cuba	20·25 N	76·35 W
123	Bayamón P. R. (Puerto Rico In.)	18·27 N	66·13 W
172	Bayan-Aul (bä'yän-oul') Sov. Un.	50·43 N	75·37 E
108	Bayard (bā'ērd) Ne.	41·45 N	103·20 W
105	Bayard WV	39·15 N	79·20 W
171	Bayburt (bä'ĭ-bŏŏrt) Tur.	40·15 N	40·10 E
104	Bay City (bā) Mi.	43·35 N	83·55 W
119	Bay City Tx.	28·59 N	95·58 W
188	Baydarag Gol (R.) Mong.	46·09 N	98·52 E
170	Baydaratskaya Guba (B.) Sov. Un.	69·20 N	66·10 E
99	Bay de Verde Can.	48·05 N	52·54 W
158	Bayern (Bavaria) (State) (bī'ērn) (bá-vâ-rĭ-á) F.R.G.	49·00 N	11·16 E
160	Bayeux (bá-yû') Fr.	49·19 N	0·41 W
109	Bayfield (bā'fēld) Wi.	46·48 N	90·51 W
173	Baykal, Ozero (Baikal, L.) (bī'käl') (bī'kôl) Sov. Un.	53·00 N	109·28 E
173	Baykals'kiy Khrebet (Baikal Mts.) Sov. Un.	53·30 N	102·00 E
172	Baykit (bī-kēt') Sov. Un.	61·43 N	96·39 E
172	Baykonur (bī-kô-nōōr') Sov. Un.	47·46 N	66·11 E
174	Baymak (båy'mäk) Sov. Un. (Urals In.)	52·35 N	58·21 E
113	Bay Mills (bā mĭlls) Mi. (Sault Ste. Marie In.)	46·27 N	84·36 W
109	Bay Mills Ind. Res. Mi.	46·19 N	85·03 W
120	Bay Minette (bā'mĭn-ĕt') Al.	30·52 N	87·44 W
197	Bayombong (bä-yôm-bông') Phil. (In.)	16·28 N	121·09 E
160	Bayonne (bá-yôn') Fr.	43·28 N	1·30 W
106	Bayonne (bā-yōn') NJ (New York In.)	40·40 N	74·07 W
119	Bayou Bodcau Res. (bī'yōō bŏd'kō) La.	32·49 N	93·22 W
113	Bayport (bā'pōrt) Mn. (Minneapolis, St. Paul In.)	45·02 N	92·46 W
165	Bayramic Tur.	39·48 N	26·35 E
158	Bayreuth (bī-roit') F.R.G.	49·56 N	11·35 E
99	Bay Roberts (bā rŏb'ērts) Can.	47·36 N	53·16 W
	Bayrūt, see Beirut		
105	Bays, L. of (bās) Can.	45·15 N	79·00 W
120	Bay St. Louis (bā' sånt lōō'ĭs) Ms.	30·19 N	89·20 W
106	Bay Shore (bā' shôr) NY (New York In.)	40·44 N	73·15 W
183	Bayt Lahm (Bethlehem) (bĕth'lê-hĕm) Jordan (Palestine In.)	31·42 N	35·13 E
119	Baytown (bā'town) Tx. (In.)	29·44 N	95·01 W
106	Bayview (bā'vū) Al. (Birmingham In.)	33·34 N	86·59 W
112	Bayview Wa. (Seattle In.)	48·29 N	122·28 W
107	Bay Village (bā) Oh. (Cleveland In.)	41·29 N	81·56 W
162	Baza (bä'thä) Sp.	37·29 N	2·46 W
171	Bazar-Dyuzi (Mt.) (bä'zár-dyōōz'ĕ) Sov. Un.	41·20 N	47·40 E
212	Bazaruto, Ilha do (I.) (bä-zä-rōō'tō) Moz.	21·42 S	36·10 E
162	Baztán (bäth-tän') Sp.	43·12 N	1·30 W
108	Beach (bēch) ND	46·55 N	104·00 W
155	Beachy Head (bēchē hĕd) Eng.	50·40 N	0·25 E
105	Beacon (bē'kŭn) NY	41·30 N	73·55 W
89	Beaconsfield (bē'kŭnz-fēld) Can. (Montreal In.)	45·26 N	73·51 W
106	Beafort Mtn. (bē'fōrt) NJ (New York In.)	41·08 N	74·23 W
118	Beals Cr. (bēls) Tx.	32·10 N	101·14 W
89	Bear Brook (R.) Can. (Ottawa In.)	45·24 N	75·15 W
111	Bear Creek (bâr krēk) Mt.	45·11 N	109·07 W
120	Bear Cr. (bâr) Al.	34·27 N	88·00 W
113	Bear Cr. Tx. (Dallas, Fort Worth In.)	32·56 N	97·09 W
117	Beardstown (bērds'toun) Il.	40·01 N	90·26 W
112	Bearhead Mtn. (bâr'hĕd) Wa. (Seattle In.)	47·01 N	121·49 W
111	Bear (L.) Id.-Ut.	41·56 N	111·10 W
95	Bear L. Can.	55·08 N	96·00 W
111	Bear R. Id.	42·17 N	111·42 W
113	Bear R. Ut. (Salt Lake City In.)	41·28 N	112·10 W
162	Beas de Segura (bā'ás dā sā-gōō'rä) Sp.	38·16 N	2·53 W
129	Beata (I.) (bĕ-ä'tä) Dom. Rep.	17·40 N	71·40 W
129	Beata, Cabo (C.) (ká'bô-bĕ-ä'tä) Dom. Rep.	17·40 N	71·20 W
117	Beatrice (bē'á-trĭs) Ne.	40·16 N	96·45 W
114	Beatty (bēt'ē) Nv.	36·58 N	116·48 W
104	Beattyville (bēt'ē-vĭl) Ky.	37·35 N	83·40 W
160	Beaucaire (bō-kâr') Fr.	43·49 N	4·37 E
161	Beaucourt (bō-kōōr') Fr.	47·30 N	6·54 E
121	Beaufort (bō'fērt) NC	34·43 N	76·40 W
121	Beaufort SC	32·25 N	80·40 W
101	Beaufort Sea Ak.	70·30 N	138·40 W
212	Beaufort West S. Afr.	32·20 S	22·45 E
89	Beauharnois (bō-är-nwä') Can. (Montreal In.)	45·23 N	73·52 W
113	Beaumont (bō'mŏnt) Ca. (Los Angeles In.)	33·57 N	116·57 W
89	Beaumont Can. (Edmonton In.)	53·22 N	113·18 W
89	Beaumont Can. (Quebec In.)	46·50 N	71·01 W
119	Beaumont Tx.	30·05 N	94·06 W
160	Beaune (bōn) Fr.	47·02 N	4·49 E
89	Beauport (bō-pôr') Can. (Quebec In.)	46·52 N	71·11 W
89	Beaupré (bō-prā') Can. (Quebec In.)	47·03 N	70·53 W
95	Beauséjour Can.	50·04 N	96·33 W
160	Beauvais (bō-vĕ') Fr.	49·25 N	2·05 E
116	Beaver (bē'vēr) Ok.	36·46 N	100·31 W
107	Beaver Pa. (Pittsburgh In.)	40·42 N	80·18 W
115	Beaver Ut.	38·15 N	112·40 W
104	Beaver (I.) Mi.	45·40 N	85·30 W
94	Beaver (R.) Can.	54·20 N	111·10 W
116	Beaver City Nb.	40·08 N	99·52 W
116	Beaver Cr. Co.	39·42 N	103·37 W

ăt; finăl; rāte; senåte; ärm; åsk; sofá; fâre; ch-choose; dh-as th in other; bē; êvent; bĕt; recĕnt; cratēr; g-go; gh-guttural g; bĭt; ĭ-short neutral; rīde; K-guttural k as ch in German ich;

PRONOUNCING INDEX

Beaver — Berettyoujfalu 257

Page	Name Pronunciation Region	Lat. °′	Long. °′
116	Beaver Cr. Ks.	39·44 N	101·05 W
108	Beaver Cr. Mt.	46·45 N	104·18 W
108	Beaver Cr. Wy.	43·46 N	104·25 W
109	Beaver Dam Wi.	43·29 N	88·50 W
111	Beaverhead Mts. (bē′vẽr-hĕd) Mt.	44·33 N	112·59 W
111	Beaverhead R. Mt.	45·25 N	112·35 W
104	Beaver Ind. Res. Mi.	45·40 N	85·30 W
112	Beaverton (bē′vẽr-tŭn) Or. (Portland In.)	45·29 N	122·49 W
134	Bebará′ (bĕ-bä-rá′) Col. (In.)	6·07 N	76·39 W
148	Bebington (bē′bĭng-tŭn) Eng.	53·20 N	2·59 W
165	Bečej (bĕ′chā) Yugo.	45·36 N	20·03 E
162	Becerreá (bā-thā′rē-ä) Sp.	42·49 N	7·12 W
210	Béchar Alg.	31·39 N	2·14 W
101	Becharof (L.) (bĕk-à-rôf) Ak.	57·58 N	156·58 W
112	Becher B. (bēch′ẽr) Can. (Seattle In.)	48·18 N	123·37 W
104	Beckley (bĕk′lĭ) WV	37·40 N	81·15 W
160	Bédarieux (bā-dà-ryû′) Fr.	43·36 N	3·11 E
89	Beddington Cr. (bĕd′ĕng tŭn) Can. (Calgary In.)	51·14 N	114·13 W
105	Bedford (bĕd′fẽrd) Can.	45·10 N	73·00 W
154	Bedford Eng.	52·10 N	0·25 W
104	Bedford In.	38·50 N	86·30 W
109	Bedford Ia.	40·40 N	94·41 W
99	Bedford Ma. (In.)	42·30 N	71·17 W
106	Bedford NY (New York In.)	41·12 N	73·38 W
107	Bedford Oh. (Cleveland In.)	41·23 N	81·32 W
105	Bedford Pa.	40·05 N	78·20 W
213	Bedford S. Afr. (Natal In.)	32·43 S	26·19 E
121	Bedford Va.	37·19 N	79·27 W
106	Bedford Hills NY (New York In.)	41·14 N	73·41 W
148	Bedworth (bĕd′wẽrth) Eng.	52·29 N	1·28 W
159	Bedzin (băN-jēn′) Pol.	50·19 N	19·10 E
117	Beebe (bē′bē) Ar.	35·04 N	91·54 W
107	Beecher (bē′chŭr) Il. (Chicago In.)	41·20 N	87·38 W
112	Beechey Hd. (bē′chĭ hĕd) Can. (Seattle In.)	48·19 N	123·40 W
107	Beech Grove (bēch grōv) In. (Indianapolis In.)	39·43 N	86·05 W
203	Beecroft Hd. (bē′krûft) Austl.	35·03 S	151·15 E
149	Beelitz (bĕ′lētz) G.D.R. (Berlin In.)	52·14 N	12·59 E
183	Be'er Sheva' (bēr-shē′bà) Isr. (Palestine In.)	31·15 N	34·48 E
183	Be'er Sheva' (R.) Isr. (Palestine In.)	31·23 N	34·30 E
218	Beestekraal S. Afr. (Johannesburg & Pretoria In.)	25·22 S	27·34 E
148	Beeston (bēs′t′n) Eng.	52·55 N	1·11 W
149	Beetz R. (bĕtz) G.D.R. (Berlin In.)	52·28 N	12·37 E
119	Beeville (bē′vĭl) Tx.	28·24 N	97·44 W
203	Bega (bā′gá) Austl.	36·50 S	149·49 E
117	Beggs (bĕgz) Ok.	35·46 N	96·06 W
160	Bègles (bĕ′gl′) Fr.	44·47 N	0·34 W
214	Begoro Ghana	6·23 N	0·23 W
184	Behala India (Calcutta In.)	22·31 N	88·19 E
92	Behm Can. Ak.	55·41 N	131·35 W
212	Beira (bā′rá) Moz.	19·46 S	34·58 E
162	Beira (Reg.) (bĕ′y-rä) Port.	40·38 N	8·(0 W
183	Beirut (Bayrūt) (bā-rōōt′) Leb. (Palestine In.)	33·53 N	35·30 E
162	Beja (bā′zhä) Port.	38·03 N	7·53 W
151	Béja Tun.	36·52 N	9·20 E
210	Bejaïa (Bougie) Alg.	36·46 N	5·00 E
162	Bejar Sp.	40·25 N	5·43 W
186	Bejestān Iran	34·30 N	58·22 E
129	Bejucal (bā-hōō-käl′) Cuba (In.)	22·08 N	82·23 W
127	Bejuco (bĕ-kōō′kō) Pan.	8·37 N	79·54 W
159	Békés (bā′kāsh) Hung.	46·45 N	21·08 E
159	Békéscsaba (bā′kāsh-chô′bô) Hung.	46·39 N	21·06 E
189	Beketova (bĕk′e-to′vá) Sov. Un.	53·23 N	125·21 E
165	Bela Crkva (bĕ′lä tsĕrk′vä) Yugo.	44·53 N	21·25 E
162	Belalcázar (bāl-äl-kä′thär) Sp.	38·35 N	5·12 W
163	Belas (bĕ′-läs) Port. (Lisbon In.)	38·47 N	9·16 W
165	Bela-Slatina (byä′la slä′tēnä) Bul.	43·26 N	23·56 E
135	Bela Vista de Goia's Braz.	16·57 S	48·47 W
196	Belawan (bå-lä′wän) Indon.	3·43 N	98·43 E
170	Belaya (R.) (byĕ′lĭ-yä) Sov. Un.	52·30 N	56·15 E
167	Belaya Tserkov′ (byĕ′lĭ-yä tsĕr′kôf) Sov. Un.	49·48 N	30·09 E
91	Belcher Is. (bĕl′chẽr) Can.	56·20 N	80·40 W
104	Belding (bĕl′dĭng) Mi.	43·05 N	85·25 W
170	Belebey (byĕ′lĕ-bā′ĭ) Sov. Un.	54·00 N	54·10 E
135	Belém (Pará) (bā-lĕN′) (pä-rä′) Braz.	1·18 S	48·27 W
115	Belen (bĕ-lân′) NM	34·40 N	106·45 W
136	Belén (bā-lān′) Par.	23·30 S	57·09 W
205	Bélep, Îsles (Is.) N. Cal.	19·30 S	160·32 E
166	Belëv (byĕl′yĕf) Sov. Un.	53·49 N	36·06 E
112	Belfair (bĕl′far) Wa. (Seattle In.)	47·27 N	122·50 W
98	Belfast (bĕl′fâst) Me.	44·25 N	69·01 W
154	Belfast N. Ire.	54·36 N	5·45 W
154	Belfast, Lough (B.) (lŏk bĕl′fâst) Ire.	54·45 N	6·00 W
161	Belfort (bā-fôr′) Fr.	47·40 N	7·50 E
185	Belgaum India	15·57 N	74·32 E
146	Belgium (bĕl′jĭ-ŭm) Eur.	51·00 N	2·52 E
167	Belgorod (byĕl′gŭ-rŭt) Sov. Un.	50·36 N	36·32 E
167	Belgorod (Oblast) Sov. Un.	50·40 N	36·42 E
167	Belgorod Dnestrovskiy (byĕl′gŭ-rŭd nyĕs-trôf′skē) Sov. Un.	46·09 N	30·19 E
	Belgrade, see Beograd		
121	Belhaven (bĕl′hā-vĕn) NC	35·33 N	76·37 W
105	Belington (bĕl′ĭng-tŭn) WV	39·00 N	79·55 W
165	Beli Timok (R.) (bĕ′lē tē′mōk) Yugo.	43·35 N	22·13 E
196	Belitung (I.) Indon.	3·30 S	107·30 E
126	Belize (bĕ-lēz′) Belize (In.)	17·31 N	88·10 W
122	Belize N.A.	17·00 N	88·40 W
126	Belize R. Belize (In.)	17·16 N	88·56 W
174	Bel′kovo (byĕl′kô-vô) Sov. Un. (Moscow In.)	56·15 N	38·49 E
173	Bel′kovskiy (I.) (byĕl-kôf′skĭ) Sov. Un.	75·52 N	133·00 E
99	Bell (I.) (bĕl) Can.	50·45 N	55·35 W
97	Bell (R.) Can.	49·25 N	77·15 W
92	Bella Bella Can.	52·10 N	128·07 W
92	Bella Coola Can.	52·22 N	126·46 W
104	Bellaire (bĕl-âr′) Oh.	40·00 N	80·45 W
119	Bellaire Tx. (In.)	29·43 N	95·28 W
185	Bellary (bĕl-lä′rē) India	15·15 N	76·56 E
136	Bella Union (bĕ′l-yä-ōō-nyô′n) Ur.	30·18 S	57·26 W
136	Bella Vista (bā′lyà vēs′tà) Arg.	27·07 S	65·14 W
136	Bella Vista Arg.	28·35 S	58·53 W
136	Bella Vista Arg. (In.)	34·18 S	58·41 W
135	Bella Vista Braz.	22·16 S	56·14 W
129	Belle-Anse Hai	18·15 N	72·00 W
99	Belle B. (bĕl) Can.	47·35 N	55·15 W
106	Belle Chasse (bĕl shäs′) La. (New Orleans In.)	29·52 N	90·00 W
104	Bellefontaine (bĕl-fŏn′tān) Oh.	40·25 N	83·50 W
113	Bellefontaine Neighbors Mo. (St. Louis In.)	38·46 N	90·13 W
108	Belle Fourche (bĕl′ fōōrsh′) SD	44·28 N	103·50 W
108	Belle Fourche (R.) Wy.	44·29 N	104·40 W
108	Belle Fourche Res. SD	44·51 N	103·44 W
161	Bellegarde-sur-Valserine (bĕl-gärd′sür-väl-sâ-rēn′) Fr.	46·06 N	5·50 E
121	Belle Glade (bĕl glād) Fl. (In.)	26·39 N	80·37 W
160	Belle Île (I.) (bĕlēl′) Fr.	47·15 N	3·30 W
99	Belle Isle, Str. of Can.	51·35 N	56·30 W
106	Belle Mead (bĕl mēd) NJ (New York In.)	40·28 N	74·40 W
99	Belleoram Can.	47·31 N	55·25 W
109	Belle Plaine (bĕl plān′) Ia.	41·52 N	92·19 W
107	Belle Vernon (bĕl vŭr′nŭn) Pa. (Pittsburgh In.)	40·08 N	79·52 W
105	Belleville (bĕl′vĭl) Can.	44·15 N	77 25 W
113	Belleville Il. (St. Louis In.)	38·31 N	89·59 W
117	Belleville Ks.	39·49 N	97·37 W
107	Belleville Mi. (Detroit In.)	42·12 N	83·29 W
106	Belleville NJ (New York In.)	40·47 N	74·09 W
109	Bellevue (bĕl′vū) Ia.	42·14 N	90·26 W
107	Bellevue Ky. (Cincinnati In.)	39·06 N	84·29 W
104	Bellevue Mi.	42·30 N	85·00 W
104	Bellevue Oh.	41·15 N	82·45 W
107	Bellevue Pa. (Pittsburgh In.)	40·30 N	80·04 W
112	Bellevue Wa. (Seattle In.)	47·37 N	122·12 W
161	Belley (bĕ-lē′) Fr.	45·46 N	5·41 E
113	Bellflower (bĕl-flou′ẽr) Ca. (Los Angeles In.)	33·53 N	118·08 W
113	Bell Gardens Ca. (Los Angeles In.)	33·59 N	118·11 W
99	Bellingham (bĕl′ĭng-hăm) Ma. (In.)	42·05 N	71·28 W
112	Bellingham Wa. (Vancouver In.)	48·46 N	122·29 W
112	Bellingham B. Wa. (Vancouver In.)	48·44 N	122·34 W
220	Bellingshausen Sea (bĕl′ĭngz houz′n) Ant.	72·00 S	80·30 W
164	Bellinzona (bĕl-ĭn-tsō′nä) Switz.	46·10 N	9·09 E
99	Bell I. Can.	50·44 N	55·35 W
106	Bellmore (bĕl-mōr) NY (New York In.)	40·40 N	73·31 W
134	Bello (bĕ′l-yô) Col. (In.)	6·20 N	75·33 W
105	Bellows Falls (bĕl′ōz fôls) Vt.	43·10 N	72·30 W
184	Bellpat Pak.	29·08 N	68·00 E
91	Bell Pen. Can.	63·50 N	81·16 W
89	Bells Corners Can. (Ottawa In.)	45·20 N	75·49 W
112	Bells Mtn. (bĕls) Wa. (Portland In.)	45·50 N	122·21 W
164	Belluno (bĕl-lōō′nō) It.	46·08 N	12·14 E
136	Bell Ville (bĕl vēl′) Arg.	32·33 S	62·36 W
212	Bellville S. Afr. (In.)	33·54 S	18·38 E
119	Bellville (bĕl′vĭl) Tx.	29·57 N	96·15 W
162	Bélmez (bĕl′mĕth) Sp.	38·17 N	5·17 W
109	Belmond (bĕl′mŏnd) Ia.	42·49 N	93·37 W
112	Belmont Ca. (San Francisco In.)	37·34 N	122·18 W
135	Belmonte (bĕl-mōn′tå) Braz.	15·58 S	38·47 W
122	Belmopan Belize	17·15 N	88·47 W
173	Belogorsk Sov. Un.	51·09 N	128·32 E
137	Belo Horizonte (bĕ′lôre-sô′n-tĕ) Braz. (Rio de Janeiro In.)	19·54 S	43·56 W
116	Beloit (bē-loit′) Ks.	39·26 N	98·06 W
109	Beloit Wi.	42·31 N	89·04 W
170	Belomorsk (byĕl-ô-môrsk′) Sov. Un.	64·30 N	34·42 E
167	Belopol′ye (byĕ′lô-pôl′yĕ) Sov. Un.	51·10 N	34·19 E
174	Beloretsk (byĕ′lō-rĕtsk) Sov. Un. (Urals In.)	53·58 N	58·25 E
168	Belorussian (S. S. R.) Sov. Un.	53·30 N	25·33 E
167	Belosarayskaya, Kosa (C.) (kô-sä′byĕ′lô-sä-räy′skä′yä) Sov. Un.	46·43 N	37·18 E
172	Belovo (bvĕ′lŭ-vû) Sov. Un.	54·17 N	86·23 E
167	Belovodsk (byĕ-lŭ-vôdsk′) Sov. Un.	49·12 N	39·36 E
170	Beloye (L.) Sov. Un.	60·10 N	38·05 E
170	Belozersk (byĕ-lŭ-zyôrsk′) Sov. Un.	60·00 N	38·00 E
148	Belper (bĕl′pẽr) Eng.	53·01 N	1·28 W
111	Belt (bĕlt) Mt.	47·11 N	110·58 W
111	Belt Cr. Mt.	47·19 N	110·58 W
119	Belton (bĕl′tŭn) Tx.	31·04 N	97·27 W
119	Belton L. Tx.	31·15 N	97·35 W
106	Beltsville (belts-vĭl) Md. (Baltimore In.)	39·03 N	76·56 W
167	Bel′tsy (bĕl′tsē) Sov. Un.	47·47 N	27·57 E
172	Belukha, Gol′tsy (Mtn.) Sov. Un.	49·47 N	86·23 E
109	Belvidere (bĕl-vē-dēr′) Il.	42·14 N	88·52 W
105	Belvidere NJ	40·50 N	75·05 W
205	Belyando (R.) (bĕl-yän′dō) Austl.	22·09 S	146·48 E
174	Belyanka (byĕl′yán-kå) Sov. Un. (Urals In.)	56·04 N	59·16 E
166	Belynichi (byĕl-ĭ-nĭ′chĭ) Sov. Un.	54·02 N	29·42 E
166	Belyy (byĕ′lē) Sov. Un.	55·52 N	32·58 E
172	Belyy (I.) Sov. Un.	73·19 N	72·00 E
174	Belyye Stolby (byĕ′lĭ-ye stôl′bĭ) Sov. Un. (Moscow In.)	55·20 N	37·52 E
149	Belzig (bĕl′tsēg) G.D.R. (Berlin In.)	52·08 N	12·35 E
120	Belzoni (bĕl-zō′nē) Ms.	33·09 N	90·30 W
212	Bembe (bĕN′bĕ) Ang.	7·00 S	14·20 E
162	Bembezar (R.) (bĕm-bā-thär′) Sp.	38·00 N	5·18 W
109	Bemidji (bē-mĭj′ĭ) Mn.	47·28 N	94·54 W
212	Bena Dibele (bĕn′á dē-bĕ′lĕ) Zaire	4·00 S	22·49 E
203	Benalla (bĕn-ăl′á) Austl.	36·30 S	146·00 E
	Benares, see Vārānasi		
162	Benavente (bā-nä-vĕn′tā) Sp.	42·01 N	5·43 W
113	Benbrook (bĕn′brōōk) Tx. (Dallas, Fort Worth In.)	32·41 N	97·27 W
113	Benbrook Res. Tx. (Dallas, Fort Worth In.)	32·35 N	97·30 W
110	Bend (bĕnd) Or.	44·04 N	121·17 W
101	Bendeleben, Mt. (bĕn-dĕl-bĕn) Ak.	65·18 N	163·45 W
218	Bender Beila Som. (Horn of Afr. In.)	9·40 N	50·45 E
218	Bender Cassim Som. (Horn of Afr. In.)	11·19 N	49·10 E
167	Bendery (bĕn-dyĕ′re) Sov. Un.	46·49 N	29·29 E
203	Bendigo (bĕn′dĭ-gō) Austl.	36·39 S	144·20 E
106	Benedict (bĕnĕ′dĭct) Md. (Baltimore In.)	38·31 N	76·41 W
158	Benešov (bĕn′ĕ-shôf) Czech.	49·48 N	14·40 E
164	Benevento (bā-nā-vĕn′tō) It.	41·08 N	14·46 E
182	Bengal, B. of (bĕn-gôl′) Asia	17·30 N	87·00 E
216	Bengamisa Zaire	0·57 N	25·10 E
183	Bengkalis (bĕng-kä′lĭs) Indon. (Singapore In.)	1·29 N	102·06 E
196	Bengkulu Indon.	3·46 S	102·18 E
216	Benguela (bĕn-gĕl′á) Ang.	12·35 S	13·25 E
154	Ben Hope (Mtn.) (bĕn hōp) Scot.	58·25 N	4·25 W
134	Beni (R.) (bā′nē) Bol.	13·41 S	67·30 W
210	Beni-Abbès (bā′nē ä-bĕs′) Alg.	30·11 N	2·13 W
163	Benicarló (bā-nē-kär-lō′) Sp.	40·26 N	0·25 E
112	Benicia (bē-nĭsh′ĭ-á) Ca. (San Francisco In.)	38·03 N	122·09 W
209	Benin Afr.	8·00 N	2·00 E
215	Benin (R.) (bĕn-ēn′) Nig.	5·55 N	5·15 E
215	Benin City Nig.	6·19 N	5·41 E
210	Beni Saf (bā′nē säf′) Alg.	35·23 N	1·20 W
216	Benito (R.) Equat. Gui.	1·35 N	10·45 E
116	Benkelman (bĕn-kĕl-mán) Ne.	40·05 N	101·35 W
164	Benkovac (bĕn′kō-váts) Yugo.	44·02 N	15·41 E
213	Ben Macdhui (Mtn.) (bĕn măk-dōō′ē) Leso-S. Afr. (Natal In.)	30·38 S	27·54 E
121	Bennettsville (bĕn′ĕts vĭl) SC	34·35 N	79·41 W
105	Bennington (bĕn′ĭng-tŭn) Vt.	42·55 N	73·15 W
106	Benns Church (bĕnz′ chûrch′) Va. (Norfolk In.)	36·47 N	76·35 W
213	Benoni (bĕ-nō′nī) S. Afr. (Johannesburg & Pretoria In.)	26·11 S	28·19 E
215	Benoy Chad	8·59 N	16·19 E
126	Benque Viejo (bĕn-kĕ bĭĕ′hō) Belize (In.)	17·07 N	89·07 W
107	Bensenville (bĕn′sĕn-vĭl) Il. (Chicago In.)	41·57 N	87·56 W
158	Bensheim (bĕns-hīm) F.R.G.	49·42 N	8·38 E
115	Benson (bĕn-sŭn) Az.	32·00 N	110·20 W
108	Benson Mn.	45·18 N	95·36 W
107	Bentleyville (bent′lē vĭl) Pa. (Pittsburgh In.)	40·07 N	80·01 W
117	Benton (bĕn′tŭn) Ar.	34·34 N	92·34 W
114	Benton Ca.	37·44 N	118·22 W
98	Benton Can.	45·59 N	67·36 W
104	Benton Il.	38·00 N	88·55 W
104	Benton Harbor (bĕn′tŭn här′bẽr) Mi.	42·05 N	86·30 W
117	Bentonville (bĕn′tŭn-vĭl) Ar.	36·22 N	94·11 W
215	Benue (R.) (bā′nōō-â) Nig.	7·55 N	8·55 E
183	Benut (R.) Mala. (Singapore In.)	1·43 N	103·20 E
104	Benwood (bĕn-wōōd) WV	39·55 N	80·45 W
165	Beograd (Belgrade) (bĕ-ô′gräd) (bĕl′gräd) Yugo.	44·48 N	20·32 E
195	Beppu (bĕ′pōō) Jap.	33·16 N	131·30 E
127	Bequia I. (bĕk-ē′ä) N. A. (In.)	13·00 N	61·08 W
183	Berakit, Tanjung (C.) Indon. (Singapore In.)	1·16 N	104·44 E
165	Berat (bĕ-rät′) Alb.	40·43 N	19·59 E
197	Berau, Teluk (B.) Indon.	2·22 S	131·40 E
136	Berazategui (bĕ-rä-zá′tĕ-gē) Arg. (Buenos Aires In.)	34·46 S	58·14 W
218	Berbera (bûr′bûr-á) Som. (Horn of Afr. In.)	10·25 N	45·05 E
215	Berbérati Cen. Afr. Emp.	4·16 N	15·47 E
160	Berck (bĕrk) Fr.	50·26 N	1·36 E
153	Berd′ansk Sov. Un.	46·45 N	36·47 E
167	Berdichev (bĕr-dē′chĕf) Sov. Un.	49·53 N	28·32 E
167	Berdyanskaya, Kosa (C.) (kô-sä′ bĕr-dyän′skä-yä) Sov. Un.	46·38 N	36·42 E
174	Berdyaush (bĕr′dyáûsh) Sov. Un. (Urals In.)	55·10 N	59·12 E
120	Berea (bē-rē′á) Ky.	37·30 N	84·19 W
107	Berea Oh. (Cleveland In.)	41·22 N	81·51 W
159	Beregovo (bĕ′rĕ-gô-vô) Sov. Un.	48·13 N	22·40 E
217	Bereku Tan.	4·27 S	35·44 E
95	Berens (R.) (bĕr′enz) Can.	52·15 N	96·30 W
95	Berens I. Can.	52·18 N	97·40 W
95	Berens River Can.	52·22 N	97·02 W
108	Beresford (bĕr′ĕs-fẽrd) SD	43·05 N	96·46 W
159	Berettyóújfalu (bĕ′rĕt-tyō-ōō′y′fô-lōō) Hung.	47·14 N	21·33 E

ng-sing; ŋ-baŋk; N-nasalized n; nŏd; cŏmmit; ōld; ôbey; ôrder; fōōd; fŏŏt; ou-out; s-soft; sh-dish; th-thin; pūre; ûnite; ûrn; stŭd; circŭs; ü-as "y" in study; ′-indeterminate vowel.

258 Bereza — Birch PRONOUNCING INDEX

Page	Name Pronunciation	Region	Lat. °′	Long. °′
159	Berëza (bĕ-rā'zà)	Sov. Un.	52·29 N	24·59 E
159	Berezhany (bĕr-yĕ'zhá-nê)	Sov. Un.	49·25 N	24·58 E
166	Berezina (R.) (bĕr-yĕ'zē-nà)	Sov. Un.	53·20 N	29·05 E
166	Berezino (bĕr-yä'zê-nô)	Sov. Un.	53·51 N	28·54 E
167	Berezna (bĕr-yôz'nà)	Sov. Un.	51·32 N	31·47 E
167	Bereznegovata	Sov. Un.	47·19 N	32·58 E
174	Berezniki (bĕr-yôz'nyê-kê)	Sov. Un. (Urals In.)	59·25 N	56·46 E
167	Berëzovka (bĕr-yôz'ôf-kà)	Sov. Un.	47·12 N	30·56 E
174	Berëzovka	Sov. Un. (Urals In.)	57·35 N	57·19 E
170	Berëzovo (bĭr-yô'zē-vû)	Sov. Un.	64·10 N	65·10 E
174	Berëzovskiy (bĕr-yô'zôf-skĭ)	Sov. Un. (Urals In.)	56·54 N	60·47 E
163	Berga (bĕr'gä)	Sp.	42·05 N	1·52 E
171	Bergama (bĕr'gä-mä)	Tur.	39·08 N	27·09 E
164	Bergamo (bĕr'gä-mō)	It.	45·43 N	9·41 E
135	Bergantín (bĕr-gän-tē'n)	Ven. (In.)	10·04 N	64·23 W
149	Bergedorf (bĕr'gē-dôrf)	F.R.G. (Hamburg In.)	53·29 N	10·12 E
158	Bergen (bĕr'gĕn)	G.D.R.	54·26 N	13·26 E
156	Bergen	Nor.	60·24 N	5·20 E
106	Bergenfield	NJ (New York In.)	40·55 N	73·59 W
149	Bergen op Zoom	Neth. (Amsterdam In.)	51·29 N	4·16 E
160	Bergerac (bĕr-zhĕ-ràk')	Fr.	44·49 N	0·28 E
161	Bergisch Gladbach (bĕrg'ĭsh-glät'bäk)	F.R.G. (Ruhr In.)	50·59 N	7·08 E
149	Berglern (bĕrgh'lĕrn)	F.R.G. (Munich In.)	48·24 N	11·55 E
213	Bergville (bĕrg'vĭl)	S. Afr. (Natal In.)	28·46 S	29·22 E
184	Berhampur	India	19·19 N	84·48 E
75	Bering Sea (bē'rĭng)	Asia-N. A.	58·00 N	175·00 W
101	Bering Str.	Ak.	64·50 N	169·50 W
167	Berislav (byĕr'ĭ-slåf)	Sov. Un.	46·49 N	33·24 E
162	Berja (bĕr'hä)	Sp.	36·50 N	2·56 W
112	Berkeley (bûrk'lĭ)	Ca. (San Francisco In.)	37·52 N	122·17 W
113	Berkeley	Mo. (St. Louis In.)	38·45 N	90·20 W
105	Berkeley Springs (bûrk'lĭ sprĭngz)	WV	39·40 N	78·10 W
148	Berkhamsted (bĕrk'hăm'stĕd)	Eng. (London In.)	51·44 N	0·34 W
107	Berkley (bûrk'lĭ)	Mi. (Detroit In.)	42·30 N	83·10 W
165	Berkovitsa (bĕ-kō'vê-tsà)	Bul.	43·14 N	23·08 E
93	Berland (R.)	Can.	54·00 N	117·10 W
162	Berlengas (Is.) (bĕr-lĕn'gàzh)	Port.	39·25 N	9·33 W
149	Berlin, East (bĕr-lēn')	G.D.R. (Berlin In.)	52·31 N	13·28 E
149	Berlin, West	F.R.G. (Berlin In.)	52·31 N	13·20 E
105	Berlin (bûr-lĭn)	NH	44·25 N	71·10 W
106	Berlin	NJ (Philadelphia In.)	39·47 N	74·56 W
213	Berlin (bĕr-lĭn)	S. Afr. (Natal In.)	32·53 S	27·36 E
109	Berlin (bûr-lĭn')	Wi.	43·58 N	88·58 W
162	Bermeja, Sierra (Mts.) (sē-ĕ'r-rä-bĕr-mĕ'hä)	Sp.	36·35 N	5·03 W
136	Bermejo (R.) (bĕr-mā'hō)	Arg.	25·05 S	61·00 W
162	Bermeo (bĕr-mā'yō)	Sp.	43·23 N	2·43 W
123	Bermuda (I.)	N.A.	32·20 N	65·45 W
158	Bern (bĕrn)	Switz.	46·55 N	7·25 E
136	Bernal (bĕr-näl')	Arg. (Buenos Aires In.)	34·27 S	58·17 W
115	Bernalillo (bĕr-nä-lē'yō)	NM	35·20 N	106·30 W
105	Bernard (L.) (bĕr-närd')	Can.	45·45 N	79·25 W
106	Bernardsville (bûr nărds'vĭl)	NJ (New York In.)	40·43 N	74·34 W
149	Bernau (bĕr'nou)	G.D.R. (Berlin In.)	52·40 N	13·35 E
158	Bernburg (bĕrn'bŏŏrgh)	G.D.R.	51·48 N	11·43 E
158	Berndorf (bĕrn'dôrf)	Aus.	47·57 N	16·05 E
104	Berne (bûrn)	In.	40·40 N	84·55 W
158	Berner Alpen (Mts.)	Switz.	46·29 N	7·30 E
161	Berneustadt (bĕr'noi'shtät)	F.R.G. (Ruhr In.)	51·01 N	7·39 E
204	Bernier (I.) (bĕr-nēr')	Austl.	24·58 S	113·15 E
158	Bernina Pizzo (Pk.)	Switz.	46·23 N	9·58 E
216	Bero (R.)	Ang.	15·10 S	12·20 E
158	Beroun (bā'rōn)	Czech.	49·57 N	14·03 E
158	Berounka R. (bĕ-rōn'kà)	Czech.	49·53 N	13·40 E
202	Berowra	Austl. (Sydney In.)	33·36 S	151·10 E
160	Berre, Étang de (L.) (ā-tôn' dĕ bâr')	Fr. (In.)	43·27 N	5·07 E
160	Berre-l' Étang (bâr'lā-tôn')	Fr. (In.)	43·28 N	5·11 E
125	Berriozabal (bā'rēō-zä-bäl')	Mex.	16·47 N	93·16 W
152	Berryan (bĕr-ē-än')	Alg.	32·50 N	3·49 E
93	Berry Creek (R.)	Can.	51·15 N	111·40 W
114	Berryessa (R.) (bĕ'rĭ ĕs'à)	Ca.	38·35 N	122·33 W
128	Berry Is.	Ba.	25·40 N	77·50 W
117	Berryville (bĕr'ē-vĭl)	Ar.	36·21 N	93·34 W
167	Bershad' (byĕr'shät)	Sov. Un.	48·22 N	29·31 E
89	Berthier	Can. (Quebec In.)	46·56 N	70·44 W
112	Bertrand (R.) (bûr'trănd)	Wa. (Vancouver In.)	48·58 N	122·31 W
105	Berwick (bûr'wĭk)	Pa.	41·05 N	76·10 W
154	Berwick (bûr'ĭk)	Scot.	55·45 N	2·01 W
107	Berwyn (bûr'wĭn)	Il. (Chicago In.)	41·49 N	87·47 W
154	Berwyn Ra.	Wales	52·45 N	3·41 W
213	Besalampy (bĕz-á-lăm-pē')	Mad.	16·48 S	40·40 E
161	Besançon (bĕ-sän-sôn)	Fr.	47·14 N	6·02 E
183	Besar, Gunong (Mt.)	Mala. (Singapore In.)	2·31 N	103·09 E
166	Besed' (R.) (byĕ'syĕt)	Sov. Un.	52·58 N	31·36 E
166	Beshenkovichi (byĕ-shĕn-kōvē'chĭ)	Sov. Un.	55·04 N	29·29 E
159	Beskides (Mts.) (bĕs'kēdz')	Czech.-Pol.	49·23 N	19·00 E
160	Bessèges (bĕ-sĕzh')	Fr.	44·20 N	4·07 E
106	Bessemer (bĕs'ē-mĕr)	Al. (Birmingham In.)	33·24 N	86·58 W
109	Bessemer	Mi.	46·29 N	90·04 W
121	Bessemer City	NC	35·16 N	81·17 W
149	Bestensee (bĕs'tĕn-zā)	G.D.R. (Berlin In.)	51·15 N	13·39 E
162	Betanzos (bĕ-tän'thōs)	Sp.	43·18 N	8·14 W
115	Betatakin Ruin (bĕt-à-tăk'ĭn)	Az.	36·40 N	110·29 W
218	Bethal (bĕth'ăl)	S. Afr. (Johannesburg & Pretoria In.)	26·27 S	29·28 E
113	Bethalto (bà-thăl'tō)	Il. (St. Louis In.)	38·54 N	90·03 W
212	Bethanien	Namibia	26·20 S	16·10 E
117	Bethany	Mo.	40·15 N	94·04 W
101	Bethel (bĕth'ĕl)	Ak.	60·50 N	161·50 W
106	Bethel	Ct. (New York In.)	41·22 N	73·24 W
105	Bethel	Vt.	43·50 N	72·40 W
107	Bethel Park	Pa. (Pittsburgh In.)	40·19 N	80·02 W
106	Bethesda (bĕ-thĕs'dà)	Md. (Baltimore In.)	39·00 N	77·10 W
105	Bethlehem (bĕth'lê-hĕm)	Pa.	40·40 N	75·25 W
218	Bethlehem	S. Afr. (Johannesburg & Pretoria In.)	28·14 S	28·18 E
	Bethlehem, see Bayt Lahm			
160	Béthune (bā-tün')	Fr.	50·32 N	2·37 E
213	Betroka (bĕ-trōk'à)	Mad.	23·13 S	46·17 E
183	Bet She'an	Isr. (Palestine In.)	32·30 N	35·30 E
98	Betsiamites	Can.	48·57 N	68·36 W
98	Betsiamites, (R.)	Can.	49·11 N	69·20 W
213	Betsiboka (R.) (bĕt-sĭ-bō'kà)	Mad.	16·47 S	46·45 E
101	Bettles Field (bĕt'tŭls)	Ak.	66·58 N	151·48 W
184	Betwa (R.) (bĕt'wà)	India	25·00 N	77·37 E
161	Betz (bĕ)	Fr. (Paris In.)	49·09 N	2·58 E
161	Betzdorf (bĕtz'dōrf)	F.R.G. (Ruhr In.)	50·47 N	7·53 E
149	Beveren	Bel. (Brussels In.)	51·13 N	4·14 E
148	Beverly (bĕv'ĕr-lĭ)	Eng.	53·50 N	0·25 W
99	Beverly	Ma. (Boston In.)	42·34 N	70·53 W
106	Beverly	NJ (Philadelphia In.)	40·03 N	74·56 W
113	Beverly Hills	Ca. (Los Angeles In.)	34·05 N	118·24 W
117	Bevier (bê-vēr')	Mo.	39·44 N	92·36 W
148	Bewdley (būd'lĭ)	Eng.	52·22 N	2·19 W
155	Bexhill (bĕks'hĭl)	Eng.	50·49 N	0·25 E
148	Bexley (bĕks'ly)	Eng. (London In.)	51·26 N	0·09 E
214	Beyla (bā'là)	Gui.	8·41 N	8·37 W
211	Beylul	Eth.	13·15 N	42·21 E
171	Beypazari (bā-pá-zä'rĭ)	Tur.	40·10 N	31·40 E
171	Beyşehir (bā-shĕ'h'r)	Tur.	38·00 N	31·45 E
171	Beyşehir Gölü (L.)	Tur.	38·00 N	31·30 E
167	Beysugskiy, Liman (B.) (lĭ-män' bĕy-sōōg'skĭ)	Sov. Un.	46·07 N	38·35 E
166	Bezhetsk (byĕ-zhĕtsk')	Sov. Un.	57·46 N	36·40 E
166	Bezhitsa (byĕ-zhĭ'tsà)	Sov. Un.	53·19 N	34·18 E
160	Béziers (bā-zyā')	Fr.	43·21 N	3·12 E
184	Bhadreswar	India (In.)	22·49 N	88·22 E
184	Bhāgalpur (bä'gŭl-pōōr)	India	25·15 N	86·59 E
188	Bhamo (bŭ-mō')	Bur.	24·00 N	96·15 E
184	Bhāngar	India (In.)	22·30 N	88·36 E
184	Bharatpur (bĕrt'pōōr)	India	27·21 N	77·33 E
184	Bhatinda (bŭ-tĭn-dà)	India	30·19 N	74·56 E
184	Bhaunagar (bäv-nŭg'ŭr)	India	21·45 N	72·58 E
185	Bhayandar	India (In.)	19·20 N	72·50 E
184	Bhilai	India	21·14 N	81·23 E
184	Bhīma (R.) (bē'mà)	India	17·15 N	75·55 E
185	Bhiwandi	India (In.)	19·18 N	73·03 E
184	Bhiwāni	India	28·53 N	76·08 E
184	Bhopāl (bō-päl)	India	23·20 N	77·25 E
184	Bhubaneswar (bōō-bû-nāsh'vûr)	India	20·21 N	85·53 E
184	Bhuj (bōōj)	India	23·22 N	69·39 E
187	Bhutan (bōō-tän')	Asia	27·15 N	90·30 E
216	Biafra, Bight of	Afr.	4·05 N	7·10 E
197	Biak (I.) (bē'āk)	Indon.	1·00 S	136·00 E
159	Biała Podlaska (byä'wä pōd-läs'kä)	Pol.	52·01 N	23·08 E
158	Białogard (byä-wō'gärd)	Pol.	54·00 N	16·01 E
159	Białystok (byä-wĭs'tōk)	Pol.	53·08 N	23·12 E
214	Biankouma	Ivory Coast	7·44 N	7·37 W
160	Biarritz (byä-rēts')	Fr.	43·27 N	1·39 W
218	Bibā (bē'bà)	Egypt (Nile In.)	28·54 N	30·59 E
120	Bibb City (bĭb' sĭ'tē)	Ga.	32·31 N	84·56 W
158	Biberach (bē'bĕräk)	F.R.G.	48·06 N	9·49 E
214	Bibiani	Ghana	6·28 N	2·20 W
98	Bic (bĭk)	Can.	48·22 N	68·42 W
104	Bicknell (bĭk'nĕl)	In.	38·45 N	87·20 W
159	Bicske (bĭsh'kĕ)	Hung.	47·29 N	18·38 E
215	Bida (bē'dä)	Nig.	9·05 N	6·01 E
98	Biddeford (bĭd'ē-fērd)	Me.	43·29 N	70·29 W
148	Biddulph (bĭd'ŭlf)	Eng.	53·07 N	2·10 W
	Bidon Cinq, see Post Maurice Cortier			
216	Bié	Ang.	12·22 S	16·56 E
159	Biebrza R. (byĕb'zhà)	Pol.	53·18 N	22·25 E
158	Biel (bēl)	Switz.	47·09 N	7·12 E
158	Bielefeld (bē'lē-fĕlt)	F.R.G.	52·01 N	8·35 E
165	Bieljina (bê-yĕ'lyē-nä)	Yugo.	44·44 N	19·15 E
164	Biella (byĕl'lä)	It.	45·34 N	8·05 E
159	Bielsk Podlaski (byĕlsk pŭd-lä'skĭ)	Pol.	52·47 N	23·14 E
196	Bien Hoa	Viet.	10·59 N	106·49 E
91	Bienville, Lac (L.)	Can.	55·32 N	72·45 W
149	Biesenthal (bē'sĕn-täl)	G.D.R. (Berlin In.)	52·46 N	13·38 E
164	Biferno (R.) (bē-fĕr'nō)	It.	41·49 N	14·46 E
216	Bifoum	Gabon	0·22 S	10·23 E
112	Big (L.) (bĭg)	Wa. (Seattle In.)	48·23 N	122·14 W
120	Big (R.)	Ar.	35·55 N	90·10 W
165	Biğa (bē'ghà)	Tur	40·13 N	27·14 E
109	Big Bay de Noc (bĭg bā dê nok')	Mi.	45·48 N	86·41 W
117	Big Bayou (bĭg' bī'yōō)	Ar.	33·04 N	91·28 W
113	Big Bear City (bĭg bâr)	Ca. (Los Angeles In.)	34·16 N	116·51 W
111	Big Belt Mts. (bĭg bĕlt)	Mt.	46·53 N	111·43 W
108	Big Bend Dam (bĭg bĕnd)	SD	44·11 N	99·33 W
118	Big Bend Natl. Park	Tx.	29·15 N	103·15 W
120	Big Black (R.) (bĭg blăk)	Ms.	32·05 N	90·49 W
117	Big Blue (R.) (bĭg blōō)	Ne.	40·53 N	97·00 W
118	Big Canyon (bĭg kăn'yŭn)	Tx.	30·27 N	102·19 W
121	Big Cypress Swp. (bĭg sī'prĕs)	Fl. (In.)	26·02 N	81·20 W
101	Big Delta (bĭg dĕl'tà)	Ak.	64·08 N	145·48 W
109	Big Fork (R.) (bĭg fôrk)	Mn.	48·08 N	93·47 W
94	Biggar	Can.	52·04 N	108·00 W
111	Big Hole (R.) (bĭg 'hōl)	Mt.	45·53 N	113·15 W
111	Big Hole Natl. Battlefield (bĭg hōl băt''l-fēld)	Mt.	45·44 N	113·35 W
111	Big Horn Mts. (bĭg hôrn)	Wy.	44·47 N	107·40 W
111	Bighorn R.	Mt.	45·50 N	107·15 W
95	Big I.	Can.	49·10 N	94·40 W
112	Big Lake (bĭg lāk)	Wa. (Seattle In.)	48·24 N	122·14 W
89	Big L.	Can. (Edmonton In.)	53·35 N	113·47 W
95	Big Mossy Pt.	Can.	53·45 N	97·50 W
104	Big Muddy (R.)	Il.	37·50 N	89·00 W
111	Big Muddy Cr. (bĭg mud'ĭ)	Mt.	48·53 N	105·02 W
214	Bignona	Senegal	12·49 N	16·14 W
94	Big Quill L.	Can.	51·55 N	104·22 W
104	Big Rapids (bĭg răp'ĭdz)	Mi.	43·40 N	85·30 W
94	Big River	Can.	53·50 N	107·01 W
115	Big Sandy (R.) (bĭg sănd'ē)	Az.	34·59 N	113·36 W
104	Big Sandy (R.)	Ky.-WV	38·15 N	82·35 W
116	Big Sandy Cr.	Co.	39·08 N	103·36 W
111	Big Sandy Cr.	Mt.	48·20 N	110·08 W
95	Bigsby I.	Can.	49·04 N	94·35 W
108	Big Sioux (R.) (bĭg sōō)	SD	44·34 N	97·00 W
118	Big Spring (bĭg sprĭng)	Tx.	32·15 N	101·28 W
108	Big Stone (L.) (bĭg stōn)	Mn.-SD	45·29 N	96·40 W
120	Big Stone Gap	Va.	36·50 N	82·50 W
111	Bigtimber (bĭg'tĭm-bĕr)	Mt.	45·50 N	109·57 W
111	Big Wood R. (bĭg wŏŏd)	Id.	43·02 N	114·30 W
164	Bihać (bē'häch)	Yugo.	44·48 N	15·52 E
184	Bihār (State) (bê-här')	India	23·48 N	84·57 E
217	Biharamulo (bê-hä-rä-mōō'lō)	Tan.	2·38 S	31·20 E
159	Bihor, Muntii (Mts.) (bē'hôr)	Rom.	46·37 N	22·37 E
214	Bijagós, Arquipélago dos (Is.) (är-kē-pä'lä-gō dôs bē-zhä-gôs)	Guinea-Bissau	11·20 N	17·10 W
185	Bijāpur	India	16·53 N	75·42 E
165	Bijelo Polje (bē'yĕ-lô pô'lyĕ)	Yugo.	43·02 N	19·48 E
116	Bijou Cr. (bē'zhōō)	Co.	39·41 N	104·13 W
184	Bīkaner (bĭ-kā'nûr)	India	28·07 N	73·19 E
194	Bikin (bê-kēn')	Sov. Un.	46·41 N	134·29 E
194	Bikin (R.)	Sov. Un.	46·37 N	135·55 E
216	Bikoro (bê-kō'rō)	Zaire	0.45 S	18·07 E
216	Bikuar, Parque Nacional do (Natl. Pk.)	Ang.	15·07 S	14·40 E
184	Bilāspur (bê-läs'pōōr)	India	22·08 N	82·12 E
196	Bilauktaung (Ra.)	Thai.	14·40 N	98·50 E
162	Bilbao (bĭl-bä'ō)	Sp.	43·12 N	2·48 W
218	Bilbays	Egypt (Nile In.)	30·26 N	31·37 E
165	Bileća (bē'lĕ-chä)	Yugo.	42·52 N	18·26 E
171	Bilecik (bē-lĕd-zhēk')	Tur.	40·10 N	29·58 E
159	Bilé Karpaty (Mts.)	Czech.	48·53 N	17·35 E
159	Biłgoraj (bēw-gō'rī)	Pol.	50·31 N	22·43 E
174	Bilimbay (bē'lĭm-bày)	Sov. Un. (Urals In.)	56·59 N	59·53 E
203	Billabong (R.) (bĭl'ă-bŏng)	Austl.	35·15 S	145·20 E
99	Billerica (bĭl'rĭk-à)	Ma. (In.)	42·33 N	71·16 W
148	Billericay	Eng. (London In.)	51·38 N	0·25 E
111	Billings (bĭl'ĭngz)	Mt.	45·47 N	108·29 W
115	Bill Williams (L.) (bĭl-wĭl'yumz)	Az.	34·10 N	113·50 W
211	Bilma (bēl'mä)	Niger	18·41 N	13·20 E
120	Biloxi (bĭ-lŏk'sĭ)	Ms.	30·24 N	88·50 W
218	Bilqās Qism Awwal	Egypt (Nile In.)	31·14 N	31·25 E
203	Bimberi Pk. (bĭm'bĕrĭ)	Austl.	35·45 S	148·50 E
197	Binaiya, Gunung (Mtn.)	Indon.	3·07 S	129·25 E
197	Binalonan (bē-nä-lô'nän)	Phil. (In.)	16·03 N	120·35 E
186	Binalud (Mtn.)	Iran	36·32 N	58·34 E
197	Biñan (bē'nän)	Phil. (In.)	14·20 N	121·06 E
158	Bingen (bĭn'gĕn)	F.R.G.	49·57 N	7·54 E
148	Bingham (bĭng'ăm)	Eng.	52·57 N	0·57 W
98	Bingham	Me.	45·03 N	69·51 W
113	Bingham Canyon	Ut. (Salt Lake City In.)	40·33 N	112·09 W
105	Binghamton (bĭng'ăm-tŭn)	NY	42·05 N	75·55 W
195	Bingo-Nada (Sea) (bĭn'gō nä-dä)	Jap.	34·06 N	133·14 E
196	Binh Dinh (bĭng'dĭng')	Viet.	13·55 N	109·00 E
203	Binnaway (bĭn'ă-wā)	Austl.	31·42 S	149·22 E
183	Bintan (I.) (bĭn'tän)	Indon. (Singapore In.)	1·09 N	104·43 E
196	Bintulu (bēn'tōō-lōō)	Mala.	3·07 N	113·06 E
210	Binzert (Bizerte) (bē-zĕrt')	Tun.	37·23 N	9·52 E
214	Bio Gorge (Val.)	Ghana	8·30 N	2·05 W
194	Bira (bē'rà)	Sov. Un.	49·00 N	133·18 E
194	Bira (R.)	Sov. Un.	48·55 N	132·25 E
184	Birātnagar (bĭ-rät'nŭ-gŭr)	Nep.	26·35 N	87·18 E
112	Birch Bay (bûrch)	Wa. (Vancouver In.)	48·55 N	122·45 W
112	Birch B.	Wa. (Vancouver In.)	48·55 N	122·52 W
95	Birch I.	Can.	52·25 N	99·55 W
90	Birch Mts.	Can.	57·36 N	113·10 W
112	Birch Pt.	Wa. (Vancouver In.)	48·57 N	122·50 W

ăt; finăl; rāte; senâte; ärm; åsk; sofà; fâre; ch-choose; dh-as th in other; bē; ēvent; bĕt; recĕnt; cratēr; g-go; gh-guttural g; bĭt; ĭ-short neutral; rīde; K-guttural k as ch in German ich;

Page	Name Pronunciation Region	Lat. °′	Long. °′
213	Bird I. (bẽrd) S. Afr. (Natal In.)	33·51 s	26·21 e
129	Bird Rock (I.) (bûrd)........Ba.	22·50 n	74·20 w
89	Birds Hill (bûrds) Can. (Winnipeg In.)	49·58 n	97·00 w
203	Birdsville (bûrdz′vĭl).......Austl.	25·50 s	139·31 e
204	Birdum (bûrd′ŭm).........Austl.	15·45 s	133·25 e
171	Birecik (bē-rĕd-zhĕk′)........Tur.	37·10 n	37·50 e
152	Bir er Ressof (bēr-ĕr-rĕ-sôf′)..Alg.	32·19 n	7·58 e
215	Bir Gara..................Chad	13·11 n	15·58 e
186	Bīrjand (bēr′jänd)...........Iran	33·07 n	59·16 e
112	Birkenfeld......Or. (Portland In.)	45·59 n	123·20 w
148	Birkenhead (bûr′kĕn-hĕd)....Eng.	53·23 n	3·02 w
149	Birkenwerder (bĕr′kĕn-vĕr-dĕr) G.D.R. (Berlin In.)	52·41 n	13·22 e
159	Bîrlad...................Rom.	46·15 n	27·43 e
106	Birmingham (bûr′mĭng-hăm) Al. (Birmingham In.)	33·31 n	86·49 w
148	Birmingham................Eng.	52·29 n	1·53 w
107	Birmingham.....Mi. (Detroit In.)	42·32 n	83·13 w
113	Birmingham Mo. (Kansas City In.)	39·10 n	94·22 w
148	Birmingham Can............Eng.	53·07 n	2·40 w
211	Bi′r Misāhah..............Egypt	22·16 n	28·04 e
215	Birnin Kebbi...............Nig.	12·32 n	4·12 e
173	Birobidzhan (bē′rō-bē-jän′) Sov. Un.	48·42 n	133·28 e
170	Birsk (bĭrsk)...........Sov. Un.	55·25 n	55·30 e
148	Birstall (bûr′stôl)..........Eng.	53·44 n	1·39 w
167	Biryuchiy (I.) (bĭr-yōō′chĭ) Sov. Un.	46·07 n	35·12 e
174	Biryulëvo (bēr-yōōl′yô-vô) Sov. Un. (Moscow In.)	55·35 n	37·39 e
172	Biryusa (R.) (bēr-yōō′sä).Sov. Un.	56·43 n	97·30 e
183	Bi′r Za′farānah Egypt (Palestine In.)	29·07 n	32·38 e
157	Biržai (bêr-zhä′ē)........Sov. Un.	56·11 n	24·45 e
115	Bisbee (bĭz′bē)..............Az.	31·30 n	109·55 w
151	Biscay, B. of (bĭs′kā′).......Eur.	45·19 n	3·51 w
121	Biscayne B. (bĭs-kān′)....Fl. (In.)	25·22 n	80·15 w
161	Bischeim (bĭsh′hīm)..........Fr.	48·40 n	7·48 e
96	Biscotasi L.................Can.	47·20 n	81·55 w
174	Biser (bē′sĕr).Sov. Un. (Urals In.)	58·24 n	58·54 e
164	Biševo (Is.) (bē′shĕ-vō).....Yugo.	42·58 n	15·50 e
114	Bishop (bĭsh′ŭp).............Ca.	37·22 n	118·25 w
119	Bishop......................Tx.	27·35 n	97·46 w
148	Bishop's Castle (bĭsh′ŏps käs′l) Eng.	52·29 n	2·57 w
121	Bishopville (bĭsh′ŭp-vĭl).......SC	34·11 n	80·13 w
210	Biskra (bēs′krá).............Alg.	34·52 n	5·39 e
108	Bismarck (bĭz′märk).........ND	46·48 n	100·46 w
197	Bismarck Arch......Pap. N. Gui.	3·15 s	150·45 e
197	Bismarck Ra.........Pap. N. Gui.	5·15 s	144·15 e
214	Bissau (bē-sä′ōō)...Guinea-Bissau	11·51 n	15·35 w
95	Bissett......................Can.	51·01 n	95·45 w
119	Bistineau (L.) (bĭs-tĭ-nō′).....La.	32·19 n	93·45 w
159	Bistrita (bĭs-trĭt-sá)........Rom.	47·09 n	24·29 e
159	Bistrita R.................Rom.	47·08 n	25·47 e
171	Bitlis (bĭt-lēs′)..............Tur.	38·30 n	42·00 e
165	Bitola (Monastir) (bē′tô-lä) (mô′nä-stêr).Yugo.	41·02 n	21·22 e
164	Bitonto (bē-tôn′tō)...........It.	41·08 n	16·42 e
111	Bitter Cr. (bĭt′ẽr)...........Wy.	41·36 n	108·29 w
158	Bitterfeld (bĭt′ẽr-fĕlt)......G.D.R.	51·39 n	12·19 e
110	Bitterroot Ra. (bĭt′ẽr-ōōt)....Mt.	47·15 n	115·13 w
111	Bitterroot R.................Mt.	46·28 n	114·10 w
167	Bityug (R.) (bĭt′yōōg)...Sov. Un.	51·23 n	40·33 e
215	Biu........................Nig.	10·35 n	12·13 e
109	Biwabik (bē-wä′bĭk)..........Mn.	47·32 n	92·24 w
195	Biwa-ko (L.) (bē-wä′kō) Jap. (Ōsaka In.)	35·03 n	135·51 e
172	Biya (R.) (bĭ′yá).......Sov. Un.	52·22 n	87·28 e
172	Biysk (bēsk)...........Sov. Un.	52·32 n	85·28 e
213	Bizana (bĭz-änä) S. Afr. (Natal In.)	30·51 s	29·54 e
	Bizerte, see Binzert		
192	Bizuta....................Mong.	46·28 n	115·10 e
164	Bjelovar (byĕ-lō′vär).......Yugo.	45·54 n	16·53 e
	Björneborg, see Pori		
156	Bjorne Fd. (byûr′nĕ fyŏrd)...Nor.	60·11 n	5·26 e
214	Bla.......................Mali	12·57 n	5·46 w
104	Black (L.) (blăk)............Mi.	45·25 n	84·15 w
105	Black (L.)..................NY	44·30 n	75·35 w
117	Black (R.)..................Ar.	35·47 n	91·22 w
96	Black (R.).................Can.	49·20 n	81·15 w
105	Black (R.)..................NY	43·45 n	75·20 w
121	Black (R.)..................SC	33·55 n	80·10 w
109	Black (R.)..................Wi.	44·07 n	90·56 w
205	Blackall (blăk′ŭl)..........Austl.	24·23 s	145·37 e
109	Black B. (blăk).............Can.	48·36 n	88·32 w
148	Blackburn (blăk′bûrn).......Eng.	53·45 n	2·28 w
101	Blackburn, Mt...............Ak.	61·50 n	143·12 w
115	Black Canyon of the Gunnison Natl. Mon. (blăk kăn′yŭn).Co.	38·35 n	107·45 w
112	Black Diamond (dī′mŭnd) Wa. (Seattle In.)	47·19 n	122·00 w
154	Blackdown Hills (blăk′doun) Eng.	50·58 n	3·19 w
109	Blackduck (blăk′dŭk)........Mn.	47·41 n	94·33 w
111	Blackfoot (blăk′fŏŏt).........Id.	43·11 n	112·23 w
93	Blackfoot Ind. Res...........Can.	50·45 n	113·00 w
111	Blackfoot Ind. Res...........Mt.	48·49 n	112·53 w
111	Blackfoot R.................Mt.	46·53 n	113·33 w
111	Blackfoot River Res...........Id.	42·53 n	111·23 w
108	Black Hills..................SD	44·08 n	103·47 w
95	Black I....................Can.	51·10 n	96·30 w
98	Black Lake.................Can.	46·02 n	71·24 w
115	Black Mesa (blăk māsá).......Az.	36·33 n	110·40 w
89	Blackmud Cr. (blăk′mŭd) Can. (Edmonton In.)	53·28 n	113·34 w
148	Blackpool (blăk′pōōl)........Eng.	53·49 n	3·02 w
115	Black Ra....................NM	33·15 n	107·55 w
128	Black River (blăk′).........Jam.	18·00 n	77·50 w
193	Black R....................Viet.	20·56 n	104·30 e
109	Black River Falls............Wi.	44·18 n	90·51 w
110	Black Rock Des. (rŏk).......Nv.	40·55 n	119·00 w
121	Blacksburg (blăks′bûrg).......SC	35·09 n	81·30 w
147	Black Sea..............Eur.-Asia	43·01 n	32·16 e
121	Blackshear (blăk′shĭr).........Ga.	31·20 n	82·15 w
121	Blackstone (blăk′stôn).........Va.	37·04 n	78·00 w
109	Black Sturgeon (R.) (stû′jŭn).Can.	49·12 n	88·41 w
202	Blacktown (blăk′toun) Austl. (Sydney In.)	33·47 s	150·55 e
98	Blackville (blăk′vĭl).........Can.	46·44 n	65·50 w
121	Blackville...................SC	33·21 n	81·19 w
214	Black Volta (Volta Noire) (R.) (vōl′tá).Afr.	8·55 n	2·30 w
120	Black Warrior (R.) (blăk wŏr′ĭ-ẽr) Al.	32·37 n	87·42 w
120	Black Warrior (R.), Locust Fk..Al.	34·06 n	86·27 w
120	Black Warrior (R.), Mulberry Fk. Al.	34·06 n	86·32 w
154	Blackwater (R.) (blăk-wô′tẽr).Ire.	52·05 n	9·02 w
117	Blackwater (R.).............Mo.	38·53 n	93·22 w
121	Blackwater (R.).............Va.	37·07 n	77·10 w
117	Blackwell (blăk′wĕl)..........Ok.	36·47 n	97·19 w
149	Bladel....Neth. (Amsterdam In.)	51·22 n	5·15 e
171	Blagodarnoye (blä′gô-där-nō′yĕ) Sov. Un.	45·00 n	43·30 e
165	Blagoevgrad (Gorna Dzhumaya) Bul.	42·01 n	23·06 e
173	Blagoveshchensk (blä′gŏ-vyĕsh′chĕnsk).Sov. Un.	50·16 n	127·47 e
174	Blagoveshchensk Sov. Un. (Urals In.)	55·03 n	56·00 e
113	Blaine (blān) Mn. (Minneapolis, St. Paul In.)	45·11 n	93·14 w
112	Blaine.......Wa. (Vancouver In.)	48·59 n	122·49 w
105	Blaine.....................WV	39·25 n	79·10 w
108	Blair (blâr).................Ne.	41·33 n	96·09 w
93	Blairmore..................Can.	49·38 n	114·25 w
105	Blairsville (blârs′vĭl).........Pa.	40·30 n	79·40 w
112	Blake (I.) (blāk)..Wa. (Seattle In.)	47·37 n	122·28 w
120	Blakely (blāk′lē)............Ga.	31·22 n	84·55 w
210	Blanc, Cap (C.).......Mauritania	20·39 n	18·08 w
161	Blanc, Mt. (môn blän).....Fr.-It.	45·50 n	6·53 e
136	Blanca, Bahia (B.) (bä-ē′ä-blän′kä).Arg.	39·30 s	61·00 w
116	Blanca Pk. (blăŋ′ká).........Co.	37·36 n	105·22 w
203	Blanche, L. (blănch).......Austl.	29·20 s	139·12 e
89	Blanche, (R.)...Can. (Ottawa In.)	45·34 n	75·38 w
107	Blanchester (blăn′chĕs-tẽr) Oh. (Cincinnati In.)	39·18 n	83·58 w
136	Blanco, C. (blăŋ′kō).........Arg.	47·08 s	65·47 w
126	Blanco, Cabo (C.) (ká′bô-blăŋ′kō) C. R.	9·29 n	85·15 w
110	Blanco, C. (blăn′kō)..........Or.	42·53 n	124·38 w
125	Blanco (R.)................Mex.	18·42 n	96·03 w
124	Blanco (R.)................Mex.	24·05 n	99·21 w
128	Blancos, Cayo (I.) (kä′yō-blăŋ′kōs).Cuba	23·15 n	80·55 w
115	Blanding...................Ut.	37·40 n	109·31 w
155	Blankenburg (blăŋ′kĕn-bōōrgh) G.D.R	51·45 n	10·58 e
149	Blankenfelde (blän′kĕn-fĕl-dĕ) G.D.R. (Berlin In.)	52·20 n	13·24 e
125	Blanquilla, Arrecife (Reef) (är-rĕ-sē′fĕ-blän-kē′l-yä).Mex.	21·32 n	97·14 w
217	Blantyre (blăn-tīyr).......Malawi	15·47 s	35·00 e
107	Blasdell (blăz′dĕl) NY (Buffalo In.)	42·48 n	78·51 w
164	Blato (blä′tō)..............Yugo.	42·55 n	16·47 e
156	Blåvands Huk (Cape) (blŏ′văns-hōk).Den.	55·36 n	8·05 e
160	Blaye-et-Ste. Luce (blā′ā-sănt-lüs′).Fr.	45·08 n	0·40 w
159	Błazowa (bwä-zhō′vá).........Pol.	49·51 n	22·05 e
217	Bleus, Monts (Mts.)........Zaire	1·10 n	30·10 e
210	Blida......................Alg.	36·33 n	2·45 e
96	Blind River (blīnd)..........Can.	46·10 n	83·09 w
104	Blissfield (blĭs-fēld)..........Mi.	41·50 n	83·50 w
148	Blithe (R.) (blīth)...........Eng.	52·22 n	1·49 w
214	Blitta......................Togo	8·19 n	0·59 e
105	Block (I.) (blŏk).............RI	41·05 n	71·35 w
92	Bloedel....................Can.	50·07 n	125·23 w
218	Bloemfontein (blōōm′fŏn-tān) S. Afr. (Johannesburg & Pretoria In.)	29·09 s	26·16 e
160	Blois (blwä).................Fr.	47·36 n	1·21 e
93	Blood Ind. Res..............Can.	49·30 n	113·10 w
109	Bloomer (blōōm′ẽr)...........Wi.	45·07 n	91·30 w
104	Bloomfield (blōōm′fēld) ....In.	39·00 n	86·55 w
109	Bloomfield..................Ia.	40·44 n	92·21 w
117	Bloomfield..................Mo.	36·54 n	89·55 w
108	Bloomfield..................Ne.	42·36 n	97·40 w
106	Bloomfield.....NJ (New York In.)	40·48 n	74·12 w
107	Bloomfield Hills.Mi. (Detroit In.)	42·35 n	83·15 w
109	Blooming Prairie (blōōm′ĭng prā′rĭ).Mn.	43·52 n	93·04 w
113	Bloomington (blōōm′ĭng-tŭn) Ca. (Los Angeles In.)	34·04 n	117·24 w
104	Bloomington.................Il.	40·30 n	89·00 w
104	Bloomington.................In.	39·10 n	86·35 w
113	Bloomington Mn. (Minneapolis, St. Paul In.)	44·50 n	93·18 w
105	Bloomsburg (blōōmz′bûrg)....Pa.	41·00 n	76·25 w
106	Blossburg (blŏs′bûrg) Al. (Birmingham In.)	33·38 n	86·57 w
105	Blossburg...................Pa.	41·45 n	77·00 w
212	Bloubergstrand.......S. Afr. (In.)	33·48 s	18·28 e
120	Blountstown (blŭnts′tun)......Fl.	30·24 n	85·02 w
158	Bludenz (blōō-dĕnts′)........Aus.	47·09 n	9·50 e
99	Blue, Mt....................Can.	50·28 n	57·11 w
107	Blue Ash (blōō ăsh) Oh. (Cincinnati In.)	39·14 n	84·23 w
109	Blue Earth (blōō ûrth).......Mn.	43·38 n	94·05 w
109	Blue Earth (R.).............Mn.	43·55 n	94·16 w
121	Bluefield (blōō′fēld)..........WV	37·15 n	81·11 w
127	Bluefields (blōō′fēldz)........Nic.	12·03 n	83·45 w
107	Blue Island......Il. (Chicago In.)	41·39 n	87·41 w
115	Blue Mesa Res...............Co.	38·25 n	107.00 w
203	Blue Mts...................Austl.	33·35 s	149·00 e
128	Blue Mts....................Jam.	18·05 n	76·35 w
110	Blue Mts....................Or.	45·15 n	118·50 w
204	Blue Mud B. (bōō mŭd)...Austl.	13·20 s	136·45 e
211	Blue Nile (Abay) (R.) (á-bä′ē).Eth.	9·45 n	37·23 e
211	Blue Nile (Al-Bahr al-Azraq) (R.) (bärĕlaz-räk′).Sud.	12·50 n	34·10 e
117	Blue Rapids (blōō răp′ĭdz)....Ks.	39·40 n	96·41 w
103	Blue Ridge (Mts.) (blōō rĭj).U. S.	35·30 n	82·50 w
93	Blue River..................Can.	52·05 n	119·17 w
113	Blue R.....Mo. (Kansas City In.)	38·55 n	94·33 w
115	Bluff.......................Ut.	37·18 n	109·34 w
106	Bluff Park..Al. (Birmingham In.)	33·24 n	86·52 w
104	Bluffton (blŭf-tŭn)............In.	40·40 n	85·15 w
104	Bluffton....................Oh.	40·50 n	83·55 w
136	Blumenau (blōō′mĕn-ou).....Braz.	26·53 s	48·58 w
183	Blumut, Gunong (Mt.) Mala. (Singapore In.)	2·03 n	103·34 e
154	Blyth (blīth)................Eng.	55·03 n	1·34 w
114	Blythe......................Ca.	33·37 n	114·37 w
117	Blytheville (blīth′vĭl).........Ar.	35·55 n	89·51 w
214	Bo.........................S.L.	7·56 n	11·21 w
197	Boac..................Phil. (In.)	13·26 n	121·50 e
126	Boaco (bô-ä′kō)..............Nic.	12·24 n	85·41 w
135	Boa Vista do Rio Branco (bō′ä vēsh′tä dōō rē′ōō brän′kōō).Braz.	2·46 n	60·45 w
210	Boa Vista I. (bō-ä-vēsh′tá) C. V. (In.)	16·01 n	23·52 w
159	Boběrka (bō′bēr-ká).....Sov. Un.	49·36 n	24·18 e
214	Bobo Dioulasso (bō′bô-dyōō-lás-sō′).Upper Volta	11·12 n	4·18 w
166	Bobr (bô′b′r)...........Sov. Un.	54·19 n	29·11 e
158	Bóbr (R.) (bŭ′br).............Pol.	51·44 n	15·13 e
167	Bobrinets (bô′brē-nyĭts).Sov. Un.	48·04 n	32·10 e
167	Bobrov (bŭb-rôf′)........Sov. Un.	51·07 n	40·01 e
167	Bobrovitsa (bŭb-rô′vē-tsá) Sov. Un.	50·43 n	31·27 e
166	Bobruysk (bŏ-brōō′ĭsk)..Sov. Un.	53·07 n	29·13 e
135	Boca del Pozo (bô-kä-dĕl-pô′zŏ) Ven. (In.)	11·00 n	64·21 w
135	Boca de Uchire (bô-kä-dĕ-ōō-chē′ rĕ).Ven. (In.)	10·09 n	65·27 w
137	Bocaina, Serra da (Mtn.) (sĕ′r-rä-dá-bô-kä′ē-nä) Braz. (Rio de Janeiro In.)	22·47 s	44·39 w
124	Bocas (bō′käs)...............Mex.	22·29 n	101·03 w
127	Bocas del Toro (bō′käs dĕl tō′rō) Pan.	9·24 n	82·15 w
159	Bochnia (bōk′nyä)...........Pol.	49·58 n	20·28 e
161	Bocholt (bō′kolt) F.R.G. (Ruhr In.)	51·50 n	6·37 e
161	Bochum (bō′kōōm) F.R.G. (Ruhr In.)	51·29 n	7·13 e
161	Bockum-Hövel (bō′kōōm-hû′fĕl) F.R.G. (Ruhr In.)	51·41 n	7·45 e
216	Bodalang..................Zaire	3·14 n	22·14 e
173	Bodaybo (bō-dī′bō).....Sov. Un.	57·12 n	114·46 e
215	Bodele (Depression) (bō-dá-lā′) Chad	16·45 n	17·05 e
150	Boden.....................Swe.	65·51 n	21·29 e
158	Boden See (L.) (bō′dĕn zā) F.R.G.-Switz.	47·48 n	9·22 e
154	Boderg (L.) (bō′dûrg).........Ire.	53·51 n	8·06 w
154	Bodmin (bŏd′mĭn)...........Eng.	50·29 n	4·45 w
154	Bodmin Moor (bŏd′mĭn mōōr) Eng.	50·36 n	4·43 w
150	Bodö (bôd′û)...............Nor.	67·13 n	14·19 e
171	Bodrum.....................Tur.	37·10 n	27·07 e
216	Boende (bō-ĕn′dá)...........Zaire	0·13 s	20·52 e
118	Boerne (bō′ẽrn)...............Tx.	29·49 n	98·44 w
213	Boesmans (R.) S. Afr. (Natal In.)	33·29 s	26·09 e
119	Boeuf R. (bĕf)................La.	32·23 n	91·57 w
214	Boffa (bôf′á)................Gui.	10·10 n	14·02 w
195	Bōfu (bō′fōō)................Jap.	34·03 n	131·35 e
119	Bogalusa (bō-gá-lōō′sá).......La.	30·48 n	89·52 w
203	Bogan (R.) (bō′gĕn)........Austl.	32·10 s	147·40 e
156	Bogense (bô′gĕn-sĕ).........Den.	55·34 n	10·09 e
127	Boggy Pk. (bŏg′ĭ-pēk) Antigua (In.)	17·03 n	61·50 w
167	Bogodukhov (bŏ-gŏ-dōō′kôf) Sov. Un.	50·10 n	35·31 e
203	Bogong, Mt.................Austl.	36·50 s	147·15 e
196	Bogor......................Indon.	6·45 s	106·45 e
166	Bogoroditsk (bŏ-gŏ′rŏ-dĭtsk) Sov. Un.	53·48 n	38·06 e
170	Bogorodsk.............Sov. Un.	56·02 n	43·40 e
174	Bogorodskoye (bô-gô-rôd′skô-yĕ) Sov. Un. (Urals In.)	56·43 n	56·53 e
134	Bogotá (bō-gō-tä′)......Col. (In.)	4·38 n	74·06 w
134	Bogotá, Rio (R.) (rē′ō-bō-gō-tä′) Col. (In.)	4·27 n	74·38 w
172	Bogotol (bŏ′gô-tŏl)......Sov. Un.	56 15 n	89·45 e
167	Bogoyavlenskoye (bŏ′gô-yäf′lĕn-skō′yĕ).Sov. Un.	48·46 n	33·19 e
171	Boguchar (bō′gōō-chär)..Sov. Un.	49·40 n	41·00 e
127	Boguete (bô-gĕ′tĕ)...........Pan.	8·54 n	82·29 w
167	Boguslav (bō′gōō-sláf)....Sov. Un.	49·34 n	30·51 e
160	Bohain-en-Vermandois (bô-ăn-ŏn-vâr-män-dwä′).Fr.	49·58 n	3·22 e
	Bohemia (Prov.), see České		
158	Bohemian For. (bō-hē′mĭ-ăn) F.R.G.	49·35 n	12·27 e
197	Bohol (I.) (bô-hôl′)..........Phil.	9·28 n	124·35 e
125	Bohom (bô-ō′m).............Mex.	16·47 n	92·42 w
218	Bohotleh (bô-hŏt′lĕ) Som. (Horn of Afr. In.)	8·15 n	46·20 e
98	Boiestown (boiz′toun).......Can.	46·27 n	66·25 w

ng-sing; ŋ-baŋk; n-nasalized n; nŏd; cŏmmit; ōld; ôbey; ôrder; fōōd; fŏŏt; ou-out; s-soft; sh-dish; th-thin; pūre; ûnite; ûrn; stŭd; circŭs; ü-as "y" in study; ′-indeterminate vowel.

Page	Name Pronunciation Region	Lat. °′	Long. °′
104	Bois Blanc (I.) (boi′ blänk)..Mi.	45·45 N	84·30 W
89	Boischâtel (bwä-shä-tĕl′) Can. (Quebec In.)	46·54 N	71·08 W
89	Bois-des-Filion (bōō-ä′dĕ-fē-yôN′) Can. (Montreal In.)	45·40 N	73·46 W
110	Boise (boi′zē)........Id.	43·38 N	116·12 W
110	Boise (R.)........Id.	43·43 N	116·30 W
116	Boise City........Ok.	36·42 N	102·30 W
95	Boissevain (bois′vān)........Can.	49·14 N	100·03 W
210	Bojador, Cabo (C.) (kȧ′bō-bō-hä-dōr′) (bŏj-ȧ-dōr′) W. Sah.	26·21 N	16·08 W
186	Bojnūrd........Iran	37·29 N	57·13 E
215	Bokani........Nig.	9·26 N	5·13 E
210	Boké (bō-kā′)........Gui.	10·58 N	14·15 W
156	Bokn Fd. (bôk″n fyôrd)........Nor.	59·12 N	5·37 E
213	Boksburg (bŏks′bûrgh)...S. Afr. (Johannesburg & Pretoria In.)	26·13 S	28·15 E
216	Bokungu........Zaire	0·41 S	22·19 E
215	Bol........Chad	13·28 N	14·43 E
215	Bolai I........Cen. Afr. Emp.	4·20 N	17·21 E
210	Bolama (bō-lä′mä).Guinea-Bissau	11·34 N	15·41 W
184	Bolan (Mt.) (bō-län′)........Pak.	30·13 N	67·09 E
124	Bolaños (bō-län′yōs)........Mex.	21·40 N	103·48 W
124	Bolaños (R.)........Mex.	21·26 N	103·54 W
184	Bolan P........Pak.	29·50 N	67·10 E
160	Bolbec (bôl-bĕk′)........Fr.	49·37 N	0·26 E
214	Bole (bō′lā)........Ghana	9·02 N	2·29 W
158	Boleslawiec (bō-lĕ-slä′vyĕts) Pol.	51·15 N	15·35 E
214	Bolgatanga........Ghana	10·46 N	0·52 W
167	Bolgrad (bŏl-grȧt)........Sov. Un.	45·41 N	28·38 E
197	Bolinao (bō-lē-nä′ō)....Phil. (In.)	16·24 N	119·53 E
197	Bolinao, C........Phil. (In.)	16·24 N	119·42 E
137	Bolívar (bō-lē′vär) Arg. (Buenos Aires In.)	36·15 S	61·05 W
134	Bolívar........Col.	1·46 N	76·58 W
117	Bolivar (bŏl′ĭ-vȧr)........Mo.	37·37 N	93·22 W
120	Bolivar........Tn.	35·14 N	88·56 W
134	Bolívar (La Columna) (Mtn.) (bō-lē′vär) (lä-kō-lōō′m-nä).Ven.	8·44 N	70·54 W
119	Bolivar Pen. (bŏl′ĭ-vȧr) Tx. (In.)	29·25 N	94·40 W
133	Bolivia (bō-lĭv′ĭ-ȧ)........S.A.	17·00 S	64·00 W
166	Bolkhov (bŏl-кôf′)........Sov. Un.	53·27 N	35·59 E
148	Bollin (R.) (bŏl′ĭn)........Eng.	53·18 N	2·11 W
148	Bollington (bôl′ĭng-tŭn)........Eng.	53·18 N	2·06 W
156	Bollnäs (bôl′nĕs)........Swe.	61·22 N	16·20 E
156	Bolmen (L.) (bôl′mĕn)........Swe.	56·58 N	13·25 E
212	Bolobo (bō′lō-bō)........Zaire	2·14 S	16·18 E
164	Bologna (bō-lōn′yä)........It.	44·30 N	11·18 E
166	Bologoye (bŏ-lŏ-gô′yĕ)...Sov. Un.	57·52 N	34·02 E
126	Bolonchenticul (bō-lôn-chĕn-tē-kōō′l).Mex. (In.)	20·03 N	89·47 W
128	Bolondrón (bō-lōn-drōn′)....Cuba	22·45 N	81·25 W
164	Bolseno, Lago di (L.) (lä′gō-dē-bôl-sā′nō).It.	42·35 N	11·40 E
170	Bol'shaya Kinel' (R.)....Sov. Un.	53·20 N	52·40 E
167	Bol'shaya Lepetikha (bŏl-shá′yá′lyĕ′pyĕ-tē′кá) Sov. Un.	47·11 N	33·58 E
167	Bol'shaya Viska (vĭs-kä′).Sov. Un.	48·34 N	31·54 E
167	Bol'shaya Vradiyevka (vrá-dyĕf′ká).Sov. Un.	47·51 N	30·38 E
174	Bol'she Ust'ikinskoye (bŏl′she ŏŏs-tyĭ-kĕn′skô-yĕ) Sov. Un. (Urals In.)	55·58 N	58·18 E
173	Bolshoy Anyuy (R.)....Sov. Un.	67·58 N	161·15 E
173	Bol'shoy Begichëv (I.)....Sov. Un.	74·30 N	114·40 E
173	Bolshoy Chuva (R.)....Sov. Un.	58·15 N	111·13 E
174	Bol'shoye Ivonino (ĭ-vô′nĭ-nō) Sov. Un. (Urals In.)	59·41 N	61·12 E
174	Bol'shoy Kuyash (bŏl′-shôy kōō′yásh) Sov. Un. (Urals In.)	55·52 N	61·07 E
167	Bolshoy Tokmak (bŏl-shôy′ tŏk-mäk′).Sov. Un.	47·17 N	35·48 E
148	Bolsover (bōl′zō-vĕr)........Eng.	53·14 N	1·17 W
163	Boltana (bôl-tä′nä)........Sp.	42·28 N	0·03 E
89	Bolton (bōl′tŭn) Can. (Toronto In.)	43·53 N	79·44 W
148	Bolton........Eng.	53·35 N	2·26 W
148	Bolton-upon-Dearne (bōl′tŭn-ŭp′ŏn-dûrn).Eng.	53·31 N	1·19 W
171	Bolu (bō′lōō)........Tur.	40·45 N	31·45 E
166	Bolva (R.) (bôl′vä)....Sov. Un.	53·30 N	34·30 E
171	Bolvadin (bŏl-vä-dēn′)........Tur.	38·50 N	30·50 E
164	Bolzano (bôl-tsä′nō)........It.	46·31 N	11·22 E
216	Boma (bō′mä)........Zaire	5·51 S	13·03 E
203	Bombala (bŭm-bä′lȧ)........Austl.	36·55 S	149·07 E
185	Bombay (bŏm-bā′)....India (In.)	18·58 N	72·50 E
185	Bombay Hbr........India (In.)	18·55 N	72·52 E
210	Bomi Hills........Lib.	7·00 N	11·00 W
137	Bom Jardim (bôn zhär-dēN′) Braz. (Rio de Janeiro In.)	22·10 S	42·25 W
137	Bom Jesus do Itabapoana (bôN-zhĕ-sōō′s-dō-ē-tá′bä-pô-á′nä).Braz. (Rio de Janeiro In.)	21·08 S	41·51 W
156	Bömlo (I.) (bûmlô)........Nor.	59·47 N	4·57 E
216	Bomongo........Zaire	1·22 N	18·21 E
137	Bom Sucesso (bôn-sōō-sĕ′sō) Braz. (Rio de Janeiro In.)	21·02 S	44·44 W
	Bomu, see Mbomou		
151	Bon, C. (bôN)........Tun.	37·04 N	11·13 E
134	Bonaire (I.) (bō-nâr′) Neth. Antilles	12·10 N	68·15 W
162	Boñar (bō-nyär′)........Sp.	42·53 N	5·18 W
99	Bonavista (bŏ-nȧ-vĭs′tȧ)....Can.	48·39 N	53·07 W
99	Bonavista B........Can.	48·45 N	53·20 W
116	Bond (bŏnd)........Co.	39·53 N	106·40 W
216	Bondo (bôn′dō)........Zaire	3·49 N	23·40 E
197	Bondoc Pen. (bôn-dŏk′) Phil. (In.)	13·24 N	122·30 E
214	Bondoukou (bŏn-dōō′kōō) Ivory Coast	8·02 N	2·48 W
128	Bonds Cay (I.) (bŏnds kē)....Ba.	25·30 N	77·45 W
	Bône, see Annaba		
196	Bone, Teluk (G.)........Indon.	4·09 S	121·00 E
196	Bone Rate, Kepulauan (I.).Indon.	6·52 S	121·45 E
136	Bonete, Cerro (Mt.) (bô′nĕtĕh çĕrrô).Arg.	27·50 S	68·35 W
137	Bonfim (bôN-fē′N) Braz. (Rio de Janeiro In.)	20·20 S	44·15 W
215	Bongor........Chad	10·17 N	15·22 E
193	Bong Son........Viet.	14·20 N	109·10 E
117	Bonham (bŏn′ăm)........Tx.	33·35 N	96·09 W
129	Bonhomme, Pic (Pk.)........Hai.	19·10 N	72·20 W
164	Bonifacio (bō-nē-fä′chō)........Fr.	41·23 N	9·10 E
164	Bonifacio, Str. of........Eur.	41·14 N	9·02 E
120	Bonifay (bŏn-ĭ-fā′)........Fl.	30·46 N	85·40 W
198	Bonin Is. (bō′nĭn)........Asia	26·30 N	141·00 E
161	Bonn (bōn).....F.R.G. (Ruhr In.)	50·44 N	7·06 E
99	Bonne B. (bŏn)........Can.	49·33 N	57·55 W
110	Bonners Ferry (bon′erz fĕr′ĭ)..Id.	48·41 N	116·19 W
113	Bonner Springs (bŏn′ĕr sprĭngz) Ks. (Kansas City In.)	39·04 N	94·52 W
117	Bonne Terre (bŏn târ′)........Mo.	37·55 N	90·32 W
93	Bonnet Pk. (bŏn′ĭt)........Can.	51·26 N	115·53 W
110	Bonneville Dam (bôn′ê-vĭl) Or.-Wa.	45·37 N	121·57 W
99	Bonnie B. (bôn′ê)........Can.	49·38 N	58·15 W
210	Bonny (bŏn′ê)........Nig.	4·29 N	7·13 E
112	Bonny Lake (bŏn′ê lăk) Wa. (Seattle In.)	47·11 N	122·11 W
93	Bonnyville (bŏn′e-vĭl)........Can.	54·16 N	110·44 W
164	Bonorva (bō-nôr′vä)........It.	40·26 N	8·46 E
196	Bonthain (bôn-tīn′)........Indon.	5·30 S	119·52 E
214	Bonthe........S. L.	7·32 N	12·30 W
197	Bontoc (bôn-tŏk′)......Phil. (In.)	17·10 N	121·01 E
128	Booby Rocks (I.) (bōō′bĭ rŏks) Ba.	23·55 N	77·00 W
121	Booker T. Washington Natl. Mon. (bŏŏk′ĕr tē wŏsh′ĭng-tŭn).Va.	37·07 N	79·45 W
149	Boom........Bel. (Brussels In.)	51·05 N	4·22 E
109	Boone (bōōn)........Ia.	42·04 N	93·51 W
117	Booneville (bōōn′vĭl)........Ar.	35·09 N	93·54 W
104	Booneville........Ky.	37·25 N	83·40 W
120	Booneville........Ms.	34·37 N	88·35 W
218	Boons........S. Afr. (Johannesburg & Pretoria In.)	25·59 S	27·15 E
106	Boonton (bōōn′tŭn) NJ (New York In.)	40·54 N	74·24 W
104	Boonville........In.	38·00 N	87·15 W
117	Boonville........Mo.	38·57 N	92·44 W
98	Boothbay Harbor (bōōth′bā här′bĕr).Me.	43·51 N	69·39 W
91	Boothia, G. of (bōō′thĭ-ȧ)....Can.	69·04 N	86·04 W
75	Boothia Pen........Can.	73·30 N	95·00 W
148	Bootle (bōōt′l)........Eng.	53·29 N	3·02 W
216	Booué........Gabon	0·06 S	11·56 E
158	Boppard (bôp′ärt)........F.R.G.	50·14 N	7·35 E
211	Bor (bôr)........Sud.	6·13 N	31·35 E
171	Bor (bōr)........Tur.	37·50 N	34·40 E
111	Borah Pk. (bō′rä)........Id.	44·12 N	113·47 W
218	Borama (bôr-á-mȧ) Som. (Horn of Afr. In.)	10·05 N	43·08 E
156	Borås (bōō′rōs)........Swe.	57·43 N	12·55 E
186	Borāzjān (bō-räz-jän′)........Iran	29·13 N	51·13 E
135	Borba (bôr′bä)........Braz.	4·23 S	59·31 W
135	Borborema, Planalto da (Plat.) (plä-nál′tô-dä-bôr-bō-rĕ′mä) Braz.	7·35 S	36·40 W
160	Bordeaux (bôr-dō′)........Fr.	44·50 N	0·37 W
105	Bordentown (bôr′dĕn-toun)....NJ	40·05 N	74·40 W
151	Bordj-bou-Arréridj (bôrj-bōō-á-rā-rĕj′).Alg.	36·03 N	4·48 E
157	Borgå (bôr′gō)........Fin.	60·26 N	25·41 E
150	Borgarnes........Ice.	64·31 N	21·40 W
116	Borger (bôr′gĕr)........Tx.	35·40 N	101·23 W
156	Borgholm (bôrg-hŏlm′)........Swe.	56·52 N	16·40 E
119	Borgne (L.) (bôrn′y′)........La.	30·03 N	89·36 W
164	Borgomanero (bôr′gō-mä-nâ′rō) It.	45·40 N	8·28 E
163	Borgo Montello (bô′r-zhō-môn-tĕ′lō) It. (Rome In.)	41·31 N	12·48 E
164	Borgo Val di Taro (bô′r-zhō-väl-dē-tá′rō).It.	44·29 N	9·44 E
112	Boring (bōring) Or. (Portland In.)	45·26 N	122·22 W
159	Borislav (bô′rĭs-lôf)....Sov. Un.	49·17 N	23·24 E
171	Borisoglebsk (bŏ-rē sô-glyĕpsk′) Sov. Un.	51·20 N	42·00 E
166	Borisov (bŏ-rē′sôf)........Sov. Un.	54·16 N	28·33 E
167	Borisovka (bŏ-rē-sôf′ká)..Sov. Un.	50·38 N	36·00 E
167	Borispol' (bo-rĭs′pol)....Sov. Un.	50·17 N	30·54 E
185	Borivli........India (In.)	19·15 N	72·48 E
162	Borja (bôr′hä)........Sp.	41·50 N	1·33 W
163	Borjas Blancas (bô′r-кäs-blä′n-käs).Sp.	41·29 N	0·53 E
161	Borken (bōr′kĕn) F.R.G. (Ruhr In.)	51·50 N	6·51 E
211	Borkou (Reg.) (bôr-kōō′)....Chad	18·11 N	18·28 E
158	Borkum I. (bōr′kōōm).....F.R.G.	53·31 N	6·50 E
156	Borlänge (bôr-lĕŋ′gĕ)........Swe.	60·30 N	15·24 E
196	Borneo (I.) (bôr′nē-ō)........Asia	0·25 N	112·39 E
156	Bornholm (I.) (bôrn-hôlm)...Den.	55·16 N	15·15 E
162	Bornos (bôr′nōs)........Sp.	36·48 N	5·45 W
167	Borodayevka........Sov. Un.	48·44 N	34·09 E
167	Boromlya (bŏ-rôm′′l-yä)..Sov. Un.	50·36 N	34·58 E
214	Boromo........Upper Volta	11·45 N	2·56 W
165	Borovan (bŏ-rô-vän′)........Bul.	43·24 N	23·47 E
166	Borovichi (bŏ-rô-vē′chê)..Sov. Un.	58·22 N	33·56 E
166	Borovsk (bô′rŏvsk)......Sov. Un.	55·13 N	36·26 E
135	Borracha, Isla la (I.) (ē′s-lä-lá-bôr-rá′chä).Ven. (In.)	10·18 N	64·44 W
204	Borroloola (bŏr-rô-lōō′lȧ)....Austl.	16·15 S	136·19 E
159	Borshchëv (bôrsh-chyôf′).Sov. Un.	48·47 N	26·04 E
160	Bort-les-Orgues (bôr-lā-zôrg)...Fr.	45·26 N	2·26 E
186	Borūjerd........Iran	33·45 N	48·53 E
167	Borzna (bôrz′ná)........Sov. Un.	51·15 N	32·26 E
173	Borzya (bôrz′yá)........Sov. Un.	50·37 N	116·53 E
164	Bosa (bō′sä)........It.	40·18 N	8·34 E
164	Bosanska Dubica (bō′sän-skä dōō′bĭt-sä).Yugo.	45·10 N	16·49 E
164	Bosanska Gradiška (bō′sän-skä grä-dĭsh′kä).Yugo.	45·08 N	17·15 E
164	Bosanski Novi (bō′s sän-skĭ nō′vē) Yugo.	45·00 N	16·22 E
164	Bosanski Petrovac (bō′sän-skĭ pĕt′rō-väts).Yugo.	44·33 N	16·23 E
165	Bosanski Šamac (bō′sän-skĭ shä′máts).Yugo.	45·03 N	18·30 E
109	Boscobel (bŏs′kō-bĕl)........Wi.	43·08 N	90·44 W
174	Boskol' (bás-kôl′) Sov. Un. (Urals In.)	53·45 N	61·17 E
149	Boskoop...Neth. (Amsterdam In.)	52·04 N	4·39 E
158	Boskovice (bŏs′kō-vē-tsĕ)....Czech.	49·26 N	16·37 E
165	Bosna (R.)........Yugo.	44·19 N	17·54 E
165	Bosnia (Reg.) (bŏs′nĭ-á)....Yugo.	44·17 N	16·58 E
216	Bosobolo........Zaire	4·11 N	19·54 E
	Bosporous (Str.), see İstanbul Boğazı		
215	Bossangoa........Cen. Afr. Emp.	6·29 N	17·27 E
215	Bossembélé........Cen. Afr. Emp.	5·16 N	17·39 E
119	Bossier City (bŏsh′ĕr)........La.	32·31 N	93·42 W
120	Boston (bôs′tŭn)........Ga.	30·47 N	83·47 W
99	Boston........Ma. (In.)	42·15 N	71·07 W
107	Boston Heights Oh. (Cleveland In.)	41·15 N	81·30 W
117	Boston Mts........Ar.	35·46 N	93·32 W
202	Botany B. (bŏt′ȧ-nĭ) Austl. (Sydney In.)	33·58 S	151·11 E
165	Botevgrad........Bul.	42·54 N	23·41 E
218	Bothaville (bō′tä-vĭl)......S. Afr. (Johannesburg & Pretoria In.)	27·24 S	26·38 E
112	Bothell (bŏth′ĕl).Wa. (Seattle In.)	47·46 N	122·12 W
150	Bothnia, G. of (bŏth′nĭ-ȧ)....Eur.	63·40 N	21·30 E
159	Botosani (bō-tō-shàn′ĭ)......Rom.	47·46 N	26·40 E
209	Botswana (bŏtswănă)........Afr.	22·10 S	23·13 E
108	Bottineau (bŏt-ĭ-nō′)........ND	48·48 N	100·28 W
161	Bottrop (bōt′trōp) F.R.G. (Ruhr In.)	51·31 N	6·56 E
135	Botucatú (bô-tōō-kä-tōō′)...Braz.	22·50 S	48·23 W
99	Botwood (bŏt′wŏŏd)........Can.	49·08 N	55·21 W
214	Bouafle (bōō-á-flā′)...Ivory Coast	6·59 N	5·45 W
214	Bouaké (bōō-á-kā′)...Ivory Coast	7·41 N	5·00 W
215	Bouar (bōō-är)....Cen. Afr. Emp.	5·57 N	15·36 E
215	Boubandjidah, Parc Natl. de (Natl. Pk.).Cam.	8·20 N	14·40 E
89	Boucherville (bōō-shä-vĕl′) Can. (Montreal In.)	45·37 N	73·27 W
214	Boucle du Baoulé, Parc Natl. de la (Natl. Pk.).Mali	13·50 N	9·15 W
210	Boudenib (bōō-dĕ-nēb′)......Mor.	32·14 N	3·04 W
109	Boudette (bōō-dĕt)........Mn.	48·42 N	94·34 W
151	Bou Dia, C. (bōō dē′ȧ))......Tun.	35·18 N	11·17 E
163	Boudouaou........Alg.	36·44 N	3·25 E
163	Boufarik (bōō-fá-rēk′)........Alg.	36·35 N	2·55 E
198	Bougainville Trench (bōō-găN-vēl′).Oceania	7·00 S	152·00 E
	Bougie, see Bejaïa		
210	Bougouni (bōō-gōō-nē′)......Mali	11·27 N	7·30 W
152	Bouira (boo-ē′rá)........Alg.	36·25 N	3·55 E
163	Bouïra-Sahary (bwē-rá sá′á-rē) Alg.	35·16 N	3·23 E
214	Bouka (R.)........Gui.	11·05 N	10·40 W
204	Boulder (bōl′dĕr)........Austl.	31·00 S	121·40 E
116	Boulder........Co.	40·02 N	105·19 W
111	Boulder (R.)........Mt.	46·10 N	112·07 W
114	Boulder City........Nv.	35·57 N	114·50 W
110	Boulder Cr........Id.	42·53 N	116·49 W
111	Boulder Pk........Id.	43·53 N	114·33 W
161	Boulogne-Billancourt (bōō-lôn′y′-bē-yäN-kōōr′) Fr. (Paris In.)	48·50 N	2·14 E
160	Boulogne-sur-Mer (bōō-lôn′y-sür-mâr′).Fr.	50·44 N	1·37 E
215	Boumba (R.)........Cam.	3·20 N	14·40 E
163	Bou-Mort, Sierra de (Mts.) (sē-ĕ′r-rä-dĕ-bō-ōō-mō′rt).Sp.	42·11 N	1·05 E
214	Bouna (bōō-nä′)......Ivory Coast	9·16 N	3·00 W
214	Bouna, Park Natl. de (Natl. Pk.).Ivory Coast	9·20 N	3·35 W
112	Boundary B. (boun′dȧ-rĭ) Can. (Vancouver In.)	49·03 N	122·59 W
114	Boundary Pk........Nv.	37·52 N	118·20 W
106	Bound Brook (bound brŏŏk) NJ (New York In.)	40·34 N	74·32 W
113	Bountiful (boun′tĭ-fŏŏl) Ut. (Salt Lake City In.)	40·55 N	111·53 W
113	Bountiful Pk. (boun′tĭ-fŏŏl) Ut. (Salt Lake City In.)	40·58 N	111·49 W
220	Bounty Is........N. Z.	47·42 S	179·05 E
210	Bourem (bōō-rĕm′)........Mali	16·43 N	0·15 W
160	Bourg-en-Bresse (bōōr-gĕN-brĕs′) Fr.	46·12 N	5·13 E
160	Bourges (bōōrzh)........Fr.	47·06 N	2·22 E
89	Bourget (bōōr-zhĕ′) Can. (Ottawa In.)	45·26 N	75·09 W
161	Bourgoin (bōōr-gwăN′)........Fr.	45·46 N	5·17 E
203	Bourke (bŭrk)........Austl.	30·10 S	146·00 E
148	Bourne (bôrn)........Eng.	52·46 N	0·22 W
154	Bournemouth (bôrn′mŭth)...Eng.	50·44 N	1·55 W
152	Bou Saada (bōō-sä′dä)......Alg.	35·13 N	4·17 E
211	Bousso (bōō-sô′)........Chad	10·33 N	16·45 E
210	Boutilimit (bōō-tē-lē-mē′) Mauritania	17·30 N	14·54 W
	Bouvert (I.), see Bouvetöen		

ăt; finȧl; rāte; senâte; ärm; ȧsk; sofȧ; fâre; ch-choose; dh-as th in other; bē; ėvent; bĕt; recĕnt; cratēr; g-go; gh-guttural g; bĭt; ĭ-short neutral; rīde; K-guttural k as ch in German ich;

Page	Name Pronunciation Region	Lat. °'	Long. °'
220	Bouvetöen (Bouvert) (I.) . . Alt. O.	54·26 S	3·24 E
164	Bovino (bō-vē'nō) It.	41·14 N	15·21 E
93	Bow (R.) (bō) Can.	50·35 N	112·15 W
108	Bowbells (bō'bĕls) ND	48·50 N	102·16 W
108	Bowdle (bōd''l) SD	45·28 N	99·42 W
205	Bowen (bō'ĕn) Austl.	20·02 S	148·14 E
106	Bowie (bōō'ĭ) (bō'ē) Md. (Baltimore In.)	38·59 N	76·47 W
116	Bowie Tx.	33·34 N	97·50 W
120	Bowling Green (bōlĭng grēn) . . Ky.	37·00 N	86·26 W
117	Bowling Green Mo.	39·19 N	91·09 W
104	Bowling Green Oh.	41·25 N	83·40 W
108	Bowman (bō'măn) ND	46·11 N	103·23 W
197	Bowokan, Pulau-Pulau (Is.) . Indon.	2·20 S	123·45 E
93	Bowron (R.) (bō'rŭn) Can.	53·20 N	121·10 W
108	Boxelder Cr. (bŏks'ĕl-dẽr) Mt.	45·35 N	104·28 W
111	Boxelder Cr. Mt.	47·17 N	108·37 W
149	Boxtel . . . . Neth. (Amsterdam In.)	51·40 N	5·21 E
216	Boyabo Zaire	3·43 N	18·46 E
89	Boyer (R.) (boi'ẽr) Can. (Quebec In.)	46·26 N	70·56 W
108	Boyer (R.) Ia.	41·45 N	95·36 W
154	Boyle (boil) Ire.	53·59 N	8·15 W
104	Boyne City Mi.	45·15 N	85·05 W
154	Boyne R. (boin) Ire.	53·40 N	6·40 W
165	Bozcaada (Tenedos) (bōz-cä'dä) (tĕ'nĕ-dŏs) . Tur.	39·50 N	26·05 E
165	Bozcaada (I.) Tur.	39·50 N	26·00 E
111	Bozeman (bōz'măn) Mt.	45·41 N	111·00 W
216	Bozene Zaire	2·56 N	19·12 E
215	Bozoum Cen. Afr. Emp.	6·19 N	16·23 E
164	Bra (brä) It.	44·41 N	7·52 E
164	Brač (I.) (bräch) Yugo.	43·18 N	16·36 E
4	Bracciano, Lago di (L.) (lä'gō-dē-brä-chä'nō) . It.	42·05 N	12·00 E
105	Bracebridge (brās'brĭj) Can.	45·05 N	79·20 W
107	Braceville (brās'vĭl) Il. (Chicago In.)	41·13 N	88·16 W
156	Bräcke (brĕk'kĕ) Swe.	62·44 N	15·28 E
107	Brackenridge (brăk'ĕn-rĭj) Pa. (Pittsburgh In.)	40·37 N	79·44 W
118	Brackettville (brăk'ĕt-vĭl) Tx.	29·19 N	100·24 W
135	Braço Maior (R.) Braz.	11·00 S	51·00 W
135	Braço Menor (R.) (brä'zō-mĕ-nō'r) . Braz.	11·38 S	50·00 W
164	Brádano (R.) (brä-dä'nō) It.	40·43 N	16·22 E
107	Braddock (brăd'ŭk) Pa. (Pittsburgh In.)	40·24 N	79·52 W
121	Bradenton (brā'dĕn-tŭn) Fl. (In.)	27·28 N	82·35 W
148	Bradfield (brăd-fēld) Eng. (London In.)	51·25 N	1·08 W
148	Bradford (brăd'fẽrd) Eng.	53·47 N	1·44 W
104	Bradford Oh.	40·10 N	84·30 W
105	Bradford Pa.	42·00 N	78·40 W
107	Bradley (brăd'lĭ) Il. (Chicago In.)	41·09 N	87·52 W
112	Bradner (brăd'nẽr) Can. (Vancouver In.)	49·05 N	122·26 W
118	Brady (brā'dĭ) Tx.	31·09 N	99·21 W
162	Braga (brä'gä) Port.	41·20 N	8·25 W
137	Bragado (brä-gä'dō) Arg. (Buenos Aires In.)	35·07 S	60·28 W
135	Bragança (brä-gän'sä) Braz.	1·02 S	46·50 W
162	Bragança Port.	41·48 N	6·46 W
137	Bragança Paulista (brä-gän'sä-pä'ōō-lē's-tà) Braz. (Rio de Janeiro In.)	22·58 S	46·31 W
89	Bragg Creek (brăg) Can. (Calgary In.)	50·57 N	114·35 W
187	Brahmaputra (R.) (brä'mà-pōō'trà) . India	26·45 N	92·45 E
187	Brāhui (Mts.) Pak.	28·32 N	66·15 E
107	Braidwood (brād'wŏŏd) Il. (Chicago In.)	41·16 N	88·13 W
167	Brăila (brē'ēlà) Rom.	45·15 N	27·58 E
109	Brainerd (brān'ẽrd) Mn.	46·20 N	94·09 W
99	Braintree (brān'trē) . . . . Ma. (In.)	42·14 N	71·00 W
106	Braithwaite (brīth'wīt) La. (New Orleans In.)	29·52 N	89·57 W
213	Brakpan (brăk'păn) S. Afr. (Johannesburg & Pretoria In.)	26·15 S	28·22 E
92	Bralorne (brā'lôrn) Can.	50·47 N	122·49 W
89	Bramalea . . . . Can. (Toronto In.)	43·48 N	79·41 W
89	Brampton (brămp'tŭn) Can. (Toronto In.)	43·41 N	79·46 W
136	Branca, Pedra (Mtn.) (pĕ'drä-brà'N-kä) Braz. (Rio de Janeiro In.)	22·55 S	43·28 W
106	Branchville (brănch'vĭl) NJ (New York In.)	41·09 N	74·44 W
121	Branchville SC	33·17 N	80·48 W
135	Branco (R.) (brāŋ'kō) Braz.	2·21 N	60·38 W
212	Brandberg (Mtn.) Namibia	21·15 S	14·15 E
149	Brandenburg (brän'dĕn-bŏŏrgh) G.D.R. (Berlin In.)	52·25 N	12·33 E
158	Brandenburg (Reg.) G.D.R.	52·12 N	13·31 E
218	Brandfort (brăn'd-fôrt) . . . . S. Afr. (Johannesburg & Pretoria In.)	28·42 S	26·29 E
95	Brandon (brăn'dŭn) Can.	49·50 N	99·57 W
105	Brandon Vt.	43·45 N	73·05 W
154	Brandon Hill (brăn-dŏn) Ire.	52·15 N	10·12 W
106	Brandywine (brăndĭ'wīn) Md. (Baltimore In.)	38·42 N	76·51 W
105	Branford (brăn'fẽrd) Ct.	41·15 N	72·50 W
159	Braniewo (brä-nyĕ'vō) Pol.	54·23 N	19·50 E
159	Brańsk (brän' sk) Pol.	52·44 N	22·51 E
89	Brantford (brănt'fẽrd) Can. (Toronto In.)	43·09 N	80·17 W
99	Bras d'Or L. (brä-dôr') Can.	45·52 N	60·50 W
135	Brasília (brä-sē'lvä) Braz.	15·49 S	47·39 W
135	Brasilia Legal (Fordlândia) (brä-sē'lyä-lĕ-gäl) (fô'rd-län-dyä) Braz.	3·45 S	55·46 W
137	Brasópolis (brä-sô'pô-lĕs) Braz. (Rio de Janeiro In.)	22·30 S	45·36 W
165	Braşov (Oraşul-Stalin) Rom.	45·39 N	25·35 E
210	Brass (brăs) Nig.	4·28 N	6·28 E
89	Bras St. Michel (R.) Can. (Quebec In.)	46·47 N	70·51 W
149	Brasschaat (bräs'κät) Bel. (Brussels In.)	51·19 N	4·30 E
107	Bratenahl (bră'tĕn-ôl) Oh. (Cleveland In.)	41·34 N	81·36 W
149	Bratislava (brä'tĭs-lä-vä) Czech. (Vienna In.)	48·09 N	17·07 E
172	Bratsk (brätsk) Sov. Un.	56·10 N	102·04 E
172	Bratskoye Vdkhr. (Res.) . Sov. Un.	56·10 N	102·05 E
167	Bratslav (brät'slàf) Sov. Un.	48·48 N	28·59 E
105	Brattleboro (brăt''l-bŭr-ô) Vt.	42·50 N	72·35 W
158	Braunau (brou'nou) Aus.	48·15 N	13·05 E
158	Braunschweig (broun'shvīgh) F.R.G.	52·16 N	10·32 E
218	Brava (brä'vä) Som. (Horn of Afr. In.)	1·20 N	44·00 E
156	Bråviken (R.) Swe.	58·40 N	16·40 E
	Bravo del Norte, Rio (R.), see Grande, Rio		
114	Brawley (brô'lĭ) Ca.	32·59 N	115·32 W
154	Bray (brā) Ire.	53·10 N	6·05 W
117	Braymer (brā'mẽr) Mo.	39·34 N	93·47 W
119	Brays Bay. (brās'bĭ'yōō) . Tx. (In.)	29·41 N	95·33 W
93	Brazeau, Mt. (bră-zō') Can.	52·33 N	117.21 W
93	Brazeau (R.) Can.	52·55 N	116·10 W
104	Brazil (brȧ-zĭl') In.	39·30 N	87·00 W
133	Brazil S. A.	9·00 S	53·00 W
133	Brazilian Highlands (Mts.) (brȧ zĭl yȧn hī-lȧndz) . Braz.	14·00 S	48·00 W
102	Brazos (R.) (brä'zōs) U. S.	33·10 N	98·50 W
118	Brazos (R.), Clear Fk. Tx.	32·56 N	99·14 W
116	Brazos (R.), Double Mountain Fk. Tx.	33·23 N	101·21 W
116	Brazos (R.), Salt Fk. (sôlt fôrk) Tx.	33·20 N	100·57 W
216	Brazzaville (brȧ-zȧ-vēl') Con.	4·16 S	15·17 E
165	Brčko (bẽrch'kō) Yugo.	44·54 N	18·46 E
159	Brda R. (bẽr-dä') Pol.	53·18 N	17·55 E
113	Brea (brē'ȧ) . Ca. (Los Angeles In.)	33·55 N	117·54 W
89	Breakeyville . . . . Can. (Quebec In.)	46·40 N	71·13 W
108	Breckenridge (brĕk'ĕn-rĭj) . . . . Mn.	46·17 N	96·35 W
118	Breckenridge Tx.	32·46 N	98·53 W
107	Brecksville (brĕks'vĭl) Oh. (Cleveland In.)	41·19 N	81·38 W
158	Břeclav (brzhĕl'läf) Czech.	48·46 N	16·54 E
154	Brecon Beacons (brĕk'ŭn bē kŭns) Wales	52·00 N	3·55 W
149	Breda (brā-dä') Neth. (Amsterdam In.)	51·35 N	4·47 E
212	Bredasdorp (brā'das-dôrp) . . S. Afr.	34·15 S	20·00 E
174	Bredy (brĕ'dĭ) . Sov. Un. (Urals In.)	52·25 N	60·23 E
158	Bregenz (brā'gĕnts) Aus.	47·30 N	9·46 E
165	Bregovo (brĕ'gō-vō) Bul.	44·07 N	22·45 E
213	Breidbach (brĕd'băk) S. Afr. (Natal In.)	32·54 S	27·26 E
150	Breidha Fd. (brā'dĭ) Ice.	65·15 N	22·50 W
161	Breil (brĕ'y') Fr.	43·57 N	7·36 E
135	Brejo (brĕ'zhōō) Braz.	3·33 S	42·46 W
156	Bremangerland (I.) (brĕ-mänger-länd) . Nor.	61·51 N	4·25 E
158	Bremen (brā-mĕn) F.R.G.	53·05 N	8·50 E
104	Bremen (brē'mĕn) In.	41·25 N	86·05 W
158	Bremerhaven (brām-ẽr-hä'fĕn) F.R.G.	53·33 N	8·38 E
112	Bremerton (brĕm'ẽr-tŭn) Wa. (Seattle In.)	47·34 N	122·38 W
149	Bremervörde (brĕ'mĕr-fûr-dĕ) F.R.G. (Hamburg In.)	53·29 N	9·09 E
89	Bremner (brĕm'nẽr) Can. (Edmonton In.)	53·34 N	113·14 W
119	Bremond (brĕm'ŭnd) Tx.	31·11 N	96·40 W
119	Brenham (brĕn'ăm) Tx.	30·10 N	96·24 W
158	Brenner P. (brĕn'ẽr) Aus.-It.	47·00 N	11·30 E
148	Brentwood (brĕnt'wŏŏd) Eng. (London In.)	51·37 N	0·18 E
105	Brentwood Md.	39·00 N	76·55 W
113	Brentwood . . . . Mo. (St. Louis In.)	38·37 N	90·21 W
107	Brentwood . . . . Pa. (Pittsburgh In.)	40·22 N	79·59 W
164	Brescia (brā'shä) It.	45·33 N	10·15 E
	Breslau, see Wroclaw		
164	Bressanone (brĕs-sä-nō'nā) It.	46·42 N	11·40 E
160	Bressuire (brĕ-swēr') Fr.	46·49 N	0·14 W
160	Brest (brĕst) Fr.	48·24 N	4·30 W
159	Brest Sov. Un.	52·06 N	23·43 E
166	Brest (Oblast) Sov. Un.	52·30 N	26·50 E
160	Bretagne, Monts de (Mts.) (mŏN-dĕ-brĕ-täN'yĕ) . Fr.	48·25 N	3·36 W
160	Breton, Pertvis (Str.) (pâr-twē'brĕ-tôN') . Fr.	46·18 N	1·43 W
120	Breton Sd. (brĕt'ŭn) La.	29·38 N	89·15 W
149	Breukelen . Neth. (Amsterdam In.)	52·09 N	5·00 E
120	Brevard (brē-värd') NC	35·14 N	82·45 W
135	Breves (brā'vĕzh) Braz.	1·32 S	50·13 W
156	Brevik (brĕ'vĕk) Nor.	59·04 N	9·39 E
203	Brewarrina (brōō-ẽr-rē'nȧ) . . Austl.	29·54 S	146·50 E
98	Brewer (brōō'ẽr) Me.	44·46 N	68·46 W
214	Brewerville Lib.	6·26 N	10·47 W
106	Brewster (brōō'stẽr) NY (New York In.)	41·23 N	73·38 W
127	Brewster, Cerro (Mtn.) (sĕ'r-rô-brōō'stẽr) . Pan.	9·19 N	79·15 W
120	Brewton (brōō'tŭn) Al.	31·06 N	87·04 W
164	Brežice (brĕ'zhĕ-tsĕ) Yugo.	45·55 N	15·37 E
165	Breznik (brĕs'nĕk) Bul.	42·44 N	22·55 E
161	Briancon (brē-äN-sôN') Fr.	44·54 N	6·39 E
160	Briare (brē-är') Fr.	47·40 N	2·46 E
112	Bridal Veil (brīd'ăl vāl) Or. (Portland In.)	45·33 N	122·10 W
128	Bridge Pt. (brĭj) Ba.	25·35 N	76·40 W
120	Bridgeport (brĭj'pôrt) Al.	34·55 N	85·42 W
106	Bridgeport . . . . Ct. (New York In.)	41·12 N	73·12 W
104	Bridgeport Il.	38·40 N	87·45 W
108	Bridgeport Ne.	41·40 N	103·06 W
104	Bridgeport Oh.	40·00 N	80·45 W
106	Bridgeport . . Pa. (Philadelphia In.)	40·06 N	75·21 W
116	Bridgeport Tx.	33·13 N	97·46 W
106	Bridgeton (brĭj'tŭn) Al. (Birmingham In.)	33·27 N	86·39 W
113	Bridgeton . . . . . Mo. (St. Louis In.)	38·45 N	90·23 W
105	Bridgeton NJ	39·30 N	75·15 W
98	Bridgetown Can.	44·51 N	65·18 W
127	Bridgetown (brĭj' toun) . Barb. (In.)	13·08 N	59·37 W
107	Bridgeville (brĭj'vĭl) Pa. (Pittsburgh In.)	40·22 N	80·07 W
203	Bridgewater (brĭj'wô-tẽr) . . . Austl.	42·50 S	147·28 E
98	Bridgewater Can.	44·23 N	64·31 W
148	Bridgnorth (brĭj'nôrth) Eng.	52·32 N	2·25 W
98	Bridgton (brĭj'tŭn) Me.	44·04 N	70·45 W
154	Bridlington (brĭd'lĭng-tŭn) . . . Eng.	54·06 N	0·10 W
161	Brie-Comte-Robert (brē-κôNt-ĕ-rō-bâr') Fr. (Paris In.)	48·42 N	2·37 E
149	Brielle . . . . Neth. (Amsterdam In.)	51·54 N	4·08 E
120	Brierfield (brī'ẽr-fēld) Al.	33·01 N	86·55 W
148	Brierfield (brī'ẽr fēld) Eng.	53·49 N	2·14 W
98	Brier I. (brī'ẽr) Can.	44·16 N	66·24 W
148	Brierley Hill (brī'ẽr-lē hĭl) . . . . Eng.	52·28 N	2·07 W
149	Brieselang (brē'zĕ-läng) G.D.R. (Berlin In.)	52·36 N	12·59 E
161	Briey (brē-ĕ') Fr.	49·15 N	5·57 E
158	Brig (brēg) Switz.	46·17 N	7·59 E
148	Brigg (brĭg) Eng.	53·33 N	0·29 W
113	Brigham City (brĭg'ăm) Ut. (Salt Lake City In.)	41·31 N	112·01 W
148	Brighouse (brĭg'hous) Eng.	53·42 N	1·47 W
203	Bright (brīt) Austl.	36·43 S	147·00 E
107	Bright (brīt) . . In. (Cincinnati In.)	39·13 N	84·51 W
148	Brightlingsea (brī't-lĭng-sē) Eng. (London In.)	51·50 N	1·00 E
106	Brighton (brīt'ŭn) Al. (Birmingham In.)	33·27 N	86·56 W
116	Brighton Co.	39·58 N	104·49 W
154	Brighton Eng.	50·47 N	0·07 W
113	Brighton . . . . Il. (St. Louis In.)	39·03 N	90·08 W
109	Brighton Ia.	41·11 N	91·47 W
162	Brihuega (brē-wā'gä) Sp.	40·32 N	2·52 W
113	Brimley (brĭm'lē) Mi. (Sault Ste. Marie In.)	46·24 N	84·34 W
165	Brindisi (brēn'dē-zē) It.	40·38 N	17·57 E
164	Brinje (brēn'yĕ) Yugo.	45·00 N	15·08 E
117	Brinkley (brĭŋk'lĭ) Ar.	34·52 N	91·12 W
112	Brinnon (brĭn'ŭn) Wa. (Seattle In.)	47·41 N	122·54 W
99	Brion (I.) (brē-ôN') Can.	47·47 N	61·29 W
160	Brioude (brē-ōōd') Fr.	45·18 N	3·22 E
203	Brisbane (brĭz' bān) Austl.	27·30 S	153·10 E
105	Bristol (brĭs'tŭl) Ct.	41·40 N	72·55 W
154	Bristol Eng.	51·29 N	2·39 W
106	Bristol . . . . . Pa. (Philadelphia In.)	40·06 N	74·51 W
106	Bristol . . . . RI (Providence In.)	41·41 N	71·14 W
121	Bristol Tn.	36·35 N	82·10 W
105	Bristol Vt.	44·10 N	73·00 W
121	Bristol Va.	36·36 N	82·00 W
107	Bristol . . . . . . Wi. (Milwaukee In.)	42·32 N	88·04 W
101	Bristol B. Ak.	58·08 N	158·54 W
154	Bristol Chan. Eng.	51·20 N	3·47 W
117	Bristow (brĭs'tō) Ok.	35·50 N	96·25 W
90	British Columbia (Prov.) (brĭt'ĭsh kŏl'ŭm-bĭ-ȧ) . Can.	56·00 N	124·53 W
218	Brits S. Afr. (Johannesburg & Pretoria In.)	25·39 S	27·47 E
212	Britstown (brĭts'toun) . . . . . S. Afr.	30·30 S	23·40 E
109	Britt (brĭt) Ia.	43·05 N	93·47 W
108	Britton (brĭt'ŭn) SD	45·47 N	97·44 W
160	Brive-la-Gaillarde (brēv-lä-gī-yärd'ĕ) . Fr.	45·10 N	1·31 E
162	Briviesca (brē-vyās'kȧ) Sp.	42·34 N	3·21 W
158	Brno (b'r'nô) Czech.	49·18 N	16·37 E
128	Broa, Ensenada de la (B.) (ĕn-sĕ-nä'dä-dĕ-lä-brō'ȧ) . Cuba	22·30 N	82·00 W
184	Broach India	21·47 N	72·58 E
120	Broad (R.) (brôd) Ga.	34·15 N	83·14 W
121	Broad (R.) NC	35·38 N	82·40 W
202	Broadmeadows (brôd'mĕd-ōz) Austl. (Melbourne In.)	37·40 S	144·53 E
107	Broadview Heights (brôd'vū) Oh. (Cleveland In.)	41·18 N	81·41 W
105	Brockport (brŏk'pōrt) NY	43·15 N	77·55 W
99	Brockton (brŏk'tŭn) . . . . Ma. (In.)	42·04 N	71·01 W
97	Brockville (brŏk'vĭl) Can.	44·35 N	75·40 W
111	Brockway (brŏk'wā) Mt.	47·24 N	105·41 W
159	Brodnica (brôd'nĭt-sȧ) Pol.	53·16 N	19·26 E
159	Brody (brô'dĭ) Sov. Un.	50·05 N	25·10 E
117	Broken Arrow (brō'kĕn ăr'ō) . . Ok.	36·03 N	95·48 W
202	Broken B. . . . . Austl. (Sydney In.)	33·34 S	151·20 E
108	Broken Bow (brō'kĕn bō) Ne.	41·24 N	99·37 W
117	Broken Bow Ok.	34·02 N	94·43 W
203	Broken Hill (brōk'ĕn) Austl.	31·55 S	141·35 E
	Broken Hill, see Kabwe		
148	Bromley (brŭm'lĭ) Eng. (London In.)	51·23 N	0·01 E
105	Bromptonville (brŭmp'tŭn-vĭl) Can.	45·30 N	72·00 W
156	Brønderslev (brûn'dẽr-slĕv) . . Den.	57·15 N	9·56 E
218	Bronkhorstspruit S. Afr. (Johannesburg & Pretoria In.)	25·50 S	28·48 E
174	Bronnitsy (brô-nyĭ'tsĭ) Sov. Un. (Moscow In.)	55·26 N	38·16 E

Page	Name Pronunciation Region	Lat. °′	Long. °′
104	Bronson (brŏn'sŭn) Mi.	41·55 N	85·15 W
89	Bronte Cr. Can. (Toronto In.)	43·25 N	79·53 W
121	Brood (R.) (brōōd) SC	34·46 N	81·25 W
107	Brookfield (brŏŏk'fēld) Il. (Chicago In.)	41·49 N	87·51 W
117	Brookfield Mo.	39·45 N	93·04 W
106	Brookhaven (brŏŏk'hāv'n) Ga. (Atlanta In.)	33·52 N	84·21 W
120	Brookhaven Ms.	31·35 N	90·26 W
110	Brookings (brŏŏk'ĭngs) Or.	42·04 N	124·16 W
108	Brookings SD	44·18 N	96·47 W
99	Brookline (brŏŏk'lĭn) Ma. (In.)	42·20 N	71·08 W
99	Brookline NH (In.)	42·44 N	71·37 W
107	Brooklyn (brŏŏk'lĭn) Oh. (Cleveland In.)	41·26 N	81·44 W
113	Brooklyn Center Mn. (Minneapolis, St. Paul In.)	45·05 N	93·21 W
107	Brook Park (brŏŏk) Oh. (Cleveland In.)	41·24 N	81·50 W
93	Brooks Can.	50·35 N	111·53 W
101	Brooks Ra. (brŏŏks) Ak.	68·20 N	159·00 W
121	Brooksville (brŏŏks'vĭl) Fl. (In.)	28·32 N	82·28 W
104	Brookville (brŏŏk'vĭl) In.	39·20 N	85·00 W
105	Brookville Pa.	41·10 N	79·00 W
120	Brookwood (brŏŏk'wŏŏd) Al.	33·15 N	87·17 W
154	Broom (B.) (brōōm) Scot.	57·59 N	5·32 W
204	Broome (brōōm) Austl.	18·00 S	122·15 E
89	Brossard Can. (Montreal In.)	45·26 N	73·28 W
128	Brothers (Is.) (brŭd'hērs) Ba.	26·05 N	79·00 W
158	Broumov (brōō'môf) Czech.	50·33 N	15·55 E
129	Brown Bk. Ba.	21·30 N	74·35 W
116	Brownfield (broun'fēld) Tx.	33·11 N	102·16 W
111	Browning (broun'ĭng) Mt.	48·37 N	113·05 W
107	Brownsboro (brounz'bô-rô) Ky. (Louisville In.)	38·22 N	85·30 W
89	Brownsburg (brouns'bûrg) Can. (Montreal In.)	45·40 N	74·24 W
107	Brownsburg. In. (Indianapolis In.)	39·51 N	86·23 W
112	Brownsmead (brounz'-mēd) Or. (Portland In.)	46·13 N	123·33 W
104	Brownstown (brounz'toun) In.	38·50 N	86·00 W
107	Brownsville (brounz'vĭl) Pa. (Pittsburgh In.)	40·01 N	79·53 W
120	Brownsville Tn.	35·35 N	89·15 W
119	Brownsville Tx.	25·55 N	97·30 W
98	Brownville Junction (broun'vĭl) Me.	45·20 N	69·04 W
118	Brownwood (broun'wŏŏd) Tx.	31·44 N	98·58 W
118	Brownwood (L.) Tx.	31·55 N	99·15 W
162	Brozas (brō'thäs) Sp.	39·37 N	6·44 W
204	Bruce, Mt. (brōōs) Austl.	22·35 S	118·15 E
104	Bruce Pen. Can.	44·50 N	81·20 W
120	Bruceton (brōōs'tŭn) Tn.	36·02 N	88·14 W
158	Bruchsal (brŏŏk'zäl) F.R.G.	49·08 N	8·34 E
158	Bruck (brŏŏk) Aus.	47·25 N	15·14 E
149	Brück (brük) G.D.R. (Berlin In.)	52·12 N	12·45 E
149	Bruck an der Leitha Aus. (Vienna In.)	48·01 N	16·47 E
89	Bruderheim (brōō'dēr-hīm) Can. (Edmonton In.)	53·47 N	112·56 W
155	Brugge Bel.	51·13 N	3·05 E
161	Brühl (brül) F.R.G. (Ruhr In.)	50·49 N	6·54 E
110	Bruneau (R.) (brōō-nō') Id.	42·47 N	115·43 W
196	Brunei (brōō-nī') Asia	4·52 N	113·38 E
161	Brünen (brü'nĕn) F.R.G. (Ruhr In.)	51·43 N	6·41 E
163	Brunete (brōō-nā'tā) Sp. (Madrid In.)	40·24 N	4·00 W
99	Brunette (I.) (brōō-nĕt') Can.	47·16 N	55·54 W
149	Brunn am Gebirge (brōōn'äm gĕ-bĭr'gĕ) Aus. (Vienna In.)	48·07 N	16·18 E
149	Brunsbüttelkoog (brōōns'büt-tĕl-kōg) F.R.G. (Hamburg In.)	53·58 N	9·10 E
121	Brunswick (brŭnz'wĭk) Ga.	31·08 N	81·30 W
98	Brunswick Me.	43·54 N	69·57 W
105	Brunswick Md.	39·20 N	77·35 W
117	Brunswick Mo.	39·25 N	93·07 W
107	Brunswick Oh. (Cleveland In.)	41·14 N	81·50 W
136	Brunswick, Pen. de Chile	53·25 S	71·15 W
205	Bruny (I.) (brōō'nē) Austl.	43·30 S	147·50 E
116	Brush (brŭsh) Co.	40·14 N	103·40 W
136	Brusque (brōō's-kōōĕ) Braz.	27·15 S	48·45 W
113	Brussels (brŭs'ĕls) Il. (St. Louis In.)	38·57 N	90·36 W
	Brussels, see Bruxelles		
149	Bruxelles (Brussels) (brü-sĕl') (brŭs'ĕls). Bel. (Brussels In.)	50·51 N	4·21 E
104	Bryan (brī'ăn) Oh.	41·25 N	84·30 W
119	Bryan Tx.	30·40 N	96·22 W
166	Bryansk (b'r-yänsk') Sov. Un.	53·12 N	34·23 E
166	Bryansk (Oblast) Sov. Un.	52·43 N	32·25 E
108	Bryant (brī'ănt) SD	44·35 N	97·29 W
112	Bryant Wa. (Seattle In.)	48·14 N	122·10 W
115	Bryce Canyon Natl. Park (brīs) Ut.	37·35 N	112·15 W
106	Bryn Mawr (brĭn mâr') Pa. (Philadelphia In.)	40·02 N	75·20 W
120	Bryson City (brīs'ŭn) NC	35·25 N	83·25 W
167	Bryukhovetskaya (b'ryŭk'ō-vyĕt-skä'yä). Sov. Un.	45·56 N	38·58 E
183	Buatan Indon. (Singapore In.)	0·45 N	101·49 E
210	Buba (bōō'bȧ) Guinea-Bissau	11·39 N	14·58 W
134	Bucaramanga (bōō-kä'rä-mäŋ'gä) Col.	7·12 N	73·14 W
197	Bucay (bōō-kī') Phil. (In.)	17·32 N	120·42 E
204	Buccaneer Arch. (bŭk-ȧ-nēr') Austl.	16·05 S	122·00 E
159	Buchach (bōō'chȧch) Sov. Un.	49·04 N	25·25 E
214	Buchanan (bû-kăn'ăn) Lib.	5·57 N	10·02 W
104	Buchanan Mi.	41·50 N	86·25 W
205	Buchanan (L.) (bû-kân'nŏn). Austl.	21·40 S	145·00 E
118	Buchanan (L.) (bû-kăn'ăn) Tx.	30·55 N	98·40 W
99	Buchans Can.	48·49 N	56·52 W
	Bucharest, see Bucureşti		
149	Buchholtz (bōōk'hōltz) F.R.G. (Hamburg In.)	53·19 N	9·53 E
107	Buck Cr. (bŭk) In. (Indianapolis In.)	39·43 N	85·58 W
105	Buckhannon (bŭk-hăn'ŭn) WV	39·00 N	80·10 W
154	Buckhaven (bŭk-hā'v'n) Scot.	56·10 N	3·10 W
154	Buckie (bŭk'ĭ) Scot.	57·40 N	2·50 W
89	Buckingham (bŭk'ĭng-ăm) Can. (Ottawa In.)	45·35 N	75·25 W
184	Buckingham (R.) (bŭk'ĭng-ăm) India	15·18 N	79·50 E
89	Buckland (bŭk'lănd) Can. (Quebec In.)	46·37 N	70·33 W
205	Buckland Tableland (Reg.) Austl.	24·31 S	148·00 E
112	Buckley (buk'lē). Wa. (Seattle In.)	47·10 N	122·02 W
98	Bucksport (bŭks'pôrt) Me.	44·35 N	68·47 W
98	Buctouche (bük-tōōsh') Can.	46·28 N	64·43 W
165	Bucureşti (Bucharest) (bōō-kōō-rĕsh'tĭ) (bōō-kȧ-rĕst'). Rom.	44·23 N	26·10 E
104	Bucyrus (bû-sī'rŭs) Oh.	40·50 N	82·55 W
159	Budapest (bōō'dȧ-pĕsht') Hung.	47·30 N	19·05 E
161	Büderich (bü'dĕ-rēĸ) F.R.G. (Ruhr In.)	51·15 N	6·41 E
184	Budge Budge India (In.)	22·28 N	88·08 E
216	Budjala Zaire	2·39 N	19·42 E
215	Buea Cam.	4·09 N	9·14 E
107	Buechel (bĕ-chûl') Ky. (Louisville In.)	38·12 N	85·38 W
161	Bueil (bwā') Fr. (Paris In.)	48·55 N	1·27 E
113	Buena Park (bwā'nȧ pärk) Ca. (Los Angeles In.)	33·52 N	118·00 W
134	Buenaventura (bwā'nä-vĕn-tōō'rȧ) Col.	3·46 N	77·09 W
129	Buenaventura Cuba (In.)	22·49 N	82·22 W
134	Buenaventura, Bahia de (B.) (bä-ē'ä-dĕ-bwā'nä-vĕn-tōō'rȧ) Col.	3·45 N	79·23 W
116	Buena Vista (bū'nȧ vĭs'tȧ) Co.	38·51 N	106·07 W
120	Buena Vista Ga.	32·15 N	84·30 W
105	Buena Vista Va.	37·45 N	79·20 W
128	Buena Vista, Bahía (B.) (bä-ē'ä-bwĕ-nä-vē's-tä). Cuba	22·30 N	79·10 W
114	Buena Vista Lake Res. (bū'nȧ vĭs'tȧ). Ca.	35·14 N	119·17 W
162	Buendia (Res.) Sp.	40·30 N	2·45 W
136	Buenos Aires (bwā'nōs ī'rās) Arg.	34·20 S	58·30 W
134	Buenos Aires Col. (In.)	3·01 N	76·34 W
127	Buenos Aires C. R.	9·10 N	83·21 W
136	Buenos Aires (Prov.) Arg.	36·15 S	61·45 W
136	Buenos Aires (L.) Arg.-Chile	46·30 S	72·15 W
161	Buer (bür) F.R.G. (Ruhr In.)	51·35 N	7·03 E
109	Buffalo (buf'ȧ lō) Mn.	45·10 N	93·50 W
107	Buffalo NY (Buffalo In.)	42·54 N	78·51 W
119	Buffalo Tx.	31·28 N	96·04 W
111	Buffalo Wy.	44·19 N	106·42 W
117	Buffalo (R.) Ar.	35·56 N	92·58 W
213	Buffalo (R.) S. Afr. (Natal In.)	28·35 S	30·27 E
120	Buffalo (R.) Tn.	35·24 N	87·10 W
119	Buffalo Bayou Tx. (In.)	29·46 N	95·32 W
109	Buffalo Cr. Mn.	44·46 N	94·28 W
90	Buffalo Head Hills Can.	57·16 N	116·18 W
89	Buford (bū'fūrd) Can. (Edmonton In.)	53·15 N	113·55 W
120	Buford (bū'fērd) Ga.	34·05 N	84·00 W
159	Bug (R.) (bōōg) Pol.	52·29 N	21·20 E
167	Bug (R.) (bōōk) Sov. Un.	48·12 N	30·13 E
134	Buga (bōō'gä) Col. (In.)	3·54 N	76·17 W
149	Buggenhout Bel. (Brussels In.)	51·01 N	4·10 E
121	Buggs Island L. NC-Va.	36·30 N	78·38 W
164	Bugojno (bōō-gō ĭ nô) Yugo.	44·03 N	17·28 E
170	Bugul'ma (bōō-gōōl'mȧ) Sov. Un.	54·40 N	52·40 E
170	Buguruslan (bōō-gōō-rōōs-lán') Sov. Un.	53·30 N	52·32 E
197	Buhi (bōō'ē) Phil. (In.)	13·26 N	123·31 E
110	Buhl (būl) Id.	42·36 N	114·45 W
109	Buhl Mn.	47·28 N	92·49 W
137	Buin (bōō-ēn') Chile (Santiago In.)	33·44 S	70·44 W
171	Buinaksk (bōō'ē-näksk) Sov. Un.	42·40 N	47·20 E
162	Bujalance (bōō-hä-län'thā) Sp.	37·54 N	4·22 W
217	Bujumbura Burundi	3·23 S	29·22 E
212	Bukama (bōō-kä'mä) Zaire	9·08 S	26·00 E
217	Bukavu Zaire	2·30 S	28·52 E
147	Bukhara (bōō-kä'rä) Sov. Un.	39·31 N	64·22 E
183	Bukitbatu Indon. (Singapore In.)	1·25 N	101·58 E
196	Bukittingg Indon.	0·25 S	100·28 E
217	Bukoba Tan.	1·20 S	31·49 E
159	Bukovina (Reg.) (bōō-kô'vĭ-nȧ) Sov. Un.	48·06 N	25·20 E
197	Bula (bōō'lä) Indon.	3·00 S	130·30 E
197	Bulalacao (bōō-lȧ-lä'kä-ō) Phil. (In.)	12·32 N	121·25 E
212	Bulawayo (bōō-lȧ-wä'yō) Rh.	20·12 S	28·43 E
101	Buldir (I.) (bŭl dĭr) Ak.	52·22 N	175·50 E
146	Bulgaria (bōōl-gā'rĭ-ă) Eur.	42·12 N	24·13 E
92	Bulkley Ra. (bŭlk'lē) Can.	54·30 N	127·30 W
162	Bullaque (R.) (bōō-lä'kȧ) Sp.	39·15 N	4·13 W
162	Bullas (bōōl'yäs) Sp.	38·07 N	1·48 W
115	Bulldog Cr. (bŭl'dŏg') Ut.	37·45 N	110·55 W
92	Bull Harbour (hăr'bēr) Can.	50·45 N	127·55 W
128	Bull Head (Mtn.) Jam.	18·10 N	77·15 W
205	Bulloo (R.) (bŭ-lōō') Austl.	25·23 S	143·30 E
112	Bull Run (R.) (bōōl) Or. (Portland In.)	45·26 N	122·11 W
112	Bull Run Res. Or. (Portland In.)	45·29 N	122·11 W
117	Bull Shoals Res. (bōōl shōlz) Ar.-Mo.	36·35 N	92·57 W
218	Bulo Burti (bōō'lō bōōr'tĭ) Som. (Horn of Afr. In.)	3·53 N	45·30 E
148	Bulphan (bōōl'făn) Eng. (London In.)	51·33 N	0·21 E
218	Bultfontein (bōōlt'fōn-tān') S. Afr. (Johannesburg & Pretoria In.)	28·18 S	26·10 E
173	Bulun (bōō-lōōn') Sov. Un.	70·48 N	127·27 E
216	Bulungu (bōō-lōōŋ'gōō) Zaire	6·04 S	21·54 E
213	Bulwer (bōōl-wēr) S. Afr. (Natal In.)	29·49 S	29·48 E
216	Bumba (bōōm'bȧ) Zaire	2·11 N	22·28 E
217	Bumire I. Tan.	1·40 S	32·05 E
197	Buna (bōō'nȧ) Pap. N. Gui.	8·58 S	148·38 E
204	Bunbury (bŭn'bŭrĭ) Austl.	33·25 S	115·45 E
203	Bundaberg (bŭn'dȧ-bûrg) Austl.	24·45 S	152·18 E
195	Bungo-Suidō (Chan.) (bōōŋ'gō sōō-ē'dō). Jap.	33·26 N	131·54 E
217	Bunia Zaire	1·34 N	30·15 E
113	Bunker Hill (bŭnk'ēr hĭl) Il. (St. Louis In.)	39·03 N	89·57 W
119	Bunkie (bŭŋ'kĭ) La.	30·55 N	92·10 W
217	Bun Plns. Ken.	0·55 N	40·35 E
215	Bununu Dass Nig.	10·00 N	9·31 E
173	Buor-Khaya, Guba (B.) Sov. Un.	71·45 N	131·00 E
173	Buor Khaya, Mys (C.) Sov. Un.	71·47 N	133·22 E
217	Bura Ken.	1·06 S	39·57 E
218	Buran (bûr'ăn) Som. (Horn of Afr. In.)	10·38 N	48·30 E
218	Burao Som. (Horn of Afr. In.)	9·20 N	45·45 E
186	Buraydah Sau. Ar.	26·23 N	44·14 E
113	Burbank (bûr'bănk) Ca. (Los Angeles In.)	34·11 N	118·19 W
205	Burdekin (R.) (bûr'dē-kĭn). Austl.	19·22 S	145·07 E
171	Burdur (bōōr-dōōr') Tur.	37·50 N	30·15 E
184	Burdwān (bōōrd-wän') India	23·29 N	87·53 E
173	Bureinskiy, Khrebet (Mts.) Sov. Un.	51·15 N	133·30 E
173	Bureya (bōōrā'ȧ) Sov. Un.	49·55 N	130·00 E
173	Bureya (R.) (bōō-rā'yä) Sov. Un.	51·00 N	130·14 E
148	Burford (bûr-fērd) Eng. (London In.)	51·46 N	1·38 W
115	Burford (L.) NM	36·37 N	107·21 W
165	Burgas (bōōr-gäs') Bul.	42·29 N	27·30 E
153	Burgaski Zaliv (G.) Bul.	42·30 N	27·40 E
213	Bur Gavo Som.	1·14 S	41·47 E
121	Burgaw (bûr'gô) NC	34·31 N	77·56 W
158	Burgdorf (bōōrg'dôrf) Switz.	47·04 N	7·37 E
149	Burgenland (State) Aus. (Vienna In.)	47·58 N	16·57 E
99	Burgeo Can.	47·36 N	57·34 W
105	Burgess Va.	37·53 N	76·21 W
118	Burgos (bōōr'gōs) Mex.	24·57 N	98·47 W
197	Burgos Phil. (In.)	16·03 N	119·52 E
162	Burgos (bōō'r-gôs) Sp.	42·20 N	3·44 W
156	Burgsvik (bōōrgs'vĭk) Swe.	57·04 N	18·18 E
184	Burhānpur (bōōr'hän-pōōr). India	21·26 N	76·08 E
197	Burias I. (bōō'rē-äs) Phil. (In.)	12·56 N	122·56 E
197	Burias Pass (bōō'rē-äs). Phil. (In.)	13 04 N	123·11 E
127	Burica, Punta (Pt.) (pōō'n-tä-bōō'rē-kä). Pan.	8·02 N	83·12 W
112	Burien (bŭ'rĭ-ĕn). Wa. (Seattle In.)	47·28 N	122·20 W
99	Burin (bûr'ĭn) Can.	47·02 N	55·10 W
99	Burin Pen. Can.	47·00 N	55·40 W
116	Burkburnett (bûrk-bûr'nĕt) Tx.	34·04 N	98·35 W
105	Burke (bûrk) Vt.	44·40 N	72·00 W
92	Burke Chan. Can.	52·07 N	127·38 W
204	Burketown (bûrk'toun) Austl.	17·50 S	139·30 E
111	Burley (bûr'lĭ) Id.	42·31 N	113·48 W
112	Burley Wa. (Seattle In.)	47·25 N	122·38 W
174	Burli Sov. Un. (Urals In.)	53·36 N	61·55 E
112	Burlingame (bûr'lĭn-găm) Ca. (San Francisco In.)	37·35 N	122·22 W
117	Burlingame Ks.	38·45 N	95·49 W
89	Burlington (bûr'lĭng-tŭn) Can. (Toronto In.)	43·19 N	79·48 W
116	Burlington Co.	39·17 N	102·26 W
109	Burlington Ia.	40·48 N	91·05 W
117	Burlington Ks.	38·10 N	95·46 W
107	Burlington Ky. (Cincinnati In.)	39·01 N	84·44 W
99	Burlington Ma. (In.)	42·31 N	71·13 W
106	Burlington NJ (Philadelphia In.)	40·04 N	74·52 W
121	Burlington NC	36·05 N	79·26 W
105	Burlington Vt.	44·30 N	73·15 W
112	Burlington Wa. (Seattle In.)	48·28 N	122·20 W
107	Burlington Wi. (Milwaukee In.)	42·41 N	88·16 W
182	Burma (bûr'mȧ) Asia	21·00 N	95·15 E
92	Burnaby Can.	49·14 N	122·58 W
118	Burnet (bûrn'ĕt) Tx.	30·46 N	98·14 W
148	Burnham on Crouch (bûrn'ăm-ŏn-krouch) Eng. (London In.)	51·38 N	0·48 E
203	Burnie (bûr'nē) Austl.	41·15 S	146·05 E
148	Burnley (bûrn'lē) Eng.	53·47 N	2·19 W
110	Burns (bûrnz) Or.	43·35 N	119·05 W
120	Burnside (bûrn'sīd) Ky.	36·57 N	84·33 W
92	Burns Lake (bûrnz lăk) Can.	54·14 N	125·46 W
98	Burnsville (bûrnz'vĭl) Can.	47·44 N	65·07 W
110	Burnt R. (bûrnt) Or.	44·26 N	117·53 W
95	Burntwood (R.) Can.	55·53 N	97·30 W
112	Burrard Inlet (bûr'ărd) Can. (Vancouver In.)	49·19 N	123·15 W
163	Burriana (bōōr-rē-ä'nä) Sp.	39·53 N	0·05 W
171	Bursa (bōōr'sȧ) Tur.	40·10 N	28·10 E
211	Būr Safājah Egypt	26·57 N	33·56 E
218	Būr Sa'īd (Port Said) Egypt (Suez In.)	31·15 N	32·19 E
161	Burscheid (bōōr'shīd) F.R.G. (Ruhr In.)	51·05 N	7·07 E
211	Būr Sūdān (Port Sudan) (sōō-dän'). Sud.	19·30 N	37·10 E
107	Burt (bûrt) NY (Buffalo In.)	43·19 N	78·45 W
104	Burt (L.) (bûrt) Mi.	45·25 N	84·45 W

ăt; finăl; rāte; senâte; ärm; ȧsk; sofȧ; fâre; ch-choose; dh-as th in other; bē; ēvent; bĕt; recĕnt; cratēr; g-go; gh-guttural g; bĭt; ĭ-short neutral; rīde; ĸ-guttural k as ch in German ich;

Page Name Pronunciation Region Lat. °′ Long. °′

112 Burton (bûr'tŭn). Wa. (Seattle In.) 47·24 N 122·28 W
148 Burton-on-Trent (bŭr'tŭn-ŏn-trĕnt). Eng. 52·48 N 1·37 W
120 Burton Res. Ga. 34·46 N 83·40 W
106 Burtonsville (bûrtŏns-vĭl) Md. (Baltimore In.) 39·07 N 76·57 W
197 Buru (I.) Indon. 3·30 S 126·30 E
218 Burullus (L.) Egypt (Nile In.) 31·20 N 30·58 E
197 Buruncan Pt. (bōō-rōōn'kän) Phil. (In.) 12·11 N 121·23 E
209 Burundi Afr. 3·00 S 29·30 E
108 Burwell (bûr'wĕl) Ne. 41·46 N 99·08 W
148 Bury (bĕr'ĭ) Eng. 53·36 N 2·17 W
173 Buryat A.S.S.R. Sov. Un. 55·15 N 112·00 E
155 Bury St. Edmunds (bĕr'ĭ-sānt ĕd'mŭndz). Eng. 52·14 N 0·44 E
136 Burzaco (bōōr-zá'kô) Arg. (Buenos Aires In.) 34·35 S 58·23 W
217 Busanga Swp. Zambia 14·10 S 25·50 E
218 Būsh (bōōsh) Egypt (Nile In.) 29·13 N 31·08 E
186 Būshehr Iran 28·48 N 50·53 E
212 Bushmanland (Reg.) (bōōsh-măn lănd). S. Afr. 29·15 S 18·45 E
117 Bushnell (bōōsh'nĕl) Il. 40·33 N 90·28 W
216 Businga (bōō-sĭŋ'gȧ) Zaire 3·20 N 20·53 E
216 Busira (R.) Zaire 0·05 S 19·20 E
159 Busk (bōō'sk) Sov. Un. 49·58 N 24·39 E
204 Busselton (bŭs'l-tŭn) Austl. 33·40 S 115·30 E
149 Bussum Neth. (Amsterdam In.) 52·16 N 5·10 E
118 Bustamante (bōōs-tä-män'tȧ). Mex. 26·34 N 100·30 W
164 Busto Arsizio (bōōs'tō är-sēd'zē-ō). It 45·47 N 8·51 E
197 Busuanga (I.) (bōō-swäŋ'gä) Phil. (In.) 12·20 N 119·43 E
216 Buta (bōō'tȧ) Zaire 2·48 N 24·44 E
213 Butha Buthe (bōō-thȧ-bōō'thȧ) Leso. (Natal In.) 28·49 S 28·16 E
120 Butler (bŭt'lēr) Al. 32·05 N 88·10 W
104 Butler In. 41·25 N 84·50 W
106 Butler Md. (Baltimore In.) 39·32 N 76·46 W
106 Butler NJ (New York In.) 41·00 N 74·20 W
105 Butler Pa. 40·50 N 79·55 W
174 Butovo (bōō-tô'vô) Sov. Un. (Moscow In.) 55·33 N 37·36 E
217 Butsha Zaire 0·57 N 29·13 E
120 Buttahatchie (R.) (bŭt-ȧ-hăch'ē) Al.-Ms. 34·02 N 88·05 W
111 Butte (būt) Mt. 46·00 N 112·31 W
213 Butterworth (bŭ tēr'wûrth) S. Afr. (Natal In.) 32·20 S 28·09 E
154 Butt of Lewis (C.) (bŭt ŏv lū'ĭs) Scot. 58·34 N 6·15 W
197 Butuan (bōō-tōō'än) Phil. 8·40 N 125·33 E
196 Butung (I.) Indon. 5·00 S 122·55 E
167 Buturlinovka (bōō-tōō'lē-nôf'ka) Sov. Un. 50·47 N 40·35 E
149 Buxtehude (bōōks-tē-hōō'dē) F.R.G. (Hamburg In.) 53·29 N 9·42 E
148 Buxton (bŭks't'n) Eng. 53·15 N 1·55 W
112 Buxton Or. (Portland In.) 45·41 N 123·11 W
170 Buy (bwē) Sov. Un. 58·30 N 41·48 E
192 Buyr Nuur (L.) (bōō'yĕr nôr) China-Mong. 47·50 N 117·00 E
165 Buzău (bōō-zĕ'ōō) Rom. 45·09 N 26·51 E
167 Buzău (R.) Rom. 45·17 N 27·22 E
211 Buzaymah Libya 25·14 N 22·13 E
171 Buzuluk (bōō-zōō-lōōk') Sov. Un. 52·50 N 52·10 E
217 Bwendi Zaire 4·01 N 26·41 E
165 Byala Bul. 43·26 N 25·44 E
Byblos, see Jubayl
159 Bydgoszcz (bĭd'gôshch) Pol. 53·07 N 18·00 E
104 Byesville (bīz-vĭl) Oh. 39·55 N 81·35 W
156 Bygdin (L.) (bügh-dēn') Nor. 61·24 N 8·31 E
156 Byglandsfjord (bügh'lănds-fyôr) Nor. 58·40 N 7·49 E
166 Bykhovo (bĭ-kô'vô) Sov. Un. 53·32 N 30·15 E
174 Bykovo (bĭ-kô'vô) Sov. Un. (Moscow In.) 55·38 N 38·05 E
172 Byrranga, Gory (Mts.) Sov. Un. 74·15 N 94·28 E
173 Bytantay (R.) (byän'tāy). Sov. Un. 68·15 N 132·15 E
159 Bytom (bĭ'tŭm) Pol. 50·21 N 18·55 E
166 Bytosh' (bĭ-tôsh') Sov. Un. 53·48 N 34·06 E
159 Bytow (bĭ'tŭf) Pol. 54·10 N 17·30 E

C

136 Caazapá (kä-zä-pä') Par. 26·14 S 56·18 W
197 Cabagan (kä-bä-gän') Phil. (In.) 17·27 N 121·50 E
197 Cabalete (I.) (kä-bä-lā'tȧ) Phil. (In.) 14·19 N 122·00 E
128 Caballones, Canal de (Chan.) (kä-nä'l-dĕ-kä-bäl-yô'nĕs). Cuba 20·45 N 79·20 W
115 Caballo Res. (kä-bä-lyō') NM 33·00 N 107·20 W
162 Cabañaquinta (kä-bän-yä-kē'n-tä) Sp. 43·10 N 5·37 W
197 Cabanatuan (kä-bä-nä-twän') Phil. (In.) 15·30 N 120·56 E
98 Cabano (kä-bä-nō') Can. 47·41 N 68·54 W
197 Cabarruyan (I.) (kä-bä-rōō'yän) Phil. (In.) 16·21 N 120·10 E
135 Cabedelo (kä-bē-dā'lōō) Braz. 6·58 S 34·49 W
125 Cabeza, Arrecife (Reef) (är-rĕ-sē'fĕ-kä-bĕ-zä). Mex. 19·07 N 95·52 W
162 Cabeza del Buey (kȧ-bā'thä dĕl bwā'). Sp. 38·43 N 5·18 W
134 Cabimas (kä-bē'mäs) Ven. 10·21 N 71·27 W
209 Cabinda (kä-bĭn'dȧ) Ang. 5·10 S 10·00 E
216 Cabinda Ang. 5·33 S 12·12 E
110 Cabinet Mts. (kăb'ĭ-nĕt) Mt. 48·13 N 115·52 W
137 Cabo Frio (kä'bô-frē'ô) Braz. (Rio de Janeiro In.) 22·53 S 42·02 W
137 Cabo Frio, Ilha do (ē'lä-dô-kä'bô frē'ô). Braz. (Rio de Janeiro In.) 23·01 S 42·00 W
97 Cabonga Res. Can. 47·25 N 76·35 W
104 Cabot Hd. (kăb'ŭt) Can. 45·15 N 81·20 W
99 Cabot Str. (kăb'ŭt) Can. 47·35 N 60·00 W
162 Cabra (käb'rä) Sp. 37·28 N 4·29 W
197 Cabra (I.) Phil. (In.) 13·55 N 119·55 E
163 Cabrera (I.) (kä-brā'rä) Sp. 39·08 N 2·57 E
162 Cabriel (R.) (kä-brē-ĕl') Sp. 39·25 N 1·20 W
114 Cabrillo Natl. Mon. (kä-brēl'yō) Ca. (In.) 32·41 N 117·03 W
135 Cabrobo' (kä-brō-bô') Braz. 8·34 S 39·13 W
136 Cabuçu (R.) (kä-bōō'-sōō) Braz. (Rio de Janeiro In.) 22·57 S 43·36 W
197 Cabugao (kä-bōō'gä-ô) Phil. (In.) 17·48 N 120·28 E
165 Čačak (chä'chȧk) Yugo. 43·51 N 20·22 E
137 Caçapava (kä'sä-pá'vȧ) Braz. (Rio de Janeiro In.) 23·05 S 45·52 W
135 Cáceres (ká'sĕ-rĕs) Braz. 16·11 S 57·32 W
162 Cáceres (ká'thā-rās) Sp. 39·28 N 6·20 W
137 Cachapoal (R.) (kä-chä-pô-ä'l) Chile (Santiago In.) 34·23 S 70·19 W
137 Cacharí (kä-chä-rē') Arg. (Buenos Aires In.) 36·23 S 59·29 W
117 Cache (R.) (kăsh) Ar. 35·24 N 91·12 W
93 Cache Creek Can. 50·48 N 121·19 W
114 Cache Cr. (kăsh) Ca. 38·53 N 122·24 W
116 Cache la Poudre (R.) (kăsh lá pōōd'r'). Co. 40·43 N 105·39 W
136 Cachi, Nevados de (Pk.) (nĕ-vá'dôs-dĕ-kȧ'chē). Arg. 25·05 S 66·40 W
136 Cachinal (kä-chē-näl') Chile 24·57 S 69·33 W
135 Cachoeira (kä-shô-ā'rä) Braz. 12·32 S 38·47 W
136 Cachoeirá do Sul (kä-shô-ā'rä-dô-sōō'l). Braz. 30·02 S 52·49 W
137 Cachoeiras de Macacu (kä-shô-ā'räs-dĕ-mä-kȧ'kōō) Braz. (Rio de Janeiro In.) 22·28 S 42·39 W
137 Cachoeiro de Itapemirim (kä-shô-ā'rô-dĕ-ē'tä-pĕmē-rē'N) Braz. (Rio de Janeiro In.) 20·51 S 41·06 W
216 Cacolo Ang. 10·07 S 19·17 E
216 Caconda (kä-kōn'dä) Ang. 13·43 S 15·06 E
98 Cacouna Can. 47·54 N 69·31 W
216 Cacula Ang. 14·29 S 14·10 E
119 Caddo (L.) (kăd'ō) La.-Tx. 32·37 N 94·15 W
124 Cadereyta (kä-dȧ-rā'tä) Mex. 20·42 N 99·47 W
118 Cadereyta Jimenez (kä-dä-rā'tä hē-mā'nāz). Mex. 25·36 N 99·59 W
163 Cadi, Sierra de (Mts.) (sē-ĕ'r-rä-dĕ-kä'dē). Sp. 42·17 N 1·34 E
197 Cadig, Mt. (kä'dēg) Phil. (In.) 14·11 N 122·26 E
104 Cadillac (kăd'ĭ-lăk) Mi. 44·15 N 85·25 W
114 Cadiz (kā'dĭz) Ca. 34·33 N 115·30 W
104 Cadiz Oh. 40·15 N 81·00 W
162 Cádiz (ká'dēz) Sp. 36·34 N 6·20 W
162 Cádiz, Golfo de (G.) (gôl-fô-dĕ-kȧ'dēz). Sp. 36·50 N 7·00 W
160 Caen (käN) Fr. 49·13 N 0·22 W
154 Caernarfon Wales 53·08 N 4·17 W
154 Caernarfon B. Wales 53·09 N 4·56 W
137 Caeté (kä'ĕ-tĕ') Braz. (Rio de Janeiro In.) 19·53 S 43·41 W
135 Caetité (kä-ȧ-tê-tā') Braz. 14·02 S 42·14 W
197 Cagayan (kä-gä-yän') Phil. 8·13 N 124·30 E
196 Cagayan (R.) Phil. 16·45 N 121·55 E
196 Cagayan Is. Phil. 9·40 N 120·30 E
196 Cagayan Sulu (I.) (kä-gä-yän sōō'lōō). Phil. 7·00 N 118·30 E
164 Cagli (käl'yē) It. 43·35 N 12·40 E
164 Cagliari (käl'yä-rē) It. 39·16 N 9·08 E
164 Cagliari, Golfo di (G.) (gôl-fô-dē-käl'yä-rē). It. 39·08 N 9·12 E
161 Cagnes (kän'y') Fr. 43·40 N 7·14 E
135 Cagua (kä'-gwä) Ven. (In.) 10·12 N 67·27 W
123 Caguas (kä'gwäs) P. R. (Puerto Rico In.) 18·12 N 66·01 W
120 Cahaba (R.) (kȧ hä-bä) Al. 32·50 N 87·15 W
216 Cahama (kä-ȧ'mä) Ang. 16·17 S 14·19 E
113 Cahokia (kȧ-hō'kĭ-ȧ) Il. (St. Louis In.) 38·34 N 90·11 W
217 Cahora-Bassa (Gorge) Moz. 15·40 S 32·50 E
160 Cahors (kȧ-ôr') Fr. 44·27 N 1·27 E
125 Cahuacán (kä-wä-kä'n). Mex. (In.) 19·38 N 99·25 W
127 Cahuita, Punta (Pt.) (pōō'n-tä-kä-wē'tȧ). C. R. 9·47 N 82·41 W
135 Caiapó, Serra do (Mts.) (sĕ'r-rä-dô-kä-yä-pô'). Braz. 17·52 S 52·37 W
128 Caibarién (kī-bä-rē-ĕn') Cuba 22·35 N 79·30 W
134 Caicedonia (kī-sĕ-dô-nēä) Col. (In.) 4·21 N 75·48 W
129 Caicos Bk. (kī'kōs) Ba. 21·35 N 72·00 W
129 Caicos Is. Turks & Caicos Is. 21·45 N 71·50 W
129 Caicos Passage (Str.) Ba. 21·55 N 72·45 W
119 Caillou B. (kȧ-yōō') La. 29·07 N 91·00 W
129 Caimanera (kī-mä-nā'rä) Cuba 20·00 N 75·10 W
197 Caiman Pt. (kī'măn) Phil. (In.) 15·56 N 119·33 E
122 Caimito, (R.) (kä-ē-mē'tô) Pan. (In.) 8·50 N 79·45 W
129 Caimito del Guayabal (kä-ē-mē'tô-dĕl-gwä-yä-bä'l) Cuba (In.) 22·42 N 82·36 W
205 Cairns (kârnz) Austl. 17·02 S 145·49 E
127 Cairo (kī'-rô) C. R. 10·06 N 83·47 W
Cairo, see Al Qāhirah
120 Cairo (kā'rō) Ga. 30·48 N 84·12 W
117 Cairo Il. 36·59 N 89·11 W
148 Caistor (kâs'tēr) Eng. 53·30 N 0·20 W
216 Caiundo Ang. 15·46 S 17·28 E
134 Cajamarca (kä-ĸä-mȧ'r-kä) Col. (In.) 4·25 N 75·25 W
134 Cajamarca (kä-hä-mär'kä) Peru 7·16 S 78·30 W
197 Cajidiocan (kä-hē-dyô'kän) Phil. (In.) 12·22 N 122·41 E
165 Čajniče (chī'nĭ-chĕ) Yugo. 43·32 N 19·04 E
113 Cajon (kȧ-hōn') Ca. (Los Angeles In.) 34·18 N 117·28 W
137 Cajuru (kȧ-zhōō'-rōō) Braz. (Rio de Janeiro In.) 21·17 S 47·17 W
164 Čakovec (chȧ'kō-vĕts) Yugo. 46·23 N 16·27 E
213 Cala (cä-lȧ) S. Afr. (Natal In.) 31·33 S 27·41 E
215 Calabar (kăl-ȧ-bär') Nig. 4·57 N 8·19 E
129 Calabazar (kä-lä-bä-zä'r) Cuba (In.) 23·02 N 82·25 W
134 Calabozo (kä-lä-bō'zō) Ven. 8·48 N 67·27 W
164 Calabria (Reg.) (kä-lä'brē-ä) It. 39·26 N 16·23 E
165 Calafat (kȧ-lȧ-fȧt') Rom. 43·59 N 22·56 E
197 Calagua Is. (kä-läg'wä). Phil. (In.) 14·30 N 123·06 E
89 Calahoo (kă-lȧ-hōō') Can. (Edmonton In.) 53·42 N 113·58 W
162 Calahorra (kä-lä-ôr'rä) Sp. 42·18 N 1·58 W
160 Calais (kȧ-lĕ') Fr. 50·56 N 1·51 E
98 Calais Me. 45·11 N 67·15 W
136 Calama (kä-lä'mä) Chile 22·17 S 68·58 W
134 Calamar (kä-lä-mär') Col. 10·24 N 75·00 W
134 Calamar Col. 1·55 N 72·33 W
197 Calamba (kä-läm'bä) Phil. (In.) 14·12 N 121·10 E
196 Calamian Group (Is.) (kä-lä-myän'). Phil. 12·14 N 118·38 E
162 Calañas (kä-län'yäs) Sp. 37·41 N 6·52 W
197 Calapan (kä-lä-pän') Phil. (In.) 13·25 N 121·11 E
153 Călărasi (kŭ-lŭ-rash'ĭ) Rom. 44·09 N 27·20 E
162 Calasparra (kä-lä-spär'rä) Sp. 38·13 N 1·40 W
162 Calatayud (kä-lä-tä-yōōdh') Sp. 41·23 N 1·37 W
197 Calauag (kä-lä-wäg') Phil. (In.) 13·56 N 122·16 E
197 Calauag B. Phil. (In.) 14·07 N 122·10 E
112 Calaveras Res. (kăl-ȧ-vĕr'ăs) Ca. (San Francisco In.) 37·29 N 121·47 W
197 Calavite, C. (kä-lä-vē'tā) Phil. (In.) 13·29 N 120·00 E
119 Calcasieu (R.) (kăl'kȧ-shū) La. 30·22 N 93·08 W
119 Calcasieu L. La. 29·58 N 93·08 W
184 Calcutta (kăl-kŭt'ȧ) India (In.) 22·32 N 88·22 E
134 Caldas (kȧ'l-däs) Col. (In.) 6·06 N 75·38 W
134 Caldas (Dept.) Col. (In.) 5·20 N 75·38 W
162 Caldas de Rainha (käl'däs dä rīn'yȧ). Port. 39·25 N 9·08 W
148 Calder (R.) (kôl'dēr) Eng. 53·39 N 1·30 W
136 Caldera (käl-dā'rä) Chile 27·02 S 70·53 W
148 Calder Can. Eng. 53·48 N 2·25 W
110 Caldwell (kôld'wĕl) Id. 43·40 N 116·43 W
117 Caldwell Ks. 37·04 N 97·36 W
104 Caldwell Oh. 39·40 N 81·30 W
119 Caldwell Tx. 30·30 N 96·40 W
89 Caledon (kăl'ē-dŏn) Can. (Toronto In.) 43·52 N 79·59 W
109 Caledonia (kăl-ē-dō'nĭ-ȧ) Mn. 43·38 N 91·31 W
154 Caledonian Can. (kăl-ē-dō'nĭ-ăn) Scot. 56·58 N 4·05 W
163 Calella (kä-lĕl'yä) Sp. 41·37 N 2·39 E
124 Calera Victor Rosales (kä-lā'rä-vē'k-tôr-rô-sȧ'lĕs). Mex. 22·57 N 102·42 W
114 Calexico (kȧ-lĕk'sĭ-kō) Ca. 32·41 N 115·30 W
89 Calgary (kăl'gȧ-rĭ) Can. (Calgary In.) 51·03 N 114·05 W
120 Calhoun (kăl-hōōn') Ga. 34·30 N 84·56 W
134 Cali (kä'lē) Col. (In.) 3·26 N 76·30 W
185 Calicut (kăl'ĭ-kŭt) India 11·19 N 75·49 E
115 Caliente (käl-yĕn'tä) Nv. 37·38 N 114·30 W
117 California (kăl-ĭ-fôr'nĭ-ȧ) Mo. 38·38 N 92·38 W
107 California Pa. (Pittsburgh In.) 40·03 N 79·53 W
102 California (State) U.S. 38·10 N 121·20 W
122 California, Golfo de (G.) (gôl-fô-dĕ-kä-lē-fôr-nyä). Mex. 30·30 N 113·45 W
159 Căliman, Munţii (Mts.) Rom. 47·05 N 24·47 E
185 Calimere, Pt. India 10·20 N 80·20 E
113 Calimesa (kă-lĭ-mā'sȧ) Ca. (Los Angeles In.) 34·00 N 117·04 W
114 Calipatria (kăl-ĭ-pȧt'rĭ-ȧ) Ca. 33·03 N 115·30 W
125 Calkini (käl-kē-nē') Mex. 20·21 N 90·06 W
203 Callabonna, L. (călă'bŏnȧ). Austl. 29·35 S 140·28 E
134 Callao (käl-yä'ô) Peru 12·02 S 77·07 W
93 Calling (L.) (kôl'ĭng) Can. 55·15 N 113·12 W
89 Calmar (kăl'mär) Can. (Edmonton In.) 53·16 N 113·49 W
109 Calmar Ia. 43·12 N 91·54 W
124 Calnalí (käl-nä-lē') Mex. 20·53 N 98·34 W
121 Calooshatchee (R.) (kȧ-loo-sȧ-hăch'ē). Fl. (In.) 26·45 N 81·41 W
126 Calotmul (käl-ôt-mōōl). Mex. (In.) 20·58 N 88·11 W
124 Calpulalpan (käl-pōō-läl'pän) Mex. 19·35 N 98·33 W
164 Caltagirone (käl-tä-jē-rō'nȧ) It. 37·14 N 14·32 E
164 Caltanissetta (käl-tä-nē-sĕt'tä). It. 37·30 N 14·02 E
216 Caluango Ang. 8·21 S 19·40 E
216 Calucinga Ang. 11·18 S 16·12 E
109 Calumet (kă-lū-mĕt') Mi. 47·15 N 88·29 W
107 Calumet, L. Il. (Chicago In.) 41·43 N 87·36 W
107 Calumet City Il. (Chicago In.) 41·37 N 87·33 W
216 Calunda Ang. 12·06 S 23·23 E
216 Caluquembe Ang. 13·47 S 14·44 E
119 Calvert (kăl'vērt) Tx. 30·59 N 96·41 W

ng-sing; ŋ-baŋk; N-nasalized n; nŏd; cŏmmit; ōld; ôbey; ôrder; fōōd; fōōt; ou-out; s-soft; sh-dish; th-thin; pūre; ûnite; ûrn; stŭd; circŭs; ü-as "y" in study; '-indeterminate vowel.

264 Calvert — Caramarca PRONOUNCING INDEX

Page	Name Pronunciation Region	Lat. °′	Long. °′
92	Calvert I. Can.	51·35 N	128·00 W
164	Calvi (käl'vē) Fr.	42·33 N	8·35 E
124	Calvillo (käl-vēl'yō) Mex.	21·51 N	102·44 W
212	Calvinia (kăl-vĭn'ĭ-ȧ) S. Afr.	31·20 S	19·50 E
162	Calzada de Calatrava (käl-zä'dä-dĕ-kä-lä-trä'vä.) Sp.	38·42 N	3·44 W
154	Cam (R.) (kăm) Eng.	52·15 N	0·05 E
128	Camagüey (kä-mä-gwā') Cuba	21·25 N	78·00 W
128	Camagüey (Prov.) Cuba	21·30 N	78·10 W
128	Camajuani (kä-mä-hwä'nē) Cuba	22·25 N	79·50 W
197	Camalig (kä-mä'lēg) Phil. (In.)	13·11 N	123·36 E
134	Camaná (kä-mä'nä) Peru	16·37 S	72·33 W
112	Camano (kä-mä'no) Wa. (Seattle In.)	48·10 N	122·32 W
112	Camano I. Wa. (Seattle In.)	48·11 N	122·29 W
118	Camargo (kä-mär gō) Mex.	26·19 N	98·49 W
126	Camarón, Cabo (C.) (kȧ'bô-kä-mä-rōn'). Hond.	16·06 N	85·05 W
112	Camas (kăm'ȧs) Wa. (Portland In.)	45·36 N	122·24 W
111	Camas Cr. Id.	44·10 N	112·09 W
135	Camatagua (kä-mä-tȧ'gwä) Ven. (In.)	9·49 N	66·55 W
184	Cambay (kăm-bā') India	22·22 N	72·39 E
196	Cambodia (kăm-bō'dĭ-ȧ) Asia	12·15 N	104·00 E
216	Cambonda, Serra (Mts.) Ang.	12·10 S	14·15 E
154	Camborne (kăm'bôrn) Eng.	50·15 N	5·28 W
160	Cambrai (käN-brĕ') Fr.	50·10 N	3·15 E
154	Cambrian Mts. (kăm'brĭ-ăn) Wales	52·05 N	4·05 W
154	Cambridge (kām'brĭj) Eng.	52·12 N	0·11 E
105	Cambridge Md.	38·35 N	76·10 W
109	Cambridge Mn.	45·35 N	93·14 W
99	Cambridge Ms. (In.)	42·23 N	71·07 W
116	Cambridge Ne.	40·17 N	100·10 W
104	Cambridge Oh.	40·00 N	81·35 W
90	Cambridge Bay Can.	69·15 N	105·00 W
104	Cambridge City In.	39·45 N	85·15 W
137	Cambuci (käm-bōō'sē) Braz. (Rio de Janeiro In.)	21·35 S	41·54 W
137	Cambuí (käm-bōō-ē') Braz. (Rio de Janeiro In.)	22·38 S	46·02 W
107	Camby (kăm'bē) In. (Indianapolis In.)	39·40 N	86·19 W
120	Camden (kăm'dĕn) Al.	31·58 N	87·15 W
117	Camden Ar.	33·36 N	92·49 W
202	Camden Austl. (Sydney In.)	34·03 S	150·42 E
98	Camden Me.	44·11 N	69·05 W
106	Camden NJ (Philadelphia In.)	39·56 N	75·06 W
121	Camden SC	34·14 N	80·37 W
216	Cameia, Parque Nacional da (Natl. Pk.). Ang.	11·40 S	21·20 E
117	Cameron (kăm'ēr-ŭn) Mo.	39·44 N	94·14 W
119	Cameron Tx.	30·52 N	96·57 W
104	Cameron WV	39·40 N	80·35 W
90	Cameron Hills Can.	60·13 N	120·20 W
209	Cameroon Afr.	5·48 N	11·00 E
215	Cameroun, Mont (Mtn.) Cam.	4·12 N	9·11 E
135	Cametá (kä-mȧ-tä') Braz.	1·14 S	49·30 W
197	Camiling (kä-mē-lĭng') Phil. (In.)	15·42 N	120·24 E
120	Camilla (kȧ-mĭl'ȧ) Ga.	31·13 N	84·12 W
162	Caminha (kä-mĭn'yȧ) Port.	41·52 N	8·44 W
135	Camoçim (kä-mô-sēN') Braz.	2·56 S	40·55 W
204	Camooweal Austl.	20·00 S	138·13 E
137	Campana (käm-pä'nä) Arg. (Buenos Aires In.)	34·10 S	58·58 W
136	Campana (I.) (käm-pän'yä). Chile	48·20 S	75·15 W
162	Campanario (käm-pä-nä'rē-ō). Sp.	38·51 N	5·36 W
163	Campanella, Punta (C.) (pōō'n-tä-käm-pä-nĕ'lä) In. (Naples In.)	40·20 N	14·21 E
137	Campanha (käm-pän-yäN') Braz. (Rio de Janeiro In.)	21·51 S	45·24 W
164	Campania (Reg.) (käm-pän'yä). It.	41·00 N	14·40 E
112	Campbell (kăm'bĕl) Ca. (San Francisco In.)	37·17 N	121·57 W
117	Campbell Mo.	36·29 N	90·04 W
220	Campbell (Is.) N.Z.	52·30 S	169·00 E
184	Campbellpore Pak.	33·49 N	72·24 E
92	Campbell River Can.	50·01 N	125·15 W
120	Campbellsville (kăm'bĕlz-vĭl). Ky.	37·19 N	85·20 W
98	Campbellton (kăm'bĕl-tŭn) Can.	48·00 N	66·40 W
202	Campbelltown (kăm'bĕl-toun) Austl. (Sydney In.)	34·04 S	150·49 E
154	Campbelltown (kăm'b'l-toun) Scot.	55·25 N	5·50 W
107	Camp Dennison (dĕ'nĭ-sŏn) Oh. (Cincinnati In.)	39·12 N	84·17 W
125	Campeche (käm-pā'chå) Mex.	19·51 N	90·32 W
122	Campeche (State) Mex.	18·55 N	90·20 W
122	Campeche, Bahía de (B.) (bä-ē'ä-dĕ-käm-pā'chā). Mex.	19·30 N	93·40 W
128	Campechuela (käm-pā-chwā'lä) Cuba	20·15 N	77·15 W
213	Camperdown (kăm'pēr-doun) S. Afr. (Natal In.)	29·14 S	30·33 E
162	Campillo de Altobuey (käm-pēl'yō dā äl-tō-bōō'ā). Sp.	39·37 N	1·50 W
135	Campina Grande (käm-pē'nä grän'dĕ). Braz.	7·15 S	35·49 W
137	Campinas (käm-pē'năzh) Braz. (Rio de Janeiro In.)	22·53 S	47·03 W
114	Camp Ind. Res. (kămp) Ca.	32·39 N	116·26 W
215	Campo (käm'pō) Cam.	2·22 N	9·49 E
134	Campoalegre (kä'm-pô-ālĕ'grĕ) Col.	2·34 N	75·20 W
164	Campobasso (käm'pô-bäs'sō) It.	41·35 N	14·39 E
137	Campo Belo Braz. (Rio de Janeiro In.)	20·52 S	45·15 W
162	Campo de Criptana (käm'pō dā krêp-tä'nä). Sp.	39·24 N	3·09 W
129	Campo Florido (kä'm-pō flô-rē'dō) Cuba (In.)	23·07 N	82·07 W
135	Campo Grande (käm-pōō grän'dĕ) Braz.	20·28 S	54·32 W
136	Campo Grande Braz. (Rio de Janeiro In.)	22·54 S	43·33 W
135	Campo Maior (käm-pōō mä-yôr') Braz.	4·48 S	42·12 W
162	Campo Maior Port.	39·03 N	7·06 W
163	Campo Real (käm'pō rå-äl') Sp. (Madrid In.)	40·21 N	3·23 W
137	Campos (kä'm-pôs) Braz. (Rio de Janeiro In.)	21·46 S	41·19 W
137	Campos do Jordão (kä'm-pôs-dô-zhôr-dou'N) Braz. (Rio de Janeiro In.)	22·45 S	45·35 W
137	Campos Gerais (kä'm-pôs-zhĕ-rȧ'es) Braz. (Rio de Janeiro In.)	21·17 S	45·43 W
212	Camps Bay (kămps). S. Afr. (In.)	33·57 S	18·22 E
106	Camp Springs (cămp sprĭngz) Md. (Baltimore In.)	38·48 N	76·55 W
118	Camp Wood (kămp wŏŏd) Tx.	29·39 N	100·02 W
94	Camrose (kăm-rōz) Can.	53·01 N	112·50 W
129	Camu (R.) (kä'mōō) Dom. Rep.	19·05 N	70·15 W
75	Canada (kăn'ȧ-dȧ) N.A.	50·00 N	100·00 W
99	Canada B. Can.	50·43 N	56·10 W
137	Cañada de Gómez (kä-nyä'dä-dĕ-gô'mĕz) Arg. (Buenos Aires In.)	32·49 S	61·24 W
116	Canadian (kȧ-nā'dĭ-ăn) Tx.	35·54 N	100·24 W
117	Canadian R. Ok.	34·53 N	97·06 W
105	Canajoharie (kăn-ȧ-jō-hăr'ē) NY	42·55 N	74·35 W
165	Çanakkale (chä-näk-kä'lĕ) Tur.	40·10 N	26·26 E
165	Çanakkale Boğazi (Dardanelles) (Str.) (chä-näk-kä'lē) (där-dȧ-nĕlz') Tur.	40·05 N	25·50 E
123	Canal Zone N.A.	9·15 N	80·30 W
105	Canandaigua (kăn-ăn-dā'gwȧ) NY	42·55 N	77·20 W
105	Canandaigua (L.) NY	42·45 N	77·20 W
122	Cananea (kä-nä-nĕ'ä) Mex.	31·00 N	110·20 W
210	Canarias, Islas (Is.) (ē's-läs-kä-nä'ryäs). Sp.	29·15 N	16·30 W
128	Canarreos, Arch. de los (Is.) (är-chē-pyĕ'lä-gô-dĕ-lôs-kä-när-rĕ'ōs). Cuba	21·35 N	82·20 W
126	Cañas (kä'-nyäs) C.R.	10·26 N	85·06 W
134	Cañasgordas (kä'nyäs-gô'r-däs) Col. (In.)	6·44 N	76·01 W
126	Cañas R. C.R.	10·20 N	85·21 W
105	Canastota (kăn-ȧs-tō'tȧ) NY	43·05 N	75·45 W
135	Canastra, Serra de (Mts.) (sĕ'r-rä-dĕ-kä-nä's-trä). Braz.	19·53 S	46·57 W
118	Canatlán (kä-nät-län') Mex.	24·30 N	104·45 W
121	Canaveral, C. Fl. (In.)	28·30 N	80·23 W
135	Canavieiras (kä-nȧ-vē-ā'räs) Braz.	15·40 S	38·49 W
203	Canberra (kăn'bĕr-ȧ) Austl.	35·21 S	149·10 E
108	Canby (kăn'bĭ) Mn.	44·43 N	96·15 W
134	Canchyauya, Cerros de (Mts.) (sĕ'r-rôs-dĕ-kän-chōō-ȧ'īä). Peru	7·30 S	74·30 W
125	Cancuc (kän-kōōk) Mex.	16·58 N	92·17 W
128	Candelaria (kän-dĕ-lä'ryä) Cuba	22·45 N	82·55 W
197	Candelaria (kän-dȧ-lä'rē-ä) Phil. (In.)	15·39 N	119·55 E
125	Candelaria (R.) (kän-dĕ-lä-ryä) Mex.	18·25 N	91·21 W
162	Candeleda (kän-dhå-lā'dhä) Sp.	40·09 N	5·18 W
	Candia, see Iráklion		
101	Candle (kăn'd'l) Ak.	65·00 N	162·04 W
108	Cando (kăn'dō) ND	48·27 N	99·13 W
197	Candon (kän-dōn') Phil. (In.)	17·13 N	120·26 E
	Canea, see Khaniá		
137	Canelones (kä-nĕ-lô-nĕs) Ur. (Buenos Aires In.)	34·32 S	56·19 W
137	Canelones (Dept.) Ur. (Buenos Aires In.)	34·34 S	56·15 W
134	Cañete (kän-yā'tå) Peru	13·06 S	76·17 W
129	Caney (kä-nā') (kā'nĭ) Cuba	20·05 N	75·45 W
117	Caney (kā'nĭ) Ks.	37·00 N	95·57 W
120	Caney (R.) Tn.	36·10 N	85·50 W
162	Cangas (kän'gäs) Sp.	42·15 N	8·43 W
162	Cangas de Narcea (kä'n-gäs-dĕ-när-sĕ-ä). Sp.	43·08 N	6·36 W
216	Cangombe Ang.	13·40 S	19·54 E
91	Caniapiscau (L.) Can.	54·10 N	71·13 E
91	Caniapiscau (R.) Can.	57·00 N	68·45 W
164	Canicatti (kä-nē-kät'tē) It.	37·18 N	13·58 E
162	Caniles (kä-nē'lås) Sp.	37·26 N	2·43 W
124	Cañitas (kän-yē'täs) Mex.	23·38 N	102·44 W
171	Çankırı (chän-kē'rē) Tur.	40·40 N	33·40 E
89	Cannell Can. (Edmonton In.)	53·35 N	113·38 W
104	Cannelton (kăn'ĕl-tŭn) In.	37·55 N	86·45 W
161	Cannes (kȧn) Fr.	43·34 N	7·05 E
98	Canning (kăn'ĭng) Can.	45·09 N	64·25 W
148	Cannock (kăn'ŭk) Eng.	52·41 N	2·02 W
148	Cannock Chase (Reg.) (kăn'ŭk chās). Eng.	52·43 N	1·54 W
109	Cannon (R.) (kăn'ŭn) Mn.	44·18 N	93·24 W
108	Cannonball (R.) (kăn'ŭn-bäl). ND	46·17 N	101·35 W
127	Caño, Isla de (I.) (ē's-lä-dĕ-kä'nō). C.R.	8·38 N	84·00 W
93	Canoe (R.) (kȧ-nōō) Can.	52·20 N	119·00 W
113	Canoga Park (kä-nō'gȧ) Ca. (Los Angeles In.)	34·07 N	118·36 W
116	Canon City (kăn'yŭn) Co.	38·27 N	105·16 W
107	Canonsburg (kăn'ŭnz-bûrg) Pa. (Pittsburgh In.)	40·16 N	80·11 W
121	Canoochee (R.) (kȧ-nōō'chē) Ga.	32·25 N	82·11 W
95	Canora (kȧ-nōrȧ) Can.	51·37 N	102·26 W
164	Canosa (kä-nō'sä) It.	41·14 N	16·03 E
127	Canouan (I.) St. Vincent (In.)	12·44 N	61·10 W
126	Cansaheab (kän-sä-ĕ-äb) Mex. (In.)	21·11 N	89·05 W
99	Canso (kăn'sō) Can.	45·20 N	61·00 W
99	Canso, C. Can.	45·21 N	60·46 W
99	Canso, Str. of Can.	45·37 N	61·25 W
162	Cantabrica, Cordillera (Mts.) (kôr-dēl-yĕ'rä-kan-tä'brē-kä). Sp.	43·05 N	6·05 W
137	Cantagalo (kän-tä-gä'lo) Braz. (Rio de Janeiro In.)	21·59 S	42·22 W
162	Cantanhede (kän-täN-yā'då). Port.	40·22 N	8·35 W
148	Canterbury (kăn'tĕr-bĕr-ē) Eng. (London In.)	51·17 N	1·06 E
205	Canterbury Bight N. Z. (In.)	44·15 S	172·08 E
128	Cantiles, Cayo (I.) (ky-ō-kän-tē'lås). Cuba	21·40 N	82·00 W
120	Canton Ga.	34·13 N	84·29 W
117	Canton Il.	40·34 N	90·02 W
99	Canton Ma. (In.)	42·09 N	71·09 W
120	Canton Ms.	32·36 N	90·01 W
117	Canton Mo.	40·08 N	91·33 W
120	Canton NC	35·32 N	82·50 W
104	Canton Oh.	40·50 N	81·25 W
105	Canton Pa.	41·50 N	76·45 W
108	Canton SD	43·17 N	96·37 W
	Canton, see Kuangchou		
198	Canton (I.) Oceania	3·50 S	174·00 W
164	Cantu (kän-tōō') It.	45·43 N	9·09 E
137	Cañuelas (kä-nyōō-ĕ'-läs) Arg. (Buenos Aires In.)	35·03 S	58·45 W
135	Canumã (R.) (kä-nōō-mȧ') Braz.	6·20 S	58·57 W
116	Canyon (kăn'yŭn) Tx.	34·59 N	101·57 W
112	Canyon (R.) Wa. (Seattle In.)	48·09 N	121·48 W
115	Canyon De Chelly Natl. Mon. Az.	36·14 N	110·00 W
115	Canyonlands Natl. Park Ut.	38·10 N	110·00 W
197	Capalonga (kä-pä-lôŋ'gä) Phil. (In.)	14·20 N	122·30 E
164	Capannori (kä-pän'nô-rē) It.	43·50 N	10·30 E
163	Caparica (kä-pä-rē'kä) Port. (Lisbon In.)	38·40 N	9·12 W
135	Capaya (R.) (kä-pä-īä). Ven. (In.)	10·28 N	66·15 W
91	Cap-Chat (kȧp-shä') Can.	48·02 N	65·20 W
98	Cap-de-la-Madeleine (kȧp dē lȧ mȧ-d'lĕn'). Can.	46·23 N	72·30 W
99	Cape Breton (I.) (kāp brĕt'ŭn) Can.	45·48 N	59·50 W
99	Cape Breton Highlands Natl. Park Can.	46·45 N	60·45 W
121	Cape Charles (kāp chärlz) Va.	37·13 N	76·02 W
214	Cape Coast Ghana	5·05 N	1·15 W
121	Cape Fear (R.) (kāp fēr) NC	34·43 N	78·41 W
212	Cape Flats (kāp flăts) S. Afr. (In.)	34·01 S	18·37 E
117	Cape Girardeau (jē-rär-dō') Mo.	37·17 N	89·32 W
105	Cape May (kāp mā) NJ	38·55 N	74·50 W
105	Cape May C.H. NJ	39·05 N	75·00 W
212	Cape of Good Hope (Prov.) (kāp ŏv gŏŏd hōp). S. Afr.	31·50 S	21·15 E
101	Cape Romanzof (rō' män zôf). Ak.	61·50 N	165·45 W
127	Capesterre Guad. (In.)	16·02 N	61·37 W
98	Cape Tormentine Can.	46·08 N	63·47 W
212	Cape Town (kāp toun) S. Afr. (In.)	33·48 S	18·28 E
210	Cape Verde Afr. (In.)	15·48 N	26·02 W
205	Cape York Pen. (kāp yôrk) Austl.	12·30 S	142·35 E
129	Cap-Haïtien (kȧp ȧ-ē-syăn') Hai.	19·45 N	72·15 W
137	Capilla de Señor (kä-pēl'yä dā sän-yôr'). Arg. (Buenos Aires In.)	34·18 S	59·07 W
97	Capitachouane (R.) Can.	47·50 N	76·45 W
115	Capitol Reef Natl. Park (kăp'ĭ-tŏl). Ut.	38·15 N	111·10 W
137	Capivari (kä-pē-vȧ'rē) Braz. (Rio de Janeiro In.)	22·59 S	47·29 W
136	Capivari (R.) Braz. (Rio de Janeiro In.)	22·39 S	43·19 W
203	Capoompeta (Mtn.) (kȧ-pōōm-pē'tȧ). Austl.	29·15 S	152·12 E
164	Capraia (I.) (kä-prä'yä) It.	43·02 N	9·51 E
164	Caprara Pt. (kä-prä'rä) It.	41·08 N	8·20 E
96	Capreol Can.	46·43 N	80·56 W
164	Caprera (I.) (kä-prā'rä) It.	41·12 N	9·28 E
163	Capri It. (Naples In.)	40·18 N	14·16 E
163	Capri, I. di (ē'-sō-lä-dē-kä'prē) It. (Naples In.)	40·19 N	14·10 E
205	Capricorn Chan. (kăp'rĭ-kôrn) Austl.	22·27 S	151·24 E
212	Caprivi Strip (Reg.) Namibia	18·00 S	22·00 E
89	Cap-Rouge (kȧp rōōzh') Can. (Quebec In.)	46·45 N	71·21 W
89	Cap-St. Ignace (kĭp săN-tē-nyȧs') Can. (Quebec In.)	47·02 N	70·27 W
164	Capua (kä'pwä) It.	41·07 N	14·14 E
124	Capulhuac (kä-pōōl-hwäk') Mex.	19·33 N	99·43 W
116	Capulin Mountain Natl. Mon. (kȧ-pū'lĭn). NM	36·15 N	103·58 W
125	Capultitlán (kä-pōō'l-tē-tlȧ'n) Mex. (In.)	19·15 N	99·40 W
134	Caquetá (R.) (kä-kā-tä') Col.	0·23 S	73·22 W
163	Carabaña (kä-rä-bän'yä) Sp. (Madrid In.)	40·16 N	3·15 E
135	Carabobo (State) (kä-rä-bô'-bô) Ven. (In.)	10·07 N	68·06 W
165	Caracal (kȧ-rȧ-kȧl') Rom.	44·06 N	24·22 E
135	Caracas (kä-rä'käs) Ven. (In.)	10·30 N	66·58 W
124	Carácuaro de Morelos (kä-rä'kwä-rō-dĕ-mô-rĕ-lôs). Mex.	18·44 N	101·04 W
137	Caraguatatuba (kä-rä-gwä-tä-tōō'bä). Braz. (Rio de Janeiro In.)	23·37 S	45·26 W
135	Carajás, Serra dos (Mts.) (sĕ'r-rä-dôs-kä-rä-zhȧ's). Braz.	5·58 S	51·45 W
134	Caramanta, Cerro (Mtn.) (sĕ'r-rô-kä-rä-mä'n-tä). Col. (In.)	5·29 N	76·01 W
136	Caramarca (kä-rä-mä'r-kä) Arg.	28·29 S	65·45 W

ăt; finăl; rāte; senâte; ärm; åsk; sofȧ; fâre; ch-choose; dh-as th in other; bē; êvent; bĕt; recĕnt; cratẽr; g-go; gh-guttural g; bĭt; ĭ-short neutral; rīde; K-guttural k as ch in German ich;

PRONOUNCING INDEX

Carandaí — Catalina 265

Page	Name	Pronunciation	Region	Lat. °′	Long. °′
137	Carandaí	(kä-rän-dàē′)	Braz. (Rio de Janeiro In.)	20·57 s	43·47 w
137	Carangola	(kä-ràn′gō′lä)	Braz. (Rio de Janeiro In.)	20·46 s	42·02 w
165	Caransebes	(kå-rån-sä′bĕsh)	Rom.	45·24 n	22·13 e
98	Caraquet	(kă-rá-kĕt′)	Can.	47·48 n	64·57 w
127	Carata, Laguna (L.)	(lä-gōō′nä-kä-rä′tä)	Nic.	13·59 n	83·41 w
127	Caratasca, Laguna (L.)	(lä-gōō′nä-kä-rä-täs′kä)	Hond.	15·20 n	83·45 w
162	Caravaca	(kä-rä-vä′kä)	Sp.	38·05 n	1·51 w
135	Caravelas	(kå-rä-vĕl′äzh)	Braz.	17·46 s	39·06 w
135	Carayaca	(kå-rä-iă′kä)	Ven. (In.)	10·32 n	67·07 w
136	Caràzinho	(kä-rá′zē-nyǒ)	Braz.	28·22 s	52·33 w
162	Carballino	(kär-bäl-yē′nō)	Sp.	42·26 n	8·04 w
162	Carballo	(kär-bäl′yō)	Sp.	43·13 n	8·40 w
112	Carbon (R.)	(kär′bŏn)	Wa. (Seattle In.)	47·06 n	122·08 w
112	Carbonado	(kår-bō-nā′dō)	Wa. (Seattle In.)	47·05 n	122·03 w
164	Carbonara, C.	(kär-bō-nä′rä)	It.	39·08 n	9·33 e
89	Carbondale	(kär′bŏn-dāl)	Can. (Edmonton In.)	53·45 n	113·32 w
117	Carbondale		Il.	37·42 n	89·12 w
105	Carbondale		Pa.	41·35 n	75·30 w
99	Carbonear	(kär-bō-nēr′)	Can.	47·45 n	53·14 w
120	Carbon Hill	(kär′bŏn hĭl)	Al.	33·53 n	87·34 w
163	Carcagente	(kär-kä-hĕn′tā)	Sp.	39·09 n	0·29 w
160	Carcans, Étang de (L.)	(ā-taN-dĕ-kär-käN)	Fr.	45·12 n	1·00 w
160	Carcassonne	(kàr-kà-sôn′)	Fr.	43·12 n	2·23 e
90	Carcross	(kär′krôs)	Can.	60·18 n	134·54 w
128	Cárdenas	(kär′dâ-näs)	Cuba	23·00 n	81·10 w
125	Cárdenas	(kä′r-dĕ-näs)	Mex.	17·59 n	93·23 w
124	Cárdenas		Mex.	22·01 n	99·38 w
128	Cardenas, Bahía de (B.)	(bä-ē′ä-dĕ-kär′dâ-näs)	Cuba	23·10 n	81·10 w
89	Cardiff	(kär′dĭf)	Can. (Edmonton In.)	53·46 n	113·36 w
154	Cardiff		Wales	51·30 n	3·18 w
154	Cardigan	(kär′dĭ-găn)	Wales	52·05 n	4·40 w
154	Cardigan B.		Wales	52·35 n	4·40 w
93	Cardston	(kärds′tŭn)	Can.	49·12 n	113·18 w
159	Carei	(kä-rĕ′)	Rom.	47·42 n	22·28 e
160	Carentan	(kä-rôN-täN′)	Fr.	49·19 n	1·14 w
104	Carey	(kā′rē)	Oh.	40·55 n	83·25 w
204	Carey (L.)	(kâr′ē)	Austl.	29·20 s	123·35 e
160	Carhaix	(kär-ĕ′)	Fr.	48·17 n	3·37 w
123	Caribbean Sea	(kăr-ĭ-bē′ăn)	N.A.-S.A.	14·30 n	75·30 w
125	Caribe, Arroyo (R.)	(är-ro′ï-kä-rē′bĕ)	Mex.	18·18 n	90·38 w
93	Cariboo Mts.	(kă′rĭ-bōō)	Can.	53·00 n	121·00 w
98	Caribou		Me.	46·51 n	68·01 w
96	Caribou (I.)		Can.	47·22 n	85·42 w
113	Caribou L.		Mn. (Duluth In.)	46·54 n	92·16 w
90	Caribou Mts.		Can.	59·20 n	115·30 w
135	Carinhanha	(kä-rĭ-nyän′yä)	Braz.	14·14 s	43·44 w
164	Carini	(kä-rē′nē)	It.	38·09 n	13·10 e
	Carinthia (State), see Kärnten				
97	Carleton Place	(kärl′tŭn)	Can.	45·15 n	76·10 w
218	Carletonville S. Afr.		(Johannesburg & Pretoria In.)	26·20 s	27·23 e
117	Carlinville	(kär′lĭn-vĭl)	Il.	39·16 n	89·52 w
154	Carlisle	(kär-lĭl′)	Eng.	54·54 n	3·03 w
104	Carlisle		Ky.	38·20 n	84·00 w
105	Carlisle		Pa.	40·10 n	77·15 w
160	Carlitte, Pic (Pk.)	(pēk′ kar-lēt′)	Fr.	42·33 n	1·56 e
164	Carloforte	(kär′lō-fôr-tå)	It.	39·11 n	8·28 e
137	Carlos Casares	(kär-lôs-kä-sä′rĕs)	Arg. (Buenos Aires In.)	35·38 s	61·17 w
154	Carlow	(kär′lō)	Ire.	52·50 n	7·00 w
118	Carlsbad	(kärlz′băd)	NM	32·24 n	104·12 w
118	Carlsbad Caverns Nat'l Park		NM	32·08 n	104·30 w
148	Carlton	(kärl′tŭn)	Eng.	52·58 n	1·05 w
113	Carlton		Mn. (Duluth In.)	46·40 n	92·26 w
104	Carlton Center	(kärl′tŭn sĕn′tēr)	Mi.	42·45 n	85·20 w
117	Carlyle	(kärlīl′)	Il.	38·37 n	89·23 w
164	Carmagnolo	(kär-mä-nyô′lä)	It.	44·52 n	7·48 e
95	Carman	(kär′măn)	Can.	49·32 n	98·00 w
154	Carmarthen	(kär-mär′thĕn)	Wales	51·50 n	4·20 w
154	Carmarthen B.	(kär-mär′thĕn)	Wales	51·33 n	4·50 w
160	Carmaux	(kår-mō′)	Fr.	44·05 n	2·09 e
106	Carmel	(kär′mĕl)	NY (New York In.)	41·25 n	73·42 w
137	Carmelo	(kär-mĕ′lo)	Ur. (Buenos Aires In.)	33·59 s	58·15 w
125	Carmen, Isla del (I.)	(ē′s-lä-dĕl-kä′r-mĕn)	Mex.	18·43 n	91·40 w
125	Carmen, Laguna del (L.)	(lä-gŏŏ′nä-dĕl-kä′r-mĕn)	Mex.	18·15 n	93·26 w
137	Carmen de Areco	(kär′mĕn′ dā ä-rā′kō)	Arg. (Buenos Aires In.)	34·21 s	59·50 w
136	Carmen de Patagones	(kä′r-mĕn-dĕ-pä-tä-gô′nĕs)	Arg.	41·00 s	63·00 w
104	Carmi	(kär′mī)	Il.	38·05 n	88·10 w
137	Carmo	(kå′r-mô)	Braz. (Rio de Janeiro In.)	21·57 s	42·06 w
137	Carmo do Rio Clara	(kä′r-mô-dô-rē′ō-klä′rä)	Braz. (Rio de Janeiro In.)	20·57 s	46·04 w
162	Carmona		Sp.	37·28 n	5·38 w
204	Carnarvon	(kär-när′vŭn)	Austl.	24·45 s	113·45 e
212	Carnarvon		S. Afr.	31·00 s	22·15 e
112	Carnation	(kär-nā′shŭn)	Wa. (Seattle In.)	47·39 n	121·55 w
163	Carnaxide	(kär-nä-shē′dĕ)	Port. (Lisbon In.)	38·44 n	9·15 w
154	Carndonagh	(kärn-dō-nä′)	Ire.	55·15 n	7·15 w
116	Carnegie	(kär-nĕg′ĭ)	Ok.	35·06 n	98·38 w
107	Carnegie		Pa. (Pittsburgh In.)	40·24 n	80·06 w
105	Carneys Point	(kär′nĕs)	NJ	39·45 n	75·25 w
158	Carnic Alps (Mts.)		Aus.-It.	46·43 n	12·38 e
163	Carnot	(kär nō′)	Alg.	36·15 n	1·40 e
215	Carnot		Cen. Afr. Emp.	5·00 n	15·52 e
154	Carnsore Pt.	(kärn′sôr)	Ire.	52·10 n	6·16 w
104	Caro	(kâ′rō)	Mi.	43·30 n	83·25 w
135	Carolina	(kä-rô-lē′nä)	Braz.	7·26 s	47·16 w
212	Carolina	(kăr-ô-lī′nȧ)	S. Afr.	26·07 s	30·09 e
126	Carolina (L.)	(kä-rō-lē′nä)	Mex. (In.)	18·41 n	89·40 w
198	Caroline Is.	(kăr′ô-līn)	Pac. Is. Trust Ter.	9·30 n	143·00 e
134	Caroni (R.)	(kä-rō′nē)	Ven.	5·49 n	62·57 w
134	Carora	(kä-rô′rä)	Ven.	10·09 n	70·12 w
153	Carpathians (Mts.)	(kär-pā′thĭ-ăn)	Eur.	49·23 n	20·14 e
165	Carpatii Meridionali (Transylvanian Alps) (Mts.)		Rom.	45·30 n	23·30 e
204	Carpentaria, G. of	(kär-pĕn-târ′ĭȧ)	Austl.	14·45 s	138·50 e
160	Carpentras	(kär-päN-träs′)	Fr.	44·04 n	5·01 e
164	Carpi		It.	44·48 n	10·54 e
120	Carabelle	(kăr′á-bĕl)	Fl.	29·50 n	84·40 w
154	Carrantuohill	(kă-răn-tōō′ĭl)	Ire.	52·01 n	9·48 w
164	Carrara	(kä-rä′rä)	It.	44·05 n	10·05 e
134	Carretas, Punta (Pt.)	(pōō′n-tä-kär-rĕ′tĕ′räs)	Peru	14·15 s	76·25 w
127	Carriacou (I.)	(kăr-ê-ȧ-kōō′)	Grenada (In.)	12·28 n	61·20 w
154	Carrick	(kăr′ĭk)	Ire.	52·20 n	7·35 w
89	Carrier	(kăr′ĭ-ēr)	Can. (Quebec In.)	46·43 n	71·05 w
120	Carriere	(kȧ-rēr′)	Ms.	30·37 n	89·37 w
104	Carriers Mills	(kăr′ĭ-ērs)	Il.	37·40 n	88·40 w
108	Carrington	(kăr′ĭng-tŭn)	ND	47·26 n	99·06 w
112	Carr Inlet	(kăr ĭn′lĕt)	Wa. (Seattle In.)	47·20 n	122·42 w
128	Carrion Crow Hbr.	(kăr′ĭŭn krō)	Ba.	26·35 n	77·55 w
162	Carrión de los Condes	(kär-rê-ōn′ dā lōs kōn′dås)	Sp.	42·20 n	4·35 w
116	Carrizo Cr.	(kär-rē′zō)	NM	36·22 n	103·39 w
118	Carrizo Springs		Tx.	28·32 n	99·51 w
115	Carrizozo	(kär-rê-zō′zō)	NM	33·40 n	105·55 w
109	Carroll	(kăr′ŭl)	Ia.	42·03 n	94·51 w
120	Carrollton	(kăr-ŭl-tŭn)	Ga.	33·35 n	84·05 w
117	Carrollton		Il.	39·18 n	90·22 w
104	Carrollton		Ky.	38·45 n	85·15 w
104	Carrollton		Mi.	43·30 n	83·55 w
117	Carrollton		Mo.	39·21 n	93·29 w
104	Carrollton		Oh.	40·35 n	81·10 w
113	Carrollton		Tx. (Dallas, Fort Worth In.)	32·58 n	96·53 w
112	Carrols	(kăr′ŭlz)	Wa. (Portland In.)	46·05 n	122·51 w
154	Carron (L.)	(kå′rŭn)	Scot.	57·25 n	5·25 w
94	Carrot (R.)		Can.	53·12 n	103·50 w
160	Carry-le-Rouet	(kä-rē′lĕ-rōō-ā′)	Fr. (In.)	43·20 n	5·10 e
171	Carsamba	(chär-shäm′bä)	Tur.	41·05 n	36·40 e
114	Carson (R.)	(kär′sŭn)	Nv.	39·15 n	119·25 w
114	Carson City		Nv.	39·10 n	119·45 w
114	Carson Sink		Nv.	39·51 n	118·25 w
134	Cartagena	(kär-tä-hā′nä)	Col.	10·30 n	75·40 w
163	Cartagena	(kär-tä-Kē′nä)	Sp.	37·46 n	1·00 w
134	Cartago	(kär-tä′gō)	Col. (In.)	4·44 n	75·54 w
127	Cartago		C. R.	9·52 n	83·56 w
162	Cartaxo	(kär-tä′shō)	Port.	39·10 n	8·48 w
106	Carteret	(kär′tē-rĕt)	NJ (New York In.)	40·35 n	74·13 w
120	Cartersville	(kär′tērs-vĭl)	Ga.	34·09 n	84·47 w
117	Carthage	(kär′thåj)	Il.	40·27 n	91·09 w
117	Carthage		Mo.	37·10 n	94·18 w
105	Carthage		NY	44·00 n	75·45 w
121	Carthage		NC	35·22 n	79·25 w
119	Carthage		Tx.	32·09 n	94·20 w
210	Carthage		Tun.	37·04 n	10·18 e
213	Carthcart	(cärth-cȧ′t)	S. Afr. (Natal In.)	32·18 s	27·11 e
91	Cartwright	(kärt′rīt)	Can.	53·36 n	57·00 w
135	Caruaru	(kä-rōō-å-rōō′)	Braz.	8·19 s	35·52 w
134	Carúpano	(kä-rōō′pä-nō)	Ven.	10·45 n	63·21 w
117	Caruthersville	(kȧ-rŭdh′ērz-vĭl)	Mo.	36·09 n	89·41 w
112	Carver	(kärv′ēr)	Or. (Portland In.)	45·24 n	122·30 w
162	Carvoeira, Cabo (C.)	(kå′bō-kär-vô-ĕ′y-rä)	Port.	39·22 n	9·24 w
107	Cary	(kă′rē)	Il. (Chicago In.)	42·13 n	88·14 w
137	Casablanca	(kä-sä-bläŋ′kä)	Chile (Santiago In.)	33·19 s	71·24 w
210	Casablanca		Mor.	33·32 n	7·41 w
137	Casa Branca	(kå′sä-brå′N-kä)	Braz. (Rio de Janeiro In.)	21·47 s	47·04 w
115	Casa Grande	(kä′sä grän′dā)	Az.	32·50 n	111·45 w
115	Casa Grande Natl. Mon.		Az.	33·00 n	111·33 w
164	Casale	(kä-sä′lā)	It.	45·08 n	8·26 e
164	Casalmaggiore	(kä-säl-mäd-jō′rā)	It.	45·00 n	10·24 e
214	Casamance (R.)	(kä-sä-mäNs′)	Senegal	12·43 n	16·00 w
205	Cascade Pt.	(kăs-kād′)	N.Z. (In.)	43·59 s	168·23 e
102	Cascade Ra.		U. S.	42·50 n	122·20 w
110	Cascade Tun.		Wa.	47·41 n	120·53 w
163	Cascais	(käs-kȧ-ēzh)	Port. (Lisbon In.)	38·42 n	9·25 w
163	Cascais, Bahía de (B.)	(bä-ē′ä-dĕ-käs-kĭ′s)	Port. (Lisbon In.)	38·41 n	9·24 w
112	Case Inlet	(kās)	Wa. (Seattle In.)	47·22 n	122·47 w
136	Caseros	(kä-sā′rôs)	Arg. (In.)	34·35 s	58·34 w
164	Caserta	(kä-zĕr′tä)	It.	41·04 n	14·21 e
104	Casey	(kā′sĭ)	Il.	39·20 n	88·00 w
110	Cashmere	(kăsh′mĭr)	Wa.	47·30 n	120·28 w
197	Casiguran	(kä-sē-gōō′rän)	Phil. (In.)	16·15 n	122·10 e
197	Casiguran Sd.		Phil. (In.)	16·02 n	121·51 e
137	Casilda	(kä-sē′l-dä)	Arg. (Buenos Aires In.)	33·02 s	61·11 w
128	Casilda		Cuba	21·50 n	80·00 w
137	Casimiro de Abreu	(kä′sē-mē′ro-dĕ-å-brĕ′ōō)	Braz. (Rio de Janeiro In.)	22·30 s	42·11 w
203	Casino	(kȧ-sē′nō)	Austl.	28·35 s	153·10 e
134	Casiquiare (R.)	(kä-sê-kyä′rā)	Ven.	2·11 n	66·15 w
163	Caspe	(käs′på)	Sp.	41·18 n	0·02 w
111	Casper	(kăs′pēr)	Wy.	42·51 n	106·18 w
170	Caspian Dep.	(kăs′pĭ-ăn)	Sov. Un.	47·40 n	52·35 e
168	Caspian Sea		Asia	40·00 n	52·00 e
105	Cass	(kăs)	WV	38·25 n	79·55 w
109	Cass (L.)		Mn.	47·23 n	94·28 w
163	Cassá de la Selva	(käs-sä′dĕ-lä-sĕl-vä)	Sp.	41·52 n	2·52 e
216	Cassai (R.)	(kä-sä′ē)	Ang.	7·30 s	21·45 e
104	Cass City	(kăs)	Mi.	43·35 n	83·10 w
89	Casselman	(kăs′′l-mån)	Can. (Ottawa In.)	45·18 n	75·05 w
108	Casselton	(kăs′′l-tŭn)	ND	46·53 n	97·14 w
137	Cássia	(kå′syä)	Braz. (Rio de Janeiro In.)	20·36 s	46·53 w
113	Cassin	(kăs′ĭn)	Tx. (San Antonio In.)	29·16 n	98·29 w
212	Cassinga	(kä-sĭŋ′gå)	Ang.	15·05 s	16·15 e
164	Cassino	(käs-sē′nō)	It.	41·30 n	13·50 e
109	Cass Lake	(kăs)	Mn.	47·23 n	94·37 w
104	Cassopolis	(kăs-ŏ′pô-lĭs)	Mi.	41·55 n	86·00 w
117	Cassville	(kăs′vĭl)	Mo.	36·41 n	93·52 w
162	Castanheira de Pêra	(käs-tän-yā′rä-dĕ-pĕ′rä)	Port.	40·00 n	8·07 w
160	Casteljaloux	(käs-tĕl-zhä-lōō′)	Fr.	44·20 n	0·04 e
163	Castellammare di Stabia	(käs-tĕl-läm-mä′rā-dē-stä′byä)	It. (Naples In.)	40·26 n	14·29 e
137	Castelli	(kås-tĕ′zhĕ)	Arg. (Buenos Aires In.)	36·07 s	57·48 w
163	Castellón de la Plana	(käs-tĕl-yô′n-dĕ-lä-plä′nä)	Sp.	39·59 n	0·05 w
160	Castelnaudary	(kås′tĕl-nō-dȧ-rē′)	Fr.	43·20 n	1·57 e
137	Castelo	(käs-tĕ′lô)	Braz. (Rio de Janeiro In.)	21·37 s	41·13 w
162	Castelo Branco	(käs-tā′lōō bräŋ′kōō)	Port.	39·48 n	7·37 w
162	Castelo de Vide	(käs-tā′lōō dĭ vē′dĭ)	Port.	39·25 n	7·25 w
160	Castelsarrasin	(kås′tĕl-så-rå-zăN′)	Fr.	44·03 n	1·05 e
164	Castelvetrano	(käs′tĕl-vê-trä′nō)	It.	37·43 n	12·50 e
134	Castilla	(kås-tē′l-yä)	Peru	5·18 s	80·40 w
162	Castilla La Nueva (Reg.)	(käs-tē′lyä lä nwā′vå)	Sp.	39·15 n	3·55 w
162	Castilla La Vieja (Reg.)	(käs-tē′lyä lä vyā′hä)	Sp.	40·48 n	4·24 w
121	Castillo De San Marcos Natl. Mon.	(käs-tē′lyā de-sän mär-kŏs)	Fl.	29·55 n	81·25 w
129	Castle (I.)	(kås′′l)	Ba.	22·05 n	74·20 w
154	Castlebar	(kås′′l-bär)	Ire.	53·55 n	9·15 w
115	Castle Dale	(kås′l dāl)	Ut.	39·15 n	111·00 w
148	Castle Donington	(dŏn′ĭng-tŭn)	Eng.	52·50 n	1·21 w
148	Castleford	(kås′l-fērd)	Eng.	53·43 n	1·21 w
93	Castlegar	(kås′′l-gär)	Can.	49·19 n	117·40 w
203	Castlemaine	(kås′′l-mān)	Austl.	37·05 s	114·10 e
115	Castle Pk.		Co.	39·00 n	106·50 w
110	Castlerock	(kås′′l-rŏk)	Wa.	46·17 n	122·53 w
109	Castle Rock Flowage (Res.)		Wi.	44·03 n	89·48 w
107	Castle Shannon	(shăn′ŭn)	Pa. (Pittsburgh In.)	40·22 n	80·02 w
107	Castleton	(kås′′l-tŏn)	In. (Indianapolis In.)	39·54 n	86·03 w
89	Castor (R.)	(kăs′tôr)	Can (Ottawa In.)	45·16 n	75·14 w
117	Castor (R.)		Mo.	36·59 n	89·53 w
160	Castres	(kås′tr′)	Fr.	43·36 n	2·13 e
127	Castries	(kås-trē′)	St. Lucia (In.)	14·01 n	61·00 w
136	Castro	(käs′trōō)	Braz.	24·56 s	50·00 w
136	Castro	(käs′tro)	Chile	42·27 s	73·48 w
162	Castro Daire	(käs′trōō dīr′ĭ)	Port.	40·56 n	7·57 w
162	Castro de Río	(käs-trô-dĕ-rē′ō)	Sp.	37·42 n	4·28 w
161	Castrop Rauxel	(käs′trōp rou′ksĕl)	F.R.G. (Ruhr In.)	51·33 n	7·19 e
162	Castro Urdiales	(käs′trō ōōr-dyä′lās)	Sp.	43·23 n	3·11 w
112	Castro Valley		Ca. (San Francisco In.)	37·42 n	122·05 w
162	Castro Verde	(käs-trō vĕr′dĕ)	Port.	37·43 n	8·05 w
164	Castrovillari	(käs′trō-vēl-lyä′rē)	It.	39·48 n	16·11 e
162	Castuera	(käs-tōō-ā′rä)	Sp.	38·43 n	5·33 w
217	Casula		Moz.	15·25 s	33·40 e
129	Cat (I.)		Ba.	25·30 n	75·30 w
126	Catacamas	(kä-tä-kä′mäs)	Hond.	14·52 n	85·55 w
137	Cataguases	(kä-tä-gwá′sĕs)	Braz. (Rio de Janeiro In.)	21·23 s	42·42 w
119	Catahoula (L.)	(kăt-ȧ-hōō′lȧ)	La.	31·35 n	92·20 w
135	Catalão	(kä-tä-louN′)	Braz.	18·09 s	47·42 w
129	Catalina (I.)	(kä-tä-lē′nä)	Dom. Rep.	18·20 n	69·00 w

ng-sing; ŋ-baŋk; N-nasalized n; nŏd; cŏmmit; ōld; ôbey; ôrder; fōōd; fŏŏt; ou-out; s-soft; sh-dish; th-thin; pūre; ûnite; ûrn; stŭd; circŭs; ü-as "y" in study; ′-indeterminate vowel.

Page	Name Pronunciation Region	Lat. °′	Long. °′
163	Cataluma (Reg.) (kä-tä-lōō′mä) Sp.	41·23 N	0·50 E
136	Catamarca (Prov.) (kä-tä-mär′kä) Arg.	27·15 S	67·15 W
197	Catanduanes (I.) (kä-tän-dwä′nĕs) Phil.	13·55 N	125·00 E
135	Catanduva (kä-tån-dōō′vä) Braz.	21·12 S	48·47 W
164	Catania (kä-tä′nyä) It.	37·30 N	15·09 E
164	Catania, Golfo di (G.) (gôl-fô-dē-kä-tä′nyä). It.	37·24 N	15·28 E
197	Catanaun (kä-tä-nä′wän) Phil. (In.)	13·36 N	122·20 E
164	Catanzaro (kä-tän-dzä′rō) It.	38·53 N	16·34 E
163	Catarroja (kä-tär-rō′hä) Sp.	39·24 N	0·25 W
121	Catawba (L.) SC	35·02 N	81·21 W
121	Catawba (R.) (kå-tô′bå) NC	35·25 N	80·55 W
125	Catazajá, Laguna de (L.) (lä-gōō′nä-dĕ-kä-tä-zä-hä′). Mex.	17·45 N	92·03 W
197	Catbalogan (kät-bä-lō′gän) Phil.	11·45 N	124·52 E
125	Catemaco (kä-tä-mä′kō) Mex.	18·26 N	95·06 W
125	Catemaco, Lago (L.) (lä′gô-kä-tā-mä′kō). Mex.	18·23 N	95·04 W
148	Caterham (kā′tĕr-ŭm) Eng. (London In.)	51·16 N	0·04 W
216	Catete (kä-tĕ′tĕ) Ang.	9·06 S	13·43 E
118	Cathedral Mt. (kå-thē′drăl) Tx.	30·09 N	103·46 W
213	Cathedral Pk. (kå-thē′drăl) S. Afr. (Natal In.)	28·53 S	29·04 E
117	Catherine, L. (kă-thĕr-ĭn) Ar.	34·26 N	92·47 W
213	Cathkin Pk. (kăth′kĭn) S. Afr. (Natal In.)	29·08 S	29·22 E
112	Cathlamet (kăth-lăm′ĕt) Wa. (Portland In.)	46·12 N	123·22 W
104	Catlettsburg (kăt′lĕts-bûrg) Ky.	38·20 N	82·35 W
122	Catoche, C. (kä-tô′chĕ) Mex.	21·30 N	87·15 W
106	Catonsville (kā′tŭnz-vĭl) Md. (Baltimore In.)	39·16 N	76·45 W
124	Catorce (kä-tôr′så) Mex.	23·41 N	100·51 W
105	Catskill (kăts′kĭl) NY	42·15 N	73·50 W
105	Catskill Mts. NY	42·20 N	74·35 W
105	Cattaraugus Ind. Res. (kăt′tă-ră-gŭs). NY	42·30 N	79·05 W
135	Catu (kå-tōō) Braz.	12·26 S	38·12 W
216	Catuala Ang.	16·29 S	19·03 E
216	Catumbela (R.) (kä′tŏm-bĕl′å) Ang.	12·40 S	14·10 E
197	Cauayan (kou-ä′yän) Phil. (In.)	16·56 N	121·46 E
134	Cauca (R.) (kou′kä) Col.	7·30 N	75·26 W
135	Caucagua (käōō-kå′gwä). Ven.(In.)	10·17 N	66·22 W
171	Caucasus Mts. (kô′kå-sŭs). Sov. Un.	43·20 N	42·00 E
95	Cauchon L. (kô-shŏn′) Can.	55·25 N	96·30 W
160	Cauderan (kō-dā-räɴ′) Fr.	44·50 N	0·40 W
89	Caughnawaga Can. (Montreal In.)	45·24 N	73·41 W
164	Caulonia (kou-lō′nyä) It.	38·24 N	16·22 E
136	Cauquenes (kou-kā′nās) Chile	35·54 S	72·14 W
134	Caura (R.) (kou′rä) Ven.	6·48 N	64·40 W
98	Causapscal Can.	48·22 N	67·14 W
92	Caution, C. (kô′shŭn) Can.	51·10 N	127·47 W
129	Cauto (R.) (kou′tō) Cuba	20·33 N	76·20 W
184	Cauvery (R.) India	11·15 N	78·06 E
136	Cava (kå′vä) Braz. (In.)	22·41 S	43·26 W
163	Cava de' Tirreni (kä′vä-dĕ-tēr-rĕ′nē). It. (Naples In.)	40·27 N	14·43 E
162	Cavado (R.) (kä-vä′dō) Port.	41·43 N	8·08 W
135	Cavalcante (kå-väl-kän′tä) Braz.	13·45 S	47·33 W
108	Cavalier (kăv-å-lēr′) ND	48·45 N	97·39 W
214	Cavally (R.) Ivory Coast-Lib.	4·40 N	7·30 W
154	Cavan (kăv′ăn) Ire.	54·01 N	7·00 W
164	Cavarzere (kä-vär′dzå-rā) It.	45·08 N	12·06 E
105	Cavendish (kăv′ĕn-dĭsh) Vt.	43·25 N	72·35 W
135	Caviana, Ilha (I.) (kä-vyä′nä) Braz.	0·45 N	49·33 W
197	Cavite (kä-vē′tä) Phil. (In.)	14·30 N	120·54 E
148	Cawood (kā′wŏŏd) Eng.	53·49 N	1·07 W
137	Caxambu (kä-shå′m-bōō) Braz. (Rio de Janeiro In.)	22·00 S	44·45 W
135	Caxias (kä′shē-äzh) Braz.	4·48 S	43·16 W
136	Caxias do Sul (kä′shē-äzh-dô-sōō′l). Braz.	29·13 S	51·03 W
163	Caxine, Cap (C.) (kăp kăk′sēn) Alg.	36·47 N	2·52 E
216	Caxito (kä-shē′tō) Ang.	8·33 S	13·36 E
134	Cayambe (kå-ïä′m-bĕ) Ec.	0·03 N	79·09 W
135	Cayenne (kā-ĕn′) Fr. Gu.	4·56 N	52·18 W
124	Cayetano Rubio (kä-yĕ-tå-nô-rōō′byô). Mex.	20·37 N	100·21 W
123	Cayey....P. R. (Puerto Rico In.)	18·05 N	66·12 W
128	Cayman Brac (I.) (kī-män′ bråk) Cayman Is.	19·45 N	79·50 W
128	Cayman Is. N. A.	19·30 N	80·30 W
128	Cay Sal Bk. (kē-săl) Ba.	23·55 N	80·20 W
105	Cayuga (L.) (kā-yōō′gå) NY	42·35 N	76·35 W
162	Cazalla de la Sierra (kä-thäl′yä-dĕ-lä-sē-ĕ′r-rä). Sp.	37·55 N	5·48 W
160	Cazaux, Étang de (L.) (ā-täɴ′ dĕ kä-zō′). Fr.	44·32 N	0·59 W
105	Cazenovia (kăz-ē-nō′vĭ-å) NY	42·55 N	75·50 W
107	Cazenovia Cr...NY (Buffalo In.)	42·49 N	78·45 W
164	Čazma (chäz′mä) Yugo.	45·44 N	16·39 E
212	Cazombo (kä-zô′m-bō) Ang.	12·25 S	22·40 E
125	Cazones (R.) (kä-zô′nĕs) Mex.	20·37 N	97·28 W
128	Cazones, Ensenada de (B.) (ĕn-sĕ-nä-dä-dĕ-kä-zō′nås). Cuba	22·05 N	81·30 W
128	Cazones, Golfo de (G.) (gôl-fô-dĕ-kä-zō′nås). Cuba	23·55 N	81·15 W
162	Cazorla (kä-thôr′lå) Sp.	37·55 N	2·58 W
162	Cea (R.) (thā′ä) Sp.	42·18 N	5·10 W
	Ceará, see Fortaleza		
135	Ceará (State) (sā-å-rä′) Braz.	5·13 S	39·43 W
135	Ceará-Mirim (sā-ä-rä′mē-rē′ɴ) Braz.	6·00 S	35·13 W
127	Cebaco, Isla (I.) (ĕ′s-lä-sä-bä′kō) Pan.	7·27 N	81·08 W
115	Cebolla Cr. (sē-bōl′yä) Co.	38·15 N	107·10 W
162	Cebollera, Sierra (Mts.) (sē-ĕ′r-rä-sĕ-bôl-yĕ-rä). Sp.	42·03 N	2·53 W
162	Cebreros (sĕ-brĕ′rôs) Sp.	40·28 N	4·28 W
197	Cebu (sā-bōō′) Phil.	10·22 N	123·49 E
107	Cecil (sē′sĭl)...Pa. (Pittsburgh In.)	40·20 N	80·10 W
109	Cedar (R.) Ia.	42·23 N	92·07 W
112	Cedar (R.)....Wa. (Portland In.)	45·56 N	122·32 W
109	Cedar (R.) West Fk. Ia.	42·49 N	93·10 W
119	Cedar Bayou Tx. (In.)	29·54 N	94·58 W
115	Cedar Breaks Natl. Mon. Ut.	37·35 N	112·55 W
109	Cedarburg (sē′dēr bûrg) Wi.	43·23 N	88·00 W
115	Cedar City Ut.	37·40 N	113·10 W
108	Cedar Cr. ND	46·05 N	102·10 W
109	Cedar Falls Ia.	42·31 N	92·29 W
120	Cedar Keys Fl.	29·06 N	83·03 W
107	Cedar Lake.....In. (Chicago In.)	41·22 N	87·27 W
107	Cedar L........In. (Chicago In.)	41·23 N	87·25 W
109	Cedar Rapids Ia.	42·00 N	91·43 W
104	Cedar Springs Mi.	43·15 N	85·40 W
120	Cedartown (sē′dēr-toun) Ga.	34·00 N	85·15 W
213	Cedarville (cêdår′vĭl) S. Afr. (Natal In.)	30·23 S	29·04 E
124	Cedral (sā-dräl′) Mex.	23·47 N	100·42 W
126	Cedros (sā′drōs) Hond.	14·36 N	87·07 W
122	Cedros (I.) Mex.	28·10 N	115·10 W
204	Ceduna (sē-dōō′nå) Austl.	32·15 S	133·55 E
164	Cefalù (chā-fä-lōō′) It.	38·01 N	14·01 E
162	Cega (R.) (thā′gä) Sp.	41·25 N	4·27 W
159	Cegléd (tsā′glād) Hung.	47·10 N	19·49 E
165	Ceglie (chĕ′lyĕ) It.	40·39 N	17·32 E
162	Cehegín (thā-å-hēn′) Sp.	38·05 N	1·48 W
129	Ceiba del Agua (sā′bä-dĕl-ä′gwä) Cuba (In.)	22·08 N	82·38 W
210	Cekhira Tun.	34·17 N	10·00 E
216	Cela (sĕ-lå) Ang.	11·25 S	15·07 E
124	Celaya (sā-lä′yä) Mex.	20·33 N	100·49 W
196	Celebes Sea Indon.	3·45 N	121·52 E
126	Celestún (sĕ-lĕs-tōō′n)..Mex. (In.)	20·57 N	90·18 W
104	Celina (sêlī′na) Oh.	40·30 N	84·35 W
164	Celje (tsĕl′yĕ) Yugo.	46·13 N	15·17 E
158	Celle (tsĕl′ĕ) F.R.G.	52·37 N	10·05 E
116	Cement (sē-mĕnt′) Ok.	34·56 N	98·07 W
197	Cenderawasih Teluk (B.)...Indon.	2·20 S	135·30 E
135	Ceniza, Pico (Mtn.) (pē′kô-sĕ-nē′zä). Ven. (In.)	10·24 N	67·26 W
160	Cenon (sĕ-nôɴ′) Fr.	44·51 N	0·33 W
119	Center (sĕn′tēr) Tx.	31·50 N	94·10 W
120	Centerhill Res. (sĕn′tēr-hĭl)....Tn.	36·02 N	86·00 W
107	Center Line (sĕn′tēr līn) Mi. (Detroit In.)	42·29 N	83·01 W
109	Centerville (sĕn′tēr-vĭl) Ia.	40·44 N	92·48 W
113	Centerville. Mn. (Minneapolis, St. Paul In.)	45·10 N	93·03 W
107	Centerville...Pa. (Pittsburgh In.)	40·02 N	79·58 W
108	Centerville SD	43·07 N	96·56 W
113	Centerville Ut. (Salt Lake City In.)	40·55 N	111·53 W
134	Central, Cordillera (Mts.) (kôr-dĕl-yĕ′rä-sĕn-trá′l)... Bol.	19·18 S	65·29 W
134	Central, Cordillera (Mts.) Col. (In.)	3·58 N	75·55 W
129	Central, Cordillera (Cibao Mts.) (kôr-dĕl-yä′rä sĕn′träl) (sē-bä′ô) Dom. Rep.	19·05 N	71·30 W
197	Central Cordillera (Mts.) (kôr-dĕl-yĕ′rä-sĕn′träl) Phil. (In.)	17·05 N	120·55 E
209	Central African Empire Afr.	7·50 N	21·00 E
122	Central America (ä-mĕr′ĭ-kå) N. A.	10·45 N	87·15 W
120	Central City (sĕn′trăl) Ky.	37·15 N	87·09 W
108	Central City (sĕn′trăl sĭ′tĭ)...Ne.	41·07 N	98·00 W
106	Central Falls (sĕn′trăl fôlz) RI (Providence In.)	41·54 N	71·23 W
104	Centralia (sĕn-trā′lĭ-å) Il.	38·35 N	89·05 W
117	Centralia Mo.	39·11 N	92·07 W
110	Centralia Wa.	46·42 N	122·58 W
170	Central Plat. Sov. Un.	55·00 N	33·30 E
106	Central Valley NY (New York In.)	41·19 N	74·07 W
113	Centreville (sĕn′tēr-vĭl) Il. (St. Louis In.)	38·33 N	90·06 W
105	Centreville Md.	39·05 N	76·05 W
197	Centro (sĕ′n-trô) Phil .(In.)	17·16 N	121·48 E
120	Century (sĕn′tû-rĭ) Fl.	30·57 N	87·15 W
	Cephalonia (I.), see Kefallinéa		
160	Céret (sā-rĕ′) Fr.	42·29 N	2·47 E
134	Cereté (sĕ-rĕ-tĕ′) Col.	8·56 N	75·58 W
164	Cerignola (chā-rē-nyô′lä) It.	41·16 N	15·55 E
164	Cerknica (tsĕr′knē-tså) Yugo.	45·48 N	14·21 E
118	Cerralvo (sĕr-räl′vō) Mex.	26·05 N	99·37 W
122	Cerralvo (I.) Mex.	24·00 N	109·59 W
134	Cerrito (sĕr-rĕ′-tô) Col. (In.)	3·41 N	76·17 W
124	Cerritos (sĕr-rē′tōs) Mex.	22·26 N	100·16 W
134	Cerro de Pasco (sĕr′rō dā päs′kō) Peru	10·45 S	76·14 W
118	Cerro Gordo, Arroyo de (är-rô-yô-dĕ-sĕ′r-rô-gôr-dō). Mex.	26·12 N	104·06 W
134	Certegui (sĕr-tĕ′gē)... Col. (In.)	5·21 N	76·35 W
197	Cervantes (sĕr-vän′tās)..Phil (In.)	16·59 N	120·42 E
162	Cervantes (thĕr-vän′tās) Sp.	42·43 N	7·04 W
162	Cervera del Río Alhama (thĕr-vā′rå dĕl rē′ō-äl-ä′mä). Sp.	42·02 N	1·55 W
163	Cerveteri (chĕr-vĕ′tĕ-rē) It. (Rome In.)	42·00 N	12·06 E
164	Cesena (chĕ′sĕ-nä) It.	44·08 N	12·16 E
157	Çēsis (sā′sĭs) Sov. Un.	57·19 N	25·17 E
158	Česká Lípa (chĕs′kä lē′pa). Czech.	50·41 N	14·31 E
158	České (Bohemia) (Prov.) (chĕs′kā) (bô-hē′mĭ-å). Czech.	49·51 N	13·55 E
158	České Budějovice (chĕs′kä bōō′dyĕ-yô-vēt-sĕ). Czech.	49·00 N	14·30 E
158	Českomoravaska Vysočina (Mts.) Czech.	49·21 N	15·40 E
165	Cesme (chĕsh′mĕ) Tur.	38·20 N	26·20 E
203	Cessnock Austl.	32·58 S	151·15 E
214	Cestos (R.) Lib.	5·40 N	9·25 W
165	Cetinje (tsĕt′in-yĕ) Yugo.	42·23 N	18·55 E
210	Ceuta (Sp.) (thā-ōō′tä) Aft.	36·04 N	5·36 W
160	Cévennes (Reg.) (sā-vĕn′) Fr.	44·20 N	3·48 E
153	Ceyhan (R.) Tur.	37·19 N	36·06 E
	Ceylon, see Sri Lanka		
112	Chabot (L.) (sha′bŏt) Ca. (San Francisco In.)	37·44 N	122·06 W
137	Chacabuco (chä-kä-bōō′kō) Arg. (Buenos Aires In.)	34·37 S	60·27 W
125	Chacaltianguis (chä-käl-tê-äŋ′gwês). Mex.	18·18 N	95·50 W
134	Chachapoyas (chä-chä-poi′yäs) Peru	6·16 S	77·48 W
136	Chaco (Prov.) (chä′kō) Arg.	26·00 S	60·45 W
115	Chaco Canyon Natl. Mon. (chä′kō). NM	35·38 N	108·06 W
174	Chad (chăd) Sov. Un. (Urals In.)	56·33 N	57·11 E
209	Chad Afr.	17·48 N	19·00 E
215	Chad, L. Afr.	13·55 N	13·40 E
121	Chadbourn (chăd′bŭrn) NC	34·19 N	78·55 W
108	Chadron (chăd′rŭn) Ne.	42·50 N	103·10 W
162	Chafarinas (C.) Mor.	35·08 N	2·20 W
117	Chaffee (chăf′ē) Mo.	37·10 N	89·39 W
186	Chāgal Hills Afg.-Pak.	29·15 N	63·28 E
166	Chagodoshcha (R.) (chä-gō-dôsh-chä). Sov. Un.	59·08 N	35·13 E
127	Chagres R. (chä′grĕs) Pan.	9·18 N	79·22 W
107	Chagrin R. (shå′grĭn) Oh. (Cleveland In.)	41·34 N	81·24 W
107	Chagrin Falls (shå′grĭn fôls) Oh. (Cleveland In.)	41·26 N	81·23 W
192	Ch'ahaerh (Reg.) (chä′här). China	44·25 N	115·00 E
186	Chāh Bahār (chä′h′ bä′här) Iran	25·18 N	60·45 E
217	Chake Chake Tan.	5·15 S	39·46 E
194	Chalantun (chä′län-tōōn′) China	47·59 N	122·56 E
126	Chalatenango (chäl-ä-tĕ-näŋ′gō) Sal.	14·04 N	88·54 W
217	Chalbi Des. Ken.	3·40 N	36·50 E
125	Chalcatongo (chäl-kä-tôŋ′gō) Mex.	17·04 N	97·41 W
124	Chalchihuites (chäl-chê-wē′tâs) Mex.	23·28 N	103·57 W
126	Chalchuapa (chäl-chwä′pä) Sal.	14·01 N	89·39 W
125	Chalco (chäl-kō) Mex. (In.)	19·15 N	98·54 W
98	Chaleur B. (shå-lûr′) Can.	47·58 N	65·33 W
148	Chalgrove (chăl′grôv) (Eng. (London In.)	51·38 N	1·05 W
193	Chaling (chä′lĭng) China	27·00 N	113·31 E
106	Chalmette (shăl-mĕt′) La. (New Orleans In.)	29·57 N	89·57 W
160	Châlons-sur-Marne (shå-lôɴ′sür-märn). Fr.	48·57 N	4·23 E
160	Châlon-sur-Saône Fr.	46·47 N	4·54 E
136	Chaltel, Cerro (Mtn.) (sĕ′r-rô-chäl′tĕl). Arg.-Chile	48·10 S	73·18 W
115	Chama (R.) (chä′mä) NM	36·19 N	106·31 W
126	Chama, Sierra de (Mts.) (sē-ĕ′r-rä-dĕ-chä-mä). Guat.	15·48 N	90·20 W
160	Chamalières (shä-mä-lyâr) Fr.	45·45 N	2·59 E
217	Chamama Malawi	12·55 S	33·43 E
184	Chaman (chŭm-än′) Pak.	30·58 N	66·21 E
184	Chambal (R.) (chŭm-bäl′) India	26·05 N	76·37 E
108	Chamberlain (chām′bēr-lĭn) SD	43·48 N	99·21 W
98	Chamberlain (L.) Me.	46·15 N	69·10 W
105	Chambersburg (chām′bērz-bûrg) Pa.	40·00 N	77·40 W
161	Chambéry (shäm-bā-rē′) Fr.	45·35 N	5·54 E
217	Chambeshi (R.) Zambia	10·35 S	31·20 E
106	Chamblee (chăm-blē′) Ga. (Atlanta In.)	33·55 N	84·18 W
89	Chambly (shäɴ-blē′) Can. (Montreal In.)	45·27 N	73·17 W
161	Chambly Fr. (Paris In.)	49·11 N	2·14 E
91	Chambord Can.	48·22 N	72·01 W
127	Chame, Punta (Pt.) (pōō′n-tä-chä′må). Pan.	8·41 N	79·27 W
126	Chamelecón (R.) (chä-mĕ-lĕ-kô′n) Hond.	15·09 N	88·42 W
161	Chamonix (shå-mô-nē′) Fr.	45·55 N	6·50 E
160	Champagne (Reg.) (shäm-pän′yĕ). Fr.	48·53 N	4·48 E
104	Champaign (shăm-pān′) Il.	40·10 N	88·15 W
184	Champdāni India (In.)	22·48 N	88·21 E
126	Champerico (chäm-på-rē′kō) Guat.	14·18 N	91·55 W
109	Champion (chăm′pĭ-ŭn) Mi.	46·30 N	87·59 W
105	Champlain, L. (shăm-plān′) NY-Vt.	44·45 N	73·20 W
161	Champlitte (shäɴ-plēt′) Fr.	47·38 N	5·28 E
125	Champotón (chäm-pō-tōn′) Mex.	19·21 N	90·43 W
125	Champotón (R.) Mex.	19·19 N	90·15 W
136	Chañaral (chän-yä-räl′) Chile	26·20 S	70·46 W
162	Chanca (R.) (chäŋ′kä)..Sp.-Port.	37·48 N	7·18 W
193	Chanchiang (Fort Bayard). China	21·20 N	110·28 E
120	Chandeleur Is. (shăn-dē-lōōr′). La.	29·53 N	88·35 W
120	Chandeleur Sd. La.	29·47 N	89·08 W
184	Chandīgarh India	30·51 N	77·13 E
91	Chandler (chăn′dlēr) Can.	48·21 N	64·41 W
117	Chandler Ok.	35·42 N	96·52 W
184	Chandrapur India	19·58 N	79·21 E
190	Chang (R.) (jäng) China	36·17 N	114·31 E
212	Changane (R.) Moz.	22·42 S	32·46 E
217	Changara Moz.	16·54 S	33·14 E
190	Ch'angch'ihuang (chäng′chē′zhōōäng). China	37·59 N	116·57 E
192	Ch'angchih China	35·58 N	112·58 E
190	Ch'angch'ing (chäng′chĭng). China	36·33 N	116·42 E

ăt; finăl; rāte; senâte; ärm; åsk; sofå; fâre; ch-choose; dh-as th in other; bē; ēvent; bĕt; recĕnt; cratĕr; g-go; gh-guttural g; bĭt; ĭ-short neutral; rīde; ĸ-guttural k as ch in German ich;

PRONOUNCING INDEX

Changch'iu — Chernovtsy 267

Page	Name / Pronunciation / Region	Lat. °'	Long. °'
190	Changch'iu (zhängchiû) China	36·50 N	117·29 E
190	Ch'angchou China	31·47 N	119·56 E
193	Changchou China	24·35 N	117·45 E
192	Ch'angch'un (Hsinking) (chäng'chōōn') (hsĭn'kĭng) China	43·55 N	125·25 E
190	Ch'anghsing Tao (I.) (chängsĭng dou). China	39·38 N	121·10 E
192	Ch'anghsintien China (In.)	39·49 N	116·12 E
193	Changhua (chäng'hwä') Taiwan	24·02 N	120·32 E
190	Changhutien (jang'hōō'dĭan) China	32·07 N	114·44 E
190	Ch'angi (jäng'yē) China	36·51 N	119·23 E
194	Changjŏn (chäng'jŭn') Kor.	38·40 N	128·05 E
192	Changkochuang China (In.)	40·09 N	116·56 E
192	Changkuangts'ai Ling (Mts.) China	43·50 N	127·55 E
190	Ch'angli (chäng'lē') China	39·46 N	119·10 E
192	Changpei (chäng'pē') China	41·12 N	114·50 E
194	Changsan Cot (I.) Kor.	38·06 N	124·50 E
193	Ch'angsha China	28·20 N	113·00 E
190	Ch'angshan Liehtao (Is.) (chäng'shän' lĭēdou). China	39·08 N	122·26 E
190	Ch'angshan Tao (I.) (chäng'shän' dou). China	37·56 N	120·42 E
190	Ch'angshu (chäng'shōō') China	31·40 N	120·45 E
193	Ch'angte (chäng'tĕ') China	29·00 N	111·38 E
193	Changting China	25·50 N	116·18 E
188	Ch'angtu (chäng'tōō') China	31·06 N	96·30 E
194	Changtu China	43·00 N	124·02 E
190	Ch'angtzu Tao (I.) (chäng'zhōō dou). China	39·02 N	122·44 E
192	Changwu (chäng'wōō') China	35·12 N	107·45 E
194	Changwu China	42·21 N	123·00 E
188	Changyeh China	38·46 N	101·00 E
190	Ch'angyüan (chäng'yü-än'). China	35·10 N	114·41 E
113	Chanhassen (shăn'hăs-sĕn) Mn. (Minneapolis, St. Paul In.)	44·52 N	93·32 W
190	Chanhua (jän'hōōä) China	37·42 N	117·49 E
146	Channel Is. (chăn'ĕl) Eur.	49·15 N	3·30 W
91	Channel-Port-aux-Basques Can.	47·35 N	59·11 W
119	Channelview (chăn'elvū). Tx. (In.)	29·46 N	95·07 W
192	Chanping China	40·12 N	116·10 E
162	Chantada (chän-tä'dä) Sp.	42·38 N	7·36 W
196	Chanthaburi Thai.	12·37 N	102·04 E
161	Chantilly (shäN-tē-yē') Fr. (Paris In.)	49·12 N	2·30 E
106	Chantilly (shăn'tĭlē) Va. (Baltimore In.)	38·53 N	77·26 W
90	Chantrey Inlet (chăn-trē) Can.	67·49 N	95·00 W
117	Chanute (shȧ-nōōt') Ks.	37·41 N	95·27 W
172	Chany (L.) (chä'nē) Sov. Un.	54·15 N	77·31 E
192	Chanyü China	44·30 N	122·30 E
193	Ch'aoan (chä'ō-än') China	23·48 N	117·10 E
190	Ch'aohsien (chou'sĭän) China	31·37 N	117·50 E
190	Chaohsien China	37·46 N	114·48 E
196	Chao Phraya, Mae Nam (R.) Thai.	16·13 N	99·33 E
190	Ch'aoshui (jĭousōōĭ) China	37·43 N	120·56 E
193	Chaot'ung (chä'ō-tōōng) China	27·18 N	103·50 E
193	Ch'aoyang (chä'ō-yäng') China	23·18 N	116·32 E
192	Ch'aoyang (Foshan) China	41·32 N	120·20 E
190	Chaoyüan (chä'ō-yü-än') China	37·22 N	120·23 E
135	Chapada, Serra da (Mts.) (sĕ'r-rä-dä-shä-pä'dä). Braz.	14·57 S	54·34 W
137	Chapadão Serra do (Mtn.) (sĕ'r-rä-dô-shä-pȧ-dou'N) Braz. (Rio de Janeiro In.)	20·31 S	46·20 W
124	Chapala (chä-pä'lä) Mex.	20·18 N	103·10 W
124	Chapala, Lago de (L.) (lä'gô-dĕ-chä-pä'lä). Mex.	20·14 N	103·02 W
124	Chapalagana (R.) (chä-pä-lä-gȧ'nä). Mex.	22·11 N	104·09 W
134	Chaparral (chä-pär-rá'l). Col. (In.)	3·44 N	75·28 W
171	Chapayevsk (châ-pī'ĕfsk). Sov. Un.	53·00 N	49·30 E
121	Chapel Hill (chăp''l hĭl) NC	35·55 N	79·05 W
112	Chaplain (L.) (chăp'lĭn) Wa. (Seattle In.)	47·58 N	121·50 W
91	Chapleau (chăp-lō') Can.	47·43 N	83·28 W
93	Chapman, Mt. (chăp'mȧn) Can.	51·50 N	118·20 W
212	Chapman's B. (chăp'mȧns bă) S. Afr. (In.)	34·06 S	18·17 E
108	Chappell (chă-pĕl') Ne.	41·06 N	102·29 W
125	Chapultenango (chä-pōōl-tē-näŋ'gō). Mex.	17·19 N	93·08 W
216	Chá Pungana Ang.	13·44 S	18·39 E
124	Charcas (chär'käs) Mex.	23·09 N	101·09 W
127	Charco de Azul, Bahía (B.) (bä-ē'ä-chä'r-kō-dĕ-ä-zōō'l). Pan.	8·14 N	82·45 W
147	Chardzhou (chĕr-jô'ōō) Sov. Un.	38·52 N	63·37 E
160	Charente (R.) (shȧ-räNt') Fr.	45·48 N	0·28 W
215	Chari (R.) (shä-rē') Chad	12·45 N	14·55 E
148	Charing (chă'rĭng) Eng. (London In.)	51·13 N	0·49 E
109	Chariton (châr'ĭ-tŭn) Ia.	41·02 N	93·16 W
117	Chariton (R.) Mo.	40·24 N	92·38 W
89	Charlemagne (shärl-mäny') Can. (Montreal In.)	45·43 N	73·29 W
155	Charleroi (shȧr-lē-rwä') Bel.	50·25 N	4·35 E
107	Charleroi (shär'lē-roi) Pa. (Pittsburgh In.)	40·08 N	79·54 W
121	Charles, C. (chärlz) Va.	37·05 N	75·48 W
89	Charlesbourg (shȧrl-bōōr') Can. (Quebec In.)	46·51 N	71·16 W
109	Charles City (chärlz) Ia.	43·03 N	92·40 W
104	Charleston (chärlz'tŭn) Il.	39·30 N	88·10 W
120	Charleston Ms.	34·00 N	90·02 W
117	Charleston Mo.	36·53 N	89·20 W
121	Charleston SC	32·47 N	79·56 W
104	Charleston WV	38·20 N	81·35 W
107	Charlestown (chärlz'toun) In. (Louisville In.)	38·46 N	85·39 W
127	Charlestown St. Kitts-Nevis-Anguilla (In.)	17·10 N	62·32 W
216	Charlesville Zaire	5·27 S	20·58 E
203	Charleville (chär'lē-vĭl) Austl.	26·16 S	146·28 E
160	Charleville Mézières (shärl-vĕl') Fr.	49·48 N	4·41 E
104	Charlevoix (shär'lē-voi) Mi.	45·20 N	85·15 W
109	Charlevoix, L. Mi.	45·17 N	85·43 W
104	Charlotte (shär'lŏt) Mi.	42·35 N	84·50 W
121	Charlotte NC	35·15 N	80·50 W
123	Charlotte Amalie (St. Thomas) (shär-lŏt'ĕ ä-mä'lĭ-ȧ). Virgin Is. (U. S. A.) (St. Thomas In.)	18·21 N	64·54 W
92	Charlotte L. Can.	52·07 N	125·30 W
121	Charlotte Hbr. Fl. (In.)	26·49 N	82·00 W
156	Charlottenberg (shär-lŭt'ĕn-bĕrg) Swe.	59·53 N	12·17 E
105	Charlottesville (shär'lŏtz-vĭl) Va.	38·00 N	78·25 W
99	Charlottetown (shär'lŏt-toun) Can.	46·14 N	63·08 W
204	Charlotte Waters (shär'lŏt). Austl.	26·00 S	134·50 E
161	Charmes (shärm) Fr.	48·23 N	6·19 E
148	Charnwood For. (chärn'wŏŏd) Eng.	52·42 N	1·15 W
89	Charny (shär-nē') Can. (Quebec In.)	46·43 N	71·16 W
184	Charol Tsho (L.) China	34·00 N	81·47 E
161	Chars (shär) Fr. (Paris In.)	49·09 N	1·57 E
187	Chārsadda (chŭr-sä'dä) Pak. (Khyber Pass In.)	34·17 N	71·43 E
205	Charters Towers (chär'tērz). Austl.	20·03 S	146·20 E
161	Chartres (shärt'r'). Fr. (Paris In.)	48·26 N	1·29 E
137	Chascomús (chäs-kō-mōōs') Arg. (Buenos Aires In.)	35·32 S	58·01 W
121	Chase City (chās) Va.	36·45 N	78·27 W
166	Chashniki (chäsh'nyē-kē). Sov. Un.	54·51 N	29·08 E
113	Chaska (chăs'kȧ) Mn. (Minneapolis, St. Paul In.)	44·48 N	93·36 W
160	Châteaubriant (shȧ-tō-brē-äN'). Fr.	47·43 N	1·23 W
160	Châteaudun (shä-tō-däN') Fr.	48·04 N	1·23 E
160	Château-Gontier (chȧ-tō'gôN' tyā'). Fr.	47·48 N	0·43 W
89	Châteauguay (chȧ-tō-gā) Can. (Montreal In.)	45·22 N	73·45 W
89	Châteauguay (R.) Can. (Montreal In.)	45·13 N	73·51 W
160	Chateauneuf-les-Martigues (shä-tō-nûf'lā-mär-tēg'ĕ) Fr. (In.)	43·23 N	5·11 E
160	Château-Renault (shȧ-tō-rē-nō') Fr.	47·36 N	0·57 E
89	Château-Richer (shȧ-tō'rē-shā') Can. (Quebec In.)	47·00 N	71·01 W
160	Châteauroux (shȧ-tō-rōō') Fr.	46·47 N	1·39 E
160	Château-Thierry (shȧ-tō'tyĕr-rē') Fr.	49·03 N	3·22 E
160	Châtellerault (shä-tĕl-rō') Fr.	46·48 N	0·31 E
109	Chatfield (chăt'fēld) Mn.	43·50 N	92·10 W
96	Chatham (chăt'ȧm) Can.	42·25 N	82·10 W
98	Chatham Can.	47·02 N	65·28 W
148	Chatham (chăt'ŭm) Eng. (London In.)	51·23 N	0·32 E
106	Chatham (chăt'ȧm) NJ (New York In.)	40·44 N	74·23 W
107	Chatham Oh. (Cleveland In.)	41·06 N	82·01 W
198	Chatham Is. N. Z.	44·00 S	178·00 W
92	Chatham Sd. Can.	54·32 N	130·35 W
101	Chatham Str. Ak.	57·00 N	134·40 W
113	Chatsworth (chătz'wûrth) Ca. (Los Angeles In.)	34·16 N	118·36 W
113	Chatsworth Res. Ca. (Los Angeles In.)	34·15 N	118·41 W
120	Chattahoochee (chăt-tȧ-hōō' chē) Fl.	30·42 N	84·47 W
120	Chattahoochee (R.) Al.-Ga.	31·17 N	85·10 W
120	Chattanooga (chăt-ȧ-nōō'gȧ) Tn.	35·01 N	85·15 W
120	Chattooga (R.) (chă-tōō'gȧ) Ga.-SC	34 47 N	83·13 W
97	Chaudière (R.) (shō-dyĕr') Can.	46·26 N	71·10 W
196	Chau Doc (shō-dŏk') Camb.	10·49 N	104·57 E
160	Chaumont (shō-môN') Fr.	48·08 N	5·07 E
161	Chaumontel (shō-mŏN-tĕl') Fr. (Paris In.)	49·07 N	2·26 E
173	Chaunskaya Guba (B.) Sov. Un.	69·15 N	170·00 E
160	Chauny (shō-nē') Fr.	49·40 N	3·09 E
166	Chausy (chou'sĭ) Sov. Un.	53·57 N	30·58 E
105	Chautauqua (L.) (shȧ-tô'kwȧ). NY	42·10 N	79·25 W
170	Chavaniga Sov. Un.	66·02 N	37·50 E
162	Chaves (chä'vĕzh) Port.	41·44 N	7·30 W
124	Chavinda (chä-vē'n-dä) Mex.	20·01 N	102·27 W
125	Chazumba (chä-zōōm'bä) Mex.	18·11 N	97·41 W
148	Cheadle (chē'd'l) Eng.	52·59 N	1·59 W
105	Cheat (R.) (chēt) WV	39·35 N	79·40 W
158	Cheb (kĕb) Czech.	50·05 N	12·23 E
174	Chebarkul (chĕ-bȧr-kûl') Sov. Un. (Urals In.)	54·59 N	60·22 E
170	Cheboksary (chyĕ-bôk-sä'rê) Sov. Un.	56·00 N	47·20 E
104	Cheboygan (shê-boi'găn) Mi.	45·40 N	84·30 W
210	Chech, Erg (Dune) Alg.	24·45 N	2·07 W
171	Chechen' (I.) (chyĕch'ĕn). Sov. Un.	44·00 N	48·10 E
190	Chech'eng (jĭŭcheng) China	34·05 N	115·19 E
	Chechiang (Prov.), see Chekiang		
117	Checotah (chê-kō'tȧ) Ok.	35·27 N	95·32 W
99	Chedabucto B. (chĕd-ȧ-bŭk-tō) Can.	45·23 N	61·10 W
196	Cheduba (I.) Bur.	18·45 N	93·01 E
94	Cheecham Hills (chēē'hăm) Can.	56·20 N	111·10 W
107	Cheektowaga (chēk-tŏ-wä'gȧ) NY (Buffalo In.)	42·54 N	78·46 W
	Chefoo, see Yent'ai		
110	Chehalis (chê-hā'lĭs) Wa.	46·39 N	122·58 W
110	Chehalis R. Wa.	46·47 N	123·17 W
194	Cheju (chĕ'jōō') Kor.	33·29 N	126·40 E
194	Cheju (Quelpart) (I.) Kor.	33·20 N	126·25 E
166	Chekalin (chĕ-kä'lĭn) Sov. Un.	54·05 N	36·13 E
190	Chekao (jĭŭgou) China	31·47 N	117·44 E
189	Chekiang (Chechiang) (Prov.) China	29·30 N	120·00 E
212	Chela, Serra da (Mts.) (sĕr'rȧ dā shā'lȧ). Ang.	15·30 S	13·30 E
110	Chelan (chê-lăn') Wa.	47·51 N	119·59 W
110	Chelan (L.) Wa.	48·09 N	120·20 W
193	Chelang Chiao (Pt.) China	22·38 N	116·00 E
163	Cheleiros (shĕ-la'rōzh) Port. (Lisbon In.)	38·54 N	9·19 W
151	Chelia (Mtn.) Alg.	35·22 N	6·47 E
163	Chéliff, Oued (R.) (ōō-ĕd shā-lēf) Alg.	36·17 N	1·22 E
172	Chelkar (chyĕl'kär) Sov. Un.	47·52 N	59·41 E
171	Chelkar (L.) Sov. Un.	50·30 N	51·30 E
172	Chelkar Tengiz (L.) (chyĕl'kär tĕn'yēz). Sov. Un.	47·42 N	61·45 E
159	Chełm (kĕlm) Pol.	51·08 N	23·30 E
159	Chełmno (kĕlm'nō) Pol.	53·20 N	18·25 E
96	Chelmsford Can.	46·35 N	81·12 W
148	Chelmsford (chĕlm's-fērd) Eng. (London In.)	51·44 N	0·28 E
99	Chelmsford Ma. (In.)	42·36 N	71·21 W
106	Chelsea (chĕl'sē) Al. (Birmingham In.)	33·20 N	86·38 W
202	Chelsea Austl. (Melbourne In.)	38·05 S	145·08 E
89	Chelsea Can. (Ottawa In.)	45·30 N	75·46 W
99	Chelsea Ma. (In.)	42·23 N	71·02 W
104	Chelsea Mi.	42·20 N	84·00 W
117	Chelsea Ok.	36·32 N	95·23 W
154	Cheltenham (chĕlt'nŭm) Eng.	51·57 N	2·06 W
106	Cheltenham (chĕltĕn-hăm) Md. (Baltimore In.)	38·45 N	76·50 W
163	Chelva (chĕl'vä) Sp.	39·43 N	1·00 W
174	Chelyabinsk (chĕl-yä-bēnsk') Sov. Un. (Urals In.)	55·10 N	61·25 E
173	Chelyuskin, Mys (C.) (chĕl-yōōs'-kĭn). Sov. Un.	77·45 N	104·45 E
217	Chemba Moz.	17·08 S	34·52 E
160	Chemillé (shē-mê-yā') Fr.	47·13 N	0·46 W
	Chemnitz, see Karl-Marx-Stadt		
105	Chemung (R.) (shê-mŭng) NY	42·20 N	77·25 W
173	Chĕn, Gora (Mtn.) Sov. Un.	65·13 N	142·12 E
184	Chenāb (R.) (chê-näb) Pak.	31·33 N	72·28 E
210	Chenachane (shē-nȧ-shän') Alg.	26·14 N	4·14 W
190	Chenchiang (jienjäng) China	32·13 N	119·24 E
110	Cheney (chē'nȧ) Wa.	47·29 N	117·34 W
190	Chengchou (jengjō) China	34·46 N	113·42 E
193	Ch'enghai China	23·22 N	116·40 E
192	Chengku China	33·05 N	107·25 E
192	Ch'engte (Jehol) (chĕng'tĕ') (rē-hōl'). China	40·50 N	117·50 E
190	Chengting (chengding) China	38·10 N	114·35 E
193	Ch'engtu (chĕng'tōō') China	30·30 N	104·10 E
190	Chengyang (chĕn'yäng') China	32·34 N	114·22 E
193	Ch'enshien China	25·40 N	113·00 E
191	Ch'entsun China (Canton In.)	22·58 N	113·14 E
192	Chentung China	45·28 N	123·42 E
193	Chenyüan (chĕn'yü-an') China	27·08 N	108·30 E
191	Chepei China (Canton In.)	23·07 N	113·23 E
134	Chepén (chĕ-pĕ'n) Peru	7·17 S	79·24 W
127	Chepo (chā'pō) Pan.	9·12 N	79·06 W
127	Chepo R. Pan.	9·10 N	78·36 W
160	Cher (R.) (shâr) Fr.	47·14 N	1·34 E
124	Cherán (chā-rän') Mex.	19·41 N	101·54 W
217	Cherangany Hills Ken.	1·25 N	35·20 E
121	Cheraw (chē'rô) SC	34·40 N	79·52 W
160	Cherbourg (shär-bōōr') Fr.	49·39 N	1·43 W
210	Cherchell (shĕr-shĕl') Alg.	36·38 N	2·09 E
170	Cherdyn' (chĕr-dyēn') Sov. Un.	60·25 N	56·32 E
172	Cheremkhovo (chĕr'yĕm-kô-vō) Sov. Un.	52·58 N	103·18 E
174	Cherëmukhovo (chĕr-yĕ-mû-kô-vō). Sov. Un. (Urals In.)	60·20 N	60·00 E
172	Cherepanovo (chĕr'yĕ pä-nô'vō) Sov. Un.	54·13 N	83·18 E
166	Cherepovets (chĕr-yĕ-pô'vyĕtz) Sov. Un.	59·08 N	37·59 E
166	Chereya (chĕr-ā'yä) Sov. Un.	54·38 N	29·16 E
152	Chergui, Chott ech (L.) chĕr gē Alg.	34·12 N	0·10 W
152	Chergui (I.) Tun.	34·50 N	11·40 E
166	Cherikov (chĕ'rē-kôf) Sov. Un.	53·34 N	31·22 E
167	Cherkassy (chĕr-kȧ'sĭ) Sov. Un.	49·26 N	32·03 E
167	Cherkassy (Oblast) Sov. Un.	48·58 N	30·55 E
172	Cherlak (chĭr-läk') Sov. Un.	54·04 N	74·28 E
174	Chermoz (chĕr-môz') Sov. Un. (Urals In.)	58·47 N	56·08 E
166	Chern' (chĕrn) Sov. Un.	53·28 N	36·49 E
167	Chërnaya Kalitva (R.) (chôr'nȧ yȧ kȧ-lēt'vȧ). Sov. Un.	50·15 N	39·16 E
167	Chernigov (chĕr-nē'gôf) Sov. Un.	51·28 N	31·18 E
167	Chernigov (Oblast) (chĕr-nē'gôf) Sov. Un.	51·23 N	31·15 E
167	Chernobay (chĕr-nō-bī') Sov. Un.	49·41 N	32·24 E
167	Chernobyl' (chĕr-nō-bĭl') Sov. Un.	51·17 N	30·14 E
172	Chernogorsk (chĕr-nŏ-gôrsk') Sov. Un.	54·01 N	91·07 E
167	Chernogovka (chĕr-nô-gôf'kȧ) Sov. Un.	47·08 N	36·20 E
174	Chernoistochinsk (chĕr-nôy-stô'chĭnsk). Sov. Un. (Urals In.)	57·44 N	59·55 E
167	Chĕrnomorskoye (chĕr-nô-môr'skô-yĕ). Sov. Un.	45·29 N	32·43 E
159	Chernovtsy (Cernăuti) (chĭr-nôf'tsē) (chĕr-nou'tsê) Sov. Un.	48·18 N	25·56 E

ng-sing; ŋ-baŋk; N-nasalized n; nŏd; cŏmmit; ōld; ôbey; ôrder; fōōd; fŏŏt; ou-out; s-soft; sh-dish; th-thin; pūre; ůnite; ûrn; stŭd; circŭs; ü-as "y" in study; '-indeterminate vowel.

268 Chernyakhovsk — Chipata PRONOUNCING INDEX

Page	Name Pronunciation Region	Lat. °'	Long. °'
157	Chernyakhovsk (chĕr-nyä'ĸôfsk) . Sov. Un.	55·38 N	21·17 E
167	Chernyanka (chĕrn-yäŋ'kä) Sov. Un.	50·56 N	37·48 E
108	Cherokee (chĕr-ô-kē') . . . Ia.	42·43 N	95·33 W
117	Cherokee . . . Ks.	37·21 N	94·50 W
116	Cherokee . . . Ok.	36·44 N	98·22 W
120	Cherokee (L.) . . . Tn.	36·22 N	83·22 W
120	Cherokee Indian Res. . . . NC	35·33 N	83·12 W
128	Cherokee Sound . . . Ba.	26·15 N	76·55 W
117	Cherokees, L. of the (chĕr-ô-kēz') . Ok.	36·32 N	95·14 W
98	Cherryfield (chĕr'ĭ-fēld) . . . Me.	44·37 N	67·56 W
112	Cherry Grove . . . Or. (Portland In.)	45·27 N	123·15 W
117	Cherryvale . . . Ks.	37·16 N	95·33 W
121	Cherryville (chĕr'ĭ-vĭl) . . . NC	35·32 N	81·22 W
173	Cherskogo, Khrebet (Mts.) Sov. Un.	66·15 N	138·30 E
166	Cherven' (chĕr'vyĕn) . . . Sov. Un.	53·43 N	28·26 E
166	Chervonoye (L.) (chĕr-vô'nô-yĕ) Sov. Un.	52·24 N	28·12 E
104	Chesaning (chĕs'ȧ-nĭng) . . . Mi.	43·10 N	84·10 W
106	Chesapeake (chĕs'ȧ-pēk) Va. (Norfolk In.)	36·48 N	76·16 W
105	Chesapeake B. . . . Md.	38·20 N	76·15 W
106	Chesapeake Beach Md. (Baltimore In.)	38·42 N	76·33 W
148	Chesham (chĕsh'ŭm) Eng. (London In.)	51·41 N	0·37 W
104	Cheshire (chĕsh'ĭr) . . . Mi.	42·25 N	86·00 W
148	Cheshire (Co.) . . . Eng.	53·16 N	2·30 W
170	Chëshskaya Guba (B.) . . . Sov. Un.	67·25 N	46·00 E
174	Chesma (chĕs'mȧ) Sov. Un. (Urals In.)	53·50 N	60·42 E
172	Chesnokovka (chĕs-nŏ-kôf'kȧ) Sov. Un.	53·28 N	83·41 E
148	Chester (chĕs'tēr) . . . Eng.	53·12 N	2·53 W
117	Chester . . . Il.	37·54 N	89·48 W
106	Chester . . . Pa. (Philadelphia In.)	39·51 N	75·22 W
121	Chester . . . SC	34·42 N	81·11 W
121	Chester . . . Va.	37·20 N	77·24 W
104	Chester . . . WV	40·35 N	80·30 W
148	Chesterfield (chĕs'tēr-fēld) . . . Eng.	53·14 N	1·26 W
205	Chesterfield, Îles . . . N. Cal.	19·38 S	160·08 E
90	Chesterfield (Inlet) . . . Can.	63·59 N	92·09 W
90	Chesterfield Inlet . . . Can.	63·19 N	91·11 W
89	Chestermere L. (chĕs'tēr-mēr) Can. (Calgary In.)	51·03 N	113·45 W
104	Chesterton (chĕs'tēr-tŭn) . . . In.	41·35 N	87·05 W
105	Chestertown (chĕs'tēr-toun) . . Md.	39·15 N	76·05 W
98	Chesuncook (L.) (chĕs'ŭn-kŏŏk) Me.	46·03 N	69·40 W
109	Chetek (chĕ'tĕk) . . . Wi.	45·18 N	91·41 W
126	Chetumal, Bahia de (B.) (bä-ē-ä dĕ chĕt-ōō-mäl') Belize (In.)	18·07 N	88·05 W
115	Chevelon Cr. (shĕv'ȧ-lŏn) . . . Az.	34·35 N	111·00 W
107	Cheviot (shĕv'ĭ-ŭt) Oh. (Cincinnati In.)	39·10 N	84·37 W
154	Cheviot Hills . . . Scot.-Eng.	55·20 N	2·40 W
161	Chevreuse (shĕ-vrûz') Fr. (Paris In.)	48·42 N	2·02 E
106	Chevy Chase (shĕvĭ chās) Md. (Baltimore In.)	38·58 N	77·06 W
211	Chew Bahir (Lake Stefanie) (stĕf-a-nē) . Eth.	4·46 N	37·31 E
110	Chewelah (chē-wē'lä) . . . Wa.	48·17 N	117·42 W
190	Cheyang (R.) (Sĭyang) . . . China	33·42 N	119·40 E
108	Cheyenne (shī-ĕn') . . . Wy.	41·10 N	104·49 W
108	Cheyenne (R.) . . . SD	44·20 N	102·15 W
108	Cheyenne River Ind. Res. . . . SD	45·07 N	100·46 W
116	Cheyenne Wells . . . Co.	38·46 N	102·21 W
184	Chhindwāra . . . India	22·08 N	78·57 E
193	Chiachi . . . China	19·10 N	110·28 E
193	Chiahsing . . . China	30·45 N	120·50 E
193	Chiai (chī'ī') . . . Taiwan	23·28 N	120·28 E
193	Chialing (R.) . . . China	30·30 N	106·20 E
193	Chian . . . China	27·15 N	115·10 E
192	Chian . . . China	41·00 N	126·04 E
190	Chiangchanchi . . . China	36·39 N	120·31 E
	Chiangshi (Prov.), see Kiangsi		
193	Chiangling . . . China	30·30 N	112·10 E
188	Chiang Mai . . . Thai.	18·38 N	98·44 E
196	Chiang Rai . . . Thai.	19·53 N	99·48 E
	Chiangsu (Prov.), see Kiangsu		
190	Chiangyen (jiäng'yĭn) . . . China	32·33 N	120·07 E
190	Chiangyin (jiäng'ĭn) . . . China	31·54 N	120·15 E
216	Chianje . . . Ang.	15·45 S	13·48 E
190	Chiantochen (jiäng'tô'jĕn) . . China	32·23 N	120·14 E
190	Chiaochou Wan (B.) (jĭou'zhĕō wän) . China	36·10 N	119·55 E
190	Chiaoho (jēou'hŭ) . . . China	38·03 N	116·18 E
192	Chiaoho . . . China	43·40 N	127·20 E
190	Chiaohsien (jēou'sĭän) . . . China	36·18 N	120·01 E
191	Ch'iaot'ou . . . China (Canton In.)	22·55 N	113·39 E
190	Chiaow Shan (Mts.) (jēou shän) China	36·59 N	121·15 E
126	Chiapa, Rio de (R.) (rē-ô-dĕ-chê-ä'pä) . Mex.	16·00 N	92·20 W
125	Chiapa de Corzo (chê-ä'pä dā kôr'zō) . Mex.	16·44 N	93·01 W
122	Chiapas (State) (chê-ä'päs) . . Mex.	17·10 N	93·00 W
125	Chiapas, Cordilla de (Mts.) (kôr-dēl-yĕ'rä-dĕ-chyä'räs) . Mex.	15·55 N	93·15 W
164	Chiari (kyä'rē) . . . It.	45·31 N	9·57 E
158	Chiasso . . . Switz.	45·50 N	8·57 E
191	Chiating . . . China (Shanghai In.)	31·23 N	121·15 E
124	Chiautla (chyä-ōōt'lȧ) . . . Mex.	18·16 N	98·37 W
164	Chiavari (kyä-vä'rē) . . . It.	44·18 N	9·21 E
193	Chiayü . . . China	33·00 N	114·00 E
195	Chiba (chē'bȧ) . . Jap. (Tōkyō In.)	35·37 N	140·08 E
195	Chiba (Pref.) . . . Jap. (Tōkyō In.)	35·47 N	140·02 E
97	Chibougamau (chē-bōō'gä-mou) Can.	49·57 N	74·23 W
97	Chibougamau (L.) . . . Can.	49·53 N	74·21 W
107	Chicago (shĭ-kô-gō) (chĭ-kȧ'gō) Il. (Chicago In.)	41·49 N	87·37 W
107	Chicago Heights (shĭ-kô'gō) (chĭ-kä'gō) . Il. (Chicago In.)	41·30 N	87·38 W
216	Chicapa (R.) (chē-kä'pä) . . . Ang.	7·45 S	20·25 E
125	Chicbul (chēk-bōō'l) . . . Mex.	18·45 N	90·56 W
98	Chic-Chocs, Mts. . . . Can.	48·38 N	66·37 W
101	Chichagof (I.) (chê-chä'gôf) . . . Ak.	57·50 N	137·00 W
126	Chichâncanab, Lago de (L.) (lä'gô-dĕ-chē-chän-kä-nä'b) Mex. (In.)	19·50 N	88·28 W
126	Chichen Itzá (Ruins) (chē-chĕ'n-ē-tsä') . Mex. (In.)	20·38 N	88·35 W
154	Chichester (chĭch'ĕs-tēr) . . . Eng.	50·50 N	0·55 W
193	Chichiang . . . China	29·05 N	106·40 E
190	Chichiashih (jĭ'jĭä'shē) . . . China	32·10 N	120·17 E
192	Ch'ich'ihaerh (Tsitsihar) . . . China	47·18 N	124·00 E
126	Chichimila (chē-chē-mē'lä) Mex. (In.)	20·36 N	88·14 W
135	Chichiriviche (chē-chē-rē-vē-chĕ) Ven. (In.)	10·56 N	68·17 W
120	Chickamauga (chĭk-ȧ-mô'gȧ) Ga.	34·50 N	85·15 W
120	Chickamauga, (L.) . . . Tn.	35·18 N	85·22 W
120	Chickasawhay (R.) (chĭk-ȧ-sô'wā) Ms.	31·45 N	88·45 W
116	Chickasha (chĭk'ȧ-shā) . . . Ok.	35·04 N	97·56 W
162	Chiclana (chê-klä'nä) . . . Sp.	36·25 N	6·09 W
134	Chiclayo (chê-klä'yō) . . . Peru	6·46 S	79·50 W
114	Chico (chē'kō) . . . Ca.	39·43 N	121·51 W
112	Chico . . . Wa. (Seattle In.)	47·37 N	122·43 W
136	Chico (R.) . . . Arg.	44·30 S	66·00 W
136	Chico (R.) . . . Arg.	49·15 S	69·30 W
197	Chico (R.) . . . Phil. (In.)	17·33 N	121·24 E
217	Chicoa . . . Moz.	15·37 S	32·24 E
125	Chicoloapan (chê-kō-lwä'pän) Mex. (In.)	19·24 N	98·54 W
125	Chiconautla (chê-kō-nä-ōō'tlȧ) Mex. (In.)	19·39 N	99·01 W
124	Chicontepec (chê-kōn'tĕ-pĕk') Mex.	20·58 N	98·08 W
105	Chicopee (chĭk'ô-pē) . . . Ma.	42·10 N	72·35 W
97	Chicoutimi (shē-kōō'tē-mē') . . Can.	48·26 N	71·04 W
126	Chicxulub (chēk-sōō-lōō'b) Mex. (In.)	21·10 N	89·30 W
91	Chidley, C. (chĭd'lĭ) . . . Can.	60·32 N	63·56 W
110	Chief Joseph Dam . . . Wa.	48·00 N	119·39 W
120	Chiefland (chēf'lȧnd) . . . Fl.	29·30 N	82·50 W
188	Ch'iehmo . . . China	38·02 N	85·16 E
190	Chiehshou Hu (L.) (jĭeh'shō hōō) China	32·59 N	119·04 E
193	Chiehyang . . . China	23·38 N	116·20 E
158	Chiem See (L.) (ĸēm zā) . . F.R.G.	47·58 N	12·20 E
190	Chienchangying (jĭan'chang'yĭng) China	40·09 N	118·47 E
190	Chienkan (R.) (jĭan'gän) . . . China	39·35 N	117·34 E
193	Chienli . . . China	29·50 N	112·52 E
193	Chienning . . . China	26·50 N	116·55 E
193	Chienou . . . China	27·10 N	118·18 E
190	Ch'ienshanchen (chĭan'shän'jen) China	31·05 N	120·24 E
193	Chienshih . . . China	30·40 N	109·45 E
193	Chienshui . . . China	23·32 N	102·50 E
190	Ch'ienwei (chĭan'wā) . . . China	40·11 N	120·05 E
164	Chieri (kyâ'rē) . . . It.	45·03 N	7·48 E
164	Chieti (kyĕ'tē) . . . It.	42·22 N	14·22 E
167	Chigirin (chê-gē'rēn) . . . Sov. Un.	49·02 N	32·39 E
124	Chignanuapan (chē'g-nä-nwä-pȧ'n) Mex.	19·49 N	98·02 W
98	Chignecto B. (shĭg-nĕk'tō) . . . Can.	45·33 N	64·50 W
101	Chignik (chĭg'nĭk) . . . Ak.	56·14 N	158·12 W
101	Chignik B. . . . Ak.	56·18 N	157·22 W
193	Chihchiang . . . China	27·25 N	109·45 E
192	Ch'ihfeng (Wulanhata) (chĭ'fûng) . China	42·18 N	118·52 E
190	Chihhochen (zhĭ'hŭ'jen) . . . China	32·32 N	117·57 E
190	Ch'ihsien (chĭ'hsyĕn') . . . China	34·33 N	114·47 E
190	Chihsien . . . China	35·25 N	114·03 E
190	Ch'ihsien . . . China	35·36 N	114·13 E
190	Chihsien . . . China	37·37 N	115·33 E
190	Chihsien . . . China	40·03 N	117·25 E
118	Chihuahua (chê-wä'wä) . . . Mex.	28·37 N	106·06 W
122	Chihuahua (State) . . . Mex.	29·00 N	107·30 W
171	Chikishlyar (chê-kêsh-lyär') Sov. Un.	37·40 N	53·50 E
190	Ch'ik'ou (chē'kō) . . . China	38·37 N	117·33 E
217	Chilanga . . . Zambia	15·34 S	28·17 E
124	Chilapa (chê-lä'pä) . . . Mex.	17·34 N	99·14 W
124	Chilchota (chêl-chō'tä) . . . Mex.	19·40 N	102·04 W
92	Chilcotin (R.) (chĭl-kō'tĭn) . . . Can.	52·20 N	124·15 W
116	Childress (chīld'rĕs) . . . Tx.	34·26 N	100·11 W
133	Chile (chē'lā) . . . S.A.	35·00 S	72·00 W
136	Chilecito (chê-lȧ-sē'tō) . . . Arg.	29·06 S	67·25 W
216	Chilengue, Serra do (Mts.) . . . Ang.	13·20 S	15·00 E
134	Chilí, Pico de (Pk.) (pē'kô-dĕ chē-lê') . Col. (In.)	4·14 N	75·38 W
122	Chilibre (chê-lē'brĕ) . . . Pan. (In.)	9·09 N	79·37 W
190	Ch'ili Hu (L.) (chē'lē hōō) China	32·57 N	118·26 E
217	Chililabombwe (Bancroft) Zambia	12·18 S	27·43 E
192	Chilin (Kirin) (chĭl'ĭn') (kĭr'ĭn) China	43·58 N	126·40 E
190	Chilip'ing (chē'lē'pĭng) . . . China	31·28 N	114·41 E
184	Chilka (L.) . . . India	19·26 N	85·42 E
92	Chilko (R.) (chĭl'kō) . . . Can.	51·53 N	123·53 W
92	Chilko L. . . . Can.	51·20 N	124·05 W
136	Chillán (chēl-yän') . . . Chile	36·44 S	72·06 W
104	Chillicothe (chĭl-ĭ-kŏth'ē) . . . Il.	41·55 N	89·30 W
117	Chillicothe . . . Mo.	39·46 N	93·32 W
104	Chillicothe . . . Oh.	39·20 N	83·00 W
93	Chilliwack (chĭl'ĭ-wăk) . . . Can.	49·10 N	121·57 W
136	Chiloé, Isla de (I.) (ē's-lä-dĕ-chē-lô-ā') . Chile	43·00 S	75·00 W
124	Chilpancingo (chēl-pän-sēŋ'gō) Mex.	17·32 N	99·30 W
109	Chilton (chĭl'tŭn) . . . Wi.	44·00 N	88·12 W
193	Chilung (Kirin) (chĭ'lung) . Taiwan	25·02 N	121·48 E
217	Chilwa, L. . . . Malawi-Moz.	15·12 S	36·30 E
112	Chimacum (chĭm'ä-kŭm) Wa. (Seattle In.)	48·01 N	122·47 W
125	Chimalpa (chē-mäl'pä) . Mex. (In.)	19·26 N	99·22 W
126	Chimaltenango (chê-mäl-tå-näŋ'gō) Guat.	14·39 N	90·48 W
124	Chimaltitan (chêmäl-tē-tän') Mex.	21·36 N	103·50 W
147	Chimbay (chĭm-bī') . . . Sov. Un.	43·00 N	59·44 E
134	Chimborazo (Mtn.) (chêm-bô-rä'zō) Ec.	1·35 S	78·45 W
134	Chimbote (chêm-bō'tå) . . . Peru	9·02 S	78·33 W
172	Chimkent (chĭm-kĕnt) . . . Sov. Un.	42·17 N	69·42 E
190	Chimo (gē'mŭ) . . . China	36·22 N	120·28 E
182	China (chī'nȧ) . . . Asia	36·45 N	93·00 E
118	China (chē'nä) . . . Mex.	25·43 N	99·13 W
126	Chinameca (Chĕ-nä-mā'kä) Sal.	13·31 N	88·18 W
	Chinan, see Tsinan		
126	Chinandega (chē-nän-dā'gä) . . Nic.	12·38 N	87·08 W
118	Chinati Pk. (chĭ-nä'tē) . . . Tx.	29·56 N	104·29 W
134	Chincha Alta (chĭn'chä äl'tä) Peru	13·24 S	76·04 W
134	Chinchas, Islas (Is.) (ē's-läs-chē'n-chäs) . Peru	11·27 S	79·05 W
192	Chincheng . . . China	35·30 N	112·50 E
190	Chinch'iao (jĭnchĭou) . . . China	31·46 N	116·46 E
203	Chinchilla (chĭn-chĭl'ȧ) . . . Austl.	26·44 S	150·36 E
162	Chinchilla (chên-chē'lyä) . . . Sp.	38·54 N	1·43 W
126	Chinchorro, Banco (Bk.) (bä'n-kô-chēn-chô'r-rō) Mex. (In.)	18·43 N	87·25 W
192	Chinchou . . . China	41·00 N	121·00 E
190	Chinchou Wan (B.) (jĭn'zhō wän) . China	39·07 N	121·17 E
212	Chinde (shēn'dĕ) . . . Moz.	17·39 S	36·34 E
194	Chin Do (I.) . . . Kor.	34·30 N	125·43 E
188	Chindwin R. (chĭn-dwĭn) . . . Bur.	23·30 N	94·34 E
190	Chinganchi (jing'än'jĭ) . . . China	34·30 N	116·55 E
190	Ch'ingch'eng (chĭng'cheng) . . China	37·12 N	117·43 E
192	Ch'ingch'eng . . . China	46·50 N	127·30 E
193	Chingchiang (jĭng'jĭang) . . . China	28·00 N	115·30 E
190	Chingchiang . . . China	32·02 N	120·15 E
190	Chingchih (jing'jĕ) . . . China	36·19 N	119·23 E
190	Ch'ingfeng (chingfeng) . . . China	35·52 N	115·05 E
188	Ch'ing Hai (Koko Nor) (L.) (kō'kô nor) . China	37·26 N	98·30 E
190	Chinghai Wan (B.) (jĭng'hăĭ wän) . China	36·47 N	122·10 E
192	Ching Ho (R.) (chĭng'hō') . . . China	34·40 N	108·20 E
193	Chinghsien (jĭng'sĭan) . . . China	26·32 N	109·45 E
190	Chinghsien . . . China	37·43 N	116·17 E
190	Ch'inghsien (chingsĭan) . . . China	38·37 N	116·48 E
192	Chinghsing . . . China	47·00 N	123·00 E
190	Ching Hu (L.) (chĭng hōō) . . China	39·00 N	115·45 E
190	Chingk'ouchen (chĭng'kō'jĕn) China	34·52 N	119·07 E
193	Chingliu . . . China	26·15 N	116·50 E
192	Chingning . . . China	35·28 N	105·50 E
217	Chingola (chĭng-gōlä) . . . Zambia	12·32 S	27·52 E
190	Ch'ingp'ing (chĭng'pĭng) . . . China	36·46 N	116·03 E
192	Chingpo Hu (L.) . . . China	44·10 N	129·00 E
191	Ch'ingp'u . . . China (Shanghai In.)	31·08 N	121·06 E
190	Ch'ingtao (Tsingtao) (tsĭng'dou) China	36·05 N	120·10 E
193	Chingtechen . . . China	29·18 N	117·18 E
212	Chinguar (chĭng-gär) . . . Ang.	12·35 S	16·15 E
210	Chinguetti (chêŋ-gĕt'ē) Mauritania	20·34 N	12·34 W
190	Ch'ingyang (chĭng'yäng) . . . China	33·25 N	118·13 E
192	Chingyang . . . China	36·02 N	107·42 E
193	Ch'ingyüan . . . China	23·43 N	113·10 E
190	Ch'ingyun (chĭng'yōōn) . . . China	37·52 N	117·26 E
192	Ch'ingyüntien . . . China (In.)	39·41 N	116·31 E
190	Chinhsiang (jĭn'sĭäng) . . . China	35·03 N	116·20 E
190	Chinhsien (jĭn'sĭän) . . . China	39·04 N	121·40 E
193	Ch'inhsien . . . China	22·00 N	108·35 E
193	Chinhua . . . China	29·10 N	119·42 E
190	Ch'inhuangtao (chĭnhōōäng'dou) China	39·57 N	119·34 E
190	Chining (jē'nĭng) . . . China	35·26 N	116·34 E
192	Chining . . . China	41·00 N	113·10 E
194	Chinju (chĭn'jōō) . . . Kor.	35·13 N	128·10 E
211	Chinko (R.) (shĭn'kô) Cen. Afr. Emp.	6·37 N	24·31 E
	Chinmen, see Quemoy		
193	Chinmu Chiao (Pt.) . . . China	18·10 N	109·40 E
113	Chino (chē'nō) Ca. (Los Angeles In.)	34·01 N	117·42 W
160	Chinon (shē-nôN') . . . Fr.	47·09 N	0·13 E
111	Chinook (shĭn-ŏŏk') . . . Mt.	48·35 N	109·15 W
112	Chinook (shĭn-ŏŏk') Wa. (Portland In.)	46·17 N	123·57 W
217	Chinsali . . . Zambia	10·34 S	32·03 E
190	Chinshachen (jĭn'shä'jĕn) . . . China	32·08 N	121·06 E
191	Chinshan China (Shanghai In.)	30·53 N	121·09 E
188	Chint'a . . . China	40·11 N	98·45 E
190	Chint'an (jĭn'tän) . . . China	31·47 N	119·34 E
212	Chinteche (chĭn-tĕ'chĕ) . . . Malawi	11·48 S	34·14 E
192	Chinyang (chĭn'yäng') . . . China	35·00 N	112·55 E
193	Chinyüh . . . China	28·40 N	120·08 E
164	Chioggia (kyôd'jä) . . . It.	45·12 N	12·17 E
191	Ch'ipao China (Shanghai In.)	31·06 N	121·16 E
217	Chipata . . . Zambia	13·39 S	32·40 E

ăt; finăl; rāte; senâte; ärm; ȧsk; sofȧ; fâre; ch-choose; dh-as th in other; bē; ēvent; bĕt; recĕnt; cratēr; g-go; gh-guttural g; bĭt; ĭ-short neutral; rīde; ĸ-guttural k as ch in German ich;

PRONOUNCING INDEX

Chipera — Civitavecchia 269

Page	Name	Pronunciation	Region	Lat. °′	Long. °′
212	Chipera	(zhê-pĕ′rä)	Moz.	15·16 S	32·30 E
120	Chipley	(chĭp′lĭ)	Fl.	30·45 N	85·33 W
98	Chipman	(chĭp′mȧn)	Can.	46·11 N	65·53 W
120	Chipola (R.)	(chĭ-pō′lȧ)	Fl.	30·40 N	85·14 W
107	Chippawa	(chĭp′ê-wä)	Can. (Buffalo In.)	43·03 N	79·03 W
108	Chippewa (R.)	(chĭp′ê-wä)	Mn.	45·07 N	95·41 W
109	Chippewa (R.)		Wi.	45·07 N	91·19 W
109	Chippewa Falls		Wi.	44·55 N	91·26 W
107	Chippewa Lake		Oh. (Cleveland In.)	41·04 N	81·54 W
98	Chiputneticook L.	(chĭ-pŏŏt-nĕt′ĭ-kŏŏk)	Can.	45·47 N	67·45 W
126	Chiquimula	(chē-kê-mōō′lä)	Guat.	14·47 N	89·31 W
126	Chiquimulilla	(chē-kē-mōō-lê′l-yä)	Guat.	14·08 N	90·23 W
134	Chiquinquira	(chê-kēŋ′kê-rä′)	Col.	5·33 N	73·49 W
137	Chiquíta, Laguna Mar (L.)	(lä-gōō′nä-mär-chê-kē′tä)	Arg. (Buenos Aires In.)	34·25 S	61·10 W
185	Chirald		India	15·52 N	80·22 E
172	Chirchik	(chĭr-chēk′)	Sov. Un.	41·28 N	69·18 E
217	Chire (R.)		Moz.	17·15 S	35·25 E
115	Chiricahua Natl. Mon.	(chĭ-rā-cä′hwä)	Az.	32·02 N	109·18 W
101	Chirikof (I.)	(chĭ′rĭ-kôf)	Ak.	55·50 N	155·35 W
127	Chiriquí, Golfo de (G.)	(gôl-fô-dĕ-chē-rê-kē′)	Pan.	7·56 N	82·18 W
127	Chiriquí, Laguna de (L.)	(lä-gŏŏ′nä-dĕ-chē-rê-kē′)	Pan.	9·06 N	82·02 W
127	Chiriqui, Punta (Pt.)	(pŏŏ′n-tä-chē-rê-kē′)	Pan.	9·13 N	81·39 W
127	Chiriqui, Volcán de (Vol.)	(vôl-kȧ′n-dĕ-chē-rê-kē′)	Pan.	8·48 N	82·37 W
127	Chiriquí Grande	(chē-rê-kē′ grän′dā)	Pan.	8·57 N	82·08 W
194	Chiri San (Mt.)	(chĭ′rĭ-sän′)	Kor.	35·20 N	127·39 E
212	Chiromo		Malawi	16·34 S	35·13 E
165	Chirpan		Bul.	42·12 N	25·19 E
127	Chirripó, Cerro (Mtn.)	(chê-rē′pō)	C. R.	9·30 N	83·31 W
127	Chirripo, Rio (R.)		C. R.	9·50 N	83·20 W
109	Chisholm	(chĭz′ŭm)	Mn.	47·28 N	92·53 W
170	Chistopol′	(chĭs-tô′pôl-y′)	Sov. Un.	55·18 N	50·30 E
173	Chita	(chê-tȧ′)	Sov. Un.	52·09 N	113·39 E
188	Ch′it′ai		China	44·07 N	89·04 E
217	Chitambo		Zambia	12·55 S	30·39 E
216	Chitembo		Ang.	13·34 S	16·40 E
101	Chitina	(chĭ-tē′nȧ)	Ak.	61·28 N	144·35 W
216	Chitokoloki		Zambia	13·50 S	23·13 E
184	Chitorgarh		India	24·59 N	74·42 E
184	Chitrāl	(chē-träl′)	Pak.	35·58 N	71·48 E
127	Chitré	(chē′trå)	Pan.	7·59 N	80·26 W
184	Chittagong	(chĭt-ȧ-gông′)	Bngl.	22·26 N	90·51 E
192	Chiualhun		China	49·59 N	127·15 E
190	Chiuch′eng	(jĭō′chĕng)	China	37·14 N	116·03 E
193	Chiuchiang		China	29·43 N	116·00 E
191	Chiuchiang		China (Canton In.)	22·50 N	113·02 E
189	Chiuchichien		China	52·23 N	121·04 E
188	Chiuchüan		China	39·46 N	98·26 E
191	Chiufenghsien		China (Shanghai In.)	30·55 N	121·38 E
190	Ch′iuhsien	(chĭō′sĭän)	China	36·43 N	115·13 E
190	Chiuhsihsien	(jĭo′sē′sĭän)	China	32·20 N	114·42 E
190	Chiuhuang (R.)	(jĭō′hooäng)	China	33·48 N	119·30 E
216	Chiumbe (R.)	(chê-ŏŏm′bå)	Ang.	9·05 S	21·00 E
190	Chiunü Shan (Mts.)	(jĭō′nü′shän)	China	35·47 N	117·23 E
164	Chivasso	(kê-väs′sō)	It.	45·13 N	7·52 E
137	Chivilcoy	(chē-vêl-koi′)	Arg. (Buenos Aires In.)	34·51 S	60·03 W
126	Chixoy (R.)	(chē-ĸoi′)	Guat.	15·40 N	90·35 W
193	Chiyang		China	26·40 N	112·00 E
193	Ch′iyao Shan (Mtn.)		China	30·00 N	108·50 E
195	Chizu	(chê-zōō′)	Jap.	35·16 N	134·15 E
115	Chloride	(klō′rīd)	Az.	35·25 N	114·15 W
159	Chmielnik	(ĸmyĕl′nêĸ)	Pol.	50·36 N	20·46 E
137	Choapa (R.)	(chō-ȧ′pä)	Chile (Santiago In.)	31·56 S	70·48 W
134	Chocó (Dept.)	(chô-kô′)	Col. (In.)	5·33 N	76·28 W
120	Choctawhatchee, B.	(chôk-tô-hăch′ê)	Fl.	30·15 N	86·32 W
120	Choctawhatchee (R.)		Fl.-Ga.	30·37 N	85·56 W
158	Chodziez	(ĸōj′yĕsh)	Pol.	52·59 N	16·55 E
136	Choele Choel	(chô-ĕ′lĕ-chôĕ′l)	Arg.	39·14 S	66·46 W
195	Chōfu	(chō′fōō′)	Jap. (Tōkyō In.)	35·39 N	139·33 E
195	Chōgo	(chō-gō)	Jap. (Tōkyō In.)	35·25 N	139·28 E
190	Chohsien	(jōōŭ′sĭän)	China	39·30 N	115·59 E
205	Choiseul, (I.)	(shwä-zûl′)	Sol. Is.	7·30 S	157·30 E
159	Chojnice	(ĸōĭ-nē-tsĕ)	Pol.	53·41 N	17·34 E
160	Cholet	(shô-lĕ′)	Fr.	47·06 N	0·54 W
192	Ch′olo (R.)		China	47·20 N	121·40 E
124	Cholula	(chō-lōō′lä)	Mex.	19·04 N	98·19 W
126	Choluteca	(chō-lōō-tā′kä)	Hond.	13·18 N	87·12 W
126	Choluteco (R.)		Hond.-Nic.	13·34 N	86·59 W
158	Chomutov	(kō′mŏŏ-tôf)	Czech.	50·27 N	13·23 E
173	Chona (R.)	(chō′nä)	Sov. Un.	60·45 N	109·15 E
134	Chone	(chô′nĕ)	Ec.	0·48 S	80·06 W
194	Chŏngjin	(chŭng-jĭn′)	Kor.	41·48 N	129·46 E
194	Chŏngju	(chŭng-jōō′)	Kor.	36·35 N	127·30 E
194	Chŏnju	(chŭn-jōō′)	Kor.	35·48 N	127·08 E
148	Chorley	(chôr′lĭ)	Eng.	53·40 N	2·38 W
174	Chornaya		Sov. Un. (Moscow In.)	55·45 N	38·04 E
134	Chorrillos	(chôr-rē′l-yōs)	Peru	12·17 S	76·55 W
159	Chortkov	(chôrt′kôf)	Sov. Un.	49·01 N	25·48 E
159	Chorzów	(kô-zhŏŏf′)	Pol.	50·17 N	19·00 E
194	Chosan	(chō-sän′)	Kor.	40·44 N	125·48 E
121	Chosen	(chō′z′n)	Fl. (In.)	26·41 N	80·41 W
194	Chōshi	(chō′shē)	Jap.	35·40 N	140·55 E
158	Choszczno	(chôsh′chnô)	Pol.	53·10 N	15·25 E
184	Chota Nagpur (Reg.)		India	23·40 N	82·50 E
111	Choteau	(shō′tō)	Mt.	47·51 N	112·10 W
190	Chou (R.)	(jēō)	China	31·59 N	114·57 E
190	Chouchiak′ou	(jêō′jĭä′kō)	China	33·39 N	114·40 E
191	Choup′u		China (Shanghai In.)	31·07 N	121·33 E
193	Choushan Arch. (Is.)	(chou′shăn)	China	30·00 N	123·00 E
190	Chouts′un	(jēō′tsōōn)	China	36·49 N	117·52 E
121	Chowan (R.)	(chô-wän′)	NC	36·13 N	76·46 W
203	Chowilla Res.		Austl.	34·05 S	141·20 E
93	Chown, Mt.	(choun)	Can.	53·24 N	119·22 W
192	Choybalsan		Mong.	47·50 N	114·15 E
205	Christchurch	(krīst′chûrch)	N. Z. (In.)	43·30 S	172·38 E
104	Christian (I.)	(krĭs′chăn)	Can.	44·50 N	80·00 W
121	Christiansburg	(krĭs′chănz-bûrg)	Va.	37·08 N	80·25 W
123	Christiansted		Vir. Is. (U. S. A.) (Puerto Rico In.)	17·45 N	64·44 W
196	Christmas (I.)		Austl.	10·35 S	105·40 E
199	Christmas (I.)		Oceania	2·20 N	157·40 W
117	Christopher	(krĭs′tô-fēr)	Il.	37·58 N	89·04 W
158	Chrudim	(ĸrōō′dyêm)	Czech.	49·57 N	15·46 E
159	Chrzanów	(ĸzhä′nŏŏf)	Pol.	50·08 N	19·24 E
190	Ch′üanch′iao	(chüän′jĭou)	China	32·06 N	118·17 E
193	Ch′üanchow		China	24·58 N	118·40 E
192	Chuangho		China	39·40 N	123·00 E
193	Ch′üanhsien		China	25·58 N	111·02 E
191	Ch′uansha		China (Shanghai In.)	31·12 N	121·41 E
136	Chubut (Prov.)	(chŏŏ-bōōt′)	Arg.	44·00 S	69·15 W
136	Chubut (R.)	(chŏŏ-bōōt′)	Arg.	43·05 S	69·00 W
190	Chuch′eng	(chŏŏ′chĕng′)	China	36·01 N	119·24 E
193	Chuchi		China	29·58 N	120·10 E
191	Chu Chiang (Pearl R.)		China (Canton In.)	23·04 N	113·28 E
190	Ch′üchou	(chü′jēō)	China	36·47 N	114·58 E
106	Chuckatuck	(chŭck ȧ-tŭck)	Va. (Norfolk In.)	36·51 N	76·35 W
127	Chucunaque (R.)	(chōō-kōō-nä′kȧ)	Pan.	8·36 N	77·48 W
166	Chudovo	(chŏŏ′dô-vô)	Sov. Un.	59·03 N	31·56 S
166	Chudskoye Oz. (Peipus, L.)	(chŏŏt′skô-yĕ)	Sov. Un.	58·43 N	26·45 E
190	Ch′üfou	(chü′fōō)	China	35·37 N	116·59 E
	Chuguchak, see T′ach′′eng				
188	Chuguchak (Reg.)	(chōō′gōō-chäk′)	China	46·09 N	83·58 E
167	Chuguyev	(chōō′gŏŏ-yĕf)	Sov. Un.	49·52 N	36·40 E
194	Chuguyevka	(chōō-gōō′yĕf-kȧ)	Sov. Un.	43·58 N	133·49 E
108	Chugwater Cr.	(chŭg′wô-tēr)	Wy.	41·43 N	104·54 W
192	Chuho		China	45·18 N	127·52 E
193	Ch′ühsien		China	28·58 N	118·58 E
190	Ch′uhsien	(chŏŏ′sĭän)	China	32·19 N	118·19 E
190	Chühsien	(jü′sĭän)	China	35·35 N	118·50 E
188	Ch′uhsiung		China	25·19 N	101·34 E
190	Chühua Tao (I.)	(jü′hŏŏȧ dou)	China	40·30 N	120·47 E
190	Chüjung	(jü′rōōng)	China	31·58 N	119·12 E
173	Chukot Natl. Okrug (Reg.)		Sov. Un.	68·15 N	170·00 E
173	Chukotskiy (Chukot) P-Ov (Pen.)		Sov. Un.	66·12 N	175·00 W
173	Chukotskoye Nagor′ye (Mts.)		Sov. Un.	66·00 N	166·00 E
114	Chula Vista	(chōō′lȧ vĭs′tȧ)	Ca. (In.)	32·38 N	117·05 W
174	Chulkovo	(chōōl-kô vô)	Sov. Un. (Moscow In.)	55·33 N	38·04 E
134	Chulucanas	(chōō-lōō-kä′näs)	Peru	5·13 S	80·13 W
172	Chulum (R.)		Sov. Un.	57·52 N	84·45 E
190	Chüma (R.)	(jü′mȧ)	China	39·37 N	115·45 E
173	Chumikan	(chōō-mē-kän′)	Sov. Un.	54·47 N	135·09 E
194	Chunchŏn	(chŏŏn-chŭn′)	Kor.	37·51 N	127·46 E
190	Chungchia Shan (Mts.)	(jŏŏng′jĭä shän)	China	32·42 N	118·19 E
193	Ch′ungch′ing (Chungking)	(ch′ungch′ing) (chŏŏng′kĭng′)	China	29·38 N	107·30 E
193	Chunghsien		China	30·20 N	108·00 E
190	Chunghsing	(jōōng′sĭng)	China	33·43 N	118·42 E
194	Chungju	(chŭng′jōō′)	Kor.	37·00 N	128·19 E
	Chungking, see Ch′ungch′ing				
193	Ch′ungming Tao (I.)		China	31·40 N	122·30 E
192	Chungwei	(chŏŏng′wā)	China	37·32 N	105·10 E
217	Chunya		Tan.	8·32 S	33·25 E
172	Chunya (R.)	(chŏŏn′yä′)	Sov. Un.	61·45 N	101·28 E
136	Chuquicamata	(chōō-kê-kä-mä′tä)	Chile	22·08 S	68·57 W
158	Chur	(kōōr)	Switz.	46·51 N	9·32 E
90	Churchill	(chûrch′ĭl)	Can.	58·50 N	94·10 W
90	Churchill, C.		Can.	59·07 N	93·50 W
95	Churchill (R.)		Can.	57·20 N	96·30 W
91	Churchill Falls		Can.	53·35 N	64·27 W
94	Churchill L.		Can.	56·12 N	108·40 W
90	Churchill Pk.		Can.	58·10 N	125·14 W
148	Church Stretton	(chûrch strĕt′ŭn)	Eng.	52·32 N	2·49 W
106	Churchton		Md. (Baltimore In.)	38·49 N	76·33 W
184	Churu		India	28·22 N	75·00 E
124	Churumuco	(chōō-rōō-mōō′kō)	Mex.	18·39 N	101·40 W
193	Ch′ushien		China	30·40 N	106·48 E
115	Chuska Mts.	(chŭs-kȧ)	Az.-NM	36·21 N	109·11 W
174	Chusovaya R.	(chōō-sô-vä′yȧ)	Sov. Un. (Urals In.)	58·08 N	58·35 E
174	Chusovoy	(chōō-sô-vôy′)	Sov. Un. (Urals In.)	58·18 N	57·50 E
172	Chust	(chŏŏst)	Sov. Un.	41·05 N	71·28 E
190	Chut′angtien	(jō′däng′dĭän)	China	31·59 N	114·13 E
170	Chuvash A. S. S. R.	(chōō′vȧsh)	Sov. Un.	55·45 N	46·00 E
118	Chuviscar (R.)	(chōō-vês-kär′)	Mex.	28·34 N	105·36 W
190	Ch′uwang	(chōō′wäng)	China	36·08 N	114·53 E
196	Chu Yang Sin (Pk.)		Viet.	12·22 N	108·20 E
190	Chüyen	(jü′yĕ)	China	35·24 N	116·05 E
107	Cicero	(sĭs′ēr-ō)	Il. (Chicago In.)	41·50 N	87·46 W
171	Cide	(jē′dĕ)	Tur.	41·50 N	33·00 E
159	Ciechanów	(tsyĕ-kä′nŏŏf)	Pol.	52·52 N	20·39 E
128	Ciego de Avila	(syā′gō dā ä′vê-lä)	Cuba	21·50 N	78·45 W
128	Ciego de Avila (Prov.)		Cuba	22·00 N	78·40 W
162	Ciempozuelos	(thyĕm-pô-thwā′lōs)	Sp.	40·09 N	3·36 W
134	Ciénaga	(syā′nä-gä)	Col.	11·01 N	74·15 W
128	Cienfuegos	(syĕn-fwā′gōs)	Cuba	22·10 N	80·30 W
128	Cienfuegos (Prov.)		Cuba	22·15 N	80·40 W
128	Cienfuegos, Bahía (B.)	(bä-ē′ä-syĕn-fwā′gōs)	Cuba	22·00 N	80·35 W
127	Ciervo, Isla de la (I.)	(ê′s-lä-dĕ-lä-syĕ′r-vô)	Nic.	11·56 N	83·20 W
159	Cieszyn	(tsyĕ′shên)	Pol.	49·47 N	18·45 E
162	Cieza	(thyā′thä)	Sp.	38·13 N	1·25 W
124	Cihuatlán	(sē-wä-tlȧ′n)	Mex.	19·13 N	104·36 W
124	Cihuatlán (R.)		Mex.	19·11 N	104·30 W
162	Cijara (Res.)		Sp.	39·25 N	5·00 W
171	Cilician Gates (P.)		Tur.	37·30 N	35·30 E
154	Cill Mantainn (Wicklow)	(kĭl män′tän) (wĭk′lō)	Ire.	52·59 N	6·06 W
116	Cimarron (R.), North Fk.		Co.	37·13 N	102·30 W
102	Cimarron R.	(sĭm-ȧ-rōn′)	U. S.	36·26 N	98·47 W
165	Cîmpina		Rom.	45·08 N	25·47 E
165	Cîmpulung		Rom.	45·15 N	25·03 E
159	Cîmpulung Moldovenesc		Rom.	47·31 N	25·36 E
163	Cinca (R.)	(thēŋ′kä)	Sp.	42·09 N	0·08 E
107	Cincinnati	(sĭn-sĭ-nȧt′ĭ)	Oh. (Cincinnati In.)	39·08 N	84·30 W
128	Cinco Balas, Cayos (Is.)	(kä′yōs-thēŋ′kō bä′läs)	Cuba	21·05 N	79·25 W
125	Cintalapa	(sên-tä-lä′pä)	Mex.	16·41 N	93·44 W
164	Cinto, Mt.	(chēn′tō)	Fr.	42·24 N	8·54 E
101	Circle	(sûr′k′l)	Ak.	65·49 N	144·22 W
104	Circleville	(sûr′k′lvĭl)	Oh.	39·35 N	83·00 W
196	Cirebon		Indon.	6·50 S	108·33 E
118	Cisco	(sĭs′kō)	Tx.	32·23 N	98·57 W
134	Cisneros	(sês-nĕ′rôs)	Col. (In.)	6·33 N	75·05 W
163	Cisterna di Latina	(chēs-tĕ′r-nä-dē-lä-tê′nä)	(Rome In.)	41·36 N	12·53 E
162	Cistierna	(thês-tyĕr′nä)	Sp.	42·48 N	5·08 W
125	Citlaltépetl (Vol.)	(sē-tlȧl-tĕ′pĕtl)	Mex.	19·04 N	97·14 W
120	Citronelle	(cĭt-rô′nēl)	Al.	31·05 N	88·15 W
164	Cittadella	(chēt-tä-dĕl′lä)	It.	45·39 N	11·51 E
164	Città di Castello	(chēt-tä′dē käs-tĕl′lō)	It.	43·27 N	12·17 E
124	Ciudad Altamirano	(syōō-dä′d-äl-tä-mē-rä′nô)	Mex.	18·24 N	100·38 W
134	Ciudad Bolívar	(syōō-dhädh′ bô-lē′vär)	Ven.	8·07 N	63·41 W
118	Ciudad Camargo (Santa Rosalia)	(syōō-dhädh′ kä-mär′gō) (sän′tȧ rō-sä′lêȧ)	Mex.	27·42 N	105·10 W
126	Ciudad Chetumal (Payo Obispo)	(syōō-dhädh′ chĕt-ōō-mäl) (pä′yō ō-bēs′pō)	Mex. (In.)	18·30 N	88·17 W
126	Ciudad Darío	(syōō-dhädh′dä′rê-ō)	Nic.	12·44 N	86·08 W
128	Ciudad de la Habana (Prov.)		Cuba	23·20 N	82·10 W
125	Ciudad de las Casas	(syōō-dä′d-dĕ-läs-kȧ′säs)	Mex.	16·44 N	92·39 W
125	Ciudad del Carmen	(syōō-dä′d-dĕl-kȧ′r-mĕn)	Mex.	18·39 N	91·49 W
124	Ciudad del Maíz	(syōō-dhädh′del mä-ēz′)	Mex.	22·24 N	99·37 W
124	Ciudad de Valles	(syōō-dhädh′dā vä′lyās)	Mex.	21·59 N	99·02 W
163	Ciudadela	(thyōō-dhä-dhā′lä)	Sp.	40·00 N	3·52 E
124	Ciudad Fernández	(syōō-dhädh′fĕr-nän′dĕz)	Mex.	21·56 N	100·03 W
124	Ciudad García	(syōō-dhädh′gär-sē′ä)	Mex.	22·39 N	103·02 W
134	Ciudad Guayana		Ven.	8·30 N	62·45 W
124	Ciudad Guzmán	(syōō-dhädh′gŏŏz-män)	Mex.	19·40 N	103·29 W
124	Ciudad Hidalgo	(syōō-dä′d-ê-dä′l-gô)	Mex.	19·41 N	100·35 W
118	Ciudad Juárez	(syōō-dhädh hwä′rāz)	Mex.	31·44 N	106·28 W
125	Ciudad Madero	(syōō-dä′d-mä-dĕ′rô)	Mex.	22·16 N	97·52 W
124	Ciudad Mante	(syōō-dä′d-mȧn′tĕ)	Mex.	22·34 N	98·58 W
124	Ciudad Manuel Doblado	(syōō-dä′d-män-wāl′ dō-blä′dō)	Mex.	20·43 N	101·57 W
122	Ciudad Obregón	(syōō-dhädh-ô-brĕ-gô′n)	Mex.	27·40 N	109·58 W
162	Ciudad Real	(thyōō-dhädh′rā-äl′)	Sp.	38·59 N	3·55 W
162	Ciudad Rodrigo	(thyōō-dhädh′rô-drē′gō)	Sp.	40·38 N	6·34 W
125	Ciudad Serdán	(syōō-dä′d-sĕr-dȧ′n)	Mex.	18·58 N	97·26 W
124	Ciudad Victoria	(syōō-dhädh′vêk-tō′rê-ä)	Mex.	23·43 N	99·09 W
164	Cividale del Friuli	(chē-vê-dä′lā-dĕl-frē-ōō′lē)	It.	46·06 N	13·24 E
164	Civitavecchia	(chē′vê-tä-vĕk′kyä)	It.	42·06 N	11·49 E

ng-sing; ŋ-baŋk; N-nasalized n; nŏd; cŏmmit; ōld; ôbey; ôrder; fōōd; fŏŏt; ou-out; s-soft; sh-dish; th-thin; pūre; ûnite; ûrn; stŭd; circŭs; ü-as "y" in study; ′-indeterminate vowel.

Page	Name Pronunciation Region	Lat. °'	Long. °'
112	Clackamas (klăc-kȧ'măs) Or. (Portland In.)	45·25 N	122·34 W
90	Claire (L.) (klâr) Can.	58·33 N	113·16 W
110	Clair Engle L. Ca.	40·51 N	122·41 W
107	Clairton (klârtŭn) Pa. (Pittsburgh In.)	40·17 N	79·53 W
120	Clanton (klăn'tŭn) Al.	32·50 N	86·38 W
104	Clare (klâr) Mi.	43·50 N	84·45 W
154	Clare (I.) Ire.	53·46 N	10·00 W
113	Claremont (klâr'mŏnt) Ca. (Los Angeles In.)	34·06 N	117·43 W
105	Claremont (klâr'mŏnt) NH	43·20 N	72·20 W
104	Claremont WV	37·55 N	81·00 W
117	Claremore (klâr'mōr) Ok.	36·16 N	95·37 W
154	Claremorris (klâr-mŏr'ĭs) Ire.	53·46 N	9·05 W
92	Clarence Str. Ak.	55·25 N	132·00 W
204	Clarence Str. (klăr'ĕns) Austl.	12·15 S	130·05 E
129	Clarence Town Ba.	23·05 N	75·00 W
117	Clarendon (klâr'ĕn-dŭn) Ar.	34·42 N	91·17 W
116	Clarendon Tx.	34·55 N	100·52 W
213	Clarens (clâ-rĕns) S. Afr. (Natal In.)	28·34 S	28·26 E
94	Claresholm (klâr'ĕs-hōlm) Can.	50·02 N	113·35 W
109	Clarinda (klȧ-rĭn'dȧ) Ia.	40·42 N	95·00 W
135	Clarines (klä-rē'nĕs) Ven. (In.)	9·57 N	65·10 W
109	Clarion (klăr'ĭ-ŭn) Ia.	42·43 N	93·45 W
105	Clarion Pa.	41·10 N	79·25 W
108	Clark (klärk) SD	44·52 N	97·45 W
104	Clark, Pt. Can.	44·05 N	81·50 W
98	Clarke City Can.	50·12 N	66·38 W
115	Clarkdale (klärk-dāl) Az	34·45 N	112·05 W
205	Clarke Ra. Austl.	20·30 S	148·00 E
111	Clark Fork (R.) Mt.	47·50 N	115·35 W
121	Clark Hill Res. (klärk-hĭl) Ga.-SC	33·50 N	82·35 W
105	Clarksburg (klärkz'bûrg) WV	39·15 N	80·20 W
120	Clarksdale (klärks-dāl) Ms.	34·10 N	90·31 W
98	Clark's Harbour (klärks) Can.	43·26 N	65·38 W
106	Clarkston (klärks'tŭn) Ga. (Altanta In.)	33·49 N	84·15 W
110	Clarkston Wa.	46·24 N	117·01 W
117	Clarksville (klärks-vĭl) Ar.	35·28 N	93·26 W
120	Clarksville Tn.	36·30 N	87·23 W
117	Clarksville Tx.	33·37 N	95·02 W
112	Clatskanie Or. (Portland In.)	46·04 N	123·11 W
112	Clatskanie (R.) (klăt-skā'nē) Or. (Portland In.)	46·06 N	123·11 W
112	Clatsop Spit (klăt-sŏp) Or. (Portland In.)	46·13 N	124·04 W
137	Cláudio (klou'-dēō) Braz. (Rio de Janeiro In.)	20·26 S	44·44 W
193	Claveria (klä-vȧ-rē'ä) Phil.	18·38 N	121·08 E
107	Clawson (klô's'n). Mi. (Detroit In.)	42·32 N	83·09 W
121	Claxton (klăks'tŭn) Ga.	32·07 N	81·54 W
120	Clay (klā) Ky.	37·28 N	87·50 W
117	Clay Center (klā sĕn'tēr) Ks.	39·23 N	97·08 W
104	Clay City (klā sĭ'tĭ) Ky.	37·50 N	83·55 W
113	Claycomo (kla-kō'mo) Mo. (Kansas City In.)	39·12 N	94·30 W
148	Clay Cross (klā krŏs) Eng.	53·10 N	1·25 W
161	Claye-Souilly (klĕ-sōō-yē') Fr. (Paris In.)	48·56 N	2·43 E
106	Claymont (klā-mŏnt) De. (Philadelphia In.)	39·48 N	75·28 W
120	Clayton (klā'tŭn) Al.	31·52 N	85·25 W
112	Clayton Ca. (San Francisco In.)	37·56 N	121·56 W
148	Clayton Eng.	53·47 N	1·49 W
113	Clayton Mo. (St. Louis In.)	38·39 N	90·20 W
116	Clayton NM	36·26 N	103·12 W
121	Clayton NC	35·40 N	78·27 W
114	Clear (L.) Ca.	39·05 N	122·50 W
154	Clear, C. (klēr) Ire.	51·24 N	9·15 W
117	Clear Boggy Cr. (klēr bŏg'ĭ krēk) Ok.	34·21 N	96·22 W
115	Clear Cr. Az.	34·40 N	111·05 W
119	Clear Cr. Tx. (In.)	29·34 N	95·13 W
111	Clear Cr. Wy.	44·35 N	106·20 W
105	Clearfield (klēr-fēld) Pa.	41·00 N	78·25 W
113	Clearfield. Ut. (Salt Lake City In.)	41·07 N	112·01 W
90	Clear Hills Can.	57·11 N	119·20 W
109	Clear Lake Ia.	43·09 N	93·23 W
112	Clear Lake Wa. (Seattle In.)	48·27 N	122·14 W
110	Clear Lake Res. Ca.	41·53 N	121·00 W
121	Clearwater (klēr-wô'tēr) Fl. (In.)	27·43 N	82·45 W
93	Clearwater (R.) Can.	52·00 N	114·50 W
93	Clearwater (R.) Can.	52·00 N	120·10 W
94	Clearwater (R.) Can.	56·10 N	110·40 W
110	Clearwater (R.) Id.	46·27 N	116·33 W
110	Clearwater (R.), Middle Fork Id.	46·10 N	115·48 W
110	Clearwater (R.), North Fork Id.	46·34 N	116·08 W
110	Clearwater (R.), South Fork Id.	45·46 N	115·53 W
110	Clearwater Mts. Id.	45·56 N	115·15 W
117	Clearwater Res. Mo.	37·20 N	91·04 W
119	Cleburne (klē'bŭrn) Tx.	32·21 N	97·23 W
148	Clee Hill (klē) Eng.	52·24 N	2·37 W
110	Cle Elum (klē ĕl'ŭm) Wa.	47·12 N	120·55 W
106	Clementon (klē'mĕn-tŭn) NJ (Philadelphia In.)	39·49 N	75·00 W
148	Cleobury Mortimer (klē'ô-bĕr'ĭ môr'tĭ-mĕr). Eng.	52·22 N	2·29 W
205	Clermont (klĕr'mŏnt) Austl.	23·02 S	147·46 E
98	Clermont Can.	47·45 N	70·20 W
160	Clermont-Ferrand (klĕr-môɴ'fĕr-răɴ'). Fr.	45·47 N	3·03 E
160	Clermont l'Hérault (klĕr-mŏɴ'lā-rō'). Fr.	43·38 N	3·22 E
120	Cleveland (klēv'lănd) Ms.	33·45 N	90·42 W
107	Cleveland Oh. (Cleveland In.)	41·30 N	81·42 W
117	Cleveland Ok.	36·18 N	96·28 W
120	Cleveland Tn.	35·09 N	84·52 W
119	Cleveland Tx.	30·18 N	95·05 W
107	Cleveland Heights Oh. (Cleveland In.)	41·30 N	81·35 W
92	Cleveland Pen. Ak.	55·45 N	132·00 W
107	Cleves (klē'vĕs) Oh. (Cincinnati In.)	39·10 N	84·45 W
154	Clew B. (klōō) Ire.	53·47 N	9·45 W
121	Clewiston (klē'wĭs-tŭn) Fl. (In.)	26·44 N	80·55 W
161	Clichy (klē-shē) Fr. (Paris In.)	48·54 N	2·18 E
154	Clifden (klĭf'dĕn) Ire.	53·31 N	10·04 W
115	Clifton (klĭf'tŭn) Az.	33·05 N	109·20 W
106	Clifton NJ (New York In.)	40·52 N	74·09 W
121	Clifton SC	35·00 N	81·47 W
119	Clifton Tx.	31·45 N	97·31 W
105	Clifton Forge Va.	37·50 N	79·50 W
120	Clinch (R.) (klĭnch) Tn.-Va.	36·30 N	83·19 W
120	Clingmans Dome (Mtn.) (klĭng'măns dōm). NC	35·37 N	83·26 W
93	Clinton (klĭn-'tŭn) Can.	51·05 N	121·35 W
104	Clinton Il.	40·10 N	88·55 W
104	Clinton In.	39·40 N	87·25 W
109	Clinton Ia.	41·50 N	90·13 W
120	Clinton Ky.	36·39 N	88·56 W
106	Clinton Md. (Baltimore In.)	38·46 N	76·54 W
99	Clinton Ma. (In.)	42·25 N	71·41 W
117	Clinton Mo.	38·23 N	93·46 W
121	Clinton NC	35·58 N	78·20 W
116	Clinton Ok.	35·31 N	98·56 W
121	Clinton SC	34·27 N	81·53 W
120	Clinton Tn.	36·05 N	84·08 W
112	Clinton Wa. (Seattle In.)	47·59 N	122·22 W
90	Clinton-Colden (L.) Can.	63·58 N	106·34 W
107	Clinton R. Mi. (Detroit In.)	42·36 N	83·00 W
109	Clintonville (klĭn'tŭn-vĭl) Wi.	44·37 N	88·46 W
104	Clio (klē'ō) Mi.	43·10 N	83·45 W
204	Cloates, Pt. (klōts) Austl.	22·47 S	113·45 E
218	Clocolan. S. Afr. (Johannesburg & Pretoria In.)	28·56 S	27·35 E
154	Clonakilty B. (klŏn-ȧ-kĭltē) Ire.	51·30 N	8·50 W
204	Cloncurry (klŏn-kŭr'ē) Austl.	20·58 S	140·42 E
154	Clonmel (klŏn-mĕl) Ire.	52·21 N	7·45 W
113	Cloquet(klô-kā'). Mn.(Duluth In.)	46·42 N	92·28 W
106	Closter (clōs'tēr) NJ (New York In.)	40·58 N	73·57 W
111	Cloud Pk. (kloud) Wy.	44·23 N	107·11 W
121	Clover (klō'vēr) SC	35·08 N	81·08 W
89	Clover Bar (klō'vēr bär) Can. (Edmonton In.)	53·34 N	113·20 W
114	Cloverdale (klō'vēr-dāl) Ca.	38·47 N	123·03 W
112	Cloverdale. Can. (Vancouver In.)	49·06 N	122·44 W
104	Cloverport (klō'vēr pōrt) Ky.	37·50 N	86·35 W
116	Clovis (klō'vĭs) NM	34·24 N	103·11 W
159	Cluj (klōōzh) Rom.	46·46 N	23·34 E
148	Clun (R.) (klŭn) Eng.	52·25 N	2·56 W
160	Cluny (klü-nē') Fr.	46·27 N	4·40 E
205	Clutha (R.) (klōō'thȧ). N. Z. (In.)	45·26 S	169·15 E
117	Clyde Ks.	39·34 N	97·23 W
104	Clyde Oh.	41·15 N	83·00 W
154	Clyde (R.) Scot.	55·35 N	3·50 W
154	Clyde, Firth of (fûrth ŏv klīd) Scot.	55·28 N	5·01 W
154	Clydebank Scot.	55·56 N	4·20 W
162	Côa (R.) (kô'ä) Port.	40·28 N	6·55 W
125	Coacalco (kō-ä-käl'kō). Mex. (In.)	19·37 N	99·06 W
115	Coachella, Can. (kō'chĕl-lȧ) Ca.	33·15 N	115·25 W
124	Coahuayana, Rio de (R.) (rē'ō-dĕ-kô-ä-wä-yä'nä). Mex.	19·00 N	103·33 W
124	Coahuayutla (kō-ä-wē'lä) Mex.	18·19 N	101·44 W
122	Coahuila (State) (kō-ä-wē'lä). Mex.	27·30 N	103·00 W
107	Coal City (kōl sĭ'tĭ) Il. (Chicago In.)	41·17 N	88·17 W
124	Coalcomán, Rio de (R.) (rê'ō-dĕ-kō-äl-kō-män'). Mex.	18·45 N	103·15 W
124	Coalcomán, Sierra de (Mts.) (syĕr'rä dā kō-äl-kō-män'). Mex.	18·30 N	102·45 W
124	Coalcomán de Matamoros (kō-äl-kō-män' dä mä-tä-mō'rôs) Mex.	18·46 N	103·10 W
94	Coaldale (kōl'dāl) Can.	49·43 N	112·37 W
114	Coaldale Nv.	38·02 N	117·57 W
117	Coalgate (kōl'gāt) Ok.	34·33 N	96·13 W
104	Coal Grove (kōl grōv) Oh.	38·20 N	82·40 W
114	Coalinga (kō-ȧ-lĭŋ'gȧ) Ca.	36·09 N	120·23 W
148	Coalville (kōl'vĭl) Eng.	52·43 N	1·21 W
123	Coamo (kō-ä'mō) P.R. (Puerto Rico In.)	18·05 N	66·21 W
134	Coari (kō-är'ē) Braz.	4·06 S	63·10 W
92	Coast Mts. (kōst) Can.	54·10 N	128·00 W
102	Coast Ranges, (Mts.) U. S.	41·28 N	123·30 W
124	Coatepec (kō-ä-tä-pĕk) Mex.	19·23 N	98·44 W
125	Coatepec Mex.	19·26 N	96·56 W
125	Coatepec Mex. (In.)	19·08 N	99·25 W
126	Coatepeque (kō-ä-tā-pā'kā). Guat.	14·40 N	91·52 W
126	Coatepeque Sal.	13·56 N	89·30 W
105	Coatesville (kōts'vĭl) Pa.	40·00 N	75·50 W
124	Coatetelco (kō-ä-tā-tĕl'kō) Mex.	18·43 N	99·47 W
105	Coaticook (kō'tĭ-kŏŏk) Can.	45·10 N	71·55 W
125	Coatlinchán (kô-ä-tlē'n-chä'n) Mex. (In.)	19·26 N	98·52 W
91	Coats (I.) (kōts) Can.	62·23 N	82·11 W
220	Coats Land (Reg.) Ant.	74·00 S	30·00 W
125	Coatzacoalcos (Puerto México) (kô-ät'zä-kô-äl'kōs) (pwĕ'r-tô-mĕ'-kē-kô). Mex.	18·09 N	94·26 W
125	Coatzacoalcos (R.) Mex.	17·40 N	94·41 W
126	Coba (Ruins) (kô'bä) Mex. (In.)	20·23 N	87·23 W
91	Cobalt (kō'bôlt) Can.	47·21 N	79·40 W
126	Cobán (kō-bän') Guat.	15·28 N	90·19 W
203	Cobar Austl.	31·28 S	145·50 E
203	Cobberas, Mt. (cŏ-bēr-ăs) Austl.	36·45 S	148·15 E
98	Cobequid Mts. Can.	45·35 N	64·10 W
154	Cobh (kôv) Ire.	51·52 N	8·09 W
134	Cobija (kô-bē'hä) Bol.	11·12 S	68·49 W
105	Cobourg (kō'bŏŏrgh) Can.	43·55 N	78·05 W
128	Cobre (R.) (kō'brā) Jam.	18·05 N	77·00 W
217	Cóbuè Moz.	12·04 S	34·50 E
158	Coburg (kō'bōōrg) F.R.G.	50·16 N	10·57 E
163	Cocentaina (kō-thān-tä-ē'nȧ) Sp.	38·44 N	0·27 W
134	Cochabamba (kō-chä-bäm'bä) Bol.	17·30 S	66·08 W
161	Cochem (kō'ĸĕm) F.R.G.	50·10 N	7·06 E
185	Cochin (kō-chĭn') India	9·58 N	76·19 E
128	Cochinos, Bahia (B.) (bä-ē'ä-kô-chê'nōs). Cuba	22·05 N	81·10 W
129	Cochinos Bks. Ba.	22·20 N	76·15 W
197	Cochinos Pt. (kô-chē'-nōs) Phil. (In.)	14·25 N	120·15 E
115	Cochita Res. NM	35·45 N	106·10 W
120	Cochran (kŏk'răn) Ga.	32·23 N	83·23 W
91	Cochrane (kŏk'răn) Can.	49·01 N	81·06 W
89	Cochrane Can. (Calgary In.)	51·11 N	114·28 W
104	Cockburn (I.) (kŏk-bûrn) Can.	45·55 N	83·25 W
106	Cockeysville (kŏk'ĭz-vĭl) Md. (Baltimore In.)	39·30 N	76·40 W
113	Cockrell Hill (kŏk'rĕl) Tx. (Dallas, Fort Worth In.)	32·44 N	96·53 W
127	Coco (Segovia) (R.) (kô-kô) (sĕ-gô'vyä) Hond-Nic.	14·55 N	83·45 W
128	Coco, Cayo (I.) (kä'-yō-kô'kô) Cuba	22·30 N	78·30 W
122	Coco, Isla del (I.) (ē's-lä-dĕl-kô-kô) C. R.	5·33 N	87·02 W
121	Cocoa (kō'kō) Fl. (In.)	28·21 N	80·44 W
121	Cocoa Beach Fl. (In.)	28·20 N	80·35 W
122	Cocoli (kŏ-kô'lē) C. Z. (In.)	8·58 N	79·36 W
115	Coconino, Plat. (kō kō nē'nō). Az.	35·45 N	112·28 W
7	Cocos (Keeling) Is. (kō'kôs) (kē'ling). Oceania	11·50 S	90·50 E
122	Coco Solito (kô-kô-sŏ-lē'tô) C. Z. (In.)	9·21 N	79·53 W
124	Cocula (kō-kōō'lä) Mex.	20·23 N	103·47 W
124	Cocula (R.) Mex.	18·17 N	99·11 W
134	Codajás (kō-dä-häzh') Braz.	3·44 S	62·09 W
135	Codera, Cabo (C.) (kȧ'bô-kō-dĕ'rä). Ven. (In.)	10·35 N	66·06 W
135	Codó (kō'dō) Braz.	4·21 S	43·52 W
164	Codogno (kô-dō'nyō) It.	45·08 N	9·43 E
127	Codrington (kŏd'rĭng-tŭn) Antigua (In.)	17·39 N	61·49 W
111	Cody (kō'dĭ) Wy.	44·31 N	109·02 W
216	Coemba Ang.	12·08 S	18·05 E
161	Coesfeld (kûs'fĕld) F.R.G. (Ruhr In.)	51·56 N	7·10 E
110	Coeur d' Alene (kûr dȧ-lān') Id.	47·43 N	116·35 W
110	Coeur d' Alene (L.) Id.	47·32 N	116·39 W
110	Coeur d' Alene (R.) Id.	47·26 N	116·35 W
117	Coffeyville (kŏf'ĭ-vĭl) Ks.	37·01 N	95·38 W
203	Coff's Harbour Austl.	30·20 S	153·10 E
213	Cofimvaba (căfĭm'vä-bȧ) S. Afr. (Natal In.)	32·01 S	27·37 E
164	Coghinas (R.) (kō'gē-nȧs) It.	40·31 N	9·00 E
160	Cognac (kôn-yak') Fr.	45·41 N	0·22 W
99	Cohasset (kô-hăs'ĕt) Ma. (In.)	42·14 N	70·48 W
105	Cohoes (kô-hōz') NY	42·50 N	73·40 W
136	Coig (kô'ĕk) (R.) Arg.	51·15 S	71·00 W
185	Coimbatore (kô-ēm-bȧ-tôr') India	11·03 N	76·56 E
162	Coimbra (kô-ēm'brä) Port.	40·14 N	8·23 W
162	Coín (kô-ēn') Sp.	36·40 N	4·45 W
163	Coina (kô-ē'nȧ). Port. (Lisbon In.)	38·35 N	9·03 W
163	Coina (R.) (kô'y-nä) Port. (Lisbon In.)	38·35 N	9·02 W
134	Coipasa, Salar de (Salt Flat) (sä-lä'r-dĕ-koi-pä'-sä). Chile	19·12 S	69·13 W
125	Coixtlahuaca (kō-ēks'tlä-wä'kä) Mex.	17·42 N	97·17 W
135	Cojedes (State) (kô-kĕ'dĕs) Ven. (In.)	9·50 N	68·21 W
129	Cojimar (kō-hê-mär'). Cuba (In.)	23·10 N	82·19 W
126	Cojutepeque (kô-hōō-tĕ-pā'kȧ) Sal.	13·45 N	88·50 W
109	Cokato (kô-kā'tō) Mn.	45·03 N	94·11 W
107	Cokeburg (kōk bûgh) Pa. (Pittsburgh In.)	40·06 N	80·03 W
203	Colac (kŏ'lȧc) Austl.	38·25 S	143·40 E
163	Colares (kō-lä'rĕs) Port. (Lisbon In.)	38·47 N	9·27 W
135	Colatina (kô-lä-tē'nä) Braz.	19·33 S	40·42 W
116	Colby (kōl'bĭ) Ks.	39·23 N	101·04 W
137	Colchagua (Prov.) (kôl-chȧ'gwä) Chile (Santiago In.)	34·42 S	71·24 W
155	Colchester (kōl'chĕs-tēr) Eng.	51·52 N	0·50 E
94	Cold L. (kōld) Can.	54·33 N	110·05 W
116	Coldwater (kōld'wô-tēr) Ks.	37·14 N	99·21 W
104	Coldwater Mi.	41·55 N	85·00 W
120	Coldwater (R.) Ms.	34·25 N	90·12 W
116	Coldwater Cr. Tx.	36·10 N	101·45 W
118	Coleman (kōl'mȧn) Tx.	31·50 N	99·25 W
213	Colenso (kŏ-lĕnz'ō) S. Afr. (Natal In.)	28·48 S	29·49 E
109	Coleraine (kōl-rān') Mn.	47·16 N	93·29 W
154	Coleraine N. Ire.	55·08 N	6·40 W
148	Coleshill (kōlz'hĭl) Eng.	52·30 N	1·42 W
109	Colfax (kōl'făks) Ia.	41·40 N	93·13 W
119	Colfax La.	31·31 N	92·42 W
110	Colfax Wa.	46·53 N	117·21 W
136	Colhué Huapi (L.) (kōl-wä'ōōȧ'pē). Arg.	45·30 S	68·45 W
218	Coligny. S. Afr. (Johannesburg) Pretoria In.)	26·20 S	26·18 E
124	Colima (kōlē'mä) Mex.	19·13 N	103·45 W
124	Colima (State) Mex.	19·10 N	104·00 W
124	Colima, Nevado de (nĕ-vä'dô-dĕ-kô-lē'mä) (Mtn.) Mex.	19·30 N	103·38 W
154	Coll (I.) (kŏl) Scot.	56·42 N	6·23 W
101	College Ak.	64·43 N	147·50 W
106	College Park (kŏl'ĕj) Ga. (Atlanta In.)	33·39 N	84·27 W
106	College Park. Md. (Baltimore In.)	38·59 N	76·58 W

ăt; finăl; rāte; senâte; ärm; åsk; sofȧ; fâre; ch-choose; dh-as th in other; bē; êvent; bĕt; recĕnt; cratēr; g-go; gh-guttural g; bĭt; ĭ-short neutral; rīde; ĸ-guttural k as ch in German ich;

PRONOUNCING INDEX

Collegeville — Corbie 271

Page	Name Pronunciation Region	Lat. °′	Long. °′
106	Collegeville (kŏl'ĕj-vĭl) Pa. (Philadelphia In.)	40·11 N	75·27 W
204	Collie (kŏl'ē) . . . . . Austl.	33·20 S	116·20 E
204	Collier B. (kŏl-yẽr) . . . . . Austl.	15·30 S	123·30 E
163	Colli Laziali (Mtn.) (kô'lē-lät-zyä'lē) . It. (Rome In.)	41·46 N	12·45 E
106	Collingswood (kŏl'ĭngz-wŏŏd) NJ (Philadelphia In.)	39·54 N	75·04 W
104	Collingwood . . . . . Can.	44·30 N	80·20 W
120	Collins (kŏl'ĭns) . . . . . Ms.	31·40 N	89·34 W
113	Collinsville (kŏl'ĭnz-vĭl) Il. (St. Louis In.)	38·41 N	89·59 W
117	Collinsville . . . . . Ok.	36·21 N	95·50 W
210	Collo (kôl'ō) . . . . . Alg.	37·02 N	6·29 E
161	Colmar (kôl'mär) . . . . . Fr.	48·03 N	7·25 E
162	Colmenar de Oreja (kôl-mā-när'dāōrā'hä) . Sp.	40·06 N	3·25 W
163	Colmenar Viejo (kôl-mā-när'vyā'hō) Sp. (Madrid In.)	40·40 N	3·46 W
	Cologne, see Köln		
134	Colombia (kô-lôm'bê-ä) . Col. (In.)	3·23 N	74·48 W
133	Colombia . . . . . S. A.	3·30 N	72·30 W
185	Colombo (kô-lôm'bō) . . . Sri Lanka	6·58 N	79·52 E
137	Colón (kō-lōn') Arg. (Buenos Aires In.)	33·55 S	61·08 W
128	Colón (kō-lô'n) . . . . . Cuba	22·45 N	80·55 W
124	Colón (kō-lōn') . . . . . Mex.	20·46 N	100·02 W
122	Colón (kŏ-lô'n) . . . . . Pan. (In.)	9·22 N	79·54 W
134	Colon, Arch. de (Galápagos Is.) (är-chê-pyĕ'l-ägô-dĕ-kō-lōn') (gä-lá'pägôs) . Ec.	0·10 S	87·45 W
127	Colón, Montañas de (Mts.) (môn-tä'n-yäs-dĕ-kŏ-lô'n) Hond.	14·58 N	84·39 W
137	Colonia (kō-lō'nê-ä) Ur. (Buenos Aires In.)	34·27 S	57·50 W
137	Colonia (Dept.) Ur. (Buenos Aires In.)	34·08 S	57·50 W
137	Colonia Suiza (kô-lô'nêä-sōōē'zä) Ur. (Buenos Aires In.)	34·17 S	57·15 W
163	Colonna (kô-lô'n-nä) . It. (Rome In.)	41·50 N	12·48 E
165	Colonne, C. di (kô-lô'n-nĕ) . . . . . It.	39·02 N	17·15 E
154	Colonsay (I.) (kŏl-ôn-sā') . . . . Scot.	56·08 N	6·08 W
136	Coloradas, Lomas (Hills) (lô'mäs-kô-lô-rä'däs) . Arg.	43·30 S	68·00 W
102	Colorado (State) . . . . . U. S.	39·30 N	106·55 W
119	Colorado (R.) . . . . . Tx.	30·08 N	97·33 W
118	Colorado City (kŏl-ô-rä'dō sĭ'tĭ) Tx.	32·24 N	100·50 W
136	Colorado, Rio (R.) . . . . . Arg.	38·30 S	66·00 W
115	Colorado Natl. Mon. . . . . . Co.	39·00 N	108·40 W
102	Colorado Plat. . . . . . U. S.	36·20 N	109·25 W
102	Colorado R. . . . . . U. S.	36·25 N	112·00 W
114	Colorado River Aqueducts . . . . Ca.	33·38 N	115·43 W
115	Colorado River Ind. Res. . . . . . Az.	34·03 N	114·02 W
128	Colorados, Arch. de los (Is.) (är-chē-pyĕ-lä-gô-dĕ-lôs-kô-lô-rä'dôs) Cuba	22·25 N	84·25 W
116	Colorado Springs (kŏl-ô-rä'dō) . Co.	38·49 N	104·48 W
125	Colotepec (R.) (kô-lô'tĕ-pĕk) Mex.	15·56 N	96·57 W
124	Colotlán' (kô-lô-tlän') . . . . . Mex.	22·06 N	103·14 W
124	Colotlán (R.) . . . . . Mex.	22·09 N	103·17 W
134	Colquechaca (kôl-kā-chä'kä) . . Bol.	18·47 S	66·02 W
111	Colstrip (kŏl'strĭp) . . . . . Mt.	45·54 N	106·38 W
113	Colton (kōl'tŭn) Ca. (Los Angeles In.)	34·04 N	117·20 W
113	Columbia (kô-lŭm'bĭ-ȧ) Il. (St. Louis In.)	38·26 N	90·12 W
120	Columbia . . . . . Ky.	37·06 N	85·15 W
106	Columbia . . . . Md. (Baltimore In.)	39·15 N	76·51 W
120	Columbia . . . . . Ms.	31·15 N	89·49 W
117	Columbia . . . . . Mo.	38·55 N	92·19 W
105	Columbia . . . . . Pa.	40·00 N	76·25 W
121	Columbia . . . . . SC	34·00 N	81·00 W
120	Columbia . . . . . Tn.	35·36 N	87·02 W
93	Columbia, Mt. . . . . . Can.	52·09 N	117·25 W
93	Columbia (R.) . . . . . Can.	51·30 N	119·00 W
90	Columbia (R.) . . . . . Can.-U. S.	46·20 N	123·00 W
104	Columbia City . . . . . In.	41·10 N	85·30 W
112	Columbia City . Or. (Portland In.)	45·53 N	112·49 W
113	Columbia Heights Mn. (Minneapolis, St. Paul In.)	45·03 N	93·15 W
93	Columbia Icefield . . . . . Can.	52·08 N	117·26 W
93	Columbia Mts. . . . . . Can.	51·30 N	118·30 W
120	Columbiana (kô-ŭm-bĭ-ă'nȧ) . . Al. .	33·10 N	86·35 W
163	Columbretes (I.) (kô-lōōm-brĕ'tĕs) . Sp.	39·54 N	0·54 E
120	Columbus (kô-lŭm'bŭs) . . . . . Ga.	32·29 N	84·56 W
104	Columbus . . . . . In.	39·15 N	85·55 W
117	Columbus . . . . . Ks.	37·10 N	94·50 W
120	Columbus . . . . . Ms.	33·30 N	88·25 W
111	Columbus . . . . . Mt.	45·39 N	109·15 W
108	Columbus . . . . . Ne.	41·25 N	97·25 W
115	Columbus . . . . . NM	31·50 N	107·40 W
104	Columbus . . . . . Oh.	40·00 N	83·00 W
119	Columbus . . . . . Tx.	29·44 N	96·34 W
109	Columbus . . . . . Wi.	43·20 N	89·01 W
129	Columbus Bk. (kô-lŭm'bŭs) . . . Ba.	22·05 N	75·30 W
104	Columbus Grove . . . . . Oh.	40·55 N	84·05 W
129	Columbus Pt. . . . . . Ba.	24·10 N	75·15 W
114	Colusa (kô-lū'sȧ) . . . . . Ca.	39·12 N	122·01 W
110	Colville (kŏl'vĭl) . . . . . Wa.	48·33 N	117·53 W
101	Colville (R.) . . . . . Ak.	69·00 N	156·25 W
110	Colville R. . . . . . Wa.	48·25 N	117·58 W
112	Colvos Pass. (kŏl'vōs) Wa. (Seattle In.)	47·24 N	122·32 W
112	Colwood (kŏl'wŏŏd) Can. (Seattle In.)	48·26 N	123·30 W
164	Comacchio (kô-mäk'kyō) . . . . . It.	44·42 N	12·12 E
124	Comala (kō-mä-lä') . . . . . Mex.	19·22 N	103·47 W
126	Comalapa (kō-mä-lä'-pä) . . . Guat.	14·43 N	90·56 W
125	Comalcalco (kō-mäl-käl'kō) . . Mex.	18·16 N	93·13 W
116	Comanche (kô-măn'chē) . . . . . Ok.	34·20 N	97·58 W
118	Comanche . . . . . Tx.	31·54 N	98·37 W
118	Comanche Cr. . . . . . Tx.	31·02 N	102·47 W
126	Comayagua (kō-mä-yä'gwä) . Hond.	14·24 N	87·36 W
121	Combahee (R.) (kŏm-bȧ-hē') . . SC	32·42 N	80·40 W
120	Comer (kŭm'ẽr) . . . . . Ga.	34·02 N	83·07 W
129	Comete, C. (kō-mā'tȧ) Turks & Caicos	21·45 N	71·25 W
184	Comilla (kô-mĭl'ä) . . . . . Bngl.	23·33 N	91·17 E
164	Comino, C. (kō-mē'nō) . . . . . It.	40·30 N	9·48 E
126	Comitán (kô-mē-tän') . . . . . Mex.	16·16 N	92·09 W
112	Commencement B. (kŏ-mĕns'mĕnt bā) Wa. (Seattle In.)	47·17 N	122·21 W
160	Commentry (kô-mäɴ-trē') . . . . Fr.	46·16 N	2·44 E
120	Commerce (kŏm'ẽrs) . . . . . Ga.	34·10 N	83·27 W
117	Commerce . . . . . Ok.	36·57 N	94·54 W
117	Commerce . . . . . Tx.	33·15 N	95·52 W
164	Como (kō'mō) . . . . . It.	45·48 N	9·03 E
164	Como, Lago di (L.) (lä'gō-dē-kō'mō) . It.	46·00 N	9·30 E
136	Comodoro Rivadavia (kō'mô-dō'rō rē-vä-dä'vê-ä) . Arg.	45·47 S	67·31 W
89	Como-Est . . . . Can. (Montreal In.)	45·27 N	74·08 W
124	Comonfort (kô-mōn-fô'rt) . . . Mex.	20·43 N	100·47 W
185	Comorin C. (kŏ'mô-rĭn) . . . . . In.	8·05 N	78·05 E
209	Comoros . . . . . Afr.	12·30 S	42·45 E
92	Comox (kō'mŏks) . . . . . Can.	49·40 N	124·55 W
125	Compainalá (kôm-pä-ē-nä-lá') Mex.	17·05 N	93·11 W
137	Companario, Cerro (Mtn.) (sĕ'r-rô-kôm-pä-nä'ryô) Arg.-Chile (Santiago In.)	35·54 S	70·23 W
160	Compiègne (kôɴ-pyĕn'y') . . . . . Fr. .	49·25 N	2·49 E
163	Comporta (kôm-pôr'tȧ) Port. (Lisbon In.)	38·24 N	8·48 W
124	Compostela (kōm-pô-stĕ'lä) . . Mex.	21·41 N	104·54 W
113	Compton (kŏmp'tŭn) Ca. (Los Angeles In.)	33·54 N	118·14 W
120	Cona (R.) (kô-nȧ) . . . . . Ga.	34·40 N	84·51 W
214	Conakry (kô-nȧ-krē') . . . . . Gui.	9·31 N	13·43 W
106	Conanicut (I.) (kŏn'ȧ-nĭ-kŭt) RI (Providence In.)	41·34 N	71·20 W
160	Concarneau (kôɴ-kär-nō') . . . . . Fr.	47·54 N	3·52 W
135	Concepción (kôn-sĕp'syōn') . . . Bol.	15·47 S	61·08 W
136	Concepción . . . . . Chile	36·51 S	72·59 W
127	Concepción . . . . . Pan.	8·31 N	82·38 W
136	Concepción . . . . . Par.	23·29 S	57·18 W
197	Concepcion . . . . . Phil. (In.)	15·19 N	120·40 E
122	Concepción (R.) . . . . . Mex.	30·25 N	112·20 W
126	Concepción (Vol.) . . . . . Nic.	11·36 N	85·43 W
126	Concepción del Mar (kôn-sĕp-syōn' dĕl mär') . Guat	14·07 N	91·23 W
118	Concepción del Oro (kôn-sĕp-syōn' dĕl ō'rō) . Mex.	24·39 N	101·24 W
136	Concepción del Uruguay (kôn-sĕp-syô'n-dĕl-ōō-rōō-gwī') . Arg.	32·31 S	58·10 W
129	Conception (I.) . . . . . Ba.	23·50 N	75·05 W
114	Conception, Pt. . . . . . Ca.	34·27 N	120·28 W
99	Conception B. (kŏn-sĕp'shŭn) Can.	47·50 N	52·50 W
118	Concho (R.) (kŏn'chō) . . . . . Tx.	31·34 N	100·00 W
118	Conchos (R.) (kōn'chōs) . . . . . Mex.	25·03 N	99·00 W
118	Conchos (R.) . . . . . Mex.	29·08 N	105·02 W
112	Concord (kŏŋ'kŏrd) Ca. (San Francisco In.)	37·58 N	122·02 W
99	Concord . . . . . Ma. (Boston In.)	42·28 N	71·21 W
105	Concord . . . . . NH	43·10 N	71·30 W
121	Concord . . . . . NC	35·23 N	80·11 W
136	Concordia (kŏn-kôr'dĭ-ȧ) . . . . . Arg.	31·18 S	57·59 W
134	Concordia . . . . . Col. (In.)	6·04 N	75·54 W
117	Concordia . . . . . Ks.	39·32 N	97·39 W
124	Concordia (kōn-kô'r-dyä) . . . . Mex.	23·17 N	106·06 W
110	Concrete (kŏn'krēt) . . . . . Wa.	48·33 N	121·44 W
108	Conde (kŏn-dē') . . . . . SD	45·10 N	98·06 W
126	Condega (kŏn-dĕ'gä) . . . . . Nic.	13·20 N	86·27 W
160	Condem (kôɴ-dĕɴ) . . . . . Fr.	43·58 N	0·22 E
160	Condé-sur-Noireau (kôɴ-dā'sür-nwä-rō') . Fr.	48·50 N	0·36 W
135	Condeúba (kōn-dā-ōō'bä) . . . . Braz.	14·47 S	41·44 W
110	Condon (kŏn'dŭn) . . . . . Or.	45·14 N	120·10 W
120	Conecun (R.) (kô-nē'kŭ) . . . . . Al.	31·05 N	86·52 W
164	Conegliano (kō-nâl-yä'nō) . . . . . It.	45·59 N	12·17 E
115	Conejos (R.) (kô-nā'hōs) . . . . . Co.	37·07 N	106·19 W
105	Conemaugh (kŏn'ĕ-mô) . . . . . Pa.	40·25 N	78·50 W
106	Coney I. (kō'nĭ) NY (New York In.)	40·34 N	73·27 W
160	Confolens (kôɴ-fä-läɴ') . . . . . Fr.	46·01 N	0·41 E
121	Congaree (R.) (kŏŋ-gȧ-rē') . . . . SC	33·53 N	80·55 W
148	Congleton (kŏŋ'g'l-tŭn) . . . . . Eng.	53·10 N	2·13 W
209	Congo (kŏŋ'gō) . . . . . Afr.	3·00 S	13·48 E
216	Congo (Zaire) (R.) . . . . . Afr.	1·10 N	18·25 E
216	Congo, Serra do (Mts.) . . . . . Ang.	6·25 S	13·50 E
	Congo, The, see Zaire		
209	Congo Basin . . . . . Zaire	2·47 N	20·58 E
148	Conisbrough (kŏn'ĭs-bŭr-ô) . . Eng.	53·29 N	1·13 W
97	Coniston . . . . . Can.	46·29 N	80·51 W
93	Conklin (kŏŋk'lĭn) . . . . . Can.	55·38 N	111·05 W
106	Conley (kŏn'lĭ) . Ga. (Atlanta In.)	33·38 N	84·19 W
154	Conn, Lough (L.) (lŏk kŏn) . . . . Ire.	53·56 N	9·25 W
154	Connacht (Reg.) (cŏn'ȧt) . . . . . Ire.	53·50 N	8·45 W
104	Conneaut (kŏn-ē-ôt') . . . . . Oh.	41·55 N	80·35 W
103	Connecticut (State) (kŏ-nĕt'ĭ-kŭt) U. S.	41·40 N	73·10 W
105	Connecticut R. . . . . . U. S.	43·55 N	72·15 W
105	Connellsville (kŏn'nĕlz-vĭl) . . . Pa.	40·00 N	79·40 W
154	Connemara, Mts. of (kŏn-nē-mȧ'rȧ) . Ire.	53·30 N	9·54 W
104	Connersville (kŏn'ẽrz-vĭl) . . . . . In.	39·35 N	85·10 W
205	Connors Ra. (kŏn'nŏrs) . . . . . Austl.	22·15 S	149·00 E
111	Conrad (kŏn'răd) . . . . . Mt.	48·11 N	111·56 W
89	Conrich (kŏn'rĭch) Can. (Calgary In.)	51·06 N	113·51 W
119	Conroe (kŏn'rō) . . . . . Tx.	30·18 N	95·23 W
137	Conselheiro Lafaiete (kôn-sĕ-lā'rô-lä-fä'ē-tĕ) Braz. (Rio de Janeiro In.)	20·40 S	43·46 W
106	Conshohocken (kŏn-shô-hŏk'ĕn) Pa. (Philadelphia In.)	40·04 N	75·18 W
197	Consolacion (kôn-sô-lā-syô'n) Phil. (In.)	16·20 N	120·21 E
128	Consolación del Sur (kōn-sô-lä-syōn') . Cuba	22·30 N	83·55 W
196	Con Son (Is.) . . . . . Viet.	8·30 N	106·28 E
112	Constance, Mt. (kŏn'stȧns) Wa. (Seattle In.)	47·46 N	123·08 W
153	Constanța (kōn-stán'tsȧ) . . . . Rom.	44·12 N	28·36 E
162	Constantina (kŏn-stän-tē'nä) Sp.	37·52 N	5·39 W
210	Constantine (kôn-stäɴ'tēn') . . . Alg.	36·28 N	6·38 E
104	Constantine (kŏn'stȧn-tēn) . . . . Mi.	41·50 N	85·40 W
136	Constitución (kōn'stĭ-tōō-syōn') Chile	35·24 S	72·25 W
106	Constitution (kŏn-stĭ-tū'shŭn) Ga. (Atlanta In.)	33·41 N	84·20 W
137	Contagem (kōn-tá'zhĕm) Braz. (Rio de Janerio In.)	19·54 S	44·05 W
124	Contepec (kōn-tĕ-pĕk') . . . . . Mex.	20·04 N	100·07 W
125	Contreras (kôn-trĕ'räs) . Mex. (In.)	19·18 N	99·14 W
90	Contwoyto (L.) . . . . . Can.	65·42 N	110·50 W
113	Converse (kŏn'vẽrs) Tx. (San Antonio In.)	29·31 N	98·17 W
117	Conway (kŏn'wā) . . . . . Ar.	35·06 N	92·27 W
105	Conway . . . . . NH	44·00 N	71·10 W
121	Conway . . . . . SC	33·49 N	79·01 W
112	Conway . . . . . Wa. (Seattle In.)	48·20 N	122·20 W
120	Conyers (kŏn'yōrz) . . . . . Ga.	33·41 N	84·01 W
184	Cooch Behār (kōōch bê-här') India	26·25 N	89·34 E
92	Cook, C. (kŏŏk) . . . . . Can.	50·08 N	127·55 W
205	Cook, Mt. . . . . . N. Z. (In.)	43·27 S	170·13 E
120	Cookeville (kŏŏk'vĭl) . . . . . Tn.	36·07 N	85·30 W
89	Cooking Lake (kŏŏk'ĭng) Can. (Edmonton In.)	53·10 N	113·08 W
89	Cooking L. . . Can. (Edmonton In.)	53·25 N	113·02 W
101	Cook Inlet . . . . . Ak.	60·50 N	151·38 W
199	Cook Is. . . . . . Oceania	19·20 S	158·00 W
205	Cook Str. . . . . . N. Z. (In.)	40·37 S	174·15 E
205	Cooktown (kŏŏk'toun) . . . . . Austl.	15·40 S	145·20 E
121	Cooleemee (kōō-lē'mē) . . . . . NC	35·50 N	80·32 W
204	Coolgardie (kōōl-gär'dē) . . . . Austl.	31·00 S	121·25 E
203	Cooma (kōō'mȧ) . . . . . Austl.	36·22 S	149·10 E
203	Coonamble (kōō-năm'b'l) . . . Austl.	31·00 S	148·30 E
185	Coonoort . . . . . India	10·22 N	76·15 E
113	Coon Rapids (kōōn) . Mn. (Minneapolis, St. Paul In.)	45·09 N	93·17 W
117	Cooper (kōōp'ẽr) . . . . . Tx.	33·23 N	95·40 W
101	Cooper Center (kōōp'ẽr sĕn'tẽr) Ak.	61·54 N	145·30 W
203	Coopers Cr. (kōō'pẽrz) . . . . . Austl.	27·32 S	141·19 E
105	Cooperstown (kōōp'ẽrs-toun) NY	42·45 N	74·55 W
108	Cooperstown . . . . . ND	47·26 N	98·07 W
203	Coorong, The (L.) (kōō'rŏng) Austl.	36·07 S	139·45 E
120	Coosa (kōō'sȧ) . . . . . Al.	32·43 N	86·25 W
120	Coosa (R.) . . . . . Al.	34·00 N	86·00 W
120	Coosawattee (R.) (kōō-sȧ-wôt'ē) Ga.	34·37 N	84·45 W
110	Coos Bay (kōōs) . . . . . Or.	43·21 N	124·12 W
110	Coos B. . . . . . Or.	43·19 N	124·40 W
203	Cootamundra (kōōtȧ-mŭnd'rȧ) Austl.	34·25 S	148·00 E
136	Copacabana (kô'pä-kȧ-bȧ'nä) Braz. (Rio de Janeiro In.)	22·57 S	43·11 W
125	Copalita (R.) (kô-pä-lē'tä) . . . Mex.	15·55 N	96·06 W
126	Copán (Ruins) (kō-pän') . . . . Hond.	14·50 N	89·10 W
119	Copano B. (kō-pän'ō) . . . . . Tx.	28·08 N	97·25 W
	Copenhagen, see København		
136	Copiapó (kō-pyä-pō') . . . . . Chile	27·16 S	70·28 W
107	Copley (kŏp'lē) Oh. (Cleveland In.)	41·06 N	81·38 W
164	Copparo (kôp-pä'rō) . . . . . It.	44·53 N	11·50 E
113	Coppell (kŏp'pĕl) Tx. (Dallas, Fort Worth In.)	32·57 N	97·00 W
101	Copper (R.) (kŏp'ẽr) . . . . . Ak.	62·38 N	145·00 W
96	Copper Cliff . . . . . Can.	46·28 N	81·04 W
109	Copper Harbor . . . . . Mi.	47·27 N	87·53 W
120	Copperhill (kŏp'ẽr hĭl) . . . . . Tn.	35·00 N	84·22 W
90	Coppermine (kŏp'ẽr-mīn) . . . . Can.	67·46 N	115·19 W
92	Copper Mtn. . . . . . Ak.	55·14 N	132·36 W
90	Copperinine (R.) . . . . . Can.	66·48 N	114·59 W
113	Copperton (kŏp'ẽr-tŭn) Ut. (Salt Lake City In.)	40·34 N	112·06 W
	Coquilhatville, see Mbandaka		
110	Coquille (kô-kēl') . . . . . Or.	43·11 N	124·11 W
136	Coquimbo (kô-kēm'bō) . . . . . Chile	29·58 S	71·31 W
137	Coquimbo (Prov.) Chile (Santiago In.)	31·50 S	71·05 W
112	Coquitlam (L.) (kō-kwĭt-lȧm) Can. (Vancouver In.)	49·23 N	122·44 W
165	Corabia (kô-rä'bĭ-ȧ) . . . . . Rom.	43·45 N	24·29 E
134	Coracora (kō'rä-kō'rä) . . . . . Peru	15·12 S	73·42 W
121	Coral Gables . . . . . Fl. (In.)	25·43 N	80·14 W
96	Coral Rapids (kŏr'ăl) . . . . . Can.	50·18 N	81·49 W
198	Coral Sea (kŏr'ăl) . . . . . Oceania	13·30 S	150·00 E
109	Coralville Res. . . . . . Ia.	41·45 N	91·50 W
203	Corangamite, L. (cŏr-ăŋg'ȧ-mīt) Austl.	38·05 S	142·55 E
107	Coraopolis (kō-rä-ŏp'ô-lĭs) Pa. (Pittsburgh In.)	40·30 N	80·09 W
164	Corato (kô'rä-tô) . . . . . It.	41·08 N	16·28 E
161	Corbeil-Essonnes (kôr-bā'yĕ-sŏn') Fr. (Paris In.)	48·31 N	2·29 E
112	Corbett (kôr'bĕt) Or. (Portland In.)	45·31 N	122·17 W
160	Corbie (kôr-bē') . . . . . Fr.	49·55 N	2·27 E

ng-sing; ŋ-baŋk; ɴ-nasalized n; nŏd; cŏmmit; ōld; ôbey; ôrder; fōōd; fŏŏt; ou-out; s-soft; sh-dish; th-thin; pūre; ûnite; ûrn; stŭd; circŭs; ü-as "y" in study; '-indeterminate vowel.

272 Corbin — Croix PRONOUNCING INDEX

Page	Name Pronunciation Region	Lat. °′	Long. °′
120	Corbin (kôr'bĭn) Ky.	36·55 N	84·06 W
148	Corby (kôr'bĭ) Eng.	52·29 N	0·38 W
136	Corcovado (Mtn.) (kôr-kô-vä'dōō) Braz. (Rio de Janeiro In.)	22·57 S	43·13 W
136	Corcovado, Golfo (G.) (kôr-kô-vä'dhō) Chile	43·40 S	75·00 W
137	Cordeiro (kôr-dā'rō) Braz. (Rio de Janeiro In.)	22·03 S	42·22 W
120	Cordele (kôr-dēl') Ga.	31·55 N	83·50 W
116	Cordell (kôr-dĕl') Ok.	35·19 N	98·58 W
75	Cordilleran Highlands (Reg.) (kōr dĭl'lŭr ǎn) N. A.	55·00 N	125·00 W
136	Córdoba (kôr'dô-vä) Arg.	30·20 S	64·03 W
125	Córdoba (kô'r-dô-bä) Mex.	18·53 N	96·54 W
162	Córdoba (kô'r-dô-bä) Sp.	37·55 N	4·45 W
136	Córdoba (Prov.) (kôr'dô-vä) Arg.	32·00 S	64·00 W
136	Córdoba, Sa. de (Mts.) Arg.	31·15 S	64·30 W
120	Cordova (kôr'dô-vȧ) Al.	33·45 N	86·11 W
101	Cordova (kôr'dô-vä) Ak.	60·34 N	145·38 W
92	Cordova B. Ak.	54·55 N	132·35 W
162	Corella (kô-rĕl-yä) Sp.	42·07 N	1·48 W
164	Corigliano (kō-rê-lyä'nō) It.	39·35 N	16·30 E
120	Corinth (kŏr'ĭnth) Ms.	34·55 N	88·30 W
	Corinth, see Kórinthos		
135	Corinto (kô-rē'n-tō) Braz.	18·20 S	44·16 W
134	Corinto Col. (In.)	3·09 N	76·12 W
126	Corinto (kōr-ĭn'to) Nic.	12·30 N	87·12 W
202	Corio Austl. (Melbourne In.)	38·05 S	144·22 E
202	Corio B. Austl. (Melbourne In.)	38·07 S	144·25 E
216	Corisco, Isal de (I.) Equat. Gui.	0·50 N	8·40 E
154	Cork (kôrk) Ire.	51·54 N	8·25 W
154	Cork Hbr. Ire.	51·44 N	8·15 W
164	Corleone (kôr-lå-ō'nā) It.	37·48 N	13·18 E
95	Cormorant L. Can.	54·13 N	100·47 W
120	Cornelia (kôr-nē'lyȧ) Ga.	34·31 N	83·30 W
218	Cornelis (R.) (kôr-nē'lĭs) S. Afr. (Johannesburg & Pretoria In.)	27·48 S	29·15 E
113	Cornell (kôr-nĕl') Ca. (Los Angeles In.)	34·06 N	118·46 W
109	Cornell Wi.	45·10 N	91·10 W
91	Corner Brook (kôr'nēr) Can.	48·57 N	57·57 W
203	Corner Inlet Austl.	38·55 S	146·45 E
	Corneto, see Tarquinia		
117	Corning (kôr'nĭng) Ar.	36·26 N	90·35 W
109	Corning Ia.	40·58 N	94·40 W
105	Corning NY	42·10 N	77·05 W
164	Corno, Monte (Mtn.) (kôr'nō) It.	42·28 N	13·37 E
128	Cornwall Ba.	25·55 N	77·15 W
105	Cornwall (kôrn'wôl) Can.	45·05 N	74·35 W
154	Cornwall Pen. (kôrn'wǎl) Eng.	50·25 N	5·04 W
134	Coro (kō'rō) Ven.	11·22 N	69·43 W
134	Corocoro (kō-rō-kō'rō) Bol.	17·15 S	68·21 W
185	Coromandel Coast (kŏr-ô-man'dĕl) India	13·30 N	80·30 E
120	Corona (kô-rō'nȧ) Al.	33·42 N	87·28 W
113	Corona Ca. (Los Angeles In.)	33·52 N	117·34 W
127	Coronada, Bahía de (B.) (bä-ē'ä-dĕ-kô-rô-nä'dō) C.R.	8·47 N	84·04 W
113	Corona del Mar (kô-rō'nȧ dĕl mär) Ca. (Los Angeles In.)	33·36 N	117·53 W
114	Coronado (kŏr-ô-nä'dō) Ca. (In.)	32·42 N	117·12 W
90	Coronation G. (kŏr-ō-nā'shŭn) Can.	68·07 N	112·50 W
136	Coronel (kō-rô-nĕl') Chile	37·00 S	73·10 W
137	Coronel Brandsen (kŏ-rô-nĕl-brȧ'nd-sĕn) Arg. (Buenos Aires In.)	35·09 S	58·15 W
136	Coronel Dorrego (kŏ-rô-nĕl-dôr-rĕ'gô) Arg.	38·43 S	61·16 W
136	Coronel Oviedo (kŏ-rô-nĕl-ô-vēĕ'dô) Par.	25·28 S	56·22 W
136	Coronel Pringles (kŏ-rô-nĕl-prēn'glĕs) Arg.	37·54 S	61·22 W
136	Coronel Suárez (kŏ-rô-nĕl-swä'rās) Arg.	37·27 S	61·49 W
203	Corowa (cŏr-ôwǎ) Austl.	36·02 S	146·23 E
126	Corozal (cŏr-ŏth-äl') Belize (In.)	18·25 N	88·23 W
119	Corpus Christi (kôr'pŭs krĭs'tē) Tx.	27·48 N	97·24 W
119	Corpus Christi B. Tx.	27·47 N	97·14 W
118	Corpus Christi L. Tx.	28·08 N	98·20 W
136	Corral (kô-räl') Chile	39·57 S	73·15 W
162	Corral de Almaguer (kô-räl'dā äl-mä-gâr') Sp.	39·45 N	3·10 W
128	Corralillo (kô-rä-lē-yō) Cuba	23·00 N	80·40 W
197	Corregidor (I.) (kô-rā-hē-dōr') Phil. (In.)	14·21 N	120·25 E
135	Correntina (kô-rĕn-tē-nȧ) Braz.	13·18 S	44·33 W
154	Corrib, Lough (L.) (lŏk kŏr'ĭb) Ire.	53·56 N	9·19 W
136	Corrientes (kō-ryĕn'tās) Arg.	27·25 S	58·39 W
136	Corrientes (Prov.) Arg.	28·45 S	58·00 W
134	Corrientes, Cabo (C.) (kȧ'bô-kō-ryĕn'tās) Col.	5·34 N	77·35 W
128	Corrientes, Cabo (C.) (kȧ'bô-kôr-rē-ĕn'tĕs) Cuba	21·50 N	84·25 W
124	Corrientes, Cabo (C.) Mex.	20·25 N	105·41 W
164	Corse, C. (kôrs) Fr.	42·59 N	9·19 E
164	Corsica (I.) (kô'r-sē-kä) Fr.	42·10 N	8·55 E
119	Corsicana (kôr-sĭ-kăn'ȧ) Tx.	32·06 N	96·28 W
124	Cortazar (kôr-tä-zär) Mex.	20·30 N	100·57 W
164	Corte (kôr'tâ) Fr.	42·18 N	9·10 E
162	Cortegana (kôr-tâ-gä'nä) Sp.	37·54 N	6·48 W
162	Cortes (kôr-tās') Sp.	36·38 N	5·20 W
128	Cortés, Ensenada de (B.) (ĕn-sĕ-nä-dä-dĕ-kôr-tās') Cuba	22·05 N	83·45 W
115	Cortez Co.	37·21 N	108·35 W
105	Cortland (kôrt'lǎnd) NY	42·35 N	76·10 W
164	Cortona (kôr-tō'nä) It.	43·16 N	12·00 E
214	Corubal (R.) Guinea-Bissau	11·43 N	14·40 W
162	Coruche (kô-rōō'she) Port.	38·58 N	8·34 W
171	Coruh (R.) (chō-rōōk') Tur.	40·30 N	41·10 E
171	Corum (chô-rōōm') Tur.	40·34 N	34·45 E
135	Corumbá (kô-rōōm-bä') Braz.	19·01 S	57·28 W
104	Corunna (kô-rŭn'ȧ) Mi.	43·00 N	84·05 W
135	Coruripe (kō-rōō-rē'pĭ) Braz.	10·09 S	36·13 W
110	Corvallis (kŏr-väl'ĭs) Or.	44·34 N	123·17 W
148	Corve (R.) (kôr'vē) Eng.	52·28 N	2·43 W
105	Corry (kŏr'ĭ) Pa.	41·55 N	79·40 W
104	Corydon (kŏr'ĭ-dŭn) In.	38·10 N	86·05 W
109	Corydon Ia.	40·45 N	93·20 W
104	Corydon Ky.	37·45 N	87·40 W
125	Cosamaloápan (kō-sä-mä-lwä'pän) Mex.	18·21 N	95·48 W
125	Coscomatepec (kôs'kōmä-tĕ-pĕk') Mex.	19·04 N	97·03 W
148	Coseley (kôs'lē) Eng.	52·33 N	2·10 W
164	Cosenza (kô-zĕnt'sä) It.	39·18 N	16·15 E
104	Coshocton (kō-shŏk'tŭn) Oh.	40·15 N	81·55 W
104	Cosigüina (Vol.) Nic.	12·59 N	83·35 W
213	Cosmoledo Group (Is.) (kŏs-mô-lā'dō) Afr.	9·42 S	47·45 E
110	Cosmopolis (kŏz-mŏp'ô-lĭs) Wa.	46·58 N	123·47 W
160	Cosne-sur-Loire (kōn-sür-lwär') Fr.	47·25 N	2·57 E
125	Cosoleacaque (kō sō lā-ä-kä'kē) Mex.	18·01 N	94·38 W
113	Costa Mesa (kŏs'tȧ mā'sȧ) Ca. (Los Angeles In.)	33·39 N	118·54 W
123	Costa Rica (kŏs'tȧ rē'kȧ) N. A.	10·30 N	84·30 W
114	Cosumnes (R.) (kŏ-sŭm'nĕz) Ca.	38·21 N	121·17 W
134	Cotabambas (kô-tä-bȧm'bäs) Peru	13·49 S	72·17 W
197	Cotabato (kō-tä-bä'tō) Phil.	7·06 N	124·13 E
125	Cotaxtla (kō-täs'tlä) Mex.	18·49 N	96·22 W
125	Cotaxtla (R.) Mex.	18·54 N	96·21 W
89	Coteau-du-Lac (cō-tō'dü-läk) Can. (Montreal In.)	45·17 N	74·11 W
89	Coteau-Landing Can. (Montreal In.)	45·15 N	74·13 W
129	Coteaux Hai.	18·15 N	74·05 W
160	Côte d'Or (hill) (kōr-dŏr') Fr.	47·02 N	4·35 E
124	Cotija de la Paz (kô-tē'-ĸä-dĕ-lä-pȧ'z) Mex.	19·46 N	102·43 W
215	Cotonou (kô-tô-nōō') Benin	6·21 N	2·26 E
134	Cotopaxi (Mtn.) (kō-tō-păk'sē) Ec.	0·40 S	78·26 W
129	Cotorro (kô-tôr-rō) Cuba (In.)	23·03 N	82·17 W
154	Cotswold Hills (kŭtz'wōld) Eng.	51·35 N	2·16 W
113	Cottage Grove (kŏt'āj grōv) Mn. (Minneapolis, St. Paul In.)	44·50 N	92·52 W
110	Cottage Grove Or.	43·48 N	123·04 W
158	Cottbus (kōtt'bōōs) G.D.R.	51·47 N	14·20 E
161	Cottian Alps (Mts.) (kŏt'ē-ŭn-ălps) Fr.-It.	44·46 N	7·02 E
108	Cottonwood (R.) (kŏt'ŭn-wŏŏd) Mn.	44·25 N	95·35 W
110	Cottonwood Cr. Ca.	40·24 N	122·50 W
129	Cotuí (kô-tōō'-ē) Dom. Rep.	19·05 N	70·10 W
118	Cotulla (kŏ-tŭl'lȧ) Tx.	28·26 N	99·14 W
161	Coubert (kōō-bâr') Fr. (Paris In.)	48·40 N	2·43 E
105	Coudersport (koŭ'dērz-port) Pa.	41·45 N	78·00 W
98	Coudres, Île aux (I.) Can.	47·17 N	70·12 W
160	Couëron (kōō-â-rôɴ') Fr.	47·16 N	1·45 W
161	Coulommiers (kōō-lô-myā') Fr. (Paris In.)	48·49 N	3·05 E
136	Coulto, Serra do (Mts.) (sĕ'r-rä-dô-kô-ōō'tô) Braz. (Rio de Janeiro In.)	22·33 S	43·27 W
108	Council Bluffs (koun'sĭl blŭf) Ia.	41·16 N	95·53 W
117	Council Grove (koun'sĭl grōv) Ks.	38·39 N	96·30 W
112	Coupeville (kōōp'vĭl) Wa. (Seattle In.)	48·13 N	122·41 W
135	Courantyne (R.) (kôr'ǎntĭn) Guy.-Sur.	4·28 N	57·42 W
92	Courtenay (cōōrt-nā') Can.	49·41 N	125·00 W
119	Coushatta (kou-shăt'ȧ) La.	32·02 N	93·21 W
160	Coutras (kōō-trä') Fr.	45·02 N	0·07 W
216	Covelo Ang.	12·06 S	13·55 E
148	Coventry (kŭv'ĕn-trĭ) Eng.	52·25 N	1·29 W
162	Covilhã (kô-vēl'yăɴ) Port.	40·18 N	7·29 W
113	Covina (kô-vē'nȧ) Ca. (Los Angeles In.)	34·06 N	117·54 W
120	Covington (kŭv'ĭng-tŭn) Ga.	33·36 N	83·50 W
104	Covington In.	40·10 N	87·15 W
107	Covington Ky. (Cincinnati In.)	39·05 N	84·31 W
119	Covington La.	30·30 N	90·06 W
104	Covington Oh.	40·10 N	84·20 W
117	Covington Ok.	36·18 N	97·32 W
120	Covington Tn.	35·33 N	89·40 W
105	Covington Va.	37·50 N	80·00 W
203	Cowal, L. (kou'ǎl) Austl.	33·30 S	147·10 E
204	Cowan, (L.) (kou'ǎn) Austl.	32·00 S	122·30 E
98	Cowansville Can.	45·13 N	72·47 W
110	Cow Cr. (kou) Or.	42·45 N	123·35 W
154	Cowes (kouz) Eng.	50·43 N	1·25 W
92	Cowichan L. Can.	48·54 N	124·20 W
110	Cowlitz (R.) (kou'lĭts) Wa.	46·30 N	122·45 W
203	Cowra (kou'rȧ) Austl.	33·50 S	148·33 E
135	Coxim (kō-shēɴ') Braz.	18·32 S	54·43 W
125	Coxquihui (kōz-kē-wē') Mex.	20·10 N	97·34 W
184	Cox's Bāzār Bngl.	21·32 N	92·00 E
134	Coyaima (kō-yȧē'mä) Col. (In.)	3·48 N	75·11 W
118	Coyame (kō-yä'mā) Mex.	29·26 N	105·05 W
118	Coyanosa Draw (kō yȧ-nō'sä) Tx.	30·55 N	103·07 W
125	Coyoacán (kô-yô-à-kän') Mex. (In.)	19·21 N	99·10 W
112	Coyote (R.) (kī'ōt) Ca. (San Francisco In.)	37·27 N	121·57 W
124	Coyuca de Benítez (kō-yōō'kä dā bā-nē'tāz) Mex.	17·04 N	100·06 W
124	Coyuca de Catalán (kō-yōō'kä dā kä-tä-län') Mex.	18·19 N	100·41 W
125	Coyutla (kō-yōō'tlä) Mex.	20·13 N	97·40 W
116	Cozad (kō'zǎd) Ne.	40·53 N	99·59 W
107	Cozaddale (kô-zǎd-dāl) Oh. (Cincinnati In.)	39·16 N	84·09 W
124	Cozoyoapan (kô-zō-yô-ä-pá'n) Mex.	16·45 N	98·17 W
126	Cozumel (kŏ-zōō-mĕ'l) Mex. (In.)	20·31 N	86·55 W
126	Cozumel, Isla de (I.) (ē's-lä-dĕ-kŏ-zōō-mĕ'l) Mex. (In.)	20·26 N	87·10 W
110	Crab Cr. (krăb) Wa.	46·47 N	119·43 W
110	Crab Cr. Wa.	47·21 N	119·09 W
213	Cradock (krä'dŭk) S. Afr. (Natal In.)	32·12 S	25·38 E
107	Crafton (krǎf'tŭn) Pa. (Pittsburgh In.)	40·26 N	80·04 W
111	Craig (krāg) Co.	40·32 N	107·31 W
165	Craiova (krȧ-yō'vȧ) Rom.	44·18 N	23·50 E
105	Cranberry (L.) (krăn'bĕr-ĭ) NY	44·10 N	74·50 W
202	Cranbourne Austl. (Melbourne In.)	38·07 S	145·16 E
93	Cranbrook (krăn'brŏŏk) Can.	49·31 N	115·46 W
106	Cranbury (krăn'bē-rĭ) NJ (New York In.)	40·19 N	74·31 W
109	Crandon (krăn'dŭn) Wi.	45·35 N	88·55 W
160	Cransac (kräɴ-zák') Fr.	44·28 N	2·19 E
106	Cranston (krǎns'tŭn) RI (Providence In.)	41·46 N	71·25 W
110	Crater L. (krā'tēr) Or.	43·00 N	122·08 W
110	Crater Lake Natl. Park Or.	42·58 N	122·40 W
111	Craters of the Moon Natl. Mon. (krā'tēr) Id.	43·28 N	113·15 W
135	Crateús (krä-tȧ-ōōzh') Braz.	5·09 S	40·35 W
135	Crato (krä'tōō) Braz.	7·19 S	39·13 W
108	Crawford (krô'fērd) Ne.	42·41 N	103·25 W
112	Crawford Wa. (Portland In.)	45·49 N	122·24 W
104	Crawfordsville (krô'fērdz-vĭl) In.	40·00 N	86·55 W
111	Crazy Mts. (krā'zĭ) Mt.	46·11 N	110·25 W
111	Crazy Woman Cr. Wy.	44·08 N	106·40 W
160	Crécy (krā-sē') Fr.	50·13 N	1·48 E
218	Crecy (krĕ-sē) S. Afr. (Johannesburg & Pretoria In.)	24·38 S	28·52 E
161	Crecy-en-Brie (krā-sē'-ĕɴ-brē') Fr. (Paris In.)	48·52 N	2·55 E
89	Credit (R.) Can. (Toronto In.)	43·41 N	79·55 W
90	Cree (L.) (krē) Can.	57·35 N	107·52 W
108	Creighton (krā'tŭn) Ne.	42·27 N	97·54 W
213	Creighton (cre-tŏn) S. Afr. (Natal In.)	30·02 S	28·52 E
160	Creil (krē'y') Fr.	49·18 N	2·28 E
164	Crema (krā'mä) It.	45·21 N	9·53 E
164	Cremona (krā-mō'nä) It.	45·09 N	10·02 E
161	Crépy-en-Valois (krā-pē'-ĕɴ-vä-lwä') Fr. (In.)	49·14 N	2·53 E
164	Cres (Tsrĕs) Yugo.	44·58 N	14·21 E
164	Cres (I.) Yugo.	44·50 N	14·31 E
121	Crescent (L.) (krĕs'ĕnt) Fl.	29·33 N	81·30 W
110	Crescent (L.) Or.	43·25 N	121·58 W
112	Crescent Beach Can. (Vancouver In.)	49·03 N	122·58 W
110	Crescent City (krĕs'ĕnt) Ca.	41·46 N	124·13 W
121	Crescent City Fl.	29·26 N	81·35 W
109	Cresco (krĕs'kō) Ia.	43·23 N	92·07 W
115	Crested Butte (krĕst'ĕd būt) Co.	38·50 N	107·00 W
113	Crestline (krĕst-līn) Ca. (Los Angeles In.)	34·15 N	117·17 W
104	Crestline Oh.	40·50 N	82·40 W
113	Crestmore (krĕst'môr) Ca. (Los Angeles In.)	34·02 N	117·23 W
93	Creston (krĕs'tŭn) Can.	49·06 N	116·31 W
109	Creston Ia.	41·04 N	94·22 W
107	Creston Oh. (Cleveland In.)	40·59 N	81·54 W
120	Crestview (krĕst'vū) Fl.	30·44 N	86·35 W
107	Crestwood (krĕst'wŏŏd) Ky. (Louisville In.)	38·20 N	85·28 W
113	Crestwood Mo. (St. Louis In.)	38·33 N	90·23 W
107	Crete (krēt) Il. (Chicago In.)	41·26 N	87·38 W
117	Crete Ne.	40·38 N	96·56 W
164	Crete (I.) Grc. (In.)	35·15 N	24·30 E
163	Creus, Cabo de (C.) (kȧ'-bô-dĕ-krĕ-ōōs) Sp.	42·16 N	3·18 E
160	Creuse (R.) (krûz) Fr.	46·51 N	0·49 E
113	Creve Coeur (krēv kōōr) Mo. (St. Louis In.)	38·40 N	90·27 W
163	Crevillente (krā-vē-lyĕn'tâ) Sp.	38·12 N	0·48 W
148	Crewe (krōō) Eng.	53·06 N	2·27 W
121	Crewe Va.	37·09 N	78·08 W
	Crimea P-Ov (Pen.), see Krymskiy		
158	Crimmitschau (krĭm'ĭt-shou) G.D.R.	50·49 N	12·22 E
116	Cripple Creek (krĭp''l) Co.	38·44 N	105·12 W
105	Crisfield (krĭs-fēld) Md.	38·00 N	75·50 W
216	Cristal, Monts de (Mts.) Gabon	0·50 N	10·30 E
137	Cristina (krēs-tē'-nä) Braz. (Rio de Janeiro In.)	22·13 S	45·15 W
134	Cristobal Colón, Pico (Pk.) (pē'kō-krēs-tô'bäl-kō-lōn') Col.	11·00 N	74·00 W
159	Crişul Alb (R.) (krē'shōōl älb) Rom.	46·20 N	22·15 E
165	Črna (R.) (ts'r'nȧ) Yugo.	41·03 N	21·46 E
165	Črna Gora (Montenegro) (Reg.) (ts'r-nȧ-gō'rȧ) (mōn-tā-nā'grō) (mōn-tĕ-nē'grō) Yugo.	42·55 N	18·52 E
164	Črnomelj (ch'r'nō-māl') Yugo.	45·35 N	15·11 E
	Croatia (Reg.), see Hrvatska		
112	Crockett (krŏk'ĕt) Ca. (San Francisco In.)	38·03 N	122·14 W
119	Crockett Tx.	31·19 N	95·28 W
106	Crofton Md. (Baltimore In.)	39·01 N	76·43 W
108	Crofton Ne.	42·44 N	97·32 W
109	Croix, Lac la (L.) (krōō-ä' läk lä) Can.-Mn.	48·19 N	91·53 W

ăt; finǎl; rāte; senâte; ärm; ȧsk; sofȧ; fâre; ch-choose; dh-as th in other; bē; ēvent; bĕt; recĕnt; cratēr; g-go; gh-guttural g; bĭt; ĭ-short neutral; rīde; ĸ-guttural k as ch in German ich;

Page	Name Pronunciation Region	Lat. °′	Long. °′
204	Croker (I.) (krō'kẽr)........Austl.	10·45 s	132·25 e
202	Cronulla (krō-nŭl'ȧ) Austl. (Sydney In.)	34·03 s	151·09 e
129	Crooked (I.)..............Ba.	22·45 n	74·10 w
99	Crooked (L.)..............Can.	48·25 n	56·05 w
92	Crooked (R.)..............Can.	54·30 n	122·55 w
110	Crooked (R.)..............Or.	44·07 n	120·30 w
117	Crooked Cr. (krŏŏk'ĕd)........Il.	40·21 n	90·49 w
110	Crooked Cr................Or.	42·23 n	118·14 w
129	Crooked Island Passage (Str.).Ba.	22·40 n	74·50 w
108	Crookston (krŏŏks'tŭn).......Mn.	47·44 n	96·35 w
104	Crooksville (krŏŏks'vĭl).......Oh.	39·45 n	82·05 w
109	Crosby (krôz'bĭ)............Mn.	46·29 n	93·58 w
108	Crosby....................ND	48·55 n	103·18 w
119	Crosby..............Tx. (In.)	29·55 n	95·04 w
105	Cross (L.) (krôs)...........Can.	44·55 n	76·55 w
119	Cross (L.)..................La.	32·33 n	93·58 w
215	Cross (R.)..................Nig.	5·35 n	8·05 e
120	Cross City..................Fl.	29·55 n	83·25 w
117	Crossett (krôs'ĕt)............Ar.	33·08 n	92·00 w
128	Cross Hbr...................Ba.	25·55 n	77·15 w
95	Cross Lake..................Can.	54·37 n	97·47 w
95	Cross L.....................Can.	54·45 n	97·30 w
106	Cross River Res. (krôs) NY (New York In.)	41·14 n	73·34 w
101	Cross Sd. (krŏs).............Ak.	58·12 n	137·20 w
104	Crosswell (krŏz'wĕl)..........Mi.	43·15 n	82·35 w
97	Crotch (R.)..................Can.	45·02 n	76·55 w
165	Crotone (krō-tô'nĕ)...........It.	39·05 n	17·08 e
106	Croton Falls Res. (krōtŭn) NY (New York In.)	41·22 n	73·44 w
106	Croton-on-Hudson (krō'tŭn-ŏn hŭd'sŭn).NY (New York In.)	41·12 n	73·53 w
109	Crow (L.)...................Can.	49·13 n	93·29 w
111	Crow Agency.................Mt.	45·36 n	107·27 w
116	Crow Cr.....................Co.	41·08 n	104·25 w
108	Crow Creek Ind. Res..........SD	44·17 n	99·17 w
111	Crow Ind. Res. (krō).........Mt.	45·26 n	108·12 w
148	Crowle (kroul)..............Eng.	53·36 n	0·49 w
119	Crowley (krou'lē)............La.	30·13 n	92·22 w
123	Crown Mtn. Vir. Is. (U. S. A.) (St. Thomas In.)	18·22 n	64·58 w
112	Crown Mtn. (kroun) Can. (Vancouver In.)	49·24 n	123·05 w
107	Crown Point (kroun point') In. (Chicago In.)	41·25 n	87·22 w
105	Crown Point.................NY	44·00 n	73·25 w
93	Crowsnest P.................Can.	49·39 n	114·45 w
109	Crow Wing (R.) (krō).......Mn.	44·50 n	94·01 w
109	Crow Wing (R.)..............Mn.	46·42 n	94·48 w
109	Crow Wing (R.), North Fork Mn.	45·16 n	94·28 w
109	Crow Wing (R.), South Fork Mn.	44·59 n	94·42 w
205	Croydon (kroi'dŭn)........Austl.	18·15 s	142·15 e
202	Croydon...Austl. (Melbourne In.)	37·48 s	145·17 e
148	Croydon.......Eng. (London In.)	51·22 n	0·06 w
106	Croydon...Pa. (Philadelphia In.)	40·05 n	74·55 w
220	Crozet Is. (krô-zĕ')........Ind. O.	46·20 s	51·30 e
128	Cruces (krōō'sās)...........Cuba	22·20 n	80·20 w
118	Cruces, Arroyo de (är-rō'yô-dĕ-krōō'sĕs).Mex.	26·17 n	104·32 w
118	Cruillas (krōō-ēl'yäs)........Mex.	24·45 n	98·31 w
128	Cruz, Cabo (C.) (kä'-bô-krōōz) Cuba	19·50 n	77·45 w
128	Cruz, Cayo (I.) (kä'yō-krōōz) Cuba	22·15 n	77·50 w
136	Cruz Alta (krōōz äl'tä)......Braz.	28·41 s	54·02 w
136	Cruz del Eje (krōō's-dĕl-ĕ-kĕ).Arg.	30·46 s	64·45 w
137	Cruzeiro (krōō-zā'rōō) Braz. (Rio de Janeiro In.)	22·36 s	44·57 w
134	Cruzeiro do Sul (krōō-zā'rōō dōō sōōl).Braz.	7·34 s	72·40 w
89	Crysler........Can. (Ottawa In.)	45·13 n	75·09 w
118	Crystal City (krĭs'tăl sĭ'tĭ)....Tx.	28·40 n	99·90 w
109	Crystal Falls (krĭs'tăl fôls)....Mi.	46·06 n	88·21 w
107	Crystal Lake (krĭs'tăl lăk) Il. (Chicago In.)	42·15 n	88·18 w
120	Crystal Springs (krĭs'tăl sprĭngz) Ms.	31·58 n	90·20 w
112	Crystal Sprs. Ca. (San Francisco In.)	37·31 n	122·26 w
159	Csongrád (chôn'gräd)......Hung.	46·42 n	20·09 e
159	Csorna (chôr'nä)..........Hung.	47·39 n	17·11 e
135	Cúa (kōō'ä)...........Ven. (In.)	10·10 n	66·54 w
125	Cuajimalpa (kwä-hĕ-mäl'pä Mex. (In.)	19·21 n	99·18 w
124	Cuale, Sierra del (Mts.) (sē-ĕ'r-rä-dĕl-kwä'lĕ).Mex.	20·20 n	104·58 w
216	Cuamato (kwä-mä'tō).......Ang.	17·05 s	15·09 e
216	Cuando (kwän'dō)..........Ang.	16·32 s	22·07 e
216	Cuando (R.)................Ang.	16·50 s	22·40 e
216	Cuangar....................Ang.	17·36 s	18·39 e
216	Cuango (Kwango) (R.) (kwäŋ'gō).Afr.	6·35 s	16·50 e
216	Cuanza (R.) (kwän'zä)......Ang.	9·05 s	13·15 e
136	Cuarto Saladillo (R.) (kwär'tō-sä-lä-dē'l-yō).Arg.	33·00 s	63·25 w
129	Cuatro Caminos (kwä'trô-kä-mē' nōs).Cuba (In.)	23·01 n	82·13 w
118	Cuatro Ciénegas (kwä'trō syā'nâ-gäs) . Mex.	26·59 n	102·03 w
126	Cuauhtemoc (kwä-ōō-tĕ-mŏk') Mex.	15·43 n	91·57 w
124	Cuautepec (kwä-ōō-tĕ-pĕk) . . Mex.	16·41 n	99·04 w
124	Cuautepec..................Mex.	20·01 n	98·19 w
125	Cuautitlán (kwä-ōō-tēt-län') Mex. (In.)	19·40 n	99·12 w
124	Cuautla (kwä-ōō'tlä).......Mex.	18·47 n	98·57 w
162	Cuba (kōō'bä)..............Port.	38·10 n	7·55 w
123	Cuba (kū'bȧ)..............N. A.	22·00 n	79·00 w

Page	Name Pronunciation Region	Lat. °′	Long. °′
135	Cubagua, Isla (I.) (ē's-lä-kōō-bä'gwä) .Ven. (In.)	10·48 n	64·10 w
216	Cubango (Okavango) (R.) (kōō-bäŋ'gō) .Ang.-Namibia	17·10 s	18·20 e
94	Cub Hills (kŭb)...........Can.	54·20 n	104·30 w
113	Cucamonga (kōō-kȧ-mŏŋ'gȧ) Ca. (Los Angeles In.)	34·05 n	117·35 w
212	Cuchi......................Ang.	14·40 s	16·50 e
118	Cuchillo Parado (kōō-chē'lyô pä-rä'dō) . Mex.	29·26 n	104·52 w
126	Cuchumatanes, Sierra de los (Mts.) Guat.	15·35 n	91·10 w
134	Cúcuta (kōō'kōō-tä).........Col.	7·56 n	72·30 w
107	Cudahy (kŭd'ȧ-hī) Wi. (Milwaukee In.)	42·57 n	87·52 w
185	Cuddalore (kŭd ȧ-lōr')......India	11·49 n	79·46 e
185	Cuddapah (kŭd'ȧ-pä)........India	14·31 n	78·52 e
204	Cue (kū)...................Austl.	27·30 s	118·10 e
162	Cuellar (kwā'lyär')...........Sp.	41·24 n	4·15 w
134	Cuenca (kwĕn'kä)............Ec.	2·52 s	78·54 w
162	Cuenca.......................Sp.	40·05 n	2·07 w
162	Cuenca, Sierra de (Mts.) (sē-ĕ'r-rä-dĕ-kwĕ'n-kä).Sp.	40·02 n	1·50 w
118	Cuencame (kwĕn-kä-mā')....Mex.	24·52 n	103·42 w
124	Cuerámaro (kwā-rä'mä-rô)...Mex.	20·39 n	101·44 w
125	Cuernavaca (kwĕr-nä-vä'kä) Mex. (In.)	18·55 n	99·15 w
119	Cuero (kwā'rō)..............Tx.	29·05 n	97·16 w
124	Cuetzalá del Progreso (kwĕt-zä-lä dĕl prō-grā'sō).Mex.	18·07 n	99·51 w
125	Cuetzalan del Progreso (kwĕt-zä-län dĕl prō-grā'sō).Mex.	20·02 n	97·33 w
162	Cuevas del Almanzora (kwĕ'väs-dĕl-äl-män-zô-rä)..Sp.	37·19 n	1·54 w
164	Cuglieri (kōō-lyâ'rē)..........It.	40·11 n	8·37 e
135	Cuiabá (kōō-yä-bä')........Braz.	15·33 s	56·03 w
125	Cuicatlán (kwē-kä-tlän')......Mex.	17·46 n	96·57 w
126	Cuilapa (kōō-ē-lä'pä).......Guat.	14·16 n	90·20 w
154	Cuillin Sd..................Scot.	57·09 n	6·20 w
216	Cuilo (R.)..................Ang.	9·15 s	19·30 e
216	Cuito (R.) (kōō-ē'tō).......Ang.	14·15 s	19·00 e
124	Cuitzeo (kwēt'zā-ō).........Mex.	19·57 n	101·11 w
124	Cuitzeo, Laguna de (L.) (lä-ōō'nä-dĕ-kwĕt'zā-ō).Mex.	19·58 n	101·05 w
129	Cul de Sac (Val.) (kōō'l-dĕ-sä'k) Dom. Rep.-Hai.	18·35 n	72·05 w
123	Culebra (I.) (kōō-lā'brä) P. R. (Puerto Rico In.)	18·19 n	65·32 w
149	Culemborg Neth. (Amsterdam In.)	51·57 n	5·14 e
205	Culgoa (R.) (kŭl-gō'ȧ)......Austl.	29·21 s	147·00 e
122	Culiacán (kōō-lyä-kä'n).....Mex.	24·45 n	107·30 w
196	Culion (kōō-lē-ōn')..........Phil.	11·43 n	119·58 e
162	Cúllar de Baza (kōō'l-yär-dĕ-bä'zä).Sp.	37·36 n	2·35 w
163	Cullera (kōō-lyā'rä)..........Sp.	39·12 n	0·15 w
213	Cullinan (kōō'lĭ-nȧn)......S. Afr. (Johannesburg & Pretoria In.)	25·41 s	28·32 e
120	Cullman (kŭl'mȧn)..........Ala.	34·10 n	86·50 w
105	Culpeper (kŭl'pĕp-ẽr)........Va.	38·30 n	77·55 w
89	Culross (kŭl'rôs) Can. (Winnipeg In.)	49·43 n	97·54 w
104	Culver (kŭl'vẽr)..............In.	41·15 n	86·25 w
113	Culver City Ca. (Los Angeles In.)	34·00 n	118·23 w
135	Cumaná (kōō-mä-nä') Ven. (In.)	10·28 n	64·10 w
89	Cumberland (kŭm'bẽr-lȧnd) Can. (Ottawa In.)	45·31 n	75·25 w
105	Cumberland.................Md.	39·40 n	78·40 w
112	Cumberland.....Wa. (Seattle In.)	47·17 n	121·55 w
109	Cumberland.................Wi.	45·31 n	92·01 w
120	Cumberland (R.)............U. S.	36·45 n	85·33 w
120	Cumberland, L..............Ky.	36·55 n	85·20 w
205	Cumberland Is..............Austl.	20·29 s	149·46 e
91	Cumberland Pen.............Can.	65·59 n	64·05 w
120	Cumberland Plat............Tn.	35·25 n	85·30 w
91	Cumberland Sd..............Can.	65·27 n	65·44 w
134	Cundinamarca (Dept.) (kōōn-dē-nä-mä'r-kä).Col. (In.)	4·57 n	74·27 w
125	Cunduacán (kōōn-dōō-ȧ-kän') Mex.	18·04 n	93·23 w
216	Cunene (Kunene) (R.) Ang.-Namibia	17·05 s	12·35 e
164	Cuneo (kōō'nā-ō).............It.	44·24 n	7·31 e
137	Cunha (kōō'nyä) Braz. (Rio de Janeiro In.)	23·05 s	44·56 w
203	Cunnamulla (kŭn-ȧ-mŭl-ȧ)..Austl.	28·00 s	145·55 e
122	Cupula, Pico (Mtn.) (pē'kō-kōō'pōō-lä).Mex.	24·45 n	111·10 w
124	Cuquío (kōō-kē'ō)...........Mex.	20·55 n	103·03 w
134	Curaçao (kōō-rä-sä'ō) (I.) Neth. Antilles	12·12 n	68·58 w
136	Curacautín (kä-rä-käōō-tē'n) . Chile	38·25 s	71·53 w
137	Curacaví (kōō-rä-kä-vē') Chile (Santiago In.)	33·23 s	71·09 w
137	Curaumilla, Punta (Pt.) (kōō-rou-mē'lyä).Chile (Santiago In.)	33·05 s	71·44 w
137	Curepto (kōō-rĕp-tô) Chile (Santiago In.)	35·06 s	72·02 w
137	Curicó (kōō-rē-kō') Chile (Santiago In.)	34·57 s	71·14 w
137	Curicó (Prov.).Chile (Santiago In.)	34·55 s	71·15 w
136	Curitiba (kōō-rē-tē'bȧ)......Braz.	25·20 s	49·15 w
128	Curly Cut Cays (Is.).........Ba.	23·40 n	77·40 w
135	Currais Novos (kōōr-rä'ēs nō-vōs).Braz.	6·02 s	36·39 w
89	Curran (kŭ-räN') Can. (Ottawa In.)	45·30 n	74·59 w
128	Current (I.) (kŭ-rĕnt)........Ba.	25·20 n	76·50 w
117	Current (R.) (kûr'ĕnt).......Mo.	37·18 n	91·21 w
213	Currie, Mt. (cŭ-rē) S. Afr. (Natal In.)	30·28 s	29·23 e

Page	Name Pronunciation Region	Lat. °′	Long. °′
121	Currituck Sd. (kûr'ĭ-tŭk).....NC	36·27 n	75·42 w
165	Curtea de Argeş (kŏŏr'tĕ-ȧ dĕ âr'zhĕsh).Rom.	45·09 n	24·40 e
116	Curtis (kûr'tĭs)..............Ne.	40·36 n	100·29 w
205	Curtis (I.).................Austl.	23·38 s	151·43 e
107	Curtisville (kûr'tĭs-vĭl) Pa. (Pittsburgh In.)	40·38 n	79·50 w
135	Curuá (R.) (kōō-rōō-ä')......Braz.	6·26 s	54·39 w
165	Ćurug (chōō'rŏŏg)...........Yugo.	45·27 n	20·26 e
216	Curunga.....................Ang.	12·51 s	21·12 e
134	Curupira, Serra (Mts.) (sĕr'rȧ kōō-rōō-pē'rȧ) Braz.-Ven.	1·00 n	65·30 w
135	Cururupu (kōō-rōō-rōō-pōō').Braz.	1·40 s	44·56 w
136	Curuzú Cuatiá (kōō-rōō-zōō' kwä-tē-ä').Arg.	29·45 s	57·58 w
135	Curvelo (kŏŏr-vĕl'ŏŏ)........Braz.	18·47 s	44·14 w
117	Cushing (kŭsh'ĭng)...........Ok.	35·58 n	96·46 w
160	Cusset (kü-sĕ')...............Fr.	46·08 n	3·29 e
108	Custer (kŭs'tẽr)..............SD	43·46 n	103·36 w
112	Custer......Wa. (Vancouver In.)	48·55 n	122·39 w
111	Custer Battlefield Nat'l. Mon. (kŭs'tẽr băt''l-fēld).Mt.	45·44 n	107·15 w
111	Cut Bank (kŭt bănk)..........Mt.	48·38 n	112·19 w
120	Cuthbert (kŭth'bẽrt).........Ga.	31·47 n	84·48 w
184	Cuttack (kŭ-tăk')............India	20·38 n	85·53 e
124	Cutzamala (R.) (kōō-tzä-mä-lä') Mex.	18·57 n	100·41 w
124	Cutzamalá de Pinzón (kōō-tzä-mä-lä'dĕ-pēn-zō'n).Mex.	18·28 n	100·36 w
216	Cuvo (R.) (kōō'vō)..........Ang.	10·55 s	14·00 e
158	Cuxhaven (kŏŏks' hä-fĕn)..F.R.G.	53·51 n	8·43 e
107	Cuyahoga Falls Oh. (Cleveland In.)	41·08 n	81·29 w
107	Cuyahoga R. (kī-ȧ-hō'gȧ) Oh. (Cleveland In.)	41·22 n	81·38 w
114	Cuyapaire Ind. Res. (kū-yȧ-pâr) Ca.	32·46 n	116·20 w
196	Cuyo Is. (kōō'yō)...........Phil.	10·54 n	120·08 e
126	Cuyotenango (kōō-yô-tĕ-näŋ'gô) Guat.	14·30 n	91·35 w
135	Cuyuni (R.) (kōō-yōō'nē) Guy.-Ven.	6·40 n	60·44 w
124	Cuyutlán (kōō-yōō-tlän')....Mex.	18·54 n	104·04 w
134	Cuzco.......................Peru	13·36 s	71·52 w
104	Cynthiana (sĭn-thĭ-ăn'ȧ).......Ky.	38·20 n	84·20 w
113	Cypress (sī'prĕs) Ca. (Los Angeles In.)	33·50 n	118·03 w
94	Cypress Hills...............Can.	49·40 n	110·20 w
94	Cypress L...................Can.	49·28 n	109·43 w
182	Cyprus (sī'prŭs)............Asia	35·00 n	31·00 e
	Cyrenaica (Prov.), see Barqah		
146	Czechoslovakia (chĕk'ô-slô-vä'kĭ-ȧ).Eur.	49·28 n	16·00 e
159	Czersk (chĕrsk)..............Pol.	53·47 n	17·58 e
159	Czestochowa (chăN-stô kô'vȧ).Pol.	50·49 n	19·10 e

D

Page	Name Pronunciation Region	Lat. °′	Long. °′
210	Dabakala (dä-bä-kä'lä) Ivory Coast	8·16 n	4·36 w
134	Dabeiba (dȧ-bā'bä).....Col. (In.)	7·01 n	76·16 w
215	Dabnou.....................Niger	14·09 n	5·22 e
112	Dabob B. (dā'bŏb) Wa. (Seattle In.)	47·50 n	122·50 w
214	Dabola......................Gui.	10·45 n	11·07 w
159	Dabrowa (dŏN-brō'vȧ).........Pol.	53·37 n	23·18 e
184	Dacca (dă'kä) (dăk'ȧ)......Bngl.	23·45 n	90·29 e
149	Dachau (dä'kou) F.R.G. (Munich In.)	48·16 n	11·26 e
89	Dacotah (dȧ-kō'tȧ) Can. (Winnipeg In.)	49·52 n	97·38 w
121	Dade City (dād).........Fl. (In.)	28·22 n	82·09 w
120	Dadeville (dād'vĭl)............Al.	32·48 n	85·44 w
184	Dādra & Nagar Haveli (Union Ter.).India	20·00 n	73·00 e
197	Daet (Mtn.) (dä'ât)....Phil. (In.)	14·07 n	122·59 e
95	Dafoe (R.)..................Can.	55·50 n	95·50 w
113	Dafter (dăf'tẽr) Mi. (Sault Ste. Marie In.)	46·21 n	84·26 w
214	Dagana (dä-gä'nä)........Senegal	16·31 n	15·30 w
215	Dagana (Reg.)...............Chad.	12·20 n	15·15 e
166	Dagda (dȧg'dȧ)...........Sov. Un.	56·04 n	27·30 e
148	Dagenham (dăg'ĕn-ăm) Eng. (London In.)	51·32 n	0·09 e
171	Dagestan (Reg.) (dä-gĕs-tän') Sov. Un.	43·40 n	46·10 e
114	Daggett (dăg'ĕt).............Ca.	34·50 n	116·52 w
197	Dagupan (dä-gōō'pän)..Phil. (In.)	16·02 n	120·20 e
161	Dahl (däl) .....F.R.G. (Ruhr In.)	51·18 n	7·33 e
211	Dahlak Arch. (Is.)..........Eth.	15·45 n	40·30 e
	Dahomey, see Benin		
195	Daigo (dī-gō)....Jap. (Ōsaka In.)	34·57 n	135·49 e
162	Daimiel Manzanares (dī-myĕl' män-zä-nä'rĕs).Sp.	39·05 n	3·36 w
	Dairen, see Lüta		
112	Dairy (R.) (dâr'ĭ) Or. (Portland In.)	45·33 n	123·04 w
112	Dairy (R.) East Fk. Or. (Portland In.)	45·40 n	123·03 w
195	Dai-Sen (Mtn.) (dī'sĕn').....Jap.	35·22 n	133·35 e

274 Dai-Tenjo-dake — Delitzsch PRONOUNCING INDEX

Page	Name Pronunciation Region	Lat. °′	Long. °′
195	Dai-Tenjo-dake (Mtn.) (dī-tĕn'jō dä-ĸä) . Jap.	36·21 N	137·38 E
195	Daitō .... Jap. (Ōsaka In.)	34·42 N	135·38 E
129	Dajabón (dä-ĸä-bō'n) .. Dom. Rep.	19·35 N	71·40 W
204	Dajarra (dȧ-jăr'ȧ) .... Austl.	21·45 S	139·30 E
214	Dakar (dȧ-kär') .... Senegal	14·40 N	17·26 W
215	Dakouraoua .... Niger	13·58 N	6·15 E
192	Dalai Nor (L.) (dä-lī'nōr) .. China	48·50 N	116·45 E
156	Dalälven (R.) .... Swe.	60·26 N	15·50 E
216	Dalatando .... Ang.	9·18 S	14·54 E
203	Dalby (dôl'bê) .... Austl.	27·10 S	151·15 E
106	Dalcour (dăl-kour) La. (New Orleans In.)	29·49 N	89·59 W
156	Dale (dä'lĕ) .... Nor.	60·34 N	5·46 E
120	Dale Hollow (L.) (dāl hŏl'ō) .. Tn.	36·33 N	85·03 W
89	Dalemead (dä'lĕ-mēd) Can. (Calgary In.)	50·53 N	113·38 W
156	Dalen (dä'lĕn) .... Nor.	59·28 N	8·01 E
218	Daleside (dāl'sīd) .... S. Afr. (Johannesburg & Pretoria In.)	26·30 S	28·03 E
89	Dalesville (dālz'vĭl) Can. (Montreal In.)	45·42 N	74·23 W
204	Daley (L.) (dā'lĭ) .... Austl.	14·15 S	131·15 E
204	Daley Waters (dā lê) .... Austl.	16·15 S	133·30 E
116	Dalhart (dăl'härt) .... Tx.	36·04 N	102·32 W
98	Dalhousie (dăl-hōō'zê) .... Can.	48·04 N	66·23 W
162	Dalías (dä-lē'äs) .... Sp.	36·49 N	2·50 W
101	Dall (I.) (dăl) .... Ak.	54·50 N	133·10 W
110	Dallas (dăl'lȧs) .... Or.	44·55 N	123·20 W
108	Dallas .... SD	43·13 N	99·34 W
113	Dallas Tx. (Dallas, Fort Worth In.)	32·45 N	96·48 W
110	Dalles Dam .... Or.	45·36 N	121·08 W
92	Dall I. .... Ak.	54·50 N	132·55 W
164	Dalmacija (Reg.) (däl-mä'tsê-yä) Yugo.	43·25 N	16·37 E
173	Dalnerechensk .... Sov. Un.	46·07 N	133·21 E
214	Daloa .... Ivory Coast	6·53 N	6·27 W
211	Dalqu (dĕl'gō) .... Sud.	20·07 N	30·41 E
89	Dalroy (dăl'roi) . Can. (Calgary In.)	51·07 N	113·39 W
205	Dalrymple, Mt. (dăl'rĭm-p'l) Austl.	21·14 S	148·46 E
120	Dalton (dôl'tŭn) .... Ga.	34·46 N	84·58 W
213	Dalton (dŏl'tŏn) . S. Afr. (Natal In.)	29·21 S	30·41 E
112	Daly City (dā'lê) Ca. (San Francisco In.)	37·42 N	122·27 W
135	Dam (däm) .... Sur.	4·36 N	54·54 W
184	Damān .... India	20·32 N	72·53 E
218	Damanhūr (dä-män-hōōr') Egypt (Nile In.)	30·59 N	30·31 E
197	Damar (I.) .... Indon.	7·15 S	129·15 E
215	Damara .... Cen. Afr. Emp.	4·58 N	18·42 E
212	Damaraland (Reg.) (dă'nȧ-rȧ-lănd) . Namibia	22·15 S	16·15 E
128	Damas Cays (Is.) (dä'mäs) .. Ba.	23·50 N	79·50 W
	Damascus, see Dimashq		
171	Damavand (Mtn.) .... Iran	36·05 N	52·05 E
216	Damba (däm'bä) .... Ang.	6·41 S	15·08 E
129	Dame Marie, Cap (C.) (dām mȧrē') . Hai.	18·35 N	74·50 W
186	Dāmghān (dām-gān') .... Iran	35·50 N	54·15 E
161	Dammartin-en-Goële (däɴ-mär-tăɴ-äɴ-gō-ĕl') . Fr. (Paris In.)	49·03 N	2·40 E
197	Dampier, Selat (Str.) (dăm'pēr) Indon.	0·40 N	131·15 E
204	Dampier Arch. (däɴ-pyâr') . Austl.	20·15 S	116·25 E
204	Dampier Land (Penin) .... Austl.	17·30 S	122·25 E
121	Dan (R.) (dån) .... NC	36·26 N	79·40 W
211	Danakil Pln. .... Eth.	12·45 N	41·01 E
214	Danané .... Ivory Coast	7·16 N	8·09 W
193	Da Nang (Tourane) .... Viet.	16·08 N	108·22 E
106	Danbury (dăn'bĕr-ĭ) Ct. (New York In.)	41·23 N	73·27 W
148	Danbury ...... Eng. (London In.)	51·42 N	0·34 E
119	Danbury .... Tx. (In.)	29·14 N	95·22 W
202	Dandenong (dăn'dē-nông) Austl. (Melbourne In.)	37·59 S	145·13 E
148	Dane (R.) (dān) .... Eng.	53·11 N	2·14 W
214	Danea .... Gui.	11·27 N	13·12 W
98	Danforth .... Me.	45·38 N	67·53 W
211	Dānglā .... Eth.	11·17 N	37·00 E
215	Dan Gora .... Nig.	11·30 N	8·09 E
214	Dani .... Upper Volta	13·43 N	0·10 W
121	Dania (dā'nĭ-ȧ) .... Fl. (In.)	26·01 N	80·10 W
166	Danilov (dä'nē-lôf) ...... Sov. Un.	58·12 N	40·08 E
165	Danilov Grad (dä'nē-lôf'gräd) Yugo.	42·31 N	19·08 E
217	Danissa Hills .... Ken.	3·20 N	40·55 E
166	Dankov (däŋ'kôf) ...... Sov. Un.	53·17 N	39·09 E
126	Danlí (dän'lē) .... Hond.	14·02 N	86·35 W
105	Dannemora (dăn-ē-mō'rȧ) .... NY	44·45 N	73·45 W
213	Dannhauser (dän'hou-zēr) S. Afr. (Natal In.)	28·07 S	30·04 E
105	Dansville (dănz'vĭl) .... NY	42·30 N	77·40 W
167	Danube, Mouths of the (dăn'ub) Rom.	45·13 N	29·37 E
153	Danube (R.) .... Eur.	43·41 N	23·35 E
99	Danvers (dăn'vērz) ...... Ma. (In.)	42·34 N	70·57 W
112	Danville (dăn'vĭl) Ca. (San Francisco In.)	37·49 N	122·00 W
104	Danville .... Il.	40·10 N	87·35 W
104	Danville .... In.	39·45 N	86·30 W
104	Danville .... Ky.	37·35 N	84·50 W
105	Danville .... Pa.	41·00 N	76·35 W
121	Danville .... Va.	36·35 N	79·24 W
150	Danzig, G. of (dån'tsĭk) ...... Pol.	54·41 N	19·01 E
183	Daphnae (Ruins) Egypt (Palestine In.)	30·43 N	32·12 E
214	Dapango .... Upper Volta	10·52 N	0·12 E
183	Dar'ā .... Syria (Palestine In.)	32·37 N	36·07 E
159	Dărăbani (dă-rä-băn'ĭ) ...... Rom.	48·13 N	26·38 E
210	Daraj .... Libya	30·12 N	10·14 E
218	Darāw (dȧ-rä'ōō) Egypt (Nile In.)	24·24 N	32·56 E
184	Darbhanga (dŭr-bŭŋ'gä) .... India	26·03 N	85·09 E
106	Darby (där'bĭ) Pa. (Philadelphia In.)	39·55 N	75·16 W
129	Darby (I.) .... Ba.	23·50 N	76·20 W
	Dardanelles (Str.), see Çanakkale Boğazı		
217	Dar-es-Salaam (där ĕs sȧ-läm') Tan.	6·48 S	39·17 E
211	Dārfūr (Prov.) (där-fōōr') .... Sud.	13·21 N	23·46 E
187	Dargai (dŭr-gä'ê) Pak. (Khyber Pass In.)	34·35 N	72·00 E
210	D'Arguin, Cap (C.) ...... Mauritania	20·28 N	17·46 W
134	Darien (dā-rĭ-ĕn') ...... Col. (In.)	3·56 N	76·30 W
106	Darien (dâ-rē-ĕn') Ct. (New York In.)	41·04 N	73·28 W
126	Darien, Cordillera de (Mts.) .. Nic.	13·00 N	85·42 W
134	Darién, Golfo del (G.) (gôl-fô-dĕl-dā-rĭ-ĕn') . N. A.-S. A.	9·36 N	77·54 W
127	Darien, Serrania del (Ra.) (sĕr-ä-nē'ä dĕl dä-rê-ĕn') . Pan.	8·13 N	77·28 W
184	Darjeeling (dŭr-jē'lĭng) ...... India	27·05 N	88·16 E
108	Darling (L.) (där'lĭng) .... ND	48·35 N	101·25 W
203	Darling (R.) .... Austl.	31·50 S	143·20 E
203	Darling Downs (Reg.) ...... Austl.	27·22 S	150·50 E
204	Darling Ra .... Austl.	30·30 S	115·45 E
154	Darlington (där'lĭng-tŭn) .... Eng.	54·32 N	1·35 W
121	Darlington .... SC	34·15 N	79·52 W
109	Darlington .... Wi.	42·41 N	90·06 W
158	Darłowo (där-lô'vô) .... Pol.	54·26 N	16·23 E
158	Darmstadt (därm'shtät) ... F.R.G.	49·53 N	8·40 E
211	Darnah .... Libya	32·44 N	22·41 E
101	Darnley B. (därn'lē) .... Ak.	70·00 N	124·00 W
162	Daroca (dä-rō-kä) .... Sp.	41·08 N	1·24 W
154	Dartmoor (därt'mōōr) .... Eng.	50·35 N	4·05 W
98	Dartmouth (därt'mŭth) ...... Can.	44·40 N	63·34 W
154	Dartmouth .... Eng.	50·33 N	3·28 W
197	Daru (I.) (dä'rōō) ... Pap. N. Gui.	9·17 S	143·13 E
164	Daruvar (där'rōō-vär) ...... Yugo.	45·37 N	17·16 E
196	Darvel B. (där'vĕl) .... Mala.	4·50 N	118·40 E
148	Darwen (där'wĕn) .... Eng.	53·42 N	2·28 W
204	Darwin (där'wĭn) .... Austl.	12·25 S	131·00 E
136	Darwin, Cordillera (Mts.) (kôr-dēl-yĕ'rä-där'wēn) Chile-Arg.	54·40 S	69·30 W
186	Daryācheh-ye Rezā'īyeh (L.) . Iran	38·07 N	45·17 E
162	Das Alturas, Serra (Mts.) (sĕ'r-rä-däs-äl-tōō'räs) . Port.	40·43 N	7·48 W
112	Dash Point (dăsh) Wa. (Seattle In.)	47·19 N	122·25 W
186	Dasht (R.) (dŭsht) .... Pak.	25·30 N	62·30 E
186	Dasht-e Kavīr Des. (dŭsht-ē-ka-vēr') . Iran	34·43 N	53·30 E
186	Dasht-e-Lūt (Des.) (dă'sht-ē-lōōt) Iran	31·47 N	58·38 E
197	Dasol B. (dä-sōl') ...... Phil. (In.)	15·53 N	119·40 E
184	Dattapukur .... India (In.)	22·45 N	88·32 E
161	Datteln (dät'tĕln) F.R.G. (Ruhr In.)	51·39 N	7·20 E
196	Datu, Tandjung (C.) ...... Indon.	2·08 N	110·15 E
157	Daugava (R.) .... Sov. Un.	56·40 N	24·40 E
166	Daugavpils (dä'ōō-gäv-pēls) Sov .Un.	55·52 N	25·32 E
95	Dauphin (dô'fĭn) .... Can.	51·09 N	100·00 W
95	Dauphin L. .... Can.	51·17 N	99·48 W
185	Dāvangere .... India	14·30 N	75·55 E
197	Davao (dä'vä-ô) .... Phil.	7·05 N	125·30 E
197	Davao G. .... Phil.	6·30 N	125·45 E
109	Davenport (dăv'ĕn-pōrt) ...... Ia.	41·34 N	90·38 W
205	Davenport .... N. Z. (In.)	37·29 S	174·47 E
110	Davenport .... Wa.	47·39 N	118·07 W
127	David (dȧ-vēdh') .... Pan.	8·27 N	82·27 W
108	David City (dā'vĭd) .... Ne.	41·15 N	97·10 W
159	David-Gorodok (dȧ-vēt' gô-rō'dôk) Sov. Un.	52·02 N	27·14 E
110	Davidson Lake (Res.) .... Wa.	46·20 N	122·10 W
117	Davis (dā'vĭs) .... Ok.	34·34 N	97·08 W
105	Davis .... WV	39·15 N	79·25 W
110	Davis L. .... Or.	43·38 N	121·43 W
114	Davis Mts. .... Tx.	30·45 N	104·17 W
220	Davis Sea .... Ant.	66·00 S	92·00 E
75	Davis Str. .... Can.	66·00 N	60·00 W
158	Davos (dä'vōs) .... Switz.	46·47 N	9·50 E
211	Dawa (R.) .... Eth.	4·34 N	41·34 E
186	Dawāsir, Wādī ad (R.) . Sau. Ar.	20·48 N	44·07 E
148	Dawley (dô'lĭ) .... Eng.	52·38 N	2·28 W
196	Dawna Ra. (dô'nȧ) .... Bur.	17·02 N	98·01 E
100	Dawson (dô'sŭn) .... Can.	64·04 N	139·22 W
120	Dawson .... Ga.	31·45 N	84·29 W
108	Dawson .... Mn.	44·54 N	96·03 W
203	Dawson (R.) .... Austl.	24·20 S	149·45 E
95	Dawson B. .... Can.	52·55 N	100·50 W
93	Dawson Creek .... Can.	55·46 N	120·14 W
101	Dawson Ra .... Can.	62·15 N	138·10 W
120	Dawson Springs .... Ky.	37·10 N	87·40 W
160	Dax (dȧks) .... Fr.	43·42 N	1·06 W
186	Dayr az Zawr (dȧ-ēr'ez-zôr') .. Syr.	35·15 N	40·01 E
218	Dayrūṭ .... Egypt (Nile In.)	27·33 N	30·48 E
107	Dayton (dā'tŭn) Ky. (Cincinnati In.)	39·07 N	84·28 W
116	Dayton .... NM	32·44 N	104·23 W
104	Dayton .... Oh.	39·45 N	84·15 W
120	Dayton .... Tn.	35·30 N	85·00 W
119	Dayton .... Tx.	30·03 N	94·53 W
110	Dayton .... Wa.	46·18 N	117·59 W
121	Daytona Beach (dā-tō'nȧ) .... Fl.	29·11 N	81·02 W
105	Dayville (dā'vĭl) .... Ct.	41·50 N	71·55 W
212	De Aar (dē-är') .... S. Afr.	30·45 S	24·05 E
108	Dead (L.) (dĕd) .... Mn.	46·28 N	96·00 W
183	Dead Sea Isr.-Jordan (Palestine In.)	31·30 N	35·30 E
108	Deadwood (dĕd'wŏŏd) .... SD	44·23 N	103·43 W
105	Deal Island (dēl-ī'lănd) ...... Md.	38·10 N	75·55 W
92	Dean (R.) (dēn) .... Can.	52·45 N	126·00 W
92	Dean Chan. .... Can.	52·33 N	127·13 W
136	Deán Funes (dĕ-ȧ'n-fōō-nĕs) . Arg.	30·26 S	64·12 W
107	Dearborn (dēr'bŭrn) Mi. (Detroit In.)	42·18 N	83·15 W
154	Dearg, Ben (Mtn.) (bĕn dŭrg) Scot.	57·48 N	4·59 W
100	Dease Str. (dēz) .... Can.	68·50 N	108·20 W
197	De Atauro (I.) (dĕ-ä-tä'ōō-rô) Indon.	8·20 S	126·15 E
114	Death Valley .... Ca.-Nv.	36·55 N	117·12 W
114	Death Valley Junction .... Ca.	36·18 N	116·26 W
114	Death Valley Natl. Mon. .... Ca.	36·34 N	117·00 W
167	Debal'tsevo (dyĕb'ăl-tsyĕ'vô) Sov. Un.	48·23 N	38·29 E
165	Debar (Dibra) (dĕ'bär) (dā'brä) Yugo.	41·31 N	20·32 E
152	Debdou (dĕb-dōō') .... Mor.	34·01 N	2·50 W
159	Deblin (dăɴ'blĭn) .... Pol.	51·34 N	21·49 E
159	Debno (dĕb-nō') .... Sov. Un.	50·24 N	25·44 E
214	Debo, Lac (L.) .... Mali.	15·15 N	4·40 W
159	Debrecen (dĕ'brĕ-tsĕn) ..... Hung.	47·32 N	21·40 E
211	Debre Markos .... Eth.	10·15 N	37·45 E
211	Debre Tabor .... Eth.	11·57 N	38·09 E
120	Decatur (dē-kā'tŭr) .... Al.	34·35 N	87·00 W
106	Decatur .... Ga. (Atlanta In.)	33·47 N	84·18 W
117	Decatur .... Il.	39·50 N	88·59 W
104	Decatur .... In.	40·50 N	84·55 W
104	Decatur .... Mi.	42·10 N	86·00 W
116	Decatur .... Tx.	33·14 N	97·33 W
160	Decazeville (dē-käz'vēl') ...... Fr.	44·33 N	2·16 E
184	Deccan (Plat.) (dĕk'ăn) ..... India	19·05 N	76·40 E
94	Deception L. .... Can.	56·33 N	104·15 W
112	Deception P. (dē-sĕp'shŭn) Wa. (Seattle In.)	48·24 N	122·44 W
158	Decin (dyĕ'chēn) .... Czech.	50·47 N	14·14 E
109	Decorah (dē-kō'rȧ) .... Ia.	43·18 N	91·48 W
	Dedeagats, see Alexandroúpolis		
174	Dedenevo (dyĕ-dyĕ'nyĕ-vô) Sov. Un. (Moscow In.)	56·14 N	37·31 E
99	Dedham (dĕd'ăm) ...... Ma. (In.)	42·15 N	71·11 W
136	Dedo do Deus (Mt.) (dĕ-dô-dō-dĕ'ōōs) Braz. (Rio de Janeiro In.)	22·30 S	43·02 W
214	Dédougou (dā-dōō-gōō') Upper Volta	12·38 N	3·28 W
154	Dee (R.) .... Scot.	57·05 N	2·25 W
154	Dee (R.) .... Wales	53·00 N	3·10 W
97	Deep River .... Can.	46·06 N	77·20 W
121	Deep (R.) (dēp) .... NC	35·36 N	79·32 W
117	Deep Fk. (R.) .... Ok.	35·35 N	96·42 W
117	Deepwater (dep-wô-tēr) ...... Mo.	38·15 N	93·46 W
98	Deer .... Me.	44·07 N	68·38 W
107	Deerfield (dēr'fēld) Il. (Chicago In.)	42·10 N	87·51 W
112	Deer Island .... Or. (Portland In.)	45·56 N	122·51 W
99	Deer Lake .... Can.	49·10 N	57·25 W
95	Deer L. .... Can.	52·40 N	94·30 W
111	Deer Lodge (dēr lŏj) .... Mt.	46·23 N	112·42 W
107	Deer Park .... Oh. (Cincinnati In.)	39·12 N	84·24 W
110	Deer Park .... Wa.	47·58 N	117·28 W
109	Deer River .... Mn.	47·20 N	93·49 W
104	Defiance (dē-fī'ăns) .... Oh.	41·15 N	84·20 W
120	DeFuniak Springs (dē fū'nĭ-ăk) Fl.	30·42 N	86·06 W
184	Deganga .... India (In.)	22·41 N	88·41 E
218	Degeh-Bur . Eth (Horn of Afr. In.)	8·10 N	43·25 E
158	Deggendorf (dĕ'ghĕn-dôrf) . F.R.G.	48·50 N	12·59 E
124	Degollado (dā-gō-lyä'dō) .... Mex.	20·27 N	102·11 W
204	DeGrey (R.) (dē grā') ...... Austl.	20·20 S	119·25 E
174	Degtyarsk (dĕg-ty'arsk) Sov. Un. (Urals In.)	56·42 N	60·05 E
185	Dehiwala-Mount Lavinia Sri Lanka	6·47 N	79·55 E
184	Dehra Dūn (dā'rōō) .... India	30·09 N	78·07 E
159	Dej (dāzh) .... Rom.	47·09 N	23·53 E
109	De Kalb (dē kălb') .... Il.	41·54 N	88·46 W
216	Dekese .... Zaire	3·27 S	21·24 E
89	Delacour (dĕ-lä-kōōr') Can. (Calgary In.)	51·09 N	113 45 W
116	Delagua (dĕl-ä'gwä) .... Co.	37·19 N	104·42 W
121	De Land (dē lănd') .... Fl.	29·00 N	81·19 W
114	Delano (dĕl'ȧ-nō) .... Ca.	35·47 N	119·15 W
115	Delano Pk. .... Ut.	38·25 N	112·25 W
109	Delavan (dĕl'ȧ-văn) .... Wi.	42·39 N	88·38 W
104	Delaware (dĕl'ȧ-wâr) .... Oh.	40·15 N	83·05 W
103	Delaware (State) .... U. S.	38·40 N	75·30 W
117	Delaware (R.) .... Ks.	39·45 N	95·47 W
105	Delaware (R.) .... U. S.	41·50 N	75·20 W
105	Delaware B. .... De.-NJ	39·05 N	75·10 W
104	Delaware Res. .... Oh.	40·30 N	83·05 E
162	Del Eje, Sierra (Mts.) (sē-ĕ'r-rä-dĕl-ĕ'kĕ) . Sp.	42·15 N	6·45 W
158	Delemont (dĕ-lā-môɴ') ...... Switz.	47·21 N	7·18 E
118	De Leon (dē lē-ŏn') .... Tx.	32·06 N	98·33 W
137	Delfínopolis (dĕl-fē'nô'pō-lēs) Braz. (Rio de Janeiro In.)	20·20 S	46·50 W
149	Delft (dĕlft) Neth. (Amsterdam In.)	52·01 N	4·20 E
155	Delfzijl .... Neth.	53·20 N	6·50 E
136	Delgada Pta. (Pt.) (pōō'n-tä-dĕl-gä'dä) . Arg.	43·46 S	63·46 W
217	Delgado, Cabo (C.) (kä'bô-dĕl-gä'dō) . Moz.	10·40 S	40·35 E
113	Delhi (dĕl'hī) .. Il. (St. Louis In.)	39·03 N	90·16 W
184	Delhi .... India	28·54 N	77·13 E
119	Delhi .... La.	32·26 N	91·29 W
184	Delhi (State) .... India	28·30 N	76·50 E
163	Del Hoyo, Sierra (Mtn.) (sē-ĕ'r-rä-dĕl-ô'yô) Sp. (Madrid In.)	40·39 N	3·56 W
158	Delitzsch (dā'lĭch) .... G.D.R.	51·32 N	12·18 E

ăt; finăl; rāte; senâte; ärm; ȧsk; sofȧ; fâre; ch-choose; dh-as th in other; bē; ēvent; bĕt; recĕnt; cratēr; g-go; gh-guttural g; bĭt; ĭ-short neutral; rīde; ĸ-guttural k as ch in German ich;

PRONOUNCING INDEX

Dell Alice — Djelfa 275

Page Name Pronunciation Region Lat. °' Long. °'

165 Dell Alice, Pt. (dĕl-ä-lē'chĕ)....It. 39·23 N 17·10 E
108 Dell Rapids (dĕl).............SD 43·50 N 96·43 W
113 Dellwood (dĕl'wo͝od) Mn. (Minneapolis, St. Paul In.) 45·05 N 92·58 W
210 Dellys (dĕ'lēs')..............Alg. 36·59 N 3·40 E
114 Del Mar (dĕl mär')......Ca. (In.) 32·57 N 117·16 W
218 Delmas (dĕl'mȧs) S. Afr. (Johannesburg & Pretoria In.) 26·08 S 28·43 E
158 Delmenhorst (dĕl'mĕn-hôrst) F.R.G. 53·03 N 8·38 E
115 Del Norte (dĕl nôrt').........Co. 37·40 N 106·25 W
173 De-Longa (I.)...........Sov. Un. 76·30 N 153·00 E
101 De Long Mts. (dē'lŏng).......Ak. 68·38 N 162·30 W
203 Deloraine (dĕ-lŭ-rān).......Austl. 41·30 S 146·40 E
104 Delphi (dĕl'fī)................In. 40·35 N 86·40 W
104 Delphos (dĕl'fŏs)..............Oh. 40·50 N 84·20 W
121 Delray Beach (dĕl-rā')....Fl. (In.) 26·27 N 80·05 W
118 Del Rio (dĕl rē'ō)............Tx. 29·21 N 100·52 W
89 Delson (dĕl'snŭ) Can. (Montreal In.) 45·24 N 73·32 W
115 Delta.......................Co. 38·45 N 108·05 W
115 Delta.......................Ut. 39·20 N 112·35 W
89 Delta Beach..Can. (Winnipeg In.) 50·10 N 98·20 W
114 Delta Mendota Can..........Ca. 37·10 N 121·02 W
165 Delvine (dĕl'vē-nȧ).........Alb. 39·58 N 20·10 E
170 Dëma (R.) (dyĕm'ä)....Sov. Un. 53·40 N 54·30 E
216 Demba...................Zaire 5·30 S 22·16 E
211 Dembidolo................Eth. 8·46 N 34·46 E
166 Demidov (dzyĕ'mē-dô'f)..Sov. Un. 55·16 N 31·32 E
115 Deming (dĕm'ĭng)...........NM 32·15 N 107·45 W
158 Demmin (dĕm'mēn)......G.D.R. 53·54 N 13·04 E
210 Demnat (dĕm-nät)..........Mor. 31·58 N 7·03 W
120 Demopolis (dē-mŏp'ō-lĭs)......Al. 32·30 N 87·50 W
107 Demotte (dē'mŏt) In. (Chicago In.) 41·12 N 87·13 W
196 Dempo, Gunung (Vol.) (dĕm'pô) Indon. 4·04 S 103·11 E
172 Dem'yanka (R.) (dyĕm-yän'kä) Sov. Un. 59·07 N 72·58 E
166 Demyansk (dyĕm-yänsk') Sov. Un. 57·39 N 32·26 E
160 Denain (dē-năn')..............Fr. 50·23 N 3·21 E
154 Denbigh (dĕn'bĭ)..........Wales 53·15 N 3·25 W
148 Denbigh (Co.)..............Wales 53·01 N 2·59 W
149 Dendermonde..Bel. (Brussels In.) 51·02 N 4·04 E
121 Dendron (dĕn'drŭn)...........Va. 37·02 N 76·53 W
174 Denezhkin Kamen, Gora (Mtn.) (dzyĕ-ŋĕ'zhkĕn kȧmĭēŋ) Sov. Un. (Urals In.) 60·26 N 59·35 E
127 D'Enfer, Pointe (Pt.)...Mart.(In.) 14·21 N 60·48 W
128 Denham, Mt.................Jam. 18·20 N 77·30 W
155 Den Helder (dĕn hĕl'dĕr)....Neth. 52·55 N 5·45 E
163 Denia (dā'nyä)...............Sp. 38·48 N 0·06 E
203 Deniliquin (dĕ-nĭl'ĭ-kwĭn)...Austl. 35·20 S 144·52 E
108 Denison (dĕn'ĭ-sŭn)...........Ia. 42·01 N 95·22 W
117 Denison......................Tx. 33·45 N 97·02 W
174 Denisovka (dĕ-nē'sof-kȧ) Sov. Un. (Urals In.) 52·26 N 61·45 E
171 Denizli (dĕn-ĭz-lē')..........Tur. 37·40 N 29·10 E
161 Denklingen (dĕn'klēn-gĕn) F.R.G. (Ruhr In.) 50·54 N 7·40 E
121 Denmark (dĕn'märk).........SC 33·18 N 81·09 W
146 Denmark...................Eur. 56·14 N 8·30 E
75 Denmark Str.............Grnld. 66·30 N 27·00 W
218 Dennilton (dĕn-ĭl-tŭn) S. Afr. (Johannesburg & Pretoria (In.) 25·18 S 29·13 E
104 Dennison (dĕn'ĭ-sŭn)........Oh. 40·25 N 81·20 W
91 De Nouvelle-France (C.)......Can. 62·03 N 74·00 W
196 Denpasar..................Indon. 8·35 S 115·10 E
148 Denton (dĕn'tŭn)...........Eng. 53·27 N 2·07 W
105 Denton......................Md. 38·55 N 75·50 W
117 Denton......................Tx. 33·12 N 97·06 W
204 D'entrecasteaux, Pt. (dăɴ-tr'kȧs-tō').Austl. 34·50 S 114·45 E
197 D'entrecasteaux Is. (dăɴ-tr'-kȧs-tō').Pap. N. Gui. 9·45 S 152·00 E
116 Denver (dĕn'vēr)............Co. 39·44 N 104·59 W
184 Deoli......................India 25·52 N 75·23 E
109 De Pere (dē pēr')...........Wi. 44·25 N 88·04 W
107 Depew (dē-pū')..NY (Buffalo In.) 42·55 N 78·43 W
104 Depue (dē pū)...............Il. 41·15 N 89·55 W
117 De Queen (dē kwēn')..........Ar. 34·02 N 94·21 W
119 De Quincy (dē kwĭn'sĭ)........La. 30·27 N 93·27 W
184 Dera Ghāzi Khān (dā'rū gä-zē' kän')......Pak. 30·09 N 70·39 E
184 Dera Ismāīl Khān (dā'rū ĭs-mä-ēl' kän') Pak. 31·55 N 70·51 E
171 Derbent (dĕr-bĕnt')......Sov. Un. 42·00 N 48·10 E
204 Derby (där'bē) (dûr'bē)....Austl. 17·20 S 123·40 E
105 Derby (dûr'bē)...............Ct. 41·20 N 73·05 W
148 Derby (där'bē).............Eng. 52·55 N 1·29 W
218 Derby (där'bĭ) S. Afr. (Johannesburg & Pretoria In.) 25·55 S 27·02 E
148 Derby (Co.) där'bē)........Eng. 53·11 N 1·30 W
218 Derdepoort S. Afr. (Johannesburg & Pretoria In.) 24·39 S 26·21 E
217 Dere, Lak (R.).............Ken. 0.45 N 40·15 E
154 Derg, Lough (B.) (lŏk dĕrg)...Ire. 53·00 N 8·09 W
119 De Ridder (dē rĭd'ēr).........La. 30·50 N 93·18 W
117 Dermott (dûr'mŏt)............Ar. 33·32 N 91·24 W
99 Derry (dâr'ĭ)..........NH (In.) 45·52 N 71·22 W
165 Derventa (dĕr'ven-tȧ)......Yugo. 45·58 N 17·58 E
203 Derwent (R.) (dĕr'wĕnt)....Austl. 42·21 S 146·30 E
148 Derwent (R.)..............Eng. 52·54 N 1·24 W
117 Des Arc (dāz ärk')...........Ar. 34·59 N 91·31 W
137 Descalvado (dĕs-käl-vá-dō) Braz. (Rio de Janeiro In.) 21·55 S 47·37 W
94 Deschambault L.............Can. 54·40 N 103·35 W
89 Deschênes.....Can. (Ottawa In.) 45·23 N 75·47 W
89 Deschenes, L....Can. (Ottawa In.) 54·25 N 75·53 W
110 Deschutes R. (dā-sho͞ot')......Or. 44·25 N 121·21 W
118 Desdemona (dĕz-dē-mō'nȧ)....Tx. 32·16 N 98·33 W
211 Dese........................Eth. 11·00 N 39·51 E
136 Deseado, Rio (R.) (rē-ō-dā-sā-ä'dhō).Arg. 46·50 S 67·45 W
127 Desirade I. (dā-zē-rȧs') Guad. (In.) 16·21 N 60·51 W
108 De Smet (dē smĕt')...........SD 44·23 N 97·33 W
109 Des Moines (dē moin')........Ia. 41·35 N 93·37 W
116 Des Moines.................NM 36·42 N 103·48 W
112 Des Moines.....Wa. (Seattle In.) 46·24 N 122·20 W
103 Des Moines (R.)............U. S. 43·45 N 94·20 W
167 Desna (R.) (dyĕs-nȧ')...Sov. Un. 51·05 N 31·03 E
136 Desolación (dĕ-sō-lä-syō'n) (I.) Chile 53·05 S 74·00 W
117 De Soto (dē sō'tō)...........Mo. 38·07 N 90·32 W
113 Des Peres (dĕs pĕr'ĕs) Mo. (St. Louis In.) 38·36 N 90·26 W
107 Des Plaines (dĕs plānz') Il. (Chicago In.) 42·02 N 87·54 W
107 Des Plaines R....Il. (Chicago In.) 41·39 N 88·05 W
158 Dessau (dĕs'ou)..........G.D.R. 51·50 N 12·15 E
158 Detmold (dĕt'mōld)......G.D.R. 51·57 N 8·55 E
107 Detroit (dē-troit') Mi. (Detroit In.) 42·22 N 83·10 W
117 Detroit.....................Tx. 33·41 N 95·16 W
108 Detroit Lakes (dē-troit' lăkz).Mn. 46·48 N 95·51 W
107 Detroit R. Can.-U. S. (Detroit In.) 42·08 N 83·07 W
159 Detva (dyĕt'vȧ)............Czech. 48·32 N 19·21 E
149 Deurne.......Bel. (Brussels In.) 51·13 N 4·27 E
149 Deutsch Wagram Aus. (Vienna In.) 48·19 N 16·34 E
89 Deux-Montagnes (dû mōɴ-tăny') Can. (Montreal In.) 45·33 N 73·54 W
89 Deux Montagnes, Lac des (L.) Can. (Montreal In.) 45·28 N 74·00 W
165 Deva (dā'vä)..............Rom. 45·52 N 22·52 E
159 Dévaványa (dā'vô-vän-yô).Hung. 47·01 N 20·58 E
171 Develi (dĕ'vȧ-lē)...........Tur. 38·20 N 35·10 E
155 Deventer (dĕv'ĕn-tēr)......Neth. 52·14 N 6·07 E
108 Devils (L.) (dĕv''lz).........ND 47·57 N 99·04 W
118 Devils (R.)..................Tx. 29·55 N 101·10 W
Devils I., see Diable, Ile du
102 Devils Lake................ND 48·10 N 98·55 W
108 Devils Lake Ind. Res.........ND 48·08 N 99·40 W
114 Devils Postpile Natl. Mon......Ca. 37·42 N 119·12 W
111 Devils Tower Natl. Mon.....Wy. 44·38 N 105·07 W
165 Devoll (R.).................Alb. 40·55 N 20·10 E
89 Devon......Can. (Edmonton In.) 53·23 N 113·43 W
218 Devon (dĕv'ŭn) S. Afr. (Johannesburg & Pretoria In.) 26·23 S 28·47 E
203 Devonport (dĕv'ŭn-pôrt....Austl. 41·20 S 146·30 E
113 Devore (dē-vôr') Ca. (Los Angeles In.) 34·13 N 117·24 W
112 Dewatto (dē-wȧt'ô) Wa. (Seattle In.) 47·27 N 123·04 W
117 Dewey (dū'ĭ)................Ok. 36·48 N 95·55 W
117 De Witt (dē wĭt')............Ar. 34·17 N 91·22 W
109 De Witt......................Ia. 41·46 N 90·34 W
148 Dewsbury (dūz'bĕr-ĭ)........Eng. 53·42 N 1·39 W
98 Dexter (dĕks'tēr)............Me. 45·01 N 69·19 W
117 Dexter......................Mo. 36·46 N 89·56 W
121 Dexter (L.)...................Fl. 29·07 N 81·24 W
186 Dezfūl.......................Iran 32·14 N 48·37 E
183 Dezhneva, Mys (East Cape) (dyĕzh'nyĭf).Sov. Un. 68·00 N 172·00 W
Dhahran, see Aẓ Ẓahrān
185 Dharamtar Cr.........India (In.) 18·49 N 72·54 E
185 Dharmavaram...............India 14·32 N 77·43 E
184 Dhaulāgīri (Mtn.) (dou-lȧ-gē'rē) Nep. 28·42 N 83·31 E
165 Dhenoúsa (I.)...............Grc. 37·09 N 25·53 E
183 Dhibān.....Jordan (Palestine In.) 31·30 N 35·46 E
165 Dhidhimótikhon...............Grc. 41·20 N 26·27 E
165 Dhodhekánisos (Dodecanese) (Is.) Grc. 38·00 N 26·10 E
184 Dhule......................India 20·58 N 74·43 E
184 Dhupgarth (Mt.)............India 27·30 N 78·27 E
164 Dia (I.) (dē'ä).........Grc. (In.) 35·27 N 25·17 E
135 Diable, Ile du (Devils I.)..Fr. Gu. 5·15 N 57·10 W
112 Diablo, Mt. (dyä'blō) Ca. (San Francisco In.) 37·52 N 121·55 W
122 Diablo Heights (dyȧ'blō) C. Z. (In.) 8·58 N 79·34 W
112 Diablo Range (Mts.) Ca. (San Francisco In.) 37·47 N 121·50 W
217 Diaca.......................Moz. 11·30 S 39·59 E
214 Diaka (R.)..................Mali 14·40 N 4·50 W
135 Diamantina..................Braz. 18·14 S 43·32 W
204 Diamantina (R.) (dī'man-tē'nȧ) Austl. 25·38 S 139·53 E
135 Diamantino (dē-ȧ-män-tē'no) Braz. 14·22 S 56·23 W
110 Diamond Pk..................Or. 43·32 N 122·08 W
129 Diana Bk. (dī'ăn'ȧ)..........Ba. 22·30 N 74·45 W
197 Diapitan B. (dyä-pē-tä'n) Phil. (In.) 16·28 N 122·25 E
Dibra, see Debar
108 Dickinson (dĭk'ĭn-sŭn).......ND 46·52 N 102·49 W
119 Dickinson (dĭk'ĭn-sŭn)...Tx. (In.) 29·28 N 95·02 W
119 Dickinson Bayou.......Tx. (In.) 29·26 N 95·08 W
120 Dickson (dĭk'sŭn)............Tn. 36·03 N 87·24 W
105 Dickson City.................Pa. 41·25 N 75·40 W
171 Dicle (R.) (dĭj'lȧ)..........Tur. 37·50 N 40·40 E
148 Didcot (dĭd'cŏt) Eng. (London In.) 51·35 N 1·15 W
214 Didiéni......................Mali 13·53 N 8·06 W
161 Die (dē).....................Fr. 44·45 N 5·22 E
90 Diefenbaker (Res.)..........Can. 51·20 N 108·10 W
94 Diefenbaker L..............Can. 51·00 N 106·55 W
129 Diego de Ocampo, Pico (Pk.) (pē'-kō-dyĕ'gō-dĕ-ō-kä'm-pō) Dom. Rep. 19·40 N 70·45 W
136 Diego Ramirez, Islas (Is.) (dē ä'gō rä-mē'rāz).Chile 56·15 S 70·15 W
213 Diego-Suarez (dē-ā'gō-swȧ'rāz) Mad. 12·18 S 49·16 E
214 Diéma......................Mali 14·32 N 9·12 W
188 Dien Bien Phan............Viet. 21·38 N 102·49 E
98 Dieppe (dē-ĕp')..............Can. 46·06 N 64·45 W
160 Dieppe.......................Fr. 49·54 N 1·05 E
117 Dierks (dērks)...............Ar. 34·06 N 94·02 W
149 Diessen (dēs'sĕn) F.R.G. (Munich In.) 47·57 N 11·06 E
149 Diest.........Bel. (Brussels In.) 50·59 N 5·05 E
98 Digby (dĭg'bĭ)...............Can. 44·37 N 65·46 W
106 Dighton (dī-tŭn) Ma. (Providence In.) 41·49 N 71·05 W
161 Digne (dēn'y')...............Fr. 44·07 N 6·16 E
160 Digoin (dē-gwăn')...........Fr. 46·28 N 4·06 E
197 Digul (R.)..................Indon. 7·00 S 140·27 E
197 Dijohan Pt. (dē-kō-än) Phil. (In.) 16·24 N 122·25 E
160 Dijon (dē-zhŏn')..............Fr. 47·21 N 5·02 E
172 Dikson (dĭk'sŏn)........Sov. Un. 73·30 N 80·35 E
211 Dikwa (dē'kwȧ)...............Nig. 12·06 N 13·53 E
197 Dili (dĭl'ē)................Indon. 8·35 S 125·35 E
152 Di Linosa I. (dē-lē-nō'sä)......It. 36·01 N 12·43 E
171 Dilizhan................Sov. Un. 40·45 N 45·00 E
101 Dillingham (dĭl'ĕng-hăm).....Ak. 59·10 N 158·38 W
111 Dillon (dĭl'ŭn)...............Mt. 45·12 N 112·40 W
121 Dillon........................SC 34·24 N 79·28 W
104 Dillon Res....................Oh. 40·05 N 82·05 W
212 Dilolo (dē-lō'lō).............Zaire 10·19 S 22·23 E
212 Dima.........................Ang. 15·45 S 20·15 E
186 Dimashq (Damascus) (dȧ-măs'kŭs).Syria 33·31 N 36·18 E
214 Dimbokro...........Ivory Coast 6·39 N 4·42 W
165 Dimbovita (R.)..............Rom. 44·43 N 25·41 E
Dimitrovo, see Pernik
215 Dimlang (Mtn.)...............Nig. 8·24 N 11·47 E
183 Dimona.......Isr. (Palestine In.) 31·03 N 35·01 E
197 Dinagat I. (dē-nä'gät).......Phil. 10·15 N 126·15 E
184 Dinājpur....................Bngl. 25·38 N 87·39 E
160 Dinan (dē-näɴ')..............Fr. 48·27 N 2·03 W
155 Dinant (dē-näɴ')............Bel. 50·17 N 4·50 E
164 Dinara Planina (Mts.) (dē'nä-rä plä'nê-nä).Yugo. 43·50 N 16·15 E
185 Dindigul....................India 10·25 N 78·03 E
197 Dingalan B. (dĭŋ-gä'län) Phil. (In.) 15·19 N 121·33 E
154 Dingle (dĭng''l)..............Ire. 52·10 N 10·13 W
154 Dingle B.....................Ire. 52·02 N 10·15 W
205 Dingo (dĭŋ'gō)............Austl. 23·45 S 149·26 E
214 Dinguiraye....................Gui. 11·18 N 10·43 W
154 Dingwall (dĭng'wôl).........Scot. 57·37 N 4·23 W
111 Dinosaur Natl. Mon. (dī'nō-sŏr) Co.-Ut. 40·45 N 109·17 W
161 Dinslaken (dēns'lä-kĕn) F.R.G. (Ruhr In.) 51·33 N 6·44 E
149 Dinteloord Neth. (Amsterdam In.) 51·38 N 4·21 E
114 Dinuba (dĭ-nū'bȧ)............Ca. 36·33 N 119·29 W
128 Dios, Cayo de (I.) (kä'yō-dĕ-dē-ōs').Cuba 22·05 N 83·05 W
214 Diourbel (dē-o͞or-bĕl')......Senegal 14·40 N 16·15 W
187 Diphu Pass (dĭ-po͞o).......China 28·15 N 96·45 E
127 Diquis (R.) (dē-kēs')........C. R. 8·59 N 83·24 W
218 Dire Dawal.Eth. (Horn of Afr. In.) 9·40 N 41·47 E
126 Diriamba (dēr-yäm'bä).......Nic. 11·52 N 86·15 W
204 Dirk Hartog (I.)............Austl. 26·25 S 113·15 E
149 Dirksland Neth. (Amsterdam In.) 51·45 N 4·04 E
203 Dirranbandi (dĭ-rä-băn'dē) Austl. 28·24 S 148·29 E
115 Dirty Devil (R.) (dûr'tĭ dĕv''l).Ut. 38·20 N 110·30 W
204 Disappointment (L.).......Austl. 23·20 S 120·20 E
112 Disappointment, C. (dĭs'ȧ-point' ment).Wa. (Portland In.) 46·16 N 124·11 W
163 D'Ischia, I. (dē'sh-kyä) It. (Naples In.) 40·26 N 13·55 E
213 Discovery (dĭs-kŭv'ēr-ĭ)l...S. Afr. (Johannesburg & Pretoria In.) 26·10 S 27·53 E
112 Discovery Is. (dĭs-kŭv'ēr-ē) Can. (Seattle In.) 48·25 N 123·13 W
218 Dishnā (dēsh'nȧ).Egypt (Nile In.) 26·08 N 32·27 E
75 Disko (dĭs'kō) (I.)..........Grnld. 70·00 N 54·00 W
121 Dismal Swp. (dĭz'mȧl).....NC-Va. 36·35 N 76·34 W
166 Disna (dēs'nȧ)..........Sov. Un. 55·34 N 28·15 E
184 Dispur.......................India 26·00 N 91·50 E
98 Disraëli (dĭs-rā'lĭ)...........Can. 45·53 N 71·23 W
103 District of Columbia.........U. S. 38·50 N 77·00 W
135 Distrito Federal (Dist.) (dēs-trē'tô-fĕ-dĕ-rä'l).Braz. 15·49 S 47·39 W
125 Distrito Federal (Dist.).....Mex. 19·14 N 99·08 W
218 Disūq (dē-so͞ok').Egypt (Nile In.) 31·07 N 30·41 E
184 Diu (dē'o͞o)................India 20·48 N 70·58 E
160 Dives (dēv)..................Fr. 49·18 N 0·05 W
197 Divilacan B. (dē-vē-lä'kän)..Phil. 17·26 N 122·25 E
137 Divinópolis (dē-vē-nô'pō-lēs) Braz. (Rio de Janeiro In.) 20·10 S 44·53 W
214 Divo...................Ivory Coast 5·50 N 5·22 W
109 Dixon (dĭks'ŭn)...............Il. 41·50 N 89·30 W
92 Dixon Ent..............Ak.-Can. 54·25 N 132·00 W
171 Diyarbakir (dē-yär-bĕk'ĭr)....Tur. 38·00 N 40·10 E
215 Dja (R.)....................Cam. 3·25 N 13·17 E
165 Djakovica...................Yugo 42·33 N 20·28 E
216 Djambala...................Con. 2·33 S 14·45 E
210 Djanet.......................Alg. 24·29 N 9·26 E
214 Djebobo (Mtn.)..............Ghana 8·20 N 0·37 E
152 Djedi (R.)...................Alg. 34·18 N 4·39 E
210 Djelfa (jĕl'fä)...............Alg. 34·40 N 3·17 E

ng-sing; ŋ-baŋk; ɴ-nasalized n; nŏd; cŏmmit; ōld; ôbey; ôrder; fo͞od; fo͝ot; ou-out; s-soft; sh-dish; th-thin; pūre; ůnite; ûrn; stŭd; circŭs; ü-as "y" in study; '-indeterminate vowel.

Page	Name Pronunciation Region	Lat. °'	Long. °'
215	Djember Chad.	10·25 N	17·50 E
152	Djerba, Ile de (I.) Tun.	33·53 N	11·26 E
210	Djerid, Chott (L.) (jĕr'ĭd) Tun.	33·15 N	8·29 E
214	Djibasso Upper Volta	13·07 N	4·10 W
214	Djibo Upper Volta	14·06 N	1·38 W
218	Djibouti (jē-bōō-tē') Djibouti (Horn of Afr. In.)	11·34 N	43·00 E
209	Djibouti Afr.	11·35 N	48·08 E
151	Djidjelli (jē-jĕ-lē') Alg.	36·49 N	5·47 E
216	Djokoumatombi Con.	0·47 N	15·22 E
216	Djoua (R.) Con.-Gabon	1·25 N	13·40 E
156	Djursholm (djōōrs'hōlm) Swe.	59·26 N	18·01 E
167	Dmitriyevka (d'mē-trê-yĕf'kȧ) Sov. Un.	47·57 N	38·56 E
167	Dmitriyev L'govskiy (d'mē'trĭ-yĕf l'gôf'skĭ) Sov. Un.	52·07 N	35·05 E
174	Dmitrov (d'mē'trôf) Sov. Un. (Moscow In.)	56·21 N	37·32 E
166	Dmitrovsk (d'mē'trôfsk) Sov. In.	52·30 N	35·10 E
167	Dnepr (Dnieper) (R.) (nē'pēr) Sov. Un.	46·47 N	32·57 E
167	Dneprodzerzhinsk (d'nyĕp'rô-zēr-shĭnsk) Sov. Un.	48·32 N	34·38 E
168	Dneprodzerzhinskoye Vdkhr Sov. Un.	49·00 N	34·10 E
167	Dnepropetrovsk (d'nyĕp'rô-pā-trôfsk) Sov. Un.	48·23 N	34·10 E
167	Dnepropetrovsk (Oblast) Sov. Un.	48·15 N	34·08 E
167	Dnepr Zaliv (B.) (dnyĕp'r zȧ'lĭf) Sov. Un.	46·33 N	31·45 E
167	Dnestr (Dniester) (R.) (nēst'rōōl) (nēs'tēr) Sov. Un.	48·21 N	28·10 E
167	Dnestrovskiy Liman (B.) Sov. Un.	46·13 N	29·50 E
	Dnieper (R.), see Dnepr		
	Dniester (R.), see Dnestr		
166	Dno (d'nô') Sov. Un.	57·49 N	29·59 E
214	Do, Lac (L.) Mali.	15·50 N	2·20 W
215	Doba Chad	8·39 N	16·51 E
106	Dobbs Ferry (dŏbz' fĕ'rê) NY (New York In.)	41·01 N	73·53 W
204	Dobbyn (dôb'ĭn) Austl.	19·45 S	140·02 E
157	Dobele (dô'bĕ-lĕ) Sov. Un.	56·37 N	23·18 E
158	Döbeln (dû'bĕln) G.D.R.	51·08 N	13·07 E
197	Doberai Jazirah (Pen.) Indon.	1·25 S	133·15 E
197	Dobo Indon.	6·00 S	134·18 E
165	Doboj (dō'boi) Yugo.	44·42 N	18·04 E
174	Dobryanka (dôb-ryän'kȧ) Sov. Un. (Urals In.)	58·27 N	56·26 E
159	Dobšina (dôp'shê-nä) Czech.	48·48 N	20·25 E
135	Doce (R.) (dō'sȧ) Braz.	19·01 S	42·14 W
128	Doce Leguas, Cayos de las (Is.) (kä'yōs-dĕ-läs-dô-sĕ-lĕ'gwäs) Cuba	20·55 N	79·05 W
124	Doctor Arroyo (dōk-tōr' är-rō'yō) Mex.	23·41 N	100·10 W
135	Dr. Ir. W. J. van Blommestein Meer (Res.) Sur.	4·45 N	55·05 W
148	Doddington (dŏd'dĭng-tŏn) Eng. (London In.)	51·17 N	0·47 E
	Dodecanese (Is.), see Dhodhekánisos		
116	Dodge City (dŏj) Ks.	37·44 N	100·01 W
105	Dodgeville (dŏj'vĭl) NY	43·10 N	74·45 W
109	Dodgeville Wi.	42·58 N	90·07 W
217	Dodoma (dō'dô-mȧ) Tan.	6·11 S	35·45 E
109	Dog (L.) (dŏg) Can.	48·42 N	89·24 W
155	Dogger Bk. (dŏg'gēr) Eur.	55·07 N	2·25 E
171	Dogubayazit Tur.	39·35 N	44·00 E
184	Dohad India	22·52 N	74·18 E
165	Doiran (L.) Grc.	41·10 N	23·00 E
195	Dōjō (dō-jō) Jap. (Ōsaka In.)	34·51 N	135·14 E
166	Dokshitsy (dôk-shētsē) Sov. Un.	54·53 N	27·49 E
197	Dolak (I.) Indon.	7·45 S	137·30 E
97	Dolbeau Can.	48·52 N	72·16 W
161	Dôle (dōl) Fr.	47·07 N	5·28 E
167	Dolgaya, Kosa (C.) (kô'sȧ dôl-gä'yä) Sov. Un.	46·42 N	37·42 E
170	Dolgiy (I.) Sov. Un.	69·20 N	59·20 E
174	Dolgoprudnyy Sov. Un. (Moscow In.)	55·57 N	37·33 E
159	Dolina (dô-lyē'nä) Sov. Un.	48·57 N	24·01 E
194	Dolinsk (dá-lēnsk') Sov. Un.	47·29 N	142·31 E
216	Dolisie Con.	4·12 S	12·41 E
128	Dollar Hbr Ba.	25·30 N	79·15 W
215	Dolo Som.	4·01 N	42·14 E
106	Dolomite (dŏl'ô-mīt) Al. (Birmingham In.)	33·28 N	86·57 W
164	Dolomitiche, Alpi (Mts.) (äl-pē-dô-lô'mē-tē'chĕ) It.	46·16 N	11·43 E
137	Dolores (dō-lō'rĕs) Arg. (Buenos Aires In.)	36·20 S	57·42 W
134	Dolores Col. (In.)	3·33 N	74·54 W
199	Dolores (dō-lō-rĕs) Phil. (In.)	17·40 N	120·43 E
118	Dolores (dō-lō'rĕs) Tx.	27·42 N	99·47 W
137	Dolores Ur. (Buenos Aires In.)	33·32 S	58·15 W
115	Dolores (R.) Co.-Ut.	38·35 N	108·50 W
124	Dolores Hidalgo (dō-lô'rĕs-ē-däl'gō) Mex.	21·09 N	100·56 W
90	Dolphin and Union Str. (dŏl'fĭn ūn'yŭn) Can.	69·22 N	117·10 W
158	Domažlice (dō'mäzh-lê-tsĕ) Czech.	49·27 N	12·55 E
161	Dombasle (dôɴ-bäl') Fr.	48·38 N	6·18 E
159	Dombóvár (dŏm'bō-vär) Hung.	46·22 N	18·08 E
160	Dôme, Puy de (Pk.) (pwē'dĕ-dôm') Fr.	45·47 N	2·54 E
134	Domeyko, Cordillera (Mts.) (kôr-dēl-yĕ'rä-dô-mā'kô) Chile	20·50 S	69·02 W
123	Dominica (dŏ-mĭ-nē'kȧ) N. A.	15·30 N	60·45 W
127	Dominica Chan N. A. (In.)	15·00 N	61·30 W
123	Dominican Republic (dô-mĭn'ĭ-kăn) N.A.	19·00 N	70·45 W
99	Dominion (dô-mĭn'yŭn) Can.	46·13 N	60·01 W
216	Domiongo Zaire	4·37 S	21·15 E
174	Domodedovo (dô-mô-dyĕ'do-vô) Sov. Un. (Moscow In.)	55·27 N	37·45 E
137	Dom Silvério (doɴ-sēl-vĕ'ryō) Braz. (Rio de Janeiro In.)	20·09 S	42·57 W
148	Don (R.) (dŏn) Eng.	53·27 N	1·34 W
148	Don (R.) Eng.	53·39 N	0·58 W
154	Don (R.) Scot.	57·19 N	2·39 W
113	Donaldson (dŏn'ăl-sŭn) Mi. (Sault Ste. Marie In.)	46·19 N	84·22 W
119	Donaldsonville (dŏn'ăld-sŭn-vĭl) La.	30·05 N	90·58 W
120	Donalsonville Ga.	31·02 N	84·50 W
158	Donawitz (dō'nȧ-vĭts) Aus.	47·23 N	15·05 E
184	Donazari Bngl.	22·18 N	91·52 E
162	Don Benito Mérida (dōn' bā-nē'tō-mĕ'rē-dä) Sp.	38·55 N	6·08 W
202	Doncaster (doŋ'kăs-tēr) Austl. (Melbourne In.)	37·47 S	145·08 E
148	Doncaster (doŋ'kăs-tēr) Eng.	53·32 N	1·07 W
216	Dondo (dōn'dō) Ang.	9·38 S	14·25 E
212	Dondo Moz.	19·33 S	34·47 E
185	Dondra Hd Sri Lanka	5·52 N	80·52 E
154	Donegal (dŏn-ê-gôl') Ire.	54·44 N	8·05 W
154	Donegal, Mts. of (dŏn-ê-gôl') Ire.	54·44 N	8·10 W
154	Donegal Bay (dŏn-ê-gôl') Ire.	54·35 N	8·36 W
167	Donets (R.) (dō-nyĕts') Sov. Un.	48·48 N	38·42 E
167	Donets Coal Basin (Reg.) (dō-nyĕts') Sov. Un.	48·15 N	38·50 E
167	Donetsk (Oblast) Sov. Un.	47·55 N	37·40 E
167	Donetsk (Stalino) (dō-nyĕts'k) (stä'lĭ-nō) Sov. Un.	48·00 N	37·35 E
204	Dongara (dôn-gă'rȧ) Austl.	29·15 S	115·00 E
196	Donggala (dôn-gä'lä) Indon.	0·45 S	119·32 E
193	Dong Hoi (dông-hō-ē') Viet.	17·25 N	106·42 E
212	Dongo (dôŋ'gō) Ang.	14·45 S	15·30 E
197	Dongon Pt. (dŏng-ôn') Phil. (In.)	12·43 N	120·35 E
216	Dongou (dôŋ-gōō') Con.	2·02 N	18·04 E
117	Doniphan (dŏn'ĭ-făn) Mo.	36·37 N	90·50 W
164	Donji Vakuf (dōn'yĭ väk'ōōf) Yugo.	44·08 N	17·25 E
118	Don Martin, Presa de (Res.) (prĕ'sä-dĕ-dôn-mär-tē'n) Mex.	27·35 N	100·38 W
98	Donnacona Can.	46·40 N	71·46 W
161	Donnemarie-en-Montois (dôn-mä-rē'ĕɴ-môɴ-twä') Fr. Paris In.)	48·29 N	3·09 E
110	Donner und Blitzen (R.) (dŏn'ēr ŏŏnt blĭ'tsĕn) Or.	42·45 N	118·57 W
213	Donnybrook (dŏ-nĭ-brŏŏk) S. Afr. (Natal In.)	29·56 S	29·54 E
107	Donora (dŏ-nō'rȧ) Pa. (Pittsburgh In.)	40·10 N	79·51 W
101	Doonerak (dōō'nē-răk) Ak.	68·00 N	150·34 W
149	Doorn Neth. (Amsterdam In.)	52·02 N	5·21 E
109	Door Pen. (dōr) Wi.	44·40 N	87·36 W
164	Dora Baltea (dō'rä bäl'tä-ä) It.	45·40 N	7·34 E
106	Doraville (dō'rȧ-vĭl) Ga. (Atlanta In.)	33·54 N	84·17 W
154	Dorchester (dôr'chĕs-tēr) Eng.	50·45 N	2·34 W
160	Dordogne (R.) (dôr-dôn'yĕ) Fr.	44·53 N	0·16 E
149	Dordrecht (dôr'drĕκt) Neth. (Amsterdam In.)	51·48 N	4·39 E
213	Dordrecht (dô'drĕκt) S. Afr. (Natal In.)	31·24 S	27·06 E
164	Dorgali (dôr'gä-lē) It.	40·18 N	9·37 E
94	Doré L. Can.	54·31 N	107·06 W
89	Dorion-Vaudreuil (dôr-yō) Can. (Montreal In.)	45·23 N	74·01 W
148	Dorking (dôr'kĭng) Eng. (London In.)	51·12 N	0·20 W
100	D'Orleans, Ile (I.) dōr-lē-äɴ', yl) Can. (Quebec In.)	46·56 N	71·00 W
107	Dormont (dôr'mŏnt) Pa. (Pittsburgh In.)	40·24 N	80·02 W
158	Dornbirn (dôrn'bĕrn) Aus.	47·24 N	9·45 E
154	Dornoch (dôr'nŏκ) Scot.	57·55 N	4·01 W
154	Dornoch Firth (dôr'nŏκ fûrth) Scot.	57·55 N	3·55 W
166	Dorogobuzh (dôrôgô'-bōō'zh) Sov. Un.	54·57 N	33·18 E
159	Dorohoi (dō-rô-hoi') Rom.	47·57 N	26·28 E
	Dorpat, see Tartu		
204	Dorre (I.) (dôr) Austl.	25·19 S	113·10 E
161	Dorsten (dōr'stĕn) F.R.G. (Ruhr In.)	51·40 N	6·58 E
161	Dortmund (dôrt'mŏŏnt) F.R.G. (Ruhr In.)	51·31 N	7·28 E
161	Dortmund-Ems Kanal (can.) (dōrt'mōōnd-ĕms' kä-näl') F.R.G. (Ruhr In.)	51·50 N	7·25 E
171	Dörtyal (dûrt'yôl) Tur.	36·50 N	36·20 E
89	Dorval (dôr-vȧl') Can. (Montreal In.)	45·26 N	73·44 W
135	Dos Caminos (dôs-kä-mê'nôs) Ven. (In.)	9·38 N	67·17 W
112	Dosewallips (R.) (dō'sê-wäl'lĭps) Wa. (Seattle In.)	47·45 N	123·04 W
162	Dos Hermanas (dōsĕr-mä'näs) Sp.	37·17 N	5·56 W
215	Dosso (dôs-ō') Niger	13·03 N	3·12 E
120	Dothan (dō'thăn) Al.	31·13 N	85·23 W
160	Douai (dōō-â') Fr.	50·23 N	3·04 E
215	Douala (dōō-ä'lä) Cam.	4·03 N	9·42 E
160	Douarnenez (dōō-är nē-nĕs') Fr.	48·06 N	4·18 W
119	Double Bayou (dŭb''l bī'yōō) Tx. (In.)	29·40 N	94·38 W
214	Douentza Mali	15·00 N	2·57 W
163	Douéra (dōō-ā'rȧ) Alg.	36·40 N	2·55 E
101	Douglas (dŭg'lăs) Ak.	58·18 N	134·35 W
115	Douglas Ar.	31·20 N	109·30 W
120	Douglas Ga.	31·30 N	82·53 W
154	Douglas (dŭg'lăs) Isle of Man	54·10 N	4·24 W
99	Douglas (dŭg'lăs) Ma. (In.)	42·04 N	71·45 W
111	Douglas (dŭg'lăs) Wy.	42·45 N	105·21 W
148	Douglas (R.) (dŭg'lăs) Eng.	53·38 N	2·48 W
120	Douglas (R.) (dŭg'lăs) Tn.	36·00 N	83·35 W
92	Douglas Chan. Can.	53·30 N	129·12 W
93	Douglas Lake Ind. Res. Can.	50·10 N	120·49 W
120	Douglasville (dŭg'lăs-vĭl) Ga.	33·45 N	84·47 W
211	Doumé (dōō-mā') Cam.	4·41 N	13·26 E
135	Dourada, Serra (Mts.) (sĕ'r-rä-dōōō-rȧ'dă) Braz.	15·11 S	49·57 W
161	Dourdan (dōōr-däɴ') Fr. (Paris In.)	48·32 N	2·01 E
162	Douro, Rio (R.) (rē'ō-dô'ōō-rô) Port.	41·03 N	8·12 W
148	Dove (R.) (dŭv) Eng.	52·53 N	1·47 W
105	Dover (dō vēr) De.	39·10 N	75·30 W
155	Dover Eng.	51·08 N	1·19 E
105	Dover NH	43·15 N	71·00 W
106	Dover NJ (New York In.)	40·53 N	74·33 W
104	Dover Oh.	40·35 N	81·30 W
218	Dover S. Afr. (Johannesburg & Pretoria In.)	27·05 S	27·44 E
155	Dover, Str. of Eur.	50·50 N	1·15 W
98	Dover-Foxcroft (dō'vēr fôks'krôft) Me.	45·10 N	69·15 W
170	Dovlekanovo (dŏv'lyĕk-ȧ-nô-vô) Sov. Un.	54·15 N	55·05 E
156	Dovre Fjell (Plat.) (dŏv'rĕ fyĕl') Nor.	62·03 N	8·36 E
113	Dow (dou) Il. (St. Louis In.)	39·01 N	90·20 W
212	Dow, L. Bots.	21·22 S	24·52 E
104	Dowagiac (dô-wô'jăk) Mi.	42·00 N	86·05 W
107	Downers Grove (dou'nērz grōv) Il. (Chicago In.)	41·48 N	88·00 W
113	Downey (dou'nĭ) Ca. (Los Angeles In.)	33·56 N	118·08 W
114	Downieville (dou'nĭ-nĭl) Ca.	39·35 N	120·48 W
116	Downs (dounz) Ks.	39·29 N	98·32 W
107	Doylestown (doilz'toun) Oh. (Cleveland In.)	40·58 N	81·43 W
210	Drâa, C. (drȧ) Mor.	28·39 N	12·15 W
210	Drâa, Oued (R.) Mor.	28·00 N	9·31 W
167	Drabov (drä'bôf) Sov. Un.	49·57 N	32·14 E
161	Drac (R.) (dräκ) Fr.	44·50 N	5·47 E
99	Dracut (drā'kŭt) Ma. (In.)	42·40 N	71·19 W
165	Draganovo (drä-gä-nō'vô) Bul.	43·13 N	25·45 E
165	Drăgăsani (drä-gä-shän'ĭ) Rom.	44·39 N	24·18 E
161	Draguignan (drä-gēn-yäɴ') Fr.	43·35 N	6·28 E
212	Drakensberg (Mts.) (drä'kĕnz-bērgh) Leso.-S. Afr.	29·15 S	29·07 E
133	Drake Passage (drāk păs'ĭj) S. A.-Ant.	57·00 S	65·00 W
165	Dráma (drä'mä) Grc.	41·09 N	24·10 E
156	Drammen (dräm'ĕn) Nor.	59·45 N	10·15 E
158	Drau (R.) (drou) Aus.	46·44 N	13·45 E
164	Drava (R.) (Drä'vä) Yugo.	46·37 N	15·17 E
164	Dravograd (Drä'vô-gräd') Yugo.	46·37 N	15·01 E
158	Drawsko Pomorskie (dräv'skō pō-mōr'skyĕ) Pol.	53·31 N	15·50 E
112	Drayton Hbr. (drā'tŭn) Wa. (Vancouver In.)	48·58 N	122·40 W
107	Drayton Plains Mi. (Detroit In.)	42·41 N	83·23 W
93	Drayton Valley Can.	53·13 N	114·59 W
188	Dre Chu (R.) China	34·11 N	96·08 E
161	Drensteinfurt (drĕn'shtīn-fōōrt) F.R.G. (Ruhr In.)	51·47 N	7·44 E
158	Dresden (drās'dĕn) G.D.R.	51·05 N	13·45 E
161	Dreux (drû) Fr. (Paris In.)	48·44 N	1·24 E
218	Driefontein S. Afr. (Johannesburg & Pretoria In.)	25·53 S	29·10 E
165	Drin (R.) (drēn) Alb.	42·13 N	20·13 E
165	Drina (R.) (drē'nä) Yugo.	44·09 N	19·30 E
165	Drinit, Pellg I (Bght.) Alb.	41·42 N	19·17 E
166	Drissa (drĭs'sä) Sov. Un.	55·48 N	27·59 E
166	Drissa (R.) Sov. Un.	55·44 N	28·58 E
106	Driver Va. (Norfolk In.)	36·50 N	76·30 W
156	Dröbak (drû'bäk) Nor.	59·40 N	10·35 E
154	Drogheda (drŏ'hē-dȧ) Ire.	53·43 N	6·15 W
159	Drogichin (drō-gē'chĭn) Sov. Un.	52·10 N	25·11 E
159	Drogobych (drô-hō'bĭch) Sov. Un.	49·21 N	23·31 E
160	Drôme (R.) (drōm) Fr.	44·42 N	4·53 E
148	Dronfield (drŏn'fēld) Eng.	53·18 N	1·28 W
93	Drumheller (drŭm-hĕl-ēr) Can.	51·28 N	112·42 W
104	Drummond (I.) (drŭm'ŭnd) Mi.	46·00 N	83·50 W
98	Drummondville (drŭm'ŭnd-vĭl) Can.	45·53 N	72·33 W
117	Drumright (drŭm'rīt) Ok.	35·59 N	96·37 W
149	Drunen Neth. (Amsterdam In.)	51·41 N	5·10 E
166	Drut' (R.) (drōōt) Sov. Un.	53·40 N	29·45 E
166	Druya (drōō'yȧ) Sov. Un.	55·45 N	27·26 E
153	Druze, Jebel (Mts.) Syria	32·40 N	36·58 E
159	Drweca R. (d'r-văn'tsȧ) Pol.	53·06 N	19·13 E
91	Dryden (drī-dĕn) Can.	49·47 N	92·50 W
202	Drysdale Austl. (Melbourne In.)	38·11 S	144·34 E
121	Dry Tortugas (I.) (tôr-tōō'gäz) Fl. (In.)	24·37 N	82·45 W
210	Dschang (dshäng) Cam.	5·34 N	10·09 E
214	Duabo Lib.	5·40 N	8·05 W
89	Duagh Can. (Edmonton In.)	53·43 N	113·24 W
123	Duarte, Pico (mtn.) (dĭŭ'ärtĕh pēcô) Dom. Rep	19·00 N	71·00 W
137	Duas Barras (dōō'äs-bȧ'r-räs) Braz. (Rio de Janeiro In.)	22·03 S	42·30 W
90	Dubawnt (L.) (dōō-bônt') Can.	63·27 N	103·30 W
90	Dubawnt (R.) Can.	61·30 N	103·49 W
186	Dubayy U. A. E.	25·18 N	55·26 E
203	Dubbo (dŭb'ō) Austl.	32·20 S	148·42 E
217	Dubie Zaire	8·33 S	28·32 E
112	Dublin (dŭb'lĭn) Ca. (San Francisco In.)	37·42 N	121·56 W

ăt; finăl; rāte; senāte; ärm; ȧsk; sofȧ; fâre; ch-choose; dh-as th in other; bē; ēvent; bĕt; recĕnt; cratēr; g-go; gh-guttural g; bĭt; ĭ-short neutral; rīde; κ-guttural k as ch in German ich;

PRONOUNCING INDEX

Dublin — East Syracuse 277

Page	Name Pronunciation Region	Lat. °′	Long. °′
120	Dublin ... Ga.	32·33 N	82·55 W
154	Dublin (Baile Atha Cliath) (bŏ′lĕŏ′hŏclē′ŏh) . Ire.	53·20 N	6·15 W
118	Dublin ... Tx.	32·05 N	98·20 W
159	Dubno (do͞o′b-nô) ... Sov. Un.	50·24 N	25·44 E
105	Du Bois (do͝o-bois′) ... Pa.	41·10 N	78·45 W
167	Dubossary (do͝o-bŏ-sä′rĭ) . Sov. Un.	47·16 N	29·11 E
171	Dubovka (do͝o-bôf′kȧ) ... Sov. Un.	49·00 N	44·50 E
174	Dubrovka (do͞o-brôf′kȧ) Sov. Un. (Leningrad In.)	59·51 N	30·56 S
165	Dubrovnik (Ragusa) (do͝o′brôv-nêk) (rä-go͞o′sä) Yugo.	42·40 N	18·10 E
166	Dubrovno (do͞o-brôf′nö) .. Sov. Un.	54·39 N	30·54 E
109	Dubuque (do͝o-būk′) ... Ia.	42·30 N	90·43 W
115	Duchesne (do͝o-shān′) ... Ut.	40·12 N	110·23 W
115	Duchesne (R.) ... Ut.	40·20 N	110·50 W
204	Duchess (dŭch′ĕs) ... Austl.	21·30 S	139·55 E
199	Ducie I. (dü-sē′) ... Oceania	25·30 S	126·20 W
120	Duck (R.) ... Tn.	35·55 N	87·40 W
112	Duckabush (R.) (dŭk′ȧ-bo͝osh) Wa. (Seattle In.)	47·41 N	123·09 W
94	Duck Lake ... Can.	52·47 N	106·13 W
95	Duck Mtn. ... Can.	51·35 N	101·00 W
120	Ducktown (dŭk′toun) ... Tn.	35·03 N	84·20 W
110	Duck Valley Ind. Res. ... Id.-Nv.	42·02 N	115·49 W
114	Duckwater Pk. (dŭk-wô-tẽr) . Nv.	39·00 N	115·31 W
134	Duda (do͞o′dä) (R.) ... Col. (In.)	3·25 N	74·23 W
172	Dudinka (do͞o-dĭn′kȧ) ... Sov. Un.	69·15 N	85·42 E
148	Dudley (dŭd′lĭ) ... Eng.	52·31 N	2·04 W
214	Duékoué ... Ivory Coast	6·45 N	7·21 W
162	Duero (R.) (dwĕ′rô) ... Sp.	41·30 N	5·10 W
104	Dugger (dŭg′ẽr) ... In.	39·00 N	87·10 W
164	Dugi Otok (I.) (do͞o′gê O′tôk) Yugo.	44·03 N	14·40 E
161	Duisburg (do͞o′ĭs-bo͝orgh) F.R.G. (Ruhr In.)	51·26 N	6·46 E
134	Duitama (do͝oê-tä′mä) ... Col.	5·48 N	73·09 W
92	Duke L (do͞ok) ... Ak.	54·56 N	131·20 W
166	Dukhovshchina (do͞o-ĸôfsh′chēnȧ) Sov. Un.	55·13 N	32·26 E
148	Dukinfield (dŭk′ĭn-fēld) ... Eng.	53·28 N	2·05 W
159	Dukla P. (do͞o′klä) ... Pol.	49·25 N	21·44 E
127	Dulce, Golfo (G.) (gōl′fô do͞ol′sā) C. R.	8·25 N	83·13 W
	Dulcigno, see Ulcinj		
161	Dülken (dül′kĕn) F.R.G. (Ruhr In.)	51·15 N	6·21 E
161	Dülmen (dül′mĕn) F.R.G. (Ruhr In.)	51·50 N	7·17 E
113	Duluth (do͝o-lo͞oth′) Mn. (Duluth In.)	46·50 N	92·07 W
183	Dūmā ... Syria (Palestine In.)	33·34 N	36·17 E
197	Dumaguete City (do͞o-mä-gā′tā) Phil.	9·14 N	123·15 E
183	Dumai ... Indon. (Singapore In.)	1·39 N	101·30 E
197	Dumali Pt. (do͞o-mä′lē) . Phil. (In.)	13·07 N	121·42 E
116	Dumas ... Tx.	35·52 N	101·58 W
154	Dumbarton (dŭm′bǎr-tŭn) ... Scot.	56·00 N	4·35 W
184	Dum-Dum ... India (In.)	22·37 N	88·25 E
154	Dumfries (dŭm-frēs′) ... Scot.	54·05 N	3·40 W
184	Dumjor ... India (In.)	22·37 N	88·14 E
106	Dumont (do͞o′mŏnt) NJ (New York In.)	40·56 N	74·00 W
218	Dumyāţ ... Egypt (Nile In.)	31·22 N	31·50 E
218	Dumyāţ, Maşabb (Chan.) Egypt (Nile In.)	31·36 N	31·45 E
159	Duna (R.) (do͝o′nä) ... Hung.	46·07 N	18·45 E
159	Dunaföldvar (do͝o′nô-fûld′vär) Hung.	46·48 N	18·55 E
159	Dunajec (R.) (do͝o-nä′yĕts) ... Pol.	49·52 N	20·53 E
159	Dunapataj (doo′nô-pô-toi) . Hung.	46·42 N	19·03 E
159	Dunaujvaros ... Hung.	46·57 N	18·55 E
174	Dunay (do͞o′nī) Sov. Un. (Leningrad In.)	59·59 N	30·57 E
167	Dunayevtsy (do͝o-nä′yĕf-tsĭ) Sov. Un.	48·52 N	26·51 E
154	Dunbar (dŭn′bär) ... Scot.	56·00 N	2·25 W
94	Dunblane (dŭn-blān′) ... Can.	51·11 N	106·52 W
104	Dunbar ... WV	38·20 N	81·45 W
92	Duncan (dŭŋ′kǎn) ... Can.	48·47 N	123·42 W
116	Duncan ... Ok.	34·29 N	97·56 W
93	Duncan (R.) ... Can.	50·30 N	116·45 W
93	Duncan Dam ... Can.	50·15 N	116·55 W
93	Duncan L. ... Can.	50·20 N	117·00 W
154	Duncansby Hd. (dŭn′kǎnz-bĭ) .. Scot.	58·40 N	3·01 W
113	Duncanville (dŭn′kȧn-vĭl) Tx. (Dallas, Fort Worth In.)	32·39 N	96·55 W
154	Dundalk (dŭn′dôk) ... Ire.	54·00 N	6·18 W
106	Dundalk ... Md. (Baltimore In.)	39·16 N	76·31 W
154	Dundalk B. (dŭn′dôk) ... Ire.	53·55 N	6·15 W
89	Dundas (dŭn-dăs′) Can. (Toronto In.)	43·16 N	79·58 W
92	Dundas I. ... Can.	54·33 N	130·55 W
107	Dundee (dŭn-dē) . Il. (Chicago In.)	42·06 N	88·17 W
154	Dundee ... Scot.	56·30 N	2·55 W
213	Dundee ... S. Afr. (Natal In.)	28·14 S	30·16 E
204	Dundras (L.) (dŭn-drȧs) ... Austl.	32·15 S	132·00 E
204	Dundras Str. (dŭn′drȧs) ... Austl.	10·35 S	131·15 E
154	Dundrum B. (dŭn-drŭm′) ... Ire.	54·13 N	5·47 W
121	Dunedin (dŭn-ē′dĭn) ... Fl. (In.)	28·00 N	82·43 W
205	Dunedin ... N. Z. (In.)	45·48 S	170·32 E
106	Dunellen (dŭn-ĕl′l′n) NJ (New York In.)	40·36 N	74·28 W
154	Dunfermline (dŭn-fẽrm′lĭn) .. Scot.	56·05 N	3·30 W
154	Dungarvin (dŭn-gȧr′vǎn) ... Ire.	52·06 N	7·50 W
112	Dungeness (dŭnj-nĕs′) Wa. (Seattle In.)	48·09 N	123·07 W
112	Dungeness (R.) .. Wa. (Seattle In.)	48·03 N	123·10 W
112	Dungeness Spit .. Wa. (Seattle In.)	48·11 N	123·03 W
160	Dunkerque (dŭɴ-kĕrk′) ... Fr.	51·02 N	2·37 E
104	Dunkirk (dŭn′kûrk) ... In.	40·20 N	85·25 W
105	Dunkirk ... NY	42·30 N	79·20 W
214	Dunkwa ... Ghana	5·22 N	1·12 W
154	Dun Laoghaire (dŭn-lā′rĕ) ... Ire.	53·16 N	6·09 W
108	Dunlap (dŭn′lǎp) ... Ia.	41·53 N	95·33 W
120	Dunlap ... Tn.	35·23 N	85·23 W
105	Dunmore (dŭn′mōr) ... Pa.	41·25 N	75·30 W
121	Dunn (dŭn) ... NC	35·18 N	78·37 W
121	Dunnellon (dŭn-ĕl′ŏn) ... Fl.	29·02 N	82·28 W
105	Dunnville (dŭn′vĭl) ... Can.	42·55 N	79·40 W
211	Dunqulah ... Sud.	19·21 N	30·19 E
110	Dunsmuir (dŭnz′mūr) ... Ca.	41·08 N	122·17 W
106	Dunwoody (dŭn-wo͝od′ĭ) Ga. (Atlanta In.)	33·57 N	84·20 W
107	Du Page R. (do͞o pāj) Il. (Chicago In.)	41·41 N	88·11 W
107	Du Page R., E. Br. Il. (Chicago In.)	41·49 N	88·05 W
107	Du Page R., W. Br. Il. (Chicago In.)	41·48 N	88·10 W
197	Dupax (do͞o′päks) ... Phil. (In.)	16·16 N	121·06 E
165	Dupnitsa (do͝op′nê-tsȧ) ... Bul.	42·15 N	23·07 E
113	Dupo (dū′pō) ... Il. (St. Louis In.)	38·31 N	90·12 W
216	Duque de Bragança (do͞o′kȧ dȧ brä-gäɴ′sä) . Ang.	9·06 S	15·57 E
136	Duque de Caxias (do͞o′kĕ-dĕ-kȧ′shyȧs) Braz. (Rio de Janeiro In.)	22·46 S	43·18 W
107	Duquesne (do͝o-kān′) Pa. (Pittsburgh In.)	40·22 N	79·51 W
117	Du Quoin (do͝o-kwoin′) ... Il.	38·01 N	89·14 W
141	Durance (R.) (dü-räɴs′) ... Fr.	43·46 N	5.52 E
104	Durand (dû-rănd′) ... Mi.	42·50 N	84·00 W
109	Durand ... Wi.	44·37 N	91·58 W
115	Durango (do͝o-răŋ′gō) ... Co.	37·15 N	107·55 W
124	Durango (do͞o-rä′n-gô) ... Mex.	24·02 N	104·42 W
122	Durango (State) ... Mex.	25·00 N	106·00 W
120	Durant (dû-rănt′) ... Ms.	33·05 N	89·50 W
117	Durant ... Ok.	33·59 N	96·23 W
162	Duratón (R.) (do͞o-rä-tōn′) ... Sp.	41·55 N	3·55 W
137	Durazno (do͞o-räz′nō) Ur. (Buenos Aires In.)	33·21 S	56·31 W
137	Durazno (Dept.) Ur. (Buenos Aires In.)	33·00 S	56·35 W
213	Durban (dûr′bǎn) S. Afr. (Natal In.)	29·48 S	31·00 E
212	Durbanville (dûr-bȧn′vĭl) S. Afr. (In.)	33·50 S	18·39 E
157	Durbe (do͞or′bĕ) ... Sov. Un.	56·36 N	21·24 E
164	Đurđevac (dūr′dyĕ-vȧts′) ... Yugo.	46·03 N	17·03 E
161	Düren (dü′rĕn) . F.R.G. (Ruhr In.)	50·48 N	6·30 E
154	Durham (dûr′ăm) ... Eng.	54·47 N	1·46 W
121	Durham ... NC	36·00 N	78·55 W
203	Durham Downs ... Austl.	27·30 S	141·55 E
165	Durrës (do͝or′ĕs) ... Alb.	41·19 N	19·27 E
105	Duryea (do͞or-yā′) ... Pa.	41·20 N	75·50 W
187	Dushanbe ... Sov. Un.	38·30 N	68·45 E
161	Düsseldorf (düs′ĕl-dôrf) F.R.G. (Ruhr In.)	51·14 N	6·47 E
149	Dussen ... Neth. (Amsterdam In.)	51·43 N	4·58 E
192	Dutalan Ula (Mtn.) ... Mong.	49·25 N	112·40 E
101	Dutch Harbor (dŭch här′bẽr) .. Ak.	53·58 N	166·30 W
112	Duvall (do͞o′vâl) . Wa. (Seattle In.)	47·44 N	121·59 W
129	Duvergé (do͞o-vĕr-hĕ′) . Dom. Rep.	18·20 N	71·20 W
112	Duwamish (R.) (do͞o-wăm′ĭsh) Wa. (Seattle In.)	47·24 N	122·18 W
	Dvina, Western, (R.), see Zapadnaya Dvina		
170	Dvinskaya Guba (G.) ... Sov. Un.	65·10 N	38·40 E
158	Dvůr Králové nad Labem (dvo͞or′ krä′lô-vā) . Czech.	50·28 N	15·43 E
184	Dwārka ... India	22·18 N	68·59 E
104	Dwight (dwīt) ... Il.	41·00 N	88·20 W
110	Dworshak Res. ... Id.	46·45 N	116·15 W
166	Dyat′kovo (dyät′kō-vō) .. Sov. Un.	53·36 N	34·19 E
107	Dyer (dī′ẽr) ... In. (Chicago In.)	41·30 N	87·31 W
120	Dyersburg (dī′ẽrz-bûrg) ... Tn.	36·02 N	89·23 W
109	Dyersville (dī′ẽrz-vĭl) ... Ia.	42·28 N	91·09 W
112	Dyes Inlet (dīz) .. Wa. (Seattle In.)	47·37 N	122·45 W
95	Dyment (dī′mĕnt) ... Can.	49·37 N	92·19 W
188	Dzabhan Gol (R.) ... Mong.	48·19 N	94·08 E
192	Dzamiin Üüde ... Mong.	44·38 N	111·32 E
213	Dzaoudzi (dzou′dzĭ) Comoro Is.	12·44 S	45·15 E
147	Dzaudzhikau (dzou-jĭ-kou′) Sov. Un.	48·00 N	44·52 E
167	Dzerzhinsk (dzhĕr-zhĭnsk′) Sov. Un.	48·24 N	37·58 E
166	Dzerzhinsk ... Sov. Un.	53·41 N	27·14 E
170	Dzerzhinsk ... Sov. Un.	56·20 N	43·50 E
172	Dzhalal-Abad (jȧ-läl′ȧ-bät′) Sov. Un.	41·13 N	73·35 E
172	Dzhambul (dzhäm-bo͞ol′) . Sov. Un.	42·51 N	71·29 E
167	Dzhankoy (dzhän′koi) ... Sov. Un.	45·43 N	34·22 E
174	Dzhetygara (dzhĕt′-gä′rȧ) Sov. Un. (Urals In.)	52·12 N	61·18 E
172	Dzhizak (dzhê′zäk) ... Sov. Un.	40·13 N	67·58 E
173	Dzhugdzhur Khrebet (Mts.) (jo͝og-jo͞or′) . Sov. Un.	56·15 N	137·00 E
159	Działoszyce (jyä-wō-shē′tsĕ) .. Pol.	50·21 N	20·22 E
126	Dzibalchén (zē-bäl-chĕ′n) Mex. (In.)	19·25 N	89·39 W
126	Dzidzantún (zēd-zän-to͞o′n) Mex. (In.)	21·18 N	89·00 W
158	Dzierzoniów (dzyĕr-zhôn′yŭf) . Pol.	50·44 N	16·38 E
126	Dzilam Gonzalez (zē-lä′m-gôn-zä′lĕz) . Mex. (In.)	21·21 N	88·53 W
126	Dzitás (zē-tȧ′s) ... Mex. (In.)	20·47 N	88·32 W
126	Dzitbalché (dzēt-bäl-chā′) Mex. (In.)	20·18 N	90·03 W
188	Dzungaria (Reg.) (dzo͝oŋ-gä′rĭ-ȧ) . China	44·39 N	86·13 E

E

Page	Name Pronunciation Region	Lat. °′	Long. °′
101	Eagle (ē′g′l) ... Ak.	64·42 N	141·20 W
104	Eagle ... WV	38·10 N	81·20 W
115	Eagle (R.) ... Co.	39·32 N	106·28 W
112	Eaglecliff (ē′g′l-klĭf) Wa. (Portland In.)	46·10 N	123·13 W
107	Eagle Cr. In. (Indianapolis In.)	39·54 N	86·17 W
109	Eagle Grove ... Ia.	42·39 N	93·55 W
98	Eagle Lake ... Me.	47·03 N	68·38 W
119	Eagle Lake ... Tx.	29·37 N	96·20 W
110	Eagle L. ... Ca.	40·45 N	120·52 W
113	Eagle Mountain L. Tx. (Dallas, Fort Worth In.)	32·56 N	97·27 W
118	Eagle Pass ... Tx.	28·49 N	100·30 W
110	Eagle Pk. ... Ca.	41·18 N	120·11 W
148	Ealing (ē′lĭng) .. Eng. (London In.)	51·29 N	0·19 W
117	Earle (ûrl) ... Ar.	35·14 N	90·28 W
120	Earlington (ûr′lĭng-tŭn) ... Ky.	37·15 N	87·31 W
121	Easley (ēz′lĭ) ... SC	34·48 N	82·37 W
122	East, Mt. ... C. Z. (In.)	9·09 N	79·16 W
113	East Alton (ôl′tŭn) Il. (St. Louis In.)	38·53 N	90·08 W
97	East Angus (ăŋ′gŭs) ... Can.	45·35 N	71·40 W
107	East Aurora (ô-rō′rȧ) NY (Buffalo In.)	42·46 N	78·38 W
119	East B. ... Tx. (In.)	29·30 N	94·41 W
149	East Berlin (bĕr-lēn′) G.D.R. (Berlin In.)	52·31 N	13·28 E
120	East Bernstadt (bûrn′stȧt) ... Ky.	37·09 N	84·08 W
155	Eastbourne (ēst′bôrn) ... Eng.	50·48 N	0·16 E
129	East Caicos (I.) (kī′kōs) Turk & Caicos Is.	21·40 N	71·35 W
205	East Cape (C.) ... N. Z. (In.)	37·37 S	178·33 E
	East Cape, see Dezhneva, Mys		
113	East Carondelet (kȧ-rŏn′dĕ-lĕt) Il. (St. Louis In.)	38·33 N	90·14 W
107	East Chicago (shĭ-kô′gō) In. (Chicago In.)	41·39 N	87·29 W
189	East China Sea ... Asia	30·28 N	125·52 E
107	East Cleveland (klēv′lănd) Oh. (Cleveland In.)	41·33 N	81·35 W
119	East Cote Blanche B. (kōt bläɴsh′) . La.	29·30 N	92·07 W
109	East Des Moines (R.) (dē moin′) Ia.	42·57 N	94·17 W
107	East Detroit (dê-troit′) Mi. (Detroit In.)	42·28 N	82·57 W
	Easter (I.), see Rapa Nui		
158	Eastern Alps (Mts.) . Aus.-Switz.	47·03 N	10·55 E
185	Eastern Ghāts (Mts.) ... India	13·50 N	78·45 E
188	Eastern Turkestan (Reg.) (to͝or-kĕ-stän′) (tûr-kĕ-stăn′) China	38·23 N	80·41 E
108	East Grand Forks (grănd fôrks) Mn.	47·56 N	97·02 W
106	East Greenwich (grĭn′ĭj) RI (Providence In.)	41·40 N	71·27 W
105	Easthampton (ēst-hămp′tŭn) .. Ma.	42·15 N	72·45 W
105	East Hartford (härt′fẽrd) ... Ct.	41·45 N	72·35 W
111	East Helena (hĕ-lē′nȧ) ... Mt.	46·31 N	111·50 W
148	East Ilsley (ĭl′slē) Eng. (London In.)	51·30 N	1·18 W
104	East Jordan (jôr′dăn) ... Mi.	45·05 N	85·05 W
113	East Kansas City (kăn′zȧs) Mo. (Kansas City In.)	39·09 N	94·30 W
118	Eastland (ēst′lănd) ... Tx.	32·24 N	98·47 W
104	East Lansing (lăn′sĭng) ... Mi.	42·45 N	84·30 W
107	Eastlawn ... Mi. (Detroit In.)	42·15 N	83·35 W
113	East Leavenworth (lĕv′ĕn-wûrth) Mo. (Kansas City In.)	39·18 N	94·50 W
104	East Liverpool (lĭv′ẽr-po͞ol) ... Oh.	40·40 N	80·35 W
213	East London (lŭn′dŭn) S. Afr. (Natal In.)	33·02 S	27·54 E
113	East Los Angeles (lōs äŋ′hȧ-lās) Ca. (Los Angeles In.)	34·01 N	118·09 W
91	Eastmain (R.) (ēst′mān) ... Can.	52·12 N	73·19 W
120	Eastman (ēst′măn) ... Ga.	32·10 N	83·11 W
106	East Millstone (mĭl′stōn) NJ (New York In.)	40·30 N	74·35 W
109	East Moline (mô-lēn′) ... Il.	41·31 N	90·28 W
115	East Nishnabotna (R.) (nĭsh-nȧ-bŏt′nȧ) . Ia.	40·53 N	95·23 W
105	Easton (ēs′tŭn) ... Md.	72·45 N	76·05 W
105	Easton ... Pa.	40·45 N	75·15 W
106	Easton L. ... Ct. (New York In.)	41·18 N	73·17 W
106	East Orange (ŏr′ĕnj) NJ (New York In.)	40·46 N	74·12 W
112	East Palo Alto Ca. (San Francisco In.)	37·27 N	122·07 W
104	East Peoria (pē-ō′rĭ-ȧ) ... Il.	40·40 N	89·30 W
107	East Pittsburgh (pĭts′bûrg) Pa. (Pittsburgh In.)	40·24 N	79·50 W
106	East Point ... Ga. (Atlanta In.)	33·41 N	84·27 W
98	Eastport (ēst′pōrt) ... Me.	44·53 N	67·01 W
106	East Providence (prŏv′ĭ-dĕns) RI (Providence In.)	41·49 N	71·22 W
148	East Retford (rĕt′fẽrd) ... Eng.	53·19 N	0·56 W
148	East Riding (Co.) (rīd′ing) ... Eng.	53·47 N	0·36 W
105	East Rochester (rŏch′ĕs-tẽr) .. NY.	43·10 N	77·30 W
113	East St. Louis (sānt lo͞o′ĭs) (lo͞o-ĭ) Il. (St. Louis In.)	38·38 N	90·10 W
168	East Siberian Sea (sī-bĭr′y′n) Sov. Un.	73·00 N	153·28 E
112	Eastsound (ēst-sound) Wa. (Vancouver In.)	48·42 N	122·42 W
105	East Stroudsburg (stroudz′bûrg) Pa.	41·00 N	75·10 W
105	East Syracuse (sĭr′ȧ-kūs) ... NY	43·05 N	76·00 W

ng-sing; ŋ-baŋk; ɴ-nasalized n; nŏd; cŏmmit; ōld; ôbey; ôrder; fo͞od; fo͝ot; ou-out; s-soft; sh-dish; th-thin; pūre; ûnite; ûrn; stŭd; circŭs; ü-as "y" in study; ′-indeterminate vowel.

278 East Tavaputs — El Paso PRONOUNCING INDEX

Page	Name Pronunciation Region	Lat. °′	Long. °′
115	East Tavaputs Plat. (tă-vă'-pŭts) Ut.	39·25 N	109·45 W
104	East Tawas (tô'wăs) Mi.	44·15 N	83·30 W
114	East Walker (R.) (wôk'ẽr) Nv.	38·36 N	119·02 W
89	East York Can. (Toronto In.)	43·41 N	79·20 W
107	Eaton (ē'tŭn) Co.	40·31 N	104·42 W
104	Eaton Oh.	39·45 N	84·40 W
107	Eaton Estates Oh. (Cleveland In.)	41·19 N	82·01 W
104	Eaton Rapids (răp'ĭdz) Mi.	42·30 N	84·40 W
120	Eatonton (ē'tŭn-tŭn) Ga.	33·20 N	83·24 W
106	Eatontown (ē'tŭn-toun) NJ (New York In.)	40·18 N	74·04 W
109	Eau Claire (ō klâr') Wi.	44·47 N	91·32 W
156	Ebeltoft (ĕ'bĕl-tŭft) Den.	56·11 N	10·39 E
105	Ebensburg Pa.	40·29 N	78·44 W
149	Ebersberg (ĕ'bĕrs-bĕrgh) F.R.G. (Munich In.)	48·05 N	11·58 E
158	Ebingen (ā'bĭng-ĕn) F.R.G.	48·13 N	9·04 E
188	Ebi Nuur (L.) (ā'bê) China	45·09 N	83·15 E
164	Eboli (ĕb'ō-lē) It.	40·38 N	15·04 E
215	Ebolowa Cam.	2·54 N	11·09 E
149	Ebreichsdorf Aus. (Vienna In.)	47·58 N	16·24 E
214	Ebrie, Lagune (Lagoon) Ivory Coast	5·20 N	4·50 W
163	Ebro, Río (R.) (rê'-ô-ā'brō) Sp.	41·30 N	0·35 W
148	Eccles (ĕk''lz) Eng.	53·29 N	2·20 W
104	Eccles WV	37·45 N	81·10 W
148	Eccleshall (ĕk''lz-hôl) Eng.	52·51 N	2·15 W
165	Eceabat (Maidos) Tur.	40·10 N	26·21 E
197	Echague (ā-chä'gwä) Phil. (In.)	16·43 N	121·40 E
127	Echandi, Cerro (Mt.) (sĕ'r-rô-ĕ-chä'nd) Pan.	9·05 N	82·51 W
95	Echimamish (R.) Can.	54·15 N	97·30 W
113	Echo Bay (ĕk'ō) Can. (Sault Ste. Marie In.)	46·29 N	84·04 W
95	Echoing (R.) (ĕk'ō-ĭng) Can.	55·15 N	91·30 W
161	Echternach (ĕk'tẽr-näk) Lux.	49·48 N	6·25 E
203	Echuca (ê-chōō'kȧ) Austl.	36·10 S	144·47 E
162	Écija (ā'thê-hä) Sp.	37·20 N	5·07 W
158	Eckernförde F.R.G.	54·27 N	9·51 E
106	Eclipse (ê-klĭps') Va. (Norfolk In.)	36·55 N	76·29 W
107	Ecorse (ê-kôrs') Mi. (Detroit In.)	42·15 N	83·09 W
133	Ecuador (ĕk'wȧ-dôr) S. A.	0·00 N	78·30 W
211	Ed Eth.	13·57 N	41·37 E
120	Eddyville (ĕd'ĭ-vĭl) Ky.	37·03 N	88·03 W
215	Ede Nig.	7·44 N	4·27 E
215	Edéa (ĕ-dā'ä) Cam.	3·48 N	10·08 E
118	Eden Tx.	31·13 N	99·51 W
113	Eden Ut. (Salt Lake City In.)	41·18 N	111·49 W
154	Eden (R.) (ē'dĕn) Eng.	54·40 N	2·35 W
148	Edenbridge (ē'dĕn-brĭj) Eng. (London In.)	51·11 N	0·05 E
148	Edenham (ē'd'n-ăm) Eng.	52·46 N	0·25 W
113	Eden Prairie (prâr'ĭ) Mn. (Minneapolis, St. Paul In.)	44·51 N	93·29 W
121	Edenton (ē'dĕn-tŭn) NC	36·02 N	76·37 W
107	Edenton Oh. (Cincinnati In.)	39·14 N	84·02 W
213	Edenvale (ēd'ĕn-vāl) S. Afr. (Johannesburg & Pretoria In.)	29·06 S	28·10 E
218	Edenville (ē'd'n-vĭl) S. Afr. (Johannesburg & Pretoria In.)	27·33 S	27·42 E
158	Eder R. (ā'dẽr) F.R.G.	51·05 N	8·52 E
121	Edgefield (ĕj'fēld) SC	33·52 N	81·55 W
108	Edgeley (ĕj'lĭ) ND	46·24 N	98·43 W
108	Edgemont (ĕj'mŏnt) SD	43·19 N	103·50 W
109	Edgerton (ĕj'ẽr-tŭn) Wi.	42·49 N	89·06 W
106	Edgewater (ĕj-wô-tẽr) Al. (Birmingham In.)	33·31 N	86·52 W
106	Edgewater Md. (Baltimore In.)	38·58 N	76·35 W
93	Edgewood (ĕj'wŏŏd) Can.	49·47 N	118·08 W
165	Édhessa Grc.	40·48 N	22·04 E
113	Edina (ê-dī'nȧ) Mn. (Minneapolis, St. Paul In.)	44·55 N	93·20 W
117	Edina Mo.	40·10 N	92·11 W
104	Edinburg (ĕd''n-bûrg) In.	39·20 N	85·55 W
118	Edinburg Tx.	26·18 N	98·08 W
154	Edinburgh (ĕd''n-bŭr-ô) Scot.	55·57 N	3·10 W
165	Edirne (Adrianople) (ĕ-dĭr'nĕ) (ā-drĭ-ăn-ō'p'l) Tur.	41·41 N	26·35 E
121	Edisto, (R.) (ĕd'ĭs-tō) SC	33·10 N	80·50 W
121	Edisto (R.), North Fk. SC	33·42 N	81·24 W
121	Edisto (R.), South Fk. SC	33·43 N	81·35 W
121	Edisto Island SC	32·32 N	80·20 W
117	Edmond (ĕd'mŭnd) Ok.	35·39 N	97·29 W
112	Edmonds (ĕd'mŭndz) Wa. (Seattle In.)	47·49 N	122·23 W
89	Edmonton Can. (Edmonton In.)	53·33 N	113·28 W
98	Edmundston (ĕd'mŭn-stŭn) Can.	47·22 N	68·20 W
119	Edna (ĕd'nȧ) Tx.	28·59 N	96·39 W
165	Edremit (ĕd-rĕ-mēt') Tur.	39·35 N	27·00 E
165	Edremit Körfezi (G.) Tur.	39·28 N	26·35 E
93	Edson (ĕd'sŭn) Can.	53·35 N	116·26 W
96	Edward (I.) (ĕd'wẽrd) Can.	48·21 N	88·29 W
217	Edward (L.) Zaire	0·25 S	29·40 E
113	Edwardsville (ĕd'wẽrdz-vĭl) Il. (St. Louis In.)	38·49 N	89·58 W
107	Edwardsville In. (Louisville In.)	38·17 N	85·53 W
113	Edwardsville Ks. (Kansas City In.)	39·04 N	94·49 W
110	Eel (R.) (ēl) Ca.	40·39 N	124·15 W
104	Eel (R.) In.	40·50 N	85·55 W
205	Efate (I.) (ā-fä'tā) New Hebr.	18·02 S	168·29 E
109	Effigy Mounds Natl. Mon. (ĕf'ĭ-jŭ mounds) Ia.	43·04 N	91·15 W
104	Effingham (ĕf'ĭng-hăm) Il.	39·05 N	88·30 W
162	Ega (R.) (ā'gä) Sp.	42·40 N	2·20 W
164	Egadi, Isole (Is.) (ĕ'sō-lĕ-ĕ'gä-dē) It.	38·01 N	12·00 E
162	Egea de los Caballeros (å-kā'å dā lōs kä-bäl-yā'rôs) Sp.	42·07 N	1·05 W
101	Egegik (ĕg'ĕ-jĭt) Ak.	58·10 N	157·22 W
159	Eger (ĕ gẽr) Hung.	47·53 N	20·24 E
	Eger (R.), see Ohře		
156	Egersund (ĕ'ghĕr-sōōn') Nor.	58·29 N	6·01 E
105	Egg Harbor (ĕg här'bẽr) NJ	39·30 N	74·35 W
148	Egham (ĕg'ăm) Eng. (London In.)	51·24 N	0·33 W
188	Egiin Gol (R.) (â-gēn') Mong.	49·41 N	100·40 E
205	Egmont, C. (ĕg'mŏnt) N. Z. (In.)	39·18 S	173·49 E
171	Egridir Gölü (L.) (ā-rĭ-dĭr') Tur.	38·10 N	30·00 E
160	Eguilles (ĕ-gwē') Fr. (In.)	43·34 N	5·21 E
209	Egypt (ē'jĭpt) Afr.	26·58 N	27·01 E
215	Eha-Amufu Nig.	6·40 N	7·46 E
162	Eibar (ā'ê-bär) Sp.	43·12 N	2·20 W
158	Eichstätt (ĭk'shtät) F.R.G.	48·54 N	11·14 E
149	Eichwalde (īĸ'väl-dĕ) G.D.R. (Berlin In.)	52·22 N	13·37 E
156	Eid (īdh) Nor.	61·54 N	6·01 E
156	Eidsberg (īdhs'bĕrgh) Nor.	59·32 N	11·16 E
156	Eidsvoll (īdhs'vôl) Nor.	60·19 N	11·15 E
158	Eifel (Plat.) (ī'fĕl) F.R.G.	50·08 N	6·30 E
204	Eighty Mile Beach Austl.	20·45 S	121·00 E
218	Eil Som. (Horn of Afr. In.)	7·53 N	49·45 E
158	Eilenburg (ī'lĕn-bŏŏrgh) G.D.R.	51·27 N	12·38 E
213	Eilliot S. Afr. (Natal In.)	31·19 S	27·52 E
158	Einbeck (īn'bĕk) F.R.G.	51·49 N	9·52 E
155	Eindhoven (īnd'hō-vĕn) Neth.	51·29 N	5·20 E
134	Eirunepé (ā-rōō-nĕ-pĕ') Braz.	6·37 S	69·58 W
158	Eisenach (ī'zĕn-äĸ) G.D.R.	50·58 N	10·18 E
158	Eisenhüttenstadt G.D.R.	52·08 N	14·40 E
158	Eisleben (īs'lā'bĕn) G.D.R.	51·31 N	11·33 E
156	Ejdfjord (ĕĭd'fyōr) Nor.	60·28 N	7·04 E
214	Ejura Ghana	7·23 N	1·22 W
125	Ejutla de Crespo (å-hōōt'lä dā krās'pō) Mex.	16·34 N	96·44 W
216	Ekanga Zaire	2·23 S	23·14 E
157	Ekenäs (Tammisaari) (ĕ'kĕ-nâs) (tám'ĭ-sä'rĭ) Fin.	59·59 N	23·25 E
149	Ekeren Bel. (Brussels In.)	51·17 N	4·27 E
216	Ekoli Zaire	0·23 S	24·16 E
156	Eksjö (ĕk'shû) Swe.	57·41 N	14·55 E
210	El Aaiún W. Sah.	26·45 N	13·15 W
163	El Affroun (ĕl ȧf-froun') Alg.	36·28 N	2·38 E
213	Elands (R.) S. Afr. (Natal In.)	31·48 S	26·09 E
218	Elands (R.) (ĕlȧnds) S. Afr. (Johannesburg & Pretoria In.)	25·11 S	28·52 E
162	El Arahal (ĕl ä-rä-äl') Sp.	37·17 N	5·32 W
152	El Asnam (Orléansville) Alg.	36·14 N	1·32 E
183	Elat Isr. (Palestine In.)	29·34 N	34·57 E
171	Elâzıg (ĕl-ä'zĕz) Tur.	38·40 N	39·00 E
120	Elba (ĕl'bȧ) Al.	31·25 N	86·01 W
164	Elba, Isola di (I.) (ê-sō lä-dē-ĕl'bȧ) It.	42·42 N	10·25 E
134	El Banco (ĕl băn'cô) Col.	8·58 N	74·01 W
162	El Barco (ĕl bär'kô) Sp.	42·26 N	6·58 W
165	Elbasan (ĕl-bä-sän') Alb.	41·08 N	20·05 E
152	El Bayadh Alg.	33·42 N	1·06 E
	Elbe (R.), see Labe		
158	Elbe (R.) (ĕl'bĕ) G.D.R.	53·47 N	9·20 E
115	Elbert, Mt. (ĕl'bẽrt) Co.	39·05 N	106·25 W
120	Elberton (ĕl'bẽr-tŭn) Ga.	34·05 N	82·53 W
160	Elbeuf (ĕl-bûf') Fr.	49·16 N	0·59 E
171	Elbistan (ĕl-bê-stän') Tur.	38·20 N	37·10 E
159	Elblag (ĕl'blăng) Pol.	54·11 N	19·25 E
162	El Bonillo (ĕl bō-nēl'yō) Sp.	38·56 N	2·31 W
89	Elbow (R.) (ĕl'bō) Can. (Calgary In.)	51·03 N	114·24 W
128	Elbow Cay (I.) Ba.	26·25 N	77·55 W
108	Elbow Lake Mn.	46·00 N	95·59 W
171	El'brus, Gora (Mt.) (ĕl'brōōs') Sov. Un.	43·20 N	42·25 E
218	El Bur Som. (Horn of Afr. In.)	4·35 N	46·40 E
171	Elburz Mts. (ĕl'bōōrz') Iran	36·30 N	51·00 E
114	El Cajon Ca. (In.)	32·48 N	116·58 W
134	El Cajon (ĕl-kä-kô'n) Col. (In.)	4·50 N	76·35 W
135	El Cambur (käm-bōōr') Ven. (In.)	10·24 N	68·06 W
119	El Campo (kăm'pō) Tx.	29·13 N	96·17 W
137	El Carmen (kȧ'r-mĕn) Chile (Santiago In.)	34·14 S	71·23 W
134	El Carmen (kȧ'r-mĕn) Col.	9·54 N	75·12 W
113	El Casco (kăs'kô) Ca. (Los Angeles In.)	33·59 N	117·08 W
114	El Centro (sĕn'trô) Ca.	32·47 N	115·33 W
112	El Cerrito (sĕr-rē'tō) Ca. (San Francisco In.)	37·55 N	122·19 W
163	Elche (ĕl'chā) Sp.	38·15 N	0·42 W
126	El Cuyo Mex. (In.)	21·30 N	87·42 W
163	Elda (ĕl'dä) Sp.	38·28 N	0·44 W
158	Elde (R.) (ĕl'dĕ) G.D.R.	53·11 N	11·30 E
210	El Djouf (Des.) (ĕl djōōf) Mauritania	21·45 N	7·05 W
109	Eldon (ĕl-dŭn) Ia.	40·55 N	92·15 W
115	Eldon Mo.	38·21 N	92·36 W
109	Eldora (ĕl-dō'rȧ) Ia.	42·21 N	93·08 W
117	El Dorado (ĕl dô-rä'dō) Ar.	33·13 N	92·39 W
104	Eldorado Il.	37·50 N	88·30 W
117	El Dorado Ks.	37·49 N	96·51 W
117	Eldorado Springs (sprĭngz) Mo.	37·51 N	94·02 W
217	Eldoret (ĕl-dô-rĕt') Ken.	0·31 N	35·17 E
124	El Ebano (ā-bä'nō) Mex.	22·13 N	98·26 W
116	Electra (ê-lĕk'trȧ) Tx.	34·02 N	98·54 W
111	Electric Pk. (ê-lĕk'trĭk) Mt.	45·03 N	110·52 W
174	Elektrogorsk (ĕl-yĕk'trô-gôrsk) Sov. Un. (Moscow In.)	55·53 N	38·48 E
174	Elektrostal (ĕl-yĕk'trô-stål) Sov. Un. (Moscow In.)	55·47 N	38·27 E
174	Elektrougli Sov. Un. (Moscow In.)	55·43 N	38·13 E
115	Elephant Butte Res. (ĕl'ê-fănt būt) NM	33·25 N	107·10 W
163	El Escorial (ĕl-ĕs-kō-ryä'l) Sp. (Madrid In.)	40·38 N	4·08 W
126	El Espino (ĕl-ĕs-pē'nō) Nic.	13·26 N	86·48 W
129	Eleuthera (I.) (ê-lū'thẽr-ȧ) Ba.	25·05 N	76·10 W
129	Eleuthera Pt. Ba.	24·35 N	76·05 W
117	Eleven Point (R.) (ê-lĕv'ĕn) Mo.	36·53 N	91·39 W
162	El Ferrol (fā-rōl') Sp.	43·30 N	8·12 W
107	Elgin (ĕl'jĭn) Il. (Chicago In.)	42·03 N	88·16 W
108	Elgin Ne.	41·58 N	98·04 W
110	Elgin Or.	45·34 N	117·58 W
154	Elgin Scot.	57·40 N	3·30 W
119	Elgin Tx.	30·21 N	97·22 W
112	Elgin Wa. (Seattle In.)	47·23 N	122·42 W
210	El Goléa (gō-lā-ä') Alg.	30·39 N	2·52 E
217	Elgon, Mt. (ĕl'gŏn) Ken.	1·00 N	34·25 E
124	El Grullo (grōōl-yō) Mex.	19·46 N	104·10 W
135	El Guapo (gwȧ'pô) Ven. (In.)	10·07 N	66·00 W
152	El Hamada (Plat.) (häm'ä-dä) Alg.	30·53 N	1·52 W
110	El Hank (Bluffs) Mauritania-Mali	23·44 N	6·45 W
135	El Hatillo (ä-tē'l-yô) Ven. (In.)	10·08 N	65·13 W
89	Elie (ē'lē) Can. (Winnipeg In.)	49·55 N	97·45 W
217	Elila (R.) (ĕ-lē'lȧ) Zaire	3·00 S	26·50 E
112	Elisa (I.) (ê-lī'sȧ) Wa. (Vancouver In.)	48·43 N	122·37 W
	Élisabethville, see Lubumbashi		
157	Elisenvaara (ā-lē'sĕn-vä'rȧ) Sov. Un.	61·25 N	29·46 E
119	Elizabeth (ê-lĭz'ȧ-bĕth) La.	30·50 N	92·47 W
106	Elizabeth NJ (New York In.)	40·40 N	74·13 W
107	Elizabeth Pa. (Pittsburgh In.)	40·16 N	79·53 W
121	Elizabeth City NC	36·15 N	76·15 W
121	Elizabethton (ê-lĭz-ȧ-bĕth'tŭn) Tn.	36·19 N	82·12 W
104	Elizabethtown (ê-lĭz'ȧ-bĕth-toun) Ky.	37·40 N	85·55 W
210	El Jadida Mor.	33·14 N	8·34 W
159	Ełk Pol.	53·53 N	22·23 E
93	Elk (R.) Can.	50·00 N	115·00 W
120	Elk (R.) Tn.	35·05 N	86·36 W
104	Elk (R.) WV	38·30 N	81·05 W
210	El Kairouan (kĕr-ōō-än) Tun.	35·46 N	10·04 E
116	Elk City (ĕlk) Ok.	35·23 N	99·23 W
104	Elkhart (ĕlk'härt) In.	41·40 N	86·00 W
116	Elkhart Ks.	37·00 N	101·54 W
119	Elkhart Tx.	31·38 N	95·35 W
109	Elkhorn (ĕlk'hôrn) Wi.	42·39 N	88·32 W
108	Elkhorn (R.) Ne.	42·06 N	97·46 W
121	Elkin (ĕl'kĭn) NC	36·15 N	80·50 W
105	Elkins (ĕl'kĭnz) WV	38·55 N	79·50 W
95	Elk I. Can.	50·45 N	96·32 W
93	Elk Island Natl. Park (ĕlk ī'lănd) Can.	53·37 N	112·45 W
110	Elko (ĕl'kō) Nv.	40·51 N	115·46 W
108	Elk Point SD	42·41 N	96·41 W
104	Elk Rapids (răp'ĭdz) Mi.	44·55 N	85·25 W
110	Elk River (rĭv'ẽr) Id.	46·47 N	116·11 W
109	Elk River Mn.	45·17 N	93·33 W
120	Elkton (ĕlk'tŭn) Ky.	36·47 N	87·08 W
105	Elkton Md.	39·35 N	75·50 W
108	Elkton SD	44·15 N	96·28 W
148	Elland (el'ănd) Eng.	53·41 N	1·50 W
115	Ellen, Mt. (ĕl'ĕn) Ut.	38·05 N	110·50 W
108	Ellendale (ĕl'ĕn-dāl) ND	46·01 N	98·33 W
110	Ellensburg (ĕl'ĕnz-bûrg) Wa.	47·00 N	120·31 W
105	Ellenville (ĕl'ĕn-vĭl) NY	41·40 N	74·25 W
89	Ellerslie (ĕl'ẽrz-lê) Can. (Edmonton In.)	53·25 N	113·30 W
148	Ellesmere (ĕlz'mẽr) Eng.	52·55 N	2·54 W
75	Ellesmere I. Can.	81·00 N	80·00 W
148	Ellesmere Port Eng.	53·17 N	2·54 W
	Ellice Is., see Tuvalu		
106	Ellicott City (ĕl'ĭ-kŏt sĭ'tê) Md. (Baltimore In.)	39·16 N	76·48 W
107	Ellicott Cr. NY (Buffalo In.)	43·00 N	78·46 W
213	Elliotdale (ĕl-ĭ-ŏt'dāl) S. Afr. (Natal In.)	31·58 S	28·42 E
96	Elliot Lake Can.	46·23 N	82·39 W
112	Elliot (ĕl'ĭ-ŭt) Wa. (Seattle In.)	47·28 N	122·08 W
116	Ellis (ĕl'ĭs) Ks.	38·56 N	99·34 W
120	Ellisville (ĕl'ĭs-vĭl) Ms.	31·37 N	89·10 W
113	Ellisville Mo. (St. Louis In.)	38·35 N	90·35 W
116	Ellsworth (ĕlz'wûrth) Ks.	38·43 N	98·14 W
98	Ellsworth Me.	44·33 N	68·26 W
220	Ellsworth Highland Ant.	77·00 S	90·00 W
158	Ellwangen (ĕl'väng-gĕn) F.R.G.	48·47 N	10·08 E
149	Elm (ĕlm) F.R.G. (Hamburg In.)	53·31 N	9·13 E
108	Elm (R.) SD	45·47 N	98·28 W
104	Elm (R.) WV	38·30 N	81·05 W
110	Elma (ĕl'mȧ) Wa.	47·02 N	123·20 W
152	El Maadid Mor.	31·32 N	4·30 W
117	Elm Cr. Tx.	33·34 N	97·25 W
113	Elmendorf (ĕl'mĕn-dôrf) Tx. (San Antonio In.)	29·16 N	98·20 W
113	Elm Fork (ĕlm fôrk) Tx. (Dallas, Fort Worth In.)	32·55 N	96·56 W
107	Elmhurst (ĕlm'hûrst) Il. (Chicago In.)	41·54 N	87·56 W
210	El Milia (mē'ä) Alg.	36·30 N	6·16 E
105	Elmira (ĕl-mī'rȧ) NY	42·05 N	76·50 W
105	Elmira Heights NY	42·10 N	76·50 W
134	El Misti (Vol.) (mē's-tē) Peru	16·04 S	71·20 W
113	El Modena (mô-dē'nô) Ca. (Los Angeles In.)	33·47 N	117·48 W
113	El Monte (mōn'tȧ) Ca. (Los Angeles In.)	34·04 N	118·02 W
115	El Morro Natl. Mon. NM	35·05 N	108·20 W
214	El Mreyyé (Des.) Mauritania	19·15 N	7·50 W
149	Elmshorn (ĕlms'hôrn) F.R.G. (Hamburg In.)	53·45 N	9·39 E
107	Elmwood Place (ĕlm'wŏŏd plās) Oh. (Cincinnati In.)	39·11 N	84·30 W
111	Elokomin (R.) (ê-lō'kō-mĭn) Wa. (Portland In.)	46·16 N	123·16 W
124	El Oro (ô-rô) Mex.	19·49 N	100·04 W
210	El Oued (wĕd') Alg.	33·23 N	6·49 E
134	El Pao (ĕl pä'ō) Ven.	8·08 N	62·37 W
126	El Paraíso (pä-rä-ē'sō) Hond.	13·55 N	86·35 W
163	El Pardo (pä'r-dō) Sp. (Madrid In.)	40·31 N	3·47 W
118	El Paso (pas'ō) Tx.	31·47 N	106·27 W

ăt; finăl; rāte; senâte; ärm; åsk; sofȧ; fâre; ch-choose; dh-as th in other; bē; êvent; bĕt; recĕnt; cratẽr; g-go; gh-guttural g; bĭt; ĭ-short neutral; rīde; ĸ-guttural k as ch in German ich;

PRONOUNCING INDEX

El Pilar — Estrondo 279

Page	Name Pronunciation	Region	Lat. °′	Long. °′
135	El Pilar (pē-lä′r)	Ven. (In.)	9·56 N	64·48 W
127	El Porvenir (pôr-vä-nēr′)	Pan.	9·34 N	78·55 W
162	El Puerto de Sta. María (pwĕr tō dā sän tä mä-rē′ä)	Sp.	36·36 N	6·18 W
127	El Real (rā-äl)	Pan.	8·07 N	77·43 W
116	El Reno (rē′nō)	Ok.	35·31 N	97·57 W
135	El Roboré (rô-bō-rĕ′)	Bol.	18·23 S	59·43 W
109	Elroy (ĕl′roi)	Wi.	43·44 N	90·17 W
101	Elsa	Can.	63·55 N	135·25 W
113	Elsah (ĕl′zȧ)	Il. (St. Louis In.)	38·57 N	90·22 W
124	El Salto (säl′tō)	Mex.	22·48 N	105·22 W
122	El Salvador	N. A.	14·00 N	89·30 W
126	El Sauce (ĕl-sä′ōō-sĕ)	Nic.	13·00 N	86·40 W
117	Elsberry (ĕlz′bĕr-ĭ)	Mo.	39·09 N	90·44 W
161	Elsdorf (ĕls′dōrf)	F.R.G. (Ruhr In.)	50·56 N	6·35 E
113	El Segundo (sĕgŭn′dō)	Ca. (Los Angeles In.)	33·55 N	118·24 W
13	Elsinore (ĕl′sĭ-nôr)	Ca. (Los Angeles In.)	33·40 N	117·19 W
113	Elsinore L.	Ca. (Los Angeles In.)	33·38 N	117·21 W
149	Elstorf (ĕls′tōrf)	F.R.G. (Hamburg In.)	53·25 N	9·48 E
202	Eltham (ĕl′thăm)	Austl. (Melbourne In.)	37·43 S	145·08 E
134	El Tigre (tē′grĕ)	Ven.	8·49 N	64·15 W
171	El′ton (L.)	Sov. Un.	49·10 N	47·00 E
113	El Toro (tō′rō)	Ca. (Los Angeles In.)	33·37 N	117·42 W
126	El Triunfo (ĕl-trē-ōō′n-fô)	Hond.	13·06 N	87·00 W
126	El Triunfo	Sal.	13·17 N	88·32 W
187	Elūru	India	16·44 N	80·09 E
115	El Vado Res.	NM	36·37 N	106·30 W
162	Elvas (ĕl′väzh)	Port.	38·53 N	7·11 W
156	Elverum (ĕl′vĕ-rōōm)	Nor.	60·53 N	11·33 E
126	El Viego (ĕl-vyĕ′kŏ)	Nic.	12·10 N	87·10 W
126	El Viejo (Vol.)	Nic.	12·44 N	87·03 W
117	Elvins (ĕl′vĭnz)	Mo.	37·49 N	90·31 W
211	El Wak (wäk′)	Ken.	3·00 N	41·00 E
107	Elwood (ĕl′wŏŏd)	Il. (Chicago In.)	41·24 N	88·07 W
104	Elwood	In.	40·15 N	85·50 W
155	Ely (ē′lĭ)	Eng.	52·25 N	0·17 E
109	Ely	Mn.	47·54 N	91·53 W
114	Ely	Nv.	39·16 N	114·53 W
107	Elyria (ē-lĭr′ĭ-ȧ)	Oh. (Cleveland In.)	41·22 N	82·07 W
157	Ema (R.) (å′mà)	Sov. Un.	58·25 N	27·00 E
156	Emån (R.)	Swe.	57·15 N	15·46 E
171	Emba (R.) (yĕm′bȧ)	Sov. Un.	46·50 N	54·10 E
134	Embalse Guri (L.)	Ven.	7·30 N	63·00 W
104	Embarrass (R.) (ĕm-băr′ăs)	Il.	39·15 N	88·05 W
89	Embrun (ĕm′brŭn)	Can. (Ottawa In.)	45·16 N	75·17 W
161	Embrun (äN-brûN′)	Fr.	44·35 N	6·32 E
217	Embu	Ken.	0·32 S	37·27 E
158	Emden (ĕm′dĕn)	F.R.G.	53·21 N	7·15 E
205	Emerald (ĕm′ēr-ăld)	Austl.	28·34 S	148·00 E
95	Emerson (ĕm′ēr-sŭn)	Can.	49·00 N	97·12 W
112	Emeryville (ĕm′ēr-ĭ-vĭl)	Ca. (San Francisco In.)	37·50 N	122·17 W
215	Emi Koussi, (Mtn.) (ā′mē kōō-sē′)	Chad	19·50 N	18·30 E
164	Emilia-Romagna (Reg.) (ā-mēl′yä rô-mà′n-yä)	It.	44·35 N	10·48 E
125	Emiliano Zapata (ĕ-mē-lyà′nô-zä-pà′tà)	Mex.	17·45 N	91·46 W
104	Eminence (ĕm′ĭ-nĕns)	Ky.	38·25 N	85·15 W
197	Emirau (I.) (ā-mē-rä′ōō)	Pap. N. Gui.	1·40 S	150·28 E
155	Emmen (ĕm′ĕn)	Neth.	52·48 N	6·55 E
161	Emmerich (ĕm′ēr-ĭk)	F.R.G. (Ruhr In.)	51·51 N	6·16 E
109	Emmetsburg (ĕm′ĕts-bûrg)	Ia.	43·07 N	94·41 W
110	Emmett (ĕm′ĕt)	Id.	43·53 N	116·30 W
111	Emmons Mt. (ĕm′ŭnz)	Ut.	40·43 N	110·20 W
118	Emory Pk. (ĕ′mô-rē pēk)	Tx.	29·13 N	103·20 W
164	Empoli (ām′pô-lē)	It.	43·43 N	10·55 E
117	Emporia (ĕm-pō′rĭ-ȧ)	Ks.	38·24 N	96·11 W
121	Emporia	Va.	37·40 N	77·34 W
105	Emporium (ĕm-pō′rĭ-ŭm)	Pa.	41·30 N	78·15 W
158	Ems R. (ĕms)	F.R.G.	52·52 N	7·16 E
158	Ems-Weser (Can.) (vā′zĕr)	F.R.G.	52·23 N	8·11 E
158	Enånger (ĕn-ôŋ′gĕr)	Swe.	61·36 N	16·55 E
122	Encantada, Cerro de la (Mtn.) (sĕ′r-rô-dĕ-lä-ĕn-kän-tä′dä)	Mex.	31·58 N	115·15 W
197	Encanto Pt. (ĕn-kän′tō)	Phil. (In.)	15·44 N	121·46 E
136	Encarnación (ĕn-kär-nä-syōn′)	Par.	27·26 S	55·52 W
124	Encarnación de Diaz (ĕn-kär-nä-syōn dà dē′äz)	Mex.	21·34 N	102·15 W
118	Encinal (ĕn′sĭ-nôl)	Tx.	28·02 N	99·22 W
134	Encontrados (ĕn-kōn-trä′dōs)	Ven.	9·01 N	72·10 W
203	Encounter B. (ĕn-koun′tēr)	Austl.	35·50 S	138·45 E
92	Endako (R.)	Can.	54·05 N	125·30 W
183	Endau (R.)	Mala. (Singapore In.)	2·29 N	103·40 E
198	Enderbury (I.) (ĕn′dĕr-bûrĭ)	Oceania	2·00 S	107·50 W
220	Enderby Land (Reg.) (ĕn′dĕr bĭl)	Ant.	72·00 S	52·00 E
108	Enderlin (ĕn′dĕr-lĭn)	ND	46·38 N	97·37 W
105	Endicott (ĕn′dĭ-kŏt)	NY	42·05 N	76·00 W
101	Endicott Mts.	Ak.	67·30 N	153·45 W
165	Enez	Tur.	40·42 N	26·05 E
105	Enfield (ĕn′fēld)	Ct.	41·55 N	72·35 W
148	Enfield	Eng. (London In.)	51·38 N	0·06 W
121	Enfield	NC	36·10 N	77·41 W
129	Engano, Cabo (C.) (kà′-bô-ĕn-gä-nô)	Dom. Rep.	18·40 N	68·30 W
196	Engaño, C. (ĕn-gän′yō)	Phil.	18·40 N	122·45 E
213	Engcobo (ĕŋ-cô-bô)	S. Afr. (Natal In.)	31·41 S	27·59 E
171	Engel′s (ĕn′gĕls)	Sov. Un.	51·20 N	45·40 E
161	Engelskirchen (ĕn′gĕls-kēr′kĕn)	F.R.G. (Ruhr In.)	50·59 N	7·25 E
116	Engelwood (ĕn′g′l-wŏŏd)	Co.	39·39 N	105·00 W
196	Enggano (I.) (ĕng-gä′nō)	Indon.	5·22 S	102·18 E
117	England (ĭŋ′glănd)	Ar.	34·33 N	91·58 W
154	England (Reg.) (ĭŋ′glănd)	U. K.	51·35 N	1·40 W
99	Englee (ĕn-glē)	Can.	50·44 N	56·06 W
106	Englewood	NJ (New York In.)	40·54 N	73·59 W
104	English (ĭn′glĭsh)	In.	38·15 N	86·25 W
91	English (R.)	Can.	50·31 N	94·12 W
151	English Chan.	Eng.	49·45 N	3·06 W
163	Énguera (ān′gārä)	Sp.	38·58 N	0·42 W
116	Enid (ē′nĭd)	Ok.	36·25 N	97·52 W
120	Enid Res.	Ms.	34·13 N	89·47 W
212	Enkeldoorn (ĕŋ′k′l-dōōrn)	Rh.	19·59 S	30·58 E
218	Enkeldoring (ĕŋ′k′l-dôr-ĭng)	S.Afr. (Johannesburg & Pretoria In.)	25·24 S	28·43 E
156	Enköping (ĕn′kû-pĭng)	Swe.	59·39 N	17·05 E
211	Ennedi (Plat.) (ĕn-nĕd′ē)	Chad.	16·45 N	22·45 E
154	Ennis (ĕn′ĭs)	Ire.	52·54 N	9·05 W
119	Ennis	Tx.	32·20 N	96·38 W
154	Enniscorthy (ĕn-ĭs-kôr′thĭ)	Ire.	52·33 N	6·27 W
154	Enniskillen (ĕn-ĭs-kĭl′ĕn)	N. Ire.	54·20 N	7·25 W
158	Enns (R.) (ĕns)	Aus.	47·37 N	14·35 E
121	Enoree (ē-nō′rē)	SC	34·43 N	81·58 W
121	Enoree, (R.)	SC	34·35 N	81·55 W
129	Enriquillo (ĕn-rē-kē′l-yô)	Dom. Rep.	17·55 N	71·15 W
129	Enriquillo, Lago (L.) (lä′gô-ĕn-rē-kē′l-yô)	Dom. Rep.	18·35 N	71·35 W
155	Enschede (ĕns′kā-dĕ)	Neth.	52·10 N	6·50 E
122	Ensenada (ĕn-sĕ-nä′dä)	Mex.	32·00 N	116·30 W
137	Enseñada	Arg. (Buenos Aires In.)	34·50 S	57·55 W
193	Enshih	China	30·18 N	109·25 E
195	Enshū-Nada (Sea) (ĕn′shōō nä-dä)	Jap.	34·25 N	137·14 E
217	Entebbe (ĕn-tĕb′ĕ)	Ug.	0·04 N	32·28 E
120	Enterprise (ĕn′tēr-prīz)	Al.	31·20 N	85·50 W
110	Enterprise	Or.	45·25 N	117·16 W
110	Entiat, L.	Wa.	45·43 N	120·11 W
160	Entraygues (ĕN-trĕg′)	Fr.	44·39 N	2·33 E
217	Entre-Rios (ĕn-trā rē′ōs)	Moz.	14·57 S	37·20 E
136	Entre Ríos (Prov.)	Arg.	31·30 S	59·00 W
215	Enugu (ĕ-nōō′gōō)	Nig.	6·27 N	7·27 E
112	Enumclaw (ĕn′ŭm-klô)	Wa. (Seattle In.)	47·12 N	121·59 W
134	Envigado (ĕn-vē-gä′dŏ)	Col. (In.)	6·10 N	75·34 W
164	Eolie, Isole (Is.) (ĕ-ô′lē-ĕ-ô′lyĕ)	It.	38·43 N	14·43 E
215	Epe	Nig.	6·37 N	3·59 E
165	Epeirus (Reg.)	Grc.	39·35 N	20·45 E
160	Epernay (ā-pĕr-nĕ′)	Fr.	49·02 N	3·54 E
161	Épernon (ā-pĕr-nôN′)	Fr. (Paris In.)	48·36 N	1·41 E
115	Ephraim (ē′frā-ĭm)	Ut.	39·20 N	111·40 W
110	Ephrata (ē frā′tȧ)	Wa.	47·18 N	119·35 W
205	Epi (ā′pē)	New Hebr.	16·59 S	168·29 E
162	Épila (ā′pē-lä)	Sp.	41·38 N	1·15 W
161	Épinal (ā-pē-nàl′)	Fr.	48·11 N	6·27 E
183	Episkopi	Cyprus (Palestine In.)	34·38 N	32·55 E
148	Epping (ĕp′ĭng)	Eng. (London In.)	51·41 N	0·06 E
216	Epupa Falls	Ang.	17·00 S	13·05 E
148	Epworth (ĕp′wûrth)	Eng.	53·31 N	0·50 W
210	Equatorial Guinea	Afr.	2·00 N	7·15 E
160	Equeurdreville (ā-kûr-dr′vēl′)	Fr.	49·38 N	1·42 W
89	Eramosa (R.) (ĕr-ȧ-mō′sȧ)	Can. (Toronto In.)	43·39 N	80·08 W
211	Erba, Jabal (Mtn.) (ĕr′bȧ)	Sud.	20·53 N	36·45 E
153	Erciyas (Mtn.)	Tur.	38·30 N	35·36 E
113	Erda (ĕr′dä)	Ut. (Salt Lake City In.)	40·41 N	112·17 W
149	Erding (ĕr′dĕng)	F.R.G. (Munich In.)	48·19 N	11·54 E
136	Erechim (ĕ-rĕ-shē′N)	Braz.	27·43 S	52·11 W
171	Ereğli (ĕ-rā′ĭ-le)	Tur.	37·40 N	34·00 E
171	Ereğli	Tur.	41·15 N	31·25 E
158	Erfurt (ĕr′fŏŏrt)	G.D.R.	50·59 N	11·04 E
165	Ergene (R.) (ĕr′gĕ-nĕ)	Tur.	41·17 N	26·50 E
162	Erges (R.) (ĕr′-zhĕs)	Port.-Sp.	39·45 N	7·01 W
157	Ergli	Sov. Un.	56·54 N	25·38 E
190	Erhlangtien (ĕr′läng′diän)	China	31·33 N	114·07 E
162	Eria (R.) (ā-rē′ä)	Sp.	42·10 N	6·08 W
116	Erick (âr′ĭk)	Ok.	35·14 N	99·51 W
117	Erie (ē′rĭ)	Ks.	37·35 N	95·17 W
105	Erie	Pa.	42·05 N	80·05 W
103	Erie, L.	U. S.-Can.	42·15 N	81·25 W
194	Erimo Saki (C.) (ā′rē-mō sä-kē)	Jap.	41·53 N	143·20 E
89	Erin (ĕ′rĭn)	Can. (Toronto In.)	43·46 N	80·04 W
211	Eritrea (Reg.) (ā-rē-trā′à)	Eth.	16·15 N	38·30 E
158	Erlangen (ĕr′läng-ĕn)	F.R.G.	49·36 N	11·03 E
107	Erlanger (ĕr′lăng-ĕr)	Ky. (Cincinnati In.)	39·01 N	84·36 W
	Ermoúpolis, see Síros			
185	Ernākulam	India	9·58 N	76·23 E
154	Erne, Upper Lough (L.) (lŏk ûrn)	N. Ire.	54·20 N	7·24 W
154	Erne, Lough (L.)	N. Ire.	54·30 N	7·40 W
91	Ernest Sound (ûr′nĭst)	Ak.	55·52 N	132·10 W
185	Erode	India	11·20 N	77·45 E
205	Eromanga (I.)	New Hebr.	18·58 S	169·18 E
119	Eros (ē′rōs)	La.	32·23 N	92·22 W
217	Errego	Moz.	16·02 S	37·14 E
152	Er Ricani	Mor.	31·09 N	4·20 W
154	Errigal, Mt. (ĕr-ĭ-gôl′)	Ire.	55·02 N	8·07 W
112	Errol Heights	Or. (Portland In.)	45·29 N	122·38 W
161	Erstein (ĕr′shtīn)	Fr.	48·27 N	7·40 E
121	Erwin (ûr′wĭn)	NC	35·16 N	78·40 W
121	Erwin	Tn.	36·07 N	82·25 W
158	Erzgebirge (Ore Mts.) (ĕrts′gĕ-bē′gĕ)	G.D.R.	50·29 N	12·40 E
171	Erzincan (ĕr-zĭn-jän′)	Tur.	39·50 N	39·30 E
171	Erzurum (ĕrz′rōōm′)	Tur.	39·55 N	41·10 E
216	Esambo	Zaire	3·40 S	23·24 E
194	Esashi (ĕs′ä-shē)	Jap.	41·50 N	140·10 E
156	Esbjerg (ĕs′byĕrgh)	Den.	55·29 N	8·25 E
162	Escairón (ĕs-kī-rō′n)	Sp.	42·34 N	7·40 W
115	Escalante (ĕs-kȧ-lăn′tē)	Ut.	37·50 N	111·40 W
115	Escalante (R.)	Ut.	37·40 N	111·20 W
118	Escalón	Mex.	26·45 N	104·20 W
120	Escambia (R.) (ĕs-kăm′bĭ-ȧ)	Fl.	30·38 N	87·20 W
109	Escanaba (ĕs-kȧ-nô′bȧ)	Mi.	45·44 N	87·05 W
109	Escanaba (R.)	Mi.	46·10 N	87·22 W
161	Esch-sur-Alzette	Lux.	49·32 N	6·21 E
158	Eschwege (ĕsh′vā-gĕ)	F.R.G.	51·11 N	10·02 E
161	Eschweiler (ĕsh′vī-lēr)	F.R.G. (Ruhr In.)	50·49 N	6·15 E
129	Escocesá, Bahia (B.) (bä-ē′ä-ĕs-kō-sĕ′sä)	Dom. Rep.	19·25 N	69·40 W
114	Escondido (ĕs-kŏn-dē′dō)	Ca.	33·07 N	117·00 W
118	Escondido, Rio (R.) (rē′ō-ĕs-kōn-dē′dô)	Mex.	28·30 N	100·45 W
127	Escondido R.	Nic.	12·04 N	84·09 W
127	Escudo de Veraguas I. (ĕs-kōō′dä dā vä-rä′gwäs)	Pan.	9·07 N	81·25 W
124	Escuinapa (ĕs-kwē-nä′pä)	Mex.	22·49 N	105·44 W
126	Escuintla (ĕs-kwēn′tlä)	Guat.	14·16 N	90·47 W
125	Escuintla	Mex.	15·20 N	92·45 W
127	Ese, Cayos de (I.)	Col.	12·24 N	81·07 W
186	Esfahān	Iran	32·38 N	51·30 E
162	Esgueva (R.) (ĕs-gĕ′vä)	Sp.	41·48 N	4·10 W
213	Eshowe (ĕsh′ô-wē)	S. Afr. (Natal In.)	28·54 S	31·28 E
214	Esiama	Ghana	4·56 N	2·21 W
104	Eskdale (ĕsk′dāl)	WV	38·05 N	81·25 W
150	Eskifjördhur (ĕs′kē-fyŭr′dōōr)	Ice.	65·04 N	14·01 W
156	Eskilstuna (å′shĕl-stü-na)	Swe.	59·23 N	16·28 E
90	Eskimo Lakes (L.) (es′kĭ-mō)	Can.	69·40 N	130·10 W
171	Eskişehir (ĕs-kê-shĕ′h′r)	Tur.	39·40 N	30·20 E
113	Esko (ĕs′kô)	Mn. (Duluth In.)	46·27 N	92·22 W
162	Esla (R.) (ĕs-lä)	Sp.	41·50 N	5·48 W
156	Eslöv (ĕs′lûv)	Swe.	55·50 N	13·17 E
134	Esmeraldas (ĕs-mȧ-räl′däs)	Ec.	0·58 N	79·45 W
129	Espada, Punta (Pt.) (pōō′n-tä-ĕs-pä′dä)	Dom. Rep.	18·30 N	68·30 W
96	Espanola (ĕs-pȧ-nō′lȧ)	Can.	46·11 N	81·59 W
127	Esparta (ĕs-pär′tä)	C. R.	9·59 N	84·40 W
204	Esperance (ĕs′pē-răns)	Austl.	33·45 S	122·07 E
128	Esperanza (ĕs-pĕ-rä′n-zä)	Cuba	22·30 N	80·10 W
163	Espichel, Cabo (C.) (kà′bō-ĕs-pĕ-shĕl′)	Port. (Lisbon In.)	38·25 N	9·13 W
134	Espinal (ĕs-pē-näl′)	Col. (In.)	4·10 N	74·53 W
135	Espinhaço, Serra do (Mts.) (sĕ′r-rä-dô-ĕs-pē-nä-sô)	Braz.	16·06 S	44·56 W
137	Espinillo, Punta (Pt.) (pōō′n-tä-ĕs-pē-nē′l-yô)	Ur. (Buenos Aires In.)	34·49 S	56·27 W
135	Espírito Santo (ĕs-pē′rē-tô-sän′tô)	Braz.	20·27 S	40·18 W
135	Espírito Santo (State)	Braz.	19·57 S	40·58 W
126	Espíritu Santo, Bahia del (B.) (bä-ē′ä-dĕl-ĕs-pē′rē-tōō-sän′tô)	Mex. (In.)	19·25 N	87·28 W
205	Espiritu Santo (I.) (ĕs-pē′rē-tōō sän′tō)	New Hebr.	15·45 S	166·50 E
126	Espita (ĕs-pē′tä)	Mex. (In.)	20·57 N	88·22 W
157	Espoo	Fin.	60·13 N	24·41 E
162	Esposende (ĕs-pō-zĕn′dā)	Port.	41·33 N	8·45 W
136	Esquel (ĕs-kĕ′l)	Arg.	42·47 S	71·22 W
112	Esquimalt (ĕs-kwī′mŏlt)	Can. (Seattle In.)	48·26 N	123·24 W
210	Essaouira	Mor.	31·34 N	9·44 W
149	Essen	Bel. (Brussels In.)	51·28 N	4·27 E
161	Essen (ĕs′sĕn)	F.R.G. (Ruhr In.)	51·26 N	6·59 E
135	Essequibo (R.) (ĕs-ā-kē′bō)	Guy.	4·26 N	58·17 W
107	Essex	Il. (Chicago In.)	41·11 N	88·11 W
106	Essex	(Md. (Baltimore In.)	39·19 N	76·29 W
99	Essex	Ma. (In.)	42·38 N	70·47 W
105	Essex	Vt.	44·30 N	73·05 W
106	Essex Fells (ĕs′ĕks fĕlz)	NJ (New York In.)	40·50 N	74·16 W
104	Essexville (ĕs′ĕks-vĭl)	Mi.	43·35 N	83·50 W
158	Esslingen (ĕs′slĕn-gĕn)	F.R.G.	48·45 N	9·19 E
102	Estacado, Llano (Plain) (yà-nō ĕs-tȧ-cȧ-dō′)	U. S.	33·50 N	103·20 W
136	Estados, Isla de los	S. A.	55·05 S	63·00 W
135	Estância (ĕs-tän′sĭ-ä)	Braz.	11·17 S	37·18 W
162	Estarreja (ĕs-tär-rā′zhä)	Port.	40·44 N	8·39 W
210	Estcourt (ĕst-coort)	S. Afr. (Natal In.)	29·04 S	29·53 E
164	Este (ĕs′tā	It.	45·13 N	11·40 E
126	Estelí (ĕs-tā-lē′)	Nic.	13·10 N	86·23 W
162	Estella (ĕs-tāl′yä)	Sp.	42·40 N	2·01 W
162	Estepa (ĕs-tā′pä)	Sp.	37·18 N	4·54 W
162	Estepona (ĕs-tå-pō′nä)	Sp.	36·26 N	5·08 W
95	Esterhazy (ĕs′tēr-hä-zē)	Can.	50·40 N	102·08 W
114	Esteros, B. (ĕs-tä′rōs)	Ca.	35·22 N	121·04 W
94	Estevan (ĕ-stē′vȧn)	Can.	49·07 N	103·05 W
92	Estevan Group (Is.)	Can.	53·05 N	129·40 W
109	Estherville (ĕs′tēr-vĭl)	Ia.	43·24 N	94·49 W
121	Estill (ĕs′tĭl)	SC	32·46 N	81·15 W
94	Eston	Can.	51·10 N	108·45 W
168	Estonian S. S. R. (ĕs-tō′nĭ-ä)	Sov. Un.	59·10 N	25·00 E
163	Estoril (ĕs-tô-rēl′)	Port. (Lisbon In.)	38·45 N	9·24 W
136	Estrêla (R.) (ĕs-trĕ′là)	Braz. (Rio de Janeiro In.)	22·39 S	43·16 W
162	Estrêla, Serra da (Mts.) (sĕr′rȧ dä ĕs-trā′lȧ)	Port.	40·25 N	7·45 W
162	Estremadura (Reg.) (ĕs-trā-mä-dōō′rȧ)	Port.	41·35 N	8·36 W
162	Estremoz (ĕs-trā-mōzh′)	Port.	38·50 N	7·35 W
135	Estrondo, Serra do (Mts.) (sĕr′rȧ dōō ĕs-trôn′dōō)	Braz.	9·52 S	48·56 W

ng-sing; ŋ-baŋk; N-nasalized n; nŏd; cŏmmit; ōld; ôbey; ôrder; fōōd; fŏŏt; ou-out; s-soft; sh-dish; th-thin; pūre; ûnite; ûrn; stŭd; circŭs; ü-as "y" in study; ′-indeterminate vowel.

Page	Name	Pronunciation	Region	Lat. °′	Long. °′
216	Esumba, Île (I.)		Zaire	2·00 N	21·12 E
159	Esztergom	(ĕs'tĕr-gōm)	Hung.	47·46 N	18·45 E
75	Etah	(ē'tă)	Grnld.	78·20 N	72·42 W
161	Étampes	(ā-tänp')	Fr. (Paris In.)	48·26 N	2·09 E
160	Étaples	(ā-tàp'l')	Fr.	50·32 N	1·38 E
89	Etchemin (R.)	(ĕch'ĕ-mĭn)	Can. (Quebec In.)	46·39 N	71·03 W
209	Ethiopa	(ê-thê-ō'pê-à)	Afr.	7·53 N	37·55 E
214	Eticoga		Guinea-Bissau	11·09 N	16·08 W
113	Etiwanda	(ĕ-tǐ-wän'dà)	Ca. (Los Angeles In.)	34·07 N	117·31 W
	Etlatongo, see San Mateo				
107	Etna	(ĕt'nà)	Pa. (Pittsburgh In.)	40·30 N	79·55 W
164	Etna, Mt. (Vol.)		It.	37·48 N	15·00 E
89	Etobicoke		Can. (Toronto In.)	43·39 N	79·34 W
89	Etobicoke Cr.		Can. (Toronto In.)	43·44 N	79·48 W
89	Etolin Str.	(ĕt ō lǐn)	Ak.	60·35 S	165·40 W
212	Etoshapan (L.)	(ĕtō'shä)	Namibia	19·07 S	15·30 E
120	Etowah	(ĕt'ō-wä)	Tn.	35·18 N	84·31 W
120	Etowah (R.)		Ga.	34·23 N	84·19 W
161	Étréchy	(ā-trā-shē')	Fr. (Paris In.)	48·29 N	2·12 E
149	Etten		Neth. (Amsterdam In.)	51·34 N	4·38 E
149	Etterbeek	(ĕt'ĕr-bāk)	Bel. (Brussels In.)	50·51 N	4·24 E
124	Etzatlán	(ĕt-zä-tlän')	Mex.	20·44 N	104·04 W
204	Eucla	(ū'klä)	Austl.	31·45 S	128·50 E
107	Euclid	(ū'klĭd)	Oh. (Cleveland In.)	41·34 N	81·32 W
117	Eudora	(u-dō'rà)	Ar.	33·07 N	91·16 W
120	Eufaula	(û-fô'là)	Al.	31·53 N	85·09 W
117	Eufaula		Ok.	35·16 N	95·35 W
117	Eufaula Res.		Ok.	35·00 N	94·45 W
110	Eugene	(û-jēn')	Or.	44·02 N	123·06 W
113	Euless	(ū'lĕs)	Tx. (Dallas, Fort Worth In.)	32·50 N	97·05 W
119	Eunice	(ū'nĭs)	La.	30·30 N	92·25 W
155	Eupen	(oi'pĕn)	Bel.	50·39 N	6·05 E
186	Euphrates (R.)	(û-frā'tēz)	Asia	36·00 N	39·30 E
160	Eure (R.)	(ûr)	Fr.	49·03 N	1·22 E
110	Eureka	(û-rē'kà)	Ca.	40·45 N	124·10 W
117	Eureka		Ks.	37·48 N	96·17 W
110	Eureka		Mt.	48·53 N	115·07 W
114	Eureka		Nv.	39·33 N	115·58 W
108	Eureka		SD	45·46 N	99·38 W
115	Eureka		Ut.	39·55 N	112·10 W
117	Eureka Springs		Ar.	36·24 N	93·43 W
186	Eurgun (Mtn.)		Iran	28·47 N	57·00 E
146	Europe	(ū'rŭp)			
121	Eustis	(ūs'tĭs)	Fl.	28·50 N	81·41 W
120	Eutaw	(ū-tä)	Al.	32·48 N	87·50 W
92	Eutsuk L.	(ōōt'sŭk)	Can.	53·20 N	126·44 W
156	Evanger	(ê-väng'ğĕr)	Nor.	60·40 N	6·06 E
107	Evanston	(ĕv'ăn-stŭn)	Il. (Chicago In.)	42·03 N	87·41 W
111	Evanston		Wy.	41·17 N	111·02 W
104	Evansville	(ĕv'ănz-vǐl)	In.	38·00 N	87·30 W
109	Evansville		Wi.	42·46 N	89·19 W
104	Evart	(ĕv'ẽrt)	Mi.	43·55 N	85·10 W
218	Evaton		S. Afr. (Johannesburg & Pretoria In.)	26·32 S	27·53 E
109	Eveleth	(ĕv'ê-lĕth)	Mn.	47·27 N	92·35 W
204	Everard (L.)	(ĕv'ēr-àrd)	Austl.	36·20 S	134·10 E
204	Everard Ra.		Austl.	27·15 S	132·00 E
184	Everest, Mt.	(ĕv'ēr-ĕst)	Nep.-China	28·00 N	86·57 E
99	Everett	(ĕv'ēr-ĕt)	Ma. (In.)	42·24 N	71·03 W
112	Everett	(ĕv'ēr-ĕt)	Wa. (Seattle In.)	47·59 N	122·11 W
91	Everett Mts.		Can.	62·34 N	68·00 W
121	Everglades	(ĕv'ēr-glādz)	Fl.	25·50 N	81·25 W
128	Everglades, The (Swp.)		Fl.	25·35 S	80·55 W
121	Everglades Natl. Park		Fl. (In.)	25·39 N	80·57 W
120	Evergreen	(ĕv'ēr-grēn)	Al.	31·25 N	87·56 W
107	Evergreen Park		Il. (Chicago In.)	41·44 N	87·42 W
113	Everman	(ĕv'ēr-măn)	Tx. (Dallas, Fort Worth In.)	32·38 N	97·17 W
112	Everson	(ĕv'ēr-sŭn)	Wa. (Vancouver In.)	48·55 N	122·21 W
162	Évora	(ĕv'ô-rä)	Port.	38·35 N	7·54 W
160	Évreux	(ā-vrû')	Fr.	49·02 N	1·11 E
165	Evrotas (R.)	(ĕv-rō'täs)	Grc.	37·15 N	22·17 E
165	Evvoia (I.)		Grc.	38·38 N	23·45 E
100	Ewa Beach	(ĕ'wä)	Hi.	21·17 N	158·03 E
211	Ewaso Ng'iro (R.)		Ken.	0·59 N	37·47 E
113	Excelsior	(ĕk-sel'sǐ-ŏr)	Mn. (Minneapolis, St. Paul In.)	44·54 N	93·35 W
117	Excelsior Springs		Mo.	39·20 N	94·13 W
154	Exe (R.)	(ĕks)	Eng.	50·57 N	3·37 W
114	Exeter	(ĕk'sê-tēr)	Ca.	36·18 N	119·09 W
154	Exeter		Eng.	50·45 N	3·33 W
105	Exeter		NH	43·00 N	71·00 W
154	Exmoor	(ĕks'mōōr)	Eng.	51·10 N	3·55 W
154	Exmouth	(ĕks'mŭth)	Eng.	50·40 N	3·20 W
204	Exmouth, G.		Austl.	21·45 S	114·30 E
99	Exploits (R.)	(ĕks-ploits')	Can.	48·50 N	56·10 W
124	Extórrax (R.)	(ĕx-tó'ráx)	Mex.	21·04 N	99·39 W
137	Extrema	(ĕs-trē'mä)	Braz. (Rio de Janeiro In.)	22·52 S	46·19 W
162	Extremadura (Reg.)	(ĕks-trā-mä-doo'rä)	Sp.	38·43 N	6·30 W
129	Exuma Sd.	(ĕk-sōō'mä)	Ba.	24·20 N	76·20 W
217	Eyasi, L.	(à-yä'sĕ)	Tan.	3·25 S	34·55 E
150	Eyja Fd.		Ice.	66·21 N	18·20 W
156	Eyrarbakki		Ice.	63·51 N	20·52 W
204	Eyre	(âr)	Austl.	32·15 S	126·20 E
203	Eyre (L.)		Austl.	28·43 S	137·50 E
204	Eyre Pen.		Austl.	33·30 S	136·00 E
136	Ezeiza	(ĕ-zā'zä)	Arg. (Buenos Aires In.)	34·36 S	58·31 W
165	Ezine	(à'zǐ-nà)	Tur.	39·47 N	26·18 E

F

Page	Name	Pronunciation	Region	Lat. °′	Long. °′
118	Fabens	(fā'bĕnz)	Tx.	31·30 N	106·07 W
156	Fåborg	(fô'bôrg)	Den.	55·06 N	10·19 E
164	Fabriano	(fä-brē-ä'nō)	It.	43·20 N	12·55 E
134	Facativá	(fä-kä-tä-tê-vá')	Col. (In.)	4·49 N	74·09 W
211	Fada	(fä'dä)	Chad	17·06 N	21·18 E
214	Fada Ngourma	(fä'dä'n gōōr'mä)	Upper Volta	12·04 N	0·21 E
173	Faddeya (I.)	(fàd'yä')	Sov. Un.	76·12 N	145·00 E
156	Faemund (L.)	(fà'mōōn)	Nor.	62·17 N	11·40 E
164	Faenza	(fä-ĕnd'zä)	It.	44·16 N	11·53 E
146	Faeroe Is.	(fā'rō)	Eur.	62·00 N	5·45 W
162	Fafe	(fä'fä)	Port.	41·30 N	8·10 W
218	Fafen (R.)		Eth. (Horn of Afr. In.)	8·15 N	42·40 E
165	Făgăraş	(fá-gà'räsh)	Rom.	45·50 N	24·55 E
156	Fagerness	(fä'ghĕr-nĕs)	Nor.	61·00 N	9·10 E
136	Fagnano (L.)	(fäk-nä'nō)	Arg.-Chile	54·35 S	68·20 W
214	Faguibine, Lac (L.)		Mali	16·50 N	4·20 W
210	Faial I.	(fä-yä'l)	Açores	38·40 N	29·19 W
218	Fā'id	(fä-yēd')	Egypt (Suez In.)	30·19 N	32·18 E
154	Fair (I.)	(fâr)	Scot.	59·34 N	1·41 W
101	Fairbanks	(fâr'bănks)	Ak.	64·50 N	147·48 W
104	Fairbury	(fâr'bĕr-ĭ)	Il.	40·45 N	88·25 W
117	Fairbury		Ne.	40·09 N	97·11 W
89	Fairchild Cr.	(fâr'chĭld)	Can. (Toronto In.)	43·18 N	80·10 W
109	Fairfax	(fâr'fäks)	Mn.	44·29 N	94·44 W
121	Fairfax		SC	32·29 N	81·13 W
106	Fairfax		Va. (Baltimore In.)	38·51 N	77·20 W
106	Fairfield	(fâr'fēld)	Al. (Birmingham In.)	33·30 N	86·50 W
202	Fairfield		Austl. (Sydney In.)	33·52 S	150·57 E
106	Fairfield		Ct. (New York In.)	41·08 N	73·22 W
104	Fairfield		Il.	38·25 N	88·20 W
109	Fairfield		Ia.	41·00 N	91·59 W
98	Fairfield		Me.	44·35 N	69·38 W
105	Fairhaven	(fâr-hā'vĕn)	Ma.	41·35 N	70·55 W
105	Fair Haven		Vt.	43·35 N	73·15 W
109	Fairmont	(fâr'mŏnt)	Mn.	43·39 N	94·26 W
105	Fairmont		WV	39·30 N	80·10 W
113	Fairmont City		Il. (St. Louis In.)	38·39 N	90·05 W
104	Fairmount		In.	40·25 N	85·45 W
113	Fairmount		Ks. (Kansas City In.)	39·12 N	95·55 W
106	Fair Oaks	(fâr ōks)	Ga. (Atlanta In.)	33·56 N	84·33 W
105	Fairport	(fâr'pōrt)	NY	43·05 N	77·30 W
104	Fairport Harbor		Oh.	41·45 N	81·15 W
116	Fairview	(fâr'vū)	Ok.	36·16 N	98·28 W
112	Fairview		Or. (Portland In.)	45·32 N	112·26 W
115	Fairview		Ut.	39·35 N	111·30 W
107	Fairview Park		Oh. (Cleveland In.)	41·27 N	81·52 W
101	Fairweather, Mt.	(fâr-wĕdh'ēr)	Can.	59·12 N	137·22 W
108	Faith	(fāth)	SD	45·02 N	120·02 W
184	Faizābād		India	26·50 N	82·17 E
123	Fajardo		P. R. (Puerto Rico In.)	18·20 N	65·40 W
197	Fakfak		Indon.	2·56 S	132·25 E
192	Fak'u		China	42·28 N	123·20 E
193	Falalise, C.		Viet.	19·20 N	106·18 E
135	Falcón (State)	(fäl-kô'n)	Ven. (In.)	11·00 N	68·28 W
105	Falconer	(fô'k'n-ēr)	NY	42·10 N	79·10 W
113	Falcon Heights	(fô'k'n)	Mn. (Minneapolis, St. Paul In.)	44·59 N	93·10 W
118	Falcon Res.	(fôk'n)	Tx.	26·47 N	99·03 W
214	Falemé (R.)	(fà-lā-mä')	Afr.	13·40 N	12·00 W
167	Faleshty	(fä-lĕsh'tĭ)	Sov. Un.	47·33 N	27·46 E
118	Falfurrias	(fäl'fōō-rē'às)	Tx.	27·15 N	98·08 W
93	Falher	(fäl'ēr)	Can.	55·44 N	117·12 W
156	Falkenberg	(fäl'kĕn-bĕrgh)	Swe.	56·54 N	12·25 E
149	Falkensee	(fäl'kĕn-zā)	G.D.R. (Berlin In.)	52·34 N	13·05 E
149	Falkenthal	(fäl'kĕn-täl)	G.D.R. (Berlin In.)	52·54 N	13·18 E
154	Falkirk	(fôl'kûrk)	Scot.	55·59 N	3·55 W
136	Falkland Is.	(fôk'lånd)	S. A.	50·45 S	61·00 W
156	Falköping	(fäl'chŭp-ĭng)	Swe.	58·09 N	13·30 E
112	Fall City		Wa. (Seattle In.)	47·34 N	121·53 W
107	Fall Cr.	(fôl)	In. (Indianapolis In.)	39·52 N	86·04 W
114	Fallon	(fäl'ŭn)	Nv.	39·30 N	118·48 W
106	Fall River		Ma. (Providence In.)	41·42 N	71·07 W
106	Falls Church		Va. (Baltimore In.)	38·53 N	77·10 W
117	Falls City		Ne.	40·04 N	95·37 W
154	Fallston	(fäls'ton)	Md. (Baltimore In.)	39·32 N	76·26 W
154	Falmouth	(fäl'mŭth)	Eng.	50·08 N	3·04 W
128	Falmouth		Jam.	18·30 N	77·40 W
104	Falmouth		Ky.	38·40 N	84·20 W
	False (B.), see Valsbaai				
183	False Divi Pt.		India	15·45 N	80·50 E
129	Falso, Cabo (C.)	(kä'bō-fäl-sō)	Dom. Rep.	17·45 N	71·55 W
156	Falster (I.)	(fäls'tĕr)	Den.	54·48 N	11·58 E
159	Fălticeni	(fûl-tê-chán'y)	Rom.	47·27 N	26·17 E
156	Falun	(fä-lōōn')	Swe.	60·38 N	15·35 E
153	Famagusta	(fä-mä-gōōs'tä)	Cyprus	35·08 N	33·59 E
136	Famatina, Sierra de (Mts.)	(sĕ-ĕ'r-rä-dĕ-fä-mä-tē'nä)	Arg.	29·00 S	67·50 W
193	Fan Ching Shan (Mts.)		China	26·40 N	107·42 E
193	Fanghsien		China	32·05 N	110·45 E
199	Fanning (I.)	(făn'ĭng)	Gilbert & Ellice Is.	4·20 N	159·00 W
89	Fannystelle	(făn'ĭ-stĕl)	Can. (Winnipeg In.)	49·45 N	97·46 W
164	Fano	(fä'nō)	It.	43·49 N	13·01 E
156	Fanø (I.)	(fän'ŭ)	Den.	55·24 N	8·10 E

Page	Name	Pronunciation	Region	Lat. °′	Long. °′
213	Farafangana	(fä-rä-fän-gä'nä)	Mad.	21·18 S	47·59 E
186	Farāh	(fä-rä')	Afg.	32·15 N	62·13 E
124	Farallón, Punta (Pt.)	(pōō'n-tä-fä-rä-lōn)	Mex.	19·21 N	105·03 W
214	Faranah	(fä-rä'nä)	Gui.	10·02 N	10·44 W
211	Farasān, Jaza'ir (Is.)		Eth.	16·45 N	41·08 E
153	Faras (R.)		Libya	30·18 N	17·19 E
153	Faregh, Wadi al (R.)	(wädĕ ĕl fä-rĕg')	Libya	30·10 N	19·34 E
205	Farewell, C.	(fâr-wĕl')	N. Z. (In.)	40·37 S	171·46 E
108	Fargo	(fär'gō)	ND	46·53 N	96·48 W
108	Far Hills	(fär hǐlz)	NJ (New York In.)	40·41 N	74·38 W
109	Faribault	(fâ'rǐ-bō)	Mn.	44·19 N	93·16 W
162	Farilhoes (Is.)	(fä-rĕ-lyônzh')	Port.	39·28 N	9·32 W
148	Faringdon	(fä'rǐng-dŏn)	Eng. (London In.)	51·38 N	1·35 W
218	Fāriskūr	(fä-rĕs-kōōr')	Egypt (Nile In.)	31·19 N	31·46 E
211	Farit, Amba (Mt.)		Eth.	10·51 N	37·52 E
159	Farkašd	(fär'käsht)	Czech.	48·00 N	17·43 E
113	Farley	(fär'lē)	Mo. (Kansas City In.)	39·16 N	94·49 W
113	Farmers Branch	(fär'mĕrz brănch)	Tx. (Dallas, Fort Worth In.)	32·56 N	96·53 W
104	Farmersburg	(fär'mĕrz-bûrg)	In.	39·15 N	87·25 W
117	Farmersville	(fär'mĕrz-vǐl)	Tx.	33·11 N	96·22 W
106	Farmingdale	(färm'ĕng-dāl)	NJ (New York In.)	40·11 N	74·10 W
106	Farmingdale		NY (New York In.)	40·44 N	73·26 W
99	Farmingham	(färm-ĭng-hăm)	Ma. (In.)	42·17 N	71·25 W
117	Farmington	(färm-ĭng-tŭn)	Il.	40·42 N	90·01 W
98	Farmington		Me.	44·40 N	70·10 W
107	Farmington		Mi. (Detroit In.)	42·28 N	83·23 W
117	Farmington		Mo.	37·46 N	90·26 W
115	Farmington		NM	36·40 N	108·10 W
113	Farmington		Ut. (Salt Lake City In.)	40·59 N	111·53 W
121	Farmville	(färm-vǐl)	NC	35·35 N	77·35 W
121	Farmville		Va.	37·15 N	78·23 W
148	Farnborough	(färn'bŭr-ô)	Eng. (London In.)	51·15 N	0·45 W
154	Farne (I.)	(färn)	Eng.	55·40 N	1·32 W
105	Farnham	(fär'năm)	Can.	45·15 N	72·55 W
148	Farningham	(fär'nǐng-ŭm)	Eng.	51·22 N	0·14 E
148	Farnworth	(färn'wŭrth)	Eng.	53·34 N	2·24 W
135	Faro (R.)	(fä'rōō)	Braz.	2·05 S	56·32 W
162	Faro		Port.	37·01 N	7·57 W
157	Fårön (I.)		Swe.	57·57 N	19·10 E
204	Farquhar, C.	(fär'kwár)	Austl.	23·50 S	112·55 E
104	Farrell	(fär'ĕl)	Pa.	41·10 N	80·30 W
184	Farrukhābād	(tŭ-rŏŏk-hä-bäd')	India	27·29 N	79·35 E
165	Fársala (Pharsalus)	(fär-sä'lä)	Grc.	39·18 N	22·25 E
156	Farsund	(fär'sōōn)	Nor.	58·05 N	6·47 E
136	Fartura, Serra da (Mts.)	(sĕ'r-rä-dä-fär-tōō'rä)	Braz.	26·40 S	53·15 W
75	Farvel, Kap (C.)		Grnld.	60·00 N	44·00 W
116	Farwell	(fär'wĕl)	Tx.	34·24 N	103·03 W
165	Fasano	(fä-zä'nō)	It.	40·50 N	17·22 E
167	Fastov	(fäs'tôf)	Sov. Un.	50·04 N	29·57 E
162	Fatima		Port.	39·36 N	9·36 E
171	Fatsa	(fät'sä)	Tur.	40·50 N	37·30 E
161	Faucilles, Monts (Mts.)	(môn' fō-sēl')	Fr.	48·07 N	6·13 E
150	Fauske		Nor.	67·15 N	15·24 E
93	Faust	(foust)	Can.	55·19 N	115·38 W
174	Faustovo		Sov. Un. (Moscow In.)	55·27 N	38·29 E
161	Faverolles	(fä-vrôl')	Fr. (Paris In.)	48·42 N	1·34 E
148	Faversham	(fä'vēr-sh'm)	Eng. (London In.)	51·19 N	0·54 E
150	Faxaflói (B.)		Ice.	64·33 N	22·40 W
120	Fayette	(fà-yĕt')	Al.	33·41 N	87·54 W
109	Fayette		Ia.	42·49 N	91·49 W
120	Fayette		Ms.	31·43 N	91·00 W
117	Fayette		Mo.	39·09 N	92·41 W
117	Fayetteville	(fà-yĕt'vǐl)	Ar.	36·03 N	94·08 W
121	Fayetteville		NC	35·02 N	78·54 W
120	Fayetteville		Tn.	35·10 N	86·33 W
214	Fazao, Forêt Classée du (For.)		Togo	8·50 N	0·40 E
184	Fazilka		India	30·30 N	74·02 E
211	Fazzān (Fezzan) (Prov.)		Libya	26·45 N	13·01 E
210	Fdérik		Mauritania	22·45 N	12·38 W
121	Fear, C.	(fēr)	NC	33·52 N	77·48 W
114	Feather (R.)	(fĕth'ĕr)	Ca.	38·56 N	121·41 W
114	Feather, Middle Fk. of (R.)		Ca.	39·34 N	121·10 W
114	Feather, North Fk. of (R.)		Ca.	40·00 N	121·20 W
148	Featherstone	(fĕdh'ēr stŭn)	Eng.	53·39 N	1·21 W
160	Fécamp	(fā-kän')	Fr.	49·45 N	0·20 E
135	Federal, Distrito (Dist.)	(dĕs-trē'tô-fĕ-dĕ-rä'l)	Ven. (In.)	10·34 N	66·55 W
112	Federal Way		Wa. (Seattle In.)	47·20 N	122·20 W
174	Fëdorovka	(fyô'dō-rôf-kä)	Sov. Un. (Moscow In.)	56·15 N	37·14 E
158	Fehmarn I.	(fĕr'märn)	F.R.G.	54·28 N	11·15 E
149	Fehrbellin	(fĕr'bĕl-lēn)	G.D.R. (Berlin In.)	52·49 N	12·46 E
137	Feia, Logoa (L.)	(lō-gōä-fĕ'yä)	Braz. (Rio de Janeiro In.)	21·54 S	41·45 W
190	Feich'eng	(fā'chĕng)	China	36·18 N	116·45 E
190	Feihsien	(fä'ê-hsyĕn')	China	35·17 N	117·59 E
135	Feira de Santana	(fĕ'ê-rä dä sänt-än'ä)	Braz.	12·16 S	38·46 W
163	Felanitx	(fä-lä-nēch')	Sp.	39·29 N	3·09 E
158	Feldkirch	(fĕld'kǐrk)	Aus.	47·15 N	9·36 E
149	Feldkirchen	(fĕld'kĕr-kĕn)	F.R.G. (Munich In.)	48·09 N	11·44 E

ăt; finăl; rāte; senâte; ärm; àsk; sofà; fâre; ch-choose; dh-as th in other; bē; ĕvent; bĕt; recĕnt; cratēr; g-go; gh-guttural g; bĭt; ĭ-short neutral; rīde; ᴋ-guttural k as ch in German ich;

Page	Name Pronunciation	Region	Lat. °′	Long. °′
126	Felipe Carrillo Puerto (fĕ-lē′pĕ-kär-rē′l-yô-pwĕ′r-tô)	Mex. (In.)	19·36 N	88·04 W
164	Feltre (fĕl′trā)	It.	46·02 N	11·56 E
213	Fénérive (fĕ-nȧ-rēv′)	Mad.	17·30 S	49·31 E
192	Fengchen (fûng′chĕn′)	China	40·28 N	113·20 E
192	Fengch'eng (fûng′chûng′)	China	40·28 N	124·03 E
193	Fengchieh	China	31·02 N	109·30 E
192	Fenghsiang	China	34·25 N	107·20 E
191	Fenghsien (fûng′hsyĕn′)	China (Shanghai In.)	30·55 N	121·26 E
190	Fenghsien	China	34·41 N	116·36 E
190	Fengjun (fĕng′yĕn)	China	39·51 N	118·06 E
190	Fengming Tao (I.) (fĕng′mĭng dou)	China	39·19 N	121·15 E
192	Fengt'ai (fûng′tī′)	China (In.)	39·51 N	116·19 E
193	Fengtu (fûng′tōō′)	China	29·58 N	107·50 E
190	Fengyang (fûng′yäng′)	China	32·55 N	117·32 E
101	Fenimore P. (fĕn-ĭ-mōr)	Ak.	51·40 N	175·38 W
104	Fenton (fĕn-tŭn)	Mi.	42·50 N	83·40 W
113	Fenton	Mo. (St. Louis In.)	38·31 N	90·27 W
192	Fenyang	China	37·20 N	111·48 E
167	Feodosiya (Kefe) (fĕ-ô-dō′sē′yȧ) (kyĕ′fĕ)	Sov. Un.	45·02 N	35·21 E
186	Ferdows	Iran	34·00 N	58·13 E
164	Ferentino (fā-rĕn-tē′nō)	It.	41·42 N	13·18 E
172	Fergana	Sov. Un.	40·16 N	72·07 E
108	Fergus Falls (fûr′gŭs)	Mn.	46·17 N	96·03 W
113	Ferguson (fûr-gŭ-sŭn)	Mo. (St. Louis In.)	38·45 N	90·18 W
214	Ferkéssédougou	Ivory Coast	9·36 N	5·12 W
164	Fermo (fĕr′mō)	It.	43·10 N	13·43 E
162	Fermoselle (fĕr-mō-sāl′yȧ)	Sp.	41·20 N	6·23 W
154	Fermoy (fûr-moi′)	Ire.	52·05 N	8·06 W
121	Fernandina Beach (fûr-năn-dē′nȧ)	Fl.	30·38 N	81·29 W
135	Fernando de Noronha, Arquipélago (Arch.) (är-kē-pĕ′lä-gô-fĕr-nän-dō-dĕ-nô-rŏ′n-yä)	Braz.	3·50 S	33·15 W
	Fernando Póo (Prov.), see Macías Nguema Biyogo			
162	Fernãn-Núñez (fĕr-nän′nōōn′yȧth)	Sp.	37·42 N	4·43 W
217	Fernâo Veloso, Baia de (B.)	Moz.	14·20 S	40·55 E
110	Ferndale (fûrn′dāl)	Ca.	40·34 N	124·18 W
107	Ferndale	Mi. (Detroit In.)	42·27 N	83·08 W
112	Ferndale	Wa. (Vancouver In.)	48·51 N	122·36 W
93	Fernie (fûr′nĭ)	Can.	49·30 N	115·03 W
112	Fern Prairie (fûrn prâr′ĭ)	Wa. (Portland In.)	45·38 N	122·25 W
202	Ferntree Gully	Austl. (Melbourne In.)	37·53 S	145·18 E
164	Ferrara (fĕr-rä′rä)	It.	44·50 N	11·37 E
163	Ferrat, Cap (C.) (kăp fĕr-rät)	Alg.	35·49 N	0·29 W
162	Ferreira do Alentejo (fĕr-rĕ′ê-rä dōō ä-lĕN-tā′zhōō)	Port.	38·03 N	8·06 W
162	Ferreira do Zezere (fĕr-rĕ′ê-rä dōō zȧ-zā′rĕ)	Port.	39·49 N	8·17 W
113	Ferrelview (fĕr′rĕl-vū)	Mo. (Kansas City In.)	39·18 N	94·40 W
134	Ferreñafe (fĕr-rĕn-yȧ′fĕ)	Peru	6·38 S	79·48 W
119	Ferriday (fĕr′ĭ-dā)	La.	31·38 N	91·33 W
151	Ferryville (fĕr-ê-vēl′)	Tun.	37·12 N	9·51 E
174	Fershampenuaz (fĕr-shȧm′pĕn-wäz)	Sov. Un. (Urals In.)	53·32 N	59·50 E
108	Fertile (fur′tĭl)	Mn.	47·33 N	96·18 W
210	Fès (fĕs)	Mor.	34·08 N	5·00 W
108	Fessenden (fĕs′ĕn-dĕn)	ND	47·39 N	99·40 W
154	Festiniog (fĕs-tĭn-ĭ-ŏg)	Wales	52·59 N	3·58 W
117	Festus (fĕst′ŭs)	Mo.	38·12 N	90·22 W
171	Fethiye (fĕt-hē′yĕ)	Tur.	36·40 N	29·05 E
91	Feuilles, Rivière aux (R.)	Can.	58·30 N	70·50 W
	Fezzan (Prov.), see Fazzān			
213	Fianarantsoa (fyȧ-nä′rȧn-tsō′ȧ)	Mad.	21·21 S	47·15 E
218	Ficksburg (fĭks′bûrg)	S. Afr. (Johannesburg & Pretoria In.)	28·53 S	27·53 E
112	Fidalgo I. (fĭ-dăl′gō)	Wa. (Seattle In.)	48·28 N	122·39 W
112	Fieldbrook (fēld′brŏŏk)	Ca.	40·59 N	124·02 W
165	Fier (fyĕr)	Alb.	40·43 N	19·34 E
154	Fife Ness (C.) (fīf′nes′)	Scot.	56·15 N	2·19 W
211	Fifth Cataract	Sud.	18·27 N	33·38 E
162	Figalo, Cap (C.) (kăp fē-gä-lô)	Alg.	35·35 N	1·12 W
160	Figeac (fē-zhȧk′)	Fr.	44·37 N	2·02 E
156	Figeholm (fē-ghĕ-hōlm)	Swe.	57·24 N	16·33 E
162	Figueira da Foz (fê-gwĕy-rä-dȧ-fô′z)	Port.	40·10 N	8·50 W
210	Figuig	Mor.	32·20 N	1·30 W
198	Fiji (fē′jē)	Oceania	18·50 S	175·00 E
126	Filadelfia (fĭl-ȧ-dĕl′fĭ-ȧ)	C. R.	10·26 N	85·37 W
174	Filatovskoye (fĭ-lä′tōf-skô-yĕ)	Sov. Un. (Urals In.)	56·49 N	62·20 E
121	Filbert (fĭl′bērt)	WV	37·18 N	81·29 W
220	Filchner Ice Shelf (fĭlk′nēr)	Ant.	80·00 S	35·00 W
165	Filiatrá	Grc.	37·10 N	21·35 E
164	Filicudi (I.) (fē′le-kōō′dē)	It.	38·34 N	14·39 E
153	Filigas (R.)	Tur.	41·10 N	32·53 E
174	Filippovskoye (fĭ-lĭ-pôf′skô-yĕ)	Sov. Un. (Moscow In.)	56·06 N	38·38 E
156	Filipstad (fĭl′ĭps-städh)	Swe.	59·44 N	14·09 E
115	Fillmore (fĭl′môr)	Ut.	39·00 N	112·20 W
216	Fimi (R.)	Zaire	2·43 S	17·50 E
89	Finch (fĭnch)	Can. (Ottawa In.)	45·09 N	75·06 W
104	Findlay (fĭnd′lȧ)	Oh.	41·05 N	83·40 W
217	Fingoè	Moz.	15·12 S	31·50 E
162	Finisterre, Cabo de (C.) (kȧ′bô-dĕ-fĭn-ĭs-târ′)	Sp.	42·52 N	9·48 W
204	Finke (R.) (fĭŋ′kê)	Austl.	25·25 S	134·30 E
146	Finland (fĭn′lănd)	Eur.	62·45 N	26·13 E
157	Finland, G. of (fĭn′lănd)	Eur.	59·35 N	23·35 E
134	Finlandia (fēn-lä′n-dêä)	Col. (In.)	4·38 N	75·39 W
90	Finlay (R.) (fĭn′lȧ)	Can.	57·45 N	125·30 W
149	Finow (fē′nōv)	G.D.R. (Berlin In.)	52·50 N	13·44 E
149	Finowfurt (fē′nō-fōōrt)	G.D.R. (Berlin In.)	52·50 N	13·41 E
158	Finsterwalde (fĭn′stēr-väl-dĕ)	G.D.R.	51·38 N	13·42 E
171	Firat (R.) (fē-rät′)	Tur.	39·40 N	38·30 E
112	Fircrest (fûr′krĕst)	Wa. (Seattle In.)	47·14 N	122·31 W
164	Firenze (Florence) (fê-rĕnt′sā)	It.	43·47 N	11·15 E
164	Firenzuola (fē-rĕnt-swô′lä)	It.	44·08 N	11·21 E
184	Fīrozpur	India	30·58 N	74·39 E
149	Fischa (R.)	Aus. (Vienna In.)	48·04 N	16·33 E
149	Fischamend Markt	Aus. (Vienna In.)	48·07 N	16·37 E
212	Fish (R.) (fĭsh)	Namibia	27·30 S	17·45 E
129	Fish Cay (I.)	Ba.	22·30 N	74·20 W
89	Fish Cr. (fĭsh)	Can. (Calgary In.)	50·52 N	114·21 W
119	Fisher (fĭsh′ēr)	La.	31·28 N	93·30 W
95	Fisher B.	Can.	51·30 N	97·16 W
92	Fisher Chan	Can.	52·10 N	127·42 W
91	Fisher Str.	Can.	62·43 N	84·28 W
95	Fishing L. (fĭsh′ĭng)	Can.	52·07 N	95·25 W
99	Fitchburg (fĭch′bûrg)	Ma. (In.)	42·35 N	71·48 W
215	Fitri, Lac (L.)	Chad	12·50 N	17·28 E
120	Fitzgerald (fĭts-jĕr′ăld)	Ga.	31·42 N	83·17 W
92	Fitz Hugh Sd. (fĭts hū)	Can.	51·40 N	127·57 W
204	Fitzroy (R.) (fĭts-roi′)	Austl.	18·00 S	124·05 E
205	Fitzroy (R.)	Austl.	23·45 S	150·02 E
204	Fitzroy Crossing	Austl.	18·08 S	126·00 E
104	Fitzwilliam (I.) (fĭts-wĭl′yŭm)	Can.	45·30 N	81·45 W
	Fiume, see Rijeka			
163	Fiumicino (fyōō-mē-chê′nô)	It. (Rome In.)	41·47 N	12·19 E
156	Fjällbacka (fyĕl′bäk-ȧ)	Swe.	58·37 N	11·17 E
156	Flaam (flôm)	Nor.	60·15 N	7·01 E
115	Flagstaff (flăg-stȧf)	Az.	35·15 N	111·40 W
213	Flagstaff (flăg′stäf)	S. Afr. (Natal In.)	31·06 S	29·31 E
105	Flagstaff (L.) (flăg-stȧf)	Me.	45·05 N	70·30 W
149	Flalow (flä′lōv)	G.D.R. (Berlin In.)	52·44 N	12·58 E
109	Flambeau (R.) (flăm-bō′)	Wi.	45·32 N	91·05 W
111	Flaming Gorge Res.	Wy.	41·13 N	109·30 W
121	Flamingo (flȧ-mĭŋ′gô)	Fl.	25·10 N	80·55 W
129	Flamingo Cay (I.) (flȧ-mĭŋ′gô)	Ba.	22·50 N	75·50 W
123	Flamingo Pt.	Vir. Is. (U. S. A.) (St. Thomas In.)	18·19 N	65·00 W
155	Flanders (Reg.) (flăn′dērz)	Fr.	50·53 N	2·29 E
108	Flandreau (flăn′drō)	SD	44·02 N	96·35 W
154	Flannan (Is.) (flăn′ăn)	Scot.	58·13 N	8·14 W
93	Flathead (R.)	Can.	49·30 N	114·30 W
111	Flathead L. (flăt′hĕd)	Mt.	47·57 N	114·20 W
111	Flathead R.	Mt.	48·45 N	114·20 W
111	Flathead R., Middle Fork	Mt.	48·30 N	113·47 W
111	Flathead R., South Fork	Mt.	48·05 N	113·45 W
107	Flat Rock (flăt rŏk)	Mi. (Detroit In.)	42·06 N	83·17 W
110	Flattery C. (flăt′ēr-ĭ)	Wa.	48·22 N	125·10 W
111	Flat Willow Cr. (flat wĭl′ô)	Mt.	46·45 N	108·47 W
156	Flekkefjord (flăk′kē-fyôr)	Nor.	58·19 N	6·38 E
104	Flemingsburg (flĕm′ĭngz-bûrg)	Ky.	38·25 N	83·45 W
158	Flensburg (flĕns′bŏŏrgh)	F.R.G.	54·48 N	9·27 E
160	Flers-del-l'Orne (flĕr-dĕ-lôrn′)	Fr.	48·43 N	0·37 W
121	Fletcher	NC	35·26 N	82·30 W
204	Flinders (Reg.) (flĭn′dērz)	Austl.	32·15 S	138·45 E
203	Flinders (I.)	Austl.	39·35 S	148·10 E
205	Flinders (R.)	Austl.	18·48 S	141·07 E
205	Flinders Rfs.	Austl.	17·30 S	149·02 E
104	Flin Flon (flĭn flŏn)	Can.	54·46 N	101·53 W
148	Flint	Wales	53·15 N	3·07 W
104	Flint	Mi.	43·00 N	83·45 W
148	Flint (Co.)	Wales	53·13 N	3·06 W
120	Flint (R.) (flĭnt)	Ga.	31·25 N	84·15 W
156	Flisen (flē′sĕn)	Nor.	60·35 N	12·03 E
104	Flora (flô′rȧ)	Il.	38·40 N	88·25 W
104	Flora	In.	40·25 N	86·30 W
120	Florala (flŏr-ăl′ȧ)	Al.	31·01 N	86·19 W
106	Floral Park (flôr′ȧl pärk)	NY (New York In.)	40·42 N	73·42 W
120	Florence (flōr′ĕns)	Al.	34·46 N	87·40 W
115	Florence	Az.	33·00 N	111·25 W
116	Florence	Co.	38·23 N	105·08 W
117	Florence	Ks.	38·14 N	96·56 W
121	Florence	SC	34·10 N	79·45 W
112	Florence	Wa. (Seattle In.)	48·13 N	122·21 W
	Florence, see Firenze			
134	Florencia (flō-rĕn′sê-ȧ)	Col.	1·31 N	75·13 W
137	Florencio Sanchez (flō-rĕn-sêō-sȧ′n-chĕz)	Ur. (Buenos Aires In.)	33·52 S	57·24 W
136	Florencio Varela (flō-rĕn′sê-o vä-rā′lä)	Arg. (Buenos Aires In.)	34·34 S	58·16 W
135	Flores (flō′rĕzh)	Braz.	7·57 S	37·48 W
126	Flores	Guat. (In.)	16·53 N	89·54 W
137	Flores (Dept.)	Ur. (Buenos Aires In.)	33·33 S	57·00 W
196	Flores (I.)	Indon.	8·14 S	121·08 E
137	Flores (R.)	Arg. (Buenos Aires In.)	36·13 S	60·28 W
196	Flores Laut (Flores Sea)	Indon.	7·09 N	120·30 E
118	Floresville (flō′rĕs-vĭl)	Tx.	29·10 N	98·08 W
135	Floriano (flō-rȧ-ä′nōō)	Braz.	6·17 S	42·58 W
136	Florianópolis (flō-rê-ä-nō′pô-lês)	Braz.	27·30 S	48·30 W
134	Florida (flō-rē′dä)	Col. (In.)	3·20 N	76·12 W
128	Florida	Cuba	22·10 N	79·50 W
106	Florida (flŏr′ĭ-dȧ)	NY (New York In.)	41·20 N	74·21 W
213	Florida	S. Afr. (Johannesburg & Pretoria In.)	26·11 S	27·56 E
137	Florida (flô-rê-dhä)	Ur. (Buenos Aires In.)	34·06 S	56·14 W
103	Florida (State) (flŏr′ĭ-dȧ)	U.S.	30·30 N	84·40 W
137	Florida (Dept.) (flô-rĕ′dhä)	Ur. (Buenos Aires In.)	33·48 S	56·15 W
205	Florida (I.)	Sol. Is.	8·56 S	159·45 E
128	Florida, Strs. of	N. A.	24·10 N	81·00 W
121	Florida B. (flŏr′ĭ-dȧ)	Fl. (In.)	24·55 N	80·55 W
121	Florida Keys (Is.)	Fl. (In.)	24·33 N	81·20 W
115	Florida Mts.	NM	32·10 N	107·35 W
118	Florido, R. (flô-rē′dō)	Mex.	27·21 N	104·48 W
149	Floridsdorf (flô′rĭds-dôrf)	Aus. (Vienna In.)	48·16 N	16·25 E
165	Florina (flô-rē′nä)	Grc.	40·48 N	21·24 E
113	Florissant (flŏr′ĭ-sănt)	Mo. (St. Louis In.)	38·47 N	90·20 W
156	Florö (flô′ü)	Nor.	61·36 N	5·01 E
108	Floyd (R.) (floid)	Ia.	42·38 N	96·15 W
116	Floydada (floi-dā′dȧ)	Tx.	33·59 N	101·19 W
107	Floyds Fk. (R.) (floi-dz)	Ky. (Louisville In.)	38·08 N	85·30 W
164	Flumendosa, R. (flōō-mĕn-dô′sä)	It.	39·45 N	9·18 E
104	Flushing (flûsh′ĭng)	Mi.	43·05 N	83·50 W
197	Fly (R.) (flī)	Pap. N. Gui.	8·00 S	141·45 E
165	Foča (fō′chä)	Yugo.	43·29 N	18·48 E
218	Fochville (fŏk′vĭl)	S. Afr. (Johannesburg & Pretoria In.)	26·29 S	27·29 E
159	Focsani (fôk-shä′nê)	Rom.	45·41 N	27·17 E
164	Foggia (fôd′jä)	It.	41·30 N	15·34 E
97	Fogo (fô′gō)	Can.	49·43 N	54·17 W
97	Fogo I.	Can.	49·40 N	54·13 W
210	Fogo I.	C. V. (In.)	14·46 N	24·51 W
158	Fohnsdorf (fōns′dôrf)	Aus.	47·13 N	14·40 E
158	Föhr I. (fûr)	F.R.G.	54·47 N	8·30 E
160	Foix (fwä)	Fr.	42·58 N	1·34 E
193	Fokang	China	23·50 N	113·35 E
215	Fokku	Nig.	11·40 N	4·31 E
216	Folgares	Ang.	14·54 S	15·08 E
164	Foligno (fô-lēn′yō)	It.	42·58 N	12·41 E
155	Folkeston	Eng.	51·05 N	1·18 E
148	Folkingham (fō′kĭng-ăm)	Eng.	52·53 N	0·24 W
121	Folkston	Ga.	30·50 N	82·01 W
116	Folsom (fŏl′sŭm)	NM	36·47 N	103·56 W
114	Folsom City	Ca.	38·40 N	121·10 W
128	Fomento (fô-mĕ′n-tō)	Cuba	21·35 N	78·20 W
134	Fómeque (fô′mĕ-kĕ)	Col. (In.)	4·29 N	73·52 W
109	Fonda (fōn′dȧ)	Ia.	42·33 N	94·51 W
109	Fond du Lac (fŏn dū lăk′)	Wi.	43·47 N	88·29 W
109	Fond du Lac Ind. Res.	Mn.	46·44 N	93·04 W
164	Fondi (fōn′dē)	It.	41·23 N	13·25 E
162	Fonsagrada (fôn-sä-grä′dhä)	Sp.	43·08 N	7·07 W
126	Fonseca, Golfo de (G.) (gôl-fô-dĕ-fôn-sā′kä)	Hond.	13·09 N	87·55 W
161	Fontainebleau (fôN-tĕn-blō′)	Fr. (Paris In.)	48·24 N	2·42 E
113	Fontana (fŏn-tă′nȧ)	Ca. (Los Angeles In.)	34·06 N	117·27 W
134	Fonte Boa (fōn′tȧ bō′ă)	Braz.	2·32 S	66·05 W
160	Fontenay-le-Comte (fôNt-nĕ′lē-kôNt′)	Fr.	46·28 N	0·53 W
161	Fontenay-Trésigny (fôN-te-hā′ tra-sēn-yē′)	Fr. (Paris In.)	48·43 N	2·53 E
111	Fontenelle Res.	Wy.	42·05 N	110·05 W
125	Fontera, Punta (Pt.) (pōō′n-tä-fôn-tĕ′rä)	Mex.	18·36 N	92·43 W
134	Fontibón (fōn-tē-bôn′)	Col. (In.)	4·42 N	74·09 W
	Foochow, see Fuchou			
213	Foothills (fŏŏt-hĭls)	S. Afr. (Johannesburg & Pretoria In.)	25·55 S	27·36 E
101	Foraker, Mt. (fôr′ȧ-kēr)	Ak.	62·40 N	152·40 W
161	Forbach (fôr′bäK)	Fr.	49·12 N	6·54 E
203	Forbes (fôrbz)	Austl.	33·24 S	148·05 E
93	Forbes, Mt.	Can.	51·52 N	116·56 W
158	Forchheim (fôrK′hīm)	F.R.G.	49·43 N	11·05 E
	Fordlândia, see Brasília Legal			
117	Fordyce (fôr′dīs)	Ar.	33·48 N	92·24 W
214	Forecariah (fōr-kȧ-rē′ä′)	Gui.	9·26 N	13·06 W
75	Forel, Mt.	Grnld.	65·50 N	37·41 W
120	Forest (fŏr′ĕst)	Ms.	32·22 N	89·29 W
108	Forest (R.)	ND	48·08 N	97·45 W
109	Forest City	Ia.	43·14 N	93·40 W
121	Forest City	NC	35·20 N	81·52 W
105	Forest City	Pa.	41·35 N	75·30 W
112	Forest Grove (grōv)	Or. (Portland In.)	45·31 N	123·07 W
106	Forest Hill	Md. (Baltimore In.)	39·35 N	76·26 W
113	Forest Hill	Tx. (Dallas, Fort Worth In.)	32·40 N	97·16 W
98	Forestville (fŏr′ĕst-vĭl)	Can.	48·45 N	69·06 W
106	Forestville	Md. (Baltimore In.)	38·51 N	76·55 W
160	Forez, Mts. du (môN dü fô-rā′)	Fr.	44·55 N	3·43 E
154	Forfar (fôr′fȧr)	Scot.	57·10 N	2·55 W
98	Forillon, Parc Natl. (Natl. Pk.)	Can.	48·50 N	64·05 W
163	Forio (Mtn.) (fô′ryō)	It. (Naples In.)	40·29 N	13·55 E
107	Forked Cr. (fôrk'd)	Il. (Chicago In.)	41·16 N	88·01 W
116	Forked Deer (R.)	Tn.	35·53 N	89·29 W
164	Forli (fôr-lē′)	It.	44·13 N	12·03 E
148	Formby (fôrm′bê)	Eng.	53·34 N	3·04 W
148	Formby Pt.	Eng.	53·33 N	3·06 W
163	Formello (fôr-mĕ′lō)	It. (Rome In.)	42·04 N	12·25 E
163	Formentera, Isla de (I.) (ê′s-lä-dĕ-fôr-mĕn-tā′rä)	Sp.	38·43 N	1·25 E
137	Formiga (fôr-mē′gȧ)	Braz. (Rio de Janeiro In.)	20·27 S	45·25 W

ng-sing; ŋ-baŋk; N-nasalized n; nŏd; cŏmmit; ōld; ôbey; ôrder; fōōd; fŏŏt; ou-out; s-soft; sh-dish; th-thin; pūre; ûnite; ûrn; stŭd; circŭs; ü-as "y" in study; ′-indeterminate vowel.

282 Formigas — Fremont PRONOUNCING INDEX

Page Name Pronunciation Region Lat. °′ Long. °′
129 Formigas Bk. (fōr-mē′gäs)...N. A. 18·30 N 75·40 W
136 Formosa (fôr-mō′sä).........Arg. 27·25 S 58·12 W
135 Formosa..................Braz. 15·32 S 47·10 W
136 Formosa (Prov.)............Arg. 24·30 S 60·45 W
217 Formosa B................Ken. 2·45 S 40·30 E
Formosa (I.), see Taiwan
135 Formosa, Serra (Mts.) (sĕ′r-rä) Braz. 12·59 S 55·11 W
183 Formosa Str. (fŏr-mō′sȧ).....Asia 24·30 N 120·00 E
174 Fornosovo (fôr-nô′sô vô) Sov. Un. (Leningrad In.) 59·35 N 30·34 E
117 Forrest City (for′ĕst sĭ′tĭ).....Ar. 35·00 N 90·46 W
205 Forsayth (fôr-sīth′)..........Austl. 18·33 S 143·42 E
156 Forshaga (fôrs′hä′gä)........Swe. 59·34 N 13·25 E
158 Forst (fôrst)............G.D.R. 51·45 N 14·38 E
120 Forsyth (fôr-sīth′)...........Ga. 33·02 N 83·56 W
111 Forsyth....................Mt. 46·15 N 106·41 W
91 Fort Albany (fôrt ôl′bȧ nĭ)...Can. 52·20 N 81·20 W
95 Fort Alexander Ind. Res.....Can. 50·27 N 96·15 W
135 Fortaleza (Ceará) (fôr′tä-lā′zȧ) (sā-ä-rä′).Braz. 3·35 S 38·31 W
115 Fort Apache Ind. Res. (ȧ-păch′ē) Az. 34·02 N 110·27 W
109 Fort Atkinson (ăt′kĭn-sŭn)....Wi. 42·55 N 88·46 W
Fort Bayard, see Chanchiang
213 Fort Beaufort (bō′fôrt) S. Afr. (Natal In.) 32·47 S 26·39 E
113 Fort Bellefontaine (bĕl-fŏn-tān′) Mo. (St. Louis In.) 38·50 N 90·15 W
111 Fort Benton (bĕn′tŭn).......Mt. 47·51 N 110·40 W
108 Fort Berthold Ind. Res. (bĕrth′ôld).ND 47·47 N 103·28 W
104 Fort Branch (brănch).........In. 38·15 N 87·35 W
100 Fort Chipewyan............Can. 58·46 N 111·15 W
116 Fort Cobb Res..............Ok. 35·12 N 98·28 W
116 Fort Collins (kŏl′ĭns).........Co. 40·36 N 105·04 W
215 Fort Crampel (krȧm-pĕl′) Cen. Afr. Emp. 6·59 N 19·11 E
213 Fort-Dauphin (dō-făɴ′).....Mad. 24·59 S 46·58 E
127 Fort-de-France (dē fräɴs) Mart. (In.) 14·37 N 61·06 W
120 Fort Deposit (dē-pŏz′ĭt).......Al. 31·58 N 86·35 W
211 Fort-de-Possel (dē pô-sĕl′) Cen. Afr. Emp. 5·03 N 19·11 E
109 Fort Dodge (dŏj).............Ia. 42·31 N 94·10 W
105 Fort Edward (wĕrd).........NY 43·15 N 73·30 W
107 Fort Erie (ē′rĭ)..Can. (Buffalo In.) 42·55 N 78·56 W
204 Fortescue (R.) (fôr′tĕs-kū)..Austl. 21·25 S 116·50 E
98 Fort Fairfield (fâr′fēld).......Me. 46·46 N 67·53 W
100 Fort Fitzgerald (fĭts-jĕr′ȧld)..Can. 59·48 N 111·50 W
95 Fort Frances (frăn′sĕs)......Can. 48·36 N 93·24 W
121 Fort Frederica Natl. Mon. (frĕd′ĕ-rĭ-kȧ).Ga. 31·12 N 85·25 W
120 Fort Gaines (gānz)..........Ga. 31·35 N 85·03 W
91 Fort George (jôrj)..........Can. 53·40 N 78·58 W
117 Fort Gibson (gĭb′sŭn)........Ok. 35·50 N 95·13 W
102 Fort Good Hope (good hōp)..Can. 66·19 N 128·52 W
154 Forth, Firth of (fûrth ôv fôrth) Scot. 56·04 N 3·03 W
211 Fort Hall (hôl).............Ken. 0·47 S 37·13 E
111 Fort Hall Ind. Res...........Id. 43·02 N 112·21 W
115 Fort Huachuca (wä-choo′kä)...Az. 31·30 N 110·25 W
89 Fortier (fôr′tyā′) Can. (Winnipeg In.) 49·56 N 97·55 W
212 Fort Jameson (jām′sŭn)...Zambia 13·35 S 32·43 E
121 Fort Jefferson Natl. Mon. (jĕf′ēr-sŭn).Fl. (In.) 24·42 N 83·02 W
212 Fort Johnston...........Malawi 14·16 S 35·14 E
98 Fort Kent (kĕnt)............Me. 47·14 N 68·37 W
112 Fort Langley (lăng′lĭ) Can. (Vancouver In.) 49·10 N 122·35 W
121 Fort Lauderdale (lô′dēr-dāl) Fl. (In.) 26·07 N 80·09 W
106 Fort Lee......NJ (New York In.) 40·50 N 73·58 W
90 Fort Liard.................Can. 60·16 N 123·34 W
129 Fort Liberté (lē-bĕr-tā′)......Hai. 19·40 N 71·50 W
120 Fort Louden (R.) (fôrt lou′dĕn) Tn. 35·52 N 84·10 W
116 Fort Lupton (lŭp′tŭn)........Co. 40·04 N 104·45 W
110 Fort McDermitt Ind. Res. (mȧk dēr′mĭt).Or. 42·04 N 118·07 W
93 Fort Macleod (mȧ-kloud′)...Can. 49·43 N 113·25 W
210 Fort MacMahon (mȧk mȧ-ôɴ′) Alg. 29·55 N 1·49 E
94 Fort McMurray (mȧk-mŭr′ĭ).Can. 56·44 N 111·23 W
90 Fort McPherson (mȧk-fŭr′s′n) Can. 67·37 N 134·59 W
109 Fort Madison (măd′ĭ-sŭn).....Ia. 40·40 N 91·17 W
121 Fort Matanzas (mä-tän′zäs)...Fl. 29·39 N 81·17 W
121 Fort Meade (mēd).......Fl. (In.) 27·45 N 81·48 W
121 Fort Mill (mĭl)..............SC 35·03 N 80·57 W
152 Fort Miribel (mē-rē-bĕl′).....Alg. 28·50 N 2·51 E
114 Fort Mohave Ind. Res. (mô-hä′vȧ) Ca. 34·59 N 115·02 W
116 Fort Morgan (môr′gȧn).......Co. 40·14 N 103·49 W
121 Fort Myers (mī′ĕrz)......Fl. (In.) 26·36 N 81·45 W
152 Fort National (fô nȧ-syō-nȧl′) Alg. 36·45 N 4·15 E
90 Fort Nelson (nĕl′sŭn)........Can. 58·57 N 122·30 W
90 Fort Nelson (R.) (nĕl′sŭn)...Can. 58·44 N 122·20 W
120 Fort Payne (pān)............Al. 34·26 N 85·41 W
111 Fort Peck (pĕk).............Mt. 47·58 N 106·30 W
108 Fort Peck Ind. Res..........Mt. 48·22 N 105·40 W
111 Fort Peck Res...............Mt. 47·52 N 106·59 W
121 Fort Pierce (pērs)........Fl. (In.) 27·25 N 80·20 W
217 Fort Portal (pôr′tȧl)........Ug. 0·40 N 30·16 E
90 Fort Providence (prŏv′ĭ-dĕns).Can. 61·27 N 117·59 W
121 Fort Pulaski Natl. Mon. (pu-lăs′kĭ).Ga. 31·59 N 80·56 W
94 Fort Qu'Appelle............Can. 50·46 N 103·55 W
101 Fort Randall (răn′d′l).......Ak. 55·12 N 162·38 W
102 Fort Randall Dam.........U. S. 42·48 N 98·35 W
90 Fort Resolution (rĕz′ō-lū′shŭn) Can. 61·08 N 113·42 W
117 Fort Riley (rī′lĭ)............Ks. 39·05 N 96·46 W
92 Fort St. James (fôrt sānt jāmz) Can. 54·26 N 124·15 W
93 Fort St. John (sānt jŏn).....Can. 56·15 N 120·51 W
184 Fort Sandeman (săn′da-mȧn) Pak. 31·28 N 69·29 E
89 Fort Saskatchewan (săs-kăt′choo-ån) Can. (Edmonton In.) 53·43 N 113·13 W
117 Fort Scott (skŏt)............Ks. 37·50 N 94·43 W
91 Fort Severn (sĕv′ērn)........Can. 56·58 N 87·50 W
171 Fort Shevchenko (shĕv-chĕn′kô) Sov. Un. 44·30 N 50·18 E
215 Fort Sibut (fôr sē-bü′) Cen. Afr. Emp. 5·44 N 19·05 E
116 Fort Sill (fôrt sĭl)...........Ok. 34·41 N 98·25 W
90 Fort Simpson (sĭmp′sŭn).....Can. 61·52 N 121·48 W
117 Fort Smith (smĭth)..........Ar. 35·23 N 94·24 W
90 Fort Smith................Can. 60·09 N 112·08 W
118 Fort Stockton (stŏk′tŭn)......Tx. 30·54 N 102·51 W
116 Fort Sumner (sŭm′nēr).......NM 34·30 N 104·17 W
121 Fort Sumter Natl. Mon. (sŭm′tēr).SC 32·43 N 79·54 W
107 Fort Thomas (tŏm′ȧs) Ky. (Cincinnati In.) 39·05 N 84·27 W
110 Fortuna (fŏr-tū′nȧ)..........Ca. 40·36 N 124·10 W
99 Fortune (fôr′tûn)...........Can. 47·04 N 55·51 W
129 Fortune (I.)................Ba. 22·35 N 74·20 W
99 Fortune B.................Can. 47·25 N 55·25 W
116 Fort Union Natl. Mon. (ūn′yŭn) NM 35·51 N 104·57 W
120 Fort Valley (văl′ĭ)...........Ga. 32·33 N 83·53 W
90 Fort Vermilion (vēr-mĭl′yŭn).Can. 58·23 N 115·50 W
212 Fort Victoria.................Rh. 20·07 S 30·47 E
104 Fortville (fôrt-vĭl)...........In. 40·00 N 85·50 W
104 Fort Wayne (wān)...........In. 41·00 N 85·10 W
154 Fort William (wĭl′yŭm)......Scot. 56·50 N 3·00 W
203 Fort William, Mt. (wĭ′lĭ-ăm).Austl. 24·45 S 151·15 E
113 Fort Worth (wûrth) Tx. (Dallas, Fort Worth In.) 32·45 N 97·20 W
101 Fort Yukon (yoo′kŏn)........Ak. 66·30 N 145·00 W
114 Fort Yuma Ind. Res. (yoo′mä).Ca. 32·54 N 114·47 W
160 Fos, Golfe de (G.) (gôlf′dĕ-fôs′) Fr. (In.) 43·22 N 4·55 E
191 Foshan.......China (Canton In.) 23·02 N 113·07 E
Foshan, see Ch'aoyang
164 Fossano (fôs-sä′nō)...........It. 44·34 N 7·42 E
113 Fossil Cr. (fŏs-ĭl) Tx. (Dallas, Fort Worth In.) 32·53 N 97·19 W
164 Fossombrone (fôs-sôm-brō′nā)..It. 43·41 N 12·48 E
116 Foss Res....................Ok. 35·38 N 99·11 W
108 Fosston (fôs′tŭn)...........Mn. 47·34 N 95·44 W
113 Fosterburg (fŏs′tēr-bûrg) Il. (St. Louis In.) 38·58 N 90·04 W
104 Fostoria (fŏs-tō′rĭ-ȧ).........Oh. 41·10 N 83·20 W
190 Fouch'eng (foo′chĕng)......China 37·53 N 116·08 E
160 Fougéres (foo-zhâr′)..........Fr. 48·23 N 1·14 W
192 Fouhsin...................China 42·05 N 121·40 E
154 Foula (I.) (fou′lȧ)..........Scot. 60·08 N 2·04 W
193 Fouling...................China 29·40 N 107·30 E
205 Foulwind, C. (foul′wĭnd) N. Z. (In.) 41·45 S 171·37 E
215 Foumban (foom-bän′).......Cam. 5·43 N 10·55 E
190 Founing (foo′nĭng).........China 33·55 N 119·54 E
116 Fountain Cr. (foun′tĭn).......Co. 38·36 N 104·37 W
113 Fountain Valley Ca. (Los Angeles In.) 33·42 N 117·57 W
117 Fourche le Fave (R.) (foorsh lä fāv′).Ar. 34·46 N 93·45 W
218 Fouriesburg (foo′rēz-bûrg)..S. Afr. (Johannesburg & Pretoria In.) 28·38 S 28·13 E
160 Fourmies (foor-mē′)..........Fr. 50·01 N 4·01 E
101 Four Mts., Is. of the (fōr).....Ak. 52·58 N 170·40 W
211 Fourth Cataract............Sud. 18·52 N 32·07 E
210 Fouta Djallon (Mts.) (foo′tä jä-lôɴ).Gui. 11·37 N 12·29 W
190 Fouts'un (foo′tsoon)........China 36·38 N 117·26 E
190 Foutzuchi (foo′tzĕ′jē).......China 33·48 N 118·13 E
190 Fouyang (foo′yäng)..........China 32·53 N 115·48 E
205 Foveaux Str. (fô-vō′)...N. Z. (In.) 46·30 S 167·43 E
116 Fowler (foul′ēr)..............Co. 38·04 N 104·02 W
104 Fowler.......................In. 40·35 N 87·20 W
204 Fowler, Pt..................Austl. 32·05 S 132·30 E
118 Fowlerton (foul′ēr-tŭn).......Tx. 28·26 N 98·48 W
112 Fox (I.) (fŏks)...Wa. (Seattle In.) 47·15 N 122·08 W
109 Fox (R.)......................Il. 41·35 N 88·43 W
109 Fox (R.).....................Wi. 44·18 N 88·23 W
99 Foxboro (fŏks′bŭrô).....Ma. (In.) 42·04 N 71·15 W
90 Foxe Basin (fŏks)..........Can. 67·35 N 79·21 W
91 Foxe Chan.................Can. 64·30 N 79·23 W
91 Foxe Pen..................Can. 64·57 N 77·26 W
101 Fox Is. (fŏks)...............Ak. 53·04 N 167·30 W
107 Fox Lake (lăk)...Il. (Chicago In.) 42·24 N 88·11 W
107 Fox L...........Il. (Chicago In.) 42·24 N 88·07 W
107 Fox Point....Wi. (Milwaukee In.) 43·10 N 87·54 W
154 Foyle, Lough (B.) (lŏk foil′)...Ire. 55·07 N 7·08 W
216 Foz do Cunene..............Ang. 17·16 S 11·50 E
163 Fraga (frä′gä)...............Sp. 41·31 N 0·20 E
128 Fragoso, Cayo (I.) (kä′yō-frä-gō′sō).Cuba 22·45 N 79·30 W
135 Franca (frä′n-kä)..........Braz. 20·28 S 47·20 W
165 Francavilla (fräŋ-kä-vēl′lä).....It. 40·32 N 17·37 E
146 France (frȧns)..............Eur. 46·39 N 0·47 E
90 Frances (L.) (frăn′sĭs).......Can. 61·27 N 128·28 W
128 Frances, Cabo (C.) (kä′bô-frän-sĕ′s).Cuba 21·55 N 84·05 W
128 Frances, Punta (Pt.) (poo′n-tä-frän-sĕ′s).Cuba 21·45 N 83·10 W
129 Frances Viejo, Cabo (C.) (kä′bô-frän′sås vyā′hō) Dom. Rep. 19·40 N 69·35 W
216 Franceville (fräɴs-vēl′)....Gabon. 1·38 S 13·35 E
108 Francis Case, L. (frăn′sĭs).....SD 43·15 N 99·00 W
137 Francisco Sales (frän-sē′s-kô-sȧ′lĕs).Braz. (Rio de Janeiro In.) 21·42 S 44·26 W
212 Francistown (frăn′sĭs-toun)..Bots. 21·17 S 27·28 E
107 Frankfort (frăŋk′fŭrt) Il. (Chicago In.) 41·30 N 87·51 W
104 Frankfort...................In. 40·15 N 86·30 W
117 Frankfort...................Ks. 39·42 N 96·27 W
104 Frankfort...................Ky. 38·10 N 84·55 W
104 Frankfort...................Mi. 44·40 N 86·15 W
105 Frankfort...................NY 43·05 N 75·05 W
218 Frankfort................S. Afr. (Johannesburg & Pretoria In.) 27·17 S 28·30 E
213 Frankfort (frănk′fōrt) S. Afr. (Natal In.) 32·43 S 27·28 E
158 Frankfurt (fräŋk′foort)...G.D.R. 52·20 N 14·31 E
149 Frankfurt (Dist.) G.D.R. (Berlin In.) 52·42 N 13·37 E
158 Frankfurt am Main.......F.R.G. 50·07 N 8·40 E
104 Franklin (frănk′lĭn)..........In. 39·25 N 86·00 W
120 Franklin....................Ky. 36·42 N 86·34 W
119 Franklin....................La. 29·47 N 91·31 W
99 Franklin...............Ma. (In.) 42·05 N 71·24 W
116 Franklin....................Ne. 40·06 N 99·01 W
105 Franklin....................NH 43·25 N 71·40 W
106 Franklin......NJ (New York In.) 41·08 N 74·35 W
104 Franklin....................Oh. 39·30 N 84·20 W
105 Franklin....................Pa. 41·25 N 79·50 W
120 Franklin....................Tn. 35·54 N 86·54 W
213 Franklin.......S. Afr. (Natal In.) 30·19 S 29·28 E
121 Franklin....................Va. 36·41 N 76·57 W
90 Franklin, Dist. of..........Can. 70·46 N 105·22 W
114 Franklin (L.)...............Nv. 40·23 N 115·10 W
110 Franklin D. Roosevelt L......Wa. 48·12 N 118·43 W
90 Franklin Mts...............Can. 65·36 N 125·55 W
107 Franklin Park....Il. (Chicago In.) 41·56 N 87·53 W
106 Franklin Square NY (New York In.) 40·43 N 73·40 W
119 Franklinton (frăŋk′lĭn-tŭn)....La. 30·49 N 90·09 W
202 Frankston..Austl. (Melbourne In.) 38·09 S 145·08 E
107 Franksville (frănkz′vĭl) Wi. (Milwaukee In.) 42·46 N 87·55 W
Franz Josef Land (Is.), see Zemlya Frantsa Iosifa
163 Frascati (fräs-kä′tē).It. (Rome In.) 41·49 N 12·45 E
107 Fraser (frā′zēr)..Mi. (Detroit In.) 42·32 N 82·57 W
203 Fraser (Great Sandy) (I.) (frā′zēr) Austl. 25·12 S 153·00 E
92 Fraser (R.)................Can. 52·20 N 122·35 W
154 Fraserburgh (frā′zēr-bûrg)...Scot. 57·40 N 2·01 W
92 Fraser Plateau..............Can. 51·30 N 122·00 W
163 Frattamaggiore (frät-tä-mäg-zhyô′rē).It. (Naples In.) 40·41 N 14·16 E
137 Fray Bentos (frī bĕn′tōs) Ur. (Buenos Aires In.) 33·10 S 58·19 W
108 Frazee (frȧ-zē′)..............Mn. 46·42 N 95·43 W
128 Fraziers Hog Cay (I.).........Ba. 25·25 N 77·55 W
161 Frechen (frĕ′kĕn) F.R.G. (Ruhr In.) 50·54 N 6·49 E
156 Fredericia (frĕdh-ĕ-rē′tsē-ȧ)..Den. 55·35 N 9·45 E
105 Frederick (frĕd′ēr-ĭk)........Md. 39·25 N 77·25 W
116 Frederick...................Ok. 34·23 N 99·01 W
96 Frederick House (R.)........Can. 49·05 N 81·20 W
118 Fredericksburg (frĕd′ēr-ĭkz-bûrg).Tx. 30·16 N 98·52 W
105 Fredericksburg..............Va. 38·20 N 77·30 W
117 Fredericktown (frĕd′ēr-ĭk-toun).Mo. 37·32 N 90·16 W
98 Fredericton (frĕd′ēr-ĭk-tŭn)..Can. 45·48 N 66·39 W
156 Frederikshavn frĕdh′ĕ-rēks-houn).Den. 57·27 N 10·31 E
156 Frederikssund (frĕdh′ĕ-rēks-soon) Den. 55·51 N 12·04 E
134 Fredonia (frē-dō′nyȧ)...Col. (In.) 5·55 N 75·40 W
117 Fredonia (frē-dō′nĭ-ȧ).........Ks. 36·31 N 95·50 W
105 Fredonia....................NY 42·25 N 79·20 W
156 Fredrikstad (frådh′rēks-ståd).Nor. 59·14 N 10·58 E
113 Freeburg (frē′bûrg) Il. (St. Louis In.) 38·26 N 89·59 W
106 Freehold (frē′hōld) NJ (New York In.) 40·15 N 74·16 W
106 Freeland (frē′lȧnd)...........Pa. 41·00 N 75·50 W
110 Freeland.........Wa. (Seattle In.) 48·01 N 122·32 W
99 Freels, C. (frēlz)............Can. 46·37 N 53·45 W
89 Freelton (frēl′tŭn) Can. (Toronto In.) 43·24 N 80·02 W
128 Freeport....................Ba. 26·30 N 78·45 W
109 Freeport (frē′pōrt)...........Il. 42·19 N 89·30 W
106 Freeport.....NY (New York In.) 40·39 N 73·35 W
113 Freeport....................Tx. 28·56 N 95·21 W
214 Freetown (frē′toun).........S. L. 8·30 N 13·15 W
162 Fregenal de la Sierra (frā-hȧ-näl′ dā lä syĕr′rä).Sp. 38·09 N 6·40 W
163 Fregene (frĕ-zhĕ′-nĕ) It. (Rome In.) 41·52 N 12·12 E
158 Freiberg (frī′bĕrgh).......G.D.R. 50·54 N 13·18 E
158 Freiburg...................G.D.R. 48·00 N 7·50 E
149 Freienried (frī′ĕn-rēd) F.R.G. (Munich In.) 48·20 N 11·08 E
136 Freirina (frå-ĭ-rē′nä)........Chile 28·35 S 71·26 W
149 Freising (frī′zĭng) F.R.G. (Munich In.) 48·25 N 11·45 E
161 Fréjus (frā-zhüs′)............Fr. 43·28 N 6·46 E
204 Fremantle (frē′măn-t′l).....Austl. 32·03 S 116·05 E
112 Fremont (frē-mŏnt′) Ca. (San Francisco In.) 37·33 N 122·00 W
104 Fremont....................Mi. 43·25 N 85·55 W
108 Fremont....................Ne. 41·26 N 96·30 W
104 Fremont....................Oh. 41·20 N 83·05 W
115 Fremont (R.)................Ut. 38·20 N 111·30 W
111 Fremont Pk.................Wy. 43·05 N 109·35 W

PRONOUNCING INDEX

French Broad — Garfield 283

Page	Name	Pronunciation	Region	Lat. °′	Long. °′
120	French Broad (R.)	(frĕnch brôd)	Tn.-NC	35·59 N	83·01 W
133	French Guiana	(gē-ä′nä)	S. A.	4·20 N	53·00 W
104	French Lick	(frĕnch lĭk)	In.	38·35 N	86·35 W
94	Frenchman (R.)		Can.	49·25 N	108·30 W
111	Frenchman Cr.	(frĕnch-măn)	Mt.	48·51 N	107·20 W
116	Frenchman Cr.		Ne.	40·24 N	101·50 W
114	Frenchman Flat		Nv.	36·55 N	116·11 W
113	French River		Mn. (Duluth In.)	46·54 N	91·54 W
93	Freshfield, Mt.	(frĕsh′fēld)	Can.	51·44 N	116·57 W
124	Fresnillo	(frās-nēl′yô)	Mex.	23·10 N	102·52 W
114	Fresno	(frĕz′nō)	Ca.	36·43 N	119·47 W
134	Fresno	(frĕs′-nô)	Col. (In.)	5·10 N	75·01 W
114	Fresno (R.)	(frĕz′nō)	Ca.	37·00 N	120·24 W
114	Fresno Slough		Ca.	36·39 N	120·12 W
158	Freudenstadt	(froi′den-shtät)	F.R.G.	48·28 N	8·26 E
203	Freycinet Pen.	(frā-sē-nĕ′)	Austl.	42·13 S	148·56 E
115	Fria (R.)	(frē-ä)	Az.	34·03 N	112·12 W
212	Fria, C.	(frĭá)	Namibia	18·15 S	12·10 E
214	Fria		Gui.	10·05 N	13·32 W
136	Frias	(frē-äs)	Arg.	28·43 S	65·03 W
158	Fribourg	(frē-bōōr′)	Switz.	46·48 N	7·07 E
113	Fridley	(frĭd′lĭ)	Mn. (Minneapolis, St. Paul In.)	45·05 N	93·16 W
158	Frieburg	(frī′bōōrgh)	F.R.G.	47·59 N	7·50 E
149	Friedberg	(frēd′bĕrgh)	F.R.G. (Munich In.)	48·22 N	11·00 E
158	Friedland	(frēt′länt)	G.D.R.	53·39 N	13·34 E
158	Friedrichshafen	(frē-drĕks-häf′ĕn)	F.R.G.	47·39 N	9·28 E
117	Friend	(frĕnd)	Ne.	40·40 N	97·16 W
119	Friendswood	(frĕnds′-wŏŏd)	Tx. (In.)	29·31 N	95·11 W
121	Fries	(frēz)	Va.	36·42 N	80·59 W
149	Friesack	(frē′säk)	G.D.R. (Berlin In.)	52·44 N	12·35 E
135	Frio, Cabo (C.)	(kä′bō-frē′ō)	Braz.	22·58 S	42·08 W
118	Frio R.		Tx.	29·00 N	99·15 W
162	Friol	(frē-ōl′)	Sp.	43·02 N	7·48 W
155	Frisian (Is.)	(frē′zhăn)	Neth.	53·30 N	5·20 E
164	Friuli-Venezia Giulia (Reg.)		It.	46·20 N	13·20 E
94	Frobisher L.	(frŏb′ĭsh′ẽr)	Can.	56·25 N	108·20 W
91	Frobisher Bay		Can.	63·48 N	68·31 W
91	Frobisher B.		Can.	62·49 N	66·41 W
148	Frodsham	(frŏdz′ăm)	Eng.	53·18 N	2·48 W
203	Frome, L.	(frōōm)	Austl.	30·40 S	140·13 E
117	Frontenac	(frŏn′tē-năk)	Ks.	37·27 N	94·41 W
125	Frontera	(frôn-tā′rä)	Mex.	18·34 N	92·38 W
160	Frontignan	(frôn-tē-nyäN′)	Fr.	43·26 N	3·45 E
111	Front Ra.	(frŭnt)	Wy.	42·17 N	105·53 W
105	Front Royal	(frŭnt)	Va.	38·55 N	78·10 W
150	Fro Sea	(frô)	Nor.	63·49 N	9·12 E
164	Frosinone	(frō-zē-nō′nâ)	It.	41·38 N	13·22 E
105	Frostburg	(frôst′bûrg)	Md.	39·40 N	78·55 W
115	Fruita	(frōōt-á)	Co.	39·10 N	108·45 W
172	Frunze	(frōōn′zĕ)	Sov. Un.	42·49 N	74·42 E
174	Fryanovo	(f′ryä′nô-vô)	Sov. Un. (Moscow In.)	56·08 N	38·28 E
174	Fryanzino	(f′ryä′zĭ-nô)	Sov. Un. (Moscow In.)	55·58 N	38·05 E
159	Frýdek	(frē′dĕk)	Czech.	49·43 N	18·22 E
158	Frydlant	(frēd′länt)	Czech.	50·56 N	15·05 E
	Fuchien (Prov.), see Fukien				
189	Fuchin	(fōō′chĭn′)	China	47·13 N	132·11 E
193	Fuchou (Foochow)	(fōō′chó)	China	26·02 N	119·18 E
190	Fuchow	(fōō′chō′)	China	39·46 N	121·44 E
195	Fuchu	(fōō′chōō)	Jap. (Tōkyō In.)	35·41 N	139·29 E
193	Fuch′un (R.)		China	29·50 N	120·00 E
126	Fuego (Vol.)	(fwā′gō)	Guat.	14·29 N	90·52 W
163	Fuencarral	(fuān-kär-räl′)	Sp. (Madrid In.)	40·29 N	3·42 W
162	Fuensalida	(fwān-sä-lē′dä)	Sp.	40·04 N	4·15 W
118	Fuente	(fwĕ′n-tĕ)	Mex.	28·39 N	100·34 W
162	Fuente de Cantos	(fwān′tå dā kän′tōs)	Sp.	38·15 N	6·18 W
163	Fuente el Saz	(fwĕn′tå ĕl säth′)	Sp. (Madrid In.)	40·39 N	3·30 W
162	Fuente-Ovejuna	(fwĕn′tå-ōvå-hōō′nä)	Sp.	38·15 N	5·30 W
162	Fuentesaúco	(fwĕn-tå-sä-ōō′kō)	Sp.	41·18 N	5·25 W
122	Fuerte, Rio del (R.)	(rê′ō-dĕl-fōō-ĕ′r-tĕ)	Mex.	26·15 N	108·50 W
135	Fuerte Olimpo	(fwĕr′tå ō-lēm-pō)	Par.	21·10 S	57·49 W
210	Fuerteventura I.	(fwĕr′tå-vĕn-tōō′rä)	Can. Is.	28·24 N	13·21 W
188	Fuhai		China	47·01 N	87·07 E
190	Fuhsien	(fōō′sĭän)	China	39·36 N	121·59 E
195	Fuji	(fōō′jē)	Jap.	35·11 N	138·44 E
195	Fuji (R.)		Jap.	35·20 N	138·23 E
195	Fujidera		Jap. (Ōsaka In.)	34·34 N	135·37 E
195	Fuji-san (Mtn.)	(fōō′jē sän)	Jap.	35·23 N	138·44 E
195	Fujisawa	(fōō′jē-sä′wa)	Jap. (Tōkyō In.)	35·20 N	139·29 E
189	Fuckien (Fuchien) (Prov.)		China	25·40 N	117·30 E
195	Fukuchiyama	(fōō′kōō-chē-yä′mä)	Jap.	35·18 N	135·07 E
195	Fukue (I.)	(fōō-kōō′ā)	Jap.	32·40 N	129·02 E
195	Fukui	(fōō′kōō-ē)	Jap.	36·05 N	136·14 E
195	Fukuoka	(fōō′kōō-ō′kå)	Jap.	33·35 N	130·23 E
195	Fukuoka		Jap. (Tōkyō In.)	31·52 N	139·31 E
194	Fukushima	(fōō′kōō-shē′mä)	Jap.	37·45 N	140·29 E
195	Fukuyama	(fōō′kōō-yä′mä)	Jap.	34·31 N	133·21 E
187	Fūlādī, Kūh-e (Mtn.)		Afg.	34·38 N	67·55 E
158	Fulda R.	(fōōl′dä)	F.R.G.	51·05 N	9·40 E
113	Fullerton	(fōōl′ẽr-tŭn)	Ca. (Los Angeles In.)	33·53 N	117·56 W
119	Fullerton		La.	31·00 N	93·00 W
108	Fullerton		Ne.	41·21 N	97·59 W
120	Fulton	(fŭl′tŭn)	Ky.	36·30 N	88·53 W
117	Fulton		Mo.	38·51 N	91·56 W
105	Fulton		NY	43·20 N	76·25 W
106	Fultondale	(fŭl′tŭn-dāl)	Al. (Birmingham In.)	33·37 N	86·48 W
195	Funabashi	(fōō′nå-bä′shē)	Jap. (Tōkyō In.)	35·43 N	139·59 E
195	Funaya	(fōō-nä′yä)	Jap. (Osaka In.)	34·45 N	135·52 E
210	Funchal	(fōōn-shäl′)	Mad. Is.	32·41 N	16·15 W
134	Fundación	(fōōn-dä-syō′n)	Col.	10·43 N	74·13 W
162	Fundão	(fōōn-douN′)	Port.	40·08 N	7·32 W
96	Fundy, B. of	(fŭn′dĭ)	Can.	45·00 N	66·00 W
96	Fundy Natl. Park		Can.	45·38 N	65·00 W
190	Funing	(fōō′nĭng′)	China	39·55 N	119·16 E
193	Funing Wan (B.)	(fōō′nĭng′)	China	26·48 N	120·35 E
215	Funtua		Nig.	11·31 N	7·17 E
217	Furancungo		Moz.	14·55 S	33·35 E
125	Furbero	(fōōr-bĕ′rô)	Mex.	20·21 N	97·32 W
166	Furmanov	(fûr-mä′nôf)	Sov. Un.	57·14 N	41·11 E
136	Furnas, Represa de (Res.)		Braz. (Rio dê Janeiro In.)	21·00 S	46·00 W
205	Furneaux Group (Is.)	(fûr′nō)	Austl.	40·15 S	146·27 E
158	Fürstenfeld	(für′stĕn-fĕlt)	Aus.	47·02 N	16·03 E
149	Fürstenfeldbruck	(fur′stĕn-fĕld′ brōōk)	F.R.G. (Munich In.)	48·11 N	11·16 E
158	Fürstenwalde	(für′stĕn-väl-dĕ)	G.D.R.	52·21 N	14·04 E
158	Fürth	(fürt)	F.R.G.	49·28 N	11·03 E
195	Furuichi	(fōō′rōō-ē′chē)	Jap. (Ōsaka In.)	34·33 N	135·37 E
195	Fusa	(fōō′sä)	Jap. (Tōkyō In.)	35·52 N	140·08 E
134	Fusagasugá	(fōō-sä-gä-sōō-gá′)	Col. (In.)	4·22 N	74·22 W
195	Fuse		Jap. (Ōsaka In.)	34·40 N	135·43 E
	Fushih, see Yenan				
195	Fushimi	(fōō′shē-mē)	Jap. (Ōsaka In.)	34·57 N	135·47 E
192	Fushun	(fōō′shōōn′)	China	41·50 N	124·00 E
192	Fusung		China	42·12 N	127·12 E
195	Futtsu	(fōō′tsōō′)	Jap. (Tōkyō In.)	35·19 N	139·49 E
195	Futtsu Misaki (C.)	(fōōt′tsōō′ mē-sä′kē)	Jap. (Tōkyō In.)	35·19 N	139·46 E
218	Fuwah	(fōō′wå)	Egypt (Nile In.)	31·13 N	30·35 E
193	Fuyang		China	30·10 N	119·58 E
192	Fuyü	(fōō′yōō)	China	45·20 N	125·00 E
156	Fyn (I.)	(fü′n)	Den.	55·24 N	10·33 E
154	Fyne (L.)	(fīn)	Scot.	56·14 N	5·10 W
156	Fyresdal Vand (L.)	(fu′rĕs-däl vän)	Nor.	59·04 N	7·55 E

G

Page	Name	Pronunciation	Region	Lat. °′	Long. °′
216	Gabela		Ang.	10·48 S	14·20 E
212	Gaborone		Bots.	24·28 S	25·59 E
210	Gabès	(gä′bĕs)	Tun.	33·51 N	10·04 E
210	Gabès, Golfe de (G.)		Tun.	32·22 N	10·59 E
215	Gabil		Chad	11·09 N	18·12 E
202	Gabin	(gŏN′bĕn)	Pol.	52·23 N	19·47 E
209	Gabon	(gá-bôN′)	Afr.	0·30 S	10·45 E
119	Gabriel R.	(gā′brĭ-ĕl)	Tx.	30·38 N	97·15 W
165	Gabrovo	(gäb′rô-vô)	Bul.	42·52 N	25·19 E
134	Gachetá	(gä-chā′tä)	Col (In.)	4·50 N	73·36 W
165	Gacko	(gäts′kô)	Yugo.	43·10 N	18·34 E
120	Gadsden	(gădz′dĕn)	Al.	34·00 N	86·00 W
167	Gadyach	(gäd-yäch′)	Sov. Un.	50·22 N	33·59 E
165	Gaesti	(gä-yĕsh′tê)	Rom.	44·43 N	25·21 E
164	Gaeta	(gä-å′tä)	It.	41·18 N	13·34 E
121	Gaffney	(găf′nĭ)	SC	35·04 N	81·47 W
210	Gafsa	(gäf′sä)	Tun.	34·16 N	8·37 E
166	Gagarin		Sov. Un.	55·32 N	34·58 E
98	Gagetown	(găj′toun)	Can.	45·47 N	66·09 W
214	Gagnoa		Ivory Coast	6·08 N	5·56 W
197	Gagrary (I.)	(gä-grä-rê)	Phil. (In.)	13·23 N	123·58 E
164	Gaïdhouronísi (I.)		Grc. (In.)	34·53 N	25·58 E
146	Gaillac-sur-Tarn	(gà-yäk′sür-tärn′)	Fr.	43·54 N	1·52 E
122	Gaillard Cut	(gä-ēl-yä′rd)	C. Z. (Panama Canal In.)	9·03 N	79·42 W
121	Gainesville	(gānz′vĭl)	Fl.	29·40 N	82·20 W
120	Gainesville		Ga.	34·16 N	83·48 W
117	Gainesville		Tx.	33·38 N	97·08 W
148	Gainsborough	(gānz′bŭr-ō)	Eng.	53·23 N	0·46 W
203	Gairdner, L.	(gård′nẽr)	Austl.	32·20 S	136·30 E
106	Gaithersburg	(gā′thẽrs′bûrg)	Md. (Baltimore In.)	39·08 N	77·13 W
217	Galana (R.)		Ken.	3·00 S	39·30 E
163	Galapagar	(gä-lä-pä-gär′)	Sp. (Madrid In.)	40·36 N	4·00 W
	Galápagos Is., see Colon, Arch. de				
154	Galashiels	(găl-á-shēlz)	Scot.	55·40 N	2·57 W
167	Galati	(gá-lätz′ĭ)	Rom.	45·25 N	28·05 E
165	Galatina	(gä-lä-tē′nä)	It.	40·10 N	18·12 E
165	Galaxidhion		Grc.	38·26 N	22·22 E
156	Galdhöpiggen		Nor.	61·37 N	8·17 E
118	Galeana	(gä-lå-ä′nä)	Mex.	24·50 N	100·04 W
109	Galena	(gá-lē′nä)	Il.	42·26 N	90·27 W
107	Galena		In. (Louisville In.)	38·21 N	85·55 W
117	Galena		Ks.	37·06 N	94·39 W
119	Galena Pk.		Tx. (In.)	29·44 N	95·14 W
122	Galera, Cerro (Mtn.)	(sĕ′r-rô-gä-lĕ′rä)	C. Z. (In.)	8·55 N	79·38 W
163	Galera (R.)	(gä-lĕ′rä)	It. (Rome In.)	41·58 N	12·21 E
134	Galeras (Vol.)	(gä-lĕ′räs)	Col.	0·57 N	77·27 W
112	Gales (R.)	(gālz)	Or. (Portland In.)	45·33 N	123·11 W
117	Galesburg	(gālz′bûrg)	Il.	40·56 N	90·21 W
109	Galesville	(gālz′vĭl)	Wi.	44·04 N	91·22 W
105	Galeton	(gāl′tŭn)	Pa.	41·45 N	77·40 W
165	Galibolu (Gallipoli)	(gē-lĭb′ô-lōō) (gá-lĭp′ô-lē)	Tur.	40·25 N	26·40 E
170	Galich	(gál′ĭch)	Sov. Un.	58·20 N	42·38 E
159	Galicia (Reg.)	(gá-lĭsh′ĭ-á)	Pol.-Sov. Un.	49·48 N	21·05 E
162	Galicia (Reg.)	(gä-lē′thyä)	Sp.	43·35 N	8·03 W
205	Galilee (L.)	(găl′ĭ-lē)	Austl.	22·23 S	145·09 E
183	Galilee, Sea of		Isr. (Palestine In.)	32·53 N	35·45 E
128	Galina Pt.	(gä-lē′nä)	Jam.	18·25 N	76·50 W
123	Galion	(găl′ĭ-ŭn)	Oh.	40·45 N	82·50 W
117	Galisteo	(gä-lĭs-tå′ō)	NM	35·20 N	106·00 W
151	Galite, La I.	(gä-lēt)	Alg.	37·36 N	8·03 E
218	Galka′yo		Som. (Horn of Afr. In.)	7·00 N	47·30 E
211	Galla (Prov.)	(gäl′lä)	Eth.	7·22 N	35·28 E
164	Gallarate	(gäl-lä-rä′tā)	It.	45·37 N	8·48 E
161	Gallardon	(gä-lär-dôN′)	Fr. (Paris In.)	48·31 N	1·40 E
117	Gallatin	(găl′á-tĭn)	Mo.	39·55 N	93·58 W
120	Gallatin		Tn.	36·23 N	86·28 W
111	Gallatin R.		Mt.	45·12 N	111·10 W
185	Galle	(gäl)	Sri Lanka	6·13 N	80·10 E
163	Gállego (R.)	(gäl-yā′gō)	Sp.	42·27 N	0·37 W
134	Gallinas, Pta. de (Pt.)	(gä-lyē′näs)	Col.	12·10 N	72·10 W
165	Gallipoli	(gäl-lē′pô-lē)	It.	40·03 N	17·58 E
	Gallipoli, see Galibolu				
104	Gallipolis	(găl-ĭ-pô-lēs)	Oh.	38·50 N	82·10 W
150	Gällivare	(yĕl-ĭ-vär′ĕ)	Swe.	68·06 N	20·29 E
162	Gallo (R.)	(gäl′yō)	Sp.	40·43 N	1·42 W
117	Gallup	(găl′ŭp)	NM	35·30 N	108·45 W
211	Galnale Doria R.		Eth.	5·35 N	40·26 E
104	Galt		Can.	43·22 N	80·19 W
154	Galty Mts.		Ire.	52·19 N	8·20 W
117	Galva	(găl′vá)	Il.	41·11 N	90·02 W
119	Galveston	(găl′vĕs-tŭn)	Tx. (In.)	29·18 N	94·48 W
119	Galveston B.		Tx.	29·39 N	94·45 W
119	Galveston I.		Tx. (In.)	29·12 N	94·53 W
154	Galway		Ire.	53·16 N	9·05 W
154	Galway B.	(gôl′wā)	Ire.	53·10 N	9·47 W
214	Gambaga	(gäm-bä′gä)	Ghana	10·32 N	0·26 W
211	Gambela	(găm-bā′lá)	Eth.	8·15 N	34·33 E
210	Gambia	(găm′bē-á)	Afr.	13·38 N	19·38 W
214	Gambia (R.) (Gambie)		Afr.	13·20 N	15·55 W
214	Gambie (R.) (Gambia)		Afr.	13·20 N	15·55 W
216	Gamboma	(gäm-bō′mä)	Con.	1·53 S	15·51 E
156	Gamleby	(gäm′lĕ-bü)	Swe.	57·54 N	16·20 E
197	Gamu	(gä-mōō′)	Phil. (In.)	17·05 N	121·50 E
184	Gandak (R.)		India	26·37 N	84·22 E
99	Gander	(găn′dẽr)	Can.	48·57 N	54·34 W
99	Gander (R.)		Can.	49·10 N	54·35 W
99	Gander L.		Can.	48·55 N	55·40 W
184	Gandhinagar		India	23·30 N	72·47 E
215	Gandi		Nig.	12·55 N	5·49 E
163	Gandia	(gän-dē′ä)	Sp.	38·56 N	0·10 W
184	Ganges, Mouths of	(găn′jēz)	India	21·18 N	88·40 E
184	Ganges (R.)	(găn′jēz)	India	24·32 N	87·58 E
164	Gangi	(gän′jē)	It.	37·48 N	14·15 E
188	Gangtok		India	27·15 N	88·30 E
111	Gannett Pk.	(găn′ĕt)	Wy.	43·10 N	109·38 W
107	Gano	(g′nô)	Oh. (Cincinnati In.)	39·18 N	84·24 W
149	Gänserndorf		Aus. (Vienna In.)	48·21 N	16·43 E
215	Ganwo		Nig.	11·13 N	4·42 E
214	Gao	(gä′ō)	Mali	16·16 N	0·03 W
161	Gap	(gáp)	Fr.	44·34 N	6·08 E
197	Gapan	(gä-pän)	Phil. (In.)	15·18 N	120·56 E
127	Garachiné	(gä-rä-chē′nå)	Pan.	8·02 N	78·22 W
127	Garachiné, Punta (Pt.)	(pōō′n-tä-gä-rä-chē′nå)	Pan.	8·08 N	78·35 W
135	Garanhuns	(gä-rän-yōōNsh′)	Braz.	8·49 S	36·28 W
117	Garber	(gár′bẽr)	Ok.	36·28 N	97·35 W
149	Garching	(gär′kĕng)	F.R.G. (Munich In.)	48·15 N	11·39 E
118	Garcia	(gär-sē′ä)	Mex.	25·90 N	100·37 W
124	Garcia de la Cadena	(dĕ-lä-kä-dĕ-nä)	Mex.	21·14 N	103·26 W
164	Garda, Lago di (L.)	(lä-gō-dē-gär′dä)	It.	45·43 N	10·26 E
160	Gardanne	(går-dån′)	Fr. (In.)	43·28 N	5·29 E
158	Gardelegen	(gär-dē-lā′ghĕn)	G.D.R.	52·32 N	11·22 E
104	Garden (I.)	(gär′d′n)	Mi.	45·50 N	85·50 W
113	Gardena	(gär-dē′nå)	Ca. (Los Angeles In.)	33·53 N	118·19 W
107	Garden City		Mi. (Detroit In.)	42·20 N	83·21 W
116	Garden City		Ks.	37·58 N	100·52 W
113	Garden Grove	(gär′d′n grōv)	Ca. (Los Angeles In.)	33·47 N	117·56 W
184	Garden Reach		India (Calcutta In.)	22·33 N	88·17 E
113	Garden River		Can. (Sault Ste. Marie In.)	46·33 N	84·10 W
184	Gardēz		Afg.	33·43 N	69·09 E
98	Gardiner	(gärd′nẽr)	Me.	44·12 N	69·46 W
111	Gardiner		Mt.	45·03 N	110·43 W
112	Gardiner		Wa. (Seattle In.)	48·03 N	122·55 W
94	Gardiner Dam		Can.	51·17 N	106·51 W
105	Gardner		Ma.	42·35 N	72·00 W
92	Gardner, Can.		Can.	53·28 N	128·15 W
101	Gareloi (I.)	(gär-lōō-ä′)	Ak.	51·40 N	178·48 W
106	Garfield	(gär′fēld)	NJ (New York In.)	40·53 N	74·06 W
113	Garfield		Ut. (Salt Lake City In.)	40·45 N	112·10 W

n -sing; ŋ-baŋk; N-nasalized n; nŏd; cŏmmit; ōld; ôbey; ôrder; fōōd; fŏŏt; ou-out; s-soft; sh-dish; th-thin; pūre; ûnite; ûrn; stŭd; circŭs; ü-as "y" in study; ′-indeterminate vowel.

284 Garfield Heights — Giresun PRONOUNCING INDEX

Page	Name Pronunciation Region	Lat. °′	Long. °′
107	Garfield Heights Oh. (Cleveland In.)	41·25 N	81·36 W
165	Gargaliánoi (gȧr-gä-lyä'nē)...Grc.	37·07 N	21·50 E
157	Gargždai (gärgzh'dī).....Sov. Un.	55·43 N	20·09 E
92	Garibaldi, Mt. (gȧr-ĭ-băl'dē)..Can.	49·51 N	123·01 W
136	Garin (gä-rē'n) Arg. (Buenos Aires In.)	34·10 S	58·44 W
217	Garissa..................Ken.	0·28 S	39·38 E
113	Garland (gär'lănd) Tx. (Dallas, Fort Worth In.)	32·55 N	96·39 W
111	Garland..................Ut.	41·45 N	112·10 W
172	Garm..................Sov. Un.	39·12 N	70·28 E
158	Garmisch-Partenkirchen (gär' mēsh pär'tĕn-kēr'kĕn)....F.R.G.	47·38 N	11·10 E
117	Garnett (gär'nĕt)..........Ks.	38·16 N	95·15 W
160	Garonne Rivière (R.) (gȧ-rôn)..Fr.	44·43 N	0·25 W
215	Garoua (gär'wä)..........Cam.	9·18 N	13·24 E
104	Garrett (găr'ĕt)..........In.	41·20 N	85·10 W
106	Garrison (găr'ĭ-sŭn) NY (New York In.)	41·23 N	73·57 W
108	Garrison..................ND	47·38 N	101·24 W
162	Garrovillas (gä-rô-vēl'yäs).....Sp.	39·42 N	6·30 W
90	Garry (L.) (găr'ĭ)..........Can.	66·16 N	99·23 W
217	Garsen..................Ken.	2·16 S	40·07 E
98	Garson..................Can.	46·34 N	80·52 W
149	Garstedt (gär'shtĕt) F.R.G. (Hamburg In.)	53·40 N	9·58 E
184	Gartok (gär-tŏk').........China	31·11 N	80·35 E
184	Garulia..............India (In.)	22·48 N	88·23 E
159	Garwolin (gär-vō'lēn)........Pol.	51·54 N	21·40 E
107	Gary (gā'rĭ)....In. (Chicago In.)	41·35 N	87·21 W
119	Garza-Little Elm Res.........Tx.	33·16 N	96·54 W
134	Garzón (gär-thōn').........Col.	2·13 N	75·44 W
197	Gasan (gä-sän')........Phil. (In.)	13·19 N	121·52 E
171	Gasan-Kuli............Sov. Un.	37·25 N	53·55 E
104	Gas City (găs)..............In.	40·30 N	85·40 W
160	Gascogne (Reg.) (gäs-kôn'yĕ).Fr.	43·45 N	1·49 W
117	Gasconade (R.) (găs-kô-nād') Mo.	37·46 N	92·15 W
204	Gascoyne (R.) (găs-koin')..Austl.	25·15 S	117·00 E
113	Gashland (găsh'-lănd) Mo. (Kansas City In.)	39·15 N	94·35 W
215	Gashua..................Nig.	12·54 N	11·00 E
161	Gasny (gäs-nē')....Fr. (Paris In.)	49·05 N	1·36 E
98	Gaspé..................Can.	48·50 N	64·29 W
98	Gaspé, Baie de (B.) (gas'pā) (gȧs-pā').Can.	48·35 N	63·45 W
98	Gaspé, Cape de (C.).........Can.	48·45 N	63·34 W
98	Gaspé, Péninsule de (Pen.)...Can.	48·23 N	65·42 W
129	Gasper Hernandez (gäs-pär' ĕr-nän'dāth).Dom. Rep.	19·40 N	70·15 W
104	Gassaway (găs'ȧ-wā).........WV	38·40 N	80·45 W
112	Gaston (găs'tŭn) Or. (Portland In.)	45·26 N	123·08 W
121	Gastonia (găs-tō'nĭ-ȧ)........NC	35·15 N	81·14 W
136	Gastre (gäs-trĕ)............Arg.	42·12 S	68·50 W
162	Gata, Cabo de (C.) (kȧ'bō-dĕ-gä'tä).Sp.	36·42 N	2·00 W
162	Gata, Sierra de (Mts.) (syĕr'rȧ dā gȧ'tä).Sp.	40·12 N	6·39 W
183	Gátes, Akrotírion (C.) Cyprus (Palestine In.)	34·30 N	33·15 E
174	Gatchina (gä-chē'nȧ) Sov. Un. (Leningrad In.)	59·33 N	30·08 E
154	Gateshead (gāts'hĕd)........Eng.	54·56 N	1·38 W
119	Gatesville (gāts'vĭl).........Mex.	31·26 N	97·34 W
89	Gatineau (gȧ'tē-nō) Can. (Ottawa In.)	45·29 N	75·38 W
89	Gatineau (R.)..Can. (Ottawa In.)	45·45 N	75·50 W
89	Gatineau, Parc de la (Natl. Pk.) Can. (Ottawa In.)	45·32 N	75·53 W
217	Gatooma (gȧ-tōō'mä)........Rh.	18·21 S	29·55 E
149	Gattendorf.....Aus. (Vienna In.)	48·01 N	17·00 E
122	Gatun (gä-tōōn')......C. Z. (In.)	9·16 N	79·25 W
122	Gatun, L..........Pan.-C. Z. (In.)	9·13 N	79·24 W
122	Gatun (R.)...........Pan. (In.)	9·21 N	79·10 W
122	Gatun Locks..........C. Z. (In.)	9·16 N	79·27 W
184	Gauhāti..................India	26·09 N	91·51 E
157	Gauja (R.) (gȧ'ōō-yȧ)...Sov. Un.	57·10 N	24·30 E
197	Gauttier-Gebergte (Mts.) (gō-tyā') Indon.	2·30 S	138·45 E
164	Gávdhos (I.) (gäv'dôs)..Grc. (In.)	34·48 N	24·08 E
108	Gavins Point Dam (gă'-vĭns).Ne.	42·47 N	97·47 W
156	Gävle (yĕv'lĕ).............Swe.	60·40 N	17·07 E
156	Gavle-bukten (B.)..........Swe.	60·45 N	17·30 E
166	Gavrilov Posad (gȧ'vrē-lôf'ka po-sȧt).Sov. Un.	56·34 N	40·09 E
166	Gavrilov-Yam (gȧ'vrē-lôf yäm') Sov. Un.	57·17 N	39·49 E
203	Gawler (gô'lēr)............Austl.	34·35 S	138·47 E
203	Gawler Ra.................Austl.	32·35 S	136·30 E
184	Gaya (gŭ'yä) (gī'ȧ).........India	24·53 N	85·00 E
210	Gaya (gä'yä)...............Nig.	11·58 N	9·05 E
104	Gaylord (gā'lôrd)............Mi.	45·00 N	84·35 W
203	Gayndah (gān'dāh)........Austl.	25·43 S	151·33 E
167	Gaysin.................Sov. Un.	48·46 N	29·22 E
	Gaza, see Ghazzah		
171	Gaziantep (gä-zē-än'tĕp).....Tur.	37·10 N	37·30 E
214	Gbarnga..................Lib.	7·00 N	9·29 W
159	Gdańsk (Danzig) (g'dänsk) (dän'tsĕg).Pol.	54·20 N	18·40 E
166	Gdov (g'dôf')...........Sov. Un.	58·44 N	27·51 E
159	Gdynia (g'dēn'yȧ)...........Pol.	54·29 N	18·30 E
116	Geary (gē'rĭ)................Ok.	35·36 N	98·19 W
214	Géba (R.)..........Guinea-Bissau	12·25 N	14·35 W
111	Gebo (gĕb'ō)................Wy.	43·49 N	108·13 W
119	Ged (gĕd)...................La.	30·07 N	93·36 W
153	Gediz (R.)..................Tur.	38·44 N	28·45 E
112	Gedney (I.) (gĕd-nē) Wa. (Seattle In.)	48·01 N	122·18 W
158	Gedser....................Den.	54·35 N	12·08 E
149	Geel..........Bel. (Brussels In.)	51·09 N	5·01 E
202	Geelong (jē-lông') Austl. (Melbourne In.)	38·06 S	144·13 E
197	Geelvink-baai (B.) (gāl'vĭnk) Indon.	2·20 S	135·30 E
215	Geidam....................Nig.	12·57 N	11·57 E
204	Geikie Ra. (gē'kē).........Austl.	17·35 S	125·32 E
158	Geislingen (gis'lĭng-ĕn).....F.R.G.	48·37 N	9·52 E
107	Geist Res. (gēst) In. (Indianapolis In.)	39·57 N	85·59 W
217	Geita.....................Tan.	2·52 S	32·10 E
149	Geldermalsen Neth. (Amsterdam In.)	51·53 N	5·18 E
161	Geldern (gĕl'dĕrn) F.R.G. (Ruhr In.)	51·31 N	6·20 E
165	Gelibolu, Yarimada (Pen.) (gĕ-lĭb'ô-lōō).Tur.	40·23 N	25·10 E
167	Gel'myazov............Sov. Un.	49·49 N	31·54 E
161	Gelsenkirchen (gĕl-zĕn-kĭrk-ĕn) F.R.G. (Ruhr In.)	51·31 N	7·05 E
183	Gemas (jĕm'ás) Mala. (Singapore In.)	2·35 N	102·37 E
216	Gemena..................Zaire	3·15 N	19·46 E
171	Gemlik (gĕm'lĭk)...........Tur.	40·30 N	29·10 E
218	Genale (R.)................Eth.	5·00 N	41·15 E
137	General Alvear (gĕ-nĕ-räl'ál-vĕ-ȧ'r).Arg. (Buenos Aires In.)	36·04 S	60·02 W
137	General Arenales (ä-rē-nä'lĕs) Arg. (Buenos Aires In.)	34·19 S	61·16 W
137	General Belgrano (bĕl-grá'nô) Arg. (Buenos Aires In.)	35·45 S	58·32 W
118	General Cepeda (sĕ-pĕ'dä)...Mex.	25·24 N	101·29 W
137	General Conesa (kô-nĕ'sä) Arg. (Buenos Aires In.)	36·30 S	57·19 W
137	General Guido (gē'dô) Arg. (Buenos Aires In.)	36·41 S	57·48 W
137	General Lavalle (lȧ-vȧ'l-yĕ) Arg. (Buenos Aires In.)	36·25 S	56·55 W
136	General Madariaga (män-dȧ-rēȧ'gä).Arg.	36·59 S	57·14 W
137	General Paz (pȧ'z) Arg. (Buenos Aires In.)	35·30 S	58·20 W
124	General Pedro Antonio Santios (pĕ'drô-än-tô'nyô-sän-tyōs). Mex.	21·37 N	98·58 W
136	General Pico (pē'kô)........Arg.	36·46 S	63·44 W
136	General Roca (rô-kä)........Arg.	39·01 S	67·31 W
136	General San Martín (sän-mȧr-tē'n) Arg. (Buenos Aires In.)	34·19 S	58·32 W
137	General Viamonte (vēä'môn-tĕ) Arg. (Buenos Aires In.)	35·01 S	60·59 W
118	General Zuazua (zwä'zwä)..Mex.	25·54 N	100·07 W
105	Genesee (R.) (jĕn-ê-sē')......NY	42·25 N	78·10 W
104	Geneseo (jē-nĕs'eō)............Il.	41·28 N	90·11 W
120	Geneva (jê-nē'vȧ)............Al.	31·03 N	85·50 W
113	Geneva..........Il. (Chicago In.)	41·53 N	88·18 W
117	Geneva....................Ne.	40·32 N	97·37 W
105	Geneva....................NY	42·50 N	77·00 W
104	Geneva....................Oh.	41·45 N	80·55 W
	Geneva, see Génève		
158	Geneva, L.................Switz.	46·28 N	6·30 E
158	Génève (Geneva) (zhē-nĕv').Switz.	46·14 N	6·04 E
167	Genichesk (gĕnē-chyĕsk') Sov. Un.	46·11 N	34·47 E
162	Genil (R.) (hȧ-nēl')..........Sp.	37·15 N	4·05 W
117	Genoa (jen'ō-ȧ).............Ne.	41·26 N	97·43 W
	Genoa, see Genova		
107	Genoa City..Wi. (Milwaukee In.)	42·31 N	88·19 W
164	Genova (Genoa) (jĕn'ō-vä).....It.	44·23 N	9·52 E
164	Genova, Golfo di (G.) (gôl-fō-dē-jĕn'ō-vä).It.	44·10 N	8·45 E
122	Genovesa (I.) (ĕ's-lä-gĕ-nō-vĕ-sä) Ec.	0·08 N	90·15 W
155	Gent......................Bel.	51·05 N	3·40 E
158	Genthin (gĕn-tēn').......G.D.R.	52·24 N	12·10 E
163	Genzano di Roma (gzhĕnt-zȧ'-nô-dē-rô'-mä) It. (Rome In.)	41·43 N	12·49 E
204	Geographe B. (jē-ô-grăf')...Austl.	33·00 S	114·00 E
204	Geographic Chan. (jēō'gră-fĭk) Austl.	24·15 S	112·50 E
171	Geokchay (gĕ-ôk'chī)....Sov. Un.	40·40 N	47·40 E
121	George (L.) (jôr-ĭj)...........Fl.	29·10 N	81·50 W
105	George (L.) (jôrj)............NY	43·40 N	73·30 W
113	George L. (jôrg) Can.-U. S. (Sault Ste. Marie In.)	46·26 N	84·09 W
107	George, L.......In. (Chicago In.)	41·31 N	87·17 W
217	George, L..................Ug.	0·02 N	30·25 E
202	Georges (R.)..Austl. (Sydney In.)	33·57 S	151·00 E
129	George Town................Ba.	23·30 N	75·50 W
135	Georgetown (jôrj'toun)......Guy.	7·45 N	58·04 W
99	Georgetown (jôr-ĭj-toun).....Can.	46·11 N	62·32 W
89	Georgetown (jôrg-toun) Can. (Toronto In.)	43·39 N	79·56 W
106	Georgetown..Ct. (New York In.)	41·15 N	73·25 W
105	Georgetown.................De.	38·40 N	75·20 W
128	Georgetown..........Cayman Is.	19·20 N	81·20 W
104	Georgetown..................Il.	40·00 N	87·40 W
104	Georgetown.................Ky.	38·10 N	84·35 W
105	Georgetown.................Md.	39·25 N	75·55 W
99	Georgetown (jôrg-toun)..Ma. (In.)	42·43 N	71·00 W
121	Georgetown (jôr-ĭj-toun).......S. C.	33·22 N	79·17 W
119	Georgetown (jôrg-toun).......Tx.	30·37 N	97·40 W
105	George Washington Birthplace Natl. Mon. (jôrj wŏsh'ĭng-tŭn) Va.	38·10 N	77·00 W
117	George Washington Carver Natl. Mon. (jôrg wăsh-ĭng-tŭn kär'vēr).Mo.	36·58 N	94·21 W
118	George West...............Tx.	28·20 N	98·07 W
103	Georgia (State) (jôr'ji-ă)....U. S.	32·40 N	83·50 W
92	Georgia, Str. of............Can.	49·20 N	124·00 W
112	Georgia, Str. of Wa. (Vancouver In.)	48·56 N	123·06 W
168	Georgian (S. S. R.)......Sov. Un.	42·17 N	43·00 E
96	Georgian B.................Can.	45·15 N	80·50 W
96	Georgian Bay Is. Natl. Pk....Can.	45·20 N	81·40 W
120	Georgiana (jôr-jē-ăn'ȧ)........Al.	31·39 N	86·44 W
204	Georgina (R.) (jôr-jē'nȧ)...Austl.	22·00 S	138·15 E
171	Georgiyevsk (gyôr-gyĕfsk') Sov. Un.	44·05 N	43·30 E
158	Gera (gā'rä).............G.D.R.	50·52 N	12·06 E
136	Geral, Serra (Mts.) (sĕr'rȧ zhȧ-räl').Braz.	28·30 S	51·00 W
153	Geral de Goiás, Serra (Mts.) (zhȧ-räl'-dĕ-gô-yȧ's).Braz.	14·22 S	45·40 W
204	Geraldton (jĕr'ăld-tŭn).....Austl.	28·40 S	114·35 E
91	Geraldton..................Can.	49·43 N	87·00 W
162	Gérgal (gĕr'gäl)..............Sp.	37·08 N	2·29 W
108	Gering (gē'rĭng).............Ne.	41·49 N	103·41 W
159	Gerlachovka Pk..........Czech.	49·12 N	20·05 E
146	German Democratic Republic Eur.	53·30 N	12·30 E
104	Germantown (jûr'mȧn-toun)..Oh.	39·35 N	84·25 W
146	Germany, Federal Republic of (jûr'mȧ-nĭ).Eur.	51·45 N	8·30 E
213	Germiston (jûr'mĭs-tŭn)...S. Afr. (Johannesburg & Pretoria In.)	26·19 S	28·11 E
197	Gerona (hā-rō'nä)......Phil. (In.)	15·36 N	120·36 E
162	Gerona (hĕ-rō'nä)............Sp.	41·55 N	2·48 E
148	Gerrards Cross (jĕr'ards krŏs) Eng. (London In.)	51·34 N	0·33 W
163	Gers (R.) (zhĕr).............Fr.	43·25 N	0·30 E
149	Gersthofen (gĕrst-hō'fĕn) F.R.G. (Munich In.)	48·26 N	10·54 E
163	Getafe (hā-tä'fȧ).Sp. (Madrid In.)	40·19 N	3·44 W
105	Gettysburg (gĕt'ĭs-bûrg)......Pa.	39·50 N	77·15 W
108	Gettysburg..................SD	45·01 N	99·59 W
161	Gevelsberg (gĕ-fĕls'bĕrgh) F.R.G. (Ruhr In.)	51·18 N	7·20 E
184	Ghāghra (R.)..............India	27·19 N	81·22 E
209	Ghana (gän'ä)..............Afr.	8·00 N	2·00 W
212	Ghanzi (gän'zē)............Bots.	21·30 S	22·00 E
210	Ghardaïa (gär-dä'ē-ä)........Alg.	32·29 N	3·38 E
184	Gharo......................Pak.	24·50 N	68·35 E
210	Ghāt.......................Libya	24·52 N	10·16 E
211	Ghazāl, Bahr al- (R.)........Sud.	9·11 N	29·37 E
215	Ghazal, Bahr el (R.) (bär ĕl ghä-zäl').Chad.	14·30 N	17·00 E
151	Ghazaouet..................Alg.	35·19 N	1·09 W
184	Ghaznī (gŭz'nē).............Afg.	33·43 N	68·18 E
183	Ghazzah (Gaza) Gaza Strip (Palestine In.)	31·30 N	34·29
159	Gheorghieni.................Rom.	46·48 N	25·30 E
159	Gherla (gĕr'lä)..............Rom.	47·01 N	23·55 E
89	Ghost Lake....Can. (Calgary In.)	51·15 N	114·46 W
210	Ghudāmis..................Libya	30·07 N	9·26 E
164	Giannutri, I. di (jän-nōō'trē)...It.	42·15 N	11·06 E
129	Gibara (hē-bä'rä)...........Cuba	21·05 N	76·10 W
212	Gibeon (gĭb'ē-ŭn).........Namibia	24·45 S	16·40 E
162	Gibraleón (hē-brä-lā-ōn')..... Sp.	37·24 N	7·00 W
151	Gibraltar (hē-bräl-tä'r).......Eur.	36·08 N	5·22 W
162	Gibraltar, Bay of.............Sp.	35·04 N	5·10 W
162	Gibraltar, Str. of.......Afr.-Eur.	35·55 N	5·45 W
104	Gibson City (gĭb'sŭn)..........Il.	40·25 N	88·20 W
204	Gibson Des.................Austl.	24·45 S	123·15 E
106	Gibson Island.Md. (Baltimore In.)	39·05 N	76·26 W
117	Gibson Res...................Ok.	36·07 N	95·08 W
119	Giddings (gĭd'ĭngz)...........Tx.	30·11 N	96·55 W
117	Gideon (gĭd'ē-ŭn)............Mo.	36·27 N	89·56 W
160	Gien (zhē-ăn')...............Fr.	47·43 N	2·37 E
158	Giessen (gēs'sĕn).........F.R.G.	50·35 N	8·40 E
89	Giffard (zhē-färd') Can. (Quebec In.)	46·51 N	71·12 W
195	Gifu (gē'fōō)................Jap.	35·25 N	136·45 E
112	Gig Harbor (gĭg).Wa. (Seattle In.)	47·20 N	122·36 W
164	Giglio, I. di (jēl'yō)..........It.	42·23 N	10·55 E
162	Gigüela (R.) (hē-gā'lä)........Sp.	39·53 N	2·54 W
162	Gijón (hē-hōn')..............Sp.	43·33 N	5·37 W
115	Gila (R.) (hē'lȧ)..............Az.	32·41 N	113·50 W
115	Gila Bend...................Az.	32·59 N	112·41 W
115	Gila Bend Ind. Res...........Az.	33·02 N	112·48 W
115	Gila Cliff Dwellings Natl. Mon. NM	33·15 N	108·20 W
115	Gila River Ind. Res...........Az.	33·11 N	112·38 W
109	Gilbert (gĭl'bērt)............Mn.	47·27 N	92·29 W
205	Gilbert (R.) (gĭl-bērt)......Austl.	17·15 S	142·09 E
92	Gilbert, Mt.................Can.	50·51 N	124·20 W
198	Gilbert Is.................Oceania	1·30 S	173·00 E
213	Gilboa, Mt. (gĭl-bōȧ) S. Afr. (Natal In.)	29·13 S	30·17 E
92	Gilford I. (gĭl'fērd)..........Can.	50·45 N	126·25 W
184	Gilgit (gĭl'gĭt)..............Pak.	35·58 N	73·48 E
92	Gil I. (gĭl)..................Can.	53·13 N	129·15 W
204	Gillen (I.) (jĭl'ĕn)..........Austl.	26·15 S	125·15 E
117	Gillett (jĭ-lĕt')...............Ar.	34·07 N	91·22 W
111	Gillette.....................Wy.	44·17 N	105·30 W
148	Gillingham (gĭl'ĭng ăm) Eng. (London In.)	51·23 N	0·33 E
104	Gilman (gĭl'măn)..............Il.	40·45 N	87·55 W
113	Gilman Hot Springs Ca. (Los Angeles In.)	33·49 N	116·57 W
119	Gilmer (gĭl'mēr).............Tx.	32·43 N	94·57 W
106	Gilmore (gĭl'môr).Ga. (Atlanta In.)	33·51 N	84·29 W
114	Gilroy (gĭl-roi')..............Ca.	37·00 N	121·34 W
197	Giluwe, Mt.........Pap. N. Gui.	6·04 S	144·00 E
95	Gimli (gĭm'lē)...............Can.	50·39 N	97·00 W
160	Gimone (R.) (zhē-mōn').......Fr.	43·26 N	0·36 E
211	Ginir.......................Eth.	7·13 N	40·44 E
164	Ginosa (jê-nō'zä)..............It.	40·35 N	16·48 E
162	Ginzo (hēn-thō')..............Sp.	42·03 N	7·43 W
164	Gioia del Colle (jō'yä dĕl kôl'lā).It.	40·48 N	16·55 E
135	Gi-Paraná (R.) (zhē-pä-rä-nä') Braz.	9·33 S	61·35 W
117	Girard (jĭ-rärd')..............Ks.	37·30 N	94·50 W
134	Girardot (hē-rär-dōt')...Col. (In.)	4·19 N	75·47 W
171	Giresun (ghĕr'ĕ-sōōn').......Tur.	40·55 N	38·20 E

ăt; finăl; rāte; senâte; ärm; ȧsk; sofȧ; fâre; ch-choose; dh-as th in other; bē; êvent; bĕt; recĕnt; cratēr; g-go; gh-guttural g; bĭt; ĭ-short neutral; rīde; K-guttural k as ch in German ich;

PRONOUNCING INDEX Giridih — Grafton 285

Page	Name	Pronunciation	Region	Lat. °'	Long. °'
184	Giridih	(jē'rē-dē)	India	24·12 N	81·18 E
160	Gironde (Est.)	(zhē-rônd')	Fr.	45·31 N	1·00 W
154	Girvan	(gûr'văn)	Scot.	55·15 N	5·01 W
205	Gisborne	(gĭz'bŭrn)	N. Z. (In.)	38·40 S	178·08 E
217	Gisenyi		Rw.	1·43 S	29·15 E
160	Gisors	(zhē-zôr')	Fr.	49·19 N	1·47 E
216	Gitambo		Zaire	4·21 N	24·45 E
212	Gitega		Burundi	3·39 S	30·05 E
165	Giurgui	(jōōr'jōō)	Rom.	43·53 N	25·58 E
160	Givet	(zhē-vĕ')	Fr.	50·80 N	4·47 E
160	Givors	(zhē-vôr')	Fr.	45·35 N	4·46 E
173	Gizhiga	(gē'zhi-gȧ)	Sov. Un.	61·59 N	160·46 E
159	Gizycko	(gĭ'zhĭ-ko)	Pol.	54·03 N	21·48 E
165	Gjinokastër		Alb.	40·04 N	20·10 E
156	Gjövik	(gyû'vĕk)	Nor.	60·47 N	10·36 E
149	Glabeek-Zuurbemde		Bel. (Brussels In.)	50·52 N	4·59 E
99	Glace Bay	(glās bā)	Can.	46·12 N	59·57 W
101	Glacier Bay Natl. Mon.	(glā'shēr)	Ak.	58·40 N	136·50 W
93	Glacier Natl. Park		Can.	51·45 N	117·35 W
110	Glacier Pk.		Wa.	48·07 N	121·10 W
112	Glacier Pt.		Can. (Seattle In.)	48·24 N	123·59 W
161	Gladbeck	(gläd'bĕk)	F.R.G. (Ruhr In.)	51·35 N	6·59 E
218	Gladdeklipkop		S. Afr. (Johannesburg & Pretoria In.)	24·17 S	29·36 E
203	Gladstone	(glăd'stōn)	Austl.	23·45 S	150·00 E
203	Gladstone		Austl.	33·15 S	138·20 E
102	Gladstone		Can.	50·15 N	98·50 W
109	Gladstone		Mi.	45·50 N	87·04 W
106	Gladstone		NJ (New York In.)	40·43 N	74·39 W
112	Gladstone		Or. (Portland In.)	45·23 N	122·36 W
104	Gladwin	(glăd'wĭn)	Mi.	44·00 N	84·25 W
164	Glamoč	(glăm'ōch)	Yugo.	44·03 N	16·51 E
158	Glarus	(glä'rōōs)	Switz.	47·02 N	9·03 E
120	Glasgow		Ky.	37·00 N	85·55 W
117	Glasgow		Mo.	39·14 N	92·48 W
111	Glasgow		Mt.	48·14 N	106·39 W
154	Glasgow	(glȧs'gō)	Scot.	55·54 N	4·25 W
107	Glassport	(glȧs'pōrt)	Pa. (Pittsburgh In.)	40·19 N	79·53 W
158	Glauchau	(glou'kou)	G.D.R.	50·51 N	12·28 E
170	Glazov	(glä'zôf)	Sov. Un.	58·05 N	52·52 E
158	Glda (R.)	(g'l'dȧ)	Pol.	53·27 N	16·52 E
148	Glen (R.)	(glĕn)	Eng.	52·44 N	0·18 W
160	Glénans, Iles de (Is.)	(ēl-dĕ-glā-näN')	Fr.	47·43 N	4·42 W
106	Glen Burnie	(bûr'nē)	Md. (Baltimore In.)	39·10 N	76·38 W
115	Glen Canyon Dam	(glĕn kăn'yŭn)	Az.	36·57 N	111·25 W
113	Glen Carbon	(kär'bŏn)	Il. (St. Louis In.)	38·45 N	89·59 W
107	Glencoe		Il. (Chicago In.)	42·08 N	87·45 W
109	Glencoe	(glĕn'kō)	Mn.	44·44 N	94·07 W
213	Glencoe	(glĕn-cō)	S. Afr. (Natal In.)	28·14 S	30·09 E
106	Glen Cove	(kōv)	NY (New York In.)	40·51 N	73·38 W
115	Glendale	(glĕn'dāl)	Az.	33·30 N	112·15 W
113	Glendale		Ca. (Los Angeles In.)	34·09 N	118·15 W
107	Glendale		Oh. (Cincinnati In.)	31·16 N	84·22 W
111	Glendive	(glĕn'dīv)	Mt.	47·08 N	104·41 W
111	Glendo		Wy.	42·32 N	104·54 W
113	Glendora	(glĕn-dō'rȧ)	Ca. (Los Angeles In.)	34·08 N	117·52 W
203	Glenelg (R.)		Austl.	37·20 S	141·30 E
107	Glen Ellyn	(glĕn ĕl'-lĕn)	Il. (Chicago In.)	41·53 N	88·04 W
203	Glen Innes	(ĭn'ĕs)	Austl.	29·45 S	152·02 E
119	Glenmora	(glĕn-mō'rȧ)	La.	30·58 N	92·36 W
110	Glenns Ferry	(fĕr'ĭ)	Id.	42·58 N	115·21 W
121	Glenville	(glĕn'vĭl)	Ga.	31·55 N	81·56 W
106	Glen Olden	(ōl'd'n)	Pa. (Philadelphia In.)	39·54 N	75·17 W
111	Glenrock	(glĕn'rŏk)	Wy.	42·50 N	105·53 W
105	Glens Falls	(glĕnz fôlz)	NY	43·20 N	73·40 W
107	Glenshaw	(glĕn'shô)	Pa. (Pittsburgh In.)	40·33 N	79·57 W
108	Glen Ullin	(glĕn'ŭl'ĭn)	ND	46·47 N	101·49 W
112	Glen Valley		Can. (Vancouver In.)	49·09 N	122·30 W
107	Glenview	(glĕn'vū)	Il. (Chicago In.)	42·04 N	87·48 W
108	Glenwood		Ia.	41·03 N	95·44 W
108	Glenwood		Mn.	45·39 N	95·23 W
115	Glenwood Springs		Co.	39·35 N	107·20 W
149	Glienicke	(glē'nē-kĕ)	G.D.R. (Berlin In.)	52·38 N	13·19 E
149	Glinde	(glĕn'dĕ)	F.R.G.(Hamburg In.)	53·32 N	10·13 E
156	Glittertinden (Mtn.)		Nor.	61·39 N	8·12 E
159	Gliwice	(gwĭ-wĭt'sĕ)	Pol.	50·18 N	18·40 E
115	Globe	(glōb)	Az.	33·20 N	110·50 W
167	Globino	(glô'bê-nō)	Sov. Un.	49·22 N	33·17 E
158	Głogów	(gwō'gōōv)	Pol.	51·40 N	16·04 E
156	Glomma (R.)	(glômmä)	Nor.	61·22 N	11·02 E
156	Glommen (R.)	(glôm'ĕn)	Nor.	60·03 N	11·15 E
149	Glonn	(glônn)	F.R.G. (Munich In.)	47·59 N	11·52 E
213	Glorieuses, Îles (Is.)		Afr.	11·28 S	47·50 E
148	Glossop	(glŏs'ŭp)	Eng.	53·26 N	1·57 W
120	Gloster	(glŏs'tēr)	Ms.	31·10 N	91·00 W
154	Gloucester	(glŏs'tēr)	Eng.	51·54 N	2·11 W
99	Gloucester		Ma. (In.)	42·37 N	70·40 W
106	Gloucester City		NJ (Philadelphia In.)	39·53 N	75·08 W
104	Glouster	(glŏs'tēr)	Oh.	39·35 N	82·05 W
99	Glover I.	(glŭv'ēr)	Can.	48·44 N	57·45 W
105	Gloversville	(glŭv'ērz-vĭl)	NY	43·05 N	74·20 W
99	Glovertown	(glŭv'ēr-toun)	Can.	48·41 N	54·02 W
166	Glubokoye	(glōō-bô-kō'yĕ)	Sov. Un.	55·08 N	27·44 E
149	Glückstadt	(glük-shtät)	F.R.G. (Hamburg In.)	53·47 N	9·25 E
167	Glukhov	(glōō'kôf')	Sov. Un.	51·42 N	33·52 E
167	Glushkovo	(glōōsh'kô-vō)	Sov. Un.	51·21 N	34·43 E
158	Gmünden	(g'mōōn'dĕn)	Aus.	47·57 N	13·47 E
159	Gniezno	(g'nyåz'nō)	Pol.	52·32 N	17·34 E
165	Gnjilane	(gnyē'lȧ-nĕ)	Yugo.	42·28 N	21·27 E
185	Goa (Ter.)	(gō'ȧ)	India	15·45 N	74·00 E
126	Goascorán	(gō-äs'kō-rän')	Hond.	13·37 N	87·43 W
211	Goba	(gō'bä)	Eth.	7·17 N	39·58 E
212	Gobabis	(gō-bä'bĭs)	Namibia	22·25 S	18·50 E
188	Gobi or Shamo (Des.)	(gō'be)	Mong.	43·29 N	103·15 E
112	Goble	(gō'b'l)	Or. (Portland In.)	46·01 N	122·53 W
161	Goch	(gōk)	F.R.G. (Ruhr In.)	51·35 N	6·10 E
184	Godāvari (R.)	(gô-dä'vŭ-rē)	India	17·42 N	81·15 E
204	Goddards Soak (Swp.)	(gŏd'ȧrdz)	Austl.	31·20 S	123·30 E
104	Goderich	(gōd'rĭch)	Can.	43·45 N	81·45 W
113	Godfrey	(gŏd'frē)	Il. (St. Louis In.)	38·57 N	90·12 W
75	Godhavn	(gōdh'hȧvn)	Grnld.	69·15 N	53·30 W
95	Gods (R.)	(gŏdz)	Can.	55·17 N	93·35 W
95	Gods Lake		Can.	54·40 N	94·09 W
75	Godthåb	(gŏt'hōōb)	Grnld.	64·10 N	51·32 W
189	Godwin Austen, Mt.	(gŏd wĭn ôs'tĕn)	Pak.	36·06 N	76·38 E
97	Goéland, Lac au (L.)		Can.	49·47 N	76·41 W
114	Goffs	(gôfs)	Ca.	34·57 N	115·06 W
109	Gogebic (L.)	(gô-gē'bĭk)	Mi.	46·24 N	89·25 W
109	Gogebic Ra.		Mi.	46·37 N	89·48 W
149	Goggingen	(gûg'gĕn-gĕn)	F.R.G. (Munich In.)	48·21 N	10·53 E
157	Gogland (I.)		Sov. Un.	60·04 N	26·55 E
215	Gogonou		Benin	10·50 N	2·50 E
124	Gogorrón	(gō-gô-rōn')	Mex.	21·51 N	100·54 W
135	Goiânia	(gô-vä'nyä)	Braz.	16·41 S	48·57 W
135	Goiás	(gô-yà's)	Braz.	15·57 S	50·10 W
135	Goiás (State)		Braz.	12·35 S	48·38 W
149	Goirle		Neth. (Amsterdam In.)	51·31 N	5·06 E
171	Göksu (R.)	(gûk'sōō')	Tur.	36·40 N	33·30 E
156	Göl	(gûl)	Nor.	60·58 N	8·54 E
121	Golax	(gō'lăks)	Va.	36·41 N	80·56 W
148	Golcar	(gŏl'kȧr)	Eng.	53·38 N	1·52 W
117	Golconda	(gŏl-kŏn'dȧ)	Il.	37·21 N	88·32 W
159	Gołdap	(gŏl'dăp)	Pol.	54·17 N	22·17 E
93	Golden		Can.	51·18 N	116·58 W
116	Golden		Co.	39·44 N	105·15 W
110	Goldendale	(gōl'dĕn-dāl)	Wa.	45·49 N	120·48 W
112	Golden Gate (Str.)	(gōl'dĕn gāt)	Ca. (San Francisco In.)	37·48 N	122·32 W
92	Golden Hinde	(hīnd)	Can.	49·40 N	125·45 W
106	Golden's Bridge		NY (New York In.)	41·17 N	73·41 W
113	Golden Valley		Mn. (Minneapolis, St. Paul In.)	44·58 N	93·23 W
114	Goldfield	(gōld'fēld)	Nv.	37·42 N	117·15 W
122	Gold Hill (Mtn.)		C. Z. (In.)	9·03 N	79·08 W
112	Gold Mtn.	(gōld)	Wa. (Seattle In.)	47·33 N	122·48 W
121	Goldsboro	(gōldz-bûr'ô)	NC	35·23 N	77·59 W
118	Goldthwaite	(gōld'thwāt)	Tx.	31·27 N	98·34 W
158	Goleniów	(gô-lĕ-nyŭf')	Pol.	53·33 N	14·51 E
173	Golets-Purpula, Gol'tsy (Mtn.)		Sov. Un.	59·08 N	115·22 E
127	Golfito	(gôl-fē'tō)	C. R.	8·40 N	83·12 W
	Golfo Dulce, see Izabal, L.				
119	Goliad	(gō-lĭ-ăd')	Tx.	28·40 N	97·12 W
197	Golo	(gō'lō)	Phil. (In.)	13·38 N	120·17 E
164	Golo (R.)		Fr.	42·28 N	9·18 E
167	Golovchino	(gō-lôf'chê-nō)	Sov. Un.	50·34 N	35·52 E
165	Golyamo Konare	(gō'lȧ-mō-kō'nä-rĕ)	Bul.	42·16 N	24·33 E
149	Golzow	(gōl'tsōv)	G.D.R. (Berlin In.)	52·17 N	12·36 E
217	Gombari	(gōōm-bä-rē)	Zaire	2·45 N	29·00 E
215	Gombe		Nig.	10·19 N	11·02 E
166	Gomel'	(go'mĕl')	Sov. Un.	52·20 N	31·03 E
166	Gomel' (Oblast)		Sov. Un.	52·18 N	29·00 E
210	Gomera I.	(gô-mā'rä)	Can. Is.	28·00 N	18·01 W
118	Gomez Farias	(gō'māz fä-rē'ás)	Mex.	24·59 N	101·02 W
118	Gómez Palacio	(pä-lä'syō)	Mex.	25·35 N	103·30 W
129	Gonaïves	(gō-nȧ-ēv')	Hai.	19·25 N	72·45 W
129	Gonaïves, Golfe des (G.)	(gō-nȧ-ēv')	Hai.	19·20 N	73·20 W
129	Gonâve, Ile De La (I.)	(gô-nàv')	Hai.	18·50 N	73·30 W
184	Gonda		India	27·13 N	82·00 E
184	Gondal		India	22·02 N	70·47 E
211	Gonder		Eth.	12·39 N	37·30 E
161	Gonesse	(gô-nĕs')	Fr. (Paris In.)	48·59 N	2·28 E
215	Goniri		Nig.	11·30 N	12·20 E
195	Gonō (R.)	(gô'nō)	Jap.	35·00 N	132·25 E
89	Gonor	(gō'nŏr)	Can. (Winnepeg In.)	50·04 N	96·57 W
213	Gonubie	(gŏn'ōō-bē)	S. Afr. (Natal In.)	32·56 S	28·02 E
124	Gonzales	(gôn-zä'lĕs)	Mex.	22·47 N	98·26 W
119	Gonzales	(gŏn-zä'lĕz)	Tx.	29·31 N	97·25 W
136	González Catán	(gōn-zä'lĕz-kä-tȧ'n)	Arg. (Buenos Aires In.)	34·31 S	58·39 W
92	Good Hope Mtn.		Can.	51·09 N	124·10 W
212	Good Hope, C. of	(kāp ov gŏŏd hôp)	S. Afr. (In.)	34·21 S	18·29 E
110	Gooding	(gŏŏd'ĭng)	Id.	42·55 N	114·43 W
104	Goodland	(gŏŏd'lănd)	In.	40·50 N	87·15 W
116	Goodland		Ks.	39·19 N	101·43 W
212	Goodwood	(gŏŏd'wŏŏd)	S. Afr. (In.)	33·54 S	18·33 E
148	Goole	(gōōl)	Eng.	53·42 N	0·52 W
108	Goose (R.)		ND	47·40 N	97·41 W
91	Goose Bay		Can.	53·19 N	60·33 W
111	Gooseberry Cr.	(gōōs-bĕr'ĭ)	Wy.	44·04 N	108·35 W
111	Goose Cr.	(gōōs)	Id.	42·07 N	113·53 W
110	Goose L.		Ca.	41·56 N	120·35 W
184	Gorakhpur	(gō'rŭk-pōōr)	India	26·45 N	82·39 E
128	Gorda, Punta (Pt.)	(pōō'n-tä-gôr-dä)	Cuba	22·25 N	82·10 W
128	Gorda Cay	(gôr'dä)	Ba.	26·05 N	77·30 W
89	Gordon	(gôr'dŭn)	Can. (Winnipeg In.)	50·00 N	97·20 W
108	Gordon		Ne.	42·47 N	102·14 W
211	Gore	(gō'rĕ)	Eth.	8·12 N	35·34 E
186	Gorgān		Iran	36·44 N	54·30 E
164	Gorgona (I.)	(gôr-gō'nä)	It.	43·27 N	9·55 E
171	Gori	(gō'rē)	Sov. Un.	42·00 N	44·08 E
149	Gorinchem	(gō'rĭn-kĕm)	Neth. (Amsterdam In.)	51·50 N	4·59 E
148	Goring	(gôr'ĭng)	Eng. (London In.)	51·30 N	1·08 W
164	Gorizia	(gô-rē'tsē-yä)	It.	44·56 N	13·40 E
170	Gorki	(gôr'kē)	Sov. Un.	56·15 N	44·05 E
170	Gor'kovskoye		Sov. Un.	56·38 N	43·40 E
166	Gor'kovskoye Vdkhr. (Res.)	(gôr-kôf-skô-yĕ)	Sov. Un.	57·38 N	41·18 E
159	Gorlice	(gôr-lē'tsĕ)	Pol.	49·38 N	21·11 E
158	Görlitz	(gŭr'lĭts)	G.D.R.	51·10 N	15·01 E
167	Gorlovka	(gôr'lôf-kȧ)	Sov. Un.	48·17 N	38·03 E
118	Gorman	(gôr'măn)	Tx.	32·13 N	98·40 W
165	Gorna-Oryakhovitsa	(gôr'nä-ôr-yĕk'ô-vē-tsȧ)	Bul.	43·08 N	25·40 E
165	Gornji Milanovac	(gôrn'yē-mē'lä-nô-väts)	Yugo.	44·02 N	20·29 E
172	Gorno-Altay Aut. Oblast		Sov. Un.	51·00 N	86·00 E
172	Gorno-Altaysk	(gôr'nŭ'ŭl-tīsk')	Sov. Un.	52·28 N	82·45 E
159	Gorodënka	(gō-rô-deŋ'kä)	Sov. Un.	48·40 N	25·30 E
170	Gorodets (Res.)		Sov. Un.	57·00 N	43·55 E
174	Gorodishche	(gô-rô'dĭsh-chĕ)	Sov. Un. (Urals In.)	57·57 N	57·03 E
167	Gorodnya	(gô-rôd''nyä)	Sov. Un.	51·54 N	31·31 E
159	Gorodok	(gô-rô-dôk')	Sov. Un.	49·37 N	23·40 E
166	Gorodok		Sov. Un.	55·27 N	29·58 E
172	Gorodok		Sov. Un.	50·30 N	103·58 E
196	Gorontalo	(gō-rōn-tä'lo)	Indon.	0·40 N	123·04 E
159	Goryn' R.	(gô'rĕn')	Sov. Un.	50·55 N	26·07 E
158	Gorzow Wielkopolski	(gō-zhōōv'vyĕl-ko-pōl'skē)	Pol.	53·44 N	15·15 E
104	Goshen	(gō'shĕn)	In.	41·35 N	85·50 W
107	Goshen		Ky. (Louisville In.)	38·24 N	85·34 W
106	Goshen		NY (New York In.)	41·24 N	74·19 W
107	Goshen		Oh. (Cincinnati In.)	39·14 N	84·09 W
115	Goshute Ind. Res.	(gō-shōōt')	Ut.	39·50 N	114·00 W
158	Goslar	(gôs'lär)	F.R.G.	51·55 N	10·25 E
135	Gospa (R.)	(gôs-pä)	Ven. (In.)	9·43 N	64·23 W
164	Gospić	(gôs'pĭch)	Yugo.	44·31 N	15·03 E
165	Gostivar	(gos'tê-vär)	Yugo.	41·46 N	20·58 E
159	Gostynin	(gôs-tē'nĭn)	Pol.	52·24 N	19·30 E
156	Göta alv (R.)	(gōĕtä ăĕl'v)	Swe.	58·11 N	12·03 E
156	Göta Can.	(yû'tȧ)	Swe.	58·35 N	15·24 E
156	Göteborg	(yû'tĕ-bôrgh)	Swe.	57·39 N	11·56 E
215	Gotel Mts.		Cam.-Nig.	7·05 N	11·20 E
126	Gotera	(gō-tä'rä)	Sal.	13·41 N	88·06 W
158	Gotha	(gō'tȧ)	G.D.R.	50·57 N	10·43 E
116	Gothenburg	(gŏth'ĕn-bûrg)	Ne.	40·57 N	100·08 W
156	Gotland (I.)		Swe.	57·35 N	17·35 E
195	Gotō-Rettō (Is.)	(gō'tō rĕt'tō)	Jap.	33·06 N	128·54 E
157	Gotska Sandön (I.)		Swe.	58·24 N	19·15 E
158	Göttingen	(gût'ĭng-ĕn)	F.R.G.	51·32 N	9·57 E
149	Gouda	(gou'dä)	Neth. (Amsterdam In.)	52·00 N	4·42 E
220	Gough (I.)	(gŏf)	Atl. O.	40·00 S	10·00 W
91	Gouin, Rés		Can.	48·15 N	74·15 W
96	Goulais (R.)		Can.	46·45 N	84·10 W
203	Goulburn	(gōl'bŭrn)	Austl.	34·47 S	149·40 E
214	Goumbati (Mtn.)		Senegal	13·08 N	12·06 W
214	Goumbou	(gōōm-bōō')	Mali	14·59 N	7·27 W
215	Gouna		Cam.	8·32 N	13·34 E
210	Goundam	(gōōn-däN')	Mali	16·29 N	3·37 W
210	Gouré	(gōō-rā')	Niger	13·53 N	10·44 E
105	Gouverneur	(gŭv-ēr-nōōr')	NY	44·20 N	75·25 W
94	Govenlock	(gŭvĕn-lŏk)	Can.	49·15 N	109·48 W
136	Governador Ilhado (I.)	(gô-vĕr-nä-dō'r-ē-lä'dô)	Braz. (Rio de Janeiro In.)	22·48 S	43·13 W
136	Governador Portela	(pōr-tĕ'lȧ)	Braz. (Rio de Janeiro In.)	22·28 S	43·30 W
135	Governador Valadares	(vä-lä-dä'rĕs)	Braz.	18·47 S	41·45 W
129	Governor's Harbour		Ba.	25·15 N	76·15 W
105	Gowanda	(gô-wŏn'dȧ)	NY	42·30 N	78·55 W
136	Goya	(gō'yä)	Arg.	29·06 S	59·12 W
148	Goyt (R.)	(goit)	Eng.	53·19 N	2·03 W
212	Graaff-Reinet	(gräf'rī'nĕt)	S. Afr.	32·10 S	24·40 E
164	Gracac	(grä'chäts)	Yugo.	44·16 N	15·50 E
165	Gračanico		Yugo.	44·42 N	18·19 E
120	Graceville	(grās'vĭl)	Fl.	30·57 N	85·30 W
108	Graceville		Mn.	45·33 N	96·25 W
126	Gracias	(grä'sē-äs)	Hond.	14·35 N	88·37 W
127	Gracias a Dios, Cabo (C.)	(kȧ'bô-grä-syäs-ä-dyô's)	Hond.	15·00 N	83·13 W
210	Graciosa I.	(grä-syô'sä)	Açores (In.)	39·07 N	27 30 W
165	Gradačac	(gra-dä'chats)	Yugo.	44·50 N	18·28 E
162	Gradelos	(grä-dĕ-lôs)	Sp.	42·38 N	5·15 W
167	Gradizhsk	(grä-dēzhsk')	Sov. Un.	49·12 N	33·06 E
162	Grado	(grä'dō)	Sp.	43·24 N	6·04 W
149	Gräfelfing	(grä'fĕl-fēng)	F.R.G. (Munich In.)	48·07 N	11·27 E
149	Grafing	(grä'fēng)	F.R.G. (Munich In.)	48·03 N	11·58 E
203	Grafton	(graf'tŭn)	Austl.	29·38 S	153·05 E
113	Grafton		Il. (St. Louis In.)	38·58 N	90·26 W
99	Grafton		Ma. (In.)	42·13 N	71·41 W

ng-sing; ŋ-baŋk; N-nasalized n; nŏd; cŏmmit; ōld; ôbey; ôrder; fōōd; fŏŏt; ou-out; s-soft; sh-dish; th-thin; pūre; ûnite; ûrn; stŭd; circŭs; ü-as "y" in study; '-indeterminate vowel.

Page	Name Pronunciation	Region	Lat. °'	Long. °'
108	Grafton............	ND	48·24 N	97·25 W
107	Grafton......Oh. (Cleveland In.)		41·16 N	82·04 W
105	Grafton............	WV	39·20 N	80·00 W
163	Gragnano (grän-yä′nô)			
		It. (Naples In.)	40·27 N	14·32 E
121	Graham (grā′ăm)........	NC	36·03 N	79·23 W
116	Graham............	Tx.	33·07 N	98·34 W
112	Graham.......Wa. (Seattle In.)		47·03 N	122·18 W
90	Graham (I.)...........	Can.	53·50 N	132·40 W
213	Grahamstown (grā′ăms′toun)			
		S. Afr. (Natal In.)	33·19 S	26·33 E
161	Graian Alps (Mts.) (grā′yăn)			
		Fr.-It.	45·17 N	6·52 E
135	Grajaú (grà-zhà-ōō′).......	Braz.	5·59 S	46·03 W
135	Grajaú (R.)...........	Braz.	4·24 S	46·04 W
159	Grajewo (grä-yä′vo).......	Pol.	53·38 N	22·28 E
137	Grama, Serra de (Mtn.)			
	(sě′r-rä-dě-grä′mà)			
		Braz. (Rio de Janeiro In.)	23·42 S	42·28 W
165	Gramada (grä′mä-dä)........	Bul.	43·46 N	22·41 E
149	Gramatneusiedl. Aus. (Vienna In.)		48·02 N	16·29 E
164	Grammichele (gräm-mě-kě′lä). It.		37·15 N	14·40 E
154	Grampian Mts. (grăm′pĭ-ăn). Scot.		56·30 N	4·55 W
126	Granada (grä-nä′dhä).......	Nic.	11·55 N	85·58 W
162	Granada (grä-nä′dä)........	Sp.	37·13 N	3·37 W
136	Gran Bajo (Pln.) (grän′bä′kŏ).Arg.		47·35 S	68·45 W
119	Granbury (grăn′bĕr-ĭ)......Tx.		32·26 N	97·45 W
105	Granby (grăn′bĭ)........Can.		45·30 N	72·40 W
117	Granby............Mo.		36·54 N	94·15 W
116	Granby............Co.		40·07 N	105·40 W
210	Gran Canaria I.			
	(grän′kä-nä′rĕ-ä).Can. Is.		27·39 N	15·39 W
136	Gran Chaco (Reg.) (grän′chá′kŏ)			
		Arg.-Par.	25·30 S	62·15 W
109	Grand (I.)........... Mi.		46·37 N	86·38 W
98	Grand (L.)........... Can.		45·17 N	67·42 W
98	Grand (L.)........... Can.		66·15 N	45·59 W
97	Grand (R.)........... Can.		43·45 N	80·20 W
104	Grand (R.)........... Mi.		42·58 N	85·13 W
117	Grand (R.)........... Mo.		39·50 N	93·52 W
108	Grand (R.)........... SD		45·40 N	101·55 W
108	Grand (R.), North Fork.....SD		45·52 N	102·49 W
108	Grand (R.), South Fork.....SD		45·38 N	102·56 W
128	Grand Bahama (I.)........Ba.		26·35 N	78·30 W
99	Grand Bank (grănd băngk). Can.		47·06 N	55·47 W
214	Grand Bassam (grän bȧ-säN′)			
		Ivory Coast	5·12 N	3·44 W
127	Grand Bourg (grän bōōr′)			
		Guad. (In.)	15·54 N	61·20 W
129	Grand Caicos (I.) (gränd kä-ē′kŏs)			
		Turks & Caicos Is.	21·45 N	71·50 W
154	Grand Canal............Ire.		53·21 N	7·15 W
	Grand Canal, see Yün Ho			
115	Grand Canyon (gränd kăn′yŭn)			
		Az.	36·05 N	112·10 W
115	Grand Canyon............Az.		35·50 N	113·16 W
115	Grand Canyon Natl. Park.....Az.		36·15 N	112·20 W
128	Grand Cayman (I.) (kā′măn)			
		Cayman Is.	19·15 N	81·15 W
110	Grand Coulee Dam (kōō′lē)..Wa.		47·58 N	119·28 W
137	Grande (R.)..Chili (Santiago In.)		35·25 S	70·14 W
125	Grande (R.)........... Mex.		17·37 N	96·41 W
137	Grande (R.)			
		Ur. (Buenos Aires In.)	33·19 S	57·15 W
138	Grande, Boca (B.)			
	(bä-ē′ä-grän′dě).Arg.		50·45 S	68·00 W
135	Grande, Boca (Est.)			
	(bŏ′kä-grä′n-dě).Ven.		8·46 N	60·17 W
122	Grande, Ciri (R.)			
	(sě′rē-grä′n′dě).Pan. (In.)		8·55 N	80·04 W
138	Grande, Cuchilla (Mts.)			
	(kōō-chē′l-yä).Ur.		33·00 S	55·15 W
137	Grande, Ilha (I.) (grän′dě)			
		Braz. (Rio de Janeiro In.)	23·11 S	44·14 W
134	Grande, Rio (R.).......Bol.		16·49 S	63·19 W
135	Grande, Rio (R.).......Braz.		19·48 S	49·54 W
102	Grande, Rio (R.) (Bravo del			
	Norte, Rio) (grän′dä).Mex.-U. S.		26·50 N	99·10 W
136	Grande, Salinas (F.)			
	(sä-lē′näs).Arg.		29·45 S	65·00 W
135	Grande, Salto (Falls)			
	(säl-tŏ).Braz.		16·18 S	39·38 W
129	Grande Cayemite, Ile (I.)....Hai.		18·45 N	73·45 W
213	Grande Comore (grä′n-dě-			
	kŏ-mŏ-rě).Comoros		11·44 N	42·38 E
126	Grande de Otoro			
	(grän′dà dā ŏ-tŏ′rŏ)....Hond.		14·42 N	88·21 W
89	Grande Pointe (gränd point′)			
		Can. (Winnipeg In.)	49·47 N	97·03 W
93	Grande Prairie (prâr′ĭ)....Can.		55·10 N	118·48 W
127	Grande R. (grän′dě).......Nic.		13·01 N	84·21 W
210	Grand Erg Occidental (Dunes)			
		Alg.	29·37 N	6·04 E
129	Grande Rivière du Nord			
	(rē-vyâr′ dü nôr′).Hai.		19·35 N	72·10 W
110	Grande Ronde R. (rônd′).....Or.		45·32 N	117·52 W
114	Gran Desierto (Des.)			
	(grän-dě-syě′r-tŏ).Mex.		32·14 N	114·28 W
127	Grande Soufriere Vol. (sōō-frē-âr′)			
		Guad. (In.)	16·06 N	61·42 W
127	Grande Terre I. (târ′).Guad. (In.)		16·28 N	61·13 W
127	Grande Vigie, Pointe de la (Pt.)			
	(gränd vē-gē′).Grande Terre (In.)		16·32 N	61·25 W
99	Grand Falls (fôlz)........Can.		56·10 N	55·40 W
95	Grandfather, Mt. (gränd-fä-thĕr′)			
		NC	36·07 N	81·48 W
116	Grandfield (gränd′fēld)......Ok.		34·13 N	98·39 W
93	Grand Forks (fôrks).......Can.		49·02 N	118·27 W
108	Grand Forks............ND		47·55 N	97·05 W
104	Grand Haven (hā′v′n)......Mi.		43·05 N	86·15 W
116	Grand Island (ī′lånd)......Ne.		40·56 N	98·20 W
107	Grand I.........NY (Buffalo In.)		43·03 N	78·58 W
115	Grand Junction (jŭngk′shŭn)..Co.		39·05 N	108·35 W

Page	Name Pronunciation	Region	Lat. °'	Long. °'
99	Grand L. (lăk)............Can.		49·00 N	57·10 W
119	Grand L............... La.		29·57 N	91·25 W
113	Grand L.......Mn. (Duluth In.)		46·54 N	92·26 W
104	Grand Ledge (lěj)........Mi.		42·45 N	84·50 W
160	Grand-Lieu, L. de (grän′-lyû).Fr.		46·00 N	1·45 W
98	Grand Manan (I.) (mȧ-nän′)..Can.		44·40 N	66·50 W
97	Grand Mère (grän mâr′).....Can.		46·36 N	72·43 W
161	Grand Morin (R.) (mô-răN′)			
		Fr. (Paris In.)	48·23 N	2·19 E
162	Grândola (grän′dô-là)......Port.		38·10 N	8·36 W
109	Grand Portage Ind. Res. (pōr′tĭj)			
		Mn.	47·54 N	89·34 W
109	Grand Portage Nat'l. Mon....Mi.		47·59 N	89·47 W
113	Grand Prairie (prě′rè)			
	Tx. (Dallas, Fort Worth In.)		32·45 N	97·00 W
115	Grand Quivira Natl. Mon.			
	(kē-vē′rà).NM		34·10 N	106·05 W
95	Grand Rapids............SD		53·08 N	99·20 W
104	Grand Rapids (răp′ĭdz).....Mi.		43·00 N	85·45 W
109	Grand Rapids............Mn.		47·16 N	93·33 W
95	Grand Rapids Forebay (Res.).Can.		53·10 N	100·00 W
98	Grand-Riviere..........Can.		48·26 N	64·30 W
111	Grand Teton Mt.........Wy.		43·46 N	110·50 W
111	Grand Teton Natl. Park (tē′tŏn)			
		Wy.	43·54 N	110·15 W
104	Grand Traverse B. (trăv′ẽrs)..Mi.		45·00 N	85·30 W
129	Grand Turk (tûrk)			
	Turks & Caicos Is.		21·30 N	71·10 W
119	Grand Turk (I.).Turks & Caicos Is.		21·30 N	71·10 W
113	Grandview (gränd′vyōō)			
	Mo. (Kansas City In.)		38·53 N	94·32 W
115	Grand Wash (R.) (wŏsh)....Az.		36·20 N	113·52 W
111	Granger (grän′jẽr).......Wy.		41·37 N	109·58 W
110	Grangeville (grānj′vĭl).....Id.		45·56 N	116·08 W
113	Granite City			
	Il. (St. Louis In.)		38·42 N	90·09 W
108	Granite Falls (fôlz)........Mn.		44·46 N	95·34 W
121	Granite Falls..........NC		35·49 N	81·25 W
112	Granite Falls....Wa. (Seattle In.)		48·05 N	121·59 W
99	Granite L............Can.		48·01 N	57·00 W
92	Granite Mt............Ak.		55·30 N	132·35 W
111	Granite Pk............Mt.		45·13 N	109·48 W
121	Graniteville (grän′ĭt-vĭl)....SC		33·35 N	81·50 W
135	Granito (grä-nē′tŏ).......Braz.		7·39 S	39·34 W
162	Granja de Torrehermosa (grän′hä			
	dä tŏr′rä-ĕr-mŏ′sä.Sp.		38·21 N	5·38 W
128	Granma (Prov.)........Cuba		20·10 N	76·50 W
156	Gränna (grěn′ä).........Swe.		58·02 N	14·38 E
163	Granollérs (grä-nŏl-yěrs′)....Sp.		41·36 N	2·19 E
134	Gran Pajonal (Marsh) (grän′-			
	pä-kō-näl′).Peru		11·14 S	71·45 W
119	Gran Piedra (Mtn.)			
	(grän-pyě′drä).Cuba		20·00 N	75·40 W
148	Grantham (grăn′tȧm).......Eng.		52·54 N	0·38 W
107	Grant Park (gränt pärk)			
	Il. (Chicago In.)		41·14 N	87·39 W
110	Grants Pass (gránts pás).....Or.		42·26 N	123·20 W
160	Granville (grän-vēl′).......Fr.		48·52 N	1·35 W
105	Granville (grăn′vĭl).......NY		43·25 N	73·15 W
95	Granville (L.)..........Can.		56·18 N	100·30 W
135	Grão Mogol (groun′ mōō-gôl′)			
		Braz.	16·34 S	42·35 W
113	Grapevine (grāp′vīn)			
	Tx. (Dallas, Fort Worth In.)		32·56 N	97·05 W
156	Gräso (I.)............Swe.		60·30 N	18·35 E
105	Grass (R.)............NY		44·45 N	75·10 W
123	Grass Cay (I.)			
	Vir. Is. (U.S.A.) (St. Thomas In.)		18·22 N	64·50 W
161	Grasse (gräs)..........Fr.		43·39 N	6·57 E
112	Grass Mtn. (grȧs)			
	Wa. (Seattle In.)		47·13 N	121·48 W
99	Grates Pt. (grāts).......Can.		48·09 N	52·57 W
160	Graulhet (grō-lě′).......Fr.		43·46 N	1·58 E
94	Gravelbourg (grăv′ĕl-bôrg)...Can.		49·53 N	106·34 W
148	Gravesend (grävz′ĕnd′)			
	Eng. (London In.)		51·26 N	0·22 E
164	Gravina (grä-vē′nä)........It.		40·48 N	16·27 E
129	Gravois, Pte. (grȧ-vwä′)....Hai.		18·00 N	74·20 W
161	Gray (grā)............Fr.		47·26 N	5·35 E
104	Grayling (grā′lĭng).......Mi.		44·40 N	84·40 W
107	Grayslake (grāz′lāk)			
	Il. (Chicago In.)		42·20 N	88·20 W
116	Grays Pk. (grāz)........Co.		39·29 N	105·52 W
167	Grayvoron (grȧ-ē′vô-rôn).Sov. Un.		50·28 N	35·41 E
158	Graz (gräts)..........Aus.		47·05 N	15·26 E
128	Great Abaco (I.) (ȧ′bä-kŏ)...Ba.		26·30 N	77·05 W
205	Great Artesian Basin (Reg.)			
	(är-tēzh-ȧn bä-sĭn).Austl.		23·16 S	143·37 E
204	Great Australian Bight			
	(ôs-trā′lĭ-ăn bīt).Austl.		33·30 S	127·00 E
128	Great Bahama Bk. (bȧ-hä′mȧ).Ba.		25·00 N	78·50 W
205	Great Barrier (I.) (băr′ĭ-ĕr)			
	N. Z. (In.)		37·00 S	175·31 E
205	Great Barrier Rf. (bȧ-rĭ-ēr rēf)			
		Austl.	16·43 S	146·34 E
102	Great Basin (grāt bā′s'n).....U. S.		40·08 N	117·10 W
90	Great Bear L. (bâr).......Can.		66·10 N	119·53 W
116	Great Bend (běnd).......Ks.		38·41 N	98·46 W
	Great Bitter, see Al Buḥayrah al			
	Murrah al Kubrā			
154	Great Blasket (Is.) (blăs′kĕt).Ire.		52·05 N	10·55 W
146	Great Britain (brĭt′n).....U. K.		56·53 N	0·02 W
127	Great Corn I...........Nic.		12·10 N	82·54 W
111	Great Divide Basin			
	(dǐ-vīd′ bā′s'n).Wy.		42·10 N	108·10 W
205	Great Dividing Ra.			
	(dǐ-vī-dǐng rănj).Austl.		35·16 S	146·38 E
96	Great Duck (I.) (dŭk).....Can.		45·40 N	83·22 W
	Greater Khingan Ra., see			
	Tahsinganling Shanmo			
109	Greater Leech Ind. Res.			
	(grät′ẽr lēch).Mn.		47·39 N	94·27 W
129	Great Exuma (I.) (ĕk-sōō′mä).Ba.		23·35 N	76·00 W

Page	Name Pronunciation	Region	Lat. °'	Long. °'
111	Great Falls (fôlz)........Mt.		47·30 N	111·15 W
121	Great Falls...........SC		34·32 N	80·53 W
129	Great Guana Cay (I.) (gwä′nä).Ba.		24·00 N	76·20 W
128	Great Harbor Cay (I.) (kē)....Ba.		25·45 N	77·50 W
129	Great Inagua (I.) (ē-nä′gwä)..Ba.		21·00 N	73·15 W
184	Great Indian Des.........India		27·35 N	71·37 E
128	Great Isaac (I.) (ī′zàk).....Ba.		26·05 N	79·05 W
212	Great Karroo (Mts.) (grät kȧ′rōō)			
		S. Afr.	32·45 S	22·00 E
212	Great Namaland (Reg.)			
		Namibia	25·45 S	16·15 E
106	Great Neck (něk)			
	NY (New York In.)		40·48 N	73·44 W
196	Great Nicobar (I.) (nĭk-ô-bär′)			
	Andaman & Nicobar Is.		7·00 N	94·18 E
128	Great Pedro Bluff (Hd.).....Jam.		17·50 N	78·05 W
75	Great Plains, The (Reg.) (plāns)			
		N. A.	45·00 N	104·00 W
129	Great Ragged (I.).........Ba.		22·10 N	75·45 W
217	Great Ruaha (R.).......Tan.		7·45 S	34·50 E
164	Great St. Bernard Pass			
	(sänt běr-närd′).Switz.-It.		45·53 N	7·15 E
128	Great Sale Cay (I.) (sāl kē)...Ba.		27·00 N	78·15 W
111	Great Salt L. (sôlt lăk).....Ut.		41·19 N	112·48 W
102	Great Sale Lake Des.......U. S.		41·00 N	113·30 W
116	Great Salt Plains Res......Ok.		36·56 N	98·14 W
116	Great Sand Dunes Natl. Mon..Co.		37·56 N	105·25 W
94	Great Sand Hills (sănd).....Can.		50·35 N	109·05 W
	Great Sandy (I.), see Fraser			
204	Great Sandy Des. (săn′dĭ)..Austl.		21·50 S	123·10 E
110	Great Sandy Des. (săn′dĭ)...Or.		43·43 N	120·44 W
101	Great Sitkin (I.) (sĭt-kĭn)...Ak.		52·18 N	176·22 W
90	Great Slave (L.) (slāv).....Can.		61·37 N	114·58 W
120	Great Smoky Mts. Natl. Park			
	(smŏk-ē).NC-Tn.		35·43 N	83·20 W
128	Great Stirrup Cay (I.) (stĭr′ŭp)			
		Ba.	25·50 N	77·55 W
204	Great Victoria Des. (vĭk-tō′rĭ-à)			
		Austl.	29·45 S	124·30 E
148	Great Waltham (wôl′thŭm)..Eng.		51·47 N	0·27 E
155	Great Yarmouth (yär-mŭth).Eng.		52·35 N	1·45 E
156	Grebbestad (grěb-bě-städh).Swe.		58·42 N	11·15 E
215	Gréboun, Mont (Mtn.)...Niger		20·00 N	8·35 E
162	Gredos, Sierra de (Mts.)			
	(syěr′rä dä grä′dŏs).Sp.		40·13 N	5·30 W
146	Greece (grēs)..........Eur.		39·00 N	21·30 E
116	Greeley (grē′lĭ).........Co.		40·25 N	104·41 W
120	Green (R.) (grēn)........Ky.		37·13 N	86·30 W
108	Green (R.)............ND		47·05 N	103·05 W
102	Green (R.)............U. S.		38·30 N	110·10 W
115	Green (R.)............Ut.		38·30 N	110·05 W
102	Green (R.)....Wa. (Seattle In.)		47·17 N	121·57 W
102	Greenbank (grēn′bănk)			
	Wa. (Seattle In.)		48·06 N	122·35 W
119	Green Bayou........Tx. (In.)		29·53 N	95·13 W
109	Green Bay...........Wi.		44·30 N	88·04 W
103	Green B............U. S.		44·55 N	87·40 W
106	Greenbelt (grēn′bĕlt)			
	Md. (Baltimore In.)		38·59 N	76·53 W
104	Greencastle (grēn-kȧs′'l)....In.		39·40 N	86·50 W
128	Green Cay (I.)..........Ba.		24·05 N	77·10 W
121	Green Cove Springs (kŏv)....Fl.		29·56 N	81·42 W
107	Greendale (grēn′dāl)			
	Wi. (Milwaukee In.)		42·56 N	87·59 W
104	Greenfield (grēn′fēld).....In.		39·45 N	85·40 W
109	Greenfield..........Ia.		41·16 N	94·30 W
105	Greenfield..........Ma.		42·35 N	72·35 W
117	Greenfield..........Mo.		37·23 N	93·48 W
104	Greenfield..........Oh.		39·15 N	83·25 W
120	Greenfield..........Tn.		36·08 N	88·45 W
89	Greenfield Park			
	Can. (Montréal In.)		45·29 N	73·29 W
107	Greenhills (grēn-hĭls)			
	Oh. (Cincinnati In.)		39·16 N	84·31 W
75	Greenland (grēn′lånd)...N. A.		74·00 N	40·00 W
112	Green Mtn....Or. (Portland In.)		45·52 N	123·24 W
116	Green Mountain Res......Co.		39·50 N	106·20 W
105	Green Mts...........Vt.		43·10 N	73·05 W
154	Greenock (grēn′ŭk).......Scot.		55·55 N	4·45 W
106	Green Pond Mtn. (pŏnd)			
	NJ (New York In.)		41·00 N	74·32 W
105	Greenport (grēn′pŏrt).....NY		41·06 N	72·22 W
115	Green River (grēn rĭv′ẽr)....Ut.		39·00 N	110·05 W
111	Green River...........Wy.		41·32 N	109·26 W
111	Green R., Blacks Fk.......Wy.		41·08 N	110·27 W
111	Green R., Hams Fk.......Wy.		41·55 N	110·40 W
120	Greensboro (grēnz′bŭro)....Al.		32·42 N	87·36 W
120	Greensboro (grēns-bûr′ŏ)....Ga.		33·34 N	83·11 W
121	Greensboro...........NC		36·04 N	79·45 W
104	Greensburg (grēnz′bŭrg)....In.		39·20 N	85·30 W
116	Greensburg (grēns-bûrg)....Ks.		37·36 N	99·17 W
105	Greensburg...........Pa.		40·20 N	79·30 W
120	Greenville (grēn′vĭl).......Al.		31·49 N	86·39 W
117	Greenville...........Il.		38·52 N	89·22 W
120	Greenville...........Ky.		37·11 N	87·11 W
214	Greenville...........Lib.		5·01 N	9·03 W
98	Greenville...........Me.		45·26 N	69·35 W
104	Greenville...........Mi.		43·10 N	85·25 W
117	Greenville...........Ms.		33·25 N	91·00 W
121	Greenville...........NC		35·35 N	77·22 W
104	Greenville...........Oh.		40·05 N	84·35 W
105	Greenville...........Pa.		41·20 N	80·25 W
121	Greenville...........SC		34·50 N	82·25 W
120	Greenville...........Tn.		36·08 N	82·50 W
117	Greenville...........Tx.		33·09 N	96·07 W
106	Greenwich (grēn-ĭch) (New York In.).Ct.		41·01 N	73·37 W
148	Greenwich (grĭn′ĭj)			
	Eng. (London In.)		51·28 N	0·00
117	Greenwood (grēn-wood′)....Ar.		35·13 N	94·15 W
107	Greenwood..In. (Indianapolis In.)		39·37 N	86·07 W
117	Greenwood...........Ms.		33·30 N	90·10 W
121	Greenwood...........SC		34·10 N	82·10 W
121	Greenwood (R.)........SC		34·17 N	81·55 W

PRONOUNCING INDEX Greenwood — Guildford 287

Page	Name Pronunciation Region	Lat. °′	Long. °′
106	Greenwood L.. NY (New York In.)	41·13 N	74·20 W
121	Greer (grēr) SC	34·55 N	81·56 W
161	Grefrath (grĕf'rät) F.R.G. (Ruhr In.)	51·20 N	6·21 E
108	Gregory (grĕg'ō-rĭ) SD	43·12 N	99·27 W
203	Gregory, L. (grĕg'ô-rê) Austl.	29·47 S	139·15 E
205	Gregory Ra. Austl.	19·23 S	143·45 E
149	Greifenberg (grī'fĕn-bĕrgh) F.R.G. (Munich In.)	48·04 N	11·06 E
158	Greifswald (grīfs'vält) G.D.R.	54·05 N	13·24 E
158	Greiz (grīts) G.D.R.	50·39 N	12·14 E
164	Gremyachinsk (grâ'myà-chĭnsk) Sov. Un. (Urals In.)	58·35 N	57·53 E
156	Grenå (grĕn'ô) Den.	56·25 N	10·51 E
120	Grenada (grê-nä'da) Ms.	33·45 N	89·47 W
123	Grenada N. A.	12·02 N	61·15 W
120	Grenada Res. Ms.	33·52 N	89·30 W
160	Grenade (grē-näd') Fr.	43·46 N	1·15 E
127	Grenadines, The (Is.) (grĕn'à-dēnz) Grenada-St. Vincent (In.)	12·37 N	61·35 W
161	Grenoble (grē-nô'bl') Fr.	45·14 N	5·45 E
108	Grenora (grê-nō'rá) ND	48·38 N	103·55 W
105	Grenville (grĕn'vĭl) Can.	45·40 N	74·35 W
127	Grenville Grenada (In.)	12·07 N	61·38 W
112	Gresham (grĕsh'ăm) Or. (Portland In.)	45·30 N	122·25 W
106	Gretna (grĕt'ná) La. (New Orleans In.)	29·56 N	90·03 W
149	Grevelingen Krammer, R. Neth. (Amsterdam In.)	51·42 N	4·03 E
165	Grevená (grĕ'vâ-nä) Grc.	40·02 N	21·30 E
161	Grevenbroich (grĕ'fen-broik) F.R.G. (Ruhr In.)	51·05 N	6·36 E
161	Grevenbrück (grĕ'fĕn-brük) F.R.G. (Ruhr In.)	51·08 N	8·01 E
99	Grey (R.) (grā) Can.	47·53 N	57·00 W
112	Grey, Pt. Can. (Vancouver In.)	49·22 N	123·16 W
111	Greybull (grā'bŏŏl) Wy.	44·28 N	108·05 W
111	Greybull R. Wy.	44·13 N	108·43 W
218	Greylingstad (grā-lĭng'shtát) S. Afr. (Johannesburg & Pretoria In.)	26·40 S	29·13 E
205	Greymouth (grā'mouth) N. Z. (In.)	42·27 S	171·17 E
203	Grey Ra. Austl.	28·40 S	142·05 E
110	Greys Hbr. (grās) Wa.	46·55 N	124·23 W
213	Greytown (grā'toun) S. Afr. (Natal In.)	29·07 S	30·38 E
	Greytown, see San Juan del Norte		
112	Grey Wolf Pk. (grā wŏŏlf) Wa. (Seattle In.)	48·53 N	123·12 W
114	Gridley (grĭd'lĭ) Ca.	39·22 N	121·43 W
120	Griffin (grĭf'ĭn) Ga.	33·15 N	84·16 W
203	Griffith (grĭf-ĭth) Austl.	34·16 S	146·10 E
107	Griffith In. (Chicago In.)	41·31 N	87·26 W
167	Grigoriopol' (grĭ'gor-i-ô'pôl) Sov. Un.	47·09 N	29·18 E
125	Grijalva (R.) (grē-häl'vä) Mex.	17·25 N	93·23 W
203	Grim, C. (grĭm) Austl.	40·43 S	144·30 E
158	Grimma (grĭm'ä) G.D.R.	51·14 N	12·43 E
89	Grimsby (grĭmz'bĭ) Can. (Toronto In.)	43·11 N	79·33 W
150	Grimsey (I.) (grĭms'ā) Ice.	66·30 N	17·50 W
156	Grimstad (grĭm-städh) Nor.	58·21 N	8·30 E
99	Grindstone Island Can.	47·25 N	61·51 W
109	Grinnel (grĭ-nĕl') Ia.	41·44 N	92·44 W
109	Griswold (grĭz'wŭld) Ia.	41·11 N	95·05 W
166	Griva (grē'và) Sov. Un.	55·51 N	26·31 E
99	Groais I. Can.	50·57 N	55·35 W
157	Grobina (grō'bĭŋa) Sov. Un.	56·35 N	21·10 E
218	Groblersdal S. Afr. (Johannesburg & Pretoria In.)	25·11 S	29·25 E
159	Grodno (grôd'nō) Sov. Un.	53·40 N	23·49 E
159	Grodzisk Masowieki (grō'jēsk mä-zō-vyĕts'ke) Pol.	52·06 N	20·40 E
158	Grodzisk Wielkopolski (grō'jēsk vyĕl-ko-pōl'skē) Pol.	52·14 N	16·22 E
119	Groesbeck (grōs'bĕk) Tx.	31·32 N	96·31 W
160	Groix, I. de (ēl dē grwä') Fr.	47·39 N	3·28 W
159	Grójec (grōō'yĕts) Pol.	51·53 N	20·52 E
158	Gronau (grō'nou) F.R.G.	52·12 N	7·05 E
155	Groningen (grō'nĭng-ĕn) Neth.	53·13 N	6·30 E
204	Groote Eylandt (I.) (grō'tē ī'länt) Austl.	13·50 S	137·30 E
212	Grootfontein (grōt'fōn-tān') Namibia	18·15 S	19·30 E
213	Groot-Kei (kē) S. Afr. (Natal In.)	32·17 S	27·30 E
212	Grootkop (Mtn.) S. Afr. (In.)	34·11 S	18·23 E
218	Groot Marico S. Afr. (Johannesburg & Pretoria In.)	25·36 S	26·23 E
218	Groot R. S. Afr. (Johannesburg & Pretoria In.)	25·13 S	26·20 E
213	Groot-Vis (R.) S. Afr. (Natal In.)	33·04 S	36·08 E
212	Groot Vloer (L.) (grōt' vlōōr') S. Afr.	30·00 S	20·16 E
99	Gros Morne (Mtn.) (grō môrn') Can.	49·36 N	57·48 W
91	Gros Morne Natl. Pk. Can.	49·45 N	59·15 W
99	Gros Pate (Mtn.) Can.	50·16 N	57·25 W
149	Gross Behnitz (grōss bĕ'nētz) G.D.R. (Berlin In.)	52·35 N	12·45 E
107	Grosse I. (grōs) Mi. (Detroit In.)	42·08 N	83·09 W
89	Grosse Isle (īl') Can. (Winnipeg In.)	50·04 N	97·27 W
158	Grossenhain (grōs'ĕn-hīn) G.D.R.	51·17 N	13·33 E
149	Grossenzersdorf Aus. (Vienna In.)	48·13 N	16·33 E
107	Grosse Pointe (point') Mi. (Detroit In.)	42·23 N	82·54 W
107	Grosse Pointe Farms (färm) Mi. (Detroit In.)	42·25 N	82·53 W
107	Grosse Pointe Park (pärk) Mi. (Detroit In.)	42·23 N	82·55 W
164	Grosseto (grôs-sā'tō) It.	42·46 N	11·09 E
158	Grossglockner Pk. (glôk'nēr) Aus.	47·06 N	12·45 E
149	Gross Höbach (hû'bäk) F.R.G. (Munich In.)	48·21 N	11·36 E
149	Gross Kreutz (kroitz) G.D.R. (Berlin In.)	52·24 N	12·47 E
161	Gross Reken (rĕ'kĕn) F.R.G. (Ruhr In.)	51·50 N	7·20 E
149	Gross Schönebeck (shō'nĕ-bĕk) G.D.R. (Berlin In.)	52·54 N	13·32 E
111	Gros Ventre R. (grōvĕn't'r) Wy.	43·38 N	110·34 W
105	Groton (grôt'ŭn) Ct.	41·20 N	72·00 W
99	Groton Ma. (In.)	42·37 N	71·34 W
108	Groton SD	45·25 N	98·04 W
165	Grottaglie (grôt-täl'yā) It.	40·32 N	17·26 E
100	Grouard Can.	55·31 N	116·09 W
99	Groveland (grōv'land) Ma. (In.)	42·45 N	71·02 W
105	Groveton (grōv'tŭn) NH	44·35 N	71·30 W
119	Groveton Tx.	31·04 N	95·07 W
171	Groznyy (grôz'nĭ) Sov. Un.	43·20 N	45·40 E
159	Grudziadz (grōō'jyôɴts) Pol.	53·30 N	18·48 E
89	Grues, Île aux (I.) (ō grü) Can. (Québec In.)	47·05 N	70·32 W
149	Grumpholds-Kirchen Aus. (Wien In.)	48·03 N	16·17 E
109	Grundy Center (grŭn'dĭ sĕn'tēr) Ia.	42·22 N	92·45 W
124	Gruñidora (grōō-nyê-dô'rō) Mex.	24·10 N	101·49 W
149	Grünwald (grōōn'väld) F.R.G. (Munich In.)	48·04 N	11·34 E
166	Gryazi (gryä'zĭ) Sov. Un.	52·31 N	39·59 E
146	Gryazovets (gryä'zô-vĕts) Sov. Un.	58·52 N	40·14 E
158	Gryfice (grĭ'fĭ-tsĕ) Pol.	53·55 N	15·11 E
158	Gryfino (grĭ'fê-nô) Pol.	53·16 N	14·30 E
127	Guabito (gwä-bē'tô) Pan.	9·30 N	82·33 W
128	Guacanayabo, Golfo de (G.) (gôl-fô-dĕ-gwä-kä-nä-yä'bō) Cuba	20·30 N	77·40 W
135	Guacara (gwá'kä-rä) Ven. (In.)	10·16 N	67·48 W
134	Guacarí (gwä-kä-rē') Col. (In.)	3·45 N	76·20 W
137	Guaçuí (gwä'sōō-ē') Braz. (Rio de Janeiro In.)	20·47 S	41·40 W
124	Guadalajara (gwä-dhä-lä-hä'rä) Mex.	20·41 N	103·21 W
162	Guadalajara (gwä-dä-lä-kä'rä) Sp.	40·37 N	3·10 W
162	Guadalcanal (gwä-dhäl-kä-näl') Sp.	38·05 N	5·48 W
205	Guadalcanal (I.) Sol. Is.	9·48 S	158·43 E
124	Guadalcázar (gwä-dhäl-kä'zär) Mex.	22·38 N	100·24 W
162	Guadalete (R.) (gwä-dhä-lā'tâ) Sp.	38·53 N	5·38 W
162	Guadalhorce (R.) (gwä-dhäl-ôr'thā) Sp.	37·05 N	4·50 W
162	Guadalimar (R.) (gwä-dhä-lē-mär') Sp.	38·29 N	2·53 W
163	Guadalope (R.) (gwä-dä-lô-pĕ) Sp.	40·48 N	0·10 W
162	Guadalquivir, Río (R.) (rē'ō-gwä-dhäl-kê-vēr') Sp.	5·57 N	6·00 W
118	Guadalupe Mex.	31·23 N	106·06 W
162	Guadalupe, Sierra de (Mts.) (syĕr'rä dā gwä-dhä-lōō'pä) Sp.	39·30 N	5·25 W
122	Guadalupe I. Mex.	29·00 N	118·45 W
118	Guadalupe Mts. NM-Tx.	32·00 N	104·55 W
118	Guadalupe Pk. Tx.	31·55 N	104·55 W
118	Guadalupe R. (gwä-dhä-lōō'pä) Tx.	29·54 N	99·03 W
162	Guadarrama, Sierra de (Mts.) (gwä-dhär-rä'mä) Sp.	41·00 N	3·40 W
163	Guadarrama (R.) (gwä-dhär-rä'mä) Sp. (Madrid In.)	40·34 N	3·58 W
123	Guadeloupe (gwä-dē-lōōp') N. A.	16·40 N	61·10 W
127	Guadeloupe Pass N. A. (In.)	16·26 N	62·00 W
128	Guadiana, Bahía de (B.) (bä-ē'ä-dĕ-gwä-dhê-ä'nä) Cuba	22·10 N	84·35 W
162	Guadiana, Rio (R.) (rē'ō-gwä-dvä'nä) Port.	37·43 N	7·43 W
162	Guadiana Alto (R.) (äl'tō) Sp.	39·02 N	2·52 W
162	Guadiana Menor (R.) (mā'nôr) Sp.	37·43 N	2·45 W
162	Guadiaro (R.) (gwä-dhê-ä rō) Sp.	37·38 N	5·25 W
163	Guadiato (R.) (gwä-dhê-ä'tō) Sp.	38·10 N	5·05 W
162	Guadiela (R.) (gwä-dhê-ā'lä) Sp.	40·27 N	2·05 W
162	Guadix (gwä-dhēsh') Sp.	37·18 N	3·09 W
135	Guaira (gwä-ē-rä) Braz.	24·03 S	44·02 W
135	Guaire (R.) (gwī'rĕ) Ven. (In.)	10·25 N	66·43 W
128	Guajaba, Cayo (I.) (kä'yō-gwä-hä'bä) Cuba	21·50 N	77·35 W
134	Guajará Mirim (gwä-zhä-rä'mē-rēɴ') Braz.	10·58 S	65·12 W
134	Guajira, Pen. de (Pen.) (pĕ-nē'ng-sōō-lä-dĕ-gwä-κē'rä) Col.-Ven.	12·35 N	73·00 W
126	Gualán (gwä-län') Guat.	15·08 N	89·21 W
137	Gualeguay (gwä-lĕ-gwä'y) Arg. (Buenos Aires In.)	33·10 S	59·20 W
137	Gualeguay (R.) Arg. (Buenos Aires In.)	32·49 S	59·05 W
137	Gualeguaychú (gwä-lâ-gwī-chōō') Arg. (Buenos Aires In.)	33·01 S	58·32 W
137	Gualeguaychú (R.) Arg. (Buenos Aires In.)	32·58 S	58·27 W
136	Gualicho, Salina (F.) (sä-lē'nä-gwä-lē'chō) Arg.	40·20 S	65·15 W
198	Guam (gwäm) Oceania	14·00 N	143·20 E
136	Guaminí (gwä-mê-nē') Arg.	37·02 S	62·21 W
134	Guamo (gwá'mō) Col. (In.)	4·02 N	74·58 W
129	Guanabacoa (gwä-nä-bä-kō'ä) Cuba (In.)	23·08 N	82·19 W
136	Guanabara, Baia de (B.) Braz. (Rio de Janeiro In.)	22·44 S	43·09 W
126	Guanacaste Cord. (Mts.) (kôr-dēl-yĕ'rä-gwä-nä-käs'tā) C. R.	10·54 N	85·27 W
122	Guanacevi (gwä-nä-sĕ-vē') Mex.	25·30 N	105·45 W
128	Guanahacabibes, Pen. de (pĕ-nēn-sōō-lä-dĕ-gwä-nä hä-kä-bē'bâs) Cuba	21·55 N	84·35 W
128	Guanajay (gwä-nä-hī') Cuba	22·55 N	82·40 W
124	Guanajuato (gwä-nä-hwä'tō) Mex.	21·01 N	101·16 W
122	Guanajuato (State) Mex.	21·00 N	101·00 W
135	Guanape (gwä-nä'pĕ) Ven. (In.)	9·55 N	65·32 W
135	Guanape (R.) Ven. (In.)	9·52 N	65·20 W
134	Guanare (gwä-nä'rā) Ven.	8·57 N	69·47 W
136	Guanduçu (R.) (gwä'n-dōō'sōō) Braz. (Rio de Janeiro In.)	22·50 S	43·40 W
128	Guane (gwä'nā) Cuba	22·10 N	84·05 W
135	Guanta (gwän'tä) Ven. (In.)	10·15 N	64·35 W
129	Guantanamo (gwän-tä'nä-mô) Cuba	20·10 N	75·10 W
129	Guantánamo (Prov.) Cuba	20·10 N	75·05 W
129	Guantanamo, Bahía de (B.) (bä-ē'ä-dĕ) Cuba	19·35 N	75·35 W
137	Guapé (gwá-pĕ) Braz. (Rio de Janeiro In.)	20·45 S	45·55 W
127	Guapiles (gwä-pē-lĕs) C. R.	10·05 N	83·54 W
136	Guapimirim (gwä-pê-mē-rē'ɴ) Braz. (Rio de Janeiro In.)	22·31 S	42·59 W
134	Guaporé (R.) (gwä-pô-rā') Bol.-Braz.	12·11 S	63·47 W
134	Guaqui (guä'kē) Bol.	16·42 S	68·47 W
163	Guara, Sierra de (Mts.) (sē-ĕ'r-rä-dĕ-gwä'rä) Sp.	42·24 N	0·15 W
135	Guarabira (gwä-rä-bē'rá) Braz.	6·49 S	35·27 W
134	Guaranda (gwä-rán'dä) Ec.	1·39 S	78·57 W
135	Guarapari (gwä-rä-pä'rê) Braz.	20·34 S	40·31 W
137	Guarapiranga, Represa do (Res.) (r'ĕ-prĕ-sä-dô-gwä'rä-pē-rá'n-gä) Braz. (Rio de Janeiro In.)	23·45 S	46·44 W
136	Guarapuava (gwä-rä-pwä'vá) Braz.	25·29 S	51·26 W
137	Guaratinguetá (guä-rä-tĭɴ-gâ-tä') Braz. (Rio de Janeiro In.)	22·49 S	45·10 W
162	Guarda (gwär'dä) Port.	40·32 N	7·17 W
162	Guarena (gwä-rā'nyä) Sp.	38·52 N	6·08 W
135	Guaribe (R.) (gwä-rê'bĕ) Ven. (In.)	9·48 N	65·17 W
135	Guárico (State) Ven. (In.)	9·42 N	67·25 W
135	Guárico (R.) Ven. (In.)	9·50 N	67·07 W
137	Guarulhos (gwá-rōō'l-yôs) Braz. (Rio de Janeiro In.)	32·28 S	46·30 W
137	Guarus (gwá'rōōs) Braz. (Rio de Janeiro In.)	21·44 S	41·19 W
134	Guasca (gwäs'kä) Col. (In.)	4·52 N	73·52 W
135	Guasipati (gwä-sê-pä'tē) Ven.	7·26 N	61·57 W
164	Guastalla (gwäs-täl'lä) It.	44·53 N	10·39 E
113	Guasti (gwäs'tĭ) Ca. (Los Angeles In.)	34·04 N	117·35 W
126	Guatemala (guä-tá-mä'lä) Guat.	14·37 N	90·32 W
122	Guatemala N. A.	15·45 N	91·45 W
135	Guatire (gwä-tê'rĕ) Ven. (In.)	10·28 N	66·34 W
137	Guaxupé (gwä-shōō-pĕ') Braz. (Rio de Janeiro In.)	21·18 S	46·42 W
128	Guayabal (gwä-yä-bä'l) Cuba	20·40 N	77·40 W
124	Guayalejo (R.) (gwä-yä-lĕ'hô) Mex.	23·24 N	99·09 W
123	Guayama (gwä-yä'mä) P. R. (Puerto Rico In.)	18·00 N	66·08 W
129	Guayamouc (R.) Hai.	19·05 N	72·00 W
134	Guayaquil (gwī-ä-kēl') Ec.	2·16 S	79·53 W
134	Guayaquil, Golfo de (G.) (gôl-fô-dĕ) Ec.	3·03 S	82·12 W
134	Guayiare (R.) (gwä-yá'rĕ) Col.	3·35 N	69·28 W
122	Guaymas (gwá'y-mäs) Mex.	27·49 N	110·58 W
129	Guayubin (gwä-yōō-bĕ'n) Dom. Rep.	19·40 N	71·25 W
126	Guazacapán (gwä-zä-kä-pän') Guat.	14·04 N	90·26 W
174	Gubakha (gōō-bä'kå) Sov. Un. (Urals In.)	58·53 N	57·35 E
164	Gubbio (gōōb'byô) It.	43·23 N	12·36 E
163	Gudar, Sierra de (Mts.) (syĕr'rä dā gōō'dhär) Sp.	40·28 N	0·47 W
156	Gudenaa (R.) Den.	56·20 N	9·47 E
156	Gudinge Fjärden (Fd.) Swe.	57·43 N	16·55 E
156	Gudvangen (gōōdh'väŋ-gĕn) Nor.	60·52 N	6·45 E
161	Guebwiller (gĕb-vê-lâr') Fr.	47·53 N	7·10 E
215	Guédi, Mont (Mtn.) Chad	12·14 N	18·58 E
210	Guelma (gwĕl'mä) Alg.	36·32 N	7·17 E
89	Guelph (gwĕlf) Can. (Toronto In.)	43·33 N	80·15 W
152	Guemar (gē-mär') Alg.	33·32 N	6·42 E
135	Güere (gwĕ'rĕ) (R.) Ven. (In.)	9·39 N	65·00 W
160	Guéret (gā-rĕ') Fr.	46·09 N	1·52 E
160	Guernsey (I.) (gûrn'zĭ) Eur.	49·27 N	2·36 W
152	Guerrara (gĕr-rä'rä) Alg.	32·50 N	4·26 E
118	Guerrero (gĕr-rā'rō) Mex.	26·47 N	99·20 W
118	Guerrero Mex.	28·20 N	100·24 W
124	Guerrero (State) Mex.	17·45 N	100·15 W
160	Gueugnon (gû-nyôɴ') Fr.	46·35 N	4·01 E
119	Gueydan (gā'dăn) La.	30·01 N	92·31 W
136	Guia de Pacobaíba (gwê'ä-dĕ-pä'kō-bī'bä) Braz. (Rio de Janeiro In.)	22·42 S	43·10 W
133	Guiana Highlands (Mts.) Braz.	3·20 N	60·00 W
125	Guichicovi (San Juan) (gwē-chê-kō'vê) Mex.	16·58 N	95·10 W
163	Guidonia (gwē-dō'nyá) It. (Rome In.)	42·00 N	12·45 E
214	Guiglo Ivory Coast	6·33 N	7·29 W
161	Guignes (gēɴ'yĕ) Fr. (Paris In.)	48·38 N	2·48 E
135	Güigüe (gwê'gwĕ) Ven. (In.)	10·05 N	67·48 W
126	Guija, L. (gē'hä) Sal.	14·16 N	89·21 W
148	Guildford (gĭl'fērd) Eng. (London In.)	51·13 N	0·34 W

ng-sing; ŋ-baŋk; ɴ-nasalized n; nŏd; cŏmmit; ōld; ôbey; ôrder; fōōd; fŏŏt; ou-out; s-soft; sh-dish; th-thin; pūre; ûnite; ûrn; stŭd; circŭs; ü-as "y" in study; '-indeterminate vowel.

288 Guilford — Hangchou

PRONOUNCING INDEX

Page	Name Pronunciation Region	Lat. °′	Long. °′
107	Guilford (gĭl'fẽrd) In. (Cincinnati In.)	39·10 N	84·55 W
162	Guimarães (gē-mä-răɴsh')...Port.	41·27 N	8·22 W
209	Guinea (gĭn'ė)...Afr.	10·48 N	12·28 W
209	Guinea, G. of...Afr.	2·00 N	1·00 E
209	Guinea-Bissau (gĭn'ė)...Afr.	12·00 N	20·00 W
128	Güines (gwē'nās)...Cuba	22·50 N	82·05 W
160	Guingamp (găɴ-gäɴ')...Fr.	48·35 N	3·10 W
128	Güira de Melena (gwē'rä dā må-lā'nä).Cuba	22·45 N	82·30 W
134	Güiria (gwê-rē'ä)...Ven.	10·43 N	62·16 W
152	Guir (R.)...Mor.-Alg.	31·55 N	2·48 W
161	Guise (guēz)...Fr.	49·54 N	3·37 E
126	Guisisil (Vol.) (gê-sê-sēl')...Nic.	12·40 N	86·11 W
184	Gujarat (State)...India	22·54 N	79·00 E
184	Gujrānwāla (gōōj-rän'va-lȧ)..Pak.	32·08 N	74·14 E
156	Gula (R.) (gōō'lȧ)...Nor.	62·55 N	10·45 E
185	Gulbarga (gŏŏl-bûr'gȧ)...India	17·25 N	76·52 E
166	Gulbene (gŏŏl-bă'nĕ)...Sov. Un.	57·09 N	26·49 E
120	Gulfport (gŭlf'pōrt)...Ms.	30·24 N	89·05 W
94	Gull Lake...Can.	50·10 N	108·25 W
92	Gull L...Can.	52·35 N	114·00 W
217	Gulu...Ug.	2·47 N	32·18 E
167	Gulyay Pole...Sov. Un.	47·39 N	36·12 E
197	Gumaca (gōō-mä-kä')...Phil. (In.)	13·55 N	122·06 E
164	Gumbeyka R. (gŏŏm-bĕy'kȧ) Sov. Un. (Urals In.)	53·20 N	59·42 E
215	Gumel...Nig.	12·39 N	9·22 E
158	Gummersbach (gŏŏm'ĕrs-bäk) F.R.G.	51·02 N	7·34 E
215	Gummi...Nig.	12·09 N	5·09 E
149	Gumpoldskirchen...Aus.	48·04 N	16·15 E
184	Guna...India	24·44 N	77·17 E
95	Gunisao (R.) (gŭn-ĭ-sā'ō)...Can.	53·40 N	97·35 W
95	Gunisao L...Can.	53·54 N	97·58 W
203	Gunnedah (gŭ'nē-dä)...Austl.	31·00 S	150·10 E
115	Gunnison (gŭn'ĭ-sŭn)...Co.	38·33 N	106·56 W
115	Gunnison...Ut.	39·10 N	111·50 W
115	Gunnison (R.)...Co.	38·30 N	106·40 W
120	Guntersville (gŭn'tĕrz-vĭl)...Al.	34·20 N	86·19 W
120	Guntersville L...Al.	34·30 N	86·20 W
149	Guntramsdorf...Aus. (Vienna In.)	48·04 N	16·19 E
185	Guntūr (gŏŏn'tōōr)...India	16·22 N	80·29 E
197	Gunungapi (I.) (gōō'nŏŏng-ä'pê) Indon.	6·52 S	127·15 E
117	Gurdon (gûr'dŭn)...Ar.	33·56 N	93·10 W
135	Gurgucia (R.) (gŏŏr-gōō'syä).Braz.	8·12 S	43·49 W
107	Gurnee (gûr'nē)...Il. (Chicago In.)	42·22 N	87·55 W
156	Gurskŏy (I.) (gōōrskûė)...Nor.	62·18 N	5·20 E
135	Gurupá (gōō-rōō-pä')...Braz.	1·28 S	51·32 W
135	Gurupi, Serra do (Mts.) (sĕ'r-rä-dô-gōō-rōō-pē').Braz.	5·32 S	47·02 W
135	Gurupí (R.) (gōō-rōō-pē')...Braz.	2·37 S	46·45 W
184	Guru Sikhar Mt...India	29·42 N	72·50 E
171	Gur'yev (gōōr'yĕf)...Sov. Un.	47·10 N	51·50 E
172	Gur'yevsk (gōōr-yĭfsk')...Sov. Un.	54·14 N	86·07 E
215	Gusau (gōō-zä'ōō)...Nig.	12·12 N	6·40 E
157	Gusev (gōō'sĕf)...Sov. Un.	54·35 N	22·15 E
214	Gushiago...Ghana	9·55 N	0·12 W
165	Gusinje (gōō-sēn'yĕ)...Yugo.	42·34 N	19·54 E
166	Gus'-Khrustal'nyy (gōōs-ᴋrōō-stäl'ny').Sov. Un.	55·39 N	40·41 E
125	Gustavo A. Madero (gōōs-tä'vô-ȧ-mä-dĕ'rô).Mex. (In.)	19·29 N	99·07 W
158	Güstrow (güs'trō)...G.D.R.	53·48 N	12·12 E
158	Gütersloh (gü'tĕrs-lo)...F.R.G.	51·54 N	8·22 E
117	Guthrie (gŭth'rĭ)...Ok.	35·52 N	97·26 W
109	Guthrie Center...Ia.	41·41 N	94·33 W
125	Gutiérrez Zamora (gōō-tĭ-âr'rāz zä-mō'rä).Mex.	20·27 N	97·17 W
109	Guttenberg (gŭt'ĕn-bûrg)...Ia.	42·48 N	91·09 W
133	Guyana (gŭy'ănă)...S. A.	7·45 N	59·00 W
116	Guymon (gī'mŏn)...Ok.	36·41 N	101·29 W
99	Guysborough (gīz'bŭr-ô)...Can.	45·23 N	61·30 W
157	Gvardeysk (gvȧr-dĕysk').Sov. Un.	54·39 N	21·11 E
215	Gwadabawa...Nig.	13·20 N	5·15 E
186	Gwādar (gwä'dŭr)...Pak.	25·15 N	62·29 E
217	Gwane (gwän)...Zaire	4·43 N	25·50 E
212	Gwelo (gwä'lō)...Rh.	19·15 S	29·48 E
217	Gwembe...Zambia	16·30 S	27·35 E
109	Gwinn (gwĭn)...Mi.	46·15 N	87·30 W
188	Gyangtse (gyäng'tsĕ')...China	29·00 N	89·28 E
184	Gyangtse...China	28·53 N	89·39 E
173	Gydan, Khrebet (Kolymskiy) (Mts.).Sov. Un.	61·45 N	155·00 E
172	Gydanskiy, P-Ov (Pen).Sov. Un.	70·42 N	76·03 E
203	Gympie (gĭm'pê)...Austl.	26·20 S	152·50 E
159	Gyöngyös (dyûn'dyûsh)...Hung.	47·47 N	19·55 E
159	Györ (dyûr)...Hung.	47·40 N	17·37 E
195	Gyōtoku (gyō'tô-kōō') Jap. (Tōkyō In.)	35·42 N	139·56 E
95	Gypsumville (jĭp'sŭm'vĭl)...Can.	51·45 N	98·35 W
159	Gyula (dyŏŏ'lä)...Hung.	46·38 N	21·18 E

H

Page	Name Pronunciation Region	Lat. °′	Long. °′
161	Haan (hän)...F.R.G. (Ruhr In.)	51·12 N	7·00 E
157	Haapamäki (häp'ä-mĕ-kē)...Fin.	62·16 N	24·20 E
157	Haapsalu (häp'sä-lŏŏ)...Sov. Un.	58·56 N	23·33 E
149	Haar (här)...F.R.G. (Munich In.)	48·06 N	11·44 E
183	Ha 'Arava (Wādī al Jayb) Isr. (Palestine In.)	30·33 N	35·10 E
149	Haarlem (här'lĕm) Neth. (Amsterdam In.)	52·22 N	4·37 E
128	Habana (Prov.) (hä-vä'nä)..Cuba	22·45 N	82·25 W
163	Habibas (C.) (hä-bē'bȧs)...Alg.	35·50 N	0·45 W
195	Habikino...Jap. (Ōsaka In.)	34·32 N	135·37 E
184	Hābra...India (In.)	22·49 N	88·38 E
194	Hachinohe (hä'chē-nō'hå)...Jap.	40·29 N	141·40 E
195	Hachiōji (hä'chê-ō'jê)...Jap.	35·39 N	139·18 E
106	Hackensack (hăk'ĕn-săk) NJ (New York In.)	40·54 N	74·03 W
186	Ḩadd, Ra's al (C.)...Om.	22·29 N	59·46 E
106	Haddonfield (hăd'ŭn-fēld) NJ (Philadelphia In.)	39·53 N	75·02 W
106	Haddon Heights (hăd'ŭn hīts) NJ (Philadelphia In.)	39·53 N	75·03 W
215	Hadejia (hä-dā'jä)...Nig.	12·30 N	9·59 E
215	Hadejia (R.)...Nig.	12·15 N	9·40 E
183	Hadera (ᴋå-dĕ'rȧ) Isr. (Palestine In.)	32·26 N	34·55 E
156	Haderslev (hä'dhĕrs-lĕv)...Den.	55·17 N	9·28 E
218	Hadibu...P. D. R. of Yem. (Horn of Afr. In.)	12·40 N	53·50 E
112	Hadlock (hăd'lŏk) Wa. (Seattle In.)	48·02 N	122·46 W
186	Ḩaḑramawt (Reg.) P. D. R. of Yem.	15·22 N	48·40 E
186	Hadur Shuayb, Jabal (Mtn.) Yemen	15·45 N	43·45 E
194	Haeju (hä'ĕ-jŭ)...Kor.	38·03 N	125·42 E
192	Haerhpin (Harbin) (här-bēn') China	45·40 N	126·30 E
150	Hafnarfjördhur...Ice.	64·02 N	21·32 W
218	Hafun, Ras (C.) (hä-fōōn') Som. (Horn of Afr. In.)	10·15 N	51·35 E
111	Hageland (hăge'lănd)...Mt.	48·53 N	108·43 W
161	Hagen (hä'gĕn).F.R.G. (Ruhr In.)	51·21 N	7·29 E
104	Hagerstown (hā'gẽrz-toun)...In.	39·55 N	85·10 W
105	Hagerstown...Md.	39·40 N	77·45 W
195	Hagi (hä'gĭ)...Jap.	34·25 N	131·25 E
160	Hague, C. de la (dē lȧ ȧg')...Fr.	49·44 N	1·55 W
	Hague, The, see 's Gravenhagen		
161	Haguenau (ȧg'nō')...Fr.	48·47 N	7·48 E
190	Haian (hāī'äɴ)...China	32·35 N	120·25 E
195	Haibara (hä'ê-bä'rä)...Jap.	34·29 N	135·57 E
192	Haich'eng...China	40·58 N	122·45 E
183	Haifa (Hefa) (hä'ē-fȧ) Isr. (Palestine In.)	32·48 N	35·00 E
193	Haifeng (hä'ê-fĕng')...China	23·00 N	115·20 E
190	Haifuchen (hāī'fōō'jĕn)...China	31·57 N	121·48 E
182	Ḩā'il (hāl)...Sau. Ar.	27·30 N	41·47 E
192	Hailaerh (Hailar) (hä-ê-lär') China	49·10 N	118·40 E
	Hailar, see Hailaerh		
111	Hailey (hā'lĭ)...Id.	43·31 N	114·19 W
97	Haileybury...Can.	47·27 N	79·38 W
117	Haileyville (hā'lĭ-vĭl)...Ok.	34·51 N	95·34 W
194	Hailin (hä'ê-lēn')...China	44·31 N	129·11 E
193	Hailing Tao (I.)...China	21·30 N	112·15 E
192	Hailun (hä'ê-lōōn')...China	47·18 N	126·50 E
192	Hailung (hä'ê-lŏŏng')...China	42·32 N	125·52 E
193	Hainan Tao (I.) (hä'e-nän'dou) China	19·00 N	111·10 E
149	Hainburg an der Donau Aus. (Vienna In.)	48·09 N	16·57 E
101	Haines (hānz)...Ak.	59·10 N	135·38 W
121	Haines City...Fl. (In.)	28·05 N	81·38 W
193	Haiphong (hī'fông') (hä'êp-hŏng) Viet.	20·52 N	106·40 E
123	Haiti (hā'tĭ)...N. A.	19·00 N	72·15 W
192	Haitien (hī'tyĕn')...China (In.)	39·59 N	116·17 E
159	Hajduböszormény (hôl'dŏŏ-bû'sûr-mān').Hung.	47·41 N	21·30 E
159	Hajduhadház (hô'ĭ-dŏŏ-hôd'häz) Hung.	47·32 N	21·32 E
159	Hajdunánás (hô'ĭ-dŏŏ-nä'näsh) Hung.	47·52 N	21·27 E
159	Hajduszoboszló (hô'ĭ-dŏŏ-sô'bôs-lō).Hung.	47·24 N	21·25 E
194	Hakodate (hä-kō-dä't å)...Jap.	41·46 N	140·42 E
195	Haku-San (Mtn.) (hä'kōō-sän') Jap.	36·11 N	136·45 E
125	Halachó (ä-lä-chō')...Mex.	20·28 N	90·06 W
211	Ḩalā'ib (hä-lä'êb)...Egypt	22·10 N	36·40 E
183	Ḩalbā...Leb. (Palestine In.)	34·33 N	36·03 E
149	Halbe (häl'bĕ) G.D.R. (Berlin In.)	52·07 N	13·43 E
158	Halberstadt (häl'bĕr-shtät) G.D.R.	51·54 N	11·07 E
197	Halcon, Mt. (häl-kōn').Phil. (In.)	13·19 N	120·55 E
156	Halden (häl'dĕn)...Nor.	59·10 N	11·21 E
148	Hale (hāl)...Eng.	53·22 N	2·20 W
100	Haleakala Crater (hä'lå-ä'kä-lä) Hi.	20·44 N	156·15 W
100	Haleakala Natl. Park...Hi.	20·46 N	156·00 W
107	Hales Corners (hālz kŏr'nẽrz) Wi. (Milwaukee In.)	42·56 N	88·03 W
148	Halesowen (hālz'ô-wĕn)...Eng.	52·26 N	2·03 W
106	Halethorpe (hāl-thôrp) Md. (Baltimore In.)	39·15 N	76·40 W
120	Haleyville (hā'lĭ-vĭl)...Al.	34·11 N	87·36 W
112	Half Moon Bay (hăf'mōōn). Ca. (San Francisco In.)	37·28 N	122·26 W
213	Halfway House (häf-wā hous) S. Afr. (Johannesburg & Pretoria In.)	26·00 S	28·08 E
149	Halfweg..Neth. (Amsterdam In.)	52·23 N	4·45 E
98	Halifax (hăl'ĭ-făks)...Can.	44·39 N	63·36 W
148	Halifax...Eng.	53·44 N	1·52 W
205	Halifax B. (hăl'ĭ-făx)...Austl.	18·56 S	147·07 E
98	Halifax Hbr...Can.	44·35 N	63·31 W
101	Halkett, C...Ak.	70·50 N	151·15 W
93	Hallam Park...Can.	52·11 N	118·46 E
194	Halla San (Mt.) (häl'lȧ-sän) Kor.	33·20 N	126·37 E
149	Halle (häl'lĕ)...Bel. (Brussels In.)	50·45 N	4·13 E
158	Halle...G.D.R.	51·30 N	11·59 E
119	Hallettsville (hăl'ĕts-vĭl)...Tx.	29·26 N	96·55 W
108	Hallock (hăl'ŭk)...Mn.	48·46 N	96·57 W
91	Hall Pen (hôl)...Can.	63·14 N	65·40 W
119	Halls Bayou...Tx. (In.)	29·55 N	95·23 W
156	Hallsberg (häls'bĕrgh)...Swe.	59·04 N	15·04 E
204	Halls Creek (hôlz)...Austl.	18·15 S	127·45 E
197	Halmahera (I.) (häl-mä-hā'rä) Indon.	0·45 N	128·45 E
197	Halmahera, Laut (Sea)...Indon.	1·00 S	129·00 E
156	Halmstad (hälm'städ)...Swe.	56·40 N	12·46 E
156	Halse Fd. (häl'sĕ fyôrd)...Nor.	63·03 N	8·23 E
117	Halstead (hôl'stĕd)...Ks.	38·02 N	97·36 W
193	Halt'an Tao (I.)...China	25·40 N	119·45 E
161	Haltern (häl'tĕrn) F.R.G. (Ruhr In.)	51·45 N	7·10 E
113	Haltom City (hôl'tŏm) Tx. (Dallas, Fort Worth In.)	32·48 N	97·13 W
	Halunrshan, see Wench'üan		
149	Halvarenbeek Neth. (Amsterdam In.)	51·29 N	5·10 E
153	Ḩamāh (hä'mä)...Syr.	35·08 N	36·53 E
186	Hamadān (hŭ-mŭ-dān')...Iran	34·45 N	48·07 E
195	Hamamatsu (hä'mä-mät'sŏŏ).Jap.	34·41 N	137·43 E
156	Hamar (hä'mär)...Nor.	60·49 N	11·05 E
191	Hamasaka (hă'mȧ-sä'kȧ)...Jap.	35·57 N	134·27 E
161	Hamborn (häm'bōrn) F.R.G. (Ruhr In.)	51·30 N	6·43 E
117	Hamburg (hăm'bûrg)...Ar.	33·15 N	91·49 W
149	Hamburg (häm'bŏŏrgh) F.R.G. (Hamburg In.)	53·34 N	10·02 E
108	Hamburg...Ia.	40·39 N	95·40 W
106	Hamburg...NJ (New York In.)	41·09 N	74·35 W
107	Hamburg...NY (Buffalo In.)	42·44 N	78·51 W
213	Hamburg (hăm'bürg) S. Afr. (Natal In.)	33·18 S	27·28 E
105	Hamden (hăm'dĕn)...Ct.	41·20 N	72·55 W
157	Hämeenlinna (hĕ'mân-lĭn-nȧ).Fin.	61·00 N	24·29 E
158	Hameln (hä'mĕln)...F.R.G.	52·06 N	9·23 E
149	Hamelwörden (hä'mĕl-vûr-dĕn) F.R.G. (Hamburg In.)	53·47 N	9·19 E
204	Hamersley Ra. (hăm'ẽrz-lê).Austl.	22·15 S	117·50 E
194	Hamhŭng (häm'hŏŏng')...Kor.	39·57 N	127·35 E
188	Hami (Qomul) (hä'mê) (kô-mōōl') China	42·58 N	93·14 E
120	Hamilton...Al.	34·09 N	88·01 W
203	Hamilton (hăm'ĭl-tŭn)...Austl.	37·50 S	142·10 E
89	Hamilton...Can. (Toronto In.)	43·15 N	79·52 W
99	Hamilton...Ma. (In.)	42·37 N	70·52 W
117	Hamilton...Mo.	39·43 N	93·59 W
111	Hamilton...Mt.	46·15 N	114·09 W
205	Hamilton...N. Z. (In.)	37·45 S	175·28 E
107	Hamilton...Oh. (Cincinnati In.)	39·22 N	84·33 W
118	Hamilton...Tx.	31·42 N	98·07 W
117	Hamilton, L...Ar.	34·25 N	93·32 W
89	Hamilton Hbr..Can. (Toronto In.)	43·17 N	79·50 W
91	Hamilton Inlet...Can.	54·20 N	56·57 W
157	Hamina (hȧ'mê-nȧ)...Fin.	60·34 N	27·15 E
121	Hamlet (hăm'lĕt)...NC	35·52 N	79·46 W
116	Hamlin (hăm'lĭn)...Tx.	32·54 N	100·08 W
161	Hamm (häm)..F.R.G. (Ruhr In.)	51·40 N	7·48 E
218	Hammanskraal (hä-mȧns-kräl') S. Afr. (Johannesburg & Pretoria In.)	25·24 S	28·17 E
149	Hamme...Bel. (Brussels In.)	51·06 N	4·07 E
149	Hamme-Oste Kanal (Can.) (hä'mĕ-ōs'tĕ kä-näl) F.R.G. (Hamburg In.)	53·20 N	8·59 E
150	Hammerfest (häm'mĕr-fĕst)..Nor.	70·38 N	23·59 E
107	Hammond (hăm'ŭnd) In. (Chicago In.)	41·37 N	87·31 W
119	Hammond...La.	30·30 N	90·28 W
112	Hammond...Or. (Portland In.)	46·12 N	123·57 W
105	Hammonton (hăm'ŭn-tŭn)...NJ	39·40 N	74·45 W
98	Hampden (hăm'dĕn)...Me.	44·44 N	68·51 W
154	Hampshire Downs (hămp'shĭr dounz).Eng.	51·01 N	1·05 W
106	Hampstead...Md. (Baltimore In.)	39·36 N	76·54 W
148	Hampstead Norris (hămp-stĕd) nŏ'rĭs).Eng. (London In.)	51·27 N	1·14 W
98	Hampton (hămp'tŭn)...Can.	45·32 N	65·51 W
109	Hampton...Ia.	42·43 N	93·15 W
106	Hampton...Va. (Norfolk In.)	37·02 N	76·21 W
106	Hampton Roads (Inlet) Va. (Norfolk In.)	36·56 N	76·23 W
210	Ḩamrā, al- Ḩammadah al- (Plat.) Libya	29·39 N	10·53 E
156	Hamrånge (häm'rông'ĕ)...Swe.	60·56 N	17·00 E
107	Hamtramck (hăm-trăm'ĭk) Mi. (Detroit In.)	42·24 N	83·03 W
186	Hāmūn-i Māshkel (L.) (hā-mōōn'ē māsh-kĕl').Pak.	28·28 N	64·13 E
194	Han (R.)...Kor.	37·10 N	127·40 E
100	Hana (hä'nä)...Hi.	20·43 N	155·59 W
128	Hanábana (R.) (hä-nä-bä'nä) Cuba	22·30 N	80·55 W
100	Hanalei B. (hä-nä-lā'ê)...Hi.	22·15 N	159·40 W
217	Hanang (Mtn.)...Tan.	4·26 S	35·24 E
158	Hanau (hä'nou)...F.R.G.	50·08 N	8·56 E
193	Han Chiang (R.)...China	25·00 N	116·35 E
192	Hanchung...China	33·02 N	107·00 E
109	Hancock (hăn'kŏk)...Mi.	47·08 N	88·37 W
93	Haney (hā-nê)...Can.	49·13 N	122·36 W
114	Hanford (hăn'fẽrd)...Ca.	36·20 N	119·38 W
188	Hangayn Nuruu (Khangai Mts.) Mong.	48·03 N	99·45 E
193	Hangchou (hăng'chō')...China	30·17 N	120·12 E

ăt; finăl; rāte; senâte; ärm; ȧsk; sofȧ; fâre; ch-choose; dh-as th in other; bē; êvent; bĕt; recĕnt; cratẽr; g-go; gh-guttural g; bĭt; ĭ-short neutral; rīde; ᴋ-guttural k as ch in German ich;

PRONOUNCING INDEX

Hangchou — Helper 289

Page	Name Pronunciation Region	Lat. °′	Long. °′
193	Hangchou Wan (B.) (hăng′chō′) China	30·20 N	121·25 E
157	Hango (häŋ′gû) Fin.	59·49 N	22·56 E
119	Hankamer (hăn′kȧ-mẽr) Tx. (In.)	29·52 N	94·42 W
193	Han Kiang (R.) (hän′kyäng′) China	31·40 N	112·04 E
108	Hankinson (häŋ′kĭn-sŭn) ND	46·04 N	96·54 W
193	Hank′ou (hän′kō′) China	30·42 N	114·22 E
204	Hann, Mt. (hän) Austl.	16·05 S	126·07 E
93	Hanna (hăn′ȧ) Can.	51·38 N	111·54 W
111	Hanna Wy.	41·51 N	106·34 W
108	Hannah ND	48·58 N	98·42 W
117	Hannibal (hăn′ĭ bǎl) Mo.	39·42 N	91·22 W
158	Hannover (hän-ō′vẽr) F.R.G.	52·22 N	9·45 E
156	Hanö-bukten (B.) Swe.	55·54 N	14·55 E
193	Hanoi (hä-noi′) Viet.	21·04 N	105·50 E
104	Hanover (hăn′ō-vẽr) Can.	44·10 N	81·05 W
99	Hanover Ma. (In.)	42·07 N	70·49 W
105	Hanover NH	43·45 N	72·15 W
105	Hanover Pa.	39·50 N	77·00 W
136	Hanover (I.) Chile	51·00 S	74·45 W
190	Hanshan (hän′shän′) China	31·43 N	118·06 E
123	Hans Lollick (I.) (häns′lôl′ĭk) Vir. Is. (U. S. A.) (St. Thomas In.)	18·24 N	64·55 W
99	Hanson (hăn′sŭn) Ma. (In.)	42·04 N	70·53 W
112	Hansville (hăns′-vĭl) Wa. (Seattle In.)	47·55 N	122·33 W
190	Hantan (hän′tän′) China	36·37 N	114·30 E
98	Hantsport (hănts′pōrt) Can.	45·04 N	64·11 W
193	Hanyang (han′yäng′) China	30·30 N	114·10 E
190	Haoch′engchi (hou′chĕng′jē) China	33·19 N	117·33 E
150	Haparanda (hä-pä-rän′dä) Swe.	65·54 N	23·57 E
106	Hapeville (hăp′vĭl) Ga. (Atlanta In.)	33·39 N	84·25 W
183	Haql Sau. Ar. (Palestine In.)	29·15 N	34·57 E
217	Har, Laga (R.) Ken.	2·15 N	39·30 E
162	Harana Sierra (Mts.) (sē-ĕ′r-rä-rä′nä) Sp.	37·17 N	3·28 W
188	Hara Nuur (L.) Mong.	47·47 N	94·01 E
211	Harar (Prov.) Eth.	8·15 N	41·00 E
188	Hara Usa (L.) Mong.	48·00 N	92·32 E
	Harbin, see Haerhpin		
104	Harbor Beach (här′bẽr bēch) Mi.	43·50 N	82·40 W
104	Harbor Springs Mi.	45·25 N	85·05 W
99	Harbour Breton (brĕt′ŭn) (brĕ-tôN′) Can.	47·29 N	55·48 W
99	Harbour Grace (grās) Can.	47·32 N	53·13 W
149	Harburg (här-bŏŏrgh) F.R.G. (Hamburg In.)	53·28 N	9·58 E
156	Hardanger Fd. (här-däng′ẽr fyôrd) Nor.	59·58 N	6·30 E
156	Hardanger Fjell (Mts.) (fyĕl′) Nor.	60·15 N	6·56 E
156	Hardanger Jöklen (Mtn.) (yû′kōōl-ĕn) Nor.	60·33 N	7·23 W
111	Hardin (här′dĭn) Mt.	45·44 N	107·36 W
213	Harding (här′dĭng) S. Afr. (Natal In.)	30·34 S	29·54 E
120	Harding (L.) Al.-Ga.	32·43 N	85·00 W
184	Hardwār (hŭr′dvär) India	29·56 N	78·06 E
114	Hardy (R.) (här′dĭ) Mex.	32·04 N	115·10 W
97	Hare B. (hâr) Can.	51·18 N	55·50 W
218	Harer (hȧ-rär′) Eth. (Horn of Afr. In.)	9·43 N	42·10 E
218	Hargeysa (här-gā′ē-sȧ) Som. (Horn of Afr. In.)	9·20 N	43·57 E
159	Harghita, Muntii (Mts.) Rom.	46·25 N	25·40 E
195	Harima-Nada (Sea) (hä′rē-mä nä-dä) Jap.	34·34 N	134·37 E
149	Haring Vliet (R.) Neth. Amsterdam In.)	51·49 N	4·03 E
118	Harlan (här′lăn) Ia.	41·40 N	95·10 W
120	Harlan Ky.	36·50 N	83·19 W
116	Harlan Co. Res. Ne.	40·03 N	99·51 W
111	Harlem (hár′lĕm) Mt.	48·33 N	108·50 W
155	Harlingen (här′lĭng-ĕn) Neth.	53·10 N	5·24 E
119	Harlingen Tx.	26·12 N	97·42 W
148	Harlow (här′lō) Eng. (London In.)	51·46 N	0·08 E
111	Harlowton (här′lō-tun) Mt.	46·26 N	109·50 W
104	Harmony (här′mō-nĭ) In.	39·35 N	87·00 W
110	Harney Basin (här′nĭ) Or.	43·26 N	120·19 W
110	Harney L. Or.	43·11 N	119·23 W
108	Harney Pk. SD	43·52 N	103·32 W
156	Härnosand (hĕr-nû-sänd) Swe.	62·37 N	17·54 E
162	Haro (ä′rō) Sp.	42·35 N	2·49 W
112	Haro Str. (hă′rō) Can.-U. S. (Seattle In.)	48·27 N	123·11 W
148	Harpenden (här′pĕn-d′n) Eng. (London In.)	51·48 N	0·22 W
116	Harper (här′pẽr) Ks.	37·17 N	98·02 W
214	Harper Lib.	4·25 N	7·43 W
112	Harper Wa. (Seattle In.)	47·31 N	122·32 W
105	Harpers Ferry (här′pẽrz) WV	39·20 N	77·45 W
97	Harricana (R.) Can.	50·10 N	78·50 W
120	Harriman (hăr′ĭ-mǎn) Tn.	35·55 N	84·34 W
105	Harrington (hăr′ĭng-tŭn) De.	38·55 N	75·35 W
186	Harri Rud (R.) Afg.	34·29 N	61·16 E
154	Harris (I.) (hăr′ĭs) Scot.	57·55 N	6·40 W
121	Harris (L.) Fl. (In.)	28·43 N	81·40 W
104	Harrisburg (hăr′ĭs-bûrg) Il.	37·45 N	88·35 W
105	Harrisburg Pa.	40·15 N	76·50 W
218	Harrismith (hă-rĭs′mĭth) S. Afr. (Johannesburg & Pretoria In.)	28·17 S	29·08 E
117	Harrison (hăr′ĭ-sŭn) Ar.	36·13 N	93·06 W
107	Harrison Oh. (Cincinnati In.)	39·16 N	84·45 W
93	Harrison L. Can.	49·31 N	121·59 W
105	Harrisonburg (hăr′ĭ-sŭn-bûrg) Va.	38·30 N	78·50 W
117	Harrisonville (hăr-ĭ-sŭn-vĭl) Mo.	38·39 N	94·21 W
113	Harrisville (hăr′ĭs-vĭl) Ut. (Salt Lake City In.)	41·17 N	112·00 W
104	Harrisville WV	39·10 N	81·05 W
104	Harrodsburg (hăr′ŭdz-bûrg) Ky.	37·45 N	84·50 W
107	Harrods Cr. (hăr′ŭdz) Ky. (Louisville In.)	38·24 N	35·33 W
148	Harrow (hăr′ō) Eng. (London In.)	51·34 N	0·21 W
149	Harsefeld (här′zĕ-fĕld′) F.R.G. (Hamburg In.)	53·27 N	9·30 E
150	Harstad (här′städh) Nor.	68·49 N	16·10 E
104	Hart (härt) Mi.	43·40 N	86·25 W
218	Hartbeesfontein S. Afr. (Johannesburg & Pretoria In.)	26·46 S	26·25 E
213	Hartbeespoortdam (L.) S. Afr. (Johannesburg & Pretoria In.)	25·47 S	27·43 E
213	Hartsbeespoort S. Afr. (Johannesburg & Pretoria In.)	25·44 S	27·51 E
120	Hartford (härt′fẽrd) Al.	31·05 N	85·42 W
117	Hartford Ar.	35·01 N	94·21 W
105	Hartford Ct.	41·45 N	72·40 W
113	Hartford Il. (St. Louis In.)	38·50 N	90·06 W
120	Hartford Ky.	37·25 N	86·50 W
104	Hartford Mi.	42·15 N	86·15 W
109	Hartford Wi.	43·19 N	88·25 W
104	Hartford City In.	40·35 N	85·25 W
148	Hartington (härt′ĭng-tŭn) Eng.	53·08 N	1·48 W
108	Hartington Ne.	42·37 N	97·18 W
154	Hartland Pt. Eng.	51·03 N	4·40 W
154	Hartlepool (här′t′l-pōōl) Eng.	54·40 N	1·12 W
217	Hartley Rh.	18·18 S	30·10 E
108	Hartley (härt′lĭ) Ia.	43·12 N	95·29 W
92	Hartley Bay Can.	53·25 N	129·15 W
95	Hart Mtn. (härt) Can.	52·25 N	101·30 W
120	Hartselle (härt′sĕl) Al.	34·24 N	86·55 W
117	Hartshorne (härts′hôrn) Ok.	34·49 N	95·34 W
121	Hartsville (härts′vĭl) SC	34·20 N	80·04 W
120	Hartwell (härt′wĕl) Ga.	34·21 N	82·56 W
120	Hartwell Res. Ga.	34·30 N	83·00 W
184	Hārua India (In.)	22·36 N	88·40 E
109	Harvard (här′vȧrd) Il.	42·25 N	88·39 W
99	Harvard Ma (In.)	42·30 N	71·35 W
116	Harvard Ne.	40·36 N	98·08 W
115	Harvard, Mt. Co.	38·55 N	106·20 W
98	Harvey Can.	45·44 N	64·46 W
107	Harvey Il. (Chicago In.)	41·37 N	87·39 W
106	Harvey La. (New Orleans In.)	29·54 N	90·05 W
108	Harvey ND	47·46 N	99·55 W
155	Harwich (här′wĭch) Eng.	51·53 N	1·13 E
184	Haryana (State) India	29·00 N	75·45 E
158	Harz Mts. (härts) G.D.R.	51·42 N	10·50 E
183	Hasā, Wādī al (R.) Jordan (Palestine In.)	30·55 N	35·50 E
195	Hashimoto (hä′shē-mō′tō) Jap.	34·19 N	135·37 E
117	Haskell (hăs′kĕl) Ok.	35·49 N	95·41 W
116	Haskell Tx.	33·09 N	99·43 W
148	Haslingden (hăz′lĭng dĕn) Eng.	53·43 N	2·19 W
156	Hassela (hăs′ĕl-ô) Swe.	62·05 N	16·46 E
149	Hasselt (häs′ĕlt) Bel. (Brussels In.)	50·56 N	5·23 E
210	Hassi Messaoud Alg.	31·17 N	6·13 E
156	Hässjö (hĕs′shû) Swe.	62·36 N	17·33 E
156	Hassleholm (häs′lĕ-hōlm) Swe.	56·10 N	13·44 E
155	Hastings (hās′tĭngz) Eng.	50·52 N	0·28 E
104	Hastings Mi.	42·40 N	85·20 W
113	Hastings Mn. (Minneapolis, St. Paul In)	44·44 N	92·51 W
116	Hastings Ne.	40·34 N	98·42 W
205	Hastings N. Z. (In.)	39·33 S	176·53 E
106	Hastings-on-Hudson (ŏn-hŭd′sŭn) NY (New York In.)	40·59 N	75·53 W
120	Hatchie (R.) (hăch′ē) Tn.	35·28 N	89·14 W
165	Hateg (kät-säg′) Rom.	45·35 N	22·57 E
148	Hatfield Broad Oak (hăt-fēld brôd ōk) Eng.	51·50 N	0·14 E
195	Hatogaya (hä′tō-gä-yä) Jap. (Tōkyō In.)	35·50 N	139·45 E
195	Hatsukaichi (hät′sōō-kä′ĕ-chē) Jap.	34·22 N	132·19 E
121	Hatteras, C. (hăt′ẽr-ȧs) NC	35·15 N	75·24 W
120	Hattiesburg (hăt′ĭz-bûrg) Ms.	31·20 N	89·18 W
161	Hattingen (hä′tĕn-gĕn) F.R.G. (Ruhr In.)	51·24 N	7·11 E
159	Hatvan (hôt′vôn) Hung.	47·39 N	19·44 E
156	Haugesund (hou′gĕ-soon′) Nor.	59·26 N	5·20 E
157	Haukivesi (L.) (hou′kē-vĕ′sē) Fin.	62·02 N	29·02 E
94	Haultain (R.) Can.	56·15 N	106·35 W
218	Hauptsrus S. Afr. (Johannesburg & Pretoria In.)	26·35 S	26·16 E
205	Hauraki, G. (hä-ōō-rä′kē) N. Z. (In.)	36·44 S	175·15 E
98	Haut, Isle au (hō) Me.	44·03 N	68·13 W
152	Haut Atlas (Mts.) Mor.	32·10 N	5·49 W
98	Hauterive Can.	49·11 N	68·16 W
100	Hauula Hi.	21·37 N	157·45 W
117	Havana (hȧ-vă′nȧ) Il.	40·17 N	90·02 W
	Havana, see La Habana		
115	Havasu L. (hăv′ȧ-sōō) Az.	34·26 N	114·09 W
158	Havel R. (hä′fĕl) G.D.R.	53·09 N	13·10 E
99	Haverhill (hā′vẽr-hĭl) Ma. (In.)	42·46 N	71·05 W
105	Haverhill NH	44·00 N	72·05 W
106	Haverstraw (hā′vẽr-strô) NY (New York In.)	41·11 N	73·58 W
158	Havlíckuv Brod Czech.	49·38 N	15·34 E
99	Havre-Bouche Boucher (hăv′rȧ-bōō-shā′) Can.	45·42 N	61·30 W
111	Havre (hăv′ẽr) Mt.	48·34 N	109·42 W
105	Havre de Grace (hăv′ẽr dē gräs′) Md.	39·35 N	76·05 W
99	Havre-St. Pierre Can.	50·15 N	63·36 W
121	Haw (R.) (hô) NC	36·17 N	79·46 W
102	Hawaii (State) U. S.	20·00 N	157·40 W
100	Hawaii (I.) (hä wī′ē) Hi.	19·50 N	157·15 W
100	Hawaiian Is. (hä-wī′ăn) U. S.	22·00 N	158·00 W
100	Hawaii Volcanoes Natl. Pk. Hi.	19·30 N	155·25 W
108	Hawarden (hā′wàr-dĕn) Ia.	43·00 N	96·28 W
100	Hawi (hä′wē) Hi.	20·16 N	155·48 W
154	Hawick (hô′ĭk) Scot.	55·25 N	2·55 W
205	Hawke B. (hôk) N. Z. (In.)	39·17 S	177·58 E
203	Hawker (hô′kẽr) Austl.	31·58 S	138·12 E
105	Hawkesbury (hôks′bĕr-ĭ) Can.	45·35 N	74·35 W
120	Hawkinsville (hô′kĭnz-vĭl) Ga.	32·15 N	83·30 W
129	Hawks Nest Pt. Ba.	24·05 N	75·30 W
108	Hawley (hô′lĭ) Mn.	46·52 N	96·18 W
148	Haworth (hā′wûrth) Eng.	53·50 N	1·57 W
186	Hawtah Sau. Ar.	15·58 N	48·26 E
113	Hawthorne (hô′thôrn) Ca. (Los Angeles In.)	33·55 N	118·22 W
114	Hawthorne Nv.	38·33 N	118·39 W
116	Haxtun (hăks′tŭn) Co.	40·39 N	102·38 W
204	Hay (R.) (hā) Austl.	23·00 S	136·45 E
90	Hay (R.) Can.	60·21 N	117·14 W
195	Hayama (hä-yä′mä) Jap. (Tōkyō In.)	35·16 N	139·35 E
195	Hayashi (hä-yä′shē) Jap. (Tōkyō In.)	35·13 N	139·38 E
115	Hayden (hā′dĕn) Az.	33·00 N	110·50 W
101	Hayes, Mt. (hāz) Ak.	63·32 N	146·40 W
105	Hayes (R.) Can.	55·25 N	93·55 W
119	Haynesville (hānz′vĭl) La.	32·55 N	93·08 W
165	Hayrabolu Tur.	41·14 N	27·05 E
100	Hay River Can.	60·50 N	115·53 W
116	Hays (hāz) Ks.	38·51 N	99·20 W
183	Haysī, Wādī al (R.) Egypt	29·24 N	34·32 E
112	Haystack Mtn. (hā-stăk′) Wa. (Seattle In.)	48·26 N	122·07 W
112	Hayward (hā′wẽrd) Ca. (San Francisco In.)	37·40 N	122·06 W
109	Hayward Wi.	46·01 N	91·31 W
120	Hazard (hăz′ȧrd) Ky.	37·13 N	83·10 W
121	Hazelhurst (hā′z′l-hûrst) Ga.	31·50 N	82·36 W
107	Hazel Park Mi. (Detroit In.)	42·28 N	83·06 W
92	Hazelton (hā′z′l-tŭn) Can.	55·15 N	127·40 W
92	Hazelton Mts. Can.	55·00 N	128·00 W
120	Hazlehurst Ms.	31·52 N	90·23 W
105	Hazleton Pa.	41·00 N	76·00 W
120	Headland (hĕd′lănd) Al.	31·22 N	85·20 W
114	Healdsburg (hēldz′bûrg) Ca.	38·37 N	122·52 W
117	Healdton (hēld′tŭn) Ok.	34·13 N	97·28 W
148	Heanor (hēn′ŏr) Eng.	53·01 N	1·22 W
220	Heard I. (hûrd) Ind. O.	53·10 S	74·35 E
119	Hearne (hûrn) Tx.	30·53 N	96·35 W
91	Hearst (hûrst) Can.	49·36 N	83·40 W
108	Heart (R.) (härt) ND	46·46 N	102·34 W
93	Heart Lake Ind. Res. Can.	55·02 N	111·30 W
99	Heart's Content (härts kŏn′tĕnt) Can.	47·52 N	53·22 W
99	Heath Pte. (hēth) Can.	49·06 N	61·45 W
117	Heavener (hēv′nẽr) Ok.	34·52 N	94·36 W
118	Hebbronville (hē′brŭn-vĭl) Tx.	27·18 N	98·40 W
115	Heber (hē′bẽr) Ut.	40·30 N	111·25 W
117	Heber Springs Ar.	35·28 N	91·59 W
111	Hebgen Res. (hĕb′gĕn) Mt.	44·47 N	111·38 W
154	Hebrides, Sea of Scot.	57·00 N	7·00 W
91	Hebron (hē′brŭn) Can.	58·11 N	62·56 W
107	Hebron In. (Chicago In.)	41·19 N	87·13 W
107	Hebron Ky. (Cincinnati In.)	39·04 N	84·43 W
117	Hebron Ne.	40·11 N	97·36 W
108	Hebron ND	46·54 N	102·04 W
	Hebron, see Al Khalīl		
156	Heby (hĭ′bü) Swe.	59·56 N	16·48 E
92	Hecate Str. (hĕk′ȧ-tē) Can.	53·00 N	131·00 W
125	Hecelchakán (ā-sĕl-chä-kän′) Mex.	20·10 N	90·09 W
95	Hecla I. Can.	51·08 N	96·45 W
156	Hedemora (hĭ-dĕ-mō′rä) Swe.	60·16 N	15·55 E
156	Hedesunda Fd. (hi-de-sōōn′dä) Swe.	60·22 N	16·50 E
148	Hedon (hĕdŭn) Eng.	53·44 N	0·12 W
149	Heemstede Neth. (Amsterdam In.)	52·20 N	4·36 E
155	Heerlen Neth.	50·55 N	5·58 E
	Hefa, see Haifa		
120	Heflin (hĕf′lĭn) Al.	33·40 N	85·33 W
158	Heide (hī′dē) F.R.G.	54·13 N	9·06 E
202	Heidelberg (hī′dĕl-bûrg) Austl. (Melbourne In.)	37·45 S	145·04 E
158	Heidelberg (hīdĕl-bĕrgh) F.R.G.	49·24 N	8·43 E
158	Heidenheim (hī′dĕn-hīm) F.R.G.	48·41 N	10·09 E
218	Heilbron (hīl′brōn) S. Afr. (Johannesburg & Pretoria In.)	27·17 S	27·58 E
158	Heilbronn (hīl′brōn) F.R.G.	49·09 N	9·16 E
161	Heiligenhaus (hī′lē-gĕn-houz) F.R.G. (Ruhr In.)	51·19 N	6·58 E
158	Heiligenstadt (hī′lē-gĕn-shtät) G.D.R.	51·21 N	10·10 E
189	Heilungkiang (Prov.) (hā-lōōng′ kyäng′) China	46·36 N	128·07 E
157	Heinola (hā-nō′lȧ) Fin.	61·13 N	26·03 E
161	Heinsberg (hīnz′bĕrgh) F.R.G. (Ruhr In.)	51·04 N	6·07 E
149	Heist-op-den-Berg Bel. (Brussels In.)	51·05 N	4·14 E
	Hejaz, see Al Ḩijāz		
150	Hekla (Vol.) (hĕk′lȧ) Ice.	63·53 N	19·37 W
159	Hel (hāl) Pol.	54·37 N	18·53 E
156	Helagsfjället (Mtn.) Swe.	62·54 N	12·24 E
117	Helena (hē-lē′nȧ) Ar.	34·33 N	90·35 W
111	Helena (hĕ-lē′nȧ) Mt.	46·35 N	112·01 W
202	Helensburgh (hĕl′ĕnz-bŭr-ô) Austl. (Sydney In.)	34·11 S	150·59 E
154	Helensburgh Scot.	56·01 N	4·53 W
156	Helge (R.) (hĕl′gĕ) Swe.	56·31 N	13·47 E
158	Helgoland I. (hĕl′gō-länd) F.R.G.	54·13 N	7·30 E
121	Hellier (hĕl′yẽr) Ky.	37·16 N	82·27 W
162	Hellín (ĕl-yĕn′) Sp.	38·30 N	1·40 W
186	Helmand (R.) (hĕl′mŭnd) Afg.	31·00 N	63·48 E
155	Helmond (hĕl′mŏnt) (ĕl′môN′) Neth.	51·35 N	5·04 E
158	Helmstedt (hĕlm′shtĕt) F.R.G.	52·14 N	11·03 E
113	Helotes (hē′lōts) Tx. (San Antonio In.)	29·35 N	98·41 W
115	Helper (hĕlp′ẽr) Ut.	39·40 N	110·55 W

ng-sing; ŋ-baŋk; N-nasalized n; nŏd; cŏmmit; ōld; ôbey; ôrder; fōōd; fŏŏt; ou-out; s-soft; sh-dish; th-thin; pūre; ůnite; ûrn; stŭd; circŭs; ü-as "y" in study; ′-indeterminate vowel.

290 Helsingborg — Hollis PRONOUNCING INDEX

Page	Name Pronunciation	Region	Lat. °'	Long. °'
156	Helsingborg (hĕl'sĭng-bôrgh)	Swe.	56·04 N	12·40 E
	Helsingfors, see Helsinki			
156	Helsingør (hĕl-sĭng-ŭr')	Den.	56·03 N	12·33 E
157	Helsinki (Helsingfors) (hĕl'sĕn-kē) (hĕl'sĭng-fôrs')	Fin.	60·10 N	24·53 E
148	Hemel Hempstead (hĕm'ĕl hĕmp'stĕd)	Eng. (London In.)	51·43 N	0·29 W
113	Hemet (hĕm'ĕt)	Ca. (Los Angeles In.)	33·45 N	116·57 W
108	Hemingford (hĕm'ĭng-fērd)	Ne.	42·21 N	103·30 W
119	Hemphill (hĕmp'hĭl)	Tx.	31·20 N	93·48 W
107	Hempstead (hĕmp'stĕd)	NY (New York In.)	40·42 N	73·37 W
119	Hempstead	Tx.	30·07 N	96·05 W
156	Hemse (hĕm'sĕ)	Swe.	57·15 N	18·25 E
156	Hemsö (I.)	Swe.	62·43 N	18·22 E
156	Hen (hĭn)	Nor.	60·14 N	10·10 E
162	Henares (R.) (å-nä'rås)	Sp.	40·50 N	2·55 W
160	Hendaye (äN-dā')	Fr.	43·20 N	1·46 W
104	Henderson (hĕn'dēr-sŭn)	Ky.	37·50 N	87·30 W
114	Henderson	Nv.	36·09 N	115·04 W
121	Henderson	NC	36·18 N	78·24 W
120	Henderson	Tn.	35·25 N	88·40 W
119	Henderson	Tx.	32·09 N	94·48 W
121	Hendersonville (hĕn'dēr-sŭn-vĭl)	NC	35·17 N	82·28 W
148	Hendon (hĕn'dŭn)	Eng. (London In.)	51·34 N	0·13 W
218	Hendrina (hĕn-drē'nå)	S. Afr. (Johannesburg & Pretoria In.)	26·10 S	29·44 E
193	Hengch'un (hĕng'chŭn')	Taiwan	22·00 N	120·42 E
155	Hengelo (hĕngĕ-lō)	Neth.	52·20 N	6·45 E
193	Henghsien	China	22·40 N	104·20 E
193	Hengshan (hĕng'shän')	China	27·20 N	112·40 E
190	Hengshui (hĕng'shōō-ē')	China	37·43 N	115·42 E
193	Hengyang	China	26·58 N	112·30 E
148	Henley on Thames (hĕn'lē ŏn tĕmz)	Eng. (London In.)	51·31 N	0·54 W
105	Henlopen, C. (hĕn-lō'pĕn)	De.	38·45 N	75·05 W
160	Hennebont (ĕn-bôN')	Fr.	47·47 N	3·16 W
218	Hennenman	S. Afr. (Johannesburg & Pretoria In.)	27·59 S	27·03 E
116	Hennessey (hĕn'ĕ-sĭ)	Ok.	36·04 N	97·53 W
149	Hennigsdorf (hĕ'nĕngz-dōrf)	G.D.R. (Berlin In.)	52·39 N	13·12 E
213	Hennops (R.) (hĕn'ŏps)	S. Afr. (Johannesburg & Pretoria In.)	25·51 S	27·57 E
213	Hennopsrivier	S. Afr. (Johannesburg & Pretoria In.)	25·50 S	27·59 E
117	Henrietta (hĕn-rĭ-ĕt'å)	Ok.	35·25 N	95·58 W
116	Henrietta (hen-rĭ-ĕ't'å)	Tx.	33·47 N	98·11 W
91	Henrietta Maria, C. (hĕn-rĭ-ĕt'å)	Can.	55·10 N	82·20 W
115	Henry Mts. (hĕn'rĭ)	Ut.	38·55 N	110·45 W
192	Henteyn Nuruu (Mts.)	Sov. Un.	49·40 N	111·00 E
110	Heppner (hĕp'nēr)	Or.	45·21 N	119·33 W
186	Herāt (hĕ-rät')	Afg.	34·28 N	62·13 E
165	Hercegovina (Reg.) (hĕr-tsĕ-gô'vē-nå)	Yugo.	43·23 N	17·52 E
89	Hercules	Can. (Edmonton In.)	53·27 N	113·20 W
161	Herdecke (hĕr'dĕ-kĕ)	F.R.G. (Ruhr In.)	51·24 N	7·26 E
127	Heredia (ā-rā'dhē-ä)	C. R.	10·04 N	84·06 W
154	Hereford (hĕrĕ'fērd)	Eng.	52·05 N	2·44 W
148	Hereford (Co.)	Eng.	52·22 N	2·52 W
106	Hereford	Md. (Baltimore In.)	39·35 N	76·42 W
116	Hereford (hĕr'ĕ-fērd)	Tx.	34·47 N	102·25 W
162	Herencia (å-rān'thē-ä)	Sp.	39·23 N	3·22 W
149	Herentals	Bel. (Brussels In.)	51·10 N	4·51 E
158	Herford (hĕr'fōrt)	F.R.G.	52·06 N	8·42 E
117	Herington (hĕr'ĭng-tŭn)	Ks.	38·41 N	96·57 W
158	Herisau (hā'rē-zou)	Switz.	47·23 N	9·18 E
149	Herk-de-Stad	Bel. (Brussels In.)	50·56 N	5·13 E
105	Herkimer (hûr'kĭ-mēr)	NY	43·05 N	75·00 W
154	Herma Ness (Prom.) (hûr'må nĕs)	Scot.	60·50 N	1·10 W
117	Hermann (hûr'mŭn)	Mo.	38·41 N	91·27 W
104	Hermansville (hûr'mŭns-vĭl)	Mi.	45·40 N	87·35 W
113	Hermantown (hĕr'mån-toun)	Mn. (Duluth In.)	46·46 N	92·12 W
218	Hermanusdorings	S. Afr. (Johannesburg & Pretoria In.)	24·08 S	27·46 E
107	Herminie (hûr-mĭ'nē)	Pa. (Pittsburgh In.)	40·16 N	79·45 W
99	Hermitage B. (hûr'mĭ-tĕj)	Can.	47·35 N	56·05 W
197	Hermit Is. (hûr'mĭt)	Pap. N. Gui.	1·48 S	144·55 E
113	Hermosa Beach (hĕr-mō'så)	Ca. (Los Angeles In.)	33·51 N	118·24 W
122	Hermosillo (ĕr-mō-sē'l-yō)	Mex.	29·00 N	110·57 W
106	Herndon (hĕrn'don)	Va. (Baltimore In.)	38·58 N	77·22 W
161	Herne (hĕr'nĕ)	F.R.G. (Ruhr In.)	51·32 N	7·13 E
156	Herning (hĕr'nĭng)	Den.	56·08 N	8·55 E
108	Heron (L.) (hĕr'ŭn)	Mn.	43·42 N	95·23 W
108	Heron Lake	Mn.	43·48 N	95·20 W
126	Herrero, Punta (pt.) (pōō'n-tä-ĕr-rĕ'rô)	Mex.	19·18 N	87·24 W
104	Herrin (hĕr'ĭn)	Il.	37·50 N	89·00 W
213	Herschel (hēr'-shĕl)	S. Afr. (Natal In.)	30·37 S	27·12 E
107	Herscher (hēr'shēr)	Il. (Chicago In.)	41·03 N	88·06 W
155	Herstal (hĕr'stäl)	Bel.	50·42 N	5·32 E
148	Hertford (hûrt'fērd)	Eng.	51·46 N	0·05 W
121	Hertford	NC	36·10 N	76·30 W
149	Hertzberg (hĕrtz'bĕrgh)	G.D.R. (Berlin In.)	52·54 N	12·58 E
183	Herzliyya	Isr. (Palestine In.)	32·10 N	34·49 E
160	Hesdin (ē-dăN')	Fr.	50·24 N	1·59 E
158	Hessen (State) (hĕs'ĕn	F.R.G.	50·16 N	8·48 E
114	Hetch Hetchy Aqueduct (hĕtch hĕt'-chĭ åk'wē-dŭkt)	Ca.	37·27 N	120·54 W
108	Hettinger (hĕt'ĭn-jēr)	ND	45·58 N	102·36 W
218	Heuningspruit	S. Afr. (Johannesburg & Pretoria In.)	27·28 S	27·26 E
218	Heystekrand	S. Afr. (Johannesburg & Pretoria In.)	25·16 S	27·14 E
148	Heywood (hā'wŏŏd)	Eng.	53·36 N	2·12 W
121	Hialeah (hī-å-lē'ăh)	Fl. (In.)	25·49 N	80·18 W
117	Hiawatha (hī-ȧ-wô'thȧ)	Ks.	39·50 N	95·33 W
115	Hiawatha	Ut.	39·25 N	111·05 W
109	Hibbing (hĭb'ĭng)	Mn.	47·26 N	92·58 W
120	Hickman (hĭk'mȧn)	Ky.	34·33 N	89·10 W
121	Hickory (hĭk'ô-rĭ)	NC	35·43 N	81·21 W
106	Hicksville (hĭks'vĭl)	NY (New York In.)	40·47 N	73·25 W
104	Hicksville	Oh.	41·15 N	84·45 W
118	Hico (hī'kō)	Tx.	32·00 N	98·02 W
114	Hidalgo (ê-dhäl'gō)	Mex.	24·14 N	99·25 W
118	Hidalgo	Mex.	27·49 N	99·53 W
122	Hidlago (State)	Mex.	20·45 N	99·30 W
118	Hidalgo del Parral (ê-dä'l-gō-dĕl-pär-rå'l)	Mex.	26·55 N	105·40 W
125	Hidalgo Yalalag (ê-dhäl'gō-yä-lä-läg)	Mex.	17·12 N	96·11 W
218	Hiedelberg	S. Afr. (Johannesburg & Pretoria In.)	26·32 S	28·22 E
210	Hierro I. (yĕ'r-rô)	Can. Is.	27·37 N	18·29 W
195	Higashimurayama	Jap. (Tōkyō In.)	35·46 N	139·28 E
195	Higashiōsaka	Jap. (Ōsaka In.)	34·40 N	135·44 E
104	Higgins (L.) (hĭg'ĭnz)	Mi.	44·20 N	84·45 W
117	Higginsville (hĭg'ĭnz-vĭl)	Mo.	39·05 N	93·44 W
104	High (I.)	Mi.	45·45 N	85·45 W
89	High Bluff	Can. (Winnipeg In.)	50·01 N	98·08 W
128	Highborne Cay (hĭbôrn kē)	Ba.	24·45 N	76·50 W
113	Highgrove (hī'grōv)	Ca. (Los Angeles In.)	34·01 N	117·20 W
119	High Island	Tx. (In.)	29·34 N	94·24 W
113	Highland (hī'lănd)	Ca. (Los Angeles In.)	34·08 N	117·13 W
117	Highland	Il.	38·44 N	89·41 W
107	Highland	In. (Chicago In.)	41·33 N	87·28 W
107	Highland	Mi. (Detroit In.)	42·38 N	83·37 W
107	Highland Park	Il. (Chicago In.)	42·11 N	87·47 W
107	Highland Park	Mi. (Detroit In.)	42·24 N	83·06 W
106	Highland Park	NJ (New York In.)	40·30 N	74·25 W
113	Highland Park	Tx. (Dallas, Fort Worth In.)	32·49 N	96·48 W
106	Highlands (hī-lăndz)	NJ (New York In.)	40·24 N	73·59 W
113	Highlands	Tx. (In.)	29·49 N	95·01 W
108	Highmore (hī'mōr)	SD	44·30 N	99·26 W
148	High Ongar (on'gēr)	Eng. (London In.)	51·43 N	0·15 E
197	High Pk.	Phil. (In.)	15·38 N	120·05 E
121	High Point	NC	35·55 N	80·00 W
93	High Prairie	Can.	55·26 N	116·29 W
113	High Ridge	Mo. (St. Louis In.)	38·27 N	90·32 W
93	High River	Can.	50·35 N	113·52 W
121	Highrock (R.) (hī'-rŏk)	NC	35·40 N	80·15 W
121	High Springs	Fl.	29·48 N	82·38 W
106	Hightstown (hīts-toun)	NJ (New York In.)	40·16 N	74·32 W
148	High Wycombe (wĭ-kŭm)	Eng. (London In.)	51·36 N	0·45 W
123	Higuero, Pta. (Pt.)	P. R. (Puerto Rico In.)	18·21 N	67·11 W
135	Higuerote (ē-gĕ-rô'-tĕ)	Ven. (In.)	10·29 N	66·06 W
129	Higüey (ê-gwĕ'y)	Dom. Rep.	18·40 N	68·45 W
157	Hiiumaa (D'Ago) (hē'ōōm-ô)	Sov. Un.	58·47 N	22·05 E
195	Hikone (hē'kô-nĕ)	Jap.	35·15 N	136·15 E
158	Hildburghausen (hĭld'bōōrg hou-zĕn)	G.D.R.	50·26 N	10·45 E
161	Hilden (hēl'dĕn)	F.R.G. (Ruhr In.)	51·10 N	6·56 E
158	Hildesheim (hĭl'dĕs-hīm)	F.R.G.	52·08 N	9·56 E
127	Hillaby, Mt. (hĭl'ȧ-bĭ)	Barb. (In.)	13·15 N	59·35 W
116	Hill City (hĭl)	Ks.	39·22 N	99·54 W
109	Hill City	Mn.	46·58 N	93·38 W
149	Hillegersberg	Neth. (Amsterdam In.)	51·57 N	4·29 E
156	Hillerød (hē'lĕ-rûdh)	Den.	55·56 N	12·17 E
117	Hillsboro (hĭlz'bŭr-ō)	Il.	39·09 N	89·28 W
117	Hillsboro	Ks.	38·22 N	97·11 W
105	Hillsboro	NH	43·05 N	71·55 W
108	Hillsboro	ND	47·23 N	97·05 W
104	Hillsboro	Oh.	39·10 N	83·40 W
110	Hillsboro	Or. (Portland In.)	45·31 N	122·59 W
119	Hillsboro	Tx.	32·01 N	97·06 W
109	Hillsboro	Wi.	43·39 N	90·20 W
89	Hillsburgh (hĭlz'bûrg)	Can. (Toronto In.)	43·48 N	80·09 W
110	Hills Creek Res.	Or.	43·41 N	122·26 W
114	Hillsdale (hĭls-dāl)	Mi.	41·55 N	84·35 W
100	Hilo (hē'lō)	Hi.	19·44 N	155·01 W
149	Hilversum (hĭl'vēr-sŭm)	Neth. (Amsterdam In.)	52·13 N	5·10 E
184	Himachal Pradesh (State)	India	36·03 N	77·41 E
187	Himalaya Mts. (hĭ-mä'lȧ-yȧ)	Asia	29·30 N	85·02 E
195	Himeji (hē'mȧ-jē)	Jap.	34·50 N	134·42 E
149	Himmelpforten (hē'mĕl-pfōr-tĕn)	F.R.G. (Hamburg In.)	53·37 N	9·19 E
129	Hinche (hēn'chå) (äNsh)	Hai.	19·10 N	72·05 W
205	Hinchinbrook (I.) (hĭn-chĭn-brōōk)	Austl.	18·23 S	146·57 W
148	Hinckley (hĭnk'lĭ)	Eng.	52·32 N	1·21 W
148	Hindley (hĭnd'lĭ)	Eng.	53·32 N	2·35 W
187	Hindu Kush (Mts.) (hĭn'dōō kōōsh')	Asia	35·15 N	68·44 E
185	Hindupur (hĭn'dōō-pōōr)	India	13·52 N	77·34 E
99	Hingham (hĭng'ăm)	Ma. (In.)	42·14 N	70·53 W
107	Hinkley (hĭnk'-lĭ)	Oh. (Cleveland In.)	41·14 N	81·45 W
162	Hinojosa (ē-nô-kô'sä)	Sp.	38·30 N	5·09 W
107	Hinsdale (hĭnz'dāl)	Il. (Chicago In.)	41·48 N	87·56 W
93	Hinton (hĭn'tŭn)	Can.	53·25 N	117·34 W
104	Hinton (hĭn'tŭn)	WV	37·40 N	80·55 W
195	Hirado (I.) (hē'rä-dō)	Jap.	33·19 N	129·18 E
195	Hirakata (hē'rä-kä'tä)	Jap. (Ōsaka In.)	34·49 N	135·40 E
195	Hiratsuka (hē-rät-sōō'kå)	Jap.	35·20 N	139·19 E
188	Hirgis Nuur (L.)	Mong.	49·18 N	94·21 E
194	Hirosaki (hē'rô-sä'kē)	Jap.	40·31 N	140·38 E
195	Hirose (hē'rô-sä)	Jap.	35·20 N	133·11 E
195	Hiroshima (hē-rô-shē'må)	Jap.	34·22 N	132·25 E
160	Hirson (ēr-sôN')	Fr.	49·54 N	4·00 E
189	Hisar	India	29·15 N	75·47 E
123	Hispaniola (I.) (hĭ'spăn-ĭ-ō-lå)	N. A.	17·30 N	73·15 W
194	Hitachi (hē-tä'chē)	Jap.	36·42 N	140·47 E
119	Hitchcock (hĭch'kŏk)	Tx. (In.)	29·21 N	95·01 W
161	Hitdorf (hēt'dōrf)	F.R.G. (Ruhr In.)	51·04 N	6·56 E
195	Hitoyoshi (hē'tô-yō'shê)	Jap.	32·13 N	130·45 E
150	Hitra (I.) (hĭträ)	Nor.	63·34 N	7·37 E
149	Hittefeld (hē'tĕ-fĕld)	F.R.G. (Hamburg In.)	53·23 N	9·59 E
195	Hiwasa (hē'wȧ-sä)	Jap.	33·44 N	134·31 E
120	Hiwassee (R.) (hī-wôs'sē)	Tn.	35·10 N	84·35 W
156	Hjälmaren (L.)	Swe.	59·07 N	16·05 E
156	Hjo (yō)	Swe.	58·19 N	14·11 E
156	Hjørring (jûr'ĭng)	Den.	57·27 N	9·59 E
159	Hlohovec (hlō'ho-vĕts)	Czech.	48·24 N	17·49 E
203	Hobart (hō'bȧrt)	Austl.	43·00 S	147·30 E
107	Hobart	In. (Chicago In.)	41·31 N	87·15 W
116	Hobart	Ok.	35·02 N	99·06 W
112	Hobart	Wa. (Seattle In.)	47·25 N	121·58 W
116	Hobbs (hŏbs)	NM	32·41 N	104·04 W
188	Hobdo Gol (R.)	Mong.	49·06 N	91·16 E
149	Hoboken (hō'bō-kĕn)	Bel. (Brussels In.)	51·11 N	4·20 E
106	Hoboken	NJ (New York In.)	40·43 N	74·03 W
156	Hobro (hô-brô')	Den.	56·38 N	9·47 E
106	Hobson (hŏb'sŭn)	Va. (Norfolk In.)	36·54 N	76·31 W
202	Hobson's B. (hŏb'sŭnz)	Austl. (Melbourne In.)	37·54 S	144·45 E
190	Hochien (hŭ'jĭän)	China	38·28 N	116·05 E
196	Ho Chi Minh City (Saigon)	Viet.	10·46 N	106·34 E
190	Hochiu	China	32·19 N	116·17 E
158	Höchst (hüKst)	F.R.G.	50·06 N	8·37 E
193	Hoch'uan	China	30·00 N	106·20 E
112	Hockinson (hŏk'-ĭn-sŭn)	Wa. (Portland In.)	45·44 N	122·29 W
126	Hoctún (ôk-tōō'n)	Mex. (In.)	20·52 N	89·10 W
104	Hodgenville (hŏj'ĕn-vĭl)	Ky.	37·35 N	85·45 W
97	Hodges Hill (Mtn.) (hŏj'ĕz)	Can.	49·04 N	55·53 W
159	Hódmezövásárhely (hōd'mĕ-zû-vô'shôr-hĕl-y')	Hung.	46·24 N	20·21 E
151	Hodna, Chott el (L.)	Alg.	35·20 N	3·27 E
159	Hodonin (hē'dô-nén)	Czech.	48·50 N	17·06 E
149	Hoegaarden	Bel. (Brussels In.)	50·46 N	4·55 E
149	Hoek van Holland	Neth. (Amsterdam In.)	51·59 N	4·05 E
194	Hoeryŏng (hwĕr'yŭng)	Kor.	42·28 N	129·39 E
161	Hoetmar (hût'mär)	F.R.G. (Ruhr In.)	51·52 N	7·54 E
158	Hof (hōf)	F.R.G.	50·19 N	11·55 E
190	Hofei (hô'fā)	China	31·51 N	117·15 E
150	Hofsjökull (Gl.) (hôfs'yü'kōōl)	Ice.	64·55 N	18·40 W
104	Hog (I.)	Mi.	45·50 N	85·20 W
120	Hogansville (hō'gănz-vĭl)	Ga.	33·10 N	84·54 W
129	Hog Cay (I.)	Ba.	23·35 N	75·30 W
129	Hogsty Rf.	Ba.	21·45 N	73·50 W
149	Hohenbrunn (hō'hĕn-brōōn)	F.R.G. (Munich In.)	48·03 N	11·42 E
161	Hohenlimburg (hō'hĕn lĕm'bōōrg)	F.R.G. (Ruhr In.)	51·20 N	7·35 E
149	Hohen Neuendorf (hō'hĕn noi'ĕn-dōrf)	G.D.R. (Berlin In.)	52·40 N	13·22 E
158	Hohe Tauern (Mts.) (hō'ĕ tou'ĕrn)	Aus.	47·11 N	12·12 E
214	Hohoe	Ghana	7·09 N	0·28 E
106	Hohokus (hō-hō-kŭs)	NJ (New York In.)	41·01 N	74·08 W
193	Hohsien	China	24·20 N	111·28 E
190	Hohsien (hō'syĕn')	China	31·44 N	118·20 E
190	Ho Hu (L.) (hŭ'hoo)	China	31·37 N	119·57 E
116	Hoisington (hoi'zĭng-tŭn)	Ks.	38·30 N	98·46 W
195	Hojo (hō'jō)	Jap.	33·58 N	132·50 E
205	Hokitika (hō-kĭ-tē'kä)	N. Z. (In.)	42·43 S	171·12 E
194	Hokkaido (I.) (hŏk'kĭ-dō)	Jap.	43·30 N	142·45 E
156	Holbaek (hôl'bĕk)	Den.	55·42 N	11·40 E
126	Holbox (ôl-bŏ'x)	Mex. (In.)	21·33 N	87·19 W
126	Holbox, Isla (I.) (ē's-lä-ôl-bŏ'x)	Mex. (In.)	21·40 N	87·21 W
115	Holbrook (hōl'brŏŏk)	Az.	34·55 N	110·15 W
99	Holbrook	Ma. (In.)	42·10 N	71·01 W
99	Holden (hōl'dĕn)	Ma. (In.)	42·21 N	71·51 W
117	Holden	Mo.	38·42 N	94·00 W
104	Holden	WV	37·45 N	82·05 W
117	Holdenville (hōl'dĕn-vĭl)	Ok.	35·05 N	96·25 W
116	Holdrege (hōl'drĕj)	Ne.	40·25 N	99·28 W
156	Hölen (hûl'ĕn)	Nor.	59·34 N	10·40 E
129	Holguín (ôl-gēn')	Cuba	20·55 N	76·15 W
129	Holguín (Prov.)	Cuba	20·40 N	76·15 W
105	Holidaysburg (hŏl'ĭ-dāz-bûrg)	Pa.	40·30 N	78·30 W
158	Hollabrunn	Aus.	48·33 N	16·04 E
104	Holland (hŏl'ănd)	Mi.	42·45 N	86·10 W
149	Hollandsch Diep (Chan.)	Neth. (Amsterdam In.)	51·43 N	4·25 E
149	Hollenstedt (hō'lĕn-shtĕt)	F.R.G. (Hamburg In.)	53·22 N	9·43 E
99	Hollis (hŏl'ĭs)	NH (In.)	42·30 N	71·29 W

ăt; finăl; rāte; senåte; ärm; åsk; sofȧ; fâre; ch-choose; dh-as th in other; bē; ēvent; bĕt; recĕnt; cratēr; g-go; gh-guttural g; bĭt; ĭ-short neutral; rīde; K-guttural k as ch in German ich;

Page	Name Pronunciation Region	Lat. °'	Long. °'
116	Hollis ... Ok.	34·39 N	99·56 W
114	Hollister (hŏl'ĭs-tẽr) ... Ca.	36·50 N	121·25 W
99	Holliston (hŏl'ĭs-tŭn) ... Ma. (In.)	42·12 N	71·25 W
104	Holly (hŏl'ĭ) ... Mi.	42·45 N	83·30 W
112	Holly ... Wa. (Seattle In.)	47·34 N	122·58 W
120	Holly Springs (hŏl'ĭ springz) .. Ms.	34·45 N	89·28 W
113	Hollywood (hŏl'ē-wŏŏd) Ca. (Los Angeles In.)	34·06 N	118·20 W
121	Hollywood ... Fl. (In.)	26·00 N	80·11 W
205	Holmes Rfs. (hōmz) ... Austl.	16·33 S	148·43 E
156	Holmestrand (hôl'mĕ-strän) .. Nor.	59·29 N	10·17 E
156	Holmsbu (hôlms'bōō) ... Nor.	59·36 N	10·26 E
156	Holmsjön (L.) ... Swe.	62·23 N	15·43 E
156	Holstebro (hôl'stĕ-brô) ... Den.	56·22 N	8·39 E
120	Holston (R.) (hōl'stŭn) ... Tn.	36·02 N	83·42 W
148	Holt (hōlt) ... Eng.	53·05 N	2·53 W
117	Holton (hōl'tŭn) ... Ks.	39·27 N	95·43 W
154	Holy (I.) (hō'lĭ) ... Wales	53·45 N	4·45 W
154	Holy (I.) ... Eng.	55·43 N	1·48 W
101	Holy Cross (hō'lĭ krôs) ... Ak.	62·10 N	159·40 W
154	Holyhead (hŏl'ē-hĕd) ... Wales	53·48 N	4·45 W
116	Holyoke (hōl'yōk) ... Co.	40·36 N	102·18 W
105	Holyoke ... Ma.	42·10 N	72·40 W
195	Homano (hō-mä'nō) Jap. (Tōkyō In.)	35·33 N	140·08 E
161	Homberg (hōm'bĕrgh) F.R.G. (Ruhr In.)	51·27 N	6·42 E
214	Hombori ... Mali	15·17 N	1·42 W
113	Home Gardens (hōm gär'd'nz) Ca. (Los Angeles In.)	33·53 N	117·32 W
113	Homeland (hōm'lănd) Ca. (Los Angeles In.)	33·44 N	117·07 W
101	Homer (hō'mẽr) ... Ak.	59·42 N	151·30 W
119	Homer ... La.	32·46 N	93·05 W
121	Homestead (hōm'stĕd) ... Fl. (In.)	25·27 N	80·28 W
113	Homestead Mi. (Sault Ste. Marie In.)	46·20 N	84·07 W
107	Homestead ... Pa. (Pittsburgh In.)	40·29 N	79·55 W
118	Homestead Natl. Mon. of America Ne.	40·16 N	96·51 W
106	Homewood (hōm'wŏŏd) Al. (Birmingham In.)	33·28 N	86·48 W
107	Homewood ... Il. (Chicago In.)	41·34 N	87·40 W
118	Hominy (hŏm'ĭ-nĭ) ... Ok.	36·25 N	96·24 W
120	Homochitto (R.) (hō-mō-chĭt'ō). Ms.	31·23 N	91·15 W
153	Homs (hōms) ... Syr.	34·42 N	36·52 E
189	Honan (Prov.) (hō'nän') ... China	33·58 N	112·33 E
134	Honda (hōn'dà) ... Col. (In.)	5·13 N	74·45 W
128	Honda, Bahía (B.) (bä-ē'ä-ô'n-dä) Cuba	23·10 N	83·20 W
118	Hondo ... Tx.	29·20 N	99·08 W
126	Hondo, Rio (R.) (hon-dō') Belize (In.)	18·16 N	88·32 W
116	Hondo (R.) ... NM	33·22 N	105·06 W
122	Honduras (hŏn-dōō'ràs) ... N. A.	14·30 N	88·00 W
122	Honduras, Gulf of ... N. A.	16·30 N	87·30 W
121	Honea Path (hŭn'ĭ pàth) ... SC	34·25 N	82·16 W
156	Hönefoss (hē'nē-fôs) ... Nor.	60·10 N	10·15 E
105	Honesdale (hōnz'dāl) ... Pa.	41·30 N	75·15 W
114	Honey (R.) (hŭn'ĭ) ... Ca.	40·11 N	120·34 W
117	Honey Grove (hŭn'ĭ grōv) ... Tx.	33·35 N	95·54 W
89	Honfleur (ôN-flûr') Can. (Quebec In.)	46·39 N	70·53 W
160	Honfleur (ôN-flûr') ... Fr.	49·26 N	0·13 E
193	Hon Gay ... Viet.	20·58 N	107·10 E
98	Honguedo, Détroit d' (Str.) .. Can.	49·08 N	63·45 W
205	Honiara ... Sol. Is.	9·15 S	159·45 E
154	Honiton (hŏn'ĭ-tŏn) ... Eng.	50·49 N	3·10 W
189	Hong Kong (hŏng' kŏng') ... Asia	21·45 N	115·00 E
100	Honolulu (hŏn-ô-lōō'lōō) ... Hi.	21·18 N	157·50 W
100	Honomu (hŏn'ô-mōō) ... Hi.	19·50 N	155·04 W
194	Honshū (I.) (hŏn'shōō) ... Jap.	36·50 N	135·20 E
110	Hood, Mt. ... Or.	45·20 N	121·43 W
112	Hood Can. (hŏŏd) Wa. (Seattle In.)	47·45 N	122·45 W
110	Hood River ... Or.	45·42 N	121·30 W
112	Hoodsport (hŏŏdz'pōrt) Wa. (Seattle In.)	47·25 N	123·09 W
184	Hoogly (R.) (hōōg'lĭ) ... India	21·35 N	87·50 E
149	Hoogstraten ... Bel. (Brussels In.)	51·24 N	4·46 E
116	Hooker (hŏŏk'ẽr) ... Ok.	36·49 N	101·13 W
126	Hool (ōō'l) ... Mex. (In.)	19·32 N	90·22 W
101	Hoonah (hōō'nä) ... Ak.	58·05 N	135·25 W
110	Hoopa Valley Ind. Res. (hōō'pà) Ca.	41·18 N	123·35 W
117	Hooper (hŏŏp'ẽr) ... Ne.	41·37 N	96·31 W
113	Hooper .. Ut. (Salt Lake City In.)	41·10 N	112·08 W
101	Hooper Bay ... Ak.	61·32 N	166·02 W
104	Hoopeston (hōōps'tŭn) ... Il.	40·35 N	87·40 W
105	Hoosick Falls (hōō'sĭk) ... NY	42·55 N	73·15 W
114	Hoover Dam (hōō'vẽr) ... Nv.	36·00 N	115·06 W
106	Hopatcong, L. (hō-păt'kong) NJ (New York In.)	40·57 N	74·38 W
101	Hope (hōp) ... Ak.	60·54 N	149·48 W
117	Hope ... Ar.	33·41 N	93·35 W
93	Hope ... Can.	49·23 N	121·26 W
108	Hope ... ND	47·17 N	97·45 W
91	Hopedale (hōp'dāl) ... Can.	55·26 N	60·11 W
99	Hopedale (hōp'dāl) ... Ma. (In.)	42·08 N	71·33 W
189	Hopeh (Prov.) ... China	39·15 N	115·40 E
126	Hopelchén (o-pĕl-chĕ'n). Mex. (In.)	19·47 N	89·51 W
91	Hopes Advance, C. (hōps ăd-vàns') Can.	61·05 N	69·35 W
204	Hopetoun (hōp'toun) ... Austl.	33·50 S	120·15 E
121	Hopewell (hōp'wĕl) ... Va.	37·14 N	77·15 W
212	Hopetown (hōp'toun) ... S. Afr.	29·35 S	24·10 E
115	Hopi Ind. Res. (hō'pē) ... Az.	36·20 N	110·30 W
113	Hopkins (hŏp'-kĭns) Mn. (Minneapolis, St. Paul In.)	44·55 N	93·24 W
120	Hopkinsville (hŏp'-kĭns-vĭl) ... Ky.	36·50 N	87·28 W
99	Hopkinton (hŏp'-kĭn-tŭn) Ma. (In.)	42·14 N	71·31 W
193	Hop'u ... China	21·28 N	109·10 E
110	Hoquiam (hō'kwĭ-ăm) ... Wa.	47·00 N	123·53 W
156	Horby (hûr'bü) ... Swe.	55·50 N	13·41 E
127	Horconcitos (ŏr-kôn-sē'-tôs) .. Pan.	8·18 N	82·11 W
218	Hordio ... Som. (Horn of Afr. In.)	10·43 N	51·05 E
158	Horgen (hôr'gĕn) ... Switz.	47·16 N	8·35 E
109	Horicon (hŏr'ĭ-kŏn) ... Wi.	43·26 N	88·40 W
186	Hormuz, Str. of (hôr'mŭz') ... Asia	26·30 N	56·30 E
	Horn, C., see Hornos, Cabo de		
205	Horn (Is.) (hôrn) ... Austl.	10·30 S	143·30 E
150	Hornavan (L.) ... Swe.	65·54 N	16·17 E
149	Horneburg (hôr'nĕ-bŏŏrgh) F.R.G. (Hamburg In.)	53·30 N	9·35 E
105	Hornell (hôr-nĕl') ... NY	42·10 N	77·40 W
90	Horn Mts. ... Can.	62·12 N	120·29 W
136	Hornos, C. de (Horn, C.) (kà'-bô-dĕ-ô'r-nôs) (kă'p-hŏr'n) Chile	56·00 S	67·00 W
202	Hornsby (hôrnz'bĭ). Austl. (Sydney In.)	33·43 S	151·06 E
156	Hornslandet (I.) ... Swe.	61·40 N	17·58 E
136	Horqueta (ŏr-kĕ'tä) ... Par.	23·20 S	57·00 W
116	Horse Cr. (hôrs) ... Co.	38·49 N	103·48 W
108	Horse Cr. ... Wy.	41·33 N	104·39 W
99	Horse Is. ... Can.	50·11 N	55·45 W
156	Horsens (hôrs'ĕns) ... Den.	55·50 N	9·49 E
112	Horseshoe B. (hôrs-shōō) Can. (Vancouver In.)	49·23 N	123·16 W
148	Horsforth (hôrs'fŭrth) ... Eng.	53·50 N	1·38 W
203	Horsham, (hôr'shăm) (hôrs'ăm) Austl.	36·42 S	142·17 E
149	Horst (hôrst) F.R.G. (Hamburg In.)	53·49 N	9·37 E
156	Horten (hôr'tĕn) ... Nor.	59·26 N	10·27 E
118	Horton (hôr'tŭn) ... Ks.	39·38 N	95·32 W
101	Horton (R.) (hôr'tŭn) ... Ak.	68·38 N	122·00 W
148	Horwich (hŏr'ĭch) ... Eng.	53·36 N	2·33 W
215	Hoséré Vokré (Mtn.) ... Cam.	8·20 N	13·15 E
193	Hoshan ... China	31·30 N	116·25 E
195	Hososhima (hō'sô-shē'mä) ... Jap.	32·25 N	131·40 E
136	Hoste (ôs'tä) (I.) ... Chile	55·20 S	70·45 W
124	Hostotipaquillo (ôs-tō-tī'pä-kēl'yō) Mex.	21·09 N	104·05 W
195	Hota (hō'tä) ... Jap. (Tōkyō In.)	35·08 N	139·50 E
188	Hotien (Khotan) (hō'tyĕn') (kō-tän'). China	37·11 N	79·50 E
129	Hoto Mayor (ô-tô-mä-yō'r) Dom. Rep.	18·45 N	69·10 W
101	Hot Springs (hŏt springs) ... Ak.	65·00 N	150·20 W
117	Hot Springs ... Ar.	34·29 N	93·02 W
108	Hot Springs ... SD	43·28 N	103·32 W
105	Hot Springs ... Va.	38·00 N	79·55 W
117	Hot Springs Natl. Park ... Ar.	34·30 N	93·00 W
129	Hotte, Massif de la (Mts.) ... Hai.	18·25 N	74·00 W
114	Hotville (hŏt'-vĭl) ... Ca.	32·50 N	115·24 W
190	Houchen (hō'jĕn') ... China	36·59 N	118·59 E
161	Houdan (ōō-dăN') .. Fr. (Paris In.)	48·47 N	1·36 E
109	Houghton (hŏ'tŭn) ... Mi.	47·06 N	88·36 W
104	Houghton (L.) ... Mi.	44·20 N	84·45 W
161	Houilles (ōō-yēs') .. Fr. (Paris In.)	48·55 N	2·11 E
98	Houlton (hōl'tŭn) ... Me.	46·07 N	67·50 W
119	Houma (hōō'mà) ... La.	29·36 N	90·43 W
214	Houndé ... Upper Volta	11·30 N	3·31 W
105	Housatonic (R.) (hōō-sà-tŏn'ĭk) Ct.-Ma.	41·50 N	73·25 W
113	House Springs (hous springs) Mo. (St. Louis In.)	38·24 N	90·34 W
120	Houston (hūs'tŭn) ... Ms.	33·53 N	89·00 W
119	Houston ... Tx. (In.)	29·46 N	95·21 W
119	Houston Ship Chan. ... Tx. (In.)	29·38 N	94·57 W
212	Houtbaai ... S. Afr. (In.)	34·03 S	18·22 E
204	Houtman Rocks (Is.) (hout'män) Austl.	28·15 S	112·45 E
154	Hove (hōv) ... Eng.	50·50 N	0·09 W
115	Hovenweep Natl. Mon. (hō'v'n-wēp). Co.-Ut.	37·27 N	108·50 W
117	Howard (hou'ărd) ... Ks.	37·27 N	96·10 W
108	Howard ... SD	44·01 N	97·31 W
148	Howden (hou'dĕn) ... Eng.	53·44 N	0·52 W
203	Howe, C. (hou) ... Austl.	37·30 S	150·40 E
104	Howell (hou'ĕl) ... Mi.	42·40 N	84·00 W
92	Howe Sd. ... Can.	49·22 N	123·18 W
89	Howick (hou'ĭk) Can. (Montreal In.)	45·11 N	73·51 W
213	Howick ... S. Afr. (Natal In.)	29·29 S	30·16 E
198	Howland (I.) (hou'lănd) .. Oceania	1·00 N	176·00 W
184	Howrah (hou'rä) ... India (In.)	22·33 N	88·20 E
93	Howse Pk. ... Can.	51·30 N	116·40 W
92	Howson Pk. ... Can.	54·25 N	127·45 W
117	Hoxie (hŏk'sĭ) ... Ar.	36·03 N	91·00 W
154	Hoy (I.) (hoi) ... Scot.	58·53 N	3·10 W
195	Hōya ... Jap. (Tōkyō In.)	35·45 N	139·35 E
192	Hoyang ... China	35·18 N	110·18 E
148	Hoylake (hoi-lāk') ... Eng.	53·23 N	3·11 W
193	Hoyüan ... China	23·48 N	114·45 E
158	Hradec Králové (hrä'dĕts krä'lô-vā). Czech.	50·14 N	15·50 E
159	Hranice (hrän'yĕ-tsĕ) ... Czech.	49·33 N	17·45 E
159	Hrinová (hrĕn'yô-vä) ... Czech.	48·36 N	19·32 E
159	Hron R. ... Czech.	48·22 N	18·42 E
159	Hrubieszów (hrōō-byā'shŏŏf) .. Pol.	50·48 N	23·54 E
164	Hrvatska (Croatia) (Reg.) (hr-väts'kä). Yugo.	45·24 N	15·18 E
191	Hsaiolung ... China (Canton In.)	22·27 N	113·26 E
188	Hsawnhsup ... Bur.	24·29 N	94·45 E
190	Hsiaching (sĭä'jĭn) ... China	36·58 N	115·59 E
190	Hsiai (sĭä'yē) ... China	34·15 N	116·07 E
193	Hsiamen (I.) ... China	24·28 N	118·20 E
193	Hsiamen (Amoy) (à-moi') ... China	24·30 N	118·10 E
192	Hsian (Sian) (shĭ'än) (syän'). China	34·20 N	109·00 E
190	Hsiang (hsē'äng') ... China	39·43 N	116·08 E
190	Hsiangch'eng ... China	33·52 N	113·31 E
192	Hsiangho (hsē'äng'-hō') China (In.)	39·46 N	116·59 E
189	Hsiaohsinganling Shanmo (Lesser Khingan Ra.). China	49·50 N	127·26 E
190	Hsiaoku Ho (R.) (sĭou'gōō hŭ) China	36·29 N	120·06 E
193	Hsiap'u ... China	27·00 N	120·00 E
190	Hsiats'un (sĭä'ts'ün) ... China	36·54 N	121·31 E
193	Hsich'ang ... China	26·50 N	102·25 E
193	Hsi Chiang (R.) ... China	22·00 N	109·18 E
191	Hsi Chiang (R.) China (Canton In.)	22·47 N	113·01 E
190	Hsichung Tao (I.) (sē'joong'dou) China	39·27 N	121·06 E
191	Hsients'unhsü. China (Canton In.)	23·10 N	113·41 E
192	Hsienyang ... China	34·20 N	108·40 E
192	Hsifeng (hsē'fĕng') ... China	42·40 N	124·40 E
190	Hsihoying (sē'hŭ'yĭng) ... China	39·58 N	114·50 E
190	Hsihsienchen (sē'sĭän'jĕn) ... China	37·21 N	119·59 E
190	Hsi Hu (L.) (sē'hōō) ... China	32·31 N	116·04 E
192	Hsiliao (R.) ... China	43·23 N	121·40 E
191	Hsinch'ang .. China (Shanghai In.)	31·02 N	121·38 E
190	Hsincheng (sĭn'jeng) ... China	34·24 N	113·43 E
190	Hsinchiachai (sĭn'jĭa'jäĭ) ... China	36·59 N	117·33 E
184	Hsinchiang (Mts.) ... China	41·52 N	81·20 E
193	Hsinchu (hsĭn'chōō') ... Taiwan	24·48 N	121·00 E
193	Hsingan ... China	25·44 N	110·32 E
190	Hsingcheng (sĭng'chĕng) ... China	40·38 N	120·41 E
190	Hsingchiawan (sĭng'jĭä'wäN) China	37·16 N	114·54 E
190	Hsinghua (sĭng'hōōà) ... China	32·58 N	119·48 E
190	Hsingt'ai (sĭng'tăĭ) ... China	37·04 N	114·33 E
190	Hsinhsiang (sĭn'sĭäng) ... China	35·17 N	113·49 E
190	Hsinhsien (sĭn'sĭäN) ... China	36·14 N	115·38 E
192	Hsinhsien ... China	38·20 N	112·45 E
193	Hsinhua ... China	27·45 N	111·20 E
193	Hsinhui ... China	22·40 N	113·08 E
188	Hsining ... China	36·52 N	101·36 E
193	Hsinkao Shan (Mtn.) ... Taiwan	23·38 N	121·05 E
	Hsinking, see Ch'angch'un		
192	Hsinmin ... China	42·00 N	122·42 E
190	Hsinp'u (sĭn'pōō) ... China	34·35 N	119·09 E
190	Hsint'ai (sĭn'tăĭ) ... China	35·55 N	117·44 E
191	Hsint'ang ... China (Canton In.)	23·06 N	113·06 E
191	Hsinti ... China (Canton In.)	22·43 N	113·20 E
190	Hsintien (sĭn'dĭäN) ... China	31·33 N	115·17 E
190	Hsinyang (sĭn'yäng) ... China	32·08 N	114·04 E
192	Hsinyeh ... China	32·40 N	112·20 E
190	Hsip'ing (sĭ'pĭng) ... China	33·21 N	114·01 E
193	Hsisha Ch'üntao (Paracel Is.) China	16·40 N	113·00 E
193	Hsishui ... China	30·30 N	115·10 E
190	Hsiungyüen ... China	40·10 N	122·08 E
190	Hsiyang (sē'yäng) ... China	37·37 N	113·42 E
193	Hsüancheng ... China	30·52 N	118·48 E
192	Hsuanhua ... China	40·35 N	115·05 E
190	Hsuanhuatien (sōōän'hōōä'dĭäN) China	31·42 N	114·29 E
190	Hsüch'ang (sü'chăng) ... China	34·02 N	113·49 E
190	Hsüchou (Süchow) ... China	34·17 N	117·10 E
190	Hsüi (sü'yē) ... China	31·02 N	113·49 E
193	Hsün Chiang (R.) ... China	23·28 N	110·30 E
134	Huacho (wä'chō) ... Peru	11·13 S	77·29 W
190	Huaian (hōōäĭ'äN) ... China	33·31 N	119·11 E
189	Huai Ho (R.) (hōōäĭ'hŭ) ... China	32·07 N	114·38 E
192	Huailai ... China	40·20 N	115·45 E
190	Huailinchen (hōōäĭlĭn'jĕn) ... China	31·27 N	117·36 E
190	Huainan ... China	32·38 N	117·02 E
190	Huaiyang (hōōäĭ'yang) ... China	33·45 N	114·54 E
190	Huaiyin (hōōäĭ'yĭn) ... China	33·34 N	118·58 E
190	Huaiyüan (hōōäĭ'yōōäN) ... China	32·53 N	117·13 E
124	Huajicori (wä-jē-kō'rē) ... Mex.	22·41 N	105·24 W
125	Huajuapan de León (wäj-wä'päm dā lā-ōn'). Mex.	17·46 N	97·45 W
115	Hualapai Ind. Res. (wäl'apī) .. Az.	35·41 N	113·38 W
115	Hualapai Mts. ... Az.	34·53 N	113·54 W
193	Hualien (hwä'lyĕn') ... Taiwan	23·58 N	121·58 E
134	Huallaga (R.) (wäl-yä'gä) ... Peru	8·12 S	76·34 W
134	Huamachuco (wä-mä-chōō'kō) Peru	7·52 S	78·11 W
125	Huamantla (wä-män'tlä) ... Mex.	19·18 N	97·54 W
216	Huambo (Nova Lisboa) ... Ang.	12·44 S	15·47 E
124	Huamuxtitlán (wä-mōōs-tē-tlän') Mex.	17·49 N	98·38 W
134	Huancavelica (wän'kä-vä-lē'kä) Peru	12·47 S	75·02 W
134	Huancayo (wän-kä'yō) ... Peru	12·09 S	75·04 W
134	Huanchaca (wän-chä'kä) ... Bol.	20·09 S	66·40 W
188	Huan Chiang (R.) ... China	36·45 N	106·30 E
190	Huangch'iao (hōōäng'chĭou). China	32·15 N	120·13 E
190	Huangch'uan (hōōäNg'chōōäN) China	32·07 N	115·01 E
189	Huang Ho (Yellow River) (hōōäng'hu). China	35·06 N	113·39 E
189	Huang Ho, Old Beds of the (R.) China	40·28 N	106·34 E
190	Huang Ho, Old Course of the (R.) China	34·28 N	116·59 E
192	Huanghoutien ... China (In.)	39·22 N	116·53 E
190	Huanghsien (hōōäNg'sĭän) .. China	37·39 N	120·32 E
190	Huangli (hōōäng'lē) ... China	31·39 N	119·42 E
191	Huanglien ... China (Canton In.)	22·53 N	113·09 E
191	Huangp'u Chiang (R.) China (Shanghai In.)	30·56 N	121·16 E
188	Huangyüan ... China	37·00 N	101·01 E
192	Huanjen ... China	41·10 N	125·30 E
134	Huánuco (wä-nōō'kō) ... Peru	9·50 S	76·17 W
134	Huanuni (wä-nōō'nē) ... Bol.	18·11 S	66·43 W
127	Huapí, Montañas de (Mts.) (môn-tä'n-yäs-dĕ-wä'-pē'). Nic.	12·35 N	84·43 W
124	Huaquechula (wä-kĕ-chōō'-lä) Mex.	18·44 N	98·37 W
134	Huaral (wä-rä'l) ... Peru	11·28 S	77·11 W

Page	Name Pronunciation Region	Lat. °'	Long. °'
134	Huarás (ōōä'rà's) Peru	9·32 S	77·29 W
134	Huascarán, Nevs. (Pk.) (wäs-kä-rän'). Peru	9·05 S	77·50 W
136	Huasco (wäs'kō) Chile	28·32 S	71·16 W
192	Huatien China	42·38 N	126·45 E
125	Huatla de Jiménez (wà'-tlä-dě-ĸē-mě'-něz). Mex.	18·08 N	96·49 W
125	Huatlatlauch (wä'tlä-tlä-ōō'ch) Mex.	18·40 N	98·04 W
125	Huatusco (wä-tōōs'kô) Mex.	19·09 N	96·57 W
124	Huauchinango (wä-ōō-chê-näŋ'gô). Mex.	20·09 N	98·03 W
127	Huaunta (wä-ōō'n-tä) Nic.	13·30 N	83·32 W
127	Huaunta, Laguna (L.) (lä-gōō'-nä-wä-ōō'n-tä). Nic.	13·35 N	83·46 W
124	Huautla (wä-ōō'tlä) Mex.	21·04 N	98·13 W
190	Huayhe Hu (L.) (hōōäī'hü'hōō) China	32·49 N	117·00 E
124	Huaynamota, Rió de (R.) (rê'ō-dě-wäy-nä-mŏ'tä). Mex.	22·10 N	104·36 W
125	Huazolotitlán (Santa María) (wäzō-lô-tlē-tlän'). Mex.	16·18 N	97·55 W
99	Hubbard (hŭb'ērd) NH (In.)	42·53 N	71·12 W
119	Hubbard Tx.	31·53 N	96·46 W
104	Hubbard (L.) Mi.	44·45 N	83·30 W
118	Hubbard Creek Res. Tx.	32·50 N	98·55 W
185	Hubli (hōō'blê) India	15·25 N	75·09 E
161	Hückeswagen (hü'kěs-vä'gěn) F.R.G. (Ruhr In.)	51·09 N	7·20 E
148	Hucknall (hŭk'năl) Eng.	53·02 N	1·12 W
148	Huddersfield (hŭd'ērz-fēld) Eng.	53·39 N	1·47 W
156	Hudiksvall (hōō'dĭks-väl) Swe.	61·44 N	17·05 E
89	Hudson (hŭd'sŭn) Can. (Montreal In.)	45·26 N	74·08 W
99	Hudson Ma. (In.)	42·24 N	71·34 W
104	Hudson Mi.	41·50 N	84·15 W
105	Hudson NY	42·15 N	73·45 W
107	Hudson Oh. (Cleveland In.)	41·15 N	81·27 W
113	Hudson Wi. (Minneapolis, St. Paul In.)	44·59 N	92·45 W
95	Hudson Bay Can.	52·52 N	102·25 W
91	Hudson B. Can.	60·15 N	85·30 W
105	Hudson Falls NY	43·20 N	73·30 W
89	Hudson Heights Can. (Montreal In.)	45·28 N	74·09 W
104	Hudson R. NY	41·55 N	73·55 W
91	Hudson Str. Can.	63·25 N	74·05 W
193	Hue (ü-ā') Viet.	16·28 N	107·42 E
162	Huebra (R.) (wĕ'brä) Sp.	40·44 N	6·17 W
126	Huehuetenango (wā-wå-tå-näŋ'gô) Guat.	15·19 N	91·26 W
124	Huejotzingo (wā-hô-tzĭŋ'gō). Mex.	19·09 N	98·24 W
124	Huejúcar (wā-hōō'kär) Mex.	22·26 N	103·12 W
124	Huejuquilla el Alto (wā-hōō-kēl'yä ĕl äl'tō). Mex.	22·42 N	102·54 W
124	Huejutla (wā-hōō'tlä) Mex.	21·08 N	98·26 W
162	Huelma (wĕl'mä) Sp.	37·39 N	3·36 W
162	Huelva (wĕl'vä) Sp.	37·16 N	6·58 W
162	Huercal-Overa (wĕr-käl' ō-vā'rä) Sp.	37·12 N	1·58 W
116	Huerfano (R.) (wâr'fȧ-nō) Co.	37·41 N	105·13 W
163	Huésca (wĕs-kä) Sp.	42·07 N	0·25 W
162	Huéscar (wās'kär) Sp.	37·50 N	2·34 W
124	Huetamo de Múñez (wā-tä'mō dā-mōōn'yĕz). Mex.	18·34 N	100·53 W
162	Huete (wā'tå) Sp.	40·09 N	2·42 W
124	Hueycatenango (wĕy-kä-tĕ-nă'n-gô). Mex.	17·31 N	99·10 W
125	Hueytlalpan (wā'ī-tläl'păn). Mex.	20·03 N	97·41 W
106	Hueytown Al. (Birmingham In.)	33·28 N	86·59 W
106	Huffman (hŭf'măn) Al. (Birmingham In.)	33·36 N	86·42 W
116	Hugh Butler (L.) Ne.	40·21 N	100·40 W
205	Hughenden (hū'ĕn-dĕn) Austl.	20·58 S	144·13 E
204	Hughes (hūz) Austl.	30·45 S	129·30 E
106	Hughesville Md. (Baltimore In.)	38·32 N	76·48 W
113	Hugo (hū'gō) Mn. (Minneapolis, St. Paul In.)	45·10 N	93·00 W
117	Hugo Ok.	34·01 N	95·32 W
116	Hugoton (hū'gō-tŭn) Ks.	37·10 N	101·28 W
192	Huhohaot'e China	41·05 N	111·50 E
124	Huichapan (wē-chä-pän') Mex.	20·22 N	99·39 W
134	Huila (Dept.) (wē'lä) Col. (In.)	3·10 N	75·20 W
134	Huila, Nevado de (Pk.) (nĕ-vä-dô-de-wē'lä). Col. (In.)	2·59 N	76·01 W
193	Huilai China	23·02 N	116·18 E
193	Huili China	26·48 N	102·20 E
125	Huimanguillo (wē-män-gēl'yō) Mex.	17·50 N	93·16 W
190	Huimin (hōōĭ mĭn) China	37·29 N	117·32 E
125	Huitzilac (ōōē't-zē-lä'k). Mex. (In.)	19·01 N	99·16 W
124	Huitzitzilingo (wē-tzē-tzē-lē'n-gō) Mex.	21·11 N	98·42 W
124	Huitzuco (wê-tzōō'kō) Mex.	18·16 N	99·20 W
125	Huixquilucan (ōōē'x-kē-lōō-kä'n) Mex. (In.)	19·21 N	99·22 W
125	Huixtla (wēs'tlä) Mex.	15·12 N	92·28 W
193	Huiyang China	23·05 N	114·25 E
193	Huk'ou (hū'kō') China	29·58 N	116·20 E
190	Hukouchi (hōōgō jē) China	33·22 N	117·07 E
192	Hulan (hōō'län') China	45·58 N	126·32 E
192	Hulan (R.) China	42·20 N	126·30 E
194	Hulin (hōō'lĭn') China	45·45 N	133·25 E
89	Hull (hŭl) Can. (Ottawa In.)	45·26 N	75·43 W
99	Hull Ma. (In.)	42·18 N	70·54 W
148	Hull (R.) Eng.	53·47 N	0·20 W
149	Hulst (hōōlst) Neth. (Amsterdam In.)	51·17 N	4·01 E
191	Huluk'eng China (Canton In.)	22·41 N	113·25 E
192	Hulutao (hōō'lōō-tä'ō) China	40·40 N	122·55 E
218	Ḩulwān (hĕl'wän). Egypt (Nile In.)	29·51 N	31·20 E

Page	Name Pronunciation Region	Lat. °'	Long. °'
123	Humacao (ōō-mä-kä'ō) P. R. (Puerto Rico In.)	18·09 N	65·49 W
124	Humaitá (ōō-mä-ē-tä') Braz.	7·37 S	62·58 W
134	Humaitá Par.	27·08 S	58·18 W
212	Humansdorp (hōō'mäns-dôrp) S. Afr.	33·57 S	24·45 E
212	Humbe (hŏŏm'bâ) Ang.	16·50 S	14·55 E
154	Humber (L.) (hŭm'bēr) Eng.	53·38 N	0·40 W
89	Humber (R.) Can. (Toronto In.)	43·53 N	79·40 W
99	Humbermouth (hŭm'bēr-mŭth) Can.	48·58 N	57·55 W
119	Humble (hŭm'b'l) Tx.	29·58 N	95·15 W
94	Humboldt (hŭm'bōlt) Can.	52·12 N	105·07 W
109	Humboldt Ia.	42·43 N	94·11 W
117	Humboldt Ks.	37·48 N	95·26 W
117	Humboldt Ne.	40·10 N	95·57 W
102	Humboldt (R.) U. S.	40·30 N	116·50 W
110	Humboldt B. Ca.	40·48 N	124·25 W
110	Humboldt R., East Fork Nv.	40·59 N	115·21 W
110	Humboldt R., North Fork Nv.	41·25 N	115·45 W
120	Humbolt Tn.	35·47 N	88·55 W
114	Humbolt Ra. Nv.	40·12 N	118·16 W
114	Humbolt Salt Marsh Nv.	39·49 N	117·41 W
114	Humbolt Sink Nv.	39·58 N	118·54 W
191	Humenchai China (Canton In.)	22·49 N	113·39 E
115	Humphreys Pk. (hŭm'frĭs) Az.	35·20 N	111·40 W
158	Humpolec (hŏŏm'pō-lĕts) Czech.	49·33 N	15·21 E
126	Humuya R. (ōō-mōō'yä) Hond.	14·38 N	87·36 W
150	Hunaflói (B.) (hōō'nä-flō'ī) Ice.	65·41 N	20·44 W
189	Hunan (Prov.) (hōō'nän') China	28·08 N	111·25 E
189	Hunch'un (hōōn'chōōn') China	42·53 N	130·34 E
165	Hunedoara (ĸōō'nĕd-wä'rà) Rom.	45·45 N	22·54 E
146	Hungary (hŭŋ'gȧ-rĭ) Eur.	46·44 N	17·55 E
203	Hungerford (hŭn'gēr-fērd) Austl.	28·50 S	144·32 E
111	Hungry Horse Res. (hŭŋ'gȧ-rĭ hôrs). Mt.	48·11 N	113·30 W
193	Hung Shui Ho (R.) (hŏŏng). China	25·00 N	107·22 E
190	Hungtse Hu (L.) (hōōngzhŭ hōō) China	33·17 N	118·37 E
158	Hunsrück (Mts.) (hōōns'rûk) F.R.G.	49·43 N	7·12 E
158	Hunte R. (hŏŏn'tē) F.R.G.	52·45 N	8·26 E
205	Hunter Is. (hŭn-tēr) Austl.	40·33 S	143·36 E
104	Huntingburg (hŭnt'ĭng-bûrg) In.	38·15 N	86·55 W
105	Huntingdon (hŭnt'ĭng-dŭn) Can.	45·10 N	74·05 W
112	Huntingdon Can. (Vancouver In.)	49·00 N	122·16 W
120	Huntingdon Tn.	36·00 N	88·23 W
148	Huntingdon and Peterborough (Co.). Eng.	52·26 N	0·19 W
104	Huntington In.	40·55 N	85·30 W
105	Huntington Pa.	40·30 N	78·00 W
104	Huntington WV	38·25 N	82·25 W
113	Huntington Beach Ca. (Los Angeles In.)	33·39 N	118·00 W
113	Huntington Park Ca. (Los Angeles In.)	33·59 N	118·14 W
106	Huntington Station NY (New York In.)	40·51 N	73·25 W
111	Huntley Mt.	45·54 N	108·01 W
120	Huntsville (hŭnts'-vĭl) Al.	34·44 N	86·36 W
105	Huntsville Can.	45·20 N	79·15 W
117	Huntsville Mo.	39·24 N	92·32 W
119	Huntsville Tx.	30·44 N	95·34 W
113	Huntsville Ut. (Salt Lake City In.)	41·16 N	111·46 W
125	Hunucmá (hōō-nōōk-mä') Mex.	21·01 N	89·54 W
190	Huolu (hōōŭ lōō) China	38·05 N	114·20 E
197	Huon G. Pap. N. Gui.	7·15 S	147·45 E
189	Hupeh (Prov.) China	31·20 N	111·58 E
183	Ḩuraydin, Wādī (R.) Egypt (Palestine In.)	30·55 N	34·12 E
104	Hurd, C. (hûrd) Can.	45·15 N	81·45 W
109	Hurley (hûr'lĭ) Wi.	46·26 N	90·11 W
136	Hurlingham (ōō'r-lēn-gäm) Arg. (Buenos Aires In.)	34·20 S	58·38 W
104	Huron (hū'rŏn) Oh.	41·20 N	82·35 W
108	Huron SD	44·22 N	98·15 W
103	Huron, L. (hū'rŏn) U. S.-Can.	45·15 N	82·40 W
109	Huron Mts. (hū'rŏn) Mi.	46·47 N	87·52 W
107	Huron R. Mi. (Detroit In.)	42·12 N	83·26 W
101	Hurricane (hŭr'ĭ-kān) Ak.	63·00 N	149·30 W
115	Hurricane Ut.	37·10 N	113·20 W
128	Hurricane Flats (Shoal) (hŭ-rĭ-kȧn flăts). Ba.	23·35 N	78·30 W
150	Húsavik Ice.	66·00 N	17·10 W
167	Husi (kōōsh') Sov. Un.	46·52 N	28·04 E
156	Huskvarna (hŏŏsk-vär'nȧ) Swe.	57·48 N	14·16 E
113	Hurst Tx. (Dallas, Ft. Worth In.)	32·48 N	97·12 W
158	Husum (hōō'zŏŏm) F.R.G.	54·29 N	9·04 E
113	Hutchins (hŭch'ĭnz) Tx. (Dallas, Fort Worth In.)	32·38 N	96·43 W
116	Hutchinson (hŭch'ĭn-sŭn) Ks.	38·02 N	97·56 W
109	Hutchinson Mn.	44·53 N	94·23 W
192	Hut'o Ho (R.) (hōō'tō'hō'). China	38·10 N	114·00 E
190	Huwu (hōō wōō) China	31·17 N	119·48 E
155	Huy (û-ē') (hû'ē) Bel.	50·33 N	5·14 E
150	Hvannadalshnukur (Mtn.) Ice.	64·09 N	16·46 W
164	Hvar (I.) (ĸhvär) Yugo.	43·08 N	16·28 E
194	Hwangju (hwäng'jōō') Kor.	38·39 N	125·49 E
106	Hyattsville (hī'ăt's-vĭl) Md. (Baltimore In.)	38·57 N	76·58 W
101	Hydaburg (hī-dă'bûrg) Ak.	55·12 N	132·49 W
148	Hyde (hīd) Eng.	53·27 N	2·05 W
185	Hyderābād (hī-dēr-å-băd'). India	17·29 N	79·28 E
184	Hyderābād (hī-dēr-å-băd'). Pak.	25·29 N	68·28 E
185	Hyderabad (State) India	23·29 N	76·50 E
161	Hyéres (ē-âr') Fr.	43·09 N	6·08 E
161	Hyéres, Iles d' (Is.) (ēl'dyâr'). Fr.	42·57 N	6·17 E
194	Hyesanjin (hyĕ'sän-jĭn') Kor.	41·11 N	128·12 E
104	Hymera (hī-mē'rȧ) In.	39·10 N	87·20 W
111	Hyndman Pk. (hīnd'măn) Id.	43·38 N	114·04 W
195	Hyōgo (Pref.) (hyō'gō) Jap. (Ōsaka In.)	34·54 N	135·15 E
100	Hythe Can.	55·20 N	119·33 W

I

Page	Name Pronunciation Region	Lat. °'	Long. °'
195	Ia (R.) (ê'ä) Jap. (Ōsaka In.)	34·54 N	135·34 E
165	Ialomita (R.) Rom.	44·37 N	26·42 E
159	Iasi (yä'shê) Rom.	47·10 N	27·40 E
197	Iba (ē'bä) Phil. (In.)	15·20 N	119·59 E
215	Ibadan (ê-bä'dän) Nig.	7·17 N	3·30 E
134	Ibagué (ê-bà-gā') Col. (In.)	4·27 N	75·13 W
165	Ibar (R.) (ē'bär) Yugo.	43·22 N	20·35 E
195	Ibaraki (ē-bä'rä-gē) Jap. (Ōsaka In.)	34·49 N	135·35 E
134	Ibarra (ê-bär'rä) Ec.	0·19 N	78·08 W
209	Iberian Pen. Port.-Sp.	41·00 N	0·07 W
98	Iberville (ê-bår-vēl') (ī'bēr-vĭl) Can.	45·14 N	73·01 W
215	Ibi (ē'bê) Nig.	8·12 N	9·45 E
135	Ibiapaba, Serra da (Mts.) (sĕ'r-rä-dä-ē-byä-pá'bä). Braz.	3·30 S	40·55 W
163	Ibiza (ê-bē'thä) Sp.	38·55 N	1·24 E
163	Ibiza, Isla de (Iviza I.) (ê's-lä-dĕ-ē-bē'zä). Sp.	39·07 N	1·05 E
217	Ibo (ē'bō) Moz.	12·20 S	40·35 E
216	Iboundji, Mont (Mtn.) Gabon	1·08 S	11·48 E
218	Ibrāhīm, Būr (B.) Egypt	29·57 N	32·33 E
186	Ibrahim, Jabal (Mtn.) Sau. Ar.	20·31 N	41·17 E
217	Ibwe Munyama Zambia	16·09 S	28·34 E
134	Ica (ē'kä) Peru	14·09 S	75·42 W
134	Icá (R.) (ē-kä') Braz.	2·56 S	69·12 W
134	Içana (ē-sä'nä) Braz.	0·15 N	67·19 W
110	Ice Harbor Dam Wa.	46·15 N	118·54 W
146	Iceland (īs'lănd) Eur.	65·12 N	19·45 W
193	Ich'ang (ē'chäng') China	30·38 N	111·22 E
195	Ichibusayama (Mt.) (ē'chê-bōō'sȧ-yä'mä). Jap.	32·19 N	131·08 E
195	Ichihara Jap. (Tōkyō In.)	35·31 N	140·05 E
195	Ichikawa (ē'chê-kä'wä) Jap. (Tōkyō In.)	35·44 N	139·54 E
195	Ichinomiya (ē'chē-nō-mē'yȧ). Jap.	35·19 N	136·49 E
195	Ichinomoto (ē-chē'nō-mō-tō) Jap. (Ōsaka In.)	34·37 N	135·50 E
167	Ichnya (ĭch'nyä) Sov. Un.	50·47 N	32·23 E
135	Icó (ê-kô') Braz.	6·25 S	38·43 W
134	Icutú, Cerro (Mtn.) (sĕ'r-rô-ê-kōō-tōō') Ven.	7·07 N	65·30 W
101	Icy C. (ī'sĭ) Ak.	70·20 N	161·40 W
117	Idabel (ī'dȧ-bĕl) Ok.	33·52 N	94·47 W
108	Idagrove (ī'dȧ-grōv) Ia.	42·22 N	95·29 W
215	Idah (ē'dä) Nig.	7·07 N	6·43 E
102	Idaho (State) (ī'dȧ-hō) U. S.	44·00 N	115·10 W
111	Idaho Falls Id.	43·30 N	112·01 W
116	Idaho Springs Co.	39·43 N	105·32 W
162	Idanha-a-Nova (ê-dän'yȧ-ä-nō'vȧ). Port.	39·58 N	7·13 W
188	Ideriin Gol (R.) Mong.	48·58 N	98·38 E
218	Idfū (êd'fōō) Egypt (Nile In.)	24·57 N	32·53 E
165	Idhra (I.) Grc.	37·20 N	23·30 E
196	Idi (ē'dê) Indon.	4·58 N	97·47 E
218	Idkū (ĕd'kōō) Egypt (Nile In.)	31·18 N	30·20 E
218	Idkū L. Egypt (Nile In.)	31·13 N	30·22 E
148	Idle (R.) (īd''l) Eng.	53·22 N	0·56 W
164	Idriaj (ē'drê-ȧ) Yugo.	46·01 N	14·01 E
213	Idutywa (ē-dōō-tī'wȧ) S. Afr. (Natal In.)	32·06 S	28·18 E
155	Ieper Bel.	50·50 N	2·53 E
164	Ierápetra Grc. (In.)	35·01 N	25·48 E
164	Iesi (yā'sê) It.	43·37 N	13·20 E
215	Ife Nig.	7·30 N	4·30 E
215	Iferouâne (ēf'rōō-än') Niger	19·04 N	8·24 E
215	Iforas, Adrar des (Mts.) (ä-drär') Alg.-Mali	19·55 N	2·00 E
217	Igalula Tan.	5·14 S	33·00 E
172	Igarka (ê-gär'kȧ) Sov. Un.	67·22 N	86·16 E
165	Ighil Izane Alg.	35·43 N	0·43 E
164	Iglesias (ē-lĕ'syōs) It.	39·20 N	8·34 E
210	Igli (ê-glē') Alg.	30·32 N	2·15 W
91	Igloolik Can.	69·33 N	81·18 W
112	Ignacio (ĭg-nā'cĭ-ō) Ca. (San Francisco In.)	38·05 N	122·32 W
136	Iguaçu (R.) (ē-gwä-sōō') Braz. (Rio de Janeiro In.)	22·42 S	43·19 W
124	Iguala (ē-gwä'lä) Mex.	18·18 N	99·34 W
163	Igualada (ê-gwä-lä'dä) Sp.	41·35 N	1·38 E
136	Iguassu (R.) (ê-gwä-sōō') Braz.	25·45 S	52·30 W
136	Iguassu Falls Braz.	25·40 S	54·16 W
137	Iguatama (ē-gwä-tá'mä) Braz. (Rio de Janeiro In.)	20·13 S	45·40 W
135	Iguatu (ê-gwä-tōō') Braz.	6·22 S	39·17 W
210	Iguidi, Erg (Dune) Alg.	26·22 N	6·53 W
197	Iguig (ē-gēg') Phil. (In.)	17·46 N	121·44 E
215	Ihiala Nig.	5·51 N	6·51 E
192	Ihsien China	41·30 N	121·15 E
190	I Ho (R.) (yē'hŭ) China	34·38 N	118·07 E
195	Iida (ē'ê-dȧ) Jap.	35·39 N	137·53 E
170	Iijoki (R.) (ē'yō'kĭ) Fin.	65·28 N	27·00 E
195	Iizuka (ē'ê-zōō-kȧ) Jap.	33·39 N	130·39 E
215	Ijebu-Ode (ê-jĕ'bōō ōdȧ) Nig.	6·50 N	3·56 E
155	IJsselmeer (L.) (ī'sĕl-mār) Neth.	52·46 N	5·14 E
157	Ikaalinen (ē'kä-lĭ-nĕn) Fin.	61·47 N	22·55 E
165	Ikaría (I.) (ē-kä'rya) Grc.	37·43 N	26·07 E
195	Ikeda (ē'kȧ-dä) Jap. (Ōsaka In.)	34·49 N	135·26 E
215	Ikerre Nig.	7·31 N	5·14 E
165	Ikhtiman (ēk'tê-män) Bul.	42·26 N	23·49 E
195	Iki (I.) (ē'kê) Jap.	33·46 N	129·44 E
195	Ikoma Jap. (Ōsaka In.)	34·41 N	135·43 E
212	Ikoma (ê-kō'mä) Tan.	2·08 S	34·47 E
174	Iksha (ĭk'shȧ) Sov. Un. (Moscow In.)	56·10 N	37·30 E
215	Ila Nig.	8·01 N	4·55 E
197	Ilagen (ê-lä'gän) Phil. (In.)	17·09 N	121·52 E
192	Ilan China	46·10 N	129·40 E

ăt; finăl; rāte; senåte; ärm; åsk; sofȧ; fâre; ch-choose; dh-as th in other; bē; êvent; bĕt; recĕnt; cratẽr; g-go; gh-guttural g; bĭt; ĭ-short neutral; rīde; ĸ-guttural k as ch in German ich;

Page	Name Pronunciation Region	Lat. °′	Long. °′
193	Ilan (ē'län')............Taiwan	24·50 N	121·42 E
159	Iława (ê-lä'vȧ)............Pol.	53·35 N	19·36 E
94	Île-á-la-Crosse............Can.	55·34 N	108·00 W
216	Ilebo (Port-Franqui)........Zaire	4·19 S	20·35 E
171	Ilek (ē'lyĕk)..........Sov. Un.	51·30 N	53·10 E
171	Ilek (R.)..............Sov. Un.	51·20 N	53·10 E
89	Île-Perrot (yl-pĕ-rōt')		
	Can. (Montreal In.)	45·21 N	73·54 W
215	Ilesha.....................Nig.	7·38 N	4·45 E
148	Ilford (ĭl'fērd)..Eng. (London In.)	51·33 N	0·06 E
154	Ilfracombe (ĭl-frȧ-kōōm')....Eng.	51·13 N	4·08 W
137	Ilhabela (ē'lä-bĕ'lä)		
	Braz. (Rio de Janeiro In.)	23·47 S	45·21 W
137	Ilha Grande, Baia de (B.)		
	(ēl'yȧ grän'dĕ)		
	Braz. (Rio de Janeiro In.)	23·17 S	44·25 W
162	Ilhavo (ēl'yȧ-vô)..........Port.	40·36 N	8·41 W
135	Ilhéus (ē-lĕ'ōōs)..........Braz.	14·52 S	39·00 W
101	Iliamna (ē-lê-ăm'nȧ).........Ak.	59·45 N	155·05 W
101	Iliamna (L.)................Ak.	59·25 N	155·30 W
101	Iliamna (Vol.)..............Ak.	60·18 N	153·25 W
172	Ilim (R.) ((ê-lyêm')......Sov. Un.	57·28 N	103·00 E
172	Ilimsk (ê-lyêmsk')........Sov. Un.	56·47 N	103·43 E
197	Ilin (I.) (ê-lyēn')......Phil. (In.)	12·16 N	120·57 E
167	Il'intsiy.................Sov. Un.	49·07 N	29·13 E
165	Iliodhrómia (I.)............Grc.	39·18 N	23·35 E
105	Ilion (ĭl'ĭ-ŭn)...............NY	43·00 N	75·05 W
188	Ili R. (ē'l'ē)............Sov. Un.	43·46 N	77·41 E
148	Ilkeston (ĭl'kĕs-tŭn)........Eng.	52·58 N	1·19 W
134	Illampu, Nevado (Pk.)		
	(nĕ-vá'dô-êl-yäm-pōō').Bol.	15·50 S	68·15 W
197	Illana B. (êl-yä-nô)........Phil.	7·38 N	123·41 E
137	Illapel (ē-zhä-pĕ'l)		
	Chile (Santiago In.)	31·37 S	71·10 W
158	Iller R. (ĭl'er)...........F.R.G.	47·52 N	10·06 E
134	Illimani, Nevado (Pk.)		
	(nĕ-vá'dô-ēl-yê-mä'nê).Bol.	16·50 S	67·38 W
103	Illinois (State) (ĭl-ĭ-noi') (ĭl-ĭ-noiz')		
	U. S.	40·25 N	90·40 W
117	Illinois (R.).................Il.	40·52 N	89·31 W
210	Illizi......................Alg.	26·35 N	8·24 E
166	Il'men', Ozero (L.) (ô'zĕ-rô el''		
	men'') (ĭl'mĕn).Sov. Un.	58·18 N	32·00 E
155	Ilmenau (R.) (ēl'mē-nou)..F.R.G.	53·20 N	10·20 E
134	Ilo........................Peru	17·46 S	71·13 W
126	Ilobasco (ê-lô-bäs'kô).........Sal.	13·57 N	88·46 W
196	Iloilo (ē-lô-ē'lō)...........Phil.	10·49 N	112·33 E
126	Ilopango, L. (ē-lô-päŋ'gō).....Sal.	13·48 N	88·50 W
215	Ilorin (ē-lô-rēn')...........Nig.	8·30 N	4·32 E
166	Ilūkste...................Sov. Un.	55·59 N	26·20 E
112	Ilwaco (ĭl-wā'kô)		
	Wa. (Portland In.)	46·19 N	124·02 W
170	Ilych (R.) (ē'l'ĭch).......Sov. Un.	62·30 N	57·30 E
195	Imabari (ē'mä-bä'rê).........Jap.	34·05 N	132·58 E
195	Imai (ê-mī')....Jap. (Ōsaka In.)	34·30 N	135·47 E
194	Iman (R.) (ê-män').....Sov. Un.	45·40 N	134·31 E
170	Imandra (L.) (ē-män'drȧ)		
	Sov. Un.	67·40 N	32·30 E
218	Imbābah (ēm-bä'bȧ)		
	Egypt (Nile In.)	30·06 N	31·09 E
136	Imbarié (ēm-bä-ryĕ')		
	Braz. (Rio de Janeiro In.)	22·38 S	43·13 W
174	Imeni Morozova		
	(ĭm-yĕ'nyĭ mô rô'zô vȧ)		
	Sov. Un. (Leningrad In.)	59·58 N	31·02 E
166	Imeni Moskvy, Kanal (Moscow		
	Can.) (kȧ-näl'ĭm-yă'		
	nĭ mŏs-kvĭ).Sov. Un.	56·33 N	37·15 E
174	Imeni Tsyurupy..........Sov. Un.		
	(Moscow In.)	55·30 N	38·39 E
174	Imeni Vorovskogo		
	Sov. Un. (Moscow In.)	55·43 N	38·21 E
194	Imienpo (yēmĭänpŭ).........China	44·59 N	127·56 E
104	Imlay City (ĭm'lā)...........Mi.	43·00 N	83·15 W
158	Immenstadt (ĭm'ĕn-shtät)..F.R.G.	47·34 N	10·12 E
218	Immerpan (ĭmĕr-pän)......S. Afr.		
	(Johannesburg & Pretoria In.)	24·29 S	29·14 E
164	Imola (ē'mô-lä).................It.	44·19 N	11·43 E
164	Imotski (ê-môts'kê)........Yugo.	43·25 N	17·15 E
135	Impameri...................Braz.	17·44 S	48·03 W
213	Impendle (ĭm-pĕnd'lȧ)		
	S. Afr. (Natal In.)	29·38 S	29·54 E
164	Imperia (êm-pā'rê-ä)..........It.	43·52 N	8·00 E
107	Imperial (ĭm-pē'rĭ-ăl)		
	Pa. (Pittsburgh In.)	40·27 N	80·15 W
114	Imperial Beach.........Ca. (In.)	32·34 N	117·08 W
115	Imperial Res..................Az.	32·57 N	114·19 W
114	Imperial Valley...............Ca.	33·00 N	115·22 W
216	Impfondo (ĭmp-fōn'dō)......Con.	1·37 N	18·04 E
187	Imphāl (ĭmp'hŭl)............India	24·42 N	94·00 E
165	Imroz (I.) (ĭm'rŏz)..........Tur.	40·10 N	25·27 E
195	Ina (R.) (ē-nä').Jap. (Ōsaka In.)	34·56 N	135·21 E
114	Inaja Ind. Res. (ê-nä'hä)......Ca.	32·56 N	116·37 W
150	Inari (L.)....................Fin.	69·02 N	26·22 E
163	Inca (ēŋ'kä)..................Sp.	39·43 N	2·53 E
171	Ince Burun (C.) (ĭn'jȧ)......Tur.	42·00 N	35·00 E
194	Inch'ŏn (ĭn'chŭn)............Kor.	37·26 N	126·46 E
164	Incudine, Mt. (Mtn.) (ēn-kōō-dē'		
	nâ) (ăɴ-kü-dēn').Fr.	41·53 N	9·17 E
156	Indalsälven (R.)............Swe.	62·50 N	16·50 E
197	Indang (ēn'däng')......Phil. (In.)	14·11 N	120·53 E
118	Indé (ēn'dā)................Mex.	25·53 N	105·15 W
117	Independence (ĭn-dê-pĕn'dĕns).Ks.	37·14 N	95·42 W
113	Independence		
	Mo. (Kansas City In.)	39·06 N	94·26 W
107	Independence.Oh. (Cleveland In.)	41·23 N	81·39 W
110	Independence..................Or.	44·49 N	123·13 W
110	Independence Mts..........Nv.	41·15 N	116·02 W
171	Inder (L.)...............Sov. Un.	48·20 N	52·10 E
182	India (ĭn'dĭ-ȧ)..............Asia	23·00 N	77·30 E
109	Indian (L.) (ĭn'dĭ-ăn).........Mi.	46·04 N	86·34 W
105	Indian (R.)...................NY	44·05 N	75·45 W
105	Indiana (ĭn-dĭ-ăn'ȧ)..........Pa.	40·40 N	79·10 W
103	Indiana (State)...........U. S.	39·50 N	86·45 W
107	Indianapolis (ĭn-dĭ-ăn-ăp'ô-lĭs)		
	In. (Indianapolis In.)	39·45 N	86·08 W
112	Indian Arm (R.) (ĭn'dĭ-ăn ärm)		
	Can. (Vancouver In.)	49·21 N	122·55 W
94	Indian Head.................Can.	50·29 N	103·44 W
96	Indian L.....................Can.	47·00 N	82·00 W
7	Indian Ocean		
109	Indianola (ĭn-dĭ-ăn-ō'lȧ).......Ia.	41·22 N	93·33 W
120	Indianola.....................Ms.	33·29 N	90·35 W
173	Indigirka (R.) (ēn-dê-gēr'kȧ)		
	Sov. Un.	67·45 N	145·45 E
122	Indio (R.) (ē'n-dyô)....Pan. (In.)	9·13 N	78·28 W
196	Indochina (Reg.) (ĭn-dô-chī'nȧ)		
	Asia	17·22 N	105·18 E
196	Indonesia (ĭn'dô-nê-zhȧ).....Asia	4·38 S	118·45 E
184	Indore (ĭn-dōr')..............India	22·48 N	76·51 E
196	Indragiri (R.) (ĭn-drȧ-jē'rē).Indon.	0·27 S	102·05 E
126	Indrāvati (R.) (ĭn-drŭ-vä'tê)		
	India	19·15 N	80·54 E
160	Indre (R.) (ăɴ'dr')...........Fr.	47·13 N	0·29 E
156	Indre Solund (I.) (ĭndrĕ-sô-lŭnd)		
	Nor.	61·09 N	4·37 E
89	Indus (ĭn'dŭs).Can. (Calgary In.)	50·55 N	113·45 W
184	Indus (R.)...................Pak.	26·43 N	67·41 E
213	Indwe (ĭnd'wȧ).S. Afr. (Natal In.)	31·30 S	27·21 E
171	Inebolu (ê-nȧ-bō'lōō)........Tur.	41·50 N	33·40 E
171	Inego (ē'nȧ-gŭ)..............Tur.	40·05 N	29·20 E
197	Infanta (ēn-făn'tä).....Phil. (In.)	14·44 N	121·39 E
197	Infanta................Phil. (In.)	15·50 N	119·53 E
162	Infantes (ēn-fän'tâs)..........Sp.	38·44 N	3·00 W
125	Inferror, Laguna (L.)		
	(lä-gōō'nä-ēn-fĕr-rôr).Mex.	16·18 N	94·40 W
125	Infiernillo, Presa de (Res.)...Mex.	18·50 N	101·50 W
162	Infiesto (ēn-fyĕ's-tô).........Sp.	43·21 N	5·24 W
215	I-n-Gall....................Niger	16·47 N	6·56 E
104	Ingersoll (ĭn'gĕr-sŏl).........Can.	43·05 N	81·00 W
205	Ingham (ĭng'ăm)............Austl.	18·45 S	146·14 E
128	Ingles, Cayos (Is.)		
	(kä-yōs-ē'n-glĕ's).Cuba	21·55 N	82·35 W
113	Inglewood (ĭn'g'l-wŏŏd)		
	Ca. (Los Angeles In.)	33·57 N	118·22 W
89	Inglewood......Can. (Toronto In.)	43·48 N	79·56 W
173	Ingoda (R.) (ēn-gō'dȧ)...Sov. Un.	51·29 N	112·32 E
158	Ingolstadt (ĭŋ'gôl-shtät)....F.R.G.	48·46 N	11·27 E
167	Ingul (R.) (ēn-gōōl')....Sov. Un.	47·22 N	32·52 E
167	Ingulets (R.) (ēn-gōōl'yĕts')		
	Sov. Un.	47·12 N	33·12 E
171	Ingur (R.) (ēn-gōōr')....Sov. Un.	42·30 N	42·00 E
212	Inhambane (ên-äm-bä'-nĕ)...Moz.	23·47 S	35·28 E
135	Inhambupe (ên-yäm-bōō'pä)		
	Braz.	11·47 S	38·13 W
212	Inharrime (ên-yär-rē'mä)....Moz.	24·17 S	35·07 E
136	Inhomirim (ē-nô-mê-rē'ɴ)		
	Braz. (Rio de Janeiro In.)	22·34 S	43·11 W
188	Ining (ē'nĭng')...............China	43·58 N	80·49 E
134	Inirida (R.) (ē-nê-rē'dä).....Col.	2·25 N	70·38 W
203	Injune (ĭn'jōōn)............Austl.	25·52 S	148·30 E
157	Inkeroinem (ĭn'kĕr-oi-nĕn)....Fin.	60·42 N	26·50 E
107	Inkster(ĭngk'stēr).Mi.(Detroit In.)	42·18 N	83·19 W
203	Innamincka (ĭnn-á'mĭn-kȧ)..Austl.	27·50 S	140·48 E
123	Inner Brass (I.) (bräs)		
	Vir. Is. (U.S.A.) (St. Thomas In.)	18·23 N	64·58 W
154	Inner Hebrides (Is.).........Scot.	57·20 N	6·20 W
188	Inner Mongolian Aut. Reg.		
	(mŏn-gō'lĭ-ăn).China	43·30 N	113·33 E
93	Innisfail....................Can.	52·02 N	113·57 W
158	Inn R. (ĭn)..............F.R.G.-Aus.	48·19 N	13·16 E
158	Innsbruck (ĭns'brŏŏk)........Aus.	47·15 N	11·25 E
195	Ino (ē'nô)...................Jap.	33·34 N	133·23 E
216	Inongo (ê-nôŋ'gō)...........Zaire	1·57 S	18·16 E
159	Inowroctaw (ē-nô-vrôts'läf)...Pol.	52·48 N	18·16 E
210	In Salah....................Alg.	27·13 N	2·22 E
115	Inscription House Ruin		
	(ĭn'skrĭp-shŭn hous rōō'ĭn).Az.	36·45 N	110·47 W
124	Inter-American Hy.		
	(ĭn'tēr ȧ-mĕr'ĭ-kăn).Mex.	22·30 N	99·08 W
109	International Falls		
	(ĭn'tēr-năsh'ŭn-ăl fôlz).Mn.	48·34 N	93·26 W
90	Inuvik......................Can.	68·40 N	134·10 W
195	Inuyama (ē'nōō-yä'mä)......Jap.	35·24 N	137·01 E
205	Invercargil (ĭn-vēr-kär'gĭl)		
	N. Z. (In.)	47·18 S	168·27 E
203	Inverel (ĭn-vēr-el')..........Austl.	29·50 S	151·32 E
113	Invergrove Hts. (ĭn'vēr-grōv)		
	Mn. (Minneapolis, St. Paul In.)	44·51 N	93·01 W
99	Inverness (ĭn-vēr-nĕs').......Can.	46·14 N	61·18 W
121	Inverness.....................Fl.	28·48 N	82·22 W
154	Inverness...................Scot.	57·30 N	4·07 W
203	Investigator Str. (ĭn-vĕst'ĭ'gā-tôr)		
	Austl.	35·33 S	137·00 E
212	Inyangani, Mt. (ên-yän-gä'nê).Rh.	18·06 S	32·37 E
114	Inyokern......................Ca.	35·39 N	117·51 W
114	Inyo Mts. (ĭn'yō)............Ca.	36·55 N	118·04 W
174	Inzer R. (ĭn'zĕr)		
	Sov. Un. (Urals In.)	54·24 N	57·17 E
216	Inzia (R.)...................Zaire	5·55 S	17·50 E
195	Iō (I.) (ē'wō)...............Jap.	30·46 N	130·15 E
165	Ioánnina (Yannina)		
	(yô-ä'nê-nȧ) (yä'nê-nȧ).Grc.	39·39 N	20·52 E
112	Ioco.........Can. (Vancouver In.)	49·18 N	122·53 W
117	Iola (ī-ō'lȧ)..................Ks.	37·55 N	95·23 W
216	Iôna, Parque Nacional do		
	(Natl. Pk.).Ang.	16·35 S	12·00 E
104	Ionia (ī-ō'nĭ-ȧ)..............Mi.	43·00 N	85·10 W
165	Ionian Is. (ī-ō'nĭ-ăn)........Grc.	39·10 N	20·05 E
153	Ionian Sea..................Eur.	38·59 N	18·48 E
165	Ios (I.) (ī'ŏs)...............Grc.	36·48 N	25·25 E
103	Iowa (State) (ī'ô-wȧ).......U. S.	42·05 N	94·20 W
109	Iowa (R.).....................Ia.	41·55 N	92·20 W
109	Iowa City.....................Ia.	41·39 N	91·31 W
109	Iowa Falls....................Ia.	42·32 N	93·16 W
116	Iowa Park....................Tx.	33·57 N	98·39 W
217	Ipala........................Tan.	4·30 S	32·53 E
159	Ipel R. (ê'pĕl)......Czech.-Hung.	48·08 N	19·00 E
134	Ipiales (ē-pê-ä'lås)...........Col.	0·48 N	77·45 W
193	Ipin (Süchow)..............China	28·50 N	104·40 E
196	Ipoh........................Mala.	4·45 N	101·05 E
203	Ipswich (ĭps'wĭch).........Austl.	27·40 S	152·50 E
155	Ipswich......................Eng.	52·05 N	1·05 E
99	Ipswich..................Ma. (In.)	42·41 N	70·50 W
108	Ipswich.......................SD	45·26 N	99·01 W
135	Ipu (ē-pōō)..................Braz.	4·11 S	40·45 W
166	Iput' (R.) (ê-pōōt')......Sov. Un.	52·53 N	31·57 E
134	Iquique (ē-kē'kĕ)...........Chile	20·16 S	70·07 W
134	Iquitos (ê-kē'tōs)...........Peru	3·39 S	73·18 W
164	Iráklion (Candia).......Grc. (In.)	35·20 N	25·10 E
182	Iran (ē-rän')................Asia	31·15 N	53·30 E
186	Iran, Plat. of...............Iran	32·28 N	58·00 E
196	Iran Mts...................Mala.	2·30 N	114·30 E
124	Irapuato (ē-rä-pwä'tō)......Mex.	20·41 N	101·24 W
182	Iraq (ē-räk')................Asia	32·00 N	42·30 E
127	Irazu Vol. (ē-rä-zōō')......C. R.	9·58 N	83·54 W
183	Irbid (ėr-bēd')		
	Jordan (Palestine In.)	32·33 N	35·51 E
171	Irbil.........................Iraq	36·10 N	44·00 E
170	Irbit (ėr-bėt')............Sov. Un.	57·40 N	63·10 E
212	Irébou (ē-rā'bōō)...........Zaire	0·40 S	17·48 E
146	Ireland (īr-lănd)............Eur.	53·33 N	13·00 W
174	Iremel', Gora (Mt.) (gȧ-rä'		
	ĭ-rĕ'mĕl).Sov. Un. (Urals In.)	54·32 N	58·52 E
213	Irene (ĭ-rē-nē)............S. Afr.		
	(Johannesburg & Pretoria In.)	25·53 S	28·13 E
172	Irgiz (ĭr-gēz')...........Sov. Un.	48·30 N	61·17 E
172	Irgiz (R.)................Sov. Un.	49·30 N	60·32 E
214	Irīgui (Reg.).....Mali-Mauritania	16·45 N	5·35 W
170	Iriklinskoye Vdkhr (Res.)		
	Sov. Un.	52·20 N	58·50 E
217	Iringa (ê-rĭŋ'gä)............Tan.	7·46 S	35·42 E
193	Iriomote Jima (I.) (ērē'-ō-mō-tā)		
	Jap.	24·20 N	123·30 E
126	Iriona (ê-rê-ō'nä)..........Hond.	15·53 N	85·12 W
154	Irish Sea (ī'rĭsh)............Eur.	53·55 N	5·25 W
172	Irkutsk (ĭr-kōōtsk')......Sov. Un.	52·16 N	104·00 E
148	Irlam (ûr'lăm)..............Eng.	53·26 N	2·26 W
129	Irois, Cap des (C.)...........Hai.	18·25 N	74·50 W
106	Irondale (ī'ērn-dăl)		
	Al. (Birmingham In.)	33·32 N	86·43 W
165	Iron Gate (Gorge)....Yugo.-Rom.	44·43 N	22·32 E
203	Iron Knob (ĭ-ăn nŏb)........Austl.	32·47 S	137·10 E
109	Iron Mountain (ī'ērn)........Mi.	45·49 N	88·04 W
109	Iron River....................Mi.	46·09 N	88·39 W
104	Ironton (ī'ērn-tŭn)...........Oh.	38·30 N	82·45 W
109	Ironwood (ī'ērn-wŏŏd)........Mi.	46·28 N	90·10 W
104	Iroquois (.R) (ĭr'ô-kwoi)....Il.-In.	40·55 N	87·20 W
91	Iroquois Falls...............Can.	48·41 N	80·39 W
195	Irō-Saki (C.) (ē'rō sä'kē).....Jap.	34·35 N	138·54 E
167	Irpen' (R.) (ĭr-pĕn')....Sov. Un.	50·13 N	29·55 E
187	Irrawaddy (R.)...............Bur.	23·27 N	96·25 E
196	Irrawaddy, Mouths of the		
	(ĭr-ȧ-wäd'ē).Bur.	15·40 N	94·32 E
188	Irrawaddy R..................Bur.	20·39 N	94·38 E
172	Irtysh (R.) (ĭr-tĭsh')......Sov. Un.	58·32 N	68·31 E
211	Irumu (ê-rōō'mōō)..........Zaire	1·30 N	29·52 E
162	Irun (ê-rōōn')................Sp.	43·20 N	1·47 W
113	Irvine (ûr'vĭn)		
	Ca. (Los Angeles In.)	33·40 N	117·45 W
154	Irvine......................Scot.	55·39 N	4·40 W
104	Irvine.......................Ky.	37·40 N	84·00 W
117	Irving (ûr'vēng)		
	Tx. (Dallas, Fort Worth In.)	32·49 N	96·57 W
106	Irvington (ûr'vēng-tŭn)		
	NJ (New York In.)	40·43 N	74·15 W
107	Irwin (ûr'-wĭn)		
	Pa. (Pittsburgh In.)	40·19 N	79·42 W
215	Isa..........................Nig.	13·14 N	6·24 E
174	Is (ēs).......Sov. Un. (Urals In.)	58·48 N	59·44 E
122	Isaacs, Mt. (ē-sä-ȧ'ks)...Pan. (In.)	9·22 N	79·01 W
124	Isabela (I.) (ê-sä-bĕ'-lä).....Mex.	21·56 N	105·53 W
134	Isabela (I.) (ē-sä-bä'lä).......Ec.	0·47 S	91·35 W
129	Isabela, Cabo (C.)		
	(kȧ'bô-ê-sä-bĕ'lä).Dom. Rep.	20·00 N	71·00 W
126	Isabella, Cord. (Mts.)		
	(kôr-dēl-yĕ'rä-ē-sä-bĕlä).Nic.	13·20 N	85·37 W
104	Isabella Ind. Res. (ĭs-ȧ-bĕl'-lȧ).Mi.	43·35 N	84·55 W
167	Isaccea (ê-säk'chä)..........Rom.	45·16 N	28·26 E
150	Isafjördhur (ēs'ȧ-fyûr-dōōr)...Ice.	66·09 N	22·39 W
216	Isangi (ê-säŋ'gē)...........Zaire	0·46 N	24·15 E
158	Isar R. (ē'zär)...............F.R.G.	48·27 N	12·02 E
164	Isarco (R.) (ê-sär'kō)..........It.	46·37 N	11·25 E
197	Isaroga Vol. (ē-sä-rō-gä)		
	Phil. (In.)	13·40 N	123·23 E
163	Ischia (ēs'kyä)....It. (Naples In.)	40·29 N	13·58 E
195	Ise (Uji-Yamada) (ĭs'hĕ)		
	(ū'gē-yä'mä'dȧ).Jap.	34·30 N	136·43 E
164	Iseo, Lago di (L.)		
	(lä-'gō-dē-ê-zĕ'ō).It.	45·50 N	9·55 E
161	Isère (R.) (ê-zâr')............Fr.	45·24 N	6·04 E
161	Iserlohn (ē'zĕr-lōn)		
	F.R.G. (Ruhr In.)	51·22 N	7·42 E
164	Isernia (ê-zĕr'nyä)............It.	41·35 N	14·14 E
195	Ise-Wan (B.) (ē'sĕ wän)......Jap.	34·49 N	136·44 E
215	Iseyin.......................Nig.	7·58 N	3·36 E
193	Ishan.......................China	24·32 N	108·42 E
194	Ishikari Wan (B.)		
	(ē'shē-kä-rē wän).Jap.	43·30 N	141·05 E
172	Ishim (ĭsh-êm')...........Sov. Un.	56·07 N	69·13 E
172	Ishim (R.)...............Sov. Un.	53·17 N	67·45 E
174	Ishimbay (ē-shēm-bī')		
	Sov. Un. (Urals In.)	53·28 N	56·02 E
190	Ishing (yēsĭng)..............China	31·26 N	119·57 E
194	Ishinomaki (ĭsh-nō-mä'kē)....Jap.	38·22 N	141·22 E
194	Ishinomaki Wan (B.)		
	(ē-shē-nō-mä'kē wän).Jap.	38·10 N	141·40 E
174	Ishly (ĭsh'lĭ).Sov. Un. (Urals In.)	54·13 N	55·55 E

294 Ishlya — James PRONOUNCING INDEX

Page Name Pronunciation Region Lat. °' Long. °'

174 Ishlya (ĭsh'lyȧ) Sov. Un. (Urals In.) 53·54 N 57·48 E
165 Ishm Alb. 41·32 N 19·35 E
218 Ishmant Egypt (Nile In.) 29·17 N 31·15 E
109 Ishpeming (ĭsh'pê-mĭng) Mi. 46·28 N 87·42 W
190 Ishui (yē suĭ) China 35·49 N 118·40 E
213 Isipingo (ĭs-ĭ-pĭŋ-gô) S. Afr. (Natal In.) 29·59 S 30·58 E
217 Isiro (Paulis) Zaire 2·47 N 27·37 E
171 İskenderun (ĭs-kĕn'dĕr-ōōn) Tur. 36·45 N 36·15 E
153 İskenderun Körfezi (G.) Tur. 36·22 N 35·25 E
171 Iskilip (ĕs'kĭ-lêp') Tur. 40·40 N 34·30 E
165 Iskūr (R.) (ĭs'k'r) Bul. 43·05 N 23·37 E
162 Isla-Cristina (ĭs'lä-krê-stē'nä) Sp. 37·13 N 7·20 W
187 Islāmābād Pak. 33·55 N 73·05 E
126 Isla Mujeres (ê's-lä-mōō-kĕ'rĕs) Mex. (In.) 21·25 N 86·53 W
95 Island L. Can. 53·47 N 94·25 W
99 Islands, B. of (ī'l*ă*ndz) Can. 49·10 N 58·15 W
154 Islay (I.) (ī'lā) Scot. 55·55 N 6·35 W
160 Isle (R.) (ēl) Fr. 45·02 N 0·29 E
148 Isle of Axholme (Reg.) (ăks'-hôm) Eng. 53·33 N 0·48 W
154 Isle of Man (măn) Eur. 54·26 N 4·21 W
109 Isle Royale Nat'l Park (īl'roi-*ă*l') U. S. 47·57 N 88·37 W
115 Isleta (ės-lā'tä) (ī-lē'tȧ) NM 34·55 N 106·45 W
98 Isle Verte (ēl vĕrt') Can. 48·01 N 69·20 W
218 Ismailia (Al Isma'īlīyah) (ēs-mä-ēl'ēȧ). Egypt (Suez In.) 30·35 N 32·17 E
218 Ismā'īlīyah Can. Egypt (Suez In.) 30·25 N 31·45 E
149 Ismaning (ēz'mä-nēng) F.R.G. (Munich In.) 48·14 N 11·41 E
218 Isnā (ės'nȧ) Egypt (Nile In.) 25·17 N 32·33 E
157 Isojärvi (L.) Fin. 61·47 N 22·00 E
171 Isparta (ė-spär'tȧ) Tur. 37·50 N 30·40 E
186 Israel Asia 32·40 N 34·00 E
112 Issaquah (ĭz'să-kwăh) Wa. (Seattle In.) 47·32 N 122·02 W
161 Isselburg (ē'sĕl-bōōrg) F.R.G. (Ruhr In.) 51·50 N 6·28 E
160 Issoire (ē-swȧr') Fr. 45·32 N 3·13 E
160 Issoudun (ē-sōō-dăn') Fr. 46·56 N 2·00 E
161 Issum (ē'sōōm) F.R.G. (Ruhr In.) 51·32 N 6·24 E
172 Issyk-Kul, Ozero (L.) Sov. Un. 42·13 N 76·12 E
184 İstādeh-ye Moqor, Ab-e (L.) Afg. 32·35 N 68·00 E
171 İstanbul (ê-stän-bōōl') Tur. 41·02 N 29·00 E
171 İstanbul Boğazı (Bosporous) (Str.) Tur. 41·10 N 29·10 E
165 Istiaía (ĭs-tyĭ'yä) Grc. 38·58 N 23·11 E
134 Istmina (ēst-mē'nä) Col. (In.) 5·10 N 76·40 W
121 Istokpoga (L.) (ĭs-tŏk-pō'gȧ) Fl. (In.) 27·20 N 81·33 W
164 Istra (pen.) (ê-strä) Yugo. 45·18 N 13·48 E
165 Istranca Dağ (Mts.) (ĭ-strän'jȧ) Bul.-Turk. 41·50 N 27·25 E
160 Istres (ēs'tr') Fr. (In.) 43·30 N 5·00 E
136 Itá (ê-tä') Par. 25·39 S 57·14 W
135 Itabaiana (ē-tä-bä-yȧ-nä) Braz. 10·42 S 37·17 W
137 Itabapoana (ē-tä'-bä-pôä'nä) Braz. (Rio de Janeiro In.) 21·19 S 40·58 W
137 Itabapoana (R.) Braz. (Rio de Janeiro In.) 21·11 S 41·18 W
137 Itabirito (ē-tä-bê-rē'tô) Braz. (Rio de Janeiro In.) 20·15 S 43·46 W
137 Itaboraí (ē-tä-bō-räē') Braz. (Rio de Janeiro In.) 22·46 S 42·50 W
135 Itabuna (ē-tä-bōō'nȧ) Braz. 14·47 S 39·17 W
137 Itacoara (ē-tä-kô'ä-rä) Braz. (Rio de Janeiro In.) 21·41 S 42·04 W
135 Itacoatiara (ē-tȧ-kwȧ-tyä'rȧ) Braz. 3·03 S 58·18 W
137 Itaguaí (ē-tä-gwä-ē') Braz. (Rio de Janeiro In.) 22·52 S 43·46 W
134 Itagüí (ē-tä'gwê) Col. (In.) 6·11 N 75·36 W
136 Itagui (R.) Braz. (Rio de Janeiro In.) 22·53 S 43·43 W
136 Itaipava (ē-tī-pȧ'-vä) Braz. (Rio de Janeiro In.) 22·23 S 43·09 W
136 Itaipu (ē-tī'pōō) Braz. (Rio de Janiero In.) 22·58 S 43·02 W
135 Itaituba (ê-tä'ī-tōō'bȧ) Braz. 4·12 S 56·00 W
136 Itajaí (ē-tä-zhī') Braz. 26·52 S 48·39 W
137 Itajubá (ē-tä-zhōō-bȧ') Braz. (Rio de Janeiro In.) 22·26 S 45·27 W
218 Itala Som. (Horn of Afr. In.) 2·45 N 46·15 E
146 Italy (ĭt'*ă*-lê) Eur. 43·58 N 11·14 E
119 Italy Tx. 32·11 N 96·51 W
136 Itambi (ē-tä'm-bê) Braz. (Rio de Janeiro In.) 22·44 S 42·57 W
195 Itami (ē'tä'mē') Jap. (Ōsaka In.) 34·47 N 135·25 E
137 Itapecerica (ē-tä-pĕ-sĕ-rē'kȧ) Braz. (Rio de Janeiro In.) 21·29 S 45·08 W
135 Itapecurú (R.) (ē-tä-pĕ-kōō-rōō') Braz. 4·05 S 43·49 W
135 Itapēcuru-Mirim (ê-tä-pĕ'kōō-rōō-mê-rēɴ') Braz. 3·17 S 44·15 W
137 Itaperuna (ē-tȧ-pâ-rōō'nä) Braz. (Rio de Janeiro In.) 21·12 S 41·53 W
137 Itapetininga (ē-tä-pĕ-tê-nē'ɴ-gä) Braz. (Rio de Janeiro In.) 23·37 S 48·03 W
135 Itapira (ē-tȧ-pē'rȧ) Braz. 20·42 S 51·19 W
137 Itapira. Braz. (Rio de Janeiro In.) 21·27 S 46·47 W
184 Itarsi India 22·43 N 77·45 E
119 Itasca (ī-tăs'kȧ) Tx. 32·09 N 97·08 W
109 Itasca (L.) Mn. 47·13 N 95·14 W
137 Itatiaia, Pico da (Pk.) (pē'-kô-dȧ-ē-tä-tyȧ'ēä) Braz. (Rio de Janeiro In.) 22·18 S 44·41 W
137 Itatiba (ē-tä-tē'bä) Braz. (Rio de Janeiro In.) 23·01 S 46·48 W
137 Itaúna (ē-tä-ōō'nä) Braz. (Rio de Janeiro In.) 20·05 S 44·35 W

137 Itaverá (ē-tä-vĕ-rȧ') Braz. (Rio de Janeiro In.) 22·44 S 44·07 W
104 Ithaca (ĭth'*ă*-kȧ) Mi. 43·20 N 84·35 W
105 Ithaca NY 42·25 N 76·30 W
165 Itháki (I.) (ē'thä-kĕ) Grc. 38·27 N 20·48 E
217 Itigi Tan. 5·42 S 34·29 E
216 Itimbiri (R.) Zaire 2·40 N 23·30 E
212 Itoko (ê-tō'kō) Zaire 1·13 S 22·07 E
218 Iţsā (ėt'sȧ) Egypt (Nile In.) 29·13 N 30·47 E
137 Itu (ê-tōō') Braz. (Rio de Janeiro In.) 23·16 S 47·16 W
190 Itu China 36·42 N 118·30 E
134 Ituango (ê-twäŋ'gō) Col. (In.) 7·07 N 75·44 W
135 Ituiutaba (ê-tōō-ēōō-tä'bä) Braz. 18·56 S 49·17 W
137 Itumirim (ē-tōō-mê-rē'ɴ) Braz. (Rio de Janeiro In.) 21·20 S 44·51 W
125 Itundujia Santa Cruz (ê-tōōn-dōō-hē'ȧ sä'n-tä krōō'z) Mex. 16·50 N 97·43 W
194 It'ung China 43·15 N 125·10 E
126 Iturbide (ē'tōōr-bē'dhȧ) Mex. (In.) 19·38 N 89·31 W
173 Iturup (I.) (ē-tōō-rōōp') Sov. Un. 45·35 N 147·15 E
136 Ituzaingo (ê-tōō-zä-ê'n-gô) Arg. (Buenos Aires In.) 34·24 S 58·40 W
149 Itzehoe (ē'tzĕ-hō) F.R.G. (Hamburg In.) 53·55 N 9·31 E
120 Iuka (ī-ū'kȧ) Ms. 34·47 N 88·10 W
137 Iúna (ē-ōō'-nä) Braz. (Rio de Janeiro In.) 20·22 S 41·32 W
172 Iva (R.) Sov. Un. 53·45 N 99·30 E
203 Ivanhoe (ĭv'ăn-hô) Austl. 32·53 S 144·10 E
159 Ivano-Frankovsk (ē-vä'nō frän-kôvsk') Sov. Un. 48·53 N 24·46 E
166 Ivanovo (ê-vä'nô-vō) Sov. Un. 57·02 N 41·54 E
166 Ivanovo (Oblast) Sov. Un. 56·55 N 40·30 E
167 Ivanpol' (ê-vän'pôl) Sov. Un. 49·51 N 28·11 E
174 Ivanteyevka (ê-vȧn-tyĕ'yĕf-kȧ) Sov. Un. (Moscow In.) 55·58 N 37·56 E
174 Ivdel' (ĭv'dyĕl) Sov. Un. (Urals In.) 60·42 N 60·27 E
Iviza I., see Ibiza, Isla de
213 Ivohibé (ê-vô-hê-bā') Mad. 22·28 S 46·59 E
209 Ivory Coast Afr. 7·43 N 6·30 W
164 Ivrea (ê-vrĕ'ä) It. 45·25 N 7·54 E
91 Ivujivik Can. 62·17 N 77·52 W
194 Iwaki (Taira) Jap. 37·03 N 140·57 E
194 Iwate Yama (Mt.) (ē-wä-tē-yä'mä) Jap. 39·50 N 140·56 E
195 Iwatsuki Jap. (Tōkyō In.) 35·48 N 139·43 E
195 Iwaya (ē'wȧ-yȧ) Jap. (Ōsaka In.) 34·35 N 135·01 E
215 Iwo Nig. 7·38 N 4·11 E
124 Ixcateopán (ēs-kä-tä-ō-pän') Mex. 18·29 N 99·49 W
149 Ixelles Bel. (Brussels In.) 50·49 N 4·23 E
125 Ixhuatán (San Francisco) (ēs-hwä-tän') Mex. 16·19 N 94·30 W
124 Ixhautlán (ēs-wȧt-län') Mex. 20·41 N 98·01 W
124 Ixmiquilpan (ēs-mê-kēl'pän) Mex. 20·30 N 99·12 W
213 Ixopo S. Afr. (Natal In.) 30·10 S 30·04 E
125 Ixtacalco (ēs-tȧ-käl'kō) Mex. (In.) 19·23 N 99·07 W
125 Ixtaltepec (Asunción) (ēs-täl-tĕ-pĕk') Mex. 16·33 N 95·04 W
125 Ixtapalapa (ēs'tä-pä-lä'pä) Mex. (In.) 19·21 N 99·06 W
125 Ixtapaluca (ēs'tä-pä-lōō'kä) Mex. (In.) 19·18 N 98·53 W
125 Ixtepec (ėks-tĕ'pĕk) Mex. 16·37 N 95·09 W
125 Ixtlahuaca (ēs-tlä-wä'kä) Mex. (In.) 19·34 N 99·46 W
125 Ixtlán de Juárez (ēs-tlän' dā hwä'râz) Mex. 17·20 N 96·29 W
124 Ixtlán del Río (ēs-tlän'dĕl rē'ō) Mex. 21·05 N 104·22 W
193 Iyang (ē'yäng') China 28·52 N 112·12 E
195 Iyo-Nada (Sea) (ē'yō nä-dä) Jap. 33·33 N 132·07 E
126 Izabal (ē'zä-bäl') Guat. 15·23 N 89·10 W
126 Izabal, L. (Golfo Dulce) (gôl'fō dōōl'sā) Guat. 15·30 N 89·04 W
126 Izalco (ē-zäl'kō) Sal. 13·50 N 89·40 W
126 Izamal (ē-zä-mä'l) Mex. (In.) 20·55 N 89·00 W
170 Izhevsk (ê-zhyĕfsk') Sov. Un. 56·50 N 53·15 E
170 Izhma (ĭzh'mȧ) Sov. Un. 65·00 N 54·05 E
170 Izhma (R.) Sov. Un. 64·00 N 53·00 E
174 Izhora R. (ēz'hô-rȧ) Sov. Un. (Leningrad In.) 59·36 N 30·20 E
167 Izmail (ēz-mȧ-ēl) Sov. Un. 45·00 N 28·49 E
171 İzmir (ĭz-mĕr') Tur. 38·25 N 27·05 E
165 Izmir Körfezi (G.) Tur. 38·43 N 26·37 E
171 Izmit (ĭz-mêt') Tur. 40·45 N 29·45 E
125 Iztaccíhuatl (Mtn.) Mex. (Mexico City In.) 19·10 N 98·38 W
195 Izu (I.) (ē'zōō) Jap. 34·32 N 139·25 E
195 Izuhara (ē'zōō-hä'rä) Jap. 34·11 N 129·18 E
195 Izumi-Ōtsu (ē'zōō-mōō ō'tsōō) Jap. (Ōsaka In.) 34·30 N 135·24 E
195 Izumo (ē'zōō-mō) Jap. 35·22 N 132·45 E

J

149 Jaachimsthal (yä'ĸēm-stäl) G.D.R. (Berlin In.) 52·58 N 13·45 E

211 Jabal, Baḩr al (R.) Sud. 7·02 N 30·45 E
184 Jabalpur India 23·18 N 79·59 E
158 Jablonec (Nad Nisou) (yäb'lô-nyĕts). Czech. 50·43 N 15·12 E
159 Jablunkov P. (yäb'lōōn-kôf) Czech. 49·31 N 18·35 E
135 Jaboatão (zhä-bô-ȧ-touɴ) Braz. 8·14 S 35·08 W
163 Jaca (hä'kä) Sp. 42·35 N 0·30 W
124 Jacala (hä-kȧ'lä) Mex. 21·01 N 99·11 W
126 Jacaltenango (hä-kȧl-tĕ-näŋ'gō) Guat. 15·39 N 91·41 W
137 Jacareí (zhä-kȧ-rĕ-ē') Braz. (Rio de Janeiro In.) 23·19 S 45·57 W
136 Jacarepaguá (zhä-kä-rȧ'pä-gwä') Braz. (Rio de Janeiro In.) 22·55 S 43·22 W
135 Jacarézinho (zhä-kä-rĕ'zê-nyô) Braz. 23·13 S 49·58 W
158 Jachymov (yä'chĭ-môf) Czech. 50·22 N 12·51 E
119 Jacinto City (hä-sĕn'tō) (jȧ-sĭn'tō) Tx. (In.) 29·45 N 95·14 W
116 Jacksboro (jăks'bŭr-ô) Tx. 33·13 N 98·11 W
120 Jackson (jăk'sŭn) Al. 31·31 N 87·52 W
114 Jackson Ca. 38·22 N 120·47 W
120 Jackson Ga. 33·19 N 83·55 W
120 Jackson Ky. 37·32 N 83·17 W
119 Jackson La. 30·50 N 91·13 W
104 Jackson Mi. 42·15 N 84·25 W
109 Jackson Mn. 43·37 N 95·00 W
120 Jackson Ms. 32·17 N 90·10 W
117 Jackson Mo. 37·23 N 89·40 W
104 Jackson Oh. 39·00 N 82·40 W
120 Jackson Tn. 35·37 N 88·49 W
202 Jackson, Port. Austl. (Sydney In.) 33·50 S 151·18 E
111 Jackson L. Wy. 43·57 N 110·28 W
120 Jacksonville (jăk'sŭn-vĭl) Al. 33·52 N 85·45 W
121 Jacksonville Fl. 30·20 N 81·40 W
117 Jacksonville Il. 39·43 N 90·12 W
119 Jacksonville Tx. 31·58 N 95·18 W
121 Jacksonville Beach Fl. 31·18 N 81·25 W
119 Jacmel (zhȧk-mĕl') Hai. 18·15 N 72·30 W
118 Jaco, L. (hä'kō) Mex. 27·51 N 103·50 W
184 Jacobābad Pak. 28·22 N 68·30 E
135 Jacobina (zhä-kô-bē'nȧ) Braz. 11·13 S 40·30 W
100 Jacques-Cartier (zhȧk'kär-tyā) Can. (Montréal In.) 45·30 N 72·39 W
98 Jacques Cartier, Mt. Can. 48·59 N 66·00 W
89 Jacques-Cartier, (R.) Can. (Quebec In.) 47·04 N 71·28 W
99 Jacques Cartier, Détroit de (Str.) Can. 50·07 N 63·58 W
98 Jacquet River (zhȧ-kĕ') (jăk'ĕt) Can. 47·55 N 66·00 W
137 Jacuí (zhä-kōō-ē') Braz. (Rio de Janeiro In.) 21·03 S 46·43 W
137 Jacutinga (zhȧ-kōō-tēn'gä) Braz. (Rio de Janeiro In.) 21·17 S 46·36 W
158 Jade B. (yä'dĕ) F.R.G. 53·28 N 8·17 E
Jadotville, see Likasi
134 Jaén (kä-ĕ'n) Peru 5·38 S 78·49 W
162 Jaen Sp. 37·45 N 3·48 W
203 Jaffa, C. (jăf'*ă*) Austl. 36·58 S 139·29 E
185 Jaffna (jäf'nȧ) Sri Lanka 9·44 N 80·09 E
128 Jagüey Grande (hä'gwā grän'dā) Cuba 22·35 N 81·05 W
183 Jahore Str. Mala. (Singapore In.) 1·22 N 103·37 E
186 Jahrom Iran 28·30 N 53·28 E
119 Jaibo (R.) (hä-ē'bō) Cuba 20·10 N 75·20 W
184 Jaipur India 27·00 N 75·50 E
184 Jaisaimer India 27·00 N 70·54 E
164 Jajce (yī'tsĕ) Yugo. 44·20 N 17·19 E
184 Jajpur India 20·49 N 86·37 E
196 Jakarta (yä-kär'tä) Indon. 6·17 S 106·45 E
150 Jakobstad (yȧ'kôb-stȧdh) Fin. 63·33 N 22·31 E
125 Jalacingo (hä-lä-sĭŋ'gō) Mex. 97·16 N 19·47 W
187 Jalālābād (jŭ-lä-lȧ-bäd) Afg. (Khyber Pass In.) 34·25 N 70·27 E
218 Jalālah al Baḩrīyah, Jabal, (Mts.) Egypt (Nile In.) 29·20 N 32·00 E
126 Jalapa (hä-lä'pȧ) Guat. 14·38 N 89·58 W
125 Jalapa de Diaz (San Felipe) (dä dē-äz') (sän fā-lē'pä). Mex. 18·06 N 96·33 W
125 Jalapa del Marqués (dĕl mär-kās'). Mex. 16·30 N 95·29 W
125 Jalapa Enríquez (ĕn-rē'kāz) Mex. 19·32 N 96·53 W
184 Jaleswar Nep. 26·50 N 85·55 E
184 Jalgaon India 21·08 N 75·33 E
124 Jalisco (hä-lēs'kō) Mex. 21·27 N 104·54 W
122 Jalisco (State) Mex. 20·07 N 104·45 W
162 Jalón (R.) (hä-lōn') Sp. 41·22 N 1·46 W
124 Jalostotitlán (hä-lōs-tē-tlān') Mex. 21·09 N 102·30 W
125 Jalpa (häl'pā) Mex. 18·12 N 93·06 W
124 Jalpa (häl'pä) Mex. 21·40 N 103·04 W
124 Jalpan (häl'pän) Mex. 21·13 N 99·31 W
125 Jaltepec (häl-tȧ-pĕk') Mex. 17·20 N 95·15 W
125 Jaltipan (häl-tȧ-pän') Mex. 17·59 N 94·42 W
124 Jaltocan (häl-tô-kän') Mex. 21·08 N 98·32 W
211 Jālū, Wāḩat (Oasis) Libya 28·58 N 21·45 E
215 Jamaare (R.) Nig. 11·50 N 10·10 E
123 Jamaica N. A. 17·45 N 78·00 W
129 Jamaica Cay (I.) Ba. 22·45 N 75·55 W
184 Jamālpur Bngl. 24·56 N 89·58 E
124 Jamay (hä-mī') Mex. 20·16 N 103·43 W
196 Jambi (mäm'bê) Indon. 1·45 S 103·28 E
165 Jambol (yȧm'bôl) Bul. 42·28 N 26·31 E
196 Jambuair, Tanjung (C.) Indon. 5·15 N 79·30 E
117 James (R.) Mo. 36·51 N 93·22 W
121 James (R.) NC 37·00 N 81·48 W
102 James (R.) U. S. 46·25 N 98·55 W
105 James (R.) Va. 37·35 N 77·50 W
91 James B. (jāmz) Can. 53·53 N 80·40 W
106 Jamesburg (jāmz'bûrg) NJ (New York In.) 40·21 N 74·26 W
129 James Pt. Ba. 25·20 N 76·30 W

ăt; fin*ă*l; rāte; senȧte; ärm; ȧsk; sofȧ; fâre; ch-choose; dh-as th in other; bē; ėvent; bĕt; recĕnt; cratẽr; g-go; gh-guttural g; bĭt; ĭ-short neutral; rīde; ĸ-guttural k as ch in German ich;

Page	Name, Pronunciation, Region	Lat. °'	Long. °'
204	James Ra. Austl.	24·15 S	133·30 E
133	James Ross (I.) Ant.	64·20 S	58·20 W
105	Jamestown (jāmz'toun) NY	42·05 N	79·15 W
108	Jamestown ND	46·54 N	98·42 W
106	Jamestown... RI (Providence In.)	41·30 N	71·21 W
213	Jamestown..... S. Afr. (Natal In.)	31·07 S	26·49 E
108	Jamestown Res. ND	47·16 N	98·40 W
125	Jamiltepec (hä-mēl-tå-pěk).. Mex.	16·16 N	97·54 W
156	Jammerbugt (B.) Den.	57·20 N	9·28 E
184	Jammu India	32·50 N	74·52 E
184	Jammu and Kashmīr (Disputed Reg.) (kȧsh-mēr'). India-Pak.	39·10 N	75·05 E
184	Jāmnagar (jäm-nŭ'gŭr) India	22·33 N	70·03 E
184	Jamshedpur (jäm'shĕd-pōōr). India	22·52 N	86·11 E
134	Jamundí (hä-mōō'n-dē'). Col. (In.)	3·15 N	76·32 W
162	Jándula (R.) (hän'dōō-lȧ) Sp.	38·28 N	3·52 W
109	Janesville (jānz'vĭl) Wi.	42·41 N	89·03 W
183	Janin ..... Jordan (Palestine In.)	32·27 N	35·19 E
150	Jan Mayen (I.) (yän mī'ĕn).. Nor.	70·59 N	8·05 W
156	Jannelund (yän'ĕ-lŏŏnd) Swe.	59·14 N	14·24 E
159	Jánoshalma (yä'nôsh-hôl-mô) Hung.	46·17 N	19·18 E
159	Janów Lubelski (yä'nōōf lŭ-bĕl'skĭ) Pol.	50·40 N	22·25 E
135	Januária (zhä-nwä'rē-ä) Braz.	15·31 S	44·17 W
190	Jaoyang (jä'ō-yäng') China	38·16 N	115·45 E
183	Japan (jȧ-păn') Asia	36·30 N	133·30 E
194	Japan, Sea of (jȧ-păn') Asia	40·08 N	132·55 E
197	Japen (I.) (yä'pĕn) Indon.	1·30 S	136·15 E
136	Japeri (zhȧ-pĕ'rē) Braz. (Rio de Janeiro In.)	22·38 S	43·40 W
134	Japurá (R.) (zhä-pōō-rä').... Braz.	1·30 S	67·54 W
119	Jarabacoa (kä-rä-bä-kô'ä) Dom. Rep.	19·05 N	70·40 W
124	Jaral del Progreso (hä-räl dĕl prô-grā'sō). Mex.	20·21 N	101·05 W
162	Jarama (R.) (hä-rä'mä) Sp.	40·33 N	3·30 W
183	Jarash ..... Jordan (Palestine In.)	32·17 N	35·53 E
128	Jardines, Banco (Bk.) (bä'n-kō-här-dē'nås). Cuba	21·45 N	81·40 W
135	Jari (R.) (zhä-rē) Braz.	0·28 N	53·00 W
160	Jarnac (zhȧr-nȧk') Fr.	45·42 N	0·09 W
159	Jarocin (yä-rō'tsyēn) Pol.	51·58 N	17·31 E
159	Jarosław (yȧ-rôs-wåf) Pol.	50·01 N	22·41 E
183	Jasin ...... Mala. (Singapore In.)	2·19 N	102·26 E
157	Jašiūnai (dzȧ-shōō-nȧ'yē). Sov. Un.	54·27 N	25·25 E
186	Jāsk (jäsk) Iran	25·46 N	57·48 E
159	Jasło (yäs'wō) Pol.	49·44 N	21·28 E
183	Jason B..... Mala. (Singapore In.)	1·53 N	104·14 E
104	Jasonville (jā'sŭn-vĭl) In.	39·10 N	87·15 W
120	Jasper (jăs'pĕr) Al.	33·50 N	87·17 W
93	Jasper Can.	52·53 N	118·05 W
120	Jasper Fl.	30·30 N	82·56 W
104	Jasper In.	38·20 N	86·55 W
108	Jasper Mn.	43·51 N	96·22 W
119	Jasper Tx.	30·55 N	93·59 W
93	Jasper Natl. Park Can.	53·09 N	117·45 W
159	Jászapáti (yäs'ô-pä-tē) Hung.	47·29 N	20·10 E
125	Jatate (R.) (hä-tä-tā') Mex.	16·30 N	91·29 W
128	Jatibonico (hä-tē-bô-nē'kō).. Cuba	22·00 N	79·15 W
163	Játiva (hä'tē-vä) Sp.	38·58 N	0·31 W
136	Jau' (zhȧ-ōō') Braz.	22·16 S	48·31 W
134	Jauja (Kä-ōō'K) Peru	11·43 S	75·32 W
124	Jaumave (hou-mä'vȧ) Mex.	23·23 N	99·24 W
157	Jaunjelgava (youn'yĕl'gȧ-vȧ) Sov. Un.	56·37 N	25·06 E
134	Javari (R.) (kȧ-vä-rē)... Col.-Peru	4·25 S	72·07 W
163	Jávea (hä-vā'ä) Sp.	38·45 N	0·07 E
196	Jawa (Java) (I.) Indon.	8·35 S	111·11 E
196	Jawa, Laut (Java Sea) Indon.	5·10 S	110·30 E
158	Jawor (yä'vôr) Pol.	51·04 N	16·12 E
159	Jaworzno (yä-vôzh'nô) Pol.	50·11 N	19·18 E
197	Jaya, Puncak (Pk.) Indon.	4·00 S	137·15 E
197	Jayapura (Sukarnapura)... Indon.	2·30 S	140·45 E
	Jayb, Wādī al (R.), see Ha 'Arava		
159	Jászberény (yäs'bĕ-rän') Hung.	47·30 N	19·56 E
183	Jazzīn .... Leb. (Palestine In.)	33·34 N	35·37 E
119	Jeanerette (jĕn-ēr-et') (zhän-rĕt') La.	29·54 N	91·41 W
152	Jebal Aures (Mts.) Alg.	35·16 N	5·53 E
210	Jebba (jĕb'ȧ) Nig.	9·07 N	4·46 E
99	Jeddore L. Can.	48·07 N	55·35 W
159	Jędrzejów (yăN-dzhā'yōōf) Pol.	50·38 N	20·18 E
120	Jefferson (jĕf'ēr-sŭn) Ga.	34·05 N	83·35 W
109	Jefferson Ia.	42·10 N	94·22 W
106	Jefferson... La. (New Orleans In.)	29·57 N	90·04 W
119	Jefferson Tx.	32·47 N	94·21 W
109	Jefferson Wi.	42·59 N	88·45 W
110	Jefferson, Mt. Or.	44·41 N	121·50 W
117	Jefferson City Mo.	38·34 N	92·10 W
111	Jefferson R. Mt.	45·37 N	112·22 W
107	Jeffersontown (jĕf'ēr-sŭn-toun) Ky. (Louisville In.)	38·11 N	85·34 W
107	Jeffersonville (jĕf'ēr-sŭn-vĭl) In. (Louisville In.)	38·17 N	85·44 W
215	Jega Nig.	12·15 N	4·23 E
	Jehol, see Ch'engte		
153	Jeib, Wadi el (R.)... Jordan-Isr.	30·30 N	35·20 E
157	Jēkabpils (yĕk'ȧb-pĭls)... Sov. Un.	56·29 N	25·50 E
158	Jelenia Góra (yĕ-lĕn'yȧ gōō'rȧ) Pol.	50·53 N	15·43 E
157	Jelgava (yĕl'gȧ-vȧ) Sov. Un.	56·39 N	23·40 E
120	Jellico (jĕl'ĭ-kō) Tn.	36·34 N	84·06 W
151	Jemmapes (zhĕ-map') Alg.	36·43 N	7·21 E
158	Jena (yā'nä) G.D.R.	50·55 N	11·37 E
190	Jench'iu (rĕnchĕō) China	38·44 N	116·05 E
121	Jenkins (jĕŋ'kĭnz) Ky.	37·09 N	82·38 W
106	Jenkintown (jĕŋ'kĭn-toun) Pa. (Philadelphia In.)	40·06 N	75·08 W
119	Jennings (jĕn'ĭngz) La.	30·14 N	92·40 W
104	Jennings Mi.	44·20 N	85·20 W
113	Jennings ...... Mo. (St. Louis In.)	38·43 N	90·16 W
135	Jequié (zhĕ-kyĕ') Braz.	13·53 S	40·06 W
135	Jequitinhonha (R.) (zhĕ-kē-tēŋ-ō'n-yä). Braz.	16·47 S	41·19 W
129	Jérémie (zhā-rȧ-mē') Hai.	18·40 N	74·10 W
135	Jeremoabo (zhĕ-rā-mō-ȧ'bō). Braz.	10·03 S	38·13 W
125	Jerez, Punta (Pt.) (pōō'n-tä-Kĕ-rāz'). Mex.	23·04 N	97·44 W
162	Jerez de la Frontera (Kĕ-rāth' dā lä frôn-tā'rä). Sp.	36·42 N	6·09 W
162	Jerez de los Caballeros (Kĕ-rath' dā lōs kä-väl-yā'rōs). Sp.	38·20 N	6·45 W
205	Jericho (jĕr'ĭ-kō) Austl.	28·38 S	146·24 E
218	Jericho (jĕr-ĭkô) S. Afr. (Johannesburg & Pretoria In.)	25·16 S	27·47 E
	Jericho, see Arīhā		
115	Jerome (jê-rōm') Az.	34·45 N	112·10 W
111	Jerome Id.	42·44 N	114·31 W
160	Jersey (I.) (jûr'zĭ) Eur.	49·13 N	2·07 W
106	Jersey City... NJ (New York In.)	40·43 N	74·05 W
105	Jersey Shore Pa.	41·10 N	77·15 W
117	Jerseyville (jĕr'zē-vĭl) Il.	39·07 N	90·18 W
183	Jerusalem (jê-rōō'sȧ-lĕm) Isr.-Jordan (Palestine In.)	31·46 N	35·14 E
121	Jesup (jĕs'ŭp) Ga.	31·36 N	81·53 W
125	Jesús Carranza (hē-sōō's-kär-rȧ'n-zä). Mex.	17·26 N	95·01 W
108	Jewel Cave Natl. Mon. SD	43·44 N	103·52 W
112	Jewell (jū'ĕl).... Or. (Portland In.)	45·56 N	123·30 W
184	Jhālawār India	24·29 N	79·09 E
184	Jhang Maghiāna Pak.	31·21 N	72·19 E
184	Jhānsi (jän'sē) India	25·29 N	78·32 E
184	Jhārsuguda India	22·51 N	86·13 E
184	Jhelum (R.) (jā'lŭm) Pak.	31·40 N	71·51 E
188	Jibhalanta Mong.	47·49 N	97·00 E
115	Jicarilla Ind. Res. (Kē-kȧ-rēl'yȧ) NM	36·45 N	107·00 W
127	Jicaron, Isla (I.) (Kē-kä-rōn'). Pan.	7·14 N	81·41 W
	Jidda, see Juddah		
159	Jiffa R. Rom.	47·35 N	27·02 E
204	Jiggalong (jĭg'ȧ-lông) Austl.	23·20 S	120·45 E
129	Jiguani (Kē-gwä-nē') Cuba	20·20 N	76·30 W
128	Jigüey, Bahía (B.) (bä-ē'ä-Kē'gwā). Cuba	22·15 N	78·10 W
190	Jihchao (rē'jou) China	35·27 N	119·28 E
158	Jihlava (yē'hlȧ-vȧ) Czech.	49·23 N	15·33 E
218	Jijiga ..... Eth. (Horn of Afr. In.)	9·15 N	42·48 E
163	Jijona (Kē-hō'nä) Sp.	38·31 N	0·29 W
211	Jilf al-Kabīr, Hadabat al (Plat.). Egypt	24·09 N	25·29 E
162	Jiloca (R.) (Kē-lō'kȧ) Sp.	41·13 N	1·30 W
126	Jilotepeque (Kē-lō-tĕ-pĕ'kĕ).. Guat.	14·39 N	89·36 W
211	Jima Eth.	7·41 N	36·52 E
165	Jimbolia (zhĭm-bô'lyä) Rom.	45·45 N	20·44 E
124	Jiménez (Kē-mā'nāz) Mex.	24·12 N	98·29 W
118	Jimenez Mex.	27·09 N	104·55 W
118	Jiménez Mex.	29·03 N	100·42 W
124	Jiménez del Téul (tĕ-ōō'l).... Mex.	21·28 N	103·51 W
105	Jim Thorpe (jĭm' thôrp') Pa.	40·50 N	75·45 W
158	Jindřichov Hradec (yĕn'd'r-zhĭ-kōōf hrä'dĕts). Czech.	49·09 N	15·02 E
217	Jinja (jĭn'jä) Ug.	0·26 N	33·12 E
126	Jinotega (Kē-nô-tā'gä) Nic.	13·07 N	86·00 W
126	Jinotepe (Kē-nô-tā'pā) Nic.	11·52 N	86·12 W
195	Jinzū-Gawa (Strm.) (jēn'zōō gä'wä). Jap.	36·26 N	137·18 E
134	Jipijapa (Kē-pê-hä'pä) Ec.	1·36 S	80·52 W
126	Jiquilisco (Kē-kē-lē's-kô) Sal.	13·18 N	88·32 W
124	Jiquilpan de Juarez (Kē-kēl'pän dā hwä'rāz). Mex.	20·00 N	102·43 W
125	Jiquipilco (hē-kē-pē'l-kô) Mex. (In.)	19·32 N	99·37 W
188	Jirgalanta Mong.	48·08 N	91·40 E
218	Jirjā (jĕr'gȧ) ..... Egypt (Nile In.)	26·20 N	31·51 E
162	Jistredo, Sierra de (Mts.) (sē-ĕ'r-rä-dĕ-Kēs-trĕ'dô). Sp.	42·50 N	6·15 W
125	Jitotol (Kē-tô-tōl') Mex.	17·03 N	92·54 W
165	Jiu (R.) Rom.	44·45 N	23·17 E
212	João Belo (zho'un-bĕ'lō) Moz.	25·00 S	33·45 E
135	João Pessoa (Paraíba) (shô-ouN' pĕ-sō'ȧ) (pä-rä-ē'bȧ). Braz.	7·09 S	34·45 W
137	João Ribeiro (zhô-uN-rē-bā'rō) Braz. (Rio de Janeiro In.)	20·42 S	44·03 W
128	Jobabo (R.) (hō-bä'bä) Cuba	20·50 N	77·15 W
89	Jock (R.) (jŏk) Can. (Ottawa In.)	45·08 N	75·51 W
124	Jocotepec (hô-kō-tȧ-pĕk').... Mex.	20·17 N	103·26 W
162	Jodar (hō'där) Sp.	37·54 N	3·20 W
184	Jodhpur (jōd'pōōr) India	26·23 N	83·00 E
157	Joensuu (yô-ĕn'sōō) Fin.	62·35 N	29·46 E
93	Joffre, Mt. (jŏ'f'r) Can.	50·32 N	115·13 W
195	Jōga-Shima (I.) (jō'gä shē'mä) Jap. (Tōkyō In.)	35·07 N	139·37 E
166	Jōgeva (yû'gĕ-vȧ) Sov. Un.	58·45 N	26·23 E
96	Joggins (jŏ'gĭnz) Can.	45·42 N	64·27 W
213	Johannesburg (yô-hän'ĕs-bōōrgh) S. Afr. (Johannesburg & Pretoria In.)	26·08 S	27·54 E
110	John Day Dam Or.	45·40 N	120·15 W
110	John Day R. (jŏn dā) Or.	44·46 N	120·15 W
110	John Day R., Middle Fork.... Or.	44·53 N	119·04 W
110	John Day R., North Fork ..... Or.	45·03 N	118·50 W
116	John Martin Res. (jŏn mär'tĭn) Co.	37·57 N	103·04 W
112	Johnson (R.) (jŏn'sŭn) Or. (Portland In.)	45·27 N	122·20 W
105	Johnsonburg (jŏn'sŭn-bûrg)... Pa.	41·30 N	78·40 W
104	Johnson City (jŏn'sŭn) Il.	37·50 N	88·55 W
105	Johnson City NY	42·10 N	76·00 W
121	Johnson City Tn.	36·17 N	82·23 W
198	Johnston (I.) (jŏn'stŭn)... Oceania	17·00 N	168·00 W
92	Johnstone St. Can.	50·25 N	126·00 W
217	Johnston Falls Afr.	10·35 S	28·50 E
105	Johnstown (jonz'toun) NY	43·00 N	74·20 W
105	Johnstown Pa.	40·20 N	78·50 W
189	Joho (Prov.) China	42·31 N	118·12 E
196	Johor (State) (jŭ-hōr') Mala.	2·15 N	103·00 E
183	Johor (R.) (jŭ-hōr') Mala. (Singapore In.)	1·39 N	103·52 E
183	Johor Bahru (bȧ-hŭ-rōō') Mala. (Singapore In.)	1·28 N	103·46 E
166	Jõhvi (yû'vĭ) Sov. Un.	59·21 N	27·21 E
160	Joigny (zhwȧn-yē') Fr.	47·58 N	3·26 E
136	Joinville (zhwăN-vēl') Braz.	26·18 S	48·47 W
160	Joinville Fr.	48·28 N	5·05 E
133	Joinville (I.) Ant.	63·00 S	53·30 W
124	Jojutla (hō-hōō'tlȧ) Mex.	18·39 N	99·11 W
150	Jökullsá (R.) (yû'kōōls-ô) Ice.	65·38 N	16·08 W
124	Jola (Kō'lä) Mex.	21·08 N	104·26 W
107	Joliet (jō-lĭ-ĕt')... Il. (Chicago In.)	41·37 N	88·05 W
97	Joliette (zhô-lyĕt') Can.	46·01 N	73·30 W
196	Jolo (hō-lō) Phil.	5·59 N	121·05 E
196	Jolo (I.) Phil.	5·55 N	121·15 E
197	Jomalig (I.) (hô-mä'lĕg). Phil. (In.)	14·44 N	122·34 E
124	Jomulco (hô-mōōl'kô) Mex.	21·08 N	104·24 W
124	Jonacatepec (hō-nä-kä-tȧ-pĕk') Mex.	18·39 N	98·46 W
157	Jonava (yō-nä'vȧ) Sov. Un.	55·05 N	24·15 E
156	Jondal (yŏn'däl) Nor.	60·16 N	6·16 E
197	Jones (jōnz) Phil. (In.)	13·56 N	122·05 E
197	Jones Phil. (In.)	16·35 N	121·39 E
117	Jonesboro (jōnz'bûro) Ar.	35·49 N	90·42 W
119	Jonesboro La.	32·14 N	92·43 W
119	Jonesville (jōnz'vĭl) La.	31·35 N	91·50 W
104	Jonesville Mi.	42·00 N	84·45 W
214	Jong (R.) S. L.	8·10 N	12·10 W
157	Joniškis (yô'nĭsh-kĭs) Sov. Un.	56·14 N	23·36 E
156	Jönköping (yûn'chû-pĭng) Swe.	57·47 N	14·10 E
97	Jonquiere (zhôN-kyâr') Can.	48·25 N	71·15 W
125	Jonuta (hô-nōō'tä) Mex.	18·07 N	92·09 W
160	Jonzac (zhôN-zȧk') Fr.	45·27 N	0·27 W
117	Joplin (jŏp'lĭn) Mo.	37·05 N	94·31 W
182	Jordan (jôr'dȧn) Asia	30·15 N	38·00 E
183	Jordan (R.). Jordan (Palestine In.)	31·58 N	35·36 E
113	Jordan R.. Ut. (Salt Lake City In.)	40·42 N	111·56 W
187	Jorhāt (jôr-hät') India	26·43 N	94·16 E
124	Jorullo, Vol. de (vôl-kȧ'n-dĕ-hô-rōōl'yō). Mex.	18·54 N	101·38 W
215	Jos Plat. (jôs) Nig.	9·53 N	9·05 E
204	Joseph Bonaparte, G. (jô'sĕf bō'nȧ-pärt). Austl.	13·30 S	128·40 E
89	Josephburg.. Can. (Edmonton In.)	53·45 N	113·06 W
89	Joseph L. (jō'sĕf lăk) Can. (Edmonton In.)	53·18 N	113·06 W
114	Joshua Tree Natl. Mon. (jô'shū-ȧ trē). Ca.	34·02 N	115·53 W
215	Jos Plat. Nig.	9·53 N	9·05 E
156	Jostedalsbreen (Gl.) (yôstĕ-däls-brĕĕn). Nor.	61·40 N	6·55 E
156	Jotun Fjell (Mts.) (yō'tōōn fyĕl') Nor.	61·44 N	8·11 E
128	Joulter's Cays (Is.) (jōl'tērz).. Ba.	25·20 N	78·10 W
161	Jouy-le-Chatel (zhwē-lĕ-shä-tĕl') Fr. (Paris In.)	48·40 N	3·07 E
128	Jovellanos (hō-vĕl-yä'nōs)... Cuba	22·50 N	81·10 W
195	Jōyō .... Jap. (Ōsaka In.)	34·51 N	135·48 E
120	J. Percy Priest Res. Tn.	36·00 N	86·45 W
190	Ju (R.) (rōō) China	33·07 N	114·18 E
124	Juan Aldama (kōōȧ'n-äl-dȧ'mä) Mex.	24·16 N	103·21 W
110	Juan de Fuca, Str. of (hwän' dā fōō'kä). Wa.-Can.	48·25 N	124·37 W
213	Juan de Nova, Île (I.) Afr.	17·18 S	43·07 E
122	Juan Diaz, (R.) (Kōōȧ'n-dē'-äz) Pan. (In.)	9·05 N	79·30 W
133	Juan Fernández, Islas de (Is.) (ē's-läs-dĕ-hwän' fĕr-nän'dāth) Chile	33·30 S	79·00 W
137	Juan L. Lacaze (hōōȧ'n-ĕ'lĕ-lä-kä'zĕ). Ur. (Buenos Aires In.)	34·25 S	57·28 W
128	Juan Luis, Cayos de (Is.) (ka-yōs-dĕ-hwän lōō-ēs'). Cuba	22·15 N	82·00 W
135	Juàzeiro (zhōōȧ'zā'rô) Braz.	9·27 S	40·28 W
135	Juazeiro do Norte (zhōōȧ'zā'rō-dô-nôr-tĕ). Braz.	7·16 S	38·57 W
136	Juárez (hōōȧ'rĕz) Arg.	37·42 S	59·46 W
211	Jūbā Sud.	4·58 N	31·37 E
218	Juba R. (jōō'bȧ) Som. (Horn of Afr. In.)	1·30 N	42·25 E
183	Jubayl (Byblos) (jōō-bĭl') Leb. (Palestine In.)	34·07 N	35·38 E
162	Júcar (R.) (hōō'kär) Sp.	39·10 N	1·22 W
128	Júcaro (hōō'kȧ-rô) Cuba	21·40 N	78·50 W
124	Juchipila (hōō-chê-pē'lȧ)... Mex.	21·26 N	103·09 W
122	Juchitán (hōō-chê-tän') Mex.	16·15 N	95·00 W
125	Juchitán de Zaragoza (hōō-chê-tän' dā thä-rä-gō'thä). Mex.	16·27 N	95·03 W
124	Juchitlán (hōō-chē-tlän) Mex.	20·05 N	104·07 W
126	Jucuapa (Kōō-kwä'pä) Sal.	13·30 N	88·24 W
186	Juddah Sau. Ar.	21·30 N	39·15 E
158	Judenburg (jōō'dĕn-bûrg) Aus.	47·10 N	14·40 E
111	Judith R. (jōō'dĭth) Mt.	47·20 N	109·36 W
193	Juian (jwĭ'än') China	27·48 N	120·40 E
126	Juigalpa (hwē-gäl'pä) Nic.	12·02 N	85·24 W
161	Juilly (zhwē-yē')... Fr. (Paris In.)	49·01 N	2·41 E
155	Juist (I.) (yōō'ēst) F.R.G.	53·41 N	6·50 E
137	Juiz de Fora (zhōō-ēzh' dā fō'rä) Braz. (Rio de Janeiro In.)	21·47 S	43·20 W
136	Jujuy (hōō-hwē') Arg.	24·14 S	65·15 W
136	Jujuy (Prov.) (hōō-hwē') Arg.	23·00 S	65·45 W
190	Jukao (rōōgou) China	32·24 N	120·33 E
213	Jukskei (R.) S. Afr. (Johannesburg & Pretoria In.)	25·58 S	27·58 E
116	Julesburg (jōōlz'bûrg) Co.	40·59 N	102·16 W
134	Juliaca (hōō-lê-ä'kä) Peru	15·26 S	70·12 W
75	Julianehåb Grnld.	60·07 N	46·20 W
161	Jülich (yü'lĕk).. F.R.G. (Ruhr In.)	50·55 N	6·22 E

ng-sing; ŋ-baŋk; N-nasalized n; nŏd; cŏmmit; ōld; ôbey; ôrder; fōōd; fŏŏt; ou-out; s-soft; sh-dish; th-thin; pūre; ûnite; ûrn; stŭd; circŭs; ü-as "y" in study; '-indeterminate vowel.

296 Julijske — Kangean
PRONOUNCING INDEX

Page	Name Pronunciation Region	Lat. °′	Long. °′
164	Julijske Alpe (Mts.) (û′lêy-skĕ′ äl′pĕ). Yugo.	46·05 N	14·05 E
184	Jullundur. India	31·29 N	75·39 E
184	Julpaiguri. India	26·35 N	88·48 E
129	Jumento Cays (Is.) (hōō-mĕn′tō) Ba.	23·05 N	75·40 W
155	Jumet (zhü-mĕ′). Bel.	50·28 N	4·30 E
162	Jumilla (hōō-mēl′yä). Sp.	38·28 N	1·20 W
109	Jump (R.) (jŭmp). Wi.	45·18 N	90·53 W
89	Jumpingpound Cr. (jŭmp-ĭng-pound). Can. (Calgary In.)	51·01 N	114·34 W
183	Jumrah. Indon. (Singapore In.)	1·48 N	101·04 E
135	Jumundá (R.) (zhōō-mōō′n-dä′) Braz.	1·33 S	57·42 W
184	Junagādh (jŏŏ-nä′gŭd). India	21·33 N	70·25 E
190	Junan (rōō Nän). China	32·59 N	114·22 E
218	Junayfah. Egypt (Suez In.)	30·11 N	32·26 E
183	Junaynah, Ra's al (Mt.) Egypt (Palestine In.)	29·02 N	33·58 E
118	Junction (jŭŋk′shŭn). Tx.	30·29 N	99·48 W
117	Junction City. Ks.	39·01 N	96·49 W
137	Jundiaí (zhōō′n-dyä-ē′) Braz. (Rio de Janeiro In.)	23·12 S	46·52 W
101	Juneau (jōō′nō). Ak.	58·25 N	134·30 W
190	Jungch'eng (jŏŏng′chĕng′). China	37·23 N	122·31 E
193	Jungchiang. China	25·52 N	108·45 E
158	Jungfrau Pk. (yŏŏng′frou). Switz.	46·30 N	7·59 E
137	Junín (hōō-nē′n) Arg. (Buenos Aires In.)	34·35 S	60·56 W
134	Junín. Col. (In.)	4·47 N	73·39 W
183	Juniyah (jōō-nē′ĕ) Leb. (Palestine In.)	33·59 N	35·38 E
150	Junkeren (Mtn.) (yōōn′kĕ-rĕn) Nor.	66·29 N	14·58 E
112	Jupiter, Mt. Wa. (Seattle In.)	47·42 N	123·04 W
99	Jupiter (R.). Can.	49·40 N	63·20 W
211	Jur (R.) (jŏŏr). Sud.	6·38 N	27·52 E
154	Jura (I.) (jōō′rȧ). Scot.	56·09 N	6·45 W
161	Jura (Mts.) (zhü-rȧ′). Switz.	46·55 N	6·49 E
154	Jura, Sd. of (jōō′rȧ). Scot.	55·45 N	5·55 W
157	Jurbarkas (yōōr-bär′käs). Sov. Un.	55·06 N	22·50 E
157	Jūrmala. Sov. Un.	56·57 N	23·37 E
134	Juruá (R.) (zhōō-rŏŏ-ä′). Braz.	5·27 S	67·39 W
135	Juruena (R.) (zhōō-rōōĕ′nä). Braz.	12·22 S	58·34 W
134	Jutaí (R.) (zhōō-tȧy). Braz.	4·26 S	68·16 W
126	Jutiapa (hōō-tê-ä′pä). Guat.	14·16 N	89·55 W
126	Juticalpa (hōō-tê-käl′pä). Hond.	14·35 N	86·17 W
124	Juventino Rosas (Kōō-vĕn-tē′nô-rŏ-säs). Mex.	20·38 N	101·02 W
61	Juvisy-sur-Orge (zhü-vê-sē′sür-ôrzh′). Fr. (Paris In.)	48·41 N	2·22 E
124	Juxtahuaca (hōōs-tlȧ-hwä′kä) Mex.	17·20 N	98·02 W
165	Južna Morava (R.) (û′zhnä mô′rä-vä). Yugo.	42·30 N	22·00 E
156	Jylland (Reg.). Den.	56·04 N	9·00 E
157	Jyväskylä) (yû′vĕs-kû-lĕ). Fin.	62·14 N	25·46 E

K

Page	Name Pronunciation Region	Lat. °′	Long. °′
217	Kaabong. Ug.	3·31 N	34·08 E
213	Kaalfontein (kärl-fŏn-tān). S. Afr. (Johannesburg & Pretoria In.)	26·02 S	28·16 E
212	Kaappunt (C.). S. Afr. (In.)	34·21 S	18·30 E
196	Kabaena (I.) (kä-bȧ-ā′nȧ). Indon.	5·35 S	121·07 E
210	Kabala (kȧ-bȧ′lȧ). S. L.	9·43 N	11·39 W
217	Kabale. Ug.	1·15 S	29·59 E
217	Kabalo (kä-bä′lō). Zaire	6·03 S	26·55 E
212	Kabambare (kä-bäm-bä′rȧ). Zaire	4·47 S	27·45 E
215	Kabba. Nig.	7·50 N	6·03 E
195	Kabe (kä′bā). Jap.	34·32 N	132·30 E
96	Kabinakagami (R.). Can.	49·00 N	84·15 W
216	Kabinda (kä-bēN′dä). Zaire	6·08 S	24·29 E
216	Kabompo (R.) (kȧ-bôm′pō) Zambia	14·00 S	23·40 E
212	Kabongo (kȧ-bông′ô). Zaire	7·58 S	25·10 E
214	Kabot. Gui.	10·48 N	14·57 W
152	Kaboudia, Ras (C.). Tun.	35·17 N	11·28 E
184	Kābul (kä′bŏŏl). Afg.	34·39 N	69·14 E
187	Kabul (R.) (kä′bŏŏl). Asia	34·44 N	69·43 E
217	Kabunda. Zaire	12·25 S	29·22 E
217	Kabwe (Broken Hill). Zambia	14·27 S	28·27 E
173	Kachuga (kȧ-chōō-gȧ). Sov. Un.	54·09 N	105·43 E
167	Kadiyevka (kȧ-dĭ-yĕf′kȧ). Sov. Un.	48·34 N	38·37 E
170	Kadnikov (käd′nê-kôf). Sov. Un.	59·30 N	40·10 E
195	Kadoma. Jap. (Ōsaka In.)	34·43 N	135·36 E
215	Kaduna (kä-dōō′nä). Nig.	10·33 N	7·27 E
215	Kaduna (R.). Nig.	9·30 N	6·00 E
214	Kaédi (kä-ā-dē′). Mauritania	16·09 N	13·30 W
100	Kaena Pt. (kä′ȧ-nä). Hi.	21·33 N	158·19 W
194	Kaesŏng (Kaijo) (kä′ĕ-sŭng) (kī′jō). Kor.	38·00 N	126·35 E
215	Kafancńan. Nig.	9·36 N	8·17 E
211	Kafia Kingi (kä′fê-ȧ kĭŋ′gê). Sud.	9·17 N	24·28 E
212	Kafue (kä′fōō). Zambia	15·45 S	28·17 E
217	Kafue (R.). Zambia	15·45 S	26·30 E
217	Kafue Flats (Pln.). Zambia	16·15 S	26·30 E
217	Kafue Natl. Pk. Zambia	15·00 S	25·35 E
217	Kafwira. Zaire	12·10 S	27·33 E
167	Kagal'nik (R.) (kä-gäl″nêk) Sov. Un.	46·58 N	39·25 E
217	Kagera (R.) (kä-gā′rȧ). Tan.	1·10 S	31·10 E
195	Kagoshima (kä′gô-shē′mȧ). Jap.	31·35 N	130·31 E
195	Kagoshima-Wan (B.) (kä′gô-shē′mä wän). Jap.	31·24 N	130·39 E
167	Kagul (ka-gŏŏl′). Sov. Un.	45·49 N	28·17 E
196	Kahayan (R.). Indon.	1·45 S	113·40 E
216	Kahemba. Zaire	7·17 S	19·00 E
217	Kahia. Zaire	6·21 S	28·24 E
117	Kahoka (kȧ-hō′kȧ). Mo.	40·26 N	91·42 W
100	Kahoolawe (I) (kä-hōō-lä′wē). Hi.	20·28 N	156·48 W
214	Kahoué, Mont (Mtn.) Ivory Coast	7·06 N	7·15 W
109	Kahshahpiwi (R.). Can.	48·24 N	90·56 W
100	Kahuku Pt. (kä-hōō′kōō). Hi.	21·50 N	157·50 W
100	Kahului. Hi.	20·53 N	156·28 W
197	Kai, Kepulauan (Is.). Indon.	5·35 S	132·45 E
183	Kaiang. Mala. (Singapore In.)	3·00 N	101·47 E
96	Kaiashk (R.). Can.	49·40 N	89·30 W
115	Kaibab Ind. Res. (kä′ē-bȧb). Az.	36·55 N	112·45 W
115	Kaibab Plat. Az.	36·30 N	112·10 W
135	Kaieteur Fall (kī-ĕ-tōōr′). Guy.	4·48 N	59·24 W
190	K'aifeng (käī′fĕng). China	34·48 N	114·22 E
	Kaijo, see Kaesong		
197	Kai Kecil (I.). Indon.	5·45 S	132·40 E
169	Kaikyō, Sōya (Str.) (sô′yȧ kȧ-ē′kĭ-ô). Sov. Un.	45·45 N	141·20 E
100	Kailua (kä′ē-lōō′ä). Hi.	21·18 N	157·43 W
100	Kailua Kona. Hi.	19·49 N	155·59 W
197	Kaimana. Indon.	3·32 S	133·47 E
195	Kainan (kä′ē-nȧn′). Jap.	34·09 N	135·14 E
215	Kainji L. Nig.	10·25 N	4·50 E
190	Kaip'ing (kī-pĭng′). China	40·25 N	122·20 E
158	Kaiserslautern (kī-zĕrs-lou′tĕrn) F.R.G.	49·26 N	7·46 E
205	Kaitaia (kä-ê-tä′ê-ȧ). N. Z. (In.)	35·30 S	173·28 E
100	Kaiwi Chan (kä′ê-wē). Hi.	21·10 N	157·38 W
193	Kaiyüan (kī′yōō-än′). China	23·42 N	103·20 E
192	Kaiyuan (kī′yōō-än′). China	42·30 N	124·00 E
101	Kaiyuh Mts. (kī-yōō′). Ak.	64·25 N	157·38 W
150	Kajaani (kä′yȧ-nê). Fin.	64·15 N	27·16 E
183	Kajang, Gunong (Mt.) Mala. (Singapore In.)	2·47 N	104·05 E
195	Kajiki (kä′jē-kê). Jap.	31·44 N	130·41 E
167	Kakhovka (kä-Kôf′kȧ). Sov. Un.	46·46 N	33·32 E
167	Kakhovskoye (L.) (kȧ-Kôf′skô-yĕ) Sov. Un.	47·21 N	33·33 E
187	Kākināda. India	16·58 N	82·18 E
101	Kaktovik (kăk-tō′vĭk). Ak.	70·08 N	143·51 W
93	Kakwa (R.) (kăk′wȧ). Can.	54·00 N	118·55 W
171	Kalach (kȧ-lȧch′). Sov. Un.	50·15 N	40·55 E
188	Kaladan (R.). Bur.	21·07 N	93·04 E
212	Kalahari Des. (kä-lä-hä′rê). Bots.	23·00 S	22·03 E
112	Kalama (kȧ-lăm′ȧ) Wa. (Portland In.)	46·01 N	122·50 W
112	Kalama (R.). Wa. (Portland In.)	46·03 N	122·47 W
165	Kalámai (kä-lä-mī′). Grc.	37·04 N	22·08 E
104	Kalamazoo (kăl-ȧ-mȧ-zōō′). Mi.	42·20 N	85·40 W
104	Kalamazoo (R.). Mi.	42·35 N	86·00 W
167	Kalanchak (kä-län-chäk′) Sov. Un.	46·17 N	33·14 E
100	Kalapana (kä-lä-pȧ′nä). Hi.	19·25 N	155·00 W
186	Kalar (Mtn.). Iran	31·43 N	51·41 E
184	Kalāt (kŭ-lät′). Pak.	29·05 N	66·36 E
196	Kalatoa (I.). Indon.	7·22 S	122·30 E
161	Kaldenkirchen (käl′dĕn-kēr-Kĕn) F.R.G. (Ruhr In.)	51·19 N	6·13 E
217	Kalemie (Albertville). Zaire	5·56 S	29·12 E
192	Kalgan (käl-gän′). China	40·45 N	114·58 E
204	Kalgoorlie (kăl-gōōr′lê). Austl.	30·45 S	121·35 E
153	Kaliakra, Nos (Pt.). Rom.	43·25 N	28·42 E
217	Kalima. Zaire	2·34 S	26·37 E
166	Kalinin (Tver) (kä-lê′nên) (tvĕr). Sov. Un.	56·52 N	35·57 E
166	Kalinin (Oblast). Sov. Un.	56·50 N	33·08 E
157	Kaliningrad (Königsberg) (kä-lĕ-nēn′grät) (kû′nĕks-bĕrgh) Sov. Un.	54·42 N	20·32 E
174	Kaliningrad (kä-lê-nēn′grät) Sov. Un. (Moscow In.)	55·55 N	37·49 E
167	Kalinkovichi (kä-lēn-ko-vē′chê) Sov. Un.	52·07 N	29·19 E
110	Kalispel Ind. Res. (kăl-ĭ-spĕl′). Wa.	48·25 N	117·30 W
111	Kalispell (kăl′ĭ-spĕl). Mt.	48·12 N	114·18 W
159	Kalisz (kä′lēsh). Pol.	51·45 N	18·05 E
217	Kaliua. Tan.	5·04 S	31·48 E
150	Kalix (R.) (kä′lēks). Swe.	67·12 N	21·41 E
156	Kalmar (käl′mär). Swe.	56·40 N	16·19 E
156	Kalmar Sund (Sd.) (käl′mär). Swe.	56·30 N	16·17 E
167	Kal'mius (R.) (käl″myōōs) Sov. Un.	47·15 N	37·38 E
149	Kalmthout. Bel. (Brussels In.)	51·23 N	4·28 E
171	Kalmyk A. S. S. R. (kȧl′mĭk) Sov. Un.	46·56 N	46·00 E
159	Kalocsa (kä′lô-chä). Hung.	46·32 N	19·00 E
100	Kalohi Chan. (kä-lō′hĭ). Hi.	20·55 N	157·15 W
217	Kaloko. Zaire	6·47 S	25·48 E
217	Kalomo (kä-lō′mō). Zambia	17·02 S	26·30 E
184	Kalsubai Mt. India	24·43 N	73·47 E
149	Kaltenkirchen (käl′tĕn-kēr-Kĕn) F.R.G. (Hamburg In.)	53·50 N	9·57 E
185	Kālu (R.). India (In.)	19·18 N	73·14 E
166	Kaluga (kȧ-lŏŏ′gä). Sov. Un.	54·29 N	36·12 E
166	Kaluga (Oblast). Sov. Un.	54·10 N	34·30 E
156	Kalundborg (kȧ-lŏŏn″bôr′). Den.	55·42 N	11·07 E
159	Kalush (kä′lŏŏsh). Sov. Un.	49·02 N	24·24 E
157	Kalvarija (käl-vä-rē′yȧ). Sov. Un.	54·24 N	23·17 E
185	Kalwa. India (Bombay In.)	19·12 N	72·59 E
174	Kal'ya (käl′yȧ) Sov. Un. (Urals In.)	60·17 N	59·58 E
185	Kalyān. India (In.)	19·16 N	73·07 E
166	Kalyazin (käl-yȧ′zēn). Sov. Un.	57·13 N	37·55 E
173	Kalyma (R.). Sov. Un.	66·32 N	152·46 E
170	Kama (L.). Sov. Un.	55·28 N	51·00 E
170	Kama (R.) (kä′mä). Sov. Un.	56·10 N	53·50 E
194	Kamaishi (kä′mä-ē′shê). Jap.	39·16 N	142·03 E
195	Kamakura (kä′mä-kōō′rä) Jap. (Tōkyō In.)	35·19 N	139·33 E
186	Kamarān (I.). P. D. R. of Yem.	15·19 N	41·47 E
184	Kāmārhāti. India (In.)	22·41 N	88·23 E
212	Kambove (käm-bō′vĕ). Zaire	10·58 S	26·43 E
173	Kamchatka, P-Ov (Pen.). Sov. Un.	55·19 N	157·45 E
173	Kamchatka (R.). Sov. Un.	54·15 N	158·38 E
161	Kamen (kä′mĕn) F.R.G. (Ruhr In.)	51·35 N	7·40 E
167	Kamenets-Podol skiy (kȧ-mă′nĕts pô-dôl′skĭ). Sov. Un.	48·41 N	26·34 E
164	Kamenjak, Rt (C.) (Kä′mĕ-nyäk) Yugo.	44·45 N	13·57 E
167	Kamenka (kä-mĕŋ′kȧ). Sov. Un.	48·02 N	28·43 E
159	Kamenka. Sov. Un.	50·06 N	24·20 E
172	Kamen'-na-Obi (kä-mĭny′nŭ ô′bē) Sov. Un.	53·43 N	81·28 E
167	Kamensk-Shakhtinskiy (kä′mĕnsk shäk′tĭn-skĭ). Sov. Un.	48·17 N	40·16 E
174	Kamensk-Ural'skiy (kä′mĕn-skĭ ōō-räl′skĭ). Sov. Un. (Urals In.)	56·27 N	61·55 E
158	Kamenz (kä′mĕnts). G.D.R.	51·16 N	14·05 E
195	Kameoka (kä′mā-ōkä) Jap. (Ōsaka In.)	35·01 N	135·35 E
184	Kȧmet (Mt.). India	35·50 N	79·42 E
158	Kamień Pomorski. Pol.	53·57 N	14·48 E
195	Kamikoma (kä′mê-kō′mä) Jap. (Ōsaka In.)	34·45 N	135·50 E
216	Kamina. Zaire	8·44 S	25·00 E
109	Kaministikwia (R.) (kȧ-mĭ-nĭ-stĭk′wĭ-ȧ). Can.	48·40 N	89·41 W
217	Kamituga. Zaire	3·04 S	28·11 E
93	Kamloops (kăm′lōōps). Can.	50·40 N	120·20 W
	Kammer, see Atter See		
184	Kampa Dzong. China	28·23 N	89·42 E
217	Kampala (käm-pä′lä). Ug.	0·19 N	32·25 E
196	Kampar-Kiri (R.) (käm′pär) Indon.	0·30 N	101·30 E
149	Kampenhout. Bel. (Brussels In.)	50·56 N	4·33 E
161	Kamp-Lintfort (kämp-lēnt′fōrt) F.R.G. (Ruhr In.)	51·30 N	6·34 E
196	Kampot (käm′pōt). Camb.	10·41 N	104·07 E
158	Kamp R. (kămp). Aus.	48·30 N	15·45 E
216	Kampene. Zaire	3·36 S	26·40 E
95	Kamsack (kăm′săk). Can.	51·34 N	101·54 W
141	Kamskoye (Res.). Sov. Un.	59·08 N	56·30 E
174	Kamskoye Vdkhr. (Res.) Sov. Un. (Urals In.)	59·03 N	56·48 E
217	Kamudilo. Zaire	7·42 S	27·18 E
100	Kamuela. Hi.	20·01 N	155·40 W
127	Kamuk, Cerro (Mt.) (sĕ′r-rô-kä-mōō′k). C. R.	9·18 N	83·02 W
194	Kamu Misaki (C.) (kä′mōō mê-sä′kē). Jap.	43·25 N	139·35 E
167	Kamyshevatskaya (kȧ-mwēsh′ĕ-vät′skä-yȧ). Sov. Un.	46·24 N	37·58 E
171	Kamyshin (kä-mwēsh′ĭn). Sov. Un.	50·08 N	45·20 E
170	Kamyshlov (kä-mēsh′lôf) Sov. Un.	56·50 N	62·32 E
193	Kan (R.) (kän). China	26·50 N	115·00 E
172	Kan (R.). Sov. Un.	56·30 N	94·17 E
115	Kanab (kăn′ăb). Ut.	37·00 N	112·30 W
115	Kanab Plat. Az.	36·31 N	112·55 W
174	Kanabeki (kȧ-nä′byĕ-kĭ) Sov. Un. (Urals In.)	57·48 N	57·16 E
101	Kanaga (I.) (kă-nă′gă). Ak.	52·02 N	117·38 W
195	Kanagawa (Pref.) (kä′nä-gä′wä) Jap. (Tōkyō In.)	35·29 N	139·32 E
195	Kanamachi (kä-nä-mä′chē) Jap. (Tōkyō In.)	35·46 N	139·52 E
216	Kananga (Luluabourg) (lōō′lōō-a-bŏŏrg′). Zaire	6·14 S	22·17 E
174	Kananikol'skoye (kȧ-nȧ-nĭ-kôl′ skô-yĕ). Sov. Un. (Urals In.)	52·48 N	57·29 E
126	Kanasín (kä-nä-sē′n). Mex. (In.)	20·54 N	89·31 W
101	Kanatak (kă-nă′tŏk). Ak.	57·35 N	155·48 W
103	Kanawha (R.) (kȧ-nô′wȧ). U. S.	37·55 N	81·50 W
195	Kanaya (kä-nä′yä) Jap. (Tōkyō In.)	35·10 N	139·49 E
153	Kanayis, Rasel (C.). Egypt	31·14 N	28·08 E
195	Kanazawa (kä′nȧ-zä′wȧ). Jap.	36·34 N	136·38 E
184	Kānchenjunga (Mtn.) (kĭn-chĭn-jŏŏn′gȧ). India-Nep.	27·30 N	88·18 E
185	Kānchipuram. India	12·55 N	79·43 E
193	Kanchou (kăn′chou). China	25·50 N	114·30 E
216	Kanda Kanda (kän′dȧ kän′dȧ) Zaire	6·56 S	23·36 E
170	Kandalaksha (kȧn-dȧ-lȧk′shȧ) Sov. Un.	67·10 N	33·05 E
170	Kandalakshskiy Zaliv (B.) Sov. Un.	66·20 N	35·00 E
157	Kandava (kän′dȧ-vȧ). Sov. Un.	57·03 N	22·45 E
215	Kandi (käN-dē′). Benin	11·08 N	2·56 E
184	Kandiāro. Pak.	27·09 N	68·12 E
184	Kandla (kŭnd′lŭ). India	23·00 N	70·20 E
185	Kandy (kän′dê). Sri Lanka	7·18 N	80·42 E
105	Kane (kān). Pa.	41·40 N	78·50 W
100	Kaneohe (kä-nā-ō′hā). Hi.	21·25 N	157·47 W
100	Kaneohe B. Hi.	21·32 N	157·40 W
167	Kanëv (kä-nyôf′). Sov. Un.	49·46 N	31·27 E
167	Kanevskaya (kȧ-nyĕf′skȧ) Sov. Un.	46·07 N	38·58 E
171	Kanevskoye Vdkhr (Res.) Sov. Un.	50·10 N	30·40 E
203	Kangaroo (I.) (kăŋ-gȧ-rŏŏ′). Austl.	36·05 S	137·05 E
186	Kangāvar (kŭŋ′gā-vär). Iran	34·37 N	46·45 E
196	Kangean, Kepulauan (I.) (käŋ′gê-än). Indon.	6·50 S	116·22 E

ăt; finăl; rāte; senâte; ärm; ȧsk; sofȧ; fâre; ch-choose; dh-as th in other; bē; êvent; bĕt; recĕnt; cratẽr; g-go; gh-guttural g; bĭt; ĭ-short neutral; rīde; K-guttural k as ch in German ich;

PRONOUNCING INDEX

Kanggye — Kellinghusen 297

Page	Name Pronunciation Region	Lat. °′	Long. °′
194	Kanggye (käng′gyĕ) Kor.	40·55 N	126·40 E
194	Kanghwa (I.) (käng′hwä) Kor.	37·38 N	126·00 E
194	Kangnŭng′nōōng) Kor.	37·42 N	128·50 E
216	Kango (käN-gō) Gabon	0·09 N	10·08 E
216	Kangowa Zaire	9·55 S	22·48 E
188	K′angting China	30·15 N	101·58 E
170	Kanin, P-Ov. (Pen.) (kȧ-nēn′) Sov. Un.	68·00 N	45·00 E
170	Kanin Nos, Mys (G.) Sov. Un.	68·40 N	44·00 E
217	Kaningo Ken.	0·49 S	38·32 E
165	Kanjiža (kä′nyē-zhä) Yugo.	46·05 N	20·02 E
107	Kankakee (kăŋ-kȧ-kē′) Il. (Chicago In.)	41·07 N	87·53 W
104	Kankakee (R.) Il.	41·15 N	88·15 W
214	Kankan (käN-käN) (kän-kän′) Gui	10·23 N	9·18 W
192	Kannan China	47·50 N	123·30 E
121	Kannapolis (kăn-ăp′ō-lĭs) NC	35·30 N	80·38 W
195	Kannoura (kä′nō-ōō′rä) Jap.	33·34 N	134·18 E
215	Kano (kä′nō) Nig.	12·00 N	8·30 E
212	Kanonkop (Mtn.) S. Afr. (In.)	33·49 S	18·37 E
116	Kanopolis Res. (kăn-ŏp′ō-lĭs) Ks.	38·44 N	98·01 W
184	Kānpur (kän′pûr) India	26·00 N	82·45 E
102	Kansas (State) (kăn′zȧs) U. S.	38·30 N	99·40 W
117	Kansas (R.) Ks.	39·08 N	95·52 W
113	Kansas City. Ks. (Kansas City In.)	39·06 N	94·39 W
113	Kansas City. Mo. (Kansas City In.)	39·05 N	94·35 W
172	Kansk Sov. Un.	56·14 N	95·43 E
194	Kansŏng Kor.	38·09 N	128·29 E
188	Kansu (Prov.) (kän-sōō′) China	39·30 N	101·30 E
196	Kan Tang (kän′täng′) Thai.	7·26 N	99·28 E
214	Kantchari Upper Volta	12·29 N	1·31 E
126	Kantunilkin (kän-tōō-nēl-kē′n) Mex. (In.)	21·07 N	87·30 W
174	Kanzhakovskiy Kamen Gora (kȧn-zhă′kôvs-kēē kămĭen) Sov. Un. (Urals In.)	59·38 N	59·12 E
193	Kaoan China	28·30 N	115·02 E
190	Kaoch′eng (kä′ō-chĕng′) China	34·56 N	114·57 E
191	Kaoch′iao...China (Shanghai In.)	31·21 N	121·35 E
193	Kaohsiung (kä-ō-syŏōng′) Taiwan	22·35 N	120·25 E
190	Kaoi (gou′yē) China	37·37 N	114·39 E
214	Kaolack Senegal	14·09 N	16·04 W
190	Kaomi (gou′mē) China	36·23 N	119·46 E
190	Kaoshun (gou′shōōn) China	31·22 N	118·50 E
190	Kaot′ang (kä′ō-täng′) China	36·52 N	116·12 E
193	Kaoteng Shan (Mtns.) China	26·30 N	110·00 E
211	Kaouar (Oasis) Niger	19·16 N	13·09 E
193	Kaoyao China	23·08 N	112·25 E
190	Kaoyu (gou′yü) Chiua	32·46 N	119·26 E
193	Kaoyu Hu (L.) (kä′ō-yōō′hōō) China	32·42 N	118·40 E
100	Kapaa Hi.	22·06 N	159·20 W
172	Kapal (kȧ-päl′) Sov. Un.	45·13 N	79·08 E
216	Kapanga Zaire	8·21 S	22·35 E
183	Kapchagay Sov. Un.	43·55 N	77·45 E
158	Kapfenberg (kȧp′fĕn-bĕrgh) Aus.	47·27 N	15·16 E
217	Kapiri Mposhi Zambia	13·58 S	28·41 E
211	Kapoeta Sud.	4·45 N	33·35 E
159	Kaposvár (kô′pôsh-vär) Hung.	46·21 N	17·45 E
194	Kapsan (käp′sän′) Kor.	40·59 N	128·22 E
196	Kapuas (Strm.) (kä′pōō-äs) Indon.	2·05 S	114·15 E
91	Kapuskasing Can.	49·28 N	82·22 W
96	Kapuskasing (R.) Can.	48·55 N	82·55 W
171	Kapustin Yar (kä′pōōs-tēn yär′) Sov. Un.	48·30 N	45·40 E
203	Kaputar, Mt. (kă-pû-tăr) Austl.	30·11 S	150·11 E
158	Kapuvár (kô′pōō-vär) Hung.	47·35 N	17·02 E
172	Kara (kärȧ) Sov. Un.	68·42 N	65·30 E
170	Kara (R.) Sov. Un.	68·30 N	65·20 E
174	Karabanovo (kä′rȧ-bȧ-nō-vô) Sov. Un. (Moscow In.)	56·19 N	38·43 E
174	Karabash (kô-rȧ-bäsh′) Sov. Un. (Urals In.)	55·27 N	60·14 E
171	Kara-Bogaz-Gol, Zaliv (B.) (kȧrȧ′ bŭ-gäs′) Sov. Un.	41·30 N	53·40 E
166	Karachev (kȧ-rȧ-chôf′) Sov. Un.	53·08 N	34·54 E
184	Karāchi Pak.	24·59 N	68·56 E
147	Karacumy (Des.) Sov. Un.	39·08 N	59·53 E
172	Karaganda (kȧ-rȧ-gän′dä) Sov. Un.	49·42 N	73·18 E
174	Karaidel (kä′rī-dĕl) Sov. Un. (Urals In.)	55·52 N	56·54 E
171	Kara-Khobda (R.) (kä-rä kôb′dȧ) Sov. Un.	50·40 N	55·00 E
187	Karakoram Pass India-Pak.	35·35 N	77·45 E
188	Karakoram Ra. (kä′rä kō′rōōm) India-Pak.	35·24 N	76·38 E
188	Karakorum (Ruins) Mong.	47·25 N	102·22 E
171	Karaköse (kä-rä-kŭ′sĕ) Tur.	39·50 N	43·10 E
168	Karakumy (kara-kum) (Des.) Sov. Un.	40·00 N	57·00 E
171	Karaman (kä-rä-män′) Tur.	37·10 N	33·00 E
205	Karamea Bght. (kȧ-rȧ-mē′ȧ bĭt) N. Z. (In.)	41·10 S	170·42 E
	Kara Sea, see Karskoye More		
195	Karatsu (kä′rȧ-tsōō) Jap.	33·28 N	129·59 E
172	Karaul (kä-rä-ōōl′) Sov. Un.	70·13 N	83·46 E
158	Karawanken Mts. Aus.	46·32 N	14·07 E
186	Karbalā′ (kŭr′bȧ-lä) Iraq	32·31 N	43·58 E
159	Karcag (kär′tsäg) Hung.	47·18 N	20·58 E
165	Kardhítsa Grc.	39·23 N	21·57 E
157	Kärdla (kĕrd′lȧ) Sov. Un.	58·59 N	22·44 E
168	Karelian (A. S. S. R.) Sov. Un.	62·30 N	32·35 E
217	Karema Tan.	6·49 S	30·26 E
172	Kargat (kär-gät′) Sov. Un.	55·17 N	80·07 E
	Karghalik, see Yehch′eng		
170	Kargopol′ (kär-gō-pōl′′) Sov. Un.	61·30 N	38·50 E
165	Kariaí Grc.	40·14 N	24·15 E
217	Kariba, L. Afr.	17·15 S	27·55 E
212	Karibib (kär′ȧ-bĭb) Namibia	21·55 S	15·50 E
185	Kārikāl (kä-rê-käl′) India	10·58 N	79·49 E
196	Karimata, Pulau-Pulau (Is.) (kä-rê-mä′tȧ) Indon.	1·08 S	108·10 E
196	Karimata, Selat (Str.) Indon.	1·15 S	107·10 E
183	Karimun Besar (I.) Indon. (Singapore In.)	1·10 N	103·28 E
196	Karimunjawa, Kepulauan (Is.) (kä′rê-mōōn-yä′vä) Indon.	5·36 S	110·15 E
218	Karin (kȧr′ĭn) Som. (Horn of Afr. In.)	10·43 N	45·50 E
197	Karkar (I.) (kär′kär) Pap. N. Gui.	4·50 S	146·45 E
172	Karkaralinsk (kär-kär-ä-lĕnsk′) Sov. Un.	49·18 N	75·28 E
186	Karkheh (R.) Iran	32·45 N	47·50 E
167	Karkinitskiy Zailv (B.) (kär-kê-net′skĭ-ē zä′lĭf) Sov. Un.	45·50 N	32·45 E
158	Karl-Marx-Stadt (Chemnitz) G.D.R.	50·48 N	12·53 E
185	Karnataka (State) India	14·55 N	75·00 E
164	Karlobag (kär-lō-bäg′) Yugo.	44·30 N	15·03 E
164	Karlovac (kär′lō-vȧts) Yugo.	45·29 N	15·16 E
167	Karlovka (kȧr′lôv-kȧ) Sov. Un.	49·26 N	35·08 E
165	Karlovo (kär′lô-vō) Bul.	42·39 N	24·48 E
158	Karlovy Vary (kär′lô-vê vä′rê) Czech.	50·13 N	12·53 E
156	Karlshamn (kärls′häm) Swe.	56·11 N	14·50 E
156	Karlskrona (kärls′krō-nä) Swe.	56·10 N	15·33 E
158	Karlsruhe (kärls′rōō-ĕ) F.R.G.	49·00 N	8·23 E
156	Karlstad (kärl′städ) Swe.	59·25 N	13·28 E
101	Karluk (kär′lŭk) Ak.	57·30 N	154·22 W
156	Karmöy (I.) (kärm-ûe) Nor.	59·14 N	5·00 E
165	Karnobat (kär-nô′bät) Bul.	42·39 N	26·59 E
158	Kärnten (Carinthia) (State) (kĕrn′tĕn) Aus.	46·55 N	13·42 E
212	Karonga (kȧ-rōŋ′gȧ) Malawi	9·52 S	33·57 E
153	Kárpathos (I.) Grc.	35·34 N	27·26 E
174	Karpinsk (kär′pĭnsk) Sov. Un. (Urals In.)	59·46 N	60·00 E
171	Kars (kärs) Tur.	40·35 N	43·00 E
172	Karsakpay (kär-säk-pī′) Sov. Un.	47·47 N	67·07 E
166	Kārsava (kär′sä-vä) Sov. Un.	56·46 N	27·39 E
187	Karshi (kär′shē) Sov. Un.	38·30 N	66·08 E
172	Karskiye Vorota, Proliv (Str.) Sov. Un.	70·30 N	58·07 E
172	Karskoye More (Kara Sea) Sov. Un.	74·00 N	68·00 E
174	Kartaly (kȧr′tá lê) Sov. Un. (Urals In.)	53·05 N	60·40 E
185	Karunagapalli India	9·09 N	76·34 E
159	Karvina Czech.	49·50 N	18·30 E
92	Kasaan Ak.	55·32 N	132·24 E
216	Kasai (R.) Zaire	3·45 S	19·10 E
217	Kasama (kȧ-sä′mȧ) Zambia	10·13 S	31·12 E
217	Kasanga (kȧ-säŋ′gȧ) Tan.	8·28 S	31·09 E
195	Kasaoka (kä′sȧ-ō′kȧ) Jap.	34·33 N	133·29 E
210	Kasba-Tadla (käs′bȧ-täd′lȧ) Mor.	32·37 N	5·57 W
217	Kasempa (kȧ-sĕm′pȧ) Zambia	13·27 S	25·50 E
217	Kasenga (kȧ-seŋ′gȧ) Zaire	10·22 S	28·38 E
217	Kasese Ug.	0·10 N	30·05 E
217	Kasese Zaire	1·38 S	27·07 E
186	Kāshān (kä-shän′) Iran	33·52 N	51·15 E
	Kashgar, see K′ashih		
188	K′ashih (Kashgar) China	39·29 N	76·00 E
195	Kashihara (kä′shê-hä′rä) Jap. (Ōsaka In.)	34·31 N	135·48 E
216	Kashiji Pln. Zambia	13·25 S	22·30 E
166	Kashin (kä-shēn′) Sov. Un.	57·20 N	37·38 E
166	Kashira (kä-shē′rȧ) Sov. Un.	54·49 N	38·11 E
195	Kashiwa (kä′shê-wä) Jap. (Tōkyō In.)	35·51 N	139·58 E
195	Kashiwara Jap. (Ōsaka In.)	34·35 N	135·38 E
170	Kashiwazaki (kä′shē-wä-zä′kê) Jap.	37·06 N	138·17 E
	Kashmir (Disputed Reg.) see Jammu and Kashmir		
184	Kashmor Pak.	28·33 N	69·34 E
174	Kashtak (käsh′tȧk) Sov. Un. (Urals In.)	55·18 N	61·25 E
166	Kasimov (kȧ-sē′môf) Sov. Un.	54·56 N	41·23 E
101	Kaskanak (kăs-kă′năk) Ak.	60·00 N	158·00 W
104	Kaskaskia (R.) (kăs-kăs′kĭ-ȧ) Il.	39·10 N	88·50 W
95	Kaskattama (R.) (kăs-kȧ-tä′mȧ) Can.	56·28 N	90·55 W
	Kaskinen, see Kaskö		
157	Kaskö (Kaskinen) (käs′kû) (käs′kē-nĕn) Fin.	62·24 N	21·18 E
174	Kasli (käs′lĭ) Sov. Un. (Urals In.)	55·54 N	60·46 E
212	Kasongo (kä-sôŋ′gō) Zaire	4·31 S	26·42 E
153	Kásos (I.) Grc.	35·20 N	26·55 E
211	Kassalā (kä-sä′lä) Sud.	15·26 N	36·28 E
158	Kassel (käs′ĕl) F.R.G.	51·19 N	9·30 E
109	Kasson (kăs′ŭn) Mn.	44·01 N	92·45 W
171	Kastamonu (kä-stȧ-mō′nōō) Tur.	41·20 N	33·50 E
164	Kastélli Grc. (In.)	35·13 N	24·11 E
153	Kastellórizon (C.) Tur.	36·01 N	30·00 E
165	Kastoría (kás-tō′rĭ-ȧ) Grc.	40·28 N	21·17 E
165	Kastron (käs′trôn) Grc.	39·52 N	25·01 E
184	Kasūr Pak.	31·10 N	74·29 E
216	Kataba Zambia	16·05 S	25·10 E
98	Katahdin, Mt. (kȧ-tä′dĭn) Me.	45·56 N	68·57 W
212	Katanga (Reg.) (kȧ-täŋ′gȧ) Zaire	8·30 S	25·00 E
204	Katanning (kȧ-tăn′ĭng) Austl.	33·45 S	117·45 E
174	Katav-Ivanovsk (kä′tȧf ĭ-vä′nôfsk) Sov. Un. (Urals In.)	54·46 N	58·13 E
174	Kateninskiy (kȧtyĕ′nĭs-kĭ) Sov. Un. (Urals In.)	53·12 N	61·05 E
165	Kateríni Grc.	40·18 N	22·36 E
217	Katete Zambia	14·05 S	32·07 E
204	Katherine (kăth′ēr-ĭn) Austl.	14·15 S	132·20 E
184	Kāthiāwār (Pen.) (kä′tyȧ-wär′) India	22·10 N	70·20 E
184	Kathmandu (kăt-măn-dōō′). Nep.	27·49 N	85·21 E
89	Kathryn (kăth′rĭn) Can. (Calgary In.)	51·13 N	113·42 W
113	Kathryn Ca. (Los Angeles In.)	33·42 N	117·45 W
184	Katihār India	25·39 N	87·39 E
214	Katiola Ivory Coast	8·08 N	5·06 W
101	Katmai Natl. Mon. (kăt′mī) Ak.	58·38 N	155·00 W
217	Katompi Zaire	6·11 S	26·20 E
216	Katopa Zaire	2·45 S	25·06 E
159	Katowice Pol.	50·15 N	19·00 E
211	Katrinah, Jabal (Mtn.) Egypt	28·43 N	34·00 E
156	Katrineholm (kȧ-trē′nĕ-hōlm) Swe.	59·01 N	16·10 E
174	Katsbakhskiy (kȧts-bäk′skĭ) Sov. Un. (Urals In.)	52·57 N	59·37 E
215	Katsina (kät′sê-nȧ) Nig.	13·00 N	7·32 E
195	Katsura (R.) (kä′tsōō-rä) Jap. (Ōsaka In.)	34·55 N	135·43 E
172	Katta-Kurgan (kȧ-tȧ-kōōr-gän′) Sov. Un.	39·45 N	66·42 E
156	Kattegat (Str.) (kăt′ĕ-gät) Eur.	56·57 N	11·25 E
217	Katumba Zaire	7·45 S	25·18 E
172	Katun′ (R.) (kȧ-tōōn′) Sov. Un.	51·30 N	86·18 E
149	Katwijkaan Zee Neth. (Amsterdam In.)	52·12 N	4·23 E
100	Kauai (I.) Hi.	22·09 N	159·15 W
100	Kauai Chan. (kä-ōō-ä′ê) Hi.	21·35 N	158·52 W
158	Kaufbeuren (kouf′boi-rĕn) F.R.G.	47·52 N	10·38 E
119	Kaufman (kôf′mǎn) Tx.	32·36 N	96·18 W
109	Kaukauna (kô-kô′nȧ) Wi.	44·17 N	88·15 W
100	Kaulakahi Chan. (kä′ōō-lȧ-kä′hê) Hi.	22·00 N	159·55 W
100	Kaunakakai (kä′ōō-nȧ-kä′kī) Hi.	21·06 N	156·59 W
157	Kaunas (Kovno) (kou′nȧs) (kôv′nô) Sov. Un.	54·52 N	23·54 E
215	Kaura Namoda Nig.	12·35 N	6·35 E
165	Kavajë (kȧ-vä′yŭ) Alb.	41·11 N	19·36 E
165	Kavála (kä-vä′lä) Grc.	40·55 N	24·24 E
165	Kavallas, Kólpos (G.) Grc.	40·45 N	24·20 E
197	Kavieng (kä-vê-ĕng′) Pap. N. Gui.	2·44 S	151·02 E
195	Kawagoe (kä-wă-gō′â) Jap. (Tōkyō In.)	35·55 N	139·29 E
195	Kawaguchi (kä-wä-gōō-chē) Jap. (Tōkyō In.)	35·48 N	139·44 E
100	Kawaikini (Mtn.) (kä-wä′ê-kĭ-nĭ) Hi.	22·05 N	159·33 W
195	Kawanishi (kä-wä′nê-shē) Jap. (Ōsaka In.)	34·49 N	135·26 E
195	Kawasaki (kä-wä-sä′kê) Jap. (Tōkyō In.)	35·32 N	139·43 E
218	Kawm Umbū Egypt (Nile In.)	24·30 N	32·59 E
214	Kaya (kä′yä) Upper Volta	13·05 N	1·05 W
196	Kayan, Selat (Strm.) Indon.	1·45 N	115·38 E
111	Kaycee (kā-sē′) Wy.	43·43 N	106·38 W
214	Kayes (kāz) Mali	14·27 N	11·26 W
171	Kayseri (kī′sĕ-rē) Tur.	38·45 N	35·20 E
113	Kaysville (kāz′vĭl) Ut. (Salt Lake City In.)	41·02 N	111·56 W
173	Kazach′ye Sov. Un.	70·46 N	135·47 E
168	Kazakh S.S.R. (kȧ-zäk′) Sov. Un.	48·45 N	59·00 E
170	Kazan′ (kȧ-zän′) Sov. Un.	55·50 N	49·18 E
167	Kazanka (kȧ-zän′kȧ) Sov. Un.	47·49 N	32·50 E
165	Kazanlŭk (kȧ′zȧn-lĕk) Bul.	42·47 N	25·23 E
167	Kazatin Sov. Un.	49·43 N	28·50 E
171	Kazbek, Gora (Mt.) (kȧz-bĕk′) Sov. Un.	42·45 N	44·30 E
186	Kāzerūn Iran	29·37 N	51·44 E
159	Kazincbarcika (kô′zĭnts-bôr-tsĭ-ko) Hung.	48·15 N	20·39 E
217	Kazungula Zambia	17·45 S	25·20 E
195	Kazusa Kameyama (kä-zōō-sä kä-mȧ′yä-mä) Jap. (Tōkyō In.)	35·14 N	140·06 E
172	Kazym (R.) (kä-zēm′) Sov. Un.	63·30 N	67·41 E
165	Kéa (I.) Grc.	37·36 N	24·13 E
100	Kealaikahiki Chan. (kā-ä′lä-ê-kä-hē′kē) Hi.	20·38 N	157·00 W
106	Keansburg (kēnz′bûrg) NJ (New York In.)	40·26 N	74·08 W
116	Kearney (kär′nĭ) Ne.	40·42 N	99·05 W
106	Kearny NJ (New York In.)	40·46 N	74·09 W
112	Keasey (kēz′ĭ) Or. (Portland In.)	45·51 N	123·20 W
171	Keban Gölü (L.) Tur.	38·20 N	39·50 E
150	Kebnekaise Mt. (kĕp′nĕ-kȧ-ēs′ĕ) Swe.	67·53 N	18·10 E
159	Kecskemét (kĕch′kĕ-māt) Hung.	46·52 N	19·42 E
196	Kedah State (kā′dä) Mala.	6·08 N	100·31 E
157	Kėdainiai (kē-dī′nĭ-ī) Sov. Un.	55·16 N	23·58 E
98	Kedgwick (kĕdj′wĭk) Can.	47·39 N	67·21 W
113	Keenbrook (kēn′brŏŏk) Ca. (Los Angeles In.)	34·16 N	117·29 W
105	Keene (kēn) NH	42·55 N	72·15 W
212	Keetmanshoop (kāt′mȧns-hōp) Namibia	26·30 S	18·05 E
115	Keet Seel Ruin (kēt sēl) Az.	36·46 N	110·32 W
109	Keewatin (kē-wä′tĭn) Mn.	47·24 N	93·03 W
100	Keewatin, Dist. of Can.	61·26 N	97·54 W
165	Kefallinía (Cephalonia) (I.) Grc.	38·08 N	20·58 E
	Kefe, see Feodosiya		
215	Keffi (kĕf′ê) Nig.	8·51 N	7·52 E
213	Kei (R.) (kā) S. Afr. (Natal In.)	32·57 S	26·50 E
157	Keila (kā′lȧ) Sov. Un.	59·19 N	24·25 E
213	Kei Mouth S. Afr. (Natal In.)	32·40 S	28·23 E
213	Keiskammahoek (kās′kämä-hōōk′) S. Afr. (Natal In.)	32·42 S	27·11 E
215	Kéita, Bahr (R.) Chad.	9·30 N	19·17 E
157	Keitele (L.) (kā′tĕ-lĕ) Fin.	62·50 N	25·40 E
100	Kekaha Hi.	21·57 N	159·42 W
218	Kelafo Eth. (Horn of Afr. In.)	5·40 N	44·00 E
183	Kelang Mala. (Singapore In.)	3·20 N	101·27 E
183	Kelang (R.) Mala. (Singapore In.)	3·00 N	101·40 E
153	Kelkit (R.) Tur.	40·38 N	37·03 E
113	Keller (kĕl′ēr) Tx. (Dallas, Fort Worth In.)	32·56 N	97·15 W
149	Kellinghusen (kĕ′lĕng-hōō-zĕn) F.R.G. (Hamburg In.)	53·57 N	9·43 E

ng-sing; ŋ-baŋk; N-nasalized n; nŏd; cŏmmit; ōld; ôbey; ôrder; fōōd; fŏŏt; ou-out; s-soft; sh-dish; th-thin; pūre; ûnite; ûrn; stŭd; circŭs; ü-as "y" in study; ′-indeterminate vowel.

298 Kellogg — Kingisepp PRONOUNCING INDEX

Page	Name Pronunciation	Region	Lat. °'	Long. °'
110	Kellogg (kĕl'ŏg)	Id.	47·32 N	116·07 W
157	Kelme' (kĕl-mâ)	Sov. Un.	55·36 N	22·53 E
215	Kélo	Chad	9·19 N	15·48 E
93	Kelowna	Can.	49·53 N	119·29 W
92	Kelsey Bay (kĕl'sê)	Can.	50·24 N	125·57 W
112	Kelso	Wa. (Portland In.)	46 09 N	122·54 W
183	Keluang	Mala. (Singapore In.)	2·01 N	103·19 E
170	Kem' (kĕm)	Sov. Un.	65·00 N	34·48 E
113	Kemah (kē'mȧ)	Tx. (In.)	29·32 N	95·01 W
172	Kemerovo	Sov. Un.	55·31 N	86·05 E
150	Kemi (kā'mê)	Fin.	65·48 N	24·38 E
150	Kemi (R.)	Fin.	67·02 N	27·50 E
195	Kemigawa (kĕ'mê-gä'wä)	Jap. (Tōkyō In.)	35·38 N	140·07 E
150	Kemijarvi (kā'mê-yĕr-vē)	Fin.	66·48 N	27·21 E
150	Kemi-joki (L.)	Fin.	66·37 N	28·13 E
111	Kemmerer (kĕm'ẽr-ẽr)	Wy.	41·48 N	110·36 W
116	Kemp (L.) (kĕmp)	Tx.	33·55 N	99·22 W
161	Kempen (kĕm'pĕn)	F.R.G. (Ruhr In.)	51·22 N	6·25 E
203	Kempsey (kĕmp'sê)	Austl.	30·59 S	152·50 E
98	Kempt (L.) (kĕmpt)	Can.	47·28 N	74·00 W
158	Kempten (kĕmp'tĕn)	F.R.G.	47·44 N	10·17 E
213	Kempton Park (kĕmp'tŏn pärk)	S. Afr. (Johannesburg & Pretoria In.)	26·07 S	28·29 E
184	Ken (R.)	India	25·00 N	79·55 E
101	Kenai (kĕ-nī')	Ak.	60·38 N	151·18 W
101	Kenai Mts.	Ak.	60·00 N	150·00 W
101	Kenai Pen.	Ak.	64·40 N	150·18 W
154	Kendal (kĕn'dȧl)	Eng.	54·20 N	1·48 W
218	Kendal	S. Afr. (Johannesburg & Pretoria In.)	26·03 S	28·58 E
104	Kendallville (kĕn'dăl-vĭl)	In.	41·25 N	85·20 W
113	Kenedy (kĕn'ĕ-dĭ)	Tx.	28·49 N	97·50 W
214	Kenema	SL.	7·52 N	11·12 W
152	Kenitra (Port Lyautey) (kĕ-nē'trȧ)	Mor.	34·21 N	6·34 W
108	Kenmare (kĕn-mâr')	ND	48·41 N	102·05 W
107	Kenmore (kĕn'mōr)	NY (Buffalo In.)	42·58 N	78·53 W
98	Kennebec (R.) (kĕn-ê-bĕk')	Me.	44·23 N	69·48 W
98	Kennebunk (kĕn-ê-buŋk')	Me.	43·24 N	70·33 W
113	Kennedale (kĕn'-ê-dāl)	Tx. (Dallas, Fort Worth In.)	32·38 N	97·13 W
	Kennedy, C., see Canaveral			
101	Kennedy, Mt.	Can.	60·25 N	138·50 W
119	Kenner (kĕn'ẽr)	La.	29·58 N	90·15 W
117	Kennett (kĕn'ĕt)	Mo.	36·14 N	90·01 W
110	Kennewick (kĕn'ê-wĭk)	Wa.	46·12 N	119·06 W
92	Kenney Dam	Can.	53·37 N	124·58 W
112	Kennydale (kĕn-nê'dāl)	Wa. (Seattle In.)	47·31 N	122·12 W
97	Kénogami (kĕn-ŏ'gä-mê)	Can.	48·26 N	71·14 W
96	Kenogamissi L.	Can.	48·15 N	81·31 W
101	Keno Hill	Can.	63·58 N	135·18 W
95	Kenora (kê-nō'rȧ)	Can.	49·47 N	94·29 W
107	Kenosha (kê-nō'shȧ)	Wi. (Milwaukee In.)	42·34 N	87·50 W
104	Kenova (kê-nō'vȧ)	WV	38·20 N	82·35 W
106	Kensico Res. (kĕn'sĭ-kō)	NY (New York In.)	41·08 N	73·45 W
104	Kent (kĕnt)	Oh.	41·05 N	81·20 W
112	Kent	Wa. (Seattle In.)	47·23 N	122·14 W
213	Kentani (kĕnt-änĭ')	S. Afr. (Natal In.)	32·31 S	28·19 E
189	Kentei Alin (Mts.) (kĕn'tā'ä-lēn')	China	45·54 N	131·45 E
188	Kentei Shan (Mts.) (kĕn'tĭ'shän')	Mong.	49·25 N	107·51 E
104	Kentland (kĕnt'lȧnd)	In.	40·50 N	87·25 W
104	Kenton (kĕn'tŭn)	Oh.	40·40 N	83·35 W
90	Kent Pen.	Can.	68·28 N	108·10 W
103	Kentucky (State) (kĕn-tŭk'ĭ)	U. S.	37·30 N	87·35 W
103	Kentucky (L.)	U. S.	36·20 N	88·50 W
103	Kentucky (R.)	U. S.	38·15 N	85·01 W
119	Kentwood (kĕnt'wo͝od)	La.	30·56 N	90·31 W
209	Kenya (kĕn'yȧ)	Afr.	1·00 N	36·53 E
217	Kenya, Mt.	Ken.	0·10 S	37·20 E
109	Kenyon (kĕn'yŭn)	Mn.	44·15 N	92·58 W
117	Keokuk (kē'ō-kŭk)	Ia.	40·24 N	91·34 W
89	Keoma (kē-ō'mȧ)	Can. (Calgary In.)	51·13 N	113·39 W
99	Kepenkeck L.	Can.	48·13 N	54·45 W
159	Kepno (kăŋ'pnō)	Pol.	51·17 N	17·59 E
185	Kerala (State)	India	16·38 N	76·00 E
203	Kerang (kê-răng')	Austl.	35·32 S	143·58 E
167	Kerch' (kĕrch)	Sov. Un.	45·20 N	36·26 E
167	Kerchenskiy Proliv (Str.) (Kerch Str.) (kĕr-chĕn'skĭ prô'lĭf)	Sov. Un.	45·08 N	36·35 E
171	Kerempe Burun (C.)	Tur.	42·00 N	33·20 E
211	Keren	Eth.	15·46 N	38·28 E
220	Kerguelen, Is. de (kĕr'gâ-lĕn)	Ind. O.	49·50 S	69·30 E
217	Kericho	Ken.	0·22 S	35·17 E
196	Kerintji, Gunung (Mtn.)	Indon.	1·45 S	101·18 E
188	Keriya (R.) (kē'rê-yä)	China	37·13 N	81·59 E
	Keriya, see Yütien			
211	Kerkenna, Îles (I.) (kĕr'kĕn-nä)	Tun.	34·49 N	11·37 E
187	Kerki (kĕr'kê)	Sov. Un.	37·52 N	65·15 E
165	Kérkira	Grc.	39·36 N	19·56 E
165	Kérkira (I.)	Grc.	39·33 N	19·36 E
198	Kermadec Is. (kẽr-măd'ĕk)	N. Z.	30·30 S	177·00 E
198	Kermadec Tonga Trench (kẽr-măd'ĕk tŏŋ'gȧ)	Oceania	23·00 S	172·30 W
186	Kermān (kĕr-män')	Iran	30·23 N	57·08 E
186	Kermānshāh (kĕr-män-shä')	Iran	34·01 N	47·00 E
114	Kern (R.)	Ca.	35·31 N	118·37 W
114	Kern, South Fork of (R.)	Ca.	35·40 N	118·15 W
114	Kern Can. (kûrn)	Ca.	36·57 N	119·37 W
214	Kérouané	Gui.	9·16 N	9·01 W
161	Kerpen (kĕr'pĕn)	F.R.G. (Ruhr In.)	50·52 N	6·42 E
94	Kerrobert	Can.	51·53 N	109·13 W
118	Kerrville (kûr'vĭl)	Tx.	30·02 N	99·07 W
154	Kerry, Mts. (kĕr'ĭ)	Ire.	51·48 N	10·02 W
189	Kerulen (R.) (kĕr'o͞o-lĕn)	Mong.	47·52 N	113·22 E
97	Kesagami L.	Can.	50·23 N	80·15 W
165	Kesan (kĕ'shȧn)	Tur.	40·50 N	26·37 E
152	Kesour, Monts des (Mts.)	Alg.	32·51 N	0·30 W
218	Kestell (kĕs'tĕl)	S. Afr. (Johannesburg & Pretoria In.)	28·19 N	28·43 E
148	Kesteven (Co.) (kĕs'tê-vĕn)	Eng.	52·57 N	0·30 W
159	Keszthely (kĕst'hĕl-lĭ)	Hung.	46·46 N	17·12 E
172	Ket' (R.) (kyĕt)	Sov. Un.	58·30 N	84·15 E
210	Keta	Ghana	6·00 N	1·00 E
183	Ketamputih	Indon. (Singapore In.)	1·25 N	102·19 E
196	Ketapang (kĕ-tȧ-päng')	Indon.	2·00 S	109·57 E
92	Ketchikan (kĕch-ĭ-kăn')	Ak.	55·21 N	131·35 W
159	Ketrzyn (kăŋ't'r-zĭn)	Pol.	54·04 N	21·24 E
148	Kettering (kĕt'ẽr-ĭng)	Eng.	52·23 N	0·43 W
104	Kettering	Oh.	39·40 N	84·15 W
93	Kettle (R.)	Can.	49·40 N	119·00 W
109	Kettle (R.) (kĕt''l)	Mn.	46·20 N	92·57 W
161	Kettwig (kĕt'vēg)	F.R.G. (Ruhr In.)	51·22 N	6·56 E
159	Kety (kăŋ tĭ)	Pol.	49·54 N	19·16 E
149	Ketzin (kĕ'tzēn)	G.D.R. (Berlin In.)	52·29 N	12·51 E
105	Keuka (L.) (kê-ū'kȧ)	NY	42·30 N	77·10 W
161	Kevelaer (kĕ'fĕ-lȧr)	F.R.G. (Ruhr In.)	51·35 N	6·15 E
109	Kewanee (kê-wä'nê)	Il.	41·15 N	89·55 W
109	Kewaunee (kê-wô'nê)	Wi.	44·27 N	87·33 W
109	Keweenaw B. (kē'wê-nô)	Mi.	46·59 N	88·15 W
109	Keweenaw Pen.	Mi.	47·28 N	88·12 W
108	Keya Paha (R.) (kē-yȧ pä'hä)	S.D.	43·11 N	100·10 W
121	Key Largo (I.)	Fl. (In.)	25·11 N	80·15 W
106	Keyport (kē'pōrt)	NJ (New York In.)	40·26 N	74·12 W
112	Keyport	Wa. (Seattle In.)	47·42 N	122·38 W
105	Keyser (kī'sẽr)	WV	39·25 N	79·00 W
121	Key West (kē wĕst')	Fl. (In.)	24·31 N	81·47 W
159	Kežmarok (kĕzh'mȧ-rôk)	Czech.	49·10 N	20·27 E
172	Khabarovo (kŭ-bȧr-ôvô)	Sov. Un.	69·31 N	60·41 E
173	Khabarovsk (kȧ-bä'rôfsk)	Sov. Un.	48·35 N	135·12 E
188	Khaidik Gol (R.) (kī'dĕk gôl)	China	42·35 N	84·04 E
172	Khakass Aut. Oblast	Sov. Un.	52·32 N	89·33 E
185	Khālāpur	India (In.)	18·48 N	73·17 E
173	Khalkha (R.)	China-Mong.	48·00 N	118·45 E
165	Khalkidhiki Khers (Pen.)	Grc.	40·30 N	23·18 E
165	Khalkís (kȧl'kĭs)	Grc.	38·28 N	23·38 E
172	Khal'mer-Yu (kŭl-myĕr'-yo͞o')	Sov. Un.	67·52 N	64·25 E
170	Khalturin (kȧl'to͞o-rēn)	Sov. Un.	58·28 N	49·00 E
184	Khambhāt, G. of	India	21·20 N	72·27 E
185	Khammam	India	17·09 N	80·13 E
184	Khānābād	Afg.	36·43 N	69·11 E
184	Khandwa	India	21·53 N	76·22 E
	Khangai Mts., see Hangayn Nuruu			
196	Khanh Hung	Viet.	9·45 N	105·50 E
164	Khaniá (Canea) (kä-nē'ä)	Grc. (In.)	35·29 N	24·04 E
164	Khaniόn, Kόlpos (G.)	Grc. (In.)	35·35 N	23·55 E
189	Khanka (L.) (kän'kȧ)	Sov. Un.	45·09 N	133·28 E
184	Khānpur	Pak.	28·42 N	70·42 E
188	Khan Tengri (kän'tĕn'grê)	China	42·10 N	80·20 E
172	Khanty-Mansiysk (kŭn-te'mŭn-sēsk')	Sov. Un.	61·02 N	69·01 E
183	Khān Yūnus	Gaza Strip (Palestine In.)	31·21 N	34·19 E
184	Kharagpur (kŭ-rŭg'po͞or)	India	22·26 N	87·21 E
167	Khar'kov (kär'kôf)	Sov. Un.	50·00 N	36·10 E
167	Khar'kov (Oblast)	Sov. Un.	49·33 N	35·55 E
170	Kharlovka	Sov. Un.	68·47 N	37·20 E
165	Kharmanli (kȧr-män'lê)	Bul.	41·54 N	25·55 E
	Khartoum, see Al Khurṭūm			
186	Khāsh	Iran	28·08 N	61·08 E
186	Khāsh (R.)	Afg.	32·30 N	64·27 E
184	Khasi Hills	India	25·38 N	91·55 E
165	Khaskovo (kȧs'kô-vô)	Bul.	41·56 N	25·32 E
173	Khatanga (kȧ-tän'gȧ)	Sov. Un.	71·48 N	101·47 E
173	Khatangskiy Zaliv (B.) (kä-täŋ'g-skê)	Sov. Un.	73·45 N	108·30 E
151	Khemis Miliana	Alg.	36·19 N	1·56 E
167	Kherson (kĕr-sôn')	Sov. Un.	46·38 N	32·34 E
167	Kherson (Oblast)	Sov. Un.	46·32 N	32·55 E
184	Khetan (R.)	India	10·57 N	78·23 E
157	Khiitola (khē'tō-lȧ)	Sov. Un.	61·14 N	29·40 E
174	Khimki (kēm'kĭ)	Sov. Un. (Moscow In.)	55·54 N	37·27 E
165	Khíos (kē'ôs)	Grc.	38·23 N	26·09 E
165	Khíos (I.)	Grc.	38·20 N	25·45 E
147	Khiva (kē'vȧ)	Sov. Un.	41·15 N	60·30 E
167	Khmel'nik	Sov. Un.	49·34 N	27·58 E
171	Khmel'nitskiy (kmĭĕ'lnē'ts-kēê)	Sov. Un.	49·29 N	26·54 E
167	Khmel'nitskiy (Oblast) (kmĕl-nēt'skĭ ôb'lȧst')	Sov. Un.	49·27 N	26·30 E
188	Khöbsögol Dalai (Koso Lake)	Mong.	51·11 N	99·11 E
166	Kholm (kôlm)	Sov. Un.	57·09 N	31·07 E
173	Kholmsk (kŭlmsk)	Sov. Un.	47·09 N	142·33 E
171	Khopër (R.) (kô'pĕr)	Sov. Un.	52·00 N	43·00 E
194	Khor (kôr')	Sov. Un.	47·50 N	134·52 E
194	Khor (R.)	Sov. Un.	47·23 N	135·20 E
164	Khóra Sfakión	Grc. (In.)	35·12 N	24·10 E
172	Khorog (kôr'ôg)	Sov. Un.	37·30 N	71·47 E
184	Khorog	Sov. Un.	37·10 N	71·43 E
167	Khorol (kô'rôl)	Sov. Un.	49·48 N	33·17 E
167	Khorol (R.)	Sov. Un.	49·50 N	33·21 E
186	Khorramshahr (kô-ram'shär)	Iran	30·36 N	48·15 E
188	Khotan (R.) (kō-tän')	China	39·09 N	81·08 E
	Khotan, see Hotien			
167	Khotin (kô'tēn)	Sov. Un.	48·29 N	26·32 E
174	Khot'Kovo (Moscow In.)	Sov. Un.	56·15 N	38·00 E
186	Khoybār	Sau. Ar.	25·45 N	39·28 E
167	Khoyniki	Sov. Un.	51·54 N	30·00 E
184	Khulna	Bngl.	22·50 N	89·38 E
186	Khūryān Mūryān (Is.)	Om.	17·27 N	56·02 E
159	Khust (ko͞ost)	Sov. Un.	48·10 N	23·18 E
171	Khvalynsk (kvȧ-lĭnsk')	Sov. Un.	52·30 N	48·00 E
186	Khvoy	Iran	38·32 N	45·01 E
187	Khyber Pass (kī'bẽr)	Pak. (Khyber Pass In.)	34·28 N	71·18 E
217	Kialwe	Zaire	9·22 S	27·08 E
217	Kiambi (kyäm'bê)	Zaire	7·20 S	28·01 E
117	Kiamichi (R.) (kyȧ-mē'chê)	Ok.	34·31 N	95·34 W
197	Kiangan (kyäŋ'gän)	Phil. (In.)	16·48 N	121·11 E
189	Kiangsi (Chiangshi) (Prov.)	China	28·15 N	116·00 E
189	Kiangsu (Chiangsu) (Prov.)	China	33·45 N	120·30 E
170	Kianta (L.) (kyȧn'tȧ)	Fin.	65·00 N	28·15 E
216	Kibenga	Zaire	7·55 S	17·35 E
217	Kibiti	Tan.	7·44 S	38·57 E
217	Kibombo	Zaire	3·54 S	25·55 E
217	Kibondo	Tan.	3·35 S	30·42 E
165	Kičevo (kē'chĕ-vô)	Yugo.	41·30 N	20·59 E
109	Kickapoo (R.) (kĭk'ȧ-po͞o)	Wi.	43·20 N	90·55 W
93	Kicking Horse P.	Can.	51·25 N	116·10 W
210	Kidal (kê-dȧl')	Mali	18·33 N	1·00 E
148	Kidderminster (kĭd'ẽr-mĭn-stẽr)	Eng.	52·23 N	2·14 W
213	Kidd's Beach (kĭdz)	S. Afr. (Natal In.)	33·09 S	27·43 E
148	Kidsgrove (kĭdz'grōv)	Eng.	53·05 N	2·30 W
158	Kiel (kēl)	F.R.G.	54·19 N	10·08 E
109	Kiel	Wi.	43·52 N	88·04 W
158	Kiel B.	F.R.G.	54·33 N	10·19 E
	Kiel Can., see Nord-Ostsee Kan.			
159	Kielce (kyĕl'tsĕ)	Pol.	50·50 N	20·41 E
149	Kieldrecht (kēl'drĕkt)	Bel. (Brussels In.)	51·17 N	4·09 E
	Kiev, see Kiyev			
167	Kiev (Oblast) (kē'yĕf) (ôb'lȧst')	Sov. Un.	50·05 N	30·40 E
171	Kievskoye Vdkhr (Res.)	Sov. Un.	51·00 N	30·20 E
214	Kiffa (kēf'ȧ)	Mauritania	16·37 N	11·24 W
212	Kigali (kê-gä'lê)	Rw.	1·59 S	30·05 E
217	Kigoma (kê-gō'mä)	Tan.	4·52 S	29·38 E
195	Kii-Suido (Chan.) (kē so͞o-ê'dō)	Jap.	33·53 N	134·55 E
194	Kikaiga (I.)	Jap.	28·25 N	130·10 E
165	Kikinda (kē'kēn-dä)	Yugo.	45·49 N	20·30 E
165	Kikladhes (Is.)	Grc.	37·30 N	24·45 E
216	Kikwit (kē'kwĕt)	Zaire	5·02 S	18·49 E
156	Kil (kĕl)	Swe.	59·30 N	13·15 E
100	Kilauea (kē-lä-o͞o-ā'ä)	Hi.	22·12 N	159·25 W
100	Kilauea Crater	Hi.	19·28 N	155·18 W
101	Kilbuck Mts. (kĭl-bŭk)	Ak.	60·05 N	160·00 W
194	Kilchu (kĭl'cho͞o)	Kor.	40·59 N	129·23 E
153	Kildare (kĭl-dār')	Ire.	53·09 N	7·05 W
216	Kilembe	Zaire	5·42 S	19·55 E
119	Kilgore	Tx.	32·23 N	94·53 W
217	Kilifi	Ken.	3·38 S	39·51 E
213	Kilimanjaro (Mtn.) (kyl-ê-măn-jä'rô)	Tan.	3·09 S	37·19 E
212	Kilimatinde (kĭl-ê-mä-tĭn'dȧ)	Tan.	5·48 S	34·58 E
217	Kilindoni	Tan.	7·55 S	39·39 E
157	Kilingi-Nõmme (kē'lĭn-gê-nôm'mĕ)	Sov. Un.	58·08 N	25·03 E
171	Kilis (kē'lês)	Tur.	36·50 N	37·20 E
167	Kiliya (kē'lyȧ)	Sov. Un.	45·28 N	29·17 E
154	Kilkenny (kĭl-kĕn-ĭ)	Ire.	52·40 N	7·30 W
165	Kilkis (kĭl'kĭs)	Grc.	40·59 N	22·51 E
154	Killala (kĭ-lä'lȧ)	Ire.	54·11 N	9·10 W
154	Killarney	Ire.	52·03 N	9·05 W
108	Killdeer (kĭl'dẽr)	ND	47·22 N	102·45 W
154	Kilmarnock (kĭl-mär'nŭk)	Scot.	55·38 N	4·25 W
154	Kilrush (kĭl'rŭsh)	Ire.	52·40 N	9·16 W
217	Kilwa Kisiwani	Tan.	8·58 S	39·30 E
213	Kilwa Kivinje	Tan.	8·43 S	39·18 E
215	Kim (R.)	Cam.	5·40 N	11·17 E
217	Kimamba	Tan.	6·47 S	37·08 E
203	Kimba (kĭm'bȧ)	Austl.	33·08 S	136·25 E
108	Kimball (kĭm-bȧl)	Ne.	41·14 N	103·41 W
108	Kimball	SD	43·44 N	98·58 W
93	Kimberley (kĭm'bẽr-lĭ)	Can.	49·41 N	115·59 W
212	Kimberley	S. Afr.	28·40 S	24·50 E
215	Kimi	Cam.	6·05 N	11·30 E
165	Kími	Grc.	38·38 N	24·05 E
165	Kímolos (I.) (kē'mô-lôs)	Grc.	36·52 N	24·20 E
166	Kimry (kĭm'rê)	Sov. Un.	56·53 N	37·24 E
216	Kimvula	Zaire	5·44 S	15·58 E
196	Kinabalu, Mt.	Mala.	5·45 N	115·26 E
104	Kincardine (kĭn-kär'dĭn)	Can.	44·10 N	81·15 W
216	Kinda	Zaire	9·18 S	25·04 E
216	Kindanba	Con.	3·44 S	14·31 E
119	Kinder (kĭn'dẽr)	La.	30·30 N	92·50 W
94	Kindersley (kĭn'dẽrz-lê)	Can.	51·27 N	109·10 W
214	Kindia (kĭn'dê-ȧ)	Gui.	10·04 N	12·51 W
170	Kinel'-Cherkassy	Sov. Un.	53·32 N	51·32 E
166	Kineshma (kê-nĕsh'mȧ)	Sov. Un.	57·27 N	41·02 E
203	King (I.) (kĭng)	Austl.	39·35 S	143·40 E
203	Kingaroy (kĭŋ'gȧ-roi)	Austl.	26·37 S	151·50 E
114	King City (kĭng sĭ'tĭ)	Ca.	36·12 N	121·08 W
89	King City	Can. (Toronto In.)	43·56 N	79·32 W
92	Kingcome Inlet (kĭng'kŭm)	Can.	50·50 N	126·10 W
116	Kingfisher (kĭng'fĭsh-ẽr)	Ok.	35·51 N	97·55 W
93	King George, Mt.	Can.	50·35 N	115·24 W
204	King George Sd. (jôrj)	Austl.	35·17 S	118·30 E
166	Kingisepp (kĭŋ-gê-sep')	Sov. Un.	59·22 N	28·38 E

ă : finăl; rāte; senâte; ärm; ȧsk; sofȧ; fâre; ch-choose; dh-as th in other; bē; ĕvent; bĕt; recĕnt; cratẽr; g-go; gh-guttural g; bĭt; ĭ-short neutral; rīde; κ-guttural k as ch in German ich;

PRONOUNCING INDEX King Leopold — Kolyberovo 299

Page	Name Pronunciation Region	Lat. °'	Long. °'
204	King Leopold Ranges (lē'ô-pōld) Austl.	16·25 S	125·00 E
115	Kingman (kĭng'măn) Az.	35·10 N	114·05 W
116	Kingman (kĭng'măn) Ks.	37·38 N	98·07 W
114	Kings (R.) Ca.	36·28 N	119·43 W
114	Kings Canyon Natl. Park (kăn'yŭn) Ca.	36·52 N	118·53 W
148	Kingsclere (kĭngs-clēr) Eng. (London In.)	51·18 N	1·15 W
203	Kingscote (kĭngz'kŭt) Austl.	35·45 S	137·32 E
155	Kings Lynn (kĭngz lĭn') Eng.	52·45 N	0·20 E
121	Kings Mt. NC	35·13 N	81·30 W
148	Kings Norton (nôr'tŭn) Eng.	52·25 N	1·54 W
204	King Sd. Austl.	16·50 S	123·35 E
106	Kings Park (kĭngz pärk) NY (New York In.)	40·53 N	73·16 W
111	Kings Pk. Ut.	40·46 N	110·20 W
121	Kingsport (kĭngz'pōrt) Tn.	36·33 N	82·36 W
203	Kingston (kĭngz'tŭn) Austl.	37·52 S	139·52 E
105	Kingston Can.	44·15 N	76·30 W
128	Kingston Jam.	18·00 N	76·45 W
105	Kingston NY	42·00 N	74·00 W
105	Kingston Pa.	41·15 N	75·50 W
112	Kingston Wa. (Seattle In.)	47·04 N	122·29 W
148	Kingston upon Hull Eng.	53·45 N	0·25 W
127	Kingstown (kĭngz'toun) St. Vincent (In.)	13·10 N	61·14 W
121	Kingstree (kĭngz'trē) SC	33·30 N	79·50 W
118	Kingsville (kĭngz'vĭl) Tx.	27·32 N	97·52 W
100	King William I. (kĭng wĭl'yăm) Can.	69·25 N	97·00 W
213	King William's Town (kĭng-wĭl'-yŭmz-toun) S. Afr. (Natal In.)	32·53 S	27·24 E
213	Kinira (R.) S. Afr. (Natal In.)	30·37 S	28·52 E
113	Kinloch (kĭn-lŏk) Mo. (St. Louis In.)	38·44 N	90·19 W
93	Kinnaird (kĭn-ärd') Can.	49·17 N	117·39 W
154	Kinnairds Hd. (kĭn-årds'hĕd) Scot.	57·42 N	3·55 W
195	Kinomoto (kē'nō-mōtō) Jap.	33·53 N	136·07 E
195	Kinosaki (kē'nō-sä'kē) Jap.	35·38 N	134·47 E
154	Kinsale Hbr. (kĭn-sāl') Ire.	51·35 N	8·17 W
216	Kinshasa (Léopoldville) Zaire	4·18 S	15·18 E
116	Kinsley (kĭnz'lĭ) Ks.	37·55 N	99·24 W
121	Kinston (kĭnz'tŭn) NC	35·15 N	77·35 W
214	Kintampo (kēn-täm'pō) Ghana	8·03 N	1·43 W
154	Kintyre Pen. Scot.	55·50 N	5·40 W
	Kioroshi, see Ōmori		
116	Kiowa (kī'ô-wȧ) Ks.	37·01 N	98·30 W
117	Kiowa Ok.	34·42 N	95·53 W
165	Kiparissía Grc.	37·17 N	21·43 E
165	Kiparissiakós Kólpos (G.) Grc.	37·28 N	21·15 E
97	Kipawa Lac (L.) Can.	46·55 N	79·00 W
217	Kipembawe (kē-pĕm-bä'wȧ) Tan.	7·39 S	33·24 E
217	Kipengere Ra. Tan.	9·10 S	34·00 E
217	Kipili Tan.	7·26 S	30·36 E
217	Kipusha Zaire	11·46 N	27·14 E
217	Kipushi Zaire	11·46 S	27·14 E
113	Kirby (kŭr'bĭ) Tx. (San Antonio In.)	29·29 N	98·23 W
119	Kirbyville (kŭr'bĭ-vĭl) Tx.	30·39 N	93·54 W
173	Kirenga (R.) (kē-rĕŋ'gȧ) Sov. Un.	56·30 N	103·18 E
173	Kirensk (kē-rĕnsk') Sov. Un.	57·47 N	108·22 E
168	Kirghiz S. S. R. (kĭr-gēz') Sov. Un.	41·45 N	74·38 E
168	Kirghiz Steppe (Plain) Sov. Un.	49·28 N	57·07 E
187	Kirgizskiy Khrebet (Kirgiz) (Mts.) Sov. Un.	37·58 N	72·23 E
216	Kiri Zaire	1·27 S	19·00 E
	Kirin, see Chilung		
192	Kirin (Chilin) (Prov.) China	43·35 N	126·40 E
148	Kirkby-in-Ashfield (kûrk'bē-ĭn-ăsh'fēld) Eng.	53·06 N	1·16 W
154	Kirkcaldy (kēr-kô'dĭ) Scot.	56·06 N	3·15 W
150	Kirkenes Nor.	69·40 N	30·03 E
148	Kirkham (kûrk'ăm) Eng.	53·47 N	2·53 W
112	Kirkland (kûrk'lănd) Wa. (Seattle In.)	47·41 N	122·12 W
96	Kirkland Lake Can.	48·14 N	80·06 W
165	Kirklareli (kêrk'lär-ĕ'lē) Tur.	41·44 N	27·15 E
117	Kirksville (kûrks'vĭl) Mo.	40·12 N	92·35 W
186	Kirkūk (kĭr-kōōk') Iraq	35·28 N	44·22 E
154	Kirkwall (kûrk'wôl) Scot.	58·58 N	2·59 W
113	Kirkwood (kûrk'wŏŏd) Mo. (St. Louis In.)	38·35 N	90·24 W
213	Kirkwood S. Afr. (Natal In.)	33·26 S	25·24 E
158	Kirn (kērn) F.R.G.	49·47 N	7·23 E
166	Kirov Sov. Un.	54·04 N	34·19 E
170	Kirov Sov. Un.	58·35 N	49·35 E
171	Kirovabad (kē-rŭ-vŭ-bät') Sov. Un.	40·40 N	46·20 E
174	Kirovgrad (kē'rŭ-vŭ-grad) Sov. Un. (Urals In.)	57·26 N	60·03 E
167	Kirovograd (kē-rŭ-vŭ-grät') Sov. Un.	48·33 N	32·17 E
167	Kirovograd (Oblast) Sov. Un.	48·23 N	31·10 E
170	Kirovsk Sov. Un.	67·40 N	33·58 E
174	Kirovsk (kê-rôfsk') Sov. Un. (Leningrad In.)	59·52 N	30·59 E
171	Kirsanov (kêr-sá'nôf) Sov. Un.	52·40 N	42·40 E
171	Kırsehir (kêr-shĕ'hēr) Tur.	39·10 N	34·00 E
215	Kirtachi Seybou Niger	12·48 N	2·29 E
184	Kirthar Ra. (kĭr-tŭr) Pak.	27·00 N	67·10 E
148	Kirton (kûr'tŭn) Eng.	53·29 N	0·35 W
150	Kiruna (kē-rōō'nä) Swe.	67·49 N	20·08 E
217	Kirundu Zaire	0·44 S	25·32 E
116	Kirwin Res. (kûr'wĭn) Ks.	39·34 N	99·04 W
195	Kiryū (kē'rĭ-ōō) Jap.	36·26 N	139·18 E
166	Kirzhach (kēr-zhák') Sov. Un.	56·08 N	38·53 E
213	Kisaki (kē-sä'kē) Tan.	7·37 S	37·43 E
164	Kisámou, Kólpos (G) Grc. (In.)	35·40 N	23·37 E
216	Kisangani (Stanleyville) Zaire	0·30 S	25·12 E
195	Kisarazu (kē'sȧ-rä'zōō) Jap. (Tōkyō In.)	35·23 N	139·55 E
172	Kiselëvsk (kē-sĭ-lyôfsk') Sov. Un.	54·05 N	86·19 E
167	Kishinëv (ke-shê-nyôf') Sov. Un.	47·02 N	28·52 E
195	Kishiwada (kē'shê-wä'dä) Jap.	34·25 N	135·18 E
174	Kishkino (kēsh'kĭ-nô) Sov. Un. (Moscow In.)	55·15 N	38·04 E
217	Kisiwani Tan.	4·08 S	37·57 E
101	Kiska (I.) (kĭs'kä) Ak.	52·08 N	177·10 E
93	Kiskatinaw (R.) Can.	55·10 N	120·20 W
95	Kiskitto L. (kĭs-kĭ'tō) Can.	54·16 N	98·34 W
95	Kiskittogisu L. Can.	54·05 N	99·00 W
159	Kiskunfélegyháza (kĭsh'kōōn-fā'lĕd-y'hä'zô) Hung.	46·42 N	19·52 E
159	Kiskunhalas (kĭsh'kōōn-hô'lôsh) Hung.	46·24 N	19·26 E
159	Kiskunmajsa (kĭsh'kōōn-mī'shô) Hung.	46·29 N	19·42 E
213	Kismayu Som.	0·18 S	42·30 E
195	Kiso-Gawa (Strm.) (kē'sō-gä'wä) Jap.	35·29 N	137·12 E
195	Kiso-Sammyaku (Mts.) (kē'sō säm'myȧ-kōō) Jap.	35·47 N	137·39 E
214	Kissidougou (kē'sē-dōō'gōō) Gui.	9·11 N	10·06 W
121	Kissimmee (kĭ-sĭm'ē) Fl. (In.)	28·17 N	81·25 W
121	Kissimmee (L.) Fl. (In.)	27·58 N	81·17 W
121	Kissimmee (R.) Fl. (In.)	27·45 N	81·07 W
150	Kistrand (kĕ'stränd) Nor.	70·29 N	25·01 E
159	Kisujszallás (kĭsh'ōō'y'sä'läsh) Hung.	47·12 N	20·47 E
217	Kisumu (kē'sōō-mōō) Ken.	0·06 S	34·45 E
214	Kita (kē'tȧ) Mali	13·03 N	9·29 W
194	Kitakami Gawa (R.) (kē'tȧ-kä'mē gä-wä) Jap.	39·20 N	141·10 E
195	Kitakyūshū (kē'tȧ-kyōō'shōō') Jap.	34·15 N	130·23 E
217	Kitale Ken.	1·01 N	35·00 E
116	Kit Carson Co.	38·46 N	102·48 W
104	Kitchener (kĭch'ĕ-nēr) Can.	43·25 N	80·35 W
216	Kitenda Zaire	6·53 S	17·21 E
211	Kitgum (kĭt'gōōm) Ug.	3·29 N	33·04 E
153	Kíthira (I.) Grc.	36·15 N	22·56 E
165	Kíthnos (I.) Grc.	37·24 N	24·10 E
92	Kitimat (kĭ'tĭ-măt) Can.	54·03 N	128·33 W
92	Kitimat (R.) Can.	53·50 N	129·00 W
92	Kitimat Ra. Can.	53·30 N	128·50 W
92	Kitlope (R.) (kĭt'lōp) Can.	53·00 N	128·00 W
195	Kitsuki (kēt'sōō-kē) Jap.	33·24 N	131·35 E
105	Kittanning (kĭ-tăn'ĭng) Pa.	40·50 N	79·30 W
106	Kittatinny Mts. (kĭ-tȧ-tĭ'nē) NJ (New York In.)	41·16 N	74·44 W
98	Kittery (kĭt'ēr-ĭ) Me.	43·07 N	70·45 W
149	Kittsee Aus. (Vienna In.)	48·05 N	17·05 E
121	Kitty Hawk (kĭt'tē hôk) NC	36·04 N	75·42 W
217	Kitunda Tan.	6·48 S	33·13 E
217	Kitwe Zambia	12·49 S	28·13 E
158	Kitzingen (kĭt'zĭng-ĕn) F.R.G.	49·44 N	10·08 E
217	Kiunga Ken.	1·45 S	41·29 E
217	Kivu, Lac (L.) Zaire	1·45 S	28·55 E
171	Kiyev (Kiev) (kē'yĕf) Sov. Un.	50·27 N	30·30 E
195	Kiyose Jap. (Tōkyō In.)	35·47 N	139·32 E
174	Kizel (kē'zĕl) Sov. Un. (Urals In.)	59·05 N	57·42 E
171	Kızıl Irmak (R.) (kĭz'ĭl ĭr-mäk') Tur.	40·15 N	34·00 E
174	Kizil'skoye (kĭz'ĭl-skô-yĕ) Sov. Un. (Urals In.)	52·43 N	58·53 E
171	Kizlyar (kĭz-lyär') Sov. Un.	44·00 N	46·50 E
195	Kizu (kē'zōō) Jap. (Ōsaka In.)	34·43 N	135·49 E
147	Kizy-Arvat (kē'zĭl-ŭr-vät') Sov. Un.	38·55 N	56·33 E
213	Klaas Smits (R.) S. Afr. (Natal In.)	31·45 S	26·33 E
149	Klaaswaal Neth. (Amsterdam In.)	51·46 N	4·25 E
158	Kladno (kläd'nō) Czech.	50·10 N	14·05 E
158	Klagenfurt (klä'gĕn-fōōrt) Aus.	46·38 N	14·19 E
157	Klaipéda (Memel) (klī'pā-dá) (mā'mĕl) Sov. Un.	55·43 N	21·10 E
110	Klamath Falls Or.	42·13 N	121·49 W
110	Klamath Mts. Ca.	42·00 N	123·25 W
110	Klamath R. Ca.	41·40 N	122·25 W
156	Klarälven (R.) Swe.	60·40 N	13·00 E
112	Klaskanine (R.) (klăs'kȧ-nīn) Or. (Portland In.)	46·02 N	123·43 W
158	Klatovy (klȧ'tô-vê) Czech.	49·23 N	13·18 E
101	Klawock (klā'wăk) Ak.	55·32 N	133·10 W
149	Kleinmachnow (klīn-mäk'nō) G.D.R. (Berlin In.)	52·22 N	13·12 E
218	Klerksdorp (klĕrks'dôrp) S. Afr. (Johannesburg & Pretoria In.)	26·52 S	26·40 E
218	Klerksraal (klĕrks'kräl) S. Afr. (Johannesburg & Pretoria In.)	26·15 N	27·10 E
166	Kletnya (klyĕt'nyȧ) Sov. Un.	52·19 N	33·14 E
166	Kletsk (klĕtsk) Sov. Un.	53·04 N	26·43 E
161	Kleve (klĕ'fĕ) F.R.G. (Ruhr In.)	51·47 N	6·09 E
110	Klickitat R. Wa.	46·01 N	121·07 W
166	Klimovichi (klē-mô-vē'chē) Sov. Un.	53·37 N	31·21 E
174	Klimovsk (klĭ'môfsk) Sov. Un. (Moscow In.)	55·21 N	37·32 E
166	Klin (klĕn) Sov. Un.	56·18 N	36·43 E
156	Klintehamn (klēn'tē-häm) Swe.	57·24 N	18·14 E
166	Klintsy (klĭn'tsĭ) Sov. Un.	52·46 N	32·14 E
218	Klip (R.) (klĭp) S. Afr. (Johannesburg & Pretoria In.)	27·18 N	29·25 E
218	Klipgat S. Afr. (Johannesburg & Pretoria In.)	25·26 S	27·57 E
156	Klippan (klyp'pȧn) Swe.	56·08 N	13·09 E
164	Ključ (klyōōch) Yugo.	44·32 N	16·48 E
158	Kłodzko (klôd'skô) Pol.	50·26 N	16·38 E
101	Klondike Reg. (klŏn'dīk) Ak.-Can.	64·12 N	142·38 W
149	Klosterfelde (klōs'tĕr-fĕl-dĕ) G.D.R. (Berlin In.)	52·47 N	13·29 E
149	Klosterneuburg (klōs-tĕr-noi'bōōrgh) Aus. (Vienna In.)	48·19 N	16·20 E
90	Kluane (L.) Can.	61·15 N	138·40 W
90	Kluane Natl. Pk. Can.	60·25 N	137·53 W
159	Kluczbork (klōōch'bŏrk) Pol.	50·59 N	18·15 E
166	Klyaz'ma (R.) (klyäz'mȧ) Sov. Un.	55·49 N	39·19 E
173	Klyuchevskaya (Vol.) (klyōō-chĕfskä'yä) Sov. Un.	56·13 N	160·00 E
174	Klyuchi (klyōō'chĭ) Sov. Un. (Urals In.)	57·03 N	57·20 E
165	Knezha (knyā'zhȧ) Bul.	43·27 N	24·03 E
108	Knife (R.) (nīf) ND	47·06 N	102·33 W
92	Knight Inlet (nīt) Can.	50·41 N	125·40 W
104	Knightstown (nīts'toun) In.	39·45 N	85·30 W
164	Knin (knēn) Yugo.	44·02 N	16·14 E
158	Knittelfeld Aus.	47·13 N	14·50 E
197	Knob Pk. (nŏb) Phil. (In.)	12·30 N	121·20 E
154	Knockmealdown Mts. (nŏk-mēl'doun) Ire.	52·13 N	8·09 W
148	Knottingley (nŏt'ĭng-lĭ) Eng.	53·42 N	1·14 W
104	Knox (nŏks) In.	41·15 N	86·40 W
92	Knox, C. Can.	54·12 N	133·20 W
109	Knoxville (nŏks'vĭl) Ia.	41·19 N	93·05 W
120	Knoxville Tn.	35·58 N	83·55 W
148	Knutsford (nŭts'fērd) Eng.	53·18 N	2·22 W
159	Knyszyn (knĭ'shĭn) Pol.	53·16 N	22·59 E
190	Ko (R.) (gōōŭ) China	33·04 N	117·16 E
195	Kobayashi (kō'bȧ-yä'shē) Jap.	31·58 N	130·59 E
195	Kōbe (kō'bĕ) Jap. (Ōsaka In.)	34·30 N	135·10 E
167	Kobelyaki (kō-bĕl-yä'kē) Sov. Un.	49·11 N	34·12 E
156	København (Copenhagen) (kû-b'n-houn') Den.	55·43 N	12·27 E
158	Koblenz (kō'blĕntz) F.R.G.	50·18 N	7·36 E
166	Kobozha (R.) (kô-bô'zhȧ) Sov. Un.	58·55 N	35·18 E
159	Kobrin (kō'brĕn') Sov. Un.	52·13 N	24·23 E
174	Kobrinskoye (kô-brĭn'skô-yĕ) Sov. Un. (Leningrad In.)	59·25 N	30·07 E
101	Kobuk (R.) (kō'bŭk) Ak.	66·58 N	158·48 W
171	Kobuleti (kô-bōō-lyā'tē) Sov. Un.	41·50 N	41·40 E
165	Kocani (kō'chä-nĕ) Yugo.	41·54 N	22·25 E
164	Kočevje (kô'chāv-ye) Yugo.	45·38 N	14·51 E
158	Kocher R. (kôk'ĕr) F.R.G.	49·00 N	9·52 E
195	Kōchi (kō'chê) Jap.	33·35 N	133·32 E
195	Kodaira Jap. (Tōkyō In.)	35·43 N	139·29 E
101	Kodiak (kō'dyăk) Ak.	57·50 N	152·30 W
101	Kodiak (I.) Ak.	57·24 N	153·32 W
211	Kodok (ko'dŏk) Sud.	9·57 N	32·08 E
214	Koforidua (kō fô-rĭ-dōō'ȧ) Ghana	6·03 N	0·17 W
195	Kōfu (kō'fōō') Jap.	35·41 N	138·34 E
195	Koga (kō'gȧ) Jap.	36·13 N	139·40 E
214	Kogan (R.) Gui.	11·30 N	14·05 W
195	Kogane (kō'gä-nȧ) Jap. (Tōkyō In.)	35·50 N	139·56 E
195	Koganei (kō'gä-nā) Jap. (Tōkyō In.)	35·42 N	139·31 E
156	Køge (kû'gĕ) Den.	55·27 N	12·09 E
156	Køge Bugt (B.) Den.	55·30 N	12·25 E
167	Kogil'nik (R.) (kô-gēl-nēk') Sov. Un.	46·08 N	29·10 E
214	Kogoni Mali	14·44 N	6·02 W
184	Koh-i Baba Mt. Afg.	39·39 N	67·09 E
187	Kohīma (kô-ē'mä) India	25·45 N	94·41 E
195	Koito (R.) (kô'ê-tō) Jap. (Tōkyō In.)	35·19 N	139·58 E
194	Kōje (I.) (kû'jĕ) Kor.	34·53 N	129·00 E
172	Kokand (kô-känt') Sov. Un.	40·27 N	71·07 E
172	Kokchetav (kôk'chĕ-täf) Sov. Un.	53·15 N	69·13 E
157	Kokemäen (R.) (kô'kĕ-mâ'ĕn) Fin.	61·23 N	22·03 E
166	Kokhma (kôk'mȧ) Sov. Un.	56·57 N	41·08 E
150	Kokkola (kôk'kô-lȧ) Fin.	63·47 N	22·58 E
104	Kokomo (kō'kô-mō) In.	40·30 N	86·20 W
	Koko Nor (L.), see Ch'ing Hai		
197	Kokopo (kô-kô'pō) Pap. N. Gui.	4·25 S	152·27 E
91	Koksoak (R.) (kôk'sô-ăk) Can.	57·42 N	69·50 W
213	Kokstad (kôk'shtät) S. Afr. (Natal In.)	30·33 S	29·27 E
190	Koku (gō'gōō) China	39·00 N	117·30 E
195	Kokubu (kō'kōō-bōō) Jap.	31·42 N	130·46 E
195	Kokuou (kô'kōō-ō'ōō) Jap. (Ōsaka In.)	34·34 N	135·39 E
	Kola Pen., see Kol'skiy P-Ov.		
185	Kolār (Kolār Gold Fields) (kôl-är') India	13·39 N	78·33 E
159	Kolárvo (kôl-ár-ōvō) Czech.	47·54 N	17·59 E
217	Kolbio Ken.	1·10 S	41·15 E
166	Kol'chugino (kôl-chōō'gē-nô) Sov. Un.	56·19 N	39·29 E
214	Kolda Sen.	12·53 N	14·57 W
156	Kolding (kŭl'dĭng) Den.	55·29 N	9·24 E
212	Kole (kō'lȧ) Zaire	3·19 S	22·46 E
170	Kolguyev (I.) (kôl-gōō'yĕf) Sov. Un.	69·00 N	49·00 E
158	Kolin (kō'lēn) Czech.	50·01 N	15·11 E
157	Kolkasrags (Pt.) (kôl-käs'rágz) Sov. Un.	57·46 N	22·39 E
161	Köln (Cologne) F.R.G. (Ruhr In.)	50·56 N	6·57 E
159	Kolno (kôw'nô) Pol.	53·23 N	21·56 E
159	Koło (kô'wô) Pol.	52·11 N	18·37 E
158	Kołobrzeg (kô-lôb'zhĕk) Pol.	54·10 N	15·35 E
174	Kolomna (kȧl-ôm'nȧ) Sov. Un. (Moscow In.)	55·06 N	38·47 E
159	Kolomyya (kō'lô-mē'yȧ) Sov. Un.	48·32 N	25·04 E
166	Kolp' (R.) (kôlp) Sov. Un.	59·29 N	35·32 E
172	Kolpashevo (kŭl pȧ shô'vȧ) Sov. Un.	58·16 N	82·43 E
174	Kolpino (kôl'pê-nô) Sov. Un. (Leningrad In.)	59·45 N	30·37 E
166	Kolpny (kôlp'nyê) Sov. Un.	52·14 N	36·54 E
170	Kol'skiy P-Ov. (Kola Pen.) Sov. Un.	67·15 N	37·40 E
170	Kolva (R.) Sov. Un.	61·00 N	57·00 E
217	Kolwezi (kōl-wĕ'zē) Zaire	10·43 S	25·28 E
174	Kolyberovo (kô-lĭ-byä'rô-vô) Sov. Un. (Moscow In.)	55·16 N	38·45 E

ng-sing; ŋ-baŋk; N-nasalized n; nŏd; cŏmmit; ōld; ôbey; ôrder; fōōd; fŏŏt; ou-out; s-soft; sh-dish; th-thin; pūre; ûnite; ûrn; stŭd; circŭs; ü-as "y" in study; '-indeterminate vowel.

300 Kolyma — Krolevets PRONOUNCING INDEX

Page	Name Pronunciation Region	Lat. °′	Long. °′
173	Kolyma (R.)............Sov. Un.	66·30 N	151·45 E
	Kolymskiy (Mts.), see Gydan, Khrebet		
172	Kolyvan' (kôl-ê-vän′)....Sov. Un.	55·28 N	82·59 E
216	Kom (R.)...........Cam.-Gabon	2·15 N	12·05 E
219	Komadorskie Ostrova (Is.) Sov. Un.	55·40 N	167·13 E
215	Komadougou Yobé (R.) Niger-Nig.	13·20 N	12·45 E
215	Komadugu Gana (R.).......Nig.	12·15 N	11·10 E
195	Komae.........Jap. (Tōkyō In.)	35·37 N	139·35 E
159	Komárno (kô′mär-nô).....Czech.	47·46 N	18·08 E
159	Komarno..............Sov. Un.	49·38 N	23·43 E
159	Komaron (kô′mä-rôm).....Hung.	47·45 N	18·06 E
212	Komatipoort (kō-mä′tê-pōrt) S. Afr.	25·21 S	32·00 E
195	Komatsu (kō-mät′sōō).......Jap.	36·23 N	136·26 E
195	Komatsushima (kō-mät′sōō-shê′mä).Jap.	34·04 N	134·32 E
217	Komeshia..................Zaire	8·01 S	27·07 E
213	Komga (kōm′gȧ) S. Afr. (Natal In.)	32·36 S	27·54 E
168	Komi (A. S. S. R.) (kômê) Sov. Un.	61·31 N	53·15 E
212	Kommetijie..........S. Afr. (In.)	34·09 S	18·19 E
188	Kommunizma, Pik (Pk.).Sov. Un.	39·46 N	71·23 E
214	Komoe (R.).........Ivory Coast	5·40 N	3·40 W
165	Komotiní..................Grc.	41·07 N	25·22 E
196	Kompong Som (Sihanoukville) Camb.	10·40 N	103·50 E
196	Kompong Thom (kŏm′pŏng-tŏm) Camb.	12·41 N	104·39 E
167	Komrat (kôm-rät′)......Sov. Un.	46·17 N	28·38 E
174	Komsomolets (kôm-sô-mô′lĕts) Sov. Un. (Urals In.)	53·45 N	63·04 E
171	Komsomolets Zaliv (B.).. Sov. Un.	45·40 N	52·00 E
173	Komsomol'sk-na-Amure (kŭm-sŭ-môlsk′nŭ-ŭ-mōōr′yĭ).Sov. Un.	50·46 N	137·14 E
167	Komsomol'skoye (kôm-sô-môl′skô-yĕ).Sov. Un.	48·42 N	28·44 E
214	Kona......................Mali	14·57 N	3·53 W
170	Konda (R.) (kôn′dȧ).....Sov. Un.	60·50 N	64·00 E
174	Kondas R. (kôn′dȧs) Sov. Un. (Urals In.)	59·30 N	56·28 E
212	Kondoa (kôn-dō′ȧ)..........Tan.	4·52 S	36·00 E
217	Kondolole.................Zaire	1·20 N	25·58 E
210	Kong (kông).........Ivory Coast	9·05 N	4·41 W
217	Kongolo (kôŋ′gō′lō).........Zaire	5·23 S	27·00 E
156	Kongsberg (kŭngs′bĕrg)......Nor.	59·40 N	9·36 E
156	Kongsvinger (kŭngs′vĭŋ-gēr)..Nor.	60·12 N	12·00 E
212	Koni (kō′nē)..............Zaire	10·32 S	27·27 E
	Königsberg, see Kaliningrad		
149	Königsbrunn (kû′nēgs-brōōn) F.R.G. (Munich In.)	48·16 N	10·53 E
149	Königs Wusterhausen (kû′nēgs vōōs′tĕr-hou-zĕn) G.D.R. (Berlin In.)	52·18 N	13·38 E
159	Konin (kô′nyên).............Pol.	52·11 N	18·17 E
165	Kónitsa (kô′nyē′tsȧ).........Grc.	40·03 N	20·46 E
165	Konjic (kôn′yēts)..........Yugo.	43·38 N	17·59 E
195	Konju....................Kor.	36·21 N	127·05 E
214	Konkouré (R.).............Gui.	10·30 N	13·25 W
184	Konnagar............India (In.)	22·41 N	88·22 E
167	Konotop (kô-nô-tôp′)....Sov. Un.	51·13 N	33·14 E
214	Konpienga (R.)......Upper Volta	11·15 N	0·35 E
159	Końskie (koin″skyĕ).........Pol.	51·12 N	20·26 E
167	Konstantinovka (kôn-stȧn-tē′nôf-kȧ).Sov. Un.	48·33 N	37·42 E
158	Konstanz (kôn′shtänts)....F.R.G.	47·39 N	9·10 E
215	Kontagora (kōn-tȧ-gō′rä).....Nig.	10·24 N	5·28 E
171	Konya (kōn′yȧ).............Tur.	36·55 N	32·25 E
93	Kootenay (R.)..............Can.	49·45 N	117·05 W
93	Kootenay L................Can.	49·35 N	116·50 W
90	Kootenay Natl. Park (kōō′tê-nȧ) Can.	51·06 N	117·02 W
195	Kōō-zan (Mtn.) (kōō′zän) Jap. (Ōsaka In.)	34·53 N	135·32 E
156	Kopervik (kô′pĕr-vêk).......Nor.	59·18 N	5·20 E
174	Kopeysk (kô-pāsk′) Sov. Un. (Urals In.)	55·07 N	61·36 E
156	Köping (chû′pĭng)..........Swe.	59·32 N	15·58 E
156	Kopparberg (kŏp′pȧr-bĕrgh)..Swe.	59·53 N	15·00 E
186	Koppeh Dāgh (Mts.)........Iran	37·28 N	58·29 E
218	Koppies..................S. Afr. (Johannesburg & Pretoria In.)	27·15 S	27·35 E
164	Koprivnica (kô′prēv-nê′tsȧ).Yugo.	46·10 N	16·48 E
159	Kopychintsy (kô-pê-chēn′tsĕ) Sov. Un.	49·06 N	25·55 E
165	Korçë (kôr′chĕ).............Alb.	40·37 N	20·48 E
164	Korčula (I.) (kôr′chōō-lȧ)...Yugo.	42·50 N	17·05 E
194	Korea B.............China-Kor.	39·18 N	123·50 E
183	Korea (kô-rē′ȧ).............Asia	38·45 N	130·00 E
194	Korean Arch...............Kor.	34·05 N	125·35 E
194	Korea Str.............Kor.-Jap.	33·30 N	128·30 E
159	Korets (kô-rĕts′)........Sov. Un.	50·35 N	27·13 E
214	Korhogo (kôr-hō′gō)..Ivory Coast	9·27 N	5·38 W
165	Korinthiakós Kólpos (G.)....Grc.	38·15 N	22·33 E
165	Kórinthos (Corinth) (kô-rên′thôs) (kŏr′ĭnth).Grc.	37·56 N	22·54 E
194	Kōriyama (kō′rê-yä′mä)......Jap.	37·18 N	140·25 E
174	Korkino (kôr′kē-nŭ) Sov. Un. (Urals In.)	54·53 N	61·25 E
158	Körmend (kûr′mĕnt).......Hung.	47·02 N	16·36 E
164	Kornat (I.) (kôr-nät′)......Yugo.	43·46 N	15·10 E
149	Korneuburg (kôr′noi-bŏŏrgh) Aus. (Vienna In.)	48·22 N	16·21 E
214	Koro......................Mali	14·04 N	3·05 W
167	Korocha (kô-rō′chȧ).....Sov. Un.	50·50 N	37·13 E
167	Korop (kō′rôp)..........Sov. Un.	51·33 N	33·54 E
167	Korosten' (kô′rôs-tĕn) ... Sov. Un.	50·51 N	28·39 E
167	Korostyshev (kô-rôs′tê-shôf) Sov. Un.	50·19 N	29·05 E
215	Koro Toro................Chad	16·05 N	18·30 E
167	Korotoyak (kô′rô-tô-yȧk′) Sov. Un.	51·00 N	39·06 E
173	Korsakov (kôr′sȧ-kôf′)...Sov. Un.	46·42 N	143·16 E
157	Korsnäs (kôrs′nĕs)...........Fin.	62·51 N	21·17 E
151	Korsør (kôrs′ûr′)............Den.	55·19 N	11·08 E
155	Kortrijk....................Bel.	50·49 N	3·10 E
173	Koryakskiy Khrebet (Mts.) Sov. Un.	62·00 N	168·45 E
167	Koryukovka (kôr-yōō-kôf′kȧ) Sov. Un.	51·44 N	32·24 E
158	Kościan (kŭsh′tsyȧn).........Pol.	52·05 N	16·38 E
159	Kościerzyna (kŭsh-tsyĕ-zhē′nȧ) Pol.	54·08 N	17·59 E
120	Kosciusko (kŏs-ĭ-ŭs′kō).......Ms.	33·04 N	89·35 W
203	Kosciusko, Mt.............Austl.	36·26 S	148·20 E
166	Kosel'sk (kô-zĕlsk′)......Sov. Un.	54·01 N	35·49 E
211	Kosha (kō′shä)..............Sud.	20·49 N	30·27 E
192	K'oshan (kō′shän′).........China	48·00 N	126·30 E
195	Koshigaya (kô′shê-gä′yä) Jap. (Tōkyō In.)	35·53 N	139·48 E
195	Koshiki-Rettō (Is.) (kō-shē′kê rȧt′tō).Jap.	31·51 N	129·40 E
184	Kosi (R.) (kô′sē)...........India	26·00 N	86·20 E
159	Košice (kō′shê-tsĕ′) .... Czech.	48·43 N	21·17 E
213	Kosmos (kŏz′mŏs).........S. Afr. (Johannesburg & Pretoria In.)	25·45 S	27·51 E
174	Kosobrodskiy (kä-sô′brôd-skĭ) Sov. Un. (Urals In.)	54·14 N	60·53 E
	Koso Lake, see Khöbsögol Dalai		
165	Kosovska Mitrovica (kô′sôv-skä′ mê′trô-vê-tsä′).Yugo.	42·51 N	20·50 E
164	Kostajnica (kôs′tä-ê-nē′tsȧ).Yugo.	45·14 N	16·32 E
218	Koster...................S. Afr. (Johannesburg & Pretoria In.)	25·52 S	26·52 E
174	Kostino (kôs′tĭ-nô) Sov. Un. (Moscow In.)	55·54 N	37·51 E
166	Kostroma (kôs-trô-mȧ′)..Sov. Un.	57·46 N	40·55 E
166	Kostroma (Oblast)......Sov. Un.	57·50 N	41·10 E
158	Kostrzyń (kôst′chên).........Pol.	52·35 N	14·38 E
174	Kos'va R. (kôs′vȧ) Sov. Un. (Urals In.)	58·44 N	57·08 E
158	Koszalin (kô-shä′lĭn).........Pol.	54·12 N	16·10 E
158	Köszeg (kû′sĕg)...........Hung.	47·21 N	16·32 E
184	Kota.....................India	25·17 N	75·49 E
196	Kota Baharu (kō′tä bä′rōō).Mala.	6·15 N	102·23 E
196	Kotabaru................Indon.	3·22 S	116·15 E
196	Kota Kinabalu............Mala.	5·55 N	116·05 E
212	Kota Kota (kō-tȧ kō-tȧ)..Malawi	12·52 S	34·16 E
183	Kota Tinggi.Mala. (Singapore In.)	1·43 N	103·54 E
165	Kotel (kō-tĕl′)..............Bul.	42·54 N	26·28 E
170	Kotel'nich (kô-tyĕl′nêch).Sov. Un.	58·15 N	48·20 E
173	Kotel'nyy (I.) (kô-tyĕl′nê) Sov. Un.	74·51 N	134·09 E
185	Kothapur.................India	16·48 N	74·15 E
157	Kotka (kŏt′kȧ)..............Fin.	60·28 N	26·56 E
170	Kotlas (kôt′lȧs).........Sov. Un.	61·10 N	46·50 E
174	Kotlin, Ostrov (I.) (ôs-trôf′ kôt′lĭn) Sov. Un. (Leningrad In.)	60·02 N	29·49 E
165	Kotor (kō′tôr).............Yugo.	42·26 N	18·48 E
166	Kotorosl' (R.) (kô-tô′rôsl) Sov. Un.	57·18 N	39·08 E
164	Kotor Varoš (kô′tôr vä′rôsh) Yugo.	44·37 N	17·23 E
167	Kotovsk (kô-tôfsk′)......Sov. Un.	47·49 N	29·31 E
190	Kotse (hŏ′zhē)............China	35·13 N	115·28 E
185	Kotte...............Sri Lanka	6·50 N	80·05 E
211	Kotto (R.).......Cen. Afr. Emp.	5·17 N	22·04 E
173	Kotuy (R.) (kô-tōō′).....Sov. Un.	71·00 N	103·15 E
101	Kotzebue (kôt′sē-bōō).........Ak.	66·48 N	162·42 W
101	Kotzebue Sd................Ak.	67·00 N	164·28 W
214	Koualé....................Mali	11·24 N	7·01 W
98	Kouchibouguac Natl. Pk.....Can.	46·53 N	65·35 W
214	Koudougou (kōō-dōō′gōō) Upper Volta	12·15 N	2·22 W
216	Kouilou (R.)...............Con.	4·00 S	12·05 E
216	Koula-Moutou............Gabon	1·08 S	12·29 E
214	Koulikoro (kōō-lê-kō′rô).....Mali	12·53 N	7·33 W
214	Koulouguidi...............Mali	13·27 N	11·30 W
215	Koumra..................Chad	8·55 N	17·33 E
214	Koundara.................Gui.	12·29 N	13·18 W
211	Koundé (kōōn-dā′) Cen. Afr. Emp.	6·08 N	14·32 E
172	Kounradskiy (kŭ-ōōn-rät′skē) Sov. Un.	47·25 N	75·10 E
214	Kouroussa (kōō-rōō′sä).......Gui.	10·39 N	9·53 W
210	Koutiala (kōō-tê-ä′lä).......Mali	12·29 N	5·29 W
157	Kouvola (kō′ŏŏ-vô-lä)........Fin.	60·51 N	26·40 E
170	Kovda (L.) (kôv′dȧ).....Sov. Un.	66·45 N	32·00 E
159	Kovel' (kō′vĕl)..........Sov. Un.	51·13 N	24·45 E
	Kovno, see Kaunas		
166	Kovrov (kôv-rôf′).......Sov. Un.	56·23 N	41·21 E
	Kowie, see Port Alfred		
193	Kowloon (kō′lōōn′)...Hong Kong	22·28 N	114·20 E
190	Koyang (gōōŭ′yäɴg).......China	33·32 N	116·10 E
165	Koynare....................Bul.	43·23 N	24·07 E
101	Koyuk (kô-yōōk′).............Ak.	65·00 N	161·18 W
101	Koyukuk (R.) (kô-yōō′kŏŏk)..Ak.	66·25 N	153·50 W
165	Kozáni....................Grc.	40·16 N	21·51 E
167	Kozelets (kôzĕ-lyĕts).....Sov. Un.	50·53 N	31·07 E
159	Kozienice (kō-zyĕ-nē′tsĕ).....Pol.	51·34 N	21·35 E
159	Koźle (kôzh′lĕ)..............Pol.	50·19 N	18·10 E
165	Kozloduy (kŭz′lô-dwē)........Bul.	43·45 N	23·42 E
195	Kōzu (I.) (kō′zōō)...........Jap.	34·16 N	139·03 E
196	Kra, Isth. of..............Thai.	9·30 S	99·45 E
213	Kraai (R.) (krā′ê) S. Afr. (Natal In.)	30·50 S	27·03 E
149	Krabbendijke Neth. (Amsterdam In.)	51·26 N	4·05 E
156	Kragerö (krä′gĕr-û).........Nor.	58·53 N	9·21 E
165	Kragujevac (krä′gōō′yĕ-vȧts) Yugo.	44·01 N	20·55 E
159	Kraków (krä′kŏŏf)...........Pol.	50·05 N	20·00 E
151	Kraljevo (kräl′ye-vô).......Yugo.	43·39 N	20·48 E
167	Kramatorsk (krȧ-mä′tôrsk) Sov. Un.	48·43 N	37·32 E
156	Kramfors (kräm′fôrs).........Swe.	62·54 N	17·49 E
164	Kranj (krän′).............Yugo.	46·16 N	14·23 E
213	Kranskop (kränz′kŏp) S. Afr. (Natal In.)	28·57 S	30·54 E
166	Krāslava (kräs′lä-vä)....Sov. Un.	55·53 N	27·12 E
158	Kraslice (kräs′lê-tsĕ).......Czech.	50·19 N	12·30 E
174	Kransnaya Gorka (kräs′nȧ-yȧ gôr′ká).Sov. Un. (Urals In.)	55·13 N	56·43 E
171	Krasnaya Sloboda.......Sov. Un.	48·25 N	44·35 E
159	Kraśnik (kräsh′nĭk)..........Pol.	50·53 N	22·15 E
174	Krasnoarmeysk (kräs′nô-ȧr-maśk′) Sov. Un. (Moscow In.)	56·06 N	38·09 E
167	Krasnoarmeyskoye......Sov. Un.	48·19 N	37·04 E
167	Krasnodar (kräs′nô-dȧr).Sov. Un.	45·03 N	38·55 E
167	Krasnodarskiy (Oblast) Province (krȧs-nô-där′skĭ ôb′lȧst) Sov. Un.	47·28 N	38·13 E
174	Krasnogorsk Sov. Un. (Moscow In.)	55·49 N	37·20 E
174	Krasnogorskiy (kräs-nô-gôr′skĭ) Sov. Un. (Urals In.)	54·36 N	61·25 E
167	Krasnograd (kräs′nô-grät) Sov. Un.	49·23 N	35·26 E
174	Krasnogvardeyskiy (krȧ′sno-gvăr-dzyē ês-kēê) Sov. Un. (Urals In.)	57·17 N	62·05 E
170	Krasnokamsk (kräs-nô-kämsk′) Sov. Un.	58·00 N	55·45 E
167	Krasnokutsk (krȧs-nô-kōōtsk′) Sov. Un.	50·03 N	35·05 E
167	Krasnosel'ye (kräs′nô-sĕl′yĕ) Sov. Un.	48·44 N	32·24 E
170	Krasnoslobodsk (kräs′nô-slôbôtsk′) Sov. Un.	54·20 N	43·50 E
174	Krasnotur'insk (krŭs-nŭ-tōō-rensk′) Sov. Un. (Urals In.)	59·47 N	60·15 E
174	Krasnoufimsk (krŭs-nŭ-ōō-fēmsk′) Sov. Un. (Urals In.)	56·38 N	57·46 E
174	Krasnoural'sk (kräs′nô-ōō-rälsk′) Sov. Un. (Urals In.)	58·21 N	60·05 E
174	Krasnousol'skiy (kräs-nô-ŏŏ-sôl′skĭ) Sov. Un. (Urals In.)	53·53 N	56·30 E
170	Krasnovishersk (kräs-nô-vêshersk′).Sov. Un.	60·22 N	57·20 E
171	Krasnovodsk (krȧs-nô-vôtsk′) Sov. Un.	40·00 N	52·50 E
172	Krasnoyarsk (kräs-nô-yȧrsk′) Sov. Un.	56·13 N	93·12 E
174	Krasnoye Selo (kräs′nŭ-yŭ sâ′lō) Sov. Un. (Leningrad In.)	59·44 N	30·06 E
166	Krasny Kholm (kräs′nê ᴋōlm) Sov. Un.	58·03 N	37·11 E
159	Krasnystaw (kräs-nê-stȧf′) ... Pol.	50·59 N	23·11 E
174	Krasnyy Bor (kräs′nê bôr) Sov. Un. (Leningrad In.)	59·41 N	30·40 E
174	Krasnyy Klyuch (kräs′nê klyûch′) Sov. Un. (Urals In.)	55·24 N	56·43 E
171	Krasnyy Kut (krȧs-nê kōōt′) Sov. Un.	50·50 N	47·00 E
196	Kratie (krȧ-tyā′)..........Camb.	12·28 N	106·06 E
174	Kratovo (krä′tô-vô) Sov. Un. (Moscow In.)	55·35 N	38·10 E
165	Kratovo (krä′tô-vô).........Yugo.	42·04 N	22·12 E
161	Krefeld (krā′fĕlt) F.R.G. (Ruhr In.)	51·20 N	6·34 E
167	Kremenchug (krĕm′ĕn-chŏŏgh′) Sov. Un.	49·04 N	33·26 E
167	Kremenchugskoye (Res.) (krĕm-ĕn-chŏŏgh′skô-ye) Sov. Un.	49·20 N	32·45 E
159	Kremenets (krĕ-mĕn-yĕts′) Sov. Un.	50·06 N	25·43 E
149	Kremmen (krĕ′mĕn) G.D.R. (Berlin In.)	52·45 N	13·02 E
149	Krempe (krĕm′pĕ) F.R.G. (Hamburg In.)	53·50 N	9·29 E
158	Krems (krĕms).............Aus.	48·25 N	15·36 E
157	Krestsy..............Sov. Un.	58·18 N	32·26 E
166	Kresttsy (krȧst′sê)......Sov. Un.	58·16 N	32·25 E
157	Kretinga (krĕ-tĭŋ′gȧ)....Sov. Un.	55·55 N	21·17 E
215	Kribi (krē′bê).............Cam.	2·57 N	9·55 E
166	Krichëv (krē′chôf).......Sov. Un.	53·44 N	31·39 E
194	Krillon, Mys (Pt.) (mĭs krĭl′ ôn) Sov. Un.	45·58 N	142·00 E
149	Krimpenald Ijssel Neth. (Amsterdam In.)	51·55 N	4·34 E
184	Krishnanagar..............India	23·29 N	88·33 E
156	Kristiansand (krĭs-tyȧn-sän″).Nor.	58·09 N	7·59 E
156	Kristianstad (krĭs-tyȧn-städ′) Swe.	56·02 N	14·09 E
156	Kristiansund (krĭs-tyȧn-sŏŏn″) Nor.	63·07 N	7·49 E
156	Kristinehamn (krês-tē′nĕ-häm′) Swe.	59·20 N	14·05 E
157	Kristinestad (krĭs-tē′nĕ-städh) Fin.	62·16 N	21·28 E
165	Kriva-Palanka (krē-vȧ-pȧ-läŋ′kȧ) Yugo.	42·12 N	22·21 E
167	Krivoy Rog (krê-voi′ rôgh′) Sov. Un.	47·54 N	33·22 E
167	Krivoye Ozero..........Sov. Un.	47·57 N	30·21 E
164	Križevci (krē′zhĕv-tsĭ)......Yugo.	46·02 N	16·30 E
164	Krk (I.) (k′rk)............Yugo.	45·06 N	14·33 E
159	Krnov (k′r′nôf)...........Czech.	50·05 N	17·41 E
156	Kröderen (krû′dĕ-rĕn).......Nor.	60·07 N	9·49 E
218	Krokodil (R.) (krŏ′kŏ-dī).. S. Afr. (Johannesburg & Pretoria In.)	24·25 S	27·08 E
167	Krolevets (krô-lĕ′vyĕts)..Sov. Un.	51·33 N	33·21 E

ăt; finăl; rāte; senâte; ärm; ȧsk; sofȧ; fâre; ch-choose; dh-as th in other; bē; êvent; bĕt; recĕnt; cratēr; g-go; gh-guttural g; bĭt; ĭ-short neutral; rīde; ᴋ-guttural k as ch in German ich;

Page	Name Pronunciation Region	Lat. °′	Long. °′
159	Kroměříž (krô'myĕr-zhēzh). Czech.	49·18 N	17·23 E
166	Kromy (krô'mê) . . . . Sov. Un.	52·44 N	35·41 E
169	Kronotskiy, Mys (C.) (krô'nôt'skĭ-ê). Sov. Un.	54·58 N	163·15 E
174	Kronshtadt (krōn'shtät) Sov. Un. (Leningrad In.)	59·59 N	29·47 E
218	Kroonstad (krōn'shtät) . . . . S. Afr. (Johannesburg & Pretoria In.)	27·40 S	27·15 E
171	Kropotkin (krå-pôt'kĭn). Sov. Un.	45·25 N	40·30 E
159	Krosno (krôs'nô) . . . . Pol.	49·41 N	21·46 E
159	Krotoszyn (krô-tō'shĭn) . . . . . . Pol.	51·41 N	17·25 E
164	Krško (k'rsh'kô) . . . . Yugo.	45·58 N	15·30 E
212	Kruger Natl. Park (krōō'gẽr) (krü'gẽr). S. Afr.	23·22 S	30·18 E
213	Krugersdorp (krōō'gẽrz-dôrp) S. Afr. (Johannesburg & Pretoria In.)	26·06 S	27·46 E
165	Krujë (krōō'yȧ) . . . . Alb.	41·32 N	19·49 E
196	Krung Thep (Bangkok) . . . . . Thai.	13·50 N	100·29 E
165	Kruševac (krōō'shĕ-vȧts) . . . Yugo.	43·34 N	21·21 E
165	Kruševo . . . . Yugo.	41·20 N	21·15 E
156	Krylbo (krül'bô) . . . . Swe.	60·07 N	16·14 E
167	Krymskaya (krĭm'skȧ-yȧ) Sov. Un.	44·58 N	38·01 E
167	Krymskaya (Oblast) . . . . . Sov. Un.	45·08 N	34·05 E
167	Krymskiy P-Ov (Crimea) (Pen.) (krēm-skĭ pô-lōō-ôs'trôf) Sov. Un.	45·18 N	33·30 E
159	Krynki (krĭn'kê) . . . . Pol.	53·15 N	23·47 E
167	Kryukov (k'r'yōō-kôf') . . . Sov. Un.	49·02 N	33·26 E
163	Ksar Chellala . . . . Alg.	35·12 N	2·20 E
163	Ksar el Boukhari . . . . Alg.	35·50 N	2·48 E
152	Ksar el Kebir . . . . Mor.	35·01 N	5·48 W
183	Kuala Klawang Mala. (Singapore In.)	2·57 N	102·04 E
183	Kuala Lumpur (kwä'lä lōōm-pōōr') Mala. (Singapore In.)	3·08 N	101·42 E
192	Kuan (kōō'än') . . . . China (In.)	39·25 N	116·18 E
190	Kuan (R.) (gōōän) . . . . China	31·56 N	115·19 E
193	Kuangchang . . . . China	25·50 N	116·18 E
191	Kuangchou (Canton) (kăn'tŏn') China (Canton In.)	23·07 N	113·15 E
193	Kuangchou Wan (B.) . . . . . . China	20·40 N	111·00 E
	Kuanghsi, see Kwangsi Chuang		
190	Kuangjao (gōōäng'rou) . . . . . China	37·04 N	118·24 E
190	Kuanglu Tao (I.) (gōōäng'lōō dou) China	39·13 N	122·21 E
190	Kuangp'ing (gōōäng'pĭng) . . China	36·30 N	114·57 E
190	Kuangshan (gōōäng'shan) . . China	32·02 N	114·53 E
193	Kuangte . . . . China	30·40 N	119·20 E
	Kuantung (Prov.), see Kwangtung		
190	Kuanhsien (gōōän'sĭän) . . . . China	36·30 N	115·28 E
190	Kuanhu (gōōän'hoo) . . . . China	34·26 N	117·59 E
190	Kuankü Shan (Mts.) (gōōän'gōō shän). China	35·20 N	117·27 E
190	Kuant'ao (gōōän'tou) . . . . . . China	36·39 N	115·25 E
192	Kuantien . . . . China	40·40 N	124·50 E
190	Kuanyün (gōōän'yün) . . . . . . China	34·28 N	119·16 E
171	Kuba (kōō'bȧ) . . . . Sov. Un.	41·05 N	48·30 E
167	Kuban' (R.) (kōō-bȧn'') . . Sov. Un.	45·10 N	37·55 E
171	Kuban (R.) . . . . Sov. Un.	45·20 N	40·05 E
153	Kuban R. . . . . Sov. Un.	45·14 N	38·20 E
170	Kubenskoye (L.) . . . . Sov. Un.	59·40 N	39·40 E
	Kucha, see Kuch'e		
188	Kuch'e (Kucha) (kō'chĕ') (kō'chä'). China	41·34 N	82·44 E
190	Kuchen (kōō'jĕn) . . . . China	33·20 N	117·18 E
190	Kuch'eng (kōō'chĕng') . . . . . China	39·09 N	115·43 E
196	Kuching (kōō'chĭng) . . . . Mala.	1·30 N	110·26 E
195	Kuchinoerabo (I.) (kōō'chê nō ĕr'ȧ-bō). Jap.	30·31 N	129·53 E
195	Kudamatsu (kōō'dȧ-mä'tsōō). Jap.	34·00 N	131·51 E
183	Kudap . . . . . Indon. (Singapore In.)	1·14 N	102·30 E
196	Kudat (kōō-dät') . . . . Mala.	6·56 N	116·48 E
157	Kudirkos Naumiestis (kōōdĭr-kôs nȧ'ōō-mē'stĭs). Sov. Un.	54·51 N	23·00 E
172	Kudymakar (kōō-dĭm-kär') Sov. Un.	58·43 N	54·52 E
190	Kuei (R.) (kōōā) . . . . China	33·30 N	116·56 E
193	Kueichih . . . . China	30·35 N	117·28 E
191	Kueichou . . . . . China (Canton In.)	22·46 N	113·15 E
	Kueichou (Prov.), see Kweichow		
193	Kueilin . . . . China	25·18 N	110·22 E
193	Kueiyang . . . . China	26·45 N	107·00 E
188	K'uerhlo . . . . China	41·37 N	86·03 E
158	Kufstein (kōōf'shtīn) . . . . Aus.	47·34 N	12·11 E
149	Kuhstedt (kōō'shtĕt) F.R.G. (Hamburg In.)	53·23 N	8·58 E
	Kuibyshev, see Kuybyshev		
212	Kuilsrivier . . . . S. Afr. (In.)	33·56 S	18·41 E
195	Kuji . . . . Jap.	33·57 N	131·18 E
195	Kujū-san (Mt.) (kōō'jōō-sän'). Jap.	33·07 N	131·14 E
165	Kukës (kōō'kĕs) . . . . Alb.	42·03 N	20·25 E
165	Kula (kōō'lȧ) . . . . Bul.	43·52 N	23·13 E
171	Kula . . . . Tur.	38·32 N	28·30 E
184	Kula Kangri Mt. . . . . China	33·11 N	90·36 E
172	Kular, Khrebet (Mts.) (kōō-lär') Sov. Un.	69·00 N	131·45 E
157	Kuldīga (kōōl'dê-gȧ) . . . . . Sov. Un.	56·59 N	21·59 E
170	Kulebaki (kōō-lĕ-bäk'ĭ) . . Sov. Un.	55·22 N	42·30 E
158	Kulmbach (klōōlm'bäk) . . . . F.R.G.	50·07 N	11·28 E
172	Kulunda (kōō-lōōn'dȧ) . . . Sov. Un.	52·38 N	74·00 E
172	Kulundinskoye (L.) . . . . . . Sov. Un.	52·45 N	77·18 E
194	Kum (R.) (kōōm) . . . . Kor.	36·50 N	127·30 E
171	Kuma (R.) (kōō'mä) . . . . . Sov. Un.	44·50 N	45·10 E
195	Kumamoto (kōō'mä-mō'tô) . . . Jap.	32·49 N	130·40 E
195	Kumano-Nada (Sea) (kōō-mä'nō nä-dä). Jap.	34·03 N	136·36 E
165	Kumanovo (kōō-mä'nô-vô) . . Yugo.	42·10 N	21·41 E
214	Kumasi (kōō-mä'sê) . . . . Ghana	6·41 N	1·35 W
215	Kumba (kōōm'bȧ) . . . . Cam.	4·38 N	9·25 E
185	Kumbakonam (kōōm'bŭ-kō'nŭm) India	10·59 N	79·25 E
165	Kumkale . . . . Tur.	39·59 N	26·10 E
215	Kumo . . . . Nig.	10·03 N	11·13 E
185	Kumta . . . . India	14·19 N	75·28 E
174	Kunashak (kû-nä'shȧk) Sov. Un. (Urals In.)	55·43 N	61·35 E
194	Kunashir (I.) (kōō-nŭ-shēr') Sov. Un.	44·40 N	145·45 E
190	Kunch'eng Hu (L.) (kōōn'chĕng hoo). China	31·36 N	120·57 E
166	Kunda (kōō'dȧ) . . . . Sov. Un.	59·30 N	26·28 E
209	Kundelungu, Plateau des (Plat.) Zaire	9·00 S	25·30 E
174	Kundravy (kōōn'drȧ-vĭ) Sov. Un. (Urals In.)	54·50 N	60·14 E
183	Kundur (I.). Indon. (Singapore In.)	0·49 N	103·20 E
216	Kunene (Cunene) (R.) Ang.-Namibia	17·05 S	12·35 E
156	Kungälv (kŭng'ĕlf) . . . . Swe.	57·53 N	12·01 E
174	Kungur (kōōn-gōōr') Sov. Un. (Urals In.)	57·27 N	56·53 E
147	Kungrad (kōōn-grät') . . . . Sov. Un.	42·59 N	59·00 E
156	Kungsbacka (kŭngs'bä-kȧ) . . . Swe.	57·31 N	12·04 E
188	K'un Lun Shan (Mts.) (kōōn'lōōn' shän'). China	35·26 N	83·09 E
193	K'unming (Yünnanfu) (kōōn' mĭng') (yûn-nän'fōō'). China	25·10 N	102·50 E
193	Kunsan (kōōn'sän') . . . . Kor.	35·54 N	126·46 E
191	K'unshan (kōōn'shän') China (Shanghai In.)	31·23 N	120·57 E
174	Kuntsëvo (kōōn-tsyō'vô) Sov. Un. (Moscow In.)	55·43 N	37·27 E
174	Kun'ya . . . . . Sov. Un. (Urals In.)	58·42 N	56·47 E
166	Kun'ya (R.) (kōōn'yȧ) . . . Sov. Un.	56·45 N	30·53 E
150	Kuopio (kōō-ô'pê-ŏ) . . . . Fin.	62·48 N	28·30 E
164	Kupa (R.) . . . . Yugo.	45·32 N	14·50 E
197	Kupang . . . . Indon.	10·14 S	123·37 E
174	Kupavna . . Sov. Un. (Moscow In.)	55·49 N	38·11 E
172	Kupino (kōō-pĭ'nô) . . . . . . Sov. Un.	54·00 N	77·47 E
137	Kupiškis (kōō-pĭsh'kĭs) . . . Sov. Un.	55·50 N	24·55 E
167	Kupyansk (kōōp-yänsk'). Sov. Un.	49·44 N	37·38 E
171	Kura (R.) (kōō'rȧ) . . . . . . Sov. Un.	41·10 N	45·40 E
188	Kurak Darya (R.) . . . . China	41·09 N	87·46 E
195	Kurashiki (kōō'rä-shē'kê) . . . . . Jap.	34·37 N	133·44 E
211	Kuraymah . . . . Sud.	18·34 N	31·49 E
195	Kurayoshi (kōō'rȧ-yō'shê) . . . . Jap.	35·25 N	133·49 E
171	Kurdistan (Reg.) (kûrd'ĭ-stăn) Tur.-Iran	37·40 N	43·30 E
211	Kurdufān (Prov.) (kôr-dô-fän') Sud.	14·08 N	28·39 E
165	Kŭrdzhali . . . . Bul.	41·39 N	25·21 E
195	Kure (kōō'rĕ) . . . . Jap.	34·17 N	132·35 E
157	Kuressaare (kōō'rĕ-sä'rĕ). Sov. Un.	58·15 N	22·26 E
172	Kurgan (kōōr-găn') . . . . . . Sov. Un.	55·28 N	65·14 E
172	Kurgan Tyube (kōōr-gän' tyōō'bĕ) Sov. Un.	38·00 N	68·49 E
195	Kurihama (kōō-rē-hä'mä) Jap. (Tōkyō In.)	35·14 N	139·42 E
173	Kuril Is. (kōō'rĭl) . . . . Sov. Un.	46·20 N	149·30 E
157	Kurisches Haff (Bay) . . . . Sov. Un.	55·10 N	21·08 E
185	Kurla . . . . India (Bombay In.)	19·03 N	72·53 E
211	Kurmuk (kōōr'mōōk) . . . . Sud.	10·40 N	34·13 E
185	Kurnool (kōōr-nōōl') . . . . India	16·00 N	78·04 E
195	Kuro (I.) kōō'rô) . . . . Jap.	30·49 N	129·56 E
202	Kurrajong . . . . Austl. (Sydney In.)	33·33 S	150·40 E
147	Kuršenai (kōōr'shȧ-nī) . . . Sov. Un.	56·01 N	22·56 E
157	Kursk (kōōrsk) . . . . Sov. Un.	51·44 N	36·08 E
157	Kursk (Oblast) (kōōrsk) . . Sov. Un.	51·30 N	35·13 E
155	Kuršumlija (kōōr'shōōm'lĭ-yȧ) Yugo.	43·08 N	21·18 E
211	Kūrtī . . . . Sud.	18·08 N	31·39 E
212	Kuruman (kōō-rōō-män') . . . S. Afr.	27·25 S	23·30 E
195	Kurume (kōō'rōō-mĕ) . . . . Jap.	33·10 N	130·30 E
195	Kururi(kōō'rōō-rê). Jap(Tōkyō In.)	35·17 N	140·05 E
174	Kusa (kōō'sȧ). Sov. Un. (Urals In.)	55·19 N	59·27 E
167	Kushchëvskaya . . . . Sov. Un.	46·34 N	39·40 E
190	Kushih (gōō'sē) . . . . China	32·11 N	115·39 E
195	Kushikino (kōō'shĭ-kē'nō) . . . Jap.	31·44 N	130·19 E
195	Kushimoto (kōō'shĭ-mō'tō) . . . Jap.	33·29 N	135·47 E
194	Kushiro (kōō'shē-rō) . . . . Jap.	43·00 N	144·22 E
172	Kush-Murun (L.) (kōōsh-mōō-rōōn'). Sov. Un.	52·30 N	64·15 E
171	Kushum (R.) (kōō-shōōm') Sov. Un.	50·30 N	50·40 E
174	Kushva (kōōsh'vȧ) Sov. Un. (Urals In.)	58·18 N	59·51 E
101	Kuskokwim (R.) . . . . Ak.	61·32 N	160·36 W
101	Kuskokwim B. (kŭs'kō-kwĭm). Ak.	59·25 N	163·14 W
101	Kuskokwim Mts. . . . . Ak.	62·08 N	158·00 W
101	Kuskovak (kŭs-kō'văk) . . . . Ak.	60·10 N	162·50 W
172	Kustanay (kōōs-tȧ-nī') . . . Sov. Un.	53·10 N	63·39 E
211	Kūstī . . . . Sud.	13·09 N	32·39 E
171	Kütahya (kû-tä'hyȧ) . . . . Tur.	39·20 N	29·50 E
171	Kutaisi (kōō-tŭ-ē'sē) . . . . . Sov. Un.	42·15 N	42·40 E
196	Kutaradja . . . . Indon.	5·30 N	95·20 E
184	Kutch, Gulf of . . . . India	22·45 N	68·33 E
184	Kutch, Rann of (Swp.) . . . . . India	23·59 N	69·13 E
149	Kutenholz (kōō'tĕn-hōlts) F.R.G. (Hamburg In.)	53·29 N	9·20 E
174	Kutim (kōō'tĭm) Sov. Un. (Urals In.)	60·22 N	58·51 E
164	Kutina (kōō'tē-nȧ) . . . . Yugo.	45·29 N	16·48 E
159	Kutno (kōōt'nô) . . . . Pol.	52·14 N	19·22 E
170	Kutno (L.) . . . . Sov. Un.	65·15 N	31·30 E
171	Kutulik (kōō tōō'lyĭk) . . Sov. Un.	53·12 N	102·51 E
159	Kuty (kōō'tê) . . . . Sov. Un.	48·16 N	25·12 E
150	Kuusamo (kōō'sȧ-mô) . . . . Fin.	65·59 N	29·10 E
166	Kuvshinovo (kōōv-shē'nô-vô) Sov. Un.	57·01 N	34·09 E
	Kuwait, see Al Kuwayt		
182	Kuwait . . . . Asia	29·00 N	48·45 E
195	Kuwana (kōō'wȧ-nȧ) . . . . Jap.	35·02 N	136·40 E
170	Kuybyshev (Kuibyshev) (kōō'ē-bĭ-shĭf). Sov. Un.	53·10 N	50·05 E
170	Kuybyshevskoye (Res.) . . Sov. Un.	53·40 N	49·00 E
190	Kuyeh (gōō'yĕ) . . . . China	39·46 N	118·23 E
174	Kuzneckovo Sov. Un. (Moscow In.)	55·29 N	38·22 E
171	Kuznetsk (kōōz-nyĕtsk') . Sov. Un.	53·00 N	46·30 E
172	Kuznetsk Basin . . . . Sov. Un.	57·15 N	86·15 E
174	Kuznetsovka (kōōz-nyĕt'sôf-kȧ) Sov. Un. (Urals In.)	54·41 N	56·40 E
166	Kuznetsovo (kōōz-nyĕt-sô'vô) Sov. Un.	56·39 N	36·55 E
174	Kuznetsy . . Sov. Un. (Moscow In.)	55·50 N	38·39 E
164	Kvarnerski Zaliv (B.) (kvär'nĕr-skĕ' zä'lêv) . Yugo.	44·41 N	14·05 E
101	Kvichak (vĭc'-hăk) . . . . Ak.	59·00 N	156·48 W
216	Kwa (R.) . . . . Zaire	3·00 S	16·45 E
214	Kwahu Plat. . . . . Ghana	7·00 N	1·35 W
216	Kwando (R.) . . . . Zambia	16·50 S	22·40 E
216	Kwango (Cuango) (R.) (kwäng'ō'). Afr.	6·35 S	16·50 E
188	Kwangsi Chuang (Aut. Reg.) China	24·00 N	108·30 E
189	Kwangtung (kuangtung) (Prov.) China	23·45 N	113·15 E
217	Kwangwazi . . . . Tan.	7·47 S	38·15 E
188	Kweichow (Kueichou) (Prov.) China	27·00 N	106·10 E
	Kweitun, see Wusu		
216	Kwenge (R.) (kwĕŋ'gĕ) . . . . . Zaire	6·45 S	18·23 E
159	Kwidzyń (kvĕ'dzĭn) . . . . Pol.	53·45 N	18·56 E
216	Kwilu (R.) (kwē'lōō) . . . . Zaire	3·22 S	17·22 E
197	Kwoka, Gunung (Mtn.) . . . . Indon.	0·45 S	132·26 E
173	Kyakhta (kyäk'tȧ) . . . . . . Sov. Un.	51·00 N	107·30 E
184	Kyang Tsho (L.) . . . . China	30·37 N	88·33 E
184	Kyayisu (R.) . . . . India	38·05 N	74·36 E
188	Kyaukpyu (chouk'pyoo') . . . . . Bur.	19·19 N	93·33 E
157	Kybartai (kē'bär-tī') . . . . Sov. Un.	54·40 N	22·46 E
193	Ky Lam . . . . Viet.	15·48 N	108·30 E
174	Kyn (kĭn') . . . Sov. Un. (Urals In.)	51·52 N	58·42 E
205	Kynuna (kī-nōō'nȧ) . . . . Austl.	21·30 S	142·12 E
217	Kyoga, L. . . . . Ug.	1·30 N	32·45 E
195	Kyōga-Saki (C.) (kyō'gä sa'kê) Jap.	35·46 N	135·14 E
194	Kyŏngju (kyŭng'yōō) . . . . Kor.	35·48 N	129·12 E
195	Kyōto (ky . 'tō') . Jap. (Ōsaka In.)	35·00 N	135·46 E
195	Kyōto (Pref.) . . . . Jap. (Ōsaka In.)	34·56 N	135·42 E
172	Kyren (kĭ-rĕn') . . . . Sov. Un.	51·46 N	102·13 E
157	Kyrön (R.) (kŭ'rô) . . . . Fin.	63·03 N	22·20 E
174	Kyrya (kēr'yȧ) Sov. Un. (Urals In.)	59·18 N	59·03 E
174	Kyshtym (kĭsh-tĭm') Sov. Un. (Urals In.)	55·43 N	60·33 E
174	Kytlym (kĭt'lĭm) Sov. Un. (Urals In.)	59·30 N	59·15 E
195	Kyūshū (I.) (kyōō'shōō') . . . . Jap.	32·27 N	131·03 E
165	Kyustendil (kyōōs-tĕn-dĭl') . . . Bul.	42·16 N	22·39 E
172	Kyzyl (kĭ zĭl) . . . . Sov. Un.	51·37 N	93·38 E
147	Kyzyl Kum, Peski (Des.) (kĭ zĭl kōōm). Sov. Un.	42·47 N	64·45 E
188	Kyzylsu (R.) . . . . China	39·26 N	74·30 E
172	Kzyl-Orda (kzĕl-ôr'dȧ) . . . Sov. Un.	44·58 N	65·45 E

L

Page	Name Pronunciation Region	Lat. °′	Long. °′
158	Laa . . . . Aus.	48·42 N	16·23 E
162	La Almunia de Doña Godina (lä'äl-mōōn'yä dā dō nyä gô-dē'nä). Sp.	41·29 N	1·22 W
134	La Asunción (lä ä-sōōn-syōn'). Ven.	11·02 N	63·57 W
136	La Banda (lä bän'dä) . . . . Arg.	27·48 S	64·12 W
124	La Barca (lä bär'kȧ) . . . . Mex.	20·17 N	102·33 W
214	Labé (lȧ-bā') . . . . Gui.	11·19 N	12·17 W
158	Labe (Elbe) (R.) (lä'bĕ) (ĕl'bĕ) Czech.	50·05 N	15·20 E
90	Laberge (L.) (lȧ-bĕrzh') . . . . . Can.	61·08 N	136·42 W
128	Laberinto de las Doce Leguas (Is.) (lä-bȧ-rēn tô dā läs dō'sā lā'gwäs). Cuba	20·40 N	78·35 W
171	Labinsk . . . . Sov. Un.	44·30 N	40·40 E
183	Labis (läb'ĭs) Mala. (Singapore In.)	2·23 N	103·01 E
163	La Bisbal (lä bēs-bäl') . . . . Sp.	41·55 N	3·00 E
197	Labo (lä'bô) . . . . Phil. (In.)	13·39 N	121·14 E
197	Labo . . . . Phil. (In.)	14·11 N	122·49 E
197	Labo, Mt. . . . . Phil. (In.)	14·00 N	122·47 E
160	Labouheyre (lȧ-bōō-âr') . . . . Fr.	44·14 N	0·58 W
136	Laboulaye (lȧ-bô'ōō-lȧ-yĕ) . . . Arg.	34·01 S	63·10 W
91	Labrador (Reg.) (lăb'rȧ-dôr) . . Can.	53·05 N	63·30 W
99	Labrador Sea . . . . Can.	50·38 N	55·00 W
134	Lábrea (lä-brā'ä) . . . . Braz.	7·28 S	64·39 W
197	Labuan (lä-bwä'n) . . . . . Phil. (In.)	13·43 N	120·07 E
196	Labuan (I.) (lä-bōō-än') . . . . . Mala.	5·28 N	115·11 E
197	Labuha . . . . Indon.	0·43 S	127·35 E
89	L'Acadie (lȧ-kȧ-dē') Can. (Montreal In.)	45·18 N	73·22 W
89	L'Acadie (R.). Can. (Montreal In.)	45·24 N	73·21 W
137	La Calera (lä-kä-lĕ-rä) Chile (Santiago In.)	32·47 S	71·11 W
136	La Calera . . . . Col. (In.)	4·43 N	73·58 W
99	Lac Allard . . . . Can.	50·38 N	63·28 W

ng-sing; ŋ-baŋk; N-nasalized n; nŏd; cŏmmit; ōld; ôbey; ôrder; fōōd; fŏŏt; ou-out; s-soft; sh-dish; th-thin; pūre; ûnite; ûrn; stŭd; circŭs; ü-as "y" in study; '-indeterminate vowel.

302 La Calle — Landes PRONOUNCING INDEX

Page	Name / Pronunciation / Region	Lat. °′	Long. °′
151	La Calle (lȧ kàl') Alg.	36·52 N	8·23 E
113	La Canada (lä kän-yä'dä) Ca. (Los Angeles In.)	34·13 N	118·12 W
125	Lacantum (R.) (lä-kän-tōō'm) Mex.	16·13 N	90·52 W
162	La Carolina (lä kä-rô-lē'nä) Sp.	38·16 N	3·48 W
125	La Catedral, Cerro (Mtn.) (sĕ'r-rô-lä-kä-tĕ-drä'l) Mex. (In.)	19·32 N	99·31 W
89	Lac-Beauport (läk-bō-pōr') Can. (Quebec In.)	46·58 N	71·17 W
185	Laccodive Is. (läk'ȧ-dīv) India	11·00 N	73·02 E
184	Laccadive Sea Asia	9·10 N	75·17 E
109	Lac Court Oreille Ind. Res. (lăk kôrt-ô-rēl) (làk kōōr tô-rā'y') Wi.	46·04 N	91·18 W
109	Lac du Flambeau Ind. Res. Wi.	46·12 N	89·50 W
126	La Ceiba (lȧ sēbä) Hond.	15·45 N	86·52 W
134	La Ceja (lä-sĕ-кä) Col. (In.)	6·02 N	75·25 W
91	Lac-Frontière Can.	46·42 N	70·00 W
170	Lacha (L.) (là'chä) Sov. Un.	61·15 N	39·05 E
158	La Chaux de Fonds (lȧ shō dē-fôn') Switz.	47·07 N	6·47 E
218	Lach Dera (R.) (läk dā'rä) Som. (Horn of Afr. In.)	0·45 N	41·26 E
89	L'Achigan (R.) (lä-shē-gän) Can. (Montreal In.)	45·49 N	73·48 W
89	Lachine (lȧ-shēn') Can. (Montreal In.)	45·26 N	73·40 W
203	Lachlan (R.) (läk'lăn) Austl.	33·54 S	145·15 E
122	La Chorrera (làchôr-rā'rä) Pan. (In.)	8·54 N	79·47 W
89	Lachute (lȧ-shōōt') Can. (Montreal In.)	45·39 N	74·20 W
161	La Ciotat (lȧ syō-tȧ') Fr.	43·13 N	5·35 E
107	Lackawanna (lak-ȧ-wŏn'ȧ) NY (Buffalo In.)	42·49 N	78·50 W
93	Lac la Biche Can.	54·46 N	112·58 W
	La Columna (Mtn.), see Bolivar		
93	Lacombe Can.	52·28 N	113·44 W
125	La Concordia (lä-kōn-kô'r-dyä) Mex.	16·07 N	92·40 W
105	Laconia (lȧ-kō'nĭ-ȧ) NH	43·30 N	71·30 W
112	La Conner (lȧ kŏn'ēr) Wa. (Seattle In.)	48·23 N	122·30 W
162	La Coruña (lä kō-rōōn'yä) Sp.	43·20 N	8·20 W
108	Lacreek (L.) (lā'krēk) SD	43·04 N	101·46 W
113	La Cresenta (lȧ krĕs'ĕnt-ȧ) Ca. (Los Angeles In.)	34·14 N	118·13 W
116	La Cross (lȧ-krôs') Ks.	38·30 N	99·20 W
109	La Crosse Wi.	43·48 N	91·14 W
126	La Cruz (lä-krōō'z) C. R.	11·05 N	85·37 W
134	La Cruz (lȧ krōōz') Col.	1·37 N	77·00 W
108	Lacs, Riviere des (R.) (rē-vyĕr' de läk) ND	48·30 N	101·45 W
97	Lac Simard, (L.) Can.	47·38 N	78·40 W
127	La Cuesta (lä-kwĕ's-tä) C. R.	8·32 N	82·51 W
162	La Culebra, Sierra de (Mts.) (sē-ĕ'r-rä-dĕ-lä-kōō-lĕ-brä) Sp.	41·52 N	6·21 W
117	La Cygne (lȧ-sēn'y') (lȧ-sēn') Ks.	38·20 N	94·45 W
104	Ladd (lăd) Il.	41·25 N	89·25 W
162	La Demanda, Sierra de (Mts.) (sē-ĕ'rä-dĕ-lä-dĕ-mä'n-dä) Sp.	42·10 N	2·35 W
163	Ladíspoli (lä-dē's-pō-lē) It. (Rome In.)	41·57 N	12·05 E
112	Ladner (lăd'nēr) Can. (Vancouver In.)	49·05 N	123·05 W
184	Lādnun (läd'nōōn) India	27·45 N	74·20 E
	Ladoga, Lake, see Ladozhskoye Ozero		
134	La Dorado (lä dō-rä'dä) Col. (In.)	5·28 N	74·42 W
157	Ladozhskoye Ozero (Ladoga, L.) (lȧ-dôsh'skô-yē ô'zĕ-rô) Sov. Un.	60·59 N	31·30 E
89	La Durantaye (lä dü-rän-tā') Can. (Quebec In.)	46·51 N	70·51 W
213	Lady Frere (lā-dē frâ'r') S. Afr. (Natal In.)	31·48 S	27·16 E
213	Lady Grey S. Afr. (Natal In.)	30·44 S	27·17 E
92	Ladysmith (lā'dĭ-smĭth) Can.	48·58 N	123·49 W
213	Ladysmith S. Afr. (Natal In.)	28·38 S	29·48 E
109	Ladysmith Wi.	45·27 N	91·07 W
197	Lae (lä'ā) Pap. N. Gui.	6·15 S	146·57 E
156	Laerdal (lâr'däl) Nor.	61·03 N	7·24 E
156	Laerdalsören (lâr'dals-û'rĕn) Nor.	61·08 N	7·26 E
156	Laesø (I.) (lâs'û) Den.	57·17 N	10·57 E
126	La Esperanza (lä ĕs-pä-rän'zä) Hond.	14·20 N	88·21 W
162	La Estrada (lä ĕs-trä'dä) Sp.	42·42 N	8·29 W
194	Lafa (lä'fä) China	43·49 N	127·19 E
160	La-Fare-les-Oliviers (lä-fär'lā-ô-lē-vyā) Fr. (In.)	43·33 N	5·12 E
120	Lafayette Al.	32·52 N	85·25 W
112	Lafayette. Ca. (San Francisco In.)	37·53 N	122·07 W
120	Lafayette (lä-fȧ-yĕt') Ga.	34·41 N	85·19 W
104	Lafayette In.	40·25 N	86·55 W
119	Lafayette La.	30·15 N	92·02 W
106	La Fayette RI (Providence In.)	41·34 N	71·29 W
161	La Ferté-Alais (lä-fĕr-tā'-ä-lā') Fr. (Paris In.)	48·29 N	2·19 E
161	La Ferté-sous-Jouarre (lȧ fĕr-tā'sōō-zhōō-är') Fr. (Paris In.)	48·56 N	3·07 E
215	Lafia Nig.	8·30 N	8·30 E
215	Lafiagi Nig.	8·52 N	5·25 E
160	La Flèche (lȧ flāsh') Fr.	47·43 N	0·03 W
160	La Flotte (lȧ flôt') Fr.	46·09 N	1·20 W
120	La Follette (lä-fŏl'ĕt) Tn.	36·23 N	84·07 W
119	Lafourche, Bay. (bä-yōō'lä-fōōrsh') La.	29·25 N	90·15 W
135	La Gaiba (lä-gī'bä) Braz.	17·54 S	57·32 W
154	Lagan (lā'gȧn) N. Ire.	54·30 N	6·00 W
156	Lagan (R.) Swe.	56·34 N	13·25 E
150	Laganes (Pt.) Ice.	66·21 N	14·02 W
122	Lagarto, R. (lä-gä'r-tô) Pan. (In.)	9·08 N	80·05 W
126	Lagartos L. (lä-gä'r-tôs) Mex. (In.)	21·32 N	88·15 W
156	Lågan (R.) (lô'ghĕn) Nor.	59·15 N	9·47 E
210	Laghouat (lä-gwät') Alg.	33·45 N	2·49 E
161	Lagny (län-yē') Fr. (Paris In.)	48·53 N	2·41 E
137	Lagoa da Prata (lȧ-gô'ä-dȧ-prä'tȧ) Braz. (Rio de Janeiro In.)	20·04 S	45·33 W
137	Lagoa Dourada (lȧ-gô'ä-dōō-rä'dä) Braz. (Rio de Janeiro In.)	20·55 S	44·03 W
197	Lagonoy (lä-gô-noi') Phil. (In.)	13·44 N	123·31 E
197	Lagonoy G. Phil. (In.)	13·34 N	123·46 E
215	Lagos (lä'gōs) Nig.	6·27 N	3·24 E
162	Lagos (lä'gōzh) Port.	37·08 N	8·43 W
124	Lagos de Moreno (lä'gōs dā mô-rā'nō) Mex.	21·21 N	101·55 W
160	La Grand' Combe (lȧ grän kȧnb') Fr.	44·12 N	4·03 E
110	La Grande (lȧ grănd') Or.	45·20 N	118·06 W
91	La Grande (R.) Can.	53·55 N	77·30 W
204	La Grange (lä grānj) Austl.	18·40 S	122.00 E
120	La Grange (lȧ-grānj') Ga.	33·01 N	85·00 W
107	La Grange Il. (Chicago In.)	41·49 N	87·53 W
104	Lagrange In.	41·40 N	85·25 W
104	La Grange Ky.	38·20 N	85·25 W
117	La Grange Mo.	40·04 N	91·30 W
107	Lagrange Oh. (Cleveland In.)	41·14 N	82·07 W
119	Lagrange Tx.	29·55 N	96·50 W
134	La Grita (lä grē'tȧ) Ven.	8·02 N	71·59 W
135	La Guaira (lä gwä'ē-rä) Ven. (In.)	10·36 N	66·54 W
162	La Guardia (lä gwär'dē-ȧ) Sp.	41·55 N	8·48 W
136	Laguna (lä-gōō'nä) Braz.	28·19 S	48·42 W
128	Laguna, Cayos (Is.) (kä'yōs-lä-gōō'nä) Cuba	22·15 N	82·45 W
197	Laguna de Bay (L.) (lă-gōō'nă dä bä'ē) Phil. (In.)	14·24 N	121·13 E
115	Laguna Ind. Res. NM	35·00 N	107·30 W
134	Lagunillas (lä-gōō-nēl'yäs) Bol.	19·42 S	63·38 W
124	Lagunillas (lä-gōō-nē'l-yäs) Mex.	21·34 N	99·41 W
129	La Habana (Havana) (lä-ä-bȧ'nä) Cuba (In.)	23·08 N	82·23 W
116	La Habra (lȧ hȧb'rȧ) Ca. (Los Angeles In.)	34·56 N	117·57 W
100	Lahaina (lä-hä'ē-nä) Hi.	20·52 N	156·39 W
160	La Haye-Descartes (lȧ ȧ-dȧ-kärt') Fr.	46·58 N	0·42 E
158	Lahn R. (län) F.R.G.	50·21 N	7·54 E
156	Laholm (lä'hôlm) Swe.	56·30 N	13·00 E
112	La Honda (lȧ hŏn'dă) Ca. (San Francisco In.)	37·20 N	122·16 W
184	Lahore (lä-hōr') Pak.	32·00 N	74·18 E
158	Lahr (lär) F.R.G.	48·19 N	7·52 E
157	Lahti (lä'tē) Fin.	60·59 N	27·39 E
193	Lai, C. Viet.	17·08 N	107·30 E
215	Lai Chad.	9·29 N	16·18 E
190	Laian (läï'än) China	32·27 N	118·25 E
190	Laichou Wan (B.) (läï'jō wän) China	37·22 N	119·19 E
160	Laigle (lĕ'gl') Fr.	48·45 N	0·37 E
193	Laipin (lī'pĭn') China	23·42 N	109·20 E
217	Laisamis Ken.	1·36 N	37·48 E
190	Laiyang (läï'yäng) China	36·59 N	120·42 E
124	Laja, Río de la (R.) (rē'ō-dĕ-lä-lȧ'кä) Mex.	20·17 N	100·57 W
128	Lajas (lä'häs) Cuba	22·25 N	80·20 W
136	Lajeado (lä-zhĕȧ'dô) Braz.	29·24 S	51·46 W
136	Lajes (lȧ'-zhĕs) Braz.	27·47 S	50·17 W
137	Lajinha (lä-zhē'nyä) Braz. (Rio de Janeiro In.)	20·08 S	41·36 W
114	La Jolla (lȧ hōl'yȧ) Ca. (In.)	32·51 N	117·16 W
114	La Jolla Ind. Res. Ca.	33·19 N	116·21 W
116	La Junta (lȧ hōōn'tȧ) Co.	37·59 N	103·35 W
119	Lake Arthur (är'thŭr) La.	30·06 N	92·40 W
120	Lake Barkley (Res.) Tn.	36·45 N	88·00 W
108	Lake Benton (bĕn'tŭn) Mn.	44·15 N	96·17 W
107	Lake Bluff (blŭf) Il. (Chicago In.)	42·17 N	87·50 W
204	Lake Brown (broun) Austl.	31·03 S	118·30 E
119	Lake Charles (chärlz') La.	30·15 N	93·14 W
121	Lake City Fl.	30·09 N	82·40 W
109	Lake City Ia.	42·14 N	94·43 W
109	Lake City Mn.	44·28 N	92·19 W
121	Lake City SC	33·57 N	79·45 W
92	Lake Cowichan (kou'ĭ-chȧn) Can.	48·50 N	124·03 W
109	Lake Crystal (krĭs'tȧl) Mn.	44·05 N	94·12 W
154	Lake Dist. (lāk) Eng.	54·25 N	3·20 W
116	Lake Elmo (ĕlmō) Mn. (Minneapolis, St. Paul In.)	45·00 N	92·53 W
107	Lake Forest (fŏr'ĕst) Il. (Chicago In.)	42·16 N	87·50 W
115	Lake Fork (R.) Ut.	40·30 N	110·25 W
109	Lake Geneva (jĕ-nē'vȧ) Wi.	42·36 N	88·28 W
91	Lake Harbour (här'bēr) Can.	62·43 N	69·40 W
114	Lake Havasu City Az.	34·27 N	114·22 W
113	Lake June (jōōn) Tx. (Dallas, Fort Worth In.)	32·43 N	96·45 W
121	Lakeland (lāk'lănd) Fl. (In.)	28·02 N	81·58 W
120	Lakeland Ga.	31·02 N	83·02 W
113	Lakeland Mn. (Minneapolis, St. Paul In.)	44·57 N	92·47 W
109	Lake Linden (lĭn'dĕn) Mi.	47·11 N	88·26 W
93	Lake Louise (lōō-ēz') Can.	51·26 N	116·11 W
109	Lake Mills (mĭlz') Ia.	43·25 N	93·32 W
107	Lakemore (lāk-mōr) Oh. (Cleveland In.)	41·01 N	81·24 W
104	Lake Odessa Mi.	42·50 N	85·15 W
110	Lake Oswego (ŏs-wē'gō) Or. (Portland In.)	45·25 N	122·40 W
105	Lake Placid NY	44·17 N	73·59 W
113	Lake Point Ut. (Salt Lake City In.)	40·41 N	112·16 W
114	Lakeport (lāk'pōrt) Ca.	39·03 N	122·54 W
108	Lake Preston (prēs'tŭn) SD	44·21 N	97·23 W
119	Lake Providence (prŏv'ĭ-dĕns) La.	32·48 N	91·12 W
109	Lake Red Rock (Res.) Ia.	41·30 N	93·15 W
108	Lake Sharpe (Res.) SD	44·30 N	100·00 W
114	Lakeside (lāk'sīd) Ca. (In.)	32·52 N	116·55 W
107	Lake Station In. (Chicago In.)	41·34 N	87·15 W
112	Lake Stevens Wa. (Seattle In.)	48·01 N	122·04 W
106	Lake Success (sŭk-sĕs') NY (New York In.)	40·46 N	73·43 W
113	Lakeview (lāk-vū') Ca. (Los Angeles In.)	33·50 N	117·07 W
110	Lakeview Or.	42·11 N	120·21 W
117	Lake Village Ar.	33·20 N	91·17 W
121	Lake Wales (wālz') Fl. (In.)	27·54 N	81·35 W
113	Lakewood (lāk'wŏŏd) Ca. (Los Angeles In.)	33·50 N	118·09 W
116	Lakewood Co.	39·44 N	105·06 W
107	Lakewood Oh. (Cleveland In.)	41·29 N	81·48 W
105	Lakewood Pa.	40·05 N	74·10 W
110	Lakewood Wa. (Seattle In.)	48·09 N	122·13 W
112	Lakewood Center Wa. (Seattle In.)	47·10 N	122·31 W
121	Lake Worth (wûrth') Fl. (In.)	26·37 N	80·04 W
113	Lake Worth Village Tx. (Dallas, Fort Worth In.)	32·49 N	97·26 W
107	Lake Zürich (tsü'rĭk) Il. (Chicago In.)	42·11 N	88·05 W
157	Lakhdenpokh'ya (l'ăk-dïe'npōкyȧ) Sov. Un.	61·33 N	30·10 E
174	Lakhtinskiy (làk-tĭn'skĭ) Sov. Un. (Leningrad In.)	59·59 N	30·10 E
108	Lakota (lȧ-kō'tȧ) ND	48·04 N	98·21 W
185	Lakshadweep (State) India	10·10 N	72·50 E
126	La Libertad (lä lē-bĕr-tädh') Guat.	15·31 N	91·44 W
126	La Libertad Guat. (In.)	16·46 N	90·12 W
126	La Libertad Sal.	13·29 N	89·20 W
137	La Ligua (lä lē'gwä) Chile (Santiago In.)	32·21 S	71·13 W
162	Lalín (lä-lē'n) Sp.	42·40 N	8·05 W
162	La Línea (lä lē'nȧ-ä) Sp.	36·11 N	5·22 W
184	Lalitpur Nep.	27·23 N	85·24 E
152	Lalla-Maghnia (lä'lä-mäg'nēȧ) Alg.	34·52 N	1·40 W
155	La Louviere (lȧ lōō-vyâr') Bel.	50·30 N	4·10 E
124	La Luz (lä lōōz') Mex.	21·04 N	101·19 W
160	La Machine (lȧ mȧ-shēn') Fr.	46·53 N	3·26 E
214	Lama-Kara Togo	9·33 N	1·12 E
97	La Malbaie (lȧ mäl-bâ') Can.	47·39 N	70·10 W
162	La Mancha (Mts.) (lä män'chä) Sp.	38·55 N	4·20 W
116	Lamar (lȧ-mär') Co.	38·04 N	102·44 W
117	Lamar Mo.	37·28 N	94·15 W
166	La Marmora, Pta. (Mtn.) (lä-mä'r-mô-rä) It.	40·00 N	9·28 E
119	La Marque (lȧ-märk) Tx. (In.)	29·23 N	94·58 W
134	Lamas (lä'mȧs) Peru	6·24 S	76·41 W
160	Lamballe (län-bäl') Fr.	48·29 N	2·36 W
216	Lambaréné (län-bȧ-rȧ-nā') Gabon	0·42 S	10·13 E
137	Lambari (läm-bȧ'rē) Braz. (Rio de Janeiro In.)	21·58 S	45·22 W
134	Lambayeque (läm-bä-yā'kā) Peru	6·41 S	79·58 W
120	Lambert (lăm'bērt) Ms.	34·10 N	90·16 W
105	Lambertville (lăm'bērt-vĭl) NJ	40·20 N	75·00 W
111	Lame Deer (lām dēr') Mt.	45·36 N	106·40 W
162	Lamego (lä-mā'gō) Port.	41·07 N	7·47 W
114	La Mesa (lä mā'sä) Ca. (In.)	32·46 N	117·01 W
134	La Mesa Col. (In.)	4·38 N	74·27 W
116	Lamesa Tx.	32·44 N	101·54 W
165	Lamía (lȧ-mē'ȧ) Grc.	38·54 N	22·25 E
197	Lamon B. (lä-mōn') Phil. (In.)	14·35 N	121·52 E
137	La Mora (lä-mō'rä) Chile (Santiago In.)	32·28 S	70·56 W
108	La Moure (lȧ mōōr') ND	46·23 N	98·17 W
137	Lampa (R.) (lä'm-pä) Chile (Santiago In.)	33·15 S	70·55 W
118	Lampasas (lăm-păs'ȧs) Tx.	31·06 N	98·10 W
118	Lampasas R. Tx.	31·18 N	98·08 W
118	Lampazos (läm-pä'zōs) Mex.	27·03 N	100·30 W
151	Lampedusa (I.) (läm-pȧ-dōō'sä) It.	35·29 N	12·58 E
149	Lamstedt (läm'shtĕt) F.R.G. (Hamburg In.)	53·38 N	9·06 E
217	Lamu (lä'mōō) Ken.	2·16 S	40·54 E
217	Lamu I. Ken.	2·25 S	40·50 E
161	La Mure (lȧ mür') Fr.	44·55 N	5·50 E
166	Lan' (R.) (làn') Sov. Un.	52·38 N	27·05 E
100	Lanai (I.) (lä-nä'ē) Hi.	20·48 N	157·06 W
100	Lanai City Hi.	20·50 N	156·56 W
184	Lanak La (P.) China	34·40 N	79·50 E
163	La Nao, Cabo de (C.) (kȧ'bô-dĕ-lä-nä'ō) Sp.	38·43 N	0·14 E
154	Lanark (lăn'ȧrk) Scot.	55·40 N	3·50 W
148	Lancashire (Co.) (lăŋ'kȧ-shĭr) Scot.	53·38 N	2·30 W
98	Lancaster (lăŋ'kȧs-tēr) Can.	45·15 N	66·06 W
154	Lancaster Eng.	54·04 N	2·55 W
104	Lancaster Ky.	37·35 N	84·30 W
99	Lancaster Ma. (In.)	42·28 N	71·40 W
105	Lancaster NH	44·25 N	71·30 W
107	Lancaster NY (Buffalo In.)	42·54 N	78·42 W
104	Lancaster Oh.	39·40 N	82·35 W
105	Lancaster Pa.	40·05 N	76·20 W
113	Lancaster Tx. (Dallas, Fort Worth In.)	32·36 N	96·45 W
109	Lancaster Wi.	42·51 N	90·44 W
192	Lanchou (län'chōō) China	35·55 N	103·55 E
160	Lançon-Provence (län-sôn'prô-văns') Fr. (In.)	43·35 N	5·08 E
212	Lândana (län-dä'nä) Ang.	5·15 S	12·07 E
158	Landau (län'dou) F.R.G.	49·13 N	8·07 E
111	Lander (lăn'dēr) Wy.	42·49 N	108·24 W
160	Landerneau (län-dĕr-nō') Fr.	48·28 N	4·14 W
160	Landes (Moorland) (Plain) (länd) Fr.	44·22 N	0·52 W

ăt; finăl; rāte; senāte; ärm; ȧsk; sofȧ; fâre; ch-choose; dh-as th in other; bē; ēvent; bĕt; recĕnt; cratēr; g-go; gh-guttural g; bĭt; ĭ-short neutral; rīde; к-guttural k as ch in German ich;

Page	Name	Pronunciation	Region	Lat. ° ′	Long. ° ′
149	Landsberg (länds'bŏŏrgh) F.R.G. (Munich In.)			48·03 N	10·53 E
154	Lands End Pt.		Eng.	50·03 N	5·45 W
158	Landshut (länts'hŏŏt)		F.R.G.	48·32 N	12·09 E
156	Landskrona (láns-krŏŏ'nä)		Swe.	55·51 N	12·47 E
120	Lanett (lá-nĕt')		Al.	32·52 N	85·13 W
192	Lanfang		China (In.)	39·31 N	116·42 E
165	Langadhás		Grc.	40·44 N	24·10 E
183	Langat (R.).Mala. (Singapore In.)			2·46 N	101·33 E
190	Langch'i (läng'che)		China	31·10 N	119·09 E
193	Langchung		China	31·40 N	106·05 E
89	Langdon (lăng'dăn) Can. (Calgary In.)			50·58 N	113·40 W
113	Langdon Mn. (Minneapolis, St. Paul In.)			44·49 N	92·56 W
89	L'Ange-Gardien (länzh gár-dyăn') Can. (Quebec In.)			46·55 N	71·06 W
156	Langeland (I.)		Den.	54·52 N	10·46 E
161	Langenthal		Switz.	47·11 N	7·50 E
149	Langenzersdorf.Aus. (Vienna In.)			48·30 N	16·22 E
156	Langesund (läng'ĕ-sŏŏn')		Nor.	58·59 N	9·38 E
156	Lang Fd. (läng'fyŏr')		Nor.	62·40 N	7·45 E
106	Langhorne (lăng'hôrn) Pa. (Philadelphia In.)			40·10 N	74·55 W
217	Langia Mts.		Ug.	3·35 N	33·35 E
150	Langjökoll (Glacier) (läng-yū'kŏŏl)		Ice.	64·40 N	20·31 W
97	Langlade (I.) St. Pierre & Miquelon			46·50 N	56·20 W
112	Langley (lăng'lĭ) Can. (Vancouver In.)			49·06 N	122·39 W
121	Langley		SC	33·32 N	81·52 W
112	Langley		Wa. (Seattle In.)	48·02 N	122·25 W
112	Langley Ind. Res. Can. (Vancouver In.)			49·12 N	122·31 W
158	Langnau (läng'nou)		Switz.	46·56 N	7·46 E
160	Lagogne (län-gŏn'y')		Fr.	44·43 N	3·50 E
160	Langon (län-gôn')		Fr.	44·34 N	0·16 W
160	Langres (läng'gr')		Fr.	47·53 N	5·20 E
160	Langres, Plateaux de (Plat.) (plä-tŏ'dĕ-län'grĕ)		Fr.	47·39 N	5·00 E
196	Langsa (läng'sä)		Indon.	4·33 N	97·52 E
196	Lang Son (läng'sŏn')		Viet.	21·52 N	106·42 E
117	L'Anguille (R.) (län-gē'y')		Ar.	35·23 N	90·52 W
106	Lanham (län'ăm) Md. (Baltimore In.)			38·58 N	76·54 W
94	Lanigan (lăn'ĭ-gán)		Can.	51·52 N	105·02 W
188	Lanisung Chiang (Mekong).China			24·45 N	100·31 E
215	Lankoviri		Nig.	9·00 N	11·25 E
105	Lansdale (lănz'dāl)		Pa.	40·20 N	75·15 W
106	Lansdowne..Pa. (Philadelphia In.)			39·57 N	75·17 W
109	L'Anse (láns)		Mi.	46·43 N	88·28 W
109	L'Anse and Vieux Desert Ind. Res. Mi.				
114	Lansford (länz'fĕrd)		Pa.	40·50 N	75·50 W
107	Lansing		Il. (Chicago In.)	41·34 N	87·33 W
109	Lansing		Ia.	43·22 N	91·16 W
113	Lansing		Ks. (Kansas City In.)	39·15 N	94·53 W
104	Lansing		Mi.	42·45 N	84·35 W
136	Lanús (lä-nōōs')		Arg. (In.)	34·27 S	58·24 W
164	Lanusei (lä-nōō-sĕ'y)		It.	39·51 N	9·34 E
196	Lanúvio (lä-nōō'vyŏ) It. (Rome In.)			41·41 N	12·42 E
196	Laoag (lä-wäg')		Phil.	18·13 N	120·38 E
189	Lao Ho (R.) (lä'ŏ hŏ')		China	43·37 N	120·05 E
196	Lao Kay (lä'ŏkä'ĕ)		Viet.	22·30 N	102·32 E
160	Laon (län)		Fr.	49·36 N	3·35 E
134	La Oroya (lä-ō-rŏ'yä)		Peru	11·30 N	76·00 W
196	Laos (lä-ōs)		Asia	20·15 N	102·00 E
127	La Palma (lä-päl'mä)		Pan.	8·25 N	78·07 W
162	La Palma		Sp.	37·24 N	6·36 W
210	La Palma I.		Can. Is.	28·42 N	19·03 W
136	La Pampa (Prov.)		Arg.	37·25 S	67·00 W
136	Lapa Rio Negro (lä-pä-rē'ō-nĕ'grō).Braz.			26·12 S	49·56 W
136	La Paz (lä päz')		Arg.	30·48 S	59·47 W
135	La Paz		Bol.	16·31 S	68·03 W
126	La Paz		Hond.	14·15 N	87·40 W
124	La Paz (lä-pá'z)		Mex.	23·39 N	100·44 W
122	La Paz		Mex.	24·00 N	110·15 W
197	La Paz		Phil. (In.)	17·41 N	120·41 E
104	Lapeer (lá-pēr')		Mi.	43·05 N	83·15 W
160	La-Penne-sur-Huveaune (la-pĕn'sür-ü-vōn').Fr. (In.)			43·18 N	5·33 E
124	La Piedad Cabadas (lä pyá-dhädh' kä-bä'dhäs).Mex.			20·20 N	102·04 W
150	Lapland (Reg.)		Eur.	68·20 N	22·00 E
137	La Plata (lä plä'tä) Arg. (Buenos Aires In.)			34·54 S	57·57 W
117	La Plata (lä plä'tá)		Mo.	40·03 N	92·28 W
115	La Plata Pk.		Co.	39·00 N	106·25 W
163	La Pobla de Lillet (lä-pŏ'blä-dĕ-lēl-yĕ't).Sp.			42·14 N	1·58 E
98	La Pocatière (lä pŏ-kä-tyär')		Can.	47·24 N	70·01 W
197	Lapog (lä-pŏg')		Phil. (In.)	17·44 N	120·28 E
99	La Poile B. (lá pwäl')		Can.	47·38 N	58·20 W
104	La Porte (lá pŏrt')		In.	41·35 N	86·45 W
107	Laporte..Oh. (Cleveland In.)			41·19 N	82·05 W
119	La Porte		Tx. (In.)	29·40 N	95·01 W
109	La Porte City		Ia.	42·20 N	92·10 W
157	Lappeenranta (lä'pēn-rän'tä)		Fin.	61·04 N	28·08 E
89	La Prairie (lá-prá-rē') Can. (Montreal In.)			45·24 N	73·30 W
165	Lapseki (läp'sá-kê)		Tur.	40·20 N	26·41 E
168	Laptev Sea (läp'tyĭf)		Sov. Un.	75·39 N	120·00 E
163	La Puebla (lä pwä'blä)		Sp.	39·46 N	3·02 E
162	La Puebla de Montalbán (lä pwä'blä dä mŏnt-äl-bän').Sp.			39·54 N	4·21 W
113	La Puente (pwĕn'tĕ) Ca. (Los Angeles In.)			34·01 N	117·57 W
159	Lapusul (R.) (lä'pōō-shōōl)		Rom.	47·29 N	23·46 E
136	La Quiaca (lä kê-ä'kä)		Arg.	22·15 S	65·44 W
164	L'Aquila (lá'kē-lä)		It.	42·22 N	13·24 E
186	Lār (lär)		Iran	27·31 N	54·12 E
202	Lara..Austl. (Melbourne In.)			38·02 S	144·24 E
210	Larache (lä-räsh')		Mor.	35·15 N	6·09 W
102	Laramie (lăr'á-mǐ)		Wy.	41·20 N	105·40 W
116	Laramie (R.)		Co.	40·56 N	105·55 W
163	L'Arba (l'är'bá)		Alg.	36·35 N	3·10 E
106	Larchmont (lärch'mŏnt) NY (New York In.)			40·56 N	73·46 W
112	Larch Mtn. (lärch) Or. (Portland In.)			45·32 N	122·06 W
162	Laredo (lá-rā'dhō)		Sp.	43·24 N	3·24 W
118	Laredo		Tx.	27·31 N	99·29 W
160	La Réole (lä rá-ōl')		Fr.	44·37 N	0·03 W
215	Largeau (lär-zhō')		Chad	17·55 N	19·07 E
128	Largo, Cayo (kä'yō-lär'gō).Cuba			21·40 N	81·30 W
108	Larimore (lär'ĭ-mōr)		ND	47·53 N	97·38 W
164	Larino (lä-rē'nō)		It.	41·48 N	14·54 E
136	La Rioja (lä rē-ōhä)		Arg.	29·18 S	67·42 W
136	La Rioja (Prov.) (lä-rē-ō'-kä).Arg.			28·45 S	68·00 W
165	Lárisa (lä'rê-sä)		Grc.	39·38 N	22·25 E
184	Lārkāna		Pak.	27·40 N	68·12 E
183	Lárnakos, Kólpos (B.) Cyprus (Palestine In.)			36·50 N	33·45 E
183	Lárnax.Cyprus (Palestine In.)			34·55 N	33·37 E
116	Larned (lär'nĕd)		Ks.	38·09 N	99·07 W
162	La Robla (lä rōb'lä)		Sp.	42·48 N	5·36 W
160	La Rochelle (lä rô-shĕl')		Fr.	46·10 N	1·09 W
160	La Roche-sur-Yon (lá rôsh'sûr-yôn').Fr.			46·39 N	1·27 W
162	La Roda (lä rō'dä)		Sp.	39·13 N	2·08 W
129	La Romona (lä-rä-mō'nä) Dom. Rep.			18·25 N	69·00 W
204	Larrey Pt. (lăr'ĕ)		Austl.	19·15 S	118·15 E
160	Laruns (lä-răns')		Fr.	42·58 N	0·28 W
156	Larvik (lär'vēk)		Nor.	59·06 N	10·03 E
135	La Sabana (lä-sä-bá'nä).Ven. (In.)			10·38 N	66·24 W
129	La Sabina (lä-sä-bē'nä) Cuba (In.)			22·10 N	82·07 W
162	La Sagra (Mtn.) (lä sä'grä)		Sp.	37·56 N	2·35 Э
115	La Sal (lá sǎl')		Ut.	38·10 N	109·20 W
107	La Salle		Il.	41·20 N	89·05 W
89	La Salle..Can. (Detroit In.)			42·14 N	83·06 W
89	La Salle..Can. (Montréal In.)			45·26 N	73·39 W
89	La Salle..Can. (Winnipeg In.)			49·41 N	97·16 W
104	La Salle		Il.	41·20 N	89·05 W
116	Las Animas (läs ä'nĭ-más)		Co.	38·03 N	103·16 W
218	Las Anod (läs än'ŏd) Som. (Horn of Afr. In.)			8·24 N	47·20 E
97	La Sarre		Can.	48·43 N	79·12 W
129	Lascahobas (läs-kä-ō'bäs)..Hai.			19·00 N	71·55 W
125	Las Cruces (läs-krōō'-sĕs).Mex.			16·37 N	93·54 W
115	Las Cruces		NM	32·20 N	106·50 W
129	La Selle, Massif De (Mts.) (lä sĕl').Hai.			18·25 N	72·05 W
136	La Serena (lä-sĕ-rē'nä).Chile			29·55 S	71·24 W
161	La Seyne-sur-Mer (lä-sân'sür-mĕr').Fr.			43·07 N	5·52 E
137	Las Flores (läs flo'rês) Arg. (Buenos Aires In.)			36·01 S	59·07 W
188	Lashio (läsh'ē-ō)		Bur.	22·58 N	98·03 E
126	Las Juntas (läs-kōō'n-täs).C. R.			10·15 N	85·00 W
218	Las Khoreh (läs kō'rä) Som. (Horn of Afr. In.)			11·13 N	48·19 E
162	Las Maismas (Reg.) (läs-mī's-mäs).Sp.			37·05 N	6·25 W
162	La Solano (lä-sô-lä'nō)		Sp.	38·56 N	3·13 W
210	Las Palmas de Gran Canaria, (läs päl'mäs).Can. Is.			28·07 N	15·28 W
127	Las Palmas		Pan.	8·08 N	81·30 W
164	La Spezia (lä spě'zyä)		It.	44·07 N	9·48 E
137	Las Piedras (läs-pyĕ'dräs) Ur. (Buenos Aires In.)			34·42 S	56·08 W
126	Las Pilas (Vol.) (läs-pē'läs)		Nic.	12·32 N	86·43 W
125	Las Rosas (läs rō thäs)		Mex.	16·24 N	92·23 W
163	Las Rozas de Madrid (läs rŏ'thas dä mä-dhrĕdh').Sp. (Madrid In.)			40·29 N	3·53 W
149	Lassee.Aus. (Vienna In.)			48·14 N	16·50 E
110	Lassen Pk. (läs'ĕn)		Ca.	40·30 N	121·32 W
110	Lassen Volcanic Natl. Park..Ca.			40·43 N	121·35 W
89	L'Assomption (läs-sôm-syôn) Can. (Montreal In.)			45·50 N	73·25 W
127	Las Tablas (läs tä'bläs)		Pan.	7·48 N	80·16 W
94	Last Mountain (läst moun'tǐn).Can.			51·05 N	105·10 W
212	Lastoursville (läs-tōōr-vēl')		Gabon	1·00 S	12·49 E
122	Las Tres Virgenes, Vol. (vē'r-hĕ-nĕs).Mex.			26·00 N	111·45 W
128	Las Tunas (Prov.)		Cuba	21·05 N	77·00 W
125	Las Vacas (läs-vá'käs)		Mex.	16·24 N	95·48 W
137	Las Vegas (läs-vě'gäs) Chile (Santiago In.)			30·50 S	70·59 W
114	Las Vegas (läs vā'gäs)		Nv.	36·12 N	115·10 W
116	Las Vegas		NM	35·36 N	105·13 W
135	Las Vegas (läs vě'gäs)..Ven. (In.)			10·26 N	64·08 W
124	Las Vigas		Mex.	19·38 N	97·03 W
136	Las Vizcachas, Meseta de (Plat.) (mě-sě'tä-dĕ-läs-vēz-kä'chás) Arg.			49·35 S	71·00 W
134	Latacunga (lä-tä-kōŏŋ'gä)..Ec.			1·02 S	78·33 W
	Latakia, see Al Lādhiqīah				
153	Latakia (lä-tä-kē'ä)		Syr.	35·10 N	35·49 E
160	La Teste-de-Buch (lä-tĕst-dĕ-büsh').Fr.			44·38 N	1·11 W
117	Lathrop (lā'thrŭp)		Mo.	39·32 N	94·21 W
	Latium, see Lazio				
161	Latoritsa R. (lá-tŏ'rĭ-tsä).Sov. Un.			48·27 N	22·30 E
112	Latourell (lá-tou'rĕl) Or. (Portland In.)			45·32 N	122·13 W
160	La Tremblade (lä-trĕn-bläd').Fr.			45·45 N	1·12 W
105	La Trobe (lá-trōb')		Pa.	40·25 N	79·15 W
91	La Tuque (lá tük')		Can.	47·27 N	72·49 W
185	Lātūr (lä-tōōr')		India	18·20 N	76·35 E
168	Latvian (R. S. R.)		Sov. Un.	57·28 N	24·29 E
203	Launceston (lôn'sĕs-tŭn)		Austl.	41·35 S	147·22 E
154	Launceston (lôn'stŏn)		Eng.	50·38 N	4·26 W
136	La Unión (lä-ōō-nyō'n)		Chile	40·15 S	73·04 W
124	La Unión (lä ōōn-nyōn')		Mex.	17·59 N	101·48 W
126	La Unión		Sal.	13·18 N	87·51 W
163	La Unión		Sp.	37·38 N	0·50 W
205	Laura (lôrá)		Austl.	15·40 S	144·45 E
166	Laura (lou'rá)		Sov. Un.	57·36 N	27·29 E
105	Laurel (lô'rĕl)		De.	38·30 N	75·40 W
106	Laurel..Md. (Baltimore In.)			39·06 N	76·51 W
120	Laurel		Ms.	31·42 N	89·07 W
111	Laurel		Mt.	45·41 N	108·45 W
112	Laurel..Wa. (Vancouver In.)			48·52 N	122·29 W
112	Laurelwood (lô'rĕl-wŏŏd) Or. (Portland In.)			45·25 N	123·05 W
121	Laurens (lô'rĕnz)		SC	34·29 N	82·03 W
75	Laurentian Highlands (Reg.) (lô'rĕn-tǐ-án).Can.			49·00 N	74·50 W
89	Laurentides Can. (Montreal In.)			45·51 N	73·46 W
164	Lauria (lou'rē-ä)		It.	40·03 N	15·02 E
121	Laurinburg (lô'rĭn-bûrg)		NC	34·45 N	79·27 W
109	Laurium (lô'rĭ-ŭm)		Mi.	47·13 N	88·28 W
158	Lausanne (lō-zän')		Switz.	46·32 N	6·35 E
196	Laut (I.)		Indon.	3·39 N	116·07 E
136	Lautaro (lou-tä'rŏ)		Chile	38·40 S	72·24 W
196	Laut Kecil, Kepulauan (Is.)		Indon.	4·44 S	115·43 E
89	Lauzon (lō-zōn') Can. (Quebec In.)			46·50 N	71·10 W
110	Lava Beds Natl. Mon. (lä'vá bĕds).Ca.			41·38 N	121·44 W
119	Lavaca R. (lä-vák'á)		Tx.	29·05 N	96·50 W
111	Lava Hot Springs		Id.	42·37 N	111·58 W
89	Laval..Can. (Montreal In.)			45·33 N	73·44 W
160	Laval (lä-väl')		Fr.	48·05 N	0·47 W
160	Lavaur (lä-vŏr')		Fr.	43·41 N	1·48 E
160	Lavaveix-les-Mines (lä-vä-vĕ'lä-mĕn').Fr.			46·05 N	2·05 E
129	La Vega (lä-vě'-gä)		Dom. Rep.	19·15 N	70·35 W
205	Lavella (I.)		Sol. Is.	7·50 S	155·45 E
164	Lavello (lä-vĕl'lō)		It.	41·05 N	15·50 E
113	La Verne (lä vûrn') Ca. (Los Angeles In.)			34·06 N	117·46 W
204	Laverton (lä'vĕr-tŭn)		Austl.	28·45 S	122·30 E
135	La Victoria (lä věk-tō'rē-ä) Ven. (In.)			10·14 N	67·20 W
120	Lavonia (lá-vō'nĭ-á)		Ga.	34·26 N	83·05 W
119	Lavon Res.		Tx.	33·06 N	96·20 W
137	Lavras (lä'vräzh) Braz. (Rio de Janeiro In.)			21·15 S	44·59 W
165	Lávrion (läv'rĭ-ôn)		Grc.	37·44 N	24·05 E
113	Lawndale (lôn'dāl) Ca. (Los Angeles In.)			33·54 N	118·22 W
214	Lawra		Ghana	10·39 N	2·52 W
107	Lawrence (lô'rĕns) In. (Indianapolis In.)			39·59 N	86·01 W
117	Lawrence Ks. (Kansas City In.)			38·57 N	95·13 W
99	Lawrence..Ma. (In.)			42·42 N	71·09 W
107	Lawrence..Pa. (Pittsburgh In.)			40·18 N	80·07 W
107	Lawrenceburg (lô'rĕns-bûrg) In. (Cincinnati In.)			39·06 N	84·47 W
104	Lawrenceburg		Ky.	38·00 N	85·00 W
120	Lawrenceburg		Tn.	35·13 N	87·20 W
120	Lawrenceville (lô'rĕns-vĭl)		Ga.	33·56 N	83·57 W
104	Lawrenceville		Il.	38·45 N	87·45 W
106	Lawrenceville..NJ (New York In.)			40·17 N	74·44 W
121	Lawrenceville		Va.	36·43 N	77·52 W
105	Lawsonia (lô-sō'nĭ-á)		Md.	38·00 N	75·50 W
116	Lawton (lô'tŭn)		Ok.	34·36 N	98·25 W
186	Lawz, Jabal al (Mtn.)		Sau. Ar.	28·46 N	35·37 E
183	Layang Layang (lä-yäng' lä-yäng').Mala. (Singapore In.)			1·49 N	103·28 E
113	Layton (lā'tŭn) Ut. (Salt Lake City In.)			41·04 N	111·58 W
157	Laždijai (läzh'dē-yǐ')		Sov. Un.	54·12 N	23·35 E
164	Lazio (Latium) (Reg.) (lä'zyŏ) (lá't-zēōom).It.			42·05 N	12·25 E
108	Lead (lēd)		SD	44·22 N	103·47 W
94	Leader		Can.	50·55 N	109·32 W
116	Leadville (lĕd'vĭl)		Co.	39·14 N	106·18 W
120	Leaf (R.) (lēf)		Ms.	31·43 N	89·20 W
119	League City (lēg)		Tx. (In.)	29·31 N	95·05 W
104	Leamington (lĕm'ĭng-tŭn)..Can.			42·05 N	82·35 W
154	Leamington (lě'mǐng-tŭn)..Eng.			52·17 N	1·25 W
148	Leatherhead (lĕdh'ĕr-hĕd) Eng. (London In.)			51·17 N	0·20 W
113	Leavenworth (lĕv'ĕn-wûrth) Ks. (Kansas City In.)			39·19 N	94·54 W
110	Leavenworth..Wa.			47·35 N	120·39 W
113	Leawood (lē'wŏŏd) Ks. (Kansas City In.)			38·58 N	94·37 W
159	Leba (lā'bä)		Pol.	54·45 N	17·34 E
183	Lebam R..Mala. (Singapore In.)			1·35 N	104·09 E
216	Lebango		Con.	0·22 N	14·49 E
113	Lebanon (lĕb'á-nŭn) Il. (St. Louis In.)			38·36 N	89·49 W
104	Lebanon		In.	40·00 N	86·30 W
120	Lebanon		Ky.	37·32 N	85·15 W
117	Lebanon		Mo.	37·40 N	92·43 W
105	Lebanon		NH	43·40 N	72·15 W
104	Lebanon		Oh.	39·25 N	84·10 W
110	Lebanon		Or.	44·31 N	122·53 W
105	Lebanon		Pa.	40·20 N	76·20 W
120	Lebanon		Tn.	36·10 N	86·16 W
186	Lebanon		Asia	34·00 N	
153	Lebanon Mts.		Leb.	33·30 N	35·32 E
167	Lebedin (lyĕ'bĕ-dên)		Sov. Un.	48·56 N	31·35 E
167	Lebedin		Sov. Un.	50·34 N	34·27 E
166	Lebedyan' (lyĕ'bĕ-dyän')		Sov. Un.	53·03 N	39·08 E
160	Le Blanc (lĕ-blän')		Fr.	46·38 N	0·59 E
129	Le Borgne (lĕ bôrn'y')		Hai.	19·50 N	72·30 W

ng-sing; ŋ-baŋk; N-nasalized n; nŏd; cŏmmit; ōld; ōbey; ôrder; fōōd; fŏŏt; ou-out; s-soft; sh-dish; th-thin; pūre; ūnite; ûrn; stŭd; circ*u*s; ü-as "y" in study; '-indeterminate vowel.

Page	Name	Pronunciation	Region	Lat. °′	Long. °′
159	Lebork	(lăn-bŏŏrk′)	Pol.	54·33 N	17·46 E
160	Le Boucau	(lĕ-bōō-kō′)	Fr.	43·33 N	1·28 W
160	Le Bouscat	(lē bōōs-kà)	Fr.	44·53 N	0·38 W
162	Lebrija	(lå-brē′hä)	Sp.	36·55 N	6·06 W
136	Lebú	(lā-bōō′)	Chile	37·35 S	73·37 W
165	Lecce	(lĕt′chā)	It.	40·22 N	18·11 E
164	Lecco	(lĕk′kō)	It.	45·52 N	9·28 E
161	Le Châtelet-en-Brie	(lĕ-shä-tĕ-lā′ ĕn-brē′)	Fr. (Paris In.)	48·29 N	2·50 E
128	Leche, Laguna de (L.)	(lā-gōō′nä-dĕ-lĕ′chĕ)	Cuba	22·10 N	78·30 W
118	Leche, Laguna de la (L.)		Mex.	27·16 N	102·45 W
161	Lechenich	(lĕ′kĕ-nĕk)	F.R.G. (Ruhr In.)	50·47 N	6·46 E
158	Lech R.	(lĕk)	F.R.G.	47·41 N	10·52 E
119	Lecompte		La.	31·06 N	92·25 W
160	Le Coteau	(lē kō-tō′)	Fr.	46·01 N	4·06 E
160	Le Creusot	(lĕkrû-zō)	Fr.	46·48 N	4·23 E
160	Lectoure	(lĕk-tōōr)	Fr.	43·56 N	0·38 E
162	Ledesma	(lå-dĕs′mä)	Sp.	41·05 N	5·59 W
93	Leduc	(lĕ-dōōk′)	Can.	53·16 N	113·33 W
109	Leech (L.)	(lēch)	Mn.	47·06 N	94·16 W
106	Leeds	(lēdz)	Al. (Birmingham In.)	33·33 N	86·33 W
148	Leeds		Eng.	53·48 N	1·33 W
108	Leeds		ND	48·18 N	99·24 W
148	Leeds and Liverpool Can.	(lĭv′ēr-pōōl)	Eng.	53·36 N	2·38 W
149	Leegebruch	(lĕh′gĕn-brōōk)	G.D.R. (Berlin In.)	52·43 N	13·12 E
148	Leek	(lēk)	Eng.	53·06 N	2·01 W
158	Leer	(lār)	F.R.G.	53·14 N	7·27 E
154	Lee R.	(lē)	Ire.	51·52 N	8·30 W
121	Leesburg	(lēz′bûrg)	Fl.	28·49 N	81·53 W
105	Leesburg		Va.	39·10 N	77·30 W
115	Lees Ferry		Az.	36·55 N	111·45 W
113	Lees Summit		Mo. (Kansas City In.)	38·55 N	94·23 W
129	Lee Stocking (I.)		Ba.	23·45 N	76·05 W
119	Leesville	(lēz′vĭl)	La.	31·09 N	93·17 W
104	Leetonia	(lē-tō′nĭ-à)	Oh.	40·50 N	80·45 W
155	Leeuwarden	(lā′wär-dĕn)	Neth.	53·12 N	5·50 E
204	Leeuwin, C.	(lōō′wĭn)	Austl.	34·15 S	114·30 E
119	Leeward Is.	(lē′wērd)	N. A.	12·25 N	62·15 W
127	Le Francois		Mart. (In.)	14·37 N	60·55 W
204	Lefroy (L.)	(lē-froi′)	Austl.	31·30 S	122·00 E
163	Leganés	(lå-gä′nås)	Sp. (Madrid In.)	40·20 N	3·46 W
197	Legaspi	(lå-gäs′pê)	Phil. (In.)	13·09 N	123·44 E
203	Legge Pk.	(lĕg)	Austl.	41·33 S	148·10 E
	Leghorn, see Livorno				
164	Legnano	(lå-nyä′nō)	It.	45·35 N	8·53 E
158	Legnica	(lĕk-nĭt′sà)	Pol.	51·13 N	16·10 E
184	Leh	(lā)	India	34·10 N	77·40 E
160	Le Havre	(lē àv′r′)	Fr.	49·31 N	0·07 E
115	Lehi	(lē′hī)	Ut.	40·25 N	111·55 W
115	Lehman Caves Natl. Mon.	(lē′măn)	Nv.	38·54 N	114·08 W
149	Lehnin	(lĕh′nēn)	G.D.R. (Berlin In.)	52·19 N	12·45 E
148	Leicester	(lĕs′tēr)	Eng.	52·37 N	1·08 W
148	Leicester (Co.)		Eng.	52·40 N	1·12 W
204	Leichhardt ,(R.)	(līk′härt)	Austl.	18·30 S	139·45 E
149	Leiden	(lī′dĕn)	Neth. (Amsterdam In.)	52·09 N	4·29 E
203	Leigh Creek	(lē krēk)	Austl.	30·33 S	138·30 E
156	Leikanger	(lī′kän′gēr)	Nor.	61·11 N	6·51 E
149	Leimuiden		Neth. (Amsterdam In.)	52·13 N	4·40 E
158	Leine R.	(lī′nĕ)	F.R.G.	51·58 N	9·56 E
154	Leinster	(lĕn-stēr)	Ire.	52·45 N	7·19 W
104	Leipsic	(līp′sĭk)	Oh.	41·05 N	84·00 W
158	Leipzig	(līp′tsĭk)	G.D.R.	51·20 N	12·24 E
162	Leiria	(lā-rē′ä)	Port.	39·45 N	8·50 W
120	Leitchfield	(lēch′fēld)	Ky.	37·28 N	86·20 W
149	Leitha (R.)		Aus. (Vienna In.)	48·04 N	16·57 E
89	Leitrim		Can. (Ottawa In.)	45·20 N	75·36 W
	Leixoes, see Matozinhos				
155	Lek (R.)	(lĕk)	Neth.	51·59 N	5·30 E
151	Lekef	(lĕkĕf′)	Tun.	36·14 N	8·42 E
216	Lékéti, Monts de la (Mts.)		Con.	2·34 S	14·17 E
156	Leksand	(lĕk′sänd)	Swe.	60·45 N	14·56 E
112	Leland	(lē′lănd)	Wa. (Seattle In.)	47·54 N	122·53 W
158	Le Locle	(lē lō′kl′)	Switz.	47·03 N	6·43 E
136	Le Maire, Estrecho de (Str.)	(ĕs-trĕ′chō-dĕ-lĕ-mī′rĕ)	Arg.	55·15 S	65·30 W
160	Le Mans	(lē män′)	Fr.	48·01 N	0·12 E
127	Le Marin		Mart. (In.)	14·28 N	60·55 W
108	Le Mars	(lē märz′)	Ia.	42·46 N	96·09 W
113	Lemay		Mo. (St. Louis In.)	38·32 N	90·17 W
197	Lemery	(lā-mā-rē′)	Phil. (In.)	13·51 S	120·55 E
183	Lemesós		Cyprus (Palestine In.)	34·39 N	33·02 E
111	Lemhi Ra. (Mts.)	(lĕm′hī)	Id.	44·35 N	113·33 W
111	Lemhi R.		Id.	44·40 N	113·27 W
108	Lemmon	(lĕm′ŭn)	SD	45·55 N	102·10 W
129	Le Môle	(lē mōl′)	Hai.	19·50 N	73·20 W
114	Lemon Grove	(lĕm′ŭn-grōv)	Ca. (In.)	32·44 N	117·02 W
107	Lemont	(lē′-mŏnt)	Il. (Chicago In.)	41·40 N	87·59 W
127	Le Moule	(lē mōōl′)	Guad. (In.)	16·19 N	61·22 W
126	Lempa R.	(lĕm′pä)	Sal.	13·20 N	88·46 W
156	Lemvig	(lĕm′vēgh)	Den.	56·33 N	8·16 E
156	Lena	(lī′nä)	Swe.	60·01 N	17·40 E
173	Lena (R.)		Sov. Un.	68·39 N	124·15 E
136	Lençóes Paulista	(lĕn-sôns′ pou-lēs′tà)	Braz.	22·30 S	48·45 W
135	Lençóis	(lĕn-sóis)	Braz.	12·38 S	41·28 W
113	Lenexa	(lē′nĕx-ă)	Ks. (Kansas City In.)	38·58 N	99·44 W
147	Lenger	(lyĭn′gyĕr)	Sov. Un.	41·38 N	70·00 E
183	Lenik (R.)		Mala. (Singapore In.)	1·59 N	102·51 E
172	Leninabad	(lĕ-nyē-nà bät′)	Sov. Un.	40·15 N	69·49 E
171	Leninakan	(lĕ-nyĕ-nà-kän′)	Sov. Un.	40·40 N	43·50 E
174	Leningrad	(lyĕ-nĕn-grät′)	Sov. Un. (Leningrad In.)	59·57 N	30·20 E
166	Leningrad (Oblast)		Sov. Un.	59·15 N	30·30 E
167	Leningradskaya	(lyĕ-nĭn-gräd′skå-yà)	Sov. Un.	46·19 N	39·23 E
174	Lenino	(lyĕ′nĭ-nô)	Sov. Un. (Moscow In.)	55·37 N	47·41 E
172	Leninogorsk	(lyĕ-nĭn ŭ gôrsk′)	Sov. Un.	50·29 N	83·25 E
171	Leninsk	(lyĕ-nēnsk′)	Sov. Un.	48·40 N	45·10 E
172	Leninsk-Kuznetski	(lyĕ-nĕnsk′ kōōz-nyĕt′skĭ)	Sov. Un.	54·28 N	86·48 E
171	Lenkoran′	(lĕn-kô-rän′)	Sov. Un.	38·52 N	48·58 E
108	Lennox	(lĕn′ŭks)	SD	43·22 N	96·53 W
121	Lenoir	(lê-nōr′)	NC	35·54 N	81·35 W
120	Lenoir City		Tn.	35·47 N	84·16 W
109	Lenox		Ia.	40·51 N	94·29 W
214	Léo		Upper Volta	11·06 N	2·06 W
158	Leoben	(lå-ō′bĕn)	Aus.	47·22 N	15·09 E
129	Léogane	(lā-ô-gan′)	Hai.	18·30 N	72·35 W
108	Leola	(lê-ō′là)	SD	45·43 N	99·55 W
99	Leominster	(lĕm′ĭn-stēr)	Ma. (In.)	42·32 N	71·45 W
109	Leon	(lē′ŏn)	Ia.	40·43 N	93·44 W
124	León	(lå-ōn′)	Mex.	21·08 N	101·41 W
126	León	(lĕ-ô′n)	Nic.	12·28 N	86·53 W
162	León	(lĕ-ô′n)	Sp.	42·38 N	5·33 W
162	Leon (Reg.)	(lĕ-ô′n)	Sp.	41·18 N	5·50 W
164	Leonforte	(lā-ôn-fôr′tä)	It.	37·40 N	14·27 E
118	Leon R.	(lē′ŏn)	Tx.	31·54 N	98·20 W
137	Leopoldina	(lā-ô-pôl-dē′nä)	Braz. (Rio de Janeiro In.)	21·32 S	42·38 W
149	Leopoldsburg		Bel. (Brussels In.)	51·07 N	5·18 E
149	Leopoldsdorf im Marchfelde	(lā′ô-pôlts-dôrf′)	Aus. (Vienna In.)	48·14 N	16·42 E
	Leopold II, L., see Mai-Ndombe				
	Léopoldville, see Kinshasa				
167	Leovo	(lå-ō′vô)	Sov. Un.	46·30 N	28·16 E
162	Lepe	(lā′pā)	Sp.	37·15 N	7·12 W
166	Lepel′	(lyĕ-pĕl′)	Sov. Un.	54·52 N	28·41 E
89	L'Épiphanie	(lā-pê-fä-nē′)	Can. (Montreal In.)	45·51 N	73·29 W
161	Le Plessis-Belleville	(lĕ-plĕ-sē′ bĕl-vēl′)	Fr. (Paris In.)	49·05 N	2·46 E
158	Lepontine Alpi (Mts.)	(lē-pŏn′tĭn)	Switz.	46·28 N	8·38 E
98	Lepreau	(lê-prō′)	Can.	45·10 N	66·28 W
172	Lepsinsh		Sov. Un.	45·32 N	80·47 E
160	Le Puy-en-Velay	(lē pwē′)	Fr.	45·02 N	3·54 E
164	Lercara	(lĕr-kä′rä)	It.	36·47 N	13·36 E
118	Lerdo	(lĕr′dō)	Mex.	25·31 N	103·30 W
211	Léré	(lā-rā′)	Chad	9·42 N	14·14 E
214	Léré		Mali	15·43 N	4·55 W
213	Leribe		Leso. (Natal In.)	28·53 S	28·02 E
163	Lérida	(lā′rē-dhä)	Sp.	41·38 N	0·37 E
125	Lerma	(lĕr′mä)	Mex.	19·49 N	90·34 W
125	Lerma		Mex. (In.)	19·17 N	99·30 W
162	Lerma	(lĕ′r-mä)	Sp.	42·03 N	3·45 W
124	Lerma (R.)		Mex.	20·14 N	101·50 W
105	Le Roy	(lē roi′)	NY	43·00 N	78·00 W
154	Lerwick	(lĕr′ĭk) (lûr′wĭk)	Scot.	60·08 N	1·27 W
89	Léry	(lā-rī′)	Can. (Montréal In.)	45·21 N	73·49 W
106	Lery, L.	(lĕ′rē)	La. (New Orleans In.)	29·48 N	89·45 W
161	Les Andelys	(lā-zäN-dē-lē′)	Fr. (Paris In.)	49·15 N	1·25 E
129	Les Cayes		Hai.	18·15 N	73·45 W
89	Les Cèdres	(lā-sĕdr′′)	Can. (Montreal In.)	45·18 N	74·03 W
165	Lesh (Alessio)	(lĕshĕ) (ä-lā′sē-ō)	Alb.	41·47 N	19·40 E
164	Lésina, Lago di (L.)	(lä′gō dē lā′zē-nä)	It.	41·48 N	15·12 E
165	Leskovac	(lĕs′kô-vàts)	Yugo.	43·00 N	21·58 E
117	Leslie	(lĕz′lĭ)	Ar.	35·49 N	92·32 W
218	Leslie		S. Afr. (Johannesburg & Pretoria In.)	26·23 S	28·57 E
170	Lesnoy	(lĕs′noi)	Sov. Un.	66·45 N	34·45 E
194	Lesogorsk	(lyĕs′ô-gôrsk)	Sov. Un.	49·28 N	141·59 E
212	Lesotho	(lĕsō′thō)	Afr.	29·45 S	28·07 E
194	Lesozavodsk	(lyĕ-sô-zà-vôdsk′)	Sov. Un.	45·21 N	133·19 E
160	Lesparre	(lē-spär)	Fr.	45·18 N	0·57 W
160	Les-Pennes-Mirabeau	(lā-pĕn′ mĭ-rä-bō′)	Fr. (In.)	43·25 N	5·19 E
160	Les Sables-d'Olonne	(lā sà′bl′dô-lŭn′)	Fr.	46·30 N	1·47 W
127	Les Saintes Is.	(lā-sănt′)	Guad. (In.)	15·50 N	61·40 W
	Lesser Khingan Ra. see Hsiaohsinganling Shanmo				
93	Lesser Slave (R.)		Can.	55·15 N	114·30 W
93	Lesser Slave L.	(lĕs′ēr slāv)	Can.	55·25 N	115·30 W
160	L'Estaque	(lĕs-täl)	Fr. (In)	43·22 N	5·20 E
161	Les Thilliers-en-Vexin	(lā-tē-yā′ ĕn-vĕ-săn′)	Fr. (Paris In.)	49·19 N	1·36 E
109	Le Sueur	(lē sōōr′)	Mn.	44·27 N	93·53 W
165	Lésvos (I.)		Grc.	39·15 N	25·40 E
158	Leszno	(lĕsh′nō)	Pol.	51·51 N	16·35 E
160	Le Teil	(lĕ tā′y′)	Fr.	44·34 N	4·39 E
93	Lethbridge	(lĕth′brĭj)	Can.	49·42 N	112·50 W
167	Letichev	(lyĕ-tê-chĕf′)	Sov. Un.	49·22 N	27·29 E
134	Leticia	(lĕ-tē′syä)	Col.	4·04 S	69·57 W
161	Letmathe	(lĕt′mät-hĕ)	F.R.G. (Ruhr In.)	51·22 N	7·37 E
160	Le Tréport	(lē-trā′pôr′)	Fr.	50·03 N	1·21 E
196	Leuser, Gulung (Mtn.)		Indon.	3·36 N	97·17 E
149	Leuven		Bel. (Brussels In.)	50·53 N	4·42 E
96	Levack		Can.	46·38 N	81·23 W
165	Levádhia		Grc.	38·25 N	22·51 E
161	Levallois-Perret	(lē-vàl-wä′pĕ-rĕ′)	Fr. (Paris In.)	48·53 N	2·17 E
150	Levanger	(lĕ-väng′ĕr)	Nor.	63·42 N	11·01 E
164	Levanna (Mtn.)	(lå-vä′nä)	Fr.-It.	45·25 N	7·14 E
204	Leveque, C.	(lê-vĕk′)	Austl.	16·26 S	123·08 E
161	Leverkusen	(lĕ′fĕr-kōō-zĕn)	F.R.G. (Ruhr In.)	51·01 N	6·59 E
212	Leverville	(lē-vā-vēl′)	Zaire	5·13 S	18·43 E
159	Levice	(lā′vĕt-sĕ)	Czech.	48·13 N	18·37 E
164	Levico	(lā′vē-kō)	It.	46·02 N	11·20 E
160	Le Vigan	(lē vē-gäN′)	Fr.	43·59 N	3·36 E
89	Lévis	(lā-vē′) (lē′vĭs)	Can. (Quebec In.)	46·49 N	71·11 W
106	Levittown	(lĕ′vĭt-toun)	Pa. (Philadelphia In.)	40·08 N	74·50 W
165	Levkás	(lyĕfkäs′)	Grc.	38·49 N	20·43 E
165	Levkás (I.)		Grc.	38·42 N	20·22 E
159	Levoča	(lā′vô-chä)	Czech.	49·03 N	20·38 E
121	Levy (L.)	(lē′vĭ)	Fl.	29·31 N	82·23 W
105	Lewes	(lōō′ĭs)	De.	38·45 N	75·10 W
154	Lewes		Eng.	50·51 N	0·01 E
154	Lewis (I.)	(lōō′ĭs)	Scot.	58·05 N	6·07 W
112	Lewis (R.) East Fk.		Wa. (Portland In.)	45·52 N	122·40 W
120	Lewisburg	(lū′ĭs-bûrg)	Tn.	35·27 N	86·47 W
104	Lewisburg	(lū′ĭs-bûrg)	WV	37·50 N	80·20 W
99	Lewis Hills		Can.	48·48 N	58·30 W
99	Lewisporte	(lū′ĭs-pōrt)	Can.	49·15 N	55·04 W
111	Lewis Ra.	(lū′ĭs)	Mt.	48·05 N	113·06 W
110	Lewis R.		Wa.	46·05 N	122·09 W
110	Lewiston	(lū′ĭs-tŭn)	Id.	46·24 N	116·59 W
98	Lewiston		Me.	44·05 N	70·14 W
107	Lewiston		NY (Buffalo In.)	43·11 N	79·02 W
111	Lewiston		Ut.	41·58 N	111·51 W
117	Lewistown	(lū′ĭs-toun)	Il.	40·23 N	90·06 W
111	Lewistown		Mt.	47·05 N	109·25 W
105	Lewistown		Pa.	40·35 N	77·30 W
104	Lexington	(lĕk′sĭng-tŭn)	Ky.	38·05 N	84·30 W
99	Lexington		Ma. (In.)	42·27 N	71·14 W
120	Lexington		Ms.	33·08 N	90·02 W
117	Lexington		Mo.	39·11 N	93·52 W
116	Lexington		Nb.	40·46 N	99·44 W
121	Lexington		NC	35·47 N	80·15 W
120	Lexington		Tn.	35·37 N	88·24 W
105	Lexington		Va.	37·45 N	79·20 W
197	Leyte (I.)	(lā′tä)	Phil.	10·35 N	125·35 E
159	Lezajsk	(lĕ′zhä-ĭsk)	Pol.	50·14 N	22·25 E
166	Lezha (R.)	(lĕ-zhä′)	Sov. Un.	58·59 N	40·27 E
160	Lézignan	(lā-zē-nyäN′)	Fr.	43·13 N	2·48 E
167	L'gov	(lgôf)	Sov. Un.	51·42 N	35·15 E
184	Lhasa	(läs′ä)	China	29·41 N	91·12 E
190	Lhsien	(yĕ′sĭäN)	China	37·09 N	119·57 E
192	Lianghsiang	(lyäng′syän′)	China (In.)	39·43 N	116·08 E
174	Lianozovo	(lĭ-a-nô′zô-vô)	Sov. Un. (Moscow In.)	55·54 N	37·36 E
190	Liaoch'eng	(lĭou′chĕng)	China	36·27 N	115·56 E
192	Liao Ho (R.)	(lyä′ō hō′)	China	41·40 N	122·40 E
189	Liaoning (Prov.)		China	41·31 N	122·11 E
190	Liaotung Pantao (Pen.)	(lĭou′dōōng bän′dou)	China	39·45 N	122·22 E
192	Liaotung Wan (B.)		China	40·25 N	121·15 E
192	Liaoyang	(lyä′ō-yäng′)	China	41·18 N	123·10 E
192	Liaoyüan	(lyä′ō-yü-än′)	China	43·00 N	124·59 E
113	Liard (R.)	(lê-är′)	Can.	59·43 N	126·42 W
134	Libano	(lē′bà-nō)	Col. (In.)	4·55 N	75·05 W
162	Libar, Sierra de (Mts.)	(sē-ĕ′r-rä-dĕ-lē-bär)	Sp.	39·42 N	5·28 W
110	Libby	(lĭb′ē)	Mt.	48·27 N	115·35 W
211	Libenge	(lê-bĕŋ′gä)	Zaire	3·39 N	18·40 E
116	Liberal	(lĭb′ēr-ăl)	Ks.	37·01 N	100·56 W
158	Liberec	(lē′bĕr-ĕts)	Czech.	50·45 N	15·06 E
209	Liberia	(lī-bē′rĭ-à)	Afr.	6·30 N	9·55 W
126	Liberia		C. R.	10·38 N	85·28 W
135	Libertad de Orituco	(lē-bĕr-tä′d-dĕ-ō-rê-tōō′kō)	Ven. (In.)	9·32 N	66·24 W
104	Liberty	(lĭb′ēr-tĭ)	In.	39·35 N	84·55 W
113	Liberty		Mo. (Kansas City In.)	39·15 N	94·25 W
121	Liberty		SC	34·47 N	82·41 W
119	Liberty		Tx.	30·03 N	94·46 W
113	Liberty		Ut. (Salt Lake City In.)	41·20 N	111·52 W
112	Liberty B.		Wa. (Seattle In.)	47·43 N	122·41 W
106	Liberty L.		Md. (Baltimore In.)	39·25 N	76·56 W
107	Libertyville	(lĭb′ēr-tĭ-vĭl)	Il. (Chicago In.)	42·17 N	87·57 W
197	Libmanan	(lĭb-mä′nän)	Phil. (In.)	13·42 N	123·04 E
213	Libode	(lĭ-bō′dĕ)	S. Afr. (Natal In.)	31·33 S	29·03 E
129	Libón, R.		Hai.	19·30 N	71·45 W
160	Libourne	(lē-bōōrn′)	Fr.	44·55 N	0·12 W
125	Libres	(lē′brās)	Mex.	19·26 N	97·41 W
216	Libreville	(lē-br′vēl′)	Gabon	0·23 N	9·27 E
106	Liburn	(lĭb′ûrn)	Ga. (Atlanta In.)	33·53 N	84·09 W
209	Libya	(lĭb′ê-ä)	Afr.	27·38 N	15·00 E
211	Libyan Des.	(lĭb′ê-ăn)	Libya	28·23 N	23·34 E
153	Libyan Plat.		Egypt	30·58 N	26·20 E
136	Licancábur, Cerro (Mtn.)	(sĕ′r-rô-lē-kän-kä′bōōr)	Chile	22·45 S	67·45 W
137	Licanten	(lē-kän-tĕ′n)	Chile (Santiago In.)	34·58 S	72·00 W
148	Lichfield	(lĭch′fēld)	Eng.	52·41 N	1·49 W
188	Lichiang		China	27·00 N	100·08 E
190	Liching	(lē′jĭn)	China	37·30 N	118·15 E
218	Lichtenburg	(lĭk′tĕn-bĕrgh)	S. Afr. (Johannesburg & Pretoria In.)	26·09 S	26·10 E
107	Lick Cr.	(lĭk)	In. (Indianapolis In.)	39·43 N	86·06 W
104	Licking (R.)	(lĭk′ĭng)	Ky.	38·30 N	84·10 W
164	Licosa, Pt.	(lē-kō′sä)	It.	40·17 N	14·40 E
159	Lida	(lē′dà)	Sov. Un.	53·53 N	25·19 E
108	Libgerwood	(lĭj′ēr-wood)	ND	46·04 N	97·10 W
156	Lidköping	(lēt′chû-pĭng)	Swe.	58·31 N	13·06 E

PRONOUNCING INDEX

Lido di Roma — Livno 305

Page Name Pronunciation Region Lat. °' Long. °'

163 Lido di Roma (Ostia Lido) (lē'dô-dē-rô'mä) (ô's-tyä-lē-dô) It. (Rome In.) 41·19 N 12·17 E
159 Lidzbark (lĭts'bärk)..........Pol. 54·07 N 20·36 E
218 Liebenbergsvlei (R.).......S. Afr. (Johannesburg & Pretoria In.) 27·35 S 28·25 E
149 Liebenwalde (lē'bĕn-väl-dĕ) G.D.R. (Berlin In.) 52·52 N 13·24 E
193 Liechou Pan-Tao (Pen.)....China 20·40 N 109·25 E
151 Liechtenstein (lĕk'tĕn-shtīn)..Eur. 47·10 N 10·00 E
155 Liège (lê-āzh')...............Bel. 50·40 N 5·30 E
193 Lienchiang................China 21·38 N 110·15 E
190 Lienshui (lĭan'sōōā)........China 33·46 N 119·15 E
189 Lienyün (lian'yün).........China 33·10 N 120·01 E
190 Lienyünchiang..............China 34·43 N 119·27 E
158 Lienz (lê-ĕnts')..............Aus. 46·49 N 12·45 E
157 Liepāja (le'pä-yä')........Sov. Un. 56·31 N 20·59 E
149 Lier...........Bel. (Brussels In.) 51·08 N 4·34 E
149 Liesing (lē'sĭng).Aus. (Vienna In.) 48·09 N 16·17 E
158 Liestal (lēs'täl)............Switz. 47·28 N 7·44 E
105 Lievre, Riviére du (R.).......Can. 45·00 N 75·25 W
216 Lifanga...................Zaire 0·19 N 21·57 E
154 Liffey R. (lĭf'ĭ)..............Ire. 53·21 N 6·35 W
205 Lifou, (I.)...............N. Cal. 21·15 S 167·32 E
197 Ligao (lê-gä'ô).........Phil. (In.) 13·14 N 123·33 E
203 Lightning Ridge...........Austl. 29·23 S 147·50 E
213 Ligonha (R.) (lê-gō'nyȧ).....Moz. 16·14 S 39·00 E
104 Ligonier (lĭg-ô-nēr)............In. 41·30 N 85·35 W
174 Ligovo (lē'gô-vô) Sov. Un. (Leningrad In.) 59·51 N 30·13 E
164 Liguria (Reg.) (lê-gōō-rē-ä)....It. 44·24 N 8·27 E
164 Ligurian Sea (lĭ-gū'rĭ-ăn).....Eur. 43·42 N 8·32 E
205 Lihou Rfs. (lê-hōō')........Austl. 17·23 S 152·43 E
193 Lihsien (lē'hsyĕn').........China 29·42 N 111·40 E
190 Lihsien....................China 38·30 N 115·38 E
190 Lihuang (lē'hōōäng)........China 31·32 N 115·46 E
100 Lihue (lê-hōō'ā)..............Hi. 21·59 N 159·23 W
157 Lihula (lē'hōō-lȧ)........Sov. Un. 58·41 N 23·50 E
217 Likasi (Jadotville)..........Zaire 10·59 S 26·44 E
166 Likhoslavl' (lyê-kôslàv''l).Sov. Un. 57·07 N 35·27 E
167 Likhovka (lyê-kôf'kȧ)....Sov. Un. 48·52 N 33·57 E
216 Likouala (R.)...............Con. 0·10 S 16·30 E
160 Lille (lēl)...................Fr. 50·38 N 3·01 E
156 Lille Baelt (str.)............Den. 55·09 N 9·53 E
156 Lillehammer (lēl'ĕ-häm'mĕr)..Nor. 61·07 N 10·25 E
156 Lillesand (lēl'ĕ-sän')........Nor. 58·16 N 8·19 E
156 Lilleström (lēl'ĕ-strûm)......Nor. 59·56 N 11·04 E
112 Lilliwaup (lĭl'ĭ-wŏp) Wa. (Seattle In.) 47·28 N 123·07 W
93 Lillooet (lĭ'lōō-ĕt)...........Can. 50·30 N 121·55 W
93 Lillooet (R.)...............Can. 49·50 N 122·10 W
217 Lilongwe (lê-lô-än).......Malawi 13·59 S 33·44 E
104 Lima (lī'mȧ).................Oh. 40·40 N 84·05 W
134 Lima (lē'mä)................Peru 12·06 S 76·55 W
162 Lima (R.)...................Port. 41·45 N 8·22 W
137 Lima Duarte (dwä'r-tě) Braz. (Rio de Janeiro In.) 21·52 S 43·47 W
111 Lima Res..................Mt. 44·45 N 112·15 W
136 Limay (lē-mä'ê) (R.)........Arg. 39·50 S 69·15 W
157 Limbazi (lēm'bä-zĭ)......Sov. Un. 57·32 N 24·44 E
184 Limbdi....................India 22·37 N 71·52 E
129 Limbé......................Hai. 19·45 N 72·30 W
158 Limburg (lem-bōōrg')......F.R.G. 50·22 N 8·03 E
156 Limedsforsen (lē'mĕs-fôrs'ĕn).Swe. 60·54 N 13·24 E
137 Limeira (lē-mā'rä) Braz. (Rio de Janeiro In.) 22·34 S 47·24 W
95 Limestone Bay (līm'stōn)....Can. 53·50 N 98·50 W
156 Limfjorden (Fd.)...........Den. 56·14 N 7·55 E
156 Limfjorden (Fd.)...........Den. 56·56 N 10·35 E
204 Limmen Bght. (lĭm'ĕn).....Austl. 14·45 S 136·00 E
165 Limni (lēm'nê)..............Grc. 38·47 N 23·22 E
165 Limnos (I.)..................Grc. 39·58 N 24·48 E
89 Limoges (lê-môzh') Can. (Ottawa In.) 45·20 N 75·15 W
160 Limoges....................Fr. 45·50 N 1·15 E
116 Limon (lī'mŏn)...............Co. 39·15 N 103·41 W
127 Limón (lê-mōn')..........C. R. 10·01 N 83·02 W
126 Limón (lē-mô'n)............Hond. 15·53 N 85·34 W
129 Limon (R.)...........Dom. Rep. 18·20 N 71·40 W
122 Limón B..............C. Z. (In.) 9·21 N 79·58 W
161 Limours (lē-mōōr')..Fr. (Paris In.) 48·39 N 2·05 E
160 Limousin, Plateaux du (Plat.) (plä-tō' dü lē-mōō-zăn').Fr. 45·44 N 1·09 E
160 Limoux (lē-mōō')............Fr. 43·03 N 2·14 E
212 Limpopo R. (lĭm-pō'pō).....Afr. 23·15 S 27·46 E
137 Linares (lê-nä'räs) Chile (Santiago In.) 35·51 S 71·35 W
118 Linares..................Mex. 24·53 N 99·34 W
162 Linares (lē-nä'rĕs)...........Sp. 38·07 N 3·38 W
137 Linares (Prov.) Chile (Santiago In.) 35·53 S 71·30 W
164 Linaro, C. (lê-nä'rä)..........It. 42·02 N 11·53 E
190 Linchang (lĭn'chäng')......China 36·19 N 114·40 E
192 Linchiang (lĭn'chäng')......China 41·45 N 127·00 E
190 Linch'ing (lĭn'chĭng).......China 36·49 N 115·42 E
193 Linch'uan................China 27·58 N 116·18 E
137 Lincoln (lĭŋ'kŭn) Arg. (Buenos Aires In.) 34·51 S 61·29 W
114 Lincoln.....................Ca. 38·51 N 121·19 W
89 Lincoln.......Can. (Toronto In.) 43·10 N 79·29 W
148 Lincoln....................Eng. 53·14 N 0·33 W
117 Lincoln......................Il. 40·09 N 89·21 W
116 Lincoln.....................Ks. 39·02 N 98·08 W
98 Lincoln......................Me. 45·23 N 68·31 W
99 Lincoln...............Ma. (In.) 42·25 N 71·19 W
117 Lincoln......................Ne. 40·49 N 96·43 W
148 Lincoln (Co.)..............Eng. 53·12 N 0·29 W
116 Lincoln, Mt.................Co. 39·20 N 106·19 W
148 Lincoln Heights (Reg.).......Eng. 53·23 N 0·39 W
107 Lincoln Park....Mi. (Detroit In.) 42·14 N 83·11 W
106 Lincoln Park..NJ (New York In.) 40·56 N 74·18 W
121 Lincolnton (lĭŋ'kŭn-tŭn).......NC 35·27 N 81·15 W
154 Lincoln Wolds (woldz').......Eng. 53·25 N 0·23 W

120 Lindale (lĭn'dāl).............Ga. 34·10 N 85·10 W
158 Lindau (lĭn'dou)..........F.R.G. 47·33 N 9·40 E
120 Linden (lĭn'dĕn)...............Al. 32·16 N 87·47 W
113 Linden.....Mo. (Kansas City In.) 39·13 N 94·35 W
106 Linden..........NJ (New York In.) 40·39 N 74·14 W
106 Lindenhurst (lĭn'dĕn-hûrst) NY (New York In.) 40·41 N 73·23 W
106 Lindenwold (lĭn'dĕn-wôld) NJ (Philadelphia In.) 39·50 N 75·00 W
156 Lindesberg (lĭn'dĕs-bĕrgh)....Swe. 59·37 N 15·14 E
155 Lindesnes (C.) (lĭn'ĕs-nĕs)....Nor. 58·00 N 7·05 E
192 Lindho...................China 40·45 N 107·30 E
217 Lindi (lĭn'dê)...............Tan. 10·00 S 39·43 E
211 Lindi R..................Zaire 1·00 N 27·13 E
218 Lindley (lĭnd'lê)............S. Afr. (Johannesburg & Pretoria In.) 27·52 S 27·55 E
149 Lindow (lēn'dōv) G.D.R. (Berlin In.) 52·58 N 12·59 E
105 Lindsay (lĭn'zê)...............Can. 44·20 N 78·45 W
116 Lindsay......................Ok. 34·50 N 97·38 W
116 Lindsborg (lĭnz'bôrg).........Ks. 38·34 N 97·42 W
148 Lindsey (Co.) (lĭn'zĭ)........Eng. 53·25 N 0·32 W
190 Lineh'ü (lĭn'chü)...........China 36·31 N 118·33 E
120 Lineville (lĭn'vĭl).............Al. 33·18 N 85·45 W
192 Linfen...................China 36·00 N 111·38 E
196 Linga, Kepulauan (Is.).....Indon. 0·35 S 105·05 E
197 Lingayen (lĭŋ'gä-yän')..Phil. (In.) 16·01 N 120·13 E
197 Lingayen G...........Phil. (In.) 16·18 N 120·11 E
158 Lingen (lĭŋ'gĕn)...........F.R.G. 52·32 N 7·20 E
193 Lingling (Yungchow).......China 26·10 N 111·40 E
190 Lingpi (lĭng'pĭ')...........China 33·33 N 117·33 E
190 Lingtienchen (ling'diän'jĕn).China 31·52 N 121·28 E
193 Lingting Yang (Can.)......China 22·00 N 114·00 E
214 Linguère (lĭŋ-gĕr')........Senegal 15·24 N 15·07 W
192 Lingwu....................China 38·05 N 106·18 E
192 Lingyüan..................China 41·12 N 119·20 E
193 Linhai....................China 28·52 N 121·08 E
192 Linhsi....................China 43·30 N 118·02 E
190 Linhuaikuan (lĭnhōōäi'gōōän) China 32·55 N 117·38 E
190 Linhuanchi (lĭn'hōōän'jē)...China 33·42 N 116·33 E
190 Lini (lĭn'yē)...............China 35·04 N 118·21 E
193 Linkao....................China 19·58 N 109·40 E
156 Linköping (lĭn'chû-pĭng).....Swe. 58·25 N 15·35 E
190 Linmingkuan (lĭn'mĭng'gōōän) China 36·47 N 114·32 E
154 Linnhe (L.) (lĭn'ê)..........Scot. 56·35 N 4·30 W
135 Lins (lê'ns)...............Braz. 21·42 S 49·41 W
106 Linthicum Heights (lĭn'thĭ-kŭm) Md. (Baltimore In.) 39·12 N 76·39 W
192 Lintien...................China 42·08 N 124·59 E
104 Linton (lĭn'tŭn)..............In. 39·05 N 87·15 W
108 Linton......................ND 46·16 N 100·15 W
193 Linwu (lĭn'wōō')..........China 25·20 N 112·30 E
190 Linying (lĭn'yĭng')........China 33·48 N 113·56 E
190 Linyü (lĭn'yü)..............China 40·01 N 119·45 E
158 Linz (lĭnts)..................Aus. 48·18 N 14·18 E
197 Lipa (lê-pä')..........Phil. (In.) 13·55 N 121·10 E
164 Lipari (lē'pä-rê)...............It. 38·29 N 15·00 E
164 Lipari (I.)....................It. 38·32 N 15·04 E
166 Lipetsk (lyē'pĕtsk)......Sov. Un. 52·26 N 39·34 E
166 Lipetsk (Oblast).........Sov. Un. 52·18 N 38·30 E
193 Lip'ing (lê'pĭng')...........China 26·18 N 109·00 E
159 Lipno (lēp'nô)...............Pol. 52·50 N 19·12 E
155 Lippe (R.) (lĭp'ĕ).........F.R.G. 51·36 N 6·45 E
158 Lippstadt (lĭp'shtät)........F.R.G. 51·39 N 8·20 E
106 Lipscomb (lĭp'skŭm) Al. (Birmingham In.) 33·26 N 86·56 W
167 Liptsy (lyēp'tsê)..........Sov. Un. 50·11 N 36·25 E
193 Lip'u.....................China 24·38 N 110·35 E
217 Lira.........................Ug. 2·15 N 32·54 E
164 Liri (R.) (lē'rē)...............It. 41·49 N 13·30 E
163 Liria (lē'ryä)................Sp. 39·35 N 0·34 W
216 Lisala (lê-sä'lä)............Zaire 2·09 N 21·31 E
163 Lisboa (Lisbon) (lêzh-bō'ä) (lĭz'bŭn).Port. (Lisbon In.) 38·42 N 9·05 W
108 Lisbon......................ND 46·21 N 97·43 W
104 Lisbon......................Oh. 40·45 N 80·50 W
Lisbon, see Lisboa
98 Lisbon Falls................Me. 43·59 N 70·03 W
154 Lisburn (lĭs'bŭrn).........N. Ire. 54·35 N 6·05 W
101 Lisburne, C.................Ak. 68·20 N 165·40 W
192 Lishih....................China 37·32 N 111·12 E
192 Lishu.....................China 43·12 N 124·18 E
192 Lishuchen.................China 45·01 N 130·50 E
193 Lishui....................China 28·28 N 120·00 E
190 Lishui (lĭ'shwĭ')...........China 31·41 N 119·01 E
191 Lishui........China (Canton In.) 23·12 N 113·09 E
160 Lisieux (lē-zyû')............Fr. 49·10 N 0·13 E
174 Lisiy Nos (lĭ'sĭy-nôs) Sov. Un. (Leningrad In.) 60·01 N 30·00 E
167 Liski (lyēs'kê)..........Sov. Un. 50·56 N 39·28 E
107 Lisle (lĭl)........Il. (Chicago In.) 41·48 N 88·04 W
161 L'Isle-Adam (lēl-ädän') Fr. (Paris In.) 49·05 N 2·13 E
203 Lismore (lĭz'môr)...........Austl. 28·48 S 153·18 E
220 Lister, Mt. (lĭs'tēr).........Ant. 78·05 S 163·00 E
183 Litani (R.)...Lib. (Palestine In.) 33·28 N 35·42 E
117 Litchfield (lĭch'fēld)...........Il. 39·10 N 89·38 W
109 Litchfield...................Mn. 45·08 N 94·34 W
107 Litchfield......Oh. (Cleveland In.) 41·10 N 82·01 W
203 Lithgow (lĭth'gō)...........Austl. 33·23 S 149·31 E
164 Lithinon, Ark. (C.).....Grc. (In.) 34·59 N 24·35 E
106 Lithonia (lĭ-thō'nĭ-ȧ) Ga. (Atlanta In.) 33·43 N 84·07 W
168 Lithuanian S. S. R. (lĭth-ū-ā'nĭ-ȧ) Sov. Un. 55·42 N 23·30 E
167 Litin (lê-tēn)...........Sov. Un. 49·16 N 28·11 E
165 Litókhoron (lē'tô-kô'rôn).....Grc. 40·05 N 22·29 E
216 Litoko....................Zaire 1·13 S 24·47 E
158 Litoměřice (lē'tô-myĕr'zhĭ-tsĕ) Czech. 50·33 N 14·10 E
158 Litomyšl (lē'tô-mêsh'l).......Czech. 49·52 N 16·14 E

217 Litoo.......................Tan. 9·45 S 38·24 E
202 Little (R.).Austl. (Melbourne In.) 37·54 S 144·27 E
120 Little (R.)..............Tn.-Mo. 36·28 N 89·39 W
119 Little R.....................Tx. 30·48 N 96·50 W
128 Little Abaco (I.) (ä'bä-kō)...Ba. 26·55 N 77·45 W
96 Little Abitibi (R.)..........Can. 50·15 N 81·30 W
220 Little America..............Ant. 78·30 S 161·30 W
196 Little Andaman I. (ăn-dȧ-măn') Andaman & Nicobar Is. 10·39 N 93·08 E
128 Little Bahama Bk. (bȧ-hā'mȧ).Ba. 26·55 N 78·40 W
111 Little Belt Mts. (bĕlt)........Mt. 47·00 N 110·50 W
111 Little Bighorn R. (bĭg-hôrn)..Mt. 45·08 N 107·30 W
Little Bitter, see Al Buḩayrah al Murrah aş Şughrāv
110 Little Bitterroot R. (bĭt'ĕr-ōōt) Mt. 47·45 N 114·45 W
116 Little Blue (R.).............Ne. 40·15 N 98·01 W
113 Little Blue R. (blōō) Mo. (Kansas City In.) 38·52 N 94·25 W
148 Littleborough (lĭt''l-bŭr-ô)...Eng. 53·39 N 2·06 W
107 Little Calumet R. (kăl-û-mĕt') Il. (Chicago In.) 41·38 N 87·38 W
128 Little Cayman (I.) (kā'mȧn) Cayman Is. 19·40 N 80·05 W
115 Little Colorado (R.) (kŏl-ō-rā'dō) Az. 36·05 N 111·35 W
106 Little Compton (kŏmp'tŏn) RI (Providence In.) 41·31 N 71·07 W
127 Little Corn I..................Nic. 12·19 N 82·50 W
129 Little Exuma (I.) (ĕk-sōō'mä).Ba. 23·25 N 75·40 W
109 Little Falls (fôlz)............Mn. 45·58 N 94·23 W
105 Little Falls..................NY 43·05 N 74·55 W
116 Littlefield (lĭt''l-fēld).........Tx. 33·55 N 102·17 W
109 Little Fork (R.) (fôrk).......Mn. 48·24 N 93·30 W
123 Little Hans Lollick (I.) (häns lŏl'lĭk).Vir. Is (U.S.A.) (St. Thomas In.) 18·25 N 64·54 W
110 Little Humboldt R. (hŭm'bōlt) Nv. 41·10 N 117·40 W
129 Little Inagua (I.) (ê-nä'gwä)..Ba. 21·30 N 73·00 W
128 Little Isaac (I.) (ĭ'zȧk)........Ba. 25·55 N 79·00 W
104 Little Kanawha (R.) (kȧ-nô'wȧ) WV 39·05 N 81·30 W
212 Little Karroo (Mts.) (kä-rōō) S. Afr. 33·50 S 21·02 E
91 Little Mecatina (R.) (mĕ cȧ tĭ nâ) Can. 52·40 N 62·21 W
107 Little Miami R. (mī-ăm'ĭ) Oh. (Cincinnati In.) 39·19 N 84·15 W
117 Little Missouri (R.) (mĭ-sōō'rĭ).Ar. 34·15 N 93·54 W
108 Little Missouri (R.)..........SD 45·46 N 103·48 W
121 Little Pee Dee (R.) (pē-dē').SC 34·35 N 79·21 W
111 Little Powder R. (pou'dēr)...Wy. 44·51 N 105·20 W
117 Little Red (R.) (rĕd).........Ar. 35·25 N 91·55 W
117 Little Red R.................Ok. 33·53 N 94·38 W
117 Little Rock (rôk).............Ar. 34·42 N 92·16 W
95 Little Sachigo L. (să'chĭ-gō)..Can. 54·09 N 92·11 W
161 Little St. Bernard P. (săntbĕr-närd') (săn bĕr-när').Fr.-It. 45·49 N 6·50 E
129 Little San Salvador (I.) (săn săl'vȧ-dôr).Ba. 24·35 N 75·55 W
108 Little Satilla (R.) (sȧ-tĭl'ȧ).....Ga. 31·43 N 82·47 W
108 Little Sioux (R.) (sōō).........Ia. 42·22 N 95·47 W
93 Little Smoky (R.) (smōk'ĭ)...Can. 55·10 N 116·55 W
111 Little Snake R. (snāk).........Co. 40·40 N 108·21 W
120 Little Tallapoosa (R.) (tăl-ȧ-pōō'sȧ).Al. 32·25 N 85·28 W
120 Little Tennessee (R.) (tĕn-ĕ-sē') Tn. 35·36 N 84·05 W
116 Littleton (lĭt''l-tŭn)..........Co. 39·34 N 105·01 W
99 Littleton..............Ma. (In.) 42·32 N 71·29 W
97 Littleton....................NH 44·15 N 71·45 W
104 Little Wabash (R.) (wô'băsh)..Il. 38·50 N 88·30 W
111 Little Wood R. (wōōd).........Id. 43·00 N 114·08 W
190 Liuan (lyōō'än')............China 31·45 N 116·29 E
193 Liuchou (lōō'chōō).........China 24·25 N 109·30 E
190 Liuho (lyōō'hō')...........China 32·22 N 118·50 E
192 Liuho.....................China 42·10 N 125·38 E
217 Liuli........................Tan. 11·05 S 34·38 E
196 Liukang Tenggaya, Kepulauan (Is.).Indon. 6·56 S 118·10 E
192 Liup'an Shan (Mts.).......China 36·20 N 105·30 E
216 Liuwa Pln................Zambia 14·30 S 22·40 E
193 Liuyang (lyōō'yäng')........China 28·10 N 113·35 E
190 Liuyüan (lū'yüän).........China 36·09 N 114·37 E
166 Līvāni (lē'vȧ-nê)........Sov. Un. 56·24 N 26·12 E
96 Lively......................Can. 46·26 N 81·09 W
101 Livengood (lĭv'ĕn-gŏŏd).......Ak. 65·30 N 148·35 W
120 Live Oak (lĭv'ōk).............Fl. 30·15 N 83·00 W
112 Livermore (lĭv'ēr-mōr) Ca. (San Francisco In.) 37·41 N 121·46 W
104 Livermore...................Ky. 37·30 N 87·05 W
202 Liverpool (lĭv'ēr-pōōl) Austl. (Sydney In.) 33·55 S 150·56 E
98 Liverpool...................Can. 44·02 N 64·41 W
148 Liverpool...................Eng. 53·25 N 2·52 W
119 Liverpool.................Tx. (In.) 29·18 N 95·17 W
101 Liverpool B.................Can. 69·45 N 130·00 W
205 Liverpool Ra................Austl. 31·47 S 31·00 E
211 Livindo R..................Gabon 1·09 N 13·30 E
120 Livingston (lĭv'ĭng-stŭn)........Al. 32·35 N 88·09 W
126 Livingston..................Guat. 15·50 N 88·45 W
113 Livingston......Il. (St. Louis In.) 38·58 N 89·51 W
111 Livingston....................Mt. 45·40 N 110·35 W
106 Livingston....NJ (New York In.) 40·47 N 74·20 W
120 Livingston....................Tn. 36·23 N 85·20 W
217 Livingstone (lĭv-ĭng-stōn)..Zambia 17·50 S 25·53 E
216 Livingstone, Chutes de (Livingstone Falls).Con.-Zaire 4·50 S 14·30 E
217 Livingstone Mts..............Tan. 9·30 S 34·10 E
217 Livingstonia (lĭv-ĭng-stō'nĭ-ȧ) Malawi 10·36 S 34·07 E
164 Livno (lēv'nô)...............Yugo. 43·50 N 17·03 E

Page	Name Pronunciation Region	Lat. °′	Long. °′
166	Livny (lēv'nē) Sov. Un.	52·28 N	37·36 E
107	Livonia (lĭ-vō-nĭ-ȧ) Mi. (Detroit In.)	42·25 N	83·23 W
164	Livorno (Leghorn) (lē-vôr'nō) (lĕg'hôrn). It.	43·32 N	11·18 E
136	Livramento (lē-vrá-mě'n-tô) Braz.	30·46 S	55·21 W
190	Liyang (lē'yäng') China	31·30 N	119·29 E
154	Lizard Pt. (lĭz'ȧrd) Eng.	49·55 N	5·09 W
161	Lizy-sur-Ourcq (lēk-sē'sür-o͞ork') Fr. (Paris In.)	49·01 N	3·02 E
149	Ljmuiden. Neth. (Amsterdam In.)	52·27 N	4·35 E
164	Ljubljana (lyo͞o'blyä'na) Yugo.	46·04 N	14·29 E
164	Ljubuški (lyo͞o'bo͞osh-kē) Yugo.	43·11 N	17·29 E
156	Ljungan (R.) Swe.	62·50 N	13·45 E
156	Ljungby (lyo͞ong'bü) Swe.	56·49 N	13·56 E
156	Ljusdal (lyo͞os'däl) Swe.	61·50 N	16·11 E
156	Ljusnan (R.) Swe.	61·55 N	15·33 E
154	Llandudno (lăn-düd'nō) Wales	53·20 N	3·46 W
154	Llanelly (lȧ-nĕl'ĭ) Wales	51·44 N	4·09 W
162	Llanes (lyä'nâs) Sp.	43·25 N	4·41 W
118	Llano (lä'nō) (lyä'nō) Tx.	30·45 N	98·41 W
118	Llano R. Tx.	30·38 N	99·04 W
134	Llanos (Reg.) (lyá'nōs). Col.-Ven.	4·00 N	71·15 W
124	Llera (lyā'rä) Mex.	23·16 N	99·03 W
162	Llerena (lyā-rā'nä) Sp.	38·14 N	6·02 W
154	Lleyn Prom. (lĭn) Wales	52·55 N	3·10 W
163	Llobregat (R.) (lyô-brě-gät'). Sp.	41·55 N	1·55 E
89	Lloyd L. (loid). Can. (Calgary In.)	50·52 N	114·13 W
96	Lloydminster Can.	53·17 N	110·00 W
163	Lluchmayor (lyo͞och-mä-yôr'). Sp.	39·28 N	2·53 E
136	Llullaillaco (Vol.) (lyo͞o-lyī-lyä'kō). Arg.	24·50 S	68·30 W
216	Loange (R.) (lō-äŋ'gä) Zaire	6·10 S	19·40 E
212	Lobatsi (lō-bä'tsē) Bots.	25·13 S	25·35 E
136	Lobería (lô-bě'rē'ä) Arg.	38·13 S	58·48 W
216	Lobito (lô-bē'tō) Ang.	12·30 S	13·34 E
174	Lobnya (lôb'nyá) Sov. Un. (Moscow In.)	56·01 N	37·29 E
137	Lobos (lō'bôs) Arg. (Buenos Aires In.)	35·10 S	59·08 W
128	Lobos, Cayo (I.) (lō'bôs) Ba.	22·25 N	77·40 W
125	Lobos, Isla de (I.) (ē's-lä-dě-lô'bōs). Mex.	21·24 N	97·11 W
134	Lobos de Tierra (I.) (lô'bō-dě-tyě'r-rä). Peru	6·29 S	80·55 W
174	Lobva (lôb'vá) Sov. Un. (Urals In.)	59·12 N	60·28 E
174	Lobva R. Sov. Un. (Urals In.)	59·14 N	60·17 E
158	Locarno (lô-kär'nō) Switz.	46·10 N	8·43 E
160	Loches (lôsh) Fr.	47·08 N	0·56 E
193	Loching China	28·02 N	120·40 E
121	Lochloosa (L.) (lŏk-lō'sȧ) Fl.	29·33 N	82·07 W
106	Loch Raven Res. Md. (Baltimore In.)	39·28 N	76·38 W
154	Lochy (L.) (lŏk'ĭ) Scot.	56·57 N	4·45 W
121	Lockhart (lŏk'härt) SC	34·47 N	81·30 W
119	Lockhart Tx.	29·54 N	97·40 W
105	Lock Haven (lŏk'hā-vĕn) Pa.	41·05 N	77·30 W
107	Lockland (lŏk'lănd) Oh. (Cincinnati In.)	39·14 N	84·27 W
89	Lockport (lŏk'pōrt) Can. (Winnipeg In.)	50·05 N	96·56 W
96	Lockeport Can.	43·42 N	65·07 W
107	Lockport Il. (Chicago In.)	41·35 N	88·04 W
107	Lockport NY (Buffalo In.)	43·11 N	78·43 W
196	Loc Ninh (lōk'nĭng') Viet.	12·00 N	106·30 E
183	Lod (lōd) Isr. (Palestine In.)	31·57 N	34·55 E
160	Lodève (lô-dĕv') Fr.	43·43 N	3·18 E
157	Lodeynoye Pole (lô-dĕy-nô'yě) Sov. Un.	60·43 N	33·24 E
94	Lodge Cr. (lŏj) Can.	49·20 N	110·20 W
111	Lodge Cr. Mt.	48·51 N	109·30 W
108	Lodgepole Cr. (lŏj'pōl) Wy.	41·22 N	104·48 W
184	Lodhran Pak.	29·40 N	71·39 E
114	Lodi (lō'dī) Ca.	38·07 N	121·17 W
164	Lodi (lô'dē) It.	45·18 N	9·30 E
107	Lodi (lō'dī) Oh. (Cleveland In.)	41·02 N	82·01 W
162	Lodosa (lô-dô'sä) Sp.	42·27 N	2·04 W
217	Lodwar Ken.	3·07 N	35·36 E
159	Łódź (wo͞odzh) Pol.	51·46 N	19·13 E
163	Loeches (lô-āch'ěs) Sp. (Madrid In.)	40·22 N	3·25 W
214	Loffa (R.) Lib.	7·10 N	10·35 W
150	Lofoten (Is.) (lô'fō-tĕn) Nor.	68·26 N	13·42 E
104	Logan (lō'gȧn) Oh.	39·35 N	82·25 W
111	Logan Ut.	41·46 N	111·51 W
104	Logan WV	37·50 N	82·00 W
90	Logan, Mt. Can.	60·54 N	140·33 W
104	Logansport (lō'gȧnz-pōrt) In.	40·45 N	86·25 W
215	Logone (R.) (lō-gō'nä) (lô-gôn') Afr.	11·15 N	15·10 E
162	Logroño (lô-grō'nyō) Sp.	42·28 N	2·25 W
162	Logrosán (lô-grô-sän') Sp.	39·22 N	5·29 W
156	Løgstør (lügh-stûr') Den.	56·56 N	9·15 E
190	Lohochai (lou'wū'jäī) China	33·35 N	114·02 E
160	Loir (R.) (lwȧr) Fr.	47·40 N	0·07 E
160	Loire (R.) Fr.	47·19 N	1·11 W
134	Loja (lō'hä) Ec.	3·49 S	79·13 W
162	Loja (lô'-kä) Sp.	37·10 N	4·11 W
216	Loka Zaire	0·20 N	17·57 E
218	Lokala Drift (lô'kä-lȧ drĭft). Bots. (Johannesburg & Pretoria In.)	24·00 S	26·38 E
217	Lokandu Zaire	2·31 S	25·47 E
167	Lokhvitsa (lôκ-vĕt'sá) Sov. Un.	50·21 N	33·16 E
217	Lokichar Ken.	2·23 N	35·39 E
217	Lokitaung Ken.	4·16 N	35·45 E
216	Lokofa-Bokolongo Zaire	0·12 N	19·22 E
215	Lokoja (lô-kō'yä) Nig.	7·47 N	6·45 E
216	Lokolama Zaire	2·34 S	19·53 E
214	Lokosso Upper Volta	10·19 N	3·40 W
211	Lol R. (lōl) Sud.	9·06 N	28·09 E
217	Loliondo Tan.	2·03 S	35·37 E
156	Lolland (lôl'än') Den.	54·41 N	11·00 E
111	Lolo Mt.	46·45 N	114·05 W
165	Lom (lōm) Bul.	43·48 N	23·15 E
113	Loma Linda (lō'mȧ lĭn'dȧ) Ca. (Los Angeles In.)	34·04 N	117·16 W
214	Loma Mansa (Mtn.) S.L.	9·13 N	11·07 W
216	Lomami (R.) Zaire	0·50 S	24·40 E
136	Lomas de Zamora (lō'mäs dā zä-mō'rä). Arg. (Buenos Aires In.)	34·31 S	58·24 W
107	Lombard (lŏm-bärd) Il. (Chicago In.)	41·53 N	88·01 W
164	Lombardia (Reg.) (lôm-bär-dē'ä). It.	45·20 N	9·30 E
197	Lomblen (I.) (lŏm-blĕn') Indon.	8·08 S	123·45 E
196	Lombok (I.) (lŏm-bŏk') Indon.	9·15 S	116·15 E
196	Lombok, Selat (Str.) Indon.	9·00 S	115·28 E
214	Lomé (lō-mā') (lō'mā) Togo.	6·08 N	1·13 E
212	Lomela (lô-mā'lȧ) Zaire	2·19 S	23·33 E
216	Lomela (R.) Zaire	0·35 S	21·20 E
118	Lometa (lô-mē'tȧ) Tx.	31·10 N	98·25 W
215	Lomie (lô-mē-ā') Cam.	3·10 N	13·37 E
113	Lomita (lō-mē'tȧ) Ca. (Los Angeles In.)	33·48 N	118·20 W
149	Lommel Bel. (Brussels In.)	51·14 N	5·21 E
154	Lomond, Loch (L.) (lŏk lō'mŭnd) Scot.	56·15 N	4·40 W
174	Lomonosov (lô-mô'nô-sof) Sov. Un. (Leningrad In.)	59·54 N	29·47 E
114	Lompoc (lŏm-pōk') Ca.	34·39 N	120·30 W
159	Lomza (lôm'zhá) Pol.	53·11 N	22·04 E
105	Lonaconing (lō-nȧ-kō'nĭng) Md.	39·35 N	78·55 W
104	London (lŭn'dŭn) Can.	43·00 N	81·20 W
148	London Eng. (London In.)	51·30 N	0·07 W
120	London Ky.	37·07 N	84·06 W
104	London Oh.	39·50 N	83·30 W
98	Londonderry (lŭn'dŭn-dĕr-ĭ). Can.	45·29 N	63·36 W
154	Londonderry N. Ire.	55·00 N	7·19 W
204	Londonderry, C. Austl.	13·30 S	127·00 E
135	Londrina (lôn-drē'nä) Braz.	21·53 S	51·17 W
104	Lonely (I.) (lōn'lĭ) Can.	45·35 N	81·30 W
114	Lone Pine Ca.	36·36 N	118·03 W
127	Lone Star Nic.	13·58 N	84·25 W
129	Long (I.) Ba.	23·25 N	75·10 W
98	Long (I.) Can.	44·21 S	66·25 W
197	Long (I.) Pap. N. Gui.	5·10 S	147·30 E
108	Long (L.) ND	46·47 N	100·14 W
112	Long (L.) Wa. (Seattle In.)	47·29 N	122·36 W
216	Longa Ang.	14·42 S	18·32 E
216	Longa (R.) (lôŋ'gȧ) Ang.	10·20 S	13·50 E
121	Long B. SC	33·30 N	78·54 W
113	Long Beach (lông bēch) Ca. (Los Angeles In.)	33·46 N	118·12 W
106	Long Beach. NY (New York In.)	40·35 N	73·38 W
106	Long Branch (lông branch) NJ (New York In.)	40·18 N	73·59 W
108	Longdon (lông'-dŭn) ND	48·45 N	98·23 W
148	Long Eaton (ē'tŭn) Eng.	52·54 N	1·16 W
154	Longford (lŏng'fērd) Ire.	53·43 N	7·40 W
113	Longhorn (lông-hôrn) Tx. (San Antonio In.)	29·33 N	98·23 W
217	Longido Tan.	2·44 S	36·41 E
92	Long I. Ak.	54·54 N	132·45 W
105	Long I. (lông) NY	40·50 N	72·50 W
105	Long Island Sd. (lông ī'lȧnd) Ct.-NY	41·05 N	72·45 W
161	Longjumeau (lôN-zhü-mō') Fr. (Paris In.)	48·42 N	2·17 E
190	Longk'ou (lo͞ong'kō) China	37·39 N	120·21 E
96	Longlac (lông'lȧk) Can.	49·41 N	86·28 W
96	Long L. Can.	49·10 N	86·45 W
108	Longlake (lông-lāk) SD	45·52 N	99·06 W
116	Longmont (lông'mŏnt) Co.	40·11 N	105·07 W
161	Longnes (lôN'yĕ) Fr. (Paris In.)	48·56 N	1·37 E
148	Longnor (lông'nôr) Eng.	53·11 N	1·52 W
108	Long Pine (lông pīn) Ne.	42·31 N	99·42 W
105	Long Pt. Can.	42·35 N	80·05 W
99	Long Pt. Can.	48·48 N	58·46 W
95	Long Pt. Can.	53·02 N	98·40 W
105	Long Point B. Can.	42·40 N	80·10 W
109	Long Prairie (lông prâr'ĭ) Mn.	45·58 N	94·49 W
99	Long Range Mts. Can.	48·00 N	58·30 W
205	Longreach (lông'rēch) Austl.	23·32 S	144·17 E
98	Long Reach (R.) Can.	45·26 N	66·05 W
202	Long Rf. Austl. (Sydney In.)	33·45 S	151·22 E
148	Longridge (lông'rĭj) Eng.	53·51 N	2·37 W
116	Longs Pk. (lôngz) Co.	40·17 N	105·37 W
148	Longton (lông'tŭn) Eng.	52·59 N	2·08 W
89	Longueuil (lôN-gû'y') Can. (Montreal In.)	45·32 N	73·30 W
110	Longview (lông-vū) Or. (Portland In.)	46·06 N	123·02 W
119	Longview Tx.	32·29 N	94·44 W
119	Longville (lông'vĭl) La.	30·36 N	93·14 W
161	Longwy (lôN-wē') Fr	49·32 N	6·14 E
196	Long Xuyen (loung' so͞o'yĕn). Viet.	10·31 N	105·28 E
117	Lonoke (lō'nōk) Ar.	34·48 N	91·52 W
161	Lons-le-Saunier (lôN-lē-sō-nyā') Fr.	46·40 N	5·33 E
137	Lontue (lōn-to͞oĕ') (R.) Chile (Santiago In.)	35·20 S	70·45 W
197	Looc (lô-ōk') Phil. (In.)	12·16 N	121·59 E
104	Loogootee In.	38·40 N	86·55 W
121	Lookout, C. (lo͝ok'out) NC	34·34 N	76·38 W
110	Lookout Pt. Res. Or.	43·51 N	122·38 W
217	Loolmalasin (Mtn.) Tan.	3·03 S	35·46 E
89	Looma (o͞o'mȧ) Can. (Edmonton In.)	53·22 N	113·15 W
154	Loop Head (lo͞op) Ire.	52·32 N	9·59 W
120	Loosahatchie (R.) (lōz-ȧ-hă'chē) Tn.	35·20 N	89·45 W
149	Loosdrechtsche Plassen (L.) Neth. (Amsterdam In.)	52·11 N	5·09 E
169	Lopatka, Mys (C.) (lô-pät'kȧ) Sov. Un.	51·00 N	156·52 E
216	Lopez, Cap (C.) Gabon	0·37 S	8·43 E
197	Lopez B. (lō'pāz) Phil. (In.)	14·04 N	122·00 E
112	Lopez I. Wa. (Seattle In.)	48·25 N	122·53 W
193	Lop'ing (lō'pĭng') China	29·02 N	117·12 E
216	Lopori (R.) (lō-pō'rē) Zaire	1·35 N	20·43 E
162	Lora (lō'rä) Sp.	37·40 N	5·31 W
107	Lorain (lô-rān') Oh. (Cleveland In.)	41·28 N	82·10 W
184	Loralai (lō-rŭ-lī') Pak.	30·31 N	68·35 E
162	Lorca (lôr'kä) Sp.	37·39 N	1·40 W
205	Lord Howe (I.) (lôrd hou). Austl.	31·44 S	157·56 E
115	Lordsburg (lôrdz'bûrg) NM	32·20 N	108·45 W
137	Lorena (lô-rā'nȧ) Braz. (Rio de Janeiro In.)	22·45 S	45·07 W
135	Loreto (lô-rā'tō) Braz.	7·09 S	45·10 W
89	Loretteville (lô-rĕt-vēl') Can. (Quebec In.)	46·51 N	71·21 W
134	Lorica (lô-rē'kä) Col.	9·14 N	75·54 W
160	Lorient (lô-rē'äN') Fr.	47·45 N	3·22 W
154	Lorne, Firth of (fûrth ŏv lôrn') Scot.	56·10 N	6·09 W
158	Lörrach (lûr'äκ) F.R.G.	47·36 N	7·38 E
113	Los Alamitos (lōs ȧl-ȧ-mē'tôs) Ca. (Los Angeles In.)	33·48 N	118·04 W
115	Los Alamos (ȧl-ȧ-môs') NM	35·53 N	106·20 W
112	Los Altos (ȧl-tôs') Ca. (San Francisco In.)	37·23 N	122·06 W
137	Los Andes (än'dĕs) Chile (Santiago In.)	32·44 S	70·36 W
113	Los Angeles (ăŋ'gĕl-ĕs) (ăn'jĕl-ĕs) (äŋ'hâ-lâs). Ca. (Los Angeles In.)	34·00 N	118·15 W
136	Los Angeles (äŋ'hâ-lâs) Chile	37·27 S	72·15 W
114	Los Angeles Aqueduct Ca.	35·12 N	118·02 W
113	Los Angeles R. Ca. (Los Angeles In.)	33·50 N	118·13 W
137	Los Bronces (lôs brō'n-sĕs) Chile (Santiago In.)	33·09 S	70·18 W
110	Loscha R. (lōs'chă) Id.	46·20 N	115·11 W
136	Los Chonos, Archipielago de (är-chē-pyĕ'lä-gô dĕ lôs chô'nôs) Chile	44·35 N	76·15 W
136	Los Estados, Isla de (I.) (ē's-lä dĕ lôs ĕs-tá'dôs). Arg.	54·45 S	64·25 W
162	Los Filabres, Sierra de (Mts.) (sē-ĕ'r-rä dĕ lôs fē-lä'brĕs). Sp.	37·19 N	2·48 W
114	Los Gatos (gä'tôs) Ca.	37·13 N	121·59 W
193	Loshan (lō'shän') China	29·40 N	103·40 E
118	Los Herreras (ĕr-rā-räs) Mex.	25·55 N	99·23 W
129	Los Ilanos (lōs ē-lä'nōs). Dom. Rep.	18·35 N	69·30 W
128	Los Indios, Cayos de (Is.) (kä'yōs dĕ lôs ē'n-dyô's). Cuba	21·50 N	83·10 W
164	Lošinj (lō'shēn') Yugo.	44·30 N	14·29 E
164	Lošinj (I.) Yugo.	44·35 N	14·34 E
174	Losino Petrovskiy Sov. Un. (Moscow In.)	55·52 N	38·12 E
163	Los Monegros (Mts.) (mô-nĕ'grōs). Sp.	41·31 N	0·18 W
113	Los Nietos (nyā'tôs) Ca. (Los Angeles In.)	33·57 N	118·05 W
128	Los Palacios Cuba	22·35 N	83·15 W
115	Los Pinos (R.) (pē'nôs) Co.-NM	36·58 N	107·35 W
124	Los Reyes (rā'yĕs) Mex.	19·35 N	102·29 W
125	Los Reyes Mex. (In.)	19·21 N	98·58 W
127	Los Santos (săn'tôs) Pan.	7·57 N	80·24 W
162	Los Santos (sän'tôs) Sp.	38·38 N	6·30 W
135	Los Teques (tĕ'kĕs) Ven. (In.)	10·22 N	67·04 W
111	Lost R. (lôst) Id.	43·56 N	113·38 W
110	Lost R. Or.	42·07 N	121·30 W
111	Lost River Mts. (rĭ'vĕr) Id.	44·23 N	113·48 W
137	Los Vilos (vē'lôs) Chile (Santiago In.)	31·56 S	71·29 W
160	Lot (R.) (lôt) Fr.	44·32 N	1·08 E
136	Lota (lŏ'tä) Chile	37·11 S	73·14 W
106	Lothian (lōth'ĭăn) Md. (Baltimore In.)	38·50 N	76·38 W
191	Lotien (lō'tyĕn') China (Shanghai In.)	31·25 N	121·20 E
217	Lotikipi Pln. Ken.	4·25 N	34·55 E
193	Loting (lō'tĭng') China	23·42 N	111·35 E
190	Lot'ing (lō'tĭng) China	39·26 N	118·53 E
158	Lötschen Tun. (lŭt'shĕn) Switz.	46·26 N	7·54 E
196	Louangphrabang (lo͞o-ang'-prä-bäng'). Laos	19·47 N	102·15 E
120	Loudon (lou'dŭn) Tn.	35·43 N	84·20 W
104	Loudonville (lou'dŭn-vĭl) Oh.	40·40 N	82·15 W
160	Loudun (lo͞o-dûN') Fr.	47·03 N	0·00
214	Louga (lo͞o'gä) Senegal	15·37 N	16·13 W
148	Loughborough (lŭf'bŭr-ô) Eng.	56·46 N	1·12 W
104	Louisa (lo͞o'ēz-ȧ) Ky.	38·05 N	82·40 W
205	Louisade Arch. (lo͞o-ĭs-äd ăr-kĭ-pĕl-ĭ-gō). Pap. N. Gui.	10·44 S	153·58 E
121	Louisberg (lo͞o'ĭs-bûrg) NC	36·05 N	79·19 W
99	Louisburg (lo͞o'ĭs-bourg) Can.	45·55 N	59·58 W
98	Louiseville Can.	46·17 N	72·58 W
91	Louis XIV, Pte. Can.	54·35 N	79·51 W
117	Louisiana (lo͞o-ē-zē-ăn'ȧ) Mo.	39·24 N	91·03 W
103	Louisiana (State) U. S.	30·50 N	92·50 W
212	Louis Trichardt (lo͞o'ĭs trĭch'ărt) S. Afr.	22·52 S	29·53 E
116	Louisville (lo͞o'ĭs-vĭl) (lo͞o'ē-vĭl) Co.	39·58 N	105·08 W
121	Louisville Ga.	33·00 N	82·25 W
107	Louisville Ky. (Louisville In.)	38·15 N	85·45 W
120	Louisville Ms.	33·07 N	89·02 W
162	Loule (lō-lā') Port.	37·08 N	8·03 W
158	Louny (lō'nē) Czech.	50·20 N	13·47 E
108	Loup (R.) (lo͞op) Ne.	41·17 N	97·58 W
108	Loup City Ne.	41·15 N	98·59 W
162	Lourdes (lo͞ord) Fr.	43·06 N	0·03 W
	Lourenço Marques, see Maputo		

ăt; finăl; rāte; senâte; ärm; ȧsk; sofȧ; fâre; ch-choose; dh-as th in other; bē; ēvent; bĕt; recĕnt; cratēr; g-go; gh-guttural g; bĭt; ĭ-short neutral; rīde; κ-guttural k as ch in German ich;

Page	Name	Pronunciation	Region	Lat. °'	Long. °'
163	Loures	(lō'rězh)	Port. (Lisbon In.)	38·49 N	9·10 W
162	Lousa	(lō'zȧ)	Port.	40·05 N	8·12 W
154	Louth	(louth)	Eng.	53·27 N	0·02 W
160	Louviers	(lōō-vyā')	Fr.	49·13 N	1·11 E
161	Louvres	(lōōv'r')	Fr. (Paris In.)	49·02 N	2·28 E
166	Lovat'	(lô-vȧt'y')	Sov. Un.	57·23 N	31·18 E
165	Lovech	(lō'věts)	Bul.	43·10 N	24·40 E
116	Loveland	(lŭv'lǎnd)	Co.	40·24 N	105·04 W
107	Loveland		Oh. (Cincinnati In.)	39·16 N	84·15 W
111	Lovell	(lŭv'ěl)	Wy.	44·50 N	108·23 W
114	Lovelock	(lŭv'lŏk)	Nv.	40·10 N	118·37 W
106	Lovick	(lŭ'vĭk)	Al. (Birmingham In.)	33·34 N	86·38 W
157	Loviisa	(lô'vē-sȧ)	Fin.	60·28 N	26·10 E
91	Low, C.	(lō)	Can.	62·58 N	86·50 W
212	Lowa	(lō'wȧ)	Zaire	1·30 S	27·18 E
107	Lowell		In. (Chicago In.)	41·17 N	87·26 W
99	Lowell		Ma. (In.)	42·38 N	71·18 W
104	Lowell		Mi.	42·55 N	85·20 W
149	Löwenberg	(lû' vĕn-běrgh)	G.D.R. (Berlin In.)	52·53 N	13·09 E
93	Lower Arrow (L.)	(ăr'ō)	Can.	49·40 N	118·08 W
	Lower Austria (State), see Niederösterreich				
108	Lower Brule Ind. Res.	(brü'lā)	SD	44·15 N	100·21 W
205	Lower Hutt	(hŭt)	N. Z. (In.)	41·08 S	175·00 E
110	Lower Klamath L.	(klăm'ȧth)	Ca.	41·55 N	121·50 W
110	Lower L.		Ca.-Nv.	41·21 N	119·53 W
106	Lower Marlboro	(lō'ēr mărl'bōrō)	Md. (Baltimore In.)	38·40 N	76·42 W
110	Lower Monumental Res.		Wa.	46·45 N	118·50 W
114	Lower Otay Res.	(ō'tā)	Ca. (San Diego In.)	32·37 N	116·46 W
109	Lower Red (L.)	(rĕd)	Mn.	47·58 N	94·31 W
	Lower Saxony (State), see Niedersachsen				
155	Lowestoft	(lō'stŏft)	Eng.	52·31 N	1·45 E
159	Łowicz	(lô'vĭch)	Pol.	52·06 N	19·57 E
159	Low Tatra Mts.		Czech.	48·57 N	19·18 E
105	Lowville	(lou'vĭl)	NY	43·45 N	75·30 W
125	Loxicha (Santa Catarina)	(lō-zē'chȧ) (sän-tä kä-tä-rē'nä)	Mex.	16·03 N	96·46 W
203	Loxton	(lôks'tŭn)	Austl.	34·25 S	140·38 E
192	Loyang		China	34·45 N	112·32 E
205	Loyauté, Iles		N. Cal.	21·17 S	168·16 E
165	Loźnica	(lôz'nē-tsȧ)	Yugo.	44·31 N	19·16 E
149	Lozorno		Czech. (Vienna In.)	48·21 N	17·03 E
167	Lozova	(lô-zō'vȧ)	Sov. Un.	48·54 N	36·17 E
167	Lozovatka	(lô-zō-vät'kä)	Sov. Un.	48·03 N	33·19 E
167	Lozovaya	(lô-zo-vä'yä)	Sov. Un.	48·27 N	38·37 E
163	Lozoya, Canal de	(kä-nä'l dě lô-thō'yä)	Sp. (Madrid In.)	40·36 N	3·41 W
217	Lualaba (R.)	(lōō-ȧ-lä'bȧ)	Zaire	1·00 S	25·45 E
217	Luama (R.)	(lōō'ä-mȧ)	Zaire	4·17 S	27·45 E
192	Luan (R.)		China	41·25 N	117·15 E
216	Luanda	(lōō-än'dä)	Ang.	8·48 S	13·14 E
212	Luanguinga (R.)	(lōō-än-gĭŋ'gȧ)	Ang.	14·00 S	20·45 E
217	Luangwa (R.)	(lōō-äŋ'gwȧ)	Zambia	11·25 S	32·55 E
190	Luanhsien	(lōōän-sĭän)	China	39·47 N	118·40 E
217	Luanshya		Zambia	13·08 S	28·24 E
162	Luarca	(lwär'kä)	Sp.	43·33 N	6·30 W
169	Lubaczów	(lōō-bä'chōōf)	Pol.	50·08 N	23·10 E
158	Lubán	(lōō'bän')	Pol.	51·08 N	15·17 E
157	Lubānas Ezers (L.)	(lōō'bä'nȧs ă'zĕrs)	Sov. Un.	56·48 N	26·30 E
197	Lubang	(lōō-bäng')	Phil. (In.)	13·49 N	120·07 E
197	Lubang (Is.)		Phil. (In.)	13·47 N	119·56 E
216	Lubango		Ang.	14·55 S	13·30 E
197	Lubao	(lōō-bä'ō)	Phil. (In.)	14·55 N	120·36 E
159	Lubartow	(lōō-bär'tōōf)	Pol.	51·27 N	22·37 E
159	Lubawa	(lōō-bä'vä)	Pol.	53·31 N	19·47 E
158	Lübben	(lüb'ěn)	G.D.R.	51·56 N	13·53 E
116	Lubbock	(lŭb'ŭk)	Tx.	33·35 N	101·50 W
98	Lubec	(lū'běk)	Me.	44·49 N	67·01 W
158	Lübeck	(lü'běk)	F.R.G.	53·53 N	10·42 E
158	Lübecker Bucht (B.)	(lü'bĕ-kĕr bōōkt)	G.D.R.	54·10 N	11·20 E
216	Lubilash (R.)	(lōō-bē-lȧsh')	Zaire	7·35 S	23·55 E
158	Lubin	(lyōō'bĭn)	Pol.	51·24 N	16·14 E
159	Lublin	(lyōō'blēn')	Pol.	51·14 N	22·33 E
167	Lubny	(lōōb'nē)	Sov. Un.	50·01 N	33·02 E
197	Lubuagan	(lōō-bwä-gä'n)	Phil. (In.)	17·24 N	121·11 E
217	Lubudi		Zaire	9·57 S	25·58 E
217	Lubudi (R.)	(lōō-bōō'dē)	Zaire	9·20 S	25·20 E
217	Lubumbashi (Élisabethville)		Zaire	11·40 S	27·28 E
217	Lucano		Ang.	11·16 S	21·38 E
164	Lucca	(lōōk'kä)	It.	43·51 N	10·29 E
154	Luce B.	(lūs)	Scot.	54·45 N	4·45 W
128	Lucea		Jam.	18·25 N	78·10 W
197	Lucena	(lōō-sā'nä)	Phil. (In.)	13·55 N	121·36 E
162	Lucena	(lōō-thā'nä)	Sp.	37·25 N	4·28 W
163	Lucena del Cid	(lōō'thā'nä dā thēdh')	Sp.	40·08 N	0·18 W
159	Lučenec	(lōō'chā-nyĕts)	Czech.	48·19 N	19·41 E
164	Lucera	(lōō-châ'rä)	It.	41·31 N	15·22 E
193	Luchi		China	28·18 N	110·10 E
190	Luchia	(lōō'jĭä)	China	32·12 N	115·53 E
190	Luchih	(lōō'jĕï)	China	31·17 N	120·54 E
193	Luchou		China	28·58 N	105·25 E
111	Lucin	(lū-sēn')	Ut.	41·23 N	113·59 W
197	Lucipara, Kepulauan (I.)	(lōō-sē-pä'rȧ)	Indon.	5·45 S	128·15 E
149	Luckenwalde	(lōōk-ĕn-väl'dě)	G.D.R. (Berlin In.)	52·05 N	13·10 E
184	Lucknow	(lŭk'nou)	India	26·54 N	80·58 E
160	Luçon	(lü-sôɴ')	Fr.	46·27 N	1·12 W
129	Lucrecia, Cabo (C.)	(kȧ'bô-lōō-krā'sē-ȧ)	Cuba	21·05 N	75·30 W
165	Luda Kamchiya (R.)		Bul.	42·46 N	27·13 E
161	Lüdenscheid	(lü'dĕn-shīt)	F.R.G. (Ruhr In.)	51·13 N	7·38 E
212	Lüderitz	(lü'dēr-ĭts) (lü'dĕ-rĭts)	Namibia	26·35 S	15·15 E
212	Lüderitz Bucht (B.)		Namibia	26·35 S	14·30 E
184	Ludhiāna		India	31·00 N	75·52 E
161	Lüdinghausen	(lü'dĕng-hou-zĕn)	F.R.G. (Ruhr In.)	51·46 N	7·27 E
104	Ludington	(lŭd'ĭng-tŭn)	Mi.	44·00 N	86·25 W
148	Ludlow	(lŭd'lō)	Eng.	52·22 N	2·43 W
107	Ludlow		Ky. (Cincinnati In.)	39·05 N	84·33 W
156	Ludvika	(loodh-vē'kȧ)	Swe.	60·10 N	15·09 E
158	Ludwigsburg	(lōōt'vêks-bōōrgh)	F.R.G.	48·53 N	9·14 E
149	Ludwigsfelde	(lōōd'vēgs-fěl-dě)	G.D.R. (Berlin In.)	52·18 N	13·16 E
158	Ludwigshafen	(lōōt'vêks-hä'fěn)	F.R.G.	49·29 N	8·26 E
158	Ludwigslust	(lōōt'vêks-lōōst)	G.D.R.	53·18 N	11·31 E
166	Ludza	(lōōd'zȧ)	Sov. Un.	56·33 N	27·45 E
212	Luebo	(lōō-ā'bō)	Zaire	5·15 S	21·22 E
217	Luena		Zaire	9·27 S	25·47 E
212	Lufira (R.)	(lōō-fē'rȧ)	Zaire	9·32 S	27·15 E
119	Lufkin	(lŭf'kĭn)	Tx.	31·21 N	94·43 W
166	Luga	(lōō'gȧ)	Sov. Un.	58·43 N	29·52 E
166	Luga (R.)		Sov. Un.	59·00 N	29·25 E
158	Lugano	(lōō-gä'nō)	Switz.	46·01 N	8·52 E
217	Lugenda (R.)	(lōō-zhĕn'dä)	Moz.	12·05 S	38·15 E
218	Lugh Ganane		Som. (Horn of Afr. In.)	3·38 N	42·35 E
154	Lugnaquilla, Mt.	(lōōk-nȧ-kwĭ-lȧ)	Ire.	52·56 N	6·30 W
164	Lugo	(lōō'gō)	It.	44·28 N	11·57 E
162	Lugo	(lōō'gō)	Sp.	43·01 N	7·32 W
165	Lugoj		Rom.	45·51 N	21·56 E
	Luhe, see Winsen				
190	Lui	(lōō-yĭ)	China	33·52 N	115·32 E
216	Luiana		Ang.	17·23 S	23·03 E
212	Luilaka (R.)	(lōō-ē-lä'kȧ)	Zaire	2·18 S	21·15 E
154	Luimneach	(lĭm'nȧk)	Ire.	52·39 N	8·35 W
124	Luis Moya	(lōōē's-mô-yä)	Mex.	22·26 N	102·14 W
137	Luján	(lōō'hän')	Arg. (Buenos Aires In.)	34·36 S	59·07 W
137	Luján (R.)		Arg. (Buenos Aires In.)	34·33 S	58·59 W
189	Lujchow Pen.		China	20·40 N	110·30 E
217	Lukanga Swp.	(lōō-käŋ'gȧ)	Zambia	14·30 S	27·25 E
216	Lukenie (R.)	(lōō-kā'nyȧ)	Zaire	3·10 S	19·05 E
212	Lukolela		Zaire	1·03 S	17·01 E
165	Lukovit	(lōō'kō-vêt')	Bul.	43·13 N	24·07 E
159	Łuków	(wōō'kōōf)	Pol.	51·57 N	22·25 E
217	Lukuga (R.)	(lōō-kōō'gȧ)	Zaire	5·50 S	27·35 E
170	Lule (R.)		Swe.	66·20 N	20·25 E
150	Luleå	(lōō-lĕ-ō)	Swe.	65·39 N	21·52 E
165	Lüleburgaz	(lü'lĕ-bōōr-gäs')	Tur.	41·25 N	27·23 E
190	Luling	(lū'lĭng)	China	39·54 N	118·53 E
119	Luling		Tx.	29·41 N	97·38 W
216	Lulonga (R.)		Zaire	1·00 S	18·37 E
112	Lulu (I.)	(lū'lōō)	Can. (Vancouver In.)	49·09 N	123·05 W
216	Lulua (R.)	(lōō'lōō-ȧ)	Zaire	15·40 S	22·07 E
	Luluabourg, see Kananga				
92	Lulu I.		Ak.	55·28 N	133·30 W
92	Lulu I.		Can.	49·09 N	123·05 W
121	Lumber (R.)	(lŭm'bĕr)	NC	35·12 N	79·35 W
120	Lumberton	(lŭm'bēr-tŭn)	Ms.	31·00 N	89·25 W
121	Lumberton		NC	34·47 N	79·00 W
137	Luminárias	(lōō-mē-nà'ryäs)	Braz. (Rio de Janeiro In.)	21·32 S	44·53 W
112	Lummi (I.)		Wa. (Vancouver In.)	48·42 N	122·43 W
112	Lummi B.	(lŭm'ĭ)	Wa. (Vancouver In.)	48·47 N	122·44 W
112	Lummi Island		Wa. (Vancouver In.)	48·44 N	122·42 W
216	Lumwana		Zambia	11·50 S	25·10 E
193	Luna	(lōō'nä)	Phil. (Manila In.)	16·51 N	120·22 E
156	Lund	(lŭnd)	Swe.	55·42 N	13·10 E
209	Lunda (Reg.)	(lōōn'dȧ)	Ang.	8·53 S	20·00 E
212	Lundi (R.)	(lōōn'dē)	Rh.	21·09 S	30·10 E
154	Lundy (I.)	(lŭn'dē)	Eng.	51·12 N	4·50 W
158	Lüneberger Heide (Reg.)	(lü'nĕ-bōōr-gĕr hī'dĕ)	F.R.G.	53·08 N	10·00 E
158	Lüneburg	(lü'nĕ-bōōrgh)	F.R.G.	53·16 N	10·25 E
160	Lunel	(lü-nĕl')	Fr.	43·41 N	4·07 E
161	Lünen	(lü'nĕn)	F.R.G. (Ruhr In.)	51·36 N	7·30 E
98	Lunenburg	(lōō'nĕn-bûrg)	Can.	44·23 N	64·19 W
99	Lunenburg		Ma. (Boston In.)	42·36 N	71·44 W
161	Lunéville	(lü-nȧ-vel')	Fr.	48·37 N	6·29 E
212	Lunga (R.)	(lōōŋ'gȧ)	Zambia	12·58 S	26·18 E
194	Lungchen	(lōōng'chĕn)	China	48·38 N	122·12 E
173	Lungchen	(lōōng'chĕn)	China	48·47 N	126·43 E
193	Lungching		China	22·20 N	107·02 E
192	Lungchingts'un	(lōōng'chĭng'tsōōn')	China	42·45 N	129·30 E
216	Lungué-Bungo (R.)		Ang.	13·00 S	21·27 E
192	Lunghsi		China	35·00 N	104·40 E
190	Lungku	(lōōng'kō)	China	34·52 N	116·48 E
191	Lungyentung		China (Canton In.)	23·12 N	113·21 E
184	Lūni (R.)		India	25·20 N	72·00 E
166	Luninets (R.)	(lōō-nēn'yets)	Sov. Un.	52·14 N	26·54 E
214	Lunsar		S. L.	8·41 N	12·32 W
192	Lupei	(lōō'pī)	China	44·35 N	120·40 E
	Lupin, see Manchouli				
136	Luque	(loo'kā)	Par.	25·18 S	57·17 W
184	Lūrah (R.)		Afg.	32·10 N	67·20 E
105	Luray	(lū-rā')	Va.	38·40 N	78·25 W
154	Lurgan	(lûr'gǎn)	N. Ire.	54·27 N	6·28 W
213	Lúrio	(lōō'rē-ō)	Moz.	13·17 S	40·29 E
217	Lúrio (R.)		Moz.	14·00 S	38·45 E
217	Lusaka		Zaire	7·10 S	29·27 E
217	Lusaka	(lōō-sä'kȧ)	Zambia	15·25 S	28·17 E
216	Lusambo	(lōō-säm'bō)	Zaire	4·58 S	23·27 E
217	Lusangi		Zaire	4·37 S	27·08 E
184	Lushai Hills		Bur.	28·28 N	92·50 E
192	Lushan		China	33·45 N	113·00 E
216	Lushiko (R.)		Zaire	6·35 S	19·45 E
213	Lushoto	(lōō-shō'tō)	Tan.	4·47 S	38·17 E
190	Lüshun (Port Arthur)	(lü'shŭn)	China	38·49 N	121·15 E
213	Lusikisiki	(lōō-sê-kê-sē'kê)	S. Afr. (Natal In.)	31·22 S	29·37 E
108	Lusk	(lŭsk)	Wy.	42·46 N	104·27 W
216	Luso	(lōō'sō)	Ang.	11·45 S	19·55 E
190	Lüta (Dairen)	(lüdȧ) (dä'lĭän)	China	38·54 N	121·35 E
190	Lut'ai	(lōō'tăi)	China	39·20 N	117·50 E
119	Lutcher	(lŭch'ēr)	La.	30·03 N	90·43 W
154	Luton	(lū'tŭn)	Eng.	51·55 N	0·28 W
159	Lutsk	(lōōtsk)	Sov. Un.	50·45 N	25·20 E
120	Luverne	(lū-vûrn')	Al.	31·42 N	86·15 W
108	Luverne	(lū-vûrn')	Mn.	43·40 N	96·13 W
217	Luvua (R.)	(lōō'vōō-ȧ)	Zaire	7·00 S	27·45 E
217	Luwingu		Zambia	10·15 S	29·55 E
120	Luxapalila Cr.	(lŭk-sȧ-pôl'ĭ-lȧ)	Al.	33·36 N	88·08 W
161	Luxembourg	(lŭk-sĕm-bûrg) (lük sän-bōōr') (look-sĕm-bōōrgh)	Lux.	49·38 N	6·30 E
146	Luxembourg		Eur.	49·30 N	6·22 E
161	Luxeuil	(lük-sû'y')	Fr.	47·49 N	6·19 E
106	Luxomni	(lŭx'ŏm-nī)	Ga. (Atlanta In.)	33·54 N	84·07 W
	Luxor, see Al Uqṣur				
192	Luya Shan (Mtn.)		China	38·50 N	111·40 E
170	Luza (R.)	(lōō'zä)	Sov. Un.	60·30 N	47·10 E
158	Luzern	(lōō-tsĕrn)	Switz.	47·03 N	8·18 E
135	Luziânia	(lōō-zyȧ'nēȧ)	Braz.	16·17 S	47·44 W
196	Luzon (I.)	(lōō-zŏn')	Phil.	17·10 N	119·45 E
193	Luzon Str.		Phil.	20·40 N	121·00 E
159	L'vov	(l'vōōf)	Sov. Un.	49·51 N	24·01 E
173	Lyakhovskiye (Is.)	(lya'kō'v-skyê)	Sov. Un.	73·45 N	145·15 E
184	Lyallpur	(lī'ăl-pûr)	Pak.	31·29 N	73·06 E
89	Lyalta		Can. (Calgary In.)	51·07 N	113·36 W
174	Lyalya R.	(lyȧ'lyȧ)	Sov. Un. (Urals In.)	58·58 N	60·17 E
165	Lyaskovets		Bul.	43·07 N	25·41 E
212	Lydenburg	(lī'dĕn-bûrg)	S. Afr.	25·06 S	30·21 E
114	Lyell, Mt.	(lī'ĕl)	Ca.	37·44 N	119·22 W
105	Lykens	(lī'kĕnz)	Pa.	40·35 N	76·45 W
159	Lyna R.	(lĭn'ȧ)	Pol.	53·56 N	20·30 E
120	Lynch	(lĭnch)	Ky.	36·56 N	82·55 W
121	Lynchburg	(lĭnch'bûrg)	Va.	37·23 N	79·08 W
112	Lynch Cove	(lĭnch)	Wa. (Seattle In.)	47·26 N	122·54 W
89	Lynden	(lĭn'dĕn)	Can. (Toronto In.)	43·14 N	80·08 W
112	Lynden		Wa. (Vancouver In.)	48·56 N	122·27 W
202	Lyndhurst		Austl. (Melbourne In.)	38·03 S	145·14 E
107	Lyndon	(lĭn'dŭn)	Ky. (Louisville In.)	38·15 N	85·36 W
105	Lyndonville	(lĭn'dŭn-vĭl)	Vt.	44·35 N	72·00 W
99	Lynn	(lĭn)	Ma. (In.)	42·28 N	70·57 W
95	Lynn Lake	(lăk)	Can.	56·51 N	100·30 W
113	Lynwood	(lĭn'wōōd)	Ca. (Los Angeles In.)	33·56 N	118·13 W
160	Lyon	(lē-ôɴ')	Fr.	45·44 N	4·52 E
121	Lyons	(lī'ŭnz)	Ga.	32·08 N	82·19 W
116	Lyons		Ks.	38·20 N	98·11 W
108	Lyons		Ne.	41·57 N	96·28 W
106	Lyons		NJ (New York In.)	40·41 N	74·33 W
105	Lyons		NY	43·05 N	77·00 W
156	Lyse Fd.	(lü'sĕ fyôr')	Nor.	58·59 N	6·35 E
156	Lysekil	(lü'sĕ-kēl)	Swe.	58·17 N	11·22 E
174	Lys'va	(lĭs'vȧ)	Sov. Un. (Urals In.)	58·07 N	57·47 E
148	Lytham	(lĭth'ăm)	Eng.	53·44 N	2·58 W
174	Lytkarino		Sov. Un. (Moscow In.)	55·25 N	37·55 E
213	Lyttelton	(lĭt'l'ton)	S. Afr. (Johannesburg & Pretoria In.)	25·51 S	28·13 E
174	Lyuban'	(lyōō'bȧn)	Sov. Un. (Leningrad In.)	59·21 N	31·15 E
167	Lyubar	(lyōō'bär)	Sov. Un.	49·56 N	27·44 E
174	Lyubertsy	(lyōō'bĕr-tsê)	Sov. Un. (Moscow In.)	55·40 N	37·55 E
166	Lyubim	(lyōō-bēm')	Sov. Un.	58·24 N	40·39 E
174	Lyublino	(lyōōb'lĭ-nô)	Sov. Un. (Moscow In.)	55·41 N	37·45 E
166	Lyudinovo	(lū-dē'novō)	Sov. Un.	53·52 N	34·28 E
188	Lyung		Mong.	47·58 N	104·52 E

M

Page	Name	Pronunciation	Region	Lat. °'	Long. °'
183	Ma'ān	(mä-än')	Jordan (Palestine In.)	30·12 N	35·45 E
156	Maarianhamina (Mariehamn)	(mä'rē-ȧn-hä'mē-na) (mȧ-rē'ĕ-hām''n)	Fin.	60·07 N	19·57 E

ng-sing; ŋ-baŋk; ɴ-nasalized n; nŏd; cŏmmit; ōld; ôbey; ôrder; fōōd; fŏŏt; ou-out; s-soft· sh-dish; th-thin; pūre; ûnite; ûrn; stŭd; circŭs; ü-as "y" in study; '-indeterminate vowel.

308 Maartensdijk — Mahone PRONOUNCING INDEX

Page	Name Pronunciation Region	Lat. °′	Long. °′
149	Maartensdijk Neth. (Amsterdam In.)	52·09 N	5·10 E
161	Maas (R.) Neth. (Ruhr In.)	51·32 N	6·07 E
155	Maastricht (mäs′trĭκt) Neth.	50·51 N	5·35 E
211	Maaten (Bishidra (Oasis) Libya	23·11 N	22·34 E
216	Mabaia Ang.	7·13 S	14·03 E
112	Mabana (mä-bä-nä) Wa. (Seattle In.)	48·06 N	122·25 W
119	Mabank (mā′bănk) Tx.	32·21 N	96·05 W
218	Mabeskraal S. Afr. (Johannesburg & Pretoria In.)	25·12 S	26·47 E
106	Mableton (mā′b′l-tŭn) Ga. (Atlanta In.)	33·49 N	84·34 W
152	Mabrouk (må-brōōk′) Alg.	29·30 N	0·20 E
210	Mabrouk Mali	19·27 N	1·16 W
218	Mabula (mä′bōō-la) S. Afr. (Johannesburg & Pretoria In.)	24·49 S	27·59 E
98	McAdam (măk-ăd′ăm) Can.	45·36 N	67·20 W
137	Macaé (mä-kä-ā′) Braz. (Rio de Janeiro In.)	22·22 S	41·47 W
106	McAfee (măk-ȧ′fē) NJ (New York In.)	41·10 N	74·32 W
135	Macaira (R.) (mä-kī′rä) Ven. (In.)	9·37 N	66·16 W
197	Macalelon (mä-kä-lā-lōn′) Phil. (In.)	13·46 N	122·09 E
117	McAlester (măk ăl′ĕs-tēr) Ok.	34·55 N	95·45 W
118	McAllen (măk-ăl′ĕn) Tx.	26·12 N	98·14 W
135	Macapá (mä-kä-pä′) Braz.	0·08 N	50·02 W
189	Macau (mȧ-kä′ōō) Asia	22·00 N	113·00 E
135	Macau (mä-kä′ōō) Braz.	5·12 S	36·34 W
129	Macaya, Pico de (Pk.) Hai.	18·25 N	74·00 W
93	McBride (măk-brīd′) Can.	53·18 N	120·10 W
106	McCalla (măk-kăl′lȧ) Al. (Birmingham In.)	33·20 N	87·00 W
118	McCamey (mȧ-kā′mĭ) Tx.	31·08 N	102·13 W
163	Maccarese (mäk-kä-rĕ′zĕ) It. (Rome In.)	41·53 N	12·13 E
120	McCaysville (mă-kāz′vĭl) Ga.	34·57 N	84·21 W
148	Macclesfield (măk″lz-fēld) Eng.	53·15 N	2·07 W
148	Macclesfield Can. (măk″lz-fēld) Eng.	53·14 N	2·07 W
121	McColl (mȧ-kól′) SC	34·40 N	79·34 W
120	McComb (mȧ-kōm′) Ms.	31·14 N	90·27 W
108	McConaughy, L. (măk kō′nō ĭ′) Ne.	41·24 N	101·40 W
116	McCook (mȧ-kŏŏk′) Ne.	40·13 N	100·37 W
121	McCormick (mȧ-kôr′mĭk) SC	33·56 N	82·20 W
154	Macdhui, Ben (Mtn.) (bĕn măk-dōō′ē) Scot.	57·06 N	3·45 W
113	Macdona (măk-dō′nȧ) Tx. (San Antonio In.)	29·20 N	98·42 W
107	McDonald (măk-dŏn′ăld) Pa. (Pittsburgh In.)	40·22 N	80·13 W
204	Macdonald (I.) (măk-dŏn′ăld) Austl.	23·40 S	127·40 E
220	McDonald I. Austl.	53·00 S	72·45 E
89	McDonald L. (măk-dŏn-ăld) Can. (Calgary In.)	51·12 N	113·53 W
204	Macdonnell Ra. (măk-dŏn′ĕl) Austl.	23·40 S	131·30 E
95	MacDowell L. (măk-dou ĕl) Can.	52·15 N	92·45 W
107	Macedonia (măs-ê-dō′nĭ-ȧ) Oh. (Cleveland In.)	41·19 N	81·30 W
165	Macedonia (Reg.) (măs-ê-dō′nĭ-ȧ) Eur.	41·05 N	22·15 E
135	Maceió (mä-sȧ-yō′) Braz.	9·33 S	35·35 W
164	Macerata (mä-chā-rä′tä) It.	43·18 N	13·28 E
203	Macfarlane, L. (mâc′fär-lān) Austl.	32·10 S	137·00 E
217	Mackinnon Road Ken.	3·44 S	39·03 E
117	McGehee (mȧ-gē′) Ar.	33·39 N	91·22 W
114	McGill (mȧ-gĭl′) Nv.	39·25 N	114·47 W
112	McGowan (măk-gou′ăn) Wa. (Portland In.)	46·15 N	123·55 W
101	McGrath (măk′grăth) Ak.	62·58 N	155·20 W
107	McGregor (măk-grĕg′ēr) Can. (Detroit In.)	42·08 N	82·58 W
109	McGregor Ia.	42·58 N	91·12 W
119	McGregor Tx.	31·26 N	97·23 W
93	McGregor (R.) Can.	54·10 N	121·00 W
89	McGregor L. (măk-grĕg′ēr) Can. (Ottawa In.)	45·38 N	75·44 W
213	Machache (Mtn.) Leso. (Natal In.)	29·22 S	27·53 E
137	Machado (mä-shá-dô) Braz. (Rio de Janeiro In.)	21·42 S	45·55 W
217	Machakos Ken.	1·31 S	37·16 E
134	Machala (mä-chä′lä) Ec.	3·18 S	78·54 W
107	McHenry (măk-hĕn′rĭ) Il. (Chicago In.)	42·21 N	88·16 W
113	Machens (măk′ĕns) Mo. (St. Louis In.)	38·54 N	90·20 W
98	Machias (mȧ-chī′ȧs) Me.	44·22 N	67·29 W
195	Machida (mä-chē′dä) Jap. (Tōkyō In.)	35·32 N	139·28 E
185	Machilīpatnam India	16·22 N	81·10 E
134	Machu Picchu (mä′chōō-pē′k-chōō) Peru	8·01 S	72·24 W
216	Macías Nguema Biyogo (Fernando Póo) (Prov.) Equat. Gui.	3·35 N	7·45 E
167	Măcin (mȧ-chēn′) Rom.	45·15 N	28·09 E
214	Macina (Depression) Mali	14·50 N	4·40 W
108	McIntosh (măk′ĭn-tŏsh) SD	45·54 N	101·22 W
205	Mackay (mȧ-kī′) Austl.	21·15 S	149·08 E
111	Mackay (măk-kā′) Id.	43·55 N	113·38 W
204	Mackay (I.) (mȧ-kī′) Austl.	22·30 S	127·45 E
90	MacKay (L.) (măk-kā′) Can.	64·10 N	112·35 W
94	Mackay (R.) Can.	56·50 N	112·30 W
112	McKay (R.) Or.	45·43 N	123·00 W
107	McKeesport (mȧ-kez′pōrt) Pa. (Pittsburgh In.)	40·21 N	79·51 W
107	McKees Rocks (mȧ-kēz′ rŏks) Pa. (Pittsburgh In.)	40·29 N	80·05 W
120	McKenzie (mȧ-kĕn′zĭ) Tn.	36·07 N	88·30 W
90	Mackenzie, Dist. of Can.	63·48 N	125·25 W
90	Mackenzie (R.) Can.	63·28 N	124·23 W
101	Mackenzie B. Ak.	69·20 N	137·10 W
90	Mackenzie Mts. (mȧ-kĕn′zĭ) Can.	63·41 N	129·27 W
110	McKenzie R. Or.	44·07 N	122·20 W
104	Mackinac, Str. of (măk′ĭ-nô) (măk′ĭ-năk) Mi.	45·50 N	84·40 W
104	Mackinaw (R.) Il.	40·35 N	89·25 W
104	Mackinaw City (măk′ĭ-nô) Mi.	45·45 N	84·45 W
101	McKinley, Mt. (mȧ-kĭn′lĭ) Ak.	63·00 N	151·02 W
117	McKinney (mȧ-kĭn′ĭ) Tx.	33·12 N	96·35 W
108	McLaughlin (mȧk-lŏf′lĭn) SD	45·48 N	100·45 W
106	McLean (mâc′lān) Va. (Baltimore In.)	38·56 N	77·11 W
104	McLeansboro (mȧ-klānz′bŭr-ô) Il.	38·10 N	88·35 W
213	Macleantown (măk-lān′toun) S. Afr. (Natal In.)	32·48 S	27·48 E
213	Maclear (mȧ-klēr′) S. Afr. (Natal In.)	31·06 S	28·23 E
90	McLennan (măk-lĭn′nȧn) Can.	55·42 N	116·54 W
92	McLeod Lake Can.	54·59 N	123·02 W
93	McLeod (R.) Can.	53·45 N	115·15 W
110	McLoughlin, Mt. (mȧk-lŏk′lĭn) Or.	42·27 N	122·20 W
118	McMillan L. (măk-mĭl′ȧn) Tx.	32·40 N	104·09 W
112	McMillin (mȧk-mĭl′ĭn) Wa. (Seattle In.)	47·08 N	122·14 W
110	McMinnville (măk-mĭn′vĭl) Or.	45·13 N	123·13 W
120	McMinnville Tn.	35·41 N	85·47 W
112	McMurray (mȧk-mŭr′ĭ) Wa. (Seattle In.)	48·19 N	122·15 W
115	McNary (mȧk-nâr′ē) Az.	34·10 N	109·55 W
119	McNary La.	30·58 N	92·32 W
110	McNary Dam Or.-Wa.	45·57 N	119·15 W
117	Macomb (mȧ-kōōm′) Il.	40·27 N	90·40 W
160	Mâcon (mä-kôɴ) Fr.	46·19 N	4·51 E
120	Macon (mā′kŏn) Ga.	32·49 N	83·39 W
120	Macon Ms.	32·07 N	88·31 W
117	Macon Mo.	39·42 N	92·29 W
117	McPherson (mȧk-fŭr′s′n) Ks.	38·21 N	97·41 W
203	Macquarie (R.) Austl.	31·43 S	148·04 E
220	Macquarie Is. (mȧ-kwŏr′ē) Austl.	54·36 S	158·45 E
120	McRae (mȧk-rā′) Ga.	32·02 N	82·55 W
120	McRoberts (mȧk-rŏb′ērts) Ky.	37·12 N	82·40 W
126	Macuelizo (mä-kwĕ-lē′zô) Hond.	15·22 N	88·32 W
183	Ma′dabā Jordan (Palestine In.)	31·43 N	35·47 E
209	Madagascar (măd-ȧ-găs′kȧr) Afr.	18·05 S	43·12 E
99	Madame (I.) (mȧ-dȧm′) Can.	45·33 N	61·02 W
185	Madanapalle India	13·06 N	78·09 E
197	Madang (mä-däng′) Pap. N. Gui.	5·15 S	145·45 E
210	Madaoua (mȧ-dou′ȧ) Niger	14·04 N	6·03 E
105	Madawaska (R.) (măd-ȧ-wôs′kȧ) Can.	45·20 N	77·25 W
122	Madden, L. C. Z. (In.)	9·15 N	79·34 W
210	Madeira, Ilha da (I.) (mä-dā′rȧ) Mad. Is.	32·41 N	16·15 W
210	Madeira, Arquipelado da (Is.) (är-kē-pĕ′lä-gō-dä-mä-dĕý-rä) Port.	33·26 N	16·44 W
134	Madeira (R.) Braz.	6·48 S	62·43 W
109	Madelia (mȧ-dē′lĭ-ȧ) Mn.	44·03 N	94·23 W
109	Madeline (I.) (măd′ĕ-lĭn) Wi.	46·47 N	91·30 W
114	Madera (mȧ-dā′rȧ) Ca.	36·57 N	120·04 W
126	Madera (Vol.) Nic.	11·27 N	85·30 W
185	Madgaon India	15·09 N	73·58 E
184	Madhya Pradesh (State) (mŭd′vŭ prŭ-dāsh′) India	22·04 N	77·48 E
117	Madill (mȧ-dĭl′) Ok.	34·04 N	96·45 W
186	Madīnat ash Sha′b P. D. R. of Yem.	12·45 N	44·00 E
216	Madingo Con.	4·07 S	11·22 E
216	Madingou Con.	4·09 S	13·34 E
120	Madison (măd′ĭ-sŭn) Fl.	30·28 N	83·25 W
120	Madison Ga.	33·34 N	83·29 W
113	Madison Il. (St. Louis In.)	38·40 N	90·09 W
104	Madison In.	38·45 N	85·25 W
117	Madison Ks.	38·08 N	96·07 W
98	Madison Me.	44·47 N	69·52 W
108	Madison Mn.	44·59 N	96·13 W
108	Madison Ne.	41·49 N	97·27 W
106	Madison NJ (New York In.)	40·46 N	74·25 W
121	Madison NC	36·22 N	79·59 W
108	Madison SD	44·01 N	97·08 W
109	Madison Wi.	43·05 N	89·23 W
111	Madison Res. Mt.	45·25 N	111·28 W
111	Madison R. Mt.	45·15 N	111·30 W
104	Madisonville (măd′ĭ-sŭn-vĭl) Ky.	37·20 N	87·30 W
113	Madisonville La.	30·22 N	90·10 W
113	Madisonville Tx.	30·57 N	95·55 W
214	Madjori Upper Volta	11·26 N	1·15 E
166	Madona (mȧ′dō′nȧ) Sov. Un.	56·50 N	26·14 E
186	Madrakah, Ra′s al (C.) Om.	18·53 N	57·48 E
185	Madras (mȧ-drȧs′) (mŭ-drŭs′) India	13·08 N	80·15 E
113	Madre, Laguna L. (lä-gōō′nä mä′drȧ) Mex.	25·08 N	97·41 W
124	Madre, Sierra (Mts.) (sē-ĕ′r-rä-mȧ′drĕ) Mex.	15·55 N	92·40 W
197	Madre, Sierra (Mts.) Phil. (In.)	16·40 N	122·10 E
136	Madre de Dios, Arch. (mȧ′drȧ dā dê-ōs′) Chile	50·40 S	76·30 W
134	Madre de Dios, Rio (R.) (rê′ō-mä′drȧ dā dê-ōs′) Bol.	12·07 S	68·20 W
124	Madre del Sur, Sierra (Mts.) (sē-ĕ′r-rä-mä′drȧ dĕlsōōr′) Mex.	17·35 N	100·35 W
109	Madrid (măd′rĭd) Ia.	41·51 N	93·48 W
163	Madrid (mä-drē′d) Sp. (Madrid In.)	40·26 N	3·42 W
162	Madridejos (mä-dhrê-dhā′hōs Sp.	39·29 N	3·32 W
110	Mad R. (măd) Ca.	40·38 N	123·37 W
217	Mado Gashi Ken.	0·44 N	39·10 E
196	Madura (I.) (mȧ-dōō′rä) Indon.	6·45 S	113·30 E
185	Madurai (mä-dōō′rä) India	9·57 N	78·04 E
136	Madureira, Serra do (Mtn.) (sĕ′r-rä-dô-mä-dōō-rā′rȧ) Braz. (Rio de Janeiro In.)	22·49 S	43·30 W
195	Maebashi (mä-ĕ-bä′shê) Jap.	36·26 N	139·04 E
163	Maella (mä-āl′yä) Sp.	41·10 N	0·07 E
128	Maestra, Sierra (Mts.) (sē-ĕ′r-rȧ-mä-ās′trä) Cuba	20·05 N	77·05 W
205	Maewo (I.) New Hebr.	15·17 S	168·16 E
212	Mafeking (mȧf′ē-kĭng) S. Afr.	25·46 S	24·45 E
217	Mafia (I.) (mä-fē′ä) Tan.	7·47 S	40·00 E
136	Mafra (mä′frä) Braz.	26·21 S	49·59 W
163	Mafra (mäf′rȧ) Port. (Lisbon In.)	38·56 N	9·20 W
173	Magadan (mȧ-gȧ-dän′) Sov. Un.	59·39 N	150·43 E
173	Magadan Oblast Sov. Un.	63·00 N	170·30 E
217	Magadi Ken.	1·54 S	36·17 E
217	Magadi (L.) (mȧ-gä′dê) Ken.	1·50 S	36·00 E
213	Magalies (R.) (mȧ-gä′lyĕs) S. Afr. (Johannesburg & Pretoria In.)	25·51 S	27·42 E
213	Magaliesberg (Mts.) S. Afr. (Johannesburg & Pretoria In.)	25·45 S	27·43 E
218	Magaliesburg S. Afr. (Johannesburg & Pretoria In.)	26·01 S	27·32 E
197	Magallanes (mä-gäl-yä′näs) Phil. (In.)	12·48 N	123·52 E
136	Magallanes, Estrecho de (Str.) (ĕs-trĕ′chô-dĕ-mä-gäl-yä′nĕs) Arg.-Chile	52·30 S	68·45 W
134	Magangué (mä-gän′gā) Col.	9·08 N	74·56 W
197	Magat (R.) (mä-gät′) Phil. (In.)	16·45 N	121·16 E
137	Magdalena (mäg-dä-lā′nä) Arg. (Buenos Aires In.)	35·05 S	57·32 W
134	Magdalena Bol.	13·17 S	63·57 W
102	Magdalena Mex.	30·34 N	110·50 W
115	Magdalena NM	34·10 N	107·45 W
136	Magdalena (I.) Chile	44·45 S	73·15 W
122	Magdalena, Bahia (B.) (bä-ē′ä-mäg-dä-lā′nä) Mex.	24·30 N	114·00 W
134	Magdalena, Rio (R.) Col.	7·45 N	74·04 W
99	Magdalen Is. (măg′dȧ-lĕn) Can.	47·27 N	61·25 W
158	Magdeburg (mäg′dĕ-bŏŏrgh) G.D.R.	52·07 N	11·39 E
136	Magé (mä-zhā′) Braz. (Rio de Janeiro In.)	22·39 S	43·02 W
164	Magenta (mȧ-jĕn′tȧ) It.	45·26 N	8·53 E
150	Mageröy (I.) (mä′ghĕr-ûê) Nor.	71·10 N	24·11 E
164	Maggiore, Lago di (L.) It.	46·03 N	8·25 E
162	Maghnia Alg.	35·07 N	2·10 W
218	Maghāghah Egypt (Nile In.)	28·38 N	30·50 E
124	Magiscatzin (mä-kês-kät-zēn′) Mex.	22·48 N	98·42 W
165	Maglaj (mȧ′glä-ê) Yugo.	44·34 N	18·12 E
165	Maglić (mäg′lêch) Yugo.	43·36 N	20·36 E
165	Maglie (mäl′yā) It.	40·06 N	18·20 E
113	Magna (măg′nȧ) Ut. (Salt Lake City In.)	40·43 N	112·06 W
174	Magnitogorsk (mȧg-nyē′tô-gôrsk) Sov. Un. (Urals In.)	53·26 N	59·05 E
117	Magnolia (măg-nō′lĭ-ȧ) Ar.	33·16 N	93·13 W
120	Magnolia Ms.	31·08 N	90·27 W
161	Magny-en-Vexin (mä-nyē′ĕɴ-vĕ-sȧɴ′) Fr. (Paris In.)	49·09 N	1·45 E
105	Magog (mȧ-gŏg′) Can.	45·15 N	72·10 W
96	Magpie (R.) Can.	50·40 N	64·30 W
98	Magpie Lac (L.) Can.	50·55 N	64·39 W
109	Magpie (R.) Can.	48·13 N	84·50 W
93	Magrath Can.	49·25 N	112·52 W
212	Magude (mä-gōō′dȧ) Moz.	24·58 S	32·39 E
188	Magwe (mŭg-wā′) Bur.	20·19 N	94·57 E
171	Mahabād Iran	36·55 N	45·50 E
211	Magahi Port (mä-hä′gê) Zaire	2·14 N	31·12 E
196	Mahakam (Strm.) Indon.	0·30 S	116·15 E
217	Mahali Mts. Tan.	6·20 S	30·00 E
213	Mahaly (mȧ-häl-ē′) Mad.	24·09 S	46·20 E
196	Mahameru, Gunung (Mtn.) Indon.	8·00 S	112·50 E
184	Mahānadi (R.) (mŭ-hä-nŭd′ē) India	20·50 N	84·27 E
213	Mahanoro (mȧ-hȧ-nô′rō) Mad.	19·57 S	48·47 E
105	Mahanoy City (mä-hȧ-noi′) Pa.	40·50 N	76·10 W
184	Mahārāshtra (State) India	19·06 N	75·00 E
183	Maḩaţţat al Qaţrānah Jordan (Palestine In.)	31·15 N	36·04 E
183	Maḩaţţat ‘Aqabat al Ḩijāzīyah Jordan (Palestine In.)	29·45 N	35·55 E
183	Maḩaţţat ar Ramlah Jordan	29·31 N	35·57 E
183	Maḩaţţat Jurf ad Darāwīsh Jordan (Palestine In.)	30·41 N	35·51 E
213	Mahavavy (R.) (mä-hä-vä′vê) Mad.	17·42 S	46·06 E
184	Mahaweli (R.) India	7·47 N	80·43 E
151	Mahdia (mä-dē′ä) (mä′dê-ȧ) Tun.	35·30 N	11·09 E
185	Mahe (mä-ā′) India	11·42 N	75·39 E
217	Mahenge (mä-hĕŋ′gä) Tan.	7·38 S	36·16 E
184	Mahi (R.) India	23·16 N	73·20 E
185	Māhīm Bay India (In.)	19·03 N	72·45 E
213	Mahlabatini (mä′lȧ-bȧ-tē′nê) S. Afr. (Natal In.)	28·15 S	31·29 E
149	Mahlow (mä′lōv) G.D.R. (Berlin In.)	52·23 N	13·24 E
108	Mahnomen (mô-nō′mĕn) Mn.	47·18 N	95·58 W
163	Mahón (mä-ōn′) Sp.	39·52 N	4·15 E
98	Mahone Bay (mȧ-hōn′) Can.	44·27 N	64·23 W
98	Mahone B. Can.	44·30 N	64·15 W

ăt; finăl; rāte; senâte; ärm; ȧsk; sofȧ; fâre; ch-choose; dh-as th in other; bē; êvent; bĕt; recĕnt; cratēr; g-go; gh-guttural g; bĭt; ĭ-short neutral; rīde; κ-guttural k as ch in German ich;

PRONOUNCING INDEX
Mahopac — Mankato 309

Page Name Pronunciation Region Lat. °′ Long. °′
106 Mahopac, L. (mā-hō′păk) NY (New York In.) 41·24 N 73·45 W
106 Mahwah (mȧ-wä′) NJ (New York In.) 41·05 N 74·09 W
148 Maidenhead (mād′ĕn-hĕd) Eng. (London In.) 51·30 N 0·44 W
148 Maidstone.....Eng. (London In.) 51·17 N 0·32 E
215 Maiduguri (mä′ē-dȧ-gōō′rê)...Nig. 11·51 N 13·10 E
134 Maigualida Sierra (Mts.) (sē-ĕ′r-rȧ-mī-gwä′lē-dē).Ven. 6·30 N 65·50 W
184 Maijdi.....Bngl. 22·59 N 91·08 E
Maikop, see Maykop
203 Main Barrier Ra. (băr′′ēr).Austl. 31·25 S 141·40 E
212 Mai-Ndombe, Lac (Leopold II, L.) Zaire 2·16 S 19·00 E
103 Maine (State) (mān).....U. S. 45·25 N 69·50 W
154 Mainland (I.) (mān-lănd) Scot. (In.) 60·19 N 2·40 W
158 Main (R.) (mīn).....F.R.G. 49·49 N 9·20 E
161 Maintenon (măN-tĕ-nôN′) Fr. (Paris In.) 48·35 N 1·35 E
213 Maintirano (mä′ên-tê-rä′nō).Mad. 18·05 S 44·08 E
158 Mainz (mīnts).....F.R.G. 49·59 N 8·16 E
210 Maio I. (mä′yo).....C. V. (In.) 15·15 N 22·50 W
137 Maipo (mī′pō) (R.) Chile (Santiago In.) 33·45 S 71·08 W
136 Maipo (Vol.).....Arg. 34·08 S 69·51 W
137 Maipú (mī′pōō′) Arg. (Buenos Aires In.) 36·51 S 57·54 W
135 Maiquetía (mī-kĕ-tē′ä)..Ven. (In.) 10·37 N 66·56 W
129 Maisí, Punta (Pt.) (pōō′n-tä-mī-sē′).Cuba 20·10 N 74·00 W
161 Maison-Rouge (mā-zôN-rōōzh′) Fr. (Paris In.) 48·34 N 3·09 E
203 Maitland (māt′lănd).....Austl. 32·45 S 151·40 E
195 Maizuru (mä-ĭ′zōō-rōō).....Jap. 35·26 N 135·15 E
196 Majene.....Indon. 3·34 S 119·00 E
211 Maji.....Eth. 6·14 N 35·34 E
Majorca I., see Mallorca, Isle de
213 Majunga (mȧ-jŭŋ′gä).....Mad. 15·12 S 46·26 E
110 Makah Ind. Res. (mȧ kī′).....Wa. 48·17 N 124·52 W
213 Makanya (mä-kän′yä).....Tan. 4·15 S 37·49 E
164 Makarska (mȧ′kär-skȧ).....Yugo. 43·17 N 17·05 E
170 Makar′yev.....Sov. Un. 57·50 N 43·48 E
Makasar, see Ujung Pandang
196 Makasar, Selat (Str.) (mȧ-kăs′ĕr) Indon. 2·00 S 118·07 E
216 Makaw.....Zaire 3·29 S 18·19 E
195 Make (I.) (mä′kȧ).....Jap. 30·43 N 130·49 E
214 Makeni.....S. L. 8·53 N 12·03 W
167 Makeyevka (mŭk-yā′ŭf-kȧ) Sov. Un. 48·03 N 38·00 E
218 Makgadikgadi Pans (L.).....Bots. 20·38 S 21·31 E
171 Makhachkala (mäk′äch-kä′lä) Sov. Un. 43·00 N 47·40 E
213 Makhaleng (R.)..Leso. (Natal In.) 29·53 S 27·33 E
165 Makhlata (mäk′lä-tä).....Bul. 43·27 N 24·16 E
217 Makindu.....Ken. 2·17 S 37·49 E
186 Makkah (Mecca) (mĕk′ȧ).Sau. Ar. 21·27 N 39·45 E
91 Makkovik.....Can. 55·01 N 59·10 W
159 Makó (mô′kō).....Hung. 46·13 N 20·30 E
216 Makokou (mȧ-kô-kōō′).....Gabon 0·34 N 12·52 E
159 Maków Mazowiecki (mä′kōōv mä-zō-vyĕts′kē).Pol. 52·51 N 21·07 E
195 Makuhari (mä-kōō-hä′rē) Jap. (Tōkyō In.) 35·39 N 140·04 E
195 Makurazaki (mä′kōō-rä-zä′kê) Jap. 31·16 N 130·18 E
215 Makurdi.....Nig. 7·45 N 8·32 E
101 Makushin (mȧ-kōō′shĭn).....Ak. 53·57 N 166·28 W
172 Makushino (mȧ-kōō-shēn′ō) Sov. Un. 55·03 N 67·43 E
185 Malabar Coast (măl′ȧ-bär)..India 11·19 N 75·33 E
216 Malabo.....Equat. Gui. 3·45 N 8·47 E
197 Malabon.....Phil. (In.) 14·39 N 120·57 E
196 Malacca, Str. of (mȧ-lăk′ȧ).....Asia 4·15 N 99·44 E
111 Malad (mȧ-läd′).....Id. 42·11 N 112·15 W
163 Maladetta (Mts.) (mä-lä-dĕt′tä) Sp. 42·30 N 0·38 E
163 Malafede (R.) (mä-lä-fĕ′dĕ) It. (Rome In.) 41·43 N 12·28 E
134 Málaga (mȧ′lä-gȧ).....Col. 6·41 N 72·46 W
162 Málaga.....Sp. 36·45 N 4·25 W
162 Málaga, Bahía de (B.) (bä-ē′ä-dĕ-mȧ′lä-gä).Sp. 36·35 N 4·10 W
162 Malagón (mä-lä-gōn′).....Sp. 39·12 N 3·52 W
205 Malaita (I.) (mȧ-lä′ē-tȧ)...Sol. Is. 8·38 S 161·15 E
211 Malakāl (mȧ-lȧ-käl′).....Sud. 9·46 N 31·54 E
174 Malakhovka (mȧ-läk′ôf-kȧ) Sov. Un. (Moscow In.) 55·38 N 38·01 E
216 Malanje (mä-läŋ-gȧ).....Ang. 9·32 S 16·20 E
210 Malanville.....Benin 12·04 N 3·09 E
98 Malapedia (R.).....Can. 48·11 N 67·08 W
127 Mala Punta (Pt.) (pōō′n-tä-mä′lä) Pan. 7·32 N 79·44 W
156 Mälaren (L.).....Swe. 59·38 N 16·55 E
91 Malartic.....Can. 48·07 N 78·11 W
92 Malaspina Str. (măl-ȧ-spē′nȧ).Can. 49·44 N 124·20 W
171 Malatya (mȧ-lä′tyȧ).....Tur. 38·30 N 38·15 E
209 Malawi.....Afr. 11·15 S 33·45 E
Malawi, L., see Nyasa, L.
196 Malaya (Reg.) (mȧ-lā′yȧ)...Mala. 3·35 N 101·30 E
166 Malaya Vishera (vê-shā′rȧ) Sov. Un. 58·51 N 32·13 E
196 Malay Pen. (mȧ-lā′) (mā′lā)..Asia 7·46 N 101·06 E
196 Malaysia (mȧ-lā′zhȧ).....Asia 4·10 N 101·22 E
154 Mal B. (măl).....Ire. 52·51 N 9·45 W
204 Malbon (măl′bŭn).....Austl. 21·15 S 140·30 E
159 Malbork (mäl′börk).....Pol. 54·02 N 19·04 E
163 Malcabran (R.) (mäl-kä-brän′) Port. (Lisbon In.) 38·47 N 8·46 W
99 Malden (môl′dĕn).....Ma. (In.) 42·26 N 71·04 W
117 Malden.....Mo. 36·32 N 89·56 W
199 Malden (I.).....Oceania 4·20 S 154·30 W
182 Maldives.....Asia 4·30 N 71·30 E
148 Maldon (môrl′dŏn) Eng. (London In.) 51·44 N 0·39 E
136 Maldonado (mäl-dŏ-nȧ′dô).....Ur. 34·54 S 54·57 W
124 Maldonado, Punta (Pt.) (pōō′n-tä).Mex. 16·18 N 98·34 W
165 Maléa, Akr. (C.).....Grc. 37·31 N 23·13 E
184 Mālegaon.....India 20·35 N 74·30 E
159 Male Karpaty (Mts.).....Czech. 48·31 N 17·15 E
205 Malekula (I.) (mä-lā-kōō′lä) New Hebr. 16·44 S 167·45 E
162 Malhão da Estrêla (Mtn.) (mäl-you′N-dä-ĕs-trĕ′lä).Sp. 40·20 N 7·38 W
110 Malheur L. (mȧ-lōōr′).....Or. 43·16 N 118·37 W
110 Malheur R. (mȧ-lōōr′).....Or. 43·45 N 117·41 W
209 Mali.....Afr. 15·45 N 0·15 W
113 Malibu (mă′lĭ-bōō) Ca. (Los Angeles In.) 34·03 N 118·38 W
217 Malimba, Monts (Mts.).....Zaire 7·45 S 29·15 E
167 Malin (mȧ-lēn′).....Sov. Un. 50·44 N 29·15 E
124 Malinalco (mä-lē-näl′kō).....Mex. 18·54 N 99·31 W
124 Malinaltepec (mä-lē-näl-tȧ-pĕk′) Mex. 17·01 N 98·41 W
213 Malindi (mä-lēn′dē).....Ken. 3·14 S 40·04 E
159 Málinec (mä′lē-nyets′).....Czech. 48·31 N 19·40 E
154 Malin Hd.....N. Ire. 55·23 N 7·24 W
217 Malindi.....Ken. 3·13 S 40·07 E
154 Malinmore Hd, (mă′lĭn-mōr)..Ire. 54·45 N 8·30 W
174 Malino (mä′lĭ-nô) Sov. Un. (Moscow In.) 55·07 N 38·12 E
167 Malinovka (mȧ-lē-nôf′kȧ).Sov. Un. 49·50 N 36·43 E
165 Malkara (mäl′kȧ-rȧ).....Tur. 40·51 N 26·52 E
165 Malko Tŭrnovo (mäl′kō-t′r′nô-vȧ).Bul. 41·59 N 27·28 E
154 Mallaig.....Scot. 56·59 N 5·55 W
218 Mallawī (mȧ-lä′wē) Egypt (Nile In.) 27·43 N 30·49 E
107 Mallet Creek (măl′ĕt) Oh. (Cleveland In.) 41·10 N 81·55 W
163 Mallorca, Isla de (Majorca I.) (ē′s-lä-dĕ-mäl-yō′r-kä).Sp. 39·18 N 2·22 E
154 Mallow (măl′ō).....Ire. 52·07 N 9·04 W
155 Malmédy (mȧl-mā-dē′).....Bel. 50·25 N 6·01 E
212 Malmesbury (mämz′bēr-ĭ)..S. Afr. 33·30 S 18·35 E
156 Malmköping (mälm′chû′pĭng) Swe. 59·09 N 16·39 E
156 Malmö (mälm′û).....Swe. 55·36 N 12·58 E
173 Malmyzh (mȧl-mēzh′)...Sov. Un. 49·58 N 137·07 E
170 Malmyzh.....Sov. Un. 56·30 N 50·48 E
166 Maloarkhangelsk (mä′lô-är-Kän′gĕlsk).Sov. Un. 52·26 N 36·29 E
197 Malolos (mä-lô′lôs).....Phil. (In.) 14·51 N 120·49 E
174 Malomal′sk (mȧ-lô-mälsk′) Sov. Un. (Urals In.) 58·47 N 59·55 E
105 Malone (mȧ-lōn′).....NY 44·50 N 74·20 W
216 Malonga.....Zaire 10·24 S 23·10 E
213 Maloti Mts......Leso (Natal In.) 29·00 S 28·29 E
166 Maloyaroslavets (mä′lô-yä-rô-slä-vyĕts).Sov. Un. 55·01 N 36·25 E
170 Malozemel′skaya Tundra (Plains) Sov. Un. 67·30 N 50·00 E
136 Malpas (măl′pȧz).....Eng. 53·01 N 2·46 W
134 Malpelo, Isla de (I.) (mäl-pä′lō) Col. 3·55 N 81·30 W
98 Malpeque B. (môl-pĕk′).....Can. 46·30 N 63·47 W
111 Malta (môl′tȧ).....Mt. 48·20 N 107·50 W
146 Malta.....Eur. 35·52 N 13·30 E
212 Maltahöhe (mäl′tä-hö′ĕ) Namibia 24·45 S 16·45 E
125 Maltrata (mäl-trä′tä).....Mex. 18·48 N 97·16 W
197 Maluku (Moluccas) (Is.)...Indon. 2·40 S 127·15 E
197 Maluku, Laut (Molucca) (Sea) Indon. 0·15 N 125·41 E
211 Malūt.....Sud. 10·30 N 32·17 E
185 Mālvan.....India 16·08 N 73·32 E
117 Malvern (măl′vērn).....Ar. 34·21 N 92·47 W
173 Malyy Anyuy (R.).....Sov. Un. 67·52 N 164·30 E
173 Malyy Lyakhovskiye (I.).Sov. Un. 74·15 N 142·30 E
173 Malyy Tamir (I.).....Sov. Un. 78·10 N 107·30 E
125 Mamantel (mä-man-tĕl′).....Mex. 18·36 N 91·06 W
106 Mamaroneck (măm′ȧ-rō-nĕk) NY (New York In.) 40·57 N 73·44 W
210 Mamau.....Gui. 10·26 N 12·07 W
217 Mambasa.....Zaire 1·21 N 29·03 E
197 Mamberamo (R.) (mäm-bȧ-rä′mō) Indon. 2·30 S 138·00 E
197 Mamburao (mäm-bōō′rä-ō) Phil. (In.) 13·14 N 120·35 E
162 Mamede, Serra de (Mts.) (sĕ′r-rä-dĕ-mä-mĕ′dĕ).Port. 39·29 N 7·11 W
210 Mamfe (mäm′fĕ).....Cam. 5·46 N 9·17 E
195 Mamihara (mä′mē-hä-rä).....Jap. 32·41 N 131·12 E
120 Mammoth Cave (măm′ŏth)...Ky. 37·10 N 86·04 W
120 Mammoth Cave Natl. Park...Ky. 37·20 N 86·21 W
111 Mammoth Hot Springs (măm′ŭth hôt sprĭngz).Wy. 44·55 N 110·50 W
185 Mamnoli.....India (In.) 19·17 N 73·15 E
134 Mamoré (R.) (mä-mō-rā′).....Bol. 13·19 S 65·27 W
214 Mampong.....Ghana 7·04 N 1·24 W
159 Mamry L. (mäm′rĭ).....Pol. 54·10 N 21·28 E
214 Man.....Ivory Coast 7·24 N 7·33 W
163 Manacor (mä-nä-kôr′).....Sp. 39·35 N 3·15 E
197 Manado.....Indon. 1·29 N 124·50 E
129 Managua (mä-nä′gwä).Cuba (In.) 22·14 N 82·17 W
126 Managua.....Nic. 12·10 N 86·16 W
126 Managua, Lago de (L.) (lä′gô-dĕ) Nic. 12·28 N 86·10 W
213 Manakara (mä-nä-kä′rŭ).....Mad. 22·17 S 48·06 E
213 Mananara (R.) (mä-nä-nä′rŭ) Mad. 23·15 S 48·15 E
213 Mananjary (mä-nän-zhä′rē)..Mad. 20·16 S 48·13 E
Manáos, see Manaus
184 Manasaroar (L.).....China 30·40 N 81·58 E
105 Manassas (mȧ-năs′ȧs).....Va. 38·45 N 77·30 W
188 Manassu.....China 44·30 N 86·00 E
135 Manaus (Manáos) (mä-nä′ōōzh) Braz. 3·01 S 60·00 W
104 Mancelona (măn-sē-lō′nȧ).....Mi. 44·50 N 85·05 W
162 Mancha Real (män′chä rā-äl′)..Sp. 37·48 N 3·37 W
174 Manchazh (män′chȧsh) Sov. Un. (Urals In.) 56·30 N 58·10 E
105 Manchester (măn′chĕs-tēr).....Ct. 41·45 N 72·30 W
148 Manchester.....Eng. 53·28 N 2·14 W
120 Manchester.....Ga. 32·50 N 84·37 W
109 Manchester.....Ia. 42·30 N 91·30 W
99 Manchester.....Ma. (In.) 42·35 N 70·47 W
113 Manchester...Mo. (St. Louis In.) 38·36 N 90·31 W
105 Manchester.....NH 43·00 N 71·30 W
104 Manchester.....Oh. 38·40 N 83·35 W
148 Manchester Ship Canal.....Eng. 53·20 N 2·40 W
192 Manchouli (Lupin) (män-chōō′lē) (lōō′pĭn).China 49·25 N 117·15 E
189 Manchuria (Reg.) (măn-chōō′rē-ȧ) China 48·00 N 124·58 E
186 Mand (R.).....Iran 28·20 N 52·30 E
156 Mandal (män′däl).....Nor. 58·03 N 7·28 E
188 Mandalav (măn′dȧ-lā).....Bur. 22·00 N 96·08 E
156 Mandalselv (R.) (män′dälsĕlv) Nor. 58·25 N 7·30 E
108 Mandan (măn′dăn).....ND 46·49 N 100·54 W
215 Mandara Mts. (män-dä′rä) Cam.-Nig. 10·15 N 13·23 E
183 Mandau Siak (R.) Indon. (Singapore In.) 1·03 N 101·25 E
217 Mandimba.....Moz. 14·21 S 35·39 E
127 Mandinga (män-dĭŋ′gä).....Pan. 9·32 N 79·04 W
184 Mandla.....India 22·43 N 80·23 E
165 Mándra (män′drä).....Grc. 38·06 N 23·32 E
213 Mandritsara (mȧn-drēt-sä′rȧ) Mad. 15·49 S 48·47 E
165 Manduria (män-dōō′rē-ä).....It. 40·23 N 17·41 E
185 Mandve.....India (In.) 18·47 N 72·52 E
185 Māndvi (mŭnd′vē).....India (In.) 19·29 N 72·53 E
184 Māndvi (mŭnd′vē).....India 22·54 N 69·23 E
185 Mandya.....India 12·40 N 77·00 E
218 Manfalūţ (män-fȧ-loot′) Egypt (Nile In.) 27·18 N 30·59 E
164 Manfredonia (män-frȧ-dô′nyä).It. 41·39 N 15·55 E
164 Manfredónia, Golfo di (G.) (gôl-fô-dē).It. 41·34 N 16·05 E
135 Mangabeiras, Chap. das (Plains) (shä-pä′däs-däs-mäŋ-gä-bē′ê-räzh).Braz. 8·05 S 47·32 W
215 Manga (Reg.).....Niger 14·00 N 11·50 E
185 Mangalore (mŭŋ-gŭ-lōr′).....India 12·53 N 74·52 E
137 Mangaratiba (män-gä-rä-tē′bȧ) Braz. (Rio de Janeiro In). 22·56 S 44·03 W
197 Mangatarem (män′gȧ-tä′rĕm) Phil. (In.) 15·48 N 120·18 E
216 Mange.....Zaire 0·54 N 20·30 E
196 Mangkalihat, Tandjoeng (C.) (mäng′kȧ-lē-hät′).Indon. 1·25 N 119·55 E
128 Mangles, Islas de (ē′s-läs-dĕ-mäŋ′glās) (măn′g′lz) Cuba 22·05 N 83·50 W
213 Mangoky (R.) (män-gō′kē)..Mad. 22·02 S 44·11 E
197 Mangole (I.).....Indon. 1·35 S 126·22 E
162 Mangualde (män-gwäl′dĕ)...Port. 40·38 N 7·44 W
136 Mangueira, L. da (L.) (män-gā′ê-rȧ).Braz. 33·15 S 52·45 W
116 Mangum (măŋ′gŭm).....Ok. 34·52 N 99·31 W
171 Mangyshlak, P.-ov. (Pen.) Sov. Un. 44·30 N 50·40 E
107 Manhattan......Il. (Chicago In.) 41·25 N 87·29 W
117 Manhattan (măn-hăt′ăn).....Ks. 39·11 N 96·34 W
113 Manhattan Beach Ca. (Los Angeles In.) 33·53 N 118·24 W
137 Manhuaçu (män-ōōá′sōō) Braz. (Rio de Janeiro In.) 20·17 S 42·01 W
137 Manhumirim (män-ōō-mê-rē′N) Braz. (Rio de Janeiro In.) 20·22 S 41·57 W
213 Mania (R.) (män′yä).....Mad. 19·52 S 46·02 E
135 Manicoré (mä-nê-kō-rā′).....Braz. 5·53 S 61·13 W
91 Manicouagane (R.).....Can. 50·00 N 68·35 W
91 Manicouagane, Lac (L.).....Can. 51·30 N 68·19 W
135 Manicuare (mä-nē-kwä′rē) Ven. (In.) 10·35 N 64·10 W
96 Manikuagen, Rivière (R.).....Can. 49·30 N 68·30 W
199 Manihiki Is. (mä′nē-hē′kē) Oceania 9·40 S 158·00 W
197 Manila (mȧ-nĭl′ȧ)......Phil. (In.) 14·37 N 121·00 E
197 Manila B.....Phil. (In.) 14·38 N 120·46 E
188 Manipur (State).....India 25·00 N 94·00 E
171 Manisa (mä′nê-sȧ).....Tur. 38·40 N 27·30 E
104 Manistee (măn-ĭs-tē′).....Mi. 44·15 N 86·20 W
104 Manistee (R.).....Mi. 44·25 N 85·45 W
109 Manistique (măn-ĭs-tēk′).....Mi. 45·58 N 86·16 W
109 Manistique (L.).....Mi. 46·14 N 85·30 W
109 Manistique (R.).....Mi. 46·05 N 86·09 W
90 Manitoba (Prov.) (măn-ĭ-tō′bȧ) Can. 55·12 N 97·29 W
95 Manitoba (L.).....Can. 51·00 N 98·45 W
94 Manito L. (măn′ĭ-tō).....Can. 52·45 N 109·45 W
109 Manitou (I.) (măn′ĭ-tōō).....Mi. 47·21 N 87·33 W
109 Manitou (L.).....Can. 49·21 N 93·01 W
104 Manitou Is.....Mi. 45·05 N 86·00 W
104 Manitoulin I. (măn-ĭ-tōō′lĭn).Can. 45·45 N 81·30 W
116 Manitou Springs.....Co. 38·51 N 104·58 W
109 Manitowoc (măn-ĭ-tô-wŏk′)...Wi. 44·05 N 87·42 W
97 Maniwaki.....Can. 46·23 N 76·00 W
134 Manizales (mä-nē-sä′lĕs).Col. (In.) 5·05 N 75·31 W
212 Manjacaze (man′yä-kä′zĕ)...Moz. 24·37 S 33·49 E
184 Mānjra (R.).....India 18·18 N 77·00 E
116 Mankato (măn-kā′tō).....Ks. 39·45 N 98·12 W
109 Mankato.....Mn. 44·10 N 93·59 W

ng-sing; ŋ-baŋk; N-nasalized n; nŏd; cŏmmit; ōld; ôbey; ôrder; fōōd; fŏŏt; ou-out; s-soft; sh-dish; th-thin; pūre; ûnite; ûrn; stŭd; circŭs; ü-as "y" in study; ′-indeterminate vowel.

310 Mankim — Marple PRONOUNCING INDEX

Page	Name Pronunciation Region	Lat. °′	Long. °′
215	Mankim....................Cam.	5·01 N	12·00 E
163	Manlleu (män-lyā′ōō).........Sp.	42·00 N	2·16 E
185	Mannar (má-när′)......Sri Lanka	9·48 N	80·03 E
184	Mannar, G. of..............India	8·47 N	78·33 E
149	Mannersdorf am Leithagebirge Aus. (Vienna In.)	47·58 N	16·36 E
158	Mannheim (män′hīm).....F.R.G.	49·30 N	8·31 E
109	Manning (măn′ĭng)...........Ia.	41·53 N	95·04 W
121	Manning....................SC	33·41 N	80·12 W
104	Mannington (măn′ĭng-tŭn)...WV	39·30 N	80·55 W
164	Mannu (R.) (mä′n-nōō).......It.	39·32 N	9·03 E
214	Mano (R.)..................Lib.	7·00 N	11·25 W
119	Man of War B..............Ba.	21·05 N	74·05 W
119	Man of War Chan............Ba.	22·45 N	76·10 W
197	Manokwari (mȧ-nŏk-wä′rē).Indon.	0·56 S	134·10 E
217	Manono..................Zaire	7·18 S	27·25 E
95	Manor (măn′ẽr).............Can.	49·36 N	102·05 W
112	Manor........Wa. (Portland In.)	45·45 N	122·36 W
185	Manori............India (In.)	19·13 N	72·43 E
161	Manosque (mȧ-nôsh′).........Fr.	43·51 N	5·48 E
89	Manotick......Can. (Ottawa In.)	45·13 N	75·41 W
163	Manresa (män-rā′sä)..........Sp.	41·44 N	1·52 E
217	Mansa.................Zambia	11·12 S	28·53 E
214	Mansabá..........Guinea-Bissau	12·18 N	15·15 W
91	Mansel (I.) (măn′sĕl).......Can.	61·56 N	81·10 W
134	Manseriche, Pongo de (Water Gap) (pŏ′n-gō-dĕ-män-sĕ-rē′chĕ).Peru	4·15 S	77·45 W
148	Mansfield (mănz′fēld).......Eng.	53·08 N	1·12 W
119	Mansfield....................La.	32·02 N	93·43 W
104	Mansfield...................Oh.	40·45 N	82·30 W
110	Mansfield..................Wa.	47·48 N	119·39 W
105	Mansfield, Mt...............Vt.	44·30 N	72·45 W
148	Mansfield Woodhouse (wŏŏd-hous).Eng.	53·08 N	1·12 W
135	Manso (R.)...............Braz.	13·30 S	51·45 W
134	Manta (män′tä).............Ec.	1·03 S	80·16 W
91	Manteno (măn-tē-nō) Il. (Chicago In.)	41·15 N	87·50 W
121	Manteo....................NC	35·55 N	75·40 W
161	Mantes-la-Jolie (mänt-ĕ-lä-zhō-lē′) Fr. (Paris In.)	48·59 N	1·42 E
115	Manti (măn′tī)..............Ut.	39·15 N	111·40 W
137	Manitqueira, Serra da (Mts.) (sĕr′rä dä män-tê-kā′ê-rȧ) Braz. (Rio de Janeiro In.)	22·40 S	45·12 W
164	Mantova (Mantua) (män′tô-vä) (măn′tū-ȧ).It.	45·09 N	10·47 E
128	Mantua (män-tōō′ä).........Cuba	22·20 N	84·15 W
113	Mantua (măn′tū-ȧ) Ut. (Salt Lake City In.)	41·30 N	111·57 W
	Mantua, see Mantova		
98	Manuan (L.) (mä-nōō′ăn)...Can.	50·36 N	70·50 W
98	Manuan (R.)...............Can.	50·15 N	70·30 W
197	Manui (Is.) (mä-nōō′ē)....Indon.	3·35 S	123·38 E
197	Manus (I.) (mä′nōōs).Pap. N. Gui.	2·22 S	146·22 E
119	Manvel (măn′vel).......Tx. (In.)	29·28 N	95·22 W
106	Manville (măn′vĭl) NJ (New York In.)	40·33 N	74·36 W
106	Manville.....RI (Providence In.)	41·57 N	71·27 W
171	Manych (R.) (mä-nĭch′)..Sov. Un.	47·00 N	41·10 E
147	Manych Dep...........Sov. Un.	46·32 N	42·44 E
171	Manych-Gudilo (Lake)..Sov. Un.	46·40 N	42·50 E
218	Manzala L.......Egypt (Nile In.)	31·14 N	32·04 E
134	Manzanares (män-sä-nä′rĕs) Col. (In.)	5·15 N	75·09 W
163	Manzanares (R.) (mänz-nä′rĕs) Sp. (Madrid In.)	40·36 N	3·48 W
163	Manzanares, Canal de (kä-nä′l-dĕ-män-thä-nä′rĕs) Sp. (Madrid In.)	40·20 N	3·38 W
128	Manzanillo (män′zä-nēl′yō)..Cuba	20·20 N	77·05 W
124	Manzanillo................Mex.	19·02 N	104·21 W
129	Manzanillo, Bahía de (B.)...Hai.	19·55 N	71·50 W
124	Manzanillo, Bahía de (B.) (bä-ē′ä-dĕ-män-zä-nē′l-yō).Mex.	19·00 N	104·38 W
127	Manzanillo, Punta (Pt.).....Pan.	9·40 N	79·33 W
194	Manzovka (mán-zhô′f-ká) Sov. Un.	44·16 N	132·13 E
215	Mao (mä′ô)...............Chad	14·07 N	15·19 E
129	Mao................Dom. Rep.	19·35 N	71·10 W
197	Maoke, Pegunungan (Mtn.) Indon.	4·00 S	138·00 E
193	Maoming..................China	21·55 N	110·40 E
125	Mapastepec (ma-päs-tȧ-pĕk′).Mex.	15·24 N	92·52 W
197	Mapia (I.) (mä′pē-ä).......Indon.	0·57 N	134·22 E
118	Mapimi (mä-pê-mē′)..........Mex.	25·50 N	103·50 W
118	Mapimi, Bolsón de (Des.) (bôl-sŏ′n-dĕ-mä-pē′mē).Mex.	27·27 N	103·20 W
94	Maple Creek (mā′p′l) (crēk).Can.	49·55 N	109·27 W
89	Maple Grove (grōv) Can. (Montreal In.)	45·19 N	73·51 W
107	Maple Heights.Oh. (Cleveland In.)	41·25 N	81·34 W
106	Maple Shade (shād) NJ (Philadelphia In.)	39·57 N	75·01 W
112	Maple Valley (văl′ê) Wa. (Seattle In.)	47·24 N	122·02 W
113	Maplewood (wŏŏd) Mn. (Minneapolis, St. Paul In.)	45·00 N	93·03 W
113	Maplewood....Mo. (St. Louis In.)	38·37 N	90·20 W
213	Mapumulo (mä-pä-mōō′lō) S. Afr. (Natal In.)	29·12 S	31·05 E
212	Maputo (Lourenço Marques).Moz.	26·50 S	32·30 E
197	Maqueda Chan. (mä-kā′dä) Phil. (In.)	13·40 N	123·52 E
212	Maquela do Zombo (mȧ-kā′lȧ dōō zôm′bōō).Ang.	6·08 S	15·15 E
109	Maquoketa (mȧ-kō-kê-tȧ).....Ia.	42·04 N	90·42 W
109	Maquoketa (R.)..............Ia.	42·08 N	90·40 W
136	Mar, Serra do (Mts.) (sĕr′rä dōō mär′).Braz.	26·30 S	49·15 W
134	Maracaibo (mä-rä-kī′bō).....Ven.	10·38 N	71·45 W
134	Maracaibo, Lago de (L.) (lä′gô-dĕ-mä-rä-kī′bō).Ven.	9·55 N	72·13 W
135	Maracay (mä-rä-käy′)..Ven. (In.)	10·15 N	67·35 W

Page	Name Pronunciation Region	Lat. °′	Long. °′
211	Marādah.................Libya	29·10 N	19·07 E
215	Maradi (mȧ-rȧ-dē′).........Niger	13·29 N	7·06 E
171	Marāgheh..................Iran	37·20 N	46·10 E
213	Maraisburg..............S. Afr. (Johannesburg & Pretoria In.)	26·12 S	27·57 E
117	Marais des Cygnes (R.).......Ks.	38·30 N	95·30 W
135	Marajó, Ilha de (I.) (mä-rä-zhō′) Braz.	0·30 S	50·00 W
217	Maralal...................Ken.	1·06 N	36·42 E
215	Marali...........Cen. Afr. Emp.	6·01 N	18·24 E
217	Marandelles (mȧ-rȧn-dĕl′ȧs)...Rh.	18·10 S	31·36 E
135	Maranguape (mä-räŋ-gwä′pĕ) Braz.	3·48 S	38·38 W
	Maranhão, see São Luis		
135	Maranhão (State) (mä-rän-youɴ) Braz.	5·15 S	45·52 W
203	Maranoa (R.) (mä-rä-nō′ä)..Austl.	27·01 S	148·03 E
163	Marano di Napoli (mä-rä′nô-dē-nȧ′pô-lē) It. (Naples In.)	40·39 N	14·12 E
134	Marañón, Rio (R.) (rê′ō-mä-rä-nyōn′).Peru	4·26 S	75·08 W
135	Marapanim (mä-rä-pä-nē′ɴ).Braz.	0·45 S	47·42 W
171	Maras (mä-räsh′)............Tur.	37·40 N	36·50 W
96	Marathon..................Can.	48·50 N	86·10 W
121	Marathon (măr′ȧ-thŏn)...Fl. (In.)	24·41 N	81·06 W
107	Marathon....Oh. (Cincinnati In.)	39·09 N	83·59 W
196	Maratua (I.)..............Indon.	2·14 N	118·30 E
124	Maravatio (mä-rä-vä′tê-ō)...Mex.	19·54 N	100·25 W
211	Marawi....................Sud.	18·07 N	31·57 E
204	Marble Bar (mär′b′l bär)...Austl.	21·15 S	119·15 E
115	Marble Can. (mär′b′l).........Az.	36·21 N	111·48 W
218	Marble Hall (hâll).........S. Afr. (Johannesburg & Pretoria In.)	24·59 S	29·19 E
99	Marblehead (mär′b′l-hĕd) Ma. (In.)	42·30 N	70·51 W
158	Marburg (mär′bŏŏrgh).....F.R.G.	50·49 N	8·46 E
216	Marca, Ponta da (Pt.).......Ang.	16·31 S	11·42 E
126	Marcala (mär-kä-lä)........Hond.	14·08 N	88·01 W
166	Marche (Reg.) (mär′kā).......It.	43·35 N	12·33 E
149	Marchegg........Aus. (Vienna In.)	48·18 N	16·55 E
144	Marchena (mär-chā′nä).......Sp.	37·20 N	5·25 W
134	Marchena (I.) (ê′s-lä-mär-chĕ′nä) Ec.	0·29 N	90·31 W
149	Marchfeld (Reg.) Aus. (Vienna In.)	48·14 N	16·37 E
117	Marceline (mär-sê-lēn′).......Mo.	39·42 N	92·56 W
137	Marcos Paz (mär-kōs′ päz) Arg. (Buenos Aires In.)	34·49 S	58·51 W
198	Marcus (I.) (mär′kŭs).......Asia	24·00 N	155·00 E
106	Marcus Hook (mär′kŭs hŏŏk) Pa. (Phildelphia In.)	39·49 N	75·25 W
105	Marcy, Mt. (mär′sê).........NY	44·10 N	73·55 W
137	Mar de Espanha (mär-dĕ-ĕs-pȧ′nyȧ) Braz. (Rio de Janeiro In.)	21·53 S	43·00 W
136	Mar del Plata (mär dĕl plä′ta).Arg.	37·59 S	57·35 W
171	Mardin (mär-dēn′)...........Tur.	37·25 N	40·40 E
205	Mare (I.) (mȧ-rā′)........N. Cal.	21·53 S	168·30 E
154	Maree (L.) (mä-rē′).........Scot.	57·40 N	5·44 W
109	Marengo (mȧ-rĕŋ′gō).........Ia.	41·47 N	92·04 W
160	Marennes (mȧ-rĕn′)..........Fr.	45·49 N	1·08 W
161	Mareuil-sur-Ourcq (mä-rû′yĕ-sür-ōōrk′).Fr. (Paris In.)	49·08 N	2·04 E
118	Marfa (mär′fȧ)..............Tx.	30·19 N	104·01 W
167	Marganets............Sov. Un.	47·41 N	34·33 E
122	Margarita (mär-gōō-rē′tä) C. Z. (In.)	9·20 N	79·55 W
135	Margarita, Isla de (I.) (mär-gȧ-rē′tä).Ven. (In.)	11·00 N	64·15 W
154	Margate (mär′gāt) ....Eng.	51·21 N	1·17 E
213	Margate (mär-gāt′) S. Afr. (Natal In.)	30·52 S	30·21 E
217	Margherita Pk...............Afr.	0·22 N	29·51 E
98	Marguerite (R.)...........Can.	50·39 N	66·42 W
170	Mari (A. S. S. R.) (mä′rē).Sov. Un.	56·20 N	48·00 E
98	Maria (mȧ-rē′ȧ)............Can.	48·10 N	66·04 W
162	Maria, Sierra de (Mts.) (sē-ĕ′r-rä-dĕ-mä-ryä).Sp.	37·42 N	2·25 W
124	María Cleofas (I.) (mä-rē′ä klā′ō-fäs).Mex.	21·17 N	106·14 W
156	Mariager (mä-rê-ägh′ẽr).....Den.	56·38 N	10·00 E
156	Mariager Fd...............Den.	56·44 N	10·32 E
124	María Magdalena (I.) (mä rē′ä mäg-dä-lā′nä).Mex.	21·25 N	106·23 W
137	Mariana (mä-ryä′nä) Braz. (Rio de Janeiro In.)	20·23 S	43·24 W
198	Mariana Is. (mä-rê-ä′nä)..Oceania	17·20 N	145·00 E
198	Mariana Trench.........Oceania	12·00 N	144·00 E
129	Marianao (mä-rê-ä-nä′ō) Cuba (In.)	23·05 N	82·26 W
117	Marianna (mā-rĭ-ăn′ȧ)........Ar.	34·45 N	90·45 W
120	Marianna...................Fl.	30·46 N	85·14 W
107	Marianna....Pa. (Pittsburgh In.)	40·01 N	80·05 W
136	Mariano Acosta (mä-rêä′nô-ä-kŏs′tä) Arg. (Buenos Aires In.)	34·28 S	58·48 W
148	Mariánské Lázně (mär′yán-skĕ′läz′nyĕ).Czech.	49·58 N	12·42 E
122	Marias, Islas (Is.) (mä-rē′äs) Mex.	21·30 N	106·40 W
111	Marias R. (mȧ-rī′ȧz).........Mt.	48·15 N	110·50 W
127	Mariato, Punta (Pt.).........Pan.	7·17 N	81·09 W
156	Maribo (mä′rê-bō)..........Den.	54·46 N	11·29 E
164	Maribor (mä′re-bôr).........Yugo.	46·33 N	15·37 E
137	Maricá (mä-rē-kä′) Braz. (Rio de Janeiro In.)	22·55 S	42·49 W
197	Maricaban (I.) (mä-rê-kä-bän′) Phil. (In.)	13·40 N	120·44 E
218	Marico R. (mä′rĭ-cô).......S. Afr. (Johannesburg & Pretoria In.)	24·53 S	26·22 E
220	Marie Byrd Land (mȧ rē′ bûrd′) Ant.	78·00 S	130·00 W

Page	Name Pronunciation Region	Lat. °′	Long. °′
156	Mariefred (mä-rē′ĕ-frĭd).....Swe.	59·17 N	17·09 E
127	Marie Galante I. (mȧ-rē′ gȧ-läɴt′) Guad. (In.)	15·58 N	61·05 W
	Mariehamn, see Maarianhamina		
156	Mariestad (mä-rē′ĕ-städ′)....Swe.	58·43 N	13·45 E
106	Marietta (mā-rĭ′-ĕt′ȧ) Ga. (Atlanta In.)	33·57 N	84·33 W
104	Marietta....................Oh.	39·25 N	81·30 W
117	Marietta....................Ok.	33·53 N	97·07 W
112	Marietta....Wa. (Vancouver In.)	48·48 N	122·35 W
172	Mariinsk (mȧ-re′ĭnsk)....Sov. Un.	56·15 N	87·28 E
157	Marijampole (mä-rê-yäm-pô′lĕ) Sov. Un.	54·33 N	23·26 E
218	Marikana (mă′-rĭ-kä-nȧ)...S. Afr. (Johannesburg & Pretoria In.)	25·40 S	27·28 E
135	Marília (mä-rē′lyȧ).........Braz.	22·02 S	49·48 W
216	Marimba...................Ang.	8·28 S	17·08 E
197	Marinduque (I.) (mä-rên-dōō′kä) Phil. (In.)	13·14 N	121·45 E
113	Marine (mȧ-rēn′).Il. (St. Louis In.)	38·48 N	89·47 W
104	Marine City.................Mi.	42·45 N	82·30 W
113	Marine L...................Mn. (Minneapolis, St. Paul In.)	45·13 N	92·55 W
113	Marine on St. Croix (ăɴ sĕɴ krōō-ä) Mn. (Minneapolis, St. Paul In.)	45·11 N	92·47 W
109	Marinette (măr-ĭ-nĕt′)........Wi.	45·05 N	87·40 W
216	Maringa (R.) (mă-riŋ′gä)......Zaire	1·15 N	20·05 E
162	Marinha Grande (mä-rēn′yȧ grän′dĕ).Port.	39·49 N	8·53 W
120	Marion (măr′ĭ-ŭn)............Al.	32·36 N	87·19 W
104	Marion.......................Il.	37·40 N	88·55 W
104	Marion......................In.	40·35 N	85·45 W
109	Marion......................Ia.	42·01 N	91·39 W
117	Marion.....................Ks.	38·21 N	97·02 W
120	Marion.....................Ky.	37·19 N	88·05 W
121	Marion.....................NC	35·40 N	82·00 W
108	Marion.....................ND	46·37 N	98·20 W
104	Marion.....................Oh.	40·35 N	83·10 W
121	Marion.....................SC	34·08 N	79·23 W
121	Marion.....................Va.	36·48 N	81·33 W
121	Marion (R.).................SC	33·25 N	80·35 W
205	Marion Rf..................Austl.	18·57 S	151·31 E
137	Mariposa (mä-rê-pô′sä) Chile (Santiago In.)	35·33 S	71·21 W
114	Mariposa Cr.................Ca.	37·14 N	120·30 W
134	Mariquita (mä-rē-kē′tä).Col. (In.)	5·13 N	74·52 W
135	Mariscal Estigarribia (mä-rēs-käl′ĕs-tē-gär-rē′byä) Par.	22·03 S	60·28 W
136	Marisco, Ponta do (Pt.) (pô′n-tä-dô-mä-rē′s-kō) Braz. (Rio de Janeiro In.)	23·01 S	43·17 W
161	Maritime Alps (Mts.) (mȧ′rĭ-tīm ălps).Fr.-It.	44·20 N	7·02 E
165	Maritsa (R.) (mä′rê-tsȧ).Grc.-Tur.	40·43 N	26·19 E
197	Mariveles...........Phil. (In.)	14·27 N	120·29 E
183	Marj Uyan...Leb. (Palestine In.)	33·21 N	35·36 E
218	Marka....Som. (Horn of Afr. In.)	1·45 N	44·47 E
188	Marka Kul′ (L.)........Sov. Un.	49·15 N	85·48 E
156	Markaryd (mär′kä-rüd)......Swe.	56·30 N	13·34 E
117	Marked Tree (märkt trē).......Ar.	35·31 N	90·26 W
149	Marken, I..Neth. (Amsterdam In.)	52·26 N	5·08 E
148	Market Bosworth (bŏz′wûrth) Eng.	52·37 N	1·23 W
148	Market Deeping (dēp′ĭng)...Eng.	52·40 N	0·19 W
148	Market Drayton (drā′tŭn)...Eng.	52·54 N	2·29 W
148	Market Harborough (här′bŭr-ô) Eng.	52·28 N	0·55 W
148	Market Rasen (rā′zĕn)......Eng.	53·23 N	0·21 W
89	Markham (märk′ȧm) Can. (Toronto In.)	43·53 N	79·15 W
220	Markham, Mt...............Ant.	82·59 S	159·30 E
167	Markovka (mȧr-kôf′kȧ)..Sov. Un.	49·32 N	39·34 E
173	Markovo (mär′kô-vô)....Sov. Un.	64·46 N	170·48 E
184	Markrāna.................India	27·08 N	74·43 E
171	Marks.................Sov. Un.	51·40 N	46·40 E
119	Marksville (märks′vĭl)........La.	31·09 N	92·05 W
149	Markt Indersdorf (märkt ēn′dĕrs-dōrf) F.R.G. (Munich In.)	48·22 N	11·23 E
158	Marktredwitz (märk-rĕd′vēts) F.R.G.	50·02 N	12·05 E
149	Markt Schwaben (märkt shvä′bĕn) F.R.G. (Munich In.)	48·12 N	11·52 E
161	Marl (märl)....F.R.G. (Ruhr In.)	51·40 N	7·05 E
106	Marlboro.....NJ (New York In.)	40·18 N	74·15 W
99	Marlborough...........Ma. (In.)	42·21 N	71·33 W
104	Marlette (mär-lĕt′)...........Mi.	43·25 N	83·05 W
119	Marlin (mär′lĭn)..............Tx.	31·18 N	96·52 W
105	Marlinton (mär′lĭn-tŭn).....WV	38·15 N	80·10 W
148	Marlow (mär′lō) Eng. (London In.)	51·33 N	0·46 W
116	Marlow.....................Ok.	34·38 N	97·56 W
128	Marls, The (Shoals) (märls)..Ba.	26·30 N	77·15 W
160	Marmande (mȧr-mänd′)........Fr.	44·30 N	0·10 E
165	Marmara (I.) (mär′mȧ-rȧ)...Tur.	40·38 N	27·35 E
171	Marmara Denizi (Sea).......Tur.	40·40 N	28·00 E
108	Marmarth (mär′mȧrth).......ND	46·19 N	103·57 W
125	Mar Muerto (L.) (mär-mōōĕ′r-tô) Mex.	16·13 N	94·22 W
149	Marne (mär′nĕ) F.R.G. (Hamburg In.)	53·57 N	9·01 E
160	Marne (R.) (märn)...........Fr.	49·08 N	3·39 E
134	Maroa (mä-rō′ä)............Ven.	2·43 N	67·37 W
213	Maroantsetra (mȧ-rō-äŋ-tsā′trȧ) Mad.	15·18 S	49·48 E
134	Maro Jarapeto (Mtn.) (mä-rō-hä-rä-pĕ′tô).Col. (In.)	6·29 N	76·39 W
213	Maromokotro (Mtn.).......Mad.	14·00 S	49·11 E
135	Maroni (R.) (mä-rō′nê) Fr. Gu.-Sur.	3·02 N	53·54 W
215	Maroua (mär′wä)..........Cam.	10·36 N	14·20 E
149	Marple (mär′p′l)...........Eng.	53·24 N	2·04 W

312 Mbamba Bay — Mesagne
PRONOUNCING INDEX

Page	Name Pronunciation Region	Lat. °′	Long. °′
217	Mbamba Bay . . . Tan.	11·17 S	34·46 E
216	Mbandaka (Coquilhatville) . . Zaire	0·04 N	18·16 E
216	Mbanza-Ngungu . . . Zaire	5·20 S	10·55 E
217	Mbarara . . . Ug.	0·37 S	30·39 E
215	Mbasay . . . Chad	7·39 N	15·40 E
217	Mbeya . . . Tan.	8·54 S	33·27 E
212	Mbigou (m-bê-gōō') . . . Gabon	2·07 S	11·30 E
216	Mbinda . . . Con.	2·00 S	12·55 E
217	Mbogo . . . Tan.	7·26 S	33·26 E
216	Mbomou (Bomu) (R.) (m'bō'mōō) Cen. Afr. Emp.-Zaire	4·50 N	23·35 E
216	Mbuji-Mayi (Bakwanga) . . . Zaire	6·09 S	23·28 E
210	Mbout (m'bōō') . . . Mauritania	16·03 N	12·31 W
217	Mchinji . . . Malawi	13·42 S	32·50 E
115	Mead, L. . . . Az.-Nv.	36·20 N	114·14 W
116	Meade (mēd) . . . Ks.	37·17 N	100·21 W
111	Meade Pk. . . . Id.	42·19 N	111·16 W
94	Meadow Lake (mĕd'ō lāk) . . . Can.	54·08 N	108·26 W
89	Meadows (mĕd'ōz) Can. (Winnipeg In.)	50·02 N	97·35 W
105	Meadville (mēd'vĭl) . . . Pa.	41·40 N	80·10 W
104	Meaford (mē'fērd) . . . Can.	44·35 N	80·40 W
91	Mealy Mts. (mē'lē) . . . Can.	53·32 N	57·58 W
203	Meandarra (mē-ăn-dä'rȧ) . . . Austl.	27·47 S	149·40 E
161	Meaux (mō) . . . Fr. (Paris In.)	48·58 N	2·53 E
125	Mecapalapa (mā-kä-pä-lä'pä) Mex.	20·32 N	97·52 W
99	Mecatina (I.) (mā-kȧ-tē'nȧ) . . Can.	50·50 N	58·33 W
99	Mecatina (R.) (mā-kȧ-tē'nȧ) . Can.	50·50 N	59·45 W
	Mecca, see Makkah		
98	Mechanic Falls (mê-kăn'ĭk) . . . Me.	44·05 N	70·23 W
105	Mechanicsburg (mê-kăn'ĭks-bûrg) . Pa.	40·15 N	77·00 W
106	Mechanicsville (mê-kăn'ĭks-vĭl) Md. (Baltimore In.)	38·27 N	76·45 W
105	Mechanicville (mêkăn'ĭk-vĭl) . . NY	42·55 N	73·45 W
149	Mechelen . . . Bel. (Brussels In.)	51·01 N	4·28 E
152	Mecheria . . . Mor.	33·30 N	0·13 W
158	Mecklenburg (Reg.) (mĕk'lĕn-bŏŏrgh) . . . G.D.R.	53·34 N	12·18 E
196	Medan (mâ-dän') . . . Indon.	3·35 N	98·35 E
136	Medanosa, Punta (Pt.) (pōō'n-tä-mĕ-dä-nô'sä) . Arg.	47·50 S	65·53 W
148	Medden (R.) (mĕd'ĕn) . . . Eng.	53·14 N	1·05 W
163	Médéa (mā-dā'ä) . . . Alg.	36·18 N	2·40 E
134	Medellín (mâ-dhĕl-yēn') . Col. (In.)	6·15 N	75·34 W
125	Medellin (mĕ-dĕl-yē'n) . . . Mex.	19·03 N	96·08 W
152	Medenine (mā-dē-nēn') . . . Tun.	33·22 N	10·33 E
99	Medfield (mĕd'fēld) . . . Ma. (In.)	42·11 N	71·19 W
99	Medford (mĕd'fērd) . . . Ma. (In.)	42·25 N	71·07 W
106	Medford . . . NJ (Philadelphia In.)	39·54 N	74·50 W
116	Medford . . . Ok.	36·47 N	97·44 W
110	Medford . . . Or.	42·19 N	122·52 W
109	Medford . . . Wi.	45·09 N	90·22 W
106	Media (mē'dĭ-ȧ) Pa. (Philadelphia In.)	39·55 N	75·24 W
159	Medias (mĕd-yäsh') . . . Rom.	46·09 N	24·21 E
110	Medical Lake (mĕd'ĭ-kăl) . . . Wa.	47·34 N	117·40 W
116	Medicine Bow Ra. (mĕd'ĭ-sĭn bō) . Co.-Wy.	40·55 N	106·02 W
111	Medicine Bow R. . . . Wy.	41·58 N	106·30 W
94	Medicine Hat (mĕd'ĭ-sĭn hăt) . Can.	50·03 N	110·40 W
111	Medicine L. (mĕd'ĭ-sĭn) . . . Mt.	48·24 N	104·15 W
116	Medicine Lodge . . . Ks.	37·17 N	98·37 W
116	Medicine Lodge (R.) . . . Ks.	37·20 N	98·57 W
105	Medina (mê-dī'nȧ) . . . NY	43·15 N	78·20 W
107	Medina . . . Oh. (Cleveland In.)	41·08 N	81·52 W
	Medina, see Al Madīnah		
162	Medina del Campo (mä-dē'nä dĕl käm'pō) . Sp.	41·18 N	4·54 W
162	Medina de Rioseco (mä-dē'nä dā rē-ō-sā'kō) . Sp.	41·53 N	5·05 W
214	Médina Gonassé . . . Sen.	13·08 N	13·45 W
118	Medina L. . . . Tx.	29·36 N	98·47 W
118	Medina R. . . . Tx.	29·45 N	99·13 W
162	Medina Sidonia (sê-dō'nyä) . . . Sp.	36·28 N	5·58 W
137	Medio (mĕ'dyô) (R.) Arg. (Buenos Aires In.)	33·40 S	60·30 W
152	Mediterranean Sea (mĕd-ĭ-tēr-ā'nê-ăn) Afr.-Asia-Eur.	36·22 N	13·25 E
151	Medjerda, Oued (R.) (wĕd mĕ-jĕr'dȧ) . Tun.	36·43 N	9·54 E
172	Mednogorsk . . . Sov. Un.	51·27 N	57·22 E
171	Medvedista (R.) (mĕd-vyĕ'dê tsȧ) . Sov. Un.	50·10 N	43·40 E
170	Medvezhegorsk (mĕd-vyĕzh'yĕ-gôrsk') . Sov. Un.	63·00 N	34·20 E
173	Medvezh'y (Is.) . . . Sov. Un.	71·00 N	161·25 E
99	Medway (mĕd'wā) . . . Ma. (In.)	42·08 N	71·23 W
166	Medyn' (mĕ-dēn') . . . Sov. Un.	54·58 N	35·53 E
167	Medzhibozh (mĕd-zhê-bōzh') Sov. Un.	49·23 N	27·29 E
204	Meekatharra (mē-kȧ-thăr'ȧ) . Austl.	26·30 S	118·38 E
115	Meeker (mēk'ēr) . . . Co.	40·00 N	107·55 W
99	Meelpaeg L. (mēl'pȧ-ĕg) . . . Can.	48·22 N	56·52 W
158	Meerane (mā-rä'nê) . . . G.D.R.	50·51 N	12·27 E
184	Meerut (mē'rŏŏt) . . . India	28·59 N	77·43 E
165	Megalópolis (mĕg-ȧ lŏ'pô-lĭs) . Grc..	37·22 N	22·08 E
167	Meganom, M. (C.) (mĭs mĕ-gȧ-nôm') . Sov. Un.	44·48 N	35·17 E
165	Mégara (mĕg'ȧ-rȧ) . . . Grc.	37·59 N	23·21 E
121	Megget (mĕg'ĕt) . . . SC	32·44 N	80·15 W
188	Meghelaya (State) . . . India	25·30 N	91·30 E
112	Megler (mĕg'lēr) Wa. (Portland In.)	46·15 N	123·52 W
166	Meglino (L.) (mȧ-glē'nô) . Sov. Un.	58·32 N	35·27 E
121	Meherrin (R.) (mê-hĕr'ĭn) . . . Va.	36·40 N	77·49 W
113	Mehlville . . . Mo. (St. Louis In.)	38·30 N	90·19 W
184	Mehsāna . . . India	23·42 N	72·23 E
160	Mehun-sur-Yèvre (mē-ŭɴ-sür-yĕvr') . Fr.	47·11 N	2·14 E
190	Meichu (mā'jĕōō) . . . China	31·17 N	119·12 E
193	Meihsien . . . China	24·20 N	116·10 E
193	Meiling Pass (mā'lĭng') . . . China	25·22 N	115·00 E
161	Meinerzhagen (mī'nĕrts-hä-gĕn) F.R.G. (Ruhr In.)	51·06 N	7·39 E
158	Meiningen (mī'nĭng-ĕn) . . . G.D.R.	50·35 N	10·25 E
158	Meiringen . . . Switz.	46·45 N	8·11 E
158	Meissen . . . G.D.R.	51·11 N	13·28 E
136	Mejillones (mâ-ᴋê-lyō'nâs) . . . Chile	23·07 S	70·31 W
216	Mekambo . . . Gabon	1·01 N	13·56 E
211	Mekele . . . Eth.	13·31 N	39·19 E
210	Meknès (mĕk'nĕs) (mĕk-nĕs') . Mor.	33·56 N	5·44 W
	Mekong (R.), see Lanisung Chiang		
196	Mekong, Mouths of the (mē'kông') . Viet.	10·09 N	107·15 E
196	Mekong R. . . . Thai.-Laos	17·53 N	103·57 E
215	Mékrou (R.) . . . Afr.	11·35 N	2·25 E
183	Melaka (Malacca) Mala. (Singapore In.)	2·11 N	102·15 E
183	Melaka (State) Mala. (Singapore In.)	2·19 N	102·09 E
202	Melbourne (mĕl'bŭrn) Austl. (Melbourne In.)	37·52 S	145·08 E
121	Melbourne . . . Fl. (In.)	28·05 N	80·37 W
148	Melbourne . . . Eng.	52·49 N	1·26 W
107	Melbourne . . Ky. (Cincinnati In.)	39·02 N	84·22 W
109	Melcher (mĕl'chēr) . . . Ia.	41·13 N	93·11 W
170	Melekess (mĕl-yĕk ĕs) . . . Sov. Un.	54·20 N	49·30 E
166	Melenki (mĕ-lyĕn'kê) . . . Sov. Un.	55·25 N	41·34 E
94	Melfort (mĕl'fôrt) . . . Can.	52·52 N	104·36 W
211	Melik, Wadi el (R.) . . . Sud.	16·48 N	29·30 E
210	Melilla (Sp.) (mā-lēl'yä) . . . Afr.	35·24 N	3·30 W
137	Melipilla (mâ-lê-pē'lyä) Chile (Santiago In.)	33·40 S	71·12 W
95	Melita . . . Can.	49·11 N	101·09 W
167	Melitopol' (mā-lê-tô'pôl-y') Sov. Un.	46·49 N	35·19 E
218	Melkrivier . . . S. Afr. (Johannesburg & Pretoria In.)	24·01 S	28·23 E
109	Mellen (mĕl'ĕn) . . . Wi.	46·20 N	90·40 W
156	Mellerud (mâl'ĕ-rōōdh) . . . Swe.	58·43 N	12·25 E
213	Melmoth . . . S. Afr. (Natal In.)	28·38 S	31·26 E
136	Melo (mā'lō) . . . Ur.	32·18 S	54·07 W
89	Melocheville (mĕ-lôsh-vēl') Can. (Montreal In.)	45·24 N	73·56 W
174	Melozha R. (myĕ'lô-zhȧ) Sov. Un. (Moscow In.)	56·06 N	38·34 E
210	Melrhir Chott (L.) (mĕl'rēr) . Alg.	33·52 N	5·22 E
99	Melrose (mĕl'rōz) . . . Ma. (In.)	42·29 N	71·06 W
109	Melrose . . . Mn.	45·39 N	94·49 W
107	Melrose Park . . . Il. (Chicago In.)	41·54 N	87·52 W
212	Melsetter (mĕl-sĕt'ēr) . . . Rh.	19·44 S	32·51 E
148	Meltham (mĕl'thăm) . . . Eng.	53·35 N	1·51 W
202	Melton (mĕl'tŭn) Austl. (Melbourne In.)	37·41 S	144·35 E
148	Melton Mowbray (mō'brâ) . . Eng.	52·45 N	0·52 W
217	Melúli (R.) . . . Moz.	16·10 S	39·30 E
161	Melun (mē-lŭɴ') . . . Fr. (In.)	48·32 N	2·40 E
216	Melunga . . . Ang.	17·16 S	16·24 E
94	Melville (mĕl'vĭl) . . . Can.	50·55 N	102·48 W
113	Melville . . . La.	30·39 N	91·45 W
205	Melville, C. . . . Austl.	14·15 S	145·50 E
204	Melville (I.) . . . Austl.	11·30 S	131·12 E
91	Melville (R.) . . . Can.	53·46 N	59·31 W
90	Melville Hills . . . Can.	69·18 N	124·57 W
91	Melville Pen . . . Can.	67·44 N	84·09 W
107	Melvindale (mĕl'vĭn-dāl) Mi. (Detroit In.)	42·17 N	83·11 W
159	Mélykút (mā'l'kōōt) . . . Hung.	46·14 N	19·21 E
213	Memba (mĕm'bȧ) . . . Moz.	14·12 S	40·35 E
	Memel, see Klaipėda		
218	Memel (mĕ'mĕl) S. Afr. (Johannesburg & Pretoria In.)	27·42 S	29·35 E
158	Memmingen (mĕm'ĭng-ĕn) . F.R.G.	47·59 N	10·10 E
135	Memo (R.) (mĕ'mō) . . . Ven. (In.)	9·32 N	66·30 W
117	Memphis (mĕm'fĭs) . . . Mo.	40·27 N	92·11 W
120	Memphis (mĕm'fĭs) . . . Tn.	35·07 N	90·03 W
116	Memphis . . . Tx.	34·42 N	100·33 W
218	Memphis (Ruins) . Egypt (Nile In.)	29·50 N	31·12 E
105	Memphremagog (L.) (mĕm'frê-mā'gŏg) . Can.	45·05 N	72·10 W
117	Mena (mē'nȧ) . . . Ar.	34·35 N	94·09 W
167	Mena (mē-nȧ') . . . Sov. Un.	51·31 N	32·14 E
202	Menangle . . . Austl. (Sydney In.)	34·08 S	150·48 E
118	Menard (mê-närd') . . . Tx.	30·56 N	99·48 W
109	Menasha (mê-năsh'ȧ) . . . Wi.	44·12 N	88·29 W
160	Mende (mäɴd) . . . Fr.	44·31 N	3·30 E
161	Menden (mĕn'dĕn) F.R.G. (Ruhr In.)	51·26 N	7·47 E
171	Menderes (R.) (mĕn'dĕr-ĕs) . Tur.	37·50 N	28·20 E
136	Mendes (mĕ'n-dĕs) . . . Braz. (In.)	22·32 S	43·44 W
110	Mendocino, C. (mĕn'dô-sē'nō) . Ca.	40·25 N	124·22 W
109	Mendota (mĕn-dō'tȧ) . . . Il.	41·34 N	89·06 W
109	Mendota (L.) . . . Wi.	43·09 N	89·41 W
136	Mendoza (mĕn-dō'sä) . . . Arg.	32·48 S	68·45 W
136	Mendoza (Prov.) . . . Arg.	35·10 S	69·00 W
203	Menindee (mĕ-nĭn-dē) . . . Austl.	32·23 S	142·30 E
112	Menlo Park (mĕn'lō pärk) Ca. (San Francisco In.)	37·27 N	122·11 W
108	Menno (mĕn'ō) . . . SD	43·14 N	97·34 W
109	Menominee (mê-nŏm'ĭ-nē) . . . Mi.	45·08 N	87·40 W
109	Menominee (R.) . . . Mi.-Wi.	45·37 N	87·54 W
107	Menomonee Falls (fôls) Wi. (Milwaukee In.)	43·11 N	88·06 W
109	Menominee Ra. . . . Mi.	46·07 N	88·53 W
107	Menomonee R. Wi. (Milwaukee In.)	43·09 N	88·06 W
109	Menomonie . . . Wi.	44·53 N	91·55 W
216	Menongue . . . Ang.	14·36 S	17·48 E
163	Menorca, Isla de (Minorca) (I.) (ê's-lä-dĕ-mĕ-nô'r-kä) . Sp.	40·05 N	3·58 E
163	Mentana (mĕn-tȧ'nä) It. (Rome In.)	42·02 N	12·40 E
196	Mentawai, Kepulauan (Is.) (mĕn-tä-vī') . Indon.	1·08 S	98·10 E
161	Menton (mäɴ-tôɴ') . . . Fr.	43·46 N	7·37 E
113	Mentone (mĕn'tŏne) Ca. (Los Angeles In.)	34·05 N	117·08 W
213	Mentz (R.) (mĕnts) S. Afr. (Natal In.)	33·13 S	25·15 E
170	Menzelinsk (mĕn'zyĕ-lênsk') Sov. Un.	55·40 N	53·15 E
204	Menzies (mĕn'zēz) . . . Austl.	29·45 S	122·15 E
118	Meogui (mâ-ō'gē) . . . Mex.	28·17 N	105·28 W
155	Meppel (mĕp'ĕl) . . . Neth.	52·41 N	6·08 E
158	Meppen (mĕp'ĕn) . . . F.R.G.	52·40 N	7·18 E
163	Mequinenza Res. . . . Sp.	41·15 N	0·35 W
164	Merabéllou, Kólpos (G.) . Grc. (In.)	35·16 N	25·55 E
117	Meramec (R.) (mĕr'ȧ-mĕk) . . . Mo.	38·06 N	91·06 W
164	Merano (mâ-rä'nō) . . . It.	46·39 N	11·10 E
99	Merasheen (I.) (mē'rȧ-shēn) . Can.	47·30 N	54·15 W
197	Merauke (mâ-rou'kā) . . . Indon.	8·32 S	140·17 E
106	Meraux (mē-ro') La. (New Orleans In.)	29·56 N	89·56 W
163	Mercato San Severino (mĕr-kȧ'tō sän sĕ-vĕ-rē'nō) It. (Naples In.)	40·34 N	14·38 E
114	Merced (mĕr-sĕd') . . . Ca.	37·17 N	120·30 W
114	Merced (R.) . . . Ca.	37·25 N	120·31 W
137	Mercedario, Cerro (Mtn.) (mĕr-sâ-dhä'rê-ō) Chile (Santiago In.)	31·58 S	70·07 W
136	Mercedes (mĕr-sā'dhās) . . . Arg.	29·04 S	58·01 W
137	Mercedes . Arg. (Buenos Aires In.)	34·41 S	59·26 W
118	Mercedes . . . Tx.	26·09 N	97·55 W
137	Mercedes . . Ur. (Buenos Aires In.)	33·17 S	58·04 W
137	Mercedita (mĕr-sĕ-dĕ'tä) Chile (Santiago In.)	33·51 S	71·10 W
112	Mercer Island (mûr'sēr) Wa. (Seattle In.)	47·35 N	122·15 W
137	Mercês (mĕr-sĕ's) Braz. (Rio de Janeiro In.)	21·13 S	43·20 N
183	Merchong (R.) Mala. (Singapore In.)	3·08 N	103·13 E
149	Merchtem . . . Bel. (Brussels In.)	50·57 N	4·13 E
89	Mercier . . . Can. (Montreal In.)	45·19 N	73·45 W
163	Mercier-Lacombe (mĕr-syā' lȧ-kôɴb) . Alg.	35·18 N	0·11 W
91	Mercy, C. . . . Can.	64·48 N	63·22 W
105	Meredith (mĕr'ê-dĭth) . . . NH	43·35 N	71·35 W
167	Merefa (mâ-rĕf'ȧ) . . . Sov. Un.	49·49 N	36·04 E
126	Merendón, Serrania de (Mts.) (sĕr-rä-nē'ä-dā mâ-rĕn-dōn') Hond.	15·01 N	89·05 W
148	Mereworth (mĕ-rĕ'wûrth) Eng. (London In.)	51·15 N	0·23 E
196	Mergui (mĕr-gē') . . . Bur.	12·29 N	98·39 E
196	Mergui Arch . . . Asia	12·04 N	97·02 E
126	Mérida . . . Mex. (Yucatan In.)	20·58 N	89·37 W
134	Mérida . . . Ven.	8·30 N	71·15 W
134	Mérida, Cordillera de (Mts.) (mĕ'rê-dhä) . Ven.	8·30 N	70·45 W
105	Meriden (mĕr'ĭ-dĕn) . . . Ct.	41·30 N	72·50 W
120	Meridian (mê-rĭd-ĭ-ăn) . . . Ms.	32·21 N	88·41 W
119	Meridian . . . Tx.	31·56 N	97·37 W
157	Merikarvia (mā'rē-kär'vê-ȧ) . Fin.	61·51 N	21·30 E
149	Mering (mĕ'rĕng) F.R.G. (Munich In.)	48·16 N	11·00 E
120	Meriwether Lewis Natl. Mon. (mĕr'ĭ-wĕth-ēr lōō'ĭs) . Tn.	35·25 N	87·25 W
118	Merkel (mûr'kĕl) . . . Tx.	32·26 N	100·02 W
157	Merkiné (mĕr'kĭ-nê) . . . Sov. Un.	54·09 N	24·10 E
149	Merksem . . . Bel. (Brussels In.)	51·15 N	4·27 E
159	Merkys R. (mär'kĭs) . . . Sov. Un.	54·23 N	25·00 E
136	Merlo (mĕr-lô) . . . Arg. (In.)	34·25 S	58·44 W
113	Merriam (mĕr-rĭ-yăm) Ks. (Kansas City In.)	39·01 N	94·42 W
113	Merriam Mn. (Minneapolis, St. Paul In.)	44·44 N	93·36 W
106	Merrick (mĕr'ĭk) NY (New York In.)	40·40 N	73·33 W
106	Merrifield (mĕr'ĭ-fēld) Va. (Baltimore In.)	38·50 N	77·12 W
109	Merrill (mĕr'ĭl) . . . Wi.	45·11 N	89·42 W
99	Merrimac (mĕr'ĭ-măk) . . Ma. (In.)	42·50 N	71·00 W
99	Merrimack . . . NH (In.)	42·51 N	71·25 W
105	Merrimack (R.) (mĕr'ĭ-măk) Ma.-NH	43·10 N	71·30 W
99	Merrimack R. . . . Ma. (In.)	42·49 N	70·44 W
93	Merritt (mĕr'ĭt) . . . Can.	50·07 N	120·47 W
119	Merryville (mĕr'ĭ-vĭl) . . . La.	30·46 N	93·34 W
211	Mersa Fatma . . . Eth.	14·54 N	40·14 E
158	Merseburg (mĕr'zĕ-bŏŏrgh) G.D.R.	51·21 N	11·59 E
148	Mersey (R.) (mûr'zê) . . . Eng.	52·52 N	2·04 W
154	Mersey (R.) . . . Eng.	53·15 N	2·51 W
171	Mersin (mĕr-sēn') . . . Tur.	37·00 N	34·40 E
183	Mersing . . . Mala. (Singapore In.)	2·25 N	103·51 E
184	Merta Road (mār'tŭ rōd) . . . India	26·50 N	73·54 E
154	Merthyr Tydfil (mûr'thēr tĭd'vĭl) . Wales	51·46 N	3·30 W
162	Mértola Almodóvar (mĕr-tô-lȧ-äl-mô-dô'vär) . . Port.	37·39 N	8·04 W
161	Méru (mā-rü') . . . Fr. (In.)	49·14 N	2·08 E
211	Meru (mā'rōō) . . . Ken.	0·01 N	37·45 E
217	Meru, Mt. . . . Tan.	3·15 S	36·43 E
135	Merume Mts. (mĕr-ü'mĕ) . . . Guy.	5·45 N	60·15 W
149	Merwerde, Kanal (Can.) Neth. (Amsterdam In.)	52·15 N	5·01 E
112	Merwin (L.) (mĕr'wĭn) Wa. (Portland In.)	45·58 N	122·27 W
171	Merzifon (mĕr'ze-fōn) . . . Tur.	40·50 N	35·30 E
161	Merzig (mĕr'tsēg) . . . F.R.G.	49·27 N	6·54 E
115	Mesa (mā'sȧ) . . . Az.	33·25 N	111·50 W
109	Mesabi Ra. (mā-sŏb'bē) . . . Mn.	47·17 N	93·04 W
165	Mesagne (mā-sän'yā) . . . It.	40·34 N	17·51 E

ăt; finăl; rāte; senâte; ärm; ȧsk; sofȧ; fâre; ch-choose: dh-as th in other; bē; êvent; bĕt; recĕnt; cratēr; g-go; gh-guttural g; bĭt; ĭ-short neutral; rīde; ᴋ-guttural k as ch in German ich;

PRONOUNCING INDEX

Mesa Verde — Mineral del Chico 313

Page	Name	Pronunciation	Region	Lat. °′	Long. °′
115	Mesa Verde Natl. Park.	(vĕr′dē)	Co.	37·22 N	108·27 W
115	Mescalero Ind. Res.	(mĕs-kä-lā′rō)	NM	33·10 N	105·45 W
211	Mesewa (Massaua)		Eth.	15·40 N	39·19 E
166	Meshchovsk	(myĕsh′chĕfsk)	Sov. Un.	54·17 N	35·19 E
115	Mesilla	(mȧ-sē′yä)	NM	32·15 N	106·45 W
215	Meskine		Chad	11·25 N	15·21 E
165	Mesolóngion	(mĕ-sô-lôŋ′gē-ôn)	Grc.	38·23 N	21·28 E
164	Messina	(mĕ-sē′nȧ)	It.	38·11 N	15·34 E
212	Messina		S. Afr.	22·17 S	30·13 E
164	Messina, Stretto di (Str.)	(strĕ′t-tô dē)	It.	38·10 N	15·34 E
165	Messíni		Grc.	37·05 N	22·00 E
165	Méssiniakós Kólpos (G.)		Grc.	36·59 N	22·00 E
165	Mesta (R.)	(mĕ-stä′)	Bul.	41·42 N	23·40 E
164	Mestre	(mĕs′trā)	It.	45·29 N	12·15 E
134	Meta (Dept.)	(mĕ′tä)	Col. (In.)	3·28 N	74·07 W
134	Meta (R.)		Col.	4·33 N	72·09 W
98	Métabetchouane (R.)	(mĕ-tȧ-bĕt-chōō-än′)	Can.	47·45 N	72·00 W
119	Metairie		La.	30·00 N	90·11 W
136	Metán	(mĕ-tá′n)	Arg.	25·32 S	64·51 W
212	Metangula		Moz.	12·42 S	34·48 E
126	Metapán	(mȧ-tä-pän′)	Sal.	14·21 N	89·26 W
89	Metcalfe	(mĕt-käf)	Can. (Ottawa In.)	45·14 N	75·27 W
112	Metchosin		Can. (Seattle In.)	48·22 N	123·33 W
124	Metepec	(mȧ-tĕ-pĕk′)	Mex.	18·56 N	98·31 W
125	Metepec		Mex. (In.)	19·15 N	99·36 W
110	Methow R.	(mĕt′hou) (mĕt hou′)	Wa.	48·26 N	120·15 W
99	Methuen	(mê-thū′ĕn)	Ma. (In.)	42·44 N	71·11 W
165	Metkovic′	(mĕt′kô-vĭch)	Yugo.	43·02 N	17·40 E
101	Metlakatla	(mĕt-lȧ-kăt′lȧ)	Ak.	55·08 N	131·35 W
117	Metropolis	(mê-trŏp′ô-lĭs)	Il.	37·09 N	88·46 W
121	Metter	(mĕt′ẽr)	Ga.	32·21 N	82·05 W
161	Mettmann	(mĕt′män)	F.R.G. (Ruhr In.)	51·15 N	6·58 E
106	Metuchen	(mĕ-tŭ′chĕn)	NJ (New York In.)	40·32 N	74·21 W
161	Metz	(mĕtz)	Fr.	49·08 N	6·10 E
124	Metztitlán	(mĕtz-têt-län′)	Mex.	20·36 N	98·45 W
215	Meuban		Cam.	2·27 N	12·41 E
160	Meuse (R.)	(mûz) (müz)	Eur.	50·32 N	5·22 E
148	Mexborough	(mĕks′bŭr-ō)	Eng.	53·30 N	1·17 W
119	Mexia	(mȧ-hē′ä)	Tx.	31·32 N	96·29 W
125	Mexicalcingo	(mĕ-kē-käl-sēn′go)	Mex. (In.)	19·13 N	99·34 W
114	Mexicali	(mȧk-sê-kä′lê)	Mex.	32·28 N	115·29 W
115	Mexican Hat	(mĕk′sĭ-kăn hăt)	Ut.	37·10 N	109·55 W
98	Mexico	(mĕk′sĭ-kō)	Me.	44·34 N	70·33 W
117	Mexico		Mo.	39·09 N	91·51 W
122	Mexico (State)	(mȧk′sê-kō)	Mex.	19·50 N	99·50 W
75	Mexico		N. A.	23·45 N	104·00 W
122	Mexico, G. of		N. A.	25·15 N	93·45 W
125	Mexico City	(mĕk′sĭ-kō)	Mex. (In.)	19·28 N	99·09 W
124	Mexticacán	(mĕs′tê-kä-kän′)	Mex.	21·12 N	102·43 W
92	Meyers Chuck		Ak.	55·44 N	132·15 W
105	Meyersdale	(mī′ẽrz-dāl)	Pa.	39·55 N	79·00 W
218	Meyerton	(mī′ẽr-tŭn)	S. Afr. (Johannesburg & Pretoria In.)	26·35 S	28·01 E
186	Meymaneh		Afg.	35·53 N	64·38 E
170	Mezen′		Sov. Un.	65·50 N	44·05 E
170	Mezen′ (R.)		Sov. Un.	65·20 N	44·45 E
160	Mézenc, Mt.	(mŏn-mā-zĕn′)	Fr.	44·55 N	4·12 E
166	Mezha (R.)	(myā′zhȧ)	Sov. Un.	55·53 N	31·44 E
161	Mézières-sur-Seine	(mā-zyâr′sür-sân′)	Fr. (In.)	48·58 N	1·49 E
159	Mezökövesd	(mĕ′zû-kû′vĕsht)	Hung.	47·49 N	20·36 E
159	Mezötur	(mĕ′zû-tōōr)	Hung.	47·00 N	20·36 E
124	Mezquital	(mȧz-kê-täl′)	Mex.	23·30 N	104·20 W
124	Mezquital (R.)		Mex.	23·07 N	104·52 W
124	Mezquitic	(mȧz-kê-tēk′)	Mex.	22·25 N	103·43 W
124	Mexquitic (R.)		Mex.	22·25 N	103·45 W
217	Mfangano I.		Ken.	0·28 S	33·35 E
174	Mga	(m′gȧ)	Sov. Un. (Leningrad In.)	59·45 N	31·04 E
213	Mgeni (R.)		S. Afr. (Natal In.)	29·38 S	30·53 E
166	Mglin	(m′glēn′)	Sov. Un.	53·03 N	32·52 E
124	Miacatlán	(mê′ä-kä-tlän′)	Mex.	18·42 N	99·17 W
125	Miahuatlán	(mê′ä-wä-tlän′)	Mex.	16·20 N	96·38 W
162	Miajadas	(mê-ä-hä′däs)	Sp.	39·10 N	5·53 W
115	Miami		Az.	33·20 N	110·55 W
121	Miami		Fl. (In.)	25·45 N	80·11 W
117	Miami		Ok.	36·51 N	94·51 W
116	Miami		Tx.	35·41 N	100·39 W
104	Miami (R.)		Oh.	39·20 N	84·45 W
121	Miami Beach		Fl. (In.)	25·47 N	80·07 W
128	Miami Drainage Can.		Fl.	26·25 N	80·50 W
104	Miamisburg	(mī-ăm′iz-bûrg)	Oh.	39·40 N	84·20 W
107	Miamitown	(mī-ăm′ĭ-toun)	Oh. (Cincinnati In.)	39·13 N	84·43 W
186	Mīāneh		Iran	37·15 N	47·13 E
197	Miangas (I.)	(myä′n-gäs)	Phil.	5·30 N	127·00 E
190	Miaochen	(mĭou′zhen)	China	31·44 N	121·28 E
193	Miaoli	(mê-ou′lĭ)	Taiwan	24·30 N	120·48 E
190	Miao Liehtao (Is.)	(miou′ lĭĕdou)	China	38·06 N	120·35 E
174	Miass	(mī-äs′)	Sov. Un. (Urals In.)	55·00 N	60·03 E
158	Miastko	(myäst′kō)	Pol.	54·01 N	17·00 E
159	Michalovce	(mē′ĸä-lôf′tsĕ)	Czech.	48·44 N	21·56 E
92	Michel Pk.		Can.	53·35 N	126·26 W
101	Michelson, Mt.	(mĭch′ĕl-sŭn)	Ak.	69·11 N	144·12 W
149	Michendorf	(mē′ĸĕn-dōrf)	F.R.G. (Berlin In.)	52·19 N	13·02 E
129	Miches	(mē′chĕs)	Dom. Rep.	19·00 N	69·05 W
103	Michigan (State)	(mĭsh′ĭ-găn)	U. S.	45·55 N	87·00 W
103	Michigan, L.		U. S.	43·20 N	87·10 W
104	Michigan City		In.	41·40 N	86·55 W
91	Michikamau (L.)		Can.	54·11 N	63·21 W
109	Michipicoten (I.)	(mĕ-shĭ-pĭ-kō′tĕn)	Can.	47·49 N	85·50 W
109	Michipicoten (R.)		Can.	47·56 N	84·42 W
109	Michipicoten Harbour		Can.	47·58 N	84·58 W
124	Michoacán (State)		Mex.	19·15 N	101·30 W
166	Michurinsk	(mĭ-chōō-rĭnsk′)	Sov. Un.	52·53 N	40·32 E
127	Mico, Punta (Pt.)	(pōō′n-tä-mē′kô)	Nic.	11·38 N	83·24 W
110	Midas	(mī′dȧs)	Nv.	41·15 N	116·50 W
212	Middleburg	(mĭd′ĕl-bûrg)	S. Afr.	31·30 S	25·00 E
218	Middleburg		S. Afr. (Johannesburg & Pretoria In.)	25·47 S	29·30 E
218	Middlewit	(mĭd′l′wĭt)	S. Afr. (Johannesburg & Pretoria In.)	24·50 S	27·00 E
92	Middle (R.)		Can.	55·00 N	125·50 W
196	Middle Andaman I.	(ăn-dȧ-măn′)	Andaman & Nicobar Is.	12·44 N	93·21 E
119	Middle Bayou		Tx. (In.)	29·38 N	95·06 W
128	Middle Bight (B.)	(bīt)	Ba.	24·20 N	77·35 W
105	Middlebury	(mĭd′l-bĕr-ĭ)	Vt.	44·00 N	73·10 W
118	Middle Concho	(kōn′chō)	Tx.	31·21 N	100·50 W
156	Middlefart	(mēd″l-färt)	Den.	55·30 N	9·45 E
108	Middle Loup (R.)	(lōōp)	Ne.	41·49 N	100·20 W
104	Middleport	(mĭd″l-pōrt)	Oh.	39·00 N	82·05 W
106	Middle River		Md. (Baltimore In.)	39·20 N	76·27 W
120	Middlesboro	(mĭd″lz-bŭr-ō)	Ky.	36·36 N	83·42 W
154	Middlesbrough (Teesside)	(mĭd″lz-brŭ)	Eng.	54·35 N	1·18 W
106	Middlesex	(mĭd″l-sĕks)	NJ (New York In.)	40·34 N	74·30 W
98	Middleton	(mĭd″l-tŭn)	Can.	44·57 N	65·04 W
148	Middleton		Eng.	53·04 N	2·12 W
101	Middleton (I.)		Ak.	59·35 N	146·35 W
105	Middletown		Ct.	41·35 N	72·40 W
105	Middletown		De.	39·30 N	75·40 W
99	Middletown		Ma. (In.)	42·35 N	71·01 W
106	Middletown		NY (New York In.)	41·26 N	74·25 W
104	Middletown		Oh.	39·30 N	84·25 W
148	Middlewich	(mĭd″l-wĭch)	Eng.	53·11 N	2·27 W
106	Midfield		Al. (Birmingham In.)	33·28 N	86·54 W
163	Midi, Canal du	(kä-näl-dü-mê-dē′)	Fr.	43·22 N	1·35 E
213	Mid Illovo	(mĭd ĭl′ô-vō)	S. Afr. (Natal In.)	29·59 S	30·32 E
105	Midland	(mĭd′lănd)	Can.	44·45 N	79·50 W
104	Midland		Mi.	43·40 N	84·20 W
118	Midland		Tx.	32·05 N	102·05 W
113	Midvale	(mĭd′vāl)	Ut. (Salt Lake City In.)	40·37 N	111·54 W
120	Midway	(mĭd′wā)	Al.	32·03 N	85·30 W
198	Midway Is.		Pac. O.	28·00 N	179·00 W
111	Midwest	(mĭd-wĕst′)	Wy.	43·25 N	106·15 W
171	Midye	(mēd′yĕ)	Tur.	41·35 N	28·10 E
158	Miedzyrzecz	(myăn-dzû′zhĕch)	Pol.	52·26 N	15·35 E
159	Mielec	(myĕ′lĕts)	Pol.	50·17 N	21·27 E
118	Mier	(myâr)	Mex.	26·26 N	99·08 W
162	Mieres	(myā′rās)	Sp.	43·14 N	5·45 W
124	Mier y Noriega	(myâr′ê nô-rê-ā′gä)	Mex.	22·28 N	100·08 W
167	Migorod		Sov. Un.	49·56 N	33·36 E
124	Miguel Auza	(mē-gĕ′l-ä-ōō′zä)	Mex.	24·17 N	103·27 W
136	Miguel Pereira	(pĕ-rā′rä)	Braz. (In.)	22·27 S	43·28 W
163	Mijares (R.)	(mē-hä′rȧs)	Sp.	40·05 N	0·42 W
195	Mikage	(mē′kȧ-gȧ)	Jap. (Ōsaka In.)	34·42 N	135·15 E
195	Mikawa-Wan (B.)	(mē′kä-wä wän)	Jap.	34·43 N	137·09 E
166	Mikhaylov	(mē-käy′lôf)	Sov. Un.	54·14 N	39·03 E
167	Mikhaylovka		Sov. Un.	47·16 N	35·12 E
171	Mikhaylovka		Sov. Un.	50·05 N	43·10 E
174	Mikhaylovka	(mê-kä′ê-lôf-kȧ)	Sov. Un. (Urals In.)	55·35 N	57·57 E
174	Mikhaylovka		Sov. Un. (Leningrad In.)	59·20 N	30·21 E
174	Mikhnëvo	(mĭk-nyô′vô)	Sov. Un. (Moscow In.)	55·08 N	37·57 E
195	Miki	(mē′kê)	Jap. (Ōsaka In.)	34·47 N	134·59 E
217	Mikindani	(mê-kên-dä′nê)	Tan.	10·17 S	40·07 E
157	Mikkeli	(mĕk′ĕ-lĭ)	Fin.	61·42 N	27·14 E
165	Míkonos (I.)		Grc.	37·26 N	25·30 E
158	Mikulov	(mĭ′kōō-lôf)	Czech.	48·47 N	16·39 E
217	Mikumi		Tan.	7·24 S	36·59 E
195	Mikuni	(mē′kōō-nê)	Jap.	36·09 N	136·14 E
195	Mikuni-Sammyaku (Mts.)	(säm′myä-kōō)	Jap.	36·51 N	138·38 E
195	Mikura (I.)	(mē′kōō-rȧ)	Jap.	33·53 N	139·26 E
109	Milaca	(mê-lăk′ȧ)	Mn.	45·45 N	93·41 W
104	Milan	(mĭ′lăn)	Mi.	42·05 N	83·40 W
117	Milan		Mo.	40·13 N	93·07 W
120	Milan		Tn.	35·54 N	88·47 W
	Milan, see Milano				
164	Milano (Milan)	(mê-lä′nō)	It.	45·29 N	9·12 E
171	Milâs	(mē′läs)	Tur.	37·10 N	27·25 E
164	Milazzo	(mê-lät′sô)	It.	38·13 N	15·17 E
108	Milbank	(mĭl′băŋk)	SD	45·13 N	96·38 W
203	Mildura	(mĭl-dū′rȧ)	Austl.	34·10 S	142·18 E
111	Miles City	(mīlz)	Mt.	46·24 N	105·50 W
105	Milford	(mĭl′fẽrd)	Ct.	41·15 N	73·05 W
105	Milford		De.	38·55 N	75·25 W
99	Milford		Ma. (In.)	42·09 N	71·31 W
107	Milford		Mi. (Detroit In.)	42·35 N	83·36 W
105	Milford		NH	42·50 N	71·40 W
107	Milford		Oh. (Cincinnati In.)	39·11 N	84·18 W
115	Milford		Ut.	38·20 N	113·05 W
154	Milford Haven	(hāv′n)	Wales	51·40 N	5·10 W
204	Miling	(mĭl″ng)	Austl.	30·30 S	116·25 E
112	Milipitas	(mĭl-ĭ-pĭ′tăs)	Ca. (San Francisco In.)	37·26 N	121·54 W
93	Milk River	(mĭlk)	Can.	49·09 N	112·05 W
111	Milk R.		Can.-U.S.	48·25 N	108·45 W
114	Mill Cr.		Ca.	40·07 N	121·55 W
89	Mill Cr.	(mĭl)	Can. (Edmonton In.)	53·13 N	113·25 W
160	Millau	(mē-yō′)	Fr.	44·06 N	3·04 E
112	Millbrae	(mĭl′brā)	Ca. (San Francisco In.)	37·36 N	122·23 W
99	Millbury	(mĭl′bẽr-ĭ)	Ma. (In.)	42·12 N	71·46 W
120	Milledgeville	(mĭl′ĕj-vĭl)	Ga.	33·05 N	83·15 W
89	Mille Îles, R. des	(rê-vyâr′ dā mēl′īl′)	Can. (Montreal In.)	45·41 N	73·40 W
109	Mille Lac Ind. Res.	(mĭl lăk′)	Mn.	46·14 N	94·13 W
109	Mille Lacs (L.)		Mn.	46·25 N	93·22 W
109	Mille Lacs, Lac des (L.)	(läk dĕ mēl läks)	Can.	48·52 N	90·53 W
121	Millen	(mĭl′ĕn)	Ga.	32·47 N	81·55 W
108	Miller	(mĭl′ẽr)	SD	44·31 N	99·00 W
167	Millerovo	(mĭl′ĕ-rô-vô)	Sov. Un.	48·58 N	40·27 E
97	Millersburg	(mĭl′ẽrz-bûrg)	Ky.	38·15 N	84·10 W
97	Millersburg		Oh.	40·35 N	81·55 W
105	Millersburg		Pa.	40·35 N	76·55 W
120	Millers Ferry Lake (Res.)		Al.	32·10 N	87·15 W
98	Millerton	(mĭl′ẽr-tŭn)	Can.	46·56 N	65·40 W
99	Millertown	(mĭl′ẽr-toun)	Can.	48·49 N	56·32 W
203	Millicent	(mĭl-ĭ-sĕnt)	Austl.	37·30 S	140·20 E
98	Millinocket	(mĭl-ĭ-nŏk′ĕt)	Me.	45·40 N	68·44 W
99	Millis	(mĭl-ĭs)	Ma. (In.)	42·10 N	71·22 W
113	Millstadt	(mĭl′stăt)	Il. (St. Louis In.)	38·27 N	90·06 W
106	Millstone (R.)	(mĭl′stōn)	NJ (New York In.)	40·27 N	74·38 W
204	Millstream	(mĭl′strēm)	Austl.	21·45 S	117·10 E
98	Milltown	(mĭl′toun)	Can.	45·13 N	67·19 W
107	Milvale	(mĭl′vāl)	Pa. (Pittsburgh In.)	40·29 N	79·58 W
112	Mill Valley	(mĭl)	Ca. (San Francisco In.)	37·54 N	122·32 W
105	Milville	(mĭl′vĭl)	NJ	39·25 N	75·00 W
117	Millwood Res.		Ar.	33·00 N	94·00 W
161	Milly-la-Forêt	(mē-yē′-la-fô-rĕ′)	Fr. (Paris In.)	48·24 N	2·28 E
212	Milnerton	(mĭl′nẽr-tŭn)	S. Afr. (In.)	33·52 S	18·30 E
108	Milnor	(mĭl′nẽr)	ND	46·17 N	97·29 W
98	Milo		Me.	44·16 N	69·01 W
	Milo (I.), see Mílos				
165	Mílos (Milo) (I.)	(mē′lŏs)	Grc.	36·45 N	24·35 E
125	Mílpa Alta	(mē′l-pä-ȧ′l-tä)	Mex. (In.)	19·11 N	99·01 W
89	Milton		Can. (Toronto In.)	43·31 N	79·53 W
120	Milton	(mĭl′tŭn)	Fl.	30·37 N	87·02 W
99	Milton		Ma. (In.)	42·16 N	71·03 W
105	Milton		Pa.	41·00 N	76·50 W
113	Milton		Ut. (Salt Lake City In.)	41·04 N	111·44 W
112	Milton		Wa. (Seattle In.)	47·15 N	122·20 W
109	Milton		Wi.	42·45 N	89·00 W
110	Milton-Freewater		Or.	45·57 N	118·25 W
107	Milwaukee		Wi. (Milwaukee In.)	43·03 N	87·55 W
107	Milwaukee R.		Wi. (Milwaukee In.)	43·10 N	87·56 W
112	Milwaukee	(mĭl-wô′kê)	Or. (Portland In.)	45·27 N	122·38 W
125	Mimiapan	(mē-myä-pȧn′)	Mex. (In.)	19·26 N	99·28 W
137	Mimoso do Sul	(mē-mô′sō-dô-sōō′l)	Braz. (Rio de Janeiro In.)	21·03 S	41·21 W
163	Mina (R.)	(mē′nȧ)	Alg.	35·24 N	0·51 E
95	Minago (R.)	(mĭ-nä′gō)	Can.	54·25 N	98·45 W
195	Minakuchi	(mē′nȧ-kōō′chê)	Jap.	34·59 N	136·06 E
128	Minas	(mē′näs)	Cuba	21·03 N	77·35 W
183	Minas		Indon. (Singapore In.)	0·52 N	101·29 E
136	Minas	(mē′näs)	Ur.	34·18 S	55·12 W
126	Minas, Sierra de las (Mts.)	(syĕr′rȧ dā läs mē′näs)	Guat.	15·08 N	90·25 W
98	Minas Basin	(mī′nȧs)	Can.	45·20 N	64·00 W
98	Minas Chan.		Can.	45·15 N	64·45 W
126	Minas de Oro	(mē′-näs-dĕ-ô-rō)	Hond.	14·52 N	87·19 W
162	Minas de Ríontinto	(mē′näs dā rē-ô-tēn′tō)	Sp.	37·43 N	6·35 W
135	Minas Gerais (State)	(mē′näzh-zhĕ-rȧ′ēs)	Braz.	17·45 S	43·50 W
135	Minas Nova	(mē′näzh nō′väzh)	Braz.	17·20 S	42·19 W
108	Minatare (L.)	(mĭn′ȧ-târ)	Ne.	41·56 N	103·07 W
125	Minatitlan	(mê-nä-tê-tlän′)	Mex.	17·59 N	94·33 W
124	Minatitlan		Mex.	19·21 N	104·02 W
195	Minato	(mē′nȧ-tô)	Jap. (Tōkyō In.)	35·13 N	139·52 E
154	Minch, The (Chan.)		Scot.	58·04 N	6·04 W
154	Minch, The Little (Chan.)	(mĭnch)	Scot.	57·35 N	6·45 W
193	Min Chiang (R.)		China	26·30 N	118·30 E
193	Min Chiang (R.)		China	29·30 N	104·00 E
197	Mindanao (I.)	(mĭn-dä-nou′)	Phil.	7·30 N	125·10 E
197	Mindanao Sea		Phil.	8·55 N	124·00 E
210	Mindelo		C. V. Is. (In.)	16·53 N	25·00 W
158	Minden	(mĭn′dĕn)	F.R.G.	52·17 N	8·58 E
119	Minden		La.	32·36 N	93·19 W
116	Minden		Ne.	40·30 N	98·54 W
197	Mindoro (I.)	(mĭn-dō′rō)	Phil. (In.)	13·04 N	121·06 E
197	Mindoro Str.		Phil. (In.)	12·28 N	120·33 E
174	Mindyak	(mēn′dyăk)	Sov. Un. (Urals In.)	54·01 N	58·48 E
106	Mineola	(mĭn-ē-ō′lȧ)	NY (New York In.)	40·43 N	73·38 W
119	Mineola		Tx.	32·39 N	95·31 W
124	Mineral del Chico	(mê-nȧ-räl′dĕl chē′kô)	Mex.	20·13 N	98·46 W

ng-sing; ŋ-baŋk; ɴ-nasalized n; nŏd; cŏmmit; ōld; ôbey; ôrder; fōōd; fŏŏt; ou-out; s-soft; sh-dish; th-thin; pūre; ûnite; ûrn; stŭd; circŭs; ü-as "y" in study; ′-indeterminate vowel.

314 Mineral del Monte — Momboyo PRONOUNCING INDEX

Page	Name Pronunciation Region	Lat. °′	Long. °′
124	Mineral del Monte (mê-nä-räl děl mōn′tâ). Mex.	20·18 N	98·39 W
171	Mineral′nyye Vody. . . . . . Sov. Un.	44·10 N	43·15 E
109	Mineral Point (mĭn′ēr-ăl) . . . . . Wi.	42·50 N	90·10 W
118	Mineral Wells (mĭn′ēr-ăl wělz) Tx.	32·48 N	98·06 W
104	Minerva (mĭ-nur′vȧ) . . . . Oh.	40·45 N	81·10 W
164	Minervino (mē-nĕr-vē′nô) . . . . . . It.	41·07 N	16·05 E
195	Mineyama (mē-nĕ-yä′mä) . . . . Jap.	35·38 N	135·05 E
98	Mingan . . . . Can.	50·18 N	64·02 W
171	Mingechaur (R.) . . . . Sov. Un.	41·00 N	47·20 E
204	Mingenew (mĭn′gĕ-nû) . . . . . Austl.	29·15 S	115·45 E
190	Mingkuang (mĭng′gōōäng) . China	32·41 N	118·00 E
104	Mingo Junction (mĭŋ′gō) . . . . . Oh.	40·15 N	80·40 W
162	Minho (Reg.) (mēn yōō) . . . . Port.	41·32 N	8·13 W
128	Minho (R.) . . . . Jam.	17·55 N	77·20 W
162	Minho, Rio (R.) (rē′ō-mē′n-yô) Port.	41·28 N	9·05 W
89	Ministik L. (mĭ-nĭs′tĭk) Can. (Edmonton In.)	53·23 N	113·05 W
215	Minna (mĭn′ȧ) . . . . Nig.	9·37 N	6·33 E
117	Minneapoli (mĭn-ê-ăp′ō-lĭ) . . . . Ks.	39·07 N	97·41 W
113	Minneapolis (mĭn-ê-ăp′ô-lĭs) Mn. (Minneapolis, St. Paul In.)	44·58 N	93·15 W
95	Minnedosa (mĭn-ê-dō′sȧ) . . . . . Can.	50·14 N	99·51 W
108	Minneota (mĭn-ê-ō′tȧ) . . . . Mn.	44·34 N	95·59 W
103	Minnesota (State) (mĭn-ê-sō′tȧ) U. S.	46·10 N	90·20 W
108	Minnesota (R.) . . . . Mn.	45·04 N	96·03 W
109	Minnetonka (L.) (mĭn-ê-tôŋ′kȧ) Mn.	44·52 N	93·34 W
115	Minnie Maud Cr. (mĭn′ĭmôd′) . Ut.	39·50 N	110·30 W
95	Minnitaki L. (mĭ′nĭ-tä′kê) . . . Can.	49·58 N	92·00 W
195	Minō (mê′nō) . . . . Jap. (Ōsaka In.)	34·49 N	135·28 E
195	Mino (R.) . . . . Jap. (Ōsaka In.)	34·56 N	135·06 E
162	Miño (R.) (mē′nyō) . . . . Sp.	42·28 N	7·48 W
104	Minonk (mī′nŏnk) . . . . Il.	40·55 N	89·00 W
107	Minooka (mĭ-nōō′kȧ) Il. (Chicago In.)	41·27 N	88·15 W
	Minorca (I.), see Menorca, Isla de		
108	Minot (mī′nŏt) . . . . ND	48·13 N	101·16 W
166	Minsk (mênsk) . . . . Sov. Un.	53·54 N	27·35 E
166	Minsk (Oblast) . . . . Sov. Un.	53·50 N	27·43 E
159	Mińsk Mazowiecki (mēn′sk mä-zô-vyĕt′skĭ) . Pol.	52·10 N	21·35 E
148	Minsterley (mĭnstēr-lē) . . . . . . Eng.	52·38 N	2·55 W
98	Minto . . . . Can.	46·05 N	66·05 W
91	Minto (L.) . . . . Can.	57·18 N	75·50 W
164	Minturno (mēn-tōōr′nō) . . . . . . It.	41·17 N	13·44 E
218	Minūf (mê-nōōf′) . Egypt (Nile In.)	30·26 N	30·55 E
172	Minusinsk (mē-nōō-sênsk′) Sov. Un.	53·47 N	91·45 E
188	Minya Konka (Mt.) (mēn′yȧ kôŋ′kȧ) . China	29·16 N	101·46 E
174	Min′yar (mēn′yȧr) Sov. Un. (Urals In.)	55·06 N	57·33 E
99	Miquelon (I.) (mĭk-ē-lôn′) St. Pierre & Miquelon	47·00 N	56·40 W
89	Miquelon L. (mĭ′kê-lôn) Can. (Edmonton In.)	53·16 N	112·55 W
124	Miquihuana (mê-kê-wä′nä) . . Mex.	23·36 N	99·45 W
159	Mir (mēr) . . . . Sov. Un.	53·27 N	26·25 E
162	Mira (R.) (mē′rä) . . . . Port.	37·29 N	8·15 W
137	Miracema (mē-rä-sĕ′mä) Braz. (Rio de Janeiro In.)	21·24 S	42·10 W
135	Mirador (mê-rä-dōr′) . . . . Braz.	6·19 S	44·12 W
134	Miraflores (mē-rä-flō′rās) . . . . . Col.	5·10 N	73·13 W
134	Miraflores . . . . Peru	16·19 S	71·20 W
122	Miraflores Locks . . . . C. Z. (In.)	9·00 N	79·35 W
129	Miragoâne (mê-rȧ-gwän′) . . . . Hai.	18·25 N	73·05 W
137	Miraí (mē-rȧ-ē′) Braz. (Rio de Janeiro In.)	21·13 S	42·36 W
113	Mira Loma (mĭ′rȧ lō′mȧ) Ca. (Los Angeles In.)	34·01 N	117·32 W
114	Miramar (mĭr′ă-mär) . . . . Ca. (In.)	32·53 N	117·08 W
160	Miramas . . . . Fr. (In.)	43·35 N	5·00 E
98	Miramichi B. (mĭr′ȧ-mē′shē) . . Can.	47·08 N	65·08 W
134	Miranda (mē-rä′n-dä) . . . Col. (In.)	3·14 N	76·11 W
135	Miranda . . . . Ven. (In.)	10·09 N	68·24 W
135	Miranda (State) . . . . Ven. (In.)	10·17 N	66·41 W
162	Miranda de Ebro (mē-rä′n-dä-dĕ-ĕ′l-brô) . Sp.	42·42 N	2·59 W
162	Miranda de Ebro (mê-rän′dä dōō-dwĕ′rô) . Port.	41·30 N	6·17 W
162	Mirandela (mê-rän-dā′lȧ) . . . . Port.	41·28 N	7·10 W
118	Mirando City (mĭr-ăn′dō) . . . . . Tx.	27·25 N	99·03 W
129	Mira Por Vos Islets (Is.) (mē′rä pōr vōs) . Ba.	22·05 N	74·30 W
129	Mira Por Vos Pass (Str.) . . . . . . Ba.	22·10 N	74·35 W
186	Mirbāt . . . . Om.	16·58 N	54·42 E
129	Mirebalais (mēr-bȧ-lĕ′) . . . . Hai.	18·50 N	72·05 W
161	Mirecourt (mēr-kōōr′) . . . . Fr.	48·20 N	6·08 E
160	Mirepoix (mēr-pwä′) . . . . Fr.	43·06 N	1·52 E
148	Mirfield (mûr′fēld) . . . . Eng.	53·41 N	1·42 W
196	Miri (mē′rē) . . . . Mala.	4·13 N	113·56 E
136	Mirim, L. (mê-rēɴ′) . . . . . Braz.-Ur.	33·00 S	53·15 W
167	Miropol′ye (mē-rô-pôl′yĕ) Sov. Un.	51·02 N	35·13 E
184	Mīrpur Khās (mēr′pōōr ᴋäs) . . Pak.	25·36 N	69·10 E
184	Mīrzāpur (mēr′zä-pōōr) . . . . . India	25·12 N	82·38 E
125	Misantla (mê-sän′tlä) . . . . Mex.	19·55 N	96·49 W
98	Miscou (I.) (mĭs′kō) . . . . Can.	47·58 N	64·35 W
98	Miscou Pt. . . . . Can.	48·04 N	64·32 W
163	Miseno, C. (mê-zĕ′nō) It. (Naples In.)	40·33 N	14·12 E
127	Misery, Mt. (mĭz′rē-ĭ) St. Kitts-Nevis-Anguilla (In.)	17·28 N	62·47 W
194	Mishan (mĭ′shäɴ) . . . . China	45·32 N	132·19 E
104	Mishawaka (mĭsh-ȧ-wôk′ȧ) . . . . In.	41·45 N	86·15 W
195	Mishima (mē′shē-mä) . . . . Jap.	35·09 N	138·56 E
136	Misiones (Prov.) (mê-syō′nās) Arg.	27·00 S	54·30 W
127	Miskito, Cayos (Is.) . . . . Nic.	14·34 N	82·30 W
159	Miskolc (mĭsh′kōlts) . . . . Hung.	48·07 N	20·50 E
197	Misol (I.) (mê-sōl′) . . . . Indon.	2·00 S	130·05 E
109	Misquah Hills (mĭs-kwä′ hĭlz) . Mn.	47·50 N	90·30 W
218	Miṣr al Jadīdah (Ruins) Egypt (Nile In.)	30·06 N	31·35 E
211	Misrātah . . . . Libya	32·23 N	14·58 E
91	Missinaibi (R.) (mĭs′ĭn-ä′ê-bê) Can.	50·27 N	83·01 W
96	Missinaibi L. . . . . Can.	48·23 N	83·40 W
113	Mission (mĭsh′ŭn) Ks. (Kansas City In.)	39·02 N	94·39 W
118	Mission . . . . Tx.	26·14 N	98·19 W
100	Mission City (sĭ′tĭ) Can. (Vancouver In.)	49·08 N	122·18 W
96	Mississagi (R.) . . . . Can.	46·35 N	83·30 W
89	Mississauga . . . . Can. (Toronto In.)	43·34 N	79·37 W
104	Mississinewa (R.) (mĭs-ĭ-sĭn′ê-wä) In.	40·30 N	85·45 W
103	Mississippi (State) (mĭs-ĭ-sĭp′ê) U. S.	32·30 N	89·45 W
105	Mississippi (L.) . . . . Can.	45·05 N	76·15 W
103	Mississippi (R.) . . . . U. S.	31·50 N	91·30 W
120	Mississippi Sd. . . . . Ms.	34·16 N	89·10 W
111	Missoula (mĭ-zōō′lȧ) . . . . Mt.	46·52 N	114·00 W
103	Missouri (State) (mĭ-sōō′rê) . . U. S.	38·00 N	93·40 W
103	Missouri (R.) . . . . U. S.	40·40 N	96·00 W
119	Missouri City . . . . Tx. (In.)	29·37 N	95·32 W
102	Missouri Coteau, (Plat.) . . . . . U. S.	47·30 N	101·00 W
108	Missouri Valley . . . . Ia.	41·35 N	95·53 W
112	Mist (mĭst) . . . . . Or. (Portland In.)	46·00 N	123·15 W
98	Mistassibi (R.) (mĭs-tȧ-sĭ′bê) . Can.	49·44 N	69·58 W
98	Mistassini (mĭs-tȧ-sĭ′nē) . . . . . Can.	48·56 N	71·55 W
91	Mistassini (L.) (mĭs-tȧ-sĭ′nê) . Can.	50·48 N	73·30 W
98	Mistassini (R.) . . . . Can.	50·02 N	72·38 W
158	Mistelbach (mĭs′tĕl-bäk) . . . . . Aus.	48·34 N	16·33 E
126	Misteriosa, L. (mēs-tĕ-ryô′sä) Mex. (In.)	18·05 N	90·15 W
164	Mistretta (mê-strĕt′tä) . . . . It.	37·54 N	14·22 E
124	Mita, Punta de (Pt.) (pōō′n-tä-dĕ-mē′tä) . Mex.	20·44 N	105·34 W
195	Mitaka (mē′tä-kä) Jap. (Tōkyō In.)	35·42 N	139·34 E
113	Mitchell (mĭch′ĕl) . Il (St. Louis In.)	38·46 N	90·05 W
104	Mitchell . . . . In.	38·45 N	86·25 W
108	Mitchell . . . . Ne.	41·56 N	103·49 W
108	Mitchell . . . . SD	43·42 N	98·01 W
205	Mitchell (R.) . . . . Austl.	15·30 S	142·15 E
121	Mitchell, Mt. . . . . NC	35·47 N	82·15 W
218	Mīt Ghamr . . . . . . Egypt (Nile In.)	30·43 N	31·20 E
165	Mitilíni . . . . Grc.	39·09 N	26·35 E
183	Mitla P. . . . . Egypt (Palestine In.)	30·03 N	32·40 E
195	Mito (mē′tō) . . . . Jap.	36·20 N	140·23 E
195	Mitsu (mēt′sōō) . . . . Jap.	34·21 N	132·49 E
158	Mittelland (can.) (mĭt′ĕl-länd) G.D.R.	52·18 N	10·42 E
149	Mittenwalde (mē′tĕn-väl-dĕ) G.D.R. (Berlin In.)	52·16 N	13·33 E
158	Mittweida (mĭt-vī′dä) . . . . . G.D.R.	50·59 N	12·58 E
217	Mitumba, Monts (Mts.) . . . . . . Zaire	10·50 S	27·00 E
174	Mityayevo (mĭt-yä′yĕ-vô) Sov. Un. (Urals In.)	60·17 N	61·02 E
195	Miura . . . . Jap. (Tōkyō In.)	35·08 N	139·37 E
167	Mius (R.) (mê-ōōs′) . . . . . Sov. Un.	47·30 N	38·48 E
195	Miwa (mē′wä) . . . Jap. (Osaka In.)	34·32 N	135·51 E
126	Mixico (mēs′kô) . . . . Guat.	14·37 N	90·37 W
124	Mixquiahuala (mēs-kê-wä′lä) . Mex.	20·12 N	99·13 W
124	Mixteco (R.) (mês-tä′kō) . . . . Mex.	17·45 N	98·10 W
195	Miyake (mē′yä-kȧ) Jap. (Ōsaka In.)	34·35 N	135·34 E
195	Miyake (I.) (mē′yä-kȧ) . . . . . . Jap.	34·06 N	139·21 E
195	Miyakonojō (mē′yȧ-kô′nô-jô) . Jap.	31·42 N	131·03 E
195	Miyazaki (mē′yä-zä′kê) . . . . . . Jap.	31·55 N	131·27 E
195	Miyoshi (mē-yō′shê′) . . . . Jap.	34·48 N	132·49 E
152	Mizdah (mēz′dä) . . . . Libya	31·29 N	13·09 E
165	Mizil (mē′zêl) . . . . Rom.	45·01 N	26·30 E
	Mizonokuchi, see Takatsu		
184	Mizoram (Union Ter.) . . . . . . India	23·25 N	92·45 E
156	Mjölby (myûl′bü) . . . . Swe.	58·20 N	15·09 E
156	Mjörn (L.) . . . . Swe.	57·55 N	12·22 E
156	Mjösa (myûsä) . . . . Nor.	60·41 N	11·25 E
156	Mjösvatn (myûs-vät′n) . . . . . . Nor.	59·55 N	7·50 E
212	Mkalama . . . . Tan.	4·07 S	34·38 E
215	Mkomazi (R.) . . S. Afr. (Natal In.)	30·10 S	3·30 E
217	Mkushi . . . . Zambia	13·40 S	29·20 E
217	Mkwaja . . . . Tan.	5·47 S	38·51 E
158	Mladá Boleslav (mlä′dä bô′lĕ-släf) Czech.	50·26 N	14·52 E
217	Mlala Hills . . . . Tan.	6·47 S	31·45 E
217	Mlanje Mts. . . . . Malawi	15·55 S	35·30 E
159	Mława (mwä′vȧ) . . . . Pol.	53·07 N	20·25 E
213	Mlazi (R.) . . . . S. Afr. (Natal In.)	29·52 S	30·42 E
165	Mljet (I.) (mlyĕt) . . . . Yugo.	42·40 N	17·45 E
214	Mo (R.) . . . . Togo	9·05 N	0·55 E
197	Moa (I.) . . . . Indon.	8·30 S	128·30 E
214	Moa (R.) . . . . S. L.	7·40 N	11·15 W
115	Moab (mō′ăb) . . . . Ut.	38·35 N	109·35 W
212	Moanda . . . . Gabon	1·37 S	13·09 E
114	Moapa River Ind. Res. (mō-ăp′ȧ) Nv.	36·44 N	115·01 W
95	Moar L. (môr) . . . . Can.	52·00 N	95·09 W
216	Mobaye (mô-bä′y′) . Cen. Afr. Emp.	4·19 N	21·11 E
117	Moberly (mō′bēr-lĭ) . . . . Mo.	39·24 N	92·25 W
93	Moberly (R.) . . . . Can.	55·40 N	121·15 W
120	Mobile (mô-bēl′) . . . . Al.	30·42 N	88·03 W
120	Mobile (R.) . . . . Al.	31·15 N	88·00 W
120	Mobile B. . . . . Al.	30·26 N	87·56 W
108	Mobridge (mō′brĭj) . . . . SD	45·32 N	100·26 W
129	Moca (mō′kä) . . . . Dom. Rep.	19·25 N	70·35 W
217	Moçambique (mō-säɴ-bē′kĕ) . Moz.	15·03 S	40·42 E
216	Moçâmedes (mô-zȧ-mĕ-dĕs) . . Ang.	15·10 S	12·09 E
212	Moçâmedes (Reg.) . . . . Ang.	16·00 S	12·15 E
186	Mocha (mō′kä) . . . . Yemen	13·11 N	43·20 E
124	Mochitlán (mō-chē-tlän′) . . . . Mex.	17·10 N	99·19 W
212	Mochudi (mō-chōō′dê) . . . . . . Bots.	24·13 S	26·07 E
217	Mocímboa da Praia (mô-sē′êm-bô-ȧ dȧ prä′ēȧ) . Moz.	11·20 S	40·21 E
110	Moclips . . . . Wa.	47·14 N	124·13 W
216	Môco, Serra (Mts.) . . . . Arg.	12·25 S	15·10 E
137	Mococa (mô-kô′kȧ) Braz. (Rio de Janeiro In.)	21·29 S	46·58 W
124	Moctezuma (môk′tâ-zōō′mä) . Mex.	22·44 N	101·06 W
217	Mocuba . . . . Moz.	16·50 S	36·59 E
213	Modderfontein . . . . S. Afr. (Johannesburg & Pretoria In.)	26·06 S	28·10 E
164	Modena (mô′dĕ-nä) . . . . It.	44·38 N	10·54 E
114	Modesto (mô-dĕs′tō) . . . . Ca.	37·39 N	121·00 W
151	Modica (mô-dē-kä) . . . . It.	36·50 N	14·43 E
149	Mödling (mûd′lĭng) Aus. (Vienna In.)	48·06 N	16·17 E
135	Moengo . . . . Sur.	5·43 N	54·19 W
115	Moenkopi . . . . Az.	36·07 N	111·13 W
161	Moers (mûrs) . . F.R.G. (Ruhr In.)	51·27 N	6·38 E
116	Moffat Tun. (môf′ăt) . . . . Co.	39·52 N	106·20 W
218	Mogadisho (mô-gȧ-dē′shō) Som. (Horn of Afr. In.)	2·08 N	45·22 E
107	Mogadore (mŏg-ȧ-dōr′) Oh. (Cleveland In.)	41·04 N	81·23 W
188	Mogaung (mô-gä′ōōng) . . . . . . Bur.	25·30 N	96·52 E
137	Mogi das Cruzes (mô-gê-däs-krōō′sĕs) Braz. (Rio de Janeiro In.)	23·33 S	46·10 W
137	Mogi-Guaçu (R.) (mô-gê-gwȧ′sōō) Braz. (Rio de Janeiro In.)	22·06 S	47·12 W
166	Mogilëv (mô-gê-lyôf′) . . . . Sov. Un.	53·53 N	30·22 E
166	Mogilëv (Oblast) (mô-gê-lyôf′) Sov. Un.	53·28 N	30·15 E
167	Mogilëv-Podol′skiy (mô-gê-lyôf) (pô-dôl′skĭ) Sov. Un.	48·27 N	27·51 E
159	Mogilno (mô-gēl′nô) . . . . Pol.	52·38 N	17·58 E
137	Mogi-Mirim (mô-gê-mē-rē′ɴ) Braz. (Rio de Janeiro In.)	22·26 S	46·57 W
217	Mogincual . . . . Moz.	15·35 S	40·25 E
188	Mogok (mô-gōk′) . . . . Bur.	23·14 N	96·38 E
115	Mogollon (mō-gô-yōn′) . . . . NM	33·25 N	108·45 W
115	Mogollon, Plat. (mō-gô-yōn′) . . Az.	34·26 N	111·17 W
218	Mogol R. (mô-gŏl) . . . . S. Afr. (Johannesburg & Pretoria In.)	24·12 S	27·55 E
162	Moguer (mô-gĕr′) . . . . Sp.	37·15 N	6·50 W
159	Mohács (mô′häch) . . . . Hung.	45·59 N	18·38 E
213	Mohale′s Hoek . . Leso. (Natal In.)	30·09 S	27·28 E
108	Mohall (mō′hôl) . . . . ND	48·46 N	101·29 W
163	Mohammadia . . . . Alg.	35·35 N	0·05 E
114	Mohave (L.) (mô-hä′vä) . . . . . . Nv.	35·23 N	114·40 W
105	Mohawk (R.) (mō′hôk) . . . . NY	43·15 N	75·20 W
213	Moheli (I.) (mô-ā-lē′) (mô-hā′lê) Comoros	12·23 S	43·38 E
184	Mohenjo-Dero (Ruins) . . . . . . Pak.	27·20 N	68·10 E
189	Moho (mō′hō′) . . . . China	53·33 N	122·30 E
150	Mo-i-Rana . . . . Nor.	65·54 N	13·15 E
157	Mõisaküla (mē̇′sȧ-kü′lä) . Sov. Un.	58·07 N	25·12 E
99	Moisie (R.) (mwȧ-zē′) . . . . Can.	50·35 N	66·25 W
160	Moissac (mwä-sȧk′) . . . . Fr.	44·07 N	1·05 E
163	Moita (mô-ē′tȧ) . Port. (Lisbon In.)	38·39 N	9·00 W
114	Mojave . . . . Ca.	35·06 N	118·09 W
114	Mojave (R.) (mô-hä′vä) . . . . . . Ca.	34·46 N	117·24 W
114	Mojave Desert . . . . Ca.	35·05 N	117·30 W
114	Mokelumne (R.) (mō-kê-lŭm′nê) Ca.	38·30 N	120·17 W
213	Mokhotlong . . . . . Leso. (Natal In.)	29·18 S	29·06 E
194	Mokp′o (mōk′pō′) . . . . Kor.	34·50 N	126·30 E
170	Moksha (R.) (mōk-shä′) . Sov. Un.	54·50 N	43·20 E
149	Mol . . . . Bel. (Brussels In.)	51·21 N	5·09 E
164	Molat (I.) (mō′lät) . . . . Yugo.	44·15 N	14·40 E
159	Moldavia (Reg.) . . . . Rom.	47·20 N	27·12 E
168	Moldavian S. S. R. . . . . Sov. Un.	48·00 N	28·00 E
156	Molde (môl′dĕ) . . . . Nor.	62·44 N	7·15 E
156	Molde Fd. (môl′dĕ fyôrd) . . . . Nor.	62·40 N	7·05 E
159	Moldova R. . . . . Rom.	47·17 N	26·27 E
212	Molepolole (mō-lȧ-pô-lō′lȧ) . . Bots.	24·15 S	25·33 E
164	Molfetta (môl-fĕt′tä) . . . . It.	41·11 N	16·38 E
137	Molina (mŏ-lē′nä) Chile (Santiago In.)	35·07 S	71·17 W
162	Molina de Aragón (mô-lē′nä dĕ ä-rä-gô′n) . Sp.	41·40 N	1·54 W
162	Molína de Segura (mô-lē′nä dĕ sĕ-gōō′rä) . Sp.	38·03 N	1·07 W
109	Moline (mô-lēn′) . . . . Il.	41·31 N	90·34 W
217	Moliro . . . . Zaire	8·13 S	30·34 E
164	Moliterno (mōl-ê-tĕr′nō) . . . . It.	40·13 N	15·54 E
134	Mollendo (mô-lyĕn′dō) . . . . Peru	17·02 S	71·59 W
101	Moller, Port (pōrt mōl′ēr) . . . . . Ak.	56·18 N	161·30 W
156	Mölndal (mûln′däl) . . . . Swe.	57·39 N	12·01 E
167	Molochnaya (R.) (mô-lôch′nȧ-yȧ) (rĕ-kä′) Sov. Un.	47·05 N	35·22 E
167	Molochnoye, Ozero (L.) (ô′zĕ-rô mô-lôch′nô-yĕ) . Sov. Un.	46·35 N	35·32 E
166	Molodechno (mô-lô-dĕch′nô) Sov. Un.	54·18 N	26·57 E
166	Molodechno (Oblast) . . . . Sov. Un.	54·27 N	27·38 E
174	Molody Tud (mō-lō-dô′ê tōō′d) Sov. Un. (Moscow In.)	55·17 N	37·31 E
166	Mologa (R.) (mô-lô′gȧ) . . Sov. Un.	58·05 N	35·43 E
100	Molokai (I.) (mō-lō kä′ê) . . . . . . Hi.	21·15 N	157·05 E
174	Molokcha R. (mô′lôk-chä) Sov. Un. (Moscow In.)	56·15 N	38·29 E
212	Molopo (R.) (mō-lō-pô) . . . . S. Afr.	27·45 S	20·45 E
95	Molson L. (mōl′sŭn) . . . . Can.	54·12 N	96·45 W
213	Molteno (môl-tä′nô) S. Afr. (Natal In.)	31·24 S	26·23 E
217	Moma . . . . Moz.	16·44 S	39·14 E
217	Mombasa (mōm-bä′sä) . . . . . . Ken.	4·03 S	39·40 E
194	Mombetsu (môm′bĕt-sōō′) . . . . Jap.	44·21 N	142·48 E
216	Momboyo (R.) . . . . Zaire	0·20 S	19·20 E

ăt; finăl; rāte; senâte; ärm; ȧsk; sofȧ; fâre; ch-choose; dh-as th in other; bē; ēvent; bĕt; recĕnt; cratēr; g-go; gh-guttural g; bĭt; ĭ-short neutral; rīde; ᴋ-guttural k as ch in German ich;

PRONOUNCING INDEX

Momence — Morehead 315

Page	Name Pronunciation Region	Lat. °′	Long. °′
107	Momence (mô-mĕns') Il. (Chicago In.)	41·09 N	87·40 W
126	Momostenango (mô-môs-tā-näŋ'gô). Guat.	15·02 N	91·25 W
126	Momotombo Nic.	12·25 N	86·43 W
197	Mompog Pass (mŏm-pŏg') Phil. (In.)	13·35 N	122·09 E
134	Mompos (mōm-pōs') Col.	8·05 N	74·30 W
156	Møn (I.) (mûn) Den.	54·54 N	12·30 E
107	Monaca (mŏ-nă'kō) Pa. (Pittsburgh In.)	40·41 N	80·17 W
151	Monaco (mŏn'ȧ-kō) Eur.	43·43 N	7·47 E
154	Monaghan (mŏn'ȧ-găn) Ire.	54·16 N	7·20 W
123	Mona Pass. (mō'nă) N. A.	18·00 N	68·10 W
92	Monarch Mtn. (mŏn'ērk) Can.	51·54 N	125·53 W
93	Monashee Mts. (mŏ-nă'shē) Can.	50·30 N	118·30 W
151	Monastir (môn-ȧs-tēr') Tun.	35·49 N	10·56 E
	Monastir, see Bitola		
167	Monastyrishche (mô-nȧs-tē-rēsh'chȧ). Sov. Un.	48·57 N	29·53 E
166	Monastyrshchina (mô-nȧs-tērsh'chĭ-nȧ). Sov. Un.	54·19 N	31·49 E
135	Monçao (mon-souN') Braz.	3·39 S	45·23 W
162	Moncayo (Mtn.) (môn-kä'yō). Sp.	41·44 N	1·48 W
170	Monchegorsk (mōn'chĕ-gôrsk) Sov. Un.	69·00 N	33·35 E
161	Mönchengladbach (mûn'kĕn gläd'bäk) F.R.G. (Ruhr In.)	51·12 N	6·28 E
162	Moncique, Serra de (Mts.) (sĕr'rä dä môn-chē'kĕ). Port.	37·22 N	8·37 W
118	Monclovra (môn-klō'vä) Mex.	26·53 N	101·25 W
98	Moncton (mŭŋk'tŭn) Can.	46·06 N	64·47 W
162	Mondego, Cabo (C.) (kȧ'bō mōn-dā'gŏŏ). Port.	40·12 N	8·55 W
162	Mondêgo (R.) (mōn-dĕ'gō) Port.	40·10 N	8·36 W
212	Mondombe (môn-dôm'bȧ) Zaire	0·45 S	23·06 E
162	Mondoñedo (môn-dô-nyā'dō) Sp.	43·35 N	7·18 W
164	Mondoví (mōn-dô'vē') It.	44·23 N	7·53 E
109	Mondovi (mŏn-dō'vĭ) Wi.	44·35 N	91·42 W
107	Monee (mŏ-nĭ) Il. (Chicago In.)	41·25 N	87·45 W
107	Monessen (mŏ-nĕs'sĕn) Pa. (Pittsburgh In.)	40·09 N	79·53 W
117	Monett (mô-nĕt') Mo.	36·55 N	93·55 W
162	Monforte de Lemos (môn-fôr'tā dĕ lĕ'môs). Sp.	42·30 N	7·30 W
215	Monga Chad.	4·12 N	22·49 E
211	Mongala R. (mŏn-gȧl'ȧ) Zaire	3·20 N	21·30 E
211	Mongalla Sud.	5·11 N	31·46 E
184	Monghyr (mŏn-gēr') India	25·23 N	86·34 E
214	Mongo (R.) S. L.	9·50 N	11·50 W
182	Mongolia (mŏŋ-gō'lĭ-ȧ) Asia	46·00 N	100·00 E
211	Mongos, Chaîne des (Mts.) Cen. Afr. Emp.	8·04 N	21·59 E
216	Mongoumba (mŏŋ-gōōm'bȧ) Cen. Afr. Emp.	3·38 N	18·36 E
216	Mongu (mŏŋ-gōō') Zambia	15·15 S	23·09 E
174	Monino Sov. Un. (Moscow In.)	55·50 N	38·13 E
217	Monkey Bay Malawi	14·05 S	34·55 E
126	Monkey River (mŭŋ'kĭ) Belize (In.)	16·22 N	88·33 W
89	Monkland (mŭngk-lănd) Can. (Ottawa In.)	45·12 N	74·52 W
216	Monkoto (môn-kō'tô) Zaire	1·38 S	20·39 E
117	Monmouth (mŏn'mŭth) (mŏn'mouth). Il.	40·54 N	90·38 W
106	Monmouth Junction (mŏn'mouth jŭngk'shŭn) NJ (New York In.)	40·23 N	74·33 W
92	Monmouth Mtn. (mŏn'mŭth). Can.	51·00 N	123·47 W
114	Mono (L.) (mō'nō) Ca.	38·04 N	119·00 W
214	Mono (R.) Togo	7·20 N	1·25 E
104	Monon (mō'nŏn) In.	40·55 N	86·55 W
105	Monongah (mô-nŏŋ'gȧ) WV	39·25 N	80·10 W
107	Monongahela (mô-nŏn-gȧ-hē'lȧ) Pa. (Pittsburgh In.)	40·11 N	79·55 W
105	Monongahela (R.) WV	39·30 N	80·10 W
165	Monopoli (mô-nô'pô-lê) It.	40·55 N	17·17 E
163	Monovar (mô-nō'vär) Sp.	38·26 N	0·50 W
164	Monreale (mōn-rȧ-ä'lā) It.	38·04 N	13·15 E
120	Monroe (mŭn-rō') Ga.	33·47 N	83·43 W
119	Monroe La.	32·30 N	92·06 W
104	Monroe Mi.	41·55 N	83·25 W
106	Monroe NY (New York In.)	41·19 N	74·11 W
121	Monroe NC	34·58 N	80·34 W
115	Monroe Ut.	38·35 N	112·10 W
112	Monroe Wa. (Seattle In.)	47·52 N	121·58 W
109	Monroe Wi.	42·35 N	89·40 W
121	Monroe (L.) Fl.	28·50 N	81·15 W
117	Monroe City Mo.	39·38 N	91·41 W
120	Monroeville (mŭn-rō'vĭl) Al.	31·33 N	87·19 W
113	Monrovia (mŏn-rō'vĭ-ȧ) Ca. (Los Angeles In.)	34·09 N	118·00 W
214	Monrovia Lib.	6·18 N	10·47 W
155	Mons (môN') Bel.	50·29 N	3·55 E
98	Monson (mŏn'sŭn) Me.	45·17 N	69·28 W
156	Mönsterås (mŭn'stĕr-ôs) Swe.	57·04 N	16·24 E
188	Montagh Ata (Mt.) China	38·26 N	75·23 E
103	Montagne Tremblante Prov. Pk. Can.	46·30 N	75·51 W
99	Montague (mŏn'tȧ-gū) Can.	46·10 N	62·39 W
104	Montague Mi.	43·30 N	86·25 W
101	Montague (I.) Ak.	60·10 N	147·00 W
197	Montalban (mōnt-äl-bän) Phil. (In.)	14·47 N	121·11 E
135	Montalbán Ven. (In.)	10·14 N	68·19 W
164	Montalcone (mōn-täl-kô'nĕ) It.	45·49 N	13·30 E
162	Montalegre (mōn-tä-lā'grĕ) Port.	41·49 N	7·48 W
102	Montana (State) (mŏn-tăn'ȧ). U.S.	47·10 N	111·50 W
162	Montánchez (mōn-tän'chȧth) Sp.	39·18 N	6·09 W
160	Montargis (môN-tȧr-zhē') Fr.	47·59 N	2·42 E
161	Montataire (môN-tȧ-târ) Fr. (Paris In.)	49·15 N	2·26 E
160	Montauban (môN-tô-bäN') Fr.	44·01 N	1·22 E
105	Montauk NY	41·03 N	71·57 W
105	Montauk Pt. (mŏn-tôk') NY	41·05 N	71·55 W
163	Montbanch (mônt-bän'ch) Sp.	41·20 N	1·08 E
160	Montbard (môN-bȧr') Fr.	47·40 N	4·19 E
161	Montbéliard (môN-bā-lyȧr') Fr.	47·32 N	6·45 E
119	Mont Belvieu (mŏnt bĕl'vū) Tx. (In.)	29·51 N	94·53 W
161	Mont Blanc Tunnel (môN bläN) Fr.-It.	45·53 N	6·53 E
160	Montbrison (môN-brē-zôN') Fr.	45·38 N	4·06 E
160	Montcalm, Pic de (Pk.) (pēk dē môN-kȧm'). Fr.	42·43 N	1·13 E
160	Montceau-les-Mines (môN-sō'lā-mēn'). Fr.	46·39 N	4·22 E
106	Montclair (mŏnt-klâr') NJ (New York In.)	40·49 N	74·13 W
160	Mont-de-Marsan (môN-dē-mȧr-säN'). Fr.	43·54 N	0·32 W
160	Montdidier (môN-dē-dyā') Fr.	49·42 N	2·33 E
137	Monte (mŏ'n-tĕ) Arg. (Buenos Aires In.)	35·25 S	58·49 W
134	Monteagudo (mōn'tā-ä-gōō'dhō) Bol.	19·49 S	63·48 W
113	Montebello (mŏn-tê-bĕl'ō) Ca. (Los Angeles In.)	34·01 N	118·06 W
89	Montebello Can. (Ottawa In.)	45·40 N	74·56 W
204	Monte Bello (Is.) Austl.	20·30 S	114·10 E
136	Monte Caseros (mŏ'n-tĕ-kä-sĕ'rôs). Arg.	30·16 S	57·39 W
126	Mont Ecillos, Cord. de (Mts.) (kôr-dēl-yĕ'rä dĕ mô'nt ĕ-sē'l-yōs). Hond.	14·19 N	87·52 W
129	Monte Cristi (mô'n-tĕ-krē's-tē) Dom. Rep.	19·50 N	71·40 W
164	Montecristo, I. di (mōn'tȧ-krēs'tō). It.	42·20 N	10·19 E
124	Monte Escobedo (mōn'tȧ ĕs-kô-bā'dhō). Mex.	22·18 N	103·34 W
163	Monteforte Irpino (môn-tĕ-fô'r-tĕ ē'r-pê'nō) It. (Naples In.)	40·39 N	14·42 E
162	Montefrío (mōn-tȧ-frē'ō) Sp.	37·20 N	4·02 W
128	Montego Bay (mŏn-tē'gō) Jam.	18·30 N	77·55 W
136	Monte Grande (mŏ'n-tĕ grän'dĕ) Arg. (Buenos Aires In.)	34·34 S	58·28 W
163	Montelavar (mōn-tĕ-lȧ-vär') Port. (Lisbon In.)	38·51 N	9·20 W
160	Montélimar (môN-tā-lē-mär') Fr.	44·33 N	4·47 E
162	Montellano (mōn-tȧ-lyä'nō) Sp.	37·00 N	5·34 W
109	Montello (mŏn-tĕl'ō) Wi.	43·47 N	89·20 W
118	Montemorelos (mōn'tȧ-mō-rā'lōs) Mex.	25·14 N	99·50 W
162	Montemor-o-Novo (môN-tĕ-môr'ŏŏ-nô'vŏŏ). Port.	38·39 N	8·11 W
	Montenegro (Reg.), see Crna Gora		
217	Montepuez Moz.	13·07 S	39·00 E
164	Montepulciano (môn'tȧ-pōōl-chä'nō). It.	43·05 N	11·48 E
160	Montereau-faut-Yonne (môN-t'rō'fō-yôn'). Fr.	48·24 N	2·57 E
114	Monterey (mŏn-tĕ-rā') Ca.	36·36 N	121·53 W
120	Monterey Tn.	36·06 N	85·15 W
114	Monterey B. Ca.	36·48 N	122·01 W
113	Monterey Park Ca. (Los Angeles In.)	34·04 N	118·08 W
134	Montería (mōn-tȧ-rē'ä) Col.	8·47 N	75·57 W
136	Monteros (mōn-tĕ'rôs) Arg.	27·14 S	65·29 W
163	Monterotondo (môn-tĕ-rô-tô'n-dô) It. (Rome In.)	42·03 N	12·39 E
118	Monterrey (mōn-tĕr-rā') Mex.	25·43 N	100·19 W
164	Monte Sant' Angelo (mô'n-tĕ sän ä'n-gzhĕ-lô). It.	41·43 N	15·59 E
110	Montesano (mŏn-tē-sä'nō) Wa.	46·59 N	123·35 W
135	Montes Claros (môn-tĕs-klä'rôs) Braz.	16·44 S	43·41 W
120	Montevallo (mŏn-tê-văl'ō) Al.	33·05 N	86·49 W
164	Montevarchi (mōn-tȧ-vär'kē) It.	43·30 N	11·45 E
137	Montevideo (mōn'tȧ-vê-dhā'ō) Ur. (Buenos Aires In.)	34·50 S	56·10 W
115	Monte Vista (mŏn'tê vĭs'tȧ) Co.	37·35 N	106·10 W
120	Montezuma (mŏn-tê-zōō'mȧ) Ga.	32·17 N	84·00 W
115	Montezuma Castle Natl. Mon. Az.	34·38 N	111·50 W
149	Montfoort. Neth. (Amsterdam In.)	52·02 N	4·56 E
161	Montfort l'Amaury (môN-fôr'lä-mō-rē') Fr. (Paris In.)	48·47 N	1·49 E
160	Montfort-sur-Meu (mŏn-fôr-sür-mû'). Fr.	48·09 N	1·58 W
120	Montgomery (mŏnt-gŭm'ēr-ĭ) Al.	32·23 N	86·17 W
104	Montgomery WV	38·10 N	81·25 W
117	Montgomery City Mo.	38·58 N	91·29 W
117	Monticello (mŏn-tĭ-sĕl'ō) Ar.	33·38 N	91·47 W
120	Monticello Fl.	30·32 N	83·53 W
120	Monticello Ga.	33·00 N	83·11 W
104	Monticello Il.	40·05 N	88·35 W
104	Monticello In.	40·40 N	86·50 W
109	Monticello Ia.	42·14 N	91·13 W
120	Monticello Ky.	36·47 N	84·50 W
98	Monticello Me.	46·19 N	67·53 W
109	Monticello Mn.	45·18 N	93·48 W
105	Monticello NY	41·35 N	74·40 W
115	Monticello Ut.	37·55 N	109·25 W
161	Montigny-lès-Metz (môN-tēn-yē'lȧ-mĕts'). Fr.	49·06 N	6·07 E
163	Montijo (môn-tē'zhō) Port. (Lisbon In.)	38·42 N	8·58 W
162	Montijo (môn-tē'hō) Sp.	38·55 N	6·35 W
127	Montijo, Bahia (B.) (bä-ē'ä mōn-tē'hō). Pan.	7·36 N	81·11 W
98	Mont-Joli (môN zhō-lē') Can.	48·35 N	68·11 W
160	Montluçon (môN-lü-sôN') Fr.	46·20 N	2·35 E
89	Montmagny (môN-mȧn-yē') Can. (Quebec In.)	46·59 N	70·33 W
89	Montmorency (mŏnt-mô-rĕn'sĭ) Can. (Quebec In.)	46·53 N	71·09 W
161	Montmorency (môN'mô-räN-sē') Fr. (Paris In.)	48·59 N	2·19 E
89	Montmorency (R.) (mŏnt-mô-rĕn'sĭ) Can. (Quebec In.)	47·30 N	71·10 W
160	Montmorillon (môN'mô-rê-yôN') Fr.	46·26 N	0·50 E
164	Montone (R.) (môn-tô'nĕ) It.	44·03 N	11·45 E
162	Montoro (môn-tō'rô) Sp.	38·01 N	4·22 W
104	Montpelier (mŏnt-pēl'yēr) In.	40·35 N	85·20 W
111	Montpelier Id.	42·19 N	111·19 W
104	Montpelier Oh.	41·35 N	84·35 W
105	Montpelier Vt.	44·20 N	72·35 W
160	Montpellier (môN-pĕ-lyā') Fr.	43·38 N	3·53 E
89	Montréal (mŏn-trê-ôl') Can. (Montréal In.)	45·30 N	73·35 W
94	Montreal L. Can.	54·20 N	105·40 W
96	Montreal (R.) Can.	47·15 N	84·20 W
97	Montreal (R.) Can.	47·50 N	80·30 W
89	Montréal-Nord Can. (Montréal In.)	45·36 N	73·38 W
158	Montreux (môn-trû') Switz.	46·26 N	6·52 E
113	Montrose (mŏnt-rōz) Ca. (Los Angeles In.)	34·13 N	118·13 W
115	Montrose (mŏn-trōz') Co.	38·30 N	107·55 W
107	Montrose Oh. (Cleveland In.)	41·08 N	81·38 W
105	Montrose (mŏnt-rōz') Pa.	41·50 N	75·50 W
154	Montrose Scot.	56·45 N	2·25 W
89	Mont-Royal Can. (Montreal In.)	47·31 N	73·39 W
98	Monts, Pointe des (Pt.) (pwănt' dā môN'). Can.	49·19 N	67·22 W
161	Mont St. Martin (môN sȧN mär-tăN'). Fr.	49·34 N	6·13 E
123	Montserrat (mŏnt-sĕ-răt') N. A.	16·48 N	63·15 W
106	Montvale (mŏnt-vāl') NJ (New York In.)	41·02 N	74·01 W
196	Monywa (mŏn'yōō-wȧ) Bur.	22·02 N	95·16 E
164	Monza (mōn'tsä) It.	45·34 N	9·17 E
163	Monzón (mōn-thōn') Sp.	41·54 N	1·09 E
119	Moody (mōō'dĭ) Tx.	31·18 N	97·20 W
218	Mooi (R.) (mōō'ĭ) S. Afr. (Johannesburg & Pretoria In.)	26·34 S	27·03 E
213	Mooi (R.) S. Afr. (Natal In.)	29·00 S	30·15 E
213	Mooirivier S. Afr. (Natal In.)	29·14 S	29·59 E
202	Moolap Austl. (Melbourne In.)	38·11 S	144·26 E
204	Moonta (mōōn'tȧ) Austl.	34·05 S	137·42 E
204	Moora (mŏŏr'ȧ) Austl.	30·35 S	116·12 E
111	Moorcroft (mōr'krôft) Wy.	44·17 N	104·59 W
204	Moore (L.) (mōr) Austl.	29·50 S	128·12 E
149	Moorenweis (mō'rĕn-vīz) F.R.G. (Munich In.)	48·10 N	11·05 E
105	Moore Res. Vt.-NH	44·20 N	72·10 W
106	Moorestown (mōrz'toun) NJ (Philadelphia In.)	39·58 N	74·56 W
107	Mooresville (mōrz'vĭl) In. (Indianapolis In.)	39·37 N	86·22 W
121	Mooresville (mōrz'vĭl) NC	35·34 N	80·48 W
108	Moorhead (mōr'hĕd) Mn.	46·52 N	96·44 W
120	Moorhead Ms.	33·25 N	90·30 W
	Moorland (Plain), see Landes		
90	Moose (L.) (mōōs) Can.	54·14 N	99·28 W
91	Moose (R.) Can.	51·01 N	80·42 W
89	Moose Creek Can. (Ottawa In.)	45·16 N	74·58 W
98	Moosehead (mōōs'hĕd) Me.	45·37 N	69·15 W
95	Moose I. Can.	51·50 N	97·09 W
94	Moose Jaw (mōōs jô) Can.	50·23 N	105·32 W
94	Moose Jaw (Cr.) Can.	50·34 N	105·17 W
94	Moose Lake Can.	53·40 N	100·28 W
95	Moose Mtn. Can.	49·45 N	102·37 W
94	Moose Mtn. Cr. Can.	49·12 N	102·10 W
105	Moosilauke (Mtn.) (mōō-sĭ-lȧ'kē). NH	44·00 N	71·50 W
149	Moosinning (mō'zē-nēng) F.R.G. (Munich In.)	48·17 N	11·51 E
95	Moosomin (mōō'sô-mĭn) Can.	50·07 N	101·40 W
91	Moosonee (mōō'sô-nê) Can.	51·20 N	80·44 W
214	Mopti (mŏp'tē) Mali	14·30 N	4·12 W
134	Moquegua (mô-kā'gwä) Peru	17·15 S	70·54 W
159	Mór (mōr) Hung.	47·51 N	18·14 E
185	Mora India (In.)	18·54 N	72·56 E
109	Mora (mō'rȧ) Mn.	45·52 N	93·18 W
116	Mora NM	35·58 N	105·17 W
162	Mora (mô-rä) Sp.	39·42 N	3·45 W
163	Mora Sp.	41·06 N	0·25 E
184	Morādābād (mô-rä-dä-bäd') India	28·57 N	78·48 E
126	Morales (mô-rä'lĕs) Guat.	15·29 N	88·46 W
213	Moramanga (mō-rä-mäŋ'gä) Mad.	18·48 S	48·09 E
129	Morant Pt. (mô-rănt') Jam.	17·55 N	76·10 W
156	Morastrand (mō'rä-stränd) Swe.	61·00 N	14·29 E
163	Morata de Tajuña (mô-rä'tä dā tä-hōō'nyä) Sp. (Madrid In.)	40·14 N	3·27 W
185	Moratuwa Sri Lanka	6·35 N	79·59 E
159	Morava (Moravia) (Prov.) (mô'rä-vä) (mō-rā'vĭ-ȧ). Czech.	49·21 N	16·57 E
158	Morava R. Czech.	49·53 N	16·53 E
	Moravia, see Morava		
135	Morawhanna (mô-rȧ-hwä'nȧ). Guy.	8·12 N	59·33 W
154	Moray Firth (mŭr'ȧ) Scot.	57·41 N	3·55 W
156	Mörbylånga (mûr'bü-lôŋ'gȧ). Swe.	56·32 N	16·23 E
95	Morden (mōr'dĕn) Can.	49·11 N	98·05 W
202	Mordialloc (môr-dĭ-ăl'ŏk) Austl. (Melbourne In.)	38·00 S	145·05 E
170	Mordvin (A.S.S.R.) Sov. Un.	54·18 N	43·50 E
154	More, Ben (Mtn.) (bĕn môr). Scot.	58·09 N	5·01 W
108	Moreau (R.) (mô-rō') SD	45·13 N	102·22 W
154	Morecambe B. (mōr'kȧm) Eng.	53·55 N	3·25 W
203	Moree (mō'rē) Austl.	29·20 S	149·50 E
104	Morehead Ky.	38·10 N	83·25 W

ng-sing; ŋ-baŋk; N-nasalized n; nŏd; cŏmmit; ōld; ôbey; ôrder; fōōd; fŏŏt; ou-out; s-soft; sh-dish; th-thin; pūre; ûnite; ûrn; stŭd; circŭs; ü-as "y" in study; '-indeterminate vowel.

316 Morehead City — Mui Ron

PRONOUNCING INDEX

Page	Name Pronunciation Region	Lat. °′	Long. °′
121	Morehead City (mōr′hĕd) NC	34·43 N	76·43 W
117	Morehouse (mōr′hous) Mo.	36·49 N	89·41 W
124	Morelia (mô-rā′lyä) Mex.	19·43 N	101·12 W
163	Morella (mô-räl′yä) Sp.	40·38 N	0·07 W
124	Morelos (mô-rā′lōs) Mex.	22·46 N	102·36 W
118	Morelos Mex.	28·24 N	100·51 W
125	Morelos Mex. (In.)	19·41 N	99·29 W
118	Morelos, R. Mex.	25·27 N	99·35 W
112	Morena, Sierra (Mt.) (syĕr′rä mô-rā′nä) Ca. (San Francisco In.)	37·24 N	122·19 W
162	Morena, Sierra (Mts.) (syĕr′rä mô-rā′nä) Sp.	38·15 N	5·45 W
115	Morenci (mô-rĕn′sĭ) Az.	33·05 N	109·25 W
104	Morenci Mi.	41·50 N	84·50 W
136	Moreno (mô-rĕ′nō) Arg. (In.)	34·25 S	58·47 W
113	Moreno Ca. (Los Angeles In.)	33·55 N	117·09 W
128	Mores (I.) (mōrz) Ba.	26·20 N	77·35 W
112	Moresby (I.) (mōrz′bĭ) Can. (Vancouver In.)	48·43 N	123·15 W
90	Moresby I. Can.	52·50 N	131·55 W
203	Moreton (I.) (môr′tŭn) Austl.	26·53 S	152·42 E
203	Moreton B. (môr′tŭn) Austl.	27·12 S	153·10 E
89	Morewood (mōr′wo͝od) Can. (Ottawa In.)	45·11 N	75·17 W
111	Morgan (môr′găn) Mt.	48·55 N	107·56 W
111	Morgan Ut.	41·04 N	111·42 W
119	Morgan City La.	29·41 N	91·11 W
104	Morganfield (môr′găn-fēld) Ky.	37·40 N	87·55 W
213	Morgan's Bay S. Afr. (Natal In.)	32·42 S	28·19 E
121	Morganton (môr′găn-tŭn) NC	35·44 N	81·42 W
105	Morgantown (môr′găn-toun) WV	39·40 N	79·55 W
187	Morga Ra. Afg. (Khyber Pass In.)	34·02 N	70·38 E
218	Morgenzon (môr′gĕnt-sŏn) S. Afr. (Johannesburg & Pretoria In.)	26·44 S	29·39 E
202	Moriac Austl. (Melbourne In.)	38·15 S	144·12 E
92	Morice L. Can.	54·00 N	127·37 W
195	Moriguchi (mō′rē-go͞o′chē) Jap. (Ōsaka In.)	34·44 N	135·34 E
89	Morinville (mō′rĭn-vĭl) Can. (Edmonton In.)	53·48 N	113·39 W
194	Morioka (mō′rē-ō′kȧ) Jap.	39·40 N	141·21 E
173	Morkoka (R.) (môr-kô′kȧ) Sov. Un.	65·35 N	111·00 E
160	Morlaix (mŏr-lĕ′) Fr.	48·36 N	3·48 W
89	Morley (mŏr′lē) Can. (Calgary In.)	51·10 N	114·51 W
161	Mormant Fr. (Paris In.)	48·35 N	2·54 E
127	Morne Diablotin, Mt. (môrn dē-ȧ-blô-tăN′) Dominica (In.)	15·31 N	61·24 W
127	Morne Gimie, Mt. (môrn′ zhē-mē′) St. Lucia (In.)	13·53 N	61·03 W
202	Mornington Austl. (Melbourne In.)	38·13 S	145·02 E
197	Morobe Pap. N. Gui.	8·03 S	147·45 E
209	Morocco (mō-rŏk′ō) Afr.	32·00 N	7·00 W
217	Morogoro (mō-rō-gō′rō) Tan.	6·49 S	37·40 E
124	Moroleón (mō-rō-lā-ōn′) Mex.	20·07 N	101·15 W
213	Morombe (mo͞o-ro͞om′bā) Mad.	21·39 S	43·34 E
136	Morón (mō-rō′n) Arg. (Buenos Aires In.)	34·24 S	58·37 W
128	Morón (mô-rōn′) Cuba	22·05 N	78·35 W
135	Morón (mô-rŏ′n) Ven. (In.)	10·29 N	68·11 W
213	Morondava (mō-rōn-dȧ′vȧ) Mad.	20·17 S	44·18 E
162	Morón de la Frontera (mô-rōn′dā läf rôn-tā′rä) Sp.	37·08 N	5·20 W
114	Morongo Ind. Res. (mō-rôŋ′gō) Ca.	33·54 N	116·47 W
212	Moroni Comoros	11·41 S	43·16 E
115	Moroni (mô-rō′nĭ) Ut.	39·30 N	111·40 W
197	Morotai (I.) (mō-rô-tä′ē) Indon.	2·12 N	128·30 E
217	Moroto Ug.	2·32 N	34·39 E
171	Morozovsk Sov. Un.	48·20 N	41·50 E
108	Morrill (mŏr′ĭl) Ne.	41·59 N	103·54 W
117	Morrilton (mŏr′ĭl-tŭn) Ar.	35·09 N	92·42 W
135	Morrinhos (mô-rēn′yōzh) Braz.	17·45 S	48·56 W
95	Morris (mŏr′ĭs) Can.	49·21 N	97·22 W
104	Morris Il.	41·20 N	88·25 W
108	Morris Mn.	45·35 N	95·53 W
95	Morris (R.) Can.	49·30 N	97·30 W
109	Morrison (mŏr′ĭ-sŭn) Il.	41·48 N	89·58 W
106	Morris Plains (mŏr′ĭs pláns) NJ (New York In.)	40·49 N	74·29 W
113	Morris Res. Ca. (Los Angeles In.)	34·11 N	117·49 W
106	Morristown (mŏr′rĭs-toun) NJ (New York In.)	40·48 N	74·29 W
120	Morristown Tn.	36·10 N	83·18 W
106	Morrisville (mŏr′ĭs-vĭl) Pa. (Philadelphia In.)	40·12 N	74·46 W
135	Morro do Chapéu (môr-o͞o do͞o-shä-pĕ′o͞o) Braz.	11·34 S	41·03 W
107	Morrow (mŏr′ō) Oh. (Cincinnati In.)	39·21 N	84·07 W
171	Morshansk (môr-shänsk′) Sov. Un.	53·25 N	41·35 E
156	Mors (I.) Den.	56·46 N	8·38 E
164	Mortara (môr-tä′rä) It.	45·13 N	8·47 E
136	Morteros (môr-tĕ′rôs) Arg.	30·47 S	62·00 W
137	Mortes, Rio das (R.) (rē′-o-däs-mô′r-tĕs) Braz. (Rio de Janeiro In.)	21·04 S	44·29 W
109	Morton Ind. Res. (mŏr′tŭn) Mn.	44·35 N	94·48 W
149	Mortsel (môr-sĕl′) Bel. (Brussels In.)	51·10 N	4·28 E
160	Morvan, Mts. du (môr-väN′) Fr.	46·45 N	4·00 E
170	Morzhovets (I.) (môr′zhô-vyĕts′) Sov. Un.	66·40 N	42·30 E
166	Mosal'sk (mō-zälsk′) Sov. Un.	54·27 N	34·57 E
110	Moscow (mŏs′kō) Id.	46·44 N	116·57 W
	Moscow, see Moskva		
	Moscow Can., see Imeni Moskvy, Kanal		
158	Mosel R. (mō′sĕl) (mô-zĕl) F.R.G.	49·49 N	7·00 E
110	Moses Lake Wa.	47·08 N	119·15 W
110	Moses L. (mō′zĕz) Wa.	47·09 N	119·30 W
218	Moses R. S. Afr. (Johannesburg & Pretoria In.)	25·17 S	29·04 E
157	Moshchnyy (Is.) (môsh′chnĭ) Sov. Un.	59·56 N	28·07 E
217	Moshi (mō′shē) Tan.	3·21 S	37·20 E
150	Mosjøen Nor.	65·50 N	13·10 E
174	Moskva (Moscow) (mŏs-kvä′) Sov. Un. (Moscow In.)	55·45 N	37·37 E
166	Moskva (Oblast) Sov. Un.	55·38 N	36·48 E
166	Moskva (R.) Sov. Un.	55·50 N	37·05 E
159	Mosonmagyaróvár Hung.	47·51 N	17·16 E
127	Mosquitos, Costa de (kôs-tä-dĕ-mŏs-kē′tō) Nic.	12·05 N	83·49 W
127	Mosquitos, Gulfo de los (G.) (go͞o′l-fô-dĕ-lôs-mŏs-kē′tōs) Pan.	9·17 N	80·59 W
156	Moss (môs) Nor.	59·29 N	10·39 E
112	Moss Beach (môs bēch) Ca. (San Francisco In.)	37·32 N	122·31 W
212	Mosselbaai (mô′sŭl bā) S. Afr.	34·06 S	22·23 E
216	Mossendjo Con.	2·57 S	12·44 E
148	Mossley (môs′lĭ) Eng.	53·31 N	2·02 W
135	Mossoró (mō-sō-ro͞o′) Braz.	5·13 S	37·14 W
120	Moss Point (môs) Ms.	30·25 N	88·32 W
158	Most (môst) Czech.	50·32 N	13·37 E
210	Mostaganem (mŏs′tä-gȧ-nĕm′) Alg.	36·04 N	0·11 E
165	Mostar (môs′tär) Yugo.	43·20 N	17·51 E
163	Móstoles (môs-tō′lās) Sp. (Madrid In.)	40·19 N	3·52 W
94	Mostoos Hills (mŏs′to͞os) Can.	54·50 N	108·45 W
126	Motagua R. (mō-tä′gwä) Guat.	15·29 N	88·39 W
156	Motala (mô-tô′lä) Swe.	58·34 N	15·00 E
154	Motherwell (mŭdh′ẽr-wĕl) Scot.	55·45 N	4·05 W
162	Motril (mô-trēl′) Sp.	36·44 N	3·32 W
126	Motul (mô-to͞o′l) Mex. (In.)	21·07 N	89·14 W
128	Mouchoir Bk. (mo͞o-shwȧr′) Ba.	21·35 N	70·40 W
129	Mouchoir Passage (Str.) Ba.	21·05 N	71·05 W
161	Moudon Switz.	46·40 N	6·47 E
214	Moudjéria Mauritania	17·53 N	12·20 W
216	Mouila Gabon	1·52 S	11·01 E
212	Mouille Pt. S. Afr. (In.)	33·54 S	18·19 E
160	Moulins (mo͞o-lăN′) Fr.	46·34 N	3·19 E
196	Moulmein (mōl-mān′) Bur.	16·30 N	97·39 E
152	Moulouya, Oued (R.) (mo͞o-lo͞o′yȧ) Mor.	34·07 N	3·27 W
120	Moultrie (mōl′trĭ) Ga.	31·10 N	83·48 W
121	Moultrie (Dam) SC	33·12 N	80·00 W
117	Mound City (mound) Il.	37·06 N	89·13 W
117	Mound City Mo.	40·08 N	95·13 W
104	Mound City Group Natl. Mon. Oh.	39·25 N	83·00 W
215	Moundon Chad	8·34 N	16·05 E
104	Moundsville (moundz′vĭl) WV	39·50 N	80·50 W
161	Mounier, Mt. (mo͞o-nyā′) Fr.	44·10 N	6·59 E
214	Mount, C. Lib.	6·47 N	11·20 W
106	Mountain Brook (moun′tĭn bro͝ok) Al. (Birmingham In.)	33·30 N	86·45 W
113	Mountain Creek L. Tx. (Dallas, Fort Worth In.)	32·43 N	97·03 W
117	Mountain Grove (grōv) Mo.	37·07 N	92·16 W
110	Mountain Home (hōm) Id.	43·08 N	115·43 W
93	Mountain Park (pärk) Can.	52·55 N	117·14 W
112	Mountain View (moun′tĭn vū) Ca. (San Francisco In.)	37·25 N	122·07 W
117	Mountain View Mo.	36·59 N	91·46 W
121	Mount Airy (âr′ĭ) NC	36·28 N	80·37 W
	Mount Athos (Reg.), see Áyion Óros		
213	Mount Ayliff (ā′lĭf) S. Afr. (Natal In.)	30·48 S	29·24 E
109	Mount Ayr (âr) Ia.	40·43 N	94·06 W
104	Mount Carmel (kär′mĕl) Il.	38·25 N	87·45 W
105	Mount Carmel Pa.	40·50 N	76·25 W
109	Mount Carroll Il.	42·05 N	89·55 W
107	Mount Clemens (klĕm′ĕnz) Mi. (Detroit In.)	42·36 N	82·52 W
98	Mount Desert (I.) (dē-zûrt′) Me.	44·15 N	68·08 W
121	Mount Dora (dō′rȧ) Fl. (In.)	28·45 N	81·38 W
202	Mount Duneed Austl. (Melbourne In.)	38·15 S	144·20 E
202	Mount Eliza Austl. (Melbourne In.)	38·11 S	145·05 E
108	Mountevideo (mōn′tȧ-vē-dhā′ō) Mn.	44·56 N	95·42 W
213	Mount Fletcher (flĕ′chẽr) S. Afr. (Natal In.)	30·42 S	28·32 E
104	Mount Forest (fŏr′ĕst) Can.	44·00 N	80·45 W
213	Mount Frere (frâr′) S. Afr. (Natal In.)	30·54 S	29·02 E
203	Mount Gambier (găm′bēr) Austl.	37·30 S	140·53 E
104	Mount Gilead (gĭl′ēăd) Oh.	40·30 N	82·50 W
107	Mount Healthy (hĕlth′ē) Oh. (Cincinnati In.)	39·14 N	84·32 W
106	Mount Holly (hŏl′ĭ) NJ (Philadelphia In.)	39·59 N	74·47 W
89	Mount Hope Can. (Toronto In.)	43·09 N	79·55 W
106	Mount Hope (hōp) NJ (New York In.)	40·55 N	74·32 W
104	Mount Hope WV	37·55 N	81·10 W
204	Mount Isa (ī′zȧ) Austl.	21·00 S	139·45 E
106	Mount Kisco (kĭs′ko) NY (New York In.)	41·12 N	73·44 W
112	Mountlake Terrace (mount lāk tĕr′ĭs) Wa. (Seattle In.)	47·48 N	122·19 W
107	Mount Lebanon (lĕb′ȧ-nŭn) Pa. (Pittsburgh In.)	40·22 N	80·03 W
101	Mount McKinley Natl. Park (mȧ-kĭn′lĭ) Ak.	63·48 N	153·02 W
204	Mount Magnet (măg-nĕt) Austl.	28·00 S	118·00 E
202	Mount Martha Austl. (Melbourne In.)	38·17 S	145·01 E
205	Mount Morgan (môr-găn) Austl.	23·42 S	150·45 E
202	Mount Moriac Austl. (Melbourne In.)	38·13 S	144·12 E
104	Mount Morris (mŏr′ĭs) Mi.	43·10 N	83·45 W
105	Mount Morris NY	42·45 N	77·50 W
214	Mt. Nimba Natl. Pk. Gui.-Ivory Coast	7·35 N	8·10 W
121	Mount Olive (ŏl′ĭv) NC	35·11 N	78·05 W
115	Mount Peale Ut.	38·26 N	109·16 W
109	Mount Pleasant (plĕz′ănt) Ia.	40·59 N	91·34 W
104	Mount Pleasant Mi.	43·35 N	84·45 W
121	Mount Pleasant SC	32·46 N	79·51 W
120	Mount Pleasant Tn.	35·31 N	87·12 W
117	Mount Pleasant Tx.	33·10 N	94·56 W
115	Mount Pleasant Ut.	39·35 N	111·20 W
107	Mount Prospect (prŏs′pĕkt) Il. (Chicago In.)	42·03 N	87·56 W
110	Mount Rainier Natl. Park (rȧ-nēr′) Wa.	46·47 N	121·17 W
90	Mount Revelstoke Natl. Park (rĕv′ĕl-stōk) Can.	51·22 N	120·15 W
105	Mount Savage (săv′āj) Md.	39·45 N	78·55 W
110	Mount Shasta (shăs′tȧ) Ca.	41·18 N	122·17 W
117	Mount Sterling (stûr′lĭng) Il.	39·59 N	90·44 W
104	Mount Sterling Ky.	38·05 N	84·00 W
109	Mount Stewart (stū′ărt) Can.	46·22 N	62·52 W
105	Mount Union (ūn′yŭn) Pa.	40·25 N	77·50 W
104	Mount Vernon (vûr′nŭn) Il.	38·20 N	88·50 W
104	Mount Vernon In.	37·55 N	87·50 W
117	Mount Vernon Mo.	37·09 N	93·48 W
106	Mount Vernon NY (New York In.)	40·55 N	73·51 W
104	Mount Vernon Oh.	40·25 N	82·30 W
106	Mount Vernon Va. (Baltimore In.)	38·43 N	77·06 W
112	Mount Vernon Wa. (Seattle In.)	48·25 N	122·20 W
190	Moup'ing (mō′pĭng) China	37·23 N	121·36 E
135	Moura (mō′rȧ) Braz.	1·33 S	61·38 W
162	Moura Port.	38·08 N	7·28 W
160	Mourenx (mo͞o-rän) Fr.	43·24 N	0·40 W
154	Mourne, Mts. (môrn) N. Ire.	54·10 N	6·09 W
215	Moussoro Chad	13·39 N	16·29 E
161	Moûtiers (mo͞o-tyâr′) Fr.	45·31 N	6·34 E
203	Mowbullan, Mt. (mō′bo͞o-lăn) Austl.	26·50 S	151·34 E
124	Moyahua (mô-yä′wä) Mex.	21·16 N	103·10 W
211	Moyale (mô-yä′lä) Ken.	3·28 N	39·04 E
214	Moyamba (mô-yäm′bä) S. L.	8·10 N	12·26 W
152	Moyen Atlas (Mts.) Mor.	32·49 N	5·28 W
161	Moyeuvre Grande Fr.	49·15 N	6·26 E
110	Moyie R. (moi′yē) Id.	48·50 N	116·10 W
134	Moyobamba (mō-yō-bäm′bä) Peru	6·12 S	76·56 W
126	Moyuta (mô-ē-o͞o′tä) Guat.	14·01 N	90·05 W
173	Moyyero (R.) Sov. Un.	67·15 N	104·10 E
209	Mozambique (mō-zăm-bēk′) Afr.	20·15 S	33·53 E
213	Mozambique Chan. (mō-zăm-bēk′) Afr.	24·00 S	38·00 E
171	Mozdok (môz-dôk′) Sov. Un.	43·45 N	44·35 E
166	Mozhaysh (mô-zhäysh′) Sov. Un.	55·31 N	36·02 E
174	Mozhayskiy (mô-zhäy′skĭ) Sov. Un. (Leningrad In.)	59·42 N	30·08 E
167	Mozyr' (mô-zür′) Sov. Un.	52·03 N	29·14 E
217	Mpanda Tan.	6·22 S	31·02 E
217	Mpika Zambia	11·54 S	31·26 E
217	Mpimbe Malawi	15·18 S	35·04 E
217	Mporokoso (′m-pō-rō-kō′sō) Zambia	9·23 S	30·05 E
217	Mpwapwa (′m-pwä′pwä) Tan.	6·21 S	36·29 E
213	Mqanduli (′m-kän′do͞o-lē) S. Afr. (Natal In.)	31·50 S	28·42 E
159	Mragowo (mräŋ′gô-vô) Pol.	53·52 N	21·18 E
210	M'sila (m′sē′lȧ) Alg.	35·47 N	4·34 E
166	Msta (R.) (m′stȧ′) Sov. Un.	58·33 N	32·08 E
166	Mstislavl' (m′stē-slävl′) Sov. Un.	54·01 N	31·42 E
217	Mtakataka Malawi	14·12 S	34·32 E
213	Mtamvuna (R.) S. Afr. (Natal In.)	30·43 S	29·53 E
213	Mtata (R.) S. Afr. (Natal In.)	31·48 S	29·03 E
166	Mtsensk (m′tsĕnsk) Sov. Un.	53·17 N	36·33 E
217	Mtwara Tan.	10·16 S	40·11 E
196	Muang Khon Kaen Thai.	16·37 N	102·41 E
196	Muang Lamphum Thai.	18·40 N	98·59 E
196	Muang Phitsanulok Thai.	16·51 N	100·15 E
196	Muang Sakon Thai.	17·00 N	104·06 E
183	Muar (R.) Mala. (Singapore In.)	2·18 N	102·43 E
217	Mubende Ug.	0·35 N	31·23 E
215	Mubi Nig.	10·18 N	13·20 E
217	Mucacata Moz.	13·20 S	39·59 E
161	Much (mo͞oK) F.R.G. (Ruhr In.)	50·54 N	7·24 E
217	Muchinga Mts. Zambia	12·40 S	30·50 E
148	Much Wenlock (mŭch wĕn′lŏk) Eng.	52·35 N	2·33 W
120	Muckalee Cr. (mŭk′ȧ lē) Ga.	31·55 N	84·10 W
112	Muckleshoot Ind. Res. (mŭck″l-sho͞ot) Wa. (Seattle In.)	47·21 N	122·04 W
217	Mucubela Moz.	16·55 S	37·52 E
135	Mucugê (mo͞o-ko͞o-zhĕ′) Braz.	13·02 S	41·19 W
109	Mud (L.) (mŭd) Mi.	46·12 N	84·32 W
114	Mud (L.) Nv.	40·28 N	119·11 W
114	Muddy (R.) (mŭd′ĭ) Nv.	36·56 N	114·42 W
117	Muddy Boggy Cr. (mŭd′ĭ bôg′ĭ) Ok.	34·42 N	96·11 W
115	Muddy Cr. (mŭd′ĭ) Ut.	38·45 N	111·10 W
203	Mudgee (mŭ-jē) Austl.	32·47 S	149·10 E
94	Mudjatik (R.) Can.	56·23 N	107·40 W
217	Mufulira Zambia	12·33 S	28·14 E
162	Mugía (mo͞o-kē′ä) Sp.	43·05 N	9·14 W
171	Muğla (mo͞og′lä) Tur.	37·10 N	28·20 E
158	Mühldorf (mül-dôrf) F.R.G.	48·15 N	12·33 E
158	Mühlhausen (mül′hou-zĕn) G.D.R.	51·13 N	10·25 E
157	Muhu (I.) (mo͞o′ho͞o) Sov. Un.	58·41 N	22·55 E
193	Mui Ron, C. Viet.	18·05 N	106·45 E

ăt; finăl; rāte; senâte; ärm; ȧsk; sofȧ; fâre; ch-choose; dh-as th in other; bē; ēvent; bĕt; recĕnt; cratẽr; g-go; gh-guttural g; bĭt; ĭ-short neutral; rīde; K-guttural k as ch in German ich;

PRONOUNCING INDEX
Muir Woods — Nakhichevan 317

Page Name Pronunciation Region Lat. °' Long. °'
114 Muir Woods Natl. Mon (mūr). Ca. 37·54 N 123·22 W
212 Muizenberg (mwĭz-ĕn-bûrg') S. Afr. (In.) 34·07 S 18·28 E
159 Mukachëvo (mōō-kȧ-chyô'vô) Sov. Un. 48·25 N 22·43 E
Mukden, see Shenyang
173 Mukhtuya (mōōk-tōō'yȧ) Sov. Un. 61·00 N 113·00 E
112 Mukilteo (mū-kĭl-tā'ō) Wa. (Seattle In.) 47·57 N 122·18 W
195 Muko (mōō'kô). Jap. (Ōsaka In.) 34·57 N 135·43 E
195 Muko (R.) (mōō'kô) Jap. (Ōsaka In.) 34·52 N 135·17 E
95 Mukutawa (R.) Can. 53·10 N 97·28 W
107 Mukwonago (mū-kwō-nȧ'gō) Wi. (Milwaukee In.) 42·52 N 88·19 W
162 Mula (mōō'lä) Sp. 38·05 N 1·12 W
158 Mulde R. (mōōl'dĕ) G.D.R. 50·30 N 12·30 E
192 Muleng China 44·32 N 130·18 E
192 Muleng (R.) China 44·40 N 130·30 E
124 Muleros (mōō-lā'rōs) Mex. 23·44 N 104·00 W
116 Muleshoe Tx. 34·13 N 102·43 W
106 Mulga (mŭl'gȧ) Al. (Birmingham In.) 33·33 N 86·59 W
99 Mulgrave (mŭl'grāv) Can. 45·37 N 61·23 W
205 Mulgrave (I.) Austl. 10·08 S 142·14 E
162 Mulhacén (Mtn.) Sp. 37·04 N 3·18 W
161 Mülheim (mül'hīm) F.R.G. (Ruhr In.) 51·25 N 6·53 E
161 Mulhouse (mü-lōōz') Fr. 47·46 N 7·20 E
154 Mull (I.) (mŭl) Scot. 56·40 N 6·19 W
110 Mullan (mŭl'ăn) Id. 47·26 N 115·50 W
196 Müller, Pegunungan (Mts.) (mül'ĕr). Indon. 0·22 N 113·05 E
154 Mullet Pen. Ire. 54·15 N 10·12 W
154 Mullinger (mŭl-ĭn-gär) Ire. 53·31 N 7·26 W
121 Mullins (mŭl'ĭnz) SC 34·11 N 79·13 W
126 Mullins River Belize (In.) 17·08 N 88·18 W
184 Multān (mōō-tän') Pak. 30·17 N 71·13 E
112 Multnomah Chan. (mŭl nō mȧ) Or. (Portland In.) 45·41 N 122·53 W
196 Mulu, Gunung (Mtn.) Mala. 3·56 N 115·11 E
217 Mulumbe, Monts (Mts.) Zaire 8·47 S 27·20 E
117 Mulvane (mŭl-vān') Ks. 37·30 N 97·13 W
217 Mumbwa (mōōm'bwä) Zambia 14·59 S 27·04 E
217 Mumias Ken. 0·20 N 34·29 E
126 Muna (mōō'nȧ) Mex. (In.) 20·28 N 89·42 W
149 München (Munich) (mün'kĕn) F.R.G. (Munich In.) 48·08 N 11·35 E
104 Muncie (mŭn'sĭ) In. 40·10 N 85·30 W
107 Mundelein (mŭn-dĕ-lĭn') Il. (Chicago In.) 42·16 N 88·00 W
134 Mundonueva, Pico de (Pk.) (pē'kô-dĕ-mōō'n-dô-nwĕ'vä) Col. (In.) 4·18 N 74·12 W
125 Muneco, Cerro (Mtn.) (sĕ'r-rô-mōō-nĕ'kō). Mex. (In.) 19·13 N 99·20 W
205 Mungana (mŭn-găn'ȧ) Austl. 17·15 S 144·18 E
217 Mungbere Zaire 2·38 N 28·30 E
113 Munger (mŭn'gẽr) Mn. (Duluth In.) 46·48 N 92·20 W
203 Mungindi (mŭn-gĭn'dē) Austl. 32·00 S 148·45 E
107 Munhall (mŭn'hôl) Pa. (Pittsburgh In.) 40·24 N 79·53 W
212 Munhango (mōōn-häŋ'gȧ) Ang. 12·15 S 18·55 E
Munich, see München
109 Munising (mū'nĭ-sĭng) Mi. 46·24 N 86·41 W
172 Munku Sardyk (Mtn.) (mōōn'kōō sär-dĭk') Sov. Un.-Mong. 51·45 N 100·30 E
197 Muños (mōōn-nyōth'). Phil. (In.) 15·44 N 120·53 E
161 Münster (mün'stẽr) F.R.G. (Ruhr In.) 51·57 N 7·38 E
107 Munster (mŭn'stẽr) In. (Chicago In.) 41·34 N 87·31 W
154 Munster (mŭn-stẽr) Ire. 52·30 N 9·24 W
196 Muntok (mōōn-tŏk') Indon. 2·05 S 105·11 E
137 Munzi Freire (mōō-nĕ'z-frā'rĕ) Braz. (Rio de Janeiro In.) 20·29 S 41·25 W
196 Muong Sing (mōō'ông-sĭng'). Laos 21·06 N 101·17 E
150 Muonio (R.) Fin.-Swe. 68·15 N 23·00 E
137 Muqui (mōō-kōō'ē) Braz. (Rio de Janeiro In.) 20·56 S 41·20 W
171 Muradiye (mōō-rä'dē-yĕ) Tur. 39·00 N 43·40 E
160 Murat (mü-rä') Fr. 45·05 N 2·56 E
171 Murat (R.) (mōō-rät') Tur. 38·50 N 40·40 E
204 Murchison (R.) (mûr'chĭ-sŭn) Austl. 26·45 S 116·15 E
217 Murchison Falls (mûr'chĭ-sŭn). Ug. 2·15 N 31·41 E
162 Murcia (mōōr'thyä) Sp. 38·00 N 1·10 W
162 Murcia (Reg.) Sp. 38·35 N 1·51 W
108 Murdo (mûr'dô) SD 43·53 N 100·42 W
159 Mureşul R. (mōō'rĕsh-ōōl). Rom. 46·02 N 21·50 E
160 Muret (mü-rĕ') Fr. 43·28 N 1·17 E
120 Murfreesboro (mûr'frēz-bŭr-ō). Tn. 35·50 N 86·19 W
141 Murgab (R.) (mōōr-gäb'). Sov. Un. 37·07 N 62·32 E
137 Muriaé (mōō-ryȧ-ĕ') Braz. (Rio de Janeiro In.) 21·10 S 42·21 W
137 Muriaé (R.) Braz. (Rio de Janeiro In.) 21·20 S 41·40 W
174 Murino (mōō'rĭ-nô) Sov. Un. (Leningrad In.) 60·03 N 30·28 E
158 Müritz See (L.) (mür'ĭts). G.D.R. 53·20 N 12·33 E
188 Murku Sardyk (Pk.) Sov. Un.-Mong. 51·56 N 100·21 E
170 Murmansk (mōōr-mänsk') Sov. Un. 69·00 N 33·20 E
170 Murom (mōō'rôm) Sov. Un. 55·30 N 42·00 E
194 Muroran (mōō'rô-rän) Jap. 42·21 N 141·05 E
162 Muros (mōō'rōs) Sp. 42·48 N 9·00 W
195 Muroto-Zaki (Pt.) (mōō'rô-tō zä'kē). Jap. 33·14 N 134·12 E
113 Murphy (mŭr'fĭ) Mo. (St. Louis In.) 38·29 N 90·29 W
120 Murphy NC 35·05 N 84·00 W
117 Murphysboro (mŭr'fĭz-bŭr-ō) Il. 37·46 N 89·21 W
120 Murray (mŭr'ĭ) Ky. 36·39 N 88·17 W
113 Murray. Ut. (Salt Lake City In.) 40·40 N 111·53 W
93 Murray (R.) Can. 55·00 N 121·00 W
121 Murray (R.) (mŭr'ĭ) SC 34·07 N 81·18 W
203 Murray Bridge Austl. 35·10 S 139·35 E
98 Murray Harbour Can. 46·00 N 62·31 W
205 Murray Reg. (mŭ'rē) Austl. 33·20 S 142·30 E
203 Murray R. Austl. 34·20 S 142·21 W
158 Mur R. (mōōr) Aus. 47·10 N 14·08 E
203 Murrumbidgee (R.) (mŭr-ŭm-bĭd'jē). Austl. 34·30 S 145·20 E
217 Murrupula Moz. 15·27 S 38·47 E
184 Murshidābād (mōōr'shē-dä-bäd') India 24·08 N 87·11 E
164 Murska Sobota (mōōr'skä sô'bô-tä). Yugo. 46·40 N 16·14 E
217 Muruasigar (Mtn.) Ken. 3·08 N 35·02 E
184 Murwāra India 23·54 N 80·23 E
203 Murwillumbah (mŭr-wĭl'lŭm-bŭ) Austl. 28·15 S 153·30 E
158 Mürz R. (mürts) Aus. 47·30 N 15·21 E
158 Murzzuschlag (mürts'tsōō-shlägh) Aus. 47·37 N 15·41 E
171 Mus (mōōsh) Tur. 38·55 N 41·30 E
165 Musala (Mtn.) Bul. 42·05 N 23·24 E
194 Musan (mōō'sän) Kor. 41·11 N 129·10 E
195 Musashino (mōō-sä'shē-nō) Jap. (Tōkyō In.) 35·43 N 139·35 E
186 Muscat (mŭs-kăt') Om. 23·23 N 58·30 E
Muscat & Oman, see Oman
109 Muscatine (mŭs-kȧ-tēn') Ia. 41·26 N 91·00 W
120 Muscle Shoals (mŭs''l shōlz) Al. 34·44 N 87·38 W
204 Musgrave Ra. (mŭs'grāv). Austl. 26·15 S 131·15 E
212 Mushie (mŭsh'ē) Zaire 3·04 S 16·50 E
215 Mushin Nig. 6·32 N 3·22 E
196 Musi (Strm.) (mōō'sē) Indon. 2·40 S 103·42 E
134 Musinga, Alto (Ht.) (ȧ'l-tô-mōō-sē'n-gä). Col. (In.) 6·40 N 76·13 W
107 Muskego L. (mŭs-kē'gō) Wi. (Milwaukee In.) 42·53 N 88·10 W
104 Muskegon (mŭs-kē'gŭn) Mi. 43·15 N 86·20 W
104 Muskegon (R.) Mi. 43·20 N 85·55 W
104 Muskegon Heights Mi. 43·10 N 86·20 W
104 Muskingum (R.) (mŭs-kĭŋ'gŭm) Oh. 39·45 N 81·55 W
117 Muskogee (mŭs-kō'gē) Ok. 35·44 N 95·21 W
105 Muskoka (L.) (mŭs-kō'kȧ) Can. 45·00 N 79·30 W
217 Musoma Tan. 1·30 S 33·48 E
197 Mussau (I.) (mōō-sä'ōō) Pap. N. Gui. 1·30 S 149·32 E
154 Musselburgh (mŭs''l-bŭr-ô). Scot. 55·55 N 3·08 W
111 Musselshell R. (mŭs''l-shĕl). Mt. 46·25 N 108·20 W
216 Mussende Ang. 10 32 S 16·05 E
216 Mussuma Ang. 14·14 S 21·59 E
171 Mustafakemalpasa Tur. 40·05 N 28·30 E
119 Mustang Bayou Tx. (In.) 29·22 N 95·12 W
116 Mustang Cr. (mŭs'tăng) Tx. 36·22 N 102·46 W
119 Mustang I. Tx. 27·43 N 97·00 W
127 Mustique I. (müs-tēk') St. Vincent (In.) 12·53 N 61·03 W
166 Mustvee (mōōst'vĕ-ĕ). Sov. Un. 58·50 N 26·54 E
189 Musu Dan (C.) (mōō'sōō dän) Kor. 40·51 N 130·00 E
194 Musu Dan (Pt.) (mōō'sōō dän) Kor. 40·48 N 129·50 E
203 Muswellbrook (mŭs'wŭl-brŏŏk) Austl. 32·15 S 150·50 E
192 Mutan (R.) China 45·30 N 129·40 E
192 Mutanchiang China 44·28 N 129·38 E
212 Mutombo Mukulu (mōō-tôm'bō mōō-kōō'lōō). Zaire 8·12 S 23·56 E
194 Mutsu Wan (B.) (mōōt'sōō wän) Jap. 41·20 N 140·55 E
99 Mutton Bay (mŭt''n) Can. 50·48 N 59·02 W
137 Mutum (mōō-tōō'm) Braz. (Rio de Janeiro In.) 19·48 S 41·24 W
172 Muyun-Kum, Peski (Des.) (mōō-yōōn' kōōm'). Sov. Un. 44·30 N 70·00 E
184 Muzaffargarh Pak. 30·09 N 71·15 E
184 Muzaffarpur India 26·13 N 85·20 E
92 Muzon, C. Ak. 54·41 N 132·44 W
118 Muzquiz (mōōz'kēz) Mex. 27·53 N 101·31 W
217 Mvomero Tan. 6·20 S 37·25 E
213 Mvoti (R.) S. Afr. (Natal. In.) 29·18 S 30·52 E
217 Mwanza (mwän'zä) Tan. 2·31 S 32·54 E
212 Mwaya (mwä'yä) Tan. 9·19 S 33·51 E
217 Mwenga Zaire 3·02 S 28·26 E
217 Mweru (L.) Zaire-Zambia 8·50 S 28·50 E
217 Mwingi Ken. 0·56 S 38·04 E
152 Mya R. (myä') Alg. 29·26 N 3·15 E
188 Myingyan (myĭng-yŭn') Bur. 21·37 N 95·26 E
196 Myinmoletkat (Pk.) Bur. 13·58 N 98·34 E
188 Myitkyina (myĭ'chē-nȧ) Bur. 25·33 N 97·25 E
159 Myjava (mûē'yȧ-vä) Czech. 48·45 N 17·33 E
194 Myohyang San (Mtn.) (myō'hyang). Kor. 40·00 N 126·12 E
150 Mýrdalsjökull (Gl.) (mür'däls-yû'kōōl). Ice. 63·34 N 18·04 W
121 Myrtle Beach (mûr't'l) SC 33·42 N 78·53 W
110 Myrtle Point Or. 43·04 N 124·08 W
166 Myshkino (mêsh'kē-nō). Sov. Un. 57·48 N 38·21 E
185 Mysore (mī-sōr') India 12·31 N 76·42 E
157 Mysovka (mē' sôf-kȧ). Sov. Un. 55·11 N 21·17 E
109 Mystic (mĭs'tĭk) Ia. 40·47 N 92·54 W
174 Mytishchi (mē-tēsh'chi) Sov. Un. (Moscow In.) 55·55 N 37·46 E
217 Mziha Tan. 5·54 S 37·47 E
217 Mzimba ('m-zĭm'bä) Malawi 11·52 S 33·34 E
213 Mzimkulu (R.). S. Afr. (Natal In.) 30·12 S 29·57 E
213 Mzimvubu (R.). S. Afr. (Natal In.) 31·22 S 29·20 E
217 Mzuzu Malawi 11·30 S 34·10 E

N

158 Naab R. (näp) F.R.G. 49·38 N 12·15 E
149 Naaldwijk. Neth. (Amsterdam In.) 52·00 N 4·11 E
100 Naalehu Hi. 19·00 N 155·35 W
157 Naantali (nän'tȧ-lê) Fin. 60·29 N 22·03 E
204 Nabberu (L.) (năb'ēr-ōō) Austl. 26·05 S 120·35 E
210 Nabeul (nā-bûl') Tun. 36·34 N 10·45 E
217 Nabiswera Ug. 1·28 N 32·16 E
218 Naboomspruit S. Afr. (Johannesburg & Pretoria In.) 24·32 S 28·43 E
183 Nābulus. Jordan (Palestine In.) 32·13 N 35·16 E
217 Nacala (nă-kȧ'lȧ) Moz. 14·34 S 40·41 E
126 Nacaome (nä-kä-ō'mȧ) Hond. 13·32 N 87·28 W
152 Naceur, Bou Mt. Mor. 33·50 N 3·55 W
193 Na Cham (nä chäm') Viet. 22·02 N 106·30 E
110 Naches R. (năch'ĕz) Wa. 46·51 N 121·03 W
158 Náchod (näk'ôt) Czech. 50·25 N 16·08 E
114 Nacimiento (R.) (nȧ-sĭ-myĕn'tô) Ca. 35·50 N 121·00 W
119 Nacogdoches (năk'ō-dō'chĕz). Tx. 31·36 N 94·40 W
118 Nadadores (nä-dä-dō'rās) Mex. 27·04 N 101·36 W
184 Nadiād India 22·45 N 72·51 E
123 Nadir Vir. Is. (U. S. A.) (St. Thomas In.) 18·19 N 64·53 W
165 Nădlac Rom. 46·09 N 20·52 E
Nad Nisou, see Jablonec
Nad Váhom, see Nové Mesto
159 Nadvornaya (näd-vōōr'nȧ-yȧ) Sov. Un. 48·37 N 24·35 E
172 Nadym (R.) (nȧ'dĭm) Sov. Un. 64·30 N 72·48 E
156 Naestved (nĕst'vĭdh) Den. 55·14 N 11·46 E
215 Nafada Nig. 11·08 N 11·20 E
218 Nafishah Egypt (Suez In.) 30·34 N 32·15 E
187 Nafūd ad Daḩy (Des.) Sau. Ar. 22·15 N 44·15 E
197 Naga (nä'gä) Phil. (In.) 13·37 N 123·12 E
195 Naga (I.) Jap. 32·09 N 130·16 E
195 Nagahama (nä'gä-hä'mä) Jap. 33·32 N 132·29 E
195 Nagahama Jap. 35·23 N 136·16 E
188 Nagaland (State) India 25·47 N 94·15 E
195 Nagano (nä'gä-nô) Jap. 36·42 N 138·12 E
195 Nagaoka (nä'gä-ō'kȧ) Jap. 37·22 N 138·49 E
195 Nagaoka Jap. (Ōsaka In.) 34·54 N 135·42 E
185 Nāgappattinam India 10·48 N 79·51 E
126 Nagarote (nä-gä-rô'tĕ) Nic. 12·17 N 86·35 W
195 Nagasaki (nä'gȧ-sä'kē) Jap. 32·48 N 129·53 E
184 Nāgaur India 27·19 N 73·41 E
174 Nagaybakskiy (nȧ-gáy-bäk'skĭ) Sov. Un. (Urals In.) 53·33 N 59·33 E
197 Nagcarlan (näg-kär-län') Phil. (In.) 14·07 N 121·24 E
185 Nāgercoil India 8·15 N 77·29 E
171 Nagornokarabakh (Reg.) (nu-gôr'nŭ-kŭ-rŭ-bäk'). Sov. Un. 40·10 N 46·50 E
195 Nagoya (nä'gō'yȧ) Jap. 35·09 N 136·53 E
184 Nāgpur (näg'pōōr) India 21·12 N 79·09 E
129 Nagua (nȧ'gwä) Dom. Rep. 19·20 N 69·40 W
197 Naguilian (nä-gwē-lē'än) Phil. (In.) 16·33 N 120·23 E
158 Nagykanizsa (nôd'y'kô'nê-shô) Hung. 46·27 N 17·00 E
159 Nagykōrōs (nôd'y'kŭ-rŭsh). Hung. 47·02 N 19·46 E
189 Naha (nä'hä) Jap. 26·02 N 127·43 E
90 Nahanni Natl. Pk. Can. 62·10 N 125·15 W
99 Nahant (nȧ-hănt) Ma. (In.) 42·26 N 70·55 W
183 Nahariyya. Isr. (Palestine In.) 33·01 N 35·06 E
171 Nahr al Khābur (R.) Syr. 35·50 N 41·00 E
163 Nahr-Ouassel (R.) (när-wä-sĕl') Alg. 35 30 N 1·55 E
136 Nahuel Huapi (L.) (nä'wål wä'pē) Arg. 41·00 S 71·30 W
126 Nahuizalco (nä-wē-zäl'kō) Sal. 13·50 N 89·43 W
197 Naic (nä-ēk) Phil. (In.) 14·20 N 120·46 E
118 Naica (nä-ē'kä) Mex. 27·53 N 105·30 W
135 Naiguatá (nī-gwä-tá'). Ven. (In.) 10·37 N 66·44 W
135 Naiguata, Pico (Mtn.) (pē'kô) Ven. (In.) 10·32 N 66·44 W
184 Naihāti India (In.) 22·54 N 88·25 E
91 Nain (nīn) Can. 56·29 N 61·52 W
154 Nairn (nârn) Scot. 57·35 N 3·54 W
217 Nairobi (nī-rō'bē) Ken. 1·17 S 36·49 E
213 Naivasha (nī-vä'shȧ) Ken. 0·47 S 36·29 E
186 Najd (Des.) Sau. Ar. 25·18 N 42·38 E
218 Naj 'Ḩammādī (näg'hä-mä'dē) Egypt (Nile In.) 26·02 N 32·12 E
194 Najin (nä'jĭn) Kor. 42·04 N 130·35 E
186 Najran (Des.) (nŭj-rän'). Sau. Ar. 17·29 N 45·30 E
194 Naju (nä'jōō) Kor. 35·02 N 126·42 E
128 Najusa (R.) (nä-hōō'sä) Cuba 21·55 N 77·55 W
192 Nakadorishima (I.) (nä'kä'dô'rê-shê'mä). Jap. 33·00 N 128·20 E
195 Nakatsu (nä'käts-ōō) Jap. 33·34 N 131·10 E
171 Nakhichevan (nȧ-kĕ-chĕ-vän') Sov. Un. 39·10 N 45·30 E

ng-sing; ŋ-baŋk; N-nasalized n; nŏd; cŏmmit; ōld; ôbey; ôrder; fōōd; fŏŏt; ou-out; s-soft; sh-dish; th-thin; pūre; ûnite; ûrn; stŭd; circŭs; ü-as "y" in study; '-indeterminate vowel.

318 Nakhodka — Negros PRONOUNCING INDEX

Page	Name Pronunciation Region	Lat. °′	Long. °′
173	Nakhodka (nŭ-kôt′kŭ) Sov. Un.	43·03 N	133·08 E
196	Nakhon Ratchasima Thai.	14·56 N	102·14 E
196	Nakhon Si Thammarat Thai.	8·27 N	99·58 E
156	Nakskov (näk′skou) Den.	54·51 N	11·06 E
159	Nakto nad Notecia (näk′wō näd nō-tĕ′chōn) Pol.	53·10 N	17·35 E
194	Naktong (R.) (näk′tŭng) Kor.	36·10 N	128·30 E
171	Nal′chik (nål-chēk′) Sov. Un.	43·30 N	43·35 E
162	Nalón (R.) (nä-lōn′) Sp.	43·15 N	5·38 W
210	Nālūt (nä-lo͞ot′) Libya	31·51 N	10·49 E
186	Namak, Daryacheh-ye (L.) Iran	34·58 N	51·33 E
109	Namakan (L.) (nă′mȧ-kăn) Mn.	48·20 N	92·43 W
186	Namakzār-e Shāhdād (L.) (nŭ-mŭk-zär′) Iran	31·00 N	58·30 E
172	Namangan (nȧ-mån-gän′) Sov. Un.	41·08 N	71·59 E
89	Namao Can. (Edmonton In.)	53·43 N	113·30 W
197	Namatanai (nä′mä-tȧ-nä′ē) Pap. N. Gui.	3·43 S	152·26 E
115	Nambe Pueblo Ind. Res. (näm′bā pwĕb′lô) NM	35·52 N	105·39 W
203	Nambour (năm′bo͞or) Austl.	26·48 S	153·00 E
196	Nam Dinh (näm dēnk′) Viet.	20·30 N	106·10 E
217	Nametil Moz.	15·43 S	39·21 E
194	Namhae (I.) (näm′hī′) Kor.	34·23 N	128·05 E
212	Namib Des. (nä-mēb′) Namibia	18·45 S	12·45 E
209	Namibia Afr.	19·30 S	16·13 E
203	Namoi (R.) (năm′oi) Austl.	30·10 S	148·43 E
152	Namous, Oued en (R.) (nȧ-mo͞os′) Alg.	31·48 N	00·19 W
110	Nampa (năm′pȧ) Id.	43·35 N	116·35 W
192	Namp′o Kor.	38·47 N	125·28 E
217	Nampuecha Moz.	13·59 S	40·18 E
217	Nampula Moz.	15·07 S	39·15 E
150	Namsos (näm′sôs) Nor.	64·28 N	11·14 E
184	Nam Tsho (L.) China	30·30 N	91·10 E
92	Namu Can.	51·03 N	127·50 W
217	Namuli, Serra (Mts.) Moz.	15·05 S	37·05 E
155	Namur (nȧ-mür′) Bel.	50·29 N	4·55 E
212	Namutoni (nä-mo͞o-tō′nē) Namibia	18·45 S	17·00 E
196	Nan, Mae Nam (R.) Thai.	18·11 N	100·29 E
125	Nanacamilpa (nä-nä-kä-mē′l-pä) Mex. (In.)	19·30 N	98·33 W
92	Nanaimo (nȧ-nī′mō) Can.	49·10 N	123·56 W
194	Nanam (nä′nän′) Kor.	41·38 N	129·37 E
195	Nanao (nä′nä-ō) Jap.	37·03 N	136·59 E
193	Nanao Tao (I.) (nä′nä-ō dou) China	23·30 N	117·30 E
193	Nanch′ang (nän′chäng′) China	28·38 N	115·48 E
193	Nancheng China	26·50 N	116·40 E
190	Nanch′enghuang Tai (I.) (nan′chĕng′ho͞oäng′dou) China	38·22 N	120·54 E
190	Nanching (Nanking) (nän′jĭng) (nän′kĭng) China	32·04 N	118·46 E
193	Nanch′ung China	30·45 N	106·05 E
161	Nancy (nän-sē′) Fr.	48·42 N	6·11 E
106	Nancy Cr. (năn′cē) Ga. (Atlanta In.)	33·51 N	84·25 W
184	Nanda Devi (Mt.) (nän′dä dā′vē) India	30·30 N	80·25 E
184	Nānded India	19·13 N	77·21 E
184	Nandurbār India	21·29 N	74·13 E
185	Nandyāl India	15·54 N	78·09 E
184	Nanga Parbat Pak.	35·20 N	74·35 E
184	Nangi India (In.)	22·30 N	88·14 E
161	Nangis (nän-zhē′) Fr. (Paris In.)	48·33 N	3·01 E
216	Nangweshi Zambia	16·26 S	23·17 E
191	Nanhsiang China (Shanghai In.)	31·17 N	121·17 E
193	Nanhsiung China	25·10 N	114·20 E
191	Nanhui China (Shanghai In.)	31·03 N	121·45 E
193	Naniana China	35·14 N	116·24 E
193	Nani Dinh Viet.	20·25 N	106·08 E
190	Nani Hu (L.) (nän′yi′ ho͞o) China	31·12 N	119·05 E
	Nanking, see Nanching		
190	Nankung (nän′ko͞ong′) China	37·22 N	115·22 E
193	Nan Ling (Mts.) China	25·15 N	111·40 E
190	Nanlo (nän′lō′) China	36·03 N	115·13 E
204	Nannine (nă-nēn′) Austl.	26·50 S	118·30 E
193	Nanning (nän′nĭng′) China	22·56 N	108·10 E
193	Nanp′an (R.) China	24·50 N	105·30 E
193	Nanp′ing China	26·40 N	118·05 E
189	Nansei-shotō (Ryukyu Islands) Jap.	27·30 N	127·00 E
106	Nansemond (năn′sê-mŭnd) Va. (Norfolk In.)	36·46 N	76·32 W
106	Nansemond R. Va. (Norfolk In.)	36·50 N	76·34 W
188	Nan Shan (Mts.) (nän′shän′) China	38·43 N	98·00 E
195	Nantai Zan (Mtn.) (nän-täê zän) Jap.	36·47 N	139·28 E
160	Nantes (nänt′) Fr.	47·13 N	1·37 W
161	Nanteuil-le-Haudouin (nän-tû-lĕ-ō-dwăn′) Fr. (Paris In.)	49·08 N	2·49 E
105	Nanticoke (năn′tĭ-kōk) Pa.	41·10 N	76·00 W
105	Nantucket (I.) (năn-tŭk′ĕt) Ma.	41·15 N	70·05 W
190	Nantung (nän′to͞ong′) China	32·02 N	120·51 E
148	Nantwich (nănt′wĭch) Eng.	53·04 N	2·31 W
192	Nanyang China	33·00 N	112·42 E
192	Nanyüan China (In.)	39·48 N	116·24 E
190	Nanyün (nän′yün′) China	38·11 N	116·37 E
193	Nao Chou (I.) China	20·58 N	110·58 E
125	Naolinco (nä-ō-lēn′kō) Mex.	19·39 N	96·50 W
165	Náousa (nä′o͞o-sȧ) Grc.	40·38 N	22·05 E
114	Napa (năp′ȧ) Ca.	38·20 N	122·17 W
105	Napanee (năp′ȧ-nē) Can.	44·15 N	77·00 W
107	Naperville (nā′pēr-vĭl) Il. (Chicago In.)	41·46 N	88·09 W
205	Napier (nā′pĭ-ēr) N. Z. (In.)	39·30 S	177·00 E
89	Napierville (nā′pĭ-ēr-vĭl) Can. (Montreal In.)	45·11 N	73·24 W
121	Naples (nā′p′lz) Fl. (In.)	26·07 N	81·46 W
	Naples, see Napoli		
134	Napo (R.) (nä′pō) Peru	1·49 S	74·20 W
104	Napoleon (nȧ-pō′lē-ŭn) Oh.	41·20 N	84·10 W
119	Napoleonville (nȧ-pō′lē-ŭn-vĭl) La.	29·56 N	91·03 W
163	Napoli (Naples) (nä′pô-lē) It. (Naples In.)	40·37 N	14·12 E
163	Napoli, Golfo di (G.) (gôl-fô-dē) It. (Naples In.)	40·29 N	14·08 E
104	Nappanee (năp′ȧ-nē) In.	41·30 N	86·00 W
195	Nara (nä′rä) Jap. (Ōsaka In.)	34·41 N	135·50 E
210	Nara Mali	15·09 N	7·27 W
195	Nara (Pref.) Jap. (Ōsaka In.)	34·36 N	135·49 E
166	Nara (R.) Sov. Un.	55·05 N	37·16 E
203	Naracoorte (nȧ-rȧ-ko͞on′tē) Austl.	36·50 S	140·50 E
185	Narasapur India	16·32 N	81·43 E
195	Narashino Jap. (Tōkyō In.)	35·41 N	140·01 E
106	Narberth (när′bûrth) Pa. (Philadelphia In.)	40·01 N	75·17 W
160	Narbonne (nȧr-bôn′) Fr.	43·12 N	3·00 E
165	Nardò (när-dô′) It.	40·11 N	18·02 E
134	Nare (nä′rĕ) Col. (In.)	6·12 N	74·37 W
159	Narew R. (nä′rĕf) Pol.	52·43 N	21·19 E
184	Narmada (R.) India	22·17 N	74·45 E
166	Naroch′ (L.) (nä′rôch) Sov. Un.	54·51 N	27·00 E
170	Narodnaya, Gora (Mtn.) (nȧ-rôd′nȧ-yȧ) Sov. Un.	65·10 N	60·10 E
166	Naro Fominsk (nä′rō-fô-mĕnsk′) Sov. Un.	55·23 N	36·43 E
157	Närpeså (R.) Fin.	62·35 N	21·24 E
202	Narrabeen (năr-ȧ-bĭn) Austl. (Sydney In.)	33·44 S	151·18 E
106	Narragansett (năr-ȧ-găn′sĕt) RI (Providence In.)	41·26 N	71·27 W
105	Narragansett B. RI	41·20 N	71·15 W
203	Narrandera (nȧ-rȧn-dē′rȧ) Austl.	34·40 S	146·40 E
204	Narrogin (năr′ô-gĭn) Austl.	33·00 S	117·15 E
166	Narva (nȧr′vȧ) Sov. Un.	59·24 N	28·12 E
197	Narvacan (när-vä-kän′) Phil. (In.)	17·27 N	120·29 E
166	Narva Jõesuu (nȧr′vȧ o͞o-ô-ä′so͞o-o͞o) Sov. Un.	59·26 N	28·02 E
150	Narvik (när′vêk) Nor.	68·21 N	17·18 E
157	Narvskiy Zaliv (B.) (nȧr′vskĭ zä′lĭf) Sov. Un.	59·35 N	27·25 E
170	Nar′yan-Mar (när′yȧn mär′) Sov. Un.	67·42 N	53·30 E
203	Naryilco (năr-ĭl′kô) Austl.	28·40 S	141·50 E
172	Narym (nä-rēm′) Sov. Un.	58·47 N	82·05 E
187	Naryn (R.) (nŭ-rĭn′) Sov. Un.	41·46 N	73·00 E
148	Naseby (nāz′bĭ) Eng.	52·23 N	0·59 W
113	Nashua (năsh′ŭ-ȧ) Mo. (Kansas City In.)	39·18 N	94·34 W
99	Nashua NH (In.)	42·47 N	71·23 W
117	Nashville (năsh′vĭl) Ar.	33·56 N	93·50 W
120	Nashville Ga.	31·12 N	83·15 W
117	Nashville Il.	38·21 N	89·42 W
104	Nashville Mi.	42·35 N	85·05 W
120	Nashville Tn.	36·10 N	86·48 W
109	Nashwauk (năsh′wôk) Mn.	47·21 N	93·12 W
165	Našice (nä′shē-tsĕ) Yugo.	45·29 N	18·06 E
159	Nasielsk (nä′syĕlsk) Pol.	52·35 N	20·50 E
170	Näsijärvi (L.) (nĕ′sē-yĕr′vē) Fin.	61·42 N	24·05 E
184	Nāsik (nä′sĭk) India	20·02 N	73·49 E
211	Nāşir (nä-zēr′) Sud.	8·30 N	33·06 E
	Nāşir, Buhayrat, see Nasser, L.		
184	Nasirābād Bngl.	24·48 N	90·28 E
184	Nasirabād India	26·13 N	74·48 E
91	Naskaupi (R.) (näs′kô-pĭ) Can.	53·59 N	61·10 W
216	′Nasondoye Zaire	10·22 S	25·06 E
92	Nass (R.) (năs) Can.	55·00 N	129·30 W
128	Nassau (năs′ô) Ba.	25·05 N	77·20 W
149	Nassenheide (nä′sĕn-hī-dĕ) G.D.R. (Berlin In.)	52·49 N	13·13 E
218	Nasser, L. (Nāşir, Buḥayrat) Egypt (Nile In.)	23·50 N	32·50 E
156	Nässjö (nĕs′shû) Swe.	57·39 N	14·39 E
197	Nasugbu (nȧ-so͞og-bo͞o′) Phil. (In.)	14·05 N	120·37 E
118	Nasworthy L. (năz′wûr-thê) Tx.	31·17 N	100·30 W
193	Nata China	19·30 N	109·38 E
127	Natá (nä-tȧ′) Pan.	8·20 N	80·30 W
134	Natagaima (nä-tä-gī′mä) Col. (In.)	3·38 N	75·07 W
135	Natal (nä-täl′) Braz.	6·00 S	35·13 W
212	Natal (Prov.) (nȧ-täl′) S. Afr.	28·50 S	30·07 E
99	Natashquan (nä-täsh′kwän) Can.	50·11 N	61·49 W
99	Natashquan (R.) Can.	50·35 N	61·35 W
120	Natchez (năch′ĕz) Ms.	1·35 N	91·20 W
119	Natchitoches (năk′ĭ-tŏsh) (nȧch-ĭ-tōsh′) La.	31·46 N	93·06 W
99	Natick (nā′tĭk) Ma. (In.)	42·17 N	71·21 W
173	National Area (Reg.) Sov. Un.	66·30 N	170·30 E
111	National Bison Ra. (Mts.) (năsh′ŭn-ăl bī′s′n) Mt.	47·18 N	113·58 W
114	National City Ca. (In.)	32·38 N	117·01 W
214	Natitingou Benin	10·19 N	1·22 E
135	Natividade (nä-tē-vē-dä′dĕ) Braz.	11·43 S	47·34 W
217	Natron, L. (nā′trŏn) Tan.	2·17 S	36·10 E
107	Natrona Hts. (nā′trō nȧ) Pa. (Pittsburgh In.)	40·38 N	79·43 W
218	Naṭrūn, Wādī an. Egypt (Nile In.)	30·33 N	30·12 E
196	Natuna Besar, Kepulauan (Is.) Indon.	3·22 N	108·00 E
115	Natural Bridges Natl. Mon. (năt′ū-răl brĭj′ĕs) Ut.	37·20 N	110·20 W
204	Naturaliste, C. (nät-ū-rȧ-lĭst′) Austl.	33·30 S	115·10 E
125	Naucalpan (nä′o͞o-käl-pȧ′n) Mex. (In.)	19·28 N	99·14 W
125	Nauchampatepetl (Mtn.) (näo͞o-chäm-pä-tĕ′pĕtl) Mex.	19·32 N	97·09 W
149	Nauen (nou′ĕn) G.D.R. (Berlin In.)	52·36 N	12·53 E
105	Naugatuck (nô′gȧ-tŭk) Ct.	41·25 N	73·05 W
197	Naujan (nä-o͞o-hän′) Phil. (In.)	13·19 N	121·17 E
158	Naumburg (noum′bo͞orgh) G.D.R.	51·10 N	11·50 E
198	Nauru Oceania	0·30 S	167·00 E
125	Nautla (nä-o͞ot′lä) Mex.	20·14 N	96·44 W
118	Nava (nä′vä) Mex.	28·25 N	100·44 W
162	Nava, L. de la Sp.	42·05 N	4·42 W
162	Nava del Rey (nä-vä dĕl rā′ē) Sp.	41·22 N	5·04 W
162	Navahermosa (nä-vä-ĕr-mō′sä) Sp.	39·39 N	4·28 W
128	Navajas (nä-vä-häs′) Cuba	22·40 N	81·20 W
115	Navajo Ind. Res. (năv′ȧ-hō) Az.-NM	36·31 N	109·24 W
115	Navajo Natl. Mon. Az.	36·43 N	110·39 W
115	Navajo Res. NM	36·57 N	107·26 W
163	Navalcarnero (nä-väl′kär-nā′rō) Sp. (Madrid In.)	40·17 N	4·05 W
162	Navalmoral de la Mata (nä-väl′mōräl′ dā lä mä′tä) Sp.	39·53 N	5·32 W
89	Navan (nă′vȧn) Can. (Ottawa In.)	45·25 N	75·26 W
136	Navarino (nä-vä-rē′nô) (I.) Chile	55·30 S	68·15 W
162	Navarra (Reg.) (nä-vär′rä) Sp.	42·40 N	1·35 W
137	Navarro (nä-vȧ′r-rō) Arg. (Buenos Aires In.)	35·00 S	59·16 W
119	Navasota (năv-ȧ-sō′tȧ) Tx.	30·24 N	96·05 W
119	Navasota R. Tx.	31·03 N	96·11 W
129	Navassa (I.) (nȧ-văs′ȧ) N. A.	18·25 N	75·15 W
162	Navia (R.) (nä-vē′ä) Sp.	43·10 N	6·45 W
137	Navidad (nä-vê-dä′d) Chile (Santiago In.)	34·57 S	71·51 W
129	Navidad Bk. (nä-vê-dädh′) Ba.	20·05 N	69·00 W
137	Navidade do Carangola (nȧ-vē-dä′dĕ-dô-kȧ-rän-gô′la) Braz. (Rio de Janeiro In.)	21·04 S	41·58 W
122	Navojoa (nä-vô-kô′ä) Mex.	27·00 N	109·40 W
165	Návplion Grc.	37·33 N	22·46 E
184	Nawābshāh (nȧ-wäb′shä) Pak.	26·20 N	68·30 E
165	Náxos (I.) (nȧk′sôs) Grc.	37·15 N	25·20 E
122	Nayarit (State) (nä-yä-rēt′) Mex.	22·00 N	105·15 W
124	Nayarit, Sierra de (Mts.) (sē-ĕ′r-rä-dĕ) Mex.	23·20 N	105·07 W
214	Naye Senegal	14·25 N	12·12 W
108	Naylor (nā′lŏr) Md. (Baltimore In.)	38·43 N	76·46 W
135	Nazaré (nä-zä-rĕ′) Braz.	13·04 S	38·49 W
162	Nazaré (nä-zä-rā′) Port.	39·38 N	9·04 W
135	Nazaré da Mata (dä-mä-tä) Braz.	7·46 S	35·13 W
118	Nazas (nä′zäs) Mex.	25·14 N	104·08 W
118	Nazas, R. Mex.	25·08 N	104·20 W
183	Nazerat Isr. (Palestine In.)	32·43 N	35·19 E
171	Nazilli (nȧ-zĭ-lē′) Tur.	37·40 N	28·10 E
174	Naziya R. (nȧ-zē′yȧ) Sov. Un. (Leningrad In.)	59·48 N	31·18 E
92	Nazko (R.) Can.	52·35 N	123·10 W
215	Ndali Benin	9·51 N	2·43 E
211	Ndélé (n′dā-lā′) Cen. Afr. Emp.	8·21 N	20·43 E
215	Ndikiniméki Cam.	4·46 N	10·50 E
215	Ndjamena (Fort-Lamy) (lȧ-mē′) Chad	12·07 N	15·03 E
212	Ndjolé (n′dzhô-lā′) Gabon	0·15 S	10·45 E
217	Ndola (n′dō′lä) Zambia	12·58 S	28·38 E
217	Ndoto Mts. Ken.	1·55 N	37·05 E
214	Ndrhamcha, Sebkha de (L.) Mauritania	18·50 N	15·15 W
217	Nduye Zaire	1·50 N	29·01 E
154	Neagh Lough (L.) (lŏk nā) N. Ire.	54·40 N	6·47 W
183	Néa Páfos. Cyprus (Palestine In.)	34·46 N	32·27 E
202	Neapean (R.) Austl. (Sydney In.)	33·40 S	150·39 E
165	Neápolis (nå-ŏp′ ô-lĭs) Grc.	36·35 N	23·08 E
164	Neápolis Grc. (In.)	35·17 N	25·37 E
101	Near Is. (nēr) Ak.	52·20 N	172·40 E
154	Neath (nēth) Wales	51·41 N	3·50 W
203	Nebine Cr. (nĕ-bēne′) Austl.	27·50 S	147·00 E
171	Nebit-Dag (nyĕ-bēt′däg′) Sov. Un.	39·30 N	54·20 E
102	Nebraska (State) (nê-brăs′kȧ) U. S.	41·45 N	101·30 W
117	Nebraska City Ne.	40·40 N	95·50 W
92	Nechako Plat. (nĭ-chă′kō) Can.	54·00 N	124·30 W
92	Nechako Ra. Can.	53·20 N	124·30 W
92	Nechako Res. Can.	53·25 N	125·10 W
92	Nechako (R.) Can.	52·45 N	124·55 W
119	Neches R. (nĕch′ĕz) Tx.	31·03 N	94·40 W
158	Neckar R. (nĕk′är) F.R.G.	49·16 N	9·06 E
136	Necochea (nā-kô-chā′ä) Arg.	38·30 S	58·45 W
167	Nedrigaylov (nĕ-drĭ-gī′lôf) Sov. Un.	50·49 N	33·52 E
99	Needham (nēd′ăm) Ma. (In.)	42·17 N	71·14 W
114	Needles (nē′d′lz) Ca.	34·51 N	114·39 W
109	Neenah (nē′nȧ) Wi.	44·10 N	88·30 W
95	Neepawa Can.	50·13 N	99·29 W
116	Nee Res. (nē) Co.	38·26 N	102·56 W
155	Neetze (R.) (nā′tzē) F.R.G.	53·04 N	11·00 E
195	Negareyama (nā′gä-rȧ-yä′mä) Jap. (Tōkyō In.)	35·52 N	139·54 E
109	Negaunee (nê-gô′nē) Mi.	46·30 N	87·37 W
183	Negeri Sembilan (State) (nā′grē-sĕm-bē-län′) Mala. (Singapore In.)	2·46 N	101·54 E
183	Negev (Des.) (nĕ′gĕv) Isr. (Palestine In.)	30·34 N	34·43 E
165	Negoi (Mtn.) (nā-goi′) Rom.	45·33 N	24·38 E
185	Negombo Sri Lanka	7·39 N	79·49 E
165	Negotin (nĕ′gô-tēn) Yugo.	44·13 N	22·33 E
196	Negrais, C. (nĕ′grĭs) Bur.	16·08 N	93·34 E
136	Negro (R.) Arg.	39·50 S	65·00 W
134	Negro, Rio (R.) (rē′ō nā′gro͞o) Braz.	0·18 S	63·21 W
162	Negro, C. (na′grô) Mor.	35·25 N	4·51 W
127	Negro, Cerro (Mt.) (sĕ′r-rô-nā′grô) Pan.	8·44 N	80·37 W
137	Negro (R.) Ur. (Buenos Aires In.)	33·17 S	58·18 W
126	Negro R. Nic.	13·01 N	87·10 W
196	Negros (I.) (nā′grōs) Phil.	9·50 N	121·45 E

ăt; finăl; rāte; senāte; ärm; åsk; sofȧ; fâre; ch-choose; dh-as th in other; bē; ėvent; bĕt; recĕnt; cratẽr; g-go; gh-guttural g; bĭt; ĭ-short neutral; rīde; K-guttural k as ch in German ich;

Page	Name Pronunciation Region	Lat. °′	Long. °′
134	Neguá (nā-gwä′) Col. (In.)	5·51 N	76·36 W
110	Nehalem R. (nē-hăl′ĕm) Or.	45·52 N	123·37 W
161	Neheim-Hüsten (nĕ′hīm) F.R.G. (Ruhr In.)	51·28 N	7·58 E
129	Neiba (nå-ē′bä) Dom. Rep.	18·30 N	71·20 W
129	Neiba, Bahai de (B.) (bä-ä′ē-dě) Dom. Rep.	18·10 N	71·00 W
129	Neiba, Sierra de (Mts.) (sē-ĕr′rä-dě) Dom. Rep.	18·40 N	71·40 W
193	Neichiang China	29·38 N	105·01 E
190	Neich′iu (nā′chĭō) China	37·17 N	114·32 E
111	Neihart (nī′hârt) Mt.	46·54 N	110·39 W
109	Neillsville (nēlz′vĭl) Wi.	44·35 N	90·37 W
134	Neira (nā′rä) Col. (In.)	5·10 N	75·32 W
158	Neisse (R.) (nēs) Pol.	51·30 N	15·00 E
134	Neiva (nå-ē′vä) (nā′vä) Col. (In.)	2·55 N	75·16 W
211	Nekemte Eth.	9·09 N	36·29 E
109	Nekoosa (nē-kōō′sȧ) Wi.	44·19 N	89·54 W
156	Neksø (něk′sû) Den.	55·05 N	15·05 E
108	Neligh (nē′lĭg) Ne.	42·06 N	98·02 W
173	Nel′kan (něl-kän′) Sov. Un.	57·45 N	136·36 E
185	Nellore (něl-lōr′) India	14·28 N	79·59 E
194	Nel′ma (něl-mä′) Sov. Un.	47·34 N	139·05 E
93	Nelson (něl′sŭn) Can.	49·29 N	117·17 W
148	Nelson Eng.	53·50 N	2·13 W
205	Nelson N. Z. (In.)	41·15 S	173·22 E
101	Nelson (I.) Ak.	60·38 N	164·42 W
203	Nelson, C. Austl.	38·29 S	141·20 E
95	Nelson (R.) Can.	56·50 N	93·40 W
114	Nelson Cr. Nv.	40·22 N	114·43 W
104	Nelsonville (něl′sŭn-vĭl) Oh.	39·30 N	82·15 W
214	Néma (nā′mä) Mauritania	16·37 N	7·15 W
113	Nemadji R. (nē-măd′jē) Wi. (Duluth In.)	46·33 N	92·16 W
157	Neman (ŋě′-mån) Sov. Un.	55·02 N	22·01 E
159	Neman R. Sov. Un.	53·28 N	24·45 E
215	Nembe Nig.	4·35 N	6·26 E
94	Nemeiban L. (nĕ-mē′bȧn) Can.	55·20 N	105·20 W
167	Nemirov (nyå-mē′rôf) Sov. Un.	48·56 N	28·51 E
160	Nemours Fr.	48·16 N	2·41 E
194	Nemuro (nā′mōō-rō) Jap.	43·13 N	145·10 E
194	Nemuro Str. Jap.	43·07 N	145·10 E
148	Nen (R.) (něn) Eng.	52·32 N	0·19 W
154	Nenagh (nē′nȧ) Ire.	52·50 N	8·05 W
101	Nenana (nå-nä′nȧ) Ak.	64·28 N	149·18 W
192	Nenchiang China	49·02 N	125·15 E
189	Nen Chiang (R.) China	47·07 N	123·28 E
190	Nengcheng China	33·15 N	116·34 E
174	Nenikyul′ (nē-nyē′kyûl) Sov. Un. (Leningrad In.)	59·26 N	30·40 E
117	Neodesha (nē-ô-dē-shô′) Ks.	37·24 N	95·41 W
117	Neosho Mo.	36·51 N	94·22 W
117	Neosho (R.) (nē-ō′shō) Ks.	38·07 N	95·40 W
182	Nepal (nĕ-pôl′) Asia	28·45 N	83·00 E
115	Nephi (nē′fī) Ut.	39·40 N	111·50 W
98	Nepisiguit (R.) (nĭ-pĭ′sĭ-kwĭt) Can.	47·25 N	66·28 W
137	Nepomuceno (nĕ-pô-mōō-sĕ′no) Braz. (Rio de Janeiro In.)	21·15 S	45·13 W
164	Nera (R.) (nā′rä) It.	42·45 N	12·54 E
160	Nérac (nā-rák′) Fr.	44·08 N	0·19 E
173	Nerchinsk (nyĕr′chĕnsk) Sov. Un.	51·47 N	116·17 E
173	Nerchinskiy Khrebet (Mts.) Sov. Un.	50·30 N	118·30 E
173	Nerchinskiy Zavod (nyĕr′chĕn-skĭzå-vôt′) Sov. Un.	51·35 N	119·46 E
166	Nerekhta (nyĕ-rĕĸ′tà) Sov. Un.	57·29 N	40·34 E
165	Neretva (R.) (nĕ′rĕt-vå) Yugo.	43·08 N	17·50 E
162	Nerja (nĕr′hä) Sp.	36·45 N	3·53 W
166	Nerl′ (R.) (nyĕrl) Sov. Un.	56·59 N	37·57 E
174	Nerskaya R. (nyĕr′skå-yå) Sov. Un. (Moscow In.)	55·31 N	38·46 E
166	Nerussa (R.) (nyå-rōō′så) Sov. Un.	52·24 N	34·20 E
154	Ness, Loch (L.) (lŏĸ nĕs) Scot.	57·23 N	4·20 W
116	Ness City (nĕs) Ks.	38·27 N	99·55 W
159	Nesterov (ŋěs′-tzhyé-rôf) Sov. Un.	50·03 N	23·58 E
157	Nesterov (nyěs-tă′rôf) Sov. Un.	54·39 N	22·38 E
165	Néstos (R.) (nās′tōs) Grc.	41·25 N	24·12 E
166	Nesvizh (nyěs′vēsh) Sov. Un.	53·13 N	26·44 E
183	Netanya Isr. (Palestine In.)	32·19 N	34·52 E
106	Netcong (nĕt′cŏnj) NJ (New York In.)	40·54 N	74·42 W
146	Netherlands (nĕdh′ĕr-lăndz) Eur.	53·01 N	3·57 E
	Netherlands Guiana, see Surinam		
91	Nettilling (L.) Can.	66·30 N	70·40 W
109	Nett Lake Ind. Res. (nĕt lāk) Mn.	48·23 N	93·19 W
163	Nettuno (nĕt-tōō′nô) It. (Rome In.)	41·28 N	12·40 E
161	Neubeckum (noi′bĕ-kōōm) F.R.G. (Ruhr In.)	51·48 N	8·01 E
158	Neubrandenburg (noi-brän′dĕn-bōōrgh) G.D.R.	53·33 N	13·16 E
158	Neuburg (noi′bōōrgh) F.R.G.	48·43 N	11·12 E
158	Neuchâtel (nû-shà-tĕl′) Switz.	47·00 N	6·52 E
158	Neuchatel, Lac de (L.) Switz.	46·48 N	6·53 E
149	Neuenhagen (noi′ĕn-hä-gĕn) G.D.R. (Berlin In.)	52·31 N	13·41 E
161	Neuenrade (noi′ĕn-rä-dĕ) F.R.G. (Ruhr In.)	51·17 N	7·47 E
160	Neufchâtel-en-Bray (nû-shä-tĕl′ĕɴ-brā′) Fr.	49·43 N	1·25 E
158	Neuhaldensleben (noi-häl′dĕns-lā′bĕn) G.D.R.	52·18 N	11·23 E
149	Neuhaus (Oste) (noi′houz) (ōz′tĕ) F.R.G. (Hamburg In.)	53·48 N	9·02 E
149	Neulengbach Aus. (Vienna In.)	48·13 N	15·55 E
158	Neumarkt (noi′märkt) F.R.G.	49·17 N	11·30 E
158	Neumünster (noi′münstĕr) F.R.G.	54·04 N	10·00 E
158	Neunkirchen (noin′kĭrĸ-ĕn) Aus.	47·43 N	16·05 E
161	Neunkirchen F.R.G.	49·21 N	7·20 E
136	Neuquén (nĕ-ōō-kān′) Arg.	38·52 S	68·12 W
136	Neuquen (Prov.) Arg.	39·40 S	70·45 W
136	Neuquén (R.) Arg.	38·45 S	69·00 W
149	Neuruppin (noi′rōō-pēn) G.D.R. (Berlin In.)	52·55 N	12·48 E
121	Neuse (R.) (nūz) NC	36·12 N	78·50 W
158	Neusiedler See (L.) (noi-zēd′lĕr) Aus.	47·54 N	16·31 E
161	Neuss (nois) F.R.G. (Ruhr In.)	51·12 N	6·41 E
158	Neustadt (noi′shtät) F.R.G.	49·21 N	8·08 E
158	Neustadt F.R.G.	54·06 N	10·50 E
158	Neustadt bei Coburg (bī kō′bōōrgh) F.R.G.	50·20 N	11·09 E
158	Neustrelitz (noi-strā′lĭts) G.D.R.	53·21 N	13·05 E
94	Neutral Hills (nū′trăl) Can.	52·10 N	110·50 W
158	Neu Ulm (noi ōō lm′) F.R.G.	48·23 N	10·01 E
89	Neuville (nū′vĭl) Can. (Quebec In.)	46·39 N	71·35 W
158	Neuwied (noi′vēdt) F.R.G.	50·26 N	7·28 E
174	Neva (R.) (nyĕ-vä′) Sov. Un. (Leningrad In.)	59·49 N	30·54 E
109	Nevada (nē-vä′dȧ) Ia.	42·01 N	93·27 W
117	Nevada Mo.	37·49 N	94·21 W
102	Nevada (State) U. S.	39·30 N	117·00 W
162	Nevada, Sierra (Mts.) (syĕr′rä nā-vä′dhä) Sp.	37·01 N	3·28 W
102	Nevada, Sierra (Mts.) (sē-ĕ′r-rä nē-vä′dȧ) U. S.	39·20 N	120·25 W
114	Nevada City Ca.	39·16 N	120·01 W
134	Nevado, Cerro el (Mtn.) (sĕ′r-rō-ĕl-nĕ-vä′dō) Col. (In.)	4·02 N	74·08 W
124	Nevado de Colima (Mtn.) (nå-vä′dhō dā kō-lē′mä) Mex.	19·34 N	103·39 W
154	Neva Stantsiya (nyĕ-vä′ stän′tsĭ-yȧ) Sov. Un. (Leningrad In.)	59·53 N	30·30 E
216	Neve, Serra da (Mts.) Ang.	13·40 S	13·20 E
166	Nevel′ (nyĕ′vĕl) Sov. Un.	56·03 N	29·57 E
135	Neveri (nĕ-vĕ-rē) (R.) Ven. (In.)	10·13 N	64·18 W
160	Nevers (nē-vâr′) Fr.	46·59 N	3·10 E
165	Nevesinje (nĕ-vĕ′sĕn-yĕ) Yugo.	43·15 N	18·08 E
154	Nevis, Ben (Mtn.) (bĕn) Scot.	56·47 N	5·00 W
127	Nevis I. (nē′vĭs) St. Kitts-Nevis-Anguilla (In.)	17·05 N	62·38 W
127	Nevis Pk. St. Kitts-Nevis-Anguilla (In.)	17·11 N	62·33 W
165	Nevrokop (nĕv′rō-kôp′) Bul.	41·35 N	23·46 E
171	Nevşehir (nĕv-shĕ′hĕr) Tur.	38·40 N	34·35 E
174	Nev′yansk (nĕv-yänsk′) Sov. Un. (Urals In.)	57·29 N	60·14 E
121	New (R.) (nū) Va.	37·20 N	80·35 W
217	Newala Tan.	10·56 S	39·18 E
107	New Albany (nû ôl′bȧ-nĭ) In. (Louisville In.)	38·17 N	85·49 W
120	New Albany Ms.	34·28 N	39·00 W
135	New Amsterdam (ăm′stĕr-dăm) Guy.	6·14 N	57·30 W
220	New Amsterdam (I.) Ind. O.	37·52 S	77·32 E
112	Newark (nū′ĕrk) Ca. (San Francisco In.)	37·32 N	122·02 W
105	Newark (nōō′ärk) De.	39·40 N	75·45 W
148	Newark (nū′ĕrk) Eng.	53·04 N	0·49 W
106	Newark (nōō′ûrk) NJ (New York In.)	40·44 N	74·10 W
105	Newark (nū′ĕrk) NY	43·05 N	77·10 W
104	Newark Oh.	40·05 N	82·25 W
104	Newaygo (nū′wā-go) Mi.	43·25 N	85·50 W
105	New Bedford (bĕd′fērd) Ma.	41·35 N	70·55 W
104	Newberg (nū′bûrg) Or.	45·17 N	122·58 W
121	New Bern (bûrn) NC	35·05 N	77·05 W
120	Newbern Tn.	36·05 N	89·12 W
109	Newberry (nū′bĕr-ĭ) Mi.	46·22 N	85·31 W
121	Newberry SC	34·15 N	81·40 W
107	New Boston (bôs′tŭn) Mi. (Detroit In.)	42·10 N	83·24 W
104	New Boston Oh.	38·45 N	82·55 W
118	New Braunfels (nū broun′fĕls) Tx.	29·43 N	98·07 W
113	New Brighton (brī′tŭn) Mn. (Minneapolis, St. Paul In.)	45·04 N	93·12 W
107	New Brighton Pa. (Pittsburgh In.)	40·34 N	80·18 W
105	New Britain (brĭt′'n) Ct.	41·40 N	72·45 W
197	New Britain (I.) Pap. N. Gui.	6·45 S	149·38 E
106	New Brunswick (brŭnz′wĭk) NJ (New York In.)	40·29 N	74·27 W
91	New Brunswick (Prov.) Can.	47·14 N	66·30 W
104	Newburg In.	38·00 N	87·25 W
117	Newburg Mo.	37·54 N	91·53 W
105	Newburgh NY	41·30 N	74·00 W
107	Newburgh Heights Oh. (Cleveland In.)	41·27 N	81·40 W
154	Newbury (nū′bĕr-ĭ) Eng.	51·24 N	1·26 W
99	Newbury Ma. (In.)	42·48 N	70·52 W
99	Newburyport (nū′bĕr-ĭ-pōrt) Ma. (In.)	42·48 N	70·53 W
205	New Caledonia Oceania	21·28 S	164·40 E
106	New Canaan (kā-nȧn) Ct. (New York In.)	41·06 N	73·30 W
98	New Carlisle (kär-līl′) Can.	48·01 N	65·20 W
203	Newcastle (nū-kás′'l) Austl.	33·00 S	151·55 E
98	Newcastle Can.	47·00 N	65·34 W
105	New Castle De.	39·40 N	75·35 W
148	Newcastle (nû-kás′'l) (nû-käs′'l) Eng.	53·01 N	2·14 W
154	Newcastle Eng.	55·00 N	1·45 W
104	New Castle In.	39·55 N	82·25 W
104	New Castle Oh.	40·20 N	82·10 W
104	New Castle Pa.	41·00 N	80·25 W
116	Newcastle Tx.	33·13 N	98·44 W
108	Newcastle Wy.	43·51 N	104·11 W
204	Newcastle Waters (wô′tērz) Austl.	17·10 S	133·25 E
104	Newcomerstown (nū′kŭm-ērz-toun) Oh.	40·15 N	81·40 W
106	New Croton Res. (krŏ′tôn) NY (New York In.)	41·15 N	73·47 W
184	New Delhi (dĕl′hī) India	28·43 N	77·18 E
108	Newell (nū′ĕl) SD	44·43 N	103·26 W
205	New England Ra. (nû ĭŋ′glănd) Austl.	29·32 S	152·30 E
101	Newenham, C. (nū-ĕn-hăm) Ak.	58·40 N	162·32 W
107	Newfane (nū-fān) NY (Buffalo In.)	43·17 N	78·44 W
91	Newfoundland (Prov.) (nū-fŭn′lănd′) (nū′fŭnd-lănd) (nû′found-lănd′) Can. (Newfoundland In.)	48·15 N	56·53 W
93	Newgate (nū′gāt) Can.	49·01 N	115·10 W
205	New Georgia (I.) (jôr′jĭ-ȧ) Sol. Is.	8·08 S	158·00 E
109	New Glasgow (glȧs′gō) Can.	45·35 N	62·36 W
197	New Guinea (I.) (gĭne) Asia	5·45 S	140·00 E
110	Newhalem (nū hă′lŭm) Wa.	48·44 N	121·11 W
103	New Hampshire (State) (hămp′shĭr) U. S.	43·55 N	71·40 W
109	New Hampton (hămp′tŭn) Ia.	43·03 N	92·20 W
213	New Hanover (hăn′ōvĕr) S. Afr. (Natal In.)	29·23 S	30·32 E
197	New Hanover (I.) Pap. N. Gui.	2·37 S	150·15 E
104	New Harmony (nū här′mô-nĭ) In.	38·10 N	87·55 W
105	New Haven (hā′vĕn) Ct.	41·20 N	72·55 W
155	Newhaven Eng.	50·45 N	0·10 E
104	New Haven (nū hāv″n) In.	41·05 N	85·00 W
205	New Hebrides (hĕb′rĭ-dēz) Oceania	16·02 S	169·15 E
148	New Holland (hŏl′ănd) Eng.	53·42 N	0·21 W
121	New Holland NC	35·27 N	76·14 W
106	New Hope Mtn. (hōp) Al. (Birmingham In.)	33·23 N	86·45 W
107	New Hudson (hŭd′sŭn) Mi. (Detroit In.)	42·30 N	83·36 W
119	New Iberia (ī-bē′rĭ-ȧ) La.	30·00 N	91·50 W
89	Newington (nū′ĕng-tŏn) Can. (Ottawa In.)	45·07 N	75·00 W
197	New Ireland (I.) (ĭr′lănd) Pap. N. Gui.	3·15 S	152·30 E
103	New Jersey (State) (jûr′zĭ) U. S.	40·30 N	74·50 W
	New Kensington (kĕn′zĭng-tŭn) Pa. (Pittsburgh In.)	40·34 N	79·35 W
117	Newkirk (nū′kûrk) Ok.	36·52 N	97·03 W
107	New Lenox (lĕn′ŭk) Il. (Chicago In.)	41·31 N	87·58 W
104	New Lexington (lĕk′sĭng-tŭn) Oh.	39·40 N	82·10 W
109	New Lisbon (lĭz′bŭn) Wi.	43·52 N	90·11 W
97	New Liskeard Can.	47·30 N	79·40 W
105	New London (lŭn′dŭn) Ct.	41·20 N	72·05 W
109	New London Wi.	44·24 N	88·45 W
117	New Madrid (măd′rĭd) Mo.	36·34 N	89·31 W
121	Newman (L.) Fl.	29·41 N	82·13 W
108	Newman's Grove (nū′mȧn grōv) Ne.	41·46 N	97·44 W
105	Newmarket (nū′mär-kĕt) Can.	44·00 N	79·30 W
104	New Martinsville (mär′tĭnz-vĭl) WV	39·35 N	80·50 W
110	New Meadows Id.	44·58 N	116·20 W
102	New Mexico (State) (mĕk′sĭ-kō) U. S.	34·30 N	107·10 W
148	New Mills (mĭlz) Eng.	53·22 N	2·00 W
107	New Munster (mŭn′stĕr) Wi. (Milwaukee In.)	42·35 N	88·13 W
120	Newnan (nū′năn) Ga.	33·22 N	84·47 W
203	New Norfolk (nôr′fŏk) Austl.	42·50 S	147·17 E
106	New Orleans (ôr′lē-ănz) La. (New Orleans In.)	30·00 N	90·05 W
104	New Philadelphia (fĭl-ȧ-dĕl′fĭ-ȧ) Oh.	40·30 N	81·30 W
205	New Plymouth (plĭm′ŭth) N. Z. (In.)	39·04 S	174·13 E
117	Newport (nū′pōrt) Ar.	35·35 N	91·16 W
202	Newport Austl. (Sydney In.)	33·39 S	151·19 E
154	Newport (nū-pôrt) Eng.	50·41 N	1·25 W
154	Newport Wales	51·36 N	3·05 W
148	Newport Eng.	52·46 N	2·22 W
107	Newport Ky. (Cincinnati In.)	39·05 N	84·30 W
98	Newport Me.	44·49 N	69·20 W
113	Newport Mn. (Minneapolis, St. Paul In.)	44·52 N	92·59 W
105	Newport NH	43·20 N	72·10 W
110	Newport Or.	44·39 N	124·02 W
106	Newport RI (Providence In.)	41·29 N	71·16 W
120	Newport Tn.	35·55 N	83·12 W
105	Newport Vt.	44·55 N	72·15 W
110	Newport Wa.	48·12 N	117·01 W
113	Newport Beach (bēch) Ca. (Los Angeles In.)	33·36 N	117·55 W
106	Newport News Va. (Norfolk In.)	36·59 N	76·24 W
109	New Prague (nū prăg) Mn.	44·33 N	93·35 W
128	New Providence (I.) (prŏv′ĭ-dĕns) Ba.	25·00 N	77·25 W
104	New Richmond (rĭch′mŭnd) Oh.	38·55 N	84·15 W
109	New Richmond Wi.	45·07 N	92·34 W
119	New Roads (rōds) La.	30·42 N	91·26 W
106	New Rochelle (rū-shĕl′) NY (New York In.)	40·55 N	73·47 W
108	New Rockford (rŏk′fōrd) ND	47·40 N	99·08 W
158	New Ross (rôs) Ire.	52·25 N	6·55 W
89	New Sarepta Can. (Edmonton In.)	53·17 N	113·09 W
191	New Shanghai China (Shanghai In.)	31·18 N	121·31 E
	New Siberian Is., see Novosibirskiye O-va		
121	New Smyrna Beach (smûr′nȧ) Fl.	29·00 N	80·57 W
205	New South Wales (State) (wālz) Austl.	32·45 S	146·14 E
89	Newton (nū′tŭn) Can. (Winnipeg In.)	49·56 N	98·04 W
148	Newton Eng.	53·27 N	2·37 W
104	Newton Il.	39·00 N	88·10 W
109	Newton Ia.	41·42 N	93·04 W

ng-sing; ŋ-baŋk; ɴ-nasalized n; nŏd; cŏmmit; ōld; ôbey; ôrder; fōōd; fŏŏt; ou-out; s-soft; sh-dish; th-thin; pūre; ûnite; ûrn; stŭd; circŭs; ü-as "y" in study; ′-indeterminate vowel.

Page	Name Pronunciation Region	Lat. °′	Long. °′
117	Newton ... Ks.	38·03 N	97·22 W
99	Newton ... Ma. (In.)	42·21 N	71·13 W
120	Newton ... Ms.	32·18 N	89·10 W
106	Newton ... NJ (New York In.)	41·03 N	74·45 W
121	Newton ... NC	35·40 N	81·19 W
119	Newton ... Tx.	30·47 N	93·45 W
107	Newtonsville (nū'tŭnz-vĭl) Oh. (Cincinnati In.)	39·11 N	84·04 W
108	Newtown (nū'toun) ... ND	47·57 N	102·25 W
107	Newtown ... Oh. (Cincinnati In.)	39·08 N	84·22 W
106	Newtown ... Pa. (Philadelphia In.)	40·13 N	74·56 W
154	Newtownards (nu-t'n-ardz') ... Ire.	54·35 N	5·39 W
109	New Ulm (ŭlm) ... Mn.	44·18 N	94·27 W
99	New Waterford (wô'tēr-fērd) Can.	46·15 N	60·05 W
112	New Westminster (wĕst'mĭn-stēr) Can. (Vancouver In.)	49·12 N	122·55 W
106	New York (yôrk) NY (New York In.)	40·40 N	73·58 W
103	New York (State) ... U. S.	42·45 N	78·05 W
205	New Zealand (zē'lănd) ... Oceania	39·14 S	169·30 E
124	Nexapa (R.) (nĕks-ä'pä) ... Mex.	18·32 N	98·29 W
195	Neya-gawa (nâ'yä gä'wä) Jap. (Ōsaka In.)	34·47 N	135·38 E
186	Neyshābūr ... Iran	36·06 N	58·45 E
174	Neyva R. (nēy'vȧ) Sov. Un. (Urals In.)	57·39 N	60·37 E
167	Nezhin (nyĕzh'ēn) ... Sov. Un.	50·03 N	31·52 E
110	Nez Perce (nĕz' pûrs') ... Id.	46·16 N	116·15 W
212	Ngami (R.) (n'gä'mē) ... Bots.	20·56 S	22·31 E
217	Ngangerabeli Pln. ... Ken.	1·20 S	40·10 E
184	Nganglaring Tsho (L.) ... China	31·42 N	82·53 E
215	Ngaoundéré (n'gōn-dâ-rā') ... Cam.	7·19 N	13·35 E
217	Ngarimbi ... Tan.	8·28 S	38·36 E
216	Ngoko (R.) ... Afr.	1·55 N	15·53 E
215	Ngol-Kedju Hill ... Cam.	6·20 N	9·45 E
213	Ngong ('n-gông) ... Ken.	1·27 S	36·39 E
216	Ngounié (R.) ... Gabon	1·15 S	10·43 E
217	Ngoywa ... Tan.	5·56 S	32·48 E
213	Ngqeleni ('ng-kĕ-lā'nē) S. Afr. (Natal In.)	31·41 S	29·04 E
215	Nguigmi ('n-gēg'mē) ... Niger	14·15 N	13·07 E
215	Ngurore ... Nig.	9·18 N	12·14 E
210	Nguru ('n-gōō'rōō) ... Nig.	12·53 N	10·26 E
217	Nguru Mts. ... Tan.	6·10 S	37·35 E
196	Nha Trang (nyä-träng') ... Viet.	12·08 N	108·56 E
210	Niafounke ... Mali	16·03 N	4·17 W
109	Niagara (nī-ăg'ȧ-rȧ) ... Wi.	45·45 N	88·05 W
107	Niagara Falls ... Can. (Buffalo In.)	43·05 N	79·05 W
107	Niagara Falls ... NY (Buffalo In.)	43·06 N	79·02 W
89	Niagara-on-the-Lake Can. (Toronto In.)	43·16 N	79·05 W
107	Niagara R. U. S.-Can. (Buffalo In.)	43·12 N	79·03 W
214	Niakaramandougou ... Ivory Coast	8·40 N	5·17 W
215	Niamey (nē-ä-mâ') ... Niger	13·31 N	2·07 E
214	Niamtougou ... Togo	9·46 N	1·06 E
217	Niangara (nē-äŋ-gá'rȧ) ... Zaire	3·42 N	27·52 E
117	Niangua (R.) (nī-ăŋ'gwȧ) ... Mo.	37·30 N	93·05 W
196	Nias (I.) (nē'äs') ... Indon.	0·58 N	97·43 E
156	Nibe (nē'bĕ) ... Den.	56·57 N	9·36 E
122	Nicaragua (nĭk-ȧ-rä'gwȧ) ... N. A.	12·45 N	86·15 W
126	Nicaragua, Lago de (L.) (lä'gô dĕ) Nic.	11·45 N	85·28 W
164	Nicastro (nê-käs'trō) ... It.	38·39 N	16·15 E
126	Nicchehabin, Punta (Pt.) (pōō'n-tä-nĕk-chĕ-ä-bê'n) Mex. (In.)	19·50 N	87·20 W
161	Nice (nēs) ... Fr.	43·42 N	7·21 E
191	Nich'engchen China (Shanghai In.)	30·54 N	121·48 E
91	Nichicun (L.) (nĭch'ĭ-kŭn) ... Can.	53·07 N	72·10 W
128	Nicholas Chan. (nĭk'ô-lȧs) ... Ba.	23·30 N	80·20 W
104	Nicholasville (nĭk'ô-lȧs-vĭl) ... Ky.	37·55 N	84·35 W
196	Nicobar Is. (nĭk-ô-bär') Andaman & Nicobar Is.	8·28 N	94·04 E
112	Nicolai Mtn. (nē-cō lī') Or. (Portland In.)	46·05 N	123·27 W
125	Nicolás Romero (nē-kō-lá's rô-mĕ'rô) . Mex. (In.)	19·38 N	99·20 W
113	Nicolet, L. (nĭ'kŏ-lĕt) Mi. (Sault Ste. Marie In.)	46·22 N	84·14 W
128	Nicolls Town ... Ba.	25·10 N	78·00 W
113	Nicols (nĭk'ĕls) Mn. (Minneapolis, St. Paul In.)	44·50 N	93·12 W
112	Nicomeki (R.) Can. (Vancouver In.)	49·04 N	122·47 W
153	Nicosia (nē-kô-sē'ȧ) ... Cyprus	35·10 N	33·22 E
126	Nicoya (nē-kō'yä) ... C. R.	10·08 N	85·27 W
126	Nicoya, Golfo de (G.) (gôl-fô-dĕ) . C. R.	10·03 N	85·04 W
126	Nicoya, Pen. de ... C. R.	10·05 N	86·00 W
	Nidaros, see Trondheim		
159	Nidzica (nê-jĕt'sȧ) ... Pol.	53·21 N	20·30 E
158	Niedere Tauern (Mts.) ... Aus.	47·15 N	13·41 E
161	Niederkrüchten (nē'dĕr-krük-tĕn) F.R.G. (Ruhr In.)	51·12 N	6·14 E
149	Niederösterreich (Lower Austria) (State) . Aus. (Vienna In.)	48·24 N	16·20 E
158	Niedersachsen (Lower Saxony) (State) (nē'dĕr-zäĸ-sĕn) . F.R.G.	52·52 N	8·27 E
214	Niélé ... Ivory Coast	10·12 N	5·38 W
215	Niellim ... Chad	9·42 N	17·49 E
158	Nienburg (nē'ĕn-bŏŏrgh) ... F.R.G.	52·40 N	9·15 E
214	Niénokoué, Mont (Mtn.) Ivory Coast	5·26 N	7·10 W
218	Nietverdiend ... S. Afr. (Johannesburg & Pretoria In.)	25·02 S	26·10 E
135	Nieuw Nickerie (nê-nē'kĕ-rē') Sur.	5·51 N	57·00 W
124	Nieves (nyā'vâs) ... Mex.	24·00 N	102·57 W
171	Niğde (nĭg'dĕ) ... Tur.	37·55 N	34·40 E
218	Nigel (nī'jĕl) ... S. Afr. (Johannesburg & Pretoria In.)	26·26 S	28·27 E
209	Niger (nī'jēr) ... Afr.	18·02 N	8·30 E
215	Niger (R.) ... Afr.	5·33 N	6·33 E
215	Niger Delta ... Nig.	4·45 N	5·20 E
209	Nigeria (nī-jē'rĭ-ȧ) ... Afr.	8·57 N	6·30 E
195	Nii (I.) (nē) ... Jap.	34·26 N	139·23 E
194	Niigata (nē'ē-gä'tȧ) ... Jap.	37·47 N	139·04 E
100	Niihau (I.) (nē'ē-hä'ōō) ... Hi.	21·50 N	160·05 E
195	Niimi (nē'mē) ... Jap.	34·59 N	133·28 E
195	Niiza ... Jap. (Tōkyō In.)	35·48 N	139·34 E
155	Nijmegen (nī'mä-gĕn) ... Neth.	51·50 N	5·52 E
195	Nikaidō (nē'ki-dō) Jap. (Ōsaka In.)	34·36 N	135·48 E
166	Nikitinka (nê-kĭ'tĭn-kȧ) .. Sov. Un.	55·33 N	33·19 E
195	Nikkō (nēk'kō) ... Jap.	36·44 N	139·35 E
167	Nikolayev (nē-kô-lä'yĕf) .. Sov. Un.	46·58 N	32·02 E
167	Nikolayev (Oblast) (ôb'lȧst) Sov. Un.	47·27 N	31·25 E
194	Nikolayevka ... Sov. Un.	48·37 N	134·49 E
174	Nikolayevka (nē-kô-lä'yĕf-kȧ) Sov. Un. (Leningrad In.)	59·29 N	29·48 E
171	Nikolayevskiy ... Sov. Un.	50·00 N	45·30 E
173	Nikolayevsk-na-Amure ... Sov. Un.	53·18 N	140·49 E
170	Nikol'sk (nê-kôlsk') ... Sov. Un.	59·30 N	45·40 E
174	Nikol'skoye (nê-kôl'skô-yĕ) Sov. Un. (Leningrad In.)	59·27 N	30·00 E
165	Nikopol (nē'kô-pŏl') ... Bul.	43·41 N	24·52 E
167	Nikopol' ... Sov. Un.	47·36 N	34·24 E
165	Nikšić (nēk'shēch) ... Yugo.	42·45 N	18·57 E
	Nīl, Nahr an-, see Nile (R.)		
137	Nilahue (R.) (nē-lȧ'wĕ) Chile (Santiago In.)	36·36 S	71·50 W
211	Nile (R.) (nīl) ... Afr.	19·15 N	32·30 E
104	Niles (nīlz) ... Mi.	41·50 N	86·15 W
104	Niles ... Oh.	41·15 N	80·45 W
185	Nileshwar ... India	12·08 N	74·14 E
185	Nilgiri Hills ... India	17·05 N	76·22 E
136	Nilópolis (nē-lô'pō-lēs) Braz. (Rio de Janeiro In.)	22·48 S	43·25 W
184	Nīmach ... India	24·32 N	74·51 E
210	Nimba, Mont (Mtn.) (nĭm'bȧ) Ivory Coast	7·40 N	8·33 W
214	Nimba Mts. ... Gui.-Ivory Coast	7·30 N	8·35 W
160	Nîmes (nēm) ... Fr.	43·49 N	4·22 E
117	Nimrod Res. (nĭm'rŏd) ... Ar.	34·58 N	93·46 W
211	Nimule (nê-mōō'lȧ) ... Sud.	3·38 N	32·12 E
216	Ninda ... Ang.	14·47 S	21·24 E
203	Ninety Mile Bch. ... Austl.	38·20 S	147·30 E
171	Nineveh (Ruins) (nĭn'ê-vȧ) ... Iraq	36·30 N	43·10 E
192	Ningan (nĭŋ'gän') ... China	44·20 N	129·20 E
190	Ningchin (nĭng'jĭn) ... China	37·39 N	116·47 E
190	Ningching (nĭng'jĭn) ... China	37·37 N	114·55 E
188	Ningerh ... China	23·14 N	101·14 E
193	Ninghai (nĭng'hī') ... China	29·20 N	121·20 E
190	Ningho (nĭng'hō') ... China	39·27 N	117·44 E
	Ningshia, see Yinch'uan		
193	Ningming ... China	22·22 N	107·06 E
193	Ningpo (nĭng-pō') ... China	29·56 N	121·30 E
188	Ningsia Hui Aut. Reg. ... China	40·18 N	104·45 E
193	Ningte ... China	26·38 N	119·33 E
192	Ningwu (nĭng'wōō') ... China	39·00 N	112·12 E
190	Ningyang (nĭng'yäng') ... China	35·46 N	116·48 E
196	Ninh Binh (nēn bēnk') ... Viet.	20·22 N	106·00 E
197	Ninigo Is. ... Pap. N. Gui.	1·15 S	143·30 E
116	Ninnescah (R.) (nĭn'ĕs-kä) ... Ks.	37·37 N	98·31 W
135	Nioaque (nēō-á'-kĕ) ... Braz.	21·14 S	55·41 W
108	Niobrara (R.) (nī-ô-brâr'ȧ) ... Ne.	42·46 N	98·46 W
214	Niokolo Koba, Parc Natl. du (Natl. Pk.) . Senegal	13·05 N	13·00 W
214	Nioro du Sahel (nê-ō'rō) ... Mali	15·15 N	9·35 W
160	Niort (nê-ôr') ... Fr.	46·17 N	0·28 W
94	Nipawin ... Can.	53·22 N	104·00 W
129	Nipe, Bahía de (B.) (bä-ē'ä-dĕ-nē'pā) . Cuba	20·50 N	75·30 W
129	Nipe, Sierra de (Mts.) (sē-ĕ'r-rȧ-dĕ) . Cuba	20·20 N	75·50 W
104	Nipigon (nĭp'ĭ-gŏn) ... Can.	48·58 N	88·17 W
96	Nipigon (L.) ... Can.	49·37 N	89·55 W
109	Nipigon B. ... Can.	48·56 N	88·00 W
98	Nipisiguit (R.) (nĭ-pĭ'sĭ-kwĭt) ... Can.	47·26 N	66·15 W
97	Nipissing (L.) (nĭp'ĭ-sĭng) ... Can.	45·59 N	80·19 W
128	Niquero (nē-kā'rō) ... Cuba	20·00 N	77·35 W
184	Nirmali ... India	26·30 N	86·43 E
165	Niš (nēsh) ... Yugo.	43·18 N	21·55 E
162	Nisa (nē'sȧ) ... Port.	39·32 N	7·41 W
165	Nišava (R.) (nē'shȧ-vȧ) ... Yugo.	43·17 N	22·17 E
195	Nishino (I.) (nēsh'ē-nō) ... Jap.	36·06 N	132·49 E
195	Nishinomiya (nēsh'ē-nô-mē'yȧ) Jap. (Ōsaka In.)	34·44 N	135·21 E
195	Nishinoomote (nēsh'ē-nô-mō'tō) Jap.	30·44 N	130·59 E
195	Nishio (nēsh'ē-ô) ... Jap.	34·50 N	137·01 E
94	Niska L. (nĭs'kȧ) ... Can.	55·35 N	108·38 W
159	Nisko (nēs'kô) ... Pol.	50·30 N	22·07 E
89	Nisku (nĭs-kū') Can. (Edmonton In.)	53·21 N	113·33 W
110	Nisqually R. (nĭs-kwôl'ĭ) ... Wa.	46·51 N	122·33 W
156	Nissan (R.) ... Swe.	57·06 N	13·22 E
156	Nisser Vand (L.) (nĭs'ĕr vän) .. Nor.	59·14 N	8·35 E
156	Nissum Fd. ... Den.	56·24 N	7·35 E
136	Niterói (nē-tĕ-rô'ĭ) Braz. (Rio de Janeiro In.)	22·53 S	43·07 W
154	Nith (R.) (nĭth) ... Scot.	55·13 N	3·55 W
159	Nitra (nē'trȧ) ... Czech.	48·18 N	18·04 E
159	Nitra R. ... Czech.	48·13 N	18·14 E
104	Nitro (nī'trō) ... WV	38·25 N	81·50 W
199	Niue (nĭ'ōō) ... Oceania	19·50 S	167·00 W
155	Nivelles (nē'vĕl') ... Bel.	50·33 N	4·17 E
160	Nivernais, Côtes de (Hills) (nē-vĕr-nĕ') . Fr.	47·40 N	3·09 E
119	Nixon (nĭk'sŭn) ... Tx.	29·16 N	97·48 W
184	Nizāmābād ... India	18·48 N	78·07 E
173	Nizhne-Angarsk (nyēzh'nyĭ-ŭngärsk') . Sov. Un.	55·49 N	108·46 E
171	Nizhne-Chirskaya (nyĭ-ŭn-gärsk') Sov. Un.	48·20 N	42·50 E
173	Nizhne-Kolymsk (kô-lĕmsk') Sov. Un.	68·32 N	160·56 E
172	Nizhneudinsk (nêzh'nyĭ-ōōdĕnsk') Sov. Un.	54·58 N	99·15 E
174	Nizhniye Sergi (nyēzh' [nyē] sĕr'gē) Sov. Un. (Urals In.)	56·41 N	59·19 E
167	Nizhniye Serogozy (nyēzh'nyĭ sĕ-rô-gô'zĭ) . Sov. Un.	46·51 N	34·25 E
174	Nizhniy Tagil (tŭgēl') Sov. Un. (Urals In.)	57·54 N	59·59 E
174	Nizhnyaya Kur'ya (nyē'zhnyȧ-yȧ koōr'yȧ) Sov. Un. (Urals In.)	58·01 N	56·00 E
174	Nizhnyaya Salda (nyē'zh[nya'ya] säl'da') Sov. Un. (Urals In.)	58·05 N	60·43 E
172	Nizhnyaya Taymyra (R.) . Sov. Un.	72·30 N	95·18 E
172	Nizhnyaya (Lower) Tunguska (R.) (tōōn-gōōs'kȧ) . Sov. Un.	64·13 N	91·30 E
174	Nizhnyaya Tura (tōō'rȧ) Sov. Un. (Urals In.)	58·38 N	59·50 E
174	Nizhnyaya Us'va (ōō'vȧ) Sov. Un. (Urals In.)	59·05 N	58·53 E
217	Njombe ... Tan.	9·20 S	34·46 E
156	Njurunda (nyōō-rōōn'dȧ) ... Swe.	62·15 N	17·24 E
217	Nkala Mission ... Zambia	15·55 S	26·00 E
213	Nkandla ('n-kănd'lȧ) S. Afr. (Natal In.)	28·40 S	31·06 E
214	Nkawkaw ... Ghana	6·33 N	0·47 W
184	Noākhāli ... Bngl.	22·52 N	91·08 E
101	Noatak (nô-ȧ'tăk) ... Ak.	67·22 N	163·28 W
101	Noatak (R.) ... Ak.	67·58 N	162·15 W
195	Nobeoka (nō-bâ-ō'kȧ) ... Jap.	32·36 N	131·41 E
104	Noblesville (nō'bl'z-vĭl) ... In.	40·00 N	86·00 W
89	Nobleton (nō'bl'tŭn) Can. (Toronto In.)	43·54 N	79·39 W
163	Nocero Inferiore (nô-chĕ'rô-ēn-fĕ-ryô'rĕ) It. (Naples In.)	40·30 N	14·38 E
124	Nochistlán (nô-chēs-tlän') ... Mex.	21·23 N	102·52 W
125	Nochixtlón (Asunción) (ä-sōōn-syōn') . Mex.	17·28 N	97·12 W
115	Nogales (nô-gä'lĕs) ... Az.	31·20 N	110·55 W
125	Nogales (nô-gä'lĕs) ... Mex.	18·49 N	97·09 W
122	Nogales ... Mex.	31·15 N	111·00 W
218	Nogal Val. (nô'gäl) Som. (Horn of Afr. In.)	8·30 N	47·50 E
167	Nogaysk (nô-gīsk') ... Sov. Un.	46·43 N	36·21 E
161	Nogent-le-Roi (nŏ-zhŏn-lĕ-rwä') Fr. (Paris In.)	48·39 N	1·32 E
160	Nogent-le-Rotrou (rō-trōō') ... Fr.	48·22 N	0·47 E
174	Noginsk (nô-gēnsk') Sov. Un. (Moscow In.)	55·52 N	38·28 E
162	Nogueira (nô-gā'rȧ) ... Sp.	42·25 N	7·43 W
163	Nogueira Pallaresa (R.) (nô-gĕ'y-rä-päl-yä-rĕ-sä) . Sp.	42·18 N	1·03 E
192	Noho (nô'hô') ... China	48·23 N	124·58 E
160	Noires, Mts. (nwȧr) ... Fr.	48·07 N	3·42 W
160	Noirmoutier, Île de (I.) (nwȧr-mōō-tyā') . Fr.	47·03 N	3·08 W
195	Nojimä-Zaki (Pt.) (nō'jê-mä zä-kê) . Jap.	35·54 N	139·48 E
104	Nokomis (nô-kō'mĭs) ... Il.	39·15 N	89·10 W
163	Nola (nô'lä) ... It. (Naples In.)	40·41 N	14·32 E
170	Nolinsk (nô-lēnsk') ... Sov. Un.	57·32 N	49·50 E
195	Noma Misaki (C.) (nō'mä mē'sä-kē) . Jap.	31·25 N	130·09 E
124	Nombre de Dios (nôm-brĕ-dĕ-dyô's) . Mex.	23·50 N	104·14 W
127	Nombre de Dios (nō'm-brĕ) .. Pan.	9·34 N	79·28 W
101	Nome (nōm) ... Ak.	64·30 N	165·20 W
90	Nonacho (L.) ... Can.	61·48 N	111·20 W
212	Nongoma (nŏn-gō'mȧ) ... S. Afr.	27·48 S	31·45 E
102	Nooksack (nŏŏk'săk) Wa. (Vancouver In.)	48·55 N	122·19 W
112	Nooksack (R.) Wa. (Vancouver In.)	48·54 N	122·31 W
149	Noorden .. Neth. (Amsterdam In.)	52·09 N	4·49 E
149	Noordwijk aan Zee Neth. (Amsterdam In.)	52·14 N	4·25 E
149	Noordzee, Kanal, (Can.) Neth. (Amsterdam In.)	52·27 N	4·42 E
90	Nootka (I.) (nōōt'kȧ) ... Can.	49·32 N	126·42 W
92	Nootka Sd. ... Can.	49·33 N	126·38 W
216	Nóqui (nô-kē') ... Ang.	5·51 S	13·25 E
194	Nor (R.) (nou') ... China	46·55 N	132·45 E
107	Nora (nō'rä) . In. (Indianapolis In.)	39·54 N	86·08 W
156	Nora ... Swe.	59·32 N	14·56 E
97	Noranda ... Can.	48·15 N	79·01 W
106	Norbeck (nōr'bĕk) Md. (Baltimore In.)	39·06 N	77·05 W
117	Norborne (nôr'bōrn) ... Mo.	39·17 N	93·39 W
113	Norco (nôr'kō) Ca. (Los Angeles In.)	33·57 N	117·33 W
106	Norcross (nôr'krôs) Ga. (Atlanta In.)	33·56 N	84·13 W
89	Nord, Riviere du (rēv-yĕr' dü nōr) Can. (Montreal In.)	45·45 N	74·02 W
93	Nordegg (nûr'dĕg) ... Can.	52·28 N	116·04 W
158	Norden (nōr'dĕn) ... F.R.G.	53·35 N	7·14 E
158	Norderney I. (nōr'dĕr-nĕy) . F.R.G.	53·45 N	6·58 E
156	Nord Fd. (nô'fyôr) ... Nor.	61·50 N	5·35 E
158	Nordhausen (nôrt'hau-zĕn) G.D.R.	51·30 N	10·48 E
158	Nordhorn (nôrt'hôrn) ... F.R.G.	52·26 N	7·05 E
150	Nord Kapp (C.) (nôr-kapp) .. Nor.	71·07 N	25·57 E

ăt; finăl; rāte; senâte; ärm; åsk; sofȧ; fâre; ch-choose; dh-as th in other; bē; ėvent; bĕt; recĕnt; cratēr; g-go; gh-guttural g; bĭt; ĭ-short neutral; rīde; ĸ-guttural k as ch in German ich;

PRONOUNCING INDEX

Nordland — Novokuznetsk 321

Page	Name, Pronunciation, Region	Lat. °'	Long. °'
112	Nordland (nôrd'lănd) Wa. (Seattle In.)	48·03 N	122·41 W
158	Nördlingen (nûrt'lĭng-ĕn)..F.R.G.	48·51 N	10·30 E
158	Nord-Ostsee Kan. (Kiel) Can. (nōrd-ōzt-zā) (kēl).....F.R.G.	54·03 N	9·23 E
158	Nordrhein-Westfalen (North Rhine-Westphalia) (State) (nŏrd'hīn-vĕst-fä-lĕn).....F.R.G.	50·50 N	6·53 E
173	Nordvik (nôrd'vĕk)......Sov. Un.	73·57 N	111·15 E
154	Nore R. (nōr)..............Ire.	52·34 N	7·15 W
120	Norfield (nôr'fēld)...........Ms.	31·24 N	90·25 W
99	Norfolk (nôr'fŏk).......Ma. (In.)	42·07 N	71·19 W
108	Norfolk....................Ne.	42·10 N	97·25 W
106	Norfolk........Va. (Norfolk In.)	36·55 N	76·15 W
198	Norfolk................Oceania	27·10 S	166·50 E
117	Norfork, L....................Ar.	36·25 N	92·09 W
124	Noria (nō'rē-ä)............Mex.	23·04 N	106·20 W
172	Noril'sk (nô rēlsk')......Sov. Un.	69·00 N	87·11 E
104	Normal (nôr'măl)...........Il.	40·35 N	89·00 W
117	Norman (nôr'măn)...........Ok.	35·13 N	97·25 W
121	Norman, L..................NC	35·30 N	80·53 W
205	Norman (R.).............Austl.	18·27 S	141·29 E
160	Normandie (Reg.) (nŏr-mäN-dē') Fr.	49·02 N	0·17 E
160	Normandie, Collines de (Hills) (kŏ-lēn'dĕ-nŏr-män-dē').Fr.	48·35 N	0·30 W
205	Normanton (nôr'măn-tŭn)..Austl.	17·45 S	141·10 E
148	Normanton..................Eng.	53·40 N	1·21 W
90	Norman Wells...............Can.	65·26 N	127·00 W
204	Nornalup (nôr-năl'ŭp)......Austl.	35·00 S	117·00 E
156	Norra Dellen (L.)..........Swe.	61·57 N	16·25 E
156	Norre Sundby (nû-rĕ-sōōn'bü) Den.	57·04 N	9·55 E
120	Norris (nŏr'ĭs)..............Tn.	36·09 N	84·05 W
120	Norris (R.)..................Tn.	36·17 N	84·10 W
106	Norristown (nŏr'ĭs-town) Pa. (Philadelphia In.)	40·07 N	75·21 W
156	Norrköping (nôr'chûp'ĭng)...Swe.	58·37 N	16·10 E
156	Norrtälje (nôr-tĕl'yĕ)........Swe.	59·47 N	18·39 E
204	Norseman (nôrs'măn)......Austl.	32·15 S	122·00 E
137	Norte, Punta (Pt.) (pōō'n-tä-nŏr'tĕ) Arg. (Buenos Aires In.)	36·17 S	56·46 W
135	Norte, Serra do (Mts.) (sĕ'r-rä-dô-nôr'te).Braz.	12·04 S	59·08 W
99	North, C....................Can.	47·02 N	60·25 W
205	North, C...............N. Z. (In.)	34·31 S	173·02 E
114	North, I......Ca. (San Diego In.)	32·39 N	117·14 W
205	North, I..............N. Z. (In.)	37·34 S	171·12 E
105	North Adams (ăd'ămz).......Ma.	42·40 N	73·05 W
204	Northam (nôr-dhăm).......Austl.	31·50 S	116·45 E
218	Northam (nôr'thăm)........S. Afr. (Johannesburg & Pretoria In.)	24·52 S	27·16 E
75	North America (à-mĕr'ĭ-kà)		
123	North American Basin (à-mĕr'ĭ-kăn).Atl. O.	23·45 N	62·45 W
204	Northampton (nôr-thămp'tŭn) Austl.	28·22 S	114·45 E
154	Northampton (nôrth-ămp'tŭn) Eng.	52·14 N	0·56 W
105	Northampton...............Ma.	42·20 N	72·45 W
105	Northampton................Pa.	40·45 N	75·30 W
148	Northampton (Co.)..........Eng.	52·25 N	0·47 W
196	North Andaman I. (ăn-dà-măn') Andaman & Nicobar Is.	13·15 N	93·30 E
99	North Andover (ăn'dô-vēr) Ma. (In.)	42·42 N	71·07 W
112	North Arm (ärm) Can. (Vancouver In.)	49·13 N	123·01 W
106	North Atlanta (ăt-lăn'tà) Ga. (Atlanta In.)	33·52 N	84·20 W
106	North Attleboro (ăt''l-bŭr-ô) Ma. (Providence In.)	41·59 N	71·18 W
104	North Baltimore (bôl'tĭ-môr)..Oh.	41·10 N	83·40 W
118	North Basque (băsk)..........Tx.	31·56 N	98·01 W
94	North Battleford (băt''l-fērd).Can.	52·47 N	108·17 W
97	North Bay....................Can.	46·13 N	79·26 W
110	North Bend (bĕnd)...........Or.	43·23 N	124·13 W
98	North Berwick (bûr'wĭk).....Me.	43·18 N	70·46 W
128	North Bght. (bĭt)............Ba.	24·30 N	77·40 W
128	North Bimini (I). (bĭ'mĭ-nē)..Ba.	25·45 N	79·20 W
	North Borneo (Reg.), see Sabah		
99	Northborough (nôrth'bûr-ô) Ma. (In.)	42·19 N	71·39 W
99	Northbridge (nôrth'brĭj) Ma. (In.)	42·09 N	71·39 W
129	North Caicos (I.) (kī'kōs).Turks & Caicos	21·55 N	72·00 W
103	North Carolina (State) (kăr-ô-lī'nà).U. S.	35·40 N	81·30 W
93	North Cascades Natl. Pk.....Wa.	48·50 N	120·50 W
128	North Cat Cay (I.)...........Ba.	25·35 N	79·20 W
104	North Chan (B.) (chăn).......Can.	46·10 N	83·20 W
154	North Chan.........N. Ire.-Scot.	55·15 N	7·56 W
121	North Charleston (chärlz'tŭn) SC	32·49 N	79·57 W
107	North Chicago (shĭ-kô'gō) Il. (Chicago In.)	42·19 N	87·51 W
107	North College Hill (kŏl'ĕj hĭl) Oh. (Cincinnati In.)	39·13 N	84·33 W
118	North Concho (kŏn'chō).......Tx.	31·40 N	100·48 W
89	North Cooking Lake (kōōk'ĭng lāk) Can. (Edmonton In.)	53·28 N	112·57 W
102	North Dakota (State) (dà-kō'tà) U. S.	47·20 N	101·55 W
154	North Downs (dounz).......Eng.	51·11 N	0·01 W
184	North Dum-Dum......India (In.)	22·38 N	88·23 E
101	Northeast C. (nôrth-ēst).......Ak.	63·15 N	169·04 W
129	Northeast Pt.................Ba.	21·25 N	73·00 W
129	Northeast Pt.................Ba.	22·45 N	73·50 W
128	Northeast Providence Chan. (prŏv'ĭ-dĕns).Ba.	25·45 N	77·00 W
158	Northeim (nôrt'hīm).......F.R.G.	51·42 N	9·59 E
128	North Elbow Cays (Is.).......Ba.	23·55 N	80·30 W
111	Northern Cheyenne Ind. Res..Mt.	45·32 N	106·43 W
	Northern Dvina (R.), see Severnaya Dvina		
154	Northern Ireland (ĭr'lănd)..U. K.	54·48 N	7·00 W
	Northern Land (Is.), see Severnaya Zemlya		
204	Northern Territory........Austl.	18·15 S	133·00 E
109	Northfield (nôrth'fēld).......Mn.	44·28 N	93·11 W
203	North Flinders, Ra. (flĭn'dērz) Austl.	31·55 S	138·45 E
155	North Foreland (fōr'lănd)....Eng.	51·20 N	1·30 E
118	North Franklin Mt. (frăŋ'klĭn).Tx.	31·55 N	106·30 W
156	North Frisian Is............Den.	55·16 N	8·15 E
122	North Gamboa (gäm-bô'ä) C. Z. (In.)	9·07 N	79·40 W
89	North Gower (gŏw'ēr) Can. (Ottawa In.)	45·08 N	75·43 W
113	North Hollywood (hŏl'ē-wŏŏd) Ca. (Los Angeles In.)	34·10 N	118·23 W
104	North Judson (jŭd'sŭn).......In.	41·15 N	86·50 W
93	North Kamloops (kăm'lōōps).Can.	50·41 N	120·22 W
113	North Kansas City (kăn'zàs) Mo. (Kansas City In.)	39·08 N	94·34 W
106	North Kingstown RI (Providence In.)	41·34 N	71·26 W
117	North Little Rock (lĭt''l rŏk)...Ar.	34·46 N	92·13 W
108	North Loup (R.) (lōōp).......Ne.	42·05 N	100·10 W
104	North Manchester (măn'chĕs-tēr) In.	41·00 N	85·45 W
113	Northmoor (nôrth'mōōr) Mo. (Kansas City In.)	39·10 N	94·37 W
95	North Moose L...............Can.	54·09 N	100·20 W
203	North Mount Lofty Ranges.Austl.	33·50 S	138·30 E
113	North Ogden (ŏg'dĕn) Ut. (Salt Lake City In.)	41·18 N	111·58 W
113	North Ogden Pk. Ut. (Salt Lake City. In.)	41·23 N	111·59 W
107	North Olmsted (ōlm-stĕd) Oh. (Cleveland In.)	41·25 N	81·55 W
116	North Pease (R.) (pēz).......Tx.	34·19 N	100·58 W
112	North Pender (I.) (pĕn'dēr) Can. (Vancouver In.)	48·48 N	123·16 W
112	North Plains (plānz) Or. (Portland In.)	45·36 N	123·00 W
108	North Platte (plăt)..........Ne.	41·08 N	100·45 W
102	North Platte, (R.)..........U. S.	41·20 N	102·40 W
104	North Pt.....................Mi.	45·00 N	83·20 W
127	North Pt.............Barb. (In.)	13·22 N	59·36 W
120	Northport (nôrth'pōrt)........Al.	33·12 N	87·35 W
106	Northport...NY (New York In.)	40·53 N	73·20 W
110	Northport....................Wa.	48·53 N	117·47 W
99	North Reading (rĕd'ĭng).Ma. (In.)	42·34 N	71·04 W
	North Rhine-Westphalia (State), see Nordrhein-Westfalen		
113	North Richland Hills Tx. (Dallas, Ft. Worth In.)	32·50 N	97·13 W
113	Northridge (nôrth'rĭdj) Ca. (Los Angeles In.)	34·14 N	118·32 W
107	North Ridgeville (rĭj-vĭl) Oh. (Cleveland In.)	41·23 N	82·01 W
107	North Royalton (roi'ăl-tŭn) Oh. (Cleveland In.)	41·19 N	81·44 W
113	North St. Paul (sânt pôl')....Mn. (Minneapolis, St. Paul In.)	45·01 N	92·59 W
94	North Saskatchewan (R.) (săn-kăch'ē-wän).Can.	52·40 N	106·45 W
150	North Sea...................Eur.	56·09 N	3·16 E
109	North Skunk (R.) (skŭnk).....Ia.	41·39 N	92·46 W
205	North Stradbroke I. (străd'brōk) Austl.	27·45 S	154·18 E
99	North Sydney (sĭd'nē).......Can.	46·13 N	60·15 W
205	North Taranaki Bght. (tä-rà-nä'kĭ bĭt).N. Z. (In.)	38·23 S	172·03 E
106	North Tarrytown (tăr'ĭ-toun) NY (New York In.)	41·05 N	73·52 W
93	North Thompson (R.)........Can.	50·50 N	120·10 W
107	North Tonawanda (tŏn-à-wŏn'dà) NY (Buffalo In.)	43·02 N	78·53 W
115	North Truchas Pks. (Mts.) (trōō'chäs).NM	35·58 N	105·37 W
99	North Twillingate (I.) (twĭl'ĭn-gāt) Can.	49·47 N	54·37 W
154	North Uist (I.) (ū'ĭst).......Scot.	57·37 N	7·22 W
98	Northumberland Str. (nôr thŭm'bēr-lănd).Can.	46·25 N	64·20 W
105	Northumberland.............NH	44·30 N	71·30 W
205	Northumberland, Is........Austl.	21·42 S	151·30 E
110	North Umpqua R. (ŭmp'kwà)..Or.	43·20 N	122·50 W
112	North Vancouver (văn-kōō'vēr) Can. (Vancouver In.)	49·19 N	123·04 W
104	North Vernon (vûr'nŭn) ...... In.	39·05 N	85·45 W
107	Northville (nôrth-vĭl) Mi. (Detroit In.)	42·26 N	83·28 W
106	North Wales (wālz) Pa. (Philadelphia In.)	40·12 N	75·16 W
204	North West C. (nôrth'wĕst).Austl.	21·50 S	112·25 E
121	Northwest Cape Fear, (R.) (cāp fēr).NC	34·34 N	79·46 W
99	North West Gander (R.) (găn'dēr) Can.	48·40 N	55·15 W
154	Northwest Highlands.......Scot.	56·50 N	5·20 W
128	Northwest Providence Chan. (prŏv'ĭ-dĕns).Ba.	26·15 N	78·45 W
90	Northwest Territories (tĕr'ĭ-tō'rĭs).Can.	64·42 N	119·09 W
155	Northwich (nôrth'wĭch)......Eng.	53·15 N	2·31 W
121	North Wilkesboro (wĭlks'bûrô).NC	36·08 N	81·10 W
109	Northwood (nôrth'wŏŏd)......Ia.	43·26 N	93·13 W
108	Northwood....................ND	47·44 N	97·36 W
111	North Wood Cr...............Wy.	44·02 N	107·37 W
112	North Yamhill (R.) (yăm' hĭl) Or. (Portland In.)	45·22 N	123·21 W
154	North York Moors (yôrk mōōrz') Eng.	54·20 N	0·40 W
89	North York....Can. (Toronto In.)	43·47 N	79·25 W
116	Norton (nôr'tŭn).............Ks.	39·40 N	99·54 W
106	Norton......Ma. (Providence In.)	41·58 N	71·08 W
121	Norton.......................Va.	36·54 N	82·36 W
101	Norton B.....................Ak.	64·22 N	162·18 W
106	Norton Res..Ma. (Providence In.)	42·01 N	71·07 W
101	Norton Sd....................Ak.	63·48 N	164·50 W
89	Norval (nôr'vål) Can. (Toronto In.)	43·39 N	79·52 W
113	Norwalk (nôr'wôk) Ca. (Los Angeles In.)	33·54 N	118·05 W
106	Norwalk......Ct. (New York In.)	41·06 N	73·25 W
104	Norwalk......................Oh.	41·15 N	82·35 W
146	Norway (nôr'wā)............Eur.	63·48 N	11·17 E
98	Norway......................Me.	44·11 N	70·35 W
109	Norway......................Mi.	45·47 N	87·55 W
95	Norway House...............Can.	53·59 N	97·50 W
150	Norwegian Sea (nôr-wē'jăn)..Eur.	66·54 N	1·43 E
99	Norwell (nôr'wĕl).......Ma. (In.)	42·10 N	70·47 W
105	Norwich (nôr'wĭch)..........Ct.	41·20 N	72·00 W
155	Norwich....................Eng.	52·40 N	1·15 E
105	Norwich......................NY	42·35 N	75·30 W
99	Norwood (nôr'wŏŏd)....Ma. (In.)	42·11 N	71·13 W
121	Norwood......................NC	35·15 N	80·08 W
107	Norwood.......Oh. (Cincinnati In.)	39·10 N	84·27 W
89	Nose Cr. (nōz).Can. (Calgary In.)	51·09 N	114·02 W
194	Noshiro (nō'shē-rô)..........Jap.	40·09 N	140·02 E
167	Nosovka (nô'sôf-kà)......Sov. Un.	50·54 N	31·35 E
213	Nossi Bé (B.) (nōō'sē bā)..Mad.	13·14 S	47·28 E
212	Nossob (R.) (nô'sŏb).....Namibia	24·15 S	19·10 E
158	Noteć R. (nô'tĕcn)..........Pol.	52·50 N	16·19 E
151	Noto (nô'tô) ....It.	36·49 N	15·08 E
156	Notodden (nōt'ôd'n).........Nor.	59·35 N	9·15 E
195	Noto-Hantō (Pen.) (nô'tō hän'tō) Jap.	37·18 N	137·03 E
98	Notre Dame, Monts (Mts.). Can.	46·35 N	70·35 W
99	Notre Dame B. (nō't'r dàm').Can.	49·45 N	55·15 W
100	Notre-Dame-des-Laurentides (dĕ-lō-räN-tēd').Can. (Quebec In.)	46·55 N	71·20 W
98	Notre-Dame-du-Lac.........Can.	47·37 N	68·51 W
104	Nottawasaga B. (nŏt'à-wà-sā'gà) Can.	44·45 N	80·35 W
91	Nottaway (R.) (nôt'à-wā)....Can.	50·58 N	78·02 W
148	Nottingham (nŏt'ĭng-ăm)....Eng.	52·58 N	1·09 W
148	Nottingham (Co.)...........Eng.	53·03 N	1·05 W
91	Nottingham I................Can.	62·58 N	78·53 W
121	Nottoway, (R.) (nôt'à-wā)....Va.	36·53 N	77·47 W
94	Notukeu Cr.................Can.	49·55 N	106·30 W
210	Nouadnibou..........Mauritania	21·02 N	17·09 W
214	Nouakchott..........Mauritania	18·06 N	15·57 W
214	Nouamrhar..........Mauritania	19·22 N	16·31 W
205	Noumea (nōō-mā'ä)........N. Cal.	22·18 S	166·48 E
98	Nouvelle (nōō-vĕl')..........Can.	48·09 N	66·22 W
211	Nouvelle Anvers (äN-vâr')...Zaire	1·42 N	19·08 E
160	Nouzonville (nōō-zôN-vēl')......Fr.	49·51 N	4·43 E
135	Nova Cruz (nō'và-krōō'z)...Braz.	6·22 S	35·20 W
217	Nova Freixo...............Moz.	14·49 S	36·33 E
137	Nova Friburgo (frē-bōōr'gōō) Braz. (Rio de Janeiro In.)	22·18 S	42·31 W
216	Nova Gaia...................Ang.	10·09 S	17·31 E
136	Nova Iguaçu (nō'vä-ē-gwä-sōō') Braz. (Rio de Janeiro In.)	22·45 S	43·27 W
137	Nova Lima (lē'mä) Braz. (Rio de Janeiro In.)	19·59 S	43·51 W
	Nova Lisboa, see Huambo		
212	Nova Mambone (nō'và-mám-bŏ'nĕ.)Moz.	21·04 S	35·13 E
164	Novara (nô-vä'rä)...........It.	45·24 N	8·38 E
137	Nova Resende Braz. (Rio de Janeiro In.)	21·12 S	46·25 W
91	Nova Scotia (Prov.) (skō'shà).Can.	44·28 N	65·00 W
165	Nova Varoš (nô'và vä'rôsh).Yugo.	43·24 N	19·53 E
157	Novaya Ladogo (nô'vá-yá lá-dô-gô).Sov. Un.	60·06 N	32·16 E
174	Novaya Lyalya (lyá'lyá) Sov. Un. (Urals In.)	59·03 N	60·36 E
167	Novaya Odessa (ô-dĕs'ä).Sov. Un.	47·18 N	31·48 E
167	Novaya Praga (prä'gá)..Sov. Un.	48·34 N	32·54 E
173	Novaya Sibir (I.) (sē-bēr') Sov. Un.	75·42 N	150·00 E
167	Novaya Vodolaga (vô-dôl'á-gá) Sov. Un.	49·43 N	35·51 E
172	Novaya Zemlya (I.) (zĕm-lyá') Sov. Un.	72·00 N	54·46 E
165	Nova Zagora (zä'gô-rà)......Bul.	42·30 N	26·01 E
163	Novelda (nō-vĕl'dä)..........Sp.	38·22 N	0·46 W
159	Nové Mesto (Nad Váhom) (nô'vĕ myĕs'tô).Czech.	48·44 N	17·47 E
159	Nové Zámky (zäm'kē).....Czech.	47·58 N	18·10 E
166	Novgorod (nôv'gô-rŏt)...Sov. Un.	58·32 N	31·16 E
166	Novgorod (Oblast)......Sov. Un.	58·27 N	31·55 E
164	Novi (nô'vē)..................It.	44·43 N	8·48 E
107	Novi (nō'vĭ).....Mi. (Detroit In.)	42·29 N	83·28 W
164	Novi Grad (gräd)..........Yugo.	44·09 N	15·34 E
117	Novinger (nŏv'ĭn-jēr)........Mo.	40·14 N	92·43 W
165	Novi-Pazar (pä-zär')........Bul.	43·22 N	27·26 E
165	Novi Pazar (pá-zär')......Yugo.	43·08 N	20·30 E
165	Novi Sad (säd')..........Yugo.	45·15 N	19·53 E
174	Novoasbest (nô-vô-ä-bĕst') Sov. Un. (Urals In.)	57·43 N	60·14 E
167	Novoaydar (nô'vô-ī-där').Sov. Un.	48·57 N	39·01 E
167	Novocherkassk (nô'vô-chĕr-kásk') Sov. Un.	47·25 N	40·04 E
167	Novogorod-Severskiy....Sov. Un.	52·01 N	33·14 E
159	Novogrudok (nô-vô-grōō'dôk) Sov. Un.	53·35 N	25·51 E
141	Novo-Kazalinsk (nô-vŭ-kŭ-zá-lyĕnsk').Sov. Un.	45·47 N	62·00 E
172	Novokuznetsk (Stalinsk) (nō'vô-kōō'z-nyĕ'tsk) (stá'lĕnsk).Sov. Un.	53·43 N	86·59 E

322 Novoladozhskiy — Ocumare del Tuy PRONOUNCING INDEX

Page Name Pronunciation Region Lat. °′ Long. °′

174 Novoladozhskiy Kanal (Can.) (nô-vô-lä'dôzh-skĭ kà-näl') Sov. Un. (Leningrad In.) 59·54 N 31·19 E
164 Novo Mesto (nôvô mas'tô) . Yugo. 45·48 N 15·13 E
167 Novomirgorod (nô'vô-mēr'gô-rôt) Sov. Un. 48·46 N 31·44 E
166 Novomoskossk . . . . Sov. Un. 54·06 N 38·08 E
167 Novomoskovsk (nô'vô-môs-kôfsk') Sov. Un. 48·37 N 35·12 E
174 Novonikol'skiy (nô'vô-nyĭ-kôl'skĭ) Sov. Un. (Urals In.) 52·28 N 57·12 E
216 Novo Redondo (nô'vŏŏ rå-dôn'dŏŏ) . Ang. 11·13 S 13·50 E
167 Novorossiysk (nô'vô-rô-sēsk') Sov. Un. 44·43 N 37·48 E
166 Novorzhev (nô'vô-rzhêv') Sov. Un. 57·01 N 29·17 E
165 Novo-Selo (nô'vô-sĕ'lô) . . . . . Bul. 44·09 N 22·46 E
172 Novosibirsk (nô'vô-sê-bērsk') Sov. Un. 55·09 N 82·58 E
173 Novosibirskiye O-va (New Siberian Is.) (no'vŭ-sĭ-bĭr'skē-ĕ) . Sov. Un. 76·45 N 140·30 E
166 Novosil' (nô'vô-sĭl) . . . . . . Sov. Un. 52·58 N 37·03 E
166 Novosokol'niki (nô'vô-sô-kôl'nê-kê) . Sov. Un. 56·18 N 30·07 E
174 Novotatishchevskiy (nô'vô-tà-tyĭsh'chĕv-skĭ) Sov. Un. (Urals In.) 53·22 N 60·24 E
167 Novoukrainka (nōvō-ōō'krà) Sov. Un. 48·18 N 31·33 E
171 Novouzensk (nô-vô-ōō-zĕnsk') Sov. Un. 50·40 N 48·08 E
166 Novozybkov (nô'vô-zēp'kôf) Sov. Un. 52·31 N 31·54 E
159 Nový Jičín (nô'vē yē'chēn) . Czech. 49·36 N 18·02 E
167 Novyy Bug (bōōĸ) . . . . . Sov. Un. 47·43 N 32·33 E
167 Novyy Oskol (ôs-kôl') . . . Sov. Un. 50·46 N 37·53 E
172 Novyy Port (nô'vē) . . . . . Sov. Un. 67·19 N 72·28 E
159 Nowa Huta (nō'vä hōō'tä) . . . . Pol. 50·04 N 20·20 E
158 Nowa Sól (nô'vá sŭl') . . . . Pol. 51·49 N 15·41 E
117 Nowata (nô-wä'tá) . . . . Ok. 36·42 N 95·38 W
203 Nowra (nou'rá) . . . . Austl. 34·55 S 150·45 E
159 Nowy Dwór Mazowiecki (nō'vĭ dvōōr mä-zo-vyĕts'ke) . Pol. 52·26 N 20·46 E
159 Nowy Sącz (nô'vê sônch') . . . . Pol. 49·36 N 20·42 E
159 Nowy Targ (tärk') . . . . Pol. 49·29 N 20·02 E
110 Noxon Res. . . . . Mt. 47·50 N 115·40 W
120 Noxubee (R.) (nŏks'ů-bē) . . . . . Ms. 33·20 N 88·55 W
162 Noya (nō'yä) . . . . Sp. 42·46 N 8·50 W
92 Noyes I. (noiz) . . . . Ak. 55·30 N 133·40 W
195 Nozaki (nō'zä-kê) . Jap. (Ōsaka In.) 34·43 N 135·39 E
213 Nqamakwe ('n-gä-mä'kwȧ) S. Afr. (Natal In.) 32·13 S 27·57 E
213 Nqutu ('n-kōō'tōō) S. Afr. (Natal In.) 28·17 S 30·41 E
214 Nsawam . . . . Ghana 5·50 N 0·20 W
215 Nsukka . . . . Nig. 6·52 N 7·24 E
213 Ntshoni (Mtn.) . S. Afr. (Natal In.) 29·34 S 30·03 E
212 Ntwetwe Pan (Salt Flat) . . . . Bots. 20·00 S 24·18 E
211 Nubah, Jibāl an-(Mts.) . . . . . . Sud. 12·22 N 30·39 E
211 Nubian Des. (nōō'bĭ-ăn) . . . . . . Sud. 21·13 N 33·09 E
134 Nudo Coropuna (Mt.) (nōō'dô kō-rō-pōō'nä) . Peru 15·53 S 72·04 W
134 Nudo de Pasco (Mt.) (dĕ pås'kô) Peru 10·34 S 76·12 W
118 Nueces R. (nů-ā'sås) . . . . Tx. 28·20 N 98·08 W
90 Nueltin (L.) (nwĕl'tin) . . . . . . Can. 60·14 N 101·00 W
126 Nueva Armenia (nwā'vä är-mā'nê-à) . Hond. 15·47 N 86·32 W
135 Nueva Esparta (State) (nwĕ'vä ĕs-pä'r-tä) . Ven. (In.) 10·50 N 64·35 W
128 Nueva Gerona (ĸĕ-rō'nä) . . . . Cuba 21·55 N 82·45 W
137 Nueva Palmira (päl-mē'rä) Ur. (Buenos Aires In.) 33·53 S 58·23 W
102 Nueva Rosita (nōōĕ'vä rô-sē'tä) Mex. 27·55 N 101·10 W
126 Nueva San Salvador (Santa Tecla) (sän' säl-vä-dōr) (sän'tä tĕ'klä) Sal. 13·41 N 89·16 W
137 Nueve de Julio (nwā'vå dā hōō'lyō) Arg. (Buenos Aires In.) 35·26 S 60·51 W
128 Nuevitas (nwā-vē'täs) . . . . . . Cuba 21·35 N 77·15 W
128 Nuevitas, Bahía de (bä-ē'ä dĕ nwā-vē'täs) . Cuba 21·30 N 77·05 W
113 Nuevo (nwā'vō) Ca. (Los Angeles In.) 33·48 N 117·09 W
118 Nuevo Laredo (lä-rā'dhō) . . . . Mex. 27·29 N 99·30 W
122 Nuevo Leon (State) (lå-ōn') . . Mex. 26·00 N 100·00 W
122 Nuevo San Juan (nwĕ'vô sän ĸōō-ä'n) . Pan. (In.) 9·14 N 79·43 W
174 Nugumanovo (nů-gů-mä'nô-vô) Sov. Un. (Urals In.) 55·28 N 61·50 E
101 Nulato (nōō-lä'tō) . . . . Ak. 64·40 N 158·18 W
204 Nullagine (nŭ-lă'jēn) . . . . Austl. 22·00 S 120·07 E
204 Nullarbor Plain (Reg.) (nŭ-lär'bôr) . Austl. 31·45 S 126·30 E
94 Numabin B. (nōō-mä'bĭn) . . . . Can. 56·30 N 103·08 W
149 Numansdorp Neth. (Amsterdam In.) 51·43 N 4·25 E
195 Numazu (nōō'mä-zōō) . . . . Jap. 35·06 N 138·55 E
137 No 1, Canal Arg. (Buenos Aires In.) 36·43 S 58·14 W
137 No. 9, Canal Arg. (Buenos Aires In.) 36·22 S 58·19 W
137 No. 12, Canal Arg. (Buenos Aires In.) 36·47 S 57·20 W
197 Numfoor . . . . Indon. 1·20 S 134·48 E
215 Nun (R.) . . . . Nig. 5·05 N 6·10 E
148 Nuneaton (nūn'ē-tŭn) . . . . Eng. 52·31 N 1·28 W
192 Nungan . . . . China 44·25 N 125·10 E
101 Nunivak (I.) (nōō'nĭ-văk) . . . . Ak. 60·25 N 167·42 W
126 Nunkiní (nōōn-kē-nê') . Mex. (In.) 20·19 N 90·14 W
101 Nunyama (nûn-yä'mà) . . Sov. Un. 65·49 N 170·32 W
164 Nuoro (nwô'rō) . . . . It. 40·29 N 9·20 E
172 Nura (R.) (nōō'rä) . . . . . . Sov. Un. 49·48 N 73·54 E
172 Nurata (nōōr'ät'à) . . . . Sov. Un. 40·33 N 65·28 E
158 Nürnberg (nürn'bĕrgh) . . . . F.R.G. 49·28 N 11·07 E
129 Nurse Cay (I.) . . . . Ba. 22·30 N 75·50 W
171 Nusabyin (nōō'sĭ-bĕn) . . . . Tur. 37·05 N 41·10 E
101 Nushagak (R.) (nū-shă-găk') . . Ak. 59·28 N 157·40 W
190 Nushan Hu (L.) (nü'shän hōō) China 32·50 N 117·59 E
187 Nushki (nŭsh'kê) . . . . Pak. 29·30 N 66·02 E
149 Nuthe R. (nōō'tê) G.D.R (Berlin In.) 52·15 N 13·11 E
106 Nutley (nŭt'lê) . NJ (New York In.) 40·49 N 74·09 W
105 Nutter Fort (nŭt'ĕr fôrt) . . . . . WV 39·15 N 80·15 W
113 Nutwood (nŭt'wŏŏd) Il. (St. Louis In.) 39·05 N 90·34 W
183 Nuwaybi 'al Muzayyinah Egypt (Palestine In.) 28·59 N 34·40 E
212 Nuweland . . . . S. Afr. (In.) 33·58 S 18·28 E
106 Nyack (nī'ăk) . NY (New York In.) 41·05 N 73·55 W
217 Nyakanazi . . . . Tan. 3·00 S 31·15 E
211 Nyala . . . . Sud. 12·00 N 24·52 E
216 Nyanga (R.) . . . . Gabon 2·45 S 10·30 E
217 Nyanza . . . . Rw. 2·21 S 29·45 E
217 Nyasa, L. (Malawi, L.) (nyä'sä) Afr. 10·45 S 34·30 E
174 Nyazepetrovsk (nyä'zĕ-pĕ-trôvsk') Sov. Un. (Urals In.) 56·04 N 59·38 E
156 Nyborg (nü'bôr'') . . . . Den. 55·20 N 10·45 E
156 Nybro (nü'brô) . . . . Swe. 56·44 N 15·56 E
188 Nyenchhen Thanglha (Mts.) China 29·55 N 88·08 E
217 Nyeri . . . . Ken. 0·25 S 36·57 E
156 Nyhem (nü'hĕm) . . . . Swe. 56·39 N 12·50 E
217 Nyika Plat . . . . Malawi 10·30 S 35·50 E
159 Nyíregyháza (nyē'rĕd-y'hä'zä) Hung. 47·58 N 21·45 E
156 Nykøbing (nü'kû-bĭng) . . . . . . Den. 56·46 N 8·47 E
156 Nykøbing Falster . . . . Den. 54·45 N 11·54 E
156 Nykøbing Sjaelland . . . . Den. 55·55 N 11·37 E
156 Nyköping (nü'chû-pĭng) . . . . . . Swe. 58·46 N 16·58 E
218 Nylstroom (nĭl'strōm) S. Afr. (Johannesburg & Pretoria In.) 24·42 S 28·25 E
203 Nymagee (nī-mà-gē') . . . . Austl. 32·17 S 146·18 E
158 Nymburk (nêm'bōōrk) . . . . . . Czech. 50·12 N 15·03 E
154 Nymphe Bk. (nĭmpf) . . . . Ire. 51·36 N 7·35 W
156 Nynäshamn (nü-nĕs-hàm'n) . . Swe. 58·53 N 17·55 E
203 Nyngan (nĭŋ'gán) . . . . Austl. 31·31 S 147·25 E
215 Nyong (R.) (nyông) . . . . Cam. 3·40 N 10·25 E
214 Nyou . . . . Upper Volta 12·46 N 1·56 W
158 Nyrány (nêr-zhä'nê) . . . . Czech. 49·43 N 13·13 E
159 Nysa (nē'sà) . . . . Pol. 50·29 N 17·20 E
Nystad, see Uusikaupunki
170 Nytva . . . . Sov. Un. 58·00 N 55·10 E
217 Myungwe . . . . Malawi 10·16 S 34·07 E
217 Nyunzu . . . . Zaire 5·57 S 28·01 E
173 Nyuya (R.) (nyōō'yà) . . . . Sov. Un. 60·30 N 111·45 E
217 Nzega . . . . Tan. 4·13 S 33·11 E
214 Nzérékoré . . . . Gui. 7·45 N 8·49 W
214 Nzi (R.) . . . . Ivory Coast 7·00 N 4·27 W

O

108 Oahe Dam (ō-á-hē) . . . . SD 44·28 N 100·34 W
108 Oahe Res. . . . . SD 45·20 N 100·00 W
100 Oahu (I.) (ō-ä'hōō) (ō'ä'hü) . . . Hi. 21·38 N 157·48 W
92 Oak Bay . . . . Can. 48·27 N 123·18 W
89 Oak Bluff (ōk blŭf) Can. (Winnipeg In.) 49·47 N 97·21 W
111 Oak Creek (ōk krēk') . . . . Co. 40·20 N 106·50 W
114 Oakdale (ōk'dāl) . . . . Ca. 37·45 N 120·52 W
104 Oakdale . . . . Ky. 38·15 N 85·50 W
119 Oakdale . . . . La. 30·49 N 92·40 W
107 Oakdale . . . . . . Pa. (Pittsburgh In.) 40·24 N 80·11 W
148 Oakengates (ōk'ĕn-gāts) . . . . . Eng. 52·41 N 2·27 W
108 Oakes (ōks) . . . . ND 46·10 N 98·50 W
98 Oakfield (ōk'fēld) . . . . Me. 46·08 N 68·10 W
106 Oakford (ōk'fōrd) Pa. (Philadelphia In.) 40·08 N 74·58 W
112 Oak Grove (grōv) Or. (Portland In.) 45·25 N 122·38 W
148 Oakham (ōk'ăm) . . . . Eng. 52·40 N 0·38 W
104 Oakharbor (ōk'här'bĕr) . . . . Oh. 41·30 N 83·05 W
112 Oak Harbor . . . . . Wa. (Seattle In.) 48·18 N 122·39 W
112 Oakland (ōk'lănd) Ca. (San Francisco In.) 37·48 N 122·16 W
108 Oakland . . . . Ne. 41·50 N 96·28 W
104 Oakland City . . . . In. 38·20 N 87·20 W
107 Oaklawn (ōk'lôn) . Il. (Chicago In.) 41·43 N 87·45 W
202 Oakleigh (ōk'lâ) Austl. (Melbourne In.) 37·54 S 145·05 E
111 Oakley (ōk'lĭ) . . . . Id. 42·15 N 135·53 W
116 Oakley . . . . Ks. 39·08 N 100·49 W
120 Oakman (ōk'măn) . . . . Al. 33·42 N 87·20 W
107 Oakmont (ōk'mŏnt) Pa. (Pittsburgh In.) 40·31 N 79·50 W
106 Oak Mtn. . . . Al. (Birmingham In.) 33·22 N 86·42 W
107 Oak Park (pärk) . Il. (Chicago In.) 41·53 N 87·48 W
112 Oak Point . . . . . Wa. (Portland In.) 46·11 N 123·11 W
120 Oak Ridge (rĭj) . . . . Tn. 36·01 N 84·15 W
89 Oakville (ōk'vĭl) Can. (Toronto In.) 43·27 N 79·40 W
89 Oakville . . . . . Can. (Winnipeg In.) 49·56 N 97·58 W
113 Oakville . . . . . Mo. (St. Louis In.) 38·27 N 90·18 W
89 Oakville Cr. . . . Can. (Toronto In.) 43·34 N 79·54 W
119 Oakwood (ōk'wŏŏd) . . . . Tx. 31·36 N 95·48 W
115 Oatman (ōt'măn) . . . . Az. 34·00 N 114·25 W
122 Oaxaca (State) (wä-hä'kä) . . . Mex. 16·45 N 97·00 W
125 Oaxaca, Sierra de (Mts.) (sē-ĕ'r-rä dĕ) . Mex. 16·15 N 97·25 W
125 Oaxaca de Juárez (ĸōōà'rĕz) . Mex. 17·03 N 96·42 W
172 Ob' (R.) . . . . Sov. Un. 62·15 N 67·00 E
96 Oba (ō'bà) . . . . Can. 48·58 N 84·09 W
195 Obama (ō'bà-mä) . . . . Jap. 35·29 N 135·44 E
154 Oban (ō'băn) . . . . Scot 56·25 N 5·35 W
215 Oban Hills . . . . Nig. 5·35 N 8·30 E
107 O'Bannon (ō-băn'nŏn) Ky. (Louisville In.) 38·17 N 85·30 W
97 Obatogamau (L.) (ō-bà-tō'găm-ô) . Can. 49·38 N 74·10 W
218 Obbia (ôb'byä) Som. (Horn of Afr. In.) 5·24 N 48·28 E
161 Oberhausen (ō'bĕr-hou'zĕn) F.R.G. (Ruhr In.) 51·27 N 6·51 E
116 Oberlin (o'bēr-lĭn) . . . . Ks. 39·49 N 100·30 W
104 Oberlin . . . . Oh. 41·15 N 82·15 W
158 Oberösterreich (Prov.) . . . . Aus. 48·05 N 13·15 E
149 Oberroth (ō'bĕr-rōt) F.R.G. (Munich In.) 48·19 N 11·20 E
149 Ober-Schleissheim (ō'bĕr-shlīs-hēm) F.R.G.(Munich In.) 48·15 N 11·34 E
197 Obi, Kepulauan (Is.) (ō'bê) . Indon. 1·25 S 128·15 E
135 Óbidos (ō'bê-dōōzh) . . . . Braz. 1·57 S 55·32 W
194 Obihiro (ō'bē-hē'rō) . . . . Jap. 42·55 N 142·50 E
120 Obion (R.) . . . . Tn. 36·10 N 89·25 W
120 Obion (R.), North Fk. (ô-bī'ŏn) Tn. 35·49 N 89·06 W
167 Obitochnaya, Kosa (C.) (kô-sä' ô-bē-tôch'nà-yà) Sov. Un. 46·32 N 36·07 E
195 Obitsu (R.) (ō'bēt'sōō) Jap. (Tōkyō In.) 35·19 N 140·03 E
218 Obock (ō-bŏk') Djibouti (Horn of Afr. In.) 11·55 N 43·15 E
166 Obol' (R.) (ō-bŏl') . . . . . . Sov. Un. 55·24 N 29·24 E
167 Oboyan' (ô-bô-yän') . . . . . Sov. Un. 51·14 N 36·16 E
172 Obskaya Guba (B.) . . . . . . Sov. Un. 67·13 N 73·45 E
214 Obuasi . . . . Ghana 6·14 N 1·39 W
167 Obukhov (ō'bōō-kôf) . . . . . Sov. Un. 50·07 N 30·36 E
174 Obukhovo . Sov. Un. (Moscow In.) 55·50 N 38·17 E
121 Ocala (ô-kä'lá) . . . . Fl. 29·11 N 82·09 W
124 Ocampo (ô-käm'pō) . . . . Mex. 22·49 N 99·23 W
134 Ocaña (ô-kän'yä) . . . . Col. 8·15 N 73·37 W
162 Ocaña (ô-kä'n-yä) . . . . Sp. 39·58 N 3·31 W
210 Occidental, Grand Erg (Dunes) Alg. 29·30 N 00·45 W
134 Occidental, Cordillera (Mts.) (kôr-dēl-yĕ'rä ôk-sê-dĕn-täl') Col. (In.) 5·05 N 76·04 W
134 Occidental, Cordillera (Mts.) Peru 10·12 S 76·58 W
122 Occidental, Sierra Madre (Mts.) (sē-ĕ'r-rä-mä'drĕ-ôk-sē-dĕn-tä'l) Mex. 29·30 N 107·30 W
114 Ocean Beach (ō'shăn bēch) Ca. (In.) 32·44 N 117·14 W
119 Ocean Bight (B.) . . . . Ba. 21·15 N 73·15 W
105 Ocean City . . . . Md. 38·20 N 75·10 W
105 Ocean City . . . . NJ 39·15 N 74·35 W
92 Ocean Falls (Fôls) . . . . Can. 52·21 N 127·40 W
202 Ocean Grove Austl. (Melbourne In.) 38·16 S 144·32 E
105 Ocean Grove (grōv) . . . . NJ 40·10 N 74·00 W
114 Oceanside (ō'shăn-sīd) . . . . Ca. 33·11 N 117·22 W
106 Oceanside . . . . NY (New York In.) 40·38 N 73·39 W
120 Ocean Springs (sprĭngs) . . . . . . Ms. 30·25 N 88·49 W
165 Ocenele Mari . . . . Rom. 45·05 N 24·17 E
167 Ochakov (ô-chä'kôf) . . . . . . Sov. Un. 46·38 N 31·33 E
188 Ochina Ho (R.) . . . . China 41·15 N 100·46 E
192 Ochir . . . . China 45·38 N 115·35 E
120 Ochlockonee R. (ŏk-lô-kō'nē) Fl.-Ga. 30·10 N 84·38 W
120 Ocilla (ô-sĭl'á) . . . . Ga. 31·36 N 83·15 W
156 Ockelbo (ôk'ĕl-bô) . . . . Swe. 60·54 N 16·35 E
121 Ocmulgee (R.) . . . . Ga. 32·35 N 83·30 W
120 Ocmulgee Natl. Mon. (ôk-mŭl'gē) Ga. 32·45 N 83·28 W
165 Ocna-Sibiului (ôk'nà-sê-byōō-lōō-ê) Rom. 45·52 N 24·04 E
129 Ocoa, Bahai de (B.) (bä-ä'ē-ô-kō'ä) Dom. Rep. 18·20 N 70·40 W
125 Ococingo (ô-kô-sē'n-gô) . . . . . Mex. 17·03 N 92·18 W
126 Ocom, L. (ô-kō'm) . . . . . Mex. (In.) 19·26 N 88·18 W
120 Oconee, (R.) (ô-kō'nē) . . . . Ga. 32·45 N 83·00 W
109 Oconomowoc (ô-kŏn'ô-mô-wŏk') Wi. 43·06 N 88·24 W
109 Oconto (ô-kŏn'tō) . . . . Wi. 44·54 N 87·55 W
109 Oconto (R.) . . . . Wi. 45·08 N 88·24 W
109 Oconto Falls . . . . Wi. 44·53 N 88·11 W
126 Ocós (ô-kōs') . . . . Guat. 14·31 N 92·12 W
126 Ocotal (ô-kô-täl') . . . . Nic. 13·36 N 86·31 W
126 Ocotepeque (ô-kô-tà-pā'kà) . Hond. 14·25 N 89·13 W
124 Ocotlán (ō-kô-tlän') . . . . Mex. 20·19 N 102·44 W
125 Ocotlán de Morelos (dā mô-rā'lōs) Mex. 16·46 N 96·41 W
125 Ocozocoautla (ô-kō'zô-kwä-ōō'tlä) Mex. 16·44 N 93·22 W
135 Ocumare del Tuy (ō-kōō-mä'rā del twē') Ven. (In.) 10·07 N 66·47 W

ăt; finăl; rāte; senâte; ärm; åsk; sofá; fâre; ch-choose; dh-as th in other; bē; êvent; bĕt; recĕnt; cratẽr; g-go; gh-guttural g; bĭt; ĭ-short neutral; rīde; ĸ-guttural k as ch in German ich;

Page	Name Pronunciation Region	Lat. °′	Long. °′
214	Oda....................Ghana	5·55 N	0·59 W
195	Odawara (ō′dȧ-wä′rä)........Jap.	35·15 N	139·10 E
156	Odda (ôdh-ȧ)..............Nor.	60·04 N	6·30 E
218	Oddur....Som. (Horn of Afr. In.)	3·55 N	43·45 E
108	Odebolt (ō′dē-bōlt)..........Ia.	42·20 N	95·14 W
162	Odemira (ō-dȧ-mē′rȧ).......Port.	37·35 N	8·40 W
171	Ödemis (û′dĕ-mēsh)........Tur.	38·12 N	28·00 E
218	Odendaalsrus (ō′dĕn-däls-rûs′) S. Afr. (Johannesburg & Pretoria In.)	27·52 S	26·41 E
156	Odense (ō′dhĕn-sĕ)..........Den.	55·24 N	10·20 E
106	Odenton (ō′dĕn-tŭn) Md. (Baltimore In.)	39·05 N	76·43 W
158	Odenwald (For.) (ō′dĕn-väld) F.R.G.	49·39 N	8·55 E
158	Oder R. (ō′dẽr)..........G.D.R.	52·40 N	14·19 E
167	Odessa (ô-dĕs′sä)........Sov. Un.	46·28 N	30·44 E
118	Odessa (ô-dĕs′ȧ)............Tx.	31·52 N	120·21 W
110	Odessa....................Wa.	47·20 N	118·42 W
167	Odessa (Oblast).........Sov. Un.	46·05 N	29·48 E
162	Odiel (R.) (ō-dē-ĕl′)..........Sp.	37·47 N	6·42 W
214	Odienné (ō-dē-ĕn-nā′) Ivory Coast	9·30 N	7·34 W
148	Odiham (ŏd′ē-ȧm) Eng. (London In.)	51·14 N	0·56 W
174	Odintsovo (ô-dēn′tsô-vô) Sov. Un. (Moscow In.)	55·40 N	37·16 E
197	Odioñgan (ō-dē-ôŋ′gän). Phil. (In.)	12·24 N	121·59 E
163	Odivelas (ō-dē-vā′lyäs) Port. (Lisbon In.)	38·47 N	9·11 W
159	Odobesti (ō-dô-bĕsh′t′)......Rom.	45·46 N	27·08 E
116	O'Donnell (ō-dŏn′ĕl)..........Tx.	32·59 N	101·51 W
159	Odorhei (ō-dôr-hā′).........Rom.	46·18 N	25·17 E
159	Odra R. (ô′drȧ).............Pol.	50·28 N	17·55 E
135	Oeiras (wȧ-ē-räzh′).........Braz.	7·05 S	42·01 W
163	Oeirás (ô-ĕ′y-rȧ′s) Port. (Lisbon In.)	38·42 N	9·18 W
109	Oelwein (ōl′wīn)..............Ia.	42·40 N	91·56 W
116	O'Fallon (ō-făl′ŭn) Il. (St. Louis In.)	38·36 N	89·55 W
111	O'Fallon Cr.................Mt.	46·25 N	104·47 W
164	Ofanto (R.) (ô-fän′tō).........It.	41·08 N	15·33 E
215	Offa.......................Nig.	8·09 N	4·44 E
158	Offenbach (ôf′ĕn-bäk)......F.R.G.	50·06 N	8·50 E
158	Offenburg (ôf′ĕn-bŏŏrgh)...F.R.G.	48·28 N	7·57 E
195	Ofuna (ō′fōō-nä). Jap (Tōkyō In.)	35·21 N	139·32 E
211	Ogaden Plat. Eth. (Horn of Afr. In.)	6·45 N	44·53 E
195	Ogaki......................Jap.	35·21 N	136·36 E
108	Ogallala (ō-gä-lä′lä)..........Ne.	41·08 N	101·44 W
215	Ogbomosho (ŏg-bô-mō′shō)...Nig.	8·08 N	4·15 E
109	Ogden (ŏg′dĕn)..............Ia.	42·10 N	94·20 W
113	Ogden...Ut. (Salt Lake City In.)	41·14 N	111·58 W
113	Ogden Pk..Ut. (Salt Lake City In.)	41·11 N	111·51 W
113	Ogden R...Ut. (Salt Lake City In.)	41·16 N	111·54 W
106	Ogdensburg (ŏg′dĕnz-bûrg) NJ (New York In.)	41·05 N	74·36 W
105	Ogdensburg..................NY	44·40 N	75·30 W
121	Ogeechee, (R.) (ô-gē′chē).....Ga.	32·35 N	81·50 W
218	Ogies....................S. Afr. (Johannesburg & Pretoria In.)	26·03 S	29·04 E
90	Ogilvie Mts. (ō′g′l-vĭ).......Can.	64·45 N	138·10 W
104	Oglesby (ō′g′lz-bĭ)............Il.	41·20 N	89·00 W
164	Oglio (R.) (ōl′yō).............It.	45·15 N	10·19 E
195	Ōgo (ō′gô).......Jap. (Ōsaka In.)	34·49 N	135·06 E
216	Ogooué (R.)...............Gabon	0·50 S	9·20 E
214	Ogou (R.)..................Togo	8·05 N	1·30 E
174	Ogudnëvo (ôg-ŏŏg-nyô′vô) Sov. Un. (Moscow In.)	56·04 N	38·17 E
164	Ogulin (ō-gōō-lēn′).........Yugo.	45·17 N	15·11 E
215	Ogwashi-Uku.................Nig.	6·10 N	6·31 E
137	O'Higgins (Prov.) (ô-kē′gēns) Chile (Santiago In.)	34·17 S	70·52 W
103	Ohio, (State) (ô′hī′ō)........U. S.	40·30 N	83·15 W
104	Ohio R.....................U. S.	37·25 N	88·05 W
121	Ohoopee (R.) (ô-hōō′pē)......Ga.	32·32 N	82·38 W
158	Ohře (Eger) R. (ōr′zhĕ) (ā′gẽr) Czech.	50·08 N	12·45 E
165	Ohrid (ō′ĸrēd)..............Yugo.	41·08 N	20·46 E
165	Ohrid (L.)............Alb.-Yugo.	40·58 N	20·35 E
195	Ōi (oi′).........Jap. (Tōkyō In.)	35·51 N	139·31 E
156	Oieren (L.) (ûĭĕrĕn).........Nor.	59·50 N	11·25 E
195	Oi-Gawa (Strm.) (ō′ē-gä′wȧ)..Jap.	35·09 N	138·05 E
105	Oil City (oil sĭ′tĭ)............Pa.	41·25 N	79·40 W
149	Oirschot..Neth. (Amsterdam In.)	51·30 N	5·20 E
160	Oise (R.) (wäz)...............Fr.	49·30 N	2·56 E
149	Oisterwijk. Neth. (Amsterdam In.)	51·34 N	5·13 E
195	Oita (ō′ē-tä)................Jap.	33·14 N	131·38 E
195	Oji (ō′jē)........Jap. (Ōsaka In.)	34·36 N	135·43 E
118	Ojinaga (ō-Kē-nä′gä)........Mex.	29·34 N	104·26 W
125	Ojitlán (San Lucas) (ōkē-tlän′) (sän-lōō′käs). Mex.	18·04 N	96·23 W
124	Ojo Caliente (ōĸō käl-yĕn′tā). Mex.	21·50 N	100·43 W
124	Ojocaliente (ô-ĸô-kä-lyĕ′n-tĕ) Mex.	22·39 N	102·15 W
128	Ojo del Toro, Pico (Pk.) (pē′kô-ô-ĸō-dĕl-tô′rô). Cuba	19·55 N	77·25 W
89	Oka (ō-kä)...Can. (Montreal In.)	45·28 N	74·05 W
171	Oka (R.) (ô-kä′)........Sov. Un.	52·10 N	35·20 E
172	Oka (R.) (ō-kä′)........Sov. Un.	53·28 N	101·09 E
170	Oka (R.) (ô-kȧ′)........Sov. Un.	55·10 N	42·10 E
212	Okahandja..............Namibia	21·50 S	16·45 E
93	Okanagan (R.) (ō′kȧ-näg′ȧn). Can.	49·06 N	119·43 W
93	Okanagan L.................Can.	50·00 N	119·28 W
210	Okano (R.) (ô′kä′nō)......Gabon	0·15 N	11·08 E
110	Okanogan...................Wa.	48·20 N	119·34 W
110	Okanogan R.................Wa.	48·36 N	119·33 W
120	Okatibbee (R.) (ō′kä-tĭb′ē)...Ms.	32·37 N	88·54 W
120	Okatoma Cr. (ô-kȧ-tō′mă)....Ms.	31·43 N	89·34 W
216	Okavango (Cubango) (R.) Ang.-S. W. Afr.	17·10 S	18·20 E
212	Okavango Swp..............Bots.	19·30 S	23·02 E
195	Okaya (ō′kȧ-yȧ)..............Jap.	36·04 N	138·01 E
195	Okayama (ō′kȧ-yä′mȧ).......Jap.	34·39 N	133·54 E
195	Okazaki (ō′kȧ-zä′kē).........Jap.	34·58 N	137·09 E
121	Okeechobee (ō-kē-chō′bē).......Fl.	27·15 N	80·50 W
121	Okeechobee, L...........Fl. (In.)	27·00 N	80·49 W
116	Okeene (ô-kēn′)..............Ok.	36·06 N	98·19 W
121	Okefenokee Swp. (ō′kē-fē-nō′kē) Ga.	30·54 N	82·20 W
117	Okemah (ô-kē′mä)...........Ok.	35·26 N	96·18 W
215	Okene......................Nig.	7·33 N	6·15 E
155	Oker (R.) (ō′kẽr).........F.R.G.	52·23 N	10·00 E
173	Okha (ŭ-ĸä′)...........Sov. Un.	53·44 N	143·12 E
174	Okhotino (ô-ĸô′tĭ-nô) Sov. Un. (Moscow In.)	56·14 N	38·24 E
173	Okhotsk (ô-ĸôtsk′).......Sov. Un.	59·28 N	143·32 E
183	Okhotsk, Sea of (ô-kôtsk′)....Asia	56·45 N	146·00 E
195	Oki Guntō (Arch.) (ō′kē gŏŏn′tō) Jap.	36·17 N	133·05 E
194	Okinawa (I.) (ō′kē-nä′wȧ)....Jap.	26·30 N	128·30 E
194	Okinawa Guntō (Is.) (gŏŏn′tō′) Jap.	26·50 N	127·25 E
195	Okino (I.) (ō′kē-nô)..........Jap.	36·22 N	133·27 E
194	Ōkino Erabu (I.) (ō-kē′nô-ȧ-rä′bōō). Jap.	27·18 N	129·00 E
102	Oklahoma (State) (ô-klȧ-hō′mȧ). U. S.	36·00 N	98·20 W
117	Oklahoma City...............Ok.	35·27 N	97·32 W
121	Oklawaha (R.) (ŏk-lȧ-wô′hô)..Fl.	29·13 N	82·00 W
117	Okmulgee (ôk-mŭl′gē).........Ok.	35·37 N	95·58 W
107	Okolona (ō-kô-lō′nȧ) Ky. (Louisville In.)	38·08 N	85·41 W
120	Okolona....................Ms.	33·59 N	88·43 W
194	Okushiri (I.) (ō′koo-shē′rē)...Jap.	42·12 N	139·30 E
215	Okuta......................Nig.	9·14 N	3·15 E
112	Olalla (ō-lä′lȧ)..Wa. (Seattle In.)	47·26 N	122·33 W
126	Olanchito (ō′län-chē′tô)....Hond.	15·28 N	86·35 W
156	Öland (I.) (û-länd′).........Swe.	57·03 N	17·15 E
113	Olathe (ô-lā′thē) Ks. (Kansas City In.)	38·53 N	94·49 W
136	Olavarría (ō-lä-vär-rē′ä)......Arg.	36·49 N	60·15 W
159	Olawa (ô-lä′vȧ).............Pol.	50·57 N	17·18 E
137	Olazcoago (ô-läz-kôä′gô) Arg. (Buenos Aires In.)	35·14 S	60·37 W
164	Olbia (ô′l-byä)...............It.	40·55 N	9·28 E
149	Olching (ōl′ĸĕng) F.R.G. (Munich In.)	48·13 N	11·21 E
128	Old Bahama Chan. (bȧ-hā′mȧ) N. A.	22·45 N	78·30 W
129	Old Bight...................Ba.	24·15 N	75·20 W
106	Old Bridge (brĭj) NJ (New York In.)	40·24 N	74·22 W
90	Old Crow (crō)..............Can.	67·51 N	139·58 W
158	Oldenburg (ôl′dĕn-bŏŏrgh). F.R.G.	53·09 N	8·13 E
105	Old Forge (fôrj).............Pa.	41·20 N	75·50 W
148	Oldham (ōld′ȧm)............Eng.	53·32 N	2·07 W
101	Old Harbor (här′bẽr).........Ak.	57·18 N	153·20 W
154	Old Head of Kinsale (ōld hĕd ŏv kĭn-sāl). Ire.	51·35 N	8·35 W
119	Old R.................Tx. (In.)	29·54 N	94·52 W
93	Olds (ōldz).................Can.	51·47 N	114·06 W
212	Old Tate...................Bots.	21·18 S	27·43 E
98	Old Town (toun)............Me.	44·55 N	68·42 W
94	Old Wives L. (wīvz)........Can.	50·56 N	106·00 W
105	Olean (ō-lē-ăn′)..............NY	42·05 N	78·25 W
159	Olecko (ô-lĕt′skô)............Pol.	54·02 N	22·29 E
173	Olekma (R.) (ô-lyĕk-mȧ′). Sov. Un.	55·41 N	120·33 E
173	Olëkminsk (ô-lyĕk-mênsk′) Sov. Un.	60·39 N	120·40 E
173	Olenëk (R.) (ô-lyĕ-nyôk′). Sov. Un.	70·18 N	121·15 E
160	Oléron Île, d' (I.) (ēl′ dō lā-rôɴ′). Fr.	45·52 N	1·58 W
159	Oleśnica (ô-lĕsh-nĭ′tsȧ).......Pol.	51·13 N	17·24 E
161	Olfen (ōl′fĕn)...F.R.G. (Ruhr In.)	51·43 N	7·22 E
173	Ol'ga (ôl′gȧ)............Sov. Un.	43·48 N	135·44 E
194	Ol'gi, Zaliv (B.) (zä′lĭf ôl′gĭ) Sov. Un.	43·43 N	135·25 E
167	Ol'gopol (ôl-gô-pôl′y′)....Sov. Un.	48·11 N	29·28 E
162	Olhão (ôl-youɴ′)...........Port.	37·02 N	7·54 W
213	Olievenhoutpoort.........S. Afr. (Johannesburg & Pretoria In.)	25·58 S	27·55 E
212	Olifants (R.) (ŏl′ĭ-fănts)....S. Afr.	23·58 S	31·00 E
165	Ólimbos...................Grc.	40·03 N	22·22 E
183	Ólimbos (Mtn.) Cyprus (Palestine In.)	34·56 N	32·52 E
124	Olinalá (ô-lē-nä-lä′).........Mex.	17·47 N	98·51 W
135	Olinda (ô-lē′n-dä)..........Braz.	8·00 S	34·58 W
163	Oliva (ô-lē′vä)...............Sp.	38·54 N	0·07 W
162	Oliva de Jerez (ô-lē′vä dā hā′rĕth) Sp.	38·33 N	6·55 W
163	Olivais (ô-lē-vȧ′ys) Port. (Lisbon In.)	38·46 N	9·06 W
104	Olive Hill (ŏl′ĭv)............Ky.	38·15 N	83·10 W
137	Oliveira (ô-lē-vā′rä) Braz. (Rio de Janeiro In.)	20·42 S	44·49 W
162	Olivenza (ō-lē-vĕn′thä)........Sp.	38·42 N	7·06 W
93	Oliver (ŏ′lĭ-vẽr).............Can.	49·11 N	119·33 W
89	Oliver......Can. (Edmonton In.)	53·38 N	113·21 W
113	Oliver (ŏ′lĭvẽr)..Wi. (Duluth In.)	46·39 N	92·12 W
89	Oliver L.....Can. (Edmonton In.)	53·19 N	113·00 W
100	Olivia (ō-lĭv′ē-ȧ)............Mn.	44·46 N	95·00 W
136	Olivos (ōlē′vōs) Arg. (Buenos Aires In.)	34·15 S	58·29 W
158	Olkusz (ôl′kōōsh)...........Pol.	50·16 N	19·41 E
134	Ollagüe (ô-lyä′gā)..........Chile	21·17 S	68·17 W
148	Ollerton (ôl′ẽr-tŭn)..........Eng.	53·12 N	1·02 W
113	Olmos Park (ōl′mŭs pärk′) Tx. (San Antonio In.)	29·27 N	98·32 W
104	Olney (ŏl′nĭ)..................Il.	38·45 N	88·05 W
112	Olney (ŏl′nē)..Or. (Portland In.)	46·06 N	123·45 W
116	Olney.......................Tx.	33·24 N	98·43 W
99	Olomane (R.) (ō′lô mȧ′nĕ)...Can.	51·05 N	60·50 W
159	Olomouc (ô′lô-mōts).......Czech.	49·37 N	17·15 E
157	Olonets (ô-lô′nĕts).......Sov. Un.	60·58 N	32·54 E
197	Olongapo..............Phil. (In.)	14·49 S	120·17 E
160	Oloron, Gave d' (Strm.) (gäv-dŏ-lŏ-rŏɴ′). Fr.	43·21 N	0·44 W
160	Oloron-Ste. Marie (ō-lô-rôɴt′săɴt mȧ-rē′). Fr.	43·11 N	1·37 W
163	Olot (ô-lōt′)..................Sp.	42·09 N	2·30 E
161	Olpe (ōl′pĕ)....F.R.G. (Ruhr In.)	51·02 N	7·51 E
167	Ol'shanka (ôl′shȧŋ-kȧ)...Sov. Un.	48·14 N	30·52 E
167	Ol'shany (ôl′shȧn-ē).....Sov. Un.	50·02 N	35·54 E
158	Olsnitz (ōlz′nētz).........G.D.R.	50·25 N	12·11 E
159	Olsztyn (ôl′shtēn)............Pol.	53·47 N	20·28 E
158	Olten (ôl′tĕn)..............Switz.	47·20 N	7·53 E
165	Oltenita (ôl-tā′nĭ-tsȧ).......Rom.	44·05 N	26·39 E
153	Olt R......................Rom.	44·09 N	24·40 E
162	Olvera (ôl-vĕ′rä).............Sp.	36·55 N	7·16 W
110	Olympia (ô-lĭm′pĭ-ȧ).........Wa.	47·02 N	122·52 W
110	Olympic Mts................Wa.	47·54 N	123·58 W
110	Olympic Natl. Park (ô-lĭm′pĭk) Wa.	47·54 N	123·00 W
110	Olympus Mt. (ô-lĭm′pŭs).....Wa.	47·43 N	123·30 W
105	Olyphant (ŏl′ĭ-fănt)...........Pa.	41·30 N	75·40 W
173	Olyutorskiy, Mys (C.) (ŭl-yōō′tŏr-skē). Sov. Un.	59·49 N	167·16 E
195	Omae-Zaki (Pt.) (ō′mä-ȧ zä′kē) Jap.	34·37 N	138·15 E
154	Omagh (ō′mä)...........N. Ire.	54·35 N	7·25 W
108	Omaha (ō′mȧ-hä)............Ne.	41·18 N	95·57 W
108	Omaha Ind. Res..............Ne.	42·09 N	96·08 W
182	Oman.....................Asia	20·00 N	57·45 E
186	Oman, G. of...............Asia	24·24 N	58·58 E
212	Omaruru (ō-mä-rōō′rōō)..Namibia	21·25 S	16·50 E
216	Omboué..................Gabon	1·34 S	9·15 E
164	Ombrone (R.) (ôm-brō′nā).....It.	42·48 N	11·18 E
	Omdurman, see UmmDurmān		
125	Omealca (ōmȧ-äl′kō)........Mex.	18·44 N	96·45 W
124	Ometepec (ô-mā-tȧ-pĕk′)....Mex.	16·41 N	98·27 W
211	Om Hajer...................Eth.	14·06 N	36·46 E
92	Omineca (R.) (ô-mĭ-nĕk′ȧ)...Can.	55·10 N	125·45 W
92	Omineca Mts................Can.	56·00 N	125·00 W
195	Ōmiya (ō′mē-yȧ). Jap. (Tōkyō In.)	35·54 S	139·38 E
126	Omoa (ô-mō′rä)............Hond.	15·43 N	88·03 W
173	Omolon (R.) (ō′mō).....Sov. Un.	67·43 N	159·15 E
195	Ōmori (Kioroshi) (ō′mô-rē) (kē′ô-rō′shē) Jap. (Tōkyō In.)	35·50 N	140·09 E
211	Omo R. (ō′mō)..............Eth.	5·54 N	36·09 E
215	Omoko.....................Nig.	5·20 N	6·39 E
126	Omotepe, Isla de (I.) (ē′s-lä-dĕ-ō-mô-tā′pȧ). Nic.	11·32 N	85·30 W
109	Omro (ŏm′rō)...............Wi.	44·01 N	89·46 W
172	Omsk (ômsk)..........Sov. Un.	55·12 N	73·19 E
195	Ōmura (ō′mōō-rȧ)...........Jap.	32·56 N	129·57 E
195	Ōmuta (ō-mōō-tȧ)...........Jap.	33·02 N	130·28 E
170	Omutninsk (ô′mōō-tēnsk). Sov. Un.	58·38 N	52·10 E
108	Onawa (ŏn-ȧ-wȧ)..............Ia.	42·02 N	96·05 W
104	Onaway....................Mi.	45·25 N	84·10 W
216	Oncócua...................Ang.	16·34 S	13·28 E
163	Onda (ōn′dä).................Sp.	39·58 N	0·13 W
159	Ondava (R.) (ōn′dȧ-vȧ)....Czech.	48·51 N	21·40 E
215	Ondo......................Nig.	7·04 N	4·47 E
192	Öndör Haan..............Mong.	47·20 N	110·40 E
170	Onega (ô-nyĕ′gȧ)........Sov. Un.	63·50 N	38·08 E
170	Onega (.R)...............Sov. Un.	63·20 N	39·20 E
	Onega, L., see Onezhskoye Ozero		
105	Oneida (ô-nī′dȧ)..............NY	43·05 N	75·40 W
105	Oneida (L.)..................NY	43·10 N	76·00 W
108	O'Neill (ō-nēl′)..............Ne.	42·28 N	98·38 W
173	Onekotan (I.) (ŭ-nyĕ-kŭ-tän′) Sov. Un.	49·45 N	153·45 E
105	Oneonta (ō-nē-ŏn′tȧ).........NY	42·25 N	75·05 W
170	Onezhskaja Guba (B.)...Sov. Un.	64·30 N	36·00 E
170	Onezhskiy, P-Ov. (Pen.)..Sov. Un.	64·30 N	37·40 E
170	Onezhskoye Ozero (Onega, L.) (ô-năsh′skô-yĕ ô′zĕ-rô). Sov. Un.	62·02 N	34·35 E
188	Ongin (ŏn′gĭn′)............Mong.	46·00 N	102·46 E
185	Ongole....................India	15·36 N	80·03 E
213	Onilahy (R.)...............Mad.	23·41 S	45·00 E
215	Onitsha (ô-nĭt′shȧ)..........Nig.	6·09 N	6·47 W
195	Onomichi (ō′nô-mē′chē)......Jap.	34·27 N	133·12 E
173	Onon (R.) (ô′nôn)........Sov. Un.	50·33 N	114·18 E
173	Onon Gol (R.) (ô′nôn)...Sov. Un.	48·30 N	110·38 E
135	Onoto (ô-nŏ′tô)........Ven. (In.)	9·38 N	65·03 W
204	Onslow (ŏnz′lō)...........Austl.	21·53 S	115·00 E
121	Onslow B. (ônz′lō)...........NC	34·22 N	77·35 W
195	Ontake San (Mtn.) (ôn′tä-kȧ sän) Jap.	35·55 N	137·29 E
113	Ontario (ŏn-tā′rĭ-ō) Ca. (Los Angeles In.)	34·04 N	117·39 W
110	Ontario....................Or.	44·02 N	116·57 W
91	Ontario (Prov.).............Can.	50·47 N	88·50 W
103	Ontario, L............U. S.-Can.	43·35 N	79·05 W
163	Onteniente (ōn-tȧ-nyĕn′tā)....Sp.	38·48 N	0·35 W
109	Ontonagon (ŏn-tô-năg′ŏn).....Mi.	46·50 N	89·20 W
195	Ōnuki (ō′nōō-kē). Jap. (Tōkyō In.)	35·17 N	139·51 E
204	Oodnadatta (ōōd′nȧ-dȧ′tȧ)..Austl.	27·38 S	135·40 E
204	Ooldea Station (ōōl-dā′ä)...Austl.	30·35 S	132·08 E
117	Oologah Res.................Ok.	36·43 N	95·32 W
149	Ooltgensplaat Neth. (Amsterdam In.)	51·41 N	4·19 E
120	Oostanaula (R.) (ōō-stȧ-nô′lȧ). Ga.	34·25 N	85·10 W
155	Oostende (ōst-ĕn′dĕ).........Bel.	51·14 N	2·55 E
149	Oosterhout. Neth. (Amsterdam In.)	51·38 N	4·52 E
155	Ooster Schelde (R.).........Neth.	51·40 N	3·40 E
92	Ootsa L....................Can.	53·49 N	126·18 W
126	Opalaca, Sierra de (Mts.) (sē-ĕ′r-rä-dĕ-ô-pä-lä′kä). Hond.	14·30 N	88·29 W
95	Opasquia (ō-păs′kwē-ȧ).......Can.	53·16 N	93·53 W
159	Opatow (ô-pä′tŏŏf)...........Pol.	50·47 N	21·25 E
159	Opava (ō′pä-vä)...........Czech.	49·56 N	17·52 E
136	Opdal (ôp′däl)..............Nor.	62·37 N	9·41 E
120	Opelika (ŏp-ē-lī′kȧ)...........Al.	32·39 N	85·23 W

ng-sing; ŋ-baŋk; ɴ-nasalized n; nŏd; cŏmmit; ōld; ôbey; ôrder; fōōd; fŏŏt; ou-out; s-soft; sh-dish; th-thin; pūre; ûnite; ûrn; stŭd; circŭs; ü-as "y" in study; '-indeterminate vowel.

324 Opelousas — Ouahigouya PRONOUNCING INDEX

Page	Name Pronunciation Region	Lat. °′	Long. °′
119	Opelousas (ŏp-ē-lōō'sȧs) La.	30·33 N	92·04 W
105	Opeongo (L.) (ŏp-ê-ŏŋ'gō) Can.	45·40 N	78·20 W
111	Opheim (ô-fīm') Mt.	48·51 N	106·19 W
101	Ophir (ō'fēr) Ak.	63·10 N	156·28 W
183	Ophir, Mt. Mala. (Singapore In.)	2·22 N	102·37 E
126	Opico (ô-pē'kō) Sal.	13·50 N	89·23 W
91	Opinaca (R.) (ŏp-ĭ-nä'kȧ) Can.	52·28 N	77·40 W
161	Opladen (ōp'lä-dĕn) F.R.G. (Ruhr In.)	51·04 N	7·00 E
215	Opobo Nig.	4·34 N	7·27 E
166	Opochka (ō-pôch'kȧ) Sov. Un.	56·43 N	28·39 E
159	Opoczno (ō-pôch'nô) Pol.	51·22 N	20·18 E
159	Opole (ô-pôl'ȧ) Pol.	50·42 N	17·55 E
159	Opole Lubelskie (ō-pō'lā lōō-bĕl'skyĕ) Pol.	51·09 N	21·58 E
	Oporto, see Pôrto		
110	Opportunity (ŏp-ŏr tū'nĭ tĭ) Wa.	47·37 N	117·20 W
167	Oposhnya (ô-pôsh'nyȧ) Sov. Un.	49·57 N	34·34 E
120	Opp (ŏp) Al.	31·18 N	86·15 W
113	Oquirrh Mts. (ō'kwēr) Ut. (Salt Lake City In.)	40·38 N	112·11 W
159	Oradea (ô-räd'yä) Rom.	47·02 N	21·55 E
152	Oran (Ouahran) (ō-rän) (ô-räN') Alg.	35·46 N	0·45 W
136	Orán (ô-rȧ'n) Arg.	23·13 S	64·17 W
117	Oran (ôr'ȧn) Mo.	37·05 N	89·39 W
203	Orange (ŏr'ĕnj) Austl.	33·15 S	149·08 E
113	Orange Ca. (Los Angeles In.)	33·48 N	117·51 W
105	Orange Ct.	41·15 N	73·00 W
160	Orange (ô-raNzh') Fr.	44·08 N	4·48 E
106	Orange NJ (New York In.)	40·46 N	74·14 W
116	Orange Tx.	30·07 N	93·44 W
135	Orange, Cabo (C.) (kȧ-bô-rȧ'n-zhĕ) Braz.	4·25 N	51·30 W
121	Orange (L.) Fl.	29·30 N	82·12 W
212	Orange (R.) Namibia-S. Afr.	29·15 S	17·30 E
121	Orangeburg (ŏr'ĕnj-bûrg) SC	33·30 N	80·50 W
128	Orange Cay (I.) (ŏr-ĕnj kē) Ba.	24·55 N	79·05 W
108	Orange City Ia.	43·01 N	96·06 W
212	Orange Free State (Prov.) S. Afr.	28·15 S	26·00 E
89	Orangeville (ŏr'ĕnj-vĭl) Can. (Toronto In.)	43·55 N	80·06 W
218	Orangeville S. Afr. (Johannesburg & Pretoria In.)	27·05 S	28·13 E
126	Orange Walk (wôl''k) Belize (In.)	18·09 N	88·32 W
197	Orani (ō-rä'nê) Phil. (In.)	14·47 N	120·32 E
149	Oranienburg (ō-rä'nē-ĕn-bŏŏrgh) G.D.R. (Berlin In.)	52·45 N	13·14 E
212	Oranjemund Namibia	28·33 S	16·20 E
165	Orastie (ô-rûsh'tyȧ) Rom.	45·50 N	23·14 E
	Oraşul-Stalin, see Braşov		
164	Orbetello (ôr-bȧ-tĕl'lō) It.	42·27 N	11·15 E
162	Orbigo (R.) (ôr-bē'gō) Sp.	42·30 N	5·55 W
203	Orbost (ôr'bŭst) Austl.	37·43 S	148·20 E
112	Orcas (I.) (ôr'kȧs) Wa. (Vancouver In.)	48·43 N	122·52 W
113	Orchard Farm (ôr'chērd färm) Mo. (St. Louis In.)	38·53 N	90·27 W
107	Orchard Park NY (Buffalo In.)	42·46 N	78·46 W
112	Orchards (ôr'chēdz) Wa. (Portland In.)	45·40 N	122·33 W
134	Orchilla (ôr-kĭl-ȧ) Ven.	11·47 N	66·34 W
108	Ord (ôrd) Ne.	41·35 N	98·57 W
204	Ord (R.) Austl.	17·30 S	128·40 E
174	Orda (ôr'dȧ) Sov. Un. (Urals In.)	56·50 N	57·12 E
162	Ōrdenes (ōr'dâ-nās) Sp.	43·46 N	8·24 W
192	Ordos Des. China	39·12 N	108·10 E
115	Ord Pk. Az.	33·55 N	109·40 W
171	Ordu (ôr'dōō) Tur.	41·00 N	37·50 E
162	Orduña (ôr-dōō'nyä) Sp.	42·59 N	3·01 W
116	Ordway (ôrd'wā) Co.	38·11 N	103·46 W
171	Ordzhonikidze (ora ghō Nĭ kĭd ze) Sov. Un.	43·05 N	44·35 E
156	Örebro (û'rĕ-brō) Swe.	59·16 N	15·11 E
174	Oredezh R. (ô'rĕ-dĕzh) Sov. Un. (Leningrad In.)	59·23 N	30·21 E
109	Oregon Il.	42·01 N	89·21 W
102	Oregon (State) U. S.	43·40 N	121·50 W
110	Oregon Caves Natl. Mon. (cāvz) Or.	42·05 N	123·13 W
112	Oregon City Or. (Portland In.)	45·21 N	122·36 W
156	Öregrund (û-rĕ-grŏŏnd) Swe.	60·20 N	18·26 E
167	Orekhov (ôr-yĕ'Kôf) Sov. Un.	47·34 N	35·51 E
166	Orekhovo-Zuyevo (ôr-yĕ'Kô-vô zōō'yĕ-vô) Sov. Un.	55·46 N	39·00 E
166	Orël (ôr-yôl') Sov. Un.	52·54 N	36·03 E
166	Orël (Oblast) Sov. Un.	52·35 N	36·08 E
167	Orel' (R.) Sov. Un.	49·08 N	34·55 E
115	Orem (ō'rĕm) Ut.	40·15 N	111·50 W
	Ore Mts., see Erzgebirge		
171	Orenburg (ô'rĕn-bŏŏrg) Sov. Un.	51·50 N	55·05 E
162	Orense (ô-rĕn'sā) Sp.	42·20 N	7·52 W
128	Organos, Sierra de los (Mts.) (sē-ĕ'r-rä-dĕ-lôs-ŏ'r-gä-nôs) Cuba	22·20 N	84·10 W
115	Organ Pipe Cactus Natl. Mon (ôr'găn pīp kăk'tŭs) Az.	32·14 N	113·05 W
137	Orgãos, Serra das (Mtn.) (sĕ'r-rä-däs-ôr-gouN's) Braz. (Rio de Janeiro In.)	22·30 S	43·01 W
167	Orgeyev (ôr-gyĕ'yĕf) Sov. Un.	47·27 N	28·49 E
188	Orhon Gol (R.) Mong.	48·33 N	103·07 E
134	Oriental, Cordillera (Mts.) (kôr-dēl-yĕ'rä ō-rê-ĕn-täl') Bol.	14·00 S	68·33 W
134	Oriental, Cordillera (Mts.) (kôr-dēl-yĕ'rä) Col. (In.)	3·30 N	74·27 W
129	Oriental, Cordillera (Mts.) (kôr-dēl-yĕ'rä-ô-ryĕ'n-täl) Dom. Rep.	18·55 N	69·40 W
122	Oriental, Sierra Madre, (Mts.) (sē-ĕ'r-rä-mä'drĕ-ô-ryĕ'n-täl') Mex.	25·30 N	100·45 W
163	Orihuela (ō'rê-wä'lä) Sp.	38·04 N	0·55 W
105	Orillia (ô-rĭl'ĭ-ȧ) Can.	44·35 N	79·25 W
111	Orin Wy.	42·40 N	105·10 W
112	Orinda Ca. (San Francisco In.)	37·53 N	122·11 W
134	Orinoco, Rio (R.) (rē'ō-ō-rĭ-nō'kō) Ven.	8·32 N	63·13 W
197	Orion (ō-rê-ōn') Phil. (In.)	14·37 N	120·34 E
184	Orissa (State) (ŏ-rĭs'ȧ) India	25·09 N	83·50 E
164	Oristano (ō-rês-tä'nō) It.	39·53 N	8·38 E
164	Oristano, Golfo di (G.) (gôl-fô-dē-ô-rês-tä'nō) It.	39·53 N	8·12 E
135	Orituco (R.) (ô-rē-tōō'kō) Ven. (In.)	9·37 N	66·25 W
135	Oriuco (R.) (ô-rêōō'kō) (R.) Ven. (In.)	9·36 N	66·25 W
157	Orivesi (L.) Fin.	62·15 N	29·55 E
125	Orizaba (ô-rê-zä'bä) Mex.	18·52 N	97·05 E
156	Orkdal (ôr'k-däl) Nor.	63·19 N	9·54 W
150	Örkedalen (ûr'kĕ-dä-lĕn) Nor.	63·13 N	9·53 E
156	Örken (L.) (ûr'kĕn) Swe.	57·11 N	14·45 E
156	Orkla (R.) (ôr'klȧ) Nor.	62·55 N	9·50 E
218	Orkney (ôrk'nĭ) S. Afr. (Johannesburg & Pretoria In.)	26·58 S	26·39 E
154	Orkney (Is.) Scot.	59·01 N	2·08 W
121	Orlando (ôr-lăn'dō) Fl. (In.)	28·32 N	81·22 W
213	Orlando (ôr-lăn-dô) S. Afr. (Johannesburg & Pretoria In.)	26·15 S	27·56 E
107	Orland Park (ôr-lăn') Il. (Chicago In.)	41·38 N	87·52 W
89	Orleans (ôr-lå-äN') Can. (Ottawa In.)	45·28 N	75·31 W
160	Orléans (ôr-lā-äN') Fr.	47·55 N	1·56 E
104	Orleans (ôr-lēnz') In.	38·40 N	86·25 W
89	Orléans, Île d' (I.) Can. (Quebec In.)	46·56 N	70·57 W
	Orléansville, see El Asnam		
121	Ormond Beach (ôr'mŏnd) Fl.	29·15 N	81·05 W
148	Ormskirk (ôrms'kērk) Eng.	53·34 N	2·53 W
89	Ormstown (ôrms'toun) Can. (Montreal In.)	45·07 N	74·00 W
160	Orne (R.) (ôrn') Fr.	49·05 N	0·32 W
159	Orneta (ôr-nyĕ'tä) Pol.	54·07 N	20·10 E
156	Ornö (I.) Swe.	59·02 N	18·35 E
150	Örnsköldsvik (ûrn'skôlts-vēk) Swe.	63·10 N	18·32 E
124	Oro, Rio del (R.) (rē'ō dĕl ō'rō) Mex.	18·04 N	100·59 W
108	Oro, Rio del (R.) Mex.	26·04 N	105·40 W
164	Orobie, Alpi (Mts.) (äl'pē-ô-rŏ'byĕ) It.	46·05 N	9·47 E
134	Orocué (ô-rô-kwā') Col.	4·48 N	71·26 W
215	Oron Nig.	4·48 N	8·14 E
154	Oronsay, Pass .of (ō'rŏn-sȧ) Scot.	55·55 N	6·25 W
164	Orosei, Golfo di (G.) (gôl-fô-dē-ō-rō-sā'ē) It.	40·12 N	9·45 E
159	Orosháza (ô-rôsh-hä'sô) Hung.	46·33 N	20·31 E
126	Orosi Vol. (ô-rō'sē) C. R.	11·00 N	85·30 W
114	Oroville (ōr'ô-vĭl) Ca.	39·29 N	121·34 W
110	Oroville Wa.	48·55 N	119·25 W
104	Orrville (ôr'vĭl) Oh.	40·45 N	81·50 W
156	Orsa (ôr'sä) Swe.	61·08 N	14·35 E
89	Orsainville Can. (Quebec In.)	46·23 N	71·17 W
156	Örsdals Vand (L.) (ûrs-däls vän) Nor.	58·39 N	6·06 E
166	Orsha (ôr'shȧ) Sov. Un.	54·29 N	30·28 E
171	Orsk (ôrsk) Sov. Un.	51·15 N	58·50 E
165	Orsova (ôr'shô-vä) Rom.	44·43 N	22·26 E
134	Ortega (ôr-tĕ'gä) Col. (In.)	3·56 N	75·12 W
162	Ortegal, Cabo (C.) (kȧ'bô-ôr-tȧ-gäl') Sp.	43·46 N	8·15 W
149	Orth Aus. (Vienna In.)	48·09 N	16·42 E
163	Orthez (ôr-tĕz') Fr.	43·29 N	0·43 W
162	Ortigueira (ôr-tê-gā'ê-rä) Sp.	43·40 N	7·50 W
112	Orting (ôrt'ĭng) . Wa. (Seattle In.)	47·06 N	122·12 W
164	Ortona (ôr-tō'nä) It.	42·22 N	14·22 E
108	Ortonville (ôr-tŭn-vĭl) Mn.	45·18 N	96·26 W
134	Oruro (ô-rōō'rō) Bol.	17·57 S	66·59 W
164	Orvieto (ôr-vyâ'tô) It.	42·43 N	12·08 E
165	Oryakhovo Bul.	43·43 N	23·59 E
156	Os (ôs) Nor.	60·24 N	5·22 E
170	Osa (ô'sȧ) Sov. Un.	57·18 N	55·25 E
127	Osa, Pen. de (ō'sä) C. R.	8·30 N	83·25 W
109	Osage (ō'sāj) Ia.	43·16 N	92·49 W
117	Osage (R.) Mo.	38·10 N	93·12 W
117	Osage City (ō'sāj sĭ'tĭ) Ks.	38·28 N	95·53 W
195	Ōsaka (ō'sä-kä) Jap. (Ōsaka In.)	34·40 N	135·27 E
195	Ōsaka (Pref.) Jap. (Ōsaka In.)	34·45 N	135·36 E
195	Ōsaka-Wan (B.) (wän) Jap.	34·34 N	135·16 E
109	Osakis (ô-sā'kĭs) Mn.	45·51 N	95·09 W
109	Osakis (L.) Mn.	45·55 N	94·55 W
117	Osawatomie (ŏs-ȧ-wăt'ō-mê) Ks.	38·29 N	94·57 W
116	Osborne (ŏz'bŭrn) Ks.	39·25 N	98·42 W
117	Osceola (ŏs-ê-ō'lȧ) Ar.	35·42 N	89·58 W
109	Osceola Ia.	41·04 N	93·45 W
117	Osceola Mo.	38·02 N	93·41 W
108	Osceola Ne.	41·11 N	97·34 W
117	Osceola Tn.	35·42 N	89·58 W
104	Oscoda (ŏs-kō'dȧ) Mi.	44·25 N	83·20 W
166	Osëtr (R.) (ô'sĕt'r) Sov. Un.	54·27 N	38·15 E
104	Osgood (ŏz'gŏŏd) In.	39·10 N	85·20 W
89	Osgoode Can. (Ottawa In.)	45·09 N	75·37 W
172	Osh (ôsh) Sov. Un.	40·28 N	72·47 E
105	Oshawa (ŏsh'ȧ-wȧ) Can.	43·50 N	78·50 W
195	Ōshima (I.) (ō'shē'mä) Jap.	34·47 N	139·35 E
108	Oshkosh (ŏsh'kŏsh) Ne.	41·24 N	102·22 W
109	Oshkosh Wi.	44·01 N	88·35 W
157	Oshmyany (ôsh-myä'nĭ) Sov. Un.	54·27 N	25·55 E
215	Oshogbo Nig.	7·47 N	4·34 E
165	Osijek (ôs'ĭ-yĕk) Yugo.	45·33 N	18·48 E
172	Osinniki (ŭ-sē'nyĭ-kē) Sov. Un.	53·29 N	85·19 E
109	Oskaloosa (ŏs-kȧ-lōō'sȧ) Ia.	41·16 N	92·40 W
156	Oskarshamn (ôs'kärs-häm'n) Swe.	57·16 N	16·24 E
156	Oskarström (ôs'kärs-strûm) Swe.	56·48 N	12·55 E
167	Oskol (R.) (ôs-kôl') Sov. Un.	51·00 N	37·41 E
156	Oslo (ôs'lō) Nor.	59·56 N	10·41 E
156	Oslo Fd (fyôrd) Nor.	59·03 N	10·35 E
162	Osma (ōs'mä) Sp.	41·35 N	3·02 W
171	Osmaniye Tur.	37·10 N	36·30 E
158	Osnabrück (ôs-nä-brük') F.R.G.	52·16 N	8·05 E
136	Osorno (ô-sō'r-nō) Chile	40·42 S	73·13 W
205	Osprey Reef (I.) (ŏs'prā) Austl.	14·00 S	146·45 E
203	Ossa, Mt. (ŏsȧ) Austl.	41·45 S	146·05 E
113	Osseo (ŏs'sē-ō) Mn. (Minneapolis, St. Paul In.)	45·07 N	93·24 W
106	Ossining (ŏs'ĭ-nĭng) NY (New York In.)	41·09 N	73·51 W
98	Ossipee (ŏs'ĭ-pê) NH	43·42 N	71·08 W
156	Ossjöen (L.) (ôs-syûĕn) Nor.	61·20 N	12·00 E
166	Ostashkov (ôs-täsh'kôf) Sov. Un.	57·07 N	33·04 E
155	Oste (R.) (ōz'tĕ) F.R.G.	53·20 N	9·19 E
167	Oster (ōs'tēr) Sov. Un.	50·55 N	30·52 E
167	Oster-dalälven (R.) Swe.	61·40 N	13·00 E
167	Oster Fd. (ûs'tēr fyôr') Nor.	60·40 N	5·25 E
167	Östersund (ûs'tēr-sŏŏnd) Swe.	63·09 N	14·49 E
167	Östhammar (ûst'häm'är) Swe.	60·16 N	18·21 E
163	Ostia Antica (ô's-tyä-än-tê'kä) It. (Rome In.)	41·46 N	12·24 E
	Ostia Lido, see Lido di Roma		
159	Ostrava Czech.	49·51 N	18·18 E
159	Ostróda (ôs'trōōt-ȧ) Pol.	53·41 N	19·58 E
167	Ostróg (ôs-trôk') Sov. Un.	50·21 N	26·40 E
167	Ostrogozhsk (ôs-trô-gôzhk') Sov. Un.	50·53 N	39·03 E
159	Ostrołeka (ôs-trô-woN'kȧ) Pol.	53·04 N	21·35 E
167	Ostropol' (ôs-trô-pôl') Sov. Un.	49·48 N	27·32 E
166	Ostrov (ôs-trôf') Sov. Un.	57·21 N	28·22 E
159	Ostrowiec Świętokrzyski (ôs-trō'vyĕts shvyĕN-tō-kzhĭ'ske) Pol.	50·55 N	21·24 E
159	Ostrów Lubelski (ôs'trŏŏf lōō'bĕl-skĭ) Pol.	51·32 N	22·49 E
159	Ostrów Mazowiecka (mä-zô-vyĕt'skä) Pol.	52·47 N	21·54 E
159	Ostrów Wielkopolski (ôs'trōōv vyĕl-kō-pōl'skē) Pol.	51·38 N	17·49 E
159	Ostrzeszów (ôs-tzhā'shōōf) Pol.	51·26 N	17·56 E
165	Ostuni (ôs-tōō'nē) It.	40·44 N	17·35 E
165	Osum (R.) (ō'sōōm) Alb.	40·37 N	20·00 E
195	Ōsumi-Guntō (Arch.) (ō'sōō-mê gōōn'tō) Jap	30·34 N	130·30 E
195	Ōsumi Kaikyō (Van Diemen) (Str.) (kāē'kyō) (văn dē'mĕn) Jap.	31·02 N	130·10 E
162	Osuna (ô-sōō'nä) Sp.	37·18 N	5·05 W
166	Osveya (ôs'vĕ-yȧ) Sov. Un.	56·00 N	28·08 E
148	Oswaldtwistle (ŏz-wȧld-twĭs''l) Eng.	53·44 N	2·23 W
105	Oswegatchie (R.) (ŏs-wê-găch'ĭ) NY	44·15 N	75·20 W
117	Oswego (ŏs-wē'gō) Ks.	37·10 N	95·08 W
105	Oswego NY	43·25 N	76·30 W
159	Oswiecim (ôsh-vyăN'tsyĭm) Pol.	50·02 N	19·17 E
194	Otaru (ō'tȧ-rōō) Jap.	43·07 N	141·00 E
134	Otavalo (ōtä-vä'lō) Ec.	0·14 N	78·16 W
212	Otavi (ô-tä'vê) Namibia	19·35 S	17·20 E
114	Otay (ō'tā) Ca. (In.)	32·36 N	117·04 W
166	Otepää (ô'tĕ-pâ) Sov. Un.	58·03 N	26·31 E
165	Othonoí (I.) Grc.	39·51 N	19·26 E
165	Óthris, Óros (Mts.) Grc.	39·00 N	22·15 E
214	Oti (R.) Ghana	9·00 N	0·10 E
91	Otish, Mts. (ô-tĭsh') Can.	52·15 N	70·20 W
212	Otjiwarongo (ŏt-jê-wȧ-rôn'gō) Namibia	20·20 S	16·25 E
164	Otočac (ō'tô-chȧts) Yugo.	44·53 N	15·15 E
174	Otradnoye (ô-trâ'd-nôyĕ) Sov. Un. (Leningrad In.)	59·46 N	30·50 E
165	Otranto (ô'trän-tô) (ô-trän'tō) It.	40·07 N	18·30 E
165	Otranto, C. di It.	40·06 N	18·32 E
165	Otranto, Strait of It.-Alb.	40·30 N	18·45 E
174	Otra R. (ôt'rȧ) Sov. Un. (Moscow In.)	55·22 N	38·20 E
104	Otsego (ŏt-sē'gō) Mi.	42·25 N	85·45 W
195	Otsu (ō'tsōō) Jap. (Ōsaka In.)	35·00 N	135·54 E
156	Ottavand (L.) (ôt'tȧ-vän) Nor.	61·53 N	8·40 E
89	Ottawa (ŏt'ȧ-wȧ) Can. (Ottawa In.)	45·25 N	75·43 W
104	Ottawa Il.	41·20 N	88·50 W
117	Ottawa Ks.	38·37 N	95·16 W
104	Ottawa Oh.	41·00 N	84·00 W
91	Ottawa (R.) Can.	46·05 N	77·20 W
91	Ottawa Is. Can.	59·50 N	81·00 W
156	Otteråen (ôt'ĕr-ôĕn) Nor.	59·13 N	7·20 E
115	Otter Cr. (ŏt'ēr) Ut.	38·20 N	111·55 W
105	Otter Cr. Vt.	44·05 N	73·15 W
112	Otter Pt. Can. (Seattle In.)	48·21 N	123·50 W
108	Otter Tail (L.) Mn.	46·21 N	95·52 W
113	Otterville (ôt'ēr-vĭl) Il. (St. Louis In.)	39·03 N	90·24 W
212	Ottery (ŏt'ēr-ĭ) S. Afr. (In.)	34·02 S	18·31 E
109	Ottumwa (ô-tŭm'wȧ) Ia.	41·00 N	92·26 W
215	Otukpa Nig.	7·09 N	7·41 E
125	Otumba (ô-tŭm'bä) Mex. (In.)	19·41 N	98·46 W
203	Otway, C. (ŏt'wā) Austl.	38·55 S	153·40 E
136	Otway, Seno (B.) (sĕ'nō-ô't-wä'y) Chile	53·00 S	73·00 W
159	Otwock (ôt'vôtsk) Pol.	52·05 N	21·18 E
103	Ouachita, (R.) U. S.	33·25 N	92·30 W
117	Ouachita Mts. (wŏsh'ĭ-tô) Ok.	34·29 N	95·01 W
211	Ouaddaï (Reg.) (wä-dī') Chad	13·04 N	20·00 E
214	Ouagadougou (wä'gȧ-dōō'gōō) Upper Volta	12·22 N	1·31 W
214	Ouahigouya (wä-ê-gōō'yä) Upper Volta	13·35 N	2·25 W

ăt; finăl; rāte; senâte; ärm; åsk; sofȧ; fâre; ch-choose; dh-as th in other; bē; êvent; bĕt; recĕnt; cratēr; g-go; gh-guttural g; bĭt; ĭ-short neutral; rīde; K-guttural k as ch in German ich;

PRONOUNCING INDEX

Ouahran — Pamiers 325

Page	Name Pronunciation Region	Lat. °′	Long. °′
	Ouahran, see Oran		
210	Oualâta (wä-lä′tä)..... Mauritania	17·11 N	6·50 W
210	Ouallene (wäl-lân′).......... Alg.	24·43 N	1·15 E
129	Ouanaminthe............... Hai.	19·35 N	71·45 W
211	Ouanda Djallé (wän′dȧ jä′lā′) Cen. Afr. Emp.	8·56 N	22·46 E
210	Ouarane (Dunes)...... Mauritania	20·44 N	10·27 W
210	Ouargla (wär′glä)............ Alg.	32·00 N	5·18 E
214	Ouarkoye........... Upper Volta	12·05 N	3·40 W
216	Oubangui (Ubangi) (R.) (o͞o-bäŋ′gê) Afr.	4·30 N	20·35 E
149	Oude Rijn (R.) Neth. (Amsterdam In.)	52·09 N	4·33 E
149	Oudewater. Neth. (Amsterdam In.)	52·01 N	4·52 E
149	Oud-Gastel. Neth. (Amsterdam In.)	51·35 N	4·27 E
152	Oudrhes, L. (Mt.).......... Mor.	32·33 N	4·49 W
212	Oudtshoorn (outs′hōrn).... S. Afr.	33·33 S	23·36 E
163	Oued Rhiou................ Alg.	35·55 N	0·57 E
163	Oued Tiélat................ Alg.	35·33 N	0·28 W
210	Oued-Zem (wĕd-zĕm′)....... Mor.	33·05 N	5·49 W
214	Ouellé.............. Ivory Coast	7·18 N	4·01 W
160	Ouessant, I. d′ (ēl-dwĕ-säN′)... Fr.	48·28 N	5·00 W
216	Ouesso.................... Con.	1·37 N	16·04 E
129	Ouest, Pt.................. Hai.	19·00 N	73·25 W
210	Ouezzane (wĕ-zan′)......... Mor.	34·48 N	5·40 W
154	Oughter (L.) (lôK oK′tĕr)..... Ire.	54·02 N	7·40 W
215	Ouham (R.).. Cen. Afr. Rep.-Chad	8·30 N	17·50 E
210	Ouidah (wē-dä′).......... Benin	6·25 N	2·05 E
210	Oujda..................... Mor.	34·41 N	1·45 W
152	Ouled Nail, Montes des (Mts.). Alg.	34·43 N	2·44 E
161	Oulins (o͞o-lȧN′).... Fr. (Paris In.)	48·52 N	1·27 E
160	Oullins (o͞o-lăN′)............. Fr.	45·44 N	4·46 E
150	Oulu (ō′lo͝o)................ Fin.	64·58 N	25·43 E
150	Oulu-jarvi (L.)............. Fin.	64·20 N	25·48 E
211	Oum Chalouba (o͞om shä-lo͞o′bä) Chad	15·48 N	20·30 E
215	Oum Hadjer............... Chad	13·18 N	19·41 E
150	Ounas (R.) (ō′nȧs).......... Fin.	67·46 N	24·40 E
148	Oundle (ôn′d′l)............ Eng.	52·28 N	0·28 W
211	Ounianga Kébir (o͞o-nê-äŋ′gȧ kē-bēr′). Chad	19·04 N	20·22 E
117	Ouray (o͞o-rā′).............. Co.	38·00 N	107·40 W
135	Ourinhos (ôo͝o-rê′nyôs)...... Braz.	23·04 S	49·45 W
162	Ourique (ō-rē′kĕ).......... Port.	37·39 N	8·10 W
137	Ouro Fino (ōŭ-rô-fē′nō) Braz. (Rio de Janeiro In.)	22·18 S	46·21 W
137	Ouro Prêto (ō′ro͝o prā′to͝o) Braz. (Rio de Janeiro In.)	20·24 S	43·30 W
154	Ouse (R.)................. Eng.	53·45 N	1·09 W
99	Outardes, Rivière aux (R.)... Can.	50·53 N	68·50 W
109	Outer (I.) (out′ēr).......... Wi.	47·03 N	90·20 W
123	Outer Brass (I.) (bräs).... Vir. Is. (U. S. A.) (St. Thomas In.)	18·24 N	64·58 W
154	Outer Hebrides (Is.)........ Scot.	57·20 N	7·50 W
94	Outlook.................. Can.	51·31 N	107·05 W
212	Outjo (ōt′yō)........... Namibia	20·05 S	17·10 E
89	Outremont (o͞o-trē-môN′) Can. (Montreal In.)	45·31 N	73·36 W
203	Ouyen (o͞o-ĕn)............ Austl.	35·05 S	142·10 E
136	Ovalle (ō-väl′yā).......... Chile	30·43 S	71·16 W
212	Ovamboland (Reg.).... S. W. Afr.	18·10 S	15·00 E
129	Ovando, Bahía de (B.) (bä-ē′ä-dĕ-ô-vä′n-dō). Cuba	20·10 N	74·05 W
162	Ovar (ô-vär′).............. Port.	40·52 N	8·38 W
149	Overijsche..... Bel. (Brussels In.)	50·46 N	4·32 E
113	Overland (ō-vēr-lănd) Mo. (St. Louis In.)	38·42 N	90·22 W
113	Overland Park Ks. (Kansas City In.)	38·59 N	94·40 W
106	Overlea (ō′vēr-lā) (ō′vēr-lē) Md. (Baltimore In.)	39·21 N	76·31 W
150	Övertornea................. Swe.	66·19 N	23·31 E
167	Ovidiopol′ (ô-vê-dê-ô′pôl′) Sov. Un.	46·15 N	03·28 E
129	Oviedo (ô-vyĕ′dō)..... Dom. Rep.	17·50 N	71·25 W
162	Oviedo (ō-vê-ā′dhō).......... Sp.	43·22 N	5·50 W
167	Ovruch (ôv′ro͝och)....... Sov. Un.	51·19 N	28·51 E
195	Owada (ō′wä-dȧ). Jap. (Tōkyō In.)	35·49 N	139·33 E
216	Owando................... Con.	0·29 S	15·55 E
105	Owasco (L.) (ō-wăs′kō)....... NY	42·50 N	76·30 W
195	Owase (ō′wä-shê)............ Jap.	34·03 N	136·12 E
105	Owego (ō-wē′gō)............. NY	42·05 N	76·15 W
109	Owen (ō′ĕn)................ Wi.	44·56 N	90·35 W
114	Owens (L.) (ō′ĕnz)........... Ca.	36·27 N	117·45 W
114	Owens (R.)................ Ca.	37·13 N	118·20 W
104	Owensboro (ō′ĕnz-bŭr-ô)...... Ky.	37·45 N	87·05 W
104	Owen Sound (ō′ĕn).......... Can.	44·30 N	80·55 W
197	Owen Stanley Ra. (stăn′lê) Pap. N. Gui.	9·00 S	147·30 E
104	Owensville (ō′ĕnz-vĭl)......... In.	38·15 N	87·40 W
117	Owensville................. Mo.	38·20 N	91·29 W
107	Owensville.... Oh. (Cincinnati In.)	39·08 N	84·07 W
104	Owenton (ō′ĕn-tŭn).......... Ky.	38·35 N	84·55 W
210	Owerri (ô-wĕr′ê)........... Nig.	5·26 N	7·04 E
106	Owings Mill (ōwĭngz mĭl) Md. (Baltimore In.)	39·25 N	76·50 W
111	Owl Cr. (oul).............. Wy.	43·45 N	108·46 W
215	Owo..................... Nig.	7·15 N	5·37 E
104	Owosso (ô-wŏs′ō)........... Mi.	43·00 N	84·15 W
110	Owyhee Mts. (ô-wī′hê)........ Id.	43·15 N	116·48 W
110	Owyhee Res................ Or.	43·27 N	117·30 W
110	Owyhee R.................. Or.	43·04 N	117·45 W
110	Owyhee R., South Fork....... Id.	42·07 N	116·43 W
95	Oxbow.................... Can.	49·12 N	102·11 W
125	Oxchuc (ôs-cho͞ok′).......... Mex.	16·47 N	92·24 W
120	Oxford (ŏks′fērd)............ Al.	33·38 N	80·46 W
97	Oxford (ŏks′fērd).......... Can.	45·44 N	63·52 W
148	Oxford........ Eng. (London In.)	51·43 N	1·16 W
99	Oxford.............. Ma. (In.)	42·07 N	71·52 W
104	Oxford..................... Mi.	42·50 N	83·15 W
120	Oxford..................... Ms.	34·22 N	89·30 W
121	Oxford..................... NC	36·17 N	78·35 W
104	Oxford..................... Oh.	39·30 N	84·45 W
95	Oxford L................... Can.	54·51 N	95·37 W
126	Oxkutzcab (ôx-ko͞o′tz-käb) Mex. (In.)	20·18 N	89·22 W
106	Oxmoor (ŏks′mo͝or) Al. (Birmingham In.)	33·25 N	86·52 W
154	Ox Mts. (ŏks)............... Ire.	54·05 N	9·05 W
114	Oxnard (ŏks′närd)........... Ca.	34·08 N	119·12 W
106	Oxon Hill (ōks′ōn hĭl) Md. (Baltimore In.)	38·48 N	77·00 W
125	Oxtotepec (ôx-tô-tĕ′pĕk) Mex. (In.)	19·10 N	99·04 W
135	Oyapock (R.) (ō-yȧ-pŏk′) Braz.-Fr. Gu.	2·45 N	52·15 W
216	Oyem (ô-yĕm) (ô-yăN′).... Gabon	1·37 N	11·35 E
173	Oymyakon (oi-myŭ-kôn′). Sov. Un.	63·14 N	142·58 E
215	Oyo (ō′yō)................ Nig.	7·51 N	3·56 E
161	Oyonnax (ô-yô-nȧks′).......... Fr.	46·16 N	5·40 E
106	Oyster Bay.. NY (New York In.)	40·52 N	73·32 W
119	Oyster Bayou.......... Tx. (In.)	29·41 N	94·33 W
119	Oyster Cr. (ois′tēr)...... Tx. (In.)	29·13 N	95·29 W
129	Ozama (R.) (ô-zä′mä).. Dom. Rep.	18·45 N	69·55 W
197	Ozamiz (ô-zä′mêz).......... Phil.	8·06 N	123·43 E
120	Ozark (ō′zärk).............. Al.	31·28 N	85·28 W
117	Ozark...................... Ar.	35·29 N	93·49 W
117	Ozarks, L. of the (ō′zärkz).... Mo.	38·06 N	93·26 W
117	Ozark Plat.................. Mo.	36·37 N	93·56 W
166	Ozëry (ô-zyô′rê)......... Sov. Un.	54·53 N	38·31 E
164	Ozieri...................... It.	40·38 N	8·53 E
159	Ozorków (ô-zôr′ko͝of).......... Pol.	51·58 N	19·20 E
125	Ozuluama (ō′zo͞o-lo͞o-ä′mä)... Mex.	21·34 N	97·52 W
125	Ozumba (ô-zo͞o′m-bä).. Mex. (In.)	19·02 N	98·48 W

P

Page	Name Pronunciation Region	Lat. °′	Long. °′
188	Paan..................... China	30·08 N	99·00 E
212	Paarl (pärl).............. S. Afr.	33·45 S	18·55 E
100	Paauilo (pä-ä-o͞o′ê-lō).......... Hi.	20·03 N	155·25 W
159	Pabianice (pä-byȧ-nē′tsĕ)..... Pol.	51·40 N	19·29 E
134	Pacaás Novos, Massiço de (Mts.) (mä-sē′sô-dĕ-pä-kȧ′s-nô′vōs) Braz.	11·03 S	64·02 W
134	Pacaraima, Serra (Mts.) (sĕr′rȧ pä-kä-rä-ē′mȧ) Braz.-Ven.	3·45 N	62·30 W
134	Pacasmayo (pä-käs-mä′yō)... Peru	7·24 S	79·30 W
188	Pach′u (pä′cho͞o′).......... China	39·50 N	78·23 E
125	Pachuca (pä-cho͞o′kä)....... Mex.	20·07 N	98·43 W
112	Pacific (pȧ-sĭf′ĭk). Wa. (Seattle In.)	47·16 N	122·15 W
112	Pacifica (pȧ-sĭf′ĭ-kä) Ca. (San Francisco In.)	37·38 N	122·29 W
114	Pacific Beach........... Ca. (In.)	32·47 N	117·22 W
114	Pacific Grove............... Ca.	36·37 N	121·54 W
199	Pacific O.		
92	Pacific Ra................. Can.	51·00 N	125·30 W
92	Pacific Rim Natl. Pk........ Can.	49·00 N	126·00 W
121	Pacolet (R.) (pā′cō-lēt)........ SC	34·55 N	81·49 W
161	Pacy-sur-Eure (pä-sē-sür-ûr′) Fr. (Paris In.)	49·01 N	1·24 E
196	Padang (pä-däng′)........ Indon.	1·01 S	100·28 E
183	Padang, Palau (I.) Indon. (Singapore In.)	1·12 N	102·21 E
183	Padang Endau Mala. (Singapore In.)	2·39 N	103·38 E
104	Paden City (pā′dĕn).......... WV	39·30 N	80·55 W
158	Paderborn (pä-dĕr-bôrn′).. F.R.G.	51·43 N	8·46 E
217	Padibe..................... Ug.	3·28 N	32·50 E
148	Padiham (păd′ĭ-hăm)........ Eng.	53·48 N	2·19 W
124	Padilla (pä-dēl′yä).......... Mex.	24·00 N	98·45 W
112	Padilla B. (pä-dĕl′lȧ) Wa. (Seattle In.)	48·31 N	122·34 W
164	Padova (Padua) (pä′dô-vä) (păd′û-ȧ). It.	45·24 N	11·53 E
119	Padre I. (pä′drā)............. Tx.	27·09 N	97·15 W
	Padua, see Padova		
120	Paducah (pȧ-dū′kȧ)........... Ky.	37·05 N	88·36 W
116	Paducah.................... Tx.	34·01 N	100·18 W
194	Paektu San (Mt.) (pâk′to͞o-sän′) China-Kor.	42·00 N	128·03 E
164	Pag (I.) (päg).............. Yugo.	44·30 N	14·48 E
196	Pagai Selatan (I.).......... Indon.	2·48 S	100·22 E
196	Pagai Utara (I.)........... Indon.	2·45 S	100·02 E
209	Pagalu (I.).......... Equat. Gui.	2·00 S	3·30 E
165	Pagasitikós Kólpos (G.)...... Grc.	39·15 N	23·00 E
117	Page...................... Az.	36·57 N	111·27 W
117	Pagosa Springs (pȧ-gō′sȧ)..... Co.	37·15 N	107·05 W
100	Pahala (pä-hä′lä)............ Hi.	19·11 N	155·28 W
183	Pahang (State) Mala. (Singapore In.)	3·02 N	102·57 E
196	Pahang R................ Mala.	3·39 N	102·41 E
121	Pahokee (pȧ-hō′kē)...... Fl. (In.)	26·45 N	80·40 W
190	Paichü (bäī′gü)............ China	33·04 N	120·17 E
192	Paich′uan................. China	47·22 N	126·00 E
157	Paide (pī′dĕ)............ Sov. Un.	58·54 N	25·30 E
192	Paiho..................... China	32·30 N	110·15 E
190	Pai Hu (L.) (bäī′ ho͞o)...... China	31·22 N	117·38 E
157	Päijänna (L.) (pĕ′ē-yĕn-nĕ)... Fin.	61·38 N	25·05 E
190	Paikouchen (bäī′gō′jen)..... China	39·08 N	116·02 E
100	Pailolo Chan. (pä-ê-lō′lō)...... Hi.	21·05 N	156·41 W
137	Paine (pī′nĕ).. Chile (Santiago In.)	33·49 S	70·44 W
104	Painesville (pānz′vĭl)......... Oh.	41·40 N	81·15 W
117	Painted Des. (pānt′ĕd)........ Az.	36·15 N	111·35 W
117	Painted Rock Res............ Az.	33·00 N	113·05 W
104	Paintsville (pānts′vĭl)........ Ky.	37·50 N	82·50 W
190	Paip′u (bäī′po͞o)........... China	32·15 N	120·47 E
193	Paise..................... China	24·00 N	106·38 E
154	Paisley (pāz′lĭ)............. Scot.	55·50 N	4·30 W
134	Paita (pä-ē′tä).............. Peru	5·11 S	81·12 W
192	Pai T′ou Shan (Mts.)....... Korea	40·30 N	127·20 E
117	Paiute Ind. Res.............. Ut.	38·17 N	113·50 W
192	Paiyü Shan (Mtns.)........ China	37·02 N	108·30 E
125	Pajápan (pä-hä′pän)........ Mex.	18·16 N	94·41 W
196	Pakanbaru............... Indon.	0·43 N	101·15 E
	Pakhoi, see Peihai		
174	Pakhra R. (päK′rá) Sov. Un. (Moscow In.)	55·29 N	37·51 E
182	Pakistan.................. Asia	28·00 N	67·30 E
	Pakistan East, see Bangladesh		
196	Pakokku (pȧ-kŏk′ko͝o)....... Bur.	21·29 N	95·00 E
164	Pakrac (pä′krȧts).......... Yugo.	45·25 N	17·13 E
159	Paks (pôksh).............. Hung.	46·38 N	18·53 E
215	Pala...................... Chad	9·22 N	14·54 E
119	Palacios (pä-lä′syōs).......... Tx.	28·42 N	96·12 W
163	Palafrogell (pä-lä-frô-gĕl)...... Sp.	41·55 N	3·09 E
164	Palagruža (Is.) (pä′lä-gro͞o′zhä) Yugo.	42·20 N	16·23 E
161	Palaiseau (pȧ-lĕ-zō′). Fr. (Paris In.)	48·44 N	2·16 E
173	Palana................. Sov. Un.	59·07 N	159·58 E
197	Palanan B. (pä-lä′nän). Phil. (In.)	17·14 N	122·35 E
197	Palanan Pt............ Phil. (In.)	17·12 N	122·40 E
184	Pālanpur (pä′lŭn-po͞or)...... India	24·08 N	73·29 E
212	Palapye (pȧ-läp′yĕ)......... Bots.	22·34 S	27·28 E
107	Palatine (păl′ȧ-tīn) Il. (Chicago In.)	42·07 N	88·03 W
121	Palatka (pȧ-lăt′kȧ)........... Fl.	29·39 N	81·40 W
197	Palau Is. (pä-lä′o͞o) Pac. Is. Trust. Ter.	7·15 N	134·30 E
197	Palauig (pȧ-lou′êg)..... Phil. (In.)	15·27 N	119·54 E
197	Palauig Pt............ Phil. (In.)	15·28 N	119·41 E
196	Palawan (I.) (pä-lä′wȧn)..... Phil.	9·50 N	117·38 E
185	Pālayankottai............. India	8·50 N	77·50 E
157	Paldiski (päl′dĭ-skĭ)...... Sov. Un.	59·22 N	24·04 E
196	Palembang (pä-lĕm-bäng′). Indon.	2·57 S	104·40 E
126	Palencia (pä-lĕn′sê-ȧ)....... Guat.	14·40 N	90·22 W
162	Palencia (pä-lĕ′n-syä)......... Sp.	42·02 N	4·32 W
125	Palenque (pä-lĕŋ′kȧ)........ Mex.	17·34 N	91·58 W
129	Palenque, Punta (Pt.) (po͞o′n-tä) Dom. Rep.	18·10 N	70·10 W
134	Palermo (pä-lĕr′mô)..... Col. (In.)	2·53 N	75·26 W
164	Palermo..................... It.	38·08 N	13·24 E
119	Palestine................... Tx.	31·46 N	95·38 W
183	Palestine (Reg.) (păl′ĕs-tīn) Asia (Palestine In.)	31·33 N	35·00 E
188	Paletwa (pŭ-lĕt′wä).......... Bur.	21·19 N	92·52 E
185	Palghāt.................. India	10·49 N	76·40 E
184	Pāli...................... India	25·53 N	73·18 E
188	Palik′un.................. China	43·43 N	92·50 E
214	Palimé.................... Togo	6·54 N	0·38 E
126	Palín (pä-lēn′)............. Guat.	14·42 N	90·42 W
110	Palisade (păl-ĭ-sād′).......... Nv.	40·39 N	116·11 W
125	Palizada (pä-lê-zä′dä)....... Mex.	18·17 N	92·04 W
184	Palk Str. (pôk)............ India	10·00 N	79·23 E
137	Palma (päl′mä) Braz. (Rio de Janeiro In.)	21·23 S	42·18 W
163	Palma, Ba. de (B.) (bä-ē′ä-dĕ). Sp.	39·24 N	2·37 E
162	Palma del Rio (dĕl rē′ō)...... Sp.	37·43 N	5·19 W
163	Palma de Mallorca (dĕ-mäl-yô′r-kä). Sp.	39·35 N	2·38 E
135	Palmares (päl-mȧ′rĕs)....... Braz.	8·46 S	35·28 W
136	Palmas (päl′mäs).......... Braz.	26·20 S	51·56 W
214	Palmas, C................. Lib.	4·22 N	7·44 W
129	Palma Soriano (sô-ré-ä′nō).. Cuba	20·15 N	76·00 W
121	Palm Beach (päm bēch′).. Fl. (In.)	26·43 N	80·03 W
135	Palmeira dos Índios (päl-mā′rä-dôs-ē′n-dyôs). Braz.	9·26 S	36·33 W
216	Palmeirinhas, Ponta das (Pt.). Arg.	9·05 S	13·00 E
163	Palmela (päl-mā′lä) Port. (Lisbon In.)	38·34 N	8·54 W
101	Palmer (päm′ēr)............. Ak.	61·38 N	149·15 W
112	Palmer......... Wa. (Seattle In.)	47·19 N	121·53 W
205	Palmerston North (päm′ēr-stŭn) N. Z. (In.)	40·21 S	175·43 E
205	Palmerville (päm′ēr-vĭl).... Austl.	16·08 S	144·15 E
121	Palmetto (pȧl-mĕt′ô)..... Fl. (In.)	27·32 N	82·34 W
129	Palmetto Pt................ Ba.	21·15 N	73·25 W
164	Palmi (päl′mē).............. It.	38·21 N	15·54 E
134	Palmira (päl-mē′rä)..... Col. (In.)	3·33 N	76·17 W
128	Palmira.................. Cuba	22·15 N	80·25 W
117	Palmyra (păl-mī′rȧ).......... Mo.	39·45 N	91·32 W
106	Palmyra.... NJ (Philadelphia In.)	40·01 N	75·00 W
199	Palmyra (I.)............ Oceania	6·00 N	162·20 W
186	Palmyra (Ruins)............ Syr.	34·25 N	38·28 E
184	Palmyras Pt............... India	20·42 N	87·45 E
147	Palmyre................... Syr.	30·35 N	37·58 E
112	Palo Alto (pä′lō äl′tō) Ca. (San Francisco In.)	37·27 N	122·09 W
116	Paloduro Cr. (pā-lô-do͞o′rô).... Tx.	36·16 N	101·12 W
183	Paloh...... Mala. (Singapore In.)	2·11 N	103·12 E
118	Paloma, L. (pä-lō′mä)....... Mex.	26·53 N	104·02 W
137	Palomo, Cerro el (Mtn.) (sĕ′r-rô-ĕl-pä-lô′mô) Chile (Santiago In.)	34·36 S	70·20 W
163	Palos, Cabo de (C.) (kȧ′bô-dĕ-pä′lôs). Sp.	39·38 N	0·43 W
113	Palos Verdes Estates (pă′lŭs vûr′dĭs) Ca. (Los Angeles In.)	33·48 N	118·24 W
110	Palouse (pȧ-lo͞oz′)........... Wa.	46·54 N	117·04 W
110	Palouse Hills.............. Wa.	46·48 N	117·47 W
110	Palouse R................. Wa.	47·02 N	117·35 W
171	Palu (pä-loo′).............. Tur.	38·55 N	40·10 E
197	Paluan (pä-lo͞o′än)..... Phil. (In.)	13·25 N	120·29 E
173	Pamamushir (I.)........ Sov. Un.	50·42 N	153·45 E
160	Pamiers (pȧ-myā′)............ Fr.	43·07 N	1·34 E

ng-sing; ŋ-baŋk; N-nasalized n; nŏd; cŏmmit; ōld; ôbey; ôrder; fo͞od; fo͝ot; ou-out; s-soft; sh-dish; th-thin; pūre; ûnite; ûrn; stŭd; circŭs; ü-as "y" in study; ′-indeterminate vowel.

326 Pamirs — Patna PRONOUNCING INDEX

Page	Name Pronunciation Region	Lat. °′	Long. °′
187	Pamirs (Plat.)..........Sov. Un.	38·14 N	72·27 E
121	Pamlico R. (păm′lĭ-kō).......NC	35·25 N	76·59 W
121	Pamlico Sd..................NC	35·10 N	76·10 W
116	Pampa (păm′pȧ)..............Tx.	35·32 N	100·56 W
136	Pampa de Castillo (Plat.) (pä′m-pä-dĕ-käs-tē′l-yô).Arg.	45·30 S	67·30 W
214	Pampana (R.)..............S. L.	8·35 N	11·55 W
197	Pampanga (R.) (päm-päŋ′gä) Phil. (In.)	15·20 N	120·48 E
136	Pampas (Reg.) (päm′päs)....Arg.	37·00 S	64·30 W
162	Pampilhosa do Botão (päm-pê-lyō′sȧ-dô-bō-to′uɴ) Port.	40·21 N	8·32 W
134	Pamplona (päm-plō′nä)......Col.	7·19 N	72·41 W
162	Pamplona (päm-plō′nä).......Sp.	42·49 N	1·39 W
105	Pamunkey (R.) (pȧ-mŭŋ′kĭ)...Va.	37·40 N	77·20 W
104	Pana (pā′nȧ).................Il.	39·25 N	89·05 W
126	Panabá (pä-nä-bä′)....Mex. (In.)	21·18 N	88·15 W
165	Panagyurishte (pȧ-nȧ-gyōō′rêsh-tĕ).Bul.	42·30 N	24·11 E
185	Panaji (Panjim)............India	15·33 N	73·52 E
123	Panamá (păn-ȧ-mä′) N. A. (Panama Canal In.)	8·35 N	81·08 W
123	Panama, G. of.............Pan.	7·45 N	79·20 W
123	Panama, Isth. of...........Pan.	9·00 N	81·00 W
127	Panama, B. of.............Pan.	8·50 N	79·08 W
120	Panama City (păn-ȧ mä′ sĭ′tĭ).Fl.	30·08 N	85·39 W
114	Panamint Ra. (păn-ȧ-mĭnt′)..Ca.	36·40 N	117·30 W
164	Panaria (Is.) (pä-nä′rē-a)......It.	38·37 N	15·05 E
164	Panaro (R.) (pä-nä′rō)........It.	44·47 N	11·06 E
196	Panay (I.) (pä-nī′)..........Phil.	11·15 N	121·38 E
165	Pančevo (pán′chĕ-vō).......Yugo.	44·52 N	20·42 E
183	Panchor....Mala. (Singapore In.)	2·10 N	102·43 E
184	Pānchur..............India (In.)	22·31 N	88·17 E
212	Panda (pän′dä′)............Zaire	10·59 S	27·24 E
171	Pandar-e Pahlavī...........Iran	37·30 N	49·30 E
128	Pan de Guajaibon (Mtn.) (pän dā gwä-jȧ-bōn′). Cuba	22·50 N	83·20 W
216	Pandu....................Zaire	5·00 N	19·15 E
157	Panevėžys (pä′nyĕ-väzh′ēs) Sov. Un.	55·44 N	24·21 E
172	Panfilov (pŭn-fĕ′lôf).....Sov. Un.	44·12 N	79·58 E
217	Panga (päŋ′gä)............Zaire	1·51 N	26·25 E
213	Pangani (pän-gä′nē).........Tan.	5·28 S	38·58 E
217	Pangani (R.)...............Tan.	4·40 S	37·45 E
191	P′angchiang..China (Canton In.)	22·57 N	113·15 E
190	Pangfou (bäng′fōō)........China	32·54 N	117·22 E
196	Pangkalpinang (päng-käl′pê-näng′) Indon.	2·11 S	106·04 E
184	Pangkong Tsho (L.).......China	33·40 N	79·30 E
91	Pangnirtung...............Can.	66·08 N	65·26 W
117	Panguitch (päŋ′gwĭch).......Ut.	37·50 N	112·30 W
184	Pānihāti......India (Calcutta In.)	22·42 N	88·23 E
137	Panimávida (pä-nē-má′vē-dä) Chile (Santiago In.)	36·44 S	71·26 W
196	Panjang, Selat (Str.).......Indon.	1·00 N	102·00 E
	Panjim, see Panaji		
192	Panshih..................China	42·50 N	126·48 E
193	Pan Si Pan (Mtn.)..........Viet.	22·25 N	103·50 E
197	Pantar (I.) (pän′tär).......Indon.	8·40 S	123·45 E
151	Pantelleria (I.) (pän-tĕl-lå-rē′ä).It.	36·43 N	11·59 E
125	Pantepec (pän-tå-pĕk′).......Mex.	17·11 N	93·04 W
124	Panuco (pä′nōō-kō).........Mex.	22·04 N	98·11 W
124	Pánuco (pä′nōō-kō)..........Mex.	29·47 N	105·55 W
124	Panuco (R.)................Mex.	21·59 N	98·20 W
118	Pánuco de Coronado (pä′nōō-kô dā kō-rô-nä′dhō) Mex.	24·33 N	104·20 W
185	Panvel..............India (In.)	18·59 N	73·06 E
126	Panzós (pän-zós′)..........Guat.	15·26 N	89·40 W
135	Pao (pà′ō) (R.)........Ven. (In.)	9·52 N	67·57 W
192	Paochang.................China	41·52 N	115·25 E
192	Paocheng.................China	33·15 N	106·58 E
192	Paochi...................China	34·10 N	106·58 E
117	Paola (pȧ-ō′lȧ)..............Ks.	38·34 N	94·51 W
104	Paoli (pȧ-ō′lĭ)................In.	38·35 N	86·30 W
106	Paoli.......Pa. (Philadelphia In.)	40·03 N	75·29 W
115	Paonia (pā-ō′nyȧ)............Co.	38·50 N	107·40 W
188	Paoshan (pä′ō-shän′).......China	25·14 N	99·03 E
191	Paoshan....China (Shanghai In.)	31·25 N	121·29 E
190	Paoti (pä′ō-tē′)............China	39·44 N	117·19 E
190	Paoting..................China	38·52 N	115·31 E
192	Paoting..................China	42·04 N	125·00 E
192	Paot′ou..................China	40·28 N	110·10 E
190	Paoying (pä′ō-yĭng)........China	33·14 N	119·20 E
159	Pápa (pä′pô).............Hung.	47·18 N	17·27 E
126	Papagayo, Golfo del (G.) (gôl-fô-dĕl-pä-pä-gá′yō).C. R.	10·44 N	85·56 W
124	Papagayo, Laguna (L.) (lä-ōō-nä).Mex.	16·44 N	99·44 W
124	Papagayo (R.) (pä-pä-gä′yō) Mex.	16·52 N	99·41 W
115	Papago Ind. Res. (pä′pä′gō)...Az.	32·33 N	112·12 W
122	Papantla de Olarte (pä-pän′tlä dā-ô-lä′r-tĕ).Mex.	20·30 N	97·15 W
125	Papatoapan (R.) (pä-pä-tô-ä-pȧ′n).Mex.	18·00 N	96·22 W
158	Papenburg (päp′ĕn-bŏŏrgh) F.R.G.	53·05 N	7·23 E
137	Papinas (pä-pē′näs) Arg. (Buenos Aires In.)	35·30 S	57·19 W
89	Papineauville (pä-pē-nō′vĕl) Can. (Ottawa In.)	45·38 N	75·01 W
197	Papua, Gulf of (păp-ōō-ȧ) Pap. N. Gui.	8·20 S	144·45 E
197	Papua New Guinea (păp-ōō-ȧ) (gĭne).Oceania	7·00 S	142·15 E
137	Papudo (pä-pōō′dô) Chile (Santiago In.)	32·30 S	71·25 W
136	Paquequer Pequeno (pä-kĕ-kĕ′r-pĕ-kĕ′nô) Braz. (Rio de Janeiro In.)	22·19 S	43·02 W
	Pará, see Belém		
135	Pará (State) (pä-rä′).......Braz.	4·45 S	53·30 W
137	Pará (pä-rä′) (R.) Braz. (Rio de Janeiro In.)	20·21 S	44·38 W
135	Pará, Rio do (R.) (rē′ō-dô-pä-rä′) Braz.	1·09 S	48·48 W
166	Para (R.)..............Sov. Un.	53·45 N	40·58 E
197	Paracale (pä-rä-kä′lå)....Phil. (In.)	14·17 N	122·47 E
136	Paracambi (pä-rä-kȧ′m-bē) Braz. (Rio de Janeiro In.)	22·36 S	43·43 W
135	Paracatu (pä-rä-kä-tōō′)....Braz.	17·17 S	46·43 W
	Paracel Is., see Hsisha Ch′üntao		
165	Paraćin (pȧ′rä-chên).......Yugo.	43·51 N	21·26 E
137	Para de Minas (pä-rä-dĕ-mē′näs) Braz. (Rio de Janeiro In.)	19·52 S	44·37 W
128	Paradise (I.)...............Ba.	25·05 N	77·20 W
110	Paradise Valley (păr′ȧ-dīs)....Nv.	41·28 N	117·32 W
134	Parados, Cerro de los (Mtn.) (sĕ′r-rô-dĕ-lôs-pä-rä′dôs) Col. (In.)	5·44 N	75·13 W
117	Paragould (păr′ȧ-gōōld).......Ar.	36·03 N	90·29 W
135	Paraguaçu (R.) (pä-rä-gwä-zōō′) Braz.	12·25 S	39·46 W
134	Paraguaná, Pen. de (Pen.) (pĕ-nĕ′ng-sōō-lä-dĕ-pä-rä-gwä-nȧ′).Ven.	12·00 N	69·55 W
133	Paraguay (păr′ȧ-gwā).......S. A.	24·00 S	57·00 W
135	Paraguay, Rio (R.) (rē′ō-pä-rä-gwä′y).S. A.	21·12 S	57·31 W
	Paraíba, see João Pessoa		
135	Paraíba (State) (pä-rä-ē′bä)..Braz.	7·11 S	37·05 W
137	Paraíba (R.) Braz. (Rio de Janeiro In.)	23·02 S	45·43 W
137	Paraíba do Sul (dô-sōō′l) Braz. (Rio de Janeiro In.)	22·10 S	43·18 W
137	Paraibuna (pä-räē-bōō′nä) Braz. (Rio de Janeiro In.)	23·23 S	45·38 W
122	Paraiso (pä-rä-ē′sō)....C. Z. (In.)	9·02 N	79·38 W
127	Paraíso...................C. R.	9·50 N	83·53 W
125	Paraíso...................Mex.	18·24 N	93·11 W
137	Paraisópolis (pä-räē-sô′pô-lēs) Braz. (Rio de Janeiro In.)	22·35 S	45·45 W
137	Paraitinga (pä-rä-ē-tē′n-gä) (R.) Braz. (Rio de Janeiro In.)	23·15 S	45·24 W
215	Parakou (pȧ-rȧ-kōō′).........Benin	9·21 N	2·37 E
135	Paramaribo (pȧ-rȧ-mȧ′rē-bō) Sur.	5·50 N	55·15 W
202	Paramatta (păr-ȧ-măt′ȧ) Austl. (Sydney In.)	33·49 S	150·59 E
160	Paramé (pȧ-rä-mā′)..........Fr.	48·40 N	1·58 W
134	Paramillo (Mtn.) (pä-rä-mē′l-yō) Col. (In.)	7·06 N	75·55 W
106	Paramus......NJ (New York In.)	40·56 N	74·04 W
173	Paramushir (I.).........Sov. Un.	50·45 N	154·00 E
183	Paran (R.).....Isr. (Palestine In.)	30·05 N	34·50 E
136	Paraná (pä-rä-nä′)...........Arg.	31·44 S	60·29 W
136	Paraná (State).............Braz.	24·25 S	52·00 W
136	Paraná, Rio (R.)............Arg.	32·15 S	60·55 W
135	Paraná (R.)...............Braz.	13·05 S	47·11 W
135	Paranaguá (pä-rä′nä-gwä′)...Braz.	25·39 S	48·42 W
135	Paranaíba (pä-rä-nȧ-ē′bȧ)...Braz.	19·43 S	51·13 W
135	Paranaíba (R.)..............Braz.	18·58 S	50·44 W
137	Parana Ibicuy (R.) (ē-bē-kōō′ē) Arg. (Buenos Aires In.)	33·27 S	59·26 W
135	Paranam..................Sur.	5·39 N	55·13 W
136	Paránápanema (R.) (pä-rä-nȧ′pä-nĕ-mä).Braz.	22·28 S	52·15 W
137	Paraopeda (R.) (pä-rä-o-pĕ′dä) Braz. (Rio de Janeiro In.)	20·09 S	44·14 W
135	Parapara (pä-rä-pä-rä)..Ven. (In.)	9·44 N	67·17 W
137	Parati (pä-rätē) Braz. (Rio de Janeiro In.)	23·14 S	44·43 W
160	Paray-le-Monial (pȧ-rĕ′lē-mô-nyäl′).Fr.	46·27 N	4·14 E
184	Pārbati (R.)...............India	24·50 N	76·44 E
158	Parchim (par′kĭm).......G.D.R.	53·25 N	11·52 E
159	Parczew (pär′chĕf)...........Pol.	51·38 N	22·53 E
135	Pardo (R.) (pär′dō).........Braz.	15·25 S	39·40 W
137	Pardo (R.) Braz. (Rio de Janeiro In.)	21·32 S	46·40 W
158	Pardubice (pär′dŏŏ-bĭt-sĕ)..Czech.	50·02 N	15·47 E
135	Parecis, Serra dos (Mts.) (sĕr′rȧ dōs pä-rȧ-sēzh′).Braz.	13·45 S	59·28 W
162	Paredes de Nava (pä-rä′dås dā nä′vä).Sp.	42·10 N	4·41 W
118	Paredón..................Mex.	25·56 N	100·58 W
97	Parent...................Can.	47·59 N	74·30 W
97	Parent, Lac (L.)...........Can.	48·40 N	77·00 W
174	Pargolovo (pár-gô′lô vô) Sov. Un. (Leningrad In.)	60·04 N	30·18 E
134	Paria, Golfo de (G.) (gôl-fô-dĕ-pä-rē-ä).Ven.	10·33 N	62·14 W
115	Paria (R.).............Az.-Ut.	37·07 N	111·51 W
124	Paricutín, Vol. (pä-rē-kōō-tē′n) Mex.	19·27 N	102·14 W
118	Parida, Rio de la (R.) (rē′ō-dĕ-lä-pä-rē′dä).Mex.	26·23 N	104·40 W
134	Parima, Serra (Mts.) (sĕr′rȧ pä-rē′mȧ).Braz.-Ven.	3·45 N	64·00 W
134	Pariñas, Punta (Pt.) (pōō′n-tä-pä-rē′n-yäs).Peru	4·30 S	81·23 W
135	Parintins (pä-rĭn-tĭnzh′).....Braz.	2·34 S	56·30 W
113	Paris (păr′ĭs)................Ar.	35·17 N	93·43 W
104	Paris.....................Can.	43·15 N	80·23 W
161	Paris (pȧ-rē′)......Fr. (Paris In.)	48·51 N	2·20 E
104	Paris.......................Il.	39·35 N	87·40 W
104	Paris......................Ky.	38·15 N	84·15 W
117	Paris......................Mo.	39·27 N	91·59 W
120	Paris......................Tn.	36·16 N	88·20 W
117	Paris......................Tx.	33·39 N	95·33 W
127	Parita, Golfo de (G.) (gôl-fô-dĕ-pä-rē′tä).Pan.	8·06 N	80·10 W
111	Park City..................Ut.	40·39 N	111·33 W
108	Parker (pär′kēr)............SD	43·24 N	97·10 W
117	Parker Dam..............Az.-Ca.	34·20 N	114·00 W
104	Parkersburg (pär′kērz-bûrg)...WV	39·15 N	81·35 W
203	Parkes (pärks)............Austl.	33·10 S	148·10 E
109	Park Falls (pärk)............Wi.	45·55 N	90·29 W
107	Park Forest......Il. (Chicago In.)	41·29 N	87·41 W
112	Parkland (pärk′lȧnd) Wa. (Seattle In.)	47·09 N	122·26 W
111	Park Ra....................Co.	40·54 N	106·40 W
109	Park Rapids................Mn.	46·53 N	95·05 W
107	Park Ridge......Il. (Chicago In.)	42·00 N	87·50 W
108	Park River.................ND	48·22 N	97·43 W
112	Parkrose (pärk′rōz) Or. (Portland In.)	45·33 N	122·33 W
213	Park Rynie....S. Afr. (Natal In.)	30·22 S	30·43 E
108	Parkston (pärks′tŭn).........SD	43·22 N	97·59 W
115	Park View (vū)...............NM	36·45 N	106·30 W
106	Parkville.....Md. (Baltimore In.)	39·22 N	76·32 W
113	Parkville....Mo. (Kansas City In.)	39·12 N	94·41 W
163	Parla (pär′lä)....Sp. (Madrid In.)	40·14 N	3·46 W
164	Parma (pär′mä)..............It.	44·48 N	10·20 E
107	Parma........Oh. (Cleveland In.)	41·23 N	81·44 W
107	Parma Heights Oh. (Cleveland In.)	41·23 N	81·36 W
135	Parnaguá (pär-nä-gwá′).....Braz.	9·52 S	44·27 W
135	Parnaíba (pär-nä-ē′bä)......Braz.	3·00 S	41·42 W
135	Parnaiba (R.)..............Braz.	3·57 S	42·30 W
165	Parnassós (Mtn.)............Grc.	38·36 N	22·35 E
149	Parndorf.......Aus. (Vienna In.)	48·00 N	16·52 E
157	Pärnu (pĕr′nōō).........Sov. Un.	58·24 N	24·29 E
157	Pärnu (R.)..............Sov. Un.	58·40 N	25·05 E
157	Pärnu Laht (B.) (läĸt)...Sov. Un.	58·15 N	24·17 E
184	Paro (pä′rô)...............Bhu.	27·30 N	89·30 E
203	Paroo (R.) (pä′rōō)........Austl.	29·40 S	144·24 E
186	Paropamisus (Mts.).........Afg.	34·45 N	63·58 E
165	Páros (pä′rôs) (pā′rŏs).......Grc.	37·05 N	25·14 E
165	Páros (I.).................Grc.	37·11 N	25·00 E
212	Parow (pă′rô)........S. Afr. (In.)	33·54 S	18·36 E
115	Parowan (păr′ô-wăn)..........Ut.	37·50 N	112·50 W
136	Parral (pär-rä′l)............Chile	36·07 S	71·47 W
118	Parral, R..................Mex.	27·25 N	105·08 W
202	Parramatta (R.) (păr-ȧ-măt′ȧ) Aust. (Sydney In.)	33·42 S	150·58 E
118	Parras (pär-räs′)...........Mex.	25·28 N	102·08 W
127	Parrita (pär-rē′tä)..........C. R.	9·32 N	84·17 W
98	Parrsboro (pärz′bŭr-ô).......Can.	45·24 N	64·20 W
104	Parry (I.) (păr′ĭ)............Can.	45·15 N	80·00 W
92	Parry, Mt..................Can.	52·53 N	128·45 W
75	Parry Is...................Can.	75·30 N	110·00 W
105	Parry Sound................Can.	45·20 N	80·00 W
92	Parsnip (R.) (pärs′nĭp).......Can.	54·45 N	122·20 W
117	Parsons (pär′s′nz)...........Ks.	37·20 N	95·16 W
105	Parsons....................WV	39·05 N	79·40 W
160	Parthenay (pȧr-t′nĕ′)..........Fr.	46·39 N	0·16 W
164	Partinico (pär-tē′nê-kô).......It.	38·02 N	13·11 E
194	Partizansk.............Sov. Un.	43·15 N	133·19 E
218	Parys (pȧ-rĭs′)..............S. Afr. (Johannesburg & Pretoria In.)	26·53 S	27·28 E
113	Pasadena (păs-ȧ-dē′nȧ) Ca. (Los Angeles In.)	34·09 N	118·09 W
106	Pasadena.......Md. (Baltimore In.)	39·06 N	76·35 W
119	Pasadena...............Tx. (In.)	29·43 N	95·13 W
120	Pascagoula (păs-kȧ-gōō′lȧ)....Ms.	30·22 N	88·33 W
120	Pascagoula (R.)..............Ms.	30·52 N	88·48 W
159	Paşcani (päsh-kän′′)........Rom.	47·46 N	26·42 E
110	Pasco (păs′kō)..............Wa.	46·13 N	119·04 W
158	Pasewalk (pä′zĕ-välk).....G.D.R.	53·31 N	14·01 E
174	Pashiya (pȧ′shĭ-yȧ) Sov. Un. (Urals In.)	58·27 N	58·17 E
194	Pashkovo (pȧsh-kô′vô)...Sov. Un.	48·52 N	131·09 E
167	Pashkovskaya (pȧsh-kôf′skȧ-yȧ) Sov. Un.	45·29 N	39·04 E
197	Pasig..................Phil. (In.)	14·34 N	121·05 E
126	Pasión, Rio de la (R.) (rē′ō-dĕ-lä-pä-syōn′).Guat. (In.)	16·31 N	90·11 W
136	Paso de los Libres (pä-sō-dĕ-lôs-lē′brĕs).Arg.	29·33 S	57·05 W
137	Paso de los Toros (tŏ′rôs) Ur. (Buenos Aires In.)	32·43 S	56·33 W
114	Paso Robles (pä′sō rō′blĕs.....Ca.	35·38 N	120·44 W
96	Pasquia Hills (păs′kwê-ȧ)....Can.	53·13 N	102·37 W
106	Passaic (pă-sā′ĭk) NJ (New York In.)	40·52 N	74·08 W
106	Passaic R.....NJ (New York In.)	40·42 N	74·26 W
98	Passamaquoddy B. (păs′ȧ-mȧ-kwŏd′ĭ).Can.	45·06 N	66·59 W
137	Passa Tempo (pä′s-sä-tĕ′m-pô) Braz. (Rio de Janeiro In.)	21·40 S	44·29 W
158	Passau (päs′ou)...........F.R.G.	48·34 N	13·27 E
120	Pass Christian (pȧs krĭs′tyĕn).Ms.	30·20 N	89·15 W
151	Passero, C. ((päs-sĕ′rô)........It.	36·34 N	15·13 E
136	Passo Fundo (pä′sŏ fōōn′dōō) Braz.	28·16 S	52·13 W
137	Passos (pä′s-sōs) Braz. (Rio de Janeiro In.)	20·45 S	46·37 W
134	Pastaza (R.) (päs-tä′zä).....Peru	3·05 S	76·18 W
134	Pasto (päs′tô)..............Col.	1·15 N	77·19 W
124	Pastora (päs-tô-rä).........Mex.	22·08 N	100·04 W
196	Pasuruan..................Indon.	7·45 S	112·50 E
157	Pasvalys (päs-vä-lēs′).....Sov. Un.	56·04 N	24·23 E
136	Patagonia (Reg.) (păt-ȧ-gō′nĭ-ȧ) Arg.	46·45 S	69·30 W
185	Pātālganga (R.).......India (In.)	18·52 N	73·08 E
106	Patapsco R. (pȧ-tăps′kō) Md. (Baltimore In.)	39·12 N	76·30 W
164	Paternò (pä-tĕr-nô′)...........It.	37·25 N	14·58 E
106	Paterson (păt′ēr-sŭn) NJ (New York In.)	40·55 N	74·10 W
111	Pathfinder Res. (păth′fīn-dēr).Wy.	42·22 N	107·10 W
184	Patiāla (pŭt-ē-ä′lŭ).........India	30·25 N	76·28 E
136	Pati do Alferes (pä-tē-dô-äl-fĕ′rĕs) Braz. (Buenos Aires In.)	22·25 S	43·25 W
184	Patna (pŭt′nŭ).............India	25·33 N	85·18 E

ăt; finăl; rāte; senåte; ärm; åsk; sofȧ; fâre; ch-choose; dh-as th in other; bē; ēvent; bĕt; recĕnt; cratēr; g-go; gh-guttural g; bĭt; ĭ-short neutral; rīde; ĸ-guttural k as ch in German ich;

PRONOUNCING INDEX

Patnanongan — Perkins 327

Page	Name Pronunciation Region	Lat. °′	Long. °′
197	Patnanongan (pät-nä-nôn'gän) Phil. (In.)	14·50 N	122·25 E
104	Patoka (R.) (pá-tō'ká) Ind.	38·25 N	87·25 W
173	Patom Plat. Sov. Un.	59·30 N	115·00 E
135	Patos (pä'tōzh) Braz.	7·03 S	37·14 W
112	Patos (pä'tōs). Wa. (Vancouver In.)	48·47 N	122·57 W
136	Patos, Lago dos (L.) (lä'gō-à dozh pä'tōzh). Braz.	31·15 S	51·30 W
135	Patos de Minas (dĕ-mē'näzh). Braz.	18·39 S	46·31 W
165	Pátrai (Patras) (pä-trī') (pä-träs') Grc.	38·15 N	21·48 E
165	Patraïkós Kólpos (G.) Grc.	38·16 N	21·19 E
	Patras, see Pátrai		
135	Patrocínio (pä-trō-sē'nê-ōō) Braz.	18·48 S	46·47 W
196	Pattani (pät'á-nê) Thai.	6·56 N	101·13 E
98	Patten (păt''n) Me.	45·59 N	68·27 W
119	Patterson (păt'ēr-sŭn) La.	29·41 N	91·20 W
105	Patton Pa.	40·40 N	78·45 W
127	Patuca, Punta (Pt.) (pōō'n-tä-pä-tōō'kä). Hond.	15·23 N	84·05 W
127	Patuca R. Hond.	15·22 N	84·31 W
105	Patuxent (R.) (pá-tŭk'sĕnt) Md.	39·10 N	77·10 W
124	Pátzcuaro (päts'kwä-rô) Mex.	19·30 N	101·36 W
124	Pátzcuaro, Lago de (L.) (lä'gô-dĕ). Mex.	19·36 N	101·38 W
126	Patzicia (pät-zê'syä) Guat.	14·36 N	90·57 W
126	Patzún (pät-zōōn') Guat.	14·40 N	91·00 W
160	Pau (pō) Fr.	43·18 N	0·23 W
160	Pau, Gave de (strm.) (gäv-dĕ). Fr.	43·33 N	0·51 W
160	Pauillac (pō-yäk') Fr.	45·12 N	0·46 W
104	Paulding (pôl'dĭng) Oh.	41·05 N	84·35 W
149	Paulinenaue (pou'lē-nĕ-nou-ĕ) G.D.R. (Berlin In.)	52·40 N	12·43 E
	Paulis, see Isiro		
135	Paulistana (pá'ōō-lēs-tá-nä) Braz.	8·13 S	41·06 W
135	Paulo Afonso, Salto (falls) (säl-tô-pou'lōō äf-fôn'sōō). Braz.	9·33 S	38·32 W
218	Paul Roux (pôrl rōō) S. Afr. (Johannesburg & Pretoria In.)	28·18 S	27·57 E
106	Paulsboro (pôlz'bē-rô) NJ (Philadelphia In.)	39·50 N	75·16 W
117	Pauls Valley (pôlz văl'ê) Ok.	34·43 N	97·13 W
134	Pavarandocito (pä-vä-rän-dô-sē'tô) Col. (In.)	7·18 N	76·32 W
174	Pavda (päv'da). Sov. Un. (Urals In.)	59·16 N	59·32 E
164	Pavia (pä-vē'ä) It.	45·12 N	9·11 E
172	Pavlodar (pàv-lô-dár') Sov. Un.	52·17 N	77·23 E
101	Pavlo'f B. (păv-lōf) Ak.	55·20 N	161·20 W
167	Pavlograd (pàv-lô-grát') Sov. Un.	48·32 N	35·52 E
167	Pavlovsk (pàv-lôfsk') Sov. Un.	50·28 N	40·05 E
174	Pavlovsk. Sov. Un. (Leningrad In.)	59·41 N	30·27 E
174	Pavlovskiy Posad (pàv-lôf'skĭ pô-sát') Sov. Un. (Moscow In.)	55·47 N	38·39 E
136	Pavuna (pä-vōō'ná) Braz. (Rio de Janeiro In.)	22·48 S	43·21 W
149	Päwesin (pă'vĕ-zēn) G.D.R. (Berlin In.)	52·31 N	12·44 E
117	Pawhuska (pô-hŭs'ká) Ok.	36·41 N	96·20 W
117	Pawnee (pô-nē') Ok.	36·20 N	96·47 W
116	Pawnee (R.) Ks.	38·18 N	99·42 W
117	Pawnee City Ne.	40·08 N	96·09 W
104	Paw Paw (pô'pô) Mi.	42·15 N	85·55 W
109	Paw Paw (R.) Mi.	42·14 N	86·21 W
106	Pawtucket (pô-tŭk'ĕt) RI (Providence In.)	41·53 N	71·23 W
165	Paxoi (I.) Grc.	39·14 N	20·15 E
104	Paxton (păks'tŭn) Il.	40·35 N	88·00 W
192	Payen (pä'yĕn') China	46·00 N	127·20 E
110	Payette (pâ-ĕt') Id.	44·05 N	116·55 W
110	Payette R. Id.	43·57 N	116·26 W
110	Payette R., North Fork Id.	44·35 N	116·10 W
110	Payette R., South Fork Id.	44·07 N	115·43 W
	Payintala, see Tungliao		
170	Pay-Khoy, Khrebet (Mts.) Sov. Un.	68·08 N	63·04 E
91	Payne (L.) (pān) Can.	59·22 N	73·16 W
109	Paynesville (pānz'vĭl) Mn.	45·23 N	94·43 W
	Payo Obispo, see Ciudad Chetumal		
136	Paysandú (pī-sän-dōō') Ur.	32·16 S	57·55 W
115	Payson (pā's'n) Ut.	40·05 N	111·45 W
165	Pazardzhik (pä-zàr-dzhek') Bul.	42·10 N	24·22 E
164	Pazin (pä'zên) Yugo.	45·14 N	13·57 E
117	Peabody (pē'bŏd-ĭ) Ks.	38·09 N	97·09 W
99	Peabody Ma. (In.)	42·32 N	70·56 W
93	Peace (R.) Can.	55·40 N	118·30 W
121	Peace Cr. (pēs) Fl. (In.)	27·16 N	81·53 W
106	Peace Dale (dāl) RI (Providence In.)	41·27 N	71·30 W
93	Peace River (rĭv'ēr) Can.	56·14 N	117·17 W
90	Peacock Hills (pē-kŏk' hĭlz) Can.	66·08 N	109·55 W
148	Peak, The (Mt.) (pēk) Eng.	53·23 N	1·52 W
204	Peak Hill Austl.	25·38 S	118·50 E
120	Pearl (R.) (pûrl) La.-Ms.	31·06 N	89·44 W
119	Pearland (pûrl'ănd) Tx. (In.)	29·34 N	95·17 W
100	Pearl Harbor Hi.	21·20 N	157·53 W
	Pearl R., see Chu Chiang		
118	Pearsall (pēr'sôl) Tx.	28·53 N	99·06 W
92	Pearse I. (pērs) Can.	54·51 N	130·21 W
213	Pearston (pē'ērstŏn) S. Afr. (Natal In.)	32·36 S	25·09 E
219	Peary Land (Reg.) (pēr'ĭ) Grnld.	82·00 N	40·00 W
116	Pease (R.) (pēz) Tx.	34·07 N	99·53 W
119	Peason (pēz''n) La.	31·25 N	93·19 W
217	Pebane (pĕ-bä'nē) Moz.	17·10 S	38·08 E
165	Peć (pĕch) Yugo.	42·39 N	20·18 E
118	Pecan Bay (pē-kăn') Tx.	32·04 N	99·15 W
135	Peçanha (pâ-kän'yá) Braz.	18·37 S	42·26 W
109	Pecatonica (R.) (pĕk-á-tŏn-ĭ-ká) Il.	42·21 N	89·28 W
170	Pechenga (pyĕ'chĕŋ-gà) Sov. Un.	69·30 N	31·10 E
170	Pechora (R.) Sov. Un.	66·00 N	52·30 E
172	Pechora Basin (pyĕ-chô'rà) Sov. Un.	67·55 N	58·37 E
170	Pechorskaya Guba (B.) Sov. Un.	68·40 N	55·00 E
115	Pecos (pā'kôs) NM	35·29 N	105·41 W
118	Pecos Tx.	31·26 N	103·30 W
102	Pecos (R.) U. S.	31·10 N	103·10 W
159	Pécs (pāch) Hung.	46·04 N	18·15 E
213	Peddie S. Afr. (Natal In.)	33·13 S	27·09 E
166	Pededze (R.) (pă'dĕd-zĕ) Sov. Un.	57·18 N	27·13 E
113	Pedley (pĕd'lē) Ca. (Los Angeles In.)	33·59 N	117·29 W
135	Pedra Azul (pā'drä-zōō'l) Braz.	16·03 S	41·13 W
135	Pedreiras (pĕ-drā'räs) Braz.	4·30 S	44·31 W
185	Pedro, Pt. (pē'drô) Sri Lanka	9·50 N	80·14 E
126	Pedro Antonio Santos (Sta. Cruz Chico) (pā'drô än-tō'nê-ô sän'tōs) (sän'tä krōōz' chē'kô) Mex. (In.)	18·55 N	88·13 W
128	Pedro Betancourt (bā-täŋ-kōrt') Cuba	22·40 N	81·15 W
136	Pedro de Valdivia (pĕ'drô-dĕ-väl-dē'vê-ä). Chile	22·32 S	69·55 W
136	Pedro do Rio (dô-rē'ô) Braz. (Rio de Janeiro In.)	22·20 S	43·09 W
135	Pedro Juan Caballero (hōōá'n-kä-bäl-yĕ'rō). Par.	22·40 S	55·42 W
122	Pedro Miguel (mê-gāl'). C. Z. (In.)	9·01 N	79·36 W
122	Pedro Miguel Locks (mê-gāl') C. Z. (In.)	9·01 N	79·36 W
135	Pedro II (pā'drōō sá-gōōn'dōō) Braz.	4·20 S	41·27 W
203	Peebinga (pê-bĭng'á) Austl.	34·43 S	140·55 E
154	Peebles (pē'b'lz) Scot.	55·40 N	3·15 W
121	Pee Dee (R.) (pē-dē') NC-SC	34·01 N	79·26 W
106	Peekskill (pēks'kĭl) NY (New York In.)	41·17 N	73·55 W
205	Pegasus B. (pĕg'á-sŭs) N. Z.	43·18 S	173·37 E
158	Pegnitz R. (pĕgh-nēts) F.R.G.	49·38 N	11·40 E
163	Pego (pā'gō) Sp.	38·50 N	0·09 W
196	Pegu (pĕ-gōō') Bur.	17·17 N	96·29 E
95	Peguis Ind. Res. Can.	51·20 N	97·35 W
188	Pegu Yoma (Mts.) (pĕ-gōō'yō'mä) Bur.	19·16 N	95·59 E
165	Pehčevo (pĕĸ'chĕ-vô) Yugo.	41·42 N	22·57 E
192	Peian (pĕ'ê-án') China	48·05 N	126·26 E
191	Pei-Chiang (R.) China (Canton In.)	22·54 N	113·08 E
190	Peich'iao (bā'chiou) China	31·03 N	121·27 E
190	Peich'enghuang Tao (I.) (bā'chĕng'hōōäng' dou). China	38·23 N	120·55 E
192	Peiching (Peking) China (In.)	39·55 N	116·23 E
93	Peigan Ind. Res. Can.	49·35 N	113·40 W
193	Peihai (Pakhoi) China	21·30 N	109·10 E
193	Peili China	19·08 N	108·42 E
	Peilintzu, see Suihua		
	Peipus, L., see Chudskoye Ozero		
190	Pei Wan (B.) (bā'wän) China	36·21 N	120·48 E
192	Peiyün Ho (R.) China (In.)	39·42 N	116·48 E
104	Pekin (pē'kĭn) Il.	40·35 N	89·30 W
	Peking, see Peiching		
190	Peking-Shih (Mun.) China	40·07 N	116·00 E
152	Pelagie, Isole I. It.	35·46 N	12·32 E
165	Pélagos (I.) Grc.	39·17 N	24·05 E
120	Pelahatchee (pĕl-á-hăch'ê) Ms.	32·17 N	89·48 W
161	Pelat, Mt. (pē-lá') Fr.	44·16 N	6·43 E
173	Peleduy (pyĕl-yĭ-dōō'ê) Sov. Un.	59·50 N	112·47 E
127	Pelee, Mt. (Vol.) (pē-lā') Mart. (In.)	14·49 N	61·10 W
104	Pelee, Pt. Can.	41·55 N	82·30 W
104	Pelee I. (pē'lê) Can.	41·45 N	82·30 W
137	Pelequén (pĕ-lĕ-kĕ'n) Chile (Santiago In.)	34·26 S	71·52 W
	Pelew (I.), see Palau		
120	Pelham (pĕl'hăm) Ga.	31·07 N	84·10 W
99	Pelham NH (In.)	42·43 N	71·22 W
109	Pelican (L.) Mn.	46·36 N	94·00 W
95	Pelican B. Can.	52·45 N	100·20 W
128	Pelican Hbr. (pĕl'ĭ-kăn) Ba.	26·20 N	76·45 W
108	Pelican Rapids (pĕl'ĭ-kăn) Mn.	46·34 N	96·05 W
109	Pella (pĕl'á) Ia.	41·25 N	92·50 W
158	Pell-Worm I. (pĕl'vōrm) F.R.G.	54·33 N	8·25 E
90	Pelly (L.) Can.	66·08 N	102·57 W
90	Pelly (R.) Can.	62·20 N	113·26 W
90	Pelly B. (pĕl'ĭ) Can.	68·57 N	91·05 W
101	Pelly Crossing Can.	62·50 N	136·50 W
90	Pelly Mts. Can.	61·50 N	133·05 W
115	Peloncillo Mts. (pĕl-ôn-sĭl'lō) Az.	32·40 N	109·20 W
165	Peloponnisos (Reg.) Grc.	37·28 N	22·14 E
136	Pelotas (pâ-lō'tăzh) Braz.	31·45 S	52·18 W
107	Pelton (pĕl'tŭn) Can. (Detroit In.)	42·15 N	82·57 W
161	Pelvoux, Mt. (pĕl-vōō') Fr.	44·56 N	6·24 E
170	Pelym (R.) Sov. Un.	60·20 N	63·05 E
121	Pelzer (pĕl'zēr) SC	34·38 N	82·30 W
183	Pemanggil (I.) Mala. (Singapore In.)	2·37 N	104·41 E
212	Pemba (pĕm'bá) Zambia	15·29 S	27·22 E
217	Pemba (I.) Tan.	5·20 S	39·57 E
217	Pemba Chan. Afr.	5·10 S	39·30 E
108	Pembina (pĕm'bĭ-ná) ND	48·58 N	97·15 W
93	Pembina (R.) Can.	53·05 N	114·30 W
95	Pembina (R.) Can.	49·08 N	98·20 W
105	Pembroke (pĕm' brōk) Can.	45·50 N	77·00 W
99	Pembroke (pĕm'brōk) Ma. (In.)	42·05 N	70·49 W
154	Pembroke Wales	51·40 N	5·00 W
185	Pen India (In.)	18·44 N	73·06 E
162	Penafiél (pā-ná-fyĕl') Port.	41·12 N	8·19 W
162	Peñafiel (pā-nyá-fyĕl') Sp.	41·38 N	4·08 W
162	Peñalara (Mtn.) (pā-nyä-lä'rä) Sp.	40·52 N	3·57 W
124	Pena Nevada, Cerro Mex.	23·47 N	99·52 W
197	Penaranda (pā-nyä-rän'dä) Phil. (In.)	15·20 N	120·59 E
162	Peñaranda de Bracamonte (pā-nyä-rän'dä dā brä-kä-mōn'tā). Sp.	40·54 N	5·11 W
163	Peña Roya (Mtn.) (pā'nyä rō'yä) Sp.	40·18 N	0·42 W
162	Peñarroya-Peublonuevo (pĕn-yär-rô'yä-pwĕ'blô-nwĕ'vô) Sp.	38·18 N	5·18 W
162	Peñas, Cabo de (C.) (kä'bô-dĕ-pā'nyäs). Sp.	43·42 N	6·12 W
136	Penas, Golfo de (gôl-fô-dĕ-pĕ'n-äs). Chile	47·15 S	77·30 W
118	Penasco R. (pā-nàs'kō) Tx.	32·50 N	104·45 W
192	Pench'i China	41·25 N	123·50 E
214	Pendembu (pĕn-dĕm'bōō) S. L.	8·06 N	10·42 W
108	Pender (pĕn'dēr) Ne.	42·08 N	96·43 W
134	Penderisco (R.) (pĕn-dĕ-rē's-kô) Col. (In.)	6·30 N	76·21 W
214	Pendjari, Parc Natl. de la (Natl. Pk.). Dahomey	11·25 N	1·30 E
110	Pendleton (pĕn'd'l-tŭn) Or.	45·41 N	118·47 W
110	Pend Oreille L. (pŏn-dô-rā') (pĕn-dô-rĕl'). Id.	48·09 N	116·38 W
110	Pend Oreille R. Wa.	48·44 N	117·20 W
135	Penedo (pâ-nā'dōō) Braz.	10·17 S	36·28 W
105	Penetanguishene (pĕn'ê-tăŋ-gĭ-shēn'). Can.	44·45 N	79·55 W
190	P'engchengchen (pĕng'chĕng'jĕn). China	36·24 N	114·11 E
190	P'englai (pĕng'lāi) China	37·49 N	120·45 E
162	Peniche (pĕ-nē'chå) Port.	39·22 N	9·24 W
107	Peninsula (pĕn-ĭn'sū-lá) Oh. (Cleveland In.)	41·14 N	81·32 W
148	Penistone (pĕn'ĭ-stŭn) Eng.	53·31 N	1·38 W
124	Penjamillo (pĕn-hä-mēl'yō) Mex.	20·06 N	101·56 W
124	Penjamo (pān'hä-mō) Mex.	20·27 N	101·43 W
148	Penk (R.) (pĕnk) Eng.	52·41 N	2·10 W
148	Penkridge (pĕnk'rĭj) Eng.	52·43 N	2·07 W
164	Penne (pĕn'nā) It.	42·28 N	13·57 E
184	Penner (R.) (pĕn'ēr) India	14·43 N	79·09 E
158	Pennine Alpi (Mts.) Switz.	46·02 N	7·07 E
154	Pennine Chain (Mts.) (pĕn-īn') Eng.	53·44 N	1·59 W
104	Pennsboro (pĕnz'bŭr-ô) WV	39·10 N	81·00 W
106	Penns Grove (pĕnz grōv) NJ (Philadelpahia In.)	39·44 N	75·28 W
103	Pennsylvania (State) (pĕn-sĭl-vā'nĭ-á). U. S.	41·00 N	78·10 W
105	Penn Yan (pĕn yăn') NY	42·40 N	77·00 W
95	Pennycutaway (R.) Can.	56·10 N	93·25 W
166	Peno (L.) (pā'nô) Sov. Un.	56·55 N	32·28 E
98	Penobscot (R.) Me.	45·00 N	68·36 W
98	Penobscot B. (pê-nŏb'skŏt) Me.	44·20 N	69·00 W
204	Penong (pê-nông') Austl.	32·00 S	133·00 E
127	Penonomé (pā-nō-nô-mā') Pan.	8·32 N	80·21 W
202	Penrith Austl. (Sydney In.)	33·45 S	150·42 E
120	Pensacola (pĕn-sá-kō'lá) Fl.	30·25 N	87·13 W
117	Pensacola Dam Ok.	36·27 N	95·02 W
124	Pensilvania (pĕn-sĕl-vá'nyä) Col. (In.)	5·31 N	75·05 W
205	Pentecost (I.) (pĕn'tê-kŏst) New Hebr.	16·05 S	168·28 E
93	Penticton Can.	49·30 N	119·35 W
154	Pentland Firth (pĕnt'lănd) Scot.	58·44 N	3·25 W
171	Penza (pĕn'zá) Sov. Un.	53·10 N	45·00 E
154	Penzance (pĕn-zăns') Eng.	50·07 N	5·40 W
158	Penzberg (pĕnts'bĕrgh) F.R.G.	47·43 N	11·21 E
173	Penzhina (R.) (pyĭn-zē-nŭ) Sov. Un.	62·15 N	166·30 E
173	Penzhino Sov. Un.	63·42 N	168·00 E
173	Penzhinskay'a Guba (B.). Sov. Un.	60·30 N	161·30 E
104	Peoria (pē-ō'rĭ-á) Il.	40·45 N	89·35 W
124	Peotillos (pā-ō-tel'yōs) Mex.	22·30 N	100·39 W
107	Peotone (pē'ô-tōn) Il. (Chicago In.)	41·20 N	87·47 W
105	Pepacton Res. (pĕp-ăc'tŭn) NY	42·05 N	74·40 W
128	Pepe, Cabo (kä'bô-pĕ'pê) (C.) Cuba	21·30 N	83·10 W
99	Pepperell (pĕp'ēr-ĕl) Ma. (In.)	42·40 N	71·36 W
165	Peqin (pĕ-kēn') Alb.	41·03 N	19·48 E
163	Perales (R.) (pā-rä'läs) Sp.	40·24 N	4·07 W
163	Perales de Tajuña (dā tä-hōō'nyä). Sp. (Madrid In.)	40·14 N	3·22 W
98	Percé (pĕr'sā') Can.	48·31 N	64·13 W
149	Perchtoldsdorf (pĕrk'tōlts-dôrf) Aus. (Vienna In.)	48·07 N	16·17 E
218	Perdekop S. Afr. (Johannesburg & Pretoria In.)	27·11 S	29·38 E
163	Perdido, Mt. (pĕr-dē'dō) Sp.	42·40 N	0·00
120	Perdido (R.) (pĕr-dī'dō) Al.-Fl.	30·45 N	87·38 W
137	Perdões (pĕr-dô'ĕs) Braz. (Rio de Janeiro In.)	21·05 S	45·05 W
134	Pereira (pà-rā'rä) Col. (In.)	4·49 N	75·42 W
167	Perekop (pĕr-â-kōp') Sov. Un.	46·08 N	33·39 E
104	Pere Marquette Mi.	43·55 N	86·10 W
167	Pereshchepino (pâ'râsh-chē'pê-nô). Sov. Un.	49·02 N	35·19 E
166	Pereslavl'-Zalesskiy (pâ-râ-slàv''l zá-lyĕs'kĭ). Sov. Un.	56·43 N	38·52 E
167	Pereyaslav (pĕ-rá-yäs'läv) Sov. Un.	50·05 N	31·25 E
137	Pergamino (pĕr-gä-mē'nō) Arg. (Buenos Aires In.)	33·53 S	60·36 W
108	Perham (pĕr'hăm) Mn.	46·37 N	95·35 W
97	Peribonca (R.) (pĕr-ĭ-bŏŋ'ká). Can.	49·10 N	71·20 W
160	Périgueux (pā-rē-gû') Fr.	45·12 N	0·43 E
134	Perija, Sierra de (Mts.) (sē-ĕ'r-rä-dĕ-pĕ-rē'ĸä). Col.	9·25 N	73·30 W
197	Perkam, Tandjung (C.) Indon.	1·20 S	138·45 E
89	Perkins (pĕr'kĕns) Can. (Ottawa In.)	45·37 N	75·37 W

328 Perlas — Pine Bluff PRONOUNCING INDEX

Page	Name Pronunciation Region	Lat. °′	Long. °′
	Perlas, Arch. de Las (är-chē-pyĕ'lä-gô-dĕ-läs-pĕr'läs) Pan.	8·29 N	79·15 W
127	Perlas, Laguna las (L.) (lä-gōō'nä-dĕ-läs). Nic.	12·34 N	83·19 W
158	Perleberg (pĕr'lē-bĕrg)....G.D.R.	53·06 N	11·51 E
174	Perm' (pĕrm). Sov. Un. (Urals In.)	58·00 N	56·15 E
	Pernambuco, see Recife		
135	Pernambuco (State) (pĕr-näm-bōō'kō). Braz.	8·08 S	38·54 W
165	Pernik (pĕr-nēk')..........Bul.	42·36 N	23·04 E
160	Peronne (pā-rôn')...........Fr.	49·57 N	2·49 E
125	Perote (pĕ-rô'tĕ)...........Mex.	19·33 N	97·13 W
194	Perouse Str.........Jap.-Sov. Un.	45·45 N	141·38 E
174	Perovo (pâ'rô-vô) Sov. Un. (Moscow In.)	55·43 N	37·47 E
160	Perpignan (pĕr-pē-nyäN')......Fr.	42·42 N	2·48 E
113	Perris (pĕr'ĭs) Ca. (Los Angeles In.)	33·46 N	117·14 W
128	Perros, Bahía (B.) (bä-ē'ä-pā'rōs) Cuba	22·25 N	78·35 W
89	Perrot Île (I.) (pĕr'ŭt) Can. (Montreal In.)	45·23 N	73·57 W
120	Perry (pĕr'ĭ)................Fl.	30·06 N	83·35 W
120	Perry......................Ga.	32·27 N	83·44 W
109	Perry......................Ia.	41·49 N	94·40 W
105	Perry......................NY	42·45 N	78·00 W
117	Perry......................Ok.	36·17 N	97·18 W
113	Perry....Ut. (Salt Lake City In.)	41·27 N	112·02 W
106	Perry Hall...Md. (Baltimore In.)	39·24 N	76·29 W
107	Perryopolis (pĕ-rē-ŏ'pô-lĭs) Pa. (Pittsburgh In.)	40·05 N	79·45 W
104	Perrysburg (pĕr ĭz-bûrg)......Oh.	41·35 N	83·35 W
116	Perryton (pĕr'ĭ-tŭn)..........Tx.	36·23 N	100·48 W
101	Perryville (pĕr-ĭ-vĭl)..........Ak.	55·58 N	159·28 W
117	Perryville..................Mo.	37·41 N	89·52 W
161	Persan (pĕr-säN')........Fr. (In.)	49·09 N	2·15 E
141	Persepolis (Ruins) (pēr-sĕp'o-lĭs) Iran	30·15 N	53·08 E
	Persia, see Iran		
186	Persian G. (pûr'zhån)........Asia	27·38 N	50·30 E
204	Perth (pûrth).............Austl.	31·50 S	116·10 E
105	Perth......................Can.	44·40 N	76·15 W
154	Perth......................Scot.	56·24 N	3·25 W
106	Perth Amboy (ăm'boi) NJ (New York In.)	40·31 N	74·16 W
161	Pertuis (pĕr-tüē')............Fr.	43·43 N	5·29 E
104	Peru (pē-rōō')...............Il.	41·20 N	89·10 W
104	Peru......................In.	40·45 N	86·00 W
133	Peru......................S. A.	10·00 S	75·00 W
164	Perugia (pā-rōō'jä)...........It.	43·08 N	12·24 E
113	Peruque (pĕ rō'kĕ) Mo. (St. Louis In.)	38·52 N	90·36 W
167	Pervomaysk (pĕr-vô-mīsk') Sov. Un.	48·04 N	30·52 E
174	Pervoural'sk (pĕr-vô-ōō-rálsk') Sov. Un. (Urals In.)	56·54 N	59·58 E
173	Pervyy Kuril'skiy Proliv (Str.) Sov. Un.	51·43 N	154·32 E
164	Pesaro (pā'zä-rō)............It.	43·54 N	12·55 E
135	Pescado (pĕs-kä'dō) (R.) Ven. (In.)	9·33 N	65·32 W
164	Pescara (pās-kä'rä)..........It.	42·26 N	14·15 E
164	Pescara (R.)................It.	42·18 N	13·22 E
171	Peschanyy, Mys (C.)....Sov. Un.	43·10 N	51·20 E
164	Pescia (pā'shä)..............It.	43·53 N	11·42 E
187	Peshāwar (pĕ-shä'wŭr) Pak. (Khyber Pass In.)	34·01 N	71·34 E
165	Peshtera...................Bul.	42·03 N	24·19 E
109	Peshtigo (pĕsh'tē-gō).........Wi.	45·03 N	87·46 W
109	Peshtigo (R.)................Wi.	45·15 N	88·14 W
141	Peski................Sov. Un.	39·46 N	59·47 E
141	Peski................Sov. Un.	44·07 N	63·17 E
174	Peski (pyâs'kĭ) Sov. Un. (Moscow In.)	55·13 N	38·48 E
162	Pêso da Régua (pā-sōō-dä-rā'gwä). Port.	41·09 N	7·47 W
126	Pespire (pâs-pē'rå).........Hond.	13·35 N	87·20 W
118	Pesqueria, R. (pās-kā-rē'å)...Mex.	25·55 N	100·25 W
124	Petacalco, Bahía de (B.) (bä-ē'ä-dĕ-pĕ-tä-käl'kô). Mex.	17·55 N	102·00 W
183	Petah Tiqwa...Isr. (Palestine In.)	32·05 N	34·53 E
114	Petaluma (pét-å-lōō'må)......Ca.	38·15 N	122·38 W
135	Petare (pĕ-tä'rĕ).......Ven. (In.)	10·28 N	66·48 W
124	Petatlán (pā-tä-tlän')........Mex.	17·31 N	101·17 W
97	Petawawa..................Can.	45·54 N	77·17 W
126	Petén, Laguna de (L.) (lä-gōō'nä-dĕ-pâ-tān') Guat. (In.)	17·05 N	89·54 W
109	Petenwell Res...............Wi.	44·10 N	89·55 W
105	Peterborough (pē'tēr-bŭr-ô)..Can.	44·20 N	78·20 W
203	Peterborough...............Austl.	32·53 S	138·58 E
148	Peterborough...............Eng.	52·35 N	0·14 W
154	Peterhead (pē-tēr-hĕd').......Scot.	57·36 N	3·47 W
105	Peter Pt....................Can.	43·50 N	77·00 W
94	Peter Pond L. (pŏnd)........Can.	55·55 N	108·44 W
101	Petersburg (pē'tērz-bûrg).....Ak.	56·52 N	133·10 W
117	Petersburg..................Il.	40·01 N	89·51 W
104	Petersburg..................In.	38·30 N	87·15 W
107	Petersburg...Ky. (Cincinnati In.)	39·04 N	84·52 W
121	Petersburg..................Va.	37·12 N	77·30 W
149	Petershagen (pĕ'tĕrs-hä-gĕn) G.D.R. (Berlin In.)	52·32 N	13·46 E
149	Petershausen (pĕ'tĕrs-hou-zĕn) F.R.G. (Munich In.)	48·25 N	11·29 E
129	Pétionville................Hai.	18·30 N	72·20 W
98	Petitcodiac (pē-tē-kô-dyȧk') Can.	45·56 N	65·10 W
127	Petite Terre I. (pē-tēt'târ') Guad. (In.)	16·12 N	61·00 W
129	Petit Goâve (pē-tē' gô-äv')...Hai.	18·25 N	72·50 W
117	Petit Jean Cr. (pē-tē'zhäN')...Ar.	35·05 N	93·55 W
216	Petit Loango.............Gabon	2·16 S	9·35 E
125	Petlalcingo (pĕ-tläl-sĕŋ'gô)...Mex.	18·05 N	97·53 W
126	Peto (pĕ'tô)...........Mex. (In.)	20·07 N	88·49 W
125	Petorca (pā-tōr'kȧ) Chile (Santiago In.)	32·14 S	70·55 W
104	Petoskey (pĕ-tŏs'kĭ)..........Mi.	45·25 N	84·55 W
183	Petra......Jordan (Palestine In.)	30·21 N	35·25 E
194	Petra Velikogo, Zaliv (B.) (zä'lĭf pĕt-rä' vĕ-lĭ'kô-vô) Sov. Un.	42·40 N	131·50 E
165	Petrich (pā'trĭch)............Bul.	41·24 N	23·13 E
115	Petrified Forest Natl. Park (pĕt'rĭ-fīd fôr'ĕst). Az.	34·58 N	109·35 W
167	Petrikovka (pyĕ'trê-kôf-kä) Sov. Un.	48·43 N	34·29 E
167	Petrikov (pyĕ'trê-kô-v)...Sov. Un.	52·09 N	28·30 E
164	Petrinja (pā'trēn-yȧ).......Yugo.	45·25 N	16·17 E
174	Petrodvorets (pyĕ-trô-dvô-ryĕts') Sov. Un. (Leningrad In.)	59·53 N	29·55 E
174	Petrokrepost' (pyĕ'trô-krĕ-pôst) Sov. Un. (Leningrad In.)	59·56 N	31·03 E
104	Petrolia (pê-trō'lĭ-ȧ).........Can.	42·50 N	82·10 W
135	Petrolina (pĕ-trō-lē'nȧ)......Braz.	9·18 S	40·28 W
149	Petronell.......Aus. (Vienna In.)	48·07 N	16·52 E
167	Petropavlovka (pyĕ'trô-päv'lôf-kȧ) Sov. Un.	48·24 N	36·23 E
174	Petropavlovka. Sov. Un. (Urals In.)	54·10 N	59·50 E
172	Petropavlovsk (pyĕ-trô-päv'lôfsk) Sov. Un.	54·44 N	69·07 E
173	Petropavlovsk-Kamchatskiy (käm-chät'skĭ). Sov. Un.	53·13 N	158·56 E
136	Petrópolis (pâ-trô-pô-lēzh') Braz. (Rio de Janeiro In.)	22·31 S	43·10 W
165	Petroseni..................Rom.	45·24 N	23·24 E
171	Petrovsk (pyĕ-trôfsk')....Sov. Un.	52·20 N	45·15 E
167	Petrovskaya (pyĕ-trôf'skȧ-yȧ) Sov. Un.	45·25 N	37·50 E
171	Petrovskoye...........Sov. Un.	45·20 N	43·00 E
173	Petrovsk-Zabaykal'skiy (pyĕ-trôfskzä-bī-käl'skĭ) Sov. Un.	51·13 N	109·08 E
157	Petrozavodsk (pyā'trô-zȧ-vôtsk') Sov. Un.	61·46 N	34·25 E
218	Petrus Steyn (pā'trōōs stän')........S. Afr. (Johannesburg & Pretoria In.)	27·40 S	28·09 E
166	Petseri (pĕt'sĕ-rê).......Sov. Un.	57·48 N	27·33 E
107	Pewaukee (pĭ-wô'kê) Wi. (Milwaukee In.)	43·05 N	88·15 W
107	Pewaukee L..Wi. (Milwaukee In.)	43·03 N	88·18 W
107	Pewee Valley (pe wē) Ky. (Louisville In.)	38·19 N	85·29 W
170	Peza (R.) (pyå'zȧ).......Sov. Un.	65·35 N	46·50 E
160	Pézenas (pā-zē-nä')...........Fr.	43·26 N	3·24 E
158	Pforzheim (pfôrts'hīm).....F.R.G.	48·52 N	8·43 E
184	Phalodi...................India	27·13 N	72·22 E
196	Phan Rang (p'hän'räng')....Viet.	11·30 N	108·43 E
	Pharsalus, see Fársala		
120	Phenix City (fē'nĭks)..........Al.	32·29 N	85·00 W
196	Phet Buri...................Thai.	13·07 N	99·53 E
120	Philadelphia (fĭl-ȧ-dĕl'phĭ-ȧ)..Ms.	32·45 N	89·07 W
106	Philadelphia. Pa. (Philadelphia In.)	40·00 N	75·13 W
108	Philip (fĭl'ĭp)................SD	44·03 N	101·35 W
	Philippeville, see Skikda		
183	Philippines (fĭl'ĭ-pēnz).......Asia	14·25 N	125·00 E
198	Philippine Sea (fĭl'ĭ-pēn).....Asia	16·00 N	133·00 E
197	Philippine Trench..........Phil.	10·30 N	127·15 E
	Philippopolis, see Plovdiv		
105	Philipsburg (fĭl'lĭps-bĕrg)......Pa.	40·55 N	78·10 W
111	Philipsburg.................Wy.	46·19 N	113·19 W
203	Phillip (I.) (fĭl'ĭp).........Austl.	38·32 S	145·10 E
183	Phillip Chan. Indon. (Singapore In.)	1·04 N	103·40 E
105	Phillipi (fĭ-lĭp'ĭ)............WV	39·10 N	80·00 W
109	Phillips (fĭl'ĭps)............Wi.	45·41 N	90·24 W
116	Phillipsburg (fĭl'lĭps-bĕrg).....Ks.	39·44 N	99·19 W
105	Phillipsburg................NJ	40·45 N	75·10 W
196	Phnom Penh (nŏm'pĕn')...Camb.	11·39 N	104·53 E
115	Phoenix (fē'nĭks).............Az.	33·30 N	112·00 W
106	Phoenix......Md. (Baltimore In.)	39·31 N	76·40 W
198	Phoenix Is...............Oceania	4·00 S	174·00 W
106	Phoenixville (fē'nĭks-vĭl) Pa. (Philadelphia In.)	40·08 N	75·31 W
196	Phu Bia (Pk.)..............Laos	19·36 N	103·00 E
196	Phu-Quoc (I.).............Camb.	10·13 N	104·00 E
196	Phuket....................Thai.	7·57 N	98·19 E
190	P'i (R.) (pē')..............China	32·06 N	116·31 E
164	Piacenza (pyä-chĕnt'sä).......It.	45·02 N	9·42 E
164	Pianosa (I.) (pyä-nō'sä)......It.	42·13 N	15·45 E
159	Piatra-Neamt (pyä'trȧ-nā-ämts') Rom.	46·54 N	26·24 E
135	Piauí (State) (pyou'ê).......Braz.	7·40 S	42·25 W
135	Piauí, Serra do (Mts.) (sĕr'rȧ dōō pyou'ê). Braz.	10·45 S	44·36 W
164	Piave (R.) (pyä'vā)...........It.	45·45 N	12·15 E
164	Piazza Armerina (pyät'sȧ är-mâ-rē'nä). It.	37·23 N	14·26 E
211	Pibor R. (pē'bôr)...........Sud.	7·21 N	32·54 E
109	Pic (R.) (pĕk)..............Can.	48·48 N	86·28 W
123	Picara Pt. (pē-kä'rä)......Vir. Is. (U. S. A.) (St. Thomas In.)	18·23 N	64·57 W
120	Picayune (pĭk'á yōōn)........Ms.	30·32 N	89·41 W
164	Piccole Alpi Dolomitche (Mts.) (pē'k-kô-le-ál'pē-dô-lô'mē-tē'chĕ) It.	46·05 N	12·17 E
163	Pic du Midi d'Ossau (Mtn.) (pĕk dü mê-dē' dôs-sō'). Fr.	42·51 N	0·25 W
117	Picher (pĭch'ēr).............Ok.	36·58 N	94·49 W
193	Pichieh..................China	27·20 N	105·18 E
137	Pichilemu (pē-chē-lĕ'mōō) Chile (Santiago In.)	34·22 S	72·01 W
125	Pichucalco (pē-chōō-käl'kô)...Mex.	17·34 N	93·06 W
125	Pichucalco (R.)..............Mex.	17·40 N	93·02 W
109	Pickerel (L.) (pĭk'ēr-ĕl).......Can.	48·35 N	91·10 W
120	Pickwick (R.) (pĭk'wĭck).......Tn.	35·04 N	88·05 W
113	Pico (pē'kô). Ca. (Los Angeles In.)	34·01 N	118·05 W
163	Pico de Aneto (Mtn.) (pē'kō-dĕ-ä-nĕ'tô). Sp.	42·35 N	0·38 E
210	Pico I. (pē'kōō)......Açores (In.)	38·16 N	28·49 W
135	Picos (pē'kōzh)............Braz.	7·13 S	41·23 W
113	Pico Rivera. Ca. (Los Angeles In.)	34·01 N	118·05 W
202	Picton (pĭk'tŭn) Austl. (Sydney In.)	34·11 S	150·37 E
98	Pictou (pĭk-tōō')............Can.	45·41 N	62·43 W
183	Pidálion, Akrotírion (C.) Cyprus (Palestine In.)	34·50 N	34·05 E
185	Pidurutalagala Mt. (pē'dōō-rōō-tä'lȧ-gä'lȧ) Sri Lanka	12·27 N	80·45 E
109	Pie (I.) (pī)................Can.	48·10 N	89·07 W
137	Piedade (pyā-dä'dĕ) Braz. (Rio de Janeiro In.)	23·42 S	47·25 W
120	Piedmont (pēd'mŏnt).........Al.	33·54 N	85·36 W
112	Piedmont. Ca. (San Francisco In.)	37·50 N	122·14 W
117	Piedmont..................Mo.	37·09 N	90·42 W
121	Piedmont..................SC	34·40 N	82·27 W
105	Piedmont..................WV	39·30 N	79·05 W
162	Piedrabuena (pyā-drä-bwā'nä). Sp.	39·01 N	4·10 W
137	Piedras, Punta (Pt.) (pōō'n-tä-pyĕ'dräs) Arg. (Buenos Aires In.)	35·25 S	57·10 W
118	Piedras Negras (pyā'dräs nā'gräs) Mex.	28·41 N	100·33 W
157	Pieksämäki (pyĕk'sĕ-mĕ-kē)..Fin.	62·18 N	27·14 E
162	Piélagos (pyā'lä-gōs).........Sp.	43·23 N	3·55 W
164	Piemonte (Reg.) (pyĕ-mô'n-tĕ). It.	44·30 N	7·42 E
218	Pienaars R..............S. Afr. (Johannesburg & Pretoria In.)	25·13 S	28·05 E
218	Pienaarsrivier............S. Afr. (Johannesburg & Pretoria In.)	25·12 S	28·18 E
108	Pierce (pērs)...............Ne.	42·11 N	97·33 W
105	Pierce.....................WV	39·15 N	79·30 W
106	Piermont (pēr'mŏnt) NY (New York In.)	41·03 N	73·55 W
108	Pierre (pēr)................SD	44·22 N	100·20 W
89	Pierrefonds...Can. (Montreal In.)	45·29 N	73·52 W
159	Pieštany (pyĕsh'tyȧ-nûĭ)...Czech.	48·36 N	17·48 E
213	Pietermaritzburg (pê-tēr-mȧ-rĭts-bûrg) S. Afr. (Natal In.)	29·36 S	30·23 E
218	Pietersburg (pē'tērz-bûrg)..S. Afr. (Johannesburg & Pretoria In.)	23·56 S	29·30 E
97	Pieton.....................Can.	44·00 N	77·15 W
212	Piet Retief (pēt rĕ-tēf')....S. Afr.	27·00 S	30·58 E
159	Pietrosul Pk...............Rom.	47·35 N	24·49 E
164	Pieve di Cadore (pyā'vȧ dē kä-dō'râ). It.	46·26 N	12·22 E
109	Pigeon (R.) (pĭj'ŭn).....Can.-Mn.	48·05 N	90·13 W
93	Pigeon L...................Can.	53·00 N	114·00 W
89	Pigeon Lake..Can. (Winnipeg In.)	49·57 N	97·36 W
117	Piggott (pĭg-ŭt)..............Ar.	36·22 N	90·10 W
125	Pijijiapan (pēkē-kê-ä'pän)...Mex.	15·40 N	93·12 W
149	Pijnacker..Neth. (Amsterdam In.)	52·01 N	4·25 E
116	Pikes Pk. (pīks)..............Co.	38·49 N	105·03 W
121	Pikeville (pīk'vĭl)............Ky.	37·28 N	82·31 W
95	Pikwitonei (pĭk'wĭ-tōn)......Can.	55·35 N	97·09 W
158	Piła (pē'lȧ).................Pol.	53·09 N	16·44 E
218	Pilansberg (pē'ȧns'bûrg)...S. Afr. (Johannesburg & Pretoria In.)	25·08 S	26·55 E
137	Pilar (pē'lär) Arg. (Buenos Aires In.)	34·27 S	58·55 W
136	Pilar.......................Par.	27·00 S	58·15 W
197	Pilar (pē'lär)...........Phil. (In.)	12·55 N	123·41 E
197	Pilar....................Phil. (In.)	17·24 N	120·36 E
135	Pilar de Goiás (dĕ-gô'yà's)...Braz.	14·47 S	49·33 W
112	Pilchuck (R.)....Wa. (Seattle In.)	48·03 N	121·58 W
112	Pilchuck Cr. (pĭl'chŭck) Wa. (Seattle In.)	48·19 N	122·11 W
112	Pilchuck Mtn....Wa. (Seattle In.)	48·03 N	121·48 W
136	Pilcomayo (R.) (pēl-cō-mī'ô)..Par.	24·45 S	69·15 W
197	Pili (pē'lê)............Phil. (In.)	13·34 N	123·17 E
159	Pilica R. (pē-lēt'sä)..........Pol.	51·00 N	19·48 E
112	Pillar Pt. (pĭl'ȧr). Can. (Seattle In.)	48·14 N	124·06 W
112	Pillar Rock....Wa. (Portland In.)	46·16 N	123·35 W
124	Pilón (R.) (pê-lōn')..........Mex.	24·13 N	99·03 W
117	Pilot Point (pī'lŭt)...........Tx.	33·24 N	97·00 W
	Pilsen, see Plzeň		
157	Piltene (pĭl'tĕ-nĕ).......Sov. Un.	57·17 N	21·40 E
124	Pimal, Cerra (Mtn.) (sĕ'r-rä-pē-mäl'). Mex.	22·58 N	104·19 W
204	Pimba (pĭm'bȧ)............Austl.	31·15 S	146·50 E
213	Pimville (pĭm'vĭl)..........S. Afr. (Johannesburg & Pretoria In.)	26·17 S	27·54 E
122	Pinacate, Cerro (Mtn.) (sĕ'r-rô-pē-nä-kä'tĕ). Mex.	31·45 N	113·30 W
197	Pinamalayan (pē-nä-mä-lä'yän) Phil. (In.)	13·04 N	121·31 E
196	Pinang....................Mala.	5·21 N	100·09 E
171	Pinarbaşi (pē'när-bä'shĭ)......Tur.	38·50 N	36·10 E
128	Pinar del Río (pē-när' dĕl rē'ō) Cuba	22·25 N	83·35 W
128	Pinar del Río (Prov.).......Cuba	22·45 N	83·25 W
197	Pinatubo (Mtn.) (pē-nä-tōō'bô) Phil. (In.)	15·09 N	120·19 E
93	Pincher Creek (pĭn'chēr krēk). Can.	49·29 N	113·57 W
117	Pinckneyville (pĭnk'nĭ-vĭl)......Il.	38·06 N	89·22 W
159	Pińczów (pēn''chōōf).........Pol.	50·32 N	20·33 E
137	Pindamonhangaba (pē'n-dä-mōnyȧ'n-gä-bä) Braz. (Rio de Janeiro In.)	22·56 S	45·26 W
128	Pinder Pt...................Ba.	26·35 N	78·35 W
165	Píndhos Oros (Mts.).........Grc.	39·48 N	21·19 E
215	Pindiga....................Nig.	9·59 N	10·54 E
92	Pine (R.) (pīn).............Can.	55·30 N	122·20 W
109	Pine (R.)...................Wi.	45·50 N	88·37 W
117	Pine Bluff (pīn blŭf).........Ar.	34·13 N	92·01 W

ăt; finăl; rāte; senâte; ärm; åsk; sofȧ; fâre; ch-choose; dh-as th in other; bē; êvent; bĕt; recĕnt; cratēr; g-go; gh-guttural g; bĭt; ĭ-short neutral; rīde; K-guttural k as ch in German ich;

Page	Name Pronunciation Region	Lat. °′	Long. °′
109	Pine City (pīn) . . . . Mn.	45·50 N	93·01 W
204	Pine Creek . . . . Austl.	13·45 S	132·00 E
114	Pine Cr. . . . . Nv.	40·15 N	116·17 W
95	Pine Falls . . . . Can.	50·35 N	96·15 W
110	Pine Forest Ra. . . . . Nv.	41·35 N	118·45 W
170	Pinega (pê-nyĕ′gȧ) . . . . . . Sov. Un.	64·40 N	43·30 E
170	Pinega (R.) . . . . Sov. Un.	64·10 N	42·30 E
106	Pine Hill (pīn hĭl) NJ (Philadelphia In.)	39·47 N	74·59 W
121	Pine Is. . . . . Fl. (In.)	24·48 N	81·32 W
121	Pine Island Sd. . . . . Fl. (In.)	26·32 N	82·30 W
106	Pine Lake Estates (lāk ĕs-tāts′) Ga. (Atlanta In.)	33·47 N	84·13 W
212	Pinelands (pīn′lănds) . . S. Afr. (In.)	33·57 S	18·30 E
113	Pine Lawn (lôn) Mo. (St. Louis In.)	38·42 N	90·17 W
92	Pine Pass . . . . Can.	55·22 N	122·40 W
108	Pine Ridge Ind. Res. (rĭj) . . . . . SD	43·33 N	102·13 W
164	Pinerolo (pē-nâ-rô′lō) . . . . It.	44·47 N	7·18 E
119	Pines, Lake o′ the . . . . Tx.	32·50 N	94·40 W
213	Pinetown (pīn′toun) S. Afr. (Natal In.)	29·47 S	30·52 E
113	Pine View Res. (vū) Ut. (Salt Lake City In.)	41·17 N	111·54 W
120	Pineville (pīn′vĭl) . . . . Ky.	36·48 N	83·43 W
119	Pineville . . . . La.	31·20 N	92·25 W
196	Ping, Mae Nam (R.) . . . . Thai.	17·54 N	98·29 E
191	Pingchoupao . . China (Canton In.)	23·01 N	113·11 E
192	Pingchüan . . . . China	40·58 N	118·40 E
183	Pinggir . . . . Indon. (Singapore In.)	1·05 N	101·12 E
193	P′ingho (pĭng′hō′) . . . . China	24·30 N	117·02 E
193	Pinghsiang . . . . China	27·40 N	113·50 E
192	Pingliang (pĭng′lyäng′) . . . . . China	35·12 N	106·50 E
193	P′inglo (pĭng′lō′) . . . . China	24·30 N	110·22 E
193	P′ingt′an . . . . China	25·30 N	119·45 E
193	Pingting (pĭng′tĭng′) . . . . China	37·50 N	113·30 E
190	P′ingtu (pĭng′tōō′) . . . . China	36·46 N	119·57 E
193	P′ingtung . . . . Taiwan	22·40 N	120·35 E
192	P′ingwu . . . . China	32·20 N	104·40 E
190	P′ingyuan (pĭng′yü-än′) . . . . China	37·11 N	116·26 E
137	Pinhal (pē-nyȧ′l) Braz. (Rio de Janeiro In.)	22·11 S	46·43 W
163	Pinhal Novo (nô vōō) Port. (Lisbon In.)	38·38 N	8·54 W
162	Pinhel (pēn-yĕl′) . . . . Port.	40·45 N	7·03 W
190	Pinhsien (pĭn′sĭän) . . . . China	38·29 N	117·58 E
192	Pinhsien . . . . China	45·40 N	127·20 E
196	Pini (I.) (pē′nê) . . . . Indon.	0·07 N	98·38 E
165	Piniós (R.) . . . . Grc.	40·33 N	21·40 E
114	Pinnacles Natl. Mon. (pĭn′ȧ-k′lz) Ca.	36·30 N	121·00 W
149	Pinneberg (pĭn′ĕ-bĕrg) F.R.G. (Hamburg In.)	53·40 N	9·48 E
112	Pinole (pĭ-nō′lē) Ca. (San Francisco In.)	38·01 N	122·17 W
128	Pinos, Isla de (I.) (ē′s-lä-dĕ-pē′nôs) . Cuba	21·40 N	82·45 W
162	Pinos-Puente (pwān′tā) . . . . Sp.	37·15 N	3·43 W
124	Pinotepa Nacional (pē-nô-tā′pä nä-syō-näl′) . Mex.	16·21 N	98·04 W
205	Pins, Ile des . . . . N. Cal.	22·44 S	167·44 E
159	Pinsk (pên′sk) . . . . Sov. Un.	52·07 N	26·05 E
134	Pinta (I.) . . . . Ec.	0·41 N	90·47 W
89	Pintendre (pĕN-täNdr′) Can. (Quebec In.)	46·45 N	71·07 W
163	Pinto (pēn′tō) . . . Sp. (Madrid In.)	40·14 N	3·42 W
94	Pinto Butte (pĭn′tō) . . . . Can.	49·22 N	107·25 W
115	Pioche (pī-ō′chē) . . . . Nv.	37·56 N	114·28 W
164	Piombino (pyôm-bē′nō) . . . . It.	42·56 N	10·33 E
111	Pioneer Mts. (pī-ō-nēr′) . . . . Mt.	45·23 N	112·51 W
159	Piotrków Trybunalski (pyōtr′kōōv trĭ-bōō-nal′skē) . Pol.	51·23 N	19·44 E
120	Piper (pī′pēr) . . . . Al.	33·04 N	87·00 W
113	Piper . . . . . . Ks. (Kansas City In.)	39·09 N	94·51 W
165	Pipéri (I.) (pē′per-ē) . . . . Grc.	39·19 N	24·20 E
115	Pipe Spring Natl. Mon. (pīp sprĭng) . Az.	36·50 N	112·45 W
108	Pipestone (pīp′stōn) . . . . Mn.	44·00 N	96·19 W
108	Pipestone Natl. Mon. . . . . Mn.	44·03 N	96·24 W
98	Pipmaucan, Rés. (pĭp-mä-kän′) Can.	49·45 N	70·00 W
104	Piqua (pĭk′wȧ) . . . . Oh.	40·10 N	84·15 W
137	Piracaia (pē-rä-kȧ′yä) Braz. (Rio de Janeiro In.)	23·04 S	46·20 W
137	Piracicaba (pē-rä-sē-kä′bä) Braz. (Rio de Janeiro In.)	22·43 S	47·39 W
137	Piraí (pē-rä-ē′) Braz. (Rio de Janeiro In.)	22·38 S	43·54 W
137	Piraíba (R.) (pä-rä-ē′bȧ) Braz. (Rio de Janeiro In.)	21·38 S	41·29 W
172	Piramida, Gol′tsy (Mtn.) Sov. Un.	54·00 N	96·00 E
164	Piran (pē-rȧ′n) . . . . Yugo.	45·31 N	13·34 E
137	Piranga (pē-rä′n-gä) Braz. (Rio de Janeiro In.)	20·41 S	43·17 W
137	Pirapetinga (pē-rä-pĕ-tē′n-gä) Braz. (Rio de Janeiro In.)	21·40 S	42·20 W
135	Pirapora (pē-rȧ-pō′rȧ) . . . . Braz.	17·39 S	44·54 W
137	Pirassununga (pē-rä-sōō-nōō′n-gä) Braz. (Rio de Janeiro In.)	22·00 S	47·24 W
135	Pirenópolis (pē-rĕ-nô′pō-lēs) . Braz.	15·56 S	48·49 W
165	Pírgos . . . . Grc.	37·51 N	21·28 E
135	Piritu, Laguna de (L.) (lä-gōō′nä-dĕ-pē-rē′tōō) Ven. (In.)	10·00 N	64·57 W
158	Pirmasens (pĭr-mä-zĕns′) . . . F.R.G.	49·12 N	7·34 E
158	Pirna (pĭr′nä) . . . . G.D.R.	50·57 N	13·56 E
165	Pirot (pē′rōt) . . . . Yugo.	43·09 N	22·35 E
115	Pirtleville (pûr′t′l-vĭl) . . . . Az.	31·25 N	109·35 W
197	Piru (pē-rōō′) . . . . Indon.	3·15 S	128·25 E
167	Piryatin (pēr-yä-tēn′) . . . . Sov. Un.	50·13 N	32·31 E
164	Pisa (pē′sä) . . . . It.	43·52 N	10·24 E
134	Pisagua (pē-sä′gwä) . . . . Chile	18·43 S	70·12 W
106	Piscataway (pĭs-kă-tă-wā) Md. (Baltimore In.)	38·42 N	76·59 W
106	Piscataway . . . NJ (New York In.)	40·35 N	74·27 W
134	Pisco (pēs′kō) . . . . Peru	13·43 S	76·07 W
134	Pisco, Bahia de (B.) (bä-ē′ä-dĕ) Peru	13·43 S	77·48 W
105	Piseco (L.) (pĭ-sā′kô) . . . . NY	43·25 N	74·35 W
158	Pisek (pē′sĕk) . . . . Czech.	49·18 N	14·08 E
164	Pisticci (pês-tē′chē) . . . . It.	40·24 N	16·34 E
164	Pistoia (pês-tô′yä) . . . . It.	43·57 N	11·54 E
162	Pisuerga (R.) (pē-swĕr′gä) . . . . . Sp.	41·48 N	4·28 W
134	Pitalito (pē-tä-lē′tō) . . . . Col.	1·45 N	75·09 W
107	Pitcairn (pĭt′kârn) Pa. (Pittsburgh In.)	40·29 N	79·47 W
199	Pitcairn . . . . Oceania	24·30 S	133·00 W
150	Pite (R.) (pē′tĕ) . . . . Swe.	66·08 N	18·51 E
150	Piteå (pē′tĕ-ô′) . . . . Swe.	65·21 N	21·10 E
165	Pitesti (pê-tĕsht′′) . . . . Rom.	44·51 N	24·51 E
204	Pithara (pĭt′ărȧ) . . . . Austl.	30·27 S	116·45 E
160	Pithiviers (pê-tē-vyā′) . . . . Fr.	48·12 N	2·14 E
106	Pitman (pĭt′mȧn) NJ (Philadelphia In.)	39·44 N	75·08 W
127	Pitons du Carbet, Mt. . . Mart. (In.)	14·40 N	61·05 W
110	Pit R. (pĭt) . . . . Ca.	40·58 N	121·42 W
213	Pitseng . . . . Leso. (Natal In.)	29·03 S	28·13 E
112	Pitt (R.) . . . . Can. (Vancouver In.)	49·19 N	122·39 W
92	Pitt I. . . . . Can.	53·35 N	129·45 W
112	Pittsburg (pĭts′bûrg) Ca. (San Francisco In.)	38·01 N	121·52 W
117	Pittsburg . . . . Ks.	37·25 N	94·43 W
117	Pittsburg . . . . Tx.	32·00 N	94·57 W
107	Pittsburgh . . . Pa. (Pittsburgh In.)	40·26 N	80·01 W
117	Pittsfield (pĭts′fēld) . . . . Il.	39·37 N	90·47 W
98	Pittsfield . . . . Me.	44·45 N	69·44 W
105	Pittsfield . . . . Ma.	42·25 N	73·15 W
105	Pittston (pĭts′tŭn) . . . . Pa.	41·20 N	75·50 W
190	P′itzuwo (Hsinchin) (pē′zhē′wŏ) (sĭn′jĭn) . China	39·25 N	122·19 E
137	Piūi (pē-ōō′ē) Braz. (Rio de Janeiro In.)	20·27 S	45·57 W
134	Piura (pē-ōō′rä) . . . . Peru	5·13 S	80·46 W
174	Piya (pē′yȧ) . . Sov. Un. (Urals In.)	58·34 N	61·12 E
113	Placentia (plă-sĕn′shĭ-ȧ) Ca. (Los Angeles In.)	33·52 N	117·50 W
99	Placentia . . . . Can.	47·15 N	53·58 W
99	Placentia B. . . . . Can.	47·14 N	54·30 W
114	Placerville (plăs′ēr-vĭl) . . . . Ca.	38·43 N	120·47 W
128	Placetas (plä-thā′täs) . . . . Cuba	22·10 N	79·40 W
105	Placid (L.) (plăs′ĭd) . . . . NY	44·20 N	74·00 W
113	Plain City (plān) Ut. (Salt Lake City In.)	41·18 N	112·06 W
107	Plainfield (plān′fēld) Il. (Chicago In.)	41·37 N	88·12 W
107	Plainfield . . . . In. (Indianapolis In.)	39·42 N	86·23 W
106	Plainfield . . . . . NJ (New York In.)	40·38 N	74·25 W
117	Plainview (plān′vū) . . . . Ar.	34·59 N	93·15 W
109	Plainview . . . . Mn.	44·09 N	93·12 W
108	Plainview . . . . Ne.	42·20 N	97·47 W
106	Plainview . . . . NY (New York In.)	40·47 N	73·28 W
116	Plainview . . . . Tx.	34·11 N	101·42 W
104	Plainwell (plan′wĕl) . . . . Mi.	42·25 N	85·40 W
89	Plaisance (plĕ-zäNs′) Can. (Ottawa In.)	45·37 N	75·07 W
129	Plana or Flat Cays (Is.) (plä′nä) Ba.	22·35 N	73·35 W
160	Plan-de-Cuques (plä-dĕ-kük′) Fr. (In.)	43·22 N	5·29 E
149	Planegg (plä′nĕg) F.R.G. (Munich In.)	48·06 N	11·27 E
117	Plano (plā′nō) . . . . Tx.	33·01 N	96·42 W
89	Plantagenet (plăN-täzh-nĕ′) Can. (Ottawa In.)	45·33 N	75·00 W
121	Plant City (plȧnt sĭ′tĭ) . . . Fl. (In.)	28·00 N	82·07 W
119	Plaquemine (pläk′mēn′) . . . . La.	30·17 N	91·14 W
162	Plasencia (plä-sĕn′thē-ä) . . . . Sp.	40·02 N	6·07 W
174	Plast (plást) . . Sov. Un. (Urals In.)	54·22 N	60·48 E
98	Plaster Rock (plȧs′tēr rŏk) . . . Can.	46·54 N	67·24 W
194	Plastun (plȧs-tōōn′) . . . . . Sov. Un.	44·41 N	136·08 E
136	Plata, R. de la (R.) (dālä plä′tä) Arg.-Ur.	34·35 S	58·15 W
164	Platani (R.) (plä-tä′nē) . . . . It.	37·26 N	13·28 E
129	Plateforme, Pte. . . . . Hai.	19·35 N	73·50 W
101	Platinum (plăt′ĭ-nŭm) . . . . Ak.	59·00 N	161·27 W
134	Plato (plä′tō) . . . . Col.	9·49 N	74·48 W
124	Platón Sánchéz (plä-tōn′ sän′chĕz) . Mex.	21·14 N	98·20 W
108	Platte (plăt) . . . . SD	43·22 N	98·51 W
117	Platte (R.) . . . . Mo.	40·09 N	94·40 W
102	Platte (R.) . . . . U. S.	40·50 N	100·40 W
109	Platteville (plăt′vĭl) . . . . Wi.	42·44 N	90·31 W
117	Plattsburg (plăts′bûrg) . . . . Mo.	39·33 N	94·26 W
105	Plattsburgh . . . . NY	44·40 N	73·30 W
108	Plattsmouth (plăts′mŭth) . . . . . Ne.	41·00 N	95·53 W
158	Plauen (plou′ĕn) . . . . G.D.R.	50·30 N	12·08 E
129	Playa de Guanabo (plä-yä-dĕ-gwä-nä′bô) Cuba (In.)	23·10 N	82·07 W
129	Playa de Santa Fe (sä′n-tä-fē′) Cuba (In.)	23·05 N	82·31 W
115	Playas (L.) (plä′yȧs) . . . . NM	31·50 N	108·30 W
125	Playa Vicente (vē-sĕn′tȧ) . . . . Mex.	17·49 N	95·49 W
125	Playa Vicente (R.) . . . . Mex.	17·36 N	96·13 W
95	Playgreen L. (plā′grēn) . . . . . . Can.	54·00 N	98·10 W
105	Pleasant (L.) (plĕz′ănt) . . . . NY	43·25 N	74·25 W
106	Pleasant Grove Al. (Birmingham In.)	33·29 N	86·57 W
112	Pleasant Hill Ca. (San Francisco In.)	37·57 N	122·04 W
117	Pleasant Hill . . . . Mo.	38·46 N	94·18 W
112	Pleasanton (plĕz′ăn-tŭn) Ca. (San Francisco In.)	37·40 N	121·53 W
117	Pleasanton . . . . Ks.	38·10 N	94·41 W
118	Pleasanton . . . . Tx.	28·58 N	98·30 W
107	Pleasant Plain (plĕz′ănt) Oh. (Cincinnati In.)	39·17 N	84·06 W
107	Pleasant Ridge . . . Mi. (Detroit In.)	42·28 N	83·09 W
107	Pleasure Ridge Park (plĕzh′ēr rĭj) Ky (Louisville In.)	38·09 N	85·49 W
113	Pleasant View (plĕz′ănt vū) Ut. (Salt Lake City In.)	41·20 N	112·02 W
106	Pleasantville (plĕz′ănt-vĭl) NY (New York In.)	41·08 N	73·47 W
205	Plenty, B. of (plĕn′tē) . . N. Z. (In.)	37·23 S	177·10 E
111	Plentywood (plĕn′tē-wŏŏd) . . . . Mt.	48·47 N	104·38 W
166	Ples (plyĕs) . . . . Sov. Un.	57·26 N	41·29 E
166	Pleshcheyevo (L.) (plĕsh-chā′yĕ-vô) . Sov. Un.	56·50 N	38·22 E
98	Plessisville (plĕ-sē′vēl′) . . . . . . Can.	46·12 N	71·47 W
159	Pleszew (plĕ′zhĕf) . . . . Pol.	51·54 N	17·48 E
161	Plettenberg (plĕ′tĕn-bĕrgh) F.R.G. (Ruhr In.)	51·13 N	7·53 E
165	Pleven (plĕ′vĕn) . . . . Bul.	43·24 N	24·26 E
165	Pljevlja (plĕv′lyä) . . . . Yugo.	43·20 N	19·21 E
159	Plock (pwôtsk) . . . . Pol.	52·32 N	19·44 E
160	Ploërmel (plō-ĕr-mĕl′) . . . . Fr.	47·56 N	2·25 W
165	Ploeşti (plō-yĕsht′′) . . . . Rom.	44·56 N	26·01 E
165	Plomárion (plō-mä′rĭ-ŏn) . . . . . Grc.	38·51 N	26·24 E
160	Plomb du Cantal (Mt.) (plôN′dükäN-täl′) . Fr.	45·30 N	2·49 E
94	Plonge, Lac la (L.) (plōNzh) . . Can.	55·08 N	107·25 W
165	Plovdiv (Philippopolis) (plôv′dĭf) (fĭl-ĭp-ŏp′ō-lĭs) . . . Bul.	42·09 N	24·43 E
125	Pluma Hidalgo (plōō′mä ē-däl′gō) Mex.	15·54 N	96·23 W
157	Plunge (plŏŏn′gä) . . . . Sov. Un.	55·56 N	21·45 E
154	Plymouth (plĭm′ŭth) . . . . Eng.	50·25 N	4·14 W
104	Plymouth . . . . In.	41·20 N	86·20 W
105	Plymouth . . . . Ma.	42·00 N	70·45 W
107	Plymouth . . . . Mi. (Detroit In.)	42·23 N	83·27 W
105	Plymouth . . . . NH	43·50 N	71·40 W
121	Plymouth . . . . NC	35·50 N	76·44 W
105	Plymouth . . . . Pa.	41·15 N	75·55 W
127	Plymouth . . . . Montserrat (In.)	16·43 N	62·12 W
109	Plymouth . . . . Wi.	43·45 N	87·59 W
166	Plyussa (R.) (plyōō′sȧ) . . . Sov. Un.	58·33 N	28·30 E
158	Plzeň (Pilsen) . . . . Czech.	49·46 N	13·25 E
214	Pô . . . . Upper Volta	11·10 N	1·09 W
164	Po, Bocche del (Mouth) (bô′chĕ-dĕl-pô′) . It.	44·57 N	12·38 E
164	Po, Fiume (R.) (fyōō′mĕ-pō) . . . It.	45·00 N	11·23 E
192	Poar . . . . China	35·10 N	113·08 E
215	Pobé (pô-bā′) . . . . Benin	6·58 N	2·41 E
117	Pocahontas (pō-kȧ-hŏn′tȧs) . . . . Ar.	36·15 N	91·01 W
109	Pocahontas . . . . Ia.	42·43 N	94·41 W
111	Pocatello (pō-kȧ-tĕl′ō) . . . . Id.	42·54 N	112·30 W
166	Pochĕp (pō-chĕp′) . . . . Sov. Un.	52·56 N	32·27 E
166	Pochinok (pô-chē′nôk) . . . . . Sov. Un.	54·14 N	32·27 E
170	Pochinski . . . . Sov. Un.	54·40 N	44·50 E
124	Pochotitán (pô-chô-tē-tä′n) . . Mex.	21·37 N	104·33 W
125	Pochutla (San Pedro) (pō-chōō′tlä) (sän pā′drō) . Mex.	15·46 N	96·28 W
105	Pocomoke City (pō-kō-mōk′) . . Md.	38·05 N	75·35 W
105	Pocono Mts. (pō-cō′nō) . . . . Pa.	41·10 N	75·05 W
137	Poços de Caldas (pō-sôs-dĕ-käl′dȧs) Braz. (Rio de Janeiro In.)	21·48 S	46·34 W
210	Poder (pô-dôr′) . . . . Senegal	16·35 N	15·04 W
172	Podkamennaya (Stony) Tunguska (R.) . Sov. Un.	61·43 N	93·45 E
174	Podol′sk (pô-dôl′′sk) Sov. Un. (Moscow In.)	55·26 N	37·33 E
167	Podvolochisk . . . . Sov. Un.	49·32 N	26·16 E
164	Poggibonsi (pôd-jē-bôn′sē) . . . . . It.	43·27 N	11·12 E
166	Pogodino (pô-gô′dê-nô) . . . Sov. Un.	54·17 N	31·00 E
194	Pohai Str. (pō′hī′) . . . . China	38·05 N	121·40 E
194	P′ohang . . . . Kor.	35·57 N	129·23 E
190	Pohsien . . . . China	33·52 N	115·47 E
190	Pohsing (pō′hsĭng′) . . . . China	37·09 N	118·08 E
127	Pointe-à-Pitre (pwăNt′ à pē-tr′) Guad. (In.)	16·15 N	61·32 W
89	Pointe-aux-Trembles (pōō-ăNt′ ō-trăNbl) Can. (Montreal In.)	45·39 N	73·30 W
89	Pointe Claire (pōō-ăNt′ klĕr) Can. (Montreal In.)	45·27 N	73·48 W
89	Pointe-des-Cascades (kăs-kädz′) Can. (Montreal In.)	45·19 N	73·58 W
89	Pointe Fortune (fôr′tūn) Can. (Montreal In.)	45·34 N	74·23 W
89	Pointe-Gatineau (pōō-ăNt′gä-tē-nō′) Can. (Ottawa In.)	45·28 N	75·42 W
216	Pointe Noire . . . . Con.	4·48 S	11·51 E
101	Point Hope (hōp) . . . . Ak.	68·18 N	166·38 W
104	Point Pleasant (plĕz′ănt) . . . . . WV	38·50 N	82·10 W
112	Point Roberts (rŏb′ērts) Wa. (Vancouver In.)	48·59 N	123·04 W
161	Poissy (pwȧ-sē′) . . . . Fr. (Paris In.)	48·55 N	2·02 E
160	Poitiers (pwȧ-tyā′) . . . . Fr.	46·35 N	0·18 E
184	Pokaran (pō′kŭr-ŭn) . . . . India	27·00 N	72·05 E
192	Pok′ot′u (pō′kô-tōō′) . . . . China	48·45 N	121·42 E
166	Pokrov (pô-krôf) . . . . Sov. Un.	55·56 N	39·09 E
167	Pokrovskoye (pô-krôf′skô-yĕ) Sov. Un.	47·27 N	38·54 E
166	Pola (R.) (pō′lä) . . . . Sov. Un.	54·44 N	31·53 E
162	Pola de Allade (dĕ-äl-yä′dĕ) . . . Sp.	43·18 N	6·35 W
162	Pola de Laviana (dĕ-lä-vyä′nä) . Sp.	43·15 N	5·29 W
146	Poland (pō′lănd) . . . . Eur.	52·37 N	17·01 E
197	Polangui (pô-län′gē) . . . . Phil. (In.)	13·18 N	123·29 E
174	Polazna (pô′láz-nȧ) Sov. Un. (Urals In.)	58·18 N	56·25 E
157	Polessk (pô′lĕsk) . . . . Sov. Un.	54·50 N	21·14 E
171	Poles′ye (Pripyat Marshes) Sov. Un.	52·10 N	27·30 E
174	Polevskoy (pô-lĕ′vs-kô′ē) Sov. Un. (Urals In.)	56·28 N	60·14 E
159	Polgár (pôl′gär) . . . . Hung.	47·54 N	21·10 E

ng-sing; ŋ-baŋk; N-nasalized n; nŏd; cŏmmit; ōld; ôbey; ôrder; fōōd; fŏŏt; ou-out; s-soft; sh-dish; th-thin; pūre; ûnite; ûrn; stŭd; circŭs; ü-as "y" in study; ′-indeterminate vowel.

330 P'oli — Portsmouth PRONOUNCING INDEX

Page	Name Pronunciation	Region	Lat. °'	Long. °'
192	P'oli (pô'lĭ)	China	45·40 N	130·38 E
164	Policastro, Golfo di (G.)	It.	41·00 N	13·23 E
161	Poligny (pō-lē-nyē')	Fr.	46·48 N	5·42 E
165	Políkhnitos	Grc.	39·05 N	26·11 E
197	Polillo (pō-lēl'yō)	Phil. (In.)	14·42 N	121·56 E
197	Polillo Is.	Phil. (In.)	15·05 N	122·15 E
197	Polillo Str.	Phil. (In.)	15·02 N	121·40 E
166	Polist' (R.) (pô'lĭst)	Sov. Un.	57·42 N	31·02 E
164	Polistena (pō-lês-tā'nä)	It.	40·25 N	16·05 E
165	Poliyiros	Grc.	40·23 N	23·27 E
172	Polkan, Gol'tsy (Mtn.)	Sov. Un.	60·18 N	92·08 E
163	Pollensa (pōl-yĕn'sä)	Sp.	39·50 N	3·00 E
126	Polochic R. (pō-lô-chēk')	Guat.	15·19 N	89·45 W
167	Polonnoye (pô'lô-nô-yĕ)	Sov. Un.	50·07 N	27·31 E
166	Polotsk (pô'lôtsk)	Sov. Un.	55·30 N	28·48 E
137	Polpaico (pôl-pà'y-kô)	Chile (Santiago In.)	33·10 S	70·53 W
111	Polson (pōl'sŭn)	Mt.	47·40 N	114·10 W
167	Poltava (pôl-tä'vä)	Sov. Un.	49·35 N	34·33 E
167	Poltava (Oblast)	Sov. Un.	49·53 N	32·58 E
166	Põltsamaa (pŏlt'sà-mä)	Sov. Un.	58·39 N	26·00 E
166	Põltsamaa (R.)	Sov. Un.	58·35 N	25·55 E
174	Polunochnoye (pô-lōō-nô'ch-nô-yĕ)	Sov. Un. (Urals In.)	60·52 N	60·27 E
172	Poluy (R.) (pôl'wē)	Sov. Un.	65·45 N	68·15 E
174	Polyakovka (pŭl-yä'kôv-kà)	Sov. Un. (Urals In.)	54·38 N	59·42 E
170	Polyarnyy (pŭl-yär'nē)	Sov. Un.	69·10 N	33·30 E
137	Pomba (pô'm-bà) (R.)	Braz. (Rio de Janeiro In.)	21·28 S	42·28 W
158	Pomerania (Reg.) (pŏm-ê-rā'nĭ-ȧ)	Pol.	53·50 N	15·20 E
156	Pomeranian B. (pō'mĕ-rä-ny-än)	G.D.R.	54·10 N	14·20 E
213	Pomeroy (pŏm'ēr-roi)	S. Afr. (Natal In.)	28·36 S	30·26 E
110	Pomeroy (pŏm'ēr-oi)	Wa.	46·28 N	117·35 W
163	Pomezia (pô-mĕ't-zyä)	It. (Rome In.)	41·41 N	12·31 E
163	Pomigliano d'Arco (pô-mē-lyà'nô-d-ä'r-kô)	It. (Naples In.)	40·39 N	14·23 E
108	Pomme de Terre (pôm dē tĕr')	Mn.	45·22 N	95·52 W
113	Pomona (pô-mō'nȧ)	Ca. (Los Angeles In.)	34·04 N	117·45 W
165	Pomorie	Bul.	42·24 N	27·41 E
184	Pomo Tsho (L.)	China	28·00 N	90·30 E
121	Pompano Beach (pŏm'pȧ-nō)	Fl. (In.)	26·12 N	80·07 W
163	Pompeii Ruins	It. (Naples In.)	40·31 N	14·29 E
106	Pompton Lakes (pŏmp'tŏn)	NJ (New York In.)	41·01 N	74·16 W
126	Pomuch (pô-mōō'ch)	Mex. (In.)	20·12 N	90·10 W
108	Ponca (pŏn'kȧ)	Ne.	42·34 N	96·43 W
117	Ponca City	Ok.	36·42 N	97·07 W
100	Ponce (pōn'sā)	P. R. (Puerto Rico In.)	18·01 N	66·43 W
185	Pondicherry (pôn-dĭ-shĕr'ē') (pŏn-dĭ-shĕr'ê)	India	11·58 N	79·48 E
185	Pondicherry (State)	India	11·50 N	74·50 E
162	Ponferrada (pôn-fĕr-rä'dhä)	Sp.	42·33 N	6·38 W
93	Ponoka (pŏ-nō'kȧ)	Can.	52·42 N	113·35 W
170	Ponoy	Sov. Un.	66·58 N	41·00 E
170	Ponoy (R.)	Sov. Un.	65·50 N	38·40 E
210	Ponta Delgada (pôn'tȧ dĕl-gä'dȧ)	Açores (In.)	37·40 N	25·45 W
136	Ponta Grossa (grō'sȧ)	Braz.	25·09 S	50·05 W
161	Pont-à-Mousson (pôɴ'tá-mōōsôɴ')	Fr.	48·55 N	6·02 E
135	Ponta Porã	Braz.	22·30 S	55·31 W
161	Pontarlier (pôɴ'tár-lyā')	Fr.	46·53 N	6·22 E
160	Pont-Audemer (pôɴ'tōd'mâr')	Fr.	49·23 N	0·28 E
161	Pontcarré (pôɴ-kà-rā')	Fr. (Paris In.)	48·48 N	2·42 E
119	Pontchartrain L. (pôɴ-shár-trăn')	La.	30·10 N	90·10 W
164	Pontedera (pōn-tā-dā'rä)	It.	43·37 N	10·37 E
162	Ponte de Sor (pōŋ'tĕ dà sōr')	Port.	39·14 N	8·03 W
148	Pontefract (pŏn'tê-frăkt)	Eng.	53·41 N	1·18 W
137	Ponte Nova (pô'n-tĕ-nô'vá)	Braz. (Rio de Janeiro In.)	20·26 S	42·52 W
162	Pontevedra (pôn-tĕ-vĕ-drä)	Sp.	42·28 N	8·38 W
	Ponthierville, see Ubundi			
104	Pontiac (pŏn'tĭ-ăk)	Il.	40·55 N	88·35 W
107	Pontiac	Mi. (Detroit In.)	42·37 N	83·17 W
196	Pontianak (pôn-tê-ä'nàk)	Indon.	0·04 S	109·20 E
183	Pontian Kechil	Mala. (Singapore In.)	1·29 N	103·24 E
171	Pontic Mts.	Turk.	41·20 N	34·30 E
160	Pontivy (pôɴ-tê-vē')	Fr.	48·05 N	2·57 W
160	Pont-l'Abbe (pôɴ-là-bā')	Fr.	47·53 N	4·12 W
161	Pontoise (pôɴ-twáz')	Fr. (Paris In.)	49·03 N	2·05 E
174	Pontonnyy (pôn'tôn-nyĭ)	Sov. Un. (Leningrad In.)	59·47 N	30·39 E
120	Pontotoc (pŏn-tô-tŏk')	Ms.	34·11 N	88·59 W
164	Pontremoli (pôn-trĕm'ô-lē)	It.	44·21 N	9·50 E
164	Ponza, Isole di (I.) (ē'sō-lĕ-dē-pōn'tsä)	It.	40·55 N	12·58 E
154	Poole (pōōl)	Eng.	50·43 N	2·00 W
106	Poolesville (poolĕs-vĭl)	Md. (Baltimore In.)	39·08 N	77·26 W
92	Pooley I. (pōō'lē)	Can.	52·44 N	128·16 W
134	Poopó, Lago de (L.) (lä'gô-dĕ-pō-ō-pô')	Bol.	18·16 S	67·57 W
134	Popayán (pō-pä-yän')	Col.	2·21 N	76·43 W
111	Poplar (pŏp'lẽr)	Mt.	48·08 N	105·10 W
117	Poplar Bluff (blŭf)	Mo.	36·43 N	90·22 W
104	Poplar Plains (plāns)	Ky.	38·20 N	83·40 W
89	Poplar Point	Can. (Winnipeg In.)	50·04 N	97·57 W
111	Poplar R.	Mt.	48·34 N	105·20 W
111	Poplar R., West Fork	Mt.	48·59 N	106·06 W
120	Poplarville (pŏp'lẽr-vĭl)	Ms.	30·50 N	89·33 W
125	Popocatépetl Volcán (Vol.) (pô-pô-kä-tā'pĕt'l)	Mex. (In.)	19·01 N	98·38 W
216	Popokabaka (pō'pô-kà-bä'kà)	Zaire	5·42 S	16·35 E
167	Popovka (pô'pôf-kà)	Sov. Un.	50·03 N	33·41 E
167	Popovka	Sov. Un.	51·13 N	33·08 E
165	Popovo (pô'pô-vō)	Bul.	43·23 N	26·17 E
184	Porbandar (pōr-bŭn'dŭr)	India	21·44 N	69·40 E
134	Porce (pôr-sĕ) (R.)	Col. (In.)	7·11 N	74·55 W
92	Porcher I. (pôr'kẽr)	Can.	53·57 N	130·30 W
162	Porcuna (pôr-kōō'nä)	Sp.	37·54 N	4·10 W
101	Porcupine (R.)	Ak.	67·00 N	143·25 W
90	Porcupine (R.)	Can.	67·38 N	140·07 W
111	Porcupine Cr. (pôr'kû-pīn)	Mt.	46·38 N	107·04 W
111	Porcupine Cr.	Mt.	48·27 N	106·24 W
95	Porcupine Hills	Can.	52·30 N	101·45 W
164	Pordenone (pōr-dà-nō'nā)	It.	45·58 N	12·38 E
164	Poreč (pô'rĕch)	Yugo.	45·13 N	13·37 E
157	Pori (Björneborg) (pô'rê) (byûr'nĕ-bôrgh)	Fin.	61·29 N	21·45 E
137	Poriúncula (po-rēōō'n-kōō-lä)	Braz. (Rio de Janeiro In.)	20·58 S	42·02 W
150	Porjus (pôr'yōōs)	Swe.	66·54 N	19·40 E
166	Porkhov (pôr'κôf)	Sov. Un.	57·46 N	29·33 E
134	Porlamar (pôr-lä-mär')	Ven.	11·00 N	63·55 W
160	Pornic (pôr-nēk')	Fr.	47·08 N	2·07 W
173	Poronaysk (pô'rô-nīsk)	Sov. Un.	49·21 N	143·23 E
158	Porrentruy (pô-räɴ-trüē')	Switz.	47·25 N	7·02 E
156	Porsgrunn (pôrs'grŏŏn')	Nor.	59·09 N	9·36 E
134	Portachuelo (pôrt-ä-chwā'lô)	Bol.	17·20 S	63·12 W
105	Portage (pôr'tāj)	Pa.	40·25 N	78·35 W
109	Portage	Wi.	43·33 N	89·29 W
113	Portage Des Sioux (dē sōō)	Mo. (St. Louis In.)	38·56 N	90·21 W
89	Portage-la-Prairie (lä-prā'rĭ)	Can. (Winnipeg In.)	49·57 N	98·25 W
92	Port Alberni (pōr äl-bĕr-nē')	Can.	49·14 N	124·48 W
162	Portalegre (pôr-tä-lā'grĕ)	Port.	39·18 N	7·26 W
116	Portales (pôr-tä'lĕs)	NM	34·10 N	103·11 W
97	Port-Alfred (ăl'frĕd)	Can.	48·20 N	70·53 W
213	Port Alfred (Kowie) (kou'ĭ)	S. Afr. (Natal In.)	33·36 S	26·55 E
92	Port Alice (ăl'ĭs)	Can.	50·23 N	127·27 W
105	Port Allegany (ăl-ē-gā'nĭ)	Pa.	41·50 N	78·10 W
110	Port Angeles (ăn'jē-lĕs)	Wa.	48·07 N	123·26 W
129	Port Antonio	Jam.	18·10 N	76·25 W
202	Portarlington	Austl. (Melbourne In.)	38·07 S	144·39 E
119	Port Arthur	Tx.	29·52 N	93·59 W
	Port Arthur, see Lüshun			
203	Port Augusta (ô-gŭs'tȧ)	Austl.	32·28 S	137·50 E
99	Port au Port B. (pôr'tō pōr')	Can.	48·41 N	58·45 W
129	Port-au-Prince (prăɴs')	Hai.	18·35 N	72·20 W
104	Port Austin (ôs'tĭn)	Mi.	44·00 N	83·00 W
99	Port aux Basques	Can.	47·36 N	59·09 W
196	Port Blair (blâr)	Andaman & Nicobar Is.	12·07 N	92·45 E
119	Port Bolivar (bŏl'ĭ-vȧr)	Tx. (In.)	29·22 N	94·46 W
98	Port Borden (bôr'dĕn)	Can.	46·15 N	63·42 W
210	Port-Bouët	Ivory Coast	5·24 N	3·56 W
98	Port-Cartier	Can.	50·01 N	66·53 W
106	Port Chester (chĕs'tẽr)	NY (New York In.)	40·59 N	73·40 W
112	Port Chicago (shĭ-kô'gō)	Ca. (San Francisco In.)	38·03 N	122·01 W
104	Port Clinton (klĭn'tŭn)	Oh.	41·30 N	83·00 W
97	Port Colborne	Can.	42·53 N	79·13 W
112	Port Coquitlam (kô-kwĭt'lȧm)	Can. (Vancouver In.)	49·16 N	122·46 W
89	Port Credit (krĕd'ĭt)	Can. (Toronto In.)	43·33 N	79·35 W
160	Port-de-Bouc (pôr-dē-bōōk')	Fr. (In.)	43·24 N	5·00 E
217	Port de Kindu	Zaire	2·57 S	25·56 E
129	Port de Paix (pĕ)	Hai.	19·55 N	72·50 W
183	Port Dickson (dĭk'sŭn)	Mala. (Singapore In.)	2·33 N	101·49 E
112	Port Discovery (B.) (dĭs-kŭv'ẽr-ĭ)	Wa. (Seattle In.)	48·05 N	122·55 W
213	Port Edward (ĕd'wẽrd)	S. Afr. (Natal In.)	31·04 S	30·14 E
98	Port Elgin (ĕl'jĭn)	Can.	46·03 N	64·05 W
213	Port Elizabeth (ê-lĭz'ȧ-bĕth)	S. Afr. (Natal In.)	33·57 S	25·37 E
120	Porterdale (pōr'tẽr-dāl)	Ga.	33·34 N	83·53 W
114	Porterville (pōr'tẽr-vĭl)	Ca.	36·03 N	119·05 W
136	Portezuelo de Tupungato (Vol.) (pôr-tĕ-zwĕ-lō-dĕ-tōō-pōō'n-gä-tô)	Arg.-Chile	33·30 S	69·52 W
	Port Francqui, see Ilebo			
112	Port Gamble (găm'bŭl)	Wa. (Seattle In.)	47·52 N	122·36 W
112	Port Gamble Ind. Res.	Wa. (Seattle In.)	47·54 N	122·33 W
216	Port-Gentil (zhäɴ-tē')	Gabon	0·43 S	8·47 E
120	Port Gibson (gĭb'sŭn)	Ms.	31·56 N	90·57 W
215	Port Harcourt (här'kŭrt)	Nig.	4·43 N	7·05 E
92	Port Hardy (här'dĭ)	Can.	50·43 N	127·29 W
99	Port Hawkesbury	Can.	45·37 N	61·21 W
204	Port Hedland (hĕd'lănd)	Austl.	20·30 S	118·30 E
110	Porthill	Id.	49·00 N	116·30 W
99	Port Hood (hŏŏd)	Can.	46·01 N	61·32 W
105	Port Hope (hōp)	Can.	43·55 N	78·10 W
104	Port Huron (hū'rŏn)	Mi.	43·00 N	82·30 W
163	Portici (pôr'tê-chê)	It. (Naples In.)	40·34 N	14·20 E
137	Portillo (pôr-tē'l-yô)	Chile (Santiago In.)	32·51 S	70·09 W
162	Portimão (pôr-tē-mo'uɴ)	Port.	37·09 N	8·34 W
106	Port Jervis (jûr'vĭs)	NY (New York In.)	41·22 N	74·41 W
183	Port Kelang	Mala. (Singapore In.)	3·00 N	101·25 E
203	Portland (pōrt'lănd)	Austl.	38·20 S	142·40 E
104	Portland	In.	40·25 N	85·00 W
98	Portland	Me.	43·40 N	70·16 W
104	Portland	Mi.	42·50 N	85·00 W
112	Portland	Or. (Portland In.)	45·31 N	123·41 W
119	Portland	Tx.	27·53 N	97·20 W
128	Portland Bight (B.)	Jam.	17·45 N	77·05 W
92	Portland Can.	Ak.	55·10 N	130·08 W
92	Portland Inlet	Can.	54·50 N	130·15 W
128	Portland Pt.	Jam.	17·40 N	77·20 W
119	Port Lavaca (lȧ-vä'kȧ)	Tx.	28·36 N	96·38 W
203	Port Lincoln (lĭŋ'kŭn)	Austl.	34·39 S	135·50 E
112	Port Ludlow (lŭd'lō)	Wa. (Seattle In.)	47·26 N	122·41 W
	Port Lyautey, see Kenitra			
203	Port Macquarie (mȧ-kwŏ'rĭ)	Austl.	31·25 S	152·45 E
112	Port Madison Ind. Res. (măd'ĭ-sŭn)	Wa. (Seattle In.)	47·46 N	122·38 W
128	Port Maria (mȧ-rī'ȧ)	Jam.	18·20 N	76·55 W
98	Port-Menier (mē-nyā')	Can.	49·49 N	64·20 W
112	Port Moody (mōōd'ĭ)	Can. (Vancouver In.)	49·17 N	122·51 W
197	Port Moresby (mōrz'bê)	Pap. N. Gui.	9·34 S	147·20 E
119	Port Neches (nĕch'ĕz)	Tx.	29·59 N	93·57 W
95	Port Nelson (nĕl'sŭn)	Can.	57·03 N	92·36 W
98	Portneuf-Sur-Mer (pôr-nûf'sür mĕr)	Can.	48·36 N	69·06 W
212	Port Nolloth (nŏl'ŏth)	S. Afr.	29·10 S	17·00 E
162	Pôrto (Oporto) (pōr'tōō)	Port.	41·10 N	8·38 W
134	Pôrto Acre (ä'krĕ)	Braz.	9·38 S	67·34 W
136	Pôrto Alegre (ä-lā'grĕ)	Braz.	29·58 S	51·11 W
216	Porto Alexandre (à-lĕ-zhän'drĕ)	Ang.	15·49 S	11·53 E
216	Porto Amboim	Ang.	11·01 S	13·45 E
217	Porto Amélia (à-mĕ'lyä)	Moz.	12·58 S	40·30 E
127	Portobelo (pōr'tô-bā'lô)	Pan.	9·32 N	79·40 W
135	Pôrto de Pedras (pā'dräzh)	Braz.	9·09 S	35·20 W
137	Pôrto Feliz (fē-lē's)	Braz. (Rio de Janeiro In.)	23·12 S	47·30 W
164	Portoferraio (pōr'tô-fĕr-rä'yō)	It.	42·47 N	10·20 E
135	Port of Spain (spān)	Trin.	10·44 N	61·24 W
164	Portogruaro (pōr'tô-grōō-ä'rō)	It.	45·48 N	12·49 E
114	Portola (pôr'tō-lá)	Ca.	39·47 N	120·29 W
135	Pôrto Mendes (mĕ'n-dĕs)	Braz.	24·41 S	54·13 W
135	Pôrto Murtinho (mōōr-tēn'yōō)	Braz.	21·43 S	57·43 W
135	Pôrto Nacional (nà-syô-näl')	Braz.	10·43 S	48·14 W
215	Porto Novo (pōr'tô-nō'vō)	Benin	6·29 N	2·37 E
112	Port Orchard (ôr'chẽrd)	Wa. (Seattle In.)	47·32 N	122·38 W
112	Port Orchard (B.)	Wa.(Seattle In.)	47·40 N	122·39 W
210	Porto Santo, Ilha de (I.) (säɴ'tōō)	Mad. Is.	32·41 N	16·15 W
135	Pôrto Seguro (sā-gōō'rōō)	Braz.	16·26 S	38·59 W
164	Porto Torres (tôr'rĕs)	It.	40·49 N	8·25 E
164	Porto-Vecchio (vĕk'ê-ô)	Fr.	41·36 N	9·17 E
134	Pôrto Velho (vāl'yōō)	Braz.	8·45 S	63·43 W
134	Portoviejo (pôr-tô-vyā'hō)	Ec.	1·11 S	80·28 W
203	Port Phillip B. (fĭl'ĭp)	Austl.	37·57 S	144·50 E
203	Port Pirie (pĭ'rê)	Austl.	33·10 S	138·00 E
90	Port Radium (rā'dē-ŭm)	Can.	66·06 N	118·03 W
128	Port Royal (B.) (roi'ăl)	Jam.	17·50 N	76·45 W
	Port Said, see Būr Sa'īd			
213	Port St. Johns (sânt jŏnz)	S. Afr. (Natal In.)	31·37 S	29·32 E
213	Port Shepstone (shĕps'tŭn)	S. Afr. (Natal In.)	30·45 S	30·23 E
154	Portsmouth (pôrts'mŭth)	Eng.	50·45 N	1·03 W
105	Portsmouth	NH	43·05 N	70·50 W
104	Portsmouth	Oh.	38·45 N	83·00 W
106	Portsmouth	Va. (Norfolk In.)	36·50 N	76·19 W

ăt; finăl; rāte; senâte; ärm; ȧsk; sofȧ; fâre; ch-choose; dh-as th in other; bē; êvent; bĕt; recĕnt; cratẽr; g-go; gh-guttural g; bĭt; ĭ-short neutral; rīde; κ-guttural k as ch in German ich;

PRONOUNCING INDEX

Portsmouth — Providence 331

Page	Name Pronunciation Region	Lat. °'	Long. °'
127	Portsmouth.......Dominica (In.)	15·33 N	61·28 W
	Port Sudan, see Būr Sūdān		
120	Port Sulphur (sŭl'fẽr).........La.	29·28 N	89·41 W
112	Port Susan (B.) (sū-zán') Wa. (Seattle In.)	48·11 N	122·25 W
121	Port Tampa (tăm'pȧ)....Fl. (In.)	27·50 N	82·30 W
112	Port Townsend (tounz'ĕnd) Wa. (Seattle In.)	48·07 N	122·46 W
112	Port Townsend (B.) Wa. (Seattle In.)	48·05 N	122·47 W
146	Portugal (pōr'tu-gȧl)........Eur.	38·15 N	8·08 W
162	Portugalete (pōr-tōō-gä-lā'tā) Sp.	43·18 N	3·05 W
216	Portugália.................Ang.	7·20 S	20·47 E
	Portuguese East Africa, see Mozambique		
	Portuguese India, see Gôa, Daman & Diu		
	Portuguese West Africa, see Angola		
160	Port Vendres (pôr vän'dr')....Fr.	42·32 N	3·07 E
203	Port Wakefield (wāk'fēld)..Austl.	34·12 S	138·10 E
106	Port Washington (wôsh'ĭng-tŭn) NY (New York In.)	40·49 N	73·42 W
109	Port Washington............Wi.	43·24 N	87·52 W
136	Posadas (pō-sä'dhäs)........Arg.	27·32 S	55·56 W
162	Posadas (pô-sä-däs).........Sp.	37·48 N	5·09 W
190	Poshan (pō'shän')..........China	36·32 N	117·51 E
166	Poshekhon 'ye Volodarsk (pô-shyĕ'kôn-yĕ vôl'ô-dȧrsk) Sov. Un.	58·31 N	39·07 E
196	Poso, Danau (L.) (pō'sō)...Indon.	2·00 S	119·40 E
174	Pospelkova (pôs-pyĕl'kô-vȧ) Sov. Un. (Urals In.)	59·25 N	60·50 E
112	Possession Sd. (pŏ-zĕsh'ŭn) Wa. (Seattle In.)	47·59 N	122·17 W
118	Possum Kingdom Res. (pŏs'ŭm kĭng'dŭm).Tx.	32·58 N	98·12 W
116	Post (pōst).................Tx.	33·12 N	101·21 W
210	Post Maurice Cortier (Bidon Cinq).Alg.	22·22 N	0·33 E
164	Postojna (pōs-tōynȧ).......Yugo.	45·45 N	14·13 E
194	Pos'yet (pos-yĕt').......Sov. Un.	42·27 N	130·47 E
117	Potawatomi Ind. Res. (pŏt-å-wä'tō mē).Ks.	39·30 N	96·11 W
218	Potchefstroom (pŏch'ĕf-strōm) S. Afr. (Johannesburg & Pretoria In.)	26·42 S	27·06 E
117	Poteau (pô-tō')..............Ok.	35·03 N	94·37 W
118	Poteet (pô-tēt)..............Tx.	29·05 N	98·35 W
164	Potenza (pô-tĕnt'sä)..........It.	40·39 N	15·49 E
164	Potenza (R.)................It.	43·09 N	13·00 E
218	Potgietersrus (pôt-kē'tērs-rûs) S. Afr. (Johannesburg & Pretoria In.)	24·09 S	29·04 E
110	Potholes Res...............Wa.	47·00 N	119·20 W
171	Poti (pô'tê)............Sov. Un.	42·10 N	41·40 E
215	Potiskum..................Nig.	11·43 N	11·05 E
106	Potomac (pô-tō'măk) Md. (Baltimore In.)	39·01 N	77·13 W
105	Potomac (R.) (pô-tō'măk)....Va.	38·15 N	76·55 W
134	Potosí (pō-tô-sē')............Bol.	19·42 S	65·42 W
117	Potosi (pŏ-tō'sĭ).............Mo.	37·56 N	90·46 W
118	Potosi, R. (pō-tô-sē')........Mex.	25·04 N	99·36 W
190	Pot'ou (bŭ''tō)..............China	38·05 N	116·35 E
126	Potrerillos (pō-trâ-rēl'yôs)..Hond.	15·13 N	87·58 W
149	Potsdam (pôts'däm) G.D.R. (Berlin In.)	52·24 N	13·04 E
105	Potsdam (pŏts'dăm).........NY	44·40 N	75·00 W
149	Potsdam (Dist.) (pôts'däm) G.D.R. (Berlin In.)	52·31 N	12·45 E
149	Pottenstein.....Aus. (Vienna In.)	47·58 N	16·06 E
148	Potters Bar (pŏt'ẽz bär) Eng. (London In.)	51·41 N	0·12 W
105	Pottstown (pŏts'toun)........Pa.	40·15 N	75·40 W
105	Pottsville (pŏts'vĭl)..........Pa.	40·40 N	76·15 W
105	Poughkeepsie (pŏ-kĭp'sê)......NY	41·45 N	73·55 W
112	Poulsbo (pōlz'bōō) Wa. (Seattle In.)	47·44 N	122·38 W
148	Poulton-le-Fylde (pōl'tŭn-lē-fīld') Eng.	53·52 N	2·59 W
137	Pouso Alegre (pō'zōō ä-lā'grĕ) Braz. (Rio de Janeiro In.)	22·13 S	45·56 W
162	Póvoa de Varzim (pō-vō'ȧ dā vär'zēn).Port.	41·23 N	8·44 W
111	Powder River..............Wy.	43·06 N	106·55 W
111	Powder R. (pou'dẽr).....Mt.-Wy.	45·18 N	105·37 W
110	Powder R...................Or.	44·55 N	117·35 W
111	Powder R., South Fk.........Wy.	43·13 N	106·54 W
111	Powell (pou'ĕl)..............Wy.	44·44 N	108·44 W
115	Powell, L...................Ut.	37·26 N	110·25 W
92	Powell L....................Can.	50·10 N	124·13 W
119	Powell Pt...................Ba.	24·50 N	76·20 W
120	Powell Res.............Ky.-Tn.	36·30 N	83·35 W
92	Powell River..............Can.	49·52 N	124·33 W
193	Poyang (pō'yäng')..........China	29·00 N	116·42 E
193	P'oyang Hu (L.)...........China	29·20 N	116·28 E
109	Poygan (R.) (poi'gȧn)........Wi.	44·10 N	89·05 W
165	Požarevac (pô'zhà'rĕ-vàts)..Yugo.	44·38 N	21·12 E
158	Poznań (pôz'nän'')..........Pol.	52·24 N	16·55 E
162	Pozoblanco (pô-thō-bläŋ'kō)...Sp.	38·23 N	4·50 W
125	Pozo Rica (pô-zô-rê'kä).....Mex.	20·32 N	97·25 W
124	Pozos (pô'zōs)..............Mex.	22·05 N	100·50 W
163	Pozuelo de Alarcón (pô-thwā'lō dā ä-lär-kōn') Sp. (Madrid In)	40·27 N	3·49 W
163	Pozzuoli (pôt-swô'lē) It. (Naples In.)	40·34 N	14·08 E
214	Pra (R.) (prȧ)...........Ghana	5·45 N	1·35 W
166	Pra (R.)...............Sov. Un.	55·00 N	40·13 E
196	Prachin Buri (prä'chēn).....Thai.	13·59 N	101·15 E
134	Pradera (prä-dĕ'rä).....Col. (In.)	3·24 N	76·13 W
160	Prades (prȧd)................Fr.	42·37 N	2·23 E
134	Prado (prädô).........Col. (In.)	3·44 N	74·55 W
113	Prado Res. (prä'dō) Ca. (Los Angeles In.)	33·45 N	117·40 W
137	Prados (prȧ'dôs) Braz. (Rio de Janeiro In.)	21·05 S	44·04 W
	Prague, see Praha		
158	Praha (Prague) (prä'hȧ) (präg) Czech.	59·05 N	14·30 E
210	Praia (prä'yȧ).........C. V. (In.)	15·00 N	23·30 W
136	Praia Funda, Ponta da (Pt.) (pôn'tä-dȧ-prä'yȧ-fōō'n-dä) Braz. (Rio de Janeiro In.)	23·04 S	43·34 W
109	Prairie du Chien (prā'rĭ dōō shēn') Wi.	43·02 N	91·10 W
89	Prairie Grove (prā'rĭ grōv) Can. (Winnipeg In.)	49·48 N	96·57 W
109	Prairie Island Ind. Res.......Mn.	44·42 N	92·32 W
89	Prairies, R. des (rē-vyâr' dā prȧ-rē') Can. (Montreal In.)	45·40 N	73·34 W
193	Pratas (Is.)..............China	20·40 N	116·30 E
164	Prato (prä'tō)................It.	43·53 N	11·03 E
160	Prats-de-Mollo (prȧ-dē-mô-lō').Fr.	42·26 N	2·36 E
116	Pratt (prăt)................Ks.	37·37 N	98·43 W
120	Prattville (prăt'vĭl)...........Al.	32·28 N	86·27 W
157	Pravdinsk..............Sov. Un.	54·26 N	20·11 E
174	Pravdinskiy (pràv-dĕn'skĭ) Sov, Un. (Moscow In.)	56·03 N	37·52 E
162	Pravia (prä'vê-ä)............Sp.	43·30 N	6·08 W
157	Pregolya (R.) (prĕ-gô'lă)..Sov. Un.	54·37 N	20·50 E
118	Premont (prê-mŏnt').........Tx.	27·20 N	98·07 W
158	Prenzlau (prĕnts'lou).....G.D.R.	53·19 N	13·52 E
159	Přerov (przhĕ'rôf)........Czech.	49·28 N	17·28 E
125	Presa Aleman (L.) (prä'sä-lĕ-mȧ'n).Mex.	18·20 N	96·35 W
125	Presa de Infiernillo (Res.)...Mex.	18·50 N	101·50 W
148	Prescot (prĕs'kŭt)..........Eng.	53·25 N	2·48 W
115	Prescott (prĕs'kŏt)..........Az.	34·30 N	112·30 W
117	Prescott....................Ar.	33·47 N	93·23 W
105	Prescott (prĕs'kŭt)..........Can.	44·45 N	75·35 W
113	Prescott (prĕs'kŏt) Wi. (Minneapolis, St. Paul In.)	44·45 N	92·48 W
108	Presho (prĕsh'ô).............SD	43·56 N	100·04 W
136	Presidencia Rogue Sáenz Peña (prĕ-sē-dĕ'n-sêȧ-rô'kĕ-sȧ'ĕnz-pĕ'n-yȧ).Arg.	26·52 S	60·15 W
135	Presidente Epitácio (prā-sê-dĕn'tĕ ā-pê-tä'syōō) Braz.	21·56 S	52·01 W
118	Presidio (prĕ-sĭ'dĭ-ô)..........Tx.	29·33 N	104·23 W
124	Presidio, Rio del (R.) (rê'ō-dĕl-prĕ-sê'dyô).Mex.	23·54 N	105·44 W
159	Prešov (prĕ'shôf)..........Czech.	49·00 N	21·18 E
165	Prespa (L.) (prĕs'pä)...Alb.-Yugo.	40·49 N	20·50 E
135	Prespuntal (R.) (prĕs-pōōn-täl') Ven. (In.)	9·55 N	64·32 W
98	Presque Isle (prĕsk'ēl')........Me.	46·41 N	68·03 W
137	Pressbaum......Aus. (Vienna In.)	48·12 N	16·06 E
214	Prestea....................Ghana	5·27 N	2·08 W
136	Preston (prĕs'tŭn)...........Eng.	53·46 N	2·42 W
111	Preston (pres'tŭn)............Id.	42·05 N	111·54 W
109	Preston (prĕs'tŭn)...........Mn.	43·42 N	92·06 W
112	Preston.........Wa. (Seattle In.)	47·31 N	121·56 W
104	Prestonburg (prĕs'tŭn-bûrg)..Ky.	37·35 N	82·50 W
136	Prestwich (prĕst'wĭch).........Eng.	53·32 N	2·17 W
213	Pretoria (prê-tō'rĭ-ȧ).......S. Afr. (Johannesburg & Pretoria In.)	25·43 S	28·16 E
213	Pretoria North (prĕ-tō'rĭ-ȧ nōord) S. Afr. (Johannesburg & Pretoria In.)	25·41 S	28·11 E
165	Préveza (prĕ'vȧ-zä)..........Grc.	38·58 N	20·44 E
101	Pribilof (Is.) (prĭ'bĭ-lof)......Ak.	57·00 N	169·20 W
165	Priboj (prē'boi)............Yugo.	43·33 N	19·33 E
115	Price (prīs)..................Ut.	39·35 N	110·50 W
115	Price (R.)...................Ut.	39·21 N	110·35 W
89	Priddis (prĭd'dĭs) Can. (Calgary In.)	50·53 N	114·20 W
89	Priddis Cr.....Can. (Calgary In.)	50·56 N	114·32 W
162	Priego (prê-ā'gō).............Sp.	37·27 N	4·13 W
157	Prienai (prê-ĕn'ī)........Sov. Un.	54·38 N	23·56 E
212	Prieska (prê-ĕs'kȧ)........S. Afr.	29·40 S	22·50 E
110	Priest L. (prēst).............Id.	48·30 N	116·43 W
110	Priest Rapids Dam...........Wa.	46·39 N	119·55 W
110	Priest Rapids Res...........Wa.	46·42 N	119·58 W
174	Priiskovaya (prĭ-ēs'kô-vȧ-yȧ) Sov. Un. (Urals In.)	60·50 N	58·55 E
164	Prijedor (prē'yĕ-dôr).......Yugo.	44·58 N	16·43 E
165	Prijepolje (prê'yĕ-pô'lyĕ)...Yugo.	43·22 N	19·41 E
165	Prilep (prē'lĕp)............Yugo.	41·20 N	21·35 E
167	Priluki (prê-lōō'kê)......Sov. Un.	50·36 N	32·21 E
157	Primorsk (prē-môrsk')...Sov. Un.	60·24 N	28·35 E
167	Primorsko-Akhtarskaya (prē-môr'skô äk-tär'skĭ-ê) Sov. Un.	46·03 N	38·09 E
213	Primrose.................S. Afr. (Johannesburg & Pretoria In.)	26·11 S	28·11 E
94	Primrose L.............Can.	54·55 N	109·45 W
94	Prince Albert (prĭns ăl'bērt)..Can.	53·12 N	105·46 W
90	Prince Albert Natl. Park.....Can.	54·10 N	105·25 W
90	Prince Albert Sd...........Can.	70·23 N	116·57 W
91	Prince Charles I. (chärlz)....Can.	67·41 N	74·10 W
91	Prince Edward I. (Prov.)....Can.	46·45 N	63·10 W
220	Prince Edward Is..........S. Afr.	46·36 S	37·57 E
98	Prince Edward Natl. Park (ĕd'wērd)...Can.	46·33 N	63·35 W
105	Prince Edward Pen..........Can.	44·00 N	77·15 W
106	Prince Frederick (prĭnce frĕdĕrĭk) Md. (Baltimore In.)	38·33 N	76·35 W
92	Prince George (jôrj).........Can.	53·51 N	122·57 W
92	Prince of Wales (I.)..........Ak.	55·47 N	132·50 W
205	Prince of Wales (I.)........Austl.	10·47 S	142·15 E
101	Prince of Wales, C. (wālz)....Ak.	65·48 N	169·08 W
92	Prince Rupert (roo'pērt).....Can.	54·19 N	130·19 W
148	Princes Risborough (prĭns'ĕz rĭz'brŭ) Eng. (London In.)	51·41 N	0·51 W
205	Princess Charlotte B. (shär'lŏt) Austl.	13·45 S	144·15 E
220	Princess Martha Coast (mär'thȧ) Ant.	72·00 S	5·00 W
92	Princess Royal Chan. (roi'ăl).Can.	53·10 N	128·37 W
92	Princess Royal I............Can.	52·57 N	128·49 W
93	Princeton (prĭns'tŭn)........Can.	49·27 N	120·31 W
104	Princeton....................Il.	41·20 N	89·25 W
104	Princeton....................In.	38·20 N	87·35 W
120	Princeton....................Ky.	37·07 N	87·52 W
109	Princeton....................Mi.	46·16 N	87·33 W
109	Princeton....................Mn.	45·34 N	93·36 W
117	Princeton....................Mo.	40·23 N	93·34 W
106	Princeton.....NJ (New York In.)	40·21 N	74·40 W
121	Princeton....................WV	37·21 N	81·05 W
109	Princeton....................Wi.	43·50 N	89·09 W
101	Prince William Sd. (wĭl'yăm)..Ak.	60·40 N	147·10 W
216	Príncipe (I.) (prēn'sê-pē).....Afr.	1·37 N	7·25 E
92	Principe Chan. (prĭn'sĭ-pē)...Can.	53·28 N	129·45 W
110	Prineville (prīn'vĭl)...........Or.	44·17 N	120·48 W
110	Prineville Res...............Or.	44·07 N	120·45 W
127	Prinzapolca (prēn-zä-pōl'kä)..Nic.	13·18 N	83·35 W
127	Prinzapolca R...............Nic.	13·23 N	84·23 W
113	Prior Lake (prī'ẽr) Mn. (Minneapolis, St. Paul In.)	44·43 N	93·26 W
157	Priozërsk (prĭ-ô'zĕrsk)...Sov. Un.	61·03 N	30·08 E
171	Pripyat (Pripet) (R.) (prē'pyät) Sov. Un.	51·50 N	29·45 E
	Pripyat Marshes, see Poles'ye		
165	Priština (prēsh'tĭ-nä).......Yugo.	42·39 N	21·12 E
120	Pritchard (prĭt'chârd)........Al.	30·44 N	87·04 W
158	Pritzwalk (prēts'välk)....G.D.R.	53·09 N	12·12 E
160	Privas (prē-väs')............Fr.	44·44 N	4·37 E
167	Privol'noye (prê'vôl-nô-yĕ) Sov. Un.	47·30 N	32·21 E
165	Prizren (prē'zrĕn)..........Yugo.	42·11 N	20·45 E
163	Procida (prô'chê-dă) It. (Naples In.)	40·31 N	14·02 E
163	Procida, I. di.....It. (Naples In.)	40·32 N	13·57 E
113	Proctor(prŏk'tẽr).Mn.(Duluth In.)	46·45 N	92·14 W
105	Proctor....................Vt.	43·40 N	73·00 W
112	Proebstel (prōb'stĕl) Wa. (Portland In.)	45·40 N	122·29 W
162	Proenca-a-Nova (prô-ān'sȧ-ä-nō'vȧ).Port.	39·44 N	7·55 W
126	Progreso (prô-grĕ'sô).......Hond.	15·28 N	87·49 W
125	Progreso (prô-grā'sō).......Mex.	21·14 N	89·39 W
118	Progreso...................Mex.	27·29 N	101·05 W
172	Prokop'yevsk..........Sov. Un.	53·52 N	86·38 E
165	Prokuplje (prô'kōōp'l-yĕ)...Yugo.	43·16 N	21·40 E
166	Pronya (R.) (prô'nyä)...Sov. Un.	54·08 N	30·58 E
166	Pronya (R.)..............Sov. Un.	54·08 N	39·30 E
135	Propriá (prō-prē-ä')..........Braz.	10·17 S	36·47 W
107	Prospect (prŏs'pĕkt) Ky. (Louisville In.)	38·21 N	85·36 W
106	Prospect Park (prŏs'pĕkt pärk) Pa. (Philadelphia In.)	39·53 N	75·18 W
110	Prosser (prŏs'ẽr).............Wa.	46·10 N	119·46 W
159	Prostějov (prŏs'tyĕ-yôf)....Czech.	49·28 N	17·08 E
112	Protection (I.) (prô-tĕk'shŭn) Wa. (Seattle In.)	48·07 N	122·56 W
166	Protoka (R.) (prôt'ô-kȧ)..Sov. Un.	55·00 N	36·42 E
165	Provadiya (prō-väd'ê-yȧ).....Bul.	43·13 N	27·28 E
104	Providence (prŏv'ĭ-dĕns)......Ky.	37·25 N	87·45 W
106	Providence...RI (Providence In.)	41·50 N	71·23 W

ng-sing; ŋ-baŋk; N-nasalized n; nŏd; cŏmmit; ōld; ôbey; ôrder; fōōd; fŏŏt; ou-out; s-soft; sh-dish; th-thin; pūre; ûnite; ûrn; stŭd; circŭs; ü-as "y" in study; '-indeterminate vowel.

332 Providence — Quakertown PRONOUNCING INDEX

Page	Name Pronunciation Region	Lat. °′	Long. °′
111	Providence ... Ut.	41·42 N	111·50 W
127	Providencia, Isla de (I.) ... Col.	13·21 N	80·55 W
119	Providenciales (I.) (prō-vē-děn-sē-ä'lâs) (prŏ-vĭ-děn'shǎlz) Turks & Caicos Is.	21·50 N	72·15 W
101	Provideniya (prô-vĭ-dă'nĭ-yȧ) Sov. Un.	64·30 N	172·54 W
105	Provincetown ... Ma.	42·03 N	70·11 W
115	Provo (prō'vō) ... Ut.	40·15 N	111·40 W
164	Prozor (prô'zôr) ... Yugo.	43·48 N	17·59 E
106	Prudence I. (pro͞o'děns) RI (Providence In.)	41·38 N	71·20 W
101	Prudhoe B. ... Ak.	70·40 N	147·25 W
159	Prudnik (pro͝od'nĭk) ... Pol.	50·19 N	17·34 E
157	Prunkkala (pro͝oṅk'ȧ-lȧ) ... Fin.	60·38 N	22·32 E
158	Prussia (Reg.) (prŭsh'ȧ) ... G.D.R.	50·43 N	8·35 E
159	Pruszków (pro͝osh'ko͝of) ... Pol.	52·09 N	20·50 E
167	Prut (R.) (pro͞ot) ... Sov. Un.	48·05 N	27·07 E
117	Pryor (prī'ẽr) ... Ok.	36·16 N	95·19 W
171	Prypeć (R.) ... Sov. Un.	51·50 N	25·35 E
159	Przedbórz (pzhěd'bo͝ozh) ... Pol.	51·05 N	19·53 E
159	Przemyśl (pzhě'mĭsh'l) ... Pol.	49·47 N	22·45 E
172	Przheval'sk (p'r-zhĭ-välsk') Sov. Un.	42·25 N	78·18 E
165	Psará (I.) (psä'rȧ) ... Grc.	38·39 N	25·26 E
167	Psël (R.) (psěl) ... Sov. Un.	49·45 N	33·42 E
165	Psevdhókavos (Pen.) ... Grc.	39·58 N	24·05 E
166	Pskov (pskôf) ... Sov. Un.	57·48 N	28·19 E
166	Pskov (Oblast) ... Sov. Un.	57·33 N	29·05 E
166	Pskovskoye Ozero (L.) (p'skôv'skô'yě ôzê-rô) . Sov. Un.	58·05 N	28·15 E
166	Ptich' (R.) (p'těch) ... Sov. Un.	53·17 N	28·16 E
164	Ptuj (ptōō'ê) ... Yugo.	46·24 N	15·54 E
193	Pucheng (po͞o'chěng') ... China	28·02 N	118·25 E
159	Puck (po͝otsk) ... Pol.	54·43 N	18·23 E
188	Pudog ... China	33·29 N	79·26 E
170	Pudozh (po͞o'dôzh) ... Sov. Un.	61·50 N	36·50 E
124	Puebla (pwā'blä) ... Mex.	19·02 N	98·11 W
124	Puebla (State) ... Mex.	19·00 N	97·45 W
162	Puebla de Don Fadrique (pwě'blä dā dōn fä-drē'kā) . Sp.	37·55 N	2·55 W
116	Pueblo (pwā'blō) ... Co.	38·15 N	104·36 W
124	Pueblo Nuevo (nwā'vô) ... Mex.	23·23 N	105·21 W
125	Pueblo Viejo (vyā'hô) ... Mex.	17·23 N	93·46 W
125	Puente Alto (pwě'n-tě ál'tô) Chile (Santiago In.)	33·36 S	70·34 W
162	Puenteareas (pwěn-tā-ä-rā'äs) . . Sp.	42·09 N	8·23 W
162	Puente Ceso (pwěn'tȧ thā'sô) . . Sp.	43·15 N	8·53 W
162	Puentedeume (pwěn-tȧ-dhȧ-o͞o'mȧ) . Sp.	43·28 N	8·09 W
162	Puente-Genil (pwěn'tȧ-hȧ-nēl') . Sp.	37·25 N	4·18 W
115	Puerco (R.) (pwěr'kō) ... NM	35·15 N	107·05 W
136	Puerto Aisén (pwě'r-tō ä'y-sě'n) Chile	45·28 S	72·44 W
125	Puerto Angel (pwě'r-tō äṅ'hâl) Mex.	15·42 N	96·32 W
127	Puerto Armuelles (pwe'r-tō är-mo͞o-ā'lyās) . Pan.	8·18 N	82·52 W
126	Puerto Barrios (pwě'r-tō bär'rê-ôs) Guat.	15·43 N	88·36 W
134	Puerto Bermúdez (pwě'r-tō běr-mo͞o'dāz) . Peru	10·17 S	74·57 W
134	Puerto Berrío (pwě'r-tō běr-rē'ō) Col. (In.)	6·29 N	74·27 W
135	Puerto Cabello (pwě'r-tō kä-běl'yō) . Ven. (In.)	10·28 N	68·01 W
127	Puerto Cabezas (pwě'r-tô kä-bā'zäs) . Nic.	14·01 N	83·26 W
136	Puerto Casado (pwě'r-tō kä-sä'dō) Par.	22·16 S	57·57 W
126	Puerto Castilla (pwě'r-tô käs-tēl'yō) . Hond.	16·01 N	86·01 W
134	Puerto Chicama (pwě'r-tō chē-kä'mä) . Peru	7·46 S	79·18 W
134	Puerto Columbia (pwěr'tô kô-lôm'bê-ȧ) . Col.	11·08 N	75·09 W
127	Puerto Cortés (pwě'r-tô kôr-tās') C. R.	9·00 N	83·37 W
126	Puerto Cortés (pwě'r-tô kôr-tās') Hond.	15·48 N	87·57 W
134	Puerto Cumarebo (pwě'r-tō ko͞o-mä-rě'bô) . Ven.	11·25 N	69·17 W
163	Puerto de Beceite (Mts.) (pwě'r-tō dě bě-sě'y-tě) . Sp.	40·43 N	0·05 W
116	Puerto de Luna (pwěr'tô dȧ lo͞o'nä) . NM	34·49 N	104·36 W
134	Puerto de Nutrias (pwě'r-tō dě no͞o-trê-äs') . Ven.	8·02 N	69·19 W
136	Puerto Deseado (pwě'r-tō dā-sȧ-ä'dhō) . Arg.	47·38 S	66·00 W
134	Puerto Eten (pwě'r-tō ě-tě'n) . Peru	6·59 S	79·51 W
127	Puerto Jimenez (pwě'r-tô Kê-mě'něz) . C. R.	8·35 N	83·23 W
137	Puerto La Cruz (pwě'r-tō lä kro͞o'z) . Ven. (In.)	10·14 N	64·38 W
162	Puertollano (pwěr-tôl-yä'nō) . . . Sp.	38·41 N	4·05 W
136	Puerto Madryn (pwě'r-tō mä-drēn') . Arg.	42·45 S	65·01 W
134	Puerto Maldonado (pwě'r-tō mäl-dō-nä'dô) . Peru	12·43 S	69·01 W
	Puerto Mexico, see Coatzacoalcos		
124	Puerto Miniso (pwě'r-tō mē-nē'sô) Mex.	16·06 N	98·02 W
136	Puerto Montt (pwě'r-tō mô'nt) Chile	41·29 S	73·00 W
136	Puerto Natales (pwě'r-tō nä-tä'lěs) Chile	51·48 S	72·01 W
134	Puerto Niño (pwě'r-tō nê'n-yô) Col. (In.)	5·57 N	74·36 W
128	Puerto Padre (pwě'r-tō pä'drā) Cuba	21·10 N	76·40 W
122	Puerto Peñasco (pwě'r-tô pěn-yä's-kô) . Mex.	31·39 N	113·15 W
136	Puerto Pinasco (pwě'r-tō pē-nȧ's-kô) . Par.	22·31 S	57·50 W
135	Puerto Píritu (pwě'r-tō pē'rē-to͞o) Ven. (In.)	10·05 N	65·04 W
129	Puerto Plata (pwě'r-tô plä'tä) Dom. Rep.	19·50 N	70·40 W
196	Puerto Princesa (pwěr-tô prên-sā'sä) . Phil.	9·45 N	118·41 E
123	Puerto Rico (pwěr'tô rē'kō) . . N. A.	18·16 N	66·50 W
123	Puerto Rico Trench ... N. A.	19·45 N	66·30 W
134	Puerto Salgar (pwě'r-tō säl-gär') . Col. (In.)	5·30 N	74·39 W
136	Puerto Santa Cruz (pwě'r-tō sän'tä kro͞oz') . . . Arg.	50·04 S	68·32 W
135	Puerto Suárez (pwě'r-tō swä'râz) . Bol.	18·55 S	57·39 W
134	Puerto Tejada (pwě'r-tō tě-Kä'dä) . Col. (In.)	3·13 N	76·23 W
124	Puerto Vallarta (pwě'r-tō väl-yär'tä) . Mex.	20·36 N	105·13 W
136	Puerto Varas (pwě'r-tō vä'räs) Chile	41·16 S	73·03 W
134	Puerto Wilches (pwě'r-tō vēl'c-hěs) . Col.	7·19 N	73·54 W
171	Pugachëv (po͞o'gȧ-chyôf) . Sov. Un.	52·00 N	48·40 E
112	Puget (pū'jět) . Wa. (Portland In.)	46·10 N	123·23 W
110	Puget Sd. ... Wa.	47·49 N	122·26 W
164	Puglia (Apulia) (Reg.) (po͞o'lyä) (ä-po͞o'lyä) . It.	41·13 N	16·10 E
190	Puhsien (po͞o'sĭän) ... China	35·43 N	115·22 E
96	Pukaskwa Natl. Pk. ... Can.	48·22 N	85·55 W
93	Pukeashun Mtn. ... Can.	51·12 N	119·14 W
183	Pukin (R.) . . Mala. (Singapore In.)	2·53 N	102·54 E
164	Pula (po͞o'lä) ... Yugo.	44·52 N	13·55 E
134	Pulacayo (po͞o-lä-kä'yō) ... Bol.	20·12 S	66·33 W
190	P'ulantien (po͞o'län'chěn') . . . China	39·23 N	121·57 E
120	Pulaski (pû-lăs'kĭ) ... Tn.	35·11 N	87·03 W
121	Pulaski ... Va.	37·00 N	81·45 W
159	Pulawy (po͞o-wä'vê) ... Pol.	51·24 N	21·59 E
184	Pulizat (R.) ... India	13·58 N	79·52 E
110	Pullman (po͝ol'măn) ... Wa.	46·44 N	117·10 W
197	Pulog (Mtn.) (po͞o'lôg) . Phil. (In.)	16·38 N	120·53 E
150	Pultusk (po͝ol'to͝osk) ... Pol.	52·40 N	21·09 E
111	Pumpkin Cr. (pŭmp'kĭn) ... Mt.	45·47 N	105·35 W
184	Punakha (po͞o-nŭk'ŭ) ... Bhu.	27·45 N	89·59 E
134	Punata (po͞o-nä'tä) ... Bol.	17·43 S	65·43 W
184	Pune ... India	18·38 N	73·53 E
184	Punjab (State) (pŭn'jäb') . . . India	31·00 N	75·30 E
134	Puno (po͞o'nô) ... Peru	15·58 S	7·02 W
136	Punta Arenas (po͞o'n-tä-ä-rě'näs) Chile	53·09 S	70·48 W
135	Punta de Piedras (po͞o'n-tä dě pyě'dräs) . Ven. (In.)	10·54 N	64·06 W
126	Punta Gorda (po͞on'tä gôr'dä) Belize	16·07 N	88·50 W
121	Punta Gorda (pŭn'tȧ gôr'dȧ) Fl. (In.)	26·55 N	82·02 W
127	Punta Gorda, Rio (R.) (po͞o'n-tä gô'r-dä) . Nic.	11·34 N	84·13 W
137	Punta Indio, Can. (po͞o'n-tä ē'n-dyô) Arg. (Buenos Aires In.)	34·56 S	57·20 W
127	Puntarenas (po͝ont-ä-rā'näs) . C. R.	9·59 N	84·49 W
134	Punto Fijo (po͞o'n-tô fē'kô) . . . Ven.	11·48 N	70·14 W
105	Punxsutawney (pŭnk-sŭ-tô'nê) . Pa.	40·55 N	79·00 W
134	Puquio (po͞o'kyô) ... Peru	14·43 S	74·02 W
172	Pur (R.) ... Sov. Un.	65·30 N	77·30 E
117	Purcell (pûr-sěl') ... Ok.	35·01 N	97·22 W
93	Purcell Mts. (pûr-sěl') ... Can.	50·00 N	116·30 W
112	Purdy (pûr'dē) . . . Wa. (Seattle In.)	47·23 N	122·37 W
124	Purépero (po͞o-rā'pȧ-rō) ... Mex.	19·56 N	102·02 W
116	Purgatoire (R.) (pûr-gȧ-twär') Colo.	37·25 N	103·53 W
184	Puri (po͞o'rê) ... India	19·52 N	85·51 E
129	Purial, Sierra de (Mts.) (sē-ě'r-rä-dě-po͞o-rê-äl') . Cuba	20·15 N	74·40 W
134	Purificacion (po͞o-rê-fê-kä-syōn') Col. (In.)	3·52 N	74·54 W
124	Purificación (po͞o-rē-fê-kä-syô'n) Mex.	19·44 N	104·38 W
124	Purificación (R.) ... Mex.	19·30 N	104·54 W
149	Purkersdorf . . . . Aus. (Vienna In.)	48·13 N	16·11 E
196	Pursat (po͝or-sät') ... Camb.	12·33 N	103·51 E
124	Puruandiro (po͞o-ro͞o-än'dê-rō) Mex.	20·04 N	101·33 W
134	Purús (R.) (po͞o-ro͞o's') ... Braz.	6·45 S	64·34 W
194	Pusan ... Kor.	35·08 N	129·05 E
174	Pushkin (po͝osh'kĭn) Sov. Un. (Leningrad In.)	59·43 N	30·25 E
174	Pushkino (po͞osh'kê-nô) Sov. Un. (Moscow In.)	56·01 N	37·51 E
166	Pustoshka (pûs-tôsh'kȧ) . . Sov. Un.	56·20 N	29·33 E
125	Pustunich (po͞os-to͞o'nêch) . . . Mex.	19·10 N	90·29 W
137	Putaendo (po͞o-tä-ěn-dô) Chile (Santiago In.)	32·37 S	70·42 W
161	Puteaux (pü-tō') . . . Fr. (Paris In.)	48·52 N	2·12 E
213	Putfontein (po͝ot'fŏn-tān) . . S. Afr. (Johannesburg & Pretoria In.)	26·08 S	28·24 E
193	P'ut'ien ... China	25·40 N	119·02 E
167	Putivl' (po͞o-tēv'l') ... Sov. Un.	51·22 N	33·24 E
125	Putla de Guerrero (po͞o'tlä-dě-gěr-rě'rō) . Mex.	17·03 N	97·55 W
105	Putnam (pŭt'nǎm) ... Ct.	41·55 N	71·55 W
172	Putorana, Gory (Mts.) . . . Sov. Un.	68·45 N	93·15 E
185	Puttalam ... Sri Lanka	8·02 N	79·44 E
134	Putumayo (R.) (po͞o-to͞o-mä'yō) Col.-Peru	1·02 S	73·50 W
191	Putung (po͞o'to͞ong') China (Shanghai In.)	31·14 N	121·29 E
196	Putung, Tandjung (C.) ... Indon.	3·35 S	111·50 E
157	Puulavesi (L.) ... Fin.	61·49 N	27·10 E
112	Puyallup (pū-ăl'ŭp) Wa. (Seattle In.)	47·12 N	122·18 W
190	P'uyang (po͞o'yäng) ... China	35·42 N	114·58 E
212	Pweto (pwā'tō) ... Zaire	8·29 S	28·58 E
172	Pyasina (R.) (pyä-sē'nȧ) . Sov. Un.	72·45 N	87·37 E
171	Pyatigorsk (pyȧ-tê-gôrsk') Sov. Un.	44·00 N	43·00 E
196	Pye ... Bur.	18·46 N	95·15 E
157	Pyhäjärvi (L.) ... Fin.	60·57 N	21·50 E
188	Pyinmana (pyên-mä'nŭ) ... Bur.	19·47 N	96·15 E
104	Pymatuning Res. (pī-mȧ-tûn'ĭng) Pa.	41·40 N	80·30 W
194	Pyŏnggang (pyŭng'gäng') ... Kor.	38·21 N	127·18 E
194	P'yŏngyang ... Kor.	39·03 N	125·48 E
114	Pyramid (L.) (pĭ'rȧ-mĭd) ... Nv.	40·02 N	119·50 W
114	Pyramid Lake Ind. Res. ... Nv.	40·17 N	119·52 W
218	Pyramids ... Egypt (Nile In.)	29·53 N	31·10 E
163	Pyrenees (Mts.) (pĭr-e-nēz') Fr.-Sp.	43·00 N	0·05 E
158	Pyrzyce (pězhĭ'tsě) ... Pol.	53·09 N	14·53 E

Q

Page	Name Pronunciation Region	Lat. °′	Long. °′
186	Qal'at Bīshah ... Sau. Ar.	20·01 N	42·30 E
211	Qallābāt ... Sud.	12·55 N	36·12 E
218	Qana el Suweis (Suez Can.) Egypt (Suez In.)	30·53 N	32·21 E
187	Qandahār ... Afg.	31·43 N	65·58 E
153	Qārah (Oasis) ... Egypt	29·28 N	26·29 E
171	Qareh Sū (R.) ... Iran	38·50 N	47·10 E
218	Qārūn, Birket (L.) Egypt (Nile In.)	29·34 N	30·34 E
211	Qasr al-Burayqah ... Libya	30·25 N	19·20 E
211	Qasr al-Farāfirah ... Egypt	27·04 N	28·13 E
211	Qaṣr Banī Walīd ... Libya	31·45 N	14·04 E
182	Qatar (kä'tȧr) ... Asia	25·00 N	52·45 E
211	Qaṭṭārah, Munkhafaḍ (Dep.) Egypt	30·07 N	27·30 E
186	Qāyen ... Iran	33·45 N	59·08 E
186	Qeshm ... Iran	26·51 N	56·10 E
186	Qeshm (I.) ... Iran	26·52 N	56·15 E
186	Qezel Owzan ... Iran	37·00 N	48·23 E
171	Qezel Owzan (R.) ... Iran	37·00 N	47·35 E
183	Qeẓi'ot . . Egypt-Isr. (Palestine In.)	30·53 N	34·28 E
183	Qiblīyah, Jabal al Jalālat al (Plat.) Egypt (Palestine In.)	28·49 N	32·21 E
218	Qifṭ (kěft) ... Egypt (Nile In.)	25·58 N	32·52 E
218	Qinā (kä'nȧ) ... Egypt (Nile In.)	26·10 N	32·48 E
218	Qinā, Wādī ... Egypt (Nile In.)	26·38 N	32·53 E
183	Qiryat Gat . . . . Isr. (Palestine In.)	31·38 N	34·36 E
183	Qiryat Shemona Isr. (Palestine In.)	33·12 N	35·34 E
186	Qom ... Iran	34·28 N	50·53 E
	Qomul see Hami		
105	Quabbin Res. (kwā'bĭn) ... Ma.	42·20 N	72·10 W
117	Quachita, L. (kwä shĭ'tô) ... Ar.	34·47 N	93·37 W
92	Quadra, Boca de, Str. (bō'kȧ dě kwŏd'rȧ) . Ak.	55·08 N	130·50 W
92	Quadra I. ... Can.	50·08 N	125·16 W
105	Quakertown (kwā'kẽr-toun) . . . Pa.	40·30 N	75·20 W

ăt; finăl; rāte; senâte; ärm; ȧsk; sofȧ; fâre; ch-choose; dh-as th in other; bē; êvent; bět; recěnt; cratẽr; g-go; gh-guttural g; bĭt; ĭ-short neutral; rīde; K-guttural k as ch in German ich;

ng-sing; ŋ-baŋk; N-nasalized n; nŏd; cŏmmit; ōld; ôbey; ôrder; fōŏd; fŏŏt; ou-out; s-soft; sh-dish; th-thin; pūre; ûnite; ûrn; stŭd; circ̣us; ü-as "y" in study; '-indeterminate vowel.

334 Rantoul — Resistencia PRONOUNCING INDEX

Page	Name Pronunciation Region	Lat. °′	Long. °′
104	Rantoul (răn-tōōl′) Il.	40·25 N	88·05 W
164	Rapallo (rä-päl′lô) It.	44·21 N	9·14 E
199	Rapa Nui (Easter) (I.) (rä′pä nōō′ē) (ēs′tēr) Chile	26·50 S	109·00 W
137	Rapel (rä-pål′) (R.) Chile (Santiago In.)	34·05 S	71·30 W
109	Rapid (R.) (răp′ĭd) Mn.	48·21 N	94·50 W
108	Rapid City SD	44·06 N	103·14 W
157	Rapla (räp′lå) Sov. Un.	59·02 N	24·46 E
105	Rappahannock (R.) (răp′ȧ-hăn′ŭk) Va.	38·20 N	75·25 W
105	Raquette (L.) (răk′ĕt) NY	43·50 N	74·35 W
159	Rara Mazowiecka (rä′rä mä-zō-vyĕts′kä) Pol.	51·46 N	20·17 E
106	Raritan R. (răr′ĭ-tăn) NJ (New York In.)	40·32 N	74·27 W
199	Rarotonga (rä′rô-tōŋ′gȧ) Cook Is.	20·40 S	163·00 W
183	Ra's an Naqb Jordan (Palestine In.)	30·00 N	35·29 E
211	Ras Dashen (Mtn.) (räs dä-shän′) Eth.	12·49 N	38·14 E
157	Raseiniai (rä-syā′nyī) Sov. Un.	55·23 N	23·04 E
186	Ra's Fartak (C.) P. D. R. of Yem.	15·43 N	52·17 E
183	Rashayya Leb. (Palestine In.)	33·30 N	35·50 E
218	Rashīd (Rosetta) (rȧ-shēd′) (rô-zĕt′ȧ) Egypt (Nile In.)	31·22 N	30·25 E
218	Rashīd, Masabb (R. Mth.) Egypt (Nile In.)	31·30 N	29·58 E
174	Rashkina (råsh′kĭ-nå) Sov. Un. (Urals In.)	59·57 N	61·30 E
167	Rashkov (räsh′kôf) Sov. Un.	47·55 N	28·51 E
186	Rasht Iran	37·13 N	49·45 E
165	Raška (räsh′kå) Yugo.	43·16 N	20·40 E
184	Ras Kuh Mtn. Pak.	34·03 N	65·10 E
171	Rasskazovo (räs-kä′sô-vô) Sov. Un.	52·40 N	41·40 E
158	Rastatt (rä-shtät) F.R.G.	48·51 N	8·12 E
174	Rastes (rås′tĕs) Sov. Un. (Urals In.)	59·24 N	58·49 E
174	Rastunovo (rås-tōō′nô-vô) Sov. Un. (Moscow In.)	55·15 N	37·50 E
162	Ras Uarc (C.) Mor.	35·28 N	2·58 W
184	Ratangarh (rŭ-tŭn′gŭr) India	28·10 N	74·30 E
196	Rat Buri Thai.	13·30 N	99·46 E
119	Ratcliff (răt′klĭf) Tx.	31·22 N	95·09 W
158	Rathenow (rä′tĕ-nō) G.D.R.	52·36 N	12·20 E
154	Rathlin (I.) (răth-lĭn) Ire.	55·18 N	6·13 W
161	Ratingen (rä′tĕn-gĕn) F.R.G. (Ruhr In.)	51·18 N	6·51 E
101	Rat Is. (răt) Ak.	51·35 N	176·48 E
184	Ratlām India	23·19 N	75·05 E
185	Ratnāgiri India	17·04 N	73·24 E
116	Raton (rȧ-tōn′) NM	36·52 N	104·26 W
110	Rattlesnake Cr. (răt″l snāk) Or.	42·38 N	117·39 W
156	Rättvik (rĕt′vēk) Swe.	60·54 N	15·07 E
158	Ratzeburger See (L.) (rä′tzĕ-bōōr-gĕr-zā) G.D.R.	53·48 N	11·02 E
137	Rauch (rá′ōōch) Arg. (Buenos Aires In.)	36·47 S	59·05 W
156	Raufoss (rou′fôs) Nor.	60·44 N	10·30 E
137	Raúl Soares (rä-ōō′l-sôä′rĕs) Braz. (Rio de Janeiro In.)	20·05 S	42·28 W
157	Rauma (rä′ōō-mȧ) Fin.	61·07 N	21·31 E
157	Rauna (rāû′nȧ) Sov. Un.	57·21 N	25·31 E
196	Raung, Gunung (Mtn.) Indon.	8·15 S	113·56 E
186	Raurkela India	22·15 N	84·53 E
157	Rautalampi (rä′ōō-tĕ-läm′pô) Fin.	62·39 N	26·25 E
159	Rava-Russkaya (rä′vȧ rōōs′kä-yȧ) Sov. Un.	50·14 N	23·40 E
164	Ravenna (rä-vĕn′nä) It.	44·27 N	12·13 E
108	Ravenna (rȧ-vĕn′ȧ) Ne.	41·20 N	98·50 W
104	Ravenna Oh.	41·10 N	81·20 W
158	Ravensburg (rä′vĕns-bōōrgh) F.R.G.	47·48 N	9·35 E
112	Ravensdale (rā′vĕnz-dāl) Wa. (Seattle In.)	47·22 N	121·58 W
204	Ravensthorpe (rā′vĕns-thôrp) Austl.	33·30 S	120·20 E
104	Ravenswood (rā′vĕnz-wŏŏd) WV	38·55 N	81·50 W
184	Rāwalpindi (rä-wŭl-pēn′dē) Pak.	33·40 N	73·10 E
186	Rawāndūz Iraq	36·37 N	44·30 E
158	Rawicz (rä′vēch) Pol.	51·36 N	16·51 E
204	Rawlina (rôr-lēnȧ) Austl.	31·13 S	125·45 E
111	Rawlins (rô′lĭnz) Wy.	41·46 N	107·15 W
136	Rawson (rô′sŭn) Arg.	43·16 S	65·09 W
137	Rawson Arg. (Buenos Aires In.)	34·36 S	60·03 W
148	Rawtenstall (rô′tĕn-stôl) Eng.	53·42 N	2·17 W
99	Ray, C. (rā) Can.	47·40 N	59·18 W
196	Raya, Bukit (Mtn.) Indon.	0·45 S	112·11 E
173	Raychikinsk (rī′chĭ-kēnsk) Sov. Un.	49·52 N	129·17 E
148	Rayleigh (rā′lê) Eng. (London In.)	51·35 N	0·36 E
93	Raymond (rā′mŭnd) Can.	49·27 N	112·39 W
110	Raymond Wa.	46·41 N	123·42 W
116	Raymondville (rā′mŭnd-vĭl) Tx.	26·30 N	97·46 W
100	Ray Mts. Ak.	65·40 N	151·45 W
119	Rayne (rān) La.	30·12 N	92·15 W

Page	Name Pronunciation Region	Lat. °′	Long. °′
124	Rayón (rä-yōn′) Mex.	21·49 N	99·39 W
213	Rayton (rā′tŭn) S. Afr. (Johannesburg & Pretoria In.)	25·45 S	28·33 E
113	Raytown (rā′toun) Mo. (Kansas City In.)	39·01 N	94·48 W
119	Rayville (rā-vĭl) La.	32·28 N	91·46 W
160	Raz, Pte. du (Pt.) (pwänt dü rä) Fr.	48·02 N	4·43 W
167	Razdel′naya (räz-dĕl′nä-yȧ) Sov. Un.	46·47 N	30·08 E
194	Razdol′noye (räz-dôl′nô-yĕ) Sov. Un.	43·38 N	131·58 E
165	Razgrad Bul.	43·32 N	26·32 E
165	Razlog (räz′lôk) Bul.	41·54 N	23·32 E
92	Razorback Mtn. (rā′zēr-băk) Can.	51·35 N	124·42 W
160	Ré, Île de (I.) (ēl dē rā′) Fr.	46·10 N	1·53 W
148	Rea (R.) (rē) Eng.	52·25 N	2·31 W
89	Reaburn (rā′bûrn) Can. (Winnipeg In.)	50·06 N	97·53 W
148	Reading (rĕd′ĭng) Eng. (London In.)	51·25 N	0·58 W
99	Reading Ma (In.)	42·32 N	71·07 W
104	Reading Mi.	41·45 N	84·45 W
107	Reading Oh. (Cincinnati In.)	39·14 N	84·26 W
105	Reading Pa.	40·20 N	75·55 W
136	Realengo (rĕ-ä-lān-gô) Braz. (Rio de Janeiro In.)	23·50 S	43·25 W
211	Rebiana (Oasis) Libya	24·10 N	22·03 E
194	Rebun (I.) (rē′bōōn) Jap.	45·25 N	140·54 E
164	Recanati (rā-kä-nä′tē) It.	43·25 N	13·35 E
204	Recherche, Arch. of the (rē-shârsh′) Austl.	34·17 S	122·30 E
166	Rechitsa (ryĕ′chēt-sȧ) Sov. Un.	52·22 N	30·24 E
135	Recife (Pernambuco) (rå-sē′fĕ) (pĕr-näm-bōō′kô) Braz.	8·09 S	34·59 W
213	Recife, Kapp (C.) (rȧ-sē′fĕ) S. Afr. (Natal In.)	34·03 S	25·43 E
136	Reconquista (rā-kôn-kēs′tä) Arg.	29·01 S	59·41 W
117	Rector (rĕk′tēr) Ar.	36·16 N	90·21 W
95	Red (R.) (rĕd) Can.-U. S.	49·11 N	97·18 W
120	Red (R.) Tn.	36·35 N	86·55 W
116	Red (R.), North Fk. Tx.	35·20 N	100·08 W
103	Red (R.) U. S.	31·40 N	92·55 W
110	Redan (rê-dăn′) (rĕd′ăn) Ga. (Atlanta In.)	33·44 N	84·09 W
110	Red Bank (băngk) NJ (New York In.)	40·21 N	74·06 W
112	Red Bluff (blŭf) Ca.	40·10 N	122·14 W
118	Red Bluff Res. Tx.	32·03 N	103·52 W
109	Redby (rĕd′bê) Mn.	47·52 N	94·55 W
109	Red Cedar (R.) (sē′dēr) Wi.	45·03 N	91·48 W
94	Redcliff (rĕd′clĭf) Can.	50·05 N	110·47 W
109	Red Cliff Ind. Res. Wi.	46·48 N	91·22 W
197	Redcliffe (rĕd′clĭf) Austl.	27·20 S	153·12 E
116	Red Cloud (kloud) Ne.	40·06 N	98·32 W
93	Red Deer (dēr) Can.	52·16 N	113·48 W
93	Red Deer (R.) Can.	52·05 N	113·00 W
94	Red Deer (R.) Can.	52·55 N	102·10 W
95	Red Deer L. Can.	52·58 N	101·28 W
111	Reddick (rĕd′dĭk) Il. (Chicago In.)	41·06 N	88·16 W
110	Redding (rĕd′ĭng) Ca.	40·36 N	122·25 W
137	Redenção da Serra (rĕ-dĕn-soun-dä-sĕ′r-rä) Braz. (Rio de Janeiro In.)	23·17 S	45·31 W
108	Redfield (rĕd′fēld) SD	44·53 N	98·30 W
119	Red Fish Bar Tx. (In.)	29·29 N	94·53 W
99	Red Indian L. (ĭn′dĭ-ăn) Can.	48·40 N	56·50 W
161	Redklinghausen (rĕk′lĭng-hou-zĕn) F.R.G. (Ruhr In.)	51·36 N	7·13 E
95	Red Lake (lāk) Can.	51·03 N	93·49 W
108	Red Lake (R.) Mn.	48·02 N	96·04 W
108	Red Lake Falls (lāk fôls) Mn.	47·52 N	96·17 W
108	Red Lake Ind. Res. Mn.	48·09 N	95·55 W
113	Redlands (rĕd′lăndz) Ca. (Los Angeles In.)	34·04 N	117·11 W
105	Red Lion (lī′ŭn) Pa.	39·55 N	76·30 W
111	Red Lodge Mt.	45·13 N	107·16 W
112	Redmond (rĕd′mŭnd) Wa. (Seattle In.)	47·40 N	122·07 W
158	Rednitz R. (rĕd′nētz) F.R.G.	49·10 N	11·00 E
108	Red Oak (ōk) Ia.	41·00 N	95·12 W
160	Redon (rē-dôn′) Fr.	47·42 N	2·03 W
136	Redonda, Isla (ē′s-lä-rĕ-dô′n-dä) Braz. (Rio de Janeiro In.)	23·05 S	43·11 W
127	Redonda I. (rĕ-dŏn′dȧ) Antigua (In.)	16·55 N	62·28 W
162	Redondela (rā-dhôn-dā′lä) Sp.	42·16 N	8·34 W
162	Redondo (rå-dôn′dōō) Port.	38·40 N	7·32 W
112	Redondo (rê-dŏn′dō) Wa. (Seattle In.)	47·21 N	122·19 W
113	Redondo Beach Ca. (Los Angeles In.)	33·50 N	118·23 W
93	Red Pass (pås) Can.	52·59 N	118·59 W
116	Red R., Prairie Dog Town Fk. (prā′rĭ) Tx.	34·54 N	101·31 W
116	Red R., Salt Fk. Tx.	35·04 N	100·31 W
188	Red R. Viet.	22·25 N	103·50 E
111	Red Rock Cr. Mt.	44·54 N	112·44 W

Page	Name Pronunciation Region	Lat. °′	Long. °′
211	Red Sea Afr.-Asia	23·15 N	37·00 E
92	Redstone (rĕd′stōn) Can.	52·08 N	123·42 W
95	Red Sucker L. (sŭk′ēr) Can.	54·09 N	93·40 W
111	Redwater Cr. Mt.	47·37 N	105·25 W
116	Red Willow Cr. Ne.	40·34 N	100·48 W
109	Red Wing Mn.	44·34 N	92·35 W
112	Redwood City (rĕd′ wŏŏd) Ca. (San Francisco In.)	37·29 N	122·13 W
109	Redwood Falls Mn.	44·32 N	95·06 W
154	Ree, Lough (B.) (lŏκ′rē′) Ire.	53·30 N	7·45 W
104	Reed City (rēd) Mi.	43·50 N	85·35 W
95	Reed L. Can.	54·37 N	100·30 W
114	Reedley (rēd′lê) Ca.	36·37 N	119·27 W
109	Reedsburg (rēdz′bûrg) Wi.	43·32 N	90·01 W
110	Reedsport (rēdz′pôrt) Or.	43·42 N	124·08 W
120	Reelfoot (R.) (rēl′fŏŏt) Tn.	36·18 N	89·20 W
161	Rees (rĕz) F.R.G. (Ruhr In.)	51·46 N	6·25 E
203	Reeves, Mt. (rēv′s) Austl.	33·50 S	149·56 E
120	Reform (rê-fôrm′) Al.	33·23 N	88·00 W
119	Refugio (rå-fōō′hyô) (rĕ-fū′jō) Tx.	28·18 N	97·15 W
158	Rega (R.) (rĕ-gä) Pol.	53·48 N	15·30 E
158	Regen R. (rā′ghĕn) F.R.G.	49·09 N	12·21 E
158	Regensburg (rā′ghĕns-bōōrgh) F.R.G.	49·02 N	12·06 E
210	Reggane Alg.	27·08 N	0·06 E
164	Reggio (rĕ′jô) It.	44·43 N	10·34 E
106	Reggio (rĕg′jĭ-ō) La. (New Orleans In.)	29·50 N	89·46 W
164	Reggio di Calabria (rĕ′jô dē kä-lä′brê-ä) It.	38·07 N	15·42 E
159	Reghin (rå-gēn′) Rom.	46·47 N	24·44 E
94	Regina (rê-jī′nȧ) Can.	50·25 N	104·39 W
119	Regla (rāg′lä) Cuba (In.)	23·08 N	82·20 W
158	Regnitz (R.) (rĕg′nētz) F.R.G.	49·50 N	10·55 E
162	Reguengos de Monsaraz (rå-gĕŋ′gōzh dā mōn-sä-räzh′) Port.	38·26 N	7·30 W
212	Rehoboth Namibia	23·10 S	17·15 E
183	Rehovot Isr. (Palestine In.)	31·53 N	34·49 E
158	Reichenbach (rī′kĕn-bäκ) G.D.R.	50·36 N	12·18 E
121	Reidsville (rēdz′vĭl) NC	36·20 N	79·37 W
148	Reigate (rī′gāt) Eng. (London In.)	51·12 N	0·12 W
160	Reims (răns) Fr.	49·16 N	4·00 E
136	Reina Adelaida, Arch. (är-chē′-pyĕ′lȧ-gô-rā′nä-ä-dĕ-lī′dä) Chile	52·00 S	74·15 W
109	Reinbeck (rīn′bĕk) Ia.	42·22 N	92·34 W
90	Reindeer (L.) (rān′dēr) Can.	57·36 N	101·23 W
94	Reindeer (R.) Can.	55·45 N	103·30 W
95	Reindeer I. Can.	52·25 N	98·00 W
95	Reindeer L. Can.	57·15 N	102·40 W
162	Reinosa (rå-ê-nō′sä) Sp.	43·01 N	4·08 W
106	Reistertown (rēs′tēr-toun) Md. (Baltimore In.)	39·28 N	76·50 W
218	Reitz S. Afr. (Johannesburg & Pretoria In.)	27·48 S	28·25 E
186	Rema, Jabal (Mtn.) Yemen	14·13 N	44·38 E
183	Rembau Mala. (Singapore In.)	2·36 N	102·06 E
134	Remedios (rĕ-mĕ′dyôs) Col. (In.)	7·03 N	74·42 W
128	Remedios (rā-mā′dhē-ōs) Cuba	22·30 N	79·35 W
127	Remedios (rĕ-mĕ′dyōs) Pan.	8·14 N	81·46 W
161	Remiremont (rē-mēr-môn′) Fr.	48·01 N	6·35 E
183	Rempang I. Indon. (Singapore In.)	0·51 N	104·04 E
161	Remscheid (rĕm′shīt) F.R.G. (Ruhr In.)	51·10 N	7·11 E
205	Rendova (I.) (rĕn′dô-vȧ) Sol. Is.	8·38 S	156·26 E
158	Rendsburg (rĕnts′bōōrgh) F.R.G.	54·19 N	9·39 E
105	Renfrew (rĕn′frōō) Can.	45·30 N	76·30 W
183	Rengam (rĕn′gäm′) Mala. (Singapore In.)	1·53 N	103·24 E
137	Rengo (rĕn′gō) Chile (Santiago In.)	34·22 S	70·50 W
167	Reni (ran′) Sov. Un.	45·26 N	28·18 E
203	Renmark (rĕn′märk) Austl.	34·10 S	140·50 E
205	Rennel (I.) (rĕn-nĕl′) Sol. Is.	11·50 S	160·38 E
160	Rennes (rĕn) Fr.	48·07 N	1·02 W
105	Rensselaer (rĕn′sĕ-lâr) NY	42·40 N	73·45 W
114	Reno (rē′nō) Nv.	39·32 N	119·49 W
164	Reno (R.) (rā′nô) It.	44·10 N	10·55 E
105	Renovo (rê-nō′vō) Pa.	41·20 N	77·50 W
104	Rensselaer (rĕn′sĕ-lâr) In.	41·00 N	87·10 W
113	Rentchler (rĕnt′chlēr) Il. (St. Louis In.)	38·30 N	89·52 W
112	Renton (rĕn′tŭn) Wa. (Seattle In.)	47·29 N	122·13 W
109	Renville (rĕn′vĭl) Mn.	44·44 N	95·13 W
89	Repentigny Can. (Montreal In.)	45·47 N	73·26 W
106	Republic (rê-pŭb′lĭk) Al. (Birmingham In.)	33·37 N	86·54 W
110	Republic Wa.	48·38 N	118·44 W
116	Republican (R.), South Fk. (rê-pŭb′lĭ-kăn) Co.	39·35 N	102·28 W
117	Republican (R.) Ks.	39·40 N	97·40 W
205	Repulse B. (rê-pŭls′) Austl.	20·56 S	149·22 E
162	Requena (rå-kā′nä) Sp.	39·29 N	1·03 W
137	Resende (rĕ-sĕ′n-dĕ) Braz. (Rio de Janeiro In.)	22·30 S	44·26 W
137	Resende Costa (kôs-tä) Braz. (Rio de Janeiro In.)	20·55 S	44·12 W
167	Reshetilovka (ryĕ′ shĕ-tē-lôf-kȧ) Sov. Un.	49·34 N	34·04 E
136	Resistencia (rä-sēs-tĕn′syä) Arg.	27·24 S	58·54 W

Page	Name Pronunciation Region	Lat. °′	Long. °′
165	Reşita (râ'shê-tà) Rom.	45·18 N	21·56 E
75	Resolute (rĕz-ô-lūt') Can.	74·41 N	95·00 W
91	Resolution (I.) (rĕz-ô-lū'shŭn) Can.	61·30 N	63·58 W
205	Resolution (I.) (rĕz-ŏl-ûshûn) N. Z. (In.)	45·43 S	166·00 E
98	Restigouche (R.) (rĕs-tê-gōōsh') Can.	47·35 N	67·35 W
134	Restrepo (rĕs-trĕ'pô) Col. (In.)	3·49 N	76·31 W
134	Restrepo Col. (In.)	4·16 N	73·32 W
126	Retalhuleu (rā-tāl-ōō-lān') Guat.	14·31 N	91·41 W
160	Rethel (r-tl') Fr.	49·34 N	4·20 E
164	Réthimnon Grc. (In.)	35·21 N	24·30 E
149	Retie Bel. (Brussels In.)	51·16 N	5·08 E
112	Retsil (rĕt'sĭl) Wa. (Seattle In.)	47·33 N	122·37 W
220	Reunion (rā-ü-nyôn') Afr.	21·06 S	55·36 E
163	Reus (rā'ōōs) Sp.	41·08 N	1·05 E
158	Reutlingen (roit'lĭng-ĕn) F.R.G.	48·29 N	9·14 E
174	Reutov (rĕ-ōōt'ôf) Sov. Un. (Moscow In.)	55·45 N	37·52 E
	Reval, see Tallinn		
174	Revda (ryâv'dá) Sov. Un. (Urals In.)	56·48 N	59·57 E
93	Revelstoke (rĕv'ĕl-stōk) Can.	51·59 N	118·12 W
127	Reventazon, R. (rå-vĕn-tä-zōn') C. R.	10·10 N	83·30 W
99	Revere (rê-vēr') Ma. (In.)	42·24 N	71·01 W
92	Revillagigedo Chan (rĕ-vĭl'a-gĭ-gē'dō) Ak.	55·10 N	131·13 W
92	Revillagigedo I. Ak.	55·35 N	131·23 W
122	Revillagigedo, Islas (I.) (ĕ's-läs-rĕ-vêl-yä-hĕ'gĕ-dô) Mex.	18·45 N	111·00 W
160	Revin (rē-văN) Fr.	49·56 N	4·34 E
184	Rewa (rā'wä) India	24·41 N	81·11 E
184	Rewāri India	28·19 N	76·39 E
111	Rexburg (rĕks'bûrg) Id.	43·50 N	111·48 W
118	Rey, L. (rā) Mex.	27·00 N	103·33 W
127	Rey, Isla del (I.) (ē's-lä-dĕl-rā'ē) Pan.	8·20 N	78·40 W
134	Reyes (rā'yĕs) Bol.	14·19 S	67·16 W
114	Reyes, Pt. Ca.	38·00 N	123·00 W
146	Reykjanes (C.) (rā'kyà-nĕs) Ice.	63·37 N	24·33 W
150	Reykjavik (rā'kyà-vēk) Ice.	64·09 N	21·39 W
118	Reynosa (rā-ê-nō'sä) Mex.	26·05 N	98·21 W
186	Rezā'īyeh (rĕ-zī'â) Iran	37·30 N	45·15 E
166	Rēzekne (rå'zĕk-nĕ) Sov. Un.	56·31 N	27·19 E
174	Rezh (rĕzh') Sov. Un. (Urals In.)	57·22 N	61·23 E
167	Rezina (ryĕzh'ĕ-nĭ) Sov. Un.	47·44 N	28·56 E
164	Rhaetien Alps (Mts.) It.	46·22 N	10·33 E
155	Rheden (rā'dĕn) Neth.	52·02 N	6·02 E
161	Rheinberg (rīn'bĕrgh) F.R.G. (Ruhr In.)	51·33 N	6·37 E
158	Rheine (rī'nĕ) F.R.G.	52·16 N	7·26 E
158	Rheinland-Pfalz (Rhineland-Palatinate) (State) F.R.G.	50·05 N	6·40 E
158	Rhein R. (rīn) F.R.G.	50·34 N	7·21 E
161	Rheydt (rĕ'yt) F.R.G. (Ruhr In.)	51·10 N	6·28 E
140	Rhine (R.) Eur.	50·34 N	7·21 E
109	Rhinelander (rīn'lăn-dēr) Wi.	45·39 N	89·25 W
149	Rhin Kanal (Can.) (rēn kä-näl') G.D.R. (Berlin In.)	52·47 N	12·40 E
149	Rhin R. (rēn) G.D.R. (Berlin In.)	52·52 N	12·49 E
106	Rhode I. RI (Providence In.)	41·31 N	71·14 W
103	Rhode Island (State) (rōd ī'lănd) U. S.	41·35 N	71·40 W
213	Rhodes (rôdz) S. Afr. (Natal In.)	30·48 S	27·56 E
209	Rhodesia (rô-dē'zhĭ-à) Afr.	17·50 S	29·30 E
165	Rhodope Mts. (rô'dô-pĕ) Bul.	42·00 N	24·08 E
154	Rhondda (rŏn'dhå) Wales	51·40 N	3·40 W
160	Rhône (R.) (rōn) Fr.	45·14 N	4·53 E
149	Rhoon Neth. (Amsterdam In.)	51·52 N	4·24 E
154	Rhum (I.) (rŭm) Scot.	57·00 N	6·20 W
135	Riachão (rê-ä-chouN') Braz.	7·15 S	46·30 W
113	Rialto (rē-ăl'tō) Ca. (In.)	34·06 N	117·23 W
183	Riau (Prov.) Indon. (Singapore In.)	0·56 N	101·25 E
196	Riau, Kepulauan (I.) Indon.	0·30 N	104·55 E
183	Riau, Selat (Str.) Indon. (Singapore In.)	0·40 N	104·27 E
162	Riaza (R.) (rê-ä'thä) Sp.	41·25 N	3·25 W
162	Ribadavia (rē-bä-dhä'vê-ä) Sp.	42·18 N	8·06 W
162	Ribadeo (rē-bä-dhā'ō) Sp.	37·32 N	7·05 W
162	Ribadesella (rē'bä-dä-sāl'yä) Sp.	43·30 N	5·02 W
217	Ribauè Moz.	14·57 S	38·17 E
154	Ribble, R. (rĭb''l) Eng.	53·10 N	3·15 W
156	Ribe (rē'bĕ) Den.	55·20 N	8·45 E
137	Ribeirão Prêto (rē-bā-rouN-prĕ'tô) Braz. (Rio de Janeiro In.)	21·11 S	47·47 W
116	Ribera (rē-bĕ'rä) NM	35·23 N	105·27 W
134	Riberalta (rē-bā-räl'tä) Bol.	11·06 S	66·02 W
109	Rib Lake (rĭb lāk) Wi.	45·20 N	90·11 W
114	Rice (rīs) Ca.	34·05 N	114·50 W
105	Rice (L.) Can.	44·05 N	78·10 W
113	Rice L. Mn. (Minneapolis, St. Paul In.)	45·10 N	93·09 W
109	Rice Lake Wi.	45·30 N	91·44 W
101	Richards I. (rĭch'ērds) Can.	69·45 N	135·30 W
113	Richards Landing (lănd'ĭng) Can. (Sault Ste. Marie In.)	46·18 N	84·02 W
113	Richardson (rĭch'ērd-sŭn) Tx. (Dallas, Fort Worth In.)	32·56 N	96·44 W
112	Richardson Wa. (Seattle In.)	48·27 N	122·54 W
90	Richardson Mts. Can.	66·58 N	136·19 W
105	Richardson Park (pärk) De.	39·45 N	75·35 W
105	Richelieu (R.) (rēsh'lyû') Can.	45·05 N	73·25 W
113	Richfield (rĭch-fēld) Mn. (Minneapolis, St. Paul In.)	44·53 N	93·17 W
107	Richfield Oh. (Cleveland In.)	41·14 N	81·38 W
115	Richfield Ut.	38·45 N	112·05 W
105	Richford (rĭch'fērd) Vt.	45·00 N	72·35 W
117	Rich Hill (rĭch hĭl) Mo.	38·05 N	94·21 W
98	Richibucto (rĭ-chĭ-bŭk'tō) Can.	46·41 N	64·52 W
120	Richland (rĭch'lănd) Ga.	32·05 N	84·40 W
110	Richland Wa.	46·17 N	119·19 W
109	Richland Center (sĕn'tēr) Wi.	43·20 N	90·25 W
205	Richmond (rĭch'mŭnd) Austl.	20·47 S	143·14 E
202	Richmond Austl. (Sydney In.)	33·36 S	150·45 E
112	Richmond Ca. (San Francisco In.)	37·56 N	122·21 W
98	Richmond Can.	45·40 N	72·07 W
89	Richmond Can. (Ottawa In.)	45·12 N	75·49 W
107	Richmond Il. (Chicago In.)	42·29 N	88·18 W
104	Richmond In.	39·50 N	85·00 W
104	Richmond Ky.	37·45 N	84·20 W
117	Richmond Mo.	39·16 N	93·58 W
119	Richmond Tx.	29·35 N	95·45 W
213	Richmond S. Afr. (Natal In.)	29·52 S	30·17 E
111	Richmond Ut.	41·55 N	111·50 W
105	Richmond Va.	37·35 N	77·30 W
112	Richmond Beach Wa. (Seattle In.)	47·47 N	122·23 W
113	Richmond Heights Mo. (St. Louis In.)	38·38 N	90·20 W
112	Richmond Highlands Wa. (Seattle In.)	47·46 N	122·22 W
89	Richmond Hill (hĭl) Can. (Toronto In.)	43·53 N	79·26 W
120	Richton (rĭch'tŭn) Ms.	31·20 N	89·54 W
104	Richwood (rĭch'wŏŏd) WV	38·10 N	80·30 W
149	Ridderkerk Neth. (Amsterdam In.)	51·52 N	4·35 E
89	Rideau (R.) Can. (Ottawa In.)	45·17 N	75·41 W
105	Rideau L. (rê-dō') Can.	44·40 N	76·20 W
106	Ridgefield (rĭj'fēld) Ct. (New York In.)	41·16 N	73·30 W
112	Ridgefield Wa. (Portland In.)	45·49 N	122·40 W
105	Rigeley (rĭj'lē) WV	39·40 N	78·45 W
107	Ridgeway (rĭj'wā) Can. (Buffalo In.)	42·53 N	79·02 W
106	Ridgewood (ridj'wŏŏd) NJ (New York In.)	40·59 N	74·08 W
105	Ridgway Pa.	41·25 N	78·40 W
95	Riding Mtn. (rīd'ĭng) Can.	50·37 N	99·37 W
90	Riding Mountain Natl. Park (rīd'ĭng) Can.	50·59 N	99·19 W
128	Riding Rocks (Is.) Ba.	25·20 N	79·10 W
213	Riebeek-Oos S. Afr. (Natal In.)	33·14 S	26·09 E
158	Ried (rēd) Aus.	48·13 N	13·30 E
158	Riesa (rē'zà) G.D.R.	51·17 N	13·17 E
164	Rieti (rē-ā'tē) It.	42·25 N	12·51 E
213	Rievleidam (L.) S. Afr. (Johannesburg & Pretoria In.)	25·52 S	28·18 E
115	Rifle (rī'f'l) Co.	39·35 N	107·50 W
157	Rīga (rē'gà) Sov. Un.	56·55 N	24·05 E
157	Riga, G. of Sov. Un.	57·56 N	23·05 E
186	Rīgān Iran	28·45 N	58·55 E
89	Rigaud (rê-gō') Can. (Montreal In.)	45·29 N	74·18 W
111	Rigby (rĭg'bê) Id.	43·40 N	111·55 W
186	Rīgestān (Reg.) Afr.	30·53 N	64·42 E
91	Rigolet (rĭg-ō-lā') Can.	54·10 N	58·40 W
157	Riihimäki Fin.	60·44 N	24·44 E
164	Rijeka (Fiume) (rĭ-yĕ'kä) Yugo.	45·22 N	14·24 E
149	Rijkevorsel Bel. (Brussels In.)	51·21 N	4·46 E
149	Rijswijk Neth. (Amsterdam In.)	52·03 N	4·19 E
159	Rika R. (rē'kà) Sov. Un.	48·21 N	23·37 E
160	Rille (R.) (rēl) Fr.	49·12 N	0·43 E
215	Rima (R.) Nig.	13·30 N	5·50 E
159	Rimavska Sobota (rē'màf-skä sô'bô-tà) Czech.	48·25 N	20·01 E
156	Rimbo (rēm'bōō) Swe.	59·45 N	18·22 E
164	Rimini (rē'mê-nē) It.	44·03 N	12·33 E
165	Rîmnicu Sărat Rom.	45·24 N	27·06 E
165	Rîmnicu-Vîlcea Rom.	45·07 N	24·22 E
98	Rimouski (rê-mōōs'kê) Can.	48·27 N	68·32 W
124	Rinc n de Romos (rên-kōn dā rô-mōs') Mex.	22·13 N	102·21 W
156	Ringkøbing (rĭng'kûb-ĭng) Den.	56·06 N	8·14 E
156	Ringkøbing Fd. Den.	55·55 N	8·04 E
156	Ringsaker (rĭngs'äk-ĕr) Nor.	60·55 N	10·40 E
156	Ringsted (rĭng'stĕdh) Den.	55·27 N	11·49 E
150	Ringvassöy (I.) (rĭng'väs-ûê) Nor.	69·58 N	16·43 E
202	Ringwood Austl. (Melbourne In.)	37·49 S	145·14 E
196	Rinjani, Gunung (Mtn.) Indon.	8·39 S	116·22 E
122	Rio Abajo (rê'ō-ä-bä'ĸō) Pan. (In.)	9·01 N	78·30 W
124	Rio Balsas (rê'ō-bäl-säs) Mex.	17·59 N	99·45 W
134	Riobamba (rē'ō-bäm-bä) Ec.	1·45 S	78·37 W
137	Rio Bonito (rē'ōō bō-nē'tōō) Braz. (Rio de Janeiro In.)	22·44 S	42·38 W
134	Rio Branco (rē'ōō bräŋ'kōō) Braz.	9·57 S	67·50 W
136	Río Branco (rīō blăncō) Ur.	32·33 S	53·29 W
135	Rio Branco (Ter.) Braz.	2·35 N	61·25 W
137	Rio Casca (rē'ō-kà's-kä) Braz. (Rio de Janeiro In.)	20·15 S	42·39 W
135	Río Chico (rê'ō chē'kŏ) Ven. (In.)	10·20 N	65·58 W
137	Rio Claro (rē'ōō klä'rōō) Braz. (Rio de Janeiro In.)	21·25 S	47·33 W
136	Río Cuarto (rē'ō kwär'tō) Arg.	33·05 S	64·15 W
137	Rio das Flores (rē'ō-däs-flô-rĕs) Braz. (Rio de Janeiro In.)	22·10 S	43·35 W
136	Rio de Janeiro (rē'ōō dā zhä-nâ'ê-rōō) Braz. (Rio de Janeiro In.)	22·50 S	43·20 W
135	Rio de Janeiro (State) Braz.	22·27 S	42·43 W
127	Río de Jesús (rê'ō-dĕ-ĸĕ-sōō's) Pan.	7·54 N	80·59 W
136	Río Dercero (rê'ō dĕr-sĕ'rô) Arg.	32·12 S	63·59 W
125	Rio Frío (rê'ō-frē'ô) Mex. (In.)	19·21 N	98·40 W
136	Río Gallegos (rē'ō gä-lā'gōs) Arg.	51·43 S	69·15 W
136	Rio Grande (rē'ōō grän'dĕ) Braz.	31·04 S	52·14 W
124	Rio Grande (rē'ō grän'dā) Mex.	23·51 N	102·59 W
118	Riogrande (rē'ō grán-dā) Tx.	26·23 N	98·48 W
115	Rio Grande (R.) (rē'ōō grän'dĕ) Co.	37·44 N	106·51 W
135	Rio Grande do Norte (State) (rē'ōō grän'dĕ dōō nôr'tĕ) Braz.	5·26 S	37·20 W
136	Rio Grande do Sul (State) (rē'ōō grän'dĕ-dô-sōō'l) Braz.	29·00 S	54·00 W
134	Ríohacha (rē'ō-ä'chä) Col.	11·30 N	72·54 W
127	Río Hato (rê'ō-ä'tô) Pan.	8·19 N	80·11 W
160	Riom (rê-ôN') Fr.	45·54 N	3·08 E
209	Rio Muni (Prov.) (rē'ō mōō'nê) Equat. Gui.	1·47 N	8·33 E
134	Ríonegro (rê'ō-nĕ'grō) Col. (In.)	6·09 N	75·22 W
136	Río Negro (Prov.) (rē'ō nā'grō) Arg.	40·15 S	68·15 W
137	Río Negro (Dept.) (rê'ō-nĕ'grō) Ur. (Buenos Aires In.)	32·48 S	57·45 W
136	Rio Negro, Embalse del (Res.) (ĕm-bä'l-sĕ-dĕl-rē'ō-nĕ'grō) Ur.	32·45 S	55·50 W
164	Rionero (rē-ō-nā'rô) It.	40·55 N	15·42 E
137	Rio Novo (rē'ō-nô'vō) Braz. (Rio de Janeiro In.)	21·30 S	43·08 W
135	Rio Pardo de Minas (rē'ō pär'dō-dĕ-mē'näs) Braz.	15·43 S	42·24 W
137	Rio Pombo (rē'ō pôm'bä) Braz. (Rio de Janeiro In.)	21·17 S	43·09 W
137	Rio Sorocaba, Represado (Res.) (rĕ-prĕ-sä-dô-rē'ō-sô-rō-kä'bä) Braz. (Rio de Janeiro In.)	23·37 S	47·19 W
134	Ríosucio (rē'ō-sōō'syô) Col. (In.)	5·25 N	75·41 W
163	Riou, Oued (R.) (ōō-ĕd rĭ-ōō) Alg.	35·45 N	1·18 E
196	Riouw, Pulau-Pulau (Is.) Indon.	0·30 N	104·55 E
135	Rio Verde (vĕr'dĕ) Braz.	17·47 S	50·49 W
124	Ríoverde (rē'ō-vĕr'dâ) Mex.	21·54 N	99·59 W
148	Ripley (rĭp'lē) Eng.	53·03 N	1·24 W
120	Ripley Ms.	34·44 N	88·55 W
120	Ripley Tn.	35·44 N	89·34 W
163	Ripoll (rê-pōl'') Sp.	42·10 N	2·10 E
109	Ripon (rĭp'ŏn) Wi.	43·49 N	88·50 W
204	Ripon (I.) Austl.	20·05 S	118·10 E
211	Ripon Falls Ug.	0·38 N	33·02 E
134	Risaralda (Dept.) Col. (In.)	6·45 S	76·00 W
205	Risdon (rĭz'dŭn) Austl.	42·37 S	147·32 E
194	Rishiri (I.) (rē-shē'rē) Jap.	45·10 N	141·08 E
183	Rishon le Ziyyon Isr. (Palestine In.)	31·57 N	34·48 E
184	Rishra India (In.)	22·42 N	88·22 E
104	Rising Sun (rīz'ĭng sŭn) In.	38·55 N	84·55 W
156	Risor (rēs'ûr) Nor.	58·44 N	9·10 E
134	Ritacuva, Alto (Mtn.) (ä'l-tô-rē-tä-kōō'vä) Col.	6·22 N	72·13 W
107	Rittman (rĭt'năn) Oh. (Cleveland In.)	40·58 N	81·47 W
110	Ritzville (rĭts'vĭl) Wa.	47·08 N	118·23 W
156	Riuvenfjell (Mts.) (rĭu-vĕn-fyĕl') Nor.	59·20 N	6·55 E
129	Riva (rē'vä) Dom. Rep.	19·10 N	69·55 W
164	Riva (rē'vä) It.	45·54 N	10·49 E
106	Riva (rī'vä) Md. (Baltimore In.)	38·57 N	76·36 W
126	Rivas (rē'väs) Nic.	11·25 N	85·51 W
160	Rive-de-Gier (rēv-dĕ-zhē-ā') Fr.	45·32 N	4·37 E
136	Rivera (rê-vā'rä) Ur.	30·52 S	55·32 W
210	River Cess (rĭv'ēr sĕs) Lib.	5·46 N	9·52 W
107	Riverdale (rĭv'ēr dāl) Il. (Chicago In.)	41·38 N	87·36 W
113	Riverdale Ut. (Salt Lake City In.)	41·11 N	112·00 W
120	River Falls Al.	31·20 N	86·25 W
109	River Falls Wi.	44·48 N	92·38 W
105	Riverhead (rĭv'ēr hĕd) NY	40·55 N	72·40 W
203	Riverina (Reg.) (rĭv-ēr-ē'nä) Austl.	34·55 S	144·30 E
92	River Jordan (jôr'dăn) Can. (Seattle In.)	48·25 N	124·03 W
113	River Oaks (ōkz) Tx. (Dallas, Fort Worth In.)	32·47 N	97·24 W
107	River Rouge (rōōzh) Mi. (Detroit In.)	42·16 N	83·09 W
95	Rivers Can.	50·01 N	100·15 W

ng-sing; ŋ-baŋk; N-nasalized n; nŏd; cŏmmit; ōld; ôbey; ôrder; fōōd; fŏŏt; ou-out; s-soft; sh-dish; th-thin; pūre; ûnite; ûrn; stŭd; circŭs ü-as "y" in study; '-indeterminate vowel.

Page	Name Pronunciation Region	Lat. °′	Long. °′
113	Riverside (rĭv′ẽr-sīd) Ca. (Los Angeles In.)	33·59 N	117·21 W
106	Riverside....NJ (Philadelphia In.)	40·02 N	74·58 W
92	Rivers Inlet.............Can.	51·45 N	127·15 W
202	Riverstone....Austl. (Sydney In.)	33·41 S	150·52 E
105	Riverton....................Va.	39·00 N	78·15 W
111	Riverton....................Wy.	43·02 N	108·24 W
160	Rivesaltes (rēv′zält′)..........Fr.	42·48 N	2·48 E
121	Riviera Beach (rĭv-ĭ-ẽr′ȧ bēch) Fl. (In.)	26·46 N	80·04 W
106	Riviera Beach. Md. (Baltimore In.)	39·10 N	76·32 W
89	Rivie're Beaudette (bō-dĕt′) Can. (Montreal In.)	45·14 N	74·20 W
98	Rivière-du-Loup (rē-vyâr′ dü lo͞o′) Can.	47·50 N	69·32 W
89	Rivière Que Barre (rēv-yĕr′ kē-bär) Can. (Edmonton In.)	53·47 N	113·51 W
98	Rivière-Trois-Pistoles (trwä′pēs-tôl′) .Can.	48·07 N	69·10 W
186	Riyadh (Ar Rīyāḍ)......Sau. Ar.	24·31 N	46·47 E
171	Rize (rē′zĕ)...............Tur.	41·00 N	40·30 E
165	Rizzuto, C. (rēt-so͞o′tô)........It.	38·53 N	17·05 E
156	Rjukan (ryo͞o′kän)..........Nor.	59·53 N	8·30 E
160	Roanne (rō-än′)..............Fr.	46·02 N	4·04 E
120	Roanoke (rō′ȧ-nōk)..........Al.	33·08 N	85·21 W
121	Roanoke....................Va.	37·16 N	79·55 W
121	Roanoke (R.)...........NC-Va.	36·17 N	77·22 W
121	Roanoke (Staunton) (R.).....Va.	37·05 N	79·20 W
121	Roanoke Rapids.............NC	36·25 N	77·40 W
121	Roanoke Rapids, L...........NC	36·28 N	77·37 W
115	Roan Plat. (rōn)............Co.	39·25 N	108·50 W
126	Roatan (rō-ä-tän′).........Hond.	16·18 N	86·33 W
126	Roatan I..................Hond.	16·19 N	86·46 W
212	Robbeneiland (I.)....S. Afr. (In.)	33·48 S	18·22 E
107	Robbins (rŏb′ĭnz). Il. (Chicago In.)	41·39 N	87·42 W
113	Robbinsdale (rŏb′ĭnz-dāl) Mn. (Minneapolis, St. Paul In.)	45·03 N	93·22 W
112	Robe (rōb)......Wa. (Seattle In.)	48·06 N	121·50 W
205	Roberts, Mt. (rŏb′ẽrts).....Austl.	32·05 S	152·30 E
110	Roberts, Pt. (rŏb′ẽrts) Wa. (Vancouver In.)	48·58 N	123·05 W
99	Robertson, Lac (L.).........Can.	51·00 N	59·10 W
214	Robertsport (rŏb′ẽrts-pōrt)...Lib.	6·45 N	11·22 W
91	Roberval (rŏb′ẽr-vǎl) (rô-bĕr-vȧl′) Can.	48·32 N	72·15 W
104	Robinson (rŏb′ĭn-sŭn).........Il.	39·00 N	87·45 W
99	Robinson's.................Can.	48·16 N	58·50 W
203	Robinvale (rŏb-ĭn′vāl)......Austl.	34·45 S	142·45 E
95	Roblin.....................Can.	51·15 N	101·25 W
93	Robson, Mt. (rŏb′sŭn).......Can.	53·07 N	119·09 W
119	Robstown (rŏbz′toun)........Tx.	27·46 N	97·41 W
163	Roca, Cabo da (C.) (kȧ′bō-dä-rō′kä) Port. (Lisbon In.)	38·47 N	9·30 W
212	Roçadas (rō-kä′däs).........Ang.	16·50 S	15·05 E
135	Rocas, Atol das (Atoll) (ä-tôl-däs-rō′kȧs). Braz.	3·50 S	33·46 W
133	Rocedos São Pedro E São Paulo (I.) (rô-zĕ′dôs-souɴ-pĕ′drō-ĕ-souɴ-päo͞o-lô). Braz.	1·50 N	30·00 W
136	Rocha (rō′chȧs).............Ur.	34·26 S	54·14 W
148	Rochdale (rŏch′dāl).........Eng.	53·37 N	2·09 W
129	Roche à Bateau (rôsh ȧ bȧ-tō′) Hai.	18·10 N	74·00 W
160	Rochefort (rôsh-fŏr′)..........Fr.	45·55 N	0·57 W
109	Rochelle (rō-shĕl′).............Il.	41·53 N	89·06 W
104	Rochester (rŏch′ĕs-tẽr)........In.	41·05 N	86·20 W
107	Rochester.......Mi. (Detroit In.)	42·41 N	83·09 W
109	Rochester...................Mn.	44·01 N	92·30 W
105	Rochester...................NH	43·20 N	71·00 W
105	Rochester...................NY	43·15 N	77·35 W
107	Rochester....Pa. (Pittsburgh In.)	40·42 N	80·16 W
109	Rock (R.).....................Il.	41·40 N	89·52 W
108	Rock (R.)....................Ia.	43·17 N	96·13 W
112	Rock (R.)......Or. (Portland In.)	45·34 N	122·52 W
112	Rock (R.)......Or. (Portland In.)	45·52 N	123·14 W
106	Rockaway (rŏck′ȧ-wā) NJ (New York In.)	40·54 N	74·30 W
202	Rockbank. Austl. (Melbourne In.)	37·44 S	144·40 E
89	Rockcliffe Park (rok′klĭf pärk) Can. (Ottawa In.)	45·27 N	75·40 W
94	Rock Cr. (rŏk).............Can.	49·01 N	107·00 W
107	Rock Cr.........Il. (Chicago In.)	41·16 N	87·54 W
111	Rock Cr.....................Mt.	46·25 N	113·40 W
110	Rock Cr.....................Or.	45·30 N	120·06 W
110	Rock Cr.....................Wa.	47·09 N	117·50 W
106	Rockdale.....Md. (Baltimore In.)	39·22 N	76·49 W
119	Rockdale (rŏk′dāl)...........Tx.	30·39 N	97·00 W
109	Rock Falls (rŏk fôlz)..........Il.	41·45 N	89·42 W
109	Rockford (rŏk′fẽrd)...........Il.	42·16 N	89·07 W
205	Rockhampton (rŏk-hămp′tŭn) Austl.	23·26 S	150·29 E
121	Rockhill (rŏk′hĭl)............SC	34·55 N	81·01 W
121	Rockingham (rŏk′ĭng-hăm).....NC	34·54 N	79·45 W
148	Rockingham For. (rok′ĭng-hăm) Eng.	52·29 N	0·43 W
109	Rock Island..................Il.	41·31 N	90·37 W
110	Rock Island Dam (ī lănd)....Wa.	47·17 N	120·33 W
89	Rockland (rŏk′lănd) Can. (Ottawa In.)	45·33 N	75·17 W
98	Rockland...................Me.	44·06 N	69·09 W
99	Rockland.............Ma. (In.)	42·07 N	70·55 W
203	Rockland Res..............Austl.	36·55 S	142·20 E
120	Rockmart (rŏk′märt).........Ga.	33·58 N	85·00 W
113	Rockmont (rŏk′mŏnt) Wi. (Duluth In.)	46·34 N	91·54 W
104	Rockport (rŏk′pōrt)..........In.	38·20 N	87·00 W
99	Rockport.............Ma. (In.)	42·39 N	70·37 W
117	Rockport....................Mo.	40·25 N	95·30 W
119	Rockport....................Tx.	28·03 N	97·03 W
108	Rock Rapids (răp′ĭdz).........Ia.	43·26 N	96·10 W
129	Rock Sd.....................Ba.	24·50 N	76·05 W
118	Rocksprings (rŏk sprĭngs).....Tx.	30·02 N	100·12 W
111	Rock Springs...............Wy.	41·35 N	109·13 W
135	Rockstone (rŏk′stôn)........Guy.	5·55 N	57·27 W
108	Rock Valley (văl′ĭ)...........Ia.	43·13 N	96·17 W
104	Rockville (rŏk′vĭl)............In.	39·45 N	87·15 W
106	Rockville.....Md. (Baltimore In.)	39·05 N	77·11 W
106	Rockville Centre (sĕn′tẽr) NY (New York In.)	40·39 N	73·39 W
117	Rockwall (rŏk′wôl)...........Tx.	32·55 N	96·23 W
109	Rockwell City (rŏk′wĕl).......Ia.	42·22 N	94·37 W
89	Rockwood (rŏk-wo͝od) Can. (Toronto In.)	43·37 N	80·08 W
98	Rockwood...................Me.	45·39 N	69·45 W
120	Rockwood...................Tn.	35·51 N	84·41 W
111	Rocky Boys Ind. Res.........Mt.	48·08 N	109·34 W
116	Rocky Ford.................Co.	38·02 N	103·43 W
106	Rocky Hill (hĭl) NJ (New York In.)	40·24 N	74·38 W
96	Rocky Island L.............Can.	46·56 N	83·04 W
121	Rocky Mount...............NC	35·55 N	77·47 W
93	Rocky Mountain House.....Can.	52·22 N	114·55 W
116	Rocky Mountain Natl. Park..Co.	40·29 N	106·06 W
75	Rocky Mts.................N. A.	50·00 N	114·00 W
107	Rocky River..Oh. (Cleveland In.)	41·29 N	81·51 W
107	Rocky R., East Br. Oh. (Cleveland In.)	41·13 N	81·43 W
107	Rocky R., West Br. Oh. (Cleveland In.)	41·17 N	81·54 W
129	Rodas (rō′dhȧs)............Cuba	22·20 N	80·35 W
148	Roden (R.) (rō′dĕn).........Eng.	52·49 N	2·38 W
112	Rodeo (rō′dē̇ō) Ca. (San Francisco In.)	38·02 N	122·16 W
118	Rodeo (rō-dā′ō)............Mex.	25·12 N	104·34 W
92	Roderick I. (rŏd′ĕ-rĭk).......Can.	52·40 N	128·22 W
160	Rodez (rô-dĕz′)...............Fr.	44·22 N	2·34 E
153	Rōdhos.....................Grc.	36·24 N	28·15 E
153	Ródhos (I.).................Grc.	36·00 N	28·29 E
159	Rodnei, Muntii (Mts.) (rôd′nĕ-ē) Rom.	47·41 N	24·05 E
166	Rodniki (rôd′nê-kê)......Sov. Un.	57·08 N	41·48 E
165	Rodonit, Kep I (C.)..........Alb.	41·38 N	19·01 E
	Rodosto, see Tekirdağ		
106	Roebling (rōb′lĭng) NJ (Philadelphia In.)	40·07 N	74·48 W
204	Roebourne (rō′bŭrn).......Austl.	20·50 S	117·15 E
204	Roebuck, B. (rō′bŭck)......Austl.	18·15 S	121·10 E
218	Roedtan.................S. Afr. (Johannesburg & Pretoria In.)	24·37 S	29·08 E
155	Roermond (ro͞or′mônt)......Neth.	51·11 N	6·00 E
155	Roeselare..................Bel.	50·55 N	3·05 E
112	Roesiger (L.) (rōz′ĭ-gẽr) Wa. (Seattle In.)	47·59 N	121·56 W
91	Roes Welcome Sd. (rōz).....Can.	64·10 N	87·23 W
166	Rogachëv (rôg′á-chyôf)..Sov. Un.	53·07 N	30·04 E
165	Rogatica (rō-gä′tē-tsä).....Yugo.	43·46 N	19·00 E
159	Rogatin (rô-gä′tĭn)......Sov. Un.	49·22 N	24·37 E
117	Rogers (rŏj-ẽrz)..............Ar.	36·19 N	94·07 W
104	Rogers City.................Mi.	45·30 N	83·50 W
120	Rogersville..................Tn.	36·21 N	83·00 W
160	Rognac (rŏn-yäk′).......Fr. (In.)	43·29 N	5·15 E
134	Rogoaguado (L.) (rō′gō-ä-gwä-dō) Bol.	12·42 S	66·46 W
167	Rogovskaya (rô-gôf′skȧ-yȧ) Sov. Un.	45·43 N	38·42 E
158	Rogózno (rô′gôzh-nô).........Pol.	52·44 N	16·53 E
110	Rogue R. (rōg)...............Or.	42·32 N	124·13 W
156	Röikenviken (rûê′kĕn-vêk-ĕn) Nor.	60·27 N	10·26 E
137	Rojas (rō′häs) Arg. (Buenos Aires In.)	34·11 S	60·42 W
125	Rojo, Cabo (C.) (rō′hō).....Mex.	21·35 N	97·16 W
123	Rojo, Cabo (C.) (rō′hō) P. R. (Puerto Rico In.)	17·55 N	67·14 W
214	Rokel (R.).................S. L.	9·00 N	11·55 W
195	Rokkō-Zan (Mtn.) (rôk′kō zän) Jap. (Osaka In.)	34·46 N	135·16 E
158	Rokycany (rô′kĭ′tsȧ-nĭ)......Czech.	49·44 N	13·37 E
134	Roldanillo (rôl-dä-nē′l-yō) Col. (In.)	4·24 N	76·09 W
117	Rolla.......................Mo.	37·56 N	91·45 W
108	Rolla.......................ND	48·52 N	99·32 W
156	Rollag (ro͞o′lägh)............Nor.	59·55 N	8·48 E
129	Rolleville...................Ba.	23·40 N	76·00 W
203	Roma (rō′mȧ)..............Austl.	26·30 S	148·48 E
213	Roma..........Leso. (Natal In.)	29·28 S	27·43 E
163	Roma (Rome) (rō′mä) (rōm) It. (Rome In.)	41·52 N	12·37 E
99	Romaine (R.) (rô-mĕn′).....Can.	51·22 N	63·23 W
159	Roman (rō′män)..........Rom.	46·56 N	26·57 E
146	Romania (rō-mā′nê-ȧ).......Eur.	46·18 N	22·53 E
121	Romano, C. (rō-mä′nō)...Fl. (In.)	25·48 N	82·00 W
128	Romano, Cayo (I.) (kä′yō-rô-mȧ′nô). Cuba	22·15 N	78·00 W
174	Romanovo (rô-mä′nô-vô) Sov. Un. (Urals In.)	59·09 N	61·24 E
160	Romans-sur-Isère (rô-mäɴ′-sür-ē-sĕr′). Fr.	45·04 N	4·49 E
197	Romblon (rōm-blōn′)...Phil. (In.)	12·34 N	122·16 E
197	Romblon (I.)...........Phil. (In.)	12·33 N	122·17 E
120	Rome (rōm)..................Ga.	34·14 N	85·10 W
105	Rome.......................NY	43·15 N	75·25 W
	Rome, see Roma		
104	Romeo (rō′mē̇-ō)............Mi.	42·50 N	83·00 W
148	Romford (rŭm′fẽrd) Eng. (London In.)	51·35 N	0·11 E
160	Romilly-sur-Seine (rô-mê-yē′sür-sān′). Fr.	48·32 N	3·41 E
124	Romita (rō-mē′tä)..........Mex.	20·53 N	101·32 W
167	Romny (rôm′nĭ).........Sov. Un.	50·46 N	33·31 E
156	Rømø (I.) (rûm′û)..........Den.	55·08 N	8·17 E
113	Romoland (rŏ′mō′lănd) Ca. (Los Angeles In.)	33·44 N	117·11 W
160	Romorantin (rô-mô-räɴ-tăɴ′)..Fr.	47·24 N	1·46 E
183	Rompin....Mala. (Singapore In.)	2·42 N	102·30 E
183	Rompin (R.). Mala. (Singapore In.)	2·54 N	103·10 E
107	Romulus (rom′ū lŭs) Mi. (Detroit In.)	42·14 N	83·24 W
154	Ronaldsay, North (I.).......Scot.	59·21 N	2·23 W
154	Ronaldsay, South (I.) (rŏn′ăld-s′ā). Scot.	59·48 N	2·55 W
111	Ronan (rō′năn)..............Mt.	47·28 N	114·03 W
135	Roncador, Serra do (Mts.) (sĕr′rȧ do͞o rôn-kä-dōr′). Braz.	12·44 S	52·19 W
162	Roncesvalles (rôn-sĕs-vä′l-yĕs). Sp.	43·00 N	1·17 W
104	Ronceverte (rŏn′sē̇-vûrt).....WV	37·45 N	80·30 W
162	Ronda (rōn′dä)..............Sp.	37·45 N	5·10 W
134	Rondônia (Ter.)............Braz.	10·15 S	63·07 W
94	Ronge, Lac la (L.) (rōnzh)...Can.	55·10 N	105·00 W
156	Rønne (rûn′ĕ)...............Den.	55·08 N	14·46 E
156	Ronneby (rōn′ĕ-bü)..........Swe.	56·13 N	15·17 E
220	Ronne Ice Shelf.............Ant.	77·30 S	38·00 W
116	Ront Ra. (Mts.) (rŏnt).......Co.	40·59 N	105·29 W
213	Roodepoort (rō′dĕ-pōrt)....S. Afr. (Johannesburg & Pretoria In.)	26·10 S	27·52 E
117	Roodhouse (ro͞od′hous).........Il.	39·29 N	90·21 W
218	Rooiberg..................S. Afr. (Johannesburg & Pretoria In.)	24·46 S	27·42 E
149	Roosendaal (rō′zĕn-däl) Neth. (Amsterdam In.)	51·32 N	4·27 E
115	Roosevelt (rōz″vĕlt)..........Ut.	40·20 N	110·00 W
115	Roosevelt (R.)...............Az.	33·45 N	111·00 W
135	Roosevelt (R.) (rō′sĕ-vĕlt)...Braz.	9·22 S	60·28 W
220	Roosevelt I.................Ant.	79·30 S	168·00 W
107	Root R.......Wi. (Milwaukee In.)	42·49 N	87·54 W
204	Roper (R.) (rōp′ẽr).........Austl.	14·50 S	134·00 E
174	Ropsha (rôp′shȧ) Sov. Un. (Leningrad In.)	59·44 N	29·53 E
160	Roquefort...................Fr.	43·59 N	3·00 E
134	Roques, Islas los (Is.).......Ven.	21·25 N	67·40 W
137	Roque Pérez (rô′kĕ-pĕ′rĕz) Arg. (Buenos Aires In.)	35·23 S	59·22 W
163	Roquetas (rô-kā′täs)..........Sp.	40·50 N	0·32 E
134	Roraima (Ter.) (rô′rīy-mä)..Braz.	2·00 N	62·15 W
135	Roraima, Mtn. (rô-rä-ē′mä) Ven.-Guy.	5·12 N	60·52 W
156	Röros (rûr′ôs)..............Nor.	62·36 N	11·25 E
158	Rorschach (rōr′shäk).......Switz.	47·27 N	9·28 E
167	Ros′ (R.) (rôs)........Sov. Un.	49·40 N	30·22 E
158	Rosa, Monte (Mt.) (mōn′tā rō′zä). It.	45·56 N	7·51 E
118	Rosales (rō-zä′läs)..........Mex.	28·15 N	100·43 W
197	Rosales (rō-sä′lĕs)........Phil. (In.)	15·54 N	120·38 E
124	Rosamorada (rō′zä-mō-rä′dhä) Mex.	22·06 N	105·16 W
125	Rosaria, Laguna (L.) (lä-go͞o′nä-rō-sȧ′ryä). Mex.	17·50 N	93·51 W
137	Rosario (rō-zä′rē-ō) Arg. (Buenos Aires In.)	32·58 S	60·42 W
135	Rosario (rô-zä′rē-o͞o)........Braz.	2·49 S	44·15 W
124	Rosario.....................Mex.	22·58 N	105·54 W
118	Rosario.....................Mex.	26·31 N	105·40 W
197	Rosario..............Phil. (In.)	13·49 N	121·13 W
137	Rosario....Ur. (Buenos Aires In.)	34·19 S	57·24 E
128	Rosario, Cayo (I.) (kä′yō-rō-sä′ryō). Cuba	21·40 N	81·55 W
136	Rosário do Sul (rô-zä′rē̇-o͞o-dô-so͞o′l). Braz.	30·17 S	54·52 W
135	Rosário Oeste (ō′ĕst′ĕ)......Braz.	14·47 S	56·20 W
112	Rosario Str.......Wa. (Seattle In.)	48·27 N	122·45 W
163	Rosas, Golfo de (G.) (gôl-fô-dĕ-rō′zäs). Sp.	42·10 N	3·20 E
161	Rosbach (rōz′bäĸ) F.R.G. (Ruhr In.)	50·47 N	7·38 E
118	Roscoe (rôs′kō)..............Tx.	32·26 N	100·38 W
108	Roseau (rô-zō′)..............Mn.	48·52 N	95·47 W

ăt; finȧl; rāte; senāte; ärm; ȧsk; sofȧ; fâre; ch-choose; dh-as th in other; bē; ēvent; bĕt; recĕnt; cratẽr; g-go; gh-guttural g; bĭt; ĭ-short neutral; rīde; ĸ-guttural k as ch in German ich;

PRONOUNCING INDEX

Roseau — Sabile 337

Page	Name Pronunciation Region	Lat. °′	Long. °′
127	Roseau...........Dominica (In.)	15·17 N	61·23 W
108	Roseau (R.)................Mn.	48·52 N	96·11 W
110	Roseberg (rōz'bûrg)..........Or.	43·13 N	123·30 W
93	Rosebud (R.) (rōz'bŭd)......Can.	51·20 N	112·20 W
111	Rosebud Cr..................Mt.	45·48 N	106·34 W
108	Rosebud Ind. Res............SD	43·13 N	100·42 W
120	Rosedale...................Ms.	33·49 N	90·56 W
112	Rosedale........Wa. (Seattle In.)	47·20 N	122·39 W
210	Roseires Res................Sud.	11·15 N	34·45 E
107	Roselle (rō-zĕl')...Il. (Chicago In.)	41·59 N	88·05 W
89	Rosemere (rōz'mēr) Can. (Montreal In.)	45·38 N	73·48 W
113	Rosemount (rōz'mount) Mn. (Minneapolis, St. Paul In.)	44·44 N	93·08 W
218	Rosendal (rô-sĕn'täl)......S. Afr. (Johannesburg & Pretoria In.)	28·32 S	27·56 E
158	Rosenheim (rō'zĕn-hīm)....F.R.G.	47·52 N	12·06 E
94	Rosetown (rōz'toun)........Can.	51·33 N	108·00 W
	Rosetta, see Rashīd		
213	Rosettenville.............S. Afr. (Johannesburg & Pretoria In.)	26·15 S	28·04 E
114	Roseville (rōz'vĭl)...........Ca.	38·44 N	121·19 W
107	Roseville........Mi. (Detroit In.)	42·30 N	82·55 W
113	Roseville...................Mn. (Minneapolis, St. Paul In.)	45·01 N	93·10 W
104	Rosiclare (rōz'ĭ-klâr)..........Il.	37·30 N	88·15 W
135	Rosignol (rŏs-ĭg-nćl)........Guy.	6·16 N	57·37 W
165	Rosiorii de Vede (rô-shôr'ê dĕ vĕ-dĕ).Rom.	44·06 N	25·00 E
156	Roskilde (rôs'kêl-dĕ)........Den.	55·39 N	12·04 E
166	Roslavl' (rôs'läv'l).......Sov. Un.	53·56 N	32·52 E
110	Roslyn (rŏz'lĭn).............Wa.	47·14 N	121·00 W
167	Rosovka...............Sov. Un.	47·14 N	36·35 E
161	Rösrath (rûz'rät) F.R.G. (Ruhr In.)	50·53 N	7·11 E
107	Ross (rôs)....Oh. (Cincinnati In.)	39·19 N	84·39 W
164	Rossano (rô-sä'nō)...........It.	39·34 N	16·38 E
89	Ross Cr.....Can. (Edmonton In.)	53·50 N	113·08 W
110	Ross Dam..................Wa.	48·40 N	121·07 W
97	Rosseau (L.) (rôs-sō')......Can.	45·15 N	79·30 W
205	Rossel (I.) (rô-sĕl')...Pap. N. Gui.	11·31 S	154·00 E
89	Rosser (rôs'sēr) Can. (Winnipeg In.)	49·59 N	97·27 W
98	Rossignol, L................Can.	44·10 N	65·10 W
95	Ross I......................Can.	54·14 N	97·45 W
93	Rossland (rôs'lănd).........Can.	49·05 N	118·48 W
214	Rosso...............Mauritania	16·30 N	15·49 W
167	Rossosh' (rôs'sŭsh)......Sov. Un.	50·12 N	39·32 E
213	Rossouw.........S. Afr. (Natal In.)	31·12 S	27·18 E
220	Ross Sea...................Ant.	76·00 S	178·00 W
220	Ross Shelf Ice..............Ant.	81·30 S	175·00 W
120	Rossville (rôs'vĭl)...........Ga.	34·57 N	85·22 W
94	Rosthern..................Can.	52·41 N	106·25 W
158	Rostock (rôs'tŭk)........G.D.R.	54·04 N	12·06 E
166	Rostov................Sov. Un.	57·13 N	39·23 E
167	Rostov (Oblast).........Sov. Un.	47·38 N	39·15 E
171	Rostov-na-Donu (rôstôv-nä-dô-nōō).Sov. Un.	47·16 N	39·47 E
150	Rösvatn (L.) (rûs-vät'n).....Nor.	65·36 N	13·08 E
120	Roswell (rôz'wĕl)............Ga.	34·02 N	84·21 W
116	Roswell....................NM	33·23 N	104·32 W
116	Rotan (rô-tăn')..............Tx.	32·51 N	100·27 W
158	Rothenburg..............F.R.G.	49·20 N	10·10 E
148	Rotherham (rŏdh'ēr-ăm).....Eng.	53·26 N	1·21 W
98	Rothesay (rôth'sâ)..........Can.	45·23 N	66·00 W
154	Rothesay..................Scot.	55·50 N	3·14 W
148	Rothwell..................Eng.	53·44 N	1·29 W
196	Roti (I.) (rō'tê)...........Indon.	10·30 S	122·52 E
203	Roto (rō'tô)...............Austl.	33·07 S	145·30 E
149	Rotterdam (rôt'ĕr-däm') Neth. (Amsterdam In.)	51·55 N	4·27 E
158	Rottweil (rōt'vīl).........F.R.G.	48·10 N	8·36 E
160	Roubaix (rōō-bĕ')............Fr.	50·42 N	3·10 E
160	Rouen (rōō-äN')..............Fr.	49·25 N	1·05 E
107	Rouge, R........Mi. (Detroit In.)	42·30 N	83·15 W
97	Rouge (R.).................Can.	46·40 N	74·50 W
89	Rouge (R.) (rōōzh) Can. (Toronto In.)	43·53 N	79·21 W
104	Rough River Res............Ky.	37·45 N	86·10 W
107	Round Lake.....Il. (Chicago In.)	42·21 N	88·05 W
99	Round Pd...................Can.	48·15 N	55·57 W
119	Round Rock.................Tx.	30·31 N	97·41 W
112	Round Top (Mtn.) (tŏp) Or. (Portland In.)	45·41 N	123·22 W
111	Roundup (round'ŭp)..........Mt.	46·25 N	108·35 W
154	Rousay (I.) (rōō'zâ).........Scot.	59·10 N	3·04 W
91	Rouyn (rōōn)..............Can.	48·22 N	79·03 W
150	Rovaniemi (rô'vȧ-nyĕ'mĭ)....Fin.	66·29 N	25·45 E
164	Rovato (rô-vä'tō)............It.	45·33 N	10·00 E
167	Roven'ki (rô-vĕn'ki')....Sov. Un.	48·06 N	39·44 E
167	Roven'ki................Sov. Un.	49·54 N	38·54 E
164	Rovereto (rō-vȧ-rā'tô).........It.	45·53 N	11·05 E
164	Rovigo (rô-vē'gô).............It.	45·05 N	11·48 E
164	Rovinj (rô'vēn')...........Yugo.	45·05 N	13·40 E
134	Rovira (rô-vē'rä)........Col. (In.)	4·14 N	75·13 W
159	Rovno (rôv'nô).........Sov. Un.	50·37 N	26·17 E
167	Rovno (Oblast).........Sov. Un.	50·55 N	27·00 E
167	Rovnoye (rôv'nô-yĕ)....Sov. Un.	48·11 N	31·46 E
217	Rovuma (Ruvuma) (R.) Moz.-Tan.	10·50 S	39·50 E
99	Rowley (rou'lē).........Ma. (In.)	42·43 N	70·53 W
113	Roxana (rŏks'ăn-nȧ) Il. (St. Louis In.)	38·51 N	90·05 W
196	Roxas (rô-xäs)..............Phil.	11·30 N	122·47 E
121	Roxboro (rŏks' bŭr-ô)........NC	36·22 N	78·58 W
214	Roxo, Cap (C.)..........Senegal	12·20 N	16·43 W
116	Roy (roi)...................NM	35·54 N	104·09 W
113	Roy......Ut. (Salt Lake City In.)	41·10 N	112·02 W
128	Royal (I.)...................Ba.	25·30 N	76·50 W
154	Royal Can. (roi-ăl)...........Ire.	53·28 N	6·45 W
213	Royal Natal Natl. Pk. (roi'ăl) S. Afr. (Natal In.)	28·35 S	28·54 E
112	Royal Oak (roi'ăl ōk) Can. (Seattle In.)	48·30 N	123·24 W
107	Royal Oak......Mi. (Detroit In.)	42·29 N	83·09 W
104	Royalton (roi'ăl-tŭn).........Mi.	42·00 N	86·25 W
160	Royan (rwä-yäN')............Fr.	45·40 N	1·02 W
160	Roye (rwä)..................Fr.	49·43 N	2·40 E
106	Royersford (rô' yĕrz-fērd) Pa. (Philadelphia In.)	40·11 N	75·32 W
120	Royston (roiz'tŭn)...........Ga.	34·15 N	83·06 W
148	Royton (roi'tŭn)............Eng.	53·34 N	2·07 W
161	Rozay-en-Brie (rô-zā-ĕN-brē') Fr. (Paris In.)	48·41 N	2·57 E
174	Rozhaya R. (rô'zhȧ-yȧ) Sov. Un. (Moscow In.)	55·20 N	37·37 E
159	Rožňava (rôzh'nyȧ-vȧ).....Czech.	48·39 N	20·32 E
171	Rtishchevo ('r-tĭsh'chĕ-vô) Sov. Un.	52·15 N	43·40 E
212	Ruacana Falls......Ang.-Namibia	17·15 S	14·45 E
217	Ruaha Natl. Pk............Tan.	7·15 S	34·50 E
205	Ruapehu (Mtn.) (rōō-ȧ-pā'hōō) N. Z. (In.)	39·15 S	175·37 E
217	Rubeho Mts.................Tan.	6·45 S	36·15 E
113	Rubidoux...Ca. (Los Angeles In.)	33·59 N	117·24 W
217	Rubondo I..................Tan.	2·10 S	31·55 E
172	Rubtsovsk..............Sov. Un.	51·31 N	81·17 E
101	Ruby (rōō'bê)...............Ak.	64·38 N	155·22 W
114	Ruby (L.)...................Nv.	40·11 N	115·20 W
114	Ruby Mts....................Nv.	40·11 N	115·36 W
111	Ruby R.....................Mt.	45·06 N	112·10 W
156	Rudkøbing (rōōdh'kûb-ĭng)..Den.	54·56 N	10·44 E
149	Rüdnitz (rüd'nētz) G.D.R. (Berlin In.)	52·44 N	13·38 E
184	Rudog (rōō'dôk)...........China	33·42 N	79·56 E
217	Rudolf, L. (rōō'dôlf)....Ken.-Eth.	3·30 N	36·05 E
155	Rudolstadt (rōō'dôl-shtät).G.D.R.	50·46 N	13·30 E
211	Rufā'ah (rōō-fä'ä)...........Sud.	14·52 N	33·30 E
160	Ruffec (rü-fĕk')..............Fr.	46·03 N	0·11 E
217	Rufiji (R.) (rōō-fē'jê).......Tan.	8·00 S	39·20 E
214	Rufisque (rü-fēsk').......Senegal	14·43 N	17·17 W
217	Rufunsa..................Zambia	15·05 S	29·40 E
110	Rufus Woods................Wa.	48·02 N	119·33 W
148	Rugby (rŭg'bê).............Eng.	52·22 N	1·15 W
108	Rugby......................ND	48·22 N	100·00 W
148	Rugeley (rōōj'lē)...........Eng.	52·46 N	1·56 W
158	Rügen (Pen.) (rü'ghĕn)...G.D.R.	54·28 N	13·47 E
157	Ruhnu-Saar (I.) (rōōnōō-sȧ'âr) Sov. Un.	57·46 N	23·15 E
158	Ruhr R. (rōōr)...........F.R.G.	51·18 N	8·17 E
124	Ruiz (rōōē'z)...............Mex.	21·55 N	105·09 W
134	Ruiz, Nevado del (Pk.) (nĕ-vȧ'dô-dĕl-rōōē'z).Col. (In.)	4·52 N	75·20 W
157	Rūjiena (rōō'yĭ-ă-nȧ)....Sov. Un.	57·54 N	25·19 E
216	Ruki (R.).................Zaire	0·05 S	18·55 E
217	Rukwa, L. (rōōk-wä').......Tan.	8·00 S	32·25 E
109	Rum (R.) (rŭm)..............Mn.	45·52 N	93·45 W
165	Ruma (rōō'mȧ)...........Yugo.	45·00 N	19·53 E
211	Rumbek (rŭm'bĕk)...........Sud.	6·52 N	29·43 E
129	Rum Cay (I.).................Ba.	23·40 N	74·50 W
98	Rumford (rŭm'fērd)...........Me.	44·32 N	70·35 W
186	Rummah, Wādī ar (R.)...Sau. Ar.	26·17 N	41·45 E
183	Rummānah..Egypt (Palestine In.)	31·01 N	32·39 E
148	Runcorn (rŭŋ'kôrn)..........Eng.	53·20 N	2·44 W
183	Rupat, Palau (I.) (rōō'pät) Indon. (Singapore In.)	1·55 N	101·35 E
183	Rupat, Selat (Str.) Indon. (Singapore In.)	1·55 N	101·17 E
111	Rupert (rōō'pērt).............Id.	42·36 N	113·41 W
91	Rupert, Rivière de (R.)......Can.	51·35 N	76·30 W
165	Ruse (Russe) (rōō'sĕ) (rōō'sĕ).Bul.	43·50 N	25·59 E
109	Rush City...................Mn.	45·40 N	92·59 W
117	Rushville (rŭsh'vĭl)............Il.	40·08 N	90·34 W
104	Rushville....................In.	39·35 N	85·30 W
108	Rushville....................Ne.	42·43 N	102·27 W
217	Rusizi (R.).................Zaire	3·00 S	29·05 E
119	Rusk (rŭsk)..................Tx.	31·49 N	95·09 W
112	Ruskin (rŭs'kĭn) Can. (Vancouver In.)	49·10 N	122·25 W
149	Russ (R.).......Aus. (Vienna In.)	48·12 N	16·55 E
135	Russas (rōō's-säs)..........Braz.	4·48 S	37·50 W
	Russe, see Ruse		
112	Russell....Ca. (San Francisco In.)	37·39 N	122·08 W
95	Russell (rŭs'ĕl)..............Can.	50·47 N	101·15 W
89	Russell........Can. (Ottawa In.)	45·15 N	75·22 W
116	Russell......................Ks.	38·51 N	98·51 W
104	Russell......................Ky.	38·30 N	82·45 W
205	Russell................N. Z. (In.)	35·38 S	174·13 E
205	Russell Is..............Sol. Is.	9·16 S	158·30 E
95	Russel L...................Can.	56·15 N	101·30 W
120	Russellville (rŭs'ĕl-vĭl)........Al.	34·29 N	87·44 W
117	Russellville.................Ar.	35·16 N	93·08 W
120	Russelville..................Ky.	36·48 N	86·51 W
114	Russian (R.) (rŭsh'ăn)........Ca.	38·59 N	123·10 W
168	Russian S. F. S. R.......Sov. Un.	61·00 N	60·00 E
218	Rustenburg (rŭs'tĕn-bûrg)..S. Afr. (Johannesburg & Pretoria In.)	25·40 S	26·15 E
119	Ruston (rŭs'tŭn).............La.	32·32 N	92·39 W
112	Ruston.........Wa. (Seattle In.)	47·18 N	122·30 W
167	Rutchenkovo (rōō-chĕn'kô-vô) Sov. Un.	47·54 N	37·36 E
162	Rute (rōō'tā)................Sp.	37·20 N	4·34 W
114	Ruth (rōōth)................Nv.	39·17 N	115·00 W
159	Ruthenia (Reg.).........Sov. Un.	48·25 N	23·00 E
121	Rutherfordton (rŭdh'ēr-fērd-tŭn) NC	35·23 N	81·58 W
105	Rutland.....................Vt.	43·35 N	72·55 W
148	Rutland (Co.)..............Eng.	52·40 N	0·37 W
106	Rutledge (rût'lĕdj) Md. (Baltimore In.)	39·34 N	76·33 W
217	Rutshuru (rōōt-shōō'rōō)....Zaire	1·11 S	29·27 E
164	Ruvo (rōō'vô)................It.	41·07 N	16·32 E
217	Ruvuma (Rovuma) (R.) Moz.-Tan.	10·50 S	39·50 E
211	Ruwenzori Mts. (rōō-wĕn-zō'rê) Afr.	0·53 N	30·00 E
166	Ruza (rōō'zȧ)...........Sov. Un.	55·42 N	36·12 E
159	Ruzhany (rōō-zhän'ĭ)....Sov. Un.	52·49 N	24·54 E
209	Rwanda.....................Afr.	2·10 S	29·37 E
174	Ryabovo (ryä'bô-vô) Sov. Un. (Leningrad In.)	59·24 N	31·08 E
166	Ryazan' (ryä-zän'')......Sov. Un.	54·37 N	39·43 E
166	Ryazan' (Oblast)........Sov. Un.	54·10 N	39·37 E
166	Ryazhsk (ryäzh'sk').....Sov. Un.	53·43 N	40·04 E
170	Rybachiy, P-Ov. (Pen.)..Sov. Un.	69·50 N	33·20 E
174	Rybatskoye (rĭ-bät'skô-yĕ) Sov. Un. (Leningrad In.)	59·50 N	30·31 E
166	Rybinsk (ry-bĭ'nsk)......Sov. Un.	58·02 N	38·52 E
166	Rybinskoye Vdkhr. (Res.) Sov. Un.	58·23 N	38·15 E
159	Rybnik (rĭb'nêk)............Pol.	50·06 N	18·37 E
167	Rybnitsa (rĭb'nêt-sȧ)....Sov. Un.	47·45 N	29·02 E
154	Ryde (rīd).................Eng.	50·43 N	1·16 W
106	Rye (rī)......NY (New York In.)	40·58 N	73·42 W
167	Ryl'sk (rêl''sk)..........Sov. Un.	51·33 N	34·42 E
194	Ryōtsu (ryōt'sōō)...........Jap.	38·02 N	138·23 E
159	Rypin (rĭ'pên)...............Pol.	53·04 N	19·25 E
	Ryukyu, see Nansei-shotō		
159	Rzeszów (zhä-shōōf).........Pol.	50·02 N	22·00 E
166	Rzhev ('r-zhĕf)..........Sov. Un.	56·16 N	34·17 E
167	Rzhishchëv ('r-zhĭsh'chĕf) Sov. Un.	49·58 N	31·05 E

S

Page	Name Pronunciation Region	Lat. °′	Long. °′
158	Saale R. (sä-lĕ)..........G.D.R.	51·14 N	11·52 E
158	Saalfeld (säl'fĕlt).........G.D.R.	50·38 N	11·20 E
158	Saar (State) (zär).........F.R.G.	49·25 N	6·50 E
158	Saarbrücken (zähr'brü-kĕn) F.R.G.	49·15 N	7·01 E
157	Saaremaa (Ezel) (I.) (sä'rĕ-mä) Sov. Un.	58·28 N	21·30 E
136	Saavedra (sä-ä-vā'drä).......Arg.	37·45 S	62·23 W
165	Šabac (shä'bäts).............Yugo.	44·45 N	19·49 E
163	Sabadell (sä-bä-dhâl').........Sp.	41·32 N	2·07 E
196	Sabah (Reg.)................Mala.	5·10 N	116·25 E
127	Saba I. (sä'bä).Neth. Antilles (In.)	17·39 N	63·20 W
128	Sabana, Arch. de (är-chē-pyĕ'lä-gô dĕ sä-bä'nä) Cuba	23·05 N	80·00 W
127	Sabana, R. (sä-bä'nä).......Pan.	8·40 N	78·02 W
129	Sabana de la Mar (sä-bä'nä dā lä mär').Dom. Rep.	19·05 N	69·30 W
135	Sabana de Uchire (sä-bà'nä dĕ ōō-chē'rĕ) Ven. (In.)	10·02 N	65·32 W
126	Sabanagrande (sä-bä'nä-grä'n-dĕ) Hond.	13·47 N	87·16 W
134	Sabanalarga (sä-bà'nä-lär'gä).Col.	10·38 N	75·02 W
134	Sabanas Páramo (Mtn.) (sä-bà'näs pà'rä-mō).Col. (In.)	6·28 N	76·08 W
125	Sabancuy (sä-bäŋ-kwē').....Mex.	18·58 N	91·09 W
196	Sabang (sä'bäng)...........Indon.	5·52 N	95·26 E
166	Sabaudia (sȧ-bou'dê-ä)........It.	41·19 N	13·00 E
117	Sabetha (sȧ-bĕth'ȧ)..........Ks.	39·54 N	95·49 W
212	Sabi (R.) (sä'bê)..............Rh.	20·18 S	32·07 E
157	Sabile (sà'bê-lĕ).........Sov. Un.	57·03 N	22·34 E

338 Sabinal — St. Isidore-de-Laprairie PRONOUNCING INDEX

Page	Name Pronunciation Region	Lat. °′	Long. °′
118	Sabinal (så-bī'nål) Tx.	29·19 N	99·27 W
128	Sabinal, Cayo (I.) (kä'yō sä-bē-näl') Cuba	21·40 N	77·20 W
122	Sabinas Mex.	28·05 N	102·30 W
118	Sabinas, R. (sä-bē'näs) Mex.	26·37 N	99·52 W
118	Sabinas, Rio (R.) (rê'ō sä-bē'näs) Mex.	27·25 N	100·33 W
118	Sabinas Hidalgo (ê-däl'gô) Mex.	26·30 N	100·10 W
119	Sabine (så-bēn') Tx.	29·44 N	93·54 W
220	Sabine, Mt. Ant.	72·05 S	169·10 E
103	Sabine (R.) U. S.	31·35 N	94·00 W
119	Sabine L. La.-Tx.	29·53 N	93·41 W
197	Sablayan (säb-lä-yän') Phil. (In.)	12·49 N	120·47 E
98	Sable, C. (sā'b'l) Can.	43·25 N	65·24 W
121	Sable, C. Fl. (In.)	25·12 N	81·10 W
97	Sables, Rivière aux (R.) Can.	49·00 N	70·20 W
160	Sablé-sur-Sarthe (säb-lā-sür-särt') Fr.	47·50 N	0·17 W
170	Sablya, Gora (Mtn.) Sov. Un.	64·50 N	59·00 E
162	Sàbor (R.) (sä-bōr') Port.	41·18 N	6·54 W
117	Sac (R.) (sôk) Mo.	38·11 N	93·45 W
105	Sacandaga Res. (sä-kăn-dâ'gà) NY	43·10 N	74·15 W
163	Sacavém (sä-kä-vĕN') Port. (Lisbon In.)	38·47 N	9·06 W
163	Sacavem (R.) Port. (Lisbon In.)	38·52 N	9·06 W
109	Sac City (sŏk) Ia.	42·25 N	95·00 W
95	Sachigo L. (săch'ĭ-gō) Can.	53·49 N	92·08 W
158	Sachsen (Reg.) (zäk'sĕn) G.D.R.	50·45 N	12·17 E
105	Sacketts Harbor (săk'ĕts) NY	43·55 N	76·05 W
98	Sackville (săk'vĭl) Can.	45·54 N	64·22 W
98	Saco (sô'kô) Me.	43·30 N	70·28 W
136	Saco (R.) (sä'kô) Braz. (Rio de Janeiro In.)	22·20 S	43·26 W
98	Saco (R.) Me.	43·53 N	70·46 W
136	Sacra Famalia do Tinguá (sä-krä fä-mä'lyä dô tên-gwà') Braz. (Rio de Janeiro In.)	22·29 S	43·36 W
114	Sacramento (săk-rá-mĕn'tō) Ca.	38·35 N	121·30 W
118	Scaramento Mex.	25·45 N	103·22 W
118	Sacramento Mex.	27·05 N	101·45 W
114	Sacramento (R.) Ca.	40·20 N	122·07 W
186	Şa'dah Yemen	16·50 N	43·45 E
93	Saddle Lake Ind. Res. Can.	54·00 N	111·40 W
112	Saddle Mtn. (săd''l) Or. (Portland In.)	45·58 N	123·40 W
187	Sadiya (sŭ-dē'yä) India	27·53 N	95·35 E
194	Sado (I.) (sä'dō) Jap.	38·05 N	138·26 E
162	Sado (R.) (sä'dōō) Port.	38·15 N	8·20 W
156	Saeby (sĕ'bü) Den.	57·21 N	10·29 E
195	Saeki (sä'â-kê) Jap.	32·56 N	131·51 E
115	Safford (săf'fērd) Az.	32·50 N	109·45 W
210	Safi (Asfi) (sä'fê) (äs'fê) Mor.	32·24 N	9·09 W
171	Safid Rud (R.) Iran	36·50 N	49·40 E
195	Saga (sä'gä) Jap.	33·15 N	130·18 E
195	Sagami-Nada (Sea) (sä'gä'mê nä-dä) Jap.	35·06 N	139·24 E
107	Sagamore Hills (săg'á-môr hĭlz) Oh. (Cleveland In.)	41·19 N	81·34 W
109	Saganaga (L.) (să-gà-nă'gà) Can.-Mn.	48·13 N	91·17 W
184	Sāgar India	23·55 N	78·45 E
104	Saginaw (săg'ĭ-nô) Mi.	43·25 N	84·00 W
113	Saginaw Mn. (Duluth In.)	46·51 N	92·26 W
113	Saginaw Tx. (Dallas, Fort Worth In.)	32·52 N	97·22 W
104	Saginaw B. Mi.	43·50 N	83·40 W
171	Sagiz (R.) (sä'gēz) Sov. Un.	48·30 N	56·10 E
105	Saguache (så-wăch') (så-gwä'chê) Co.	38·05 N	106·10 W
105	Sagauche Cr. Co.	38·05 N	106·40 W
129	Sagua de Tánamo (sä-gwä dĕ tá'nä-mō) Cuba	20·40 N	75·15 W
128	Sagua la Grande (sä-gwä lä grä'n-dĕ) Cuba	22·45 N	80·05 W
115	Saguaro Natl. Mon. (säg-wä'rō) Az.	32·12 N	110·40 W
96	Saguenay (R.) (săg-ē-nā') Can.	48·20 N	70·15 W
163	Sagunto (sä-gōōn'tō) Sp.	39·40 N	0·17 W
209	Sahara Des. (sá-hä'rá) Afr.	23·44 N	1·40 W
152	Saharan Atlas (Mts.) Mor.-Alg.	32·51 N	1·02 W
184	Sahāranpur (sŭ-hä'rŭn-pōōr') India	29·58 N	77·41 E
113	Sahara Village (sá-hä'rá) Ut. (Salt Lake City In.)	41·06 N	111·58 W
184	Sāhiwāl Pak.	30·43 N	73·04 E
124	Sahuayo de Dias Mex.	20·03 N	102·43 W
210	Saïda (sä'ê-dä) Alg.	34·51 N	00·07 E
	Saigon, see Ho Chi Minh City		
195	Saijō (sä'ê-jô) Jap.	33·55 N	133·13 E
157	Saimaa (sä'ĭ-mä) Fin.	61·24 N	28·45 E
124	Sain Alto (sä-ēn' äl'tō) Mex.	23·35 N	103·13 W
89	St. Adolphe (sânt a'dŏlf) (săN' tá-dôlf') Can. (Winnipeg In.)	49·40 N	97·07 W
160	St. Affrique (săN' tá-frēk') Fr.	43·58 N	2·52 E
202	St. Albans (sânt ôl'bănz) Austl. (Melbourne In.)	37·44 S	144·47 E

Page	Name Pronunciation Region	Lat. °′	Long. °′
148	St. Albans Eng. (London In.)	51·44 N	0·20 W
105	St. Albans Vt.	44·50 N	73·05 W
104	St. Albans WV	38·20 N	81·50 W
154	St. Albans Hd. Eng.	50·34 N	2·00 W
89	St. Albert (sânt ăl'bērt) Can. (Edmonton In.)	53·38 N	113·38 W
160	St. Amand Montrond (săN't á-mäN' môN-rôN') Fr.	46·44 N	2·28 E
213	St. André, Cap (C.) Mad.	16·15 S	44·31 E
89	St. André-Est. Can. (Montreal In.)	45·33 N	74·19 W
120	St. Andrew, B. Fl.	30·20 N	85·45 W
98	St. Andrews Can.	45·05 N	67·03 W
154	St. Andrews Scot.	56·20 N	2·40 W
99	St. Andrew's Chan. (ăn'drōōz) Can.	46·06 N	60·28 W
89	St. Anicet (sĕNt ä-nē-sĕ') Can. (Montreal In.)	45·07 N	74·23 W
113	St. Ann (sânt ăn') Mo. (St. Louis In.)	38·44 N	90·23 W
98	Ste. Anne (săNt' àn') (sânt ăn') Can.	46·55 N	71·46 W
107	St. Anne Il. (Chicago In.)	41·01 N	87·44 W
127	Ste. Anne Guad. (In.)	16·15 N	61·23 W
89	Ste.-Anne (R.) Can. (Quebec In.)	47·07 N	70·50 W
89	Ste. Anne-de-Beaupré (dē bō-prā') Can. (Quebec In.)	47·02 N	70·56 W
89	Ste. Anne-des-Plaines (dā plĕN) Can. (Montreal In.)	45·46 N	73·49 W
99	St. Anns B. (ănz) Can.	46·20 N	60·30 W
128	St. Ann's Bay Jam.	18·25 N	77·15 W
89	St. Anselme (săN' täN-sĕlm') Can. (Quebec In.)	46·37 N	70·58 W
99	St. Anthony (säN ăn'thô-nê) Can.	51·24 N	55·35 W
111	St. Anthony (sânt ăn'thô-nê) Id.	43·59 N	111·42 W
89	St. Antoine-de-Tilly Can. (Quebec In.)	46·00 N	71·31 W
197	St. Antonio, Mt. Phil. (In.)	13·23 N	122·00 E
89	St. Apollinaire (săN' tá-pôl-ê-nâr') Can. (Quebec In.)	46·36 N	71·30 W
161	St. Arnoult-en-Yvelines (sàN-tär-nōō'ĕN-nēv-lēn') Fr. (Paris In.)	48·33 N	1·55 E
89	St. Augustin-de-Québec (sĕn tō-güs-tēn') Can. (Quebec In.)	46·45 N	71·27 W
89	St. Augustin-Deux-Montagnes Can. (Montreal In.)	45·38 N	73·59 W
121	St. Augustine (sânt ô'gŭs-tēn) Fl.	29·53 N	81·21 W
89	Ste. Barbe (sânt bärb') Can. (Montreal In.)	45·14 N	74·12 W
127	St. Barthelemy I. Guad. (In.)	17·55 N	62·32 W
154	St. Bees Hd. (sânt bēz' hĕd) Eng.	54·30 N	3·40 W
89	St. Benoit (sĕN bĕ-nōō-ä') Can. (Montreal In.)	45·34 N	74·05 W
106	St. Bernard (bēr-närd') La. (New Orleans In.)	29·52 N	89·52 W
107	St. Bernard Oh. (Cincinnati In.)	39·10 N	84·30 W
93	St. Bride Mt. (sânt brīd) Can.	51·30 N	115·57 W
154	St. Brides B. (sânt brīdz') Wales	51·17 N	4·45 W
160	St. Brieuc (săN' brēs') Fr.	48·32 N	2·47 W
89	St. Bruno (brū'nō) Can. (Montreal In.)	45·31 N	73·40 W
89	St. Canut (săN' kà-nū') Can. (Montreal In.)	45·43 N	74·04 W
98	St. Casimir (kà-zē-mēr') Can.	46·45 N	72·34 W
89	St. Catharines (kăth'à-rĭnz) Can. (Toronto In.)	43·10 N	79·14 W
127	St. Catherine, Mt. Grenada (In.)	12·10 N	61·42 W
160	St. Chamas (sàN-shä-mä') Fr. (In.)	43·32 N	5·03 E
160	St. Chamond (săN' shà-môN') Fr.	45·30 N	4·17 E
89	St. Charles (săN' shärlz') Can. (Quebec In.)	46·47 N	70·57 W
107	St. Charles (sânt chärlz') Il. (Chicago In.)	41·55 N	88·19 W
104	St. Charles Mi.	43·20 N	84·10 W
109	St. Charles Mn.	43·56 N	92·05 W
113	St. Charles Mo. (St. Louis In.)	38·47 N	90·29 W
89	St. Charles, Lac (L.) Can. (Quebec In.)	46·56 N	71·21 W
104	St. Clair (sânt klâr) Mi.	42·55 N	82·30 W
104	St. Clair (L.) Can.-Mi.	42·25 N	82·30 W
104	St. Clair (R.) Can.-Mi.	42·45 N	82·25 W
89	Ste. Claire Can. (Quebec In.)	46·36 N	70·52 W
107	St. Clair Shores Mi. (Detroit In.)	42·30 N	82·54 W
161	St. Claude (săN' klōd') Fr.	46·24 N	5·53 E
89	St. Clet (săNt' klā') Can. (Montreal In.)	45·22 N	74·21 W
121	St. Cloud (sânt kloud') Fl. (In.)	28·13 N	81·17 W
109	St. Cloud Mn.	45·33 N	94·08 W
89	St. Constant (kŏn'stănt) Can. (Montreal In.)	45·23 N	73·34 W
213	St. Croix I. (săN krwă) S. Afr. (Natal In.)	33·48 S	25·45 E
123	Saint Croix (I.) (sânt kroi') Vir. Is. (U. S. A.) (Puerto Rico In.)	17·40 N	64·43 W
98	St. Croix (R.) (kroi') Can.-Me.	45·28 N	67·32 W
109	St. Croix Ind. Res. Wi.	45·40 N	92·21 W

Page	Name Pronunciation Region	Lat. °′	Long. °′
109	St. Croix R. (sânt kroi') Mn.-Wi.	45·00 N	92·44 W
89	St. Damien-de-Buckland (sânt dā'mê-ĕn) Can. (Quebec In.)	46·37 N	70·39 W
89	St. David (dā'vĭd) Can. (Quebec In.)	46·47 N	71·11 W
154	St. David's Hd. Wales	51·54 N	5·25 W
161	St.-Denis (săN'dē-nē') Fr. (Paris In.)	48·26 N	2·22 E
161	St. Dié (dê-ā') Fr.	48·18 N	6·55 E
160	St. Dizier (dê-zyā') Fr.	48·49 N	4·55 E
89	St. Dominique (sĕN dō-mē-nēk') Can. (Montreal In.)	45·19 N	74·09 W
89	St. Edouard-de-Napierville (sĕN-tĕ-dōō-är') Can. (Montreal In.)	45·14 N	73·31 W
101	St. Elias, Mt. (sânt ê-lī'ăs) Can.	60·25 N	141·00 W
160	St. Étienne Fr.	45·26 N	4·22 E
89	St. Etienne-de-Lauzon (săN' tā-tyĕn') Can. (Quebec In.)	46·39 N	71·19 W
89	Ste. Euphémie (sĕNt û-fĕ-mē') Can. (Quebec In.)	46·47 N	70·27 W
89	St. Eustache (săN' tû-stàsh') Can. (Montreal In.)	45·34 N	73·54 W
89	St. Eustache Can. (Winnipeg In.)	49·58 N	97·47 W
127	St. Eustatius I. (sânt u-stā'shŭs) Neth. Antilles (In.)	17·32 N	62·45 W
89	Ste. Famille (săN't fà-mē'y') Can. (Quebec In.)	46·58 N	70·58 W
99	St. Félicíen (săN fā-lê-syăN') Can.	48·39 N	72·28 W
98	Ste. Felicite Can.	48·54 N	67·20 W
89	St. Féréol (fa-rā-ôl') Can. (Quebec In.)	47·07 N	70·52 W
164	St. Florent, Golfe de (G.) Fr.	42·55 N	9·08 E
160	St. Florent-sur-Cher (săN' flô-räN'sür-shâr') Fr.	46·58 N	2·15 E
160	St. Flour (săN flōōr') Fr.	45·02 N	3·09 E
89	Ste. Foy (săNt fwä) Can. (Quebec In.)	46·47 N	71·18 W
117	St. Francis (R.) Ar.	35·56 N	90·27 W
105	St. Francis L. (săN frăn'sĭs) Can.	45·00 N	74·20 W
89	St. François (săN'fräN-swä') Can. (Quebec In.)	47·01 N	70·49 W
218	St. François de Boundji Con.	1·03 S	15·22 E
89	St. Francois Xavier Can. (Winnepeg In.)	49·55 N	97·32 W
160	St. Gaudens (gō-dăNs') Fr.	43·07 N	0·43 E
117	Ste. Genevieve (sânt jĕn'ĕ-vēv) Mo.	37·58 N	90·02 W
203	St. George (sânt jôrj') Austl.	28·02 S	148·40 E
98	St. George (săN jôrj') Can.	45·08 N	66·49 W
89	St. George (săN'zhôrzh') Can. (Toronto In.)	43·14 N	80·15 W
121	St. George (sânt jôrj') SC	33·11 N	80·35 W
115	St. George Ut.	37·05 N	113·40 W
101	St. George (I.) Ak.	56·30 N	169·40 W
99	St. George, C. Can.	48·28 N	59·15 W
120	St. George, C. Fl.	29·30 N	85·20 W
99	St. George's (jôrj'ĕs) Can.	48·26 N	58·29 W
135	St. Georges Fr. Gu.	3·48 N	51·47 W
127	St. Georges Grenada (In.)	12·02 N	61·57 W
99	St. Georges B. Can.	45·49 N	61·45 W
99	St. George's B. Can.	48·20 N	59·00 W
154	St. George's Chan. (jôr-jĕz) Eng.-Ire.	51·45 N	6·30 W
161	St. Germain-en-Laye (săN' zhĕr-măN-äN-lā') Fr. (Paris In.)	48·53 N	2·05 E
89	St. Gervais (zhĕr-vĕ') Can. (Quebec In.)	46·43 N	70·53 W
160	St. Girons (zhē-rôN') Fr.	42·58 N	1·08 E
158	St. Gotthard Tun. (sânt gôthărd) (săN gô-tár') Switz.	46·38 N	8·55 E
99	St. Gregory, Mt. (sânt grĕg'ĕr-ê) Can.	49·19 N	58·13 W
209	St. Helena Atl. O.	16·01 S	5·16 W
212	St. Helenabaai (B.) Afr.	32·25 S	17·15 E
148	St. Helens (sânt hĕl'ĕnz) Eng.	53·27 N	2·44 W
112	St. Helens (hĕl'ĕnz) Or. (Portland In.)	45·52 N	122·49 W
110	St. Helens, Mt. Wa.	46·13 N	122·10 W
160	St. Helier (hyĕl'yĕr) Jersey	49·12 N	2·06 W
89	St. Henri (săN' hĕN'rê) Can. (Quebec In.)	46·41 N	71·04 W
89	St. Hubert Can. (Montreal In.)	45·29 N	73·24 W
105	St. Hyacinthe (săN' tê-ä-săNt') (sânt hī'à-sĭnth) Can.	45·35 N	72·55 W
98	St.-Ignace Can.	46·42 N	70·30 W
109	St. Ignace (sânt ĭg'nàs) Mi.	45·51 N	84·39 W
109	St. Ignace (I.) (săN' ĭg'nàs) Can.	48·47 N	88·14 W
98	St. Irenee (săN' tē-rā-nā') Can.	47·34 N	70·15 W
89	St. Isidore-de-Laprairie (saN' tē-zē-dōr') (sânt ĭz'ĭ-dôr) Can. (Montreal In.)	45·18 N	73·41 W

ăt; finăl; rāte; senâte; ärm; åsk; sofá; fâre; ch-choose; dh-as th in other; bē; êvent; bĕt; recĕnt; cratēr; g-go; gh-guttural g; bĭt; ĭ-short neutral; rīde; K-guttural k as ch in German ich;

PRONOUNCING INDEX St. Isidore-de-Prescott — Salado de los Nadadores 339

Page	Name Pronunciation Region	Lat. °'	Long. °'
89	St. Isidore-de-Prescott (săN' ĭz'ĭ-dôr-prĕs-kŏt) Can. (Ottawa In.)	45·23 N	74·54 W
89	St. Isidore-Dorchester (dŏr-chĕs'tĕr) . Can. (Quebec In.)	46·35 N	71·05 W
113	St. Jacob (jā-kŏb) . Il. (St. Louis In.)	38·43 N	89·46 W
109	St. James (sånt jāmz') Mn.	43·58 N	94·37 W
107	St. James Mo.	37·59 N	91·37 W
92	St. James, C. Can.	51·58 N	131·00 W
89	St. Janvier (săN' zhän-vyā') Can. (Montreal In.)	45·43 N	73·56 W
105	St. Jean (săN' zhäN') Can.	45·20 N	73·15 W
89	St. Jean Can. (Quebec In.)	46·55 N	70·54 W
97	St. Jean, Lac (L.) Can.	48·35 N	72·00 W
89	St. Jean-Chrysostome (krĭ-zōs-tōm') . Can. (Quebec (In.)	46·43 N	71·12 W
160	St. Jean-d'Angely (däN-zhå-lē') Fr.	45·56 N	0·33 W
160	St. Jean de Luz (dē lüz') Fr.	43·23 N	1·40 W
89	St. Jérôme (sånt jĕ-rōm') (săN zhā-rōm') Can. (Montreal In.)	45·47 N	74·00 W
89	St. Joachim-de-Montmorency (sånt jō'ȧ-kĭm) Can. (Quebec In.)	47·04 N	70·51 W
98	St. John (sånt jŏn) Can.	45·16 N	66·03 W
107	St. John In. (Chicago In.)	41·27 N	87·29 W
116	St. John Ks.	37·59 N	98·44 W
108	St. John ND	48·57 N	99·42 W
98	St. John (R.) Can.	46·39 N	67·40 W
99	St. John B. Can.	50·54 N	57·08 W
99	St. John, C. Can.	50·00 N	55·32 W
99	St. John I. Can.	50·49 N	57·14 W
123	St. John (I.) Vir. Is. (U. S. A.) (Puerto Rico In.)	18·16 N	64·48 W
91	St. John (R.) N.A.	45·15 N	67·40 W
99	St. John's (jŏns) Can.	47·34 N	52·43 W
115	St. Johns (jŏnz) Az.	34·30 N	109·25 W
104	St. Johns Mi.	43·05 N	84·35 W
127	St. Johns Antigua (In.)	17·07 N	61·50 W
121	St. Johns (R.) Fl.	29·54 N	81·32 W
105	St. Johnsbury (jŏnz'bĕr-ē) Vt.	44·25 N	72·00 W
98	St. Joseph (jō'zhûf) Can.	46·17 N	70·52 W
104	St. Joseph Mi.	42·05 N	86·30 W
117	St. Joseph (sånt jô-sĕf) Mo.	39·44 N	94·49 W
127	St. Joseph Dominica (In.)	15·25 N	61·26 W
104	St. Joseph (I.) Can.	46·15 N	83·55 W
91	St. Joseph (L.) (jō'zhûf) Can.	51·31 N	90·40 W
104	St. Joseph (R.) (sånt jō'sĕf) Mi.	41·45 N	85·50 W
120	St. Joseph, B. (jō'zhûf) Fl.	29·48 N	85·26 W
97	St. Joseph-de-Beauce (sĕN zhō-zĕf'dĕ bōs) . Can.	46·18 N	70·52 W
89	St. Joseph-du-Lac (sĕN zhō-zĕf' dü läk) Can. (Montreal In.)	45·32 N	74·00 W
119	St. Joseph I. (sånt jô-sĕf) Tx.	27·58 N	96·50 W
160	St. Junien (săN'zhü-nyăN') Fr.	45·53 N	0·54 E
89	Ste. Justine-de-Newton (sånt jŭs-tēn') Can. (Montreal In.)	45·22 N	74·22 W
154	St. Kilda (I.) (kĭl'dȧ) Scot.	57·10 N	8·32 W
123	St. Kitts (I.) (sānt kĭtts) St. Kitts-Nevis-Anguilla	17·24 N	63·30 W
89	St. Lambert (săN' läN-bĕr') (sånt lăm'bĕrt) Can. (Montreal In.)	45·29 N	73·29 W
89	St. Lambert-de-Lévis Can. (Quebec In.)	46·35 N	71·12 W
89	St. Laurent (săN'lō-rän) Can. (Montreal In.)	45·31 N	73·41 W
135	St. Laurent Fr. Gu.	5·27 N	53·56 W
89	St. Laurent-d'Orleans Can. (Quebec In.)	46·52 N	71·00 W
99	St. Lawrence (sānt lô'rĕns) Can.	46·55 N	55·23 W
101	St. Lawrence (I.) (sånt lô'rĕns) . Ak.	63·10 N	172·12 W
99	St. Lawrence, Gulf of Can.	48·00 N	62·00 W
91	St. Lawrence R. (Fleuve St.-Laurent) . Can.-U. S.	48·24 N	69·30 W
89	St. Lazare (săN'lȧ-zȧr') Can. (Quebec In.)	46·39 N	70·48 W
89	St. Lazare-de-Vaudreuil Can. (Montreal In.)	45·24 N	74·08 W
161	St. Léger-en-Yvelines (sȧN-lā-zhě'ěN-nēv-lēn') Fr. (Paris In.)	48·43 N	1·45 E
98	St. Leonard (sånt lĕn'ȧrd) Can.	47·10 N	67·56 W
89	St. Léonard Can. (Montreal In.)	45·36 N	73·35 W
106	St. Leonard Md. (Baltimore In.)	38·29 N	76·31 W
160	St. Léonard-de-Noblat (săN' lā-ô-nár'dē-nô-blá') . Fr.	45·51 N	1·30 E
160	St.-Lô (săN'lō') Fr.	49·08 N	1·07 W
104	St. Louis (sånt lōō'ĭs) Mi.	43·25 N	84·35 W
113	St. Louis (sånt lōō'ĭs) (lōō'ē) Mo. (St. Louis In.)	38·39 N	90·15 W
214	St.-Louis Senegal	16·02 N	16·30 W
89	St. Louis, Lac (L.) (săN' lōō-ē') Can. (Montreal In.)	45·24 N	73·51 W
109	St. Louis (R.) (sånt lōō'ĭs) Mn.	46·57 N	92·58 W
89	St. Louis-de-Gonzague (săN' lōō ē') Can. (Montreal In.)	45·13 N	74·00 W
113	St. Louis Park Mn. (Minneapolis, St. Paul In.)	44·56 N	93·21 W
123	St. Lucia N. A.	13·54 N	60·40 W
127	St. Lucia Chan. (lū'shĭ-ȧ) N. A. (In.)	14·15 N	61·00 W
121	St. Lucie Can. (lū'sê) Fl. (In.)	26·57 N	80·25 W
154	St. Magnus B. (măg'nŭs) Scot.	60·25 N	2·09 W
160	St. Maixent (săN' mĕk-säN') Fr.	46·25 N	0·12 W
160	St. Malo (săN' mȧ-lō') Fr.	48·40 N	2·02 W
160	St. Malo, Golfe de (G.) (gôlf-dĕ-săN-mä-lō') . Fr.	48·50 N	2·49 W
129	St. Marc (săN' mȧrk') Hai.	19·10 N	72·40 W
129	St.-Marc, Canal de (Chan.) Hai.	19·05 N	73·15 W
161	St. Marcellin (mär-sĕ-lăN') Fr.	45·08 N	5·15 E
213	Ste.-Marie, Île (I.) Mad.	16·58 S	50·15 E
213	Ste. Marie, Cap (C.) Mad.	25·31 S	45·00 E
161	Ste. Marie aux Mines (sȧN'tĕ-mä-rē'ō-mēn') . Fr.	48·14 N	7·08 E
98	Ste. Marie-Beauce (săNt'mȧ-rē') Can.	46·27 N	71·03 W
110	St. Maries (sånt mā'rēs) Id.	47·18 N	116·34 W
106	St. Margarets . Md. (Baltimore In.)	39·02 N	76·30 W
89	Ste. Martine . . Can. (Montreal In.)	45·14 N	73·37 W
127	St. Martin I. (mär'tĭn) Guad.-Neth-Antilles (In.)	18·06 N	62·54 W
98	St. Martins (mär'tĭnz) Can.	45·21 N	65·32 W
119	St. Martinville (mär'tĭn-vĭl) La.	30·08 N	91·50 W
93	St. Mary (R.) (mā'rê) Can.	49·25 N	113·00 W
93	St. Mary (Res.) Can.	49·30 N	113·00 W
214	St. Mary, C. Gam.	13·28 N	16·40 W
203	St. Marys (mā'rêz) Austl.	41·40 S	148·10 E
104	St. Marys Can.	43·15 N	81·10 W
121	St. Marys Ga.	30·43 N	81·35 W
117	St. Mary's Ks.	39·12 N	96·03 W
104	St. Mary's Oh.	40·30 N	84·25 W
105	St. Marys Pa.	41·25 N	78·30 W
104	St. Marys WV	39·20 N	81·15 W
121	St. Marys (R.) Ga.-Fl.	30·37 N	82·05 W
98	St. Mary's B. Can.	44·20 N	66·10 W
99	St. Mary's B. Can.	46·50 N	53·47 W
99	St. Marys Is. Can.	50·19 N	59·17 W
113	St. Marys R. Can.-U. S. (Sault Ste. Marie In.)	46·27 N	84·33 W
121	St. Mathew (măth'ū) SC	33·40 N	80·46 W
101	St. Matthew (I.) Ak.	60·25 N	172·10 W
107	St. Matthews (măth'ūz) Ky. (Louisville In.)	38·15 N	85·39 W
161	St. Maur-des-Fossés . Fr. (Paris In.)	48·48 N	2·29 E
98	St. Maurice (R.) (săN' mô-rēs') (sånt mô'rĭs) . Can.	47·20 N	72·55 W
101	St. Michael (sånt mī'kĕl) Ak.	63·22 N	162·20 W
89	St. Michel (săN'mê-shĕl') Can. (Quebec In.)	46·52 N	70·54 W
129	St. Michel-de-l'Atalaye Hai.	19·25 N	72·20 W
89	St. Michel-de-Napierville Can. (Montreal In.)	45·14 N	73·34 W
161	St. Mihiel (săN' mē-yĕl') Fr.	48·53 N	5·30 E
160	St. Mitre (săN mēt-rĕ) Fr. (In.)	43·27 N	5·02 E
158	St. Moritz (sånt mō'rĭts) (zäŋkt mō'rēts) Switz.	46·31 N	9·50 E
160	St. Nazaire (săN'nȧ-zȧr') Fr.	47·18 N	2·13 W
89	St. Nérée (nā-rā') Can. (Quebec In.)	46·43 N	70·43 W
89	St. Nicolas (ne-kō-lä') Can. (Quebec In.)	46·42 N	71·32 W
129	St. Nicolas, Cap (C.) Hai.	19·45 N	73·35 W
160	St. Omer (săN'tô-mâr') Fr.	50·44 N	2·16 E
98	St. Pascal (sĕN pȧ-skȧl') Can.	47·32 N	69·48 W
93	St. Paul (sånt pôl') Can.	53·59 N	111·17 W
113	St. Paul Mn. (Minneapolis, St. Paul In.)	44·57 N	93·05 W
108	St. Paul Ne.	41·13 N	98·28 W
101	St. Paul (I.) Ak.	57·10 N	170·20 W
214	St. Paul (R.) Lib.	7·10 N	10·00 W
99	St. Paul I. Can.	47·15 N	60·10 W
220	St. Paul I. Ind. O.	38·43 S	77·31 E
113	St. Paul Park (pärk) Mn. (Minneapolis, St. Paul In.)	44·51 N	93·00 W
121	St. Pauls (pôls) NC	34·47 N	78·57 W
109	St. Peter (pē tēr) Mn.	44·20 N	93·56 W
160	St. Peter Port Guernsey	49·27 N	2·35 W
121	St. Petersburg (pē'tērz-bûrg) Fl. (In.)	27·47 N	82·38 W
89	Ste. Pétronille (sĕNt pĕt-rō-nēl') Can. (Quebec In.)	46·51 N	71·08 W
89	St. Philémon (sĕN fēl-mōN') Can. (Quebec In.)	46·41 N	70·28 W
89	St. Philippe-d'Argenteuil (săn'fe-lēp') Can. (Montreal In.)	45·20 N	73·28 W
89	St. Philippe-de-Lapairie Can. (Montreal In.)	45·38 N	74·25 W
127	St. Pierre (săn'pyâr') . . Mart. (In.)	14·45 N	61·12 W
99	St. Pierre (I.) St. Pierre & Miquelon	46·47 N	56·11 W
98	St. Pierre, Lac (L.) Can.	46·07 N	72·45 W
99	St. Pierre & Miquelon N. A.	46·53 N	56·40 W
89	St. Pierre-d'Orléans Can. (Quebec In.)	46·53 N	71·04 W
89	St. Pierre-Montmagny Can. (Quebec In.)	46·55 N	70·37 W
89	St. Placide (plăs'ĭd) Can. (Montreal In.)	45·32 N	74·11 W
160	St. Pol-de-Léon (săN-pô'dĕ-lā-ôN') Fr.	48·41 N	4·00 W
158	St. Pölten (zäŋkt-pûl'tĕn) Aus.	48·12 N	15·38 E
160	St. Quentin (săN'kän-tăN') Fr.	49·52 N	3·16 E
89	St. Raphaël (rä-fȧ-ĕl') Can. (Quebec In.)	46·48 N	70·46 W
98	St. Raymond (săN' rā-môN') (sånt rā'mŭnd) Can.	46·50 N	71·51 W
89	St. Rédempteur (săN rā-dāNp-tûr') Can. (Quebec In.)	46·42 N	71·18 W
89	St. Rémi (sĕN rĕ-mē') Can. (Montreal In.)	45·15 N	73·36 W
89	St. Romuald-d'Etchemin (sĕN rŏ'mōō-ăl) Can. (Quebec In.)	46·45 N	71·14 W
127	Ste. Rose Guad. (In.)	16·19 N	61·45 W
160	Saintes Fr.	45·44 N	0·41 W
89	Ste. Scholastique (skô-lȧs-tēk') Can. (Montreal In.)	45·39 N	74·05 W
160	St. Servan-sur-Mer (sĕr-väN') . . Fr.	48·37 N	1·59 W
98	St. Siméon Can.	47·51 N	69·55 W
89	St. Stanislas-de-Kostka (sĕN stä-nēs-läz' de kōst'kä) Can. (Montreal In.)	45·11 N	74·08 W
98	St. Stephen (stē'vĕn) Can.	45·12 N	66·17 W
89	St. Sulpice Can. (Montreal In.)	45·50 N	73·21 W
89	St. Thérèse-de-Blainville (tĕ-rĕz' dĕ blĕN-vēl') Can. (Montreal In.)	45·38 N	73·51 W
104	St. Thomas (tŏm'ȧs) Can.	42·45 N	81·15 W
	St. Thomas, see Charlotte Amalie		
123	St. Thomas (I.) Vir. Is. (U. S. A.) (St. Thomas In.)	18·22 N	64·57 W
123	St. Thomas Hbr. (tŏm'ȧs) . . Vir. Is. (U. S. A.) (St. Thomas In.)	18·19 N	64·56 W
89	St. Timothée (tē-mô-tā') Can. (Montreal In.)	45·17 N	74·03 W
161	St. Tropez (trô-pĕ') Fr.	43·15 N	6·42 E
89	St. Valentin (vȧl-ĕn-tīn) Can. (Montreal In.)	45·07 N	73·19 W
160	St. Valéry (vȧ-lā-rē') Fr.	50·10 N	1·39 E
89	St. Vallier (väl-yā') Can. (Quebec In.)	46·54 N	70·49 W
158	St. Veit (zäŋKt vĭt') Aus.	46·46 N	14·20 E
98	St. Victor (vĭk'tēr) Can.	46·09 N	70·56 W
123	St. Vincent N. A.	13·20 N	60·50 W
203	St. Vincent, G. (vĭn'sĕnt) Austl.	34·55 S	138·00 E
127	St. Vincent Pass N. A. (In.)	13·35 N	61·10 W
94	St. Walburg Can.	53·39 N	109·12 W
160	St. Yrieix (ē-rē-ĕ) Fr.	45·30 N	1·08 E
195	Saitama (Pref.) (sī'tä-mä) Jap. (Tōkyō In.)	35·52 N	139·40 E
174	Saitbaba (sá-ĕt'bá-bȧ) Sov. Un. (Urals In.)	54·06 N	56·42 E
134	Sajama, Nevada (Pk.) (nĕ-vȧ'dä-sä-hȧ'mä) . Bol.	18·13 S	68·53 W
195	Sakai (sä'kä-ê) Jap. (Ōsaka In.)	34·34 N	135·28 E
195	Sakaiminato Jap.	35·33 N	133·15 E
186	Sakākah Sau. Ar.	29·58 N	40·03 E
108	Sakakawea, Lake ND	47·49 N	101·58 W
217	Sakania (sȧ-kä'nĭ-ȧ) Zaire	12·45 S	28·34 E
171	Sakarya (R.) (sȧ-kär'yȧ) Tur.	40·10 N	31·00 E
194	Sakata (sä'kä-tä) Jap.	38·56 N	139·57 E
194	Sakchu (säk'chōō) Kor.	40·29 N	125·09 E
173	Sakhalin (I.) (sȧ-kȧ-lēn') . . Sov. Un.	51·52 N	144·15 E
157	Šakiai (shä'kĭ-ī) Sov. Un.	54·59 N	23·05 E
193	Sakishima-Gunto (Is.) (sä'kê-shē'ma gōōn'tō') . Jap.	24·25 N	125·00 E
171	Sakmara (R.) Sov. Un.	52·00 N	56·10 E
106	Sakomet R. (sä-kō'mĕt) RI (Providence In.)	41·32 N	71·11 W
195	Sakurai Jap. (Ōsaka In.)	34·31 N	135·51 E
95	Sakwaso L. (sȧ-kwȧ'sō) Can.	53·01 N	91·55 W
128	Sal, Cay (I.) (kē săl) Ba.	23·45 N	80·25 W
171	Sal (R.) (sȧl) Sov. Un.	47·20 N	42·10 E
156	Sala (sô'lä) Swe.	59·56 N	16·34 E
164	Sala Consilina (sä'lä kôn-sê-lē'nä) It.	40·24 N	15·38 E
114	Salada, Laguna (L.) (lä-gōō'nä-sä-lä'dä) . Mex.	32·34 N	115·45 W
137	Saladillo (sä-lä-dēl'yō) Arg. (Buenos Aires In.)	35·38 S	59·48 W
126	Salado (sä-lä'dhō) Hong.	15·44 N	87·03 W
136	Salado (sä-lä'dō) (R.) Arg.	26·05 S	63·35 W
137	Salado (R.) Arg. (Buenos Aires In.)	35·53 S	58·12 W
125	Salado (R.) (sä-lä'dô) Mex.	18·30 N	97·29 W
118	Salado, Rio (R.) (rê'ō) Mex.	26·55 N	99·36 W
113	Salado Cr. . . Tx. (San Antonio In.)	29·23 N	98·25 W
118	Salado de los Nadadores Rio (R.) (dĕ-lôs-nä-dä-dō'rĕs) . Mex.	27·26 N	101·35 W

ng-sing; ŋ-baŋk; N-nasalized n; nŏd; cŏmmit; ōld; ôbey; ôrder; fōōd; fŏŏt; ou-out; s-soft; sh-dish; th-thin; pūre; ûnite; ûrn; stŭd; circŭs; ü-as "y" in study; '-indeterminate vowel.

Page	Name	Pronunciation	Region	Lat. ° ′	Long. ° ′
135	San Casimiro (kä-sē-mē′rō)		Ven. (In.)	10·01 N	67·02 w
164	San Cataldo (kä-täl′dō)........		It.	37·30 N	13·59 E
129	Sánchez (sän′chĕz)....		Dom. Rep.	19·15 N	69·40 w
124	Sanchez, Río de los (R.)	(rē′ō-dĕ-lôs)	Mex.	20·31 N	102·29 w
124	Sánchez Román (Tlaltenango)	(rô-mä′n) (tlä′l-tĕ-nän-gô)	Mex.	21·48 N	103·20 w
162	San Clemente (sän klä-mĕn′tä)		Sp.	39·25 N	2·24 w
114	San Clemente (I.).............		Ca.	33·02 N	118·36 w
129	San Cristobal (krĕs-tō′bäl)		Dom. Rep.	18·25 N	70·05 w
126	San Cristóbal...............		Guat.	15·22 N	90·26 w
134	San Cristóbal...............		Ven.	7·43 N	72·15 w
134	San Cristobal (I.)...........		Ec.	1·05 S	89·15 w
205	San Cristobal (I.)...........		Sol. Is.	10·47 S	162·17 E
164	San Croce, C. (krô′chä).......		It.	37·15 N	15·18 E
128	Sancti Spiritus	(säŋk′tē spē′rē-tōos)	Cuba	21·55 N	79·25 w
128	Sancti Spiritus (Prov.)......		Cuba	22·05 N	79·20 w
160	Sancy, Puy de (Pk.)	(pwē-dĕ-sȧn-sē′)	Fr.	45·30 N	2·53 E
122	Sand (I.) (sănd).Or. (Portland In.)			46·16 N	124·01 w
109	Sand (I.)...................		Wi.	46·03 N	91·09 w
218	Sand (R.)...................		S. Afr. (Johannesburg & Pretoria In.)	28·09 S	26·46 E
213	Sand (R.).......S. Afr. (Natal In.)			28·30 S	29·30 E
195	Sanda (sän′dä)...Jap. (Ōsaka In.)			34·53 N	135·14 E
196	Sandakan (sȧn-dä′kȧn)....Mala.			5·51 N	118·03 E
154	Sanday (I.) (sănd′ä)........Scot.			59·17 N	2·25 w
148	Sandbach (sănd′băch)......Scot.			53·08 N	2·22 w
156	Sandefjord (sän-dĕ-fyôr′)....Nor.			59·09 N	10·14 E
112	San de Fuca (de-fōō-cä)		Wa. (Seattle In.)	48·14 N	122·44 w
115	Sanders................Az.			35·13 N	109·20 w
118	Sanderson (săn′dĕr-sŭn)......Tx.			30·09 N	102·24 w
120	Sandersville (săn′dĕrz-vĭl)....Ga.			32·57 N	82·50 w
156	Sandhammar, C.	(sänt′häm-mȧr).Swe.		55·24 N	14·37 E
108	Sand Hills (Reg.) (sănd)......Ne.			41·57 N	101·29 w
106	Sand Hook (sănd hŏŏk)		NJ (New York In.)	40·29 N	74·05 w
148	Sandhurst (sănd′hŭrst)		Eng. (London In.)	51·20 N	0·48 w
114	San Diego (săn dê-ā′gô)..Ca. (In.)			32·43 N	117·10 w
116	San Diego................Tx.			27·47 N	98·13 w
114	San Diego (R.)............Ca.			32·53 N	116·57 w
124	San Diego de la Unión	(sän dê-ā-gô dä lä ōō-nyōn′)	Mex.	21·27 N	100·52 w
119	Sandies Cr. (sănd′ēz)........Tx.			29·13 N	97·34 w
113	San Dimas (săn dě-mäs)		Ca. (Los Angeles In.)	34·07 N	117·49 w
116	San Dimas (dě-mäs′).......Mex.			24·08 N	105·57 w
156	Sandnes (sänd′nĕs)..........Nor.			58·52 N	5·44 E
212	Sandoa (sän-dō′ȧ)..........Zaire			9·39 S	23·00 E
159	Sandomierz (sȧn-dô′myĕzh)...Pol.			50·39 N	21·45 E
164	San Donà di Piave	(sän dô nä′ dē pyä′vē)	It.	45·38 N	12·34 E
188	Sandoway (sän-dô-wī′)......Bur.			18·24 N	94·28 E
110	Sandpoint (sănd point)........Id.			48·17 N	116·34 w
202	Sandringham		Austl. (Melbourne In.)	37·57 S	145·01 E
164	Sandrio (sä′n-dryô)..........It.			46·11 N	9·53 E
117	Sand Springs (sănd sprĭnz)....Ok.			36·08 N	96·06 w
204	Sandstone (sănd′stōn)......Austl.			28·00 S	119·25 E
107	Sandstone................Mn.			46·08 N	92·53 w
106	Sandusky (săn-dŭs′kē)		Al. (Birmingham In.)	33·32 N	86·50 w
104	Sandusky................Mi.			43·25 N	82·50 w
104	Sandusky................Oh.			41·25 N	82·45 w
104	Sandusky (R.)............Oh.			41·10 N	83·20 w
104	Sandwich (sănd′wĭch)........Il.			41·35 N	88·53 w
112	Sandy (sănd′ē)..Or. (Portland In.)			45·24 N	122·16 w
113	Sandy....Ut. (Salt Lake City In.)			40·36 N	111·53 w
112	Sandy (R.)......Or. (Portland In.)			45·24 N	122·17 w
203	Sandy C................Austl.			24·25 S	153·10 E
111	Sandy Cr................Wy.			42·08 N	109·35 w
106	Sandy Hook (hŏŏk)		Ct. (New York In.)	41·25 N	73·17 w
89	Sandy L.....Can. (Edmonton In.)			53·46 N	113·58 w
99	Sandy L................Can.			49·16 N	57·00 w
95	Sandy L................Can.			53·00 N	93·07 w
119	Sandy Point............Tx. (In.)			29·22 N	95·27 w
102	Sandy Pt....Wa. (Vancouver In.)			48·48 N	122·42 w
106	Sandy Springs (springz)		Ga. (Atlanta In.)	33·55 N	84·23 w
137	San Enrique (sän-ĕn-rē′kĕ)		Arg. (Buenos Aires In.)	35·47 S	60·22 w
136	San Estanislao (ĕs-tä-nĕs-lä′ô).Par.			24·38 S	56·20 w
126	San Esteban (ĕs-tĕ′bän)....Hond.			15·13 N	85·53 w
197	San Fabian (fä-byä′n)..Phil. (In.)			16·14 N	120·28 E
137	San Felipe (fä-lē′pä)		Chile (Santiago In.)	32·45 S	70·43 w
124	San Felipe (fĕ-lē′pĕ)......Mex.			21·29 N	101·13 w
124	San Felipe................Mex.			22·21 N	105·26 w
134	San Felipe (fĕ-lē′pĕ)......Ven.			10·13 N	68·45 w
114	San Felipe, Cr. (sän fĕ-lēp′ȧ)..Ca.			33·10 N	116·03 w

Page	Name	Pronunciation	Region	Lat. ° ′	Long. ° ′
128	San Felipe, Cayos de (Is.)	(kä′yōs-dĕ-sän-fĕ-lē′pĕ)	Cuba	22·00 N	83·30 w
163	San Felíu de Guixols	(sän fä-lē′ōō dä gĕ-hôls)	Sp.	41·45 N	3·01 E
133	San Felix, Isla de (I.)	(ē′s-lä-dĕ-sän fä-lēks′)	Chile	26·20 S	80·10 w
162	San Fernanda (fĕr-nä′n-dä)....		Sp.	36·28 N	6·13 w
136	San Fernando (fĕr-nä′n-dō)		Arg. (Buenos Aires In.)	34·11 S	58·34 w
113	San Fernando (fĕr-nän′dō)		Ca. (Los Angeles In.)	34·17 N	118·27 w
137	San Fernando.Chile (Santiago In.)			36·36 S	70·58 w
118	San Fernando (fĕr-nän′dō)...Mex.			24·52 N	98·10 w
197	San Fernando (sän fĕr-nä′n-dō)		Phil. (In.)	16·38 N	120·19 E
134	San Fernando de Apure	(sän-fĕr-nä′n-dō-dĕ-ä-pōō′rä)	Ven.	7·46 N	67·29 w
134	San Fernando de Atabapo	(dĕ-ä-tä-bä′pô).Ven.		3·58 N	67·41 w
163	San Fernando de Henares	(dĕ-ä-nä′räs).Sp. (Madrid In.)		40·23 N	3·31 w
118	San Fernando R.	(sän fĕr-nän′dō).Mex.		25·07 N	98·25 w
156	Sånfjället (Mtn.)...........Swe.			62·19 N	13·30 E
89	Sanford (sän′fĕrd)		Can. (Winnipeg In.)	49·41 N	97·27 w
121	Sanford (sän′fôrd)......Fl. (In.)			28·46 N	80·18 w
98	Sanford (sän′fĕrd).........Me.			43·26 N	70·47 w
121	Sanford................NC			35·26 N	79·10 w
136	San Francisco (sän frän′sĭs′kō)		Arg.	31·23 S	62·09 w
112	San Francisco		Ca. (San Francisco In.)	37·45 N	122·26 w
126	San Francisco.............Sal.			13·48 N	88·11 w
	San Francisco, see Ixhuatán				
115	San Francisco (R.).........NM			33·35 N	108·55 w
112	San Francisco B. (săn frän′sĭs′kō)		Ca. (San Francisco In.)	37·45 N	122·21 w
122	San Francisco del Oro (dĕl ō′rō)		Mex	27·00 N	106·37 w
124	San Francisco del Rincón	(dĕl rĕn-kōn′).Mex.		21·01 N	101·51 w
135	San Francisco de Macaira	(dĕ-mä-kī′rä).Ven. (In.)		9·58 N	66·17 w
129	San Francisco de Macoris	(dä-mä-kō′rĕs).Dom. Rep.		19·20 N	70·15 w
129	San Francisco de Paula	(dä pou′lä).Cuba (In.)		23·04 N	82·18 w
113	San Gabriel	(săn gä-brē-ĕl′) (gä′brē-ĕl)	Ca. (Los Angeles In.)	34·06 N	118·06 w
124	San Gabriel Chilac	(sän-gä-brē-ĕl-chē-läk′).Mex.		18·19 N	97·22 w
113	San Gabriel Mts.		Ca. (Los Angeles In.)	34·17 N	118·03 w
113	San Gabriel Res.		Ca. (Los Angeles In.)	34·14 N	117·48 w
113	San Gabriel R.		Ca. (Los Angeles In.)	33·47 N	118·06 w
117	Sangamon (R.) (săn′gȧ-mŭn)...Il.			40·08 N	90·08 w
114	Sanger (săng′ĕr)...........Ca.			36·42 N	119·33 w
158	Sangerhausen (säng′ĕr-hou-zĕn)		G.D.R.	51·28 N	11·17 E
215	Sangha (R.).............Afr.			2·40 N	16·10 E
197	Sangihe (sä′gē-ē).......Indon.			3·30 N	125·30 E
134	San Gil (sän-kē′l)..........Col.			6·32 N	73·13 w
164	San Giovanni in Fiore	(sän jô-vän′nē ēn fyô′rä).It.		39·15 N	16·40 E
163	San Giuseppe Vesuviano	(sän-zhē̄ōō-sē′p-pĕ-vĕ-sōō-vyä′nô).It. (Naples In.)		40·36 N	14·31 E
194	Sangju (säng′jōō′).........Kor.			36·20 N	128·07 E
185	Sāngli.................India			16·56 N	74·38 E
215	Sangmélima.............Cam.			2·56 N	11·59 E
162	Sangonera (R.) (sän-gō-nä′rä)..Sp.			37·43 N	1·58 w
113	San Gorgonio Mt. (săn gôr-gō′nĭ-ō)		Ca. (Los Angeles In.)	34·06 N	116·50 w
100	Sangre De Cristo, Range	(säng′ĕr-de-krēs-tō).U. S.		37·45 N	105·50 w
112	San Gregoria (sän grĕ-gôr′ȧ)		Ca. (San Francisco In.)	37·20 N	122·23 w
164	Sangro (R.) (säŋ′grô)........It.			41·38 N	13·56 E
162	Sangüesa (sän-gwĕ′sä)........Sp.			42·36 N	1·15 w
190	Sanho (sän′hō)..........China			39·59 N	117·06 E
121	Sanibel I. (săn′ĭ-bĕl).....Fl. (In.)			26·26 N	82·15 w
126	San Ignacio.........Belize (In.)			17·11 N	89·04 w
	San Iledfonso, see Villa Alta				
197	San Ildefonso, C.	(sän-ĕl-dĕ-fôn-sô).Phil. (In.)		16·03 N	122·10 E
162	San Ildefonso o la Granja	(ō lä grän′khä).Sp.		40·54 N	4·02 w
136	San Isidro (ē-sē′drô)		Arg. (Buenos Aires In.)	34·13 S	58·31 w
127	San Isidro..............C. R.			9·24 N	83·43 w
113	San Jacinto (săn jȧ-sĭn′tō)		Ca. (Los Angeles In.)	33·47 N	116·57 w
197	San Jacinto (sän hä-sēn′tō)		Phil. (In.)	12·33 N	123·43 E

Page	Name	Pronunciation	Region	Lat. ° ′	Long. ° ′
119	San Jacinto (R.), West Fork...Tx.			30·35 N	95·37 w
113	San Jacinto R.		Ca. (Los Angeles In.)	33·44 N	117·14 w
119	San Jacinto R...............Tx.			30·25 N	95·05 w
137	San Javier (sän-hä-vē′ĕr)		Chile (Santiago In.)	35·35 S	71·43 w
125	San Jerónimo..........Mex. (In.)			19·31 N	98·46 w
124	San Jerónimo de Juárez	(hä-rō′nĕ-mô dä hwä′räz).Mex.		17·08 N	100·30 w
135	San Joaquin (hô-ä-kē′n).Ven. (In.)			10·16 N	67·47 w
114	San Joaquin (R.) (sän hwä-kēn′)		Ca.	37·10 N	120·51 w
114	San Joaquin Valley..........Ca.			36·45 N	120·30 w
136	San Jorge, Golfo (G.)	(gôl-fô-sän-кō′r-кĕ).Arg.		46·15 S	66·45 w
135	San José (sän hô-sä′)........Bol.			17·54 S	60·42 w
112	San Jose (sän hô-sä′)		Ca. (San Francisco In.)	37·20 N	121·54 w
127	San Jose (sän hô-sä′).......C. R.			9·57 N	84·05 w
126	San José...............Guat.			13·56 N	90·49 w
197	San José..........Phil. (In.)			12·22 N	121·04 E
197	San José..........Phil. (In.)			14·49 N	120·47 E
197	San José..........Phil. (In.)			15·49 N	120·57 E
137	San José (hô-sĕ′)		Ur. (Buenos Aires In.)	34·20 S	56·43 w
137	San José (Dept.)		Ur. (Buenos Aires In.)	34·17 S	56·23 w
122	San Jose (I.) (кō-sĕ′).......Mex.			25·00 N	110·35 w
115	San Jose (R.) (sän hô-sĕ′)...NM			35·15 N	108·10 w
137	San José (R.) (sän-hô-sĕ′)		Ur. (Buenos Aires In.)	34·05 S	56·47 w
127	San Jose, Isla de (I.)	(ē′s-lä-dĕ-sän hô-sä′).Pan.		8·17 N	79·20 w
136	San José de Feliciano	(dä lä ĕs-kē′nä).Arg.		30·26 S	58·44 w
135	San José de Gauribe	(sän-hô-sĕ′dĕ-gáōō-rē′bĕ).Ven. (In.)		9·51 N	65·49 w
129	San Jose de las Lajas	(sän-кō-sĕ′dĕ-läs-lä′käs).Cuba (In.)		22·13 N	82·10 w
124	San José Iturbide	(ē-tōōr-bē′dē).Mex.		21·00 N	100·24 w
136	San Juan (hwän′)..........Arg.			31·36 S	68·29 w
134	San Juan (hōōä′n)........Col. (In.)			3·23 N	73·48 w
129	San Juan (sän hwän′)..Dom. Rep.			18·50 N	71·15 w
197	San Juan (sän-кōōä′n)..Phil. (In.)			14·30 N	121·14 E
197	San Juan..........Phil. (In.)			16·41 N	120·20 E
123	San Juan (sän hwän′)		P. R. (Puerto Rico In.)	18·30 N	66·10 w
	San Juan, see Guichicovi				
	San Juan, see Mazatlán				
136	San Juan (Prov.)...........Arg.			31·00 S	69·30 w
123	San Juan, Cabezas de (C.)		P. R. (Puerto Rico In.)	18·29 N	65·30 w
216	San Juan, Cabo (C.)..Equat. Gui.			1·08 N	9·23 E
128	San Juan, Pico (Pk.)	(pĕ′kô-sän-kōōä′n).Cuba		21·55 N	80·00 w
125	San Juan, Rio (R.)	(sän-hōō-än′).Mex.		18·10 N	95·23 w
118	San Juan, Rio (R.)	(rē′ō-sän-hwän′).Ut.		37·10 N	110·30 w
115	San Juan Mts.		Ut.	37·10 N	110·30 w
136	San Juan Bautista	(sän hwän′ bou-tēs′tä).Par.		26·48 S	57·09 w
124	San Juan Capistrano	(sän-hōō-än′ kä-pês-trä′nô).Mex.		22·41 N	104·07 w
114	San Juan Cr. (săn hwän′)....Ca.			35·24 N	120·12 w
118	San Juan de Guadalupe	(sän hwan dä gwä-dhä-lōō′pä).Mex.		24·37 N	102·43 w
127	San Juan del Norte (Greytown)	(dĕl nôr-tä) (grā′toun).Nic.		10·55 N	83·44 w
127	San Juan del Norte Bahia de (B.)	(bä-ē′ä-dĕ-sän hwän dĕl nôr′tä).Nic.		11·12 N	83·40 w
124	San Juan de los Lagos	(sän-hōō-än′dä los lä′gôs).Mex.		21·15 N	102·18 w
124	San Juan de los Lagos (R.)	(dä los lä′gôs).Mex.		21·13 N	102·12 w
135	San Juan de los Morros	(dĕ-lôs-mô′r-rôs).Ven. (In.)		9·54 N	67·22 w
124	San Juan del Rio (dĕl rē′ô)..Mex.			21·20 N	99·59 w
118	San Juan del Rio	(sän hwän del rē′ô).Mex.		24·47 N	104·29 w
126	San Juan del Sur (dĕl sōōr)...Nic.			11·15 N	85·53 w
118	San Juan de Sabinas	(sän-sä-bē′näs).Mex.		27·56 N	101·23 w
125	San Juan Evangelista	(sän-hōō-ä′n-ä-väŋ-kä-lēs′tä).Mex.		17·57 N	95·08 w
112	San Juan I......Wa. (Seattle In.)			48·28 N	123·08 w
112	San Juan Is. (sän hwän)		Can. (Vancouver In.)	48·49 N	123·14 w
125	San Juan Ixtenco (ĕx-tĕ′n-kô)		Mex.	19·14 N	97·52 w
128	San Juan Martinez	(sän kōō ä′n-mär-tē′nĕz).Cuba		22·15 N	83·50 w
115	San Juan Mts. (san hwän′)....Co.			37·50 N	107·30 w

ăt; fīnăl; rāte; senâte; ärm; ȧsk; sofȧ; fâre; ch-choose; dh-as th in other; bē; ĕvent; bĕt; recĕnt; cratēr; g-go; gh-guttural g; bǐt; ĭ-short neutral; rīde; ᴋ-guttural k as ch in German ich;

ng-sing; ŋ-baŋk; N-nasalized n; nŏd; cŏmmit; ōld; ôbey; ôrder; fōōd; fŏŏt; ou-out; s-soft; sh-dish; th-thin; pūre; ûnite; ûrn; stŭd; circǔs; ü-as "y" in study; '-indeterminate vowel.

ăt; fĭnăl; rāte; senâte; ärm; ásk; sofá; fâre; ch-choose; dh-as th in other; bē; ĕvent; bĕt; recĕnt; cratēr; g-go; gh-guttural g; bĭt; ĭ-short neutral; rīde; к-guttural k as ch in German ich

PRONOUNCING INDEX

Schwelm — Serpukhov 345

Page	Name	Pronunciation	Region	Lat. °′	Long. °′
161	Schwelm	(shvĕlm)	F.R.G. (Ruhr In.)	51·17 N	7·18 E
158	Schwenningen	(shvĕn'ĭng-ĕn)	F.R.G.	48·04 N	8·33 E
158	Schwerin	(shvě-rēn')	G.D.R.	53·36 N	11·25 E
158	Schweriner See (L.)	(shvě'rē-nĕr zā)	G.D.R.	53·40 N	11·06 E
161	Schwerte	(shvĕr'tĕ)	F.R.G. (Ruhr In.)	51·26 N	7·34 E
149	Schwielow L.	(shvē'lōv)	G.D.R. (Berlin In.)	52.20 N	12·52 E
158	Schwyz	(schēts)	Switz.	47·01 N	8·38 E
164	Sciacca	(shê-äk'kä)	It.	37·30 N	13·09 E
154	Scilly (Is.)	(sĭl'ê)	Eng.	49·56 N	6·50 W
104	Scioto (R.)	(sī-ō'tō)	Oh.	39·10 N	82·55 W
99	Scituate	(sĭt'ū-āt)	Ma. (In.)	42·12 N	70·45 W
111	Scobey	(skō'bê)	Mt.	48·48 N	105·29 W
112	Scoggin	(skŏ'gĭn)	Or. (Portland In.)	45·28 N	123·14 W
89	Scotch (R.)	(skŏch)	Can. (Ottawa In.)	45·21 N	74·56 W
110	Scotia	(skō'shá)	Ca.	40·29 N	124·06 W
154	Scotland	(skŏt'lănd)	U. K.	57·05 N	5·10 W
108	Scotland		SD	43·08 N	97·43 W
121	Scotland Neck	(nĕk)	NC	36·06 N	77·25 W
105	Scotstown	(skŏts'toun)	Can.	45·35 N	71·15 W
90	Scott, C.	(skŏt)	Can.	50·47 N	128·26 W
110	Scott, Mt.		Or.	42·55 N	122·00 W
112	Scott, Mt.		Or. (Portland In.)	45·27 N	122·33 W
113	Scott Air Force Base		Il. (St. Louis In.)	38·33 N	89·52 W
213	Scottburgh	(skŏt'bŭr-ô)	S. Afr. (Natal In.)	30·18 S	30·42 E
116	Scott City		Ks.	38·28 N	100·54 W
106	Scottdale	(skŏt' dāl)	Ga. (Atlanta In.)	33·47 N	84·16 W
220	Scott Is.		Ant.	67·00 S	178·00 E
220	Scott Ra.		Ant.	68·00 S	55·00 E
108	Scottsbluff	(skŏts'blŭf)	Ne.	41·52 N	103·40 W
108	Scotts Bluff Natl. Mon.		Ne.	41·45 N	103·47 W
95	Scottsboro	(skŏts'bŭro)	Al.	34·40 N	86·03 W
104	Scottsburg	(skŏts' bûrg)	In.	38·40 N	85·50 W
203	Scottsdale	(skŏts'dāl)	Austl.	41·12 S	147·37 E
95	Scottsville	(skŏts'vĭl)	Ky.	36·45 N	86·10 W
104	Scottville		Mi.	44·00 N	86·20 W
105	Scranton	(skrăn'tŭn)	Pa.	41·45 N	75·45 W
105	Scugog (L.)	(skū'gôg)	Can.	44·05 N	78·55 W
148	Scunthorpe	(skŭn'thôrp)	Eng.	53·36 N	0·38 W
	Scutari, see Shkodër				
165	Scutari (R.)	(skōō'tä-rê)	Alb.	42·14 N	19·33 E
121	Sea, Is.	(sē)	Ga.-SC	31·21 N	81·05 W
112	Seabeck	(sē'bĕck)	Wa. (Seattle In.)	47·38 N	122·50 W
106	Sea Bright	(sē brīt)	NJ (New York In.)	40·22 N	73·58 W
119	Seabrook	(sē'brŏŏk)	Tx.	29·34 N	95·01 W
105	Seaford	(sē'fērd)	De.	38·35 N	75·40 W
116	Seagraves	(sē'grāvs)	Tx.	32·51 N	102·38 W
90	Seal (R.)		Can.	59·08 N	96·37 W
113	Seal Beach		Ca. (Los Angeles In.)	33·44 N	118·06 W
129	Seal Cays (Is.)		Turks & Caicos Is.	21·10 N	71·45 W
129	Seal Cays (Is.)		Ba.	22·40 N	75·55 W
212	Seal I.	(sēl)	S. Afr. (In.)	34·07 S	18·36 E
119	Sealy	(sē'lê)	Tx.	29·46 N	96·10 W
117	Searcy	(sûr'sê)	Ar.	35·13 N	91·43 W
114	Searles (L.)	(sûrl's)	Ca.	35·44 N	117·22 W
98	Searsport	(sērz'pōrt)	Me.	44·28 N	68·55 W
110	Seaside	(sē'sīd)	Or.	45·59 N	123·55 W
112	Seattle	(sê-ăt''l)	Wa. (Seattle In.)	47·36 N	122·20 W
126	Sebaco	(sĕ-bä'kô)	Nic.	12·50 N	86·03 W
98	Sebago	(sê-bā'gō)	Me.	43·52 N	70·20 W
122	Sebastion Vizcaino, Bahia (B.)	(bä-ē'ä-sĕ-bäs-työ'n-vês-kä-ē'nô)	Mex.	28·45 N	115·15 W
114	Sebastopol	(sê-bås'tô-pôl)	Ca.	38·27 N	122·50 W
196	Sebatik (I.)		Indon.	3·52 N	118·14 E
211	Sebderat		Eth.	15·30 N	36·45 E
216	Sébé (R.)		Gabon	0·45 S	13·30 E
165	Sebes		Rom.	45·58 N	23·34 E
104	Sebewaing	(se'bê-wăng)	Mi.	43·45 N	83·25 W
166	Sebezh	(syě'bězh)	Sov. Un.	56·16 N	28·29 E
171	Sebinkarahisar		Tur.	40·15 N	38·10 E
162	Sebkha bou Areg (Marsh)		Mor.	35·09 N	3·02 W
163	Sebkhan d'Oran (L.)		Alg.	35·28 N	0·28 W
158	Sebnitz	(zěb'nēts)	G.D.R.	51·01 N	14·16 E
163	Seborbe	(sě-bôr-dě)	Sp.	39·50 N	0·30 W
152	Sebou, Oued R.		Mor.	34·23 N	5·18 W
104	Sebree	(sê-brē')	Ky.	37·35 N	87·30 W
121	Sebring	(sē'brĭng)	Fl. (In.)	27·30 N	81·26 W
104	Sebring		Oh.	40·55 N	81·05 W
164	Secchia (R.)	(sĕ'kyä)	It.	44·25 N	10·25 E
125	Seco (R.)	(sĕ'kô)	Mex.	18·11 N	93·18 W
117	Sedalia		Mo.	38·42 N	93·12 W
160	Sedan	(sē-däN)	Fr.	49·49 N	4·55 E
117	Sedan	(sê-dăn')	Ks.	37·07 N	96·08 W
183	Sedom		Isr. (Palestine In.)	31·04 N	35·24 E
112	Sedro Woolley	(sē'drô-wŏŏl'ê)	Wa. (Seattle In.)	48·30 N	122·14 W
157	Seduva	(shĕ'dŏŏ-vá)	Sov. Un.	55·46 N	23·45 E
212	Seekoevlei (L.)	(zā'kŏŏf-lī)	S. Afr. (In.)	34·04 S	18·33 E
149	Seestall	(zā'shtäl)	F.R.G. (Munich In.)	47·58 N	10·52 E
152	Sefrou	(sĕ-frōō')	Mor.	33·49 N	4·46 W
170	Seg (L.)	(syĕgh)	Sov. Un.	64·00 N	33·30 E
183	Segamat	(sā'gá-mát)	Mala. (Singapore In.)	2·30 N	102·49 E
215	Segbana		Benin	10·56 N	3·42 E
214	Ségou	(sā-gōō')	Mali	13·27 N	6·16 W
134	Segovia	(sĕ-gô'vēä)	Col. (In.)	7·08 N	74·42 W
162	Segovia	(så-gō'vê-ä)	Sp.	40·58 N	4·05 W
	Segovia (R.), see Coco				
163	Segre (R.)	(så'grā)	Sp.	41·54 N	1·10 E
101	Seguam (I.)	(sē'gwäm)	Ak.	52·16 N	172·10 W
101	Seguam P.		Ak.	52·20 N	173·00 W
215	Séguédine		Niger	20·12 N	12·59 E
214	Séguéla	(sā-gā-lä')	Ivory Coast	7·57 N	6·40 W
118	Seguin	(sĕ-gēn')	Tx.	29·35 N	97·58 W
101	Segula (I.)	(sē-gū'lá)	Ak.	52·08 N	178·35 E
163	Segura (R.)	(så-gōō'rä)	Sp.	38·07 N	0·33 W
162	Segura, Sierra de (Mts.)	(sē-ě'r-rä-dě)	Sp.	38·05 N	2·45 W
162	Segura (R.)		Sp.	38·24 N	2·12 W
184	Sehwān		Pak.	26·33 N	67·51 E
129	Seibo	(sĕ'y-bō)	Dom. Rep.	18·45 N	69·05 W
116	Seiling		Ok.	36·09 N	98·56 W
157	Seinäjoki	(så'ē-nĕ-yô'kê)	Fin.	62·47 N	22·50 E
160	Seine, Baie de la (B.)	(bī dĕ lä sån)	Fr.	49·37 N	0·53 W
96	Seine (R.)	(sån)	Can.	49·04 N	91·00 W
89	Seine (R.)	(sån)	Can. (Winnipeg In.)	49·48 N	96·30 W
160	Seine, Rivière (R.)	(rēv-yâr')	Fr.	49·21 N	1·17 E
136	Seio do Venus (Mtn.)	(sĕ-yô-dô-vĕ'nōōs)	Braz. (Rio de Janeiro In.)	22·28 S	43·12 W
163	Seixal	(så-ê-shäl')	Port. (Lisbon In.)	38·38 N	9·06 W
217	Sekenke		Tan.	4·16 S	34·10 E
214	Sekondi-Takoradi	(sĕ-kôn'dê tä-kô-rä'dê)	Ghana	4·59 N	1·43 W
211	Sekota		Eth.	12·47 N	38·59 E
183	Selangor (State)	(så-län'gōr)	Mala. (Singapore In.)	2·53 N	101·29 E
165	Selanoutsi	(sål'á-nôv-tsĭ)	Bul.	43·42 N	24·05 E
197	Selaru (I.)		Indon.	8·30 S	130·30 E
196	Selatan, Tandjung (C.)	(så-lä'tän)	Indon.	4·09 S	114·40 E
101	Selawik	(sē-lá-wĭk)	Ak.	66·30 N	160·09 W
196	Selayar (I.)		Indon.	6·15 S	121·15 E
156	Selbu (L.)	(sĕl'bōō)	Nor.	63·18 N	11·55 E
148	Selby	(sĕl'bê)	Eng.	53·47 N	1·03 W
101	Seldovia	(sĕl-dō'vê-á)	Ak.	59·26 N	151·42 W
173	Selemdzha (R.)	(så-lĕmt-zhä')	Sov. Un.	52·28 N	131·50 E
173	Selenga (R.)	(sĕ lĕŋ gä')	Sov. Un.	51·00 N	106·40 E
188	Selenge Gol. (R.)		Mong.	49·04 N	102·23 E
173	Selennyakh (R.)	(sĕl-yĭn-yäk)	Sov. Un.	67·42 N	141·45 E
161	Sélestat	(sē-lē-stä')	Fr.	48·16 N	7·27 E
210	Selibaby	(så-lê-bá-bē')	Mauritania	15·21 N	12·11 W
166	Seliger (L.)	(sĕl'lê-gĕr)	Sov. Un.	57·14 N	33·18 E
184	Seling Tsho (L.)		China	31·55 N	89·00 E
166	Selizharovo	(så'lê-zhä'rô-vô)	Sov. Un.	56·51 N	33·28 E
95	Selkirk	(sĕl'kûrk)	Can.	50·09 N	96·52 W
90	Selkirk Mts.		Can.	51·00 N	117·40 W
112	Selleck	(sĕl'ĕck)	Wa. (Seattle In.)	47·22 N	121·52 W
107	Sellersburg	(sĕl'ĕrs-bûrg)	In. (Louisville In.)	38·25 N	85·45 W
173	Sellya Khskaya, Guba (B.)	(sĕl-yäk'sKá-yá)	Sov. Un.	72·30 N	136·00 E
120	Selma	(sĕl'má)	Al.	32·25 N	87·00 W
114	Selma		Ca.	36·34 N	119·37 W
121	Selma		NC	35·33 N	78·16 W
113	Selma		Tx. (San Antonio In.)	29·33 N	98·19 W
120	Selmer		Tn.	35·11 N	88·36 W
149	Selsingen	(zĕl'zĕn-gĕn)	F.R.G. (Hamburg In.)	53·22 N	9·13 E
212	Selukwe	(sê-lŭk'wê)	Rh.	19·34 S	30·03 E
110	Selway R.	(sĕl'wå)	Id.	46·07 N	115·12 W
90	Selwyn (L.)	(sĕl'wĭn)	Can.	59·41 N	104·30 W
165	Seman (R.)		Alb.	40·48 N	19·53 E
196	Semarang	(sĕ-mä'räng)	Indon.	7·03 S	110·27 E
196	Semarinda		Indon.	0·30 S	117·10 E
	Semendria, see Smederevo				
167	Semënovka	(sĕ-myôn'ôf-kä)	Sov. Un.	52·10 N	32·34 E
196	Semeru, Gunung (Mtn.)		Indon.	8·06 S	112·55 E
112	Semiahmoo Ind. Res.		Can. (Vancouver In.)	49·01 N	122·43 W
112	Semiahmoo Spit	(sĕm'ĭ-á-mōō)	Wa. (Vancouver In.)	48·59 N	122·52 W
101	Semichi Is.	(sē-mē'chī)	Ak.	52·40 N	174·50 W
111	Seminoe Res.	(sĕm'ĭ nô)	Wy.	42·08 N	107·10 W
117	Seminole	(sĕm'ĭ-nōl)	Ok.	35·13 N	96·41 W
118	Seminole		Tx.	32·43 N	102·39 W
121	Seminole Ind. Res.		Fl. (In.)	26·19 N	81·11 W
121	Seminole Ind. Res.		Fl. (In.)	27·05 N	81·25 W
120	Seminole, L.		Fl.-Ga.	30·57 N	84·46 W
172	Semipalatinsk	(sĕ'mê-pá-lá-tyēnsk')	Sov. Un.	50·28 N	80·29 E
101	Semisopochnoi (I.)	(sĕ-mē-så-pōsh' noi)	Ak.	51·45 N	179·25 W
172	Semiyarskoye	(sĕ'mê-yär'skô-yĕ)	Sov. Un.	51·03 N	78·28 E
211	Semliki R.	(sĕm'lê-kē)	Ug.-Zaire	0·45 N	29·36 E
	Semlin, see Zemun				
158	Semmering P.	(sĕm'ĕr-ĭng)	Aus.	47·39 N	15·50 E
171	Semnān		Iran	35·30 N	53·30 E
135	Senador Pompeu	(sĕ-nä-dōr-pôm-pĕ'ōō)	Braz.	5·34 S	39·18 W
120	Senatobia	(sĕ-ná-tō'bê-á)	Ms.	34·36 N	89·56 W
194	Sendai	(sĕn-dī')	Jap.	38·18 N	141·02 E
117	Seneca	(sĕn'ĕ-ká)	Ks.	39·49 N	96·03 W
120	Seneca		SC	34·40 N	82·58 W
106	Seneca		Md. (Baltimore In.)	39·04 N	77·20 W
105	Seneca (L.)		NY	42·30 N	76·55 W
105	Seneca Falls		NY	42·55 N	76·55 W
209	Senegal	(sĕn-ĕ-gôl')	Afr.	14·53 N	14·58 W
214	Sénégal (R.)		Afr.	16·00 N	14·00 W
218	Senekal	(sĕn'ĕ-kál)	S. Afr. (Johannesburg & Pretoria In.)	28·20 S	27·37 E
158	Senftenberg	(zĕnf'tĕn-bĕrgh)	G.D.R.	51·32 N	14·00 E
213	Sengunyane (R.)		Leso (Natal In.)	29·35 S	28·08 E
135	Senhor do Bonfim	(sĕn-yôr dô bôN-fē'N)	Braz.	5·21 S	40·09 W
164	Senigallia	(så-nê-gäl'lyä)	It.	43·42 N	13·16 E
164	Senj	(sĕn')	Yugo.	44·58 N	14·55 E
150	Senja (I.)	(sĕnyä)	Nor.	69·28 N	16·10 E
161	Senlis	(säN-lēs')	Fr. (Paris In.)	49·13 N	2·35 E
211	Sennar Dam		Sud.	13·38 N	33·38 E
91	Senneterre		Can.	48·20 N	77·22 W
166	Senno	(syĕ'nô)	Sov. Un.	54·48 N	29·43 E
160	Sens	(säNs)	Fr.	48·05 N	3·18 E
126	Sensuntepeque	(sĕn-sōōn-tå-pā'kå)	Sal.	13·53 N	88·34 W
165	Senta	(sĕn'tä)	Yugo.	45·54 N	20·05 E
195	Senzaki	(sĕn'zä-kē)	Jap.	34·22 N	131·09 E
	Seoul, see Sŏul				
183	Sepang		Mala. (Singapore In.)	2·43 N	101·45 E
136	Sepetiba, Baia de (B.)	(bäē'ä dĕ så-pâ-tē'bá)	Braz. (Rio de Janeiro In.)	23·01 S	43·42 W
197	Sepik (R.)	(sĕp-ēk')	Pap. N. Gui.	4·07 S	142·40 E
160	Septèmes-les-Vallons	(sĕ-tâm'la-vä-ôN')	Fr. (Marseille In.)	43·25 N	5·23 E
129	Septentrional, Cordillera (Mts.)	(kôr-dēl-yĕ'rä sĕp-tĕn-tryô-nä'l)	Dom. Rep.	19·50 N	71·15 W
161	Septeuil	(sĕ-tû')	Fr. (Paris In.)	48·53 N	1·40 E
98	Sept-Îles	(sĕ-tēl')	Can.	50·12 N	66·23 W
120	Sequatchie (R.)	(sē-kwăch'ê)	Tn.	35·33 N	85·14 W
112	Sequim	(sē'kwĭm)	Wa. (Seattle In.)	48·05 N	123·07 W
112	Sequim B.		Wa. (Seattle In.)	48·04 N	122·58 W
114	Sequoia Natl. Park	(sê-kwoi'á)	Ca.	36·34 N	118·37 W
155	Seraing	(sĕ-răN')	Bel.	50·38 N	5·28 E
197	Seram (I.)		Indon.	2·45 S	129·30 E
184	Serāmpore		India (Calcutta In.)	22·44 N	88·21 E
196	Serang	(så-räng')	Indon.	6·13 S	106·10 E
183	Seranggung		Indon. (Singapore In.)	0·49 N	104·11 E
	Serbia (Reg.), see Srbija				
171	Serdobsk	(sĕr-dôpsk')	Sov. Un.	52·30 N	44·20 E
159	Sered		Czech.	48·17 N	17·43 E
167	Seredina-Buda	(sĕ-rå-dē'ná-bōō'dá)	Sov. Un.	52·11 N	34·03 E
183	Seremban	(sĕr-ĕm-bän')	Mala. (Singapore In.)	2·44 N	101·57 E
217	Serengeti Natl. Pk.		Tan.	2·20 S	34·50 E
217	Serengeti Pln.		Tan.	2·40 S	34·55 E
212	Serenje	(sĕ-rĕn'yê)	Zambia	13·12 S	30·49 E
218	Serenli	(så-rĕn'lê)	Som. (Horn of Afr. In.)	2·28 N	42·15 E
	Seres, see Sérrai				
159	Seret		Czech.	48·17 N	17·43 E
159	Seret		Rom.	47·58 N	26·01 E
159	Seret R.	(sĕr'ĕt)	Sov. Un.	49·45 N	25·30 E
172	Sergeya Kirova (I.)	(sĕr-gyĕ'yá kê'rô-vå)	Sov. Un.	77·30 N	86·10 E
135	Sergipe (State)	(sĕr-zhē'pĕ)	Braz.	10·27 S	37·04 W
170	Sergiyevsk		Sov. Un.	53·58 N	51·00 E
165	Sérifos		Grc.	37·10 N	24·32 E
165	Sérifos (I.)		Grc.	37·42 N	24·17 E
137	Serodino	(sĕ-rô-dē'nō)	Arg. (Buenos Aires In.)	32·36 S	60·56 W
136	Seropédica	(sĕ-rô-pĕ'dē-kä)	Braz. (Rio de Janeiro In.)	22·44 S	43·43 W
174	Serov	(syĕ-rôf')	Sov. Un. (Urals In.)	59·36 N	60·30 E
212	Serowe	(sĕ-rō'wĕ)	Bots.	22·18 S	26·39 E
162	Serpa	(sĕr-pä)	Port.	37·56 N	7·38 W
166	Serpukhov	(syĕr'pōō-kôf)	Sov. Un.	54·53 N	37·27 E

346 Serrai — Shetland
PRONOUNCING INDEX

Page	Name Pronunciation	Region	Lat. °′	Long. °′
165	Sérrai (Seres) (sĕr′rĕ) (sĕr′ĕs)	Grc.	41·06 N	23·36 E
118	Serranias Del Burro (sĕr-rä-nē′äs dĕl bōō′r-rô)	Mex.	29·39 N	102·07 W
135	Serrinha (sĕr-rēn′yȧ)	Braz.	11·43 S	38·49 W
162	Serta (sĕr′tȧ)	Port.	39·48 N	8·01 W
135	Sertânia (sĕr-tá′nyä)	Braz.	8·28 S	37·13 W
137	Sertãozinho (sĕr-toun-zē′n-yô)	Braz. (Rio de Janeiro In.)	21·10 S	47·58 W
183	Serting (R.)	Mala. (Singapore In.)	3·01 N	102·32 E
136	Seruí (sĕ-rōō-ē′)	Braz. (Rio de Janeiro In.)	22·40 S	43·08 W
217	Sese Is.	Ug.	0·30 S	32·30 E
164	Sesia (R.) (sâz′yä)	It.	45·33 N	8·25 E
163	Sesimbra (sĕ-sē′m-brä)	Port. (Lisbon In.)	38·27 N	9·06 W
213	Sesmyl (R.)	S. Afr. (Johannesburg & Pretoria In.)	25·51 S	28·06 E
164	Sestri Levante (sĕs′trē lâ-vän′tȧ)	It.	44·15 N	9·24 E
174	Sestroretsk (sĕs-trô-rĕtsk)	Sov. Un. (Leningrad In.)	60·06 N	29·58 E
174	Sestroretskiy Razliv, Ozero (L.) (ô′zĕ-rô sĕs-trô′ rĕts-kĭ-räz′lĭf)	Sov. Un. (Leningrad In.)	60·05 N	30·07 E
195	Seta (sĕ′tä)	Jap. (Ōsaka In.)	34·58 N	135·56 W
160	Sète (sĕt)	Fr.	43·24 N	3·42 E
135	Sete Lagoas (sĕ-tĕ lä-gô′äs)	Braz.	19·23 S	43·58 W
210	Setif (sâ-tēf′)	Alg.	36·18 N	5·21 E
195	Seto (sĕ′tō)	Jap.	35·11 N	137·07 E
195	Seto-Naikai (Sea) (sĕ′tô nī′kī)	Jap.	33·50 N	132·25 E
210	Settat (sĕt-ät′) (sē-tȧ′)	Mor.	33·02 N	7·30 W
212	Sette-Cama (sĕ-tĕ-kä-mä′)	Gabon.	2·29 S	9·40 E
128	Settlement Pt. (sĕt′l-mĕnt)	Ba.	26·40 N	79·00 W
218	Settlers (sĕt′lẽrs)	S. Afr. (Johannesburg & Pretoria In.)	24·57 S	28·33 E
195	Settsu	Jap. (Osaka In.)	34·46 N	135·33 E
163	Setúbal (sâ-tōō′bäl)	Port. (Lisbon In.)	30·32 N	8·54 W
162	Setúbal, B. de (bä-ē′ä)	Port.	38·27 N	9·08 W
95	Seul, Lac (L.) (läk sûl)	Can.	50·20 N	92·30 W
156	Sevalen (L.) (sĕ′vä-lĕn)	Nor.	62·19 N	10·15 E
171	Sevan (L.) (syĭ-vän′)	Sov. Un.	40·10 N	45·20 E
167	Sevastopol′ (Akhiar) (syĕ-vȧs-tô′pôl″) (äĸ′yár)	Sov. Un.	44·34 N	33·34 E
	Seven Is., see Shichitō			
148	Sevenoaks (sĕ-vĕn-ôks′)	Eng. (London In.)	51·16 N	0·12 E
174	Severka R. (sâ′vĕr-kȧ)	Sov. Un. (Moscow In.)	55·11 N	38·41 E
91	Severn (R.) (sĕv′ẽrn)	Can.	55·21 N	88·42 W
154	Severn (R.)	Eng.	51·42 N	2·25 W
106	Severna Park (sĕv′ẽrn-ȧ)	Md. (Baltimore In.)	39·04 N	76·33 W
170	Severnaya Dvina (Northern Dvina (R.)	Sov. Un.	63·00 N	42·40 E
169	Severnaya Zemlya (Northern Land) (Is.) (sĕ-vyĭr-nī′u zĭ-m′lyä′)	Sov. Un.	79·33 N	101·15 E
174	Severoural′sk (sĕ-vyĭ-rŭ-ōō-rälsk′)	Sov. Un. (Urals In.)	60·08 N	59·53 E
115	Sevier (L.) (sê-vēr′)	Ut.	38·55 N	113·10 W
115	Sevier R.	Ut.	39·25 N	112·20 W
115	Sevier R., East Fork	Ut.	37·45 N	112·10 W
134	Sevilla (sĕ-vē′l-yä)	Col. (In.)	4·16 N	75·56 W
162	Sevilla (sâ-vēl′yä)	Sp.	37·29 N	5·58 W
107	Seville (sĕ′vĭl)	Oh. (Cleveland In.)	41·01 N	81·45 W
165	Sevlievo (sĕv′lyĕ-vô)	Bul.	41·02 N	25·05 E
160	Sèvre Nantaise (R.) (sâ′vrĕ nän-tâz′)	Fr.	47·00 N	1·02 W
160	Sèvre Niortaise (R.) (sâ′vr′ nyôr-tâz′)	Fr.	46·23 N	1·05 W
166	Sevsk (syĕfsk)	Sov. Un.	52·08 N	34·28 E
101	Seward (sū′ȧrd)	Ak.	60·18 N	149·28 W
117	Seward	Ne.	40·55 N	97·06 W
101	Seward Pen.	Ak.	65·40 N	164·00 W
136	Sewell (sĕ′ōō-ĕl)	Chile	34·01 S	70·18 W
107	Sewickley (sê-wĭk′lê)	Pa. (Pittsburgh In.)	40·33 N	80·11 W
125	Seybaplaya (sā-ê-bä-plä′yä)	Mex.	19·38 N	90·40 W
20	Seychelles (sā-shĕl′)	Afr.	5·20 S	55·10 E
150	Seydhisfjördhur (sā′dēs-fyûr-dōōr)	Ice.	65·21 N	14·08 W
126	Seyé (sĕ-yĕ′)	Mex. (In.)	20·51 N	89·22 W
153	Seyhan (R.)	Tur.	37·28 N	35·40 E
167	Seym (R.) (sĕym)	Sov. Un.	51·23 N	33·22 E
97	Seymour (sē′mōr)	In.	38·55 N	85·55 W
109	Seymour	Ia.	40·41 N	93·03 W
116	Seymour	Tx.	33·35 N	99·16 W
213	Seymour (sē′môr)	S. Afr. (Natal In.)	32·33 S	26·48 E
213	Sezela	S. Afr. (Natal In.)	30·33 S	30·37 W
164	Sezze (sĕt′sȧ)	It.	41·32 N	13·30 E
210	Sfaz (sfäks)	Tun.	34·51 N	10·45 E
165	Sfîntu-Gheorghe	Rom.	45·53 N	25·49 E
149	's Gravenhage (The Hague) ('s ĸrä′vĕn-hä′ĸĕ) (häg)	Neth. (Amsterdam In.)	52·05 N	4·16 E
189	Sha (R.) (shä)	China	33·33 N	114·30 E
190	Sha (R.)	China	34·47 N	118·27 E
190	Sha (R.)	China	39·26 N	122·08 E
212	Shabani	Rh.	20·15 S	30·28 E
174	Shablykino (sháb-lē′kĭ-nô)	Sov. Un. (Moscow In.)	56·22 N	38·37 E
191	Shaching	China (Canton In.)	22·44 N	113·48 E
220	Shackleton Shelf Ice (shăk″l-tŭn)	Ant.	65·00 S	100·00 E
106	Shades Cr. (shādz)	Al. (Birmingham In.)	33·20 N	86·55 W
106	Shades Mtn.	Al. (Birmingham In.)	33·22 N	86·51 W
215	Shagamu	Nig.	6·51 N	3·39 E
184	Shāhjahānpur (shä-jŭ-hän′pōōr)	India	27·58 N	79·58 E
192	Shaho (shä-hō′)	China (In.)	40·08 N	116·16 E
186	Shahrezā (shä-rā′zā)	Iran	31·47 N	51·47 E
171	Shahsavār	Iran	36·40 N	51·00 E
107	Shaker Hts. (shā′kẽr)	Oh. (Cleveland In.)	41·28 N	81·34 W
167	Shakhty (shäĸ′tē)	Sov. Un.	47·41 N	40·11 E
215	Shaki	Nig.	8·39 N	3·25 E
113	Shakopee (shăk′ô-pe)	Mn. (Minneapolis, St. Paul In.)	44·48 N	93·31 W
211	Shala L. (shä′lȧ)	Eth.	7·34 N	39·00 E
186	Shām, Jabal ash (Mtn.)	Om.	23·01 N	57·45 E
211	Shambe (shäm′bȧ)	Sud.	7·08 N	30·46 E
186	Shammar, Jabal (Mts.) (jĕb′ĕl shŭm′ár)	Sau. Ar.	27·13 N	40·16 E
211	Shamo (L.)	Eth.	5·58 N	37·00 E
105	Shamokin (shȧ-mō′kĭn)	Pa.	40·45 N	76·30 W
116	Shamrock (shăm′rŏk)	Tx.	35·14 N	100·12 W
212	Shamva (shäm′vȧ)	Rh.	17·18 S	31·35 E
211	Shandī	Sud.	16·44 N	33·29 E
107	Shandon (shăn-dŭn)	Oh. (Cincinnati In.)	39·20 N	84·13 W
190	Shangch′eng (shäng′chĕng)	China	31·47 N	115·22 E
190	Shangchialin (shäng′jĭä′lĭn)	China	38·20 N	116·05 E
190	Shangch′iu (shäng′chĭō)	China	34·24 N	115·39 E
191	Shanghai (shäng′hī′)	China (Shanghai In.)	31·14 N	121·27 E
191	Shanghaihsien	China (Shanghai In.)	31·02 N	121·24 E
190	Shanghai Shih (Mun.)	China	31·30 N	121·45 E
190	Shangho (shäng′hŏ)	China	37·18 N	117·10 E
193	Shangjao	China	28·25 N	117·58 E
190	Shangts′ai (shäng′tsī′)	China	33·16 N	114·16 E
192	Shangtu	China	41·38 N	113·22 E
	Shanhsi (Prov.), see Shansi			
190	Shanhsien (shän′hsyĕn′)	China	34·47 N	116·04 E
106	Shannon (shăn′ŭn)	Al. (Birmingham In.)	33·23 N	86·52 W
154	Shannon R. (shăn′ŏn)	Ire.	52·30 N	9·58 W
188	Shanshan (shän′shän′)	China	42·51 N	89·53 E
189	Shansi (Shanhsi) (Prov.)	China	37·30 N	112·00 E
173	Shantar (I.) (shän′tär)	Sov. Un.	55·13 N	138·42 E
193	Shant′ou (Swatow) (swä′tō′)	China	23·20 N	116·40 E
189	Shantung (Prov.)	China	36·08 N	117·09 E
193	Shantung Pantao (Pen.)	China	37·00 N	120·10 E
193	Shantung Pt. (shän′tōōng′)	China	37·28 N	122·40 E
193	Shaohsing	China	30·00 N	120·40 E
193	Shaokuan	China	24·58 N	113·42 E
190	Shaopo (shou′pō′)	China	32·33 N	119·30 E
190	Shaopo Hu (L.) (shou′pŏ′hōō)	China	32·07 N	119·13 E
174	Shapki (shäp′kĭ)	Sov. Un. (Leningrad In.)	59·36 N	31·11 E
204	Shark B. (shärk)	Austl.	25·30 S	113·00 E
99	Sharon (shăr′ŏn)	Ma. (In.)	42·07 N	71·11 W
104	Sharon	Pa.	41·15 N	80·30 W
116	Sharon Springs	Ks.	38·51 N	101·45 W
107	Sharonville (shăr′ŏn vĭl)	Oh. (Cincinnati In.)	39·16 N	84·24 W
107	Sharpsburg (shärps′bûrg)	Pa. (Pittsburgh In.)	40·30 N	79·54 W
186	Sharr, Jabal (Mtn.)	Sau. Ar.	28·00 N	36·07 E
193	Shashih	China	30·20 N	112·18 E
110	Shasta, Mt.	Ca.	41·35 N	122·12 W
110	Shasta L. (shăs′tȧ)	Ca.	40·51 N	122·32 W
170	Shatsk (shȧtsk)	Sov. Un.	54·00 N	41·40 E
116	Shattuck (shăt′ŭk)	Ok.	36·16 N	99·53 W
94	Shaunavon	Can.	49·40 N	108·25 W
120	Shaw (shô)	Ms.	33·36 N	90·44 W
109	Shawano (shȧ-wô′nô)	Wi.	44·41 N	88·13 W
91	Shawinigan	Can.	46·32 N	72·46 W
113	Shawnee (shô-nē′)	Ks. (Kansas City In.)	39·01 N	94·43 W
117	Shawnee	Ok.	35·20 N	96·54 W
104	Shawneetown (shô′nē-toun)	Il.	37·40 N	88·05 W
193	Shayang	China	31·00 N	112·38 E
159	Shchara (R.) (sh-chä′rȧ)	Sov. Un.	53·17 N	25·12 E
174	Shchëlkovo (shchĕl′kô-vô)	Sov. Un. (Moscow In.)	55·55 N	38·00 E
167	Shchëtovo (shchĕ′tô-vô)	Sov. Un.	48·11 N	39·13 E
167	Shchigry (shchē′grē)	Sov. Un.	51·52 N	36·54 E
167	Shchors (shchôrs)	Sov. Un.	51·38 N	31·58 E
174	Shchuch′ye Ozero (shchōōch′yĕ ô′zĕ-rō)	Sov. Un. (Urals In.)	56·31 N	56·35 E
184	Sheakhala	India (In.)	22·47 N	88·10 E
218	Shebele R. (shā′bâ-lē)	Eth. (Horn of Afr. In.)	6·07 N	43·10 E
218	Shebelle (R.)	Som. (Horn of Afr. In.)	1·38 N	43·50 E
109	Sheboygan (shê-boi′găn)	Wi.	43·45 N	87·44 W
109	Sheboygan Falls	Wi.	43·43 N	87·51 W
183	Shechem (Ruins)	Jordan (Palestine In.)	32·15 N	35·22 E
92	Shedin Pk. (shĕd′ĭn)	Can.	55·55 N	127·32 W
98	Shediac (shĕ′dê-ăk)	Can.	46·13 N	64·32 W
154	Sheelin (L.) (shē′lĭn)	Ire.	53·46 N	7·34 W
148	Sheerness (shēr′nĕs)	Eng. (London In.)	51·26 N	0·46 E
120	Sheffield (shĕf′fēld)	Al.	35·42 N	87·42 W
89	Sheffield	Can. (Toronto In.)	43·20 N	80·13 W
148	Sheffield	Eng.	53·23 N	1·28 W
107	Sheffield	Oh. (Cleveland In.)	41·26 N	82·05 W
107	Sheffield Lake	Oh. (Cleveland In.)	41·30 N	82·03 W
190	Shehsien (shĕ′hsyĕn′)	China	36·34 N	113·42 E
154	Shehy, Mts.	Ire.	51·46 N	9·45 W
170	Sheksna (R.) (shĕks′nȧ)	Sov. Un.	59·50 N	38·40 E
173	Shelagskiy, Mys (C.) (shĭ-läg′skē)	Sov. Un.	70·08 N	170·52 E
117	Shelbina (shĕl-bī′nȧ)	Ar.	39·41 N	92·03 W
104	Shelburn (shĕl′bŭrn)	In.	39·10 N	87·30 W
98	Shelburne	Can.	43·46 N	65·19 W
105	Shelburne	Can.	44·04 N	80·12 W
107	Shelby (shĕl′bê)	In. (Chicago In.)	41·12 N	87·21 W
104	Shelby	Mi.	43·35 N	86·20 W
120	Shelby	Ms.	33·56 N	90·44 W
111	Shelby	Mt.	48·35 N	111·55 W
121	Shelby	NC	35·16 N	81·35 W
104	Shelby	Oh.	40·50 N	82·40 W
104	Shelbyville (shĕl′bê-vĭl)	Il.	39·20 N	88·45 W
104	Shelbyville	In.	39·30 N	85·45 W
104	Shelbyville	Ky.	38·10 N	85·15 W
120	Shelbyville	Tn.	35·30 N	86·28 W
186	Shelbyville Res.	Il.	39·30 N	88·45 W
108	Sheldon (shĕl′dŭn)	Ia.	43·10 N	95·50 W
119	Sheldon	Tx. (In.)	29·52 N	95·07 W
173	Shelekhova, Zaliv (B.)	Sov. Un.	60·00 N	156·00 E
101	Shelikof Str. (shĕ′lê-kôf)	Ak.	57·56 N	154·20 W
94	Shellbrook	Can.	53·15 N	106·22 W
111	Shelley (shĕl′lê)	Id.	43·24 N	112·06 W
109	Shellrock (R.) (shĕl′rŏk)	Ia.	43·25 N	93·19 W
166	Shelon′ (R.) (shä′lôn)	Sov. Un.	57·50 N	29·40 E
105	Shelton (shĕl′tŭn)	Ct.	41·15 N	73·05 W
116	Shelton	Ne.	40·46 N	98·41 W
110	Shelton	Wa.	47·14 N	123·05 W
174	Shemakha (shĕ-mȧ-kä′)	Sov. Un. (Urals In.)	56·16 N	59·19 E
171	Shemakha	Sov. Un.	40·35 N	48·40 E
117	Shenandoah (shĕn-ăn-dō′ȧ)	Ia.	40·46 N	95·23 W
105	Shenandoah	Pa.	40·50 N	76·15 W
105	Shenandoah	Va.	38·30 N	78·30 W
105	Shenandoah Natl. Park	Va.	38·35 N	78·25 W
105	Shenandoah (R.)	Va.	38·55 N	78·05 W
190	Shenchiu (shenchĭō)	China	33·11 N	115·06 E
215	Shendam	Nig.	8·53 N	9·32 E
190	Shengfang (shengfäng)	China	39·05 N	116·40 E
	Shenhsi (Prov.), see Shensi			
190	Shenhsien (shen′sĭän)	China	38·02 N	115·33 E
174	Shenkursk (shĕn-kōōrsk′)	Sov. Un.	62·10 N	43·08 E
192	Shenmu	China	38·55 N	110·35 E
188	Shensi (Shenhsi) (Prov.)	China	35·30 N	109·10 E
190	Shentse (shen′zhŏ)	China	38·12 N	115·12 E
192	Shenyang (Mukden) (shĕn′yäng′) (mōōk′dĕn)	China	41·45 N	123·22 E
184	Sheopur	India	25·37 N	78·10 E
89	Shepard (shĕ′pȧrd)	Can. (Calgary In.)	50·57 N	113·55 W
167	Shepetovka (shĕ-pĕ-tôf′kȧ)	Sov. Un.	50·10 N	27·01 E
203	Shepparton (shĕp′ăr-tŭn)	Austl.	36·15 S	145·25 E
99	Sherborn (shûr′bŭrn)	Ma. (In.)	42·15 N	71·22 W
214	Sherbro I.	S. L.	7·30 N	12·55 W
105	Sherbrooke	Can.	45·24 N	71·54 W
148	Sherburn (shûr′bŭrn)	Eng.	53·47 N	1·15 W
159	Shereshevo (shĕ-rĕ-shĕ-vô)	Sov. Un.	52·31 N	24·08 E
117	Sheridan (shĕr′ĭ-dăn)	Ar.	34·19 N	92·21 W
110	Sheridan	Or.	45·06 N	123·22 W
111	Sheridan	Wy.	44·48 N	106·56 W
117	Sherman (shĕr′măn)	Tx.	33·39 N	96·37 W
174	Sherna R. (shĕr′nȧ)	Sov. Un. (Moscow In.)	56·08 N	38·45 E
95	Sherridon	Can.	55·10 N	101·10 W
149	's Hertogenbosch (sĕr-tō′ghĕn-bôs)	Neth. (Amsterdam In.)	51·41 N	5·19 E
112	Sherwood	Or. (Portland In.)	45·21 N	122·50 W
148	Sherwood For.	Eng.	53·11 N	1·07 W
93	Sherwood Park	Can.	53·31 N	113·19 W
154	Shetland (Is.) (shĕt′lănd)	Scot.	60·35 N	2·10 W

ăt; finăl; rāte; senâte; ärm; ȧsk; sofȧ; fâre; ch-choose; dh-as th in other; bē; ēvent; bĕt; recĕnt; cratẽr; g-go; gh-guttural g; bĭt; ĭ-short neutral; rīde; ĸ-guttural k as ch in German ich;

PRONOUNCING INDEX

Shevchenko — Silverton 347

Page	Name	Pronunciation	Region	Lat. °′	Long. °′
186	Shevchenko		Sov. Un.	44·00 N	51·10 E
211	Shewa Gimira		Eth.	7·13 N	35·49 E
108	Sheyenne (R.)	(shī-ĕn')	ND	46·42 N	97·52 W
104	Shiawassee (R.)	(shī-ȧ-wôs'ē)	Mi.	43·15 N	84·05 W
186	Shibām	(shē'bäm)	P. D. R. of Yem.	16·02 N	48·40 E
218	Shibīn al Kawn	(shē-bēn'ĕl kōm')	Egypt (Nile In.)	30·31 N	31·01 E
218	Shibīn al Qanāṭir	(kȧ-nä'tēr)	Egypt (Nile In.)	30·18 N	31·21 E
195	Shichitō (Seven Is.)	(shē'chē-tō)	Jap.	34·18 N	139·28 E
111	Shields R.	(shēldz)	Mt.	45·54 N	110·40 W
148	Shifnal	(shĭf'năl)	Eng.	52·40 N	2·22 W
190	Shih (R.)	(shē hŏ)	China	32·09 N	114·11 E
190	Shihchiachuang		China	38·04 N	114·31 E
190	Shihchiangchen	(shē'kĭäng'zhen)	China	32·16 N	120·59 E
191	Shihch'iao		China (Canton In.)	22·56 N	113·22 E
190	Shihchiu Hu (L.)	(shē'jĭō'hōō)	China	31·29 N	119·07 E
192	Shihlung		China	23·05 N	113·58 E
190	Shihohienfou		China	31·27 N	117·51 E
191	Shiht'ou		China (Canton In.)	23·01 N	113·23 E
190	Shihts'un	(shē'chōōen)	China	33·47 N	117·18 E
190	Shihtzu Shan (Mts.)	(shē'jē shän)	China	37·17 N	121·38 E
191	Shihwan		China (Canton In.)	23·01 N	113·04 E
193	Shihwanta Shan (Mtns.)		China	22·10 N	107·30 E
192	Shihwei Pk.		China	47·11 N	119·59 E
184	Shikārpur		Pak.	27·51 N	68·52 E
195	Shiki	(shē'kē)	Jap. (Tōkyō In.)	35·50 N	139·35 E
195	Shikoku (I.)	(shē'kō'kōō)	Jap.	33·43 N	133·33 E
173	Shilka (R.)	(shĭl'kȧ)	Sov. Un.	53·00 N	118·45 E
184	Shilla (Mt.)		India	37·18 N	78·17 E
184	Shillong	(shēl-lông')	India	25·39 N	91·58 E
113	Shiloh	(shī'lō)	Il. (St. Louis In.)	38·34 N	89·54 W
195	Shimabara	(shē'mä-bä'rä)	Jap.	32·46 N	130·22 E
195	Shimada	(shē'mä-dä)	Jap.	34·49 N	138·13 E
195	Shimizu	(shē'mē-zōō)	Jap.	35·00 N	138·29 E
195	Shimminato	(shēm'mē'nä-tō)	Jap.	36·47 N	137·05 E
195	Shimoda	(shē'mō-dȧ)	Jap.	34·41 N	138·58 E
185	Shimoga		India	13·59 N	75·38 E
217	Shimoni		Ken.	4·39 S	39·23 E
195	Shimonoseki	(shē'mō-nō-sĕ'kē) (shē-mō-nō'sĕ-kĭ)	Jap.	33·58 N	130·55 E
195	Shimo-Saga	(shē'mō sä'gä)	Jap. (Ōsaka In.)	35·01 N	135·41 E
154	Shin, Loch (L.)	(lŏĸ shĭn)	Scot.	58·08 N	4·02 W
195	Shinagawa-Wan (B.)	(shē'nä-gä'wä wän)	Jap. (Tōkyō In.)	35·37 N	139·49 E
195	Shinano-Gawa (Strm.)	(shē-nä'nō gä'wä)	Jap.	36·43 N	138·22 E
195	Shingū	(shĭn'gōō)	Jap.	33·43 N	135·59 E
195	Shinji (L.)	(shĭn'jē)	Jap.	35·23 N	133·05 E
217	Shinkolobwe		Zaire	11·02 S	26·35 E
211	Shinyanga	(shĭn-yäŋ'gä)	Tan.	3·40 S	33·26 E
194	Shiono Misaki (C.)	(shē-ō'nō mē'sä-kē)	Jap.	33·20 N	136·10 E
128	Ship Channel Cay (I.)	(shĭp chă-nĕl kē)	Ba.	24·50 N	76·50 W
148	Shipley	(shĭp'lē)	Eng.	53·50 N	1·47 W
98	Shippegan	(shĭ'pē-găn)	Can.	47·45 N	64·42 W
98	Shippegan I.		Can.	47·50 N	64·38 W
105	Shippenburg	(shĭp'ĕn bûrg)	Pa.	40·00 N	77·30 W
98	Shipshaw (R.)	(shĭp'shô)	Can.	48·50 N	71·03 W
183	Shiqma (R.)		Isr. (Palestine In.)	31·31 N	34·40 E
195	Shirane-san (Mtn.)	(shē'rä'nȧ-sän')	Jap.	35·44 N	138·14 E
194	Shira Saki (C.)	(shē'rä sä'kē)	Jap.	41·25 N	142·10 E
212	Shirati	(shē-rä'tē)	Tan.	1·15 S	34·02 E
186	Shīrāz	(shē-räz')	Iran	29·32 N	52·27 E
217	Shire (R.)	(shē'rȧ)	Malawi	16·20 S	35·05 E
167	Shirokoye	(shē'rô-kô-yĕ)	Sov. Un.	47·40 N	33·18 E
101	Shishaldin Vol.	(shī-shăl'dĭn)	Ak.	54·48 N	164·00 W
107	Shively	(shīv'lē)	Ky. (Louisville In.)	38·11 N	85·47 W
184	Shivpuri		India	25·31 N	77·46 E
183	Shivta, Horvot (Ruins)		Isr. (Palestine In.)	30·54 N	34·36 E
115	Shivwits (Shebit) Ind. Res.	(shĭv'wĭts) (shĕ'bĭt)	Ut.	37·10 N	113·50 W
115	Shivwits Plat.		Az.	36·13 N	113·42 W
99	Shirley	(shûr'lē)	Ma. (In.)	42·33 N	71·39 W
195	Shizuki	(shĭ'zōō-kē)	Jap.	34·29 N	134·51 E
195	Shizuoka	(shē'zōō'ōkȧ)	Jap.	34·58 N	138·24 E
166	Shklov	(shklôf)	Sov. Un.	54·11 N	30·23 E
165	Shkodër (Scutari)	(shkô'dûr) (skōō'tȧrē)	Alb.	42·04 N	19·30 E
194	Shkotovo	(shkô'tô-vô)	Sov. Un.	43·15 N	132·21 E
117	Shoal Cr.	(shōl)	Il.	38·37 N	89·25 W
95	Shoal L.		Can.	49·32 N	95·00 W
104	Shoals	(shōlz)	In.	38·40 N	86·45 W
195	Shōdo (I.)	(shō'dō)	Jap.	34·27 N	134·27 E
185	Sholāpur	(shō'lä-pōōr)	India	17·42 N	75·51 E
107	Shorewood	(shōr'wŏŏd)	Wi. (Milwaukee In.)	43·05 N	87·54 W
111	Shoshone	(shô-shōn'ē)	Id.	42·56 N	114·24 W
111	Shoshone L.		Wy.	44·17 N	110·50 W
111	Shoshone R.		Wy.	44·20 N	109·28 W
111	Shoshoni		Wy.	43·14 N	108·05 W
167	Shostka	(shôst'kȧ)	Sov. Un.	51·51 N	33·31 E
190	Sh'ouchang	(shō'zhäng)	China	35·59 N	115·52 E
190	Shouhsien		China	32·36 N	116·45 E
190	Shoukuang	(shō'gōōäng)	China	36·53 N	118·45 E
167	Shpola	(shpô'lȧ)	Sov. Un.	49·01 N	31·36 E
119	Shreveport	(shrēv'pôrt)	La.	32·30 N	93·46 W
148	Shrewsbury	(shrōōz'bĕr-ĭ)	Eng.	52·43 N	2·44 W
99	Shrewsbury		Ma. (In.)	42·18 N	71·43 W
148	Shropshire (Co.)	(shrŏp'shĕr)	Eng.	52·36 N	2·45 W
128	Shroud Cay (I.)	(shroud)	Ba.	24·20 N	76·40 W
192	Shuangch'eng		China	45·18 N	126·18 E
190	Shuangho	(shōōäng hŏ)	China	31·33 N	116·48 E
189	Shuangliao		China	43·37 N	123·30 E
190	Shuanglunho	(shōōäng'lōōĕn'hŏ)	China	31·50 N	115·07 E
192	Shuangyang		China	43·28 N	125·45 E
109	Shullsburg	(shŭlz'bûrg)	Wi.	42·35 N	90·16 W
190	Shulyehehen	(shōōlĭĕhŭhĕn)	China	36·08 N	114·07 E
101	Shumagin (Is.)	(shōō'mȧ-gēn)	Ak.	55·22 N	159·20 W
165	Shumen		Bul.	43·15 N	26·54 E
193	Shunan	(shōō'nän')	China	29·38 N	119·00 E
101	Shungnak	(shŭng'nȧk)	Ak.	66·55 N	157·20 W
192	Shuni	(shōōn'yĭ)	China (In.)	40·09 N	116·38 E
188	Shunning	(shŭ'nĭng')	China	24·34 N	99·49 E
191	Shunte		China (Canton In.)	22·50 N	113·15 E
174	Shunut, 'Gora (Mt.)	(gȧ-rä shōō'nōōt)	Sov. Un. (Urals In.)	56·33 N	59·45 E
186	Shuqrah		P. D. R. of Yem.	13·32 N	46·02 E
186	Shūrāb (R.)	(shōō räb)	Iran	31·08 N	55·30 E
194	Shuri	(shōō'rē)	Jap.	26·10 N	127·48 E
171	Shur R.	(shōōr)	Iran	35·40 N	50·10 E
186	Shūshtar	(shōōsh'tŭr)	Iran	31·50 N	48·46 E
93	Shuswap L.	(shōōs'wŏp)	Can.	50·57 N	119·15 W
166	Shuya	(shōō'yȧ)	Sov. Un.	56·52 N	41·23 E
190	Shuyang	(shōō yäng)	China	34·09 N	118·47 E
193	Shweba		Bur.	22·23 N	96·13 E
	Shyaulyay, see Šiauliai				
194	Siakin (L.)	(sĭä'jĭn)	China	42·25 N	132·45 E
183	Siak Ketjil (R.)		Indon. (Singapore In.)	1·01 N	101·45 E
183	Siaksriinderapura	(sê-äks'rĭ ĕn'drȧ-pōō'rä)	Indon. (Singapore In.)	0·48 N	102·05 E
184	Siālkot	(sê-äl'kōt)	Pak.	32·39 N	74·30 E
	Sian, see Hsian				
190	Siaowu Shan (Mts.)	(sĭou'wōō shän)	China	39·48 N	114·52 E
165	Siátista	(syä'tĭs-ta)	Grc.	40·15 N	21·32 E
197	Siau (I.)		Indon.	2·40 N	126·00 E
157	Šiauliai (Shyaulyay)	(shê-ou'lê-ī)	Sov. Un.	55·57 N	23·19 E
174	Sibay	(sē'báy)	Sov. Un. (Urals In.)	52·41 N	58·40 E
164	Šibenik	(shê-bā'nēk)	Yugo.	43·44 N	15·55 E
182	Siberia (Reg.)		Asia	57·00 N	97·00 E
196	Siberut (I.)	(sē'bȧ-rōōt)	Indon.	1·22 S	99·45 E
184	Sibī		Pak.	29·41 N	67·52 E
216	Sibiti	(sê-bê-tē')	Con.	3·41 S	13·21 E
165	Sibiu	(sê-bĭ-ōō')	Rom.	45·47 N	24·09 E
108	Sibley	(sĭb'lē)	Ia.	43·24 N	95·33 W
196	Sibolga	(sê-bō'gȧ)	Indon.	1·45 N	98·45 E
187	Sibsāgar	(sēb-sŭ'gŭr)	India	26·47 N	94·45 E
196	Sibuti		Phil.	4·40 N	119·30 E
197	Sibuyan (I.)	(sē-bōō-yän')	Phil. (In.)	12·19 N	122·25 E
196	Sibuyan Sea		Phil.	12·43 N	122·38 E
196	Sicapoo (Mtn.)	(sē-kä-pōō')	Phil.	18·05 N	121·03 E
151	Sicily (I.)	(sĭs'ĭ-lē)	It.	37·38 N	13·30 E
126	Sico R.	(sē-kō)	Hond.	15·32 N	85·42 W
134	Sicuaní	(sē-kwä'nē)	Peru	14·12 S	71·12 W
218	Sidamo (Prov.)	(sē-dä'mō)	Eth.	5·08 N	37·45 E
164	Siderno Marina	(sê-dĕr'nô mä-rē'nä)	It.	38·18 N	16·19 E
164	Sídheros, Akr. (C.)		Grc. (In.)	35·19 N	26·20 E
165	Sidhiró Kastron		Grc.	41·13 N	23·27 E
163	Sidi-Aïsa		Alg.	35·53 N	3·44 E
211	Sīdī Barrānī		Egypt	31·41 N	26·09 E
210	Sidi bel Abbès	(sē'dē-bĕl ȧ-bĕs')	Alg.	35·15 N	0·43 W
210	Sidi Ifni	(ēf'nē)	Mor.	29·22 N	10·15 W
220	Sidley, Mt.	(sĭd'lē)	Ant.	77·25 S	129·00 W
92	Sidney		Can.	48·39 N	123·24 W
111	Sidney	(sĭd'nē)	Mt.	47·43 N	104·07 W
108	Sidney		Ne.	41·10 N	103·00 W
104	Sidney		Oh.	40·20 N	84·10 W
120	Sidney Lanier, L.	(lăn'yēr)	Ga.	34·27 N	83·56 W
214	Sido		Mali	11·40 N	7·36 W
	Sidon, see Ṣaydā				
183	Sidr, Wādī (R.)		Egypt (Palestine In.)	29·43 N	32·58 E
159	Siedlce	(syĕd''l-tsĕ)	Pol.	52·09 N	22·20 E
161	Siegburg	(zēg'bōōrgh)	F.R.G. (Ruhr In.)	50·48 N	7·13 E
161	Siegen	(zē'ghĕn)	F.R.G. (Ruhr In.)	50·52 N	8·01 E
149	Sieghartskirchen		Aus. (Vienna In.)	48·16 N	16·00 E
158	Sieg R.	(zēg)	F.R.G.	50·51 N	7·53 E
159	Siemiatycze	(syĕm'yä'tê-chĕ)	Pol.	52·26 N	22·52 E
159	Siemionówka	(sĕĕ-mĕō'nôf-kä)	Pol.	52·53 N	23·50 E
196	Siem Reap	(syĕm'rā'äp)	Camb.	13·32 N	103·54 E
164	Siena	(sê-ĕn'ä)	It.	43·19 N	11·21 E
159	Sieradz	(syĕ'rädz)	Pol.	51·35 N	18·45 E
162	Siero	(syā'rō)	Sp.	43·24 N	5·39 W
159	Sierpc	(syĕrpts)	Pol.	52·51 N	19·42 E
118	Sierra Blanca	(sē-ĕ'rȧ blaŋ-kä)	Tx.	31·10 N	105·20 W
115	Sierra Blanca Pk.	(blăn'kȧ)	NM	33·25 N	105·50 W
209	Sierra Leone	(sê-ĕr'rä lā-ō'nȧ)	Afr.	8·48 N	12·30 W
113	Sierra Madre	(mä'drē)	Ca. (Los Angeles In.)	34·10 N	118·03 W
118	Sierra Mojada	(sē-ĕ'r-rä-mô-кä'dä)	Mex.	27·22 N	103·42 W
165	Sífnos (I.)		Grc.	36·58 N	24·30 E
156	Sigdal	(sēgh'däl)	Nor.	60·01 N	9·35 E
160	Sigean	(sē-zhŏɴ')	Fr.	43·02 N	2·56 E
109	Sigeurney	(sē-gûr-nĭ)	Ia.	41·16 N	92·10 W
159	Sighet	(sē-gât')	Rom.	47·57 N	23·55 E
159	Sighisoara	(sē-gê-shwä'rȧ)	Rom.	46·11 N	24·48 F
150	Siglufjördhur		Ice.	66·06 N	18·45 W
171	Signakhi		Sov. Un.	41·45 N	45·50 E
113	Signal Hill	(sĭg'nȧl hĭl)	Ca. (Los Angeles In.)	33·48 N	118·11 W
134	Sigsig	(sēg-sēg')	Ec.	3·05 S	78·44 W
156	Sigtuna	(sēgh-tōō'nȧ)	Swe.	59·40 N	17·39 E
128	Siguanea, Ensenada de la (B.)	(ĕn-sĕ-nä-dä-dĕ-lä-sê-gwä-nā'ä)	Cuba	21·45 N	83·15 W
126	Siguatepeque	(sē-gwȧ'tĕ-pĕ-kĕ)	Hond.	14·33 N	87·51 W
162	Sigüenza	(sē-gwĕ'n-zä)	Sp.	41·03 N	2·38 W
214	Siguiri	(sê-gê-rē')	Gui.	11·25 N	9·10 W
171	Siirt	(sĭ-ērt')	Tur.	38·00 N	42·00 E
217	Sikalongo		Zambia	16·46 S	27·07 E
214	Sikasso	(sê-käs'sō)	Mali	11·19 N	5·40 W
117	Sikeston	(sīks'tŭn)	Mo.	36·50 N	89·35 W
173	Sikhote Alin', Khrebet (Mts.)	(se-кô'ta a-lēn')	Sov. Un.	45·00 N	135·45 E
165	Sikinos (I.)	(sĭ'kĭ-nōs)	Grc.	36·45 N	24·55 E
184	Sikkim (State)		India	27·42 N	88·25 E
159	Siklós	(sĭ'klōsh)	Hong.	45·51 N	18·18 E
162	Sil (R.)	(sē'l)	Sp.	42·20 N	7·13 W
197	Silang	(sê-läng')	Phil. (In.)	14·14 N	120·58 E
124	Silao	(sê-lä'ō)	Mex.	20·56 N	101·25 W
184	Silchar	(sĭl-chär')	India	24·52 N	92·50 E
218	Silent Valley	(sī'lĕnt vă'lē)	S. Afr. (Johannesburg & Pretoria In.)	24·32 S	26·40 E
121	Siler City	(sī'lēr)	NC	35·45 N	79·29 W
159	Silesia (Reg.)	(sĭ-lē'shȧ)	Pol.	50·58 N	16·53 E
171	Silifke		Tur.	36·20 N	34·00 E
153	Silistra	(sê-lēs'trȧ)	Bul.	44·01 N	27·13 E
156	Siljan (R.)	(sēl'yän)	Swe.	60·48 N	14·28 E
156	Silkeborg	(sĭl'kĕ-bôr')	Den.	56·10 N	9·33 E
89	Sillery	(sēl'-re')	Can. (Quebec In.)	46·46 N	71·15 W
117	Siloam Springs	(sĭ-lōm)	Ar.	36·10 N	94·32 W
216	Siloana Plns.		Zambia	16·55 S	23·10 E
124	Silocayoápan	(sē-lô-kä-yô-ȧ'pän)	Mex.	17·29 N	98·09 W
119	Silsbee	(sĭlz' bē)	Tx.	30·19 N	94·09 W
157	Šilutė	(shĭ-lōō'tȧ)	Sov. Un.	55·23 N	21·26 E
137	Silva Jardim	(sē'l-vä-zhär-dêɴ)	Braz. (Rio de Janeiro In.)	22·40 S	42·24 W
112	Silvana	(sĭl-vän'ȧ)	Wa. (Seattle In.)	48·12 N	122·16 W
135	Silvânia	(sēl-vȧ'nyä)	Braz.	16·43 S	48·33 W
184	Silvassa		India	20·10 N	73·00 E
117	Silver (L.)		Mo.	39·38 N	93·12 W
112	Silverado	(sĭl-vēr-ä'dō)	Ca. (Los Angeles In.)	33·45 N	117·40 W
129	Silver Bk.		Ba.	20·40 N	69·40 W
129	Silver Bank Passage (Str.)		Ba.	20·40 N	70·20 W
109	Silver Bay		Mn.	47·24 N	91·07 W
115	Silver City	(sĭl'vēr sĭ'tĭ)	NM	32·45 N	108·20 W
127	Silver City		Pan.	9·20 N	79·54 W
105	Silver Creek	(crēk)	NY	42·35 N	79·10 W
115	Silver Cr.		Az.	34·30 N	110·05 W
107	Silver Cr.		In. (Louisville In.)	38·20 N	85·45 W
107	Silver Cr., Muddy Fk.		In. (Louisville In.)	38·26 N	85·52 W
112	Silverdale	(sĭl'vēr-dāl)	Wa. (Seattle In.)	49·39 N	122·42 W
107	Silver Lake	(lāk)	Wi. (Milwaukee In.)	42·33 N	88·10 W
107	Silver L.		Wi. (Milwaukee In.)	42·35 N	88·08 W
106	Silver Spring	(sprĭng)	Md. (Baltimore In.)	39·00 N	77·00 W
112	Silver Star Mtn.		Wa. (Portland In.)	45·45 N	122·15 W
92	Silverthrone Mtn.	(sĭl'vēr-thrōn)	Can.	51·31 N	126·06 W
115	Silverton	(sĭl'vēr-tŭn)	Co.	37·50 N	107·40 W
107	Silverton		Oh. (Cincinnati In.)	39·12 N	84·24 W
110	Silverton		Or.	45·02 N	122·46 W
213	Silverton		S. Afr. (Johannesburg & Pretoria In.)	25·45 S	28·13 E

ng-sing; ŋ-baŋk; ɴ-nasalized n; nŏd; cŏmmit; ōld; ôbey; ôrder; fōōd; fŏŏt; ou-out; s-soft; sh-dish; th-thin; pūre; ûnite; ûrn; stŭd; circŭs; ü-as "y" in study; '-indeterminate vowel.

348 Silves — Snake PRONOUNCING INDEX

Page	Name Pronunciation Region	Lat. °'	Long. °'
162	Silves (sēl'vĕzh) Port.	37·15 N	8·24 W
110	Silvies R. (sĭl'vēz) Or.	43·44 N	119·15 W
174	Sim (sĭm) Sov. Un. (Urals In.)	55·00 N	57·42 E
216	Simba Zaire	0·36 N	22·55 E
105	Simcoe (sĭm'kō) Can.	42·50 N	80·20 W
105	Simcoe (L.) Can.	44·30 N	79·20 W
196	Simeulue (I.) Indon.	2·27 N	95·30 E
167	Simferopol' (Akmechet) (sêm-fĕ-rô'pôl') (ák-mĕch'ĕt) Sov. Un.	44·58 N	34·04 E
153	Simi (I.) Grc.	36·27 N	27·41 E
112	Similk Beach (sē'mĭlk) Wa. (Seattle In.)	48·27 N	122·35 W
184	Simla (sĭm'là) India	31·09 N	77·15 E
159	Simleul-Silvaniei (shêm-lā'ōōl-sêl-vä'nyĕ-ê) Rom.	47·14 N	22·46 E
128	Simms Pt. Ba.	25·00 N	77·40 W
125	Simojovel (sê-mō-hō-vĕl') Mex.	17·12 N	92·43 W
157	Simola (sē'mô-là) Fin.	60·55 N	28·06 E
137	Simonésia (sē-mô-nĕ'syä) Braz. (Rio de Janeiro In.)	20·04 S	41·53 W
93	Simonette (R.) (sĭ-mŏn-ĕt') Can.	54·15 N	118·00 W
212	Simonstad S. Afr. (In.)	34·11 S	18·25 E
92	Simood Sound Can.	50·45 N	126·25 W
158	Simplon P. (sĭm'plŏn) (săN-plôN') Switz.	46·13 N	7·53 E
158	Simplon Tun. It.-Switz.	46·16 N	8·20 E
109	Simpson (I.) Can.	48·43 N	87·44 W
204	Simpson Des. (sĭmp-sŭn) Austl.	24·40 S	136·40 E
156	Simrishamn (sēm'rês-häm'n) Swe.	55·35 N	14·19 E
174	Sim R. Sov. Un. (Urals In.)	55·00 N	57·42 E
119	Sims Bayou (sĭmz bī-yōō') Tx. (In.)	29·37 N	95·23 W
189	Simushir (I.) (se-mōō'shēr) Sov. Un.	47·15 N	150·47 E
165	Sinaia (sĭ-nä'yȧ) Rom.	45·20 N	25·30 E
211	Sinai Pen. (sī'nī) Egypt	29·24 N	33·29 E
197	Sinait (sē-nä'ēt) Phil. (In.)	15·54 N	120·28 E
122	Sinaloa (State) (sē-nä-lô-ä) Mex.	25·15 N	107·45 W
194	Sinanju (sĭ'nän-jōō') Kor.	39·39 N	125·41 E
171	Sinap Tur.	42·00 N	35·05 E
134	Sincé (sēn'sā) Col.	9·15 N	75·14 W
134	Sincelejo (sēn-sā-lā'hō) Col.	9·12 N	75·30 W
112	Sinclair Inlet (sĭn-klâr') Wa. (Seattle In.)	47·31 N	122·41 W
92	Sinclair Mills Can.	54·02 N	121·41 W
157	Sindi (sēn'dê) Sov. Un.	58·20 N	24·40 E
167	Sinel'nikovo (sē'nyĕl-nē'kô'vô) Sov. Un.	49·19 N	35·33 E
162	Sines (sē'nȧzh) Port.	37·57 N	8·50 W
183	Singapore (sĭn'gȧ-pōr') Singapore (Singapore In.)	1·18 N	103·52 E
183	Singapore Asia (Singapore In.)	1·22 N	103·45 E
183	Singapore Str. Indon. (Singapore In.)	1·14 N	104·20 E
165	Singitikós Kólpos (G.) Grc.	40·15 N	24·00 E
188	Singu (sĭn'gŭ) Bur.	22·37 N	96·04 E
167	Siniye Lipyagi (sēn'ê-ĕ lēp'yä-gê) Sov. Un.	51·24 N	38·29 E
164	Sinj (sēn') Yugo.	43·42 N	16·39 E
211	Sinjah Sud.	13·09 N	33·52 E
188	Sinkiang Uighur (Aut. Reg.) China	40·15 N	82·15 E
174	Sin'kovo (sĭn-kô'vô) Sov. Un. (Moscow In.)	56·23 N	37·19 E
135	Sinnamary Fr. Gu.	5·15 N	57·52 W
164	Sinni (R.) (sēn'nē) It.	40·05 N	16·15 E
218	Sinnūris Egypt (Nile In.)	29·25 N	30·52 E
136	Sino, Pedra de (Mtn.) (pĕ'drä-dô-sē'nô) Braz. (Rio de Janeiro In.)	22·27 S	43·02 W
217	Sinoia (sĭ-noi'ȧ) Rh.	17·22 S	30·12 E
149	Sint Niklaas Bel. (Brussels In.)	51·10 N	4·07 E
119	Sinton (sĭn'tŭn) Tx.	28·03 N	97·30 W
163	Sintra (sên'trȧ) Port. (Lisbon In.)	38·48 N	9·23 W
119	Sint Truiden Bel. (Brussels In.)	50·49 N	5·14 E
194	Sinŭiju (sĭ'nōōĭ-jōō) Kor.	40·04 N	124·33 E
174	Sinyavino (sĭn-yä'vĭ-nô) Sov. Un. (Leningrad In.)	59·50 N	31·07 E
166	Sinyaya (R.) (sên'yȧ-yȧ) Sov. Un.	56·40 N	28·20 E
167	Sinyukha (R.) (sē'nyŏŏ-ĸȧ) Sov. Un.	48·34 N	30·49 E
158	Sion (sē'ôN') Switz.	46·15 N	7·17 E
108	Sioux City (sōō) Ia.	42·30 N	96·25 W
108	Sioux Falls (fôlz) SD	43·33 N	96·43 W
95	Sioux Lookout Can.	50·06 N	91·55 W
134	Sipí (sē-pē') Col. (In.)	4·39 N	76·38 W
90	Sipiwesk Can.	55·27 N	97·24 W
120	Sipsey (R.) (sĭp'sē) Al.	33·26 N	87·42 W
196	Sipura (I.) Indon.	2·15 S	99·33 E
124	Siqueros (sē-kā'rōs) Mex.	23·19 N	106·14 W
127	Siquia, R. (sē-kē'ä) Nic.	12·23 N	84·36 W
151	Siracusa (sē-rä-koo'sä) It.	37·02 N	15·19 E
184	Sirājganj (sĭ-räj'gŭnj) Bngl.	24·23 N	89·43 E
126	Sirama (sē-rä-mä) Sal.	13·23 N	87·55 W
93	Sir Douglas, Mt. (sûr dŭg'lăs) Can.	50·44 N	115·20 W
204	Sir Edward Pellew Group (Is.) (pĕl'ū) Austl.	15·15 S	137·15 E
159	Siretul R. Rom.	46·10 N	27·18 E
186	Sirhān, Wadi (R.) Sau. Ar.	31·02 N	37·16 E
165	Síros (Ermoúpolis) Grc.	37·30 N	24·56 E
165	Síros (I.) Grc.	37·23 N	24·55 E
184	Sirsa India	29·39 N	75·02 E
93	Sir Sandford, Mt. (sûr sănd'fērd) Can.	51·40 N	117·52 W
157	Sirvintos (shēr'vĭn-tôs) Sov. Un.	55·02 N	24·59 E
93	Sir Wilfrid Laurier, Mt. (sûr wĭl'frĭd lôr'yēr) Can.	52·47 N	119·45 W
164	Sisak (sē'sȧk) Yugo.	45·29 N	16·20 E
125	Sisal (sē-säl') Mex.	21·09 N	90·03 W
114	Sisquoc (R.) (sĭs'kwŏk) Ca.	34·47 N	120·13 W
108	Sisseton (sĭs'tŭn) SD	45·39 N	97·04 W
186	Sistān, Daryacheh-ye (L.) Iran-Afg.	31·45 N	61·15 E
161	Sisteron (sēst'rôN') Fr.	44·10 N	5·55 E
104	Sisterville (sĭs'tēr-vĭl) WV	39·30 N	81·00 W
164	Sitía (sē'tĭ-ȧ) Grc. (In.)	35·09 N	26·10 E
101	Sitka (sĭt'kȧ) Ak.	57·08 N	135·18 W
148	Sittingbourne (sĭt-ĭng-bôrn) Eng. (London In.)	51·20 N	0·44 E
196	Sittwe Bur.	20·09 N	92·54 E
171	Sivas (sē'väs) Tur.	39·50 N	36·50 E
167	Sivash (L.) (sē'vȧsh) Sov. Un.	45·55 N	34·42 E
171	Siverek (sē'vĕ-rĕk) Tur.	37·50 N	39·20 E
157	Siverskaya (sē'vĕr-skȧ-yȧ) Sov. Un.	59·17 N	30·03 E
211	Siwah (Oasis) (sē'wä) Egypt	29·33 N	25·11 E
127	Sixaola R. (sē-ĸä-ō'lä) (sĕk-sȧ-ō'lȧ) C. R.	9·31 N	83·07 W
211	Sixth Cataract Sud.	16·26 N	32·44 E
156	Sjaelland (I.) (shĕl'lăn') Den.	55·34 N	11·35 E
165	Sjenica (syĕ'nē-tsȧ) Yugo.	43·15 N	20·02 E
167	Skadovsk (skä'dôfsk) Sov. Un.	46·08 N	32·54 E
156	Skagen (skä'ghĕn) Den.	57·43 N	10·32 E
156	Skagen (Pt.) Den.	57·43 N	10·31 E
156	Skagerrak (Str.) (skä-ghĕ-räk') Eur.	57·43 N	8·28 E
112	Skagit B. (skăg'ĭt) Wa. (Seattle In.)	48·20 N	122·32 W
110	Skagit R. Wa.	48·29 N	121·52 W
101	Skagway (skăg-wā) Ak.	59·30 N	135·28 W
156	Skälderviken (B.) Swe.	56·20 N	12·25 E
173	Skalistyy, Golets (Mtn.) Sov. Un.	57·28 N	119·48 E
112	Skamania (skȧ-mā'nĭ-ȧ) Wa. (Portland In.)	45·37 N	112·03 W
112	Skamokawa Wa. (Portland In.)	46·16 N	123·27 W
156	Skanderborg (skän-ĕr-bôr') Den.	56·04 N	9·55 E
105	Skaneateles (skăn-ē-ăt'lĕs) NY	42·55 N	76·25 W
105	Skaneateles (L.) NY	42·50 N	76·20 W
156	Skänninge (shĕn'ĭng-ĕ) Swe.	58·24 N	15·02 E
156	Skanör (skän'ûr) Swe.	55·24 N	12·49 E
165	Skantzoúra (Is.) (skän'tsōō-rä) Grc.	39·03 N	24·05 E
156	Skara (skä'rȧ) Swe.	58·25 N	13·24 E
92	Skeena (R.) (skē'nă) Can.	54·10 N	129·40 W
92	Skeena Mts. Can.	56·00 N	128·00 W
213	Skeerpoort S. Afr. (Johannesburg & Pretoria In.)	25·49 S	27·45 E
213	Skeerpoort (R.) S. Afr. (Johannesburg & Pretoria In.)	25·58 S	27·41 E
135	Skeldon (skĕl'dŭn) Guy.	5·49 N	57·15 W
150	Skellefte (R.) (shĕl'ĕ-ftĕ) Swe.	65·18 N	19·08 E
150	Skellefteå (shĕl'ĕf-tē-å') Swe.	64·47 N	20·48 E
156	Skern (R.) (skĕrn) Den.	55·56 N	8·52 E
154	Skerries (Is.) (skĕr'ēz) Wales	53·30 N	4·59 W
174	Skhodnya Sov. Un. (Moscow In).	55·57 N	37·21 E
174	Skhodnya R. (skôd'nyȧ) Sov. Un. (Moscow In.)	55·55 N	37·16 E
165	Skíathos (I.) (skē'ȧ-thôs) Grc.	39·15 N	23·25 E
154	Skibbereen (skĭb'ēr-ēn) Ire.	51·32 N	9·25 W
92	Skidegate (inlet) (skĭ'-dĕ-gāt') Can.	53·15 N	132·00 W
119	Skidmore (skĭd'môr) Tx.	28·16 N	97·40 W
156	Skien (skē'ĕn) Nor.	59·13 N	9·35 E
159	Skierniewice (skyĕr-nyĕ-vēt'sĕ) Pol.	51·58 N	20·13 E
92	Skihist Mtn. Can.	50·11 N	121·54 W
152	Skikda (Philippeville) Alg.	36·58 N	6·51 E
218	Skilpadfontein S. Afr. (Johannesburg & Pretoria In.)	25·02 S	28·50 E
165	Skíros Grc.	38·53 N	24·32 E
165	Skiros (I.) Grc.	38·50 N	24·43 E
156	Skive (skē'vĕ) Den.	56·34 N	8·56 E
150	Skjalfandá (R.) (skyäl'fänd-ô) Ice.	65·24 N	16·40 W
150	Skjerstad (skyĕr-städ) Nor.	67·12 N	15·37 E
164	Škofja Loka (shkôf'yȧ lō'kȧ) Yugo.	46·10 N	14·20 E
107	Skokie (skō'kē) Il. (Chicago In.)	42·02 N	87·45 W
112	Skokomish Ind. Res. (skō-kō'mĭsh) Wa. (Seattle In.)	47·22 N	123·07 W
159	Skole (skô'lĕ) Sov. Un.	49·03 N	23·32 E
165	Skópelos (I.) (skô'pȧ-lôs) Grc.	39·04 N	23·31 E
166	Skopin (skô'pēn) Sov. Un.	53·49 N	39·35 E
165	Skopje (skôp'yĕ) Yugo.	42·02 N	21·26 E
156	Skövde (shûv'dĕ) Swe.	58·25 N	13·48 E
173	Skovorodino (skô'vô-rô'dĭ-nô) Sov. Un.	53·53 N	123·56 E
98	Skowhegan (skou-hē'găn) Me.	44·45 N	69·27 W
164	Skradin (skrä'dên) Yugo.	43·49 N	17·58 E
156	Skreia (skrā'ä) Nor.	60·40 N	10·55 E
156	Skudeneshavn (skōō'dĕ-nes-houn') Nor.	59·10 N	5·19 E
156	Skulerud (skōō'lĕ-rōōdh) Nor.	59·40 N	11·30 E
115	Skull Valley Ind. Res. (skŭl) Ut.	40·25 N	112·50 W
120	Skuna, (R.) (skû'nȧ) Ms.	33·57 N	89·36 W
109	Skunk (R.) (skŭnk) Ia.	41·12 N	92·14 W
157	Skuodas (skwô'dȧs) Sov. Un.	56·16 N	21·32 E
156	Skurup (skû'rōōp) Swe.	55·29 N	13·27 E
167	Skvira (skvē'rȧ) Sov. Un.	49·43 N	29·41 E
158	Skwierzyna (skvê-ĕr'zhĭ-nȧ) Pol.	52·35 N	15·30 E
154	Skye (I.) (skī) Scot.	57·25 N	6·17 W
112	Skykomish (R.) (skī'kō-mĭsh) Wa. (Seattle In.)	47·50 N	121·55 W
136	Skyring, Seno (B.) (sĕ'nô-s-krē'ng) Chile	52·35 S	72·30 W
156	Slagese Den.	55·25 N	11·19 E
196	Slamet, Gunung (Mtn.) (slä'mĕt) Indon.	7·15 S	109·15 E
165	Slănic (slŭ'nēk) Rom.	45·13 N	25·56 E
109	Slate (I.) (slāt) Can.	48·38 N	87·14 W
117	Slater (slāt'ēr) Mo.	39·13 N	93·03 W
165	Slatina (slä'tē-nä) Rom.	44·26 N	24·21 E
116	Slaton (slā'tŭn) Tx.	33·26 N	101·38 W
90	Slave (R.) (slāv) Can.	59·40 N	111·21 W
172	Slavgorod (slȧf'gō-rôt) Sov. Un.	52·58 N	78·43 E
165	Slavonija (Reg.) (slä-vô'nē-yä) Yugo.	45·29 N	17·31 E
164	Slavonska Požega (slä-vôn'skä pô'zhĕ-gä) Yugo.	45·18 N	17·42 E
165	Slavonski Brod (slä-vôn'skê brôd) Yugo.	45·10 N	18·01 E
167	Slavuta (slȧ-vōō'tȧ) Sov. Un.	50·18 N	27·01 E
167	Slavyansk (slȧv'yänsk') Sov. Un.	48·52 N	37·34 E
167	Slavyanskaya (slȧv-yȧn'skȧ-yȧ) Sov. Un.	45·14 N	38·09 E
108	Slayton (slā'tŭn) Mn.	44·00 N	95·44 W
148	Sleaford (slē'fērd) Eng.	53·00 N	0·25 W
109	Sleepy Eye (slēp'ĭ ī) Mn.	44·17 N	94·44 W
119	Slidell (slī-dĕl') La.	30·17 N	89·47 W
149	Sliedrecht Neth. (Amsterdam In.)	51·49 N	4·46 E
154	Sligo (slī'gō) Ire.	54·17 N	8·19 W
156	Slite (slē'tĕ) Swe.	57·41 N	18·47 E
165	Sliven (slē'vĕn) Bul.	42·41 N	26·20 E
106	Sloatsburg (slōts'bŭrg) NY (New York In.)	41·09 N	74·11 W
157	Slobodka (slô'bôd-kȧ) Sov. Un.	54·34 N	26·12 E
170	Slobodskoy (slô'bôt-skoi) Sov. Un.	58·48 N	50·02 E
157	Sloka (slô'kȧ) Sov. Un.	56·57 N	23·37 E
159	Slonim (swō'nêm) Sov. Un.	53·05 N	25·19 E
148	Slough (slou) Eng. (London In.)	51·29 N	0·36 W
	Slovakia (Prov.), see Slovensko		
164	Slovenija (Reg.) (slô-vĕ'nê-yä) Yugo.	45·58 N	14·43 E
159	Slovensko (Slovakia) (Prov.) (slô-vĕn'skô) (slô-väk'ĭ-ȧ) Czech.	48·40 N	19·00 E
159	Sluch' (R.) Sov. Un.	50·56 N	26·48 E
164	Sluderno (slōō-dĕr'nô) It.	46·38 N	10·37 E
164	Slunj (slōōn') Yugo.	45·08 N	15·46 E
159	Slupsk (swōōpsk) Pol.	54·28 N	17·02 E
166	Slutsk (slōōtsk) Sov. Un.	53·02 N	27·34 E
154	Slyne Head (slīn) Ire.	53·25 N	10·05 W
117	Smackover (smăk'ô-vēr) Ar.	33·22 N	92·42 W
165	Smederevo (Semendria) (smĕ'dĕ-rĕ-vô) (sĕ-mĕn'drĭ-ȧ) Yugo.	44·39 N	20·54 E
165	Smederevska Palanka (smĕ-dĕ-rĕv'skä pä-län'kä) Yugo.	44·21 N	21·00 E
156	Smedjebacken (smĭ'tyĕ-bä-kĕn) Swe.	60·09 N	15·19 E
167	Smela (smyā'là) Sov. Un.	49·14 N	31·52 E
167	Smeloye (smyā'lô-ĕ) Sov. Un.	50·55 N	33·36 E
105	Smethport (smĕth'pōrt) Pa.	41·50 N	78·25 W
148	Smethwick (Warley) (In.) Eng.	52·30 N	2·01 W
166	Smiltene (smēl'tĕ-nĕ) Sov. Un.	57·26 N	25·57 E
93	Smith (smĭth) Can.	55·10 N	114·02 W
112	Smith (I.) Wa. (Seattle In.)	48·20 N	122·53 W
116	Smith Center (sĕn'tēr) Ks.	39·45 N	98·46 W
92	Smithers (smĭth'ērs) Can.	54·47 N	127·10 W
121	Smithfield (smĭth'fēld) NC	35·30 N	78·21 W
111	Smithfield Ut.	41·50 N	111·49 W
104	Smithland (smĭth'lănd) Ky.	37·10 N	88·25 W
121	Smith Mountain Lake (Res.) Va.	37·00 N	79·45 W
119	Smith Point Tx. (In.)	29·32 N	94·45 W
111	Smith R. Mt.	47·00 N	111·20 W
97	Smiths Falls (smĭths) Can.	44·55 N	76·05 W
203	Smithton (smĭth'tŭn) Austl.	40·55 S	145·12 E
113	Smithton Il. (St. Louis In.)	38·24 N	89·59 W
119	Smithville (smĭth'vĭl) Tx.	30·00 N	97·08 W
212	Smitswinkelvlakte S. Afr. (In.)	34·16 S	18·25 E
114	Smoke Creek Des. (smōk crēk) Nv.	40·28 N	119·40 W
93	Smoky (R.) (smōk'ĭ) Can.	55·30 N	117·30 W
117	Smoky Hill (R.) (smōk'ĭ hĭl) Ks.	38·40 N	97·32 W
156	Smöla (I.) (smûlä) Nor.	63·16 N	7·40 E
166	Smolensk (smô-lyĕnsk') Sov. Un.	54·46 N	32·03 E
166	Smolensk (Oblast) Sov. Un.	55·00 N	32·18 E
165	Smyadovo Bul.	43·04 N	27·00 E
105	Smyrna (smûr'nȧ) De.	39·20 N	75·35 W
106	Smyrna Ga. (Atlanta In.)	33·53 N	84·31 W
101	Snag (snăg) Can.	62·18 N	140·30 W
109	Snake (R.) (snāk) Mn.	45·58 N	93·20 W

ăt; finăl; rāte; senâte; ärm; ȧsk; sofȧ; fâre; ch-choose; dh-as th in other; bē; êvent; bĕt; recĕnt; cratēr; g-go; gh-guttural g; bĭt; ĭ-short neutral; rīde; ĸ-guttural k as ch in German ich;

PRONOUNCING INDEX

Snake — South 349

Page	Name Pronunciation Region	Lat. °′	Long. °′
110	Snake (R.)....Wa.	46·35 N	117·20 W
115	Snake Ra....Nv.	39·20 N	114·15 W
111	Snake R., Henrys Fork....Id.	43·52 N	111·55 W
109	Snake River Pln. (rĭv′ẽr)....Id.	43·08 N	114·46 W
128	Snap Pt....Ba.	23·45 N	77·30 W
115	Sneffels Pk. (snĕf′ĕlz)....Co.	38·00 N	107·50 W
89	Snelgrove (snĕl′grōv) Can. (Toronto In.)	43·44 N	79·50 W
159	Sniardwy L. (snyärt′vĭ)....Pol.	53·46 N	21·59 E
156	Snöhetta (Mtn.) (snû-hĕttä)..Nor.	62·18 N	9·12 E
112	Snohomish (snô-hō′mĭsh) Wa. (Seattle In.)	47·55 N	122·05 W
112	Snohomish (R.)..Wa. (Seattle In.)	47·53 N	122·04 W
112	Snoqualmie (snō qwäl′mē) Wa. (Seattle In.)	47·32 N	121·50 W
110	Snoqualmie R....Wa.	47·32 N	121·53 W
167	Snov (R.) (snôf)....Sov. Un.	51·38 N	31·38 E
154	Snowdon, Mt. (snō′dŭn)....Wales	53·05 N	4·04 W
105	Snow Hill (hĭl)....Md.	38·15 N	75·20 W
95	Snow Lake....Can.	54·50 N	100·10 W
205	Snowy Mts. (snō′ê)....Austl.	36·17 S	148·30 E
116	Snyder (snī′dẽr)....Ok.	34·40 N	98·57 W
118	Snyder....Tx.	32·48 N	100·53 W
148	Soar (R.) (sōr)....Eng.	52·44 N	1·09 W
211	Sobat R. (sō′bȧt)....Sud.	9·04 N	32·02 E
166	Sobinka (sô-bĭŋ′kȧ)....Sov. Un.	55·59 N	40·02 E
195	Sobo Zan (Mt.) (sō′bô zän)...Jap.	32·47 N	131·27 E
135	Sobral (sô-brä′l)....Braz.	3·39 S	40·16 W
159	Sochaczew (sô-ĸä′chĕf)....Pol.	52·14 N	20·18 E
188	Soch′e (Yarkand) (sō′chĕ) (yär-känt′).China	38·15 N	77·15 E
171	Sochi (sôch′ĭ)....Sov. Un.	43·35 N	39·50 E
199	Society Is. (sô-sī′ĕ-tê) Fr. Polynesia	15·00 S	157·30 W
125	Socoltenango (sô-kôl-tĕ-näŋ′gō) Mex.	16·17 N	92·20 W
137	Socorro (sô-kô′r-rō) Braz. (Rio de Janeiro In.)	22·35 S	46·32 W
134	Socorro (sô-kôr′rō)....Col.	6·23 N	73·19 W
115	Socorro....NM	34·05 N	106·55 W
218	Socotra I. (sô-kō′trȧ) P. D. R. of Yem. (Horn of Afr. In.)	13·00 N	52·30 E
162	Socuellamos (sô-kōō-āl′yä-môs) Sp.	39·18 N	2·48 W
114	Soda (L.) (sō′dȧ)....Ca.	35·12 N	116·25 W
112	Soda Pk....Wa. (Portland In.)	45·53 N	122·04 W
111	Soda Springs (sprĭngz)....Id.	42·39 N	111·37 W
156	Söderhamn (sû-dẽr-häm′′n)...Swe.	61·20 N	17·00 E
156	Söderköping....Swe.	58·30 N	16·14 E
156	Södertälje (sû-dẽr-tĕl′yĕ)....Swe.	59·12 N	17·35 E
192	Sodi Soruksum (Mtn.)....China	37·20 N	102·00 E
211	Sodo....Eth.	7·03 N	37·46 E
156	Södra Dellen (L.)....Swe.	61·45 N	16·30 E
158	Soest (zōst)....F.R.G.	51·35 N	8·05 E
	Sofia, see Sofiya		
165	Sofiya (Sofia) (sô′fê-yȧ) (sô′fê-ȧ) Bul.	42·43 N	23·20 E
167	Sofiyevka (sô-fē′yĕf-kȧ)...Sov. Un.	48·03 N	33·53 E
195	Soga (sō′gä)....Jap (Tōkyō In.)	35·35 N	140·08 E
134	Sogamoso (sô-gä-mô′sō)....Col.	5·42 N	72·51 W
156	Sogndal (sôghn′dȧl)....Nor.	58·20 N	6·17 E
156	Sogndal....Nor.	61·14 N	7·04 E
156	Sogne Fd. (sôgn′ĕ fyôrd)....Nor.	61·09 N	5·30 E
166	Sogozha (R.) (sô′gō-zhȧ)..Sov. Un.	58·35 N	39·08 E
160	Soissons (swä-sôɴ′)....Fr.	49·23 N	3·17 E
195	Sōka (sō′kä)....Jap. (Tōkyō In.)	35·50 N	139·49 E
159	Sokal (sô′käl′)....Sov. Un.	50·28 N	24·20 E
171	Soke (sû′kĕ)....Tur.	37·40 N	27·10 E
214	Sokodé (sô-kô-dā′)....Togo	8·59 N	1·08 E
159	Sokolka (sô-kōōl′kȧ)....Pol.	53·23 N	23·30 E
210	Sokolo (sô-kô-lō′)....Mali	14·51 N	6·09 W
214	Sokone....Senegal	13·53 N	16·22 W
215	Sokoto (sō′kô-tō)....Nig.	13·04 N	5·16 E
159	Sokotów Podlaski (sô-kô-wōōf′ pŭd-lä′skĭ).Pol.	52·24 N	22·15 E
125	Sola de Vega (San Miguel) (sō′lä dā vā′gä) (sän mê-gāl′) Mex.	16·31 N	96·58 W
197	Solana (sō-lä′nä)....Phil. (In.)	17·40 N	121·41 E
202	Solander, C....Austl. (Sydney In.)	34·03 S	151·16 E
197	Solano (sō-lä′nō)....Phil. (In.)	16·31 N	121·11 E
134	Soledad (sŏ-lĕ-dä′d)....Col.	10·47 N	75·00 W
124	Soledad Díez Gutierrez (sô-lâ-dhädh′dē′äz gōō-tyā′rĕz) Mex.	22·19 N	100·54 W
110	Soleduck R. (sōl′dŭk)....Wa.	47·59 N	124·28 W
126	Solentiname, Islas de (Is.) (ē′s-läs-dĕ-sô-lĕn-tê-nä′mȧ).Nic.	11·15 N	85·16 W
148	Solihull (sō′lĭ-hŭl)....Eng.	52·25 N	1·46 W
174	Solikamsk (sô-lē-kȧmsk′) Sov. Un. (Urals In.)	59·38 N	56·48 E
134	Solimões, Rio (R.) (rē′ō-sô-lē-mô′ĕs).Braz.	2·45 S	67·44 W
161	Solingen (zō′lĭng-ĕn) F.R.G. (Ruhr In.)	51·10 N	7·05 E
156	Sollefteå (sôl-lĕf′tĕ-ô)....Swe.	63·06 N	17·17 E
163	Sóller (sō′lyĕr)....Sp.	39·45 N	2·40 E
171	Sol′-Iletsk....Sov. Un.	51·10 N	55·05 E
160	Sologne (Reg.) (sō-lōn′yĕ)....Fr.	47·36 N	1·53 E
126	Solola (sô-lō′lä)....Guat.	14·45 N	91·12 W
198	Solomon Is. (sŏ′lō-mŭn)...Oceania	7·00 S	148·00 E
116	Solomon R....Ks.	39·24 N	98·19 W
116	Solomon R. North Fk....Ks.	39·34 N	99·52 W
116	Solomon R., South Fk....Ks.	39·19 N	99·52 W
107	Solon (sō′lŭn)..Oh. (Cleveland In.)	41·23 N	81·26 W
158	Solothurn (zō′lō-thōōrn)....Switz.	47·13 N	7·30 E
170	Solov′etskiy (I.)....Sov. Un.	65·10 N	35·40 E
164	Šolta (I.) (shôl′tä)....Yugo.	43·20 N	16·15 E
158	Soltau (sôl′tou)....F.R.G.	53·00 N	9·50 E
166	Sol′tsy (sôl′tsê)....Sov. Un.	58·04 N	30·13 E
192	Solun (sô-lōōn′)....China	47·32 N	121·18 E
105	Solvay (sŏl′vā)....NY	43·05 N	76·10 W
156	Sölvesborg (sûl′vĕs-bôrg)....Swe.	56·04 N	14·35 E
170	Sol′vychegodsk (sôl′vê-chĕ-gôtsk′) Sov. Un.	61·18 N	46·58 E
154	Solway Firth (sŏl′wāfûrth′) Eng.-Scot.	54·42 N	3·55 W
217	Solwezi....Zambia	12·11 S	26·25 E
209	Somalia (sō-ma′lē-ȧ)....Afr.	3·28 N	44·47 E
217	Somanga....Tan.	8·24 S	39·17 E
165	Sombor (sôm′bôr)....Yugo.	45·45 N	19·10 E
124	Sombrerete (sōm-brå-rā′tȧ)..Mex.	23·38 N	103·37 W
135	Sombrero, Cayo (C.) (kä-yô-sôm-brĕ′rô).Ven. (In.)	10·52 N	68·12 W
120	Somerset (sŭm′ẽr-sĕt)....Ky.	37·05 N	84·35 W
106	Somerset....Ma. (Providence In.)	41·46 N	71·05 W
105	Somerset....Pa.	40·00 N	79·05 W
113	Somerset...Tx. (San Antonio In.)	29·13 N	98·39 W
213	Somerset East..S. Afr. (Natal In.)	32·44 S	25·36 E
98	Somersworth (sŭm′ẽrz-wûrth).NH	43·16 N	70·53 W
114	Somerton (sŭm′ẽr-tŭn)....Az.	32·36 N	114·43 W
99	Somerville (sŭm′ẽr-vĭl)..Ma. (In.)	42·23 N	71·06 W
106	Somerville....NJ (New York In.)	40·34 N	74·37 W
120	Somerville....Tn.	35·14 N	89·21 W
119	Somerville....Tx.	30·21 N	96·31 W
159	Somesul R. (sô-mȧ′shōōl)....Rom.	47·43 N	23·09 E
163	Somma Vesuviana (sôm′mä vā-zōō-vê-ä′nä) It. (Naples In.)	40·38 N	14·27 E
160	Somme (R.) (sŏm)....Fr.	50·02 N	2·04 E
149	Sommerfeld (zō′mẽr-fĕld) G.D.R. (Berlin In.)	52·48 N	13·02 E
202	Sommerville Austl. (Melbourne In.)	38·14 S	145·10 E
126	Somoto (sô-mō′tō)....Nic.	13·28 N	86·37 W
136	Somuncurá, Meseta de (Plat.) (mĕ-sĕ′tä-dĕ-sô-mōō′n-kōō-rá′) Arg.	41·15 S	68·00 W
184	Son (R.) (sōn)....India	24·40 N	82·35 E
127	Soná (sō′nä)....Pan.	8·00 N	81·19 W
194	Sŏnchŏn (sŭn′shŭn)....Kor.	39·49 N	124·56 E
213	Sondags (R.)...S. Afr. (Natal In.)	33·17 S	25·14 E
156	Sønderborg (sûn′′er-bôrgh)...Den.	54·55 N	9·47 E
158	Sondershausen (zôn′dẽrz-hou′zĕn) G.D.R.	51·17 N	10·45 E
193	Song Ca (R.)....Viet.	19·15 N	105·00 E
217	Songea (sôn-gā′ȧ)....Tan.	10·41 S	35·39 E
194	Sŏngjin (sŭng′jĭn′)....Kor.	40·38 N	129·10 E
196	Songkhla (sông′klä′)....Thai.	7·09 N	100·34 E
217	Songwe....Zaire	12·25 S	29·40 E
158	Sonneberg (sôn′ĕ-bĕrgh)...G.D.R.	50·20 N	11·14 E
114	Sonora (sô-nō′rȧ)....Ca.	37·58 N	120·22 W
118	Sonora....Tx.	30·33 N	100·38 W
122	Sonora (State)....Mex.	29·45 N	111·15 W
122	Sonora (R.)....Mex.	28·45 N	111·35 W
114	Sonora Pk....Ca.	38·22 N	119·39 W
162	Sonseca (sôn-sā′kä)....Sp.	39·41 N	3·56 W
134	Sonsón (sôn-sôn′)....Col. (In.)	5·42 N	75·28 W
126	Sonsonate (sōn-sô-nä′tȧ)....Sal.	13·46 N	89·43 W
197	Sonsorol Is. (sŏn-sō-rōl′) Pas. Is. Trust Ter.	5·03 N	132·33 E
190	Soochow (Wuhsien) (sōō′jō) (wōō′sĭän).China	31·19 N	120·37 E
112	Sooke Basin (sŏŏk) Can. (Seattle In.)	48·21 N	123·47 W
113	Soo Locks (sōō lŏks)..Can.-U. S.	46·30 N	84·30 W
134	Sopetrán (sô-pĕ-trä′n)...Col. (In.)	6·30 N	75·44 W
156	Sopot (sô′pôt)....Pol.	54·26 N	18·25 E
158	Sopron (shŏp′rôn)....Hung.	47·41 N	16·36 E
164	Sora (sô′rä)....It.	41·43 N	13·37 E
156	Sör Aurdal (sŭr äür-däl)....Nor.	60·54 N	9·24 E
162	Sorbas (sôr′bäs)....Sp.	37·05 N	2·07 W
125	Sordo (R.) (sô′r-dō)....Mex.	16·39 N	97·33 W
97	Sorel (sô-rĕl′)....Can.	46·01 N	73·07 W
203	Sorell, C....Austl.	42·10 S	144·50 E
164	Soresina (sō-rȧ-zē′nä)....It.	45·17 N	9·51 E
162	Soria (sō′rê-ä)....Sp.	41·46 N	2·28 W
137	Soriano (sŏ-rēä′nô) (Dept.) Ur. (Buenos Aires In.)	33·25 S	58·00 W
137	Sorocaba (sô-rô-kä′bȧ) Braz. (Rio de Janeiro In.)	23·29 S	47·27 W
167	Soroki (sō-rō′kĕ)....Sov. Un.	48·09 N	28·17 E
197	Sorong (sō-rông′)....Indon.	1·00 S	131·20 E
166	Sorot′ (R.) (sō-rō′tzh)....Sov. Un.	57·08 N	29·23 E
217	Soroti (sō-rō′tê)....Ug.	1·43 N	33·37 E
150	Söröy (I.) (sûr′ûê)....Nor.	70·37 N	20·58 E
162	Sorraia (R.) (sôr-rī′ȧ)....Port.	38·55 N	8·42 W
163	Sorrento (sôr-rĕn′tō) It. (Naples In.)	40·23 N	14·23 E
197	Sorsogon (sôr-sôgōn′)....Phil.	12·51 N	124·02 E
157	Sortavala (sôr′tä-vä-lä)...Sov. Un.	61·43 N	30·40 E
192	Sŏsan (sŭ′sän)....Korea	36·40 N	126·25 E
167	Sosna (R.) (sôs′nȧ)....Sov. Un.	50·33 N	38·15 E
167	Sosnitsa (sôs-nê′tsȧ)....Sov. Un.	51·30 N	32·29 E
172	Sosnogorsk....Sov. Un.	63·13 N	54·09 E
159	Sosnowiec (sôs-nô′vyĕts)....Pol.	50·17 N	19·10 E
194	Sosunova, Mys (Pt.) (mĭs sô′sōō-nôf′ȧ).Sov. Un.	46·28 N	138·06 E
174	Sos′va R. (sôs′vȧ) Sov. Un. (Urals In.)	59·55 N	60·40 E
170	Sos′va (R.) (sôs′vȧ)....Sov. Un.	63·10 N	63·30 E
215	Sota (R.)....Benin	11·10 N	3·20 E
124	Sota la Marina (sô-tä-lä-mä-rē′nä) Mex.	22·45 N	98·11 W
125	Soteapan (sō-tȧ-ä′pän)....Mex.	18·14 N	94·51 W
124	Soto la Marina, Rio (R.) (rê′ō-sō′tō lä mä-rē′nä).Mex.	23·55 N	98·30 W
126	Sotuta (sô-tōō′tä)....Mex. (In.)	20·35 N	89·00 W
216	Souanké....Con.	2·05 N	14·03 E
135	Soublette (sŏ-ōō-blĕ′tĕ)..Ven. (In′)	9·55 N	66·06 W
164	Soúdhas, Kolpós (G.)...Grc. (In.)	35·33 N	24·22 E
165	Souflion....Grc.	41·12 N	26·17 E
127	Soufriere (sōō-frê-âr′) St. Lucia (In.)	13·50 N	61·03 W
127	Soufríere, Mt....St. Vincent (In.)	13·19 N	61·12 W
127	Soufrière (Vol.)...Montserrat (In.)	16·43 N	62·10 W
151	Souk-Ahras (sōōk-ä-räs′)....Alg.	36·18 N	8·19 E
194	Sŏul (Seoul)....Kor.	37·35 N	127·03 E
94	Sounding Cr. (soun′dĭng)....Can.	51·35 N	111·00 W
218	Sources, Mt. aux (môɴ′tō sōōrs′) Leso.-S. Afr. (Natal In.)	28·47 S	29·04 E
162	Soure (sōr-ĕ)....Port.	40·04 N	8·37 W
99	Souris (sōō′rē′)....Can.	46·20 N	62·17 W
95	Souris....Can.	49·38 N	100·15 W
95	Souris (R.)....Can.	49·10 N	102·00 W
119	Sourlake (sour′lāk)....Tx.	30·09 N	94·24 W
210	Sousse (sōōs)....Tun.	36·00 N	10·39 E
160	Soustons (sōōs-tôɴ′)....Fr.	43·46 N	1·22 W
121	South (R.)....NC	34·49 N	78·33 W
209	South Africa....Afr.	28·00 S	24·50 E
106	South Amboy (south′ăm′boi) NJ (New York In.)	40·28 N	74·17 W
133	South America		
154	Southampton (south-ămp′tŭn) Eng.	50·54 N	1·30 W
105	Southampton....NY	40·53 N	72·24 W
91	Southampton I....Can.	64·38 N	84·00 W
196	South Andaman I. (ăn-dȧ-măn′) Andaman & Nicobar Is.	11·57 N	93·24 E
204	South Australia (State) (ôs-trā′lĭ-ȧ).Austl.	29·45 S	132·00 E
129	South B....Ba.	20·55 N	73·35 W
104	South Bend (bĕnd)....In.	41·40 N	86·20 W
110	South Bend (bĕnd)....Wa.	46·39 N	123·48 W
128	South Bight (B.)....Ba.	24·20 N	77·35 W
128	South Bimini (I.) (bē′mê-nê)..Ba.	25·40 N	79·20 W
99	Southborough (south′bŭr-ô) Ma. (In.)	42·18 N	71·33 W
121	South Boston (bôs′tŭn)....Va.	36·41 N	78·55 W
105	Southbridge (south′brĭj)....Ma.	42·05 N	72·00 W
129	South Caicos (I.) (kī′kōs) Turks & Caicos	21·30 N	71·35 W
197	South C....Pap. N. Gui.	10·40 S	149·00 E
103	South Carolina (State) (kăr-ô-lī′nȧ).U. S.	34·15 N	81·10 W
148	South Cave (cāv)....Eng.	53·45 N	0·35 W
104	South Charleston (south chärlz′tŭn).WV	38·20 N	81·40 W
196	South China Sea (chī′nȧ)....Asia	15·23 N	114·12 E
202	South Cr....Austl. (Sydney In.)	33·43 S	167·00 E
102	South Dakota (State) (dȧ-kō′tȧ) U. S.	44·20 N	101·55 W
154	South Downs (dounz)....Eng.	50·55 N	1·13 W
184	South Dum-Dum....India (In.)	22·36 N	88·25 E
205	Southeast, C....Austl.	43·47 S	146·03 E
148	Southend-on-Sea (south-ĕnd′) Eng. (London In.)	51·33 N	0·41 E
205	Southern Alps (Mts.) (sŭ-thûrn ălps).N. Z. (In.)	44·08 S	169·18 E
204	Southern Cross....Austl.	31·13 S	119·30 E
93	Southern Indian (L.) (sŭth′ẽrn ĭn′dĭ-ăn).Can.	56·46 N	98·57 W
121	Southern Pines (sŭth′ẽrn pīnz).NC	35·10 N	79·23 W
154	Southern Uplands (ŭp′lăndz).Scot.	55·15 N	4·28 W
115	Southern Ute Ind. Res. (ūt)...Co.	37·05 N	108·23 W
	Southern Yemen, see Yemen, People′s Democratic Republic of		
107	South Euclid (ū′klĭd) Oh. (Cleveland In.)	41·30 N	81·34 W
104	South Fox (I.) (fŏks)....Mi.	45·25 N	85·55 W
113	South Gate (gāt) Ca. (Los Angeles In.)	33·57 N	118·13 W
133	South Georgia (I.) (jôr′jȧ).Falk Is.	54·00 S	37·00 W
104	South Haven (hāv′′n)....Mi.	42·25 N	86·15 W
121	South Hill....Va.	36·44 N	78·08 W
95	South Indian Lake....Can.	56·50 N	99·00 W
105	Southington (sŭdh′ĭng-tŭn)....Ct.	41·35 N	72·55 W
205	South I....N. Z. (In.)	43·15 S	167·00 E

350 South Loup — Staraya Kupavna PRONOUNCING INDEX

Page	Name Pronunciation Region	Lat. °′	Long. °′
108	South Loup (R.) (lo͞op).......Ne.	41·21 N	100·08 W
99	South Merrimack (mĕr'ĭ-măk) NH (In.)	42·47 N	71·36 W
107	South Milwaukee (mĭl-wô'kê) Wi. (Milwaukee In.)	42·55 N	87·52 W
95	South Moose L.............Can.	53·51 N	100·20 W
89	South Nation (R.) (nā'shŭn) Can. (Ottawa In.)	45·12 N	75·07 W
128	South Negril Pt. (nå-grēl')...Jam.	18·15 N	78·25 W
113	South Ogden (ŏg'dĕn) Ut. (Salt Lake City In.)	41·12 N	111·58 W
98	South Paris (păr'ĭs).........Me.	44·13 N	70·32 W
107	South Park (pärk) Ky. (Louisville In.)	38·06 N	85·43 W
113	South Pasadena (păs-å-dē'nå) Ca. (Los Angeles In.)	34·06 N	118·08 W
115	South Pease (R.) (pēz).......Tx.	33·54 N	100·45 W
112	South Pender (I.) (pĕn'dẽr) Can. (Vancouver In.)	48·45 N	123·09 W
120	South Pittsburgh (pĭts'bûrg)..Tn.	35·00 N	85·42 W
102	South Platte (R.) (plăt).....U. S.	40·40 N	102·40 W
96	South Porcupine...........Can.	48·28 N	81·13 W
104	South Pt..................Mi.	44·50 N	83·20 W
127	South Pt...............Barb. (In.)	13·00 N	59·43 W
203	Southport (south'pōrt).....Austl.	27·57 S	153·27 E
121	Southport.................NC	35·55 N	78·02 W
148	Southport (south'pôrt)......Eng.	53·38 N	3·00 W
107	Southport...In. (Indianapolis In.)	39·40 N	86·07 W
98	South Portland (pōrt-lănd)...Me.	43·37 N	70·15 W
112	South Prairie (prā'rĭ) Wa. (Seattle In.)	47·08 N	122·06 W
113	South Range (rānj) Wi. (Duluth In.)	46·37 N	91·59 W
106	South River (rĭv'ẽr) NJ (New York In.)	40·27 N	74·23 W
106	South R........Ga. (Atlanta In.)	33·40 N	84·15 W
113	South St. Paul.............Mn. (Minneapolis, St. Paul In.)	44·54 N	93·02 W
113	South Salt Lake (sôlt lāk) Ut. (Salt Lake City In.	40·44 N	111·53 W
133	South Sandwich Is. (sănd'wĭch) Falk. Is.	58·00 S	27·00 W
133	South Sandwich Trench S. A.-Ant.	55·00 S	27·00 W
112	South San Francisco (săn frăn-sĭs'kô) Ca. (San Francisco In.)	37·39 N	122·24 W
94	South Saskatchewan (R.) (săs-kach'ĕ-wän).Can.	53·15 N	105·05 W
154	South Shields (shēldz).......Eng.	55·00 N	1·22 W
154	South Shropshire Hills (shrŏp'shĭr).Eng.	52·30 N	3·02 W
108	South Sioux City (so͞o sĭt'ê)...Ne.	42·28 N	96·26 W
205	South Taranaki Bight (tä-rä-nä'kê).N. Z. (In.)	39·27 S	171·44 E
93	South Thompson (R.) (tŏmp'sŭn).Can.	50·41 N	120·21 W
113	Southton (south'tŭn) Tx. (San Antonio In.)	29·18 N	98·26 W
154	South Uist (I.) (û'ĭst).......Scot.	57·15 N	7·24 W
110	South Umpqua R. (ŭmp'kwå).Or.	43·00 N	122·54 W
148	Southwell (south'wĕl).......Eng.	53·04 N	0·56 W
	South West Africa, see Namibia		
205	Southwest C..........N. Z. (In.)	47·17 S	167·12 E
98	Southwest Miramichi (R.) (mĭr å-mê'shē).Can.	46·35 N	66·17 W
129	Southwest Pt...............Ba.	23·55 N	74·30 W
128	Southwest Pt...............Ba.	25·50 N	77·10 W
157	Sovetsk (Tilsit) (sô-vyĕtsk') Sov. Un.	55·04 N	21·54 E
173	Sovetskaya Gavan' (sŭ-vyĕt'skī-u gä'vŭn').Sov. Un.	48·59 N	140·14 E
182	Soviet Union (sō-vĭ-ĕt')..Eur.-Asia	60·30 N	64·00 E
148	Sow (R.) (sou).............Eng.	52·45 N	2·12 W
194	Sōya Misaki (C.) (sō'yå mê'sä-kē) Jap.	45·35 N	141·25 E
166	Sozh (R.) (sôzh)........Sov. Un.	52·17 N	31·00 E
165	Sozopol (sôz'ô-pôl').........Bul.	42·18 N	27·50 E
155	Spa (spä)..................Bel.	50·30 N	5·50 E
146	Spain (spān)...............Eur.	40·15 N	4·30 W
108	Spalding (spôl'dĭng).........Ne.	41·43 N	98·23 W
112	Spanaway (spăn'å-wā) Wa. (Seattle In.)	47·06 N	122·26 W
105	Spangler (spăng'lẽr).........Pa.	40·40 N	78·50 W
115	Spanish Fork (spăn'ĭsh fôrk) Ut.	40·10 N	111·40 W
128	Spanish Town.............Jam.	18·00 N	76·55 W
114	Sparks (spärks).............Nv.	39·34 N	119·45 W
106	Sparrows Point (spăr'ōz) Md. (Baltimore In.)	39·13 N	76·29 W
120	Sparta (spär'tå)............Ga.	33·16 N	82·59 W
117	Sparta.....................Il.	38·07 N	89·42 W
104	Sparta.....................Mi.	43·10 N	85·45 W
120	Sparta.....................Tn.	35·54 N	85·26 W
109	Sparta.....................Wi.	43·56 N	90·50 W
	Sparta, see Spárti		
106	Sparta Mts...NJ (New York In.)	41·00 N	74·38 W
121	Spartanburg (spär'tăn-bûrg)..SC	34·57 N	82·13 W
162	Spartel (C.) (spär-tĕl')......Mor.	35·48 N	5·50 W
165	Spárti (Sparta).............Grc.	37·07 N	22·28 E
164	Spartivento, C. (spär-tê-vĕn'tô).It.	37·55 N	16·09 E
164	Spartivento, C..............It.	38·54 N	8·52 E
166	Spas-Demensk (spås dyĕ-mĕnsk') Sov. Un.	54·24 N	34·02 E
166	Spas-Klepiki (spås klĕp'ê-kê) Sov. Un.	55·09 N	40·11 E
173	Spassk-Dal'niy (spŭsk'däl'nyē) Sov. Un.	44·30 N	133·00 E
166	Spassk-Ryazanskiy (ryä-zän'skĭ) Sov. Un.	54·24 N	40·21 E
164	Spátha, Akr. (C.).......Grc. (In.)	35·42 N	24·45 E
106	Spaulding (spôl'dĭng) Al. (Birmingham In.)	33·27 N	86·50 W
99	Spear, C. (spēr)............Can.	47·32 N	52·32 W
108	Spearfish (spēr'fĭsh)..........SD	44·28 N	103·52 W
107	Speed (spēd)...In. (Louisville In.)	38·25 N	85·45 W
107	Speedway (spēd'wā) In. (Indianapolis In.)	39·47 N	86·14 W
149	Speicher L. (shpī'кẽr) F.R.G. (Munich In.)	48·12 N	11·47 E
104	Spencer (spĕn'sẽr)............In.	39·15 N	86·45 W
109	Spencer.....................Ia.	43·09 N	95·08 W
121	Spencer....................NC	35·43 N	80·25 W
104	Spencer....................WV	38·55 N	81·20 W
203	Spencer G. (spĕn'sẽr) ......Austl.	34·20 S	136·55 E
149	Sperenberg (shpĕ'rĕn-bĕrgh) G.D.R. (Berlin In.)	52·09 N	13·22 E
165	Sperkhiós (R.)..............Grc.	38·54 N	22·02 E
154	Sperrin Mts. (spĕr'ĭn).....N. Ire.	54·55 N	6·45 E
158	Spessart (Mts.) (shpĕ'särt).F.R.G.	50·07 N	9·32 E
154	Spey (L.) (spā).............Scot.	57·25 N	3·29 W
158	Speyer (shpī'ẽr)..........F.R.G.	49·18 N	8·26 E
218	Sphinx (Pyramid) (sfĭnks) Egypt (Nile In.)	29·57 N	31·08 E
149	Spijkenisse Neth. (Amsterdam In.)	51·51 N	4·18 E
164	Spinazzola (spê-nät'zô-lä)......It.	40·58 N	16·05 E
110	Spirit Lake (spĭr'ĭt)...........Id.	47·58 N	116·51 W
109	Spirit Lake (lāk).............Ia.	43·25 N	95·08 W
159	Spišská Nová Ves (spēsh'skä nō'vä vĕs).Czech.	48·56 N	20·35 E
	Spitsbergen (Is.), see Svalbard		
158	Spittal (shpê-täl')...........Aus.	46·48 N	13·28 E
164	Split (splêt)...............Yugo.	43·30 N	16·28 E
95	Split L....................Can.	56·08 N	96·15 W
110	Spokane (spōkăn')...........Wa.	47·39 N	117·25 W
110	Spokane R..................Wa.	47·47 N	118·00 W
164	Spoleto (spô-lā'tō)...........It.	42·44 N	12·44 E
117	Spoon (R.) (spo͞on)...........Il.	40·36 N	90·22 W
109	Spooner (spo͞on'ẽr)...........Wi.	45·50 N	91·53 W
165	Sporádhes (Is.)..............Grc.	38·55 N	24·05 E
106	Spotswood (spŏtz'wo͝od) NJ (New York In.)	40·23 N	74·22 W
110	Sprague R. (sprāg)..........Or.	42·30 N	121·42 W
196	Spratly (I.) (sprăt'lê).......China	8·38 N	11·54 E
121	Spray (sprā)................NC	36·30 N	79·44 W
158	Spree R. (shprā)..........G.D.R.	51·53 N	14·08 E
158	Spremberg (shprĕm'bĕrgh).G.D.R.	51·35 N	14·23 E
117	Spring (R.).................Ar.	36·25 N	91·35 W
212	Springbok (sprĭng'bŏk).....S. Afr.	29·35 S	17·55 E
114	Spring, Cr. (sprĭng).........Nv.	40·18 N	117·45 W
119	Spring Cr...................Tx.	30·03 N	95·43 W
118	Spring Cr...................Tx.	31·08 N	100·50 W
99	Springdale.................Can.	49·30 N	56·05 W
117	Springdale (sprĭng'dāl)........Ar.	36·10 N	94·07 W
107	Springdale...Pa. (Pittsburgh In.)	40·33 N	79·46 W
116	Springer (sprĭng'ẽr)..........NM	36·21 N	104·37 W
115	Springerville................Az.	34·08 N	109·17 W
116	Springfield (sprĭng'fēld).......Co.	37·24 N	102·04 W
109	Springfield.................Mn.	44·14 N	94·59 W
110	Springfield..................Or.	44·01 N	123·02 W
117	Springfield..................Il.	39·46 N	89·37 W
104	Springfield.................Ky.	37·35 N	85·10 W
105	Springfield.................Ma.	42·05 N	72·35 W
117	Springfield.................Mo.	37·13 N	93·17 W
104	Springfield.................Oh.	39·55 N	83·50 W
120	Springfield..................Tn.	36·30 N	86·53 W
105	Springfield..................Vt.	43·20 N	72·35 W
212	Springfontein (sprĭng'fôn-tīn) S. Afr.	30·16 S	25·45 E
99	Springhill (sprĭng-hĭl').......Can.	45·39 N	64·03 W
114	Spring Mts..................Nv.	36·18 N	115·49 W
213	Springs (sprĭngs)..........S. Afr. (Johannesburg & Pretoria In.)	26·16 S	28·27 E
89	Springstein (sprĭng'stīn) Can. (Winnipeg In.)	49·49 N	97·29 W
106	Springton Res. (sprĭng-tŭn) Pa. (Philadelphia In.)	39·57 N	75·26 W
202	Springvale.Austl. (Melbourne In.)	37·57 N	145·09 E
114	Spring Valley..........Ca. (In.)	32·46 N	117·01 W
104	Springvalley (sprĭng-văl'ĭ)......Il.	41·20 N	89·15 W
109	Spring Valley...............Mn.	43·41 N	92·26 W
106	Spring Valley.NY (New York In.)	41·07 N	74·03 W
115	Springville (sprĭng-vĭl)........Ut.	40·10 N	111·40 W
202	Springwood...Austl. (Sydney In.)	33·42 S	150·34 E
89	Spruce Grove (spro͞os grōv) Can. (Edmonton In.)	53·32 N	113·55 W
116	Spur (spûr).................Tx.	33·29 N	100·51 W
105	Squam (L.) (skwôm).........NH	43·45 N	71·30 W
92	Squamish (skwŏ'mĭsh).......Can.	49·42 N	123·09 W
92	Squamish (R.)..............Can.	50·10 N	124·30 W
164	Squillace, Gulfo di (G.) (go͞o'l-fô-dē skwêl-lä'châ).....It.	38·44 N	16·47 E
165	Srbija (Serbia) (Reg.) (sr bê-yä) (sĕr'bê-ä).Yugo.	44·05 N	20·35 E
165	Srbobran (s'r'bô-brän').....Yugo.	45·32 N	19·50 E
173	Sredne-Kolymsk (s'rĕd'nyĕ kô-lêmsk').Sov. Un.	67·49 N	154·55 E
174	Sredne Rogartka (s'red'nå-ya) (rô gär'tkå) Sov. Un. (Leningrad In.)	59·49 N	30·20 E
174	Sredniy Ik (R.) (srĕd'nĭ ĭk) Sov. Un. (Urals In.)	55·46 N	58·50 E
174	Sredniy Ural (Mts.) (o͝o'rål) Sov. Un. (Urals In.)	57·47 N	59·00 E
159	Śrem (shrĕm)...............Pol.	52·06 N	17·01 E
165	Sremska Karlovci (srĕm'skê kär'lov-tsê).Yugo.	45·10 N	19·57 E
165	Sremska Mitrovica (srĕm'skä mê'trô-vê-tsä').Yugo.	44·59 N	19·39 E
173	Sretensk (s'rĕ'tĕnsk).....Sov. Un.	52·13 N	117·39 E
182	Sri Lanka (Ceylon)..........Asia	8·45 N	82·30 E
184	Srīnagar (srē-nŭg'ŭr)........India	34·11 N	74·49 E
159	Sroda (shrô'då).............Pol.	52·14 N	17·17 E
	Ssuch'uan (Prov.), see Szechwan		
193	Ssuen....................China	24·50 N	108·18 E
190	Ssuhsien (sŭ'sĭän)..........China	33·29 N	116·57 E
188	Ssumao...................China	22·56 N	101·07 E
193	Ssŭnan...................China	27·50 N	108·30 E
192	Ssup'ing..................China	43·05 N	124·24 E
190	Ssushui (sĕ'so͞oĭ)..........China	35·40 N	117·17 E
191	Ssut'uan....China (Shanghai In.)	30·57 N	121·43 E
149	Stabroek......Bel. (Brussels In.)	51·20 N	4·21 E
149	Stade (shtä'dĕ) F.R.G. (Hamburg In.)	53·36 N	9·28 E
150	Stadhur....................Ice.	65·08 N	20·56 W
156	Städjan (Mtn.) (stĕd'yän)...Swe.	61·53 N	12·50 E
148	Stafford (stăf'fẽrd).........Eng.	52·48 N	2·06 W
116	Stafford....................Ks.	37·58 N	98·37 W
148	Stafford (Co.)..............Eng.	52·45 N	2·00 W
149	Stahnsdorf (shtäns'dôrf) G.D.R. (Berlin In.)	52·22 N	13·10 E
	Stalin, see Varna		
	Stalinabad, see Dushanbe		
	Stalingrad, see Volgograd		
	Stalino, see Donetsk		
167	Stalino (Oblast) (stä'lĭ-nô) (ôb'låst).Sov. Un.	47·54 N	37·13 E
172	Stalino, Pik (Mtn.)......Sov. Un.	39·00 N	72·15 E
	Stalinsk, see Novokuznetsk		
148	Stalybridge (stā'lê-brĭj)......Eng.	53·29 N	2·03 W
109	Stambaugh (stăm'bô)........Mi.	46·03 N	88·38 W
106	Stamford (stăm'fẽrd) Ct. (New York In.)	41·03 N	73·32 W
148	Stamford...................Eng.	52·39 N	0·28 W
116	Stamford....................Tx.	32·57 N	99·48 W
149	Stammersdorf (shtäm'ĕrs-dôrf) Aus. (Vienna In.)	48·19 N	16·25 E
117	Stamps (stămps).............Ar.	33·22 N	93·31 W
117	Stanberry (stan'bĕr-ê).......Mo.	40·12 N	94·34 W
218	Standerton (stăn'dẽr-tŭn)..S. Afr. (Johannesburg & Pretoria In.)	26·57 S	29·17 E
108	Standing Rock Ind. Res. (stănd'ĭng rŏk).ND	47·07 N	101·05 W
148	Standish (stăn'dĭsh).........Eng.	53·36 N	2·39 W
120	Stanford (stăn'fẽrd).........Ky.	37·29 N	84·40 W
213	Stanger (stăŋ-ger) S. Afr. (Natal In.)	29·22 S	31·18 E
156	Stangvik Fd. (stang'vêk fyôrd) Nor.	62·54 N	8·55 E
128	Staniard Creek..............Ba.	24·50 N	77·55 W
114	Stanislaus (R.) (stăn'ĭs-lô)....Ca.	38·10 N	120·16 W
98	Stanley (stăn'lê)............Can.	46·17 N	66·44 W
136	Stanley...............Falk. Is.	51·46 S	57·59 W
108	Stanley....................ND	48·20 N	102·25 W
109	Stanley....................Wi.	44·56 N	90·56 W
216	Stanley Falls...............Zaire	0·30 N	25·12 E
215	Stanley Pool (L.)...........Zaire	4·07 S	15·40 E
184	Stanley Res. (stăn'lê)........India	12·07 N	77·27 E
	Stanleyville, see Kisangani		
126	Stann Creek (stăn krēk) Belize (In.)	17·01 N	88·14 W
173	Stanovoy Khrebet (Mts.) (stŭn-å-voi').Sov. Un.	56·12 N	127·12 E
113	Stanton (stăn'tŭn) Ca. (Los Angeles In.)	33·48 N	118·00 W
108	Stanton....................Ne.	41·57 N	97·15 W
118	Stanton....................Tx.	32·08 N	101·46 W
112	Stanwood (stăn'wo͝od) Wa. (Seattle In.)	48·14 N	122·23 W
109	Staples (stā'p'lz)............Mn.	46·21 N	94·48 W
120	Stapleton...................Al.	30·45 N	87·48 W
146	Stara Planina (Balkan Mts.) Bul.	42·50 N	24·45 E
174	Staraya Kupavna (stä'rå-yå kû-päf'nå) Sov. Un. (Moscow In.)	55·48 N	38·10 E

ăt; finăl; rāte; senâte; ärm; åsk; sofå; fâre; ch-choose; dh-as th in other; bē; ēvent; bĕt; recĕnt; cratẽr; g-go; gh-guttural g; bĭt; ĭ-short neutral; rīde; к-guttural k as ch in German ich;

PRONOUNCING INDEX

Staraya Russa — Such'ien 351

Page	Name Pronunciation Region	Lat. °′	Long. °′
166	Staraya Russa (stä'rȧ-yȧ rōōsȧ) Sov. Un.	57·58 N	31·21 E
165	Stara Zagora (zä'gô-rȧ) Bul.	42·26 N	25·37 E
89	Starbuck (stär'bŭk) Can. (Winnipeg In.)	49·46 N	97·36 W
158	Stargard Szczeciński (shtär'gärt shchĕ-chyn'skē) Pol.	53·19 N	15·03 E
166	Staritsa (stä'rē-tsȧ) Sov. Un.	56·29 N	34·58 E
121	Starke (stärk) Fl.	29·55 N	82·07 W
116	Starkville (stärk'vĭl) Co.	37·06 N	104·34 W
120	Starkville Ms.	33·27 N	88·47 W
149	Starnberg (shtärn-bĕrgh) F.R.G. (Munich In.)	47·59 N	11·20 E
167	Starobel'sk (stä-rô-byĕlsk') Sov. Un.	49·19 N	38·57 E
166	Starodub (stä-rô-drōōp') Sov. Un.	52·25 N	32·49 E
159	Starograd Gdański (stä'rō-grad gdĕn'skē) Pol.	53·58 N	18·33 E
167	Staro-Konstantinov (stä'rô kôn-stȧn-tē'nôf) Sov. Un.	49·45 N	27·12 E
167	Staro-Minskaya (stä'rô mĭn'skȧ-yȧ) Sov. Un.	46·19 N	38·51 E
167	Staro-Shcherbinovskaya Sov. Un.	46·38 N	38·38 E
174	Staro-Subkhangulovo (stäro-sōōb-kan-gōō'lōvō) Sov. Un. (Urals In.)	53·08 N	57·24 E
174	Staroutkinsk (stȧ-rô-ōōt'kĭnsk) Sov. Un. (Urals In.)	57·14 N	59·21 E
167	Staroverovka Sov. Un.	49·31 N	35·48 E
154	Start Pt. (stärt) Eng.	50·14 N	3·34 W
159	Stary Sacz (stä-rē sôŋch') Pol.	49·32 N	20·36 E
167	Staryy Oskol (stä'rē ôs-kôl') Sov. Un.	51·18 N	37·51 E
158	Stassfurt (shtäs'fōōrt) G.D.R.	51·52 N	11·35 E
159	Staszów (stä'shōōf) Pol.	50·32 N	21·13 E
105	State College (stāt kŏl'ĕj) Pa.	40·50 N	77·55 W
113	State Line (līn) Mn. (Duluth In.)	46·36 N	92·18 W
106	Staten I. (stăt'ĕn) NY (New York In.)	40·35 N	74·10 W
121	Statesboro (stāts'bŭr-ô) Ga.	32·26 N	81·47 W
121	Statesville (stāts'vĭl) NC	34·45 N	80·54 W
113	Staunton (stôn'tŭn) Il. (St. Louis In.)	39·01 N	89·47 W
105	Staunton Va.	38·10 N	79·05 W
156	Stavanger (stä'väng'ĕr) Nor.	58·59 N	5·44 E
112	Stave (R.) (stāv) Can. (Vancouver In.)	49·12 N	122·24 W
148	Staveley (stāv'lē) Eng.	53·17 N	1·21 W
149	Stavenisse Neth. (Amsterdam In.)	51·35 N	3·59 E
171	Stavropol' Sov. Un.	45·05 N	41·50 E
158	Stawno (swav'nō) Pol.	54·21 N	16·38 E
116	Steamboat Springs (stēm'bōt') Co.	40·30 N	106·48 W
167	Steblëv (styĕp'lyôf) Sov. Un.	49·23 N	31·03 E
109	Steel (R.) (stēl) Can.	49·08 N	86·55 W
105	Steelton (stēl'tŭn) Pa.	40·15 N	76·45 W
149	Steenbergen Neth. (Amsterdam In.)	51·35 N	4·18 E
110	Steens Mts. (stēnz) Or.	42·15 N	118·52 W
204	Steep Pt. (stēp) Austl.	26·15 N	112·05 E
	Stefaniee, L., see Chew Bahir		
107	Steger (stē'gĕr) Il. (Chicago In.)	41·28 N	87·38 W
158	Steiermark (Styria) (State) (shtī'ĕr-märk) Aus.	47·22 N	14·40 E
90	Steinbach Can.	49·32 N	96·41 W
150	Steinkjer (stĕin-kyĕr) Nor.	64·00 N	11·19 E
112	Stella (stĕl'ȧ) Wa. (Portland In.)	46·11 N	123·12 W
98	Stellarton (stĕl'ȧr-tŭn) Can.	45·34 N	62·40 W
158	Stendal (shtĕn'däl) G.D.R.	52·37 N	11·51 E
171	Stepanakert (styĕ'pän-ȧ-kĕrt) Sov. Un.	39·50 N	46·40 E
203	Stephens, Port (stē'fĕns) Austl.	32·43 N	152·55 E
99	Stephenville (stē'vĕn-vĭl) Can.	48·33 N	58·35 W
172	Stepnyak (styĭp-nyäk') Sov. Un.	52·37 N	70·43 E
161	Sterkrade (shtĕr'krädĕ) F.R.G. (Ruhr In.)	51·31 N	6·51 E
213	Sterkstroom S. Afr. (Natal In.)	31·33 S	26·36 E
116	Sterling (stûr'lĭng) Co.	40·38 N	103·14 W
109	Sterling Il.	41·48 N	89·42 W
116	Sterling Ks.	38·11 N	98·11 W
99	Sterling Ma. (In.)	42·26 N	71·41 W
118	Sterling Tx.	31·53 N	100·58 W
174	Sterlitamak (styĕr'lē-ta-mäk') Sov. Un. (Urals In.)	53·38 N	55·56 E
159	Šternberk (shtĕrn'bĕrk) Czech.	49·44 N	17·18 E
	Stettin, see Szczecin		
158	Stettiner Haff (L.) (shtĕ'tē-nĕr häf) G.D.R.	53·47 N	14·02 E
93	Stettler Can.	52·19 N	112·43 W
104	Steubenville (stū'bĕn-vĭl) Oh.	40·20 N	80·40 W
112	Stevens (L.) (stē'vĕnz) Wa. (Seattle In.)	47·59 N	122·06 W
109	Stevens Point Wi.	44·30 N	89·35 W
111	Stevensville (stē'vĕnz-vĭl) Mt.	46·31 N	114·03 W
90	Stewart (R.) (stū'ĕrt) Can.	63·27 N	138·48 W
205	Stewart I. N. Z. (In.)	46·50 S	168·06 E
98	Stewiacke (stū'wē-ăk) Can.	45·08 N	63·21 W
218	Steynsrus (stīns'rōōs) S. Afr. (Johannesburg & Pretoria In.)	27·58 S	27·33 E
158	Steyr (shtīr) Aus.	48·03 N	14·24 E
90	Stikine (R.) (stĭ-kēn') Can.	58·17 N	130·10 W
90	Stikine Ranges Can.	59·05 N	130·00 W
112	Stillaguamish (R.) Wa. (Seattle In.)	48·11 N	122·18 W
112	Stillaguamish (R.), South Fk. (stĭl-ȧ-gwä'mĭsh) Wa. (Seattle In.)	48·05 N	121·59 W
113	Stillwater (stĭl'wô-tēr) Mn. (Minneapolis, St. Paul In.)	45·04 N	92·48 W
111	Stillwater Mt.	45·23 N	109·45 W
117	Stillwater Ok.	36·06 N	97·03 W
114	Stillwater Ra. Nv.	39·43 N	118·11 W
110	Stillwater R. Mt.	48·47 N	114·40 W
165	Štip (shtĭp) Yugo.	41·43 N	22·07 E
154	Stirling (stûr'lĭng) Scot.	56·05 N	3·59 W
89	Stittsville (stĭts'vĭl) Can. (Ottawa In.)	45·15 N	75·54 W
156	Stjördalshalsen (styûr-däls-hälsĕn) Nor.	63·26 N	11·00 E
109	Stockbridge Munsee Ind. Res. (stŏk'brĭdj mŭn-sē) Wi.	44·49 N	89·00 W
149	Stockerau (shtô'kĕ-rou) Aus. (Vienna In.)	48·24 N	16·13 E
98	Stockholm (stŏk'hōlm) Me.	47·05 N	68·08 W
156	Stockholm (stôk'hôlm') Swe.	59·23 N	18·00 E
148	Stockport (stŏk'pôrt) Eng.	53·24 N	2·09 W
114	Stockton (stŏk'tŭn) Ca.	37·56 N	121·16 W
154	Stockton Eng.	54·35 N	1·25 W
116	Stockton Ks.	39·26 N	99·16 W
109	Stockton (I.) Wi.	46·56 N	90·25 W
118	Stockton Plat Tx.	30·34 N	102·35 W
117	Stockton Res. Mo.	37·40 N	93·45 W
156	Stöde (stû'dĕ) Swe.	62·26 N	16·35 E
148	Stoke-on-Trent (stōk-ŏn-trĕnt) Eng.	53·01 N	2·12 W
159	Stokhod (R.) (stō-kōd) Sov. Un.	51·24 N	25·20 E
165	Stolac (stô'läts) Yugo.	43·03 N	17·59 E
173	Stolbovoy (Is.) (stôl-bô-voi') Sov. Un.	73·43 N	133·05 E
159	Stolin (stô'lēn) Sov. Un.	51·54 N	26·52 E
161	Stommeln (shtō'mĕln) F.R.G. (Ruhr In.)	51·01 N	6·46 E
156	Stömstad Swe.	58·58 N	11·09 E
148	Stone Eng.	52·54 N	2·09 W
89	Stoneham (stōn'ȧm) Can. (Quebec In.)	46·59 N	71·22 W
99	Stoneham Ma. (Boston In.)	42·30 N	71·05 W
154	Stonehaven (stōn'hā-v'n) Scot.	56·57 N	2·09 W
106	Stone Mountain (stōn) Ga. (Atlanta In.)	33·49 N	84·10 W
89	Stonewall (stōn'wôl) Can. (Winnipeg In.)	50·09 N	97·21 W
120	Stonewall Ms.	32·08 N	88·44 W
89	Stoney Creek (stō'nē) Can. (Toronto In.)	43·13 N	79·45 W
105	Stonington (stōn'ĭng-tŭn) Ct.	41·20 N	71·55 W
114	Stony Cr. (stō'nē) Ca.	39·28 N	122·35 W
89	Stony Indian Res. Can. (Calgary In.)	51·10 N	114·45 W
89	Stony Mountain Can. (Winnipeg In.)	50·05 N	97·13 W
89	Stony Plain (stō'nē plān) Can. (Edmonton In.)	53·02 N	114·00 W
89	Stony Plain Ind. Res. Can. (Edmonton In.)	53·29 N	113·48 W
106	Stony Point NY (New York In.)	41·13 N	73·58 W
156	Storå (R.) Den.	56·22 N	8·35 E
170	Stora Lule (R.) (stōō'rä lōō'lĕ) Swe.	67·00 N	19·30 E
156	Stord (I.) (stôrd) Nor.	59·54 N	5·15 E
156	Store Baelt (Str.) Den.	55·25 N	10·50 E
150	Stören (stûrĕn) Nor.	62·58 N	10·21 E
156	Store Sotra (Sartor) (stô-rĕ-sô'-trȧ) (sär'tôr) Nor.	60·24 N	4·35 E
156	Stor Fd. (stôr fyôrd) Nor.	62·17 N	6·19 E
213	Stormberg (Mts.) (stôrm'bûrg) S. Afr. (Natal In.)	31·28 S	26·35 E
109	Storm Lake Ia.	42·39 N	95·12 W
123	Stormy Pt. (stôrm'ē) Vir. Is. (U. S. A.) (St. Thomas In.)	18·22 N	65·01 W
154	Stornoway (stôr'nô-wā) Scot.	58·13 N	6·21 W
159	Storozhinets (stô-rô'zhēn-yĕts) Sov. Un.	48·10 N	25·44 E
156	Störsjo (stôr'shû) Swe.	62·49 N	13·08 E
156	Störsjoen (L.) (stôr-syûĕn) Nor.	61·32 N	11·30 E
156	Störsjon (L.) Swe.	63·06 N	14·00 E
156	Storvik (stôr'vĕk) Swe.	60·37 N	16·31 E
99	Stoughton (stō'tŭn) Ma. (In.)	42·07 N	71·06 W
109	Stoughton Wi.	42·54 N	89·15 W
155	Stour (R.) (stour) Eng.	52·09 N	0·29 E
148	Stourbridge (stour'brĭj) Eng.	52·27 N	2·08 W
99	Stow (stō) Ma. (In.)	42·56 N	71·31 W
107	Stow Oh. (Cleveland In.)	41·09 N	81·26 W
218	Straatsdrif S. Afr. (Johannesburg & Pretoria In.)	25·19 S	26·22 E
154	Strabane (stră-băn') N. Ire.	54·59 N	7·27 W
161	Straelen (shtră'lĕn) F.R.G. (Ruhr In.)	51·26 N	6·16 E
205	Strahan (strā'ăn) Austl.	42·08 S	145·28 E
158	Strakonice (strä'kô-nyê-tsĕ) Czech.	49·18 N	13·52 E
165	Straldzha (sträl'dzhȧ) Bul.	42·37 N	26·44 E
158	Stralsund (shräl'sōōnt) G.D.R.	54·18 N	13·04 E
156	Strand (stränd) Nor.	59·05 N	5·59 E
154	Strangford, Lough (B.) (lôk străng'fērd) Ire.	54·30 N	5·34 W
156	Strängnas (strĕng'nĕs) Swe.	59·23 N	16·59 E
154	Stranraer (străn-rär') Scot.	54·55 N	5·05 W
161	Strasbourg (strȧs-bōōr') Fr.	48·36 N	7·49 E
104	Stratford (străt'fērd) Can.	43·20 N	81·05 W
105	Stratford Ct.	41·10 N	73·05 W
154	Stratford Eng.	52·13 N	1·41 W
109	Stratford Wi.	44·16 N	90·02 W
92	Strathcona Prov. Pk. Can.	49·40 N	125·50 W
158	Straubing (strou'bĭng) F.R.G.	48·52 N	12·36 E
158	Strausberg (strous'bĕrgh) G.D.R.	52·35 N	13·50 E
115	Strawberry (R.) Ut.	40·05 N	110·55 W
110	Strawberry Mts. (strô'bĕr'ĭ) Or.	44·19 N	119·20 W
118	Strawn (strôn) Tx.	32·38 N	98·28 W
104	Streator (strē'tēr) Il.	41·05 N	88·50 W
108	Streeter ND	46·40 N	99·22 W
89	Streetsville (strētz'vĭl) Can. (Toronto In.)	43·34 N	79·43 W
165	Strehaia (strĕ-kä'yȧ) Rom.	44·37 N	23·13 E
174	Strel'na (strĕl'nȧ) Sov. Un. (Leningrad In.)	59·52 N	30·01 E
148	Stretford (strĕt'fērd) Eng.	53·25 N	2·19 W
197	Strickland (R.) (strĭk'lănd) Pap. N. Gui.	6·15 S	142·00 E
149	Strijen Neth. (Amsterdam In.)	51·44 N	4·32 E
165	Strimonikós Kólpos (G.) Grc.	40·40 N	23·55 E
164	Strómboli (Vol.) (strôm'bô-lē) It.	38·46 N	15·16 E
174	Stromyn (strô'mĭn) Sov. Un. (Moscow In.)	56·02 N	38·29 E
120	Strong (R.) (strông) Ms.	32·03 N	89·42 W
107	Strongsville (strôŋgz'vĭl) Oh. (Cleveland In.)	41·19 N	81·50 W
154	Stronsay (I.) (strŏn'sā) Scot.	59·09 N	2·35 W
105	Stroudsburg (stroudz'bûrg) Pa.	41·00 N	75·15 W
156	Struer Den.	56·29 N	8·34 E
166	Strugi Krasnyye (strōō'gĭ krä's-ny'yĕ) Sov. Un.	58·14 N	29·10 E
165	Struma (R.) (strōō'mȧ) Bul.	41·55 N	23·05 E
165	Strumica (strōō'mĭ-tsȧ) Yugo.	41·26 N	22·38 E
174	Strunino Sov. Un. (Moscow In.)	56·23 N	38·34 E
104	Struthers (strŭdh'ērz) Oh.	41·00 N	80·35 W
149	Struvenhütten (shtrōō'vĕn-hü-tĕn) F.R.G. (Hamburg In.)	53·52 N	10·04 E
218	Strydpoortberge (Mts.) S. Afr. (Johannesburg & Pretoria In.)	24·08 N	29·18 E
159	Stryy (strē') Sov. Un.	49·16 N	23·51 E
159	Strzelce Opolskie (stzhĕl'tsĕ o-pŏl'skyĕ) Pol.	50·31 N	18·20 E
159	Strzelin (stzhĕ-lĭn) Pol.	50·48 N	17·06 E
159	Strzelno (stzhăl'nô) Pol.	52·37 N	18·10 E
121	Stuart (stū'ērt) Fl. (In.)	27·10 N	80·14 W
109	Stuart Ia.	41·31 N	94·20 W
101	Stuart (I.) Ak.	63·25 N	162·45 W
112	Stuart (I.) Wa. (Vancouver In.)	48·42 N	123·10 W
92	Stuart L. Can.	54·32 N	124·35 W
204	Stuart Ra. Austl.	29·00 S	134·30 E
196	Stung Treng (stōōng'trĕng') Camb.	13·36 N	106·00 E
149	Stupava Czech. (Vienna In.)	48·17 N	17·02 E
159	Stupsk (swōōpsk) Pol.	54·28 N	17·02 E
89	Sturgeon (R.) Can. (Edmonton In.)	53·41 N	113·46 W
109	Sturgeon (R.) Mi.	46·43 N	88·43 W
109	Sturgeon Bay Wi.	44·50 N	87·22 W
95	Sturgeon B. Can.	52·00 N	98·00 W
91	Sturgeon Falls Can.	46·19 N	79·49 W
104	Sturgis Ky.	37·35 N	88·00 W
104	Sturgis Mi.	41·45 N	85·25 W
108	Sturgis SD	44·25 N	103·31 W
204	Sturt Cr. Austl.	19·40 S	127·40 E
107	Sturtevant (stŭr'tĕ-vănt) Wi. (Milwaukee In.)	42·42 N	87·54 W
213	Stutterheim (stŭrt'ĕr-hīm) S. Afr. (Natal In.)	32·34 S	27·27 E
117	Stuttgart (stŭt'gärt) Ar.	34·30 N	91·33 W
158	Stuttgart (shtōōt'gärt) F.R.G.	48·48 N	9·15 E
150	Stykkisholmur Ice.	65·00 N	21·48 W
159	Styr' R. (stêr) Sov. Un.	51·44 N	26·07 E
	Styria, see Steiermark		
193	Suao (sōō'ou) Taiwan	24·35 N	121·45 E
184	Subarnarakha (R.) India	22·38 N	86·26 E
157	Subata (sōō'bȧ-tȧ) Sov. Un.	56·02 N	25·54 E
197	Subic (sōō'bĭk) Phil. (In.)	14·52 N	120·15 E
197	Subic B. Phil. (In.)	14·41 N	120·11 E
165	Subotica (sōō'bô'tē-tsȧ) Yugo.	46·06 N	19·41 E
217	Subugo (Mtn.) Ken.	1·40 S	35·49 E
106	Succasunna (sŭk'kȧ-sŭn'nȧ) NJ (New York In.)	40·52 N	74·37 W
159	Suceava (sōō-chȧ-ä'vȧ) Rom.	47·39 N	26·17 E
159	Suceava R. Rom.	47·45 N	26·10 E
159	Sucha (sōō'Kȧ) Pol.	49·44 N	19·40 E
125	Suchiapa (sōō-chē-ä'pä) Mex.	16·38 N	93·08 W
125	Suchiapa (R.) Mex.	16·27 N	93·26 W
190	Such'ien (sü'chĭän) China	33·57 N	118·17 E

ng-sing; ŋ-baŋk; N-nasalized n; nŏd; cŏmmit; ōld; ôbey; ôrder; fōōd; fŏŏt; ou-out; s-soft; sh-dish; th-thin; pūre; ûnite; ûrn; stŭd; circŭs; ü-as "y" in study; '-indeterminate vowel.

352 Suchitoto — Swan Hill
PRONOUNCING INDEX

Page Name Pronunciation Region Lat. °′ Long. °′

126 Suchitoto (sōō-chê-tō'tō) . . . Sal. 13·58 N 89·03 W
Süchow, see Hsüchou
Süchow, see Ipin
112 Sucia Is. (sōō'sê-ȧ) Wa. (Vancouver In.) 48·46 N 122·54 W
134 Sucio (R.) (sōō'syô) . . . Co. (In.) 6·55 N 76·15 W
154 Suck (sŭk) . . . Ire. 53·34 N 8·16 W
134 Sucre (sōō'krā) . . . Bol. 19·06 S 65·16 W
135 Sucre (State) (sōō'krĕ) . . Ven. (In.) 10·18 N 64·12 W
129 Sud, Canal du (Chan.) . . . Hai. 18·40 N 73·15 W
89 Sud, Rivière du (rê-vyâr'dü süd') Can. (Québec In.) 46·56 N 70·35 W
174 Suda (sōō'dá) . Sov. Un. (Urals In.) 56·58 N 56·45 E
166 Suda (R.) (sōō'dȧ) . . . Sov. Un. 59·24 N 36·40 E
186 Sudair (sŭ-dä'ĕr) . . . Sau. Ar. 25·48 N 46·28 E
209 Sudan . . . Afr. 14·00 N 28·00 E
215 Sudan (Reg.) (sōō-dän') . . . Afr. 15·00 N 7·00 E
91 Sudbury (sŭd'bĕr-ê) . . . Can. 46·28 N 81·00 W
99 Sudbury . . . Ma. (In.) 42·23 N 71·25 W
158 Sudetes (Mts.) . . . Czech. 50·41 N 15·37 E
166 Sudogda (sōō'dôk-dȧ) . . . Sov. Un. 55·57 N 40·29 E
166 Sudost' (R.) (sōō-dôst') . . Sov. Un. 52·43 N 33·13 E
167 Sudzha (sōōd'zhȧ) . . . Sov. Un. 51·14 N 35·11 E
163 Sueca (swā'kä) . . . Sp. 39·12 N 0·18 W
92 Suemez I. . . . Ak. 55·17 N 133·21 W
Suez, see As Suways
218 Suez, G. of (sōō-ĕz') Egypt (Suez In.) 29·53 N 32·33 E
Suez Can., see Qana el Suweis
106 Suffern (sŭf'fērn) NY (New York In.) 41·07 N 74·09 W
106 Suffolk (sŭf'ŭk) . . Va. (Norfolk In.) 36·43 N 76·35 W
104 Sugar (Cr.) . . . In. 39·55 N 87·10 W
116 Sugar City . . . Co. 38·12 N 103·42 W
113 Sugar Creek Mo. (Kansas City In.) 39·07 N 94·27 W
117 Sugar Cr. (shōōg'ĕr) . . . Il. 40·14 N 89·28 W
113 Sugar I. . Mi. (Sault Ste. Marie In.) 46·31 N 84·12 W
203 Sugarloaf Pt. (sōōgĕr'lôf) . . . Austl. 32·19 S 153·04 E
95 Suggi L. . . . Can. 54·22 N 102·47 W
183 Suhaymī, Wādī as (R.) Egypt (Palestine In.) 29·48 N 33·12 E
158 Suhl (zōōl) . . . G.D.R. 50·37 N 10·41 E
190 Suhsien (sōō'sĭän) . . . China 33·37 N 117·51 E
193 Suichuan (Mtn.) . . . China 26·25 N 114·10 E
190 Suichung (sōōĭ'jōōng) . . . China 40·22 N 120·20 E
173 Suifenho (swā'fŭn'hŭ') . . . China 44·47 N 131·13 E
192 Suihua (Peilintzu) . . . China 46·38 N 126·50 E
190 Suining (sōō'ê-nĭng') . . . China 33·54 N 117·57 E
137 Suipacha (swê-pä'chä) Arg. (Buenos Aires In.) 34·45 S 59·43 W
190 Suip'ing (sōō'ê-pĭng) . . . China 33·09 N 113·58 E
154 Suir R. (sūr) . . . Ire. 52·20 N 7·32 W
112 Suisun B. (sōō-ê-sōōn') Ca. (San Francisco In.) 38·07 N 122·02 W
195 Suita (sōō'ê-tä) . . Jap. (Ōsaka In.) 34·45 N 135·32 E
192 Suite . . . China 37·32 N 110·12 E
106 Suitland (sōōt'lănd) Md. (Baltimore In.) 38·51 N 76·57 W
188 Suiyuan (Prov.) (sōō'ê-yän') China 41·31 N 107·04 E
196 Sukabumi . . . Indon. 6·52 S 106·56 E
196 Sukadana . . . Indon. 1·15 S 110·30 E
195 Sukagawa (sōō'kä-gä'wä) . . . Jap. 37·08 N 140·07 E
Sukarnapura, see Jayapura
166 Sukhinichi (sōō'κē'nê-chê) Sov. Un. 54·07 N 35·18 E
170 Sukhona (R.) (sōō-κô'nȧ) Sov. Un. 59·30 N 42·20 E
174 Sukhoy Log (sōō'kôy lôg) Sov. Un. (Urals In.) 56·55 N 62·03 E
171 Sukhumi (sōō-kōōm') . . . Sov. Un. 43·00 N 41·00 E
184 Sukkur (sŭk'ŭr) . . . Pak. 27·49 N 68·50 E
92 Sukkwan I. . . . Ak. 55·05 N 132·45 W
174 Suksun (sōōk'sōōn) Sov. Un. (Urals In.) 57·08 N 57·22 E
195 Sukumo (sōō'kōō-mô) . . . Jap. 32·58 N 132·45 E
93 Sukunka (R.) . . . Can. 55·00 N 121·50 W
197 Sula, Kepulauan (I.) . . . Indon. 2·20 S 125·20 E
167 Sula (R.) (sōō-lȧ') . . . Sov. Un. 50·36 N 33·13 E
126 Sulaco R. (sōō-lä'kō) . . . Hond. 14·55 N 87·31 W
184 Sulaimān Ra. (sōō-lä-ê-män') Pak. 29·47 N 69·10 E
171 Sulak (R.) (sōō-lȧk') . . . Sov. Un. 43·30 N 47·00 E
196 Sulawesi (Celebes) (Is.) . . . Indon. 2·15 S 120·30 E
156 Suldals Vand (L.) (sŭl-däls vän) Nor. 59·35 N 6·59 E
174 Suleya (sōō-lĕ'ya) Sov. Un. (Urals In.) 55·12 N 58·52 E
149 Sulfeld (zōōl'fĕld) F.R.G. (Hamburg In.) 53·48 N 10·13 E
167 Sulina (sōō-lē'nȧ) . . . Rom. 45·08 N 29·38 E
150 Sulitelma (Mtn.) (sōō-lê-tyĕl'mȧ) Nor.-Swe. 67·03 N 16·09 E
134 Sullana (sōō-lyä'nä) . . . Peru 4·57 N 80·47 W
120 Sulligent (sŭl'ĭ-jĕnt) . . . Al. 33·52 N 88·06 W
104 Sullivan (sŭl'ĭ-văn) . . . Il. 41·35 N 88·35 W
104 Sullivan . . . In. 39·05 N 87·20 W
117 Sullivan . . . Mo. 38·13 N 91·09 W
164 Sulmona (sōōl-mō'nä) . . . It. 42·02 N 13·58 E
188 Sulo . . . China 41·29 N 80·15 E
188 Sulo Ho (R.) . . . China 40·53 N 94·55 E
117 Sulphur (sŭl'fŭr) . . . Ok. 34·31 N 96·58 W
117 Sulphur (R.) . . . Tx. 33·26 N 95·06 W
117 Sulphur Springs (sprĭngz) . . . Tx. 33·09 N 95·36 W
112 Sultan (sŭl'tăn) . Wa. (Seattle In.) 47·52 N 121·49 W
112 Sultan (R.) . . . Wa. (Seattle In.) 47·55 N 121·49 W
124 Sultepec (sōōl-tȧ-pĕk') . . . Mex. 18·50 N 99·51 W
196 Sulu Arch. (sōō'lōō) . . . Phil. 5·52 N 122·00 E
153 Suluntah . . . Libya 32·39 N 21·49 E
196 Sulu Sea . . . Phil. 8·25 N 119·00 E
195 Suma (sōō'mä) . . . Jap. (Ōsaka In.) 34·39 N 135·08 E
112 Sumas (sū'mȧs) Wa. (Vancouver In.) 49·00 N 122·16 W
196 Sumatera (Sumatra) (I.) (sōō-mä-trȧ) . Indon. 2·06 N 99·40 E
196 Sumba (I.) (sŭm'bȧ) . . . Indon. 9·52 S 119·00 E
216 Sumba, Île (I.) . . . Zaire 1·44 N 19·32 E
196 Sumbawa (I.) (sōōm-bä'wä) Indon. 9·00 S 118·18 E
196 Sumbawa-Besar . . . Indon 8·32 S 117·20 E
217 Sumbawanga . . . Tan. 7·58 S 31·37 E
159 Sümeg (shü'mĕg) . . . Hung. 46·59 N 17·19 E
195 Sumida (R.) (sōō'mê-dä) . . . Jap. 36·01 N 139·24 E
137 Sumidouro (sōō-mê-dō'rōō) Braz. (Rio de Janeiro In.) 22·04 S 42·41 W
195 Sumiyoshi (sōō'mê-yō'shê) Jap. (Ōsaka In.) 34·43 N 135·16 E
110 Summer L. (sŭm'ĕr) . . . Or. 42·50 N 120·35 W
93 Summerland (sŭ'mĕr-lănd) . . Can. 49·39 N 117·33 W
98 Summerside (sŭm'ĕr-sīd) . . . Can. 46·25 N 63·47 W
121 Summerton (sŭm'ĕr-tŭn) . . . SC 33·37 N 80·22 W
121 Summerville (sŭm'ĕr-vĭl) . . . SC 33·00 N 80·10 W
107 Summit (sŭm'mĭt) Il. (Chicago In.) 41·47 N 87·48 W
106 Summit . . . N.J. (New York In.) 40·43 N 74·21 W
110 Summit Lake Ind. Res. . . . Nv. 41·35 N 119·30 W
115 Summit Pk. . . . Co. 37·20 N 106·40 W
112 Sumner (sŭm'nĕr) Wa. (Seattle In.) 47·12 N 122·14 W
158 Šumperk (shōōm'pĕrk) . . . Czech. 49·57 N 17·02 E
120 Sumrall (sŭm'rôl) . . . Ms. 31·25 N 89·34 W
121 Sumter (sŭm'tĕr) . . . SC 33·55 N 80·21 W
167 Sumy (sōō'mĭ) . . . Sov. Un. 50·54 N 34·47 E
167 Sumy (Oblast) . . . Sov. Un. 51·02 N 34·05 E
111 Sunburst . . . Mt. 48·53 N 111·55 W
105 Sunbury (sŭn'bĕr-ê) . . . Pa. 40·50 N 76·45 W
196 Sunda Is. . . . Indon. 9·00 S 108·40 E
156 Sundals Fd. (sōōn'däls) . . . Nor. 62·50 N 7·55 E
111 Sundance (sŭn'dăns) . . . Wy. 44·24 N 104·27 W
184 Sundarbans (Swp.) (sōōn'dĕr-bŭns) . Bngl.-India 21·50 N 89·00 E
196 Sunda Selat (Str.) . . . Indon. 5·45 S 106·15 E
196 Sunda Trench (sōōn'dä) . . . Indon. 9·45 S 107·30 E
204 Sunday Str. (sŭn'dā) . . . Austl. 15·50 S 122·45 E
156 Sundbyberg (sōōn'bü-bĕrgh) . Swe. 59·24 N 17·56 E
154 Sunderland (sŭn'dĕr-lănd) . . . Eng. 54·55 N 1·25 W
106 Sunderland . . . Md. (Baltimore In.) 38·41 N 76·36 W
156 Sundsvall (sōōnds'väl) . . . Swe. 62·24 N 19·19 E
120 Sunflower, (R.) (sŭn-flou'ĕr) . . . Ms. 32·57 N 90·40 W
192 Sungari Res. (sōōn'gȧ-rē) . . . China 42·55 N 127·50 E
Sungari (R.), see Sung Hua
191 Sungchiang . . China (Shanghai In.) 31·01 N 121·14 E
189 Sung Hua (R.) (Sungari) (sōōn'gȧ-rē) . China 46·09 N 127·53 E
192 Sungtzu (Mtn.) . . . China 39·40 N 114·50 E
171 Sungurlu (sōōn'gōōr-lōō') . . . Tur. 40·08 N 34·20 E
184 Sun Kosi (R.) . . . Nep. 27·13 N 85·52 E
113 Sunland (sŭn-lănd) Ca. (Los Angeles In.) 34·16 N 118·18 W
156 Sunne (sōōn'ĕ) . . . Swe. 59·51 N 13·07 E
148 Sunninghill (sŭnĭng'hĭl) Eng. (London In.) 51·23 N 0·40 W
113 Sunnymead (sŭn'ĭ-mēd) Ca. (Los Angeles In.) 33·56 N 117·15 W
115 Sunnyside . . . Ut. 39·35 N 110·20 W
110 Sunnyside . . . Wa. 46·19 N 120·00 W
112 Sunnyvale (sŭn-nê-văl) Ca. (San Francisco In.) 37·23 N 122·02 W
112 Sunol (sōō'nŭl) Ca. (San Francisco In.) 37·36 N 122·53 W
111 Sun R. (sŭn) . . . Mt. 47·34 N 111·53 W
113 Sunset (sŭn-sĕt) Ut. (Salt Lake City In.) 41·08 N 112·02 W
115 Sunset Crater Natl. Mon. (krā'tĕr) . Az. 35·20 N 111·30 W
202 Sunshine . . Austl. (Melbourne In.) 37·47 S 144·50 E
173 Suntar (sōōn-tȧr') . . . Sov. Un. 62·14 N 117·49 E
214 Sunyani . . . Ghana 7·20 N 2·20 W
157 Suoyarvi (sōō'ô-yĕr'vê) . . Sov. Un. 62·12 N 32·29 E
115 Superior (su-pē'rĭ-ĕr) . . . Az. 33·15 N 111·10 W
116 Superior . . . Ne. 40·04 N 98·05 W
113 Superior . . . Wi. (Duluth In.) 46·44 N 92·06 W
111 Superior . . . Wy. 41·45 N 108·57 W
125 Superior, Laguna (L.) (lä-gōō'nȧ sōō-pä-rê-ōr') . Mex. 16·20 N 94·55 W
91 Superior, L. . . . Can.-U. S. 47·38 N 89·20 W
113 Superior Village . . Wi. (Duluth In.) 46·38 N 92·07 W
194 Sup'ung Res. (sōō'pōōng) Kor.-China 40·35 N 126·00 E
112 Suquamish (sōō-gwä'mĭsh) Wa. (Seattle In.) 47·44 N 122·34 W
183 Şūr (Tyre) (sōōr) (tīr) Leb. (Palestine In.) 33·16 N 35·13 E
186 Sūr . . . Om. 22·23 N 59·28 E
196 Surabaya . . . Indon. 7·23 S 112·45 E
196 Surakarta . . . Indon. 7·35 S 110·45 E
159 Šurany (shōō'rá-nû') . . . Czech. 48·05 N 18·11 E
203 Surat (sū-rāt) . . . Austl. 27·18 S 149·00 E
184 Surat (sōō'rŭt) . . . India 21·08 N 73·22 E
196 Surat Thani . . . Thai. 8·59 N 99·14 E
166 Surazh (sōō-rȧzh') . . . Sov. Un. 53·02 N 32·27 E
166 Surazh . . . Sov. Un. 55·24 N 30·46 E
160 Surgères (sür-zhâr') . . . Fr. 46·06 N 0·51 W
172 Surgut (sōōr-gōōt') . . . Sov. Un. 61·18 N 73·38 E
196 Surin . . . Thai. 14·59 N 103·57 E
133 Surinam (sōō-rê-näm') . . . S A. 4·00 N 56·00 W
218 Surud Ad (Mtn.) Som. (Horn of Afr. In.) 10·40 N 47·23 E
195 Suruga-Wan (B.) (sōō'rōō-gä wän) . Jap. 34·52 N 138·36 E
211 Surt . . . Libya 31·14 N 16·37 E
153 Surt, Khalij (G.) . . . Afr. 31·30 N 18·28 E
164 Susa (sōō'sä) . . . It. 45·01 N 7·09 E
195 Susa . . . Jap. 34·40 N 131·39 E
164 Sušac (sōō'shäts) . . . Yugo. 44·31 N 14·15 E
164 Sušak (sōō'shȧk) . . . Yugo. 45·20 N 14·24 E
164 Sušak (I.) . . . Yugo. 42·45 N 16·30 E
195 Susaki (sōō'sä-kê) . . . Jap. 33·23 N 133·16 E
101 Susitna (sōō-sĭt'nȧ) . . . Ak. 61·28 N 150·28 W
101 Susitna (R.) . . . Ak. 62·00 N 150·28 W
105 Susquehanna (sŭs'kwê-hăn'ȧ) . . Pa. 41·55 N 73·35 W
105 Susquehanna (R.) . . . Pa. 39·50 N 76·20 W
107 Sussex . . . Wi. (Milwaukee In.) 43·08 N 88·12 W
98 Sussex (sŭs'ĕks) . . . Can. 45·43 N 65·31 W
106 Sussex . . . NJ (New York In.) 41·12 N 74·36 W
193 Susung (sōō'sōōng') . . . China 30·18 N 116·08 E
202 Sutherland (sŭdh'ĕr-lănd) Austl. (Sydney In.) 34·02 S 151·04 E
212 Sutherland (sŭ'thĕr-lănd) . . . S. Afr. 32·25 S 20·40 E
184 Sutlej (R.) (sŭt'lĕj) . . . Pak.-India 30·15 N 72·25 E
148 Sutton (sut''n) . . Eng. (London In.) 51·21 N 0·12 W
99 Sutton . . . Ma. (In.) 42·09 N 71·46 W
148 Sutton Coldfield (kōld'fēld) . . Eng. 52·34 N 1·49 W
148 Sutton-in-Ashfield (ĭn-ăsh'fēld) Eng. 53·07 N 1·15 W
213 Suurberge (Mts.) S. Afr. (Natal In.) 33·15 S 25·32 E
195 Suwa (sōō'wä) . . . Jap. 36·03 N 138·08 E
95 Suwannee L. . . . Can. 56·08 N 100·10 W
159 Suwatki (sōō-vou'kê) . . . Pol. 54·05 N 22·58 E
120 Suwannee (R.) (sōō-wô'nê) . Fl.-Ga. 29·42 N 83·00 W
218 Suways al Ḩulwah, Tur'at as (Can.) . Egypt (In.) 30·15 N 32·20 E
166 Suzdal' (sōōz'dȧl) . . . Sov. Un. 56·26 N 40·29 E
194 Suzu Misaki (C.) (sōō'zōō mê'sä-kê) . Jap. 37·30 N 137·35 E
168 Svalbard (Spitsbergen) (Is.) (sväl'bärt) (spĭts'bûr-gĕn) . Eur. 77·00 N 20·00 E
156 Svaneke (svä'nĕ-kĕ) . . . Den. 55·08 N 15·07 E
167 Svatovo (svä'tô-vô) . . . Sov. Un. 49·23 N 38·10 E
156 Svedala (svĕ'dä-lä) . . . Swe. 55·29 N 13·11 E
156 Sveg . . . Swe. 62·03 N 14·22 E
156 Svelvik (svĕl'vĕk) . . . Nor. 59·37 N 10·18 E
157 Švenčionys . . . Sov. Un. 55·09 N 26·09 E
156 Svendborg (svĕn-bôrgh) . . . Den. 55·05 N 10·35 E
112 Svensen (svĕn'sĕn) Or. (Portland In.) 46·10 N 123·39 W
174 Sverdlovsk (svĕrd-lôfsk') Sov. Un. (Urals In.) 56·50 N 61·10 E
194 Svetlaya (svyĕt'lȧ-yȧ) . . . Sov. Un. 46·09 N 137·53 E
165 Svilajnac (svē'lȧ-ê-nȧts) . . . Yugo. 44·12 N 21·14 E
165 Svilengrad (svĕl'ĕn-grȧt) . . . Bul. 41·44 N 26·11 E
170 Svir' (R.) . . . Sov. Un. 60·55 N 33·40 E
157 Svir Kanal (can.) (kȧ-näl') Sov. Un. 60·10 N 32·40 E
165 Svishtov (svēsh'tôf) . . . Bul. 43·36 N 25·21 E
166 Svisloch' (svēs'lôκ) . . . Sov. Un. 53·38 N 28·10 E
158 Svitavy . . . Czech. 49·46 N 16·28 E
159 Svitsa (R.) (svĭ-tsȧ) . . . Sov. Un. 49·09 N 24·10 E
173 Svobodnyy (svô-bôd'nĭ) . . Sov. Un. 51·28 N 128·28 E
150 Svolvaer (svôl'vĕr) . . . Nor. 68·15 N 14·29 E
173 Svyatoy Nos, Mys (C.) (svyŭ'toi nôs) . Sov. Un. 72·18 N 139·28 E
148 Swadlincote (swŏd'lĭn-kōt) . . . Eng. 52·46 N 1·33 W
205 Swain Rfs. (swān) . . . Austl. 22·12 S 152·08 E
121 Swainsboro (swānz'bŭr-ô) . . . Ga. 32·37 N 82·21 W
212 Swakopmund (svä'kôp-mōōnt) (swȧ'kôp-mōōnd) . Namibia 22·40 S 14·30 E
154 Swale (R.) (swāl) . . . Eng. 54·12 N 1·30 W
148 Swallowfield (swŏl'ô-fēld) Eng. (London In.) 51·21 N 0·58 W
99 Swampscott (swŏmp'skŏt) Ma. (In.) 42·28 N 70·55 W
202 Swan, I. (swŏn) Austl. (Melbourne In.) 38·15 S 144·41 E
204 Swan (R.) . . . Austl. 31·30 S 126·30 E
95 Swan (R.) . . . Can. 51·58 N 101·45 W
203 Swan Hill . . . Austl. 35·20 S 143·30 E

ăt; finăl; rāte; senâte; ärm; åsk; sofȧ; fâre; ch-choose; dh-as th in other; bē; ēvent; bĕt; recĕnt; cratĕr; g-go; gh-guttural g; bĭt; ĭ-short neutral; rīde; κ-guttural k as ch in German ich;

ng-sing; ŋ-baŋk; N-nasalized n; nŏd; cŏmmit; ōld; ôbey; ôrder; fōōd; fŏŏt; ou-out; s-soft; sh-dish; th-thin; pūre; ûnite; ûrn; stŭd; circŭs; ü-as "y" in study; '-indeterminate vowel.

ăt; fināl; rāte; senāte; ärm; ásk; sofá; fâre; ch-choose; dh-as th in other; bē; ĕvent; bĕt; recĕnt; cratĕr; g-go; gh-guttural g; bĭt; ĭ-short neutral; rīde; к-guttural k as ch in German ich;

PRONOUNCING INDEX
Tarrejon de Ardoz — Tepeji del Rio 355

Page	Name Pronunciation Region	Lat. °'	Long. °'
163	Tarrejón de Ardoz (tär-rĕ-кô'n-dĕ-är-dôz) Sp. (Madrid In.)	40·28 N	3·29 W
106	Tarrytown (tăr'ĭ-toun) NY (New York In.)	41·04 N	73·52 W
171	Tarsus (tȧr'sōōs) (tär'sŭs) Tur.	37·00 N	34·50 E
136	Tartagal (tär-tä-gȧ'l) Arg.	23·31 S	63·47 W
153	Tartous (tȧr-tōōs') Egypt	34·54 N	35·59 E
166	Tartu (Dorpat) (tär'tōō) (dôr'pät) Sov. Un.	58·23 N	26·44 E
195	Tarumi (tä'rōō-mē) Jap. (Ōsaka In.)	34·38 N	135·04 E
166	Tarusa (tä-rōōs'ȧ) Sov. Un.	54·43 N	37·11 E
113	Tarzana (tär-ză'ȧ) Ca. (Los Angeles In.)	34·10 N	118·32 W
190	Tashanchen (dä'sähn'jĕn) China	34·17 N	119·17 E
147	Tashauz (tŭ-shŭ-ōōs') Sov. Un.	41·50 N	59·45 E
172	Tashkent (tȧsh'kĕnt) Sov. Un.	41·23 N	69·04 E
205	Tasman B. (tăz'măn) N. Z. (In.)	39·11 S	173·22 E
203	Tasmania (State) (tăz-mā'nĭ-ȧ) Austl.	38·20 S	146·30 E
205	Tasmania (I.) Austl.	41·28 S	142·30 E
203	Tasman Pen. Austl.	43·00 S	148·30 E
198	Tasman Sea Oceania	29·30 S	155·00 E
124	Tasquillo (täs-kē'lyō) Mex.	20·34 N	99·21 W
210	Tassili-n-Ajjer (Plat.) (tȧs'ē-lē ä'jĕr) Alg.	25·40 N	6·57 E
170	Tatar (A. S. S. R.) (tȧ-tär') Sov. Un.	55·30 N	51·00 E
172	Tatarsk (tȧ-tärsk') Sov. Un.	55·15 N	75·00 E
173	Tatar Str. Sov. Un.	51·00 N	141·45 E
112	Tater Hill (Mtn.) (tāt'ēr hĭl) Or. (Portland In.)	45·47 N	123·02 W
195	Tateyama (tä'tē-yä'mä) Jap.	35·04 N	139·52 E
92	Tatlow, Mt. Can.	51·23 N	123·52 W
159	Tatra Mts. Czech.-Pol.	49·15 N	19·40 E
193	Tattien Ting (Mtn.) China	22·25 N	111·20 E
193	Tatu Ho (R.) China	29·20 N	103·30 E
137	Tatuí (tä-tōō-ē') Braz. (Rio de Janeiro In.)	23·21 S	47·49 W
192	Tat'ung (tä'tōōng') China	40·00 N	113·30 E
137	Taubaté (tou-bȧ-tā') Braz. (Rio de Janeiro In.)	23·03 S	45·32 W
158	Tauern Tun. Aus.	47·12 N	13·17 E
212	Taung (tä'ōōng) S. Afr.	27·25 S	29·45 E
106	Taunton (tän'tŭn) Ma. (Providence In.)	41·54 N	71·03 W
106	Taunton R. RI (Providence In.)	41·50 N	71·02 W
155	Taunus (Mts.) (tou'nōōz) F.R.G.	50·15 N	8·33 E
205	Taupo, L. (tä'ōō-pō) N. Z. (In.)	38·38 S	175·27 E
157	Taurage (tou'rȧ-gā) Sov. Un.	55·15 N	22·18 E
	Taurus Mts., see Toros Dağlari		
162	Tauste (tä-ōōs'tȧ) Sp.	41·55 N	1·15 W
172	Tavda (tȧv-dȧ') Sov. Un.	58·00 N	64·44 E
170	Tavda (R.) Sov. Un.	59·20 N	63·28 E
161	Taverny (tȧ-vĕr-nē') Fr. (Paris In.)	49·02 N	2·13 E
125	Taviche (tä-vē'chĕ) Mex.	16·43 N	96·35 W
162	Tavira (tä-vē'rȧ) Port.	37·09 N	7·42 W
196	Tavoy Bur.	14·04 N	98·19 E
171	Tavşanli (tȧv'shän-lĭ) Tur.	39·30 N	29·30 E
119	Tawakoni (L.) Tx.	32·51 N	95·59 W
195	Tawaramoto (tä'wä-rä-mô-tô) Jap. (Ōsaka In.)	34·33 N	135·48 E
104	Tawas City Mi.	44·15 N	83·30 W
104	Tawas Pt. (tô'wȧs) Mi.	44·15 N	83·25 W
190	Tawen (R.) (dä'wĕn) China	35·58 N	116·53 E
196	Tawitawi Group (Is.) (tä'wē-tä'wē) Phil.	4·52 N	120·35 E
211	Tawkar Sud.	18·28 N	37·46 E
124	Taxco de Alarcón (täs'kō dĕ ä-lär-kô'n) Mex.	18·34 N	99·37 W
154	Tay, Firth of (fûrth ŏv tā) Scot.	56·26 N	2·45 W
154	Tay (L.) Scot.	56·25 N	5·07 W
154	Tay (R.) Scot.	56·35 N	3·37 W
197	Tayabas B. (tä-yä'bäs) Phil. (In.)	13·44 N	121·40 E
172	Tayga (tī'gä) Sov. Un.	56·12 N	85·47 E
173	Taygonos, Mys (Taigonos) (C.) Sov. Un.	60·37 N	160·17 E
119	Taylor Tx.	30·35 N	97·25 W
115	Taylor, Mt. NM	35·20 N	107·40 W
104	Taylorville (tā'lēr-vĭl) Il.	39·30 N	89·20 W
186	Taymā Sau. Ar.	27·45 N	38·55 E
173	Taymyr (Taimyr) (L.) (tī-mĭr') Sov. Un.	74·13 N	100·45 E
172	Taymyr, P-Ov (Taimyr) (Pen.) Sov. Un.	75·15 N	95·00 E
172	Tayshet (Taishet) (tī-shĕt') Sov. Un.	56·09 N	97·49 E
172	Taytay (tī-tī) Phil.	10·37 N	119·10 E
193	Tayü China	25·20 N	114·20 E
197	Tayung (tä-yōōng') Phil. (In.)	16·01 N	120·45 E
172	Taz (R.) (tȧz) Sov. Un.	67·15 N	80·45 E
210	Taza (tä'zä) Mor.	34·08 N	4·00 W
172	Tazovskoye Sov. Un.	66·58 N	78·28 E
171	Tbilisi ('tbĭl-yē'sē) Sov. Un.	41·40 N	44·45 E
216	Tchibanga (chē-bäŋ'gä) Gabon	2·51 S	11·02 E
214	Tchien Lib.	6·04 N	8·08 W
215	Tchigai, Plat. du (Plat.) Chad-Niger	21·20 N	14·50 E
159	Tczew (t'chĕf') Pol.	54·06 N	18·48 E
126	Teabo (tĕ-ä'bô) Mex. (In.)	20·25 N	89·14 W
119	Teague (tēg) Tx.	31·39 N	96·16 W
125	Teapa (tā-ä'pä) Mex.	17·35 N	92·56 W
210	Tébessa (tā'bĕs'ä) Alg.	35·27 N	8·13 E
183	Tebing Tinggi (I.) (teb'ĭng-tĭng'gä) Indon. (Singapore In.)	0·54 N	102·39 E
124	Tecalitlán (tā-kä-lē-tlän') Mex.	19·28 N	103·17 W
214	Techiman Ghana	7·35 N	1·56 W
124	Tecoanapa (tāk-wä-nä-pä') Mex.	16·33 N	98·46 W
126	Tecoh (tĕ-kô) Mex. (In.)	20·46 N	89·27 W
124	Tecolotlán (tā-kô-lô-tlän') Mex.	20·13 N	103·57 W
125	Tecolutla (tā-kô-lōō'tlä) Mex.	20·33 N	97·00 W
125	Tecolutla (R.) Mex.	20·16 N	97·14 W
124	Tecomán (tā-kô-män') Mex.	18·53 N	103·53 W
125	Tecómitl (tĕ-kŏ'mētl) Mex. (In.)	19·13 N	98·59 W
124	Tecozautla (tā'kô-zä-ōō'tlä) Mex.	20·33 N	99·38 W
124	Tecpan de Galeana (tĕk-pän' dā gä-lā-ä'nä) Mex.	17·13 N	100·41 W
125	Tecpatán (tĕk-pä-tá'n) Mex.	17·08 N	93·18 W
124	Tecuala (tĕ-kwä-lä) Mex.	22·24 N	105·29 W
159	Tecuci (ta-kōōch') Rom.	45·51 N	27·30 E
107	Tecumseh (tē-kŭm'sē) Can. (Detroit In.)	42·19 N	82·53 W
104	Tecumseh Mi.	42·00 N	84·00 W
118	Tecumseh Ne.	40·21 N	96·09 W
117	Tecumseh Ok.	35·18 N	96·55 W
154	Tees (R.) (tēz) Eng.	54·40 N	2·10 W
	Teesside, see Middlesbrough		
134	Tefé (tĕf-ā') Braz.	3·27 S	64·43 W
195	Teganuna (L.) (tā'gä-nōō'nä) Jap. (Tōkyō In.)	35·50 N	140·02 E
126	Tegucigalpa (tå-gōō-sē-gäl'pä) Hond.	14·08 N	87·15 W
114	Tehachapi Mts. (tē-hă-shā'pĭ) Ca.	34·50 N	118·55 W
92	Tehentlo L. Can.	55·11 N	125·00 W
186	Tehrān (tĕ-hrän') Iran	35·45 N	51·30 E
190	Tehsien (dŭ'sĭän) China	37·28 N	116·17 E
193	Tehua China	25·30 N	118·15 E
125	Tehuacan (tā-wä-kän') Mex.	18·27 N	97·23 W
125	Tehuantepec (Sto. Domingo) (tȧ-wän-tȧ-pĕk') (sän-tô dô-mē'n-gô) Mex.	16·20 N	95·14 W
122	Tehuantepec, Golfo de (G.) (gôl-fô dĕ) Mex.	15·45 N	95·00 W
125	Tehuantepec, Istmo de (Isth.) (ē'st-mô dĕ) Mex.	17·55 N	94·35 W
125	Tehuantepec (R.) Mex.	16·30 N	95·23 W
124	Tehuehuetla Arroyo (R.) (tĕ-wĕ-wĕ'tlä är-rō-yō) Mex.	17·54 N	100·26 W
124	Tehuitzingo (tā-wē-tzĭŋ'gō) Mex.	18·21 N	98·16 W
216	Teixeira de Sousa Ang.	10·42 S	22·12 E
162	Tejeda, Sierra de (Mts.) (sē-ĕ'r-rä dĕ tĕ-kĕ'dä) Sp.	36·55 N	5·57 W
162	Tejo, Rio (R.) (rē-ōtä'hōō) Port.	39·23 N	8·01 W
125	Tejúpan (Santiago) (tĕ-кōō-pä'n) (sän-tyȧ'gô) Mex.	17·39 N	97·34 W
124	Tejúpan, Punta (Pt.) (pōō'n-tä) Mex.	18·19 N	103·30 W
124	Tejupilco de Hidalgo (tȧ-hōō-pēl'kō dā ē-dhäl'gō) Mex.	18·52 N	100·07 W
108	Tekamah (tē-kā'mȧ) Ne.	41·46 N	96·13 W
126	Tekax de Alvaro Obregon (tĕ-kä'x dĕ ȧ'l-vä-rô-brĕ-gô'n) Mex. (In.)	20·12 N	89·11 W
211	Tekeze (R.) Eth.	13·38 N	38·00 E
165	Tekirdağ (Rodosto) (tĕ-kēr'dägh') Tur.	41·00 N	27·28 E
126	Tekit (tĕ-kē't) Mex. (In.)	20·35 N	89·18 W
110	Tekoa (tē-kō'ȧ) Wa.	47·15 N	117·03 W
126	Tela (tā'lä) Hond.	15·45 N	87·25 W
126	Tela, Bahia de (B.) (bä-ē'ä dĕ) Hond.	15·53 N	87·29 W
183	Telapa Burok, Gunong (Mt.) Mala. (Singapore In.)	2·51 N	102·04 E
171	Telavi Sov. Un.	42·00 N	45·20 E
183	Tel Aviv-Yafo (tĕl-ä-vēv'jä'fȧ) Isr. (Palestine In.)	32·03 N	34·46 E
90	Telegraph Creek (tĕl'ē-gràf) Can.	57·59 N	131·22 W
167	Teleneshty (tyĕ-le-nĕsht'i) Sov. Un.	47·31 N	28·22 E
114	Telescope Pk. (tĕl'ē skōp) Ca.	36·12 N	117·05 W
135	Teles Pirez (R.) (tĕ-lĕs pē'rĕz) Braz.	8·28 S	57·07 W
183	Telesung Indon. (Singapore In.)	1·07 N	102·53 E
126	Telica (Vol.) (tå-lē'kä) Nic.	12·38 N	86·52 W
188	Telii Nuur (L.) China	45·49 N	86·08 E
214	Télimélé Gui.	10·54 N	13·02 W
104	Tell City (tĕl) In.	38·00 N	86·45 W
101	Teller (tĕl'ēr) Ak.	65·17 N	166·28 W
134	Tello (tĕ'l-yô) Col. (In.)	3·05 N	75·08 W
115	Telluride (tĕl'ū-rīd) Co.	37·55 N	107·50 W
183	Telok Datok Mala. (Singapore In.)	2·51 N	101·33 E
124	Teloloapan (tā'lô-lô-ä'pän) Mex.	18·19 N	99·54 W
170	Tel'pos-Iz, Gora (Mtn.) (tyĕl'pôs-ēz') Sov. Un.	63·50 N	59·20 E
157	Telšiai (tĕl'sha'ē) Sov. Un.	55·59 N	22·17 E
149	Teltow (tĕl'tō) G.D.R. (Berlin In.)	52·24 N	13·12 E
183	Telukletyak Indon. (Singapore In.)	1·53 N	101·45 E
214	Tema Ghana	5·38 N	0·01 E
124	Temascalcingo (tā'mäs-käl-sĭŋ'gō) Mex.	19·55 N	100·00 W
124	Temascaltepec (tā'mäs-käl-tȧ pĕk) Mex.	19·00 N	100·03 W
126	Temax (tĕ'mäx) Mex. (In.)	21·10 N	88·51 W
171	Temir (tyĕ'mēr) Sov. Un.	49·10 N	57·15 E
172	Temir-Tau Sov. Un.	50·08 N	73·13 E
97	Témiscaming (tē-mĭs'kȧ-mĭng) Can.	46·40 N	78·50 W
98	Temiscouata (L.) (tĕ'mĭs-kōō-ä'tä) Can.	47·40 N	68·50 W
125	Temoaya (tĕ-mô-ä-yä) Mex. (In.)	19·28 N	99·36 W
136	Temperley (tĕ'm-pĕr-lā) Arg. (In.)	34·32 S	58·24 W
164	Tempio Pausania (tĕm'pē-ō pou-sä'nē-ä) It.	40·55 N	9·05 E
119	Temple (tĕm'p'l) Tx.	31·06 N	97·20 W
113	Temple City Ca. (Los Angeles In.)	34·07 N	118·02 W
89	Templeton (tĕm'p'l-tŭn) Can. (Ottawa In.)	45·29 N	75·37 W
158	Templin (tĕm-plēn') G.D.R.	53·08 N	13·30 E
124	Tempoal (R.) (tĕm-pô-ä'l) Mex.	21·38 N	98·23 W
167	Temryuk (tyĕm-ryŏŏk') Sov. Un.	45·17 N	37·21 E
136	Temuco (tå-mōō'kō) Chile	38·46 S	72·38 W
174	Temyasovo (tĕm-yä'sô-vô) Sov. Un. (Urals In.)	53·00 N	58·06 E
126	Tenabó (tĕ-nä-bŏ') Mex. (In.)	20·05 N	90·11 W
185	Tenāli India	16·10 N	80·32 E
124	Tenamaxtlán (tā'nä-mäs-tlän') Mex.	20·13 N	104·06 W
124	Tenancingo (tȧ-nän-sēŋ'gō) Mex.	18·54 N	99·36 W
125	Tenango (tȧ-näŋ'gō) Mex. (In.)	19·09 N	98·51 W
196	Tenasserim (tĕn-ăs'ēr-ĭm) Bur.	12·09 N	99·01 E
167	Tenderovskaya Kosa (C.) (tĕn-dĕ-rôf'skȧ-yȧ kô-sä') Sov. Un.	46·12 N	31·17 E
	Tenedos, see Bozcaada		
215	Tenéré (Des.) Niger	19·23 N	10·15 E
210	Tenerife I. (tå-nå-rē'fā) (tĕn-ēr-ĭf') Can. Is.	28·41 N	17·02 W
151	Ténés (tā-nĕs') Alg.	36·28 N	1·22 E
190	T'enghsien (tĕng'hsē-ĕn') China	35·07 N	117·08 E
172	Tengiz (L.) (tyĭn-gēz') Sov. Un.	50·45 N	68·39 E
195	Tenjin (tĕn'jēn) Jap. (Ōsaka In.)	34·54 N	135·04 E
217	Tenke (tĕŋ'kȧ) Zaire	11·26 S	26·45 E
117	Tenkiller Ferry Res. (tĕn-kĭl'ēr) Ok.	35·42 N	94·47 W
214	Tenkodogo (tĕŋ-kô-dō'gô) Upper Volta	11·47 N	0·22 W
112	Tenmile (R.) (tĕn mīl) Wa. (Vancouver In.)	48·52 N	122·32 W
204	Tennant Creek (tĕn'ănt) Austl.	19·45 S	134·00 E
103	Tennessee (State) (tĕn-ĕ-sē') U. S.	35·50 N	88·00 W
103	Tennessee (L.) U. S.	35·35 N	88·20 W
120	Tennessee (R.) U. S.	35·10 N	88·20 W
120	Tennille (tĕn'ĭl) Ga.	32·55 N	86·50 W
137	Teno (tĕ'nô) (R.) Chile (Santiago In.)	34·55 S	71·00 W
203	Tenora (tĕn-ôrȧ) Austl.	34·23 S	147·33 E
125	Tenosique (tā-nô-sē'kā) Mex.	17·27 N	91·25 W
195	Tenri Jap. (Ōsaka In.)	34·36 N	135·50 E
195	Tenryū-Gawa (Strm.) (tĕn'ryōō'gä'wä) Jap.	35·16 N	137·54 E
119	Tensas R. (tĕn'sô) La.	31·54 N	91·30 W
120	Tensaw (R.) (tĕn'sô) Al.	30·45 N	87·52 W
203	Tenterfield (tĕn'tēr-fēld) Austl.	29·00 S	152·06 E
121	Ten Thousand, Is. (tĕn thou'zănd) Fl. (In.)	25·45 N	81·35 W
124	Teocaltiche (tā'ô-käl-tē'chā) Mex.	21·27 N	102·38 W
125	Teocelo (tā-ô-sā'lō) Mex.	19·22 N	96·57 W
124	Teocuitatlán de Corona (tā'ô-kwē'tä-tlän' dā kô-rō'nä) Mex.	20·06 N	103·22 W
135	Teófilo Otoni (tĕ-ô'fē-lō-tô'nē) Braz.	17·49 S	41·18 W
124	Teoloyucan (tā'ô-lô-yōō'kän) Mex.	19·43 N	99·12 W
125	Teopisca (tā-ô-pēs'kä) Mex.	16·30 N	92·33 W
125	Teotihuacán (tĕ-ô-tē-wȧ-kȧ'n) Mex. (In.)	19·40 N	98·52 W
125	Teotitlán del Camino (tā-ô-tē-tlän' dĕl kä-mē'nô) Mex.	18·07 N	97·04 W
124	Tepalcatepec (tā'päl-kä-tā'pĕk) Mex.	19·11 N	102·51 W
124	Tepalcatepec (R.) Mex.	18·54 N	102·25 W
124	Tepalcingo (tā'päl-sēŋ'gō) Mex.	18·34 N	98·49 W
124	Tepatitlan de Morelos (tā-pä-tē-tlän' dā mô-rä'los) Mex.	20·15 N	102·47 W
125	Tepeaca (tā-pā-ä'kä) Mex.	18·57 N	97·54 W
124	Tepecoacuilco de Trujano (tā'pā-kō'ä-kwēl'kō dā trōō-hä'nō) Mex.	19·15 N	99·29 W
124	Tepeji del Rio (tā-pā-кe' dĕl rē'ō) Mex.	19·55 N	99·22 W

ng-sing; ŋ-baŋk; ɴ-nasalized n; nŏd; cŏmmit; ōld; ōbey; ôrder; fōōd; fŏŏt; ou-out; s-soft; sh-dish; th-thin; pūre; ûnite; ûrn; stŭd; circŭs; ü-as "y" in study; '-indeterminate vowel.

Page	Name Pronunciation Region	Lat. °′	Long. °′
125	Tepelmeme (tā'pĕl-mā'mā) Mex.	17·51 N	97·23 W
125	Tepetlaoxtoc (tā'pâ-tlä'ōs-tōk') Mex. (In.)	19·34 N	98·49 W
124	Tepezala (tā-pâ-zä-lä') Mex.	22·12 N	102·12 W
124	Tepic (tā-pēk') Mex.	21·32 N	104·53 W
190	Tep'ing (dŭ'pĭng) China	37·28 N	116·57 E
174	Tëplaya Gora (tyôp'lá-yá gô-rá) Sov. Un. (Urals In.)	58·32 N	59·08 W
158	Teplice Sanov (tĕp'lĭ-tsĕ shä'nôf) Czech.	50·39 N	13·50 E
125	Teposcolula (San Pedro y San Pablo) (tā-pôs-kô-lōō'lä) (sän pā'drō ē sän pä'blō) Mex.	17·33 N	97·29 W
134	Tequendama, Salto de (Falls) (sä'l-tô dĕ tĕ-kĕn-dä'mä) Col. (In.)	4·34 N	74·18 W
124	Tequila (tâ-kē'lä) Mex.	20·53 N	103·48 W
125	Tequisistlán (R.) (tĕ-kē-sês-tlá'n) Mex.	16·20 N	95·40 W
124	Tequisquiapan (tâ-kēs-kê-ä'pän) Mex.	20·33 N	99·57 W
163	Ter (R.) (tĕr) Sp.	42·04 N	2·52 E
214	Téra Niger	14·01 N	0·45 E
162	Tera (R.) (tā'rä) Sp.	42·05 N	6·24 W
164	Teramo (tā'rä-mô) It.	42·40 N	13·41 E
161	Terborg (tĕr-bōrg) Neth. (Ruhr In.)	51·55 N	6·23 E
171	Tercan (tĕr'jän) Tur.	39·40 N	40·12 E
210	Terceira I. (tĕr-sā'rä) Açores (In.)	38·49 N	26·36 W
159	Terebovlya (tĕ-rä'bôv-lyá) Sov. Un.	49·18 N	25·43 E
171	Terek (R.) Sov. Un.	43·30 N	45·10 E
174	Terenkul' (tĕ-rĕn'kōōl) Sov. Un. (Urals In.)	55·38 N	62·18 E
135	Teresina (tĕr-å-sē'ná) Braz.	5·04 S	42·42 W
136	Teresópolis (tĕr-ā-sô'pō-lēzh) Braz. (Rio de Janeiro In.)	22·25 S	42·59 W
170	Teriběrka (tyĕr-ê-byôr'ká) Sov. Un.	69·00 N	35·15 E
171	Terme (tĕr'mĕ) Tur.	41·05 N	42·00 E
187	Termez (tyĕr'mĕz) Sov. Un.	37·19 N	67·20 E
164	Termini (tĕr'mê-nê) It.	37·58 N	13·39 E
125	Términos, Laguna de (L.) (lä-gōō'nä dĕ ĕ'r-mē-nôs) Mex.	18·37 N	91·32 W
164	Termoli (tĕr'mô-lê) It.	42·00 N	15·01 E
148	Tern (R.) (tûrn) Eng.	52·49 N	2·31 W
197	Ternate (tĕr-nä'tā) Indon.	0·52 N	127·25 E
164	Terni (tĕr'nê) It.	42·38 N	12·41 E
159	Ternopol' (tēr-nō-pōl') Sov. Un.	49·32 N	25·36 E
194	Terpeniya, Zaliv (B.) (zä'lĭf tĕr-pă'nĭ-yá) Sov. Un.	49·10 N	143·05 E
173	Terpeniya, Mys (C.) Sov. Un.	48·44 N	144·42 E
92	Terrace (tĕr'ĭs) Can.	54·31 N	128·35 W
164	Terracina (tĕr-rä-chē'nä) It.	41·18 N	13·14 E
99	Terra Nova Natl. Park Can.	48·37 N	54·15 W
89	Terrebonne (tĕr-bŏn') Can. (Montréal In.)	45·42 N	73·38 W
119	Terrebonne B. La.	28·55 N	90·30 W
104	Terre Haute (tĕr-ê hōt') In.	39·25 N	87·25 W
119	Terrell (tĕr'ĕl) Tx.	32·44 N	96·15 W
112	Terrell Wa. (Vancouver In.)	48·53 N	122·44 W
113	Terrell Hills (tĕr'ĕl hĭlz) Tx. (San Antonio In.)	29·28 N	98·27 W
155	Terschelling (I.) (tĕr-skĕl'ĭng) Neth.	53·25 N	5·12 E
162	Teruel (tâ-rōō-ĕl') Sp.	40·20 N	1·05 W
165	Tešanj (tĕ'shän') Yugo.	44·36 N	17·59 E
149	Teschendorf (tĕ'shĕn-dōrf) G.D.R. (Berlin In.)	52·51 N	13·10 E
125	Tesecheacan (tĕ-sĕ-chĕ-ä-kä'n) Mex.	18·10 N	95·41 W
101	Teshekpuk (L.) (tē-shĕk'pŭk) Ak.	70·18 N	152·36 W
194	Teshio Dake (Mt.) (tĕsh'ê-ō-dä'kā) Jap.	44·00 N	142·50 E
194	Teshio Gawa (R.) (tĕsh'ê-ô gä'wä) Jap.	44·35 N	144·55 E
188	Tesiin Gol (R.) Mong.	50·14 N	94·30 E
101	Teslin (tĕs-lĭn) Can.	60·10 N	132·30 W
90	Teslin (L.) Can.	60·12 N	132·08 W
90	Teslin (R.) Can.	61·18 N	134·14 W
92	Tessalon Can.	46·20 N	83·35 W
216	Tessaoua (tĕs-sä'ōō-ä) Niger	13·53 N	7·53 E
149	Tessenderlo Bel. (Brussels In.)	51·04 N	5·08 E
154	Test (R.) (tĕst) Eng.	51·10 N	2·20 W
164	Testa del Gargano (Pt.) (tās'tä dĕl gär-gä'nō) It.	41·48 N	16·13 E
92	Tetachuck L. Can.	53·20 N	125·50 W
217	Tete (tā'tĕ) Moz.	16·13 S	33·35 E
93	Tête Jaune Cache (tĕt'-zhōn-kăsh) Can.	52·57 N	119·26 W
96	Tetepiskaw, Lac (L.) Can.	51·02 N	69·23 W
167	Teterev (R.) (tyĕ'tyĕ-rĕf) Sov. Un.	50·35 N	29·18 E
158	Teterow (tā'tĕ-rō) G.D.R.	53·46 N	12·33 E
166	Teteven (tĕt'ĕ-ven') Bul.	42·57 N	24·15 E
111	Teton R. (tē'tŏn) Mt.	47·54 N	111·37 W
210	Tetouan Mor.	35·42 N	5·34 W
165	Tetovo (tā'tō-vô) Yugo.	42·01 N	21·00 E
194	Tetyukhe-Pristan (tĕt-yōō'ĸĕ prĭ-stän') Sov. Un.	44·21 N	135·44 E
170	Tetyushi (tyĕt-yōō'shĭ) Sov. Un.	54·58 N	48·40 E
149	Teupitz (toi'pētz) G.D.R. (Berlin In.)	42·08 N	13·37 E
164	Tévere (Tiber) (R.) (tā'vâ-rā) (tī'bēr) It.	42·30 N	12·14 E
183	Teverya Isr. (Palestine In.)	32·48 N	35·32 E
99	Tewksbury (tūks'bĕr-ĭ) Ma. (In.)	42·37 N	71·14 W
92	Texada I. Can.	49·40 N	124·24 W
117	Texarkana (tĕk-sär-kăn'á) Ar.	33·26 N	94·02 W
117	Texarkana Tx.	33·26 N	94·04 W
102	Texas (State) U. S.	31·00 N	101·00 W
119	Texas City Tx. (In.)	29·23 N	94·54 W
124	Texcaltitlán (tās-käl'tê-tlän') Mex.	18·54 N	99·51 W
155	Texel (I.) (tĕk'sĕl) Neth.	53·10 N	4·45 E
125	Texcoco (tās-kō'kō) Mex. (In.)	19·31 N	98·53 W
125	Texistepec (tĕk-sēs-tā-pĕk') Mex.	17·51 N	94·46 W
125	Texmelucan (tās-mâ-lōō'kän) Mex. (In.)	19·17 N	98·26 W
117	Texoma, L. (tĕk'ō-mă) Ok.	34·03 N	96·28 W
213	Teyateyaneng Leso. (Natal In.)	29·11 S	27·43 E
166	Teykovo (tĕy-kô-vô) Sov. Un.	56·52 N	40·34 E
125	Teziutlán (tâ-zē-ōō-tlän') Mex.	19·48 N	97·21 W
124	Tezontepec (tâ-zōn-tâ-pĕk') Mex.	19·52 N	98·48 W
124	Tezontepec de Aldama (dā äl-dä'mä) Mex.	20·19 N	99·19 W
184	Tezpur India	26·42 N	92·52 E
90	Tha-anne (R.) Can.	60·50 N	96·56 W
213	Thabana Ntlenyana (Mtn.) Leso. (Natal In.)	29·28 S	29·17 E
218	Thabazimbi S. Afr. (Johannesburg & Pretoria In.)	24·36 S	27·22 E
182	Thailand Asia	16·30 N	101·00 E
196	Thailand, G. of Asia	11·37 N	100·46 E
196	Thale Luang (L.) Thai.	7·51 N	99·39 E
148	Thame (tām) Eng. (London In.)	51·43 N	0·59 W
104	Thames (R.) (tĕmz) Can.	42·40 N	81·45 W
155	Thames (R.) Eng.	51·26 N	0·54 E
153	Thamit R. Libya	30·39 N	16·23 E
185	Thāna (thä'nŭ) India (In.)	19·13 N	72·58 E
185	Thāna Cr. India (In.)	19·03 N	72·58 E
188	Thanglha Ri (Mts.) China	33·15 N	89·07 E
193	Thanh-Hoa (tän'hō'á) Viet.	19·46 N	105·42 E
185	Thanjāvūr India	10·51 N	79·11 E
161	Thann (tän) Fr.	47·49 N	7·05 E
161	Thaon-les-Vosges (tä-ôɴ-lā-vōzh') Fr.	48·16 N	6·24 E
203	Thargomindah (thár'gō-mĭn'dá) Austl.	27·58 S	143·57 E
165	Thásos (I.) (thă'sôs) Grc.	40·41 N	24·53 E
123	Thatch Cay (I.) (thăch) Vir. Is. (U. S. A.) (St. Thomas In.)	18·22 N	64·53 W
158	Thaya R. (tä'yá) Aus.-Czech.	48·48 N	15·40 E
117	Thayer (thâ'ēr) Mo.	36·30 N	91·34 W
	Thebes, see Thivai		
218	Thebes (Ruins) (thēbz) Egypt (Nile In.)	25·47 N	32·39 E
112	The Brothers (Mtn.) (brŭth'ērs) Wa. (Seattle In.)	47·39 N	123·08 W
94	The Coteau (Hills) Can.	51·10 N	107·30 W
110	The Dalles (dălz) Or.	45·36 N	121·10 W
197	The Father (Mtn.) Pap. N. Gui.	5·10 S	151·55 E
	The Hague, see 's Gravenhage		
184	Thelum Pak.	32·59 N	73·43 E
202	The Oaks Austl. (Sydney In.)	34·04 S	150·36 E
203	Theodore (thē'ō'dôr) Austl.	24·51 S	150·09 E
115	Theodore Roosevelt Dam (thē-ô-dōr rōō-sá-vĕlt) Az.	33·46 N	111·25 W
108	Theodore Roosevelt Natl. Mem. Park ND	47·20 N	103·42 W
95	The Pas (pä) Can.	53·50 N	101·15 W
93	The Rajah (Mtn.) Can.	53·15 N	118·31 W
111	Thermopolis (thēr-mŏp'ô-lĭs) Wy.	43·38 N	108·11 W
203	The Round Mtn. Austl.	30·17 S	152·19 E
165	Thessalía (Reg.) Grc.	39·50 N	22·09 E
91	Thessalon Can.	46·11 N	83·37 W
165	Thessaloníki (thĕs-sá-lô-nē'kê) Grc.	40·38 N	22·59 E
98	Thetford Mines (thĕt'fērd mīns) Can.	46·05 N	71·20 W
213	The Twins (Mtn.) (twĭnz) Leso.-S. Afr. (Natal In.)	30·09 S	28·29 E
218	Theunissen S. Afr. (Johannesburg & Pretoria In.)	28·25 S	26·44 E
95	Thibaudeau (tĭ'bŏ-dō') Can.	57·05 N	94·08 W
119	Thibodaux (tê-bô-dō') La.	29·48 N	90·48 W
108	Thief (L.) (thēf) Mn.	48·32 N	95·46 W
108	Thief (R.) Mn.	48·18 N	96·07 W
108	Thief River Falls (thēf rĭv'ēr fôlz) Mn.	48·07 N	96·11 W
160	Thiers (tyâr) Fr.	45·51 N	3·32 E
214	Thiès (tê-ĕs') Senegal	14·48 N	16·56 W
217	Thika Ken.	1·03 S	37·05 E
184	Thimbu Bhu.	27·33 N	89·42 E
150	Thingvallavatn (L.) Ice.	64·12 N	20·22 W
161	Thionville (tyôɴ-vēl') Fr.	49·23 N	6·31 E
211	Third Cataract Sud.	19·53 N	30·11 E
156	Thisted (tēs'tĕdh) Den.	56·57 N	8·38 E
150	Thisti Fd. (tēs'têl) Ice.	66·29 N	14·59 W
203	Thistle (I.) (thĭs''l) Austl.	34·55 S	136·11 E
165	Thivai (Thebes) Grc.	38·20 N	23·18 E
150	Thjörsá (R.) (tyûr'sá) Ice.	64·23 N	19·18 W
149	Tholen Neth. (Amsterdam In.)	51·32 N	4·11 E
116	Thomas (tŏm'ăs) Ok.	35·44 N	98·43 W
105	Thomas WV	39·15 N	79·30 W
120	Thomaston (tŏm'ăs-tŭn) Ga.	32·51 N	84·17 W
120	Thomasville (tŏm'ăs-vĭl) Al.	31·55 N	87·43 W
121	Thomasville NC	35·52 N	80·05 W
92	Thomlinson, Mt. Can.	55·33 N	127·29 W
95	Thompson Can.	55·48 N	97·59 W
93	Thompson (R.) Can.	50·15 N	121·20 W
117	Thompson (R.) Mo.	40·32 N	93·49 W
110	Thompson Falls Mt.	47·35 N	115·20 W
121	Thomson (tŏm'sŭn) Ga.	33·28 N	82·29 W
205	Thomson (R.) (tŏm-sŏn) Austl.	29·30 S	143·07 E
217	Thomson's Falls Ken.	0·02 N	36·22 E
161	Thonon-les-Bains (tô-nôɴ'lā-băɴ') Fr.	46·22 N	6·27 E
150	Thórisvatn (L.) Ice.	64·02 N	19·09 W
148	Thorne (thôrn) Eng.	53·37 N	0·58 W
104	Thorntown (thôrn'tŭn) In.	40·05 N	86·35 W
89	Thorold (thō'rōld) Can. (Toronto In.)	43·13 N	79·12 W
160	Thouars (tōō-är') Fr.	47·00 N	0·17 W
105	Thousand Is. (thou'zănd) NY-Can.	44·15 N	76·10 W
165	Thrace (Reg.) (thrās) Grc.-Tur.	41·20 N	26·07 E
148	Thrapston (thrăp'stŭn) Eng.	52·23 N	0·32 W
111	Three Forks (thrē fôrks) Mt.	45·56 N	111·35 W
104	Three Oaks (thrē ōks) Mi.	41·50 N	86·40 W
214	Three Points, C. Ghana	4·45 N	2·06 W
104	Three Rivers Mi.	42·00 N	83·40 W
75	Thule Grnld.	76·34 N	68·47 W
158	Thun (tōōn) Switz.	46·46 N	7·34 E
96	Thunder Bay Can.	48·28 N	89·12 W
109	Thunder B. (thŭn'dēr) Can.	48·29 N	88·52 W
94	Thunder Hills Can.	54·30 N	106·00 W
158	Thuner See (L.) Switz.	46·40 N	7·30 E
118	Thurber (thûr'bēr) Tx.	32·30 N	98·23 W
158	Thüringen (Thuringia) (former state or region) (tü'rĭng-ĕn) G.D.R.	51·07 N	10·45 E
154	Thurles (thûrlz) Ire.	52·44 N	7·45 W
148	Thurrock (thŭ'rŏk) Eng. (London In.)	51·28 N	0·19 E
205	Thursday (I.) (thûrz-dā) Austl.	10·17 S	142·23 E
89	Thurso (thŭr'sô) Can. (Ottawa In.)	45·36 N	75·15 W
154	Thurso Scot.	58·35 N	3·40 W
220	Thurston Pen. (thûrs'tŭn) Ant.	71·20 S	98·00 W
212	Thysville (tēs-vēl') Zaire	5·08 S	14·58 E
197	Tiaong (tē-ä-ông') Phil. (In.)	13·56 N	121·20 E
210	Tiaret Alg.	35·28 N	1·15 E
136	Tibagi (tē'bá-zhē) Braz.	24·40 S	50·35 W
211	Tibasti, Sarir (Des.) Chad	24·00 N	16·30 E
215	Tibati Cam.	6·27 N	12·38 E
	Tiber (R.), see Tevere		
211	Tibesti Massif (Mts.) Chad	20·40 N	17·48 E
188	Tibet, Plat. of (tĭ-bĕt') China	32·22 N	83·30 E
188	Tibetan Aut. Reg. (tĭ-bĕt'on) China	31·15 N	84·48 E
183	Tibnīn Leb. (Palestine In.)	33·12 N	35·23 E
112	Tiburon (tē-bōō-rōn') Ca. (San Francisco In.)	37·53 N	122·27 W
129	Tiburon Hai.	18·35 N	74·25 W
122	Tiburón (I.) Mex.	28·45 N	113·10 W
127	Tiburon, Cabo (C.) (kà'bô) Pan.	8·42 N	77·19 W
112	Tiburon I. Ca. (San Francisco In.)	37·52 N	122·26 W
197	Ticaco Pass (tē-kä-kô) Phil. (In.)	12·38 N	123·50 E
197	Ticao (I.) (tê-kä'ō) Phil. (In.)	12·40 N	123·30 E
148	Tickhill (tĭk'ĭl) Eng.	53·26 N	1·06 W
105	Ticonderoga (tī-kŏn-dēr-ō'gá) NY	43·50 N	73·30 W
126	Ticul (tē-kōō'l) Mex. (In.)	20·22 N	89·32 W
156	Tidaholm (tē'dá-hōlm) Swe.	58·11 N	13·53 E
148	Tideswell (tīdz'wĕl) Eng.	53·17 N	1·47 W
210	Tidikelt (Reg.) (tē-dê-kĕlt') Alg.	25·53 N	2·11 E
214	Tidjikdja (tê-jĭk'jä) Mauritania	18·33 N	11·25 W
192	T'iehling (tyâ'lĭng) China	42·18 N	123·50 E
163	Tielmes (tyâl-mâs') Sp. (Madrid In.)	40·15 N	3·20 W
193	Tien Ch'ih (L.) (tyĕn) China	24·58 N	103·18 E
190	T'ienching (Tientsin) (tyĕn'tsĕn') China	39·08 N	117·14 E
149	Tienen Bel. (Brussels In.)	50·49 N	4·58 E
190	Tienerhwan (dĭän'ĕ'hōōän) China	31·39 N	114·08 E
190	Tienfou (dĭän'fōō) China	31·53 N	117·28 E
190	T'ienma Shan (Mts.) (tĭän'mä shän) China	36·02 N	117·57 E
193	Tienmen (tyĕn'mĕn) China	30·40 N	113·10 E
193	Tienpai China	21·30 N	111·20 E
193	T'ienpao China	23·18 N	106·40 E
	Tien-Shan (Mts.), see Tyan' Shan'		
190	Tienshan Hu (L.) (dĭän'shän'hōō) China	31·08 N	120·30 E
192	T'ienshui China	34·25 N	105·40 E
192	T'ientsaokang China	45·58 N	126·00 E

Page Name Pronunciation Region Lat. °′ Long. °′

Tientsin, see T'ienching
190 Tietsin-Shih (Mun.)........China 39·30 N 117·13 E
193 T'ientung................China 23·32 N 107·10 E
156 Tierp (tyĕrp)..............Swe. 60·21 N 17·28 E
213 Tierpoort...............S. Afr. (Johannesburg & Pretoria In.) 25·53 S 28·26 E
125 Tierra Blanca (tyĕ'r-rä-blä'n-kä) Mex. 18·28 N 96·19 W
136 Tierra del Fuego (Reg.) (tyĕr'rä dĕl fwā'gô).Chile-Arg. 53·50 S 68·45 W
162 Tiétar (R.) (tê-ā'tär).........Sp. 39·56 N 5·44 W
137 Tietê (tyā-tā') Braz. (Rio de Janeiro In.) 23·08 S 47·42 W
135 Tieté (R.).................Braz. 20·46 S 50·46 W
104 Tiffin (tĭf'ĭn)................Oh. 41·10 N 83·15 W
120 Tifton (tĭf'tŭn)..............Ga. 31·25 N 83·34 W
112 Tigard (tī'gärd).Or. (Portland In.) 45·25 N 122·46 W
98 Tignish (tĭg'nĭsh)............Can. 46·57 N 64·02 W
174 Tigoda R. (tē'gô-dȧ) Sov. Un. (Leningrad In.) 59·29 N 31·15 E
136 Tigre (tê'grĕ)..........Arg. (In.) 34·09 S 58·35 W
134 Tigre (R.)..................Peru 2·20 S 75·41 W
212 Tigres, Península dos (Pen.) (pĕ-nē'ŋ-sōō-lä-dôs-tê'grĕs).Ang. 16·30 S 11·45 E
186 Tigris (R.).................Asia 34·45 N 44·10 E
183 Tīh, Jabal at (Mts.) Egypt (Palestine In.) 29·23 N 34·05 E
125 Tihuatlán (tê-wä-tlän')......Mex. 20·43 N 97·34 W
114 Tijuana (tê-hwä'nä)....Mex. (In.) 32·32 N 117·02 W
136 Tijuca, Pico da (Mtn.) (pē'kō-dä-tê-zhōō'kȧ) Braz. (Rio de Janeiro In.) 22·56 S 43·17 W
126 Tikal (Ruins) (tê-käl').Guat. (In.) 17·16 N 89·49 W
171 Tikhoretsk (tê-κôr-yĕtsk') Sov. Un. 45·55 N 40·05 E
166 Tikhvin (têκ-vēn')......Sov. Un. 59·36 N 33·38 E
186 Tikrīt......................Iraq 34·36 N 43·31 E
173 Tiksi (têk-sē')...........Sov. Un. 71·42 N 128·32 E
149 Tilburg (tĭl'bûrg) Neth. (Amsterdam In.) 51·33 N 5·05 E
214 Tilemsi, Vallée du (Val.).....Mali 17·50 N 0·25 E
173 Tilichiki (tyĭ-le-chĭ-kê)...Sov. Un. 60·49 N 166·14 E
167 Tiligul (R.) (tē'lĭ-gûl)....Sov. Un. 47·25 N 30·27 E
210 Tillabéry (tē-yȧ-bā-rē')..... Niger 14·14 N 1·30 E
110 Tillamook (tĭl'ȧ-mŏŏk)........Or. 45·27 N 123·50 W
110 Tillamook B.................Or. 45·32 N 124·26 W
156 Tillberga (tēl-bĕr'ghȧ).......Swe. 59·40 N 16·34 E
97 Tillsonburg (tĭl'sŭn-bûrg)....Can. 42·50 N 80·50 W
Tilsit, see Sovetsk
167 Tim (têm).............Sov. Un. 51·39 N 37·07 E
205 Timaru (tĭm'á-rōō)....N. Z. (In.) 44·26 S 171·17 E
167 Timashevskaya (tĕmă-shĕfs-kä'yă).....Sov. Un. 45·47 N 38·57 E
119 Timbalier B. (tĭm'bȧ-lēr)......La. 28·55 N 90·14 W
112 Timber (tĭm'bēr) Or. (Portland In.) 45·43 N 123·17 W
210 Timbo (tĭm'bō).............Gui. 10·41 N 11·51 W
Timbuktu, see Tombouctou
156 Time (tē'mĕ)...............Nor. 58·45 N 5·39 E
214 Timétrine Monts (Mts.).....Mali. 19·50 N 0·30 W
210 Timimoun (tē-mê-mōōn').....Alg. 29·14 N 0·22 E
214 Timiris, Cap (C.).....Mauritania 19·23 N 16·32 W
165 Timis (R.)................Rom. 45·28 N 21·06 E
91 Timiskaming Station (tê-mĭs'kȧ-mĭng).Can. 46·41 N 79·01 W
91 Timmins (tĭm'ĭnz)..........Can. 48·25 N 81·22 W
121 Timmonsville (tĭm'ŭnz-vĭl)....SC 34·09 N 79·55 W
197 Timor (I.) (tê-mōr').......Indon. 10·08 S 125·00 E
198 Timor Sea..................Asia 12·40 S 125·00 E
165 Timoşoara................Rom. 45·44 N 21·21 E
115 Timpanogos Cave Natl. Mon. (tĭ-măn'ō-gŏz).Ut. 40·25 N 111·45 W
119 Timpson (tĭmp'sŭn)..........Tx. 31·55 N 94·24 W
173 Timpton (R.) (têmp'tôn).Sov. Un. 57·15 N 126·35 E
218 Timsāh (L.) (tĭm'sä) Egypt (Suez In.) 30·34 N 32·22 E
129 Tina, Monte (Mtn.) (mô'n-tē-tē'nȧ).Dom. Rep. 18·50 N 70·40 W
213 Tina (R.) (tē'nȧ) S. Afr. (Natal In.) 30·50 S 28·44 E
135 Tinaguillo (tê-nä-gē'l-yō) Ven. (In.) 9·55 N 68·18 W
183 Tīnah, Khalīj at (G.) Egypt (Palestine In.) 31·06 N 32·42 E
210 Tindouf (tên-dōōf')..........Alg. 27·43 N 7·44 W
183 Tinggi, Palau (I.) Mala. (Singapore In.) 2·16 N 104·16 E
190 T'ingho (dĭng'hŭ)..........China 37·45 N 118·29 E
190 Tinghsien (dĭng'sĭän).......China 38·30 N 115·00 E
190 Tinghsing (dĭng'sĭng).......China 39·18 N 115·50 E
214 Tingi Mts..................S. L. 9·00 N 10·50 W
191 Tinglin.....China (Shanghai In.) 30·53 N 121·18 E
134 Tingo María (tēn'gô-mä-rē'ä).Peru 9·15 S 76·04 W
214 Tingréla............Ivory Coast 10·29 N 6·24 W
156 Tingsryd (tĭngs'rüd)..........Swe. 56·32 N 14·58 E
190 Tingtzu Wan (B.) (dĭng'tze wän) China 36·33 N 121·06 E
124 Tinguindio Paracho (tēn'kē'n-dyō-pärä-chô).Mex. 19·38 N 102·02 W
137 Tinguiririca (R.) (tē'n-gē-rē-rē'kä) Chile (Santiago In.) 36·48 S 70·45 W
190 Tingyüan (tĭng'yü-än').....China 32·32 N 117·40 E
107 Tinley Park (tĭn'lē) Il. (Chicago In.) 41·34 N 87·47 W
156 Tinnosset (tĕn'nôs'sĕt).......Nor. 59·44 N 9·00 E
156 Tinnsjö (tĭnnsyû)...........Nor. 59·55 N 8·49 E
136 Tinogasta (tē-nô-gäs'tä)......Arg. 28·07 S 67·30 W
165 Tínos (I.)..................Grc. 37·45 N 25·12 E
210 Tinrhert, Plat. du...........Alg. 27·30 N 7·30 E
187 Tinsukia (tin-sōō'kĭ-ȧ)......India 27·18 N 95·29 E
115 Tintic (tĭn'tĭk)...............Ut. 39·55 N 112·15 W
214 Tio, Pic de (Pk.)............Gui. 8·55 N 8·55 W
183 Tioman (I.) Mala. (Singapore In.) 2·25 N 104·30 E
126 Tipitapa (tē-pê-tä'pä)........Nic. 12·14 N 86·05 W
126 Tipitapa R..................Nic. 12·13 N 85·57 W
120 Tippah Cr., (R.) (tĭp'pȧ).....Ms. 34·43 N 88·15 W
104 Tippecanoe (R.) (tĭp-ê-kȧ-nōō') In. 40·55 N 86·45 W
154 Tipperary (tĭ-pē-râ'rê)........Ire. 52·28 N 8·13 W
117 Tippo Bay. (tĭp'ō bīōō')......Ms. 33·35 N 90·06 W
104 Tipton......................In. 40·15 N 86·00 W
109 Tipton......................Ia. 41·46 N 91·10 W
165 Tirane (tê-rä'nä)...........Alb. 41·18 N 19·50 E
164 Tirano (tê-rä'nō).............It. 46·12 N 10·09 E
167 Tiraspol' (tê-räs'pôl')....Sov. Un. 46·52 N 29·38 E
171 Tire (tē'rĕ)..................Tur. 38·05 N 27·48 E
154 Tiree (I.) (tī-rē')...........Scot. 56·34 N 6·30 W
165 Tîrgovişte..................Rom. 44·54 N 25·29 E
165 Tîrgu-Jiu...................Rom. 45·02 N 23·17 E
159 Tîrgu-Mureş.................Rom. 46·33 N 24·35 E
159 Tîrgu Neamt.................Rom. 47·14 N 26·23 E
159 Tîrgu-Ocna..................Rom. 46·18 N 26·38 E
159 Tîrgu Săcuesc...............Rom. 46·04 N 26·06 E
184 Tirich Mir (Mt.).............Pak. 36·50 N 71·48 E
174 Tirlyanskiy (tĭr-lyän'skĭ) Sov. Un. (Urals In.) 54·13 N 58·37 E
165 Tírnavos....................Grc. 39·50 N 22·14 E
159 Tîrnăveni...................Rom. 46·19 N 24·18 E
158 Tirol (State) (tê-rōl')........Aus. 47·13 N 11·10 E
164 Tirso (R.) (tēr'sô)............It. 40·15 N 9·03 E
185 Tiruchchirāppalli (tĭr'ōō-chĭ-rä'pȧ-lĭ).India 10·49 N 78·48 E
185 Tirunelveli................India 8·53 N 77·43 E
185 Tiruppur..................India 11·11 N 77·08 E
94 Tisdale (tĭz'dāl)............Can. 52·51 N 104·04 W
184 Tista (R.)..................India 26·03 N 88·52 E
165 Tisza (R.) (tĭ'sä)..........Yugo. 45·50 N 20·13 E
159 Tisza R. (tē'sä)...........Hung. 46·30 N 20·08 E
184 Titāgarh............India (In.) 22·44 N 88·23 E
134 Titicaca, Lago (L.) (lä'gô-tē-tê-kä'kä).Bol.-Peru 16·12 S 70·33 W
134 Titiribi (tē-tē-rē-bê')....Col. (In.) 6·05 N 75·47 W
217 Tito, Lagh (R.).............Ken. 2·25 N 39·05 E
165 Titograd....................Yugo. 42·25 N 20·42 E
165 Titovo Užice (tê'tô-vô ōō'zhĕ-tsĕ) Yugo. 43·51 N 19·53 E
165 Titov Veles (tê'tôv vĕ'lĕs)..Yugo. 41·42 N 21·50 E
216 Titule......................Zaire 3·17 N 25·32 E
121 Titusville (tī'tŭs-vĭl).....Fl. (In.) 28·37 N 80·44 W
105 Titusville....................Pa. 40·40 N 79·40 W
161 Titz (tētz)......F.R.G. (Ruhr In.) 51·00 N 6·26 E
106 Tiverton (tĭv'ēr-tŭn) RI (Providence In.) 41·38 N 71·11 W
163 Tívoli (tē'vô-lê)....It. (Rome In.) 41·58 N 12·48 E
126 Tixkokob (tēx-kō-kō'b). Mex. (In.) 21·01 N 89·23 W
124 Tixtla de Guerrero (tē'x-tlä-dĕ-gĕr-rĕ'rô).Mex. 17·36 N 99·24 W
196 Tizard Bk. and Rf. (tĭz'ȧrd).China 10·51 N 113·20 E
126 Tizimín (tē-zē-mê'n)...Mex. (In.) 21·08 N 88·10 W
210 Tizi-Ouzou (tē'zê-ōō-zōō')....Alg. 36·44 N 4·04 E
135 Tiznados (R.) (têz-nä'dôs) Ven. (In.) 9·53 N 67·49 W
210 Tiznit (têz-nēt).............Mor. 29·52 N 9·39 W
125 Tlacolula de Matamoros (tlä-kô-lōō'lä dā mätä-mō'rôs) Mex. 16·56 N 96·29 W
125 Tlacotálpan (tlä-kô-täl'pän) Mex. 18·39 N 95·40 W
124 Talcotepec (tlä-kô-tȧ-pĕ'k)..Mex. 17·46 N 99·57 W
125 Tlacotepec..................Mex. 18·41 N 97·40 W
124 Tlacotepec..................Mex. 19·11 N 99·41 W
125 Tláhuac (tlä-wäk').....Mex. (In.) 19·16 N 99·00 W
124 Tlajomulco de Zúñiga (tlä-hô-mōō'l-ko-dĕ-zōō'n-yē-gä) Mex. 20·30 N 103·27 W
124 Tlalchapa (tläl-chä'pä)......Mex. 18·26 N 100·29 W
125 Tlalixcoyan (tlä-lēs'kô-yän').Mex. 18·53 N 96·04 W
125 Tlalmanalco (tläl-mä-nä'l-kô) Mex. (In.) 19·12 N 98·48 W
125 Tlalnepantia (tläl-nĕ-pȧ'n-tyä) Mex. (In.) 19·32 N 99·13 W
125 Tlalnepantla (tläl-nȧ-pän'tlä) Mex. (In.) 18·59 N 99·01 W
125 Tlalpan (tläl-pä'n).....Mex. (In.) 19·17 N 99·10 W
124 Tlalpujahua (tläl-pōō-κä'wä).Mex. 19·50 N 100·10 W
Tlaltenango, see Sánchez Román
124 Tlapa (tlä'pä)..............Mex. 17·30 N 98·09 W
125 Tlapacoyan (tlä-pä-kô-yá'n).Mex. 19·57 N 97·11 W
124 Tlapaneco (R.) (tlä-pä-nĕ'kô) Mex. 17·59 N 98·44 W
124 Tlapehuala (tlä-pȧ-wä'lä)....Mex. 18·17 N 100·30 W
124 Tlaquepaque (tlä-kĕ-pä'kĕ)..Mex. 20·39 N 103·17 W
124 Tlatlaya (tlä-tlä'yä)........Mex. 18·36 N 100·14 W
124 Tlaxcala (tläs-kä'lä)........Mex. 19·16 N 98·14 W
124 Tlaxcala (State)............Mex. 19·30 N 98·15 W
124 Tlaxco (tläs'kō)............Mex. 19·37 N 98·06 W
125 Tlaxiaco Sta. Maria Asunción (tläk-sē-ä'kō sän'tä mä-rē'ä ä-sōōn-syōn').Mex. 17·16 N 95·41 W
125 Tlayacapan (tlä-yä-kä-pȧ'n) Mex. (In.) 18·57 N 99·00 W
210 Tlemcen (tlĕm-sĕn').........Alg. 34·53 N 1·21 W
92 Tlevak Str...................Ak. 55·03 N 132·58 W
159 Tlumach (t'lû-mäch')....Sov. Un. 48·47 N 25·00 E
129 Toa (R.) (tō'ä).............Cuba 20·25 N 74·35 W
111 Toana Ra. (Mts.) (tō-ȧ-nō')...Nv. 40·45 N 114·11 W
129 Toar, Cuchillas de (Mtn.) (kōō-chê'l-lyäs-dĕ-tô-ä'r).Cuba 18·20 N 74·50 W
123 Tobago (I.) (tô-bā'gō)......N. A. 11·15 N 60·30 W
92 Toba Inlet..................Can. 50·20 N 124·50 W
162 Tobarra (tô-bär'rä)...........Sp. 38·37 N 1·42 W
172 Tobol (R.) (tô-bôl')......Sov. Un. 56·02 N 65·30 E
172 Tobol'sk (tô-bôlsk')......Sov. Un. 58·09 N 68·28 E
134 Tocaima (tô-kä'y-mä)...Col. (In.) 4·28 N 74·38 W
135 Tocantinópolis (tō-kän-tē-nŏ'pō-lēs).Braz. 6·27 S 47·18 W
135 Tocantins (R.) (tō-kän-tēns').Braz. 3·28 S 49·22 W
120 Toccoa (tŏk'ô-ȧ).............Ga. 34·35 N 83·20 W
120 Toccoa (R.).................Ga. 34·53 N 84·24 W
195 Tochigi (tō'chē-gĭ)..........Jap. 36·25 N 139·45 E
190 T'ochi Tao (I.) (tōōŭ'jē dou) China 38·11 N 120·45 E
126 Tocoa (tō-kô'ä)............Hond. 15·37 N 86·01 W
136 Tocopilla (tō-kô-pēl'yä).....Chile 22·03 S 70·08 W
135 Tocuyo de la Costa (tô-kōō'yō-dĕ-lä-kôs'tä) Ven. (In.) 11·03 N 68·24 W
195 Toda...........Jap. (Tōkyō In.) 35·48 N 139·42 E
148 Todmorden (tŏd'môr-dĕn)... Eng. 53·43 N 2·05 W
214 Tóecé..............Upper Volta 11·50 N 1·16 W
92 Tofino (tô-fē'nō)...........Can. 49·09 N 125·54 W
156 Töfsingdalens (Natl. Park)...Swe. 62·09 N 13·05 E
195 Tōgane (tō'gä-nā)...........Jap. 35·29 N 140·16 E
196 Togian, Kepulauan (Is.)...Indon. 0·20 S 122·00 E
209 Togo (tō'gō)................Afr. 8·00 N 0·52 E
174 Toguzak R. (tô'gōō-zák) Sov. Un. (Urals In.) 53·40 N 61·42 E
121 Tohopekaliga (L.) (tō'hô-pē'kȧ-lĭ'gȧ).Fl. (In.) 28·16 N 81·09 W
190 To'Hu (L.) (tōōŭ'hōō)......China 33·07 N 117·25 E
157 Toijala (toi'yȧ-lȧ)...........Fin. 61·11 N 21·46 E
195 Toi-Misaki (C.) (toi mê'sä-kê).Jap. 31·20 N 131·20 E
114 Toiyabe Ra. (toi'yă-bē)......Nv. 38·59 N 117·22 W
194 Tokachi Gawa (R.) (tō-kä'chê gä'wä).Jap. 43·10 N 142·30 E
159 Tokaj (tô'kô-ê)............Hung. 48·06 N 21·24 E
194 Tokara Guntō (Is.) (tō-kä'rä gŏōn'tō').Jap. 29·45 N 129·15 E
194 Tokara Kaikyo (Str.) (tô'kä-rä kī'kyō).Jap. 30·20 N 129·50 E
171 Tokat (tô-κät')..............Tur. 40·20 N 36·30 E
198 Tokelau Is. (tō-kê-lä'ōō)..Oceania 8·00 S 176·00 W
172 Tokmak (tôk'mȧk)........Sov. Un. 42·44 N 75·41 E
195 Tokorozawa (tô'kô-rô-zä'wä) Jap. (Tōkyō In.) 35·47 N 139·29 E
194 Tokuno (I.) (tô-kōō'nō).....Jap. 27·42 N 129·25 E
195 Tokushima (tō'kōō'shē-mä)...Jap. 34·06 N 134·31 E
195 Tokuyama (tō'kōō'yä-mä)....Jap. 34·04 N 131·49 E
195 Tōkyō (tō'kê-ō)..Jap. (Tōkyō In.) 35·41 N 139·44 E
195 Tōkyō (Pref.)...Jap. (Tōkyō In.) 35·42 N 139·40 E
195 Tōkyō-Wan (B.) (tō'kyō wän) Jap. (Tōkyō In.) 35·32 N 139·56 E
165 Tolbukhin...................Bul. 43·33 N 27·52 E
124 Tolcayuca (tôl-kä-yōō'kä)...Mex. 19·55 N 98·54 W
109 Toledo (tô-lē'dō).............Ia. 41·59 N 92·35 W
104 Toledo......................Oh. 41·40 N 83·35 W
110 Toledo......................Or. 44·37 N 123·58 W
162 Toledo (tô-lĕ'dô)............Sp. 39·53 N 4·02 W
162 Toledo, Montes de (Mts.) (mô'n-tĕs-dĕ-tô-lĕ'dô).Sp. 39·33 N 4·40 W
103 Toledo Bend Res..........La.-Tx. 31·30 N 93·30 W
134 Tolima (Dept.) (tô-lē'mä) Col. (In.) 4·07 N 75·20 W
134 Tolima, Nevado del (Pk.) (nĕ-vä-dô-dĕl-tô-lē'mä).Col. (In.) 4·40 N 75·20 W
124 Tolimán (tô-lê-män')........Mex. 20·54 N 99·54 W
148 Tollesbury (tōl'z-bĕrĭ) Eng. (London In.) 51·46 N 0·49 E
164 Tolmezzo (tôl-mĕt'zō).........It. 46·25 N 13·03 E
165 Tolmin (tôl'mên)...........Yugo. 46·12 N 13·45 E
159 Tolna (tôl'nô)..............Hung. 46·25 N 18·47 E
196 Tolo, Teluk (B.) (tō'lō)....Indon. 2·00 S 122·06 E
162 Tolosa (tô-lō'sä).............Sp. 43·10 N 2·05 W
112 Tolt (R.) (tōlt)..Wa. (Seattle In.) 47·13 N 121·49 W

Page	Name / Pronunciation	Region	Lat. °′	Long. °′
104	Toluca (tô-lōō'kȧ)	Il.	41·00 N	89·10 W
125	Toluca (tô-lōō'kä)	Mex. (In.)	19·17 N	99·40 W
125	Toluca, Nevado de (Mtn.) (nĕ-vä-dô-dĕ-tô-lōō'kä)	Mex. (In.)	19·09 N	99·42 W
192	Tolun	China	42·12 N	116·15 E
170	Tolyatti	Sov. Un.	53·30 N	49·10 E
172	Tom' (R.)	Sov. Un.	55·33 N	85·00 E
109	Tomah (tō'mȧ)	Wi.	43·58 N	90·31 W
109	Tomahawk (tŏm'ȧ-hôk)	Wi.	45·27 N	89·44 W
167	Tomakovka (tô-mä'kôf-kȧ)	Sov. Un.	47·49 N	34·43 E
162	Tomar (tō-mär')	Port.	39·36 N	8·26 W
159	Tomashevka (tô-mȧ'shĕf-kȧ)	Sov. Un.	51·34 N	23·37 E
159	Tomaszow Lubelski (tô-mä'shŏŏf lōō-bĕl'skĭ)	Pol.	50·20 N	23·27 E
159	Tomaszów Mazowiecki (tô-mä'shŏŏf mä-zô'vyĕt-skĭ)	Pol.	51·33 N	20·00 E
124	Tomatlán (tô-mä-tlȧ'n)	Mex.	19·54 N	105·14 W
124	Tomatlán (R.)	Mex.	19·56 N	105·14 W
214	Tombadonkéa	Gui.	11·00 N	14·23 W
135	Tombador, Serra do (Mts.) (sĕr'rȧ dŏŏ tōm-bä-dôr')	Braz.	11·31 S	57·33 W
120	Tombigbee (R.) (tŏm-bĭg'bē)	Al.	31·45 N	88·02 W
137	Tombos (tô'm-bōs)	Braz. (Rio de Janeiro In.)	20·53 S	42·00 W
214	Tombouctou (Timbuktu) (tôm-bōōk-tōō')	Mali	16·46 N	3·01 W
115	Tombstone (tōōm'stōn)	Az.	31·40 N	110·00 W
156	Tomelilla (tô'mĕ-lēl-lä)	Swe.	55·34 N	13·55 E
162	Tomelloso (tō-mål-lyō'sō)	Sp.	39·09 N	3·02 W
196	Tomini, Teluk (B.) (tô-mē'nē)	Indon.	0·10 N	121·00 E
173	Tommot (tŏm-mŏt')	Sov. Un.	59·13 N	126·22 E
172	Tomsk (tŏmsk)	Sov. Un.	56·29 N	84·57 E
125	Tonalá (tō-nä-lä')	Mex.	16·05 N	93·45 W
124	Tonala	Mex.	20·38 N	103·14 W
125	Tonalá (R.)	Mex.	18·05 N	94·08 W
107	Tonawanda (tôn-ȧ-wŏn'dȧ)	NY (Buffalo In.)	43·01 N	78·53 W
107	Tonawanda Cr.	NY (Buffalo In.)	43·05 N	78·43 W
148	Tonbridge (tŭn-brij)	Eng. (London In.)	51·11 N	0·17 E
195	Tonda (tôn'dä)	Jap. (Ōsaka In.)	34·51 N	135·38 E
195	Tondabayashi (tôn-dä-bä'yä-shē)	Jap. (Ōsaka In.)	34·29 N	135·36 E
197	Tondano (tôn-dä'nō)	Indon.	1·15 N	124·50 E
156	Tønder (tûn'nĕr)	Den.	54·47 N	8·49 E
125	Tondlá	Mex.	16·04 N	93·57 W
195	Tone (R.) (tō'nē)	Jap. (Tōkyō In.)	35·55 N	139·57 E
195	Tone-Gawa (Strm.) (tô'nĕ gä'wa)	Jap.	36·12 N	139·19 E
198	Tonga (tŏŋ'gȧ)	Oceania	18·50 S	175·20 W
215	Tongo	Cam.	5·11 N	14·00 E
136	Tongoy (tōn-goi')	Chile	30·16 S	71·29 W
	Tongue of Arabat (Spit), see Arabatskaya Strelka			
128	Tongue of the Ocean (Chan.) (tŭng ŏv thē ōshŭn)	Ba.	24·05 N	77·20 W
111	Tongue R. (tŭng)	Mt.	45·08 N	106·40 W
211	Tonj R. (tônj)	Sud.	6·18 N	28·33 E
184	Tonk (Tŏŋk)	India	26·13 N	75·45 E
117	Tonkawa (tŏŋ'kȧ-wô)	Ok.	36·42 N	97·19 W
193	Tonkin, Gulf of (tôn-kăn')	Viet.	20·30 N	108·10 E
196	Tonle Sap (L.) (tôn'lā säp')	Camb.	13·03 N	102·49 E
160	Tonneins (tô-năɴ')	Fr.	44·24 N	0·18 E
158	Tönning (tû'nēng)	F.R.G.	54·20 N	8·55 E
114	Tonopah (tō-nô-pä')	Nv.	38·04 N	117·15 W
156	Tönsberg (tûns'bĕrgh)	Nor.	59·19 N	10·25 E
125	Tonto (R.) (tōn'tō)	Mex.	18·15 N	96·13 W
115	Tonto Cr.	Az.	34·05 N	111·15 W
115	Tonto Natl. Mon. (tôn'tô)	Az.	33·33 N	111·08 W
113	Tooele (tōō-ĕl'ē)	Ut. (Salt Lake City In.)	40·33 N	112·17 W
193	Toohsien	China	25·30 N	111·32 E
203	Toowoomba (tōō wōōm'bȧ)	Aust.	27·32 S	152·10 E
113	Topanga (tō'păn-gȧ)	Ca. (Los Angeles In.)	34·05 N	118·36 W
117	Topeka (tô-pē'kȧ)	Ks.	39·02 N	95·41 W
125	Topilejo (tô-pē-lĕ'hô)	Mex. (In.)	19·12 N	99·09 W
115	Topock	Az.	34·40 N	114·20 W
159	Topol'čany (tô-pôl'chä-nü)	Czech.	48·38 N	18·10 E
122	Topolobampo (tō-pō-lô-bä'm-pô)	Mex.	25·45 N	109·00 W
165	Topolovgrad	Bul.	42·05 N	26·19 E
110	Toppenish (tôp'ĕn-ĭsh)	Wa.	46·22 N	120·00 W
214	Tora, Île (I.)	Mauritania	19·50 N	16·45 W
99	Torbay (tôr-bā')	Can.	47·40 N	52·43 W
	Torbay, see Torquay			
203	Torbreck, Mt. (tôr-brĕk)	Austl.	37·05 S	146·55 E
104	Torch (L.) (tôrch)	Mi.	45·00 N	85·30 W
156	Töreboda (tû'rĕ-bō'dä)	Swe.	58·44 N	14·04 E
155	Torhout	Bel.	51·01 N	3·04 E
134	Toribío (tô-rē-bē'ô)	Col. (In.)	2·58 N	76·14 W
195	Toride (tô'rē-dä)	Jap. (Tōkyō In.)	35·54 N	104·04 E
164	Torino (Turin) (tô-rē'no) (tū'rĭn)	It.	45·05 N	7·44 E
150	Torino (R.) (tôr'nĭ-ô)	Fin.-Swe.	67·00 N	23·50 E
162	Tormes (R.) (tōr'mās)	Sp.	41·12 N	6·15 W
150	Torne (R.) (tôr'nĕ)	Swe.	67·29 N	21·44 E
150	Torne Träsk (L.) (tôr'nĕ trĕsk)	Swe.	68·10 N	20·36 E
91	Torngat Mts.	Can.	59·18 N	64·35 W
150	Tornio (tôr'nĭ-ô)	Fin.	65·55 N	24·09 E
98	Toro, Lac (L.)	Can.	46·53 N	73·46 W
165	Toronaíos Kólpos (G.)	Grc.	40·10 N	23·35 E
89	Toronto (tô-rŏn'tō)	Can. (Toronto In.)	43·40 N	79·23 W
104	Toronto	Oh.	40·30 N	80·35 W
118	Toronto, L. (lä'gô-tô-rô'n-tō)	Mex.	27·35 N	105·37 W
166	Toropets (tô'rô-pyĕts)	Sov. Un.	56·31 N	31·37 E
171	Toros Dağlari (Taurus Mts.) (tô'rŭs)	Tur.	37·00 N	32·40 E
163	Torote (R.) (tô-rō'tä)	Sp. (Madrid In.)	40·36 N	3·24 W
156	Torp (tôrp)	Swe.	62·30 N	16·04 E
	Torpen, see Åmot			
154	Torquay (Torbay) (tôr-kē')	Eng.	50·30 N	3·26 W
134	Torra, Cerro (Mtn.) (sĕ'r-rô-tŏ'r-rä)	Col. (In.)	4·41 N	76·22 W
113	Torrance (tŏr'rănc)	Ca. (Los Angeles In.)	33·50 N	118·20 W
163	Torre Annunziata (tôr'rā ä-nōōn-tsē-ä'tä)	It. (Naples In.)	40·31 N	14·27 E
162	Torre de Cerredo (Mtn.) (tôr'rå dā thå-rā'dhō)	Sp.	43·10 N	4·47 W
163	Torre del Greco (tôr'rå dĕl grā'kô)	It. (Naples In.)	40·32 N	14·23 E
162	Torrejoncillo (tôr'rā-hōn-thē'lyō)	Sp.	39·54 N	6·26 W
162	Torrelavega (tôr-rā'lä-vā'gä)	Sp.	43·22 N	4·02 W
164	Torre Maggiore (tôr'rā mäd-jō'rā)	It.	40·41 N	15·18 E
203	Torrens, L. (tŏr-ĕns)	Austl.	30·07 S	137·40 E
163	Torrente (tôr-rĕn'tā)	Sp.	39·25 N	0·28 W
118	Torreon (tôr-rå-ōn')	Mex.	25·32 N	103·26 W
163	Torre-Pacheco (tôr-rĕ-pä-chĕ'kô)	Sp.	37·44 N	0·58 W
205	Torres Is. (tôr'rĕs) (tŏr'ĕz)	New Hebr.	13·18 N	165·59 E
114	Torres Martinez Ind. Res. (tôr'ĕz mär-tē'nĕz)	Ca.	33·33 N	116·21 W
162	Tôrres Novas (tôr'rĕzh nō'väzh)	Port.	39·28 N	8·37 W
197	Torres Str. (tôr'rĕs)	Austl.	10·30 S	141·30 E
162	Tôrres Vedras (tôr'rĕzh vā'dräzh)	Port.	39·08 N	9·18 W
163	Torrevieja (tôr-rā-vyā'hä)	Sp.	37·58 N	0·40 W
187	Torrijos (tôr-rē'hōs)	Phil. (In.)	13·19 N	122·06 E
105	Torrington (tŏr'ĭng-tŭn)	Ct.	41·50 N	73·10 W
108	Torrington	Wy.	42·04 N	104·11 W
162	Torro (tô'r-rō)	Sp.	41·27 N	5·23 W
156	Torsby (tôrs'bü)	Swe.	60·07 N	12·56 E
156	Torshälla (tôrs'hĕl-ä)	Swe.	59·26 N	16·21 E
150	Tórshavn (tôrs-houn')	Faer.	62·00 N	6·55 W
123	Tortola (I.) (tôr-tō'lä)	Vir. Is. (Br.) (Puerto Rico In.)	18·34 N	64·40 W
164	Tortona (tôr-tō'nä)	It.	44·52 N	8·52 W
163	Tortosa (tôr-tō'sä)	Sp.	40·59 N	0·33 E
163	Tortosa, Cabo de (C.) (kȧ'bô-dĕ-tôr-tō-sä)	Sp.	40·42 N	0·55 E
129	Tortue, Canal de la (Chan.) (tôr-tü')	Hai.	20·05 N	73·20 W
129	Tortue, Ile de la (I.)	Hai.	20·10 N	73·00 W
89	Tortue, Rivière de la (R.) (lä tōr-tü')	Can. (Montreal In.)	45·12 N	73·32 W
135	Tortuga, Isla la (I.) (ē's-lä-lä-tôr-tōō'gä)	Ven. (In.)	10·55 N	65·18 W
159	Toruń (tō'rōōn')	Pol.	53·01 N	18·37 E
166	Tõrva (t'r'vȧ)	Sov. Un.	58·02 N	25·56 E
154	Tory (I.) (tō'rē)	Ire.	55·17 N	8·10 W
166	Torzhok (tôr'zhôk)	Sov. Un.	57·03 N	34·53 E
195	Tosa-Wan (B.) (tō'sä wän)	Jap.	33·14 N	133·39 E
164	Toscana (Reg.) (tôs-kä'nä)	It.	43·23 N	11·08 E
174	Tosna R. Sov. Un.	(Leningrad In.)	59·38 N	30·52 E
174	Tosno (tôs'nô)	Sov. Un. (Leningrad In.)	59·32 N	30·52 E
136	Tostado (tôs-tȧ'dô)	Arg.	29·10 S	61·43 W
171	Tosya (tôz'yȧ)	Tur.	41·00 N	34·00 E
162	Totana (tô-tä-nä)	Sp.	37·45 N	1·28 W
170	Tot'ma (tôt'mȧ)	Sov. Un.	60·00 N	42·20 E
135	Totness	Sur.	5·51 N	56·17 W
126	Totonicapán (tô-tō-nē-kä'pän)	Guat.	14·55 N	91·20 W
137	Totoras (tô-tô'räs)	Arg. (Buenos Aires In.)	32·33 S	61·13 W
195	Totsuka (tōt'sōō-kä)	Jap.	35·24 N	139·32 E
148	Tottenham (tŏt'ĕn-ȧm)	Eng. (London In.)	51·35 N	0·06 W
195	Tottori (tô'tô-rē)	Jap.	35·30 N	134·15 E
210	Touat (Oases) (tōō'ät)	Alg.	27·22 N	0·38 W
214	Touba	Ivory Coast	8·17 N	7·41 W
214	Touba	Senegal	14·51 N	15·53 W
210	Toubkal Jebel (Mtn.)	Mor.	31·15 N	7·46 W
214	Tougan	Upper Volta	13·04 N	3·04 W
210	Touggourt (tōō-gōōrt') (tōō-gōōr')	Alg.	33·09 N	6·07 E
152	Touil R. (tōō-ēl')	Alg.	34·42 N	2·16 E
161	Toul (tōōl)	Fr.	48·39 N	5·51 E
98	Toulnustouc (R.)	Can.	50·23 N	67·55 W
161	Toulon (tōō-lôɴ')	Fr.	43·09 N	5·54 E
160	Toulouse (tōō-lōōz')	Fr.	43·37 N	1·27 E
196	Toungoo (tŏ-ōōŋ-gōō')	Bur.	19·00 N	96·29 E
	Tourane, see Da Nang			
160	Tourcoing (tōōr-kwăɴ')	Fr.	50·44 N	3·06 E
161	Tournan-en-Brie (tōōr-näɴ-ĕɴ-brē')	Fr. (Paris In.)	48·45 N	2·47 E
160	Tours (tōōr)	Fr.	47·23 N	0·39 E
211	Touside, Pic (Pk.) (tōō-sē-dā')	Chad	21·10 N	16·30 E
156	Tovdalselv (R.) (tôv-däls-ĕlv)	Nor.	58·23 N	8·16 E
105	Towanda (tô-wän'dȧ)	Pa.	41·45 N	76·30 W
119	Town Bluff L.	Tx.	30·52 N	94·30 W
108	Towner (tou'nĕr)	ND	48·21 N	100·24 W
99	Townsend (toun'zĕnd)	Ma. (In.)	42·41 N	71·42 W
111	Townsend	Mt.	46·19 N	111·35 W
112	Townsend, Mt.	Wa. (Seattle In.)	47·52 N	123·03 W
135	Townsville (tounz'vĭl)	Austl.	19·18 S	146·50 E
106	Towson (tou'sŭn)	Md. (Baltimore In.)	39·24 N	76·36 W
196	Towuti, Danau (L.) (tô-wōō'tē)	Indon.	3·00 S	121·45 E
118	Toyah (tô'yȧ)	Tx.	31·19 N	103·46 W
195	Toyama (tō'yä-mä)	Jap.	36·42 N	137·14 E
195	Toyama-Wan (B.)	Jap.	36·58 N	137·16 E
195	Toyohashi (tō'yô-hä'shē)	Jap.	34·44 N	137·21 E
195	Toyonaka (tō'yô-nä'kȧ)	Jap. (Ōsaka In.)	34·47 N	135·28 E
152	Tozeur (tô-zûr')	Tun.	33·59 N	8·11 E
162	Trabancos (R.) (trä-bäŋ'kōs)	Sp.	41·15 N	5·13 W
171	Trabzon (tråb'zōn)	Tur.	41·00 N	39·45 E
114	Tracy (trā'sē)	Ca.	37·45 N	121·27 W
98	Tracy	Can.	46·00 N	73·13 W
108	Tracy	Mn.	44·13 N	95·37 W
120	Tracy City	Tn.	35·15 N	85·44 W
162	Trafalgar, Cabo de (C.) (kȧ'bô-dĕ-trä-fäl-gä'r)	Sp.	36·10 N	6·02 W
213	Trafonomby (Mtn.)	Mad.	24·32 S	46·35 E
93	Trail (trāl)	Can.	49·06 N	117·42 W
149	Traisen (R.)	Aus. (Vienna In.)	48·15 N	15·55 E
149	Traiskirchen	Aus. (Vienna In.)	48·01 N	16·18 E
157	Trakai (trȧ-kāy)	Sov. Un.	54·38 N	24·59 E
159	Trakiszki (trȧ-kē'-sh-kē)	Pol.	54·16 N	23·07 E
154	Tralee (trȧ-lē')	Ire.	52·16 N	9·20 W
156	Tranas (trăn'ôs)	Swe.	58·03 N	14·56 E
184	Tranbonsha (Mt.)	China	35·27 N	86·25 E
162	Trancoso (träŋ-kō'sōō)	Port.	40·46 N	7·23 W
197	Trangan (I.) (träŋ'gän)	Indon.	6·52 S	133·30 E
164	Trani (trä'nē)	It.	41·15 N	16·25 E
141	Transcaucasia (Reg.)	Sov. Un.	41·17 N	44·30 E
188	Trans Himalaya Mts. (trăns'hĭ-mä'lȧ-yȧ)	China	30·25 N	83·43 E
212	Transvaal (Prov.) (trăns-väl')	S. Afr.	24·21 S	28·18 E
159	Transylvania (Reg.) (trăn-sĭl-vā'nĭ-ȧ)	Rom.	46·30 N	22·35 E
	Transylvanian Alps (Mts.), see Carpatii Meridionali			
164	Trapani (trä'pä-nē)	It.	38·02 N	12·34 E
161	Trappes (tråp)	Fr. (Paris In.)	48·47 N	2·01 E
203	Traralgon (trȧ'răl-gŏn)	Austl.	38·15 S	146·33 E
214	Trarza (Reg.)	Mauritania	17·35 N	15·15 W
164	Trasimeno, Lago (L.) (lä'gō trä-sê-mā'nō)	Ir.	43·00 N	12·12 E
162	Tras os Montes (Mts.) (träzh'ōzh mōn'tāzh)	Port.	41·33 N	7·13 W
162	Trasparga (träs-pär-gä)	Sp.	43·13 N	7·50 W
158	Traun R. (troun)	Aus.	48·10 N	14·15 E
158	Traunstein (troun'stīn)	F.R.G.	47·52 N	12·38 E
108	Traverse, L. (trăv'ērs)	Mn.-SD	45·46 N	96·53 W
104	Traverse City	Mi.	44·45 N	85·40 W
164	Travnik (träv'nēk)	Yugo.	44·13 N	17·43 E
112	Treasure I. (trĕzh'ēr)	Ca. (San Francisco In.)	37·49 N	122·22 W
149	Trebbin (trĕ'bēn)	G.D.R. (Berlin In.)	52·13 N	13·13 E
158	Třebič (t'rzhĕ'bēch)	Czech.	49·13 N	15·53 E
165	Trebinje (trå'bēn-yĕ)	Yugo.	42·43 N	18·21 E
158	Trebisov (trĕ'bē-shôf)	Czech.	48·36 N	21·32 E
158	Třeboň (t'rzhĕ'bôn')	Czech.	49·00 N	14·48 E
205	Tregrosse Is. (trê-grōs')	Austl.	18·08 S	150·53 E
136	Treinta y Tres (trå-ĕn'tä ē trās')	Ur.	33·14 S	54·17 W
160	Trélazé (trā-lȧ-zā')	Fr.	47·27 N	0·32 W
136	Trelew (trē'lū)	Arg.	43·15 S	65·25 W
156	Trelleborg	Swe.	55·24 N	13·07 E
154	Tremadoc B. (trĕ-mă'dŏk)	Wales	52·43 N	4·27 W
164	Tremiti, Isole di (Is.) (ē'sō-lĕ dēträ-mĕ'tē)	It.	42·07 N	16·33 E
159	Trenčín (trĕn'chēn)	Czech.	48·52 N	18·02 E

ăt; finăl; rāte; senâte; ärm; ȧsk; sofȧ; fâre; ch-choose; dh-as th in other; bē; êvent; bĕt; recĕnt; cratēr; g-go; gh-guttural g; bĭt; ĭ-short neutral; rīde; ĸ-guttural k as ch in German ich;

PRONOUNCING INDEX

Trenque Lauquen — T'ulufan 359

Page	Name Pronunciation Region	Lat. °′	Long. °′
136	Trenque Lauquén (trĕn′kĕ-là′ōō-kĕ′n). Arg.	35·50 S	62·44 W
97	Trent (R.) (trĕnt) Can.	44·15 N	77·55 W
154	Trent (R.) Eng.	53·05 N	1·00 W
148	Trent and Mersey Can. (trĕnt) (mûr zē). Eng.	53·11 N	2·24 W
164	Trento (trĕn′tô) It.	46·04 N	11·07 E
164	Trento (Reg.) It.	46·16 N	10·47 E
91	Trenton (trĕn′tŭn) Can.	44·05 N	77·35 W
99	Trenton Can.	45·37 N	62·38 W
107	Trenton Mi. (Detroit In.)	42·08 N	83·12 W
117	Trenton Mo.	40·05 N	93·36 W
106	Trenton NJ (New York In.)	40·13 N	74·46 W
120	Trenton Tn.	35·57 N	88·55 W
99	Trepassey (trê-păs′ê) Can.	46·44 N	53·22 W
99	Trepassey B. Can.	46·40 N	53·20 W
136	Tres Arroyos (trās′är-rō′yōs). Arg.	38·18 S	60·16 W
137	Três Coracoes (trĕ′s kō-rä-zō′ĕs) Braz. (Rio de Janeiro In.)	21·41 S	45·14 W
125	Tres Cumbres (trĕ′s kōō′m-brĕs) Mex. (In.)	19·03 N	99·14 W
135	Três Lagoas (trĕ′s lä-gô′äs) . . Braz.	20·48 S	51·42 W
135	Três Marias, Represa (Res.) (rĕ-prä′sä trĕs′ mä-rē′äs). Braz.	18·15 S	45·30 W
134	Tres Morros, Alto de (Mtn.) (ä′l-tō dĕ trĕ′s mô′r-rôs) Col. (In.)	7·08 N	76·10 W
137	Três Pontas (trĕ′s pô′n-täs) Braz. (Rio de Janeiro In.)	21·22 S	45·30 W
216	Três Pontas, Cabo das (C.) . . Ang.	10·23 S	13·32 E
137	Três Rios (trĕ′s rē′ōs) Braz. (Rio de Janeiro In.)	22·07 S	43·13 W
89	Très-St. Rédempteur (săN rā-dāNp-tûr′) Can. (Montreal In.)	45·26 N	74·23 W
149	Treuenbrietzen (troi′ĕn-brē-tzĕn) G.D.R. (Berlin In.)	52·06 N	12·52 E
164	Treviglio (trā-vē′lyô) It.	45·30 N	9·34 E
164	Treviso (trĕ-vê′sō) It.	45·39 N	12·15 E
188	Triangle, The (Reg.) Asia	26·00 N	98·00 E
218	Trichardt (trĭ-kärt′) S. Afr.	26·32 N	29·16 E
164	Trieste (trê-ĕs′tā) It.	45·39 N	13·48 E
164	Trieste, G. of It.	45·38 N	13·40 E
162	Trigueros (trê-gā′rōs) Sp.	37·23 N	6·50 W
184	Trigu Tsho (L.) China	28·47 N	91·37 E
165	Tríkkala Grc.	39·33 N	21·49 E
197	Trikora, Puncak (Pk.) Indon.	4·15 S	138·45 E
107	Trim Cr. (trĭm) Il. (Chicago In.)	41·19 N	87·39 W
185	Trincomalee (trĭŋ-kô-mȧ-lē′) Sri Lanka	8·39 N	81·12 E
148	Tring (trĭng) . . . Eng. (London In.)	51·46 N	0·40 W
134	Trinidad (trē-nê-dhädh′) Bol.	14·48 S	64·43 W
116	Trinidad (trĭn′ĭdăd) Co.	37·11 N	104·31 W
128	Trinidad (trē-nê-dhädh′) Cuba	21·50 N	80·00 W
137	Trinidad . . . Ur. (Buenos Aires In.)	33·29 S	56·55 W
128	Trinidad, Sierra de (Mts.) (sē-ĕ′r-rȧ dĕ trê-nē-dä′d). Cuba	21·50 N	79·55 W
135	Trinidad (I.) (trĭn′ĭ-dăd) Trin.	10·00 N	61·00 W
123	Trinidad and Tobago (trĭn′ĭ-dăd) (tō-bā′gō). N. A.	11·00 N	61·00 W
133	Trinidade, Ilha da (I.) (ē′lä dä trē-nē-dä-dĕ). Braz.	21·00 S	32·00 W
122	Trinidad R. Pan. (In.)	8·55 N	80·01 W
125	Trinitaria (trē-nē-tä′ryä) Mex.	16·09 N	92·04 W
127	Trinité Mart. (In.)	14·47 N	61·00 W
99	Trinity (trĭn′ĭ-tê) Can.	48·59 N	53·55 W
119	Trinity Tx.	30·52 N	95·27 W
101	Trinity (Is.) Ak.	56·25 N	153·15 W
116	Trinity (R.), East Fk. Tx.	33·24 N	96·42 W
117	Trinity (R.), West Fk. Tx.	33·22 N	98·26 W
99	Trinity B. Can.	48·00 N	53·40 W
110	Trinity R. Ca.	40·50 N	123·20 W
119	Trinity R. Tx.	30·50 N	95·09 W
164	Trino (trē′nô) It.	45·11 N	8·16 E
120	Trion (trī′ŏn) Ga.	34·32 N	85·18 W
	Tripoli, see Ţarābulus		
	Tripoli, see Tarābulus		
165	Tripolis (trĭ′pô-lĭs) Grc.	37·32 N	22·32 E
	Tripolitania (Prov.), see Tarābulus		
108	Tripp (trĭp) SD	43·13 N	97·58 W
184	Tripura (State) India	24·00 N	92·00 E
220	Tristan da Cunha Is. (três-tän′dä kōōn′yȧ). Alt. O.	35·30 S	12·15 W
135	Triste, Golfo (G.) (gôl-fô trĕ′s-tĕ) Ven. (In.)	10·40 N	68·05 W
106	Triticus Res. (trī tĭ-cŭs) NY (New York In.)	41·20 N	73·36 W
185	Trivandrum (trê-vŭn′drŭm). India	8·34 N	76·58 E
159	Trnava (t′r′nȧ-vȧ) Czech.	48·22 N	17·34 E
197	Trobriand Is. (trō-brê-ănd′) Pap. N. Gui.	8·25 S	151·45 E
164	Trogir (trô′gēr) Yugo.	43·32 N	16·17 E
91	Trois-Rivières (trwä′rē-vyâr′) Can.	46·21 N	72·35 W
174	Troitsk (trô′ĕtsk) Sov. Un. (Urals In.)	54·06 N	61·34 E
172	Troitsko-Pechorsk (trô′ĭtsk-ô-pyĕ-chôrsk′). Sov. Un.	62·18 N	56·07 E
167	Troitskoye Sov. Un.	47·39 N	30·16 E
156	Trollhättan (trôl′hĕt-ĕn) Swe.	58·17 N	12·17 E
156	Trollheim (Mts.) (trôll-hĕĭm). Nor.	62·48 N	9·05 E
150	Tromsö (trôm′sû) Nor.	69·38 N	19·12 E
114	Trona (trō′nȧ) Ca.	35·49 N	117·20 W
136	Tronador, Cerro (Mtn.) (sĕ′r-rô trō-nä′dôr). Arg.	41·17 S	71·56 W
124	Troncoso (trôn-kô′sō) Mex.	22·43 N	102·22 W
156	Trondheim (Nidaros) (trôn′hâm) (nē′dhä-rôs). Nor.	63·25 N	11·35 E
156	Trosa (trô′sä) Swe.	58·54 N	17·25 E
91	Trout (L.) Can.	51·16 N	92·46 W
90	Trout (L.) Can.	61·10 N	121·30 W
110	Trout Cr. Or.	42·18 N	118·31 W
112	Troutdale (trout′dāl) Or. (Portland In.)	45·32 N	122·23 W
109	Trout Lake Mi.	46·20 N	85·02 W
95	Trout L. Can.	51·13 N	93·20 W
160	Trouville (trōō-vēl′) Fr.	49·23 N	0·05 E
120	Troy (troi) Al.	31·47 N	85·46 W
113	Troy Il. (St. Louis In.)	38·44 N	89·53 W
117	Troy Ks.	39·46 N	95·07 W
117	Troy Mo.	38·56 N	99·57 W
110	Troy Mt.	48·28 N	115·56 W
105	Troy NY	42·45 N	73·45 N
121	Troy NC	35·21 N	79·58 W
104	Troy Oh.	40·00 N	84·10 W
165	Troy (Ruins) Tur.	39·59 N	26·14 E
160	Troyes (trwä) Fr.	48·18 N	4·03 E
	Trst, see Trieste		
165	Trstenik (t′r′stĕ-nêk) Yugo.	43·36 N	20·00 E
166	Trubchëvsk (trōōp′chĕfsk) Sov. Un.	52·36 N	32·46 E
	Trucial States, see United Arab Emirates		
114	Truckee (trŭk′ê) Ca.	39·20 N	120·12 W
114	Truckee (R.) Ca.-Nv.	39·25 N	120·07 W
202	Truganina. Austl. (Melbourne In.)	37·49 N	144·44 E
134	Trujillo (trōō-κē′l-yō) . . . Col. (In.)	4·10 N	76·20 W
126	Trujillo (trōō-κēl′yō) Hond.	15·55 N	85·58 W
134	Trujillo Peru	8·08 S	79·00 W
162	Trujillo (trōō-κē′l-yô) Sp.	39·27 N	5·50 W
134	Trujillo Ven.	9·15 N	70·28 W
124	Trujillo (R.) Mex.	23·12 N	103·10 W
129	Trujin, L. (trōō-κēn′) . . Dom. Rep.	17·45 N	71·25 W
117	Trumann (trōō′măn) Ar.	35·41 N	90·31 W
165	Trŭn (trŭn) Bul.	42·49 N	22·39 E
98	Truro (trōō′rō) Can.	45·22 N	63·16 W
154	Truro Eng.	50·17 N	5·05 W
106	Trussville (trŭs′vĭl) Al. (Birmingham In.)	33·37 N	86·37 W
115	Truth or Consequences (trōōth ŏr kŏn′sē-kwĕn-sĭs). NM	33·10 N	107·20 W
158	Trutnov (trōōt′nôf) Czech.	50·36 N	15·36 E
158	Trzcianka (tchyän′kȧ) Pol.	53·02 N	16·27 E
158	Trzebiatow (tchĕ-byä′tōō-v) . . Pol.	54·03 N	15·16 E
188	Tsaidam Swp. (tsī′däm) China	37·19 N	94·08 E
192	Ts'aiyü China (In.)	39·39 N	116·36 E
121	Tsala Apopka (R.) (tsä′lȧ ă-pŏp′kȧ). Fl.	28·57 N	82·11 W
190	Ts'anghsien (chäng′sĭän) China	38·21 N	116·53 E
191	Ts'angmen . . . . China (Canton In.)	22·42 N	113·09 E
	Tsangwu, see Wuchou		
190	Tsaochuang (jou′jōōäng) . . . China	34·51 N	117·34 E
190	Ts'aohsien (tsou′sĭän) China	34·48 N	115·33 E
188	Tsast Bogda Ula (Mt.) Mong.	46·44 N	92·34 E
217	Tsavo Natl. Pk. Ken.	2·35 S	38·45 E
112	Tsawwassen Ind. Res. Can. (Vancouver In.)	49·03 N	123·11 W
172	Tselinograd (tsĕ′lē-nô-grä′d) Sov. Un.	51·10 N	71·43 E
191	Tsengch'en . . . China (Canton In.)	23·18 N	113·49 E
174	Tsentral'nyy-Kospashskiy (tsĕn-träl′nyĭ-kôs-pȧsh′skĭ) Sov. Un. (Urals In.)	59·03 N	57·48 E
216	Tshela (tshā′lȧ) Zaire	4·59 S	12·56 E
216	Tshikapa (tshê-kä′pä) Zaire	6·25 S	20·48 E
216	Tshofa Zaire	5·14 S	25·15 E
216	Tshuapa (R.) Zaire	10·15 S	21·25 E
213	Tsiafajovona (Mtn.) Mad.	19·17 S	47·27 E
171	Tsimlyanskiy (Res.) (tsym-lyă′ns-kēē). Sov. Un.	47·50 N	43·40 E
190	Tsinan (Chinan) (je′nän) . . . China	36·40 N	117·01 E
188	Tsinghai (Prov.) (jĭng′hāī) . . China	36·14 N	95·30 E
	Tsingtao, see Ch'ingtao		
213	Tsiribihina (R.) (tsē′rê-bē-hê-nä′) Mad.	19·45 S	43·30 E
213	Tsitsa (R.) (tsē′tsȧ) S. Afr. (Natal In.)	31·28 S	28·53 E
	Tsitsihar, see Ch'ich'ihaerh		
213	Tsolo (tsō′lō) . . S. Afr. (Natal In.)	31·19 S	28·47 E
213	Tsomo . . . . S. Afr. (Natal In.)	32·03 S	27·49 E
213	Tsomo (R.) . . . S. Afr. (Natal In.)	31·53 S	27·48 E
195	Tsu (tsōō) Jap.	34·42 N	136·31 E
195	Tsuchiura (tsōō′chê-ōō-rä) . . . Jap.	36·04 N	140·09 E
195	Tsuda (tsōō′dä) . . Jap. (Ōsaka In.)	34·48 N	135·43 E
194	Tsugaru Kaikyō (str.) (tsōō′gä-rōō kī′kyō). Jap.	41·25 N	140·20 E
212	Tsumeb (tsōō′mĕb) Namibia	19·10 S	17·45 E
195	Tsunashima (tsōō′nä-shê′mä) Jap. (Tōkyō In.)	35·32 N	139·37 E
193	Ts'unghua China	23·30 N	113·40 E
190	Tsunhua (zhōōn′hooä) China	40·12 N	117·55 E
195	Tsuruga (tsōō′rōō-gä) Jap.	35·39 N	136·04 E
195	Tsurugi San (Mtn.) (tsōō′rōō-gê sän). Jap.	33·52 N	134·07 E
194	Tsuruoka (tsōō′rōō-ō′kä) Jap.	38·43 N	139·51 E
195	Tsurusaki (tsōō′rōō-sä′kê) . . . Jap.	33·15 N	131·42 E
195	Tsu Shima (I.) (tsōō shē′mä) . . Jap.	34·28 N	129·30 E
195	Tsushima Kaikyō (Str.) (tsōō′shê-mä kī′kyō). Asia	33·52 N	129·30 E
195	Tsuwano (tsōō′wȧ-nô′) Jap.	34·28 N	131·47 E
195	Tsuyama (tsōō′yä-mä′) Jap.	35·05 N	134·00 E
162	Tua (R.) (tōō′ä) Port.	41·23 N	7·18 W
112	Tualatin (R.) (tōō′ȧ-lā-tĭn) Or. (Portland In.)	45·25 N	122·54 W
199	Tuamotu (Low), Arch. (tōō-ä-mō′tōō). Fr. Polynesia	19·00 S	141·20 W
197	Tuao (tōō-ä-ō) Phil. (In.)	17·44 N	121·26 E
171	Tuapse (tōō′áp-sĕ) Sov. Un.	44·00 N	39·10 E
210	Tuareg (Reg.) Alg.	21·26 N	2·51 E
136	Tubarão (tōō-bä-rouN′) Braz.	28·23 S	48·56 W
158	Tübingen (tü′bĭng-ĕn) F.R.G.	48·33 N	9·05 E
174	Tubinskiy (tû bĭn′skĭ) Sov. Un. (Urals In.)	52·53 N	58·15 E
211	Tubruq Libya	32·03 N	24·04 E
135	Tucacas (tōō-kä′käs) . . . Ven. (In.)	10·48 N	68·20 W
106	Tucker (tŭk′ẽr) . . Ga. (Atlanta In.)	33·51 N	84·13 W
115	Tucson (tōō-sŏn′) Az.	32·15 N	111·00 W
136	Tucumán (tōō-kōō-män′) Arg.	26·52 S	65·08 W
136	Tucumán (Prov.) Arg.	26·30 S	65·30 W
116	Tucumcari (tōō′kŭm-kâr-ê) . . . NM	35·11 N	103·43 W
134	Tucupita (tōō-kōō-pē′tä) Ven.	9·00 N	62·09 W
135	Tucuruí (tōō-kōō-tōō-ē′) Braz.	3·34 S	49·44 W
162	Tudela (tōō-dhā′lä) Sp.	42·03 N	1·37 W
120	Tugaloo (R.) (tŭg′ȧ-lōō). Ga.-SC	34·35 N	83·05 W
213	Tugela (R.) (tōō-gel′ȧ) S. Afr. (Natal In.)	28·50 S	30·52 E
213	Tugela Ferry . . S. Afr. (Natal In.)	28·44 S	30·27 E
104	Tug Fork (R.) (tŭg) WV	37·50 N	82·30 W
197	Tuguegarao (tōō-gā-gȧ-rä′ō) Phil. (In.)	17·37 N	121·44 E
190	T'uhsieh (R.) (tōō′hăĭ) China	37·05 N	166·56 E
218	Tuinplaas S. Afr. (Johannesburg & Pretoria In.)	24·54 S	28·46 E
113	Tujunga (tōō-jŭŋ′gȧ) Ca. (Los Angeles In.)	34·15 N	118·16 W
174	Tukan (tōō′kȧn) Sov. Un. (Urals In.)	53·52 N	57·25 E
197	Tukangbesi, Kepulauan (Is.) Indon.	6·00 S	124·15 E
211	Tūkrah Libya	32·34 N	20·47 E
90	Tuktoyaktuk (tōōk-tō-yäk′tōōk) Can.	69·32 N	132·37 W
170	Tukum (tōō′kōōm) Sov. Un.	57·00 N	22·50 E
157	Tukums (tōō′kōōms) Sov. Un.	56·57 N	23·09 E
212	Tukuyu (tōō-kōō′yȧ) Tan.	9·13 S	33·43 E
112	Tukwila (tŭk′wĭ-lȧ) Wa. (Seattle In.)	47·28 N	122·16 W
124	Tula (tōō′lä) Mex.	20·04 N	99·22 W
166	Tula (tōō′lȧ) Sov. Un.	54·12 N	37·37 E
166	Tula (Oblast) Sov. Un.	53·45 N	37·19 E
124	Tula (R.) (tōō′lä) Mex.	20·40 N	99·27 W
205	Tulagi (I.) (tōō-lä′gē) Sol. Is.	9·15 S	160·17 E
112	Tulalip (tū-lă′lĭp). Wa. (Seattle In.)	48·04 N	122·18 W
112	Tulalip Ind. Res. . Wa. (Seattle In.)	48·06 N	122·16 W
124	Tulancingo (tōō-län-sĭŋ′gō) . . Mex.	20·04 N	98·24 W
196	Tulangbawang (R.) Indon.	4·17 S	105·00 E
114	Tulare (tōō-lä′rȧ) (tul-âr′) Ca.	36·12 N	119·22 W
114	Tulare Basin Ca.	35·57 N	120·18 W
115	Tularosa (tŭl-ȧ-rō′zȧ) NM	33·05 N	106·05 W
134	Tulcán (tōōl-kän′) Ec.	0·44 N	77·52 W
167	Tulcea (tōōl′chȧ) Rom.	45·10 N	28·47 E
167	Tul'chin (tōōl′chĕn) Sov. Un.	48·42 N	28·53 E
124	Tulcingo (tōōl-sĭŋ′gō) Mex.	18·03 N	98·27 W
114	Tule (R.) (tōō′lȧ) Ca.	36·08 N	118·50 W
213	Tuléar (tōō-lā-är′) Mad.	20·16 S	43·44 E
114	Tule River Ind. Res. (tōō′lȧ) . . Ca.	36·05 N	118·35 W
212	Tuli (tōō′lê) Rh.	20·58 S	29·12 E
116	Tulia (tōō′lĭ-ȧ) Tx.	34·32 N	101·46 W
125	Tulijá (R.) (tōō-lē-κä′) Mex.	17·28 N	92·11 W
101	Tulik Vol. (tōō′lĭk) Ak.	53·28 N	168·10 W
183	Tūlkarm (tōōl kärm) Jordan (Palestine In.)	32·19 N	35·02 E
120	Tullahoma (tŭl-ȧ-hō′mȧ) Tn.	35·21 N	86·12 W
154	Tullamore (tŭl-ȧ-mōr′) Ire.	53·15 N	7·29 W
160	Tulle (tül) Fr.	45·15 N	1·45 E
149	Tulln (tōōln) . . . Aus. (Vienna In.)	48·21 N	16·04 E
149	Tullner Feld (Reg.) Aus. (Vienna In.)	48·20 N	15·59 E
125	Tulpetlac (tōōl-pȧ-tlăk′) Mex. (Mexico City In.)	19·33 N	99·04 W
117	Tulsa (tŭl′sȧ) Ok.	36·08 N	95·58 W
134	Tuluá (tōō-lōō-ȧ′) Col. (In.)	4·06 N	76·12 W
188	T'ulufan (Turfan) (tōō′lōō-fän′) (tōōr-fän′). China	43·06 N	88·41 E

ng-sing; ŋ-baŋk; N-nasalized n; nŏd; cŏmmit; ōld; ôbey; ôrder; fōōd; fŏŏt; ou-out; s-soft; sh-dish; th-thin; pūre; ûnite; ûrn; stŭd; circŭs; ü-as "y" in study; ′-indeterminate vowel.

360 Tulum — Udskaya PRONOUNCING INDEX

Page	Name Pronunciation Region	Lat. °′	Long. °′
126	Tulum (to͞o-lo͞o′m) . . . . . Mex. (In.)	20·17 N	87·26 W
172	Tulun (to͝o-lo͞on′) . . . . Sov. Un.	54·29 N	100·43 E
115	Tumacacori Natl. Mon. (to͞o-mä-kä′kå-rē) . Az.	31·36 N	110·20 W
134	Tumaco (to͞o-mä′kô) . . . . Col.	1·41 N	78·44 W
126	Tuma R. (to͞o′mä) . . . . Nic.	13·07 N	85·32 W
216	Tumba, Lac (L.) (to͝om′bä) . . Zaire	0·50 S	17·45 E
134	Tumbes (to͞o′m-bĕs) . . . . Peru	3·39 S	80·27 W
124	Tumbiscatío (to͞om-bê-skå-tē′ō) Mex.	18·32 N	102·23 W
112	Tumbo (I.) . . Can. (Vancouver In.)	48·49 N	123·04 W
192	T'umen (to͞o′mĕn) . . . . China	43·00 N	129·50 E
194	Tumen (R.) . . . . China	42·08 N	128·40 E
135	Tumeremo (to͞o-må-rā′mō) . . Ven.	7·15 N	61·28 W
185	Tumkūr . . . . India	13·22 N	77·05 E
135	Tumuc-Humac Mts. (to͞o-mo͝ok′o͞o-mäk′) . S. A.	2·15 N	54·50 W
128	Tunas de Zaza (to͞o′näs dā zä′zä) Cuba	21·40 N	79·35 W
154	Tunbridge Wells (tŭn′brĭj welz′) Eng.	51·05 N	0·09 E
172	Tundra (Reg.) . . . . Sov. Un.	70·45 N	84·00 E
217	Tunduru . . . . Tan.	11·07 S	37·21 E
189	Tung (R.) . . . . China	24·13 N	115·08 E
190	Tunga (do͞ong′ä) . . . . China	36·11 N	116·16 E
184	Tungabhadra Res. . . . . India	15·26 N	75·57 E
193	T'ungan (to͞on′gän′) . . . . China	24·48 N	118·02 E
190	T'ungch'engi (to͞ong′chĕng′yē) China	36·21 N	116·14 E
189	T'ungchiang . . . . China	47·38 N	132·54 E
190	Tungeh'angshou (to͞ong′chäng′shō) China	38·21 N	114·41 E
190	Tunghai (do͞ong′hăī) . . . . China	34·35 N	119·05 E
192	T'ungho . . . . China	45·58 N	128·40 E
193	Tunghsiang . . . . China	28·18 N	116·38 E
192	Tunghsien . . . . . China (Peking In.)	39·55 N	116·40 E
190	Tung Hu (L.) (to͞ong′ ho͞o′) . China	32·22 N	116·32 E
193	Tungjen (to͝ong′jĕn′) . . . . China	27·45 N	109·12 E
191	Tungkuan . . . . China (Canton In.)	23·03 N	113·14 E
192	T'ung-Kuan . . . . China	34·48 N	110·25 E
190	Tungkuang (do͞ong′go͞oäng) . China	37·54 N	116·33 E
193	T'ungku Chiao (Pt.) . . . . China	19·40 N	111·15 E
192	Tungliao (Payintala) . . . . China	43·30 N	122·15 E
190	Tungming (to͝ong′mĭng′) . . . . China	35·16 N	115·06 E
190	Tungpa (to͞ong′bä) . . . . China	31·40 N	119·02 E
190	Tungpa . . . . China	35·56 N	116·19 E
192	T'ungpei (to͞ong′på) . . . . China	48·00 N	126·48 E
190	Tungping (to͞ong′pĭng) . . . . . China	35·50 N	116·24 E
190	Tungp'ing Hu (L.) (ho͞o) . . . China	36·06 N	116·24 E
190	Tungt'antien (do͞ong′tän′dĭän) China	35·26 N	116·54 E
193	Tungt'ing Hŭ (L.) (to͞ong′tĕng′ ho͞o) . China	29·10 N	112·30 E
190	Tungwen (R.) (do͞ong′wĕn) . China	36·24 N	119·00 E
192	Tunhua . . . . China	48·18 N	128·10 E
185	Tuni . . . . India	17·29 N	82·38 E
120	Tunica (tū′nĭ-kȧ) . . . . Ms.	34·41 N	90·23 W
210	Tunis (tū′nĭs) . . . . Tun.	36·59 N	10·06 E
151	Tunis, Golfe de (G.) . . . . Tun.	37·06 N	10·43 E
209	Tunisia (tu-nĭzh′ĕ-ȧ) . . . . Afr.	35·00 N	10·11 E
134	Tunja (to͞o′n-hä) . . . . Col.	5·32 N	73·19 W
105	Tunkhannock (tŭnk-hăn′ŭk) . . Pa.	41·35 N	75·55 W
112	Tunnel (R.) (tŭn′ĕl) Wa. (Seattle In.)	47·48 N	123·04 W
114	Tuolumne (R.) (twô-lŭm′nê) . . . Ca.	37·35 N	120·37 W
173	Tuostakh (R.) . . . . Sov. Un.	67·09 N	137·30 E
135	Tupã (to͞o-pä) . . . . Braz.	21·47 S	50·33 W
120	Tupelo (tū′pê-lō) . . . . Ms.	34·14 N	88·43 W
135	Tupinambaranas, Ilha (I.) (ē′lä-to͞o-pē-näN-bä-rä′näs) . Braz.	3·04 S	58·09 W
134	Tupiza (to͞o-pē′zä) . . . . Bol.	21·26 S	65·43 W
105	Tupper Lake (tŭp′ēr) . . . . NY	44·15 N	74·25 W
134	Tuquerres (to͞o-kĕ′r-rĕs) . . . . . . Col.	1·12 N	77·44 W
172	Tura (to͝or′ȧ) . . . . Sov. Un.	64·08 N	99·58 E
141	Tura (R.) . . . . Sov. Un.	57·15 N	64·23 E
124	Turbio (R.) (to͞or-byô) . . . . Mex.	20·28 N	101·40 W
134	Turbo (to͞o′bō) . . . . Col.	8·02 N	76·43 W
159	Turciansky Svätý Martin (to͝or′chyan-skū′svä′tû′ mär′tyēn) . Czech.	49·02 N	18·48 E
159	Turda (to͝or′dȧ) . . . . Rom.	46·35 N	23·47 E
	Turfan, see T'ulufan		
188	Turfan Depression . . . . China	42·16 N	90·00 E
213	Turffontein . . . . S. Afr. (Johannesburg & Pretoria In.)	26·15 S	28·03 E
172	Turgay (to͝or′gī) . . . . Sov. Un.	49·42 N	63·39 E
147	Turgayka (R.) (to͝or-gī′kä) Sov. Un.	49·44 N	66·15 E
165	Tŭrgovishte . . . . Bul.	43·14 N	26·36 E
171	Turgutlu . . . . Tur.	38·30 N	27·20 E
157	Türi (tü′rĭ) . . . . Sov. Un.	58.49 N	25·29 E
162	Turia (R.) (to͞o′ryä) . . . . Sp.	40·12 N	1·18 W
124	Turicato (to͞o-rê-kä′tō) . . . . . . Mex.	19·03 N	101·24 W
128	Turiguano (I.) (to͞o-rê-gwä′nō) Cuba	22·20 N	78·35 W
	Turin, see Torino		
159	Turka (to͝or′kä) . . . . Sov. Un.	49·10 N	23·02 E
172	Turkestan (tûr-kĕ-stăn′) (to͝or-kĕ-stan′) . Sov. Un.	42·40 N	65·00 E
168	Turkestan (Reg.) . . . . Sov. Un.	43·27 N	62·14 E
182	Turkey . . . . Eur.-Asia	38·45 N	32·00 E
109	Turkey (R.) (tûrk′ê) . . . . Ia.	43·20 N	92·16 W
168	Turkmen (S. S. R.) (to͞ork-mĕn′) Sov. Un.	40·46 N	56·01 E
129	Turks I. Pass. . Turks & Caicos Is.	21·15 N	71·25 W
123	Turks (Is.) (tûrks) Turks & Caicos Is.	21·40 N	71·45 W
157	Turku (Åbo) (to͝or′ko͞o) (ô′bô) . Fin.	60·28 N	22·12 E
114	Turlock (tûr′lŏk) . . . . Ca.	37·30 N	120·51 W
126	Turneffe (I.) (tûr-nĕf′fê) . Belize (In.)	17·25 N	87·43 W
113	Turner (tûr′nēr) Ks. (Kansas City In.)	39·05 N	94·42 W
128	Turner Sd. . . . . Ba.	24·20 N	78·05 W
214	Turners Pen. . . . . S.L.	7·20 N	12·40 W
149	Turnhout (tŭrn-hout′) Bel. (Brussels In.)	51·19 N	4·58 E
158	Turnov (to͝or′nôf) . . . . Czech.	50·36 N	15·12 E
165	Turnu Măgurele (to͝or′no͝o mŭ-go͞o-rĕ′ly′) . Rom.	43·54 N	24·49 E
165	Turnu-Severin (sĕ-vĕ-rēn′) . . Rom.	44·37 N	22·38 E
128	Turquino, Pico de (Pk.) (pē′kō dā to͞or-kē′nō) . Cuba	20·00 N	76·50 W
127	Turrialba (to͞or-ryä′l-bä) . . . . C. R.	9·54 N	83·41 W
165	Turski Trstenik . . . . Bul.	43·26 N	24·50 E
147	Turtkul' (to͝ort-ko͞ol′) . . . . Sov. Un.	41·28 N	61·02 E
95	Turtle (R.) . . . . Can.	49·20 N	92·30 W
119	Turtle B. . . . . Tx. (In.)	29·48 N	94·38 W
108	Turtle Cr. . . . . SD	44·40 N	98·53 W
108	Turtle Mountain Ind. Res. . . . ND	48·45 N	99·57 W
108	Turtle Mts. . . . . ND	48·57 N	100·11 W
172	Turukhansk (to͞o-ro͞o-känsk′) Sov. Un.	66·03 N	88·39 E
159	Turya R. (to͞or′yȧ) . . . . . . Sov. Un.	51·18 N	24·55 E
120	Tuscaloosa (tŭs-kȧ-lo͞o′sȧ) . . . . . Al.	33·10 N	87·35 W
110	Tuscarora (tŭs-kȧ-rō′rȧ) . . . . . . Nv.	41·18 N	116·15 W
107	Tuscarora Ind. Res. NY (Buffalo In.)	43·10 N	78·51 W
104	Tuscola (tŭs-kō-lȧ) . . . . Il.	39·50 N	88·20 W
120	Tuscumbia (tŭs-kŭm′bĭ-ȧ) . . . . Al.	34·41 N	87·42 W
193	Tushan (do͞o′shän) . . . . China	25·50 N	107·42 E
190	Tushan . . . . China	31·38 N	116·16 E
174	Tushino (to͞o′shĭ-nô) Sov. Un. (Moscow In.)	55·51 N	37·24 E
120	Tuskegee (tŭs-kē′gê) . . . . Al.	32·25 N	85·40 W
190	T'ussuk'ou (to͞o′sē′kō) . . . . . China	36·19 N	117·37 E
113	Tustin (tŭs′tĭn) Ca. (Los Angeles In.)	33·44 N	117·49 W
166	Tutayev (to͞o-tȧ-yĕf′) . . . . Sov. Un.	57·53 N	39·34 E
148	Tutbury (tŭt′bēr-ê) . . . . Eng.	52·52 N	1·51 W
185	Tuticorin (to͞o-tê-kô-rĭn′) . . . . India	8·51 N	78·09 E
125	Tutitlan (to͞o-tē-tlä′n) . . Mex. (In.)	19·38 N	99·10 W
135	Tutóia (to͞o-tō′yȧ) . . . . Braz.	2·42 S	42·21 W
165	Tutrakan . . . . Bul.	44·02 N	26·36 E
117	Tuttle Creek Res. . . . . Ks.	39·30 N	96·38 W
158	Tuttlingen (to͝ot′lĭng-ĕn) . . . F.R.G.	47·58 N	8·50 E
120	Tutwiler (tŭt′wĭ-lēr) . . . . Ms.	34·01 N	90·25 W
172	Tuva Aut. Oblast . . . . Sov. Un.	51·15 N	90·45 E
198	Tuvalu . . . . Oceania	5·20 S	174·00 E
186	Tuwayq, Jabal (Mts.) . . . . Sau. Ar.	20·45 N	46·30 E
106	Tuxedo Park (tŭk-sē′dō pärk) NY (New York In.)	41·11 N	74·11 W
148	Tuxford (tŭks′fērd) . . . . Eng.	53·14 N	0·54 W
124	Tuxpan (to͞os′pän) . . . . Mex.	19·34 N	103·22 W
125	Túxpan . . . . Mex.	20·57 N	97·26 W
125	Túxpan (R.) (to͞os′pän) . . . . . Mex.	20·55 N	97·52 W
125	Túxpan, Arrecife (Rf.) (är-rĕ-sē′fĕ-to͞o′x-pä′n) . Mex.	21·01 N	97·12 W
125	Tuxtepec (to͞os-tȧ-pĕk′) . . . . . Mex.	18·06 N	96·09 W
125	Tuxtla Gutiérrez (to͞os′tlä go͞o-tyâr′rĕs) . Mex.	16·44 N	93·08 W
150	Tuy . . . . Sp.	42·07 N	8·49 W
135	Tuy (to͞o′ê) (R.) . . . . Ven. (In.)	10·15 N	66·03 W
127	Tuyra R. (to͞o-ē′rȧ) . . . . Pan.	7·55 N	77·37 W
193	Tuyün (to͞o′yün′) . . . . China	26·18 N	107·40 E
171	Tuz Gölü (L.) . . . . Tur.	39·00 N	33·30 E
115	Tuzigoot Natl. Mon. . . . . Az.	34·40 N	111·52 W
165	Tuzla (to͝oz′lȧ) . . . . Yugo.	44·33 N	18·46 E
156	Tvedestrand (tvĭ′dhĕ-stränd) . Nor.	58·39 N	8·54 E
156	Tveitsund (tvåt′so͝ond) . . . . . . Nor.	59·03 N	8·29 E
	Tver, see Kalinin		
146	Tvertsa (L.) (tvĕr′tsȧ) . . . Sov. Un.	56·58 N	35·22 E
154	Tweed (R.) (twēd) . . . . Scot.	55·32 N	2·35 W
218	Tweeling (twē′lĭng) . . . . S. Afr. (Johannesburg & Pretoria In.)	27·34 S	28·31 E
107	Twelvemile Cr. (twĕlv′mīl) NY (Buffalo In.)	43·13 N	78·58 W
89	Twenty Mile Cr. (twĕn′tĭ mīl) Can. (Toronto In.)	43·09 N	79·49 W
148	Twickenham (twĭk′′n-ăm) Eng. (London In.)	51·26 N	0·20 W
99	Twillingate (twĭl′ĭn-gāt) . . . . Can.	49·39 N	54·46 W
111	Twin Bridges (twĭn brĭ-jĕz) . . . Mt.	45·34 N	112·17 W
111	Twin Falls (fôls) . . . . Id.	42·33 N	114·29 W
107	Twinsburg (twĭnz′bûrg) Oh. (Cleveland In.)	41·19 N	81·26 W
114	Twitchell Res. . . . . Ca.	34·50 N	120·10 W
116	Two Butte Cr. (to͞o būt) . . . . . . Co.	37·39 N	102·45 W
109	Two Harbors . . . . Mn.	47·00 N	91·42 W
117	Two Prairie Bay (prā′rĭ bī o͞o′) . Ar.	34·48 N	92·07 W
109	Two Rivers (rĭv′ērz) . . . . Wi.	44·09 N	87·36 W
202	Tyabb . . . . . Austl. (Melbourne In.)	38·16 S	145·11 E
159	Tyachev (tyä′chĕf) . . . . . . Sov. Un.	48·01 N	23·42 E
188	Tyan' Shan' (Tien-Shan) (Mts.) Sov. Un.-China	42·00 N	78·46 E
167	Tyasmin (R.) (tyȧs-mĭn′) . Sov. Un.	49·14 N	32·23 E
213	Tylden (tĭl-dĕn) S. Afr. (Natal In.)	32·08 S	27·06 E
148	Tyldesley (tĭldz′lê) . . . . Eng.	53·32 N	2·28 W
108	Tyler (tī′lēr) . . . . Mn.	44·18 N	96·08 W
119	Tyler . . . . Tx.	32·21 N	95·19 W
120	Tylertown (tī′lēr-toun) . . . . Ms.	31·08 N	90·06 W
108	Tyndall (tĭn′dȧl) . . . . SD	42·58 N	97·52 W
173	Tyndinskiy . . . . Sov. Un.	55·22 N	124·45 E
154	Tyne (R.) (tīn) . . . . Eng.	54·59 N	1·56 W
154	Tynemouth (tīn′mŭth) . . . . . . Eng.	55·04 N	1·39 W
156	Tynest (tün′sĕt) . . . . Nor.	62·17 N	10·45 E
99	Tyngsboro (tĭnj-bûr′ô) . . Ma. (In.)	42·40 N	71·27 W
	Tyre, see Şūr		
156	Tyri Fd. (tü′rê) . . . . Nor.	60·03 N	10·25 E
115	Tyrone (tī′rōn) . . . . NM	32·40 N	108·20 W
105	Tyrone . . . . Pa.	40·40 N	78·15 W
203	Tyrrell, L. (tir′ĕll) . . . . Austl.	35·12 S	143·00 E
151	Tyrrhenian Sea (tĭr-rē′nĭ-ȧn) . . . It.	40·10 N	12·15 E
157	Tyrvää (tür′vȧ) . . . . Fin.	61·19 N	22·51 E
171	Tyub-Karagan, Mys (C.) . Sov. Un.	44·30 N	50·10 E
172	Tyukalinsk (tyo͞o-kȧ-lĭnsk′) Sov. Un.	56·03 N	71·43 E
173	Tyukyan (R.) (tyo͝ok′yȧn) Sov. Un.	65·42 N	116·09 E
171	Tyuleniy (I.) . . . . Sov. Un.	44·30 N	48·00 E
172	Tyumen' (tyo͞o-mĕn′) . . . . Sov. Un.	57·02 N	65·28 E
172	Tyura-Tam . . . . Sov. Un.	46·00 N	63·15 E
126	Tzucacab (tzo͞o-kä-kä′b) Mex. (In.)	20·06 N	89·03 W
190	Tz'uhsien (tsĕ′sĭän) . . . . China	36·22 N	114·23 E
190	Tzupo . . . . China	36·48 N	118·04 E
193	Tzu Shui (R.) (tso͞o) . . . . China	26·50 N	111·00 E
190	Tzuya (R.) (zhĕ′yä) . . . . China	38·38 N	116·31 E
190	Tzuyang (tsĕ′yäng) . . . . China	35·35 N	116·50 E

U

Page	Name Pronunciation Region	Lat. °′	Long. °′
152	Uarc, Ras (C.) . . . . Mor.	35·31 N	2·45 W
134	Uaupés (wä-o͞o′pās) . . . . Braz.	0·02 S	67·03 W
137	Ubá (o͞o-bȧ′) Braz. (Rio de Janeiro In.)	21·08 S	42·55 W
216	Ubangi (Oubangui) (R.) (o͞o-băŋ′gê) . Afr.	4·30 N	20·35 E
137	Ubatuba (o͞o-bȧ-to͞o′bȧ) Braz. (Rio de Janeiro In.)	23·25 S	45·06 W
162	Ubeda (o͞o′bȧ-dä) . . . . Sp.	38·01 N	3·23 W
135	Uberaba (o͞o-bȧ-rä′bȧ) . . . . . . Braz.	19·47 S	47·47 W
135	Uberlândia (o͞o-bĕr-lȧ′n-dyä) Braz.	18·54 S	48·11 W
212	Ubombo (o͞o-bôm′bô) . . . . . . S. Afr.	27·33 S	32·13 E
196	Ubon Ratchathani (o͞o′bŭn rä′chätá-nē) . Thai.	15·15 N	104·52 E
167	Ubort' (R.) (o͞o-bôrt′) . . . . Sov. Un.	51·18 N	27·43 E
162	Ubrique (o͞o-brē′kȧ) . . . . Sp.	36·43 N	5·36 W
188	Ubsa Nuur (L.) . . . . Mong.	50·29 N	93·32 E
217	Ubundi (Ponthierville) . . . . . . Zaire	00·21 S	25·29 E
134	Ucayali (R.) (o͞o′kä-yä′lē) . . . . Peru	8·58 S	74·13 W
149	Uccle (ü′kl′) . . . . Bel. (Brussels In.)	50·48 N	4·17 E
174	Uchaly (û-chä′lĭ) Sov. Un. (Urals In.)	54·22 N	59·28 E
172	Uch-Aral (o͞och′ȧ-ral′) . . . . Sov. Un.	46·14 N	80·58 E
195	Uchiko (o͞o′chê-kō) . . . . Jap.	33·30 N	132·39 E
195	Uchinoura (o͞o′chê-nô-o͞o′rȧ) Jap.	31·16 N	131·03 E
174	Uchinskoye Vodokhranilishche L. (o͞och-ēn′skô-yĕ vô-dô-Krȧ-nĭ′lĭ-shchĕ) Sov. Un. (Moscow In.)	56·08 N	37·44 E
194	Uchiura-Wan (B.) (o͞o′chê-o͞o′rä wän) . Jap.	42·20 N	140·44 E
	Uch Turfan, see Wushih		
173	Uchur (R.) (o͞o-cho͞or′) . . . Sov. Un.	58·27 N	131·34 E
173	Uda (R.) (o͞o′dȧ) . . . . Sov. Un.	52·28 N	110·51 E
173	Uda (R.) . . . . Sov. Un.	53·54 N	131·29 E
184	Udaipur (o͞o-dŭ′ê-po͝or) . . . . India	24·41 N	73·41 E
167	Uday (R.) (o͞o-dī′) . . . . Sov. Un.	50·45 N	32·13 E
156	Uddevalla (o͞od′dĕ-väl-ȧ) . . . . . Swe.	58·21 N	11·55 E
164	Udine (o͞o′dĕ-nȧ) . . . . It.	46·05 N	13·14 E
172	Udmurt (A. S. S. R.) . . . . . Sov. Un.	57·00 N	53·00 E
196	Udon Thani . . . . Thai.	17·31 N	102·51 E
135	Udskaya Guba (B.) . . . . . . Sov. Un.	55·00 N	136·30 E

ăt; finȧl; rāte; senȧte; ärm; ȧsk; sofȧ; fâre; ch-choose; dh-as th in other; bē; êvent; bĕt; recĕnt; cratẽr; g-go; gh-guttural g; bĭt; ĭ-short neutral; rīde; K-guttural k as ch in German ich;

ng-sing; ŋ-baŋk; N-nasalized n; nŏd; cŏmmit; ōld; ôbey; ôrder; fōōd; fŏŏt; ou-out; s-soft; sh-dish; th-thin; pūre; ûnite; ûrn; stŭd; circŭs; ü-as "y" in study; '-indeterminate vowel.

362 Ust'-Kishert' — Vashon PRONOUNCING INDEX

Page	Name Pronunciation Region	Lat. °'	Long. °'
174	Ust'-Kishert' (ŏŏst kĕ'shĕrt) Sov. Un. (Urals In.)	57·21 N	57·13 E
170	Ust'-Kulom (kŏŏ'lŭn)....Sov. Un.	61·38 N	54·00 E
173	Ust'-Maya (mà'yȧ)......Sov. Un.	60·33 N	134·43 E
173	Ust' Olenëk............Sov. Un.	72·52 N	120·15 E
173	Ust-Ordynskiy (ŏŏst-ôr-dyēnsk'ĭ) Sov. Un.	52·47 N	104·39 E
173	Ust' Penzhimo..........Sov. Un.	63·00 N	165·10 E
172	Ust' Port (ŏŏst'pôrt')....Sov. Un.	69·20 N	83·41 E
170	Ust'-Tsil'ma (tsĭl'mà)....Sov. Un.	65·25 N	52·10 E
173	Ust'-Tyrma (tor'mà).....Sov. Un.	50·27 N	131·17 E
174	Ust'Uls (ŏŏls).Sov. Un. (Urals In.)	60·35 N	58·32 E
168	Ust'-Urt, Plato (Plat.) (ŏŏrt) Sov. Un.	44·03 N	54·58 E
166	Ustyuzhna (yōōzh'nà)...Sov. Un.	58·49 N	36·19 E
195	Usuki (ōō'sōō-kē')...........Jap.	33·06 N	131·47 E
126	Usulutan (ōō-sōō-lä-tän').....Sal.	13·22 N	88·25 W
125	Usumacinta (R.) (ōō'sōō-mä-sēn'tō).Mex.	18·24 N	92·30 W
174	Us'va (ōōs'và) Sov. Un. (Urals In.)	58·41 N	57·38 E
102	Utah (State) (ū'tô).........U. S.	39·25 N	112·40 W
115	Utah (L.)...................Ut.	40·10 N	111·55 W
185	Utan...............India (In.)	19·27 N	72·43 E
115	Ute Mtn. Ind. Res..........NM	36·57 N	108·34 W
157	Utena (ōō'tā-nä)........Sov. Un.	55·32 N	25·40 E
213	Utete (ōō-tā'tā)............Tan.	8·05 S	38·47 E
107	Utica (ū'tĭ-kȧ)..In. (Louisville In.)	38·20 N	85·39 W
105	Utica.......................NY	43·05 N	75·10 W
162	Utiel (ōō-tyâl')..............Sp.	39·34 N	1·13 W
107	Utika (ū'tĭ-kȧ)...Mi. (Detroit In.)	42·37 N	83·02 W
95	Utik L....................Can.	55·16 N	96·00 W
94	Utikuma L................Can.	55·50 N	115·25 W
126	Utila I. (ōō-tē'lä).........Hond.	16·07 N	87·05 W
195	Uto (ōō'tō')...............Jap.	32·43 N	130·39 E
149	Utrecht (ü'trĕĸt) (ū'trĕkt) Neth. (Amsterdam In.)	52·05 N	5·06 E
162	Utrera (ōō-trā'rä)............Sp.	37·12 N	5·48 W
156	Utsira (I.) (ŭtsĭrä)..........Nor.	59·21 N	4·50 E
195	Utsunomiya (ōōt'sōō-nō-mē-yà') Jap.	36·35 N	139·52 E
196	Uttaradit..................Thai.	17·47 N	100·10 E
184	Uttarpara-Kotrung India (Calcutta In.)	22·40 N	88·21 E
184	Uttar Pradesh (State) (ōōt-tär-prä-dĕsh).India	27·00 N	80·00 E
148	Uttoxeter (ŭt-tôk'sē-tēr).....Eng.	52·54 N	1·52 W
123	Utuado (ōō-tōō-ä'dhō) P. R. (Puerto Rico In.)	18·16 N	66·40 W
157	Uusikaupunki (Nystad) (ōō'sĭ-kou'pŏŏŋ-kĭ) (nü'städh) Fin.	60·48 N	21·24 E
118	Uvalde (ū-văl'dē)...........Tx.	29·14 N	99·47 W
174	Uvel'skiy (ŏŏ-vyĕl'skĭ) Sov. Un. (Urals In.)	54·27 N	60·22 E
217	Uvinza..................Tan.	5·06 S	30·22 E
12	Uvira (ōō-vē'rä)...........Zaire	3·28 S	29·03 E
166	Uvod' (R.) (ŏŏ-vôd')......Sov. Un.	56·52 N	41·03 E
213	Uvongo Beach..S. Afr. (Natal In.)	30·49 S	30·23 E
195	Uwajima (ōō-wä'jē-mä)......Jap.	33·12 N	132·35 E
99	Uxbridge (ŭks'brĭj).....Ma. (In.)	42·05 N	71·38 W
126	Uxmal (Ruins) (ōō'x-mä'l) Mex. (In.)	20·22 N	89·44 W
174	Uy R. (ōōy)..Sov. Un. (Urals In.)	54·05 N	62·11 E
174	Uyskoye (ûy'skô-yĕ) Sov. Un. (Urals In.)	54·22 N	60·01 E
134	Uyuni (ōō-yōō'nē)...........Bol.	20·28 S	66·45 W
134	Uyuni, Salar de (Salt Flat) (sä-lär-dĕ).Bol.	20·58 S	67·09 W
168	Uzbek S. S. R. (ŏŏz-bĕk').Sov. Un.	42·42 N	60·00 E
171	Uzen, Bol'shoy (R.).....Sov. Un.	49·50 N	49·35 E
167	Uzh (R.) (ōōzh).........Sov. Un.	51·07 N	29·05 E
159	Uzhgorod (ōōzh'gô-rôt)..Sov. Un.	48·38 N	22·18 E
165	Uzunköpru (ōō'zōōn'kû-prü)..Tur.	41·17 N	26·42 E
	V		
212	Vaal (R.) (väl)............S. Afr.	28·15 S	24·30 E
218	Vaaldam (L.).............S. Afr. (Johannesburg & Pretoria In.)	26·58 S	28·37 E
218	Vaalplaas..................S. Afr. (Johannesburg & Pretoria In.)	25·39 S	28·56 E
218	Vaalwater..................S. Afr. (Johannesburg & Pretoria In.)	24·17 S	28·08 E
157	Vaasa (vä'sà)...............Fin.	63·06 N	21·39 E
159	Vác (väts).................Hung.	47·46 N	19·10 E
129	Vache, Ila À (I.) (väsh)......Hai.	18·05 N	73·40 W
150	Vadsö (vädh'sû).............Nor.	70·08 N	29·52 E
156	Vadstena (väd'stĭ'nà)........Swe.	58·27 N	14·53 E
158	Vaduz (vä'dŏŏts)..........Liech.	47·10 N	9·32 E
170	Vaga (R.) (va'gà).......Sov. Un.	61·55 N	42·30 E
156	Vågsöy (I.)................Nor.	61·58 N	4·44 E
159	Vah R. (väĸ)..............Czech.	48·07 N	17·52 E
184	Vaigai (R.)................India	10·20 N	78·13 E
172	Vakh (R.) (vàĸ).........Sov. Un.	61·30 N	81·33 E
165	Valachia (Reg.).............Rom.	44·45 N	24·17 E
89	Valcartier-Village (väl-kärt-yĕ' vē-läzh') Can. (Quebec In.)	46·56 N	71·28 W
166	Valdai Hills (vàl-dī' gô'rĭ) Sov. Un.	57·50 N	32·35 E
166	Valday (Valdai) (vàl-dī').Sov. Un.	57·58 N	33·13 E
162	Valdecañas Res..............Sp.	39·15 N	5·30 W
157	Valdemārpils............Sov. Un.	57·22 N	22·34 E
163	Valdemorillo (väl-då-mô-rēl'yō) Sp. (Madrid In.)	40·30 N	4·04 W
162	Valdepeñas (väl-då-pān'yäs)...Sp.	38·46 N	3·22 W
162	Valderaduey (R.) (väl-dĕ-rä-dwĕ'y).Sp.	41·39 N	5·35 W
136	Valdés, Pen. (vàl-dĕ's).......Arg.	42·15 S	63·15 W
101	Valdez (văl'dĕz).............Ak.	61·10 N	146·18 W
163	Valdilecha (väl-dē-lā'chä) Sp. (Madrid In.)	40·17 N	3·19 W
136	Valdivia (väl-dē'vä)........Chile	39·47 S	73·13 W
134	Valdivia (väl-dē'vēä)....Col. (In.)	7·10 N	75·26 W
97	Val-d' Or..................Can.	48·03 N	77·50 W
120	Valdosta (văl-dŏs'tȧ)..........Ga.	30·50 N	83·18 W
162	Valdovino (väl-dô-vē'nō)......Sp.	43·36 N	8·05 W
110	Vale (vāl)...................Or.	43·59 N	117·14 W
135	Valença (vä-lĕn'sȧ).........Braz.	13·43 S	38·58 W
160	Valence-sur-Rhône (vä-lĕɴs-sür-rōn').Fr.	44·56 N	4·54 E
162	Valencia (vä-lĕ'n-syä).......Port.	42·03 N	8·36 W
163	Valencia (vä-lĕn'thē-ä).......Sp.	39·26 N	0·23 W
162	Valencia....................Sp.	39·34 N	7·13 W
135	Valencia (vä-lĕn'syä)....Ven. (In.)	10·11 N	68·00 W
163	Valencia (Reg.) (vä-lĕn'thē-ä)..Sp.	39·08 N	0·43 W
154	Valencia (I.) (vȧ-lĕn'shȧ).....Ire.	51·55 N	10·26 W
135	Valencia, Lago de (L.)..Ven. (In.)	10·11 N	67·45 W
160	Valenciennes (vȧ-läɴ-syĕn')....Fr.	50·24 N	3·36 E
108	Valentine (vȧ läɴ-tē-nyē')....Ne.	42·52 N	100·34 W
134	Valera (vä-lĕ'rä)...........Ven.	9·12 N	70·45 W
174	Valerianovsk (vȧ-lĕ-rĭ-ä'nôvsk) Sov. Un. (Urals In.)	58·47 N	59·34 E
213	Valhalla (vàl-hăl-ȧ)........S. Afr. (Johannesburg & Pretoria In.)	25·49 S	28·09 E
111	Valier (vă-lēr')..............Mt.	48·17 N	112·14 W
165	Valjevo (väl'yà-vô)........Yugo.	44·17 N	19·57 E
166	Valka (väl'gà)..........Sov. Un.	57·47 N	26·03 E
167	Valki (väl'kē)..........Sov. Un.	49·49 N	35·40 E
126	Valladolid (väl-yä-dhô-lēdh') Mex. (In.)	20·39 N	88·13 W
162	Valladolid (väl-yä-dhô-lēdh')...Sp.	41·41 N	4·41 W
163	Vall de Uxo' (väl-dĕ-ōōx-ô')...Sp.	39·50 N	0·15 W
134	Valle (Dept.) (vä'l-yĕ)...Col. (In.)	4·03 N	76·13 W
114	Valle, Arroyo del (ä-rō'yō dĕl väl'yà).Ca.	37·36 N	121·43 W
163	Vallecas (väl-yā'käs) Sp. (Madrid In.)	40·23 N	3·37 W
118	Valle de Allende (väl'yā dā äl-yĕn'dà).Mex.	26·55 N	105·25 W
124	Valle de Bravo (brä'vô).....Mex.	19·12 N	100·07 W
135	Valle de Guanape (vä'l-yĕ-dĕ-gwä-nä'pĕ) Ven. (In.)	9·54 N	65·41 W
134	Valle de la Pascua (lä-pä's-kōōä) Ven.	9·12 N	65·08 W
124	Valle de Santiago (sän-tē-ä'gô) Mex.	20·23 N	101·11 W
134	Valledupar (dōō-pär')........Col.	10·13 N	73·39 W
134	Valle Grande (grän'dä).......Bol.	18·27 S	64·03 W
112	Vallejo (vä-yā'hō) (vă-lā'hō) Ca. (San Francisco In.)	38·06 N	122·15 W
124	Vallejo, Sierra de (Mts.) (sē-ĕ'r-rä-dĕ-väl-yĕ'ĸō).Mex.	21·00 N	105·10 W
136	Vallenar (väl-yà-när').......Chile	28·39 S	70·52 W
163	Vallerano (R.) (vä-lĕ-rä'nō) It. (Rome In.)	41·46 N	12·29 E
152	Valletta (väl-lĕt'ä).........Malta	35·50 N	14·29 E
113	Valle Vista (văl'yȧ vĭs'tȧ) Ca. (Los Angeles In.)	33·45 N	116·53 W
108	Valley City.................ND	46·55 N	97·59 W
107	Valley City (văl'ĭ) Oh. (Cleveland In.)	41·14 N	81·56 W
117	Valley Falls.................Ks.	39·25 N	95·26 W
89	Valleyfield (văl'ē-fēld) Can. (Montréal In.)	45·16 N	74·09 W
91	Valleyfield.................Can.	45·05 N	74·00 W
113	Valley Park (văl'ē pärk) Mo. (St. Louis In.)	38·33 N	90·30 W
106	Valley Stream (văl'ĭ strēm) NY (New York In.)	40·39 N	73·42 W
164	Valli di Comácchio (L.) (vä'lē-dē-kô-mä'chyô).It.	44·38 N	12·15 E
129	Vallière (väl-yâr')...........Hai.	19·30 N	71·55 W
137	Vallimanca (R.) (väl-yē-mä'n-kä) Arg. (Buenos Aires In.)	36·21 S	60·55 W
163	Valls (väls)..................Sp.	41·15 N	1·15 E
157	Valmiera (vàl'myĕ-rà)...Sov. Un.	57·34 N	25·54 E
160	Valognes (vȧ-lôn'y')..........Fr.	49·32 N	1·30 W
	Valona, see Vlorë		
137	Valparaíso (väl'pä-rä-ē'sô) Chile (Santiago In.)	33·02 S	71·32 W
104	Valparaiso (văl-pȧ-rā'zô)......In.	41·25 N	87·05 W
124	Valparaiso.................Mex.	22·49 N	103·33 W
137	Valpariso (Prov.) Chile (Santiago In.)	32·58 S	71·23 W
160	Valréas (väl-rà-ä')............Fr.	45·25 N	4·56 E
218	Vals (R.).................S. Afr. (Johannesburg & Pretoria In.)	27·32 S	26·51 E
197	Vals, Tandjung (C.).......Indon.	8·30 S	137·15 E
212	Valsbaai (False Bay)..S. Afr. (In.)	34·14 S	18·35 E
174	Valuyevo (vȧ-lōō'yĕ-vô) Sov. Un. (Moscow In.)	55·34 N	37·21 E
167	Valuyki (vȧ-lŏŏ-ē'kē)....Sov. Un.	50·14 N	38·04 E
162	Valverde del Camino (väl-vĕr-dĕ-dĕl-kä-mē'nō).Sp.	37·34 N	6·44 W
184	Vambanād (R.)............India	10·00 N	76·03 E
171	Van (vȧn)..................Tur.	38·04 N	43·10 E
117	Van Buren (văn bū'rĕn).......At.	35·26 N	94·20 W
98	Van Buren..................Me.	47·09 N	67·58 W
104	Vanceburg (văns'bûrg).......Ky.	38·35 N	83·20 W
112	Vancouver (văn-ĸōō'vēr) Can. (Vancouver In.)	49·16 N	123·06 W
112	Vancouver.....Wa. (Portland In.)	45·37 N	122·40 W
92	Vancouver I...............Can.	49·50 N	125·05 W
92	Vancouver Island Ra........Can.	49·25 N	125·25 W
104	Vandalia (văn-dā'lĭ-ȧ).........Il.	39·00 N	89·00 W
117	Vandalia...................Mo.	39·19 N	91·30 W
218	Vanderbijlpark............S. Afr. (Johannesburg & Pretoria In.)	26·43 S	27·50 E
92	Vanderhoof.................Can.	54·01 N	124·01 W
	Van Diemen (Str.), see Ōsumi Kaikyō		
204	Van Diemen, C. (văndē'mĕn) Austl.	11·05 S	130·15 E
204	Van Diemen G.............Austl.	11·50 S	131·30 E
124	Vanegas (vä-nĕ'gäs).........Mex.	23·54 N	100·54 W
156	Vänern (L.)................Swe.	58·52 N	13·17 E
156	Vänersborg (vĕ'nērs-bôr')....Swe.	58·24 N	12·15 E
213	Vanga (väŋ'gä).............Ken.	4·38 S	39·10 E
185	Vangani.............India (In.)	19·07 N	73·15 E
171	Van Gölü (L.)..............Tur.	38·45 N	43·00 E
118	Van Horn....................Tx.	31·03 N	104·50 W
89	Vanier.........Can. (Ottawa In.)	45·27 N	75·39 W
104	Van Lear (văn lēr')..........Ky.	37·45 N	82·50 W
160	Vannes (vàn)................Fr.	47·42 N	2·46 W
113	Van Nuys (văn nīz') Ca. (Los Angeles In.)	34·11 N	118·27 W
197	Van Rees, Pegunungan (Mtn.) Indon.	2·30 S	138·45 E
157	Vantaan (R.)...............Fin.	60·25 N	24·43 E
104	Van Wert (văn wûrt')........Oh.	40·50 N	84·35 W
156	Vara (vä'rä)...............Swe.	58·17 N	12·55 E
164	Varakļāni..............Sov. Un.	56·38 N	26·46 E
164	Varallo (vä-räl'lô)............It.	45·44 N	8·14 E
184	Vārānasi (Benares).........India	25·25 N	83·00 E
150	Varanger Fd. (vä-räng'gĕr)...Nor.	70·05 N	30·53 E
164	Varano, Lago di (L.) (lä'gō-dē-vä-rä'nô).It.	41·52 N	15·55 E
164	Varaždin (vä'räzh'dĕn).....Yugo.	46·17 N	16·20 E
164	Varazze (vä-rät'sā)...........It.	44·23 N	8·34 E
156	Varberg (vär'bĕrg).........Swe.	57·06 N	12·16 E
165	Vardar (R.) (vär'där).......Yugo.	41·40 N	21·50 E
156	Varde (vär'dĕ)..............Den.	55·39 N	8·28 E
150	Vardö (värd'û)..............Nor.	70·23 N	30·43 E
196	Varella, C...................Viet.	12·58 N	109·50 E
157	Varėna (vä-rā'nà).......Sov. Un.	54·16 N	24·35 E
89	Varennes (vȧ-rĕn') Can. (Montréal In.)	45·41 N	73·27 W
165	Varěs (vä'rĕsh)............Yugo.	44·10 N	18·20 E
164	Varese (vä-rā'sā).............It.	45·45 N	8·49 E
137	Varginha (vär-zhē'n-yä) Braz. (Rio de Janeiro In.)	21·33 S	45·25 W
157	Varkaus (vär'kous)..........Fin.	62·19 N	27·51 E
174	Varlamovo (vár-lȧ'mô-vô) Sov. Un. (Urals In.)	54·37 N	60·41 E
165	Varna (Stalin) (vär'nȧ) (stä'lĭn) Bul.	43·14 N	27·58 E
174	Varna.......Sov. Un. (Urals In.)	53·22 N	60·59 E
156	Värnamo (vĕr'nȧ-mô)........Swe.	57·11 N	13·45 E
158	Varnsdorf (värns'dôrf).....Czech.	50·54 N	14·36 E
121	Varnville (värn'vĭl)...........SC	32·49 N	81·05 W
89	Vars (värz).....Can. (Ottawa In.)	45·21 N	75·21 W
167	Varvaropolye (vár'vár'ô-pô-lyĕ) Sov. Un.	48·38 N	38·37 E
185	Vasa.................India (In.)	19·20 N	72·47 E
162	Vascongadas (Reg.) (väs-kôn-gä'däs).Sp.	42·35 N	2·46 W
170	Vashka (R.)............Sov. Un.	63·20 N	47·50 E
112	Vashon (văsh'ŭn) Wa. (Seattle In.)	47·27 N	122·28 W

ăt; finȧl; rāte; senâte; ärm; ȧsk; sofȧ; fâre; ch-choose; dh-as th in other; bē; ēvent; bĕt; recĕnt; cratēr; g-go; gh-guttural g; bĭt; ĭ-short neutral; rīde; ĸ-guttural k as ch in German ich;

PRONOUNCING INDEX

Vashon Heights — Victoria 363

Page	Name Pronunciation Region	Lat. °′	Long. °′
112	Vashon Heights (hītz) Wa. (Seattle In.)	47·30 N	122·28 W
112	Vashon I. . . . . Wa. (Seattle In.)	47·27 N	122·27 W
167	Vasil'kov (vá-sêl'-kôf') . . . Sov. Un.	50·10 N	30·22 E
159	Vaslui (vás-lōō'ē) . . . . Rom.	46·39 N	27·49 E
104	Vassar (văs'ēr) . . . . Mi.	43·25 N	83·35 W
136	Vassouras (väs-sō'räzh) Braz. (Rio de Janeiro In.)	22·25 S	43·40 W
156	Västanfors (vĕst'án-fôrs) . . . . . Swe.	59·59 N	15·49 E
156	Västerås (vĕs'tĕr-ôs) . . . . Swe.	59·39 N	16·30 E
156	Väster-dalälven (R.) . . . . Swe.	61·06 N	13·10 E
156	Västervik (vĕs'tĕr-vēk) . . . . . . Swe.	57·45 N	16·35 E
164	Vasto (väs'tô) . . . . It.	42·06 N	12·42 E
172	Vasyugan (R.) (vás-yōō-gán') Sov. Un.	58·52 N	77·30 E
163	Vatican City (Cittádel Vaticano) (văt'ĭ-kăn sĭt'ē) (chē-tá'del vä-tē-kä'nô) . Eur. (Rome In.)	41·54 N	12·22 E
164	Vaticano, C. (vä-tē-kä'nô) . . . . . It.	38·38 N	15·52 E
150	Vatnajökull (Gl.) (vät'ná-yû-kōōl) Ice.	64·34 N	16·41 W
213	Vatomandry (vä-tōō-män'drē) Mad.	18·53 S	48·13 E
159	Vatra Dornei (vät'rȧ dôr'nā') Rom.	47·22 N	25·20 E
156	Vättern (L.) . . . . Swe.	58·15 N	14·24 E
89	Vandreuil (vô-drû'y') Can. (Montreal In.)	45·24 N	74·02 W
112	Vaugh (vôn) . . . . Wa. (Seattle In.)	47·21 N	122·47 W
89	Vaughan . . . . . . Can. (Toronto In.)	43·47 N	79·36 W
116	Vaughn . . . . NM	34·37 N	105·13 W
134	Vaupés (R.) (vá'ōō-pĕ's) . . . . . Col.	1·18 N	71·14 W
156	Vaxholm (väks'hôlm) . . . . Swe.	59·26 N	18·19 E
156	Växjo (vĕks'shû) . . . . Swe.	56·53 N	14·46 E
170	Vaygach (I.) (vī-gäch') . . . Sov. Un.	70·00 N	59·00 E
135	Veadeiros, Chapadas dos (Mts.) (shä-pä'däs-dôs-vē-á-dā'rōs) Braz.	15·20 S	48·43 W
156	Veblungsnares (vib'lōōngs-nĕs) Nor.	62·33 N	7·46 E
165	Vedea (R.) (vå'dyȧ) . . . . Rom.	44·25 N	24·45 E
137	Vedia (vĕ'dyä) Arg. (Buenos Aires In.)	34·29 S	61·30 W
104	Veedersburg (vē'dērz-bûrg) . . . . In.	40·05 N	87·15 W
125	Vega de Alatorre (vā'gä dā ä-lä-tōr'rå) . Mex.	20·02 N	96·39 W
129	Vega Real (Mts.) (vĕ'gä-rĕ-ä'l) Dom. Rep.	19·30 N	71·05 W
150	Vegen (I.) (vĕ'ghĕn) . . . . Nor.	65·38 N	10·51 E
94	Vegreville . . . . Can.	53·30 N	112·03 W
185	Vehār L. . . . . India (In.)	19·11 N	72·52 E
137	Veinticinco de Mayo (vå-ēn'tē-sēn'kō dā mä'yō) Arg. (Buenos Aires In.)	35·26 S	60·09 W
162	Vejer (vā-kĕr') . . . . Sp.	36·15 N	5·58 W
156	Vejle (vī'lĕ) . . . . Den.	55·41 N	9·29 E
161	Velbert (fĕl'bĕrt) F.R.G. (Ruhr In.)	51·20 N	7·03 E
164	Velebit (Mts.) (vā'lĕ-bĕt) . . . Yugo.	44·25 N	15·23 E
161	Velen (fĕ'lĕn) . . . F.R.G. (Ruhr In.)	51·54 N	7·00 E
162	Vélez-Málaga (vā'lāth-mä'lä-gä) Sp.	36·48 N	4·05 W
162	Vélez Rubio (rōō'bē-ō) . . . . Sp.	37·38 N	2·05 W
164	Velika Kapela (Mts.) (vĕ'lē-kä kä-pĕ'lä) . Yugo.	45·03 N	15·20 E
165	Velika Morava (R.) (mô'rä-vä) Yugo.	44·20 N	21·10 E
165	Velika Tŭrnovo . . . . Bul.	43·06 N	25·38 E
166	Velikaya (R.) (vå-lē'kå-yå) Sov. Un.	57·25 N	28·07 E
159	Velikiy Bychkov (vĕ-lē'kē bōōch-kôf') . Sov. Un.	47·59 N	24·01 E
166	Velikiye Luki (vyē-lē'-kyê lōō'ke) Sov. Un.	56·19 N	30·32 E
170	Velikiy Ustyug (vå-lē'kĭ ōōs-tyōōg') . Sov. Un.	60·45 N	46·38 E
166	Velikoye (vå-lē'kô-yĕ) . . . . Sov. Un.	57·21 N	39·45 E
166	Velikoye (L.) . . . . Sov. Un.	57·00 N	36·53 E
166	Velizh (vå'lēzh) . . . . Sov. Un.	55·37 N	31·11 E
158	Velke Meziřičí (vĕl'kā mĕzh''r-zhyĭ-chĭ) . Czech.	49·21 N	16·01 E
205	Vella (I.) (vāl'yä) . . . . Sol. Is.	8·00 S	156·42 E
163	Velletri (vĕl-lā'trē) . It. (Rome In.)	41·42 N	12·48 E
185	Vellore (vĕl-lōr') . . . . India	12·57 N	79·09 E
174	Vels (vĕls) . . . Sov. Un. (Urals In.)	60·35 N	58·47 E
170	Vel'sk (vĕlsk) . . . . Sov. Un.	61·00 N	42·18 E
149	Velten (fel'tĕn) G.D.R. (Berlin In.)	52·41 N	13·11 E
174	Velya R. (vĕl'yá) Sov. Un. (Moscow In.)	56·23 N	37·54 E
134	Venadillo (vĕ-nä-dē'l-yō) . Col. (In.)	4·43 N	74·55 W
124	Venado (vå-nä'dō) . . . . Mex.	22·54 N	101·07 W
136	Venado Tuerto (vĕ-nä'dô-tōōĕ'r-tô) . Arg.	33·28 S	61·47 W
160	Vendée, Collines de (hills) (kō-lēn' dĕ väN-dā') . Fr.	46·44 N	0·17 W
160	Vendôme (väN-dōm') . . . . Fr.	47·46 N	1·05 E
164	Veneto (Reg.) (vĕ-nĕ'tô) . . . . It.	45·58 N	11·24 E
166	Venëv (vĕn-ĕf') . . . . Sov. Un.	54·19 N	38·14 E
164	Venezia (Venice) (vå-nāt'sē-ä) . It.	45·25 N	12·18 E
164	Venezia, Golfo di (G.) (gôl-fô-dē-vå-nāt'sē-ä) . It.	45·23 N	13·00 E
133	Venezuela (vĕn-ē-zwē'lȧ) . . . . . S. A.	8·00 N	65·00 W
134	Venezuela, Golfo de (G.) (gôl-fô-dĕ) . Ven.	11·34 N	71·02 W
101	Veniaminof, Mt. . . . . Ak.	56·12 N	159·20 W
113	Venice (vĕn'ĭs) Ca. (Los Angeles In.)	33·59 N	118·28 W
113	Venice . . . . Il. (St. Louis In.)	38·40 N	90·10 W
	Venice, see Venezia		
161	Venlo . . . . Neth. (Ruhr In.)	51·22 N	6·11 E
157	Venta (R.) (vĕn'tå) . . . . . . Sov. Un.	57·05 N	21·45 E
136	Ventana, Sierra de la (Mts.) (sē-ĕ'r-rä-dĕ-lä-vĕn-tá'nä) . Arg.	38·00 S	63·00 W
218	Ventersburg (vĕn-tērs'bûrg) . S. Afr. (Johannesburg & Pretoria In.)	28·06 S	27·10 E
218	Ventersdorp (vĕn-tērs'dôrp) S. Afr. (Johannesburg & Pretoria In.)	26·20 S	26·48 E
164	Ventimiglia (vĕn-tē-mēl'yä) . . . . It.	43·46 N	7·37 E
105	Ventnor (vĕnt'nēr) . . . . NJ	39·20 N	74·25 W
157	Ventspils (vĕnt'spēls) . . . . Sov. Un.	57·24 N	21·41 E
134	Ventuari (R.) (vĕn-tōōȧ'rē) . . . Ven.	4·47 N	65·56 W
114	Ventura (vĕn-tōō'rȧ) . . . . Ca.	34·18 N	119·18 W
174	Venukovsky (vĕ-nōō'kôv-skĭ) Sov. Un. (Moscow In.)	55·10 N	37·26 E
124	Venustiano Carranza (vĕ-nōōs-tyä'nō-kär-rä'n-zä) Mex.	19·44 N	103·48 W
125	Venustiano Carranzo (kär-rä'n-zô) Mex.	16·21 N	92·36 W
136	Vera (vĕ-rä) . . . . Arg.	29·22 S	60·09 W
162	Vera (vā'rä) . . . . Sp.	37·18 N	1·53 W
122	Vera Cruz (State) (vā-rä-krōōz') Mex.	20·30 N	97·15 W
125	Veracruz . . . . Mex.	19·13 N	96·07 W
184	Verāval (vĕr'ŭ-väl) . . . . India	20·59 N	70·49 E
164	Vercelli (vĕr-chĕl'lē) . . . . It.	45·18 N	8·27 E
89	Verchères (vĕr-shâr') Can. (Montréal In.)	45·46 N	73·21 W
115	Verde (R.) (vûrd) . . . . Az.	34·04 N	111·40 W
129	Verde, Cap (C.) . . . . Ba.	22·50 N	75·00 W
129	Verde, Cay (I.) . . . . Ba.	22·00 N	75·05 W
125	Verde (R.) . . . . Mex.	16·05 N	97·44 W
124	Verde (R.) . . . . Mex.	20·50 N	103·00 W
124	Verde (R.) . . . . Mex.	21·48 N	99·50 W
197	Verde (I.) (vĕr'dā) . . . . . Phil. (In.)	13·34 N	121·11 E
197	Verde Island Pass. (vĕr'dē) Phil. (In.)	13·36 N	120·39 E
113	Verdemont (vûr'dē-mŏnt) Ca. (Los Angeles In.)	34·12 N	117·22 W
158	Verden (fĕr'dĕn) . . . . F.R.G.	52·55 N	9·15 E
117	Verdigris (R.) (vûr'dē-grēs) . . . Ok.	36·50 N	95·29 W
89	Verdun (vĕr'dŭN') Can. (Montréal In.)	45·27 N	73·34 W
160	Verdun (vâr-dûN') . . . . Fr.	49·09 N	5·21 E
218	Vereeniging (vĕ-rā'nĭ-gĭng) . S. Afr. (Johannesburg & Pretoria In.)	26·40 S	27·56 E
218	Verena (vĕr-ĕn ȧ) . . . . S. Afr. (Johannesburg & Pretoria In.)	25·30 S	29·02 E
166	Vereya (vĕ-rå'yȧ) . . . . Sov. Un.	55·21 N	36·08 E
162	Vergara (vĕr-gä'rä) . . . . Sp.	43·08 N	2·23 W
162	Verin (vå-rēn') . . . . Sp.	41·56 N	7·26 W
174	Verkhne Chusovskiye Gorodki (vyĕrk'nyĕ chōō-sôv'skĭ-ye gå-rôd'ki) . Sov. Un. (Urals In.)	58·13 N	75·06 E
173	Verkhne-Kamchatsk (vyĕrk'nyĕ kåm-chatsk') Sov. Un.	54·42 N	158·41 E
174	Verkhne Neyvinskiy (nā-vĭn'skĭ) Sov. Un. (Urals In.)	57·17 N	60·10 E
174	Verkhne Ural'sk (ŏŏ-ralsk') Sov. Un. (Urals In.)	53·53 N	59·15 E
167	Verkhneye (vyĕrK'nĕ-yĕ) . Sov. Un.	48·53 N	38·29 E
174	Verkhniy Avzyan (vyĕrk'nyĕ åv-zyån') Sov. Un. (Urals In.)	53·32 N	57·30 E
174	Verkhniye Kigi (vyĕrk'nĭ-yĕ kĭ'gĭ) Sov. Un. (Urals In.)	55·23 N	58·37 E
174	Verkhniy Ufaley (ŏŏ-fá'lā) Sov. Un. (Urals In.)	56·04 N	60·15 E
174	Verkhnyaya Pyshma (vyĕrk'nyä-yä pōōsh'nå) Sov. Un. (Urals In.)	56·57 N	60·37 E
174	Verkhnyaya Salda (säl'då) Sov. Un. (Urals In.)	58·03 N	60·33 E
172	Verkhnyaya Tunguska (Angara) (R.) (tōōn-gōōs'kå) . Sov. Un.	58·13 N	97·00 E
174	Verkhnyaya Tura (tōō'rå) Sov. Un. (Urals. In.)	58·22 N	59·51 E
174	Verkhnyaya Yayva (yäy'vå) Sov. Un. (Urals In.)	59·28 N	59·38 E
174	Verkhotur'ye (vyĕr-kô-tōōr'yĕ) Sov. Un. (Urals In.)	58·52 N	60·47 E
173	Verkhoyansk (vyĕr-Kô-yänsk') Sov. Un.	67·43 N	133·33 E
173	Verkhoyanskiy Khrebet (Mts.) (vyĕr-Kô-yänsk') . Sov. Un.	67·45 N	128·00 E
93	Vermilion (vẽr-mĭl'yŭn) . . . . . Can.	53·22 N	110·51 W
109	Vermilion (L.) . . . . Mn.	47·49 N	92·35 W
93	Vermilion (R.) . . . . Can.	53·30 N	111·00 W
98	Vermilion (R.) . . . . Can.	47·30 N	73·15 W
104	Vermilion (R.) . . . . Il.	41·05 N	89·00 W
109	Vermilion (R.) . . . . Mn.	48·09 N	92·31 W
94	Vermilion Hills . . . . Can.	50·43 N	106·50 W
109	Vermilion Ra. . . . . Mn.	47·55 N	91·59 W
108	Vermillion . . . . SD	42·46 N	96·56 W
108	Vermillion (R.) . . . . SD	43·54 N	97·14 W
119	Vermillion B. . . . . La.	29·47 N	92·00 W
103	Vermont (State) (vẽr-mŏnt') . U. S.	43·50 N	72·50 W
111	Vernal (vûr'nȧl) . . . . Ut.	40·29 N	109·40 W
212	Verneuk Pan (L.) (vĕr-nŭk') S. Afr.	30·10 S	21·46 E
113	Vernon (vŭr'nŭn) Ca. (Los Angeles In.)	34·01 N	118·12 W
93	Vernon (vĕr-nôN') . . . . Can.	50·18 N	119·15 W
89	Vernon . . . . Can. (Ottawa In.)	45·10 N	75·27 W
104	Vernon (vûr'nŭn) . . . . In.	39·00 N	85·40 W
106	Vernon . . . . NJ (New York In.)	41·12 N	74·29 W
116	Vernon . . . . Tx.	34·09 N	99·16 W
121	Vero Beach (vē'rō) . . . . Fl. (In.)	27·36 N	80·25 W
165	Véroia . . . . Grc.	40·30 N	22·13 E
164	Verona (vā-rō'nä) . . . . It.	45·28 N	11·02 E
112	Vernonia (vûr-nō'nyȧ) Or. (Portland In.)	45·52 N	123·12 W
161	Versailles (vĕr-sī'y') . Fr. (Paris In.)	48·48 N	2·07 E
104	Versailles (vẽr-sālz') . . . . Ky.	38·05 N	84·45 W
117	Versailles . . . . Mo.	38·27 N	92·52 W
214	Vert, Cap (C.) . . . . Senegal	14·43 N	17·30 W
213	Verulam (vĕ-rōō-lăm) S. Afr. (Natal In.)	29·39 S	31·08 E
155	Verviers (vĕr-vyā') . . . . Bel.	50·35 N	5·57 E
167	Vesëloye (vĕ-syô'lô-yĕ) . . . Sov. Un.	46·59 N	34·56 E
157	Vesijärvi (L.) . . . . Fin.	61·09 N	25·10 E
161	Vesoul (vē-sōōl') . . . . Fr.	47·38 N	6·11 E
106	Vestavia Hills Al. (Birmingham In.)	33·26 N	86·46 W
150	Vester Aalen (Is.) (vĕs'tēr ô'lĕn) Nor.	68·54 N	14·03 E
150	Vestfjord . . . . Nor.	67·33 N	12·59 E
150	Vestmannaeyjar (vĕst'män-ä-ā'yär) . Ice.	63·12 N	20·17 W
163	Vesuvio (vesuvius) (Mtn.) (vĕ-sōō'vyä) . It. (Naples In.)	40·35 N	14·26 E
166	Ves'yegonsk (vĕ-syĕ-gônsk') Sov. Un.	58·42 N	37·09 E
159	Veszprem (vĕs'prām) . . . . Hung.	47·05 N	17·53 E
159	Vesztö (vĕs'tû) . . . . Hung.	46·55 N	21·18 E
166	Vetka (vyĕt'kå) . . . . Sov. Un.	52·36 N	31·05 E
156	Vetlanda (vĕt-län'dä) . . . . Swe.	57·26 N	15·05 E
170	Vetluga (vyĕt-lōō'gå) . . . . Sov. Un.	57·50 N	45·42 E
170	Vetluga (R.) . . . . Sov. Un.	56·50 N	45·50 E
165	Vetovo (vā'tô-vô) . . . . Bul.	43·42 N	26·18 E
165	Vetren (vĕt'rĕn') . . . . Bul.	42·16 N	24·04 E
218	Vet R. (vĕt) . . . . S. Afr. (Johannesburg & Pretoria In.)	28·25 S	26·37 E
104	Vevay (vē'vā) . . . . In.	38·45 N	85·05 W
161	Veynes (vān'') . . . . Fr.	44·31 N	5·47 E
160	Vézère (R.) (vā-zer') . . . . Fr.	45·01 N	1·00 E
134	Viacha (vēȧ'chȧ) . . . . Bol.	16·43 S	68·16 W
164	Viadana (vē-ä-dä'nä) . . . . It.	44·55 N	10·30 E
117	Vian (vī'ăn) . . . . Ok.	35·30 N	95·00 W
135	Viana (vē-ä'nä) . . . . Braz.	3·09 S	44·44 W
162	Viana del Bollo (vē-ä'nä dĕl bôl'yô) . Sp.	42·10 N	7·07 W
162	Viana do Alentejo (vē-ä'nȧ dōō ä-lĕN-tā'hōō) . Port.	38·20 N	8·02 W
162	Viana do Castélo (dōō käs-tā'lōō) Port.	41·41 N	8·45 W
196	Viangchan . . . . Laos	18·07 N	102·33 E
162	Viar (R.) (vē-ä'rä) . . . . Sp.	38·15 N	6·08 W
164	Viareggio (vē-ä-rĕd'jô) . . . . It.	43·52 N	10·14 E
156	Viborg (vē'bôr) . . . . Den.	56·27 N	9·22 E
164	Vibo Valentia (vē'bô-vä-lĕ'n-tyä) It.	38·47 N	16·06 E
163	Vicálvero (vē-kä'l-vĕ-rō) Sp. (Madrid In.)	40·25 N	3·37 W
136	Vicente López (vē-sĕ'n-tĕ-lô'pĕz) Arg. (Buenos Aires In.)	34·15 S	58·29 W
164	Vicenza (vē-chĕnt'sä) . . . . It.	45·33 N	11·33 E
163	Vich (vēch) . . . . Sp.	41·55 N	2·14 E
166	Vichuga (vē-chōō'gȧ) . . . . Sov. Un.	57·13 N	41·58 E
160	Vichy (vē-shē') . . . . Fr.	46·06 N	3·28 E
104	Vicksburg (vĭks'bûrg) . . . . Mi.	42·10 N	85·30 W
120	Vicksburg . . . . Ms.	32·20 N	90·50 W
137	Viçosa (vē-sô'sä) Braz. (Rio de Janeiro In.)	23·46 S	42·51 W
137	Victoria (vēk-tô'rēä) Arg. (Buenos Aires In.)	32·36 S	60·09 W
92	Victoria (vĭk-tō'rĭ-ȧ) . . . . Can.	48·26 N	123·23 W
136	Victoria (vēk-tô-rēä) . . . . Chile	38·15 S	72·16 W
193	Victoria (vĭk-tō'rĭ-ȧ) . . Hong Kong	22·10 N	114·18 E
134	Victoria (vēk-tô'rēä) . . . . Col. (In.)	5·19 N	74·54 W
215	Victoria (vĭk-tō'rĭ-ȧ) . . . . Cam.	4·01 N	9·12 E
197	Victoria (vēk-tô-ryä) . . . Phil. (In.)	15·34 N	120·41 E
119	Victoria (vĭk-tō'rĭ-ȧ) . . . . Tx.	28·48 N	97·00 W
121	Victoria . . . . Va.	36·57 N	78·13 W

ng-sing; ŋ-baŋk; N-nasalized n; nŏd; cŏmmit; ōld; ôbey; ôrder; fōōd; fŏŏt; ou-out; s-soft; sh-dish; th-thin; pūre; ûnite; ûrn; stŭd; circŭs; ü-as "y" in study; '-indeterminate vowel.

ăt; finăl; rāte; senăte; ärm; àsk; sofá; fâre; ch-choose; dh-as th in other; bē; ěvent; bĕt; recĕnt; cratēr; g-go; gh-guttural g; bĭt; ĭ-short neutral; rīde; ᴋ-guttural k as ch in German ich;

Page	Name Pronunciation Region	Lat. °′	Long. °′
165	Visoko (vē'sô-kô) Yugo.	43·59 N	18·10 E
165	Vistonís (L.) (vēs'tô-nĭs) Grc.	40·58 N	25·12 E
	Vistula (R.), see Wisla		
165	Vitanovac (vē'tä'nô-vàts) Yugo.	43·44 N	20·50 E
166	Vitebsk (vē'tyĕpsk) Sov. Un.	55·12 N	30·16 E
166	Vitebsk (Oblast) Sov. Un.	55·05 N	29·18 E
164	Viterbo (vê-tĕr'bō) It.	42·24 N	12·08 E
173	Vitim (vē'têm) Sov. Un.	59·22 N	112·43 E
173	Vitim (R.) (vē'têm) Sov. Un.	56·12 N	115·30 E
174	Vitino (vē'tĭ-nô) Sov. Un. (Leningrad In.)	59·40 N	29·51 E
135	Vitória (vê-tō'rê-ä) Braz.	20·09 S	40·17 W
162	Vitoria (vē-tô-ryä) Sp.	42·43 N	2·43 W
135	Vitória de Conquista (-dä-kōn-kwē's-tä) Braz.	14·51 S	40·44 W
160	Vitré (vē-trā') Fr.	48·09 N	1·15 W
160	Vitrolles (vē-trōl') Fr. (In.)	43·27 N	5·15 E
160	Vitry-le-François (vē-trē'lĕ-fräN-swà') Fr.	48·44 N	4·34 E
151	Vittoria (vê-tô'rê-ô) It.	37·01 N	14·31 E
164	Vittorio (vê-tô'rê-ô) It.	45·59 N	12·17 E
197	Vitu Is. (vē'tōō) Pap. N. Gui.	4·45 S	149·50 E
162	Vivero (vê-vā'rō) Sp.	43·39 N	7·37 W
119	Vivian (vĭv'ĭ-ăn) La.	32·51 N	93·59 W
165	Vize (vē'zĕ) Tur.	41·34 N	27·46 E
185	Vizianagaram India	18·10 N	83·29 E
149	Vlaardingen (vlär'dĭng-ĕn) Neth. (Amsterdam In.)	51·54 N	4·20 E
166	Vladimir (vlà-dyē'mēr) Sov. Un.	56·08 N	40·24 E
166	Vladimir (Oblast) (vlä-dyē'mēr) Sov. Un.	56·08 N	39·53 E
194	Vladimiro-Aleksandrovskoye (vlà-dyē'mē-rô à-lĕk-sän'drôf-skô-yĕ) Sov. Un.	42·50 N	133·00 E
159	Vladimir-Volynskiy (vlà-dyē'mēr vô-lēn'skĭ) Sov. Un.	50·50 N	24·20 E
173	Vladivostok (vlà-dê-vôs-tök') Sov. Un.	43·06 N	131·47 E
165	Vlasenica (vlä'sĕ-nêt'sà) Yugo.	44·11 N	18·58 E
165	Vlasotinci (vlä'sô-tēn-tsĕ) Yugo.	42·58 N	22·08 E
155	Vlieland (I.) (vlē'länt) Neth.	53·19 N	4·55 E
155	Vlissingen (vlĭs'sĭng-ĕn) Neth.	51·30 N	3·34 E
165	Vlorë (Valona) (vlō'rŭ) Alb.	40·28 N	19·31 E
158	Vltana R. Czech.	49·24 N	14·18 E
170	Vodl (L.) (vôd''l) Sov. Un.	62·20 N	37·20 E
212	Voël (R.) S. Afr.	32·52 S	25·12 E
164	Voghera (vô-gā'rä) It.	44·58 N	9·02 E
213	Vohémar (vô-ā-mär') Mad.	13·35 S	50·05 E
112	Voight (R.) Wa. (Seattle In.)	47·03 N	122·08 W
214	Voinjama Lib.	8·25 N	9·45 W
163	Voiron (vwà-rôN') Fr.	45·23 N	5·48 E
94	Voisin, Lac (L.) (vwô'-zĭn) Can.	54·13 N	107·15 W
165	Voïviïs (L.) Grc.	39·34 N	22·50 E
167	Volchansk (vôl-chänsk') Sov. Un.	50·18 N	36·56 E
167	Volch'ya (R.) (vôl-chyä') Sov. Un.	49·42 N	34·39 E
134	Volcán Misti (Vol.) Peru	16·04 S	71·20 W
171	Volga (R.) (vôl'gä) Sov. Un.	47·30 N	46·20 E
171	Volga, Mouths of the Sov. Un.	46·00 N	49·10 E
171	Volgograd (Stalingrad) (vŏl-gō-grä't) (stá'lên-grat) Sov. Un.	48·40 N	42·20 E
171	Volgogradskoye (Res.) (vôl-gô-grad'skô-yĕ) Sov. Un.	51·10 N	45·10 E
166	Volkhov (vôl'kôf) Sov. Un.	59·54 N	32·21 E
166	Volkhov (R.) Sov. Un.	58·45 N	31·40 E
159	Volkovysk (vôl-kô-vêsk') Sov. Un.	53·11 N	24·29 E
174	Volodarskiy (vô-lô-där'skĭ) Sov. Un. (Leningrad In.)	59·49 N	30·06 E
166	Vologda (vô'lôg-dà) Sov. Un.	59·12 N	39·52 E
166	Vologda (Oblast) Sov. Un.	59·00 N	37·26 E
167	Volokonovka (vô-lô-kô'nôf-kà) Sov. Un.	50·28 N	37·52 E
166	Volokolamsk (vô-lô-kôlàmsk) Sov. Un.	56·02 N	35·58 E
165	Vólos (vô'lôs) Grc.	39·23 N	22·56 E
166	Volozhin (vô'lô-shên) Sov. Un.	54·04 N	26·38 E
171	Vol'sk (vôl'sk) Sov. Un.	52·10 N	47·00 E
214	Volta, L. (vôl'tà) Ghana	7·10 N	0·30 W
214	Volta (R.) Ghana	6·05 N	0·30 E
214	Volta Blanche (R.) Upper Volta	11·30 N	0·40 W
214	Volta Noire (Black Volta) (R.) Afr.	10·30 N	2·55 W
137	Volta Redonda (vōl'tä-rā-dôn'dä) Braz. (Rio de Janeiro In.)	22·32 S	44·05 W
164	Volterra (vôl-tĕr'rä) It.	43·22 N	10·51 E
164	Voltri (vōl'trē) It.	44·25 N	8·45 E
164	Volturno (R.) (vôl-tōōr'nô) It.	41·12 N	14·20 E
166	Volzhskoye (L.) (vôl'sh-skô-yĕ) Sov. Un.	56·43 N	36·18 E
113	Von Ormy (vŏn ôr'mê) Tx. (San Antonio In.)	29·18 N	98·36 W
166	Vōōpsu (vōōp'-sōō) Sov. Un.	58·06 N	27·30 E
149	Voorberg Neth. (Amsterdam In.)	52·04 N	4·21 E
213	Voortrekkerhoogte S. Afr. (Johannesburg & Pretoria In.)	25·48 S	28·10 E
166	Vop' (R.) (vôp) Sov. Un.	55·20 N	32·40 E
150	Vopnafjördhur Ice.	65·43 N	14·58 W
158	Vorarlberg (Prov.) Aus.	47·20 N	9·55 E
156	Vordingborg (vôr'dĭng-bôr) Den.	55·10 N	11·55 E
165	Voríai (Is.) Grc.	39·12 N	24·03 E
165	Vorios Evvíkós Kólpos (G.) Grc.	38·48 N	23·02 E
170	Vorkuta (vôr-kōō'tà) Sov. Un.	67·28 N	63·40 E
157	Vormsi (I.) (vôrm'sĭ) Sov. Un.	59·06 N	23·05 E
171	Vorona (R.) (vô-rô'na) Sov. Un.	51·50 N	42·00 E
170	Voron'ya (R.) (vô-rô'nyà) Sov. Un.	68·20 N	35·20 E
167	Voronezh (vô-rô'nyĕzh) Sov. Un.	51·39 N	39·11 E
167	Voronezh (Oblast) Sov. Un.	51·10 N	39·13 E
166	Voronezh (R.) Sov. Un.	52·17 N	39·32 E
159	Voronovo (vô'rô-nô-vô) Sov. Un.	54·07 N	25·16 E
174	Vorontsovka (vô-rônt'sôv-kà) Sov. Un. (Urals In.)	59·40 N	60·14 E
171	Voroshilovgrad Sov. Un.	48·34 N	39·18 E
167	Voroshilovgrad (Oblast) Sov. Un.	49·08 N	38·37 E
166	Võrts-Järv (L.) (vôrts yärv) Sov. Un.	58·15 N	26·12 E
166	Võru (vô'rû) Sov. Un.	57·50 N	26·58 E
174	Vorya R. (vôr'yà) Sov. Un. (Moscow In.)	55·55 N	38·15 E
161	Vosges (Mts.) (vōzh) Fr.	48·09 N	6·57 E
174	Voskresensk (vôs-krĕ-sĕnsk') Sov. Un. (Moscow In.)	55·20 N	38·42 E
156	Voss (vôs) Nor.	60·40 N	6·24 E
174	Vostryakovo Sov. Un. (Moscow In.)	55·23 N	37·49 E
170	Votkinsk (vôt-kēnsk') Sov. Un.	57·00 N	54·00 E
170	Votkinskoye Vdkhr (Res.) Sov. Un.	57·30 N	55·00 E
162	Vouga (R.) (vō'gà) Port.	40·43 N	7·51 W
160	Vouziers (vōō-zyā') Fr.	49·25 N	4·40 E
156	Voxna älv (R.) Swe.	61·30 N	15·24 E
109	Voyageurs Natl. Park Mn.	48·30 N	92·40 W
170	Vozhe (L.) (vôzh'yĕ) Sov. Un.	60·40 N	39·00 E
167	Voznesensk (vôz-nyĕ-sĕnsk') Sov. Un.	47·34 N	31·22 E
168	Vrangelya (Wrangel) (I.) Sov. Un.	71·25 N	173·38 E
165	Vranje (vrän'yĕ) Yugo.	42·33 N	21·55 E
165	Vratsa (vrät'tsà) Bul.	43·12 N	23·31 E
165	Vrbas (v'r'bäs) Yugo.	45·34 N	19·43 E
164	Vrbas (R.) Yugo.	44·25 N	17·17 E
160	Vrchlabi (v'r'chlä-bê) Czech.	50·32 N	15·51 E
218	Vrede (vrĭ'dĕ) (vrēd) S. Afr. (Johannesburg & Pretoria In.)	27·25 S	29·11 E
218	Vredefort (vrĭ'dĕ-fôrt) (vrēd'fōrt) S. Afr. (Johannesburg & Pretoria In.)	27·00 S	27·21 E
149	Vreeswijk Neth. (Amsterdam In.)	52·00 N	5·06 E
165	Vršac (v'r'shàts) Yugo.	45·08 N	21·18 E
159	Vrutky (vrōōt'kê) Czech.	49·09 N	18·55 E
212	Vryburg (vrī'bûrg) S. Afr.	26·55 S	29·45 E
212	Vryheid (vrī'hīt) S. Afr.	27·43 S	30·58 E
159	Vsetín (fsĕt'yēn) Czech.	49·21 N	18·01 E
174	Vsevolozhskiy (vsyĕ'vôlô'zh-skĕē) Sov. Un. (Leningrad In.)	60·01 N	30·41 E
128	Vuelta Abajo (Mts.) (vwĕl'tä ä-bä'hō) Cuba	22·20 N	83·45 W
149	Vught Neth. (Amsterdam In.)	51·38 N	5·18 E
165	Vukovar (vŏŏ'kô-vär) Yugo.	45·20 N	19·00 E
104	Vulcan (vŭl'kăn) Mi.	45·45 N	87·50 W
164	Vulcano (I.) (vōōl-kä'nô) It.	38·23 N	15·00 E
165	Vŭlchedrŭm Bul.	43·43 N	23·29 E
157	Vyartsilya (vyàr-tsē'lyà) Sov. Un.	62·10 N	30·40 E
170	Vyatka (R.) (vyàt'kà) Sov. Un.	58·25 N	51·25 E
194	Vyazemskiy (vyà-zĕm'skĭ) Sov. Un.	47·29 N	134·39 E
166	Vyaz'ma (vyàz'mà) Sov. Un.	55·12 N	34·17 E
170	Vyazniki (vyàz'nê-kê) Sov. Un.	56·10 N	42·10 E
157	Vyborg (Viipuri) (vwē'bôrk) Sov. Un.	60·43 N	28·46 E
170	Vychegda (R.) (vê'chĕg-dă) Sov. Un.	61·40 N	48·00 E
170	Vym (R.) (vwēm) Sov. Un.	63·15 N	51·20 E
174	Vyritsa (vē'rĭ-tsà) Sov. Un. (Leningrad In.)	59·24 N	30·20 E
166	Vyshnevolotskoye (L.) (vŭy'sh-ŋĕ'vôlôt's-kô'yĕ) Sov. Un.	57·30 N	34·27 E
166	Vyshniy Volochëk (vêsh'nyĭ vôl-ô-chĕk') Sov. Un.	57·34 N	34·35 E
158	Vyskov (vêsh'kôf) Czech.	49·17 N	16·58 E
158	Vysoké Mýto (vû'sô-kā mû'tô) Czech.	49·58 N	16·07 E
166	Vysokovsk (vĭ-sô'kôfsk) Sov. Un.	56·16 N	36·32 E
170	Vytegra (vû'tĕg-rà) Sov. Un.	61·00 N	36·20 E
170	Vyur Sov. Un.	57·55 N	27·00 E

W

Page	Name Pronunciation Region	Lat. °′	Long. °′
215	W, Parcs Nationaux du (Natl. Pk.) Dahomey-Niger	12·20 N	2·40 E
214	Wa Ghana	10·04 N	2·29 W
155	Waal (R.) (väl) Neth.	51·46 N	5·00 E
149	Waalwijk Neth. (Amsterdam In.)	51·41 N	5·05 E
93	Wabamuno (wŏ'bă-mŭn) Can.	53·33 N	114·28 W
93	Wabasca (wŏ-bás'-kă) Can.	56·00 N	113·53 W
104	Wabash (wô'băsh) In.	40·45 N	85·50 W
104	Wabash (R.) Il.-In.	38·00 N	88·00 W
109	Wabasha (wä'bă-shô) Mn.	44·24 N	92·04 W
95	Wabowden (wă-bō'-d'n) Can.	54·55 N	98·38 W
159	Wabrzeźno (vôŋ-bzĕzh'nô) Pol.	53·17 N	18·59 E
121	Waccamaw (R.) (wăk'ă-mô) SC	33·47 N	78·55 W
120	Waccasassa B. (wă-kă-să'să) Fl.	29·02 N	83·10 W
149	Wachow (vä'kōv) G.D.R. (Berlin In.)	52·32 N	12·46 E
119	Waco (wā'kō) Tx.	31·35 N	97·06 W
116	Waconda Lake (Res.) Ks.	39·45 N	98·15 W
195	Wadayama (wä'dä'yä-mä) Jap.	35·19 N	134·49 E
155	Waddenzee (Sea) Neth.	53·00 N	4·50 E
92	Waddington, Mt. (wŏd'dĭng-tŭn) Can.	51·23 N	125·15 W
94	Wadena Can.	51·57 N	103·50 W
109	Wadena (wŏ-dē'nă) Mn.	46·26 N	95·09 W
121	Wadesboro (wādz'bŭr-ô) NC	34·57 N	80·05 W
183	Wādī Mūsā. Jordan (Palestine In.)	30·19 N	35·29 E
121	Wadley (wŏd'lê) Ga.	32·54 N	82·25 W
211	Wad Madani (wäd mĕ-dä'nê) Sud.	14·27 N	33·31 E
159	Wadowice (và-dô'vēt-sĕ) Pol.	49·53 N	19·31 E
107	Wadsworth (wŏdz'wŭrth) Oh. (Cleveland In.)	41·01 N	81·44 W
91	Wager B. (wā'jēr) Can.	65·48 N	88·19 W
203	Wagga Wagga (wôg'ă wôg'ă) Austl.	35·10 S	147·30 E
117	Wagoner (wăg'ŭn-ēr) Ok.	35·58 N	95·22 W
116	Wagon Mound (wăg'ŭn mound) NM	35·59 N	104·45 W
159	Wagrowiec (vôŋ-grô'vyĕts) Pol.	52·47 N	17·14 E
100	Wahiawa Hi.	21·30 N	158·03 W
108	Wahoo (wä-hōō') Ne.	41·14 N	96·39 W
108	Wahpeton (wô'pê-tŭn) ND	46·17 N	96·38 W
100	Waialua (wä'ê-ä-lōō'ä) Hi.	21·33 N	158·08 W
100	Waianae (wä'ê-à-nä'ä) Hi.	21·25 N	158·11 W
158	Waidhofen (vīd'hôf-ĕn) Aus.	47·58 N	14·46 E
173	Waigeo (I.) (wä-ê-gä'ô) Indon.	0·07 N	131·00 E
191	Waikang (wăī'käng) China (Shanghai In.)	31·23 N	121·11 E
205	Waikato (R.) (wä'ê-kä'to) N. Z. (In.)	38·00 S	175·47 E
203	Waikerie (wā'kēr-ē) Austl.	34·15 S	140·00 E
100	Wailuku (wä'ê-lōō'kōō) Hi.	20·55 N	156·30 W
100	Waimanalo (wä-ê-mä'nä-lo) Hi.	21·19 N	157·53 W
100	Waimea (wä-ê-mā'ä) Hi.	21·56 N	159·38 W
184	Wainganga (R.) (wä-ēn-gŭŋ'gä) India	20·24 N	79·41 E
196	Waingapu Indon.	9·32 S	120·00 E
101	Wainwright (wān-rīt) Ak.	74·40 N	159·00 W
93	Wainwright Can.	52·49 N	110·52 W
100	Waipahu (wä'ê-pä'hōō) Hi.	21·20 N	158·02 W
113	Waiska R. (wă-ĭz-kă) Mi. (Sault Ste. Marie In.)	46·20 N	84·38 W
110	Waitsburg (wāts'bûrg) Wa.	46·17 N	118·08 W
195	Wajima (wä'jê-mà) Jap.	37·23 N	136·56 E
217	Wajir Ken.	1·45 N	40·04 E
195	Wakamatsu (wä-kä'mät-sōō) Jap.	33·54 N	130·44 E
96	Wakami (R.) Can.	47·43 N	82·22 W
195	Wakasa-Wan (B.) (wä'kä-sä wän) Jap.	35·43 N	135·39 E
205	Wakatipu (R.) (wä-kä-tē'pōō) N. Z. (In.)	44·24 S	169·00 E
195	Wakayama (wä-kä'yä-mä) Jap.	34·14 N	135·11 E
198	Wake (I.) (wāk) Oceania	19·25 N	167·00 E
116	Wa Keeney (wô-kē'nê) Ks.	39·01 N	99·53 W
89	Wakefield (wāk-fēld) Can. (Ottawa In.)	45·39 N	75·55 W
148	Wakefield Eng.	53·41 N	1·25 W
99	Wakefield Ma. (In.)	42·31 N	71·05 W
109	Wakefield Mi.	46·28 N	89·55 W
108	Wakefield Ne.	42·15 N	96·52 W
106	Wakefield RI (Providence In.)	41·26 N	71·30 W
121	Wake Forest (wāk fŏr'ĕst) NC	35·58 N	78·31 W
195	Waki (wä'kê) Jap.	34·05 N	134·10 E
194	Wakkanai (wä'kä-nä'ê) Jap.	45·19 N	141·43 E
212	Wakkerstroom (vák'ēr-strōm) (wăk'ēr-strōōm) S. Afr.	27·19 S	30·04 E
96	Wakonassin (R.) Can.	46·35 N	82·10 W
158	Wałbrzych (väl'bzhûk) Pol.	50·46 N	16·16 E
98	Waldoboro (wôl'dô-bŭr-ô) Me.	44·06 N	69·22 W
110	Waldo L. (wôl'dō) Or.	43·46 N	122·10 W

ng-sing; ŋ-baŋk; N-nasalized n; nŏd; cŏmmit; ōld; ôbey; ôrder; fōōd; fŏŏt; ou-out; s-soft; sh-dish; th-thin; pūre; ûnite; ûrn; stŭd; circŭs; ü-as "y" in study; '-indeterminate vowel.

366 Waldorf — Wayland PRONOUNCING INDEX

Page	Name	Pronunciation	Region	Lat. °'	Long. °'
106	Waldorf	(wăl'dŏrf)	Md. (Baltimore In.)	38·37 N	76·57 W
113	Waldron		Mo. (Kansas City In.)	39·14 N	94·47 W
112	Waldron (I.)		Wa. (Vancouver In.)	48·42 N	123·02 W
101	Wales	(wālz)	Ak.	65·35 N	168·14 W
154	Wales		U. K.	52·12 N	3·40 W
214	Walewale		Ghana	10·21 N	0·48 W
158	Wałez	(välch)	Pol.	53·61 N	16·30 E
203	Walgett	(wôl'gĕt)	Austl.	30·00 S	148·10 E
220	Walgreen Coast	(wôl'grēn)	Ant.	73·00 N	110·00 W
120	Walhalla	(wŏl-hăl'ȧ)	SC	34·45 N	83·04 W
217	Walikale		Zaire	1·25 S	28·03 E
109	Walker	(wôk'ẽr)	Mn.	47·06 N	94·37 W
109	Walker	(wôk'ẽr)	Mn.	47·06 N	94·37 W
114	Walker (R.)		Nv.	39·07 N	119·10 W
112	Walker, Mt.		Wa. (Seattle In.)	47·47 N	122·54 W
95	Walker L.		Can.	54·42 N	96·57 W
114	Walker L.		Nv.	38·46 N	118·30 W
114	Walker River Ind. Res.		Nv.	39·06 N	118·20 W
111	Walkerville	(wôk'ẽr-vĭl)	Mt.	46·20 N	112·32 W
110	Wallace	(wŏl'ås)	Id.	47·27 N	115·55 W
96	Wallaceburg		Can.	42·39 N	82·25 W
202	Wallacia		Austl. (Sydney In.)	33·52 S	150·40 E
110	Wallapa B.	(wŏl ȧ pă)	Wa.	46·39 N	124·30 W
203	Wallaroo	(wŏl-ȧ-rōō)	Austl.	33·52 S	137·45 E
148	Wallasey	(wŏl'ȧ-sē)	Eng.	53·25 N	3·03 W
110	Walla Walla	(wŏl'ȧ wŏl'ȧ)	Wa.	46·03 N	118·20 W
107	Walled Lake	(wôl'd lāk)	Mi. (Detroit In.)	42·32 N	83·29 W
211	Wallel, Tulu (Mt.)		Eth.	9·00 N	34·52 E
148	Wallingford	(wŏl'ĭng-fẽrd)	Eng. (London In.)	51·34 N	1·08 W
105	Wallingford		Vt.	43·30 N	72·55 W
198	Wallis Is.		Oceania	13·00 S	176·10 E
119	Wallisville	(wŏl'ĭs-vĭl)	Tx. (In.)	29·50 N	94·44 W
110	Wallowa	(wôl'ō-wȧ)	Or.	45·34 N	117·32 W
110	Wallowa Mts.		Or.	45·10 N	117·22 W
110	Wallowa R.		Or.	45·28 N	117·28 W
110	Wallula		Wa.	46·08 N	118·55 W
154	Walney (C.)	(wôl'nē)	Eng.	54·04 N	3·13 W
113	Walnut	(wôl'nŭt)	Ca. (Los Angeles In.)	34·00 N	117·51 W
117	Walnut (R.)		Ks.	37·28 N	97·06 W
115	Walnut Canyon Natl. Mon.		Az.	35·10 N	111·30 W
112	Walnut Creek		Ca. (San Francisco In.)	37·54 N	122·04 W
113	Walnut Cr.		Tx. (Dallas, Fort Worth In.)	32·37 N	97·03 W
117	Walnut Ridge	(rĭj)	Ar.	36·04 N	90·56 W
99	Walpole	(wôl'pōl)	Ma. (In.)	42·09 N	71·15 W
105	Walpole		NH	43·05 N	72·25 W
148	Walsall	(wôl-sôl)	Eng.	52·35 N	1·58 W
116	Walsenburg	(wôl'sĕn-bûrg)	Co.	37·38 N	104·46 W
120	Walter F. George Res.		Al.-Ga.	32·00 N	85·00 W
116	Walters	(wôl'tẽrz)	Ok.	34·21 N	98·19 W
99	Waltham	(wôl'thăm)	Ma. (In.)	42·22 N	71·14 W
148	Walthamstow	(wôl'tăm-stō)	Eng. (London In.)	51·34 N	0·01 W
105	Walton		NY	42·10 N	75·05 W
148	Walton-le-Dale	(lē-dāl')	Eng.	53·44 N	2·40 W
212	Walvis Bay	(wôl'vĭs)	S. Afr.	22·50 S	14·30 E
109	Walworth	(wôl'wŭrth)	Wi.	42·33 N	88·39 W
216	Wamba (R.)		Zaire	5·30 N	17·05 E
117	Wamego	(wŏ-mē'gō)	Ks.	39·13 N	96·17 W
213	Wami (R.)	(wä'mē)	Tan.	6·31 S	37·17 E
97	Wanapitei L.		Can.	46·45 N	80·45 W
106	Wanaque	(wŏn'ȧ-kū)	NJ (New York In.)	41·03 N	74·16 W
106	Wanaque Res.		NJ (New York In.)	41·06 N	74·20 W
190	Wanchih	(wän'chĭ')	China	31·11 N	118·31 E
203	Wandoan		Austl.	26·09 S	149·51 E
149	Wandsbek	(vänds'bĕk)	F.R.G. (Hamburg In.)	53·34 N	10·07 E
148	Wandsworth	(wôndz'wûrth)	Eng.	51·26 N	0·12 W
205	Wanganui	(wôŋ'gȧ-nōō'ē)	N. Z. (In.)	39·53 N	175·01 E
203	Wangaratta	(wŏŋ'gȧ-răt'ȧ)	Austl.	36·23 N	146·18 E
194	Wangching	(wäng'chēng)	China	43·14 N	129·33 E
190	Wangch'ingt'o	(wäng'chĭng'tōō')	China	39·14 N	116·56 E
158	Wangeroog I.	(vän'gĕ-rōg)	F.R.G.	53·49 N	7·57 E
193	Wanhsien	(wän'hsyĕn')	China	30·48 N	108·22 E
190	Wanhsien	(wän'sĭän)	China	38·51 N	115·10 E
217	Wankie	(wă 'kē)	Rh.	18·22 S	26·29 E
148	Wantage	(wŏn'tȧj)	Eng. (London In.)	51·33 N	1·26 W
106	Wantagh		NY (New York In.)	40·41 N	73·30 W
193	Wantsai		China	28·05 N	114·25 E
203	Waodoan	(wŏd'ŏn)	Austl.	26·12 S	149·52 E
104	Wapakoneta	(wä'pȧ-kō-nĕt'ȧ)	Oh.	40·35 N	84·10 W
94	Wapawekka Hills	(wŏ'pă-wĕ'-kă-hĭlz)	Can.	54·45 N	104·20 W
94	Wapawekka L.		Can.	54·55 N	104·40 W
109	Wapello	(wŏ-pĕl'ō)	Ia.	41·10 N	91·11 W
95	Wapesi L.	(wŏ-pĕ'-zē)	Can.	50·34 N	92·21 W
117	Wappapello Res.	(wă'pȧ-pĕl-lō)	Mo.	37·07 N	90·10 W
105	Wappingers Falls	(wŏp'ĭn-jẽrz)	NY	41·35 N	73·55 W
109	Wapsipinicon (R.)	(wŏp'sĭ-pĭn'ĭ-kŏn)	Ia.	42·16 N	91·35 W
195	Warabi	(wä'rä-bē)	Jap. (Tōkyō In.)	35·50 N	139·41 E
184	Warangal	(wŭr'ăŋ-gȧl)	India	18·03 N	79·45 E
204	Warburton, The (R.)	(wŏr'bûr-tŭn)	Austl.	27·30 S	138·45 E
183	Wardān, Wādī (R.)		Egypt (Palestine In.)	29·22 N	33·00 E
92	Ward Cove		Ak.	55·24 N	131·43 W
218	Warden	(wôr'dĕn)	S. Afr. (Johannesburg & Pretoria In.)	27·52 N	28·59 E
184	Wardha	(wŭr'dä)	India	20·46 N	78·42 E
104	War Eagle	(wôr ē'g'l)	WV	37·30 N	81·50 W
158	Waren	(vä'rĕn)	F.R.G.	53·32 N	12·43 E
161	Warendorf	(vä'rĕn-dōrf)	F.R.G. (Ruhr In.)	51·57 N	7·59 E
203	Warialda		Austl.	29·32 S	150·34 E
212	Warmbad	(värm'bäd) (wôrm'băd)	Namibia	28·25 S	18·45 E
218	Warmbad		S. Afr. (Johannesburg & Pretoria In.)	24·52 S	28·18 E
112	Warm Beach	(wôrm)	Wa. (Seattle In.)	48·10 N	122·22 W
110	Warm Springs Ind. Res.	(wôrm sprĭnz)	Or.	44·55 N	121·30 W
110	Warm Springs Res.		Or.	43·42 N	118·40 W
156	Warnemünde	(vär'nĕ-mün-dĕ)	G.D.R.	54·11 N	12·04 E
110	Warner Ra. (Mts.)		Ca.-Or.	41·30 N	120·17 W
158	Warnow R.	(vär'nō)	G.D.R.	53·51 N	11·55 E
203	Warracknabeal		Austl.	36·20 S	142·28 E
203	Warragamba Res.		Austl. (Sydney In.)	33·40 S	150·00 E
205	Warrego (R.)	(wôr'ē-gō)	Austl.	27·13 S	145·58 E
117	Warren	(wŏr'ĕn)	Ar.	33·37 N	92·03 W
89	Warren		Can. (Winnipeg In.)	50·08 N	97·32 W
104	Warren		In.	40·40 N	85·25 W
107	Warren		Mi. (Detroit In.)	42·33 N	83·03 W
108	Warren		Mn.	48·11 N	96·44 W
104	Warren		Oh.	41·15 N	80·50 W
112	Warren		Or. (Portland In.)	45·49 N	122·51 W
105	Warren		Pa.	41·50 N	79·10 W
106	Warren		RI (Providence In.)	41·44 N	71·14 W
107	Warrendale	(wŏr'ĕn-dāl)	Pa. (Pittsburgh In.)	40·39 N	80·04 W
117	Warrensburg	(wŏr'ĕnz-bûrg)	Mo.	38·45 N	93·42 W
121	Warrenton	(wŏr'ĕn-tŭn)	Ga.	33·26 N	82·37 W
112	Warrenton		Or. (Portland In.)	46·10 N	123·56 W
105	Warrenton		Va.	38·45 N	77·50 W
210	Warri	(wär'ē)	Nig.	5·33 N	5·43 E
148	Warrington		Eng.	53·22 N	2·30 W
120	Warrington	(wŏr'ĭng-tŭn)	Fl.	30·21 N	87·15 W
203	Warrnambool	(wôr'năm-bōōl)	Austl.	36·20 S	142·28 E
109	Warroad	(wôr'rōd)	Mn.	48·55 N	95·20 W
205	Warrumbungle Ra.	(wôr'ŭm-bŭŋ-g'l)	Austl.	31·18 S	150·00 E
117	Warsaw	(wôr'sô)	Il.	40·21 N	91·26 W
104	Warsaw		In.	41·15 N	85·50 W
105	Warsaw		NY	42·45 N	78·10 W
121	Warsaw		NC	35·00 N	78·07 W
	Warsaw, see Warszawa				
148	Warsop	(wôr'sŭp)	Eng.	53·13 N	1·05 W
159	Warszawa (Warsaw)	(vȧr-shä'vȧ)	Pol.	52·15 N	21·05 E
158	Warta R.	(vär'tȧ)	Pol.	52·35 N	15·07 E
213	Wartburg		S. Afr. (Natal In.)	29·26 S	30·39 E
203	Warwick	(wŏr'ĭk)	Austl.	28·05 S	152·10 E
98	Warwick		Can.	45·58 N	71·57 W
154	Warwick		Eng.	52·19 N	1·46 W
106	Warwick		NY (New York In.)	41·15 N	74·22 W
106	Warwick		RI (Providence In.)	41·42 N	71·27 W
148	Warwick (Co.)		Eng.	52·22 N	1·34 W
113	Wasatch Mts.	(wô'săch)	Ut. (Salt Lake City In.)	40·45 N	111·46 W
115	Wasatch Plat.		Ut.	38·55 N	111·40 W
102	Wasatch Ra.		U. S.	39·10 N	111·30 W
213	Wasbank		S. Afr. (Natal In.)	28·27 S	30·09 E
110	Wasco	(wäs'kō)	Or.	45·36 N	120·42 W
109	Waseca	(wô-sē'kȧ)	Mn.	44·04 N	93·31 W
155	Wash, The (Est.)	(wŏsh)	Eng.	53·00 N	0·20 E
98	Washburn	(wŏsh'bŭrn)	Me.	46·46 N	68·10 W
109	Washburn		Wi.	46·41 N	90·55 W
111	Washburn, Mt.		Wy.	44·55 N	110·10 W
106	Washington	(wŏsh'ĭng-tŭn)	DC (Washington DC In.)	38·50 N	77·00 W
120	Washington		Ga.	33·43 N	82·46 W
104	Washington		In.	38·40 N	87·10 W
109	Washington		Ia.	41·17 N	91·42 W
117	Washington		Ks.	39·48 N	97·04 W
117	Washington		Mo.	38·33 N	91·00 W
121	Washington		NC	35·32 N	77·01 W
107	Washington		Pa. (Pittsburgh In.)	40·10 N	80·14 W
102	Washington (State)		U. S.	47·30 N	121·10 W
105	Washington, Mt.		NH	44·15 N	71·15 W
112	Washington, L.		Wa. (Seattle In.)	47·34 N	122·12 W
109	Washington (I.)		Wi.	45·18 N	86·42 W
104	Washington Court House		Oh.	39·30 N	83·25 W
113	Washington Park		Il. (St. Louis In.)	38·38 N	90·06 W
116	Washita (R.)	(wŏsh'ĭ-tô)	Ok.	35·33 N	99·16 W
112	Washougal	(wŏ-shōō'gȧl)	Wa. (Portland In.)	45·35 N	122·21 W
112	Washougal (R.)		Wa. (Portland In.)	45·38 N	122·17 W
159	Wasilkow	(vȧ-sēl'kŏŏf)	Pol.	53·12 N	23·13 E
95	Waskaiowaka L.	(wŏ'skă-yō'wŏ-kă)	Can.	56·30 N	96·20 W
95	Wass L.	(wŏs)	Can.	53·40 N	95·25 W
161	Wassenberg	(vä'sĕn-bĕrgh)	F.R.G. (Ruhr In.)	51·06 N	6·07 E
114	Wassuk Ra.	(wȧs'sŭk)	Nv.	38·58 N	119·00 W
97	Waswanipi, Lac (L.)		Can.	49·35 N	76·15 W
123	Water (I.)	(wô'tẽr)	Vir. Is. (U. S. A.) (St. Thomas In.)	18·20 N	64·57 W
218	Waterberge (Mts.)	(wôrtẽr'bûrg)	S. Afr. (Johannesburg & Pretoria In.)	24·25 S	27·53 E
121	Waterboro	(wô'tẽr-bûr-ō)	SC	32·50 N	80·40 W
105	Waterbury	(wô'tẽr-bĕr-ē)	Ct.	41·30 N	73·00 W
129	Water Cay (I.)		Ba.	22·55 N	75·50 W
89	Waterdown	(wô'tẽr-doun)	Can. (Toronto In.)	43·20 N	79·54 W
121	Wateree (R.)	(wô'tẽr-ē)	SC	34·40 N	80·48 W
154	Waterford	(wô'tẽr-fẽrd)	Ire.	52·20 N	7·03 W
107	Waterford		Wi. (Milwaukee In.)	42·46 N	88·13 W
149	Waterloo		Bel. (Brussels In.)	50·44 N	4·24 E
97	Waterloo	(wô-tẽr-lōō')	Can.	43·30 N	80·40 W
97	Waterloo		Can.	45·25 N	72·30 W
117	Waterloo		Il.	38·19 N	90·08 W
107	Waterloo		Ia.	42·30 N	92·22 W
106	Waterloo		Md. (Baltimore In.)	39·11 N	76·50 W
105	Waterloo		NY	42·55 N	76·50 W
90	Waterton-Glacier Intl. Peace Park	(wô'ter-tŭn-glā'shûr)	Mt.-Can.	48·55 N	114·10 W
93	Waterton Lakes Nat. Pk.		Can.	49·05 N	113·50 W
99	Watertown	(wô'tẽr-toun)	Ma. (In.)	42·22 N	71·11 W
105	Watertown		NY	44·00 N	75·55 W
108	Watertown		SD	44·53 N	97·07 W
107	Watertown		Wi.	43·13 N	88·40 W
120	Water Valley	(văl'ē)	Ms.	34·08 N	89·38 W
98	Waterville		Me.	44·34 N	69·37 W
107	Waterville		Mn.	44·10 N	93·35 W
110	Waterville		Wa.	47·38 N	120·04 W
105	Watervliet	(wô'tẽr-vlēt')	NY	42·45 N	73·54 W
148	Watford	(wŏt'fŏrd)	Eng. (London In.)	51·38 N	0·24 W
94	Wathaman L.		Can.	56·55 N	103·43 W
	Watling (I.), see San Salvador				
148	Watlington	(wŏt'lĭng-tŭn)	Eng. (London In.)	51·37 N	1·01 W
116	Watonga	(wŏ-tôŋ'gȧ)	Ok.	35·50 N	98·26 W
217	Watsa	(wät'sä)	Zaire	3·03 N	29·32 E
104	Watseka	(wŏt-sē'kȧ)	Il.	40·45 N	87·45 W
107	Watson	(wŏt'sŭn)	In. (Louisville In.)	38·21 N	85·42 W
90	Watson Lake		Can.	60·18 N	128·50 W
114	Watsonville	(wŏt'sŭn-vĭl)	Ca.	36·55 N	121·46 W
161	Wattenscheid	(vä'tĕn-shīd)	F.R.G. (Ruhr In.)	51·30 N	7·07 E
113	Watts	(wŏts)	Ca. (Los Angeles In.)	33·56 N	118·15 W
120	Watts Bar (R.)	(bär)	Tn.	35·45 N	84·49 W
108	Waubay	(wô'bā)	SD	45·19 N	97·18 W
121	Wauchula	(wô-chōō'lȧ)	Fl. (In.)	27·32 N	81·48 W
107	Wauconda	(wô-kŏn'dȧ)	Il. (Chicago In.)	42·15 N	88·08 W
107	Waukegan	(wŏ-kē'găn)	Il. (Chicago In.)	42·22 N	87·51 W
107	Waukesha	(wô'kē-shô)	Wi. (Milwaukee In.)	43·01 N	88·13 W
109	Waukon	(wô kŏn)	Ia.	43·15 N	91·30 W
109	Waupaca	(wô-păk'ȧ)	Wi.	44·22 N	89·06 W
109	Waupun	(wô-pŭn')	Wi.	43·37 N	88·45 W
116	Waurika	(wô-rē'kȧ)	Ok.	34·09 N	97·59 W
109	Wausau	(wô'sô)	Wi.	44·58 N	89·40 W
109	Wausaukee	(wô-sô'kē)	Wi.	45·22 N	87·58 W
104	Wauseon	(wô'sē-ŏn)	Oh.	41·30 N	84·10 W
109	Wautoma	(wô-tō'mȧ)	Wi.	44·04 N	89·11 W
107	Wauwatosa	(wô-wȧ-t'ō'sȧ)	Wi. (Milwaukee In.)	43·03 N	88·00 W
155	Waveney (R.)	(wāv'nē)	Eng.	52·27 N	1·17 E
109	Waverly	(wā'vẽr-lē)	Ia.	42·43 N	92·29 W
213	Waverly		S. Afr. (Natal In.)	31·54 S	26·29 E
120	Waverly		Tn.	36·04 N	87·46 W
211	Wāw		Sud.	7·41 N	28·00 E
96	Wawa		Can.	47·59 N	84·47 W
211	Wāw al-Kabir		Libya	25·23 N	16·52 E
95	Wawanesa	(wŏ'wŏ-nē'să)	Can.	49·36 N	99·41 W
104	Wawasee (L.)	(wô-wô-sē')	In.	41·25 N	85·45 W
119	Waxahachie	(wăk-sȧ-hăch'ē)	Tx.	32·23 N	96·50 W
121	Waycross	(wā'krôs)	Ga.	31·11 N	82·24 W
120	Wayland	(wā'lănd)	Ky.	37·25 N	82·47 W
99	Wayland		Ma. (In.)	42·23 N	71·22 W

ăt; finăl; rāte; senāte; ärm; åsk; sofȧ; fâre; ch-choose; dh-as th in other; bē; ēvent; bĕt; recĕnt; cratẽr; g-go; gh-guttural g; bĭt; ĭ-short neutral; rīde; K-guttural k as ch in German ich;

Page	Name Pronunciation	Region	Lat. °′	Long. °′
107	Wayne	Mi. (Detroit In.)	42·17 N	83·23 W
108	Wayne	Ne.	42·13 N	97·03 W
106	Wayne	NJ (New York In.)	40·56 N	74·16 W
106	Wayne	Pa. (Philadelphia In.)	40·03 N	75·22 W
121	Waynesboro (wānz'bŭr-ô)	Ga.	33·05 N	82·02 W
105	Waynesboro	Pa.	39·45 N	77·35 W
105	Waynesboro	Va.	38·05 N	78·50 W
105	Waynesburg (wānz'bûrg)	Pa.	39·55 N	80·10 W
120	Waynesville (wānz'vĭl)	NC	35·28 N	82·58 W
116	Waynoka (wā-nō'kȧ)	Ok.	36·34 N	98·52 W
113	Wayzata (wā-zä-tȧ)	Mn. (Minneapolis, St. Paul In.)	44·58 N	93·31 W
184	Wazīrbad	Pak.	32·39 N	74·11 E
95	Weagamow L. (wē'ăg-ă-mou)	Can.	52·53 N	91·22 W
154	Weald, The (Reg.) (wēld)	Eng.	50·58 N	0·15 W
116	Weatherford (wĕ-dhēr-fērd)	Ok.	85·32 N	98·41 W
119	Weatherford	Tx.	32·45 N	97·46 W
148	Weaver (R.) (wē'vēr)	Eng.	53·09 N	2·31 W
110	Weaverville (wē'vēr-vĭl)	Ca.	40·44 N	122·55 W
117	Webb City	Mo.	37·10 N	94·26 W
113	Weber R.	Ut. (Salt Lake City In.)	41·13 N	112·07 W
99	Webster	Ma. (In.)	42·04 N	71·52 W
108	Webster	SD	45·19 N	97·30 W
109	Webster City	Ia.	42·28 N	93·49 W
113	Webster Groves (grōvz)	Mo. (St. Louis In.)	38·36 N	90·22 W
105	Webster Springs (sprĭngz)	WV	38·30 N	80·20 W
220	Weddell Sea (wĕd'ĕl)	Ant.	73·00 S	45·00 W
149	Wedel (vā'dĕl)	F.R.G. (Hamburg In.)	53·35 N	9·42 E
92	Wedge Mtn. (wĕj)	Can.	50·10 N	122·50 W
98	Wedgeport (wĕj'pōrt)	Can.	43·44 N	65·59 W
148	Wednesfield (wĕd''nz-fēld)	Eng.	52·36 N	2·04 W
110	Weed (wēd)	Ca.	41·35 N	122·21 W
213	Weenen (vā'nĕn)	S. Afr. (Natal In.)	28·52 S	30·05 E
155	Weert	Neth.	51·16 N	5·39 E
149	Weesp	Neth. (Amsterdam In.)	52·18 N	5·01 E
159	Wegorzewo (vôŋ-gô'zhĕ-vô)	Pol.	54·14 N	21·46 E
159	Wegrow (vôŋ'grōōf)	Pol.	52·23 N	22·02 E
190	Wei (R.) (wā)	China	35·47 N	114·27 E
192	Weich'ang (wā'chäng')	China	41·50 N	118·00 E
190	Weifang	China	36·43 N	119·08 E
190	Weihai (wa'hăī')	China	37·30 N	122·05 E
192	Wei Ho (R.)	China	34·00 N	108·10 E
188	Weihsi (wā'hsē')	China	27·27 N	99·30 E
190	Weihsien (wā'hsyĕn')	China	36·59 N	115·17 E
158	Weilheim (vīl'hīm')	F.R.G.	47·50 N	11·06 E
158	Weimar (vī'mär)	G.D.R.	50·59 N	11·20 E
192	Weinan	China	34·32 N	109·40 E
205	Weipa	Austl.	12·25 S	141·54 E
95	Weir River (wēr-rĭv-ēr)	Can.	56·49 N	94·04 W
104	Weirton (wēr'tŭn)	WV	40·25 N	80·35 W
110	Weiser (wē'zēr)	Id.	44·15 N	116·58 W
110	Weiser R.	Id.	44·26 N	116·40 W
190	Weishih (wā'shē)	China	34·23 N	114·12 E
158	Weissenburg (vī'sĕn-bōōrgh)	F.R.G.	49·04 N	11·20 E
158	Weissenfels (vī'sĕn-fĕlz)	G.D.R.	51·13 N	11·58 E
159	Wejherowo (vā-hĕ-rô'vô)	Pol.	54·36 N	18·15 E
121	Welch (wĕlch)	WV	37·24 N	81·28 W
121	Weldon (wĕl'dŭn)	NC	36·24 N	77·36 W
117	Weldon (R.)	Mo.	40·22 N	93·39 W
117	Weleetka (wē-lēt'kȧ)	Ok.	35·19 N	96·08 W
203	Welford (wĕl'fērd)	Austl.	25·08 S	144·43 E
218	Welkom (wĕl'kŏm)	S. Afr. (Johannesburg & Pretoria In.)	27·57 S	26·45 E
107	Welland (wĕl'ănd)	Can. (Buffalo In.)	42·59 N	79·13 W
154	Welland (R.)	Eng.	52·38 N	0·40 W
99	Wellesley (wĕlz'lē)	Ma. (In.)	42·18 N	71·17 W
204	Wellesley Is.	Austl.	16·15 S	139·25 E
203	Wellington (wĕl'lĭng-tŭn)	Austl.	32·40 S	148·50 E
148	Wellington	Eng.	52·42 N	2·30 W
117	Wellington	Ks.	37·16 N	97·24 W
205	Wellington	N. Z. (In.)	41·15 S	174·45 E
104	Wellington	Oh.	41·10 N	82·10 W
116	Wellington	Tx.	34·51 N	100·12 W
136	Wellington (I.) (ōō'ĕ'lĕng-tŏn)	Chile	49·30 S	76·30 W
204	Wells (wĕlz)	Austl.	26·35 S	123·40 E
93	Wells	Can.	53·06 N	121·34 W
104	Wells	Mi.	45·50 N	87·00 W
109	Wells	Mn.	43·44 N	93·43 W
110	Wells	Nv.	41·07 N	115·04 W
105	Wellsboro (wĕlz'bŭ-rô)	Pa.	41·45 N	77·15 W
104	Wellsburg (wĕlz'bûrg)	WV	40·10 N	80·40 W
110	Wells Res.	Wa.	48·05 N	119·45 W
104	Wellston (wĕlz'tŭn)	Oh.	39·05 N	82·30 W
117	Wellsville (wĕlz'vĭl)	Mo.	39·04 N	91·33 W
105	Wellsville	NY	42·10 N	78·00 W
104	Wellsville	Oh.	40·35 N	80·40 W
111	Wellsville	Ut.	41·38 N	111·57 W
158	Wels (vĕls)	Aus.	48·10 N	14·01 E
154	Welshpool (wĕlsh'pōōl)	Wales	52·44 N	3·10 W
218	Welverdiend (vĕl-vēr-dēnd')	S. Afr. (Johannesburg & Pretoria In.)	26·23 S	27·16 E
148	Welwyn Garden City (wĕl'ĭn)	Eng. (London In.)	51·46 N	0·17 W
148	Wem (wĕm)	Eng.	52·51 N	2·44 W
217	Wembere (R.)	Tan.	4·35 S	33·55 E
190	Wenan Wa (Swp.) (wĕn'än' wä)	China	38·56 N	116·29 E
110	Wenatchee (wē-năch'ē)	Wa.	47·24 N	120·18 W
110	Wenatchee Mts.	Wa.	47·28 N	121·10 W
193	Wench'ang	China	19·32 N	110·42 E
214	Wenchi	Ghana	7·42 N	2·07 W
193	Wenchou (wĕn'chō)	China	28·00 N	120·40 E
192	Wench'üan (Halunrshan)	China	47·10 N	120·00 E
211	Wendo	Eth.	6·37 N	38·29 E
111	Wendorer	Ut.	40·47 N	114·01 W
89	Wendover (wĕn-dōv'ēr)	Can. (Ottawa In.)	45·34 N	75·07 W
148	Wendover	Eng. (London In.)	51·44 N	0·45 W
99	Wenham (wĕn'ăm)	Ma. (In.)	42·36 N	70·53 W
106	Wenonah (wĕn'ō-nȧ)	NJ (Philadelphia In.)	39·48 N	75·08 W
193	Wenshan	China	23·20 N	104·15 E
190	Wenshang (wĕn'shäng)	China	35·43 N	116·31 E
190	Wenshussu (wĕn'shōō'sĕ)	China	31·55 N	114·47 E
188	Wensu (Aksu) (wĕn'sōō') (äk'sōō')	China	41·45 N	80·30 E
155	Wensum (R.) (wĕn'sŭm)	Eng.	52·45 N	1·08 E
190	Wenteng (wĕn'tĕng')	China	37·14 N	122·03 E
203	Wentworth (wĕnt'wûrth)	Austl.	24·03 S	141·53 E
212	Wepener (wē'pĕn-ēr) (vā'pĕn-ēr)	S. Afr.	29·43 S	27·04 E
149	Werder (vĕr'dĕr)	G.D.R. (Berlin In.)	52·23 N	12·56 E
211	Were Ilu	Eth.	10·39 N	39·21 E
161	Werl (vĕrl)	F.R.G. (Ruhr In.)	51·33 N	7·55 E
161	Werne (vĕr'nĕ)	F.R.G. (Ruhr In.)	51·39 N	7·38 E
149	Werneuchen (vĕr'hoi-kĕn)	G.D.R. (Berlin In.)	52·38 N	13·44 E
158	Werra R. (vĕr'ä)	F.R.G.	51·16 N	9·54 E
202	Werribee	Austl. (Melbourne In.)	37·54 S	144·40 E
202	Werribee (R.)	Austl. (Melbourne In.)	37·40 S	144·37 E
158	Wertach R. (vĕr'täk)	F.R.G.	48·12 N	10·40 E
161	Weseke (vĕ'zĕ-kĕ)	F.R.G. (Ruhr In.)	51·54 N	6·51 E
161	Wesel (vā'zĕl)	F.R.G. (Ruhr In.)	51·39 N	6·37 E
158	Weser R. (vā'zĕr)	F.R.G.	53·08 N	8·35 E
118	Weslaco (wĕs-lā'kō)	Tx.	26·10 N	97·59 W
97	Weslemkoon (L.)	Can.	45·02 N	77·25 W
99	Wesleyville (wĕs'lē-vĭl)	Can.	49·09 N	53·34 W
204	Wessel (Is.) (wĕs'ĕl)	Austl.	11·45 S	136·25 E
218	Wesselsbron (wĕs'ĕl-brŏn)	S. Afr. (Johannesburg & Pretoria In.)	27·51 S	26·22 E
108	Wessington Springs (wĕs'ĭng-tŭn)	SD	44·06 N	98·35 W
122	West, Mt.	C. Z. (In.)	9·10 N	79·52 W
107	West Allis (wĕst-ăl'ĭs)	Wi. (Milwaukee In.)	43·01 N	88·01 W
113	West Alton (ôl'tŭn)	Mo. (St. Louis In.)	38·52 N	90·13 W
119	West B.	Tx. (In.)	29·11 N	95·03 W
109	West Bend (wĕst bĕnd)	Wi.	43·25 N	88·13 W
184	West Bengal (State) (bĕn-gôl')	India	23·30 N	87·30 E
149	West Berlin (bĕr-lēn')	F.R.G. (Berlin In.)	52·31 N	13·20 E
120	West Blocton (blŏk'tŭn)	Al.	33·05 N	87·05 W
99	Westborough (wĕst'bŭr-ô)	Ma. (In.)	42·17 N	71·37 W
99	West Boylston (boil'stŭn)	Ma. (In.)	42·22 N	71·46 W
104	West Branch (wĕst brȧnch)	Mi.	44·15 N	84·10 W
148	West Bridgford (brĭj'fērd)	Eng.	52·55 N	1·08 W
148	West Bromwich (wĕst brŭm'ĭj)	Eng.	52·32 N	1·59 W
98	Westbrook (wĕst'brŏŏk)	Me.	43·41 N	70·23 W
109	Westby (wĕst'bē)	Wi.	43·40 N	90·52 W
129	West Caicos (I.) (käē'kō) (kī'kōs)	Turks & Caicos	21·40 N	72·30 W
204	West Cape Howe (C.)	Austl.	35·15 S	117·30 E
107	West Chester (chĕs'tēr)	Oh. (Cincinnati In.)	39·20 N	84·24 W
106	West Chester	Pa. (Philadelphia In.)	39·57 N	75·36 W
107	West Chicago (chĭ-kä'gō)	Il. (Chicago In.)	41·53 N	88·12 W
121	West Columbia (cŏl'ŭm-bē-ȧ)	SC	33·58 N	81·05 W
119	West Columbia	Tx.	29·08 N	95·39 W
119	West Cote Blanche B. (kōt blänch)	La.	29·30 N	92·17 W
113	West Covina (wĕst kō-vē'nȧ)	Ca. (Los Angeles In.)	34·04 N	117·55 W
109	West Des Moines (dē moin')	Ia.	41·35 N	93·42 W
109	West Des Moines (R.)	Ia.	42·52 N	94·32 W
128	West End	Ba.	26·40 N	78·55 W
148	Westerham (wĕ'stēr'ŭm)	Eng. (London In.)	51·15 N	0·05 E
149	Westerhorn (vĕs'tĕr-hōrn)	F.R.G. (Hamburg In.)	53·52 N	9·41 E
149	Westerlo	Bel. (Brussels In.)	51·05 N	4·57 E
105	Westerly (wĕs'tēr-lē)	RI	41·25 N	71·50 W
158	Western Alps (Mts.)	Switz.-Fr.	46·19 N	7·03 E
204	Western Australia (State) (ôs-trā'lĭ-ȧ)	Austl.	24·15 S	121·30 E
154	Western Downs	Eng.	50·50 N	2·25 W
185	Western Ghāts (Mts.)	India	17·35 N	74·00 E
105	Western Port (wĕs'tērn pōrt)	Md.	39·30 N	79·00 W
209	Western Sahara (sȧ-hä'rȧ)	Afr.	23·05 N	15·33 W
198	Western Samoa	Oceania	14·30 S	172·00 W
168	Western Siberian Lowland	Sov. Un.	63·37 N	72·45 E
104	Westerville (wĕs'tēr-vĭl)	Oh.	40·10 N	83·00 W
158	Westerwald (For.) (vĕs'tĕr-väld)	F.R.G.	50·35 N	7·45 E
105	Westfield (wĕst'fēld)	Ma.	42·05 N	72·45 W
106	Westfield	NJ (New York In.)	40·39 N	74·21 W
106	Westfield (wĕst'fēld)	NY	42·20 N	79·40 W
99	Westford (wĕst'fērd)	Ma. (In.)	42·35 N	71·26 W
106	West Frankfort (frăŋk'fŭrt)	Il.	37·55 N	88·55 W
148	West Ham	Eng. (London In.)	51·30 N	0·00
105	West Hartford (härt'fērd)	Ct.	41·45 N	72·45 W
117	West Helena (hĕl'ĕn-ȧ)	Ar.	34·32 N	90·39 W
123	West Indies (Reg.) (ĭn'dēz)	N. A.	19·00 N	78·30 W
113	West Jordan (jôr'dăn)	Ut. (Salt Lake City In.)	40·37 N	111·56 W
148	West Kirby (kûr'bē)	Eng.	53·22 N	3·11 W
104	West Lafayette (lä-fȧ-yĕt')	In.	40·25 N	86·55 W
107	Westlake	Oh. (Cleveland In.)	41·27 N	81·55 W
218	Westleigh (wĕst-lē)	S. Afr. (Johannesburg & Pretoria In.)	27·39 S	27·18 E
109	West Liberty (wĕst lĭb'ēr-tĭ)	Ia.	41·34 N	91·15 W
112	West Linn (lĭn)	Or. (Portland In.)	45·22 N	122·37 W
93	Westlock (wĕst'lŏk)	Can.	54·09 N	113·52 W
117	West Memphis	Ar.	35·08 N	90·11 W
113	Westminster (wĕst'mĭn-stēr)	Ca. (Los Angeles In.)	33·45 N	117·59 W
105	Westminster	Md.	39·40 N	76·55 W
120	Westminster	SC	34·38 N	83·10 W
89	Westmount (wĕst'mount)	Can. (Montréal In.)	45·29 N	73·36 W
99	West Newbury (nū'bēr-ē)	Ma. (In.)	42·47 N	70·57 W
107	West Newton (nū'tŭn)	Pa. (Pittsburgh In.)	40·12 N	79·45 W
106	West New York (nû yŏrk)	NJ (New York In.)	40·47 N	74·01 W
117	West Nishnabotna (R.) (nĭsh-nȧ-bŏt'nȧ)	Ia.	40·56 N	95·37 W
99	Weston (wĕs'tŭn)	Ma. (In.)	42·22 N	71·18 W
104	Weston	WV	39·00 N	80·30 W
218	Westonaria	S. Afr. (Johannesburg & Pretoria In.)	26·19 S	27·38 E
154	Weston-super-Mare (wĕs'tŭn sū'pēr-mā'rē)	Eng.	51·23 N	3·00 W
106	West Orange (wĕst ŏr'ĕnj)	NJ (New York In.)	40·46 N	74·14 W
121	West Palm Beach (päm bēch)	Fl. (In.)	26·44 N	80·04 W
120	West Pensacola (pĕn-sȧ-kō'lȧ)	Fl.	30·24 N	87·18 W
112	West Pittsburg (pĭts'bûrg)	Ca. (San Francisco In.)	38·02 N	121·56 W
117	Westplains (wĕst-plānz')	Mo.	36·42 N	91·51 W
120	West Point	Ga.	32·52 N	85·10 W
120	West Point	Ms.	33·36 N	88·39 W
108	Westpoint	Ne.	41·50 N	96·00 W
106	West Point	NY (New York In.)	41·23 N	73·58 W
113	West Point	Ut. (Salt Lake City In.)	41·07 N	112·05 W
105	West Point	Va.	37·25 N	76·50 W
106	Westport (wĕst'pōrt)	Ct. (New York In.)	41·07 N	73·22 W
154	Westport	Ire.	53·44 N	9·36 W
112	Westport (wĕst'pôrt)	Or. (Portland In.)	46·08 N	123·22 W
154	Westray (I.) (wĕs'trā)	Scot.	59·19 N	3·05 W
92	West Road (R.) (rōd)	Can.	53·00 N	124·00 W
113	West St. Paul (sânt pôl')	Mn. (Minneapolis, St. Paul In.)	44·55 N	93·05 W
129	West Sand Spit (I.)	Ba.	21·25 N	72·10 W
155	West Schelde (R.)	Neth.	51·25 N	3·30 E
112	West Slope	Or. (Portland In.)	45·30 N	122·46 W
115	West Tavaputs Plat. (wĕst tăv'ȧ-pōōts)	Ut.	39·45 N	110·35 W
104	West Terre Haute (tĕr-ē hōt')	In.	39·30 N	87·30 W
109	West Union (ūn'yŭn)	Ia.	42·58 N	91·48 W
119	West University Place	Tx. (In.)	29·43 N	95·26 W
107	Westview (wĕst'vū)	Oh. (Cleveland In.)	41·21 N	81·54 W
107	West View	Pa. (Pittsburgh In.)	40·31 N	80·02 W
99	Westville (wĕst'vĭl)	Can.	45·34 N	62·43 W
104	Westville	Il.	40·00 N	87·40 W
103	West Virginia (State) (wĕst vēr-jĭn'ĭ-ȧ)	U. S.	39·00 N	80·50 W
114	West Walker (R.) (wôk'ēr)	Ca.	38·25 N	119·25 W
106	West Warwick (wŏr'ĭk)	RI (Providence In.)	41·42 N	71·31 W
106	Westwego (wĕst-wē'gō)	La. (New Orleans In.)	29·55 N	90·09 W

ng-sing; ŋ-baŋk; N-nasalized n; nŏd; cŏmmit; ōld; ôbey; ôrder; fōōd; fŏŏt; ou-out; s-soft; sh-dish; th-thin; pūre; ûnite; ûrn; stŭd; circŭs; ü-as "y" in study; '-indeterminate vowel.

368 Westwood — Wilton PRONOUNCING INDEX

Page	Name Pronunciation Region	Lat. °′	Long. °′
114	Westwood (wĕst′wŏŏd) Ca.	40·18 N	121·00 W
113	Westwood Ks. (Kansas City In.)	39·03 N	94·37 W
99	Westwood Ma. (In.)	42·13 N	71·14 W
106	Westwood NJ (New York In.)	40·59 N	74·02 W
203	West Wyalong (wī′alông) Austl.	34·00 S	147·20 E
197	Wetar (I.) (wĕt′ár) Indon.	7·34 S	126·00 E
93	Wetaskiwin (wĕ-tăs′kê-wŏn) Can.	52·58 N	113·22 W
113	Wetmore (wĕt′mōr) Tx. (San Antonio In.)	29·34 N	98·25 W
161	Wettin (vĕ′tēn) F.R.G. (Ruhr In.)	51·23 N	7·23 E
120	Wetumpka (wê-tŭmp′kȧ) Al.	32·33 N	86·12 W
161	Wetzlar (vets′lär) F.R.G.	50·35 N	8·30 E
197	Wewak (wā-wäk′) Pap. N. Gui.	3·19 S	143·30 E
117	Wewoka (wê-wō′kȧ) Ok.	35·09 N	96·30 W
154	Wexford (wĕks′fērd) Ire.	52·20 N	6·30 W
148	Weybridge (wā′brĭj) Eng. (London In.)	51·20 N	0·26 W
94	Weyburn (wā′-bûrn) Can.	49·41 N	103·52 W
211	Weyib (R.) Eth.	6·25 N	41·21 E
154	Weymouth (wā′mŭth) Eng.	50·37 N	2·34 W
99	Weymouth Ma. (In.)	42·44 N	70·57 W
107	Weymouth Oh. (Cleveland In.)	41·11 N	81·48 W
128	Whale Cay (I.) Ba.	24·50 N	77·45 W
128	Whale Cay Chans. Ba.	26·45 N	77·10 W
154	Wharfe (R.) (hwôr′fê) Eng.	54·01 N	1·53 W
106	Wharton (hwôr′tŭn) NJ (New York In.)	40·54 N	74·35 W
119	Wharton Tx.	29·19 N	96·06 W
109	What Cheer (hwŏt chēr) Ia.	41·23 N	92·24 W
112	Whatcom, L. (hwät′kŭm) Wa. (Portland In.)	48·44 N	123·34 W
93	Whatshan L. (wŏt′-shăn) Can.	50·00 N	118·03 W
111	Wheatland (hwēt′lănd) Wy.	42·04 N	104·52 W
107	Wheaton (hwē′tŭn) Il. (Chicago In.)	41·52 N	88·06 W
106	Wheaton Md. (Baltimore In.)	39·05 N	77·05 W
108	Wheaton Mn.	45·48 N	96·29 W
115	Wheeler Pk. Nv.	38·58 N	114·15 W
107	Wheeling (hwēl′ĭng) Il. (Chicago In.)	42·08 N	87·54 W
104	Wheeling WV	40·05 N	80·45 W
137	Wheelwright (ŏŏē′l-rē′gt) Arg. (Buenos Aires In.)	33·46 S	61·14 W
112	Whidbey I. (hwĭd′bê) Wa. (Seattle In.)	48·13 N	122·50 W
106	Whippany (hwĭp′á-nē) NJ (New York In.)	40·49 N	74·25 W
120	Whistler (hwĭs′lēr) Al.	30·46 N	88·07 W
97	Whitby (hwĭt′bê) Can.	43·50 N	79·00 W
148	Whitchurch (hwĭt′chûrch) Eng.	52·58 N	2·49 W
97	White (L.) Can.	45·15 N	76·35 W
96	White (L.) Can.	48·47 N	85·50 W
96	White (R.) Can.	48·34 N	85·46 W
117	White (R.) Ar.	34·32 N	91·11 W
115	White (R.) Co.	40·10 N	108·55 W
104	White (R.) In.	39·15 N	86·45 W
108	White (R.) SD	43·41 N	99·48 W
108	White (R.), South Fork SD	43·13 N	101·04 W
116	White (R.) Tx.	36·25 N	102·20 W
105	White (R.) Vt.	43·45 N	72·35 W
114	White, Mt. Ca.	37·38 N	118·13 W
99	White B. Can.	50·00 N	56·30 W
113	White Bear Lake Mn. (Minneapolis, St. Paul In.)	45·05 N	93·01 W
113	White Bear L. Mn. (Minneapolis, St. Paul In.)	45·04 N	92·58 W
95	White Bear Ind. Res. Can.	49·15 N	102·15 W
119	White Castle La.	30·10 N	91·09 W
112	White Center Wa. (Seattle In.)	47·31 N	122·21 W
104	White Cloud Mi.	43·35 N	85·45 W
93	Whitecourt (wĭt′-côrt) Can.	54·09 N	115·41 W
108	White Earth (R.) ND	48·30 N	102·44 W
108	White Earth Ind. Res. Mn.	47·18 N	95·42 W
109	Whiteface (R.) (whĭt′fās) Mn.	47·12 N	92·13 W
105	Whitefield (hwĭt′fēld) NH	44·20 N	71·35 W
111	Whitefish (hwĭt′fĭsh) Mt.	48·24 N	114·25 W
109	Whitefish (B.) Mi.	46·36 N	84·50 W
109	Whitefish (R.) Mi.	46·12 N	86·56 W
95	Whitefish B. Can.	49·26 N	94·14 W
107	Whitefish Bay Wi. (Milwaukee In.)	43·07 N	77·54 W
117	White Hall Il.	39·26 N	90·23 W
104	Whitehall (hwĭt′hôl) Mi.	43·20 N	86·20 W
105	Whitehall NY	43·30 N	73·25 W
154	Whitehaven (hwĭt′hā-vĕn) Eng.	54·35 N	3·30 W
112	Whitehorn, Pt. (hwĭt′hôrn) Wa. (Vancouver In.)	48·54 N	122·48 W
90	Whitehorse (whĭt′hôrs) Can.	60·39 N	135·01 W
119	White L. La.	29·40 N	92·35 W
98	White Mts. Me.	44·22 N	71·15 W
105	White Mts. NH	42·20 N	71·05 W
108	Whitemouth (L.) Can.	49·14 N	95·40 W
211	White Nile (Abyad, Al-Bahr al-) (R.) Sud.	14·00 N	32·35 E
109	White Otter (L.) Can.	49·15 N	91·48 W
90	White P. Ak.-Can.	59·35 N	135·03 W
106	White Plains NY (New York In.)	41·02 N	73·47 W
96	White River Can.	48·38 N	85·23 W
104	White R., East Fork In.	38·45 N	86·20 W
110	White R. Wa.	47·07 N	121·48 W
115	White River Plat. Co.	39·45 N	107·50 W
112	White Rock Can. (Vancouver In.)	49·01 N	122·49 W
113	Whiterock Res. (hwĭt′rŏk) Tx. (Dallas, Fort Worth In.)	32·51 N	96·40 W
92	Whitesail L. (whīt′-sāl) Can.	53·30 N	127·00 W
115	White Sands Natl. Mon. NM	32·50 N	106·20 W
170	White Sea Sov. Un.	66·00 N	40·00 E
113	White Settlement Tx. (Dallas, Fort Worth In.)	32·45 N	97·28 W
111	White Sulphur Springs Mt.	46·32 N	110·49 W
213	White Umfolzi (R.) (ŭm-fô-lō′zê) S. Afr. (Natal In.)	28·12 S	30·55 E
121	Whiteville (hwĭt′vĭl) NC	34·18 N	78·45 W
214	White Volta (R.) Ghana	9·40 N	1·10 W
109	Whitewater (whĭt-wŏt′ēr) Wi.	42·49 N	88·40 W
108	Whitewater (L.) Can.	49·14 N	100·39 W
121	Whitewater B. Fl. (In.)	25·16 N	80·21 W
111	Whitewater Cr. Mt.	48·50 N	107·50 W
95	Whitewater L. Can.	49·15 N	100·20 W
107	Whitewater R. In. (Cincinnati In.)	39·19 N	84·55 W
120	Whitewell (hwĭt′wĕl) Tn.	35·11 N	85·31 W
117	Whitewright (hwĭt′rīt) Tx.	33·33 N	96·25 W
154	Whitham (R.) (wĭth′ăm) Eng.	53·08 N	0·15 W
107	Whiting (hwĭt′ĭng) In. (Chicago In.)	41·41 N	87·30 W
99	Whitinsville (hwĭt′ĕns-vĭl) Ma. (In.)	42·06 N	71·40 W
99	Whitman (hwĭt′măn) Ma. (In.)	42·05 N	70·57 W
121	Whitmire (hwĭt′mīr) SC	34·30 N	81·40 W
114	Whitney, Mt. Ca.	36·34 N	118·18 W
119	Whitney L. (hwĭt′nê) Tx.	32·02 N	97·36 W
148	Whitstable (wĭt′stáb'l) Eng. (London In.)	51·22 N	1·03 E
205	Whitsunday (I.) (hwĭt′s'n-dā) Austl.	20·16 S	149·00 E
113	Whittier (hwĭt′ĭ-ēr) Ca. (Los Angeles In.)	33·58 N	118·02 W
213	Whittlesea (wĭt′l′sē) S. Afr. (Natal In.)	32·11 S	26·51 E
148	Whitworth (hwĭt′wŭrth) Eng.	53·40 N	2·10 W
203	Whyalla (hwī-ăl′ȧ) Austl.	33·00 S	137·32 E
92	Whymper, Mt. (wĭm′-pēr) Can.	48·57 N	124·10 W
96	Wiarton (wī′ăr-tŭn) Can.	44·45 N	80·45 W
117	Wichita (wĭch′ĭ-tô) Ks.	37·42 N	97·21 W
116	Wichita (R.) Tx.	33·50 N	99·38 W
116	Wichita Falls (fôls) Tx.	33·54 N	98·29 W
154	Wichita Mts. Ok.	34·48 N	98·43 W
154	Wick (wĭk) Scot.	58·25 N	3·05 W
106	Wickatunk (wĭk′ă-tŭnk) NJ (New York In.)	40·21 N	74·15 W
115	Wickenburg Az.	33·58 N	112·44 W
107	Wickliffe (wĭk′klĭf) Oh. (Cleveland In.)	41·37 N	81·29 W
	Wicklow, see Cill Mantainn		
154	Wicklow Mts. (wĭk′lō) Ire.	52·49 N	6·20 W
112	Wickup Mtn. (wĭk′ŭp) Or. (Portland In.)	46·06 N	123·35 W
105	Wiconisco (wĭ-kŏn′ĭs-kō) Pa.	43·35 N	76·45 W
104	Widen (wī′dĕn) WV	38·25 N	80·55 W
148	Widnes (wĭd′nĕs) Eng.	53·21 N	2·44 W
158	Wieden (vē′dĕn) F.R.G.	49·41 N	12·09 E
159	Wieliczka (vyĕ-lēch′kȧ) Pol.	49·58 N	20·06 E
159	Wieluń (vyĕ′lōōn′) Pol.	51·13 N	18·33 E
149	Wien (Vienna (vēn) (vê-ĕn′ä) Aus. (Vienna In.)	48·13 N	16·22 E
149	Wien (State) Aus. (Vienna In.)	48·11 N	16·23 E
158	Wiener Neustadt (vē′nĕr noi′shtät) Aus.	47·48 N	16·15 E
149	Wiener Wald (For.) Aus. (Vienna In.)	48·09 N	16·05 E
159	Wieprz, R. (vyĕpzh) Pol.	51·25 N	22·45 E
119	Wiergate (wēr′gāt) Tx.	31·00 N	93·42 W
158	Wiesbaden (vēs′bä-dĕn) F.R.G.	50·05 N	8·15 E
148	Wigan (wĭg′ăn) Eng.	53·33 N	2·37 W
120	Wiggins (wĭg′ĭnz) Ms.	30·51 N	89·05 W
154	Wight, Isle of (I.) (wīt) Eng.	50·44 N	1·17 W
117	Wilber (wĭl′bēr) Ne.	40·29 N	96·57 W
117	Wilburton (wĭl′bēr-tŭn) Ok.	34·54 N	95·18 W
203	Wilcannia (wĭl-cān-ĭȧ) Austl.	31·30 S	143·30 E
149	Wildau (vēl′dou) G.D.R. (Berlin In.)	52·20 N	13·39 E
149	Wildberg (vēl′bĕrgh) G.D.R.(Berlin In.)	52·52 N	12·39 E
94	Wildcat Hill (wīld′kăt) Can.	53·17 N	102·30 W
93	Wildhay (R.) (wīld′-hā) Can.	53·15 N	117·20 W
113	Wildomar (wĭl′dô-mär) Ca. (Los Angeles In.)	33·35 N	117·17 W
108	Wild Rice (R.) Mn.	47·10 N	96·40 W
108	Wild Rice (R.) ND	46·10 N	97·12 W
113	Wild Rice L. Mn. (Duluth In.)	46·54 N	92·10 W
158	Wild Spitze Pk. Aus.	46·49 N	10·50 E
105	Wildwood NJ	39·00 N	74·50 W
116	Wiley (wī′lê) Co.	38·08 N	102·41 W
218	Wilge R. (wĭl′jê) S. Afr. (Johannesburg & Pretoria In.)	25·38 S	29·09 E
218	Wilge R. S. Afr. (Johannesburg & Pretoria In.)	27·27 S	28·46 E
205	Wilhelm, Mt. Pap. N. Gui.	5·58 S	144·58 E
135	Wilhelmina Gebergte (Mts.) Sur.	4·30 N	57·00 W
158	Wilhelmshaven (vēl-hĕlms-hä′fĕn) F.R.G.	53·30 N	8·10 E
149	Wilhemina, Kanal (can.) Neth. (Amsterdam In.)	51·37 N	4·55 E
105	Wilkes-Barre (wĭlks′băr-ê) Pa.	41·15 N	75·50 W
220	Wilkes Land Ant.	71·00 S	126·00 E
112	Wilkeson (wĭl-kē′sŭn) Wa. (Seattle In.)	47·06 N	122·03 W
94	Wilkie (wĭlk′ē) Can.	52·25 N	108·43 W
107	Wilkinsburg (wĭl′kĭnz-bûrg) Pa. Pittsburgh In.)	40·26 N	79·53 W
110	Willamette R. Or.	44·15 N	123·13 W
104	Willard (wĭl′ȧrd) Oh.	41·00 N	82·50 W
113	Willard Ut. (Salt Lake City In.)	41·24 N	112·02 W
115	Willcox (wĭl′kŏks) Az.	32·15 N	109·50 W
134	Willemstad Neth. Antilles	12·12 N	68·58 W
148	Willesden (wĭlz′dĕn) Eng. (London In.)	51·31 N	0·17 W
93	W. A. C. Bennett Dam Can.	56·01 N	122·10 W
204	William Creek (wĭl′yăm) Austl.	28·45 S	136·20 E
115	Williams (wĭl′yămz) Az.	35·15 N	112·15 W
128	Williams (I.) Ba.	25·30 N	78·30 W
120	Williamsburg (wĭl′yămz-bûrg) Ky.	36·42 N	84·09 W
107	Williamsburg Oh. (Cincinnati In.)	39·04 N	84·02 W
121	Williamsburg Va.	37·15 N	76·41 W
93	Williams Lake Can.	52·08 N	122·09 W
104	Williamson (wĭl′yăm-sŭn) WV	37·40 N	82·15 W
105	Williamsport Md.	39·35 N	77·45 W
105	Williamsport Pa.	41·15 N	77·05 W
121	Williamston (wĭl′yămz-tŭn) NC	35·50 N	77·04 W
121	Williamston SC	34·36 N	82·30 W
104	Williamstown (wĭl′yămz-toun) WV	39·20 N	81·30 W
107	Williamsville (wĭl′yăm-vĭl) NY (Buffalo In.)	42·58 N	78·46 W
105	Willimantic (wĭl-ĭ-măn′tĭk) Ct.	41·40 N	72·10 W
119	Willis (wĭl′ĭs) Tx.	30·24 N	95·29 W
205	Willis Is. Austl.	16·15 S	150·30 E
108	Williston (wĭl′ĭs-tŭn) ND	48·08 N	103·38 W
92	Williston, L. Can.	55·40 N	123·40 W
93	Willmar (wĭl′mär) Mn.	45·07 N	95·05 W
107	Willoughby (wĭl′ô-bê) Oh. (Cleveland In.)	41·39 N	81·25 W
111	Willow Cr. (wĭl′ô) Mt.	48·45 N	111·34 W
110	Willow Cr. Or.	44·21 N	117·34 W
106	Willow Grove Pa. (Philadelphia In.)	40·07 N	75·07 W
107	Willowick (wĭl′ô-wĭk) Oh. (Cleveland In.)	41·39 N	81·28 W
212	Willowmore (wĭl′ô-môr) S. Afr.	33·15 S	23·37 E
107	Willow Run (wĭl′ô rŭn) Mi. (Detroit In.)	42·16 N	83·34 W
114	Willows (wĭl′ōz) Ca.	39·32 N	122·11 W
117	Willow Springs (sprĭngz) Mo.	36·59 N	91·56 W
213	Willowvale (wĭ-lô′vāl) S. Afr. (Natal In.)	32·17 S	28·32 E
119	Wills Point (wĭlz point) Tx.	32·42 N	96·02 W
113	Wilmer (wĭl′mēr) Tx. (Dallas, Fort Worth In.)	32·35 N	96·40 W
107	Wilmette (wĭl-mĕt′) Il. (Chicago In.)	42·04 N	87·42 W
203	Wilmington Austl.	32·39 S	138·07 E
113	Wilmington (wĭl′mĭng-tŭn) Ca. (Los Angeles In.)	33·46 N	118·16 W
106	Wilmington De. (Philadelphia In.)	39·45 N	75·33 W
107	Wilmington Il. (Chicago In.)	41·19 N	88·09 W
99	Wilmington Ma. (In.)	42·34 N	71·10 W
121	Wilmington NC	34·12 N	77·56 W
104	Wilmington Oh.	39·20 N	83·50 W
104	Wilmore (wĭl′mōr) Ky.	37·50 N	84·35 W
148	Wilmslow (wĭlmz′ lō) Eng.	53·19 N	2·14 W
	Wilno, see Vilnius		
218	Wilpoort S. Afr. (Johannesburg & Pretoria In.)	26·57 S	26·17 E
117	Wilson (wĭl′sŭn) Ar.	35·35 N	90·02 W
121	Wilson NC	35·42 N	77·55 W
117	Wilson Ok.	34·09 N	97·27 W
120	Wilson, L. Al.	34·45 N	86·58 W
120	Wilson (R.) Al.	34·53 N	87·28 W
202	Wilson, Pt. Austl. (Melbourne In.)	38·05 S	144·31 E
113	Wilson, Mt. Ca. (Los Angeles In.)	34·15 N	118·06 W
111	Wilson Pk. Ut.	40·46 N	110·27 W
203	Wilson's Prom. (wĭl′sŭnz) Austl.	39·05 S	146·50 E
113	Wilsonville (wĭl′sŭn-vĭl) Il. (St. Louis In.)	39·04 N	89·52 W
149	Wilstedt (vēl′shtĕt) F.R.G. (Hamburg In.)	53·45 N	10·04 E
149	Wilster (vēl′stēr) F.R.G. (Hamburg In.)	53·55 N	9·23 E
106	Wilton (wĭl′tŭn) Ct. (New York In.)	41·11 N	73·25 W

ăt; finăl; rāte; senâte; ärm; ȧsk; sofȧ; fâre; ch-choose; dh-as th in other; bē; êvent; bĕt; recĕnt; cratēr; g-go; gh-guttural g; bĭt; ĭ-short neutral; rīde; K-guttural k as ch in German ich;

PRONOUNCING INDEX

Wilton — Wulanhata 369

Page	Name Pronunciation Region	Lat. °′	Long. °′
108	Wilton....................ND	47·09 N	100·47 W
204	Wiluna (wĭ-lōō'nȧ).........Austl.	26·35 S	120·25 E
104	Winamac (wĭn'ȧ măk).........In.	41·05 N	86·40 W
218	Winburg (wĭm-bûrg).......S. Afr. (Johannesburg & Pretoria In.)	28·31 S	27·02 E
113	Winchester (wĭn'chĕs-tẽr) Ca. (Los Angeles In.)	33·41 N	117·06 W
154	Winchester.................Eng.	51·04 N	1·20 W
110	Winchester..................Id.	46·14 N	116·39 W
104	Winchester..................In.	40·10 N	84·50 W
104	Winchester.................Ky.	38·00 N	84·15 W
99	Winchester......Ma. (Boston In.)	42·28 N	71·09 W
105	Winchester.................NH	42·45 N	72·25 W
115	Winchester..................Tn.	35·11 N	86·06 W
105	Winchester..................Va.	39·10 N	78·10 W
105	Windber (wĭnd'bẽr)..........Pa.	40·15 N	78·45 W
108	Wind Cave Natl. Park........SD	43·36 N	103·53 W
115	Winder (wīn'dẽr)............Ga.	33·58 N	83·43 W
154	Windermere (wĭn'dẽr-mēr)...Eng.	54·25 N	2·59 W
93	Windfall (wĭnd'fôl).........Can.	54·11 N	116·15 W
105	Windham (wĭnd'ăm)..........Ct.	41·45 N	72·05 W
99	Windham.......NH (Boston In.)	42·49 N	71·21 W
212	Windhoek (vĭnt'hŏŏk)....Namibia	22·05 S	17·10 E
107	Wind L......Wi. (Milwaukee In.)	42·49 N	88·06 W
118	Wind Mtn...................NM	32·02 N	105·30 W
109	Windom (wĭn'dŭm)..........Mn.	43·50 N	95·04 W
203	Windora (wĭn-dō'rȧ).......Austl.	25·15 S	142·50 E
111	Wind R.....................Wy.	43·17 N	109·02 W
111	Wind River Ind. Res.........Wy.	43·07 N	109·08 W
111	Wind River Ra..............Wy.	43·19 N	109·47 W
202	Windsor (wĭn'zẽr) Austl. (Sydney In.)	33·37 S	150·49 E
107	Windsor.......Can. (Detroit In.)	42·19 N	83·00 W
98	Windsor...................Can.	44·59 N	64·08 W
99	Windsor...................Can.	48·57 N	55·40 W
116	Windsor....................Co.	40·27 N	104·51 W
148	Windsor.......Eng. (London In.)	51·27 N	0·37 W
117	Windsor....................Mo.	38·32 N	93·31 W
98	Windsor....................Vt.	43·30 N	72·25 W
121	Windsor....................NC	35·58 N	76·57 W
123	Windward Is. (wind'wẽrd)...N. A.	12·45 N	61·40 W
129	Windward Pass............N. A.	19·30 N	74·20 W
94	Winefred L.................Can.	55·30 N	110·35 W
117	Winfield...................Ks.	37·14 N	97·00 W
111	Winifred (wĭn ĭ frĕd).........Mt.	47·35 N	109·20 W
91	Winisk (R.)................Can.	54·30 N	86·30 W
118	Wink (wĭŋk)................Tx.	31·48 N	103·06 W
95	Winkler (wĭnk'lẽr)..........Can.	49·11 N	97·56 W
214	Winneba (wĭn'ē-bȧ).......Ghana	5·25 N	0·36 W
109	Winnebago (wĭn'ē-bā'gō).....Mn.	43·45 N	94·08 W
109	Winnebago, L...............Wi.	44·09 N	88·10 W
108	Winnebago Ind. Res..........Ne.	42·15 N	96·06 W
110	Winnemucca (wĭn-ē-mŭk'ȧ)...Nv.	40·59 N	117·43 W
114	Winnemucca (L.).............Nv.	40·06 N	119·07 W
108	Winner (wĭn'ẽr)..............SD	43·22 N	99·50 W
107	Winnetka (wĭ-nĕt'kȧ) Il. (Chicago In.)	42·07 N	87·44 W
111	Winnett (wĭn'ĕt)............Mt.	47·01 N	108·20 W
119	Winnfield (wĭn'fēld).........La.	31·56 N	92·39 W
109	Winnibigoshish (L.) (wĭn'ĭ-bĭ-gō'shĭsh).Mn.	47·30 N	93·45 W
89	Winnipeg (wĭn'ĭ-pĕg) Can. (Winnipeg In.)	49·53 N	97·09 W
95	Winnipeg, L................Can.	52·00 N	97·00 W
90	Winnipeg (R.)..............Can.	52·20 N	95·54 W
95	Winnipeg Beach............Can.	50·31 N	96·58 W
95	Winnipegosis (wĭn'ĭ-pē-gō'sĭs).Can.	51·39 N	99·56 W
95	Winnipegosis (L.)...........Can.	52·30 N	100·00 W
105	Winnipesaukee (L.) (wĭn'ē-pē-sô'kē).NH	43·40 N	71·20 W
119	Winnsboro (wĭnz'bŭr'ô).......La.	32·09 N	91·42 W
121	Winnsboro..................SC	34·29 N	81·05 W
117	Winnsboro..................Tx.	32·56 N	95·15 W
89	Winona (wĭ-nō'nȧ) Can. (Toronto In.)	43·13 N	79·39 W
109	Winona.....................Mn.	44·03 N	91·40 W
120	Winona.....................Ms.	33·29 N	89·43 W
105	Winooski (wĭ-nōōs-kē)........Vt.	44·30 N	73·10 W
149	Winsen (Luhe) (vēn'zĕn) (lōō'hĕ) F.R.G. (Hamburg In.)	53·22 N	10·13 E
148	Winsford (wĭnz'fẽrd)........Eng.	53·11 N	2·30 W
115	Winslow (wĭnz'lō)............Az.	35·00 N	110·45 W
112	Winslow........Wa. (Seattle In.)	47·38 N	122·31 W
105	Winsted (wĭn'stĕd)...........Ct.	41·55 N	73·05 W
148	Winster (wĭn'stẽr)..........Eng.	53·08 N	1·38 W
121	Winston-Salem (wĭn stŭn-sā'lĕm) NC	36·05 N	80·15 W
213	Winterberge (Mts.) S. Afr. (Natal In.)	32·18 S	26·25 E
121	Winter Garden (wĭn'tẽr gär'd'n) Fl. (In.)	28·32 N	81·35 W
92	Winter Harbour............Can.	50·31 N	128·02 W
121	Winter Haven (hā'vĕn)...Fl. (In.)	28·01 N	81·38 W
95	Wintering L. (wĭn'tẽr-ĭng)...Can.	55·24 N	97·42 W
121	Winter Park (pärk)......Fl. (In.)	28·35 N	81·21 W
118	Winters (wĭn'tẽrz)...........Tx.	31·59 N	99·58 W
109	Winterset (wĭn'tẽr-sĕt)........Ia.	41·19 N	94·03 W
161	Winterswijk.....Neth. (Ruhr In.)	51·58 N	6·44 E
158	Winterthur (vĭn'tĕr-tōōr)...Switz.	47·30 N	8·32 E
213	Winterton.....S. Afr. (Natal In.)	28·51 S	29·33 E
98	Winthrop (wĭn'thrŭp)........Me.	44·19 N	70·00 W
99	Winthrop..............Ma. (In.)	42·23 N	70·59 W
109	Winthrop...................Mn.	44·31 N	94·20 W
205	Winton (wĭn-tŭn)..........Austl.	22·17 S	143·08 E
161	Wipperfürth (vĕ'pĕr-fürt) F.R.G. (Ruhr In.)	51·07 N	7·23 E
148	Wirksworth (wûrks'wûrth)...Eng.	53·05 N	1·35 W
103	Wisconsin (State) (wĭs-kŏn'sĭn) U. S.	44·30 N	91·00 W
109	Wisconsin (R.)..............Wi.	43·14 N	90·34 W
109	Wisconsin Dells.............Wi.	43·38 N	89·46 W
109	Wisconsin Rapids...........Wi.	44·24 N	89·50 W
108	Wishek (wĭsh'ĕk)............ND	46·15 N	99·34 W
159	Wisla (Vistula) R. (vēs'wȧ) (vĭs'tû-lȧ).Pol.	52·48 N	19·02 E
159	Wisloka R. (vēs-wô'kȧ).......Pol.	49·55 N	21·26 E
135	Wismar (wĭs'mȧr)...........Guy.	5·58 N	58·15 W
158	Wismar (vĭs'mär).........G.D.R.	53·53 N	11·28 E
108	Wisner (wĭz'nẽr).............Ne.	42·00 N	96·55 W
161	Wissembourg (vē-säɴ-bōōr')...Fr.	49·03 N	7·58 E
117	Wister, L. (vĭs'tẽr)...........Ok.	35·02 N	94·52 W
218	Witbank (wĭt-băŋk)........S. Afr. (Johannesburg & Pretoria In.)	25·53 S	29·14 E
213	Witberg (Mtn.) S. Afr. (Natal In.)	30·32 S	27·18 E
148	Witham (wĭdh'ăm) Eng. (London In.)	51·48 N	0·37 E
148	Witham (R.)...............Eng.	53·11 N	0·20 W
107	Withamsville (wĭdh'ămz-vĭl) Oh. (Cincinnati In.)	39·04 N	84·16 W
121	Withlacoochee (R.) (wĭth-lȧ-kōō'chē).Fl. (In.)	28·58 N	82·30 W
120	Withlacoochee (R.)..........Ga.	31·15 N	83·30 W
113	Withrow (wĭdh'rō)...........Mn. (Minneapolis, St. Paul In.)	45·08 N	92·54 W
148	Witney (wĭt'nē) Eng. (London In.)	51·45 N	1·30 W
104	Witt (vĭt)....................Il.	39·10 N	89·15 W
161	Witten (vē'tĕn).F.R.G. (Ruhr In.)	51·26 N	7·19 E
158	Wittenberg (vē'tĕn-bĕrgh).G.D.R.	51·53 N	12·40 E
158	Wittenberge (vĭt-ĕn-bĕr'gē) G.D.R.	52·59 N	11·45 E
158	Wittlich (vĭt'lĭk)..........F.R.G.	49·58 N	6·54 E
213	Witu (wē'tōō)..............Ken.	2·18 S	40·28 E
213	Witwatersberg (Mts.) (wĭt-wôr-tẽrz-bûrg).S. Afr. (Johannesburg & Pretotia In.)	25·58 S	27·53 E
218	Witwatersrand (Ridge) (wĭt-wôr'tẽrs-rănd).S. Afr. (Johannesburg & Pretoria In.)	25·55 S	26·27 E
159	Wkra R. (f'krȧ).............Pol.	52·40 N	20·35 E
159	Wloclawek (vwô-tswä'vĕk)....Pol.	52·38 N	19·08 E
159	Wlodawa (vwô-dä'vä)........Pol.	51·33 N	23·33 E
159	Wloszczowa (vwôsh-chô'vä)...Pol.	50·51 N	19·58 E
99	Woburn (wōō'bŭrn) (wō'bŭrn) Ma. (In.)	42·29 N	71·10 W
149	Woerden..Neth. (Amsterdam In.)	52·05 N	4·52 E
148	Woking........Eng. (London In.)	51·18 N	0·33 W
148	Wokingham (wô'kĭng-hăm) Eng. (London In.)	51·23 N	0·50 W
113	Wolcott (wōl'kŏt) Ks. (Kansas City In.)	39·12 N	94·47 W
105	Wolf (I.) (wŏŏlf)...........Can.	44·10 N	76·25 W
120	Wolf (R.)...................Ms.	30·45 N	89·36 W
109	Wolf (R.)...................Wi.	45·14 N	88·45 W
158	Wolfenbüttel (vôl'fĕn-büt-ĕl) F.R.G.	52·10 N	10·32 E
107	Wolf L..........Il. (Chicago In.)	41·39 N	87·33 W
111	Wolf Point (wŏŏlf point).....Mt.	48·07 N	105·40 W
149	Wolfratshausen (vôlf'räts-hou-zĕn) F.R.G. (Munich In.)	47·55 N	11·25 E
158	Wolfsburg (vôlfs'bŏŏrgh)...F.R.G.	52·30 N	10·37 E
98	Wolfville (wŏŏlf'vĭl).........Can.	45·05 N	64·22 W
158	Wolgast (vôl'gäst)..........G.D.R.	54·04 N	13·46 E
213	Wolhuterskop............S. Afr. (Johannesburg & Pretoria In.)	25·41 S	27·40 E
149	Wolkersdorf....Aus. (Vienna In.)	48·24 N	16·31 E
90	Wollaston (L.) (wŏŏl'ăs-tŭn)..Can.	58·15 N	103·20 W
90	Wollaston Pen..............Can.	70·00 N	115·00 W
203	Wollongong (wŏŏl'ŭn-gŏng).Austl.	34·26 S	151·05 E
159	Wolomin (vō-wō'mēn)........Pol.	52·19 N	21·17 E
94	Wolseley...................Can.	50·25 N	103·15 W
148	Wolstanton (wŏŏl-stăn'tŭn)..Eng.	53·02 N	2·13 W
149	Woltersdorf (vōl'tĕrs-dōrf) G.D.R. (Berlin In.)	52·07 N	13·13 E
148	Wolverhampton (wŏŏl'vẽr-hămp-tŭn).Eng.	52·35 N	2·07 W
218	Wolwehoek..............S. Afr. (Johannesburg & Pretoria In.)	26·55 S	27·50 E
194	Wŏnsan (wŭn'sän')..........Kor.	39·08 N	127·24 E
203	Wonthaggi (wônt-hăg'ē)....Austl.	38·45 S	145·42 E
108	Wood (wŏŏd)................SD	43·26 N	100·25 W
108	Woodbine (wŏŏd'bīn).........Ia.	41·44 N	95·42 W
106	Woodbridge (wŏŏd'brĭj') NJ (New York In.)	40·33 N	74·18 W
90	Wood Buffalo Natl. Park....Can.	59·50 N	118·53 W
113	Woodburn (wŏŏd'bûrn) Il. (St. Louis In.)	39·03 N	90·01 W
110	Woodburn...................Or.	45·10 N	122·51 W
106	Woodbury (wŏŏd'bẽr-ē) NJ (Philadelpahi In.)	39·50 N	75·14 W
113	Woodcrest (wŏŏd'krĕst) Ca. (Los Angeles In.)	33·53 N	117·18 W
112	Woodinville (wŏŏd'ĭn-vĭl) Wa. (Seattle In.)	47·46 N	122·09 W
114	Woodland (wŏŏd'lănd)........Ca.	38·41 N	121·47 W
112	Woodland.....Wa. (Portland In.)	45·54 N	122·45 W
113	Woodland Hills Ca. (Los Angeles In.)	34·10 N	118·36 W
197	Woodlark (I.) (wŏŏd'lärk) Pap. N. Gui.	9·07 S	152·00 E
107	Woodlawn Beach (wŏŏd'lôn bēch) NY (Buffalo In.)	42·48 N	78·51 W
94	Wood Mountain............Can.	49·14 N	106·20 W
113	Wood River.....Il. (St. Louis In.)	38·52 N	90·06 W
204	Woodroffe, Mt. (wŏŏd'rŭf)..Austl.	26·05 S	132·00 E
121	Woodruff (wŏŏd'rŭf)..........SC	34·43 N	82·03 W
204	Woods (L.) (wŏŏdz)........Austl.	18·00 S	133·18 E
103	Woods, L. of the.......Can.-Mn.	49·25 N	93·25 W
113	Woods Cross (krôs) Ut. (Salt Lake City In.)	40·53 N	111·54 W
104	Woodsfield (wŏŏdz-fēld)......Oh.	39·45 N	81·10 W
112	Woodson (wŏŏdsŭn) Or. (Portland In.)	46·07 N	123·20 W
98	Woodstock (wŏŏd'stŏk)......Can.	43·10 N	80·50 W
98	Woodstock..................Can.	46·09 N	67·34 W
148	Woodstock.....Eng. (London In.)	51·48 N	1·22 W
109	Woodstock...................Il.	42·20 N	88·29 W
105	Woodstock..................Va.	38·55 N	78·25 W
105	Woodsville (wŏŏdz'vĭl).......NH	44·10 N	72·00 W
120	Woodville (wŏŏd'vĭl).........Ms.	31·06 N	91·11 W
119	Woodville...................Tx.	30·48 N	94·25 W
116	Woodward (wŏŏd'wôrd)......Ok.	36·25 N	99·24 W
148	Woolwich (wŏŏl'ĭj) Eng. (London In.)	51·28 N	0·05 E
203	Woomera (wŏŏm'ẽrȧ)......Austl.	31·15 S	136·43 E
106	Woonsocket (wōōn-sŏk'ĕt) RI (Providence In.)	42·00 N	71·30 W
108	Woonsocket.................SD	44·03 N	98·17 W
104	Wooster (wŏŏs'tẽr)..........Oh.	40·50 N	81·55 W
154	Worcester (wŏŏ'stẽr)........Eng.	52·09 N	2·14 W
99	Worcester.............Ma. (In.)	42·16 N	71·49 W
212	Worcester (wŏŏs'tẽr).......S. Afr.	33·35 S	19·31 E
148	Worcester (Co.) (wŏŏ'stẽr)...Eng.	52·24 N	2·15 W
113	Worden (wôr'dĕn) Il. (St. Louis In.)	38·56 N	89·50 W
154	Workington (wûr'kĭng-tŭn)..Eng.	54·40 N	3·30 W
148	Worksop (wûrk'sŏp) (wûr'sŭp) Eng.	53·18 N	1·07 W
111	Worland (wûr'lănd)..........Wy.	44·02 N	107·56 W
158	Worms (vōrms)............F.R.G.	49·37 N	8·22 E
202	Worona Res...Austl. (Sydney In.)	34·12 S	150·55 E
107	Worth (wûrth)...Il. (Chicago In.)	41·42 N	87·47 W
117	Worth L. Tx. (Dallas, Fort Worth In.)	32·48 N	97·32 W
119	Wortham (wûr'dhăm)........Tx.	31·46 N	96·22 W
154	Worthing (wûr'dhĭng)........Eng.	50·48 N	0·29 W
104	Worthington (wûr'dhĭng-tŭn)..In.	39·05 N	87·00 W
108	Worthington................Mn.	43·38 N	95·36 W
197	Wowoni (I.) (wō-wō'nē)....Indon.	4·05 S	123·45 E
148	Wragby (răg'bē).............Eng.	53·17 N	0·19 W
101	Wrangell (rănōgĕl)...........Ak.	56·28 N	132·25 W
101	Wrangell, Mt................Ak.	61·58 N	143·50 W
101	Wrangell Mts...........Ak.-Can.	62·28 N	142·40 W
154	Wrath, C. (răth)............Scot.	58·34 N	5·01 W
116	Wray (rā)...................Co.	40·06 N	102·14 W
137	Wreak (R.) (rēk)...........Eng.	52·45 N	0·59 W
205	Wreck Rfs. (rĕk)...........Austl.	22·00 S	155·52 E
148	Wrekin, The (Mt.) (rĕk'ĭn)....Eng.	54·20 N	2·33 W
121	Wrens (rĕnz)................Ga.	33·15 N	82·25 W
99	Wrentham......Ma. (Boston In.)	42·04 N	71·20 W
148	Wrexham (rĕk'săm)........Wales	53·03 N	3·00 W
107	Wrights Corners (rītz kôr'nẽrz) NY (Buffalo In.)	43·14 N	78·42 W
121	Wrightsville (rīts'vĭl).........Ga.	32·44 N	82·44 W
159	Wroclaw (Breslau) (vrôtsläv) (brĕs'lou).Pol.	51·07 N	17·10 E
148	Wrotham (rōōt'ŭm) Eng. (London In.)	51·18 N	0·19 E
159	Wrzesnia (vzhăsh'nyȧ).......Pol.	52·19 N	17·33 E
193	Wuch'ang (wōō'chäng').....China	30·32 N	114·25 E
192	Wuch'ang.................China	44·59 N	127·00 E
190	Wuchi (wōō'jē).............China	38·12 N	114·57 E
190	Wuchiang (wōō'jĭäng)......China	31·10 N	120·38 E
190	Wuch'iao (wōō'chĭou)......China	37·37 N	116·29 E
192	Wuch'ing (wōō'chĭng').China (In.)	39·32 N	116·51 E
193	Wu Chin Shan.............China	18·48 N	109·30 E
193	Wuchou (Tsangwu) (wōō'chō') China	23·32 N	111·25 E
193	Wuhan....................China	30·30 N	114·15 E
190	Wuhsi (wōō'sē).............China	31·36 N	120·17 E
	Wuhsien, see Soochow		
193	Wuhsing...................China	30·38 N	120·10 E
190	Wuhu (wōō'hōō')...........China	31·22 N	118·22 E
193	Wui Shan (Mts.)...........China	26·38 N	116·35 E
194	Wulachieh (wōō'kä-ĸē'ȧ)...China	44·08 N	126·25 E
	Wulanhata, see Ch'ihfeng		

ng-sing; ŋ-baŋk; ɴ-nasalized n; nŏd; cŏmmit; ōld; ôbey; ôrder; fōōd; fŏŏt; ou-out; s-soft; sh-dish; th-thin; pūre; ûnite; ûrn; stŭd; circŭs; ü-as "y" in study; '-indeterminate vowel.

Page	Name	Pronunciation	Region	Lat. °'	Long. °'
196	Wu Liang Shan (Mts.)		China	23·07 N	100·45 E
190	Wulitien (wōō'lē'dīän)		China	32·09 N	114·17 E
188	Wulunuch'i (Urunchi)		China	43·49 N	87·43 E
149	Wünsdorf (vüns'dorf)		G.D.R. (Berlin In.)	52·10 N	13·29 E
115	Wupatki Nat'l Mon		Ariz.	35·35 N	111·45 W
193	Wup'ing (wōō'pǐng)		China	25·05 N	116·01 E
161	Wuppertal (vŏŏp'ĕr-täl)		F.R.G. (Ruhr In.)	51·16 N	7·14 E
193	Wu R. (wōō')		China	27·30 N	108·00 E
158	Würm See (L.) (vürm zā)		F.R.G.	47·58 N	11·30 E
161	Würselen (vür'zĕ-lĕn)		F.R.G. (Ruhr In.)	50·49 N	6·09 E
158	Würzburg (vürts'bŏŏrgh)		F.R.G.	49·48 N	9·57 E
158	Wurzen (vŏŏrt'sĕn)		G.D.R.	51·22 N	12·45 E
188	Wushih (Uch Turfan) (wōō'shǐ) (ōōch' tŏŏr-fän')		China	41·13 N	79·08 E
149	Wustermark (vōōs'tĕr-märk)		G.D.R. (Berlin In.)	52·33 N	12·57 E
149	Wustrau (vōōst'rou)		G.D.R. (Berlin In.)	52·51 N	12·51 E
188	Wusu (Kweitun) (wōō'sōō') (kwā'tōōn)		China	44·28 N	84·07 E
191	Wusung (wōō'sōōng)		China (Shanghai In.)	31·23 N	121·29 E
149	Wuustwezel		Bel. (Brussels In.)	51·23 N	4·36 E
190	Wuwei (wōō'wā')		China	31·19 N	117·53 E
190	Wuyuch'ang		China	33·18 N	120·15 E
189	Wuyün (wōō-yün')		China	48·51 N	130·06 E
107	Wyandotte (wī'ăn-dŏt)		Mi. (Detroit In.)	42·12 N	83·10 W
148	Wye (wī)		Eng. (London In.)	51·12 N	0·57 E
148	Wye (R.)		Eng.	53·14 N	1·46 W
117	Wymore (wī'mōr)		Ne.	40·09 N	96·41 W
212	Wynberg (wĭn'bĕrg)		S. Afr. (In.)	34·00 S	18·28 E
204	Wyndham (wĭnd'ăm)		Austl.	15·30 S	128·15 E
117	Wynne (wĭn)		Ar.	35·12 N	90·46 W
117	Wynnewood (wĭn'wŏŏd)		Ok.	34·39 N	97·10 W
117	Wynona (wī-nō'nȧ)		Ok.	36·33 N	96·19 W
94	Wynyard (wĭn'yĕrd)		Can.	51·47 N	104·10 W
107	Wyoming (wī-ō'mǐng)		Oh. (Cincinnati In.)	39·14 N	84·28 W
102	Wyoming (State)		U. S.	42·50 N	108·30 W
111	Wyoming Ra.		Wy.	42·43 N	110·35 W
148	Wyre For. (wīr)		Eng.	52·24 N	2·24 W
158	Wysokie Mazowieckie (vĕ-sō'kyĕ mä-zō-vyĕts'kyĕ)		Pol.	52·55 N	22·42 E
158	Wyszkow (vĕsh'kŏŏf)		Pol.	52·35 N	21·29 E
121	Wytheville (wĭth'vĭl)		Va.	36·55 N	81·06 W

X

Page	Name	Pronunciation	Region	Lat. °'	Long. °'
128	Xagua, Banco (Bk.) (bä'n-kō-sä'gwä)		Cuba	21·35 N	80·50 W
161	Xanten (ksän'tĕn)		F.R.G. (Ruhr In.)	51·40 N	6·28 E
165	Xanthi		Grc.	41·08 N	24·53 E
212	Xau, L.		Bots.	21·15 S	24·38 E
126	Xcalak (sä-lä'k)		Mex. (In.)	18·15 N	87·50 W
104	Xenia (zē'nǐ-ȧ)		Oh.	39·40 N	83·55 W
124	Xicotencatl (sē-kō-tĕn-kät'l)		Mex.	32·00 N	98·58 W
124	Xilitla (sē-lē'tlä)		Mex.	21·24 N	98·59 W
135	Xingú (R.) (zhēṇ-gōō')		Braz.	6·20 S	52·34 W
124	Xochihuehuetlan (sō-chē-wĕ-wĕ-tlä'n)		Mex.	17·53 N	98·29 W
125	Xochimilco (sō-chē-mēl'kō)		Mex. (In.)	19·05 N	99·06 W

Y

Page	Name	Pronunciation	Region	Lat. °'	Long. °'
193	Yaan		China	30·00 N	103·20 E
159	Yablonitskiy Pereval (P.) (yȧb-lŏ'nǐt-skǐ pĕ-rĕ-väl')		Sov. Un.	48·20 N	24·25 E
173	Yablonovyy Khrebet (Mts.) (yȧ-blŏ-nô-vĕ')		Sov. Un.	51·15 N	111·30 E
195	Yachiyo		Jap. (Tōkyō In.)	35·43 N	140·07 E
112	Yacolt (yȧ'kōlt)		Wa. (Portland In.)	45·52 N	122·24 W
112	Yacolt (Mt.)		Wa. (Portland In.)	45·52 N	122·27 W
120	Yacona (R.) (yȧ'cō nä)		Ms.	34·13 N	89·30 W
136	Yacuiba (yä-kōō-ē'bà)		Arg.	22·02 S	63·44 W
121	Yadkin (R.) (yăd'kǐn)		NC	36·12 N	80·40 W
211	Yafran		Libya	31·57 N	12·04 E
167	Yagotin (yä'gô-tēn)		Sov. Un.	50·18 N	31·46 E
128	Yaguajay (yä-guä-hä'ē)		Cuba	22·20 N	79·20 W
195	Yahagi-Gawa (Strm.) (yä'hä-gē gä'wä)		Jap.	35·16 N	137·22 E
191	Yahu		China (Canton In.)	23·19 N	113·17 E
124	Yahualica (yä-wä-lē'kä)		Mex.	21·08 N	102·53 W
190	Yahungch'iao (yä'hōōng'chǐou)		China	39·45 N	117·52 E
193	Yaihsien		China	18·20 N	109·10 E
125	Yajalon (yä-hä-lōn')		Mex.	17·16 N	92·20 W
174	Yakhroma (yäk'rô-ma)		Sov. Un. (Moscow In.)	56·17 N	37·30 E
174	Yakhroma R.		Sov. Un. (Moscow In.)	56·15 N	37·38 E
110	Yakima (yăk'ǐmȧ)		Wa.	46·35 N	120·30 W
110	Yakima R. (tăk'ǐ-mȧ)		Wa.	46·48 N	120·22 W
216	Yakoma		Zaire	4·05 N	22·27 E
195	Yaku (I.) (yä'kōō)		Jap.	30·15 N	130·41 E
173	Yakut A.S.S.R.		Sov. Un.	65·21 N	117·13 E
101	Yakutat (yȧk'ōō-tȧt)		Ak.	59·32 N	139·35 W
173	Yakutsk (yȧ-kōōtsk')		Sov. Un.	62·13 N	129·49 E
194	Yal (R.) (yäl)		China	48·20 N	122·35 E
104	Yale		Mi.	43·05 N	82·45 W
117	Yale		Ok.	36·07 N	96·42 W
110	Yale Res.		Wa.	46·00 N	122·20 W
211	Yalinga (yȧ-lǐṇ'gȧ)		Cen. Afr. Emp.	6·56 N	23·22 E
120	Yalobusha (R.) (yȧ-lô-bŏŏsh'ȧ)		Ms.	33·48 N	90·02 W
171	Yalta (yäl'tä)		China (Canton In.) Sov. Un.	44·29 N	34·12 E
194	Yalu (Amnok) (R.)		China-Kor.	41·20 N	126·35 E
188	Yalung Chiang (R.) (yä'lōōng')		China	32·29 N	98·41 E
172	Yalutorovsk (yä-lōō-tô'rôfsk)		Sov. Un.	56·42 N	66·32 E
195	Yamada (yä'mȧ-dȧ)		Jap.	33·37 N	133·39 E
194	Yamagata (yä-mä'gä-tȧ)		Jap.	38·12 N	140·24 E
195	Yamaguchi (yä-mä'gōō-chē)		Jap.	34·10 N	131·30 E
172	Yamal, P-ov (Pen.) (yä-mäl')		Sov. Un.	71·15 N	70·00 E
174	Yamantau, Gora (Mt.) (gä-rä' yä' man-tàw)		Sov. Un. (Urals In.)	54·16 N	58·08 E
129	Yamasá (yä-mä'sä)		Dom. Rep.	18·50 N	70·00 W
195	Yamasaki (yä'mä'sä-kē)		Jap.	35·01 N	134·33 E
195	Yamasaki		Jap. (Osaka In.)	34·53 N	135·41 E
195	Yamashina (yä'mä-shē'nä)		Jap. (Osaka In.)	34·59 N	135·50 E
195	Yamashita (yä'mä-shē'tä)		Jap. (Osaka In.)	34·53 N	135·25 E
195	Yamato		Jap. (Tōkyō In.)	35·28 N	139·28 E
195	Yamato-Kōriyama		Jap. (Osaka In.)	34·39 N	135·48 E
195	Yamato-takada (yä'mä-tô tä'kä-dä)		Jap. (Osaka In.)	34·31 N	135·45 E
134	Yambi, Mesa de (mě'sä-dě-yȧ'm-bē)		Col.	1·55 N	71·45 W
197	Yamdena (I.)		Indon.	7·23 S	130·30 E
188	Yamdrog Tsho (L.)		China	29·11 N	91·26 E
188	Yamethin (yǔ-mē'thĕn)		Bur.	20·14 N	96·27 E
112	Yamhill (yäm'hǐl)		Or. (Portland In.)	45·20 N	123·11 W
174	Yamkino (yäm'kǐ-nô)		Sov. Un. (Moscow In.)	55·56 N	38·25 E
203	Yamma Yamma, L. (yäm'ȧ yäm'ȧ)		Austl.	26·15 S	141·30 E
173	Yamsk (yämsk)		Sov. Un.	59·41 N	154·09 E
184	Yamuna (R.)		India	26·50 N	80·10 E
173	Yana (R.) (yä'nä)		Sov. Un.	69·42 N	135·45 E
203	Yanac (yăn'ák)		Austl.	36·10 S	141·30 E
195	Yanagawa (yä-nä'gä-wä)		Jap.	33·11 N	130·24 E
184	Yanam (yǔnǔm')		India	16·48 N	82·15 E
186	Yanbu'		Sau. Ar.	23·57 N	38·02 E
216	Yandongi		Zaire	2·51 N	22·16 E
190	Yangch'eng Hu (L.) (yäng'chĕng'hŏō)		China	31·30 N	120·31 E
193	Yangchiang		China	21·52 N	111·58 E
190	Yangchiaokou (yang'jēou'gō)		China	36·17 N	118·53 E
190	Yangchiat'an (yäng'jēä'tän)		China	31·43 N	115·53 E
189	Yangchou		China	32·24 N	119·24 E
190	Yangchüan		China	37·52 N	113·36 E
193	Yangch'un (yäng'chōōn')		China	22·08 N	111·48 E
190	Yangerhchuang (yäng'ē'jōōäng)		China	38·18 N	117·31 E
190	Yangho (yäng'hǔ)		China	33·48 N	118·23 E
190	Yanghsin (yäng'sǐn)		China	37·37 N	117·34 E
192	Yangkochuang		China (Peking In.)	40·10 N	116·48 E
190	Yangku (yäng'kōō')		China	36·06 N	115·46 E
190	Yangsanmu (yäng'sän'mōō)		China	38·28 N	117·18 E
189	Yangtze (R.) (yäng'tse)		China	30·30 N	117·25 E
194	Yangyang (yäng'yäng')		Kor.	38·02 N	128·38 E
108	Yankton (yănk'tǔn)		SD	42·51 N	97·24 W
174	Yannina, see Ioánnina				
174	Yanychi (yä'nǐ-chǐ		Sov. Un. (Urals In.)	57·42 N	56·24 E
211	Yao (yä'ō)		Chad	12·50 N	17·38 E
195	Yao		Jap. (Osaka In.)	34·37 N	135·76 E
215	Yaoundé (yä-ōōn-dä')		Cam.	3·52 N	11·31 E
198	Yap (yäp) (I)		Pac. Is. Trust Ter.	11·00 N	138·00 E
129	Yaque del Norte (R.) (yä'kȧ dĕl nôr'tä)		Dom. Rep.	19·40 N	71·25 W
129	Yaque del Sur (R.) (yä-kĕ-dĕl-sōō'r)		Dom. Rep.	18·35 N	71·05 W
122	Yaqui (R.) (yä'kē)		Mex.	28·15 N	109·40 W
135	Yaracuy (State) (yä-rä-kōō'ē)		Ven. (In.)	10·10 N	68·31 W
203	Yaraka (yȧ-räk'ȧ)		Austl.	24·50 S	144·08 E
170	Yaransk (yä-ränsk')		Sov. Un.	57·18 N	48·05 E
211	Yarda (Well) (yär'dȧ)		Chad	18·29 N	19·13 E
184	Yarkand (R.) (yär-känt')		India	36·11 N	76·10 E
98	Yarmouth (yär'mǔth)		Can.	43·50 N	66·07 W
174	Yaroslavka (yȧ-rô-släv'kä)		Sov. Un. (Urals In.)	55·52 N	57·59 E
166	Yaroslavl' (yȧ-rô-släv''l)		Sov. Un.	57·57 N	39·54 E
166	Yaroslavl' (Oblast)		Sov. Un.	58·05 N	38·05 E
170	Yarra-to (L.) (yȧ'rô-tô')		Sov. Un.	68·30 N	71·30 E
166	Yartsevo (yär'tsyĕ-vô)		Sov. Un.	55·04 N	32·38 E
172	Yartsevo		Sov. Un.	60·13 N	89·52 E
134	Yarumal (yä-rōō-mäl')		Col. (In.)	6·57 N	75·24 W
159	Yasel'da R. (yä-syŭl'dä)		Sov. Un.	53·13 N	25·53 E
159	Yasinya		Sov. Un.	48·17 N	24·21 E
129	Yateras (yä-tä'räs)		Cuba	20·00 N	75·00 W
117	Yates Center (yäts)		Ks.	37·53 N	95·44 W
90	Yathkyed (L.) (yȧth-kī-ĕd')		Can.	62·41 N	98·00 W
195	Yatsuga-take (Mtn.) (yät'sōō-gä dä'kä)		Jap.	36·01 N	138·21 E
195	Yatsushiro (yät'sōō'shē-rô)		Jap.	32·30 N	130·35 E
217	Yatta Plat.		Ken.	1·55 S	38·10 E
124	Yautepec (yä-ōō-tä-pĕk')		Mex.	18·53 N	99·04 W
159	Yavorvo (yä'vô-rô'yĕ)		Sov. Un.	49·56 N	23·24 E
195	Yawata (yä'wä-tä)		Jap. (Osaka In.)	34·52 N	135·43 E
195	Yawatahama (yä'wä'tä'hä-mä)		Jap.	33·24 N	132·25 E
216	Yayama		Zaire	1·16 S	23·07 E
186	Yazd		Iran	31·59 N	54·03 E
120	Yazoo (R.) (yä'zōō)		Ms.	32·30 N	90·40 W
120	Yazoo City		Ms.	32·50 N	90·18 W
196	Ye (yā)		Bur.	15·13 N	97·52 E
106	Yeadon (yē'dǔn)		Pa. (Philadelphia In.)	39·56 N	75·16 W
162	Yecla (yā'klä)		Sp.	38·35 N	1·09 W
166	Yefremov (yě-frä'môf)		Sov. Un.	53·08 N	38·04 E
166	Yegor'yevsk (yě-gôr'yĕfsk)		Sov. Un.	55·23 N	38·59 E
188	Yehch'eng (Karghalik) (yě'chĕng)		China	37·30 N	79·26 E
170	Yelabuga (yě-lä'bŏō-gà)		Sov. Un.	55·50 N	52·18 E
171	Yelan		Sov. Un.	50·50 N	44·00 E
166	Yelets (yě-lyĕts')		Sov. Un.	52·35 N	38·28 E
174	Yelizavetpol'skiy (yě'lǐ-za-vĕt-pôl-skĭ)		Sov. Un. (Urals In.)	52·51 N	60·38 E
173	Yelizavety, Mys (C.) (yě'lǐg-sä-vyě'tä)		Sov. Un.	54·28 N	142·59 E
154	Yell (I.) (yěl)		Scot.	60·35 N	1·27 W
120	Yellow (R.)		Fl.	30·33 N	86·53 W
93	Yellowhead Pass (yěl'ô-hěd)		Can.	52·52 N	118·35 W
90	Yellowknife (yěl'ô-nīf)		Can.	62·29 N	114·38 W
	Yellow R., see Huang Ho				
192	Yellow Sea		Asia	35·20 N	122·15 E
111	Yellowstone L.		Wy.	44·27 N	110·03 W
111	Yellowstone Natl. Park (yěl'ô-stōn)		Wy.	44·45 N	110·35 W
111	Yellowstone R.		Mt.	46·28 N	105·39 W
111	Yellowstone R., Clark Fk.		Mt.	46·55 N	109·05 W
111	Yellowtail Res.		Mt.-Wy.	45·00 N	108·10 W
166	Yel'nya (yěl'nyȧ)		Sov. Un.	54·34 N	33·12 E
174	Yemanzhelinsk (yě-mán-zhä'lǐnsk)		Sov. Un. (Urals In.)	54·47 N	61·24 E
182	Yemen (yěm'ĕn)		Asia	15·45 N	44·30 E
182	Yemen, People's Democratic Republic of		Asia	14·45 N	46·45 E
170	Yemetsk		Sov. Un.	63·28 N	41·28 E
167	Yenakiyevo (yě-nä'kǐ-yě-vô)		Sov. Un.	48·14 N	38·12 E
192	Yenan (yěn'än')		China	36·35 N	109·32 E
188	Yenan (Fushih)		China	36·46 N	109·15 E
187	Yenangyaung (yä'nän-d oung)		Bur.	20·27 N	94·59 E
190	Yench'eng (yěn'chĕng)		China	33·23 N	120·11 E
190	Yencheng (yěn'chěng)		China	33·38 N	113·59 E
188	Yench'i (yěn'chǐ)		China	42·14 N	86·28 E
192	Yenchi		China	42·55 N	129·35 E
190	Yenchiaha (yen'jēä'hä)		China	31·47 N	114·50 E
190	Yenchianchi (yěn'jēä'jē)		China	32·51 N	115·57 E
190	Yenching (yěn'jǐn)		China	35·09 N	114·13 E

ăt; fĭnȧl; rāte; senâte; ärm; ȧsk; sofȧ; fâre; ch-choose; dh-as th in other; bē; ĕvent; bĕt; recĕnt; cratēr; g-go; gh-guttural g; bĭt; ĭ-short neutral; rīde; ᴋ-guttural k as ch in German ich;